THE
ALL ENGLAND
LAW REPORTS
2003

Volume 3

Editor-in-Chief
CRAIG ROSE   Barrister

Editor
KAREN WIDDICOMBE   Solicitor

Members of the LexisNexis Group worldwide

United Kingdom	LexisNexis UK, a Division of Reed Elsevier (UK) Ltd, Halsbury House, 35 Chancery Lane, LONDON, WC2A 1EL, and 4 Hill Street, EDINBURGH EH2 3JZ
Argentina	LexisNexis Argentina, BUENOS AIRES
Australia	LexisNexis Butterworths, CHATSWOOD, New South Wales
Austria	LexisNexis Verlag ARD Orac GmbH & Co KG, VIENNA
Canada	LexisNexis Butterworths, MARKHAM, Ontario
Chile	LexisNexis Chile Ltda, SANTIAGO DE CHILE
Czech Republic	Nakladatelství Orac sro, PRAGUE
France	Editions du Juris-Classeur SA, PARIS
Germany	LexisNexis Deutschland GmbH, FRANKFURT and MUNSTER
Hong Kong	LexisNexis Butterworths, HONG KONG
Hungary	HVG-Orac, BUDAPEST
India	LexisNexis Butterworths, NEW DELHI
Ireland	LexisNexis, DUBLIN
Italy	Giuffrè Editore, MILAN
Malaysia	Malayan Law Journal Sdn Bhd, KUALA LUMPUR
New Zealand	LexisNexis Butterworths, WELLINGTON
Poland	Wydawnictwo Prawnicze LexisNexis, WARSAW
Singapore	LexisNexis Butterworths, SINGAPORE
South Africa	LexisNexis Butterworths, DURBAN
Switzerland	Stämpfli Verlag AG, BERNE
USA	LexisNexis, DAYTON, Ohio

A CIP Catalogue record for this book is available from the British Library.

Printed and bound in Great Britain by William Clowes Ltd, Beccles and London

ISBN for the complete set of volumes: 0 406 85159 X
for this volume:

ISBN 0-406-96515-3

9 780406 965158

Visit LexisNexis UK at www.lexisnexis.co.uk

House of Lords

The Lord High Chancellor of Great Britain:
Lord Falconer of Thoroton

Lords of Appeal in Ordinary

Lord Bingham of Cornhill
Lord Nicholls of Birkenhead
Lord Steyn
Lord Hoffmann
Lord Hope of Craighead
Lord Hutton

Lord Saville of Newdigate
Lord Hobhouse of Woodborough
Lord Millett
Lord Scott of Foscote
Lord Rodger of Earlsferry
Lord Walker of Gestingthorpe

Court of Appeal

The Lord High Chancellor of Great Britain

The Lord Chief Justice of England and Wales: Lord Woolf
(President of the Criminal Division)

The Master of the Rolls: Lord Phillips of Worth Matravers
(President of the Civil Division)

The President of the Family Division: Dame Elizabeth Butler-Sloss

The Vice-Chancellor: Sir Robert Andrew Morritt

Lords Justices of Appeal

Sir Paul Joseph Morrow Kennedy
Sir Simon Denis Brown (Vice-President of the
    Civil Division)
Sir Christopher Dudley Roger Rose
    (Vice-President of the Criminal Division)
Sir Peter Leslie Gibson
Sir Robin Ernest Auld
Sir Malcolm Thomas Pill
Sir William Aldous
Sir Alan Hylton Ward
Sir Konrad Hermann Theodor Schiemann
Sir Mathew Alexander Thorpe
Sir Mark Howard Potter
Sir Henry Brooke
Sir Igor Judge (Deputy Chief Justice)
Sir George Mark Waller
Sir John Frank Mummery
Sir Charles Barrie Knight Mantell
Sir John Murray Chadwick
Sir Richard Joseph Buxton

Sir Anthony Tristram Kenneth May
    (Vice-President of the Queen's
    Bench Division)
Sir Simon Lane Tuckey
Sir Anthony Peter Clarke
Sir John Grant McKenzie Laws
Sir Stephen John Sedley
Sir Jonathan Hugh Mance
Dame Brenda Marjorie Hale
Sir David Nicholas Ramsey Latham
Sir John William Kay
Sir Bernard Anthony Rix
Sir Jonathan Frederic Parker
Dame Mary Howarth Arden
Sir David Wolfe Keene
Sir John Anthony Dyson
Sir Andrew Centlivres Longmore
Sir Robert John Anderson Carnwath
Sir Thomas Scott Gillespie Baker
Dame Janet Hilary Smith
Sir Roger John Laugharne Thomas (appointed
    14 July 2003) (Senior Presiding Judge for
    England and Wales)

High Court of Justice

The Lord High Chancellor of Great Britain
The Lord Chief Justice of England
The President of the Family Division
The Vice-Chancellor
The Senior Presiding Judge for England and Wales
The puisne judges of the High Court

Chancery Division

The Lord High Chancellor of Great Britain
The Vice-Chancellor

Sir John Edmund Frederic Lindsay
Sir Edward Christopher Evans-Lombe
Sir Robin Raphael Hayim Jacob
Sir William Anthony Blackburne
Sir Gavin Anthony Lightman
Sir Colin Percy Farquharson Rimer
Sir Hugh Ian Lang Laddie
Sir Timothy Andrew Wigram Lloyd
Sir David Edmund Neuberger

Sir Andrew Edward Wilson Park
Sir Nicholas Richard Pumfrey
Sir Michael Christopher Campbell Hart
Sir Lawrence Anthony Collins
Sir Nicholas John Patten
Sir Terrence Michael Elkan Barnet Etherton
Sir Peter Winston Smith
Sir Kim Martin Jordan Lewison

Queen's Bench Division

The Lord Chief Justice of England

Sir Stuart Neil McKinnon
Sir Douglas Dunlop Brown
Sir Michael Morland
Sir Roger John Buckley
Sir Peter John Cresswell
Sir Christopher John Holland
Sir Richard Herbert Curtis
Sir Anthony David Colman
Sir John Thayne Forbes
Sir Michael Alexander Geddes Sachs
Sir Stephen George Mitchell
Sir Rodger Bell
Sir Michael Guy Vicat Harrison
Sir William Marcus Gage
Sir Thomas Richard Atkin Morison
Sir Andrew David Collins
Sir Maurice Ralph Kay
Sir Anthony Hooper
Sir Alexander Neil Logie Butterfield
Sir George Michael Newman

Sir David Anthony Poole
Sir Martin James Moore-Bick
Sir Gordon Julian Hugh Langley
Sir Roger John Laugharne Thomas (appointed
    Lord Justice of Appeal 14 July 2003)
Sir Robert Franklyn Nelson
Sir Roger Grenfell Toulson
Sir Michael John Astill
Sir Alan George Moses
Sir David Eady
Sir Jeremy Mirth Sullivan
Sir David Herbert Penry-Davey
Sir Stephen Price Richards
Sir David William Steel
Sir Charles Antony St John Gray
Sir Nicolas Dusan Bratza
Sir Michael John Burton
Sir Rupert Matthew Jackson
Dame Heather Carol Hallett
Sir Patrick Elias

[continued on next page]

Queen's Bench Division *(continued)*

Sir Richard John Pearson Aikens
Sir Stephen Robert Silber
Sir John Bernard Goldring
Sir Peter Francis Crane
Dame Anne Judith Rafferty
Sir Geoffery Douglas Grigson
Sir Richard John Hedley Gibbs
Sir Richard Henry Quixano Henriques
Sir Stephen Miles Tomlinson
Sir Andrew Charles Smith
Sir Stanley Jeffrey Burnton
Sir Patrick James Hunt
Sir Christopher John Pitchford
Sir Brian Henry Leveson
Sir Duncan Brian Walter Ouseley
Sir Richard George Bramwell McCombe
Sir Raymond Evan Jack

Sir Robert Michael Owen
Sir Colin Crichton Mackay
Sir John Edward Mitting
Sir David Roderick Evans
Sir Nigel Anthony Lamert Davis
Sir Peter Henry Gross
Sir Brian Richard Keith
Sir Jeremy Lionel Cooke
Sir Richard Alan Field
Sir Christopher John Pitchers
Sir Colman Maurice Treacy
Sir Peregrine Charles Hugo Simon
Sir Roger John Royce
Dame Laura Mary Cox
Sir Adrian Bruce Fulford
Sir Jack Beatson
Sir Michael George Tugendhat

Family Division

The President of the Family Division

Sir Robert Lionel Johnson
Dame Joyanne Winifred Bracewell
Sir Jan Peter Singer
Sir Nicholas Allan Roy Wilson
Sir Nicholas Peter Rathbone Wall
Sir Andrew Tristram Hammett Kirkwood
Sir Hugh Peter Derwyn Bennett
Sir Edward James Holman
Dame Mary Claire Hogg

Sir Christopher John Sumner
Sir Anthony Philip Gilson Hughes
Sir Arthur William Hessin Charles
Sir David Roderick Lessiter Bodey
Dame Jill Margaret Black
Sir James Lawrence Munby
Sir Paul James Duke Coleridge
Sir Mark Hedley

Official Judgment Numbers
and
Paragraph References

Since 11 January 2001, official judgment numbers have been given to all judgments delivered in the House of Lords, Privy Council, both divisions of the Court of Appeal and the Administrative Court. All such judgments have fixed paragraph numbering, as do judgments delivered on or after 11 January 2001 in those parts of the High Court which did not then adopt the system of official judgment numbers (see Practice Note (judgments: neutral citation) [2001] 1 All ER 193 for the Court of Appeal and the High Court). On 14 January 2002 the system of judgment numbers was extended to all parts of the High Court (see Practice Direction (High Court judgments: neutral citation) [2002] 1 All ER 351). We have adopted the following practice in respect of judgments with official judgment numbers and official paragraph numbering:

- The official judgment number is inserted immediately beneath the case name;
- Official paragraph numbers are in bold in square brackets;
- Holding references in the headnotes, and any other cross-references, are to an official paragraph number, not to a page of the report;
- When such a judgment is subsequently cited in another report,

   (i) the official judgment number is inserted before the usual report citations in the case lists and on the first occasion when the case is cited in the text. Thereafter, only the report citations are given;

   (ii) All 'at' references are to the official paragraph number rather than to a page of a report, with the paragraph number in square brackets but not in bold;

   (iii) The 'at' reference is only given in conjunction with the first report cited; eg [2001] 4 All ER 159 at [16], [2001] AC 61. If an 'at' reference is included on the first occasion when the case is cited, it also appears alongside the official judgment number.

For the avoidance of doubt, these changes do not apply to reports of judgments delivered before 11 January 2001 or to the citation of such cases in other reports.

CITATION

These reports are cited thus:

[2003] 3 All ER

REFERENCES

These reports contain references to the following major works of legal reference described in the manner indicated below.

Halsbury's Laws of England

The reference 14 *Halsbury's Laws* (4th edn) para 185 refers to paragraph 185 on page 90 of volume 14 of the fourth edition of *Halsbury's Laws of England*.

The reference 15 *Halsbury's Laws* (4th edn reissue) para 355 refers to paragraph 355 on page 283 of reissue volume 15 of the fourth edition of *Halsbury's Laws of England*.

The reference 7(1) *Halsbury's Laws* (4th edn) (1996 reissue) para 9 refers to paragraph 9 on page 24 of the 1996 reissue of volume 7(1) of the fourth edition of *Halsbury's Laws of England*.

Halsbury's Statutes of England and Wales

The reference 14 *Halsbury's Statutes* (4th edn) (2003 reissue) 734 refers to page 734 of volume 14 of the fourth edition of *Halsbury's Statutes of England and Wales*.

The reference 40 *Halsbury's Statutes* (4th edn) (2001 reissue) 269 refers to page 269 of the 2001 reissue of volume 40 of the fourth edition of *Halsbury's Statutes of England and Wales*.

Halsbury's Statutory Instruments

The reference 14 *Halsbury's Statutory Instruments* (2001 issue) 201 refers to page 201 of the 2001 issue of volume 14 of the grey volumes series of *Halsbury's Statutory Instruments*.

Cases reported in volume 3

Page

Page

x

Digest of cases reported in volume 3

House of Lords petitions

This list, which covers the period 25 June 2003 to 31 July 2003, sets out all cases which have formed the subject of a report in the All England Law Reports in which an Appeal Committee of the House of Lords has, subsequent to the publication of that report, refused leave to appeal. Where the result of a petition for leave to appeal was known prior to the publication of the relevant report a note of that result appears at the end of the report.

Cranfield v Bridgegrove Ltd [2003] 3 All ER 129. Leave to appeal refused 31 July 2003 (Lord Hoffmann, Lord Scott of Foscote and Lord Walker of Gestingthorpe).

Holder v Law Society [2003] 3 All ER 62. Leave to appeal refused 31 July 2003 (Lord Hoffmann, Lord Scott of Foscote and Lord Walker of Gestingthorpe).

Grady v Prison Service [2003] 3 All ER 745. Leave to appeal refused 8 July 2003 (Lord Steyn, Lord Hoffmann and Lord Walker of Gestingthorpe).

South Bucks District Council v Porter
Chichester District Council v Searle and others
Wrexham County Borough Council v Berry
[2003] UKHL 26

HOUSE OF LORDS

LORD BINGHAM OF CORNHILL, LORD STEYN, LORD CLYDE, LORD HUTTON AND LORD SCOTT OF FOSCOTE

7, 8, 9, APRIL, 22 MAY 2003

Town and country planning – Enforcement of planning control – Unauthorised development of land – Power of court to grant injunction restraining breach of planning control – Whether court required to exercise independent judgment on planning issues and hardship when considering whether to grant injunction – Guidance on exercise of power – Town and Country Planning Act 1990, s 187B.

The three appeals concerned the enforcement of planning control against gipsies who were occupying lands in the areas of the respective local authorities without planning permission to do so. In each case the local planning authority had sought an injunction under s 187B of the Town and Country Planning Act 1990. That section provided: '(1) Where a local planning authority consider it necessary or expedient for any actual or apprehended breach of planning control to be restrained by injunction, they may apply to the court for an injunction, whether or not they have exercised or are proposing to exercise any of their other powers under this part. (2) On an application under subsection (1) the court may grant such an injunction as the court thinks appropriate for restraining the breach …' Those injunctions were granted and the gipsies appealed to the Court of Appeal. The authorities argued that the judge exercising his s 187B discretion was more or less bound to grant an injunction unless the authority's application could be shown to be flawed on *Wednesbury* grounds and that it was not until the stage of committal for breach of an injunction that a court was entitled to reach an independent view on proportionality. They also contended that the court's role was unaffected by the Human Rights Act 1998. The Court of Appeal determined that the judge on a s 187B application was not required, nor even entitled, to reach his own independent view of the planning merits of each case, however, he should not grant injunctive relief unless he had considered for himself all questions of hardship for the defendant and his family. The court also held that it would not be consistent with the duty under s 6(1) of the 1998 Act to act

compatibly with the European Convention for the Protection of Human Rights
and Fundamental Freedoms 1950 (as set out in Sch 1 to the 1998 Act) without
considering the question of proportionality. The authorities appealed.

Held – The jurisdiction of the court under s 187B of the 1990 Act was an original
not a supervisory jurisdiction, and in all cases the court had to decide whether in
all the circumstances it was just and proportionate, in the Convention sense, to
exercise its discretion under the section to grant the relief sought against the
particular defendant. Moreover, the word 'may' in s 187B(2) applied not only to
the terms of any injunction a court might grant, but also to the decision as to
whether it should grant any injunction. No single test could be prescribed as to
when the court's discretion, which was not unfettered, would be exercised in
favour of granting an injunction from those in which it would not. Like every
other judicial discretion it had to be exercised judicially with due regard to the
purpose for which the power was conferred, namely to permit abuses to be
curbed and urgent solutions provided where those were called for. Furthermore,
an application by an authority under s 187B was not an invitation to the court to
exercise functions allocated elsewhere. Thus it could never be appropriate for the
court to hold that planning permission should not have been refused or that an
appeal against an enforcement notice should have succeeded or that an authority
should have had different spending priorities. Nevertheless, the court was not
precluded from entertaining issues not related to planning policy or judgment.
All would depend on the particular facts, and the court had always, of course, to
act on evidence including whether the authority had taken account of the
personal circumstances of the defendant and any hardship an injunction might
cause. The guidance given by the Court of Appeal was judicious and accurate in
all respects. Accordingly the appeals would be dismissed (see [20], [27]–[31], [38],
[50], [53], [56], [73], [75], [86], [93], [104], below.

    Mole Valley DC v Smith, Reigate and Banstead BC v Brown (1992) 90 LGR 557 and
Hambleton DC v Bird [1995] 3 PLR 8 disapproved.

    Decision of the Court of Appeal [2002] 1 All ER 425 affirmed.

Notes

For injunctions restraining breaches of planning control, see 46 *Halsbury's Laws*
(4th edn reissue) para 684.

    For the Town and Country Planning Act 1990, s 187B, see 46 *Halsbury's Statutes*
(4th edn) (1998 reissue) 698.

Cases referred to in opinions

A-G (on the relation of Hornchurch UDC) v Bastow [1957] 1 All ER 497, [1957] 1 QB
    514, [1957] 2 WLR 340.
A-G v Chaudry [1971] 3 All ER 938, [1971] 1 WLR 1614, CA.
Associated Provincial Picture Houses Ltd v Wednesbury Corp [1947] 2 All ER 680,
    [1948] 1 KB 223, CA.
Basildon DC v Secretary of State for the Environment, Transport and the Regions [2001]
    JPL 1184.
Buckley v UK (1996) 23 EHRR 101, [1996] ECHR 20348/92, ECt HR and E Com
    HR.
Castanho v Brown & Root (UK) Ltd [1981] 1 All ER 143, [1981] AC 557, [1980]
    3 WLR 991, HL.
Chapman v UK (2001) 10 BHRC 48, (2001) 33 EHRR 399, ECt HR.

City of London Corp v Bovis Construction Ltd [1992] 3 All ER 697, CA.

a *East Barnet UDC v British Transport Commission* [1961] 3 All ER 878, [1962] 2 QB 484, [1962] 2 WLR 134.

Gouriet v Union of Post Office Workers [1977] 3 All ER 70, [1978] AC 435, [1977] 3 WLR 300, HL.

Guildford BC v Smith [1994] JPL 734, CA.

b *Hambleton DC v Bird* [1995] 3 PLR 8, CA.

Liddell's Settlement Trusts, Re, Liddell v Liddell [1936] 1 All ER 239, [1936] Ch 365, CA.

Manchester Corp v Connolly [1970] 1 All ER 961, [1970] Ch 420, [1970] 2 WLR 746, CA.

Mole Valley DC v Smith, Reigate and Banstead BC v Brown (1992) 90 LGR 557, CA.

c *Pioneer Aggregates (UK) Ltd v Secretary of State for the Environment* [1984] 2 All ER 358, [1985] AC 132, [1984] 3 WLR 32, HL.

R (on the application of Alconbury Developments Ltd) v Secretary of State for the Environment, Transport and the Regions [2001] UKHL 23, [2001] 2 All ER 929, [2001] 2 WLR 1389.

d *R v Basildon DC, ex p Clarke* [1996] JPL 866.

R v Lincolnshire CC, ex p Atkinson (1995) 8 Admin LR 529.

R v Wicks [1997] 2 All ER 801, [1998] AC 92, [1997] 2 WLR 876, HL.

Sheffield City Council v Smart, Central Sunderland Housing Co Ltd v Wilson [2002] EWCA Civ 4, [2002] LGR 467.

e *Tesco Stores Ltd v Secretary of State for the Environment* [1995] 2 All ER 636, [1995] 1 WLR 759, HL.

Waverley BC v Hilden [1988] 1 All ER 807, [1988] 1 WLR 246.

Westminster City Council v Great Portland Estates plc [1984] 3 All ER 744, [1985] AC 661, [1984] 3 WLR 1035, HL.

f
Cases also referred to in list of authorities

Ayres v Secretary of State for the Environment (1997) 74 P & CR 246.

Brind v Secretary of State for Home Dept [1991] 1 All ER 720, [1991] 1 AC 969, [1991] 2 WLR 588, HL.

Bristol City Council v Lovell [1998] 1 All ER 775, [1998] 1 WLR 446, HL.

g *Brown v Stott (Procurator Fiscal, Dunfermline)* [2001] 2 All ER 97, [2001] 2 WLR 817, PC.

Bryan v UK (1995) 21 EHRR 342, [1995] ECHR 19178/91, ECt HR.

Buckingham CC v North West Estates plc [2003] JPL 414.

Jennison v Baker [1972] 1 All ER 997, [1972] 2 QB 52, [1972] 2 WLR 429, CA.

h *Miles v Secretary of State for the Environment* [1999] CA Transcript 1495.

R (on the application of Samaroo) v Secretary of State for the Home Dept [2001] EWCA Civ 1139, [2001] UKHRR 1150.

R v Clarke [2002] EWCA Crim 753, [2002] JPL 1372.

R v DPP, ex p Kebeline, R v DPP, ex p Rechachi [1999] 4 All ER 801, [2000] 2 AC 326, [1999] 3 WLR 972, HL.

j *R v Secretary of State for the Home Dept, ex p Daly* [2001] UKHL 26, [2001] 3 All ER 433, [2001] 2 AC 532, [2001] 2 WLR 1622.

Runa Begum v Tower Hamlets London Borough Council [2003] UKHL 5, [2003] 1 All ER 731, [2003] 2 WLR 388.

Runnymeade BC v Harwood [1994] 1 PLR 22, CA.

Tandrige DC v Delaney [2000] 1 PLR 11.

Wrexham County BC v National Assembly for Wales [2002] EWHC 2414 (Admin), [2002] All ER (D) 77 (Oct).

Appeals

South Bucks DC v Porter

The defendant, South Bucks District Council, appealed with permission of the House of Lords Appeal Committee given on 18 March 2002 from a decision of the Court of Appeal (Simon Brown, Peter Gibson and Tuckey LJJ) on 12 October 2001 ([2001] EWCA Civ 1549, [2002] 1 All ER 425, [2002] 1 WLR 1359) allowing the appeal of the claimant, Linda Porter, from the decision of Burton J on 27 January 2000 granting South Bucks District Council, an injunction under s 187B of the Town and Country Planning Act 1990 requiring the claimant within one year to cease using land at Willow Tree Farm, Iver, Buckinghamshire for stationing caravans and storage and business purposes, to demolish various outbuildings and to remove the hardstanding. The facts are set out in the opinion of Lord Bingham of Cornhill.

Chichester DC v Searle and ors

The defendant, Chichester District Council, appealed with permission of the House of Lords Appeal Committee given on 18 March 2002 from a decision of the Court of Appeal (Simon Brown, Peter Gibson and Tuckey LJJ) on 12 October 2001 ([2001] EWCA Civ 1549, [2002] 1 All ER 425, [2002] 1 WLR 1359) allowing the appeal of the claimants, Darren Searle, Danny Keet and Kim Searle, from the decision of Judge Barratt QC at the Chichester County Court on 30 June 2000 granting Chichester District Council an injunction under s 187B of the Town and Country Planning Act 1990 prohibiting the residential use of certain land by the claimants and requiring them within 28 days to remove mobile homes, certain other structures and the hardcore base. The facts are set out in the opinion of Lord Bingham of Cornhill.

Wrexham County BC v Berry

The defendant, Wrexham County Borough Council, appealed with permission of the House of Lords Appeal Committee given on 18 March 2002 from a decision of the Court of Appeal (Simon Brown, Peter Gibson and Tuckey LJJ) on 12 October 2001 ([2001] EWCA Civ 1549, [2002] 1 All ER 425, [2002] 1 WLR 1359) allowing the appeal of the claimant, Michael Berry, from the decision of McCombe J on 12 February 2001 granting Wrexham County Borough Council, an injunction under s 187B of the Town and Country Planning Act 1990 requiring the claimant to remove all caravans and vehicles off land lying within the Green Barrier near Wrexham. The facts are set out in the opinion of Lord Bingham of Cornhill.

Timothy Straker QC and *Ian Albutt* (instructed by *Sharpe Pritchard* as agents for *Lynne Reardon*, Slough) for South Bucks.

Charles George QC and *Stephen Cottle* (instructed by the *Community Law Partnership*, Birmingham) for Mrs Porter.

Timothy Straker QC and *Robin Green* (instructed by *Sharpe Pritchard* as agents for *Michael J Kelley*, Chichester) for Chichester.

Mr Searle did not appear.

a *Timothy Straker QC* and *Robin Green* (instructed by *Sharpe Pritchard* as agents for *Anthony Williams*, Wrexham) for Wrexham.

Charles George QC and *Stephen Cottle* (instructed by the *Community Law Partnership*, Birmingham) for Mr Berry.

b Their Lordships took time for consideration.

22 May 2003. The following opinions were delivered.

LORD BINGHAM OF CORNHILL.

c [1] My Lords, on 12 October 2001 the Court of Appeal (Simon Brown, Peter Gibson and Tuckey LJJ) ([2001] EWCA Civ 1549, [2002] 1 All ER 425, [2002] 1 WLR 1359) allowed three appeals and dismissed one. The dismissal of the fourth of these appeals (*Hertsmere BC v Harty*) has not been challenged and that case need not be mentioned further. The appellants before the Court of Appeal in each of the three cases now before the House were gipsies complaining of

d injunctions granted against them at first instance on the application of local planning authorities under s 187B of the Town and Country Planning Act 1990. For reasons given by Simon Brown LJ in a judgment with which the other members of the court agreed (at [60], [61]) the gipsies' appeals were allowed and the cases were remitted to the respective trial courts for redetermination. By leave of the House the three local authorities now appeal to it, challenging the

e guidance given by the Court of Appeal on the grant of injunctions under s 187B. The correctness of that guidance is the central issue in these appeals.

[2] Although the Court of Appeal described (at [5]) the facts of these particular cases as of secondary importance only, because the issue raised is one of principle, it is none the less relevant to record the facts in brief summary and to note factual

f developments in the period of 18 months since the Court of Appeal gave judgment.

MR BERRY

[3] Mr Berry bought land near Wrexham, within the Green Barrier, the Welsh equivalent of the Green Belt, in August 1994. The land is within the area of the

g Wrexham County Borough Council. His applications for planning permission to live on the land with his wife and six children were refused in October 1994, December 1995 and July 1999. He and his family were then living on a local authority site at Croesnewydd, but in September 1999 that site was closed and they were evicted. They transferred to another local authority site nearby at

h Ruthin Road but were subjected to violence at the hands of other residents of the site and in September 2000 moved to the land which Mr Berry owned. The local authority warned him that he had no planning permission to use the site in this way, and called on him to rectify this breach of planning control. His solicitor was instructed to say that Mr Berry would apply for planning permission. The local authority however resolved to issue an enforcement notice and seek an

j injunction. The application for an injunction was made on 26 October 2000. The hearing of this application was stayed to await the outcome of an application pending in the European Court of Human Rights (*Chapman v UK* (2001) 10 BHRC 48). On 12 February 2001 the application came before McCombe J, who granted an injunction requiring Mr Berry to remove himself and his caravans and vehicles from the site on or before 20 April 2001. Mr Berry's appeal against this decision was allowed by the Court of Appeal in the decision under appeal. He had by this time, following the grant of the injunction, again applied for planning permission *a* which had again (July 2001) been refused. This refusal prompted the local authority to issue the enforcement notice authorised some ten months earlier, which it did on 31 July 2001. Mr Berry appealed both against the refusal of planning permission and against issue of the enforcement notice. On 18 June 2002 (well after the decisions of the judge and the Court of Appeal) both appeals *b* succeeded. The local authority's challenge to those decisions was rejected by Sullivan J in the Administrative Court but awaits a further hearing by the Court of Appeal.

[4] There was evidence before McCombe J, to which he referred in his judgment (p 10), that Mr Berry had a history of cardiac illness. He had had a severe heart attack in about 1997. He remained under the care of a consultant *c* cardiologist. His symptoms of chest pain were largely controlled by medication, but occasional emergencies required his admission to hospital.

[5] No site was available for occupation by Mr Berry and his family within the local authority's area, except at Ruthin Road.

d

MR SEARLE AND OTHERS

[6] In May 2000 Mr Searle (whom it is unnecessary to distinguish from his co-respondents) bought land within the area of the Chichester District Council from a Mrs Collins for £14,000. She had previously applied for planning permission for residential occupation of the land but had been refused. The land was not within a Green Belt but was in an area where development was closely *e* controlled. Mr Searle was told by the local authority that planning permission was needed to move a mobile home on to the land, and gave more than one assurance that he would not do so, but by 12 June 2000 he had moved two such homes on to the site. He requested a form to apply for planning permission and asked that enforcement action be deferred, but on 19 June the local authority *f* resolved to apply for the grant of an injunction. On 22 June application was made and on 30 June an injunction was granted by Judge Barratt QC, who ordered that both mobile homes be removed forthwith. The Court of Appeal allowed Mr Searle's appeal against that order in the decision now under appeal. After that date, the local authority issued an enforcement notice and Mr Searle appealed against the issue of that notice and also against the refusal of planning permission. *g* It seems that an inquiry was held, the outcome of which is unknown to the House. But Mr Searle and his co-respondents have not appeared to resist the local authority's appeal to the House or uphold the decision of the Court of Appeal. This appeal therefore raises the same issue of principle as those of Mr Berry and Mrs Porter, but whatever the outcome of the appeal there can in this case be no *h* question of remitting the matter to the trial judge or re-imposing the injunction, which is understood to have been overtaken by events.

MRS PORTER

[7] Mrs Porter has lived with her partner in a caravan on a site within the *j* Green Belt at Iver in Buckinghamshire since 1985 when she bought the land. It is within the area of the South Buckinghamshire District Council. She has never had planning permission to live on the site, which her partner has used for breeding and dealing in horses. Applications for planning permission made by her in 1988, 1992, 1993 and 1997 were refused, and her appeals against these refusals were either withdrawn (1992, 1993) or dismissed (1998). Enforcement

a notices were issued in 1987 and 1993: she was fined for non-compliance with the earlier of these notices in 1988; her appeal against the latter was dismissed in 1994. In September 2000 a further application for planning permission was refused, but she appealed and following a public inquiry in January 2002 an inspector, in February 2002, allowed her appeal and granted her planning permission limited to her personal occupation and requiring removal of her caravan as soon as she
b no longer needed it. The reason given by the inspector was that—

> 'The status of [Mrs Porter] as a gipsy, the lack of an alternative site for her to go to in the area and her chronic ill health constitute very special circumstances which are, in this case, sufficient to override national and statutory development GB policies.'

c The local authority challenged the inspector's decision in the Administrative Court before Judge Rich QC in September 2002, but unsuccessfully. Permission was given to the local authority to appeal to the Court of Appeal against his decision, and on 19 May 2003 the appeal was allowed. Meanwhile, however, the present proceedings had been initiated. The local authority provisionally decided,
d subject to legal advice, to seek an injunction on 13 January 1999. Application was duly made on 1 December 1999 and on 27 January 2000 Burton J granted an injunction requiring Mrs Porter to cease to use the land for the stationing of caravans on or before 27 January 2001. It was Mrs Porter's appeal against that decision which led to the judgment now under appeal before the House. It will be noted that planning permission had not been granted to Mrs Porter when
e Burton J and the Court of Appeal made their respective decisions.

[8] Mrs Porter was born in 1942. There was evidence before the trial judge that she suffered from chronic asthma, severe generalised osteo-arthritis and chronic urinary tract infection. Her mobility was poor as a result of her osteo-arthritis and asthma. She suffered from depression and was taking
f painkillers, antibiotics, antidepressants and medication for her asthma. Her general practitioner considered that eviction from the site would be detrimental to her health, which has worsened over the last few years.

[9] There were three residential gipsy sites within the local authority's area, but all of them were full and had long waiting lists; there would be a delay of up to three years before a pitch was likely to become available.

g

PLANNING CONTROL

[10] Over the past 60 years there has been ever-increasing recognition of the need to control the use and development of land so as to prevent inappropriate development and protect the environment. This is, inevitably, a sensitive
h process, since it constrains the freedom of private owners to use their own land as they wish. But it is a very important process, since control, appropriately and firmly exercised, enures to the benefit of the whole community.

[11] It is unnecessary for present purposes to do more than identify the rudiments of the current planning regime, now largely found in the 1990 Act.
j The cornerstone of this regime, regulated by ss 55–106B in Pt III of the Act, is the requirement in s 57(1) that planning permission be obtained for the carrying out of any development of land as defined in s 55. Applications are made to, and in the ordinary way determined in the first instance by, local planning authorities, which are local bodies democratically elected and accountable. The responsibility of the local community for managing its own environment is integral to the system. But the local planning authority's decision is not final. An appeal against

its decision lies to the Secretary of State, on the merits, which will be investigated by an expert, independent inspector empowered to hold an inquiry at which evidence may be received and competing interests heard before advice is tendered to the Secretary of State. The final decision on the merits rests with the Secretary of State, a political officeholder answerable to Parliament. The courts have no statutory role in the granting or refusing of planning permission unless, on purely legal grounds, it is sought to challenge an order made by the local planning authority or the Secretary of State: in such event s 288 of the Act grants a right of application to the High Court. In addition, there exists the general supervisory jurisdiction of the High Court, which may in this field as in others be invoked to control decisions which are made in bad faith, or perversely, or unfairly or otherwise unlawfully. But this is not a jurisdiction directed to the merits of the decision under review.

[12] The second crucial instrument of control provided by the Act is the enforcement notice, which local planning authorities are empowered to issue by s 172 where it appears to them that there has been a breach of planning control and that it is expedient to issue a notice. Once the notice has taken effect, it amounts to a mandatory order to do what the notice specifies as necessary to remedy the breach (s 173). Failure to comply may be penalised, on summary conviction, by a substantial fine, and on conviction on indictment by an unlimited fine (s 179(8)). Persistent non-compliance may give rise to repeated convictions (s 179(6)). The coercive effect of an enforcement notice may be reinforced by a stop notice, which the local planning authority may (save in the case of buildings used as dwelling houses) serve if they consider it expedient that any relevant activity should cease before the expiry of the period for compliance (s 183). Failure to comply may be visited with the same penalties as on non-compliance with an enforcement notice (s 187(2)), and persistent non-compliance may give rise to repeated convictions (s 187(1A)). Again, however, the local planning authority's decision on enforcement is not final: a right of appeal to the Secretary of State lies against an enforcement notice (s 174). On appeal the merits of the planning situation may be fully explored and an application for planning permission may be made (s 174(2)(a)). In this instance also the control regime is entrusted to democratically-accountable bodies, the local planning authority and the Secretary of State. The role of the court is confined to determining a challenge on a point of law to a decision of the Secretary of State (s 289), and to its ordinary supervisory jurisdiction by way of judicial review.

[13] The means of enforcement available to local planning authorities under the 1990 Act and its predecessors, by way of enforcement orders, stop orders and criminal penalties, gave rise to considerable dissatisfaction. There were a number of reasons for this, among them the delay inherent in a process of application, refusal, appeal, continued user, enforcement notice, appeal; the possibility of repeated applications, curbed but not eliminated by s 70A of the 1990 Act; and the opportunities for prevarication and obstruction which the system offered. In the case of gipsies, the problem was compounded by features peculiar to them. Their characteristic lifestyle debarred them from access to conventional sources of housing provision. Their attempts to obtain planning permission almost always met with failure: statistics quoted by the European Court of Human Rights in *Chapman v UK* (2001) 10 BHRC 48 at 65–66 (para 66) showed that in 1991, the most recent year for which figures were available, 90% of applications made by gipsies had been refused whereas 80% of all applications had been granted. But for many years the capacity of sites authorised for occupation by gipsies has fallen

a well short of that needed to accommodate those seeking space on which to station their caravans. Sedley J alluded to this problem in *R v Lincolnshire CC, ex p Atkinson* (1995) 8 Admin LR 529 at 533, in a passage quoted in *Chapman*'s case (2001) 10 BHRC 48 at 59–60 (para 45):

b 'It is relevant to situate this new and in some ways Draconic legislation in its context. For centuries the commons of England provided lawful stopping places for people whose way of life was or had become nomadic. Enough common land had survived the centuries of enclosure to make this way of life still sustainable, but by section 23 of the Caravan Sites and Control of Development Act 1960 local authorities were given power to close the commons to travellers. This they proceeded to do with great energy, but c made no use of the concomitant power given to them by section 24 of the same Act to open caravan sites to compensate for the closure of the commons. By the Caravan Sites Act 1968, therefore, Parliament legislated to make the section 24 power a duty, resting in rural areas upon county councils rather than district councils (although the latter continued to possess the d power to open sites). For the next quarter of a century there followed a history of non-compliance with the duties imposed by the Act of 1968, marked by a series of decisions of this court holding local authorities to be in breach of their statutory duty, to apparently little practical effect. The default powers vested in central government, to which the court was required to defer, were rarely if ever used.'

e The essential problem was succinctly stated in a housing research summary, 'Local Authority Powers for Managing Unauthorised Camping' (Office of the Deputy Prime Minister, No 90, 1998, updated 4 December 2000):

f 'The basic conflict underlying the "problem" of unauthorised camping is between gipsies/travellers who want to stay in an area for a period but have nowhere they can legally camp, and the settled community who, by and large, do not want gipsies/travellers camped in their midst. The local authority is stuck between the two parties, trying to balance the conflicting needs and often satisfying no one.'

g [14] The perceived inadequacy of local authorities' enforcement powers led them to seek injunctive relief, whether in a relator action in the name of the Attorney General (as in *A-G (on the relation of Hornchurch UDC) v Bastow* [1957] 1 All ER 497, [1957] 1 QB 514, a case involving caravans but not gipsies), or by invoking the general injunctive power of the court (as in *Manchester Corp v* h *Connolly* [1970] 1 All ER 961, [1970] Ch 420), or, later, under s 222 of the Local Government Act 1972 as in *Waverley BC v Hilden* [1988] 1 All ER 807, [1988] 1 WLR 2466 and *Mole Valley DC v Smith* (1992) 90 LGR 557). Dissatisfaction with the efficacy of measures to enforce planning control however persisted, and in July 1988 Mr Robert Carnwath QC was asked by the Secretary of State to j examine the scope and effectiveness of existing enforcement provisions and recommend improvements.

[15] In his report ('Enforcing Planning Control', February 1989), Mr Carnwath acknowledged (p 21 (para 1.1)) that the enforcement system had received a consistently bad press ever since the beginning of modern planning control in 1947. He recognised (p 24 (para 2.8)) that—

'The enforcement system therefore cannot be too rigid. There will always be difficult cases where there is a need to balance the interests of enforcement against the individual circumstances of a business or individual. The system needs to be flexible enough to accommodate such cases, while providing the teeth to secure effective action where it is justified. There will always be disagreement as to where the line is to be drawn.'

Mr Carnwath considered (p 41 (para 2.22)) that the best approach lay in recognition of the injunction as a back-up to the normal statutory remedies, since 'Use of the Courts ensures that both sides are fully protected, and that the remedies can be adapted to suit the needs of the case'. He favoured a formalisation and clarification, but not a significant extension, of the existing law, to give statutory recognition to this 'useful weapon in the planning armoury' (p 41 (2.23)). His recommendation on this matter was expressed in these terms (pp 85–86):

'10.1 As explained above (chapter 5, section 2), injunctions have proved a useful back-up to the statutory system in difficult cases. However, there are still doubts about the circumstances in which the remedy is available. In particular, it is unclear to what extent it is available to restrain an actual or threatened breach of planning control before it has become a criminal offence (following service of an enforcement notice or stop notice).

10.2 In my view the authority should be able to apply for an injunction in respect of any breach or threatened breach of planning control, whether or not an enforcement notice or stop notice has been served. There are likely to be two sets of circumstances where it will be especially useful. First, it can provide an urgent remedy in cases where there is a serious threat to amenity, to deal with either a threatened breach (before a stop notice can be served) or an actual breach (for example, where there are problems in preparing an effective enforcement and stop notice in time). Secondly, it can provide a stronger back-up power in cases where the existing remedies have proved, or are thought likely to be, inadequate. The latter function is well recognised in existing case-law, and has a precedent, for example, in section 58(8) of the Control of Pollution Act 1974.

10.3 I think it would be a mistake to attempt to prescribe too closely the circumstances in which the remedy would be available, or the forms of order which could be granted. Experience of decisions over the last few years (see Chapter 5 above) shows that the merit of the remedy is its flexibility and its ability to evolve to meet changing needs. What is required is its recognition in the Act as a normal back-up to the other remedies, and acceptance that it is for the authority to judge (subject to the ordinary judicial review criteria of reasonableness) when its use is appropriate. The court already has a wide discretion as to the terms on which an order is to be made. In cases where an order is made in advance of an enforcement or stop notice, the terms could include an undertaking by the authority to serve such notices, so that the ordinary procedures would be available for determining the merits and protecting the recipient.'

[16] Legislative effect was given to Mr Carnwath's recommendation by s 187B, inserted into the 1990 Act by s 3 of the Planning and Compensation Act 1991, which became effective on 2 January 1992. The correct interpretation and application of this section lie at the heart of these appeals. It provides:

a
'*Injunctions restraining breaches of planning control.*—(1) Where a local planning authority consider it necessary or expedient for any actual or apprehended breach of planning control to be restrained by injunction, they may apply to the court for an injunction, whether or not they have exercised or are proposing to exercise any of their other powers under this Part.

b
(2) On an application under subsection (1) the court may grant such an injunction as the court thinks appropriate for the purpose of restraining the breach.

(3) Rules of court may provide for such an injunction to be issued against a person whose identity is unknown.

(4) In this section "the court" means the High Court or the county court.'

c
[17] Since the enactment of the section the Department of the Environment has given guidance to local planning authorities on the exercise of enforcement powers which, although inadmissible to construe the section, throws light on what was officially understood to be its effect. Thus in circular 21/91 ('Planning and Compensation Act 1991: Implementation of the Main Enforcement Provisions', 16 December 1991) it was stated:

d
'7 The decision whether to grant an injunction is always solely a matter for the court, in its absolute discretion in the circumstances of any case. Nevertheless, it is unlikely that the court will grant an injunction unless all the following criteria are satisfied:- (1) the LPA [local planning authority] have taken account of what appear to be the relevant considerations in deciding that it is necessary or expedient to initiate injunctive proceedings;

e
(2) there is clear evidence that a breach of planning, listed building, or conservation area control, or unauthorised work on a protected tree, has already occurred, or is likely to occur, on land in the LPA's area; (3) injunctive relief is a commensurate remedy in the circumstances of the particular case ... Even when all these criteria are satisfied, the court may

f
decide that the circumstances of the case do not, on the balance of convenience, justify granting an injunction. If an injunction is granted, the court may suspend its effect until a specified later date.'

This advice was substantially repeated in circular 10/97 ('Enforcing Planning

g
Control: Legislative Provisions and Procedural Requirements', 31 July 1997, paras 5.5–5.10), with the substitution of 'proportionate' for 'commensurate' but again with reference to the 'absolute' discretion of the court. In ch 9 of Enforcing Planning Control: Good Practice Guide for Local Planning Authorities (1997), the Department of Environment, Transport and the Regions addressed the topic again:

h
'*The personal nature of injunctive proceedings*
9.9.   Unlike an enforcement notice or a stop notice, a planning enforcement injunction is not primarily directed at the parcel of land on which the breach of control is taking place. Injunctive proceedings are

j
"personal" in the sense that the LPA seeks to obtain an order from the court to restrain a person, or a number of people, who must each be cited by name in the LPA's application, from carrying on the breach. It follows that, in assessing what is called "the balance of convenience" in the decision whether to grant injunctive relief on the LPA's application, the court will have to weigh the public interest (which the LPA represents) against the private interest of the person or people whom the LPA seek to restrain. This differs

from, for example, the process of an enforcement appeal where the
decision-maker is concerned with whether the appeal should succeed on its
legal or planning merits. And, even if the court concludes that an
interlocutory injunction should be granted, its effect may be suspended for a
specified period so that the defendant has time in which to make suitable
alternative arrangements for whatever activity is to be restrained. The court
may require the plaintiff (the LPA) and the defendant to appear in person at
the end of an initial period of suspension of an injunction, so that the balance
of convenience can be reassessed.'

THE COURT OF APPEAL DECISION

[18] In the Court of Appeal separate teams of counsel represented the
appellant gipsies and the respondent local authorities and the submissions made
on each side were not to identical effect. Simon Brown LJ summarised the
gipsies' argument (see [2002] 1 All ER 425 at [29]–[34]). In broad summary the
argument, in all essentials the argument repeated by Mr Charles George QC in
the House, was to the following effect. Section 187B gives the judge a discretion,
to be exercised as an original jurisdiction not a review power. Since injunctions
are likely to prove the most effective way of remedying breaches of planning
control, because attended by the most severe sanctions, including imprisonment,
they should be granted only where plainly appropriate and where the court is
willing to contemplate the imposition of severe penalties. If the court is unwilling
to commit it should be unwilling to enjoin. In cases such as Mole Valley DC v Smith
(1992) 90 LGR 557 and Hambleton DC v Bird [1995] 3 PLR 8 the court had taken
too narrow a view of its discretion. The court—

'would only be prepared to grant injunctive relief in cases which the court
itself regarded as clear, cases where it was quite satisfied first that the
planning authority (whether the district council or the Secretary of
State/inspector on appeal) had properly reached a final conclusion that the
gipsies' continuing occupation of the site could no longer be tolerated in
the public interest, and secondly that it was appropriate to enforce their
removal by injunction even though, in a case where no alternative sites were
available, that would drive the gipsies either onto the roads, into
homelessness accommodation (see Chapman v UK (2001) BHRC 48 at 62–63
(para 54)) or, on non-compliance with the injunction, into prison.' (See
[2002] 1 All ER 425 at [31].)

Whatever the position before the Human Rights Act 1998, the court must now
address the issues arising under art 8(2) of the European Convention for the
Protection of Human Rights and Fundamental Freedoms 1950 (as set out in Sch 1
to the 1998 Act) and reach its own decision on whether the gipsies' removal from
the site is proportionate to the public interest in preserving the environment.
This did not mean that the court would pay no heed to the decisions of local
planning authorities: issues as to whether or not planning permission should be
granted are exclusively a matter for them, and the planning history of the site,
including any recent decisions, will be highly relevant. Respect should be
accorded to the decisions of a democratically accountable body. But it is still for
the court to reach its own independent conclusion on the proportionality of the
relief sought to the object to be attained.

a **[19]** In the Court of Appeal Mr Timothy Straker QC represented the three local authorities now before the House and Simon Brown LJ summarised (at [35]) his essential argument as being—

> *b* 'that the judge exercising his s 187B jurisdiction is more or less bound to grant an injunction unless the local planning authority's application can be shown to be flawed on *Wednesbury* grounds [see *Associated Provincial Picture Houses Ltd v Wednesbury Corp* [1947] 2 All ER 680, [1948] 1 KB 223].'

c The court's function is supervisory. The power to grant an injunction should be exercised in support of planning control. The *Mole Valley* and *Hambleton* cases were rightly decided. Not until the stage of committal for breach of an injunction is the court entitled to reach an independent view on proportionality. At the injunction stage the court should consider only whether the gipsies should leave the site, not whether they should suffer serious penalty if they fail to do so. The court's role is unaffected by the 1998 Act. Reliance was placed on the decision of the House in *R (on the application of Alconbury Developments Ltd) v Secretary of State for the Environment, Transport and the Regions* [2001] UKHL 23, [2001] 2 All ER 929,

d [2001] 2 WLR 1389.

[20] The Court of Appeal's ruling on the approach to s 187B was expressed in five paragraphs of Simon Brown LJ's judgment, which I must quote in extenso:

'THE APPROACH TO SECTION 187B

e [38] I would unhesitatingly reject the more extreme submissions made on either side. It seems to me perfectly clear that the judge on a s 187B application is not required, nor even entitled, to reach his own independent view of the planning merits of the case. These he is required to take as decided within the planning process, the actual or anticipated breach of

f planning control being a given when he comes to exercise his discretion. But it seems to me no less plain that the judge should not grant injunctive relief unless he would be prepared if necessary to contemplate committing the defendant to prison for breach of the order, and that he would not be of this mind unless he had considered for himself all questions of hardship for the defendant and his family if required to move, necessarily including,

g therefore, the availability of suitable alternative sites. I cannot accept that the consideration of those matters is, as Burton J suggested was the case in the pre-1998 Act era, "entirely foreclosed"' at the injunction stage. Questions of the family's health and education will inevitably be of relevance. But so too, of course, will countervailing considerations such as the need to enforce

h planning control in the general interest and, importantly therefore, the planning history of the site. The degree and flagrancy of the postulated breach of planning control may well prove critical. If conventional enforcement measures have failed over a prolonged period of time to remedy the breach, then the court would obviously be the readier to use its own, more coercive powers. Conversely, however, the court might well be

j reluctant to use its powers in a case where enforcement action had never been taken. On the other hand, there might be some urgency in the situation sufficient to justify the pre-emptive avoidance of an anticipated breach of planning control. Considerations of health and safety might arise. Preventing a gipsy moving onto the site might, indeed, involve him in less hardship than moving him out after a long period of occupation. Previous planning decisions will always be relevant; how relevant, however, will inevitably depend on a variety of matters, including not least how recent they are, the extent to which considerations of hardship and availability of alternative sites were taken into account, the strength of the conclusions reached on land use and environmental issues, and whether the defendant had and properly took the opportunity to make his case for at least a temporary personal planning permission.

[39] Relevant too will be the local authority's decision under s 187B(1) to seek injunctive relief. They, after all, are the democratically-elected and accountable body principally responsible for planning control in their area. Again, however, the relevance and weight of their decision will depend above all on the extent to which they can be shown to have had regard to all the material considerations and to have properly posed and approached the art 8(2) questions as to necessity and proportionality.

[40] Whilst it is not for the court to question the correctness of the existing planning status of the land, the court in deciding whether or not to grant an injunction (and, if so, whether and for how long to suspend it) is bound to come to some broad view as to the degree of environmental damage resulting from the breach and the urgency or otherwise of bringing it to an end. In this regard the court need not shut its mind to the possibility of the planning authority itself coming to reach a different planning judgment in the case.

[41] True it is, as Mr McCracken [counsel for Hertsmere BC] points out, that, once the planning decision is taken as final, the legitimate aim of preserving the environment is only achievable by removing the gipsies from site. That is not to say, however, that the achievement of that aim must always be accepted by the court to outweigh whatever countervailing rights the gipsies may have, still less that the court is bound to grant injunctive (least of all immediate injunctive) relief. Rather I prefer the approach suggested by the 1991 circular: the court's discretion is absolute and injunctive relief is unlikely unless properly thought to be "commensurate"—in today's language, proportionate. The *Hambleton* approach seems to me difficult to reconcile with that circular. However, whatever view one takes of the correctness of the *Hambleton* approach in the period prior to the coming into force of the 1998 Act, to my mind it cannot be thought consistent with the court's duty under s 6(1) to act compatibly with convention rights. Proportionality requires not only that the injunction be appropriate and necessary for the attainment of the public interest objective sought—here the safeguarding of the environment—but also that it does not impose an excessive burden on the individual whose private interests—here the gipsy's private life and home and the retention of his ethnic identity—are at stake.

[42] I do not pretend that it will always be easy in any particular case to strike the necessary balance between these competing interests, interests of so different a character that weighing one against the other must inevitably be problematic. This, however, is the task to be undertaken by the court and, provided it is undertaken in a structured and articulated way, the appropriate conclusion should emerge.'

MOLE VALLEY DC v SMITH

a

[21] Before considering the merits of the competing arguments and the correctness of the guidance given by the Court of Appeal, account should be taken of earlier Court of Appeal authority. *Mole Valley DC v Smith* (1992) 90 LGR 557 was one of two appeals heard and reported together. The other was *Reigate and Banstead BC v Brown*, which involved different gipsies and a different

b (although neighbouring) local authority.

[22] In the *Mole Valley* case the gipsies appealed against the grant of an injunction by Hoffmann J at first instance under s 222 of the 1972 Act. The facts disclosed (at 565–566) a history of unsuccessful enforcement by the local planning authority and non-compliance by the gipsies over several years. The principal issue before the Court of Appeal was whether the gipsies could successfully resist

c eviction by the local planning authority on the ground that a different body, the county council, had fallen down on its statutory duty to provide enough pitches to accommodate the gipsies seeking them (see (1992) 90 LGR 557 at 559–560). Lord Donaldson of Lymington MR held (at 568) that they could not, a conclusion shared by Balcombe LJ (at 569) and Stuart-Smith LJ (at 570). Lord Donaldson of

d Lymington MR approved (at 567) a passage in the judgment of Hoffmann J where he had said:

'There can be no doubt that requiring [the defendants] to leave the site would cause considerable hardship. This court, however, is not entrusted with a general jurisdiction to solve social problems. The striking of a balance

e between the requirements of planning policy and the needs of these defendants is a matter which, in my view, has been entrusted to other authorities.'

The Court of Appeal did not approach this case as one turning on hardship to the

f gipsies, which was not relied on as a ground of appeal. No reference was made to age, infirmity, ill-health or the reasonable needs of children. The Court of Appeal furthermore understood (at 563) that a number of additional pitches would become available in the reasonably near future, declined to shorten the period allowed by the judge for complying with the injunction (at 568–569) and envisaged that in deciding whether to enforce the injunction the local planning

g authority would have regard to the availability of alternative authorised pitches 'very shortly thereafter' (at 569).

[23] In the *Reigate and Banstead* case the principal issue was the same (see (1992) 90 LGR 557 at 559–560) but the evidence of unsuccessful enforcement and non-compliance was even stronger (at 563–565). There was little prospect of

h additional pitches becoming available in this area in the near future (see (1992) 90 LGR 557 at 563). In this case the gipsies did rely on what they claimed (at 559) would be exceptional hardship if interlocutory relief were granted pending trial, but no allusion was made to this ground of appeal in the judgments and no reference was made to the personal circumstances of the gipsies. The court

j granted the same period of suspension (at 568–569), and made (at 569) the same observation about enforcement, envisaging, it would seem, that these gipsies would take advantage of the additional pitches expected to become available nearby.

[24] The ratio of both decisions was that the problems confronting the gipsies, the local planning authorities and the county council—

'are social in nature and fall to be solved in the context of town and country planning policies. These are matters ultimately for the Secretary of State, subject only to the court's supervisory jurisdiction by means of judicial review which is not invoked in these proceedings.' (See (1992) 90 LGR 557 at 566.)

HAMBLETON DC v BIRD

[25] In this case ([1995] 3 PLR 8) the local authority appealed against the refusal of the trial judge to grant an injunction under s 187B to restrain the respondent gipsies, a large family, from continuing to use land, which they owned, for the purpose of siting residential caravans. The gipsies had used the site, in breach of planning control, for a number of years. Applications for planning permission had been refused and an enforcement notice had proved ineffective, as had prosecutions for non-compliance (see [1995] 3 PLR 8 at 9–11). In declining to grant an injunction the judge had referred to the financial burden on the local authority of housing the gipsies, money which the judge plainly thought could be better spent (see [1995] 3 PLR 8 at 12), and he considered it wrong to grant an injunction, which would cause 'gross disruption to no great public benefit' when the gipsies were contemplating a further planning application which might arguably succeed (see [1995] 3 PLR 8 at 12).

[26] Giving the leading judgment in the Court of Appeal, Pill LJ made detailed reference to the *Mole Valley* case, and also to a decision of Scott J in *Waverley BC v Hilden* [1988] 1 All ER 807 at 821–822, [1988] 1 WLR 246 at 264. He criticised (at 15) the trial judge for taking it upon himself to assess the benefits and disbenefits to the public as a whole and to exercise the policy function of planning and housing authorities. He also held (at 15) that the possibility of a future grant of planning permission was not a legitimate reason for refusing an injunction to restrain a breach of the law. These errors were held to vitiate the judge's exercise of discretion, and exercising a fresh discretion Pill LJ thought it clear that an injunction should be granted, a conclusion with which Sir Ralph Gibson (at 16) and Balcombe LJ (at 18) agreed. In the course of his judgment Pill LJ made no reference to hardship. He accepted (at 12) that at the date of trial no alternative site was available, although Sir Ralph Gibson (at 17) thought it clear that such a site would before long become available, and he discounted the gipsies' objections to it.

SECTION 187B

[27] The jurisdiction of the court under s 187B is an original, not a supervisory, jurisdiction. The supervisory jurisdiction of the court is invoked when a party asks it to review an exercise of public power. A local planning authority seeking an injunction to restrain an actual or apprehended breach of planning control does nothing of the kind. Like other applicants for injunctive relief it asks the court to exercise its power to grant such relief. It is of course open to the defendant, in resisting the grant of an injunction, to seek to impugn the local authority's decision to apply for an injunction on any of the conventional grounds which may be relied on to found an application for judicial review. As Carnwath J observed in *R v Basildon DC, ex p Clarke* [1996] JPL 866 at 869:

'If something had gone seriously wrong with the procedure, whether in the initiation of the injunction proceedings or in any other way, it was

a
difficult to see why the County Court judge could not properly take it into account in the exercise of his discretion to grant or refuse the injunction.'

But a defendant seeking to resist the grant of an injunction is not restricted to reliance on grounds which would found an application for judicial review.

[28] The court's power to grant an injunction under s 187B is a discretionary
b power. The permissive 'may' in sub-s (2) applies not only to the terms of any injunction the court may grant but also to the decision whether it should grant any injunction. It is indeed inherent in the concept of an injunction in English law that it is a remedy that the court may but need not grant, depending on its judgment of all the circumstances. Underpinning the court's jurisdiction to grant an injunction is s 37(1) of the Supreme Court Act 1981, conferring power to do so
c 'in all cases in which it appears to the court to be just and convenient to do so'. Thus the court is not obliged to grant an injunction because a local authority considers it necessary or expedient for any actual or apprehended breach of planning control to be restrained by injunction and so makes application to the court. No assistance is gained from *R v Wicks* [1997] 2 All ER 801, [1998] AC 92,
d relied on by the local authorities, where it was held to be too late to challenge an enforcement notice in criminal proceedings, a situation quite unlike the present.

[29] The court's discretion to grant or withhold relief is not however unfettered (and by quoting the word 'absolute' from the 1991 circular ([2002] 1 All ER 425 at [41]) Simon Brown LJ cannot have intended to suggest that it was). The discretion of the court under s 187B, like every other judicial discretion, must
e be exercised judicially. That means, in this context, that the power must be exercised with due regard to the purpose for which the power was conferred: to restrain actual and threatened breaches of planning control. The power exists above all to permit abuses to be curbed and urgent solutions provided where these are called for. Since the facts of different cases are infinitely various, no
f single test can be prescribed to distinguish cases in which the court's discretion should be exercised in favour of granting an injunction from those in which it should not. Where it appears that a breach or apprehended breach will continue or occur unless and until effectively restrained by the law and that nothing short of an injunction will provide effective restraint (*City of London Corp v Bovis Construction Ltd* [1992] 3 All ER 697 at 714), that will point strongly towards the
g grant of an injunction. So will a history of unsuccessful enforcement and persistent non-compliance, as will evidence that the defendant has played the system by wilfully exploiting every opportunity for prevarication and delay, although s 187B(1) makes plain that a local planning authority, in applying for an injunction, need not have exercised nor propose to exercise any of its other
h enforcement powers under Pt VII of the Act. In cases such as these the task of the court may be relatively straightforward. But in all cases the court must decide whether in all the circumstances it is just to grant the relief sought against the particular defendant.

[30] As shown above the 1990 Act, like its predecessors, allocates the control of development of land to democratically-accountable bodies, local planning
j authorities and the Secretary of State. Issues of planning policy and judgment are within their exclusive purview. As Lord Scarman pointed out in *Pioneer Aggregates (UK) Ltd v Secretary of State for the Environment* [1984] 2 All ER 358 at 363, [1985] AC 132 at 141, 'Parliament has provided a comprehensive code of planning control'. In *R (on the application of Alconbury Developments Ltd) v Secretary of State for the Environment, Transport and the Regions* [2001] UKHL 23 at [48], [60], [75], [129],

[132], [139]–[140], [159], [2001] 2 All ER 929 at [48], [60], [75], [129], [132],
[139]–[140], [159], [2001] 2 WLR 1389 the limited role of the court in the planning
field is made very clear. An application by a local planning authority under s 187B
is not an invitation to the court to exercise functions allocated elsewhere. Thus
it could never be appropriate for the court to hold that planning permission
should not have been refused or that an appeal against an enforcement notice
should have succeeded or (as in *Hambleton DC v Bird* [1995] 3 PLR 8) that a local
authority should have had different spending priorities. But the court is not
precluded from entertaining issues not related to planning policy or judgment,
such as the visibility of a development from a given position or the width of a
road. Nor need the court refuse to consider (pace the *Hambleton* case) the
possibility that a pending or prospective application for planning permission may
succeed, since there may be material to suggest that a party previously
unsuccessful may yet succeed, as the cases of Mr Berry and Mrs Porter show. But
all will depend on the particular facts, and the court must always, of course, act
on evidence.

[31] In *Westminster City Council v Great Portland Estates plc* [1984] 3 All ER 744
at 750, [1985] AC 661 at 670 Lord Scarman drew attention to the relevance to
planning decisions, on occasion, of personal considerations:

> 'Personal circumstances of an occupier, personal hardship, the difficulties
> of businesses which are of value to the character of a community are not
> to be ignored in the administration of planning control. It would be
> inhuman pedantry to exclude from the control of our development the
> human factor. The human factor is always present, of course, indirectly as
> the background to the consideration of the character of land use. It can,
> however, and sometimes should, be given direct effect as an exceptional or
> special circumstance. But such circumstances, when they arise, fall to be
> considered not as a general rule but as exceptions to a general rule to be
> met in special cases. If a planning authority is to give effect to them, a
> specific case has to be made and the planning authority must give reasons
> for accepting it. It follows that, though the existence of such cases may be
> mentioned in a plan, this will only be necessary where it is prudent to
> emphasise that, notwithstanding the general policy, exceptions cannot be
> wholly excluded from consideration in the administration of planning
> control.'

Ouseley J made the same point more recently in *Basildon DC v Secretary of State for
the Environment, Transport and the Regions* [2001] JPL 1184, an appeal under s 288
of the 1990 Act, when he said (at 1193 (para 33)):

> 'From that analysis I conclude, first, that quite apart from any
> considerations of common humanity, the needs of these particular gypsy
> families were a material consideration because they had a need for this
> development in this location. Those personal circumstances entitled the
> Secretary of State to have regard to them as relevant to the decision he had
> to make in the public interest about the use of the land for the stationing of
> residential caravans. Their particular need for stability in the interest of the
> education of the younger children can also reasonably be seen as an aspect of
> the wider land use interest in the provision of gypsy sites, which interest
> includes the need for stable educational opportunities. There is also a public

a   interest in the planning system providing stable educational opportunities
         for gypsy families, including these gypsy families.'

Thus the Secretary of State was entitled to have regard to the personal
circumstances of the gipsies, as he did in the cases of Mr Berry and Mrs Porter.
When application is made to the court under s 187B, the evidence will usually
b   make clear whether, and to what extent, the local planning authority has taken
account of the personal circumstances of the defendant and any hardship an
injunction may cause. If it appears that these aspects have been neglected and on
examination they weigh against the grant of relief, the court will be readier to
refuse it. If it appears that the local planning authority has fully considered them
and none the less resolved that it is necessary or expedient to seek relief, this will
c   ordinarily weigh heavily in favour of granting relief, since the court must accord
respect to the balance which the local planning authority has struck between
public and private interests. It is, however, ultimately for the court to decide
whether the remedy sought is just and proportionate in all the circumstances, and
there is force in the observation attributed to Václav Havel, no doubt informed
by the dire experience of central Europe: 'The Gypsies are a litmus test not of
d   democracy but of civil society' (quoted by McCracken and Jones, counsel for
Hertsmere in the fourth appeal, 'Article 8 ECHR, Gypsies, and Some Remaining
Problems after *South Buckinghamshire*' [2003] JPL 382 at 396, fn 99).

[32] When granting an injunction the court does not contemplate that it will
be disobeyed (see *Re Liddell's Settlement Trusts, Liddell v Liddell* [1936] 1 All ER 239
e   at 247–248, [1936] Ch 365 at 373–374; *Castanho v Brown & Root (UK) Ltd* [1981]
1 All ER 143 at 150, [1981] AC 557 at 574). Apprehension that a party may disobey
an order should not deter the court from making an order otherwise appropriate:
there is not one law for the law-abiding and another for the lawless and truculent.
When making an order, the court should ordinarily be willing to enforce it if
f   necessary. The rule of law is not well served if orders are made and disobeyed
with impunity. These propositions however rest on the assumption that the
order made by the court is just in all the circumstances and one with which the
defendant can and reasonably ought to comply, an assumption which ordinarily
applies both when the order is made and when the time for enforcement arises.
Since a severe financial penalty may be imposed for failure to comply with an
g   enforcement notice, the main additional sanction provided by the grant of an
injunction is that of imprisonment. The court should ordinarily be slow to make
an order which it would not at that time be willing, if need be, to enforce by
imprisonment. But imprisonment in this context is intended not to punish but to
induce compliance, reinforcing the requirement that the order be one with which
h   the defendant can and reasonably ought to comply. The court ought not to face
the dilemma addressed by Staughton LJ in *Guildford BC v Smith* [1994] JPL 734 at
739.

[33] There is no reason to doubt that *Mole Valley DC v Smith* (1992) 90 LGR 557
and *Hambleton DC v Bird* [1995] 3 PLR 8 were rightly decided on their facts, but
they should now be read subject to this opinion.
j

ARTICLE 8 OF THE EUROPEAN CONVENTION ON HUMAN RIGHTS
[34] If s 187B is interpreted and applied in accordance with the principles
adumbrated in the foregoing paragraphs, it is very questionable whether art 8 of
the convention has any bearing on the court's approach to an application under
the section. But since the European Court of Human Rights has given judgment

in two cases involving gipsies in the United Kingdom, brief reference should be
made to those cases. In both it was effectively common ground that enforcement
action by the local planning authority to secure the removal of the gipsy from a
site involved an interference by a public authority with the gipsy's right to respect
for her home, that such interference was in accordance with the law and that the
measures pursued aims entitled to recognition under the convention as
legitimate. The issue was whether measures were 'necessary in a democratic
society' or, differently expressed, whether the means employed to pursue those
legitimate aims were proportionate.

[35] In *Buckley v UK* (1996) 23 EHRR 101 at 120 (paras 84–86) the Commission
concluded, by a narrow majority, that the measures were excessive and
disproportionate. Even allowing for the margin of appreciation enjoyed by the
national authorities, the Commission found that the interests of the applicant
outweighed the general interest. The court, also by a majority, took the opposite
view: it concluded (at 132 (para 84)) that the responsible planning authorities had
arrived at their decision after weighing in the balance the various competing
interests at issue; that it was not for the court to sit in appeal on the merits of that
decision; that the reasons relied on by the planning authorities were relevant and
sufficient; and that the means employed to achieve the legitimate aims pursued
could not be regarded as disproportionate.

[36] A majority of the court again rejected the complaint of the applicant in
Chapman v UK (2001) 33 EHRR 399. The report of this case contains a helpful and
detailed summary of the factual background and also makes reference to the
Framework Convention for the Protection of National Minorities (ETS no 157),
which the United Kingdom ratified and which came into force in May 1998 (the
framework convention) (see also (2001) 10 BHRC 48). In this case the
Commission found, by a majority, that there had been no violation of
Mrs Chapman's rights under art 8 ((2001) 10 BHRC 48 at 66 (para 69)), and a
majority of the court agreed (at 75 (para 115)). The court recognised (at 67 (para
73)) that Mrs Chapman's occupation of her caravan was an integral part of her
ethnic identity as a gipsy but acknowledged (at 70 (para 92)) that as a
supranational court it was ill-equipped to assess matters within the proper
purview of national authorities and did not accept (at 71 (para 94)) that a
consensus had emerged on the practical steps necessary to give effect to the
framework convention. It envisaged (at 71 (para 95)) that problems might arise
under art 14 if gipsies were treated differently from non-gipsies. In rejecting
Mrs Chapman's complaint the court (at 74 (para 113)) was not persuaded that
there were no alternatives available to her other than remaining in occupation of
land without planning permission in a Green Belt area and held (at 75 (para 115)):

'The humanitarian considerations which might have supported another
outcome at national level cannot be used as the basis of a finding by the court
which would be tantamount to exempting the applicant from the
implementation of the national planning laws and obliging governments to
ensure that every gipsy family has available for its use accommodation
appropriate to its needs. Furthermore, the effect of these decisions cannot
on the facts of this case be regarded as disproportionate to the legitimate aim
being pursued.'

[37] These cases make plain that decisions properly and fairly made by
national authorities must command respect. They also make plain that any
interference with a person's right to respect for her home, even if in accordance

a with national law and directed to a legitimate aim, must be proportionate. As a public authority, the English court is prohibited by s 6(1) and (3)(a) of the Human Rights Act 1998 from acting incompatibly with any convention right as defined in the Act, including art 8. It follows, in my opinion, that when asked to grant injunctive relief under s 187B the court must consider whether, on the facts of the case, such relief is proportionate in the convention sense, and grant relief only if

b it judges it to be so. Although domestic law is expressed in terms of justice and convenience rather than proportionality, this is in all essentials the task which the court is in any event required by domestic law to carry out. I should add that while nothing in the Court of Appeal judgment in *Sheffield City Council v Smart, Central Sunderland Housing Co Ltd v Wilson* [2002] EWCA Civ 4, [2002] LGR 467 is, as I read it, inconsistent with what is said above, I should be wary of concluding

c that any action by a public authority seeking possession of residential property occupied by a defendant engages the operation of art 8.

CONCLUSION

[38] The guidance given by the Court of Appeal in the judgment of Simon

d Brown LJ quoted in [20], above was in my opinion judicious and accurate in all essential respects and I would endorse it.

[39] In the Berry case the Court of Appeal concluded ([2002] 1 All ER 425 at [49]) that the trial judge had erred in regarding *Chapman's* case as effectively determinative of the application before him. I find no fault with that conclusion. I would accordingly dismiss this appeal with costs, and affirm the Court of

e Appeal's order that the matter be remitted to the Queen's Bench Division for the underlying application for an injunction to be determined.

[40] In the Searle case I would again dismiss the appeal, but with no order for costs and no order for remission. The Court of Appeal was entitled to conclude (at [44]) that the trial judge had taken too restricted a view of the discretion which

f he was called upon to exercise.

[41] In the Porter case I would dismiss the appeal and make the same orders as in the Berry case. The judge was wrong to regard all questions of hardship as 'entirely foreclosed' by the *Mole Valley* and *Hambleton* decisions, as the Court of Appeal rightly held (at [43]).

[42] I have had the advantage of reading in draft the opinions of my noble and

g learned friends with which I agree.

LORD STEYN.

[43] My Lords, the question is how s 187B of the Town and Country Planning Act 1990 (as inserted in the 1990 Act by the Planning and Compensation Act 1991)

h should be interpreted. Section 187B reads as follows:

> '(1) Where a local planning authority consider it necessary or expedient for any actual or apprehended breach of planning control to be restrained by injunction, they may apply to the court for an injunction, whether or not they have exercised or are proposing to exercise any of their other powers

j
> under this Part.
>
> (2) On an application under subsection (1) the court may grant such an injunction as the court thinks appropriate for the purpose of restraining the breach.
>
> (3) Rules of court may provide for such an injunction to be issued against a person whose identity is unknown.

(4) In this section "the court" means the High Court or the county court.'

a

The Civil Procedure Rules 1998 make the provision contemplated by sub-s (3): RSC Ord 110, r 1; CCR, Ord 49, r 7.

[44] The question of interpretation before the Court of Appeal ([2001] EWCA Civ 1549, [2002] 1 All ER 425, [2002] 1 WLR 1359) was whether (as three local planning authorities contended) it is beyond the power of the court under s 187B(2) to take into account in the exercise of its discretion the hardship likely b to be caused by an injunction to vacate land in the case of a defendant who was in ill health and had nowhere else to go. Counsel for the local authorities acknowledged that in accordance with the law as stated in *Westminster City Council v Great Portland Estates plc* [1984] 3 All ER 744, [1985] AC 661 such matters are relevant to the decisions of local authorities and the Secretary of State. c Overruling first instance decisions the Court of Appeal held that such matters may also be relevant to the exercise of the discretion of the court under s 187B and it remitted the decisions for rehearing at first instance. The local authorities now challenge the decision of the Court of Appeal.

[45] The setting of s 187B is as follows. By the 1980s it had become a notorious fact that determined individuals and enterprises could, by playing the system d with the aid of lawyers, frustrate the implementation of valid planning decisions for many years. It was not only old people in caravans which caused the problem. More frequently flagrant and persistent breaches were perpetrated by entrepreneurs for commercial profit. It is true that the 1990 Act provides for a system of enforcement notices which if ignored may lead to a prosecution e (s 171A). The 1990 Act also contains provisions for the service of stop notices (s 183(1)). These powers were supported by the power of the Attorney General on relation of a local authority to claim an injunction restraining a breach of planning law (see *A-G (on the relation of Hornchurch UDC) v Bastow* [1957] 1 All ER 497, [1957] 1 QB 514). This power was supplemented by s 222 of the Local Government Act 1972 as amended. Section 222(1) provides: f

> 'Where a local authority consider it expedient for the promotion or protection of the interests of the inhabitants of their area—(a) they may prosecute or defend or appear in any legal proceedings and, in the case of civil proceedings, may institute them in their own name, and (b) they may, in their own name, make representations in the interests of the inhabitants g at any public inquiry held by or on behalf of any Minister or public body under any enactment.'

There was nevertheless a strong perception that the planning system was systematically abused and that it required more effective enforcement.

[46] This led to the Report by Robert Carnwath QC, entitled 'Enforcing h Planning Control', which was published in February 1989. Paragraph 10.3 of the Report described the supplemental function of injunctions:

> 'I think it would be a mistake to attempt to prescribe too closely the circumstances in which the remedy would be available, or the forms of order j which could be granted. Experience of decisions over the last few years ... shows that the merit of the remedy is its flexibility and its ability to evolve to meet changing needs. What is required is its recognition in the Act as a normal back-up to the other remedies, and acceptance that *it is for the authority to judge (subject to the ordinary judicial review criteria of reasonableness) when its use is appropriate.* The court already has a wide discretion as to the

a terms on which an order is to be made. In cases where an order is made in advance of an enforcement or stop notice, the terms could include an undertaking by the authority to serve such notices, so that the ordinary procedures would be available for determining the merits and protecting the recipient.' (My emphasis.)

b Mr Carnwath's recommendation was:

'Recommendation (11) I recommend that there be an express power for authorities exercising planning functions to apply to the High Court or County Court for an injunction to restrain any threatened or actual breach of planning control (whether or not an enforcement or stop notice has been served), where they consider it necessary or expedient in order to prevent *c* serious damage to amenity or otherwise to supplement the powers available under the Act.'

It will be noted that the language of s 187B follows the wording of recommendation 11 to a substantial extent.

d [47] Counsel for the local authorities fastened on to the italicised words in para 10.3 to argue that it is the exclusive task of democratically elected planning authorities to weigh issues of personal hardship against the public interest in enforcing planning law. Taken in isolation there may be some logical force in this argument. The main emphasis of the Carnwath Report was on the public interest in enforcing planning. But Mr Carnwath did not ignore considerations of personal hardship. In para 2.8 (p 24) he said:

e personal hardship. In para 2.8 (p 24) he said:

'The enforcement system ... cannot be too rigid. There will always be difficult cases where there is a need to balance the interests of enforcement against the individual circumstances of a business or individual. The system needs to be flexible enough to accommodate such cases, while providing the *f* teeth to secure effective action where it is justified. There will always be disagreement as to where the line is to be drawn.'

In para 2.22 (p 41) he observed that 'use of the courts ensures that both sides are fully protected'. In para 4.2 (p 58) he emphasised the value of 'a flexible system of interim remedies—based on the balance of convenience'. The support for the *g* position of the local authorities in the Carnwath Report is therefore fragile.

[48] Next, counsel for the local authorities relied on dicta in the House of Lords, in diverse contexts, which emphasise that, subject to judicial review, the planning system is essentially one administered by democratically elected authorities: see *Pioneer Aggregates (UK) Ltd v Secretary of State for the Environment* *h* [1984] 2 All ER 358, [1985] AC 132; *Tesco Stores Ltd v Secretary of State for the Environment* [1995] 2 All ER 636, [1995] 1 WLR 759; *R v Wicks* [1997] 2 All ER 801, [1998] AC 92; *R (on the application of Alconbury Developments Ltd) v Secretary of State for the Environment, Transport and the Regions* [2001] UKHL 23, [2001] 2 All ER 929, [2001] 2 WLR 1389. These dicta do not directly or by useful analogy throw any light on the amplitude of the court's jurisdiction to grant an injunction operating *j* in personam requiring a defendant to vacate land.

[49] Counsel for the local authorities put forward a related point based on the structure of the 1990 Act. He submitted in his printed case, and in oral argument, that it is for the local planning authority to determine whether an injunction is appropriate, and for the court, exercising a limited review jurisdiction, to grant an injunction in terms suited to restricting the relevant breach. I would reject this

argument. It depends on interpolating words into the language of s 187B(2) which are ill-suited to the context. Under s 187B(2) the court is not exercising a review jurisdiction: the coercive power conferred by statute is an original jurisdiction. Moreover, the remedy is an equitable one, which prima facie carries with it the notion of a broad discretion.

[50] The starting point must be the language of s 187B read in the context of its purpose viz in the words of the Carnwath Report that 'use of the courts ensures that both sides are fully protected' (p 41 (para 2.22)). The argument of the local authorities that consideration of questions of hardship by them means that this aspect may not be considered by the court under s 187B sits uneasily with the breadth of the statutory language. The critical provision is sub-s (2) which provides that the court *may* grant such an injunction *as the court thinks appropriate* for the purpose of restraining the breach. 'May' does not mean 'shall'. The notion of 'appropriate' relief necessarily involves an exercise of judgment weighing the factors for and against the grant of an injunction. There is not a hint of the restriction of the court's ordinary powers to consider logically relevant countervailing considerations at the stage of the grant of an injunction.

[51] The local authority is empowered to apply for an injunction under s 187B(1) whenever it considers it 'necessary or expedient' to do so. I would not accept a tentative suggestion in argument that 'or' in this phrase could be read as 'and'. In my view the local authority may apply for an injunction if it considers it 'expedient', that is convenient, to do so. It is not in doubt that the local authority may take into consideration questions of hardship. But the independent criterion of expediency suggests that the intent was that the local authority is entitled to take the view that notwithstanding marked personal hardship 'we will put the matter before the court for it to decide on all countervailing issues'. The *Encyclopaedia of Planning Law and Practice*, vol 2 (para P187B.09) rightly points out that s 187B(1) is only 'a deliberately loose entry barrier and is not the criterion upon which the court is required to act'.

[52] Procedural considerations pull in the same direction. There may be a delay between the decision of the local authority and the hearing of application for an injunction by the court. During this period the personal circumstances of a defendant may change adversely, eg the individual may suffer a stroke or a heart attack. On the interpretation of the local authorities the solution is the contrived one that the matter should be adjourned for the local authority to reconsider the decision already taken. If the Court of Appeal's decision is correct, the solution is simple and straightforward: the court will consider the case in the round as it is presented to it on the day of the hearing.

[53] There is an even more important factor to be taken into account. The terms of an injunction must be strictly observed. The potential penalties upon a breach of an injunction are considerable. The local authorities argue that, while personal hardship may not be taken into account by the court considering the grant of an injunction, the court will be able to do so in considering what penalties to impose in committal proceedings. The concession is, of course, inevitable. But it results in the situation that, even in a case where the judge would not contemplate sending a defendant to prison for a breach, he must nevertheless impose an injunction carrying that threat. Such an approach does not advance the rule of law. It tends to bring the law into disrepute. In the Court of Appeal Simon Brown LJ found the right balance. He observed:

a   'It seems to me perfectly clear that the judge on a s 187B application is not
required, nor even entitled, to reach his own independent view of the
planning merits of the case. These he is required to take as decided within
the planning process, the actual or anticipated breach of planning control
being given when he comes to exercise his discretion. But it seems to me no
less plain that the judge should not grant injunctive relief unless he would be
b   prepared if necessary to contemplate committing the defendant to prison for
breach of the order, and that he would not be of this mind unless he had
considered for himself all questions of hardship for the defendant and his
family if required to move, necessarily including, therefore, the availability
of suitable alternative sites. I cannot accept that the consideration of those
matters is, as Burton J suggested [in *South Buckinghamshire DC v Porter*] was
c   the case in the pre-1998 Act era, "entirely foreclosed" at the injunction stage.
Questions of the family's health and education will inevitably be of
relevance. But so too, of course, will countervailing considerations such as
the need to enforce planning control in the general interest and, importantly
therefore, the planning history of the site. The degree and flagrancy of the
d   postulated breach of planning control may well prove critical.' (See [2002]
1 All ER 425 at [38], [2002] 1 WLR 1359 at [38].)

I would endorse this approach. In short the granting of an injunction under
s 187B is an equitable remedy and the court has a wide discretion.

     [54] A series of circulars issued by the Department of Environment, and its
e   successor the Department of the Environment, Transport and the Regions, have
since 1991 emphasised the width of the power of the court and that injunctive
relief must be a commensurate remedy in the particular case: circular 21/91 dated
16 December 1991 (para 7); circular 18/94 dated 23 November 1994; circular
10/97, dated 31 July 1997 (para 5.10); DETR guidance dated 26 July 2000 (para 9).
f   Section 187B came into force on 2 January 1992 (see Planning and Compensation
Act 1991 (Commencement No 5 and Transitional Provisions) Order 1991,
SI 1991/2905). But it received the Royal Assent on 25 July 1991. These circulars
are not relevant to the construction of s 187B: they were not part of the
contemporary materials available to Parliament when the legislation was passed.
g   On the other hand, they may arguably have some value as persuasive evidence of
the workability of the interpretation preferred by the Court of Appeal. It is
unnecessary, however, to rely on these materials in the present case.

     [55] That leaves two Court of Appeal decisions which undoubtedly assist the
argument of the local authorities. The first is *Mole Valley DC v Smith* (1992)
90 LGR 557. The defendants, who were gipsies, had persistently flouted planning
h   laws in respect of caravan sites. They relied on the fact that the city council was
in undoubted breach of its statutory duty to gipsies by failing to provide sufficient
sites for them. Lord Donaldson of Lymington MR relied on a dictum of
Hoffmann J at first instance which was to the following effect (at 567):

j   'There can be no doubt that requiring [the defendants] to leave the site
would cause considerable hardship. This court, however, is not entrusted
with a general jurisdiction to solve social problems. The striking of a balance
between the requirements of planning policy and the needs of these
defendants is a matter which, in my view, has been entrusted to other
authorities.'

With the agreement of the other members of the court the Master of the Rolls
dismissed the appeal against the grant of an injunction.   *a*

[56] The second decision is *Hambleton DC v Bird* [1995] 3 PLR 8. Despite
persistent breaches of the planning laws the judge had refused to grant an
injunction requiring the defendants to vacate certain land. The Court of Appeal
held that the judge had misdirected himself by taking into consideration the
merits of the planning decision and whether a further application for planning   *b*
permission might be successful; and he wrongly considered the availability of
alternative accommodation for the respondents, the evidence that the official site
was unsuitable, and the hardship to the respondents (see [1995] 3 PLR 8 at 17).
There are passages in the judgments which suggest that under s 187B hardship is
legally *irrelevant* to the exercise of the court's discretion.

[57] These decisions pre-date the coming into operation of the Human Rights   *c*
Act 1998. But even under domestic law the dicta were in my view too austere in
so far as they appeared to suggest that even great hardship was irrelevant. A civil
society requires a fairer and more balanced approach. There was insufficient
allowance for the equitable nature of the remedy and the width of the discretion.
On this ground alone these decisions of the Court of Appeal should no longer to   *d*
be treated as controlling.

[58] In any event, the new landscape of the 1998 Act requires a different
perspective. Article 8 of the European Convention for the Protection of Human
Rights and Fundamental Freedoms 1950 (as set out in Sch 1 to the 1998 Act)
contains a fundamental right. It reads:
                                                                              e
> '1. Everyone has the right to respect for his private and family life, his
> home and his correspondence.
> 2. There shall be no interference by a public authority with the exercise of
> this right except such as is in accordance with the law and is necessary in a
> democratic society in the interests of national security, public safety or the
> economic well-being of the country, for the prevention of disorder or crime,   *f*
> for the protection of health or morals, or for the protection of the rights and
> freedoms of others.'

It is unlawful for the court to act in a way which is incompatible with a
convention right (s 6(1)). Even if it had previously been possible to ignore great
or marked hardship in the exercise of discretion under s 187B—a hypothesis   *g*
which I do not accept—such an approach is no longer possible. Sometimes,
perhaps more often than not, the interference with a convention right may be
justified on public interest grounds. But effective protection of a convention right
requires the court to approach the matter in a structured fashion in accordance
with the principle of proportionality. What in the context of the present case is   *h*
required was explained by Simon Brown LJ in terms on which I cannot improve.
He said:

> 'Proportionality requires not only that the injunction be appropriate and
> necessary for the attainment of the public interest objective sought—here
> the safeguarding of the environment—but also that it does not impose an   *j*
> excessive burden on the individual whose private interests—here the gipsy's
> private life and home and the retention of his ethnic identity—are at stake.'
> (See [2002] 1 All ER 425 at [41].)

Plainly, the protection of the relevant convention right would not be effectively
protected by leaving it to local authorities acting under s 187B(1) to consider

a matters of hardship under art 8. It follows that, whatever their earlier status, the reasoning in the *Mole* and *Hambleton* decisions are no longer authoritative or helpful.

[59] For the reasons given by my noble and learned friend Lord Bingham of Cornhill, as well as the reasons I have given, I would make the orders proposed by Lord Bingham.

b

LORD CLYDE.

[60] My Lords, these three appeals concern the enforcement of planning control against gipsies who were occupying lands in the areas of the respective local authorities without planning permission to do so. The respondents in one
c of the appeals, that of *Chichester DC v Searle* and others did not present argument at the hearing because they have sold the lands in question and left them. In each of the two remaining cases planning permissions have been given at least to secure the occupation by the respective respondents but these are currently under appeal. The issue before this House relates to the granting of injunctions against the respective respondents under s 187B of the Town and Country
d Planning Act 1990.

[61] Section 187B provides:

'(1) Where a local planning authority consider it necessary or expedient for any actual or apprehended breach of planning control to be restrained by injunction, they may apply to the court for an injunction, whether or not
e they have exercised or are proposing to exercise any of their other powers under this Part.

(2) On an application under subsection (1) the court may grant such an injunction as the court thinks appropriate for the purpose of restraining the breach.'

f

[62] It is undisputed that under sub-s (2) the court has a discretion. What is in dispute is the extent of that discretion, in particular with regard to the possible effects of an injunction on the defendants by way of hardship. The appellants contend that the role of the court is essentially a supervisory one. On their approach, if the local authority have considered the question of the possible
g hardship to the defendants, and all other relevant factors, the court may not explore such matters but must accept the conclusion reached by the authority. The respondents argue that the particular point of dispute in the present cases is whether the court may consider the consequences of the injunction for the defendants in deciding whether or not to grant it. They contend that at the very
h least the court may properly have regard to the possible hardship for the defendants. The issue thus raises questions about the precise scope of the discretion given to the court by s 187B(2).

[63] It may be noted at the outset that the section is talking about an injunction. This is not a new remedy created by Parliament but a familiar and
j long-established form of remedy in English law. What the section did was to give an express statutory power for local planning authorities to apply to the court for that remedy and a discretion in the court to grant it. The power was given expressly to local planning authorities, so that this remedy may not be sought under the statute by anyone else. Parliament imposed an express pre-condition for the application upon the authority, namely that it must consider it necessary or expedient for an actual or apprehended breach of planning control to be

restrained by injunction. That initial step of consideration is one which they must
have taken before they can make the application and it serves as an initial restraint
on the power to make the application under the Act. It does not seem to me to
bear upon the problem of the scope of the court's discretion. I note in passing
that we are not required in the present case to explore the application of the
possibly overlapping tests of 'necessary or expedient'.

[64] Subsection (1) may be seen as widening the availability of the power to
apply in providing that the application may be made whether or not the authority
have exercised or are proposing to exercise any of the other powers in Pt VII of
the Act. That includes in particular the power to issue a planning contravention
notice under s 171C, an enforcement notice under s 172, a breach of condition
notice under s 187A, and a stop notice under s 183. But that does not mean that
the court may not take account of the facts regarding any other remedy
which the authority have pursued or the fact that they have not pursued any
other remedy. In my view the provisions in sub-s (1) all relate to the power in the
authority to make the application. They do not cast any direct light on
the question of the scope of the discretion given to the court in sub-s (2) in the
granting or withholding of the remedy. The authority have to decide in
accordance with the statute to make the application for an injunction but it is for
the court to decide whether or not to grant it and the decision to make the
application cannot determine that question.

[65] Since the remedy which the court was expressly permitted to grant under
sub-s (2) was a familiar remedy under English law it might be expected that in
dealing with an application for such a remedy the court would adopt the same
approach and apply the same tests as it has always done in relation to injunctions.
The jurisdiction expressly conferred upon the court by sub-s (2) is plainly an
original jurisdiction. It is not presented as a means of appeal or of review of the
decision to enforce planning control or of the decision to apply for an injunction.
On the face of it there seems no reason why the court should not take into
account what effect an injunction might have on the personal circumstances of
the defendant.

[66] Counsel for the appellants laid stress on the final phrase of s 187B(2) 'for
the purpose of restraining the breach'. As a matter of the construction of the
subsection this phrase does not seem to me to circumscribe the power of the
court so as to make the whole choice of action dependant upon the consideration
of whether or not an injunction would serve the purpose of restraining the
breach. If that was the intention of the final phrase then it would be hard to
imagine any case in which an injunction would not be granted. In every case an
injunction operates to restrain the breach. But the court is not compelled to grant
an injunction. The subsection only empowers that to be done. I cannot read into
the phrase any limitation upon the matters to which the court may have regard
in exercising its discretion nor can I find there an indication that the court's role
is intended to be a supervisory one. The importance of the phrase to my mind is
in directing the court to the purposes which any injunction must be designed to
achieve. The injunction which is permitted by the subsection is 'such' injunction
as will serve the stated purposes. The phrase indicates the kind of injunction, the
terms of the order, if any, which may be granted. It does not resolve the question
how far the court's discretion may go.

[67] The principal theme in the appellants' argument as it seemed to me was
the concern that the court should not trespass into areas with which it has no
concern. I certainly accept that it is for the planning authorities and not for the

a courts to see to the preparation and administration of plans and policies for the use of land. What uses should or should not be allowed of lands within the area of the authority, what developments should or should not be permitted to take place upon such lands, are questions for the planning authorities and not for courts of law to resolve. The expression 'planning matters' may be too uncertain a use of language in this context. I also find the expression 'planning code' which

b was sometimes used in the argument lacking in precision. The expression 'planning merits' seems to me to be more exact, but I would prefer to identify the forbidden ground as comprising matters of 'planning judgment'.

[68] The factors which require to be considered in the making of a planning judgment are potentially many and varied. They include matters relating to the economic and social needs of the locality, the interests of the public and of the

c individual members of it who live there, the preservation of the environment and the protection of amenity. Lord Hoffmann observed in *Tesco Stores Ltd v Secretary of State for the Environment* [1995] 2 All ER 636 at 657, [1995] 1 WLR 759 at 780:

> 'If there is one principle of planning law more firmly settled than any other, it is that matters of planning judgment are within the exclusive province of
d >   the local planning authority or the Secretary of State.'

The courts may consider the legality of a planning judgment but not the merits of the planning decision. In *R (on the application of Alconbury Developments Ltd) v Secretary of State for the Environment, Transport and the Regions* [2001] UKHL 23, [2001] 2 All ER 929, [2001] 2 WLR 1389 this distinction was recognised and held

e to be consistent with art 6(1) of the European Convention for the Protection of Human Rights and Fundamental Freedoms 1950 (as set out in Sch 1 to the Human Rights Act 1998). If the courts were to embark upon a reassessment of matters of planning judgment they would, to use the language of Lord Hoffmann in *R v Wicks* [1997] 2 All ER 801 at 818, [1998] AC 92 at 120 be subverting the

f whole scheme of the Act.

[69] Planning authorities will in particular require to consider the human factor. In *Westminster City Council v Great Portland Estates plc* [1984] 3 All ER 744 at 750, [1985] AC 661 at 670 Lord Scarman observed:

> 'Personal circumstances of an occupier, personal hardship, the difficulties
g >   of businesses which are of value to the character of a community are not to be ignored in the administration of planning control.'

Certainly in the enforcement of planning control these personal and human factors must be taken into account. They will also play a part in the earlier stages of the drawing up of plans and policies as well, of course, in the decisions in

h individual cases whether or not some particular permission should or should not be granted.

[70] But the enforcement of the planning decisions which have been reached by planning authorities does not in my view strictly involve the exercise of a planning judgment. The statutory provisions relating to enforcement are set out

j in a distinct part of the 1990 Act, Pt VII. They are in a broad sense 'planning matters'. Indeed the initiative to enforce planning control under these provisions lies with the authority. In deciding whether to take action in the event of a breach of planning control the authority will require to weigh a variety of factors which go beyond the considerations of the planning judgment in the light of which the plans were made and permissions granted or refused. The factors will now include the seriousness of the breach and its effect in the particular case. The

authority will also require to consider which of the various methods of
enforcement provided by the statute they should adopt. Enforcement notices
and stop notices are courses which the authority may take at their own hand. So
also is the breach of condition notice introduced by s 187A. But the injunction
provided for by s 187B requires the intervention of the court. Parliament has
expressly given the power to grant this particular form of remedy to the court.
The authority must decide that the course is 'necessary or expedient', but it is for
the court, not for them, to issue the order.

[71] In exercising its power the court must not reassess matters which are the
subject of a planning judgment. But that does not mean that the factors which
have been considered by the authority in making their planning judgment may
not be properly taken into account by the court in deciding whether or not to
grant this particular remedy. In looking at the factors which weighed with the
authority the court is not embarking upon a reassessment of what was decided as
matter of planning judgment but entering upon the different exercise of deciding
whether the circumstances are such as to warrant the granting of the particular
remedy of an injunction.

[72] It is said that if the court was enabled to take into account matters which
have been considered by the planning authority in deciding whether a particular
development was acceptable in planning terms and the court refused an
injunction it would in effect be granting a temporary planning permission for the
development. But the analogy is not exact. The authority might be able to take
fresh steps for enforcement on a more secure basis than that on which they had
attempted to do so before. They could also seek enforcement if any change of
circumstances occurred. So the defendant does not truly enjoy any protective
permission. The temporary relief which he may enjoy is no different from the
relief which he would achieve through a successful challenge by judicial review
and the propriety of the court granting review of an invalid decision by the local
authority should not be open to criticism on the ground that the court is granting
some kind of temporary permission to the person who applied for review.

[73] Accordingly in my view s 187B(2) allows and has always allowed the
court in the exercise of its discretion in granting an injunction to weigh up the
public interest in securing the enforcement of planning policy and planning
decisions against the private interests of the individuals who are allegedly in
breach of planning control. In particular I would hold that it is open to the court
to consider questions of hardship, particularly as regards health, arising out of the
effect on such individuals of a grant of an injunction. In that regard I do not
consider the observations contrary to that view in *Mole Valley DC v Smith, Reigate
and Banstead BC v Brown* (1992) 90 LGR 557 and more particularly in *Hambleton DC
v Bird* [1995] 3 PLR 8 to be sound.

[74] Those two cases were decided before the 1998 Act came into effect. The
requirement imposed by s 6(1) of that Act on a court to whom an application for
an injunction is made under s 187B of the 1990 Act now makes it a matter of
statutory necessity for the court in any case where art 8 of the convention applies
to see whether the test of proportionality is satisfied before an injunction is
granted. Counsel for the appellants sought assistance from the decision of the
Court of Appeal in *Sheffield City Council v Smart, Central Sunderland Housing Co Ltd
v Wilson* [2002] EWCA Civ 4, [2002] LGR 467. But that case was dealing with
non-secure tenancies under s 193 of the Housing Act 1996 and it may be noted by
way of distinction that Laws LJ said (at [31]):

a
'In my judgment it is important to notice that the regimes of secure tenancies and of planning control (engaged in the gipsy cases), require the court to adjudicate upon the specific merits or otherwise of coercive action in the individual case ...'

b
Counsel also argued that the court did not require itself to apply a test of proportionality where the regime was already compliant with the convention. But while the scheme of the planning legislation may comply with the convention the application of particular provisions of it in particular circumstances gives rise to distinct and separate questions which are not solved merely by reference to the general regime.

c
[75] So far as the particular cases before us are concerned I gratefully adopt the account of the facts which has been set out in the speech of my noble and learned friend Lord Bingham of Cornhill. In that regard I would point out that the circumstances of the two cases where the respondents have contested the appeal before us are quite special. In each case the respondent owns the land in question and while the two pieces of land lie respectively in an area of Green Belt or Green Barrier it is not suggested that there is any urgent environmental problem. In

d
each case there are problems of health and lack of alternative accommodation made more problematic as the respondents are gipsies where considerations of humanity may be particularly acute owing to their particular traditions and lifestyle. That their cases are far from hopeless on the merits is reflected in the fact that they have each been granted a planning permission, although since the

e
hearing before us I understand that an appeal by the local authority in Mrs Porter's case has been upheld. These considerations give a particular force to the proposition that an injunction may be an inappropriate remedy. But that these particular cases have that force should not be understood as diminishing in any way the value of the means of enforcement of planning control provided by s 187B. One reason for its introduction was to reduce the risk of the system for

f
the enforcement of planning control being abused. It remains a potent weapon for that purpose and no doubt in other cases its use to support and back up the other methods of control will be found to be appropriate.

[76] However in the present case I consider that the Court of Appeal proceeded upon the correct approach and I agree with the decision which they reached. I agree in particular with their criticism of the decision in the case of

g
Berry whose facts in my view can be distinguished from those in *Chapman v UK* (2001) 10 BHRC 48. I would accordingly dismiss the three appeals which are before us.

h
LORD HUTTON.
[77] My Lords, I have had the advantage of reading in draft the speeches of my noble and learned friends Lord Bingham of Cornhill and Lord Steyn and I am in full agreement with the reasons which they give for dismissing these appeals. I will only add a few observations of my own relating to the issue of personal hardship.

j
[78] The appeals are concerned with the problem which arises when the enforcement of planning control would result in considerable personal hardship to the occupier of the site against whom the enforcement is to take place. The present cases are examples of the difficulties which arise when it is desirable on planning grounds relating to the amenity of the area to stop the use of land as a site for a caravan or mobile home, but when an injunction under s 187B of the

Town and Country Planning Act 1990 ordering the cessation of such use would
cause severe hardship to the person who lives in the caravan or mobile home
because of his or her age or ill health.

[79] Section 187B of the 1990 Act provides:

'(1) Where a local planning authority consider it necessary or expedient
for any actual or apprehended breach of planning control to be restrained by
injunction, they may apply to the court for an injunction, whether or not
they have exercised or are proposing to exercise any of their other powers
under this Part.

(2) On an application under subsection (1) the court may grant such an
injunction as the court thinks appropriate for the purpose of restraining the
breach.'

[80] In his judgment in the Court of Appeal (with which Peter Gibson and
Tuckey LJJ agreed)) Simon Brown LJ stated ([2001] EWCA Civ 1549 at [4], [2002]
1 All ER 425 at [4], [2002] 1 WLR 1359) that the central issue for determination on
the appeals was the extent to which the court itself on a s 187B application should
exercise an independent judgment in deciding whether or not to grant an
injunction. After a careful consideration of the authorities Simon Brown LJ stated
(at [38]–[42]) his opinion as to the approach which a court should take on an
application for an injunction under s 187B in cases such as the present ones, which
have been set out in full in the speech of Lord Bingham.

[81] Mr Straker QC, for the appellants, submitted that the Court of Appeal
erred in departing from the approach taken by that court in earlier decisions that
it is not for a court to weigh competing interests in planning matters. Parliament
had entrusted to local planning authorities, which are democratically elected
bodies, the task of weighing such interests and the decisions of those authorities
are subject to an appeal on the merits to the Secretary of State who is answerable
to Parliament. Therefore it is not the concern of a court to carry out that function
and to decide where the balance lies between the interests of the defendant
occupier and the wider community. If, on an application under s 187B, a local
planning authority proves a breach of planning control, an injunction should be
granted unless it can be shown that its decision to enforce planning control is
invalid on *Wednesbury* grounds (see *Associated Provincial Picture Houses Ltd v
Wednesbury Corp* [1947] 2 All ER 680, [1948] 1 KB 223). The purpose of the court
is to assist in the enforcement of planning control, not to make planning decisions
itself.

[82] Mr Straker cited a number of decisions in support of this submission:
Pioneer Aggregates (UK) Ltd v Secretary of State for the Environment [1984] 2 All ER
358, [1985] AC 132; *Tesco Stores Ltd v Secretary of State for the Environment* [1995]
2 All ER 636, [1995] 1 WLR 759; *R (on the application of Alconbury Developments Ltd)
v Secretary of State for the Environment, Transport and the Regions* [2001] UKHL 23,
[2001] 2 All ER 929, [2001] 2 WLR 1389. The statement which most strongly
supports the appellants' argument is the observation of Lord Hoffmann in the
Tesco Stores case [1995] 2 All ER 636 at 657, [1995] 1 WLR 759 at 780:

'The fact that the law regards something as a material consideration
therefore involves no view about the part, if any, which it should play in the
decision-making process. This distinction between whether something is a
material consideration and the weight which it should be given is only one
aspect of a fundamental principle of British planning law, namely that the

a   courts are concerned only with the legality of the decision-making process
and not with the merits of the decision. If there is one principle of planning
law more firmly settled than any other, it is that matters of planning
judgment are within the exclusive province of the local planning authority
or the Secretary of State.'

b   [83] However the issue which lies at the heart of this case is what in
Westminster City Council v Great Portland Estates plc [1984] 3 All ER 744, [1985] AC
661 Lord Scarman termed 'the human factor'. The cases on which Mr Straker
relied related to matters of planning policy and the planning merits of particular
cases and were not concerned with cases where the question of human hardship
arose. On this issue the speech of Lord Scarman (with which the other members
c   of the House concurred) provides clear guidance. In the *Great Portland Estates*
case a question arose as to whether in formulating a plan for the development of
the use of land under the Town and Country Planning Act 1971 a city council
should have regard to the interests of individual occupiers of premises. In his
speech Lord Scarman considered the extent to which the human factor can be
taken into account in planning decisions. He cited ([1984] 3 All ER 744 at
d   749–750, [1985] AC 661 at 669) the observation of Lord Parker CJ in *East Barnet
UDC v British Transport Commission* [1961] 3 All ER 878 at 884, [1962] 2 QB 484 at
491 that 'what one is really considering is the character of the use of the land, not
the particular purpose of a particular occupier'. He said ([1984] 3 All ER 744 at
750, [1985] AC 661 at 670) that 'a planning purpose is one which relates to the
e   character of the use of land' and stated:

'However, like all generalisations Lord Parker CJ's statement has its own
limitations. Personal circumstances of an occupier, personal hardship, the
difficulties of businesses which are of value to the character of a community
are not to be ignored in the administration of planning control. It would be
f   inhuman pedantry to exclude from the control of our development the
human factor. The human factor is always present, of course, indirectly as
the background to the consideration of the character of land use. It can,
however, and sometimes should, be given direct effect as an exceptional or
special circumstance. But such circumstances, when they arise, fall to be
considered not as a general rule but as exceptions to a general rule to be met
g   in special cases.' (See [1984] 3 All ER 744 at 750, [1985] AC 661 at 670.)

[84] In his judgment Simon Brown LJ ([2002] 1 All ER 425 at [38]) drew a
distinction between the planning merits of a case on the one hand and the
hardship which would be suffered by a defendant and his family on the other. He
held that it was not for the judge to decide purely planning matters—this was a
h   matter for the local planning authority, but that it was right for the judge to take
into account the human factor, stating:

'It seems to me perfectly clear that the judge on a s 187B application is not
required, nor even entitled, to reach his own independent view of the
j   planning merits of the case. These he is required to take as decided within
the planning process, the actual or anticipated breach of planning control
being a given when he comes to exercise his discretion. But it seems to me
no less plain that the judge should not grant injunctive relief unless he would
be prepared if necessary to contemplate committing the defendant to prison
for breach of the order, and that he would not be of this mind unless he had
considered for himself all questions of hardship for the defendant and his

family if required to move, necessarily including, therefore, the availability
of suitable alternative sites.'

[85] As Lord Scarman recognised in his speech in the *Great Portland Estates* case
that the human factor is sometimes a distinct and additional factor to be viewed
separately from ordinary planning considerations and that on occasions it should
be given direct effect as an exceptional or special circumstance, I think that Simon
Brown LJ was right to make the distinction he did between purely planning
considerations and the human factor, and that he was also right to hold that the
human factor should be taken into account in deciding whether planning control
should be enforced by the granting of an injunction.

[86] I do not accept Mr Straker's submission that it is not appropriate for a
court to take into account and weigh against purely planning considerations the
hardship which the defendant would suffer if he or she were forced to move from
the site. It is clear that s 187B gives the court an original jurisdiction which it is to
exercise as it thinks right. Subsection (2) states that the court 'may' grant such an
injunction as the court 'thinks appropriate' for the purpose of restraining the
breach. Therefore it is not for the court to act merely as a rubber stamp to
endorse the decision of the local planning authority to stop the user by the
particular defendant in breach of planning control. Moreover the court is as well
placed as the local planning authority to decide whether the considerations
relating to the human factor outweigh purely planning considerations; the
weight to be attached to the personal circumstances of a defendant in deciding
whether a coercive order should be made against him is a task which is constantly
performed by the courts.

[87] Article 8 of the European Convention for the Protection of Human
Rights and Fundamental Freedoms 1950 (as set out in Sch 1 to the Human Rights
Act 1998 provides:

'1. Everyone has the right to respect for his private and family life, his
home and his correspondence.
2. There shall be no interference by a public authority with the exercise of
this right except such as is in accordance with the law and is necessary in a
democratic society in the interests of national security, public safety or the
economic well-being of the country, for the prevention of disorder or crime,
for the protection of health or morals, or for the protection of the rights and
freedoms of others.'

In *Buckley v UK* (1996) 23 EHRR 101 the European Court of Human Rights held
that the fact that a gipsy was living in a caravan on a site in breach of planning
control did not disentitle her from claiming that the caravan was her 'home'
within the meaning of art 8. Simon Brown LJ held (at [41]) that under s 6(1) of
the 1998 Act a court hearing an application for an injunction under s 187B must
act in a way which is compatible with the right given by art 8. In my opinion he
was right to do so because s 187B requires the court to decide on the facts of the
individual case whether it is appropriate to grant an injunction which, in cases
such as these, will require the defendant to leave his or her home.

[88] The learned Lord Justice (at [38]–[42]) gave what, in my respectful
opinion, is clear and helpful guidance as to the factors which a court hearing a
s 187B application should take into account, which included the following. He
stated (at [38]):

a

'Questions of the family's health and education will inevitably be of relevance. But so too, of course, will countervailing considerations such as the need to enforce planning control in the general interest and, importantly therefore, the planning history of the site. The degree and flagrancy of the postulated breach of planning control may well prove critical. If conventional enforcement measures have failed over a prolonged period of

b

time to remedy the breach, then the court would obviously be the readier to use its own, more coercive powers.'

And (at [39]):

c

'Relevant too will be the local authority's decision under s 187B(1) to seek injunctive relief. They, after all, are the democratically elected and accountable body principally responsible for planning control in their area. Again, however, the relevance and weight of their decision will depend above all on the extent to which they can be shown to have had regard to all the material considerations and to have properly posed and approached the

d

article 8(2) questions as to necessity and proportionality.'

In *Chapman v UK* (2001) 10 BHRC 48 at 72–73 the European Court of Human Rights stated:

e

'102. Where a dwelling has been established without the planning permission which is needed under the national law, there is a conflict of interest between the right of the individual under art 8 of the convention to respect for his or her home and the right of others in the community to environmental protection ... When considering whether a requirement that the individual leave his or her home is proportionate to the legitimate aim pursued, it is highly relevant whether or not the home was established

f

unlawfully. If the home was lawfully established, this factor would self-evidently be something which would weigh against the legitimacy of requiring the individual to move. Conversely, if the establishment of a home in a particular place was unlawful, the position of the individual objecting to an order to move is less strong. The court will be slow to grant protection to those who, in conscious defiance of the prohibitions of the law, establish

g

a home on an environmentally protected site. For the court to do otherwise would be to encourage illegal action to the detriment of the protection of the environmental rights of other people in the community.

103. A further relevant consideration, to be taken into account in the first place by the national authorities, is that if no alternative accommodation is

h

available, the interference is more serious than where such accommodation is available. The more suitable the alternative accommodation is, the less serious is the interference constituted by moving the applicant from his or her existing accommodation.

104. The evaluation of the suitability of alternative accommodation will

j

involve a consideration of, on the one hand, the particular needs of the person concerned—his or her family requirements and financial resources—and, on the other hand, the rights of the local community to environmental protection. This is a task in respect of which it is appropriate to give a wide margin of appreciation to national authorities, who are evidently better placed to make the requisite assessment.'

[89] I consider that the factors stated by Simon Brown LJ properly reflect the considerations which in *Chapman's* case the European Court stated should be taken into account and that a court which follows the guidance given by him will be acting compatibly with art 8.

[90] Whilst I do not express a concluded opinion on the point which was not the subject of detailed argument before the House, I see no reason to doubt the view expressed by Laws LJ in *Sheffield City Council v Smart, Central Sunderland Housing Co Ltd v Wilson* [2002] EWCA Civ 4 at [40], [41], [2002] LGR 467 at [40], [41] that there are some statutory regimes under which the balance of interests arising under art 8(2) has in all its essentials been struck by the legislature and under which a court, before ordering a defendant to give up possession of accommodation where he has been living, is not obliged to adjudicate upon the specific merits of coercive action in an individual case.

[91] Mr George QC, for the respondents, submitted that Simon Brown LJ had gone too far in stating that the judge on a s 187B application was not entitled to reach his own independent view on the planning merits of the case. He advanced the submission that, whilst it would be right for the judge to accord great deference to the decision of the local planning authority on matters of planning policy such as whether an area of land should be kept as an open space or should be used for the building of houses, the judge was not bound by its decision on every aspect of planning control. Thus, for example, if the local planning authority decided to enforce the removal of some unsightly structure because it spoilt the view of a number of houses, it would be open for the judge to differ from that decision if it were proved that no house had a view of the structure.

[92] In stating that the judge should not come to a decision on the planning merit of the case I think that Simon Brown LJ was intending to give effect to the principle stated by Lord Hoffmann in *Tesco Stores Ltd v Secretary of State for the Environment* [1995] 2 All ER 636 at 657, [1995] 1 WLR 759 at 780 and was not considering the unusual type of case suggested by Mr George. In my opinion the judge is not precluded from deciding some factual issue, such as that instanced by counsel. But I think that such cases would be rare and I consider that a judge should be alert to ensure that he does not embark on the determination of an issue which would, in reality, involve him in the assessment of planning considerations which lie within the ambit of the functions of the local planning authority.

[93] Accordingly for the reasons which I have given, and also for the reasons given by Lord Bingham and Lord Steyn, I would dismiss these appeals.

LORD SCOTT OF FOSCOTE.

[94] My Lords, the issue of importance raised by these three appeals relates to the function of the court and the criteria the court should apply when dealing with an application by a local planning authority, made under s 187B of the Town and County Planning Act 1990, for an injunction to restrain a breach of planning control. I have had the advantage of reading in advance the opinions of my noble and learned friends Lord Bingham of Cornhill, Lord Steyn, Lord Clyde and Lord Hutton and need not repeat what they have said about the facts of the three cases and about the background to and the reasons for the enactment of s 187B.

[95] I respectfully agree that the jurisdiction exercised by the court on an application under s 187B is an original, as opposed to a supervisory, jurisdiction. The section did not, however, confer a new jurisdiction. It had been settled law

a for many years that the court had jurisdiction to grant a civil law remedy by way of injunction in order to enforce the public law, except in cases where statute had expressly or by necessary implication removed the jurisdiction. In *A-G v Chaudry* [1971] 3 All ER 938 at 947, [1971] 1 WLR 1614 at 1624 Lord Denning MR said:

b 'Whenever Parliament has enacted a law and given a particular remedy for the breach of it, such remedy being in an inferior court, nevertheless the High Court always has reserve power to enforce the law so enacted by way of an injunction or declaration or other suitable remedy. The High Court has jurisdiction to ensure obedience to the law whenever it is just and convenient so to do.'

c [96] The principle was confirmed by this House in *Gouriet v Union of Post Office Workers* [1977] 3 All ER 70, [1978] AC 435 but their Lordships emphasised that the jurisdiction was one 'of great delicacy and ... to be used with caution' ([1977] 3 All ER 70 at 83, [1978] AC 435 at 481 per Lord Wilberforce).

[97] Absent some special statutory authorisation, an application for an injunction to enforce the public law has to be brought by the Attorney General. In *A-G (on the relation of Hornchurch UDC) v Bastow* [1957] 1 All ER 497 at 500, [1957] 1 QB 514 at 519 Devlin J described the Attorney General as 'the only authority who has a right to bring a civil suit on the infringement of public rights'. This principle, too, was confirmed by the House in *Gouriet's* case. However, s 222 of the Local Government Act 1972 empowered local authorities to institute civil actions in their own name where they considered it 'expedient for the promotion or protection of the interests of the inhabitants of their area ...' Post 1972, therefore, an application by a local planning authority for an injunction to enforce the planning law could be made in an action brought by the local authority in its own name. Previously the action had to be a relator action brought in the name and with the consent of the Attorney General. But the nature of the application for an injunction was not changed by the advent of locus standi for the local authority to sue in its own name. Nor were the criteria to be applied by the court in deciding whether or not to grant the injunction altered. The criteria remained those expressed in s 37 of the Supreme Court Act 1981 (and its predecessor, s 45 of the Judicature Act 1925), which empowered the High Court to grant an injunction: 'in all cases in which it appears to the court to be just and convenient to do so.'

[98] Section 187B, providing specifically in relation to planning controls an authority to bring proceedings that previously had been provided generally by s 222 of the 1972 Act, authorised a local planning authority to apply for an injunction in support of planning law where the local planning authority 'consider it necessary or expedient for any actual or apprehended breach of planning control to be restrained by injunction' (sub-s (1)). The criteria of 'necessary or expedient' relate to the decision of the local authority to apply for the injunction. They take the place of criteria set out in s 222 of the 1972 Act. They are not criteria which apply to the court's decision whether or not to grant the injunction. Section 187B(2) says that on an application under sub-s (1) the court 'may grant such an injunction as the court thinks appropriate for the purpose of restraining the breach'. This language does not, in my opinion, add to or subtract from the criteria expressed in s 37 of the 1981 Act. The grant of the injunction must be 'just and convenient'. If the grant of the injunction cannot satisfy this test it can hardly be thought 'appropriate' to grant it.

[99] The criteria that govern the grant by the court of the injunction make *a* clear, in my opinion, that the court must take into account all or any circumstances of the case that bear upon the question whether the grant would be 'just and convenient'. Of particular importance, of course, will be whether or not the local planning authority can establish not only that there is a current or apprehended breach of planning control but also that the ordinary statutory means of enforcement are not likely to be effective in preventing the breach or *b* bringing it to an end. In a case in which the statutory procedure of enforcement notice, prosecution for non-compliance and exercise by the authority of such statutory self-help remedies as are available had not been tried and where there was no sufficient reason to assume that, if tried, they would not succeed in dealing with the breach, the local planning authority would be unlikely to succeed in persuading the court that the grant of an injunction would be just and *c* convenient.

[100] In deciding whether or not to grant an injunction under s 187B the court does not turn itself into a tribunal to review the merits of the planning decisions that the authority, or the Secretary of State, has taken. The purpose of the injunction would be to restrain the alleged breach of planning controls and the *d* court could not in my opinion properly refuse an injunction simply on the ground that it disagreed with the planning decisions that had been taken. If the court thought that there was a real prospect that an appeal against an enforcement notice or a fresh application by the defendant for the requisite planning permission might succeed, the court could adjourn the injunction application until the planning situation had become clarified. But where the planning *e* situation is clear and apparently final the court would, in my opinion, have no alternative but to consider the injunction application without regard to the merits of the planning decisions.

[101] It does not, however, follow that once the planning situation is clear and apparently final it is not open to the court to take into account the personal *f* circumstances of the defendant and the hardship that may be caused if the planning controls are enforced by an injunction. Planning controls are imposed as a matter of public law. The local planning authority in seeking to enforce those controls is not enforcing any private rights of its own. If a local authority mortgagee is seeking an order for possession against the mortgagor, or a local authority landlord is seeking an order for possession against a tenant, or a local *g* authority landowner is seeking an order to remove squatters or to restrain trespass, the local authority is seeking an order to enforce its private property rights. It is as well entitled to do so as is a private mortgagee, landlord or landowner. The function of the court in civil litigation of that character is, in my opinion, to give effect to the private rights that the local authority claimant is *h* seeking to enforce. But an application for an injunction under s 187B, or any other application for an injunction in aid of the public law is different. As Lord Wilberforce said in *Gouriet's* case, the jurisdiction to grant such injunctions is one of great delicacy and to be used with caution.

[102] I respectfully agree with the criticism expressed by my noble and learned *j* friend Lord Steyn of the two Court of Appeal authorities particularly relied on by the appellant planning authorities (see [2002] 1 All ER 425 at [55]–[57] of his opinion). The hardship likely to be caused to a defendant by the grant of an injunction to enforce the public law will always, in my opinion, be relevant to the court's decision whether or not to grant the injunction. In many, perhaps most, cases the hardship prayed in aid by the defendant will be of insufficient weight to

a counter balance a continued and persistent disobedience to the law. There is a strong general public interest that planning controls should be observed and, if not observed, enforced. But each case must depend upon its own circumstances.

[103] The manner in which the Court of Appeal approached the issue, as evidenced by the judgment of Simon Brown LJ (at [38]–[42]), cited by my noble and learned friend Lord Bingham of Cornhill, was, in my respectful opinion,

b correct.

[104] For these reasons, as well as those to be found in the opinions of my noble and learned friends with all of which I am in agreement, I too would dismiss these appeals and make the orders proposed by Lord Bingham.

Appeals dismissed.

Dilys Tausz   Barrister.

R v Cooksley
R v Stride
R v Cook
Attorney General's Reference (No 152 of 2002)

[2003] EWCA Crim 996

COURT OF APPEAL, CRIMINAL DIVISION

LORD WOOLF CJ, GAGE AND MOSES JJ

31 MARCH, 3 APRIL 2003

Road traffic – Dangerous driving – Causing death by dangerous driving or by careless driving when under influence of drink or drugs – Sentence – Guidelines.

(1) An immediate custodial sentence will generally be necessary in respect of a person who has been convicted of causing death by dangerous driving. Aggravating factors include (a) consumption of drugs (including legal medication known to cause drowsiness) or alcohol; (b) excessive speed, racing, competitive driving or 'showing off'; (c) disregard of warnings from fellow passengers; (d) a prolonged, persistent, and deliberate course of very bad driving; (e) aggressive driving, eg driving much too close to the vehicle in front, persistent inappropriate attempts to overtake or cutting in after overtaking; (f) driving while unavoidably distracted, eg by reading or by use of a mobile telephone (especially if hand-held); (g) driving when knowingly suffering from a medical condition that significantly impairs driving skills; (h) driving when knowingly deprived of adequate sleep or rest; (i) driving a poorly maintained or dangerously loaded vehicle, especially where that has been motivated by commercial concerns; (j) other offences committed at the same time, eg driving without ever holding a licence, driving while disqualified, driving without insurance, driving while a learner without supervision, taking a vehicle without consent, driving a stolen vehicle; (k) previous convictions for motoring offences, particularly offences involving bad driving or the consumption of excessive alcohol before driving; (l) more than one person killed as a result of the offence, especially if the offender knowingly puts more than one person at risk or the occurrence of multiple death is foreseeable; (m) serious injury to one or more victims in addition to any death(s); (n) behaviour at the time of the offence, eg failing to stop, falsely claiming that one of the victims was responsible for the crash or trying to throw the victim off the bonnet by swerving in order to escape; (o) causing death in the course of dangerous driving in an attempt to avoid detection or apprehension; and (p) committing the offence while on bail (see [15], [21], below).

(2) Mitigating factors include (a) a good driving record; (b) the absence of previous convictions; (c) a timely plea of guilty; (d) genuine shock or remorse (which may be greater if the victim is either a close relation or a friend); (e) the offender's age (but only in cases where lack of driving experience has contributed to the commission of the offence); and (f) the fact that the offender has also been seriously injured as a result of the offence, but only very serious, or life-changing, injury should have a significant effect on the sentence (see [15], [20], below).

a (3) In cases where there are no aggravating circumstances, the starting point for adult offenders, even when there is a plea of guilty, is a custodial sentence of perhaps 12 to 18 months, a custodial sentence only being avoidable if there are exceptional mitigating features. A starting point of two to three years is appropriate for an offence involving a momentary dangerous error of judgment or a short period of bad driving but which has been aggravated by an habitually

b unacceptable standard of driving on the part of the offender (aggravating factors (j) or (k)), by the death of more than one victim or serious injury to other victims (aggravating factors (l) and (m)) or by the offender's irresponsible behaviour at the time of the offence (aggravating factors (n) to (p)). It is possible to foresee circumstances, particularly where more than one of those aggravating factors are present, where five years may be appropriate. When the standard of

c the offender's driving is more highly dangerous (as indicated, for example, by the presence of one or two of aggravating factors (a) to (i)), a sentence of four to five years is the starting point in a contested case. For contested cases involving an extremely high level of culpability on the offender's part, the starting point is six years (see [21]–[23], [25], [26], [28], [29], below).

d (4) For sentencing purposes, cases of causing death by careless driving when under the influence of drink or drugs do not form a separate category to cases of causing death by dangerous driving. It will be perfectly possible for sentencing judges to fit such cases into one of the guideline categories set out above (see [34], below).

e (5) Matters relevant to fixing the length of the driving disqualification for the offence of causing death by dangerous driving will be much the same as the factors already listed. Bans of two years or so will be appropriate where the offender has a good driving record and the offence results from a momentary error of judgment. Longer bans of between three and five years are appropriate where, having regard to the circumstances of the offence and the offender's record, it is clear that the

f offender tends to disregard the rules of the road or drives carelessly or inappropriately. Bans of between five and ten years may be used where the offence itself, and the offender's record, show that he represents a real and continuing danger to other road users. Disqualification for life is a highly exceptional course, but may be appropriate in a case where the danger represented by the offender is an extreme and indefinite one (see [40]–[42], below).

g

Notes

For causing death by dangerous driving or by careless driving when under the influence of drink or drugs, see 40(2) *Halsbury's Laws* (4th edn reissue) paras 673, 682.

h
Cases referred to in judgment

A-G's Ref (No 26 of 1999) [2000] 1 Cr App R (S) 394, CA.
A-G's Ref (No 56 of 2002) [2002] EWCA Crim 2292, [2003] 1 Cr App R (S) 476.
A-G's Ref (No 58 of 2000) [2001] 2 Cr App R (S) 102, CA.
R v Boswell [1984] 3 All ER 353, [1984] 1 WLR 1047, CA.
j R v Braid [2002] EWCA Crim 737, [2002] 2 Cr App R (S) 509.
R v Brown [2001] EWCA Crim 2108, [2002] 1 Cr App R (S) 504.
R v Browning [2001] EWCA Crim 1831, [2002] 1 Cr App R (S) 377.
R v Corkhill [2001] EWCA Crim 2683, [2002] 2 Cr App R (S) 60.
R v France [2002] EWCA Crim 1419, [2003] 1 Cr App R (S) 108.
R v Jenkins [2001] EWCA Crim 242, [2001] 2 Cr App R (S) 265.

R v Locke (1995) 16 Cr App R (S) 795, CA.

R v Mallone [1996] 1 Cr App R (S) 221, CA.

R v Newton (1982) 77 Cr App R 13, CA.

R v Noble [2002] EWCA Crim 1713, [2003] 1 Cr App R (S) 312.

R v Pettipher (1989) 11 Cr App R (S) 321, CA.

R v Pimm [1994] RTR 391, DC.

R v Roche [1999] 2 Cr App R (S) 105, CA.

R v Shepherd, R v Wernet [1994] 2 All ER 242, [1994] 1 WLR 530, CA.

Appeals against sentence and application for leave to refer sentence

R v Cooksley

Robert Charles Cooksley appealed against the sentence of four years' imprisonment and six years' disqualification from driving imposed on him by Judge David Wynn Morgan in the Crown Court at Cardiff on 10 September 2002 for an offence of causing death by careless driving when under the influence of drink. The facts are set out in the judgment of the court.

R v Stride

Ian Paul Stride appealed against the sentence of two-and-a-half years' imprisonment and five years' disqualification from driving imposed on him by Judge Balston in the Crown Court at Maidstone on 13 September 2002 for an offence of causing death by dangerous driving. The facts are set out in the judgment of the court.

R v Cook

Neil Terence John Cook appealed against the sentence of seven years' detention imposed on him by the Recorder of Liverpool (Judge David Clarke QC) in the Crown Court at Liverpool on 27 September 2002 for two offences of causing death by dangerous driving. The facts are set out in the judgment of the court.

Attorney General's Reference (No 152 of 2002)

The Attorney General applied under s 36 of the Criminal Justice Act 1988 for leave to refer to the Court of Appeal as unduly lenient the sentence of 12 months' imprisonment suspended for two years and disqualification from driving for four years imposed on the respondent, Richard James Crump, by Judge Sessions in the Crown Court at Chichester on 29 November 2002 for an offence of causing death by dangerous driving. The facts are set out in the judgment of the court.

Hilary Roberts (assigned by the *Registrar of Criminal Appeals*) for Cooksley.
Stephen Morley (instructed by *Pattinson & Brewer*, Maidstone) for Stride.
Gerald Baxter (assigned by the *Registrar of Criminal Appeals*) for Cook.
Nicholas Hilliard (instructed by the *Treasury Solicitor*) for the Attorney General.
Geoffrey Mercer QC (instructed by *Bennett Griffin*, Worthing) for Crump.

Cur adv vult

a 3 April 2003. The following judgment of the court was delivered.

LORD WOOLF CJ.

[1] This judgment relates to three appeals against sentence and one Attorney General's reference. The appeals and the reference have been listed together to enable us to decide whether we should issue fresh guidelines as to sentencing for
b the offence of causing death by dangerous driving and careless driving when under the influence of drink or drugs in view of the advice of the Sentencing Advisory Panel (the panel) of February 2003 (the advice) which recommended that there should be new guidelines. In his foreword, the chairman of the panel, Professor Martin Wasik, pointed out:

c   'This offence causes particular difficulty for sentencers. By definition, it is one which always gives rise to extremely serious harm: the death of at least one victim (and in some cases serious injury to others). Understandably this often leads to calls from victims' families, and from the wider community, for tough sentencing. On the other hand, an offender sentenced for causing
d   death by dangerous driving did not *intend* to cause death or serious injury, even in the extreme case where he or she deliberately drove for a prolonged period with no regard for the safety of others. The Panel believes that new guidelines will help sentencers to strike an appropriate balance between the level of culpability of the offender and the magnitude of the harm resulting
e   from the offence. The Panel drew up its initial proposals on the basis that the outcome of an offence, including the number of people killed, was relevant to the sentence, but that the *primary* consideration must always be the culpability of the offender. That was supported by the majority of respondents to our consultation paper, and it remains our view. Two of the detailed points in the Panel's advice deserve particular mention. One is the
f   significance of multiple deaths. Although the number of people killed is often a matter of chance, there are (as some of our consultees pointed out to us) cases where the offender has knowingly put more than one person at risk, or where the occurrence of multiple deaths was reasonably foreseeable. In such cases, we recommend that the occurrence of more than one death should be treated as a more seriously aggravating factor. The second point
g   is the inclusion of "driving when knowingly deprived of adequate sleep or rest" in the list of factors that would aggravate the seriousness of an offence. Under previous sentencing guidelines, "briefly dozing at the wheel" was seen as an example of a "momentary dangerous error of judgment", indicating a less serious offence. The Panel's view (again supported by consultees) is that
h   falling asleep is more likely to aggravate than mitigate the seriousness of an offence, because drivers do not normally fall asleep without warning, and the proper course of action for a motorist who feels drowsy is to stop driving and rest.'

j [2] Mr Nicholas Hilliard appears on behalf of the Attorney General on the reference. In addition, he has assisted the court by making submissions on the advice of the panel. He has referred to paras 1.1–1.3 of the Department of Transport's paper *Tomorrow's roads: safer for everyone. The Government's road safety strategy and casualty reduction targets for 2010* (1 March 2000). Those paragraphs provide:

'1.1   Road accidents cause immense human suffering. Every year, around
3,500 people are killed on Britain's roads and 40,000 are seriously injured. In *a*
total, there are over 300,000 road casualties, in nearly 240,000 accidents, and
about fifteen times that number of non-injury incidents. This represents a
serious economic burden; the direct cost of road accidents involving deaths
or injuries is thought to be in the region of £3 billion a year.

1.2   Nevertheless, Britain has had—relatively speaking—remarkable *b*
success in reducing road casualties. And this is despite the vast growth in
traffic since the beginning of the last century. In 1930 there were only 2.3
million motor vehicles in Great Britain, but over 7,000 people were killed in
road accidents. Today, there are over 27 million vehicles on our roads but
far fewer road deaths.

1.3   In 1987 a target was set to reduce road casualties by one-third by 2000 *c*
compared with the average for 1981–85. We have more than achieved this
target for reducing deaths and serious injuries. Road deaths have fallen by
39% and serious injuries by 45% and we are now one of the safest countries
in Europe and indeed the world. However, there has not been any such
steep decline in the number of accidents, nor in the number of slight injuries, *d*
although improvements in vehicle design have helped to reduce the severity
of injuries to car occupants.'

[3] He drew our attention to para 12 of the advice, which indicates that driving
offences causing death are among those most frequently referred by the Attorney
General to this court because he considers that the sentence at trial was unduly *e*
lenient. The Attorney General is in favour of fresh guidelines being issued. We have
come to the conclusion that the following guidelines should be issued. They are
based upon the advice, the terms of which in general we accept. The new
guidelines shall come into force forthwith and should be applied by courts when
passing sentence from the date of this judgment. *f*

[4] The advice refers to the possibility of the maximum sentence being
increased for causing death by dangerous driving by Parliament. This guidance
is given on the basis of the existing maximum penalty which is ten years'
imprisonment. In addition, disqualification for a minimum period of two years
and endorsement of the offender's licence are obligatory and the offence carries
3–11 penalty points. The offender must also be required to pass an extended *g*
driving test before his licence can be restored.

[5] The offence of causing 'the death of another person by driving a
mechanically propelled vehicle dangerously on a road or other public place' was
created by s 1 of the Road Traffic Act 1988, as substituted by s 1 of the Road
Traffic Act 1991. The maximum penalty for this offence was originally five years' *h*
imprisonment but this was increased to the present maximum of ten years by the
Criminal Justice Act 1993.

[6] The significant distinction between the former offence of causing death by
reckless driving and reckless driving is that the new offences do not require
evidence of the offender's state of mind as the test is now objective. When a *j*
person is to be regarded as driving dangerously for the purposes of both offences
is now contained in s 2A of the 1988 Act (inserted into that Act by the 1991 Act).
That section provides that a person is to be regarded as driving dangerously if:

'(1) ... (a) the way he drives falls *far below* what would be expected of a
competent and careful driver, and (b) it would be obvious to a competent

a
and careful driver that driving in that way would be dangerous.' (My emphasis.)

A person is also to be regarded as driving dangerously if 'it would be obvious to a competent and careful driver that driving the vehicle in its current state would be dangerous' (see s 2A(2)).

b
[7] Section 2A(3) further provides that in determining what would be expected of and obvious to a competent and careful driver regard must be had not only to the circumstances of which he could be expected to be aware, but also to *any circumstances shown to have been within the knowledge of the accused*. This last provision does introduce a subjective element into the offence of driving a vehicle in a dangerous state but this does not materially alter the objective nature of the

c
offence as a whole.

[8] Dangerous driving has to be distinguished from careless and inconsiderate driving (see s 3 of the 1988 Act) and causing death by careless driving when under the influence of drink or drugs (see s 3A of the 1988 Act). The former offence is a summary offence for which the offender is not subject to imprisonment and has

d
a maximum penalty of a level 4 fine (currently £2,500). Disqualification is discretionary and the offence carries 3–9 penalty points. The latter offence is indictable only and subject to the same maximum penalty of ten years' imprisonment.

[9] There is still the offence of motor manslaughter in relation to which a sentence of life imprisonment can be imposed. It is also an offence to which s 2

e
of the Crime (Sentences) Act 1997 applies so that in the absence of exceptional circumstances relating either to the offender or to his offences a mandatory sentence of imprisonment for life must be imposed if the offender has a previous conviction for a 'serious offence'.

[10] Where death is not a consequence of the dangerous driving, then the maximum penalty is two years' imprisonment. As that offence can still result in

f
catastrophic injuries being caused by an accident we agree with the advice that—

'Under the present structure there is an unduly large gap between the maximum of two years for dangerous driving … and 10 years for an offence in which the same standard of driving has, by chance, resulted in death.'

g
Like the panel, we therefore welcome the proposed five-year maximum for the basic offence of dangerous driving. We do not see the same need to increase the maximum of ten years' imprisonment for death by dangerous driving, particularly as the offence of motor manslaughter still remains. That offence being reserved for situations where on the facts there was a very high risk of the

h
driving resulting in death (see *R v Pimm* [1994] RTR 391).

[11] Before referring to the guidelines, we would make the following points about sentencing for death by dangerous driving. (i) Although the offence is one which does not require an intention to drive dangerously or an intention to injure, because before an offender can be convicted of dangerous driving, his

j
driving has to fall 'far below' the standard of driving that would be expected of a competent and careful driver and the driving must be such that it would be obvious to the same competent and careful driver that driving in that way would be dangerous, it will usually be obvious to the offender that the driving was dangerous and he therefore deserves to be punished accordingly. (ii) In view of the much heavier sentence which can be imposed where death results as compared with those cases where death does not result, it is clear that Parliament

regarded the consequences of the dangerous driving as being a relevant
sentencing consideration so that if death does result this in itself can justify a
heavier sentence than could be imposed for a case where death does not result.
(iii) Where death does result, often the effects of the offence will cause grave
distress to the family of the deceased. The impact on the family is a matter that
the courts can and should take into account. However, as was pointed out by
Lord Taylor of Gosforth CJ in *R v Shepherd, R v Wernet* [1994] 2 All ER 242 at 245,
[1994] 1 WLR 530 at 536:

> '… we wish to stress that human life cannot be restored, nor can its loss be
> measured by the length of a prison sentence. We recognise that no term of
> months or years imposed on the offender can reconcile the family of a
> deceased victim to their loss, nor will it cure their anguish.'

(iv) A factor that courts should bear in mind in determining the sentence which
is appropriate is the fact that it is important for the courts to drive home the
message as to the dangers that can result from dangerous driving on the road. It
has to be appreciated by drivers the gravity of the consequences which can flow
from their not maintaining proper standards of driving. Motor vehicles can be
lethal if they are not driven properly and this being so, drivers must know that if
as a result of their driving dangerously a person is killed, no matter what the
mitigating circumstances, normally only a custodial sentence will be imposed.
This is because of the need to deter other drivers from driving in a dangerous
manner and because of the gravity of the offence.

[12] Prior to the increase in the maximum period of imprisonment to ten
years and when the offence was still causing death by *reckless driving* this court
gave a guideline judgment in *R v Boswell* [1984] 3 All ER 353, [1984] 1 WLR 1047.
The legislative changes since that time have meant the guidance in that case is out
of date. However, in the case of *R v Shepherd* to which reference has already been
made the court indicated that the list of aggravating and mitigating circumstances
set out in *R v Boswell* were still relevant, but that where a driver had driven with
selfish disregard for the safety of other road users or of his passengers or with a
degree of recklessness, instead of the appropriate sentence being two years or
more, sentences of upwards of five years would be appropriate. As is pointed out
by the advice, the import of that decision is that bad cases should be dealt with at
least twice as severely as before but without necessarily affecting sentencing in
cases which previously attracted shorter custodial terms or making custodial
sentences more likely in those cases where custody would not previously have
been considered necessary. In practice, however, it is clear that there has been an
upward trend across the range of cases, and, in particular that non-custodial
sentences are rarely used.

ASSESSING THE SERIOUSNESS OF AN OFFENCE
[13] In the advice the panel expresses their view in these terms:

> '13. The key problem for a sentencer dealing with this offence is the
> tension between the outcome of the offence (which is inevitably the death of
> at least one victim) and the degree of the offender's culpability. The Panel's
> provisional view, that the offender's culpability should be the dominant
> component in the sentencing exercise but that the outcome of the offence
> should have some effect, was strongly endorsed by the majority of
> respondents to the consultation paper. The Panel understands the view of

a   the minority, that causing death is invariably a very serious crime, but reaffirms its initial view that culpability must be the dominant factor when the offence involves no intention to kill or injure.'

[14] As we have made clear, in accord with the view of the minority referred to in the advice, we accept that causing death is invariably a very serious crime. None the less, we do not dissent from the panel's view that culpability must be *b*   the dominant factor when assessing as precisely as possible just where in the level of serious crimes the particular offence comes.

[15] The panel sets out a series of aggravating and mitigating factors. These are more extensive than those that were set out in *R v Boswell*. We adopt them but stress that they should not be regarded as an exhaustive statement of the *c*   factors. In addition it is important to appreciate that the significance of the factors can differ. There can be cases with three or more aggravating factors, which are not as serious as a case providing a bad example of one factor. They are as follows.

d   *Aggravating factors*

'14. … *Highly culpable standard of driving at time of offence*

(a) the consumption of drugs (including legal medication known to cause drowsiness) or of alcohol, ranging from a couple of drinks to a "motorised pub crawl"

e   (b) greatly excessive speed; racing; competitive driving against another vehicle; "showing off"

(c) disregard of warnings from fellow passengers

(d) a prolonged, persistent and deliberate course of very bad driving

(e) aggressive driving (such as driving much too close to the vehicle in *f*   front, persistent inappropriate attempts to overtake, or cutting in after overtaking)

(f) driving while the driver's attention is avoidably distracted, e.g. by reading or by use of a mobile phone (especially if hand-held)

(g) driving when knowingly suffering from a medical condition which *g*   significantly impairs the offender's driving skills

(h) driving when knowingly deprived of adequate sleep or rest

(i) driving a poorly maintained or dangerously loaded vehicle, especially where this has been motivated by commercial concerns

Driving habitually below acceptable standard

h   (j) other offences committed at the same time, such as driving without ever having held a licence; driving while disqualified; driving without insurance; driving while a learner without supervision; taking a vehicle without consent; driving a stolen vehicle

(k) previous convictions for motoring offences, particularly offences which *j*   involve bad driving or the consumption of excessive alcohol before driving

Outcome of offence

(l) more than one person killed as a result of the offence (especially if the offender knowingly put more than one person at risk or the occurrence of multiple deaths was foreseeable)

(m) serious injury to one or more victims, in addition to the death(s)

Irresponsible behaviour at time of offence

(n) behaviour at the time of the offence, such as failing to stop, falsely claiming that one of the victims was responsible for the crash, or trying to throw the victim off the bonnet of the car by swerving in order to escape

(o) causing death in the course of dangerous driving in an attempt to avoid detection or apprehension

(p) offence committed while the offender was on bail.'

Mitigating factors

'22. ... (a) a good driving record;

(b) the absence of previous convictions;

(c) a timely plea of guilty;

(d) genuine shock or remorse (which may be greater if the victim is either a close relation or a friend);

(e) the offender's age (but only in cases where lack of driving experience has contributed to the commission of the offence), and

(f) the fact that the offender has also been seriously injured as a result of the accident caused by the dangerous driving.'

[16] Having referred to the aggravating factors, the panel deals with specific situations which have been considered in recent authorities. One such situation is what the panel describes as 'avoidable distractions'. The example given, supported by the case of *R v Browning* [2001] EWCA Crim 1831, [2002] 1 Cr App R (S) 377 is the use of mobile phones when driving. In *R v Browning* the defendant was a lorry driver who veered off the road and killed a man in a lay-by while sending a text message. This court upheld the custodial sentence of five years. In giving the judgment of the court Mance LJ made a statement which we would endorse. He said (at [27]):

'The use of a mobile phone to read and to compose text messages while driving is a highly perilous activity. Even the use of a handheld mobile phone by a driver whilst moving, a much too common feature of driving today, is self-evidently risky. But the risks of reading and composing text messages appear to us of a wholly different order and to be, to use the judge's word, of the most "blatant" nature.'

We would respectfully endorse those words. In that case Browning had pleaded guilty but there had to be a *Newton* hearing (see *R v Newton* (1982) 77 Cr App R 13). Browning's evidence was not accepted so he was not entitled to full credit for his plea. The sentence of five years for an offender of good character and who was remorseful was upheld. *R v Browning* provides a useful example of what we would regard as being the current appropriate level of sentencing.

[17] Explaining their inclusion as an aggravating factor at (h), driving when knowingly deprived of sleep or rest, the panel was right to draw attention to the observations of this court in *A-G's Ref (No 26 of 1999)* [2000] 1 Cr App R (S) 394. There it was said that falling asleep at the wheel usually involves a period during which a driver is conscious of drowsiness and difficulty in keeping his or her eyes open and the fact that the proper course for a driver in such a position to adopt is to stop driving and rest.

Multiple deaths

a [18] The panel then discusses the authorities in respect of multiple deaths and in particular the case of *R v Pettipher* (1989) 11 Cr App R (S) 321 and *R v France* [2002] EWCA Crim 1419, [2003] 1 Cr App R (S) 108. We agree with the conclusion of the panel that the number of deaths resulting from dangerous driving is relevant to the length of sentence. There are cases in which the
b defendant, if, for example, he is a coach driver who drives after being deprived of sleep or under the influence of alcohol, must be taken to appreciate that the consequence could be that there will be more than one death if he is involved in an accident. Certainly in that situation, multiple deaths will be a more seriously aggravating feature.

c [19] Even where there is no reason to suggest that the defendant is knowingly putting more than one person at risk, the fact that the consequences of dangerous driving are particularly serious, for example, involving multiple deaths is a relevant factor as to the length of sentence. That is the view that will be taken by the public. However, we are certainly not suggesting that the sentence should be multiplied according to the number of persons who sadly lose their life. It is still
d necessary to regard the offender's culpability in relation to the driving as the dominant component in the sentencing exercise. While the sentence is increased to reflect more than one death the sentence must remain proportionate to the nature of an offence which does not involve any intent to injure.

The offender's own injuries

e [20] The advice relies on the case of *R v Mallone* [1996] 1 Cr App R (S) 221 for suggesting that a sentence can be reduced because of the extent of the offender's own injuries if the injuries are serious. We agree this is a relevant consideration. The injuries can make the sentence of imprisonment a greater punishment than usual. His injuries are also in themselves a punishment and should bring home to the offender, in the most direct possible way, what can be the consequences of
f dangerous driving. We however, also agree with the panel that the fact that the offender has been injured should not automatically be treated as a mitigating factor and that only 'very serious, or life changing, injury' should have a *significant* effect on the sentence. Some indication of the scale of the effect is provided by the facts of *R v Mallone*. The offender had a very severe head injury,
g severe facial injuries, he lost the sight of his right eye and his right little finger, and there was continuing loss of use of his right arm and leg. On appeal this court reduced the sentence from five to four years but in doing so were taking into account, not only the injuries, but the fact that the trial judge had erroneously sentenced the appellant on the basis he had consumed an excessive amount
h of alcohol.

LENGTH OF SENTENCE

No aggravating circumstances

j [21] As in the case of sentencing for any offence a sentence of imprisonment should only be imposed if necessary and then for no longer than necessary. In these cases an immediate custodial sentence will generally be necessary. The starting point for causing death by dangerous driving should be a short custodial sentence of perhaps 12 to 18 months. That is the approach that should be adopted even when there is a plea of guilty, though the plea of guilty will justify the appropriate reduction in the length of sentence. This is in relation to an adult

offender. We regard as an example of this approach the case of *R v Brown* [2001]
EWCA Crim 2108, [2002] 1 Cr App R (S) 504. In *R v Brown* the defendant
momentarily fell asleep while driving his van in daylight, drifted across the road
and collided head-on with a car travelling in the opposite direction, killing a
passenger in it. The mitigating factors were a guilty plea, previous good
character with an impeccable driving record and the fact that the offender
displayed genuine shock and remorse. In addition, the effect on the appellant's
life and family was devastating. This court reduced the sentence to nine months'
imprisonment.

[22] *R v Brown* makes it clear that in order to avoid a custodial sentence there
have to be exceptional mitigating features. As exceptional features, the panel
refer to the case of *R v Jenkins* [2001] EWCA Crim 242, [2001] 2 Cr App R (S) 265.
In that case the defendant was 16 years old with learning difficulties who lost
control of a motorcycle because of its dangerous condition and his pillion
passenger, who was his best friend, was killed. He pleaded guilty because it
would have been obvious to a competent and careful driver that the condition of
his vehicle was dangerous. He was sentenced to detention and a training order
for 12 months but the Court of Appeal, while agreeing that the custodial sentence
was warranted, 'as a justifiable statement of society's abhorrence to dangerous
driving and the use of dangerous vehicles on a public road', took into account that
the defendant was not competent to maintain the bike and the fact that his mental
condition prevented him from fully appreciating its dangerous condition. In the
circumstances, there having been delay in the case coming to trial, a two-year
supervision order was substituted. There obviously can be other exceptional
situations and we consider it preferable not to try and anticipate what
those situations will be. It is sufficient to emphasise that they have to be
exceptional.

Intermediate culpability

[23] As against that case, the panel states and we would agree, that:

'30. An offence involving a momentary dangerous error of judgment or a
short period of bad driving may be aggravated by a habitually unacceptable
standard of driving on the part of the offender (factors (j) or (k) in paragraph
14 above), by the death of more than one victim or serious injury to other
victims (factors (l) and (m) in paragraph 14) or by the offender's irresponsible
behaviour at the time of the offence (factors (n) to (p) in paragraph 14). The
presence of one or more of these features could indicate a sentence within
the higher range, up to three years.'

Accordingly, our *starting* point is two to three years. We do, however, qualify the
panel's advice to this extent that we foresee circumstances, particularly where
there is more than one of the factors present referred to above, where five years
could be appropriate if, for example, there is more than one victim.
Unfortunately, because of the range of the variety of facts it is not possible to
provide more precise guidelines.

[24] The panel refer to the case of *R v Braid* [2002] EWCA Crim 737, [2002] 2
Cr App R (S) 509. In *R v Braid* the offender during daylight and in good conditions
overtook a lorry while approaching a blind bend and collided head-on with an
approaching car. A passenger in the car was killed and in addition the driver of
the other vehicle suffered injuries which would permanently affect his mobility.
This is therefore a case where factor (m) applied and culpability was aggravated

a by serious injury to another victim in addition to the death of the deceased. The offender pleaded guilty. He was 20 years of age and of good character. The sentencing judge noted he had driven very badly over a short distance. This court endorsed the view of the sentencing judge that personal circumstances did not weigh heavily in the balance in these cases. The public were entitled to require the courts to reflect the loss of life and to demonstrate that dangerous
b driving was a serious social evil, which if death results would lead to a substantial custodial sentence. The appellant should have appreciated that he was approaching a blind corner and that he could not see far enough to ensure that he could pass the articulated lorry safely. In reducing the sentence to 18 months' detention in a young offenders institution, the court was, as it said, reflecting the many mitigating features. However, it also said that the case did not display any
c of the aggravating features. This would not be true in relation to the present guidelines and if the guidelines had been in force, we would not have expected the court to interfere with the period of two years' detention imposed by the trial judge.

d *Higher culpability*
[25] In relation to offences of higher culpability the panel states:

'32. When the standard of the offender's driving is more highly dangerous (as would be indicated, for example, by the presence of one or two of factors (a) to (i) in the list at paragraph 14 above), the Panel suggests that the
e appropriate starting point would be a custodial sentence within the range from two to five years. The exact level of sentence would be determined by the dangerousness of the driving and by the presence or absence of other aggravating or mitigating factors.'

[26] As a *starting point* we consider a bracket of two to five years is too wide.
f We suggest that sentencers should take as a *starting point* four to five years in relation to a contested case of this type. There will be cases which will involve higher sentences than five years because they are bad examples and cases, particularly where there is a plea, where the sentence will be less than four years where there are significant mitigating factors.

g [27] The approach that we have just indicated is consistent with the approach of this court in *A-G's Ref (No 58 of 2000)* [2001] 2 Cr App R (S) 102; a sustained course of dangerous driving at excessive speeds, 50 mph in a 30 mph area, was involved in that case. The offender had also consumed alcohol, although it was unclear whether this contributed to the offence. While driving on the wrong side of the road the offender collided head-on with a motorcyclist who was killed. In addition
h a seven-year-old pillion passenger suffered leg injuries. The offender was an unqualified driver and he had left the scene of the crash immediately although he gave himself up to the police on the following day. On a guilty plea, this court increased the sentence to three-and-a-half years. That sentence included an allowance for double jeopardy, but for that allowance the sentence would not have
j been less than four years.

Most serious culpability
[28] Here, what this panel state is as follows:

'34. The Panel suggests that custodial sentences over five years should be reserved for cases involving an extremely high level of culpability on the offender's part. This might be indicated by the presence of three or more of aggravating factors (a) to (i), although an exceptionally bad example of a single aggravating feature could be sufficient to place an offence in this category. A sentence close to the maximum would be appropriate in a case displaying a large number of these features, or where there were other aggravating factors.'

[29] The panel do not give a starting point. We feel it would be helpful if we suggest again in a contested case a *starting point* of six years otherwise we endorse what the panel states.

[30] The panel gave as an example the case of *R v Corkhill* [2001] EWCA Crim 2683, [2002] 2 Cr App R (S) 60 where an offender was sentenced to seven years' detention. The Court of Appeal agreed this was a bad case but described it as 'not among the very worse' and reduced the sentence to five years. Bearing in mind that Corkhill was 19 years old and pleaded guilty, we see it as consistent with our *starting point*.

[31] As an example of the most serious case justifying a total custodial sentence of the maximum of ten years we refer, as did the panel, to *R v Noble* [2002] EWCA Crim 1713, [2003] 1 Cr App R (S) 312. The Court of Appeal made it clear in that case, that the maximum sentence was justified not simply by the number of deaths but by the range of other aggravating factors, including driving at an excessive speed while about two-and-a-half times over the alcohol limit and then seeking to avoid responsibility by claiming one of the victims had been driving.

STARTING POINTS

(A) *Death by dangerous driving*

[32] We have set out four *starting points*; no aggravating circumstances—12 to 18 months; intermediate culpability—two to three years; higher culpability—four or five years and most serious culpability—six years or over. We make clear that *starting points* only indicate where a person sentencing should start from when seeking to determine what should be the appropriate sentence. There is, however, a danger in relation to the higher *starting points* of the sentencer, if he is not careful, double accounting. The sentencer must be careful not to use the same aggravating factors to place the sentence in a higher category and then add to it because of the very same aggravating features.

[33] In making our recommendations as to *starting points*, we have made the allowance we consider appropriate for the fact that those who commit offences of dangerous driving which result in death are less likely, having served their sentence, to commit the same offence again. Apart from their involvement in the offence which resulted in death, they can be individuals who would not otherwise dream of committing a crime. They, unlike those who commit crimes of violence, also do not intend to harm their victims.

(B) *Careless driving under the influence of drink*

[34] We have not, so far, mentioned the level of sentencing in cases of causing death by careless driving when under the influence of drink. The panel have not advised that such cases should form a separate category. We agree. The driving may not exhibit the aggravating factors set out in (a) to (i) of para 14 of the panel's advice. In some cases, the only aggravating factor will be the amount of alcohol consumed. In other cases, there may be the aggravating factor of disregarding a

a warning from a fellow passenger or knowingly driving a poorly maintained vehicle. There may be previous motoring convictions. There will also be cases where the driving is itself of significance in determining the appropriate sentence. As was made clear in *R v Locke* (1995) 16 Cr App R (S) 795, it is not necessary to have an additional count of death by dangerous driving before the full culpability of the offender's driving is taken into account in determining the right sentence.
b It will be perfectly possible for sentencing judges to fit cases of causing death by careless driving when under the influence of drink into one of the four guideline categories which we propose.

THE VIEWS OF THE VICTIMS' FAMILIES

c **[35]** Here, the panel refer to the practice statement of 16 October 2001 (see *Practice Direction (criminal proceedings: victim personal statements)* [2001] 4 All ER 640, [2001] 1 WLR 2038). The panel also refers to the case of *R v Roche* [1999] 2 Cr App R (S) 105 where the court accepted that they could as an act of mercy reduce a sentence if relatives of a victim indicated that the punishment imposed on the offender was aggravating their distress. The panel also refers to the fact
d that in that case Lord Bingham of Cornhill CJ said (at 109): '… the court is not swayed by demands for vengeance and has to be very cautious in paying attention to pleas for mercy.'

[36] The last case to which we should refer because it was helpfully drawn to our attention by Mr Hilliard, on behalf of the Attorney General, is *A-G's Ref (No 56 of 2002)* [2002] EWCA Crim 2292, [2003] 1 Cr App R (S) 476. In that case
e the offender who was aged 37 pleaded guilty to two counts of causing death by careless driving when over the prescribed limit. He was sentenced to two years' imprisonment on each count concurrently as well as being disqualified for three years.

[37] In that case a family had been driving in another vehicle at about 2.30 am
f in the morning on the M1 motorway. Although how the accident occurred was not precisely established, it seems that the likely cause was the fact that the offender had fallen asleep and this caused his vehicle to collide with another vehicle travelling in the same direction and that vehicle then spun off the motorway killing the front seat passenger and the rear offside passenger and
g the rear nearside passenger. They were all members of the same family. The offender had been drinking and his blood alcohol concentration would have been, at the time of the accident, somewhere in the region of 105 mg of alcohol in 100 ml of blood. The number of persons injured and the fact that the offender had been drinking were relied upon by the Attorney General as aggravating features but there were mitigating features, namely the offender had pleaded
h guilty and shown genuine remorse, he was a man of good character, 37 years of age in responsible employment. The fact that the case was a result of a momentary inattention and not a prolonged course of bad driving was also relied upon.

j **[38]** In giving the judgment of the court Kay LJ pointed out (at [24]) that—

'sentences that would have been deemed appropriate 10 years ago now would not begin to be considered to be right. Sentences have been very substantially increased.'

Kay LJ added (at [25]):

'This was a case in which there was no prolonged course of bad driving
over and above that which is inevitably present in a case of this kind, namely,   *a*
that any driving with excess alcohol is serious bad driving. If you drive with
excess alcohol late at night, one of the possibilities is that it will increase the
chances that you will fall asleep at the wheel. Those who fall asleep at the
wheel, whether from excess alcohol or otherwise, represent an enormous
danger to other road users. Accordingly, it is incumbent upon all to ensure   *b*
that they do not place themselves in a position where that is likely to
happen.'

[**39**] He also referred (at [26]) to the fact that—

'falling asleep is not generally something that happens in a moment. It is
normally the end product of a process of feeling tired and people do have the   *c*
opportunity to stop and avoid an accident when they start to feel that they
are falling asleep.'

The court did not therefore regard the case as one of momentary inattention.
However, it was not the worst driving. In addition the blood alcohol level was not
particularly high. However, the court went on to say, where more than one death   *d*
is caused and where permanent serious injuries added to the factor of the number
of deaths, those are matters that must be given some weight in the sentencing
process. The fact that there were the deaths and one very serious injury was not in
any way the result the driver intended and therefore the degree to which there is an
increase in sentence for such factors is not generally thought to be very marked.   *e*
None the less the authorities clearly establish that it is an important factor that has
to be borne in mind. The court therefore took the view that a sentence in the
brackets of four to five years should be imposed in a case of that sort. We
respectfully agree.

DISQUALIFICATION   *f*
[**40**] As we have already indicated disqualification is mandatory for a
minimum period of two years. The main purpose of disqualification is as the
panel advised, 'forward looking and preventative rather than backward looking
and punitive'. It is designed to protect road users in the future from an offender
who had shown himself to be a real risk on the roads. We do, however, accept   *g*
that for the offender being disqualified is a real punishment. The panel suggests
the risk represented by the offender is reflected in the level of culpability which
attaches to his driving so that matters relevant to fixing the length of the driving
disqualification for the offence of causing death by dangerous driving will be
much the same as those factors we have listed already. We agree with this
suggestion.   *h*
[**41**] We accept the advice of the panel as to the length of bans. We do so
notwithstanding the fact that the panel adopts three bans of seriousness whereas
in respect of imprisonment we have adopted four categories. We consider the
advice in relation to disqualification is sufficiently precise.
[**42**] The advice was in the following terms: *j*

'42. While those convicted of causing death by dangerous driving are likely
to regard disqualification as an onerous part of the punishment for the offence,
the main purpose of disqualification is forward-looking and preventative,
rather than backward-looking and punitive. A driving ban is designed to
protect road users in the future from an offender who, through his conduct on

a this occasion, and perhaps other occasions, has shown himself to be a real risk on the roads. In general, the Panel suggests, the risk represented by the offender is reflected in the level of culpability which attaches to his driving, so that matters relevant to fixing the length of the driving disqualification for the offence of causing death by dangerous driving will be much the same as those appearing in the list of aggravating factors for the offence itself. Shorter bans

b of two years or so will be appropriate where the offender had a good driving record before the offence and where the offence resulted from a momentary error of judgment. Longer bans, between 3 and 5 years, will be appropriate where, having regard to the circumstances of the offence and the offender's record, it is clear that the offender tends to disregard the rules of the road, or to drive carelessly or inappropriately. Bans between 5 and 10 years may be

c used where the offence itself, and the offender's record, show that he represents a real and continuing danger to other road users. Disqualification for life is a highly exceptional course, but may be appropriate in a case where the danger represented by the offender is an extreme and indefinite one. [R v Noble [2003] 1 Cr App R (S) 312] was described by the Court of Appeal as "one of those rare cases" where disqualification for life was necessary in order to

d protect the public.'

[43] We do not agree that the length of the ban should be tailored to take into account the anticipated date of early release of the offender. On the other hand we accept that to extend the ban for a substantial period after release can be

e counter-productive particularly if it is imposed on an offender who is obsessed with cars or who requires a driving licence to earn his or her living because it may tempt the offender to drive while disqualified.

[44] The balancing of these conflicting considerations is very much the responsibility of the sentencer. In doing so the balancing exercise will require the sentencer to take into account the requirement which now exists that an order

f must be made that the offender is required to pass an extended driving test.

[45] We can now turn to the individual cases.

ROBERT CHARLES COOKSLEY

The facts

g [46] In the Crown Court at Newport on 20 August 2002 this appellant changed his plea from not guilty to guilty on a count of causing death by careless driving when under the influence of drink. On 10 September 2002 he was sentenced to a term of four years' imprisonment, disqualified from driving for six years and ordered to take an extended re-test following a disqualification period. He appeals

h by leave of the single judge. The facts are as follows. At about 8.25 pm on 1 September 2001 the appellant was driving along the A48 towards Newport when he ran into a cyclist travelling in the same direction. Immediately before the accident the driver of a car which was following the appellant's car noticed the appellant's car braking in a quick but controlled manner. The car behind the

j appellant's car pulled out to overtake and as it did so the front-seat passenger noticed that the appellant's car had hit the cyclist. That car pulled up and the driver and his passenger returned to the scene of the accident. The appellant was trying to resuscitate the cyclist and his female passenger was hysterical. An ambulance and the police were called. The injured cyclist was removed from the scene in the ambulance but later died. Police officers at the scene smelt alcohol on the breath of the appellant and his passenger. The appellant's passenger told police officers that

she and the appellant had started drinking at 11.00 am and they were on their way
from one public house to another when the accident occurred. She said that she
had told the appellant that he should not be driving but had gone along with him
to avoid a row. Both she and the appellant tested positive on a roadside breath test
but later at the police station the appellant refused to provide either a specimen of
breath or blood for analysis. Following a plea and directions hearing, at which the
appellant pleaded not guilty, the prosecution served the evidence of an expert who
had made a back calculation from the roadside breath test relating to the amount of
alcohol which it was alleged the appellant had consumed before the accident. In his
opinion the appellant must have consumed at least nine pints of beer before
the accident although the appellant admitted to consuming only four pints. The
defence instructed its own expert and it suffices to note that the accuracy of
the prosecution expert's evidence ultimately was not challenged and the appellant
pleaded guilty. He is now aged 46 and has a number of previous convictions which
include in 1994 a conviction for driving with excess alcohol and in 2001 for failing
to stop after an accident.

[47] On behalf of the appellant, it is submitted that apart from the consumption
of alcohol there was an absence of serious culpability. Counsel submits that there
is no evidence of the appellant's car meandering or wandering across the road.
There is no evidence of excessive speed and the appellant remained at the scene of
the accident. Further, it is submitted that the judge failed to give sufficient credit
for the appellant's guilty plea and remorse shown by him.

Our conclusions

[48] In our judgment the submissions on the lack of culpability fail to address the
gravity of the case against the appellant, namely that he had consumed such a
quantity of alcohol as to cause him to fail to see the cyclist in time or at all. In
addition, there is the aggravating feature that he had driven notwithstanding a
warning from his passenger that he should not do so. In our judgment this was
a bad case of causing death by careless driving when under the influence of drink.
The appellant had spent a good part of the day drinking. He was warned not to
drive by his passenger. Clearly, he cannot have seen the cyclist in time to avoid the
accident. For these reasons his judgment must have been seriously affected by
alcohol. In our opinion this case falls into the third category of seriousness or higher
culpability, and notwithstanding the appellant's guilty plea, for which only limited
credit was due, and the fact that this was a case of careless driving, the sentence was
not manifestly excessive.

The result

[49] This appeal must be dismissed.

IAN PAUL STRIDE

The facts

[50] This appellant appeals against a sentence of two-and-a-half years'
imprisonment imposed in the Crown Court at Maidstone on 13 September 2002
following a trial at which he was convicted of causing death by dangerous
driving. He was disqualified from driving for five years and until an extended
re-test is taken.

[51] The appellant has been a professional lorry driver for over 20 years. On
16 December 2000 he had started work at 3 pm. He drove to a garage in Kent to

a make a delivery and left that garage at 5.36 pm. After driving a distance of only 19 miles, taking him some 22 minutes, an accident occurred on the M20 motorway. Two vehicles were stationary on the hard shoulder. One of them had broken down and a Peugeot 405 had parked behind the other car in order to assist. There were approximately seven people standing on the verge of the hard shoulder at the time, some were getting into the rear of the Peugeot. As the

b appellant's tanker approached, it slowly veered off the main carriageway onto the hard shoulder and into collision with the rear of the Peugeot. Tragically Richard Foord, in the back of the Peugeot at the time, was killed. The appellant told the police and maintained at trial that he had a sneezing fit causing him to leave the road.

[52] It is apparent that the trial judge directed the jury that if the explanation

c for the accident might have been that the appellant had sneezed, he should be acquitted. But if the jury was sure that, as the prosecution contended, the appellant had fallen asleep he should be convicted.

[53] The jury convicted and accordingly the judge sentenced him on the basis that the appellant had fallen asleep. It is conceded on behalf of the appellant that

d the judge was entitled to take that view.

[54] The appellant is 43 and of good character. He volunteered that he had been convicted of a traffic offence approximately 20 years ago and more recently of a minor speeding offence. A number of witnesses gave evidence and wrote of his honesty, integrity and hard work. The pre-sentence report spoke of the fact that he had been traumatised by the accident. In his sentencing remarks the judge

e accepted that there were no aggravating features.

Our conclusions

[55] This, as we have said, was a case where a driver fell asleep at the wheel. Usually, as we have indicated at [17], above, this will be an aggravating feature.

f Sleep is normally preceded by a period of drowsiness and difficulty in keeping the eyes open. But this was an unusual case. The appellant had not been driving for any lengthy period. Nor had he been working throughout the day. There was no reason why he should anticipate becoming tired, let alone falling asleep. In those circumstances we take the view that the judge was correct in declining to identify any aggravating feature and in particular we do not think this is a case

g where the driver was knowingly deprived of adequate sleep or rest.

[56] On the other hand, there was powerful personal mitigation. In those circumstances we do not think this case falls within our intermediate category of two to three years. It was a rare case of a driver momentarily and unexpectedly falling asleep at the wheel. In those circumstances we take the view that it falls

h within the lowest category and a sentence of 18 months' imprisonment was appropriate.

[57] Additionally, we take the view that disqualification for driving for a period of five years was too long. Disqualification is primarily intended to provide a safeguard to the public for the future. In the light of this professional

j driver's good driving record we take the view that protection of the public does not require disqualification for five years and for that period we substitute a period of three years' disqualification.

The result

[58] Accordingly in this case the appeal is allowed by substituting for the period of two-and-a-half years of imprisonment a period of 18 months'

imprisonment and for the disqualification of five years a period of three years and
until an extended re-test is taken.

a

NEIL TERENCE JOHN COOK

The facts

[59] This appellant was sentenced by the Recorder of Liverpool on 27
September 2002 to a total of seven years' detention in a young offenders
institution for two offences of causing death by dangerous driving. He had
pleaded guilty earlier. The appellant is aged 20. The facts demonstrate that these
offences were of the most serious kind.

b

[60] On 17 May 2002 at about 4 am the appellant was driving a Volvo
motorcar. It was not his own and he was unable to identify the owner. There
were five passengers in the car. He was driving the car on a dual carriageway in
Liverpool in respect of which there was a 30 mph speed limit. The area was
known as dangerous and there were signs along it reading 'Speed Kills' and 'Slow
Down Please'. His speed was estimated at between 68 and 73 mph at the time of
the accident. As he approached a sharp left hand bend he lost control. The car
hit the left hand kerb, rose into the air, struck a tree and crashed through the
gardens of three houses demolishing a wall and a bay window. A passenger
sitting in the rear and another passenger sitting in the front passenger seat were
killed immediately. One other passenger suffered a large cut on her head, a
fractured forearm and a chipped vertebrae at the top of her neck. Another
passenger sustained serious head injuries requiring intensive support on a
respirator and a fifth passenger suffered a fractured hip.

c

d

e

[61] The appellant had a bad driving record which included three previous
offences of driving whilst disqualified. He was driving whilst disqualified at the
time of these offences.

[62] As the Recorder of Liverpool noted in his sentencing remarks the only
mitigation was that he had pleaded guilty when the case first came into the
Crown Court and had expressed sorrow and remorse. There was graphic
evidence of the impact his driving had had upon the relatives of the deceased.

f

[63] It was argued on this appellant's behalf that whilst there were significant
aggravating features, deriving from the manner of his driving and the fact that he
was disqualified, insufficient allowance had been made for the age of this
appellant and his plea of guilty. Our attention was drawn to the decision of
this court in *R v Corkhill* [2002] 2 Cr App R (S) 60 in which a sentence of seven
years' detention was reduced to five years having regard to the early plea of guilty
and the appellant's youth.

g

h

Our conclusions

[64] In our judgment this case was worse. Two young people were killed and
others suffered severe injuries as a result of this appellant's deliberate decision to
drive at dangerous speed in order to impress his fellow passengers.

[65] Having regard to the appellant's sustained driving at speed and the fact
that he was disqualified, we place this case within the most severe culpability
category. The appellant drove persistently at an excessive speed in order to show
off to his fellow passengers, aggravating features as identified by the panel at
para 14(b). However, this appellant is entitled to some credit for his plea even
though it was not entered at the earliest time. The conclusion we have reached
is that a sentence of seven years for a person of the appellant's age is an

j

a excessively high sentence and a sentence of six years' detention will appropriately meet the requirements of punishment and deterrence for this serious offence.

The result

[**66**] Accordingly, we allow the appeal and quash the sentence of seven years and instead impose a sentence of six years' detention.

b

RICHARD CRUMP

[**67**] On 26 September 2002 in the Crown Court at Chichester, the defendant, Richard James Crump was convicted of causing death by dangerous driving. On 29 November 2002 he was sentenced to 12 months' imprisonment suspended for two years. He was disqualified from driving for four years, ordered to take an *c* extended driving test and ordered to pay £200 towards the costs of the prosecution. Her Majesty's Attorney General applies under s 36 of the Criminal Justice Act 1988 for leave to refer the sentence to this court for review because he considers it was unduly lenient. We grant leave.

d *The facts*

[**68**] The facts were as follows. At about 12.30 pm on 18 January 2001 the defendant was driving his Peugeot motorcar south along South Farm Road, Worthing approaching a railway crossing. He had two passengers in his car. At the same time Hannah O'Leary, aged 86, was walking in South Farm Road in the vicinity of the railway crossing. As the defendant approached the crossing *e* the signalman activated the warning bells and crossing lights sequence. The sequence was that yellow lights come on for three seconds and the audible warning started. After three seconds red lights start to flash. After another seven-and-a-half seconds the facing barriers start to descend. A pedestrian saw the Peugeot drive over the railway line as the barriers descended. His evidence was that the defendant *f* had to cross into the opposite carriageway on the north side of the line and 'shimmy' his way diagonally across the crossing to get through. The pedestrian described the vehicle as travelling too fast. At the same time a taxi driven by Liberato Dichello approached the crossing from the south side as the lights flashed and the gates started to come down. He saw Mrs O'Leary step into the road off the east pavement. He stopped his vehicle short of where she was crossing so that *g* she could cross in front of his taxi. His evidence was that she had reached about halfway across the lane when the Peugeot vehicle came over the crossing at an angle and struck her. By then the crossing gates were halfway down and the car was at an angle in order to avoid the gate. Mr Dichello thought that the car was travelling at more than 30 mph. The defendant stopped the Peugeot a short *h* distance from the point of impact. At the scene he spoke to a police officer saying: 'I had to make a snap decision. I was confronted by a red light and she stepped out from the side of the road in front of me.' A little later when he was sitting alone in the back of a police car the defendant received a telephone call on his mobile from one of his passengers. The defendant's side of the conversation was recorded by a *j* video system inside the police car. He said: 'Yeh, well, this is your fault. You know that don't you? Do you know that? No? [Pause.] Go on, give it loads. Go on, you can do it. Go on. Yeh, anyway.'

[**69**] Later when interviewed he said that he thought he was probably travelling at about 40 mph. He had not noticed the flashing lights and the warning bells and had been unaware of the crossing until one of his passengers had said 'Quick, go, there's a crossing'. He said that—

'It was like a split [second] decision thing ... I wasn't expecting there to be
a train crossing there and I've kind of obviously gone through it whilst its   a
coming down at some point, not realised it, someone said "there's a barrier
, coming down" and then this woman just stepped out in front of me.'

Re-interviewed on 22 March 2001 Crump estimated his speed at 30 to 35 mph.

[70] As a result of the impact Mrs O'Leary sustained multiple injuries and on   b
14 February 2001 she died in hospital as a result of heart failure brought on by
the injuries.

[71] The defendant is now aged 30. He had three previous convictions for
speeding the last of which was in 1997.

The reports   c

[72] Before the judge there was a pre-sentence report and two medical
reports. All these reports comment on the sincerity of expressions of remorse by
the defendant. The medical reports show that the defendant suffers from a severe
and disabling eczema.   This condition requires treatment by a daily bath
containing an emollient and the application of steroid ointment and moisturising   d
creams.   From time to time the defendant has to be admitted to hospital for
in-patient treatment. A psychiatrist reported that the defendant showed signs of
post-traumatic stress disorder which he suspected had caused the defendant to
develop a dependence on prescribed sleeping tablets and anti-anxiety drugs.

[73] The judge sentenced the defendant on the basis that he had approached   e
the crossing travelling at a speed in the mid-30s. He said that it was implicit from
his direction and the jury's verdict that the defendant having seen the warning
lights decided to go on and take the various risks involved in not stopping. For
this reason he had to drive an 'S' course along the road in order to pass under the
barrier on his side of the road.   The judge concluded that only a custodial
sentence was justified but that the interplay between the defendant's   f
psychological make-up and his medical difficulties were such as to constitute
exceptional circumstances enabling him to suspend the sentence.

The submissions

[74] The Attorney General contends that the following aggravating features   g
were present. (1) The defendant failed to heed the warning bells and lights
which would have been evident for some time. (2) The defendant ran the risk of
his vehicle blocking the railway line if he had not managed to drive under the
crossing gates. (3) The defendant had three previous convictions for speeding.

[75] The Attorney General accepts that the following mitigating factors were   h
present. (1) Apart from road traffic offences the defendant had no other previous
convictions. (2) The defendant was in poor health. He suffered from severe
eczema and had experienced some symptoms of post-traumatic stress disorder
after the incident. (3) The defendant was remorseful for what he had done.

[76] Mr Hilliard submitted that, on the judge's findings, this was a case of the   j
defendant taking a deliberate risk by attempting to cross the railway crossing as
the barriers were descending. He pointed to the risk of disastrous consequences
which might have occurred if the defendant's vehicle had been trapped on the
crossing. He submitted that the sentence of 12 months was unduly low and that the
starting point should have been two-and-a-half years in prison. From this starting
point some allowance could properly be made for the defendant's personal

a mitigation but the mitigation was not such as to amount to exceptional circumstances enabling the court to suspend the sentence.

[77] Mr Geoffrey Mercer QC representing the defendant before us, as he did in the lower court, submitted that, ignoring the defendant's medical condition, the sentence was not unduly lenient. He submitted that there were no aggravating features and that the decision to drive over the crossing as the barriers were

b descending was a split-second decision amounting to no more than an error of judgment. He further submitted that, in view of the defendant's medical condition, the judge was justified in suspending the sentence of imprisonment.

Our conclusions

[78] The Attorney General should have leave.

c [79] We are of the opinion that the sentence passed was unduly lenient. In our judgment the aggravating feature in this case is the deliberate risk which the defendant took in deciding to drive across the railway crossing as the barriers were descending. In order to do so it was inevitable that he had to drive onto the wrong side of the road. There was the considerable risk that if he failed to pass under the second barrier he might cause a very serious accident involving a train. In our

d judgment his driving was such that it came into the second intermediate category to which we have referred; that is the two to three year bracket. In the circumstances, we accept the Attorney General's submission that the starting point was two-and-a-half years. Taking into account the defendant's considerable remorse and the other personal mitigation save for his medical condition in our

e view the appropriate sentence would have been two years.

[80] However, in our judgment, the judge was entitled to suspend the sentence. He had seen the defendant give evidence. The defendant's medical condition was undoubtedly serious and difficult to treat. In the course of his sentencing remarks the judge was handed a letter from the prison authorities in which it was stated that

f in principle the prison medical services would be able to give the prescribed level of care which the defendant's condition required. The judge found that in reality the Prison Service would, at the least, have extreme difficulty in coping with the defendant's condition. Having carefully read the medical reports, in our view, the judge was quite entitled to reach that conclusion and, as he stated, as an act of humanity to suspend the sentence. In addition, we have been told by counsel

g that the effect of having this appeal hanging over his head, has caused the defendant's eczema to deteriorate. We take the view that having regard to the principle of double jeopardy it would in any event now be wrong to direct an immediate sentence of imprisonment.

[81] Accordingly the sentence will be varied to a term of two years'

h imprisonment suspended for two years. The period of disqualification will remain unaltered as will the order that when the period of disqualification has expired before he drives again the defendant must take an extended test.

Cooksley's appeal dismissed. Stride's and Cook's appeals allowed. Leave granted to Attorney General and sentence varied as indicated.

j

Lynne Townley   Barrister.

Holder v Law Society

[2003] EWCA Civ 39

COURT OF APPEAL, CIVIL DIVISION

ALDOUS, CARNWATH LJJ AND SIR CHRISTOPHER STAUGHTON

21, 24 JANUARY 2003

Solicitor – Law Society – Intervention – Compliance of Law Society's intervention procedure with human rights legislation – Human Rights Act 1998, Sch 1, Pt II, art 1.

Human rights – Right to peaceful enjoyment of possessions – Intervention in solicitor's practice – Compliance of Law Society's intervention procedure with human rights legislation – Human Rights Act 1998, Sch 1, Pt II, art 1.

The Law Society intervened in the claimant's practice as a solicitor under the provisions of the Solicitors Act 1974. The claimant applied to the court for an order directing the society to withdraw the notice of intervention. On an application by the society for summary judgment, the master dismissed the claim. The claimant appealed, on the ground, inter alia, that the society's intervention power, either generally or as applied in the instant case, infringed his rights under art 1[a] of the First Protocol to the European Convention for the Protection of Human Rights and Fundamental Freedoms 1950 (as set out in Sch 1 to the Human Rights Act 1998), which provided that every person was entitled to the peaceful enjoyment of his possessions. The judge held that, apart from issues under the 1998 Act, the society's intervention had been entirely justified; that whilst the power of intervention was not of itself contrary to the 1998 Act, that power could in some cases infringe the right to possession, the question essentially being one of fact and degree; and that, on the evidence in the instant case, it was not possible to conclude that there was no real prospect of the claimant establishing that his human rights had been infringed. Accordingly, he allowed the appeal and directed that the matter go to trial. The society, in reliance on the public interest exception in art 1, appealed on the ground that the judge had been wrong to find that the intervention procedure raised any issue under the 1998 Act.

Held – The intervention procedure had been recognised as draconian in some respects, but necessary for the protection of the public interest, and the courts had repeatedly emphasised the balancing exercise that the procedure involved. There was no material difference between that and the fair balance required by art 1, nor any arguable ground for thinking that the margin allowed to the legislature had been crossed, particularly having regard to the deference which was properly paid to an Act of Parliament, as compared to an administrative decision. The society also had a margin of discretion, but the court had a separate duty to consider the merits of the case, while paying due regard to the views of the society as the relevant professional body. That met any 'fair balance' requirement. As the judge had found that, viewed by reference to the 1974 Act itself, the society's intervention had been entirely justified, that should have led

---

a   Article 1 is set out at [28], below

a him to uphold the society's view as to where the balance lay on the facts of the instant case. Accordingly, the master's order would be restored and the society would be granted summary judgment (see [31]–[33], [36], [39], below).

Sporrong and Lonnroth v Sweden (1983) 5 EHRR 35, *Holy Monasteries v Greece* [1994] EHRR 1, *Giles v Law Society* (1995) 8 Admin LR 105, *Dooley v Law Society* (15 September 2000, unreported), *R (on the application of Farrakhan) v Secretary of State*
b *for the Home Department* [2002] 4 All ER 289, *International Transport Roth GmbH v Secretary of State for the Home Department* [2002] 3 WLR 344 considered.

Decision of Peter Smith J [2002] All ER (D) 378 (Jul) reversed.

Notes

c For circumstances in which the Law Society may intervene in a solicitor's practice, see 44(1) *Halsbury's Laws* (4th edn reissue) para 479.

For the Human Rights Act 1998, s 7, Sch 1, Pt II, art 1, see 7 *Halsbury's Statutes* (4th edn) (2002 reissue) 505, 525.

Cases referred to in judgments

d *Airey v Ireland* (1979) 2 EHRR 305, [1979] ECHR 6289/73, ECt HR.
Buckley v Law Society (No 2) [1984] 3 All ER 313, [1984] 1 WLR 1101.
Dooley v Law Society (15 September 2000, unreported), Ch D.
Giles v Law Society (1996) 8 Admin LR 105, CA.
Holy Monasteries v Greece (1994) 20 EHRR 1, [1994] ECHR 13029/87, ECt HR.
e *International Transport Roth GmbH v Secretary of State for the Home Dept* [2002] EWCA Civ 158, [2002] 3 WLR 344.
Parker v Camden London BC, Newman v Camden London BC [1985] 2 All ER 141, [1986] Ch 162, [1985] 3 WLR 47, CA.
Pine v Law Society [2001] EWCA Civ 1574.
R (on the application of Farrakhan) v Secretary of State for the Home Dept [2002] EWCA
f Civ 606, [2002] 4 All ER 289, [2002] QB 1391, [2002] 3 WLR 481.
Sporrong v Sweden (1983) 5 EHRR 35, [1982] ECHR 7151/75, ECt HR.
Wilson Smith v Law Society (29 March 1999, unreported).
Wright v Law Society (4 September 2002, unreported), Ch D.
X v UK (1983) 6 EHRR 136, E Com HR.

g
Cases also cited or referred to in skeleton arguments

Campbell v UK (1992) 15 EHRR 137, ECt HR.
F v Switzerland (1987) 10 EHRR 411, ECt HR.
Potter v Law Society (20 December 1999, unreported), Ch D.
h *Pybus v Office for the Supervision of Solicitors* [2001] All ER (D) 164 (Dec).
R v Law Society, ex p Mortgage Express Ltd [1997] 2 All ER 348, CA.
Van Marle v Netherlands (1986) 8 EHRR 483, ECt HR.

Appeal

j The defendant, the Law Society, appealed from the decision of Peter Smith J on 25 July 2002 ([2002] All ER (D) 378 (Jul)) allowing the appeal of the claimant, David Herman Holder, from the decision of Master Price on 30 August 2001 dismissing his application to the High Court on 26 June 2001 for an order directing the Law Society to withdraw the notice of intervention of 15 June 2001 in respect of the claimant's practice. The facts are set out in the judgment of Carnwath LJ.

Timothy Dutton QC and *Nicholas Peacock* (instructed by *Wright Son & Pepper*) for
the Law Society.

Philip Engelman and *Roger Pezzani* (instructed by *Teacher Stern Selby*) for the
claimant.

Cur adv vult

24 January 2003. The following judgments were delivered.

CARNWATH LJ.

[1] On Friday, 15 June 2001 the Law Society resolved to intervene in the
practice of the claimant under the Solicitors Act 1974. On 26 June the claimant
applied to the High Court for an order directing the Law Society to withdraw the
notice of intervention. No further steps were taken pursuant to that application,
until 2 August when the Law Society applied for summary judgment under CPR
Pt 24. On 30 August Master Price made an order dismissing the claim. The
appeal which was heard by Peter Smith J almost a year later, led to him allowing
the appeal on 25 July 2002 and directing that the claim should go to trial. The Law
Society now appeals against that order.

[2] In fairness to both the master and the judge, I record that, for reasons
which have not been satisfactorily explained, the judge was not given a note of
the master's reasoning, and may therefore have had the impression that it was
dealt with more cursorily than was in fact the case. A subsequent note of the
judgment, based on solicitors' notes and approved by the master, has been shown
to us, from which it is clear that the matter was fully considered by the master.

BACKGROUND

[3] I can take the material facts from the judge's findings. I do not understand
them to be significantly in dispute. I record that Mr Engelman (for Mr Holder)
said that his client did not admit dishonesty, although he admitted reasonable
grounds to suspect dishonesty. I also note Mr Holder's evidence as to the difficult
circumstances of his early life, which led to him being admitted as a solicitor
relatively late at the age of 37, and to the problems he experienced thereafter in
establishing himself. The judge held ([2002] EWHC 1559 (Ch), [2002] All ER (D)
378 (Jul)):

> '[9] The claimant is a solicitor who was admitted to the roll in 1994. In
> November 1996 he became a partner with a John Baskin and they practised
> under the style "Baskin & Co". The practice was not set up as a true
> partnership. The claimant described the structure as "sort of individual
> within the partnership". Despite the appearance of being in partnership, he
> stated that they had "separate bank accounts and separate overdraft
> facilities", although the accounts certified to LS were based on the average of
> their two branches.
>
> [10] Under the Solicitors Practice Rules 1990 (practice r 13) it is forbidden
> for a solicitor to be a sole practitioner unless and until he is more than three
> years qualified. The claimant in his evidence is describing an arrangement
> which appears to be designed to circumvent the rule by an arrangement
> which, to the outside world and the LS, would appear as a partnership,
> whereas he and Mr Baskin were, in reality, operating as individual sole
> traders.

a

[11] From August 2000 the claimant practised on his own account.

[12] On 8 June 2001 a Mr AS Becconsall an Investigation Compliance Officer of the OSS (the Office of Supervision of Solicitors) began an inspection into the claimant's books and accounts. That inspection revealed:

(1) That in breach of rr 32 and 33 of the SAR he had not maintained any client account records since 31 March 2000 (14 months); nor could he

b   produce client bank account statements and paying-in books (r 33). The claimant admits this. The submission by Mr Dutton QC that the absence of an accounting system of itself puts client funds at risk is well made.

(2) There was an agreed *minimum* cash shortfall on client account at £200,950 comprising £60,000 on the client account of SKT Charitable Trust and £140,950 nominally in the client account of Hilary Simmonds. The

c   claimant admitted this and that he agreed it with Mr Becconsall at the time of the inspection and in my judgment does not challenge these findings in any credible way.

(3) The claimant also told Mr Becconsall that he had withdrawn money from client account for his own purposes to reduce his liabilities to

d   moneylenders.

(4) The claimant was substantially in debt to two moneylenders, Jack Steinberg £220,000 and George Rothschild £266,000. He would obtain money from them, which he would put into the office or client account, and he would issue post-dated cheques for the amount of the loan paying 2% per month in cash as interest.

e

(5) He accepted in statements made to Mr Becconsall his calculation of the claimant's debts as being £680,000 at least, excluding the client accounts shortage of £200,950. The creditors include his professional liability insurers (SIF and St Paul's), VAT, PAYE, Inland Revenue and National Insurance.'

f

[4] The judge also made findings on the reasons for Mr Holder's problems:

'[13] The reason for his serious financial problems was that he put himself massively in debt to fringe moneylenders. This he admitted both to Mr Becconsall and in his evidence. In his first witness statement he stated that he became unable to continue any longer, or repay them for some months before the intervention. Further, although he did not believe the

g   lenders monies were client funds (first witness statement para 21) he admits that he signed letters on the headed notepaper which were to be used by the lenders in claims on the Law Society Compensation Fund saying that the monies could fall within the definition of "client monies". The compensation fund exists primarily to compensate those who have lost their

h   money ie client monies at the hands of dishonest solicitors. A letter falsely describing the monies as clients monies when the claimant did not believe them to be so, is the LS contended serious dishonesty as it could be used to mislead the Compensation Fund to the advantage of both the claimant and those from whom he had been borrowing money ...'

j

[5] He rejected Mr Engelman's attempt to challenge this interpretation of the letter. He thought Mr Holder's state of mind was clear from his own evidence. Mr Holder had said (at paras 21–22 of his first statement):

'In or about latter part of 2000, I could not continue any longer and was unable to pay the two gentleman referred to. I began to receive various threats, which included reporting me to the Law Society. In those

circumstances, and not knowing where to turn, and being let down by
everyone, I was forced into signing letters, which the gentlemen thought
they could use by claiming the funds loaned from the Compensation Fund
... I realised that the end was inevitable and started to wind down the
practice. I became considerably depressed, and it was after I had considerably
wound down the practice, in order to protect my clients, that I went to
(solicitors) with the view to disclose everything to the Law Society.'

He added that there were still some 'active client files', and that, if the
intervention were set aside, he would have 'financial assistance from my local
community whom I have considerably assisted in the past to set me up again'.
However there was, and is, no substantial evidence to support this hope. We
were also told that Mr Holder is currently awaiting trial on charges of theft
relating to his dealings in May 2001, but that fact cannot of course affect our view
of the matter.

[6] Mr Becconsall's findings were set out in a report dated 14 June 2001 to
David Middleton, head of the Investigation Enforcement of the Office for the
Supervision of Solicitors (OSS). On the following day (Friday, 15 June) the
chairman of the Compliance and Supervision Committee of the Law Society,
acting under delegated powers, resolved to exercise the powers of intervention
under Sch 1 to the Act, to vest the practice moneys in the society and to require
the claimant to deliver practice documents to the society's agent. The stated
grounds were under paras 1(1)(a) and (c). The notice was sent by recorded
delivery on 15 June and arrived on Monday, 18 June. Mr Holder first learnt of the
intervention on the Friday as a result of a telephone call to Mr Becconsall's office.

[7] The judge, rightly in my view, concluded that apart from issues under the
Human Rights Act 1998, to which I shall come, the intervention of the Law
Society was entirely justified. He said:

'[34] In the light of the above evidence the following appear to be
incontrovertible.
  1. The claimant was in serious breach of various of the SAC and had been
for many months.
  2. He had probably removed a large amount of money from his client
account. Like Mr Dutton QC I view the letters from the supposed clients
attached to his third witness statement with scepticism.
  3. He was involved with moneylenders and had substantial debts to them
which led him to make a potentially fraudulent misuse of the Solicitors
Compensation Fund.
  4. The claimant did not dispute in any credible way any of those
allegations.
  [35] It follows from the above absent a human rights claim, the
intervention of the LS was in my judgment entirely justified ...'

[8] Before turning to those issues, it is necessary to note a comment made by
the judge about what he thought was the apparent lack of urgency in the exercise
of the powers. He said:

'[36] I should observe however, that whilst the intervention was made
under the chairman's urgent emergency powers as set out above, the actual
intervention did not proceed, so far as I can see, with an urgency that
required an immediate intervention. I say that because the LS did not, for
example, go to court to bolster the intervention powers. They made no

a attempt to serve the intervention notice on the day they made the decision; they were content that it be sent in the post. Those matters show that whilst this case is serious, as any intervention by definition must be serious, and whilst there was dishonesty, they did not believe that there was an *immediate* potential for clients to lose money. The conclusion I draw from their report is that the dishonesty had already been complete and that was the basis for

b the intervention.'

THE STATUTE

[9] The society's powers of intervention are set out in Sch 1 to the Solicitors Act 1974. The relevant grounds in this case were reason to suspect dishonesty on

c the part of a solicitor (para 1(1)(a)) and failure to comply with the accounts rules (para 1(1)(c)). Paragraph 6(1) confers the power, by resolution, to provide for the vesting in the society of money held by the solicitor 'in connection with his practice'. Such money is, on the making of the resolution, held by the society 'upon trust for the persons beneficially entitled'.

[10] The society is required to serve on the solicitor, and 'any other person

d having possession of' money to which the resolution applies, a certified copy of the resolution, and 'a notice prohibiting the payment out of any such sums of money' (para 6(3)). It appears from the evidence of Mr Middleton (unsurprisingly), that the notice on the solicitor is normally served after notice has been served on his bank, thereby effectively freezing his accounts. However,

e there appears to be no specific evidence that this happened in the present case.

[11] Paragraph 6(4) provides that the person served with a notice may within eight days of service, on not less than 48 hours' notice, 'apply to the High Court for an order directing the Society to withdraw the notice'. If the court makes such an order, it has power 'also to make such other order with respect to the matter as it may think fit' (para 6(5)).

f [12] By para 9 the society may give notice requiring the production or delivery of documents held by the solicitor in connection with his practice. Again there is provision for the solicitor to apply to the court for re-delivery of the documents (para 9(8)).

[13] Where intervention powers have been exercised on the grounds of

g suspected dishonesty or breach of accounting rules the exercise of the power operates immediately to suspend any practising certificate of the solicitor for the time being in force (1974 Act, s 15(1)(a)). The solicitor may before the certificate expires apply to the society to terminate the suspension, and if the society refuses he may appeal to the Master of the Rolls (s 16).

h [14] The nature and characteristics of the intervention jurisdiction have been discussed in a number of cases, starting with *Buckley v Law Society (No 2)* [1984] 3 All ER 313, [1984] 1 WLR 1101 (Megarry V-C), and most recently in this court, in *Giles v Law Society* (1996) 8 Admin LR 105. It has been recognised that it is a 'draconian' jurisdiction, necessary to protect the public interest, but balanced by the right to apply to the court. As Sedley LJ said in *Giles's* case (at 118–119):

j 'The manifest purpose of sch. 1 to the Solicitors Act 1974 … is to create an *ex parte* procedure leading where appropriate to intervention, the consequences of which are undoubtedly drastic and potentially terminal for a solicitor's practice. Where an intervention is persisted with, para. 6(4) of sch. 1 provides for a solicitor to be heard on an application made within eight days to the court for an order directing the Law Society to withdraw the

notice prohibiting payment out of money held by solicitors save with the
leave of the court. Since this is the key intervention power, at least in cases   *a*
of suspected dishonesty, it is realistic to describe the sub-paragraph as
conferring jurisdiction upon the court to direct the Law Society to withdraw
from the intervention. On such an application it is for the court to decide
whether or not to direct withdrawal on the then material before it … it is by
common consent a matter for the court's judgment (I prefer not to use the   *b*
word discretion in this context) whether it should direct withdrawal—a
judgment which may be significantly, though not conclusively, affected by
the Law Society's own view of the facts, since on the view taken by the
professional body charged with the regulation of solicitors' practices is itself
a relevant evidential factor to which the judge not only can but must have
regard.'   *c*

[15] The court itself conducts 'a two-stage process'. Its role was summarised
by Neuberger J in *Dooley v Law Society* (15 September 2000, unreported):

'First it must decide whether the grounds under para 1 are made out; in this
case, primarily, whether there are grounds for suspecting dishonesty.   *d*
Secondly, if the court is so satisfied, then it must consider whether in the light
of all the evidence before it the intervention should continue. In deciding the
second question, the court must carry out a balancing exercise between the
need in the public interest to protect the public from dishonest solicitors and
the inevitably very serious consequences to the solicitor if the intervention
continues.'   *e*

[16] Finally, it should not be thought that the protracted progress of the
present proceedings is in any way typical. Where necessary the procedure can
operate very quickly. By way of illustration, we were referred to one case (*Wilson
Smith v Law Society* (29 March 1999, unreported)) where the judge gave a   *f*
temporary injunction by telephone on the day before the proposed intervention
to enable the matter to be considered in court the following morning. In another
recent case to which I shall return (*Wright v Law Society* (4 September 2002,
unreported)), an interim injunction was granted to preserve the position pending
the full hearing a few days later. The judge recorded the speed with which all the
parties had worked, including the submission of skeleton arguments by e-mail   *g*
over the weekend.

THE HUMAN RIGHTS ISSUE
[17] Before the judge it was submitted by Mr Engelman (appearing then as
now for Mr Holder) that the intervention power, either generally or as applied in   *h*
this case, infringed Mr Holder's right to 'peaceful enjoyment of his possessions'
under art 1 of the First Protocol to the European Convention for the Protection
of Human Rights and Fundamental Freedoms 1950, as applied by the Human
Rights Act 1998, and that in addition there had been a breach of the claimant's
right to a fair hearing under art 6. As to the latter, the judge, who as I said did not
have a note of the master's judgment, considered that there had not been a fair   *j*
hearing on that occasion, but he considered that the right of appeal to him was
sufficient to cure any such defect.
[18] As to art 1, the judge rejected Mr Engelman's broad submission that
'under no circumstances' could the power of intervention be justified, because of
its effect in destroying the practice of the solicitor. The judge said:

a

'[38] For reasons which I will give in this judgment I do not accept Mr Engelman's submission as widely based as it is. It seems to me that balancing the rights of the individual against the rights of the public and the state interest in seeing that the conduct of solicitors is maintained to the highest professional standards of integrity, the power of intervention is a necessary power and the power *of itself* is not contrary to Human Rights Act

b

1998. However, I do accept an alternative submission that the power can in some cases infringe the right to possession but it is essentially a question of fact and degree in each case.'

Later in his judgment he expanded on what he saw as the 'draconian' features of the intervention power:

c

'[68] The effect of an intervention is admittedly draconian. It seems to me that the effect of the intervention would, in reality, render it at the very least, difficult, if not impossible, for a solicitor to collect outstanding fees and, more importantly, work in progress. In respect of the latter there are undoubtedly cases where solicitors work on an entire fee basis.

d

Conveyancing transactions, for example, are regularly carried out on such a basis. Commercial or business transactions are similarly carried out on the basis of a fee quoted for doing a particular job. The result of an intervention will prevent the solicitor from carrying on the contract. It means that the solicitor will have discharged himself with the result that the solicitor will no

e

longer be able to carry out the duties. He will thus lose his entitlement to a fee and, according to well known principles of entire contracts, would not be able to claim a quantum meruit.

[69] As a matter of practicality it seems to me that the claimant's evidence as to the difficulties of collection are made out. Whilst Mr Dutton QC said the LS will afford documents, or rather copies of documents, to enable

f

collections to be made, I can well foresee (and this has been my experience in the interventions where I have been involved) that the destruction of the practice causes the clients to be scattered to the winds and the recoverability of monies made virtually impossible.'

g

[19] He then considered whether such effects could be justified under art 1. He said:

'[70] Is that necessary? In some cases it may be necessary because it might be a necessary evil to correct a much greater one. The more interesting question is, is it *always* necessary? In that case I am not convinced that it can

h

be said that an intervention in the way in which the procedure is currently permitted to be exercised, is always necessary. It follows from that analysis that if the procedure was not necessary in that way, and it resulted in the interference in the right to possession of property, the procedure itself will infringe the claimant's human rights. I do not see that it can be said that

j

there is no other alternative. If a report for example, is prepared along the lines of the present case there would have been no difficulty in making an appointment at short notice to go to court for an order for an intervention or some lesser order if the court thought that appropriate. There would then be an independent review and the court (like a search order or a freezing order) would act on the evidence. If the evidence was made out, there would be an independent review of the procedure. Intervention in a full blown way

might be required on occasions. Alternatively the court might feel a lesser
intervention (such as a receiver, a manager) would be appropriate ...'   *a*

[20] He thought the appointment of a receiver would have considerable
advantages over the intervention procedure:

'[71] There are considerable advantages in my view to this process vis-à-vis
LS [the Law Society], the SCF [the Solicitors Compensation Fund] and the   *b*
clients. First, client continuity would not be affected in the same way.
Second, the receiver would be able to carry on the practice and attempt to
deal with the client's cases. I accept there may be instances where that might
not be possible, but an independent receiver would be able to make a rapid
assessment as occurs in many other cases of receivership and/or liquidation.
Mr Dutton QC suggested that the receivers would be require indemnity   *c*
form the LS. I am not persuaded as to that. Receivers and managers in the
case of insolvency regularly fail to obtain indemnities from their appointers
but look usually only to the assets. But even if he is right, that would be
deployed by the LS as an argument before the judge to justify an intervention
as opposed to a receivership.   *d*
[72] Third, a receiver would be in a position to take immediate steps to
preserve goodwill and work in progress for the general benefit of the
creditors, the LS, the SCF and possibly the claimant. I do not see any
disadvantages in that process save in an exceptional case where the LS feels
immediate action is necessary. It seems to me that if a system can operate
which has the same, or even better benefits, but has the possibility of   *e*
preserving property, which would otherwise be destroyed or lost, that leads
to two conclusions. First, that is a fairer system. Second, that the present
system is not only unfair but is an infringement of the claimant's human
rights.'

Accordingly he concluded: *f*

'[79] ... On the evidence before me at the moment I cannot conclude that
there is no real prospect of the claimant establishing that his human rights
have been infringed. I say that because it seems to me that the procedure in
the present case was not necessarily the only way to address the problem. I
do not see why a receivership could not have been contemplated as an   *g*
adjunct to the intervention powers in advance of the intervention or in
tandem with the intervention.'

[21] The Law Society has been understandably concerned at the implications
of the judgment of Peter Smith J for the exercise of its intervention powers. It *h*
intervenes in approximately 100 solicitors' practices per year, of which a
substantial proportion are cases of suspected dishonesty. Furthermore, it does
not consider that the alternative procedure proposed by the judge is in fact
available in law, even if otherwise desirable (which it disputes).

[22] More recently, Judge Behrens in *Wright's* case declined to follow the
reasoning of Peter Smith J. He said: *j*

'The Law Society has to take into account the public interest in deciding
whether to exercise its powers of intervention at all. The public interest
requires a balance to be struck between the draconian effect of intervention
and the matters referred to earlier in this judgment. Second I have
considerable doubts about the jurisdiction of the court to adopt the sort of

a
solution envisaged by Peter Smith J in paras 70 and 71 of his judgment. Intervention in its full form is the statutory remedy entrusted by Parliament to the Law Society in order to regulate the profession. It is not, in view, open to the courts to devise a different and less draconian remedy. I cannot, for my part, see that the court would have power to appoint a Receiver in an application by the Law Society to determine whether there ought to be an
b
intervention or not.

Neither counsel were able to point me to any express power in any statute authorising the appointment of a Receiver or the more limited intervention referred to in Peter Smith J's judgment. It seems to me that if such a power is to exist it should be provided for by Parliament.'

c

THE ISSUES IN THIS COURT

[23] Mr Dutton QC, for the Law Society, submits that the judge was wrong to find that the intervention procedure raised any issue under the 1998 Act, and in particular that he was wrong to think that there was an alternative procedure.
d
Mr Engelman, on the other hand, repeats his submission that the intervention procedure itself offends art 1, and he supports the judge's finding of the possibility of a breach on the facts of this case.

[24] Mr Engelman also makes a submission on art 6, which I can deal with briefly. He refers to Mr Holder's evidence of the difficulties he had, in June 2001, in obtaining legal assistance, once his accounts had been in effect frozen. Relying
e
on the decision of the European Court of Human Rights in *Airey v Ireland* (1979) 2 EHRR 305, Mr Engelman submits that his client's lack of means to employ a lawyer meant that his right of access to a court was effectively denied. However, a similar argument was rejected by this court in the same legal context in *Pine v Law Society* [2001] EWCA Civ 1574 (15 October 2001). Sir Andrew Morritt V-C,
f
referred to *Airey*'s case, and to its interpretation by the Commission in *X v UK* (1983) 6 EHRR 136. He noted that the principle distilled by the Commission from the decision of the court in *Airey*'s case was that—

> 'only in exceptional circumstances, namely where the withholding of legal aid would make the assertion of a civil claim practically impossible, or where
g
> it would lead to obvious unfairness of the proceedings can such a right be invoked by virtue of art 6(1) of the convention.'

[25] It had been contended for Mr Pine that—

> 'the possible consequences were so serious for the solicitor that
h
> disciplinary proceedings should be placed towards the criminal end of the spectrum of civil proceedings in deciding what is and is not fair ... (and) that it was obviously unfair to take and pursue disciplinary proceedings with such immediate and future consequences for the livelihood of a solicitor, particularly where his lack of means stems from the Law Society's own acts in connection with those proceedings, unless at the same time provision is
j
> made for the impecunious solicitor to receive legal advice and representation if he wanted it at no expense to himself.'

[26] Sir Andrew Morritt V-C rejected this submission:

> 'I do not accept this submission. It is clear from the passage I have quoted from *Airey*'s case in [9], above that, at least in proceedings in which a party

may appear in person, the requirements of art 6 with respect to legal advice
and representation depend on the facts of any given case.'

Having reviewed the facts of the case he said:

> 'The procedure was not complex. The relevant facts were within the
> knowledge of Mr Pine. Mr Pine was a solicitor experienced in commercial
> litigation. Mr Pine had ample opportunity to indicate any defences he might
> wish to advance. In my judgment neither the seriousness of the likely
> consequences nor the emotional involvement of Mr Pine, which is not
> apparent from his letters to have been a debilitating factor anyway, when
> considered in the light of the absence of legal advice or representation, gave
> rise to any unfairness.'

[27] I see no reason to take a different view in this case. Mr Holder was a
solicitor who specialised in litigation. He had been closely involved in the
investigation, and had fairly admitted most of the relevant facts. There was
nothing particularly complex about the issues, and there is no evidence that he
would have had any difficulty in understanding them, or presenting his case to
the court.

ARTICLE 1
[28] Article 1 of the First Protocol to the European Convention on Human
Rights is in these terms:

> 'Every natural or legal person is entitled to the peaceful enjoyment of his
> possessions. No one shall be deprived of his possessions except in the public
> interest and subject to the conditions provided for by law and by the general
> principles of international law.
> The preceding provisions shall not, however, in any way impair the right
> of a State to enforce such laws as it deems necessary to control the use of
> property in accordance with the general interest or to secure the payment of
> taxes or other contributions or penalties.'

Mr Dutton did not dispute that the intervention involved an interference with
Mr Holder's peaceful enjoyment of his possessions; but he of course relied on the
public interest justification, which is also emphasised by the English cases on the
interpretation of the 1974 Act.

[29] Mr Engelman referred to the principles laid down by the Strasbourg court
for the application of the public interest test:

> '... the Court must determine whether a fair balance was struck between
> the demands of the general interest of the community and the requirements
> of the protection of the individual's fundamental rights.' (See *Sporrong v
> Sweden* (1983) 5 EHRR 35 at 52 (para 69).)

> '... there must be a reasonable relationship of proportionality between the
> means employed and the aim sought to be realised by any measure depriving
> a person of his possessions.' (See *Holy Monasteries v Greece* (1994) 20 EHRR 1
> at 48 (para 70).)

He submitted that if, as the judge found, the more draconian features of the
intervention procedure were not 'necessary', the requirement of 'proportionality'
was not satisfied.

a [30] With respect to the submission, and to the judge, this approach ignores the 'all important' factor, when considering issues of proportionality, of the 'margin of appreciation or discretion' or 'area of judgment' allowed to the legislator and the decision-maker (see, for example, *R (on the application of Farrakhan) v Secretary of State for the Home Dept* [2002] EWCA Civ 606 at [67], [2002] 4 All ER 289 at [67], [2002] QB 1391; and the review of the principles in

b *International Transport Roth GmbH v Secretary of State for the Home Dept* [2002] EWCA Civ 158, [2002] 3 WLR 344). This aspect was not mentioned by the judge, although it was referred to in Mr Engelman's written submissions to him. In para [70] (quoted above) he appears to have approached the matter on the basis that it was for the court to determine what was 'necessary' in the public interest, and in doing so to compare other possible procedures devised by the court. In

c my view, this was fundamentally wrong.

[31] In the present case, the 'margin' arises at two stages: first, the discretion allowed to the legislature in establishing the statutory regime, and, secondly, the discretion of the Law Society as the body entrusted with the decision in an individual case. (In the former case, the only remedy for exceeding the 'margin'

d may be a 'declaration of incompatibility' under the 1998 Act.) The intervention procedure, now contained in the 1974 Act, is long-established (dating back to 1941, in its earliest form), and has been reviewed by the court on many occasions. As appears from the cases to which I have referred, it has been recognised as 'draconian' in some respects, but necessary for the protection of the public interest; and the courts have repeatedly emphasised the 'balancing exercise'

e which it involves. I see no material difference between this and the 'fair balance' which art 1 requires. Nor do I see any reason why the 1998 Act should be thought to have changed anything. There has long been a right of individual petition to the Strasbourg court for breaches of the convention, but we have not been referred to any questioning of the intervention procedure under art 1. I see no

f arguable grounds for thinking that the margin allowed to the legislature has been crossed, particularly having regard to the deference which is properly paid to an Act of Parliament, as compared to an administrative decision (see the *Roth* case [2002] 3 WLR 344 at [26], [83] per Laws LJ).

[32] Having reached that point, the Law Society's actions must be judged by reference to the procedure laid down by Parliament, not to some hypothetical

g alternative procedure. This makes it unnecessary to rule on Mr Dutton's submission that the alternative procedure suggested by the judge, involving an application to the court for a receiver, was not in fact available to the society. He referred to *Parker v Camden London BC, Newman v Camden London BC* [1985] 2 All ER 141, [1986] Ch 162, where this court held that the wide power to appoint a

h receiver and manager, under the Supreme Court Act 1981, s 37, could not properly be used to supplant the management powers given by Parliament to the housing authority. We do not need to decide whether that case provides guidance as to the availability of that power to support the very different functions of the Law Society. In any event, if the intervention procedure on its

j own had been found to be non-compliant, it might be necessary, to avoid incompatibility, to 'read in' such a power (applying the beneficial interpretation required under the 1998 Act, s 3).

[33] The Law Society also has a 'margin of discretion', but the court has a separate duty to consider the merits of the case, in accordance with the principles I have discussed, while paying due regard, as Sedley LJ said (see *Giles's* case above), to the views of the Law Society, as the relevant professional body. As I

have said, this meets any 'fair balance' requirement. The judge found that, viewed by reference to the 1974 Act itself, the society's intervention was 'entirely justified'. I agree. In my view, that should have led him to have upheld the society's view as to where the balance lay on the facts of this case.

[34] As I have noted, the judge mentioned the perceived problem of collecting outstanding fees, particularly in relation to work in progress on contracts on 'an entire fee basis', and the difficulties of access to documents. Mr Engelman does not claim that Mr Holder in fact had work in progress of this kind, and there is evidence that the society has been willing to permit supervised access to the documents when required. In my view these are not factors which could possibly affect the overall judgment.

[35] Finally, I should comment on the passage in which the judge suggested that there was no 'immediate' urgency, and his reliance on the fact that the society had been 'content' that the notice should be sent by post. The evidence of Mr Middleton, the officer responsible, was as follows:

'Of particular relevance in this context is the substantial amount of money owed to fringe money-lenders, the fact that he is in sole charge of his client account and that substantial sums had already taken from that client account together with his admissions. There was an obvious risk that should further monies be available to Mr Holder in his client account prior to the intervention he might have sought to remove those monies prior to the intervention taking place.'

This was in my view an entirely reasonable assessment. I do not think the judge was justified in reading anything into the fact that notice was served by post to arrive on the Monday, particularly since it was the resolution which led to money vesting in the Law Society; and it would be the notice to the bank (not to the solicitor) which would normally be the most critical step in preventing dissipation.

[36] For these reasons, I would allow the appeal and restore the order of the master.

SIR CHRISTOPHER STAUGHTON.

[37] I agree that this appeal should be allowed, on the ground that there was never any prospect of the Law Society's intervention being set aside. The claimant, a solicitor and sole practitioner, did not keep the accounts which the Law Society required him to keep. There was a deficit on his client account of £200,950; he owed £200,000 and £266,000 to moneylenders; and there were reasonable grounds for suspecting that he had been fraudulent in connection with his practice. If ever there was a case where it was desirable in the public interest that the Law Society should intervene in a solicitor's practice, this was that case. It is the habitual task of solicitors to have in their charge in the course of their practice large sums of their clients' money. They must be honest and reliable people.

[38] In the exercise of its powers of intervention the Law Society must of course comply with the European Convention for the Protection of Human Rights and Fundamental Freedoms 1950 (as set out in Sch 1 to the Human Rights Act 1998). I can imagine circumstances where the Law Society might be found not to have complied with the convention, or with the 1998 Act. After all, a solicitor whose practice is the object of an intervention loses his practising certificate, and in all probability his livelihood as well. The provisions for

a bringing an intervention to an end are very unlikely to restore the solicitor's goodwill and his prosperity. If it comes about that the intervention was mistaken or unjustified, there is a risk that the solicitor will suffer a substantial loss without recourse to any remedy. In practice this may never happen; but it is a cause for concern. However, not in this case.

b **ALDOUS LJ.**
     [**39**] I also agree.

Appeal allowed.

James Brooks   Barrister.

Schmidt v Rosewood Trust Ltd   *a*
[2003] UKPC 26

PRIVY COUNCIL

LORD NICHOLLS OF BIRKENHEAD, LORD HOPE OF CRAIGHEAD, LORD HUTTON, LORD
HOBHOUSE OF WOODBOROUGH AND LORD WALKER OF GESTINGTHORPE   *b*

17–19 FEBRUARY, 27 MARCH 2003

Trust and trustee – Disclosure of trust documents – Isle of Man – Whether dependent
upon proprietary interest of beneficiary – Whether object of mere power entitled to
disclosure.   *c*

Powers of trustee – Discretionary trusts – Isle of Man – Distinctions between trusts and
powers.

The settlor died intestate and letters of administration were granted to his son, *d*
the claimant. The defendant company was the sole trustee of two settlements, the
subject matter of the proceedings. The claimant applied for disclosure of trust
accounts and information about the trust assets by virtue of the discretionary
interests or expectations which the claimant claimed that he had, and that his
father had had during his life, under the two settlements. The High Court of the
Isle of Man ordered, inter alia, that the defendant should provide certain *e*
information and make extensive disclosure of unredacted documents. The
defendant appealed to the Staff of Government Division of the Isle of Man on
the ground, inter alia, that the claimant was not a beneficiary under the two
settlements, and that his father was never more than a mere object of a power
who as such had no entitlement to trust documents or information. The *f*
defendant's appeal was allowed and the claimant appealed to the Privy Council.
The defendant contended that a beneficiary's right to disclosure of trust
documents should be classified as a proprietary right and that no object of a mere
power could have any such right, because he had no proprietary interest in the
trust property.   *g*

Held – It was fundamental to the law of trusts that the court had jurisdiction to
supervise and, if appropriate, intervene in the administration of a trust, including
a discretionary trust. The right to seek disclosure of trust documents was one
aspect of the court's inherent jurisdiction to supervise, and if necessary to
intervene in, the administration of trusts. The right to seek the court's *h*
intervention did not depend on entitlement to a fixed and transmissible interest.
The object of a discretion (including a mere power) might also be entitled to
protection from a court of equity, although the circumstances in which he might
seek protection, and the nature of the protection he might expect to obtain,
would depend on the court's discretion. However, no beneficiary had any *j*
entitlement as of right to disclosure of anything which could plausibly be
described as a trust document. Especially when there were issues as to personal
or commercial confidentiality, the court might have to balance the competing
interests of beneficiaries, the trustees themselves, and third parties. Disclosure
might have to be limited and safeguards might have to be put in place. In the
circumstances the appeal would be allowed and the matter remitted to the High

a Court for further consideration in light of the Board's judgment (see [51], [52],
   [66], [67], [69], below).

Notes
For the answering of inquiries by strangers see 48 *Halsbury's Laws* (4th edn) (2000
reissue) para 857.

b
Cases referred to in judgment
A-G of Ontario v Stavro (1994) 119 DLR (4th) 750, Ont HC.
AT & T Istel Ltd v Tully [1992] 3 All ER 523, [1993] AC 45, [1992] 3 WLR 344, HL;
   rvsg [1992] 2 All ER 28, [1992] QB 315, [1992] 2 WLR 112, CA.
Butt, Re, Butt v Kelson [1952] 1 All ER 167, [1952] Ch 197, CA.
c *Chaine-Nickson v Bank of Ireland* [1976] IR 393, Ir HC.
Clarke v Earl of Ormonde (1821) Jac 108, 37 ER 791, [1814–23] All ER Rep 329.
Cowin, Re, Cowin v Gravett (1886) 33 Ch D 179.
Gartside v IRC [1968] 1 All ER 121, [1968] AC 553, [1968] 2 WLR 277, HL.
Gestetner Settlement, Re, Barnett v Blumka [1953] 1 All ER 1150, [1953] Ch 672,
d   [1953] 2 WLR 1033.
Gulbenkian's Settlement Trusts, Re, Whishaw v Stephens, [1968] 3 All ER 785, [1970]
      AC 408, [1968] 3 WLR 1127, HL; *affg* sub nom *Re Gulbenkian's Settlement Trusts,
      Hacobian v Maun* [1967] 3 All ER 15, [1968] Ch 126, [1967] 3 WLR 1112, CA.
Hartigan Nominees Pty Ltd v Rydge (1992) 29 NSWLR 405, NSW CA.
Hay's Settlement Trusts, Re [1981] 3 All ER 786, [1982] 1 WLR 202.
e *Howard de Walden (Lord) v IRC* [1942] 1 All ER 287, [1942] 1 KB 389, CA.
Londonderry's Settlement, Re, Peat v Walsh [1964] 3 All ER 855, [1965] Ch 918, CA.
Manisty's Settlement, Re, Manisty v Manisty [1973] 2 All ER 1203, [1974] Ch 17,
      [1973] 3 WLR 341.
McPhail v Doulton [1970] 2 All ER 228, [1971] AC 424, [1970] 2 WLR 1110, HL; *rvsg*
f   in part sub nom *Re Baden's Deed Trusts, Baden v Smith* [1969] 1 All ER 1016,
      [1969] 2 Ch 388, [1969] 3 WLR 12, CA.
Mettoy Pension Trustees Ltd v Evans [1991] 2 All ER 513, [1990] 1 WLR 1587.
Morice v Bishop of Durham (1805) 10 Ves 522, 32 ER 947, [1803–13] All ER Rep 451,
      LC.
Murphy's Settlements, Re, Murphy v Murphy, [1998] 3 All ER 1, [1999] 1 WLR 282.
g *Nelson, Re, Norris v Nelson* (1918) [1928] Ch 920n, CA.
O'Rourke v Darbishire [1920] AC 581, [1920] All ER Rep 1, HL.
Randall v Lubrano (31 October 1975, unreported), NSW SC.
Rouse v IOOF Australia Trustees Ltd (1999) 2 ITELR 289, Aust SC.
Saunders v Vautier (1841) 4 Beav 115, 49 ER 282, Rolls Ct; *affd* (1841) Cr&Ph 240,
h   41 ER 482, [1835–42] All ER Rep 58, LC.
Smith, Re, Public Trustee v Aspinall [1928] Ch 915, [1928] All ER Rep 520.
Spellson v George (1987) 11 NSWLR 300, NSW SC.
Tillott, Re, Lee v Wilson [1892] 1 Ch 86.
Vestey's (Lord) Exors v IRC [1949] 1 All ER 1108, HL.
j *Whitrick (decd), Re, Sutcliffe v Sutcliffe* [1957] 2 All ER 467, [1957] 1 WLR 884, CA.

Cases also cited in argument
Armitage v Nurse [1997] 2 All ER 705, [1998] Ch 241, [1997] 3 WLR 1046, CA.
Breadner v Granville-Grossman [2000] 4 All ER 705, [2001] Ch 523, [2001] 2 WLR 593.
Brooks' Scttlement Trusts, Re, Lloyds Bank Ltd v Tillard [1939] 3 All ER 920, [1939]
   Ch 993.

Fairbairn (decd), Re [1967] VR 633, Vic SC.

Gilchrist, Ex p, Re Armstrong (1886) 17 QBD 521, CA.

Jones v Torin (1833) 6 Sim 225, 53 ER 589.

Leek (decd), Re, Darwen v Leek [1967] 2 All ER 1160, [1967] Ch 1061, [1967] 3 WLR 576; *affd* [1968] 1 All ER 793, [1969] 1 Ch 563, [1968] 2 WLR 1385, CA.

Millar v Hornsby (2000) 3 ITELR 81, Vic SC.

Norwich Pharmacal Co v Customs and Excise Comrs [1973] 2 All ER 943, [1974] AC 133, [1973] 3 WLR 164, HL.

Saxone Shoe Co Ltd's Trust Deed, Re, Re Abbott's Will Trusts, Abbott v Pearson [1962] 2 All ER 904, [1962] 1 WLR 943.

Talbot v Marshfield (1865) 2 Dr & Sm 549, 62 ER 728.

Tierney v King [1983] 2 Qd R 580, Qld SC.

Wynne v Humberston (1858) 27 Beav 421, 54 ER 165.

Appeal

Vadim Schmidt appealed with special leave granted on 19 September 2001 from a decision of the Staff of Government Division of the High Court of the Isle of Man (Deemster M Kerruish QC and GF Tattersall QC sitting as a Judge of Appeal) dated 26 February 2001 ((2001) 3 ITELR 734) allowing the appeal of the respondent, Rosewood Trust Ltd, from the order of Deemster Cain QC in the High Court of the Isle of Man on 19 November 1999, requiring the respondent to provide information concerning two settlements known as the Angora Trust and the Everest Trust in which the appellant claimed to be interested on his own behalf and as administrator of the estate of his late father, Vitali Schmidt.

Alan Steinfeld QC and *Marcus Staff* (instructed by *Lane & Partners* as agents for Cains, Isle of Man) for the appellant.

David Brownbill and *Michael Gibbon* (instructed by *Saunders & Co* as agents for Simocks, Isle of Man) for the respondent.

The Board took time for consideration.

27 March 2003. The following judgment of the Board was delivered.

LORD WALKER OF GESTINGTHORPE.

INTRODUCTION

[1] It has become common for wealthy individuals in many parts of the world (including countries which have no indigenous law of trusts) to place funds at their disposition into trusts (often with a network of underlying companies) regulated by the law of, and managed by trustees resident in, territories with which the settlor (who may be also a beneficiary) has no substantial connection. These territories (sometimes called tax havens) are chosen not for their geographical convenience (indeed face-to-face meetings between the settlor and his trustees are often very inconvenient) but because they are supposed to offer special advantages in terms of confidentiality and protection from fiscal demands (and, sometimes from problems under the insolvency laws, or laws restricting freedom of testamentary disposition, in the country of the settlor's domicile). The trusts and powers contained in a settlement established in such circumstances may give no reliable indication of who will in the event benefit from the settlement. Typically it will contain very wide

a discretions exercisable by the trustees (sometimes only with the consent of a so-called protector) in favour of a widely-defined class of beneficiaries. The exercise of those discretions may depend on the settlor's wishes as confidentially imparted to the trustees and the protector. As a further cloak against transparency, the identity of the true settlor or settlors may be concealed behind some corporate figurehead.

b [2] All these considerations may encourage a settlor to entrust substantial funds to an apparently secure and confidential offshore shelter. But the very same features may, as this case strikingly illustrates, present problems to the close relatives of a settlor who dies unexpectedly, as did Mr Vitali Schmidt (Mr Schmidt), the co-settlor of two Isle of Man settlements called the Angora Trust and the Everest Trust.

c [3] The main issue on this appeal is the claim of Mr Schmidt's son Vadim, the appellant, to obtain trust accounts and other information from the trustees of the two settlements. The sole trustee of each settlement is Rosewood Trust Ltd (Rosewood), an Isle of Man company which is in business as a provider of corporate and trustee services. It is the respondent to the appeal. The appellant's claim for

d disclosure of accounts and other information has been made in two capacities, that is both personally and as the administrator of Mr Schmidt's estate. Mr Schmidt died intestate in Moscow on 31 August 1997 and letters of administration to his estate in the Isle of Man were granted to the appellant on 17 August 1998.

[4] Before any summary of the trusts and powers of the settlements it is

e appropriate to say something about the background to this litigation, and the evidence which was before the lower courts. When Mr Schmidt died (according to the appellant's evidence, unexpectedly and alone at his Moscow apartment) the appellant was 19 years of age (he was born on 28 September 1977). He was entitled to share in his father's estate together with his mother Svetlana and his paternal grandmother, Alisa. He has deposed that he has devoted his time and resources to

f tracing the assets of his father's estate. His father was a senior executive director of Lukoil, which is the largest oil company in Russia and one of the largest oil companies in the world. The appellant believes that his efforts to trace his father's assets (in Liechtenstein, Austria, Cyprus and the Isle of Man) have been frustrated by some of his father's co-directors.

g [5] In June 1998 the appellant commenced proceedings (the 1998 proceedings) in the Isle of Man against Rosewood, its directors and several other defendants. In the 1998 proceedings the appellant alleged breach of trust and breach of fiduciary duty. He obtained an ex parte order made on 10 July 1998 (and varied by consent on 16 July 1998) prohibiting Rosewood and other defendants from dealing with

h assets comprised directly or indirectly in the Angora Trust and the Everest Trust. The order also provided for extensive disclosure of information.

[6] The appellant commenced the present proceedings by petition on 1 June 1999. His case, as set out in an affidavit sworn by him on 7 June 1999, is that the disclosure made to him pursuant to the ex parte order 'raised more questions than

j it answered', especially as parts of some disclosed documents had been obliterated. It appears that over $US 105m was received by the two settlements between their creation and 1998. The appellant deposed that sums totalling about $US 14·6m had been paid to him (as his father's administrator) between August and October 1998. These sums were not accepted by him by way of compromise of the claims made in the 1998 proceedings, and he believed them to represent only a fraction of Mr Schmidt's total entitlement under the two settlements. The appellant has

obtained a lengthy accountants' report dated 4 June 1999 from Ernst & Young   a
setting out alleged deficiencies and inconsistencies in the material provided.

[7] The appellant's present proceedings seek fuller disclosure of trust accounts
and information about the trust assets, not by way of discovery in the 1998
proceedings but by virtue of the discretionary interests or expectations which the
appellant claims that he himself has, and that his late father had during his life,
under the two settlements. The present proceedings were initially attacked by   b
Rosewood as being an abuse of process, but that submission was rejected at first
instance and was not pursued on Rosewood's appeal to the Staff of Government
Division (see (2001) 3 ITELR 734).

[8] That is only a brief summary of the background to the litigation. It has many
features which might be thought to prompt further questions. However neither   c
side has suggested that the settlements should be regarded as sham documents, or
as documents entered into for illegal purposes. It is unnecessary to try to go further,
at this stage, into the origins of the settlements. Indeed it would not be possible to
go much further since the judgments below are very short on any findings of fact,
and the record before the Board does not contain all the affidavit evidence sworn in
the two sets of proceedings. It appears that Rosewood does not accept that   d
Mr Schmidt was a settlor of either settlement. Certainly he was not named as a
settlor. But (in responses filed in the High Court of the Isle of Man) Rosewood has
described Pacquerette Ltd (Pacquerette), the named settlor, as 'simply a nominee'
and has stated that Mr Schmidt 'was involved in the setting up' of each trust.
Rosewood also stated in its answer that its involvement was 'simply to receive and   e
pay out such funds as [Mr Schmidt] chose to channel through the Isle of Man'. In
the absence of other evidence that justifies the conclusion that he was one of those
who joined in causing the settlements to be made and funded, and was in substance
a co-settlor.

THE TERMS OF THE SETTLEMENTS   f

[9] The Angora Trust was executed on 6 April 1992 between (1) Pacquerette and
(2) Lorne House Trust Ltd (Lorne House). The Everest Trust was executed on
20 June 1995 between Pacquerette and Lorne House. Lorne House (an Isle of Man
company apparently controlled by the same persons as Rosewood) retired from the
trusteeship of both settlements, and Rosewood was appointed as sole trustee in its   g
place, on 3 May 1997.

[10] The Angora Trust and the Everest Trust are in similar but by no means
identical form. The convenient course is to summarise the trusts and powers of the
Angora Trust and then identify the points of difference in the Everest Trust.

[11] Clause 1 of the Angora Trust contains definitions. Some are self-   h
explanatory but the following should be noted. (1) 'The Trust Period' and 'the
Accumulation Period' are both defined as the period of 80 years from the execution
of the settlement (and that period is by cl 2 the perpetuity period permitted by the
law of the Isle of Man) subject to powers for the trustees to terminate either period
before the expiration of 80 years. (2) 'The Beneficiaries' are defined as the Royal   j
National Lifeboat Institution (the RNLI) and the persons listed in the second
schedule. That schedule (originally copied in a redacted form, but later without
redaction) contains the names of Mr Schmidt and other Lukoil senior executives.
(3) 'The Protector' is defined as Mr Schmidt 'or any other person holding the office
of Protector hereunder'. Clause 3 provides for the settlement to be regulated by the
law of the Isle of Man, subject to a power for trustees to change the proper law.

a

[12] Clauses 4, 5, 6 and 7 contain the dispositive trusts and powers affecting the trust fund. These present some difficulties of construction but their general effect is as follows. (1) Clause 4(1) contains a wide power of appointment exercisable by the trustees, with the prior written consent of the protector, by deed executed during the trust period. The objects of the powers are all or any one or more of the beneficiaries, subject to certain restrictions set out in the proviso to cl 4(1). Some of

b

these restrictions relate to United States taxation and need not be set out in detail, but it is notable that provisos (ee) and (ff) are as follows:

> '(ee) no distribution of income shall be made to any beneficiary who has not attained the age of twenty-one years except in payment of educational or necessary medical expenses or for the alleviation of hardship.

c

> (ff) no distribution of capital shall be made to any beneficiary who has not attained the age of twenty-five years except in payment of educational or necessary medical expenses or for the alleviation of hardship.'

(2) Clause 7 contains a comparable power (except that the consent of the protector is not required) for the trustees to make transfers to other settlements benefiting all

d

or any of the beneficiaries. (3) Clause 5 contains a power for the trustees to accumulate income during the accumulation period.

[13] It is cll 4(2) and 6 which present the difficulties of construction. Clause 4(2) is in the following terms:

e

> '(2) Upon the death of any Beneficiary the Trustee shall hold that portion of the Trust Fund to which the deceased Beneficiary had been entitled during his lifetime UPON TRUST for such person or persons as the deceased Beneficiary had notified the Trustee in writing and in the absence of such notification for that person or those persons whom the Trustee believes to be the closest surviving relative or relatives of the deceased Beneficiary.'

f

The problem here is that unless and until the trustees have exercised their power of appointment under cl 4(1) in such a way as to give any of the beneficiaries a fixed entitlement (for instance, a life interest in some fraction of the trust fund) the reference to 'that portion of the Trust Fund to which the deceased Beneficiary had been entitled during his lifetime' is inapposite.

g

[14] Clause 6 is in the following terms:

> 'Subject as aforesaid the Trustee shall hold the Trust Fund and the income thereof so far as not effectively dealt with pursuant to the foregoing trusts and powers UPON TRUST for such purposes as are according to the laws of the Isle of Man or any subsequent forum of administration.'

h

The problem here is that there is a gap. It is possible to conjecture (especially by reference to the comparable clause of the Everest Trust) that the gap should be filled by 'charitable' (or 'charitable and public') but it would be a strong thing for any court to fill the gap as part of a process of construction (as opposed to

j

rectification).

[15] The remaining clauses of the Angora Trust contain wide administrative and other powers and provisions, mostly in a familiar form. The following call for mention. (1) Clause 29 enables a sole corporate trustee to act, and cll 28 and 29 together provide for the remuneration of trustees. (2) Clauses 30, 31 and 32 provide for the devolution (and possible lapse) of the functions of the protector (since Mr Schmidt's death, Mr Alexander Djparidze has been appointed as protector).

(3) Clause 33 confers on the protector the power of appointing and removing
trustees, and (in sub-cl (c), which also seems to have a gap)— a

'power to require the Trustee or Trustees upon request information relating
to the Trust including minutes accounts documents papers records or other
information no matter how maintained or any part thereof whether specified
or in general.'
b

(4) Clause 34 gives the trustees power to have the trust accounts audited and ends
with the words 'and any Beneficiary may require such an audit'. (5) Clause 38 gives
the trustees power to release or restrict their own powers.

[16] The principal points of difference in the Everest Trust are as follows.
(1) Clauses 1, 2 and 4 correspond to cll 1, 2 and 3 respectively of the Angora Trust
except that (i) the definition of 'the Beneficiaries' includes any person or charity c
added under cl 3; (ii) the same definition refers to a second schedule which was
apparently never included in the deed, but the names of Lukoil senior executives
were added in manuscript at the end of the deed (the full list has never been
disclosed, but it included Mr Schmidt); and (iii) the protector was named as Mr Ralif
Safin. (2) Clause 3.3 confers on the trustees power exercisable by written d
instrument during the trust period to add to the class of beneficiaries 'any person
or persons or class or classes of person (including an individual then unborn) or
charity' other than a current trustee or (while the trustees are resident in the Isle of
Man) any Isle of Man resident. Other provisions in cl 3 permit the trustees to
exclude beneficiaries and permit a person (if sui juris) to exclude himself. (3) Clause
5(a) contains a wide power of appointment very similar to that in cl 4(1) of the e
Angora Trust, except that the provisos are different (in particular, they do not refer
to United States tax nor do they refer to benefits for persons under 21 or 25 years of
age). There is no cl 5(b). (4) Clause 6 contains, in default of and subject to any
appointment under cl 5, (i) a discretionary trust of income in favour of the
beneficiaries, subject to (ii) a proviso containing a power for the trustees to f
accumulate income during the accumulation period. (5) Clauses 7 and 8
correspond to cll 6 and 7 respectively of the Angora Trust, except that the apparent
gap in cl 6 of the Angora Trust is in cl 7 of the Everest Trust filled by the words 'both
charitable and public as the Trustee shall from time to time determine'. (6) Clause
35 of the Everest Trust (corresponding to cl 34 of the Angora Trust) does not
include the final words 'and any Beneficiary may require such an audit'. g

[17] Each settlement contained (in its first schedule) particulars of the property
initially settled. In the Angora Trust this was 50 ordinary shares in Nizam Ltd, a
company incorporated in the Republic of Ireland. The first schedule to the Everest
Trust has never been fully disclosed, but it included two $US1 shares in a company
called Petragonis Ltd (Petragonis). The Ernst & Young report contains some h
further information (but, the appellant says, incomplete information) about the
web of companies (incorporated in different parts of the world) apparently
associated with the two settlements. For present purposes it is sufficient to identify
a company called Gingernut Ltd (Gingernut) and Petragonis as to the two
companies which were used as the principal vehicles for the distribution to or for j
the benefit of Mr Schmidt of funds from the Angora Trust and the Everest Trust
respectively. These two companies were apparently the source of the sums
distributed to the appellant, as Mr Schmidt's personal representative, in 1998.

[18] Before leaving the terms of the two settlements there is one further
feature of the Angora Trust which calls for mention, although the weight to be
attached to it is a matter for debate. An unredacted copy of the Angora Trust

a found by the appellant with his father's papers shows that the second schedule originally contained eight names. Mr Schmidt's name was followed by the words 'as to a three-tenths share (30%)'. Each of the other seven names was followed by the words 'as to a one-tenth share (10%)'. All the references to fractional shares were crossed through (but so as to remain legible). In addition four of the names had been crossed through, and one further name had been

b added in manuscript (without any reference to a share). This feature, together with the other problematic points on the Angora Trust already mentioned, gives much force to the submission of Mr Steinfeld QC (for the appellant) that the settlement was 'cobbled together'. Mr Brownbill (for Rosewood) agreed that the settlement appeared to contain mistakes.

[19] On 23 June 1992 Mr Schmidt wrote to Lorne House as trustee of the Angora
c Trust a letter (the Angora letter) in the following terms:

> 'I understand that I am a beneficiary of the Angora Trust. If I should die prior to the termination of the Trust I wish any portion to which I might have been entitled to be held upon trust for [and then he gave the appellant's name and date and place of birth].'

d

[20] On 31 October 1995 Mr Schmidt wrote to Lorne House as trustee of the Everest Trust a letter (the Everest letter) in the following terms:

> 'The Everest Trust. While I recognise the discretionary powers vested in you as Trustees of the above Trust, it would be my wish if I were to die prior
e > to the termination of the Trust that my share of the trust property be given to Vadim Schmidt.'

[21] There are some indications (in particular in Rosewood's answer, which was later amended in this respect) that Rosewood initially accepted the Angora letter as an effective exercise of a power conferred on Mr Schmidt by cl 4(2) of the Angora
f Trust. However Rosewood's present position is that neither letter had any legal effect.

THE PROCEEDINGS BELOW

[22] The appellant's petition first came before Deemster Cain on 5 October 1999. It was supported by the appellant's affidavit of 7 June 1999 already mentioned.
g Rosewood had an opportunity to put in evidence but did not do so. The time for argument was limited and the deemster indicated that he was not going to make an order at that hearing. But he gave a short ex tempore judgment declining to dismiss the petition as an abuse of process. He indicated that in principle Rosewood as trustee must make disclosure to its beneficiaries—'each beneficiary', he said, 'is
h entitled to know what the trustees have done with the money'—but that he was concerned about the confidentiality of third parties. He made the helpful suggestion that disclosure might be made, not to the appellant himself, but to the appellant's legal or accountancy advisers. He adjourned the matter to see whether the parties could agree a form of order.

j [23] The parties were unable to agree on the form of order and the matter came back to the deemster on 19 November 1999 when he made an order. The order as finally drawn up is elaborate, running to nine pages of typescript and including (in its second schedule) the names of over 60 companies (or other legal entities) established in different parts of the world. The essential provisions of the order were for Rosewood to make extensive disclosure of unredacted documents and to provide information to three named members of the firm of Ernst & Young (the

inspectors) on the inspectors and their lawyers giving undertakings to hold all
the disclosed documents and information in confidence, to be used only for
purposes authorised by the order. It is not necessary, for present purposes, to go
further into the detail of the order.

[24] Rosewood appealed to the Staff of Government Division and the appeal
was heard by Deemster Kerruish QC and Mr GF Tattersall QC (sitting as a Judge of
Appeal) on several dates between January and April 2000. The court heard but
rejected an application by Rosewood to adduce further evidence. It gave a reserved
judgment on 26 February 2001 allowing the appeal and setting aside the order of
Deemster Cain (see (2001) 3 ITELR 734).

[25] Rosewood had initially put forward four grounds of appeal. The first, abuse
of process, was not proceeded with; the second and third raised points as to the
extent and efficacy of the safeguards for confidentiality embodied in the order; and
the fourth related to costs. But a week before the appeal hearing Rosewood asked
for permission to amend its grounds of appeal and to contend that the appellant was
not a beneficiary in any sense of the word under the two settlements, and that his
father, Mr Schmidt, was never more than 'a mere object of a power who as such
had no entitlement to trust documents or information'. The amendment was
allowed even though it necessitated an adjournment and allowed Rosewood to run
a quite different case from that which it had put forward below.

[26] Most of the judgment of the Staff of Government Division is concerned
with the point of principle raised in the new ground of appeal. Since it allowed the
appeal on that ground, it did not go far into the other grounds of appeal. But
the court indicated (at [65]) that if it had concluded that the deemster had
jurisdiction to make the order appealed from, it would have 'felt constrained to
exercise [its] discretion in favour of, in principle, making an order for disclosure'.
The court noted (at [66]) that it had not found it necessary to consider—

'firstly, the privacy and confidentiality of the other beneficiaries of the
settlement; secondly, the scope of the order; and thirdly the appointment of
the [appellant's, ie Vadim Schmidt's] lawyers [which seems to be a mistake for
"accountants"] as inspectors.'

Her Majesty in Council gave special leave to appeal on 19 September 2001.

ISSUES OF CONSTRUCTION
[27] Before turning to the point of law which is the main issue on this appeal it
is convenient to clear the ground by referring briefly to some preliminary issues of
construction which were not argued below, but which were to some extent
debated before the Board. Three of these relate to the Angora Trust, and two can
be dealt with quite briefly. (1) The appellant's printed case contended that cl 4(1)
contains not a power of appointment, but a discretionary trust. Mr Steinfeld rightly
did not seek to develop this contention in his oral submissions, although he did not
formally abandon it. It is a hopeless argument. (2) The gap in cl 6 may well have
been intended to be filled by a reference to charity, but it would be a strong thing
for the court to fill the gap as part of a process of construction (see for instance
Re Whitrick (decd), Sutcliffe v Sutcliffe [1957] 2 All ER 467, [1957] 1 WLR 884). The
trustees could at any time fill the gap, if they thought fit, by appointing an ultimate
trust to the RNLI. But it is not necessary to pursue the point because it has no
practical bearing on the outcome of the appeal. (3) The effect (if any) of cl 4(2), in
conjunction with the Angora letter, is however potentially of very great
importance, and it must be considered more fully.

a [28] Both sides agree that the Angora Trust is a badly-drafted document. It may be that the Lukoil executives who caused it to be brought into existence had an inadequate understanding of its effect. The deleted reference to fixed shares in the second schedule strongly suggests that they may not have seen the settlement as conferring on the trustees the very wide discretions which it appears to confer.

b [29] Mr Steinfeld submitted that each of the putative settlors should be regarded as having been in some sense entitled to the funds which he caused to be brought into the settlement, and that this enabled cl 4(2) to be given a sensible meaning. The alternative, he said, would be that the settlement would become a sort of tontine for the longest-living settlor, an absurd result which cannot have been intended.

c [30] Mr Brownbill submitted that cl 4(2) was obviously a mistake of some sort, and that it would do unacceptable violence to the language of the settlement to treat Mr Schmidt as having been entitled to a portion of the trust fund during his lifetime, when he was never more than a mere object of a discretionary power of appointment.

d [31] Their Lordships take the view that they cannot decide this issue of construction, for two reasons. First, it is a question which is likely to be of acute concern to the other beneficiaries interested under the Angora Trust, but they are not at present parties to the proceedings. The other beneficiaries (or at any rate a representative of them in respect of whom a representation order could be made) would have to be joined and given the opportunity of making submissions on the point of construction. They would then be bound by any order deciding the point.

e The second reason for the Board to refrain from deciding the point at this stage is that there is insufficient evidence (and no findings below) as to the surrounding circumstances (or 'matrix of fact') in which the settlement was made.

[32] The Board does not therefore express any view on this issue of construction, beyond stating that it (unlike the point on cl 4(1)) is arguable.

f Mr Steinfeld's proposed construction does do some violence to the language of cl 4(2), but the modern approach of the court is not to reject any part of a legal document as meaningless without first trying hard to give it a sensible meaning: see the observations of Lord Upjohn in *Re Gulbenkian's Settlement Trusts, Whishaw v Stephens* [1968] 3 All ER 785 at 791, [1970] AC 508 at 522 (on appeal from *Re Gulbenkian's Settlement Trusts, Hacobian v Maun* [1967] 3 All ER 15, [1968] Ch 126).

g The appellant may take steps to have the proceedings reconstituted and to have this issue of construction determined in the High Court of the Isle of Man. But unless and until he takes that course and succeeds in his argument, it cannot be assumed that the appellant in his personal capacity is a beneficiary (in any sense) under the Angora Trust.

h [33] In relation to the Everest Trust the appellant in his personal capacity is no more than a possible object of the very wide power to add beneficiaries conferred by cl 3.3. The Everest letter provides clear evidence of Mr Schmidt's wishes and confirms (as would in any case be fairly evident) that the appellant may have a particularly strong claim on the trustees' discretion. But neither the Everest letter nor any other document put in evidence had any further effect on his status as a possible beneficiary, and ultimately Mr Steinfeld did not contend otherwise.

j

DISCLOSURE TO DISCRETIONARY BENEFICIARIES: THE BACKGROUND

[34] Counsel have very properly referred the Board to a considerable number of authorities, some of them going back to the early years of the nineteenth century. It is appropriate to reflect that during the long period covered by these authorities

(but especially during the second half of the twentieth century) the forms and functions of settlements have changed to a degree which would have astonished *a* Lord Eldon LC. By the 1930s high rates of personal taxation led some wealthy individuals to make settlements which enabled funds to be accumulated in the hands of overseas trustees or companies (see for instance *Lord Vestey's Exors v IRC* [1949] 1 All ER 1108). This practice increased enormously with the introduction of capital gains tax in 1965. But increasingly stringent anti-avoidance measures *b* encouraged legal advisers to devise forms of settlement under which the true intended beneficiaries were not clearly identified in the settlement. Indeed their interests or expectations were often barely perceptible. Rarely did a beneficiary take an indefeasibly vested interest with an ascertainable market value. Tax avoidance is therefore one element which has strongly influenced the forms of settlements; and once the offshore tax-avoidance industry has acquired standard *c* forms its inclination is to use them, subject perhaps to some more or less skilful adaptation, even for clients whose aim is not to avoid United Kingdom taxation.

[35] There is another element, also linked (though less directly) to taxation, which has encouraged the inclusion in settlements of very widely defined classes of beneficiaries. After the 1939–45 war estate duty was charged in the United *d* Kingdom at very high rates, with much less generous reliefs for agricultural and business property than those now available. A wealthy landowner or businessman might be advised that the safest way to preserve his fortune was to give most of it away, while he was still in the prime of life, to trustees of an irrevocable settlement in discretionary form under which the settlor himself was not a beneficiary. It is not surprising that a settlor in such a position should wish to cover as comprehensively *e* as he could all possible current and future claims on his bounty, since he was being asked to make an immediate, irrevocable disposition of much of his wealth, rather than being able to review from time to time the ambulatory dispositions in his will and codicils. But his lawyers might also advise him that the most natural expressions for defining discretionary objects of his bounty (such as 'relatives', 'old *f* friends', 'dependants' or 'persons with moral claims') were of doubtful legal efficacy. So there was a tendency to define the class in the widest possible terms. The process can be seen in a long line of cases starting with *Re Gestetner Settlement, Barnett v Blumka* [1953] 1 All ER 115, [1953] Ch 672. It led to *Re Manisty's Settlement, Manisty v Manisty* [1973] 2 All ER 1203, [1974] Ch 17, upholding the validity of an 'intermediate' power comparable to that in cl 3.3 of the Everest Trust (that is, a *g* power to add as beneficiaries anyone in the world apart from a very small class of excluded persons).

[36] The Board have to consider what rights or claims to disclosure the appellant has, either personally or as his father's personal representative, under two badly drafted settlements whose terms have been moulded by the sort of influences *h* mentioned above. One possible reaction would be that Mr Schmidt and his colleagues have made their bed and they must lie on it; if they have deliberately entered into a web of camouflage, it is hardly for anyone claiming through them to complain that the position is not transparent. As Lord Greene MR observed, giving the judgment of the court in *Lord Howard de Walden v IRC* [1942] 1 All ER 287 at 289, *j* [1942] 1 KB 389 at 397 if a taxpayer plays with fire it scarcely lies in his mouth to complain of burnt fingers. However, the Board consider that that inclination must be resisted. As already noted, it has not been suggested that the settlements are shams, or tainted with illegality. It is fundamental to the law of trusts that the court has jurisdiction to supervise and if appropriate intervene in the administration of a trust, including a discretionary trust. As Holland J said in the Australian case of

a *Randall v Lubrano* (31 October 1975, unreported) cited by Kirby P in *Hartigan Nominees Pty Ltd v Rydge* (1992) 29 NSWLR 405 at 416:

> '... no matter how wide the trustee's discretion in the administration and application of a discretionary trust fund and even if in all or some respects the discretions are expressed in the deed as equivalent to those of an absolute owner of the trust fund, the trustee is still a trustee.'

b

DISCRETIONARY TRUSTS AND POWERS

[37] Several of the numerous authorities referred to by counsel have been concerned with the general characteristics of interests (or rights) under discretionary trusts (on the one hand) and mere powers (of a dispositive
c character) conferred on trustees in their fiduciary capacity (on the other hand). It is convenient to refer to these before coming to the authorities directly concerned with disclosure of trust documents or information.

[38] In the important case of *McPhail v Doulton* [1970] 2 All ER 228, [1971] AC 424 the House of Lords finally settled the vexed question of whether the test for validity, in point of certainty of objects, is the same for trusts and powers, or
d whether the test for trusts is more demanding. It held the test to be the same. That general question arose in the context of a provision (which the Court of Appeal took to be a power, but the House of Lords held to be a trust) for trustees to distribute income 'to or for the benefit of any of the officers and employees or ex-officers or ex-employees of [a named company] or to any relatives or
e dependants of any such persons' (with a power for the trustees to hold up income which did not, as the House of Lords held, prevent the trustees distributing the retentions as income) (see [1970] 2 All ER 228 at 228, [1971] AC 424 at 428).

[39] That was the context in which Lord Wilberforce ([1970] 2 All ER 228 at 240, [1971] AC 424 at 448–449) made some general observations which, although
f fairly lengthy, need to be set out in full:

> '... some general observations, or reflections, may be permissible. It is striking how narrow and in a sense artificial is the distinction, in cases such as the present, between trusts or as the particular type of trust is called, trust powers, and powers. It is only necessary to read the learned judgments in the Court of Appeal ([1969] 1 All ER 1016, [1969] 2 Ch 388) to see that what
g to one mind may appear as a power of distribution coupled with a trust to dispose of the undistributed surplus, by accumulation or otherwise, may to another appear as a trust for distribution coupled with a power to withhold a portion and accumulate or otherwise dispose of it. A layman and, I suspect, also a logician would find it hard to understand what difference there is. It
h does not seem satisfactory that the entire validity of a disposition should depend on such delicate shading. And if one considers how in practice reasonable and competent trustees would act, and ought to act, in the two cases, surely a matter very relevant to the question of validity, the distinction appears even less significant. To say that there is no obligation to exercise a
j mere power and that no court will intervene to compel it, whereas a trust is mandatory and its execution may be compelled, may be legally correct enough, but the proposition does not contain an exhaustive comparison of the duties of persons who are trustees in the two cases. A trustee of an employees' benefit fund, whether given a power or a trust power, is still a trustee and he would surely consider in either case that he has a fiduciary duty; he is most likely to have been selected as a suitable person to

administer it from his knowledge and experience, and would consider he has
a responsibility to do so according to its purpose. It would be a complete *a*
misdescription of his position to say that, if what he has is a power
unaccompanied by an imperative trust to distribute, he cannot be controlled
by the court unless he exercised it capriciously, or outside the field permitted
by the trust (cf Farwell on Powers (3rd Edn, 1916, p 10)). Any trustee would
surely make it his duty to know what is the permissible area of selection and *b*
then consider responsibly, in individual cases, whether a contemplated
beneficiary was within the power and whether, in relation to other possible
claimants, a particular grant was appropriate. Correspondingly a trustee
with a duty to distribute, particularly among a potentially very large class,
would surely never require the preparation of a complete list of names,
which anyhow would tell him little that he needs to know. He would *c*
examine the field, by class and category; might indeed make diligent and
careful enquiries, depending on how much money he had to give away and
the means at his disposal, as to the composition and needs of particular
categories and of individuals within them; decide on certain priorities or
proportions, and then select individuals according to their needs or *d*
qualifications. If he acts in this manner, can it really be said that he is not
carrying out the trust? Differences there certainly are between trusts (trust
powers) and powers, but as regards validity should they be so great as that in
one case complete, or practically complete ascertainment is needed, but not
in the other? Such distinction as there is would seem to lie in the extent of
the survey which the trustee is required to carry out; if he has to distribute *e*
the whole of a fund's income, he must necessarily make a wider and more
systematic survey than if his duty is expressed in terms of a power to make
grants. But just as, in the case of a power, it is possible to underestimate the
fiduciary obligation of the trustee to whom it is given, so, in the case of a trust
(trust power), the danger lies in overstating what the trustee requires to *f*
know or to enquire into before he can properly execute his trust. The
difference may be one of degree rather than of principle; in the well-known
words of Sir George Farwell (Farwell on Powers (3rd Edn, 1916, p 10)) trusts
and powers are often blended, and the mixture may vary in its ingredients.'

[40] This passage gives a very clear and eminently realistic account of both the *g*
points of difference and the similarities between a discretionary trust and a
fiduciary dispositive power. The outstanding point of difference is of course that
under a discretionary trust of income distribution of income (within a reasonable
time) is mandatory, the trustees' discretion being limited to the choice of the
recipients and the shares in which they are to take. If there is a small, closed class *h*
of discretionary objects who are all sui juris, their collective entitlement gives
them a limited power of disposition over the income subject to the discretionary
trust, as is illustrated by *Re Smith, Public Trustee v Aspinall* [1928] Ch 915, [1928]
All ER Rep 520 and *Re Nelson, Norris v Nelson* (1918) [1928] Ch 920n. But the
possibility of such a collective disposition will be rare, and on his own the object *j*
of a discretionary trust has no more of an assignable or transmissible interest than
the object of a mere power.

[41] Apart from the test for certainty being the same and the fact that an
individual's interest or right is non-assignable, there are other practical
similarities between the positions of the two types of object. Either has the
negative power to block a family arrangement or similar transaction proposed to

a   be effected under the rule in *Saunders v Vautier* (1841) 4 Beav 115, 49 ER 282
    (unless in the case of a power the trustees are specially authorised to release, that
    is to say extinguish, it). Both have a right to have their claims properly considered
    by the trustees. But if the discretion is exercisable in favour of a very wide class
    the trustees need not survey mankind from China to Peru (as Harman J, echoing
    Dr Johnson, said in *Re Gestetner Settlement* [1953] 1 All ER 1150 at 1155–1156,
b   [1953] Ch 672 at 688–689) if it is clear who are the prime candidates for the
    exercise of the trustees' discretion.

    [42]   That thought was developed by Templeman J in *Re Manisty's Settlement*
    [1973] 2 All ER 1203, [1974] Ch 17, although he was mainly concerned to contrast
    the exercise by trustees of an intermediate power (in the sense mentioned above)
    with the exercise by trustees of a wide special power. He said ([1973] 2 All ER
c   1203 at 1211, [1974] Ch 17 at 27) that a wide power, whether special or
    intermediate, does not negative or prohibit a sensible approach by trustees to the
    consideration and exercise of their powers. After referring to some very
    well-known observations by Lord Eldon LC in *Morice v Bishop of Durham* (1805) 10
    Ves 522 at 539, [1803–13] All ER Rep 451 at 458, Templeman J continued:

d   'Nor does an intermediate power break the principles laid down by Lord
         Eldon LC in the passage which I have read because, in relation to a power
         exercisable by the trustees at their absolute discretion, the only "control"
         exercisable by the court is the removal of the trustees, and the only "due
         administration" which can be "directed" is an order requiring the trustees to
e   consider the exercise of the power, and in particular a request from a person
         within the ambit of the power.' (See [1973] 2 All ER 1203 at 1211–1212,
         [1974] Ch 17 at 27–28.)

    However in *Mettoy Pension Trustees Ltd v Evans* [1991] 2 All ER 513 at 549,
    [1990] 1 WLR 1587 at 1617–1618, Warner J (after referring to Lord Wilberforce's
f   observations in *McPhail v Doulton* [1970] 2 All ER 228 at 247, [1971] AC 424 at
    456–457 and to some authorities not cited in *Re Manisty's Settlement*) took a broader
    view of the court's power to intervene in the case of a fiduciary dispositive power.

DISCLOSURE TO DISCRETIONARY BENEFICIARIES: A PROPRIETARY BASIS?

g   [43]   Much of the debate before the Board addressed the question whether a
    beneficiary's right or claim to disclosure of trust documents should be regarded
    as a proprietary right. Mr Brownbill argued that it should be classified in that
    way, and from that starting point he argued that no object of a mere power could
    have any right or claim to disclosure, because he had no proprietary interest in
    the trust property. Mr Brownbill submitted that this point has been conclusively
h   settled by the decision of the House of Lords in *O'Rourke v Darbishire* [1920] AC
    581, [1920] All ER Rep 1. It is therefore useful to go straight to that case to see
    what it did decide.

    [44]   The facts of the case were unusual. Sir Joseph Whitworth, a man of
    considerable wealth, had died in 1887. In 1884 he had made a will appointing
j   three executors and leaving his residuary estate to charity. By a codicil made in
    1885 he altered his will to leave his ultimate residue to his executors for their own
    benefit, with a precatory expression of his wishes that it should be used for
    charitable purposes. Two further codicils executed in 1886 extended the scope of
    the first codicil's gift to the executors. Sir Joseph's intestate successors would
    have been Mrs Uniacke (as to realty) and Mrs Uniacke and Mrs McGowan (as to
    personalty). Mrs McGowan threatened to challenge the will and codicils, but in

1889 there was a compromise between all interested parties. Then in 1916, after
Mrs Uniacke, Mrs McGowan and the executors had all died, Mrs Uniacke's *a*
administrator (Mr O'Rourke) sought to challenge both the will and codicils and
the compromise, alleging fraud by Mr Darbishire (who was one of the executors
and had been Sir Joseph's solicitor). Mr O'Rourke sought to obtain disclosure of
documents containing legal advice given to Sir Joseph during his lifetime, and to
his executors after his death.   *b*

[45] The House of Lords dismissed Mr O'Rourke's appeal, primarily because he
had not made out even a prima facie case that the will and codicils were invalid, or
that the communications had been promoting fraud. Viscount Finlay ([1920] AC
581 at 603, [1920] All ER Rep 1 at 6) referred to Mr O'Rourke's reliance on a
'proprietary right' and Lord Sumner ([1920] AC 581 at 617, [1920] All ER Rep 1 at
12) referred to 'what has been called the "proprietary" ground'. Lord Parmoor said: *c*

> 'A cestui que trust, in an action against his trustees, is generally entitled to
> the production for inspection of all documents relating to the affairs of the
> trust. It is not material for the present purpose whether this right is to be
> regarded as a paramount proprietary right in the cestui que trust, or as a right *d*
> to be enforced under the law of discovery, since in both cases an essential
> preliminary is either the admission, or the establishment, of the status on
> which the right is based.' (See [1920] AC 581 at 619–620, [1920] All ER Rep 1
> at 13.)

[46] It is on what was said by Lord Wrenbury that Mr Brownbill most relied. *e*
Lord Wrenbury said:

> 'If the plaintiff is right in saying that he is a beneficiary and if the documents
> are documents belonging to the executors as executors, he has a right to
> access to the documents which he desires to inspect upon what has been
> called in the judgments in this case a proprietary right. The beneficiary is *f*
> entitled to see all trust documents because they are trust documents and
> because he is a beneficiary. They are in this sense his own. Action or no
> action, he is entitled to access to them. This has nothing to do with
> discovery. The right to discovery is a right to see someone else's documents.
> The proprietary right is a right to access to documents which are your own.'
> (See [1920] AC 581 at 626–627, [1920] All ER Rep 1 at 17.)   *g*

On the facts of the case, what Lord Wrenbury said was very apposite. If
Mr O'Rourke was right in his claim, the executors had had no proper legal or
equitable title to Sir Joseph's estate. The grant of probate to them should have
been revoked and Mr O'Rourke (together with the representatives of *h*
Mrs McGowan) would have been entitled to the whole of the estate, including
any documents which formed part of it.

[47] The same can be said of the earliest authority to which the Board was
referred, the decision of Lord Eldon LC in *Clarke v Earl of Ormonde* (1821) Jac 108,
[1814–23] All ER Rep 329. Under private Acts of Parliament real estate in Ireland *j*
was vested in trustees in trust to raise money to pay the debts of Walter Marquis
of Ormonde, and subject to that trust for the Marquis in fee simple. In those
circumstances it is hardly surprising that Lord Eldon LC ((1821) Jac 108 at
119–120) referred to the Marquis' estate in fee simple before observing: 'But he
would have the right to say to the trustees, What estates have you sold? What
debts have you paid?'

a [48] In *Re Cowin, Cowin v Gravett* (1886) 33 Ch D 179 a beneficiary with a vested future interest in one-eighth of a testator's residuary trust fund, subject to his mother's interest during widowhood, wished to mortgage his interest and for that reason sought inspection of the title deeds to the trust property. North J made an order for inspection but rejected the notion that the beneficiary had an absolute right. He quoted (at 185) from the then current edition of *Lewin on*
b *Trusts* (8th edn, 1885) p 975: 'All documents held by the trustee in that character must be produced by him to the *cestuis que trust*, who in equity are the true owners.' But North J clearly considered that the particular interest of an individual beneficiary might in some circumstances run counter to the collective interest of the beneficiaries as a body. He said (at 187):

c   'I do not say that he is entitled as of right, but only that he is entitled under the circumstances, because there might be a state of circumstances under which the right to production would not exist.'

Chitty J took a similar approach in *Re Tillott, Lee v Wilson* [1892] 1 Ch 86, noting (at 89) that a trustee is not bound to give a beneficiary information about a share
d in which he has no interest.

[49] In *Re Londonderry's Settlement, Peat v Walsh* [1964] 3 All ER 855, [1965] Ch 918, the Court of Appeal had to consider one of the most important limitations on the right to disclosure of trust documents, that is the need to protect confidentiality in communications between trustees as to the exercise of their dispositive discretions, and in communications made to the trustees by other
e beneficiaries. That issue can alternatively be seen as an inquiry whether such confidential communications are indeed trust documents. The judgments of the three members of the court (Harman, Danckwerts and Salmon LJJ) are not easy to reconcile. All three referred to *O'Rourke v Darbishire* but Harman and Danckwerts LJJ found that Lord Wrenbury's general observations gave little assistance on the
f issue which concerned them. Only Salmon LJ ([1964] 3 All ER 855 at 862, [1965] Ch 918 at 937) expressly adopted the proprietary basis of the principle.

[50] Lord Wrenbury's observations in *O'Rourke v Darbishire* have also been cited in several Australian cases, and they were referred to by Lord Lowry in *AT & T Istel Ltd v Tully* [1992] 3 All ER 523 at 540, [1993] AC 45 at 65. The Board does not find it surprising that Lord Wrenbury's observations have been so often
g cited, since they are a vivid expression of the basic distinction between the right of a beneficiary arising under the law of trusts (which most would regard as part of the law of property) and the right of a litigant to disclosure of his opponent's documents (which is part of the law of procedure and evidence). But the Board cannot regard it as a reasoned or binding decision that a beneficiary's
h right or claim to disclosure of trust documents or information must always have the proprietary basis of a transmissible interest in trust property. That was not an issue in *O'Rourke v Darbishire*.

[51] Their Lordships consider that the more principled and correct approach is to regard the right to seek disclosure of trust documents as one aspect of the
j court's inherent jurisdiction to supervise, and if necessary to intervene in, the administration of trusts. The right to seek the court's intervention does not depend on entitlement to a fixed and transmissible beneficial interest. The object of a discretion (including a mere power) may also be entitled to protection from a court of equity, although the circumstances in which he may seek protection, and the nature of the protection he may expect to obtain, will depend on the court's discretion: see Lord Wilberforce in *Gartside v IRC* [1968] 1 All ER 121 at

134, [1968] AC 553 at 617–618 and in *McPhail v Doulton* [1970] 2 All ER 228 at 247,
[1971] AC 424 at 456–457, Templeman J in *Re Manisty's Settlement* [1973] 2 All ER *a*
1203 at 1211–1212, [1974] Ch 17 at 27–28 and Warner J in *Mettoy Pension Trustees
Ltd v Evans* [1991] 2 All ER 513 at 549, [1990] 1 WLR 1587 at 1617–1618.
Mr Brownbill's submission to the contrary effect tends to prove too much, since
he would regard the object of a discretionary trust as having a proprietary interest
even though it is not transmissible (except in the special case of collective action *b*
taken unanimously by all the members of a closed class).

[52] Their Lordships are therefore in general agreement with the approach
adopted in the judgments of Kirby P and Sheller JA in the Court of Appeal of New
South Wales in *Hartigan Nominees Pty Ltd v Rydge* (1992) 29 NSWLR 405. That
was a case concerned with disclosure of a memorandum of wishes addressed to
the trustees by Sir Norman Rydge (who was in substance, but not nominally, the *c*
settlor). Kirby P said (at 421–422):

'I do not consider that it is imperative to determine whether that document
is a "trust document" (as I think it is) or whether the respondent, as a
beneficiary, has a proprietary interest in it (as I am also inclined to think he
does). Much of the law on the subject of access to documents has *d*
conventionally been expressed in terms of the "proprietary interest" in the
document of the party seeking access to it. Thus, it has been held that a
cestui que trust has a "proprietary right" to seek all documents relating to the
trust: see *O'Rourke v Darbishire* ([1920] AC 581 at 601, 603, [1920] All ER Rep
1 at 5). This approach is unsatisfactory. Access should not be limited to *e*
documents in which a proprietary right may be established. Such rights may
be *sufficient*; but they are not *necessary* to a right of access which the courts
will enforce to uphold the cestui que trust's entitlement to a reasonable
assurance of the manifest integrity of the administration of the trust by the
trustees. I agree with Professor HAJ Ford's comment, in his book (with
Mr WA Lee) *Principles of the Law of Trusts*, 2nd ed (1990) Sydney, Law Book *f*
Co, at 425, that the equation of rights of inspection of trust documents with
the beneficiaries' equitable rights of property in the trust assets "gives rise to
far more problems than it solves" (at p 425): "... The legal title and rights to
possession are in the trustees: all the beneficiary has are equitable rights
against the trustees ... The beneficiary's rights to inspect trust documents are *g*
founded therefore not upon any equitable proprietary right which he or she
may have in respect of those documents but upon the trustee's fiduciary duty
to keep the beneficiary informed and to render accounts. It is the extent of
that duty that is in issue. The equation of the right to inspect trust
documents with the beneficiary's equitable proprietary rights gives rise to *h*
unnecessary and undesirable consequences. It results in the drawing of
virtually incomprehensible distinctions between documents which are trust
documents and those which are not; it casts doubts upon the rights of
beneficiaries who cannot claim to have an equitable proprietary interest in
the trust assets, such as the beneficiaries of discretionary trusts; and it may
give trustees too great a degree of protection in the case of documents, *j*
artificially classified as not being trust documents, and beneficiaries too great
a right to inspect the activities of trustees in the case of documents which are,
equally artificially, classified as trust documents."'

[53] Mahoney JA (at 435) favoured the proprietary basis but recognised that it
extended to information of a non-documentary kind. Sheller JA (at 444)

a considered that inquiry as to an applicant's proprietary interest was 'if not a false, an unhelpful trail'. All three members of the court expressed reservations about the reasoning and conclusions in *Re Londonderry's Settlement*.

[54] It will be observed that Kirby P said that for an applicant to have a proprietary right might be sufficient, but was not necessary. In the Board's view it is neither sufficient nor necessary. Since *Re Cowin* well over a century ago the
b court has made clear that there may be circumstances (especially of confidentiality) in which even a vested and transmissible beneficial interest is not a sufficient basis for requiring disclosure of trust documents; and *Re Londonderry's Settlement* and more recent cases have begun to work out in some detail the way in which the court should exercise its discretion in such cases. There are three such areas in which the court may have to form a discretionary judgment:
c whether a discretionary object (or some other beneficiary with only a remote or wholly defeasible interest) should be granted relief at all; what classes of documents should be disclosed, either completely or in a redacted form; and what safeguards should be imposed (whether by undertakings to the court, arrangements for professional inspection, or otherwise) to limit the use which
d may be made of documents or information disclosed under the order of the court.

[55] The proprietary basis of a beneficiary's right to disclosure was fully argued before the Staff of Government Division, which accepted ((2001) 3 ITELR 734 at [35]) the submission (made on behalf of the appellant) that a proprietary interest, although often found, was not necessary. On this part of the case the
e Board agrees with the conclusion reached by the Staff of Government Division, and does not accept the criticisms of it put forward by Mr Brownbill. It has nevertheless been necessary to look at the authorities in some detail, because they lead on to part of the Staff of Government Division's judgment (at [42]–[60]) in which the court reached the conclusion that Deemster Cain had no jurisdiction
f to make the order for disclosure which he did make. In reaching that conclusion the court distinguished (or treated as unhelpful) a number of cases, of which the most important are *Chaine-Nickson v Bank of Ireland* [1976] IR 393, *Spellson v George* (1987) 11 NSWLR 300, *Hartigan Nominees Pty Ltd v Rydge* (1992) 29 NSWLR 405, *A-G of Ontario v Stavro* (1994) 119 DLR (4th) 750 and *Re Murphy's Settlements, Murphy v Murphy* [1998] 3 All ER 1, [1999] 1 WLR 282.

g

DISCLOSURE TO DISCRETIONARY BENEFICIARIES: THE RECENT CASES

[56] *Chaine-Nickson v Bank of Ireland* [1976] IR 393 was a decision of the High Court of Ireland (Kenny J). It was concerned with an application for disclosure of accounts and other information made by the beneficiary of what was described
h as a discretionary trust. But the report does not give an adequate summary of the trust. The only dispositive provision set out verbatim looks more like a power than a trust, as it begins 'upon trust to pay, divide or apply the whole or such part (if any) of the income and capital respectively thereof as [the trustees] shall from time to time in their absolute and uncontrolled discretion think fit'. It appears
j that initially the settlement infringed the rule against perpetuities and had to be corrected, but again the summary is terse.

[57] After stating the general rule that a beneficiary with a vested interest is entitled to disclosure Kenny J continued (at 396):

'However, in the case of a discretionary trust, none of the potential beneficiaries have any right to be paid capital or income. All the trust fund is held by the trustees in this case on discretionary trusts and, if the plaintiff is not entitled to the trust accounts and particulars of the investments, it *a* follows that none of the potential beneficiaries have a valid claim to any information from the trustees. The result is that the trustees are not under an obligation to account to anyone in connection with their management of the trust fund. This logical conclusion from the defendants' argument leads to remarkable consequences. The amount of remuneration to which the trustees are entitled is specified in the settlement and the potential *b* beneficiaries have an interest in seeing that the amount is not exceeded, for they are the persons who will ultimately benefit by payments of capital and income. The defendants' contention, however, has the result that they do not have to account for or disclose the amount of their remuneration. This seems to me to be contrary to the basic concept of a trustee being accountable for his management of the trust fund.'   *c*

[58] The Staff of Government Division seem to have regarded *Chaine-Nickson's* case as a special and unusual case, in that there would normally be some beneficiary who had a fixed interest in default of exercise of the trustees' discretion, and who would be in a position to require disclosure of accounts. But offshore settlements do very commonly, for reasons already noted, have no *d* ascertained beneficiary with a fixed interest and a real economic stake in the enforcement of the trustees' fiduciary duties. The Staff of Government Division was, with respect, too ready to dismiss *Chaine-Nickson's* case as untypical and unhelpful. The contrary view does indeed lead to remarkable results.

[59] *Spellson v George* (1987) 11 NSWLR 300 was a decision of the Equity Division *e* of the Supreme Court of New South Wales (Powell J). The plaintiff (who had recently been divorced) was suing both on his own account and on behalf of his children for information about four separate settlements made by members of his ex-wife's family, three of which had apparently been wound up. Much of the report is concerned with the plaintiff's right to sue on behalf of his children without the concurrence of their joint guardian. However there is at the end of the *f* judgment of Powell J (at 315–316) a valuable discussion of the authorities and the underlying principle (though the clarity of the discussion is slightly marred by the expressions 'power' and 'trust' being used almost interchangeably). The whole passage merits study. The conclusion (at 316) is as follows:

'The question then is, whether a person whose status is only that of a *g* potential object of the exercise of a discretionary power can properly be regarded as one of the cestuis que trust of the relevant trustee. I do not doubt that he can, and should, properly be so regarded, for although it is true to say that, unless, and until, the trustee exercises his discretion in his favour, he has no right to receive, and enjoy, any part of the capital or income of the trust *h* fund, it does not follow that, until that time arises, he has no rights against the trustee. On the contrary, it is clear that the object of a discretionary trust, even before the exercise of the trustee's discretion in his favour, does have rights against the trustee (see, eg, *Gartside v Inland Revenue Commissioners* ([1968] 1 All ER 121 at 127, [1968] AC 553 at 605–606) per Lord Reid, ([1968] *j* 1 All ER 121 at 134, [1968] AC 553 at 617–618) per Lord Wilberforce)—those rights, so it seems to me, are not restricted to the right to have the trustee bona fide consider whether or not to exercise his (the trustee's) discretion in his (the object's) favour, but extend to the right to have the trust property properly managed and to have the trustee account for his management, a view, I am glad to say, which appears to have been shared by both Holland J

a   in *Randall v Lubrano* (31 October 1974, unreported) and Kenny J in
    Chaine-Nickson v Bank of Ireland ([1976] IR 393).'

[60] The Staff of Government Division quoted the above paragraph (and the
preceding paragraph) from Powell J's judgment and criticised him for having
given no reasons (apart from referring to *Randall v Lubrano* and *Chaine-Nickson's*

b   case) for his extension of the discretionary object's rights to a right to require the
    trustees to account for their trusteeship. Their Lordships regard this criticism as
    surprising and unwarranted. Powell J had avowedly begun with first principles
    ([1987] 11 NSWLR 300 at 315):

c   '... the fundamental proposition that one of the essential elements of a
        private trust, be it a discretionary trust or some other form of trust, is that the
        trustee is subject to a personal obligation to hold, and to deal with, the trust
        property for the benefit of some identified, or identifiable, person or group
        of persons.'

d   From there he had proceeded to the trustees' correlative duty to account. The
    observations of Lord Reid and Lord Wilberforce in *Gartside v IRC* [1968] 1 All ER
    121 at 127, 134, [1968] AC 553 at 605–606, 617–618, were naturally directed to a
    discretionary object's rights in respect of distribution of income from the trust fund,
    because (in the context of construing the estate duty legislation) that is what the
    case was about (cf Sir Robert Megarry V-C in *Re Hay's Settlement Trusts* [1981] 3 All

e   ER 786 at 793, [1982] 1 WLR 202 at 210, 'so far as relevant to the case before me').

[61] The *Hartigan Nominees* case was, as already noted, a case about a settlor's
letter of wishes. There was two main issues: whether the letter of wishes should
be disclosed, despite its confidential nature; and how much weight trustees, in
exercising their discretions, should give to a letter of wishes. Much of the

f   discussion of well-known authorities was in the context of the second question.
    For present purposes the case is of most interest for the division of opinion in the
    Court of Appeal of New South Wales on whether a beneficiary's right or claim to
    disclosure of documents is proprietary in nature (see [52]–[54], above). In its
    comments on the case the Staff of Government Division mentioned only the
    judgment of Mahoney JA, who was in a minority on this point (although in

g   the majority as to the outcome of the appeal). For the reasons already mentioned
    their Lordships prefer the views, as to the true basis for ordering disclosure, of
    Kirby P and Sheller JA.

[62] The fourth of the cases considered by the Staff of Government Division,
in this part of its judgment, was *A-G of Ontario v Stavro* (1994) 119 DLR (4th) 750.

h   In that case Lederman J had to consider an application for disclosure made by a
    beneficiary with a contingent interest in an unadministered estate. He referred
    to the argument for a proprietary basis and (echoing Sheller JA in the *Hartigan
    Nominees* case) considered (at 756) that it 'leads one astray'. The case is not
    directly in point, but it is in line with the prevailing view in Australia as it emerges

j   from *Spellson v George* and the *Hartigan Nominees* case (the point has recently been
    left open by the Full Court of the Supreme Court of South Australia, in the
    context of a commercial trust resembling a unit trust, in *Rouse v IOOF Australia
    Trustees Ltd* (1999) 2 ITELR 289).

[63] Finally there is the decision of Neuberger J in *Re Murphy's Settlements*
[1998] 3 All ER 1, [1999] 1 WLR 282. That case was concerned with a beneficiary's
right to obtain information (as to the identity of the trustees) from the settlor

himself but Neuberger J discussed the position of the plaintiff as a discretionary *a* object and stated:

> 'The facts that in this case the plaintiff is merely within the class of discretionary beneficiaries (as opposed to being someone with a vested beneficial interest in the trust property) and that there is no suggestion of wrongdoing on the part of the trustees, appears to me to go to the question of whether to exercise the discretion [to exercise what the judge called the *b* equitable jurisdiction], rather than whether the discretion exists at all.' (See [1998] 3 All ER 1 at 10, [1999] 1 WLR 282 at 290.)

[64] The Staff of Government Division found this of no assistance, stating that it was based on a concession and that the judge did not have the benefit of any detailed analysis or submissions. However in considering whether to accept the *c* concession Neuberger J did (like Powell J in *Spellson v George*) start from first principles; and his discussion ([1998] 3 All ER 1 at 10, [1999] 1 WLR 282 at 291) of the principles to be derived from the authorities, from *Morice v Bishop of Durham* (1805) 10 Ves 522, [1803–13] All ER Rep 457 to *Chaine-Nickson*'s case, appears to the Board to be illuminating and helpful. *d*

[65] To this review of the authorities considered by the Staff of Government Division it is appropriate to add three footnotes. (1) The Board were also assisted by references to a number of leading textbooks. Of the leading English works on trusts *Lewin on Trusts* (17th edn, 2000) appears to favour the proprietary approach and *Underhill and Hayton's Law Relating to Trusts and Trustees* (15th edn, 1995) the alternative approach. But each has a balanced survey of the cases and neither *e* takes an extreme position. (2) Neither side made any submissions seeking to distinguish between trust documents and documents relating to the affairs of a company controlled by the trustees (see for instance *Re Butt, Butt v Kelson* [1952] 1 All ER 167, [1952] Ch 197). This may have represented a realistic decision made by the trustees in the light of how the two settlements were in fact administered. *f* (3) Mr Steinfeld did not base himself on the final words of cl 34 of the Angora Trust, or on any other express provision of either settlement. Mr Brownbill made some brief submissions based on the protector's powers to obtain documents and information. These points may conceivably bear on the exercise of the court's discretion but they cannot in the Board's view go to the issue of jurisdiction. *g*

CONCLUSION

[66] Their Lordships have already indicated their view that a beneficiary's right to seek disclosure of trust documents, although sometimes not inappropriately described as a proprietary right, is best approached as one aspect of the court's inherent jurisdiction to supervise (and where appropriate intervene *h* in) the administration of trusts. There is therefore in their Lordships' view no reason to draw any bright dividing line either between transmissible and non-transmissible (that is, discretionary) interests, or between the rights of an object of a discretionary trust and those of the object of a mere power (of a fiduciary character). The differences in this context between trusts and powers *j* are (as Lord Wilberforce demonstrated in *McPhail v Doulton* [1970] 2 All ER 228, [1971] AC 424) a good deal less significant than the similarities. The tide of Commonwealth authority, although not entirely uniform, appears to be flowing in that direction.

[67] However the recent cases also confirm (as had been stated as long ago as *Re Cowin* (1886) 33 Ch D 179) that no beneficiary (and least of all a discretionary

a object) has any entitlement as of right to disclosure of anything which can plausibly be described as a trust document. Especially when there are issues as to personal or commercial confidentiality, the court may have to balance the competing interests of different beneficiaries, the trustees themselves and third parties. Disclosure may have to be limited and safeguards may have to be put in place. Evaluation of the claims of a beneficiary (and especially of a discretionary object) may be an

b important part of the balancing exercise which the court has to perform on the materials placed before it. In many cases the court may have no difficulty in concluding that an applicant with no more than a theoretical possibility of benefit ought not to be granted any relief.

[68] It would be inappropriate for the Board to go much further in attempting to give the High Court of the Isle of Man guidance as to the future conduct of this

c troublesome matter. But their Lordships can, without trespassing on the High Court's discretion, summarise their views on the different components of the appellant's claims. (1) It seems to be common ground that during Mr Schmidt's lifetime substantial distributions were made for his benefit, all or most by allocation of funds to the two companies (Gingernut and Petragonis) which were regarded as

d being (in some sense) Mr Schmidt's. The appellant as Mr Schmidt's personal representative does not accept that these funds have been fully accounted for. His contention is that in respect of allocated funds Mr Schmidt ceased to be a mere discretionary object, and became absolute owner. On the face of it the appellant (as personal representative) seems to have a powerful case for the fullest disclosure in respect of these funds. (2) The appellant as personal representative would also, on

e the face of it, have a strong claim to disclosure of documents or information relevant to the issue whether, but for breaches of fiduciary duty (such as for instance overcharging) more funds would have been available for distribution to Mr Schmidt, and would or might have been allocated to him in practice. The Board express no view whatever as to whether the appellant has a case for overcharging

f or any other breach of fiduciary duty. But claims of that sort have been put forward in the 1998 proceedings, and the possibility must be noted in order to make the position clear. (3) As regards the appellant's personal claims under the Angora Trust since his father's death, his status as beneficiary of any sort depends on the issue of construction discussed at [28]–[32], above. (4) As regards the Everest Trust, the appellant is a possible object of the very wide power in cl 3.3 (see [33], above),

g but an object who may be regarded (especially in view of the Everest letter) as having exceptionally strong claims to be considered.

[69] Their Lordships will therefore humbly advise Her Majesty that the appeal should be allowed, the order of Deemster Cain restored and the matter remitted to the High Court of the Isle of Man for further consideration in the light of the

h Board's judgment.

[70] Rosewood must pay the appellant's costs before the Staff of Government Division and before the Board. The High Court will determine whether (and if so to what extent and out of which funds) Rosewood should be entitled to reimbursement of those costs out of the trust property. The appellant does not

j contend that Rosewood acted unreasonably but does contend that in this litigation it has in substance acted for its own benefit (see RSC Ord 48A, rr 3(3) and 6(2)).

Appeal allowed.

Neneh Munu   Barrister.

Pegram Shopfitters Ltd v Tally Weijl (UK) Ltd

[2003] EWHC 984 (TCC)

QUEEN'S BENCH DIVISION (TECHNOLOGY AND CONSTRUCTION COURT)

JUDGE ANTHONY THORNTON QC

14 FEBRUARY 2003

Building contract – Adjudication – Award – Jurisdiction to make award – Parties accepting existence of construction contract but disputing its conditions – Appointment of adjudicator under statutory scheme – Meaning of 'enables a party to give notice at any time of his intention to refer a dispute to adjudication' – Whether adjudicator having jurisdiction – Scheme for Construction Contracts (England and Wales) Regulations 1998 – Housing Grants, Construction and Regeneration Act 1996, s 108.

The claimant undertook refurbishment works for the defendant. A dispute arose as to the final account and the claimant referred the matter to an adjudicator under the statutory scheme contained in the Scheme for Construction Contracts (England and Wales) Regulations 1998, pursuant to s 108(1)[a] of the Housing Grants, Construction and Regeneration Act 1996. The defendant disputed the adjudicator's jurisdiction on the basis, inter alia, that the contract was on JCT standard terms which met the requirements of s 108(2) of the Act so as to displace the statutory scheme with its own. That subsection provided that 'the contract shall (a) enable a party to give notice at any time of his intention to refer a dispute to adjudication; (b) provide a timetable with the object of securing the appointment of the adjudicator and referral of the dispute to him within 7 days of such notice.' By s 108(5) if the contract did not comply with those requirements, the adjudication provision of the statutory scheme applied. The adjudicator accepted jurisdiction under the statutory scheme and made an award in the claimant's favour. The defendant refused to pay and the claimant brought proceedings to enforce the award. An issue arose as to whether the adjudicator's award was unenforceable by reason of lack of jurisdiction.

Held – Having regard to the context of the right to refer a dispute arising under a construction contract to adjudication under s 108(1), which included a dispute as to which terms were incorporated into that contract, the words 'the contract shall (a) enable' and 'the contract … shall (b) provide' in s 108(2) of the 1996 Act meant that the contract should both contain the provisions required by s 108(2), and should contain them in a manner that enabled their applicability to be readily ascertained without dispute. If there was such a dispute, then the contract did not comply with s 108, and the statutory scheme applied in default. That was so even if it subsequently emerged from the decision of the adjudicator that the terms of the contract did in fact comply with the requirements of s 108. Without such an extended construction, effect could not be given to the underlying right of a party to refer all disputes arising under a construction contract to adjudication. It followed that, in the instant case, the adjudicator had had jurisdiction.

---

a   Section 108, so far as material, is set out at [15], below

a   Accordingly, his decision was enforceable and there would be judgment for the claimant (see [25]–[31], below).

Notes

For the jurisdiction of an adjudicator, see 4(3) *Halsbury's Laws* (4th edn reissue) para 214.

b   For the Housing Grants, Construction and Regeneration Act 1996, s 108, see 11 *Halsbury's Statutes* (4th edn) (2000 reissue) 289.

Case referred to in judgment

C & B Scene Concept Design Ltd v Isobars Ltd [2002] EWCA Civ 46, (2002) 82 ConLR
c   154, CA.

Cases referred to in skeleton arguments

Ballast plc v The Burrell Co (Construction Management) Ltd (21 June 2001, unreported), Ct of Sess.
Brogden v Metropolitan Railway Co (1877) 2 App Cas 666, HL.
d   *Charnock v Liverpool Corp* [1968] 3 All ER 473, [1968] 1 WLR 1498, CA.
Christiani and Neilson Ltd v The Lowry Centre Development Co Ltd (16 June 2000, unreported), QBD.
Fastrack Contractors Ltd v Morrison Construction Ltd (2000) 75 ConLR 33.
Glencot Development and Design Co Ltd v Ben Barrett & Son [2001] BLR 207.
e   *Joinery Plus Ltd (in admin) v Laing Ltd* [2002] All ER (D) 201 (Jan).
Macob Civil Engineering Ltd v Morrison Construction Ltd (1994) 64 ConLR 1.
Project Consultancy Group v Trustees of the Gray Trust [1999] BLR 377.
Sherwood & Casson Ltd v Mackenzie [2000] 2 TCLR 418.

Claim

f   By Pt 8 claim form dated 23 January 2003, the claimant, Pegram Shopfitters Ltd, sought the enforcement of an award of an adjudicator, Mr CD Morris, dated 16 August 2002 requiring the defendant, Tally Weijl (UK) Ltd to pay to the claimant the sum of £95,483·78, interest of £11,717·97 and the adjudicator's fees, arising out of a dispute in relation to remuneration for work carried out by the
g   claimant for the defendant. The facts are set out in the judgment.

Jeremy Hyam (instructed by *Field Seymour Parkes*, Reading) for the claimant.
Abdul Jinadu (instructed by *Maxwell Batley*) for the defendant.

h   JUDGE ANTHONY THORNTON QC.

INTRODUCTION
    [1] The claimant seeks to enforce the award of an adjudicator which the defendant declines to pay on the grounds that it was decided without jurisdiction.
j   The underlying background to that decision was refurbishment works being carried out by the claimant shopfitters at a new Tally Weijl retail clothing store in Oxford Street, London W1N 9HB. The refurbishment works were carried out between June and September 2000 and, following practical completion, disputes as to the value of that work arose which the claimant referred to adjudication having elected to adopt the statutory scheme rules (Scheme for Construction Contracts (England and Wales) Regulations 1998, SI 1998/649) concerned with

the appointment of, and the procedure to be adopted by, the adjudicator. The
claimant sought the nomination of an adjudicator from the Association of
Independent Construction Adjudicators. Mr CD Morris was nominated and he
published his decision on 16 August 2002 in which he decided that the claimant
should be paid £95,483·78, interest of £11,717·97 and the adjudicator's fees. No
reasons were asked for prior to the publication of that decision so that the
decision is unreasoned.

[2] The defendant has declined to pay the sums directed to be paid. Two
jurisdictional grounds are taken by the defendant. First, it is contended that there
was no construction contract in existence between the parties and, hence, no
construction contract underlay or gave rise to the claimant's statutory
entitlement to an adjudication as to the disputes concerning the true value of its
work. Secondly, it is alleged that if there was a construction contract in existence,
that contract was different in content to the construction contract found to exist
by the adjudicator. In consequence, that contract incorporated different
adjudication rules into any adjudication arising out of that contract to those
adopted by the adjudicator and, thus, the adjudicator was appointed and the
adjudication was conducted by reference to the wrong rules and in contravention
of the parties' agreement as to the procedural rules that would apply. On this
additional ground, therefore, the defendant contended that the adjudication was
conducted without jurisdiction.

[3] If the defendant makes good either ground of alleged lack of jurisdiction,
the decision is a nullity and is unenforceable. However, the claimant contends
that the adjudicator had referred to him the question of what was the true value
of its work and as to what were the applicable terms incorporated into the
construction contract both parties accepted was in existence. Thus, the
adjudicator correctly proceeded on the basis that there was a construction
contract underlying both the disputes referred to him and his appointment, that
its terms did not clearly and unequivocally incorporate any adjudication
procedural rules and that, in consequence, the scheme rules applied. In any case,
the application of the wrong rules, if the adjudicator applied the wrong rules, did
not amount to an error which undermined his jurisdiction and the resulting
decision was still valid. In summary, any error as to the terms of the contract or
as to the applicable procedural adjudication rules was an error of law within the
adjudicator's jurisdiction and did not render the decision unenforceable.

[4] Since the defendant failed to pay the decision as directed, these
proceedings were instituted on 23 January 2003 in the form of a CPR Pt 8 claim
form. The claimant seeks summary judgment for the sums directed to be paid.

THE CONSTRUCTION CONTRACT

[5] The dispute as to the adjudicator's jurisdiction involves a consideration of
whether the parties entered into a construction contract at all and, if so, what
conditions of contract were incorporated into that construction contract. Since
detailed evidence was adduced that was directed to these questions, I will
summarise it although I leave over for further consideration whether I should
make my own findings on these questions which, if the adjudicator had
jurisdiction, were ones that were essentially for him to decide.

[6] The work on site started on 9 June 2000. Prior to that, no contract
documents had been prepared and no tendering process had been undertaken.
The claimant had been introduced to the defendant by the project architect a
short time before work started and invited to undertake the shopfitting work

a   which was to be undertaken at great speed and with an immediate start on site. The contract documentation would be produced and agreed and a contract entered into as work proceeded. At the first project meeting held on 15 June 2000, it was agreed, in a non-contractual sense, that the work would be subject to a form of prime cost contract and that the claimant and the consultants would produce an agreed schedule of work. It was also agreed that a letter of intent

b   would be provided by the defendant, pending final agreement as to the terms of the contract.

[7] During June and July 2000 the claimant undertook the strip out work without any clear-cut letter of intent having been provided. The nearest that the defendant got to providing such a letter was by a letter dated 7 July 2000 in which the defendant wrote to the claimant instructing it to carry out the works subject

c   to a term that the form of the contract would be the JCT Standard Form of Prime Cost Contract (1998 edn) (JCT PC 98). However, this was immediately responded to by the claimant in a letter dated 10 July 2002 addressed to the architect declining to enter into a contract which incorporated these conditions and instead offering its own conditions which had already been sent to the

d   defendant.

[8] The claimant became increasingly concerned at the lack of any contractual basis for the work it was carrying out, particularly once the stripping out work was completed and the refurbishment work, involving the employment of subcontractors, had started. On 21 July 2000, the claimant faxed the defendant and asked for formal instructions and an agreement by which it could continue

e   the work. The fax sought a particular assurance regarding payment. The claimant reiterated these concerns at a subsequent site meeting held on 27 July 2000. On the following day, the claimant sent to the defendant four marked up plans showing the partitions that it had been asked to install with a budget price included. This document was signed by an authorised representative of the

f   defendant. This jointly signed document is relied on by the claimant as giving rise to the construction contract. It also relies on its standard conditions sent previously to the defendant which contained a term that the defendant's acceptance of any quotation would confirm its agreement to all conditions contained in that standard conditions document.

g   [9] The defendant, soon afterwards on 2 August 2000, sent the claimant a finalised letter of appointment which was in similar terms to that sent on 7 July 2000, thereby seeking to incorporate the JCT PC 98 terms and, if already applicable, seeking to exclude the claimant's standard terms. The letter contained a requirement that the claimant should confirm its agreement to the terms of the letter by returning the enclosed copy signed where indicated but this copy was

h   neither signed nor returned by the claimant. No further communication of note occurred concerning the terms of the contract under which the work was being carried out.

[10] On the basis of these exchanges, the claimant contended that the contract was formed by its offer contained in its quotation of 28 July 2000 read with the

j   earlier communication enclosing its standard conditions and the defendant's acceptance of both constituted by its signature on that quotation.

[11] The defendant contended that, at best, the joint signatures on the document of 28 July 2000 could only have related to, and given rise to, a construction contract concerning the partitions. Since the quotation made no reference to earlier communications or to the claimant's conditions, these conditions could not be regarded as applying to any of the claimant's work. In

consequence, the other work could only have been subject to the letter dated 2
August 2000 and that the claimant's failure to sign and return a copy did not
preclude a contract coming into being.

[12] The claimant disputed the defendant's contentions, particularly on the
ground that, since a contact was already in being, its failure to sign and return the
offer contained in the letter dated 2 August 2000 was the clearest possible
indication that it was not agreeing to be bound by that proposed contract and
remained bound by the earlier contract.

[13] It can be seen from this summary that it was not clear-cut or obvious
which set of conditions, namely the claimant's conditions or JCT PC 98, had been
incorporated into the construction contract but that there was in existence a
construction contract of some kind. Thus, one of the disputes requiring
resolution was as to which set of conditions had been incorporated since that the
answer to that question would determine whether the basis of valuation and
payment was in accordance with the claimant's rates and quotations or by
reference to a prime cost. Unless a pure question of jurisdiction as to whether or
not a contract existed at all arises, a court ought ordinarily not to decide a
disputed question in enforcement proceedings since that question has been left,
by the terms of the statutory jurisdiction of the adjudicator, for decision by the
adjudicator.

THE DISPUTE REFERRED TO THE ADJUDICATOR
[14] The claimant had submitted a final account to the defendant in March
2002 claiming a sum of £144,706·64 plus VAT as being outstanding. Having failed
to obtain what it regarded as a proper response to this document, it served a
notice of adjudication on the defendant dated 3 July 2002 to the effect that the
dispute between the parties was to be settled by the process of adjudication in
accordance with the provisions of the Housing Grants, Construction and
Regeneration Act 1996. The notice enclosed a copy of the claimant's application
to the Association of Independent Construction Adjudicators as a nominating
body, for the appointment of an adjudicator. The nature of the dispute was stated
to be 'Valuation and payment of Final Account'.

THE JURISDICTION OF THE ADJUDICATOR
[15] The jurisdictional questions raised by the defendant in relation to the
decision of the adjudicator arise out of the statutory basis for the adjudication.
This is set out in ss 108 and 114 of the 1996 Act which provide:

'(1) A party to a construction contract has the right to refer a dispute
arising under the contract for adjudication under a procedure complying
with this section.

For this purpose "dispute" includes any difference.

(2) The contract shall—(a) enable a party to give notice at any time of his
intention to refer a dispute to adjudication; (b) provide a timetable with the
object of securing the appointment of the adjudicator and referral of the
dispute to him within 7 days of such notice ...

(5) If the contract does not comply with the requirements of subsections (1)
to (4), the adjudication provisions of the Scheme for Construction Contracts
apply ...

a
114. ...—(1) The Minister shall by regulations make a scheme ("the Scheme for Construction Contracts") containing provision about the matters referred to in the preceding provisions of this Part.'

The relevant scheme is set out in the Scheme for Construction Contracts (England and Wales) Regulations 1998, SI 1998/649 (the Scheme).

b
[16] It has been seen that the parties were contending for one or other of two sets of conditions as having been incorporated into the contract which both parties accepted was a construction contract. The claimant contended that its conditions were incorporated and the defendant that JCT PC 98 were incorporated. Both parties accepted that if the claimant's conditions were incorporated, that the requirements for adjudication provided for by s 108 were
c
not met so that the adjudication would be governed by the Scheme whereas, given the detailed provisions for adjudication contained in JCT PC 98, if those conditions prevailed, the adjudication would be governed by the contractual provisions and not by the Scheme provisions. Since these provisions, whether the Scheme or the contractual, governed all questions of appointment, timescales and procedure, it is vital to know which applied. Surprisingly, the defendant did
d
not put in evidence the details of either set of rules and merely confined its submissions to the general proposition that the 'right' set of adjudication provisions had to be used for all questions of appointment and procedure for the adjudication to be correctly constituted and for the decision to be within jurisdiction and enforceable.

e
NO CONSTRUCTION CONTRACT
[17] Turning to the history of the adjudication, the starting point is the reaction of the defendant on being informed that Mr Morris had been appointed as adjudicator. On receiving that information, the defendant's solicitors wrote to him with a copy to the claimant's solicitors on 16 July 2002 in the following terms:
f

'If there is a construction contract between [the defendant] and the [claimant] then it is in the JCT Standard Form of Prime Cost Contract 1998. The appointment of the applicant was confirmed, at the latest, by a letter dated 2 August 2000 specifying the form of contract. As we understand it, you have been nominated by the [claimant] pursuant to the Scheme for
g
Construction Contracts (England and Wales) Regulations 1998. However, if there is to be an adjudication then the nomination process and the rules of adjudication should follow the JCT procedure. It follows that we can neither accept your jurisdiction, nor sign the Deed of Appointment. You will note that we are copying this letter to the [claimant's] solicitors and it may be that
h
they will now be willing to withdraw your nomination and proceed correctly, in accordance with the contract. If [the claimant] will not withdraw your nomination and if you are minded to proceed then [the defendant] will wish to participate without prejudice to their objection to your jurisdiction and under protest.'

j
[18] To this letter, the claimant's solicitors replied to the adjudicator as follows:

'[The claimant] refute the statements contained in this letter to the effect that they are bound by the JCT Standard Form of Prime Cost Contract. This form of contract was rejected in express terms by [the claimant] as you will see in the statement of dispute. The only agreement in writing or otherwise

that exists between the parties is dated 28 July 2000 which is [the claimant's]
letter of that date incorporating their conditions duly signed and returned by
[the defendant]. There can be no question regarding your jurisdiction in this
matter the Scheme clearly applies.'

[19] The adjudicator, although his decision did not contain reasons, set out the
procedural history of the adjudication in his decision. This included the following
passage:

'The [defendant] wrote on 26 July 2002 "if despite our objections you
decide to proceed with the adjudication then we reserve the right to make
submissions on the matters put before you without prejudice to our
challenge to your jurisdiction". This sentiment was expressed in further
communications and submissions made by the [defendant]. At para 2.3 of
the statement of response the [defendant] states that "the [defendant] does
not consent to or grant the adjudicator the authority to determine the issue
of jurisdiction".'

[20] The defendant's written submissions for this summary judgment hearing
clearly set out the nature of the jurisdictional challenge mounted by the
defendant to the adjudicator's appointment and decision. These stated:

'3.1 The defendant's primary contention is that the adjudicator did not
have the jurisdiction to adjudicate or determine the dispute purportedly
referred to him by the claimant. The referral to adjudication and the
nomination of the adjudicator were purportedly made pursuant to the term
of the Scheme for Construction Contracts Regulations (England and Wales)
1998 ("the Scheme"). The claimant contends that the provisions of the
Scheme applied by reason of their implication into its standard conditions of
sale which it contend applied to the works.
3.2 The defendant denies that the claimant's conditions of sale applied to
the works. The defendant avers that the Works were carried out pursuant to
the terms of the JCT Prime Cost 1998 Standard Form of contract ("JCT PC
98"). JCT PC 98 complies with the provisions of ss 108(1)–(4) of the 1996 Act)
therefore it follows that there is no scope for the implication therein of the
provisions of the Scheme.
3.3 The defendant avers that: (i) JCT PC 98 applied to the work carried out
by the claimant. Therefore, in purporting to act pursuant to the terms of the
Scheme, the adjudicator was acting without jurisdiction because he failed to
determine the dispute referred to him under the actual conditions between
the parties.'

[21] It is clear from these extracts that: (1) Each party was contending that
there was a written construction contract in being. However, whereas the
claimant was contending for one based on its own conditions of sale, the
defendant was contending for one based on JCT PC 98. (2) The defendant was
contending that the applicable rules for the appointment of the adjudicator and
for the procedure to be followed in the adjudication on appointment were those
set out in JCT PC 98. The claimant was contending that since there were no
standard conditions incorporated into the construction contract and that the only
conditions incorporated were ones containing no rules of appointment or
procedure, the statutory implication arose. This, being s 108 of the 1996 Act,
provides that if the construction contract does not contain specific minimum

a   terms relating to the conduct of the adjudication, 'the adjudication provisions of
the Scheme for Construction Contracts apply'.

[22] The adjudicator clearly understood that these were the rival contentions
of the parties since his decision contains this clearly stated passage:

b   '2.01 The [claimant] and [defendant] agree that there is a contract in place
for the construction works carried out by the [claimant] between 8 June 2000
and 30 September 2000 at 368–370 Oxford Street, London W1N 9HB.

2.02 There is dispute between the parties as to the precise form of contract
…

2.05 Clause 108(1) of the 1996 Act specifically limits the scope of an
adjudication to "a dispute arising under the contract".

c   2.06 By extension, a dispute arising about the formation of a contract is
beyond the valid scope of an arbitration (sic), and no decision has been made
in that regard.'

[23] The defendant now contends that there was no contract at all, that the
parties' relationship was purely a non-contractual one that, in consequence,

d   the claimant's only entitlement to payment was for a quantum meruit and
that the adjudicator lacked jurisdiction since there was no construction contract
in writing in place under and by virtue of which the claimant could refer resulting
disputes to adjudication.

[24] The jurisdictional challenge that the defendant mounted before the
adjudicator was mounted on the premise that there was in existence a

e   construction contract between the parties since that challenge was to this effect:

'under our contract with the claimant, we are entitled to an adjudicator
appointment procedure and to an adjudication in conformity with our
contractual agreement. We are not required to submit to an adjudication

f   conducted under a different procedure since that procedure would only be
applicable if the terms of the construction contract contended for by the
claimant, which are different from the terms that we contend for, are
applicable.'

It would be diametrically opposite to that approach for the defendant now to
contend that there was no contract at all between the parties.

g   [25] It is not open to the defendant to advance this contention in these
enforcement proceedings. As recorded by the adjudicator in his decision, the
defendant accepted that there was a contract in being between the parties for the
refurbishment work carried out by the claimant and based its submissions to him
on that basis. This application and the adjudication should be considered on the

h   basis that both parties accepted that a construction contract was in place since the
decision is premised on that commonly accepted understanding and it would be
inequitable if the defendant was now entitled to reprobate from its position
before the adjudicator. Moreover, for the purposes of these enforcement
proceedings, the defendant is estopped from resiling from that position having

j   adopted it before the adjudicator.

ADJUDICATION RULES

[26] At first sight, the defendant's contentions pose an intractable logical
puzzle. The puzzle is as to how an adjudication can start at all in the
circumstances of this case. The puzzle arises in this way: both parties accept that
there is a construction contract and that each party is, in consequence entitled to

call for an adjudication of disputes arising under that contract. However, each
party contends for different terms and different appointment procedures arising
out of those terms. Thus, one of the disputes requiring resolution by the
adjudicator is which terms were incorporated into the construction contract.
Since an adjudicator's appointment must be made in conformity with the
relevant contractual terms and since the adjudicator cannot determine his own
jurisdiction, particularly where, as here, the defendant expressly states that he is
not being given jurisdiction to determine his own jurisdiction, it would seem that
the adjudicator is hamstrung since he cannot determine whether or not he should
proceed to hear and decide the dispute in question. However, each party is none
the less entitled to an immediate adjudication to resolve which terms were
incorporated into the construction contract that they both accepted governed
their relationship. It is clearly within the scope of an adjudicator's jurisdiction to
determine whether particular documents were incorporated into the
construction contract under which he was appointed and out of which the
dispute arises (see *C & B Scene Concept Design Ltd v Isobars Ltd* [2002] EWCA Civ
46, (2002) 82 ConLR 154 particularly at [21]–[30] per Sir Murray Stuart-Smith).

[27] On a careful analysis, however, the situation is not as puzzling as it seems
on first sight. It is important to take into account the precise basis of the statutory
jurisdiction of the adjudicator. As already set out, this is derived from s 108(1) of
the 1996 Act. That provides that 'a party to a construction contract has the right
to refer a dispute arising under the contract for adjudication under a procedure
complying with this section'. It follows that, since both parties agree that their
relationship was governed by a construction contract, each of them has the right
to refer disputes arising under that contract to adjudication. It would be
surprising if that right could be thwarted because the parties could not agree as to
which set of conditions had been incorporated into the contract or which set of
adjudication provisions should apply. If the defendant's contentions are accepted,
in a situation where it was not obvious which adjudication provisions should
apply, even though it was accepted by both parties that their relationship was
governed by a construction contract, it would not be possible to embark on an
adjudication without first seeking a determination from the court to that
question despite the statutory entitlement to an immediate and speedy
adjudication.

[28] Section 108, as has been seen, provides that the construction contract
shall enable a party to give notice at any time of his intention to refer a dispute to
adjudication and shall provide a timetable with the object of securing the
appointment of an adjudicator and referral of the dispute to him within seven
days of such notice. The section continues:

'(5) If the contract does not comply with the requirements of subsections
(1) to (4) [which include the provisions I have just summarised], the
adjudication provisions of the Scheme for Construction Contracts apply.'

[29] If the parties enter into their construction contract in such a way that its
terms are not clearly and unquestionably capable of being identified, because, as
here, the negotiations consisted of a series of offers and counter-offers and no
complete and composite set of contract documents was ever identified and
signed, the parties have not produced a construction contract whose terms
enable a party to give notice at any time of his intention to refer a dispute to
adjudication nor have they provided a contractual timetable with the object of
securing the appointment of an adjudicator within seven days of such a notice.

a   Indeed, without an adjudication, the manner of giving notice to refer a dispute to adjudication and the means of appointing, and the timetable for the appointment of, the adjudicator that are provided for in the contract cannot be ascertained.

[30] In those circumstances, s 108 of the 1996 Act provides that the Scheme shall apply since the contract does not comply with the statutory requirement that it should enable a party to give notice at any time of his intention to refer a *b* dispute to adjudication nor does it provide an appropriate timetable for an appointment within seven days of such a notice. A construction contract whose terms cannot be readily ascertained by both parties does not enable these essential formalities to be undertaken in the requisite timetable. A contract only enables these things to be done if it not only provides for them but also provides for them in a form that precludes any reasonable argument as to its terms *c* concerning the adjudication which both parties have the right to demand and have instituted in a limited timetable.

[31] This conclusion arises from the use of the words 'the contract shall enable' and 'the contract shall provide' in s 108(2)(a) and (b) of the 1996 Act. These words, in the context of the mandatory requirement that a party has the *d* right to refer a dispute arising under a construction contract, which includes a dispute as to which terms are included in the contract, to adjudication, mean that the contract shall both contain the required provisions and shall contain them in a manner and form that enables their applicability to be readily ascertained without dispute. If there is a dispute as to their applicability, the contract does not enable a party to give the requisite notice of an intention to refer a dispute to *e* adjudication with the result that the contract does not comply with s 108(1) and that the adjudication provisions of the Scheme apply in default. This is so even if it subsequently emerges from the decision of the adjudicator that the terms of the construction contract did, in fact, comply with the requirements of s 108(1). Unless this extended construction of s 108 is applied by a court, effect cannot be *f* given to the underlying mandatory requirement that a party has the right to refer all disputes arising under the construction contract to adjudication.

CONCLUSION

[32] It follows that the adjudicator was appointed to determine disputes arising under a construction contract and, correctly, was both appointed under *g* the Scheme and then applied the Scheme to that adjudication. Thus, the jurisdictional challenges to his appointment and decision fail and his decision is enforceable. There is to be judgment for the claimant.

Order accordingly.

Martyn Gurr   Barrister.

Sandeman Coprimar SA v Transitos y Transportes Integrales SL and others

[2003] EWCA Civ 113

COURT OF APPEAL, CIVIL DIVISION

LORD PHILLIPS OF WORTH MATRAVERS MR, RIX AND SCOTT BAKER LJJ

20, 21 JANUARY, 11 FEBRUARY 2003

Carriers – Contract – Carriage of goods – Compensation for loss of goods – International carriage of goods by road – Goods of no intrinsic value – Owner guaranteeing tax authorities for loss of goods – Liability under contract of carriage and sub-contracts – Whether guarantee payment constituting charge in respect of carriage of goods – Carriage of Goods by Road Act 1965, Schedule, art 23(4).

The claimant company imported Scotch whisky into Spain. Each bottle of spirits released onto the Spanish market bore a paper seal which indicated that excise duty had been paid. The seals, which were issued by the Spanish authorities to producers or importers, had no intrinsic value, but their recipients were required to give a guarantee to the tax authorities that they would not be used illicitly. If the seals were not used for their proper purpose, or returned within six months, the guarantor was required to pay the equivalent of the duty that would have been recovered on the bottles to which the seals should have been attached. The first defendant agreed with the claimant that it would carry a consignment of 456,000 seals from Spain to Scotland. The first defendant sub-contracted the contract of carriage to the third defendant. The third defendant consolidated the consignment of seals with other goods bound for the United Kingdom and contracted with an English company to carry the consolidated cargo from Spain to the premises of the second defendant in England. The third defendant instructed the fourth defendant to arrange the on-carriage of the seals to Scotland and the fourth defendant agreed with the second defendant that it would arrange that on-carriage. The second defendant agreed with the fifth defendant that it would transport the seals to Scotland. The seals arrived at the second defendant's premises, but never reached Scotland. The claimant commenced proceedings in respect of the loss of the seals, the greater part of its claim relating to the amount payable to the Spanish tax authorities under the guarantee. The judge held, inter alia, that while the first defendant was liable to the claimant under the Convention on the Contract for the International Carriage of Goods by Road[a] (CMR) (set out in the Schedule to the Carriage of Goods by Road Act 1965), there was no privity of contract between the claimant and either the second or third defendants since the first defendant had not made out a consignment note as required by art 34 of the CMR; that the first defendant (which was insolvent and had taken no part in the proceedings) was liable for the guarantee payment because it had been aware of the nature of the seals and the consequences that would attend their loss; that the guarantee payment came within the definition of 'other charges in respect of the carriage of the goods' in art 23(4) of the CMR; and that although the second and third defendants were liable to the claimant in

***

a The Convention on the Contract for the International Carriage of Goods by Road, so far as material, is set out in the annex

a bailment, if art 23(4) were to apply to them, the guarantee payment was too
remote to be recoverable from them at common law. The claimant appealed
against the decision that the second and third defendants were not liable in
respect of the guarantee payment, and the third defendant cross-appealed,
arguing that it was not liable to the claimant at all.

b **Held** – The appeal would be dismissed and the cross-appeal allowed for the
following reasons—
(1) The judge had been correct in holding that the liability to make the
guarantee payment was too remote to be recoverable from the second or third
defendant as damages in negligence or conversion. However, he had erred in
holding that the guarantee payment fell within the definition of 'other charges in
c respect of the carriage of the goods' in art 23(4) of the CMR. The liability under
the guarantee was not a duty payable in respect of the goods carried, but was
rather a liability arising under a guarantee as a result of the claimant's inability to
account for the seals (see [31]–[35], [38], [39], [42], [69], below); *James Buchanan &
Co Ltd v Babco Forwarding and Shipping (UK) Ltd* [1977] 3 All ER 1048 distinguished.
d (2) The judge had been wrong to hold that the third defendant was liable to
the claimant as bailee of the seals. The third defendant was not the first
carrier, the last carrier or the carrier performing that portion of the carriage
during which the loss had occurred. The claimant could not therefore contend
that the third defendant remained susceptible to suit in relation to the loss of the
seals after they had been transferred to a successive carrier (see [42], [48], [66],
e [69], below).

Notes
For compensation payable by a carrier, see 5(1) *Halsbury's Laws* (4th edn reissue)
para 561.
f For the Carriage of Goods by Road Act 1965, Schedule, art 23(4), see
38 *Halsbury's Statutes* (4th edn) (2001 reissue) 152.

Cases referred to in judgment
Buchanan (James) & Co Ltd v Babco Forwarding and Shipping (UK) Ltd [1977] 3 All ER
  1048, [1978] AC 141, [1977] 3 WLR 907, HL; *affg* [1977] 1 All ER 518, [1977] QB
g 208, [1977] 2 WLR 107, CA.
CIA Portorafti Commerciale SA v Ultramar Panama Inc, The Captain Gregos (No 2)
  [1990] 2 Lloyd's Rep 395, CA.
*Elder, Dempster & Co Ltd v Paterson, Zochonis & Co, Griffiths Lewis Steam Navigation
  Co v Paterson, Zochonis & Co Ltd* [1924] AC 522, [1924] All ER Rep 135, HL.
h *Gilchrist Watt & Sanderson Pty Ltd v York Products Ltd* [1970] 3 All ER 825, [1970]
  1 WLR 1262, PC.
*Hispanica de Petroleos SA v Vencedora Oceanica Navegacion SA, The Kapetan Marcos
  NL (No 2)* [1987] 2 Lloyd's Rep 321.
Johnson Matthey & Co Ltd v Constantine Terminals Ltd [1976] 2 Lloyd's Rep 215.
j *Kuwait Airways Corp v Iraq Airways Co (No 3)* [2001] 1 All ER (Comm) 557, [2002]
  2 AC 883, [2001] 3 WLR 1117, CA; *affd* [2002] UKHL 19, [2002] 3 All ER 209,
  [2002] 2 AC 883, [2002] 2 WLR 1353.
Morris v CW Martin & Sons Ltd [1965] 2 All ER 725, [1966] 1 QB 716, [1965] 3 WLR
  276, CA.
New Zealand Shipping Co Ltd v AM Satterthwaite & Co Ltd, The Eurymedon [1974]
  1 All ER 1015, [1975] AC 154, [1974] 2 WLR 865, PC.

Overseas Tankship (UK) Ltd v Morts Docks and Engineering Co Ltd, The Wagon Mound
   [1961] 1 All ER 404, [1961] AC 388, [1961] 2 WLR 126, PC.

Pioneer Container, The, KH Enterprise (cargo owners) v Pioneer Container (owners)
   [1994] 2 All ER 250, [1994] 2 AC 324, [1994] 3 WLR 1, PC.

Scruttons Ltd v Midland Silicones Ltd [1962] 1 All ER 1, [1962] AC 446, [1962] 2 WLR
   186, HL.

Singer Co (UK) Ltd v Tees and Hartlepool Port Authority [1988] 2 Lloyd's Rep 164.

Wilson v Darling Island Stevedoring and Lighterage Co Ltd (1955) 95 CLR 43, Aus HC.

Appeal and cross-appeal

Sandeman Coprimar SA (Seagram) appealed with the permission of Judge
Hegarty QC sitting as a deputy judge of the Mercantile Court at Liverpool
granted on 22 November 2001 from his order of 6 July 2001 that the second
defendant, Bradford Cargo Terminals Ltd (BCT), was not liable for sums payable
by Seagram to the Spanish tax authorities. The third defendant, Spain TIR
Centro Transportes Internacionales SA (Spain-TIR), cross-appealed from a
finding of liability against it. The first defendant, Transitos y Transportes
Integrales SL (TTI), was insolvent and took no part in the hearing. Claims against
the fourth defendant, Interserve International Freight plc, and the fifth defendant,
Joda Freight, were discontinued. The facts are set out in the judgment of the
court.

Michael Nolan (instructed by *DLA*) for Seagram.

Nigel Meeson QC (instructed by *Hill Dickinson*) for BCT.

Michael Coburn (instructed by *Thomas Cooper & Stibbard*) for Spain-TIR.

Cur adv vult

11 February 2003. The following judgment of the court was delivered.

LORD PHILLIPS OF WORTH MATRAVERS MR.

[1] This is an appeal from the judgment delivered by Judge Hegarty QC at
Liverpool on 6 July 2001 and perfected subsequently. It is brought with the
permission of Judge Hegarty granted on 22 November 2001. It relates to the loss of
some unusual goods in the course of international carriage by road. The appellants
(Seagram) owned those goods. The judge held that three of the defendants who
were involved in the carriage were responsible for the loss. In consequence of the
loss of the goods, Seagram had to pay Ptas 113,324,310, equivalent to some
£420,000, under a guarantee given to the Spanish tax authorities. This
represented almost the entirety of their claim. The judge held that Seagram was
entitled to recover this sum from the first defendants (Transitos y Transportes
Integrales SL (TTI)). TTI are, however, insolvent and took no part in the hearing.
The judge held that the second defendants (Bradford Cargo Terminals Ltd
(BCT)) and the third defendants (Spain TIR Centro Transportes
Internacionales SA (Spain-TIR)), while liable to Seagram for loss of the goods,
were not liable for this sum. It is against that finding that Seagram appeal. By a
cross-appeal Spain-TIR, for their part, deny that they are under any liability at all.

[2] The facts of this case raise many and complex issues. In resolving those
issues the judgment appealed against ran to 117 pages. Happily, not all
those issues are raised before us. None the less this appeal illustrates the

a problems that arise when parties to international carriage by road depart from the scheme laid down under the relevant international convention.

THE FACTS

[3] The following facts are extracted from the judgment of Judge Hegarty. They are not contentious.

b [4] Seagram is a company incorporated in Spain by the name Sandeman Coprimar SA. The company trades under the name Seagram Espana. Seagram imports Scotch whisky into Spain.

[5] Spain imposes excise duties on spirits, including whisky, which become payable when the liquor is released from a bonded warehouse or some other similar suspensive regime. Accordingly, where whisky is imported into Spain
c from the United Kingdom, no United Kingdom duty is payable but Spanish duty is payable on importation into Spain or release from bond. When liquor is released onto the Spanish market, each bottle bears a paper seal of a particular design and bearing a serial number. This is in the form of a strip which is affixed to both sides of the neck of the bottle and runs over the cork or the cap. The
d technical word for this is 'precinta', which can be translated as 'tax seal'.

[6] The presence of a tax seal on a bottle indicates that excise duty has been paid. Tax seals are issued by the Spanish authorities to producers or importers. No charge is made for these seals and they have no intrinsic value. If used illicitly, however, these seals can facilitate the evasion of duty. Those to whom they are issued are required to give a guarantee to the tax authorities to guard against this
e eventuality. If the seals are not used for their proper purpose, namely the sealing of bottles on which duty has been paid, or alternatively returned within six months, the guarantor is called upon to pay the equivalent of the duty that would have been recovered on the bottles to which the seals should, in the normal course of events, have been attached.

f [7] At or about the beginning of August 1994 Seagram entered into an oral agreement with TTI that TTI would carry nine cartons containing a total of 456,000 tax seals from Madrid to the premises of Chivas Brothers Ltd (Chivas) in Paisley, Scotland. On 4 August TTI entered into a sub-contract with Spain-TIR under which the latter agreed to carry nine cartons of 'precintas para botellas de licor' (seals for bottles of spirits) from Madrid to Paisley. TTI arranged for the
g seals to be collected from Seagram's agents in Madrid and delivered to Spain-TIR's premises for the purposes of on-carriage.

[8] Spain-TIR, in their turn, sub-contracted this carriage. They did so in the following manner. Having received the nine cartons, they consolidated these with other goods bound for the United Kingdom. They then contracted with an
h English company, BJ Waters Ltd, to carry the consolidated cargo from their premises in Madrid to the premises of BCT in Bradford. Spain-TIR prepared a consignment note in respect of the consolidated cargo covering carriage from their depot in Madrid to BCT's premises. On this the seals were described as 'precintos botellas'.

j [9] Spain-TIR instructed agents, a company of freight forwarders called Interserve International Freight plc (Interserve) to arrange for the on-carriage to Paisley. Interserve were, at one stage, joined as fourth defendants to the action, but the claim against them was discontinued. Interserve agreed with BCT that the latter would arrange for the on-carriage of the seals from their premises in Bradford to Paisley. They sent an unloading list to BCT prior to the arrival of the cargo, which described the seals as '9 cartons botels'. BCT agreed with Joda

Freight (Joda), a transportation company based in Keighley, that they would transport the cartons on to Chivas's premises in Paisley. Joda were joined as fifth defendants to the action. *a*

[10] The cartons never reached Chivas. It was common ground that they had got as far as BCT. One of the issues that the judge had to resolve was whether BCT lost the cartons or whether BCT delivered them to Joda, who then lost them. The judge found that they were never delivered to Joda, but lost by BCT. *b* There is no appeal against that finding.

THE JUDGE'S FINDINGS

[11] English law in relation to international carriage by road was significantly altered by the Carriage of Goods by Road Act 1965. That Act gave statutory effect to the Convention on the Contract for the International Carriage of Goods *c* by Road (CMR) (as set out in the Schedule to the 1965 Act). The effect of the CMR on the rights and liabilities of the parties lies at the root of this appeal. We have annexed the relevant provisions of the CMR to this judgment.

[12] The scheme of the CMR, where successive carriers perform carriage covered by a single contract, is that each successively becomes party to this *d* contract as a result of accepting the goods and the consignment note relating to them—see art 34 of the CMR. The consignment note sets out the terms of the single contract, and a copy of it travels with the goods.

[13] In the present case TTI never made out a consignment note. In these circumstances the judge held that there was no privity of contract between *e* Seagram and either Spain-TIR or BCT. We turn to explain the basis upon which the judge found that each of these three companies was under a liability, albeit not the identical liability, to Seagram.

THE LIABILITY OF TTI

[14] Although TTI never made out the consignment note required by art 4 of *f* the CMR, the contract between Seagram and TTI was none the less subject to the provisions of the CMR. Articles 1 and 4 so provide. The judge held that it followed that TTI were liable for the loss of the seals in the course of transit to their contractual destination, namely Paisley. No challenge is made to this conclusion.
g

THE LIABILITY OF SPAIN-TIR

[15] The judge, after a lengthy consideration of the authorities, concluded that Spain-TIR was not brought into contractual relationship with Seagram. Accordingly, they did not rank as a 'successive carrier' under art 34 of the CMR. They took possession of the goods as sub-contractors under their contract with TTI. That *h* contract was, itself, subject to the CMR, by virtue of art 1, but Seagram were not party to it. In these circumstances the judge held that 'whether or not TTI was expressly or by implication authorised to create a sub-bailment, Seagram is entitled to treat Spain-TIR as bailee of the seals'.

[16] The judge held that Spain-TIR's responsibility as bailee for the care of the *j* seals persisted until Spain-TIR delivered the seals to Paisley, in accordance with Spain-TIR's contract with TTI. The transfer of possession of the seals to BCT, under a further sub-contract, did not relieve Spain-TIR of responsibility to Seagram for the care of the seals. The judge held that it followed that Spain-TIR had the same liability as BCT for the loss of the seals.

THE LIABILITY OF BCT

a [17] The judge held:

> 'Like Spain-TIR, BCT voluntarily accepted the custody of the seals for
> reward and would, therefore, appear to have owed Seagram the duties of a
> bailee. In my judgment, that analysis would apply even if, as contended on
> behalf of Seagram, the sub-bailment to BCT was not expressly or by
b > implication authorised by Seagram.'

[18] The judge held that the only claim that Seagram was entitled to pursue
against Spain-TIR and BCT was in bailment. Negligence on the part of BCT was
to be inferred from the loss of the seals, and on this basis BCT was in breach of
bailment. Furthermore, the loss of the seals by BCT amounted to a conversion
c of them, both at common law and by virtue of the provisions of s 2(2) of the Torts
(Interference with Goods) Act 1977. Spain-TIR was in identical breach of duty.

THE MEASURE OF DAMAGE

[19] The judge first considered the measure of damage at common law and
then went on to consider the effect of art 23 of the CMR.
d

LIABILITY AT COMMON LAW

[20] The judge held that the seals had no intrinsic value at all. In so far as
Seagram were entitled to damages, this was in respect of consequential loss.
English principles of remoteness applied. To be recoverable, loss had to be of a
e type that was reasonably foreseeable. Carriage charges thrown away fell into this
category. Each of the three defendants was liable in respect of these. They
amounted to Ptas 42,550, the equivalent of less than £200.

[21] So far as the liability to the Spanish authorities under the guarantee was
concerned, the judge found that TTI were aware of the nature of the seals and
the consequences that would attend their loss, so that TTI were liable to Seagram
f for this. The same was not true of either Spain-TIR or BCT. On the evidence
neither of those companies could reasonably have appreciated either the nature
of the goods that were in the cartons nor the financial consequences to
Seagram of their loss.

g ARTICLE 23

[22] Article 23 of the CMR lays down the measure of compensation
recoverable where a carrier is liable under the convention for the loss of the
goods carried. The starting point under art 23(1) is that the carrier is liable for
the value of the goods at the place and time at which they were accepted
for carriage. In addition, under art 23(4), 'Customs duties and other charges
h incurred in respect of the carriage of the goods shall be refunded'. The judge held
that the sums payable under the guarantee constituted such charges provided,
but only provided, that they satisfied the English law test of remoteness. In the
case of TTI they did so. It followed from this finding that TTI had a contractual
liability under art 23 that mirrored the common law liability found by the judge.
j So far as Spain-TIR and BCT were concerned, if art 23(4) were to apply to them,
it would impose no liability in respect of sums payable under the guarantee for,
in their case, these were too remote.

[23] We have used the conditional tense in this last sentence, because the
judge expressed the view that whether or not art 23 applied was a matter for
the election by Spain-TIR and BCT, and it was open to them to exercise that

election even after his judgment. This finding was based upon the permissive
terms of art 28(2), which the judge held applied to each of these defendants. It *a*
was up to them whether to invoke the provisions of art 23. If they did so, they
would become subject to all the provisions of that article.

THE ISSUES RAISED ON THE APPEAL
[24] The following issues arise on this appeal. (i) Was the judge correct to *b*
hold that the guarantee payment was too remote to be recovered from Spain-TIR
or BCT at common law? Seagram contend that he was not. Spain-TIR and BCT
support his finding. (ii) If the guarantee payment was not too remote, did it
constitute part of the value of the seals? Seagram contends that it did not.
Spain-TIR and BCT contend that it did. (iii) Was the judge correct to hold that
the guarantee payment fell within the definition of 'other charges' under *c*
art 23(4)? Spain-TIR and BCT contend that he was not. Seagram support his
finding. (iv) Was the judge correct to hold that 'other charges' under art 23(4)
could only be recovered if not too remote under English law? Seagram contend
that he was not. Spain-TIR and BCT support his finding. (v) Was the judge
correct to hold that Spain-TIR were liable to Seagram as bailees of the seals? *d*
Spain-TIR contend that he was not. Seagram support his finding. (vi) Was the
judge correct to hold that BCT were liable to Seagram as bailees of the seals? BCT
contend that he was not. Seagram support his finding. (vii) Was the judge
correct to indicate that Spain-TIR and BCT could elect whether to rely on art 23,
but that if they did so would be bound by all its provisions? Seagram contend that
Spain-TIR and BCT have no right to elect, but are bound by all the provisions of *e*
art 23. Spain-TIR and BCT contend that they enjoy a right to elect to rely on
those provisions of art 23 which limit their liability.

WAS THE JUDGE CORRECT TO HOLD THAT THE GUARANTEE PAYMENT WAS TOO
REMOTE TO BE RECOVERED FROM SPAIN-TIR AND BCT AT COMMON LAW?
[25] The judge cited *Overseas Tankship (UK) Ltd v Morts Docks and Engineering* *f*
Co Ltd, The Wagon Mound [1961] 1 All ER 404, [1961] AC 388 as laying down the
following test of remoteness in the law of negligence:

'A negligent tortfeasor is not responsible for all the direct consequences of
his negligence, but only for such damage as ought reasonably to have been *g*
foreseen. There are two relevant qualifications to that general principle.
Firstly, the test of reasonable foreseeability in tort is generally more stringent
and less favourable to the wrongdoer than the similar test in contract.
Secondly, so long as the general nature of the damage in question was
reasonably foreseeable, it is immaterial that the precise extent of the damage,
or the precise manner in which it was caused, may not themselves have been *h*
foreseeable.'

[26] So far as the law of conversion is concerned, the judge adopted the
following passage from the decision of the Court of Appeal in *Kuwait Airways Corp v
Iraq Airways Co (No 3)* [2001] 1 All ER (Comm) 557 at 628, [2002] 2 AC 883 at 1030 *j*
(para 538):

'It appears to us that as the law now stands, in conversion cases a court has
to ask whether at the time of the conversion the type of loss that occurred (as
opposed to the precise manner in which it occurred) was reasonably
foreseeable.'

a [27] On behalf of Seagram, Mr Nolan did not challenge these tests. He submitted, however, that the judge had misapplied them. He put his case in a number of ways. First he relied upon the fact that BCT had no idea what was in the cartons. This was of the nature of their business. All kinds of goods came into their possession, often imprecisely described. In these circumstances BCT could not be heard to say that any type of loss was unforeseeable.

b [28] There can be problems in applying a test of foreseeability to carriers who handle consolidated containers of many different varieties of goods. Some would argue that one of the objects of the CMR convention was to make such an exercise superfluous. There is, however, no such problem on the facts of this case. No carrier without specific knowledge of the nature of 'precintas' and of the guarantee that has to be given to the Spanish authorities in exchange for their

c release, could envisage that the loss of a number of cartons could give rise to the type of liability experienced by Seagram in this case. Mr Nolan submitted that the loss in this case was of the same type as the loss that occurs when dutiable spirits are stolen and duty has to be paid on them. We shall be dealing with this suggested analogy in a different context later in this judgment. Suffice it to say

d that we do not accept it. The liability in this case was not analogous to duty payable on the goods carried.

[29] Mr Nolan submitted that when a number of items are lost, the owner will foreseeably suffer a financial loss in respect of each item. In this case a payment had to be made under the guarantee in respect of each seal. It followed, argued Mr Nolan, that the loss was of a type foreseeable as the consequence of the loss

e of goods carried. This contention is unsound. The fact that one kind of damage occurs item by item does not render another kind of damage that also occurs item by item similar in type.

[30] Finally, Mr Nolan argued that because the guarantee payment fell within the express definition of 'other charges' in art 23(4), the payment in question was

f of a type expressly contemplated by the CMR conditions. BCT contracted on CMR conditions and, therefore, could not be heard to suggest that this type of loss was not readily foreseeable. We have yet to deal with the issue of whether the guarantee payment did fall within the definition of 'other charges'. If the judge was right that it did, this was only by giving the meaning of that phrase so wide a compass that it embraced liabilities of types that were not reasonably

g foreseeable. We reject the suggestion that so wide a meaning of 'charges' could embrace a single 'type' of damage when applying the common law test of remoteness.

[31] We are in no doubt that the liability to make the guarantee payment was too remote to be recoverable from Spain-TIR or BCT as damages in negligence

h or conversion.

IF THE GUARANTEE PAYMENT WAS NOT TOO REMOTE, DID IT CONSTITUTE PART OF THE VALUE OF THE SEALS?

[32] The argument that the guarantee payment formed part of the value of the

j seals was advanced by Spain-TIR and BCT by way of alternative to their primary case that the payment was too remote to be recoverable at all. If this alternative case had succeeded, they would have sought to invoke the limit of liability provided by art 23(3) of the CMR. Having regard to the answer that we have given to the previous question, this issue does not arise. We will, however, deal with it shortly, for the answer further supports our conclusion that the guarantee payment was too remote to be recovered. The guarantee was exacted

to guard against the possibility that the seals might be misused so as to deprive a
the Spanish authorities of excise duty payable on liquor sold in Spain. The
evidence was that, if it could be demonstrated that the seals had been destroyed,
the guarantee would not be called. Thus it was not inevitable that loss of the seals
would result in payment under the guarantee. For instance, if the seals had been
destroyed by fire, no payment would have been exacted. This demonstrates that
the liability under the guarantee formed no part of the value of the seals. It arose b
as a consequence of their loss by reason (i) of the undertaking given under the
guarantee and (ii) of the circumstances in which the loss occurred.

WAS THE JUDGE CORRECT TO HOLD THAT THE GUARANTEE PAYMENT FELL WITHIN
THE DEFINITION OF 'OTHER CHARGES' UNDER ART 23(4)?

[33] In making his finding the judge held that he was bound to follow the c
decision of the House of Lords in *James Buchanan & Co Ltd v Babco Forwarding and
Shipping (UK) Ltd* [1977] 3 All ER 1048, [1978] AC 141. Mr Coburn, on behalf of
Spain-TIR challenged that conclusion, arguing that the judge felt himself unduly
constrained by that decision.

[34] The *Buchanan* case concerned the theft of a consignment of whisky that d
was being carried under CMR terms, from the plaintiffs' bonded warehouse in
Glasgow to Teheran. Its value, in bond, was £7,000. Had it been exported from
the United Kingdom no excise duty would have been payable. It was, however,
stolen from a lorry park in London, while in the course of transit. In these
circumstances the plaintiffs became liable under s 85 of the Customs and Excise e
Act 1952 to pay excise duty on the whisky in the sum of some £30,000. The
plaintiffs contended that the value of the whisky included the £30,000 duty, so
that it could be recovered under art 23(2) of the CMR. This contention was
rejected by both the Court of Appeal ([1977] 1 All ER 518, [1977] QB 208) and the
House of Lords, a result which underpins our conclusion in [32], above, were
underpinning needed. f

[35] For present purposes, the crucial issue was that raised by the plaintiffs as
an alternative argument. Was the liability to duty recoverable as falling within
'the carriage charges, Customs duties and other charges incurred in respect of the
carriage of the goods' under art 23(4)? In the absence of authority, we would
have answered this question in the negative. It seems to us that one object of the g
CMR is to make a clear apportionment of risk arising in the course of
international carriage by road, so as to facilitate insurance and avoid double
insurance. A natural reading of art 23 would seem to us to impose liability on the
carrier for the value of the goods when the carriage begins, subject to the art 23(3)
limit, together with charges incidental to the carriage of the goods, including h
customs duties. Such charges, typically, are foreseeable and form an increment
to the value of the goods. Article 23(6) refers to entitlement to higher
compensation under arts 24 and 26. Article 26 would seem designed to enable a
consignor to impose liability on the carrier for a value exceeding the art 23(3)
limit and for possible consequential loss—a liability compensated for by a j
surcharge and which, by virtue of being declared, can be insured against by
the carrier.

[36] The minority in the House of Lords resolved the issue as we would have
done. The majority, however, did not. They upheld the judgment of the Court
of Appeal, though not that court's reasoning, in concluding that the liability to
excise duty constituted 'other charges' under art 23(4). Their reasoning can be

a   derived from the following passages. Lord Wilberforce ([1977] 3 All ER 1048 at 1054, [1978] AC 141 at 154) said:

> 'I find that the judgment of Master Jacob carries conviction. The duty, he says, became chargeable having regard to the way in which the goods were carried by the appellants. "In respect of" is wide enough to include the way in which the goods were carried, miscarried or lost. I think this is right—and
>
> *b*   I do not consider that it is answered by saying that the charge would not have arisen if the thieves had exported the goods or if the whisky had flowed away. No doubt this is true but the fact that an exemption might have arisen does not prevent the charge which did arise from being "in respect of the carriage". The appellants' duty was to carry the whisky to the port of
>
> *c*   embarkation—their failure to do so might, or might not, bring a charge into existence. But if it did, I think it right to say that the charge was in respect of the carriage.'

Lord Dilhorne ([1977] 3 All ER 1048 at 1057, [1978] AC 141 at 158) said:

> *d*   'If "in respect of" is given the broad interpretation of "in consequence of", content can be given to the words in question. They will clearly cover a far wider ambit than carriage charges. While it would not be right to seek to import common law doctrines into the convention, it cannot be right, in my opinion, to construe "in respect of" as meaning "for" with the result that the article would read "carriage charges ... and other charges for carriage". They
>
> *e*   must be given a wider meaning than that and in my opinion the right meaning to give them is that in the context in which they appear they mean "in consequence of" or "arising out of".'

Lord Salmon ([1977] 3 All ER 1048 at 1059, 1060, [1978] AC 141 at 160, 161) said:

> *f*   'Were the charges for excise duty which the respondents have been obliged to pay incurred in "respect of the carriage of the goods"? No doubt these words are flexible and somewhat imprecise, but, especially as they appear in an international convention relating to commercial affairs, they should not be construed pedantically or rigidly but sensibly and broadly. So construed, I agree with the view expressed by Master Jacob in his judgment
>
> *g*   that they are wide enough to include "in consequence of the way in which the goods were carried by the appellants". They were certainly carried in such a way as caused the respondents to be charged with £30,000 in respect of excise duty ... My Lords, in my view, the language of art 23 is capable of bearing and does bear the meaning attached to it by Master Jacob. This
>
> *h*   meaning accords with both reason and justice. An excise duty of £30,000 has become chargeable against the respondent exporters solely because of the fault of the appellant carriers' servant for which the carriers are vicariously liable. Reason and justice seem to demand that the burden of paying the £30,000 should rest on the shoulders of the carriers rather than on those of the innocent exporters.'

j

[37] Each of the majority proceeded on the basis that art 23 was the only route by which liability for excise tax could be recovered. None made any reference to art 26. Their speeches extend the meaning of the words 'in respect of the carriage' to embrace 'in consequence of the miscarriage'.

[38] The decision in the *Buchanan* case is critically discussed in Professor Clarke's book, *International Carriage of Goods by Road: CMR* (3rd edn, 1997)

pp 368–373 (para 98) and in *Hill & Messent on CMR: Contracts for the International Carriage of Goods by Road* (3rd edn, 2000) pp 202–209 (paras 9.25–9.34). Each suggests that the approach of the majority of the House of Lords must be subject to some restriction. We shall refer to some of the observations of the authors of these works when we come to address the next issue. Nor is the decision one which lies happily with the approach to the ambit of art 23 of the courts of most of the other signatories to the convention, France being an exception. For our part we do not consider that the decision should be applied any more widely by the courts of this country than respect for the doctrine of precedent requires.

[39] The judge held:

'I find it impossible to make any rational distinction between the statutory liability for duty which was the subject matter of that case and the liability under the guarantee in the present case.'

We do not agree. In the *Buchanan* case the excise duty payable was a charge on the goods carried. It was, as a matter of English law, an automatic consequence of the loss of the goods within the jurisdiction. It could be said to be similar in kind to the customs duty payable upon importation of the goods into another country. The liability under the guarantee in this case is not a duty payable in respect of the goods carried. It is a liability arising under a guarantee that arose as a result of the inability of Seagram to account for the seals. Not only is the liability a more remote consequence of the loss of the seals than is excise duty payable on whisky that is stolen, as to which see the next issue, but it does not, in our view, fall within the meaning of a 'charge incurred in respect of the carriage of the goods'. For this reason we hold that payment under the guarantee is not recoverable under art 23(4). Was the judge correct to hold that 'other charges' under art 23(4) could only be recovered if not too remote under English law?

[40] The judge adopted and applied the following passage from Professor Clarke's work (p 371 (para 98)):

'The trouble with the broad view is that it makes it difficult for the carrier to estimate exposure to liability. Whereas there is a monetary limit on the amount of liability for loss, damage or delay to the goods, there is no limit in the CMR on the amount of compensation that can be awarded for "other charges". Inevitably, some kind of rule is required to identify those charges which are "in consequence of" the carriage and those which are not. In the CMR the question was not anticipated and has not been answered. An answer must be found in national law, and found, it appears, in rules of causation and remoteness. In terms of causation, charges will be recoverable under English law if they were incurred as part of a reasonable response to the threat posed by the carrier's breach of the contract of carriage. In terms of remoteness, charges will be recoverable if they are losses of a type which the carrier should reasonably have contemplated would be incurred in the event of his breach of the contract of carriage.'

[41] *Hill & Messent* (p 204 (para 9.31)) make a similar suggestion that the 'width of expression' used by the House of Lords should only be applied to expenses that were within the actual or constructive knowledge of the carrier 'so they could be held liable without offending normal rules of remoteness'.

[42] Because we have distinguished the *Buchanan* case it is not necessary for us to rule whether these expressions of view are correct and we shall not do so. We sympathise with the perceived need to restrict the scope of the *Buchanan* case. At

a the same time we think it unfortunate if that decision imports the application of English principles of remoteness. This does not seem appropriate, for the scheme of the CMR contemplates an identical liability imposed on a succession of carriers. On the facts of the present case, the judge found that TTI were liable in respect of the guarantee payment, but that Spain-TIR and BCT were not. Had they all been linked to a single CMR contract this would have led to problems
b when art 38 fell to be applied.

WAS THE JUDGE CORRECT TO HOLD THAT SPAIN-TIR WERE LIABLE TO SEAGRAM AS BAILEES OF THE SEALS?

[43] This issue arises on a cross-appeal by Spain-TIR. Only the liability for the carriage charges now turns on the issue, and that is a liability which seems likely
c ultimately to fall on BCT. The issue is, however, an important one because, together with the seventh issue, it calls for consideration of the legal nature of a sub-bailment on terms. This takes us into deep waters.

[44] The starting point is to review the circumstances in which Spain-TIR became involved with the carriage of the seals. This requires some elaboration
d of the facts that we set out at the beginning of this judgment.

[45] The head contract of carriage was between Seagram and TTI and it was, by operation of law, subject to the CMR. Spain-TIR agreed with TTI to carry the seals from Madrid to Paisley. This contract also was subject to the CMR by operation of law. TTI gave Spain-TIR written instructions which identified the sender as
e Seagram and the consignee as Chivas. Spain-TIR issued a CMR consignment note which named the sender as Spain-TIR and the consignee as BCT. Spain-TIR sub-contracted to BJ Waters the carriage from their depot to BCT's premises in Bradford. This contract, also, was subject to the CMR by operation of law. Interserve, as Spain-TIR's agents agreed with BCT that BCT would carry the seals to their destination at Paisley. This agreement was on CMR terms, both because
f the contract between Interserve and BCT so provided and because BCT received the seals with, and on the terms of, the consignment note prepared by Spain-TIR.

[46] The judge recorded the concession by Mr Nolan on behalf of Seagram that Spain-TIR were entitled to invoke art 28 of the CMR and avail themselves of
g those provisions of the CMR which fixed or limited the compensation due. The judge held that, in the light of this concession, it was not necessary for him to decide whether Spain-TIR would have been entitled to rely upon those provisions under the doctrine of 'bailment on terms'. Findings made by the judge in relation to BCT bear, however, on that question.

h [47] The judge found that TTI must be regarded as having, at least by implication, authorised Spain-TIR to sub-contract to BCT performance of the last leg of the journey. Mr Nolan conceded that BCT also were entitled to invoke art 28 of the CMR. The judge went on to hold:

j   'I would not have been prepared to hold that Seagram had expressly forbidden any sub-bailment of the seals. In those circumstances, given the likelihood of consolidation and deconsolidation and the very widespread practice of sub-contracting all or part of contracts for the international carriage of goods by road, I would have been prepared, if the matter had not been resolved by concession, to hold that Seagram had impliedly consented to a sub-bailment of the seals. It would, I think, almost inexorably have

followed that its consent would have extended to a sub-bailment on the
terms of the CMR, given the international nature of the carriage.'

It necessarily follows from this that the judge would have been prepared to hold
that Seagram had impliedly consented to a sub-bailment by TTI to Spain-TIR on
terms of the CMR.

[48] In our judgment the judge was justified for the reasons that he gave in
concluding that both Spain-TIR and BCT had taken possession of the goods as
bailees on terms of the CMR. It remains to consider the implications of this.

[49] Mr Coburn submitted that it was not open to Seagram to sue Spain-TIR
for breach of bailment for two reasons. He submitted that, under principles of
common law, Spain-TIR were not liable for breach of bailment because they
were not in possession of the seals at the time of their loss. He further submitted
that because both the contract between Seagram and TTI and the contract
between TTI and Spain-TIR were governed by the CMR, the CMR applied
generally to regulate the rights and liabilities of these three parties. In these
circumstances, art 36 applied and Spain-TIR could not be sued by Seagram
because they were not the first carrier, the last carrier or the carrier performing
that portion of the carriage during which the event causing the loss occurred.

[50] Turning to the position at common law, Mr Coburn submitted that
where a contractual bailee of goods sub-bails them to A, who in turn sub-sub-bails
them to B, who loses them, the bailee will be liable to the owner for breach of a
non-delegable duty of care, but A will have no liability, being neither in
possession of the goods at the time of their loss nor party to the contract under
which they were bailed.

[51] The basis upon which the judge found Spain-TIR liable as bailees was,
that having voluntarily accepted possession of the goods for onward carriage to
Paisley, and entrusted to BCT part of the responsibilities that they had assumed,
they were liable for the loss of the goods caused by the default of BCT.

[52] We have difficulty with the judge's analysis, having regard to his finding
that Seagram authorised Spain-TIR to sub-contract to BCT. The basis of this
finding was that Seagram consented to a chain of sub-contracts that was a typical
feature of CMR carriage. Why in these circumstances should a greater liability
be imposed upon Spain-TIR than that incidental to being a link in the chain of
successive carriers under a single CMR contract? Why should Spain-TIR not be
entitled to rely on art 36?

[53] This question requires consideration of the manner in which a
sub-bailment on terms operates. The doctrine was first clearly stated by Lord
Denning MR in *Morris v CW Martin & Sons Ltd* [1965] 2 All ER 725, [1966] 1 QB
716. That case involved the sub-bailment to the defendants, with the consent of
the owner, the plaintiff, of a fur stole that had been delivered to the bailee for
cleaning. The fur stole was converted by a servant of the sub-bailee. The
contract between the bailee and the sub-bailee contained exempting conditions.
The Court of Appeal held that the defendants, as sub-bailees for reward, owed
the plaintiff the same duty to take reasonable care of the fur that was owed by the
bailee. They were liable for the default of their servant. The exempting
conditions did not, on their true construction, exempt from liability for the loss.
In these circumstances it was unnecessary to decide whether they applied as
between the plaintiff and the defendants. Lord Denning MR expressed the view
that in such circumstances the owner was bound by the conditions as if he had

a expressly or impliedly consented to the bailee making a sub-bailment containing those conditions, but not otherwise.

[54] This doctrine was approved and applied by Steyn J in *Singer Co (UK) Ltd v Tees and Hartlepool Port Authority* [1988] 2 Lloyd's Rep 164. It also received approval by members of the Court of Appeal in *Hispanica de Petroleos SA v Vencedora Oceanica Navegacion SA, The Kapetan Marcos NL (No 2)* [1987] 2 Lloyd's

b Rep 321 and *CIA Portorafti Commerciale SA v Ultramar Panama Inc, The Captain Gregos (No 2)* [1990] 2 Lloyd's Rep 395.

[55] In *Johnson Matthey & Co Ltd v Constantine Terminals Ltd* [1976] 2 Lloyd's Rep 215, Donaldson J adopted a different approach to the entitlement of a sub-bailee to rely, as against the bailor, upon the terms upon which the bailee had sub-bailed the goods to him. The sub-bailees in that case sought to rely upon

c their standard conditions to provide a defence in respect of their loss of a consignment of silver belonging to the plaintiffs. Donaldson J first observed that it was probably possible to hold, following the approach of Lord Denning MR in *Morris'* case, that there had been a bailment on terms with the consent of the plaintiffs. He went on to hold, however, that such consent was unnecessary. He

d explained (at 222) the basis of this:

> 'But the plaintiffs cannot prove the bailment upon which, in my judgment, they must rely, without referring to terms upon which the silver was received by [the first defendants] from [the second defendant]. These terms establish (a) that [the first defendants] were bailees for reward but also
>
e > (b) that the implied duties of such a bailee were qualified by exceptions. And, despite Mr. Wadsworth's vigorous argument to the contrary, I really do not see how the plaintiffs can rely upon one part of the contract while ignoring the other. Consent seems to me to be relevant only between the bailor and head bailee. If the sub-bailment is on terms to which the bailor consented, he has no cause of action against the head bailee. If it was not, the sub-bailee
f > is still protected, but if the bailor is damnified by the terms of the sub-bailment he has a cause of action against the head bailee.'

[56] *Morris'* case and the *Johnson Matthey* case received detailed analysis in the decision of the Privy Council, delivered by Lord Goff of Chieveley in *The Pioneer Container, KH Enterprise (cargo owners) v Pioneer Container (owners)* [1994] 2 All ER

g 250, [1994] 2 AC 324. In that case the plaintiffs engaged carriers to ship goods by sea under bills of lading which gave the carriers authority to sub-contract 'on any terms'. The carriers sub-contracted to the defendant ship owners on terms which included a Taiwanese exclusive jurisdiction clause. The issue was whether this clause was binding as between the plaintiffs and the defendants.

h [57] Lord Goff first considered the relationship between the plaintiffs and the sub-bailee. On this he found authoritative guidance in the decision of the Privy Council in *Gilchrist Watt & Sanderson Pty Ltd v York Products Ltd* [1970] 3 All ER 825, [1970] 1 WLR 1262. There, the defendants were stevedores who had lost two cases of clocks that they had received as sub-bailees of the shipowners, who

j owed a duty to deliver them to the plaintiffs under the bills of lading. The Privy Council held that the defendants were liable to the plaintiffs, in that, as Lord Pearson observed ([1970] 3 All ER 825 at 829, [1970] 1 WLR 1262 at 1267), they—

> 'took on themselves an obligation to the plaintiffs to exercise due care for the safety of the goods, although there was no contractual relation or attornment between the defendants and the plaintiffs.'

[58] Following this decision, Lord Goff held that there was a 'collateral bailment' between the plaintiffs and the defendant shipowners. He then turned to consider the terms of this bailment. He approved the doctrine formulated by Lord Denning MR in *Morris'* case, adding this comment on the relevance of 'consent':

> 'It must be assumed that, on the facts of the case, no direct contractual relationship has been created between the owner and the sub-bailee, the only contract created by the sub-bailment being that between the bailee and the sub-bailee. Even so, if the effect of the sub-bailment is that the sub-bailee voluntarily receives into his custody the goods of the owner and so assumes towards the owner the responsibility of a bailee, then to the extent that the terms of the sub-bailment are consented to by the owner, it can properly be said that the owner has authorised the bailee so to regulate the duties of the sub-bailee in respect of the goods entrusted to him, not only towards the bailee but also towards the owner.' (See *The Pioneer Container* [1994] 2 All ER 250 at 259, [1994] 2 AC 324 at 339.)

[59] Lord Goff went on to state ([1994] 2 All ER 250 at 259–260, [1994] 2 AC 324 at 339–340) that this doctrine did not turn on estoppel, nor on contract:

> 'Such a conclusion, finding its origin in the law of bailment rather than the law of contract, does not depend for its efficacy either on the doctrine of privity of contract, or on the doctrine of consideration. That this may be so appears from the decision of the House of Lords in *Elder, Dempster & Co Ltd v Paterson, Zochonis & Co, Griffiths Lewis Steam Navigation Co v Paterson, Zochonis & Co Ltd* [1924] AC 522, [1924] All ER Rep 135. In that case, shippers of cargo on a chartered ship brought an action against the shipowners for damage caused to the cargo by bad stowage, for which the shipowners were responsible. It is crucial to observe that the cargo was shipped under charterers' bills of lading, so that the contract of carriage contained in or evidenced by the bills of lading was between the shippers and the charterers. The shipowners nevertheless sought to rely, as against the shippers, upon an exception in the bill of lading which protected the charterers from liability for damage due to bad stowage. It was held that the shipowners were entitled to do so, the preferred reason upon which the House so held (see *Scruttons Ltd v Midland Silicones Ltd* [1962] 1 All ER 1 at 8, [1962] AC 446 at 470 per Viscount Simonds, following the opinion of Fullagar J in *Wilson v Darling Island Stevedoring and Lighterage Co Ltd* (1955) 95 CLR 43 at 78) being found in the speech of Lord Summer where he said ([1924] AC 522 at 564, [1924] All ER Rep 135 at 155): "... in the circumstances of this case the obligations to be inferred from the reception of the cargo for carriage to the United Kingdom amount to a bailment upon terms, which include the exceptions and limitations of liability stipulated in the known and contemplated form of bill of lading." Of course, there was in that case a bailment by the shippers direct to the shipowners, so that it was not necessary to have recourse to the concept of sub-bailment. Even so, notwithstanding the absence of any contract between the shippers and the shipowners, the shipowners' obligations as bailees were effectively subject to the terms upon which the shipowners implicitly received the goods into their possession. Their Lordships do not imagine that a different conclusion would have been reached in the *Elder, Dempster* case if the shippers had delivered the goods,

a not directly to the ship, but into the possession of agents of the charterers
who had, in their turn, loaded the goods on board; because in such
circumstances, by parity of reasoning, the shippers may be held to have
impliedly consented that the sub-bailment to the shipowners should be on
terms which included the exemption from liability for bad stowage.'

b [60] Lord Goff then turned to the decision in the *Johnson Matthey* case. He held
that the analysis of Donaldson J was unsound, being contrary to *Morris'* case and the
Gilchrist Watt case. The exposition of the law that followed merits citation in full:

'In addition, the conclusion of Donaldson J that consent is relevant *only*
between the owner and the bailee is inconsistent with the reasoning of Lord
Denning MR in [*Morris'* case] when he expressed the opinion that the bailor
c is bound by the terms of the sub-bailment to which he has consented but not
otherwise. Their Lordships have already expressed their agreement with the
approach of Lord Denning MR on this point. Indeed, as they see it, once it
is recognised that the sub-bailee, by voluntarily taking the owner's goods
into his custody, ipso facto becomes the bailee of those goods vis-à-vis the
d owner, it must follow that the owner's rights against the sub-bailee will only
be subject to terms of the sub-bailment if he has consented to them, ie if he
has authorised the bailee to entrust the goods to the sub-bailee on those
terms. Such consent may, as Lord Denning MR pointed out, be express or
implied; and in this context the sub-bailee may also be able to invoke, where
e appropriate, the principle of ostensible authority. In truth, at the root of this
question lies a doctrinal dispute of a fundamental nature, which is
epitomised in the question—is it a prerequisite of a bailment that the bailor
should have consented to the bailee's possession of the goods?   An
affirmative answer to this question (which is the answer given by Bell *Modern
Law of Personal Property in England and Ireland* (1989) pp 88–89) leads to the
f conclusion that, if the owner seeks to hold a sub-bailee responsible to him as
bailee, he has to accept all the terms of the sub-bailment, warts and all; for
either he will have consented to the sub-bailment on those terms or, if not,
he will (by holding the sub-bailee liable to him as bailee) be held to have
ratified all the terms of the sub-bailment. A negative answer to the question
is however supported by other writers, notably by [*Palmer on Bailment*
g (2nd edn, 1991) p 31 and following], where Professor Palmer cites a number
of examples of bailment without the consent of the owner, and by Professor
Tay in her article "The essence of bailment" (1966) 5 Syd LR 239. On this
approach, a person who voluntarily takes another person's goods into his
custody holds them as bailee of that person (the owner); and he can only
h invoke, for example, terms of a sub-bailment under which he received the
goods from an intermediate bailee as qualifying or otherwise affecting his
responsibility to the owner if the owner consented to them. It is the latter
approach which, as their Lordships have explained, has been adopted by
English law and, with English law, the law of Hong Kong. Their Lordships
j wish to add that this conclusion, which flows from the decisions in [*Morris'*
case] and the *Gilchrist Watt* case, produces a result which in their opinion is
both principled and just. They incline to the opinion that a sub-bailee can
only be said for these purposes to have voluntarily taken into his possession
the goods of another if he has sufficient notice that a person other than the
bailee is interested in the goods so that it can properly be said that (in
addition to his duties to the bailee) he has, by taking the goods into his

custody, assumed towards that other person the responsibility for the goods
which is characteristic of a bailee. This they believe to be the underlying
principle. Moreover, their Lordships do not consider this principle to impose
obligations on the sub-bailee which are onerous or unfair, once it is
recognised that he can invoke against the owner terms of the sub-bailment
which the owner has actually (expressly or impliedly) or even ostensibly
authorised. In the last resort the sub-bailee may, if necessary and appropriate,
be able to invoke against the bailee the principle of warranty of authority.'
(See *The Pioneer Container* [1994] 2 All ER 250 at 261–262, [1994] 2 AC 324 at
341–342.)

[61] Thus far the cases that we have considered have been those in which the
sub-bailee has sought to rely upon conditions which reduced his liability or, in
The Pioneer Container, were beneficial to him. What if some of the terms agreed
between the bailee and the sub-bailee increase the liability of the sub-bailee
beyond that arising under the common law? Can the bailor enforce such
conditions against the sub-bailee? Professor Palmer in his work, *Bailment*
(2nd edn, 1991) p 1329 addresses this question:

'Occasionally, the terms of the sub-bailment will cast upon the sub-bailee
a greater responsibility for the safety of the goods than would exist at
common law. These terms are clearly enforceable by the intermediate party
since he will enjoy a contractual relationship with the sub-bailee. Even if the
sub-bailment is gratuitous the sub-bailee will apparently be bound by his
promise to the intermediary, because a gratuitous bailee seems capable of
enlarging his duty at common law. The more immediate question is
whether such additional duties are directly enforceable by the owner against
the sub-bailee. In certain circumstances such enforcement should be
possible. If the terms of a sub-bailment can be invoked to reduce the
common law duties that are owed by the sub-bailee to the owner, they
should be relevant to establish a responsibility that is greater. The criterion
would be whether such additional duties were an integral part of the
owner-sub-bailee relationship, and essential to its efficacy, or were merely
incidental. The sub-bailee should therefore be liable to the owner for the
non-performance of any duty which represents one of the central terms or
understandings upon which he was allowed to assume possession.'

This is one possible solution to the problem, but not the only one.

[62] We draw attention to the observations of Lord Goff in the passage cited
above that, were it correct that consent of the bailor was a prerequisite of a
bailment, any resulting bailment would be subject to 'all the terms of the
sub-bailment, warts and all'. It seems to us that it must follow from this,
and indeed that it should logically be the case, that where a bailor consents to and
thereby authorises a sub-bailment on terms, all the terms agreed between the
bailee and the sub-bailee, in so far as these are applicable to the relationship of
the bailor and the sub-bailee, apply as between the bailor and the sub-bailee.

[63] It seems to us that this result also follows from the application of the
principles of the law of contract. Lord Goff's authoritative analysis in *The Pioneer
Container* traces the origin of 'bailment on terms' to principles of the law of
bailment that do not turn on contract, but this does not exclude the possibility
that the law of contract may have a role to play in this area. The principles of the
law of bailment have always overlapped with those of the law of contract, for

a   bailment and contract often go hand in hand. Where a bailee has the consent, and thus the authority, of the bailor to enter into a sub-bailment on particular terms and does so, and where those terms purport to govern the relationship not merely between the sub-bailee and the bailee, but between the sub-bailee and the bailor, it seems to us that all the elements of a collateral contract binding the sub-bailee and the bailor will be present, for there will be privity, via the

b   agency of the bailee, and no difficulty in identifying consideration, at least if the terms are capable of resulting in benefit to each of the parties. It is easier to identify a contract in such circumstances than in the circumstances which led the Privy Council to identify one in *New Zealand Shipping Co Ltd v AM Satterthwaite & Co Ltd, The Eurymedon* [1974] 1 All ER 1015, [1975] AC 154.

c   [64] These considerations are very relevant in the present case. The judge has found that Seagram implicitly authorised the conclusion of a chain of contracts on CMR terms. The CMR conditions, which applied as between Seagram and TTI required that, if there was such a contractual chain, all links in it should be welded to a single contract by transfer of the goods and the consignment note. TTI produced no consignment note but, as each link in the chain was formed, there was

d   agreement between the immediate parties that the contract should be on CMR terms. It seems to us that in these circumstances the sub-bailment of each party in the chain was on terms of all the CMR conditions, whether by application of the doctrine of bailment on terms or under principles of the law of contract.

[65] Thus we consider that the judge was correct to rule that Spain-TIR and

e   BCT could not rely upon those of the CMR conditions which limited or fixed their liability without being bound by other relevant CMR conditions. On our analysis, however, no right to elect was open to them. The CMR conditions were applicable as a consequence of the seals being bailed to them on the terms of those conditions.

f   [66] On this basis, we find that Mr Coburn was correct to submit that art 36 applied. It was not open to Seagram to sue Spain-TIR in that Spain-TIR was not the first carrier, the last carrier or the carrier performing that portion of the carriage during which the loss occurred. They came into possession of the goods in circumstances where they were authorised to sub-bail them on CMR terms. Seagram cannot, in these circumstances, contend that Spain-TIR remains

g   susceptible to suit in relation to loss of the seals after they had been transferred to a successive carrier.

WAS THE JUDGE CORRECT TO HOLD THAT BCT WERE LIABLE TO SEAGRAM AS BAILEES OF THE SEALS?

h   [67] BCT did not challenge the finding that they were liable for the carriage costs of the cartons containing the seals. By their respondents' notice they contended, however, that, if liability for the guarantee payment was imposed by virtue of art 23(4), they were not liable for this because they were not bailees of the seals themselves. This argument was based upon the proposition that a

j   person who comes into possession of goods will not be constituted bailee of them if, unknown to him, they have properties which give them an unforeseeably elevated value—see the discussion in *Palmer* p 436 and following. As we have held that BCT is under no liability in respect of the guarantee payment, either under the terms of the CMR or at common law, this issue does not arise. We would add that the terms of art 23 do not seem to us to give any scope for the application of the doctrine in question.

WAS THE JUDGE CORRECT TO INDICATE THAT SPAIN-TIR AND BCT COULD ELECT
WHETHER TO RELY ON ART 23, BUT THAT IF THEY DID SO THEY WOULD BE BOUND BY
ALL ITS PROVISIONS?

[68] We have already answered this question in [65], above. The judge
approached the question on the premise that Spain-TIR and BCT fell into the
category of persons for whom art 28(2) makes provision. On our analysis, any
liability falling on Spain-TIR or BCT was not 'extra-contractual' within the
meaning of that term in art 28(2), but arose because they were subject, whether
by contract or the law of bailment, to those provisions of the CMR which both
impose and restrict liability.

[69] For the reasons that we have given, Seagram's appeal will be dismissed
and Spain-TIR's cross-appeal will be allowed.

Appeal dismissed. Cross-appeal allowed.

Kate O'Hanlon   Barrister.

ANNEX

CONVENTION ON THE CONTRACT FOR THE INTERNATIONAL CARRIAGE OF
GOODS BY ROAD

'CHAPTER I
SCOPE OF APPLICATION
Article 1

1. This Convention shall apply to every contract for the carriage of goods
by road in vehicles for reward, when the place of taking over of the goods and
the place designated for delivery, as specified in the contract, are situated in
two different countries, of which at least one is a Contracting country,
irrespective of the place of residence and the nationality of the parties ...

CHAPTER II
PERSONS FOR WHOM THE CARRIER IS RESPONSIBLE
Article 3

For the purposes of this Convention the carrier shall be responsible for the
acts and omissions of his agents and servants and of any other persons of whose
services he makes use for the performance of the carriage, when such agents,
servants or other persons are acting within the scope of their employment, as
if such acts or omissions were his own.

CHAPTER III
CONCLUSION AND PERFORMANCE OF THE CONTRACT OF CARRIAGE
Article 4

The contract of carriage shall be confirmed by the making out of a
consignment note. The absence, irregularity or loss of the consignment note
shall not affect the existence or the validity of the contract of carriage which
shall remain subject to the provisions of this Convention.

Article 5

1. The consignment note shall be made out in three original copies signed
by the sender and by the carrier. These signatures may be printed or
replaced by the stamps of the sender and the carrier if the law of the country in
which the consignment note has been made out so permits. The first copy

a

shall be handed to the sender, the second shall accompany the goods and the third shall be retained by the carrier ...

Article 6

1. The consignment note shall contain the following particulars:

b

(a) the date of the consignment note and the place at which it is made out;

(b) the name and address of the sender;

(c) the name and address of the carrier;

(d) the place and the date of taking over of the goods and the place designated for delivery;

(e) the name and address of the consignee;

c

(f) the description in common use of the nature of the goods and the method of packing, and, in the case of dangerous goods, their generally recognised description;

(g) the number of packages and their special marks and numbers;

(h) the gross weight of the goods or their quantity otherwise expressed;

d

(i) charges relating to the carriage (carriage charges, supplementary charges, customs duties and other charges incurred from the making of the contract to the time of delivery);

(j) the requisite instructions for Customs and other formalities;

(k) a statement that the carriage is subject, notwithstanding any clause to the contrary, to the provisions of this Convention ...

e

CHAPTER IV
LIABILITY OF THE CARRIER
Article 17

1. The carrier shall be liable for the total or partial loss of the goods and for damage thereto occurring between the time when he takes over the goods and

f

the time of delivery, as well as for any delay in delivery ...

Article 23

1. When, under the provisions of this Convention, a carrier is liable for compensation in respect of total or partial loss of goods, such compensation shall be calculated by reference to the value of the goods at the place and time

g

at which they were accepted for carriage.

2. The value of the goods shall be fixed according to the commodity exchange price or, if there is no such price, according to the current market price or, if there is no commodity exchange price or current market price, by reference to the normal value of goods of the same kind and quality.

h

3. Compensation shall not, however, exceed 8.33 units of account [SDRs] per kilogram of gross weight short.

4. In addition, the carriage charges, Customs duties and other charges incurred in respect of the carriage of the goods shall be refunded in full in case of total loss and in proportion to the loss sustained in case of partial loss, but no

j

further damage shall be payable ...

6. Higher compensation may only be claimed where the value of the goods or a special interest in delivery has been declared in accordance with articles 24 and 26.

7. The unit of account mentioned in this Convention is the Special Drawing Right as defined by the International Monetary Fund. The amount mentioned in paragraph 3 of this article shall be converted into the national currency of the

State of the Court seised of the case on the basis of the value of that currency
on the date of the judgment or the date agreed upon by the Parties] ...

Article 26

1. The sender may, against payment of a surcharge to be agreed upon, fix
the amount of a special interest in delivery in the case of loss or damage or of
the agreed time-limit being exceeded, by entering such amount in the
consignment note.

2. If a declaration of a special interest in delivery has been made,
compensation for the additional loss or damage proved may be claimed, up to
the total amount of the interest declared, independently of the compensation
provided for in articles 23, 24 and 25 ...

Article 28

1. In cases where, under the law applicable, loss, damage or delay arising out
of carriage under this Convention gives rise to an extra-contractual claim, the
carrier may avail himself of the provisions of this Convention which exclude
his liability or which fix or limit the compensation due.

2. In cases where the extra-contractual liability for loss, damage or delay of
one of the persons for whom the carrier is responsible under the terms of
article 3 is in issue, such person may also avail himself of the provisions of this
Convention which exclude the liability of the carrier or which fix or limit the
compensation due ...

CHAPTER VI
PROVISIONS RELATING TO CARRIAGE PERFORMED BY SUCCESSIVE CARRIERS
Article 34

If carriage governed by a single contract is performed by successive road
carriers, each of them shall be responsible for the performance of the whole
operation, the second carrier and each succeeding carrier becoming a party to
the contract of carriage, under the terms of the consignment note, by reason
of his acceptance of the goods and the consignment note.

Article 35

1. A carrier accepting the goods from a previous carrier shall give the latter a
dated and signed receipt. He shall enter his name and address on the second
copy of the consignment note. Where applicable, he shall enter on the
second copy of the consignment note and on the receipt reservations of the kind
provided for in article 8, paragraph 2 ...

Article 36

Except in the case of a counter-claim or a set-off raised in an action
concerning a claim based on the same contract of carriage, legal proceedings in
respect of liability for loss, damage or delay may only be brought against the
first carrier, the last carrier or the carrier who was performing that portion of
the carriage during which the event causing the loss, damage or delay
occurred; an action may be brought at the same time against several of these
carriers ...

Article 38

If one of the carriers is insolvent, the share of the compensation due from
him and unpaid by him shall be divided among the other carriers in proportion
to the share of the payment for the carriage due to them.'

a # Cranfield and another v Bridgegrove Ltd and other appeals
[2003] EWCA Civ 656

b COURT OF APPEAL, CIVIL DIVISION
WARD, WALLER AND DYSON LJJ
13, 14 MARCH, 14 MAY 2003

c *Claim form – Service – Extension of time for service – Rule of procedure empowering court to grant post-expiry application for extension of time for serving claim form where court 'unable to serve' form within prescribed period – Whether court having jurisdiction to grant extension in cases where it had failed to serve due to neglect – CPR 7.6(3)(a).*

d *Claim form – Service – Dispensing with service – Guidance on exercise of discretion – CPR 6.9.*

Claim form – Service – Service on company – Statutory provision permitting company to be served at its registered office – Rule of procedure requiring document to be served on solicitor if authorised to accept service and notifying serving party that he was so authorised – Inter-relationship between statutory provision and rule of procedure – Companies Act 1985, s 725(1) – CPR 6.2, 6.4.

e

Claim form – Service – Service on individual at usual or last known residence – Rule of procedure requiring document to be served at individual's usual or last known residence if no solicitor acting for that person and no address given for service – Whether service
f *under that rule could be bad notwithstanding that conditions precedent satisfied – CPR 6.5(6).*

In the first of five appeals to the Court of Appeal raising issues on the service of claim forms, the claimants sent two such forms to the county court with a request that they be issued and served on the defendant. The court duly issued the claim
g forms, but forgot to serve them within the four-month period prescribed by the CPR. The claimants subsequently applied for an order extending the time for service, relying on CPR 7.6(3)(a)[a] which empowered the court to grant such an extension if, inter alia, it had been 'unable to serve' the claim form. The district judge dismissed the application, but his decision was reversed on appeal by the
h circuit judge. The defendant appealed, contending that r 7.6(3)(a) applied only where the court had attempted to serve the claim form or had at least applied its mind to the question whether or not to serve. That contention was adopted by the defendant in the second appeal. In that case, the claimant's solicitors had taken the draft claim form to the county court for issue. The court official took
j the view that the court should serve the claim form, but informed the claimant's solicitors that it would be necessary to obtain a letter from the defendant's solicitors confirming that they would accept service. Although the claimant's solicitors received such a letter a few weeks later, they did not forward it to the court for a further three months. By that time, only four days remained before

---

a   Rule 7.6 is set out at [1], below

the expiry of the prescribed period for service, but the claimant's solicitors failed
to impress upon the court the urgency of the situation. The court failed to serve *a*
the claim form within the prescribed period, but the district judge subsequently
granted orders extending the time for service. Those orders were set aside by
another district judge, and that decision was upheld by the circuit judge. The
claimant appealed.

In the third appeal, the claimant's solicitors should have served the claim form *b*
on the defendant personally since no solicitor had been authorised to accept
service. Instead, they sent a draft claim form to the defendant's insurers a few
days before the last day for service. The defendant subsequently applied to strike
out the proceedings on the ground that they had never been properly served.
The district judge granted the application, but his decision was reversed by the
circuit judge who dispensed with service in the exercise of his discretion under *c*
CPR 6.9[b]. On the defendant's appeal, the Court of Appeal was required to
determine whether the case fell within the scope of that discretion.

In the fourth appeal, the claimant was injured while working for the defendant
company. He instructed solicitors who asked the company's insurers to confirm
details of the solicitors nominated to accept service. Those solicitors *d*
subsequently wrote to the claimant's solicitors, confirming that they had
instructions to accept service. In such circumstances, CPR 6.4(2)[c], which formed
part of the rule dealing with personal service, required the document to be served
on the solicitor. However, r 6.2(1)[d] provided that the rules in CPR Pt 6 were to
apply except where, inter alia, any other enactment made a different provision, *e*
while r 6.2(2) provided that a company could be served by any method permitted
under Pt 6 as an alternative to the method of service set out in s 725(1)[e]of the
Companies Act 1985. Under that provision, a document could be served on a
company by, inter alia, sending it by post to the company's registered office.
Shortly before the expiry of the time prescribed for service, the claimant's
solicitors purported to serve the claim form by sending it by first class post to the *f*
company's registered office. The district judge subsequently set aside service,
holding that the claim form had not been served on the company's solicitors
before the expiry of the prescribed period and that service on the company itself
was not sufficient. The claimant's appeal was allowed by the circuit judge who
dispensed with service under r 6.9. On the company's appeal, the issue arose as *g*
to whether there had, in fact, been valid service under s 725(1) of the 1985 Act. In
resolving that issue, the Court of Appeal considered the inter-relationship
between s 725(1) and the CPR, and whether, as the company contended, the
claimant had elected to proceed by way of service on the company's solicitors
under the CPR.

In the fifth appeal, the claimant was injured in a road traffic accident. Since the *h*
insurance position of the other driver, H, was uncertain, the claimant's solicitors
intimated a claim to the Motor Insurers' Bureau (MIB). The latter were informed
by inquiry agents that H had recently left the address shown on the electoral
register (the address) and that his whereabouts were unknown. MIB
subsequently informed the claimant's solicitors that H had left the address. *j*
Nineteen months later, the claim form was issued. A few days before the expiry

b   Rule 6.9 is set out at [1], below
c   Rule 6.4 is set out at [78], below
d   Rule 6.2, so far as material, is set out at [77], below
e   Section 725(1) is set out at [75], below

a of the four-month period for service, the claim form was sent by first class post to H at the address, purportedly in accordance with CPR 6.5(6)[f]. Under that rule, a document had to be transmitted to, or left, at the usual or last known residence of the party to be served if no solicitor was acting for that party and he had not given an address for service. There was no doubt that the address was H's last known address. Nevertheless, MIB, which had been joined as second defendant,

b contended on a subsequent application that the claim form had not been served on H within the prescribed period. That contention was accepted by the district judge who held that it could not be doing justice between the parties to serve at the last known address, without making further inquiry, over two years after H had vacated it. The claimant appealed.

c **Held** – (1) On its true construction, CPR 7.6(3)(a) was not confined to cases where the court had attempted to serve the claim form or had applied its mind to the question whether or not to serve. The words 'unable to serve' in that provision included all cases where the court had failed to serve the claim form, and accordingly the court had jurisdiction to extend time for service where it had

d failed to serve in time through mere neglect. In most cases where the real cause of the failure to serve in time was court neglect, it would be appropriate to grant an extension of time if the claimant had acted promptly in making the application for an extension. There would, however, be some cases where, although court neglect had contributed to the failure to serve in time, the real cause had been the conduct of the claimant or the claimant's legal representative. In such cases, the

e court would often decide not to exercise its discretion to extend the time for service, but each case would turn on its own facts. In the first appeal, the court's neglect had been the real cause of the failure to serve in time, and accordingly the defendant's appeal would be dismissed. In the second appeal, however, failures by the claimant's solicitors had been the real reason why the claim form had not

f been served within the prescribed period. It followed that it would not be appropriate to extend time for service under r 7.6(3)(a), and the claimant's appeal would be dismissed (see [21], [29], [30], [37], [38], [48], [51], below).

(2) The discretion to dispense with service of the claim form under CPR 6.9 could be exercised only in exceptional circumstances, and should not be exercised in circumstances such as those in the third appeal. Unlike the document issued

g by the court, the draft claim form was not stamped with the court seal, and it did not contain a statement of truth. Nor had the draft claim form been sent to the defendant or to a solicitor authorised to accept service on his behalf. It had been sent to the defendant's insurers who had no such authority. There had been significant departures from the rules as to the permitted methods of service.

h They were not mere technicalities. Accordingly, the third appeal would be allowed (see [56], [60], [61], below); *Anderton v Clwyd CC* [2002] 3 All ER 813 applied.

(3) A claimant could serve a claim form on a defendant company either by one of the methods permitted by s 725(1) of the 1985 Act or by serving it in

j accordance with one of the methods permitted by the CPR. They were true alternatives. That was made clear by CPR 6.2(2). If a defendant had not given an address for service, a claimant could choose whether to follow the s 725(1) or the CPR route for service. Moreover, although it was possible for the parties to make a binding contract whereby the claimant agreed to serve the claim form by one

---

f   Rule 6.5, so far as material, is set out at [95], below

route rather than the other, there had been no such agreement in the fourth
appeal. Rather, the parties had agreed that, if the claimant decided to effect a
personal service under CPR 6.4, he would serve on the company's solicitors
rather than on the company. It followed that the service on the company's
registered office by first class post had been good service. Accordingly, the fourth
appeal would be dismissed (see [83]–[86], [89], below); *Nanglegan v Royal Free
Hampstead NHS Trust* [2001] 3 All ER 793 distinguished. b

(4) If the two conditions precedent for the operation of CPR 6.5(6) were
satisfied, the document had to be sent, in the case of an individual, to his usual or
last known residence. The rule was plain and unqualified. There was no basis for
holding that, if the two conditions were satisfied, and the document was sent to
that address, that would not amount to good service. Accordingly, the fifth c
appeal would be allowed (see [102], [104], below).

Notes

For service on a company, see 7(2) *Halsbury's Laws* (4th edn) (1996 reissue)
para 1146, and for extension of time for serving the claim form, rules about
service generally, personal service and dispensing with service, see 37 *Halsbury's* d
Laws (4th edn reissue) paras 306, 316, 319, 325.

For the Companies Act 1985, s 725, see 8 *Halsbury's Statutes* (4th edn) (1999
reissue) 588.

Cases referred to in judgment e

Allison (Kenneth) Ltd (in liq) v AE Limehouse & Co (a firm) [1991] 4 All ER 500, [1992]
2 AC 105, [1991] 3 WLR 671, HL.

Anderton v Clwyd CC [2002] EWCA Civ 933, [2002] 3 All ER 813, [2002] 1 WLR
3174.

Elmes v Hygrade Food Products plc [2001] EWCA Civ 121, [2001] All ER (D) 158 f
(Jan).

Godwin v Swindon BC [2001] EWCA Civ 1478, [2001] 4 All ER 641, [2002] 1 WLR
997.

Ladd v Marshall [1954] 3 All ER 745, [1954] 1 WLR 1489, CA.

Montgomery Jones & Co v Liebenthal & Co [1898] 1 QB 487, CA. g

Nanglegan v Royal Free Hampstead NHS Trust [2001] EWCA Civ 127, [2001] 3 All ER
793, [2002] 1 WLR 1043.

Vinos v Marks & Spencer plc [2001] 3 All ER 784, CA.

Wilkey v BBC [2002] EWCA Civ 1561, [2002] 4 All ER 1177, [2003] 1 WLR 1. h

Appeals

Cranfield and anor v Bridgegrove Ltd

The defendant, Bridgegrove Ltd, appealed from the decision of Judge Hull QC in j
Guildford County Court on 25 January 2002 allowing an appeal by the claimants,
Michael David Cranfield and Barbara Priscilla Cranfield, from the decision of
District Judge Darbyshire on 24 September 2001 dismissing the claimants'
application for an extension of time for serving the claim forms in their
proceedings against the defendant. The facts are set out in the judgment of the
court.

a

Claussen v Yeates

The claimant, Peter Claussen, appealed from the decision of Judge Butter QC in Central London County Court on 9 May 2001 dismissing his appeal from the order of District Judge Haselgrove on 21 September 2000 setting aside the orders of District Judge Langley on 18 April and 29 June 2000 extending the time for service of the claim form in the claimant's proceedings against the defendant,
b   Stephen Michael Yeates. The facts are set out in the judgment of the court.

McManus v Sharif

The defendant, Mrs R Sharif, appealed from the decision of Judge Hornby in Bow County Court on 28 October 2002 allowing an appeal by the claimant, Chrystalla
c   McManus, from the order of District Judge Gregory on 9 July 2002 striking out the claimant's proceedings against the defendant. The facts are set out in the judgment of the court.

Murphy v Staples UK Ltd

d   The defendant, Staples UK Ltd, appealed from the decision of Judge Armitage QC in Manchester County Court on 13 October 2002 allowing an appeal by the claimant, Lee Murphy, from the order of District Judge Hugman on 7 May 2002 setting aside the purported service of the claim form. The facts are set out in the judgment of the court.

e
Smith v Hughes and anor

The claimant, Aidan Thomas Smith, appealed from the order of District Judge Duerden in Bury County Court on 3 December 2002 dismissing his proceedings against the defendants, David Hughes and the Motor Insurers Bureau (MIB). David Hughes took no part in the proceedings. The facts are set out in the
f   judgment of the court.

Jonathan Gaunt QC (instructed by *DFM Beckman*) for the appellant defendant in the first appeal.
Charles Phipps (instructed by *Clyde & Co,* Guildford) for the respondent claimants
g   in the first appeal.
Jalil Asif (instructed by *Traymans*) for the appellant claimant in the second appeal.
Hugh Hamill (instructed by *Vizards Wyeth,* Dartford) for the respondent defendant in the second appeal.
Stephen Stewart QC and *Steven Snowden* (instructed by *Edward Duthie*) for the
h   appellant defendant in the third appeal.
John Ross QC and *Nicholas Yell* (instructed by *Kenneth Elliott & Rowe,* Romford) for the respondent claimant in the third appeal.
Christopher Purchas QC and *Gerwyn Samuel* (instructed by *Branton Edwards,* Manchester) for the appellant defendant in the fourth appeal.
j   *Nigel Tozzi QC* (instructed by *Horwich Farrelly,* Manchester) for the respondent claimant in the fourth appeal.
Gordon Exall (instructed by *Graham Leigh Pfeffer & Co,* Bury) for the appellant claimant in the fifth appeal.
Peter Gregory (instructed by *Weightman Vizards*) for the MIB.

Cur adv vult

14 May 2003. The following judgment of the court was delivered.

a

DYSON LJ.

INTRODUCTION
[1] The interpretation and application of CPR 6.9 (power of the court to dispense with service) and CPR 7.6 (extension of time for serving a claim form) continue to cause difficulty despite several recent attempts by this court to elucidate the relevant principles. There are before the court five appeals which raise several issues relating to these two rules. It is convenient to set out the relevant provisions at the very outset:

b

'**6.9** ... (1) The court may dispense with service of a document.

c

(2) An application for an order to dispense with service may be made without notice ...

7.6 ... (1) The claimant may apply for an order extending the period within which the claim form may be served.

(2) The general rule is that an application to extend the time for service must be made—(a) within the period for serving the claim form specified by rule 7.5; or (b) where an order has been made under this rule, within the period for service specified by that order.

d

(3) If the claimant applies for an order to extend the time for service of the claim form after the end of the period specified by rule 7.5 or by an order made under this rule, the court may make such an order only if—(a) the court has been unable to serve the claim form; or (b) the claimant has taken all reasonable steps to serve the claim form but has been unable to do so; and, (c) in either case, the claimant has acted promptly in making the application.'

e

[2] CPR 7.5(2) provides that '[t]he general rule is that a claim form must be served within 4 months after the date of issue'.

f

[3] Before we discuss the issues that arise, we need to refer to the recent decisions of this court that bear on the questions that we have to decide.

[4] In *Vinos v Marks & Spencer plc* [2001] 3 All ER 784, it was decided that, after the expiry of the time limit for service of a claim form, the court has no power to extend the time for service if the circumstances fall outside r 7.6(3). May LJ said (at 790 (para 20)):

g

'If you then look up from the wording of the rules and at a broader horizon, one of the main aims of the CPR and their overriding objective is that civil litigation should be undertaken and pursued with proper expedition. Criticism of Mr Vinos' solicitors in this case may be muted and limited to one error capable of being represented as small; but there are statutory limitation periods for bringing proceedings. It is unsatisfactory with a personal injury claim to allow almost three years to elapse and to start proceedings at the very last moment. If you do, it is in my judgment generally in accordance with the overriding objective that you should be required to progress the proceedings speedily and within time limits. Four months is in most cases more than adequate for serving a claim form. There is nothing unjust in a system which says that, if you leave issuing proceedings to the last moment and then do not comply with this particular time requirement and do not satisfy the conditions in r 7.6(3), your claim is lost and a new claim will be statute-barred.'

h

j

a
[**5**] In *Elmes v Hygrade Food Products plc* [2001] EWCA Civ 121, [2001] All ER (D) 158 (Jan), it was held that, where a claim form is served in time but is incorrectly served (in that case on the defendants' insurers instead of on the defendants themselves), there is no power in the court under CPR 3.10(b) (remedy of errors of procedure) or CPR 6.8 (service by an alternative method) retrospectively to remedy the error by deeming good service to have been effected by an alternative

b
method not permitted by the rules. A similar conclusion was reached in *Nanglegan v Royal Free Hampstead NHS Trust* [2001] EWCA Civ 127, [2001] 3 All ER 793, [2002] 1 WLR 1043, where service had been incorrectly effected on the defendant rather than its solicitors: the defendant had given its solicitors' address for service (see CPR 6.5(2)).

[**6**] *Godwin v Swindon BC* [2001] EWCA Civ 1478, [2001] 4 All ER 641, [2002]

c
1 WLR 997 was principally concerned with the interpretation of CPR 6.7(1) (rules for deemed service). But the court also said (at [50] per May LJ) that r 6.9 cannot be invoked to dispense with service 'when what would be done is in substance that which r 7.6(3) forbids'.

[**7**] In *Anderton v Clwyd CC* [2002] EWCA Civ 933, [2002] 3 All ER 813, [2002]

d
1 WLR 3174, a different view was expressed as to the scope of r 6.9. The judgment of the court was given by Mummery LJ. He said (at [2]):

> 'Now that the disputed interpretations of the CPR have been resolved by *Godwin*'s case and by this judgment, there will be very few (if any) acceptable excuses for future failures to observe the rules for service of a claim form.

e
> The courts will be entitled to adopt a strict approach, even though the consequences may sometimes appear to be harsh in individual cases.'

[**8**] He summarised the legal position (at [3]) as including the following:

> '... (b) the fact that the claim form has actually been received by, and come

f
> to the attention of, the defendant or his solicitor through the post, by fax or by means other than personal service within the period of four months allowed by r 7.5(2) is legally irrelevant to ascertaining the day of service, as deemed by r 6.7; (c) if an application for an extension of time is issued by the claimant after the end of the period of service, the court will rarely have power under r 7.6(3) to grant an extension of time and only in the most

g
> exceptional circumstances will it be proper to exercise its discretion under r 6.9 to dispense with service ...'

[**9**] The conclusions of the court on the scope of r 6.9 were stated as follows:

> '[55] On this point we conclude that the r 6.9 is sufficiently widely worded

h
> to entitle the court to dispense retrospectively with service of the claim form in an appropriate case (cf the obiter view of Simon Brown LJ in *Elmes v Hygrade Food Products plc* [2001] All ER (D) 158 (Jan)). The vast majority of applications, in which it will be appropriate to make an order to dispense with service, will be for prospective orders sought and granted before the end of the period for service. As a general rule applications made for

j
> retrospective orders to dispense with service will be caught by the reasoning in *Godwin*'s case. There may, however, be exceptional cases in which it is appropriate to dispense with service without undermining the principle in *Godwin*'s case that r 6.9 should not be used to circumvent the restrictions on granting extensions of time for service as laid down in r 7.6(3) and thereby validate late service of the claim form.

[56] In our judgment there is a sensible and relevant distinction, which was not analysed or recognised in *Godwin's* case, between two different kinds of case.

[57] First, an application by a claimant, who has not even attempted to serve a claim form in time by one of the methods permitted by r 6.2, for an order retrospectively dispensing with service under r 6.9. The claimant still needs to serve the claim form in order to comply with the rules and to bring it to the attention of the defendant. That case is clearly caught by *Godwin's* case as an attempt to circumvent the limitations in r 7.6(3) on the grant of extensions of time for service of the claim form.

[58] Second, an application by a claimant, who has in fact already made an ineffective attempt in time to serve a claim form by one of the methods allowed by r 6.2, for an order dispensing with service of the claim form. The ground of the application is that the defendant does not dispute that he or his legal adviser has in fact received, and had his attention drawn to, the claim form by a permitted method of service within the period of four months, or an extension thereof. In the circumstances of the second case the claimant does not need to serve the claim form on the defendant in order to bring it to his attention, but he has failed to comply with the rules for service of the claim form. His case is not that he needs to obtain permission to serve the defendant out of time in accordance with the rules, but rather that he should be excused altogether from the need to prove service of the claim form in accordance with the rules. The basis of his application to dispense with service is that there is no point in requiring him to go through the motions of a second attempt to complete in law what he has already achieved in fact. The defendant accepts that he has received the claim form before the end of the period for service of the claim form. Apart from losing the opportunity to take advantage of the point that service was not in time in accordance with the rules, the defendant will not usually suffer prejudice as a result of the court dispensing with the formality of service of a document, which has already come into his hands before the end of the period for service. The claimant, on the other hand, will be prejudiced by the refusal of an order dispensing with service as, if he is still required to serve the claim form, he will be unable to do so because he cannot obtain an extension of time for service under r 7.6(3).

[59] In the exercise of the dispensing discretion it may also be legitimate to take into account other relevant circumstances, such as the explanation for late service, whether any criticism could be made of the claimant or his advisers in their conduct of the proceedings and any possible prejudice to the defendant on dispensing with service of the claim form.'

[10] The court then turned to consider the five appeals that were before it. Two are of some relevance to the issues which we have to consider. In *Chambers v Southern Domestic Electrical Services Ltd*, the claim form was sent by first class post to the defendant's solicitors on 12 July 2001, and it actually arrived on the next day, which was the last day for service. By virtue of r 6.7(1), service was irrebuttably deemed to have taken place on 14 July, and there were no grounds for extending the time for service under r 7.6(3). Since the claim form had been received by, and had come to the attention of, the defendant's solicitor (who was the correct person on whom to effect service) before the end of the four-month

a period for service, the court regarded the case as 'exceptional', and dispensed with service under r 6.9.

[11] In *Dorgan v Home Office*, the period for service expired on 11 August 2001 (a Saturday). At 4.02 pm on 10 August, the claim form was sent by fax by the claimant's solicitor. The receipt of the fax by the defendant's solicitor (again the person authorised to accept service) was recorded as commencing at 4.03 pm.

b The defendant's solicitor read the fax and made a telephone call about it to the claimant's solicitor soon thereafter. The claim form was deemed to be served on 13 August (a Monday), since r 6.7(1) provides that, if a fax is transmitted before 4 pm on a business day, it is deemed to be served on that day, but in any other case, it is deemed to be served on the business day after the day on which it is transmitted. The application to dispense with service was made promptly after

c the claimant's solicitor was notified that it was not accepted that there had been effective service of the claim form. The court made an order dispensing with service.

[12] The last in the series of cases to which it is necessary to refer is *Wilkey v BBC* [2002] EWCA Civ 1561, [2002] 4 All ER 1177, [2003] 1 WLR 1. The claim form

d was delivered to the defendant's legal department at 2 pm on 28 February 2001, the last day for service. By virtue of r 6.7(1), the claim form was deemed to have been served on 1 March. This court allowed an appeal by the claimant against the decision of the judge refusing to dispense with service under r 6.9. Giving the leading judgment, Simon Brown LJ referred to *Anderton v Clwyd CC* [2002] 3 All ER 813 at [55]–[59]. He conveniently described cases where the claimant has

e sought to serve the claim form by a permitted method of service and the form has in fact been received by the defendant before the end of the period for service as 'category 2 cases', a category, as he put it, 'not previously recognised by the authorities' (see [2002] 4 All ER 1177 at [3]).

[13] Simon Brown LJ proposed a solution to the possible problem identified in

f the July 2002 edition of Civil Procedure News (29 July 2002), which, responding to *Anderton*'s case, had commented (p 11):

> 'It is to be feared a disproportionate amount of time and effort may have to be expended by procedural judges dealing with applications based on this aspect of the *Anderton* case.'

g

[14] He expressed his solution in the following terms:

> '[18] … In category 2 cases which, like the present (and, as I am led to believe, like a number of other appeals now awaiting hearing in this court), involve deemed late service before this court's decision in *Anderton*'s case the

h r 6.9 dispensing power should ordinarily be exercised in the claimant's favour unless the defendant can establish either that he would suffer prejudice (apart, obviously, from the loss of his Limitation Act defence) or some other good reason why the power should not be exercised. Merely to establish that the claimant has been guilty of avoidable delay in either the

j issue, or the service, of the claim form, or both, would not generally constitute such good reason. There will always have been some avoidable delay. Similarly, the fact that the claim looks unpromising would not generally be a good reason for refusing to exercise the dispensing power in a pre-*Anderton* category 2 case. In a post-*Anderton* case, however, the dispensing power should, in my judgment, ordinarily *not* be exercised in the claimant's favour. These cases, albeit within category 2 and therefore in one

sense to be regarded as exceptional, to my mind fall foul of para [2] of the
court's judgment in *Anderton*'s case. In these cases "a strict approach" should
generally be adopted.

[19] This approach, in my judgment, will not only provide a useful guide
as to how the court may be expected to exercise its discretion in these cases,
but it also follows such guidance on the point as the judgment in *Anderton*'s
case affords. It would mean that the court in post-*Anderton* cases, quite
logically, would be the readier to reject the claimant's explanation for late
service and to criticise his conduct of proceedings, both of these being
identified in *Anderton*'s case [2002] 3 All ER 813 at [59] as relevant
considerations.

[20] This approach also provides a complete answer to [counsel for the
defendant's] superficially persuasive argument that to apply *Anderton*'s case
as the appellants submit is appropriate, namely, as if it creates a presumption
in favour of dispensing orders in all category 2 cases, would effectively
destroy the deemed service rule, since virtually every case of service by
physical delivery of the claim form on the last day of the permitted period
would involve actual receipt in time, and thus the exercise of the dispensing
power. If, as I would hold, the presumption arises in only pre-*Anderton* cases,
the deemed service rule, and the highly desirable certainty which it provides,
will continue to apply in all but the most exceptional post-*Anderton* cases.'

THE GENERIC ISSUES

[15] In all the cases that are before us, the time for service of the claim form
expired before 3 July 2002, the date on which judgment was handed down in
Anderton's case. They were all, therefore, what Simon Brown LJ called
'pre-*Anderton* cases'. The following generic issues arise. (a) Where the claim
form is to be served by the court (see CPR 6.3), is the court 'unable to serve' it
within the meaning of r 7.6(3)(a) if, simply through oversight on its part, it fails to
serve it in time? (b) If the words 'unable to serve the claim form' cannot be
construed to embrace the circumstances described in (a), should the court be
willing in principle to dispense with service in such a case? (c) Can a claim form
be served on a defendant limited company at its registered office pursuant to
s 725(1) of the Companies Act 1985 where the defendant has previously notified
the claimant that its solicitors will accept service under r 6.4(2)? (d) Where a
claim form is purportedly served in time, by a method of service permitted by
r 6.2, but on the wrong person (not being in accordance with r 6.4), are there any,
and if so what, circumstances in which the court ought to be willing in principle
to dispense with service?

[16] Issues (a) and (b) arise in *Cranfield and anor v Bridgegrove Ltd* and *Claussen v
Yeates*. Issue (c) arises in *Murphy v Staples UK Ltd*. Issue (d) arises in *McManus
v Sharif*. In *McManus*' case, service was purportedly on the defendant's insurers
within the four-month period: it should have been on the defendant himself. The
position is more complex in *Murphy*'s case, but as will appear, issue (d) also arises
contingently in that appeal. In *Murphy*'s case, service was purportedly effected on
the defendant. There is an issue as to whether it should have been effected on the
defendant's solicitor who had been authorised to accept service on the
defendant's behalf.

[17] The issue that arises in *Smith v Hughes and anor* is the meaning of 'usual or
last known residence', being the place for service of an individual where no

a solicitor is acting for the party to be served, and the party has not given an address for service (see r 6.5(6)).

THE MEANING OF RULE 7.6(3)(A)

[18] Mr Gaunt QC (whose submissions are adopted by Mr Hamill) submits that, when read in their context, the words 'has been unable to serve' do not
b apply to a situation where the court has not even tried to effect service. Rule 7.6(3)(a) is directed to the situation where the court has decided to adopt one of the methods of service permitted by r 6.2, and has encountered an impediment which prevents it from effecting service of the claim form. It is not a necessary condition of being unable to serve that the court should have taken all reasonable steps to serve (contrast the position under r 7.6(3)(b)). It is
c sufficient that the court has been prevented from serving by its chosen permitted method of service. The court must have attempted to serve, or at least applied its mind to the question whether or not to serve. Thus, Mr Gaunt accepts that the following are examples of cases where it can properly be said that the court 'has been unable to serve': (a) it has tried and failed to serve, (b) it has not
d attempted to serve because it wishes to serve by post, but is prevented from doing so because it has not been given the address for service by the claimant, or (c) it is prevented from serving by lack of resources.

[19] As a matter of ordinary language, Mr Gaunt submits, it is not possible to say that someone has been unable to serve a document if he has not even tried to serve it. As he put it, if a process server is instructed to serve a claim form, and
e he fails even to try to serve the document, he cannot honestly say that he has been unable to serve the document.

[20] He submits that the CPR are intended to be read as a coherent code, and seeks support for his submissions in the fact that the word 'unable' appears three times in the rules relating to the service of documents. First, in r 6.11, where the
f court, if 'unable' to serve a document must 'send a notice of non-service stating the method attempted to the party who requested service'. In this context, it is clear that the word 'unable' denotes an unsuccessful attempt to serve. Secondly, in r 7.6(3)(b), which speaks of the claimant having taken all reasonable steps to serve the claim form, but having been 'unable' to do so. This too clearly denotes an unsuccessful attempt to serve. And thirdly, in r 7.6(3)(a), Mr Gaunt submits
g that r 7.6(3)(a) relates back to r 6.11 where the court will have notified the party requesting service that its attempt to serve has been unsuccessful.

[21] We do not accept Mr Gaunt's submissions as to the meaning of r 7.6(3)(a). If they are correct, there is undoubtedly in our view a most regrettable lacuna in the CPR, and one for which there is no rational explanation. There is
h no sensible reason why it should have been intended to exclude from the power to extend time under r 7.6(3)(a) those cases where the court has simply failed to effect service in time. The consequences of a failure to serve the claim form in time can be disastrous for a claimant as several of the cases that are before us amply demonstrate. Service by the court is the general rule (see r 6.3). The
j possibility that the court will from time to time fail to serve through neglect is a real one. Why should it have been intended to give the court the power to extend time when the court has tried to serve and has been prevented from doing so by some impediment, but not where the failure to serve has occurred as a result of mere oversight?

[22] The answer given by Mr Gaunt and Mr Hamill is that the perceived lacuna does not in fact exist. They say that the CPR provide adequate

mechanisms to alert a claimant as to the possibility that the court has failed to
serve the claim form, so that there is no need to adopt a strained interpretation of
r 7.6(3)(a) to cover the situation of non-service by the court through mere
neglect. Thus, r 6.14(1) provides that where a claim form is served by the court,
the court must send the claimant a notice 'which will include the date when the
claim form is deemed to be served under rule 6.7'. If the claimant does not
receive such a notice, he is put on inquiry. Alternatively, if the court has tried but
failed to serve, it is required to send a notice of non-service under r 6.11. In this
way, submit counsel, the CPR provide a system which should be foolproof. If a
claimant does not receive a notice under r 6.11 or a notice under r 6.14(1), then
he or she should be aware that the claim form may not have been served, and
should make inquiry of the court to ascertain the position. In the rare case where
the court mistakenly sends the claimant a notice under r 6.14(1) stating that it has
served the claim form when it has not in fact done so, Mr Gaunt and Mr Hamill
submit that a claimant will in principle be entitled to an extension of time under
r 7.6(3)(b). If, contrary to these submissions, the CPR do not provide a foolproof
system to protect claimants from court error, then they will have an
unanswerable right of action against the Lord Chancellor for damages.

[23] We reject the submission that the CPR provide a claimant with sufficient
protection against the possibility that the court has simply failed to serve the
claim form by neglect, and that this is the reason why r 7.6(3)(a) does not deal
with that situation. It may be that a competent solicitor, conscientiously acting
in the interests of a claimant, is under a duty to communicate with the court if he
or she does not receive a notice under rr 6.11 or 6.14(1) within a reasonable time
of the date of the issue of the claim form. But that is not a sufficient reason for
concluding that, if Mr Gaunt and Mr Hamill are right as to the construction of
r 7.6(3)(a), there is no lacuna in the CPR. First, many claimants are litigants in
person. The CPR must, so far as possible, be construed in a way which achieves
justice for claimants who are unrepresented as well as those who have the benefit
of legal representation. It is unreal to suppose that litigants in person will be alive
to the possible significance of the absence of a notice under rr 6.11 or 6.14(1).
Secondly, we reject the argument that, where a claimant is misled by the court
into believing that the claim form has been served when it has not been served,
he can apply for an extension of time for service under r 7.6(3)(b) on the footing
that he has taken all reasonable steps to serve the claim form, but has been unable
to do so. It seems to us that the obvious and natural construction of r 7.6(3) is that
sub-para (a) is concerned with cases where service is to be by the court, and
sub-para (b) is concerned with cases where service is to be by the claimant. We
do not consider that a claimant can invoke r 7.6(3)(b) in a case where service is to
be by the court. Thirdly, if it were thought that rr 6.11 and 6.14(1) provided
sufficient protection against the consequences of the court's inability to serve, it
is difficult to see why there should be any need for r 7.6(3)(a) at all. It is clear that
it was not thought that rr 6.11 and 6.14(1) do afford sufficient protection. It was
therefore necessary to give the court the power to extend time where the court
has been unable to effect service of the claim form within the four-month period.
And there is no reason to suppose that it was intended that the court should have
this power where the court has failed to serve in some circumstances (ie those
suggested by Mr Gaunt and Mr Hamill) and not in others (failure through mere
neglect).

[24] We conclude, therefore, that, if the submissions of Mr Gaunt and
Mr Hamill are correct, there is a serious lacuna in the CPR for which there is no

a rational justification. It is, of course, possible that the case of failure by the court to serve by neglect was simply overlooked by the draftsman. Unless compelled to do so by clear words, we are unwilling to adopt a construction of the rule which (a) recognises the existence of a lacuna for which there is no rational justification and (b) will inevitably result in injustice to claimants for which there is no justification. Indeed, we would go further. If the argument of Mr Gaunt is
b correct, then the CPR permit the court, by its neglect, to deny claimants access to the court altogether. It would be truly remarkable if the CPR permitted an extension of time where the court has been unable to serve in time where the court has not been at fault, but not where there had been a failure to serve the claim form in time through mere oversight. In view of the special status of the common law right of access to the courts, the court should construe the CPR as
c having that effect only if compelled to do so.

[**25**] Since 2 October 2000, the Human Rights Act 1998 has been in force. The proceedings in *Cranfield and anor v Bridgegrove Ltd* are ones to which the 1998 Act applies. The 1998 Act does not, however, apply to the case of *Claussen v Yeates*. We shall consider the true meaning of r 7.6(3)(a) first without regard to the
d 1998 Act.

[**26**] In our judgment, the words 'has been unable to serve' do not bear the restricted meaning for which Mr Gaunt and Mr Hamill contend. At first sight, there seems to be force in the submission that it is a misuse of language to say that someone has been unable to do something which he has not even attempted to do. But the word 'unable' does not necessarily connote that there has been a
e failed attempt. Indeed, this seems to be conceded by Mr Gaunt, since he accepts that 'unable to serve' includes the case where the court has decided that it will not attempt to serve, for example, because it does not have the address for service, or it does not have the resources required to effect service. In our judgment, Mr Gaunt is right to accept that it is not a misuse of language to say that someone
f has been unable to do X when he has not even attempted to do X. Mr Phipps draws attention to CPR PD 44 (para 13.8) which provides:

> 'If a summary assessment of costs is appropriate but the court awarding costs is unable to do so on the day, the court must give directions as to a further hearing before the same judge.'

g In this situation, the court is 'unable' to do something which it does not even attempt to do, because it knows that it will not be able to do it. There is no question of a failed attempt. The court simply does not do it. This may be because the court believes that it will not be possible to do it within court hours. Or it may be that the court does not do it because it does not wish to do it. The
h judge may want to leave court early that day because he has another engagement, or because he is tired. The important point is that, for whatever reason, the court is not able to do the summary assessment of costs on the day.

[**27**] The fact that 'unable' does not necessarily connote that there has been a failed attempt is important. Once the focus shifts from a failed attempt, it
j becomes clear that the real emphasis is on what happens. If it is not a misuse of language to say that the court was unable to do X because (for whatever reason) it did not wish to do X, then we do not consider that it is a misuse of language to say that the court was unable to do X because it simply failed to do X. In each case, the court could have done X, but did not do it.

[**28**] Nor do we consider that the contextual points made by Mr Gaunt assist his interpretation. We accept that there is a clear link between rr 6.11 and

7.6(3)(a). But we do not consider that the reference in r 6.11 to a notice of non-service 'stating the method attempted' assists in the interpretation of *a* r 7.6(3)(a). Indeed, since Mr Gaunt concedes that the court 'has been unable to serve' even where it has not attempted service, for example because it does not have the address for service, it is impossible to see how even on his argument r 6.11 assists in the resolution of the question at issue. Nor does r 7.6(3)(b) assist in the interpretation of r 7.6(3)(a).   *b*

[29] We conclude, therefore, even without regard to the 1998 Act, the words 'has been unable to serve' in r 7.6(3)(a) include all cases where the court has failed to serve, including mere oversight on its part. It is therefore unnecessary to consider the position under the 1998 Act. If it had been necessary to do so, we would not have hesitated to adopt what might be considered to be a linguistically strained interpretation in order to read r 7.6(3)(a) in a way which is compatible *c* with art 6 of the European Convention for the Protection of Human Rights and Fundamental Freedoms 1950 (as set out in Pt I of Sch 1 to the 1998 Act), so as to ensure that litigants are not denied access to the courts, where it is the fault of the courts that the claim form has not been served in time.

[30] The court does, therefore, have the jurisdiction to extend time for service *d* under r 7.6(3)(a) where the court fails through neglect to serve in time. It must in all cases decide how to exercise the discretion conferred by the rule. We suggest that in most cases where the real cause of the failure to serve in time is court neglect, it will be appropriate to grant an extension of time if the claimant has acted promptly in making the application (see r 7.6(3)(c)). But there will be *e* some cases where, although court neglect has contributed to the failure to serve in time, the real cause has been the conduct of the claimant or the claimant's legal representative. In such cases, the court will often decide not to exercise its discretion to extend the time for service. But each case will turn on its own facts.

THE SCOPE OF RULE 6.9   *f*

[31] The decisions in *Anderton v Clwyd CC* [2002] 3 All ER 813, [2002] 1 WLR 3174 and *Wilkey v BBC* [2002] 4 All ER 1177, [2003] 1 WLR 1 have clarified the relationship between rr 6.9 and 7.6. In pre-*Anderton* cases, the court may exercise its discretion to dispense with service retrospectively where the claim form, although deemed by r 6.7(1) to be served out of time, has in fact been received by *g* the defendant or his legal adviser 'by a permitted method of service' within the four-month period (see *Anderton*'s case (at [58])). In the post-*Anderton* cases, the court will ordinarily not exercise its discretion to dispense with service even in such a case (see *Wilkey*'s case). It is clear from these two decisions that the basic rule is that the power to dispense with service should not be used to undermine the principle enunciated in *Godwin v Swindon BC* [2001] 4 All ER 641, [2002] *h* 1 WLR 997 that service should not be dispensed with retrospectively to circumvent the restrictions on granting extensions of time laid down in r 7.6(3). The exception recognised in *Anderton*'s case (confined to pre-*Anderton* cases) is where the claim form has been received within the four-month period by a 'permitted method of service'. Mummery LJ used this phrase, or an equivalent *j* phrase, three times in [57] and [58] of the judgment. Rule 6.2 provides:

'(1) A document may be served by any of the following methods—(a) personal service, in accordance with rule 6.4; (b) first class post; (c) leaving the document at a place specified in rule 6.5; (d) through a document exchange in accordance with the relevant practice direction; or

a
(e) by fax or other means of electronic communication in accordance with the relevant practice direction.'

[32] In *Anderton's* case, the court did not have to consider whether the exception might also apply in a case where there has been some comparatively minor departure from the permitted method of service. An example of what might fairly be described as a minor departure is where the claim form has been

b
sent by second class post (instead of first class post), and has been sent to the right person at the right address and has been received within the four-month period. We do not think that we are bound by *Anderton's* case and *Wilkey's* case to hold that a court could not properly exercise its discretion to dispense with service in such a case. In our view, it is not appropriate to attempt to provide an exhaustive

c
guide to the circumstances in which it is proper to dispense with service of a claim form retrospectively under r 6.9, whether in pre-*Anderton* cases, or in post-*Anderton* cases. We hope that what we say at [49] and [50], below in relation to *Claussen v Yeates*, at [56]–[60], below in relation to *McManus v Sharif*, and at [87] and [88], below in relation to *Murphy v Staples UK Ltd* will provide guidance as to the correct approach to be adopted at least in circumstances similar to those that

d
occurred in those cases. We wish to underline the exceptional nature of the power to dispense with service in such cases. The court was at pains to emphasise this point in both *Anderton's* case and *Wilkey's* case. The principle in *Godwin's* case is important, and must not be subverted. It will be subverted unless the power to dispense with service retrospectively is confined to truly exceptional cases.

e
CRANFIELD V BRIDGEGROVE LTD
[33] The claimants are the tenants of property at Brinscombe Crescent, Godalming. They hold under two leases, both of which were due to expire on 28 September 2001. They carry on the business of a general store at the premises, where they employ approximately 20 employees. On 20 November 2000, the

f
defendant gave notice under s 25 of the Landlord and Tenant Act 1954 terminating the tenancies on 28 September 2001. The notices stated that an application for a new tenancy would not be opposed. On 12 February 2001, the claimants' solicitors sent two claim forms to the Guildford County Court with a request that they be issued and served on the defendant at the address provided.

g
On 15 February, the court issued the two claim forms. The court sent formal notices to the solicitors that the forms had been issued on 15 February. These notices were in the Form N209, which is a standard form containing inter alia the following words:

h
'The court sent it [the claim form] with a copy of your witness statement(s) to the defendant by first class post on [   ] and it will be deemed served on [   ]. The defendant has until [   ] to reply.'

In both notices, these words were struck out, and the following words added in manuscript: 'your application is with the District Judges for directions'. These

j
notices were received by the solicitors on 17 February.
[34] The time for service of the claim forms expired on 15 April 2001. On 23 August, solicitors acting on behalf of the respondent wrote to the claimants' solicitors stating that no proceedings had been served. Accordingly, they said, the leases would terminate on 28 September and the respondent would then require vacant possession. Mr Falvert-Smith was dealing with the matter on behalf of the claimants. He immediately telephoned the court. What he was told was

confirmed in the court's letter dated 24 August, which stated that the claim forms had not been served:

> 'The copies of the claim form that were to be served were put on the Court file by mistake. Please accept the Court's apologies for this mishap. The Court will send out the service copies today. I apologise for any inconvenience caused.'

On the same day, the claimants' solicitors sent copies of the claim form to the respondents' solicitors, and on the following day the court sent the service copies to them too.

[35] On 18 September 2001, the claimants applied for an extension of time for service of the claim forms until 15 October on the grounds that—

> 'the failure to effect service of the claim form was due to an error of the court and not as a result of any neglect or default on the part of the claimants. In the circumstances, the claimants have taken all reasonable steps to serve the claim form within the time limited by CPR 7.5.'

On 24 September, District Judge Darbyshire dismissed the applications. He applied r 7.6(3), and considered that it could not be said that the court or the claimants had been 'unable' to serve within the requisite time for service. He was bound by *Vinos v Marks & Spencer plc* [2001] 3 All ER 784, and therefore compelled to dismiss the applications. No application was made to dispense with service.

[36] On 25 January 2002, Judge Hull QC allowed the claimants' appeal. He noted that, by reason of the decision in *Godwin v Swindon BC* [2001] 4 All ER 641, he had no power to dispense with service under r 6.9. He then turned to r 7.6(3)(a) and construed 'unable' as including circumstances in which the court had simply failed to serve by incompetence or oversight. Accordingly, he held that the court had been unable to serve the claim forms. Next, he considered whether the claimants had acted promptly in making their applications. He said that the solicitors were instructed promptly, and that they acted promptly on discovering that the claim forms had not been served. He thought that it was 'going too far' to expect the solicitors to badger the court and seek confirmation that service had been effected, and effected in time. He said that they were entitled to assume that all was well, and that all had been done in accordance with the rules. He then considered the exercise of his discretion, and concluded that the obvious prejudice to the claimants that would result if he did not extend time outweighed any prejudice that the defendant would suffer if he did extend time. For these reasons, he allowed the appeal.

[37] For the reasons expressed earlier in this judgment, Judge Hull construed r 7.6(3)(a) correctly. Mr Gaunt has criticised the conduct of the claimants' solicitors, and submitted that the real cause of the problem was their assumption that the court would have served the claim form, although they did not receive a notice under rr 6.10 or 6.14(1). But the defendant was only given permission to appeal on the point of construction, and not the judge's exercise of discretion. In any event, we should say that we see no basis on which the exercise of discretion could be challenged. In our judgment, this was a case where the real cause of the failure to serve in time was the court's neglect. That conclusion is not undermined by the fact that it is possible to argue that the claimants' solicitors were at fault in failing to appreciate that there might be a problem, and in failing to ascertain the position before the time for service had expired.

[38] We therefore dismiss this appeal.

CLAUSSEN V YEATES

a   [39] Mr Claussen was injured in a road accident on 7 October 1996. He instructed solicitors, Traymans, on 29 October. Liability has never been seriously in issue, and the defendant's insurers have made a voluntary interim payment of damages in respect of the value of the claimant's moped. Finalisation of the claimant's case on quantum was delayed because his recovery was protracted, and the prognosis was not clear. The defendant's insurers were kept informed by
b   the claimant's solicitors about the progress of the claim. On 29 July 1999, Traymans sent a number of reports and documents to the insurers, and made a Pt 36 offer. The insurers replied on 6 August that they wished to have their own medical examination of the claimant, and an appointment was made for 23 September. On 24 August, Mr Mutti (the partner at Traymans dealing with
c   the case on behalf of the claimant) wrote asking whether the insurers would nominate solicitors to accept service. By letter dated 27 August, the insurers nominated A E Wyeth and Co (Wyeth), but did not provide their address.

    [40] On 30 September, Traymans notified the insurers that proceedings would be issued, and said that there would then be four months in which to resolve the
d   matter before it became necessary to serve particulars of claim. A draft claim form was then prepared for issue, and a trainee solicitor took it to the Central London County Court on 5 October 1999. She had been instructed by Mr Mutti to retrieve the claim form after it had been issued, so that it could be served by Traymans. The claim form, which was issued on 5 October, gave the defendant's address as 'Stephen Michael Yeates c/o A E Wyeth & Co, solicitors, DX 31904,
e   Dartford'. In view of the address 'c/o Wyeth', the court official took the view that the court should serve the claim form, and that a letter from Wyeth would be needed confirming that they would accept service. The trainee solicitor was, however, given a sealed copy of the claim form by the court.

    [41] On 5 October, Mr Mutti wrote to Wyeth at their Dartford address,
f   saying: 'Proceedings were issued on the 5th October 1999, but we do not propose to serve them at present, as we anticipate that this matter is likely to settle.' Wyeth replied on 20 October stating that service would be accepted at their London office, and asking for a copy of the sealed summons in 'confirmation of the commencement of the proceedings'. At the request of Wyeth, on 9 November Traymans sent them at that address a copy of the claim form as
g   issued. On 15 November, Wyeth wrote asking Traymans to 'ensure that when service is effected and if you intend to ask us to accept service on the defendant's behalf, the appropriate documentation is sent to this firm's London office'.

    [42] Thereafter, little happened until a date (which the judge was prepared to assume was 1 February 2000) when a letter was sent by Traymans to the court
h   addressed to the court manager with the correct title and number of the action. It stated:

        'Please find enclosed Notice of Issue of Legal Aid Certificate, Particulars of Claim and Claimant's Schedule of Loss in respect of this case which was issued in October of last year. Could you please place a copy on your file and
j   serve the Defendant via his solicitors in due course. We attach a copy of a letter from the Defendant's solicitors confirming that they will accept service.'

    [43] This was the first time that Traymans had provided the court with the confirmation that it had sought on 5 October 1999 that Wyeth would accept service. The last date for service was 5 February. Traymans also wrote on

1 February to Wyeth saying that they had lodged the documents with the court
which 'no doubt will serve these in due course', and enclosing copies. Nothing
happened until 4 April when Traymans tried to find out the position, and learnt
that Wyeth had not heard from the court. Mr Mutti telephoned the court, and
was told that the matter had been 'put on hold awaiting a letter confirming that
Wyeth would accept service'. Mr Mutti pointed out that such a letter had been
enclosed with his letter of 1 February. The member of the court staff confirmed
that this was shown on the computer record. The file and letters of 1 February
and 5 April (in which Traymans said that the time for service had passed) were
placed before District Judge Langley, who on 18 April made an order that the
time for service of the claim form, particulars of claim and response pack be
extended to 26 May.

[44] On 19 June, Traymans wrote to the court and to Wyeth to find out
whether the claim form had been served. On learning that it had not been served,
they wrote to District Judge Langley expressing their concern, and asking her to
look into the matter urgently. On 29 June, she ordered that the time for service
be extended to 31 July 2000.

[45] On 2 August, Wyeth issued an application that the orders dated 18 April
and 29 June be set aside, and that the claim form and the purported service of it
be set aside. On 21 September, District Judge Haselgrove acceded to this
application. The claimant appealed to the judge. In a reserved judgment given
on 9 May 2001, Judge Butter QC dismissed the appeal.

[46] Before Judge Butter, it was common ground between the parties that, in
the light of *Vinos v Marks & Spencer plc* [2001] 3 All ER 784, there was no residual
discretion to extend time or to cure procedural irregularities. Accordingly, the
claimant had to bring himself within r 7.6(3) in order to obtain an extension of
time. There was no application to dispense with service. The central parts of the
judgment are these:

'[12] The defendant contended that upon a proper construction of
r 7.6(3)(a) it was necessary for the court to have attempted to serve but been
unable to do so, that in the present case the court had done nothing because
it was waiting for information which it had made plain that it required, that
in any event Traymans could themselves have served the claim form, that
although arguably the responsibility for service lay with the court after
1 February 2000 the court was given less than four days to do so, and that it
could not fairly be said that the claimant had taken all reasonable steps to
serve the form.

[13] The following additional matters may be noted. Traymans were
entitled to insist that they would serve the claim form. They must have been
aware that there was no question of the court serving it without the
confirmation which the court required. Their trainee solicitor was given a
sealed copy of the form on 5 October 1999 and a copy of this was in fact sent
by Traymans to Wyeth on 9 November though, in the light of the
contemporaneous correspondence, counsel for the claimant has not sought
to argue that this constituted service. (Particulars of claim would have had
to be served within 14 days unless time was extended.) On 1 February 2000,
Traymans' letter to the court did not refer to the fact that the claim form had
not been served and did not convey any sense of urgency. The court receives
many thousands of letters and other documents every week and it is entirely
unrealistic to assume that the court will almost immediately effect service.

There is no evidence as to what consideration was given to the documents handed in on 1 February but the position is that it would not have been appropriate for the court to serve the form after 5 February as time had not been extended. Although the claimant's representatives seek to rely upon the fact that no notice of non-service was sent by the court (under r 6.11), it should be borne in mind that where service is effected, the court will send out a certificate of service under r 6.14 in relation to this claim form, and notification of receipt of an acknowledgment of service in relation to the particulars of claim under r 10.4. In the present case no step appears to have been taken by Traymans between 1 February and 4 April 2000. No application was at any stage issued in accordance with r 7.6(4) and CPR PD 7.8, despite the requirement among other things of the need for evidence, though it may be that District Judge Langley was or would have been entitled to dispense with the filing of an application notice pursuant to r 23.3(2).

[14] In overall terms, District Judge Haselgrove accepted the submissions of the defendant summarised in [12], above. I consider that he was right to accept them. The natural interpretation of r 7.6(3)(a) is that the court has attempted to serve the claim form but has been unable to do so. If support for this view is needed, it is to be found in the wording of r 6.11 which requires this court if unable to serve to "state the method attempted". Whatever sympathy one may have for the claimant, the interpretation put forward by his counsel involves an unnaturally strained interpretation upon the wording of the rule. The claimant therefore fails in respect of r 7.6(3)(a). District Judge Haselgrove was in my view also correct in concluding that the claimant did not satisfy the requirements of r 7.6(3)(b) where the emphasis is on the claimant as distinct from the court. Here the claimant took no step at all after 5 October 1999 to serve the claim form and I do not see that he can come within r 7.6(3)(b) by saying that he handed documents to the court on 1 February 2000. It is unnecessary for me to decide the point but I should say that I have considerable reservations as to whether the claimant can be said to have complied with r 7.6(3)(c) and (4).'

[47] For the reasons that we have already given, Judge Butter misinterpreted r 7.6(3)(a). It was open to him to extend the time for service if he considered that court neglect was the real cause of the failure to serve the claim form in time, and that, applying the overriding objective, an extension of time was appropriate in all the circumstances. Since the judge did not exercise his discretion under r 7.6(3)(a), it is necessary for us to do so now.

[48] In our view, it was failures by Traymans that were the real reason why the claim form was not served within the four-month period in this case. They knew that the court would not serve the claim form until it received a letter from Wyeth confirming that they would accept service. Mr Mutti received such a letter early during the four-month period. No explanation has been given as to why that letter was not sent to the court until 1 February. If it had been sent shortly after it had been received by Traymans in October 1999, there is no reason to suppose that the court would not have effected service long before 5 February 2000. Nor does Mr Mutti explain why, having waited until 1 February to send the letter from Wyeth, he wrote to the court asking them to serve the defendant 'in due course'. He should have impressed on the court the urgency of the situation (which was entirely of his own making), and asked it to make sure

that the claim form was served by 5 February. We would agree with the
comment of Judge Butter that, since the court receives many thousands of letters
every week, 'it is entirely unrealistic to assume that the court will almost
immediately effect service'. In these circumstances, we do not consider that the
conduct of the court was the real reason why the claim form was not served in
time. We do not, therefore, think that this is a case in which it would be right to
extend time for service under r 7.6(3)(a).

[49] Mr Asif submits in the alternative that we should make an order under
r 6.9 dispensing with service. He says that the case is analogous to the category 2
cases recognised in *Anderton v Clwyd CC* [2002] 3 All ER 813, [2002] 1 WLR 3174.
He relies in particular on the fact that on 9 November 1999, Traymans sent a copy
of the claim form as issued to Wyeth. Thus a copy was sent by a permitted
method of service to the person authorised to accept service at the address given
for service. He submits, therefore, that the case falls within the scope of the
category 2 cases identified in *Anderton*'s case at [58], and that, since this is a
pre-*Anderton* case, it is one in which it is appropriate in principle to make an order
under r 6.9. We cannot accept this submission. In the two cases which succeeded
in *Anderton*'s case, what was sent was the original claim form that had been issued
by the court, and it was clear that the claim forms were purportedly being served,
albeit that they were deemed to be served out of time. The recipient knew that,
on the assumption that what was sent amounted to valid service, time started to
run from the date of service of the claim form for certain purposes. Thus, for
example, unless the claim form stated that particulars of claim were to follow, the
time for acknowledgement of service was 14 days after service of the claim form
(see r 10.3(1)(b)).

[50] But in the present case, Traymans did not purport to serve the claim form
by sending the copy to Wyeth on 9 November. There was no question of time
starting to run from the date of service of that copy. On the contrary, Traymans
made it clear that they were not proposing to serve the claim form on
9 November, and this was well understood by Wyeth (see their letter of
15 November). Traymans knew that they would eventually be asking the court
to serve the claim form in due course, and that is precisely what they asked the
court to do on 1 February. Nor did Traymans purport to serve the claim form on
1 February 2000. By their letter of that date, they made it clear that the claim
form would be served by the court 'in due course' ie at some unspecified future
date. In our view, this case does not fall within the exceptional category of cases
identified in *Anderton*'s case ([2002] 3 All ER 813 at [58]). It would be quite
inappropriate to make an order dispensing with service here.

[51] For these reasons, the appeal is dismissed.

MCMANUS V SHARIF

[52] The claimant suffered substantial injuries on 26 February 1998 when the
defendant's car mounted the pavement and collided with her. Shortly thereafter,
the claimant instructed solicitors, Ronald Prior & Co (Priors). On 14 May 1998,
Priors wrote to the defendant's insurers, KGM Motor Policies at Lloyds (KGM)
inviting them to admit liability. On 2 June, KGM replied confirming that 'for the
purposes of negotiations liability is not in dispute'. During the following
two years, negotiations proceeded, and the insurers made a modest interim
payment, and met various expenses that were incurred by the claimant. But no
final settlement was reached.

a [53] The limitation period was due to expire on 26 February 2001. Priors issued a claim form (without particulars of claim or accompanying documents) on 19 February 2001. They requested that the service copy be remitted to them for service, and this was done. The last day for service of the claim form was, therefore, Tuesday 19 June. On Friday 15 June, Priors sent KGM 'by way of service' an unsigned and unsealed copy of the claim form together with

b particulars of claim and a schedule of losses. These documents were received by KGM on 18 June. In their letter dated 15 June which enclosed the documents, Priors wrote:

> 'The writer has left the sealed Claim Form at home, as he was working on this case last night. We therefore enclose copy Claim Form, and will fax the
c   sealed version on Monday.'

In fact, what they sent was not a copy of the claim form that had been issued, but a draft claim form. By r 6.4(1), the claim form and particulars of claim should have been served on the defendant personally: no solicitor had been authorised to accept service so as to bring r 6.4(2) into play, and there had been no prior
d agreement between the parties that service would be effected on KGM. By letter dated 22 June, KGM informed Priors that they 'would like you to serve our insured direct'. On 25 June, Priors purported to effect personal service of all the papers on the defendant at her home address.

[54] KGM instructed solicitors on behalf of the defendant. On 3 July 2001,
e they wrote to Priors pointing out that they had not indicated that they were willing to accept service, and that the defendant should have been served personally. No further steps were taken in the proceedings until the defendant's solicitors issued an application on 21 February 2002 to strike out the claim on the grounds that proper service of the proceedings had never been effected on the defendant. The application was heard by District Judge Gregory on 26 June. It
f was conceded on behalf of the claimant that there had not been proper service. Counsel appearing for the claimant sought to rely on an alleged agreement that the defendant would meet the claim and that he was thereby estopped from seeking the protection of the CPR to avoid liability. In a reserved judgment given on 9 July, this submission was rejected by District Judge Gregory. Since no other argument had been put forward on behalf of the claimant, the district judge felt
g constrained to accede to the defendant's application and strike out the claim. As he saw it, the claimant had not complied with r 7.5, and, in view of *Vinos v Marks & Spencer plc* [2001] 3 All ER 784 and *Elmes v Hygrade Food Products plc* [2001] All ER (D) 158 (Jan), had little or no prospect of obtaining an extension of time under r 7.6. The attention of District Judge Gregory was not drawn to r 6.9 at the date
h of the hearing (which pre-dated *Anderton*'s case), and no application was made to him for an order to dispense with service. The district judge refused permission to appeal. He was not made aware of the decision in *Anderton*'s case. On 31 July, Judge Bradbury granted permission to appeal limited to the issue of whether District Judge Gregory should have considered r 6.9 and exercised his discretion
j to dispense with service of the claim form. It is evident that, in giving permission to appeal, Judge Bradbury was heavily influenced by *Anderton*'s case.

[55] On 28 October 2002, Judge Hornby allowed the claimant's appeal. The appeal proceeded as if District Judge Gregory had held that he had no jurisdiction to dispense with service under r 6.9, so that it was appropriate for Judge Hornby to decide whether to dispense with service for himself. The judge cited extensively from *Anderton v Clwyd CC* [2002] 3 All ER 813, and referred in

particular to [57] and [58] of the judgment. We should set out the whole of his
conclusion: *a*

'In the light of *Anderton's* case it is clear in my judgment that the court has
a discretion to exercise which can be exercised retrospectively in exceptional
circumstances without undermining the principle in *Godwin v Swindon BC*
[2001] 4 All ER 641, [2002] 1 WLR 997. Plainly, the exercise of such discretion
must have regard to the overriding principles of CPR Pt 1. In the instant case   *b*
the arguments seem to me to be finely balanced. On the one hand it is said
that by serving the defendant's insurers the claimant does not fall within the
exception described in [58]. The claimant knew the defendant's name and
address, that she or her solicitors should be served within the four-month
period. No applications were made under rr 7.6, 6.8 or 6.9. The claimants   *c*
were risking disaster by serving on the last day. The defendants would be
wrongfully deprived of the Limitation Act 1980. On the other hand, the
defendant's insurers were aware of the claim within three months as
contrasted by the facts in *Anderton's* case and had admitted liability 18 days
later. They looked after the defendant's interests throughout and were in
substantial proactive negotiations. Medical reports had been disclosed and   *d*
offers of settlement made. It was submitted that to draw a distinction
between the defendant's insurers and her legal advisers was a technical point
devoid of merit when the defendant's interests were fully protected by her
insurers throughout. Moreover, applying the principles of CPR Pt 1, if the
claim were to be struck out the claimant, whose claim was substantial, was   *e*
not guaranteed success against her first solicitors. She would be proceeding
against a party who had formerly represented her. There was likely to be
considerable delay overall and much extra expense. The added complexities
caused by the different nature of the claim were a factor and a reallocation of
further court resources to new proceedings should be borne in mind. I
remind myself that the district judge impliedly indicated that if he had had a   *f*
discretion he would probably have exercised it in favour of the claimant in
all the circumstances. I have weighed up carefully the rival arguments which
I have outlined briefly above. Both counsel put their arguments admirably.
After careful consideration and reminding myself of the way the Court of
Appeal considered the cases of Chambers and Dorgan in *Anderton's* case I am   *g*
persuaded that the balance just tips in favour of the claimant and that my
discretion should therefore be exercised in favour of the claimant for the
reasons advanced by Mr Yell and set out fully in this judgment. Accordingly,
this appeal shall be allowed.'

[56] In our judgment, Judge Hornby should not have made an order under   *h*
r 6.9 in this case. He took too liberal a view of the scope of the discretion
conferred on the court by the rule. He did not pay sufficient regard to the fact
that, even in category 2 cases (of which this is an example), the discretion may be
exercised only in exceptional circumstances, and the court should be very slow
indeed to dispense with service retrospectively in circumstances which fall   *j*
outside those mentioned in *Anderton's* case ([2002] 3 All ER 813 at [58]) to which
we have referred at [9], above.
[57] The circumstances of the present case fell outside the scope of *Anderton's*
case (at [58]) in a number of respects. First, what was purportedly served was not
the claim form issued by the court or a photocopy of that document, but a draft
claim form. Thus, unlike the document issued by the court, it was not stamped

a with the court seal, and it did not contain a statement of truth. Rule 7.5 provides that, after a claim form has been issued, '*it* must be served on the defendant' (my emphasis).

[**58**] Secondly, Priors made it clear to KGM that they understood that they were not serving the claim form, because they said that they would fax it on 18 June. Thirdly, the draft claim form was not sent to the defendant or a solicitor

b authorised to accept service on behalf of the defendant as permitted by r 6.4. It was sent to the defendant's insurers, who had no authority to accept service on behalf of the defendant. This is not a mere technical point. Mr Ross QC makes the point that in *Anderton*'s case, the court referred to the fact that the claim form had in fact been received by the defendant or 'his legal adviser' by a permitted method of service as critical to whether the circumstances were exceptional so as

c to bring the r 6.9 power into play after the time for service has expired. He submits that the term 'legal adviser' (which does not appear in the CPR) must have been deliberately chosen in preference to the terms 'legal representative' or 'solicitor' (which do appear), and must have been intended to include, for example, insurers who are conducting the defence as KGM were in the present

d case. We do not agree. In *Anderton*'s case, the court referred three times to the receipt of a claim form 'by a permitted method of service'. In our view, when using the term 'legal adviser', the court was clearly referring to a solicitor, since personal service on a defendant under the CPR is only permitted if it is effected on the defendant, or on a solicitor authorised to accept service (see rr 6.4 and 6.5). We note that in *Anderton*'s case (at [3]), the court spoke of the claim form having

e been received by, and come to the attention of 'the defendant or his solicitor'. It is clear that the terms 'legal adviser' and 'solicitor' were used interchangeably. In any case, we do not think that an insurer, whose interest does not necessarily coincide with that of the insured defendant, can properly be described as the defendant's legal adviser, even where no solicitor has been appointed to act on

f his behalf.

[**59**] Thirdly, the draft claim form was not sent to an address given for service in accordance with r 6.5.

[**60**] We do not rule out the possibility that the power to dispense with service of the claim form should be exercised in circumstances which do not fall squarely within those described in *Anderton*'s case: see further discussion at [87] and [88],

g below. But wherever the boundary for the exercise of this exceptional jurisdiction is to be drawn, we have no doubt that it should not be exercised in a case such as this. There were significant departures from the rules as to the permitted mode of service. They were not mere technicalities.

[**61**] For these reasons, we would allow this appeal.

h
MURPHY V STAPLES UK LTD

[**62**] The claimant suffered personal injuries as the result of an accident at work on 22 November 1998. He was employed by the defendant as a part-time shelf stacker, and was injured when the bottom of a ladder that he was

j descending slipped from under him. He instructed Horwich Farrelly (Horwich) to act as his solicitors soon after the accident. On 28 May 1999, Horwich wrote to the defendant's insurers asking them to 'confirm details of solicitors nominated to accept service of proceedings on behalf of your insured'. On 2 June 1999, the defendant's insurers replied saying that their inquiries into liability were continuing, but that if Horwich wanted to issue proceedings at this stage, their solicitors, Branton Edwards (Branton), would accept service. On 9 June, Branton

wrote to Horwich confirming that they had instructions to accept service, asking
for an advance copy of the claimant's medical report, and suggesting the
possibility of a jointly instructed expert.

[63] Thereafter, Horwich continued to prepare the claimant's claim. On
21 November 2001 (one day before the expiry of the limitation period), the claim
form was issued. On 15 March 2002, Horwich purported to serve the claim form
by first class post together with particulars of claim, schedule of damages and
medical reports. This was done by serving the defendant at its registered office.
The accompanying letter recited the fact that Horwich had been in
correspondence with the defendant's insurers and Branton, and continued: 'we
would respectfully suggest that the enclosed documentation be forwarded
immediately' to Branton. On the same day, Horwich sent to Branton by first class
post copies of all the documents that were purportedly served on the defendant,
including a copy of the claim form that had been issued by the court. The
accompanying letter informed Branton that the documents had been 'served
today on your client's registered office'.

[64] Although the defendant apparently did forward the original documents
to Branton, they had not been received by that firm by 26 March when Branton
wrote to Horwich stating that the purported service was defective because it
should have been effected on them, and not on the defendant. On 3 April 2002,
Branton issued an application to set aside the purported service of the claim form
on the grounds that it was not in accordance with r 6.5. There was no
cross-application to dispense with service under r 6.9, and no evidence was filed
on behalf of the claimant. In a judgment given on 7 May 2002, Deputy District
Judge Hugman acceded to the defendant's application, and ordered that service
be set aside. The district judge referred to *Godwin v Swindon BC* [2001] 4 All ER
641, [2002] 1 WLR 997 and *Nanglegan v Royal Free Hampstead NHS Trust* [2001]
3 All ER 793, [2002] 1 WLR 1043, and held that the only question before him was
whether there had been service on Branton on or before 21 March. Service on
the defendant itself would not suffice. He concluded that service had been
effected on the defendant at its registered office, and that the sending of 'courtesy'
copies of the documents to Branton on 15 March or some subsequent date prior
to 26 March did not amount to service on Branton.

[65] In view of *Godwin's* case and *Nanglegan's* case, counsel for the claimant
did not seek to persuade Deputy District Judge Hugman to extend the time for
service retrospectively. Despite the absence of an application, the deputy district
judge considered whether to dispense with service. He said, however, that this
was an 'ordinary case, where the service of a claim form is something which is
physically achieved'. To dispense with service would 'fly in the face of the Court
of Appeal's views'. He refused, therefore, to dispense with service.

[66] The claimant appealed with the permission of Judge Holman. The appeal
was heard by Judge Armitage QC who gave a reserved judgment on
13 October 2002. The claimant applied for permission to adduce evidence before
the judge. This evidence comprised a statement by David Spencer dated
20 May 2002 to which was appended a number of documents which showed
some important aspects of the procedural history. Mr Spencer is a solicitor with
Horwich who has had the conduct of this litigation on behalf of the claimant.

[67] Before Judge Armitage, the claimant did not challenge the decisions by
Deputy District Judge Hugman that (a) the claim form had been served on the
defendant, and (b) the sending of 'courtesy' copies on Branton did not amount to
service on the solicitors. As regards r 6.9, Judge Armitage said that on the

material available to the deputy district judge, and in the light of the law as it
stood at the time, the decision not to dispense with service was clearly correct. In
the light of *Anderton v Clwyd CC* [2002] 3 All ER 813, however, an issue arose as to
whether the decision under r 6.9 was correct.

[68] Judge Armitage first had to decide whether to admit the evidence of
Mr Spencer. He approached this question by applying the principles in *Ladd v
Marshall* [1954] 3 All ER 745, [1954] 1 WLR 1489. He said that he found the failure
to adduce any evidence on behalf of the claimant before Deputy District Judge
Hugman 'difficult to understand'. He concluded that it had not been
demonstrated that the evidence could not have been obtained with reasonable
diligence. He decided not to admit the evidence.

[69] Judge Armitage then addressed the various points made by Mr Halliday,
counsel then appearing on behalf of the claimant, in support of the submission
that service should be dispensed with under r 6.9. He rejected the submission
that he should infer that the claimant had a strong case on liability. A point was
made based on the fact that an expert plastic surgeon had been jointly instructed
by the parties in 1999. The judge considered that this was 'not the same as
negotiations to settle or upon quantification, subject to liability or after
admission, but does indicate a significant awareness of the likely issues on
damages'. The third point relied on by Mr Halliday was that there had been an
interim payment and a substantial offer in relation to liability. This was
demonstrated by the evidence of Mr Spencer, but, having refused to admit this
evidence, Judge Armitage refused to take it into account. The fourth point made
by Mr Halliday was that the solicitors had been instructed on behalf of the
defendant 30 months before service was effected. The judge dismissed this as a
'thoroughly bad point'. The problems arose because the claimant's solicitors left
service until the last moment, and then failed to look at their file to see upon
whom service was to be effected.

[70] Judge Armitage took the next two points together. These were that the
defendant and its solicitors were aware of the contents of the claim form and the
other documents before the date for service had expired. As to this, the judge
said:

'On any view both the defendants and their solicitors had actual
knowledge of the existence and content of the claim form within a few days
of the deadline for service, possibly before, but possibly after it. Albeit not
good service the defendants and their insurer's solicitors had actual
knowledge of the claim and its content.'

[71] The remaining substantive points went to the question of where the
balance of prejudice lay. Judge Armitage said:

'In my judgment that balance comes down heavily in favour of allowing
the action to proceed. The defendants will suffer the prejudice of losing a
cast iron defence to a claim of which they had fair and timely notice. Service
was procedurally ineffective, but was not demonstrably actually ineffective.
The defendant's ability to contest the claim (on liability and quantum) on its
merits, is unaffected by the claimant's decision to proceed at the very last
moment. There is no evidence to suggest that that decision was made on
tactical grounds, that is to say with the intention of causing problems for the
defendants in their defence to the claim.'

[72] Judge Armitage summarised his conclusion in these terms:

'In my judgment the circumstances are exceptional. This was a technical error. It was easily avoidable, but has no more than technical consequences for the defendants compared with potentially very grave consequences for the claimant. Any relevant delay was insignificant. The claimant and/or his solicitors have not performed their obligations under the rules as to time, as to service or in this appeal with any great credit. They have been fortunate in what may be seen as the merciful decision of the Court of Appeal in *Anderton's* case. Although not wrong at the time it was made, I allow the claimant's appeal against the district judge's order on the basis that the decision was wrong having regard to the subsequent declaration of the court's powers concerning dispensing with service of a claim form, by the Court of Appeal in *Anderton's* case.'

Accordingly, he allowed the claimant's appeal.

[73] Permission to appeal to this court was given on the question whether in a pre-*Anderton* case, the category of 'exceptional' cases where service may be dispensed with retrospectively under r 6.9 is restricted to cases where there has been an unsuccessful attempt to serve at the address for service.

[74] But we need first to deal with the point raised by Waller LJ during the course of argument that the sending of the claim form by first class post to the defendant's registered office on 15 March constituted good service pursuant to s 725(1) of the Companies Act 1985, such that there was no need to invoke r 6.9 at all. Mr Tozzi QC adopted this as part of his submissions. Mr Purchas QC protested that it had been conceded below that there had not been service on the defendant in accordance with r 6.5, and the suggestion that service had been effected under s 725(1) had not been raised, and that it was too late for the point to be taken now. But we decided that it would be unsatisfactory to determine this appeal on a false basis. Any prejudice caused to the defendant by the fact that the point was taken so late could be met by an appropriate order for costs, and giving the defendant time to submit further submissions in writing on the new point. Since the end of the hearing we have received written submissions from both parties on the point.

[75] Mr Tozzi submits as follows. Section 725(1) of the 1985 Act provides: 'A document may be served on a company by leaving it at, or sending it by post to, the company's registered office.'

[76] Section 7 of the Interpretation Act 1978 provides:

'Where an Act authorises or requires any document to be served by post ... then, unless the contrary intention appears, the service is deemed to be effected by properly addressing, pre-paying and posting a letter containing the document and, unless the contrary is proved, to have been effected at the time at which the letter would be delivered in the ordinary course of post.'

[77] Rule 6.1 provides that the rules in CPR Pt 6 apply to the service of documents 'except where—(a) any other enactment, a rule in another Part, or a practice direction makes a different provision'. Rule 6.2(1) provides the methods by which service may be effected, viz by personal service in accordance with r 6.4, by first class post, by leaving the document at a place specified in r 6.5, through a document exchange, or by fax or other electronic communication. Rule 6.2(2) provides:

a
'A company may be served by any method permitted under this Part as an alternative to the methods of service set out in—(a) section 725 of the Companies Act 1985 (service by leaving a document at or posting it to an authorised place); (b) section 695 of that Act (service on overseas companies); and (c) section 694A of that Act (service of documents on companies incorporated outside the UK and Gibraltar and having a branch
b   in Great Britain).'

[78] Rule 6.4 contains the following provisions relating to personal service:

'(1) A document to be served may be served personally, except as provided in paragraph (2).
(2) Where a solicitor—(a) is authorised to accept service on behalf of a
c   party; and (b) has notified the party serving the document in writing that he is so authorised, a document must be served on the solicitor, unless personal service is required by an enactment, rule, practice direction or court order.
(3) A document is served personally on an individual by leaving it with that individual.
d   (4) A document is served personally on a company or other corporation by leaving it with a person holding a senior position within the company or corporation.'

[79] Rule 6.5 deals with the address for service. Rule 6.5(2) requires a party to give an address for service within the jurisdiction. Rule 6.5(4) provides that '[a]ny
e   document to be served (a) by first class post ... must be sent or transmitted to, or left at, the address given by the party to be served'. Rule 6.5(6) provides that where—

'(a) no solicitor is acting for the party to be served; and (b) the party has not given an address for service, the document must be sent or transmitted to, or
f   left at, the place shown in the following table.'

The table shows the place for service according to the nature of the party to be served. It includes as the place for service of a company registered in England and Wales either the '[p]rincipal office of the company' or '[a]ny place of business of the company within the jurisdiction which has a real connection with the claim'.
g   [80] In this case, service was effected using the statutory procedure. Mr Tozzi submits that the fact that service by post pursuant to the 1985 Act overlaps with service by first class post under r 6.2(1)(b) is immaterial. Service by first class post is a permitted method of service. Accordingly, service on the company at its registered office was good service. The case of *Nanglegan v Royal Free Hampstead*
h   *NHS Trust* [2001] 3 All ER 793 can be distinguished, since the defendant in that case was not a company. Alternatively it was wrongly decided.
[81] The submissions on behalf of the defendant may be summarised as follows. A defendant company may be served under s 725(1) of the 1985 Act, under the CPR or in such other way as may be agreed between the parties: see *Kenneth Allison Ltd (in liq) v AE Limehouse & Co (a firm)* [1991] 4 All ER 500 at 506,
j   [1992] 2 AC 105 at 116–117 per Lord Bridge of Harwich, with whom Lords Lowry, Templeman and Jauncey agreed. Lord Bridge said:

'I do not see any difficulty in holding that the kind of ad hoc agreement in question is legally effective. If one party, knowing that another wishes to serve process upon him, requests or authorises the other to do so in a particular way which is outside the rules and the other does so, then, unless

the rules themselves prohibit consensual service, the party so served cannot
be heard to say that the service was not valid. Thus, I have no doubt that, if *a*
the circumstances of the present case had come before the court in 1898, the
validity of the service would have been affirmed. The crucial question is
whether subsequent changes in the Rules of the Supreme Court have
introduced just such a prohibition of consensual service outside the rules as
was unsuccessfully contended for in *Montgomery Jones & Co v Liebenthal & Co* *b*
[1898] 1 QB 487.'

[82] This presupposes that r 6.2(2) and s 725(1) provide alternative, and not
concurrent, methods of service. Where a choice or election is made as to the
method of service to be employed, then both parties are bound by it. Once the
CPR is engaged by an effective election, the parties know when the court *c*
timetable will start to run, because the claimant will have served a certificate of
service specifying the deemed date of service. In this way, certainty is achieved.
On the facts of the present case, the claimant by his solicitors elected to proceed
by way of service on the defendant's solicitors under the CPR, rather than under
s 725(1). At no time prior did the claimant seek to resile from the election. The *d*
defendant also relies on *Nanglegan*'s case.

[83] Our conclusion on this issue is as follows. A claimant may serve the claim
form on a defendant company either by leaving it at, or by sending it by post to,
the company's registered office, or by serving it in accordance with one of the
methods permitted by the CPR. They are true alternatives. That is made clear
by r 6.2(2). There are differences between the two methods. For example, *e*
service under s 725(1) may be by second class post. Rule 6.1 provides for service
by first class post. Service under s 725(1) is deemed to have been effected at the
time at which the letter would be delivered 'in the ordinary course of post' (see
s 7 of the 1978 Act) *unless the contrary is proved*. Rule 6.7 provides that, where
service is by first class post, the document is irrebuttably deemed to have been *f*
served on the second day after it was posted. Another difference is that service
under s 725(1) must be by leaving the document at, or posting it to, the registered
office. Rule 6.2(1) provides for five permitted methods of service.

[84] If a defendant has not given an address for service, a claimant may choose
whether to follow the s 725(1) or the CPR route for service. In *Nanglegan*'s case,
it was held that, where a defendant elects to give his address for service, and *g*
nominates his solicitor to accept service, r 6.5(4) requires personal service to be
effected upon the nominated solicitor, and not on the defendant. As Thorpe LJ
put it ([2001] 3 All ER 793 at 797, [2002] 1 WLR 1043 at 1047): 'There will be many
instances in which a defendant does not want service either at his residence or at
his place of business.' But in that case, the court was not concerned with the *h*
interplay between s 725(1) and the CPR, which expressly recognise alternative
methods.

[85] We accept that it is possible for the parties to make a binding contract
whereby the claimant agrees to serve the claim form by the CPR route rather
than under s 725(1) or vice versa. But we do not consider that the effect of the *j*
letters dated 28 May, 2 and 9 June 1999 was to deny to the claimant the option of
serving under s 725(1) of the 1985 Act. In our judgment, the true effect of these
letters was not a binding promise by the claimant to serve on the solicitors under
r 6.4(2). Rather, it was that the parties agreed that, *if* the claimant decided to
effect personal service under r 6.4, then they would serve on the defendant's
solicitors rather than on the company under r 6.4(4). The *Kenneth Allison* case is

a authority for the proposition that an ad hoc agreement for service not permitted by the CPR is legally effective. We do not consider that it assists in the resolution of the issue which arises here.

[86] Our conclusion, therefore, is that the service on the company's registered office by first class post on 15 March 2002 was good service.

b [87] In these circumstances, it is not necessary to decide whether Judge Armitage was right to dispense with service under r 6.9. However, in view of the importance of giving some guidance as to the scope of r 6.9 in cases such as this, we shall express our opinion on this issue on the footing that (contrary to the view just expressed) service should have been on the defendant's solicitors under r 6.4(2). In our judgment, on that hypothesis, the circumstances identified by the judge did not make this an 'exceptional' case within the letter or the spirit of
c *Anderton v Clwyd CC* [2002] 3 All ER 813, [2002] 1 WLR 3174 and *Wilkey v BBC* [2002] 4 All ER 1177, [2003] 1 WLR 1. But we wish to emphasise the following features. It is clear that a copy of the claim form as issued was sent to Branton on 15 March 2002. In other words, a copy of the right document was sent to the right person at the right address and, if r 6.7 applied, it was deemed to have been served
d before the expiry of the four-month period. Moreover, Branton were informed by Horwich that the original documents had been served on the defendant's registered office that same day. The only flaw in the process was that Horwich sent a copy of the issued claim form, rather than the original document itself. In this regard, it is to be noted that, if Horwich had sent the issued claim form to
e Branton by fax, that would have been good service. A document received by fax is a copy document. The circumstances revealed by this case do not precisely satisfy the criteria in *Anderton*'s case: Branton received a document served by one of the permitted methods of service (ie by first class post on the right person at the right address), but it was a copy of the document that should have been served.

f [88] In these very unusual circumstances, had it been necessary to do so, we would have decided that it was right to dispense with service under r 6.9. It is possible that the relationship between service under s 725(1) and service under the CPR was not fully understood, and that the importance of serving on the party to be served the original claim form that has been issued (rather than a
g copy) was not appreciated. But in future the significance of these points will have to be taken into account. Errors of this kind will generally not be regarded as good reasons for making an order under r 6.9. In stipulating a strict approach for the future in such circumstances, we have been guided by what was said in *Anderton*'s case and *Wilkey*'s case.

h [89] But for the reasons that we have given, this appeal is dismissed.

SMITH V HUGHES

[90] The claimant was injured in a road traffic accident on 18 December 1997. It seems that he was driving the car of his mother, Mrs E Smith. They both
j instructed the same firm of solicitors, Graham Leigh Pfeffer & Co (GLP). In his statement dated 30 September 2002, Ian Wolstenholme, a legal executive employed by GLP, explains that the insurance position of Mr Hughes was somewhat uncertain. By a letter dated 30 March 1998, Budget Insurance Services (Budget) said that Mr Hughes was not insured. Thereupon, GLP intimated a claim to the Motor Insurers Bureau (MIB), and entered into correspondence with London & Edinburgh Insurance Co (L & E) who were agents for the MIB.

[91] In April 1999, inquiry agents instructed by the MIB reported that Mr Hughes had left the address shown on the electoral register in about February 1999, and that his then current whereabouts were unknown. That address was 45 Whitworth Close, Birchwood, Warrington, Cheshire. On 19 May 1999, GLP wrote to the MIB, sending a completed application form, which, it is assumed, was an application form for an MIB agreement to be put in place in connection with this claim. On 25 May, the MIB wrote to GLP a letter in respect of the claim by Mrs Smith, saying that the inquiry agent had established that Mr Hughes had left his address in about February, adding that (a) they were awaiting confirmation from the police whether a formal accident report was 'available to clarify the insurance position and liability'; and (b) 'your client' (ie Mrs Smith) had not provided any description of the circumstances of the accident which would be required before any consideration could be given to the claim.

[92] The insurance position remained uncertain. But in about November 1999, Budget confirmed that Mr Hughes was not insured, and the Norwich Union, having merged with L & E, took over the conduct of the case on behalf of the MIB.

[93] The claim form was issued on 14 December 2000. So far as GLP were concerned, they continued to receive contradictory signals from Budget and the Norwich Union, and the insurance position remained unclear. On 10 April 2001, the claim form, particulars of claim and all relevant associated documentation were sent by first class post to Mr Hughes at 45 Whitworth Close, Birchwood, Warrington, Cheshire. The documents were not returned by the Post Office to GLP. On 15 August 2001, the MIB was joined as second defendant. On 21 August 2002, MIB made an application requesting that the court decide as a preliminary issue whether the MIB could have any liability to the claimant. The basis of the application was its contention that the claim form had not been served on Mr Hughes within the four-month period for service.

[94] The application was heard by District Judge Duerden, who gave judgment on 3 December 2002. He decided that the claim form had not been served on Mr Hughes on 12 April 2001, and dismissed the claim against both defendants. One of the issues of fact that he had to resolve was whether a letter similar to that sent by the MIB to GLP on 25 May 1999 in respect of Mrs Smith's claim had been sent by them to GLP in respect of the claimant's claim. Mr Wolstenholme asserted in his statement that the letter dated 25 May sent in respect of Mrs Smith's claim was sent to another member of the GLP legal team, and that no similar letter was received in relation to this claim, nor was a copy of the inquiry agent's report ever received by GLP. District Judge Duerden said that he was satisfied on balance that there was one person, whose reference was MBT, who was dealing with both claims.

[95] Having made that finding, the district judge turned to the question of service. He referred to r 6.5 (which deals with address for service), and in particular r 6.5(6) which provides that, where no solicitor is acting for the party to be served, and the party has not given an address for service, if the document is to be served on an individual, it must be sent or transmitted to, or left at his or her 'usual or last known residence'. There was no doubt in this case that Mr Hughes' last known residence was the address to which the claim form was sent on 10 April 2001. It was not suggested by the MIB that there was any other subsequent known address for Mr Hughes. District Judge Duerden referred to r 6.8 which provides:

a

'(1) Where it appears to the court that there is a good reason to authorise service by a method not permitted by these Rules, the court may make an order permitting service by an alternative method.

(2) An application for an order permitting service by an alternative method—(a) must be supported by evidence; (b) may be made without notice.

b

(3) An order permitting service by an alternative method must specify—(a) the method of service; and (b) the date when the document will be deemed to be served.'

[96] He said that it was 'reasonably incumbent' on a solicitor faced with a letter in the terms of the MIB letter dated 25 May 1999 to 'contemplate' an
c application for service by an alternative method under r 6.8. The most obvious alternative method would have been by service on the MIB. GLP failed to take this course even though 'they knew that sending it to the last known address of the first defendant would not result in service'. The conclusion of District Judge Duerden is encapsulated in the following passage:

d

'However generous a reading one makes of the rules and however persuasive the Court of Appeal's decision in *Anderton*'s case may be and I do not seek for a moment to detract from that; I do recognise it as a very useful decision in procedural matters as it accentuates the need for certainty but however persuasive that may be, to purport to serve at the last known
e address two years and some after the defendant has vacated it without making further inquiry cannot be doing justice between the parties. It cannot be expected that the first defendant will get to know of those proceedings and that is the purpose of service.'

In the result, he held that Mr Hughes had not been served.
f [97] On behalf of the claimant, Mr Exall submits as follows. Service on the last known residence of an individual is good service. The rules are clear and there are no grounds for construing them in any other way. Alternatively, he relies on rr 6.10 and 6.14 and the fact that the claim form was not returned undelivered to support the presumption that service had taken place. Rule 6.14(2) provides that, where the claim form is served by the claimant, he must file a certificate of service
g within seven days of service of the claim form. Rule 6.10 provides that, where a rule requires a certificate of service, the certificate must state (a) that the document has not been returned undelivered, and (b) where service is by post, the date of posting.

[98] Mr Exall submits that the district judge should have applied the
h fundamental principle to be derived from *Anderton v Clwyd CC* [2002] 3 All ER 813, [2001] 1 WLR 3174 namely that the rules for service are designed to provide certainty. In r 6.7, this is achieved by providing rules for the time when service is deemed to be effected which are not rebuttable by evidence as to when the documents are actually received. So too in relation to the address for service,
j certainty is achieved by a rule which permits service on a person's last known residence. This is a sensible pragmatic rule designed to deal with the situation which occurs where a defendant does not give an address for service as required by r 6.5(2). Moreover, the potential injustice to a defendant who has been served at his last known residence is, to some extent at least, mitigated by r 13.5(2). This provides that if a claimant who has entered judgment subsequently has good reason to believe that the particulars of claim did not reach the defendant before

the claimant entered judgment, he must file a request for the judgment to be set
aside, and apply to the court for directions.

[99] In any event, Mr Exall submits that the district judge fell into error in
relation to the facts of the case itself. The evidence did not establish that
Mr Hughes was not living at the address in April 2001. It was not reasonable to
infer from the fact that he left the address in February 1999 that he was not living
there in April 2001. All the more so in view of the fact that the documents were
not returned undelivered by the Post Office to GLP.

[100] On behalf of the MIB, Mr Gregory supports the reasoning of the district
judge. He submits that District Judge Duerden was entitled to hold that GLP, as
solicitors to the claimant, were fixed with the knowledge of the contents of the
letter of 25 May 1999. GLP cannot realistically have believed that the address
45 Whitworth Close could fairly be described as Mr Hughes' 'usual' residence, or
his 'last known residence', since it was known that this was not his residence, and
had not been his residence since February 1999. Accordingly, if they sent the
documentation to that address on 10 April 2001, GLP did so in the knowledge
that it would not be received by Mr Hughes. Mr Gregory submits that it is
implicit in r 6.5 that there is a reasonable belief on the part of the person
purporting to serve the documentation that it will come to the attention of its
intended recipient at the address served. There is nothing in *Anderton's* case
which compels the conclusion for which the claimant contends.

[101] It seems that there is some doubt as to the meaning and effect of r 6.5(6)
where service is effected on an individual at his last known residence. The notes
to the White Book (*Civil Procedure* (Autumn 2002 edn)) vol I, p 133 include the
following:

> 'The CPR do not make it clear whether service by post to a defendant's last
> known address at which he no longer resides, and the defendant does not in
> fact receive the claim, is good service.'

[102] In our judgment, the position is clear. There are two conditions
precedent for the operation of the provisions of r 6.5(6), namely that (a) no
solicitor is acting for the party to be served, and (b) the party has not given an
address for service. If those conditions are satisfied, then the rule states that the
document to be sent *must* be sent or transmitted to, or left at, the place shown in
the table. In the case of an individual, that means at his or her usual or last known
residence. The rule is plain and unqualified. We see no basis for holding that, if
the two conditions are satisfied, and the document is sent to that address, that
does not amount to good service. The rule does not say that it is not good service
if the defendant does not in fact receive the document. If that had been intended
to be the position, the rule would have said so in terms. Nor can we see any basis
for holding that, if the claimant knows or believes that the defendant is no longer
living at his or her last known residence, service may not be effected by sending
the claim form, or leaving it at, that address. That would be to fly in the face of
the clear words of the rule. The rule is intended to provide a clear and
straightforward mechanism for effecting service where the two conditions
precedent to which we have referred are satisfied.

[103] As we have said, there is no suggestion in this case that 45 Whitworth
Close was not Mr Hughes' last known residence. If the MIB had disputed the
claimant's claim that this was Mr Hughes' last known residence, then difficult
questions might have arisen. In particular, is the rule concerned with the
claimant's actual knowledge, or is it directed at the knowledge which, exercising

a reasonable diligence, he or she could acquire? We incline to the latter view, but, as we have said, the point does not arise on this appeal.

[104] But for the reasons that we have given, in our judgment District Judge Duerden misinterpreted r 6.5(6), and the appeal must be allowed.

First, second and fourth appeals dismissed, but third and fifth appeals allowed.

Melanie Martyn   Barrister.

Masterman-Lister v Brutton & Co
Masterman-Lister v Jewell and another
[2002] EWCA Civ 1889

COURT OF APPEAL, CIVIL DIVISION

KENNEDY, POTTER AND CHADWICK LJJ

12–15 NOVEMBER, 19 DECEMBER 2002

Practice – Parties – Capacity – Claimant suffering brain damage as result of road traffic accident – Claimant compromising action – Claimant seeking to sue solicitors advising him to compromise – Claimant seeking to re-open issue of capacity – Whether claimant a 'patient' under the rules of the court – Whether burden of proof on claimant to show inability of managing or administering his affairs – Test to be applied to determine whether capacity in issue – Time at which issue of capacity to be raised – RSC Ord 80, r 10 – CPR Pt 21.

The claimant was born in 1963. In 1980, he was involved in a serious road traffic accident and suffered severe brain damage. The defendants were instructed to issue a claim. In 1987, the claimant accepted an offer to compromise the action. The claimant had attempted to work after the accident, but was only able to perform menial tasks and had not worked since 1989. He lived with his parents until 1992, when he purchased his own house. In late 1993, the claimant, having been told by the defendants that his claim could not be re-opened issued a writ for damages for negligence and/or breach of contract in relation to the defendants' conduct of his litigation. The statement of claim was not served until May 1996, and the defendants in their defence asserted that the claim was statute-barred. In 1997, the claimant was advised by a consultant in neuropsychiatric rehabilitation that he was, and had been since the accident a patient within the meaning of s 94(2) of the Mental Health Act 1983, namely a person who was incapable by reason of mental disorder of managing and administering his property and affairs. The claimant then sought to reopen the settlement of his personal injury action on the basis that it had never received the approval of the court, as was required at the relevant time pursuant to RSC Ord 80, r 10. That rule which defined the term 'patient' was replaced by CPR 21.1(2)(b). A trial of a preliminary issue, in relation to both actions was ordered, as to whether the claimant had been a 'patient' within the meaning of RSC Ord 80 and/or CPR Pt 21 at any time since September 1980. The judge ruled that the court should only take over the individual's function of decision making when it was shown on the balance of probabilities that the individual did not have the capacity sufficiently to understand, absorb and retain information, including advice, relevant to the matters in question sufficiently to enable him or her to make decisions based upon such information. He then considered the evidence and concluded that since 1983 at the latest, the claimant had been fully capable of managing and administering his property and affairs and therefore was not a 'patient' for the purposes of either the Act, Ord 80 or CPR Pt 21. The claimant appealed. On appeal issues arose as to the burden of proof; the test for determining capacity to litigate and compromise; and the time at which the issue of capacity should be raised.

a **Held** – (1) The burden of proof rested on those asserting incapacity. The fact that there was evidence that as a result of a head injury sustained in an accident it was agreed that the claimant was incapable of managing his property and affairs did not mean that he could rely on the presumption of continuance. Although there was no requirement in Ord 80 of CPR Pt 21 that a judicial officer had to consider medical evidence or be satisfied as to incapacity before a person could be treated

b as a patient, following the implementation of the Human Rights Act 1988, in order that a party was not deprived of his civil rights by being treated as a patient, the court should always, as a matter of practice, at the first convenient opportunity, investigate the question of capacity whenever there was any reason to suspect that it might be absent. That meant that, even where the issue did not

c seem to be contentious, a district judge who was responsible for case management would almost certainly require the assistance of a medical report before being able to be satisfied that incapacity existed (see [17], below).

(2) For the purposes of Ord 80 and Pt 21, the test to be applied to determine a person's capacity was issue-specific. What had to be considered was whether the

d party to legal proceedings was capable of understanding, with the assistance of such proper explanation from legal advisers and experts in other disciplines as the case might require, the issues on which his consent or decision was likely to be necessary in the course of those proceedings. If the party had capacity to understand that which he needed to understand in order to pursue or defend a

e claim there was no reason why the law, whether substantive or procedural, should require the interposition of a next friend or litigation friend. Moreover, a person should not be held unable to understand the information relevant to a decision if he could understand an explanation of that information in broad terms and simple language. Furthermore, he should not be regarded as unable to make a rational decision merely because the decision which he did, in fact, make was a

f decision which would not be made by a person of ordinary prudence (see [26], [27], [55], [62], [64]–[69], [75], [78], below); *White v Fell* (12 November 1987, unreported) considered.

(3) Normally no problem arose as to when the issue of capacity should be raised. It raised itself. However, if the claimant lacked capacity and, without any

g fault on anyone's part, no-one recognised that fact, the court could regularise the position retrospectively. Under CPR 21.3(4) any step taken before a child or patient had a litigation friend was to be of no effect, unless the court otherwise ordered. Provided everyone had acted in good faith and here had been no manifest disadvantage to the party subsequently found to have been a patient at

h the relevant time the court could not refuse to regularise the position. To do otherwise would be unjust and contrary to the overriding objective of the CPR, but in any given case the ultimate decision had to depend on the particular facts. Nevertheless, finality in litigation was also important, and the rules as to capacity were not designed to provide a vehicle for re-opening litigation which having

j apparently been properly conduct had for long been understood to be at an end (see [30], [31], below).

(4) In the instant case, the judge had used the correct approach and had been entitled, on the evidence, to come to the conclusion that the claimant had been fully capable of managing and administering his property and affairs (see [54], [84], below).

Notes

a

For mental disorder and legal incapacity see 30 *Halsbury's Laws* (4th edn reissue) para 1421, and for limitation of action in cases of legal incapacity see 28 *Halsbury's Laws* (4th edn reissue) para 867.

For the Limitation Act 1980, ss 28, 38, see 24 *Halsbury's Statutes* (4th edn) (1998 reissue) 727, 741.

For the Mental Health Act 1983, ss 1(2), 94(2), see 28 *Halsbury's Statutes* (4th *b* edn) (2001 reissue) 834, 962.

Cases referred to in judgment

Ball v Mannin (1829) 3 Bli NS 1, 6 ER 569.
Banks v Goodfellow LR 5 QB 549, [1861–73] All ER Rep 47.   *c*
Beall v Smith (1873) 9 Ch App 85.
Beaney, Re [1978] 2 All ER 595, [1978] 1 WLR 770.
C (adult: refusal of treatment), Re [1994] 1 All ER 819, [1994] 1 WLR 290.
CAF, Re (23 March 1962, unreported).
Cumming, Re (1852) 1 De GM&G 537.   *d*
Durham v Durham (1885) 10 PD 80.
F v West Berkshire Health Authority (Mental Health Act Commission intervening) [1989] 2 All ER 545, [1990] 2 AC 1, [1989] 2 WLR 1025, HL.
Gibbons v Wright (1954) 91 CLR 423, Aust HC.
Hart v O'Connor [1985] 2 All ER 880, [1985] AC 1000, [1985] 3 WLR 214, PC.   *e*
Harwood v Baker (1840) 3 Moo PCC 282, 13 ER 117, PC.
Imperial Loan Co v Stone [1892] 1 QB 599, CA.
K Re, Re F [1988] 1 All ER 358, [1988] Ch 310, [1988] 2 WLR 781.
Leather v Kirby [1965] 2 All ER 441, [1965] 2 QB 367, [1965] 2 WLR 1318, CA.
Manches v Trimborn (1946) 115 LJKB 305.   *f*
Mason v Mason [1972] 3 All ER 315, [1972] 3 WLR 405.
MB (an adult: medical treatment), Re [1997] 2 FCR 541, CA.
Molton v Camroux (1849) 4 Exch 17, 154 ER 1107, Ex Ch.
Park's Estate, Re, Park v Park [1953] 2 All ER 408, [1954] P 89, [1953] 3 WLR 307, affd; [1953] 2 All ER 1411, [1954] P 112, [1953] 3 WLR 1012, CA.
S (FG), Re [1973] 1 All ER 273, [1973] 1 WLR 178.   *g*
W (Enduring Power of Attorney), Re [2001] 4 All ER 88, [2001] Ch 609, [2001] 2 WLR 957, CA.
W v L [1973] 3 All ER 884, [1974] QB 711, [1973] 3 WLR 859, CA.
White v Fell (12 November 1987, unreported).   *h*
Winterwerp v Netherlands (1979) 2 EHRR 387, [1979] ECHR 6301/73, ECtHR.

Appeal

The claimant, Martin Joseph Masterman-Lister, appealed with permission of Wright J from his decision on 15 March 2002 ([2002] EWCA Civ 1889, [2002] *j* All ER (D) 297 (Dec)) in relation to a preliminary issue, set out [1], below, ordered to be determined by Master Murray on 29 March 2000, arising out of two claims brought by the claimant against (i) Brutton & Co and (ii) Gordon Jewell and Home County Dairies in respect of personal injury resulting from a road traffic accident on 9 September 1980. The facts are set out in the judgment of Kennedy LJ.

a Brian Langstaff QC, Patricia Hitchcock and Anna Beale (instructed by Stewarts) for
   the appellant.
   Robin De Wilde QC and Nick Brown (instructed by Blake Lapthorn, Portsmouth) for
   Brutton & Co.
   Richard Methuen QC and Hugh Hamill (instructed by Clarke Willmott,
   Southampton) for Mr Jewell and Home Counties Dairies.
b Robert Francis QC for the Official Solicitor.

                                                                    Cur adv vult

   19 December 2002. The following judgments were delivered.

c KENNEDY LJ.
   [1] This is an appeal by the claimant from a decision of Wright J ([2002] EWHC
   417 (QB), [2002] All ER (D) 247 (Mar)) in relation to a preliminary issue namely:

        'Whether the claimant has been a patient within the meaning of RSC
        Order 80 and/or Part 21 of the CPR at any time since the 8th September 1980
d   and, if so, what are the period or periods when the claimant has been a
        patient between the 8th September 1980 to date.'

   On 29 March 2000 Master Murray ordered the trial of that issue in relation to
   both of the claimant's actions, and after a lengthy hearing in January and
   February 2002 the judgment was delivered on 15 March 2002.
e

   BACKGROUND
   [2] For this section of my judgment I am indebted to the judgment of the trial
   judge. The claimant was born on 24 July 1963, and on 9 September 1980, when
   riding a motorcycle to his work as an engineering apprentice, he collided with a
f milk float driven by Mr Jewell, an employee of Home Counties Dairies. The
   claimant sustained very severe injuries, including a serious head injury. He was
   in hospital for over three months and when he returned to work in June 1981 he
   was only able to perform routine clerical work, which he continued to perform
   until March 1989 when he resigned. He has barely worked since that date.
   [3] The claimant's parents consulted a solicitor, Mr Wilks of Brutton & Co,
g soon after the accident, and on 24 December 1980 proceedings were commenced
   against Mr Jewell and Home Counties Dairies. It took some time to gather
   together the medical reports and the information in relation to financial loss, so
   the statement of claim was not served until 7 September 1985. The defence
   denied liability and alleged contributory negligence which counsel for the
h claimant had advised could be assessed as high as 50%. In October 1985 there was
   a payment into court, which was not accepted, but on 11 September 1987 the
   payment into court was increased to £70,000. Two days previously the claimant,
   his father and his solicitor had attended a lengthy conference with his counsel in
   London. At that time counsel had valued the claim at £117,000 on full liability,
j and recommended serious consideration of any payment into court representing
   half of that sum.
   [4] Nevertheless the claimant was not happy with the offer of £70,000, and on
   13 September 1987 he wrote to Mr Wilks. As the judge said, the letter asked three
   relevant and sensible questions as to the effect of delaying an acceptance. The
   claimant's father said in evidence that the letter, although physically written by
   the claimant, was largely dictated to him by his father, and that seems to be borne

out by the entry for that day in the claimant's diary, but the entry also says that
he and his father 'discussed all the possibilities of my court case' including
'accepting their present offer or waiting a while'.

[5]   On 15 September 1987 there was a conference at the offices of
Brutton & Co in Fareham attended by Mr Wilks, the claimant, both his parents,
and Mr Boot, a financial director of the claimant's father's company and a family
confidante. The payment into court was fully discussed. The attendance note of
the solicitor records that the claimant, with the advice of his parents, instructed
the solicitor to tell the other side that if a further £10,000 was paid into court the
claimant would accept it. Mr Wilks did as instructed. The defendants' solicitors
took instructions from their clients, and were authorised to pay a further £6000
provided there was acceptance within 24 hours. The claimant's father was
telephoned and was, it seems, delighted. The claimant was markedly less
enthusiastic but after considering the offer overnight he agreed to accept it, and
the action was therefore settled for £76,000 and costs.

[6]   For a time the claimant remained at home but in 1992, three years after he
had given up work, he used £55,000 of his capital to buy a house. There he lives
alone relying for income on state benefits. It was common ground before the
judge that because of his physical and mental disabilities he is very unlikely ever
to be able to obtain worthwhile remunerative employment.

[7]   In late 1993 the claimant, having been told by Brutton & Co that his claim
could not be reopened, consulted his brother-in-law Mr Knowles, who is a
solicitor, and on 17 December 1993 a writ was issued against Brutton & Co for
damages for negligence and/or breach of contract in relation to their conduct of
his litigation. The statement of claim was not served until 21 May 1996, and not
surprisingly the defence which was served on 6 February 1997 asserts that the
claim is statute-barred.

[8]   In June 1997 the claimant was examined by Dr Martyn Rose, a consultant
in neuro-psychiatric rehabilitation. His view was and is that ever since the time
of his accident the claimant has been a 'patient', within the meaning of s 94(2) of
the Mental Health Act 1983, that is to say a person who 'is incapable, by reason
of mental disorder, of managing and administering his property and affairs'. The
claimant then sought to reopen the settlement of his claim in the original
proceedings on the basis that it has never received the approval of the court, as
then required by RSC Ord 80, r 10 (now CPR 21.10). Thus in March 2000
Master Murray ordered the trial of the same preliminary issue in relation to both
actions.

RSC ORD 80

[9]   The present CPR did not become effective until April 1999, so in this case
we are primarily concerned with the previous provisions relating to litigants
under a disability which were to be found in RSC Ord 80. Within that Order, r 1
read:

'In this Order—
"the Act" means the Mental Health Act 1983;
"patient" means a person who, by reason of mental disorder within the
meaning of the Act, is incapable of managing and administering his property
and affairs;
"person under disability" means a person who is an infant or a patient.'

a Before I look more closely at that definition of a patient it is worth noting some of the consequences of being a patient. Rule 2(1) provides: 'A person under disability may not bring, or make a claim in, any proceedings except by his next friend'. Rule 2(3) provides: 'A next friend or guardian ad litem of a person under disability must act by a solicitor'. Rule 10 provides:

b 'Where in any proceedings money is claimed by or on behalf of a person under disability, no settlement, compromise or payment and no acceptance of money paid into court, whenever entered into or made, shall so far as it relates to that person's claim be valid without the approval of the Court.'

c The claimant was an infant when he began his action against Mr Jewell and Home Counties Dairies in December 1980. That disability was recognised and his father agreed to act and did act as next friend, so the proceedings were properly instituted. On 24 July 1981 the claimant reached the age of 18, and on 17 August 1981 he served notice of adoption in relation to his action. At that stage it had not occurred to anyone that the claimant might still be under a disability because he might be a patient for the purposes of RSC Ord 80, r 1. At no time d prior to 1987 did any doctor raise that possibility, although Professor McLellan now says that it was implicit in his reports of October 1984 and September 1997. The claimant's solicitor, Mr Wilks, was an experienced personal injuries lawyer, and the possibility did not occur to him; nor did it occur to Mr Walker, the experienced personal injuries counsel who was instructed, and Mr Langstaff QC, who has appeared for the claimant before us, has made it clear that the lawyers e originally instructed are not now being criticised for failing to recognise that the claimant might be a patient. Nonetheless, Mr Langstaff contends, as it was contended by Mrs Cox QC, as she then was, in the court below that at all times from the accident onwards the claimant was a patient who could only litigate or continue to litigate by his next friend, and who could only settle a claim with the f approval of the court.

What does the definition mean?

[10] Mental disorder is defined in s 1(2) of the 1983 Act, and it seems to be common ground that if at any material time the claimant was incapable of managing and administering his property and affairs that was by reason of mental g disorder within the meaning of the Act. So what is meant by being 'incapable of managing and administering his property and affairs?' The same wording can be found in s 94(2) in Pt VII of the 1983 Act which deals with the powers of the Court of Protection to manage the property and affairs of patients. Section 94(2) provides:

h 'The functions of the judge under this Part of this Act shall be exerciseable where, after considering medical evidence, he is satisfied that a person is incapable, by reason of mental disorder, of managing and administering his property and affairs; and a person as to whom the judge is so satisfied is referred to in this Part of this Act as a patient.'

j Although the grounds of appeal begin with the assertion in para 1(a) that the judge erred in law in that he applied the wrong test for capacity, and various criticisms are made of the way in which he formulated the test, it emerged after Mr Langstaff had concluded his submissions as to the law that there is no criticism of the judge's formulation. What is criticised is his application of the law as he found it to be to the evidence in the case. Nevertheless permission to appeal was

given by the trial judge because there is an important issue of law involved in
relation to which there has been no previous decision of this court, and for that *a*
reason we have had the benefit of submissions from Mr Robert Francis QC on
behalf of the Official Solicitor, so I do need to look at the legal position with some
care.

Capacity at different times and in different contexts   *b*

[11] Although as I have said, we are primarily concerned with whether or not
the claimant was a patient for the purposes of RSC Ord 80, r 1 in September 1987,
it is also necessary to consider his capacity at other times and in other contexts
since that date.

[12] First, it has to be recognised that someone who is treated as a patient for   *c*
the purposes of RSC Ord 80, r 1, who litigates by a next friend, is not necessarily
and may never become accepted by the Court of Protection as a patient pursuant
to s 94(2) of the 1983 Act. As is clear from the wording of s 94(2) the jurisdiction
of the Court of Protection is only exercised when, after considering medical
evidence, a nominated judge is satisfied as to the person's incapacity. Under
Ord 80, r 1 no judicial officer has to consider medical evidence or be satisfied as   *d*
to incapacity before a person can be treated as a patient. So the judge was in error
when he indicated [2002] All ER (D) 247 (Mar) at [29] that where a person was so
treated there was a 'consequent involvement of the Court of Protection'.
However that error had no effect whatsoever on the judge's conclusions and I
need say no more about it.   *e*

[13] Secondly, the issue of incapacity arises in relation to the claimant's ability
to sue his former solicitors during the six years after September 1987, and the
relevant provision is to be found in s 28(1) of the Limitation Act 1980 which
reads—

'... if on the date when any right of action accrued for which a period of   *f*
limitation is prescribed by this Act, the person to whom it accrued was under
a disability, the action may be brought at any time before the expiration of
six years from the date when he ceased to be under a disability or died
(whichever first occurred) notwithstanding that the period of limitation has
expired.'   *g*

Section 38(2) and (3) provide:

'(2) For the purposes of this Act a person shall be treated as under a
disability while he is an infant, or of unsound mind.
(3) For the purposes of subsection (2) above a person is of unsound mind if   *h*
he is a person who, by reason of mental disorder within the meaning of the
Mental Health Act 1983, is incapable of managing and administering his
property and affairs.'

Section 38(4) deals with circumstances when a person is to be conclusively   *j*
presumed to be of unsound mind, generally speaking when detained in hospital.

[14] Thirdly, the question arises of the claimant's capacity in relation to the
commencement and conduct of the two actions which are before us. It is
Mr Langstaff's contention that the claimant is a patient as defined by CPR
21.1(2)(b) which provides:

a
'"patient" means a person who by reason of mental disorder within the meaning of the Mental Health Act 1983 is incapable of managing and administering his own affairs.'

The wording, it will be noted, differs slightly from the wording in RSC Ord 80, r 1, in that the title of the 1983 Act is set out in full, and the words 'property and affairs' are replaced by 'own affairs'. Mr Francis submits that the change may have some significance.

b

Capacity is important

[15] Quite apart from personal injury litigation it is clear that the issue of capacity is important to the Official Solicitor who, we are told, acts at any one time for about 1700 'patients' in civil and family proceedings. An unknown number of other persons also act as litigation friends. In the Court of Protection 15,000 applications to register enduring powers of attorney are received each year on the ground that the donees have reason to believe that the donors are incapable of managing their property and affairs, and at any given time the Court of Protection has jurisdiction over a large number of estates of patients.

c

d

Business affairs, presumptions and the burden of proof

[16] There is no definition in the 1983 Act or in the Rules of the Supreme Court or in the Civil Procedure Rules to assist as to the meaning of 'incapable of managing and administering his ... affairs' but in *F v West Berkshire Health Authority (Mental Health Act Commission intervening)* [1989] 2 All ER 545 at 554, [1990] 2 AC 1 at 59, per Lord Brandon of Oakbrook, it was held that Pt VII of the 1983 Act, which includes s 94(2), does not extend to physical care and/or treatment. It includes 'only business matters, legal transactions and other dealings of a similar kind'.

e

f
[17] It is common ground that all adults must be presumed to be competent to manage their property and affairs until the contrary is proved, and that the burden of proof rests on those asserting incapacity. Mr Langstaff submitted that where, as in the present case, there is evidence that as a result of a head injury sustained in an accident the doctors who have been consulted agree that for a time the claimant was incapable of managing his property and affairs he can rely on the presumption of continuance. That I would not accept. Of course, if there is clear evidence of incapacity for a considerable period then the burden of proof may be more easily discharged, but it remains on whoever asserts incapacity. Furthermore it has to be recognised that when a person is treated as a patient, whether or not as a result of an order of the court, he is thereby deprived of civil rights, in particular his right to sue or defend in his own name, and his right to compromise in litigation without the approval of the court. They are important rights, long cherished by English law and now safeguarded by the European Convention for the Protection of Human Rights and Fundamental Freedoms 1950 (as set out in Sch 1 to the Human Rights Act 1998). In *Re Cumming* (1852) 1 De GM&G 537, Knight Bruce LJ said at 557:

g

h

j

'It is the right of an English person to require that the free use of his property, and personal freedom, shall not be taken from him on the ground of alleged lunacy, without being allowed the opportunity of establishing his sanity or denying his insanity before a jury as a contesting party, not merely as a subject of inquiry.'

Neither RSC Ord 80 nor CPR 21.1 seem to meet that requirement, which is underlined by arts 6 and 8 of the convention. In *Winterwerp v Netherlands* (1979) 2 EHRR 387, [1979] ECHR 6301/73, a Dutch national detained in hospital complained that his detention had divested him of his capacity to administer his property, and thus there had been determination of his civil rights and obligations without the guarantee of a judicial procedure, as laid down in art 6(1) of the convention. That complaint was accepted by the European Court of Human Rights, but neither Ord 80 nor CPR 21.1 contains any requirement for a judicial determination of the question of whether or not capacity exists. Mr Francis submits, and I accept, that this is a matter which should be considered by the Rules Committee, and meanwhile courts should always, as a matter of practice, at the first convenient opportunity, investigate the question of capacity whenever there is any reason to suspect that it may be absent (e g significant head injury) other than in cases where there has already been an order pursuant to s 94(2) of the 1983 Act. That means that, even where the issue does not seem to be contentious, a district judge who is responsible for case management will almost certainly require the assistance of a medical report before being able to be satisfied that incapacity exists. In this respect, an admission said to have been made by a person alleged to lack capacity cannot be regarded as being of great weight because of his or her alleged incapacity. The judge may consider that he would be assisted by seeing the person alleged to lack capacity, a view expressed by Wright J in this case. In my view it would be wrong to attempt to compel that person to attend, but the judge can always make his view clear, and in most cases that indication, together with a reminder as to the burden of proof, should suffice.

If capacity is in issue how should it be decided?

[18] In 1962 Wilberforce J in *Re CAF* (23 March 1962, unreported), held that, when considering a person's capacity to manage and administer his property and affairs, it is necessary to have regard to the complexity and importance of that person's property and affairs. This has been a matter of some debate in Australia, where there has been a suggestion that the test might be that of ability to deal in a reasonably competent fashion with the ordinary affairs of man, but in *White v Fell* (12 November 1987, unreported) where the issue of capacity arose in the context of limitation, Boreham J said at page 9–10 of the transcript:

'The expression "incapable of managing her own affairs and property" must be construed in a common sense way as a whole. It does not call for proof of complete incapacity. On the other hand, it is not enough to prove that the plaintiff is now substantially less capable of managing her own affairs and property than she would have been had the accident not occurred. I have no doubt that the plaintiff is quite incapable of managing unaided a large sum of money such as the sort of sum that would be appropriate compensation for her injuries. That, however, is not conclusive. Few people have the capacity to manage all their affairs unaided ... It may be that she would have chosen, and would choose now, not to take advice, but that is not the question. The question is: is she capable of doing so? To have that capacity she requires first the insight and understanding of the fact that she has a problem in respect of which she needs advice ... Secondly, having identified the problem, it will be necessary for her to seek an appropriate adviser and to instruct him with sufficient clarity to enable him to understand the problem and to advise her appropriately ... Finally, she needs

a
sufficient mental capacity to understand and to make decisions based upon, or otherwise give effect to, such advice as she may receive.'

So the whole test was related to the individual plaintiff and her immediate problems. That was the approach adopted by Wright J in the present case, and before us everyone has accepted it to be the right approach. Mr Francis submits that the change in the wording from RSC Ord 80 to CPR 21.1 emphasises the
b
need to focus on the litigation under consideration rather than the whole of the claimant's business affairs and, although it could be argued that a different approach has to be taken in relation to s 28(1) of the 1980 Act, the words used relate the disability to the specific right of action.

[19] An application to the Court of Protection under Pt VII of the 1983 Act is
c
different. There the judge must consider the totality of the property and affairs of the alleged patient, and no doubt if it is shown that he lacks the capacity to manage a significant part of his affairs the court will be prepared to act, exercising control in such a way that the patient continues to have control in relation to matters which he can handle.

d
[20] The decision of Boreham J in *White*'s case ([2002] All ER (D) 247 (Mar)) gives a clear indication of how he thought that capacity should be judged in the context of personal injuries litigation, and Wright J followed the same path. He said (at [29]) that the court should only take over the individual's function of decision-making—

e
'... when it is shown on the balance of probabilities that such person does not have the capacity sufficiently to understand, absorb and retain information (including advice) relevant to the matters in question sufficiently to enable him or her to make decisions based upon such information.'

f
[21] Mr Langstaff does not take issue with that approach, but he submits that, when the decision has to be made in relation to a claimant in existing or contemplated personal injuries litigation, what has to be considered is not only the part which a litigant must play in litigation up to the time when judgment will be delivered, but also his capacity thereafter to manage any proceeds of litigation. In this respect the focus must be on the capacity or ability of the individual and
g
not upon the actual outcome. A litigant who meets the criteria for capacity should still be regarded as a patient even if it can be shown that he has in fact made wise decisions and taken good advice. What he has done is relevant but not determinative in considering whether the criteria are or were satisfied at the relevant time.

h
[22] There is no reported English decision directly concerned with the capacity to litigate and compromise but the courts have considered capacity in other contexts, for example the capacity to make a will (*Bankes v Goodfellow* [1870] LR 5 QB 549). In the limitation case of *Leather v Kirby* [1965] 2 All ER 441 at 444, [1965] 2 QB 367 at 384, Lord Denning MR found that the plaintiff had no insight
j
at all into his mental state. 'He was not capable of instructing a solicitor properly. He certainly was not capable of exercising any reasonable judgment on a possible settlement.' Accordingly the action should have been started by a next friend. It was not, but that was put right at the trial when at the suggestion of the judge a next friend was appointed.

[23] In *Re Beaney* [1978] 2 All ER 595 at 601, [1978] 1 WLR 770 at 774 the court was concerned with the validity of a gift made by a donor suffering from senile

dementia, Mr Martin Nourse QC, sitting as deputy judge of the Chancery
Division, said:

> 'The degree or extent of understanding required in respect of any
> instrument is relative to the particular transaction which it is to effect. In the
> case of a will the degree required is always high. In the case of a contract, a
> deed made for consideration or a gift inter vivos, whether by deed or
> otherwise, the degree required varies with the circumstances of the
> transaction. Thus, at one extreme, if the subject-matter and value of a gift
> are trivial in relation to the donor's other assets a low degree of
> understanding will suffice. But, at the other, if its effect is to dispose of the
> donor's only asset of value and thus for practical purposes to pre-empt the
> devolution of his estate under his will or on his intestacy, then the degree of
> understanding required is as high as that required for a will, and the donor
> must understand the claims of all potential donees and the extent of the
> property to be disposed of.'

[24] In *Re C (adult: refusal of treatment)* [1994] 1 All ER 819 at 822, [1994] 1 WLR
290 at 292 a paranoid schizophrenic sought an injunction to prevent the
amputation of his infected leg without his written consent, and Thorpe J said:

> 'For the patient offered amputation to save life, there are three stages to the
> decision: (1) to take in and retain treatment information, (2) to believe it and
> (3) to weigh that information, balancing risks and needs.'

[25] In the subsequent medical treatment case of *Re MB (an adult: medical
treatment)* [1997] 2 FCR 541 at 553–554, Butler-Sloss LJ said:

> 'A person lacks capacity if some impairment or disturbance of mental
> functioning renders the person unable to make a decision whether to
> consent to or to refuse treatment. That inability to make a decision will
> occur when
>
> (a) The patient is unable to comprehend and retain the information which
> is material to the decision, especially as to the likely consequences of having
> or not having the treatment in question.
>
> (b) The patient is unable to use the information and weigh it in the balance
> as part of the process of arriving at the decision.'

[26] Mr Langstaff's formulation of that test for present purposes was that there
must be: (1) understanding, and (2) retention of matters relevant to the decision,
followed by (3) evaluation. Mr Francis submitted that a person's ability to
manage his or her property and affairs requires an ability to make and
communicate, and where appropriate give effect to, all decisions required in
relation to them. So the mental abilities required include the ability to recognise
a problem, obtain and receive, understand and retain relevant information,
including advice; the ability to weigh the information (including that derived
from advice) in the balance in reaching a decision, and the ability to communicate
that decision. Mr Francis further submits that the court should have regard to the
complexity of decisions under consideration but not to the court's own valuation
of the gravity of those decisions because it is not for the court to decide in a
non-medical treatment case what is or is not serious in the life of the person
before it. To that extent he is critical of the use by Wright J of the word
'sufficiently' at [29] of his judgment and also of the judge's failure specifically to

a refer to the ability to weigh information in the balance. Whilst I agree with the approach put forward by Mr Francis, I do not accept his criticisms of the trial judge. In my judgment the judge's use of the word 'sufficiently' was appropriate on each occasion, and the concept articulated by the judge of having sufficient information to enable one to make decisions based on that information is simply another way of referring to the ability to weigh information in the balance.

b [27] What, however, does seem to me to be of some importance is the issue-specific nature of the test; that is to say the requirement to consider the question of capacity in relation to the particular transaction (its nature and complexity) in respect of which the decisions as to capacity fall to be made. It is not difficult to envisage claimants in personal injury actions with capacity to deal with all matters and take all 'lay client' decisions related to their actions up to and

c including a decision whether or not to settle, but lacking capacity to decide (even with advice) how to administer a large award. In such a case I see no justification for the assertion that the claimant is to be regarded as a patient from the commencement of proceedings. Of course, as Boreham J said in White's case, capacity must be approached in a common sense way, not by reference to each

d step in the process of litigation, but bearing in mind the basic right of any person to manage his property and affairs for himself, a right with which no lawyer and no court should rush to interfere.

Causation and other matters

[28] Where a lack of capacity to manage property and affairs is demonstrated

e the court will have to determine whether the incapacity is due to mental disorder as defined in the 1983 Act. As indicated in [10], above that is not a problem in this case, and I therefore decline to comment on the way in which mental illness was defined in *W v L* [1973] 3 All ER 884 at 890, [1974] QB 711 at 719.

[29] The conclusion that in law capacity depends on time and context means

f that inevitably a decision as to capacity in one context does not bind a court which has to consider the same issue in a different context. A person may be a patient for purposes of RSC Ord 80, r 1 or CPR 21.1, but not for the purposes of s 94(2), and any medical witness asked to assist in relation to capacity therefore needs to know the area of the alleged patient's activities in relation to which his advice is sought. The final decision as to capacity, it is agreed, rests with the court but, in

g almost every case, the court will need medical evidence to guide it.

When should the issue of capacity be raised?

[30] Normally no problem arises as to when the issue of capacity should be raised. It raises itself. A responsible solicitor acting for a claimant or defendant

h has doubts about the capacity of his client, and seeks a medical opinion. If the opinion suggests that the client lacks the necessary capacity then the solicitor arranges for the appointment of a litigation friend. Sometimes the doubts may arise in relation to an opponent acting in person, and then it may be appropriate to bring the issue of capacity before the court. Maybe, as suggested by

j Mr Methuen QC, for Mr Jewell and Home Counties Dairies, it would help if the initiating court forms (N1 and N9) or the personal injuries protocol were to contain some material drawing attention to the issue of capacity, and it certainly seems desirable for some change to be made so that a person cannot, as at present, become a patient for the purposes of CPR 21.1 without knowing what is going on. That could be achieved by requiring that, unless the court otherwise orders, anyone intending to become a litigation friend without a court order served upon the intended patient notice of his intention to act as litigation friend, and a copy of the certificate of suitability, so that the intended patient is then in the same position that he would be in were there to be an application for a litigation friend to be appointed by order of the court (see CPR 21 PD 3.3(2)). But what if, as is said to have been the case here, the claimant did lack capacity but, without any fault on anyone's part, no one recognised that fact? RSC Ord 80 and CPR 21 are worded in such a way as to indicate that in that event the litigation is ineffective and decisions made in the course of litigation are invalid—see, for example, Ord 80, rr 2(1) and 10, CPR 21.2(1) and 21.10(1), but CPR 21.3(4) does suggest a solution. It provides: 'Any step taken before a child or patient has a litigation friend shall be of no effect unless the court otherwise orders.'

[31] So a court can regularise the position retrospectively, and that was also possible under the RSC (see *Leather v Kirby* [1965] 2 All ER 441, [1965] 2 QB 367). Provided everyone has acted in good faith and there has been no manifest disadvantage to the party subsequently found to have been a patient at the relevant time I cannot envisage any court refusing to regularise the position. To do otherwise would be unjust and contrary to the overriding objective of the CPR, but in any given case the ultimate decision must depend on the particular facts. In the context of litigation rules as to capacity are designed to ensure that claimants and defendants who would otherwise be at a disadvantage are properly protected, and in some cases that parties to litigation are not pestered by other parties who should be to some extent restrained. However, finality in litigation is also important, and the rules as to capacity are not designed to provide a vehicle for reopening litigation which having apparently been properly conducted (whatever the wisdom of the individual decisions in relation to it) has for long been understood to be at an end.

THE FACTS—CRITICISMS

[32] I turn now to what is really at the heart of the claimant's case, namely the way in which the judge applied the law to the evidence. Mr Langstaff, and Miss Hitchcock in reply, make a number of criticisms, which I can summarise as follows: (1) The judge failed to have sufficient regard to and failed to address the agreed consequences of the serious head injury, namely serious memory deficit, dysexecutive syndrome and pain. The medical evidence, it is said, was not properly analysed. (2) The judge failed to focus on the ability of the claimant to make decisions at the relevant time, and instead looked at outcomes, at decisions made with the benefit of close parental support. (3) The judge failed to distinguish between, on the one hand the acknowledged ability of the claimant to deal with lesser problems such as handling relatively small sums of money, and on the other hand his contested ability to make appropriate decisions in relation to, for example, large sums. (4) The judge failed to give sufficient weight not only to the claimant's medical witnesses but also to his lay witnesses, namely his parents, Mr Vetterlein and Mr Chidgey. (5) The judge gave too much weight to the claimant's diaries and too little weight to other evidence indicative of impaired decision-making capacity. In order to evaluate these criticisms it is necessary to look first at what was common ground, the outline history, and the extent to which the experts disagreed before turning to look at the evidence and the judge's evaluation.

Common ground and medical reports

a

[33] The accident in which the claimant was injured having happened in September 1980 when he was 17 years of age, the claimant returned to work after about nine months. His orthopaedic injuries and his frontal lobe injury meant that it was impossible for him to return to work as an engineering apprentice, but he was given routine clerical work, and his claim for damages for personal
b injuries against the driver of the milk float and that driver's employers was pursued. That meant that the claimant was in reasonably regular contact with his then solicitor, Mr Wilks, an experienced personal injuries lawyer, and was examined by a number of doctors. With the possible exception of Professor McLellan no one is known to have voiced any misgivings about his capacity to
c manage his own affairs, including in particular the litigation upon which he was then embarked.

[34] In September 1987 that litigation was brought to an end in circumstances to which I have already referred. The claimant was then working for British Aerospace and living at home. In 1989 he gave up his job and in 1992 he moved to
d his own house. He then began the present proceedings, and in June 1997 he was examined by Dr Martyn Rose, to whose reports I have already referred (see [8], above). Over the next four-and-a-half years the claimant was examined by a total of six consultants, including Dr Rose. Dr Moffatt, a neurologist, and Dr Powell, a clinical psychologist, were, like Dr Rose, instructed by the claimant's present solicitors. Broadly speaking their expertise was matched by that of
e Dr Jacobson, a neuro-psychiatarist, Dr Roberts, a neurologist, and Dr Leng, a neuro-psychologist, all of whom were instructed by solicitors acting for the defendants. In preparation for the trial the doctors were paired off by reference to their areas of expertise, and in January 2002 each pair of doctors produced a joint report indicating what could and could not be agreed. The reports indicate a large
f measure of agreement as to the nature of the head injury and its effects, and I quote short extracts from each joint report:

(1) Dr Rose and Dr Jacobson

g   'Dr Jacobson considers that the claimant regained capacity because the aggravating effects of depression on cognitive functions lessened as his depression improved. Dr Jacobson notes that the bulk of cognitive recovery after brain injury occurs in the first two years, with small diminishing degrees of further recovery in year three, and the time point of regaining capacity at
h   up to three years is marked by resolution of depression and reaching a plateau of cognitive recovery.

        Dr Rose does not accept that the claimant regained capacity. Neither does he believe that before 1984 capacity was caused by fluctuating moods. He believes that Mr Masterman-Lister's cognitive abilities will always have been
j   significantly effected to the point of rendering him a patient within the meaning of the 1983 Mental Health Act, and that the fluctuating mood will have simply added to the level of incapacity.'

The report then goes on to deal with the significance of the claimant's diaries and other evidence in relation to the claimant's life since 1980, about which the doctors were not agreed.

(2) Dr Moffatt and Dr Roberts

They agreed that:

a

'He sustained a severe brain injury in a road accident on 9 September 1980 due to concussion and anoxic brain damage or both. He has been left with little in the way of physical disabilities or impairment of his general intellectual functions as a result, but has remained with an unreliable memory, his abilities to organise his life and affairs are affected, and his personality changed.

b

The tests carried out earlier after the head injury and more recently by four neuro-psychologists have all confirmed a memory impairment without evidence of general intellectual deterioration. All three neuro-psychologists who have tested him recently have found some impairment of functions generally accepted to be subserved by the frontal lobes of the brain.'

c

They disagreed 'about the extent to which the brain injury has affected his ability to manage his affairs since the accident.' Again there was consideration of the diaries, and the evidence from other sources.

d

(3) Dr Leng and Dr Powell

After expressing similar views as to the head injury and its effects their joint report states:

'We agree that his neuro-psychological test performance is not so bad that the results speak for themselves and utterly rule out his having capacity.

e

Conversely his neuro-psychological test performance is not so preserved that it can be taken for granted that he has capacity.

Rather, the neuro-psychological test results should be seen as one strand of evidence, certainly raising the issue of capacity but needing to be considered in conjunction with all other sources of evidence.

In other words, at this level of deficit of test performance, some patients will have capacity, and some will not, depending on the entirety of evidence and on the precise circumstances.

f

We fully understand that ultimately it is a decision for the court as to whether he is capable of managing his own affairs, but we have formed our own view of all the material and Dr Leng leans to the view that he does have capacity and Dr Powell leans to the view that he does not.

g

In brief, Dr Leng feels that the diary entries and letters seem to demonstrate sufficent capacity to manage his own affairs, and that there is no reason to suppose that he was not also so capable at the time of accepting the offer of settlement (i e by the time the settlement was accepted his recovery had long since plateaued). On the other hand, Dr Powell feels that the diaries were not compiled with the intent of collecting evidence on capacity, but even so, the diaries and letters do yield evidence of rigidity of thinking, poor judgment, immaturity, cognitive deficit and vulnerability, which when taken in conjunction with the deficit of mind evident on tests, indicates that he needs the Court of Protection to safeguard his interests.'

h

j

[35] The last joint report, in particular, highlights the point that in this case the medical evidence on testing does not speak for itself. Test results are one strand of evidence, to be considered by the court with all other sources, and as to the conclusion which should be reached it is clear that the experienced consultants were not agreed. They were all called to give evidence at the trial, and it can be

a seen from the transcripts of evidence that their positions remained very much as they had been before the trial began.

The medical evidence at trial

[36] Mr Langstaff drew our attention to passages in the transcripts of the evidence of Dr Powell and Dr Moffatt which emphasised the importance of the
b memory deficit and its impact upon the decision-making process. He pointed out, rightly, that Dr Roberts accepts that as a result of his head injury the claimant is vulnerable. He said so in his letter of 14 March 2001. Dr Roberts would like to see the claimant 'contributing to a discussion of his financial needs with other trustees, who will not allow him to have full control'. But it is important to see how that letter goes on. Dr Roberts continued:
c

'It is not my view that this makes him incapable of understanding and managing his life otherwise without supervision. The question is clearly one of degree, which is not appropriately assessed by judging everyone with some impairment of frontal lobe function as incapable of managing their affairs.'
d

[37] Dr Powell in his report of 5 June 2001 said that the claimant:

'Needs supervision in managing any large sum of money. Therefore, by definition, he was incapable of deciding for himself whether the offer he was made in settlement of his claim was fair or not.'
e

That, as Mr Langstaff concedes, is a total non-sequitur.

[38] Mr Langstaff submitted that Dr Roberts' conclusion that for many years the claimant has not been a patient within the meaning of RSC Ord 80, r 1 is attributable to the doctor's rejection of the paternalism of the Court of Protection, and he further submitted that Dr Leng and Dr Jacobson relied not on
f clinical examination or medical assessment of injury, but rather on their view of the diaries even though Dr Leng described the entries as shallow, repetitive, banal and immature. Mr Langstaff submitted that at the end of the day the judge had a lot of evidence of incapacity coming not only from the doctors but also from the claimant's parents and friends, which was met only by reference to the
g diaries. I am afraid that I regard that as a misrepresentation of the position. Each of the doctors was plainly attempting to assist the court by evaluating the position overall, recognising that at the end of the day it was for the judge, in the light of the all of the evidence, to reach a conclusion. This was not a case where there was a strong case for the claimant which called for an answer. It was, on the contrary, a case where capacity had to be assessed in relation to a spectrum, and
h that is neatly illustrated by one answer given by Dr Moffatt when asked about the distinction between his evidence and that of Dr Roberts. He said:

'I suppose really at the end of the day the distinction is … Dr Roberts seems to suggest that a form of benign paternalism is easily sufficient to support this man and … I would plump for the more Draconian approach.'
j

Non-medical evidence at trial

[39] The claimant did not give evidence but his parents did, and so did two of his friends, Mr Vetterlein and Mr Chidgey. The court also heard from Professor McLellan and Mr Wilks. Mr Langstaff invited our attention to the evidence of Mr Vetterlein where he describes the claimant as being unable to weigh up the

pros and cons. He said of the plaintiff 'you can almost see the cogs not meshing' and he spoke of the claimant's failure to make progress with applications for benefits. Similarly, Mr Chidgey said that the claimant is 'not able to cope with complex situations or things were there is more than one element ... he also has a tendency to see what he can see very much in black and white.' Mr Langstaff submitted that the evidence of Mr Vetterlein and Mr Chidgey and the other lay evidence was important evidence which the judge failed sufficiently to analyse.

[40] In addition to the oral evidence the judge had before him a mass of documentary evidence, including in particular the claimant's diaries kept throughout the relevant period, and his letters. From those sources Mr Langstaff drew our attention to seven entries which, he submitted, demonstrated the claimant's lack of capacity in relation to matters of substance:

'(1) On 1 November 1987, soon after his claim was settled, the claimant wrote in his diary that he would give every single penny he had away to be able to go out with a girl with whom he was then infatuated.

(2) On 29 December 1987 the claimant took a different girl to a shop and bought her a music centre. We were told that it cost £336·70.

(3) On 25 April 1989 the claimant recorded receiving a very troubling letter from the Vegan Society which was in financial difficulty. He went to the building society where his money was invested, and drew £500, £125 for a life membership and £375 as a donation.

(4) On 25 September 1990 the claimant was interviewed at Lymington Police Station after taking part in an anti-hunt demonstration during the course of which a van had been burnt. Part of the police record of the interview reads:

"He tried to explain that the two girls had nothing to do with the arson but were unfortunate in that they happened to be with him. He offered to pay all of any subsequent claim for compensation."

It was submitted to us that his offer was indicative of financial irresponsibility. It could, of course, have been a very sensible and responsible attempt to avert a prosecution.

(5) In a letter to a friend written in July 1994 the claimant explained how he had caused trouble at a site office of some builders. The police had to be called and the claimant told the duty sergeant that his brother-in-law was a London solicitor and that he had numerous dealing[s] with legal matters before. Whatever view one takes of the conduct as recorded it is difficult to see how it can be said to demonstrate any lack of capacity.

(6) In another letter written in December 1994 the claimant describes breaking the release valve of a pressure cooker, and going to buy a replacement. He lost it on the way home and got another one next day. He then found the one that he had lost, and found a spare one at home.

(7) On 28 April 1996 in another letter the claimant records being criticised by a girl friend because he had overstocked his freezer with some items (i e vol-au-vent cases and vegan sausages). Plainly he was not keeping proper control of the contents of his freezer, as he acknowledged.'

[41] Mr Langstaff also reminded us that after leaving British Aerospace the claimant was at times unrealistic when seeking employment, regarding himself, for example, as capable of using ladders.

The judge's approach

a
[42] Having dealt with matters of law the judge turned to the evidence, and he began with the medical evidence, pointing out what was agreed. There was, as the judge recorded ([2002] All ER (D) 247 (Mar) at [32]), a 'significant impairment of executive function ... compounded by a very serious deficit of memory'. To some extent the claimant could compensate for his defective memory by using
b
his diary and keeping lists, but the judge went on to point out:

'The dysexecutive syndrome itself involves changes in personality such as obsessionality, immaturity, rigidity of thinking, eccentricity and emotional outbursts. The effect of this syndrome is to impair his ability to organise his life and to plan many of his everyday functions. On the other hand, it is again
c
accepted on all sides that the nature of the damage to Martin's brain is such that his pre-accident level of intelligence is very largely preserved. It is further agreed that Martin's condition has remained essentially unchanged since about 1983.'

[43] The judge then listed (at [33]) ten factors identified by Dr Powell and
d Dr Rose as indicative of lack of capacity. I need not recite the list. That paragraph ends:

'Dr Powell adds that when these deficits are coupled with self centred thinking and a rigidity of approach his relationships with other people and with the problems of life "don't mesh". I have to observe, however, that not
e all these matters will engage, even indirectly, with business and similar matters.'

[44] The failure to 'mesh' was of course the point made by Mr Vetterlein, whose evidence together with that of Mr Chidgey illustrated those effects of the dysexecutive syndrome which the judge recognised to be agreed.
f
[45] The judge then considered the equivocal test performances, and Dr Powell's acceptance that the claimant was very much a borderline case. Dr Rose was more emphatic, but the judge found that to be attributable to his approach to the concept of protection, the purpose of which he regarded as being to protect individuals from making foolish mistakes. That was borne out by a
g passage from the evidence of Dr Rose to which our attention was invited. The judge also noted that Dr Rose did not take into account when assessing capacity the availability of advice, although he did consider whether the claimant understood the need to obtain advice. The judge (at [35]) then made reference to the evidence of Dr Jacobson, Dr Moffatt and Dr Roberts, who all believed that the claimant's brain injuries 'may have contributed to his obsessive and rigid
h behaviour, but have not determined his interests'. Dr Rose did not agree. He considered that the claimant's eccentricities are the direct result of the brain injuries. The judge then compared the experience of the medical witnesses in relation to that issue, and for that reason preferred the view of the majority.

[46] The judge then went on to look at Dr Roberts' suggestion that when
j dealing with a large sum the claimant would benefit from reliable trustees and found, for the reasons which he gave (at [36]), that Dr Roberts 'was thinking in terms of wisdom and not understanding' so the evidence of Dr Roberts did not assist the claimant's case.

[47] The judge (at [37]) then looked at the differing ways in which the doctors looked at the diaries, and concluded thus:

'Having spent many days reviewing the diaries and the letters I am satisfied
that this material taken in conjunction with the other evidence as to how
Martin has functioned over the past twenty years is of very considerable
assistance to me in reviewing the opinions expressed by the doctors and in
assessing to what extent their differing views have been justified in practice.'

After that the judge looked at the medical evidence obtained in relation to the
original action, and the evidence of Professor McLellan, before turning to look at
non-medical evidence.

[48] Mr and Mrs Lister the judge found to be 'enormously protective' of the
claimant and that led them both, to some degree at least, to exaggerate his
difficulties. The judge gave an example of exaggeration which I need not repeat,
and went on to outline the nature of the parents' concerns, including those
related to veganism and animal rights. Before us there is no criticism of that
review. The judge's reference to the evidence of Mr Vetterlein and Mr Chidgey
does not include those passages in their evidence to which I have referred earlier
in this judgment, but, as I have indicated, the judge was alive to the points
illustrated by their evidence because he referred to them when dealing with the
medical evidence.

[49] The judge then considered the evidence of Mr Wilks, including his
evidence that the claimant spent one-and-a-half hours providing a witness
statement, and the fact that the claimant was to be called as a witness if his claim
had not been settled. Mr Wilks dealt in detail with his contact with his client, and
with the way in which the settlement was arrived at. Notably the claimant's
father is recorded (at [58]) as accepting that had he not been available—

'... Martin would very probably have accepted the offer of investment
advice that Mr. Wilks had made to him, and failing him, would probably
have consulted his bank manager.'

The judge examined the evidence as to how the claimant managed his bank
account, and his credit card, and noted no change for the worse when the
claimant left home and moved into his own house.

[50] The judge also noted that on a number of occasions from 1983 onwards
the claimant was involved in civil litigation, often with the assistance of his
solicitor brother-in-law Mr Knowles without there being any suggestion of lack
of capacity. In 1992 when buying his house the claimant arranged his own
bridging loan.

[51] As to the £500 to the Vegan Society on which Mr Langstaff still relies, the
judge pointed out that the society is a consuming passion of the claimant and
added: 'I cannot see that such an act of generosity could be possibly be interpreted
as irrational, or in any way supporting a suggestion that he was unfit to manage
his affairs.' The claimant has more than once been on the council of the society.

[52] The judge gave an example of the claimant acting responsibly to protect
young girls, and in the final section of his judgment reviewed the claimant's
letters, including a most impressive letter to his nephew which, as the judge said,
was a letter that any adult could be proud of writing. Miss Hitchcock invited our
attention to other letters. I have read those, but the point made by the judge is a
valid one. Any adult might also be proud of the claimant's achievement with the
Samaritans.

[53] The judge said (at [74])—

'... the evidence of the last 20 years enables me to arrive with confidence at certain conclusions. So far as the ordinary incidents of life are concerned such as feeding and caring for himself and the ordinary incidents of day to day living, Martin is perfectly capable of looking after himself with a minimum of outside assistance. When greater problems present themselves he is able to recognise that such problems exist, and his reasoning faculties enable him to deal with a good many of them himself. Where more formidable problems arise he recognises that they exist, is able to recognise that he needs external advice to deal with them and is able to go to appropriate sources for such advice—generally his mother and father, but his sources are by no means limited to them ... while the mental disorders identified by the various medical experts in the present proceedings are of such a nature that, if present to a sufficiently severe degree, are undoubtedly capable of rendering a sufferer incapable of managing his property and affairs, the conclusion that I have come to on all the evidence before me is that the degree and extent to which Martin suffers from such disabilities falls far short of that standard.'

MY CONCLUSION

[54] I have gone through the judgment at some length in order to demonstrate that there is no substance in the criticisms that are now being made. As Mr de Wilde QC for Brutton & Co pointed out, there were other achievements of the claimant to which the judge did not refer (ie learning to drive, learning to type and obtaining two passes at O-Level). But the judge did spell out and give proper weight to the medical evidence as to the effects of the head injury. He was fully alive to the fact that what he was investigating was capacity not outcomes, although of course outcomes can often cast a flood of light on capacity, as they did in this case. The judge was also alive to the distinction between management of day-to-day affairs and the management of more serious problems. That very distinction is highlighted in the part of para [74] of the judgment which is quoted above. In the judgment every witness, medical and lay, was considered. Of course not everything they said was recited, but no significant point seems to have been overlooked, and for the reasons which he gave the judge was fully entitled to evaluate the contemporaneous evidence from the diaries and the letters as he did. Indeed there is so little in the seven points identified by Mr Langstaff that the selection in no way undermines the judge's approach. In the course of his judgment the judge dealt with fiscal control, including the odd items of relatively large expenditure. The loss of a pressure cooker valve and the overstocking of a freezer may well be examples of the claimant's problem with his memory, but they are also examples of mishaps which can occur to those who do not have his handicaps. Certainly neither they nor the unrealistic job application can be regarded as matters casting doubt upon the judge's conclusion that since 1983 at the latest the claimant has been fully capable of managing and administering his property and affairs. That, as it seems to me, is a sufficient answer to the preliminary issue, and I would therefore dismiss this appeal.

POTTER LJ.

[55] I agree. Having seen in draft the judgment of Chadwick LJ, I am also indebted to, and agree with, his exegesis of the position under RSC Ord 80, as now embodied in CPR 21, against the background of the general law in relation to mental capacity.

CHADWICK LJ.

a

[56] I agree that these appeals must be dismissed for the reasons set out by Kennedy LJ. But the issues raised are of general importance—as well as being of great importance to the claimant and his parents—and I have thought it appropriate to add some observations of my own.

[57] English law requires that a person must have the necessary mental capacity if he is to do a legally effective act or make a legally effective decision for b himself. Illustrations of the requirement are found in relation to the making of testamentary dispositions (*Harwood v Baker* (1840) 3 Moo PCC 282, *Banks v Goodfellow* LR 5 QB 549, [1861–73] All ER Rep 47), the execution of voluntary deeds (*Ball v Mannin* (1829) 3 Bli NS 1, 6 ER 569, *Re Beaney* [1978] 2 All ER 595, [1978] 1 WLR 770), the entry into marriage (*Durham v Durham* (1885) 10 PD 80, c *Re Park's Estate* [1953] 2 All ER 408, [1954] P 89), the consent to a decree of divorce (*Mason v Mason* [1972] 3 All ER 315, [1972] 3 WLR 405) and the consent to or refusal of medical treatment (*Re C (adult: refusal of treatment)* [1994] 1 All ER 819, [1994] 1 WLR 290, *Re MB (an adult: medical treatment)* [1997] 2 FCR 541, [1997] Fam Law 542). In such cases, the disposition or consent, if made or given without the necessary mental capacity, is void and of no effect. The position is otherwise d in the case of a bargain made for consideration. There the rule is that a contract made by a person without the necessary mental capacity is voidable against the other party; but only if it is shown that the other party knew of the lack of capacity—see *Molton v Camroux* (1848) 2 Exch 487, (1849) 4 Exch 17, *Imperial Loan Co v Stone* [1892] 1 QB 599, *Hart v O'Connor* [1985] 2 All ER 880, [1985] AC 1000. e

[58] The authorities are unanimous in support of two broad propositions. First, that the mental capacity required by the law is capacity in relation to the transaction which is to be effected. Second, that what is required is the capacity to understand the nature of that transaction when it is explained. Those two propositions find expression in the passage from the judgment of Mr Martin Nourse QC in *Re Beaney* [1978] 2 All ER 595 at 601, [1978] 1 WLR 770 at 774 to f which Kennedy LJ has referred. But they can be traced from much earlier authority. In *Ball v Mannin* (1829) 3 Bli NS 1 at 12 and 22, 6 ER 569, the House of Lords upheld a direction to the jury that what was required was that a person should be (at 21) 'capable of understanding what he did by executing the deed in question when its general import was fully explained to him'. In *Harwood v Baker* g (1840) 3 Moo PCC 282 at 290, the Judicial Committee of the Privy Council explained that—

> '... in order to constitute a sound disposing mind, a Testator must not only be able to understand that he is by his Will giving the whole of his property to one object of his regard; but that he must also have capacity to h comprehend the extent of his property, and the nature of the claims of others, whom, by his Will, he is excluding from all participation in that property ...'

In *Manches v Trimborn* (1946) 115 LJKB 305, Hallett J pointed out that the answer to the question whether the mental capacity necessary to render the consent of j the party concerned a real consent was present in any particular case would depend on the nature of the transaction. The cases were reviewed by the High Court of Australia in *Gibbons v Wright* (1954) 91 CLR 423. Sir Owen Dixon CJ, in a passage at 438, to which Mr Nourse QC referred in *Re Beaney* ([1978] 2 All ER 595 at 601, [1978] 1 WLR 770 at 774), stated the principle in these terms—

a

'... the mental capacity required by the law in respect of any instrument is relative to the particular transaction which is being effected by means of the instrument, and may be described as the capacity to understand the nature of that transaction when it is explained.'

The same test was applied by this court in *Re Park's Estate* [1953] 2 All ER 1411 at 1430, [1954] P 112 at 127. Singleton LJ said:

b

'Was the deceased on the morning of May 30, 1949, capable of understanding the nature of the contract into which he was entering, or was his mental condition such that he was incapable of understanding it? In order to ascertain the nature of the contract of marriage a man must be mentally capable of appreciating that it involves the responsibilities normally attaching to marriage. Without that degree of mentality, it cannot be said that he understands the nature of the contract.'

c

[59] In *Re K, Re F* [1988] 1 All ER 358 at 361, [1988] Ch 310 at 313, Hoffmann J treated as 'well established' the proposition that—

d

'... capacity to perform a juristic act exists when the person who purported to do the act had at the time the mental capacity, with the assistance of such explanation as he may have been given, to understand the nature and effect of that particular transaction'.

He cited *Re Beaney* [1978] 2 All ER 595, [1978] 1 WLR 770 as authority. That passage was approved by this court in *Re W (Enduring Power of Attorney)* [2001] 4 All ER 88, [2001] Ch 609.

e

[60] The broad propositions are not in doubt. The question of difficulty in any particular case is likely to be whether the party does have the mental capacity, with the assistance of such explanation as he may be given, to understand the nature and effect of the particular transaction. In *Re C (adult: refusal of treatment)* [1994] 1 All ER 819, [1994] 1 WLR 290, Thorpe J rejected what had been described as 'the minimal competence test'—the capacity to understand in broad terms the nature and effect of the proposed treatment—in favour of a more specific test. As he put it ([1994] 1 All ER 819 at 824, [1994] 1 WLR 290 at 295):

f

g

'... the question to be decided is whether it has been established that C's capacity is so reduced by his chronic mental illness that he does not sufficiently understand the nature, purpose and effects of the proffered amputation.'

[61] Hoffmann J addressed the same point in *Re K, Re F* [1988] 1 All ER 358, [1988] Ch 310. He allowed an appeal against the decision of the Master of the Court of Protection refusing registration to an enduring power of attorney on the ground that the donor, although capable of understanding the nature of the power, was herself incapable by reason of mental disorder of managing her property and affairs at the time that she executed the power. He held ([1988] 1 All ER 358 at 362, [1988] Ch 310 at 315) that—

h

j

'... there is no logical reason why, though unable to exercise her powers, [the donor] could not confer them on someone else by an appropriate juristic act. The validity of that act depends on whether she understood its nature and effect, and not on whether she would hypothetically have been able to perform all the acts which it authorised.'

But he went on to consider what was meant by understanding the nature and effect of the power. He said ([1988] 1 All ER 358 at 363, [1988] Ch 310 at 316): *a*

> '... I do not think that it would be sufficient if he realised only that it gave cousin William power to look after his property. Counsel as amicus curiae helpfully summarised the matters which the donor should have understood in order that he can be said to have understood the nature and effect of the power: first, if such be the terms of the power, that the attorney will be able *b* to assume complete authority over the donor's affairs; second, if such be the terms of the power, that the attorney will in general be able to do anything with the donor's property which the donor could have done; third, that the authority will continue if the donor should be or become mentally incapable; fourth, that if he should be or become mentally incapable, the power will be *c* irrevocable without confirmation by the court. I do not wish to prescribe another form of words in competition with the explanatory notes prescribed by the Lord Chancellor, but I accept the summary of counsel as amicus curiae as a statement of the matters which should ordinarily be explained to the donor whatever the precise language which may be used and which the evidence should show he has understood.' *d*

[62] The authorities to which I have referred provide ample support for the proposition that, at common law at least, the test of mental capacity is issue specific: that, as Kennedy LJ has pointed out, the test has to be applied in relation to the particular transaction (its nature and complexity) in respect of which the question whether a party has capacity falls to be decided. It is difficult to see why, *e* in the absence of some statutory or regulatory provision which compels a contrary conclusion, the same approach should not be adopted in relation to the pursuit or defence of litigation.

[63] Litigation is conducted in accordance with rules of court. It is no surprise, therefore, that the Rules of the Supreme Court (RSC) have made provision, since *f* first promulgated in the First Schedule to the Supreme Court of Judicature Act 1875, for the conduct of actions by and against persons of unsound mind. Order XVIII of those rules provided that, in all cases where persons of unsound mind not so found by inquisition might have sued or been sued before the Supreme Court of Judicature Act 1873, they might sue in any action by their next friend 'in manner practised in the Court of Chancery' before the 1873 Act and might defend *g* any action by their guardian ad litem. The practice in the Court of Chancery before 1873 was explained in the judgment of James LJ in *Beall v Smith* (1873) 9 Ch App 85 at 91–92:

> 'The law of the Court of Chancery undoubtedly is that in certain cases *h* where there is a person of unsound mind, not so found by inquisition, and therefore incapable of invoking the protection of the Court, that protection may in proper cases, and if and so far as may be necessary and proper, be invoked on his behalf by any person as his next friend ... It is not by reason of the incompetency, but notwithstanding the incompetency, that the Court of Chancery entertains the proceedings.' *j*

[64] The RSC were made under the power conferred by s 99(1) of the Judicature Act 1925 (now found in s 84(1) and (2) of the Supreme Court Act 1981). The power is to regulate and prescribe practice and procedure. There is no reason to think that the rule-making body intended—or had power—to alter the substantive law as to the test of mental capacity applicable in relation to the

a pursuit or defence of legal proceedings; and, as I have said, no reason to think that that test was not the issue-specific test long recognised by the common law.

[65] RSC Ord 80, r 2(1) provided that a person under disability might not bring proceedings except by his next friend and might not defend proceedings except by his guardian ad litem. Subject to anything to be inferred from the use of the defined phrase 'person under disability', there is nothing in that sub-rule which

b alters the general law. The pursuit and defence of legal proceedings are juristic acts which can only be done by persons having the necessary mental capacity; and the court is concerned not only to protect its own process but to provide protection to both parties to litigation which comes before it. A defendant is entitled to expect that he will not be required to defend proceedings brought against him by a person of unsound mind acting without a next friend. Order 80,

c r 2(2) was facilitative: it provided that anything which in the ordinary conduct of the proceedings is required or authorised to be done by a party to proceedings shall or may, if the party is a person under a disability, be done by his next friend or guardian ad litem.

[66] RSC Ord 80, r 3(2) provided that (save in particular cases) an order

d appointing a person as next friend or guardian ad litem was not necessary. That, as it seems to me, is of some significance. The rule-making body plainly contemplated, and intended, that the question whether a party was required to act through a next friend or guardian ad litem (as the case might be) should, in the ordinary case, be determined by the party himself or by those caring for him; perhaps with the advice of a solicitor but without the need for inquiry by the

e court. Order 80, r 2(3) required that a next friend or guardian ad litem must act by a solicitor; and r 3(8)(i) required that, in such a case, the solicitor was to file a certificate certifying that he believed the party to be a patient, with his grounds of belief. But there was no requirement, as such, in the rules for the filing or consideration of medical evidence. If the rule were to work in practice, the test

f of mental capacity should be such that, in the ordinary case, the need for a next friend or guardian ad litem should be readily recognised by an experienced solicitor.

[67] RSC Ord 80, r 10(1) provided that, where in any proceedings money was claimed by a person under disability, no settlement or compromise of the claim should be valid without the approval of the court. That requirement supplements

g the general law as to bargains with persons of unsound mind—as explained in *Imperial Loan Co v Stone* [1892] 1 QB 599 and *Hart v O'Connor* [1985] 2 All ER 880, [1985] AC 1000. Absent that rule, a defendant sued by a person whom he knew to be of unsound mind—because, for example, the claimant was an adult acting by a next friend—could not safely compromise the claim by a payment. There

h was a risk that the compromise would be set aside. In that context, the rule may be seen as facilitative; it enables a binding compromise to be made. It is also, when read in conjunction with Ord 80, r 12, protective of the claimant's interests—in that the court is concerned both to approve the compromise and to give directions as to how the money paid under the compromise shall be dealt

j with.

[68] RSC Ord 80, rr 10 and 12 must be read in the context of r 2. The hypothesis underlying rr 10 and 12, as it seems to me, is that the claimant who is under a disability will bring his claim by a next friend, as r 2 requires; so that the defendant, and the court, will be on notice that rr 10 and 12 are engaged. To my mind it is not self-evident that rr 10 and 12 have any application where the claimant brings a claim in contravention of r 2—so that, in the eyes of the

defendant and the court, he is asserting that he is not under a disability. If rr 10 and 12 were intended to apply in such a case (which I doubt) then it would be open to question whether the rule making body had power to change the substantive law expounded in *Imperial Loan Co v Stone* and *Hart v O'Connor*. The question does not arise on this appeal; and will not arise in these proceedings if (as I would hold) the appeal should be dismissed. It is unnecessary to decide it. But it may well be that an important assumption which underlies the present appeal—that, if the claimant were under disability in September 1987, the compromise into which he entered must be set aside—would prove, on examination, to be ill-founded.

[69] As I have said, subject to anything to be inferred from the use of the defined phrase 'person under disability', there is nothing in RSC Ord 80 which purports to alter the substantive law as to the test of mental capacity applicable in relation to the pursuit or defence of legal proceedings; and no reason to think that the rule making body intended—or had power—to make such an alteration. '[P]erson under disability' is defined to mean 'a person who is an infant or a patient': and 'patient' means 'a person who, by reason of mental disorder within the meaning of the [Mental Health Act 1983], is incapable of managing and administering his property and affairs.' It is plain that the lack of capacity which brings a person within the definition of 'patient' for the purposes of the rules must be attributable to mental disorder as defined by the Act; but it is necessary to consider what, if any, further relevance the 1983 Act may have in relation to the test of mental capacity applicable to the pursuit or defence of legal proceedings.

[70] The jurisdiction formerly exercised by the Crown as parens patriae in relation to persons who, by reason of unsound mind, were unable to manage their property or affairs ceased to be exercisable on the coming into force, on 1 November 1960, of the Mental Health Act 1959 and the revocation of the last warrant by which that jurisdiction had been assigned to the Lord Chancellor and the judges of the Chancery Division—see the observations of Lord Brandon of Oakbrook in *F v West Berkshire Health Authority (Mental Health Act Commission intervening)* [1989] 2 All ER 545 at 552–553, [1990] 2 AC 1 at 57–58. Since 1960 the position has been governed by the provisions of the 1959 Act (subsequently repealed and replaced by the 1983 Act) and the common law—[1989] 2 All ER 545 at 553, [1990] 2 AC 1 at 58.

[71] At the time when the RSC were made s 103(1)(h) of the 1959 Act (now s 96(1)(i) of the 1983 Act) conferred power on the judges nominated for the purposes of Pt VIII of that Act (now Pt VII of the 1983 Act), and on the Master, Deputy Master and nominated officers of the Court of Protection, to give directions for the conduct of legal proceedings in the name of a patient or on his behalf. In that context 'patient' means a person in respect of whom the judge exercising the power is satisfied, after considering medical evidence, that he is incapable, by reason of mental disorder, of managing and administering his property and affairs—see s 101 of the 1959 Act (now s 94(2) of the 1983 Act). Where such directions are given, the person authorised under the Act is entitled to be next friend or guardian ad litem—see RSC Ord 80, r 3(3). But what if the Court of Protection has not become involved?

[72] The relationship between the jurisdiction of the Court of Protection to order and give directions for, or to authorise, legal proceedings in the name or on behalf of, a patient within the meaning of s 101 of the 1959 Act (as it then was) on the one hand and rules of court providing for the appointment of a next friend or guardian ad litem for a person under disability on the other hand was considered

a   by Ungoed Thomas J in *Re S (FG)* [1973] 1 All ER 273, [1973] 1 WLR 178. He pointed out that persons under disability, for the purposes of the rules of court, could include persons incapable of managing and administering their property and affairs who were not 'patients' for the purposes of the 1959 Act. The reason was that the rules of court did not contain or impose the requirement of judicial satisfaction after the consideration of medical evidence. So there is no reason

b   why the test of mental capacity, when applied to the power to pursue or defend legal proceedings, should necessarily lead to the same conclusion as it will when applied in order to determine whether the same person is or is not a patient within the 1983 Act. Although the test is probably the same test—see the observation attributed to Sir Raymond Jennings QC and approved by Wilberforce J in *In re CAF* (23 March 1962, unreported) but noted in *Heywood &*

c   *Massey: Court of Protection Practice* (13th edn, 2002) para 2.006—the 'property and affairs' in relation to which the test falls to be applied are likely to be different. It is, I think, rare for a judge of the Court of Protection to be asked to exercise the power to give directions or authority in relation to the conduct of legal proceedings (under s 96(1)(i) of the 1983 Act) in isolation; it will be more usual for

d   that power to be invoked in conjunction with, or following, the appointment of a receiver under s 99(1)—see s 99(2) of the Act. In that context 'property and affairs' will extend to the whole of the person's property and affairs; not just to the affairs encompassed by the litigation.

[73]   In *F v West Berkshire Health Authority (Mental Health Act Commission intervening)* [1989] 2 All ER 545, [1990] 2 AC 1 it was held that, although the

e   expression 'the affairs of patients'—taken by itself and without regard to the context in which it appears—was capable of extending to medical treatment, it must be construed, in the context of Pt VII of the 1983 Act, as including only 'business matters, legal transactions and other dealings of a similar kind'—see Lord Brandon's observations ([1989] 2 All ER 545 at 554, [1990] 2 AC 1 at 59). In

f   my view the expression 'property and affairs' should be given the same meaning in the context of RSC Ord 80. It is pertinent to have in mind that the relevant inquiry, in the context of that rule, is whether a person has the mental capacity which the law requires in a person who is to be permitted to pursue or defend legal proceedings without the interposition of a next friend or guardian ad litem

g   (as the case may be). The answer to that inquiry does not turn on whether or not the person has the requisite mental capacity to make some other legally effective decision.

[74]   The point is illustrated by the outcome in *Re C (adult: refusal of treatment)* [1994] 1 All ER 819, [1994] 1 WLR 290. C had been admitted to a secure hospital

h   as a patient under Pt III of the 1983 Act. He was subsequently diagnosed as suffering from gangrene in the foot. Acting by his next friend he sought an injunction to restrain the hospital from amputating. Thorpe J held that C had the requisite mental capacity to make a decision to refuse treatment. As he put it, ([1994] 1 All ER 819 at 824, [1994] 1 WLR 290 at 295):

j   'Although his general capacity is impaired by schizophrenia, it has not been established that he does not sufficiently understand the nature, purpose and effects of the treatment he refuses. Indeed, I am satisfied that he has understood and retained the relevant treatment information, that in his own way he believes it, and that in the same fashion he has arrived at a clear choice.'

Nevertheless, it was never in doubt that C was a patient for the purposes of the
procedural rule which required that his suit could not have been brought except
with the interposition of a next friend. There is no inconsistency between the
requirement that a party to legal proceedings comply with RSC Ord 80 and a
decision that he has an understanding of the nature, purpose and effects of the
medical treatment which is under consideration in those proceedings. The test
is issue specific; and, when applied to different issues, it may yield different
answers.

[75] For the purposes of RSC Ord 80—and, now, CPR 21—the test to be
applied, as it seems to me, is whether the party to legal proceedings is capable of
understanding, with the assistance of such proper explanation from legal advisers
and experts in other disciplines as the case may require, the issues on which his
consent or decision is likely to be necessary in the course of those proceedings. If
he has capacity to understand that which he needs to understand in order to
pursue or defend a claim, I can see no reason why the law—whether substantive
or procedural—should require the interposition of a next friend or guardian ad
litem (or, as such a person is now described in the CPR, a litigation friend).

[76] That approach seems to me consistent with the approach adopted by this
court in *Leather v Kirby* [1965] 2 All ER 441, [1965] 2 QB 367, a decision on whether
a claimant was of 'unsound mind' for the purposes of what was then s 22 of the
Limitation Act 1939 (now replaced by s 28 of the Limitation Act 1980). A person
is of 'unsound mind' for the purposes of the 1980 Act if he is 'a person who, by
reason of mental disorder within the meaning of the Mental Health Act 1983, is
incapable of managing and administering his property and affairs' (see s 38(3)).
The language is the same as that used in RSC Ord 80, r 1; and there is good reason
why the test should be the same in each context—see the observations of
Danckwerts LJ in *Leather v Kirby* ([1965] 2 All ER 441 at 445, [1965] 2 QB 367 at
385). In upholding the trial judge's decision that the claimant was of unsound
mind—so as to prevent the relevant period of limitation from running against
him—Lord Denning MR, said ([1965] 2 All ER 441 at 444, [1965] 2 QB 367 at 384):

> 'After a time he was to some extent able to appreciate (from being told by
> others) something of what had happened to him, and indeed to his scooter.
> But he could not concentrate on it for any length of time. Not long enough
> to be able to appreciate the nature and extent of any claim that he might
> have. In particular he had no insight at all into his own mental state. He was
> not capable of instructing a solicitor properly. He certainly was not capable
> of exercising any reasonable judgment on a possible settlement.'

The features which Lord Denning MR identified in that passage are features
which, as it seems to me, would lead, plainly, to a conclusion that the claimant
was a person under a disability for the purposes of RSC Ord 80.

[77] The same approach was adopted by Boreham J in *White v Fell*
(12 November 1987, unreported). In that case, also, it was necessary to decide
whether the claimant had been incapable of managing her property and affairs in
the context of a Limitation Act defence. The judge identified three features to
which he thought it appropriate to have regard. First, the need for the claimant
to have 'insight and understanding of the fact that she has a problem in respect of
which she needs advice'. Second, the need to be able to instruct an appropriate
adviser 'with sufficient clarity to enable him to understand the problem and
advise her appropriately'. Third, the need 'to understand and make decisions
based upon, or otherwise give effect to, such advice as she may receive'.

a Boreham J accepted that the claimant was 'now quite incapable of managing unaided a large sum of money such as the sort of sum that would be appropriate compensation for her injuries'. Further, he accepted that, if she succeeded in her claim for compensation 'as almost inevitably she will', she would need to 'take, consider and act upon appropriate advice'; but that she might choose not to take advice. He accepted that 'she may not understand all the intricacies of litigation,
b or of a settlement, or of a wise investment policy'. But he was satisfied that, nevertheless, the claimant had not been shown to be incapable of managing her affairs. She had had the necessary understanding to take the decisions which she needed to take in relation to a claim for compensation.

[78] Wright J held that he should follow that approach in the present case. He
c rejected the submission, advanced on behalf of the claimant, that a finding of incapacity was required 'if the effect of the injury to his brain renders [the claimant] vulnerable to exploitation or at the risk of the making of rash or irresponsible decisions' (see [2002] EWHC 417 (QB) at [24], [2002] All ER (D) (Mar) at [24]). I think that he was right to do so. The courts have ample powers to protect those who are vulnerable to exploitation from being exploited; it is
d unnecessary to deny them the opportunity to take their own decisions if they are not being exploited. It is not the task of the courts to prevent those who have the mental capacity to make rational decisions from making decisions which others may regard as rash or irresponsible.

[79] The judge found assistance in recommendations made by the Law
e Commission in 1995, in Pt III of its report *Mental Incapacity* (Law Com no 232). The report drew attention (at paras 3.16 and 3.17) to the need that a person should be able both: (i) to understand and retain the information relevant to the decision which has to be made (including information about the reasonably foreseeable consequences of deciding one way or another or of failing to make any decision), and (ii) to use that information in the decision-making process. I
f think that he was right to have regard to those recommendations. I think he was right, also, to have in mind the qualifications (expressed in paras 3.18 and 3.19 of the report) that a person should not be held unable to understand the information relevant to a decision if he can understand an explanation of that information in broad terms and simple language; and that he should not be regarded as unable
g to make a rational decision merely because the decision which he does, in fact, make is a decision which would not be made by a person of ordinary prudence.

[80] It had appeared from the grounds of appeal annexed to the appellant's notice in these appeals that the appellant would contend that the judge 'erred in law in that he applied the wrong test for capacity and in formulating the test'; had
h 'uncritically followed the narrow approach applied by Boreham J in *White v Fell*' had failed to address 'the robust criticisms of this test' made on behalf of the appellant; and had failed 'to take into account the importance of risk and vulnerability'. When giving permission for an appeal to this court the judge expressed the view that there was an important point of law involved.

j [81] It was a matter of some surprise, therefore, that counsel for the appellant disclaimed any intention to advance a fundamental attack on the judge's approach as a matter of law. The furthest he sought to go was to submit that the judge ought to have taken into account, when deciding whether the claimant had had the requisite capacity to pursue a claim in legal proceedings, the fact that (as alleged) the claimant would plainly not have had the requisite capacity to manage and administer a large award of damages.

[82] It might have been thought that an obvious difficulty in the way of that
submission, in the present case, was the fact that the claimant had taken what   *a*
were accepted to be sensible decisions in the management of the not
inconsiderable sum which he had received under the compromise in 1987. But it
was said that the question whether he had capacity to take those decisions was
not to be answered solely by reference to outcomes. I accept that as conceptually
correct. For the same reason that—as the Law Commission pointed out—a   *b*
person is not to be regarded as unable to make a rational decision merely because
the decision which he does make is one which would not be made by a person of
ordinary prudence, so he is not to be regarded as having capacity merely because
the decision appears rational. But, to my mind, outcomes are likely to be
important (although not conclusive) indicators of the existence, or lack, of
understanding.   *c*

[83] More pertinently, I reject the submission that a person who would be
incapable of taking investment decisions in relation to a large sum received as
compensation is to be held, for that reason, to be incapable of pursuing a claim
for that compensation. I accept that capacity to pursue a claim requires capacity
to take a decision to compromise that claim; and that capacity to compromise   *d*
requires an understanding of what the effects of a compromise will be—in
particular, an understanding that it will be necessary to deal with the
compensation monies in a way which will provide for the future. But that does
not, as it seems to me, require an understanding as to how that will be done. As
Hoffmann J pointed out in *Re K, Re F* [1988] 1 All ER 358 at 362, [1988] Ch 310 at
315, there is no logical reason why a person who understands that something   *e*
needs to be done, but who does not have the requisite understanding to do it for
himself, should not confer on another the power to do what needs to be done.

[84] In my view the judge identified correctly the principles which he had to
apply in addressing the issue which was before him. Kennedy LJ has explained
why the criticism that the judge failed to apply those principles to the facts must   *f*
be rejected. I agree. The application of those principles led the judge to a
conclusion which he was entitled to reach. For my part, I find it of particular
significance that, in this case, two experienced solicitors acting for the claimant in
litigation did not recognise the need for the appointment of a next friend; and that
no criticism is made of either in that respect. These appeals should be dismissed.
          g

Appeal dismissed.

Dilys Tausz   Barrister.

a Inter Lotto (UK) Ltd v Camelot Group plc
[2003] EWHC 1256 (Ch)

CHANCERY DIVISION

LADDIE J

b

20, 21 MAY, 6 JUNE 2003

Trade mark – Registration – Effect of registration – Whether owner of registered trade mark having statutory right to use mark overriding another person's common law passing off rights – Trade Marks Act 1994, s 9(1).

c

Trade mark – Infringement – Effect of infringement – Whether infringement of trade mark in itself constituting wrongdoing of sufficient depravity to engage doctrine of ex turpi causa.

d The claimant was engaged in the business of operating lotteries. It alleged that, since August 2001, it had promoted and organised the running of lotteries in relation to which it had used the trade mark 'HOT PICK'. It also claimed to have built up a reputation and goodwill in the mark. The defendant managed another lottery under an operating licence. By its terms, all intellectual property rights relating to that lottery were owned by the licensor and licensed to the defendant.

e On 17 October 2001 the defendant caused the licensor to apply to register the name 'HOTPICKS' as a trade mark (the HOTPICKS mark). The claimant alleged that in July 2002 the defendant launched a new lottery game under or by reference to the HOTPICKS mark. It brought proceedings against the defendant for, inter alia, passing off, alleging that HOTPICKS was confusingly similar to HOT PICK, that the defendant's activities had resulted in confusion in the market place and that

f claimant was entitled to rely on the goodwill built up by its alleged use of the HOT PICK mark from August 2001 until the defendant started using the HOTPICKS mark in July 2002. On the determination of a preliminary issue, the defendant contended that its ownership of the HOTPICKS mark gave it a statutory right to use it, and that that right overrode any common law passing off rights which the

g claimant might have. In so contending, it relied on s 9(1)[a] of the Trade Marks Act 1994 which provided that the proprietor of a registered trade mark had exclusive rights in the trade mark which were infringed by use of the trade mark in the United Kingdom without his consent. The defendant also contended that all use of the claimant's mark after the registration date was to be treated as unlawful, and that

h accordingly the claimant was precluded, under the doctrine of ex turpi causa, from relying upon any reputation or goodwill generated by such unlawful use in support of its passing off claim. The defendant therefore contended that 17 October 2001, not July 2002, was the cut-off date for assessing the claimant's reputation and goodwill for the purposes of its passing off claim.

j **Held** – (1) Section 9(1) of the 1994 Act did not give the owner of a registered trade mark a right to use that mark which overrode another person's passing off rights. The contention to the contrary involved a misreading of that provision and a basic flaw in the appreciation of what was achieved by registration.

---

a   Section 9(1) is set out at [31], below

Section 9(1) did not stipulate that the proprietor of the registered mark had an
exclusive right to use the mark. It stipulated that he had the exclusive rights in   *a*
the trade mark which were infringed by the use of the trade mark without his
consent. In other words, registered trade marks, like all other statutory
intellectual property rights, did not give a right to the proprietor to use, but rather
the right to exclude others from using in a manner that was prohibited by the Act.
If the legislature had intended to bestow on the owner of a registered trade mark   *b*
an entitlement to override the rights of others, it could and should have done so
expressly. It followed in the instant case that the defendant had not acquired, by
registration, any entitlement to use the HOTPICKS mark, but only the right to
prevent others infringing (see [35], [39], [40], below); *Re Lyle & Kinahan Ltd's
Application* (1907) 24 RPC 249 applied.

(2) Trade mark infringement did not without more amount to wrongdoing of   *c*
such a level of depravity as to engage the doctrine of ex turpi causa. Although
there might be cases where the nature of the infringement was so flagrant and
clearly and knowingly wrongful that a court might refuse to allow a claimant to
rely on his goodwill and reputation, the only wrongdoing alleged in the instant
case was the fact of the wrongdoing. It followed that the relevant date for   *d*
assessing the claimant's reputation and goodwill for its claim in passing off was
the date upon which the defendant started using the mark in relation to its lottery
product, not the date of the application for registration (see [45], [47], below).

Notes
For rights conferred by registered trade mark and for circumstances in which a   *e*
claimant might be to disentitled to protection in a passing off action, see 48
Halsbury's Laws (4th edn) (2000 reissue) paras 79, 339.

For the Trade Marks Act 1993, s 9, see 48 *Halsbury's Statutes* (4th edn) (2001
reissue) 119.

f

Cases referred to in judgment
Bile Bean Manufacturing Co v Davidson (1906) 23 RPC 725, Ct of Sess.
Burberrys v JC Cording & Co Ltd (1909) 26 RPC 693.
Faulder & Co Ltd v O and G Rushton Ltd (1903) 20 RPC 477, CA.
Fisons Ltd v EJ Godwin (Peat Industries) Ltd [1976] RPC 653.
ICL Ltd v Berk Pharmaceuticals Ltd [1981] FSR 1.   *g*
Leather Cloth Co Ltd v American Leather Cloth Co Ltd (1865) 11 HL Cas 523, 11 ER
    1435, HL.
Lyle & Kinahan Ltd's Application, Re (1907) 24 RPC 249, CA.
Millington v Fox (1838) 3 My & Cr 338, 40 ER 956.
Mitchell v Henry (1880) 15 Ch D 181, CA.   *h*
Montgomery v Thompson [1891] AC 217, HL.
Newman v Pinto (1887) 4 RPC 508, CA.
Orr Ewing v Registrar of Trade-Marks (1879) 4 App Cas 479, HL.
Perry v Truefitt (1842) 6 Beav 66, 49 ER 749.
Saville Perfumery Ltd v June Perfect Ltd and FW Woolworth & Co Ltd (1941) 58 RPC   *j*
    147, HL.

Cases referred to in skeleton arguments
Anheuser-Busch Inc v Budejovicky Budvar NP (t/a Budweiser Budvar Brewery) [1984]
    FSR 413, CA.

a *Ansul BV v Ajax Brandbeveiliging BV* Case C-40/01 (2003) Transcript (judgment), 11 March 2003.

Arthur Martin (Sales) Ltd v Electra Mechanics (1975) Ltd (1986) 13 IPR 122, NZ HC.

Barlow and Jones v Jabez Johnson & Co (1890) 7 RPC 395, CA.

Barnsley Brewery Co Ltd v RBNB [1997] FSR 462.

British Telecommunications plc v One In A Million Ltd [1998] 4 All ER 476, [1999] 1
b WLR 903, CA.

Bryant v Heyde (1886) 7 NSWR 72, NSW SC.

Cadbury Schweppes Pty Ltd v Pub Squash Co Pty Ltd [1981] 1 All ER 213, [1981] 1
WLR 193, PC.

Campomar Sociedad Ltda v Nike International Ltd (2000) 169 ALR 677, Aust HC.

Denny (Henry) & Sons Ltd v United Biscuits (UK) Ltd [1981] FSR 114.
c *Eli Lilly & Co Ltd v Chelsea Drug Chemical Co Ltd* [1966] RPC 14.

General Electric Co v The General Electric Co Ltd [1972] 2 All ER 507, [1972] 1 WLR
729, HL.

Harris v Ogg (1884) 5 NSWR 114, NSW SC.

Intercontex v Schmidt [1988] FSR 575.

d *Johnson & Son (Loughborough) Ltd v W Puffer & Co Ltd* (1930) 47 RPC 95.

Keary Developments Ltd v Tarmac Construction Ltd [1995] 3 All ER 534, CA.

Lecouturier v Rey [1910] AC 262, HL.

Levi Strauss & Co v Tesco Stores Ltd [2002] EWHC 1556 (Ch), [2003] RPC 319.

Luxembourg v Linster Case C-287/98 [2000] ECR I-6917, ECJ.

e *McGregor-Doniger Inc v Sterling McGregor Ltd* [1981] FSR 299.

New South Wales Dairy Corp v Murray Goulburn Co-operative Co Ltd (1989) 14 IPR
26, Aust Fed Ct; *affd* (1990) 18 IPR 385, Aust HC.

Nicholson & Sons Ltd's Application (1931) 48 RPC 227, CA.

Parkinson (Sir Lindsay) & Co Ltd v Triplan Ltd [1973] 2 All ER 273, [1973] QB 609,
[1973] 2 WLR 632, CA.
f *Penney (JC) Co Inc v Penneys Ltd* [1975] FSR 367, CA.

Pontiac Marina Pte Ltd v CDL Hotels International Ltd [1998] FSR 839, Singapore
CA.

Sen Sen Co v Britten [1899] 1 Ch 692.

Silhouette International Schmied GmbH & Co KG v Hartlauer Handelsgesellschaft mbH
g Case C-355/96 [1998] All ER (EC) 769, [1999] Ch 77, [1998] 3 WLR 1218, [1998]
ECR I-4799, ECJ.

Star Industrial Co Ltd v Yap Kwee Kor (t/a New Star Industrial Co) [1976] FSR 256,
PC.

Sunshine Leisure Products (NZ) Ltd v Great Outdoors Co Ltd [1986] 2 NZLR 183, NZ
h HC.

Thorne (R) & Sons Ltd v Pimms Ltd, Re Pimms' Trade Mark (1909) 26 RPC 221.

Upper Assam Tea Co v Herbert & Co (1889) 7 RPC 183, CA.

Van Zeller v Mason, Cattley & Co (1907) 25 RPC 37.

Whirlpool Trade Mark [1997] FSR 905, India SC.

j *Zino Davidoff SA v A & G Imports Ltd, Levi Strauss & Co v Tesco Stores Ltd, Levi
Strauss & Co v Costco Wholesale UK Ltd* Joined cases C-414–C-416/99 [2002] All
ER (EC) 55, [2002] Ch 109, [2002] 2 WLR 321, [2001] ECR I-8691.

Preliminary issue

By order of Patten J on 19 March 2003, the court was required to determine a
preliminary issue, set out at [9], below, in proceedings for, inter alia, passing off

brought by the claimant, Inter Lotto (UK) Ltd, against the defendant, Camelot
Group plc. The facts are set out in the judgment.

Geoffrey Hobbs QC and *Philip Roberts* (instructed by *McDermott Will & Emery*) for
   Inter Lotto.
Michael Silverleaf QC and *Michael Hicks* (instructed by *Jones Day Gouldens*) for
   Camelot.

Cur adv vult

6 June 2003. The following judgment was delivered.

LADDIE J.
   [1] This is the judgment on the trial of a preliminary issue ordered by consent
by Patten J on 19 March 2003. The claimant, Inter Lotto (UK) Ltd (Inter Lotto),
is engaged in the business of running lotteries on behalf of a number of charities.
The defendant is Camelot Group plc (Camelot). It also runs lotteries. In
particular it manages the National Lottery under an operating licence from the
National Lottery Commission (NLC).
   [2] By claim form dated 9 January of this year, Inter Lotto brought
proceedings for trade mark infringement and passing off against Camelot. For
present purposes it is only the passing off claim which is of interest. In substance
Inter Lotto alleges that continuously since 4 August 2001 it has promoted and
organised the running of lotteries throughout the country in relation to which it
has used the trade mark 'HOT PICK'. It claims to have built up a reputation and
goodwill in that mark. It alleges that from about 7 July 2002, Camelot launched
a new lottery game under or by reference to the trade mark 'HOTPICKS'. It
alleges that HOTPICKS is confusingly similar to HOT PICK and that the
defendant's activities have resulted in confusion in the market place and
constitute passing off.
   [3] Camelot raises a number of defences. For example it says that Inter Lotto
did not use HOT PICK as a mark for a lottery and, if it did, it did not start
promoting the mark until much later than it claims and that, for various reasons
which are not relevant to the current application, Camelot's activities have not
and will not cause any or any significant damage to Inter Lotto. However, central
to the current application are the defences arising out of Camelot's use of a
registered trade mark. By the terms of its operating licence, all intellectual
property rights relating to the National Lottery are owned by NLC and licensed
to the operator, Camelot. On 17 October 2001 Camelot caused NLC to apply to
register the name HOTPICKS as a trade mark under application number 2283392
(the '392 mark). It was advertised for opposition on 7 August 2002. Inter Lotto
opposed on 7 November 2002. That opposition in the Trade Marks Registry is
currently stayed pending the outcome of the current application. A number of
other trade mark applications were made and, in some cases, opposed. They can
be ignored for present purposes.
   [4] Camelot was exclusively licensed by NLC to use the '392 mark on 24 April
2002. It pleads that its use of the registered trade mark gives it a number of
defences. The only ones relevant to this application are pleaded as follows:

   '11. In the premises: (a) by reason of the provisions of s 9 of the Trade
   Marks Act 1994 and the NLC licences, the defendant has at all material times
   had the exclusive rights in [the '392 mark] ... (c) by reason of the provisions

a
of ss 9, 10(1), 10(2) and 30 of the 1994 Act and the provisions of the NLC licences, upon the premises of the particulars of claim (namely that the word HOTPICKS so resembles the words HOT PICK when used in relation to lotteries as to give rise to confusion), the claimant's use of the words HOT PICK in relation to its lottery game is and always has been unlawful and may therefore not be relied upon by the claimant in support of any action for

b
passing off against the defendant which is the lawful user of the trade marks the subject of [the '392 mark] ...

13. ... By reason of the facts and matters set out in para 11 above, no goodwill or reputation in the words HOT PICK can accrue to the claimant and the claimant may not rely upon any use it may have made of the words HOT PICK in relation to any case made against the defendant.'

c
[5] The effect of these pleas may be summarised as follows. Because of the exclusive rights which will exist in NLC's trade mark, all use of Inter Lotto's mark after the date of registration is to be treated as unlawful. As a result, Inter Lotto cannot rely upon any reputation or goodwill generated by such unlawful use (ie after 17 October 2001) in support of its passing off case. This was the way in

d
which Mr Silverleaf QC put his client's case:

'The claimant's use of its mark is unlawful and cannot found an action. If the defendant is entitled to the benefit of a valid trade mark registration, it has the exclusive right to use the mark. It follows that the claimant's use of the same mark is unlawful. On this basis alone the claim for passing off should fail: ex turpi causa non oritur actio. There has to be a nexus between

e
the illegality and the claim for passing off: *ICL Ltd v Berk Pharmaceuticals Ltd* [1981] FSR 1. However, it is difficult to think of a closer nexus than that the use relied upon in support of a passing off claim is an infringement of a trade mark registration. The effect of an unlawfully acquired reputation has been raised before and it has been held that such a reputation is incapable of

f
supporting a claim for passing off.'

[6] The point is emphasised in a supplementary skeleton argument served by Mr Silverleaf shortly before the hearing. In response to a large number of authorities cited in the claimant's skeleton argument by Mr Hobbs QC, who

g
appears for Inter Lotto, Mr Silverleaf expressed his client's position as follows:

'The defendant's case is based upon the proposition that a valid trade mark registration *which is of such scope as to prevent the specific user relied upon by the claimant to support its claim for passing off* entitles the defendant to restrain the claimant from infringing his registration and is therefore a bar to the passing

h
off claim.'

[7] Thus, because Inter Lotto's use of its mark after 17 October 2001 was unlawful, it was, per se, incapable of giving rise to any goodwill and reputation which a court would be prepared to protect. The date of registration of Camelot's mark therefore acts as a guillotine. Only rights accrued before then

j
can be taken into account in support of Inter Lotto's case of passing off.

[8] Inter Lotto's case is that it can rely on all the goodwill built up by its alleged use of the HOT PICK mark from 4 August 2001 until Camelot commenced using HOTPICKS in July 2002. It is not disputed that, absent the special defence which is central to this application, it is the date when the defendant started using its mark which is relevant for determining the passing off claim. On the other hand

Mr Hobbs accepts that if Camelot's plea is good in law, so that it can only rely on the reputation and goodwill generated in the period prior to the date of application to register the '392 mark, that is to say prior to 17 October 2001, this could have a significant impact on his client's passing off claim since it would need to demonstrate the development of sufficient reputation and goodwill in a few months at the very early stages of its use of the HOT PICK mark. Mr Hobbs argues that the defendant's plea is bad in law. Inter Lotto can rely on the later and more extensive use which it alleges.

[9] It is against that background that the parties agreed to the making of the consent order requiring the determination of the following preliminary issue:

'Is 17 October 2001 (the date on which the NLC applied under application number 2283392 to register the designation HOTPICKS as a trade mark) the relevant date at which the claimant's reputation and goodwill for its claim in passing off falls to be assessed?'

[10] Before considering the arguments advanced by the parties, it is necessary to have a clear understanding of what is in issue. I have already referred to the relevant pleadings in the defence and passages in Mr Silverleaf's skeleton arguments. However the nature of Camelot's case changed significantly during the course of the hearing.

[11] It is possible to formulate a defence to the passing off action in two ways. First, it could be said that Inter Lotto has no enforceable goodwill and reputation. If that is the case, the claim will fail. Inter Lotto will have no rights which it can assert. The sword is taken from its hand. Second, it could be said that, even if Inter Lotto does have enforceable goodwill and reputation, Camelot cannot be restrained because it has an overriding *entitlement* to do the acts of which complaint is made. In such a case Camelot would have a personal shield. As can be seen from the pleadings and extracts from its skeleton arguments above, the plea advanced on behalf of Camelot was of the first type. The numerous authorities relied on by Mr Hobbs addressed the second type of defence. Because they did so, Mr Silverleaf said they were irrelevant and did not deal with the point he was raising. However, during the course of his speech he changed position. He asserted that Camelot's ownership of the '392 mark provided it with an entitlement to use it. He said that his client had a 'better' claim than Inter Lotto to the marks in suit. He said that the issue was one of priority of rights and 'hierarchy'. His client's right to use its registered trade mark overrode any common law rights Inter Lotto might have.

[12] Although this second type of defence is not what is pleaded by Camelot, Mr Hobbs did not object to Mr Silverleaf raising it. He says that both defences are bad in law.

[13] At the forefront of his argument Mr Hobbs relies on s 2(2) of the Trade Marks Act 1994:

'No proceedings lie to prevent or recover damages for the infringement of an unregistered trade mark as such; but nothing in this Act affects the law relating to passing off.'

[14] At its simplest, Mr Hobbs argues that there are here on the assumed facts, two distinct rights; NLC's and Camelot's in NLC's mark and Inter Lotto's in its reputation and goodwill built up by use. Although they may, in some circumstances, overlap, they are not the same and one is not superior to the other. There is no hierarchy. Each has to be considered on its own merits. The

a existence of Camelot's registration does not interfere with his client's right to sue to protect the goodwill and reputation which it has built up by activity in the market place. Mr Silverleaf argues that Mr Hobbs has misconstrued the section.

[15] This application concerns some important but quite basic issues of intellectual property law. Each side argues that its position is supported by or consistent with s 2(2) of the 1994 Act when construed in its historical context. For
b that reason, the history of trade mark and passing off causes of action is a convenient starting point.

THE ORIGINS AND DEVELOPMENT OF PASSING OFF AND TRADE MARK RIGHTS

[16] An erudite discussion of the development of the law of passing off and trade marks is to be found in Wadlow *The Law of Passing-Off* (2nd edn, 1995)
c pp 9–31 (paras 1.05–1.15). For present purposes, the following summary is sufficient.

[17] Two or more centuries ago, the cause of action in passing off was dependent upon proof of fraud. With time, this requirement disappeared, at least in one form of the action, and it became dependent upon proof, inter alia, of
d misrepresentation. An early example of this is *Millington v Fox* (1838) 3 My & Cr 338, 40 ER 956. As Wadlow points out, by 1842 the term 'passing off' was in use and the principles of the cause of action were defined by Lord Langdale MR in *Perry v Truefitt* (1842) 6 Beav 66 at 73, 49 ER 749 at 752 in terms which are familiar to the modern practitioner:

e 'I think that the principle on which both the Courts of law and of Equity proceed, in granting relief and protection in cases of this sort, is very well understood. A man is not to sell his own goods under the pretence that they are the goods of another man; he cannot be permitted to practise such a deception, nor to use the means which contribute to that end. He cannot therefore be allowed to use names, marks, letters, or other *indicia*, by which
f he may induce purchasers to believe, that the goods which he is selling are the manufacture of another person. I own it does not seem to me that a man can acquire property in a name or mark; but whether he has or not a property in the name or the mark, I have no doubt that another person has not a right to use that name or mark for the purposes of deception, and in
g order to attract to himself that course of trade, or that custom, which, without that improper act, would have flowed to the person who first used, or was alone in the habit of using the particular name or mark.'

[18] Much the same thing was said by Parker J in a well-known passage in *Burberrys v JC Cording & Co Ltd* [1909] 26 RPC 693 at 701:

h 'The principles of law applicable to a case of this sort are well known. On the one hand, apart from the law as to trade marks, no one can claim monopoly rights in the use of a word or name. On the other hand, no one is entitled by the use of any word or name, or indeed in any other way, to represent his goods as being the goods of another to that other's injury. If an
j injunction be granted restraining the use of a word or name, it is no doubt granted to protect property, but the property, to protect which it is granted, is not property in the word or name, but property in the trade or good-will which will be injured by its use.'

[19] The ambit of the cause of action may well have expanded but not in a way which has any impact on the issues I have to consider. The above passages are of

significance because they are early examples of the courts highlighting one of the
crucial differences between passing off and trade mark rights. Under the former, *a*
the claimant acquires no property in his name or mark. The cause of action is
dependent on deception of the customer. Misappropriation of the name or mark
by the defendant may be the means by which that deception has been facilitated,
but that does not mean that the claimant owns the mark.

[20] In a series of case in the middle of the nineteenth century, Lord Westbury *b*
held that there was a right of property in trade marks. Wadlow describes this as
follows (p 18 (para 1.09)):

> 'While the common law still required fraud, equity did not confine itself to
> relaxing the standard of dishonesty required before it would intervene. In a
> series of cases Lord Westbury L.C. "surprised the profession" [see *Newman v* *c*
> *Pinto* (1887) 4 RPC 508 per Fry LJ] by holding that there was a right of
> property in trade marks which was transmissible and enforceable even
> against innocent infringement. Perhaps Lord Westbury would also have
> recognised property in trade names, and if so the whole of the law of
> passing-off as it was then understood could have been re-interpreted in terms
> of infringement of property rights as opposed to misrepresentation. That, *d*
> however, was not to happen. The law of trade marks was put on a statutory
> basis, the law of passing-off continued in terms of misrepresentation, and the
> idea of passing-off protecting a property right was largely rejected or
> forgotten until the twentieth century. In retrospect, passing-off and trade
> mark infringement may be seen as separate torts which to some extent *e*
> evolved out of the same historical authorities, just as copyright and breach of
> confidence cannot always be distinguished in early cases on piracy of
> unpublished literary works.'

[21] The statutory basis of trade mark law referred to by Wadlow started with
the Trade Marks Registration Act 1875. As its name suggests, it was designed to *f*
put in place a registration system for trade marks. To encourage traders to use
this, it provided at s 1:

> '... from and after the first day of July one thousand eight hundred and
> seventy-six a person shall not be entitled to institute any proceeding to
> prevent the infringement of any trade mark as defined by this Act until and *g*
> unless such trade mark is registered in pursuance of this Act.'

[22] The provisions of the 1875 Act were amplified by the Trade Marks
Registration Amendment Act 1876. As far as I am aware, at the time no one
suggested that the provisions of these Acts had any impact on the cause of action
in passing off which were not based on a claim to a property right in the name or *h*
mark.

[23] Once these Acts were passed, infringement proceedings could only be
brought in respect of new marks which were registered. However, in respect of
trade marks which were in use before the 1875 Act but in respect of which
registration had been refused, the common law action for infringement of the *j*
unregistered mark continued (see *Orr Ewing v Registrar of Trade-Marks* (1879) 4
App Cas 479). In the meantime, passing off actions were unaffected. An
argument to the contrary appears to have been dismissed in *Mitchell v Henry*
(1880) 15 Ch D 181. In any event the provisions of s 1 of the 1875 Act were, in
substance, repeated in s 42 of the Trade Marks Act 1905:

a   'No person shall be entitled to institute any proceeding to prevent or to recover damages for the infringement of an unregistered trade mark unless such trade mark was in use before the thirteenth of August one thousand eight hundred and seventy-five, and has been refused registration under this Act. The Registrar may, on request, grant a certificate that such registration has been refused.'

b   [24] Furthermore, an entirely new provision was added in s 45:

'Nothing in this Act contained shall be deemed to affect rights of action against any person for passing off goods as those of another person or the remedies in respect thereof.'

c   [25] One of the leading textbooks of the day, Kerly *The Law of Trade Marks and Trade Names* (3rd edn, 1908) expressed the view that the latter section merely stated expressly what was already the law. Other textbooks of the time said the same thing. Kerly illustrated the point by referring to the 'Stone Ales' case, *Montgomery v Thompson* [1891] AC 217. Thompson had a registered 'Stone Ale' as a trade mark. He sued a competitor, Mr Montgomery. The mark was removed
d   from the register. Notwithstanding that, Thompson succeeded in an action to restrain Mr Montgomery from using the mark in relation to his beer. The cause of action in passing off was independent of the trade mark rights. A very similar case was *Faulder & Co Ltd v O and G Rushton Ltd* (1903) 20 RPC 477. Kerly discussed the differences between a trade mark infringement action and a passing
e   off action (p 343):

'… where an injunction is granted to restrain the use of a mark calculated to pass off the defendant's goods as those of the plaintiff, by reason of its resemblance to his unregistered mark, it should be so limited as to leave it open for the defendant to use any part, or the whole, of the plaintiff's
f   unregistered mark, if he can do so, in any manner which is not calculated to lead to deception.'

[26] That passage is as applicable today as it was in 1908. Because the action in passing off protects the reputation and goodwill of a trader, not his names, marks or get up per se, a rival trader can, in theory, use those names, marks or
g   get up as long as he does so in a way which does not lead to deception. See, for example, *Fisons Ltd v EJ Godwin (Peat Industries) Ltd* [1976] RPC 653. In this respect there is a difference between passing off and trade mark rights as explained by Lord Greene MR in *Saville Perfumery Ltd v June Perfect Ltd and FW Woolworth & Co Ltd* (1941) 58 RPC 147 at 162:

h   'I now turn to the claim based on passing-off. It does not necessarily follow that a trader who uses an infringing mark upon goods is also guilty of passing-off. The reason is that in the matter of infringement, as I have already pointed out, once a mark is used as indicating origin, no amount of added matter intended to show the true origin of the goods can affect the
j   question. In the case of passing-off, on the other hand, the defendant may escape liability if he can show that the added matter is sufficient to distinguish his goods from those of the plaintiff. Such proof may be very difficult, but theoretically at any rate the result may be as I have stated.'

[27] Thus, the effect of s 45 of the 1905 Act was to confirm what was already the law, namely that the rights created by registration of a trade mark were

different to those protected by passing off proceedings and, for that reason, the
legislation relating to the former had no impact on the latter.

[28] In the Trade Marks Act 1938, ss 42 and 45 were brought together and
re-enacted as s 2:

'No person shall be entitled to institute any proceeding to prevent, or to
recover damages for, the infringement of an unregistered trade mark, but
nothing in this Act shall be deemed to affect rights of action against any
person for passing off ... or the remedies thereof.'

[29] It is not suggested that this changed the law. The provision in the
1994 Act is, in substance, identical. Once again, neither Mr Silverleaf nor
Mr Hobbs suggested that it changed the law.

[30] Consistent with this history, s 2(2) of the 1994 Act is an unpromising start
for the defendant. Its argument is that the existence of the '392 trade mark
registration gives rise to a per se overriding of Inter Lotto's ability to protect its
reputation and goodwill by means of passing off proceedings. If correct, the
rights created under trade mark legislation would 'affect the law relating to
passing off' or, at the least, affect its practical application. However there is
nothing to suggest that the legislature had in mind the problem in this case,
namely a clash of competing rights. What the section and its predecessors were
primarily concerned with was whether the owner of a registered trade mark was
capable of owning and enforcing, at the same time, rights to sue in passing off.
The section, consistent with cases like *Montgomery v Thompson* [1891] AC 217,
confirms that a trader who has built up a reputation and goodwill in his business
is entitled to protect it by passing off proceedings, whether or not *he* has also
acquired trade mark registrations in respect of any names or marks used in
relation to that business. As far as I can tell, no one appears to have argued that
the exclusive right given by registration overrode passing off rights. There is no
reason to believe that that type of argument was in the mind of the legislature
when s 45 of the 1938 Act and its equivalent in later Acts were being drafted. For
this reason I think it is necessary to look more closely at the two defences raised
by Camelot.

DOES CAMELOT HAVE A RIGHT TO USE THE '392 MARK WHICH OVERRIDES
INTER LOTTO'S RIGHTS?

[31] Camelot's argument is based upon the provisions of s 9(1) of the 1994 Act:

'The proprietor of a registered trade mark has exclusive rights in the trade
mark which are infringed by use of the trade mark in the United Kingdom
without his consent. The acts amounting to infringement, if done without
the consent of the proprietor, are specified in section 10.'

[32] Mr Silverleaf says that, in the light of this provision, the owner of (or
licensee under) a registered trade mark has a statutory right to use it. This cannot
be taken away. Passing off rights are 'inferior' and cannot be used to impugn or
restrict that entitlement. He says the matter is purely hierarchical. The person
with the better title succeeds. He also prays in aid ss 22 and 27 of the 1994 Act
which provide that a registered trade mark is personal property and also treat
applications for trade marks in the same way. He says that if a trade mark is a
property which entitles the owner to exclude others from infringing it, it must
carry with it the right to stop others from preventing the owner from using it
himself.

a   [33] To understand the impact of this argument, it is useful to bear in mind some of the other differences between the right to protect reputation and goodwill by passing off proceedings and the rights acquired under a trade mark registration. The essential characteristic of the former is that it is built up by use. If the use stops, the reputation and goodwill will wither and die. Once it is dead, passing off proceedings will not avail the claimant. If there has only been a small
b   amount of use, the reputation and goodwill may be insufficient to justify protection and, even if it is, if the use ceases such reputation and goodwill as was generated is likely to dissipate quickly. On the other hand it is possible and common to obtain registrations for marks which have never been used. Although the 1994 Act requires the applicant for a registered trade mark to state that the mark is being used or that he has a bona fide intention to use it the only
c   encouragement to keep to the latter intention is to be found in s 46. This provides that a mark may be taken off the register if it is not used for a continuous period of five years. It is not necessary for present purposes to determine whether removal after such a period of non-use is mandatory or, as was the case under the 1938 Act, discretionary. Another, but related, difference is that the proprietor
d   chooses in respect of what goods or services he wants to register his mark. Even if the mark is used by the proprietor in relation to some goods or services, it is possible and common to register marks in respect of a much wider group of goods and services on which it will never be used.

        [34] The practical application of Mr Silverleaf's argument can be explained by reference to a notional example. A trader starts to use a trade mark 'X'. He uses
e   it extensively in relation to particular goods and builds up a valuable reputation and goodwill. At the same time another trader applies to register 'X' as a trade mark which he does not use in respect of the same class of goods. At the outset, each trader is ignorant of the existence of the other. After four-and-a-half years, the second trader decides to start using his registered mark. He learns of the first
f   trader and sues for infringement. The second trader sues for passing off. Mr Silverleaf argues that not only does the second trader succeed on the infringement proceedings, but the first trader cannot succeed in passing off. The result is that the second trader is entitled to take all the goodwill and reputation which the first trader had built up. Indeed, if Mr Silverleaf's argument is correct, it is difficult to see why he limited himself to saying that the guillotine on Inter
g   Lotto's reputation comes down on 17 October 2001. Even if Inter Lotto had built up an enormous reputation and goodwill before that date, according to this argument, Camelot is 'entitled' to use its registered trade mark.

        [35] In my view Mr Silverleaf's argument is untenable. It involves a misreading of s 9(1) of the 1994 Act and a basic flaw in the appreciation of what
h   registration achieves. The section does not stipulate that the proprietor of the registered mark has an 'exclusive right to use' the mark. It stipulates that he has the 'exclusive rights in the trade mark which are infringed by use of the trade mark in the United Kingdom without his consent'. In other words, registered trade marks, like all other statutory intellectual property rights do not give a right
j   to the proprietor to use, but give him the right to exclude others from using. The types of activities which can be prohibited by the existence of a registered trade mark are those which are set out in s 10 of the 1994 Act. None of this gives rise to an entitlement to the proprietor to use.

        [36] The point is explained particularly clearly in Professor Cornish's admirable book *Intellectual Property* (3rd edn, 1996) pp 5–6 (para 1-04):

'One characteristic shared by all types of intellectual property to date is that the rights granted are essentially negative: they are rights to stop others *a* doing certain things—rights in other words to stop pirates, counterfeiters, imitators and even in some cases third parties who have independently reached the same ideas, from exploiting them without the licence of the rightowner. Some aspects of intellectual property confer positive entitlements, such as the right to be granted a patent or register a trade mark *b* upon fulfilling the requisite conditions; but these are essentially ancillary. The fact that intellectual property gives a right to control the activities of others has a number of implications, often inadequately understood. The rightowner does not need the right in order to exploit a market for its goods or services: a patent is not a pre-condition to exploiting one's own invention. By way of corollary, the right gives no liberty to ignore the rights of other *c* individuals (including their intellectual property) or to override public liabilities ...'

[37] This is true across the whole field of intellectual property. The exclusive rights given in a copyright work do not mean that the owner of that copyright is entitled to use his work even though it infringes some prior author's rights. *d* Similarly in the field of patents, it has never been the law that the owner of an improvement patent has an entitlement to use his invention even in breach of the prior patent in respect of which his invention is an improvement. Indeed, patent legislation contains express provisions to allow the owner of an improvement patent, in very limited circumstances, to obtain a compulsory licence, for which *e* he will have to pay, under the master patent. Furthermore, how far does this entitlement go? Does it allow the owner of a statutory intellectual property right to override public health laws, the law of libel and so on?

[38] Mr Silverleaf did not shy away from this problem. I put to him in the course of argument a hypothetical case where the registered trade mark consists of a fancy label or the shape of a container. In the first it involves the wholesale *f* unlicensed copying of someone else's copyright drawings and in the latter it is a breach of someone else's registered design or unregistered design right. I asked if the proprietor of the registered mark is entitled to override these conflicting rights. His answer was Yes.

[39] In my view Mr Silverleaf's proposition is bad in law. His client has *g* acquired no entitlement to use the '392 mark by registration. It has only acquired the right to prevent others infringing. A number of the cases cited by Mr Hobbs support that view. I need only refer to one of them, *Re Lyle & Kinahan Ltd's Application* (1907) 24 RPC 249 at 262 per Buckley LJ:

'The registration of a Trade Mark does not confer any right at all of the *h* description there pointed to, but it does confer a right, and the only right is the right to prevent anybody else from using that Trade Mark as a mark for their goods, but it does not give the registered owner of the Trade Mark any right to use that Trade Mark if the Trade Mark would deceive. I conceive that if at the date when application is made to register a Trade Mark there is *j* no ground of objection upon the footing that it will be calculated to deceive, and if subsequently by alterations in the character of the business of the two parties respectively the use of the Trade Mark will be calculated to deceive and a passing-off action were brought by one party against the other, it would be no defence at all on the part of the owner of the registered Trade Mark to say—"Deception or no deception I am entitled to do it because that

a
is my registered Trade Mark." That could not be advanced for one moment. In other words, the registration of a Trade Mark does not confer any right to do that which could not have been done irrespective of the Trade Mark, in the sense of doing any acts which would be competition in business. The only right which it confers is a right to restrain others from using that Trade Mark.'

b
[40] Had the legislature intended to bestow on the owner of a registered trade mark (or any other intellectual property right) an entitlement to override the rights of others it could and should have done so expressly. An example of this is to be found in the Trade Marks Act 1938 which provided that use of a registered trade mark could not amount to an infringement of another registered trade
c mark (see s 4(4)). A similar provision is to be found in the 1994 Act (see s 11(1)). However even that limited and express statutory right may be open to challenge since it is said by the claimant to be inconsistent with the provisions of the First Council Directive (EEC) 89/104 (to approximate the laws of the member states relating to trade marks) (OJ 1989 L40 p 1) (the Trade Mark Directive).
d Furthermore Mr Silverleaf's argument is difficult to reconcile with s 48(1) which provides:

> 'Where the proprietor of an earlier trade mark or other earlier right has acquiesced for a continuous period of five years in the use of a registered trade mark in the United Kingdom, being aware of that use, there shall cease
e to be any entitlement on the basis of that earlier trade mark or other right ... (b) to oppose the use of the later trade mark in relation to the goods or services in relation to which it has been so used ...'

[41] This proceeds on the basis that the owner of the earlier right (for example Inter Lotto as owner of its rights to protect its goodwill) *is* entitled to sue the
f proprietor of the later trade mark if the use of the latter has not been continuous or has not been for five years or if the owner of the earlier mark was ignorant of the later use of the registered trade mark. In other words the owner of the registered trade mark does not have an entitlement to use his mark in the face of earlier competing rights owned by someone else.

g
IS INTER LOTTO PRECLUDED FROM RELYING ON REPUTATION AND GOODWILL BUILT UP ON THE BACK OF USE OF THE TRADE MARK WHICH, IN THE CIRCUMSTANCES PRESUMED FOR THIS APPLICATION, CONSTITUTED INFRINGEMENT OF THE '392 MARK?

[42] Mr Silverleaf's argument is encapsulated in the extract from his skeleton argument set out in [5] and [6], above. Taken at face value, this would produce
h strange and far-reaching results. First, if a trader cannot rely upon goodwill or reputation built up on trade which is 'unlawful' in the sense used by Mr Silverleaf, it would follow that it should be incapable of being relied on against any competitor. Thus it would be a defence to a passing off action to show that the claimant's use infringed a third party's trade marks. Since there has been an
j explosion of registration of marks, both national and Community, covering ever wider classes of goods and services, in many cases it would be open to the defendant to run this point. Furthermore, if infringement of a trade mark makes the use 'unlawful' and, for that reason, undeserving of protection in a court of law, why should the unlawfulness be limited to infringement of trade mark? If the use relied on by the claimant could be said to infringe someone else's copyright, design rights or be libellous why should he be any more entitled to rely

on his goodwill and reputation than if his unlawfulness consisted of infringement
of a registered trade mark?

[43] In the course of argument Mr Silverleaf addressed some of these points.
First he said that this defence would only be open to the proprietor of the
infringed right. Second he said that the weakness in the claimant's ability to rely
on its reputation and goodwill only arises once the owner of the infringed right
has lodged a claim of infringement. As far as I could tell, both of these were
arguments of expediency. There was no discernible principle which would
justify cutting down the ex turpi rule in this way. As Mr Hobbs said, if
Mr Silverleaf were right, the claimant's goodwill and reputation would be
simultaneously lawful and protectable against third parties but unlawful and not
protectable against the owner of the registered trade mark.

[44] There is nothing in this defence either. The underlying principle of
ex turpi causa is that the behaviour of the party has been so heinous that the court
will not assist it. In the case of trade marks and passing off, occasionally the courts
have held that the claimant's rights have been built up or supported fraudulently.
In those cases the court will not support the claim. Examples include *Bile Bean
Manufacturing Co v Davidson* (1906) 23 RPC 725 and *Leather Cloth Co Ltd v American
Leather Cloth Co Ltd* (1865) 11 HL Cas 523 at 542, 11 ER 1435 at 1443–1444 in
which Lord Kingsdown said:

> 'Nobody doubts that a trader may be guilty of such misrepresentations
> with respect to his goods, as to amount to a fraud upon the public, and to
> disentitle him on that ground, as against a rival trader, to the relief in a court
> of equity which he might otherwise claim. What would constitute a
> misrepresentation of this description, may in particular cases be a reasonable
> subject of doubt, and it was in the present case the ground of the difference
> between the two judgments under consideration. The general rule seems to
> be that the mis-statement of any material fact calculated to deceive the
> public, will be sufficient for the purpose.'

[45] Relevant considerations include the following. First, whether or not a
party's behaviour has been so bad as to merit exclusion from protection by the
court is an issue of fact. Second, the wrongdoing has to be substantial and go to
the heart of the right sued on. In my view it is unarguable that trade mark
infringement without more amounts to wrongdoing of such a level of depravity
as to engage the doctrine. Calling Inter Lotto's actions 'unlawful' as Mr Silverleaf
did on many occasions, does not alter its character. There may be cases where
the nature of the infringement is so flagrant and clearly and knowingly wrongful
that a court might refuse to allow the claimant to rely on his goodwill and
reputation. For example, a trader who sells through street markets counterfeit
versions of sound recordings and DVDs bearing a famous trade mark might not
be allowed to rely on his sales to maintain a passing off action against another
counterfeiter who has come onto the market after him. But there is nothing like
that here. The only wrongdoing alleged is the fact of infringement of the
'392 mark (assuming, of course, that it is infringed). As I have said, the argument
is that there is a per se disentitlement from relying on Inter Lotto's goodwill and
reputation as and from the date on which Camelot applied to register the
'392 mark. It should be borne in mind that there is no suggestion of dishonesty
or flagrancy here, not least because it appears that Inter Lotto was using its mark
months before Camelot applied to register its mark and a year before Camelot
started to use it.

[**46**] Mr Silverleaf says that it is absurd that Inter Lotto should be allowed to sue his client for passing off. He say that Inter Lotto is trying to say that Camelot cannot use its registered mark. First, this is a mischaracterisation of Inter Lotto's case. It is only saying that Camelot cannot use its mark in a way which will lead to deception and confusion. If Camelot can avoid those problems, it can continue to use the '392 mark. Second, whatever the impact of the '392 registration on Inter Lotto, I can see nothing absurd or even surprising in Inter Lotto being able to prevent its reputation and goodwill (assuming for this purpose that the allegations made in its pleadings are borne out at the trial) being appropriated by Camelot.

[**47**] It follows that the preliminary issue is answered in the negative. The relevant date for assessing Inter Lotto's reputation and goodwill for its claim in passing off is the date upon which Camelot started using that mark in relation to its lottery product.

[**48**] I should mention that both Mr Hobbs and Mr Silverleaf made reference to the provisions of the Trade Mark Directive in the course of their submissions. Each said that his arguments were consistent with, or not inconsistent with, that legislation. For the reasons set out above, the answer to the preliminary question is clear as a matter of domestic law. In those circumstances it is not necessary to consider the Community legislation.

Order accordingly.

Celia Fox   Barrister.

R v G and another

[2002] EWCA Crim 1992

COURT OF APPEAL, CRIMINAL DIVISION
DYSON LJ, SILBER J AND JUDGE BEAUMONT QC
16, 17 JULY 2002

Criminal law – Damage to property – Recklessness whether property would be destroyed or damaged – Recklessness – Arson – Test to be applied in deciding whether defendant reckless – Whether defendant's act had created obvious risk that property would be destroyed or damaged – Whether obviousness of risk to be determined according to characteristics of particular defendant – Whether age of defendant to be taken into account in determining obviousness of risk – Whether failure to take account of defendant's age breaching right to fair trial – Criminal Damage Act 1971, s 1 – Human Rights Act 1998, Sch 1, Pt I, art 6(1).

The defendants, aged 11 and 12 respectively, set fire to bundles of newspapers, threw them under a large bin, and left them to burn. The bin was set alight and the fire spread to a shop and adjoining buildings. Damage estimated at £1m was caused. In interview, the defendants said that they had thought that the newspapers would burn themselves out, and that it had never crossed their minds that there was a risk that fire would spread to the buildings. They were charged with arson being reckless as to whether or not property would be destroyed or damaged, contrary to s 1(1) and (3) of the Criminal Damage Act 1971. At the start of the trial the judge ruled, on the basis of previous binding authority, that the test that the jury had to apply in deciding whether the defendants had been reckless as to whether the property would be destroyed or damaged was whether they had done an act which had in fact created an obvious risk that property would be destroyed or damaged, and whether, when they had done the act, they had either not given any thought to the possibility of there being such a risk, or had recognised that there was some risk involved and had nevertheless gone on to do it. He further ruled that the question whether there was an obvious risk of the property being damaged had to be assessed by reference to the reasonable man, and not to a person endowed with the characteristics of the defendants. He directed the jury in accordance with that ruling, telling them that no allowance was made by the law for the youth of the defendants, for their lack of maturity, or for their own inability, if such the jury found it to be, to assess what was going on. The defendants were convicted, and appealed against their convictions on the grounds (i) that the judge had erred in his ruling as to the correct test to be applied, and that he should have held that that test did not apply to children; and/or (ii) that if that test would otherwise apply to children, it was incompatible with art 6[a] of the European Convention for the Protection of Human Rights and Fundamental Freedoms 1950 (as set out in Sch 1 to the Human Rights Act 1998).

Held – (1) The test to be applied in a case of reckless arson was whether the defendant had done an act which had in fact created an obvious risk that property would be destroyed or damaged, and whether, when he had done the act, he had

a Article 6 is set out at [24], below

a either not given any thought to the possibility of there being such a risk, or had recognised that there was some risk involved and had nevertheless gone on to do it. That test was objective, in that the question whether there was an obvious risk of the property being damaged had to be assessed by reference to the ordinarily prudent person, no other qualities or characteristics being relevant. The judge had, accordingly, directed the jury correctly (see [20], [23], below); *R v Caldwell*
b [1981] 1 All ER 961 applied.

(2) A provision which defined the mental element that was a necessary ingredient of an offence was plainly a matter of substantive law, not a matter of procedure, since it was part of the very definition of what constituted the offence. Article 6 of the convention was not concerned with the fairness of provisions of substantive law. Accordingly, the fairness of the test to be applied in cases of
c reckless arson, in so far as it applied to children, was not justiciable under art 6; *Z v UK* [2001] 2 FCR 246 considered.

Notes
For destroying or damaging property see 11(1) *Halsbury's Laws* (4th edn reissue)
d para 594.

For the Criminal Damage Act 1971, s 1, see 12 *Halsbury's Statutes* (2000 reissue) 522.

For the Human Rights Act 1998, Sch 1, Pt I, see 7 *Halsbury's Statutes* (4th edn) (2002 reissue) 554.

e **Cases referred to in judgment**
Ashingdane v UK (1985) 7 EHRR 528, [1985] ECHR 8225/78, ECt HR.
Barbera v Spain (1988) 11 EHRR 360, [1988] ECHR 10588/83, ECt HR.
Elliott v C (a minor) (1983) 77 Cr App R 103, DC.
R v Caldwell [1981] 1 All ER 961, [1982] AC 341, [1981] 2 WLR 509, HL.
f *R v Coles* (1995) 1 Cr App R 157, CA.
R v Cunningham [1957] 2 All ER 412, [1957] 2 QB 396, [1957] 3 WLR 76, CCA.
R v Lawrence [1981] 1 All ER 974, [1982] AC 510, [1981] 2 WLR 524, HL.
R v Miller [1983] 1 All ER 978, [1983] 2 AC 161, [1983] 2 WLR 539, HL.
R v Reid [1992] 3 All ER 673, [1992] 1 WLR 793, HL.
R v Stephen Malcolm R (1984) 79 Cr App R 334, CA.
g *R v Stephenson* [1979] 2 All ER 1198, [1979] QB 695, [1979] 3 WLR 193, CA.
Salabiaku v France (1988) 13 EHRR 379, [1988] ECHR 10589/83, ECt HR.
Z v UK (2001) 10 BHRC 384, ECt HR.

h **Appeal**
The appellants, AG and SR, appealed with leave from their conviction on 23 March 2001 in the Crown Court at Aylesbury before Judge Maher and a jury, of a single offence of arson, causing damage to property being reckless as to whether such property would be damaged, contrary to s 1(1) and (3) of the Criminal Damage Act 1971. The facts are set out in the judgment of Dyson LJ.
j

Andrew Jefferies (assigned by the *Registrar of Criminal Appeals*) for G.
Alan Newman QC and *Isobel Ascherson* (assigned by the *Registrar of Criminal Appeals*) for R.
Richard Whittam and *Basil Hillman* (instructed by the *Crown Prosecution Service*) for the Crown.

Cur adv vult

a

17 July 2002. The following judgment of the court was delivered.

DYSON LJ.

[1] On 23 March 2001 in the Crown Court at Aylesbury before Judge Maher
and a jury, the appellants were convicted of a single offence of arson, causing   b
damage to property being reckless as to whether such property would be
damaged, contrary to s 1(1) and (3) of the Criminal Damage Act 1971. On
20 April, they were each sentenced to a one-year supervision order. At the time
of the offences, AG was 11 years of age, and SR 12. They appeal against their
convictions with the leave of the single judge.

[2] In *R v Caldwell* [1981] 1 All ER 961 at 967, [1982] AC 341 at 354, Lord   c
Diplock (with whom Lords Keith of Kinkel and Roskill agreed) said that a person
charged with an offence under s 1(1) of the 1971 Act is 'reckless as to whether any
such property would be destroyed or damaged' if—

> '(1) he does an act which in fact creates an obvious risk that property will
> be destroyed or damaged and (2) when he does the act he either has not   d
> given any thought to the possibility of there being any such risk or has
> recognised that there was some risk involved and has none the less gone on
> to do it.'

We shall refer to this as 'the *Caldwell* test'. Earlier in his speech, Lord Diplock had   e
made it clear that his exposition of the requirements of recklessness was made by
reference to the 'ordinary prudent individual'. The defendant in that case was an
adult.

[3] At the start of the trial the judge ruled that he had to direct the jury to apply
the *Caldwell* test, and that whether there was an obvious risk of the property being
damaged was to be assessed by reference to the reasonable man, and not a person   f
endowed with the characteristics of the defendants. The judge summed up in
accordance with this ruling. He said that 'the ordinary reasonable bystander is an
adult ... He has got in his mind that stock of everyday information which one
acquires in the process of growing up'. A little later he said: 'no allowance is made
by the law for the youth of these boys or their lack of maturity or their own
inability, if such you find it to be, to assess what was going on.'   g

[4] The appeal raises one issue only, and it is an important issue. It is argued
on behalf of both appellants that the judge was wrong to rule that the *Caldwell* test
was the correct test to apply. He should have held that it (a) does not apply to
children; and/or (b) if it would otherwise apply to children, it is incompatible
with art 6 of the European Convention for the Protection of Human Rights and   h
Fundamental Freedoms 1950 (as set out in Sch 1 to the Human Rights Act 1998).
He should, therefore, have held that, at least in the case of a defendant who is a
young child, art 6 requires it to be a necessary condition of recklessness that the
relevant risk be obvious to the particular defendant, and not merely to the
ordinary reasonable bystander. Before we examine the arguments in more detail,   j
we should briefly set out the facts.

[5] On the night of 21 August 2000, the appellants were out camping. At about
3.45 am on 22 August, they got into the yard at the back of the Co-op shop in NP
where they opened up bundles of newspapers. They set some of them alight, and
threw the burning newspapers under a large wheelie-bin where they left them to
burn. The bin was set alight, and the fire spread to the shop. The shop and some

a adjoining buildings caught fire. Approximately £1m damage was caused. At their first interview, the boys denied any involvement. In their second interview, they admitted what had happened, and said that they thought that the lit newspapers would burn themselves out on the concrete floor. They said that it never crossed their minds that there was a risk that the fire would spread to the building.

b THE AUTHORITIES
[6] We start with an examination of the relevant authorities. First, *R v Caldwell* [1981] 1 All ER 961, [1982] AC 341 itself. Lord Diplock, with whom Lords Keith and Roskill agreed, gave the leading speech. He said:

c 'My Lords, I see no warrant for making any such assumption in an Act whose declared purpose is to revise the then existing law as to offences of damage to property, not to perpetuate it. "Reckless" as used in the new statutory definition of the mens rea of these offences is an ordinary English word. It had not by 1971 become a term of legal art with some more limited esoteric meaning than that which it bore in ordinary speech, a meaning which surely includes not only deciding to ignore a risk of harmful
d consequences resulting from one's acts that one has recognised as existing, but also failing to give any thought to whether or not there is any such risk in circumstances where, if any thought were given to the matter, it would be obvious that there was. If one is attaching labels, the latter state of mind is neither more nor less "subjective" than the first. But the label solves nothing. It is a statement of the obvious; mens rea is, by definition, a state of mind of
e the accused himself at the time he did the physical act that constitutes the actus reus of the offence; it cannot be the mental state of some non-existent, hypothetical person. Nevertheless, to decide whether someone has been "reckless" as to whether harmful consequences of a particular kind will result from his act, as distinguished from his actually intending such harmful
f consequences to follow, does call for some consideration of how the mind of the ordinary prudent individual would have reacted to a similar situation. If there were nothing in the circumstances that ought to have drawn the attention of an ordinary prudent individual to the possibility of that kind of harmful consequence, the accused would not be described as "reckless" in the natural meaning of that word for failing to address his mind to the
g possibility; nor, if the risk of the harmful consequences was so slight that the ordinary prudent individual on due consideration of the risk would not be deterred from treating it as negligible, could the accused be described as "reckless" in its ordinary sense if, having considered the risk, he decided to ignore it.' (See [1981] 1 All ER 961 at 966, [1982] AC 341 at 353–354.)

h
[7] A little later, appears the passage that we have already set out at [2], above.
[8] *R v Caldwell* was concerned with an offence under s 1(1) of the 1971 Act. In *R v Lawrence* [1981] 1 All ER 974, [1982] AC 510, the House of Lords had to consider recklessness for the purpose of an offence of reckless driving. Lord Diplock dealt with the question of recklessness and said ([1981] 1 All ER 974 at
j 982, [1982] AC 510 at 526–527):

'I turn now to the mens rea. My task is greatly simplified by what has already been said about the concept of recklessness in criminal law in *R v Caldwell*. Warning was there given against adopting the simplistic approach of treating all problems of criminal liability as soluble by classifying the test of liability as being either "subjective" or "objective". Recklessness on the

part of the doer of an act does presuppose that there is something in the
circumstances that would have drawn the attention of an ordinary prudent
individual to the possibility that his act was capable of causing the kind of
serious harmful consequences that the section which creates the offence was
intended to prevent, and that the risk of those harmful consequences
occurring was not so slight that an ordinary prudent individual would feel
justified in treating them as negligible. It is only when this is so that the doer
of the act is acting "recklessly" if, before doing the act, he either fails to give
any thought to the possibility of there being any such risk or, having
recognised that there was such risk, he nevertheless goes on to do it. In my
view, an appropriate instruction to the jury on what is meant by driving
recklessly would be that they must be satisfied of two things: first, that the
defendant was in fact driving the vehicle in such a manner as to create an
obvious and serious risk of causing physical injury to some other person who
might happen to be using the road or of doing substantial damage to
property; and, second, that in driving in that manner the defendant did so
without having given any thought to the possibility of there being any such
risk or, having recognised that there was some risk involved, had none the
less gone on to take it. It is for the jury to decide whether the risk created by
the manner in which the vehicle was being driven was both obvious and
serious and, in deciding this, they may apply the standard of the ordinary
prudent motorist as represented by themselves. If satisfied that an obvious
and serious risk was created by the manner of the defendant's driving, the
jury are entitled to infer that he was in one or other of the states of mind
required to constitute the offence and will probably do so; but regard must
be given to any explanation he gives as to his state of mind which may
displace the inference.'

[9] All subsequent attempts in cases under s 1(1) of the 1971 Act to distinguish
R v Caldwell, and to persuade the court not to apply the *Caldwell* test have failed.
Thus, in *Elliott v C (a minor)* (1983) 77 Cr App R 103, the Divisional Court applied
the test to the case of a 14-year-old girl who was in a remedial class at school. The
court held that the phrase 'creates an obvious risk' means that the risk must have
been obvious to a reasonably prudent person, and not necessarily to the
defendant. The justices had found that the risk that the fire that had been started
by the defendant would cause damage would not have been obvious 'having
regard to the age and understanding of the defendant, her lack of experience of
dealing with inflammable spirit, and the fact that she must have been tired and
exhausted at the time' (see (1983) 77 Cr App R 103 at 117). They therefore
dismissed the information. The Divisional Court allowed the prosecutor's
appeal on the ground that the justices had failed to apply the *Caldwell* test.
Robert Goff LJ expressed his unhappiness about this result. Nevertheless, he said
(at 118–119):

'Here again, it would be unrealistic if I were to disguise the fact that I am
well aware that the statement of principle by Lord Diplock in *R. v.
CALDWELL* has been the subject of comment, much of it critical, in articles
written by jurists; and that I have studied certain of these articles with
interest. I find it striking that the justices, in reaching their conclusion in the
present case, have done so (no doubt in response to an argument advanced
on the defendant's behalf) by imposing upon Lord Diplock's statement of
principle a qualification similar to one considered by Professor Glanville

a

Williams in his article "Recklessness Redefined" in [1981] C.L.J. 252, 270-271. This is that a defendant should only be regarded as having acted recklessly by virtue of his failure to give any thought to an obvious risk that property would be destroyed or damaged, where such risk would have been obvious *to him* if he had given any thought to the matter. However, having studied Lord Diplock's speech, I do not think it would be consistent with his

b

reasoning to impose any such qualification. I say that not only because this qualification does not appear in terms in his conclusion which I have already quoted, but also because, when considering earlier in his speech Professor Kenny's definition of recklessness (which he rejected as being too narrow), Lord Diplock expressly adverted to the fact that that definition presupposed that "if thought were given to the matter by the doer before the act was

c

done, it would have been apparent *to him* that there was a real risk of its having the relevant harmful consequences." It seems to me that, having expressly considered that element in Professor Kenny's test, and having (as I think) plainly decided to omit it from his own formulation of the concept of recklessness, it would not now be legitimate for an inferior court, in a case

d

under this particular subsection, to impose a qualification which had so been rejected by Lord Diplock himself. It follows that for that reason alone I do not feel able to uphold the reasoning of the magistrates in the present case.'

[10] The case of *R v Stephen Malcolm R* (1984) 79 Cr App R 334 concerned a defendant who was 15 years of age. It was accepted on his behalf that *R v Caldwell*

e

[1981] 1 All ER 961, [1982] AC 341 prevented the court from asking the question whether the defendant was aware of the risk. But it was argued (at 340) that the court could ask the question whether a 'person of the age of the defendant and with his characteristics which might be relevant to his ability to foresee the risk, would have appreciated it'. The judgment of the court was given by Ackner LJ. He held that it was not open to this court to accept this suggested modified

f

departure from the full rigour of the *Caldwell* test. He did not think (at 341) that this '*via media* was for one moment in the mind of Lord Diplock'. Ackner LJ did not disguise his regret in reaching this conclusion.

[11] Another attempt to distinguish *R v Caldwell* was made in *R v Coles* [1995] 1 Cr App R 157. But before we consider that case, we need to refer to the House

g

of Lords' decision in *R v Reid* [1992] 3 All ER 673, [1992] 1 WLR 793. This was a reckless driving case. The summing up had contained a direction using the very words stated by Lord Diplock in *R v Lawrence* [1981] 1 All ER 974 at 982, [1982] AC 510 at 526 as being 'an appropriate instruction' on what is meant by driving recklessly. It was submitted that the definition of recklessness in *R v Lawrence* was incorrect, and that their Lordships should depart from it. This they refused to do.

h

They endorsed the reasoning in *R v Caldwell* and *R v Lawrence* that responsibility in the criminal law should extend beyond those who appreciate the risks they run to those who culpably fail to do so. But there are passages in the speeches on which Mr Newman relies as indicating a possible softening of Lord Diplock's formulation in *R v Lawrence*. In particular, Lord Keith said ([1992] 3 All ER 673 at

j 675, [1992] 1 WLR 793 at 796):

'The substance of Lord Diplock's formulation of a specimen jury direction is accordingly apt, in my opinion, to cover the generality of cases. But I do not rule out that in certain cases there may be special circumstances which require it to be modified or added to, for example where the driver acted under some understandable and excusable mistake or where his capacity to

appreciate risks was adversely affected by some condition not involving fault
on his part. There may also be cases where the driver acted as he did in a
sudden dilemma created by the actions of others. The specific certified
question as to whether the jury should always be directed in the ipsissima
verba of Lord Diplock's formulation I would answer in the negative. In
some cases when the only relevant issue is one of disputed fact it may not be
necessary to use it all. In others it may require to be modified or adapted to
suit the circumstances of the case.'

[12] We would also refer to the speech of Lord Goff of Chieveley ([1992] 3 All
ER 673 at 690, [1992] 1 WLR 793 at 813) and the speech of Lord
Browne-Wilkinson ([1992] 3 All ER 673 at 696, [1992] 1 WLR 793 at 819).

[13] But it is important to emphasise that these are no more than dicta which,
as was said by Stewart Field and Mervyn Lynn in their article 'Capacity,
Recklessness and the House of Lords' [1993] Crim LR 127, are 'a possible signpost
to future refinement of the test for *Caldwell/Lawrence* recklessness'. Moreover,
various of the speeches indicated that what was said about recklessness in *R v Reid*
was directed only at the offence of reckless driving. Thus Lord Ackner: [1992]
3 All ER 673 at 683, [1992] 1 WLR 793 at 805. Lord Goff ([1992] 3 All ER 673 at 685,
[1992] 1 WLR 793 at 807) said that the case was not directly concerned with the
meaning of the word 'reckless' in s 1(1) of the 1971 Act. Lord Browne-Wilkinson
([1992] 3 All ER 673 at 675 at 694, [1992] 1 WLR 793 at 816–817) said that he did not
accept that the constituent elements of recklessness must be the same in all
statutes. He identified three factors which could lead to the conclusion that
recklessness in the offence of reckless driving did not bear the same meaning as
recklessness in s 1 of the 1971 Act.

[14] We can now return to *R v Coles* (1995) 1 Cr App R 157. The appellant in
that case was 15 years of age. The defence wished to call expert evidence from a
psychologist on the capacity of the appellant to foresee the risks involved in his
actions, and submitted that the test of recklessness should be subjective. The trial
judge refused to allow the evidence and rejected the submission as to the correct
test for recklessness. The defendant pleaded guilty and appealed to this court.
The appeal was dismissed. Hobhouse LJ gave the judgment of the court. He
reviewed the authorities, including *R v Reid*. He said that the request by the
defence to substitute in the first leg of the *Caldwell* direction 'a defendant aged 11
with low intellectual functioning' for the usual reference to the 'reasonable
prudent man' was 'misconceived'. It showed confusion between actus reus and
mens rea (see (1995) 1 Cr App R 157 at 163). The first leg provided an objective
criterion which the defendant's act must satisfy, and his mental state was
irrelevant on that point. The appellant then sought to argue that the facts
required a qualification to the second leg of the *Caldwell* direction so as to require
the jury to consider the culpability of the particular defendant having regard to
his capacity to foresee the relevant risk (see (1995) 1 Cr App R 157 at 163).
Hobhouse LJ accepted that proof of an obvious risk was not necessarily proof of
recklessness: the jury must listen to the defendant's explanations, which might
show that he did not fall within either of the two state of mind in the second leg
of the *Caldwell* direction (see (1995) 1 Cr App R 157 at 165). The matter was not,
however, free of authority. *R v Miller* [1983] 1 All ER 978, [1983] 2 AC 161 was
authority for the view that for proof of recklessness, there is no need to prove any
actual appreciation on the part of the defendant of the relevant risk (see (1995) 1
Cr App R 157 at 166). The qualification suggested to the *Caldwell* test was the

a   same as had been rejected in *Elliott v C (a minor)* (1983) 77 Cr App R 103. As
    regards *R v Reid*, Hobhouse LJ noted that in that case a further attempt had been
    made, in the context of reckless driving, to depart from the formulations of Lord
    Diplock in *R v Caldwell* and *R v Lawrence*, and said ((1995) 1 Cr App R 157 at 168):

b   'The essence of the argument being advanced was the same as the
        underlying argument advanced before us—that it is inconsistent with a
        proper approach to criminal responsibility to exclude a subjective
        qualification of the *Caldwell* formulation. The House of Lords in reasoned
        judgments rejected those arguments. Even if it were open to this court to do
        so, it is not appropriate that this Court should accede to an invitation to
        reformulate the law of recklessness when it has so recently been confirmed,
c   after full consideration, by a decision of the House of Lords.'

    A CONSIDERATION OF THE PROBLEM WITHOUT REFERENCE TO ART 6 OF THE
    CONVENTION
        [15] Mr Newman QC submits as follows. The *Caldwell* test is not binding on
    us in this case because the facts here are materially different from the facts in *R v
d   Caldwell*. The ratio of *R v Caldwell* is that the test propounded by Lord Diplock
    only applies to defendants who are adults who have no relevant disability. That
    is why he referred repeatedly in his speech to the 'ordinary prudent individual'.
    He did not have in mind young children, who although in general terms are old
    enough to have criminal responsibility, may not be of sufficient age to be able to
e   have the understanding and foresight of an adult. Nor did he have in mind
    persons, of whatever age, who suffer from some relevant mental or physical
    disability. In short, the House of Lords only had to consider the case of the
    ordinary prudent individual, and the application of the *Caldwell* test is confined to
    such persons.
        [16] The central question that arises is: to whom must the risk mentioned in
f   the first leg of the test be 'obvious'? Mr Newman submits that it must be obvious
    either to the defendant in the particular case, or to a reasonably prudent person
    endowed with the age and other characteristics of the defendant that are relevant
    to his or her being able to appreciate the existence of the risk. He says that it is
    irrational to take what is obvious to a reasonably prudent adult as the yardstick
g   by which to measure what is obvious to a young child or a person with relevant
    disabilities. Lord Diplock could not have intended this.
        [17] Mr Newman makes the point that the *Caldwell* test has been subjected to
    frequent and sustained criticism, particularly in academic writings. One example
    will suffice. In the current edition of *Smith and Hogan's Criminal Law* (10th edn,
h   2002) pp 81–82 the authors say:

        'The test works harshly in these cases of young people. In the case of
        adults, it will do so in the case of those who lack the capacities of the ordinary
        prudent person. In [*R v Stephenson* [1979] 2 All ER 1198, [1979] QB 695] a
        tramp sheltered in a hollow in a haystack. Feeling cold, he lit a fire in the
j   hollow. The haystack was destroyed. Any reasonable person would have
        been aware of the risk but Stephenson was suffering from schizophrenia and
        may not have been aware of it. Because this was not clearly left to the jury,
        the court—pre-*Caldwell*—quashed his conviction. Even if he had stopped to
        think it is possible that, because of his condition, he might not have realised
        that there was a risk of damage. *Stephenson* appears to be overruled by
        Caldwell. How far are we to go in ignoring abnormalities? Is a blind man to

be held to have recklessly damaged property because he was unaware of a risk which would have been obvious to a sighted person? And what about temporary handicaps – the person who strikes a match, being unaware because of his heavy cold, that the premises reek with petrol fumes? *Caldwell*, as interpreted in *Elliott v C* and *R v Stephen Malcolm R*, appears to be a slippery slope to intolerable injustice with no obvious exit. If it would have appeared to the reasonably prudent person that there was an obvious risk, it is immaterial that a person with expert knowledge not possessed by the defendant would have known that there was no, or no serious, risk. A person may act, reckless to whether life is endangered, without there being in fact any danger to life.'

[18] We readily acknowledge the force of the criticisms that have been made of the *Caldwell* test. They were adverted to in *Elliott v C (a minor)* (1983) 77 Cr App R 103 and *R v Stephen Malcolm R* (1984) 79 Cr App R 334. The *Caldwell* test has been criticised and has not been applied in a number of Commonwealth jurisdictions. All this we accept. The question for us is whether it is open to us to hold that the *Caldwell* test should not have been applied in this case. We are in no doubt that it is not.

[19] First, it seems to us that in *R v Caldwell*, Lord Diplock was propounding a test at a high level of generalisation, which he intended to apply at least to all cases under s 1 of the 1971 Act. He considered the definition of recklessness given by Professor Kenny in the first edition of his *Outlines of Criminal Law* (1901) in the context of offences which are committed 'maliciously' and which was approved in *R v Cunningham* [1957] 2 All ER 412, [1957] 2 QB 396, viz:

'In any statutory definition of a crime "malice" must be taken ... as requiring either (i) an actual intention to do the particular *kind* of harm that in fact was done, or (ii) recklessness as to whether such harm should occur or not (i.e. the accused has foreseen that the particular kind of harm might be done, and yet has gone on to take the risk of it).'

[20] This test unquestionably does focus on the state of mind of the particular defendant who is before the court. But Lord Diplock rejected this as the test to be applied to recklessness in s 1(1) of the 1971 Act. The passage which we have already quoted at [6], above, refers three times to the 'ordinary prudent individual'. Although Lord Diplock criticised the use of the labels 'subjective' and 'objective', it is clear that he opted for what it is convenient to call the 'objective' test. There is nothing in his speech to indicate that he considered that any qualities or characteristics were relevant other than that the person should be ordinarily prudent. A number of characteristics may affect a person's ability to see a risk for what it is: he may be too young, or too old; he may be of poor intelligence or suffer from some relevant psychological condition; or from physical disabilities which impair his ability to appreciate the existence of a risk. If Lord Diplock had considered that any of these factors was relevant to the obviousness of the risk, he would have said so. He would not have repeatedly referred to the ordinary prudent individual.

[21] But secondly, even if we entertained some doubt as to the intended scope of the *Caldwell* test, we are in any event bound by previous authority to reject Mr Newman's submissions. It is true that the decision in *Elliott*'s case is not binding on this court. But the carefully considered judgments of Robert Goff LJ and Glidewell J are of great persuasive force. We bear in mind that Robert

a Goff LJ said (at 116–117) that he allowed the appeal simply because he felt constrained to do so by *R v Caldwell*, although the result was one about which he was unhappy. The decisions in *R v Stephen Malcolm R* (1984) 79 Cr App R 334 and *R v Coles* (1995) 1 Cr App R 157 are binding on this court. Mr Newman submits that these decisions are simply wrong and should not be followed.

b [22] We do not feel able to accept this submission. It seems to us that Professor Elliott put the matter accurately in his article 'Endangering Life by Destroying or Damaging Property' [1997] Crim LR 382 at 387:

c 'Thus, in the absence of further recourse to the House of Lords, it is still the law that a defendant charged with criminal damage who gives no thought to an obvious risk is prima facie reckless. He is allowed to explain his failure to give thought, which may in rare cases be held to be non-culpable, but evidence of lack of capacity to see the risk will not prevent a finding of recklessness. The objective criterion which his conduct must satisfy is that it suggests to an ordinary prudent individual the possibility of a non-negligible risk of the relevant harm occurring.'

d We should add that we do not consider that *R v Reid* [1992] 3 All ER 673, [1992] 1 WLR 793 requires us to arrive at a different result. First, *R v Reid* was analysed in *R v Coles* with the result to which we have earlier referred. We are bound by *R v Coles*, and that is sufficient reason for saying that *R v Reid* does not advance Mr Newman's argument. Secondly, in *R v Reid* their Lordships made it clear that they were dealing with reckless driving, and not with s 1(1) of the 1971 Act.

e Thirdly, both *Elliott's* case and *R v Stephen Malcolm R* were cited in *R v Reid*. No mention is made of either decision in any of the speeches in *R v Reid*. If the House of Lords considered that those decisions were wrong, it is most surprising that they did not say so.

f [23] In our judgment, it is for the House of Lords to decide whether the time has come to revisit the *Caldwell* test. Although we see great force in the criticisms of the first leg of the *Caldwell* test that have been made, it is not open to this court to depart from it. Accordingly, we reject the first route by which Mr Newman seeks to challenge the convictions in this case.

ARTICLE 6 OF THE CONVENTION

g [24] Article 6 of the convention provides:

'1. In the determination of his civil rights and obligations or of any criminal charge against him, everyone is entitled to a fair and public hearing within a reasonable time by an independent and impartial tribunal established by law. Judgment shall be pronounced publicly but the press and public may be

h excluded from all or part of the trial in the interest of morals, public order or national security in a democratic society, where the interests of juveniles or the protection of the private life of the parties so require, or to the extent strictly necessary in the opinion of the court in special circumstances where publicity would prejudice the interests of justice.

j 2. Everyone charged with a criminal offence shall be presumed innocent until proved guilty according to law.

3. Everyone charged with a criminal offence has the following minimum rights:
(a) to be informed promptly, in a language he understands and in detail, of the nature and cause of the accusation against him;
(b) to have adequate time and facilities for the preparation of his defence;

(c) to defend himself in person or through legal assistance of his own choosing or, if he has not sufficient means to pay for legal assistance, to be given it free when the interests of justice so require;

(d) to examine or have examined witnesses against him and to obtain the attendance and examination of witnesses on his behalf under the same conditions as witnesses against him;

(e) to have the free assistance of an interpreter if he cannot understand or speak the language used in court.'

[25] Mr Newman advances the following propositions: (a) to judge the moral and legal culpability of a child by reference to the understanding and life experience of an adult is irrational and, therefore, unfair; (b) the *Caldwell* test is disproportionately harsh given the serious consequences that can potentially flow from a conviction of an offence under s 1(1) of the 1971 Act (detention for life); and (c) the *Caldwell* test effectively renders an offence under s 1(1) an offence of strict liability in the case of a child, because a child is incapable of advancing a defence based on his or her immaturity and lack of understanding.

[26] He contends that art 6 is not restricted to ensuring procedural fairness. In any event, it is not helpful to classify provisions as procedural on the one hand and substantive on the other hand. Whether a provision is substantive or procedural in form is often a 'matter of chance', since it depends on how the national legislature has chosen to frame the provision. Mr Newman illustrates his point by the following example:

'... if, instead of containing the word *"reckless"* in the offence-creating provision, there had been a separate provision of law which stated: "as regards criminal trials, children are presumed to have the same mental development and experience in life as adults" such provision would have been labelled "procedural" rather than 'substantive" ...'

The European Court of Human Rights does not attach importance to such labelling, but looks at 'the proceedings ... as a whole' and asks whether they comply with art 6 (see *Barbera v Spain* (1988) 11 EHRR 360 at 384–385 (para 68)).

[27] In our judgment, Mr Newman's submissions are misconceived. We fully accept that art 6 should be given a broad and purposive interpretation. But it seems to us that it is clear, even without the assistance of Strasbourg jurisprudence, that on any natural reading of it, art 6 is not concerned with the fairness of provisions of *substantive* law. It contains three distinct elements: access to a court; provisions regarding the organisation and constitution of the court; and minimum standards of fairness concerning the conduct of proceedings. Mr Newman argues that the phrase 'a fair hearing', which appears in the body of the article, is sufficient to include the fairness of substantive law. But if the article is read as a whole, we have no doubt that this phrase does not bear the weight for which Mr Newman contends.

[28] The distinction between procedural and substantive law is clear and important. It is not a matter of mere 'labelling'. A provision which defines the mental element or mens rea that is a necessary element of an offence is plainly not a matter of procedure. It is a matter of substantive law since it is part of the very definition of what constitutes the offence. There is a difference in kind between the requirement for, and definition of, a mental element of an offence (substantive), and the means by which the existence of such a mental element may be proved (procedural).

a   [29] It is a matter for the contracting state to choose how to define the essential elements of an offence. Thus, it has been established that an offence of strict liability, as opposed to one requiring a mental element, does not violate art 6(2). In *Salabiaku v France* (1988) 13 EHRR 379 at 387 (para 27), the European Court of Human Rights said:

b   'As the Government and the Commission have pointed out, in principle the Contracting States remain free to apply the criminal law to an act where it is not carried out in the normal exercise of one of the rights protected under the Convention and, accordingly, to define the constituent elements of the resulting offence. In particular, and again in principle, the Contracting States may, under certain conditions, penalise a simple or objective fact as c   such, irrespective of whether it results from criminal intent or from negligence. Examples of such offences may be found in the laws of the Contracting States.'

[30] The European Court of Human Rights has made it clear on a number of occasions that art 6 is not concerned with the fairness of substantive law. The d   case of *Z v UK* (2001) 10 BHRC 384 is a recent and important example. The applicants' claims against a local authority for negligently failing to protect them against abuse at the hands of their parents had been struck out in the United Kingdom courts as disclosing no cause of action. They complained, inter alia, that there had been a breach of art 6 because they had been denied access to a court. It was held by the European Court of Human Rights that there had been e   no breach. The court recognised the distinction between substantive law (which is not a matter for art 6) and procedural law (which is). Thus they said (at 405–406 (para 87)):

'The court recalls its constant case law to the effect that: "Article 6(1) extends only to *contestations* (disputes) over (civil) 'rights and obligations' f   which can be said, at least on arguable grounds, to be recognised under domestic law; it does not itself guarantee any particular content for (civil) 'rights and obligations' in the substantive law of the Contracting States" ... It will however apply to disputes of a "genuine and serious nature" concerning the actual existence of the right as well as to the scope or manner in which it g   is exercised.'

[31] Later they said (at 408 (para 98)):

'As it has recalled above in para 87 it is a principle of convention case law that art 6 does not in itself guarantee any particular content for civil rights h   and obligations in national law, although other articles such as those protecting the right to respect for family life (art 8) and the right to property ... may do so.'

[32] Finally, they said (at 408–409):

j   '100. In the present case, the court is led to the conclusion that the inability of the applicants to sue the local authority flowed not from an immunity but from the applicable principles governing the substantive right of action in domestic law. There was no restriction on access to the court of the kind contemplated in *Ashingdane v UK* (1985) 7 EHRR 528.

101. The applicants may not therefore claim that they were deprived of any right to a determination on the merits of their negligence claims. Their

claims were properly and fairly examined in light of the applicable domestic legal principles concerning the tort of negligence. Once the House of Lords had ruled on the arguable legal issues that brought into play the applicability of art 6(1) of the convention ... the applicants could no longer claim any entitlement under art 6(1) to obtain any hearing concerning the facts. As pointed out above, such a hearing would have served no purpose, unless a duty of care in negligence had been held to exist in their case. It is not for this court to find that this should have been the outcome of the striking out proceedings since this would effectively involve substituting its own views as to the proper interpretation and content of domestic law.'

[33] The position is quite clear. So far as art 6 is concerned, the fairness of the provisions of the substantive law of the contracting states is not a matter for investigation. The content and interpretation of domestic substantive law is not engaged by art 6. It may, however, be engaged by other articles of the convention. Thus, for example, if the penalty for an offence under s 1(1) of the 1971 Act were *fixed* at the current maximum of life imprisonment, then there would be an overwhelming case for saying that it amounted to 'inhuman or degrading treatment punishment' contrary to art 3.

[34] On the other hand, the means by which a person's substantive civil rights are vindicated by the courts of the contracting states, and the means by which those courts try a person charged with a substantive criminal offence are susceptible to scrutiny under art 6. We are in no doubt that the fairness of the *Caldwell* test, in so far as it is applied to children, is not justiciable under art 6.

[35] Mr Newman has been unable to cite any decision of the European Court of Human Rights which supports the proposition that art 6 is concerned with fairness of substantive law. We do not consider that the decision in *Barbera v Spain* (1988) 11 EHRR 360 affords any support for Mr Newman's contrary submissions. That was a case which concerned allegations of bias in the court and procedural unfairness. There was no complaint that the substantive offences on which they faced trial were themselves unfair. It was in that context that what the court said at para 68 (at 384–385) must be considered. They said:

'As a general rule, it is for the national courts, and in particular the court of first instance, to assess the evidence before them as well as the relevance of the evidence which the accused seeks to adduce. The Court must, however, determine—and in this it agrees with the Commission—whether the proceedings considered as a whole, including the way in which prosecution and defence evidence was taken, were fair as required by Article 6(1). For this purpose it will consider in turn the various grounds of complaint before it.'

[36] For these reasons, these appeals must be dismissed.

Appeals dismissed.

Lynne Townley   Barrister.

a
Cinderella Rockerfellas Ltd v Rudd
[2003] EWCA Civ 529

COURT OF APPEAL, CIVIL DIVISION

POTTER, CHADWICK AND TUCKEY LJJ

b

3, 4 FEBRUARY, 11 APRIL 2003

Rates – Rateable occupation – Rateable hereditament – Chattels enjoyed with land –
Vessel used as floating nightclub – Vessel permanently secured to land – Vessel's owner
licensed to use land for such purpose – Whether rateable.

c

The company operated and occupied a nightclub situated upon a floating vessel
which at all material times was moored and berthed on a river under licence. The
vessel was moored to the quay and held in position over the riverbed by means
of ropes and chains secured to capstans on the quayside. On an appeal by the
d company against two entries in the valuation list relating to the vessel, the local
valuation tribunal directed that the entries should be deleted on the ground that
the vessel was not rateable. The valuation officer appealed to the Lands Tribunal,
which held, applying the principle that although a chattel was not a rateable
hereditament by itself, it might become rateable together with land if placed on
a piece of land and enjoyed with it in such circumstances and with such a degree
e of permanence that the chattel and the land could together be regarded as one
unit of occupation, that the vessel was rateable. The company appealed,
contending that the absence of vertical connection to the riverbed effectively
prevented the presence of the floating vessel from being regarded as itself a
method of occupation of the land beneath, and that the absence of any adaptation
of the vessel or its integration and enjoyment with the adjacent land preserved its
f separate character as a chattel.

Held – The principle that a chattel placed upon a piece of land, enjoyed with that
land and enhancing its value, could with that land form a rateable hereditament
while remaining in law a chattel, was apt to apply in a case where the chattel was
g a floating vessel placed upon land covered with water. The question whether the
chattel had a direct physical connection to that part of the land which lay
vertically beneath it was highly relevant to, and would generally be definitive of,
the question whether the chattel occupied and/or was enjoyed with land
comprised within the hereditament identified. However, a permanently moored
h vessel, moored in position over part of a riverbed licensed to the owner for that
purpose, even without such a physical connection, could in appropriate
circumstances be enjoyed with the riverbed beneath and enhance its value. In the
instant case, by means of horizontal connection to the adjacent quay which
together with the riverbed formed part of the same hereditament, the vessel was
permanently secured in a position above and within a part of the riverbed which
j was licensed to the company for the very purpose for which it was used. In those
circumstances the Lands Tribunal had been entitled to find that the vessel was
rateable, and the appeal would, accordingly, be dismissed (see [42], [43], [62]–[65],
below).

London CC v Wilkins (Valuation Officer) [1956] 3 All ER 38, *Field Place Caravan*
Park Ltd v Harding (Valuation Officer) [1966] 3 All ER 247 applied. *Assessor for*

Glasgow v Gilmartin 1920 SC 488, *Assessor for Glasgow v RNVR Club (Scotland)* 1974
SC 67, *Comr of Rating and Valuation v Yiu Lian Machinery Repairing Works Ltd* [1985]
2 HKC 517 considered.

Notes
For the non-domestic rating of moorings, artificial watercourses, towing-paths
and harbours, see 39(1) *Halsbury's Laws* (4th edn reissue) para 629.

Cases referred to in judgments
Anderson Grice & Co Ltd v Angus Assessor [1962] RA 590, LVAC.
Cory v Bristow (1877) 2 App Cas 262, [1874–80] All ER Rep 136, HL.
Earby's Case (1633) 2 Bulst 354, 80 ER 1180.
Electric Telegraph Co v Salford Overseers (1855) 11 Exch 181, 156 ER 795.
Felgate (Valuation Officer) v Lotus Leisure Enterprises Ltd [2000] RA 89.
Field Place Caravan Park Ltd v Harding (Valuation Officer) [1966] 3 All ER 247, [1966]
    2 QB 484, [1966] 3 WLR 198, CA.
Glasgow (Assessor for) v Gilmartin 1920 SC 488, LVAC.
Glasgow (Assessor for) v RNVR Club (Scotland) 1974 SC 67, LVAC.
Laing (John) & Son Ltd v Kingswood Assessment Committee [1949] 1 All ER 224,
    [1949] 1 KB 344, CA.
Lancashire Telephone Co v Manchester Overseers (1884) 13 QBD 700; *affd* (1884)
    14 QBD 267, CA.
London CC v Wilkins (Valuation Officer) [1956] 3 All ER 38, [1957] AC 362, [1956]
    3 WLR 505, HL.
Menzies (John) & Co Ltd v Assessor for Edinburgh 1937 SC 784, LVAC.
Renfrewshire (Assessor for) v Mitchell 1965 SC 271, Ct of Sess.
Ryan Industrial Fuels Ltd v Morgan (Valuation Officer) [1965] 3 All ER 465, [1965]
    1 WLR 1347, CA.
Smith's Dock Co Ltd v Tynemouth Corp [1908] 1 KB 315, DC.
Thomas (Valuation Officer) v Witney Aquatic Co Ltd [1972] RA 493.
Westminster City Council v Southern Rly Co [1936] 2 All ER 322, [1936] AC 511, HL.
Whenman v Clark [1916] 1 KB 94, CA.
Woodbury (Valuation Officer) v The Yard Arm Club Ltd [1990] 1 EGLR 237; *affd* sub
    nom *Westminster City Council v Woodbury (Valuation Officer)* [1991] 2 EGLR 173,
    CA.
Yiu Lian Machinery Repairing Works Ltd v Comr of Rating and Valuation [1982] HKC
    55, HK Lands Trib; *affd* sub nom *Comr of Rating and Valuation v Yiu Lian
    Machinery Repairing Works Ltd* [1985] 2 HKC 517, Hong Kong CA.

Appeal
Cinderella Rockerfellas Ltd, owner and occupier of a nightclub situated on a
floating vessel known as the Tuxedo Royale, moored and berthed on the River
Tyne at Hillgate Quay, Gateshead, Tyne and Wear, appealed with permission
granted by Peter Gibson LJ on 4 September 2002 from the decision of the Lands
Tribunal (George Bartlett QC, President) dated 13 June 2002 ([2002] RA 131)
allowing two consolidated appeals by the respondent valuation officer, Peter
James Rudd, from the decision of the Tyne and Wear Valuation Tribunal that
two entries in the valuation list relating to the vessel should be deleted on the
ground that the vessel was not rateable. The facts are set out in the judgment of
Potter LJ.

a *David Widdicombe QC* and *Robert Walton* (instructed by *Richmonds,* Newcastle-upon-Tyne) for the company.
Timothy Mould (instructed by the *Solicitor of Inland Revenue*) for the valuation officer.

Cur adv vult

b 11 April 2003. The following judgments were delivered.

POTTER LJ.

INTRODUCTION

c [1] This is an appeal by Cinderella Rockerfellas Ltd (the appellants) the operators and occupiers of a nightclub situated upon a floating vessel, the Tuxedo Royale (the vessel) which at all material times was moored and berthed on the River Tyne at Hillgate Quay, Gateshead. They appeal against the decision of the Lands Tribunal (George Bartlett QC, President) dated 13 June 2002 ([2002] RA 131) whereby the Lands Tribunal allowed two consolidated appeals by the

d valuation officer against decisions of the Tyne and Wear Valuation Tribunal. The latter tribunal had, on appeals by the appellants, directed that two entries 'River and riverbed occupied by floating nightclub, moorings, car park and premises' and '"Tuxedo Royale", Hillgate Quay, Gateshead, Tyne and Wear' should be deleted on the ground that the vessel was not rateable.

e [2] The appeal thus raises the question of the rateability of floating vessels in the English law of rating and, incidentally, whether it diverges from Scottish law.

THE FACTS

[3] The material facts as agreed between the parties before the Lands Tribunal were as follows. I have indicated in square brackets certain additional matters not mentioned in the agreed facts but which were not in dispute on the appeal.

f [4] The vessel was built in 1964. It is 350 feet long, 54 feet in the beam and has a gross registered tonnage of 5888. Then known as Sol Express, it operated as a passenger and drive-on vehicle ferry until 1988 when it was modified for its present use and renamed. It was moored at Hillgate Quay from 1989 to 1999 under licence granted to the appellants by the Crown Estate Commissioners (the

g commissioners). The first licence, dated 26 January 1990 (the 1990 licence), granted for a period of five years from 26 November 1988 the right to place and maintain on and over the foreshore and bed of the River Tyne adjoining Hillgate Quay, in the position indicated on the plan and annexed licence, the vessel or such replacement vessel as might be approved by the licensor. [The plan attached

h showed the vessel in position in the river beside the quay within a rectangular marked area closely drawn around the vessel indicating the extent of the foreshore and river bed licensed.] By cl 2(11) the vessel was not to be used for any purpose 'save as an entertainment complex comprising restaurants, bars and disco function rooms exhibitions and like users'. Clause 3(4) stipulated:

j   'Nothing herein is to be construed as conferring on the Licensee the right to the exclusive use of any part of the said foreshore or bed of the River Tyne and the Commissioners shall be at liberty to grant such interest rights and easements in or over the same as the Commissioners shall think fit provided only that the placing and maintenance of the Vessel in accordance with this Licence is not thereby prevented.'

[5] Thereafter there was no interference by the licensor with the appellants' use of the parts of the foreshore or bed of the river to which the licence related and the commissioners granted no additional rights during the term of the 1990 licence. By licence dated 23 November 1994 the commissioners granted rights to the respondents in similar terms to those in the 1990 licence save that cl 3(4) was omitted. The vessel was used in compliance with cl 2(11) throughout the period of both licences.

[6] The 1·52 acres of land which contained the Hillgate Quay frontage on its northern boundary was the subject of a lease for ten years from 26 November 1983 originally made between Gateshead Borough Council (the council) and a company called Riverzest Ltd, which became vested in the appellants. The lease included the right to use the frontage for the purpose of berthing a vessel previously known as the SS Caledonian Princess or any other vessel in the appellants' ownership which the council might authorise in writing as an alternative to the named vessel. There was a prohibition against using the quay structure for any other purposes and a requirement that the vessel should be used as a restaurant, licensed premises, hotel, disco and conference centre. Clause 3(g) required the lessee to use the surface of the quay area for the parking of customers' private vehicles in properly marked out parking areas.

[7] By a lease dated 21 November 1994 the council granted the appellants a further 12-year term from 26 November 1993 upon terms not materially different from those in the previous lease. Again, at all material times, the quay structure, vessel and quay areas were used within the purposes provided by the leases.

[8] The vessel was moved to the quay and held in position over the river bed by means of ropes and chains secured to capstans on the quayside. It was subject to tidal movement. It remained secured at its berth from 1989 to 1999, only being moved from its position once for the purpose of demonstrating that it could be moved away from its mooring. On that occasion it was moved by being towed by tugs. In 1999 it was moved to the River Tees for similar use, before being replaced at Gateshead by a similar vessel.

[9] The main accommodation on the vessel consisted of bars, offices, a restaurant, a café/diner and adjoining discotheque, a main discotheque holding up to 700 people, a kitchen, toilets, two private function suites, storage areas and a cellar on the lower deck. Access to the vessel was by means of four metal gangways on the quay. [The gangways were strongly constructed of steel, totally enclosed and capable of moving on the quayside as the vessel rose and fell with the tide.] The car park was used as a private car park for the purposes of the appellant's business use of the vessel. The vessel generated its own electricity and there was no mains connection. It was not connected to a public sewer, but instead had tanks that were emptied and serviced by a private contractor. There was a water supply to the quay and from there to the vessel by means of a hose. There was a telephone connection.

[10] The vessel had a full justices' on-licence and an entertainment licence granted by the local authority. It was registered in the Registry of British Ships. Permission to moor it at Hillgate Quay was granted by the Port of Tyne Authority, subject to requirements relating to lighting, the need for a competent ship keeper on constant duty and other matters.

THE DECISION OF THE LANDS TRIBUNAL
[11] The Lands Tribunal resolved the issue whether the vessel was rateable by applying the principle stated by Lord Denning MR in *Field Place Caravan Park Ltd*

a *v Harding (Valuation Officer)* [1966] 3 All ER 247 at 250, [1966] 2 QB 484 at 497–498 in which, basing himself upon *London CC v Wilkins (Valuation Officer)* [1956] 3 All ER 38, [1957] AC 362, Lord Denning MR stated:

b 'The correct proposition today is that, although a chattel is not a rateable hereditament by itself, nevertheless it may become rateable together with land, if it is placed on a piece of land and enjoyed with it in such circumstances and with such a degree of permanence that the chattel with the land can together be regarded as one unit of occupation.'

[12] Applying that principle, the Lands Tribunal held that the vessel was rateable for the reasons set out in its decision ([2002] RA 131 at [21]):

c 'The fact that the Tuxedo Royale is a vessel is no bar to rateability. In the normal way a vessel, as a mobile chattel, is not rateable. As the Sol Express the whole function of the vessel lay in its mobility, its ability to move and to transport passengers and vehicles. Moored under the Tyne Bridge, on the other hand, it was the immobility of the Tuxedo Royale that enabled it to
d perform its new role as a nightclub. The fact that it had been designed to propel itself across the sea and to transport passengers and goods ceased to have any significance other than to add to its attractiveness in its new and wholly different role. Its moorings were intended to ensure that the vessel stayed in position, eliminating all movement except for the small amount that would inevitably arise from the tidal nature of the river. The occupation
e by the ratepayers of the vessel, the river bed and quay had the same characteristics in terms of permanence and exclusiveness as in the case of a nightclub contained in a building on dry land. The vessel, is, in my judgment, undoubtedly rateable.'

f [13] In coming to its decision, the Lands Tribunal referred to its own previous decision in *Felgate (Valuation Officer) v Lotus Leisure Enterprises Ltd* [2000] RA 89 and observed that the vessel was rateable for the same reasons that a vessel called the Lotus was rateable in that case.

THE RELEVANT LAW
g [14] The unit of property which is the subject of rating is 'the hereditament'. By s 64(1) of the Local Government Finance Act 1988—

'A hereditament is anything which, by virtue of the definition of hereditament in section 115(1) of the [General Rate Act 1967], would have
h been a hereditament for the purposes of that Act had this Act not been passed.'

[15] Section 115(1) of the 1967 Act provided:

'... "hereditament" means property which is or may become liable to a
j rate, being a unit of such property which is, or would fall to be, shown as a separate item in the valuation list.'

[16] Section 64(4) of the 1988 Act provides:

'A hereditament is a relevant hereditament if it consists of property of any of the following descriptions—(a) lands ...'

[17] 'Land' is not defined in the 1988 Act. However, by virtue of s 5 of and Sch 1 to the Interpretation Act 1978, 'land' in an Act of Parliament passed after 1978 includes land covered by water.

[18] Section 41(1) and (2) of the 1988 Act requires the valuation officer for a billing authority, such as the respondent in this case, to compile and maintain local rating lists on 1 April 1990 and on 1 April every fifth year afterwards.

[19] By s 42(1)—

'A local non-domestic rating list must show, for each day in each chargeable financial year for which it is in force, each hereditament which fulfils the following conditions on the day concerned—(a) it is situated in the authority's area, (b) it is a relevant non-domestic hereditament ...'

[20] From the origins of rating in 1601 as provided for in the Poor Relief Act 1601, the liability to be rated rested upon the occupier of the property concerned: see *Earby's Case* (1633) 2 Bulst 354, 80 ER 1180. The position is still the same, save for specific statutory provision first made in 1966 for rates to be chargeable on certain unoccupied properties. A ratepayer's liability in respect of occupied hereditaments now arises from the express provision contained in s 43(1) of the 1988 Act:

'A person (the ratepayer) shall as regards a hereditament be subject to a non-domestic rate in respect of a chargeable financial year if the following conditions are fulfilled in respect of any day in the year—(a) on the day the ratepayer is in occupation of all or part of the hereditament, and (b) the hereditament is shown for the day in a local non-domestic rating list in force for the year.'

[21] *Earby's Case* also decided that assessments under the 1601 Act 'ought to be made according to the visible estate of the inhabitants there, both real *and personal*'. Although largely ignored in practice by rating authorities, the rateability of inhabitants for personal property (ie chattels) was only abolished by the Poor Rate Exemption Act 1840. Since that date therefore, the liability of the occupier has been limited to hereditaments in the nature of land, and no chattel is rateable per se.

[22] A ship is a floating chattel. Prior to 1840 ships were rated in the parish which was regarded as their home. Thereafter they ceased to be rated. However, a line of decisions including such cases as *Cory v Bristow* (1877) 2 App Cas 262, [1874–80] All ER Rep 136 and *Smith's Dock Co Ltd v Tynemouth Corp* [1908] 1 KB 315 held that the owners of vessels or floating structures used for commercial purposes while fixed in position on a long-term basis over moorings on the river bed could for rating purposes be treated as the occupiers of those moorings and the part of the river bed in which they were situated.

[23] In parallel, a line of authority developed in relation to structures and other chattels on or connected with land held in occupation whereby, albeit not part of that land, such chattels were rated with it on the basis that they were enjoyed with the land and enhanced its value. These authorities related to such chattels as telegraph posts and wires (see *Electric Telegraph Co v Salford Overseers* (1855) 11 Exch 181, 156 ER 795), telephone wires (see *Lancashire Telephone Co v Manchester Overseers* (1884) 13 QBD 700), showcases and kiosks at a railway station (see *Westminster City Council v Southern Railway Co* [1936] 2 All ER 322, [1936] AC 511) and a number of cases concerned temporary huts and structures erected by builders upon construction sites. The principle underlying those

a decisions was examined and made clear in *London CC v Wilkins (Valuation Officer)* [1956] 3 All ER 38, [1957] AC 362. In that case it was claimed that four builders' moveable huts, erected as temporary structures on a site for 18 months, only one of which was moved from one part of the site to the other during that period, were chattels and therefore not rateable. The House of Lords held that the question whether or not the structures had lost their character as chattels was not
b decisive as the test of rateability, nor was the conscious intention of the contractors to attach or not to attach them to the soil. These were no more than factors which fell to be considered and the test of rateability was whether there was evidence that the structures, occupied for a period which was not transient, were enjoyed with the land and enhanced its value. Viscount Kilmuir LC stated ([1956] 3 All ER 38 at 44, [1957] AC 362 at 373–374):
c
> '... the test of rateability is whether there is evidence that the structures were enjoyed with the land and enhanced its value. In considering this, the intention of the erector and the other elements of annexation, period, size, quality, amenities and purpose are all material. All these factors are important, but intention, and certainly what I may call the "conscious
d element" in intention, is no more than one factor and its importance is not overriding. The question is eminently one of fact ...'

[24] Lord Radcliffe said ([1956] 3 All ER 38 at 46–47, [1957] AC 362 at 378):

> 'No one supposes, of course, that a man is rateable in respect of the
e enjoyment of chattels as he is in respect of the occupation of land. But, on the other hand, I think that that is a long way from saying that the presence of chattels on land can never be a relevant factor either in determining the assessment of the rateable value of a hereditament or in determining whether there is a rateable occupation or not ... I think it equally well
f established that a structure placed on another person's land can with it form a rateable hereditament, even though the structure remains in law a chattel and as such the property of the person who placed it there. It has been habitual practice to treat gas and water pipes, drains and sewers, telegraph posts placed in, and telegraph or telephone wires placed over, land as being themselves rateable subjects. Yet I do not think that there is any foundation
g for supposing that when the undertaker, equipped either with the licence of the owner of the soil or with statutory powers, affixes his apparatus to a building or lays it in or on the soil the law regards him as thereby making it part of the freehold.'

[25] Later he stated ([1956] 3 All ER 38 at 47, 48, [1957] AC 362 at 380):
h
> 'When the owners of pipes, cables, posts, etc., are rated as occupiers they are rated in respect of those things themselves, by means of which they occupy land, not merely in respect of the land that is occupied; just as in *Cory v. Bristow* ((1877) 2 App Cas 262, [1874–80] All ER Rep 136), it was the
j moorings themselves that were treated as the rateable hereditament ... In my opinion, the present case really centres round the question whether the sheds, erected on a building site by a building contractor for the purpose of his operations, involve such a degree of permanency in his occupation as to make it a rateable one. I have no doubt that, in considering this, it is at any rate relevant to ascertain to what extent and in what way these constructions have been made a fixed part of the site on which they stand, for the more

casually they are attached the less likely it is that the occupation of them will
be found to be a permanent one. In this sense it may be of some importance   *a*
to inquire whether they are chattels or not; but to make the whole issue of
rateability depend on the bare issue, for instance, whether a particular
structure has or has not foundations in the ground which give it a measure
of lateral as well as subjacent support would be to use a legal distinction for
a purpose for which it was never intended.'   *b*

[26] In *Field Place Caravan Park Ltd v Harding (Valuation Officer)* [1966] 3 All ER
247, [1966] 2 QB 484 the Court of Appeal considered the rateability of a residential
caravan site. The caravans were on wheels and retained their mobility although
they were jacked up to keep them stable. The Court of Appeal upheld the
decision of the Lands Tribunal confirming the entries of the caravans in the   *c*
valuation list. In giving the leading judgment, Lord Denning MR having
considered the observations of Viscount Kilmuir LC and Lord Radcliffe in
Wilkins' case, stated the proposition applicable to the facts of the case before him
as set out at [11], above.

[27] In the light of certain submissions made for the appellants to which I refer
below, it is pertinent to observe that in relation to the Scottish case of *Assessor for*   *d*
Glasgow v Gilmartin (1920) SC 488 in which it was held that a small hut which
could be moved on wheels was not rateable in Scottish law, Lord Denning MR
observed that the provisions of the relevant Scottish Acts were different from the
relevant English provisions. Salmon LJ also observed ([1966] 3 All ER 247 at 254,
[1966] 2 QB 484 at 503):   *e*

'To my mind that decision turned entirely on the statute which governed
the law of rating in Scotland and which had no application to any of the
matters we have to consider. In my judgment the fact that the structure in
question happens to be a caravan on wheels rather than a hut or bungalow
is material only to a consideration of the question whether or not the   *f*
occupation of the caravan dweller is transient. That question does not arise
in this case, because it is conceded that it would be impossible to say that the
occupation of these caravan dwellers was so transient as to be incapable of
constituting rateable occupation. As was pointed out in [*Westminster City
Council v Southern Railway Co* [1936] 2 All ER 322, [1936] AC 511], in rating, as
distinct perhaps from tax law, the courts look to the substance and not the   *g*
form.'

[28] The effect of those authorities was considered by the Lands Tribunal in
Woodbury (Valuation Officer) v The Yard Arm Club Ltd [1990] 1 EGLR 237 in relation
to a vessel, the Hispaniola, moored in the River Thames to two steel piles called   *h*
dolphins fore and aft, each embedded in the river bed. The vessel was connected
to the dolphins by steel horns which permitted it to rise and fall with the tide but
prevented forward, rearward or lateral movement. The vessel was also anchored
to the river bed fore and aft, a subsidiary chain going to the embankment wall.
The vessel was used as a restaurant and was permanently connected to all main
services for that purpose. Access to the vessel from the embankment was via a   *j*
metal canopied gangway. The vessel and its moorings were owned by the club
authorised to operate it, whereas the river bed was owned by the Port of London
Authority which had granted the club a licence to place and retain the vessel with
its piles etc in the position which it occupied. By s 178(1) of the Port of London
Act 1968, land vested in the port authority (which included the bed of the river

a   beneath the vessel) was exempt from rating or inclusion in any valuation list. The decision of the Lands Tribunal turned upon that last point. Giving judgment the President (VG Wellings QC) stated (at 239):

b   'I cannot accept that the dolphins and the vessel are land. They and the anchors which rest on the river bed are chattels. Nevertheless, on the facts of the present appeal it is clear, and I hold, that the club by means of the vessel, its dolphins and anchors is in occupation of that part of the river bed over which it is moored and permanently so. That part of the river bed together with the vessel would thus be a rateable hereditament or part of a rateable hereditament if section 178 of the Port of London Act 1968 had no application: see *Cory* v *Bristow* ((1877) 2 App Cas 262, [1874–80] All ER Rep

c   136). In other words, the relevant parts of the river bed, together with the chattels, that is to say the vessel, the dolphins and the anchors constitute a unit of occupation: see *per* Lord Denning MR in *Field Place Caravan Park* v *Harding* ([1966] 3 All ER 247 at 250, [1966] 2 QB 484 at 498). However on the authority of *Whenman* v *Clark* ([1916] 1 KB 94), that unit of occupation is not rateable because of the operation of section 178 of the Port of London Act

d   1968.'

[29] Mr Wellings also considered an alternative submission that, by reason of the connection by the horizontal chains and gangways to the river wall, the vessel was rateable together with the part of the river wall in question which was owned by the Greater London Council. Counsel for the club answered that submission

e   by saying that chattels could only be rateable if they were in, on or over rateable land and that the relation between the land and the chattels must be vertical and not horizontal. Mr Wellings observed:

f   'I think that that observation is correct, but whether it is so or not, it appears to me that it is not possible for the vessel to occupy part of the river bed, as I have held it to do, and part of the river wall as well. Moreover, I agree with [counsel for the club] that, if paramountcy comes into question, it is the river bed which is the more important because the vessel derives its stability therefrom and without that stability could not be used as a floating restaurant ...'

g   [30] On appeal, Lloyd LJ in upholding the decision of the Lands Tribunal observed ([1991] 2 EGLR 173 at 175):

'I confess that, like the Lands Tribunal, I find some difficulty in the concept of lateral occupation by a chattel, if indeed occupation by a chattel is the right

h   test. But for reasons which will appear, I do not find it necessary to resolve that difficulty ... Such authority as there is seems to suggest that the Hispaniola does not occupy the Victoria Embankment in any relevant sense, though I accept, of course, that it was attached to the embankment fore and aft by chains and that it was permanently connected to all the main services

j   ... Similarly, in *Thomas (Valuation Officer)* v *Witney Aquatic Co Ltd* ([1972] RA 493), the hereditament was described as "lake, club house and premises" with a rateable value of £250. The club house was floating on the surface of the lake. It was argued, first, that "lake" was not an adequate description of the land beneath the water and, second, that the ratepayers were not in rateable occupation of the club house, as it was a chattel. Both arguments were rejected. It was held that the club house was enjoyed with the lake and

so with the land beneath the lake and was therefore part of the rateable
hereditament so described. So the educated reader would, *prima facie*, at any
rate, take "the premises" as a reference to the land comprising the river bed
and not the embankment. If that is so, then [counsel for the rating authority]
is in difficulty, for by section 178(1) of the Port of London Act of 1968 the
river bed is not rateable.'

[31] In concurring, Mann LJ said (at 177):

'... if it be supposed that the bed of the river is occupied by means of the
Hispaniola being held above it by the embedded dolphins, then that
occupation would not be a rateable occupation of the bed because of
section 178 of the 1968 Act. The correctness of the supposition does not fall
for decision. However, on the facts as found, I am of the view that it would
be a correct identification of the only land which could be said to be enjoyed
through the vessel. In common with Lloyd LJ and with Mr Wellings, I doubt
whether one can occupy land by means of a chattel which is not on, under
or above that land.'

[32] The decision in *Thomas (Valuation Officer) v Witney Aquatic Co Ltd* [1972]
RA 493 referred to by Lloyd LJ was a decision of the Lands Tribunal in respect of
a club house floating upon a lake over which the ratepayer had rights of use for
sporting and boating activities and to maintain a floating club house which was
moored to three steel barges in turn moored to the land. The club house was also
made fast to the land by two wire hawsers and kept at a fixed distance from the
land by two gangways, being moved in winter months to an island in the lake.
The disputed hereditament was described as 'lake, club house and premises'.

[33] In finding that the floating club house was a chattel enjoyed with the land
and therefore rateable as part of the hereditament, the tribunal relied on the
words of Lord Russell of Killowen in *Westminster City Council v Southern
Railway Co* [1936] 2 All ER 322 at 326, [1936] AC 511 at 529:

'Subject to special enactments, people are rated as occupiers of land, land
being understood as including not only the surface of the earth but all strata
above or below. The occupier, not the land, is rateable; but, the occupier is
rateable in respect of the land which he occupies.'

[34] The tribunal added (at 505):

'The expression "land" is in my opinion wide enough to include water
lying on the surface of the earth, so that the lake in the present case is capable
of being part of the hereditament, if it satisfies the other tests of rateability,
and in those circumstances I consider that the word "lake" would be a proper
description of that part of the hereditament.'

[35] In *Felgate (Valuation Officer) v Lotus Leisure Enterprises Ltd* [2000] RA 89, to
which I have already referred in [13], above, the valuation officer had entered in
the rating list a floating restaurant called the Lotus moored at Millwall Dock as
'dock bed, floating restaurant, moorings and premises'. The Lands Tribunal was
concerned to decide whether such rateable hereditament had been correctly
identified. The vessel was a steel hull without means of propulsion or steering
with a superstructure erected to contain the restaurant. It was permanently
moored in position connected to the dock wall by three hawsers at the bow and
two at the stern, each looped over bollards. There were two further connections

a to the dock wall by means of steel hawsers and the vessel was connected to all main services. Access was by means of four wooden and steel gangways resting on rollers to allow for the vertical movement of the water in the dock. The vessel was permanently in position save that it was moved on two occasions each year from its mooring by a tug to the other side of the dock for the purpose of undertaking essential maintenance in an operation which lasted no more than a
b few hours.

[36] It was submitted for the valuation officer that the owners were the occupiers of a hereditament comprising the part of the dock bed over which the vessel was moored and the water beneath the Lotus. *Field Place Caravan Park Ltd v Harding (Valuation Officer)* [1966] 3 All ER 247, [1966] 2 QB 484 was relied on. It was submitted for the owners that there could be no occupation of the bed of a
c river or a dock by a vessel floating above it without some kind of permanent fixture to the bed concerned. The President of the Lands Tribunal (George Bartlett QC) conducted a wide-ranging review of the relevant authorities, including that of the Scottish Lands Valuation Appeal Court in *Assessor for Glasgow v RNVR Club (Scotland)* 1974 SC 67 and that of the Hong Kong Court of
d Appeal in *Comr of Rating and Valuation v Yiu Lian Machinery Repairing Works Ltd* [1985] 2 HKC 517. In the former case a ship used as a club and moored to a quay in the Clyde in physical circumstances remarkably similar to this case, was held not to be 'heritable' in nature and therefore not rateable under Scottish law. In the latter case, floating dry docks in Hong Kong harbour were held to be not sufficiently connected with a piece of land to be rateable under the wording of the
e relevant Ordinance in Hong Kong.

[37] Applying the principle laid down in the *Field Place Caravan Park* case, George Bartlett QC said as follows ([2000] RA 89 at 100–101):

> '25. Applying this principle, therefore, whether the vessel is rateable
f depends on whether it is placed on a piece of land and enjoyed with it in such circumstances and with such a degree of permanence that the chattel with the land can together be regarded as one unit of occupation. "Enjoyed with" the land means no more than that the chattel, although not forming part of the realty, must have some real connection with the land on which it rests (see *(Ryan Industrial Fuels Ltd v Morgan (Valuation Officer)* [1965] 3 All ER 465,
g [1965] 1 WLR 1347)).
>
> 26. The fact that the vessel is floating does not in my judgment prevent it from forming part of a hereditament. Solicitor for the respondent company accepts that this is so and does not suggest that the tribunal was wrong in *Woodbury (Valuation Officer) v The Yard Arm Club Ltd* ([1990] 1 EGLR 237) in
h treating The Hispaniola as part of a hereditament extending upwards from the bed of the river. The crucial point, on his argument, is that the vessel here is not attached fore and aft to dolphins and to anchors in the bed of a river but is secured to moorings on the dock side. This distinction does not seem to me to be significant.
>
j 27. The relevant circumstances are in my judgment these. Although it is a vessel, the essential function of The Lotus is to remain stationary and attached to the dock side to provide a static, landbased facility as a restaurant. Apart from the fact that it floats, it is not designed for movement and has no means of propulsion. It has in fact remained stationary for over six years with the exception of the occasions, twice a year for a few hours, when it is towed across the dock for maintenance purposes. It enjoys all main services.

Its presence excludes the potential use for a similar purpose by anyone else of the dock bed beneath it or the dock side alongside it. It is enjoyed with the *a* dock bed and the dock side in that it is supported by the dock bed in conjunction with the water above it and it is secured to moorings on the dock side.

28. In these circumstances I am satisfied that the valuation officer is correct in identifying as a rateable hereditament the dock bed, the floating *b* restaurant and its moorings. Physically the hereditament consists in my view of the dock bed immediately beneath the vessel, the space above it that is filled with water, the vessel itself and its moorings on the dock side. The fact that there is water immediately beneath the vessel is only of relevance, it seems to me, to the extent that the vessel could become more mobile if it were not secured ... The occupation of the respondent company fulfils all *c* the ingredients of rateable occupation. Actual use is made of the dock bed for the support of the vessel through the medium of the water above it; the occupation is plainly of benefit to the respondent company; in view of the fact that the vessel is continuously secured in position (apart from the few hours when it is moved for maintenance) and has remained in the same *d* position for a number of years, the occupation is undoubtedly permanent; and in my judgment, it is also exclusive. The harbour authority can no doubt be said to use all the dock bed and the space above it, including the area beneath the vessel, in that it controls the volume of water within the dock, but this does not interfere with the use that the respondent company makes of the dock bed, which is exclusive for their purposes, and, in my view, is *e* plainly paramount.'

THE SUBMISSIONS OF THE PARTIES

[38] For the appellants, Mr Widdicombe QC accepts that the principle which *f* fell to be applied by the Lands Tribunal in this case, was that propounded by the House of Lords in *London CC v Wilkins (Valuation Officer)* [1956] 3 All ER 38, [1957] AC 362 and Lord Denning MR in the *Field Place Caravan Park* case to the effect that chattels may be rateable with land and together form a rateable hereditament if they are enjoyed with the land and enhance its value. However, he points out that the context in which the principle was propounded was one in *g* which the House of Lords and the Court of Appeal were concerned with chattels/structures which were physically placed upon land but insufficiently attached to become fixtures. Mr Widdicombe also accepts that in principle (though only in rare cases), the test propounded may be apt to extend to a floating structure or vessel. However, he submits that that can only be so in a case where *h* such structure or vessel is immovable and physically connected to the land with which it is said to form a rateable hereditament.

[39] Mr Widdicombe submits that a floating ship is a chattel so far conceptually removed from 'lands' that, if it is to be treated as part of a rateable hereditament a high degree of connection and/or adaptation should be sought *j* before so regarding it. He submits that in this case no such element is present. He submits that the absence of *vertical* connection to the river bed effectively prevents the presence of the floating vessel from being regarded as itself a method of occupation of the land beneath; and the absence of any adaptation of the vessel or its integration and enjoyment with the adjacent land, preserves its separate character as a chattel, enjoyed as such.

a [40] In this respect Mr Widdicombe places heavy reliance upon the Scottish and Hong Kong cases to which I have already referred and submits that the Lands Tribunal fell into error in distinguishing them.

[41] Mr Mould for the respondents submits that the Lands Tribunal was right to apply the principle succinctly stated by Lord Denning MR in the *Field Place Caravan Park* case and, by applying that principle, to find that the vessel was *b* rateable property for the reasons which it gave.

[42] Mr Mould submits that the principle that a chattel placed upon a piece of land, enjoyed with that land and enhancing its value, can with that land form a rateable hereditament, while remaining in law a chattel, is apt to apply in a case where the chattel is a floating vessel placed upon land covered with water: see the Interpretation Act 1978 (see [17], above), the observation of Lord Russell in *c* *Westminster City Council v Southern Railway Co* [1936] 2 All ER 322 at 366, [1936] AC 511 at 529 and the decisions of the Lands Tribunal in *Thomas (Valuation Officer) v Witney Aquatic Co Ltd* [1972] RA 493 (see [32]–[34], above) and *Felgate (Valuation Officer) v Lotus Leisure Enterprises Ltd* [2000] RA 89 (see [35]–[37], above).

[43] Mr Mould accepts that, in relation to the question whether the chattel *d* (a) occupies and / or (b) is enjoyed with land comprised within the hereditament identified, the question whether the land has a direct physical connection to that part of the land which lies vertically beneath it, is highly relevant and will generally be definitive. However, he submits that, in the case of a permanently moored vessel, moored in position over a part of the river bed licensed to the owner for that purpose, even without such a physical connection it is in *e* appropriate circumstances possible to provide an affirmative answer to the question whether the vessel is enjoyed with the river bed beneath and enhances its value. In this case, by means of horizontal connection to the adjacent quay which together with the river bed formed part of the same hereditament, the vessel was permanently secured in a position above and within a part of the river *f* bed which was licensed to the appellants for the very purpose for which it was used and was in fact used for no other purpose. In those circumstances the Lands Tribunal was entitled to find that the four conditions of rateable occupation were in fact satisfied.

g DISCUSSION

[44] The four conditions of rateable occupation as set out in *John Laing & Son Ltd v Kingswood Assessment Committee* [1949] 1 All ER 224 at 232, [1949] 1 KB 344 at 357 and approved in *Wilkins'* case are: (i) actual occupational possession (which involves actual as opposed to intended user of the land in question); *h* (ii) occupation or possession which is exclusive (ie if the occupier can exclude all other persons from using the land in the same way as he does); (iii) occupation or possession which is of some value or benefit to the occupier/possessor; (iv) occupation or possession which has a sufficient quality of permanence: see generally *Ryde on Rating and the Council Tax* (2003) pp 58–59 (paras 61–62).

j [45] The cases culminating in *Wilkins'* case and the *Field Place Caravan Park* case which developed the principle that chattels may be rateable if enjoyed with the land and enhancing its value have also made clear that the placing of a valuable chattel in or on land may itself be all that is required by way of occupation of the lands to render the chattel and the land together a rateable hereditament.

[46] Assuming for a moment that condition (i) can be satisfied, in the sense that the Lands Tribunal was entitled to hold that the vessel could properly be

regarded as occupying the river bed beneath (see further below), there seems to me no room for doubt that conditions (ii)–(iv) were satisfied in this case.

[47] So far as condition (ii) is concerned, when a person occupies land in respect of which he has no *title* to the exclusive occupation or possession but his occupation is exclusive *in fact*, then he is rateable in respect of that occupation. It seems to me that the question is identical to that enunciated by Lord Russell in the *Westminster City Council* case [1936] 2 All ER 322 at 328, [1936] AC 511 at 532, namely whether the person sought to be rated has the enjoyment of the land 'to the substantial exclusion of all other persons'. As made clear in that case, the relevant question is: what in fact is the occupation in respect of which the person is said to be rateable. In that respect, it is immaterial whether the title to occupy is attributable to a lease or a licence (see [1936] 2 All ER 322 at 329, [1936] AC 511 at 533). The substance of the document granting the right of occupation is highly material; however, what is material is not so much the precise terms of the grant but whether the occupation is in fact greater or lesser than the terms convey. It is also the position that the reservation by the grantor of a right which is never exercised and could not be fully exercised without destroying the grant is to be disregarded (see [1936] 2 All ER 322 at 353, [1936] AC 511 at 567 per Lord Wright MR).

[48] The factual position in this case, as already indicated, was that the vessel between 1990 and 1999, under successive licences from the commissioners, occupied a fixed position in the river, immediately above the area of the foreshore and river bed the subject of the licence. While the licence stated that its terms were not to be construed as giving exclusive use of the disputed area to the appellants, the liberty of the commissioners to grant elsewhere any rights or easements over the relevant land was limited by the proviso that it should not thereby prevent the placing and maintenance of the vessel in accordance with the licence. Nor, as the agreed facts stated, were any other or 'rival' rights granted by the commissioners during the entire period that the vessel was moored in position under the terms of the licence. In these circumstances it is clear that *if* the vessel could be properly regarded in occupation of the river bed beneath, it was de facto in exclusive occupation.

[49] So far as condition (iii) is concerned, it is plain that the occupation was of great value and benefit to the appellants as occupiers. Equally, so far as condition (iv) was concerned, there was a period of occupation of some nine years with a single brief interruption on some unspecified date when the vessel was temporarily removed from its mooring by tugs. I therefore return to consider condition (i).

[50] Throughout a period of nine years, the vessel was placed in position over the licensed area of river bed beneath. While the principle stated in *London CC v Wilkins (Valuation Officer)* [1956] 3 All ER 38, [1957] AC 362 and *Field Place Caravan Park Ltd v Harding (Valuation Officer)* [1966] 3 All ER 247, [1966] 2 QB 484 dealt with structures which were physically placed *upon* dry land, and there were not in this case any moorings within the river bed by which the vessel could be said to occupy the river bed (cf *Cory v Bristow* (1877) 2 App Cas 262, [1874–80] All ER Rep 136), it does not seem to me that the interposition of water between the vessel and the river bed of itself acted in any significant manner to deprive the appellants of occupation of the area of the river bed the subject of the licence. The 'permanent' presence of the vessel was sufficient to constitute de facto exclusive occupation of that part of the river bed. That view seems to me entirely consistent with the observations of Lloyd and Mann LJJ in the case of the

a Hispaniola (*Westminster City Council v Woodbury (Valuation Officer)* [1991] 2 EGLR 173) quoted at [30] and [31], above.

[51] Mr Widdicombe submits that such a conclusion is at odds with the Scottish and Hong Kong cases to which I have already referred. I therefore turn briefly to those authorities.

[52] In the Scottish case *Assessor for Glasgow v RNVR Club (Scotland)* 1974 SC 67,
b in which the physical facts were remarkably similar, the Lands Valuation Appeal Court was concerned with the question whether a former naval vessel refitted for use as a club was 'heritable' or not in Scottish law. It should at once be observed that the entry in the valuation roll under consideration simply referred to the subject of the valuation as 'Description: Club. Situation: Custom House Quay'.
c Thus there was no reference to, or consideration of, the relationship of the vessel to the river bed beneath or to any land save the adjoining quay to which it was secured. Indeed it does not appear that there had been any licence granted to the vessel's owners in respect of the river bed of the kind with which we are concerned.

[53] In giving the leading judgment, Lord Fraser adopted the approach taken
d by Lord Fleming in *John Menzies & Co v The Assessor for Edinburgh* 1937 SC 784 and followed by Lord Kilbrandon in *Assessor for Renfrewshire v Mitchell* 1965 SC 271, by asking the question first whether the subject structure belonged to a class or genus which was prima facie heritable. He rejected the submission of counsel that there was a genus 'club' into which the vessel could be conveniently placed
e and stated (1974 SC 67 at 72):

'In my opinion the general character of this structure is plainly, and obviously, that of a ship. It began its life as a ship and unquestionably continued as such until 1947, and it still retains much of its original appearance and character. Above all it shares with other ships the essential
f characteristic that it habitually floats on water. Nobody has suggested that a ship is *prima facie* heritable and I do not think such a suggestion could reasonably be made. If one starts from that position, the question is whether there are special facts about this ship which distinguish it from other ships and make it heritable and not moveable. It undoubtedly has many unusual features. Perhaps the most prominent of these is that it has been moored at
g its present position for 16 or 17 years and that its owners have no intention of moving it in the foreseeable future. But that does not take the matter far, because it is settled that, if a thing is by its nature moveable, the mere passage of time will not make it heritable, even though it is never in fact moved: *Anderson Grice & Co Ltd v. Assessor for Angus* [1962] RA 590. The connections
h of the various services, and especially of gas, are consistent with and indeed indicative of the intention to keep the ship where it is. Further its use as a clubhouse in the middle of Glasgow is an unusual use for a ship. But, in my opinion, these factors are not enough to outweigh its general character of moveability.'

j [54] Later in his judgment he observed (at 72–73):

'... I do not think that a floating ship, even if permanently moored in one place, could enter the roll as being lands or heritages, except perhaps if there was a high degree of mutual adaptation between the ship and the berth at which it was moored.'

[55] Lord Avonside was of similar opinion, as was Lord Keith. He said
(at 73–74):   a

    'The subjects of appeal were designed and constructed as a ship, and they
    rest not upon land but upon water. This is the outstanding characteristic of
    the subjects. In my opinion this characteristic necessarily involves that the
    subjects are *prima facie* moveable. The other circumstances of the case are   b
    not, in my view, sufficient to warrant the inference that the subjects have
    become heritable by attachment to, or mutual adaptation with, heritable
    property.'

[56] It is thus apparent that the approach of the Scottish courts places great
emphasis upon the general character of the structure for the purpose of its   c
classification as either heritable or moveable: see also *Armour's Valuation for
Rating* (5th edn, 1985) pp 227–232 (paras 9-01–9-08), where the observation
appears that—

    'reference to English authority in this field is inappropriate and could be   d
    misleading, since the separate considerations of the heritability of the subject
    and the rateability of the occupation are not clearly distinguished in the
    English cases.'

Since the *RNVR Club* case was decided on the basis of Scottish law and turned
entirely on whether or not the vessel was 'moveable', I do not think it affords   e
Mr Widdicombe any useful support in this appeal.

[57] The same is true of the decision of the Hong Kong Lands Tribunal in *Yiu
Lian Machinery Repairing Works Ltd v Comr of Rating and Valuation* [1982] HKC 55
in which the President of the tribunal (Judge Cruden), following the decision in
the *RNVR Club* case held that, before the floating dry docks concerned could be   f
rateable as chattels enjoyed with the land, there would have to be a high degree
of mutual adaptation between the vessels and the berth at which they were
moored. Judge Cruden observed (at 72):

    'I appreciate that even in the absence of sufficient physical or legal
    connection between the vessels as chattels and the land to satisfy Hong Kong   g
    requirements, the position in England might be different. For the English
    criterion of occupation and liability for rates flowing from the mere existence
    of a unit of occupation would be sufficient for floating docks together with
    the land—either sea bed or shore—to form one unit of occupation and so to
    constitute a rateable hereditament. However, I am satisfied that the unit of   h
    occupation has no place in Hong Kong rating law.'

[58] On appeal ([1985] 2 HKC 517) the Hong Kong Court of Appeal held, in
the words of the headnote, that having regard to the history of the legislation in
Hong Kong, it could not be said that the English rule that the value of chattels
was to be included as part of the land itself was, on a proper construction of the   j
wording of the Ordinance, applicable in Hong Kong, where a stricter course
prevailed; only the land itself or any building or part thereof were rateable and
the Lands Tribunal's decision that none of the dry docks was sufficiently
connected with a piece of land to be taken into account in estimating its rateable
value would not be disturbed.

a [59] The particular observation upon which Mr Widdicombe has placed emphasis is the following:

'We find ourselves unable to accept the proposition that a vessel which floats in the sea many feet above a piece of land is properly said to be enjoyed with it or to enhance its value. If that is so, then the same must be said in respect, for example, of an advertising balloon attached by wire to dry land, b or even perhaps to a block in the sea bed off a popular holiday resort. Both the balloon and the vessel are of course connected to the land, but the connection is not for the purpose of enjoying or enhancing the land. It is simply to prevent either getting lost or into difficulties. Objects left free in air or on water are inclined to stray unless properly tethered. Builders huts c and caravans set upon jacks do not.' (See [1985] 2 HKC 517 at 526.)

[60] I do not find those observations telling or indeed accurate in relation to the facts of this case. As I have already indicated, it does not seem to me that the mere fact that a vessel floats on water above the land (ie the river bed), per se d prevents it from being a chattel enjoyed with the land and which enhances its value. Nor, if it is secured permanently in position by horizontal attachment to adjacent land forming part of the same hereditament, is it vital that the vessel should be directly secured or connected to the land beneath. In such circumstances, the purpose and function of the horizontal attachment is to e confine the vessel to the area of the licensed land beneath, thereby enjoying that land (albeit supported by the water above it) as a permanent means of support by which means the river bed, together with the adjacent quay as part of the same hereditament, is enhanced in value.

[61] The analogy of an advertising balloon connected by a single wire and free f to float to and fro, unrelated to or constrained by the area of the land beneath and plainly incapable of amounting to occupation of it, seems to me inapt. This is an area in which analogies are on the whole unhelpful. However, in the example given, a more appropriate analogy would be that of a barrage balloon permanently tethered in a stationary position by guy ropes with a platform suspended from it just above the land beneath and in permanent use as a g nightclub dance floor, approached by a heavy metal ramp or ramps resting on the ground. Be that as it may, as the court went on to observe, whether a chattel is sufficiently connected with a piece of land to be taken into account in estimating its rateable value is essentially a question of fact in every case.

h CONCLUSION

[62] There is no suggestion in this case that the Lands Tribunal misstated or misunderstood any of the primary facts in relation to the position, purpose or function of the Tuxedo Royale or the nature or extent of the hereditament the subject of their decision. Nor is it suggested that they misstated or j misunderstood the principles of law applicable to those facts save as to the degree of connection and/or adaptation of the vessel necessary to amount to occupation of the land in question. In that respect, I accept the submissions of Mr Mould set out at [41]–[43], above and the conclusion of the Lands Tribunal as stated in [12], above.

[63] I would therefore dismiss this appeal.

CHADWICK LJ.
[64] I agree.

a

TUCKEY LJ.
[65] I also agree.

Appeal dismissed. Permission to appeal refused.

b

Kate O'Hanlon   Barrister.

a Westminster City Council v O'Reilly and others
[2003] EWHC 485 (Admin)

b QUEEN'S BENCH DIVISION (ADMINISTRATIVE COURT)

MACKAY J

21, 28 FEBRUARY 2003

Licensing – Permitted hours – Special hours certificate – Premises for which music and dancing licence in force for part of premises – Whether possible to have special hours
c *certificate in force for whole premises – Licensing Act 1964, s 77A.*

The licensees had the benefit of a justices' on-licence in relation to the ground and basement floors of a building. A music and dancing licence (MDL) was granted in respect of the basement under s 52 of the Local Government Act 1963. A
d provisional special hours certificate (SHC) was also granted pursuant to s 77A[a] of the Licensing Act 1964 which covered both the basement and the ground floor. Section 77A(1) provided that a provisional hours certificate would be issued where 'the licensing justices are satisfied … (a) that the premises are … (ii) premises for which a music and dancing licence is in force.' The concluding words of the section empowered justices, if they were satisfied that 'part only of
e the premises is intended to be used' for music and dancing, to grant an SHC 'for that part'. The matter came before the justices who confirmed the provisional SHC. The local authority, concerned that the justices' ruling would open the door to late night bars, appealed by way of case stated. The authority contended (i) that the SHC could not apply to the ground floor since there was no MDL in force in relation to that floor. It argued that to hold otherwise would require the
f word 'premises' where it appeared in s 77A(1)(a)(ii) to be construed, not as the whole of the licensed premises, but as 'the licensed premises or any part of them'; (ii) that the concluding words of the section were apt to cover the facts of the instant case where part only of the premises and not both floors was intended to be used for music and dancing. Therefore the discretion that was in the hands of
g the justices was restricted to granting, if all other matters were proved to their satisfaction, a provisional SHC 'for that part'; and (iii) that the interdependence of the MDL and the SHC were well illustrated by s 81[b] of the 1964 Act which provided that if at any time while a SHC was in force there was not also a MDL in force for the premises to which or part of which the SHC related, the SHC would be revoked. The licensees argued that there was no reason why two sets
h of premises, that covered by the SHC and that covered by the MDL, had necessarily to be coterminous, provided the justices were otherwise satisfied that s 77A was met, and that since s 81(2) existed to cope with cases of abuse by enabling the police to apply to revoke the SHC, the resultant scheme was sensible, workable and appropriate.
j

Held – On the true construction of s 77A of the 1964 Act there could be no special hours certificate in relation to an area that was not already covered by a music

---

a   Section 77A, so far as material, is set out at [9], below
b   Section 81, so far as material, is set out at [16], below

and dancing licence. If, at (1)(a)(ii) 'the premises' (a word which up to that point *a* in the section, and after that point in the section, was plainly used to refer to the premises covered by the justices' liquor licence) was to have some different meaning, namely the whole premises or any part of them, then the draftsman would have said so, as he had in two other places in the s 77A. Further, the concluding words were there to reinforce what the section had already said: that an SHC could not be granted in respect of a physical area which was not itself *b* covered by an MDL. Moreover, while s 81(2) provided a mechanism for policing SHCs, that was no sort of reason for opening the doors any wider than was necessary to the possibility of abuse of them. It followed that both the grant of a provisional SHC and its confirmation was wrong in law. Accordingly, the appeal would be allowed (see [25]–[31], below).

c

Notes
For special hours certificates, see 26 *Halsbury's Laws* (4th edn reissue) para 245.
   For the Licensing Act 1964, s 77A, see 24 *Halsbury's Statutes* (1998 reissue) 426.

Cases referred to in judgment *d*
Customs and Excise Comrs v Griffith [1924] 1 KB 735, [1924] All ER Rep 744, CA.
R v Crown Court at Stafford, ex p Shipley [1998] 2 All ER 465, [1998] 1 WLR 1438, CA.
Richards v Bloxham (Binks) (1968) 66 LGR 739, DC.
Spring House (Freehold) Ltd v Mount Cook Land Ltd [2001] EWCA Civ 1833, [2002] 2 All ER 822. *e*

Case referred to in skeleton arguments
Northern Leisure plc v Schofield [2001] 1 All ER 660, [2001] 1 WLR 1196.

Case stated *f*
The City of Westminster appealed by way of case stated from the decision of the Licensing Committee sitting at Horseferry Road Magistrates' Court on 7 May 2002 confirming and making final a provisional special hours certificate granted on 18 December 2001 in favour of Richard Thomas O'Reilly, Luca Cordiglien, Stephen Fleury and Mark Robert Young, relating to the ground and basement floors of a restaurant and bar complex known as the Elysium in *g* Glasshouse Street, London W1. The question for the opinion of the High Court is set out at [6], below. The facts are set out in the judgment of the court.

James Rankin (instructed by *Colin Wilson*) for the appellants.
John Saunders QC and *Andrew Evans* (instructed by *Jeffrey Green Russell*) for the *h* respondents.

cur adv vult

28 February 2003. The following judgment of the court was delivered.

j

MACKAY J.
   [1] Part of the Café Royal complex at Glasshouse Street, London W1, is known under the style 'Elysium'. On the ground floor there is a reception area, bar and servery, and a kitchen. At the basement level there is a second kitchen, a restaurant and a lounge. Entrances to both floors are to be found at the level

a of the ground floor. There are two: one in Regent Street and one in Glasshouse Street itself. Access to the basement is internal; that is to say, through the ground floor.

[2] The licensing history relating to Elysium is as follows. There was a provisional justices' on-licence in existence in respect of both ground and basement floors which was declared final on 4 May 2002. It is subject to certain

b conditions which are not material to this appeal. On 18 December 2001 the licensing committee for South Westminster granted a provisional special hours certificate (SHC) pursuant to s 77A of the Licensing Act 1964, to which I will have to return. As they say in their case stated, that certificate covered both the basement and the ground floor, as were depicted in certain plans deposited with them. Also on that date a provisional music and dancing licence (MDL)

c was granted by Westminster City Council (Westminster) under s 52 of the London Government Act 1963. One condition of the MDL, as granted, was that it allowed the premises to remain open till 1 am. There was an appeal by the licensees to the Crown Court, which resulted in that terminal time limit being extended to 3 am. The MDL was made the subject of a full grant on

d 7 May 2002, to expire after 31 October 2002. It said on its face that it licensed the use of the basement of the premises for music and dancing subject to certain conditions, not all of which are relevant for the purposes of this appeal. The first condition allowed the premises to remain open for the purpose of this licence up to 3 am on Mondays to Saturdays. Mr Saunders QC, on behalf of the licensees, harbours reservations—indeed, I think he would put it higher than

e that—as to whether the restriction apparent on the face of the MDL as being to the basement only should have appeared on it, but realistically accepts, for the purpose of my task today, that I can only proceed on the basis that the MDL was issued with that restriction.

[3] This is an appeal by way of case stated. The stated case discloses further

f facts which are relevant and which have required substantial amendment by consent in the light of further investigations undertaken after I granted a short adjournment of this appeal last week. All the references in the stated case to plans 105E and 106A as being the approved deposited plans are agreed to be wrong and should read as referring to plans 105F and 106D. The significance of that difference for the purposes of this appeal is that on the latter set of plans

g it was made plain that the area in respect of which the SHC was sought was both floors. Also there were physical modifications of the structure of the premises apparent in those plans and those were approved, all contrary to what was said in the case as stated by the justices.

h [4] Additionally, on 30 April 2002 an environmental health officer for Westminster wrote to the justices drawing their attention to the fact that the MDL related to the basement only; but other evidence before me is to the effect that the justices' clerk now has no record of that letter having been received. On 3 May Westminster wrote again to the justices reiterating that position. The evidence from the justices' clerk is that after the hearing which is

j questioned in this appeal (that is to say, the hearing of 7 May) she found this letter attached to papers relevant to the application, but there was no file note to indicate that the letter had been brought to the attention of the justices at the hearing. Paragraph 4 of the stated case was to the effect that Westminster, among others, had raised no objection to the grant of the application at the hearing. That must now be read subject to further agreed amendments of the

case to the effect that a representative of Westminster did attend the hearing
and drew the attention of the justices to the content of the letter of 3 May 2002. *a*
Whether that actually constituted an objection properly so called is a rather fine
point and one not necessary to be decided, it seems to me, by me today.

[5] This, therefore, is an appeal by way of case stated against the decision of
the licensing committee, sitting at Horseferry Road Magistrates' Court on 7
May 2002, by which the provisional SHC granted on 18 December 2001 was *b*
confirmed and made final. As I have already stated, but should repeat, that
related to both floors of Elysium, whereas the MDL covered the basement
only. The justices expressed their conclusions in this way:

> 'We were of the opinion that as the premises were licensed for
> intoxicating liquor, that a local authority music and dancing licence was in *c*
> force and that those parts of the premises to which the SHC was to apply
> had been completed in accordance with the approved deposited plans the
> provisional grant of the SHC should be declared final in accordance with
> s 77A(3).'

[6] They framed the following question for the opinion of this court: *d*

> 'Whether we were correct in law in declaring the provisional SHC under
> s 77A(3) of the 1964 Act final and thereby, an extension in the permitted
> hours until 3 a m in respect of a part of the premises for which there was no
> public entertainment licence in force.'

The four persons named as the successful licensees in the final certificate are the *e*
respondents to this appeal. They support the justices' decision and would
answer this question affirmatively.

[7] At an earlier hearing it seemed that there was to be an argument by the
respondents as to the lack of standing of Westminster to make this appeal under
s 111 of the Magistrates' Courts Act 1980. But that no longer being pursued, it *f*
is necessary to look at the substantive issue in dispute.

[8] The original s 77 of the 1964 Act allowed for the grant of an SHC in
respect of licensed premises which were, among other things, 'structurally
adapted, and bona fide used, or intended to be used', for music and dancing and
substantial refreshment. There was seen to be a disadvantage to this scheme in
that the intending operator of premises who hoped to benefit from the grant of *g*
such a certificate had to take something of a gamble. He had to acquire and
structurally adapt his premises in the hope that the justices would, in their
discretion, grant him an SHC on completion. Though he could acquire a
provisional justices' on-licence and a provisional MDL, he could not acquire a
provisional SHC. So in 1996 there was added by amendment to the 1964 Act a *h*
new s 77A which provided for such a provisional grant.

[9] As s 77A is at the heart of this appeal, I must read its relevant parts:

> '(1) Where, on an application made by a person interested in any premises
> of in respect of which a grant or provisional grant of a justices' licence has been
> made and which are to be, or are in the course of being, constructed, altered or *j*
> extended, the licensing justices are satisfied—(a) that the premises are ...
> (ii) premises for which a music and dancing licence is in force, (b) that the
> whole or any part of the premises is intended to be used, and, if completed
> in accordance with plans deposited with the licensing justices, will be
> structurally adapted, for the purpose of providing for persons resorting to

a   the premises ... (ii) ... music and dancing and substantial refreshment, to which the sale of intoxicating liquor is ancillary, the licensing justices may make a provisional grant, with or without limitations, of a special hours certificate for the premises or, if they are satisfied that part only of the premises is intended to be used or will be adapted as mentioned in paragraph (b) of this subsection, for that part.'

b   [10] In this case, when such an application was made under this section and granted on 18 December 2001, the position was as follows. First, the whole of the premises known as Elysium (that is to say, the ground and basement floors) were licensed premises within the meaning of that section. Secondly, an MDL was in force, not for the whole of the premises, but for part of them, namely the basement only. Thirdly, that part of the premises, and not the whole of them, was intended to be used for, and was structurally adapted for providing, music, dancing and substantial refreshment, to which the sale of intoxicating liquor was ancillary. In the event the justices granted a provisional SHC in respect of the whole premises; that is to say, both floors.

d   [11] Westminster argue that, as it is the case that the ground floor does not have the benefit of an MDL and it cannot be, or have been, the intention to provide music and dancing facilities on that floor, the justices had no power to grant an SHC, provisional or final, in respect of that floor. They only had power to grant an SHC of either kind in respect of the area covered by the MDL, namely the basement.

e   [12] The respondents argue that there is nothing in the words of the statute or in logic which requires that the physical area of the building (to use a neutral term) covered by the SHC has to be coterminous with the area where music and dancing is permitted by licence, provided that such facilities are properly provided elsewhere on the premises.

f   [13] Putting more flesh on the bones of those respective arguments, Westminster's case starts from the point (which is not contentious) that the word 'premises', where it appears, as it does, in many parts of the statute, is a word which is flexible as to its meaning, even protean; that is to say, capable of bearing different meanings according to the context in which it finds itself. If authority were needed for that, they say, there is the authority of the Court of Appeal—in a very different kind of case—in *Spring House (Freehold) Ltd v Mount Cook Land Ltd* [2001] EWCA Civ 1833 at [28], [2002] 2 All ER 822 at [28], where so much is stated. In *Customs and Excise Comrs v Griffith* [1924] 1 KB 735 at 746–747, [1924] All ER Rep 744 at 750 Scrutton LJ, considering this problem in the specific context of licensed premises, said:

h   '... I do not find anything in the Licensing Act which limits the word "premises" to an entire building. In my opinion any part of a building which is defined by metes and bounds is "premises" in respect of which a licence can be granted, provided it is in the justices' opinion structurally adapted for the sale of liquor.'

j   Hence the limitation of the MDL to part of the larger premises (which can be perceived, for example, in s 82 of the 1964 Act), says Mr Rankin, shows how within a set of licensed premises one part of those larger premises can be treated for certain purposes as separate premises.

[14] The governing principle (if there is one single principle) which must always be held in mind when considering SHCs, and s 77A in particular, was

expressed by Simon Brown LJ, in *R v Crown Court at Stafford, ex p Shipley* [1998] 2 All ER 465 at 482, [1998] 1 WLR 1438 at 1456 in this way:

a

> 'During whatever hours of trading are permitted by the SHC the drinking must "on the whole" be ancillary to the provision of food and/or entertainment; an SHC should not be granted to an ordinary public house so as to turn it into a "late night pub".'

b

Westminster in this case fear that the result of the justices' order will be to do just that: to open the door to the creation, deliberate or otherwise, of a late-night bar pure and simple on the ground floor of Elysium.

[15] Looking at the words of s 77A itself, Mr Rankin argues that, for the respondents' opposition to his appeal to succeed, 'premises', where it appears at sub-s (1)(a)(ii), must be construed, not as the whole of the licensed premises, which is its meaning in the body of sub-s (1), but as 'the licensed premises or any part of them'. Secondly, he draws my attention particularly to the concluding words of the section empowering justices—

c

> 'if they are satisfied that *part only* of the premises is intended to be used or will be adapted as mentioned in paragraph (b) of this subsection, *for that part*.' (My emphasis.)

d

He says those words are apt to cover the facts of this case, where part only of the premises (that is to say, the basement) and not both floors was intended to be used or adapted for music and dancing and substantial refreshment. Therefore the discretion that was in the hands of the justices was restricted to granting, if all other matters were proved to their satisfaction, a provisional SHC 'for that part'; that is to say, the basement. These, he says, are plain words and they mean quite simply what they say.

e

[16] He says that the link between or the interdependence of the MDL and the SHC are well illustrated by s 81. In its relevant parts that section reads:

f

> '(1) If at any time while a special hours certificate is in force there is not also in force for the premises to which or part of which the certificate relates ... (b) where the special hours certificate is granted by virtue of section ... 77A(3)(b)(ii) of this Act, a music and dancing licence ... the special hours certificate shall thereby be revoked ...

g

> (2) At any time while a special hours certificate for any premises or part of premises is in force, the chief officer of police may apply to the licensing justices ... for the revocation of the certificate on the ground that, while the certificate has been in force—(a) the premises have not, or the part has not, been used as mentioned in section ... 77A ... or that on the whole the persons resorting to the premises or part are there, at times when the sale or supply of intoxicating liquor there is lawful by virtue only of the certificate, for the purpose of obtaining intoxicating liquor rather than for an appropriate purpose ...'

h

'Appropriate purpose' is defined as dancing and the obtaining of refreshments other than intoxicating liquor.

j

[17] So under the first subsection, if for any reason the MDL dies (expiry, revocation or whatever) and it was one which related to the premises or the part to which the SHC relates, the SHC dies with it and is automatically revoked. The SHC for the whole of the premises or part of the premises has no

a capacity for independent life unless underpinned by an MDL which has, says Mr Rankin, to cover the same area as it. The SHC can relate to a narrower area than the MDL, he argues, but the position cannot be reversed. So far as sub-s (2) is concerned, the words in sub-s (2)(a) 'the premises have not, or the part has not, been used ...' give grounds to the police to make an application to revoke, as does the fact that, as a matter of fact, the premises as a whole have *b* not, or the part in question has not, been used 'on the whole' for appropriate purposes.

[18] Mr Saunders points to this and says that this gives Westminster just the protection against the coming into being of a late-night bar on the ground floor which it says it fears; and that is undoubtedly right. But Westminster say, for the purposes of construing s 77A, that its value is that it underlines how *c* interrelated the SHC and the MDL are and that underpinning any premises or any part of any premises to which an SHC is attached must also be found an MDL.

[19] The respondents' argument, as I have said, is that there is no reason in logic or law why the two sets of premises, that covered by the SHC and that *d* covered by the MDL, must necessarily be coterminous. Just as, argues Mr Saunders, within premises which are undoubtedly covered by an MDL not every square metre will be intended to be, or capable of being, used, for example, for dancing over, or for eating at, or even for either, so it will be with premises used more widely: there will be separate areas; there will be bars and sitting-out places where no question of dancing arises. If justices are otherwise *e* satisfied that s 77A is met (and it is to be noted that the sale of intoxicating liquor has to be ancillary to the provision of music, dancing and substantial refreshment) and since s 81 exists to cope with cases of abuse, the resultant scheme is perfectly sensible, workable and appropriate.

[20] He invites me to take this approach, that I should look at the premises *f* as a whole, both floors, and answer the questions posed by s 77A: are there sufficient facilities for dancing and sufficient facilities for eating, such that they evidence an intention by the would-be holder of an SHC that any drinking on the premises, viewed as a whole, can properly be viewed as likely to be ancillary to those purposes? Take, for example, a position where one had a basement entirely devoted to a dance floor and a ground floor entirely devoted to the *g* provision of a restaurant and bar. Why should it be necessary, he argues, to have an MDL covering both floors, when there would have been no question of the ground floor being used for the dancing area, but that otherwise the project would easily fit within the structure and framework of s 77A. So he argues, returning to what I might call his problems in s 77A, that I should view *h* sub-s (1)(a)(ii) as in effect asking this question of the justices: is there an MDL applicable to some part of these premises? The words in the concluding sentence of s (1) 'part only of the premises' are there to cover a situation (which both sides accept as a possibility, if the facts were such as to demand it) where the SHC sought relates to some area which is in fact smaller than that covered *j* by the MDL.

[21] He reminds me of the classic and general authority in this case of *Richards v Bloxham (Binks)* (1968) 66 LGR 739 at 744–745, which illustrates the principles on which a s 81(2) revocation may take place. Where on the whole customers resort to premises covered by the SHC, in the words of Lord Parker CJ, 'to consume intoxicating liquor and not either to dance or to have

substantial refreshment', then that is a ground on which the justices in their
discretion may revoke the licence.   *a*

[22] I have not found this an easy issue to resolve, free, as it is, of direct
authority, despite the clear and helpful submissions from both counsel. But my
conclusion is that I prefer the appellants' arguments for the following three
main reasons.

[23] The first is the reading of s 77A itself and the two problem areas, as I   *b*
have called them and indicated. If, at sub-s (1)(a)(ii), the 'premises' (a word
which up to that point in the section, and after that point in the section, is
plainly used to refer to the premises covered by the justices' liquor licence; that
is to say, in this case both floors) was to have some different meaning, namely
the whole premises or any part of them, then the simple answer, to my mind,   *c*
is that the draftsman could have said so, and would have said so, as he did in
two other places in this very section.

[24] Secondly, the concluding words could indeed be apt to cover a situation
where the part of the premises covered by the SHC was smaller rather than
larger than the part covered by the MDL. Such a situation, while being far from
impossible to envisage, must surely be, in relative terms, a rare occurrence. A   *d*
much more likely interpretation of these words is that they are there to
reinforce what the section has already said: that an SHC must not issue in
respect of a physical area which is not itself covered by an MDL. I comfort
myself in this conclusion by the realisation which I have reached that this
would secure more effectively, in my judgment, the objectives of the section,   *e*
while at the same time avoiding the risks of the 'late-night bar', against the
creation of which the justices have to be alive at all times.

[25] Thirdly, while s 81(2) does indeed provide a mechanism for policing
SHCs, that, in my judgment, is no sort of reason for opening the door any wider
than is necessary to the possibility of abuse of them. By this I do not mean   *f*
abuse by these licensees or, indeed, any licensees in general. It would be quite
possible to envisage, as Mr Saunders effectively invites me to envisage, the
ground floor of these premises being used as some kind of ancillary sitting-out
area by resting dancers and / or postprandial drinkers. But however sincere the
intentions of the licensee, it would be equally possible to see the ground floor
of these premises being regularly resorted to, on an off-the-street basis, by   *g*
late-night drinkers who might well be entirely indifferent to—perhaps even
ignorant of—the facilities on offer below their feet. To leave that to be dealt
with by police action, and burden the enforcement system with the task of
disentangling whether 'on the whole' the persons resorting are there for the
purpose of drinking rather than an appropriate purpose, would be an   *h*
undesirable result if its prospect can be lessened. The situation created by the
present grant seems to me almost bound to lead to such problems.

[26] In form this appeal lies against the justices' decision of 7 May 2002 in
making the provisional grant a final one and therefore acting under s 77A(3). I
have not set out the terms of that subsection. I do not think I need to do so.   *j*
But they include a requirement for the justices to be 'satisfied, in relation to the
premises to which the certificate relates ... that they are, or are part of ...
premises for which a music and dancing licence is in force'.

[27] It is accepted for the purposes of this appeal that if, in my judgment, the
provisional grant was in error, as in my judgment it was, then the final grant

a too must be equally wrong in law. I would therefore answer the question asked in the negative.

[**28**] The result is that, for the avoidance of doubt, I make a formal declaration that the SHC granted by the justices on 7 May 2002 applies to the basement floor only of the premises known as Elysium, Glasshouse Street, London W1, and to no other part.

b [**29**] To that extent, this appeal is allowed.

Appeal allowed. Permission to appeal granted.

Martyn Gurr   Barrister.

Re Salvage Association

[2003] EWHC 1028 (Ch)

CHANCERY DIVISION

BLACKBURNE J

15 APRIL, 9 MAY 2003

Company – Administration order – Jurisdiction – Association incorporated by Royal Charter – Insolvency Act 1986, ss 1(4), 8(7).

The members of the general committee of an association incorporated by Royal Charter in 1876, applied for an administration order for the purposes of the approval of a voluntary arrangement and/or a more advantageous realisation of its assets than would be effected on a winding up. An issue arose as to the court's jurisdiction to make an administration order under Pt II of the Insolvency Act 1986 in respect of the association and its ability to enter into a company voluntary arrangement available under Pt I of that Act. With effect from 31 May 2002, s 8(7)[a] of the Act provided that a reference to a 'company' includes a reference to a company in relation to which an administration order may be made by virtue of art 3[b] of Council Regulation (EC) 1346/2000 (on Insolvency Proceedings) (the regulation) and s 1(4)[c] provided that a reference to a 'company' includes a reference to a company in relation to which a proposal for a voluntary arrangement may be made by virtue of art 3 of the regulation. Article 2(d)[d] of the regulation defined 'court' as 'the judicial body or any other competent body of a member state empowered to open insolvency proceedings'.

Held – The jurisdiction of the court to make an administration order applied to companies in the extended sense referred to in art 3, namely 'company or legal person'. The association was just such a company: the Royal Charter by which it was incorporated was effective to constitute the association a legal person separate from its members, enjoying perpetual succession, having a common seal, capable of suing and being sued in the courts and having power, in addition to the particular powers set out in the Charter, to do all matters and things incidental or appertaining to a body corporate. The centre of the association's main interests was in the European Union, and, more particularly, in the United Kingdom with the result that the regulation applied and art 3(1) allocated jurisdiction for the main proceedings to the United Kingdom. Further, s 1(4) created domestic law jurisdiction to open company voluntary arrangement proceedings in the jurisdiction in relation to a legal person such as the association. Adopting a broad interpretation of the definition of the expression 'court' in art 2(d) there was power in the association to enter into a voluntary arrangement with its creditors. It followed that the court had jurisdiction to make an administration order in relation to the association and might properly do so for

---

a   Section 8(7) is set out at [8], below
b   Article 3, so far as material, is set out at [9], below
c   Section 1(4) is set out at [16], below
d   Article 2(d), so far as material, is set out at [19], below

a the purpose, inter alia, of approving a company voluntary arrangement (see [14], [17], [24], below).

    Re BRAC Rent-A-Car International Inc [2003] 2 All ER 201 applied.

Notes

For the power of the court to make an administration order see 7(3) *Halsbury's Laws* (4th edn) (1996 reissue) para 2081.

b   For the Insolvency Act 1986, ss 1, 8, see 4 *Halsbury's Statutes* (4th edn) (1996 reissue) 736, 743.

Case referred to in judgment

BRAC Rent-A-Car International Inc, Re [2003] EWHC 128 (Ch), [2003] 2 All ER 201,
c   [2003] 1 WLR 1421.

Cases referred to in skeleton argument

Glaser (W&A) Ltd, Re [1994] BCC 199.
International Bulk Commodities Ltd, Re [1993] 1 All ER 361, [1993] Ch 77, [1992] 3
d   WLR 238.

Application

The general committee of The Salvage Association petitioned for an administration order under s 8(1) of the Insolvency Act 1986 in respect of its business affairs. The facts are set out in the judgment.

e

Gabriel Moss QC (instructed by *Lawrence Graham*) for the applicant.

Cur adv vult

f

15 April 2003. Blackburne J announced that the application would be granted for reasons to be given later.

9 May 2003. The following judgment was delivered.

g **BLACKBURNE J.**

INTRODUCTION

    [1] On 15 April 2003, in the course of a busy interim applications list, I made an order placing The Salvage Association in administration with a view to the
h approval of a voluntary arrangement and (or alternatively) a more advantageous realisation of its assets than would be effected on a winding up. I did so on the petition of the members of the Association's general committee. As the petition raised what are, to some extent, novel questions of jurisdiction under the Insolvency Act 1986, I indicated that I would set out in writing the reasons why I
j was satisfied that the court had jurisdiction to make the order. I now set out those reasons. I begin with some background.

    [2] The Salvage Association is an association of members incorporated by Royal Charter. Its original Charter was granted in 1867. The incorporated body was given the name 'The Association for the Protection of Commercial Interests as respects Wrecked and Damaged Property'. In 1971 the 1867 Charter was revoked and replaced by a new Royal Charter. It was renamed 'The Salvage

Association'. Its principal objects have been to protect the interests of members and others in respect of shipping, cargoes and marine, non-marine and aviation *a* insurance; and to carry out salvage operations, including in particular surveys of shipping, cargoes and investigations into the causes of loss, damage or injury to such interests. Its membership has comprised Lloyds' underwriters and insurance companies.

[3] For reasons which it is unnecessary to relate the Association concluded in *b* late 2000 that its core surveying business was unlikely in the future to generate sufficient profit. In March 2001 it sold its business to a subsidiary of British Maritime Technology. The Association's intention was to conclude a solvent wind-down of its activities, settle outstanding liabilities in full, and, at the end of this process, surrender its Royal Charter. A surplus for distribution to members was expected. *c*

[4] Among its liabilities are funding obligations owed to a pension scheme known as The Salvage Association Retirement Benefits Plan for Surveyors. The Plan was set up to provide for the surveyors employed by the Association. In late December 2001 it became apparent that the Association's liability to the Plan was several times greater than the £1·4m for which provision had been made in its *d* financial projections: £1·4m was twice the estimated deficiency of which the Association was aware at the time of the sale of its business in March 2001.

[5] With the co-operation of members willing to enter into compromises of claims they have arising out of moneys which the Association has collected on their behalf, there is a very good prospect of securing a satisfactory resolution of the Association's financial difficulties through a voluntary arrangement. The *e* arrangement would involve members with claims against the Association abandoning a percentage of those claims, thereby enabling the Association to satisfy a greater proportion of its liability to the Plan. The hope is that, by means of a voluntary arrangement implemented under the protection of an administration, the Association may be enabled to wind itself down in a manner satisfactory to its *f* creditors and befitting an organisation established by Royal Charter which has operated throughout its long life as a valued vehicle of the London marine insurance market.

[6] These proposals, amply demonstrated as achievable by the evidence before the court, presuppose two matters: first, that the court's jurisdiction to make an administration order under Pt II of the 1986 Act and, second, that the *g* ability to enter into a company voluntary arrangement, available under Pt I of the 1986 Act, extend, in both cases, to an association incorporated by Royal Charter. There is no precise authority covering either point. After hearing argument from Mr Gabriel Moss QC appearing on behalf of the Association instructed by Messrs Lawrence Graham and being satisfied that the necessary jurisdiction existed, I *h* made an order placing the Association in administration and appointed Ian Christopher Oakley Smith and Mark Charles Batten of PricewaterhouseCoopers to be the joint administrators. As I have mentioned, I indicated when making that order that I would set out in writing why I was satisfied that the necessary jurisdiction existed. *j*

ADMINISTRATION

[7] It has for long been a matter of controversy whether the reference to a 'company' in s 8(1)—the provision which empowers the court to make an administration order in relation to a company—includes unregistered companies which could be wound up under the 1986 Act. There are arguments both ways

a
(see, for example, *Lightman & Moss, the Law of Receivers and Administrators of Companies* (3rd edn, 2000) (paras 25-045–25-048) favouring an interpretation which would extend the meaning of 'company' to include foreign unregistered companies; but see Smart, *Cross-Border Insolvency* (2nd edn, 1998) pp 130–136 concluding that Pt II of the 1986 Act is confined to registered companies).

b
[8] With effect from 31 May 2002, however, the 1986 Act has contained in s 8(7) a provision making clear that a reference to a 'company' in Pt II goes beyond a company registered under the Companies Acts. Inserted by reg 5 of the Insolvency Act 1986 (Amendment) (No 2) Regulations 2002, SI 2002/1240 (the 2002 regulations), s 8(7) is as follows:

c
'In this Part a reference to a company includes a reference to a company in relation to which an administration order may be made by virtue of Article 3 of the EC Regulation.'

The reference is to Council Regulation (EEC) 1346/2000 on Insolvency Proceedings (OJ 2000 L160 p 1) (the regulation).

[9] Article 3, so far as material, is as follows:

d
'1. The courts of the Member State within the territory of which the centre of a debtor's main interests is situated shall have jurisdiction to open insolvency proceedings. In the case of a company or legal person, the place of the registered office shall be presumed to be the centre of its main interests in the absence of proof to the contrary.

e
2. Where the centre of the debtor's main interests is situated within the territory of a Member State, the courts of another Member State shall have jurisdiction to open insolvency proceedings against that debtor only if he possesses an establishment within the territory of that other Member State.'

f
Article 2(a) defines 'insolvency proceedings' as 'the collective proceedings' listed in Annex A. The proceedings so listed include (in relation to the United Kingdom) administration.

g
[10] The operation of s 8(7) was recently considered by Lloyd J in *Re BRAC Rent-A-Car International Inc* [2003] EWHC 128 (Ch), [2003] 2 All ER 201, [2003] 1 WLR 1421. That case concerned a company incorporated in Delaware which had its registered office in the United States. It had never traded in the United States. Its operations were conducted almost entirely in the United Kingdom. It was registered under the Companies Acts as an overseas company. The question was whether there was jurisdiction under Pt II of the 1986 Act to make an administration order in relation to it. This turned on whether the jurisdiction to open insolvency proceedings conferred by art 3 of the regulation is limited, in the case of legal persons, to those incorporated within the European Union. Lloyd J,

h
for reasons which I need not set out, held that it was not. He rejected a submission that, as regards the expression '... a company or legal person ...' appearing in art 3(1), the regulation was confined to entities incorporated in a relevant member state. Since, in that case, the company had been incorporated in the United States, the submission, if accepted, would have denied the English courts jurisdiction.

j
[11] The significance of that decision, for present purposes, is that, in the case of 'main proceedings'—which are the relevant proceedings in this case—then, provided the centre of main interests of the company is within the United Kingdom, jurisdiction in relation to the various types of insolvency proceedings set out in Annex A to the regulation (so far as capable of relating to a company)

is allocated to the United Kingdom and it matters not where the company was
incorporated (whether in a member state or elsewhere in the world). Assuming *a*
Re BRAC was correctly decided, the question which arises is whether s 8(7) is only
effective in relation to companies incorporated outside the United Kingdom,
leaving it to United Kingdom domestic law to determine whether, as regards a
company incorporated within the jurisdiction (and irrespective of the location of
that company's centre of main interests), it has jurisdiction to open any and if so *b*
what insolvency proceedings in relation to that company.

[12] Mr Moss submitted that, assuming that the purpose of the amendment to
s 8 was to avoid discrimination against European Union companies in other
member states in the application English domestic law once international
jurisdiction was allocated to the United Kingdom under the regulation, it would
have made no sense for Parliament to have used the criterion of place of *c*
registration in clarifying domestic law jurisdiction when the regulation itself had
rejected it in favour of the concept of the 'centre of main interests'. On the
contrary, he said, it makes sense to regard an European Union company for the
purposes of English domestic law jurisdiction as one which has its centre of main
interests in the European Union (including the United Kingdom) and to ignore *d*
the place of incorporation. I agree. It would be odd if a company which had the
centre of its main interests in the United Kingdom could be the subject of an
administration order if incorporated anywhere in the world other than in the
United Kingdom but could not be if, although a 'company' within the extended
meaning of that expression ('... company or legal person ...') and assuming (but
without deciding) that the operation of Pt II of the 1986 Act (ignoring s 8(7)) is *e*
confined to companies registered under the Companies Act 1985 or one of its
statutory predecessors, it happened not to be a company registered under one of
those Acts.

[13] Mr Moss submitted that I should follow the decision in *Re BRAC* unless I
considered it to be plainly wrong. In so submitting Mr Moss nevertheless pointed *f*
to what he said was an error in the judge's discussion of s 8(7). He emphasised
that the error did not in any way affect the conclusion in that case or the
reasoning which led to it. This was Lloyd J's reference (at [9]) to s 8(7) being
'strictly speaking, unnecessary because the [regulation] ... has direct effect in all
the member states (except Denmark ...) as of 31 May 2002'. Mr Moss said that
this implied, incorrectly, that the regulation lays down criteria for the making of *g*
administration orders. This, he submitted, was wrong since art 4(2) of the
regulation expressly provides that the domestic law criteria for 'opening'
proceedings are to be governed by the law of the state of opening, in this case
English domestic law. What s 8(7) does, he submitted, is to clarify (or extend,
according to one's view of previous law) English domestic law to state that *h*
whenever the courts in the United Kingdom have international jurisdiction under
art 3 they also have domestic law jurisdiction. Subject to that minor criticism, the
validity of which I accept, I respectfully find persuasive the reasoning which led
Lloyd J to his conclusion in *Re BRAC* and I am content therefore to follow his
decision. *j*

[14] Applying s 8(7) and the decision in *Re BRAC* there is plainly jurisdiction to
make an administration order in this case. The centre of the Association's main
interests is in the European Union and, more particularly, in the United Kingdom
with the result that the regulation (as regards the proceedings which it covers)
applies and art 3(1) allocates jurisdiction for main proceedings to the United
Kingdom. Administration is within the list of insolvency proceedings covered by

a the article. Finally, s 8(7) makes clear that the jurisdiction of the English court to make an administration order applies to companies in the extended sense ('company or legal person') referred to in art 3(1). The Association is just such a company: the Royal Charter by which it was incorporated was effective to constitute the Association a legal person separate from its members, enjoying perpetual succession, having a common seal, capable of suing and being sued in
b the courts and having power, in addition to the particular powers set out in the Charter, to do all matters and things incidental or appertaining to a body corporate.

COMPANY VOLUNTARY ARRANGEMENT

[15] That brings me to the further jurisdictional question which is whether the
c ability to enter into a company voluntary arrangement under Pt I of the 1986 Act extends to unregistered companies.

[16] Here also an amendment to the 1986 Act has been made, effective from 31 May 2002, this time by reg 4 of the 2002 regulations. This provides for the insertion of a new subsection—sub-s (4)—into s 1 of the 1986 Act. Following the
d same formula as appears in s 8(7), s 1(4) is as follows:

> 'In this Part a reference to a company includes a reference to a company in relation to which a proposal for a voluntary arrangement may be made by virtue of Article 3 of the EC Regulation.'

e 'Voluntary arrangements under insolvency legislation' are among the insolvency proceedings (applicable to the United Kingdom) set out in Annex A.

[17] In my judgment, for the same reasons as apply in relation to the making of an administration order, s 1(4) creates domestic law jurisdiction to open company voluntary arrangement proceedings in this jurisdiction in relation to a legal person such as the Association. It therefore follows that the same factors
f which operate to confer jurisdiction to make an administration order under Pt II in respect of the Association apply no less to the ability of the Association to enter into a voluntary arrangement with its creditors under Pt I.

[18] I should nevertheless mention one particular matter to which Mr Moss drew my attention. It concerns the apparent assumption in art 3(1), evident from its wording, that the jurisdiction to open insolvency proceedings with which that
g article is concerned relates to proceedings by reference to 'the courts of the Member State'.

[19] Article 2(d) defines 'court' for the purposes of the regulation as meaning:

> '... the judicial body or any other competent body of a Member State
h empowered to open insolvency proceedings or to take decisions in the course of such proceedings ...'

[20] The reference to insolvency proceedings is, as art 2(a) explains (and has already been mentioned), to the collective proceedings listed in Annex A. In the case of the United Kingdom they include 'Voluntary arrangements under
j insolvency legislation'. They also include 'Creditors' voluntary winding up (with confirmation by the court)' as well as administration and other forms of collective insolvency regime. At first blush it might appear difficult to fit the concept of the 'opening' of insolvency proceedings 'by the court' or some 'other competent body of a Member State' to the process by which a company voluntary arrangement is commenced, or for that matter, to a creditors' voluntary liquidation. A voluntary arrangement is set in motion by a decision of a meeting of the company's creditors

payable on costs by the defendant to the claimant, Kimberley Caroline Powell, acting by her father and next friend Leslie John Powell, arising out of a claim for damages for personal injury, should run from the date upon which judgment was entered, rather than the date upon which damages were quantified. The facts are set out in the judgment of Kay LJ.

Ralph Lewis QC (instructed by *Lloyd and Cooper*, Leominster) for the claimant.
David Holland (instructed by *Beachcroft Wansbroughs*, Winchester) for the defendant.

LORD PHILLIPS OF WORTH MATRAVERS MR.
[1] I shall ask Kay LJ to give a short judgment which will make it quite plain why this appeal has been disposed of in this way.

KAY LJ.
[2] This is an appeal from the decision of Master Rogers given on 31 July 2002 by which he ruled that interest payable by the defendant to the claimant on the entire costs of the action should run from 1 June 1994, the date upon which judgment was entered for the claimant for damages to be assessed, rather than the much later date upon which damages were quantified.

[3] The case was an action claiming damages for personal injury suffered soon after birth by the claimant, an infant. She was born on 26 June 1986 at the defendant's hospital in Hereford. Her care following her birth was alleged to be negligent, as a result of which she suffered severe brain damage. Legal aid was obtained to pursue a claim and proceedings commenced in June 1989.

[4] In April 1994 liability was admitted and judgment was entered by consent in the following terms: 'That the plaintiff do recover against the defendants damages to be assessed and costs.'

[5] In June 2001 the issue of quantum was resolved by the parties. On 11 June Judge Nicholl, sitting as a judge of the High Court, approved a gross award of £2,175,000 inclusive of £250,000 interim payments. Clause F of the terms of settlement which formed part of the approval, and which was made an order of the court, provided:

'The defendant pay the claimant's costs to be subject to detailed assessment (if not agreed) on the standard basis and in accordance with Reg 107 of the Civil Legal Aid (General) Regulations 1989 [SI 1989/339], the claimant's solicitors waiving any claim to further costs.'

[6] On 31 July 2002 the matter of costs came before Master Rogers. He decided to consider as a preliminary point the date from which interest on the costs should run. The contention advanced on behalf of the claimant was that the interest on the costs ran from April 1994 when the judgment for damages to be assessed was entered. On behalf of the defendant it was argued that the correct date was June 2001 when the judgment for the agreed measure of damages was entered. As Master Rogers observed, the consequences of the claimant's contention were 'fairly startling'. He calculated that if the costs were of the order of £200,000, interest would amount to approximately £156,000 if the claimant was right.

[7] The argument advanced before Master Rogers on behalf of the claimant, was based upon s 17 of the Judgments Act 1838 which, following amendment

a by art 3 of the Civil Procedure (Modification of Enactments) Order 1998, SI 1998/2940, provides: 'Every judgment debt shall carry interest ... from such time as shall be prescribed by rules of court until the same shall be satisfied ...'

[8] Section 18 of the 1838 Act makes an order for costs a judgment debt within the meaning of s 17. CPR 40.8(1) provides:

b   'Where interest is payable on a judgment pursuant to section 17 of the Judgments Act 1838 or section 74 of the County Courts Act 1984, the interest shall begin to run from the date that judgment is given unless—(a) a rule in another Part or a practice direction makes different provision; or (b) the court orders otherwise.'

c [9] The contention on behalf of the claimant was that the judgment of April 1994 ordered the defendant to pay the costs of the action. It was argued that the interest on the costs ran from that date.

[10] On behalf of the defendant it was submitted that the date of the order giving rise to the entitlement to costs was 11 June 2001, the date of the infant *d* settlement approval hearing when damages were assessed. If that argument was not to be accepted, it was contended that, even if interest on the costs incurred in relation to liability ran from the earlier date, interest on costs in determining quantum should run from the latter date.

[11] Neither party suggested to Master Rogers that he had any power to order that the costs run from any different date. Master Rogers concluded on *e* the arguments presented to him that the date from which the interest ran was the date when the original judgment had been entered, June 1994. He clearly recognised that this decision would seem unjust to the defendant in that interest would be carried on a substantial part of the costs for many years before those costs were actually incurred, but he felt compelled by the 1838 Act, as *f* subsequently interpreted by the courts, to reach such a conclusion.

[12] Unfortunately, neither party drew to the attention of Master Rogers the provisions of CPR 44.3(6)(g), which provides:

     'The orders which the court may make under this rule include an order that a party must pay ... (g) interest on costs from or until a certain date, *g*   including a date before judgment.'

[13] There was thus no need in law for Master Rogers to find himself in the legal straitjacket that the parties had suggested. He had a discretion which enabled him to look at the dates when the costs had been incurred, and to come to a conclusion in relation to the payment of interest that fitted the justice of *h* the circumstances of the particular case. He did not do so because he was not made aware of the possibility of that course. It becomes immediately apparent that the decision that he made cannot stand.

[14] Having considered the matter, counsel for the parties (neither of whom appeared before Master Rogers) have now appreciated that that is the situation. *j* They have discussed what would be a fair order pursuant to the rule to which we have referred, and they have been able to agree terms. In those circumstances it is unnecessary for us to consider the matter any further, just as it is unnecessary to consider the rather difficult questions as to what would have been the position under the old law, which now happily is a part of legal history.

Held – The 1990 Act authorised the authority to license IVF treatment with PGD *a* for the purpose of tissue typing, subject to such conditions as it considered appropriate. When concern as to the characteristics of any child that she might bear might inhibit a woman from bearing a child, IVF treatment coupled with PGD that would eliminate that concern could properly be said to be 'for the purpose of assisting women to carry children'. The activities that the authority had licensed in the instant case were the same as those it regularly licensed for the *b* purpose of assisting women to bear children free of hereditary diseases. The difference was as to the desired characteristics identified by the biopsy. That difference might be critical in determining whether or not the authority would decide to license the activities in question. That difference could not, however, be critical in determining whether or not the treatment, including the PGD, was 'for the purpose of enabling women to carry children'. Whether the PGD had the *c* purpose of producing a child free from genetic defects, or of producing a child with stem cells matching a sick or dying sibling, the IVF treatment that included the PGD constituted treatment 'for the purpose of enabling women to carry children'. Moreover, when the object of the treatment was to enable a woman to bear a child with a tissue type that would enable stem cells to be provided to a *d* sick sibling, an embryo would only be suitable for the purpose of being placed within her if it would lead to the birth of a child with the tissue type in question (see [48]–[50], [93], [96], [97], [145], [146], below).

Decision of Maurice Kay J [2003] 2 All ER 105 reversed.

Notes *e*
For prohibitions on the use of embryos and licences for treatment, see 30 *Halsbury's Laws* (4th edn reissue) paras 59, 61–62.

For the Human Fertilisation and Embryology Act 1990, ss 2, 3, Sch 2, para 1, see 28 *Halsbury's Statutes* (4th edn) (2001 reissue) 291, 332.

f

Cases referred to in judgments
R (on the application of Quintavalle) v Secretary of State for Health [2003] UKHL 13, [2003] 2 All ER 113, [2003] 2 WLR 692.
Pepper (Inspector of Taxes) v Hart [1993] 1 All ER 42, [1993] AC 593, [1992] 3 WLR 1032, HL.
Royal College of Nursing of the UK v Dept of Health and Social Security [1981] 1 All ER *g* 545, [1981] AC 800, [1981] 2 WLR 279, HL.

Cases referred to in skeleton arguments
Black-Clawson International Ltd v Papierwerke Waldhof-Aschaffenburg AG [1975] 1 All *h* ER 810, [1975] AC 591, [1975] 2 WLR 513, HL.
NHS Trust A v M, NHS Trust B v H [2001] 1 All ER 801, [2001] Fam 348, [2001] 2 WLR 942.
R v Radio Authority, ex p Bull [1997] 2 All ER 561, [1998] QB 294, [1997] 3 WLR 1094, CA.

j

Appeal
The Human Fertilisation and Embryology Authority (HFEA) appealed with permission of Maurice Kay J given on 20 December 2002 from his decision of the same date ([2003] 2 All ER 105) giving judgment in favour of the respondent, Josephine Quintavalle, acting on behalf of Comment on Reproductive Ethics, in

a judicial review proceedings concerning the power of the HFEA to grant licences for tissue typing under para 1 of Sch 2 to the Human Fertilisation and Embryology Act 1990. The facts are set out in the judgment of Lord Phillips of Worth Matravers MR.

b *David Pannick QC* and *Dinah Rose* (instructed by *Morgan Cole*, Cardiff) for the appellant.

James Dingemans QC and *Martin Chamberlain* (instructed by *Coningsbys*, Surrey) for the respondent.

James Eadie (instructed by *Department of Work and Pensions*) for the Secretary of State for Health as Intervener.

c *Cur adv vult*

16 May 2003. The following judgments were delivered.

LORD PHILLIPS OF WORTH MATRAVERS MR.

d [1] Mr and Mrs Hashmi have five children. The fourth, a son, Zain was born with a blood disorder known as beta thalassaemia major. By the time that he was two and a half years old this had reduced him to a parlous condition, requiring him to take a daily cocktail of drugs and to submit to regular blood transfusions in hospital in order to remain alive. His life expectancy is uncertain. Mrs Hashmi *e* had been aware that she had a genetic predisposition to producing children with this disorder and, when pregnant with Zain had undergone prenatal testing to see whether, if she carried Zain to term, he would be born with the disorder. The test failed to disclose that this was indeed the position.

[2] Zain's condition might be cured by a transplant of stem cells from someone with matching tissue. The stem cells could be supplied from blood *f* taken from the umbilical cord of a newborn child, or from bone marrow. The most likely source of matching tissue would be a sibling, for statistically Mrs Hashmi has one chance in four of producing a child with matching tissue, although the odds are somewhat longer of producing such a child who is not affected with beta thalassaemia major. None of Zain's three elder siblings have *g* tissue that matches his.

[3] Mrs Hashmi resolved to have another child, in the hope that it would have matching tissue. She conceived, but prenatal testing showed that the child would have beta thalassaemia major, so she underwent an abortion. She conceived again, and a healthy son was born, but unfortunately his tissue did not match that of Zain. *h*

[4] At this point Mrs Hashmi met Dr Simon Fishel, the managing and scientific director of Centres for Assisted Reproduction Ltd (CARE). CARE is the largest single provider of in vitro fertilisation (IVF) services in the United Kingdom. It provides these services at various locations both to NHS and private patients. Dr Fishel told Mrs Hashmi of a procedure, at the cutting edge of technology, that *j* had been developed at the Reproductive Genetics Institute (RGI) in Chicago in the United States and which might provide the solution to her problem. In summary, that procedure would include the following stages. (i) The fertilisation 'in vitro' of a number of eggs taken from Mrs Hashmi with sperm taken from her husband to form embryos. (ii) The removal from the developing embryo of a single cell by a biopsy. (iii) The examination of that cell using

molecular genetics to see whether the embryo carried the beta thalassaemia disease. This process is commonly described as 'Pre-implantation Genetic Diagnosis' (PGD). (iv) Use simultaneously of the same process to identify whether the embryo had the same tissue type as Zain. Because this process involves examination of proteins known as human leukocyte antigens (HLA), this form of PGD is described as 'HLA typing'. I shall refer to it by the more popular phrase of 'tissue typing'. (v) Jettison of embryos found by this analysis to be either disease bearing or of a different HLA type to Zain and implantation in the womb of Mrs Hashmi of an embryo shown to be disease free and of the same HLA as Zain.

[5] Mrs Hashmi asked Dr Fishel whether it would be possible for her to be impregnated in this country with an embryo created and selected in this way. IVF treatment can only be carried out in this country under licence issued by the appellant, the Human Fertilisation and Embryology Authority (HFEA), pursuant to the Human Fertilisation and Embryology Act 1990. For some years PGD screening against genetic disease had been carried out as part of IVF treatment licensed by the HFEA. Tissue typing had never, however, been carried out as part of such treatment and Dr Fishel considered that this procedure required express authorisation under licence from HFEA. After careful consideration of the implications, CARE applied to the HFEA for a ruling as to whether an IVF clinic could properly apply for a licence to administer treatment including tissue typing.

[6] The HFEA announced their decision in a press release on 13 December 2001. They would be prepared in principle to grant a licence for treatment that included tissue typing, subject to a number of conditions. The HFEA decided that tissue typing should only be permitted where PGD was already necessary to avoid the passing on of a serious genetic disorder. They also decided that licences permitting PGD in conjunction with tissue typing should only be granted on a case by case basis. Such licences would only be granted subject to the following conditions. (a) The condition of the affected child should be severe or life threatening, of a sufficient seriousness to justify the use of PGD. (b) The embryos should themselves be at risk of the condition affecting the child. (c) All other possibilities of treatment and sources of tissue for the affected child should have been explored. (d) The techniques should not be available where the intended recipient is a parent. (e) The intention should be to take only cord blood for the purposes of the treatment. (f) Appropriate counselling should be given to the parents. (g) Families should be encouraged to take part in follow-up studies. (h) Embryos should not be genetically modified to provide a tissue match.

[7] In accordance with this decision, on 22 February 2002, the HFEA granted a licence to Park Hospital operated by CARE in Nottingham to carry out IVF treatment that included PGD for 'beta thalassaemia in conjunction with HLA typing for patients known as Mr and Mrs H'.

[8] Mr and Mrs Hashmi then made two attempts to produce a child by IVF treatment involving PGD and tissue typing. In the first IVF was effected at Park Hospital. Fifteen embryos were produced. The biopsied cells from those were then flown to RGI in Chicago for genetic analysis, while the embryos were frozen awaiting the results. Only one embryo proved to have an exact tissue match, but it carried the beta thalassaemia disease. Mr and Mrs Hashmi travelled to RGI for the second attempt. Ten embryos were produced. Two of these proved disease free and to have a tissue match with Zain. One was implanted in Mrs Hashmi,

a   but no pregnancy resulted. Mr and Mrs Hashmi were prevented from a further attempt by the judgment that is the subject of this appeal.

THE SCIENCE INVOLVED

[9] Dr Fishel in his witness statement described how PGD in conjunction with tissue typing is carried out by the RGI. There is no need to attempt to describe
b   the entire process; it suffices to identify the following two stages. (i) About three days after in vitro fertilisation, when the embryo has sub-divided into eight cells, one of these cells is removed by a biopsy. (ii) The genetic material in the cell is then tested with a genetic probe, the DNA sequence of which has been so prepared as to identify whether there is a tissue match and whether the embryonic tissue contains any form of thalassaemia disease.
c
THE CHALLENGE

[10] The respondent, Josephine Quintavalle, acts on behalf of Comment on Reproductive Ethics (CORE). CORE is a group whose purpose is 'to focus and facilitate debate on ethical issues arising from human reproduction and, in particular, assisted reproduction'. Absolute respect for the human embryo is a
d   principal tenet of CORE. The respondent sought and obtained permission to seek judicial review of the HFEA's decision announced on 13 December 2001. She challenged that decision on the ground that the HFEA had no power to issue a licence that permitted the use of HLA typing to select between healthy embryos. Her challenge succeeded. On 20 December 2002 Maurice Kay J gave
e   judgment in her favour, quashing the HFEA's decision (see [2003] 2 All ER 105).

[11] Maurice Kay J gave permission to appeal against his judgment to this court because of the importance of the issue of whether tissue typing can lawfully be licensed by the HFEA. The Secretary of State for Health was concerned that the judgment has wider implications—in particular that it puts in doubt the legitimacy of the beneficial practice of PGD screening for genetic diseases.
f   Accordingly the Secretary of State obtained permission to intervene to support the HFEA's appeal.

THE ACT

[12] The 1990 Act was passed 'to make provision in connection with human
g   embryos and any subsequent development of such embryos; to prohibit certain practices in connection with embryos and gametes; to establish a Human Fertilisation and Embryology Authority', and for other purposes.

[13] The following provisions of the Act are particularly material:

'2.—(1) In this Act ...

h   "treatment services" means medical, surgical or obstetric services provided to the public or a section of the public for the purpose of assisting women to carry children ...

Activities governed by the Act

3. *Prohibitions in connection with embryos.*—(1) No person shall—(a) bring about the creation of an embryo, or (b) keep or use an embryo, except in
j   pursuance of a licence ...

5. *The Human Fertilisation and Embryology Authority.*—(1) There shall be a body corporate called the Human Fertilisation and Embryology Authority ...

Scope of licences

11. *Licences for treatment, storage and research.*—(1) The Authority may grant the following and no other licences—(a) licences under paragraph 1 of

Schedule 2 to this Act authorising activities in the course of providing
treatment services, (b) licences under that Schedule authorising the storage
of gametes and embryos, and (c) licences under paragraph 3 of that Schedule
authorising activities for the purposes of a project of research ...

Licence conditions

12. *General conditions.*—The following shall be conditions of every licence
granted under this Act—(a) that the activities authorised by the licence shall
be carried on only on the premises to which the licence relates and under the
supervision of the person responsible ...

13. *Conditions of licences for treatment.*—(1) The following shall be
conditions of every licence under para 1 of Sch 2 to this Act ...

(5) A woman shall not be provided with treatment services unless account
has been taken of the welfare of any child who may be born as a result of the
treatment (including the need of that child for a father), and of any other
child who may be affected by the birth ...

SCHEDULE 2

ACTIVITIES FOR WHICH LICENCES MAY BE GRANTED

Licences for treatment

1.—(1) A licence under this paragraph may authorise any of the following
in the course of providing treatment services—(a) bringing about the
creation of embryos in vitro, (b) keeping embryos, (c) using gametes,
(d) practices designed to secure that embryos are in a suitable condition to be
placed in a woman or to determine whether embryos are suitable for that
purpose, (e) placing any embryo in a woman, (f) mixing sperm with the egg
of a hamster, or other animal specified in directions, for the purpose of
testing the fertility or normality of the sperm, but only where anything
which forms is destroyed when the test is complete and, in any event, not
later than the two cell stage, and (g) such other practices as may be specified
in, or determined in accordance with, regulations.

(2) Subject to the provisions of this Act, a licence under this paragraph
may be granted subject to such conditions as may be specified in the licence
and may authorise the performance of any of the activities referred to in
sub-paragraph (1) above in such manner as may be so specified.

(3) A licence under this paragraph cannot authorise any activity unless it
appears to the Authority to be necessary or desirable for the purpose of
providing treatment services ...

Licences for research

3.—(1) A licence under this paragraph may authorise any of the
following—(a) bringing about the creation of embryos *in vitro*, and
(b) keeping or using embryos, for the purposes of a project of research
specified in the licence.

(2) A licence under this paragraph cannot authorise any activity unless it
appears to the Authority to be necessary or desirable for the purpose
of—(a) promoting advances in the treatment of infertility, (b) increasing
knowledge about the causes of congenital disease, (c) increasing knowledge
about the causes of miscarriages, (d) developing more effective techniques of
contraception, or (e) developing methods for detecting the presence of gene
or chromosome abnormalities in embryos before implantation, or for such
other purposes as may be specified in regulations.

a
(3) Purposes may only be so specified with a view to the authorisation of projects of research which increase knowledge about the creation and development of embryos, or about disease or enable such knowledge to be applied ...

(6) No licence under this paragraph shall be granted unless the Authority is satisfied that any proposed use of embryos is necessary for the purposes of
b
the research ...

General

4.—(1) A licence under this Schedule can only authorise activities to be carried on on premises specified in the licence and under the supervision of an individual designated in the licence.

c
(2) A licence cannot—(a) authorise activities falling within both para 1 and para 3 above, (b) apply to more than one project of research, (c) authorise activities to be carried on under the supervision of more than one individual, or (d) apply to premises in different places.'

[14] For present purposes it is important to note the following scheme of the
d Act. Section 3 prohibits the creation or use of an embryo except in pursuance of a licence. Section 11 restricts the power of the HFEA to grant licences by reference to the provisions of Sch 2. Schedule 2 sets out lists of activities which may be authorised by a licence and makes provision for adding to these by regulations. So far as treatment is concerned, the HFEA is, however, subject to the overriding restriction that it cannot authorise any activity unless it appears
e necessary or desirable for the purpose of providing 'treatment services'.

THE ISSUES BEFORE THE JUDGE

[15] Before Maurice Kay J two issues were canvassed. (i) Does genetic analysis of a cell taken from an embryo involve the 'use of an embryo'? (ii) Is genetic analysis for the purpose of tissue typing 'necessary or desirable for the
f purpose of providing treatment services'?

[16] The first issue arose out of the submission on behalf of the HFEA that tissue typing did not require a licence because it was performed on a cell extracted from an embryo rather than the embryo itself. The HFEA accepted that the removal of the cell by a biopsy constituted 'use of an embryo', but submitted that
g testing the cell thereafter did not constitute such use. Mrs Quintavalle contended that tissue typing did constitute 'use of an embryo' and, in consequence, could not be carried on without a licence.

[17] The second issue arose only if the HFEA failed on the first issue. In that event the HFEA contended that they could lawfully licence such use in that tissue
h typing was 'desirable for the purpose of rendering treatment services'. The HFEA argued that the relevant test was whether the activity under consideration was 'at least desirable for the overall purpose of providing fertility treatment'.

[18] Mrs Quintavalle relied upon the definition of 'treatment services' and submitted that it could not be said that tissue typing was for the purpose of those services. The purpose of tissue typing was not to 'assist women to carry children'
j but to ensure that a child born to a particular woman would have tissue that was compatible with the tissue of a sibling.

THE JUDGMENT OF MAURICE KAY J

[19] The judge held against the HFEA on both issues. There were a number of reasons why he held that tissue typing involved the use of an embryo,

including the fact that it was inconceivable that Parliament intended to leave an
activity such as tissue typing, which had potential for misuse, outside the control
of the Act. As to the second issue he observed that tissue typing of an embryo had
no impact on the ability of a woman to carry the embryo after implantation. In
those circumstances it could not be said that tissue typing was 'necessary or
desirable for the purpose of assisting a woman to carry a child'.

THE ISSUES BEFORE US

[20] Mr Pannick QC, who appeared for the HFEA, accepted that the first issue
considered by Maurice Kay J did not go to the heart of the case. He recognised
that the primary object of carrying out a biopsy of each embryo was to carry out
tissue typing of the cell that was removed. It was common ground that the
biopsy involved 'using' the embryo. If the tissue typing was not carried out 'for
the purpose of assisting a woman to carry a child', then the biopsy could not be
said to be for that purpose either. More broadly Mr and Mrs Hashmi's case
demonstrated the true nature of treatment involving tissue typing. The primary
object of the entire treatment, comprehending creation of the embryo, biopsy for
PGD and tissue typing, the analysis of the cell removed by the biopsy and the
implantation of the embryo, if it proved to be free of disease and a tissue match
for Zain, was to produce a child whose umbilical cord would provide the stem
cells which might save Zain's life. The vital question was whether this treatment
was 'for the purpose of assisting a woman to carry a child'.

[21] Mr Pannick submitted that the answer to this question was Yes. He
submitted that the judge had wrongly concluded that treatment services had to
have as their sole object the assistance of the physical process of producing a
child. IVF coupled with PGD was a practice aimed at enabling women to have
children free of hereditary diseases. Analysis of the Act, and of background
material to which it was legitimate to have resort, demonstrated that treatment
services extended to embrace PGD designed to prevent the implantation of
embryos which would result in the birth of a children carrying genetic defects.
Such screening assisted a woman to carry a child because it gave her the
knowledge that the child would not be born handicapped. Without such
knowledge some women who carried genetic diseases would not be prepared to
have children. In the same way tissue typing would assist Mrs Hashmi to carry a
child, for her wish to do so was conditional upon knowing that the birth of that
child would be capable of saving the life and health of Zain.

[22] Mr Pannick accepted that under this reasoning PGD with the object of
ensuring that a child had certain characteristics for purely social reasons might
also be said to be 'for the purpose of assisting women to carry children' but
submitted that it was for the HFEA to control PGD to ensure that this was not
used for purposes which were ethically objectionable. That accorded with the
scheme of the Act. It was only practices that were unquestionably objectionable
that were prohibited by the legislation. PGD for the purpose of avoiding genetic
defects was not objectionable at all.

[23] Mr Pannick accepted that it would not be enough for him to show that
tissue typing was a practice that assisted women to carry children. He had to
show that a biopsy with the object of tissue typing was one of the specific
activities listed in para 1(1) of Sch 2. He submitted that it fell within '(d) practices
designed to secure that embryos are in a suitable condition to be placed in a
woman or to determine whether embryos are suitable for that purpose'.

a Suitability could have regard to the desired characteristics of the child that would be produced by the embryo.

[24] Mr Dingemans QC, for Mrs Quintavalle, challenged these submissions. He did not abandon the primary submission that 'treatment services' only extended to services designed to assist women in overcoming problems in conceiving and carrying a child to term. Most of his energies were, however,

b directed to an alternative argument. Even if PGD for the purpose of screening out genetic defects fell within the definition of 'treatment services', such a practice differed in principle from PGD screening designed to reject healthy and viable embryos because they lacked some desired characteristic. While the former might be said to assist a woman in carrying a child the latter certainly could not.

c

BACKGROUND MATERIAL

[25] Maurice Kay J did not consider it necessary to resort to background material when interpreting the Act but before us both parties devoted much time to exploring the history of the legislation. I have found this a helpful exercise

d because that history bears closely on the issue of construction that we have to resolve. The House of Lords in *R (on the application of Quintavalle) v Secretary of State for Health* [2003] UKHL 13, [2003] 2 All ER 113, [2003] 2 WLR 692 recently considered another issue of construction of the Act raised by Mrs Quintavalle and Lord Bingham of Cornhill gave the following summary of the legislative history and purpose of the Act. This is a good starting point.

e

'[11] The birth of the first child resulting from in vitro fertilisation in July 1978 prompted much ethical and scientific debate which in turn led to the appointment in July 1982 of a Committee of Inquiry under the chairmanship of Dame Mary Warnock DBE to—

f

"consider recent and potential developments in medicine and science related to human fertilisation and embryology; to consider what policies and safeguards should be applied, including consideration of the social, ethical and legal implications of these developments; and to make recommendations."

g

The committee reported in July 1984 (*Report of the Committee of Inquiry into Human Fertilisation and Embryology* (Cmnd 9314) (the Warnock Report)). A White Paper was published in November 1987 *Human Fertilisation and Embryology: A Framework for Legislation* (Cm 259) when the Department of

h Health and Social Security recognised (para 6) "the particular difficulties of framing legislation on these sensitive issues against a background of fast-moving medical and scientific development".

[12] There is no doubting the sensitivity of the issues. There were those who considered the creation of embryos, and thus of life, in vitro to be either sacrilegious or ethically repugnant and wished to ban such activities

j altogether. There were others who considered that these new techniques, by offering means of enabling the infertile to have children and increasing knowledge of congenital disease, had the potential to improve the human condition, and this view also did not lack religious and moral arguments to support it. Nor can one doubt the difficulty of legislating against a background of fast-moving medical and scientific development. It is not

often that Parliament has to frame legislation apt to apply to developments
at the advanced cutting edge of science.

[13] The solution recommended and embodied in the 1990 Act was not to
ban all creation and subsequent use of live human embryos produced in vitro
but instead, and subject to certain express prohibitions of which some have
been noted above, to permit such creation and use subject to specified
conditions, restrictions and time limits and subject to the regimes of control
briefly described in [4] above. The merits of this solution are not a matter for
the House in its judicial capacity. It is, however, plain that while Parliament
outlawed certain grotesque possibilities (such as placing a live animal
embryo in a woman or a live human embryo in an animal), it otherwise
opted for a strict regime of control. No activity within this field was left
unregulated. There was to be no free for all.'

[26] Neither party now suggests that tissue typing is an activity that is left
unregulated by the Act. The issue is whether it is absolutely prohibited by the
Act, whether it is an activity that the Secretary of State could by regulation permit
to be licensed but has not yet done so, or whether it is a practice which can be
licensed because it falls within para 1(1)(d) of Sch 2. A more detailed analysis of
the background material is needed to assist in resolving this issue.

THE WARNOCK REPORT

[27] The first eight chapters of the *Report of the Committee of Inquiry into Human
Fertilisation and Embryology* (Cmnd 9314) (the Warnock Report) address techniques
for the alleviation of infertility. Chapter 9 is headed 'The Wider Use of these
Techniques'. This addresses the problem of hereditary diseases. It contemplates
the possibility of avoiding transmission of a gender linked hereditary disease by
PGD screening for gender to avoid implantation of embryos with the vulnerable
gender. It states:

'We see no reason why, if a method of selecting the sex of a child before
fertilisation is developed, this should not be offered to couples who have
good medical reasons for choosing the sex of their child.'

The report goes on to consider the possibility of gender selection for purely social
reasons and concludes that it is not possible to make positive recommendations
on this issue other than that the acceptability of such a practice should be kept
under review.

[28] Chapter 12 of the report is headed 'Possible Future Developments in
Research'. This opens with the following comments:

'There is a number of specific techniques and procedures involving the use
of human embryos which have caused much public anxiety. Many of these
have not yet reached the stage where they are practical possibilities. We
believe that our recommendations for the regulation of research will allay
much of that anxiety, as it will be the duty of the proposed licensing body
(13.3) to keep these and other new techniques under constant review;
indeed, in some instances our proposals will preclude certain developments
altogether. It is important, however to consider whether further restrictions
are required, although it must be borne in mind that we cannot foresee all
possible developments.'

a [29] The chapter specifically considers the possibility of embryonic biopsy followed by PGD in order to diagnose whether an embryo is genetically abnormal and concludes that this is unlikely to become feasible for a considerable time.

[30] Chapter 13 of the report recommends the establishment of a new statutory licensing authority both to regulate those infertility services which should be subject to control and to licence research involving the use of embryos
b in circumstances where this is justified by the objectives of the research.

THE WHITE PAPER

[31] The White Paper (*Human Fertilisation and Embryology: A Framework for Legislation* (Cm 259)), produced after consultation on the Warnock Report, announced the government's intention to create a statutory licensing authority.
c As recommended in the Warnock Report one function of this authority would be to licence the provision of 'infertility services'. So far as research was concerned, however, the consultation process had disclosed strongly conflicting views. The government proposed to leave it to Parliament to decide whether the authority's role should extend to licensing embryo research, or whether such research
d should be absolutely prohibited.

[32] The White Paper set out in an annex the arguments for and against permitting the licensing of research. Arguments in favour included:

e
'49. It is argued that the greatest potential benefits of research involving human embryos lie in the prevention of congenital disorders. Studies of eggs, sperm and early embryos may lead to ways of preventing some chromosomal abnormalities developing. Also, in the future, those who support research envisage the development of techniques including embryo biopsy which might allow the very early detection of embryos which had single gene or chromosome defects which would result in seriously abnormal babies. In the UK some 7,000 babies a year (about 1 per cent of all
f babies) are born with an obvious single gene inherited defect. Pre-implantation "diagnosis" could ultimately result in some fall in that number.'

A footnote explained:

g
'1. Male infertility is the sole cause in about 30 per cent of cases of infertility and it is a factor in some others.

2. The technique of embryo biopsy could extend the use of IVF from treating infertile couples to those at risk of passing on an hereditary handicap. It would involve the removal and culture of one or two cells from an embryo still in vitro and need not affect the subsequent development of
h the embryo. It could, however, give the possibility in some instances of rejecting defective embryos in favour of healthy ones and reducing the number of requests for abortion on grounds of fetal abnormality. Attempts are also being made to develop non-invasive techniques for detecting defective embryos.'

j [33] The White Paper commented:

'29. The key distinction in the debate surrounding embryo research appears to be between the use of an embryo with the intention of achieving (with that embryo) a successful pregnancy leading to a healthy baby; and its use for other reasons (eg improvement of knowledge about disease). Those who are opposed to all research involving human embryos argue that

procedures which lead to the destruction of the embryo or which make it
unsuitable for transfer to a woman should not be permitted in any
circumstances. Procedures which do not damage the embryo, or which are
actively beneficial to it, do not give the same cause for concern even though
such procedures may form part of what some would regard as a programme
of research (for example the observation of embryos developing in different
nutrient fluids prior to transfer to a woman.)

30. The Government therefore proposes that the alternative draft clauses
which will be made available to Parliament should be along the following
lines:

It will be a criminal offence to carry out any procedures on a human
embryo other than those aimed at preparing the embryo for transfer to the
uterus of a woman: or those carried out to ascertain the suitability of that
embryo for the intended transfer.

Except as part of a project specifically licensed by the SLA, it will be a
criminal offence to carry out any procedures on a human embryo other than
those aimed at preparing the embryo for transfer to the uterus of a woman
or those carried out to ascertain the suitability of that embryo for the
intended transfer.'

[34] The latter is plainly the origin of the provision that ultimately became
para 1(1)(d) of Sch 2. It is to be noted that 'suitability' is not defined, but that
procedures carried out to ascertain suitability for transfer were considered to be
appropriate for licensing, whether or not embryo research was prohibited.

PROCEEDINGS IN PARLIAMENT

[35] The Bill that became the Act was introduced in the House of Lords on
22 November 1989. As presaged in the White Paper there were alternative draft
provisions, one which permitted the licensing of research and one which
prohibited this. On the second reading on 7 December 1989 the clause permitting
embryo research was carried by 154 votes. The second reading in the House of
Commons took place on 2 April and the third reading on 23 April 1990. Proposed
amendments imposing a ban on embryo research were heavily defeated. By the
time of the third reading it was known that Dr Robert Winston had successfully
implanted female embryos after genetically screening out male embryos which
were, or might have been, affected with gender linked genetic disorders.

[36] In the course of debate on the third reading, Mr Kenneth Clarke, the
Secretary of State for Health, remarked (171 Official Report (6th series) col 37):

'Not all reproductive technologies are aimed at helping infertile couples to
have children. Some are designed to help people to have healthy normal
children by allowing a range of congenital diseases and handicaps to be
detected prenatally by pre-implantation diagnosis. The possibility of
preventing genetic disease is one of the reasons most frequently cited in
support of embryo research.'

Mr Clarke was then addressed by Mrs Ann Winterton, who was opposed to
embryo research. She was anxious to refute the suggestion that a ban on research
would lead to a ban on PGD screening for hereditary defects. She asked him to
confirm that 'Sch 2, para 1(d) would allow such pre-implantation screening for
genetic handicaps to continue even if today we voted for a ban on destructive
embryo research'. Mr Clarke confirmed (at col 38) that '[t]hat treatment, now

a that it is being developed, could be continued if the amendments were agreed to'. Mrs Winterton later made the same point again and it was subsequently repeated by others.

DISCUSSION

b [37] Maurice Kay J did not find it appropriate to consider whether the Act permits PGD screening for hereditary diseases. Mr Pannick's argument founded on this question as a stepping stone to the construction for which he contended. It seems to me not merely appropriate but necessary to consider the implications of any suggested construction on the position of screening for hereditary diseases. As I have shown, this practice was an important feature of the context in which the Act was passed.

c [38] Mr Pannick submitted that para 3(2)(b) of Sch 2 was significant. This permits the licensing of embryo research activities for the purpose of 'developing methods for detecting the presence of gene or chromosome abnormalities in embryos before implantation'. Mr Pannick argued that it would be strange if Parliament approved research to develop a method for achieving an objective

d which was prohibited elsewhere in the Act. The clear inference of permitting such research was that Parliament approved of PGD to avoid implantation of embryos carrying genetic defects. The phrase 'for the purpose of assisting women to carry children' and of 'suitable for that purpose' in Sch 2, para 1(1)(d) had to be read so as to embrace that activity.

e [39] I found this argument persuasive. The Warnock Report recommended permitting the licensing of existing techniques of infertility treatment. It went on to consider wider uses of IVF to screen out hereditary diseases. It was in favour of gender selection to screen out gender linked diseases, which was the only form of PGD screening which seemed likely to prove feasible in the immediate future. It anticipated the remote possibility of PGD involving single cell biopsy of the

f type with which this appeal is concerned, and recommended permitting regulated research. The White Paper left open the question of whether research under licence should be permitted. The decision turned essentially on whether the potential benefits from research outweighed the ethical objection to creating and then destroying human embryos. Foremost in the potential benefits was the possibility of preventing the passing on of hereditary diseases to children.

g [40] Parliament chose to permit the licensing of research. It makes little sense for Parliament, at the same time, to prohibit reaping the benefit of that research, even under licence.

[41] The matter is, in my judgment, put beyond doubt by the statement made

h by the Secretary of State in the course of Parliamentary debate. This is one of those rare cases where, under the application of the principle in *Pepper (Inspector of Taxes) v Hart* [1993] 1 All ER 42, [1993] AC 593, it is legitimate to resort to such material. The minister made an express statement to Parliament upon the very issue of construction under consideration and it is clear that the issue in question was of particular concern to Parliament.

j [42] The question remains whether the two vital phrases 'for the purpose of assisting women to carry children' and 'designed to secure that the embryo is suitable for the purpose of being placed in a woman' are appropriate to describe the object of IVF treatment which is designed not to assist the processes of fertilisation and gestation, but to ensure that the child which is produced by those processes is healthy.

[43] My initial reaction to the meaning of 'for the purpose of assisting women
to carry children' was the same as that of Maurice Kay J. The phrase naturally *a*
suggests treatment designed to assist the physical processes from fertilisation to
the birth of a child. But if the impediment to bearing a child is concern that it may
be born with a hereditary defect, treatment which enables women to become
pregnant and to bear children in the confidence that they will not be suffering
from such defects can properly be described as 'for the purpose of assisting *b*
women to carry children'. I believe that it is appropriate to give it this meaning
in order sensibly to reconcile the provisions of the Act that deal with treatment
and those that deal with research. I also think that it is legitimate when deciding
to adopt this construction to have regard to the fact that the more narrow
alternative construction would render unlawful a practice which has been carried
on for over a decade and which is patently beneficial. It is also legitimate to have *c*
regard to Mr Clarke's statement to Parliament.

[44] What of the actual process of biopsy and PGD—can that properly be said
to be 'designed to secure that the embryo is suitable for the purpose of being
placed in a woman'? Here I agree with Mr Pannick that, once satisfied that the
treatment as a whole is for the purpose of enabling a woman to carry a child, no *d*
further problem arises. The word 'suitable' takes its meaning from its context.
Where the object of the treatment is to enable a woman to bear a child confident
that it will not carry a hereditary defect, an embryo will only be suitable for the
purpose of being placed within her if it is free of that defect. PGD is thus designed
to secure that the embryo is suitable for this purpose. The reassurance which
Mr Clarke gave to Parliament was not one which did violence to the language of *e*
para 1(i)(d) of Sch 2.

[45] I should add that Mr Dingemans suggested that it was possible to
accommodate PGD testing within the narrow construction of the Act reached by
Maurice Kay J on the basis that embryos with genetic defects are more prone to
result in miscarriage. Mr Eadie, for the Secretary of State, sought permission to *f*
adduce evidence from a geneticist, Professor Alexander Raeburn, that shows that
some hereditary diseases do not affect the development of the embryo within the
woman. If it mattered, I would have had regard to this evidence, but there is
ample other evidence which shows that the primary concern about genetic
defects was and is not that they imperil the pregnancy but that they lead to the
birth of children carrying the defects. *g*

TISSUE TYPING

[46] I said that Mr Pannick used the question of whether the Act permitted
PGD screening as a stepping stone to the construction of the Act for which he
contended. It remains to consider whether this stepping stone takes him safely *h*
to his destination.

'TREATMENT FOR THE PURPOSE OF ASSISTING WOMEN TO BEAR CHILDREN'

[47] The discussion thus far had led me to the following conclusion. When
concern as to the characteristics of any child that she may bear may inhibit a
woman from bearing a child, IVF treatment coupled with PGD that will *j*
eliminate that concern can properly be said to be 'for the purpose of assisting
women to carry children'. When the Act was passed women who had reason to
fear that they would give birth to children with genetic defects were probably the
only section of the population for whom it was envisaged that IVF treatment
could be justified on this basis. No evidence suggests that the wish of a woman

a to bear a child in order to provide a source of stem cells for a sick or dying sibling was anticipated at that time. Such a wish is now the reality, and the case of Mr and Mrs Hashmi is not unique.

[48] The activities that the HFEA has licensed in the case of Mr and Mrs Hashmi, are the same as those it has regularly licensed for the purpose of assisting women to bear children free of hereditary diseases: (i) creation of
b embryos; (ii) biopsies of the embryos; (iii) analysis of the cells removed by biopsy by the use of a DNA probe in order to identify those embryos likely to produce children with desired characteristics; and (iv) implantation of those embryos. The difference is as to the desired characteristics. That difference may be critical in determining whether or not the HFEA will decide to license the activities in
c question. I cannot see, however, that the difference can be critical in determining whether or not the treatment, including the PGD, is 'for the purpose of enabling women to carry children'. My conclusion is that whether the PGD has the purpose of producing a child free from genetic defects, or of producing a child with stem cells matching a sick or dying sibling, the IVF treatment that includes the PGD constitutes 'treatment for the purpose of assisting women to bear
d children'.

'DESIGNED TO SECURE THAT THE EMBRYO IS SUITABLE FOR THE PURPOSE OF BEING PLACED IN THE WOMAN'

[49] Just as in the case of PGD screening for genetic defects, the meaning of 'suitable' falls to be determined having regard to its context. When the object of
e the treatment is to enable a woman to bear a child with a tissue type that will enable stem cells to be provided to a sick sibling, an embryo will only be suitable for the purpose of being placed within her if it will lead to the birth of a child with the tissue type in question. Accordingly I conclude that the HFEA was right to decide that the Act authorised it to licence IVF treatment with PGD for the
f purpose of tissue typing subject to such conditions as it considered appropriate.

CONCLUSION

[50] IVF treatment can help women to bear children when they are unable to do so by the normal process of fertilisation. Screening of embryos before implantation enables a choice to be made as to the characteristics of the child to
g be born with the assistance of the treatment. Whether and for what purposes such a choice should be permitted raises difficult ethical questions. My conclusion is that Parliament has placed that choice in the hands of the HFEA. For the reasons that I have given I would allow this appeal.

h SCHIEMANN LJ.

[51] The advances of science have made possible in vitro fertilisation and the creation of embryos outside the human body. Those embryos can be used for experimental and other purposes. They can, even after use for experimental or other purposes, be implanted inside a woman. All this, for which the common
j law made no special provision, gave rise to a considerable amount of public anxiety. Some wished to prevent the creation of such embryos in vitro. Others considered that the benefits to be gained by such creation outweighed the disbenefits. By the Human Fertilisation and Embryology Act 1990 Parliament decided in principle not to forbid the creation of embryos in vitro and their subsequent use but to regulate what could be done.

[52] The Act provided for the setting up of the Human Fertilisation and Embryology Authority with a general power to keep under review information about embryos and about the provision of treatment services and activities governed by the Act. Part of the regulatory mechanism established by the Act is the issue of licences by or on behalf of the Authority.

[53] The underlying task which faces the court in the present case is one of construction of this Act. It is clear from the Act that Parliament itself has regulated some matters: other matters it has left to be regulated by the Authority. We have to decide whether the issue of a licence to permit tissue typing in order to test an embryo for tissue compatibility with a sibling affected by a particular disorder is in principle open to the Authority. The judge held it was not. For reasons which I shall endeavour to set out I respectfully differ.

[54] The structure of the Act is as follows.

SOME ACTIVITIES ARE FORBIDDEN OUTRIGHT

[55] Parliament has made the decision that the activities enumerated in s 3(2) and (3) of the Act are unacceptable in any circumstances.

[56] Section 3(2) provides: 'No person shall place in a woman—(a) a live embryo other than a human embryo, or (b) any live gametes other than human gametes.'

[57] Section 3(3) provides:

'A licence cannot authorise—(a) keeping or using an embryo after the appearance of the primitive streak, (b) placing an embryo in any animal, (c) keeping or using an embryo in circumstances in which regulations forbid its keeping or use, or (d) replacing a nucleus of a cell of an embryo with a nucleus taken from a cell of any person, embryo or subsequent development of an embryo.'

[58] Section 41(1) provides:

'A person who—(a) contravenes section 3(2) ... of this Act, or (b) does anything which by virtue of section 3(3) of this Act, cannot be authorised by a licence is guilty of an offence and liable on conviction on indictment to imprisonment for a term not exceeding ten years ...'

SOME ACTIVITIES ARE FORBIDDEN UNLESS DONE IN PURSUANCE OF A LICENCE

[59] Some activities are forbidden unless done in pursuance of a licence or of a direction given by the Authority—see s 3(1) and s 23(3).

[60] Section 3(1) provides: 'No person shall—(a) bring about the creation of an embryo, or (b) keep or use an embryo except in pursuance of a licence ...'

[61] A person who contravenes s 3(1) is guilty of an offence carrying a lesser maximum penalty of two years' imprisonment—see s 41(2) and (4).

THE LICENSING REGIME

[62] Parliament has imposed inhibitions on what a licence can authorise. The phraseology imposing those inhibitions is sometimes in positive form.

[63] Thus s 11 indicates that the only activities for which licences may be granted are—(a) activities in the course of providing treatment services, (b) storage and (c) research. From that one can deduce that Parliament has decided that licences may not be granted for other activities.

a [64] The phraseology is sometimes in negative form forbidding outright the licensing of some types of activity. I have drawn attention to the outright prohibitions in s 3(3) on what can be authorised. But there are other inhibitions.

[65] Thus para 1(4) provides that a licence can not authorise altering the genetic structure of any cell while it forms part of an embryo. Schedule 2, para 4(2) sets out further inhibitions on what a licence can do.

b [66] The phraseology is sometimes in the form of forbidding an activity unless certain preconditions are satisfied. One example of this legislative technique is provided by Sch 2, para 1(3) which in my judgment is the crucial provision in this appeal. It provides that: 'A licence under this paragraph cannot authorise any activity unless it appears to the Authority to be necessary or desirable for the purpose of providing treatment services.' I shall return to this paragraph later.

c [67] There seems to me no practical differences between inhibitions imposed in the negative and those imposed in the positive form.

[68] One should note that Parliament has not imposed any express obligation on the Authority to grant a licence in any prescribed circumstances.

d WHAT A LICENCE CAN AUTHORISE

[69] By contrast with the *inhibitions* as to what may be done and as to what may be authorised by a licence, sub-paras 1(1) and (2) of the second Schedule set out what *may* be authorised by a licence. A provision to which reference has been made in the argument is the following:

e '1 (1) A licence under this paragraph may authorise any of the following in the course of providing treatment services ... (d) practices designed to secure that embryos are in a suitable condition to be placed in a woman or to determine whether embryos are suitable for that purpose ...'

f THE DECISION UNDER ATTACK

[70] The decision of the Authority which was quashed by the judge was the decision in principle to allow tissue typing to be used in conjunction with preimplantation genetic diagnosis for serious genetic diseases. It was made clear by the press release that, before this technique could be used in treatment, g approval would be required from an Authority licence committee which would consider applications on a case by case basis and that licences would be subject to strict conditions. A licence has indeed been issued designed to assist Mr and Mrs Hashmi to have a further child which will not suffer from the genetic disease from which Zain suffers and whose tissue is compatible with his. The validity of h that licence is, however, not directly in issue before us.

[71] The whole process envisaged by the Authority was: (i) the removal of a cell from an embryo created by in vitro fertilisation; (ii) the testing of that cell to see both (a) whether the embryo carries a genetic disorder and (b) whether the embryo enjoys tissue compatibility with a sibling affected with that disorder; and (iii) where it was established that the embryo both did not carry the genetic j disorder and enjoyed tissue compatibility, the implantation of the embryo in the mother of the affected sibling. Hereafter I shall refer to this whole process as the process in issue.

ANALYSIS: SCHEDULE 2, SUBPARAGRAPH 1(3)

[72] It is convenient at this point to set the relevant subparagraph again:

'1 (3) A licence under this paragraph cannot authorise any activity unless it appears to the Authority to be necessary or desirable for the purpose of providing treatment services.'

[73] The crucial question for the court is whether the process in issue could lawfully appear to the Authority as being necessary or desirable for providing treatment services.

[74] The definition of treatment services appears in s 2(1). This provides:

'In this Act ...
"treatment services" means medical, surgical or obstetric services provided to the public or a section of the public for the purposes of assisting women to carry children.'

[75] Incorporating that definition into para 1(3) of the second Schedule leads to the following result:

'A licence under this paragraph cannot authorise any activity unless it appears to the Authority to be necessary or desirable *for the purpose of providing medical, surgical or obstetric services provided to the public or a section of the public* for the purpose of assisting women to carry children.'

[76] All parties, faced with this inelegant amalgam, have proceeded on the basis that the issues before us can be resolved more easily by simply ignoring the words which I have placed in italics. I agree that this seems the most sensible approach. The primary question can thus be phrased thus: *can the process in issue lawfully appear to the authority as necessary or desirable for the purpose of assisting a woman to carry a child?*

SOME BACKGROUND CONSIDERATIONS

[77] It is clear that Parliament decided to permit the creation in vitro and subsequent use of embryos in some circumstances for some purposes. There is therefore not the absolute ban on this type of activity, which undoubtedly some would have wished. There is, however, an absolute ban on certain segments of this type of activity which are absolutely prohibited as being ethically objectionable in all circumstances and thus within what it is convenient to call a prohibited area.

[78] The dispute between the parties has centred on whether the process in issue falls within the prohibited area or within the area which is to be regulated by the Authority.

[79] The ethical concerns which underlie this legislation are concerns about (a) the creation of embryos and (b) the use of embryos. Four separate matters fall for consideration: (i) the creation of the embryos; (ii) their use in the course of carrying out the biopsies and also (so it is argued) the testing procedures in relation to the extracted cell; (iii) the implantation of an embryo after tests have revealed that it does not suffer from a genetic defect and its tissue is compatible with that of a sibling; and (iv) allowing embryos which did not suffer from a genetic defect to perish because their tissue is not so compatible.

[80] It is a commonplace practice in one in vitro fertilisation cycle to create several embryos. One is then implanted. The others are stored ready for implantation in a later cycle if a further attempt to achieve pregnancy is needed. If however a pregnancy results and there is no wish for a further pregnancy, the other embryos are allowed to perish. This is so even though there is no reason

a to suspect any abnormalities in them. Paragraphs 44–48 of the White Paper *Human Fertilisation and Embryology: A Framework for Legislation* (Cm 259) make clear that the government did not regard this as always unacceptable. Section 17 of the Act seeks to ensure that proper arrangements are made for the disposal of embryos that have been allowed to perish.

b [81] It seems to me that the creation of embryos with the knowledge that some perfectly healthy embryos will deliberately be allowed to perish was not regarded by Parliament as always unacceptable. The contrary has not been argued.

[82] Further, it seems to me that the use of an embryo by implantation after tests have revealed that it does not suffer from a genetic defect was not regarded by Parliament as always unacceptable in itself. Again, the contrary has not been argued.

c [83] Allowing embryos which do not suffer from a genetic defect to perish was also not regarded by Parliament as always unacceptable. Again the contrary has not been argued.

[84] The submissions have concentrated on the concern identified in [79](ii), above. This relates to two matters. It has not been argued before us that the use *d* of an embryo by carrying out of a biopsy to extract one cell was itself regarded by Parliament as always unacceptable. The evidence is that this process need not harm the embryo from which the cell has been extracted.

[85] There is in my judgment no indication in the Act that the carrying out of tests on cells extracted from an embryo was regarded by Parliament as *e* unacceptable as such. Again the contrary has not been argued although I think that Mr Dingemans wished to leave the point open.

[86] It is clear that amongst the purposes for which embryos are permitted to be used are projects of research specified in the licence: Sch 2, para 3(1). Amongst those purposes can be developing methods for detecting the presence of gene or chromosome abnormalities in embryos before implantation, increasing *f* knowledge about the causes of congenital disease and other serious disease and enabling such knowledge to be applied in developing treatments for serious disease: see Sch 2, para 3(2) and the Human Fertilisation and Embryology (Research Purposes) Regulations 2001, SI 2001/188. These are all matters which Parliament has permitted the Authority to sanction.

g
CONCLUSION

[87] The analysis undertaken in the preceding paragraphs indicates that Parliament was not opposed in principle to doing to an embryo any of the things which are likely to happen to it if the decision of the Authority is implemented. On the other hand Parliament did not sanction a free-for-all. No part of the *h* process in issue (with the possible exception of carrying out tests on the extracted cells) can lawfully be done without a licence granted by an Authority specially set up by Parliament to supervise developments in this field. The phraseology of para 1(3) immediately points to the Authority as the primary decision taker.

[88] One of the tasks of that Authority was to determine whether the process *j* in issue appeared to it to be necessary or desirable for the purposes of assisting a woman to carry a child. That involved the Authority in determining whether the process in issue would assist a woman to carry a child and, if so, whether it was necessary or desirable for that purpose.

[89] In my judgment it was lawfully open to the Authority to come to the conclusion that the process in issue would assist some women, who would

otherwise refrain from conception or abort either spontaneously or deliberately, to carry a child.

[90] Further in my judgment it was lawfully open to the Authority to come to the conclusion that the process in issue was necessary or desirable for that purpose.

[91] I therefore consider that the Authority's decision in principle does not infringe para 1(3) of the second Schedule.

[92] It remains to consider whether the sanctioning of the process in issue is inhibited by para 1(1)(d) of the Schedule.

[93] Since the process in issue does not offend against sub-para 1(3) it follows that it will be done for the purpose of assisting a woman to carry a child. If that be so, it will also be done 'in the course of providing treatment services' and thus fall within the opening words of para 1(1).

[94] It does not appear to me that the separation out of various activities in the latter part of para 1(1) presents any further difficulties if I am right in my conclusions so far.

[95] The creation of the embryo in vitro is expressly listed. So is the placing of an embryo in the woman.

[96] Once one accepts, as I do, that the process in issue can in some circumstances lawfully be regarded by the Authority as desirable for the purpose of assisting a woman to carry a child, then this implies in my judgment that the concept of suitability in para 1(1)(d) is wide enough to embrace ensuring that the embryo does not suffer from a genetic defect and tissue incompatibility. I therefore consider that the remaining proposed activities fall comfortably within the phrase 'practices designed to determine whether embryos are suitable' for the purpose of implantation.

[97] For these reasons I would allow this appeal.

[98] I point out in conclusion that Parliament did not impose upon the Authority any express obligation to sanction the grant of licences even if what was proposed was indubitably necessary for the purpose of assisting a woman to carry a child. That seems to me to dispose of much of the force of the argument that if what has been sanctioned in principle here and licensed in one case is lawful, then licensing activities for the purpose of social selection is an unavoidable consequence. If the decision of the Authority is upheld in the present case it does not mean that parents have a right to in vitro fertilisation for social selection purposes.

MANCE LJ.

INTRODUCTION

[99] The facts of this case excite great sympathy. But the issue is one of law. It involves the construction of the Human Fertilisation and Embryology Act 1990, in the context of scientific developments which go beyond any specifically envisaged at the time of the Act. Mr and Mrs Hashmi presently have five children, one of whom, Zain, suffers from a potentially fatal blood disorder, beta thalassaemia, so that he produces no or inadequate red blood cells. His condition fluctuates, sometime giving great cause for concern, but giving him, even at the best of times, a quality of life which is described as 'extremely miserable' in relation to the other children. His future is uncertain. He may live to his 30s or even early 40s on evolving medication and frequent blood transfusions; he could become allergic to medication, which could itself be life-threatening; and he

a might at any time develop fairly rapid organ failure. All this could be cured by a successful stem cell transplant from a matched donor, after which Zain could achieve a relatively normal life.

[100] A matching donor may sometimes be found in the form of an existing relative willing to assist, or in a donor bank. Failing success in one of these ways, Dr Fishel, the Hashmi's clinical embryologist, explains that consultants
b commonly suggest the delivery of a sibling matching the sick child. Following the birth of such a sibling, stem cell blood can be recovered from the umbilical cord and donated to the sick child. This procedure does not in any way invade the new child's body. Mrs Hashmi has tried to give birth to a matching sibling on two occasions. This has led to one pregnancy being terminated because of the presence of beta thalassaemia and to the birth of the Hashmi's son, Haris, who is
c not however a tissue match for Zain.

[101] Against that background the Centre for Assisted Reproduction Ltd at the Park Hospital, Nottingham (the care clinic) applied to the Human Fertilisation and Embryo Authority (HFEA) on 27 September 2001 for a licence to perform a Preimplantation Genetic Diagnosis (PGD), including thereby screening for beta
d thalassaemia and tissue (or human leukocyte antigen) typing for Mr and Mrs Hashmi. The term PGD is in the previous sentence used in a wide sense to include tissue typing. The documents before us show that the term is sometimes used in a narrower sense to cover simply testing for genetic defects. The proposal was for embryos created by in vitro fertilisation (IVF) to be biopsied and for the biopsied
e material to be transported to Chicago for screening and tissue typing. In November 2001 a committee of the HFEA and (as it had become) the Human Genetics Commission had approved such screening 'where there is a significant risk of a serious genetic disorder being present in the embryo', but had 'agreed that there were sufficient ethical difficulties' with tissue typing 'that it should be subject to further discussion before its use was considered'. Despite this, the
f HFEA received favourable advice from its ethics committee on 22 November 2001 on the proposal relating to Mr and Mrs Hashmi. After discussing this, the HFEA at its meeting on 29 November 2001 concluded that, in circumstances where there would have in any event to be a biopsy to screen for beta thalassaemia, the HFEA might in very rare circumstances and under strict controls, permit further testing of cells derived from the embryo, including in
g particular tissue typing. That decision was announced by press release dated 13 December 2001. The present proceedings were brought by Josephine Quintavalle on behalf of Comment on Reproductive Ethics (Core) on 5 March 2003, seeking an order quashing the HFEA's decision and declaring that a licence granted by the HFEA cannot authorise practices designed to test an embryo for
h tissue-compatibility with an affected sibling.

[102] After consideration by the HFEA the care clinic's application led to the grant of a licence on 22 February 2003 for various listed activities to be carried out under the supervision of Mr Simon Thornton, including IVF, PGD and Preimplantation Genetic Screening for Aneuploidy.
j [103] The licence is subject to extensive conditions, set out in Annex A, which in turn refers to Annexes B, C and D. In particular, s (5)(a) of Annex A provides that, with respect to any PGD programme, it is a condition 'that PGD may only be carried out for those disorders specifically listed in the PGD licences Annex C to the licence'. Annex C provides for 'Sexing for X-linked diagnosis' in respect of haemophilia, Duchenne muscular dystrophy and Linz syndrome, for 'Specific

diagnosis' in respect of cystic fibrosis, beta thalassaemia, sickle cell anaemia and
chromosomal translocation and for the following 'Special Category': a
'ß-thalassaemia in conjunction with HLA typing for patients known as Mr and
Mrs H'.

[104] All these tests appear in Annex C under the general heading of PGD.
Screening for genetic defects and tissue typing both involve a detailed genetic
analysis using the same cells taken from an embryo by biopsy. But genetic b
screening for abnormalities such as beta thalassaemia can be undertaken without
at the same time undertaking tissue typing.

[105] A note to Annex C refers back to Annex A, ss 4 and 5 for additional
conditions relating to PGD. Section 4 makes it a condition with respect to any
programme involving blastomere/polar body biopsy:

c

'(b) that no embryo or material removed from it may be subjected to a test
which supplies genetic information about the embryo that is not listed in an
annex to this licence or specifically approved by a licence committee in any
particular case.

(c) that no embryo may be transferred to a woman where that embryo, or d
any material removed from it or from the gametes that produced it, has been
subject to a test, which supplies genetic information about the embryo, that
is not specifically listed in an Annex to this licence or not specifically
approved by a licence committee in any particular case.

(d) that centres should not use any information derived from tests on an
embryo, or any material removed from it or from the gametes that produced e
it, to select embryos of a particular sex for social reasons.'

[106] The licence is capable on its face of covering any number of treatments,
save for its (unprecedented) inclusion, in Annex C, of the 'Specific Category'
referring to Mr and Mrs Hashmi. Two unsuccessful IVF procedures had been f
undertaken by the time the present case brought by Mrs Quintavalle came before
Maurice Kay J for hearing. On 20 December 2002 ([2003] 2 All ER 105) he gave
judgment quashing the decision in principle announced by the HFEA on
13 December 2001. The present appeal is brought by the HFEA with the support
of the Secretary of State for Health. The arguments have developed before us
along rather different lines to those raised before the judge. g

THE HUMAN FERTILISATION AND EMBRYOLOGY ACT 1990

[107] I need not repeat the statutory scheme, which has been set out by Lord
Phillips of Worth Matravers MR. The relevant starting point consists in the
prohibitions under s 3(1) on bringing about the creation of an embryo (defined in h
s 1(2) as meaning creation outside the human body) or use of an embryo, except
in pursuance of a licence. A licence can only authorise activities 'in the course of',
and which appear to the HFEA to be necessary or desirable 'for the purpose of',
'providing treatment services': see s 11 and Sch 2, paras 1(1) and (3). Treatment
services are defined by s 2(2) as 'medical, surgical or obstetric services provided
to the public or a section of the public for the purpose of assisting women to carry j
children'. Treatment services extend beyond the activities for which any licence
would be required. There are of course many medical, surgical and obstetric
services (including advice, medicine and hospital facilities) 'for the purpose of
enabling women to carry children' which do not involve the creation outside the
human body, or the keeping or use, of an embryo.

a [108] The House of Lords in *R (on the application of Quintavalle) v Secretary of State for Health* [2003] UKHL 13, [2003] 2 All ER 113, [2003] 2 WLR 692 has recently considered the statutory scheme. Lord Bingham of Cornhill (with whose speech Lord Steyn, Lord Hoffmann and Lord Scott of Foscote all agreed) identified the Act (at [4]) as imposing three levels of control:

b 'The highest is that contained in the Act itself. As is apparent, for example from s 3(2) and (3), the Act prohibits certain activities absolutely, a prohibition fortified by a potential penalty of up to ten years' imprisonment (s 41(1)). The next level of control is provided by the Secretary of State, who is empowered to make regulations for certain purposes subject (so far as relevant here) to an affirmative resolution of both Houses of Parliament (s 45(1), (4)). Pursuant

c to s 3(3)(c) the Secretary of State may make regulations prohibiting the keeping or use of an embryo in specified circumstances. The third level of control is that exercised by the Authority. Section 3(1) prohibits the creation, keeping or use of an embryo except in pursuance of a licence, and the Act contains very detailed provisions governing the grant, revocation and

d suspension of licences and the conditions to which they may be subject: see, among other references, ss 11–22 of and Sch 2 to the Act. A power is also conferred on the Authority to give binding directions: ss 23–24.'

[109] The House of Lords had, as we have, to grapple with at first sight contrasting rules that a statute always bears the meaning that it had when

e Parliament passed it and that a statute is always speaking, and with the difficulty that arises in deciding whether a modern invention or activity falls within statutory language used at a time when it did not exist. The House approved Lord Wilberforce's description (in *Royal College of Nursing of the UK v Dept of Health and Social Security* [1981] 1 All ER 545 at 564–565, [1981] AC 800 at 822) of the

f court's role in this situation:

'In interpreting an Act of Parliament it is proper, and indeed necessary, to have regard to the state of affairs existing, and known by Parliament to be existing, at the time. It is a fair presumption that Parliament's policy or intention is directed to that state of affairs. Leaving aside cases of omission

g by inadvertence, this being not such a case when a new state of affairs, or a fresh set of facts bearing on policy, comes into existence, the courts have to consider whether they fall within the parliamentary intention. They may be held to do so if they fall within the same genus of facts as those to which the expressed policy has been formulated. They may also be held to do so if there can be detected a clear purpose in the legislation which can only be

h fulfilled if the extension is made. How liberally these principles may be applied must depend on the nature of the enactment, and the strictness or otherwise of the words in which it has been expressed. The courts should be less willing to extend expressed meanings if it is clear that the Act in question was designed to be restrictive or circumscribed in its operation rather than

j liberal or permissive. They will be much less willing to do so where the new subject matter is different in kind or dimension from that for which the legislation was passed. In any event there is one course which the courts cannot take under the law of this country: they cannot fill gaps, they cannot by asking the question, "What would Parliament have done in this current case, not being one in contemplation, if the facts had been before it?",

attempt themselves to supply the answer, if the answer is not to be found in
the terms of the Act itself.'

a

TISSUE TYPING AS USE OF AN EMBRYO

[110] The prohibition in s 3 on creation or use without a licence relates to any
'embryo'. Under s 1(1), except where otherwise stated, embryo means 'a live
human embryo where fertilisation is complete', but also includes 'an egg in the
process of fertilisation'. The judge concluded that tissue typing itself involved use
of an embryo. The most substantial reasons the judge gave were that Parliament
could not have intended to leave an activity such as tissue typing outside the
direct control of the Act, and that Sch 2, para 1(1)(d) covers practices designed to
secure the suitable condition, or to determine the suitability, of embryos to be
placed in a woman. The judge's view would have significant practical
consequences. Under s 12(a) (though subject to the possibility of directions
under s 24, sub-ss (3) and (4) in particular) a licence must provide that the
activities which it authorises shall be carried on only on the premises to which the
licence relates and under the supervision of the person responsible, ie here at the
care clinic under Mr Thornton's supervision. On the judge's view, the
transporting of embryonic cell material to a laboratory outside the care clinic (eg
to Chicago, as in this case) would, at least in the absence of any relevant
qualifying directions, be impermissible.

b

c

d

[111] I do not consider that the judge's view was correct. An embryo is
distinct from embryonic cell material, which is extracted from an embryo leaving
the embryo free to continue to develop. Section 3A(1) with its distinction
between an embryo and female cells taken or derived from an embryo also
confirms this. The points made by the judge overlook the fact that the creation
outside the human body, biopsying and implantation of an embryo all fall within
s 3. They can all only take place under a licence, which may impose strict
conditions regarding the nature of any testing permissible in respect of any
embryonic cell material removed from such an embryo. Clause (d) also controls
the purpose for which any such biopsy must take place, a point to which I will
return. The fact that *some* practices (eg a biopsy) designed to secure the suitable
condition, or determine the suitability, of embryos to be placed in a woman
involve use of an embryo does not mean that *all* practices for such a purpose
involve 'use' of the embryo, or therefore require to be licensed as activities under
para 1(1) of Sch 2. The language of the HFEA's press notice and licence are open
to the forensic comment that at points they equate embryonic cells with an
embryo from which they have been removed, and treat PGD (including here
both screening and tissue typing) as activities themselves requiring to be licensed.
But these documents cannot construe for us the true scope of the legislative
provisions.

e

f

g

h

CREATION AND BIOPSYING OF AN EMBRYO FOR THE PURPOSE OF ANY FORM OF PGD

[112] The central issues are thus whether the activities of bringing about the
creation by IVF of an embryo and, particularly, its biopsying are activities capable
of being licensed, when the purpose is to test embryonic cells removed from the
embryo by PGD, including tissue typing, and only to place the embryo in the
relevant woman if the embryo is both free from genetic disorder and has tissue
compatible with an existing sibling.

j

[113] These issues turn, firstly, upon the definition of 'treatment services' in
s 2(1) as 'medical, surgical or obstetric services provided to the public or a section

a of the public for the purpose of assisting women to carry children'. Licences may (as stated in [107], above) only be granted authorising activities which satisfy the two initial criteria, that they are 'in the course of', and appear to the HFEA to be necessary or desirable 'for the purpose of', providing treatment services (s 11 and Sch 2, paras 1(1) and (3)).

b [114] Treatment services are already defined by s 2(1) to include a required purpose (that 'of assisting women to carry children'). Schedule 2, para 1(3), in providing that any activity must appear to the HFEA necessary or desirable for the purpose of services for that purpose, is to say the least inelegant. There is a duplication of 'purposes' if the full definition is read into para 1(3). It does not make sense to consider whether an activity (consisting for example of 'placing an embryo in a woman') is necessary or desirable for the purpose of providing

c medical services for the purpose of assisting women to carry children. The intention must be that the activity should appear to the HFEA to be necessary or desirable for the simple purpose of assisting women to carry children. The true function of Sch 2, para 1(3) is to establish the standard by which the HFEA must form its judgment as to whether an activity should be licensed.

d [115] Provided an activity meets the two initial criteria, and in the absence of any regulation under Sch 2, para 1(1)(g), it must also fall within one of the particular heads of Sch 2, para 1(1). The most relevant one is (d)—'practices designed ... to determine whether embryos are suitable for that purpose' (viz 'to be placed in a woman'). Part of cl (d) was relied on in the claim form, but it was not relied on as a bar to the HFEA's objection by the judge, or it seems raised as

e such in argument before him. There was no respondent's notice seeking to raise it before us. Nevertheless, it was referred to before us and is important to consider. Curiously, the only relevant argument raised in the claim form related to the initial words of cl (d) 'in a suitable condition to be placed in a woman'. The claim form submitted, firstly and correctly, that these words focus on condition;

f secondly, that they are only concerned with 'those characteristics of the embryo which *in objective terms* render it unsuitable to be placed *in any woman*'; and thirdly that any contrary interpretation would permit the HFEA to license selection for characteristics such as sex, intelligence or hair colour. The first submission ignores the critical later words 'practices designed ... to determine whether embryos are suitable for that purpose'. These words go on any view wider than

g the condition of the embryo, to allow some consideration of its inherent characteristics or qualities. I return to the second submission in [127], below and to the third in [145], below.

THE PERMISSIBILITY OF SCREENING OUT GENETIC DEFECTS?

h [116] The judge said that the case did not require him to resolve whether not only tissue typing, but also PGD, in the limited sense of screening to avoid use of any embryo showing genetic defects, was unlawful. But, in deciding in Mrs Quintavalle's favour, he interpreted 'treatment services' in a way which, the HFEA submits, could present obstacles to screening of embryos for genetic defects, as well as to the taking of decisions not to implant particular embryos

j based on the results of such screening. The judge associated the concept of 'assisting women to carry children' with problems arising from 'an impaired ability to conceive or to carry a child through pregnancy to full term and birth', and observed that the carrying of a child would be 'wholly unaffected by the tissue typing'. By focusing on the single question whether the woman could conceive and carry a child to full term and birth, the judge on one view eliminated

the possibility of any test the main purpose or effect of which could be said to
determine whether the child would, after its birth, be healthy or suffer from, or
be the carrier of, some abnormality, as well as the possibility of deciding against
the implantation of a particular embryo because of any abnormality detected that
would affect the viability of the embryo while being carried.

[117] It is doubtful whether so limited an interpretation was advanced to the
judge. The skeleton argument lodged on Mrs Quintavalle's behalf in the
Administrative Court contains these passages:

> '15. ... (c) Parliament was aware of the possibility of genetic testing by
> embryonic biopsy and, in the light of that knowledge, provided that a licence
> could authorise "practices designed to ... determine whether embryos are
> suitable" to be placed in a woman: see Sch 2, para 1(1)(d) ...
>
> (e) But there are some activities which Parliament placed beyond the reach
> of regulations ... [Sch 2, para 1(3)] ensures that any such [genetic] testing
> must be carried out for the purpose of assisting women to carry children (eg
> by screening out embryos with a genetic defect) and *not* for any other
> purpose—for example, to allow parents to choose a male or female child or
> (to take another more extreme example) to choose a baby with a preferred
> eye or hair colour.'

[118] Those passages regarding Parliament's knowledge and intentions are
amply born out by the information regarding research which took place and
came to Parliament's attention during the Parliamentary process as well as by the
debate recorded in Hansard, to which Lord Phillips MR has referred. Before us,
Mr Dingemans QC for Mrs Quintavalle sought to reconcile the judge's words
with the general permissibility of genetic testing. He submitted that the judge's
formulation would not restrict genetic testing to screen out abnormalities, because
abnormal genetic conditions involve a greater risk of problems in carriage and
birth, even though this risk may not materialise in any particular case. He drew
attention, as the only relevant evidence, to a passage in the witness statement of
Dr Fishel, to the effect that most chromosomal abnormalities 'are not compatible
with normal foetal development'. On that basis, he submitted (in the words of
his skeleton argument) that 'If it is right that most defects cause an embryo to be
non-viable, the dire consequences predicted by the [HFEA] do not follow'. The
Secretary of State sought to put before us fresh evidence from Professor Raeburn,
at which it was agreed that we could look provisionally (or de bene esse). It was
that chromosomal abnormalities are likely significantly to impair the viability of
an embryo, whereas the majority of conditions caused by single gene
abnormalities (which we were told include beta thalassaemia) do not affect the
viability of an embryo, but almost always have a major postnatal impact.

[119] Had Professor Raeburn's evidence appeared critical to this appeal, I
would have been reluctant, in view of the importance of the issue, to proceed
without it and without admitting in reply any further evidence that the
respondent might have been able to adduce. But we know, as Dr Fishel's
statement tells us, that some abnormalities are compatible with normal foetal
development. One has also to ask whether Parliament can have intended to limit
the assistance given to women to carry children to treatment for infertility,
including treatment to determine the viability of an embryo for implantation,
carriage to and birth at term; or whether Parliament must be taken to have had a
broader concern for the health of the child after birth and future generations.

a   Children with inherited genetic problems are of course loved and receive exceptional care from their families, as in the case of Zain. That does not however bear directly on the question whether it is open to a family to choose that the potential mother in the family should not conceive a child who may suffer disability, pain and perhaps an early death or who as a carrier may expose his or her own children to the same fate.

b   [120] The legislation contains a number of indications telling against any limitation of focus to mere viability. First, Parliament resolved the choice left to it as a result of the White Paper of November 1987 (*Human Fertilisation and Embryology: A Framework for Legislation* (Cm 259) para 30) in favour of permitting research under licence on embryos. It therefore included s 11(1)(c) and Sch 2, para 3. Under Sch 2, para 3 such licences may authorise creation and use of
c embryos 'for the purpose of ... (e) developing methods for detecting the presence of gene or chromosome abnormalities in embryos before implantation' or for other purposes which might be specified in regulations 'with a view to the authorisation of projects of research which increase knowledge about the creation and development of embryos, or about disease, or enable such
d knowledge to be applied'. Regulations permitting licences for the purposes of increasing knowledge about the development of embryos and about serious disease and of enabling any such knowledge to be applied in developing treatments for serious disease have now been made (the Human Fertilisation and Embryology (Research Purposes) Regulations 2001, SI 2001/188). While it is theoretically possible that Parliament intended to permit research into methods
e of detecting abnormalities, or into applications of knowledge acquired about disease, which it would be impermissible to licence for practical use unless the Act was amended, it seems improbable that it was contemplated that research, a particularly contentious matter, should be permissible into methods and applications the use of which in practice Parliament had decided to exclude.

f   [121] Second, under Sch 2, para 1(1)(f) licences may be granted authorising the mixing of sperm 'for the purpose of testing the fertility or normality of the sperm'.

  [122] Third, there is some support in s 13(5) for a conclusion that Parliament cannot have limited its sights to matters going to the viability of an embryo for
g the purpose of being implanted, carried to term and born as a child. It is true that s 13(5) is a condition which must be included in every licence under Sch 2, para 1 (and is included in the licence relating to Mr and Mrs Hashmi), and that its role is to require the treating body, here the care clinic, to take account of the welfare of every child who may be born as a result of the treatment and of any other child who may be affected by the birth. This is a requirement that must not only apply
h before, but continue throughout the administration of treatment services. On the respondent's case it is not a requirement which the clinic can fulfil in one most effective way, by screening to avoid the implantation of an embryo which has or may have a genetic abnormality which would affect the child after birth (and, potentially, also affect siblings, in cases where the birth of such a child might
j impose heavy stress on the family generally). In short, s 13(5) points towards a wider concern for the future child and siblings, which is better served if the legislation is read as permitting such screening.

  [123] Fourth, I note that 'treatment services' are defined as 'medical, surgical and obstetric services provided to the public or a section of the public'. Although their purpose must be to assist women to carry children, they are not services

provided exclusively to women. The potential father is someone to whom such services may be being provided, and whose natural concerns about future health and welfare would be expected to be relevant (cf also s 28). This too tends to point against any conclusion that the legislation focuses solely on the woman's narrow physical ability to become pregnant and give birth.

[124] I turn to the Warnock Report, which inspired much of the subsequent Act. The judge did not consider it appropriate to have regard to this report, but the relevance of it and the subsequent White Paper as background, and of the mischiefs intended to be addressed as indicated by these documents, is confirmed by the House of Lords' reasoning in the first *Quintavalle* case. The Warnock committee took a positive view towards the wider use of techniques (then in their infancy) as a facility or service available in cases other than infertility (ch 9). Chapter 9.2 dealt with the transmission of hereditary disease 'which may be severely handicapping to the next generation, either because the individual has the condition or is a carrier'. The committee also identified among these techniques sex selection for 'couples who have good medical reasons for choosing the sex of their child' (ch 9.11), while observing that, 'if an efficient and easy method of ensuring the conception of a child of a particular sex became available, it is likely that some couples would wish to make use of it for purely social reasons', which could affect not only the individual family and the children involved, but society as a whole (ch 9.11). While 'dubious' about the use of sex selection techniques on a wide scale, the committee did not find it possible to make any positive recommendations. It considered that the whole question of the acceptability of sex selection should be kept under review, and referred in this context to ch 13, where it recommended the establishing of an authority such as the HFEA.

[125] The White Paper focuses on the issue of research, on which the government proposed to leave Parliament with a choice. But it contemplated expressly (in paras 29–30) that embryos could under the proposed legislation be screened by PGD, so as to achieve 'successful pregnancy leading to a healthy baby', that embryos would only be implanted 'if suitable', and that they would be allowed 'to perish where they were not to be transferred (eg because an abnormality had been detected)'. As I shall demonstrate in more detail (in [135]–[139], below), the White Paper does not suggest that any different approach than that adopted in the Warnock Report was being taken to the particular wider techniques on which the Warnock Report had commented in its ch 9.

[126] I am in these circumstances left in no real doubt that the concept of 'medical, surgical or obstetric services ... for the purpose of assisting women to carry children' was intended to embrace not merely services to assist women physically to carry to term and give birth, but also services to assist them to give birth to children who would be normal and healthy during their lives and would in turn be able to have normal and healthy children. I have equally little difficulty in concluding that the words 'practices designed ... to determine whether embryos are suitable for that purpose [namely to be placed in a woman]' in Sch 2, para 1(1)(d) were intended to embrace PGD in the form of screening to avoid the use of any embryo with an abnormality which might affect the viability of the embryo if implanted or which might affect any resulting child either during that child's own life or any future generation because the child would be a carrier. 'Suitable' is explained in *Longman's Dictionary of the English Language* as 'meeting the requirements of a use, purpose, or situation'. But here the statute only

a identifies the next step or immediate purpose, leaving it to those interpreting it to ascertain from its background and other terms the more distant purposes and wider context that may admissibly be taken into account when judging suitability.

[127] The initial words of para 1(1)(d)—'Practices designed to secure that embryos are in a suitable condition to be placed in a woman'—focus on the need to protect the embryo's condition, by for example keeping and treating it in an

b appropriate way. The second half of para 1(1)(d) deals in a more general way with the 'suitability' of the embryo to be placed in 'a woman'. The abstract and impersonal way in which this is expressed is explicable because the paragraph is dealing with practices that may and will usually be authorised by a licence granted to a clinic in general terms for classes of activity in relation to women who have not yet been ascertained. It does not follow from this formulation that

c the suitability of an embryo for implantation is to be assessed objectively without reference to the particular woman in whom it is to be placed. That would make no sense. The compatibility of the particular embryo with the particular mother must, at least, be a fundamental consideration.

[128] I add this consideration. To see the legislation as interested only in

d women's ability successfully to experience the physical process of pregnancy and birth would seem to me to invert the significance of the human wish to reproduce. Just as 'placing an embryo in a woman' is only a first step towards a successful pregnancy, so pregnancy and the experience of birth are steps towards an expanded family life, not an end in themselves.

e THE PERMISSIBILITY OF TISSUE TYPING?

[129] This brings me to the more difficult question whether the concepts of 'treatment services' and 'practices suitable … to determine whether embryos are suitable' to be placed in a woman cover the present case. Mr Eadie for the Secretary of State submitted that this question does not arise in circumstances like those of Mr and Mrs Hashmi, with which the HFEA's decision announced on

f 13 December 2001 was also concerned. A biopsy is necessary in any event for the legitimate purpose of testing embryonic cells to screen out beta thalassaemia. Taking the opportunity to test the same cells to check for tissue compatibility with an affected sibling would not itself constitute an activity requiring a licence and would not affect the legitimacy of the licensed activity of taking a biopsy to

g screen out beta thalassaemia. In Mr Eadie's skeleton argument, this argument was put on the basis that the HFEA was only prepared to permit tissue typing tests 'where the genetic test (the dominant and necessary purpose of the biopsy) is to take place'.

[130] Mr Pannick QC (while not adopting Mr Eadie's present argument in

h other respects) did submit that there was no evidence that Mr and Mrs Hashmi would not want another child in any event (provided only that the child was free of an abnormality such as beta thalassaemia). If necessary, I would infer that Mr and Mrs Hashmi would, in their whole family's interests, decide against having another child unless they could be confident of realising their hopes to improve the whole family's life by curing Zain. But, whether this is so or not, the

j present proceedings relate to a decision by the HFEA announced in December 2001 which was directed to circumstances where both screening out of a genetic defect and tissue typing were (and in the case of Mr and Mrs Hashmi are) important purposes of an intended biopsy. If one looks at the actual licence granted to the care clinic in respect of Mr and Mrs Hashmi, this also confirms that, whatever other longer term decision might or might not be taken, the biopsy envisaged by the HFEA's decision and the care clinic licence had a dual purpose, which was to authorise both PGD to screen out abnormalities *and* tissue typing. Indeed, Mrs Hashmi in her powerful oral plea before us underlined her family's desire to save Zain, while stressing the protection that any new child brought into the family home would enjoy.

[131] Where a biopsy has two basic purposes of this kind, I do not, as presently advised, think that a licence can be given for it, if one of those purposes falls outside those permitted under s 2(1) and Sch 2, para 1(1)(d). Mr Pannick was therefore right in my view to accept that in such circumstances the HFEA has to establish that each of these purposes can properly be regarded as being 'for the purpose of assisting women to carry children' and as falling within the concept of 'practices ... designed to determine whether embryos are suitable' to be placed in a woman. The former phrase is the primary control, which only Parliament can relax. The latter concept would be capable of expansion within the limits of the former phrase, by the Secretary of State making regulations under Sch 2, para 1(1)(g) and s 45(1) of the Act.

[132] It follows from [129]–[131], above that whether a biopsy for the purpose of tissue typing is *capable* of being licensed cannot depend upon whether or not a biopsy is also intended for the purpose of PGD screening for genetic abnormalities. The HFEA by its decision announced in December 2001 and by its licence to the care clinic restricted tissue typing to cases where a biopsy was anyway necessary to screen out genetic abnormalities. But that was a restriction introduced not because the HFEA regarded the Act as requiring it to limit any licence in this way, but because the HFEA, exercising its judgment, considered that the invasive procedure of a biopsy should only be undertaken on an embryo if it was necessary in the first instance from the point of view of the embryo, in other words to confirm the embryo's genetic normality. If a biopsy was necessary in any event on that ground, then there was no objection to allowing it for the further purpose of tissue testing.

[133] For reasons that I have already considered in relation to PGD screening to exclude abnormalities, the assistance to women to carry children which the Act contemplates is not limited to assistance in the narrow physical operation of becoming pregnant and giving birth. It extends to assistance in ensuring that any child born will so far as possible be free of genetic defects and not be a carrier of some hereditary problem which could affect a future generation. Considerations relating to the future well-being of yet-to-be-born children will weigh heavily with any prospective parents. So too will any effect that a new child would be likely to have on an existing sibling. Families which cannot, for financial reasons or because of the needs of an existing sibling, accommodate another child, may take steps to avoid having one. Families may equally have another child with the idea in mind that he or she will be company for an existing child. Such considerations may no doubt also play a significant role in the clinical judgment, about the welfare of any child who may be born and of any other child who may be affected by the birth, which is contemplated by s 13(5) of the Act. Whilst that subsection probably had primarily in mind consideration of any adverse effects on the welfare of the future or any existing child, the language does not exclude positive effects. The relevant considerations may indeed point in opposite directions. For example, it might be to the benefit of an existing child to have a companion, but there might be a countervailing risk to the welfare of the new child in the form of some hereditary disability.

a [134] It is, however, at the core of the respondent's case that the services which may be provided do not extend to assisting women to carry children selected for particular characteristics unrelated to any abnormality. Screening out genetic abnormalities is one thing. Screening out certain normal characteristics is another. The crucial distinction has been put as being between 'screening out abnormalities' and 'screening in preferences'. That distinction

b raises a spectre of eugenics and 'designer babies'. But it is a crude over-simplification to view this case as being about 'preferences'. The word suggests personal indulgence or predilection and the luxury of a real choice. But there is no element of whim in the circumstances that the HFEA had it in mind to licence in December 2001, and Mr and Mrs Hashmi are not seeking to indulge themselves. The case is about a family's reaction, understandable in the light of

c current scientific possibilities, to a cruel fate which one of its members is suffering and will continue to suffer, without a successful stem cell transplant. Ethical concerns that a child to be born might be used as a vehicle, or would not be valued and loved were, for good reason in the circumstances as they appear, not at the forefront of any submissions made to us in the present case. Other

d concerns, for example regarding any increase in the numbers of embryos that might be discarded, were raised. But I do not regard any of them as in any way decisive, or as having any relevance approaching that which attaches to the Warnock Report and White Paper, which evidence the immediate background to the legislation and the aspects of IVF which were being addressed. On the HFEA's and the Secretary of State's case, such ethical concerns as may be raised

e by the presently proposed procedures fall appropriately to be addressed by the HFEA and the care clinic in the exercise of their respective functions.

[135] Returning to the discussion in the Warnock Report, ch 9.11, on sex selection (see [124], above), the present circumstances lie conceptually between the two poles of 'good medical reasons' for tests, by which the Warnock

f committee was referring simply to medical reasons affecting children yet to be born, and testing for 'purely social reasons' which the Warnock committee said would 'obviously affect the individual family and the children involved, and would also have implications for society as a whole'. However they lie far closer in spirit in my view to the former pole that to the latter. There are here good medical reasons for screening any embryo, although they do not relate to any

g future child's health. The concerns to which the HFEA's decision and the licence for Mr and Mrs Hashmi are directed are anything but 'purely social', relating as they do to the health of a sibling and the well-being of the whole family. What matters in any event is that the Warnock committee proposed in ch 9.11 of its report to leave even the general question of the acceptability of sex selection to

h the authority which it recommended should be established.

[136] Mr Dingemans submitted that the Warnock committee had elsewhere made clear that the legislation should prohibit absolutely any development such as the presently proposed tissue typing. He referred to ch 12.16. The committee in ch 12 anticipated the future development of various techniques (among them

j in ch 12.11 cloning by embryo-splitting, in ch 12.12–12.13 embryonic biopsy to identify any abnormality and in ch 12.14 nucleus substitution). In ch 12.15, it anticipated a possible further technique to identify and replace a defective gene. Then, in ch 12.16, the committee said this:

'Public anxiety about these techniques centres, not so much on their possible therapeutic use, but on the idea of the deliberate creation of human beings with specific characteristics. This has overtones of selective breeding. We regard such techniques as purely speculative but believe that any developments in these fields are precluded by the controls we have already recommended ...'

It added:

'We would go further. We recommend that the proposed licensing body promulgates guidance on what types of research, apart from those prohibited by law, would be unlikely to be considered ethically acceptable in any circumstances and therefore would not be licensed. We envisage this guidance being reviewed from time to time to take account of both changes in scientific knowledge and changes in public attitudes.'

[137] When speaking of 'such techniques' as purely speculative, it is not clear that the Warnock committee had in mind all the possible future techniques previously discussed, or whether it was referring to techniques with 'overtones of selective breeding'. But, assuming that it was speaking of all the possible future techniques, its reference to 'the controls we have already recommended' did not contemplate that all such techniques would be absolutely prohibited under the legislation. The 'controls' in question were to consist of a combination of absolute prohibitions (see eg ch 12.8 and 9) and the performance by the proposed licensing body of its function. See also ch 12.1, where the committee said that:

'We believe that our recommendations for the regulation of research will allay much of that anxiety, as it will be the duty of the proposed licensing body (13.3) to keep these and other new techniques under constant review; indeed, in some instances our proposals will preclude certain developments altogether.'

[138] In these circumstances, I see no inconsistency between chs 9.11 and 12.16 of the Warnock Report.

[139] One of the potential future techniques to which the Warnock Report referred without recommending any absolute prohibition was embryo-splitting (ch 12.11). Lord Bingham noted this as a point of some relevance when he concluded in *Quintavalle*'s case [2003] 2 All ER 113 at [18] that the Act permitted the licensing of cloning by cell nuclear replacement (CNR), involving implanting a replacement nucleus in an unfertilised egg, as distinct from replacing the nucleus of an already fertilised embryo. The White Paper did, however, go further than the Warnock Report in two other areas—by recommending absolute prohibitions of nucleus substitution and of techniques aimed at modifying the genetic constitution of an embryo. Lord Bingham inferred in *Quintavalle*'s case that s 3(3)(d) of the Act was enacted to give effect to this White Paper recommendation. It is in my opinion of considerable relevance to this appeal that neither Warnock nor the White Paper recommended any absolute prohibition in relation to embryonic testing or in relation to sex selection for reasons unrelated to the child-to-be-born's medical condition.

[140] Mr Pannick also pointed out that the effect of s 4(1)(b) (which contains a limited extension of protection beyond embryos to sperm) is to enable use in the course of providing treatment services (as defined in s 2(1)) to prospective parents together of sperm sorted to select sex. That is not to say that the same approach governs sex selection in relation to embryos. It clearly does not. Embryos enjoy on any view a higher level of protection, and, when their use is permissible at all,

a it is only under the control of the HFEA. But it is at least clear that there is no absolute bar on sex selection in all circumstances.

[141] The Act was framed at a time when PGD to screen out disabilities was understood as a possibility, and was (as I have concluded) contemplated in certain of its provisions. In contrast, tissue typing and other techniques to screen out certain normal characteristics were only speculative possibilities at the time of the

b Act. That the distinction between these procedures may itself be debatable, as Mr Pannick exemplified by taking the instances of dyslexia and deafness, does not really help, since problems of scope on any view arise. But it can be said that the concept of 'services ... for the purpose of assisting women to carry children' seems on its face wide enough to embrace some forms of activity in relation to healthy embryos, eg testing to ensure that the right sperm and egg had been used,

c although the considerations here differ from those presently under consideration.

[142] More importantly, once it is recognised that the concept of 'services ... for the purpose of assisting women to carry children' extends beyond purely physical problems affecting the viability of the embryo during pregnancy and birth, and allows the screening of embryos for genetic abnormalities, it becomes

d clear that such services may have regard to prospective parents' and society's concern for others and for the future. The concept is in other words to be read in a general, rather than a restrictive sense. If that is so, I see no basis for drawing a line which excludes the services envisaged by the decision announced on 13 December 2001. The assistance to carry a child provided can be viewed either

e as assistance to have a child whose addition to the family could, without any invasion of tissue, bring very special benefits for a sibling and for the family as a whole and who would be expected to be valued correspondingly, or more narrowly as assistance to the parents in giving them crucial information to decide whether the potential mother should go ahead to have an embryo placed in her. In whichever way the assistance is viewed, I regard it as coming within the

f statutory concept of 'services ... for the purpose of assisting women to carry children'.

[143] Where Parliament intended to put absolute limits in the fields of potential scientific development identified by the Warnock Report and White Paper, it did so expressly, as in s 3(2) and (3). Notably it did not include any

g absolute prohibition in the area of sex selection for 'social purposes'. The inference is that even this was left to be regulated by the licensing authority with the assistance of clinics (on which licences must under the Act impose conditions extending well beyond the purely medical or surgical to matters of general welfare). The present circumstances involve a form of selection which is much less obviously problematic than, and very far removed from, selection for social

h purposes. But, as I have stressed, what matters is that the HFEA's judgment of the desirability of the proposed treatment services has not, as such, been challenged, if it lay within its powers to make it at all. I would therefore hold that it was, in circumstances such as those faced by the Hashmis, open to the HFEA under the Act to conclude that a biopsy for the purpose of selecting an embryo

j with tissue compatible with that of a very sick child was an activity necessary or desirable for the purpose of treatment services as defined.

[144] Viewing the issue in terms of the guidance provided by Lord Wilberforce's formulation ([109], above), a biopsy for the purpose of tissue typing is, in the wider sense, a form of PGD. Its direct purpose is to establish the embryo's genetic makeup and in that light to decide whether or not it should be implanted.

The differences between the testing of embryonic cells for abnormality and for tissue typing lies in the precise aspects of the genetic makeup tested and in the factors taken into account when deciding whether to implant. In the one case, it may be said, the procedures are with a view to ensuring the health of the child to be or of future generations, while in the other they are to promote the health of a sibling and the general welfare of the existing family. The taxonomy of statutory provisions may offer no easy answer (cf the difference of judicial opinion in the *Royal College of Nursing* case itself), but I would regard these as differences falling in Lord Wilberforce's terms within the same genus (even if not the same species) of facts as those to which the expressed statutory policy has been formulated. Indeed, I would go further for reasons which I have already indicated. The background (in the form of the Warnock Report and White Paper) supports the view that Parliament envisaged the possibility or likelihood of future developments (even though it could not know precisely what they would be) and positively intended to bring all such procedures within the sphere of the HFEA, with the exception of those specifically prohibited.

[145] It remains to consider Sch 2, para 1(1)(d). I have rejected the suggestion that this clause is only concerned with characteristics which in objective terms render an embryo unsuitable to be placed in *any* woman ([127], above). The compatibility of the particular embryo with the particular woman is fundamental. Clause (d) also enables a clinic and parents to consider before implantation not merely whether the embryo can viably be implanted and carried to term, but also whether the future child will himself or herself be healthy or a carrier of an hereditary disease which may affect future generations ([126]–[128], above). I have further concluded that a biopsy for the purpose of tissue typing and of enabling a choice to be made regarding implantation based on the compatibility of the embryo's tissue with that of a sibling is capable of constituting a service for the purpose of assisting woman to carry children ([142], above). But is suitability for placement in a woman, in contrast to treatment services, to be judged only by considering whether the embryo is viable and capable of leading to a healthy child who will not be a carrier of an hereditary disease? If it is, there is still the possibility of the Secretary of State widening the ambit of licensable activities by regulation under Sch 2, para 1(1)(g). Nevertheless, I consider it improbable that this was a distinction or a limitation that Parliament intended at this point to introduce by the bare requirement that a licensed practice should be designed to determine whether an embryo was suitable to be implanted. As I have observed, that requirement leaves open the more distant purposes and wider context by reference to which suitability may be judged ([126], above). Having concluded that the concept of treatment services embraces the situation addressed by the HFEA's decision announced on 13 December 2001, it is natural also to regard the concept of suitability as apt to do so. Tissue typing is aimed at providing assistance matching the felt and perceived needs of the family as a whole and the parents and siblings in particular. The HFEA must already bear their interests in mind when determining whether to issue any licence. The HFEA, when granting any licence, may, in the exercise of its powers under s 11 and Sch 2, para 1(1) and (2), limit in such way as it considers appropriate the practices which it licenses or the purposes for which they may be undertaken—as it in fact did (see [105], above). Clinics are bound to have regard to the interests of siblings as well as those of any child-to-be-born under s 13(5) when providing any treatment services; and their performance of that role is

a likely to be assisted by information obtained from tissue typing. I conclude that the suitability of the embryo to be placed in a (particular) woman may be considered in the context of objectively established aims and perceived needs relating to the child-to-be-born's parents and to an affected sibling, of the kind that the HFEA had in mind in reaching its decision announced on 13 December 2001 and in later granting the care clinic's licence.

b
CONCLUSION
[146] I would for these reasons hold that the appeal succeeds. I would accordingly set aside the order whereby the judge quashed the HFEA's decision in principle announced on 13 December 2001 to allow tissue typing to test an embryo for tissue compatibility with an affected sibling.

c
Appeal allowed.

Kate O'Hanlon   Barrister.

Skidmore v Dartford & Gravesham NHS Trust

[2003] UKHL 27

HOUSE OF LORDS

LORD BINGHAM OF CORNHILL, LORD STEYN, LORD CLYDE, LORD HUTTON AND LORD SCOTT OF FOSCOTE

10 APRIL, 22 MAY 2003

Medical practitioner – Disciplinary proceedings – Procedure – Categorisation of proceedings – Whether professional or personal conduct – Department of Health Circular HC(90)9.

The employee was a consultant surgeon employed by the trust. Whilst he was performing keyhole surgery on a patient, a major artery was punctured and there was a large loss of blood. The operation had to be converted to open surgery and was eventually completed successfully. The patient's husband sought an explanation from the patient relations manager who in turn asked for the employee's comments. The thrust of his explanation was to blame the episode on a faulty instrument and to suggest that the blood loss was normal. The trust brought a charge of personal misconduct against the employee alleging that he had sought to deliberately mislead the patient and her family, the community health council and the chief executive through a series of statements and correspondence which he knew to be untrue. Department of Health Circular HC(90)9, a contractual disciplinary code, was incorporated into the employee's contract. It provided for a difference in procedure depending on whether the case involved allegations of 'professional conduct' or 'personal conduct'. The former was governed by a judicialised procedure under the circular. The latter was governed by less formal disciplinary procedures without, amongst other things, the right of legal representation. Personal conduct was defined as 'performance or behaviour of practitioners due to factors other than those associated with the exercise of medical or dental skills' and professional conduct was defined as 'performance or behaviour of practitioners arising from the exercise of medical or dental skills'. At the disciplinary hearing before the trust's chief executive the question whether the proceedings were properly constituted or whether the case should have been dealt with under the circular was argued as a preliminary point. The chief executive decided that the allegations were of personal and not professional misconduct and that as a result she had jurisdiction to deal with the complaint. She concluded that the employee had lied and that he should be dismissed with immediate effect. The employee applied to an employment tribunal alleging unfair dismissal. The tribunal dismissed the complaint and the employee's appeal was dismissed by the Employment Appeal Tribunal on the ground that the case against him was essentially of a personal nature. On the employee's appeal, the Court of Appeal held that the decision of the employer had to comply with the terms of the contract and that the decision of the trust on categorisation was wrong since the case was one involving professional conduct. The trust appealed to the House of Lords.

a **Held** – A purposive construction of the circular and common sense considerations pointed towards a broad interpretation of professional conduct. When in a doctor/patient relationship a doctor committed deliberate misconduct it might come within the category of professional conduct. Lies told by a doctor to a patient about important details of an operation could amount to professional conduct. In such a case the medical practitioner was professing to

b speak as a doctor about a matter covered by his medical skills. Accordingly in breach of contract the trust adopted the wrong procedure. The decision of the Employment Appeal tribunal would be quashed and the matter remitted to an employment tribunal to reconsider the complaint of unfair dismissal on the basis that the trust employed the wrong procedure (see [1], [19], [20], [22]–[24], [29], [30], below).

c   *Saeed v Royal Wolverhampton Hospitals NHS Trust* [2001] ICR 903 considered.
Decision of the Court of Appeal [2002] All ER (D) 52 (Jan) affirmed.

Notes
For the contractual basis for disciplinary powers, see 16 *Halsbury's Laws* (4th edn)
d (2000 reissue) para 408.

Cases referred to in opinions
Associated Provincial Picture Houses Ltd v Wednesbury Corp [1947] 2 All ER 680, [1948] 1 KB 223, CA.
Bhanot v South West London & St George's Mental Health NHS Trust [2000] Lloyd's
e   Rep Med 324.
Brown v GIO Insurance Ltd [1998] Lloyd's Rep IR 201, CA.
Chatterjee v City and Hackney Community Services NHS Trust (1998) 49 BMLR 55.
Kramer v South Bedfordshire Community Health Care Trust (1995) 30 BMLR 34.
Niarchos (London) Ltd v Shell Tankers Ltd [1961] 2 Lloyd's Rep 496.
f *R v Secretary of State for Health and Trent Regional Health Authority, ex p Guirguis* [1990] IRLR 30, CA.
Saeed v Royal Wolverhampton Hospitals NHS Trust [2001] ICR 903, CA; *affg* [2000] Lloyd's Rep Med 331.
West of England Shipowners Mutual Insurance Association (Luxembourg) v Cristal Ltd, The Glacier Bay [1996] 1 Lloyd's Rep 370, CA.
g

Cases also referred to in list of authorities
A County Council v W (Disclosure) [1997] 1 FLR 574.
Dzumhur v Redbridge Healthcare NHS Trust (3 March 2000, unreported).
Investors Compensation Scheme Ltd v West Bromwich Building Society [1998] 1 All ER
h   98, [1998] 1 WLR 896, HL.

Appeal
Dartford & Gravesham NHS Trust appealed with permission of the Appeal Committee of the House of Lords given on 30 May 2002 from the decision of the
j Court of Appeal (Keene, Aldous LJJ and Sir Christopher Slade) on 15 January 2002 ([2002] EWCA Civ 18, [2002] ICR 403) allowing an appeal by the respondent, Frederick David Skidmore, from the decision of the Employment Appeal Tribunal on 22 February 2001, dismissing his appeal from the decision of an industrial tribunal on 4 August 1999 that the correct procedure had been adopted for his dismissal from his employment with the appellant. The facts are set out in the opinion of Lord Steyn.

Michael Douglas QC (instructed by *Brachers*) for the trust.
Timothy Barnes QC and *Angus Moon* (instructed by *Radcliffes Le Brasseur*) for the employee.

Their Lordships took time for consideration.

22 May 2003. The following opinions were delivered.

LORD BINGHAM OF CORNHILL.
[1] My Lords, I have had the advantage of reading in draft the opinion of my noble and learned friend Lord Steyn. I am in full agreement with it and I would accordingly dismiss the appeal and make the order which he proposes.

LORD STEYN.

(I) THE QUESTIONS
[2] My Lords, this appeal raises important issues in respect of hospital disciplinary proceedings. The context is a contractual disciplinary code. Specifically, the issues arise because of the incorporation of Department of Health Circular HC(90)9 *Disciplinary Procedures for Hospital and Community Medical and Dental Staff* dated March 1990 (Circular HC(90)9) in most hospital doctors' contracts. Circular HC(90)9 governed the hospital sector of the National Health Service before the creation of autonomous trusts under the National Health Service and Community Care Act 1990. It is still in use by autonomous NHS trusts. The disciplinary code provides for a difference in procedure depending on whether the case involves allegations of 'professional conduct' or 'personal conduct'. The former is governed by a judicialised procedure under Circular HC(90)9. The latter is governed by less formal disciplinary procedures without, amongst other things, the right of legal representation. Inevitably this relatively complex structure gives rise to issues of demarcation concerning the category in which a particular case falls. Not surprisingly, this has given rise to legal problems and criticism: compare Raymond 'The Employment Rights of the NHS Hospital Doctor' in Dyer *Doctors, Patients and the Law* (1992) p 194; the Department of Health consultation paper dated November 1999 entitled *Supporting Doctors, Protecting Patients: A consultation paper on preventing, recognising and dealing with poor clinical performance of doctors in the NHS in England*; and the NHS Executive's *A summary of the responses to 'Supporting Doctors, Protecting Patients'* (2001) section 4. There has been a difference of judicial view reflected in a number of decisions to which it will be necessary to turn. Two questions dominate the debate. They are: (1) Who decides on the categorisation of a case? (2) How is the line between professional and personal conduct to be drawn? Both these questions arise in the present appeal.

(II) THE OPERATION AND THE AFTERMATH
[3] In April 1997 Mr Skidmore was a consultant surgeon at the Joyce Green Hospital. On 3 April 1997 Mr Skidmore operated on Mrs A for the removal of a gall bladder. The method was keyhole surgery. During the surgical procedure the patient's left iliac artery was punctured by a sharp three-pronged instrument. There was a large loss of blood. The operation had to be converted to open surgery. A surgeon, who had been operating in an adjacent theatre, was called to assist. There was a short period of cardio-pulmonary resuscitation. The patient

a had eight units of blood transfused during the operation and two further units transfused post-operatively. On any view it was a serious episode with potential life-threatening implications. But the operation was eventually completed successfully and Mrs A made a complete recovery.

[4] Mrs A's husband sought an explanation from the patient relations manager who in turn asked for Mr Skidmore's comments. In two meetings Mr Skidmore
b gave his explanation first to Mrs A and then to Mrs A and her husband. The thrust of his explanation was to blame the episode on a faulty instrument and to suggest that the blood loss was normal, viz only two units, and that Mrs A had not arrested or required resuscitation. This version of events was in conflict with the contemporaneous notes of the operation made by the anaesthetist. In a written response Mr Skidmore expanded on his oral explanations.
c

(III) THE DISCIPLINARY PROCEEDINGS

[5] Following further exchanges and investigations, the Dartford & Gravesham NHS Trust (the trust) made a charge of personal misconduct against Mr Skidmore. The outline statement alleged that Mr Skidmore—

d 'sought to deliberately mislead:
—The patient and her family
—community health council
—the chief executive
through a series of statements and correspondence which he knew to be
e untrue ... Mr Skidmore set out to deceive the patient, her husband, the community health council and her GP about the actual events that occurred in theatre and subsequently ... Mr Skidmore set out to deceive the chief executive with information he knew not to be true.'

The trust had decided that this charge was properly a charge in respect of
f personal conduct within the meaning of the disciplinary code.

[6] On 27 and 28 October 1997 the hearing took place before the trust's chief executive. Dr Barker of the Medical Protection Society represented Mr Skidmore and Dr Key represented the management. The question whether the proceedings were properly constituted or whether the case should have been dealt with under the Circular HC(90)9 procedure governing professional conduct was argued as a
g preliminary point. The chief executive decided that the allegations were of personal and not professional misconduct and that as a result she had jurisdiction to deal with the complaint. Oral evidence was then heard from witnesses on behalf of both parties. On 20 November 1997 the chief executive delivered her reasoned decision. She concluded that Mr Skidmore had falsely told Mr and
h Mrs A that two units had been transfused in the theatre when in truth eight units had been transfused and that he had stated as a fact that the instrument was faulty and had been returned to the manufacturer for inspection when this was clearly not the case. She concluded that Mr Skidmore had lied and had continued to be untruthful when he appeared before her. She decided that he should be dismissed
j with immediate effect.

[7] Mr Skidmore appealed to an appeal panel of the trust board. On 2 December 1997 an appeal panel consisting of the trust chairman, the finance director, and three non-executive directors heard the appeal. The question of the correct procedure was again dealt with as a preliminary point. After hearing submissions the panel decided that the allegations were properly dealt with under the internal disciplinary procedures. The hearing continued. The chief executive gave evidence

before the panel and was cross-examined by Mr Skidmore's representative, Dr Panting. The panel also heard evidence from Mr Skidmore, two witnesses who had given evidence below and also a local general practitioner who had not. On 18 December 1997 the panel delivered its decision. It found that Mr Skidmore's conduct constituted gross misconduct and that summary dismissal had been appropriate.

[8] Annex C of Circular HC(90)9 requires the Secretary of State on application to refer to a panel the question whether an applicant's appointment is being terminated on the sole ground of personal misconduct. Mr Skidmore appealed under Annex C. By letter dated 11 June 1998 the Secretary of State rejected the appeal on the basis that he had no jurisdiction in accordance with the decision of the Court of Appeal in *R v Secretary of State for Health and Trent Regional Health Authority, ex p Guirguis* [1990] IRLR 30, as Mr Skidmore had been dismissed without notice.

(IV) THE PROCEEDINGS ALLEGING UNFAIR DISMISSAL

[9] Mr Skidmore then applied to an industrial tribunal (now an employment tribunal) alleging unfair dismissal. The grounds of his application were twofold, viz that the wrong procedures had been adopted and that the complaint was without substance. On 4 August 1999 the tribunal dismissed the application by a majority.

[10] Mr Skidmore appealed to the Employment Appeal Tribunal (EAT) on a number of grounds. One ground was that the wrong procedure had been adopted. On 22 February 2001 the EAT dismissed the appeal ([2001] ICR 911). Relying on decisions of Lightman J in *Kramer v South Bedfordshire Community Health Care Trust* (1995) 30 BMLR 34 and *Chatterjee v City and Hackney Community Services NHS Trust* (1998) 49 BMLR 55, the EAT took the view that, absent bad faith or *Wednesbury* unreasonableness (see *Associated Provincial Picture Houses Ltd v Wednesbury Corp* [1947] 2 All ER 680, [1948] 1 KB 223), the employer's decision on categorisation was final. In any event, the EAT concluded that the case against Mr Skidmore was essentially of a personal nature.

(V) THE COURT OF APPEAL DECISION

[11] In an unreserved judgment, given on 15 January 2002 by Keene LJ with the agreement of Aldous LJ and Sir Christopher Slade, the Court of Appeal unanimously allowed Mr Skidmore's appeal ([2002] EWCA Civ 18, [2002] ICR 403). Following a recent decision of the Court of Appeal in *Saeed v Royal Wolverhampton Hospitals NHS Trust* [2001] ICR 903, Keene LJ held that the decision of the employer must comply with the terms of the contract. Keene LJ further held that on the facts the decision of the employer on categorisation was wrong: the case was one involving professional conduct. The appeal before the House challenges the decision of the Court of Appeal on both points. Before directly addressing these issues it is necessary to set out critical features of Circular HC(90)9 and to explain the conflict of judicial decisions.

(VI) CIRCULAR HC(90)9

[12] Circular HC(90)9 is a lengthy document. For present purposes it is only necessary to set out a few extracts from it. The circular draws a distinction between 'personal conduct', 'professional conduct' and 'professional competence'. Those categories of allegations of misconduct are defined in para 3 of the circular as follows:

a
'PERSONAL CONDUCT—Performance or behaviour of practitioners due to factors other than those associated with the exercise of medical or dental skills.

PROFESSIONAL CONDUCT—Performance or behaviour of practitioners arising from the exercise of medical or dental skills.

b
PROFESSIONAL COMPETENCE—Adequacy of performance of practitioners related to the exercise of their medical or dental skills and professional judgment.'

Circular HC(90)9 then provides (Annex B):

c
'There are broadly three types of case which may involve medical or dental staff: (a) cases involving personal conduct; (b) cases involving professional conduct; (c) cases involving professional competence. *It is for the Authority to decide under which category a case falls.* Guidance on the definition of each category is given in paragraph 3 of the Circular.' (See above; my emphasis.)

d
In cases involving personal conduct Annex B provides that 'the position of a doctor or dentist is no different from that of other health service staff'. With regard to cases involving professional misconduct and professional incompetence, Annex B of Circular HC(90)9 provides in para 8 that the panel (consisting usually of three members) should have a legally-qualified chairman. Moreover in such cases Annex B of Circular HC(90)9 provides, inter alia, in para 12 for the following further procedural rights:

e

f
'The practitioner should have the right to appear personally before the investigating panel and to be represented (either by a lawyer ... or otherwise), and to hear all the evidence presented to the panel. He should have the right to cross-examine all witnesses and to produce his own witnesses, and they and he may also be subjected to cross-examination.'

By contrast the internal procedure applicable to cases of personal conduct contains no such safeguards and is generally more informal.

g
[13] Since the hearing of the present case in the Court of Appeal, counsel for Mr Skidmore has unearthed the genesis of Circular HC(90)9. While the distinction between professional and personal conduct goes back to 1956, the disciplinary arrangements presently reflected in Circular HC(90)9 were the result of the deliberations of a joint working party which published a report in August 1988 entitled *Disciplinary Procedures for Hospital and Community Doctors and Dentists.* The joint working party was made up of representatives of the health departments, the NHS and the professions. It was set up to 'review disciplinary procedures for hospital and community doctors and dentists' and specifically to 'consider the scope, operation and effectiveness of the disciplinary procedures' in Circular HM(61)112. Paragraph 3 of the report reads:

h

j
'The Working Party recognised the professions' concerns that disciplinary procedures for senior doctors and dentists must ensure that the grounds for dismissal have been fully justified, since a specialist who has been dismissed from an NHS post on professional grounds would be unlikely to find alternative employment elsewhere. The professions felt that the procedures used should be sufficiently weighty to reflect both the long periods of training and competitive selection processes which doctors have undergone

before appointment to senior posts, and also the potential gravity of the
outcome of such procedures.'

The recommendations of the working party were accepted and gave rise to
Circular HC(90)9 which was published by the Department of Health in March 1990.
The terms contained in Circular HC(90)9 were imposed upon doctors by reg 3 of
the National Health Service (Remuneration and Conditions of Service)
Regulations 1991, SI 1991/481. It is now part of the employment contract of
Mr Skidmore and of the employment contracts of almost all NHS hospital
doctors. It will be necessary to return to the significance of the report for the
purpose of Circular HC 90(9) (see [20], below).

(VII) THE CASE LAW

[14] Concentrating at this stage on the issue of whose decision determines the
categorisation of a case, I now turn to the directly relevant case law as matters
stood at the time of the Court of Appeal judgment. In a carefully reasoned
judgment in *Kramer v South Bedfordshire Community Health Care Trust* (1995) 30
BMLR 34 Lightman J (at 38) approached the problem as follows:

> 'As an implied term of [the] contract of employment, the trust in making
> this decision must act in good faith and (I would also think) reach a decision
> which the trust could reasonably reach. If the trust can be shown to have
> acted in breach of this term, its decision may be challenged on that ground,
> but (subject to this important proviso) its decision stands. There can
> otherwise be no reason to include in the contract this provision that
> categorisation is a matter for the trust. Unlike [counsel for the doctor], I
> cannot regard this provision as otiose or find any significance in the fact that
> the impact of the provision was not appreciated by the trust's legal advisers
> until I raised it. The decision of the trust cannot be impugned merely
> because the employee or the court would have characterised the case
> differently or considers the trust's characterisation is wrong, or because the
> trust has given no reasons (in particular in a case like the present where no
> reasons were sought and no complaint has been made of lack of reasons prior
> to the hearing). The trust in this case decided that the charges were of
> personal misconduct and accordingly that the procedure appropriate to
> proceedings for personal misconduct should be adopted. This decision can
> only be impugned on grounds of lack of good faith or unreasonableness in
> reaching this determination on the part of the trust.'

In all material respects this decision was made on the same contractual terms as
are to be found in the contract before the House. In *Chatterjee v City and Hackney
Community Services NHS Trust* (1998) 49 BMLR 55 Lightman J followed his earlier
decision in *Kramer's* case. In *Bhanot v South West London & St George's Mental
Health NHS Trust* [2000] Lloyd's Rep Med 324 at 328 Bell J disagreed. He observed:

> 'This is an action for breach of contract and what I am deciding is whether
> on the information before me the case of breach of contract is sufficiently
> strong to make the order which the claimant seeks.'

At first instance in *Saeed v Royal Wolverhampton Hospitals NHS Trust* [2000] Lloyd's
Rep Med 331, Gage J preferred the approach of Lightman J. On the facts Gage J
found that the allegation of indecent assault during a medical examination against
a senior house officer was one of personal conduct. The Court of Appeal ([2001]
ICR 903) agreed with Gage J on the latter point and dismissed the appeal. Hale LJ

a (with whom Dame Elizabeth Butler-Sloss P and Potter LJ agreed) defined the first issue as follows (at 907): 'Who decided into which category the case fell, and on what basis could the court interfere with that decision?' Hale LJ commenced her judgment by saying:

b
> '12   One might have thought that the answer to the first issue was obvious. The employer who is contemplating disciplinary action against an employee has to decide which procedure should be followed. If the employee thinks that the employer has made the wrong choice, he can try to have it changed in advance or seek damages after the event. The court will have to perform its usual task of construing the contract and applying it to the facts of the case.

c
> 13   Unfortunately the issue has been clouded by the introduction of public law concepts into an ordinary contractual situation ...'

She then discussed the conflicting dicta at first instance and expressed her preference for the general approach of Bell J. She concluded (at 908 (para 17)):

d
> 'Of course the employer has to decide which procedure to follow. But the employer has to take that decision in accordance with the terms of the contract ... the trust will be in breach of contract if [the definitions in Circular HC(90)9] are not properly applied.'

Taking the view that an indecent assault by a doctor during an examination of a
e patient cannot amount to a charge of professional misconduct she held that the appeal should be dismissed.

(VIII)   ISSUE NO 1: WHO DECIDES?
   [15] Counsel for the trust invited the House to adopt the approach of Lightman J on the first issue. For reasons which can be explained shortly it is not
f possible to adopt this course. It is common ground, and rightly so, that no public law issues are involved and that the questions before the House must be resolved within the framework of the contract between Mr Skidmore and the trust. That is so despite the fact that a public body is involved. Prima facie therefore the position is as follows. The trust is entitled to decide what disciplinary route should be followed. That decision must, however, comply with the terms of the
g contract. If a non-conforming decision is taken and acted upon, there is a breach of contract resulting in the usual remedies. The only escape from this position would be if it could be shown that the parties agreed upon wording in their contract making it clear that the employer's decision would be final thereby excluding the role of the court except, of course, in cases of bad faith or possibly
h the absence of reasonable grounds for the decision. There is no such provision in the present contract. It does, of course, provide that 'It is for the authority to decide under which category a case falls'. This provision merely states the obvious: the trust must take the initial decision to commence the appropriate disciplinary procedure. It is, however, quite insufficient to exclude the normal
j consequences of a failure to follow the agreed contractual procedures. If there has been a breach by the trust in adopting the wrong procedure, Mr Skidmore is entitled to appropriate relief. So far I am in general agreement with the approach of the Court of Appeal in *Saeed*'s case.
   [16] There is, however, one aspect of the analysis of the Court of Appeal which I cannot accept. Hale LJ observed that the issue has been clouded by the introduction of public law concepts into an ordinary contractual situation. That

is not how Lightman J approached the matter in *Kramer v South Bedfordshire Community Health Care Trust* (1995) 30 BMLR 34 and *Chatterjee v City and Hackney Community Services NHS Trust* (1998) 49 BMLR 55. On the contrary, he expressly based his reasoning on an implied term of the contract of employment. He said that there 'can otherwise be no reason to include in the contract this provision that categorisation is a matter for the trust'. The likelihood is that Lightman J had in mind decided cases where the court interpreted a contractual term dependent on the exercise of the will of one party as by implication restricted to a decision taken in good faith and on reasonable grounds, e g a clause entrusting a decision as to the adequacy of performance to the absolute discretion of one party. The foundation of such an implication is to satisfy the reasonable expectations of the parties. Some examples of such cases are to be found in the judgment of McNair J in *Niarchos (London) Ltd v Shell Tankers Ltd* [1961] 2 Lloyd's Rep 496 at 507–509; see also Lewison *The Interpretation of Contracts* (2nd edn, 1997) pp 347–350 (para 12.03). There are other recent examples of special provisions: see *West of England Shipowners Mutual Insurance Association (Luxembourg) v Cristal Ltd, The Glacier Bay* [1996] 1 Lloyd's Rep 370 ('the sole judge') and *Brown v GIO Insurance Ltd* [1998] Lloyd's Rep IR 201 ('the sole judge'). The mistake of the judge in *Kramer*'s case and *Chatterjee*'s case was to place a weight upon a contractual provision which it was incapable of bearing. There was no agreement to entrust the issue to the final decision of the trust. There was no warrant for the term the judge implied. The contract was entirely workable on the basis that the trust had to decide on categorisation but it had to do so in accordance with the contract.

[**17**] I would reject the challenge of the trust to the decision of the Court of Appeal on the first point.

(IX) ISSUE NO 2: WHICH CATEGORY?

[**18**] It is now necessary to consider how the case against Mr Skidmore should be categorised. The starting point must be the proper interpretation of the definitions contained in the disciplinary code. It seems right to treat the definitions of professional conduct ('behaviour of practitioners arising from the exercise of medical or dental skills') and professional competence ('adequacy of performance of practitioners related to the exercise of their medical or dental skills and professional judgment') as the primary categories. Personal conduct is the residual category consisting of 'behaviour ... due to factors *other* than those associated with the exercise of medical or dental skills' (my emphasis). If a case is properly to be categorised as involving professional conduct or competence, the judicialised disciplinary route under Circular HC(90)9 is obligatory. That is so even if the case could also be said to amount to personal misconduct.

[**19**] For present purposes it is unnecessary to examine the distinction between professional conduct and professional competence. It is common ground that professional competence is not a relevant category. The line drawn between professional conduct and personal conduct is conduct 'arising from the exercise of medical or dental skills' and 'other' conduct. How this distinction should in practice be applied must now be considered. The structure of the disciplinary code set out in Circular HC(90)9 is a classic case requiring a broad and purposive interpretation enabling sensible procedural decisions to be taken. It would, for example, be surprising if a case where a doctor embarked on an intimate medical examination of a woman, which he knew to be wholly unnecessary, necessarily fell outside the scope of what may constitute professional misconduct. After all,

a in such a case, the doctor is using his position as a hospital doctor to perpetrate an act of serious professional misconduct. I cannot, therefore, agree with the ruling in *Saeed v Royal Wolverhampton Hospitals NHS Trust* [2001] ICR 903 at 910 (para 24) that an indecent assault committed by a doctor during a medical examination cannot constitute professional misconduct within the code. It is a case of a doctor misusing his ostensible medical skills for improper purposes. In

b my view it falls within the scope of professional misconduct within the definition. Relying on the text of Circular HC(90)9 I take the view that a purposive construction, and commonsense considerations, point towards a broad interpretation of professional conduct.

[20] Since the decision in *Saeed's* case and the hearing in the Court of Appeal

c there has become available the joint working party report (*Disciplinary Procedures for Hospital and Community Doctors and Dentists* (August 1998)) setting out the reasons for the line drawn between professional and personal misconduct. The emphasis is on the serious consequences for a doctor of an adverse decision, making a doctor dismissed on professional grounds virtually unemployable. In my view this background material reinforces a broad interpretation of Circular

d HC(90)9 notably in respect of what may amount to professional misconduct. It supports the interpretation that when in a doctor/patient relationship a doctor commits deliberate misconduct it may come within the category of professional conduct.

[21] Keene LJ concluded that the allegations against Mr Skidmore fell within

e the category of professional conduct and that was the appropriate machinery to be used. He explained ([2002] ICR 403):

> '[32] … First, the applicant was lying about the performance by him of an operation. The operation did not merely provide the occasion or opportunity for his misconduct, as happens in some cases where a medical
>
> f examination of a patient provides an opportunity for an indecent assault, to take a familiar example. The operation here was the subject matter of the lie, and the conduct on the part of the applicant would not have taken place but for the exercise of his medical skills in the course of the operation. It comes into a different category from lies told about a matter not involving
>
> g his medical skills, such as, for example, whether he had been having an affair with a member of the nursing staff.
>
> [33] Secondly, the history of this matter shows that it was seen as part of the applicant's professional duty to respond to the complaint by Mr A and to communicate with the patient and his general practitioner, and in due course
>
> h with the chief executive. He was patently expected to respond to the letter from the patient relations manager and the enclosed complaint. Indeed, any surgeon would be expected to explain to a patient what had happened during the course of an operation if something untoward or unexpected had taken place, as the GMC booklet "Good Medical Practice" indicates. Such an
>
> j explanation surely is to be regarded as conduct arising from the exercise of his medical skills. The doctor in such a situation is acting in the course of fulfilling a professional responsibility. In the same way, it is part of a consultant's normal responsibility to keep a patient's general practitioner informed of the success or failure of an operation which he has conducted. So the letter of 21 April 1997 to the general practitioner is to be seen as arising from the exercise of the applicant's medical skills during the operation.

[34] Thirdly, it is to my mind relevant that the allegations against the applicant raised issues which, at least to a degree, needed medical experience or expertise for their determination. I have in mind in particular the applicant's attempted explanation of how he confused the number of units of blood transfused. Despite Mr Douglas's attempts to persuade us to the contrary, it seems to me that some medical experience was required to give proper consideration to that proffered explanation. The internal disciplinary procedure does not necessarily involve anyone with medical experience determining such an issue. The independent procedure under the Circular does. That too points towards the proper categorisation of the allegations here.'

This reasoning is irresistible.

[22] Given the interpretation, which I have adopted, it is in truth self-evident that lies told by a doctor to a patient about important details of an operation can amount to professional conduct. After all in such a case the medical practitioner is professing to speak as a doctor about a matter covered by his medical skills. The argument to the contrary on behalf of the trust must be rejected.

(X) THE OUTCOME

[23] I conclude that in breach of contract the trust adopted the wrong procedure. I would therefore dismiss the appeal. In the result the decision of the EAT is quashed and the matter is remitted to an employment tribunal to reconsider the complaint of unfair dismissal on the basis that the trust employed the wrong procedure.

LORD CLYDE.

[24] My Lords, I agree that the appeal should be dismissed for the reasons set out in the speech of my noble and learned friend Lord Steyn. I add a few words of my own merely in the hope of giving assistance in the future application of the scheme of categories of conduct set out in the Department of Health Circular HC(90)9 *Disciplinary Procedures for Hospital and Community Medical and Dental Staff* (Circular HC(90)9).

[25] Paragraph 3 of Circular HC(90)9 explains that authorities had sometimes had great difficulty in defining the nature of the conduct in question. The expressions 'personal conduct', 'professional conduct' and 'professional competence' required in particular concentration upon the particular words 'personal' and 'professional' and the making of some kind of distinction between them. Clearly these terms would be hard to apply precisely and grey areas could easily be identified where the terms could overlap. Those difficulties were sought to be overcome by Circular HC(90)9. The guidance which it gave had the effect of moving the attention away from the former expressions and onto the agreed definitions of the categories of conduct. One importance of this was that the words 'personal' and 'professional' are no longer of importance in themselves. The new guidance would work equally well if the three categories were identified as 'type A conduct', 'type B conduct' and 'type C conduct'. The expressions 'personal conduct' and 'professional conduct' and 'professional competence' have become simply labels, serving only to identify categories which have now been fully defined.

[26] The categories must be taken to be exhaustive of all kinds of conduct which might attract disciplinary attention. While it is a threefold categorisation there are only two forms of procedure which may follow. The expression 'due

a to factors associated with' is not a very happy one. But to make the scheme coherent and exhaustive of all cases which may be subject to disciplinary procedure the two main cases must be those where the conduct is due to factors associated with the exercise of medical or dental skills and those where the conduct is due to factors other than those associated with the exercise of medical or dental skills. That latter case is labelled 'personal conduct' and attracts the b procedure appropriate for such cases. If the conduct is due to factors associated with the exercise of medical or dental skills it will fall into one or other of the two groups which bear the respective labels of 'professional conduct' and 'professional competence'. In relation to the task of making a choice between the second and third kinds of conduct, consideration has to be given to the matters of adequacy and professional judgment which characterise the third kind of c conduct. But that choice is not of consequence for the basic distinction in procedure. Both the second and the third kinds of conduct call for the more elaborate processing of the case.

[27] While I do not for a moment suggest that there is only one way in which one must go about the task of deciding which category applies in any particular d case, I would prefer first to ask the question whether the conduct complained of is due to factors associated with the exercise of medical or dental skills. One must look at the conduct in question and ask whether it has come about through factors associated with the exercise of medical or dental skills. I agree with my noble and learned friend Lord Steyn that a broad approach is appropriate. If there is such an association then the further question may be asked whether it is a e matter of conduct or of competence within the meaning of the second and third definitions. If it does not fall into the third category as a matter of the adequacy of the performance of a practitioner related to the exercise of medical or dental skills and professional judgment then it must fall into the second category. But in either case the more elaborate procedure will have to be followed. If on the other f hand there is no such association then the case will be one for the less elaborate procedure designed for cases in the category of 'personal conduct'.

[28] Approaching the present case in this way it seems to me clear beyond doubt that the conduct in question was due to factors associated with the respondent's exercise of medical skills and so did not qualify under the heading of 'personal conduct'.

g

LORD HUTTON.

[29] My Lords, I have had the advantage of reading in draft the opinion of my noble and learned friend Lord Steyn. For the reasons he has given, with which I am in full agreement, I too would dismiss this appeal and make the order which h he proposes.

LORD SCOTT OF FOSCOTE.

[30] My Lords, I have had the advantage of reading in advance the opinion of my noble and learned friend, Lord Steyn. For the reasons he has given, with j which I agree, I too would dismiss this appeal and make the order proposed.

Appeal dismissed.

Celia Fox   Barrister.

Sepet and another v Secretary of State for the Home Department

[2003] UKHL 15

HOUSE OF LORDS

LORD BINGHAM OF CORNHILL, LORD STEYN, LORD HOFFMANN, LORD HUTTON AND LORD RODGER OF EARLSFERRY

4–6 FEBRUARY, 20 MARCH 2003

Immigration – Leave to enter – Refugee – Asylum – Fear of persecution by applicant for refugee status – Conscientious objection to military service – Whether international law recognising right of conscientious objection to military service for purpose of establishing refugee status – Convention and Protocol relating to the Status of Refugees 1951, art 1A(2).

The applicants were Turkish nationals of Kurdish origin, each of whom claimed asylum in the United Kingdom on the ground that they would be liable, if returned to Turkey, to perform compulsory military service, on pain of imprisonment if they refused. Neither of them claimed to have a conscientious objection to military service in all circumstances, or an objection based on religious belief, each rather objecting because of political opposition to the policies of the then Turkish government in relation to the Kurdish people, and because of a wish not to be required to participate in actions, possibly involving atrocities and abuse of human rights, against their own people. Their claims for asylum were rejected by the Secretary of State, and challenges to his decision were successively rejected by a special adjudicator (who found that there was no likelihood that either applicant would be required to engage in military action contrary to the basic rules of human conduct), the Immigration Appeal Tribunal and the Court of Appeal. They appealed to the House of Lords, contending that there was an internationally recognised fundamental right to refuse to undertake military service on grounds of conscience which brought them within the definition of refugees in art 1A(2)[a] of the Convention and Protocol relating to the Status of Refugees 1951 as having a well-founded fear of being persecuted for reasons of race, religion, nationality, membership of a particular social group or political opinion.

Held – There was currently no legal rule binding in international law which recognised a right to conscientious objection to military service, such as would give rise to a good case for refugee status if it were not respected. While the reach of an international human rights convention was not forever determined by the intentions of those who originally framed it, there was no material which established an extant right of absolute or partial conscientious objection. Accordingly, the appeals would be dismissed (see [11], [20], [24], [53], [55], [56], [58], below).

Per curiam. In deciding whether an asylum applicant has been or would be persecuted for convention reasons, the decision maker will begin by considering

---

a Article 1A(2), so far as material, is set out at [2], below.

a   the reason in the mind of the persecutor for inflicting the persecutory treatment. He will then ask if that is the real reason, or whether there is some other effective reason (see [23], [24], [56], [59], below).

Notes

b   For asylum and the meaning of 'refugee', see 4(2) *Halsbury's Laws* (4th edn) (2002 reissue) paras 238, 239.

Cases referred to in opinions

A v Minister for Immigration and Ethnic Affairs (1997) 2 BHRC 143, Aust HC.

A v Switzerland (1984) 38 DR 219, E Com HR.

A-G of Canada v Ward [1993] 2 SCR 689, Can SC.

c   *Autio v Finland* (1991) 72 DR 245, E Com HR.

Canas-Segovia v Immigration and Naturalization Service (1990) 902 F 2d 717, US Ct of Apps (9th Cir).

Canas-Segovia v Immigration and Naturalization Service (1992) 970 F 2d 599, US Ct of Apps (9th Cir).

d   *Chen Shi Hai v Minister for Immigration and Multicultural Affairs* [2000] HCA 19, (2000) 201 CLR 293, Aust HC.

Ciric v Canada (Minister of Employment and Immigration) [1994] 2 FC 65, Can Fed Ct.

Erduran v Minister for Immigration and Multicultural Affairs [2002] FCA 814, Aust Fed Ct.

Gillette v US (1970) 401 US 437, US SC.

Goodwin v UK [2002] 2 FCR 577, ECt HR.

e   *Grandrath v Germany* (1965) 8 YB 324, E Com HR.

Grandrath v Germany (1967) 10 YB 626, Committee of Ministers of the Council of Europe.

Heudens v Belgium App No 24630/94 (22 May 1995, unreported), E Com HR.

Horvath v Secretary of State for the Home Dept [2000] 3 All ER 577, [2001] 1 AC 489,

f   [2000] 3 WLR 379, HL.

Immigration and Naturalization Service v Elias-Zacarias (1992) 502 US 478, US SC.

Johansen v Norway (1985) 44 DR 155, E Com HR.

LTK v Finland (1985) 94 ILR 396, UN HR Committee.

Minister for Immigration and Multicultural Affairs v Ibrahim [2000] HCA 55, (2000) 204 CLR 1, Aust HC.

g   *Minister for Immigration and Multicultural Affairs v Yusuf* [2001] HCA 30, (2001) 206 CLR 323, Aust HC.

Omoruyi v Secretary of State for the Home Dept [2001] Imm AR 175, CA.

Qureshi v Victoria University of Manchester (1996) [2001] ICR 863, EAT.

R v Immigration Appeal Tribunal, ex p Shah [1997] Imm AR 145; *rvsd* [1998] 4 All ER

h   30, [1998] 1 WLR 74, CA; *rvsd* [1999] 2 All ER 545, [1999] 2 AC 629, [1999] 2 WLR 1015, HL.

R v Secretary of State for the Home Dept, ex p Adan, R v Secretary of State for the Home Dept, ex p Aitseguer [2001] 1 All ER 593, [2001] 2 AC 477, [2001] 2 WLR 143, HL; *affg* [1999] 4 All ER 774, [2001] 2 AC 477, [1999] 3 WLR 1274, CA.

j   *Refugee Appeal No 72635/01* (6 September 2002, unreported), NZ Refugee Status Appeals Authority.

Sandralingham v Secretary of State for the Home Dept, Rajendrakumar v Immigration Appeal Tribunal [1996] Imm AR 97, CA.

Sivakumar v Secretary of State for the Home Dept [2001] EWCA Civ 1196, [2002] INLR 310; *affd* [2003] UKHL 14, [2003] 2 All ER 1097, [2003] 1 WLR 840.

Thlimmenos v Greece App No 34369/97 (4 December 1998, unreported), E Com HR; (2001) 31 EHRR 411, ECt HR.

Tsirlis v Greece (1998) 25 EHRR 198, ECt HR.

X v Austria (1973) 43 CD 161, E Com HR.

Zolfagharkhani v Canada (Minister of Employment and Immigration) [1993] FC 540, Can Fed Ct.

Cases referred to in list of authorities

Adan v Secretary of State for the Home Dept [1997] 2 All ER 723, [1997] 1 WLR 1107, CA.

Alonzo v US Immigration and Naturalization Service (1990) 915 F 2d 546, US Ct of Apps (9th Cir).

Applicant N 403 v Minister for Immigration and Multicultural Affairs [2000] FCA 1088, Aust Fed Ct.

Atibo v Immigration Officer, London (Heathrow) Airport [1978] Imm AR 93, IAT.

Brown v Stott (Procurator Fiscal, Dunfermline) [2001] 2 All ER 97, [2001] 2 WLR 817, PC.

Bugdaycay v Secretary of State for the Home Dept [1987] 1 All ER 940, [1987] AC 514, [1987] 2 WLR 606, HL.

C v UK (1983) 37 DR 142, E Com HR.

Castillo v Immigration and Naturalization Service (1991) 951 F 2d 1117, US Ct of Apps (9th Cir).

Castioni, Re [1891] 1 QB 149, [1886–90] All ER Rep 640, DC.

Church v Secretary of State for the Home Dept (5 April 1982, unreported).

Dwomoh v Sava (1988) 696 F Supp 970, US DC (SD NY).

Fadil v Secretary of State for the Home Dept [2001] Imm AR 392, CA.

IS v Bulgaria App No 32438/96 (6 April 2000, unreported), ECt HR.

Israelian v Minister for Immigration and Multicultural Affairs [1998] FCA 447, Aust Fed Ct.

Jain v Secretary of State for the Home Dept [2000] Imm AR 76, CA.

Järvinen v Finland (1990) 118 ILR 137, UN HR Committee.

Kalashnikov v Russia App No 47095/99 (15 July 2002, unreported), ECt HR.

R (Kariharan) v Secretary of State for the Home Dept [2002] EWCA Civ 1102, [2003] QB 933, [2002] 3 WLR 1783.

Kolczynski, Re [1955] 1 All ER 31, sub nom *R v Governor of Brixton Prison, ex p Kolzynski* [1955] 1 QB 540, [1955] 2 WLR 116, DC.

Legal Consequences for States of the Continued Presence of South Africa in Namibia (South West Africa) (1971) ICJ Rep 16, ICJ.

Magyari v Minister for Immigration and Multicultural Affairs [1997] FCA 417, Aust Fed Ct.

Mehenni v Minister for Immigration and Multicultural Affairs [1999] FCA 789, Aust Fed Ct.

Mijoljevic v Minister for Immigration and Multicultural Affairs [1999] FCA 834, Aust Fed Ct.

Montoya v Secretary of State for the Home Dept [2002] EWCA Civ 620, [2002] INLR 399.

Nagarajan v London Regional Transport [1999] 4 All ER 65, [2000] 1 AC 501, [1999] 3 WLR 425, HL.

Nicaragua v USA (1986) 76 ILR 349, ICJ.

North Sea Continental Shelf Cases (1969) 41 ILR 29, ICJ.

Paramananthan v Minister for Immigration and Multicultural Affairs [1998] FCA 1693, (1998) 94 FCR 28, Aust Fed Ct.

Peers v Greece (2001) 33 EHRR 1192, ECt HR.

Petrovski v Secretary of State for the Home Dept [1993] Imm AR 134, IAT.

Prior v Canada [1988] 2 FC 371, Can Fed Ct.

R (on the application of Yogathas) v Secretary of State for the Home Dept, R (on the application of Thangarasa) v Secretary of State for the Home Dept [2001] EWCA Civ *a*   1611, [2001] All ER (D) 121 (Sep); *affd* [2002] UKHL 36, [2002] 4 All ER 800, [2002] 3 WLR 1276.

R v Secretary of State for the Home Dept, ex p Hashem [1987] Imm AR 577.

R v Secretary of State for the Home Dept, ex p Mehari [1994] 2 All ER 494, [1994] QB 474, [1994] 2 WLR 349.

R v Secretary of State for the Home Dept, ex p Robinson [1997] 4 All ER 210, [1998] QB
b   929, [1997] 3 WLR 1162, CA.

R v Secretary of State for the Home Dept, ex p Sivakumaran (UN High Comr for Refugees intervening) [1988] 1 All ER 193, [1988] AC 958, [1988] 2 WLR 92, HL.

R v Zausmer (1911) 7 Crim App R 41.

Schtraks v Government of Israel [1962] 3 All ER 529, [1964] AC 556, [1962] 3 WLR 1013, HL.

c   *Selective Draft Law Cases* (1917) 245 US 366, US SC.

South West Africa Cases [1966] ICJ Rep 1, ICJ.

Stefanov v Bulgaria App No 32438/96 (3 May 2001, unreported), ECt HR.

T v Secretary of State for the Home Dept [1996] 2 All ER 865, [1996] AC 742, [1996] 2 WLR 766, HL.

d   *V v Netherlands* (1984) 39 DR 267, E Com HR.

Appeals

The applicants, Yasin Sepet and Erdem Bulbul, appealed with permission of the Appeal Committee of the House of Lords given on 21 November 2001 from the decision of the Court of Appeal (Waller, Laws and Jonathan Parker LJJ) on 11 May
e   2001 ([2001] EWCA Civ 681, [2001] Imm AR 452) dismissing their appeals from the decision of the Immigration Appeal Tribunal (Collins J and PR Moulden) on 18 May 2000 dismissing their appeals from (i) the determination of a special adjudicator (JRLG Varcoe CMG) on 19 February 1998 dismissing Mr Sepet's appeal from the decision of the respondent, the Secretary of State for the Home
f   Department, on 29 September 1993 refusing his application for asylum in the United Kingdom, and (ii) the special adjudicator's determination on 27 February 1998 dismissing Mr Bulbul's appeal from the Secretary of State's decision on 11 July 1996 refusing his application for asylum in the United Kingdom. The United Nations High Commissioner for Refugees intervened in the proceedings. The facts are set out in the opinion of Lord Bingham of Cornhill.

g
Andrew Nicol QC and *Rick Scannell* (instructed by *Deighton Guedalla*) for Mr Sepet.

Andrew Nicol QC and *Nadine French* (instructed by *Birnberg Peirce & Partners*) for Mr Bulbul.

John Howell QC and *Mark Shaw QC* (instructed by the *Treasury Solicitor*) for the
h   Secretary of State.

Nicholas Blake QC and *Tim Eicke* (instructed by *Wesley Gryk*) for the High Commissioner.

Their Lordships took time for consideration.

j   20 March 2003. The following opinions were delivered.

LORD BINGHAM OF CORNHILL.

[1] My Lords, the issue in this appeal is whether the applicants, both of them Turkish nationals of Kurdish origin, should have been granted asylum on the ground that they were refugees within the meaning of art 1A(2) of the Geneva

Convention relating to the Status of Refugees (Geneva, 28 July 1951; TS 39 (1953); Cmnd 9171) (the 1951 convention) and the 1967 Protocol to that convention (New York, 31 January 1967; TS 15 (1969); Cmnd 3906). The ground upon which asylum was claimed related to their liability, if returned to Turkey, to perform compulsory military service on pain of imprisonment if they refused. Their claims for asylum were rejected by the respondent Secretary of State, and challenges to his decisions were successively rejected by the Special Adjudicator (Mr JRLG Varcoe CMG), the Immigration Appeal Tribunal (Collins J and Mr PR Moulden) ([2000] Imm AR 445) and the Court of Appeal (Waller, Laws and Jonathan Parker LJJ) ([2001] EWCA Civ 681, [2001] Imm AR 452). In argument before the House, as in the Court of Appeal, helpful submissions were made on behalf of the United Nations High Commissioner for Refugees.

[2] By s 8(1) of the Asylum and Immigration Appeals Act 1993 (in force at the relevant time):

'A person who is refused leave to enter the United Kingdom under the 1971 [Immigration] Act may appeal against the refusal to a special adjudicator on the ground that his removal in consequence of the refusal would be contrary to the United Kingdom's obligations under the [1951] Convention.'

Paragraph 334 of the Immigration Rules (1994) (HC 395) expands the language of the subsection:

'An asylum applicant will be granted asylum in the United Kingdom if the Secretary of State is satisfied that: (i) he is in the United Kingdom ... and (ii) he is a refugee, as defined by the Convention and Protocol; and (iii) refusing his application would result in his being required to go ... in breach of the Convention and Protocol, to a country in which his life or freedom would be threatened on account of his race, religion, nationality, political opinion or membership of a particular social group.'

These last words reproduce some of the language of the 1951 convention itself, made in direct response to what was then very recent history. Thus the preamble to that convention referred to the rights and freedoms recognised in the Universal Declaration of Human Rights (Paris, 10 December 1948; UNTS 2 (1949); Cmd 7226) approved in 1948 and recorded that the United Nations had 'on various occasions manifested its profound concern for refugees and endeavoured to assure refugees the widest possible exercise of these fundamental rights and freedoms'. For purposes of the 1951 convention a refugee was defined by art 1A(2) to mean any person who—

'owing to well-founded fear of being persecuted for reasons of race, religion, nationality, membership of a particular social group or political opinion, is outside the country of his nationality and is unable or, owing to such fear, is unwilling to avail himself of the protection of that country ...'

In the very extensive discussion of this definition the five grounds specified have conveniently come to be known as 'convention reasons'. Article 1 of the convention also contains, at art 1F, an important exclusion:

'The provisions of this Convention shall not apply to any person with respect to whom there are serious reasons for considering that: (a) he has committed a crime against peace, a war crime, or a crime against humanity, as defined in the international instruments drawn up to make provision in

a
respect of such crimes; (b) he has committed a serious non-political crime outside the country of refuge prior to his admission to that country as a refugee; (c) he has been guilty of acts contrary to the purposes and principles of the United Nations.'

[3] In any asylum case the facts are all important and these cases are no
b exception. The first applicant, now aged 32, has not claimed to have a conscientious objection to bearing arms, serving his country or donning a uniform. His objections to military service stemmed from his political opposition to the policies of the then Turkish government and from his wish not to be required to participate in actions, including atrocities, which he alleged to be
c perpetrated against his own people in the Kurdish areas of the country. The special adjudicator accepted that this applicant's reluctance to perform military service stemmed from his genuine political opinions, but found no reasonable likelihood that he would be required to engage in military action contrary to the basic rules of human conduct, even assuming that he was required to serve in a predominantly Kurdish area of Turkey. This applicant's wish to avoid military
d service was at least one of his reasons for leaving Turkey (which he did in 1990). He would still be regarded as liable for conscription on his return and might be charged with the offence of draft evasion, not having returned sooner. Any further refusal on his part would almost certainly lead to the preferment of charges against him.

e [4] The second applicant is now 25. He arrived in the United Kingdom in 1996. He later claimed that he would have received his call-up papers in August 1997 and become liable to call-up in about February 1998. He would be liable to be apprehended on his return to Turkey and to face a charge of draft evasion if he continued to refuse to serve. He has not claimed that he would refuse to wear
f uniform in all circumstances. His objection to performing military service related to his general antipathy towards the policy of the then Turkish government to oppose self-determination for the Kurdish people. He also feared that he might be sent to the operational area and required to take part in military action, possibly involving atrocities and abuse of human rights, against his own people.
g The special adjudicator found that this applicant's objection was not one of moral conviction but, rather, stemmed from his political views. He found no reasonable likelihood that this applicant would be required to engage in, or be associated with, acts offending against the basic rules of human conduct.

[5] Turkish law at present provides no non-combatant alternative to military
h service. Draft evaders are liable to a prison sentence of between six months and three years. On completion of the sentence the offender is required to undertake his military service. It is an agreed fact that those who refuse to perform military service in Turkey (including Kurds) are not subject to disproportionate or excessive punishment, in law or in fact, as a result of their refusal. Draft evaders are liable to
j prosecution and punishment irrespective of the reasons prompting their refusal.

[6] The task of the House is to interpret the 1951 convention and, having done so, apply it to the facts of the applicants' cases, between which it is unnecessary to distinguish. In interpreting the convention the House must respect arts 31 and 32 of the Vienna Convention on the Law of Treaties (Vienna, 23 May 1969; TS 58 (1980); Cmnd 7964):

'ARTICLE 31

General rule of interpretation

1. A treaty shall be interpreted in good faith in accordance with the ordinary meaning to be given to the terms of the treaty in their context and in the light of its object and purpose.

2. The context for the purpose of the interpretation of a treaty shall comprise, in addition to the text, including its preamble and annexes: (a) any agreement relating to the treaty which was made between all the parties in connexion with the conclusion of the treaty; (b) any instrument which was made by one or more parties in connexion with the conclusion of the treaty and accepted by the other parties as an instrument related to the treaty.

3. There shall be taken into account, together with the context: (a) any subsequent agreement between the parties regarding the interpretation of the treaty or the application of its provisions; (b) any subsequent practice in the application of the treaty which establishes the agreement of the parties regarding its interpretation; (c) any relevant rules of international law applicable in the relations between the parties.

4. A special meaning shall be given to a term if it is established that the parties so intended.

ARTICLE 32

Supplementary means of interpretation

Recourse may be had to supplementary means of interpretation, including the preparatory work of the treaty and the circumstances of its conclusion, in order to confirm the meaning resulting from the application of article 31, or to determine the meaning when the interpretation according to article 31: (a) leaves the meaning ambiguous or obscure; or (b) leads to a result which is manifestly absurd or unreasonable.'

It is plain that the convention has a single autonomous meaning, to which effect should be given in and by all member states, regardless of where a decision falls to be made (see *R v Secretary of State for the Home Dept, ex p Adan, R v Secretary of State for the Home Dept, ex p Aitseguer* [2001] 1 All ER 593, [2001] 2 AC 477). It is also, I think, plain that the convention must be seen as a living instrument in the sense that while its meaning does not change over time its application will. I would agree with the observation of Sedley J in *R v Immigration Appeal Tribunal, ex p Shah* [1997] Imm AR 145 at 152:

'Unless it [the convention] is seen as a living thing, adopted by civilised countries for a humanitarian end which is constant in motive but mutable in form, the Convention will eventually become an anachronism.'

I would also endorse the observation of Laws LJ in *R v Secretary of State for the Home Dept, ex p Adan, R v Secretary of State for the Home Dept, ex p Aitseguer* [1999] 4 All ER 774 at 795, [2001] 2 AC 477 at 500:

'It is clear that the signatory states intended that the convention should afford continuing protection for refugees in the changing circumstances of the present and future world. In our view the convention has to be regarded as a living instrument: just as, by the Strasbourg jurisprudence, the European Convention on Human Rights is so regarded.'

a [7] To make good their claim to asylum as refugees it was necessary for the applicants to show, to the standard of reasonable likelihood or real risk, (1) that they feared, if they had remained in or were returned to Turkey, that they would be persecuted, (2) for one or more of the convention reasons, and (3) that such fear was well founded. Although it is no doubt true, as stated in *Sandralingham v Secretary of State for the Home Dept, Rajendrakumar v Immigration Appeal Tribunal*

b [1996] Imm AR 97 at 109, that the 1951 convention definition raises a single composite question, analysis requires consideration of the constituent elements of the definition. At the heart of the definition lies the concept of persecution. It is when a person, suffering or fearing persecution in country A, flees to country B that it becomes the duty of country B to afford him (by the grant of asylum) the protection denied him by or under the laws of country A. History provides many

c examples of racial, religious, national, social and political minorities (sometimes even majorities) which have without doubt suffered persecution. But it is a strong word. Its dictionary definitions (save in their emphasis on religious persecution) accord with popular usage: '... the infliction of death, torture, or penalties for adherence to a religious belief or an opinion as such, with a view to

d the repression or extirpation of it ...'; 'A particular course or period of systematic infliction of punishment directed against the professors of a (religious) belief ...': *Oxford English Dictionary* (2nd edn, 1989). Valuable guidance is given by Professor Hathaway *The Law of Refugee Status* (1991) p 112, in a passage relied on by Lord Hope of Craighead in *Horvath v Secretary of State for the Home Dept* [2000] 3 All ER 577 at 581, [2001] 1 AC 489 at 495:

e
'In sum, persecution is most appropriately defined as the sustained or systemic failure of state protection in relation to one of the core entitlements which has been recognised by the international community.'

In this passage Professor Hathaway draws attention to a second requirement, no
f less important than that of showing persecution: the requirement to show, as a condition of entitlement to recognition as a refugee, that the persecution feared will (in reasonable likelihood) be for one or more of the five convention reasons. As Dawson J pointed out in the High Court of Australia in *A v Minister for Immigration and Ethnic Affairs* (1997) 2 BHRC 143 at 160:

g
'By including in its operative provisions the requirement that a refugee fear persecution, the convention limits its humanitarian scope and does not afford universal protection to asylum seekers. No matter how devastating may be epidemic, natural disaster or famine, a person fleeing them is not a refugee within the terms of the convention. And by incorporating the five
h convention reasons the convention plainly contemplates that there will even be persons fearing persecution who will not be able to gain asylum as refugees.'

[8] There is compelling support for the view that refugee status should be accorded to one who has refused to undertake compulsory military service on the
j grounds that such service would or might require him to commit atrocities or gross human rights abuses or participate in a conflict condemned by the international community, or where refusal to serve would earn grossly excessive or disproportionate punishment (see, for example, *Zolfagharkhani v Canada (Minister of Employment and Immigration)* [1993] FC 540, *Ciric v Canada (Minister of Employment and Immigration)* [1994] 2 FC 65, *Canas-Segovia v Immigration and*

Naturalization Service (1990) 902 F 2d 717, *UNHCR Handbook on Procedures and Criteria for Determining Refugee Status* (paras 169, 171)). But the applicants cannot, on the facts as found, bring themselves within any of these categories. Nor have they been found to have a rooted objection to all military service of any kind, or an objection based on religious belief. Their unwillingness to serve is based on their strong and sincere opposition to the policy of the Turkish government towards their own Kurdish community. There can be no doubt that the applicants' fear of the treatment which they will receive if they are returned to Turkey and maintain their refusal to serve is well founded: it is the treatment described in [5], above. The crucial question is whether the treatment which the applicants reasonably fear is to be regarded, for purposes of the 1951 convention, as persecution for one or more of the convention reasons.

[9] The core of the applicants' argument in the Court of Appeal was summarised by Laws LJ ([2001] Imm AR 452 at [19]) in these terms:

'(i) There exists a fundamental right, which is internationally recognised, to refuse to undertake military service on grounds of conscience. (ii) Where an individual, motivated by genuine conscientious grounds, refuses to undertake such service and the state offers no civilian or non-combative alternative, the prospect of his prosecution and punishment for evading the draft would if carried into effect amount to persecution for a Convention reason within article 1A(2) (assuming, what is not in contention in these cases, that the nature of the punishment would be sufficiently severe to amount to potential persecution). (iii) Proposition (ii) applies alike to cases of absolute and partial conscientious grounds; and the [applicants], on the proved or admitted facts, are refugees according to this reasoning.'

This was the thrust of the applicants' case before the House also. The key is to be found in submission (i): for while discriminatory infringement of a recognised human right may not necessarily constitute persecution for convention reasons, Mr Nicol QC for the applicants accepted that there could be no persecution for convention reasons without discriminatory infringement of a recognised human right. So it is necessary to investigate whether the treatment which the applicants reasonably fear would infringe a recognised human right.

[10] The leading international human rights instruments, literally interpreted, give little assistance to the applicants' argument. The Universal Declaration of Human Rights in 1948 prohibited slavery or servitude (art 4) and declared a right to freedom of thought, conscience and religion, including a right to manifest religion or belief publicly or privately (art 18), but it made no express reference to a right of conscientious objection. A very similar right to freedom of thought, conscience and religion is embodied in the European Convention on Human Rights and Fundamental Freedoms 1950 (as set out in Sch 1 to the Human Rights Act 1998) (the ECHR) (art 9) and in the International Covenant on Civil and Political Rights (New York, 19 December 1966; TS 6 (1977); Cmnd 6702) (the ICCPR) (art 18). Each of these instruments also (in arts 4 and 8 respectively) outlaws slavery, servitude and forced or compulsory labour. But in art 8(3)(c) of the ICCPR it is expressly provided that 'forced or compulsory labour' shall not include: '(ii) Any service of a military character and, in countries where conscientious objection is recognized, any national service required by law of conscientious objectors ...' Despite minor differences of wording, art 4(3)(b) of the ECHR is to identical effect. At the time when these provisions were drafted

a and adopted, it was plainly contemplated that there could be states, parties to the respective conventions, which did not recognise a right of conscientious objection and did not provide a non-combatant alternative to compulsory military service. Articles 4(3)(b) of the ECHR and 8(3)(c) of the ICCPR have not been amended by international agreement, and there has been no later convention recognising or defining or regulating a right of conscientious
b objection.

[11] For reasons on which I have already touched, the reach of an international human rights convention is not forever determined by the intentions of those who originally framed it. Thus, like the Court of Appeal, the House was appropriately asked to consider a mass of material illustrating the movement of international opinion among those concerned with human rights
c and refugees in the period, now a very significant period, since the major relevant conventions were adopted. A large number of these materials were listed by Waller LJ ([2001] Imm AR 452 at [194]), and they were also considered at length by Laws LJ. From these materials it is plain that several respected human rights bodies have recommended and urged member states to recognise a right of
d conscientious objection to compulsory military service, to provide a non-combatant alternative to it and to consider the grant of asylum to genuine conscientious objectors. But resolutions and recommendations of this kind, however sympathetic one may be towards their motivation and purpose, cannot themselves establish a legal rule binding in international law. I shall accordingly confine my attention to five documents which seem to me most directly relevant
e in ascertaining the point which international opinion has now reached.

[12] Mention must first be made of the *UNHCR Handbook* which, subject to minor editing, dates from 1979 and is recognised as an important source of guidance on matters to which it relates. It is necessary to quote paras 167–174:

f 'Deserters and persons avoiding military service

167. In countries where military service is compulsory, failure to perform this duty is frequently punishable by law. Moreover, whether military service is compulsory or not, desertion is invariably considered a criminal offence. The penalties may vary from country to country, and are not normally regarded as persecution. Fear of prosecution and punishment for
g desertion or draft-evasion does not in itself constitute well-founded fear of persecution under the definition. Desertion or draft-evasion does not, on the other hand, exclude a person from being a refugee, and a person may be a refugee in addition to being a deserter or draft-evader.

168. A person is clearly not a refugee if his only reason for desertion or
h draft-evasion is his dislike of military service or fear of combat. He may, however, be a refugee if his desertion or evasion of military service is concomitant with other relevant motives for leaving or remaining outside his country, or if he otherwise has reasons, within the meaning of the definition, to fear persecution.

j 169. A deserter or draft-evader may also be considered a refugee if it can be shown that he would suffer disproportionately severe punishment for the military offence on account of his race, religion, nationality, membership of a particular social group or political opinion. The same would apply if it can be shown that he has well-founded fear of persecution on these grounds above and beyond the punishment for desertion.

170. There are, however, also cases where the necessity to perform
military service may be the sole ground for a claim to refugee status, ie when
a person can show that the performance of military service would have
required his participation in military action contrary to his genuine political,
religious or moral convictions, or to valid reasons of conscience.

171. Not every conviction, genuine though it may be, will constitute a
sufficient reason for claiming refugee status after desertion or draft-evasion.
It is not enough for a person to be in disagreement with his government
regarding the political justification for a particular military action. Where,
however, the type of military action, with which an individual does not wish
to be associated, is condemned by the international community as contrary
to basic rules of human conduct, punishment for desertion or draft-evasion
could, in the light of all other requirements of the definition, in itself be
regarded as persecution.

172. Refusal to perform military service may also be based on religious
convictions. If an applicant is able to show that his religious convictions are
genuine, and that such convictions are not taken into account by the
authorities of his country in requiring him to perform military service, he
may be able to establish a claim to refugee status. Such a claim would, of
course, be supported by any additional indications that the applicant or his
family may have encountered difficulties due to their religious convictions.

173. The question as to whether objection to performing military service
for reasons of conscience can give rise to a valid claim to refugee status
should also be considered in the light of more recent developments in this
field. An increasing number of States have introduced legislation or
administrative regulations whereby persons who can invoke genuine
reasons of conscience are exempted from military service, either entirely or
subject to their performing alternative (ie civilian) service. The introduction
of such legislation or administrative regulations has also been the subject of
recommendations by international agencies. In the light of these
developments, it would be open to Contracting States, to grant refugee
status to persons who object to performing military service for genuine
reasons of conscience.

174. The genuineness of a person's political, religious or moral
convictions, or of his reasons of conscience for objecting to performing
military service, will of course need to be established by a thorough
investigation of his personality and background. The fact that he may have
manifested his views prior to being called to arms, or that he may already
have encountered difficulties with the authorities because of his convictions,
are relevant considerations. Whether he has been drafted into compulsory
service or joined the army as a volunteer may also be indicative of the
genuineness of his convictions.'

Some of these paragraphs may very readily be accepted. The paragraph most
helpful to the applicants is para 170. But this appears to be qualified by para 171,
which immediately follows and is much less helpful to the applicants. Less
helpful also is para 172, in its tentative suggestion that a person 'may be able to
establish a claim to refugee status'. The same comment may be made of para 173:
'... it would be open to Contracting States, to grant refugee status ...' Read as a
whole, these paragraphs do not in my opinion provide the clear statement which
the applicants need.

[13] The applicants understandably placed reliance on General Comment 22
(30 July 1993) of the United Nations Human Rights Committee, which in para 11
said (with reference to art 18 of the ICCPR):

> '11. Many individuals have claimed the right to refuse to perform military
> service (conscientious objection) on the basis that such right derives from
> their freedoms under article 18. In response to such claims, a growing
> number of States have in their laws exempted from compulsory military
> service citizens who genuinely hold religious or other beliefs that forbid the
> performance of military service and replaced it with alternative national
> service. The Covenant does not explicitly refer to a right to conscientious
> objection, but the Committee believes that such a right can be derived from
> article 18, inasmuch as the obligation to use lethal force may seriously
> conflict with the freedom of conscience and the right to manifest one's
> religion or belief. When this right is recognized by law or practice, there
> shall be no differentiation among conscientious objectors on the basis of the
> nature of their particular beliefs; likewise, there shall be no discrimination
> against conscientious objectors because they have failed to perform military
> service. The Committee invites States parties to report on the conditions
> under which persons can be exempted from military service on the basis of
> their rights under article 18 and on the nature and length of alternative
> national service.'

This is perhaps the nearest one comes to a suggestion that a right of conscientious
objection can be derived from art 18 of the ICCPR. But it is, again, a somewhat
tentative suggestion ('believes that such a right can be derived'), and the
Committee implicitly acknowledges that there are member states in which a
right of conscientious objection is not recognised by law or practice. Thus while
the thrust of the Committee's thinking is plain, one finds no clear assertion of
binding principle.

[14] I turn next to the Joint Position adopted by the Council of the European
Union on the harmonised application of the term 'refugee' in art 1 of the 1951
convention (see OJ 1996 L63 p 2). Paragraph 10 (p 6) of this Joint Position was
entitled 'Conscientious objection, absence without leave and desertion' and
reads:

> 'The fear of punishment for conscientious objection, absence without
> leave or desertion is investigated on an individual basis. It should in itself be
> insufficient to justify recognition of refugee status. The penalty must be
> assessed in particular in accordance with the principles set out in point 5. In
> cases of absence without leave or desertion, the person concerned must be
> accorded refugee status if the conditions under which military duties are
> performed themselves constitute persecution. Similarly, refugee status may
> be granted, in the light of all the other requirements of the definition, in cases
> of punishment of conscientious objection or deliberate absence without
> leave and desertion on grounds of conscience if the performance of his
> military duties were to have the effect of leading the person concerned to
> participate in acts falling under the exclusion clauses in Article 1F of the
> Geneva Convention ...'

The reference to 'point 5' appears to refer most specifically to sub-para 5.1.2(b)
which reads:

'*Discriminatory punishment*

    Punishment or the threat thereof on the basis of a universally applicable *a* criminal law provision will be discriminatory if persons who breach the law are punished but certain persons are subject to more severe punishment on account of characteristics likely to lead to the award of refugee status. The discriminatory element in the punishment imposed is essential. Persecution may be deemed to exist in the event of a disproportionate sentence, provided *b* that there is a link with one of the grounds of persecution referred to in Article 1A.'

This statement recognises the grounds for claiming asylum to which I have referred in [8], above. But it goes no further, and the statement is prefaced by a rider that 'it shall not bind the legislative authorities or affect decisions of the *c* judicial authorities of the member states'.

    [15] I refer next to the Charter of Fundamental Rights of the European Union, which includes art 10:

'Freedom of thought, conscience and religion

    1. Everyone has the right to freedom of thought, conscience and religion. *d* This right includes freedom to change religion or belief and freedom, either alone or in community with others and in public or in private, to manifest religion or belief, in worship, teaching, practice and observance.

    2. The right to conscientious objection is recognised, in accordance with the national laws governing the exercise of this right.' *e*

While para 1 is said to derive, as it plainly does, from art 9 of the ECHR, para 2 is said to derive from national constitutional traditions. The applicants' difficulty is that national laws and national constitutional traditions may, or may not, recognise a right of conscientious objection; in any event, the Treaty of Nice expressly acknowledged that the status of the Charter of Fundamental Rights was *f* a matter to be addressed thereafter.

    [16] Lastly, in this context I would refer to a draft directive of the Council of the European Union (dated 28 November 2002) on minimum standards for the qualification of third country nationals as refugees. Since the draft may be amended, and may never be adopted, it must be received with caution. But since it is seeking to harmonise member states' interpretation of the requirements of *g* art 1A(2) of the 1951 convention, and since (although provisional) it represents the most recent statement on this subject which the House has seen, it seems to me to deserve attention. Chapter III concerns the qualification for being a refugee and art 11 (entitled 'Acts of persecution') provides:

    '1. Acts considered as persecution within the meaning of Article 1A of the *h* Geneva Convention must: (a) be sufficiently serious by their nature or repetition as to constitute a severe violation of basic human rights, in particular the rights from which derogation cannot be made under Article 15(2) of the European Convention for the Protection of Human Rights and Fundamental Freedoms; or (b) be an accumulation of various measures, *j* including violations of human rights which is sufficiently severe as to affect an individual in a similar manner as mentioned in sub-paragraph (a).

    2. Acts of persecution, which can be qualified as such in accordance with paragraph 1, can inter alia take the form of ... (e) prosecution or punishment for refusal to perform military service in a conflict, where performing

a military service would include crimes or acts falling under the exclusion clauses as set out in Article 14, paragraph 2 …'

Article 14 is entitled 'Exclusion' and provides in para (2):

b 'A third country national … is excluded from being a refugee where there are serious reasons for considering that: (a) he or she has committed a crime against peace, a war crime, or a crime against humanity, as defined in the international instruments drawn up to make provision in respect of such crimes; (b) he or she has committed a serious non-political crime outside the country of refuge prior to his or her admission as a refugee; which means the time of issuing a residence permit based on the granting of refugee status; particularly cruel actions, even if committed with an allegedly political

c objective, may be classified as serious non-political crimes; (c) he or she has been guilty of acts contrary to the purposes and principles of the United Nations as set out in the Preamble and Articles 1 and 2 of the Charter of the United Nations.'

d This statement plainly affords a narrower ground for claiming asylum than some of the statements quoted above. It may be thought too narrow and may no doubt be widened in the course of negotiation. But it makes it hard for the applicants to show that there is clear international recognition of the right for which they contend, at any rate as of now. This temporal limitation is important, since international opinion is dynamic and the House cannot do more than give effect

e to what it understands to be the current position.

[17] It is necessary to consider whether the applicants' contention finds compelling support in the decided cases. There are undoubtedly authorities on which they can properly rely, notably *Canas-Segovia v Immigration and Naturalization Service* (1990) 902 F 2d 717, *Canas-Segovia v Immigration and Naturalization Service* (1992) 970 F 2d 599 and *Erduran v Minister for Immigration and Multicultural Affairs*

f [2002] FCA 814. But the first of these decisions is in my opinion open to the criticism made of it by Jonathan Parker LJ ([2001] Imm AR 452 at [147]–[150]), and the second does not sit altogether comfortably with the decision of the majority of the High Court of Australia in *Minister for Immigration and Multicultural Affairs v Yusuf* [2001] HCA 30, (2001) 206 CLR 323. They can scarcely

g be said to constitute a settled body of judicial opinion. Against them must be set a line of decisions of the European Commission on Human Rights which have, at least until recently, held the right asserted by the applicants to be excluded by art 4(3)(b) of the ECHR (see *Grandrath v Germany* (1965) 8 YB 324, *Grandrath v Germany* (1967) 10 YB 626, *X v Austria* (1973) 43 CD 161, *A v Switzerland* (1984) 38 DR 219, *Johansen v Norway* (1985) 44 DR 155, *Autio v Finland* (1991) 72 DR 245 and

h *Heudens v Belgium* App No 24630/94 (22 May 1995, unreported)). The applicants drew support from the dissent of one Commission member in *Tsirlis v Greece* (1998) 25 EHRR 198 at 224–226, a dissent which was repeated and elaborated, with a greater body of support, in the report of the Commission adopted on 4 December 1998 in the case of *Thlimmenos v Greece* App No 34369/97

j (4 December 1998, unreported) (paras 3, 4). This dissenting view was not however adopted by the European Court of Human Rights when the case came before it ((2000) 31 EHRR 411). Whether the imposition of sanctions on conscientious objectors to compulsory military service might, notwithstanding art 4(3)(b) of the ECHR, infringe the right to freedom of thought, conscience and religion guaranteed by art 9(1) was a point which the court (at 424, 426 (paras 43,

53)) expressly left open. I am in respectful agreement with the detailed analysis of this authority made by Jonathan Parker LJ ([2001] Imm AR 452 at [124]–[139]). While, therefore, there are indications of changed thinking among a minority of members of the Commission, there is as yet no authority to support the applicants' contention.

[18] It is not in my opinion necessary to explore the circumstances in which the practice of states may give rise to a right commanding international recognition, since the evidence before the House does not disclose a uniformity of practice. It is no doubt true that the dependence of modern warfare on sophisticated weaponry and technological skill has lessened the need for mass armies and so diminished the dependence of some states on conscription. Thus in Europe several states currently have no conscription, and of those that do the great majority recognise a right of conscientious objection. But figures based on a 1998 report by War Registers International show a somewhat different picture worldwide. Of 180 states surveyed, some form of conscription was found to exist in 95. In 52 of those 95 states the right of conscientious objection was found not to be recognised at all. In a further seven of those 95 states there was no known provision governing a right of conscientious objection. In the remaining 36 states the right of conscientious objection appeared to be recognised to some extent. It could not, currently, be said that there is de facto observance of anything approaching a uniform rule.

[19] In the course of his judgment, Laws LJ ([2001] Imm AR 452 at [23]–[24]) quoted the works of two respected authorities on refugee law, Professor Hathaway *The Law of Refugee Status* (1991) and Professor Goodwin-Gill *The Refugee in International Law* (2nd edn, 1996). It is unnecessary to repeat his citations, also relied on before the House. It is however noteworthy that Professor Hathaway (at p 182) describes the right to conscientious objection as 'an emerging part of international human rights law' and Professor Goodwin-Gill observes (at p 55) that 'The international community nevertheless appears to be moving towards acceptance of a right of conscientious objection.' Both, in short, discern movement towards recognition of a right, but neither suggests it has yet been achieved. In a report prepared for the appeal of the first applicant, it is true, Professor Goodwin-Gill went a little further (see the judgment of Laws LJ ([2001] Imm AR 452 at [25])); but even then he suggests what states ought to do, and suggests that recognition of a right of conscientious objection ought to derive from the protection given to freedom of conscience by customary international law and universal human rights treaties. The problem, to my mind, is that the treaties have treated compulsory military service as an exception from the forced labour prohibition without making any other provision, and I do not think there is, as yet, a new consensus.

[20] On the main issue to which this opinion has so far been addressed, the Court of Appeal was divided. Of absolute conscientious objectors Laws LJ concluded (at [79]):

'In the result, I would hold that there is no material to establish a presently extant legal rule or principle which vouchsafes a right of absolute conscientious objection, such that where it is not respected, a good case to refugee status under the Convention may arise. No such putative rule or principle is to be found in the Convention's international autonomous meaning or common standard.'

a Turning to partial conscientious objectors he reached (at [84]) a similar conclusion:

> 'It is plain, however, that no matter how clear the political basis for a partial objection may be, there is in such a case no more of an international underpinning, by treaty or customary law, to quicken the objector's claim into a legal right than in the case of the absolute objector. In my judgment, therefore, such a claim is stillborn for all the reasons I have already given.'

b

Jonathan Parker LJ (at [100]) shared his view. Waller LJ took a view more favourable in principle to the applicants. Of absolute objectors he said (at [201]):

c
> 'Thus if someone can show that he/she is a genuine conscientious objector, that he/she is to be conscripted into a military in a state that simply does not recognise the possibility of such conscientious belief, and that he/she will be prosecuted as a result, in my view he/she will have established a well-founded fear of persecution for a Convention reason. That however does not dispose of the appeals before us.'

d
His opinion (at [208]) in the case of partial objectors was similar:

> 'In my view thus a partial objector *may* be able to show a deep-seated conscientious reason why he/she should not be conscripted by reference to the fact that he/she will be required to take part in a war against his/her own ethnic community, and may show an infringement of article 9(1), but it takes
e more than mere disagreement with a policy that allows Kurds to be conscripted to fight Kurds to establish that position.'

Thus although there was agreement on the outcome, there was disagreement on the intervening steps. Despite my genuine respect for the care and thoroughness
f with which Waller LJ has put forward his conclusions, and with a measure of reluctance since they may well reflect the international consensus of tomorrow, I feel compelled to accept the view of the Court of Appeal majority on the state of the law today as revealed by the abundant materials before us. That conclusion is fatal to the success of these appeals, which I would accordingly dismiss.

g
[21] This conclusion makes it strictly unnecessary to determine a further issue raised by the respondent Secretary of State, but since the House heard full argument and the issue is one of great practical importance I think it desirable to express an opinion. It was argued that, in deciding whether an asylum applicant had been or would be persecuted for convention reasons—

h
> 'the examination of the circumstances should be approached from the perspective of the persecutor, since that is the perspective that is determinative in inciting the persecution (see *A-G of Canada v Ward* [1993] 2 SCR 689 at 747).'

j Support for this approach is found in *Immigration and Naturalization Service v Elias-Zacarias* (1992) 502 US 478, a decision very strongly criticised by Professor Hathaway (see 'The Causal Nexus in International Refugee Law' (2002) 23 Mich J Int'l L 207). The Court of Appeal unanimously rejected this argument ([2001] Imm AR 452 at [92], [154], [182])) and some of the authorities point towards a more objective approach (see *Chen Shi Hai v Minister for Immigration and*

Multicultural Affairs [2000] HCA 19, (2000) 201 CLR 293 at 304, 313 (paras 33, 65),
Refugee Appeal No 72635/01 (6 September 2002, unreported) paras 167–173)).

[22] I would express the test somewhat differently from the Court of Appeal
in this case. In his judgment in *Sivakumar v Secretary of State for the Home Dept*
[2001] EWCA Civ 1196 at [23], [2002] INLR 310 at [23], Dyson LJ stated: 'It is
necessary for the person who is considering the claim for asylum to assess
carefully the real reason for the persecution.' This seems to me to be a clear,
simple and workmanlike test which gives effect to the 1951 convention provided
that it is understood that the reason is the reason which operates in the mind of
the persecutor and not the reason which the victim believes to be the reason for
the persecution, and that there may be more than one real reason. The
application of the test calls for the exercise of an objective judgment. Decision
makers are not concerned (subject to a qualification mentioned below) to explore
the motives or purposes of those who have committed or may commit acts of
persecution, nor the belief of the victim as to those motives or purposes. Having
made the best assessment possible of all the facts and circumstances, they must
label or categorise the reason for the persecution. The qualification mentioned is
that where the reason for the persecution is or may be the imputation by the
persecutors of a particular belief or opinion (or, for that matter, the attribution of
a racial origin or nationality or membership of a particular social group) one is
concerned not with the correctness of the matter imputed or attributed but with
the belief of the persecutor: the real reason for the persecution of a victim may be
the persecutor's belief that he holds extreme political opinions or adheres to a
particular faith even if in truth the victim does not hold those opinions or belong
to that faith. I take this approach to reflect that put forward by McHugh J in
Minister for Immigration and Multicultural Affairs v Ibrahim [2000] HCA 55, (2000)
204 CLR 1 at 33 (para 102):

> 'In this case, among the questions which the Tribunal should have asked
> were (a) what harm does the applicant fear on his return to Somalia? (b) is
> that fear well-founded? (c) *why* will the applicant be subjected to that harm?
> and (d) if the answer to (c) is "because of his membership of a particular
> social group", would the harm constitute persecution for the purpose of the
> Convention?'

Treatment is not persecutory if it is treatment meted out to all and is not
discriminatory (see *A v Minister for Immigration and Ethnic Affairs* (1997) 2 BHRC
143 at 168 per McHugh J). The question held to be appropriate in the field of
racial discrimination in *Qureshi v Victoria University of Manchester* (1996) [2001] ICR
863 at 874, suitably adapted to the particular case, is in my view apt in this context
also: 'Were racial grounds an effective cause of the difference in treatment?'

[23] However difficult the application of the test to the facts of particular
cases, I do not think that the test to be applied should itself be problematical. The
decision-maker will begin by considering the reason in the mind of the persecutor
for inflicting the persecutory treatment. That reason would, in this case, be the
applicants' refusal to serve in the army. But the decision maker does not stop
there. He asks if that is the real reason, or whether there is some other effective
reason. The victims' belief that the treatment is inflicted because of their political
opinions is beside the point unless the decision-maker concludes that the holding
of such opinions was the, or a, real reason for the persecutory treatment. On the
facts here, that would not be a tenable view, since it is clear that anyone refusing

a to serve would be treated in the same way, whatever his personal grounds for refusing.

LORD STEYN.

[24] My Lords, I have had the privilege of reading the opinion of Lord Bingham of Cornhill. I am in complete agreement with it. For the reasons he has *b* given I would also dismiss the appeals.

LORD HOFFMANN.

[25] My Lords, the applicants are Kurdish Turks who came to this country at the ages of 19 and 18 respectively. They were shortly to become liable under *c* Turkish law to military service. On arrival in the United Kingdom they claimed asylum on various grounds, of which the only one now relied upon is a fear that if returned to Turkey they would be prosecuted for refusing to enlist. They claim that their refusal was on the ground of their deeply held political objections to the policies of the then Turkish government towards the Kurdish minority. This, they say, was sufficient to entitle them to asylum because punishment for *d* refusing military service on such grounds would be persecution for reasons of their political opinions within the meaning of the Geneva Convention relating to the Status of Refugees (Geneva, 28 July 1951; TS 39 (1953); Cmnd 9171) (the 1951 convention).

[26] I emphasise that the case is put simply on the basis that they would be *e* liable to punishment for refusing to perform military service. This is because of two important findings of fact by the special adjudicator which are now not challenged and which form part of the agreed statement of facts. The first is that the penalty for draft evasion (a prison sentence of six months to three years) is not disproportionate or excessive. The second is that there is no reasonable likelihood that the applicants would have been required to engage in military *f* action contrary to basic rules of human conduct, whether against Kurds or anyone else.

[27] The Secretary of State says that in these circumstances there is nothing wrong or unusual in Turkey having compulsory military service and suitable penalties for disobedience. If the applicants refuse to serve, the state is entitled to *g* punish them, not for their political opinions but for failing to enlist. Their political opinions may be the reason why they refuse to serve but they are not the reason why they will be punished. They are free to hold whatever opinions they please about Turkish policy towards the Kurds as long as they report for duty. Putting the same point in a different way, imposing a punishment for failing to comply with a universal obligation of this kind is not persecution.

h **[28]** Mr Nicol QC, who appeared for the applicants, says that it is not so simple. Treating some group of people in the same way as everyone else may be persecuting them if their group has a right to be treated differently. For example, in *Thlimmenos v Greece* (2001) 31 EHRR 411 the appellant was refused appointment as a chartered accountant pursuant to a general law which *j* disqualified anyone who had been convicted of felony. The applicant's felony had been a refusal to do military service on the ground of his religious convictions as a Jehovah's Witness. The European Court of Human Rights held (at 424–425 (para 44)) that the disqualification infringed the anti-discrimination provisions of art 14 of the European Convention on Human Rights and Fundamental Freedoms 1950 (as set out in Sch 1 to the Human Rights Act 1998) (the ECHR) because it failed to treat his felony, committed because of his religious principles, *a* differently from ordinary felonies:

> 'The right not to be discriminated against in the enjoyment of the rights guaranteed under the Convention is also violated when States without an objective and reasonable justification fail to treat differently persons whose situations are significantly different.' *b*

[29] The right guaranteed under the convention in respect of which there had been discrimination was the freedom of religion guaranteed by art 9. The court found that failure to treat the applicant differently had no objective justification. The conviction had no relevance to his suitability as an accountant and he had already been punished by a prison sentence for his refusal to do military service. *c*

[30] *Thlimmenos v Greece* therefore supports the proposition that, at any rate for the purposes of art 14, a law of general application may have a discriminatory effect if it contains no exceptions for people who have a right to be treated differently. But I note in passing that the court, while holding that Thlimmenos had a right to be treated differently in respect of qualification as an accountant, *d* expressed no view on the point which arises in this case, namely whether he would have had a right to be treated differently in respect of his obligation to perform military service. That would have required an altogether different assessment of objective justification.

[31] I shall consider later whether this principle of discrimination by failing to treat different cases differently can be fitted into the language of the 1951 *e* convention. Accepting for the moment that it can, I pass on to the next stage in Mr Nicol's argument, which is to show that it applies to laws imposing a general obligation to do military service. The question here is whether people who object to such service on conscientious religious or political grounds have a human right to be excused. *f*

[32] Mr Nicol accepts that ordinarily a conscientious religious or political objection is not a reason for being entitled to treat oneself as absolved from the laws of the state. In many western countries, including the United Kingdom, civil disobedience is an honourable tradition which goes back to Antigone. It may be vindicated by history—think of the suffragettes—but often what makes it *g* honourable and demonstrates the strength of conviction is willingness to accept the punishment. (That is not to agree with Socrates that it would necessarily be dishonourable to try to avoid punishment.) The standard moral position is summarised by Ronald Dworkin in *Taking Rights Seriously* (1977) pp 186–187:

> 'In a democracy, or at least a democracy that in principle respects *h* individual rights, each citizen has a general moral duty to obey all the laws, even though he would like some of them changed. He owes that duty to his fellow citizens, who obey laws that they do not like, to his benefit. But this general duty cannot be an absolute duty, because even a society that is in principle just may produce unjust laws and policies, and a man has duties *j* other than his duties to the state. A man must honour his duties to his God and to his conscience, and if these conflict with his duty to the state, then he is entitled, in the end, to do what he judges to be right. If he decides that he must break the law, however, then he must submit to the judgment and punishment that the state imposes, in recognition of the fact that his duty to

a his fellow citizens was overwhelmed but not extinguished by his religious or moral obligations.'

[33] This suggests that while the demonstrator or objector cannot be morally condemned, and may indeed be praised, for following the dictates of his conscience, it is not necessarily unjust for the state to punish him in the same way as any other person who breaks the law. It will of course be different if the law
b itself is unjust. The injustice of the law will carry over into its enforcement. But if the law is not otherwise unjust, as conscription is accepted in principle to be, then it does not follow that because his objection is conscientious, the state is not entitled to punish him. He has his reasons and the state, in the interests of its citizens generally, has different reasons. Both might be right.

c [34] That is certainly the view we would take of someone who, for example, refused to pay part of his taxes because he felt he could not conscientiously contribute to military expenditure, or insisted on chaining herself to a JCB because she thought it was morally offensive to destroy beautiful countryside to build a new motorway. As judges we would respect their views but might feel it necessary to punish them all the same. Whether we did so or not would be
d largely a pragmatic question. We would take into account their moral views but would not accept an unqualified moral duty to give way to them. On the contrary we might feel that although we sympathised and even shared the same opinions, we had to give greater weight to the need to enforce the law. In deciding whether or not to impose punishment, the most important
e consideration would be whether it would do more harm than good. This means that the objector has no right not to be punished. It is a matter for the state (including the judges) to decide on utilitarian grounds whether to do so or not. As Ronald Dworkin said in *A Matter of Principle* (1985) p 114: 'Utilitarianism may be a poor general theory of justice, but it states an excellent necessary condition for a just punishment.'

f [35] Mr Nicol was, I think, inclined to accept these principles as correct for most forms of civil disobedience. Conscientious objection to a law is not enough to make punishment unjust. It is not a reason why the objector has a right to be treated differently. But he said that military service was different. An obligation to kill people was something which the state could not justly impose upon
g anyone who had a deeply held objection to doing so.

[36] The difficulty about this argument is that it is accepted that in general the state does have the right to impose upon its citizens an obligation to kill people in war. It would of course be different if they were being asked to commit war crimes; in such a case, anyone could legitimately object. But ordinary army
h service, though demanding and often inconvenient, sometimes unpleasant and occasionally dangerous, is in many countries (and was in many more, including the United Kingdom) part of the citizen's ordinary duty.

[37] Mr Nicol did not offer a rational ground for distinguishing between objection to military service and objection to other laws. One might feel intuitively that some such ground might be constructed around the notion of the
j sanctity of life, although I am not sure that even that could be described as rational. In any event, it would not have served Mr Nicol's purpose because it does not form the basis of these applicants' objections. They would have no objection to fighting in a war for a Turkish (or Kurdish) government of the right political complexion. He appealed instead to the practice of nations and the opinions of jurists, which he says support the proposition that conscientious

objection to military service on any religious or political ground should be recognised.

[38] The question in this appeal is the meaning of the term 'refugee' in the 1951 convention. That in turn raises the question of what is meant by 'persecuted'. Mr Nicol says that if people are subjected to punishment which would be regarded as discriminatory by reference to their fundamental human rights, they are being persecuted. If those fundamental rights relate to their religious beliefs or political opinions, then they are being persecuted for reasons of those beliefs or opinions. My Lords, I have not attempted to examine all aspects of these propositions but for present purposes I am content to accept them. I shall therefore consider whether punishing conscientious objectors is an infringement of their fundamental human rights to freedom of conscience and opinion.

[39] How does one establish the scope of fundamental human rights for the purposes of an international convention such as the 1951 convention? Many state parties to the 1951 convention are also parties to human rights conventions, such as the ECHR and the International Covenant on Civil and Political Rights (New York, 19 December 1966; TS 6 (1977); Cmnd 6702) (the ICCPR). Mr Nicol says that the current state of human rights as expressed in those and other similar conventions is the best guide to their content for the purposes of the 1951 convention.

[40] Mr Howell QC, who appeared for the Secretary of State, said that the question was whether a right of conscientious objection had become part of customary international law. For that purpose there had to have been a general and consistent practice of states which was recognised as conforming to a legal obligation (see *Oppenheim's International Law* (9th edn, 1992) vol 1 pp 27–31 (ed Jennings and Watts)). There was plainly no such settled practice relating to conscientious objection. There are many countries, of which I shall mention some in a moment, which do not recognise it.

[41] I do not think it is possible to apply the rules for the development of rules of international law concerning the relations of states with each other (for example, as to how boundaries should be drawn) to the fundamental human rights of citizens against the state. There are unhappily many fundamental human rights which would fail such a test of state practice and the 1951 convention is itself a recognition of this fact. In my opinion a different approach is needed. Fundamental human rights are the minimum rights which a state ought to concede to its citizens. For the purpose of deciding what these minimum rights are, international instruments are important even if many state parties in practice disregard them. (The African Charter on Human and People's Rights, adopted in 1981, is perhaps a conspicuous example.) But the instruments show recognition that such rights *ought* to exist. The delinquent states do not normally deny this; they usually pretend that they comply. Equally, the fact that many states openly deny this existence of a human right is not necessarily a reason for saying that it does not exist. One may think, so much the worse for them. But state practice is nevertheless important because it is difficult to assert the existence of a universal fundamental human right disavowed by many states which take human rights seriously.

[42] As I have said, there are many countries which do not, or did not until relatively recently, recognise any form of conscientious objection. Those that do are not agreed on the grounds upon which it should be allowed. The Rapporteur

a of the Committee on Legal Affairs and Human Rights of the Council of Europe reported on 4 May 2001 on 'Exercise of the right of conscientious objection to military service in Council of Europe member states' (para 24): 'Grounds for exemption from military service range from a very limited list of reasons to a very broad interpretation of the concept of conscience.'

b [43] In the United Kingdom, for example, some forms of conscientious objection were recognised in both World Wars; the practice of the tribunals which decided claims to conscientious objector status does not appear to have been uniform.   Likewise in the United States conscientious objection is recognised, but the statutory grounds are more specific: the objection must be to all war and not merely to the particular war for which one is being conscripted. This ruled out people who did not object to serving in defence of their country *c* but thought that the Vietnam War, for example, was immoral.   In France conscientious objection was not recognised until 1963, after the end of the Algerian War, and in Germany it was recognised in the new 1949 constitution after the end of the 1935–45 war, when the German Army was in abeyance.   On the other hand, in many countries there is conscription and no conscientious *d* objection.

[44] What conclusions can one draw from these mixed data?   It seems to me that even in Europe and the United States, the recognition of conscientious objection, sometimes as a prelude to the abolition of conscription, does not demonstrate any recognition of a principle that conscientious objectors have a *e* moral right to be treated differently.   On the contrary, I think that practice supports Dworkin's view that recognition of the strength of the objector's religious, moral or political feelings is only part of a complex judgment that includes the pragmatic question as to whether compelling conscientious objectors to enlist or suffer punishment will do more harm than good.   Among the other relevant factors are the following: first, martyrs attract sympathy, *f* particularly if they suffer on religious grounds in a country which takes religion seriously; secondly, unwilling soldiers may not be very effective; thirdly, they tend to be articulate people who may spread their views in the ranks; fourthly, modern military technology requires highly trained specialists and not masses of unskilled men.

g [45] I pass then from state practice to the opinions of jurists.   There seems little doubt that the framers of the ICCPR and the ECHR did not think that the conventions conferred a right to conscientious objection.   That is shown by the provisions of art 8(c)(ii) of the ICCPR and art 4(3)(b) of the ECHR which speak, in a different context, of countries 'where conscientious objection is recognised'. *h* That clearly indicates that the framers thought there might be state parties to the convention in which conscientious objection was not recognised.   Of course that is not by any means conclusive.   The framers of the post-Civil War amendments to the constitution of the United States did not think that they were inconsistent with segregation, but the courts in the mid-twentieth century decided that they were.   The broad concepts of human rights do not change in meaning: 'respect *j* for … private life' always means the area of personal autonomy which the state must concede to the individual, but each generation of judges must give its own content to such concepts.   They may think that the framers of the instrument were wrong in their assumptions or that the extent of the area of personal autonomy has changed with changes in the values of society (see *Goodwin v UK* [2002] 2 FCR 577).   Perhaps even more important, there may be changes in what is perceived to be the appropriate balance between one human right (eg respect for private life) and another (eg freedom of expression by newspapers) or the extent to which a human right needs to be qualified in the interests of good government or on other utilitarian grounds.

[46] In the present case, the human right relied upon as founding a right to conscientious objection is the freedom of thought, conscience and religion (see art 18 of the ICCPR and art 9 of the ECHR). Although both articles give an unqualified right to hold religious opinions and to manifest that belief in 'worship, observance, practice and teaching', the right to manifest a religion or belief in other ways may be limited so far as 'necessary to protect public safety, order, health, or morals or the fundamental rights and freedoms of others'. The framers of the covenants appear to have believed, as I have said, that public safety was a legitimate reason for not allowing a religion or belief to be manifested by refusal to do military service. So the question is whether that is no longer the right view to take.

[47] The changes in the nature of warfare which I mentioned earlier do not seem to me a reason for recognising an international human right to conscientious objection. They only strengthen the pragmatic reasons, in countries which have high technology armies but still have conscription, for not punishing conscientious objection. But that is a matter of policy, not principle. It is no reason for saying that a country which needs a citizen army to defend itself is obliged to put the conscience of a conscript before the needs of national defence and, perhaps as important, the principle of equality of sacrifice among citizens.

[48] The notion that there is such a human right seems to be of recent origin. In *LTK v Finland* (1985) 94 ILR 396 the United Nations Human Rights Committee established under the ICCPR said flatly that 'the Covenant does not provide for the right to conscientious objection'. But in 1993 the committee issued 'General Comment 22' on 30 July 1993 in which it tentatively changed its mind and said:

'11. Many individuals have claimed the right to refuse to perform military service (conscientious objection) on the basis that such right derives from their freedoms under article 18. In response to such claims, a growing number of States have in their laws exempted from compulsory military service citizens who genuinely hold religious or other beliefs that forbid the performance of military service and replaced it with alternative national service. The Covenant does not explicitly refer to a right to conscientious objection, but the Committee believes that such a right can be derived from article 18, inasmuch as the obligation to use lethal force may seriously conflict with the freedom of conscience and the right to manifest one's religion or belief.'

[49] There are two observations to be made. First, the fact that (a) people claim a right to conscientious objection under art 18 and (b) a growing number of states concede a right to conscientious objection, does not by any means demonstrate that they recognise that such a right exists under art 18. It may show no more than that their military requirements make it sensible to tolerate some form of conscientious objection. Secondly, the statement that an obligation to use lethal force may 'seriously conflict with freedom of conscience etc' does not even attempt to explain why such an obligation should be distinguished from other legal obligations which may similarly conflict.

a [50] The European Court of Human Rights has never found it necessary to decide whether art 9 (the equivalent of art 18 of the ICCPR) entails a right of conscientious objection but the European Commission on Human Rights has considered the matter several times. On all the occasions when it considered that it was necessary to decide the point, it has said that art 9 does not (see, for example, *Autio v Finland* (1991) 72 DR 245 referring to earlier cases). In *Tsirlis v*
b *Greece* (1998) 25 EHRR 198 at 224 there was a single dissent from Mrs Liddy, who distinguished cases in which the action does not 'actually express the belief concerned' (like chaining oneself to the railings outside Parliament) or 'has no specific conscientious implications in itself' (like paying tax). I find it hard to see the principle upon which these distinctions are made: they appear to involve questions of degree. There is no reason why a religion should not require one to
c chain oneself to railings, not pay tax or fight a holy war and to say that such beliefs would be irrational or contrary to the public interest would seem to me to miss the point. However, Mrs Liddy gained five more votes for a similar dissent in *Thlimmenos v Greece* App No 34369/97 (4 December 1998, unreported), and there the matter stands.

d [51] Finally there is the recently adopted Charter of Fundamental Rights of the European Union which provides in art 10(2) that '[t]he right to conscientious objection is recognised, in accordance with the national laws governing the exercise of this right'. The reference to national laws enabled the European institutions which proclaimed the Charter (the legal status of which is still undecided) to avoid defining the nature of the right but this makes it difficult to
e provide a coherent theory as to why the right should exist. Is it based upon particular respect for a religious or philosophical belief in the sanctity of life? In that case, it should be confined to objections, as in the United States, to all wars and perhaps only to combatant roles in the forces. Or is it more broadly based on political objection to particular operations? In that case, how should it be
f distinguished from other aspects of government policy? It is difficult to escape the conclusion that this provision was adopted because all the member states either had no conscription or did not foresee a situation in which it would be necessary to force deeply unwilling recruits into their armed forces.

[52] If one turns to consider what the European Union considers would amount to a violation of fundamental rights by other nations, a different story
g emerges. On 4 March 1996 the Council of the European Union adopted, pursuant to the 'Third Pillar' provisions of art K.3 of the Maastricht Treaty (now art 31 EU), a Joint Position on the interpretation of the 1951 convention (OJ 1996 L63 p 2). Point 10 said that fear of punishment for conscientious objection should in itself be insufficient to justify recognition of refugee status. It might however
h amount to persecution if the punishment was discriminatory, if the conditions under which service had to be performed amounted in themselves to persecution or if they would require the applicant to commit war crimes or the like. A similar position is adopted in the current draft of a Council Directive on refugees which was approved at the Justice and Home Affairs Council on 28 November 2002.
j These documents suggest that the European Union does not accept that a failure to recognise conscientious objection is a discriminatory breach of the fundamental human rights of the objectors.

[53] In my opinion, therefore, the applicants have not made out their case for saying that there exists a core human right to refuse military service on conscientious grounds which entails that punishment of persons who hold such

views is necessarily discriminatory treatment. The existence of such a right is not
supported by either a moral imperative or international practice.   *a*

[54] This conclusion makes it unnecessary to decide whether Mr Nicol is right
in saying that, for the purposes of the 1951 convention, to apply a general law
imposing significant punishment on people who have a human right to be treated
differently because of their conscientious opinions amounts to persecution on the
grounds that they hold those opinions, or whether, as the Secretary of State says,   *b*
it is a complete answer that the Turkish authorities are not concerned with their
political opinions but only with their refusal to enlist. My present inclination is
to agree with Laws LJ that it would be inconsistent to say that a general
conscription law which did not make an exception for conscientious objectors
was an infringement of their fundamental human rights but that punishing
conscientious objectors under such a law was not persecution for reasons of their   *c*
opinions. The bizarre case of *Omoruyi v Secretary of State for the Home Dept* [2001]
Imm AR 175 was different. Mr Omoruyi was not claiming that by virtue of his
Christianity he had a human right to be treated differently from other Nigerians
in being allowed to bury his father's body. Everyone had such a right. He was
claiming that having to comply with the demands of a criminal gang was harder   *d*
on him because he was a Christian. Whether or not that was the case, it did not
mean that the reason why he was subjected to the demand or not excepted from
the demand had anything to do with his religion.

[55] I would therefore dismiss the appeal.

LORD HUTTON.   *e*

[56] My Lords, I have had the advantage of reading in draft the speech of my
noble and learned friend Lord Bingham of Cornhill. I am in full agreement with
it and for the reasons which he gives I, too, would dismiss these appeals.

LORD RODGER OF EARLSFERRY.   *f*

[57] My Lords, my noble and learned friends Lord Bingham of Cornhill and
Lord Hoffmann have explained that, until now, with only minor exceptions the
relevant bodies have been unwilling to affirm the existence in international law
of a right to object to military service on grounds of conscience. Those bodies
have preferred, at most, to commend to states that they should recognise such a   *g*
right within their domestic legal order. The reluctance to go further doubtless
reflects the real difficulty of identifying the scope of any right that all states would
have to recognise, whatever their circumstances. It is not obvious, for example,
that the recognition in peacetime of a right to exemption from military service on
grounds of conscience raises precisely the same issues as the recognition of such
a right by a state which is fighting for its very survival, which, lacking more   *h*
sophisticated weapons, requires all the manpower it can muster and which may
not be in a position to scrutinise applications for exemption. The dilemma of the
conscientious objector asserting a right to exemption in an hour of national peril
is correspondingly the more exquisite.

[58] The applicants do not object to performing military service in all   *j*
circumstances. This only makes defining the scope of the right which they assert
more problematical. In *Gillette v US* (1970) 401 US 437, in a powerful opinion
delivered at the height of the controversy over the selective draft for military
service in Vietnam, Marshall J analysed the particular difficulties of recognising
anything short of an absolute objection to military service. He drew attention to

a the inevitable competition between the values of conscientious objection and of equality of sacrifice, a competition that has to be resolved while bearing in mind that in practice an extensive right of conscientious objection will tend to be asserted by the educated and articulate rather than by the less fortunate members of society. States with different histories, different social mixes and different political, cultural, religious or philosophical values may legitimately differ as to

b how such a sensitive issue should be determined. It is hardly surprising therefore that no universal solution which all must follow has so far been identified. In these circumstances, for the reasons given by Lord Bingham and Lord Hoffmann I agree that the House cannot recognise the supposed core human right for which the applicants contend. The appeals must accordingly be dismissed.

     [59] I also agree with what Lord Bingham has said about the way in which
c decision makers should determine the reasons for the persecution which an applicant fears.

Appeals dismissed.

Kate O'Hanlon   Barrister.

CMA CGM SA v
Beteiligungs-Kommanditgesellschaft
MS 'Northern Pioneer'
Schiffahrtgesellschaft mbH & Co and
others

[2002] EWCA Civ 1878

COURT OF APPEAL, CIVIL DIVISION

LORD PHILLIPS OF WORTH MATRAVERS MR, RIX AND DYSON LJJ

19 NOVEMBER, 18 DECEMBER 2002

Arbitration – Award – Leave to appeal against award – Appeal against refusal of leave to appeal to Court of Appeal – Principles to be applied – Arbitration Act 1996, s 69.

Arbitration proceedings were commenced between the owners and charterers of container ships which had been chartered under the New York Produce Exchange form of time charter. Clause 31[a] of each of the charterparties was a war cancellation clause and the proceedings raised the question whether the charterers had validly cancelled the charters pursuant to cl 31. The arbitrators found that they had not. The charterers sought permission to appeal to the Commercial Court from that decision pursuant to s 69[b] of the Arbitration Act 1996, contending that the arbitrators had erred in relation to issues of law. The judge refused permission to appeal against the arbitrators' award because he was of the view that the criteria set out in s 69(3)(b), which included that leave should be given only on a question of law that the tribunal had been asked to determine, precluded such permission, since the critical question raised by the charterers, namely whether cl 31 was subject to an implied condition that the right to cancel had to be exercised within a reasonable time of its accrual, had not been explored before the arbitrators. However, in relation to four issues of law he granted permission to appeal to the Court of Appeal against his decision. The appeal raised the following questions: (i) whether the judge had applied the correct principles when granting permission to appeal to the Court of Appeal; (ii) whether the judge had applied the correct principles when refusing permission to appeal against the arbitrators' award; and (iii) whether the judge had correctly applied those principles.

Held – (1) Permission to appeal to the Court of Appeal against the refusal of permission to appeal to the High Court should be granted only in cases where a decision to grant or refuse permission to appeal to the High Court in the particular case called for elucidation as to the manner of the application of the statutory criteria laid down in s 69 of the 1996 Act. In the instant case, the judge had not identified any uncertainty as to the manner in which the statutory criteria should be applied, had not pointed to any uncertainty in the criteria and had not suggested any respect in which he might have misapplied the criteria. It followed that he had not applied the correct principles in granting leave to appeal to the

---

a   Clause 31, so far as is material, is set out at [2], below
b   Section 69, so far as is material, is set out at [10], below

a Court of Appeal (see [12]–[16], below); *Antaios Cia Naviera v Salen Rederierna AB, The Antaios* [1984] 3 All ER 229 applied.

(2) Since the judge had held that the finding of the arbitrators on the question he had identified as critical was not a finding on a question which the tribunal was asked to determine within the meaning of s 69(3)(b), his decision to refuse permission to appeal from the arbitrators' award was inevitable. He had b therefore applied the correct principles, as laid down by s 69(3), to the question whether permission should have been granted to appeal against the arbitrators' award (see [24]–[27], below).

(3) In so far as the judge's refusal of permission was founded on s 69(3)(b), it was not well founded. There were, however, other considerations which justified his decision. Before the judge could grant permission to appeal, s 69 c required that the judge should find (i) that the decision of the arbitrators on the existence of an implied term was obviously wrong or that the point was one of general public importance and that the decision of the arbitrators was at least open to serious doubt and (ii) that reversing the decision of the arbitrators on the point would substantially affect the rights of one or more of the parties. It could d not be said in the instant case that the arbitrators' decision was obviously wrong, nor that it was open to serious doubt. Had the arbitrators applied the principles of election, waiver and estoppel, they would have concluded that those precluded the right to cancel the charterparty after a period of delay as long as that in the instant case. Moreover, the determination of the question was not one which would substantially affect the rights of the parties, and the question was not one e of general public importance. Accordingly, the appeal would be dismissed (see [36]–[38], [55], [56], [65], below); *Antaios Cia Naviera v Salen Rederierna AB, The Antaios* [1984] 3 All ER 229 applied.

Notes

f For appeal from an arbitration award on a point of law, see Supp to 2 *Halsbury's Laws* (4th edn reissue) paras 690–713.4.

Cases referred to in judgment

Antaios Cia Naviera SA v Salen Rederierna AB, The Antaios [1984] 3 All ER 229, [1985] g AC 191, [1984] 3 WLR 592, HL; *affg* [1983] 3 All ER 777, [1983] 1 WLR 1362, CA; *affg* [1983] 2 Lloyd's Rep 473.

Associated Provincial Picture Houses Ltd v Wednesbury Corp [1947] 2 All ER 680, [1948] 1 KB 223, CA.

Edwards (Inspector of Taxes) v Bairstow [1955] 3 All ER 48, [1956] AC 14, [1955] 3 WLR h 410, HL.

Kawasaki Kisen Kabushiki Kaisha and Belships Co Ltd, Skibsaksjeselskap, Re An Arbitration between [1939] 2 All ER 108.

Kawasaki Kisen Kabushiki Kaisha of Kobe v Bantham Steamship Co Ltd [1939] 1 All ER 819, [1939] 2 KB 544, CA.

j *Mardorf Peach & Co Ltd v Attica Sea Carriers Corp of Liberia, The Laconia* [1977] 1 All ER 545, [1977] AC 850, [1977] 2 WLR 286, HL.

North Range Shipping Ltd v Seatrans Shipping Corp [2002] EWCA Civ 405, [2002] 2 All ER (Comm) 193, [2002] 1 WLR 2397.

Petraco (Bermuda) Ltd v Petromed International SA [1988] 3 All ER 454, [1988] 1 WLR 896, CA.

Peyman v Lanjani [1984] 3 All ER 703, [1985] Ch 457, [1985] 2 WLR 154, CA.

Pioneer Shipping Ltd v BTP Tioxide Ltd, The Nema [1981] 2 All ER 1030, [1982] AC
724, [1981] 3 WLR 292, HL.   *a*
Scandinavian Trading Tanker Co AB v Flota Petrolera Ecuatoriana, The Scaptrade
    [1981] 2 Lloyd's Rep 425; *affd* [1983] 1 All ER 301, [1983] QB 529, [1983] 2 WLR
    248, CA; *affd* [1983] 2 All ER 763, [1983] 2 AC 694, [1983] 3 WLR 203, HL.

Appeal   *b*
The claimant charterers, CMA CGM SA, appealed from the order of Tomlinson J
on 2 July 2002 refusing them permission to appeal pursuant to s 69 of the
Arbitration Act 1996 from an award of arbitrators (Sir Christopher Staughton,
Adrian Hamilton QC and Kenneth Rokison QC). On 16 July 2002 Tomlinson J
granted permission to appeal from that order to the Court of Appeal pursuant to
s 69. The respondent owners (claimants in the arbitration) were Beteiligungs-KG   *c*
MS 'Northern Pioneer' Schiffahrtsgesellschaft mbH & Co, Beteiligungs-KG MS
'Northern Reliance' Schiffahrtsgesellschaft mbH & Co, Beteiligungs-KG MS
'Northern Faith' Schiffahrtsgesellschaft mbH & Co, Beteiligungs-KG MS 'Northern
Honour' Schiffahrtsgesellschaft mbH & Co and Beteiligungs-KG MS 'Northern
Dignity' Schiffahrtsgesellschaft mbH & Co. The facts are set out in the judgment   *d*
of the court.

Philippa Hopkins (instructed by *Ince & Co*) for the charterers.
Stephen Kenny (instructed by *Holman Fenwick & Willan*) for the owners.

                                                                    Cur adv vult   *e*

18 December 2002. The following judgment of the court was delivered.

LORD PHILLIPS OF WORTH MATRAVERS MR.

INTRODUCTION   *f*
    [1] This appeal arises out of and relates to an award of three eminent
commercial arbitrators, Sir Christopher Staughton, Mr Adrian Hamilton QC and
Mr Kenneth Rokison QC. The arbitration raised the question of whether
charterers of four vessels under the New York Produce Exchange (NYPE) form
of charter had validly cancelled those charters pursuant to the war cancellation
clause. The arbitrators held that they had not. The charterers sought permission   *g*
to appeal to the Commercial Court against that decision, contending that the
arbitrators had erred in relation to seven issues of law. They did so pursuant to
s 69 of the Arbitration Act 1996. By order dated 2 July 2002 Tomlinson J refused
permission to appeal. On 16 July 2002 he granted permission to appeal to this
court against his decision in relation to four issues. So far as we are aware, this is   *h*
the first time that permission to appeal to this court has been granted pursuant to
s 69 of the 1996 Act. The appeal raises three issues. (1) Did Tomlinson J apply
the correct principles when granting permission to appeal to this court? (2) Did
Tomlinson J apply the correct principles when refusing permission to appeal
against the arbitrators' award? (3) Did Tomlinson J correctly apply the latter   *j*
principles?
    [2] The respondents (the owners), who were the claimants in the arbitration,
are five German limited liability partnerships each of which owns one container
ship. They chartered these vessels under the NYPE form of time charter, with
amendments up to 12 June 1981, to a company of which the appellants (the
charterers), who were the respondents in the arbitration, are the universal

a successor. Clause 31 of each of the charterparties was a war cancellation clause which provided, so far as material, as follows:

> 'In the event of the outbreak of war (whether there be a declaration of war or not) between any two or more of the following countries: The United States of America, the United Kingdom, France, Russia, the People's Republic of China, Federal Republic of Germany and any country of the EEC or in the event of the nation under whose flag the vessel sails becoming involved in war (whether there be a declaration of war or not), either the Owners or the charterers may cancel this charter ...'

b

[3] The charters were for lengthy terms and, from 1996 to 1999, container line rates fell. In September 1997 the charters were varied, to accommodate the

c charterers. Notwithstanding this variation the charterers had, in March 1999, a powerful commercial motive for terminating the charters. It was in March 1999 that a military operation began in Kosovo in which Germany participated as a member of the North Atlantic Treaty Organization (NATO). In relation to this, the arbitrators found the following facts:

d

> 'The particular operation with which we are concerned started on 24 March 1999. Germany participated as a member of NATO. Under the German constitution, the German Bundestag approved German participation in the operation. From 24 March 1999, this participation involved the deployment of ten Tornado ECR aircraft and four Tornado Recce aircraft of
> e the German Air Force, initially mainly suppressing Yugoslav air defences, and reconnaissance, and later switching to other targets. During the second half of April the intensity of the operation, including Germany's participation increased considerably. We conclude, however, that the operation was one operation, starting on 24 March 1999, and the increase in Germany's
> f participation was one of scale or tempo, rather than in the nature of Germany's involvement.'

[4] By notice dated 29 April 1999 the charterers purported to terminate each of the charterparties on the ground that Germany, under whose flag the vessels sailed, had become involved in war in Kosovo and Yugoslavia.

g [5] The arbitrators found that the cancellation of the charterparties was invalid for reasons which included the following: (1) (by a majority) that the events in Kosovo did not constitute 'war' within the meaning of that word in cl 31; (2) (by the same majority) that if events in Kosovo did constitute war, Germany was not 'involved' in that war within the meaning of that word in cl 31;

h (3) that under cl 31, the right to cancel a charter had to be exercised within a reasonable time of the event in question; (4) the charterers had not given notice of cancellation within a reasonable time of the alleged involvement of Germany in the alleged war.

[6] The issues in respect of which the charterers sought permission to appeal and which we shall have to consider, having regard to the terms upon which

j Tomlinson J gave leave to appeal to us, are the following:

> '(i) Whether on a proper construction of cl 31 of the charterparties, the expression "[a] nation ... becoming involved in war" in that clause is apt to encompass circumstances in which a nation participates in a military operation as a member of NATO (or another international body).
> (ii) Whether the option to cancel given by cl 31 of the charterparties arose

only in the event that the war in question, or the flag state's involvement in
that war, had an impact on the trading or operations of the vessel or vessels
concerned. (iii) Whether (a) there was implied into cl 31 of the charterparties
any term to the effect that the right to cancel the charterparties pursuant to
that clause had to be exercised by the giving of a notice within a particular
time frame or (b) there was no such implied term and the right to cancel
could be lost only as the result of an election by the party concerned. (iv) If
there was an implied term, whether the term in question was that the right
to cancel had to be exercised (a) by notice given within a reasonable time of
its accrual (and in particular within a few days thereof) or (b) before such
time had elapsed as to make the other party believe that no such right would
be exercised.'

SECTION 69 AND ITS HISTORY

[7] The regime under which decisions of arbitrators were brought before the
High Court by case stated was radically altered by the Arbitration Act 1979, s 1 of
which provided, in so far as material:

'(1) In the Arbitration Act 1950 ... section 21 (statement of case ...) shall
cease to have effect and, without prejudice to the right of appeal conferred
by subsection (2) below, the High Court shall not have jurisdiction to set
aside or remit an award on an arbitration agreement on the ground of errors
of fact or law on the face of the award.
(2) Subject to subsection (3) below, an appeal shall lie to the High Court
on any question of law arising out of an award made on an arbitration
agreement; and on the determination of such an appeal the High Court may
... (a) confirm, vary or set aside the award ...
(3) An appeal under this section may be brought by any of the parties to
the reference—(a) with the consent of all the other parties to the reference;
or (b) ... with the leave of the court.
(4) The High Court shall not grant leave under subsection (3)(b) above
unless it considers that, having regard to all the circumstances, the
determination of the question of law concerned could substantially affect the
rights of one or more of the parties to the arbitration agreement ...
(7) No appeal shall lie to the Court of Appeal from a decision of the High
Court on an appeal under this section unless—(a) the High Court or the
Court of Appeal gives leave; and (b) it is certified by the High Court that the
question of law to which its decision relates either is one of general public
importance or is one which for some other special reason should be
considered by the Court of Appeal ...'

[8] In *Pioneer Shipping Ltd v BTP Tioxide Ltd, The Nema* [1981] 2 All ER 1030,
[1982] AC 724 the House of Lords gave guidance as to the circumstances in which
permission to appeal to the High Court from the decision of an arbitrator should
be given. In relation to the construction of a 'one-off' clause, permission should
not be given unless, in the opinion of the court, the arbitrator was obviously
wrong. In dealing with the approach to standard clauses, Lord Diplock said
([1981] 2 All ER 1030 at 1040, [1982] AC 724 at 743):

'For reasons already sufficiently discussed, rather less strict criteria are in
my view appropriate where questions of construction of contracts in
standard terms are concerned. That there should be as high a degree of legal
certainty as it is practicable to obtain as to how such terms apply on the

occurrence of events of a kind that it is not unlikely may reproduce themselves in similar transactions between other parties engaged in the same trade is a public interest that is recognised by the 1979 Act, particularly in s 4. So, if the decision of the question of construction in the circumstances of the particular case would add significantly to the clarity and certainty of English commercial law it would be proper to give leave in a case sufficiently substantial to escape the ban imposed by the first part of s 1(4), bearing in mind always that a superabundance of citable judicial decisions arising out of slightly different facts is calculated to hinder rather than to promote clarity in settled principles of commercial law. But leave should not be given, even in such a case, unless the judge considered that a strong prima facie case had been made out that the arbitrator had been wrong in his construction; and when the events to which the standard clause fell to be applied in the particular arbitration were themselves one-off events stricter criteria should be applied on the same lines as those that I have suggested as appropriate to one-off clauses.'

[9] Three years later, Lord Diplock had occasion to revert to this topic in *Antaios Cia Naviera SA v Salen Rederierna AB, The Antaios* [1984] 3 All ER 229 at 235, [1985] AC 191 at 203–204:

'My Lords, I think that your Lordships should take this opportunity of affirming that the guideline given in *The Nema* [1981] 2 All ER 1030 at 1040, [1982] AC 724 at 743 that, even in a case that turns on the construction of a standard term, "leave should not be given ... unless the judge considered that a strong prima facie case had been made out that the arbitrator had been wrong in his construction" applies even though there may be dicta in other reported cases at first instance which suggest that on some question of the construction of that standard term there may among commercial judges be two schools of thought. I am confining myself to conflicting dicta, not decisions. If there are conflicting decisions, the judge should give leave to appeal to the High Court, and whatever judge hears the appeal should in accordance with the decision that he favours give leave to appeal from his decision to the Court of Appeal with the appropriate certificate under s 1(7) as to the general public importance of the question to which it relates; for only thus can be attained that desirable degree of certainty in English commercial law which s 1(4) of the 1979 Act was designed to preserve.'

[10] Section 69 of the 1996 Act has replaced the *Nema* guidelines with statutory criteria, as follows:

'(1) Unless otherwise agreed by the parties, a party to arbitral proceedings may (upon notice to the other parties and to the tribunal) appeal to the court on a question of law arising out of an award made in the proceedings ...
(2) An appeal shall not be brought under this section except—(a) with the agreement of all the other parties to the proceedings, or (b) with the leave of the court ...
(3) Leave to appeal shall be given only if the court is satisfied—(a) that the determination of the question will substantially affect the rights of one or more of the parties, (b) that the question is one which the tribunal was asked to determine, (c) that, on the basis of the findings of fact in the award—(i) the decision of the tribunal on the question is obviously wrong, or (ii) the question is one of general public importance and the decision of the tribunal

is at least open to serious doubt, and (d) that, despite the agreement of the parties to resolve the matter by arbitration, it is just and proper in all the circumstances for the court to determine the question.

(4) An application for leave to appeal under this section shall identify the question of law to be determined and state the grounds on which it is alleged that leave to appeal should be granted.

(5) The court shall determine an application for leave to appeal under this section without a hearing unless it appears to the court that a hearing is required.

(6) The leave of the court is required for any appeal from a decision of the court under this section to grant or refuse leave to appeal.'

[11] The statutory criteria are clearly strongly influenced by the *Nema* guidelines. They do not, however, follow these entirely. We have concluded that they open the door a little more widely to the granting of permission to appeal than the crack that was left by Lord Diplock. We shall elaborate on this conclusion later in this judgment.

[12] Section 69(6) reproduces, in effect, s 1(6A) of the 1979 Act, which provided:

'Unless the High Court gives leave, no appeal shall lie to the Court of Appeal from a decision of the High Court—(a) to grant or refuse leave under subsection (3)(b) ...'

Lord Diplock, in a speech with which the other members of the House concurred, considered the principles to be applied under this subsection in *The Antaios* ([1984] 3 All ER 229 at 236–237, [1985] AC 191 at 205):

'... leave to appeal to the Court of Appeal should be granted by the judge under s 1(6A) only in cases where a decision whether to grant or to refuse leave to appeal to the High Court under s 1(3)(b) in the particular case in his view called for some amplification, elucidation or adaptation to changing practices of existing guidelines laid down by appellate courts, and that leave to appeal under s 1(6A) should *not* be granted in any other type of case. Judges should have the courage of their own convictions and decide for themselves whether, applying existing guidelines, leave to appeal to the High Court under s 1(3)(b) ought to be granted or not. In the sole type of case in which leave to appeal to the Court of Appeal under s 1(6A) may properly be given the judge ought to give reasons for his decision to grant such leave so that the Court of Appeal may be informed of the lacuna, uncertainty or unsuitability in the light of changing practices that the judge has perceived in the existing guidelines; moreover, since the grant of leave entails also the necessity for the application of *Edwards (Inspector of Taxes) v Bairstow* [1955] 3 All ER 48, [1956] AC 14 principles by the Court of Appeal in order to examine whether the judge had acted within the limits of his discretion, the judge should also give the reasons for the way in which he had exercised his discretion.'

[13] Nothing in s 69 of the 1996 Act affords any grounds for departing from these principles. On the contrary, the fact that, as we have indicated, s 69 opens a little more widely the door to granting permission to appeal from the award of an arbitrator is all the more reason why the judge's decision on the application for such permission should be final.

a

[14] Tomlinson J refused the charterers' application for permission to appeal to the Commercial Court because he was firmly of the view that the statutory criteria set out in s 69(3) of the 1996 Act precluded the grant of permission. He did so notwithstanding that he had identified issues in relation to the proper construction of a standard war cancellation clause, such as cl 31, that were
b 'obviously of general public importance'. In granting permission to appeal to this court in relation to his decision he explained why he did so:

'However, on the issues relating to the war cancellation clause, I grant leave to appeal from my decision pursuant to s 69(6) of the 1996 Act, in order
c that the Court of Appeal may consider whether I have misapplied the statutory criteria or have approached them inappropriately inflexibly given the general public importance of the underlying question of the proper approach to the construction of a standard war cancellation clause, and, if it thinks it appropriate, give guidance.'

d [15] The observations of Lord Diplock in *The Antaios*, which we have set out in [12], above, fall to be applied, subject to this qualification. The guidelines are no longer judge-made—they are statutory criteria. There is no scope for amplifying or adapting them in the light of changing practices. To the extent that there is scope for elucidation as to the manner of their application, it may be appropriate to grant permission to appeal. Subject to this, if the judge decides
e that the statutory criteria for granting permission to appeal are not satisfied, he should not grant permission to appeal against that decision. His decision on the merits of the application for permission to appeal should be final.

[16] Tomlinson J did not identify any uncertainty as to the manner in which the statutory criteria should be applied. It was his clear view that they precluded
f the grant of permission to appeal. He did not point to any uncertainty in the criteria. He did not suggest any respect in which he might have misapplied the criteria. We detect that he hoped that this court might find a way to ease the rigorous restriction that the criteria impose on review by the Commercial Court of important issues of law arising in arbitrations. Lord Diplock would not, we think, have approved the grant of permission to appeal for such a motive and nor
g do we. We shall, however, take advantage in due course of the opportunity to consider the extent to which some of Lord Diplock's observations in *The Antaios* can be reconciled with the statutory criteria.

SOME COMMENTS ON PROCEDURE
h [17] Before considering the principles applied by Tomlinson J we wish to say a word about the procedure adopted in this case. In accordance with sub-ss 4 and 5 of s 69 the charterers applied in writing for permission to appeal. The claim form in which they did so set out clearly and concisely, albeit over ten pages, their grounds of appeal. This claim form was accompanied by a witness statement
j from Mr Deering, the charterers' solicitor. This included three detailed pages of 'background to the dispute' for the alleged purpose of satisfying Tomlinson J that determination of the questions in issue would substantially affect the rights of the parties—see s 69(3)(a). This was unnecessary and inappropriate. The rights of the parties are those at issue in the arbitration and s 69(3)(a) is designed to ensure that permission to appeal will not be given in relation to issues which have no

substantial impact on those rights. What appears to have been a lengthy plea 'ad misericordiam' as to the charterers' financial plight was uncalled for.

[18] Exhibited to Mr Deering's statement were 137 pages of exhibits, which included not merely the award but a considerable volume of background material, including the charterers' skeleton argument at the arbitration (45 pages).

[19] Mr Leir of the owners' solicitors responded with 28 pages of argument against the grant of permission to appeal. Mr Deering felt it necessary to respond to this with a further 13 pages, including the assertion that his clients were not aware of their right to cancel the charters until two days before they did so—a statement which raises a number of questions but which, so it seems to us, was not likely to be of any assistance to Tomlinson J.

[20] In *North Range Shipping Ltd v Seatrans Shipping Corp* [2002] EWCA Civ 405, [2002] 2 All ER (Comm) 193, [2002] 1 WLR 2397 this court held that a judge, when refusing permission to appeal under s 69 of the 1996 Act, was required by virtue of art 6 of the European Convention for the Protection of Human Rights and Fundamental Freedoms 1950 (as set out in Sch 1 to the Human Rights Act 1998) to give sufficient reasons to enable the losing party to understand why the judge had reached his decision, although the court emphasised that such reasons could be very short. To this extent Lord Diplock's guidance in *The Antaios* is no longer followed.

[21] Tomlinson J, in refusing permission to appeal, gave very adequate reasons for his decision in two-and-a-half closely typed pages, which were faxed to the parties on 13 June 2002. On 20 June the charterers' solicitors faxed to the judge a three-page 'application for further consideration', joining issue with some of the judge's conclusions. Not surprisingly, this provoked a three-page riposte from the owners' solicitors, to which the charterers' solicitors responded.

[22] Because his order refusing permission to appeal had not yet been drawn up, the judge considered it appropriate to consider this correspondence. He commented:

'I cannot think that the Court of Appeal envisaged that the giving of reasons should lead to a potentially never-ending process in which it is suggested that, for one reason, or another, the judge's decision is wrong. In the ordinary way the proper forum in which to debate the question whether a first instance judge has made an incorrect decision is in the Court of Appeal, not by way of application to the judge to reconsider his decision. I would accept that there may be cases in which it may be appropriate to draw to the attention of the court that it has apparently proceeded upon a misapprehension or otherwise failed to have regard to a relevant consideration. I do not however accept that the present is such a case.'

[23] We sympathise with the judge's comments. More fundamentally, we view the whole saga that we have just described with dismay. The statutory requirement that applications for permission to appeal should be paper applications unless the court otherwise directs must surely have been intended to simplify the procedure and to save the court's time. That requirement reflects the fact that the criteria for the grant of permission to appeal are clear-cut and easy to apply. They do not require the drawing of fine lines, nor will they usually give much scope for the court to require assistance in the form of submissions or advocacy. If this case reflects current practice, and we apprehend that it may, then the procedure has got out of hand and is at odds with both the spirit of the legislation and the ethos of the Commercial Court. Any written submissions

a placed before the court in support of an application for permission to appeal from findings in an arbitral award should normally be capable of being read and digested by the judge within the half-hour that, under the old regime, used to be allotted for such applications.

b DID TOMLINSON J APPLY THE CORRECT PRINCIPLES WHEN REFUSING PERMISSION TO APPEAL AGAINST THE ARBITRATORS' AWARD?

[24] For an appeal against the award to succeed, the charterers would have to reverse three separate findings of the arbitrators in relation to cl 31 of the charterparty: (1) that operations in Kosovo were not 'war'; (2) that Germany was not 'involved'; and (3) that the charterers had been required to give notice of cancellation within a reasonable time and had failed to do so.

c [25] In his reasons for refusing permission to appeal, Tomlinson J observed that the first two issues involved mixed fact and law and that the proper approach to the construction of clauses such as cl 31 was a question of general public importance. He did not, expressly, consider whether the majority decision of the tribunal on these two issues was at least open to serious doubt. This was perhaps

d because even if there were grounds for challenge in relation to these two issues, such challenge would not affect the result, or the rights of the parties, unless the unanimous decision of the arbitrators on the third issue could be attacked. As to that issue, the challenge that the charterers sought to bring was to the finding of the arbitrators that, as a matter of law, the charterers had to exercise any right to cancel that they enjoyed within a reasonable time.

e [26] Tomlinson J held that this challenge was not open to the charterers because the question was not 'one which the tribunal was asked to determine': see s 69(3)(b). He further held that there were alternative bases upon which the time that elapsed before the charterers gave notice of cancellation might have been relevant: (1) implied term, (2) waiver/election and estoppel. These latter

f alternatives were not explored before the arbitrators. As we understand his judgment, it was because questions of waiver/election and estoppel were not explored before the arbitrators that Tomlinson J concluded that it was not open to the charterers to challenge the arbitrators' finding that, by reason of an implied term, notice of cancellation had to be given within a reasonable time.

g [27] Given Tomlinson J's conclusion that the arbitrators were not asked to determine the critical question his decision that the application for permission to appeal must be refused was inevitable. He applied the correct principles, as laid down by s 69(3). Whether the manner of his application of those principles is open to attack remains to be considered.

h DID TOMLINSON J CORRECTLY APPLY THE PRINCIPLES GOVERNING PERMISSION TO APPEAL FROM AN ARBITRATION AWARD?

[28] In *Antaios Cia Naviera SA v Salen Rederierna AB, The Antaios* [1984] 3 All ER 229, [1985] AC 191 Lord Diplock observed, in the passage that we have quoted at [12], above, that in performing the task which confronts us, the Court of Appeal

j had to apply *Edwards (Inspector of Taxes) v Bairstow* [1955] 3 All ER 48, [1956] AC 14 in order to decide 'whether the judge had acted within the limits of his discretion'. This demonstrates that our task is essentially one of judicial review. In so far as Tomlinson J has made findings of law, we can review them. In so far as he has made findings of fact, or exercised a discretion, the familiar *Wednesbury* test falls to be applied (*Associated Provincial Picture Houses Ltd v Wednesbury Corp* [1947] 2 All ER 680, [1948] 1 KB 223).

'THE QUESTION IS ONE THAT THE ARBITRATORS WERE ASKED TO DETERMINE'

[29] Section 69(3)(b) is an addition to the *Nema* guidelines, resolving a   *a*
difference of view between the Commercial Court and the Court of Appeal in
Petraco (Bermuda) Ltd v Petromed International SA [1988] 3 All ER 454, [1988] 1 WLR
896. In his decision giving permission to appeal to this court, Tomlinson J
commented 'the critical question was not even raised faintly'. On behalf of the
charterers, Miss Hopkins challenged this finding. It is first necessary to identify   *b*
what Tomlinson J considered to be 'the critical question'.

[30] The issues that we have set out in [6], above, were four of seven issues
that the charterers identified in their claim form in order to comply with s 69(4)
of the 1996 Act. On analysis, we consider that the 'critical question' identified by
Tomlinson J was issue (iii). We so find having regard to the following passage
from his reasons for refusing permission to appeal: *c*

> 'I do not believe that it would be a proper exercise of my statutory
> discretion to give leave to appeal in circumstances where the arbitrators have
> unanimously concluded that any right to cancel which the charterers may
> have enjoyed was not exercised within a reasonable time and was thus lost.
> The applicants recognise that even were they successful on all issues relating   *d*
> to the war cancellation clause, there would have to be a remission to the
> arbitrators for them to consider whether CMA had waived or had elected not
> to exercise the option to cancel, that being a question which they had not
> been asked to determine at the hearing. The arbitrators find that CMA
> would have known of and been able to assess the well-publicised events   *e*
> within a few days. CMA adduced no evidence to lay a foundation for an
> argument that they could not be taken to have waived or elected not to
> exercise the option to cancel because they were unaware of the existence of
> that right, and they seem at the hearing to have argued only very faintly
> against the necessity to imply a term that the right must be exercised within
> a reasonable time. What was described by their counsel as "the more   *f*
> interesting question" was the nature of the term, a reflection of the debate
> whether the term should be formulated such that the right of cancellation is
> to be exercised within a reasonable time or before such lapse of time as
> would make the other party think that the right would not be exercised.
> That strikes me as an arid debate since I cannot think that the formulation of   *g*
> the term in these different ways can lead to a different outcome, and it would
> appear that CMA's counsel came close to accepting this when he suggested
> that the latter, "Davenport" formulation [Brian Davenport QC and Michele
> White 'Last voyage orders – again: The Gregos' [1994] Lloyd's MCLQ 154],
> encapsulates the test for determining what is a reasonable time. Another
> way of putting the same point is that if within a reasonable time within   *h*
> which to ascertain that war had broken out and within which to decide the
> question whether, seeing that war had broken out, it was in their interests to
> continue to implement the contract or not, one party does not give to the
> other notice of cancellation, the other party is entitled to conclude that the
> existence of the war will not be relied upon as giving rise to the right to   *j*
> cancel. The short point is therefore that the arbitrators were not asked to
> analyse the matter in terms of waiver/election and evidence was not
> deployed before them concerning CMA's awareness or lack of awareness as
> to the existence of a right to cancel. The resolution of the question in fact left
> to the arbitrators was an objective determination of fact peculiarly within
> the province of the arbitrators. I conclude that it is inappropriate to give

a
leave to appeal on the issues arising out of the war cancellation clause. The questions raised are either questions the determination of which will not substantially affect the rights of one or more of the parties or are questions which the tribunal was not asked to determine.'

b
[31] Miss Hopkins' submissions on this point can be summarised as follows: (1) the arbitrators had held that cl 31 was subject to an implied condition that the right to cancel had to be exercised within a reasonable time of its accrual; (2) the charterers had challenged before the arbitrators the existence of this implied condition; (3) it followed that the question of whether there was an implied term was one which 'the tribunal was asked to determine'; (4) it was the charterers' case that mere inaction would not constitute an election, estoppel or waiver, however long it continued; (5) it was for the owners, not the charterers, to raise
c
any averments of estoppel, waiver or election. They had not done so.

[32] In support of her submission that the question of an implied term was before the arbitrators, Miss Hopkins relied upon: (i) The charterers' skeleton argument at the arbitration. This included in the issues to be determined: 'Did the option have to be exercised within any particular time? If so, did CMA
d
exercise it within time?' The answer to these issues, suggested by the skeleton, was: 'It is not necessary to imply a term limiting the time during which the option has to be exercised. Wars wax and wane and are unpredictable'. (ii) A passage of discussion between the charterers' counsel and Sir Christopher Staughton in the course of the former's submissions:

e
'Mr Haddon-Cave: Question 3 on p 7, did the option have to be exercised within a reasonable time and if so was it exercised within a reasonable time? And his estoppel point. I see the force on why it might be thought that there was an implied term, but it's not necessarily so because, as Mr Hamilton pointed out yesterday, the character of the war changes and you may wish
f
at some stage in the war to exercise the option, you may not.

Sir Christopher Staughton: Are you allowed to wait and see what sort of war it is going to be?

Mr Haddon-Cave: There is no reason why the parties could not have intended that to be the case.

g
Sir Christopher Staughton: If it's established that you have to exercise the option within a reasonable time, why should you be allowed a licence to decide what's a reasonable time for you?

Mr Haddon-Cave: That's the issue—is it necessary to imply a term? I quite see the force of that point as an option; I don't argue the point terribly forcefully, there is an authority to that effect, so I don't dwell on it or accept
h
it. The more interesting question, perhaps, is what is the nature of that term, and I suggest that it is as Mr Davenport suggests on p 160 of his article, that the option probably has to be exercised before such time has elapsed that will leave the other party to think that no notice of termination was going to be exercised.'

j
(iii) The charterers' written closing argument, which simply repeated the matters in their skeleton argument to which we have referred at (i), above.

[33] In their award the arbitrators made the following finding:

'An option to cancel a charterparty in the event of war must be exercised within a reasonable time of the event in question. In *Re An Arbitration between Kawasaki Kisen Kabushiki Kaisha and Belships Co Ltd, Skibsaksjeselskap*

[1939] 2 All ER 108, Branson J said, in respect of the Japan/China war (at 183): "... the charterers and the shipowners would be entitled here to a reasonable time within which to ascertain that war had broken out, and within which to consider and decide the question whether or not, seeing that war had broken out, they thought it was in their interest to continue to implement the contract."'

[34] We consider that in making this finding the arbitrators were determining a question which they had been 'asked to determine'. It is true that Mr Haddon-Cave QC had virtually conceded the point, but we consider that he did enough to prevent being shut out under s 69(3)(b) from seeking to appeal against the arbitrators' finding on the point.

[35] No doubt because Mr Haddon-Cave challenged the implication of a term so faintly, no questions of election, waiver or estoppel appear to have been explored at the arbitration, although the cryptic statement 'and his estoppel point' in the passage that we have quoted at [32](ii), above, suggests that estoppel may have received at least a passing reference in the submissions made on behalf of the owners. In these circumstances, we do not consider that the fact that issues of election, waiver or estoppel were not explored is a bar, by virtue of s 69(3)(b), to the grant of permission to appeal issue (iii) set out at [6], above.

[36] All of this leads us to conclude, not without hesitation, that, in so far as Tomlinson J's refusal of permission to appeal was founded on s 69(3)(b), it was not well founded. None the less, if the charterers had intended to make a serious challenge to the implication of a term, we consider that they should have laid the ground for this more thoroughly. It may well be that Mr Haddon-Cave concluded that the arbitrators would feel obliged, or inclined, to follow *Re An Arbitration between Kawasaki Kisen Kabushiki Kaisha and Belships Co Ltd, Skibsaksjeselskap* [1939] 2 All ER 108. None the less we think that it would have been open to him to urge them strenuously not to do so in the light of subsequent developments in the law, so as to make it plain that this was a live issue and one that would, if necessary, form the basis of a challenge before the Commercial Court. Had he done so, this would almost undoubtedly have been met with alternative allegations of election, waiver and estoppel, and these matters would have been explored. As it is, were the charterers to be given permission to appeal to the Commercial Court and there to succeed on the ground that the arbitrators were wrong to find an implied term and that issues of election, waiver and estoppel remained to be resolved, the matter would have to be remitted to the arbitrators for further consideration. This fact would, in our opinion, have justified Tomlinson J in declining to give permission to appeal on the ground that s 69(3)(d) was not satisfied. There were, however, other considerations that, in our opinion, justified the judge in refusing permission to appeal.

[37] Before he could grant permission to appeal s 69 required that the judge should find (1) that the decision of the arbitrators on the existence of an implied term was obviously wrong or that the point was one of general public importance and that the decision of the arbitrators was at least open to serious doubt and (2) that reversing the decision of the arbitrators on the point would substantially affect the rights of one or more of the parties. We turn to consider these criteria.

WAS THE DECISION OF THE ARBITRATORS THAT THERE WAS AN IMPLIED TERM OBVIOUSLY WRONG?

[38] As we shall show shortly, there is scope for argument as to whether the arbitrators were correct in finding that cl 31 was subject to an implied term that

a the right to cancel had to be exercised within a reasonable time, but it cannot be said that the arbitrators were obviously wrong to follow the decision in the *Belships* case, and Miss Hopkins did not submit to the contrary.

WAS THE DECISION OF THE ARBITRATORS THAT THERE WAS AN IMPLIED TERM OPEN TO SERIOUS DOUBT?

b [39] The *Belships* case, which the arbitrators followed, concerned a clause in a charterparty which gave owners and charterers the option of cancelling the charterparty if one of a number of specified countries became 'engaged in war' with any other of those countries. It was submitted to Branson J that, so long as a state of war continued, the option given by this clause remained open. He rejected that submission. He held that there was a term to be implied that the

c option would have to be exercised within a reasonable time. In so finding he applied the test of whether, as a matter of business efficacy, it was necessary to imply such a term.

[40] Cases dealing with the operation of war cancellation clauses are rare. More common are cases dealing with the right to withdraw a vessel from a charterparty for non-payment of hire. Those cases all agree that such a right has

d to be exercised within a reasonable time of the non-payment, but they do not agree on the juridical basis for such a requirement. As an alternative to an implied term, principles of election, waiver and estoppel have been advanced as the explanation. These principles can raise difficult theoretical questions as to the manner of their application—see *Scandinavian Trading Tanker Co AB v Flota Petrolera*

e *Ecuatoriana, The Scaptrade* [1981] 2 Lloyd's Rep 425 at 430, although they do not appear to have done so in practice. We believe that there is a good reason for this, as we shall explain. Having regard to the different theories to which we have referred above, it is at least arguable that there is a serious doubt as to whether the juridical basis of the requirement to exercise a right to withdraw from a charter within a reasonable time is an implied term. For the reasons which follow

f we do not need to express a final view on this matter.

DOES IT MATTER?

[41] Is the question of whether the arbitrators were right to follow the *Belships* case in implying a term 'a question of general public importance'? If they were wrong, will this 'substantially affect the rights' of the parties? Miss Hopkins

g submits that the answer to both questions is Yes. This is because it is her case that the mere passage of time will not give rise to the implication of an election or a waiver or to an estoppel. Thus, she argues, it is only the implication of a term that can give rise to a requirement to give notice of cancellation within a reasonable time.

h [42] Miss Hopkins' submission echoes one which was advanced in *The Antaios*. Indeed, there are close parallels between this case and *The Antaios* which it is helpful to identify before proceeding further. In the present case there were two relevant issues before the arbitrators. The first was as to the true construction of the war cancellation clause in the NYPE charter. We shall call this issue 'the

j construction issue'. The second was as to whether the right to cancel the charter had been lost as a result of the passage of time. We shall call this issue 'the time issue'.

[43] *The Antaios* also involved a purported cancellation of a time charter on the NYPE form. In that case it was the owners who had purported to terminate the charter by withdrawing their vessel. They relied upon cl 5, which provided 'on any breach of this charterparty owners shall be at liberty to withdraw the vessel ...'

There was an issue as to whether the words 'any breach' meant 'any breach at all'
or 'any repudiatory breach'. We shall call this 'the construction issue'. The *a*
arbitrators held that the words meant 'any repudiatory breach', that the breach
relied upon by the owners was not repudiatory and that, therefore, the owners
had had no right to withdraw the vessel.

[44] Owners in *The Antaios* learned of the breach by the charterers on 7 May
1980 but did not purport to withdraw their vessel until 20 May. There was an *b*
issue as to whether this period of delay had resulted in the loss by the owners of
their right (if right there was) to withdraw the vessel. We shall call this issue 'the
time issue'. The arbitrators held in favour of the charterers on this issue also.
The time issue in *The Antaios* raised precisely the same questions as the time issue
in the present case. We turn to consider the treatment of those questions in
The Antaios. *c*

[45] An application for permission to appeal pursuant to the 1979 Act was
made to Staughton J, and the decision of the arbitrators on the time issue can be
deduced from the report of his judgment (see [1983] 2 Lloyd's Rep 473). The
arbitrators held that there was an implied term that the right to withdraw would
be exercised within a reasonable time. A reasonable time would have been two *d*
days, and certainly not as long as 13 days, and thus any right to withdraw was lost.
The arbitrators also held, however, that there was no conduct on the part of the
owners that amounted to affirmation or election during that 13-day period.

[46] In seeking permission to appeal to the Commercial Court, counsel for the
owners argued that the arbitrators had been wrong to imply a term. The right to
withdraw would only have been lost by waiver, and on the arbitrators' findings *e*
there had been no waiver. Staughton J examined the authorities and concluded
that they demonstrated quite clearly 'that lapse of a reasonable time does deprive
the owner of the right to withdraw' (see [1983] 2 Lloyd's Rep 473 at 475). He
went on to hold that what mattered was the arbitrators' conclusion that the right
to withdraw was lost, not the manner in which they described that right. Once *f*
they had found as a fact that a reasonable time had expired, their conclusion was
inevitable.

[47] So far as the construction issue was concerned, Staughton J observed that
the arbitrators' finding was at odds with one, if not two, expressions of view by
commercial judges. Had that been the only issue he would have been minded to
give permission to appeal. As, however, he considered that the arbitrators' *g*
conclusion on the time issue was correct, and this was determinative of the result,
permission to appeal would be refused. Subsequently Staughton J gave permission
to appeal against his decision for the sole purpose of permitting the Court of
Appeal to consider whether his approach had been correct in principle.

[48] The Court of Appeal ([1983] 3 All ER 777, [1983] 1 WLR 1362) were *h*
unanimous in holding that Staughton J had acted correctly in principle in giving
permission to appeal to the Court of Appeal against his own decision. By a
majority they held that his decision to refuse permission to appeal to the
Commercial Court against the award of the arbitrators was also correct. They
did so on the basis that the arbitrators had correctly held that the owners had to *j*
exercise their right (if right they had) to withdraw the vessel within a reasonable
time and that, whatever the juridical basis for this requirement, the arbitrators'
findings that a reasonable time had elapsed was inviolable.

[49] The following are the material passages in the leading judgment of
Sir John Donaldson MR ([1983] 3 All ER 777 at 782–784, [1983] 1 WLR 1362
at 1370–1371):

'I now turn to the substance of the appeal. In *Mardorf Peach & Co Ltd v Attica Sea Carriers Corp of Liberia, The Laconia* [1977] 1 All ER 545, [1977] AC 850 Lord Wilberforce, with the agreement of Lord Salmon, said, obiter, that notice of withdrawal must be given within a reasonable time after the default and that what is a reasonable time is essentially a matter for the arbitrators. As a general proposition this is hardly open to challenge, but somewhat different views have been expressed on why this should be the case. Two theories in particular have been aired, namely that the rule stems from an implied term of the contract or that delay in exercising the right will amount to waiver or create an estoppel. In the present case the owners knew of the default on 7 May 1980 and indicated to the charterers that any delay in withdrawing the vessel would be without prejudice to their right to do so. The arbitrators took the view that such an indication prevented the owners' conduct amounting to a waiver of their rights of creating any estoppel. However, they espoused the implied term explanation for the legal result declared in *The Laconia* and held that the owners had lost any right to withdraw the vessel ... I know of no authority for the proposition, and I do not think that I have ever heard it suggested before, that a shipowner can extend the time for reaching a decision whether or not to withdraw beyond what is reasonable in all the circumstances by the simple device of announcing that his failure to decide is without prejudice to his rights ... If counsel for the owners is right, and the owner can extend his option to withdraw the vessel in this way, chaos would result. Ships would be hove to at sea or tied up in port, no one knowing whether they were going to perform the chartered service. Counsel for the owners answers this by saying that when the next hire comes due, or when the owner has to accept or reject instructions from the charterers, he will have to make up his mind. I am not sure that this is necessarily so, because if counsel is right I do not see why he should not continue to perform the charterparty in all respects while at the same time proclaiming that none of this was to be taken as being an election to affirm the contract. So far as accepting payment of hire is concerned, if this must inevitably amount to an affirmation of the contract, it must be remembered that hire is sometimes paid only monthly. An interval of nearly a month before the owners could be forced to elect would be wholly unacceptable commercially. This is not to say that a declaration such as was made by the owners in this case can never have any effect. As Lloyd J pointed out in *The Scaptrade* ([1981] 2 Lloyd's Rep 425 at 430), what time is reasonable may well be affected by matters known only to the owners. Being in ignorance of these matters, charterers might reasonably conclude after x days that the owners were not going to withdraw the vessel and in such circumstances I can well understand it being held that the owners had waived their right to withdraw or were estopped from asserting it. If on the other hand the owners made their problems known to the charterers or indicated that they were not abandoning their rights, they may thereby retain their right of withdrawal for a longer period than x days, being such period as was reasonable in all the circumstances, including the special problems which were afflicting them. Thus waiver or an implied term are not alternatives. The implied term may well set a limit on the owners' rights and waiver may cut down those rights, but the concept of waiver is only appropriate where the person "waiving" is giving up some right. In the instant appeal the owners are contending that by "waiver" they acquired something which they would not otherwise have had, namely a right to withdraw the vessel after the expiry of a reasonable time.'

[50] In concurring with the result proposed by Sir John Donaldson MR, Fox LJ held, on the authority of *Mardorf Peach & Co Ltd v Attica Sea Carriers Corp of Liberia, The Laconia* [1977] 1 All ER 545, [1977] AC 850, that there was no doubt as to the existence of the rule that a right to withdraw must be exercised within a reasonable time. He continued ([1983] 3 All ER 777 at 788, [1983] 1 WLR 1362 at 1376–1377):

'I do not think that the fact that doubt or dispute exists as to the basis of the rule is, by itself, a sufficient reason for giving leave to appeal to the High Court. If the decision was probably right, whatever the basis of the rule, it was proper to refuse leave ... I turn then to consider what would be the consequence in this case of a resolution of the question of the basis of the rule as stated by Lord Wilberforce in *The Laconia*. Resolution in favour of the implied term theory would leave matters as they are since the arbitrators proceeded upon that basis. The question, therefore, is what would be the consequence of resolution in favour of the "election" theory. As I understand the reasons of the arbitrators, the only materiality of the "election" basis is that, if it be right, the fact that the owners indicated that the delay after 7 May would be without prejudice to their right to terminate demonstrated that there was no election by the owners to affirm the contract. I cannot see how the mere unilateral assertion of the owners that delay after 7 May was to be without prejudice to their rights can affect the matter. If the owners can do that, the rule, whatever its basis, is largely useless. I can see that there might be circumstances in which the owners could not reasonably be expected to make up their mind at once and that if they bring that to the notice of the charterers (who might not otherwise be aware of it) they could reserve their position. That, however, is a quite different matter and goes generally to the question of reasonableness. I would suppose that the question of reasonableness must be determined in the light of all the circumstances. One does not look at it exclusively from the point of view of either side. But, be that as it may, if the owners' right to withdraw must be exercised within a reasonable time I do not see how they can extend the "reasonable time" simply by their own choice; though they could no doubt extinguish or reduce their rights by waiver. Apart from the "without prejudice" point, the arbitrators, as I read the reasons, do not suggest that the juridical basis of the rule would have affected their finding of fact on the question of reasonable time and I do not think it would.'

[51] In the House of Lords Lord Diplock gave the following endorsement to the decision of Staughton J and the majority of the Court of Appeal in a short passage ([1984] 3 All ER 229 at 234, [1985] AC 191 at 201–202):

'Staughton J, however, indicated that but for the "reasonable time" point he would have been strongly minded to give leave to appeal on the construction of the NYPE withdrawal clause since this was in a standard form which is widely used and conflicting judicial dicta are to be found as to the meaning which the arbitrators had ascribed to the expression "any breach of this Charter Party" appearing in the clause. Staughton J, however, noted in his reasons for refusing leave that, while there were alternative jurisprudential concepts from which the requirement that notice of

a   withdrawal should be given within a reasonable time might be derived,
ie "implied term" of the contract and "waiver", both of which concepts had
been referred to indifferently by Lord Wilberforce in *Mardorf Peach & Co Ltd v
Attica Sea Carriers Corp of Liberia, The Laconia* [1977] 1 All ER 545, [1977] AC
850 (a case which dealt only with withdrawal in default of punctual and
regular payment of the hire), whichever concept were applied to the facts of
b   the instant case it would lead to the same result; and although the arbitrators
had plumped for "implied term" and excluded "waiver", the grounds which
they said precluded the existence of waiver were in the view of Staughton J
and of the majority of the Court of Appeal (which is also shared by me) quite
manifestly wrong.'

c   As the other members of the House of Lords agreed with Lord Diplock's speech,
this passage would seem to determine that principles of waiver are capable of
resulting in the loss of a right to withdraw from a charter through effluxion of
time alone.

    [52] The passages that we have just quoted do not afford much assistance to
d   identifying (1) how it is that the doctrines of election, waiver and estoppel are
capable of producing a 'rule' that a right to avoid a charter must be exercised
within a reasonable time, nor (2) to identifying the considerations that are
relevant to determining what is a 'reasonable time' and whether these are the
same when considering an implied term as when considering election, waiver
and estoppel. Our own conclusions are as follows.

e   [53] A time charterparty is a joint adventure. The shipowner provides the use
of his ship in accordance with orders given by the charterer. The charterer pays
hire for the services provided by the shipowner. The suggestion that such a
charter may permit a prolonged period during which one or both of the parties
remains at liberty to terminate the charter is in conflict with business efficacy, as
f   so forcefully demonstrated by Sir John Donaldson MR at [49], above. If
circumstances arise giving rise to a right to terminate the charter business efficacy
requires that the right be exercised promptly. If the shipowner continues to
provide the services of his ship, or the charterer continues to make use of those
services beyond such time as would reasonably be needed to react to those
circumstances, the inference will normally be that he has decided not to exercise
g   the right to terminate the charter. In such circumstances the principles of
election, waiver and estoppel will normally preclude the party in question from
thereafter terminating the charter. Thus the requirements of business efficacy
that justify the implication of a term that the right to withdraw be exercised
within a reasonable time will normally produce the same result as a consequence
h   of the application of the principles of election, waiver, and estoppel.

    [54] Principles of election, waiver and estoppel can, however, sometimes be
difficult to apply. Miss Hopkins has demonstrated that to us by an attempt to rely
upon the difficult case of *Peyman v Lanjani* [1984] 3 All ER 703, [1985] Ch 457, in
support of the surprising submission that the charterers in this case could not lose
j   their right to cancel the charter until they received legal advice that they had such
a right. *The Antaios* provides another example of those difficulties, for it was not
clear to Ackner LJ, who dissented in the Court of Appeal, that the owners' right
to withdraw was barred by principles of election, waiver or estoppel. In the light
of such potential difficulties, it seems to us that there is a strong case for the
implication of the term found by Branson J in the *Belships* case. As we stated
earlier, however, this is not a question which it is necessary for us to resolve.

[55] At the end of the day the question for us, applying the template of *The Antaios*, is whether, on the facts of this case, the decision of the arbitrators that the charterers were out of time for exercising a right to cancel the charter was 'open to serious doubt'. We are in no doubt that it was not. The following are our reasons. A delay in purporting to cancel the charterparty for over a month from the date of the events alleged to have given rise to the right to cancel was only consistent with a determination to continue with the charterparty despite those events. Had the arbitrators applied the principles of election, waiver and estoppel we are confident that they would have concluded that these precluded the right to cancel the charterparty after so long a period of delay. Thus the juridical basis upon which the arbitrators found that the right to cancel had to be exercised within a reasonable time did not impact upon their decision.

[56] For these reasons we do not consider that determination of the question of whether the arbitrators were right to imply the term which they applied would substantially affect the rights of the parties. Nor do we consider that the question is one which is of general public importance. It follows that this appeal must be dismissed.

[57] Thus, in order to resolve this appeal, it has not proved necessary to decide whether, if the construction issue had stood alone, it would have been open to Tomlinson J to have granted permission to appeal to the Commercial Court against the majority arbitrators' finding on that issue. This question raises, however, consideration of the extent to which the criteria in s 69 of the 1996 Act have departed from the *Nema* guidelines and this is a matter upon which we believe it would be helpful to give guidance.

THE DEPARTURE FROM THE *NEMA* GUIDELINES

[58] In *The Antaios* Sir John Donaldson MR considered the question raised by Staughton J of whether, where the commercial judge had formed the view that the arbitrators were probably right, the fact that the Court of Appeal might take a different view was any ground for granting permission to appeal to the High Court. He answered this question ([1983] 3 All ER 777 at 782, [1983] 1 WLR 1362 at 1369–1370):

'My answer to this question is that it is not if his appreciation that the Court of Appeal might take a different view has no more solid a basis than that this is in the nature of appellate courts and that if the Court of Appeal did take a different view and the parties were sufficiently persistent his own view might equally well be affirmed by the House of Lords. It is quite different if there are known to be differing schools of thought, each claiming their adherents amongst the judiciary, and the Court of Appeal, given the chance, might support either the school of thought to which the judge belongs or another school of thought. In such a case leave to appeal to the High Court should be given, provided that the resolution of the issue would substantially affect the rights of the parties (s 1(4) of the 1979 Act) *and* the case qualified for leave to appeal to the Court of Appeal under s 1(7) of the 1979 Act as no doubt it usually would. I add this additional qualification because there is no point in the judge giving leave when he has little doubt that the arbitrator is right and that, despite adversarial argument, he will affirm the award, unless he is also prepared to enable the Court of Appeal to resolve the conflict of judicial opinion.'

Fox LJ agreed with him ([1983] 3 All ER 777 at 788–789, [1983] 1 WLR 1362 at 1377–1378).

a [59] In [9], above, we have quoted what we have described as the gloss placed by Lord Diplock on his *Nema* guidelines. He went on to explain his reasons for differing from the views of Sir John Donaldson MR ([1984] 3 All ER 229 at 235–236, [1985] AC 191 at 204):

b 'Decisions are one thing; dicta are quite another. In the first place they are persuasive only, their persuasive strength depending on the professional reputation of the judge who voiced them. In the second place, the fact that there can only be found dicta but no conflicting decisions on the meaning of particular words or phrases appearing in the language used in a standard term in a commercial contract, especially if, like the NYPE withdrawal clause, it has been in common use for very many years, suggests either that *c* a choice between the rival meanings of those particular words or phrases that are espoused by the conflicting dicta is not one which has been found in practice to have consequences of sufficient commercial importance to justify the cost of litigating the matter or that businessmen who enter into contracts containing that standard term share a common understanding as to what those particular words and phrases were intended by them to mean. It was *d* strenuously urged on your Lordships that, wherever it could be shown by comparison of judicial dicta that there were two schools of thought among commercial judges on any question of construction of a standard term in a commercial contract, leave to appeal from an arbitral award which involved that question of construction would depend on which school of thought was *e* the one to which the judge who heard the application adhered. Maybe it would; but it is in the very nature of judicial discretion that within the bounds of "reasonableness" in the wide *Wednesbury* sense of that term, one judge may exercise the discretion one way whereas another judge might have exercised it in another; it is not peculiar to s 1(3)(b). It follows that I do not agree with Sir John Donaldson MR where in the instant case he says that *f* leave should be given under s 1(3)(b) to appeal to the High Court on a question of construction of a standard term on which it can be shown that there are two schools of thought among puisne judges where the conflict of judicial opinion appears in dicta only (see [1983] 3 All ER 777 at 782, [1983] 1 WLR 1362 at 1369–1370). This would not normally provide a reason for *g* departing from the *Nema* guidelines which I have repeated earlier in this speech.'

[60] The reasoning in this passage would have precluded Tomlinson J from giving permission to appeal on the construction issue unless he had formed the view that the arbitrators' decision on that issue was probably wrong. We do not, however, consider that this part of the *Nema* guidelines survives the provisions of *h* s 69. The criterion for granting permission to appeal in s 69(3)(c)(ii) is that the question should be one of general public importance and that the decision of the arbitrators should be *at least open to serious doubt*. These words impose a test which is broader than Lord Diplock's requirement that permission to appeal should not be given 'unless the judge considered that a strong prima facie case *j* had been made out that the arbitrator had been wrong in his construction'. Section 69(3)(c)(ii) is consonant with the approach of Sir John Donaldson MR in *The Antaios*.

[61] The guideline of Lord Diplock which has been superseded by s 69(3)(c)(ii) was calculated to place a particularly severe restraint on the role of the Commercial Court and higher courts in resolving issues of commercial law of general public importance. This is because the likelihood of conflicting judicial

decisions in relation to such issues, where they related to standard clauses in widely used charterparties containing arbitration clauses, was greatly reduced by the guideline itself. We consider that the facts of this case demonstrate that changing circumstances can raise issues of general public importance in relation to such clauses that are not covered by judicial decision.

[62] The nature of international conflict has changed over the years. The changes underlie the construction issue. The reasoning of the majority arbitrators on this issue was as follows. (1) There is no technical meaning of the word 'war'. It must be construed in a commonsense way—see *Kawasaki Kisen Kabushiki Kaisha of Kobe v Bantham Steamship Co Ltd* [1939] 1 All ER 819 at 826, [1939] 2 KB 544 at 558–559. (2) 'War' is to be distinguished from 'warlike activities and hostilities short of war' dealt with in cl 23(a) of the charter. 'War' means a war between nation states. (3) A businessman applying common sense in the context of cl 31 would not regard the NATO operation in Kosovo as a war. (4) Members of NATO participating in a NATO operation are not 'involved' in the operation as a nation.

[63] The minority arbitrator, Sir Christopher Staughton, thought that the majority arbitrators had asked the wrong question. They should have asked whether a businessman would have said that there was a war in Kosovo in March and April 1999, to which the answer would have been Yes. Germany, in his view, was 'involved' in the Kosovo conflict.

[64] The difference of view between the experienced arbitrators in this case provides, of itself, ground for contending that the decision of the majority is 'at least open to serious doubt'. We conclude that, had it not been for the fact that the arbitrators' conclusion on the 'time' issue rendered the question academic, it would have been open to Tomlinson J, in accordance with s 69 of the 1996 Act, to follow his inclination and give permission to appeal.

[65] For the reasons that we have given, this appeal will be dismissed.

Appeal dismissed.

Kate O'Hanlon   Barrister.

a

Coppard v Customs and Excise Commissioners

[2003] EWCA Civ 511

b

COURT OF APPEAL, CIVIL DIVISION
THORPE, SEDLEY AND MANCE LJJ
25 MARCH, 9 APRIL 2003

c

Judge – Judge in fact – De facto doctrine – Meaning of doctrine – Whether de facto judge 'a tribunal established by law' – Human Rights Act 1998, Sch 1, Pt I, art 6(1).

Proceedings in the Queen's Bench Division went to trial before a circuit judge authorised to deal with the business of the Technology and Construction Court. By an oversight, the statutory power of the Lord Chancellor to authorise circuit judges to sit as justices of the High Court, which was routinely exercised on the
d appointment of circuit judges to the Technology and Construction Court, had not been exercised, although the judge was well qualified to sit. The judge found against the claimant on all substantive points. Subsequently, the claimant discovered that the judge had not been authorised to sit as a High Court Judge. He therefore appealed contending that (i) the judge knew or ought to have known that he was not a High Court judge in law and that accordingly he was
e not one de facto; and (ii) that in any event he was not 'a tribunal established by law' as required by art 6(1)[a] of the European Convention for the Protection of Human Rights and Fundamental Freedoms 1950 (as set out in Sch 1 to the Human Rights Act 1998). The Court of Appeal was therefore required to consider the meaning of the de facto doctrine and whether that doctrine was compatible with
f art 6.

Held – (1) On the true meaning of the de facto doctrine, a person who was believed, and believed himself, to have the necessary judicial authority would be regarded in law as possessing such authority. Thus the doctrine could not validate the acts, or ratify the authority, of a person who, though believed by the world to
g be a judge of the court in which he sat, knew that he was not. A person who lacked authority included a person who had shut his eyes to the fact that he lacked authority when it was obvious, but not a person who had neglected to find it out. In the instant case, the judge neither knew nor ought to have known that he was not authorised to sit as a judge of the High Court. Accordingly, the judge was a
h de facto judge of the High Court and his judgment therefore a judgment of the High Court (see [18], [24], [32], [40], below); *Fawdry and Co (a firm) v Murfitt (Lord Chancellor intervening)* [2003] QB 104 considered.

(2) A de facto judge was 'a tribunal established by law' for the purposes of art 6 of the convention. Such a judge was a tribunal whose authority was established
j by common law since the de facto doctrine validated the office of the judge rather than his acts. That doctrine matched the substantive content of the phrase 'established by law'. It did not ratify the acts of usurpers or operate arbitrarily. It was limited, in effect, to the correction of mistakes of form rather than of substance. In those circumstances, the convention did not require the disqualification

---

a   Article 6, so far as material, is set out at [26], below

of a judge purely because his authority had not been formally established before
he sat.   It followed in the instant case that the judge had been a tribunal   *a*
established by law.   Accordingly, the appeal would be dismissed (see [32], [35],
[36], [39], [40] below).

Notes
For independent tribunals established by law, see 8(2) *Halsbury's Laws* (4th edn   *b*
reissue) para 140.
    For the Human Rights Act 1998, Sch 1, Pt I, art 6, see 7 *Halsbury's Statutes* (4th
edn) (2002 reissue) 554.

Cases referred to in judgment
A v B (a company) [2002] EWCA Civ 337, [2002] 2 All ER 545, [2002] 3 WLR 542.   *c*
Aldridge, Re (1897) 15 NZLR 361, NZ CA.
Fawdry and Co (a firm) v Murfitt (Lord Chancellor intervening) [2002] EWCA Civ 643,
    [2003] QB 104, [2002] 3 WLR 1354.
Locabail (UK) Ltd v Bayfield Properties Ltd [2000] 1 All ER 65, [2000] QB 451, [2000]
    2 WLR 870, CA.   *d*
Manitoba Language Rights under the Manitoba Act 1870, Reference re (1985) 19 DLR
    (4th) 1, Canada SC.
State v Carroll (1871) 38 Conn 449, Connecticut SC.
Sunday Times v UK (1979) 2 EHRR 245, [1979] ECHR 6538/74, ECt HR.
Zand v Austria (1978) 15 DR 70, E Com HR.
                                                                                     e

Cases referred to in skeleton arguments
Abbot of Fountaine's case (1431) 9 H VI 33.
Adams v Adams (A-G intervening) [1970] 3 All ER 572, [1971] P 188, Div.
Bagot's Case (1469) YB 9 Edw 4.
Curtin v Barton (1893) 139 NY 505, NY CA.   *f*
De Cubber v Belgium (1984) 7 EHRR 236, [1984] ECHR 9186/80, E Ct HR.
Delcourt v Belgium (1970) 1 EHRR 355, [1970] ECHR 2689/65, E Ct HR.
EE v Federal Republic of Germany App No 18889/91 (14 October 1992, unreported),
    E Com HR.
Gahan v Lafitte (1842) 3 Moo PCC 382, PC.
Golder v UK (1975) 1 EHRR 524, [1975] ECHR 4451/70, E Ct HR.   *g*
Harris v Jays (1599) 4 Co Rep 30a, 76 ER 956.
Hodgetts v Baker (1890) 34 Sol Jo 584, Ch D.
Knowles v Luce (1579) Moore KB 109, 72 ER 473.
Medicaments and Related Classes of Goods (No 2), Re [2001] ICR 564, [2001] 1 WLR
    700, CA.   *h*
Pfeifer v Austria (1992) 14 EHRR 692, [1990] ECHR 11855/95, E Ct HR.
Porrett, Re [1891] 2 Ch 433, CA.
R v Bedford Level Corp (1805) 6 East 356, 102 ER 1323.
R v Gough [1993] 2 All ER 724, [1993] AC 646, [1993] 2 WLR 883, HL.
R v Sussex Justices, ex p McCarthy [1924] 1 KB 256, [1923] All ER Rep 233,DC.   *j*
Sayers v Clarke Walker (a firm) [2002] EWCA Civ 645, [2002] 3 All ER 490, [2002] 1
    WLR 3095, CA.
Stieringer v Germany App No 28899/95 (25 November 1996, unreported), E Com HR.
Stubbings v UK (1996) 1 BHRC 316, E Ct HR.
Tameside Metropolitan BC v Grant [2002] 3 FCR 238, [2002] Fam 194, [2002] 2 WLR 376.
Walker v UK (2000) 29 EHRR CD 276, E Ct HR.

a *Whitfield v A-G* [1989] LRC (Const) 248, Bah SC.
   Yorkshire Bank plc v Hall [1999] 1 All ER 879, [1999] 1 WLR 1713, CA.

Appeal

The claimant, Edgar John Coppard, appealed with permission of the Court of
Appeal (Judge and Mummery LJJ) granted on 5 November 2002 from the decision
b of Judge Richard Seymour QC in the Queen's Bench Division on 23 January 2001
([2001] All ER (D) 148 (Jan)), awarding him nominal damages only in his
proceedings for breach of contract against the defendant, the Customs and Excise
Commissioners. The Lord Chancellor intervened in the appeal. The facts are set
out in the judgment of the court.

c *Duncan Macpherson* (instructed by *Johnson Sillett Bloom*) for Mr Coppard.
   Michael Patchett-Joyce (instructed by the *Solicitor for Customs and Excise*) for the
       commissioners.
   Philip Sales (instructed by the *Treasury Solicitor*) for the Lord Chancellor.

Cur adv vult

d
9 April 2003. The following judgment was delivered.

SEDLEY LJ.
   [1] This is a judgment of the court.

e
THE ISSUE
   [2] This appeal raises an issue of some constitutional importance. It can be
framed without levity in the question: when is a judge not a judge?
   [3] The facts giving rise to it can be shortly stated. Mr Coppard sued the
Commissioners of Customs and Excise (the commissioners) in the Queen's
f Bench Division of the High Court for damages for breach of a contract which
they had entered into with him for deferred payments of value added tax. The
breach had resulted in the commissioners making him bankrupt, and they
admitted liability for any damage it had caused. The case therefore went to trial
on damages alone. It was listed for hearing before Judge Richard Seymour QC,
who after a two-day hearing delivered a reserved judgment on 23 January 2001
g ([2001] All ER (D) 148 (Jan)), finding against Mr Coppard on all substantive
questions and awarding him nominal damages of £2 for the admitted breach. He
refused permission to appeal, and were it not for subsequent developments the
case would not have reached this court.
   [4] What Mr Coppard subsequently discovered, however, was that Judge
h Seymour was not authorised to sit as a judge of the High Court. The office he held
was that of circuit judge. In that capacity he was authorised by the Lord Chancellor,
pursuant to s 68 of the Supreme Court Act 1981, to deal with what was known as
Official Referees' business and is now the business of the Technology and
Construction Court (TCC), a limb of the High Court; but that was all.
j [5] The Lord Chancellor has power under s 9(1) of the 1981 Act to authorise
circuit judges to sit as justices of the High Court. This power is routinely
exercised on the appointment of a circuit judge to the TCC, but by a most
regrettable oversight it had not been exercised in respect of Judge Seymour or (as
has now been ascertained) Judge Toulmin QC. Accordingly it is accepted both
by the commissioners and by counsel for the Lord Chancellor that the judge sat
and adjudicated in Mr Coppard's case without legal authority.

[6] Before considering the consequences of this, it is right to say that the judgment Judge Seymour delivered was of high quality and legally impeccable. The sole reason why this court (Judge and Mummery LJJ) gave conditional permission to appeal after refusal on the papers by Latham LJ was that his position raised a question of general importance which was not resolved by authority.

TIME

[7] It is first necessary to deal with the condition upon which permission was granted: that this court must be satisfied by affidavit evidence that it is right to enlarge the time for appealing.

[8] Mr Coppard can be exonerated of any delay until the last week of August 2001, when he finally learnt from the Lord Chancellor's Department what Judge Seymour's legal status had been at the time of trial and judgment. From then until 12 June 2002, when the appellant's notice was finally lodged, he deposes that he was occupied in seeking funds, first—unsuccessfully, despite a favourable opinion of counsel—from the Legal Services Commission, then privately. He finally remortgaged his house on 29 May 2002 and within a fortnight had issued his appellant's notice.

[9] It is in the interests of public justice, at least as much as in Mr Coppard's interests, that the present issue should be resolved. It is only if to do so at this distance of time would unjustifiably damage or jeopardise the position of others that we would be disposed to refuse to enlarge time, and we do not see such a situation here. Neither the commissioners nor the intervener takes any point on time. In all these circumstances we enlarge the time for appealing to the date of the appellant's notice.

THE NATURE OF THE CHALLENGE

[10] In his amended grounds Mr Duncan Macpherson puts his case with simplicity and clarity. His premise is that Judge Seymour knew or ought to have known that he was not authorised to sit as a judge of the High Court. It follows, he contends, that when he tried this High Court case Judge Seymour was a judge neither in law nor in fact. He submits, both consequently and independently, that Judge Seymour did not constitute a tribunal established by law within art 6 of the European Convention for the Protection of Human Rights and Fundamental Freedoms 1950 (as set out in Sch 1 to the Human Rights Act 1998), and that his judgment should be set aside and the damages claim reheard by a properly constituted tribunal.

[11] Some important elements of this process of reasoning are uncontentious. It is common ground, for the reasons I have given, that Judge Seymour was in law not a judge of the High Court. If in addition he was not a High Court judge de facto, it will follow that his judgment, not being a judgment of the High Court at all, is a nullity and has to be set aside as of right. In this event art 6 will add nothing. But if Judge Seymour was, in the eye of English law, a High Court judge in fact, with the result that his judgment is valid at common law, the question will arise whether the obligation of the state under s 6 of the 1998 Act to act compatibly with the convention rights would be violated by the common law's recognition of a judgment not given by 'a tribunal established by law'.

[12] The contention of Mr Philip Sales for the Lord Chancellor is that in answering the first question we will be answering the second—in other words, that 'law' in art 6 includes common law; but if he is wrong, as Mr Macpherson

a   says he is on authority and principle, then on this further and alternative ground the appeal must succeed. If Mr Sales is held to be right, however, Mr Macpherson seeks to fall back on a further argument: that in that case the common law, by treating an invalid assumption of jurisdiction as valid, itself offends against art 6. But we do not think that this argument is on analysis a true fallback. It is the same answer as Mr Macpherson gives to Mr Sales' proposition that a judge in fact is a

b   judge in law, namely that art 6 will not accommodate such a proposition even if the common law does.

[13] The one answer to the appeal which in our judgment is unacceptable in principle is that advanced, perhaps more out of hope than out of conviction, by counsel for the commissioners, Mr Michael Patchett-Joyce, that the want of authority was a simple error of procedure which by virtue of CPR 3.10 does not

c   of itself invalidate any step taken on the basis of it. It would do little for the rule of law and for constitutional propriety to relegate an issue as important as qualification for judicial office to the realm of procedure.

[14] So the two key questions are: (i) Did Judge Seymour sit and give judgment as a judge in fact of the High Court? (i) Did he in that event constitute

d   a tribunal established by law?

THE LAW

[15] The concept of a judge in fact (de facto) is an ancient one. It is not confined to judges but has been extended to offices, including the monarchy itself, which have been exercised by persons later held not to have lawfully

e   occupied them. The central requirement for the operation of the doctrine is that the person exercising the office must have been reputed to hold it. Given this, Wade and Forsyth *Administrative Law* (8th edn, 2000) pp 291–292, describe the doctrine in this way:

f   'In one class of cases there is a long-standing doctrine that collateral challenge is not to be allowed: where there is some unknown flaw in the appointment or authority of some officer or judge. The acts of the officer or judge may be held to be valid in law even though his own appointment is invalid and in truth he has no legal power at all.'

g   [16] Recently this court in *Fawdry and Co (a firm) v Murfitt (Lord Chancellor intervening)* [2002] EWCA Civ 643, [2003] QB 104, [2002] 3 WLR 1354 considered some of the implications of the doctrine so stated. The case concerned a different situation from the present because the judge who had sat was held to have been a judge in law, albeit for reasons which had been unknown to her. But had this

h   not been the case, it would have been necessary to consider whether she had been a judge in fact, and the court looked at this question contingently. All three members of the court were troubled by the possibility that the principle might be so broad as to validate the acts of someone who knew perfectly well, although the litigants did not, that he or she had no authority to adjudicate. Neither Mr Philip Sales (who appeared in that case, as in this, for the Lord Chancellor as

j   intervener) nor the court was content with the idea that the doctrine could go so far; and more than one authority suggested that it did not. Thus in *Re Aldridge* (1897) 15 NZLR 361 at 372, Richmond J said:

    'It may well be that the principle which validates the acts of a Judge *de facto* cannot be invoked for their own protection by any who wilfully abuse the office, still less by mere usurpers.'

[17] This question, although not determinative, was considered by this court in the *Fawdry* case. Hale LJ, giving the leading judgment, said ([2003] QB 104 at [30]):

> 'But what if the court usher had been persuaded to sit and everyone in court had behaved as if he were entitled to do so? There must come a point at which, whatever the public perception, there is no basis for applying the de facto doctrine. The dividing line between what is and is not sufficient "colour" in borderline cases may not be as clear as one would like, but fortunately the point does not arise for decision here.'

Sedley LJ said (at [43]):

> 'In the present state of authority the position of the usurper, in the sense of someone who discharges an office in the actual or constructive knowledge that he has no title to it, is in my view uncertain. If the purpose of the de facto doctrine is the maintenance of stability and confidence in the legal system and the prevention of technical disputes about the formalities of appointment, it might well be said that a sufficiently clearly reputed tenure of office should not be open to challenge even on the ground of the purported officer's knowledge of his own incapacity. Yet, as Mr Sales's response on behalf of the Lord Chancellor confirms, it goes entirely against the grain to validate the acts of someone who knows, even if the world does not, that he is not qualified to hold the office he is exercising.'

Ward LJ (at [60]–[61]) declined to speculate on the acts of an impostor beyond expressing the tentative view that the judgment of a knowing impostor is a nullity, and that likewise the decision of a judge exercising a jurisdiction he knew he did not possess would be 'a decision that never was'.

[18] For reasons which will become apparent when we turn to art 6 of the convention, it is necessary in this case, in contrast to the *Fawdry* case, not simply to form a view but to reach a conclusion on this question. We would hold that the de facto doctrine cannot validate the acts, nor therefore ratify the authority, of a person who, though believed by the world to be a judge of the court in which he sits, knows that he is not. We accept, on well-known principles, that a person who knows he lacks authority includes a person who has shut his eyes to that fact when it is obvious, but not a person who has simply neglected to find it out. We will call such a person a usurper.

WAS THE JUDGE A USURPER?

[19] Is it arguable that Judge Seymour was such a person? There is now before the court a witness statement of Emma Millicent Robinson, a barrister in the Government Legal Service, who recounts that she spoke to Judge Seymour on 26 February 2003 about this case. She says:

> 'The judge told me that he was appointed as a judge of the TCC in July 2000. This was his first full-time judicial appointment. The judge recalled that, on his appointment, the judge in charge of the TCC lists (then Dyson J) explained that, during the times when the judge had unexpected capacity in his TCC list, he would be expected to volunteer to assist in the Queen's Bench Division or the Chancery Division of the High Court. The judge explained that he understood he did have authority to sit in the Queen's

a Bench Division and Chancery Division by virtue of his appointment as a TCC judge alone and that no further authorisation was required.'

She goes on to explain that the TCC is part of the High Court, and that a judge appointed to that court has authority by virtue of s 68 of the 1981 Act to hear and decide TCC business.

b [20] Mr Macpherson accepts this statement as an admissible and factual account of the state of the judge's knowledge. Mr Sales submits that the judge himself is not open to questioning about it: see *Locabail (UK) Ltd v Bayfield Properties Ltd* [2000] 1 All ER 65 at 75, [2000] QB 451 at 477. Mr Macpherson has not sought to debate this, but he submits that as evidence it is simply not good enough: Judge Seymour knew that no s 9 authority had been issued to him and c should have known that being assigned under s 68 to the TCC did not by itself have the effect that he assumed it did. In so far as this was a matter of fact, there was no error on the judge's part: he knew the facts. In so far as it was an error of law, Mr Macpherson first submitted, it cannot be a proper foundation for the de facto doctrine. He accepted, however, that if this were right the leading New d Zealand case of *Re Aldridge* (1897) 15 NZLR 361 could not have gone the way it did, and for that reason abandoned the point.

[21] It is important nevertheless that this court should not accept such a concession, at least when it is not dictated by binding authority, without considering whether it is rightly made. We are not bound by *Aldridge's* case, and e in spite of its high standing in the common law on this topic, it is apparent both from it and from the present case that the common law does not—or not yet—have all the answers. The reason why, even so, we would accept the concession is that the basis of the de facto doctrine is not the nature but the occurrence of a mistake as to the judicial authority of the individual concerned.

f [22] The argument is in our view not advanced by the distinction that Mr Macpherson has sought to make between an error as to appointment and an error as to authority. His suggestion is that cases such as *Aldridge's* case and *State v Carroll* (1871) 38 Conn 449 depended on the judge's belief that he had been appointed, not simply (as in the present case) that he had authority. This seems to us a distinction without a difference in the present context.

g [23] The statute law which authorises some judges, in virtue of their appointment, to exercise one aspect only of the High Court's jurisdiction and requires them to be given separate authority to exercise other aspects of it, is piecemeal and complicated. It is unfortunate but unsurprising that Judge Seymour assumed that his appointment to the TCC, a limb of the High Court, h gave him power to sit elsewhere in the High Court without further authorisation. It certainly did not amount, in our judgment, either to knowledge of his own incapacity or to wilful blindness to it.

[24] We hold that Judge Seymour neither knew nor ought to have known, in the sense that he was ignoring the obvious or failing to make obvious inquiries, j that he was not authorised to sit as a judge of the High Court. There is uncontested evidence that but for an oversight in the Lord Chancellor's Department he would have been formally authorised under s 9 of the 1981 Act. He was well qualified to sit. This is therefore not a case of usurpation, nor of lack of the requisite competence or qualification. On established principles of law, Judge Seymour was a judge in fact of the High Court and his judgment therefore a judgment of the High Court.

ARTICLE 6 OF THE CONVENTION

[25] But this is an end of the appeal only if, as Mr Sales submits is the case, the validation of Judge Seymour's status (not merely of his judgment) at common law is cognate with his establishment by law as a tribunal for the purposes of art 6. Mr Macpherson submits that it is not: he argues that the doctrine of de facto authority validates acts done under colour of a supposed but legally non-existent authority, but that it does not create authority in law where none existed—indeed its very premise is the non-existence of true authority in law. Thus in the leading Canadian case *Reference re Manitoba Language Rights under the Manitoba Act 1870* (1985) 19 DLR (4th) 1, the Supreme Court of Canada, which had had the benefit of wide-ranging citation of common law authority, said (at 28):

> 'The application of the *de facto* doctrine is, however, limited to validating acts which are taken under invalid authority: it does not validate the authority under which the acts took place.'

[26] Article 6 begins:

> '1. In the determination of his civil rights and obligations or of any criminal charge against him, everyone is entitled to a fair and public hearing within a reasonable time by an independent and impartial tribunal established by law.'

By s 6 of the 1998 Act:

> '(1) It is unlawful for a public authority to act in a way which is incompatible with a Convention right ...
> (3) In this section "public authority" includes ... a court or tribunal ...'

[27] Two important questions thus arise. (i) Does the de facto doctrine validate the act or the office? (ii) If it is the latter, is this a sufficient compliance with the requirement of art 6 that a person's civil rights are to be determined by a tribunal established by law?

[28] We put the questions in this way because it is correctly conceded by Mr Sales that if Judge Seymour's acts alone are validated, this is insufficient to comply with art 6: the tribunal itself will by definition not have been established by law. We put them in this order for an equally important reason. The true ambit of the de facto doctrine cannot logically be determined by the requirements of art 6: to do this would be to adjust the common law defensively, not to declare it objectively. It is one thing to bring the substantive doctrines of the common law into harmony with the convention in the manner described by this court in *A v B (a company)* [2002] EWCA Civ 337 at [4], [2002] 2 All ER 545 at [4], [2002] 3 WLR 542. It is another for a legal system to hold itself to be convention-compliant by ratifying what would otherwise be non-compliant.

DOES THE DE FACTO DOCTRINE VALIDATE THE ACT OR THE OFFICE?

[29] Mr Macpherson, to whose industry we are very much indebted, cites a series of persuasive rulings from other common law jurisdictions. Of these, it is sufficient to refer to the judgment of Butler CJ (with whom the other members of the court agreed) in the Supreme Court of Connecticut in *State v Carroll* (1871) 38 Conn 449 at 471:

> 'An officer *de facto* is one whose acts, though not those of a lawful officer, the law, upon principles of policy and justice, will hold valid so far as they

a   involve the interests of the public and third persons, where the duties of the office were exercised [irregularly].'

[30] There is no need for further citation because Mr Sales accepts that there is no authoritative statement of the de facto doctrine which suggests, at least in terms, that it validates the office and not merely acts done under colour of it. His
b   argument, echoing his submissions in *Fawdry and Co (a firm) v Murfitt (Lord Chancellor intervening)* [2003] QB 104, is that the former is nevertheless its true logic. Dramatic though this proposition is in the face of centuries of restatements of the doctrine throughout the common law world, it seems to us to be right. The point powerfully made by Mr Macpherson, that the very premise of the de facto doctrine is that there was no legal authority, is not necessarily an answer to
c   it, for the true analysis may be that the judge in fact *becomes* a judge in law by the operation of the doctrine, and that this is why his acts are valid.

[31] The question whether the de facto doctrine validates the act or the office was left open in the *Fawdry* case. Hale LJ, whose judgment contains an indispensable account of the origins and development of this branch of the law,
d   concluded (at [36]), albeit with expressed hesitation, that since 'there must be some basis for the authority assumed by the judge ... the rule can be regarded as validating the establishment of the tribunal as well as the acts it performs'. In *Reference re Manitoba Language Rights under the Manitoba Act 1870* (1985) 19 DLR (4th) 1, it is noteworthy that the Supreme Court of Canada went on to conclude
e   that the doctrine of necessity permitted it to hold temporarily valid, pending proper re-enactment, the body of legislation which it had found to be constitutionally invalid. In other words, because legal certainty and administrative stability could not tolerate the vacuum, the court itself possessed authority to confer interim validity on Manitoba's legislation.

f   [32] It seems to us that Mr Sales' analysis makes sense of an otherwise intractable—indeed a logically unintelligible—theory which appears to predicate the validity of a judgment on the very invalidity of its author's office. In its place it postulates, in the interests of certainty and finality, that a person who is believed and believes himself to have the necessary judicial authority will be regarded in law as possessing such authority. If this is the true meaning of the de facto
g   doctrine of jurisdiction, as we would hold it is, then the first question of compatibility with art 6 is answered. The judge in fact is a tribunal whose authority is established by the common law.

DOES A JUDGE IN FACT COME WITHIN ART 6?

h   [33] The answer to the question of convention-compliance, in our judgment, depends on at least two things: first, what the substantive content of the phrase 'established by law' is; and secondly, whether the de facto doctrine, even in the shape in which we have now construed it, matches that content.

ESTABLISHED BY LAW
j   [34] There is no decision of either the European Court of Human Rights or the European Commission of Human Rights which deals comprehensively with the content of the expression 'established by law'. But in *Zand v Austria* (1978) 15 DR 70 at 80 (para 69) the Commission of Human Rights, in debating the status of the Austrian labour courts, which had been set up only under elective ministerial powers, said that the object and purpose of the provision was—

'that the judicial organization in a democratic society must not depend on
the discretion of the Executive, but that it should be regulated by law
emanating from Parliament.'

The Court of Human Rights has made it clear (see *Sunday Times v UK* (1979) 2
EHRR 245) that law declared by the courts ranks for these purposes with that
made by Parliament. We do not consider, however, that this passage in *Zand's*
case (which s 2 of the 1998 Act requires us to take into account) answers the
question. First of all, it is addressed to the issue then before the Commission of
Human Rights, which concerned the use of ministerial powers to create
courts—hence the focus on the executive. Secondly, it seems to us that
independence from the executive is what the word 'independent' in art 6(1) is
principally concerned with. Thirdly, and perhaps most importantly, it is plain
that much more than this is involved in the concept of a tribunal established by
law. Among other things, the purpose (especially when one remembers the
period of European history of which the convention was intended to mark a
definitive end) is to ensure that justice is administered by, and only by, the
prescribed exercise of the judicial power of the state, not by ad hoc 'people's
courts' and the like. Such a principle must be fundamental to any concept of the
rule of law. Implicit in it is that the composition and authority of a court must
not be arbitrary.

COMPATIBILITY WITH THE CONVENTION

[35] This brings us to the second question: does the de facto doctrine meet this
standard? To the extent that, as we hold, it validates the authority of the tribunal
and not merely its acts, it does. But Mr Macpherson submits that it does not
exclude, as it needs to, a validation of the authority of a person who is so
incompetent to sit that to ratify him in office would amount to arbitrariness or
irrationality offensive to the rule of law.

[36] This argument is in very large part already addressed by our holding that
the doctrine cannot validate the authority of a usurper, for it will be a rare case in
which an incompetent person who lacks legal authority does not know that he or
she ought not to be sitting as a judge. The freak case of a person without either
professional competence or legal authority who believes despite his
incompetence that he is authorised to sit as a judge can be addressed if and when
it arises. What matters to the present issues is that the de facto doctrine ratifies
the authority only of persons believed by themselves and the world to possess the
judicial power they are exercising. It does not protect people who have deluded
themselves or others into thinking they have authority.

[37] But there is a second and more troubling ground on which
Mr Macpherson contends that a judge in fact is not a tribunal established by law.
'Established' in his contention requires a tribunal to have been established by the
time the individual's civil rights and obligations come before it. We are not
disposed to accept Mr Sales' argument that the common law gives de facto
tribunals this legal status proleptically. To accept this would be to establish, in
effect, a prior dispensation for avoidable error, with undesirable consequences for
legal certainty and good administration. If the de facto doctrine establishes a
tribunal by law, it seems to us that it does so by recognising the authority, in an
appropriate and legally controlled situation, of what would otherwise not be a
lawful tribunal.

[38] The convention itself is silent on this question. So is the International
Covenant on Civil and Political Rights (New York, 16 December 1966; TS 6

a (1977); Cmnd 6702), though by art 14(1) it adds the adjective 'competent' to the requisite qualities of a tribunal established by law. But art 47 of the Charter of Fundamental Rights of the European Union (OJ 2000 C364 p 1), a non-binding instrument adopted by the United Kingdom and the other member states in December 2000, says: 'Everyone is entitled to a fair and public hearing within a reasonable time by an independent and impartial tribunal previously established

b by law.' This reproduces the language of art 6(1) of the convention with the striking addition of the word 'previously'. If it were part of the language of the convention we might well have been driven to hold that the de facto doctrine did not comply with it. But is it, as Mr Macpherson urges, implicit in the convention? No jurisprudence of the Commission or Court of Human Rights indicates that it is, but that could be because the question has not yet come before either body.

c [39] We remind ourselves that the convention is not a United Kingdom statute, and that we should be concerned less with close analysis of its language than with the principles which animate it. We remind ourselves that the legal system of every member state will contain ways of dealing with errors and omissions in the appointment of persons to judicial office, whether by ratifying

d or by nullifying what has happened. Provided that the United Kingdom's legal response, at least as it has developed in England and Wales, is not such as to ratify the acts of usurpers or to operate arbitrarily and is limited, in effect, to the correction of mistakes of form rather than of substance—and in our judgment it meets all these tests—we do not consider that the convention requires the disqualification of a judge purely because his authority was not formally

e established before he sat.

CONCLUSION
[40] A person who sits as a judge of the High Court of England or Wales in the circumstances in which Judge Seymour sat is in our judgment a judge in fact and a tribunal established by law. In spite, therefore, of the novel and difficult issues

f which this appeal has raised, it must be dismissed.

Appeal dismissed.

Kate O'Hanlon   Barrister.

Khiaban v Beard

a

[2002] EWCA Civ 358

COURT OF APPEAL, CIVIL DIVISION
WARD AND DYSON LJJ
10 MARCH 2003

b

Practice – Claim – Value of claim – Whether court having power to require claimant to claim sums which he had chosen not to include in his claim form or pleadings – CPR 26.8(2).

c

The claimant's car was damaged in a collision with the defendant's car. The repair costs of £756 were borne by the claimant's insurer, subject to an insurance excess of £125. In order to keep a minimum the costs of proposed proceedings by the claimant against the defendant, the parties' insurers entered into a memorandum of understanding by which they agreed to abide by the court's decision as to liability in relation to a claim by the claimant to recover the excess. The court's decision would thus determine which insurer would bear the repair costs. Pursuant to that memorandum, the claimant's insurers (being subrogated to the claimant's rights against the defendant) brought proceedings against the defendant in the claimant's name, claiming £155 (ie the £125 excess plus some miscellaneous expenses). After the existence of the memorandum was confirmed to the court, the district judge, acting of her own motion, ordered the claimant to file and serve amended particulars of claim reflecting 'the true value' of the claim. By those amended particulars, the claimant deleted the claim for miscellaneous expenses, but left the claim for £125 unamended. The district judge subsequently struck out the proceedings, holding that the amended particulars of claim did not reflect the value of the claim since they failed to include the full cost of the repairs. On a subsequent application by the claimant to set aside the strike out order, the district judge drew a distinction between subrogated and non-subrogated costs and held that it was for the court to assess the true value of the claim. In reaching that conclusion, she relied on CPR 26.8(2)[a] which provided that, when deciding the track for a claim, it was for the court to assess its financial value. The district judge dismissed the application, and the claimant appealed to the Court of Appeal. On the appeal, the court was required to determine whether, in the context of the CPR, a 'claim' included claims not before the court.

d

e

f

g

Held – In the context of the CPR, the word 'claim' only covered that which the claimant sought to recover through the court, and it was never used in a context which suggested that it included claims which had not been brought before the court in legal proceedings. There was nothing in the general law which positively obliged a claimant to include in his pleaded case all the claims which he could arguably advance against a defendant. Nor was there any such requirement in the CPR. In particular, there was nothing in the language of CPR 26.8 to indicate that the court was concerned with the value of items which were not being

h

j

---

a   Rule 26.8, so far as material, provides: '(1) When deciding the track for a claim, the matters to which the court shall have regard include—(a) the financial value ... of the claim ...
(2) It is for the court to assess the financial value of a claim ...'

a claimed. The court had no power to increase the financial value of a claim in respect of items of claim that had been included in the claim form and the particulars of claim. Still less did it have the power to increase the claim to include items of claim that the claimant had chosen not to include at all. It followed in the instant case that there was nothing in the CPR to justify the decision of the district judge to order the claimant to increase his claim to include

b the repair costs. Nor was there any reason for distinguishing between subrogated and non-subrogated claims. The parties had done nothing objectionable. The real issue between them was liability, and the parties had been entitled to simplify the claim, limiting the amount claimed to £125. In so doing, they had acted in accordance with the overriding objective in that expense had been saved and the case could be dealt with proportionately. Accordingly, the appeal would be

c allowed (see [12]–[18], [20]–[22], below).

Notes

d For the requirement for the court to assess the financial value of the claim when allocating a case to a track, see 37 *Halsbury's Laws* (4th edn reissue) para 470.

Cases referred to in judgments

B (infants), Re [1965] 2 All ER 651n, [1965] 1 WLR 946.
Henderson v Henderson (1843) 3 Hare 100, 67 ER 313, [1843–60] All ER Rep 378.

Appeal

e The claimant, Mr Khiaban, appealed with permission of District Judge Stephenson from her order in Barnet County Court on 11 February 2002, giving effect to her decision of 25 January 2002, dismissing the claimant's application for an order setting aside an order made by the district judge on 5 November 2001 striking out the claimant's proceedings for damages against the defendant, Tony Beard. The

f facts are set out in the judgment of Dyson LJ.

Michael Ashe QC and *Constance Mahoney* (instructed by *Websters*) for the claimant. The defendant did not appear.

g **DYSON LJ** (giving the first judgment at the invitation of Ward LJ).

[1] This is an appeal from the order of District Judge Stephenson made on 11 February 2002 sitting at Barnet County Court whereby she dismissed the claimant's application to set aside her order dated 5 November 2001 by which she had struck out the claimant's claim on the grounds that the amended particulars

h of claim did not reflect the full value of his claim. She gave the claimant permission to appeal against her decision of 11 February, and directed that the appeal be transferred to Judge Paul Collins at the Central London County Court. Judge Collins considered that the issue raised by this appeal involved an important point of principle or practice such as to justify the transfer of the appeal

j to the Court of Appeal under CPR Pt 52, r 14(1)(a).

[2] The action concerns a road traffic accident which occurred on 27 March 2000. As a result of the collision between the vehicles of the two parties, the claimant's vehicle had to be repaired at a cost of £755·89 (including value added tax). The claimant paid an insurance excess of £125, but subject to this, the repair costs were borne by his insurer. The parties' insurers entered into a memorandum

of understanding (MOU) by which they agreed to abide by the court's decision as
to liability in relation to the claimant's claim to recover the excess from the
defendant: the court's decision would determine which insurer would bear the
repair costs. Pursuant to the MOU, on 13 December 2000, the claimant's insurer
(being subrogated to the claimant's rights against the defendant) issued a claim
against the defendant in the name of the claimant. By the claim form, the
claimant claimed damages which were quantified at £155·73. This sum
comprised £125 in respect of the insurance policy excess, and £25 for
miscellaneous expenses.

[3] On 14 July 2001, District Judge Stephenson of her own motion ordered:

'1. By 8 August 2001 the following party or parties will disclose any
written or oral agreement between their insurers to refund to the other side's
insurers the full cost of vehicle repairs if the insurance policy excess is
recovered as a consequence of these proceedings:
Parties: claimant and defendant.'

[4] On 3 August, the defendant's solicitors confirmed to the court the
existence of the MOU. On 17 August, District Judge Stephenson, again acting of
her own motion, ordered the claimant to file and serve amended particulars
of claim reflecting 'the true value' of the claim together with the appropriate
court fee by 4 pm on 14 September, and that 'in default the claim be struck out'.
On 13 September, the claimant served his amended claim form and particulars of
claim. By his amended particulars of claim, he deleted the claim for
miscellaneous expenses, but left the claim for £125 unamended. He added the
following words:

'The claimant is comprehensively insured with AXA Insurance and they
have paid for the repairs to the vehicle on or about 28th April 2000 in the sum
of £738·90. It has been agreed between the claimant and the defendant
insurers that they will abide by the courts decision and keep their claim for
the repairs to the claimant's vehicle out of the proceedings to keep the costs
to a minimum.'

[5] On 5 November, the district judge struck out the claim for breach of the
order of 17 August. The order recited that the district judge found that the
amended particulars of claim did not reflect the full value of the claim as they did
not include the full cost of vehicle repairs. Brief reasons were annexed to her
order. They stated:

'(a) The value of a claim determines the level of a court fee. This is set out
in the County Court Fees Order 1999, SI 1999/689. Schedule 1, para 1.1
refers to commencement of proceedings "to recover a sum of money". If the
proceedings have been brought to determine whether a sum of money, that
is the full vehicle repair costs, should be paid, the full court fee should be
paid. (b) Under CPR 26.8 when deciding the track for a claim, the matters
to which the court shall have regard include "(a) the financial value, if any,
of the claim". If a claim is to determine liability for a repair bill the court
must know the amount of money in issue, that is the total of the bill, not just
a segment of it, in other words not just the excess. (c) No provision under
the CPR is cited which enables litigants to understate their claims by
agreement in order to minimize costs.'

a

[6] On 7 November, the claimant gave notice of his intention to apply for an order that the order of November should be set aside on the grounds that the particulars of claim did reflect the full value of the claim. At the hearing on 25 January 2002, the claimant was represented by Mrs Mahoney. The defendant did not appear and was not represented. At the conclusion of the argument, the district judge gave her ruling, but the order was not drawn up until 11 February.

b

[7] The district judge said that a distinction was to be drawn between a subrogated claim, and one which was not subrogated. It was quite clear in this case that 'what was in dispute' between the two insurers was the total cost of the repair costs. She considered that CPR 26.8(2), which provides that, when deciding the track for a claim, it is for the court to assess the financial value of a claim, supported her view that it was for the court to determine the true value of

c

a claim. She said:

'The difficulty arises with regard to subrogated claims where the outstanding issue of the vehicle excess is used as a peg for the insurance companies to hang their proceedings on with regard to liability. What the insurance companies want is simply the decision as to liability so that,

d

between themselves, be the true cost of what is in dispute £200, £2,000, or whatever, they will get the decision of the court on liability in order to decide who pays up for the full cost of vehicle repairs.'

[8] And later:

e

'The small claims track is particularly wide and it is, it appears, being utilised by insurance companies to get the county courts to make decisions on liability, whatever the size of the claim that they have between themselves, just on the basis of sometimes £100, £125 or £200 excess claims.'

[9] She then touched on the question of court fees, and said:

f

'The other point which I grappled with is what is the role of the court with regard to the payment of the fees when it comes to the decisions of the judiciary. Is it a judicial function to consider whether a higher fee should have been paid because the true value of the claim is much higher? Or is it nothing to do with the judiciary?'

g

[10] She concluded by saying that she had not been persuaded to set aside her order. She thought that there may be a lacuna in the CPR, and as I have said, gave permission to appeal.

DISCUSSION

h

[11] As before the district judge, so too before this court, the defendant has not appeared and has not been represented. We have, however, been greatly assisted by Mr Michael Ashe QC who appears on behalf of the claimant. Largely for the reasons advanced by Mr Ashe, I consider that the decision of the district judge cannot be supported. The word 'claim' is not defined in the CPR: see *Civil Procedure* (the White Book) (Autumn 2002) vol 1, p 527 (para 25.12.4) which states:

j

'Rule 2.3(1) defines "defendant" as a person against whom a claim is made. The word "claim" is not defined. When used as a noun in other rules it usually refers to the whole of the case in question (see, for example, r.8.1 and r.26.2) or to a separate cause of action raised in proceedings (see, for example, r.7.3). It therefore appears that, under r.25.12, as under the

pre-CPR provision (RSC O.23) a claimant is not entitled to apply for security
for costs solely in respect of some interim application initiated by the
defendant, for example an application under Pt 17 to amend his defence or
under Pt 18 for further information as to the Particulars of Claim (for a case
authority on the pre-CPR provision, see [Re B (Infants) [1965] 2 All ER 651n,
[1965] 1 WLR 946]).'

[12] But, although the CPR appear to afford the word 'claim' different
meanings according to the context in which it appears, nowhere is it used in a
context which suggests that it includes claims which are not brought before the
court in legal proceedings. Thus, in the context of a road traffic case, 'claim'
should be construed as meaning a demand made formally through the court by
the claimant for a sum to be paid to him or her by the defendant. As Mr Ashe puts
it in his skeleton argument—

'"claim" in the context of the CPR cannot be said to include any amount
which one party may hope to retrieve from another party as a result of a
private agreement between the two. It can only cover what the claimant
seeks to recover through the court'.

[13] A claimant may have various reasons for not including in his claim heads
of damages to which he would arguably be entitled, if he established liability. He
may decide that the cost of proving a head of loss is disproportionate to the sum
that he thinks he is likely to recover. Or he may decide that the evidence that
would have to be adduced in order to prove a head of loss would cause him
embarrassment which he wishes to avoid. Or he may decide not to seek to
recover a head of loss because he is confident that it will be made good to him by
a third party. A claimant is fully entitled to decide what to include in his claim. If
he excludes a head of loss from his claim, and he is awarded judgment on his
pleaded claim, he will normally be precluded as a matter of law from
subsequently starting proceedings to recover the excluded head of loss: see
Henderson v Henderson (1843) 3 Hare 100, [1843–60] All ER Rep 378. That is the
chance that a claimant must take if he excludes from his claim sums which he
could claim from the defendant. But there is nothing in the general law which
positively obliges a claimant to include in his pleaded case all the claims which he
could arguably advance against a defendant.

[14] The question that arises, therefore, is whether there is anything in the
CPR which justifies the conclusion reached by the district judge. It would be very
surprising if there were, since such an interference in the autonomy of a claimant
to decide what to include in his claim would be a very serious matter indeed.
CPR 16.3 provides, so far as material:

'Statement of value to be included in the claim form
(1) This rule applies where the claimant is making a claim for money.
(2) The claimant must, in the claim form, state—(a) the amount of money
which he is claiming; (b) that he expects to recover—(i) not more than
£5,000; (ii) more than £5,000 but not more than £15,000; or (iii) more than
£15,000; or (c) that he cannot say how much he expects to recover.'

[15] The reference to 'the amount of money which he is claiming' supports
the view that the amount 'claimed' by a claimant is limited for the purposes of
the CPR to what is in the claim form. There is nothing in CPR 16.3 to suggest

a that the court is in any way concerned with the question whether the claimant should be claiming more than he is in fact claiming.

[16] The district judge was much influenced by CPR 26.8, which deals with matters relevant to allocation to a track. It provides that, when allocating a claim to a track, the court must have regard, inter alia, to its 'financial value'. But there is nothing in the language of CPR 26.8 to indicate that the court is concerned with
b the value of items which are *not* being claimed. Indeed, r 26.8(2)(a) goes so far as to require the court to disregard items which *are* being claimed, but which are not in dispute. The amount 'in dispute' must be limited to that which is included in the claim form or particulars of claim, and is (a) an amount for which the defendant does not admit liability, or (b) a sum in respect of an item forming part of the claim for which judgment has not been entered: see CPR PD 26, para 7.4.
c [17] Nor does CPR PD 26, para 7.3(1) support the conclusion of the district judge. It states: 'Rule 26.8(2) provides that it is for the court to assess the financial value of a claim.' CPR PD 26, para 7.3 amplifies CPR 26.8(2). In particular, PD 26, para 7.3(2) provides:

d   'Where the court believes that the amount the claimant is seeking exceeds what he may reasonably be expected to recover it may make an order under rule 26.5(3) directing the claimant to justify the amount.'

[18] This provision is directed at the case where the court believes that the value of a claim may be overstated. If the draftsman of CPR 26.8 had intended
e that the court should have the power to increase the value of a claim, it would have been provided for here. In my judgment, the court does not have the power to increase the financial value of a claim in respect of items of claim that are included in the claim form and particulars of claim. Still less does it have power to increase the claim to include items of claim that the claimant has chosen not to include at all.
f [19] As has been seen, the district judge made reference to the court fees, although it is not clear what part, if any, the impact of the amount claimed on court fees played in her reasoning. County Court Fees Order 1999, SI 1999/689, Sch 1, para 1.1 provides that the court is only entitled to demand fees in relation to 'the sum claimed'. Thus, for example, where the sum claimed does not exceed
g £200, the fee payable is £27. As Mr Ashe submits, it is no part of the judicial function to extract from the parties the maximum possible amount of court fees at the cost of forcing a claimant to claim more than he wishes to claim.

[20] In my judgment, therefore, there is nothing in the CPR which justified the decision of the district judge to order the claimant to increase his claim to include the repair costs. Nor is there any reason for distinguishing between
h subrogated and non-subrogated claims. There is nothing objectionable in what the parties did in the present case. Even if the claimant had included the full claim in his claim form and/or particulars of claim, its value would still have been well under £5,000, and, therefore, on the face of it, a case suitable for the small claims track. In any event, the real issue between the parties was liability. The parties
j were entitled to simplify the claim, and limit the amount claimed to £125. In so doing, they have acted in accordance with the overriding objective in that expense has been saved and the case can be dealt with proportionately. If the issue of liability were complex and not suitable for the small claims track, then it would be open to the court to allocate the case to a different track: see CPR PD 26, para 8.1.

[21] I would, therefore, allow this appeal. The district judge was wrong to
strike out the claim on the basis that the claim form and the particulars of claim *a*
as amended did not reflect the full value of the claim. Nor was she entitled to
make an order that the claimant must amend his claim form and particulars of
claim to increase the value of the claim. I would set aside the orders of
5 November 2001 and 11 February 2002, and reinstate the claim.

b

WARD LJ.
[22] I agree.

Appeal allowed.

James Brooks   Barrister.

a
JI MacWilliam Co Inc v Mediterranean Shipping Co SA
The Rafaela S
[2003] EWCA Civ 556

b

COURT OF APPEAL, CIVIL DIVISION
PETER GIBSON, RIX LJJ AND JACOB J
17, 24 JANUARY, 16 APRIL 2003

c *Shipping – Bill of lading – Carriage of goods by sea – Hague Rules – Straight bill of lading – Rules applying to contracts 'covered by a bill of lading or any similar document of title' – Status of straight bill of lading – Carriage of Goods By Sea Act 1971, s 1(4) – Hague Rules, art I(b).*

d The shipper consigned four containers of printing machinery to the claimant. It was shipped on vessels owned by or demise chartered to the defendant. The bill of lading issued by the defendant named the claimant as the consignee and indicated that the bill was non-negotiable, ie it was a 'straight' bill of lading, and the goods could not be transferred by indorsement of the bill. The defendant agreed to carry the goods from the port of loading to the port of discharge which
e was identified as Felixstowe. The bill also provided that if a final destination were specified the defendant, acting as shippers agent, would arrange for transport from the port of discharge to the destination. Boston, United States, was specified as the final destination. The goods were carried from Durban, South Africa to Felixstowe, where they were discharged and subsequently reshipped to Boston. The goods were damaged and proceedings were issued in England. At
f arbitration, the issue arose as to whether the Carriage of Goods By Sea Act 1971 applied, which, by s 1(3)[a], applied 'where the port of shipment is a port in the United Kingdom'. Accordingly the question arose as to whether the shipment from South Africa to the United States of America was governed by one contract of carriage or two. If the Act did apply, then s 1(4) (derived from art I(b)[b] of the
g Hague Rules) applied the Rules if the contract of carriage 'expressly or by implication [provided] for the issue of a bill of lading or any similar document of title'. The question therefore arose as to whether a straight bill of lading was a 'bill of lading or any similar document of title'. The arbitrators concluded that the shipment was governed by one contract of carriage and that, in any event, a straight bill of lading was not a 'bill of lading' within the Act. The claimant
h appealed to the judge, who concluded that there had been two separate contracts, but upheld the arbitrators' decision that a straight bill was not a 'bill of lading', and accordingly dismissed the appeal. The claimant appealed to the Court of Appeal on the ground that a straight bill of lading was a 'bill of lading' within s 1(4) of the Act, and also within art I(b) of the Rules.

j

Held – (1) The carriage of the goods from England to the United States of America was under a separate contract of carriage to that from South Africa to

---

a   Section 1, so far as material, is set out at [4] and [82], below
b   Article I, so far as material, is set out at [50], below

England. There was nothing to extend the defendant's responsbility as carrier beyond Felixstowe. It was not contracted to carry the goods to Boston until it entered into a new arrangement to on-carry the goods from Felixstowe. Accordingly, there had been a 'port of shipment' within England, and the judge had been correct to conclude that the Act applied (see [24], [25], [27], [28], [156], [159], below).

(2) A straight bill of lading, although non-negotiable, was to be viewed as a bill of lading within the meaning of the Rules. The Rules were concerned with the content of a contract of carriage in circumstances where such a contract as found in a bill of lading might come to affect a third party into whose hands such a bill was transferred. A named consignee under a straight bill, unless he was the same person as the shipper, was as much a third party as a named consignee under a classic bill. A straight bill, in practice, was used just like a classic bill, as a document against which payment was required and the transfer of which thus marked the intended transfer of property. The shipper and his bankers and insurers needed the same protection as the shipper under a classic bill; and the consignee himself and his insurers in turn needed to have rights against the carrier under the contract of carriage. The practice was also that a straight bill was written on the form of an otherwise classic bill, and required production of the bill on delivery. Furthermore, a straight bill was in principle, function and form much closer to a classic negotiable bill than to a non-negotiable receipt (see [135]–[139], [151], [156], [159], below).

(3) A straight bill of lading, having to be produced to obtain delivery, was also a document of title. There was no reason why a document which had to be produced to obtain possession of the goods should not be regarded, in an international convention, as a document of title (see [145], [146], [159] below).

The claimant's appeal would accordingly be allowed.

Per curiam. Even in the absence of an express provision requiring a straight bill of lading to be produced to obtain delivery, it is in principle a document of title (see [145], [156], [159], below).

Notes

For bills of lading, see 43(2) *Halsbury's Laws* (4th edn reissue) paras 1532–1541.

For the Carriage of Goods by Sea Act 1971, s1, see 39 *Halsbury's Statutes* (4th edn) (1995 reissue) 370, 375.

Cases referred to in judgments

Anders Maersk, The [1986] 1 Lloyd's Rep 483, Hong Kong HC.

Barclays Bank Ltd v Customs and Excise Comrs [1963] 1 Lloyd's Rep 81.

Brij, The [2001] 1 Lloyd's Rep 431, Hong Kong HC.

Browner International Ltd v Monarch Shipping Co Ltd, The European Enterprise [1989] 2 Lloyd's Rep 185.

Carlberg v Wemyss Coal Co Ltd 1915 SC 616, Ct of Sess.

Cia Portorafti Commerciale SA v Ultramar Panama Inc, The Captain Gregos [1990] 3 All ER 967, CA.

Duke of Yare, The (10 April 1997, unreported).

Gardano & Giampari v Greek Petroleum George Mamidakis & Co [1961] 3 All ER 919, [1962] 1 WLR 40.

Glyn Mills Currie & Co v East and West India Dock Co (1882) 7 App Cas 591, [1881–5] All ER Rep 674, HL.

a *Henderson (CP) & Co v Comptoir d'Escompte de Paris* (1873) LR 5 PC 253, PC.
Hugh Mack & Co Ltd v Burns & Laird Lines Ltd (1944) 77 Ll L Rep 377, NI CA.
International Air and Sea Cargo GmbH v The Chitral (Owners) [2000] 1 All ER (Comm) 932.
Kum v Wah Tat Bank Ltd [1971] 1 Lloyd's Rep 439, PC.
Kuwait Petroleum Corp v I & D Oil Carriers Ltd, The Houda [1994] 2 Lloyd's Rep 541, CA.
b *Lickbarrow v Mason* (1787) 2 Term Rep 63, 100 ER 35, [1775–1802] All ER Rep 1.
Marlborough Hill, The v Alex Cowan & Sons Ltd [1921] 1 AC 444, PC.
Maurice Desgagnes, The [1977] 1 Lloyd's Rep 290, Can Fed Ct.
McCarren & Co Ltd v Humber International Transport Ltd and Truckline Ferries (Poole) Ltd, The Vechscroon [1982] 1 Lloyd's Rep 301.
Motis Exports Ltd v Dampskibsselskabet AF 1912, A/S [1999] 1 All ER (Comm) 571;
c *affd* [2000] 1 All ER (Comm) 91, CA.
MSC Magallanes, The (16 May 2002, unreported), Rennes CA.
Olivine Electronics Pte Ltd v Seabridge Transport Pte Ltd [1995] 3 SLR 143, Singapore HC.
Parsons Corp v CV Scheepvaartonderneming Happy Ranger [2002] 1 All ER (Comm) 176; *rvsd* [2002] EWCA Civ 694, [2002] 2 All ER (Comm) 24.
d *SA Sucre Export v Northern River Shipping Ltd, The Sormovskiy 3068* [1994] 2 Lloyd's Rep 266.
Sanders v Maclean (1883) 11 QBD 327, CA.
Stafford Allen & Sons Ltd v Pacific Steam Navigation Co [1956] 1 Lloyd's Rep 104; *affd* [1956] 2 All ER 716, [1956] 1 WLR 629, CA.
Stag Line Ltd v Foscolo, Mango & Co Ltd [1932] AC 328, [1931] All ER Rep 666, HL.
e *Stettin, The* (1889) 14 PD 142.
Sze Hai Tong Bank Ltd v Rambler Cycle Co Ltd [1959] 3 All ER 182, [1959] AC 576, [1959] 3 WLR 214, PC.
Thrige v United Shipping Co Ltd (1924) 18 Ll L Rep 6, CA.
Voss v APL Co Pte Ltd [2002] 2 Lloyd's Rep 707, Singapore CA.

f
Appeal

The claimant, JI MacWilliam Co Inc, appealed with permission granted by Mance LJ on 19 June 2002 from the decision of Langley J on 17 April 2002 ([2002] EWHC 593 (Comm)) dismissing its appeal from an award by Messrs Hamsher, Mabbs and Moss on 30 May 2001 in an arbitration between the claimant and the *g* defendant, Mediterranean Shipping Co SA, on a preliminary issue arising out of claims for damage to cargo. The facts are set out in the judgment of Rix LJ.

Alistair Schaff QC (instructed by *Clyde & Co*) for the claimant.
Simon Croall (instructed by *Duval Vassiliades*) for the defendant.
h
Cur adv vult

16 April 2003. The following judgments were delivered.

RIX LJ.
j [1] In 1924 the international maritime community enacted a convention, the International Convention for the Unification of Certain Rules of Law relating to Bills of Lading (Brussels, 25 August 1924; TS 17 (1931); Cmd 3806), intended to regulate the minimum terms by which international shipping contracts of carriage of goods by sea should be governed. That convention, although signed at Brussels, derived, with amendments, from a set of standard rules originally

designed for incorporation into bills of lading as a matter of contract which were
negotiated at The Hague in 1922. Thus the rules came to be known as the Hague *a*
Rules. By art I(b) those rules applied only to contracts of carriage 'covered by a
bill of lading or any similar document of title'. It is a matter of some surprise that
nearly 80 years later the meaning of that phrase is still controversial. Indeed new
forms of shipping documents appear to have caused in recent years an increasing
number of cases to reach the courts raising the question whether a bill of lading *b*
consigned to a named consignee, a so-called 'straight bill of lading', is a bill of
lading within the meaning of the Rules. A straight bill of lading is to be contrasted
with an 'order' or bearer bill of lading, each of which permits the transferability
of the bill to any number of transferees in succession, respectively by
indorsement or delivery. This form of transferability has also traditionally, but
idiosyncratically, been referred to as 'negotiability'. *Scrutton on Charterparties and* *c*
Bills of Lading (20th edn, 1996) p 185, explains the point well:

> 'Note 1 "Negotiable" as a term of art describes an instrument which can
> give to a transferee a better title than that possessed by the transferor. A bill
> of lading is not "negotiable" in this sense: the indorsee does not get a better
> title than his assignor. Indeed a bill of lading is "negotiable" only in a *d*
> popular, and not in a technical, sense. For it is "negotiable" to the same
> extent as a cheque marked "not negotiable", *i.e* it is "transferable".'

The effect of a negotiable bill of lading has been famously described by Bowen LJ
in *Sanders v Maclean* (1883) 11 QBD 327 at 341:
e
> 'A cargo at sea while in the hands of the carrier is necessarily incapable of
> physical delivery. During this period of transit and voyage, the bill of lading
> by the law merchant is universally recognised as its symbol, and the
> indorsement and delivery of the bill of lading operates as a symbolical
> delivery of the cargo. Property in the goods passes by such indorsement and *f*
> delivery of the bill of lading, whenever it is the intention of the parties that
> the property should pass, just as under similar circumstances the property
> would pass by an actual delivery of the goods ... It is a key which in the hands
> of a rightful owner is intended to unlock the door of the warehouse, floating
> or fixed, in which the goods may chance to be.'

g
A straight bill of lading, on the other hand, requires delivery of the goods to the
named consignee and (subject to the shipper's ability to redirect the goods)
to no other.

[2] The present appeal concerns such a straight bill of lading, under which the
shipper, Coniston International Machinery Ltd, of Liverpool (Coniston), consigned *h*
four containers of printing machinery to J I MacWilliam Co Inc, of Boston,
United States of America (MacWilliam). MacWilliam had purchased the
machinery from Coniston under a sale contract cif Boston. The machinery was
carried on two vessels each of which was owned by or demise chartered to
Mediterranean Shipping Co SA, of Geneva (MSC). One vessel, the Rosemary,
carried the machinery from Durban in South Africa to Felixstowe in England, *j*
where it was discharged and subsequently reshipped. The other vessel, the
Rafaela S, carried the machinery from Felixstowe to its final destination at
Boston. On the way, it was badly damaged. The parties to the appeal, which
arises, via the Commercial Court, out of a London arbitration, are MacWilliam
and MSC. The business issue between the parties is whether the contract of

a carriage contained in or evidenced by the bill of lading prescribed a package limitation under the Hague Rules, the Hague-Visby Rules, or the United States Carriage of Goods by Sea Act 1936 (the United States Act). The Hague-Visby Rules are an amended version of the Hague Rules, introduced by the Protocol signed at Brussels on 23 February 1968. They contain a more liberal package limitation. The United States Act reflects the earlier limitation regime of the
b Hague Rules and would limit any recovery to $US 500 per package.

   [3] The straight bill of lading issued by MSC to Coniston at Durban on 18 December 1989 (the date, now more than 13 years ago, may be noted) is the only contract document in evidence relating to the carriage. If it governed the complete voyage to Boston, then its terms relate directly to that second leg on which the machinery was damaged. If, however, the position is that it only
c governed the first leg to Felixstowe, then no second bill of lading to cover the on-carriage to Boston was ever issued. It is nevertheless common ground that, in such a case, the carriage on that second leg would be governed by a second contract in the same form as the Durban-Felixstowe bill of lading, mutatis mutandis, in other words by a straight bill of lading.

d [4] At this stage it is still a matter of mere assumption that MacWilliam has title to sue and that MSC is liable at all for the damaged machinery. However, the parties have decided to determine the package limitation regime as a preliminary issue in the arbitration. That issue ultimately turns on whether the compulsory regime of the Carriage of Goods by Sea Act 1971, which gives to the Hague-Visby Rules the force of law 'where the port of shipment is a port in the
e United Kingdom' (see s 1(3)), applies to the second leg of the voyage, that from Felixstowe to Boston. MacWilliam submits that the 1971 Act's regime does apply, MSC submits that it does not. That difference in turn raises three questions of some refinement. The first of these is whether the relevant contract of carriage is a single contract from Durban to Boston, or whether the carriage as
f a whole was covered by two separate contracts, one governing the voyage from Durban to Boston and the other governing the on-voyage from Felixstowe to Boston. The second question, however, is whether the separate contract of carriage which would in that case govern the second leg from Felixstowe to Boston was a contract which 'expressly or by implication provides for the issue of a bill of lading or any similar document of title' (see s 1(4) of the 1971 Act). Seeing
g that it is common ground that such a contract would have been in the form of a straight bill of lading, the second question is simply whether a straight bill of lading is a 'bill of lading or any similar document of title' within the meaning of the 1971 Act. Since that phrase goes back ultimately to the Hague Rules, the parties are agreed that the second question is asking whether a straight bill of
h lading is a bill of lading or similar document of title within the meaning of the Hague Rules. If it is not, it is again common ground that the more liberal package regime of the Hague-Visby Rules does not apply.

   [5] The third question only arises if, on the contrary, the second leg was governed by a contract within s 1(4) of the 1971 Act and asks whether, whatever
j the answer to the first question, and even if therefore there was a single contract for the whole carriage from Durban to Boston, there nevertheless was a 'port of shipment ... in the United Kingdom' within the meaning of s 1(3) of the 1971 Act, namely Felixstowe. MacWilliam submits that there was and that the answer to the first question is therefore ultimately irrelevant. This third question has tended to be obscured below, possibly because it was considered to be bound up with the

first question, as I think MSC views it to be, but also perhaps because, in the light
of both the arbitrators' and Langley J's decision on the straight bill of lading   *a*
question, neither the first nor the third questions were decisive.

[6] Thus it was that the arbitrators (Messrs Mabbs, Hamsher and Moss)
defined only two issues in their award as follows: 'Was the shipment from
Durban to Boston governed by one contract of carriage or two?' and 'Was the
[straight] bill of lading a "bill of lading" within [the 1971 Act]?'   *b*

[7] The answers given by the arbitrators were 'One' and 'No' respectively.
Therefore MacWilliam failed, on two separate grounds, to avoid the United
States Act's $US 500 per package regime. The arbitrators did not separately address
MacWilliam's submission that Felixstowe was in any event a 'port of shipment'.

[8] Permission was given to appeal the award to the Commercial Court
([2002] EWHC 593 (Comm), [2002] 2 Lloyd's Rep 403), where Langley J upheld   *c*
the arbitrators' answer on the bill of lading issue, and therefore dismissed the
appeal, but went on to express his views for differing from the arbitrators on the
one contract or two issue. In his view there were two separate contracts. He,
however, defined this issue (at [4]) in a way which incorporated MacWilliam's
further 'port of shipment' submission, as follows: *d*

> 'Whether, as the buyers [Macwilliam] also contended, the "port of
> shipment" for the carriage of the goods pursuant to that "bill of lading" was
> a port in the United Kingdom (namely Felixstowe) within s. 1(3) of (the 1971
> Act) ("issue 2"). Issue 2 itself depended upon whether there was a single
> contract of shipment from Durban to Boston or two contracts of carriage   *e*
> from Durban to Felixstowe and Felixstowe to Boston.'

[9] Permission was again given to MacWilliam to take a second appeal to the
Court of Appeal. By a respondent's notice MSC has sought to uphold Langley J's
order dismissing the appeal from the award on the alternative ground that the
arbitrators were also right on the one contract or two issue.   *f*

[10] The three questions argued on the appeal are very different. The one
contract or two issue is a question of construction on the wording of the bill of
lading. The straight bill of lading issue is a question of general significance with
potentially far-reaching implications. The 'port of shipment' issue has barely
been addressed below, but appears to be a mixed question of statutory   *g*
interpretation and fact. The arbitrators and Langley J dealt with the bill of lading
issue first. However, it will not be reached at all unless there is a 'port of
shipment' within the United Kingdom. It is therefore logical, but also convenient,
to take the two questions which relate to the 'port of shipment' first. It is as well
to settle the form of the contract (one contract or two) before asking what its   *h*
effect is in the light of international convention or domestic statute. In any event,
however, I need to begin by setting out the terms of the straight bill of lading.

THE STRAIGHT BILL OF LADING
[11] The face of the bill of lading contained a series of numbered boxes, in
which various details were typed. There was also printed material, as well as   *j*
several stamped provisions. The document as a whole was headed 'Original
BILL OF LADING' and it was given a number in a box headed 'B/L NO'.

[12] The numbered boxes had printed titles asking for appropriate details to be
supplied. Thus box (1) was headed 'Shipper' and had Coniston's name and
address inserted in it. Box (2) was headed 'Consignee: (B/L not negotiable unless

a "ORDER OF")': it referred to MacWilliam's name and address but did not contain the additional words 'order of'. That was what made the document a straight bill of lading. The terms of box (2), both the printed words and the absence of 'order of' in the typed-in provisions, are the linchpin of MSC's argument on the bill of lading issue. Box (6) was headed 'Vessel' and referred to 'ROSEMARY'. Box (7) gave the 'Port of Loading' as 'DURBAN'; box (8) the 'Port

b of discharge' as 'FELIXSTOWE'. Box (9) was headed 'Final destination (through transport)' and referred to 'BOSTON'. Against the number (9) was an asterisk, picked up further down the page by the printed information—'If box 5 and/or 9 filled out, this is a through Bill of Lading (see clause 3)'. This provision together with cl 3 (see [17], below) is central to the one contract or two issue. Box (10) was headed 'On-carriage' but was left blank. Box (11) was headed 'Number of

c Original Bs/L' and was filled out '3 (THREE)'. Box (13) contained the 'particulars furnished by shipper'.

[13] Further unnumbered boxes, left blank, were headed 'Specification of freight and charges', 'Declared Value (See Clause 21)' and 'Signed for the merchants (Compulsory for Italy, Belgium and France)'.

d [14] In a box above the boxes for 'Place and date of issue' (where 'DURBAN' and '18 December 1989' were inserted) and 'Signed for the Master ... as Agents' (where an agent's stamp and signature were inserted) were three printed paragraphs dealing with receipt, agreement and attestation. The last of these, in essentially standard form, reads as follows:

e   'In WITNESS whereof the number of Original Bills of Lading stated above [viz three] all of this tenor and date, has been signed, one of which being accomplished, the others to stand void. One of the Bills of Lading must be surrendered duly endorsed in exchange for the goods or delivery order.'

[15] Although the freight box was left empty, another box headed 'Freight
f Payable at:' was completed with the typed word 'DESTINATION'; but another copy of the bill had that word crossed through in manuscript and the word 'Felixstowe' written above it. The words 'FREIGHT PAYABLE DESTINATION' were also typed in the centre of the particulars of the goods.

[16] There were also two stamped provisions which were relevant to the one contract or two issue, namely 'On-Carriage to BOSTON to be arranged by
g M.S.C. Agents' (the word 'Boston' was written into a blank space in this stamp), and 'Cargo to be cleared by U.S. Custom at port of discharge'.

[17] The reverse of the form contained standard conditions in typically small print. It will be sufficient to set out the following:

h   'This contract is between the Merchant and the Master, acting on behalf of the Carrier. Wherever the term "Merchant" occurs in this Bill of Lading (hereinafter "B/L") it shall be deemed to include the Shipper, the Consignee, the holder of the B/L, the receiver and the owner of the goods. "Carrier" shall mean the vessel and her owner or demise charterer for whom the Master has entered into this contract ... MSC shall act as agent of the owner
j   or demise charterer in arranging the transport covered by this B/L ...

     1. PARAMOUNT CLAUSE. It is mutually agreed that this Bill of Lading shall have effect subject to the provisions of the International Convention relating to Bills of Lading dated Brussels 25th August 1924 (hereinafter called "Hague Rules"). The Hague Rules shall not apply where ... this bill of lading is subject to any compulsorily applicable enactment, including Hague-Visby

Rules, based on said Hague Rules, 1924. If goods are shipped to or from the
United States, this bill of lading shall be subject to US Carriage of Goods by   *a*
Sea Act 1936. The Carrier's published tariff is incorporated herein and made
part of this contract.

2. LAW AND JURISDICTION. Claims and disputes arising under or in
connection with this B/L shall be referred to arbitration in London or such
other place as the Carrier in his sole discretion shall designate ... English law   *b*
shall be applied, unless some other law is compulsorily applicable, except
that claims and disputes relating to cargo carried to or from the United States
shall be subject to the sole jurisdiction of the US in the US District Court,
Southern District of New York, and US law shall be applied.

3. SUBSTITUTION OF VESSEL, THROUGH TRANSPORT,   *c*
TRANSSHIPMENT AND FORWARDING. The Carrier agrees to carry the
goods from the Port of Loading to the Port of Discharge, and shall have the
right at its sole discretion to substitute other vessels, feederships, lighters or
other modes of transport for the vessel named herein (Box 6). If boxes 5
and/or 9 are filled out, the Carrier will, acting as shipper's agent, only
arrange for transport of the cargo by other carriers from the place of origin   *d*
to Port of Loading and/or from Port of Discharge to destination, and during
such segments of Through Transport, handling and storage of the goods
shall be subject to the freight contracts and tariffs of the other carriers. It is
expressly understood that the Carrier's liability as "carrier" applies only from
the Port of Loading to Port of Discharge under this B/L, and only while the
goods remain in its actual custody and control, whether as Carrier or bailee ...   *e*

21. CLAIMS VALUATION, PACKAGE LIMITATION, TIME-BAR ...
Neither the carrier nor the ship shall in any event be or become liable for any
loss or damage to or in connection with goods in an amount exceeding
Pounds Sterling 100 of lawful tender in the U.K. per package or unit, unless
the nature and the value of such goods have been declared by the merchant   *f*
before shipment and inserted in the B/L. But declaration of value for the
purpose of calculation of freight shall not be considered a declaration in the
above sense. This limitation of liability shall apply to all contractual claims
as well as to any claims arising from other causes. In case goods are shipped
to or from the United States, the carrier's liability shall be limited to $500 per   *g*
package or customary freight unit, unless excess value is inserted on the face
hereof and extra charge paid.'

ONE CONTRACT OR TWO?

[18] The arbitrators considered that there was only one contract. Their   *h*
reasoning started with the words on the face of the form that 'this is a through
Bill of Lading', which they considered confirmed the bill's appearance as a 'classic
through transport bill' covering the entire carriage from port of loading at
Durban to final destination at Boston. There was further support in the fact that
freight was only payable at destination, presumably in a single sum (the
arbitrators actually state that 'freight was paid in one lump sum'), and in the   *j*
background sale contract 'cif Boston' which emphasised that intermediate
arrangements were of limited if any significance to the shipper and consignee.
There remained the stipulation that Felixstowe was the port of discharge
together with cl 3. The arbitrators interpreted these provisions, however, as
merely giving to MSC the option of making alternative provisions on a second leg

a from Felixstowe to final destination. For that leg MSC was entitled to delegate the obligation to another carrier or to complete the carriage itself. Where MSC opted to complete the carriage itself, it did so under its original contract.

[19] Langley J ([2002] 2 Lloyd's Rep 403) came to the opposite conclusion. This was, I think, essentially based on his reading of cl 3 (together with the relevant box entries) as providing for two separate contracts, rather than a single *b* contract under which MSC exercised an option to complete a single voyage by means of transshipment at an intermediate port.

[20] On this appeal, Mr Simon Croall, on behalf of MSC, has submitted that the arbitrators were right essentially for the reasons given by them. Properly construed in its entirety, the bill of lading issued at Durban evidenced a contract *c* of carriage to ship cargo from Durban to Boston with an option to sub-contract parts of the carriage and in particular the leg from Felixstowe to Boston. Although cl 3 said nothing about MSC performing that second leg as a carrier in its own ships, as distinct from arranging for transport as the shipper's agent, it was common ground that MSC was entitled to arrange such on-carriage in its own ships. Where it did so, it was still performing the original contract of carriage *d* under a single through bill of lading for a freight which had been agreed for the whole carriage payable in one sum at final destination in Boston.

[21] Mr Alistair Schaff QC, on the other hand, on behalf of MacWilliam, has supported the conclusion of the judge. He has emphasised that the expression 'through bill of lading' must itself take its colour from the other contractual provisions and in this case predominantly from cl 3. That clause, when read *e* together with the relevant boxes on the front of the bill, does not provide for a single contract of carriage but for two separate contracts, one from Durban to Felixstowe and the other from Felixstowe to Boston. It may be true that MSC was entitled to arrange that second contract to be with itself, but that should not disguise the fact that such an arrangement must be viewed in exactly the same *f* light as a new contract arranged through MSC's agency with a different carrier. If the latter would be a separate contract with a separate port of shipment, then so must be the former arrangement. Otherwise the regime under the bill of lading would change depending on the manner in which MSC exercised its option. If it arranged on-carriage with itself, then there would be a single contract *g* for a voyage from Durban to Boston, with transshipment at Felixstowe, and United States law and jurisdiction would apply under cl 2 and the United States Act would apply under the penultimate sentence of cl 1. If on the other hand, MSC arranged on-carriage with another carrier, then the contract would only be for shipment from Durban to Felixstowe, not to the United States, and London arbitration and English law would apply under cl 2, and there would be a port of *h* shipment within the United Kingdom which, subject to the straight bill of lading issue, would also invoke the compulsory regime of the 1971 Act. However, law, jurisdiction and the applicable shipping regime must, it was submitted, be established at the outset of the contract, and could not 'float' dependent on subsequent events.

j [22] Two authorities have been cited as throwing some light on this issue. In *Stafford Allen & Sons Ltd v Pacific Steam Navigation Co* [1956] 1 Lloyd's Rep 104 it would seem that the first carrier's bill of lading provided for shipment at Corinto in Nicaragua, discharge and transshipment at Cristobal (in the Canal Zone) by a named 'on carrier' and a final destination in London. A special clause, cl 11, dealt with the circumstances of transshipment, to the effect that the first carrier made

arrangements for the transshipment and on-carriage 'solely as the forwarding
agent of the shipper and without any other responsibility whatsoever' and that
the transshipment and on-carriage would be subject to 'all the provisions of the
regular form of bill of lading' of the second carrier. No further bill of lading was
issued, but the second carrier did have a regular form of bill of lading. The
plaintiff's cargo was damaged on the second leg and it sued the second carrier.
The issue was whether the regime terms of the first carrier's bill of lading applied
throughout the voyage to London, or whether the terms of the second carrier's
regular bill of lading applied. Sellers J held that the second carrier's terms applied.
Nothing more is known about the terms of the first carrier's bill of lading, for
instance as to the freight provisions.

[23] In *The Anders Maersk* [1986] 1 Lloyd's Rep 483, a decision of the Hong
Kong High Court, the bill of lading stated that the port of shipment was
Baltimore and the port of discharge was Shanghai. The bill gave the carrier a
right of transshipment, which it exercised at Hong Kong. It appears to have been
described as a through bill of lading. It made no express reference to Hong Kong
at all. The plaintiffs' cargo was damaged between Hong Kong and Shanghai. The
issue was whether Hong Kong was the 'port of shipment' for the purposes of the
Hong Kong equivalent of the 1971 Act. Mayo J held that transshipment was not
the same as shipment, and that there had been only one port of shipment and that
was Baltimore. Therefore, under the bill of lading terms, the United States Act's
$US 500 per package limitation applied. Mayo J said (at 486):

'Unless reference is made to the contract between the parties, there would
always be a likelihood that there would be an element of uncertainty. The
shipper of goods may have no knowledge of the arrangements being made
by the carrier, and it would put the shipper in an invidious position if he
could only establish his rights by a subsequent re-construction of events
which took place without his knowledge. I entirely reject Mr. Tong's
argument that shipment includes transhipment. All the references to
shipment in the rules are consistent with shipment being confined to the
initial shipment referred to in the bill of lading.'

[24] In my judgment, the present case is closer to the situation in the *Stafford
Allen* case than in *The Anders Maersk*. MSC's bill of lading specifically identifies
Felixstowe as the port of discharge. It is true that Boston is also identified as the
ultimate destination (as was London in the *Stafford Allen* case) and that the bill
states that it is therefore a 'through Bill of Lading': but for the meaning of that
loose and ambiguous expression (see *Scrutton* pp 369–371) one is immediately
referred by the bill's own language ('If box 5 and/or 9 filled out, this is a through
Bill of Lading (see clause 3)') to cl 3. That clause then sets out the limits of MSC's
obligations as a carrier under its bill. 'The Carrier agrees to carry the goods from
the Port of Loading to the Port of Discharge.' Felixstowe, not Boston, is the port
of discharge. MSC therefore did not agree to carry the goods to Boston. For the
purposes of that voyage to Felixstowe it is entitled to substitute other vessels etc.
If box 9 is filled in with a final destination, then 'the Carrier will, acting as
shipper's agent, only arrange for transport of the cargo by other carriers ... from
Port of discharge to destination', just as in the *Stafford Allen* case the first carrier
acted only as an agent in arranging the on-carriage by the second carrier. Clause 3
continues: 'and during such segments of Through Transport, handling and
storage of the goods shall be subject to the freight contracts and tariffs of the other

a carriers', again as in the *Stafford Allen* case the on-carriage from Cristobal was subject to the second carrier's 'regular bill of lading'. The next sentence in cl 3 begins with special emphasis—'It is expressly understood'—and continues 'that the Carrier's liability as "carrier" applies only from Port of Loading to Port of Discharge under this B/L ...' That is consistent with the point made in the first sentence of the clause, but underlines it by stressing that MSC's liability as a *b* carrier ends at Felixstowe. The clause continues: 'and only while the goods remain in its actual custody and control, whether as Carrier or bailee'. Mr Croall submits that the machinery remained in MSC's custody and control on the Rafaela S on the voyage from Felixstowe to Boston, but that submission ignores the point that the second half of this sentence is an additional limitation on MSC's liability.

c [25] There is nothing in cl 3 to extend MSC's responsibility as carrier beyond Felixstowe. It may be common ground that there was nothing to prevent MSC making a further arrangement for another MSC vessel to perform the on-carriage from Felixstowe, but that is not to be derived from cl 3 itself. In these circumstances, unless some other part of the bill of lading has a preponderant and *d* overriding effect, superseding cl 3, I cannot see how it can be said that the contract evidenced by the bill is a contract of carriage (as distinct from a contract *for* carriage) beyond Felixstowe.

[26] Do then the references to freight being payable at destination or anything else on the face of the bill transform the situation? I do not think so. The actual freight arrangements are not known, but the freight tariffs of MSC and any other *e* carriers were incorporated into the bill by language within cll 1 and 3. In practice, however, the freight will have been agreed, probably with Coniston, as part of the background to the sale and carriage. It was obviously not intended in practice for MacWilliam, the buyer, to pay for the freight element of its purchase twice. Nevertheless each carrier would have its remedy against the 'merchant' for *f* freight in accordance with its incorporated tariff, save to the extent that such rights arising under a general incorporation may have been superseded by any special arrangement. Then there is the stamped legend 'On-carriage to Boston to be arranged by M.S.C. agents': that is consistent with cl 3. Finally there is the stamp: 'Cargo to be cleared by U.S. Custom at port of discharge' but that, if a reference to a port in the United States, cannot displace the parties' choice of *g* Felixstowe as the port of discharge, and must be understood to refer instead to port of final destination.

[27] For these reasons, I conclude that although MSC was contracted to arrange on-carriage to Boston, it was not contracted to carry the machinery to Boston until it entered into a new arrangement at some stage, the details of which *h* are not reported, to on-carry the goods from Felixstowe. That was a separate contract of carriage, which entitled the shipper to demand a bill of lading and therefore, subject to the straight bill of lading issue, meant that the contract was 'covered by a bill of lading' for the purposes of art I of the Hague or Hague-Visby Rules: see *Parsons Corp v CV Scheepvaartonderneming Happy Ranger* [2002] EWCA *j* Civ 694, [2002] 2 All ER (Comm) 24.

'PORT OF SHIPMENT'

[28] It is convenient to take this issue at this stage, since it is now apparent that it is in truth closely connected with the one contract or two issue. If there are two contracts, then it is hard to see how Felixstowe is not to be regarded as the 'port

of shipment' for the purpose of the second contract. The bill of lading which the
shipper would have been entitled to have issued to it would presumably have
stated Felixstowe as the port of shipment. This would not have been a mere case
of transshipment at an intermediate stage of a single contract of carriage, as in
The Anders Maersk [1986] 1 Lloyd's Rep 483.

[29] If, on the other hand, the first question had been determined in favour of
a single contract, then it may be that the port of shipment issue would not have
been so obviously decided in favour of Durban rather than Felixstowe, seeing
that the single contract would still have referred to Felixstowe as a port of
discharge. If Felixstowe was a port of discharge it could, I suppose, be argued that
it was also a port of shipment. However, it would in truth be a port of
reshipment. I suspect, therefore, that the answer would have been to regard
Durban as the critical port of shipment, otherwise all the problems of a single
contract governed by a changing regime, highlighted in Mr Schaff's submissions,
would ensue. It is not perhaps impossible to have different parts of a single
contract governed by a different legal regime, including a different proper law,
although I think that this is more familiar to civil law jurisprudence than to the
common law, and I would be sceptical about inferring any such intention on the
part of the parties. However, this discussion merely emphasises that ultimately
this question could be a matter of statutory interpretation rather than contractual
construction. These are waters that the submissions of counsel have not entered.
Since it is not necessary to decide whether Felixstowe would be a 'port of
shipment' within the meaning of s 1(3) of the 1971 Act on the hypothesis of a
single contract of carriage, I would prefer to leave the question undetermined.

[30] The critical question is now whether a straight bill of lading is within the
regime of the Hague Rules and thus within the regime of the 1971 Act as well.

IS A STRAIGHT BILL OF LADING A 'BILL OF LADING OR ANY SIMILAR DOCUMENT OF TITLE'?

[31] The submissions of the parties on this issue are essentially
straightforward, but have little point of contact. On behalf of MSC, Mr Croall
submits that negotiability, or more properly speaking transferability, that is to say
the ability to transfer the rights and liabilities under the bill of lading contract by
indorsement or delivery to a succession of transferees, is essential to the nature
and meaning of a 'bill of lading' properly so-called. It is only such a document
that can be called a 'document of title' or at any rate a 'similar document of title',
for only such a document is capable of transferring title to the goods concerned.
That this is so can be traced back to the time when the law merchant developed
the bill of lading and recognised in it a universal custom as to its nature. That this
remains the position to this day is confirmed by the Law Commission's and the
Scottish Law Commission's report *Rights of Suit in Respect of Carriage of Goods by
Sea* (1991) (Law Com no 196, Scot Law Com no 130) (the Law Commission
report) and the ensuing Carriage of Goods by Sea Act 1992, which treat a straight
bill of lading as if it were a sea waybill and not a bill of lading. The earlier 1971 Act
also treated 'a bill of lading' and 'a non-negotiable document' separately in
s 1(6)(a) and (b). As for the Hague Rules themselves, their travaux préparatoires
demonstrate that in 1924 those responsible for the formulation of the rules,
consistently with the law both before and since, regarded transferability as the
essence of a bill of lading.

[32] On behalf of MacWilliam, however, Mr Schaff submits that all this is to
ignore matters of greater significance. Although a straight bill of lading cannot be

a transferred down a series of transferees, it can be transferred at any rate once, namely to the named consignee, and that for the purpose of that limited transfer it performs all the functions of a transferable bill of lading. It is a 'document of title' both for that reason and in any event because the consignee cannot obtain possession of the goods without its presentation (see the attestation clause set out at [14], above). Moreover, the Hague Rules are not concerned with transferability

b per se, but with securing an international regime of minimum standards as to the substance of the bill of lading contract, so as to protect parties who are not privy to its negotiation themselves but are nevertheless bound by its terms by reason of its transfer to them.   That is why as between immediate parties to a charterparty the Hague Rules regime does not apply and they therefore retain complete freedom of contract. However, the Hague Rules' rationale applies

c equally to the first transferee even if he is also the only possible and last transferee: he, like any subsequent transferee, is not in privity with the shipowner prior to transfer. Moreover, since the Hague Rules are an international convention, they should not be construed too narrowly according to domestic English concepts. In this connection, the MSC bill of lading 'looks and smells' like a bill of lading.

d As for the travaux préparatoires, they demonstrate that straight bills of lading were recognised in 1924, and that the Hague Rules were intended to embrace them. As for the Law Commission report and the 1992 Act, they come too late to affect the issue, and in any event proceed on a view of English law which either reflects too narrow and domestic a view or may even have proceeded upon a mistake. Thus at least since the Bill of Lading Act 1855 a straight bill of lading was

e treated in exactly the same way, despite its limited transferability, as a fully 'negotiable' bill.

[**33**] Mr Croall seeks to answer some of these points as follows. He submits that a first transferee is not to be treated as a 'third party' to the original bill of lading contract since he is an immediate party to an underlying sale of goods

f contract with the shipper and thus can influence the terms of the contract of carriage. As for the attestation clause, he submits that it only applies where the bill of lading is 'negotiable' and that 'duly endorsed' in it therefore means 'duly endorsed as appropriate', which would not be the case where the bill is filled in as a straight bill. As for the 1855 Act, that did not apply to straight bills of lading precisely because they were not fully transferable.

g [**34**] The arbitrators agreed with MSC's position. Thus in their reasons they argued as follows:

> '21. We were not impressed by the argument put forward on behalf of the claimants that the Hague-Visby Rules apply to straight-consigned bills of
> *h* lading because a purposive construction of such conventions is necessary to give effect to the basic intention of redressing the imbalance of bargaining power between carriers and cargo interests. As we have already noted, we regard the primary objective of such international conventions as being to protect the interests of third parties to whom bills of lading can be expected to be negotiated but who do not have any say in the initial bargaining process
> *j* which leads to the issuing of the bill of lading.
>
> 22. It did not seem to us to assist the claimants to argue that the bill in this case must be presumed to be a bill of lading properly so described since it stated that it was a bill of lading and resembled in all superficial respects a bill of lading. The fact was that it was on a printed form which was clearly intended to be used for *both* negotiable and non-negotiable bills. The

distinction between negotiable bills of lading and straight-consigned bills or waybills is fundamental and whilst counsel for the respondents was able to refer us to a number of decisions which appeared to support his proposition that the touchstone of the distinction between these two types of bills was that one was a negotiable instrument, the endorsement and delivery of which could affect the property [in] the goods shipped, counsel for the claimants did not seem able to find any persuasive support for his position on the authorities. We found ourselves inescapably drawn to the conclusion that the bill of lading in this case was a straight-consigned bill of lading which was not a document of title.'

[35] In the Commercial Court ([2002] 2 Lloyd's Rep 403) Langley J also agreed with Mr Croall's submissions. Langley J put the matter thus:

'[21] In my judgment Mr. Croall is right and Mr. Schaff wrong in these submissions. A "document of title" in this context is, I think, the antithesis of a document which can evidence the title of only one person. It is general not specific to one person. It is a document by which goods can be transferred by endorsement and delivery of the document itself. A straight consigned bill of lading is not such a document. Indeed the parties to this bill have a choice, exercisable by inclusion in Box (2) of the words "Order of" before naming the consignee, whether or not to constitute the bill a document of title in the sense to which I have referred.

[22] While in terms of strict analysis Mr. Schaff is right that no binding authority has determined the question, the consistent and overwhelming burden of judicial and other legal sources is against his submission.

[23] The established definition of a bill of lading includes the characteristics of "transferability" of title to the goods: Scrutton on Charterparties, 20th ed., art. 2, pp. 1–2; Benjamin's Sale of Goods, 5th ed. par. 18–007; Carver on Bills of Lading, 1st ed. pars 6–007 and 6–014. The Law Commission Report (Law Com No 196) which led to the Carriage of Goods by Sea Act, 1992 noted, at par. 2.50, that a straight consigned bill of lading was not a document of title at common law. The terms of the 1992 Act itself reflect that in s. 1(2). I also agree with Mr. Croall that the *travaux préparatoires* for the Hague Rules support the same conclusion. So, too, do the terms of s. 1(6)(b) of COGSA, 1971 itself which make express provision for circumstances in which "a non-negotiable document" may result in application of the Rules.'

[36] In the light of these arguments it is necessary to seek to interpret the Hague Rules by reference not only to their background and own terms and purposes, but also to the subsequent viewpoints expressed in authorities, statutes and textbooks.

THE BACKGROUND TO THE HAGUE RULES

[37] A good place to start is the 1855 Act. This provided in part as follows:

'WHEREAS by the custom of merchants, a bill of lading of goods being transferable by endorsement, the property in goods may thereby pass to the endorsee, but nevertheless all rights in respect of the contract contained in the bill of lading continue in the original shipper or owner; and it is expedient that such rights should pass with the property ...

1. *Consignees, and endorsees of bills of lading empowered to sue.*—Every consignee of goods named in a bill of lading, and every endorsee of a bill of

a
lading, to whom the property in the goods therein mentioned shall pass upon or by reason of such consignment or endorsement, shall have transferred to and vested in him all rights of suit, and be subject to the same liabilities in respect of such goods as if the contract contained in the bill of lading had been made with himself.'

b
[38] It will be noted first, that the preamble begins by citing the concept of a transferable bill of lading which by the custom of merchants passes property by its indorsement, but secondly, that s 1 extends the idea of passing contractual rights with the property not only to indorsees but also to consignees 'named in a bill' where property in the goods passes 'by reason of such consignment'. Mr Croall, who is concerned to submit that the expression 'bill of lading' can *only*

c
properly refer to a fully transferable bill and cannot describe a straight consigned bill, is forced to submit that the expression 'Every consignee named in a bill of lading' does not embrace a bill of lading which is neither an 'order' bill nor a bearer bill. It might be said that this limitation is not immediately apparent in the width of the language used ('*Every consignee ... named*' (my emphasis)), nor in the purpose of this limitation. Why would Parliament not wish a named consignee

d
under a straight bill of lading to have contractual rights and liabilities under the bill of lading passed to him as well as the property in the goods?

[39] In *CP Henderson & Co v Comptoir d'Escompte de Paris* (1873) LR 5 PC 253 the Privy Council had to consider a 'bill of lading ... in the usual form, with this difference, that the words "or order or assigns" are omitted'. The Privy Council

e
was prepared to assume that such a bill was not a negotiable instrument. It said (at 259–260):

'It has been argued that, notwithstanding the omission of these words, this bill of lading was a negotiable instrument, and there is some authority at *nisi prius* for that proposition; but, undoubtedly, the general view of the

f
mercantile world has been for some time that, in order to make bills of lading negotiable, some such words as "or order or assigns" ought to be in them.'

[40] On the basis of this assumption, the question for decision was the effect of the onward indorsement of such a bill by the consignee to the defendant bank in circumstances where the shipper and consignee had privately agreed that the

g
proceeds of sale of the goods should be remitted to London as security for an advance made by the shipper to the consignee. It was held that such indorsement gave the bank only an equitable right to the goods, but that the bank subsequently added to that a legal title when possession of the goods was actually delivered to it. In such a case, whose title was to be preferred, that of Henderson

h
the shipper, or that of the bank, the indorsee? That depended on whether the bank had any notice of the trust in favour of Henderson. It was argued that the omission of the usual words 'or order or assigns' put the bank on inquiry, but that argument was rejected. It was held first, that there was no evidence as to why the words were omitted, and secondly, that even if the omission had been

j
observed, it would not have amounted to notice of the arrangement. This litigation did not involve a shipowner and thus cannot throw any direct light on the problem under discussion. It seems however that as late as 1873 the significance of the words 'or order' for the negotiability of a bill of lading was still regarded as unsettled; that such a document, even though assumed not to be a negotiable instrument, was still referred to throughout the Privy Council's opinion as a 'bill of lading'; and that even the use of such a bill did not prevent its

indorsement passing an equitable title. There is little support in such treatment for regarding the expression 'bill of lading' as reserved in some way exclusively *a* for the admittedly usual form of a bill to order.

[41] The researches of Mr Croall, for which I am grateful, have produced an extract from the first edition of Carver's *A Treatise on the Law relating to the Carriage of Goods by Sea* (1885) p 464 (para 481). He there described the bill of lading as—

b

'generally a negotiable instrument, carrying with it the right to demand and have possession of the goods described in it ... But in order that it may have this character, it must, it seems, purport on the face of it to be negotiable ... It usually states that delivery is to be to the "order or assigns" of the consignee, or of the shipper; and words of this kind seem to be essential to the negotiability.'   *c*

[42] Carver then went on to refer to the *Henderson* case. What may be observed about this description is the careful language that whereas the words 'order or assigns' seem essential to negotiability in the stated sense, it is not suggested that negotiability is essential to the existence of a bill of lading; and *d* Carver was cautious to say that the bill of lading was 'generally' a negotiable instrument.

[43] In *The Marlborough Hill v Alex Cowan & Sons Ltd* [1921] 1 AC 444 the question was whether a document, described within itself as a bill of lading but written less usually in the form of a receipt of goods *for* (rather than *of*) shipment, was a bill of lading for the purposes of the Admiralty Court Act 1861, which set *e* out the jurisdiction of the Admiralty Court for an action in rem. The claim had been brought by consignees or indorsees of such documents, which provided for delivery to the shipper's order. The Privy Council held that it was a bill of lading within the meaning of the Act. Among the incidents of the document noted in the speech of Lord Phillimore was that it purported to be negotiable. It seems to *f* me that the observations of Lord Phillimore offer some assistance to both sides of the argument. Mr Croall prays in aid the comment (at 452) that 'If this document is a bill of lading, it is a negotiable instrument'. On the other hand, Mr Schaff points to passages which stress other incidents of the document as being standard for a bill of lading, such as detailed terms and conditions in familiar form; the fact that the document is called a bill of lading many times in the course *g* of such provisions and that it is made subject to the United States Harter Act 1893 (the Harter Act); the fact that it provides that 'If required by the shipowner, one signed bill of lading, duly endorsed, must be surrendered on delivery of the goods'; and that it 'ends in the time honoured form', viz 'In witness whereof the master or agent of said vessel has signed three bills of lading, all of this tenor and *h* date, of which if one is accomplished, the others shall be void' (see [1921] 1 AC 444 at 452–453). I do not for my part read Lord Phillimore as saying that negotiability is essential to the existence of a bill of lading nor even that it was its defining aspect. If that was so, he would not have to look further. He was rather emphasising that the document would work as merchants would expect a bill of lading to work. Thus he said (at 452):   *j*

'Money can be advanced upon it, and business can be done in the way in which maritime commerce has been carried on for at least half a century, throughout the civilised world. Both parties have agreed to call this a bill of lading; both, by its terms have entered into obligations and acquired rights a such as are proper to a bill of lading. All the other incidents in its very detailed language are such as are proper to such a document.'

[44] In my judgment this tells one nothing as to whether a non-negotiable bill of lading could not properly be called such. Indeed, it would be a remarkable thing if a claim by a consignee under a non-negotiable bill of lading would not merit falling under the admiralty jurisdiction.

b [45] In 1924, on the eve of the Hague Rules, *Thrige v United Shipping Co Ltd* (1924) 18 Ll L Rep 6 suggests that at any rate in England (for the position in the United States, see below) the use of a straight bill of lading was regarded as unusual and its ramifications still unsettled. The plaintiff Thrige was a Danish seller of machinery to a purchaser in England, the Victoria Co. The terms of sale

c were cash against documents. Thrige used a Danish line to carry the machinery and took a straight bill of lading which named the Victoria Co as the consignee without any reference to 'or order or assigns'. The goods were discharged at Harwich and proceeded by rail to London, where the Great Eastern Railway delivered them to the Victoria Co without production of the bill of lading, and Thrige, whose documents had not been taken up, thereby lost the value of the

d shipment. The role of the defendant line in this matter was obscure: at any rate the actual decision in the case was that no cause of action had been shown against it at all, since it acted as a mere agent without possession of the goods. However, the interest of the case for present purposes is that, of all judges, Scrutton LJ himself was intrigued by the issues which might have arisen if the carrier itself,

e the Danish line, had been sued. He described the bill of lading (at 8) as being 'in a very odd and unusual form' in that it was taken neither to the shipper's nor to the consignee's order. At any rate he appears to have been quite comfortable in describing the document as a bill of lading. He went on to say (at 9):

f 'That renders it unnecessary to decide the question which I personally feel considerable interest in, i.e., as to whether, when a bill of lading is made out to a consignee and the property passes on shipment, the shipowner who delivers to the named consignee without production of the bill of lading is or is not guilty of any breach of contract. It is not necessary to decide it; and I only wish to say that if the *Stettin* case (1889), 14 PD 142, decides there is such a duty, I think the *Stettin* case may require consideration. I am not expressing

g a final opinion, but I do not at present agree that with a statement in the simple form that I have stated it, where the property is passed on shipment and the bill of lading is to a named consignee, the agent of the shipowner gets into any difficulties if he delivers to the named consignee without production of such bill of lading. It is also unnecessary to determine whether such bill of

h lading is or is not a negotiable instrument.'

[46] There are a number of separate strands for consideration in that dictum. One raises the question whether the proper analysis of a sale cash against documents is that property passes on shipment (subject to a vendor's lien) or whether property does not pass until the exchange of payment and documents.

j Another is the question, which I will consider separately below, whether a carrier under a straight bill of lading is entitled to deliver the goods to the named consignee without production of the bill of lading. On the submissions in this court there is a dispute both as to this issue in itself and also as to whether, if production of the bill of lading remains necessary, this by itself makes a straight bill a 'similar document of title'. What for the present is of particular interest, however, is that as late as 1924 even so hugely experienced a figure as Scrutton LJ himself should be expressing uncertainty as to the effect of a straight bill of lading. *a*

THE UNITED STATES LAW PRIOR TO THE HAGUE RULES

[47] In the United States, on the other hand, the straight bill of lading was sufficiently recognised at a relatively early stage as to be given specific treatment in the Pomerene Bills of Lading Act 1916 (USC title 49) (the Pomerene Act). It is *b* defined (s 2) as a bill in which it is stated that the goods are consigned or destined to a specified person. Such a bill 'shall have placed plainly upon its face by the carrier issuing it 'nonnegotiable' or "not negotiable"' (see s 6). Section 29 provides:

> 'A bill may be transferred by the holder by delivery, accompanied with an *c* agreement, express or implied, to transfer the title to the bill or to the goods represented thereby ...'

Section 32 provides:

> 'A person to whom a bill has been transferred, but not negotiated, acquires thereby as against the transferor the title to the goods, subject to the terms *d* of any agreement with the transferor. If the bill is a straight bill such person also acquires the right to notify the carrier of the transfer to him of such bill and thereby to become the direct obligee of whatever obligations the carrier owed to the transferor of the bill immediately before notification ...'

[48] It appears that under United States law a straight bill of lading within the *e* Pomerene Act is subject to the minimum contractual standards of the Harter Act, s 1 of which applied the Act's scope to 'any bill of lading or shipping document'. The Harter Act was a leading precursor of the Hague Rules.

THE HAGUE RULES   *f*

[49] *Scrutton* pp 404–417 contains helpful 'Introductory Notes' concerning the history of the Hague Rules both in their original and in their amended form (the Hague-Visby Rules). I would extract the following (pp 404–405):

> 'At common law the shipowner, whether he carried the goods under a charterparty or under a bill of lading, could modify his prima facie liability as *g* carrier as much as he wished, and in the course of years the protective exceptions in these documents increased both in number and complexity to such an extent that a careful scrutiny of the documents became necessary in order to ascertain what rights they conferred against the shipowner. So far as charterparties were concerned this was unobjectionable; the decreased *h* liabilities enabled the shipowner to carry at a lower rate of freight and the charterer had ample opportunity of ascertaining the terms of his contract. With bills of lading, however, different considerations arose. Not only were they contracts of carriage but they were also documents of title, which by virtue of mercantile custom and the Bills of Lading Act 1855, passed freely from hand to hand as part of the currency of trade conferring on their holder *j* both rights and liabilities. Thus consignees, bankers and others who had not been parties to the original contract and had no effective control over its terms, became interested in the bill of lading without having had any real opportunity of examining its terms or assessing the value of the security it afforded. In the years before and immediately after the 1914–18 War, as the

a
terms of bills of lading became more diverse, the need for standardisation
became more and more insistent and an increasing demand was made on the
part of importers and exporters for the imposition by legislation, on the lines
of the American Harter Act 1893, of certain minimum liabilities of
sea-carriers who issued bills of lading.'

b
[50] The distinction drawn between the freedom of contract which was
unobjectionable as between immediate parties to a contract of carriage and the
need for protection for subsequent transferees is the explanation for a number of
the provisions of the Hague Rules. I need to set out the following extracts:

'ARTICLE I
c
... (b) "Contract of carriage" applies only to contracts of carriage covered
by a bill of lading or any similar document of title, in so far as such document
relates to the carriage of goods by sea, including any bill of lading or any
similar document as aforesaid issued under or pursuant to a charterparty
from the moment at which such bill of lading or any similar document of title
d
regulates the relations between a carrier and a holder of the same ...

ARTICLE V
... The provisions of these Rules shall not be applicable to charterparties,
but if bills of lading are issued in the case of a ship under a charterparty they
e
shall comply with the terms of these Rules ...

ARTICLE VI
Notwithstanding the provisions of the preceding Articles, a carrier, master
or agent of the carrier, and a shipper shall in regard to any particular goods
f
be at liberty to enter into any agreement in any terms as to the responsibility
and liability of the carrier for such goods ... provided that in this case no bill
of lading has been or shall be issued and that the terms agreed shall be
embodied in a receipt which shall be a non-negotiable document and shall be
marked as such. Any agreement so entered into shall have full legal effect:
Provided that this Article shall not apply to ordinary commercial shipments
g
made in the ordinary course of trade, but only to other shipments where the
character or condition of the property to be carried or the circumstances,
terms and conditions under which the carriage is to be performed, are such
as reasonably to justify a special agreement.'

h
[51] Thus, arts I(b) and V make it plain both that the Hague Rules do not apply
to charterparties at all (because they are only contracts between immediate
parties) and that they only apply to bills of lading issued under a charterparty once
they have started to regulate the relations between the carrier and a bill of lading
holder. This latter rule reflects the doctrine that when a bill of lading is issued to
a shipper who is also in charterparty relations with the carrier, then as long as the
j
bill of lading remains in the shipper's hands it operates only as a receipt and does
not in the least affect the contractual regime under the charterparty: once,
however, the bill of lading is transferred into the hands of a third party, then it
springs into life as a separate contract of carriage, which is why it must comply at
the outset with the requirements of the Hague Rules. *Scrutton* (p 424) mentions
as an example of 'the moment' from which a bill of lading issued under a

charterparty regulates the relations between a carrier and the bill's holder as *a*
being—

> 'if the charterer ships goods and takes a bill of lading making the goods
> deliverable to a named consignee, the time when the bill of lading is
> delivered to the consignee.'

Unless this text is written on the assumption that a bill of lading must by *b*
definition be negotiable, that reads very much like the case of a straight bill of
lading.

[52] This court was not addressed by counsel as to the significance of art VI.
I would therefore be reluctant to place too much weight on its terms. It seems to
me, however, to be saying that a shipper and a carrier may agree any terms for
carriage provided that (i) no bill of lading is issued, (ii) the terms agreed are *c*
embodied in a document described instead as a 'receipt' and marked as
'non-negotiable', and (iii) the shipments concerned are of a special nature such as
reasonably to justify a special agreement. This article effectively renders such an
exceptional, permissive regime one that exists only at the fringes of carriage by
sea. It gives no support to the hypothesis that a straight bill of lading dealing with *d*
ordinary commercial shipments would lie outside the international minimum
standards of the Hague Rules.

[53] It may be noted that when the Hague Rules were scheduled to the
Carriage of Goods by Sea Act 1924, s 4 of the latter disapplied the final proviso of
art VI in relation to any carriage of goods from one port in Great Britain or
Northern Ireland to any other such port (or in the Irish Free State), so that in *e*
relation to such shipments art VI, which begins with the paramount words
'Notwithstanding the provisions of the preceding articles', entitles the shipper
and carrier to operate in a regime of complete freedom of contract in relation to
goods of any kind, provided only that no bill of lading is issued and instead the
terms of carriage are embodied in a receipt marked as non-negotiable. *f*

THE INTERPRETATION OF THE HAGUE RULES

[54] It is by now well recognised that English statutes which give effect to
international conventions need to be interpreted with the international origin of
the rules well in mind. In *Stag Line Ltd v Foscolo, Mango & Co Ltd* [1932] AC 328,
[1931] All ER Rep 666, with reference to the Hague Rules themselves as *g*
incorporated into the 1924 Act, Lord Atkin said ([1932] AC 328 at 342–343, [1931]
All ER Rep 666 at 673):

> 'It will be remembered that the Act only applies to contracts of carriage of
> goods outwards from ports of the United Kingdom: and the rules will often
> have to be interpreted in the courts of the foreign consignees. For the *h*
> purpose of uniformity it is, therefore, important that the Courts should apply
> themselves without any predilection for the former law, always preserving
> the right to say that words used in the English language which have already
> in the particular context received judicial interpretation may be presumed to
> be used in the sense already judicially imputed to them.' *j*

[55] And Lord MacMillan famously said ([1932] AC 328 at 350, [1931] All ER
Rep 666 at 677):

> 'As these rules must come under the consideration of foreign Courts it is
> desirable in the interests of uniformity that their interpretation should not be

a   rigidly controlled by domestic precedents of antecedent date, but rather that the language of the rules should be construed on broad principles of general acceptation.'

THE TRAVAUX PRÉPARATOIRES OF THE HAGUE RULES

[56] Both Mr Schaff and Mr Croall relied on the travaux préparatoires as
b pointing in their favour, while both recognised that in this area 'only a bull's eye counts'. The arbitrators tended to think that they supported Mr Croall's position, for they said:

> '... it did seem to us to be clear that there was nothing in these records of
> the discussions leading to the convention to suggest that the expression "bill
> of lading" in the strict legal sense was intended to extend to documents
c > which were not negotiable. This was perhaps not surprising, since our
> understanding is that the overwhelming concern of the international body
> which were responsible for this convention was to ensure that the progress
> of international trade was promoted by safe-guarding the rights of third
> parties to whom bills of lading might be negotiated.'
d

[57] I would readily agree with the last sentiment, but this passage tends to beg two or even three questions at the heart of this case: one is whether, there was in 1924 a 'strict legal sense' limiting the expression 'bill of lading' to a negotiable document: Scrutton LJ's dictum in *Thrige v United Shipping Co Ltd* (1924) 18 Ll L Rep 6 at 9 would suggest there was not. The second is whether the
e logic of the legislators of the Hague Rules did not extend to all third parties to whom bills of lading might be transferred, such as a named consignee. The third is whether too narrow a domestic view of things is in any event the correct approach.

[58] Langley J ([2002] 2 Lloyd's Rep 403 at [23] (see [35], above)) also
f considered that the travaux préparatoires supported Mr Croall. It appears, however, that both the arbitrators and the judge had less of the material than was available in this court.

[59] As often occurs, the travaux préparatoires are rich in ambiguity. I am not sure that either party has scored a bull's eye. What, however, does I think emerge, and does so with some clarity, is that the assembled representatives were
g anxious to preserve freedom of contract for immediate parties and protection for third parties (that is not in dispute); that the case of straight bills of lading was discussed in conference, without it must be said an unequivocal result; but also that it is impossible to find any clear statement of an intention to exclude straight bills of lading from the protection of the Hague Rules. I shall try to indicate the
h basis of these conclusions.

[60] At the London Conference held in October 1922 (see Sturley *The legislative history of the Carriage of Goods by Sea Act and the travaux préparatoires of the Hague Rules* (1990)) a question was asked as to bills of lading issued under charterparties where shipper and receiver are the same person (ie as I suppose,
j where the shipment is between two branches of the same organisation): what if the bill of lading was not negotiated? Sir Leslie Scott (recently Solicitor-General) said (vol 2, p 391) that in such a case the bill of lading remained a mere receipt and the contract was to be found in the charterparty—

> 'and it is only when it is negotiated ... and gets into the hands of a third
> party that it will represent the conditions of carriage ... I have always

understood up to now that the intention, at The Hague and subsequently,
always has been in those cases [ordinary charterparty shipments] to leave
freedom of contract unaffected.'

The chairman (Sir Henry Duke, President of the Probate, Divorce and Admiralty
Division) said (vol 2, p 395):

'At The Hague the view was that there was business which was between
two individuals, and with which the Bankers and Insurers and the world at
large had nothing to do, where the shipper was the receiver of the goods and
was intended to be, and that you need not legislate about them ...'

[61] That was on 10 October. On 24 October, a discussion was initiated which
focused on the 'bill of lading as a negotiable document, bearing the clause "to
order"' and the role of a subsequent holder 'who took no part in its drafting'
(vol 1, p 349). At one point, however, there was this exchange (vol 1, pp 352–353):

'**Mr. de Rousiers.**—That is what we understand by *"connaissement
négociable"* (negotiable bill of lading) or *"connaissement à personne dénommée"*
(bill of lading for a designated person). In fact, negotiable bills are the vast
majority.

Mr. Beecher.—In so far as I understand **Sir Leslie Scott**, he seems to
believe that these rules, as they are defined, only apply to bills of lading that
are negotiated or negotiable. But the opinion of the London Conference was
(and in my opinion, that is essential) that these rules apply to all bills of lading
whether negotiable or not. I am told that a bill of lading that is not deemed
negotiable in England is so on the Continent.

The Chairman [Mr. Louis Franck].—Not negotiable, but simply
transferable under the rules concerning the transfer of civil obligations
according to law.

Mr. Beecher.—But **Sir Leslie Scott** seems to be mistaken about what we
understand as the subject of these rules. This is why I want to know whether
the rules apply to all bills of lading indiscriminately, whether negotiable or
not.

The Chairman.—What does the Harter Act say on the matter?

Mr. Beecher.—It applies to all bills of lading indiscriminately.

Sir Leslie Scott.—It is the same here. The rules apply to all bills of lading,
but there is nothing in the convention that says that when a charterer by
means of his charter party receives a bill of lading from the shipowner, it
constitutes a new contract between him and the shipowner.'

[62] That exchange, between, as it appears, representatives of the United
Kingdom, France and the United States, would seem to be directly in point and
favours Mr Schaff. On the other hand, just a few pages on (p 385), Mr Franck
raises the same question again, with specific reference to art I(b):

'Let us now return to article 1(b), which we had left to one side. With all
possible respect to the authors of this proposal, I do not find it very clear. Do
you intend to exclude those bills of lading called, *"connaissements à personne
dénommée"* (bills of lading for a denominated person).'

[63] To which Sir Leslie Scott replies: 'I believe the French delegation
considers the drafting adequate.' It is not clear whether Sir Leslie Scott is saying,
consistently with his answer a few short pages before, 'Yes, as the French

a delegation itself accepts', or whether he is simply failing to answer the question. It would make more sense to suppose the former.

[64] So far, these materials were not before the arbitrators or Langley J. They assist Mr Schaff. Indeed, the exchange quoted at [61], above, taken by itself, could be described as a 'bull's eye'. The balance of the materials discussed below, however, were before the arbitrators and/or Langley J.

b [65] The conference resumed in October 1923 in Brussels. There was a discussion as to the meaning of 'any similar document of title' in art I(b) (vol 1, pp 432–433):

'**Mr. Berlingieri** indicated that this idea was expressed in the comments of the German delegation, where it said "document giving to the legitimate c holder the right to the goods carried."

Sir Leslie Scott added that it was a document that could be negotiated with a banker.

Mr. Ripert asked if one might apply these rules to a nominal (ie a straight) bill of lading?

d **The Chairman** replied that one could, except when it was a matter of a non-negotiable bill of lading. In such a case article 6 (see [50], above) would apply.

Mr. Ripert verified that the rules did not apply to a bill of lading that was non-negotiable and felt that this should be pointed out in article 1.

Sir Leslie Scott observed that that happened in article 6.'

e
[66] A few lines later the question was asked what a 'similar document of title' might be. Sir Leslie Scott gave a mate's receipt as an example and added: 'The desire was to avoid the possible side-stepping of the convention by the parties through the adoption of a similar document that was not called a bill of lading.'

[67] As far as it goes, this passage might seem to assist Mr Croall rather than f Mr Schaff, but it is difficult to interpret, possibly because of terminological uncertainties. A distinction is made between a negotiable and a non-negotiable straight bill. Since a straight or nominal bill is by definition one made out to a named consignee only, what is the difference? It could perhaps depend on the use to which the straight bill is put. Where it is not used with a contract of sale, as g where the shipper and receiver are the same person, or perhaps two different companies within the same group, then there might be no question of any transfer of title. Where, however, the bill of lading is used as part of international trade, for instance under a cif sale under which title is not intended to pass save against payment for the documents, then although the bill, not being an 'order' or bearer bill, is not negotiable in the full sense, ie repeatedly transferable, it is h transferable once. It may be that 'negotiable' is being used in these passages both in the sense of meaning fully transferable and in the sense of limited transferability. That would at any rate explain why Scrutton LJ in *Thrige v United Shipping Co Ltd* (1924) 18 Ll L Rep 6 was uncertain whether a straight bill of lading was to be regarded as a negotiable instrument or not (see [45], above). Moreover, j the reference to the future art VI is interesting, for that is not concerned with bills of lading at all, and is limited to shipments outside the ordinary course of commerce. It is very difficult indeed to think that straight bills were thought of as falling within that description.

[68] It is also interesting to note that in Sir Leslie Scott's view the expression 'or any similar document of title' was intended as an anti-avoidance device. As

such it is a useful one, for where the document can affect title, it has the capacity *a*
to affect third parties, who, of course are the object of the conference's concern.

[69] I think that my understanding of these texts is supported by a further
discussion a few pages on (vol 1, pp 435–436) about the language in art I(b) 'from
the moment' etc. Article I(b) says 'from the moment at which such bill of lading
or similar document of title regulates the relations between a carrier and a holder
of the same'. Various expressions were canvassed, such as 'from the moment the *b*
bill of lading is negotiated' and 'from the moment it is remitted to a third party'.
The trouble with the latter was the possibility that a third party 'might be an
agent of the shipper'; moreover, where goods were simply sent abroad by a
shipper to its own factory, 'there is no third-party interest'. It may not be a
coincidence that the enigmatic word 'negotiated' was passed by. At any rate the
chairman, Mr Franck, remarked—   *c*

> 'that it would be up to the courts to decide in each case if there was a bill
> of lading, that is to say, a document representing the goods on board a
> specific ship giving title to delivery.'

My understanding is also supported by this passage (vol 1, p 441):   *d*

> '**The Chairman** stated that as soon as a bill of lading could be negotiated,
> and placed in the possession of a holder, it should conform to the Hague
> Rules ... No one carried goods without a bill of lading, except in cases that
> were altogether out of the ordinary, which there is no point discussing here,
> because the question posed is purely theoretical. In general, the shipper had *e*
> a bill of lading, and he needed this document of title to receive the goods at
> their destination, to prove his rights toward the captain, to insure the goods,
> to get credit. *What one more often sees, perhaps, are straight bills of lading, but in
> every case there was a bill of lading or similar document of title.*' (My emphasis.)

[70] On the other hand, as a matter of counterpoint there is the following *f*
passage (from a subsequent day's session) in Mr Croall's favour (vol 1,
pp 477–478):

> '**The Chairman [Mr. Loder]** noted that in the convention everything
> concerning the bill of lading had been regulated and that article 6 had been
> inserted later to show that in this case there was freedom of contract. From *g*
> the time when the bill of lading was negotiable (sic negotiated?), the
> convention applied. But if there was no bill of lading, it did not apply and
> freedom of contract still existed.
>
> **Sir Leslie Scott** attested that the scope of the convention was just that
> indicated by **Mr. Loder**. The possibility existed of issuing a non-negotiable
> document. Here the term "bill of lading" meant an ordinary bill of lading, *h*
> that is to say, negotiable.
>
> **Mr. Berlingieri** wanted there to be understanding on the meaning of the
> word negotiable. He would prefer the word "non-transferable" instead of
> "non-negotiable" because a straight bill of lading could be a negotiable bill of
> lading provided the transfer formalities were fulfilled. One might therefore *j*
> evade the convention by always creating a straight bill of lading and by later
> fulfilling the formalities required for transfer.
>
> **Mr. Franck** believed that the concept of the first conference had been for
> the bill of lading to be "to bearer" or "to order." If it were a straight bill of
> lading, one might allow transfer by the normal method. It should not be

a feared that, by means of transfer under general law, one could evade this provision.'

However, almost immediately another representative, Mr Sohr, noted that—

b 'the express goal of article 3 (sic art III, r 8) had been to prevent frauds and agreements like those indicated by **Mr. Berlingieri**. It was evident that one could not evade the convention by creating a straight bill of lading and by having recourse to civil transfer. It was still necessary that it should not apply to ordinary commercial cargoes since the last paragraph (sic of art VI) expressly prevented it.'

c [71] That is a statement in Mr Schaff's favour, for it makes a plain distinction between the subject matter of art VI and the ordinary case of a straight bill of lading.

[72] This led to a further discussion of the purpose of art VI. Mr Franck returned (vol 1, pp 478–479) to the charge:

d 'But what was established was that there was no way of evading, by means of this text, the chief object of the convention, which was to protect negotiable bills of lading "to order".

The Chairman re-affirmed this point of view. The convention only regulated the question of bills of lading. If one was not issued, the absolute freedom of the parties remained. But if one created a bill of lading, it was

e necessary to do so according to the rules decreed by the convention.

Mr. Ripert wanted a clear statement on two points. In France there was an important trade with the United States, which imported typewriters, industrial machines, etc. This trade was carried out by firms that shipped these machines to themselves or their branch offices with no intention of

f transferring the bills of lading to third parties. It should be understood that it was permissible to issue a nominal bill of lading for these machines that did not include the clause "to order" and to which the rules did not apply.

Sir Leslie Scott pointed out that the *rules always applied to ordinary commercial cargoes*. (My emphasis.)

Mr. Ripert asked what should be understood by exceptional cargoes.

g **Sir Leslie Scott** cited some examples. Aboard was a cargo of cotton damaged by seawater and there was a desire to reship what remained of this damaged cargo. Another example might be the shipment of a product containing some new material when it was not known whether this cargo would suit the ship, for which it might be dangerous. That was an

h experimental shipment. It was the beginning of what would perhaps later become an ordinary trade, but for the time being it was still an exceptional cargo.'

j [73] It seems to me that this passage confirms, what appears to me the natural construction of art VI, that straight bills of lading were not intended to fall within it. This passage also demonstrates that although a bill of lading under which a shipper ships to himself (the French example of the typewriter trade) would, for reasons quite outside art VI, lie beyond the rules since such a bill of lading would remain a mere receipt, nevertheless, where ordinary commercial cargoes were concerned, the rules were intended to bite, even if, as I would hazard, the bill of lading was a straight (nominal) one.

[74] This is I think confirmed by a further passage, the last that I will cite, a page later (vol 1, p 480) as follows:

> 'Mr. Ripert felt that that was not enough because the nominal bill of lading in France could be transferred. Would it be necessary to make the bill of lading completely non-transferable (sic to fall within art VI)?
>
> Sir Leslie Scott stated that a nominal bill of lading fell just as much under the convention as any other bill of lading, even if it had not been transferred.'

[75] In sum, I would regard this material as showing that at the heart of the Conference's concern was the archetypal fully negotiable, ie repeatedly transferable, bill of lading, which of course was the paradigm case of a document of title and an instrument which therefore would come into the hands of third parties. Such a document was the prime focus of the Hague Rules. On the other hand there were a number of other cases where it is clear that the representatives intended the rules to be disapplied: such as the charterparty, such as the bill of lading issued under a charterparty to a shipper in whose hands it remained a mere receipt, such as a mere receipt marked non-negotiable in the context of out of the ordinary shipments, and such as a bill of lading which could never come into the hands of a third party as a document of title because it was consigned by a shipper only to himself. That left the question: what of a straight bill of lading, which was not a mere receipt in the hands of the original shipper, which was not a consignment by a shipper to himself, and which was not an extraordinary shipment, but an ordinary contract of carriage in international trade pursuant to a sale contract under whose terms title was to remain with the seller/shipper until transfer of the shipping documents, such a document as was in every sense like an 'order' bill of lading save that the shipment was consigned to a named consignee and thus could only be transferred once? At the end of the day, I do not think that there is anything in the travaux préparatoires which I have seen which unequivocally states that such a case is outside the scope of the Hague Rules, and there is much in that material which points in the opposite direction.

AUTHORITIES FROM THE HAGUE RULES TO THE 1971 ACT

[76] It took the best part of 20 years for a British court to consider the question of a non-negotiable document by reference to the Hague Rules and then it fell to the Northern Ireland Court of Appeal to do so, in *Hugh Mack & Co Ltd v Burns & Laird Lines Ltd* (1944) 77 Ll L Rep 377. The shipment was of men's clothing from Belfast to Glasgow, carried pursuant to a consignment note and receipt stamped 'Non-negotiable'. The consignment note named consignees in Scotland and stated: 'Please receive for forwarding per Burns and Laird Lines' steamers the undernoted goods ...'. These documents were retained by the shipper. The goods were damaged and the shipper claimed against the carrier, which relied on terms incorporated into its receipt. The shipper said that the Hague Rules applied by virtue of the 1924 Act. The claim failed on two grounds. The first was that the consignment note and receipt was not a bill of lading or any similar document of title; the second was that in any event the parties had freedom of contract under art VI as amended in the case of coastal trade within the British Isles and Ireland by s 4 of the 1924 Act. As to the first point Andrews LCJ said (at 383):

> 'Such a receipt, even if it can be properly described as a "document of title," is not "similar to" a bill of lading. It has none of its characteristics. It is different in form; it is given at a different time; it bears no stamp; it does not

a   acknowledge the goods to be on board any particular ship, nor, indeed, does
    it acknowledge a shipment on board at all; it is retained by the consignor, not
    sent to the consignee; above all, it is not a negotiable instrument, the
    indorsement and delivery of which may affect the property in the goods
    shipped.'

b   [77] Mr Croall relies on that 'above all'; but of course a document which was
    retained and was never intended to be sent to the consignee as a symbol of the
    goods could never have affected the property in the goods. It is plain, moreover,
    that the receipt was never treated as a 'bill of lading' of any kind, nor *similar* to
    one.

    [78] *Gardano & Giampari v Greek Petroleum George Mamidakis & Co* [1961] 3 All ER
c   919, [1962] 1 WLR 40 is another of the small number of cases in English law which
    are concerned with straight bills of lading. The shipment in that case was made
    by Greek Petroleum under a c&f sale contract with the Greek Ministry of
    Commerce and pursuant to a charterparty between Greek Petroleum and the
    claimant shipowner, Gardano. The bill of lading simply named the Greek
    Ministry as consignee. The shipowner argued, in reliance on s 1 of the Bills of
d   Lading Act 1855 (see [37], above) that the shipper had lost its title to sue as a result
    of the transfer of the bill of lading to the consignee. That argument failed on a
    number of grounds, one of which was that s 1 of the 1855 Act did not operate
    where property had passed under the express terms of the sale contract *not* on or
    by reason of the consignment but ex the loading installation. If, however,
e   Mr Croall were correct in his submissions, s 1 could never have applied in any
    event. But for the special terms of the sale contract, however, McNair J would
    have treated it as a typical cif or c&f contract, which he described in these terms
    ([1961] 3 All ER 919 at 924, [1962] 1 WLR 40 at 52):

        'It is quite true that in an ordinary contract of sale in the traditional c.i.f or
f   c. & f. form the seller discharges his obligations as regards delivery by
        tendering a bill of lading covering the goods. It is not necessary for me here
        to state all the qualifications involved, but the transaction is essentially one
        which has been correctly described as a sale of goods performed by delivery
        of documents, and in the normal way the property passes when the
        documents are taken up.'
g
    [79] This question was further discussed in the Privy Council in *Kum v Wah
    Tat Bank Ltd* [1971] 1 Lloyd's Rep 439 at 446. The documents in that case were
    mate's receipts stated to be consigned to a named consignee and marked
    'non-negotiable'. The case was decided on a different point, but Lord Devlin said:

h   'It is well settled that "Negotiable", when used in relation to a bill of lading,
        means simply transferable. A negotiable bill of lading is not negotiable in the
        strict sense; it cannot, as can be done by the negotiation of a bill of exchange,
        give to the transferee a better title than the transferor has got, but it can by
        endorsement and delivery give as good a title. But it has never been settled
j   whether delivery of a non-negotiable bill of lading transfers title or
        possession at all. The bill of lading obtains its symbolic quality from the
        custom found in *Lickbarrow v. Mason* ((1787) 2 Term Rep 63, 100 ER 35) and
        that is a custom which makes bills of lading "negotiable and transferable" by
        endorsement and delivery or transmission. To the same effect the Bills of
        Lading Act, 1855, recites that a bill of lading is by the custom of merchants

"transferable by endorsement". There appears to be no authority on the effect of a non-negotiable bill of lading. This is not surprising. When consignor and consignee are also seller and buyer, as they most frequently are, the shipment ordinarily serves as delivery (Sale of Goods Act, 1893, sect. 32(1)) and also as an unconditional appropriation of the goods (sect. 18, rule 5(2)) which passes the property. So as between seller and buyer it does not usually matter whether the bill of lading is a document of title or not.'

[80] So the point remained undecided. However, I understand Lord Devlin here to be speaking purely generally about the sale of goods issue. I can see no reason why as between a seller and a buyer under a cif sale the usual principle discussed by McNair J in the *Gardano & Giampari* case does not apply, even in the case of a straight bill. The seller does not wish to part with property unless the buyer pays for the documents, and the seller/shipper who is left with both goods and documents wishes to be protected against losing his goods to a consignee who is allowed to take delivery of them from the ship without production of a bill of lading.

[81] *The Maurice Desgagnes* [1977] 1 Lloyd's Rep 290 is a decision of the Canada Federal Court. The issue was whether a document, which was not described as a bill of lading, was not issued by or with the authority of the carrier, and which recorded shipment by Canadian General Electric Co at Barrie, Ontario, of goods consigned *to itself* at St John's, Newfoundland, was a bill of lading within the meaning of the Hague Rules as scheduled to the Canadian Carriage of Goods by Water Act 1970. Reference was made to *Hugh Mack & Co Ltd v Burns & Laird Lines Ltd* (1944) 77 Ll L Rep 377. Dube J concluded as follows (at 296):

'The document before the Court is not titled "bill of lading" and there is nothing to indicate that the carrier intended it to be a bill of lading. In fact, the defendant carrier in his defence alleges it did not issue a bill of lading. The document has to be considered as a mere receipt given by the forwarder to the shipper, and not a negotiable bill of lading issued by the shipowner and signed by the master or other agent in authority.'

Although relied on by Mr Croall, I do not think that this case takes the matter any further forward at all.

THE CARRIAGE OF GOODS BY SEA ACT 1971
[82] The 1971 Act was the medium by which the Hague-Visby Rules were introduced to English law. As in the case of the 1924 Act, the 1971 Act required a 'bill of lading or any similar document of title'. However, the concept of a 'receipt which is a non-negotiable document marked as such' and which 'expressly provides that the Rules are to govern the contract as if the receipt were a bill of lading' makes its entrance. The relevant provisions are s 1(4) and (6), as follows:

'(4) Subject to subsection (6) below, nothing in this section shall be taken as applying anything in the Rules to any contract for the carriage of goods by sea, unless the contract expressly or by implication provides for the issue of a bill of lading or any similar document of title ...

(6) Without prejudice to Article X(c) of the Rules, the Rules shall have the force of law in relation to—(a) any bill of lading if the contract contained in or evidenced by it expressly provides that the Rules shall govern the contract,

a   and (b) any receipt which is a non-negotiable document marked as such if the contract contained in or evidenced by it is a contract for the carriage of goods by sea which expressly provides that the Rules are to govern the contract as if the receipt were a bill of lading, but subject, where paragraph (b) applies, to any necessary modifications and in particular with the omission of Article III of the Rules of the second sentence of paragraph 4 and of
b   paragraph 7.'

[83] As for the Hague-Visby Rules scheduled to the 1971 Act, arts I(b), V, and VI remained as they had done under the Hague Rules.

[84] The concept of a receipt which is a non-negotiable document marked as such derives from art VI of the Hague Rules: but there, as in the same article of
c   the Hague-Visby Rules, it was a means for contracting out of the Hague Rules; whereas under s 1(6) it is an alternative means for incorporating the Hague Rules. However, s 4 of the 1924 Act, which disapplied the final proviso of art VI in the case of coastal voyages, now disappears.

[85] Mr Croall relies on the concept of a non-negotiable receipt in s 1(6) as being an indication that a bill of lading within the meaning of the 1971 Act, and
d   therefore, it is suggested, within the meaning of the Hague Rules themselves, is something different from a straight bill of lading. The arbitrators and the judge indorsed that submission. However, I am not convinced by this reasoning. A non-negotiable receipt is not prima facie the same thing as a straight bill of lading. A premise to the contrary would mean that all talk of a straight bill of lading is
e   incoherent, a contradiction in terms, and that would make nonsense of much of the discussion of the issue which I have cited above. There was no investigation in counsel's submissions into the origins of the distinction drawn in s 1(6), but I would hazard that it derives from the previous concepts of art VI and s 4 of the 1924 Act. Article VI says that you are only very exceptionably permitted to avoid issuing a bill of lading where otherwise you would be required to do so, and thus
f   to take yourself outside the Hague Rules, but that when entitled to do so you have to do so in a very clear manner, avoiding the language of bill of lading and making it clear that the document concerned, described as a receipt, is non-negotiable. It is clear from the terms of art VI above and from the travaux préparatoires that art VI is not covering the ground of a straight bill of lading.
g   Section 4 of the 1924 Act said that you could use that device in less restricted circumstances, namely in all coasting voyages between ports in the British Isles including all of Ireland. Section 1(6) of the 1971 Act now provided that the same technique could be used not only to take you outside the Hague Rules but, where the document also makes it clear that the Hague-Visby Rules are to govern as if the document were a bill of lading, to bring you back inside the Hague Rules.
h   It appears that such documents are in use on short journeys, such as cross-Channel trips, where it is not necessary or practicable to employ a bill of lading surrender of which by the receiver is required to obtain delivery of the goods. Nevertheless, there is no inevitable desire in such a trade to stand outside the terms of the Hague Rules; and so special provision was made to allow such
j   documents to come back within the regime of the Hague Rules. See *McCarren & Co Ltd v Humber International Transport Ltd and Truckline Ferries (Poole) Ltd, The Vechscroon* [1982] 1 Lloyd's Rep 301, where the document covered the carriage of sides of pork from Poole to Cherbourg and was described as a 'commercial vehicle movement order'; and *Browner International Ltd v Monarch Shipping Co Ltd, The European Enterprise* [1989] 2 Lloyd's Rep 185, where the

carriage was of a refrigerated tractor trailer from Dover to Calais under a document described as a consignment note/waybill in respect of a contract which expressly provided that no bill of lading would be issued. It would be quite understandable that the United Kingdom, with its enormous trade between its own islands and the continent, might wish to make special provision for such circumstances.

UP TO THE CARRIAGE OF GOODS BY SEA ACT 1992

[86] In *Cia Portorafti Commerciale SA v Ultramar Panama Inc, The Captain Gregos* [1990] 3 All ER 967 there was a claim in tort by purchasers of a cargo of oil which had been carried under bills of lading which incorporated the Hague-Visby Rules. There was an alleged theft of part of the cargo, and the question was whether art III, r 6 of the Hague-Visby Rules barred the claim on the ground that it had not been brought within one year. The Court of Appeal held that it could not finally determine the issue on the present facts, because it was not yet clear whether the claimants were parties to the bills. It was in this context that Bingham LJ said (at 976–977):

'As s 1(4) of the 1971 Act and art I, para (b) and art X of the rules in particular make clear, the bill of lading is the bedrock on which this mandatory code is founded. A bill of lading is a contractual document with certain commercially well-known consequences when indorsed and transferred. It is not clear to me why the code should treat the existence of a bill of lading as a matter of such central and overriding importance if the code is to apply with equal force as between those who are not parties to the contract which the bill contains or evidences.'

[87] I mention this citation only because it has been relied on in a subsequent case (see [109], below) concerning straight bills of lading as a definitive statement of the meaning of a bill of lading, viz that only a fully negotiable bill which can be transferred by indorsement down a line of transferees is capable of being a bill of lading within the meaning of the Hague Rules. However, it seems to me that all that Bingham LJ was doing, in the context of a case involving receivers of cargo when it was still uncertain whether they had become parties to the bills in question, was to emphasise that a bill of lading, when indorsed and transferred, remained a contractual document to the terms of which subsequent parties were capable of becoming contractually bound as parties to it by 'commercially well-known consequences'. There is of course no doubt that such a negotiable bill is a paradigm example of a bill of lading. The question remains whether a straight bill of lading, albeit it is capable of being transferred only once to a named consignee, and then by delivery rather than indorsement, also comes within the designation of being a bill of lading.

[88] The 1992 Act was preceded by the Law Commission report. Unlike the 1924 and 1971 Acts, the 1992 Act was not concerned with the *content* of a contract for the carriage of goods by sea, but, like the 1855 Act, with the *transfer* of rights and liabilities under it. The 1855 Act, which had tied such transfer to the concept of property passing at the identical time and by reason of a consignment or indorsement, had been shown by the pressure of factual situations to be causing difficult problems relating to title to sue the carrier. For these purposes, in the course of its report the Law Commission not surprisingly discussed the concept

a of a bill of lading. Under the heading 'Definition of bill of lading', the Commission
wrote (para 2.50):

> 'We have also opted against a definition of "bill of lading", just as there is
> no definition under the 1855 Act or the Factors Acts. Under the present law,
> a bill of lading is usually identified by reference to its three functions, i.e. that
b > it is a receipt for the goods, that it usually evidences the contract of carriage
> and that it may be a document of title (at least until complete delivery of the
> goods has been made to the person entitled thereto). However, to attempt
> a definition, which would necessarily be elaborate would, we feel, be
> counterproductive, particularly as there are many documents which are
> called bills of lading but which are not bills of lading properly so-called: for
c > instance, a standard ocean "shipped" bill of lading is radically different from
> a so-called "house" bill of lading, which is really no more than a merchant's
> delivery order. However, clause 1(2) of the Bill stipulates that a bill of lading
> must be transferable, thus following the preamble to the 1855 Act. A
> "straight" consigned bill of lading, such as one made out "to X" without any
d > such words as "to order", *is not a document of title at common law.* It will
> therefore merely be a receipt for the goods and, in the absence of a
> charterparty, will usually evidence (in the hands of the shipper) or contain (in
> the hands of a third party) the terms of the contract of carriage. *Hence, it will
> resemble a sea waybill, apart from the fact that a sea waybill will not normally be
e > presented to the ship to obtain delivery.* The main practical consequence of
> "straight" bills of lading not satisfying clause 1(2) of the Bill is that they will
> not fall within the ambit of clause 4 of the Bill, relating to the conclusive
> nature of a bill of lading in the hands of a lawful holder. Were a "straight"
> bill of lading to be a bill of lading for the purposes of the Bill, it would mean
> that the holder thereof would have the benefit of clause 4 whereas the
f > consignee named in the sea waybill would not. *Apart from being inconsistent
> with the Hague-Visby Rules, this would be an anomalous result given that "straight"
> bills of lading and sea waybills are much the same type of document save that the sea
> waybill is not required to obtain delivery.* The contrary argument is that sea
> waybills should come within the ambit of clause 4, an argument which we
g > have rejected for the reasons given below. In conclusion, we require that a
> bill of lading must be transferable to fall within the Bill. Where a bill of lading
> is not transferable, it will undoubtedly fall within the definition of sea waybill
> to be found in clause 1(3) of the Bill.' (My emphases.)

h [89] I have italicised certain passages on which particular emphasis has been
placed by counsel, and which are the subject of dispute. The footnote
accompanying the statement that a straight bill of lading 'is not a document of
title at common law' cites *Benjamin's Sale of Goods* (3rd edn, 1987) p 903
(para 1446). The footnote accompanying the statement that for a straight bill of
lading to be a bill of lading would be inconsistent with the Hague-Visby Rules
j refers to s 1(6) of the 1971 Act and says that that provision—

> 'distinguishes bills of lading and non-negotiable (meaning non-transferable)
> receipts, into which latter category sea waybills or straight bills of lading are
> capable of falling: see (*Browner International Ltd v Monarch Shipping Co Ltd,
> The European Enterprise* [1989] 2 Lloyd's Rep 185) ...'

[90] Mr Schaff relies on the distinction made between a straight bill of lading *a* and a sea waybill to the effect that the former is, although the latter is not, 'required to obtain delivery'. Mr Schaff submits, moreover, that on that basis a straight bill of lading is in any event a document of title similar to a bill of lading within the meaning of the Hague Rules.

[91] In accordance with the recommendations of the Law Commission, the 1992 Act makes a distinction between bills of lading and sea waybills in the *b* following terms of s 1(2) and (3):

'(2) References in this Act to a bill of lading—(a) do not include references to a document which is incapable of transfer either by indorsement or, as a bearer bill, by delivery without indorsement; but (b) subject to that, do include references to a received for shipment bill of lading.   *c*

(3) References in this Act to a sea waybill are references to any document which is not a bill of lading but—(a) is such a receipt for goods as contains or evidences a contract for the carriage of goods by sea; and (b) identifies the person to whom delivery of the goods is to be made by the carrier in accordance with that contract.'   *d*

[92] It follows that, for the purposes of the 1992 Act, a straight bill of lading cannot be a bill of lading within s 1(2) above, but will be a sea waybill within s 1(3). That, however, will not affect the essence of the subject matter of the 1992 Act, for in either case rights under the respective document can be transferred to the named person to whom delivery is to be made, in the case of the bill of lading *e* if he is its 'lawful holder', and liabilities can then be transferred to that person if he takes or demands delivery of the goods: see s 2 (dealing with rights), s 3 (dealing with liabilities) and s 5(2) (dealing with the meaning of the holder of a bill of lading). When those sections are read, it is perfectly obvious why the more complicated case of the classic bill of lading has been dealt with separately, and *f* the more simple case of the straight bill of lading and/or sea waybill has been addressed in different terms: but both are dealt with essentially to the same ends.

[93] Section 5(5), moreover, states that the 1992 Act takes effect 'without prejudice to the application, in relation to any case, of the rules (the Hague-Visby Rules)' which have the force of law under the 1971 Act. Section 6(2) repeals the 1855 Act.   *g*

[94] Thus the 1992 Act is drafted on the basis that a straight bill of lading is not a bill of lading for the purposes of the 1992 Act, but leaves open the question for the purposes of the Hague and Hague-Visby Rules and the 1971 Act.

FROM THE 1992 ACT TO DATE   *h*

[95] In the last decade or so a number of cases have been coming to court concerning straight bills of lading. It is not clear why there is this recent proliferation of such cases, as compared with the paucity of them over the previous 150 years or so. It may have something to do with changes in the documentary forms used in connection with carriage by sea. This may in turn *j* have been influenced by the terms of the 1992 Act. The question has arisen in connection with such forms as to whether the Hague-Visby Rules apply. That question has been looked at from the point of view of whether the straight bill of lading is a bill of lading, and also from the point of view of whether the document is a 'similar document of title'. The latter question has been seen possibly to

a depend on whether the consignee is obliged to present the document in order to obtain delivery of the goods.

[96] In that connection, it is established law that at any rate in the case of a classic (negotiable) bill of lading the obligation of the ship is to deliver only against its surrender: see *SA Sucre Export v Northern River Shipping Ltd, The Sormovskiy 3068* [1994] 2 Lloyd's Rep 266 and *Motis Exports Ltd v Dampskibsselskabet AF 1912, A/S*
b [1999] 1 All ER (Comm) 571 (affirmed in the Court of Appeal [2000] 1 All ER (Comm) 91). The relevant authorities are collected in those judgments. It is sufficient to quote from them as follows. In *The Sormovskiy 3068* Clarke J said ([1994] 2 Lloyd's Rep 266 at 274):

c   'It makes commercial sense to have a simple rule that in the absence of an express term of the contract the master must only deliver the cargo to the holder of the bill of lading who presents it to him. In that way both the shipowners and the persons in truth entitled to possession of the cargo are protected by the terms of the contract.'

[97] In *The Motis*, where the issue was whether the carrier was excused if he
d without negligence delivered against a forged bill of lading, Stuart-Smith LJ said ([2000] 1 All ER (Comm) 91 at 98 (para 19)):

        'But it has been established for well over a century that under a bill of lading contract, a shipowner is both entitled and bound to deliver the goods against production of an original bill of lading, provided he has no notice of
e   any other claim or better title to the goods (see *Glyn Mills Currie & Co v East and West India Dock Co* (1882) 7 App Cas 591, [1881–5] All ER Rep 674, *The Stettin* (1889) 14 PD 142, *Carlberg v Wemyss Coal Co Ltd* 1915 SC 616 at 624, *Sze Hai Tong Bank Ltd v Rambler Cycle Co Ltd* and particularly the passage I have cited ([1959] 3 All ER 182 at 184, [1959] AC 576 at 586), *Barclays Bank Ltd v
f   Customs and Excise Comrs* [1963] 1 Lloyd's Rep 81 and *Kuwait Petroleum Corp v I & D Oil Carriers Ltd, The Houda* [1994] 2 Lloyd's Rep 541, esp at 550, 552–553 and 556). It seems probable that the importance of this obligation stems from the negotiable nature of the bill of lading.'

[98] Mr Croall emphasises that last sentence. Mance LJ said (at 100 (para 8)):

g   'Looking at the matter more broadly, the issue is one of risk. A shipowner issues bills of lading to serve as the key to the goods, and ought usually to be well placed to recognise its own bills of lading ... the bill of lading serves, as it seems to me, an important general role in representing and securing both title and physical possession of goods; although skilled fraud may not be
h   uncommon, the shipowners' construction ... would appear to ... undervalue the importance which both parties must be taken to have attached to the ship's obligation to deliver against presentation of original bills of lading.'

[99] Mr Schaff emphasises the general principle or philosophy apparent in the citations from the judgments of Clarke J and Mance LJ. He also submits that,
j against the background of that principle and philosophy, the last sentence in the citation from the judgment of Stuart-Smith LJ should not be understood too narrowly. The traditional importance of the presentation of a bill of lading may *stem* from its negotiable nature, since the ability to transfer a bearer bill of lading merely by delivery or an 'order' bill of lading merely by indorsement means that the carrier cannot know, save by presentation of the bill, who is ultimately

entitled to delivery. However, once the principle is established, then the requirement of presentation ought to apply in any case where the carrier cannot be certain who is entitled to delivery: and that must apply at least to any bill in which the obligation to present the bill in order to obtain delivery is written into the contract—as Mr Schaff submits is the case here, as shown by the attestation clause. After all, in a case where the shipper requires to be paid cash against documents before he is willing to release the bill of lading, the fact that he has named the consignee cannot make any difference.

[100] In this connection *The Stettin* (1889) 14 PD 142 is of some interest, especially as it is a leading case, cited for instance in both *The Sormovskiy 3068* and *The Motis*. The bill of lading there was issued by the owners of a German flag vessel and covered carriage from London to Stettin. It was made out to a named consignee, S Mendelsohn, 'or to his or their assigns'. Mendelsohn was the agent for Julius Manasse in Breslau, and was instructed by the shipper that on arrival in Stettin he was to arrange for the goods to be sent on by lighter to Manasse in Breslau. No bill of lading was produced by Mendelsohn for delivery, however, and it seems that the shipper was not paid by Manasse. The shipper sued the carrier for misdelivery of the goods. It appears to have been common ground that the bill of lading was governed by German law, of which there was evidence. The defendant shipowner's evidence (at 145) was to the effect that where there was a named consignee 'or order' but the consignee did not indorse the bill (as in that case), the effect was the same as a straight bill of lading ('namens connossement'), viz the shipowner could deliver to the consignee *without* production of a bill of lading unless told by the shipper not to do so, taking the risk, presumably as against an indorsee, of whether there had been an indorsement or not. The shipper's German law evidence (at 144), however, was that whether the bill was to be regarded as an 'order' bill or a straight bill, the law was the same, viz delivery without production of the bill of lading was *not* permitted. Butt J gave a short judgment and said (at 147):

'German advocates have been called on both sides, but, as they differ, I must, in this divergence of opinion, decide what, in the result, the German law appears to me to be. Having considered the reasons given by these advocates for their opinions, I have come to the conclusion that, on this point, German law does not essentially differ from English law. According to English law and the English mode of conducting business, a shipowner is not entitled to deliver goods to the consignee without production of the bill of lading. I hold that the shipowner must take the consequences ...'

[101] It seems to me that against the background of the evidence of German law which Butt J was there considering, he was speaking generally of the situation whether the naming of the consignee rendered the applicable rule that of an order bill or a straight bill. I accept that on the facts both German advocates were agreed that the bill of lading in question was an order bill. If, however, the judge had decided the case simply on that basis, then I assume he would have said so. It will be recalled, however, that in *Thrige v United Shipping Co Ltd* (1924) 18 Ll L Rep 6 Scrutton LJ had said that in the case of a straight bill it was an open question whether delivery could be made without production of the bill of lading, but that he was doubtful whether at any rate in a case where property passed on shipment *The Stettin* was good authority (see [45], above).

a [**102**] This then is the background to a series of modern cases. The first of them comes from Singapore—*Olivine Electronics Pte Ltd v Seabridge Transport Pte Ltd* [1995] 3 SLR 143. The straight bill of lading in question covered the carriage of a shipment of television sets from Singapore to Russia. The bill of lading contained a clause materially identical to the attestation clause in the present case ('must be surrendered duly endorsed in exchange for the goods').

b Goh Joon Seng J (at 149) did not consider the shipper's claim for summary judgment for damages for delivery without production of the bill of lading as unanswerable, since the point was still 'somewhat open'.

[**103**] The researches of counsel have brought to light a Dutch case decided in 1997, *The Duke of Yare* (10 April 1997, unreported). Three trailers were shipped from Scheveningen to Great Yarmouth consigned to a named consignee

c (GE Plastics). The goods were damaged and one issue, although not necessarily decisive of the case, was whether the Hague-Visby Rules were compulsorily applicable by Dutch law. That in turn seems to have depended on whether the document which either had been issued or ought to have been issued was a 'bill of lading or any similar document of title'. The exemplar document was a

d straight bill or 'rektacognossement'. The court said that such a document—

> *e* 'exists alongside the bearer or order bill of lading. The fact that a straight bill of lading cannot be treated in the same way as a bearer or order bill of lading does not detract from the fact that the present straight bill of lading meets the legal requirements to be considered as such. As opposed to a non-negotiable sea waybill—said document not normally considered a "similar document" in English and Dutch literature—the holder of a straight bill of lading has the exclusive right to delivery of the goods, therefore delivery of the bill of lading is a requirement for obtainment of the load.'

f [**104**] It would seem from this that the Dutch court would regard a straight bill of lading as a bill of lading within the meaning of the Hague-Visby Rules and also considers that its surrender is necessary to obtain delivery of the goods.

[**105**] In *International Air and Sea Cargo GmbH v The Chitral* (*Owners*) [2000] 1 All ER (Comm) 932 the Pakistan National Shipping Corp bill of lading named Al Ghaith as consignee of goods carried on the defendant's vessel from Bremen to Dubai.

g Goods were damaged during the voyage. The bill of lading was otherwise in conventional form, but the box in which the consignee was to be named said 'If order state notify party' and no notify party was stated. Al Ghaith had nevertheless indorsed the bill to another party. It was submitted by the defendant carrier that Al Ghaith, having indorsed the bill, had no title to sue. Al Ghaith said

h that its indorsement was ineffective because, since no notify party had been stated, the bill was not to order but a straight bill of lading. The carrier said that the bill remained an order bill because the general printed language of the bill said that delivery was to be 'unto the above-mentioned consignee or to his or their assigns'. David Steel J rejected that argument. He considered (at 938 (para 19)) that the form was drafted to permit its use either as a straight or order bill, and

j that therefore the more general language 'consignee or … assigns' should be understood as subject to the implicit words 'as applicable'. Mr Croall relies on this approach for submitting that the attestation clause with its reference to 'duly endorsed' should be similarly understood as subject to the implicit words 'as appropriate', and that where the form is used as a straight bill this clause is simply inapplicable.

[106] That submission was accepted by the arbitrators and by Langley J, in reliance on *The Chitral*. However, *The Chitral* was distinguished in *Parsons Corp v CV Scheepvaartonderneming Happy Ranger* [2002] 2 All ER (Comm) 24 at [28]–[29] on the basis that in that case there was nothing in any consignee or notify box, other than the mere absence of the words 'or to order', to suggest that the bill was not negotiable. It seems to me that the present case is again different. It is not in dispute that the bill of lading, as filled out, was not an 'order' bill. It follows that it could not be 'duly endorsed'. But even if the bill had been a classic negotiable bill made out to a named consignee 'or order', there is nothing to require it to have been indorsed where it is simply transferred to the consignee (see *Benjamin's Sale of Goods* (6th edn, 2002) p 973 (para 18-012)). Therefore, on any view the words 'duly endorsed' are subject to the understanding 'if applicable'. The position remains that the bill of lading stated that one of its three originals, all of which were in fact issued, 'must be surrendered ... in exchange for the goods'. And why not? In that way the carrier will be assured that he is not delivering to a person without title if the shipper has withheld the bill for the usual reason that he has not been paid; and the shipper will be assured that the goods will not be delivered unless he has been content to transfer the bill. It is not as though a shipper under a straight bill of lading, as well as under an order bill, cannot withhold the goods, or even redirect them, at any rate if notice is given to the carrier: see *Benjamin* (6th edn) pp 973–974 (para 18-013) and pp 979–980 (paras 18-018 to 18-019). This is because, although the shipper's contract with the carrier under a straight bill is to deliver to the named consignee, it is construed as a contract to deliver as provided in the bill or as the shipper may direct. Although notice may be required to redirect delivery of the goods, there may well be a dispute about the giving of such a notice and in the meantime a condition of surrender of the bill of lading is the traditional and safe way of policing such matters; and litigation is avoided.

[107] *The Brij* [2001] 1 Lloyd's Rep 431 was decided in the Hong Kong High Court. The facts of this case were complicated, because two different sets of bills of lading had been issued for shipments from China to Venezuela. As between the claimant shipper and a freight forwarder called WTW, *order* bills were issued to the claimant naming the receiver/buyer's agent, Amaya, as the 'notify' party, but leaving the consignee simply 'to order' (the 'Talent bills'). As between WTW and the ship's operator, however, a further set of bills was issued, but only to WTW and not to the claimant, under which the goods were consigned to Amaya (the 'CAVN bills'). WTW retained the CAVN bills (they were 'not meant to be negotiable or to be negotiated' but were 'kept in a drawer and not meant to be used'), because they regarded the operative carriage contract as evidenced by the Talent bills, and it was the Talent bills which were forwarded by the claimant under its sale contract to obtain payment from its buyer (see [2001] 1 Lloyd's Rep 431 at 434). In Venezuela, the goods were delivered to Amaya without production of any bill of lading. The claimant sued on the CAVN bills, not on the Talent bills. Waung J held that the claim in contract under the CAVN bills failed on the ground that the claimant was not a party to them. The claimant also sued in tort and the judge seems to have regarded that issue as dependent on the question whether the CAVN bills were 'Straight bills or not'. He found that these bills were straight bills, even though the consignee box said 'or order', apparently on the basis that the surrounding circumstances showed that they were never

a intended to be used. With respect, that seems to me to be a different question from the proper construction of the bills.

[108] Mr Croall, however, relied on *The Brij* for acceptance there found (also at 434) of the proposition, for which the judge cited *Benjamin's Sale of Goods* (5th edn, 1997) p 989–990 (para 18-014), that under a straight bill the carrier is bound to deliver to the named consignee without production of the bill. It may
b be noted, however, that this statement of *Benjamin* is at odds with the Law Commission's view (cited at [88], above) that a straight bill differs from a sea waybill in that the former does require its production in order to obtain delivery of the goods. I shall have to refer below to the debate on the subject of straight bills to be found in various textbooks. For the present I would merely comment first, that *The Brij* does not provide any reasoning, other than its reliance on
c *Benjamin*, to support the proposition in issue; and secondly, that because of its special facts I do not think that *The Brij* is really of any assistance to the current debate.

[109] In *Parsons Corp v CV Scheepvaartonderneming Happy Ranger* [2002] 1 All ER (Comm) 176 at first instance Tomlinson J, to whom neither *The Chitral* nor
d *The Brij* seem to have been cited for they are not mentioned in his judgment, appears (at [23] and [27]) to have founded his decision that a straight bill of lading is not a bill of lading within the meaning of the Hague-Visby Rules on the passage from the judgment of Bingham LJ in *Cia Portorafti Commerciale SA v Ultramar Panama Inc, The Captain Gregos* [1990] 3 All ER 967 which I have cited at [86], above. However, for the reasons which I have sought to explain at [87], above
e I do not think that Bingham LJ there had the problem of a straight bill of lading in mind.

[110] *Voss v APL Co Pte Ltd* [2002] 2 Lloyd's Rep 707 is a decision of the Singapore Court of Appeal. Mr Voss shipped a Mercedes from Hamburg to Busan, South Korea, using APL as his carrier. APL issued a bill of lading which
f named the buyer in the consignee box without the words 'to order'. The bill of lading also provided:

> 'A set of 3 originals of this bill of lading is hereby issued by the Carrier. Upon surrender to the Carrier of any one negotiable bill of lading, properly endorsed, all others shall stand void.'

g
[111] Despite that language, it was not disputed (at 709 (para 10)) that the bill of lading was a straight, non-negotiable, bill. Nor (at 721 (para 49)) does any specific reliance appear to have been placed on the second sentence just cited, as distinct from the issue of the bill in a set of three originals. The full set of bills at all times remained with Mr Voss, for the buyer did not pay. The Mercedes was
h released to the buyer without production of the bill of lading. The submissions before the court covered much of the same ground as this present appeal. In a careful judgment, Chao Hick Tin JA, reviewed much of the material considered here either above or (in the case of textbooks) below, including the *Rafaela S* itself at first instance ([2002] 2 Lloyd's Rep 403) and other citations not here mentioned.
j The question posed (at 715 (para 1)) was 'whether, in relation to a straight bill of lading ... the shipowner may deliver [to the named consignee] without production of the BL'. The submission of the carrier (at 717 (para 15)), citing *Scrutton* p 39 was that a straight bill of lading was in this respect like a sea waybill, where delivery is made to the named consignee on proof of his identity. The submission of the claimant, however, was that production of a straight bill of

lading is necessary. That submission appears to have been made and considered
as a matter of principle, and not in reliance on the bill's language quoted above
('Upon surrender to the carrier' etc). Chao Hick Tin JA commented, accurately
as I would understand the position (at 717 (para 16)):

> 'The advantage of resorting to a sea waybill is that it avoids the problems
> arising from the late arrival of the documentation; its contents can be telexed
> to the destination. Sea waybills are often used in trades involving short sea
> voyages, where the carrying ship may arrive at its destination before the
> shipping documents do.'

[112] It is as well to bear in mind that the Singapore Court of Appeal was not
concerned with the question whether a straight bill is a bill of lading for the
purpose of the Hague or Hague-Visby Rules, but only with the more limited
question whether production of a straight bill is necessary for delivery of the
goods. On that question the court's judgment concluded as follows (at 721–722):

> '48. At the end of the day, it seems to us that the issue must be resolved on
> the basis of contract law and the intention of the parties. The entire
> argument of the appellants is that a straight BL is the same as a sea waybill.
> While it is true that a BL, devoid of the characteristic of negotiability, is
> substantially similar in effect to that of a sea waybill, that is [not] to say that
> they are the same. If the parties had intended to create a sea waybill they
> would have done so. Ordinarily, the main characteristics of a BL are twofold.
> First, it is negotiable (i.e. transferable). Second, it is a document of title,
> requiring its presentation to obtain delivery of the cargo. In the case of a
> straight bill, while the characteristic of transferability is absent, there is no
> reason why one should thereby infer that the parties had intended to do
> away with the other main characteristic, i.e. delivery upon presentation. As
> the Judge below noted, while one cannot indorse a straight bill to transfer
> constructive possession of the cargo, it does not necessarily follow that the
> straight bill does not impose a contractual term obligating the carrier to
> require its production to obtain delivery.
>
> 49. It seems to us that clear words must be present to imply that the
> parties intended the instrument to be treated, in all respects, as if it were a sea
> waybill and that its presentation by the named consignee is not necessary.
> Indeed, if the parties had wanted to have a sea waybill they could have quite
> easily adopted that format. They would not have issued a BL with three
> originals. By issuing the instrument as a BL, it must mean that they wished
> to retain all the other features of a BL, other than the characteristic of
> transferability ...
>
> 51. Secondly, even looking at the matter from the perspective of the
> market place, there is much to commend the rule that even in respect of a
> straight bill presentation of it is a prerequisite to obtaining delivery. If
> nothing else, the advantage of this rule is that it is simple to apply. It is
> certain. It would prevent confusion and avoid the shipowners and/or their
> agents having to decide whether a bill is a straight bill or an order bill
> [e.g., *The Happy Ranger* ([2002] 2 All ER (Comm) 24)], and run the risk
> attendant thereto if the determination they make on that point should turn
> out to be erroneous. The rule would obviate such wholly unnecessary
> litigation ...

a

52. Thirdly, to accept the arguments put forward by APL is to envisage two broad categories of documents which could be used by shippers. The first option is the negotiable BL; in such a situation, delivery of the goods can only be made upon presentation of the BL. The second option for shippers is to use a non-negotiable straight BL or sea waybill; here, the straight BL or waybill need not be produced for delivery of the goods. In essence, APL's

b

scheme envisages that as long as the shipping document is non-negotiable on its face, presentation of the original BL or sea waybill is unnecessary for delivery. We think that this approach is overly restrictive for an unpaid seller who wishes to use a non-negotiable BL while retaining his security for payment.

c

53. Indeed, to hold that a straight BL is not the same as a sea waybill has the advantage of providing such a seller, or in the case of documentary credit, the bank, with some security against default by the buyer, and the buyer of some assurance that the seller has shipped the cargo before he is required to make payment. In short, it gives both the buyer and the seller where they, for their own reasons, want only a straight BL to be issued, a fair measure of protection. That was what Mr. Voss wanted: payment before

d

delivery by carrier. In contrast, the sea waybill is only a contract of carriage whereby the carrier undertakes to deliver the cargo to the person identified by the shipper as entitled to take delivery of the cargo. The sea waybill is retained by the shipper and all the consignee need show to take delivery is proof of his identity. It is a receipt, not a document of title. It, unlike a BL,

e

cannot be used as a security to obtain financing.'

[113] Thus the Singapore Court of Appeal here put forward three reasons for its decision. The first, is that one of the two critical features of a classic bill of lading is that it is a document of title in the sense that its presentation is necessary to obtain possession of the goods: in the absence of clear words or good reason,

f

that feature should be regarded as surviving in the case of a straight bill of lading. The second, is that such a rule is a good, simple and certain rule: reference was here made to Clarke J in *SA Sucre Export v Northern River Shipping Ltd, The Sormovskiy 3068* [1994] 2 Lloyd's Rep 266 at 274. The third, is that such a rule better protects the interests of a seller (and his bank) and buyer.

g

[114] Mr Schaff relies on this decision for its demonstration that a straight bill of lading is still, in any event, a document of title. Mr Croall submits that the reasoning is flawed in its reliance on the assumption that a straight bill of lading can survive as a document of title in the absence of negotiability, and that in any event a non-negotiable bill is not a 'similar' document of title for the very reason that it is not negotiable.

h

[115] The final authority relied on before us is a French one, *The MSC Magallanes* (16 May 2002, unreported), a decision of the Court of Appeal of Rennes. The carriage in this case was from Anvers to Durban. Straight bills of lading were issued by the carrier, MSC, and sent by the shipper to the consignee, who was an agent for the buyer. The shipper then decided to divert delivery and

j

notified the carrier to this effect. Nevertheless, the goods were delivered to the consignee, and by the consignee to the buyer. The shipper claimed against the carrier for misdelivery, but failed. The shipper appears to have argued that the bills, not being negotiable, were not documents of title but similar to sea waybills, and that therefore it was open to it to divert the goods even after the bills' transfer, on the basis that the carrier's contract was with it and the carrier was

therefore obliged to follow its instructions. The court, however, considered that
the bills, albeit 'nominative and non-negotiable', were bills of lading and *a*
documents of title for all that, and obliged delivery against and only against their
production. The ratio of the decision appears therefore to be in the following
paragraphs:

> 'In effect, [the shipper] having given the original bills of lading and *b*
> documents of title of the merchandise to [the consignee], MSC could only
> follow the instructions given by the legitimate bearer of the bills of lading,
> these documents giving rights. Having lost possession of the bills of
> lading, [the shipper] no longer had the power to change the instructions
> given to the carrier regarding the destination of the merchandise being
> transported ...' *c*

[116] Thus the French Court of Appeal, like the Singapore Court of Appeal,
and the Dutch court, appears to have considered that a straight bill of lading
remains a document of title, and that its production is necessary for delivery of
the goods.

d

THE TEXTBOOKS

[117] The textbooks which cover this subject provide a rich field for inquiry,
and I will try to put the dispute between Mr Schaff and Mr Croall as to the
deployment of the opinions of their learned and scholarly authors as
straightforwardly as I can.

e

[118] It is common ground that the textbooks cite negotiability of the order or
bearer bill of lading as being the essence of what, for clarity of exposition, may be
called a classic bill of lading. Such a bill is also a document of title, because it is
the key to the goods in what has been described as a floating warehouse, and
under a classic bill of lading that key can be passed on, at any rate until the
contract of carriage is fulfilled, again and again. The essential issue for present *f*
purposes is whether a straight bill of lading is sufficiently like a classic 'negotiable'
bill of lading to be regarded as a bill of lading under the Hague-Visby Rules.
Another way, perhaps, of putting the issue is whether the essence of a bill of
lading as a document of title is that the key has to be capable of being passed again
and again, or whether it is sufficient that it can be passed at least once. In that
connection it seems to be common ground that a document which does not have *g*
to be produced to the carrier to obtain delivery of the goods cannot be called a
document of title. Mr Croall submits, however, that only a document of title
which is fully transferable and therefore 'negotiable' can be called a 'similar'
document of title. That, however, it seems to me, is to beg the question. If
'negotiability' is existentially critical to a bill of lading, then it is unnecessary to *h*
ask separately whether a straight bill of lading is a document of title, because even
if it is, it will not be 'similar'.

[119] It seems to me that it is unhelpful to cite passages in the textbooks which
describe the features of a classic bill of lading. By definition, such passages will
refer to its negotiability. The important passages will be those which describe the *j*
features of a straight bill of lading.

[120] *Scrutton* does not consider the position of a straight bill of lading, save to
point out (p 37) that (i) under the 1992 Act, by definition, a straight bill of lading
can only be a sea waybill, and (ii) that because a sea waybill within the meaning
of the 1992 Act has not at present been established as a document of title by

a mercantile custom, therefore it must be doubtful whether it is within the Hague-Visby Rules.

[121] *Benjamin's Sale of Goods* has a more extensive treatment of the subject. Significantly, the treatment has changed between the fifth edition of 1997 and the sixth edition of 2002. In the fifth edition (pp 989–990 (para 18-014)) this is said, under a heading which mentions both straight bills and sea waybills:

b
> 'It is not easy to find a suitable term in English law to refer to such bills ...
> The essential point is that documents of the present kind differ from order and bearer bills in that they are not transferable by indorsement (where necessary) and delivery. Sea waybills fall into the category of documents of the present kind and the expression "sea waybills" will be used to refer to
c them in the following discussion, while the expression "bills of lading" will be used to refer to order or bearer bills. Two things follow from the fact that a document of this kind is not transferable by indorsement and delivery. First, the consignee (if in possession of the document) cannot, by purporting to transfer it in this way, impose on the carrier a legal obligation to deliver the goods to another person. Secondly, the shipper cannot oblige the carrier
d to deliver the goods to a different consignee from the one named merely by indorsing and delivering the bill to that other person; for under a straight bill the carrier is entitled and bound to deliver the goods to the originally named consignee without production of the bill, so that, when he delivers the goods, he may have no means of knowing of the purported transfer of the
e bill. This difficulty cannot arise in the case of an order bill, under which the goods are deliverable only on production of the bill.'

It is similarly stated (p 1023 (para 18-044)) that a straight bill or sea waybill—

f
> 'is not a symbol of the goods because the carrier is entitled and bound to deliver the goods to the named consignee without production of the bill. It follows that a carriage document will not be a document of title in the common law sense if it is expressed on its face to be "non-negotiable".'

[122] I have four comments on these passages. First, understandably in the light of the 1992 Act straight bills are included with sea waybills: but this
g categorisation obscures what may be an important difference between them for the purpose of the Hague-Visby Rules. Secondly, the statement that a shipper under a non-negotiable bill cannot oblige the carrier to deliver to someone other than the named consignee merely by indorsing and delivering the bill to another person is true: but that tells you only that the bill is not negotiable and not that the carrier is bound to deliver to the named consignee without production of the
h bill. Thirdly, that no authority is mentioned for that last proposition. And fourthly, that it would seem to be accepted that if, contrary to that last proposition, the consignee of a straight bill did have to produce the bill to obtain possession of the goods, then such a bill could be described as a document of title.

[123] In the sixth edition, however, these passages have been developed and
j altered. The equivalent paragraphs to 18-014 and 18-044 of the fifth edition are now numbered 18-017 and 18-059. They have become too lengthy to quote in full here, but it may be noted that they discuss some of the recent jurisprudence on straight bills including both this case and *Voss v APL Co Pte Ltd*, each at first instance (see eg footnotes 4 and 98). Points to note, however, are: (i) that the proposition that a straight bill need not be produced by the consignee in order to

take delivery of the goods is founded in the contrast with an order bill on the basis
that where a bill may be transferred by order a carrier can never know to whom   *a*
to deliver unless the bill is produced; but (ii) that production of a straight bill may
nevertheless be required by contractual provision under it; and (iii) that it is now
allowed that the definitional contrasts of the 1992 Act (and the 1971 Act) do not
necessarily mean that 'sea waybills, or similar non-transferable documents,
cannot be bills of lading for any legal purposes whatsoever'. So it is expressly   *b*
contemplated that a straight bill may yet be a document of title for the 'wholly
distinct' purpose of the Hague-Visby Rules (pp 1015–1016 (para 18-059)):

> 'Indeed, to apply the same tests for these two purposes comes dangerously
> close to the similar link between contractual and proprietary issues made in
> the Bills of Lading Act 1855, a link which was found to be unsatisfactory and   *c*
> which was therefore severed by the Carriage of Goods by Sea Act 1992.
> There may be no policy reasons against subjecting parties to a contract
> contained in or evidenced by a "straight" bill to the contractual regime of the
> Rules; indeed, the 1971 Act specifically provides that, by the use of
> appropriate words, the Rules can be made applicable to a "non-negotiable"   *d*
> receipt containing or evidencing a contract for the carriage of goods by sea.
> But the policy reasons for (or against) applying the Rules to "straight" bills or
> "non-negotiable" receipts have nothing to do with the question whether
> such documents are documents of title in the common law sense.'

[124] *Carver on Bills of Lading* (1st edn, 2001) deals with straight bills (pp 4–6   *e*
(paras 1-007 to 1-009) and p 244 (para 6-007)). The distinguished editors of *Carver*,
Professor Sir Guenter Treitel QC and Professor Francis Reynolds QC, are
common to the authorship of *Benjamin*, and the treatment in *Carver* and in the
latest edition of *Benjamin* is broadly similar. Thus it may be noted that it is stated
(p 244 (para 6-007)) that no production of a bill of lading is necessary for delivery
under a straight bill, but that it is acknowledged (p 5 (para 1-008)) that the   *f*
definitions and distinctions of the 1971 and 1992 Acts 'apply only for the purposes
of the Acts in which they occur and not for the purposes of other legislation or of
rules of common law ...'. There is a full and interesting discussion of the English
statutory and common law meanings of 'document at title' (pp 239–242
(paras 6-001 to 6-003)). It is submitted there that the common law meaning is   *g*
derived from proof of mercantile custom and thus limited narrowly to negotiable
bills of lading, whereas the statutory use of the expression is broader and extends
for instance to all those documents listed in s 1(4) of the Factors Act 1889, which
include 'any bill of lading ... and any other document used in the ordinary course
of business as proof of the possession or control of goods ...'. This is an area of   *h*
debate which counsel have acknowledged by citation of these passages, but into
which they have not led us. I would be reluctant to go there without adversarial
argument, but I would again hazard the view that the question of 'document of
title' within the meaning of the Hague Rules is bound up with the question
whether 'bill of lading' is there limited to a negotiable bill. If it is, then there is
perhaps good reason to think that 'any similar document of title' is also being   *j*
used in a limited sense. If, however, it is not, then there may be less reason to
think that the latter expression is also so limited. In this connection it is well to
remind oneself that the Hague Rules are an international convention and that
English common or statutory law is not determinative. On the contrary, it is
salutary to bear in mind that the courts of France, Holland and Singapore have

a determined that a straight bill of lading does require to be produced for delivery
   of the goods and on that basis have been prepared to describe such documents as
   documents of title.

   [125] *Voyage Charters* (2nd edn, 2001) by Cooke, Young, Taylor, Kimball,
   Martowski and Lambert describes the issue of surrender of a straight bill of lading
   as 'an open question' (p 480 (para 18.143)):

b   'The one way in which a straight bill of lading differs from an ordinary sea
       waybill is that, being on a bill of lading form, it usually contains words, such
       as "one of which being accomplished the others to be void" which indicate
       that it is to be surrendered on delivery. It is an open question whether the
       carrier under a straight bill is entitled or obliged to deliver to the named
c   consignee without production of the bill or whether, as in the case of a
       transferable bill, he should only deliver upon its presentation.'

   The same work states (p 484 (paras 18.158–18.159)):

       'Bills of lading often provide expressly that the goods are to be discharged
       or delivered upon, and only upon, the surrender of the bill of lading and the
d   standard formula "one of which being accomplished the others to be void' is
       to the same effect. Furthermore, the status of the bill of lading as a document
       of title imposes the same requirements … The present trend of authority
       greatly favours a clear, simple and strict rule obliging a carrier to require the
       surrender of a bill of lading before effecting delivery …'

e **[126]** Gaskell *Bills of Lading: Law and Contracts* (2001) helpfully sets out
   numerous sea waybill forms (pp 726–740 (paras 22.34–22.56)). The BIMCO Blank
   Back Form begins (para 22.35): 'This Liner Waybill which is not a document of
   title …'. It continues (para 22.47): 'The goods will be delivered to the Party
   named as Consignee or its authorised agent, on production of proof of identity
f without any documentary formalities …'. The Genwaybill states (para 22.36):
   'This Waybill is a non-negotiable document. It is not a bill of lading …'. It
   contains the same passage about delivery as just cited above (para 22.48). The
   text points out (pp 419, 420 (paras 14.23, 14.24)) that—

       'In practice, most sea waybills contain express terms allowing delivery
g   merely on proof of identity, without any production of documents such as
       the waybill itself … It is unclear whether a carrier is obliged to deliver to the
       consignee named in a document which is expressly described as a "straight
       bill", even *without* production of that bill. *Rights of Suit* [ie the Law Commission
       report] seems to assume that a straight bill does have to be presented, while
       it is accepted that a waybill does not. It is submitted that the view of *Benjamin*
h   is to be preferred, on the basis that there is no real distinction between a
       waybill and a straight bill, and that neither are needed to obtain delivery of
       the goods (*unless* the contract so requires).'

   [127] One possible answer to the current case, of course, is that the Rafaela S
j form of bill of lading, when used as a straight bill, *did so require*. In that context
   Gaskell comments as follows (p 420 (para 14.25)):

       'In practice, most of the standard form bills [ie bills of lading, *not* waybills]
       (which are mainly designed to be negotiable) do contain express terms which
       singly or together provide that a bill is to be surrendered before goods will
       be delivered. There is no apparent distinction, as a matter of construction,

between cases where the bill is made out to order and when it is consigned
"straight" to a named consignee. Thus, the express terms on the surrender   *a*
of bills such as Conlinebill or the P & O Nedlloyd Bill states that "an original
bill of lading, duly endorsed, *must* be surrendered ...". This clause is to be
found on the face of most bills. It might be said that the reference to "duly
endorsed" indicates that the term only applies to negotiable and not straight
bills. The better view is probably that the carrier is only requiring that any   *b*
bill presented should apparently entitle the holder to claim delivery (as with
a bearer bill), so there is no reason to restrict the application of the clause to
negotiable bills when it is well known that the forms could easily be used as
non-negotiable documents, e.g. straight consigned bills.'

There Gaskell is in effect discussing this very case, and rejecting Mr Croall's   *c*
submission that the attestation clause should be regarded as inapplicable.

[128] In any event, I cannot forbear remarking, by reference to the forms of
sea waybill set out in *Gaskell*, that in practice those forms are quite distinct from
the (hybrid, order or straight) bill of lading form used in the present case (or in
International Air and Sea Cargo GmbH v The Chitral (Owners) [2000] 1 All ER   *d*
(Comm) 932 and *Parsons Corp v CV Scheepvaartonderneming Happy Ranger* [2002]
2 All ER (Comm) 24). Whatever the intricacies of the law as discussed in this
judgment, I do not regard it as a happy matter that the omission of adding the
words 'or order' in the consignee box in this case (or the omission to add a notify
party in the form used in *The Chitral*), either of which could well have happened
without any deliberation at all, should have the effect of transforming a   *e*
contractual document which in every respect looks and reads like a bill of lading
into a sea waybill, when a sea waybill commonly takes a totally different form.

[129] *Schmitthoff's Export Trade: The Law and Practice of International Trade*
(10th edn, 2000) states a view (p 292 (para 15-038)) with which Mr Croall submits
Benjamin, Carver and *Gaskell* are at variance, to the effect that—   *f*

'Logically, the function of the bill of lading as a document of title is distinct
from its negotiable quality. Even a bill of lading which is not made
negotiable operates as a document of title, because the consignee named
therein can only claim delivery of the goods from the shipowner if able to
produce the bill of lading. However, the great practical value of the bill of   *g*
lading as a means of making goods in transit rapidly transferable is due to the
customary combination of the two features of the bill, namely its
quasi-negotiability and its function as a document of title.'

[130] I am uncertain to what extent this passage is at variance with the other   *h*
authors. All the textbooks would seem to accept that *if* the goods under a straight
bill can only be properly delivered against production of the bill, then it *is* a
document of title. There is disagreement, however, as to whether that hypothesis
is correct. Again, I am not sure to what extent that disagreement depends on the
assumption that a straight bill has nothing to say expressly about use of the
document to obtain delivery. Everyone seems to be agreed that if a straight bill   *j*
expressly provides, as it commonly does, that its surrender is required for delivery
to take place, then it is a document of title.

[131] Finally, Tetley *Marine Cargo Claims* (3rd edn, 1988) casts a comparative
eye over the jurisprudence of many countries. Professor Tetley QC states
(p 183) that—

a
'*The named or nominate bill of lading* provides for delivery of the goods to a
named person, without also specifying "to order or assigns". The nominate
bill of lading is a document of title but is not negotiable. The named
consignee may obtain delivery of the goods from the carrier upon surrender
of the original nominate bill of lading to the carrier.'

b
He also says (p 184):

'In the case of a nominate bill, the bill and the title to the goods thereunder
can only be transferred once, i.e. from the shipper to the consignee.
Thereafter the title to the goods covered by the nominate bill cannot be
transferred by the mere delivery of the bill itself …'

c
[132] He points out (p 995) that the United States straight bill under the
Pomerene Act is a hybrid, having certain of the qualities of a document of title,
and yet it need not be presented to take delivery.

[133] Mr Croall submitted that the textbooks were almost uniformly in favour
of the carrier's case. However, in my judgment the position is more complex and
mixed, and it can also be said that, on the basis that the bill of lading expressly
d
requires its surrender to obtain delivery, there is something like uniformity in the
opposite direction.

CONCLUSIONS

[134] The first question is whether a straight bill of lading, but otherwise in the
e
form of any classic bill of lading, is a bill of lading within the meaning of the
Hague Rules. If it is, then, it has not been suggested that it should have a different
meaning under the 1971 Act, for all that the treatment of the distinction between
a bill of lading and a non-negotiable receipt in its s 1(6) may be seen, in retrospect,
as a harbinger of the distinction between a bill of lading and a sea waybill to be
found in s 1 of the 1992 Act. It is common ground that the point is open. It is
f
open today. It was open and uncertain immediately before the agreement of the
Hague Rules.

[135] In my judgment, a straight bill of lading, for all that it is non-negotiable,
should be viewed as a bill of lading within the meaning of the Hague Rules. I say
that for the following reasons.

g
[136] First, the Hague Rules are predominately concerned with the content of
a contract of carriage in circumstances where such a contract as found in a bill of
lading may come to affect a third party into whose hands such a bill is transferred.
It seems to me to be plain as a matter of common sense but also on a review of
the material cited in this judgment, that in this connection a named consignee
under a straight bill of lading, unless he is the same person as the shipper, is as
h
much a third party as a named consignee under a classic bill. Therefore I would
view such a named consignee under a straight bill as prima facie within the
concern of the Hague Rules.

[137] Secondly, while it is I suppose true that a straight bill of lading can be
used in circumstances where there is no intention of transferring it to the
j
consignee, the authorities considered demonstrate that in practice it is used, just
like a classic bill, as a document against which payment is required and the
transfer of which thus marks the intended transfer of property. Therefore, as
Professor Tetley says, its nature is that, although it cannot be transferred more
than once, for it is not negotiable, it can be transferred by delivery (just like a
classic bill) to the named consignee. In these circumstances, the shipper and his

bankers and insurers need the same protection as the shipper under a classic bill;
and the consignee himself and his insurers in turn need to have rights against the
carrier under the contract of carriage. I can see no reason why straight bills of
lading have not always been within the 1855 Act. Those needs are in any event
recognised under the 1992 Act.

[138] Thirdly, whatever may be the position as a matter of principle and in the
absence of express agreement, the practice appears to be that a straight bill of
lading, unlike a mere sea waybill, is written on the form of an otherwise classic
bill and requires production of the bill on delivery, and therefore transfer to a
consignee to enable him to obtain delivery. (In this respect the position of a
straight bill under the Pomerene Act appears to be different, but even so the
Harter Act, one of the forerunners of the Hague Rules, would seem to cover
straight as well as negotiable bills.)

[139] Fourthly, suppose the question is asked, in the context of the Hague
Rules, in these terms: what of the straight bill? Is this a 'bill of lading' or, being
non-negotiable, something else, more akin to a non-negotiable receipt? Then, as
it seems to me, the straight bill of lading is in principle, function, and form much
closer to a classic negotiable bill, than to a non-negotiable receipt, which, to judge
from art VI of the Hague Rules, was viewed as something far more exotic.

[140] Fifthly, the travaux préparatoires of the Hague Rules, despite lacking
unequivocal cogency, to my mind are not only consistent with the view I would
prefer, but go far to support it.

[141] Sixthly, I am unimpressed by the argument derived from the terms of
the 1971 and 1992 Acts. They may reflect a developing English view about how
to categorise bills of lading and non-negotiable receipts and sea waybills, but, as
the learned authors of *Benjamin* and *Carver* point out, they are ultimately dealing
with different purposes. In any event, I do not see how they can control the
meaning of the Hague Rules, which are not only much earlier, but also of
international and not merely domestic scope.

[142] The next question is as to the effect of the attestation clause in the bill of
lading in the present case. Is it applicable only to the use of the bill in its
negotiable form, or does it survive to control its use as a straight bill? In my
judgment, for the reasons stated in [106], above and in *Gaskell* (see [127], above),
the attestation clause is to be construed as applicable in either event. If it had been
intended that it should not apply when the bill was used in non-negotiable form,
then it could very easily have said so. Against the background of the common
forms of sea waybills, it is truly remarkable that it does not say so.

[143] The third question is, then, whether such a straight bill of lading, which
has to be produced to obtain delivery, is a document of title? In my judgment it
is. I consider that the authorities and textbooks discussed above support that
view. Whatever the history of the phrase in English common or statutory law
may be, I see no reason why a document which has to be produced to obtain
possession of the goods should not be regarded, in an international convention,
as a document of title. It is so regarded by the courts of France, Holland and
Singapore.

[144] Is it a 'similar' document of title? If I am right to consider that
negotiability is not a necessary requirement of a 'bill of lading' within the
meaning of the Hague Rules, then plainly it is. But I also think that the good sense
of regarding a straight bill whose production is required for delivery of the goods

a as a document of title in turn supports the answer to the prior question of whether a straight bill is a 'bill of lading'.

[145] The final question is whether a straight bill of lading is in principle a document of title, even in the absence of an express provision requiring its production to obtain delivery? It would seem that *Voss v APL Co Pte Ltd* [2002] 2 Lloyd's Rep 707 concluded that it was (at any rate if it is issued in traditional *b* form in three originals). That was also the view of the Law Commission. It is unnecessary to decide the point, but in my judgment it is. It seems to me to be undesirable to have a different rule for different kinds of bills of lading—which I think was the view of Butt J in *The Stettin* (1889) 14 PD 142 as well. It is true, as *Benjamin* states, that in the case of a negotiable bill the carrier needs to have the bill produced in order to be able to police the question of who is entitled to *c* delivery. Yet an analogous problem arises with a straight bill. A shipper needs the carrier to assist him in policing his security in the retention of the bill. He is entitled to redirect the consignment on notice to the carrier, and, although notice is required, a rule of production of the bill is the only safe way, for the carrier as well as the shipper, to police such new instructions. In any event, if proof of *d* identity is necessary, as in practice it is, what is wrong with the bill itself as a leading form of proof? That is of course an inconvenient rule where the carriage is very short, as in cross-Channel shipments, and that is why sea waybills are used in such trades. But it is clear that straight bills are used in intercontinental carriage and therefore the inconvenience argument fades.

[146] I am not unhappy to come to these conclusions. It seems to me that the *e* use of these hybrid forms of bill of lading is an unfortunate development and has spawned litigation in recent years in an area which for the previous century or so has not caused any real difficulty. Carriers should not use bill of lading forms if what they want to invite shippers to do is to enter into sea waybill type contracts. It may be true that ultimately it is up to shippers to ensure that the boxes in these *f* hybrid forms are filled up in the way that best suits themselves; but in practice I suspect that serendipity often prevails. In any event, these forms invite error and litigation, which is best avoided by a simple rule.

RESULT

[147] For these reasons, I conclude that this was a bill of lading or similar *g* document of title to which the Hague-Visby Rules applied. In the circumstances I would allow this appeal.

JACOB J.

[148] This appeal depends first upon the meaning and effect of the document *h* entitled 'Bill of Lading'. It ends with these words:

> 'In WITNESS whereof the number of Original Bills of Lading stated above … all of this tenor and date, has been signed, one of which being accomplished, the others to stand void. One of the Bills of Lading must be surrendered duly endorsed in exchange for the goods or delivery order.'

j

[149] Unless the last sentence is taken as struck out or meaningless, the consignee will not be given the goods by the carrier unless he produces an original bill of lading. No one disputes that would be so if the two little words 'Order of' had been added after the name and address of the consignee in the relevant box. I can see no reason why their omission from that box should have

such a striking-out effect on the sentence in question. Langley J said ([2002] EWHC 593 (Comm) at [27], [2002] 2 Lloyd's Rep 403 at [27]):

> 'But I would add that in any event I do not think the printed words in the bill of lading requiring surrender of the bill against delivery of the goods can bear even the weight which Mr. Schaff seeks to put on them. MSC were obliged to deliver the cargo to and only to the consignees. That obligation and the concomitant entitlement of the consignees is not affected by whether or not the consignee has or surrenders the bill of lading. It is a consequence of the agreement between MSC and the shipper to be found in the fact that the bill of lading names the consignee without the words "Order of". Nor does MSC need the protection of delivering only in exchange for the bill of lading as it would with a transferable bill ... I also agree with the arbitrators that delivery against the bill of lading was not necessary.'

[150] I do not follow this. It is true that without these words the carrier could fulfil his obligation by delivery to the named consignee. But these words add more to the arrangement—that the consignee is not to be given the goods unless he produces an original bill. In practice he will not be able to do that unless he has paid for the goods and been given an original in exchange. The consignor had a real interest in ensuring that the right to possession (which is really what is meant by 'title' here) did not pass until he puts an original bill into the hands of the consignee. That is of course also true in the case of an order bill which in fact has not been indorsed over to a third party: the original consignee cannot obtain delivery without the original bill. Putting it another way, it is not only the carrier who gets protection from the bill. So also does the shipper. I can see no reason why the carrier under this bill would be permitted to make delivery to the named consignee without surrender of an original bill. So the bill is not a mere receipt.

[151] It follows, I think, that the bill is a document of title in the sense that its transfer to the consignee entitles the latter to delivery and is essential to that entitlement. Moreover a consignee who had been given the bill could demonstrate his title to third parties by its production. What he could not do is to transfer title simply by indorsing the bill. He could in principle transfer entitlement *as between him and a third party* by a separate arrangement between him and the third party, for instance by executing a fresh document (whether bill or deed or whatever). That would not affect the position of the carrier—he remains bound to deliver to the named consignee and none other.

[152] That being the effect of the bill, I turn to consider whether it is a *bill of lading or any similar document of title* within the meaning of s 1(4) of the Carriage of Goods by Sea Act 1971. That phrase itself derives from art I(b) of the Hague-Visby Rules, scheduled to the Act. Self-evidently it has the same meaning as in those rules. The goods were damaged en route. The consignee/buyers sue the carriers for negligence. If the bill is within the meaning then the Hague-Visby Rules apply with the consequence that liability cannot be capped by anything in the contract of carriage (see art III, para 8). (I note in passing that is somewhat bizarre that the buyers' very title to sue stems from the bill yet it is said that the bill is not a document of title for the purposes of the 1971 Act and the Hague-Visby Rules.)

[153] What then is the purpose of those rules? It is to provide protection from onerous terms in the contract of carriage. The carriers submit that such protection is only to be provided if there is a document of title in the sense of a

a document which can be used to convey title generally—a conventional order bill of lading being the paradigm example. But I do not see why. Ask the question 'who is to be given protection?' An order bill protects not only the indorsee(s) of the bill but also the original consignee. I can see no rational reason for giving such a consignee protection but not a consignee who is not able to transfer title by indorsement.

b [154] There is another way of looking at it. Suppose the consignee had a say in the terms of the bill of lading. If he wanted the goods purely for himself (for instance special purpose machinery, as may well be the case here) rather than for dealing in (as might be the case with a commodity cargo) there is no reason why he would want the goods delivered to his order. Yet, on the respondent's argument, unless he asked for those magic words he loses protection. That

c would be far from self-evident to an ordinary businessman and would be a quite illogical consequence.

[155] A number of academic authors have, particularly in the last 20 years or so, written opinions to the contrary, as indeed did the Law Commission. But, with respect, I do not find in them a sufficient explanation of why the consignee's

d protection against onerous terms in the contract of carriage, or the consignor's protection in respect of receiving his money before delivery, should depend on whether it is a straight or order bill.

[156] Accordingly I would allow the appeal on the first point. As to the points raised on the cross-appeal I agree with Rix LJ and have nothing to add.

e
PETER GIBSON LJ.

[157] In *Parsons Corp v CV Scheepvaartonderneming Happy Ranger* [2002] EWCA Civ 694 at [31], [2002] 2 All ER (Comm) 24 at [31] Tuckey LJ said that the question whether a straight bill of lading was a bill of lading or similar document of title within the meaning of s 1(4) of the Carriage of Goods by Sea Act 1971 and the

f Hague/Hague-Visby Rules was not an easy point. He commented that it would be unwise to assume that the statements in the textbooks (which suggested a negative answer to that question) were correct, and that comment was underlined by Rix LJ (at [49]). Tuckey LJ was unwilling to decide the point in a case in which it did not call for decision. The point does call for decision on this

g appeal, in which we have had the benefit of admirable argument from Mr Schaff QC for MacWilliam and Mr Croall for MSC. I would pay tribute to their industrious researches which have resulted in all the relevant material being put before us.

[158] Although we are differing from Langley J and from the arbitrators,

h Rix LJ's judgment, with which I am in respectful agreement, is so comprehensive that, subject only to one matter, there is nothing which I would wish to add. That matter relates to the fact that I was a signatory in 1991 to the joint report of the Law Commission and the Scottish Law Commission on *Rights of Suit in Respect of Carriage of Goods by Sea* (1991) (Law Com no 196, Scot Law Com no 130) (the joint report), on which Langley J relied in reaching his conclusion that the straight bill

j of lading used in this case was not a bill of lading within the meaning of s 1(4). As will be apparent from my agreement with Rix LJ's judgment, I am afraid that I now take a different view of some of the statements in para 2.50 of the joint report. Although Dr Eric Clive of the Scottish Law Commission observed in footnote 1 to para 1 of his Note of Partial Dissent that it was at least arguable that a straight bill of lading was a bill of lading for the purposes of the Hague-Visby

All England Law Reports [2003] 3 All ER

Rules, I have to say that I do not recall much, if any, discussion on this topic within the Commissions or with the distinguished consultants who assisted the Commissions in the preparation of the joint report. The textbook authorities at that time appeared to be consistent and clear.

[159] However, in the light of the material now put before us as analysed by Rix LJ and for the reasons given by him I too would allow this appeal.

Appeal allowed.

James Brooks   Barrister.

1 May 2003. Rix LJ granted permission to appeal.

a R (on the application of U) v Metropolitan Police Commissioner

R (on the application of R) v Durham Constabulary

b [2002] EWHC 2486 (Admin)

QUEEN'S BENCH DIVISION (DIVISIONAL COURT)

LATHAM LJ AND FIELD J

c 12, 13, 29 NOVEMBER 2002

Criminal law – Young offender – Final warning scheme – Young offenders suspected of committing indecent assaults – Police failing to warn offenders that administration of final warning leading to entry on sex offenders register – Whether scheme complying with convention rights – Crime and Disorder Act 1998, ss 65, 66 – Human Rights Act 1988, Sch 1, Pt I, art 6.

The claimants, who were both aged 15, were interviewed by the police on suspicion of committing indecent assaults on young girls. The respective police authorities determined that the circumstances justified giving final warnings as *e* provided for by the Final Warning Scheme established by ss 65[a] and 66[b] of the Crime and Disorder Act 1998, as amended by s 56 of the Criminal Justice and Court Services Act 2000. The Home Office guidance, which was in effect at the relevant time, provided that a reprimand or warning could only be given if the young person made a clear and reliable admission to all elements of the offence, having been made aware of the consequences of such an admission. There was, *f* however, no requirement for the young person to consent to a reprimand or final warning. The guidance also advised, that in giving a warning the officer should make clear that if the offence was one covered by the Sex Offenders Act 1997, the young person would be required to register under that Act. Neither claimant was made aware of that requirement and they accordingly applied for judicial review *g* contending that the Act and the guidance did not comply, inter alia, with art 6[c] of the European Convention for the Protection of Human Rights and Fundamental Freedoms 1950 (as set out in Sch 1 to the Human Rights Act 1998). The Secretary of State, the interested party, accepted that art 6 was engaged, but submitted: (i) that it was engaged only until such time as the police were satisfied under *h* s 65(1)(e) that it would not be in the public interest for the offender to be prosecuted since that brought to an end the criminal charge in the same way as discontinuance of proceedings; and (ii) that there was no breach of art 6(2) because there was no conviction.

j **Held** – The administration of a reprimand or warning under s 65 of the Crime and Disorder Act 1998 was the determination of a criminal charge within the meaning of art 6 of the convention. The phrase 'criminal charge' had an

---

a   Section 65, so far as material, is set out at [7], below
b   Section 66, so far as material, is set out at [7], below
c   Article 6, so far as material, is set out at [32], below

autonomous meaning under the convention, was determined by reference to
substance rather than form and included official notification given to an
individual by the competent authority of an allegation that he had committed a
criminal offence. Prima facie, therefore, the claimants were entitled to a fair trial
of the allegations made against them attended by all the guarantees which were
required by the convention. That did not mean, however, that the procedures
for cautions, reprimands and final warnings were necessarily in breach of art 6.
Indeed the scheme was not itself unlawful as there was nothing in the Act which
required the police to proceed without the consent of the offender. The vice lay
with the guidance, and the practice adopted pursuant to that guidance. Provided,
therefore, there was an effective waiver procedure requiring such consent by the
offender, and his or her parent, carer or other appropriate adult, there would be
conformity with the convention. Moreover, it might be that if an offender had
made a free and reliable admission in the full knowledge of the consequences, the
court could, on the facts, conclude that informed consent had been given.
Nevertheless, to rely on implied consent, would not be a sufficient safeguard of
an offender's convention rights, particularly where the scheme was targeted at
children and young persons. In the instant cases, although decisions were taken
not to prosecute, the claimants had been required to subject themselves to a
procedure which had the effect of publicly pronouncing their guilt of the offence
of indecent assault. It followed that they had been denied a right to a trial of the
charges against them, and been declared guilty by an administrative process.
Accordingly the decisions would be quashed (see [35]–[39], below).

Notes

For effects of reprimands and warnings on young offenders, see 5(3) *Halsbury's
Laws* (4th edn reissue) para 1604.

For the Crime and Disorder Act 1998, ss 65, 66, see 6 *Halsbury's Statutes* (4th
edn) (1999 reissue) 785–787.

For the Human Rights Act 1998, Sch 1, Pt I, art 6, see 7 *Halsbury's Statutes* (4th
edn) (2002 reissue) 554.

Cases referred to in judgment

Deweer v Belgium (1980) 2 EHRR 439, [1980] ECHR 6903/75, ECt HR.
R v Greater Manchester Police, ex p R (2000) Independent, 23 October, DC.
R v Metropolitan Police Comr, ex p Thompson [1997] 1 WLR 1519, DC.

Cases also cited or referred to in skeleton arguments

Engel v Netherlands (No 2) (1976) 1 EHRR 706, ECt HR.
Ezeh v UK (2002) 12 BHRC 589, ECt HR.
H and M v DPP [1998] Crim LR 653, CA.
Malmstrom v Sweden (1983) 38 DR 18.
R v Court [1988] 2 All ER 221, [1989] AC 28, [1988] 2 WLR 1071, HL.
R (Bibi) v Newham London BC, R (Al-Nashed) v Newham London BC [2001] EWCA
Civ 607, [2002] 1 WLR 237.
Van Raalte v Netherlands (1997) 24 EHRR 503, [1997] ECHR 20060/92, ECt HR.
Wandsworth London BC v Michalak [2002] EWCA Civ 271, [2002] 4 All ER 1136,
[2003] 1 WLR 617.
X v Austria (1980) 19 DR 213.

a   **Applications for judicial review**

R (on the application of U) v Metropolitan Police Commissioner
The claimant, U, proceeding by his mother and litigation friend, applied for
judicial review of the decision of a police constable in the employ of the
defendant, the Metropolitan Police Commissioner, to issue the final warning
b   administered to the claimant on 12 February 2002 pursuant to s 65 of the Crime
and Disorder Act 1998, following allegations of indecent assault, and his
subsequent decision to refuse to quash the decision on 14 March 2002. The facts
are set out in the judgment of the court.

c   *R (on the application of R) v Durham Constabulary*
The claimant, R, proceeding by his father and litigation friend, applied for judicial
review of the decision of a police constable in the employ of the defendant, the
Durham Constabulary, to issue the final warning administered to the claimant on
23 January 2002 pursuant to s 65 of the Crime and Disorder Act 1998, following
allegations of indecent assault. The facts are set out in the judgment of the court.
d

Marc Willers (instructed by *Parker Arrenberg Dawson & Cobb*) for the applicant U.
Geoff Knowles (instructed by *Gordon Brown Associates*, Chester-le-Street) for the
    applicant R.
Anne Studd (instructed by *David Hamilton*) for the defendant in the case of U and
e   (instructed by *Chris Southey*, Durham) for the defendant in the case of R.
Steven Kovats (instructed by the *Treasury Solicitor*) for the Secretary of State for the
    Home Department, the interested party.

Cur adv vult

f   29 November 2002. The following judgment was delivered.

LATHAM LJ.
    [1] This judgment is the judgment of the court. These two applications raise
important questions of principle and practice in relation to the final warning
g   scheme (the scheme) established by ss 65 and 66 of the Crime and Disorder Act
1998, as amended by s 56 of the Criminal Justice and Court Services Act 2000.
The scheme is part of the strategy devised to prevent offending and re-offending
by children and young persons. Its aim is to divert children and young persons
from their offending behaviour before they enter the court system. It replaced,
for children and young persons, the systems of cautions which had previously
h   been in place with a more structured approach intended to prevent re-offending.
Depending on the seriousness of the offence, a reprimand is normally given for a
first offence and a final warning for a second offence; thereafter the young
offender should generally be charged. Following a final warning, the police have
a statutory duty to refer the young offender to a youth offending team in order
j   to determine whether or not to provide an intervention programme. The
procedures are governed by the provisions of the 1998 Act, and guidance issued
under that Act by the Home Office.
    [2] As we have said, the scheme replaced for young offenders the system of
cautions which remains in place for all other offenders. This latter system is
informal, in the sense that it is not underpinned by any statutory provision. The

procedures are governed by Home Office circular 18/1994. The critical difference
between this system and the scheme is that, under the circular, a caution can only
be given if the offender gives his informed consent to being cautioned. Under the
scheme, neither the 1998 Act, nor the guidance given by the Home Office makes
any provision for such consent. Neither a caution, nor a reprimand or final
warning, can, however, be given unless the offender has admitted the relevant
offence or offences.

[3] In the two applications with which we are concerned the claimants, both
15 at the relevant time, were suspected of having committed indecent assaults on
young girls; in U's case on a station platform; in R's case, at school. Both
applicants were interviewed and, it is accepted, admitted that they had
committed indecent assaults. They claim, however, that those admissions were
the result of inducements rendering them unreliable. The respective police
authorities determined that the circumstances justified giving final warnings,
which were duly administered. The claimants were then required to register
under the provisions of the Sex Offenders Act 1997, a consequence of a final
warning of which neither was aware prior to its administration. The defendant
disputes the circumstances in which it is said that the admissions were made; and
the claimant U led evidence before us that after the final warning had been
administered, the officer administering it so acted as to give rise to a legitimate
expectation that the decision to administer the warning would be reconsidered.
It is accepted on behalf of both defendants that neither of the claimants was asked
whether he consented to the administration of the final warning. And in U's case
it is accepted that the decision was not in fact reconsidered.

[4] We therefore have to resolve three separate issues. (a) In relation to each
claimant, we have to determine whether or not the defendants were entitled to
rely on the admissions. This does not raise any new issue of principle. It is
accepted on behalf of the defendants that unless they can establish that the
admissions were reliable, in the sense of not having been obtained by reason of
an inducement, then one of the preconditions for the administration of a final
warning would not have been met. (b) In the case of U, we have to determine
whether the evidence supports the assertion that he had a legitimate expectation
as to the way his case would be dealt with which was not met by the police, so as
to justify this court in concluding that he had been unfairly dealt with. (c) We
have to consider the important submission made on behalf of both claimants that
the 1998 Act and the guidance given by the Home Office in relation to the scheme
do not comply with arts 6, 8 and 14 of the European Convention on Human
Rights and Fundamental Freedoms 1950 (as set out in Sch 1 to the Human Rights
Act 1998) in that it is not a precondition of the administration of a final warning
that an offender should have given his informed consent to that course being
adopted. The particular vice about which both claimants complain is that at no
stage was either of them informed of the fact that the administration of the final
warning would result in a requirement to register under the 1997 Act.

[5] With those preliminary observations we propose to set out the relevant
statutory provisions, the terms of the circular and the guidance given by the
Home Office before dealing with the factual and legal issues raised by these
applications.

CAUTIONS

[6] Paragraph 2 of the circular provides:

a

'DECISION TO CAUTION

2. A formal caution is a serious matter. It is recorded by the police; it should influence them in their decision whether or not to institute proceedings if the person should offend again; and it may be cited in any subsequent court proceedings. In order to safeguard the offender's interests, the following conditions must be met before a caution can be administered—

—there must be *evidence of the offender's guilt* sufficient to give a realistic prospect of conviction;

—the offender must *admit the offence;*

—the offender (or, in the case of a juvenile, his parents or guardian) must understand the significance of a caution and give *informed consent* to being cautioned.'

THE 1998 ACT (AS AMENDED)

[7]

'**65.** *Reprimands and warnings.*—(1) Subsections (2) to (5) below apply where—(a) a constable has evidence that a child or young person ("the offender") has committed an offence; (b) the constable considers that the evidence is such that, if the offender were prosecuted for the offence, there would be a realistic prospect of his being convicted; (c) the offender admits to the constable that he committed the offence; (d) the offender has not previously been convicted of an offence; and (e) the constable is satisfied that it would not be in the public interest for the offender to be prosecuted.

(2) Subject to subsection (4) below, a constable may reprimand the offender if the offender has not previously been reprimanded or warned.

(3) The constable may warn the offender if—(a) the offender has not previously been warned; or (b) where the offender has previously been warned, the offence was committed more than two years after the date of the previous warning and the constable considers the offence to be not so serious as to require a charge to be brought; but no person may be warned under paragraph (b) above more than once.

(4) Where the offender has not been previously reprimanded, the constable shall warn rather than reprimand the offender if he considers the offence to be so serious as to require a warning.

(5) The constable shall—(a) where the offender is under the age of 17, give any reprimand or warning in the presence of an appropriate adult; and (b) explain to the offender and, where he is under that age, the appropriate adult in ordinary language—(i) in the case of a reprimand, the effect of subsection (5)(a) of section 66 below; (ii) in the case of a warning, the effect of subsections (1), (2), (4) and (5)(b) and (c) of that section, and any guidance issued under subsection 3 of that section.

(6) The Secretary of State shall publish, in such a manner as he considers appropriate, guidance as to—(a) the circumstances in which it is appropriate to give reprimands or warnings, including criteria for determining—(i) for the purposes of subsection (3)(b) above, whether an offence is not so serious as to require a charge to be brought; and (ii) for the purposes of subsection (4) above, whether an offence is so serious as to require a warning … (b) the category of constable by whom reprimands and warning may be

given; and (c) the form which reprimands and warning are to take and the
manner in which they are to be given and recorded ...

(9) Any reference (however expressed) in any enactment passed before or
in the same Session as this Act to a person being cautioned shall be
construed, in relation to any time after that commencement, as including a
reference to a child or young person being reprimanded or warned.

66. *Effect of reprimands and warning.*—(1) Where a constable warns a
person under section 65 above, he shall as soon as practicable refer the person
to a youth offending team.

(2) A youth offending team—(a) shall assess any person referred to them
under subsection (1) above; and (b) unless they consider it inappropriate to
do so, shall arrange for him to participate in a rehabilitation programme.

(3) The Secretary of State shall publish, in such manner as he considers
appropriate, guidance as to—(a) what should be included in a rehabilitation
programme arranged for a person under subsection (2) above; (b) the
manner in which any failure by a person to participate in such a programme
to be recorded; and (c) the persons to whom any such failure be notified.

(4) Where a person who has been warned under section 65 above is
convicted of an offence committed within two years of the warning, the
court by or before which he is so convicted—(a) shall not make an order
under subsection (1)(b) (conditional discharge) of section 12 of the Powers of
Criminal Courts (Sentencing) Act 2000 in respect of the offence unless it is of
the opinion that there are exceptional circumstances relating to the offence
or offender which justify its doing so; and (b) where it does so, it will state in
open court that it is of that opinion and why it is.

(5) The following, namely—(a) any reprimand of a person under
section 65 above; (b) any warning of a person under that section; and (c) any
report of a failure by a person to participate in a rehabilitation programme
arranged for him under subsection (2) above, may be cited in criminal
proceedings in the same circumstances as a conviction of the person may be
cited.

(6) In this section "rehabilitation programme" means a programme the
purpose of which is to rehabilitate participants and to prevent them from
re-offending.'

THE 1997 ACT

[8]

'**1.** *Sex offenders subject to notification requirements.*—(1) A person becomes
subject to the notification requirements of this Part if, after the
commencement of this Part ... (c) in England and Wales or Northern
Ireland, he is cautioned by a constable in respect of such an offence which, at
the time the caution is given, he has admitted.'

[9] The 1998 Act extends this category to those who have been reprimanded
or warned under that Act. The consequence, so far as children and young
persons who have been so reprimanded or warned is that the notification
requirements where the offence is of indecent assault, the offence with which we
are concerned, lasts for two-and-a-half years: see ss 1(4) and 4(2) of the 1997 Act.

HOME OFFICE GUIDANCE

a

[10] The guidance which was in effect at the relevant time included the following when dealing with the administration of a reprimand or warning:

'73. In giving a warning, the officer should specify the offence(s) which has lead to it and make clear that ... If the offence is one covered by the Sex Offenders Act 1997, the young person is required to register with the police for inclusion in the Sex Offenders Register (para. 77 below) ...

b

77. The Sex Offenders Act 1997 requires those convicted or cautioned for certain sex offences to notify the police of their details – this now includes offenders who are given a reprimand or warning for offences listed in that Act. The police officer must explain to a young offender and their appropriate adult that on receiving a reprimand or warning for such an offence they will be required to register with the police for inclusion on the sex offenders register. Where the YOT carries out a prior assessment of the young offender who has been reported for a sex offence this is an opportunity for them to explain about the register to the offender and his or her parents.'

c

d

[11] In the current guidance, published in November 2002, those provisions are essentially replicated. However, in dealing with the requirement that the young person must admit the offence, it provides:

e

'4.12 A reprimand or warning can be given only if the young person makes a clear and reliable admission to all elements of the offence. This should include an admission of dishonesty and intent, where applicable.

4.13 Unlike adult cautions, the young person does not "consent" to a reprimand or final warning. Under the legislation, it is a matter for the police to decide the appropriate disposal in accordance with the statutory criteria.

f

4.14 Young people and their parents/carers or other appropriate adults should have access to the information and the options available including the final warning scheme so that they can make an informed decision before the question as to whether they admit the offence is put to them. For instance they should be aware that the police will decide the appropriate disposal under the final warning scheme in the light of the statutory criteria. The status of a reprimand or final warning should also be explained, including:

g

• the fact that a record will be kept for a minimum of five years or until the offender reaches 18 years of age whichever is the longer;

• that it can be cited in criminal proceedings;

h

• in some cases made available to employers;

• if the offence is listed under the Sex Offenders Act 1997, that a reprimand or final warning will also be require them to register with the police for inclusion in the sex offenders register ...'

j GENERALLY

[12] The practical effect of these provisions is that a reprimand or warning is not a conviction, but is entered on the police national computer (PNC) and is therefore available for those who are entitled to inspect the contents of that computer. In particular the information is therefore available to local authorities in the exercise of their powers in relation to education and care of children.

THE FACTS

a

The claimant U

[13] Two girls complained that they had been indecently assaulted by being inappropriately touched on 16 May 2001 at New Cross Gate train station. U was arrested on 14 November 2001 and was bailed to return to the police station for interview on 24 November 2001, when he was accompanied by a solicitor, *b* Mrs Gale. He was interviewed, and denied both allegations. He was bailed again to attend an identification parade. On 25 January 2002 U, again accompanied by Mrs Gale, was identified by one of the two girls but not the other. After the identification, there was a conversation between Mrs Gale and PC Wratten in which, according to Mrs Gale, PC Wratten indicated that if U was minded to admit the matter then he would be re-interviewed and provided that he made *c* admissions on tape, the matter would be dealt with by way of a final warning. She then saw U and told him what PC Wratten had said. She explained the effect of a final warning, but did not tell him of the requirements under the 1997 Act, of which she was herself at the time unaware. She told us that U was concerned about going to court because it would take time. She told him that although that *d* was understandable, it was not a basis on which he should make such a major decision. She advised him that a final warning would be less detrimental to him than a conviction.

[14] U was then interviewed on tape. He admitted that he had been on the platform at New Cross Gate at the time, and that he had put his hand up a girl's skirt and pinched her. He stated that he had not said this before because he was *e* scared. He said that he understood that it was wrong. After the interview, PC Wratten said that he would grant bail to U to return to the police station, which Mrs Gale and U understood to be for the purposes of administering the final warning.

[15] After that attendance, Mrs Gale wrote a note which reads: *f*

'Attend PC Ratten [sic]
He has checked with the girls and their parents and the Sergeant and takes the view that the matter is suitable for a final warning. I attended the client and reported the above. "U" indicated that he was willing to admit the offence on tape in consideration of getting a final warning. He decided to do *g* this
—to avoid lengthy proceedings
—to avoid the risk of a conviction thereby acquiring a criminal record.'

[16] PC Wratten told us that after the positive identification, he spoke to his *h* sergeant and they decided that U should be re-interviewed. He spoke to Mrs Gale. He said that he told her the only disposal option was to charge U but that if an admission was made then there would be a further option, that of a warning. He denied having said to Mrs Gale that if U admitted the offence, he would be given a warning. His evidence was that this was a decision which could not be made by him, but had to be made by him in conjunction with his sergeant. *j*

[17] Having heard both Mrs Gale and PC Wratten give evidence, we are satisfied PC Wratten's recollection is not correct. Mrs Gale made it clear to us that she did not consider at the time that PC Wratten was doing anything wrong, indeed she considered that he was being helpful. None the less she was satisfied that she had been given an assurance that if U admitted the offence, he would be

a given a final warning. Her evidence is fully borne out by the contents of her note; and we accept it.

[18] U eventually attended at Southwark Police Station for the purposes of the administration of the final warning. The matter had been transferred from PC Wratten to PC Sharpe, who was a police officer trained in the administration of such warnings. U arrived early with his foster mother. PC Sharpe was not
b aware that Mrs Gale was due to attend. He accordingly administered the warning. Mrs Gale unfortunately arrived late, as did U's natural mother who had also been informed of U's appointment. By then U and his foster mother had left. Mrs Gale and U's mother met PC Sharpe who informed them of what had happened. U's mother became extremely upset. She said that she was not in favour of the final warning having been administered. PC Sharpe, according to
c Mrs Gale, then informed U's mother that U had been told to attend at Catford Police Station to sign on the sex offenders register. This upset U's mother further. PC Sharpe, according to Mrs Gale, then said that he could always cancel the final warning and he would not complete the paperwork until U's mother had had an opportunity to hear the admission which U had made. PC Sharpe told us that as
d he had not given any promise to either Mrs Gale or to U's mother but had been prepared to delay completing the paperwork to give U's mother an opportunity to hear the admissions U had made on tape. He told us that he had waited for five days and then notified the PNC of the warning.

[19] We have come to the conclusion that PC Sharpe did not give to either Mrs Gale or to U's mother any unequivocal promise which could give rise to a
e legitimate expectation of a sort which would justify this court in concluding that there had been any unfairness in the way in which U had been dealt with. The warning had been properly administered. PC Sharpe was seeking to cope as best he could, with what had undoubtedly become a fraught situation.

[20] On 14 February 2002, Mrs Gale wrote to U asking him to contact her to
f discuss what had happened. U went to see her on 28 February 2002. He told her that he had only admitted the offence to receive a final warning and that he was in fact not guilty. He made it clear that he was not happy about going on the sex offenders register for a period of two-and-a-half years. Despite being advised that if the final warning was set aside, the matter would probably go to court and he might be convicted, he said that he had decided that he wanted the final warning
g cancelled and that he wanted the matter to go to court. It was in those circumstances that the judicial review proceedings were commenced.

R's claim

h [21] In November 2001, a number of girls made complaints of what they considered to be indecent assaults by R. They were all girls who were at school with R and made their complaints originally to the school itself. As a result R was excluded from school. The complaints were reported to the police. Five girls were interviewed on videotape; and their complaints were sufficiently serious for the police to investigate. In January 2002, WPC Cummins, now detective
j constable, telephoned R's stepfather asking him if he would be prepared to take R to the police station for interview. His evidence was that in the course of that telephone conversation, he asked what was likely to happen. He told us that at that time the family were under considerable stress, and R himself was in a very distraught state. The stepfather's evidence was that WPC Cummins had told him that the parents did not want the matter to go any further and that because

R had no criminal record or history of behaviour of this type, depending on admissions that he made, he would be likely to be given a 'caution'. Accordingly *a* he was prepared to take R to the police station. R was interviewed on 11 January 2002. He told us that he was at no time told what the consequences of a caution might be. In particular he was not told that one of the consequences would be a requirement to register under the 1997 Act. He said that in the light of what he had been told by WPC Cummins, he did not consider it necessary to obtain legal *b* advice. Had he been told of the consequence of a caution he would undoubtedly have done so.

[22] During the course of the interview, R admitted to what he described as 'horseplay', such as pinging bra straps, and touching the girls on the bottom playfully, which he did not consider to have any sexual connotation; none the less he admitted having touched girls on the breast. It is not suggested on behalf of R *c* that the contents of the interview do not constitute admissions of indecent assault. It is clear that they do.

[23] DC Cummins told us that she had certainly spoken to R's stepfather to ask him if he was willing to accompany R to the police station. She said, however, that she had at no stage given any indication to R's stepfather as to the possibility *d* of a final warning until after the interview. She was adamant that at no time before then was any indication given to R's stepfather of what the possible outcomes of any interview might be. Having heard both R's stepfather and DC Cummins, we are satisfied that she did not at any stage before the interview give any indication that if R made admissions in interview, he would receive a *e* caution or final warning. The contents of the interview are themselves instructive. It is plain that in large part, R was seeking to minimise what had happened. There is nothing to suggest that he was making any admissions in order to obtain some benefit for himself.

[24] The final warning was given to R on 29 January 2002. His stepfather told us that he was not then told of the consequence of a final warning, namely that R *f* would have to register under the 1997 Act. It was only when the youth offending team came to his home later in February 2002 that that requirement was made plain. There is no doubt that he reacted strongly to this information. Despite the fact that it is suggested that he had been provided with information at the time of the final warning as to this requirement, we are satisfied from the evidence of *g* those who were there at the time, that neither he nor his wife were aware of that information until the attendance of the youth offending team. It was as a result of what he was then told that he saw solicitors and these proceedings were commenced.

THE ISSUES *h*

[25] The second issue which we have identified, which relates to U only, we have already disposed of in dealing with the facts. As we have said, there is no factual basis upon which U could claim that he had a legitimate expectation that his final warning would be reconsidered which would justify this court in intervening. *j*

[26] Before dealing with the first and third issues, it is worth putting them in their context. The underlying complaint in these proceedings is that neither claimant was made aware at any time during the procedure that the consequences of a final warning would be a requirement to register under the 1997 Act. Mrs Gale told us frankly that she had not known of this requirement.

a Had she known, she may well have given advice to U in different terms. As far as R is concerned, his stepfather told us that he would have sought legal advice, particularly as it was hoped that R would join the forces on leaving school and he would have wanted to discover whether the effect of registering under the 1997 Act would create a problem. Leaving aside the legal niceties for the moment, both claimants say that it is simply unfair to obtain an admission of an offence and

b then proceed administratively to what is in effect a public declaration of guilt, with the particular consequences for those charged with sex offences, without at any stage spelling out those consequences. It is submitted that, at the very least, those consequences should have been spelt out before each of the claimants was interviewed. The main thrust, however, of the claimants' submissions is that no final warning should have been given without the express informed consent of

c the claimants.

[27] Turning then to the first issue, it is common ground that the police are not entitled to rely, when determining whether or not to administer a reprimand or a final warning, on an admission procured by way of an inducement so rendering the admission unreliable. This court so held in *R v Metropolitan Police*

d *Comr, ex p Thompson* [1997] 1 WLR 1519. In that case a police inspector determined that a caution was the appropriate way of dealing with an offender and then, on interview, asked him whether he was willing to accept a caution, telling him that by accepting the caution he was admitting the offence. The court held that the cautioning procedure was predicated upon a reliable admission and genuine consent. The court considered that as a result there were, essentially,

e two vices in the procedure in fact adopted. First, the consent thereby obtained could not be said to have constituted a reliable admission. Second, the procedure had conflated two separate steps in a proper cautioning process. The admission of guilt was a precondition to a decision to administer a caution; and accordingly there should have been an admission before formal consideration was given to

f proceeding by way of caution.

[28] In the case of U, our conclusions of fact are such that both vices exist in his case. PC Wratten together with the sergeant, had decided that a final warning was an appropriate disposal before interviewing U. But, more important, that had been conveyed to Mrs Gale in circumstances which were clearly capable of amounting to an inducement when that information was relayed to U. In all the

g circumstances, we consider that the admission was not a reliable admission and could not, accordingly, properly found a decision to administer a final warning.

[29] The position is different in the case of R. We are satisfied that there was no inducement offered to R prior to or at the time of his making the relevant admissions. Accordingly, the police were entitled to rely on them. However,

h that still leaves the question of the effect of the fact that nothing was said about the consequences that might flow from those admissions. In *R v Greater Manchester Police, ex p R* (2000) Independent, 23 October, this question arose under the procedure for administering cautions. At the time that the applicant in that case admitted the offence, he was not made aware of the requirement to

j register under the 1997 Act in the event of a caution. He and his father were, however, made aware of that requirement at the time that they were asked to consent to a caution. The court held that the police, in informing them of the requirement before asking for the consent to a caution, had satisfied the requirement of the circular to obtain informed consent and that the caution was accordingly lawful. The court, however, said that it would have been preferable

if that requirement had been made clear before the interview in which the
admission was made. Laws LJ, in agreeing with the lead judgment of Rafferty J,
said:

> 'There is no escape from the application of the notification provisions
> contained in the 1997 Act to caution juveniles. On the facts here the police
> should certainly have made that clear on 17 June. I desire only to emphasise
> my respectful view that the decision of this court in *Ex p Thompson* was not
> intended to discourage recourse to sensible and practical exchanges between
> police, suspect and the legal advisor in a case where a caution is in prospect
> in appropriate disposal of the case, but it is of the greatest importance that a
> caution should not be offered as an inducement for the making of a
> confession.'

[30] Paragraph 4.14 of the new Home Office guidance, which we have set out
(see [11], above) is clearly intended to address this problem, which is more acute
in the context of the scheme in the light of the fact that informed consent is not a
precondition of a reprimand or final warning. The new guidance meets the first
of the complaints of the claimants to which we referred in [25], above. Further,
provided that the information is conveyed to the child or young person and those
with him in a way which does not give any indication that an admission will result
in a reprimand or final warning, the formula proposed could not amount to an
inducement rendering any admission unreliable. There is no doubt, however,
that the police must be scrupulously careful not to give any indication as to the
likely form of disposal in the event of an admission, because if they do they run
the risk that any admission upon which they subsequently rely will be open to
challenge.

[31] However, we do not consider that that failure to warn of the
consequences of a reprimand or a final warning could render the decision to
reprimand or administer a final warning unlawful as a matter of domestic law.
The preconditions set out in the 1998 Act and the guidance in effect at the time
were met in R's case. And the scheme, as defined by the 1998 Act and the
guidance does not require the young offender's consent. The most important
question of principle in this case is whether or not this consequence gives rise to
a breach of any of the provisions of the convention, which is the third issue which
we have to determine.

[32] It is the claimants' contention that the scheme even as presently devised
does not conform to the requirements of art 6, art 8 and art 14 of the convention.
These provide as follows:

> 'Article 6
>
> Right to a fair trial
> 1. In the determination of his civil rights and obligations or of any criminal
> charge against him, everyone is entitled to a fair and public hearing within a
> reasonable time by an independent and impartial tribunal established by law ...
> 2. Everyone charged with a criminal offence shall be presumed innocent
> until proved guilty according to law ...

a

Article 8

Right to respect for private and family life
1. Everyone has the right to respect for his private and family life, his home and his correspondence.

b
2. There shall be no interference by a public authority with the exercise of this right except such as is in accordance with the law and is necessary in a democratic society in the interests of national security, public safety or the economic well-being of the country, for the prevention of disorder or crime, for the protection of health or morals, or for the protection of the rights and freedoms of others …

c

Article 14

Prohibition of discrimination
The enjoyment of the rights and freedoms set forth in this Convention

d
shall be secured without discrimination on any ground such as sex, race, colour, language, religion, political or other opinion, national or social origin, association with a national minority, property, birth or other status.'

[**33**] The first and main submission on behalf of the claimants is that the whole process involved in the scheme is subject to the provisions of art 6. It is submitted

e
that for the purposes of that article, the process constitutes the determination of a criminal charge within the meaning of that phrase in the convention, requiring its determination by an independent and impartial tribunal. It is accepted that this does not give the claimants an absolute right to a trial. The police would be entitled at any time to discontinue proceedings against them. But, they submit, this is not what the scheme involves. The scheme results in what is in effect a

f
public declaration of guilt by an administrative process and accordingly breaches both art 6(1) and (2). It would be otherwise, it is accepted, if the claimants had given informed consent to disposal of the matter under the scheme so that they could properly be said to have waived their art 6 rights. As for art 8, it is submitted that the requirements resulting from a reprimand or final warning are capable of affecting the claimants' private and family life, and, even if

g
proportionate, are discriminatory, in that adults, who are subject to the system of cautions are given the opportunity to decide whether or not to accept a caution, whereas children and young persons are not. Further the scheme discriminates between adults and children and young persons by denying to the latter the right to consent, so that they are discriminated against in relation to their arts 6 and 8

h
rights.

[**34**] The Secretary of State, who appears because of the potential challenge to the legislation, accepts that art 6 is engaged, but submits that it is engaged only until such time as the police are satisfied under s 65(1)(e) of the 1998 Act that it would not be in the public interest for the offender to be prosecuted. It is

j
submitted that this brings to an end the criminal charge in the same way as discontinuance of proceedings. Further, it is submitted that there is no breach of art 6(2) because there has been no conviction. It is accepted that art 8 is also engaged, but it is submitted that in so far as there is interference with the individual's private or family life, that interference is proportionate in the public interest. As to art 14, it is submitted that there is no question of discrimination.

The system of cautions and the scheme are different in kind. The scheme is a structured approach to the problems presented specifically by children and young persons and cannot be equated to the system of cautions for adults.

[35] We have no doubt that the Secretary of State is right to concede that art 6 is engaged. The phrase 'criminal charge' has an autonomous meaning under the convention, which is determined by reference to substance rather than form. In *Deweer v Belgium* (1980) 2 EHRR 439 at 459 (para 46), the court defined it as 'the official notification given to an individual by the competent authority of an allegation that he has committed a criminal offence'.

[36] Prima facie, therefore, the claimants were entitled to a fair trial of the allegations made against them attended by all the guarantees which are required by the convention. There is, however, no doubt that that is not an absolute right. The police would have been entitled to decide not to prosecute and discontinue the proceeding: see *Deweer's* case (at 460–461 (para 49)). But that is not what happened in the present case. Although the decision was taken not to prosecute, the claimants were required to subject themselves to a procedure which had the effect of publicly pronouncing their guilt of the offence of indecent assault. That was the consequences of the final warnings being recorded on the PNC, so that the fact of the final warnings became available not only in the event of future offending, but also to all those who have access to the PNC. It seems to us that these consequences prima facie constituted a breach of art 6(1) and (2). The claimants were denied a right to a trial of the charges against them, and declared guilty by an administrative process.

[37] That does not mean, however, that the procedures for cautions, reprimands and final warnings are necessarily in breach of art 6. It would be unfortunate if they were. For they provide significant advantages both to the public, and to the individual offender. They constitute a sensible means of ensuring that resources are not wasted on cases where the paraphernalia of the court appearance is unnecessary given the character of the individual and the nature of the charge; and in the case of the scheme, this has the further clear policy objective of seeking to prevent re-offending by children and young persons. From the offender's point of view, it results in the matter being dealt with expeditiously and does not result in a conviction, which undoubtedly has more serious consequences than a caution, reprimand or final warning.

[38] The European Court of Human Rights recognised in *Deweer's* case, (again at 460–461 (para 49)), that the domestic legal systems of the contracting states frequently provide mechanisms by which a person may waive his right to have his case dealt with by a court. However, the court stated that any such mechanism must be looked at with care so as to ensure that any waiver has not been the result of constraint. Accordingly the scheme, and the system of cautions, can only conform with the convention if their procedures can properly be said to amount to such a waiver. In our view an effective waiver requires informed consent by the offender to the procedure being adopted, as in the case of cautions. This conclusion does not, however, mean that the scheme itself is unlawful in the sense that the 1998 Act does not conform with the convention. There is nothing in the 1998 Act which requires the police to proceed without the consent of the offender. The vice lies in the guidance, and the practice adopted pursuant to that guidance. In the two cases with which we are concerned, there has clearly been no informed consent, so that there has been a breach of the claimants' art 6 rights. Accordingly the decisions must be quashed. In these

a circumstances, we do not consider that it is necessary to come to any conclusion as to the arguments based upon arts 8 and 14.

[**39**] However, the conclusion that we have reached that informed consent is required before the procedure can comply with art 6 does not mean that in every case where a reprimand or final warning has been given, there has been a breach of the offender's convention rights. The procedure adopted by the police may

b well in any particular case have resulted in informed consent being given. For example, where an offender has made a free and reliable admission in the full knowledge of the consequences, it may well be that the court could on the facts conclude that informed consent has indeed been given. But to rely on implied consent in that way would not, in our view, be a sufficient safeguard of an offender's convention rights, particularly bearing in mind the fact that the

c scheme is targeted at children and young persons. The appropriate practice must be to ensure that before a reprimand or final warning is administered, the offender and his or her parent, carer or other appropriate adult should be told of the consequences, and asked whether or not they consent to that course being taken.

d
Applications granted.

Dilys Tausz   Barrister.

SCT Finance Ltd v Bolton

[2002] EWCA Civ 56

COURT OF APPEAL (CIVIL DIVISION)

WALLER, RIX LJJ AND WILSON J

16 JANUARY 2002

Costs – Order for costs – Discretion – Judge ordering detailed assessment of costs on standard basis – Judge placing quantified limit on costs unsuccessful defendant should pay – Whether placing of limit within judge's discretion – CPR 1.1(2)(c), 44.3 – CPR PD 44.

Costs – Third party – Assessment of third party costs – Presence of party ultimately paying costs at assessment hearing – Action to be taken where party ultimately paying costs not present at assessment hearing – CPR 3.1(7).

The defendant purchased a car by way of hire purchase. The distributors, V, had sold the car to the dealers, H, who arranged a hire purchase arrangement through the claimant company. As a result of problems he was experiencing with the car, the defendant ceased payments to the claimant. The claimant issued proceedings for the outstanding balance of £351. The defendant issued a defence and a counterclaim for damages. In order better to defend the counterclaim, the claimant issued Pt 20 proceedings against H. In turn, H issued Pt 20 proceedings against V for the same purpose. Judgment was given on the claim, and the counterclaim was dismissed. The judge went on to make an order for costs. Estimated bills of costs were provided by the claimant in the sum of £9,000, by H in the sum of £24,000 and by V in the sum of £18,000. The judge ruled that the costs of each Pt 20 defendant should move up the line of defendants, with the result that the bill of costs of the claimant would include those of both H and V. The judge directed himself that, by CPR 44.3(6), he had the power to limit the costs in some way. He ruled that the costs of the claimant, which would include those of H and V, should be subject to a detailed assessment on the standard basis and paid by the defendant, but that the defendant's liability would be limited to £15,000, because the costs had been allowed to escalate out of proportion to the amount at stake, and also because of the defendant's limited means. The claimant appealed on the grounds that the imposition of such a limit was wrong in law or beyond a reasonable exercise of the judge's discretion.

Held – Although CPR 44.3(6) did not specifically cover an order placing a limit on costs, the rule was not exhaustive of the orders it was possible to make, and there was no doubt that by virtue of CPR 44.3(1)(b) a court could validly identify a quantified ceiling on costs. However, because the judge had ordered a detailed assessment of costs on the standard basis, only those costs which were proportionate would be allowed under CPR 44. Moreover, by virtue of CPR PD 44, the provisions of, inter alia, CPR 1.1(2)(c), which stated that cases should be dealt with in a way proportionate to the financial position of each party, were to be applied. It followed, therefore, that the judge's attempt to allow for a perceived lack of proportion to the amount in issue and to the defendant's means by limiting the amount payable was unprincipled, since that same lack of proportion was already fully allowed for by virtue of detailed assessment on a standard basis *a* having been ordered. The limit on the amount payable by the defendant would therefore be removed, and the defendant would be liable for all the costs of the claimant as assessed on the standard basis (see [25], [36], [40], [47], [52], [54], below).

Per curiam. Where litigation involves a chain of Pt 20 parties and costs are ordered to move up the line of defendants with a final order against one party, all

b such costs should be assessed together and the party ultimately paying such costs should be present at the assessment hearing. Where such a party is not present, it is possible to use CPR 3.1(7) to revoke such an assessment and allow a new assessment by a district judge (see [56]–[59], below).

Notes
c
For the assessment of costs and factors to be taken into account in deciding the amount of costs, see 10 *Halsbury's Laws* (4th edn reissue) paras 22, 23.

Case referred to in judgments
Johnson v Ribbins (Sir Francis Pittis & Son (a firm), third party) [1977] 1 All ER 806,
d   [1977] 1 WLR 1458, CA.

Appeal
The claimant, SCT Finance Ltd (the hire-purchase company) appealed from the decision of Judge Elly in the Reading County Court on 9 March 2001, whereby he

e allowed the hire-purchase company's claim against the defendant, John Bolton, in respect of arrears of instalments owing on a motor car, dismissed the defendant's counterclaim and limited the costs recoverable by the claimant to £15,000. The facts are set out in the judgment of Wilson J.

f *Rosana Bailey* (instructed by *Sechiari, Clark & Mitchell,* Cardiff) for the hire-purchase company.
The defendant appeared in person.

WALLER LJ.
   [1] I will ask Wilson J to deliver the first judgment.
g

WILSON J.
   [2] This is an appeal brought with leave of the single Lord Justice from the county court in relation to costs. As such, it is overcast, from start to finish, by the heavy burden faced by any appellant in establishing that the judge's decision
h falls outside the discretion in relation to costs conferred upon him under CPR 44.3(1). For reasons of general policy, namely that it is undesirable for further costs to be incurred in arguing about costs, this court discourages such appeals by interpreting such discretion very widely.

   [3] The appeal is brought by SCT Finance Ltd (the hire-purchase company)
j from the order of Judge Elly in the Reading County Court on 9 March 2001. Before the judge were proceedings brought by the hire-purchase company against Mr Bolton, who, in April 1995, had bought from it a car on terms as to hire purchase. As a result of a counterclaim made by Mr Bolton, the hire-purchase company issued a CPR Pt 20 claim against WR Hammant Ltd (the dealers) through whom Mr Bolton had bought the car. As a result of the Pt 20 claim

against them, the dealers in turn issued a Pt 20 claim against Volkswagen Group UK Ltd (the distributors) who had sold the car to them.

[4] The substantive result of the proceedings, against which there is no appeal, was that judgment be given on the claim by the hire-purchase company against Mr Bolton in the sum of £351; and that the counterclaim and the two successive claims under Pt 20 be dismissed. Then came the orders for costs. They were: (a) that the distributors' costs be paid by the dealers, subject to detailed assessment on the standard basis; (b) that the dealers' costs be paid by the hire-purchase company, subject to detailed assessment on the standard basis and so as to include the costs payable by the dealers pursuant to (a); and (c) that the hire-purchase company's costs be paid by Mr Bolton, subject to detailed assessment on the standard basis and so as to include the costs payable by the hire-purchase company pursuant to (b) but subject also to (i) postponement referable to costs incurred while Mr Bolton was in receipt of public funds for the prosecution of his counterclaim; and (ii) an overall ceiling of £15,000.

[5] The hire-purchase company accepts the validity of the limitation at (i), made pursuant to what is now s 11 of the Access to Justice Act 1999. Mr Bolton appears to have been publicly funded for the prosecution of his counterclaim between about November 1999 and February 2000, namely before the vast bulk of the costs had been incurred by any of the other parties. So the hire-purchase company does not expect that the effect of that limitation will be to postpone recovery of any significant amount of its costs. Its appeal is against the limitation at (ii), namely the overall ceiling of £15,000. In circumstances in which the estimates placed before the judge of the costs of the distributors were about £18,000, of the dealers were about £24,000 and of the hire-purchase company itself referable to the counterclaim were about £9,000, the hire-purchase company alleges that, in imposing a ceiling of £15,000 upon its recovery against Mr Bolton, the judge exceeded the generous ambit of his discretion.

[6] The story begins in April 1995 when Mr Bolton informed the dealers that he wanted to buy a new SEAT Cordoba 1.6 CLX motor car on hire purchase. SEAT cars are manufactured in Spain, in effect by Volkswagen. The dealers arranged the purchase through the hire-purchase company. So the dealers bought the car from the distributors and sold it to the hire-purchase company, who leased it to Mr Bolton; and in May 1995 Mr Bolton took delivery of it. It had then travelled 30 miles.

[7] Mr Bolton, including his family, used the car extensively. By May 1996 he had travelled over 21,000 miles in it; and by May 2000 he had travelled 110,000 miles in it.

[8] In the years following his acquisition of the car, Mr Bolton had a number of problems with its brakes. Inspections and repairs were undertaken. Late in 1996 he complained to the dealers about an alleged design fault in the brakes. The dealers caused an officer of the distributors' technical division to inspect it. There the matter seemed to rest.

[9] In January 1998 Mr Bolton ceased to make his monthly payments to the hire-purchase company. He had come to the view that the new car which he had contracted to buy in April 1995 on hire purchase should have been fitted with an air bag and an air-conditioning unit. By letter dated 14 May 1998, SEAT UK disabused him of the validity of that view. But, erroneously (as it was later to transpire), it added that, though bought in April 1995, the car that was sold to him would have been built to the specification set in June 1994. Mr Bolton later

a   discovered that under such specification the car should have been fitted with a sun roof and with a driver's seat the height of which was adjustable. In the interim, however, namely with effect from July 1998, he resumed payments to the hire-purchase company. He again stopped making such payments in January 1999.

b   [10] In July 1999 the hire-purchase company issued the proceedings against Mr Bolton in the Reading County Court in respect of arrears of instalments. The claim was for £917. By his defence in August 1999, Mr Bolton correctly pointed out that there had been a duplication in the calculation of the claim amounting to £266, which reduced it to £651. Indeed, following the issue of the proceedings, he paid a further £300 against what was owed, thereby reducing it to £351. More importantly Mr Bolton filed a counterclaim for damages not exceeding £10,000,

c   by which he claimed that: (a) in lacking a sun roof and an adjustable driver's seat, the car was not in accordance with the specification for which he had contracted; and (b) in relation to problems with the brakes, rear wheel bearings and wiring faults in the boot, the car had been neither of merchantable quality nor fit for its purpose at the time of its acquisition in 1995.

d   [11] The hire-purchase company filed a defence to the counterclaim. For obvious reasons it had no internal knowledge of the matters raised in the counterclaim. Before, however, issuing proceedings under Pt 20 against the dealers, it sought to compromise the litigation with Mr Bolton. By letters in January 2000, expressly made under CPR Pt 36, Mr Bolton, through his then solicitors, offered to settle the litigation for a net payment to him of £3,000 and,

e   by contrast, the hire-purchase company offered to settle it on the basis that neither party should make any payment to the other. Neither offer was acceptable to the other. Thereupon, namely in April 2000, the hire-purchase company issued Pt 20 proceedings against the dealers. This move prompted the proceedings issued in July 2000 by the dealers, again under Pt 20, against the

f   distributors. By these successive proceedings, Mr Bolton's complaints about the nature and quality of the car which he had acquired over four years earlier were passed down the contractual line for the distributors to answer.

[12] Following issue of its proceedings, the hire-purchase company's claim had been allocated to the fast track. In July 2000, however, that company,

g   apparently worried by the escalation of costs, issued an application for the proceedings to be re-allocated to the small claims track. It argued that, even on Mr Bolton's case, his counterclaim had a value of not more than £5,000. It seems that it was the dealers who opposed re-allocation to the small claims track. At all events the district judge directed that the proceedings should remain in the fast track and indeed that, in the event of failure to reach agreement, whether

h   between the experts who had by then been consulted on behalf of Mr Bolton and of the two Pt 20 defendants referable to the matters raised by the counterclaim or between Mr Bolton and the hire-purchase company referable to the amount of the claim, the proceedings should be re-allocated to the multi-track.

[13] In November 2000 Mr Bolton wrote to the effect that he refused to agree

j   the amount of the claim against him and that he had instructed his expert not to consider material produced (as he said, late) by the expert for the Pt 20 defendants. The result was that the proceedings were indeed re-allocated to the multi-track, down which they travelled to hearing and judgment on 7, 8 and 9 March 2001. Separate counsel appeared for the hire-purchase company, the dealers and the distributors. Mr Bolton, by then without public funding, appeared in person.

[14] By his substantive judgment dated 8 March, the judge, without difficulty, computed the value of the claim at £351. The difficulties for Mr Bolton in advancing a counterclaim about the nature or quality of a car purchased over four years earlier and after he had travelled over 100,000 miles in it were obvious. In fact when, outside court, the two experts were at last in a position to discuss matters, they agreed that in 1995 the car had been fit for its purpose and of merchantable quality. Further evidence from the distributors led them and the judge to accept that, contrary to the letter from SEAT UK dated 14 May 1998, neither a sun roof nor an adjustable driver's seat was within the specification of the model offered for sale to the public and sold to Mr Bolton in April 1995. So, at the end of the second day of the hearing, for those reasons alone, the judge dismissed the counterclaim.

[15] On the third day the judge addressed the issues of costs. Before him had been placed the three estimates of costs referable to the counterclaim and to its consequential proceedings under Pt 20, to which I have already referred and which amounted in all to about £51,000.

[16] Early in his substantive judgment at the end of the second day, the judge had, reasonably, used strong language by which to draw attention to the disparity between the costs incurred and the sums at stake in the proceedings. He said:

'Unfortunately, because there was a counterclaim made, which was limited in its amount to £10,000 in total, the finance company joined in the garage, the garage have joined in the manufacturers and, on the basis of what has been put before me up to now in respect of costs, we have a situation where we have costs claims before me of something of the order of over £50,000. On top of that there is whatever Mr Bolton may have personally expended on his solicitors and, on top of that, whatever has been paid under the legal aid scheme, as it then was, to those solicitors. I have to say that it is a very unattractive situation in which we find ourselves, where somebody is going to pick up bills for something of the order of £50,000 in costs—whether that turns out to be Mr Bolton or whether it turns out to be to be one of the other parties to the proceedings, but however the cake is cut, there is still that amount of money which has been spent on a debt which started on a claim of just under £1,000. It has been accepted it was overcalculated because of a double charge for fees, and should have been started at £651, in respect of which £300 has since been paid. I do not know what anybody who is not a lawyer sitting in this court could be thinking about when they hear that, for sake of £350 outstanding, somebody is picking up bills totalling over £50,000. It is a monstrous situation. But that is the position in which I am told we find ourselves here.'

[17] In his judgment on costs the judge first addressed the distributors' claim for costs and decided that, notwithstanding that the letter dated 14 May 1998, for which they had in effect been responsible, had been the source of protracted confusion, they should be paid their costs. He also decided that the dealers should be paid their costs. But by whom should the costs of the distributors and the dealers be paid? The hire-purchase company argued that in each case any order for such costs should be made directly against Mr Bolton. But the distributors and the dealers each argued that any such order should go up the line, i e that the costs of the distributors be paid by the dealers and that the costs of the latter be paid by the hire-purchase company.

[18] Accepting that he had a discretion to favour either route, the judge chose the latter. He held that, in that it had been reasonable for the dealers to join the distributors, the costs awarded to them against the hire-purchase company should include the costs payable by them to the distributors. Of the costs payable under each of these two orders, he directed detailed assessment on the standard basis. He added:

> 'I have remarked on the size of the bills. As I have said already, and I repeat for the sake of clarity, they do look high. They certainly look high against the amounts which are at stake. But that does not mean to say that they are not justifiable. That is a matter which the district judge will have to determine. I leave to the district judge the determination of the question of whether or not they should be reduced having regard to the overall requirement that costs should bear some relative resemblance to the claim which they are being incurred to meet.'

[19] Then the judge addressed the claim for costs made by the hire-purchase company against Mr Bolton referable to the counterclaim, it being in effect agreed that it should receive only fixed costs referable to the claim. The judge concluded that, in that Mr Bolton had lost the counterclaim, it was clearly right in principle that he should pay the hire-purchase company its costs thereof on the standard basis. He reminded himself of the statutory protection for Mr Bolton referable to costs incurred while he was publicly funded. He concluded that it had been reasonable for the hire-purchase company to issue proceedings under Pt 20 against the dealers, with the result that such costs as were awarded to the hire-purchase company should include such costs as it was required to pay to the dealers. He continued as follows:

> 'The only remaining question is whether or not I should have regard to any sort of limit on the costs, because I do have to take into account the various circumstances which are set out in CPR 44.3 with regard to costs. For example, conduct of the parties, whether a party has succeeded in part of his case, and so forth. I also can, under r 44.3(6), make an order which is a power of limiting the costs in some way. It does seem to me that it is right that I should do that in this case. I am concerned about the fact that all this expense has been incurred. Whilst I have to acknowledge that I cannot say that Hammants, nor Volkswagen, or either of them, should not have been joined into the proceedings, it does seem to me that, in doing so, and in the general conduct of these proceedings, the costs have been allowed to escalate out of proportion to the amounts at stake. It seems to me that it is right, in dealing with a litigant—and this is not just a case of because Mr Bolton is in person and is clearly not a man of means—that I make this decision. But it does seem to me that there ought to be an overall limit on his liability. I would put that at the sum of £15,000. In doing that, I have related that to the amounts which are said to have been at stake on the counterclaim and also the fact of the number of parties involved.'

[20] From that passage I collect two reasons for the judge's imposition of the ceiling of £15,000. The main reason was that 'the costs have been allowed to escalate out of proportion to the amounts at stake'. But the judge added: ' ... this is not just a case of because Mr Bolton is in person and is clearly not a man of means ...'

[21] The use of the word 'just' suggests to me that Mr Bolton's perceived lack of means was a subsidiary reason for the decision.

[22] One of the major points made on behalf of the hire-purchase company in this appeal is that there is an anomaly written across this part of the judge's order. He was, in reality, addressing three sets of costs for which ultimately Mr Bolton was to be liable; and his concern was that they had escalated out of proportion to the amounts at stake. Yet, *if* it was appropriate for him so to do, the judge allowed for this factor against only one of the successful parties, being, I might add, that party whose estimate of costs was lowest. The costs payable to the distributors and to the dealers, both in effect by the hire-purchase company, were not the subject of a ceiling; but those payable to the hire-purchase company were the subject of a ceiling and at first sight a very low one. If, for the sake of argument, this was the appropriate mechanism by which the judge would cut out such costs as were out of proportion to the amounts at stake, the effect was that the costs of the distributors and of the dealers escaped his knife and that the consequence of any lack of proportionality in the amount of their costs was visited upon the hire-purchase company.

[23] The judge was right to conclude that the normal principle is that the costs of successful defendants brought in under what is now Pt 20 of the CPR pass up the line to the principal defendant: see *Johnson v Ribbins (Sir Francis Pittis & Son (a firm), third party)* [1977] 1 All ER 806, [1977] 1 WLR 1458. Indeed in the present type of case it can be argued that, in the configuration of contracts entered into in April 1995, it was the hire-purchase company who chose to enter into a contract with the private individual with all the attendant risks of irrecoverability of the costs of any forensic conflict with him.   Nevertheless, had it been appropriate for the judge to have placed some ceiling on Mr Bolton's liability for the three sets of costs, there was a strong argument that his discretion should have been so exercised as to make the three orders for costs directly against him, each the subject of a ceiling in terms of a figure or a percentage.

[24] The bigger question, however, is whether any ceiling was appropriate at all.

[25] In this regard it is necessary to address certain of the provisions in r 44.3, as indeed the judge purported to do. As he rightly observed, the general discretion to make an order for costs under para (1) includes, by virtue of para (6)(b), an order for 'a stated amount in respect of another party's costs'. There has been discussion this morning as to whether those words are apt to cover an order for detailed assessment subject to the ceiling of a stated amount. It may be that, on a strict view, they are not thus apt. But para (6) identifies seven types of order which the general discretion under para (1), derived from s 51(1) of the Supreme Court Act 1981, is said only to 'include'. Paragraph (1)(b) of r 44.3 provides that the court has discretion as to the amount of costs payable by one party to another; and I have no doubt that a court can properly identify the amount thus payable as being such costs as are calculated by detailed assessment but subject to a quantified ceiling. So in my view the judge had ample discretion to make the order which he did.

[26] But the manner by which such discretion should be exercised is subject to other paragraphs of the rule. The starting point is to be collected from para (2):

'If the court decides to make an order about costs—(a) the general rule is that the unsuccessful party will be ordered to pay the costs of the successful party; but (b) the court may make a different order.'

a

[**27**] Paragraph (4) provides:

> 'In deciding what order (if any) to make about costs, the court must have regard to all the circumstances, including—(a) the conduct of all the parties; (b) whether a party has succeeded on part of his case, even if he has not been wholly successful; and (c) any payment into court or admissible offer to settle made by a party which is drawn to the court's attention (whether or not made in accordance with Part 36).'

b

[**28**] The reference to the conduct of the parties in para (4)(a) is amplified in para (5) in terms which it is unnecessary to set out.

[**29**] One of Miss Bailey's complaints on behalf of the hire-purchase company is that the judge failed to discharge his duty under para (4). She says in particular

c

that he failed to advert to the fact, which was clearly brought to his attention, that in January 2000, before the significant costs had been incurred, Mr Bolton had refused to accept the Pt 36 offer of her client, whereunder both claim and counterclaim be discontinued with no order for costs. In my view there is considerable force in that point. Although para (4) does not purport to provide a

d

comprehensive definition of the circumstances relevant to the exercise of the discretion, a proper consideration of all three factors there particularised affords no ammunition whatever for Mr Bolton in opposing full application of the general rule.

[**30**] In my view, however, there is a more fundamental objection to the judge's imposition of the ceiling. The objection is born of the fact that he had

e

already ordered that all three sets of the costs of the successful parties be subject to detailed assessment on the standard basis. What then is the standard basis under the CPR? Rule 44.4 provides as follows:

> '(1) Where the court is to assess the amount of costs (whether by summary

f

> or detailed assessment) it will assess those costs—(a) on the standard basis; or (b) on the indemnity basis, but the court will not in either case allow costs which have been unreasonably incurred or are unreasonable in amount …
>
> (2) Where the amount of costs is to be assessed on the standard basis, the court will—(a) only allow costs which are proportionate to the matters in issue; and (b) resolve any doubt which it may have as to whether costs were

g

> reasonably incurred or reasonable and proportionate in amount in favour of the paying party.'

[**31**] Therefore, under the standard basis, costs can be allowed only if they are proportionate to the matters in issue. That means, as is made clear by r 44.5(1)(a), that both the nature of the work in respect of which the costs were incurred and

h

the amount of such costs must be proportionate.

[**32**] Section 11.1 of the practice direction (CPR PD 44) supplementary to Pt 44 explains the operation in this respect of rr 44.4 and 44.5:

> 'In applying the test of proportionality the court will have regard to

j

> rule 1.1(2)(c). The relationship between the total of the costs incurred and the financial value of the claim may not be a reliable guide. A fixed percentage cannot be applied in all cases to the value of the claim in order to ascertain whether or not the costs are proportionate.'

[**33**] Rule 1.1(2)(c) provides that dealing with a case justly, in accordance with the overriding objective of the rules, includes, so far as is practicable—

'dealing with the case in ways which are proportionate—(i) to the amount
of money involved; (ii) to the importance of the case; (iii) to the complexity
of the issues; and (iv) to the financial position of each party ...'

[34] Thus the principal effect of the judge's decision, clearly correct, to direct
assessments of costs on the standard, rather than the indemnity, basis was to
require the costs assessor to disallow costs which, on an overall rather than
mechanical view, were disproportionate to the matters in issue and indeed to
disallow them if he remained in doubt on the point. Interestingly, even the
financial position of Mr Bolton was, to some extent, to figure in that inquiry by
virtue of r 1.1(2)(c)(iv).

[35] In the course of argument Waller LJ canvassed with Miss Bailey whether
it could be considered proportionate to the matters in issue for her client and both
the Pt 20 defendants all to have briefed separate counsel for the hearing.
Miss Bailey indicated that there were, or may have been, conflicts which required
the three parties to have separate representation. Nevertheless that is the sort of
feature to which I would expect any inquiry into proportionality to pay close
regard.

[36] It follows, in my view, that the ceiling of £15,000 imposed by the judge
was, with respect, unprincipled. It purported to make allowance for perceived
lack of proportion in the amount of the costs in circumstances where his
directions for standard assessments had already made full allowance for any such
lack of proportion. The ceiling would have effect only to the extent that the costs
assessor had been satisfied that costs which were proportionate to the matters in
issue had been incurred in a sum exceeding £15,000. The effect of the ceiling
would in that event be to excise from Mr Bolton's liability the excess element of
the proportionate costs and would thus be contrary to the judge's primary reason
for imposing it. Furthermore, to the limited, and in my view controversial,
extent to which it was proper for the judge also to have regard to Mr Bolton's
perceived lack of means, that factor would also figure in the assessor's appraisal
of proportionality.

[37] Mr Bolton has filed a respondent's notice by which he seeks to uphold the
judge's ceiling by reference to arguments not referred to by the judge.

[38] Mr Bolton, who has appeared, as he did before the judge, in person before
us and who has addressed us with great clarity and civility, complains, first of all,
that the hire-purchase company failed to comply with the majority of the
interlocutory directions which had been made in the proceedings. The only clear
example of this alleged default is its failure to serve its expert's report and
statements from its witnesses of fact and to give disclosure within various dates
prior to 22 December 1999 which had been set in an order dated 14 October 1999.
That related to the period prior to the issue of the Pt 20 proceedings; and it must
not be forgotten that the hire-purchase company had no internal knowledge of
the matters raised in the counterclaim. Indeed it is clear that during the period of
that delay it was making what may now be seen to have been a very reasonable
offer to settle the proceedings prior to any significant proliferation of costs. In my
view it cannot be said that its failure to meet those deadlines had any significant
impact on the development of the litigation.

[39] Mr Bolton's other arguments are that, in seeking at a hearing in February
2000 to obtain permission to issue its Pt 20 proceedings against the dealers, the
hire-purchase company misrepresented part of the procedural history to the
district judge and that, having secured such permission, it failed by some three

a weeks to issue the proceedings within the time which he set. These might have
been regarded as insubstantial points, not related to the proliferation of costs, had
it not been for a suggestion by Mr Bolton, hotly disputed by the hire-purchase
company, that the misrepresentation, if such it was, was deliberate and that its
failure to issue within the time set, which is far from established to my
satisfaction, was sought to be masked by a fax document which the hire-purchase
b company forged. These two suggestions of serious forensic misconduct were
articulated by Mr Bolton before the judge. Had they been established to his
satisfaction, they would, I have no doubt, have figured in his judgment and
probably have been reflected to some extent in his award. In my view it is
impossible for this court to proceed on the footing of the accuracy of those
suggestions.

c
[**40**] I therefore propose that this appeal be allowed and that the provision
which imposed the ceiling of £15,000 upon Mr Bolton's liability for costs be set
aside.

[**41**] It remains for me only to add a footnote arising from the fact, of which
Miss Bailey told us this morning, that a detailed assessment of the costs of the
d dealers was purported to be conducted by a district judge on 2 November 2001.
The purported assessment has resulted in a certificate that the hire-purchase
company is obliged to pay the dealers' costs in a sum of about £17,000.

[**42**] The assessment seems to me to be both curious and unfortunate.

[**43**] It is curious because, as Miss Bailey assures us, it does not purport to
e include the liability of the dealers for the costs of the distributors, which of course
fall, under the order of the circuit judge, to be included in the sum payable to the
dealers by the hire-purchase company. In other words the district judge was
presumably addressing a bill in a total analogous to the estimate of £24,000 placed
by the dealers before the circuit judge; and the effect of his assessment was
f apparently to reduce that bill by about £7,000. This court is not in a position to
comment upon whether such a reduction properly reflects the exercise which fell
to be undertaken by the district judge, particularly with regard to proportionality.

[**44**] The assessment is also unfortunate because Mr Bolton tells us that he was
given no notice of it; and that the bill of costs which was the foundation of it was
never served upon him. It would have been clear to the district judge, from
g perusal of the circuit judge's order, that in principle the ultimate payer of all the
costs was Mr Bolton. So, whether or not he was aware that the ceiling imposed
by the circuit judge was under appeal, the district judge should, in my view, have
ordered that Mr Bolton be treated as a 'relevant person' within r 47.6(2) and
section 32.10(1)(c) of the practice direction supplementary to it. As such a person,
h he should have been served by the dealers with notice of commencement and
with their bill and, in the event of his serving points of dispute, he should have
been given notice of the assessment hearing.

[**45**] I also consider that it would have been far preferable for the district judge
to consider the matters of proportionality and of reasonableness in a
j contemporaneous assessment of all sets of costs of the three successful parties. It
is unclear why, for example, the costs of the distributors have not been the
subject of assessment. It goes without saying that, if such is to be explained by
reference to some agreement as to the amount of their costs reached with the
dealers and with the hire-purchase company, Mr Bolton, who has not been party
to it, would still in any event be entitled to the protection of a detailed assessment.

[46] In the above circumstances, and on the basis that the asserted absence of service on Mr Bolton is true, I would expect the circuit judge to be receptive to an application by Mr Bolton for permission to appeal against the assessment and for an extension of time for doing so.

a

RIX LJ.

[47] I agree. The judge, by his order for costs, in the knowledge that some *b* £50,000 had been estimated as incurred in costs by the hire-purchase company, the dealer and the distributor, permitted full recovery by the dealer and the distributor, for whose costs the hire-purchase company would become liable, but prevented the hire-purchase company from recovering any more than a maximum of £15,000 against Mr Bolton.

c

[48] Whatever justice this may have done to Mr Bolton, it was a prima facie injustice to the hire-purchase company as between it and the dealer and the distributor, unless perchance the judge had been able to conclude that, and had articulated reasons why, the litigation had been conducted in such a way as to justify such a prima facie anomaly. But he articulated no reasons to explain this anomaly.

d

[49] In making such an order for costs, CPR 44.3(4) requires the judge ('must') have regard to all circumstances, including the conduct of all the parties and any admissible offer to settle made by a party which is drawn to the court's attention.

[50] However, the judge, in that part at the end of his judgment on costs in which he imposed the £15,000 ceiling, made no criticism of the hire-purchase *e* company's conduct, nor did he take into account Mr Bolton's threefold refusal to accept a drop-hands offer made to him at an early stage by the hire-purchase company. Nor did the judge have regard to the facts (a) that the hire-purchase company's estimate of costs was substantially less than the estimate of either the dealer or the distributor, and (b) that, on the merits of Mr Bolton's counterclaim, the hire-purchase company was merely piggy in the middle and *f* that the real dispute involved the dealer and the distributor.

[51] In these circumstances the judge failed, in my judgment, to take into account all that he was required to take into account, and arrived at an order for costs which was wholly unreasonable and unjust as against the hire-purchase company.

g

[52] For these reasons, in addition to those given by my Lord, I would allow this appeal and remove the £15,000 ceiling contained in the judge's order.

[53] The question of proportionality, as well as that of the reasonableness of the costs claimed, all rolled up as they are into the hire-purchase company's costs, must, in the event, be resolved at the assessment stage. In that connection I hope *h* that the assessment of the dealer's costs will prove to be no ultimate impediment to a fair and just resolution of the ultimate assessment of all the parties' costs which Mr Bolton will have to pay.

WALLER LJ.   *j*

[54] I also agree that, having allowed for the recovery of costs up the chain, as the judge had done, without any cap on any individual claim, it was wholly wrong to cap the recovery of the hire-purchase company so far as Mr Bolton was concerned, and I agree with the reasons given by both Wilson J and Rix LJ for that result.

a [55] I would just add, however, a word on an aspect which has concerned me and which relates to the footnote to the judgment of Wilson J.

[56] Where litigation has involved a chain of CPR Pt 20 parties, and where costs orders are made up a chain, with a final order being made incorporating all those costs against one party, two things seem to me to be obvious. First, when making an assessment of those costs, where questions of proportionality and *b* reasonableness will arise, all such costs should be assessed together. Second, it seems to me to be obvious that the ultimate payer has the most interest in arguing questions of reasonableness or questions of proportionality.

[57] Now, without the final costs certificate that we were shown this morning in relation to the dealer's costs, there would be no difficulty in dealing with these costs in accordance with those obvious points. But what of this final cost *c* certificate? Does it place any impediment? It seems to me that one might rely on CPR 3.1(7). That is a provision which says: 'A power of the court under these Rules to make an order includes a power to vary or revoke the order.'

[58] I cannot find referred to in the notes to the CPR, a decision which I understand to exist of Neuberger J's, which essentially says that you cannot *d* construe that power as allowing any court at any time simply to reverse itself if it happens to change its mind. With respect I follow the logic of that decision, and I am not seeking to suggest that there is anything wrong with Neuberger J's view.

[59] But where, as in this case, one has a situation where one party was not present when the assessment took place, and was indeed, as I have sought to suggest, the party with the most interest in being entitled to argue about *e* proportionality and reasonableness, it seems to me possible that r 3.1(7) could be invoked. I would suggest indeed that the parties should be sensible, and see the logic that Mr Bolton should have been present, and should go, by agreement, before the district judge to set aside that final certificate.

[60] If the parties cannot agree, or if the district judge cannot be persuaded to *f* use that power, then I agree with Wilson J that the only other course is for there to be an appeal from that order. Again I would hope that a circuit judge would give permission to appeal, even if it is out of time, having regard to the fact that Mr Bolton only heard of the existence of that final costs order today when the matter was produced before us.

g [61] The position then should be that the costs judge should be able to consider all the bills of the distributor, the dealer and the hire-purchase company together, and should be able to consider questions of proportionality and reasonableness, and should, in particular, be able to consider whether it was really right that three lots of lawyers were necessary to be present to fight this case against Mr Bolton.

h [62] I perhaps should add one footnote to this footnote, which is that, of course, as the judge was concerned about the enormity of costs that were incurred in relation to a very small claim, I, too, am concerned that by inviting a further process of assessment of costs, one is inviting a further incurring of costs in relation to the assessment of costs in relation to the fighting of a very small *j* claim. Maybe the only answer to that is for the parties to consider the questions of proportionality and reasonableness for themselves, and consider whether it is not possible to reach some form of agreement in relation to costs so that those further costs are not incurred.

[63] That, I should say, would only be possible if Mr Bolton sees, as I suggest he should see, that if he had accepted a CPR Pt 36 offer now many months ago,

all these costs could have been saved, and we would not be here today. Thus he
would have to accept that a considerable proportion of the costs must be borne *a*
by him.

Appeal allowed.

James Brooks   Barrister.

a
Warriner v Warriner
[2002] EWCA Civ 81

COURT OF APPEAL, CIVIL DIVISION
MUMMERY, LATHAM AND DYSON LJJ
b 24 JANUARY 2002

Damages – Personal injury – Amount of damages – Discount rate for future pecuniary loss – Statutory provision permitting court to take into account rate of return different from that prescribed by Lord Chancellor if it were 'more appropriate to the case in question' – Meaning of 'more appropriate in the case in question' – Damages Act 1996, s 1 – Damages (Personal Injury) Order 2001.

c

After suffering serious brain damage in an accident, the claimant, who had a life expectancy of a further 46 years, brought a claim for damages in excess of £3m—a sum based on a discount rate of 2%. Under s 1(1)[a] of the Damages Act 1996, the
d court was required, when determining the rate to be expected from the investment of a sum awarded as damages for future pecuniary loss in an action for personal injury, to take into account such rate of return as might from time to time be prescribed by the Lord Chancellor. Section 1(2) provided that sub-s (1) did not prevent the court taking a different rate of return into account if any party to the proceedings showed that it was 'more appropriate to the case in question'.
e Pursuant to s 1(1), the Lord Chancellor prescribed a single discount rate of 2.5%. In setting that rate, the Lord Chancellor stated that it would eliminate the scope for uncertainty and argument about the applicable rate, and that he particularly had in mind larger awards that were intended to cover longer periods. At a case management conference, the judge made an order permitting the claimant to
f adduce an expert report which concluded that 2% was the more appropriate discount rate for the quantification of her future losses. The defendant appealed, contending that the report did not raise a prima facie case for a rate of 2% rather than 2.5%. The claimant contended that a lower rate was appropriate because of her long life expectancy and the size of her claim. In considering those submissions, the Court of Appeal was required to provide guidance as to the
g meaning of the phrase 'more appropriate in the case in question' in s 1(2) of the 1996 Act.

Held – In deciding whether a rate different from that prescribed by the Lord Chancellor in the 2001 order was 'more appropriate in the case in question'
h within the meaning of s 1(2) of the 1996 Act, the court had to have regard to the reasons given by him in arriving at that rate. If the case in question fell into a category that the Lord Chancellor had taken into account and/or there were special features of the case which (i) were material to the choice of the rate of return and (ii) were shown, from an examination of the Lord Chancellor's
j reasons, not to have been taken into account, then a different rate of return might be 'more appropriate'. If s 1(2) were construed in that way, it was likely that there would be comparatively few cases in which that provision would be successfully invoked, at least while the 2.5% rate and the Lord Chancellor's reasons for it continued to apply. Such a construction accorded with and promoted the policy

---

a   Section 1, so far as material, is set out at [9], below

considerations which informed the Lord Chancellor's decision to choose the single rate of 2.5%, namely that the certainty of such a rate was desirable, that it would facilitate settlements and that it would result in saving the expense of expert evidence at trial. In the instant case, the circumstances relied upon by the claimant were not sufficient, even arguably, to justify applying a discount rate of 2% rather than 2.5%. Claims by claimants with life expectancies of between 30 and 50 years were not uncommon. Nor were claims in the range of £2m to £3m. Claims of that kind were included in the category which the Lord Chancellor particularly had in mind when setting the rate at 2.5%, and the expert report had not identified any special features which took the case outside the classes of case that the Lord Chancellor had taken into account. Accordingly, the appeal would be allowed (see [33], [35], [37], [39]–[41], [43]–[47], below).

Wells v Wells, Thomas v Brighton Health Authority, Page v Sheerness Steel Co plc [1998] 3 All ER 481 and *Warren v Northern General Hospital NHS Trust (No 2)* [2000] 1 WLR 1404 considered.

Notes
For calculating future pecuniary loss in personal injury cases, see 12(1) *Halsbury's Laws* (4th edn reissue) para 881.

For the Damages Act 1996, s 1, see 13 *Halsbury's Statutes* (4th edn) (2000 reissue) 616.

For the Damages (Personal Injury) Order 2001, see 5 *Halsbury's Statutory Instruments* (2002 issue) 482.

Cases referred to in judgments
Warren v Northern General Hospital NHS Trust (No 2) [2000] 1 WLR 1404, CA.
Wells v Wells, Thomas v Brighton Health Authority, Page v Sheerness Steel Co plc [1998] 3 All ER 481, [1999] 1 AC 345, [1998] 3 WLR 329, HL.

Cases also cited or referred to in skeleton arguments
Butani v Camden London BC [2000] CA Transcript 1112, CA.
Page v Smith [1995] 2 All ER 736, [1996] AC 155, [1995] 2 WLR 644, HL.
Skrine & Co v Euromoney Publications plc [2001] EWCA Civ 1479, [2001] All ER (D) 134 (Oct).
Thomas v Wignall [1987] 1 All ER 1185, [1987] QB 1098, [1987] 2 WLR 930, CA.
Van Oudenhoven v Griffin Inns Ltd [2000] 1 WLR 1413, CA.

Appeal
The defendant, Geoffrey Warriner, appealed from the order of Judge Murphy QC, sitting as a judge of the High Court on 22 October 2001, permitting the parties to adduce expert forensic accountancy evidence in relation to the discount rate to be applied in a claim for damages for personal injury brought by the claimant, Dianna Wendy Warriner. The facts are set out in the judgment of Dyson LJ.

John Leighton Williams QC and *Anthony Seys Llewellyn* (instructed by *Beachcroft Wansbroughs*) for the defendant.
Laura Cox QC and *Patricia Hitchcock* (instructed by *Irwin Mitchell*, Sheffield) for the claimant.

MUMMERY LJ.
[1] I will ask Dyson LJ to give the first judgment.

DYSON LJ.

a

[2] The claimant suffered serious brain damage in a road traffic accident on 20 February 1998. It is said on her behalf that she currently has a life expectancy of 46 years. Her affairs are now administered by the Court of Protection. She commenced proceedings against the defendant in 1998. The defendant has admitted liability, but quantum remains in issue.

b

[3] A case management conference was held on 22 October 2001 by Judge Murphy QC sitting as a deputy judge of the High Court. The claimant wished to rely on the expert evidence of Mr Hogg dated 19 October 2001. In his report, Mr Hogg states that in his opinion multipliers assessed on the basis of a 2·5% discount rate are unfair for claimants who are awarded large sums of damages which are expected to compensate them for future losses over a long period of

c

time. It is his opinion that in cases such as that of this claimant, the appropriate discount rate for the quantification of future losses is 2%, and not 2·5%, the figure stated by Lord Irvine of Lairg LC in the Damages (Personal Injury) Order 2001, SI 2001/2301 (the 2001 order) that was made on 25 June 2001, and to which I shall come shortly. Mr Hogg's report was first disclosed to the defendant at the

d

hearing of the case management conference. The judge made various case management decisions. These included an order that:

'1. Evidence from a forensic accountant being necessary, the parties have permission to adduce evidence from forensic accountants dealing with the issue of the discount rates to be applied when assessing future loss

e

multipliers.'

[4] Mr Hogg's report was duly served on the defendant on 22 October.

[5] The defendant had objected to the order permitting forensic accountancy evidence in relation to the discount rate issue on the grounds that the application was too late. It was said that it was wrong to allow evidence on an issue of such

f

great importance and complexity to be admitted so shortly before the trial, which at that time was due to start on 14 November. No objection was taken on 22 October on the basis that the evidence should not have been admitted because it did not support a case that had real prospects of success that the discount rate should be 2% rather than 2·5%.

g

[6] On 26 October, the claimant served a revised schedule of damages based on a 2% discount rate. The schedule pleads substantial sums under heads which are typical for this type of case, including claims for the cost of future care and for loss of future earnings. On the basis of a 2% discount rate, the total sum claimed is in excess of £3m. On any view, this is a substantial claim. It was conceded on behalf of the defendant before the judge that it was worth more than £1m.

h

[7] On 29 October, an application was made to the judge on behalf of the defendant that he should reconsider his decision to permit evidence from expert accountants as to the correct discount rate. But the judge held that, since the order of 22 October had been drawn up, he had no jurisdiction to reconsider the matter. It is clear, however, that even if he had reconsidered the matter, he

j

would not have reached a different conclusion, since he refused the defendant permission to appeal his earlier decision. He gave these reasons for refusing permission to appeal:

'The claimant asserted that this was an exceptional case for the purposes of the discount rate to be applied. Section 1(2) of the Act contemplates there being exceptional cases. The difference in damages could be as much as

£500,000. I gave permission for the evidence to be heard and permitted the [defendant] reasonable time for obtaining [his] own expert. Overriding principle applies.'

[8] He adjourned the hearing of the trial of quantum until February 2002. The defendant was later given permission to appeal against the decision of 22 October by Hale LJ.

[9] The Act to which the judge was referring was the Damages Act 1996, which so far as material provides:

'1.—(1) In determining the return to be expected from the investment of a sum awarded as damages for future pecuniary loss in an action for personal injury the court shall, subject to and in accordance with the rules of court made for the purposes of this section, take into account such rate of return (if any) as may from time to time be prescribed by an order made by the Lord Chancellor.

(2) Subsection (1) above shall not however prevent the court taking a different rate of return into account if any party to the proceedings shows that it is more appropriate in the case in question.'

[10] As I have said, on 25 June 2001 Lord Irvine LC made the 2001 order prescribing a rate of 2·5%. His reasons for selecting that figure were published on 27 June. The following day, an error in calculating the figure for the three-year average yield on index-linked government stock (ILGS) which formed an important part of Lord Irvine LC's decision was brought to his attention. On 27 July, Lord Irvine LC published fresh reasons for the figure of 2·5% based on the accurate three-year average yield.

[11] It is necessary to refer to some passages in Lord Irvine's reasons. He said that he had decided to set a single rate to cover all cases:

'It will eliminate scope for uncertainty and argument about the applicable rate. Similarly, I consider it is preferable to have a fixed rate, which promotes certainty and which avoids the complexity and extra costs that a formula would entail ...'

[12] He recognised that the rate would be bound to be applied in a range of different circumstances over a period of time: that was why he set the rate to the nearest 0·5%. He said that he had decided that he should—

'set a rate which should obtain for the foreseeable future. I consider it would be very detrimental to the reasonable certainty which is necessary to promote the just and efficient resolution of disputes (by settlement as well as by hearing in court) to make frequent changes to the discount rate. Therefore, whilst I will remain ready to review the discount rate whenever I find there is a significant and established change in the relevant real rates of return to be expected, I do not propose to tinker with the rate frequently to take account of every transient shift in market conditions.'

[13] Later he said:

'Setting a single rate to cover all cases, whilst highly desirable for the reasons given above, has the effect that the discount rate has to cover a wide variety of different cases, and claimants with widely differing personal and financial characteristics. Moreover, as has become clear from the consultation exercise (including responses by expert financial analysts to questions which

a

I posed them), the real rate of return on investments of any character (including investments in Index-Linked Government Securities) involves making assumptions for the future about a wide variety of factors affecting the economy as a whole, including for example the likely rate of inflation. In these circumstances, it is inevitable that any approach to setting the discount rate must be fairly broad-brush. Put shortly, there can be no single "right"

b

answer as to what rate should be set. Since it is in the context of larger awards, intended to cover longer periods, that there is the greatest risk of serious discrepancies between the level of compensation and the actual losses incurred if the discount rate set it not appropriate, I have had this type of award particularly in mind when considering the level at which the discount rate should be set.'

c

[14] Lord Irvine LC then explained in some detail why he had alighted on 2.5% rather than any other rate. He took a simple average of ILGS yields at an assumed rate of inflation of 3%, and arrived at an average gross yield of 2·46%. He concluded, therefore, that the net average yield on ILGS as adjusted to take account of tax lies in the range of 2% to 2·5%. Given that the rate was to be set

d

to the nearest 0·5%, the choice lay between 2% and 2·5%. He then explained in detail why he opted for 2·5% rather than 2%. In summary, he gave these reasons: (a) the market in ILGS was at present distorted, so that the prevailing yields were artificially low; (b) the Court of Protection, even in the wake of the decision of the House of Lords in *Wells v Wells, Thomas v Brighton Health Authority, Page v*

e

Sheerness Steel Co plc [1998] 3 All ER 481, [1999] 1 AC 345 had continued to invest on behalf of claimants in multi-asset portfolios, such that real rates of return well in excess of 2·5% could be expected; and (c) it was likely that 'real' claimants with large awards of compensation would not be advised to invest solely or even primarily in ILGS, but rather in a mixed portfolio.

[15] Finally Lord Irvine said:

f

'Finally, in deciding that a single rate of 2.5% should have been set by me on 25 June 2001, I have borne in mind that it will, of course, remain open for the Courts under section 1(2) of the Damages Act 1996 to adopt a different rate in any particular case if there are exceptional circumstances which justify it in doing so.'

g

[16] I turn now to Mr Hogg's report.

[17] Mr Hogg referred to Lord Irvine's rate of 2.5% and said that Lord Irvine had based his reasoning on the average gross redemption yield on ILGS in the previous three years. In section 3 of his report, taking Lord Irvine's gross yield

h

figure of 2·46%, he considered the impact of taxation on the claimant's case on the assumption of different levels of award. He arrived at returns net of tax of 1·86%, 1·97% and 2·12% on the basis of awards of £2·75m, £2m and £1m respectively.

[18] In section 4, he adapted the gross yield of 2·46% to the claimant's circumstances. The only circumstance that he identified was her 46-year life

j

expectancy. He noted that Lord Irvine had given equal weighting to the yields of each of the 12 ILGS stocks that he had taken into account in arriving at his figure of 2·46%, and said that in the case of this claimant the portfolio of ILGS should be weighted towards stocks with the longest maturity dates. He said (para 4.4):

'The weighting adopted by the Lord Chancellor may give a fair result for some claimants but not for those whose damages have to last for long

periods. As Mrs Warriner's damages have to last 46 years her portfolio of
ILGS would be heavily weighted towards the stocks with the longest *a*
maturity dates. I illustrate this in the following table.'

[19] He then set out a table showing an estimated gross yield of 2·18% for
Mrs Warriner over a 46-year period on the basis of what Mr Hogg considered to
be more realistic weightings. He increased this to 2·21% to take account of the *b*
fact that her claim for loss of earnings was in respect of a shorter period than her
claim for care costs. Finally, Mr Hogg took taxation into account and said that
she would achieve a net return of 1·63% on an award of 2·75m invested in ILGS,
1·74% on £2m and 1·885% on £1m. He set out his conclusions at section 5. These
included:

c

'5.4 In my opinion the method adopted by the Lord Chancellor for
arriving at the gross ILGS yield is unfair for claimants whose damages have
to last for a long period.'

[20] On behalf of the defendant, Mr Leighton Williams QC submits that the
judge should not have allowed the claimant to adduce the evidence of Mr Hogg *d*
on the discount rate issue because (a) the application for permission to admit it
was too late and (b) the claimant has not in any event raised a prima facie case for
a rate of 2% rather than 2·5%. Counsel did not develop his first ground. The
decision of the judge was an exercise of discretion in case management. It is
common ground that this court will not interfere with the exercise of case
management powers unless it is shown that the decision that is challenged was *e*
plainly wrong. In my judgment, this decision was not plainly wrong on the
grounds that the application was too late. I say no more about the first ground of
appeal.

[21] I turn to the substantive ground that was developed by Mr Leighton
Williams. He submits that it is not open to the claimant to seek to show by means *f*
of the evidence of Mr Hogg that Lord Irvine LC has fixed a rate that is 'wrong' or
'unfair'. The rate of 2·5% is now law, and must be applied until and unless it is
changed, subject only to showing that this rate is not appropriate in the case in
question under s 1(2) of the 1996 Act. The present case, where it is said that the
claimant has a life expectancy of 46 years, is not unusual and is typical of cases *g*
that Lord Irvine had 'particularly in mind' when setting the rate at 2·5%. A
central purpose of having a fixed rate for all types of cases is to achieve certainty.
It is only in a very exceptional case that a different rate should be adopted.

[22] Mr Leighton Williams refers to *Warren v Northern General Hospital NHS
Trust (No 2)* [2000] 1 WLR 1404. That was a case decided after *Wells v Wells* [1998]
3 All ER 481, [1999] 1 AC 345 (in which the House of Lords had laid down the *h*
guideline rate of 3%), but before Lord Irvine LC set the rate at 2·5%. In *Warren's*
case, the claimant contended that damages should be assessed on the basis of a
discount rate of 2% rather than 3% in accordance with *Wells'* case. The argument
was that the discount rate should be reduced to counteract the effect of the higher
rate tax on the award. The Court of Appeal rejected the argument. *j*
Stuart-Smith LJ gave the judgment of the court. He said ([2000] 1 WLR 1404 at
1408 (para 13)):

'The need for certainty to facilitate settlements coupled with the
undesirability of extensive evidence from accountants, actuaries or
economists with a view to persuading the courts to change the discount rate,

a   militates strongly against any court seeking to do so before the Lord
           Chancellor has acted under the Act of 1996.'

[23] He said (at 1411 (para 17)) that in *Wells'* case, the House of Lords came
down firmly in favour of an overall rate of 3% 'save in very exceptional cases', and
that this must mean that funds which fall within 0·5% of the norm of 3% should
not be regarded as exceptional, let alone very exceptional. The court rejected the
b   argument that the fact that the claim was in excess of £3m made it exceptional so
as to justify a departure from the 3% norm.

[24] Although *Warren's* case was decided before Lord Irvine LC prescribed the
2·5% rate, Mr Leighton Williams relies on it as showing that there is nothing
exceptional about the present case, and that there is no real prospect that the trial
c   judge would award damages on the basis of a discount rate other than 2·5%.
Accordingly, the judge was in error in making the order permitting evidence to
be adduced by forensic accountants.

[25] Mr Leighton Williams criticises Mr Hogg for failing to take into account
all of the reasons given by Lord Irvine for prescribing the rate of 2·5%; in
particular, he makes the point that Mr Hogg focused exclusively on Lord Irvine's
d   reference to the average gross yield of 2·46% without also recognising that Lord
Irvine took a number of other factors into account in arriving at his rate of 2·5%.
He also submits that Mr Hogg has not identified any features of the present case
which make it one to which s 1(2) of the 1996 Act should apply.

[26] On behalf of the claimant, Miss Cox QC submits that the decision that is
e   challenged on this appeal is a case management decision, and that the court
should only interfere with it if satisfied that the judge was plainly wrong. She says
that the question of whether the discount rate should be 2% or 2·5% is one that
should be determined by the judge at trial after hearing expert evidence.
Mr Hogg has raised at least a prima facie case for 2% on the facts of the present
case. The difference between an award on the basis of 2% and an award on the
f   basis of 2·5% is very substantial.

[27] She submits that s 1(2) of the 1996 Act does not require the claimant to
show that there are exceptional circumstances which justify a lower rate than
2·5%. All that the claimant has to show is that a lower rate is 'more appropriate
in the case in question'. The claimant does not attack the rate chosen by Lord
g   Irvine. She does, however, say that a lower rate is more appropriate by reason of
the particular circumstances of the case. These are the combination of a long life
expectancy and a claim for damages in excess of £3m. She submits that
Mr Hogg's report raises a prima facie case, or a case that has a real prospect of
success, and that the particular circumstances of the claimant's case make it more
appropriate to use a rate of 2% than 2·5%. It is at least arguable that the claimant
h   will not receive full and just compensation if her award is based on the 2·5% rate.
It would be wrong in principle to prevent the trial judge from hearing evidence
and a full argument on the point.

CONCLUSION
j   [28] In *Wells'* case [1998] 3 All ER 481, [1999] 1 AC 345 the House of Lords laid
down a guideline discount rate of 3% that was to be applied generally until Lord
Irvine LC prescribed a rate pursuant to s 1(1) of the 1996 Act. Their Lordships
recognised that a single rate was a somewhat rough and ready instrument, but they
embraced it on policy grounds. These grounds were that the certainty of such a
rate was desirable, would facilitate settlements, and result in saving the expense of
expert evidence at trial: see per Lord Lloyd of Berwick [1998] 3 All ER 481 at 493,

[1999] 1 AC 345 at 373, and per Lord Steyn who said ([1998] 3 All ER 481 at 506, [1999] 1 AC 345 at 388):

> 'My Lords, until the Lord Chancellor takes action under his statutory powers it is essential that there should be a firm and workable principle. It should be general and simple in order to enable settlement negotiations and litigation to be conducted with the benefit of a reasonable degree of predictability of the likely outcome of a case. While acknowledging an element of arbitrariness in any figure, I am content to adopt about 3% as the best present net figure. For my part I would derive that rate from the net average return index-linked government securities over the past three years. While this figure of about 3% should not be regarded as immutable, I would suggest that only a marked change in economic circumstances should entitle any party to reopen the debate in advance of a decision by the Lord Chancellor. The effect of the decision of the House on the discount rate, together with the availability of the Ogden tables, should be to eliminate the need in future to call actuaries, accountants and economists in such cases.'

[29] Lord Clyde said ([1998] 3 All ER 481 at 514, [1999] 1 AC 345 at 397):

> 'The certainty of the result should produce economies in achieving agreement and settlement which should outweigh any rough edges of imprecision. Of course such a formula should not be seen as set in stone. It can serve as a general guide, open to modification and adjustment to meet the demands of particular cases.'

[30] Finally, Lord Hutton said ([1998] 3 All ER 481 at 519, [1999] 1 AC 345 at 404):

> 'I further consider that in order to promote and facilitate settlements and to simplify the assessment of damages in actions which come on for trial the rate of 3% taken by this House in the present appeals should be applied in other cases notwithstanding fluctuations in the return on ILGS until the Lord Chancellor prescribes a different rate pursuant to his power under s 1 of the Damages Act 1996 or unless there is a very considerable change in economic circumstances.'

[31] These policy considerations were articulated and applied by this court in *Warren's* case [2000] 1 WLR 1404, as has already been seen. In that case, the court interpreted *Wells'* case as saying that the overall rate of 3% should be applied save in 'very exceptional cases'.

[32] The same policy considerations informed Lord Irvine LC's decision to choose the single rate of 2·5%. This is clear from the passages that I have already quoted from his reasons published on 27 July 2001. It is also clear that, in arriving at the figure of 2·5%, he took into account the fact that it remains open to the court under s 1(2) of the 1996 Act to adopt a different rate if there are 'exceptional circumstances which justify it in doing so'. These policy considerations are no less important since Lord Irvine prescribed the 2·5% rate on 25 June 2001 than they were before.

[33] We are told that this is the first time that this court has had to consider the 1996 Act, and that guidance is needed as to the meaning of 'more appropriate in the case in question' in s 1(2). The phrase 'more appropriate', if considered in isolation, is open-textured. It prompts the question: by what criteria is the court to judge whether a different rate of return is more appropriate in the case in

a question? But the phrase must be interpreted in its proper context, which is that Lord Irvine LC has prescribed a rate pursuant to s 1(1) and has given very detailed reasons explaining what factors he took into account in arriving at the rate that he has prescribed. I would hold that in deciding whether a different rate is more appropriate in the case in question, the court must have regard to those reasons. If the case in question falls into a category that Lord Irvine did not take into

b account and/or there are special features of the case which (a) are material to the choice of rate of return and (b) are shown from an examination of Lord Irvine's reasons not to have been taken into account, then a different rate of return may be 'more appropriate'.

[34] Miss Cox criticises Lord Irvine LC for using the phrase 'exceptional circumstances' at the end of his reasons when referring to s 1(2) of the 1996 Act.

c So did Lord Brennan in the debate in the House of Lords on 29 November 2001 when an opposition motion that the order be revoked and a rate of 2% be substituted was rejected (see 629 HL Official Report (cols 531–532). It is true that the phase 'exceptional circumstances' does not appear in the 1996 Act. But in my judgment Lord Irvine must have meant by 'exceptional circumstances' no more

d than special circumstances not taken into account by him in fixing the rate of 2·5%. If 'exceptional circumstances' is understood in that way, the phase is, in my view, a helpful explanation of the meaning of the subsection.

[35] If s 1(2) is interpreted in this way, it is likely that it will be in comparatively few cases that s 1(2) will be successfully invoked, at any rate as long as the 2·5% rate and Lord Irvine's reasons for it continue to apply. The construction that I

e have given to s 1(2) seems to me to accord with and promote the policy considerations to which I have already referred. A generous and open-ended interpretation of s 1(2) would undermine the policy that was clearly articulated by Lord Irvine in his reasons, and by the courts before that.

[36] I turn now to consider whether the report of Mr Hogg raises a case that

f has a real prospect of success of showing that a lower rate than 2·5% is more appropriate in this case.

[37] Miss Cox relies on the fact that the claimant has a life expectancy of 46 years and that the sum claimed was in excess of £3m. In my view, these circumstances are not sufficient, even arguably, to justify applying a discount rate of 2% rather than 2·5%. I note in passing that in *Warren*'s case the claimant had

g a life expectancy of 47 years and the sum awarded at trial on the basis of the 3% rate was £3·1m. The court rejected the argument that the case was exceptional such that, on application of the principles stated in *Wells*' case, a rate lower than 3% should be adopted. In *Warren*'s case, it was argued (as before us) that, unless a lower rate was taken, the claimant would be undercompensated and suffer

h injustice. The response of the court was that prudent investment of a very large fund could take care of all but the most exceptional circumstances.

[38] One of the factors taken into account by Lord Irvine in arriving at a rate of 2·5% was that prudent investment by the Court of Protection would enable a rate of return at or above 2·5% to be achieved comfortably. Of greater

j importance is the fact that, as has been seen from one of the passages that I have quoted earlier, Lord Irvine was alive to the very point that Miss Cox makes, namely that it is in the context of larger awards intended to cover longer periods that there is the greatest risk of serious discrepancies between the level of compensation and the actual losses incurred if the discount rate set is not appropriate. Lord Irvine said in terms that he had this type of award 'particularly in mind' when considering the level at which the discount rate should be set.

[39] Miss Cox makes the valid point that Lord Irvine does not say what he meant by 'larger awards, intended to cover longer periods'. How large? How long? But claims by claimants with life expectancies of between 30 and 50 years are by no means uncommon, nor are claims in the range of £2m to £3m. I cannot accept that claims of this kind were not included in the category which Lord Irvine had particularly in mind when setting the rate at 2·5%. In my judgment Mr Hogg has not identified any special features of this case which take it outside the classes of case that Lord Irvine took into account when fixing the rate. In truth, it seems to me that, despite Miss Cox's disavowal, Mr Hogg's report is, on analysis, more a criticism of Lord Irvine's rate itself. It is noteworthy that on Mr Hogg's approach, the net return for the claimant even if her award were no more than £1m would be below 2% and would, in his view, justify invoking s 1(2).

[40] To summarise, therefore, I consider that there is nothing in the particular facts of this that makes it more appropriate to apply a lower rate than 2·5%. I would allow the appeal on this basis. It is true that this involves interfering with a case management decision. But the argument before the judge was limited to the delay point, although he made reference to s 1(2) in his judgment. Of particular significance is the fact that he was not shown Lord Irvine's reasons, and did not have the benefit of the detailed submissions that were made by counsel in this court.

LATHAM LJ.

[41] I agree. In this area certainty is extremely important. It enables cases to be settled with confidence, and it produces fairness as between litigants.

[42] Prior to the making of the Damages (Personal Injury) Order 2001, SI 2001/2301 by Lord Irvine of Lairg LC under the Damages Act 1996, the court applied the conventional discount rate (for many years 4·5% and latterly 3%) across the board, save in exceptional circumstances: see *Wells v Wells, Thomas v Brighton Health Authority, Page v Sheerness Steel Co plc* [1998] 3 All ER 481, [1999] 1 AC 345 and *Warren v Northern General Hospital NHS Trust (No 2)* [2000] 1 WLR 1404. Nothing in the 1996 Act suggests to me that it was Parliament's intention that this general policy should in any way be diluted. That, indeed, is clearly the view of Lord Irvine, as set out in the reasons that he gave. In that I consider him to have been correct.

[43] It is against that policy background, therefore, that the words in s 1(2) of the 1996 Act fall to be construed. The phrase 'more appropriate', as explained by Dyson LJ, has to be read in conjunction with the reasons given by Lord Irvine LC for choosing the particular rate of return that he has. It follows that it is difficult to see how a case falling squarely within the category of case envisaged by Lord Irvine, in which he has given a reasoned justification for the prescribed rate, could be said to be one in relation to which that prescribed rate is inappropriate in the absence of special features.

[44] Turning to the present appeal, it is clear that the judge's decision was made without the benefit of Lord Irvine's reasons. We are, therefore, entitled to consider afresh the appropriate order to make. Although the court should always be careful when seeking to restrict the ambit of evidence, it can and should do so if there is no real prospect of the evidence having any effect on the issues to be tried. The evidence of Mr Hogg raises no special features which take this case outside the category of those in receipt of large awards specifically referred to by Lord Irvine in his reasons, as explained by Dyson LJ. Lord Irvine explains fully

a why he considered that the 2·5% rate of return is appropriate for them, and refers to the fact that proper advice is likely to result in a wider spread of investment than solely in index-linked stock. Lord Irvine indeed went further in his reasons for prescribing the rate of 2·5% than merely his calculation based upon the rate of return from index-linked stock. Mr Hogg's report makes no reference to those matters and does not seek to deal with them in any way.

b [45] It follows, in my judgment, that there is no material before the court to suggest that 2·5% is inappropriate. It follows that the report of Mr Hogg would have no effect on the issue before the court.

[46] Accordingly I would allow the appeal.

MUMMERY LJ.

c [47] I agree with both judgments. The appeal is allowed.

Appeal allowed.

James Brooks   Barrister.

R v Threapleton
[2001] EWCA Crim 2892

COURT OF APPEAL, CRIMINAL DIVISION

WALLER LJ, ROUGIER AND STANLEY BURNTON JJ

20 NOVEMBER, 19 DECEMBER 2001

Sentence – Confiscation order – Order for costs – Judge making costs order before determination of amount payable under confiscation order – Whether order for costs lawful – Criminal Justice Act 1988, s 72.

The defendant was charged with corruptly giving a bribe to a local government employee. He was convicted at a retrial, and in August 2000 was sentenced to 18 months' imprisonment (reduced on appeal in December 2000 to 12 months' imprisonment), and ordered to pay £15,000 towards the costs of the prosecution. In January 2001 a confiscation order was made against him under the Criminal Justice Act 1988 in the sum of £15,000. The defendant appealed, inter alia, against the costs order, on the ground that it was unlawful because: (i) being an 'order for payment' within s 72(5)(b)[a] of the 1988 Act it should not, by reason of s 72A(9)[b], have been made until after the making of the confiscation order, and (ii) that by making the confiscation order after the costs order, the judge had been unable to fulfil his duty under s 72(5) to take the confiscation order into account when making the order for costs. It was submitted on behalf of the Crown that the same costs order could lawfully have been made by the judge in January 2001, and that the court should exercise its power under s 11(3) of the Criminal Appeal Act 1968 to make an order for costs that could have been made by the Crown Court on that occasion.

Held – Having regard to the provisions of s 72 of the 1988 Act, the costs order was one that could not lawfully have been made. On the assumption that s 11(3) of the 1968 Act conferred on the court the power to make an order which could have been made by the Crown Court, it would not, however, be right for the court to exercise that power. To do so would be to condone the fact that the requirements of the 1988 Act had not been complied with. Those requirements were not merely formal: they were intended to ensure that the determination of the amount payable under a confiscation order had priority over any order which came within s 72(5)(b). The amount payable under the confiscation order depended on the defendant's realisable property, or the amount that might be realised at the time the order was made, and the effect of the statutory procedure was that such property should not have been depleted by an order for costs when the determinations required for the making of a confiscation order were made. In the instant case it was not certain that, had the correct procedure been followed, the same order for costs would have been made. The judge would in all probability have determined that a greater sum be paid under the confiscation order, since at that stage the defendant's property would not have been depleted by, nor would it have been liable to be depleted by, any previous costs order. Accordingly, the costs order made by the judge would be quashed (see [20], [22], below).

---

a   Section 72(5) is set out at [16], below

b   Section 72A(9) is set out at [18], below

Notes

a   For the making of a confiscation order, see 11(2) *Halsbury's Laws* (4th edn reissue), para 1285.

For the Criminal Justice Act 1988, s 72, see 12 *Halsbury's Statutes* (4th edn) (2002 reissue) 951.

b   **Cases referred to in judgments**

R v Efionayi (1994) 16 Cr App R (S) 380, CA.
R v Ross [2001] EWCA Crim 560, [2001] 2 Cr App Rep (S) 484.

Appeal and application

c   The appellant, Michael Threapleton, appealed with leave granted by Judge Heppel QC from his order of 4 August 2000 in the Crown Court at Hull, requiring the appellant to pay the sum of £15,000 towards the costs of his prosecution for bribery following his conviction on 27 July 2000 and applied for leave to appeal against a confiscation order made by Judge Heppel QC sitting in the Crown Court at Hull on 26 January 2001 made under the Criminal Justice Act
d   1988 in the sum of £15,000. The facts are set out in the judgment of the court.

Peter Binder (assigned by the *Registrar of Criminal Appeals*) for the appellant.
Nicholas Dean (instructed by the *Crown Prosecution Service*) for the Crown.

e   20 November 2001. The court announced that the appeal would be allowed and the application for leave to appeal would be refused for reasons to be given later.

19 December 2001. The following judgment of the court was delivered.

f   **STANLEY BURNTON J.**

[1] The court has before it: (a) the appellant's appeal, with leave of the single judge, against a costs order made against him by Judge Heppel QC on 4 August 2000, ordering him to pay the sum of £15,000 towards the costs of the prosecution; (b) an application by the appellant for leave to appeal against a confiscation order made under the Criminal Justice Act 1988 by Judge Heppel on
g   26 January 2001 in the same sum of £15,000.

[2] At the conclusion of the hearing of the appeal and the application for leave to appeal, we stated that the appeal against the costs order would be allowed and we refused leave to appeal against the confiscation order. We said that we would give our reasons in writing, and we now do so.

h

THE PROCEEDINGS IN THE CROWN COURT

[3] On 27 July 2000 at the Crown Court at Hull the appellant was convicted at a retrial before Judge Heppel of corruptly giving a bribe to a Roger Dearnley, an employee of Doncaster Metropolitan Borough Council. The particulars of the
j   offence specified in the indictment as amended were as follows:

'Michael Threapleton, on or about 5 February 1993 corruptly gave Roger Dearnley who at that time held public office in the employment of Doncaster Metropolitan Borough Council, a gift, reward or advantage namely a Fiat Uno motor car, registration number J640 AWB, as a reward for business contracts on behalf of Doncaster Metropolitan Borough Council being awarded to Executive Security Limited by Roger Dearnley or with his assistance or as an inducement to Roger Dearnley to award or assist in awarding further contracts to Executive Surveillance and Security Ltd.'   *a*

[4] The appellant was sentenced to 18 months' imprisonment, subsequently reduced by the Court of Appeal to 12 months. His co-accused Roger Dearnley was also convicted of corruption. The other, Roger Bodill, had been acquitted at an earlier trial.

[5] On 4 August 2000 Judge Heppel made the costs order against the appellant   *b* referred to above.

[6] On 19 December 2000 the full court allowed the appellant's appeal against sentence to the extent of reducing the term of imprisonment to one of 12 months. His appeal against the costs order was adjourned pending the conclusion of the confiscation proceedings.   *c*

[7] On 26 January 2001 Judge Heppel made the confiscation order referred to above.

THE FACTS

[8] About September 1990 Dearnley began work as a principal valuer for the   *d* Doncaster Metropolitan Borough Council (Doncaster MBC). He reported to a chief valuation officer, but still had important responsibilities for property managed by Doncaster MBC. One of the properties Dearnley managed was known as the Mexborough Business Centre, and he was responsible for letting out business units, collecting rent and security services. In June 1991 Dearnley had instructed one of his staff to invite tenders for security services at the   *e* Mexborough Business Centre and a number of companies were approached. Executive Security Contracts Ltd (ESC), run by a man named Dack was not approached. The parent company of ESC was EFM Holdings Group, and Threapleton was a director.

[9] On 2 August 1991, Doncaster MBC received a letter from ESC addressed to Dearnley quoting a rate of £4·00 per hour. The previous company, which had   *f* been charging £3·60 per hour, was dismissed and ESC were appointed to take over the security contract. No formal contract ever seemed to be drawn up, and ESC simply began to invoice Doncaster MBC for the services they provided. At the time ESC were expecting to invoice Doncaster MBC for about £36,000 p a, but the amounts paid grew each year. In the year 1991–1992 Doncaster MBC   *g* paid £52,000, in 1992–1993 that grew to about £130,000 and in 1993–1994 to about £385,000. Dearnley was involved in authorising much of that expenditure.

[10] Once ESC started working for Doncaster MBC it was well placed to take on other work offered by the council. From August 1991 Doncaster MBC paid ESC and Executive Surveillance and Security Ltd (ESSL) approximately £1m. Beyond invoices   *h* the business generated little by way of documentation or formal agreements.

[11] By late 1992 and early 1993 Dearnley had built up a close link with ESC and he proposed that a more sophisticated security system be set up at the Mexborough Business Centre. It was about this time that Dearnley was introduced to Threapleton, who was planning to set up ESSL.

[12] At about this time Dearnley had a car which he described as 'a banger'.   *j* He could not afford to buy a new car, but was entitled to apply to Doncaster MBC for a loan to purchase a car. In December 1992 he applied for a loan, which was supported by an invoice from Imola Sports Ltd. This was another company in the EFM group, which was run by Mr Bodill. On 4 December 1992, Dearnley signed an agreement with Doncaster MBC to borrow £5,445 to purchase a Fiat Uno motor car. He returned the cheque and a second cheque was issued. In

a February 1993, Threapleton purchased a Fiat Uno motor car from GT Cars and arranged payment of a finance agreement through his personal bank account. He gave the vehicle to Dearnley who paid nothing for the vehicle or the use of it. When Dearnley was required to provide information regarding his purchase of the car he maintained the pretence that he had used the loan to purchase the Fiat Uno. He in fact used the money obtained to clear a number of debts.

b [13] In February 1993, Threapleton set up ESSL and took with him many of the staff from ESC and a number of their existing clients, including Doncaster MBC. No formal tendering process took place.

[14] In June 1993 two elderly-persons homes closed. At the instigation of Dearnley ESSL took over guarding those premises. The rate paid to ESSL, as agreed and arranged through Dearnley, was higher than the rate paid to the *c* previous companies. Dearnley also helped ESSL obtain the contract for a video surveillance system at Mexborough Business Centre. Only ESSL quoted for the work. As part of wider investigations, the police began to look at ESSL's dealing with Doncaster MBC.

[15] The appeal against the costs order is put on two bases. The first is that *d* the order was unlawful: it is submitted that no costs order should have been made until after the making of the confiscation order, if any.

[16] Section 72(5) of the Criminal Justice Act 1988 reads as follows:

e 'Where a court makes a confiscation order against a defendant in any proceedings, it shall be its duty, in respect of any offence of which he is convicted in those proceedings, to take account of the order before—(a) imposing any fine upon him; (b) making any order involving any payment by him, other than an order under section 35 of the Powers of Criminal Courts Act 1973 (compensation orders); or (c) … but subject to that shall leave the order out of account in determining the appropriate sentence or other manner of dealing with him.'

f

[17] The order for costs in this case was an order for payment by him within s 72(5)(b).

[18] Section 72(5) is modified by s 72A in cases where the court postpones the determinations that are required by s 71 (namely whether the defendant has benefited from any relevant criminal conduct and the amount to be recovered in *g* his case) for specified periods as permitted by s 72A, and sentences the defendant before making a confiscation order as permitted by s 72A(7). The court proceeded under s 72A in the present case, and the court proceeded to sentence the appellant before making the confiscation order. Section 72A(8) and (9) are as follows:

h '(8) Where the court has so proceeded—(a) subsection (1) of section 71 above shall have effect as if the words from "before sentencing" onwards were omitted; (b) that section shall further have effect as if references to an offence that will be taken into consideration in determining any sentence included references to an offence that has been to taken into account; and *j* (c) section 72(5) above shall have effect as if after "determining" there were inserted "in relation to any offence in respect of which he has not been sentenced or otherwise dealt with".

(9) In sentencing, or otherwise dealing with, the defendant in respect of the offence, or any of the offences, concerned at any time during the specified period, the court shall not—(a) impose any fine on him; or (b) make any such order as is mentioned in s 72(5)(b) or (c) above.'

The 'specified period' is the period, following conviction, of the postponement of the determinations of the defendant's benefit and the amount to be recovered from him: see s 72A(1).

[19] Mr Binder submitted that the confiscation order must be made before any order for costs. Here it was made afterwards. The judge was accordingly unable to fulfil his duty under s 72(5) by taking it into account when making the order for costs. More obviously, the order was made in breach of the prohibition in s 72A(9). He also submitted that the costs order was a wrongful exercise of the judge's discretion.

[20] Mr Dean conceded, as was inevitable, that the judge should not have made the costs order before making the confiscation order. It follows that the order was one that could not lawfully have been made, and that it must be quashed: cf R v Ross [2001] EWCA Crim 560, [2001] 2 Cr App Rep (S) 484.

[21] We mention that the relevant provisions of the 1988 Act were not brought to the judge's attention by counsel. We emphasise that it is the duty of counsel for both the prosecution and the defence to bring such provisions to the attention of the court, and they should have done so on 4 August 2000 when the judge raised the possibility of his making an order for costs before dealing with confiscation.

[22] Mr Dean submitted that although the order made on 4 August 2000 had to be quashed, the same order could lawfully have been made by the judge on 26 January 2001; that this court has power under s 11(3) of the Criminal Appeal Act 1968 to make an order for costs that could have been made by the Crown Court on that occasion; that in view of the identity of the sums ordered to be paid as costs and under the confiscation order this court could be confident that if no costs order had been made by the judge on 4 August 2000 he would have made the same order on 26 January 2001; and that this court should therefore make the same order for costs as that made on 4 August 2000. Assuming that s 11(3) of the 1968 Act does confer such power on this court, we do not think that it would be right to exercise it. To do so would be to condone the fact that the requirements of the 1988 Act were not complied with. Those requirements are not merely formal: they are intended to ensure that the determination of the amount payable under a confiscation order has priority over, in this case, an order for the payment of costs. The amount payable under the confiscation order depended on the realisable property of the defendant (or 'the amount that might be realised at the time the order [was] made' (see s 71(6)), and the effect of the statutory procedure is that that property should not have been depleted by an order for costs when the determinations required for the making of a confiscation order are made. Furthermore, we are not satisfied that if the correct procedure had been followed, the same order for costs would have been made. The judge would in all probability have determined that a greater sum be paid by the appellant under the confiscation order, since at that stage his realisable property had not been depleted by, or was not liable to be depleted by, any previous costs order.

[23] In view of our decision on the first point, it is unnecessary to deal with the question of the judge's exercise of discretion, other than to say that, apart from the failure to comply with the requirements of the 1988 Act, we see no basis for interfering with his decision.

THE CONFISCATION ORDER

[24] The appeal against the confiscation order is put on the basis that the judge was bound to proceed on the basis of the version of the facts charged before the jury most favourable to the defendant. The way in which the count was left to

a the jury created alternative bases upon which the jury could convict. On the basis of the first alternative facts charged, the car was given as reward for business contracts awarded in the past to ESC, Mr Dack's company. On this basis, it is argued, the appellant derived no benefit from the corrupt act, and indeed the Crown did not allege that he had. On the alternative facts charged, the appellant derived benefit from the moneys received by his company, ESSL, as a result of

b the corrupt gift of the car to Dearnley. Mr Binder submitted that since the judge had no way of knowing the basis of the jury's verdict, he was required to adopt the view of the facts most favourable to the accused.

[25] The judge decided he was bound as a matter of strict law to approach the question of whether or not the appellant benefited from the corruption and to what extent in the way that Mr Binder submitted, the way most favourable to the

c accused. He turned therefore to the argument that the appellant only intended to reward Dearnley for past favours done and that he therefore received no benefit from those favours.

[26] The judge held that the test under s 71(4) of the 1988 Act is an objective one and the accused's intention is therefore irrelevant: if any benefit in fact

d accrued to the accused, and the facts of the case taken globally pointed to a causal link between the offence and that benefit, then the accused had in fact benefited as a result of the offence within the terms of the section. He found that even if the car was given as a reward for past services to ESC it led to the promotion of the interests of ESSL with consequential advantage to Threapleton. He said:

e   'Mr Grenfell, for the appellant, argues: to the extent that the defendant may have gained from the placing by the council of contracts with Executive Surveillance and Security Ltd, he would not have gained those benefits from the commission of the offence as he intended it should be committed, that is to say simply by rewarding Dearnley for past favours done for Executive

f   Security Contracts Ltd. In my judgment that approach is wrong in law. The test under s 71(4) of the Criminal Justice Act 1988 is a purely objective one. The way in which the defendant may have intended to commit the offence, and whether he intended to get something out of it, or what he intended to get out of it, is irrelevant. If benefit in fact inures to the defendant, and the facts globally taken in the case point to a causal link between the offence and

g   the benefit, then in my judgment he has received benefit "as a result of" the offence. In my judgment, even if the car was given as a reward, or a thank you, to Dearnley for services to Executive Security Contracts Ltd, it did, on my findings of fact, lead to the promotion of the interests of Executive Surveillance and Security Ltd, with consequential advantage to Threapleton.

h   In my judgment, the overwhelming thrust of the totality of the evidence pointed that way, particularly when one considers the time at which the car was given, in the context of the setting-up of the second company. And, indeed, to hold that no benefit flowed from the reward given to Dearnley for past services would, in my judgment, be to fly in the face of common sense

j   in the circumstances of this case.'

[27] The judge calculated the benefit by reference to the evidence led at trial on behalf of the appellant that the contracts placed by Doncaster MBC with ESSL amounted to 25% of the company's turnover. During the period from the gift to arrest the prosecution calculated the benefit to the company, to Threaplcton, as £308,000. This comprised partly consultancy fees and partly payments to the company for purchases that were to the benefit of the appellant personally. The

judge, adopting a broad-brush approach, reduced this sum to £260,000, of which
25% were derived from trading with the local authority resulting from the
corrupt gift. The judge therefore calculated the appellant's benefit as the sum of
£65,000. That calculation is not challenged on behalf of the appellant: the
submission made on his behalf is that no such calculation was permissible.
Having considered the assets available (ie the relevant realisable property of the
appellant), the judge took account of the costs order he had made and the legal
costs the appellant had incurred in his defence, and made an order for the
payment of the sum of £15,000.

[28] We reject the submission that in making a confiscation order the judge is
bound to approach the case on the version of the facts before the jury most
favourable to the defendant. *R v Efionayi* (1994) 16 Cr App R (S) 380, relied upon
by Mr Binder, was concerned with sentencing in the strict sense of the word, ie a
sentence of imprisonment. The principle applied in the context of that case does
not apply in the present context. Section 71 of the 1988 Act imposes a duty on the
court to make the determinations specified in sub-ss (1A), (1B) and (6), ie whether
the defendant has benefited from any relevant criminal conduct, the amount of
that benefit and the amounts that might be realised at the time the order is made.
In the case of the Crown Court, the court there means the trial judge, and does
not include the jury. The same determinations fall to be made under s 72A, where
the determinations are postponed. The fact that the determinations are separate
from the trial process itself is emphasised by s 71(7A) of the 1988 Act, which
provides that the standard of proof required to determine any question arising
under Pt VI of the Act is that applicable in civil proceedings.

[29] In any event, however, the question required to be answered in this case
was not whether the car was a gift for past favours or an inducement for future
favours, but whether the offender benefited from the conduct of which he was
found guilty, and if so, by sub-s (6), the amount of that benefit and the amount
appearing to the court to be the amount that might be realised when the order
was made. Those are the questions that the judge addressed. The jury were not
concerned whether, if they found that the car was given as a reward for past
services, its gift had resulted in subsequent financial benefit for the appellant, or
whether, if they found that the car was given as an inducement to Dearnley to
award or assist in awarding further contracts to ESSL, Dearnley had in fact
awarded or assisted in awarding such contracts to ESSL, and if he did whether and
to what extent the appellant benefited from that.

[30] The question required to be determined by the judge was not whether
the car was a gift for past favours or an inducement for future favours, but
whether the offender benefited from the conduct of which he was found guilty,
ie the corrupt gift of the car to Dearnley, and if so, by sub-s (6), the amount of that
benefit and the amount appearing to the court to be the amount that might be
realised when the order is made. Those are the questions that the judge
addressed. In doing so, he assumed that a valid costs order had been made against
the appellant; but that incorrect assumption led to a smaller confiscation order
than would otherwise have been made.

[31] It follows that there are no grounds for impugning the confiscation order.

Appeal allowed, application for leave to appeal refused.

Lynne Townley   Barrister.

Société Eram Shipping Co Ltd and others v Compagnie Internationale de Navigation
[2003] UKHL 30

HOUSE OF LORDS

LORD BINGHAM OF CORNHILL, LORD NICHOLLS OF BIRKENHEAD, LORD HOFFMANN, LORD HOBHOUSE OF WOODBOROUGH AND LORD MILLETT

17, 18 MARCH, 12 JUNE 2003

Execution – Third party debt order – Debts owing or accruing from foreign judgment debtors – Third party bank incorporated and resident in Hong Kong but having place of residence in England – Judgment debtors having accounts with third party bank in Hong Kong – Whether court having jurisdiction to make third party debt order final – CPR 72.4(2).

The judgment creditor, a Romanian company, obtained judgment in a French court against the judgment debtors, a company and an individual resident in Hong Kong. The judgment debtors did not satisfy the judgment and the judgment creditor registered it in the High Court under the provisions of the Civil Jurisdiction and Judgments Act 1982. One or other of the judgment debtors held an account in Hong Kong with the third party, a bank. The debt due from the third party to the judgment debtors on that account was situated in Hong Kong and was governed by the laws of Hong Kong. The judgment creditor successfully applied, without notice, to the High Court for an interim third party debt order under CPR 72.4(2)[a] in respect of the debt owed by the third party to the judgment debtors in Hong Kong. At a hearing to decide whether the interim third party order should be made final, the judge declined to make a final order, and set aside the interim order. He considered that the third party would be at risk of having to pay twice, once in London and again in Hong Kong, and was reluctant to exercise jurisdiction over foreigners in relation to their conduct outside the territorial jurisdiction of the court. The judgment creditor's appeal to the Court of Appeal was allowed. The court discounted the risk that the third party might have to pay twice, and placed reliance on the existence of a restitutionary remedy available to the third party in Hong Kong. The third party appealed to the House of Lords.

Held – It was not open to the court to make a third party debt order under CPR Pt 72 in a case where it was clear or it appeared that the making of the order would not discharge the debt of the third party to the judgment debtor according to the law which governed that debt. If, however, the English court did have jurisdiction to make such an order, the objections to its exercising such a jurisdiction to do so would be very strong on grounds of principle, comity and convenience. The importance which the Court of Appeal had attached to the supposed availability to the third party of a restitutionary remedy in Hong Kong if the third party made or was compelled to make payment to the judgment creditor under an English order appeared to reflect some misunderstanding of the procedure. The order took effect against the property of the judgment debtor. The property

---

a   CPR 72.4(2) is set out at [12], below

of the third party was in no way involved, save by the diminution of its debt to
the judgment debtor. If the effect of an order in the instant case would be to
compel the third party to disburse its own funds, that would be a very clear
indication that the order was one which should never have been made. The
order of the Court of Appeal would accordingly be set aside and the judge's order
restored (see [26]–[31], [54], [59], [62]–[65], [68]–[70], [84], [107]–[109], [113],
below.

Decision of the Court of Appeal [2001] 2 All ER (Comm) 721 reversed.

Notes

For third party debt orders, see 17(1) *Halsbury's Laws* (4th edn reissue) paras 251, 266.

Cases referred to in opinions

Anisminic Ltd v Foreign Compensation Commission [1969] 1 All ER 208, [1969] 2 AC
147, [1969] 2 WLR 163, HL; *rvsg* [1967] 2 All ER 986, [1968] 2 QB 862, [1967]
3 WLR 382, CA.

Babanaft International Co SA v Bassatne [1989] 1 All ER 433, [1990] Ch 13, [1989]
2 WLR 232, CA.

Ballantine v Golding (1784) Cooke's Bankrupt Laws 419.

Baltic Shipping v Translink Shipping Ltd [1995] 1 Lloyd's Rep 673.

Bartley v Hodges (1861) 1 B & S 375, 121 ER 754.

Bonalumi v Secretary of State for the Home Dept [1985] 1 All ER 797, [1985] QB 675,
[1985] 2 WLR 722, CA.

Burrows v Jemino (1726) 2 Stra 733, 93 ER 815.

Chatterton v Watney (1881) 17 Ch D 259, CA.

Choice Investments Ltd v Jeromnimon (Midland Bank Ltd, garnishee) [1981] 1 All ER
225, [1981] QB 149, [1980] 2 WLR 80, CA.

Combined Weighing and Advertising Machine Co, Re (1889) 43 Ch D 99, CA.

*Deutsche Schachtbau-und Tiefbohrgesellschaft mbH v Shell International Petroleum Co
Ltd (t/a Shell International Trading Co)* [1988] 2 All ER 833, [1990] 1 AC 295,
[1988] 3 WLR 230, HL.

Ellis v M'Henry (1871) LR 6 CP 228.

Galbraith v Grimshaw [1910] 1 KB 339; *affd* [1910] AC 508.

Gardiner v Houghton (1862) 2 B & S 743, 121 ER 1247.

General Horticultural Co, Re, ex p Whitehouse (1886) 32 Ch D 512.

International Tin Council, Re [1987] 1 All ER 890, [1987] Ch 419, [1987] 2 WLR 1229.

Interpool Ltd v Galani [1987] 2 All ER 981, [1988] QB 738, [1987] 3 WLR 1042, CA.

Joachimson (N) v Swiss Bank Corp [1921] 3 KB 110, [1921] All ER Rep 92, CA.

Kuwait Oil Tanker Co SAK v Qabazard [2003] UKHL 31, [2003] 3 All ER 501, [2003]
3 WLR 14.

Lewis v Owen (1821) 4 B & Ald 654, 106 ER 1076.

Liberian Insurance Agency Inc v Mosse [1977] 2 Lloyd's Rep 560.

London (Mayor etc) v Cox (1867) LR 2 HL 239.

London Corp v London Joint Stock Bank (1881) 6 App Cas 393, HL.

MacKinnon v Donaldson Lufkin & Jenrette Securities Corp [1986] 1 All ER 653, [1986]
Ch 482, [1986] 2 WLR 453.

Martin v Nadel (Dresdner Bank, garnishees) [1906] 2 KB 26, [1904–7] All ER Rep 827, CA.

Odwin v Forbes (1817) Buck 57, PC.

Phillips v Allan (1828) 8 B & C 477, 108 ER 1120.

Phillips v Eyre (1870) LR 6 QB 1, Ex Ch.

Potter v Brown (1804) 5 East 124, 102 ER 1016.

a Pritchett v English and Colonial Syndicate [1899] 2 QB 428, CA.
Quelin v Moisson (1828) 1 Knapp 265, 12 ER 320.
R v Grossman (1981) 73 Cr App R 302, CA.
R v Jameson [1896] 2 QB 425.
Rasu Maritima SA v Perusahaan Pertambangan Minyak Dan Gas Bumi Negara (Pertamina) and Government of Indonesia (as interveners) [1977] 3 All ER 324,
b [1978] QB 644, [1977] 3 WLR 518, CA.
Richardson v Richardson (National Bank of India Ltd, garnishee) [1927] P 228, [1927] All ER Rep 92.
Rogers v Whiteley [1892] AC 118, HL; affg (1889) 23 QBD 236.
SCF Finance Co Ltd v Masri (No 3) [1987] 1 All ER 194, [1987] QB 1028, [1987] 2 WLR 81, CA.
c Smith v Buchanan (1800) 1 East 6, 102 ER 3.
Swiss Bank Corp v Boehmische Industrial Bank [1923] 1 KB 673, CA.
Wood v Dunn (1866) LR 2 QB 73.
Zoneheath Associates Ltd v China Tianjin International Economic and Technical Co-operative Corp [1994] CLC 348.

d
Cases also referred to in list of authorities
Airbus Industrie GIE v Patel [1998] 2 All ER 257, [1999] 1 AC 119, [1998] 1 WLR 686, HL.
AS-Autoteile Service GmbH v Malhé Case 220/84 [1985] ECR 2267.
Bank of China v NBM LLC [2001] EWCA Civ 1933, [2002] 1 All ER 717, [2002] 1 WLR 844.
e Camdex International Ltd v Bank of Zambia [1996] 3 All ER 431, [1998] QB 22, [1996] 3 WLR 759, CA.
Chase Manhattan Bank NA v FDC Co Ltd [1985] HKC 470, HK CA.
Colquhoun v Brooks (1888) 21 QBD 52, CA; affd (1889) 14 App Cas 493, [1886–90] All ER Rep 1063, HL.
f Damayanti Kantilal Doshi V Indian Bank [1999] 4 SLR 1, Sing CA.
Denilauler v SNC Couchet Frères Case 125/79 [1980] ECR 1553, ECJ.
Kuwait Oil Tanker Co SAK v Qabazard [2002] EWCA Civ 34, [2001] 1 All ER (Comm) 351.
Libyan Arab Foreign Bank v Bankers Trust Co [1989] 3 All ER 252, [1989] QB 728, [1989] 3 WLR 314.
g Owens Bank Ltd v Bracco [1992] 2 All ER 193, [1992] 2 AC 443, [1992] 2 WLR 621, HL.
Power Curber International Ltd v National Bank of Kuwait SAK [1981] 3 All ER 607, [1981] 1 WLR 1233, CA.
Reichert v Dresdner Bank AG Case C-261/90 [1992] ECR I-2149.
Rossano v Manufacturers Life Insurance Co Ltd [1962] 2 All ER 214, [1963] 2 QB 352, h [1962] 3 WLR 157.
Soinco SACI v Novokuznetsk Aluminium Plant [1998] 2 Lloyd's Rep 337, CA.
Tai Hing Cotton Mill Ltd v Liu Chong Hing Bank Ltd [1985] 2 All ER 947, [1986] AC 80, [1985] 3 WLR 317, PC.
Vinall v De Pass [1892] AC 90, HL.

j
Appeal
The appellant third party, Hong Kong and Shanghai Banking Corp Ltd (HSBC), appealed with permission of the Appeal Committee of the House of Lords given on 21 August 2002 from a decision of the Court of Appeal (Schiemann, Mance and Keene LJJ) on 7 August 2001 ([2001] EWCA Civ 17, [2001] 2 All ER (Comm) 721) allowing the appeal of the respondent judgment creditor, Société Eram Shipping

Co Ltd, from the decision of Tomlinson J on 23 January 2001 ([2001] 1 All ER
(Comm) 843) whereby he refused to make a garnishee order (now a third party
debt order) made on 4 April 2000 against the judgment debtors, Compagnie
Internationale de Navigation, Société Ocean Link Ltd and Mr Yoon Sei Wha, and
against HSBC, absolute. The facts are set out in the opinion of Lord Bingham of
Cornhill.

John Higham QC and *Christopher Harrison* (instructed by *Stephenson Harwood*) for
the third party.
Hugo Page (instructed by *Penningtons*) for the judgment creditor.
The judgment debtors did not appear.

Their Lordships took time for consideration.

12 June 2003. The following opinions were delivered.

LORD BINGHAM OF CORNHILL.
[1] My Lords, this appeal is against the making of what was formerly called a
garnishee order absolute but is now called a final third party debt order. When
they were begun the proceedings were governed by a procedure since replaced
by a procedure very similar in substance but expressed in different language, and
I shall so far as possible use the new terminology. The feature of the order which
gives rise to controversy is that it was made in relation to a foreign debt. The
House is called upon to consider the power of the English court to make an order
in such a case and, if there is power, the manner in which it should be exercised.
[2] The appellant is the Hong Kong and Shanghai Banking Corp Ltd, a
company incorporated in Hong Kong and carrying on a banking business there
and elsewhere. It has a branch in London and is registered in England under s 691
of the Companies Act 1985. The appellant would formerly have been called 'the
garnishee' but is now to be called 'the third party', by which term I shall describe it.
[3] Société Eram Shipping Co Ltd is a Romanian shipping company. I shall
refer to it as 'the judgment creditor'.
[4] Société Oceanlink Ltd and Mr Yoon Sei Wha are a company and an
individual resident in Hong Kong. I shall refer to them as 'the judgment debtors'.
A third company against which the judgment creditor also issued proceedings
may be ignored for present purposes. The judgment debtors have played no part
in these proceedings at any stage.
[5] The judgment creditor claimed demurrage against the judgment debtors
and obtained judgment against them in the Brest Commercial Court for some
$US 101,000 and 5,000 French francs. The judgment debtors did not satisfy the
judgment and the judgment creditor registered it in the Queen's Bench Division
of the High Court under the provisions of the Civil Jurisdiction and Judgments
Act 1982.
[6] One or other of the judgment debtors holds an account in Hong Kong with
the third party. The debt due from the third party to the judgment debtors on
this account is situated in Hong Kong and is governed by the law of Hong Kong.
[7] The judgment creditor could have obtained a third party debt (or
garnishee) order in Hong Kong against the third party in respect of the debt due
from the third party to the judgment debtors. Under the law and procedure of
Hong Kong it was open to the judgment creditor to obtain such an order after
applying to the Hong Kong court for registration and enforcement of the Brest

a   judgment or after suing in Hong Kong on the judgment registered in the Queen's Bench Division. The judgment creditor did not adopt those procedures. Instead, it applied to the High Court in England for an interim third party debt order (then called a garnishee order nisi) in respect of the debt owed by the third party to the judgment debtors in Hong Kong. The application was made in the usual way without notice to the third party, and an order was made that all debts accruing

b   to the judgment debtors from the third party be attached to answer the Brest judgment registered in the High Court; and also that the third party attend on an application by the judgment creditor that the third party pay to the judgment creditor the debt due from the third party to the judgment debtors or so much thereof as might be sufficient to satisfy the judgment and the costs of the third party debt order (or garnishee) proceedings.

c   [8] A hearing took place before Tomlinson J sitting in the Commercial Court to decide whether the interim third party debt order should be made final (or the garnishee order nisi be made absolute). The undisputed evidence was that under the law and procedure of Hong Kong a third party debt (or garnishee) order made in England did not have the effect of extinguishing the third party's (or

d   garnishee's) Hong Kong debt to a judgment debtor in Hong Kong. Nor would the Hong Kong court give effect to an English third party debt (or garnishee) order by reciprocal enforcement or action. Having reviewed the authorities, the judge declined to make a final third party debt order and he set aside the interim order. His essential reasons (elaborated in a very convincing judgment) were, first, that he considered the third party to be at risk of having to pay twice (once

e   in London in compliance with the English order if made, and again in Hong Kong at the suit of the judgment debtors), and secondly out of reluctance to exercise jurisdiction over foreigners in relation to their conduct outside the territorial jurisdiction of the court (see [2001] 1 All ER (Comm) 843). On appeal by the judgment creditor the Court of Appeal (Schiemann, Mance and Keene LJJ)

f   reversed the judge's decision (see [2001] EWCA Civ 1317, [2001] 2 All ER (Comm) 721). In a judgment of the court delivered by Mance LJ the risk that the third party might have to pay twice was discounted and reliance was placed on the existence of a restitutionary remedy available to the third party in Hong Kong.

[9] The third party challenges the Court of Appeal judgment, contending that the English court had no jurisdiction to make an order in this case and that, if it

g   did, it should have exercised its discretion against making an order. The judgment creditor rejects these contentions, submitting that the Court of Appeal reached the correct conclusions for the reasons which it gave.

THE ATTACHMENT OF DEBTS

h   [10] As many a claimant has learned to his cost, it is one thing to recover a favourable judgment; it may prove quite another to enforce it against an unscrupulous defendant. But an unenforceable judgment is at best valueless, at worst a source of additional loss. This was a problem which our Victorian forebears addressed with characteristic energy and pragmatism. The Judgments Acts of 1838 and 1840 allowed choses in action to be taken in execution. Then, in

j   the Common Law Procedure Act 1854, a new garnishee procedure was introduced. The essential features of this procedure were laid down in ss 61–63 and 65 of the Act:

'**61.** It shall be lawful for a Judge, upon the *ex parte* Application of such Judgment Creditor, either before or after such oral Examination, and upon Affidavit by himself or his Attorney stating that Judgment has been

recovered, and that it is still unsatisfied, and to what Amount, and that any
other Person is indebted to the Judgment Debtor, and is within the
Jurisdiction, to order that all Debts owing or accruing from such third Person
(hereinafter called the Garnishee) to the Judgment Debtor shall be attached
to answer the Judgment Debt; and by the same or any subsequent Order it
may be ordered that the Garnishee shall appear before the Judge or a Master
of the Court, as such Judge shall appoint, to show Cause why he should not
pay the Judgment Creditor the Debt due from him to the Judgment Debtor,
or so much thereof as may be sufficient to satisfy the Judgment Debt.

62. Service of an Order that debts due or accruing to the Judgment Debtor
shall be attached, or Notice thereof to the Garnishee, in such Manner as the
Judge shall direct, shall bind such Debts in his Hands.

63. If the Garnishee does not forthwith pay into Court the Amount due
from him to the Judgment Debtor or an Amount equal to the Judgment
Debt, and does not dispute the Debt due or claimed to be due from him to
the Judgment Debtor, or if he does not appear upon Summons, then the
Judge may order Execution to issue, and it may be sued forth accordingly,
without any previous Writ or Process, to levy the Amount due from such
Garnishee towards Satisfaction of the Judgment Debt …

65. Payment made by or Execution levied upon the Garnishee under any
such Proceeding as aforesaid shall be a valid Discharge to him as against the
Judgment Debtor to the Amount paid or levied, although such Proceeding
may be set aside or the Judgment reversed.'

[11] The procedure so established was regulated by the Rules of Court
scheduled to the Supreme Court of Judicature Act 1875 when that Act took effect,
and by the Rules of the Supreme Court promulgated in 1883 when those replaced
them. In each of these codes of rules Ord 45 regulated garnishee proceedings.
When the rules were revised in 1965 (Rules of the Supreme Court (Revision) 1965,
SI 1965/1776, made under s 99 of the Supreme Court of Judicature (Consolidation)
Act 1925), Ord 45 was substantially reproduced as Ord 49. It is apparent from the
terms of rr 1(1) and (2), 3 and 8 of this order as last amended in 1981 that the
nature of the 1854 procedure remained essentially unchanged:

'*Attachment of debt due to judgment debtor*

1.—(1) Where a person (in this order referred to as "the judgment
creditor") has obtained a judgment or order for the payment by some other
person (in this order referred to as "the judgment debtor") of a sum of money
amounting in value to at least £50, not being a judgment or order for the
payment of money into court, and any other person within the jurisdiction
(in this order referred to as "the garnishee") is indebted to the judgment
debtor, the court may, subject to the provisions of this order and of any
enactment, order the garnishee to pay the judgment creditor the amount of
any debt due or accruing due to the judgment debtor from the garnishee, or
so much thereof as is sufficient to satisfy that judgment or order and the costs
of the garnishee proceedings.

(2) An order under this rule shall in the first instance be an order to show
cause, specifying the time and place for further consideration of the matter,
and in the meantime attaching such debt as is mentioned in paragraph (1) or
so much thereof as may be specified in the order, to answer the judgment or

a order mentioned in that paragraph and the costs of the garnishee proceedings.

Service and effect of order to show cause

3.—(1) Unless the court otherwise directs, an order under rule 1 to show cause must be served—(a) on the garnishee personally, at least 15 days before the time appointed thereby for the further consideration of the

b matter; and (b) on the judgment debtor, at least 7 days after the order has been served on the garnishee and at least 7 days before the time appointed by the order for the further consideration of the matter.

(2) Such an order shall bind in the hands of the garnishee as from the service of the order on him any debt specified in the order or so much thereof as may be so specified.

c *Discharge of garnishee*

8. Any payment made by a garnishee in compliance with an order absolute under this order, and any execution levied against him in pursuance of such an order, shall be a valid discharge of his liability to the judgment debtor to the extent of the amount paid or levied notwithstanding that the

d garnishee proceedings are subsequently set aside or the judgment or order from which they arose reversed.'

[12] CPR Pt 72 came into effect on 25 March 2002. Entitled 'Third Party Debt Orders', this part replaced Ord 49. But although the terminology was changed, the nature of the procedure was not, as is clear from rr 72.1(1), 72.2(1) and (2),

e 72.4 and 72.9:

'72.1   *Scope of this Part and interpretation*

(1) This Part contains rules which provide for a judgment creditor to obtain an order for the payment to him of money which a third party who is within the jurisdiction owes to the judgment debtor …

f 72.2   *Third party debt order*

(1) Upon the application of a judgment creditor, the court may make an order (a "final third party debt order") requiring a third party to pay to the judgment creditor—(a) the amount of any debt due or accruing due to the judgment debtor from the third party; or (b) so much of that debt as is

g sufficient to satisfy the judgment debt and the judgment creditor's costs of the application.

(2) The court will not make an order under paragraph 1 without first making an order (an "interim third party debt order") as provided by rule 72.4(2) …

h 72.4   *Interim third party debt order*

(1) An application for a third party debt order will initially be dealt with by a judge without a hearing.

(2) The judge may make an interim third party debt order—(a) fixing a hearing to consider whether to make a final third party debt order; and

j (b) directing that until that hearing the third party must not make any payment which reduces the amount he owes the judgment debtor to less than the amount specified in the order.

(3) An interim third party debt order will specify the amount of money which the third party must retain, which will be the total of—(a) the amount of money remaining due to the judgment creditor under the judgment or

order; and (b) an amount for the judgment creditor's fixed costs of the
application, as specified in the relevant practice direction.

(4) An interim third party debt order becomes binding on a third party
when it is served on him.

(5) The date of the hearing to consider the application shall be not less
than 28 days after the interim third party debt order is made ...

72.9 Effect of final third party offer

(1) A final third party debt order shall be enforceable as an order to pay
money.

(2) If—(a) the third party pays money to the judgment creditor in
compliance with a third party debt order; or (b) the order is enforced against
him, the third party shall, to the extent of the amount paid by him or realised
by enforcement against him, be discharged from his debt to the judgment
debtor.

(3) Paragraph (2) applies even if the third party debt order, or the original
judgment or order against the judgment debtor, is later set aside.'

[13] As the cited provisions made clear, the procedure has from the beginning
made provision for a two-stage process, first an order nisi or interim order, then
an order absolute or final order. The decided cases leave no room for doubt
about the legal effect of each of these orders.

[14] Section 62 of the 1854 Act describes the order nisi as binding the judgment
debtor's chose in action in the hands of the garnishee. The effect of the order, as
Chitty J put in *Re General Horticultural Co, ex p Whitehouse* (1886) 32 Ch D 512 at
515, is 'to give the judgment creditor execution against the debts owing to his
debtor'. In *Rogers v Whiteley* [1892] AC 118 at 121 Lord Halsbury LC spoke of the
order attaching all debts, and Lord Watson (at 122) said:

'The effect of an order attaching "all debts" owing or accruing due by [the
garnishee] to the judgment debtor is to make the garnishee custodier for the
Court of the whole funds attached; and he cannot, except at his own peril,
part with any of those funds without the sanction of the Court.'

As Lord Morris put it (at 123):

'... all debts due and owing by the above-named garnishee are attached to
answer the judgment creditor's demand—that is, they are all captured for
the purpose of afterwards answering that demand.'

In *Galbraith v Grimshaw* [1910] 1 KB 339, Farwell LJ pointed out that the order
nisi—

'does not, it is true, operate as a transfer of the property in the debt, but it
is an equitable charge on it, and the garnishee cannot pay the debt to any one
but the garnishor without incurring the risk of having to pay it over again to
the creditor.'

Atkin LJ made the same point in *Joachimson (N) v Swiss Bank Corp* [1921] 3 KB 110
at 131, [1921] All ER Rep 92 at 102: 'The service of the order nisi binds the debt in
the hands of the garnishee—that is, it creates a charge in favour of the judgment
creditor.' The point was again made by Lord Denning MR in *Choice Investments
Ltd v Jeromnimon (Midland Bank Ltd, garnishee)* [1981] 1 All ER 225 at 227, [1981]
QB 149 at 155:

a

'[Service of the order nisi] prevents the bank from paying the money to its customer until the garnishee order is made absolute, or is discharged ... The money at the bank is then said to be "attached" ... But the "attachment" is not an order to pay. It only freezes the sum in the hands of the bank until the order is made absolute or is discharged. It is only when the order is made absolute that the bank is liable to pay.'

b

[15] The effect of the order absolute has been similarly explored in the authorities. It was pointed out in *Re Combined Weighing and Advertising Machine Co* (1889) 43 Ch D 99 that the order does not operate as a transfer of the garnishee's debt but attaches the debt and confers a right of execution only. Cotton LJ explained in *Chatterton v Watney* (1881) 17 Ch D 259 at 262:

c

'The effect of a garnishee order is to bind the debt attached and to prevent the creditor from receiving it; and when it is made absolute it gives the judgment creditor a right to recover payment from the garnishee, and by rule 8 it is provided that payment made by the garnishee under the proceeding shall be a valid discharge to him as against the judgment debtor.

d

There is nothing in the terms of the General Order to affect any security for the debt, it only takes away the right of the judgment debtor to receive the money and gives the judgment creditor a right to receive it. It has not the effect of transferring the security, nor does it give the person who obtained the garnishee order any right to the security or any claim against the land comprised in it.'

e

Lindley MR defined the effect of the order absolute very succinctly in *Pritchett v English and Colonial Syndicate* [1899] 2 QB 428 at 433:

'... the order is, in substance, not an order to pay a debt, but an order on the garnishees, the syndicate, to hand over something in their hands belonging to [the judgment debtor] to [the judgment creditor].'

f

[16] In a much-quoted passage of his judgment in *Ellis v M'Henry* (1871) LR 6 CP 228 at 234, Bovill CJ sitting in the Court of Common Pleas said:

g

'In the first place, there is no doubt that a debt or liability arising in any country may be discharged by the laws of that country, and that such a discharge, if it extinguishes the debt or liability, and does not merely interfere with the remedies or course of procedure to enforce it, will be an effectual answer to the claim, not only in the courts of that country, but in every other country. This is the law of England, and is a principle of private international law adopted in other countries. It was laid down by Lord King, in *Burrows v. Jemino* ((1726) 2 Stra 733); by Lord Mansfield, in *Ballantine v. Golding* ((1784) Cooke's Bankrupt Laws 419); by Lord Ellenborough, in *Potter v. Brown* ((1804) 5 East 124, 102 ER 1016); by the Privy Council, in *Odwin v. Forbes* ((1817) Buck 57); and in *Quelin v. Moisson* ((1828) 1 Knapp 265 at 266, 12 ER 320); and by the Court of Queen's Bench in the case of *Gardiner v. Houghton* ((1862) 2 B & S 743, 121 ER 1247); and by the Court of Exchequer Chamber, in the elaborate judgment delivered by my Brother Willes, in *Phillips v. Eyre* ((1870) LR 6 QB 1 at 28). Secondly, as a general proposition, it is also true that the discharge of a debt or liability by the law of a country other than that in which the debt arises, does not relieve the debtor in any other country: *Smith v. Buchanan* ((1800) 1 East 6, 102 ER 3); *Lewis v. Owen* ((1821) 4 B & Ald

h

j

654); *Phillips* v. *Allan* ((1828) 8 B & C 477, 108 ER 1120); *Bartley* v. *Hodges* ((1861) 1 B & S 375, 121 ER 754).'

This statement remains good law. In *Martin v Nadel* (*Dresdner Bank, garnishees*) [1906] 2 KB 26, [1904–7] All ER Rep 827, where a garnishee order was sought in England against the London branch of a German bank to attach a balance owed to the judgment debtor by the Berlin branch of the bank, Vaughan Williams LJ said ([1906] 2 KB 26 at 29):

'It appears to me to be clear that a garnishee order is of the nature of an execution, and is governed by the lex fori; and by international law an execution which has been carried into effect in a foreign country under foreign law, and has taken away part of a man's property, is not recognised as binding. There can be no doubt that under the rules of international law the Dresdner Bank could not set up, in an action in Berlin, the execution levied in this country in respect to this debt. If we consider the converse case it is clear, to my mind, that we should take that view of a similar transaction occurring abroad.'

Stirling LJ was of the same mind ([1906] 2 KB 26 at 31):

'On the facts of this case the debt of the bank to Nadel would be properly recoverable in Germany. That being so, it must be taken that the order of this Court would not protect the bank from being called on to pay the debt a second time.'

It is evident that the Hong Kong law and procedure (recorded in [8], above) which deny recognition to a third party debt or garnishee order made in England in relation to a debt sited in Hong Kong is not an unusual or idiosyncratic rule but one which reflects general international practice.

[17] The House was referred to no reported case in which the English court has made a final third party debt order or garnishee order absolute in relation to a foreign debt, although (with one exception) the refusal has been put on discretionary grounds; and discretion has been exercised against the making of an order even where the debt to be attached is situated in this country where it has appeared that the third party, despite the discharge of its debt to the judgment debtor as a matter of English law, may be at risk elsewhere of compulsion to pay a second time.

[18] In *Martin v Nadel*, to which reference has already been made, an absolute order was refused because the garnishee bank was at risk of having to pay twice and the making of an order in such circumstances was 'inequitable' and 'contrary to natural justice' ([1906] 2 KB 26 at 30–31). In *Swiss Bank Corp v Boehmische Industrial Bank* [1923] 1 KB 673 the situation was different, because the debt was situated here in England. Bankes LJ pointed out this distinction and its importance (at 678–679):

'If the debt is situate, or in other words if it is properly recoverable, in this country, then it would be discharged by payment under an order of our Courts and the garnishee need have no fear of being required to pay it a second time; but if the debt is situate, that is properly recoverable, in a foreign country, then it is not discharged by payment in this country under an order of the Courts of this country, and the debtor may be called upon to pay it over again in the foreign country. There is no doubt as to the effect of payment made under a garnishee order here. It is clearly a discharge pro

a
tanto of the debt ... There is a vital distinction between the facts of that case [*Martin v Nadel*] and the facts of the present case ... That was a debt situate in Berlin, being properly recoverable in Berlin. That was the debt sought to be garnished. Here the debt sought to be garnished was a debt situate in England being properly recoverable in England. In this case the debt can be properly discharged in England. In *Martin v Nadel* the debt could be properly
b
discharged only in Berlin.'

Scrutton LJ (at 680–681) said that—

'the Court will not make absolute a garnishee order where it will not operate to discharge the garnishee in whole or pro tanto from the debt; it will not expose him to the risk of having to pay the debt or part of it twice over.'

c
Scrutton LJ considered this (at 681) to be 'well established as a principle of discretion on which the Court acts'.

[19] The exception mentioned in [17], above, is found in *Richardson v Richardson* (*National Bank of India Ltd, garnishee*) [1927] P 228, [1927] All ER Rep 92, in which
d
a bank owed debts to a judgment debtor customer on accounts held both in London and in Africa. It was accepted that the former were subject to a garnishee order. The dispute concerned the latter. Hill J said ([1927] P 228 at 235, [1927] All ER Rep 92 at 96):

'The bank is no doubt indebted to the judgment debtor and the bank is
e
within the jurisdiction. The Order deals with the case where "any other person is indebted to the judgment debtor and is within the jurisdiction". But both in principle and upon authority, that means "is indebted within the jurisdiction and is within the jurisdiction". The debt must be properly recoverable within the jurisdiction. In principle, attachment of debts is a form of execution, and the general power of execution extends only to
f
property within the jurisdiction of the Court which orders it. A debt is not [properly] within the jurisdiction if it cannot be recovered here.'

Hill J was accordingly ([1927] P 228 at 236, [1927] All ER Rep 92 at 96)—

'of opinion that moneys held by the bank to the credit of the judgment
g
debtor at the African branches cannot be made the subject of a garnishee order, for they are not a debt recoverable within the jurisdiction.'

He went on to hold that, if he was wrong in that conclusion, he would exercise his discretion against the making of an order.

h
[20] In *SCF Finance Co Ltd v Masri (No 3)* [1987] 1 All ER 194, [1987] QB 1028, the Court of Appeal (Slade and Ralph Gibson LJJ and Sir John Megaw) differed from the view taken by Hill J, while accepting ([1987] 1 All ER 194 at 205, [1987] QB 1028 at 1044) that in a case where the garnishee was not indebted within the jurisdiction that might be relevant to the exercise of the court's discretion. Since, in that case, the debt in question was an English debt, the court's jurisdiction in
j
relation to foreign debts did not fall for decision. Nor did it in *Interpool Ltd v Galani* [1987] 2 All ER 981, [1988] QB 738, which concerned the examination of a judgment debtor under RSC Ord 48 and not the making of a garnishee order under Ord 49. As Balcombe LJ observed at the end of the judgment of the court (given on behalf of Lloyd LJ and himself) ([1987] 2 All ER 981 at 985, [1988] QB 738 at 743):

'The use of Ord 48, in English enforcement proceedings, in order to
discover the *existence* of foreign assets, does not confer, or purport to confer,   *a*
jurisdiction on the English court in relation to enforcement proceedings in
any other country in which those assets may be situate.'

But, referring to the absence of any requirement in Ord 49, r 1(1) that the
garnished debt as well as the garnishee must be properly within the jurisdiction,   *b*
the court made reference to the *SCF Finance* case and described the decision in
Richardson v Richardson as 'no longer good law' ([1987] 2 All ER 981 at 983, [1988]
QB 738 at 741).

[21] Reference should be made to the decision of the House in *Deutsche
Schachtbau- und Tiefbohrgesellschaft mbH v Xas Al-Khaimah National Oil Co* [1988]
2 All ER 833, [1990] 1 AC 295. That case concerned a garnishee order absolute   *c*
made in respect of a debt situated in England, and the House was not called upon
to consider the position where foreign debts were in issue. But a majority of the
House agreed with the opinion of Lord Goff of Chieveley, who referred ([1988]
2 All ER 833 at 850, [1990] 1 AC 295 at 350) to the court's 'discretionary power to
make a garnishee order absolute' and concluded that it would be 'inequitable'   *d*
([1988] 2 All ER 833 at 853, 854–855, [1990] 1 AC 295 at 353, 355) to do so—

'where the payment by the garnishee under the order absolute will not
necessarily discharge his liability under the attached debt, there being a real
risk that he may be held liable in some foreign court to pay a second time.'
(See [1988] 2 All ER 833 at 854–855, [1990] 1 AC 295 at 355.)   *e*

Unsurprisingly, in the light of these authorities, the English court continued to
exercise its discretion against the making of orders in relation to debts with a
foreign situs: see, for example, *Zoneheath Associates Ltd v China Tianjin International
Economic and Technical Co-operative Corp* [1994] CLC 348.

f

EXTRA-TERRITORIAL JURISDICTION

[22] In the course of argument before the House on this appeal, attention was
drawn to a line of authority not directly related to garnishee or third party debt
orders but bearing on the exercise by the English court of powers affecting the
conduct of foreigners outside its jurisdiction. *R v Grossman* (1981) 73 Cr App R 302   *g*
concerned an application made against Barclays Bank in London to obtain
inspection of an account held at a branch of the bank in the Isle of Man. The Civil
Division of the Court of Appeal (Lord Denning MR, Shaw and Oliver LJJ) which
determined the application was later held to have lacked jurisdiction to do so (see
Bonalumi v Secretary of State for the Home Dept [1985] 1 All ER 797, [1985] QB 675)
but no doubt has been thrown on the opinions expressed (see (1981) 73 Cr App R   *h*
302 at 308–309). The Manx branch was to be considered a different entity from
the bank's head office in London and any order in respect of the production of the
books should be made by the Manx court and not the English court. Otherwise
there was a risk of jurisdictional conflict which must be avoided. *R v Grossman*
was cited and relied on by Hoffmann J in *MacKinnon v Donaldson Lufkin & Jenrette*   *j*
Securities Corp [1986] 1 All ER 653, [1986] Ch 482, where a plaintiff in an English
action had obtained an order against an American bank, served on its London
office, requiring production of books and papers at its New York head office.
Hoffmann J pointed out the distinction between 'personal jurisdiction (ie who
can be brought before the court)' and 'subject matter jurisdiction (ie to what
extent the court can claim to regulate the conduct of those persons)' ([1986] 1 All ER

a 653 at 657, [1986] Ch 482 at 493). He held ([1986] 1 All ER 653 at 658, [1986] Ch 482 at 493):

> 'In principle and on authority it seems to me that the court should not, save in exceptional circumstances, impose such a requirement upon a foreigner, and, in particular, upon a foreign bank. The principle is that a state should refrain from demanding obedience to its sovereign authority by foreigners in
b > respect of their conduct outside the jurisdiction.'

The judge went on ([1986] 1 All ER 653 at 658, [1986] Ch 482 at 494) to explain the rationale of the principle:

> 'The need to exercise the court's jurisdiction with due regard to the
c > sovereignty of others is particularly important in the case of banks. Banks are in a special position because their documents are concerned not only with their own business but with that of their customers. They will owe their customers a duty of confidence regulated by the law of the country where the account is kept. That duty is in some countries reinforced by criminal sanctions and sometimes by "blocking statutes" which specifically forbid the
d > bank to provide information for the purpose of foreign legal proceedings (compare s 2 of our Protection of Trading Interests Act 1980). If every country where a bank happened to carry on business asserted a right to require that bank to produce documents relating to accounts kept in any other such country, banks would be in the unhappy position of being forced
e > to submit to whichever sovereign was able to apply the greatest pressure.'

[23] Similar reticence was approved by the Court of Appeal (Kerr, Neill and Nicholls LJJ) when considering worldwide Mareva injunctions in *Babanaft International Co SA v Bassatne* [1989] 1 All ER 433, [1990] Ch 13. The court accepted that there was nothing to preclude English courts from granting Mareva-type
f injunctions against defendants extending to assets outside the jurisdiction, but insisted ([1989] 1 All ER 433 at 444, [1990] Ch 13 at 32 per Kerr LJ) that—

> 'there can be no question of such orders operating directly upon the foreign assets by way of attachment, or upon third parties, such as banks, holding the assets. The effectiveness of such orders for these purposes can
g > only derive from their recognition and enforcement by the local courts, as should be made clear in the terms of the orders to avoid any misunderstanding suggesting an unwarranted assumption of extraterritorial jurisdiction.'

Nicholls LJ was similarly concerned ([1989] 1 All ER 433 at 453, [1990] Ch 13 at
h 44) at the 'extraterritorial vice' of unqualified orders. He pointed out ([1989] 1 All ER 433 at 454, [1990] Ch 13 at 46):

> 'The enforcement of the judgment in other countries, by attachment or like process, in respect of assets which are situated there is not affected by the order. The order does not attach those assets. It does not create, or purport
j > to create, a charge on those assets, nor does it give the plaintiff any proprietary interest in then. The English court is not attempting in any way to interfere with or control the enforcement process in respect of those assets.'

As is well known, this judgment was reflected in what became the standard form of Mareva injunction order, until further protection was afforded to those holding overseas assets of persons subject to Mareva injunctions pursuant to the judgment of Clarke J in *Baltic Shipping v Translink Shipping Ltd* [1995] 1 Lloyd's Rep 673.

CONCLUSION

[24] To resolve the issues arising between the judgment creditor and the third party in this appeal it is in my opinion necessary to return to very basic first principles. A garnishee or third party debt order is a proprietary remedy which operates by way of attachment against the property of the judgment debtor. The property of the judgment debtor so attached is the chose in action represented by the debt of the third party or garnishee to the judgment debtor. On the making of the interim or nisi order that chose in action is (as it has been variously put) bound, frozen, attached or charged in the hands of the third party or garnishee. Subject to any monetary limit which may be specified in the order, the third party is not entitled to deal with that chose in action by making payment to the judgment debtor or any other party at his request. When a final or absolute order is made the third party or garnishee is obliged (subject to any specified monetary limit) to make payment to the judgment creditor and not to the judgment debtor, but the debt of the third party to the judgment debtor is discharged pro tanto.

[25] As appears from the provisions of primary and subordinate legislation cited in [10]–[12], above, the discharge of the third party or garnishee on making payment to the judgment debtor under a final or absolute order has been an integral feature of this procedure from the beginning. In s 65 of the 1854 Act, in Ord 45, rr 8 and 7 of the 1875 and 1883 rules respectively, in Ord 49, r 8 of the 1965 rules and in CPR 72.9 the discharge of the third party or garnishee has been expressed as a necessary consequence of the making of the order ('shall').

[26] It is not in my opinion open to the court to make an order in a case, such as the present, where it is clear or appears that the making of the order will not discharge the debt of the third party or garnishee to the judgment debtor according to the law which governs that debt. In practical terms it does not matter very much whether the House rules that the court has no jurisdiction to make an order in such a case or that the court has a discretion which should always be exercised against the making of an order in such a case. But the former seems to me the preferable analysis, since I would not accept that the court has power to make an order which, if made, would lack what has been legislatively stipulated to be a necessary consequence of such an order. I find myself in close agreement with the opinion of Hill J in *Richardson v Richardson*, subject only to the qualification (of little or no practical importance) that an order may be made relating to a chose in action sited abroad if it appears that by the law applicable in that situs the English order would be recognised as discharging pro tanto the liability of the third party to the judgment debtor. If (contrary to my opinion) the English court had jurisdiction to make an order in a case such as the present, the objections to its exercising a discretion to do so would be very strong on grounds of principle, comity and convenience: it is contrary in principle to compel a bank to pay out money owed by a customer if its liability to its customer is not reduced to the same extent; it is inconsistent with the comity owed to the Hong Kong court to purport to interfere with assets subject to its local jurisdiction; and the judgment creditor has a straightforward and readily available means of enforcing its judgment against the assets of the judgment debtors in Hong Kong.

[27] It is of course true, as the judgment creditor argued and as was accepted in the *SCF Finance* case [1987] 1 All ER 194 at 205, [1987] QB 1028 at 1044, that the

a legislation has from the beginning stipulated that the third party or garnishee should be within the jurisdiction but not that the debt to be attached should be within the jurisdiction. This seems to me a point of very little weight. The language used in 1854 has, until very recently, been reproduced with remarkably little change, and I think it rather unlikely that Parliament in 1854 was directing its mind to garnishees served within the jurisdiction but owing debts to the

b judgment debtor abroad. Since no order attaching a foreign chose in action has been made in any reported case, there can have been no pressing need for the Rules Committee to clarify any suggested ambiguity in the rules.

[28] The Court of Appeal attached importance to the supposed availability to the third party of a restitutionary remedy in Hong Kong if the third party made (or was compelled to make) payment to the judgment creditor under an English

c order. This appears to me, with respect, to reflect some misunderstanding of the procedure. For, as already emphasised, the order takes effect against the property of the judgment debtor. Its effect is to enable the judgment creditor to take the property of the judgment debtor. The property of the third party is in no way involved, save by the diminution of its debt to the judgment debtor. Yet a

d disbursement of its own resources, compelled by law, is the ground relied on to support the third party's putative claim against the judgment debtors in Hong Kong. If, as in my opinion would be so, the effect of an order in this case would be to compel the third party to disburse its own funds, that would be a very clear indication that the order was one which should never have been made. The judge's reasoning on this point was, in my opinion, entirely sound.

e [29] The Court of Appeal also placed reliance on the third party's standard terms and conditions. It is unnecessary to set these out. They do not entitle the third party to make deductions from the judgment debtors' account which are not authorised by the law applicable to that account. They do not, in other words, override the rule that an English third party debt or garnishee order is not

f recognised in Hong Kong.

[30] At first instance the judge treated the issue before him as one of discretion, as on existing authority he was bound to do, and gave compelling reasons why an absolute order should not be made. I would for my part accept those reasons did I not consider that he had no jurisdiction to make an absolute order. I would allow the third party's appeal with costs in the Court of Appeal

g and before the House, set aside the order of the Court of Appeal and restore the order of the judge in so far as it set aside the garnishee order nisi, ordered that there be no absolute order and awarded costs to the third party, summarily assessed, against the judgment creditor.

h **LORD NICHOLLS OF BIRKENHEAD.**

[31] My Lords, I have had the opportunity of reading in draft the speeches of my noble and learned friends Lord Bingham of Cornhill and Lord Hoffmann. For the reasons they give, with which I agree, I too would allow this appeal.

j **LORD HOFFMANN.**

[32] My Lords, the question in this appeal is whether the court can make a third party debt order under CPR Pt 72 in respect of a foreign debt. By a foreign debt, I mean for present purposes a debt which is payable in a foreign country and governed by the foreign law. Different considerations may apply in cases in which one of these conditions is missing but I put them aside because the facts of the present case are both simple and typical. The judgment creditor is seeking to

enforce a French judgment which has been registered in this country. It wishes
to use the third party debt procedure to execute against money standing to the
debtor's credit in an account with the Hong Kong and Shanghai Banking Corp Ltd
(the bank) at its principal office in Hong Kong. The credit balance is a debt payable
by the bank to the debtor in Hong Kong and governed by Hong Kong law.

[33] Part 72 came into force on 25 March 2002, replacing RSC Ord 49
(garnishee proceedings), under which provisions the judgment creditor's
application was made on 3 April 2000. But there is no material difference
between the two sets of rules. Rule 72.2(1) gives the court power to order a third
party to pay to the judgment creditor 'the amount of any debt due or accruing
due to the judgment debtor from the third party'. RSC Ord 49, r 1(1) provided
that if a person within the jurisdiction (the garnishee) was 'indebted to the
judgment debtor', the court could order him to pay the debt to the judgment
creditor. Rule 72.9(2) now provides that, if the third party pays money to the
judgment creditor in compliance with the order, he shall to that extent 'be
discharged from his debt to the judgment debtor'. Likewise, RSC Ord 49, r 8
provided that any payment made by a garnishee in compliance with an order
'shall be a valid discharge of his liability to the judgment creditor to the extent of
the amount paid'.

[34] So despite its very recent enactment and modern language, the third
party debt order is a process of execution which goes back far into English legal
history. RSC Ord 49 is derived from the provisions of ss 61 to 70 of the Common
Law Procedure Act 1854. These provisions were enacted on the recommendation
of the *Second Report of the Royal Commission on the Superior Courts of Common Law*
(1853), which included Jervis CJ, Martin B, Sir Alexander Cockburn and the future
Bramwell B and Willes J. The commissioners said (p 38):

> '[W]e may suggest, that the remedies of creditors against the property of
> their debtors might be made more extensive by enabling a creditor after
> judgment to attach debts and monies of his debtor in the hands of third
> persons, and so obtain satisfaction of his judgment. We are not aware of any
> process, either in the superior courts of law or equity, in suits between
> subject and subject, by which this can directly be done, though the course of
> proceeding under writs of execution at the suit of the crown, and by way of
> foreign attachment in the mayor's court of London and some other cities, as
> well as in the courts of many foreign countries, shows that such a remedy
> would be practicable and useful.'

[35] The procedure called foreign attachment, to which the commissioners
referred and on which the procedure under the 1854 Act was modelled, had
existed by immemorial custom in London and other cities. The custom had been
certified by the Recorder of London in 1481 but went back much further;
enthusiastic City historians traced it to the Roman occupation and even to the
laws of Troy (see *London (Mayor etc) v Cox* (1867) LR 2 HL 239 at 256).

[36] Foreign attachment of debts was primarily an interlocutory process to
compel the defendant's appearance and provide security for judgment but, in the
event of default by a defendant, it was also a process of execution. Besides being
a model for the 1854 garnishee order, foreign attachment as an interlocutory
process had further offspring in the shape of the Mareva injunction: see Lord
Denning MR in *Rasu Maritima SA v Perusahaan Pertambangan Minyak Dan Gas
Bumi Negara (Pertamina) and Government of Indonesia (as interveners)* [1977] 3 All ER

a   324 at 331, [1978] QB 644 at 657–658. But the attachment of foreign debts raises similar issues of principle at whatever stage in the proceedings the debts are attached and the decisions on the scope of foreign attachment are therefore still relevant.

[37] Exorbitant claims of jurisdiction by the Mayor of London's Court, allegedly founded upon the custom of foreign attachment, were challenged in *b*   *London (Mayor etc) v Cox* (1867) LR 2 HL 239.   The result of that case was overdetermined because none of the three parties resided in the City and neither the judgment debt nor the garnishee's debt had accrued there. The House of Lords held that the court had no jurisdiction to grant a foreign attachment and issued a writ of prohibition.   The principal ground of decision was that the Mayor's Court, being a local court, could not establish jurisdiction over *c*   a non-resident defendant merely by serving a garnishee notice upon another non-resident who was physically present in the City and was alleged to owe him a debt. But Willes J, who gave the opinion of the judges which was adopted by the House, also dealt (at 268) with the position of the garnishee whose foreign debt to the judgment debtor the court was purporting to attach:

d
> 'A foreign banker, of whom as banker it may be said *"pecunia est alter sanguis"*, passing through *London,* may be called upon, at the suit of some other foreigner, of whom he never heard, and the validity of whose claim he is not to be permitted to dispute, to pay in *London* in cash what he might at home have paid in paper; and if, to get rid of annoyance, or relying upon *e*   English justice, he pays, his customer may afterwards insist … in a foreign court that the debt or the party was not subject to the jurisdiction.'

[38] The second ground of decision was therefore (at 274–275) that a foreign attachment could not be made against a garnishee merely on account of his physical presence in the jurisdiction:

f
> 'It appears, therefore, to be in accordance with authority and good sense to hold that a man who could not be sued in *London* by his own creditor cannot by the mere act of using the Queen's highway through the *City* … become liable to be stayed there under the custom of the place by the alleged creditor of his creditor.'

g   [39] In *London Corp v London Joint Stock Bank* (1881) 6 App Cas 393 the scope of foreign attachment again came before the House of Lords. This time the question was whether a corporation could be a garnishee. The House decided that it could not because, according to the custom, the only means of compulsion which could be used to obtain payment of the debt from a garnishee was his physical *h*   detention. It followed that there was no way of making a corporation pay. This meant that if it did pay, it would not be able to defend a subsequent claim by his creditor on the ground that it had been compelled by law to pay. The House decided that this was fatal to the use of foreign attachment, because it was essential to the procedure that the payment by the garnishee should discharge its *j*   debt to the judgment debtor. 'The garnishee', said Lord Blackburn (at 415)—

> 'if he is to be obliged to pay the money, must be discharged from paying it to his creditor. Now the garnishee cannot, according to the authorities, or to reason, set himself free towards his creditor by making any voluntary payment: it must be a compulsory payment; a payment under compulsion of law or else he is not discharged.'

[40] Lord Watson likewise said (at 421):

'In considering the merits of that part of the case it is very necessary to keep in view that which has been already referred to by both my noble and learned friends, namely, that it is of the essence of this custom that execution may follow upon the order directed to the garnishee, in the event of his not obeying that order and failing to hand over the goods of the defendant, or to pay the money of the defendant to the plaintiff. That is necessary, because the courts of law have held that, unless he so deliver or pay under compulsion, he is not discharged. The custom would not be a reasonable one unless it went the length of affording protection to the garnishee when he obeys the order of the court.'

[41] This objection that a corporate debtor could not be compelled to satisfy a foreign attachment did not of course apply to post-judgment attachment under the statutory garnishee procedure, which by then was contained in Ord 45 of the Rules of Court scheduled to the Supreme Court of Judicature Act 1875. The rules made express provision for ordinary execution against a garnishee who did not pay, whether he was a corporate or a natural person. And, as I have mentioned, they also provided expressly that a garnishee who paid under the order should be discharged from his debt. But the question is whether, in the case of a foreign debt, these provisions are sufficient to satisfy the principle that the garnishee can be made to pay only if he will be discharged from payment to his creditor.

[42] This was the question considered by the Court of Appeal in the important case of *Martin v Nadel (Dresdner Bank, garnishees)* [1906] 2 KB 26, [1904–7] All ER Rep 827. The judgment debtor lived in Berlin, where he maintained an account with the Dresdner Bank. Judgment was entered against him in an action in London; he appealed unsuccessfully to the Court of Appeal and then to the House of Lords, which required him to give security for costs by depositing £200 in court and providing a bank recognisance for £500. The latter was provided by the bank's London branch against the security of the same amount deposited with the branch in Berlin. The appeal was dismissed and the costs paid out of the money in court and £300 paid by the London branch under the recognisance. This left the judgment debtor with just under £200 in his account in Berlin. The judgment creditor obtained a garnishee order against the bank attaching the balance in Berlin. But the bank appealed and the Court of Appeal set the order aside.

[43] Counsel for the bank argued that the German courts might recognise the judgment against Mr Nadel, because he had submitted to the jurisdiction, but not the garnishee order 'which forms part of a code relating to execution'. Counsel for the judgment creditor argued that the balance was not really a foreign debt because Nadel could have sued for it in England as money had and received to his use.

[44] Vaughan Williams LJ said ([1906] 2 KB 26 at 29):

'It appears to me to be clear that a garnishee order is of the nature of an execution, and is governed by the lex fori; and by international law an execution which has been carried into effect in a foreign country under foreign law, and has taken away part of a man's property, is not recognized as binding. There can be no doubt that under the rules of international law the Dresdner Bank could not set up, in an action in Berlin, the execution levied in this country in respect to this debt.'

a **[45]** It would, I think, have been open to the Court of Appeal to say that when RSC Ord 45, r 2 referred to 'all debts' owing or accruing from a third party, they did not include foreign debts—at any rate, not foreign debts in the sense in which I have been using that expression. It is true that the language is entirely general, but, as Millett J said in *Re International Tin Council* [1987] 1 All ER 890 at 901, [1987] Ch 419 at 450:

b
> 'It is one thing to give effect to plain and unambiguous language in a statute. It is quite another to insist that general words must invariably be given their fullest meaning and applied to every object which falls within their literal scope, regardless of the probable intentions of Parliament.'

c **[46]** Against the background of private international law and the principles which garnishee proceedings had inherited from foreign attachment, there were good arguments for saying that foreign debts did not fall within the scope of the rule. But the Court of Appeal did not take this course. Instead, it said that the judgment creditor did not have a right to a garnishee order ex debito justitiae. It *d* was a matter of discretion and the court should not make an order when it would be inequitable to do so. Both Vaughan Williams LJ and Stirling LJ said that it would be inequitable to make an order which left the bank still liable to an action in Berlin.

[47] *Martin v Nadel* was distinguished by the Court of Appeal in *Swiss Bank Corp v Boehmische Industrial Bank* [1923] 1 KB 673, in which the Swiss bank had *e* obtained an English judgment against a bank in Prague. It executed upon the judgment by a garnishee order against the Prague bank's account with the London Merchant Bank in London. Again there was no problem about the jurisdiction of the English court to enter judgment: the Prague bank had submitted to the jurisdiction. But the London Merchant Bank appealed against *f* the garnishee order on the ground that it could still be held liable for the same debt in Prague. Bankes LJ said that the debt owed by the London bank, being properly recoverable in England, was situated in England and therefore discharged by compliance with the garnishee order, not only as a matter of English law but under international law which it could be assumed would be *g* applied in all other countries. In *Martin v Nadel*, on the other hand, the debt was situated in Germany and as a matter of international law would not be treated anywhere outside England as having been discharged by an English garnishee order. Scrutton LJ (at 680–681) again identified the matter as being one of discretion:

h
> 'The court will not make absolute a garnishee order where it will not operate to discharge the garnishee in whole or pro tanto from the debt; it will not expose him to the risk of having to pay the debt or part of it twice over. That is well established as a principle of discretion on which the court acts.'

[48] In *Richardson v Richardson*, however, Hill J gave the principle a harder *j* edge. Mrs Richardson had divorced her husband living in East Africa and obtained an order for costs. To enforce it, she applied for a garnishee order against his money in the Mombasa and Dar-es-Salaam branches of the National Bank of India, which had its head office in London. The judge said ([1927] P 228 at 235, [1927] All ER Rep 92 at 96) that 'in principle and upon authority', the words 'is indebted to the judgment debtor' in RSC Ord 45 meant 'is indebted within the jurisdiction':

'In principle, attachment of debts is a form of execution, and the general
power of execution extends only to property within the jurisdiction of the
Court which orders it. A debt is not property within the jurisdiction if it
cannot be recovered here. As a matter of authority, the case of *Martin v.
Nadel*, as explained by *Swiss Bank Corporation v Boehmische Industrial Bank*, and
the decision and judgments in that case show that the Order does not apply
unless the debt is properly recoverable within the jurisdiction.'

[49] The question of whether the matter was one of jurisdiction or discretion
was considered by the Court of Appeal in the *SCF Finance* case. Leggatt J gave
judgment against Mr Masri for over $US900,000. His wife had $US400,000 in an
account with the London branch of the United Arab Bank. The judge held that
she was estopped from denying that this money belonged beneficially to
Mr Masri. Leggatt J treated the money as a debt owed by the wife to the husband
and made a garnishee order against it. The difficulty was that both of them lived
in Jordan and so, it was said, the debt was a foreign debt, situate and recoverable
in Jordan. But, said Ralph Gibson LJ ([1987] 1 All ER 194 at 205–206, [1987] QB
1028 at 1044):

'[The issue estoppel] has established that, as between the two of them and
as a matter of English law, the debt due from the Arab Bank, which is a debt
arising in this country, is due to the first defendant and therefore available to
be attached in satisfaction of the judgment debt due from him to the
plaintiffs. Nothing ... has given us the least reason to suppose that the
second defendant could be at any risk of being ordered to pay the debt a
second time to her husband.'

[50] As I read this passage, the court was treating the garnishee order as
operating, not so much on a debt between wife and husband, but on the debt
owed by the bank, which Mrs Masri was estopped from claiming was owed to her
rather than the judgment debtor. On this basis the debt was clearly not a foreign
debt and there was no difficulty about the attachment. The court did, however,
say that it thought Hill J was wrong in *Richardson's* case to say that there was no
jurisdiction to attach foreign debts. It was, as the court had said in *Martin v Nadel*,
a matter of discretion. This view was repeated by Balcombe LJ giving the
judgment of the court in *Interpool Ltd v Galani* [1987] 2 All ER 981 at 983, [1988]
QB 738 at 741.

[51] In *Deutsche Schachtbau-und Tiefbohrgesellschaft mbH v Shell International
Petroleum Co Ltd (t/a Shell International Trading Co)* [1988] 2 All ER 833, [1990] 1 AC
295 Hobhouse J said that one could confidently regard *Martin v Nadel* as
establishing that—

'if in accordance with the conflict of law rules recognised by the English
courts, the garnishee order absolute will not suffice to discharge the liability
of the garnishee and the garnishee will continue to be exposed to a risk of
being held liable for the debt by a foreign court of competent jurisdiction, a
garnishee order will not be made.'

[52] What was more controversial was whether one should assume that
foreign courts would act in accordance with recognised conflict of laws rules or
whether one should also refuse to make a garnishee order if there appeared a risk
that the garnishee, although discharged in accordance with English conflict rules,
would be exposed to a second claim in a foreign court which did not give effect

a to them. On this point the House of Lords were divided, Lord Templeman taking the former view and the other members of the House the latter. Lord Oliver of Aylmerton said ([1988] 2 All ER 833 at 845, [1990] 1 AC 295 at 343):

b 'It has to be recognised that a debt is a species of property which may be recoverable by legal process from a debtor in more than one jurisdiction and it would be entirely inequitable that the garnishee should, by process in different jurisdictions properly conducted in accordance with the local law, be compelled to pay twice over in order that a judgment with which he has no connection whatever should be satisfied at his expense. If the reality is that this is likely to be the result, the fact that the particular foreign legal process is not one which commends itself to our jurisprudence is really *c* immaterial.'

[53] In analysing the authorities, Lord Goff of Chieveley said that the question was always whether it would be inequitable to make the garnishee order absolute. It would generally be inequitable to do so if the garnishee would have to pay the debt twice over. In deciding whether this might happen, the normal *d* assumption was that any foreign court, in accordance with general principles of private international law, would treat the debt as discharged if three conditions were satisfied: (1) the English court had international jurisdiction to enter judgment against the debtor; (2) the situs of the debt was England; and (3) the effect of payment under the garnishee order in English law was to discharge the debt. Lord Goff then considered whether this assumption should be made in *e* every case: was compliance with the three criteria both necessary and sufficient? Lord Goff did not express a view as to whether compliance was necessary, although he noted the court in *Martin v Nadel* had not simply applied the three criteria as a matter of private international law but had considered whether in fact a payment under the garnishee order would be recognised by a court in Berlin as *f* discharging the local debt. This suggests that if the evidence of foreign law had shown that, contrary to the general principles of private international law, the foreign court would have treated the debt as discharged, it would have been acceptable to make the garnishee order absolute. But the real issue in the case was whether compliance was sufficient. Lord Goff said ([1988] 2 All ER 833 at 854–855, [1990] 1 AC 295 at 355) that it was not:
g

'[T]he principle which is here being applied is that a garnishee order absolute should not be made where it is inequitable to do so, and further that it is accepted in the authorities that it is inequitable so to do where the payment by the garnishee under the order absolute will not necessarily discharge his liability under the attached debt, there being a real risk that he *h* may be held liable in some foreign court to pay a second time. To deprive the garnishee of the benefit of this equity merely because the court which may hold him liable a second time is not acting in accordance with accepted principles of international law would not be right, especially bearing in mind that the garnishee is a wholly innocent party who has been dragged into *j* somebody else's dispute, and that the judgment creditor has the opportunity of seeking elsewhere for assets of the judgment debtor which he may seize in satisfaction of the judgment debt.'

[54] My Lords, so far I have been considering the matter, as almost all the authorities have done, as one of fairness and equity between the parties. But there is another dimension. The execution of a judgment is an exercise of

sovereign authority. It is a seizure by the state of an asset of the judgment debtor to satisfy the creditor's claim. And it is a general principle of international law that one sovereign state should not trespass upon the authority of another, by attempting to seize assets situated within the jurisdiction of the foreign state or compelling its citizens to do acts within its boundaries.

[55] In the modern world, banking is perhaps the strongest illustration of the importance of mutual respect for national sovereignties. There are nearly 500 foreign banks in London, to say nothing of British banks with branches overseas. Banking is a highly regulated activity and each head office or branch has to comply with the laws of the jurisdiction in which it operates. If the courts of one country in which a bank operates exercise no restraint about using their sovereign powers of compulsion in relation to accounts maintained with that bank at branches in other countries, conflict and chaos is likely to follow.

[56] There is already a hint of this in Willes J's example of the foreign banker (*cuius pecunia est alter sanguis*) who was entitled to say *civis Romanus* (or wherever) *sum* and not be mulcted by foreign attachment in the City of London on account of an alleged debt owing at his foreign place of business. But sensitivity to foreign sovereignty appears most clearly in the rules which have been developed for that younger offspring of foreign attachment, the Mareva injunction or freezing order. Unlike the case of its elder sibling, there is no question of a freezing order putting a bank in the position of having to pay twice. Nevertheless, unless carefully limited, a freezing order applying to foreign banking debts can put the bank in the position of having to choose between being in contempt of an English court and having to dishonour its obligations under a law which does not regard the English order as a valid excuse.

[57] So in *Babanaft International Co SA v Bassatne* [1989] 1 All ER 433 at 446, [1990] Ch 13 at 35 the late Kerr LJ, who was a master of international commercial law, said:

'Unqualified Mareva injunctions covering assets abroad can never be justified, either before or after judgment, because they involve an exorbitant assertion of jurisdiction of an in rem nature over third parties outside the jurisdiction of our courts.'

[58] The result was that freezing orders have been tailored to make it clear, first, that they do not affect anyone outside the jurisdiction unless enforced by a court of the relevant country and, secondly, that they do not prevent third parties such as foreign banks, which have an English presence and are therefore subject to the jurisdiction, from complying with what they reasonably believe to be their obligations under the law of the situs or proper law of the debt or any order of a local court: see *Baltic Shipping v Translink Shipping Ltd* [1995] 1 Lloyd's Rep 673.

[59] The conclusion I draw from this survey of principle and authority is that there are strong reasons of principle for not making a third party debt order in respect of a foreign debt. I agree with my noble and learned friend Lord Millett that the application of such principles is not at all the same as the exercise of a discretion. To that extent, the references to a discretion in cases like the *SCF Finance* case and *Interpool Ltd v Galani* [1987] 2 All ER 981, [1988] QB 738 are misleading. On the other hand, a principle is not the same as a statutory rule restricting the jurisdiction. It may have to give way to some other overriding principle. But I find it hard to think what such a principle might be. Until this case there was no reported instance in which the normal principle had not been applied.

a   [60] That brings me to the judgments in the present case. The bank produced uncontradicted evidence that by Hong Kong law the garnishee order would not discharge the debt owing by the bank to the judgment debtor in Hong Kong. Tomlinson J refused to make the order absolute on the ground that the bank would be at risk of having to pay its customer again in Hong Kong. But the Court of Appeal reversed his decision and granted the order.

b   [61] In a judgment given by Mance LJ the Court of Appeal reasoned as follows: (1) the Hong Kong court would recognise the underlying judgment in the French court; (2) it would therefore recognise that the judgment debtor was indebted to the creditor; (3) if the bank paid pursuant to the garnishee order, it would have paid the judgment debtor's debt under compulsion of law; (4) a person who pays the debt of another under compulsion of law can claim
c   reimbursement by a restitutionary action; (5) this applies equally when the compulsion is applied by a foreign law; (6) Hong Kong law on this point can be assumed to be the same as English law; (7) therefore if the bank were sued by the judgment debtor in Hong Kong it could set off its restitutionary claim and would not have to pay twice; (8) there was no infringement of Hong Kong sovereignty
d   because the bank was being required to pay in England, not Hong Kong.

[62] The argument does not lack novelty and ingenuity but I respectfully think it is flawed because it travesties the nature of a third party debt order. The essence of such an order is that it is execution in rem against the property of the judgment debtor, against a res or chose in action which belongs to him and which is within the jurisdiction of the court making the order. As the Royal
e   Commissioners said in 1853, it is an attachment of 'monies of [the] debtor in the hands of third persons' (see [34], above). It is true that once the judgment debtor's chose in action has been captured or attached, the court will realise it or turn it to account by ordering the third party to pay the debt to the judgment creditor. But that is a process of realisation in the same way as the sale of a chattel
f   belonging to the debtor which has been taken in execution. It is not a personal claim against the third party. The third party pays with his own money only in the same sense as a bank upon which a cheque has been drawn by a customer in credit pays with its own money. But the substance of the matter is that the judgment creditor is paid with the debtor's money, as the drawee of the cheque is paid with the customer's money.
g   [63] The discharge of the third party's indebtedness effected by CPR 72.9(2) (formerly RSC Ord 49, r 8) is therefore an essential part of the execution. As Lord Blackburn said in *London Corp v London Joint Stock Bank* (1881) 6 App Cas 393 at 415, the garnishee, 'if he is to be obliged to pay the money, must be discharged from paying it to his creditor'. It is this which ensures that the creditor is paid
h   with the debtor's money and not the third party's.

[64] It is not in my opinion an adequate substitute for this protection to argue that if the third party has to pay out of his own money, he will acquire a restitutionary claim in personam which he can set off against the debt. In the domestic context, such a claim is impossible. As Tomlinson J said in this case
j   ([2001] 1 All ER (Comm) 843 at 851):

'The fact that it is ... of the essence of the procedure that the garnishee thereby obtains a good discharge against his own creditor means that he has no need of a restitutionary claim against his creditor ... Indeed, it can readily be seen that it would in fact be wholly inimical to the structure of the garnishee jurisdiction if ... a garnishee were by payment to the judgment

creditor to obtain the right to a restitutionary claim against the judgment
debtor ... A claim in restitution could only be consistent with the garnishee   *a*
remaining liable to the judgment debtor ...'

[65] Paradoxically, therefore, the restitutionary claim postulated by the Court
of Appeal can exist only in a foreign law. In the present case, the Court of Appeal
inferred its existence in the law of Hong Kong from the decision of Donaldson J   *b*
in *Liberian Insurance Agency Inc v Mosse* [1977] 2 Lloyd's Rep 560, in which he began
his judgment by saying that the facts were probably unique and that he certainly
hoped they were. That is not a promising introduction if one is looking for
universally applicable principles of law. The facts were that Liberian insurance
brokers had been held liable in a Liberian court to pay a cargo claim alleged to be
owing to the insured plaintiff by underwriters in London. The brokers were   *c*
obliged to satisfy the claim in Liberia. Having done so, they sued the underwriters
in London on the ground that they had paid their debt under compulsion of law.
Donaldson J said that compulsion under a foreign law could found a
restitutionary claim but dismissed the action on the ground that the underwriters
would have had a good defence to a claim by the insured.   *d*

[66] The claim against the brokers, whatever its merits, was an ordinary in
personam contractual claim over which the Liberian court undoubtedly had
jurisdiction. It is therefore not surprising that Donaldson J was prepared to
recognise it as creating a legal obligation to pay. But there is no in personam
claim against the bank in this case. The bank owes the judgment creditor
nothing. The third party debt jurisdiction is, as I have said, execution in rem   *e*
against the chose of action. If the English court has no jurisdiction over the debt,
I do not understand why a foreign court should recognise the third party's
obligation to pay as having been under compulsion of law. Under generally
accepted conflict of law rules, it is simply an unlawful seizure. The notion that
one can justify the attachment of a foreign debt by imputing to the foreign law   *f*
recognition of an exorbitant order for the purpose of founding a claim of payment
under compulsion of law is in my opinion quite unreal.

[67] The Court of Appeal rejected the suggestion that it was infringing the
sovereignty of Hong Kong by saying that it was not ordering the bank to do
anything in Hong Kong. All it had to do was to pay money in London. On this
ground it distinguished cases like *R v Grossman* (1981) 73 Cr App R 302 and   *g*
MacKinnon v Donaldson Lufkin & Jenrette Securities Corp [1986] 1 All ER 653, [1986]
Ch 482 in which courts had refused to order banks to produce information about
accounts held in foreign jurisdictions. But this distinction depends upon treating
the third party debt order simply as an order against the bank instead of what it
really is, namely, a process of execution by the attachment of property of the   *h*
judgment debtor. Once the true nature of the order is understood, it becomes
plain that an order in respect of a foreign debt is an attempt to levy execution on
an asset in the foreign jurisdiction, which infringes the principle of international
law applied in *R v Grossman* and *Mackinnon's* case.

[68] I would therefore regard this as a straightforward case governed by   *j*
Martin v Nadel (Dresdner Bank, garnishees) [1906] 2 KB 26, [1904–7] All ER Rep 827.
In cases in which the debt is plainly foreign, I find it hard to imagine a case in
which such an order could be made. I do not find the example of the Panamanian
debt given by the Court of Appeal persuasive. It was said that if the third party
owing money to the judgment debtor was a Panamanian company which had no
assets other than an account in a bank in London, it would be justifiable to make

a the order and execute against the third party's assets in London. But that would still leave the Panamanian company exposed to proceedings by the judgment debtor in Panama to recover the same debt. I do not see why it would be equitable to put the Panamanian company, which has nothing to do with the basic dispute, into a position of insolvency in Panama so that the creditor's claim can be satisfied in London.

b [69] For these reasons I would allow the appeal and discharge the garnishee order.

LORD HOBHOUSE OF WOODBOROUGH.

[70] My Lords, in full agreement with the opinions of my noble and learned friends Lord Bingham of Cornhill and Lord Hoffmann, I too would allow the c appeal and make the order proposed. I am also in broad agreement with what my noble and learned friend Lord Millett is to say in his opinion.

[71] I will, however, add two observations relevant to this and similar cases. The first relates to the situs of a debt. In the present case there is no dispute that the situs of the relevant debt is Hong Kong and not England. (The same is true, d mutatis mutandis, in the parallel case concerning UBS AG (see *Kuwait Oil Tanker Co SAK v Qabazard* [2003] UKHL 31, [2003] 3 All ER 501).) But it is still necessary to understand why this is so. Stirling LJ in *Martin v Nadel (Dresdner Bank, garnishees)* [1906] 2 KB 26 at 31, like others before and since, found it most appropriate to refer to the work *Dicey and Morris on the Conflict of Laws*. I will do the same, using the thirteenth edition (2000).

e [72] Rule 112 states that 'choses in action generally are situate in the country where they are properly recoverable or can be enforced'. The text amplifies this in relation to debts, saying, 'a debt is [generally] situate in the country where the debtor resides ... It may not, however, be the only place: English courts may take jurisdiction against non-residents on the basis of temporary presence', or under f the CPR or the Brussels or Lugano Conventions. Nevertheless, this possibility does not make the debt situate in England if the debtor is not resident here. But, generally speaking, 'for the purpose of determining situs, a corporation is resident wherever it carries on business' (pp 925–926):

g > 'Where ... the debtor has two or more places of residence and the creditor either expressly or impliedly stipulates for payment at one of them, then the debt will be there situate. This refinement is important in connection with bank accounts where (as in English law) under the applicable law of the contract between banker and customer the bank's obligation to repay is performable primarily at the branch where the account is kept, and h accordingly in such a case all accounts kept at a particular branch are to be held there situate ... Where the debtor has more than one place of residence but there is no express or implied promise to pay at any one of them then the debt is situate at that place of residence where it would be paid in the ordinary course of business.' (See pp 926–927.)

j [73] The third party debtor, garnishee, is a corporation. It is incorporated in Hong Kong where it presumably has its head management. But it has places of business in England and is registered as an overseas company under Pt XXIII of the Companies Act 1985. The English courts accordingly have jurisdiction. The company can be served within the jurisdiction and has one or more places of business here. If the company were an ordinary trading company and the debt it owed to the judgment debtor an ordinary commercial debt, say, payment for a service rendered or goods supplied, the judgment debtor could have sued the company and recovered the debt in England and could have argued that the company had sufficient residence here to make England the or a situs of the debt. But, with banks and the debts of banks to their customers, the debt is, absent some special agreement, repayable at the branch where the customer's account is kept and the situs of the debt is in that country. This has a double significance. It is part of and defines the substantive obligation of the bank to its customer and it identifies the situs of the debt for the purposes of private international law. The authorities cited, in particular *London (Mayor etc) v Cox* (1867) LR 2 HL 239, *Martin v Nadel, Swiss Bank Corp v Boehmische Industrial Bank* [1923] 1 KB 673 and *Richardson v Richardson (National Bank of India Ltd, garnishee)* [1927] P 228, [1927] All ER Rep 92, demonstrate this. The recognition of what is the substantive obligation of the bank is an essential part of the analysis.

[74] In the present case (and in the UBS AG case (see *Kuwait Oil Tanker Co SAK v Qabazard*, [2003] 3 All ER 501)), the third party debtor is a bank and the debt (or alleged debt) is one owing by the bank to its customer (the judgment debtor) at a branch in another country. This is an important fact because to make a garnishee or third party debt order requiring payment of the debt in this country (probably also translating it into sterling) is to impose on the bank an obligation which it has never assumed. It is not an obligation which the customer (the judgment debtor) could have asserted let alone enforced against the bank. This shows the fundamental objection to the reasoning and decision of the Court of Appeal. Nothing could be a better illustration of the disregard of this truth than the order actually made by the Court of Appeal which would convert the bank's relationship to its customer from that of banker and customer to that of claimant and respondent in restitution litigation. Nor is maintaining respect for the actual obligation of the bank an academic point. There may be a whole number of practical reasons why the bank's contract must be respected: local law, local regulation, currencies, tax, exchange control, insolvency rules, confidentiality and so on. One can also ask why is it that the judgment creditor is so reluctant to enforce his judgment in the country where the debt is payable which in the present case it is accepted that it could have easily done. But the most important point is that the order would purport to enforce a supposed right which did not exist and the judgment debtor did not possess. This is unprincipled and in the true sense exorbitant. Another way of stating the same point is that the application for the third party debt (garnishee) order lacked subject matter.

[75] The other additional observation I would make is that the possible question of subject-matter jurisdiction is always important. There are relatively few examples in English procedural law but the present case is one of them for the reasons my noble and learned friends have already given. Subject-matter jurisdiction also has a major role under the Brussels and Lugano Conventions. A garnishee or third party debt order will result in an enforceable liability in personam of the third party to the judgment creditor which is amenable to execution (*Re Combined Weighing and Advertising Machine Co* (1889) 43 Ch D 99; *Pritchett v English and Colonial Syndicate* [1899] 2 QB 428), but it does not follow that only personal jurisdiction is relevant as is illustrated by *Babanaft International Co SA v Bassatne* [1989] 1 All ER 433, [1990] Ch 13. This is the misunderstanding which has led to the erroneous dicta in *SCF Finance Co Ltd v Masri (No 3)* [1987] 1 All ER 194, [1987] QB 1028 and *Interpool Ltd v Galani* [1987] 2 All ER 981, [1988] QB 738 and the mistaken criticism of what Hill J said in *Richardson v Richardson*. It is unfortunate also that what Lord Goff said in *Deutsche Schachtbau-und*

a *Tiefbohrgesellschaft mbH v Shell International Petroleum Co Ltd (t/a Shell International Trading Co)* [1988] 2 All ER 833, [1990] 1 AC 295 should have been cited without having regard to what that case was about. The debt was a commercial debt with an admitted situs in England. It was properly recoverable in England and the order made by the English court would discharge the debt. The question which arose was the exceptional one whether there was a real and substantial risk that b the garnishee, Shell, would nevertheless, in a foreign country, be compelled to pay the debt again. This did not raise a question of jurisdiction or lack of subject matter but more simply the, in that case, difficult question whether it was equitable in the discretion of the court to make the garnishee order. Lord Goff was not expressing a view about the question which the present appeal raises.

c
LORD MILLETT.

[76] My Lords, the question in this appeal is whether an English court can properly make a garnishee order absolute (now known as a final third party debt order) in respect of a foreign debt, in this case a sum standing to the credit of the judgment debtor in an overseas bank account and so situate abroad.

d
[77] In formulating the question in this way I have deliberately avoided using the slippery word 'jurisdiction', a word which is 'used in a variety of senses and takes its colour from its context' (*Anisminic Ltd v Foreign Compensation Commission* [1967] 2 All ER 986 at 994, [1968] 2 QB 862 at 889 per Diplock LJ). The expression 'the jurisdiction of the court' connotes its authority to decide a case or make an e order having legal effect. But it is possible to distinguish between two different senses in which the expression is used. The first is where the jurisdiction of the court is statutory or is excluded or limited by statute. Two examples may be given. One occurs because statute has given the county court exclusive jurisdiction to make a possession order against the tenant of rent-controlled property, with the result that the ordinary jurisdiction of the High Court to make f such an order is excluded. The present case provides a second example, for under the terms of the relevant rules of court the power of the court to make a third party debt order is and always has been expressly limited to the case where the third party (garnishee) is within the jurisdiction, with the result that the power of the court to make such an order against a third party who is outside the g jurisdiction is excluded. In such cases, where the limits of the court's jurisdiction are imposed ab extra, the lines of demarcation are defined. The court has jurisdiction within the prescribed limits and none outside them.

[78] But the word 'jurisdiction' is also used in a different sense to connote the territorial reach of the legislative powers of Parliament and the adjudicative h powers of the court. In these cases jurisdictional limits are self-imposed as a matter of principle and in order to conform to the norms of international law. In his book *Further Studies in International Law* (1990) p 4, Dr Mann wrote:

'International jurisdiction is an aspect or an ingredient or a consequence of j sovereignty ... laws extend so far as, but no further than, the sovereignty of the State which puts them into force nor does any legislator normally intend to enact laws which apply to or cover persons, facts, events or conduct outside the limits of his State's sovereignty. This is a principle or, perhaps one should say, an observation of universal application. Since every State enjoys the same degree of sovereignty, jurisdiction implies respect for the corresponding rights of other States. To put it differently, jurisdiction

involves both the right to exercise it within the limits of the State's
sovereignty and the duty to recognise the same right of other States.   *a*

Or, to put the same idea in positive and negative form, the State has the
right to exercise jurisdiction within the limits of its sovereignty, but is not
entitled to encroach upon the sovereignty of other States.'

[79] The principle was succinctly stated by Lord Russell of Killowen CJ in *R v*   *b*
Jameson [1896] 2 QB 425 at 430. In describing the canon of statutory construction
that, if another construction be possible, general words in an Act of Parliament
will not be construed as applying to foreigners in respect of acts done by them
outside the dominions of the enacting power, he observed:

'That is a rule based on international law by which one sovereign power is   *c*
bound to respect the subjects and the rights of all other sovereign powers
outside its own territory.'

[80] The near universal rule of international law is that sovereignty, both
legislative and adjudicative, is territorial, that is to say it may be exercised only in
relation to persons and things within the territory of the state concerned or in   *d*
respect of its own nationals. But in terms of domestic law these limits are
self-imposed. A sovereign legislature has power under its domestic law to
disregard them and a court of 'unlimited jurisdiction' (that is to say one which has
power to decide the limits of its own jurisdiction) cannot be said to lack power to
do so. Where the court observes the limits imposed by international law it may
be a matter for debate whether it has no jurisdiction or has a jurisdiction which it   *e*
refrains from exercising as a matter of principle. But it needs to be appreciated
that, whether the court disclaims jurisdiction or merely declines to exercise it, it
does so as a matter of principle and not of discretion.

[81] I make no excuse for labouring this point, because the issue in the present
case has been seen as turning on the distinction between 'jurisdiction' and   *f*
'discretion', whereas in truth it turns on the distinction between the court's duty
to disclaim or decline jurisdiction as a matter of principle and its power to do so
as a matter of discretion.

[82] In the present case the debt in question consists of a sum standing to the
credit of the judgment debtor in an account at a bank in Hong Kong. Like many
international banks, the bank has a branch in London and is accordingly within   *g*
the jurisdiction of the English court. The Court of Appeal, reversing Tomlinson J,
held that a third party debt order could properly be made against it. It observed
that the requirement that the third party be within the jurisdiction of the court
was the only express jurisdictional requirement in the Rules, and this was
satisfied. There was no requirement that the debt itself be situate here. Prima   *h*
facie, therefore, the court had jurisdiction to make the order.

[83] The Court of Appeal reasoned that in making the order it was merely
exercising in personam jurisdiction against a third party within the jurisdiction. It
acknowledged that the order would not have the usual consequence of
extinguishing the debt owing by the third party to the judgment debtor, since the   *j*
evidence showed that the courts of Hong Kong would not recognise or give effect
to the English order. But it followed that the order would not have extra-
territorial effect. The English court would not be entrenching on the jurisdiction
of the courts of Hong Kong, since it would not order the bank to do anything in
Hong Kong. It would merely order the bank to pay a sum of money to the
judgment creditor in England, and leave it to the bank to recoup itself out of the

a sum standing in its books to the credit of the judgment debtor. There would be no difficulty in its doing so, since it could rely on the law of restitution (which was the same in Hong Kong as in England) and the terms of its banking contract with the judgment debtor to allow the necessary set-off. Clearly the English court ought not to make an order if there were any danger that the third party might be called upon to pay twice. But this was a matter of discretion, not jurisdiction.

b [84] My Lords, this reasoning is coherent and intelligible, and if it reflected the true nature of a third party order I would accept it. But an immediate question presents itself. What justification can there possibly be for ordering the third party to discharge the judgment debt out of its own money? The third party is a stranger to the transaction which gave rise to the judgment debt. Before the order was made it was under no obligation to the judgment creditor, with whom c it may have transacted no business and of whom it may have had no knowledge. On the Court of Appeal's analysis the order of the English court creates the obligation which it then compels the third party to satisfy. The only justification which is put forward for this extraordinary process is that the third party is indebted in a like sum to the judgment debtor. But since, as the Court of Appeal d accepts, that debt is not extinguished by the order, it is impossible to see how its existence can serve to justify the process.

[85] The order in the present case was made under RSC Ord 49, the terms of which have been set out by my noble and learned friend Lord Bingham of Cornhill and which I need not repeat. As he has shown, it was in substantially the same terms as its predecessors and can be traced back to the Common Law e Procedure Act 1854. The editorial introduction to Ord 49 in the White Book explained the order as follows:

> 'If a judgment debtor is owed money by another, the judgment creditor can obtain an order that that other (referred to in O.49 as "the garnishee") should discharge the debt by payment direct to the judgment creditor.'

f An introductory note to Ord 49 described its object in the following terms:

> 'It should always be borne in mind that the object and intention of the process is to render "debts" as a form of property available in execution. This marks both the nature of the process and its limitations.'

g [86] These two passages indicate the true nature of a third party debt order. It is a process of execution which enables a judgment creditor to obtain satisfaction of his judgment debt out of money owed to the judgment debtor. The court does not order the third party to pay the judgment creditor out of its own money, but to discharge the debt which it owes to the judgment debtor by payment of that h debt to the judgment creditor. The subject matter of execution is a chose in action, which like land cannot be seized; but the procedure is modelled on the process of obtaining execution against land with such modifications as are necessary to reflect the difference in the nature of the asset. As in the case of land execution is effected in two stages. The first stage takes the form of an order nisi j (or interim order) which creates a charge on the asset to be executed against and gives the judgment creditor priority over other claimants to the asset; and the second stage takes the form of an order absolute (or final order) which brings about the realisation of the asset and the payment of the proceeds to the judgment creditor.

[87] That this is the nature of the process appeared plainly from the wording of ss 61 and 62 of the 1854 Act. Section 61 authorised the court to order that debts

owing to the judgment debtor 'be attached to answer the judgment debt'; and
s 62 provided that service of the order nisi on the garnishee 'shall bind such debts
in his hands'. The word 'attached' still appeared in Ord 49, r 1(2), which provided
that the order nisi should have the effect of 'attaching' the debt to answer the
judgment. The 'attachment' of a chose in action is the equivalent of the seizure
of a tangible asset. A third party debt order 'attaches', that is to say appropriates,
the debt owing to the judgment debtor to answer the judgment debt. This is the
classic method of creating an equitable charge over a debt or fund. It creates a
proprietary interest by way of security in the debt or fund and gives priority to
the claim of the judgment creditor to have his debt paid out of the fund before all
other claims against it including that of the judgment debtor himself. Order 49,
r 8 provided that any payment made by the garnishee in compliance with an order
absolute should operate to discharge pro tanto its liability to the judgment debtor.

[88] Two things follow. First, a third party debt order is not an in personam
order against the third party; it has proprietary consequences and takes effect as
an order in rem against the debt owed by the third party to the judgment debtor.
Secondly, the discharge of the debt is an integral part of the scheme of the order,
which first creates and then realises a proprietary interest in the debt and makes
the proceeds available to the judgment creditor.

[89] The process has been so described in numerous authorities. In *Chatterton v
Watney* (1881) 17 Ch D 259 at 260 Sir George Jessel MR said that the effect of a
garnishee order 'is to declare the debt bound'; while Cotton LJ, rejecting the idea
that the order operates to assign the debt to the judgment creditor, said (at 262)
that—

> 'The effect of a garnishee order is to bind the debt attached and to prevent
> the creditor from receiving it; and when it is made absolute it gives the
> judgment creditor a right to recover payment from the garnishee, and by
> rule 8 it is provided that payment made by the garnishee under the
> proceeding shall be a valid discharge to him as against the judgment debtor.
> There is nothing in the terms of the General Order to affect any security for
> the debt, it only takes away the right of the judgment debtor to receive the
> money and gives the judgment creditor a right to receive it.'

[90] In *Re General Horticultural Co, ex p Whitehouse* (1886) 32 Ch D 512 at 515
Chitty J said that the effect of an order nisi 'was to give the judgment creditor
execution against the debts owing to his debtor' and held that the rule was settled
that the order charged only 'what the judgment debtor can himself honestly deal
with'. This was clearly seen as a rule of law and not a matter of discretion.

[91] In *Rogers v Whiteley* (1889) 23 QBD 236 Lindley LJ considered the case
where money in the bank account included money of which the judgment debtor
was trustee. That money, Lindley LJ said (at 238), could not be ordered to be paid
to the judgment creditor who obtained the charging order: 'he can only obtain
payment out of the debtor's own money'.

[92] In the same case the House of Lords held that a garnishee order nisi which
was unlimited in amount made against a bank attached the whole of the money
in the account, and that the bank was entitled to dishonour cheques which
the judgment debtor drew on the balance over and above the amount of the
judgment debt. Lord Watson said ([1892] AC 118 at 122):

'The effect of an order attaching "all debts" owing or accruing due by him to the judgment debtor is to make the garnishee custodier for the court of the whole funds attached; and he cannot, except at his own peril, part with any of those funds without the sanction of the court.'

Lord Morris said that on the plain meaning of the order in that case (at 123):

'… all debts due and owing by the above-named garnishee are attached to answer the judgment creditor's demand—that is, they are all captured for the purpose of afterwards answering that demand.'

Their Lordships observed that it would be open to the judge to frame the order so that the amount of the debts attached should be limited to an amount sufficient to answer the judgment, and that in that particular case he ought to have done so. That suggestion has been adopted in the modern form of order.

[93] In *Galbraith v Grimshaw* [1910] 1 KB 339 at 343 Farwell LJ stated in terms that a garnishee order nisi creates an equitable charge on the debt owed by the bank to the judgment debtor. In that case the judgment debtor had become bankrupt in Scotland after the making of an order nisi but before an order absolute. Farwell LJ said (at 344):

'It is said that the debt is now the property of the plaintiff as the trustee in the bankruptcy of the judgment debtors; but it is property which is subject to a charge, and there is nothing in the Scotch Act which entitles the trustee to receive that property until he has paid off that charge.'

Affirming the decision of the Court of Appeal Lord MacNaghten said ([1910] AC 508 at 512) that the Scottish Court—

'must take the assets of the bankrupt such as they were at [the date of the bankruptcy] and with all the liabilities to which they were then subject. The debt attached by the order nisi was at the date of the sequestration earmarked for the purpose of answering a particular claim—a claim which in due course would have ripened into a right.'

[94] The position would have been different had it been an English bankruptcy by reason of s 45 of the Bankruptcy Act 1883 (now s 183 of the Insolvency Act 1986). This gives an executing judgment creditor priority in the bankruptcy of the judgment debtor provided that execution is complete before the commencement of the bankruptcy. It is to be observed that s 183, like its predecessors, provides that execution against a debt is completed when the debt is received, not when the judgment debt is satisfied. The two are, of course, supposed to take place at the same time; but if the third party is compelled to satisfy the judgment debt without obtaining a release of its own indebtedness to the bankrupt, it will be at risk of having its right of recoupment reduced to a right of proof in the bankruptcy.

[95] In *Joachimson (N) v Swiss Bank Corp* [1921] 3 KB 110 at 131, [1921] All ER Rep 92 at 102 Atkin LJ repeated that service of the order nisi 'binds the debt in the hands of the garnishee—that is, it creates a charge in favour of the judgment creditor'.

[96] The two-stage process was explained by Lord Denning MR in characteristically simple language in *Choice Investments Ltd v Jeromnimon (Midland Bank Ltd, garnishee)* [1981] 1 All ER 225 at 226–227, [1981] QB 149 at 154–155:

'The word "garnishee" is derived from the Norman-French. It denotes one
who is required to "garnish", that is, to furnish a creditor with the money to
pay off a debt. A simple instance will suffice. A creditor is owed £100 by a
debtor. The debtor does not pay. The creditor gets judgment against him
for the £100. Still the debtor does not pay. The creditor then discovers that
the debtor is a customer of a bank and has £150 at his bank. The creditor can
get a "garnishee" order against the bank by which the bank is required to pay
into court or direct to the creditor, *out of its customer's £150* [my emphasis],
the £100 which he owes to the creditor. There are two steps in the process.
The first is a garnishee order nisi. Nisi is Norman-French (*sic*). It means
"unless". It is an order upon the bank to pay the £100 to the judgment
creditor or into court within a stated time, *unless* there is some sufficient
reason why the bank should not do so. Such reason may exist if the bank
disputes its indebtedness to the customer for some reason or other ... On
making the payment, the bank gets a good discharge from its indebtedness
to its own customer—just as if he himself directed the bank to pay it. If it is
a deposit on seven-days' notice, the order nisi operates as the notice.'

[97] These passages are inconsistent with the notion that the order merely
operates in personam against the person of the judgment creditor and has no
effect upon the debt itself; many of the cases would have been decided differently
if this were the case. A third party debt order requires the third party to pay the
debt it owes to the judgment debtor to the judgment creditor instead—which has
no adverse consequences to it—not merely to pay a sum equal to the debt out of
its own pocket, which could be seriously prejudicial to its interests. This is what
justifies the order, as Lindley LJ explained in *Pritchett v English and Colonial
Syndicate* [1899] 2 QB 428 at 433:

'It is quite true that before that order was made there was no debt owing
by [the third party] to [the judgment creditor]: the debt was owing by [the
judgment debtor]; and the order is, in substance, not an order to pay a debt,
but an order on the [third party] to hand over something in their hands
belonging to [the judgment debtor] to [the judgment creditor].'

The discharge of the debt owed by the third party to the judgment debtor is not,
therefore, merely a fortunate consequence of the order but a necessary and
integral part of it. It is what justifies the making of the order and makes it a
process of execution against the assets of the judgment debtor.

[98] If the debt is situate and payable overseas, however, it is beyond the
territorial reach of our courts. The books contain many statements to this effect.
In *Ellis v M'Henry* (1871) LR 6 CP 228 at 234 Bovill CJ said:

'In the first place, there is no doubt that a debt or liability arising in any
country may be discharged by the laws of that country, and that such a
discharge, if it extinguishes the debt or liability, and does not merely interfere
with the remedies or course of procedure to enforce it, will be an effectual
answer to the claim, not only in the courts of that country, but in every other
country. This is the law of England, and is a principle of private international
law adopted in other countries ... Secondly, as a general proposition, it is also
true that the discharge of a debt or liability by the law of a country other than
that in which the debt arises, does not relieve the debtor in any other country ...'

a
[99] Time and again in the early nineteenth century the English courts held
that a debt payable in England was not discharged by a foreign bankruptcy. In
Smith v Buchanan (1800) 1 East 6 at 11, 102 ER 3 at 5 Kenyon CJ expostulated:

b
'It might as well be contended that if the State of Maryland had enacted
that no debts due from its own subjects to the subjects of England should be
paid, the plaintiff would have been bound by it. This is the case of a contract
lawfully made by a subject in this country, which he resorts to a Court of
Justice to enforce; and the only answer given is that a law has been made in
a foreign country to discharge these defendants from their debts on
condition of their having relinquished all their property to their creditors.
But how is that an answer to a subject of this country suing on a lawful
c
contract made here? How can it be pretended that he is bound by a condition
to which he has given no assent either express or implied?'

[100] Before the present case a garnishee order has been sought against a
foreign debt in only two reported cases, and in neither case was the application
successful. In *Martin v Nadel (Dresdner Bank, garnishees)* [1906] 2 KB 26, [1904–7]
d All ER Rep 827 the order was sought against the London branch of a German
bank where the judgment debtor maintained an account. The application was
refused. Vaughan Williams LJ said ([1906] 2 KB 26 at 29):

'There can be no doubt that under the rules of international law the
Dresdner Bank could not set up, in an action in Berlin, the execution levied
e
in this country in respect to this debt. If we consider the converse case it is
clear, to my mind, that we should take that view of a similar transaction
occurring abroad.'

Stirling LJ said ([1906] 2 KB 26 at 31):

f
'Mr Dicey, at p 318 of his treatise on the Conflict of Laws, points out the
rule of law that debts or choses in action are generally to be looked upon as
situate in the country where they are properly recoverable or can be
enforced. On the facts of this case the debt of the bank to Nadel would be
properly recoverable in Germany. That being so, it must be taken that the
order of this court would not protect the bank from being called on to pay
g
the debt a second time.'

[101] In *Richardson v Richardson (National Bank of India Ltd, garnishee)* [1927]
P 228, [1927] All ER Rep 92, where a garnishee order was sought against bank
accounts in Kenya and Tanganyika. Hill J refused to make the order, holding that
h he had no jurisdiction to make it. The debts, he said, 'cannot be made the subject
of a garnishee order, for they are not a debt recoverable within the jurisdiction'.
[102] *Martin v Nadel* was distinguished in *Swiss Bank Corp v Boehmische
Industrial Bank* [1923] 1 KB 673 because the debt was payable in England. Bankes LJ
explained that the distinction was critical (at 678–679):

j
'The decision of that question depends upon where the debt sought to be
attached is situate. If the debt is situate, or in other words if it is properly
recoverable, in this country, then it would be discharged by payment under
an order of our Courts and the garnishee need have no fear of being required
to pay it a second time; but if the debt is situate, that is properly recoverable,
in a foreign country, then it is not discharged by payment in this country
under an order of the Courts of this country, and the debtor may be called

upon to pay it over again in the foreign country. There is no doubt as to the
effect of payment made under a garnishee order here. It is clearly a discharge *a*
pro tanto of the debt ... That was a debt situate in Berlin, being properly
recoverable in Berlin. That was the debt sought to be garnished. Here the
debt sought to be garnished was a debt situate in England being properly
recoverable in England. In this case the debt can be properly discharged in
England. In *Martin v Nadel* the debt could be properly discharged only in Berlin.' *b*

Scrutton LJ (at 680–681) referred to—

'the decision in *Martin v Nadel,* that the court will not make absolute a
garnishee order where it will not operate to discharge the garnishee in whole
or pro tanto from the debt; it will not expose him to the risk of having to pay *c*
the debt or part of it twice over. That is well established as a principle of
discretion on which the court acts.'

[103] By this time the law was regarded as settled. Whatever the theoretical
extent of the court's jurisdiction, in practice it would not make a third party order
where the debt was situate abroad, because (in the words of Scutton LJ) 'it' (that *d*
is to say the order) 'will not operate to discharge the garnishee in whole or pro
tanto from the debt'.

[104] Unfortunately what had become the settled practice of the court for
more than 50 years has been put in doubt in more recent cases: *SCF Finance Co Ltd v
Masri (No 3)* [1987] 1 All ER 194, [1987] QB 1028 and *Interpool Ltd v Galani* [1987]
2 All ER 981, [1988] QB 738. In neither case did the question arise for decision. *e*
The former concerned a debt which was (or was treated as being) situate in
England, while the latter concerned the examination of the judgment debtor
under RSC Ord 48 and not the making of a garnishee order under Ord 49. In each
case the Court of Appeal held that there was no requirement that the debt owing
to the judgment debtor must be properly recoverable within the jurisdiction. *f*
The court would not make an order where the debt was recoverable abroad if this
would expose the third party to the risk of having to pay the debt or part of it
twice over, but this was a matter of discretion not jurisdiction. To resist an order
the third party would have to show that the risk was a real and substantial one.
In so far as *Richardson v Richardson* was authority to the contrary it was to be taken
as no longer good law. *g*

[105] In *Deutsche Schachtbau-und Tiefbohrgesellschaft mbH v Shell International
Petroleum Co Ltd (t/a Shell International Trading Co)* [1988] 2 All ER 833, [1990] 1 AC
295, which also concerned a debt situate in England, Lord Goff of Chieveley
referred in passing ([1988] 2 All ER 833 at 850, [1990] 1 AC 295 at 350) to the
court's 'discretionary power to make a garnishee order absolute' and said ([1988] *h*
2 All ER 833 at 854–855, [1990] 1 AC 295 at 355) that it would be 'inequitable' to
make such an order where there was 'a real risk that [the third party] may be held
liable in some foreign court to pay a second time'. There is no doubt, of course,
that the court's power to make an order in the case of an English debt is
discretionary. The present question is different. It is whether its power to refuse *j*
an order in the case of a foreign debt is discretionary. Lord Goff was not
concerned with such a question. More significantly, Lord Goff enumerated the
conditions on which he would expect a foreign court to give effect to an order of
the English court. One of them was that the debt was situate in England.

[106] My Lords, I think that the more recent cases are based on a misreading
of the judgments of the Court of Appeal in *Martin v Nadel* and the *Swiss Bank* case.

a It is true that in the former case Vaughan Williams LJ ([1906] 2 KB 26 at 30) refused the order on the ground that it would be 'inequitable' to order the third party to pay the money to the execution creditor when the payment 'would leave [it] still liable to an action to recover the same debt brought in a competent court' abroad; while Stirling LJ ([1906] 2 KB 26 at 31) held that it would be 'inequitable and contrary to natural justice' to make an order which 'would not protect the

b [third party] from being called on to pay the debt a second time'. In the latter case Scrutton LJ ([1923] 1 KB 673 at 681) put the matter as a 'principle of discretion on which the court acts' in one passage, but he said elsewhere (at 683) that *Martin v Nadel* was a case where 'the debt was not an English debt and was not one on which the English courts could exercise jurisdiction'.

[107] But it is not just a matter of language. The reasoning in those cases does
c not support the gloss which has been put upon them. The judgments were directed to the territorial reach of the court's jurisdiction, and were founded on the rule of international law that a debt can be discharged only by the law of the place where it is recoverable. There was no attempt to evaluate the risk that the third party might be compelled to pay twice. It was enough that the English

d court could not itself protect the third party and discharge the debt by the force of its own order. In *Martin v Nadel* Vaughan Williams LJ placed reliance on the statement of Channell B giving the judgment of the Exchequer Chamber in *Wood v Dunn* (1866) LR 2 QB 73 at 80 that—

e 'the law will never compel a person to pay a sum of money a second time which he had paid once under the sanction of a court *having competent jurisdiction* ...' (My emphasis.)

[108] This is an important qualification. Just as the English court would not regard a foreign court as being a court of competent jurisdiction to discharge a debt recoverable here, so a foreign court would not regard our court as
f competent to discharge a debt recoverable there; and that was sufficient in itself to preclude the making of the order in respect of a foreign debt. Although in places this was described as a matter of discretion and in other places as a matter of principle, I think that the rationale was based on principle.

[109] However that may be, I have no doubt that the issue should be regarded
g as one of principle. Our courts ought not to exercise an exorbitant jurisdiction contrary to generally accepted norms of international law and expect a foreign court to sort out the consequences. I do not share the Court of Appeal's confidence that the bank would have a restitutionary remedy under the law of Hong Kong. The cases indicate that it would not have such a remedy under English law in the converse case; compulsion of law connotes compliance with

h the order of a court of competent jurisdiction. It cannot safely be assumed that a foreign court would regard compliance with an order of a court whose jurisdiction it did not recognise as a sufficient basis for a restitutionary claim. Nor do I understand how a bank can properly debit a customer's account if it is not authorised to do so by the law which governs the account.

j [110] But it goes further than this. A restitutionary claim normally yields a personal remedy not a proprietary one. If the third party debt order does not have extra-territorial effect in the place where the account is kept, then the account itself is not affected by the order. Such an order cannot give priority in the judgment debtor's bankruptcy or over other execution creditors in the foreign jurisdiction. Indeed, having regard to the terms of s 183 of the Insolvency Act 1986, I do not see how it would prevail even against an English bankruptcy.

The order must, as the Court of Appeal appreciated, operate in personam and compel the third party to make payment out of its own money with only such rights of recourse against the judgment debtor as the foreign court or the English law of bankruptcy may allow.

[111] But this would not be to execute the judgment against the assets of the judgment debtor. It would not be a process of execution at all. As I have explained, the discharge of the debt owed by the third party to the judgment debtor is not merely a normal consequence of the order but the critical feature which makes the process one of execution. If the court cannot discharge the debt by force of its own order, it cannot make the order. If the debt is situate abroad, the court should not seek to evaluate the risk of the third party being compelled to pay twice. The only relevant question is whether the foreign court would regard the debt as automatically discharged by the order of the English court. Since this would be most unusual, it would be for the judgment creditor to establish.

[112] I wish to add one thing more. RSC Ord 49 has now been replaced by CPR Pt 72, which is cast in more modern language. It is common ground that, as the editorial introduction states, the basic purpose of the rule remains unchanged. Unfortunately all reference to attachment has been dropped, and there is no longer any indication that the order has proprietary consequences. The words which formerly created an equitable charge at the interim stage have been replaced by a power to grant an injunction, which is normally a personal remedy. The straightforward language of Pt 72 is deceptive. Its true nature cannot easily be understood without a knowledge of its history and antecedents. I do not, with respect, regard this as an altogether satisfactory state of affairs.

[113] For these reasons, and for the further reasons contained in the speeches of my noble and learned friends Lord Bingham of Cornhill and Lord Hoffmann, I would allow the appeal, set aside the order of the Court of Appeal, and dismiss the application for a garnishee order.

Appeal allowed.

Kate O'Hanlon   Barrister.

a # Kuwait Oil Tanker Co SAK and another v Qabazard and another
[2003] UKHL 31

b HOUSE OF LORDS
LORD BINGHAM OF CORNHILL, LORD NICHOLLS OF BIRKENHEAD, LORD HOFFMANN, LORD HOBHOUSE OF WOODBOROUGH AND LORD MILLETT
17–19 MARCH, 12 JUNE 2003

Execution – Third party debt order – Debts owing or accruing from foreign judgment
c *debtors – Third party bank incorporated and registered in Switzerland but having place of business in England – Judgment debtors having accounts with third party bank in London and Switzerland – Whether court having jurisdiction to make third party debt order final – Civil Jurisdiction and Judgments Act 1982, s 3A, Sch 3C, art 16(5).*

d Judgment was given against the judgment debtor in the Commercial Court in 1998. An appeal was dismissed in 2000. Since then the judgment creditor had been trying to find assets of the judgment debtor against which to execute. The judgment creditor suspected that the judgment debtor might have money in accounts at a branch of the third party bank. On an application by the judgment creditor for a third party debt order to be made absolute, the judge said it was *e* clear that the relevant accounts, if any, were in Switzerland. The third party argued that the court had no jurisdiction to make a third party debt order (i) because of the provisions of art 16(5)[a] of the Convention on Jurisdiction and the Enforcement of Judgments in Civil and Commercial Matters 1988 (the Lugano Convention) (as set out in Sch 3C to the Civil Jurisdiction and Judgments *f* Act 1982), to which Switzerland and the United Kingdom were parties; and (ii) because it would be inequitable to make a third party debt order which would have the consequence of requiring the third party to pay the judgment creditor any money which might be standing to the credit of the judgment debtor in Switzerland, since it would be at risk of having to pay twice. The judge said that on balance he did not think that the Lugano Convention deprived him of *g* jurisdiction, but that there was a real risk that the third party would be exposed to proceedings by the judgment debtor and to other sanctions under Swiss law. He therefore dismissed the application and discharged the interim third party debt order. The judgment creditor appealed. The Court of Appeal held that art 16(5) was no obstacle to the exercise of the jurisdiction as the place where the *h* third party debt order was being enforced was England. On the question whether the third party was likely to have to pay twice, the court remitted the matter to the judge for further consideration as to whether Swiss law would recognise a restitutionary claim which the third party would be able to set off against a claim for payment of the debt. The third party appealed.

j **Held** – (1) It was not correct to characterise the third party debt order as a claim in personam made against the third party in England. It was enforcement of the judgment in rem against the debt, which in the instant case was situated in Switzerland. Article 16(5) therefore conferred exclusive jurisdiction on Switzerland (see [5]–[8], [16], [18]–[20], below).

---

a   Article 16(5), so far as material, is set out at [4], below

(2) The Swiss debts, if any, were foreign debts and would not be discharged by
compliance with the English order. Accordingly, the judge's order discharging
the third party debt order would be restored (see [8], [17]–[20], below); *Société
Eram Shipping Co Ltd v Compagnie Internationale de Navigation* [2003] 3 All ER 465
applied.

Decision of the Court of Appeal [2002] 1 All ER (Comm) 351 reversed.

Notes
For third party debt orders, see 17(1) *Halsbury's Laws* (4th edn reissue)
paras 251–266.

For the Civil Jurisdiction and Judgments Act 1982, Sch 3C, art 16(5), see
11 *Halsbury's Statutes* (4th edn) (2000 reissue) 1210.

Cases referred to in opinions
AS-Autoteile Service GmbH v Malhé Case 220/84 [1985] ECR 2267, ECJ.
Babanaft International Co SA v Bassatne [1989] 1 All ER 433, [1990] Ch 13, [1989]
   2 WLR 232, CA.
Denilauler v Snc Couchet Frères Case 125/79 [1980] ECR 1553, ECJ.
Reichert v Dresdner Bank AG Case C-261/90 [1992] ECR 1-2149, ECJ.
Société Eram Shipping Co Ltd v Compagnie Internationale de Navigation [2003] UKHL
   30, [2003] 3 All ER 465, [2003] 3 WLR 21; *rvsg* [2001] EWCA Civ 1317, [2001] 2
   All ER (Comm) 721.

Cases also referred to in list of authorities
Airbus Industrie GIE v Patel [1998] 2 All ER 257, [1999] 1 AC 119, [1998] 2 WLR 686, HL.
Baltic Shipping Co v Translink Shipping Ltd and Translink Pacific Shipping Ltd [1995]
   1 Lloyd's Rep 673.
Bank of China v NBM LLC [2001] EWCA Civ 1933, [2002] 1 All ER 717, [2002]
   1 WLR 844.
Camdex International Ltd v Bank of Zambia (No 3) [1997] CLC 714, CA.
Chase Manhattan Bank NA v FDC Co Ltd [1985] 2 HKC 470, Hong Kong CA.
Chatterton v Watney (1881) 17 Ch D 259, CA.
Choice Investments Ltd v Jeromnimon (Midland Bank Ltd, garnishee) [1981] 1 All ER
   225, [1981] QB 149, [1981] 2 WLR 80, CA.
Colquhoun v Brooks (1888) 21 QBD 52, CA; *affd* (1889) 14 App Cas 493, [1886–90]
   All ER Rep 1063, HL.
Damayanti Kantilal Doshi v Indian Bank [1999] 4 SLR 1, Sing CA.
Deutsche Schachtbau- und Tiefbohrgesellschaft mbH v Ras Al Khaimah National Oil Co
   [1987] 2 All ER 769, [1990] 1 AC 295, [1987] 3 WLR 1023, CA; *rvsd* [1988] 2 All ER
   833, [1990] 1 AC 295, [1988] 3 WLR 230, HL.
Ellis v M'Henry (1871) LR 6 CP 228.
Galbraith v Grimshaw [1910] 1 KB 339, CA; *affd* [1910] AC 508, [1908–10] All ER
   Rep 561, HL.
General Horticultural Co, Re, ex p Whitehouse (1886) 32 Ch D 512.
Interpool Ltd v Galani [1987] 2 All ER 981, [1988] QB 738, [1987] 3 WLR 1042, CA.
Joachimson (N) v Swiss Bank Corp [1923] 3 KB 110, [1921] All ER Rep 92, CA.
Kuwait Oil Tanker Co SAK v Qabazard [2002] EWCA Civ 34, [2002] 1 All ER
   (Comm) 351.
Liberian Insurance Agency Inc v Mosse [1977] 2 Lloyd's Rep 560.
Libyan Arab Foreign Bank v Bankers Trust Co [1989] 3 All ER 252, [1989] QB 728,
   [1989] 3 WLR 314.

a *MacKinnon v Donaldson Lufkin & Jenrette Securities Corp* [1986] 1 All ER 653, [1986]
       Ch 482, [1986] 2 WLR 453.
     Martin v Nadel (Dresdner Bank, garnishees) [1906] 2 KB 26, [1904–7] All ER Rep 827, CA.
     Owens Bank Ltd v Bracco (No 2) Case C-129/92 [1994] 1 All ER 336, [1994] QB 509,
       [1994] 2 WLR 759, [1994] ECR I-117, ECJ.
     Power Curber International Ltd v National Bank of Kuwait SAK [1981] 3 All ER 607,
b   [1981] 1 WLR 1233, CA.
     Pritchett v English and Colonial Syndicate [1899] 2 QBD 428, CA.
     R v Grossman (1981) 73 Cr App R 302, CA.
     Richardson v Richardson (National Bank of India Ltd, garnishees) [1927] P 228, [1927]
       All ER Rep 92.
     Rogers v Whiteley (1889) 23 QBD 236, CA; *affd* [1892] AC 118, [1891–4] All ER Rep
c   682, HL.
     Rossano v Manufacturers Life Insurance Co Ltd [1962] 2 All ER 214, [1963] 2 QB 352,
       [1962] 3 WLR 157.
     SCF Finance Co Ltd v Masri (No 3) (Masri, garnishee) [1987] 1 All ER 194, [1987] QB
       1028, [1987] 2 WLR 81, CA.
d *Soinco SACI and Eural KFT v Novokuznetsk Aluminium Plant (No 2)* [1998] 2 Lloyd's
       Rep 346, CA.
     Swiss Bank Corp v Boehmische Industrial Bank [1923] 1 KB 673, CA.
     Tai Hing Cotton Mill Ltd v Liu Chong Hing Bank Ltd [1985] 2 All ER 947, [1986] AC
       80, [1985] 3 WLR 317, PC.
e *Vinall v De Pass* [1892] AC 90, HL.
     *Zoneheath Associates Ltd v China Tianjin International Economic and Technical
       Co-operative Corp* [1994] CLC 348.

Appeal

f UBS AG appealed with the permission of the Appeal Committee of the House of
Lords given on 1 July 2002 from the order of the Court of Appeal (Peter Gibson,
Laws and Longmore LJJ) on 25 January 2002 ([2002] 1 All ER (Comm) 351)
allowing the appeal of the judgment creditors, Kuwait Oil Tanker Co SAK and
Sitka Shipping Inc (KOTC), from the order of Langley J on 23 March 2001 ([2001]
IL Pr 719) whereby he decided not to make absolute a garnishee order (now a
third party debt order) against the London branch of UBS AG in respect of
g accounts held by the judgment debtors, Hassan Ali Hassan Qabazard and Abdul
Fattah Al-Bader. The facts are set out in the opinion of Lord Hoffmann.

Laurence Rabinowitz QC (instructed by *Allen & Overy*) for UBS.
Mark Hoyle and *David Holloway* (instructed by *Waterson Hicks*) for KOTC.
h The judgment debtors did not appear.

Their Lordships took time for consideration.

j 12 June 2003. The following opinions were delivered.

LORD BINGHAM OF CORNHILL.
   [1] My Lords, I gratefully adopt and need not repeat the account given by
my noble and learned friend Lord Hoffmann of the facts, history and issues in
this appeal.
   [2] For reasons given by the House in *Société Eram Shipping Co Ltd v Compagnie
Internationale de Navigation* [2003] UKHL 30, [2003] 3 All ER 465 I think it clear that

the English court had no jurisdiction to make a garnishee order absolute in this case. Had the matter been one of discretion there were strong reasons for not making such an order, and Langley J was right to decline to do so. *a*

[3] This case, however, differs from the *Société Eram* case in one significant respect: that the United Kingdom is a party to the Lugano Convention on Jurisdiction and the Enforcement of Judgments in Civil and Commercial Matters 1988 (as set out in Sch 3C to the Civil Jurisdiction and Judgments Act 1982), *b* incorporated into English law by s 3A of the Civil Jurisdiction and Judgments Act 1982 as amended (the Lugano Convention), and Switzerland (where the chose in action which the judgment creditors seek to attach is situated) is also a party. Thus the question of jurisdiction to make the order sought must be considered not simply as one of English law or private international law as applied in England and Wales but as one governed, or potentially governed, by obligations binding *c* on the United Kingdom by virtue of international convention.

[4] Two provisions of the Lugano Convention are relevant. First, art 16(5) confers 'exclusive jurisdiction, regardless of domicile ... in proceedings concerned with the enforcement of judgments' on 'the courts of the Contracting State in which the judgment has been or is to be enforced'. Secondly, art 19 *d* provides:

'Where a court of a Contracting State is seised of a claim which is principally concerned with a matter over which the courts of another Contracting State have exclusive jurisdiction by virtue of Article 16, it shall declare of its own motion that it has no jurisdiction.' *e*

Thus if the order which the judge was asked to make in this case involved the enforcement of a judgment he had no choice but to accept jurisdiction if the United Kingdom was the contracting state in which the judgment was to be enforced or renounce jurisdiction in favour of Switzerland if it was not.

[5] The opinions of the House in the *Société Eram* case indicate that *f* Switzerland is the state in which enforcement will take place because it is there that the debt is situated upon which it is sought to execute. English authority points towards that conclusion: see, for example, *Babanaft International Co SA v Bassatne* [1989] 1 All ER 433 at 446, 454, [1990] Ch 13 at 35, 46. While the House was referred to no foreign authority which could be said to show international *g* endorsement of that approach, such material as there is appears to support it rather than otherwise.

[6] In his authoritative report on the Brussels Convention on Jurisdiction and the Enforcement of Judgments in Civil and Commercial Matters 1968 (as set out in Sch 1 to the 1982 Act) (the Brussels Convention) (OJ 1979 C59 p 1), Mr Jenard *h* commented (p 36) on art 16(5) of that convention (which is in the same terms in the Lugano Convention) in these terms:

'Enforcement of judgments
Article 16(5) provides that the courts of the State in which a judgment has been or is to be enforced have exclusive jurisdiction in proceedings *j* concerned with the enforcement of that judgment. What meaning is to be given to the expression "proceedings concerned with the enforcement of judgments"? It means those proceedings which can arise from "recourse to force, constraint or distraint on movable or immovable property in order to ensure the effective implementation of judgments and authentic instruments". Problems arising out of such proceedings come within the exclusive

a jurisdiction of the courts for the place of enforcement. Provisions of this kind appear in the internal law of many Member States.'

The recourse to which the author refers would, on facts such as those here, take place in Switzerland. The judgment of the European Court of Justice in *Denilauler v Snc Couchet Frères* Case 125/79 [1980] ECR 1553 was not directed to the interpretation of art 16(5), but the observations (at 1570 (para 16)) would apply

b with added force to execution:

'The courts of the place or, in any event, of the Contracting State, where the assets subject to the measures sought are located, are those best able to assess the circumstances which may lead to the grant or refusal of the measures sought or to the laying down of procedures and conditions which

c the plaintiff must observe in order to guarantee the provisional and protective character of the measures ordered.'

The opinion of the Advocate General (Lenz) in *AS-Autoteile Service GmbH v Malhé* Case 220/84 [1985] ECR 2267 at 2271 was to similar effect:

d 'Furthermore, the particular areas which fall under Article 16, certain disputes regarding tenancies, companies, registers, industrial property and the enforcement of judgments, are matters which, because of their particular difficulty or complexity, require that the court having jurisdiction should be particularly familiar with the relevant national law.'

e *Reichert v Dresdner Bank AG* Case C-261/90 [1992] ECR 1-2149 was a case concerned with art 16(5) of the Brussels Convention, among other articles. In the course of its judgment the European Court of Justice said (at 2182 (para 26)):

'From that point of view it is necessary to take account of the fact that the essential purpose of the exclusive jurisdiction of the courts of the place in

f which the judgment has been or is to be enforced is that it is only for the courts of the Member State on whose territory enforcement is sought to apply the rules concerning the action on that territory of the authorities responsible for enforcement.'

g It would appear that very much the same considerations of principle, comity and convenience as underlie the English law are reflected in the jurisprudence on the Brussels and Lugano Conventions also.

[7] I would accordingly allow the appeal and make the order which Lord Hoffmann proposes.

h **LORD NICHOLLS OF BIRKENHEAD.**

[8] My Lords, I have had the opportunity of reading in draft the speeches of my noble and learned friends Lord Bingham of Cornhill and Lord Hoffmann. I agree that, for the reasons they give, this appeal should be allowed.

j **LORD HOFFMANN.**

[9] My Lords, Mr Qabazard conspired with others to defraud the Kuwait Oil Tanker Co SAK and Sitka Shipping Inc (KOTC) of large sums of money. On 16 November 1998 Moore-Bick J gave judgment against him for over $US130m. An appeal was dismissed in May 2000 ([2000] 2 All ER (Comm) 271). Since then, KOTC have been trying to find assets of Mr Qabazard against which to execute. By December 2000 they had found and recovered a mere £140,000.

[10] Ten years earlier Mr Qabazard, in his own name and also under an alias, maintained accounts with UBS AG (UBS, formerly Union Bank of Switzerland) in London and Geneva. Documents obtained by KOTC showed that in November 1990 he transferred $US34·5m from his London account to his Swiss account. KOTC suspected that he might still have money in accounts at one or other of the branches of UBS. On 19 December 2000 KOTC issued an application under RSC Ord 49, r 2 for a garnishee order in respect of all debts due from UBS to Mr Qabazard. On 21 December 2000 Tomlinson J made an order nisi under r 1(2) calling upon UBS to show cause as to why the order should not be made absolute. The order nisi was served upon UBS at its branch office in London. UBS responded with a witness statement by its legal counsel saying that: (1) the London branch held no account in the name of Mr Qabazard or his alias and (2) UBS was prohibited by Swiss law from disclosing whether he had an account at a branch in Switzerland.

[11] The application to make the garnishee order absolute was heard by Langley J on 23 March 2001 ([2001] IL Pr 719). The judge said that it was clear that the relevant accounts, if any, were in Switzerland. Nothing had been found in England. So the question was whether an English court should make a garnishee order in respect of money held by the judgment debtor in a Swiss bank account.

[12] UBS argued that the court had no jurisdiction to make such an order because art 16(5) of the Lugano Convention on Jurisdiction and the Enforcement of Judgments in Civil and Commercial Matters 1988 (as set out in Sch 3C to the Civil Jurisdiction and Judgments Act 1982) (the Lugano Convention), to which Switzerland and the United Kingdom are parties, provides that 'in proceedings concerned with the enforcement of judgments, the courts of the Contracting State in which the judgment has been or is to be enforced' shall have exclusive jurisdiction. The attachment of money in a Swiss bank account was enforcement of the judgment in Switzerland and therefore within the exclusive jurisdiction of the Swiss courts.

[13] In the alternative, UBS said that it would be inequitable to make a garnishee order which had the consequence of requiring it to pay KOTC any money which might be standing to the credit of Mr Qabazard in Switzerland because UBS would be at risk of having to pay twice. RSC Ord 49, r 8 provides that payment by a garnishee under an order absolute is a valid discharge of his liability to the judgment debtor. But, under general rules of private international law, the discharge cannot affect a debt which (like money in a Swiss bank account) is neither situate in England nor governed by English law. It would not provide UBS with a defence to a claim by Mr Qabazard in a Swiss court.

[14] Langley J said that, 'on balance', he did not think that the Lugano Convention deprived him of jurisdiction. A garnishee order against UBS in London would not infringe Swiss sovereignty by applying a foreign enforcement procedure within its jurisdiction. It operated only indirectly on the Swiss account. But he accepted that on the evidence of the Swiss conflict of laws and its banking laws, there was a real risk that UBS would be exposed to proceedings by Mr Qabazard and to other sanctions under Swiss law. He therefore dismissed the application to make the garnishee order absolute and discharged it.

[15] By the time the case came before the Court of Appeal, a different constitution had decided *Société Eram Shipping Co Ltd v Compagnie Internationale de Navigation* [2001] EWCA Civ 1317, [2001] 2 All ER (Comm) 721, which is the subject of the other appeal in which your Lordships are giving judgment today. Following that decision, Longmore LJ, who gave the judgment of the court, held that the place where the garnishee order was being enforced was England. It was

a there that UBS was being required to pay. Article 16(5) was therefore no obstacle to the exercise of jurisdiction. On the contrary, it conferred exclusive jurisdiction upon the English court. On the question of whether UBS was likely to have to pay twice, the Court of Appeal remitted the matter to the judge for further consideration as to whether Swiss law would recognise a restitutionary claim such as the court in the *Société Eram* case had considered that the garnishee would

b be able to set off against a claim for payment of the debt.

[16] My Lords, I think it is clear that neither of these reasons can stand with the judgments which have been given today in the *Société Eram* case ([2003] UKHL 30, [2003] 3 All ER 465). It is not correct to characterise the garnishee or third party debt order as a claim in personam made against the third party in England. It is enforcement of the judgment in rem against the debt, which in this case is

c situated in Switzerland. Article 16(5) therefore confers exclusive jurisdiction on Switzerland and it is understandable that UBS's Swiss law expert should have said that a Swiss court would regard the order as an infringement of its sovereignty. Indeed, the judgment of the Court of Appeal produces the extraordinary result that the courts of any member state in which UBS maintains a branch have

d exclusive jurisdiction under art 16(5) to make a garnishee or similar order in respect of a debt in Switzerland—a strange form of exclusivity.

[17] The other point is also governed by your Lordships' judgment in the *Société Eram* case. The Swiss debts, if any, are foreign debts and will not be discharged by compliance with the English order. So even without art 16(5), Langley J was right not to make the order.

e [18] I would therefore allow the appeal and restore the order of Langley J discharging the garnishee order.

LORD HOBHOUSE OF WOODBOROUGH.

[19] My Lords, for the reasons given by my noble and learned friends Lord Bingham of Cornhill and Lord Hoffmann, I too would allow the appeal and make

f the order proposed.

LORD MILLETT.

[20] My Lords, I have had the advantage of reading in draft the speeches of my noble and learned friends, Lord Bingham of Cornhill and Lord Hoffmann. I agree

g with them, and for the reasons they give I too would allow the appeal.

[21] The case is governed by the decision of your Lordships in *Société Eram Shipping Co Ltd v Compagnie Internationale de Navigation* [2003] UKHL 30, [2003] 3 All ER 465, but is a fortiori. The debt is situate in Switzerland, like the United Kingdom a party to the Lugano Convention on Jurisdiction and the Enforcement of

h Judgments in Civil and Commercial Matters 1988 (as set out in Sch 3C to the Civil Jurisdiction and Judgments Act 1982) (the Lugano Convention). The case is therefore governed by art 16(5) of the Lugano Convention, which is given the force of law in the United Kingdom by s 3A of the Civil Jurisdiction and Judgments Act 1982. In the present case, therefore, the limits of the court's jurisdiction to enforce its judgments are not a matter of self-restraint, but are imposed from without by convention and

j statute. Since the judgment creditor is seeking to execute a judgment against the property and not the person of the judgment debtor, and the property in question is situate in another convention state, the court is bound to decline jurisdiction.

Appeal allowed.

Kate O'Hanlon   Barrister.

R v Sekhon and others
R v McFaul
R v Knights and another
[2002] EWCA Crim 2954

COURT OF APPEAL, CRIMINAL DIVISION
LORD WOOLF CJ, HOLLAND AND KEITH JJ
4, 5 NOVEMBER, 16 DECEMBER 2002

Sentence – Confiscation order – Postponement of confiscation proceedings – Whether non-compliance with statutory procedural requirements for postponement of confiscation proceedings going to court's jurisdiction – Whether court having to specify period of postponement when deciding to postpone confiscation proceedings – Criminal Justice Act 1988, s 72A.

Where it is necessary to postpone confiscation proceedings brought under the Criminal Justice Act 1988, all that is strictly required, under s 72A[a] of the Act, to give the court jurisdiction is a decision to postpone. Such a decision requires no particular form of words. When the court is considering whether to postpone confiscation proceedings and whether there are exceptional circumstances justifying a postponement extending beyond the period otherwise prescribed, the issues arising are of the same type that courts are regularly required to determine when engaged in case management, and strict compliance with procedural requirements relating to issues of that nature would not normally be expected to go to jurisdiction. Any default on the judge's part can be satisfactorily dealt with on appeal when it is to be expected that the court will examine the circumstances and not focus on technicalities. The issue will be: what does justice require having regard to the Parliamentary code? Similarly, a failure to specify a period of postponement can be made a matter of complaint by appeal to the Court of Appeal after a confiscation order has been made, and the order can be quashed if justice so requires. However, the statement of a period of postponement is not critical for establishing jurisdiction, and the order will stand if no injustice is involved (see [37], [48], below).

R v Palmer (No 1) [2003] 1 Cr App R (S) 572 disapproved.

R v Miranda [2000] 2 Cr App R (S) 347, *R v Davies* [2002] 1 WLR 1806 and *R v Martin* [2002] 2 Cr App R (S) 122 doubted.

Notes
For confiscation orders, see 11(2) *Halsbury's Laws* (4th edn reissue) para 1284.

Section 72A of the Criminal Justice Act 1988 has been repealed with effect from 24 March 2003 by the Proceeds of Crime Act 2002, s 456, Sch 11, para 17(2)(a).

Cases referred to in judgment
A-G's Ref (No 3 of 1999) [2001] 1 All ER 577, [2001] 2 AC 91, [2001] 2 WLR 56, HL.
Brayhead (Ascot) Ltd v Berkshire CC [1964] 1 All ER 149, [1964] 2 QB 303, [1964] 2 WLR 507, DC.

---

a   Section 72A is set out at [11], below

a   Liverpool Borough Bank v Turner (1861) 30 LJ Ch 379, 45 ER 715, LC.
   London and Clydeside Estates Ltd v Aberdeen DC [1979] 3 All ER 876, [1980] 1 WLR
      182, HL.
   R v Barwick [2001] 1 Cr App R (S) 445, CA.
   R v Cole [1998] All ER (D) 142, (1998) Independent, 30 April, CA.
   R v Copeland [2002] EWCA Crim 736, [2002] 2 Cr App R (S) 512.
b   R v Davies [2001] EWCA Crim 2902, [2002] 1 WLR 1806.
   R v Farooki (1983) 77 Cr App R 257, CA.
   R v Immigration Appeal Tribunal, ex p Jeyeanthan, Ravichandran v Secretary of State for
      the Home Dept [1999] 3 All ER 231, [2000] 1 WLR 354, CA.
   R v Kelly [2000] 2 Cr App R (S) 129, CA.
c   R v Lingham [2001] 1 Cr App R (S) 158, CA.
   R v Martin [2001] EWCA Crim 2761, [2002] 2 Cr App R (S) 122.
   R v Miranda [2000] 2 Cr App R (S) 347, CA.
   R v Palmer (No 1) [2002] EWCA Crim 2202, [2003] 1 Cr App R (S) 572.
   R v Phillips [2001] EWCA Crim 2790, [2002] 2 Cr App R (S) 49.
   R v Pisciotto [2002] EWCA Crim 1592, [2003] 1 Cr App R 68.
d   R v Ross [2001] EWCA Crim 560, [2001] 2 Cr App R (S) 484.
   R v Sheerin (1976) 64 Cr App R 68, CA.
   R v Soffe (1982) 75 Cr App R 133, CA.
   R v Spring Hill Prison Governor, ex p Sohi [1988] 1 All ER 424, [1988] 1 WLR 596, DC.
   R v Steele, R v Shevki [2001] 2 Cr App R (S) 178, CA.
e   R v Tuegel [2000] 2 All ER 872, CA.
   R v Urbanowski [1976] 1 All ER 679, [1976] 1 WLR 455, CA.

Appeals and applications for leave to appeal

f   *R v Sekhon and ors*
Daljit Singh Sekhon, Shangara Singh and Satnam Singh appealed, and Gurdev
Singh Dhnoay applied for leave to appeal, against the confiscation orders made
against them under the Criminal Justice Act 1988 by Judge Wood in the Crown
Court at Newcastle-upon-Tyne on 9 June 1999 following their pleas of guilty in
September 1998 to offences of cheating the public revenue. The facts are set out
g   in the judgment of the court.

                                 R v McFaul
Kevin McFaul applied for leave to appeal against the confiscation order made
against him under the Drug Trafficking Act 1994 by Judge Clifton in the Crown
h   Court at Liverpool on 10 April 2000 following his conviction on 8 November 1999
of an offence of conspiracy to supply diamorphine. The facts are set out in the
judgment of the court.

                              R v Knights and anor
j   Richard Michael Knights and Kevin Maguire appealed against the confiscation
orders made against them under the Criminal Justice Act 1988 by Judge Haworth
in the Crown Court at Kingston-upon-Thames on 30 July 2001 following Knights'
plea of guilty on 10 July 2000 to an offence of being knowingly concerned in
dealing with goods which were chargeable with duty and had not been paid with
intent to defraud, and Maguire's conviction of the same offence on 12 October
2000. The facts are set out in the judgment of the court.

Balbir Singh (instructed by *Murria Solicitors*, Birmingham) for Sekhon.

Avtar Bhatoa (instructed by *Bassra Solicitors*, Bradford) for Shangara Singh.

Robert Rhodes QC and *Simon Taylor* (instructed by *Pannone & Partners*, Manchester) for Satnam Singh.

Sunit Sandhu (instructed by *Harbans Singh*, Birmingham) for Dhnoay.

Jason Smith (instructed by *Brian Jackson & Co*, Liverpool) for McFaul.

Christopher Campbell-Clyne (instructed by *Harkavys*) for Knights.

Jo Boothby (instructed by *Clive Gomes*) for Maguire.

David Perry and *John Muir* (instructed by the *Solicitor for Customs and Excise*) for the Crown in the cases of Sekhon, Shangara Singh, Satnam Singh and Dhnoay.

Michael Brompton (instructed by the *Solicitor for Customs and Excise*) for the Crown in the cases of Knights and Maguire.

Cur adv vult

16 December 2002. The following judgment of the court was delivered.

LORD WOOLF CJ.

INTRODUCTION

[1] One of the most successful weapons which can be used to discourage offences that are committed in order to enrich the offenders is to ensure that if the offenders are brought to justice, any profit which they have made from their offending is confiscated. It is therefore not surprising that Parliament has repeatedly enacted legislation designed to enable the courts to confiscate the proceeds of crime.

[2] Regrettably a series of cases have come before the courts recently which reveal that the prosecuting authorities, including the advocates appearing for them, have been attaching far too little significance to ensuring that confiscation proceedings are effective. A series of cases have resulted in orders for the confiscation of substantial sums being set aside for the failure to adhere to procedural requirements that are often of a technical nature.

[3] Furthermore, until Mr Perry was instructed to appear in the present cases, on behalf of the prosecution, important arguments as to the effect of non-compliance with procedural requirements were not placed before the courts.

[4] These repeated failures on the part of prosecuting authorities should not be allowed to continue. The sort of mistakes being made are apparent from the cases to which it will be necessary to refer in this judgment which relates to appeals arising out of three prosecutions. The first prosecution is in respect of Daljit Singh Sekhon, Satnam Singh, Shangara Singh and Gurdev Singh Dhnoay. The second prosecution relates to Kevin McFaul and the third prosecution to Richard Michael Knights and Kevin Maguire.

[5] It is convenient before turning to the circumstances of these cases to set out the statutory framework. It is also desirable to consider the large body of case law that has accumulated around that legislation. In relation to both the legislation and the case law we are indebted to Mr Perry for the account that he provided. In the description that we now provide, we rely heavily on his extremely helpful submissions. It is necessary to refer to the successive legislation because even in relation to the same trial different legislation can apply to different defendants because of the dates on which their respective provisions came into force.

THE BACKGROUND TO THE LEGISLATION

[6] *The 1988 Act: an overview of the provisions.* (i) The Hodgson Committee report *The Profits of Crime and their Recovery* (1984) made a number of recommendations which form the background to confiscation provisions in the Criminal Justice Act 1988. It is the 1988 Act as subsequently amended with which we are concerned in these appeals. (ii) The report recommended the repeal of the criminal bankruptcy order and its replacement with a sentence of confiscation designed to catch the profits of major crime. Following these recommendations, a confiscation regime was introduced in relation to drug trafficking by the Drug Trafficking Offences Act 1986. As well as including the powers of restraint and confiscation, that Act also contained a statutory assumption to the effect that a drug trafficker's assets were the proceeds of crime and therefore liable to confiscation. (iii) The 1988 Act introduced a new power to make a confiscation order in the case of certain crimes other than drug trafficking offences. The confiscation provisions in the 1988 Act, as originally enacted, applied mainly to offenders in the Crown Court and only in cases where the defendant had benefited by at least £10,000 from the offence (see s 71). In such cases the maximum amount of the confiscation order was the amount of the benefit or the extent of the realisable property, whichever was the lesser. (iv) The procedure for making a confiscation order involved the prosecution serving a notice (see s 72) and, thereafter, was subject to a procedure requiring further statements and counter-statements to establish the extent of the defendant's benefit (see s 73). (v) Section 74 provided rules for calculating the 'amount that might be realised' and contains provisions designed to defeat sham transactions. (vi) Confiscation orders were to be enforced as unpaid fines (see s 75) but it was also provided that a receiver might be appointed to realise the defendant's property in order to apply it in satisfaction of the order (see ss 80–82). (vii) The pre-trial restraint of property was provided for in ss 76–79. Two forms of order were introduced. First, a restraint order, which may be used to prevent dealing with designated property and, secondly, the charging order which may be used to impose a charge on designated property to preserve assets for a future confiscation order. (viii) The provisions of the 1988 Act most relevant to the issues raised in these appeals are ss 71 and 72 that are in Pt VI of the Act. We refer to them initially in their unamended form.

SECTION 71 OF THE 1988 ACT

[7] Section 71, so far as material, provides as follows:

'(1) The Crown Court and a magistrates' court shall each have power, in addition to dealing with an offender in any other way, to make an order under this section requiring him to pay such sum as the court thinks fit.

(2) The Crown Court may make such an order against an offender where—(a) he is found guilty of any offence to which this Part of this Act applies; and (b) it is satisfied—(i) that he has benefited from that offence or from that offence taken together with some other offence of which he is convicted in the same proceedings, or which the court takes into consideration in determining his sentence, and which is not a drug trafficking offence; and (ii) that his benefit is at least the minimum amount ...

(4) For the purposes of this Part of this Act a person benefits from an offence if he obtains property as a result of or in connection with its commission and his benefit is the value of the property so obtained.

(5) Where a person derives a pecuniary advantage as a result of or in connection with the commission of an offence, he is to be treated for the purposes of this Part of this Act as if he had obtained as a result of or in connection with the commission of the offence a sum of money equal to the value of the pecuniary advantage.

(6) The sum which an order made by a court under this section requires an offender to pay must be at least the minimum amount, but must not exceed—(a) the benefit in respect of which it is made; or (b) the amount appearing to the court to be the amount that might be realised at the time the order is made, whichever is the less.

(7) For the purposes of this Part of this Act the minimum amount is £10,000 ...'

Thus, by reason of s 71, before a court had power to make a confiscation order the court had to be satisfied that the defendant had benefited by at least £10,000. This followed a recommendation made by the Hodgson Committee which had been in favour of limiting the power to make confiscation orders by reference to a sum of money so as to prevent its operation in impracticable small cases.

SECTION 72 OF THE 1988 ACT

[8] Section 72, so far as material, provides:

'(1) A court shall not make a confiscation order unless the prosecutor has given written notice to the court to the effect that it appears to him that, were the court to consider that it ought to make such an order, it would be able to make an order requiring the offender to pay at least the minimum amount.

(2) If the prosecutor gives the court such a notice, the court shall determine whether it ought to make a confiscation order ...

(4) If the court determines that it ought to make such an order, the court shall, before sentencing or otherwise dealing with the offender in respect of the offence or, as the case may be, any of the offences concerned, determine the amount to be recovered in his case by virtue of this section and make a confiscation order for that amount specifying the offence or offences ...'

Under s 72(1) and (2) the procedure for making an order was dependent on the prosecution giving notice that there were likely to be sufficient assets to meet it. Where such a notice was given, the court was bound to consider the making of an order. By s 71(4) the court was required to determine the amount to be recovered and make a confiscation order before sentencing or otherwise dealing with the offender.

THE CRIMINAL JUSTICE ACT 1993

[9] Part III of the Criminal Justice Act 1993 (ss 27–35) made significant changes to Pt VI of the 1988 Act. The principal changes that were made to the confiscation regime were twofold: (i) the standard of proof required to determine any question as to whether a person had benefited, and whether his benefit was at least the minimum amount and the amount to be recovered, was to be that applicable in civil proceedings (see s 71(7A) of the 1988 Act as inserted by s 27 of the 1993 Act); (ii) the court was given power to postpone a determination of the amount which might be recovered until after the court had sentenced the defendant (see s 72A of the 1988 Act as inserted by s 28 of the 1993 Act).

a [10] The power to order postponement was enacted to give the sentencing court the flexibility to sentence the offender, so that he might not be left in a state of uncertainty, before proceeding to confiscation. Under the 1988 Act in its original form (and under the Drug Trafficking Offences Act 1986 in its original form) the sentencing court was prevented from proceeding to sentence until the court had gone through the procedural steps involved in confiscation. This often
b meant that sentence was adjourned for a considerable period of time in order to enable the parties to prepare and present evidence and arguments.

SECTION 72A OF THE 1988 ACT
[11] Section 72A, (in its unamended form) so far as material, provides as follows:

c
(1) Where a court is acting under section 71 above but considers that it requires further information before—(a) determining whether the defendant has benefited as mentioned in s 71(2)(b)(i) above; (b) determining whether his benefit is at least the minimum amount; or (c) determining the amount to be recovered in his case by virtue of s 72 above, it may, for the
d purposes of enabling that information to be obtained, postpone making that determination for such period as it may specify.
(2) More than one postponement may be made under subsection (1) above in relation to the same case.
(3) Unless it is satisfied that there are exceptional circumstances, the court shall not specify a period under subsection (1) above which—(a) by itself; or
e (b) where there have been one or more previous postponements under subsection (1) above or (4) below, when taken together with the earlier specified period or periods, exceeds six months beginning with the date of conviction.
(4) Where the defendant appeals against his conviction, the court may, on
f that account—(a) postpone making any of the determinations mentioned in subsection (1) above for such period as it may specify; or (b) where it has already exercised its powers under this section to postpone, extend the specified period.
(5) A postponement or extension under subsection (1) or (4) above may be made—(a) on application by the defendant or the prosecutor; or (b) by
g the court of its own motion.
(6) Unless the court is satisfied that there are exceptional circumstances, any postponement or extension under subsection (4) above shall not exceed the period ending three months after the date on which the appeal is determined or otherwise disposed of.
h (7) Where the court exercises its powers under subsection (1) or (4) above, it may nevertheless proceed to sentence, or otherwise deal with, the defendant in respect of the offence or any of the offences concerned.
(8) Where the court has so proceeded, section 72 above shall have effect as if—(a) in subsection (4), the words from "before sentencing" to "offences
j concerned" were omitted; and (b) in subsection (5), after "determining" there were inserted "in relation to any offence in respect of which he has not been sentenced or otherwise dealt with".
(9) In sentencing, or otherwise dealing with, the defendant in respect of the offence, or any of the offences, concerned at any time during the specified period, the court shall not—(a) impose any fine on him; or (b) make any such order as is mentioned in s 72(5)(b) or (c) above.

(10) In this section references to an appeal include references to an
application under section 111 of the Magistrates' Courts Act 1980 (statement
of case by magistrates' court).

(11) In this section, "the date of conviction" means—(a) the date on
which the defendant was convicted of the offence concerned, or (b) where
he was convicted in the same proceedings, but on different dates, of two or
more offences which may be taken together for the purposes of
subsection (2) or, as the case may be, (3) of section 71 above, the date of the
latest of those convictions.'

Section 72A gave the sentencing court the power to postpone the confiscation
proceedings. The court may order one or several postponements providing the
total period does not exceed six months from the date of conviction, though even
then that time limit can be extended if there are 'exceptional circumstances'.

THE PROCEEDS OF CRIME ACT 1995

[12] The 1988 Act was further amended by the Proceeds of Crime Act 1995.
(It had also been amended by the Criminal Justice and Public Order Act 1994, but
the amendments effected by that Act are not directly material to the issues raised
in these appeals.)

[13] Section 1 of the 1995 Act made a number of changes to s 71 of the 1988
Act and these changes may be summarised as follows: (i) a *duty* was placed upon
the court to exercise its powers to embark upon confiscation proceedings in every
case in which written notice had been given by the prosecutor; (ii) the court was
given a *power* to institute confiscation proceedings of its own volition; (iii) the
minimum figure of £10,000 was abolished. Thus, s 71(1) of the 1988 Act now
provides:

'(1) Where an offender is convicted, in any proceedings before the Crown
Court or a magistrates' court, of an offence of a relevant description, it shall
be the duty of the court—(a) if the prosecutor has given written notice to the
court that he considers that it would be appropriate for the court to proceed
under this section, or (b) if the court considers, even though it has not been
given such notice, that it would be appropriate for it so to proceed, to act as
follows before sentencing or otherwise dealing with the offender in respect
of that offence or any other relevant criminal conduct.'

[14] Section 2 of the 1995 Act inserted s 72AA into the 1988 Act to provide for
confiscation in relation to a course of criminal conduct.

[15] Section 3 of the 1995 Act amended s 73 of the 1988 Act (effect of provision
of statement by prosecutor) and provided for the service on the court and
defendant of statements from the prosecutor.

[16] Section 4 of the 1995 Act inserted s 73A into the 1988 Act so as to
empower the court to order the defendant to provide information to assist it in
carrying out its functions under Pt VI of the 1988 Act.

[17] Sections 5–10 of the 1995 Act amended the 1988 Act in relation to such
matters as the review and revision of confiscation orders, the enforcement of
confiscation orders and the variation of confiscation orders.

[18] Part VI of the 1988 Act came into force on 3 April 1989. The amendments
made by the 1993 Act, which were of a procedural nature, came into force on
3 February 1995 (see the Criminal Justice Act 1993 (Commencement No 8) Order
1995, SI 1995/43); the amendments made by the 1995 Act came into force on
1 November 1995 (see the Proceeds of Crime Act 1995 (Commencement) Order

a 1995, SI 1995/2650). The amendments to the 1988 Act made by the 1995 Act apply when the offences of which the accused is convicted were committed on or after 1 November 1995.

THE HUMAN RIGHTS ACT 1998

[19] In addition to the domestic legislation, in the *Sekhon* appeal there is
b reliance on art 6 of the European Convention for the Protection of Human Rights and Fundamental Freedoms 1950 (as set out in Sch 1 to the 1998 Act). However, because of the conclusions which we have come to it is not necessary to deal with this issue.

THE ARGUMENT ON THE LEGISLATION

c [20] In all the cases before us the argument turned on whether the confiscation proceedings had taken place in accordance with the procedure set out in the 1988 Act in the amended form appropriate to the particular appellant. It was only when Mr Perry came on the scene that the prosecution case was advanced in what we are satisfied is the appropriate manner by the following
d issues. (i) Did the confiscation proceedings take place in accordance with the procedures set out in the 1988 Act, and, in particular, did the sentencing judge properly postpone the confiscation hearing? (ii) If the confiscation proceedings did not take place in accordance with the procedures set out in the 1988 Act, were the confiscation orders in each case nevertheless lawfully made?

[21] Before examining the statutory provisions further, let us try to explain
e why the second issue is all important when considering whether a court has been deprived of jurisdiction to make a confiscation order.

(i) The starting point is that the court is seized of a general criminal jurisdiction over the proceedings. The confiscation proceedings are ancillary to the main proceedings.

f (ii) The courts have been given by Parliament jurisdiction to make confiscation orders where a defendant has been found guilty and a defendant has benefited from the crime of which he has been found guilty.

(iii) It is in those circumstances obvious that what Parliament intends is that a confiscation order should be made by the court, if a defendant has been found guilty and has benefited from his crime, absent any indication to the contrary.

g (iv) Parliament can make provision itself as to the procedure to be followed before a confiscation order is made or it can give the power to another body, such as a rule committee, to lay down rules of procedure. However, in criminal proceedings those rules are frequently contained in primary legislation, but they remain none the less rules of procedure.

h (v) The purpose of rules of procedure is not usually to give or take away a court's jurisdiction. It is the substantive provisions of the legislation creating the power or duty of the court which have given the jurisdiction, here under sub-ss (1) and (2) of s 71 above. What the procedural provisions are doing is to provide a convenient and just machinery enabling the court to exercise its
j jurisdiction.

(vi) The procedural provisions can be, but usually are not, conditions that have to be fulfilled to give the court jurisdiction. More usually procedural provisions do no more than: (a) enable the court if they are not complied with to make orders to require something to be done if it has not been done in accordance with the statutory provisions or (b) in the same circumstances to dismiss the proceedings.

(vii) Neither (a) nor (b) above happens automatically in the absence of the proceedings being abandoned. What is required is for the court to come to a decision (usually on the application of the prosecution or defence) to take action (a) or (b) above. What action the court takes will depend on what is just in all the circumstances.

(viii) If there is no application made (see sub-para (vii), above) but the next steps set out in the procedural provisions take place, the step that is not taken as it should have been can usually be ignored. It is no longer relevant even though Parliament has said it 'must' or 'should' be taken. This is because its objective of moving the procedure forward is no longer required. We would not regard this outcome to involve a 'waiver'.

(ix) It is because of the matters set out in sub-para (viii), above, that procedural steps usually do not go to jurisdiction. The difficulty arises because Parliament does not often expressly indicate what procedural steps are to result in proceedings becoming, in effect, a nullity if they are not taken. It is left to the courts to infer what Parliament intended to happen if a procedural requirement is not complied with. Deducing what Parliament intended can be difficult. It may be helpful if it is remembered that (a) the use of mandatory terms is far from decisive and (b) substantive provisions giving the court its jurisdiction are not to be automatically defeated in the ordinary way by non-compliance with procedural requirements unless this is necessary to achieve the statutory purpose.

[22] It is unfortunate that the second issue was not previously advanced on behalf of the Crown. Mr Perry submits there are two facets to the second issue, the first being that breaches of apparently absolute statutory requirements do not necessarily deprive the court of jurisdiction and the second is dependent on the doctrine of waiver. That doctrine plays no part in our decisions in these appeals but we recognise that in other cases it could be important.

[23] In relation to the second issue Mr Perry submits that if even the most trivial breach of an apparently absolute requirement had the effect of vitiating the relevant proceedings the consequences would be out of all proportion. Here, he relies upon *Bennion on Statutory Interpretation* (3rd edn, 1997) and the following statement of principle (p 31):

'Where a requirement arises under a statute, the court, charged with the task of enforcing the statute, needs to decide what consequence Parliament intended should follow from failure to implement the requirement. This is an area where legislative drafting has been markedly deficient. Drafters find it easy to use the language of command. They say that a thing "shall" be done. Too often they fail to consider the consequence when it is not done. What is not thought of by the drafter is not expressed in the statute. Yet the courts are forced to reach a decision. It would be draconian to hold that in every case failure to comply with the relevant requirement invalidates the thing done. So the courts' answer has been to devise a distinction between mandatory and directory duties.'

[24] He also refers to numerous authorities which deal with the distinction between 'mandatory and directory duties' including in relation to the time limit specified in the Crown Court Rules 1982, SI 1982/1109 (see *R v Urbanowski* [1976] 1 All ER 679, [1976] 1 WLR 455, *R v Spring Hill Prison Governor, ex p Sohi* [1988] 1 All ER 424, [1988] 1 WLR 596) and as to the time for preferring a bill of indictment in the Indictment (Procedure) Rules 1971, SI 1971/2084 (see *R v Sheerin* (1976)

a 64 Cr App R 68, *R v Soffe* (1982) 75 Cr App R 133 and *R v Farooki* (1983) 77 Cr App R 257).

[25] There is no doubt that difficulties for courts exist in applying the distinction between mandatory requirements, on the one hand, and directory requirements on the other. Even if the terms 'directory' and 'mandatory' are not used the problem remains of answering the question: 'What is the effect of *b* non-compliance with procedural requirements?' What is necessary as indicated by Lord Campbell LC in *Liverpool Borough Bank v Turner* (1861) 30 LJ Ch 379 at 381, 45 ER 715 at 718, is 'to try to get at the real intention of the legislature, by carefully attending to the whole scope of the statute to be construed'.

[26] In a case in which the Secretary of State had failed to apply for leave to appeal on the form prescribed by statutory instrument, the Court of Appeal (Civil *c* Division) in the case of *R v Immigration Appeal Tribunal, ex p Jeyeanthan, Ravichandran v Secretary of State for the Home Dept* [1999] 3 All ER 231 at 235–236, [2000] 1 WLR 354 at 359 took very much the same view in a judgment of Lord Woolf MR. What was stated is as follows:

d 'Because of what can be the very undesirable consequences of a procedural requirement which is made so fundamental that any departure from the requirement makes everything that happens thereafter irreversibly a nullity it is to be hoped that provisions intended to have this effect will be few and far between. In the majority of cases, whether the requirement is categorised as directory or mandatory, the tribunal before whom the defect is properly *e* raised has the task of determining what are to be the consequences of failing to comply with the requirement in the context of all the facts and circumstances of the case in which the issue arises. In such a situation that tribunal's task will be to seek to do what is just in all the circumstances (see *Brayhead (Ascot) Ltd v Berkshire CC* [1964] 1 All ER 149, [1964] 2 QB 303 applied by the House of Lords in *London and Clydeside Estates Ltd v* *f* *Aberdeen DC* [1979] 3 All ER 876, [1980] 1 WLR 182).'

This statement has since had the benefit of the endorsement of Lord Steyn in the House of Lords in *A-G's Ref (No 3 of 1999)* [2001] 1 All ER 577 at 583, [2001] 2 AC 91 at 117.

g [27] In relation to the procedural requirements which Parliament has imposed it is possible fairly readily to come to certain conclusions. These are as follows. (i) Since the 1988 Act was passed, Parliament has been attaching increasing importance to courts being in a position to make confiscation orders. For that reason it has relaxed the requirements of the order having to be made as part of the original sentencing process. In the 1988 Act in its unamended form, the court *h* was unable to proceed to sentence until the court had gone through the procedural steps and dealt with confiscation. The subsequent amendments gave the court power to adjourn sentencing but care was taken to specify the limits on the power to postpone its decision to order confiscation. (See s 28 of the 1993 Act and the terms of s 72A of the 1988 Act inserted by s 28.) This process was *j* continued by the 1995 Act which extended the court's powers. (ii) Parliament was intent on ensuring that wherever practicable the process of making a confiscation order and sentencing should be linked. It can be readily understood why Parliament should have adopted this course. After all, it is important that the defendant should know as soon as practicable what are the consequences to him of his conviction. Parliament, therefore, when it did relax the requirements did tend to require the court to be satisfied that if it was to grant a postponement or extension there were 'exceptional circumstances' to justify this (see e g s 72A(3) and (6)).

[28] On the other hand we suggest that it would not have been the intention of Parliament to exclude the jurisdiction of the court in relation to the making of confiscation orders because of procedural defects of a technical nature that caused no injustice to the defendant. In this context it is interesting to note that certainly this is not Parliament's intention now. The most recent legislation in this area is the Proceeds of Crime Act 2002. Section 14(11) of that Act provides:

'A confiscation order must not be quashed only on the ground that there was a defect or omission in the procedure connected with the application for or the granting of a postponement.'

[29] We would expect a procedural failure only to result in a lack of jurisdiction if this was necessary to ensure that the criminal justice system served the interests of justice and thus the public or where there was at least a real possibility of the defendant suffering prejudice as a consequence of the procedural failure.

[30] Having set out this general approach, it is convenient to return to the procedural requirements themselves. Here it is important to note that s 71 of the 1988 Act is dealing with the jurisdiction of the court. It does contain provisions which undoubtedly have to be complied with to give the court jurisdiction to make an order. The defendant must have been found guilty of the required offence. In addition, the court must be satisfied that the offender has benefited from the offence to the required extent. Section 72, on the other hand, is dealing with procedure and procedural requirements do not usually go to jurisdiction.

[31] Notwithstanding the actual language of s 72(1) which read literally is mandatory in its terms, we would not regard it as likely that Parliament would, for example, be concerned to deprive the court of jurisdiction because of defects in the contents of the written notice which is required by s 72(1). The notice, which does not have to be given to the defendant, starts the procedure and avoids the court being involved in confiscation proceedings if the prosecutor thinks that the court would not be able to order the defendant to pay more than £10,000. Furthermore, once the 1995 Act was in force, this is the almost inevitable conclusion because not only was the court required to exercise its powers when a notice had been given it had power to exercise its powers of its own volition.

[32] It seems to us that the non-jurisdictional nature of the requirements of s 72 is supported by the decision of the Court of Appeal in *R v Urbanowski* [1976] 1 All ER 679, [1976] 1 WLR 455. That was a case in which the court was considering s 7(4) of the Courts Act 1971 which provides:

'The trial of a person committed by a magistrates' court ... (b) shall, unless the Crown Court has otherwise ordered, begin not later than the expiration of the prescribed period beginning with the date of his committal ...'

[33] Rule 19 of the Crown Court Rules 1971, SI 1971/1292 prescribed a period of 56 days. Scarman LJ in giving judgment said of the subsection ([1976] 1 All ER 679 at 681, [1976] 1 WLR 455 at 458):

'It seems to us plain that s 7(4) of the 1971 Act is primarily addressed to the Crown Court, and obliges the court to take steps to ensure that cases are begun within the prescribed period. Accordingly in our view this provision, being addressed to the court and its officials, is directory and not mandatory;

a   and it follows from that view of the subsection that it is open to the Crown
     Court to grant an extension of time if it thinks fit after the expiration of the
     prescribed period.'

THE CASE LAW
       [34] Having made these general observations it is next important to look at
b   the relevant case law. The general effect of the decisions on postponement of the
     confiscation proceedings can be summarised as follows: (i) the postponement
     of confiscation proceedings must be ordered by a judicial decision (see *R v Steele,
     R v Shevki* [2001] 2 Cr App R (S) 178, *R v Ross* [2001] EWCA Crim 560, [2001] 2 Cr
     App R (S) 484); (ii) whilst no particular form of words is required, the decision to
     postpone must be made manifest (*R v Steele* and *R v Ross*).
c   [35] Turning to individual cases, the case which it is convenient to take first,
     because it contains a statement in the judgment of the court given by Judge LJ
     with which we would respectfully agree, is *R v Cole* [1998] All ER (D) 142, (1998)
     Independent, 30 April. It was a case where the trial judge had become ill after a
     difficult and complex trial. The issue was whether this constituted exceptional
     circumstances in parallel legislation dealing with drug trafficking. Judge LJ
d   stated:

         '... s 3 therefore creates a convenient code which permits the court to pass
         an appropriate sentence before having determined whether to make a
         confiscation order under s 2, and simultaneously maintains the necessary
         control over the process which could otherwise become protracted and
e   ultimately unfair ... The court should normally deal with a confiscation
         order within six months of the conviction. In exceptional circumstances this
         period may be exceeded. The judgment whether circumstances are
         exceptional or not must be made by the court considering whether to make
         a confiscation order, and the decision must be made before the six-month
f   period has elapsed ... here the judge was in hospital on the date when he had
         indicated that he would determine the confiscation issue. Of course it might
         have been the defendant who was ill and unfit to attend court. For that
         matter it might equally have been counsel who the defendant wished to
         appear for him. Having studied the statutory code we do not consider that
         it was intended or drafted so as to preclude the listing officer making sensible
g   arrangements for the conduct of Crown Court business, normally after
         discussion with the trial judge or the resident judge ...'

       [36] This subject was again addressed by Judge LJ in *R v Steele* [2001] 2 Cr App
     R (S) 178 to which we have already referred (see [34], above). This is a case also
h   decided under the Drug Trafficking Act 1994 rather than under the 1988 Act.
     However, Judge LJ again sets out what should be the general approach which is
     relevant to the similar statutory provisions we are considering. He said (at 194):

         'Confiscation orders should normally form part of the ordinary sentencing
         process. For lack of appropriate information, this will often be impractical.
j   If the conditions in section 3(1) or section 3(4) are satisfied, and within six months
         of conviction, the court may decide that the determination should be
         postponed. Unless the circumstances are exceptional this should not extend
         beyond six months after conviction. These decisions involve the court's
         discretion, judicially exercised when the statutory conditions are present,
         taking full account of the preferred statutory sequence as well as the express
         direction in the statute that save in exceptional circumstances confiscation

determinations should not be postponed for more than six months after
conviction. So far as practicable, adjournments which would have the effect *a*
of postponing the determination beyond that period, or in exceptional cases,
beyond the period envisaged when the decision to postpone was made,
should be avoided. Nevertheless when the circumstances in an individual
case compel an adjournment which would have this effect, then whether or
not the information gathering process has been completed, it may be *b*
ordered, for example, to take account of illness on one side or the other, or
the unavailability of the judge, without depriving a subsequent order for
confiscation of its validity.'

[37] We refer to both of the judgments of Judge LJ. As it appears to us, they
make it clear that the consideration of whether there should be a postponement *c*
of the confiscation proceedings and whether there are exceptional circumstances
involve just the type of issue that courts regularly are required to determine when
engaged in case management. The strict compliance with procedural requirements
relating to issues of this nature would not normally be expected to go to
jurisdiction. The provisions tell the judge the order in which he must deal with
matters and the considerations he must have in mind. Any default by the judge *d*
can be satisfactorily dealt with on appeal when it is to be expected that the court
would examine the circumstances and not focus on technicalities. The issue
would be, what did justice require, having regard to the Parliamentary code. The
court would take into account, as Mr Campbell-Clyne on behalf of Knights urges,
'the draconian' nature of the proceedings so far as the defendant is concerned. *e*

[38] We turn next to *R v Ross* [2001] 2 Cr App R (S) 484, in which the Court of
Appeal (Potter LJ, Stanley Burnton J and Judge Sir Rhys Davies QC (the Recorder
of Manchester)) considered the situation of a judge who had passed sentence and
then postponed the confiscation proceedings under the 1994 Act. The confiscation
order was quashed. Potter LJ stated (at [18]):
f
'In our judgment, section 2 and section 3 of the Act lay down a clear and
mandatory sequence to be followed in a case such as the present when a
defendant appears before the Crown Court to be sentenced in respect of one
or more drug trafficking offences, and either the prosecution makes a request
within section 2(i)(a), or the court considers it is appropriate to proceed *g*
under section 2. We say mandatory because of the first five words of
section 2(2) ["The court shall first determine …"].'

He went on to state (at [25]):

'… section 3(1) confers a discretion on the court to postpone making a *h*
determination. It is only if that discretion is exercised, by making an order
for the postponement of a determination, that sections 3(7) and (8) permit
sentence to be passed before the determination is made … the exercise of
that discretion requires a judicial decision. No particular form of words is
required, but the decision to postpone must be made manifest and, in
particular, it must specify the period of the postponement, which cannot go *j*
beyond six months from the date of conviction unless the circumstances are
exceptional.'

[39] This case is in part inconsistent with what we have said earlier. However,
the court dealt with the question of whether the language was mandatory but did
not ask itself what was the effect of non-compliance with the language. That

a court did not have the benefit of Mr Perry's argument. Even this authority requires no more than that there should be a decision made to postpone the confiscation hearing. The nature of the decision and its form are not treated as critical. We understand Potter LJ as indicating that as long as there is a decision to postpone that is all that matters. In other words the decision gives the court jurisdiction. Other matters go to the nature of that decision and could

b appropriately be dealt with on appeal. *R v Phillips* [2001] EWCA Crim 2790, [2002] 2 Cr App R (S) 49 can be explained in the same way.

[**40**] The next case to which we should refer is *R v Davies* [2001] EWCA Crim 2902, [2002] 1 WLR 1806. In that case it was decided that when ordering a postponement under s 3 of the 1994 Act it is necessary to specify the period of the postponement. In giving the judgment of the court, Pitchford J, explaining the

c statutory scheme under the 1994 Act, stated:

'[26] Before sentence is passed the court must, if asked by the prosecution, or of its own motion if it considers it appropriate, act under section 2 to determine whether the defendant has benefited from drug trafficking, and, if

d so, determine the amount to be recovered from the defendant …

[27] Where the court is acting under section 2 but considers it requires further information before making either determination, it may postpone the determination for such period as it may specify …

[28] The second use of the word "may" in section 3(1) means, in this context, "must" … In our view, the mandatory nature of the requirement is

e established by reading section 3(1) together with section 3(3) …

[29] The plain purpose of the section is to place time limits on the determination proceedings. Had Parliament intended merely to set a period within which, subject to exceptional circumstances, the determination must be made, it could, and in our view would, have explicitly so provided. The

f whole section, particularly subsection (3), is structured upon the assumption that the setting of a period or periods for postponement will take or has taken place. Without the setting of a period under subsection (1), the limitation imposed by subsection (3) does not bite. It follows that either Parliament intended that there should be no limitation when the court chooses not to specify the period or it intended that the court should specify a period in

g every case. In our view the latter construction is inevitable.

[30] In expressing its decision under section 3(1), no particular form of words is required, provided that the decision of the court is made before sentence and that the decision of the court is manifest.'

h [**41**] This reasoning of Pitchford J is impeccable but it does not follow that, if this reasoning is correct, Parliament intended that the setting of the period of postponement was a condition precedent to the court's jurisdiction. We would respectfully doubt the correctness of this decision if it means the court inevitably is without jurisdiction because of a failure to specify a date to which there is to be

j a postponement even if the application in fact is heard within the required period.

[**42**] We question whether if the argument advanced before us by Mr Perry had been advanced the decision would have been the same. The trial court, or failing the trial court, the appeal court could have fully protected the interests of the defendant. If the confiscation order was made within the period permitted by the 1994 Act we would suggest it is unnecessary by implication to read a requirement into the statutory code which that statutory code does not specify.

[43] In this connection we would prefer the approach of Rix LJ in *R v Copeland* [2002] EWCA Crim 736, [2002] 2 Cr App R (S) 512. In that case it was held by the Court of Appeal (Rix LJ, Leveson J and Sir Richard Tucker) that a failure to specify a period of postponement did not deprive the Crown Court of jurisdiction to make a confiscation order. The Court of Appeal referred to the decision in *R v Ross* and stated (at [17]):

'We are troubled by the reference in *Ross* to the fact that the court must specify the period in light of the fact that the statute makes no such requirement and that it did not, as we would observe, provide that the court shall specify such a period. The decision in *Ross* was of course based on facts very different to the facts of the present case. In that case before sentence the Crown originally said there would be no inquiry. It subsequently said that there might be a request for an inquiry and the whole matter was left in the air whether there would be any inquiry at all. That is quite different from the facts of the present case.'

[44] However, in *R v Pisciotto* [2002] EWCA Crim 1592, [2003] 1 Cr App R 68 (Keene LJ, Davis J and Judge John Griffith Williams (the Recorder of Cardiff)) it was decided that a failure to specify the period of the postponement was fatal to the making of a confiscation order and the reasoning in *R v Davies* was to be preferred to the reasoning in *R v Copeland*. We respectfully disagree and would prefer the reasoning in *R v Copeland*.

[45] There are two authorities which suggest that the Crown Court retains a general power to postpone or adjourn confiscation proceedings, for a period that is limited only by its own discretion as to whether or not there are exceptional circumstances and whether or not the offender is sentenced for the offence prior to the confiscation proceedings. The two decisions are *R v Tuegel* [2000] 2 All ER 872 and *R v Lingham* [2001] 1 Cr App R (S) 158.

[46] In *R v Tuegel* (Rose LJ, Tucker and Elias JJ) it was held ([2000] 2 All ER 872 at 893, 894) that a judge 'has inherent power at common law to adjourn the whole or part of the sentencing exercise' and that the power was 'not subject to any specific common law time limit'. In that case a confiscation order made under the 1988 Act, outside the six-month time limit, was upheld on the basis that the sentencing court and counsel had proceeded on the basis that there were exceptional circumstances which justified a confiscation order being made outside the six-month period.

[47] In *R v Lingham* [2001] 1 Cr App R (S) 158 the Court of Appeal held that a court may postpone making a confiscation order for a period of more than six months from the date of conviction if the postponement is for a purpose other than that of obtaining information. Speaking for the Court of Appeal, Jowitt J stated (at 161):

'Leaving aside section 3 of the Drug Trafficking Act 1994, a court is entitled to make its own decision about when an application relating to a case of which it is seized should be heard and whether it should be adjourned. It must act judicially. Subsections (1) and (3) of section 3 are all to be considered against this background. For the legitimacy of this approach see [*R v Tuegel* [2000] 2 All ER 872 at 894].'

[48] The authorities, to which we have referred so far, do not deal with the question of waiver and in view of our conclusions, it is not necessary for us to give detailed consideration to waiver. However, even without waiver, in our opinion

a all that is strictly required in order to give the court jurisdiction where a postponement is necessary is that there should be a decision to postpone. This requires no particular form of words. We are not persuaded that the statement of a period of postponement is critical for establishing jurisdiction. It is not a condition precedent for there to be jurisdiction. If there is a failure to specify then this could be a matter of complaint by appeal to the Court of Appeal after a

b confiscation order has been made. Then the Court of Appeal could, if justice so required, quash the confiscation order. If, however, no injustice was involved, the confiscation order would stand.

[49] Before leaving the authorities we should refer to two more cases. The first of those cases is *R v Kelly* [2000] 2 Cr App R (S) 129. In that case the judgment of the court was given by Laws LJ. In the course of his judgment which related

c to a confiscation order made under the 1994 Act Laws LJ, after having been referred to *R v Tuegel,* said (at 137):

'Nothing is plainer than that a postponement under section 3(1) is constituted, and only constituted, by a judicial decision unless there is something wholly exceptional that must be taken and done in open court

d and reasons there given for it.'

[50] In *R v Kelly* nothing was said about exceptional circumstances. No period was specified under s 3(1). In our judgment nothing capable of being called a judicial decision was arrived at under s 3(1) on that day. In those circumstances it was decided that the confiscation order was made without jurisdiction. There

e being no decision at all in that case, we would not question the correctness of the decision.

[51] The second is *R v Palmer (No 1)* [2002] EWCA Crim 2202, [2003] 1 Cr App R (S) 572. In *R v Palmer* a confiscation order in the total sum of £33,243,812·46 had been made on 23 April 2002. In this court Rix LJ presided. The court quashed the

f confiscation order. Two notices under s 72 had been served by the prosecution. As to the first, Rix LJ indicated (at [57]) that the court had 'anxiously considered' the submissions that despite inaccuracies it was valid. He observed that he saw the strength in the Crown's case 'that in substance everyone knew where they were going' and that it was clear to all that the appellant was a wealthy man who had profited enormously from his fraud but he concluded 'albeit with reluctance',

g that the judge was right to find that the first notice was invalid and that the second notice could not make up for its deficiencies. He was of the opinion that the first notice, not having been valid, a second notice served after the confiscation proceedings had commenced could not cure the absence of an effective notice at the outset. The consequence was that it was not possible for the trial court to

h postpone the confiscation proceedings and proceed to sentence.

[52] The first notice in *R v Palmer* referred to the wrong section. The explanation as the court pointed out was that it was drafted with the 1995 provisions in mind when that Act was not in force at the relevant time. So the notice referred to the amended s 71(1)(a) when it should have referred to s 72(1)

j (the 1995 Act did not apply to the proceedings). In addition, it did not refer to the fact that if an order was made it would at least be for £10,000, which in Palmer's case was hardly likely to be in issue. The errors were due to the notice being on a standard form developed for use when the 1995 provisions applied. Neither the court nor the defendant, if they had seen the notice, would have been under any doubt that the prosecution thought this was a case where confiscation proceedings should continue. It is difficult to conceive that Parliament intended that technical failures of this sort should affect the jurisdiction of the court to make a confiscation order.

    [53] The Court of Appeal was, however, without the benefit of the argument advanced before us by Mr Perry. Furthermore, they were influenced by two decisions given by this court which shared the same disadvantage. Those decisions being R v Martin [2001] EWCA Crim 2761, [2002] 2 Cr App R (S) 122 and R v Miranda [2000] 2 Cr App R (S) 347.

    [54] After the decision in R v Palmer, counsel appearing for the Crown abandoned the Crown's right to appeal. In those circumstances when Mr Perry, on behalf of the Crown, sought leave to appeal, the court took the view that there was no power to grant leave to appeal.

    [55] The question that remains is what is the status of R v Palmer and the other authorities on which it was based. What has happened is that as part of the normal common law process, decision has followed decision extending the principle that there is no jurisdiction if there is a procedural failure from one aspect to another of the confiscation process. R v Palmer is only significant because it dealt with the use of a notice designed for use under a later Act being used as a notice under an earlier Act. Even though the wrong notice was used it could still achieve and did achieve its primary objective of initiating confiscation proceedings. Yet a defendant who had been otherwise properly subjected to a confiscation order in excess of £30m had that order quashed. This is a result that Parliament could not have intended.

    [56] For one constitution of this court to hold that a series of cases have been decided per incuriam, is not a course to be lightly taken. There is now new legislation which contains the section to which we have referred above which is designed to prevent repetition of the problem. There are, however, no doubt other cases in the pipeline which could be affected by the earlier authorities which did not consider Mr Perry's argument. In these circumstances we feel it right to indicate that in our view R v Palmer is wrongly decided and should not be followed and each of the earlier cases to which we have referred should be examined with care to see whether in fact it can be said they should be regarded as doing any more than deciding that there should be a decision to postpone confiscation proceedings, however generally expressed, prior to the completion of sentencing an offender, if confiscation proceedings are to take place after sentencing.

THE APPEALS OF DALJIT SINGH SEKHON, SATNAM SINGH, SHANGARA SINGH AND GURDEV SINGH DHNOAY

    [57] We turn to the individual appeals and set out the sequence of events in the appeals of Daljit Singh Sekhon, Satnam Singh, Shangara Singh and Gurdev Singh Dhnoay. (i) Daljit Singh Sekhon, Satnam Singh and Gurdev Singh Dhnoay pleaded guilty to an offence of conspiracy to cheat the public revenue. The offence occurred between 1 August 1994 and 30 November 1995. The relevant statutory scheme in this case is the 1988 Act as amended by the 1993 Act. (ii) Satnam Singh pleaded guilty to an offence of conspiracy to cheat the public revenue on indictment T971094. The offence occurred between 1 August 1994 and 30 November 1995. The relevant statutory scheme in his case is the 1988 Act as amended by the 1993 Act. (iii) Shangara Singh pleaded guilty to an offence of conspiracy to cheat the public revenue on indictment T980773. The offence occurred between 1 November 1996 and 30 June 1997. The relevant statutory scheme in his case is the 1988 Act as amended by the 1993 Act and the 1995 Act.

a [58] In the case of the appellant Shangara Singh the statutory scheme is that which applied after 1 November 1995, including the 1995 Act, whereas the cases of the other appellants were governed by the 1988 Act as amended by the 1993 Act only. However, this makes no material difference to the issues that we have to consider.

b [59] Unlike the other appellants we are now considering Gurdev Singh Dhnoay does not have leave to appeal and he is seeking leave to appeal out of time. We extend time and grant him leave to appeal. The facts of the offences are unimportant, as the appellants all pleaded guilty at the Crown Court at Newcastle in September 1998. Briefly the case arose from the appellants' different roles in the importation or diversion on a large scale of alcoholic goods on which no duty had been paid. The total revenue evaded was calculated to be
c about £5,555,600.

[60] The chronology of events can again be conveniently taken from Mr Perry's submissions. (i) The sentencing hearing was adjourned and took place on 17 and 18 December 1998. (ii) In advance of the sentencing hearing, by a letter dated 8 October 1998, the judge and the appellants Daljit Singh Sekhon, Satnam Singh
d and Shangara Singh were notified by the prosecution that this was a suitable case in which to proceed under Pt VI of the 1988 Act.

[61] The sequence of events thereafter was as follows: (i) on 17 December 1998, counsel for the prosecution opened the facts against Daljit Singh Sekhon, Satnam Singh and Gurdev Singh Dhnoay; (ii) on 18 December 1998, counsel for
e the prosecution opened the facts against Shangara Singh; (iii) Judge Wood passed sentence; (iv) counsel for the prosecution then raised the question of confiscation in open court; (v) the confiscation hearing was adjourned to February 1999; (vi) the confiscation hearing was listed for hearing on 19 February 1999 and on that date, in the cases of Daljit Sekhon, Satnam Singh and Gurdev Singh Dhnoay, having found exceptional circumstances, Judge Wood postponed the hearing for
f four months; (vii) the case of Shangara Singh was listed on 2 March 1999 and Judge Wood postponed the matter on the basis of his ruling on 19 February 1999; (viii) the confiscation hearing took place on 7, 8 and 9 June 1999 and Judge Wood made confiscation orders against all of the appellants; (ix) further hearings took place on 12 and 13 August 1999, at which hearings Judge Wood reconsidered the
g confiscation order made against Gurdev Singh Dhnoay and made a confiscation order in the case of Daljit Singh Sekhon.

[62] It appears that the appellants were notified of the prosecution's intention to proceed with confiscation proceedings. A restraining order was made prohibiting the appellants from dealing with certain assets on 16 December 1998.
h On 17 and 18 December 1998 they appeared at the Crown Court for sentence and (with the possible exception of Shangara) they were sentenced on 18 December 1998. No mention was made of the postponement of the confiscation proceedings before sentence. After sentence, as appears from the transcript, counsel for the prosecution raised the issue of confiscation proceedings and the procedure to be
j adopted and clearly had s 72A in mind since he referred to a period of six months. No question was raised as to the need for exceptional circumstances to exist if the adjournment was to be for more than six months. The trial judge, Judge Wood, indicated that the matter should be heard initially in February though the parties considered that it might have subsequently been adjourned to a later date.

[63] Clearly what happened did not comply with the procedure set out in s 72A because that section contemplates the decision to postpone being made

prior to the passing of sentence. On the evidence which is before us that did not
happen. Thus there was a clear contravention of s 72(4) of the 1988 Act.   *a*

[64] It has to be accepted that subject to there being a decision to postpone, it
was intended that the confiscation order should be made before sentence.
Whereas other procedural requirements may not be critical, that there should be
a postponement of the making of the confiscation order when there is power to
do so, is fundamental to the exercise of the jurisdiction to make a confiscation   *b*
order. In these cases, therefore, in accord with the earlier decisions, we accept
that the effect of non-compliance was intended by Parliament to go to
jurisdiction subject to any possible argument as to waiver. In the result,
therefore, there having been no postponement or even purported decision to
postpone until after sentence the confiscation orders were made without
jurisdiction, the orders have therefore to be quashed. To this extent the appeals   *c*
will be allowed.

THE APPLICATION OF KEVIN MCFAUL

[65] McFaul was a party to the conspiracy which involved Keith Ross which
was the subject of the decision in *R v Ross* [2001] 2 Cr App R (S) 484. The facts of   *d*
his case are indistinguishable from those in *R v Ross* but he made no application
to appeal until the decision in *R v Ross* was brought to his attention. As in the case
we have just been considering, in McFaul's case as well there had not been any
decision to postpone until after he was sentenced on 9 November 1999. In his
case, the relevant legislation was ss 2 and 3 of the 1994 Act. However, there is no
material difference between the legislation in that Act and s 72A of the 1988 Act.   *e*

[66] Although there was considerable delay in the application for leave to
appeal we do not consider it would be right bearing in mind what has happened
to his co-accused to allow the confiscation order which was made in the case of
McFaul to stand. Accordingly, we grant him leave to appeal and allow his appeal
against the confiscation order which was made and quash that confiscation order.   *f*

[67] In both the first case and McFaul's case we have not dealt with any
question of waiver since in our judgment it would be wrong to do so when it was
raised at a later date.

THE APPEALS OF RICHARD MICHAEL KNIGHTS AND KEVIN MAGUIRE

[68] On 10 July 2000, in the Crown Court at Kingston-upon-Thames, Knights   *g*
pleaded guilty to being knowingly concerned in dealing with goods which were
chargeable with duty which had not been paid with intent to defraud contrary to
s 170(1)(b) of the Customs and Excise Management Act 1979. On 12 October
2000 Maguire was convicted of the same offence. On 17 October both were
sentenced.   *h*

[69] On 30 July 2001 before the same court a confiscation order was made
against Knights in the sum of £139,260 and in the case of Maguire, in the sum of
£114,930.

[70] One of the grounds of appeal relied upon by Maguire, but not originally
by Knights, was that a confiscation order was made in the course of proceedings   *j*
which were invalid by reason of the circumstances of their initiation and
postponement under s 72 of the 1988 Act. This point was subsequently adopted
by Knights, so in both cases it is necessary to see whether the points taken as to
the jurisdiction to make the order have any validity. However, in the case of
Knights and Maguire there had been a hearing on the day prior to the appellants
being sentenced and the trial judge, Judge Haworth, set a timetable for

a sentencing and confiscation. Judge Haworth ordered the prosecution to serve its
statement in the confiscation proceedings by 11 December 2000 with a mention
hearing on 4 January 2001. On the latter date Judge Haworth set a date of 23
January 2001 for the confiscation hearing, having decided that his unavailability
until that date amounted to exceptional circumstances.

b [71] We have before us the transcripts dealing with the different proceedings
before the trial judge. It is clear from those transcripts that on 16 October 2000
there was discussion with regard to a timetable for confiscation proceedings
before sentencing. Judge Haworth was wrongly told on 16 October by counsel
that the six months ran from sentence rather than conviction but this does not
matter as it did not affect the order which the judge made. Clearly he considered
that the proceedings should be postponed starting from the date of conviction.

c The need for postponement would be greater from the later date of sentence.
Furthermore, it is apparent that he did postpone the proceedings. Much
argument took place before us as to whether there was postponement to a
specific date because the date which was being selected was a date for, in effect,
further directions. However, in our judgment as long as the parties are clearly

d envisaging that the process was to take place within the timescale provided for by
s 72A, that is sufficient.

[72] On 4 January 2001 it was common ground that the parties were not in a
position to deal with matters then and sensibly and appropriately Judge Haworth
adjourned the matter to the last date on which he would be sitting in January,
namely 23 January.

e [73] Where, as here, there have been complex proceedings, it would be
wholly inappropriate for any judge but the trial judge to deal with the
confiscation proceedings unless that was unavoidable. In our judgment Judge
Haworth was entitled to postpone the confiscation proceedings in the way that
he did bearing in mind his availability.

f [74] Accordingly in our judgment there is nothing in the procedural points
which have been raised by these appellants and we can now turn to the final
issues raised in these appeals, namely the extent to which they had benefited from
the crime which they committed. We turn first to the law.

THE LAW

g [75] This involves provisions of the 1988 Act as amended by the 1993 Act and
the 1995 Act:

'**71.** … (4) For the purposes of this Part of this Act a person benefits from
an offence if he obtains property as a result of or in connection with its
commission and his benefit is the value of the property so obtained …

h (6) Subject to subsection (1C) above the sum which an order made by a
court under this section requires an offender to pay shall be equal to—(a) the
benefit in respect of which it is made; or (b) the amount appearing to the
court to be the amount that might be realised at the time the order is made,
whichever is the less.

j (7A) The standard of proof required to determine any question arising
under this Part of this Act as to—(a) whether a person has benefited from any
offence, or … (c) the amount to be recovered in his case … shall be that
applicable in civil proceedings.'

[76] These provisions were helpfully discussed in *R v Barwick* [2001] 1 Cr App
R (S) 445 at 453:

'We stress that the scheme of the Act requires the court to perform two distinct and discrete tasks. First, to determine the benefit. Secondly, to determine the amount that might be realised at the time the order is made, which may be very different. Further, the amount that might be realised may be quite unrelated to the identifiable proceeds of the offence, *e.g.* a lottery win, inheritance, or other lawfully acquired property. In the end, the task of the court at the second stage is to determine the amount "appearing to the court" to be the amount that might be realised. But once the benefit has been proved, it is permissible and ought normally to be the approach of the court, to conclude that the benefit remains available until the defendant proves otherwise; subject to the issue of changes in the value of money to which we now turn.'

THE HEARING

[77] It fell to Judge Haworth to make rulings pursuant to these provisions on 30 July 2001 having heard evidence during several preceding days, the witnesses being both appellants, Mrs Knights (the wife of the first appellant) and Mr Rodger, a co-defendant. The first rulings were as to the respective benefits that accrued to the appellants by reason of their criminal activities. As to this, he ruled that the benefit obtained by Mr Knights amounted to £139,260 and that obtained by Mr Maguire amounted to £114,930.

[78] These rulings are not the subject of current appeal. It is conceded that evidence had been put before Judge Haworth from which he could fairly infer benefits in such sums. That said, two features of the relevant judgment merit mention. First, the rulings necessarily involved total rejection of the respective appellants as witnesses of truth. Knights had contended that the benefit obtained through active participation in a fraud involving the evasion of £3·6m duty on the importation of some 36 tonnes of cigarettes was no more than £5,000. Maguire's statement in response to the prosecutor's statement failed to acknowledge any benefit at all as accruing from his similarly active participation save, possibly, for cash amounting to £19,800 found at his home following arrest. In the course of submissions we gathered that when under cross-examination he seemingly conceded that £4,000 utilised to pay off an overdraft was an obtained benefit.

[79] Secondly, at the time of this ruling and referring to the respective benefits as found, Judge Haworth added:

'There is no evidence that either of these defendants used any of this money to make purchases or fund an extravagant lifestyle. I have no doubt whatsoever that each has his nest egg salted away.'

[80] Having made these rulings Judge Haworth heard further submissions from, respectively, counsel for each appellant and for the Crown and then made additional rulings as to the amounts now due for payment as provided for by s 71(6). The totality of the rulings merits citation:

'Well dealing with each case, as far as Mr Knights is concerned he has the following realisable assets. His share of the equity of the house, £35,000; and the Abbey account £57·41; and his benefit from this enterprise, £139,260, which makes a total realisable asset of £178,699. I do not think it is likely that Mr Knights has spent any of the benefit figure at all. As I have said I am satisfied it is salted away, therefore in his case, I make a confiscation order of the lesser of the two sums, that is the benefit figure, £139,260 with a three-year term imprisonment in default. In Mr Maguire's case I find his

a   realisable assets to be the equity in Chichester Terrace, £46,250, the Abbey
     account, £25; the benefit from this enterprise, £114,930 less the £4,000 that
     was paid into the bank on the 22 November 1997. Therefore his total
     realisable assets are £157,205. I make the confiscation order in the sum of
     £114,930 with three years' imprisonment in default.'

b   [81] Following this ruling Judge Haworth was prevailed upon to clarify his
     ruling with respect to Mr Maguire, doing so as follows:

         'I wanted to make it clear if I did not do so already that I make the same
         finding in respect of Maguire that I did in respect of Knights namely that I do
         not think it likely that he has spent any of the benefits and am satisfied that
         he has salted them away.'
c

     THESE APPEALS
     [82] Mr Boothby, counsel for Mr Maguire, made the principal submission,
     effectively on behalf of both appellants. He invited us to hold that in these latter
     rulings Judge Haworth's exercise of discretion was outwith the parameters set by
d   s 71 and in any event wholly unreasonable so that we could and should set it
     aside. By reference to s 71(6), if the judge was holding that each man was
     currently retaining his respective benefit as identified in the first rulings then
     references to other realisable assets were otiose, thus betraying muddled
     thinking. If in each case the other realisable assets were material to his
     deliberation then perhaps it was his findings as to benefits being 'salted away' that
e   were open to challenge. In any event there was no attempt made by way of these
     rulings to address the appellants' individual circumstances nor indeed to address
     the submissions earlier made to him by counsel. Given evidence that Mr Knights
     lived frugally whereas Mr Maguire spent money liberally, the judge should have
     explained his decision that their present financial positions were comparable—
f   absent such explanation there had to be a doubt as to a finding that each had
     'salted away' their respective benefit.
     [83] This court is critical of the content of the rulings under appeal. They are
     so short as to be labelled cursory. They do not in terms address the issues then
     raised in submissions and the content owes nothing to s 71(6) and (7A). It is not
     surprising that they have spawned these appeals and this, Mr Boothby's principal
g   submission, has commanded our careful attention. However, in the event we
     cannot accept it. We remind ourselves that Judge Haworth had had every
     opportunity to form views as to the appellants and as to their respective disposal
     of such benefits as accrued from their fraudulent conduct. Thus he had had
     several recent days of evidence in turn preceded by the evidence given at the trial.
h   It was on the basis of such views that he rejected each man's evidence and
     asserted in the course of his first rulings that each had in fact 'salted away' his
     accrued benefit. Given these findings of fact, effectively beyond challenge before
     this appellate court, the second rulings became inevitable. It is a pity that Judge
     Haworth did not say as much, and it is a pity that he qualified the simplicity of his
j   approach by identifying realisable assets other than the respective accrued
     benefits, that is, assets that lay outwith s 71(6). That said, we have his findings of
     fact, such amply founded by his receipt of evidence and they serve to sustain the
     rulings under appeal.
     [84] Other subsidiary points were taken. Should the judge have asserted in his
     first rulings that the respective benefits had been 'salted away'? And should not
     there have been a forensic pause following the first rulings so as to allow the

appellants to, as it were, focus upon the scope for realising the now identified
benefits? Neither point carries any weight. The finding made in the course of the *a*
first rulings might strictly have been better made by way of the second rulings but
both sets of rulings reflect the same receipt of evidence and evidential overlap
between the issue as to amount of benefit and the issue as to realisable assets must
be on occasions inevitable. As to the second point there should be no need for
honest and candid defendants to delay preparation and presentation of a case as *b*
to realisable assets until there is a ruling as to accrued benefit.

[85] The respective appeals against the rulings as to realisable assets are
rejected and the appeals of both these appellants are dismissed.

*Appeals allowed in the cases of Sekhon, Shangara Singh and Satnam Singh. Applications
for leave to appeal granted and appeals allowed in the cases of Dhnoay and McFaul.* *c*
Appeals dismissed in the cases of Knights and Maguire.

Lynne Townley   Barrister.

a

R v Simpson
[2003] EWCA Crim 1499

COURT OF APPEAL, CRIMINAL DIVISION
LORD WOOLF CJ, KENNEDY LJ, MITCHELL, HALLETT AND PITCHERS JJ

b 12, 23 MAY 2003

Precedent – Court of Appeal – Criminal Division – Doctrine of stare decisis not applied with same rigidity as in Civil Division of Court of Appeal.

c
Sentence – Confiscation order – Application for confiscation order – Whether non-compliance with statutory procedural requirements going to court's jurisdiction – Criminal Justice Act 1988, ss 71, 72 – Proceeds of Crime Act 1995, s 16(5).

The appellant pleaded guilty to offences involving VAT fraud and was sentenced to a total of 30 months' imprisonment. A confiscation order in the sum of
d £209,351·24 was made under s 71[a] of the Criminal Justice Act 1988. The appellant appealed against the confiscation order on the ground, inter alia, that the judge had had no jurisdiction to make it because the notice served on the court by the prosecution was not in the form required by s 72(1)[b] of the 1988 Act, and that by virtue of s 16(5)[c] of the Proceeds of Crime Act 1995, since one of the offences to which he had pleaded guilty had been committed before 1 November 1995, the
e amendment to s 72 made by s 1 of the 1995 Act providing that service of a notice was no longer necessary, did not apply. He submitted that the application of s 16(5) was not limited to offences on which the confiscation order was based. The appellant further argued that the court should not follow a recent decision of the Court of Appeal (the recent decision), in which the court, in holding that
f non-compliance with the statutory procedure did not go the court's jurisdiction to postpone confiscation proceedings, had disapproved a previous decision (the previous decision) in which a confiscation order had been quashed because a valid s 72 notice had not been served. The appellant argued, inter alia, that it had not been open to the court making the recent decision to conclude that the previous decision was irregular and for that reason should not be followed.

g

Held – (1) A degree of discretion remained in the Court of Appeal, Criminal Division to decide whether or not a previous decision should be treated as a binding precedent in future, when there were grounds for saying that that decision was wrong. The doctrine of stare decisis did not apply as rigidly to the
h Court of Appeal in its criminal jurisdiction as in its civil jurisdiction. Whilst there might be a case for restricting the discretion to cases where the departure from authority was in favour of an accused, that should not apply where, as in the instant case, a defendant wished to rely upon a wrongly decided case to provide a technical defence. The law had been misapplied and misunderstood in the
j previous decision, because the court had not had the opportunity to consider all the authorities which had been considered in the recent decision. There were ample grounds for regarding the previous decision as irregular and therefore not binding on the court. There was no doubt that the recent decision applied to the

---

a   Section 71, so far as material, is set out at [7], below
b   Section 72, so far as material, is set out at [8], below
c   Section 16, so far as material, is set out at [12], below

instant case, and that, accordingly, any defects in the notice had not deprived the
sentencing judge of jurisdiction to make the confiscation order (see [32]–[34],
[37], [38], [56], below); dicta of Diplock LJ in *R v Gould* [1968] 1 All ER 849 at 851
applied; *R v Sekhon, R v McFaul, R v Knights* [2003] 3 All ER 508 approved; *R v
Palmer (No 1)* [2003] 1 Cr App R (S) 572 disapproved.

(2) Section 16(5) had to be construed as applying to an offence in respect of
which a confiscation order was or could be sought. To interpret the section
otherwise would lead to absurd results. The appeal would therefore be dismissed
(see [19], [56], below).

Notes

For decisions of the Court of Appeal as authorities, see 37 *Halsbury's Laws*
(4th edn reissue), para 1242.

Section 16(5) of the Proceeds of Crime Act 1995 has been repealed with effect
from 24 March 2003 by the Proceeds of Crime Act 2002, s 457, Sch 12.

Cases referred to in judgment

Critchell v Lambeth BC [1957] 2 All ER 417, [1957] 2 QB 535, [1957] 3 WLR 108, CA.
DPP v Merriman [1972] 3 All ER 42, [1973] AC 584, [1972] 3 WLR 545, HL.
Mirehouse v Rennell (1833) 1 Cl & Fin 527, 6 ER 1015, HL.
R v Ahmed (8 February 2000, unreported), CA.
R v Barwick [2001] 1 Cr App R (S) 445, CA.
R v Copeland [2002] EWCA 736, [2002] Cr App R (S) 512.
R v Gould [1968] 1 All ER 849, [1968] 2 QB 65, [1968] 2 WLR 643, CA.
R v Martin [2001] EWCA Crim 2761, [2002] 2 Cr App R (S) 122.
R v Miranda [2000] 2 Cr App R (S) 347, CA.
R v Newsome, R v Browne [1970] 3 All ER 455, [1970] 2 QB 711, [1970] 3 WLR 586, CA.
R v Newton (1982) 77 Cr App R 13, CA.
R v Palmer (No 1) [2002] EWCA Crim 2202, [2003] 1 Cr App R (S) 572.
R v Sekhon, R v McFaul, R v Knights [2002] EWCA Crim 2954, [2003] 3 All ER 508.
R v Taylor [1950] 2 All ER 170, [1950] 2 KB 368, CA.
Young v Bristol Aeroplane Co Ltd [1944] 2 All ER 293, [1944] KB 718, CA.

Case referred to in skeleton arguments

Bryers v Canadian Pacific Steamships Ltd [1956] 3 All ER 560, [1957] 1 QB 134, [1956]
3 WLR 776, CA; *affd sub nom Canadian Pacific Steamships v Bryers* [1957] 3 All ER
572, [1958] AC 485, [1957] 3 WLR 993, HL.

Appeal

Ian McDonald Simpson appealed from the confiscation order made against him
under the Criminal Justice Act 1988 by Judge Balston in the Crown Court at
Maidstone on 1 February 2002 following his pleas of guilty on 8 January 2001 to
value added tax offences and cheating the public revenue. The facts are set out in
the judgment of the court.

Raymond Walker QC and *Simon Taylor* (assigned by the *Registrar of Criminal
Appeals*) for Simpson.
Jonathan Fisher QC and *John Law* (instructed by the *Solicitor for Customs & Excise*)
for the Crown.

Cur adv vult

a 23 May 2002. The following judgment of the court was delivered.

LORD WOOLF CJ.

INTRODUCTION

[1] This is yet a further appeal involving a confiscation order. The confiscation
b order was made under the provisions of the Criminal Justice Act 1988 by Judge
Balston in the Crown Court at Maidstone on 1 February 2002.

[2] On 8 January 2001 the appellant, Ian McDonald Simpson, had pleaded
guilty on re-arraignment to two counts involving value added tax (VAT) offences
(counts 4 and 6), two counts of producing a false document for the purposes of
VAT (counts 5 and 14), one count of cheating the public revenue (count 16) and
c one count of being knowingly concerned in the fraudulent evasion of VAT
(count 18). Following a *Newton* hearing (see *R v Newton* (1982) 77 Cr App R 13)
before the same court, on 1 May 2001 the appellant was sentenced to 30 months'
imprisonment on count 6 and to concurrent sentences of 12 months' imprisonment
on each of the other counts.

d [3] The confiscation order which is the subject of the appeal was made under
s 71 of the 1988 Act. The sum of £209,351·34 was ordered to be confiscated with
a sentence of 18 months' imprisonment in default of payment. The appellant was
also ordered to pay £15,000 towards the costs of the prosecution. There were two
other alleged offenders, one was acquitted and the other, Kenneth Anthony
Young was prosecuted in Scotland and sentenced to five years' imprisonment on
e each count concurrent. In addition, a confiscation order was made in the sum of
£26,000.

[4] The frauds involved taking advantage of the special cash accounting
scheme which can be used for making VAT returns. The scheme was introduced
to give relief to small businesses which would otherwise have to pay VAT
charged on a transaction before the business had received payment from its
f customer. The scheme also took advantage of the fact that a business may
legitimately purchase goods and services from a subsidiary, this involving what is
known for VAT purposes as 'outsourcing'. A number of bogus outsourcing
agreements were deployed in carrying out the frauds.

[5] The grounds of appeal fall into two categories. First, there are those in
g relation to Judge Balston's jurisdiction to make the confiscation order and
secondly, there are those which relate to the amount of the confiscation order. It
is the grounds of appeal which relate to jurisdiction which explain the
constitution of this court. The Crown's contention is that the jurisdictional
points are of no substance because of the decision of this court (Lord Woolf CJ,
h Holland and Keith JJ) in the case of *R v Sekhon, R v McFaul, R v Knights* [2002]
EWCA Crim 2954, [2003] 3 All ER 508, which clearly establishes that the points
are without substance. However, Mr Raymond Walker QC, who together with
Mr Simon Taylor, appears on behalf of the appellant contends that the decision
in *R v Sekhon* wrongly indicates that the decision of this court in *R v Palmer (No 1)*
[2002] EWCA Crim 2202, [2003] 1 Cr App R (S) 572 was wrongly decided and that
j earlier cases applied in *R v Palmer* 'should be examined with care' (see *R v Sekhon*
at [56]). It was the decision in *R v Palmer* that caused the appellant to amend his
notice of appeal to raise the jurisdiction points. No leave to appeal has yet been
granted to the appellant in respect of the jurisdiction points. However, this court
can and does give leave for them to be argued. It should not be thought that we
are giving leave because we consider that there is any substance in the jurisdiction
points. We only give leave so as to enable the appellant to have a possibility of

appealing further by applying to this court to certify a point of law and then
applying to this court or the House of Lords for leave to appeal to the House of *a*
Lords. If there is no further appeal, it is our hope that this decision will put an end
to the string of appeals which are continuing to come before this court. There
have already been at least ten decisions in which *R v Sekhon* has been applied.

THE JURISDICTIONAL ISSUE   *b*
[6] The fact that the relevant provisions of the 1988 Act have been the subject
of a number of amendments has contributed to the problem. Powers of
confiscation appear in similar terms in the Drug Trafficking Act 1994 and they
have also been the subject of amendment and give rise to the same problems.
The legislative history is set out in *R v Sekhon* (at [6]–[18]) and it is not necessary
to repeat that history. It is sufficient for the purposes of the present appeal to set *c*
out the relevant terms of ss 71 and 72 of the 1988 Act as it was originally enacted.
[7] The provisions of s 71 so far as relevant were as follows:

> '(1) The Crown Court and a magistrates' court shall each have power, in
> addition to dealing with an offender in any other way, to make an order
> under this section requiring him to pay such sum as the court thinks fit.   *d*
> (2) The Crown Court may make such an order against an offender
> where—(a) he is found guilty of any offence to which this Part of this Act
> applies; and (b) it is satisfied—(i) that he has benefited from that offence or
> from that offence taken together with some other offence of which he is
> convicted in the same proceedings, or which the court takes into *e*
> consideration in determining his sentence, and which is not a drug trafficking
> offence; and (ii) that his benefit is at least the minimum amount ...
> (4) For the purposes of this Part of this Act a person benefits from an
> offence if he obtains property as a result of or in connection with its
> commission and his benefit is the value of the property so obtained.
> (5) Where a person derives a pecuniary advantage as a result of or in *f*
> connection with the commission of an offence, he is to be treated for the
> purposes of this Part of this Act as if he had obtained as a result of or in
> connection with the commission of the offence a sum of money equal to the
> value of the pecuniary advantage.
> (6) The sum which an order made by a court under this section requires *g*
> an offender to pay must be at least the minimum amount, but must not
> exceed—(a) the benefit in respect of which it is made; or (b) the amount
> appearing to the court to be the amount that might be realised at the time
> the order is made, whichever is the less.
> (7) For the purposes of this Part of this Act the minimum amount is *h*
> £10,000 ...'

[8] Section 72, so far as material, provided:

> '(1) A court shall not make a confiscation order unless the prosecutor has
> given written notice to the court to the effect that it appears to him that,
> were the court to consider that it ought to make such an order, it would be *j*
> able to make an order requiring the offender to pay at least the minimum
> amount.
> (2) If the prosecutor gives the court such a notice, the court shall
> determine whether it ought to make a confiscation order ...
> (4) If the court determines that it ought to make such an order, the court
> shall, before sentencing or otherwise dealing with the offender in respect of

a the offence or, as the case may be, any of the offences concerned, determine the amount to be recovered in his case by virtue of this section and make a confiscation order for that amount specifying the offence or offences.'

[9] Under s 72(1) and (2) the procedure for making an order was dependent on the prosecution giving a notice that there were likely to be sufficient assets to meet it. Where such a notice was given, the court was bound to consider the
b making of an order. By s 71(4) the court was required to determine the amount to be recovered and make a confiscation order before sentencing or otherwise dealing with the offender.

[10] Sections 71 and 72 were amended by the Criminal Justice Act 1993, the Criminal Justice and Public Order Act 1994 and the Proceeds of Crime Act 1995.
c It is the amendments which were made by the 1995 Act which are relevant to the argument which is advanced on behalf of the appellant. Section 1 of the 1995 Act amended s 71(1)–(3). It did so in terms described in the decision in *R v Sekhon, R v McFaul, R v Knights* [2003] 3 All ER 508 at [13] as follows:

d '(i) a *duty* was placed upon the court to exercise its powers to embark upon confiscation proceedings in every case in which written notice had been given by the prosecutor; (ii) the court was given a *power* to institute confiscation proceedings of its own volition; (iii) the minimum figure of £10,000 was abolished. Thus, s 71(1) of the 1988 Act now provides:
e "(1) Where an offender is convicted, in any proceedings before the Crown Court or a magistrates' court, of an offence of a relevant description, it shall be the duty of the court—(a) if the prosecutor has given written notice to the court that he considers that it would be appropriate for the court to proceed under this section, or (b) if the court considers, even though it has not been given such notice, that it would be appropriate for it so to proceed, to act as follows before sentencing or otherwise dealing with the offender in respect
f of that offence or any other relevant criminal conduct."'

[11] The 1995 Act also repealed s 72(1)–(4). The other amendments made were briefly summarised in *R v Sekhon* as follows:

'[14] Section 2 of the 1995 Act inserted s 72AA into the 1988 Act to provide
g for confiscation in relation to a course of criminal conduct.
[15] Section 3 of the 1995 Act amended s 73 of the 1988 Act (effect of provision of statement by prosecutor) and provided for the service on the court and defendant of statements from the prosecutor.
[16] Section 4 of the 1995 Act inserted s 73A into the 1988 Act so as to
h empower the court to order the defendant to provide information to assist it in carrying out its functions under Pt VI of the 1988 Act.
[17] Sections 5–10 of the 1995 Act amended the 1988 Act in relation to such matters as the review and revision of confiscation orders, the enforcement of confiscation orders and the variation of confiscation orders.'

j [12] The commencement of s 1 of the 1995 Act, which amended s 71 of the 1988 Act, was provided for in s 16 of that Act. Subsections (5) and (6) of s 16 provide:

'(5) Section 1 above shall not apply in the case of any proceedings against any person where that person is convicted in those proceedings of an offence which was committed before the commencement of that section.

(6) Sections 8(1) and 9 above shall not apply where the offence, or any of
the offences, in respect of which the confiscation order was made was
committed before the commencement of section 1 above.' *a*

[13] Section 72, prior to being amended by the 1995 Act, required in
mandatory terms, if a literal construction of the section is adopted, the service of
a notice on the court setting out the information stated in s 72(1). However, after
the 1995 Act came into force that notice was no longer necessary because the *b*
court could act on its own motion (see s 71(1)(b) as amended).

[14] Mr Walker argues that in view of the language of s 72 prior to the
amendments of the 1995 Act the court did not have jurisdiction to make a
confiscation order unless: (i) a notice which complies with s 72(1) was served and
(ii) *none of the offences* on which the appellant is indicted and convicted were *c*
committed before 1 November 1995.

[15] On the facts of this case Mr Walker has to advance this submission
because he can only rely on count 6 of the indictment for arguing that the 1995
Act was not in force at the relevant time and count 6 was not a count on which
the confiscation order was based. While Mr Walker accepts that this is the *d*
position, he points to the language of s 16(5) of the 1995 Act which he contends
does not limit the restriction of the application of s 16(5) to offences on which a
confiscation order is based.

[16] In support of the appellant's argument reliance was placed upon the
decision of this court in the case of *R v Ahmed* (8 February 2000, unreported)
(Kennedy LJ, Goldring J and Sir Charles McCullough). Sir Charles McCullough *e*
in giving judgment in that case said:

'22. In these proceedings there were three offences in the three counts.
Count 3 within a period wholly after 1 November 1995. The other two,
counts 1 and 2, were in relation to periods partly before and partly after that
date. In each of those instances there were overt acts committed in *f*
pursuance of the existence of the relevant conspiracy both before and after
that date, 1 November 1995.

23. Counsel's submission is that as the conspiracies in counts 1 and 2 ran
from 1 January 1995, the offences in counts 1 and 2 were being committed
both before and after 1 November 1995. That being so in these proceedings *g*
the appellant was "convicted ... of an offence which was committed before
[1 November 1995]". We agree. It follows that the judge had the *discretion*
to make an order in the full agreed sum of £40,000 or a lesser sum or none at
all.' (My emphasis.)

h

[17] However, when those paragraphs are read as a whole, it is clear that
Sir Charles was not seeking to say anything different from what we have
indicated is the position. Sir Charles made it plain that the court was not
'persuaded that these arguments would or might persuade the judge to do other
than he did'.

[18] Reliance was also placed upon the case of *R v Martin* [2001] EWCA Crim *j*
2761, [2002] 2 Cr App R (S) 122. It is said that the approach of Sir Charles was
approved in that later case. However, that does not provide any further
assistance to the appellant. The only other point, that it is important not to
ignore in relation to *R v Ahmed*, is that unlike here, there was no issue in that case
that the conspiracies were ones to which the 1995 Act could not apply. The dates
in the counts of the indictment reflected the actual dates.

a [19] Mr Walker's submission, if correct, means that in this case if the appellant had been acquitted on count 6 the confiscation order would be subject to the 1995 Act but because he was convicted of count 6 the confiscation order cannot be made. This is obviously an absurd result and we have no doubt that Mr Jonathan Fisher QC, who appeared on behalf of the Crown, is right in his contention that s 16(5) is not intended to produce this very strange consequence.

b In our judgment s 16(5) has to be applied so that after the word 'offence' there appears, the words 'in respect of which a confiscation order is or could be sought' as proposed in the admirable skeleton argument prepared by Mr David Barnard who appeared on behalf of the Crown before Mr Fisher was instructed.

[20] Before coming to Mr Walker's principal point on behalf of the appellant there is the further problem that he faces. This is that while count 6, in the particulars of the offence, refers to 16 October 1995, because that is the date on the invoice which is relied upon by the Crown as the initial act constituting the offence, it is clear from the evidence that the invoice was created on 19 November 1995. So in fact, the offence was committed after 1 November 1995. In any event the argument of the appellant, that the 1995 Act cannot be relied upon, fails on the facts.

d

THE IRREGULARITY (PER INCURIAM) ISSUE

[21] This is the issue which is of considerable significance and explains why it was thought appropriate to have a decision by a court constituted by the five judges who are hearing this appeal. We will deal with the issue as succinctly as we can but we recognise the broad importance of the issue in relation to both

e statutory construction and the doctrine of precedent.

[22] Initially, it is necessary to identify the limited nature of the dispute between the parties. The issue in dispute is (on the assumption that s 1 of the 1995 Act was not in force) does the fact that the notice that was served on the court by the prosecution was not in the form required by s 72 of the 1988 Act mean that the court had no jurisdiction to make a confiscation order? This the

f appellant contends is the position. This is the argument notwithstanding that the Crown had already informed the court prior to the service of the notice that the figure suggested as being the amount that the appellant benefited from the fraud far exceeded the statutory minimum amount of £10,000. In addition, the issue as to jurisdiction was not raised by the appellant prior to the confiscation order

g being made.

[23] Mr Walker contends that this court should not follow the decision in *R v Sekhon* in so far as it casts doubt upon the decision in *R v Palmer (No 1)* [2003] 1 Cr App R (S) 572. In support of this submission he advances three separate arguments. First, he submits that the issue as to the correctness of the decision in *R v Palmer* was not canvassed during the hearing in *R v Sekhon*. This submission

h is the result of his being misinformed as to what happened at the hearing of *R v Sekhon*. Mr Walker's junior, Mr Simon Taylor, was also junior counsel for Mr Satnam Singh in *R v Sekhon*. Mr Walker, no doubt as a result of what he had been told by Mr Taylor, was under the impression that there had been no argument as to the correctness of the decision in *R v Palmer* on the appeal in *R v*

j Sekhon. This impression was wrong. It is perhaps to be explained by the fact that at the beginning of the hearing in *R v Sekhon* the court indicated that it was proposing to allow the appeals in the case of Mr Taylor's client and his co-defendants who were involved in his appeal. Accordingly, the court indicated it was not necessary for the legal advisers of those appellants to attend during the argument relating to the other appellants who were also involved in the appeal. The appeals of the other three appellants then proceeded and it was in relation to those appeals that the effect of the decision in *R v Palmer* was contested. However, unusually since unless Mr Perry was able to persuade us otherwise, those appeals would have to be allowed as well, by agreement Mr Perry advanced his arguments on behalf of the Crown prior to the appellants advancing their argument. The right approach to the law was, however, fully canvassed. There is therefore no substance in this point.

[24] After the course of events in *R v Sekhon* had been discussed, Mr Walker turned to his argument that it had not been open to the court in *R v Sekhon* to conclude that *R v Palmer* had been decided irregularly and for that reason should not be followed. As to this, there was a striking division between the views of the parties since Mr Barnard in his skeleton argument on behalf of the Crown contended that *R v Sekhon* itself was a binding precedent as to the status of *R v Palmer* and this court should refuse to go behind the *R v Sekhon* decision.

[25] Mr Walker, when developing his submissions, relies on 37 *Halsbury's Laws* (4th edn reissue) para 1242 as to the situations in which it is appropriate for the Court of Appeal to depart from a decision otherwise binding on the court. The situations are stated to be: (i) where the court has acted in ignorance of a previous decision of its own court or a court of co-ordinate jurisdiction which covered the case before it. If this is the case the court must decide which case to follow; (ii) where the court has acted in ignorance of a decision of the House of Lords; (iii) where the court has given its decision in ignorance of the terms of a statute or a rule having statutory force; or (iv) where in exceptional and rare cases, the court is satisfied that there has been a manifest slip or error and there is no prospect of an appeal to the House of Lords.

[26] He also refers to two further passages in the same paragraph of *Halsbury's Laws* as to the Court of Appeal (Criminal Division). The first stating that a full Court of Appeal has no greater powers than the usual constitution of the court of three judges and, except in the cases mentioned above has no power to overrule a previous decision of the court. The other citation is that—

'In its criminal jurisdiction the Court of Appeal applies the same principles as on the civil side, but recognises that there are exceptions (a) where the applicant is in prison and in the full court's opinion wrongly so; (b) where the court thinks the law was misunderstood or misapplied; and (c) where the full court is carrying out its duty to lay down principles and guidelines in relation to sentencing.'

[27] These statements from *Halsbury's Laws* are unexceptional and are soundly based upon the authorities to which they refer. Prominent among them is the decision in *Young v Bristol Aeroplane Co Ltd* [1944] 2 All ER 293, [1944] KB 718. However, the paragraphs in *Halsbury's Laws* should not be read as if they are contained in a statute. The rules as to precedent reflect the practice of the courts and have to be applied bearing in mind that their objective is to assist in the administration of justice. They are of considerable importance because of their role in achieving the appropriate degree of certainty as to the law. This is an important requirement of any system of justice. The principles should not, however, be regarded as so rigid that they cannot develop in order to meet contemporary needs.

[28] One of the earliest statements on the rationale underpinning this doctrine was made by Parke J (see *Mirehouse v Rennell* (1833) 1 Cl & Fin 527 at 546, 6 ER 1015 at 1023) when he stated:

a

'Our common-law system consists in the applying to new combinations of circumstances those rules of law which we derive from legal principles and judicial precedents; and for the sake of attaining uniformity, consistency and certainty, *we must apply those rules, where they are not plainly unreasonable and inconvenient, to all cases which arise*; and we are not at liberty to reject them, and to abandon all analogy to them, in those to which they have not yet been

b

judicially applied, because we think that the rules are not as convenient and reasonable as we ourselves could have devised.' (My emphasis.)

[29] In Lord Greene MR's judgment in *Young's* case [1944] 2 All ER 293 at 300, [1944] KB 718 at 729, Lord Greene was careful to provide for a degree of flexibility. He stated:

c

'We do not think that it would be right to say that there may not be other cases of decisions given *per incuriam* in which this court might properly consider itself entitled not to follow an earlier decision of its own.'

[30] The House of Lords is in a special position because it is, so far as this

d

jurisdiction is concerned, the final court of appeal in both criminal and civil matters, but the reasons for it departing from its previous practice are worth repeating. They appear in the *Practice Statement (Judicial Precedent)* [1966] 3 All ER 77, [1966] 1 WLR 1234:

e

'Their lordships regard the use of precedent as an indispensable foundation upon which to decide what is the law and its application to individual cases. It provides at least some degree of certainty upon which individuals can rely in the conduct of their affairs, as well as a basis for orderly development of legal rules. Their lordships nevertheless recognise that too rigid adherence to precedent may lead to injustice in a particular case and also unduly restrict the proper development of the law. They propose therefore to modify their

f

present practice and, while treating former decisions of this House as normally binding, to depart from a previous decision when it appears right to do so. In this connexion they will bear in mind the danger of disturbing retrospectively the basis on which contracts, settlements of property and fiscal arrangements have been entered into and also the especial need for certainty as to the criminal law. This announcement is not intended to affect

g

the use of precedent elsewhere than in this House.'

[31] The passage from *Halsbury's Laws* makes a distinction between the position of the Criminal and Civil Divisions of the Court of Appeal but there is no general power in the Court of Appeal (Criminal Division) equivalent to that

h

contained in the practice statement.

[32] That the position in the criminal jurisdiction of the Court of Appeal should be different from that in the civil is derived from the judgment of Diplock LJ in *R v Gould* [1968] 1 All ER 849 at 851, [1968] 2 QB 65 at 68–69. The relevant passage reads as follows:

j

'In its criminal jurisdiction, which it has inherited from the Court of Criminal Appeal, the Court of Appeal does not apply the doctrine of stare decisis with the same rigidity as in its civil jurisdiction. If on due consideration we were to be of opinion that the law had been either misapplied or misunderstood in an earlier decision of this court, or its predecessor the Court of Criminal Appeal, we should be entitled to depart from the view as to the law expressed in the earlier decision notwithstanding that the case could not be brought within any of the exceptions laid down in *Young* v. *Bristol Aeroplane Co., Ltd.* ([1944] 2 All ER 293, [1944] KB 718) as justifying the Court of Appeal in refusing to follow one of its own decisions in a civil case (*R. v. Taylor* ([1950] 2 All ER 170, [1950] 2 KB 368)). A fortiori we are bound to give effect to the law as we think it is if the previous decision to the contrary effect is one of which the ratio decidendi conflicts with that of other decisions of this court or its predecessors of co-ordinate jurisdiction.'

[33] What Lord Diplock said in *R v Gould* has to be read in the light of his later comment in *DPP v Merriman* [1972] 3 All ER 42 at 58, [1973] AC 584 at 605. There he stated:

'These decisions it rightly treated as binding, for although the Criminal Division of the Court of Appeal is not so strictly bound by its own previous decisions as is the Civil Division, its liberty to depart from a precedent which it is convinced was erroneous is restricted to cases where the departure is in favour of the accused. This would not be the case in the instant appeal.'

[34] There is nothing to suggest in *DPP v Merriman* that Lord Diplock was reminded of what he said in *R v Gould*. We appreciate that there may be a case for not interpreting the law contrary to a previous authority in a manner that would mean that an offender who otherwise would not have committed an offence would be held to have committed an offence. However, we do not understand why that should apply to a situation where a defendant, as here, wishes to rely upon a wrongly decided case to provide a technical defence. While justice for a defendant is extremely important, justice for the public at large is also important. So is the maintenance of confidence in the criminal justice system. If the result in *R v Palmer (No 1)* [2003] 1 Cr App R (S) 572 had to be applied to other cases even though the Court of Appeal had acted in ignorance of the appropriate approach this would indeed, reveal a most unattractive picture of our criminal justice system's ability to protect the public.

[35] Here we prefer the approach indicated in *Bennion on Statutory Interpretation* (4th edn, 2002) p 134 which states:

'The basis of the *per incuriam* doctrine is that a decision given in the absence of relevant information cannot safely be relied on. This applies whenever it is at least probable that if the information had been known the decision would have been affected by it.'

[36] It is now convenient to refer to another argument advanced by Mr Walker. He submits that the issue raised in *R v Sekhon, R v McFaul, R v Knights* [2003] 3 All ER 508 was not the same issue as that in *R v Palmer* and therefore that the views in *R v Sekhon* about *R v Palmer* should not be regarded as necessary for the decision in *R v Sekhon*. This argument of Mr Walker misses the point. Although *R v Sekhon* was dealing with another procedural failure, namely the need to postpone the confiscation proceedings to a specific date, the approach to interpretation required in both cases was the same. If *R v Palmer* was correctly decided, then the same approach would have also applied to the contested issue in *R v Sekhon*. As Lord Evershed MR said in *Critchell v Lambeth BC* [1957] 2 All ER 417 at 424, [1957] 2 QB 535 at 545:

'I think that it would be wrong for this court to introduce into a matter already complicated enough, and made complicated by what I cannot help feeling to be the imperfections of the drafting of these Acts, refinements and narrow distinctions between cases which might fall under one section rather than another of the same legislation.'

a [37] This court considers that the law was misunderstood and misapplied in *R v Palmer*. In *R v Palmer* the court did not have the opportunity to consider all the authorities which were considered in *R v Sekhon*. There was also before *R v Palmer* conflicting decisions, including another decision of this court with Rix LJ presiding in *R v Copeland* [2002] EWCA 736, [2002] Cr App R (S) 512. The combination of these features provided in our judgment ample grounds for this court to regard the decision b in *R v Palmer* as being irregular and therefore not binding upon this court. We do not, however, accept the contention of Mr Barnard that this court was not entitled to look behind the decision in *R v Sekhon*. The normal position is that courts will not do so but they undoubtedly have a residual discretion to do so.

[38] In addition, it is not wholly without significance that the present court is constituted by five members of the Court of Appeal (Criminal Division). We c consider a degree of discretion remains in this court to decide whether a previous decision should be treated as a binding precedent in future or not when there are grounds for saying that the decision is wrong. In exercising that residual discretion, the constitution of the court is of relevance. We would here refer to the judgment of Widgery LJ in the five-judge court in *R v Newsome, R v Browne* d [1970] 3 All ER 455, [1970] 2 QB 711. There the court was dealing with the question of a guideline judgment on sentence. In that case, as in *R v Sekhon* there was good reason to adopt a flexible approach. In *R v Sekhon* the court made it clear that the discretion to depart from a previous precedent was not to be exercised lightly and we endorse that restrictive and cautious approach.

[39] It is, however, relevant to note in relation to the Court of Appeal e (Criminal Division) that there can be situations when a wrong decision of the Criminal Division can create a greater problem than decisions of the Civil Division with regard to appealing to the House of Lords. There are many situations where in practice there is little prospect of an appeal to the House of Lords because of the requirements, prior to an appeal, of a certificate that there f is a point of law of general public importance involved (see s 33 of the Criminal Appeal Act 1968) and the absence of a right to appeal after an acquittal. For example, if a judge of first instance is bound by a decision of the Criminal Division and as a result a defendant is acquitted there will be no right to appeal from that acquittal so there can be no confiscation proceedings that will be subject to appeal, as an order can only be made after the defendant has been convicted. In g addition, there will be little if any prospect of the Attorney General being entitled to refer the case to the Court of Appeal never mind the House of Lords if a judge refuses to make a confiscation order. So here, if *R v Palmer* had been allowed to stand notwithstanding that it was indeed wrongly decided, the consequences are that in a future case there could be considerable difficulty in obtaining a decision h from the Lords. The only conceivable route would appear to be a reference to the Court of Appeal in the later case by the Attorney General under his powers to refer an unduly lenient sentence. However, it is doubtful that the refusal to make a confiscation order on the grounds of lack of jurisdiction is in fact an unduly lenient sentence. However, we do not finally decide this point.

j [40] There is no doubt that if the decision of this court in *R v Palmer* represents the law then it provides very considerable assistance to the appellant, subject to the points made earlier. However, in *R v Sekhon* in relation to the case of *R v Palmer* it was stated as follows:

'[51] The second is *R v Palmer (No 1)* [2002] EWCA Crim 2202, [2003] 1 Cr App R (S) 572. In *R v Palmer* a confiscation order in the total sum of £33,243,812·46 had been made on 23 April 2002. In this court Rix LJ presided.

The court quashed the confiscation order. Two notices under s 72 had been served by the prosecution. As to the first, Rix LJ indicated that the court had "anxiously considered" the submissions that despite inaccuracies it was valid. He observed that he saw the strength in the Crown's case "that in substance everyone knew where they were going" and that it was clear to all that the appellant was a wealthy man who had profited enormously from his fraud but he concluded "albeit with reluctance", that the judge was right to find that the first notice was invalid and that the second notice could not make up for its deficiencies. He was of the opinion that the first notice, not having been valid, a second notice served after the confiscation proceedings had commenced could not cure the absence of an effective notice at the outset. The consequence was that it was not possible for the trial court to postpone the confiscation proceedings and proceed to sentence.

[52] The first notice in *R v Palmer* referred to the wrong section. The explanation as the court pointed out was that it was drafted with the 1995 provisions in mind when that Act was not in force at the relevant time. So the notice referred to the amended s 71(1)(a) when it should have referred to s 72(1) (the 1995 Act did not apply to the proceedings). In addition, it did not refer to the fact that if an order was made it would at least be for £10,000, which in Palmer's case was hardly likely to be in issue. The errors were due to the notice being on a standard form developed for use when the 1995 provisions applied. Neither the court nor the defendant, if they had seen the notice, would have been under any doubt that the prosecution thought this was a case where confiscation proceedings should continue. It is difficult to conceive that Parliament intended that technical failures of this sort should affect the jurisdiction of the court to make a confiscation order.

[53] The Court of Appeal was, however, without the benefit of the argument advanced before us by Mr Perry. Furthermore, they were influenced by two decisions given by this court which shared the same disadvantage. Those decisions being *R v Martin* [2001] EWCA Crim 2761, [2002] 2 Cr App R (S) 122 and *R v Miranda* [2000] 2 Cr App R (S) 347 ...

[55] The question that remains is what is the status of *R v Palmer* and the other authorities on which it was based. What has happened is that as part of the normal common law process, decision has followed decision extending the principle that there is no jurisdiction if there is a procedural failure from one aspect to another of the confiscation process. *R v Palmer* is only significant because it dealt with the use of a notice designed for use under a later Act being used as a notice under an earlier Act. Even though the wrong notice was used it could still achieve and did achieve its primary objective of initiating confiscation proceedings. Yet a defendant who had been otherwise properly subjected to a confiscation order in excess of £30m had that order quashed. This is a result that Parliament could not have intended.

[56] For one constitution of this court to hold that a series of cases have been decided per incuriam, is not a course to be lightly taken. There is now new legislation which contains the section to which we have referred above which is designed to prevent repetition of the problem. There are, however, no doubt other cases in the pipeline which could be affected by the earlier authorities which did not consider Mr Perry's argument. In these circumstances we feel it right to indicate that in our view *R v Palmer* is wrongly decided and should not be followed and each of the earlier cases to which we have referred should be examined with care to see whether in fact it can be said they should be regarded as doing any more than deciding that

a

there should be a decision to postpone confiscation proceedings, however generally expressed, prior to the completion of sentencing an offender, if confiscation proceedings are to take place after sentencing.'

[41] We have no doubt we should apply these paragraphs of the judgment in *R v Sekhon*. They are fatal to the arguments of the appellant on the jurisdiction

b issue. Any defects in the notice did not deprive the trial judge of jurisdiction.

THE AMOUNT OF THE CONFISCATION ORDER

[42] Next and finally we turn to the complaints concerning Judge Balston's approach to two aspects of the merits of making a confiscation order. First, it is said that he erred in including the sum of £115,000 in the benefit figure and

c second, it is said that Judge Balston erred in his approach to the assessment of the appellant's realisable assets. The judge made a confiscation order for the full amount of the benefit—namely, £209,351·34.

[43] The benefit of £115,000 is said to have arisen in this way. In the autumn of 1996 the appellant and Young embarked upon a joint enterprise to cheat the

d public revenue by means of the 'outsourcing companies' fraud. Arising out of his fraudulent transactions Young paid the appellant a total of £38,779·70 by way of commissions. That is not disputed nor is it disputed that that money fell to be included as a 'benefit' of the appellant.

[44] After Customs and Excise had searched Young's premises in March 1997

e and effectively brought an end to the fraud, Young transferred £115,000 to the appellant who in turn transferred it to a Swiss account. It is not disputed that the money represented the profit from the fraud. It is said on behalf of the appellant that the purpose of the transfer was to enable the appellant to invest the money on behalf of Young. The appellant subsequently in June and August 1997 repaid a total of £35,000 to Young but retained the balance of £80,000. When the

f appellant applied for an individual voluntary arrangement, Young was shown as a creditor. Did the transfer of £115,000 constitute a benefit for the appellant arising from the offence alleged in count 16? The answer to that question depends upon whether, under s 71(4) of the 1988 Act (as amended), that money was a benefit obtained by the appellant 'as a result of or in connection with' the commission of an offence. On behalf of the appellant it is said first that the

g £115,000 was outside the scope of the joint fraudulent enterprise involving the appellant and Young and second that the circumstances in which the appellant had obtained control of this money were such that it cannot be described as a benefit obtained 'as a result of or in connection with' the offence.

h [45] We have unhesitatingly concluded that the appellant did 'obtain' this money 'as a result of or in connection with' the offence charged in count 16 and that accordingly to that extent he had benefited from the offence. There was the clearest evidence before the judge that this money was obtained as a result of or in connection with the offence of cheating the public revenue because it represented a part of the proceeds of the fraud upon which together the appellant

j and Young had embarked. The fact that by virtue of some private arrangement part of the proceeds passed from Young's hands into the appellant's is neither here nor there. When that occurred he 'obtained' the property and the value of the property determined the extent of his benefit.

[46] As to the judge's assessment of the appellant's realisable assets, it is settled law (see *R v Barwick* [2001] 1 Cr App R (S) 445) that the onus of proving the 'benefit' obtained is upon the prosecution. If a defendant wishes to contend that

the amount which can be realised falls short of the benefit figure the burden is upon him to establish that to the civil standard. The court said (at 453):

'... the scheme of the Act requires the court to perform two distinct and discrete tasks. First, to determine the benefit. Secondly, to determine the amount that might be realised at the time the order is made, which may be very different. Further, the amount that might be realised may be quite unrelated to the identifiable proceeds of the offence, e.g. a lottery win, inheritance, or other lawfully acquired property. In the end, the task of the court at the second stage is to determine the amount "appearing to the court" to be the amount that might be realised. But once the benefit has been proved, it is permissible and ought normally to be the approach of the court, to conclude that the benefit remains available until the defendant proves otherwise; subject to the issue of changes in the value of money ...'

[47] That approach was clearly adopted by Judge Balston:

'Turning to the question of what assets are realisable for the purpose of making a confiscation order, the accepted approach of the court is to conclude that the benefit remains available until the defendant proves otherwise. This places on him the burden of proving that the realisable assets available to him are less than the benefit he has been found to have received. He must prove it on the civil standard of proof.'

[48] Over the following 15 pages of transcript Judge Balston proceeded to give clear and unassailable reasons for concluding that the appellant had failed to make a full disclosure of his assets. Furthermore Judge Balston was 'satisfied that he has other assets which may well exceed the deductions he is claiming' by way of living and business expenses.

[49] In the result it is not surprising that Judge Balston was unable to conclude that the appellant had satisfied him on a balance of probability that the value of his benefit exceeded the value of his realisable assets. In this case, unlike in many, Judge Balston was not confronted with an acceptance on the part of the prosecution that the value of the realisable assets (whatever it might be) fell far short of the benefit figure. It was the prosecution's case here that the assets did exceed the benefit figure and that one significant component of his realisable assets was his equitable interest in the matrimonial home at 80 London Road, Hailsham. The appellant claimed that his wife arranged the mortgage and purchased the property herself in the late 1980s. He maintained he had no interest in it. It is true that the property was registered in the name of his wife. Judge Balston, however, investigated the background to this transaction in some detail. He concluded that some years earlier (in the early 1980s)—

'There was an agreement between the defendant and his wife that for the future they would so arrange their affairs that their assets would be unassailable by the defendant's creditors.'

[50] Although not accepted by the defence the prosecution's valuation of the property was £402,500. There were two endowment policies charged to the building society with a surrender value of about £61,799. It was calculated that following repayment of the mortgages and the costs of the sale there should be an equity of £205,746. Contrary to the appellant's contention the prosecution claimed he had a 50% interest in the equity. The assets thus available from this source alone amounted to £102,873.

a [51] Quite apart from not accepting either the figures or the fact of his interest in the property the appellant further claimed that Barclays Bank had a charge on the property. As to that Judge Balston while accepting that a caution was registered against the title, declined to allow any reduction, attributable to the charge, from the value of this realisable asset. He said:

b 'There is no evidence that has been placed before me that confirms that the debt to the bank has not been paid. There is no evidence to tell me how the debt was originally incurred. It could, for example, have arisen from a guarantee by Mrs Simpson of a debt owed by the defendant to the bank. There is no evidence as to the amount now due under the charging order, if indeed the money has not been paid. The onus is upon the defendant to

c satisfy me about these matters. He has not done so.'

[52] Further, as to the policies Judge Balston said:

d 'It is further contended by the defence that the surrender value of the life policies is not an asset available to the defendant. I disagree. He has supplied no details of these policies other than the surrender values. The inference that I draw from their existence is that they are additional security for the payment of the mortgages and that when the mortgages are redeemed or the policies mature, the proceeds will go towards extinguishing the mortgage debt.'

e [53] Finally as to whether or not the appellant did have an equitable interest in the property Judge Balston said:

f 'I have also concluded that he has an equitable interest in the house and land at Hamelsham Manor, not only because of his interest in the proceeds of sale of 13 Howlett Drive but also because he has failed to satisfy me as to the origin of the moneys he says were found by Mrs Simpson. Additionally, his statement that he was paying rent for the use of the property by his business is again unsupported by any evidence and if it is true, is a contribution to the mortgage repayments in disguise.'

g [54] The appellant's wife did not give evidence. Of her absence from the witness box Judge Balston said this:

h 'One witness who might greatly have helped the court is Mrs Simpson. I am told there are matrimonial problems between her and the defendant, but one might have expected her to have been called to give evidence as, if what the defendant tells me about her part in this affair is true, her evidence could have been expected to be of assistance to the defendant.'

[55] We find it is impossible to fault Judge Balston's approach to this particular issue. His reasons for rejecting the appellant's claim as to the extent of his assets seem to us to be unanswerable and in our judgment the conclusion that the

j appellant had failed to satisfy Judge Balston that the confiscation order should be other than in the sum of the benefit figure was inevitable.

[56] Accordingly, the appeal is dismissed.

Appeal dismissed.

Sanchia Pereira   Barrister.

Inland Revenue Commissioners v Bebb Travel plc

[2003] EWCA Civ 563

COURT OF APPEAL, CIVIL DIVISION

WARD, MAY AND ARDEN LJJ

24 MARCH, 16 APRIL 2003

Employment – Remuneration – National minimum wage – Non-compliance – Whether compliance officer having power to serve enforcement notice in respect of employer's failure to pay national minimum wage to former workers – National Minimum Wage Act 1998, s 19.

A compliance officer acting for and on behalf of the Revenue concluded that the respondent employer had not paid the national minimum wage to certain former workers. Section 19(1)[a] of the National Minimum Wage Act 1998 provided that if an officer was of the opinion that a worker who 'qualifies' for the national minimum wage had not been remunerated for any pay reference period by his employer at a rate at least equal to the national minimum wage, the officer could serve an enforcement notice requiring the employer to remunerate the worker for pay reference periods ending on or after the date of the notice at a rate equal to the national minimum wage. Section 19(2) provided that an enforcement notice could 'also' require 'the employer' to pay to 'the worker' the difference between the wages received and the minimum wage in respect of the employer's previous failure to remunerate the worker at a rate at least equal to the national minimum wage. The officer issued an enforcement notice under s 19, requiring the employer to pay the former workers the difference between the wages received and the national minimum wage. The employer appealed to an employment tribunal, contending that the notice was invalid since it did not relate to any pay reference period for present workers ending on or after the date of service of the notice, but only to past pay periods in respect of past workers. The tribunal allowed the appeal and rescinded the notice. That decision was upheld by the Employment Appeal Tribunal. The Revenue appealed to the Court of Appeal, contending, inter alia, that s 19(1) could be construed to refer to workers who had ceased to be employed, and that s 19(2) was not dependent on the power to issue an enforcement notice provided by s 19(1), but rather empowered the service of an independent enforcement notice, relating to a worker no longer employed by an employer.

Held – On the true construction of s 19 of the 1998 Act, a valid enforcement notice could only relate to present workers in respect of present and future wages, and also, if appropriate, in respect of past wages. There was thus no power to issue an enforcement notice in respect of past workers for past pay. The use of the present tense in 'qualifies' in s 19(1) was deliberate. Construed in its context, it made no sense to say that an individual was a qualifying worker when he was in fact a past worker. The emphasis on the present was confirmed by that part of s 19(1) which set out the terms of the enforcement notice that the officer

---

a   Section 19 is set out at [12], below

a was empowered to serve. The notice could require payment of the minimum wage for the current and future period. Current and future periods could only relate to present workers. Moreover, s 19(2) was not a freestanding provision. 'The employer' and 'the worker' in sub-s (2) were those referred to in sub-s (1), leading to the conclusion that the enforcement notice referred to in sub-s (2) was the same as that referred to in sub-s (1). The dependency of sub-s (2) on sub-s (1)

b was conclusively demonstrated by permitting the enforcement notice 'also' to require the employer to pay up for his past failures to remunerate properly. The ordinary natural meaning of 'also' was 'in addition'. Under sub-s (1) present and future payments of the national minimum wage could be required in respect of a present worker, and under sub-s (2) past payments could also be required to be paid, ie past in addition to present and future. Accordingly, the appeal would be

c dismissed (see [23]–[25], [27], [31], [34], [35], [38]–[44], below).

Decision of the Employment Appeal Tribunal [2002] 4 All ER 534 affirmed.

Notes

For the power of an officer to issue an enforcement notice, see 16 *Halsbury's Laws*
d (4th edn) (2000 reissue) para 186.

For the National Minimum Wage Act 1998, s 19, see 16 *Halsbury's Statutes* (4th edn) (2000 reissue) 895.

Cases referred to in judgments

A-G's Ref (No 1 of 1988) [1989] 2 All ER 1, [1989] AC 971, [1989] 2 WLR 729, HL.
e *M (a minor) (care orders: threshold conditions), Re* [1994] 3 All ER 298, [1994] 2 AC 424, [1994] 3 WLR 558, HL.

Appeal

The Inland Revenue Commissioners appealed with permission of the
f Employment Appeal Tribunal (Judge J R Reid QC, G Mills and P A L Parker CBE) from its decision on 16 August 2002 ([2002] 4 All ER 534) dismissing their appeal from the decision of an employment tribunal sitting at Cardiff, and sent to the parties on 11 September 2001, rescinding an enforcement notice under s 19 of the National Minimum Wage Act 1998 served on the respondent, Bebb Travel plc,
g on 6 October 2000. The facts are set out in the judgment of Ward LJ.

John Cavanagh QC and *Jennifer Eady* (instructed by the *Solicitor of Inland Revenue*) for the Inland Revenue.
Daniel Oudkerk (instructed by *Dechert*) for Bebb.

h *Cur adv vult*

16 April 2003. The following judgments were delivered.

WARD LJ.

j [1] This is an appeal about the enforcement procedure available under the National Minimum Wage Act 1998. The employment tribunal decided in a decision promulgated on 11 September 2001 that an enforcement notice served under the 1998 Act be rescinded and on 16 August 2002 the Employment Appeal Tribunal (the appeal tribunal) upheld that decision (see [2002] 4 All ER 534). Because the point was thought to be 'one of some general significance', the appeal tribunal granted permission to appeal.

THE STATUTORY BACKGROUND

[2] The 1998 Act came into force on 1 April 1999. It gives 'workers' the right to be paid at least the national minimum wage as fixed from time to time by the National Minimum Wage Regulations 1999, SI 1999/584. At the time with which we are concerned the minimum wage was £3·60 per hour but it has since risen to £4·20 and will rise again in October to £4·50 an hour. 'Worker' is defined by s 54(3) of the 1998 Act to mean: '… an individual who has entered into or works under (or, where the employment has ceased, worked under)—(a) a contract of employment …' One notes that worker thus defined includes the individual whose employment has ceased and for convenience I shall call such a person a 'past worker' to distinguish him or her from the individual currently working under a contract of employment (a 'present worker').

[3] In order to determine whether an individual is being paid the national minimum wage, it is necessary to determine the hourly rate of pay. This is calculated as an average hourly rate in respect of a 'pay reference period' which is either one month or, if the worker is paid by reference to a shorter period than a month, that shorter period (see reg 10). Where remuneration is received at some date after the pay reference period during which it was earned, e g bonus pay or commission, then the 1999 regulations provide that it is to be allocated to the period during which it was earned rather than that when it was received. The regulations provide a detailed set of rules for calculating pay and hours for the purposes of the 1998 Act, including detailed rules on how various types of payment are to be treated (see regs 30–37) and as to how different categories of work are to be treated (see regs 15–29A).

[4] Employers are under a duty to keep records in respect of each worker for a minimum of three years so as to be able to demonstrate that the worker is being paid at a rate at least equal to the national minimum wage (see reg 38). A right to inspect those records is provided both to the individual worker who suspects that he has not been paid the national minimum wage (see s 10 of the 1998 Act) and to an enforcement officer (see s 14). The officers are appointed by the Secretary of State and he has arranged that the Inland Revenue shall provide those officers.

[5] These officers are given wide-ranging powers. In addition to having the right to inspect records, they may demand that information be given to them and they may even enter premises to exercise those powers. Relevantly for the purpose of this appeal, the officers are given power to issue enforcement notices under s 19 and if that notice is not complied with then the officer has a power to sue for wages on behalf of the worker (see s 20) or serve a penalty notice (see s 21).

[6] The worker is given a range of new rights. Under s 17 the worker is to be taken to be entitled under his contract to be paid as additional remuneration any shortfall between his contractual wage and the minimum wage. He is able to enforce that right by action taken in the county court. The worker is also given the right not to suffer detriment (see s 23) and can enforce that right by proceeding in the employment tribunal. Dismissal may be automatically regarded as unfair (see s 25).

[7] Just to emphasise the seriousness of this legislation, s 31 creates an offence for refusing or wilfully neglecting to pay the minimum wage and an employer guilty of the offence is liable to a fine not exceeding level 5 on the standard scale i e not exceeding £5,000. In civil proceedings the ordinary burden of proof is

a reversed because it is presumed that the individual qualifies for the minimum wage unless the contrary is established.

THE ORIGINS OF THIS DISPUTE

[8] Bebb Travel plc (Bebb) operates a coach service. It employed stewards and stewardesses on the coaches to carry out various tasks for the company for which

b they received their basic pay. The actual hourly rate of remuneration calculated in accordance with the 1999 regulations was below the applicable hourly rate of national minimum wage. The stewards and stewardesses were, however, allowed by Bebb to provide and sell refreshments on the coach and to retain any profits made from those sales but to bear any losses. They were treated for that purpose as self-employed persons.

c [9] In February and in May 2000 a national minimum wage compliance officer acting for and on behalf of the Inland Revenue visited Bebb's premises and examined the wage records. In May 2000 Bebb dismissed all its stewards and stewardesses. It is not suggested in this case that the dismissal was in any way related to the officer's visits: in fact Bebb had good and proper cause to terminate

d this arrangement and all the workers were properly paid redundancy in accordance with their rights.

[10] The compliance officer visited again in September and having formed the opinion that the workers had not been paid the minimum wage, he issued an enforcement notice under s 19 of the 1998 Act on 6 October 2000. That enforcement notice related to 25 of the former stewards and stewardesses. All

e had long since ceased to work for Bebb, some for a very long time, for example one lady ended her employment with the company in April 1999. The enforcement notice required Bebb to pay each of the workers sums due to them under s 17 of the 1998 Act (the difference between the wages received and the minimum wage). The sums due ranged from £26·52 to £4,892·45, the total

f shortfall being £37,649·43. Bebb was required to pay that sum by 13 October 2000. The company was informed of its right to appeal but was also informed that failure to comply with the notice might result in the company becoming liable to pay the financial penalty under s 21 of the 1998 Act. That penalty accrued at the rate of £7·40 [sic] in respect of each worker to whom the failure to comply related for each day that Bebb failed to comply with the whole or part of

g the notice. The penalties due to date would therefore be in the region of £160,000.

THE APPEAL TO THE EMPLOYMENT TRIBUNAL

[11] Bebb exercised the right of appeal given under the 1998 Act and sought

h an order that the enforcement notice be rescinded. Bebb contended that the enforcement notice was invalid as it did not relate to any pay reference period for present workers ending on or after the date of service of the notice but only to past pay periods in respect of past workers. The argument depends upon the proper construction of s 19 of the 1998 Act.

j THE SECTIONS OF THE 1998 ACT BEARING UPON THE POINT

[12] Section 19 lies at the heart of the appeal. It provides as follows:

'*Power of officer to issue enforcement notice.*—(1) If an officer acting for the purposes of this Act is of the opinion that a worker who qualifies for the national minimum wage has not been remunerated for any pay reference period by his employer at a rate at least equal to the national minimum wage,

the officer may serve a notice (an "enforcement notice") on the employer
requiring the employer to remunerate the worker for pay reference periods
ending on or after the date of the notice at a rate equal to the national
minimum wage.

(2) An enforcement notice may also require the employer to pay to the
worker within such time as may be specified in the notice the sum due to the
worker under section 17 above in respect of the employer's previous failure
to remunerate the worker at a rate at least equal to the national minimum
wage.

(3) The same enforcement notice may relate to more than one worker
(and, where it does so, may be so framed as to relate to workers specified in
the notice or to workers of a description so specified).

(4) A person on whom an enforcement notice is served may appeal
against the notice before the end of the period of four weeks following the
date of service of the notice.

(5) An appeal under subsection (4) above lies to an employment tribunal.

(6) On an appeal under subsection (4) above, the employment tribunal
shall dismiss the appeal unless it is established—(a) that, in the case of the
worker or workers to whom the enforcement notice relates, the facts are
such that an officer who was aware of them would have had no reason to
serve any enforcement notice on the appellant; or (b) where the enforcement
notice relates to two or more workers, that the facts are such that an officer
who was aware of them would have had no reason to include some of the
workers in any enforcement notice served on the appellant; or (c) where the
enforcement notice imposes a requirement under subsection (2) in relation
to a worker,—(i) that no sum was due to the worker under section 17 above;
or (ii) that the amount specified in the notice as the sum due to the worker
under that section is incorrect; and in this subsection any reference to a
worker includes a reference to a person whom the enforcement notice
purports to treat as a worker.

(7) Where an appeal is allowed by virtue of paragraph (a) of subsection (6)
above, the employment tribunal shall rescind the enforcement notice.

(8) If, in a case where subsection (7) above does not apply, an appeal is
allowed by virtue of paragraph (b) or (c) of subsection (6) above—(a) the
employment tribunal shall rectify the enforcement notice; and (b) the
enforcement notice shall have effect as if it had originally been served as so
rectified.

(9) The powers of an employment tribunal in allowing an appeal in a case
where subsection (8) above applies shall include power to rectify, as the
tribunal may consider appropriate in consequence of its decision on the
appeal, any penalty notice which has been served under section 21 below in
respect of the enforcement notice.

(10) Where a penalty notice is rectified under subsection (9) above, it shall
have effect as if it had originally been served as so rectified.'

[13] Section 19(2) refers to s 17. Section 17 provides:

'(1) If a worker who qualifies for the national minimum wage is
remunerated for any pay reference period by his employer at a rate which is
less than the national minimum wage, the worker shall be taken to be
entitled under his contract to be paid, as additional remuneration in respect
of that period, the amount described in subsection (2) below.

a
(2) That amount is the difference between—(a) the relevant remuneration received by the worker for the pay reference period; and (b) the relevant remuneration which the worker would have received for that period had he been remunerated by the employer at a rate equal to the national minimum wage.

(3) In subsection (2) above, "relevant remuneration" means remuneration
b
which falls to be brought into account for the purposes of regulations under section (2) above.'

[14] It is perhaps necessary to refer to other sections in a little detail. Section 20 gives power to the officer to sue on behalf of the worker:

c
'(1) If an enforcement notice is not complied with in whole or in part, an officer acting for the purposes of this Act may, on behalf of any worker to whom the notice relates,—(a) present a complaint under section 23(1)(a) of the Employment Rights Act 1996 (deductions from worker's wages in contravention of section 13 of that Act) to an employment tribunal in respect of any sums due to the worker by virtue of section 17 above; or ...

d
(c) commence other civil proceedings for the recovery, on a claim in contract, of any sums due to the worker by virtue of section 17 above.

(2) The powers conferred by subsection (1) above for the recovery of sums due from an employer to a worker shall not be in derogation of any right which the worker may have to recover such sums by civil proceedings.'

e
[15] Section 21 provides for a financial penalty for non-compliance. By sub-s (1) it gives the officer satisfied that there has been a failure to comply with the enforcement notice power to serve a penalty notice requiring the employer to pay a financial penalty to the Secretary of State. Subsection (3) provides:

'The amount of the financial penalty shall be calculated at a rate equal to
f
twice the hourly amount of the national minimum wage (as in force at the date of the penalty notice) in respect of each worker to whom the failure to comply relates for each day during which the failure to comply has continued in respect of the worker.'

There was some confusion about the application of these penalty provisions.
g
Mr John Cavanagh QC, who appeared for the Inland Revenue, was minded at first to contend that the penalty related only to the period between the time of failure to pay under the enforcement notice and the time of the penalty notice but he later received instructions from the Inland Revenue confirming that the Inland Revenue were of the view that the penalties would continue to be payable day after day until payment was actually made. It is a view with which I agree.
h
Subsection (8) provides that any sums received by the Secretary of State by virtue of this section shall be paid into the consolidated fund. Mr Cavanagh therefore accepts that this is a penal provision with the consequence that if there are two reasonable constructions to be given to the 1998 Act, the court should adopt the more lenient construction. But this applies only where the court is left in real
j
doubt about the true meaning.

[16] Mr Daniel Oudkerk, for Bebb, draws our attention to s 28(1) which provides:

'Where in any civil proceedings any question arises as to whether an individual qualifies *or qualified* at any time for the national minimum wage, it shall be presumed that the individual qualifies or, as the case may be,

qualified at that time for the national minimum wage unless the contrary is
established.' (My emphasis.)   *a*

[17] In my judgment it is also necessary to refer closely to some of the
definitions. I have already given the definition of 'worker'. Section 55(1)
provides:

'In this Act, unless the context otherwise requires—"enforcement notice" *b*
shall be construed in accordance with section 19 above ... "person who
qualifies for the national minimum wage" shall be construed in accordance
with section 1(2) above; and related expressions shall be construed
accordingly ...'

Section 1(2) provides: *c*

'A person qualifies for the national minimum wage if he is an individual
who—(a) is a worker; (b) is working, or ordinarily works, in the United
Kingdom under his contract; and (c) has ceased to be of compulsory school age.'

Section 1(1) is also relevant as also providing that whole raison d'etre for the 1998 Act: *d*

'A person who qualifies for the national minimum wage shall be
remunerated by his employer in respect of his work in any pay reference
period at a rate which is not less than the national minimum wage.'

THE DECISION OF THE EMPLOYMENT TRIBUNAL   *e*
[18] The essential findings of the employment tribunal were these:

'7. ... In our view the wording of s 19(1) is clear. We can see no ambiguity.
The subsection empowers the officer to serve a notice where he is of the
opinion that the worker "qualifies" for the national minimum wage. That is
in the present. The situation with which this case is concerned does not
relate to workers who qualified when the enforcement notice was issued. It *f*
relates to past workers who in the past had qualified for the national
minimum wage.
8. Also the wording to remunerate "for pay reference periods ending on
or after the date of the notice" could hardly be clearer. The empowering
subsection is concerned purely with pay reference periods subsisting in the *g*
month leading up to the notice or after the notice. In the present case there
was no pay reference period subsisting in the month leading up to the date
when the notice was served. There had not been one for four-and-a-half
months ...
10. ... Subsection (2) does not empower an officer to serve notice. It *h*
merely empowers him to include previous failures in a validly served notice.
There is nothing in sub-s (2) capable of altering the clear meaning of
sub-s (1). It merely adds to it as is clearly indicated by use of "also", and by
reference not to *a* worker and *an* employer but '*the*' worker and '*the*'
employer, who can only be the worker and employer referred to in sub-s (1)
where the worker "qualifies" in the present.'   *j*

[19] The employment tribunal concluded that Bebb had established that an
officer aware of the fact that there had been no pay reference periods for
four-and-a-half months prior to the date of the issue of the notice would have had
no reason to serve a notice on that date. Accordingly the tribunal allowed Bebb's
appeal and rescinded the notice.

THE DECISION OF THE APPEAL TRIBUNAL

a   [20] The appeal tribunal ([2002] 4 All ER 534) dismissed the Inland Revenue's appeal. Theirs was a carefully reasoned judgment delivered by Judge JR Reid QC. He carefully analysed the language and concluded that, although there were oddities in the 1998 Act, these did not persuade the appeal tribunal that the employment tribunal were wrong. One of the oddities of the 1998 Act they noted

b   was that an officer bringing civil proceedings could be met by a Limitation Act defence, but the daily penalty under s 21 for failing to pay the statute-barred amount would continue to run until payment. Another oddity was that if there were two workers who were underpaid and one left just before the pay period to which the enforcement notice related, then the notice can require back payments to the one who has stayed on but not to the one who has left. Their conclusion

c   (at [20]) was:

'Subsection (2) provides a summary way of obtaining underpayments for existing workers. It was not intended to enable or require enforcement officers to investigate and initiate recovery proceedings for workers who had long since moved on.'

d

THE INLAND REVENUE'S SUBMISSIONS

    [21] I hope I do justice to Mr Cavanagh's sustained submissions by summarising them as follows. (i) Section 19(1) is in two parts. The first describes the threshold for its operation, viz the officer being of the opinion that a worker who qualifies has not received the national minimum wage. If the threshold is met then the

e   second part describes the power the officer may exercise, viz to serve an enforcement notice requiring the employer to remunerate the worker. (ii) He accepts that if s 19(2) gives a separate power not parasitic upon s 19(1), then s 19(2) must be read as if the first part of s 19(1) is imported into it. (iii) He has to accept that, because s 19(1) is concerned with the requirement that the

f   employer remunerate the worker for a pay reference period which ends on or after the date of the notice, it must necessarily therefore contemplate payment to a worker who is in employment at the time of that pay reference period, ie a present worker. Nevertheless he submits it can (not necessarily must) also be construed to refer to workers who have ceased to be employed. Section 19(1) does look back because it contemplates the power to issue enforcement notices

g   being given in respect of past failures to pay the minimum wage in that: (a) 'has not been remunerated' contemplates a past event; (b) 'for *any* pay reference period' (my emphasis) makes it plain that the operation of the subsection is not confined to present and/or future pay reference periods, and must be capable of referring to past periods; (c) in any event it may not be possible to determine that

h   there has been a failure to pay the minimum wage in respect of a current period if, as is possible, part of the remuneration is to be made in the future, for example, by way of a bonus. The officer would in those circumstances have to be looking back at past performance. (iv) 'Worker' as defined in s 54(3) includes a worker whose employment has ceased and so the worker who qualifies must include the

j   past worker. (v) 'Qualifies' has a timeless effect so that it can include: (a) those currently employed where a current failure to pay can be demonstrated; (b) those currently employed where a past failure only can be shown and who were qualified at that time in the past; and also (c) those no longer qualified at present but who were qualified at some time in the past. (vi) Even though his construction strains the natural meaning of the words, it is not an impossible construction: compare the way the House of Lords construed the words 'is

suffering ... significant harm' in s 31(2) of the Children Act 1989 and decided that
in that instance 'is' means 'was': see *Re M (a minor) (care orders: threshold conditions)*
[1994] 3 All ER 298, [1994] 2 AC 424. (vii) Section 19(2) is not dependent upon
the power to issue the enforcement notice provided by s 19(1). If it were, s 19(2)
would read 'the enforcement notice' not 'an enforcement notice'. (viii) If s 19(2)
was intended to be parasitic, the legislature would have said 'an enforcement
notice under s 19(1)' or words to that effect to make the position clear. (ix) 'May
also' are permissive words which do not connote any necessary dependency
upon s 19(1). 'Also' for this purpose means 'further, in addition, besides, too'.
Section 19(2) should be read in the sense that besides the circumstances which
might apply under s 19(1) an enforcement notice may be issued in the
circumstances envisaged by s 19(2). As the skeleton argument puts it: ' "I may run
and I may also jump" does not imply that the two actions must be carried out
simultaneously or that one is necessarily dependent upon the other.' (x) 'The
employer' and 'the worker' in s 19(2) refer not to the employer and the worker
described in s 19(1) but to the employer and worker under s 17. (xi) The
language of s 19(1) and (2) is at least ambiguous. A construction should therefore
be given which best gives effect to the purpose of the 1998 Act. (xii) Even if, as
he concedes, the enforcement provisions of ss 19 and 21 are penal in their effect,
the court must still adopt a purposive approach notwithstanding a strained
meaning to the language results. See the approach adopted in *A-G's Ref (No 1 of
1988)* [1989] 2 All ER 1, [1989] AC 971. (xiii) The purpose is to protect a
vulnerable body of workers especially those in the 'fringe economy'. These
workers being vulnerable through lack of knowledge of their rights,
impecuniosity, or the sheer disadvantage of the misfortune of being menial, the
reservation to them of a right to issue proceedings themselves is an insufficient
protection. That is the mischief which is cured by providing an independent
enforcement procedure taken by a third party. That protects the underpaid
workers from being victimised in one way or another, for example, by dismissal
or refusal to re-engage or from the reluctance of a new employer to engage a
known 'troublemaker'. Past workers are just as entitled to protection as present
workers. (xiv) The appeal tribunal's construction produced the recognised
'oddity' that an unscrupulous employer—and there is no suggestion whatever in
this case that Bebb is an unscrupulous employer—can evade the consequences of
an enforcement notice by sacking their workers as soon as inquiries by an
enforcement officer create the obvious risk that notice will follow in due course.

BEBB'S SUBMISSIONS

[22] Mr Oudkerk submits: (i) Section 19(1) clearly contemplates operation in
respect of current workers and s 19(1) cannot apply to former workers.
(ii) 'Qualifies' in the clause 'a worker who qualifies' is expressed in the present
tense. The present tense is appropriate for s 19(1). The words mean what they
say. Where the legislature wished to refer to a worker who was qualified, the
1998 Act says so (see s 28). (iii) Since s 19(1) defines an 'enforcement notice', the
words 'an enforcement notice' in s 19(2) must refer to the same enforcement
notice contemplated by s 19(1). The exercise of the power must be as prescribed
by s 19(1) which is confined to current workers. (iv) 'The employer' and 'the
worker' in s 19(2) also refer back to s 19(1). (v) In the phrase 'may also require',
'also' means in addition to the requirements capable of being imposed under
s 19(1). (vi) Since the obligation under the enforcement notice is to pay remuneration
to the worker, the Inland Revenue's construction would place a potentially

a impossible burden on the employer where the workers have disappeared, especially if, as is the case, there is no time limit for the issue of the enforcement notice and so steps can, at least in theory, be taken years after the cessation of employment and even years after the obligation to keep records has expired. (vii) No statutory purpose can be divined for s 19(1) and (2). (viii) The former employee is not without his remedy: he or she can sue in the county court.

b (ix) Workers who suffer 'detriment' are given rights under ss 23–25.

MY ANALYSIS OF THE POSITION

[23] I start with s 19(1). I agree that the first part sets out what conditions must exist to give the officer the power to serve the enforcement notice. He must be of the opinion that 'a worker who qualifies for the national minimum wage' has

c not been properly remunerated 'for any pay reference period'. Use of the present tense in 'qualifies' was deliberate: where the draughtsman wished to distinguish between the present tense and the past tense, he was capable of making the distinction explicit (see s 28). There is a further indication that the present tense is intended. The clause 'a worker who qualifies for the national minimum wage'

d is defined in s 55 which refers back to s 1(2). That too is couched in the present tense—'a person qualifies … if he *is* an individual who—(a) *is* a worker' (my emphasis). Because the whole clause is defined the defined meaning must prevail and it cannot, in my judgment, be permissible to take the word 'worker' out of the clause and give it the different meaning conferred by s 54(3). Construed in its context—'a worker who qualifies'—it makes no sense to say that an individual is

e a qualifying worker when he is in fact a past worker.

[24] The emphasis on the present is confirmed by the second part of s 19(1) which sets out the terms of the enforcement notice the officer is empowered to serve. That enforcement notice may require the employer to remunerate the worker 'for pay reference periods ending on or after the date of the notice', ie to

f require payment of the minimum wage for the current and future period. Current and future pay periods can only relate to present workers. They cannot be made to apply to past workers. The view of the employment tribunal was correct.

[25] As for s 19(2), I accept Mr Cavanagh's point that any dependence upon s 19(1) would have been clear if s 19(2) had referred to '*the* enforcement notice', as opposed to '*an* enforcement notice'. 'An enforcement notice' by itself more

g naturally suggests some notice other than the notice referred to in sub-s (1). Mr Cavanagh accepts, however, and he is right to accept, that this is but one straw in the wind. Other straws are blown more strongly in the opposite direction. The employment notice under s 19(2) may also require '*the* employer

h to pay to *the* worker' the sums due (my emphasis). If s 19(2) was free-standing, it is impossible to know who that employer and that worker is. The more natural meaning is then they are the employer and worker referred to in sub-s (1), leading to the conclusion that the enforcement notice referred to in sub-s (2) is the same enforcement notice referred to in sub-s (1).

j [26] Then there is the reference to 'the sum due to the worker under section 17 above'. Section 17 applies to 'a worker who qualifies for the national minimum wage', which brings in ss 55 and 1(2), and, for the reasons already given, this is a reference to a present worker, not a past worker.

[27] The dependency of sub-s (2) on sub-s (1) is to my mind conclusively demonstrated by permitting the enforcement notice 'also' to require the employer to pay up for his past failures to remunerate properly. The ordinary

natural meaning of 'also' is 'in addition'. Under sub-s (1) present and future
payments of the national minimum wage can be required in respect of a present
worker and under sub-s (2) past payments can also be required to be paid, ie past
in addition to present and future.

[28] In my judgment there is a problem with the Inland Revenue's contention
that 'also' means 'besides' in the sense that if 'besides' the enforcement notice
issued under s 19(1), a 'further'—and necessarily different—enforcement notice can
be issued under s 19(2). The problem, as it seems to me, is that if s 19(2) is
independent of s 19(1) then there is no indication in the language of s 19(2), read
in isolation, of the threshold that has to be crossed before the notice can be issued.
'Enforcement notice' is a defined phrase and s 55 requires it to be construed in
accordance with s 19. Section 19(1) contains the real clue because in s 19(1) the
notice which the officer is empowered to serve is given a special meaning—'the
officer may serve a notice (an "enforcement notice")'. Consequently 'an
enforcement notice', whether for the purpose of sub-ss (1) or (2) is the notice the
officer may serve if he is of the opinion that the worker is a worker who qualifies.
We are back to the present tense and to the restriction explicit in sub-s (1) that 'an
enforcement notice' can only relate to a present worker not a past worker.

[29] Subsection (4) gives a person on whom an enforcement notice is
served—which must include an enforcement notice served under sub-s (2)—the
right to appeal against 'the notice'. On an appeal the employment tribunal shall
dismiss the appeal unless it is established under sub-s (6)(a) that in the case of the
worker to whom the enforcement notice relates, the facts are such that an officer
who was aware of them would have no reason to serve any enforcement notice
on the appellant. So the enforcement notice served under s 19(2) is to be judged
against the facts of which the officer should have been aware. This must be a
reference to the threshold requirement in s 19(1) that he be of the opinion that
there is a worker who qualifies for the national minimum wage and that that
worker is not being properly remunerated. Everything points to the precondition
for the service of the notice set by sub-s (1) being carried into sub-s (2). It is all
one of a piece.

[30] Mr Cavanagh has to accept that some preconditions have to be implied
into sub-s (2) and he concedes that the first part of sub-s (1) must be implied into
sub-s (2). As soon as he does that, his case is dead. If, for reasons I have set out,
the worker who qualifies for sub-s (1) purposes is and can only be a present
worker, then it seems to me impossible when construing the word 'qualifies' if
imported into sub-s (2), to mean 'qualified'. The same word cannot mean
different things in one section of the Act.

[31] In the result I am in no doubt about the meaning to be given to s 19. A
valid enforcement notice can only relate to present workers in respect of present
and future wages (see sub-s (1)) and also, if appropriate, their past wages (see
sub-s (2)). There is no power to issue an enforcement notice in respect of past
workers for past pay.

[32] Because I am not in doubt as to the meaning, I do not need to gauge in
the tortuous attempt to find a *particular* purpose for s 19(1) and (2). This is an Act
'to make provision for and in connection with a national minimum wage'. Its
purpose is obvious in the sense that the 1998 Act is there to boost the wages of a
menial group who are inevitably disadvantaged and vulnerable to exploitation.
They are likely to be unable easily to assert their rights and a proper purpose of
the 1998 Act is undoubtedly to enable enforcement to be taken by an independent
officer on their behalf. I find it impossible, however, to identify any particular

a mischief which so afflicts past workers that any ambiguity in s 19 would have to be construed to include them. Mr Oudkerk convinces me that an employer could be placed at such severe disadvantage if years after the event he is required to pay past workers, often itinerant workers, when he would have no idea where they are nor the means ever to find them. Yet if he does not pay he is subject to penalties. That would be an odd state of affairs. A scheme to assist the current

b workforce works no injustice. These are, however, idle musings on my part. I could not divine a specific purpose if I had to, but fortunately I do not have to try.

[33] I do not know if I am entitled to derive wry amusement from the fact, or whether I should simply ignore the fact, that there is already a Bill before Parliament which will introduce an amendment to s 19 by inserting the following:

c

'(2A) If an officer acting for the purposes of this Act is of the opinion that a worker who has at any time qualified for the national minimum wage has not been remunerated for any pay reference period (whether ending before or after the coming into force of this subsection) by his employer at a rate at least equal to the national minimum wage, the officer may serve on the

d employer an enforcement notice which imposes a requirement under subsection (2) above in relation to the worker, whether or not a requirement under subsection (1) above is, or may be, imposed in relation to that worker (or any other worker to whom the notice relates).

(2B) An enforcement notice may not impose a requirement under

e subsection 2 above in respect of any pay reference period ending more than six years before the date on which the notice is served.'

[34] That seems clear enough. It is as if the employment tribunal had marked the Parliamentary draftsman's essay and suggested he should try again. But I should not tease. All I should do is dismiss the appeal.

f

MAY LJ.

[35] I agree that this appeal should be dismissed for the reasons given by Ward LJ, whose account of the facts and circumstances of this appeal I gratefully adopt. I agree that the Employment Appeal Tribunal (the appeal tribunal)

g reached the correct conclusion for the correct reasons. I record briefly in my own words my reasons for rejecting Mr Cavanagh QC's submission that s 19(2) of the National Minimum Wage Act 1998 should be construed as empowering a free-standing enforcement notice.

[36] Section 19 of the 1998 Act provides:

h

'(1) If an officer acting for the purposes of this Act is of the opinion that a worker who qualifies for the national minimum wage has not been remunerated for any pay reference period by his employer at a rate at least equal to the national minimum wage, the officer may serve a notice (an "enforcement notice") on the employer requiring the employer to

j remunerate the worker for pay reference periods ending on or after the date of the notice at a rate equal to the national minimum wage.

(2) An enforcement notice may also require the employer to pay to the worker within such time as may be specified in the notice the sum due to the worker under section 17 above in respect of the employer's previous failure to remunerate the worker at a rate at least equal to the national minimum wage.'

[37] The respondent, Bebb Travel plc (Bebb), contends and the appeal
tribunal held that the requirement in s 19(2) could only be made in an *a*
enforcement notice served under s 19(1). The Inland Revenue contend that
s 19(2) empowers the service of an independent enforcement notice, relating to a
worker no longer employed by an employer, requiring the former employer to
pay to the worker a sum due to the worker for the employer's previous failure to
remunerate the worker at a rate at least equal to the national minimum wage. *b*
Mr Cavanagh accepts that this requires a strained construction of s 19(1) and (2).
But he submits that his strained construction should be adopted so as not to
defeat what he maintains is the purpose of the legislation.

[38] In my judgment, the construction for which Bebb contends is plainly
correct. I do not consider that Mr Cavanagh's construction can be strained even
as a possible construction of the two subsections read in the context of the statute *c*
as a whole. In addition, the purpose for which Mr Cavanagh needs to contend is
not, in my view, apparent from the statute itself and there is no external material
from which that purpose can be gleaned. The general purpose of the statute is
obvious, that is to require employers to pay their workers remuneration at a rate
which is not less than the national minimum wage. Section 19 is however *d*
concerned with enforcement. It is one only of four possible means of
enforcement. Mr Cavanagh's purpose has to be that Parliament intended that
an enforcement officer should be able to serve an enforcement notice in relation
to past failures by an employer in relation to workers who had ceased to be
employed by the employer when the enforcement notice is served.
Mr Cavanagh gave an array of possible reasons why this may have been *e*
Parliament's purpose. But in my view the Parliamentary purpose may equally
have been that enforcement notices should mainly be used to require employers
to comply with the legislation in relation to their existing employees for the
future. There would then be sense in enabling an enforcement notice for that
first purpose also to address past failures. Just as Mr Cavanagh had reasons why *f*
the purpose for which he contended might have been the Parliamentary
intention, so Mr Oudkerk, counsel for Bebb, pointed to the penal nature of these
provisions and employers' difficulties in complying with an enforcement notice
for past failures relating to workers who had long since left and might be difficult
to trace. In my view, Mr Cavanagh's purpose assumes the construction of the
section for which he contends. There is no other material from which that *g*
purpose could be derived.

[39] It is accepted that the enforcement notice in s 19(1) has to relate to an
existing worker, because it has to require the employer to remunerate the worker
at a rate equal to the national minimum wage for pay reference periods ending
on or after the date of the notice. This also, in my view, derives from the *h*
expression 'a worker who qualifies for the national minimum wage'. As Ward LJ
pointed out during the hearing, that expression is defined in s 55 so that it is to be
construed in accordance with s 1(2). Section 1(2) defines a person who qualifies
for the national minimum wage as an individual who *is* a worker. Mr Cavanagh
struggled to extricate himself from the present tense use of 'qualifies' in s 19(1). *j*
He did not in my view succeed. Section 28(1), in using the expression 'whether
an individual qualifies or qualified', shows that this statute refers to past
qualification when it intends to do so. I accept Mr Cavanagh's submission that
the trigger for service of an enforcement notice under s 19(1) has to be a past
failure to remunerate the worker at a rate at least equal to the national minimum
wage. But that derives, not from a strained meaning of the word 'qualifies', but

a from the natural meaning of the succeeding words 'has not been remunerated for any pay reference period by his employer at a rate at least equal to the national minimum wage'.

[40] There are the following additional clear indications in favour of Bebb's construction. Section 19(1) defines 'enforcement notice' as a notice requiring the employer to remunerate the worker for pay reference periods ending on or after

b the date of the notice at a rate equal to the national minimum wage. The expression thus defined has to have the defined meaning when it appears in s 19(2). The use of the definite article for 'the employer' and 'the worker' in s 19(2) plainly refer back to 'a worker' and 'his employer' in s 19(1). Mr Cavanagh's attempt to take these definite articles back to s 17 was not remotely persuasive. The expression 'may also' connotes that a s 19(1) enforcement notice may also

c deal with previous failures to remunerate the worker at a rate at least equal to the national minimum wage. These words in their context do not relate to a free-standing enforcement notice independent of a notice under s 19(1). If that had been the intention, the structure of the material now in two subsections would naturally have been different. The two different kinds of enforcement

d notice would naturally have been subordinated grammatically to a single introductory expression.

[41] For these reasons, in my judgment Bebb's construction of these subsections is plainly correct.

ARDEN LJ.

e [42] For the reasons given below, I agree that s 19(2) of the National Minimum Wage Act 1998 is supplemental to s 19(1) and that accordingly the powers conferred by the former subsection can only be used where the enforcement notice also satisfies s 19(1).

[43] In my judgment, an enforcement notice can be served under s 19(1) only

f if the officer forms the requisite opinion about a person who is then a worker in relation to the employer on whom it is proposed to serve the enforcement notice. This follows from the fact that under s 19(1) the worker must be a person 'who qualifies for the national minimum wage'. The use of the present tense is clear and can be contrasted with the use of the words 'qualifies or qualified at any time for the national minimum wage' in s 28(1). Under s 19(1) the question whether

g the worker also had to be qualified at the date he was remunerated below the required rate is left silent. If he is required also to be qualified at that date, the requirement is implicit and is not to be found in the word 'qualifies', which is plainly in the present tense.

[44] Furthermore, an enforcement notice for the purpose of the opening

h clause of s 19(2) is defined by s 19(1). It is—

> 'a notice … on the employer requiring the employer to remunerate the worker for pay reference periods ending on or after the date of the notice at a rate equal to the national minimum wage.'

j This demonstrates that s 19(2) cannot confer a free-standing power to serve an enforcement notice. The use of the definite article 'the' with the words 'employer' and 'worker' support the conclusion that the employer and worker have just been identified, that is in s 19(1) and not (as submitted) in s 17. In addition, my preferred construction gives the word 'also' in s 19(2) its normal meaning. It confers one option and one option only: that of *adding* a stipulation about past defaults to the enforcement notice dealing with the future. It does not

provide an alternative approach. On the Inland Revenue's construction, the
word 'also' has to mean 'further or alternatively'. *a*

[45] Moreover, Mr Cavanagh QC, for the Inland Revenue, accepts that even
if s 19(2) is a free-standing power the officer must still be of the opinion described
in the opening words of s 19(1). However, he goes on to submit that, under that
requirement as it applies to s 19(1), it must be the officer's opinion that 'a worker
who *qualified* for the national minimum wage has not been remunerated' for the *b*
relevant period at the appropriate rate. It need hardly be observed that it would
be odd, if s 19(2) is a free-standing provision, for it to be silent about the essential
precondition of its operation, especially if that precondition has not only to be
imported from s 19(1) but modified. I am not disposed to accept the submission
which confers on the word 'qualifies' such chameleon-like character. In particular,
I do not accept Mr Cavanagh's submission that it is a word of 'universal tense' *c*
(whatever that may mean) or that (in the alternative) the true construction of
'qualifies' in s 19(1) is 'qualified'.

[46] I do not consider the conclusion that s 19(2) is not free-standing to be
absurd as the Inland Revenue submits. It was open to Parliament to determine
that the class of low paid workers who would benefit from s 19 should not be the *d*
whole class of such persons, but only a limited part of such class, principally
current employees. Such an approach could not be said to be irrational: on the
contrary it would be consistent with a policy of placing a limit on the need for the
public resources to be devoted to the service of enforcement notices and the
taking of steps under s 20. Such a policy is also supported by the absence of time
limits in ss 19 and 21. It would also afford some practical recognition of the *e*
difficulties for an employer in maintaining records and tracing past employees in
order to make shortfall payments to them. There is certainly nothing in the 1998
Act to compel the conclusion that Parliament must have intended that the whole
class should benefit, and in my judgment the Inland Revenue would need to
show that to establish that it was right to depart from the plain meaning of s 19 *f*
so as to make s 19(2) a free-standing power.

[47] I have reached the above conclusion simply by interpreting s 19 in the
context of the 1998 Act. For my part, I do not find it necessary to apply any
presumption against the Inland Revenue's construction. It is enough, in my
view, to give s 19 its fair interpretation.

g

Appeal dismissed.

Melanie Martyn   Barrister.

a
Marcq v Christie Manson & Woods Ltd (trading as Christie's)
[2003] EWCA Civ 731

b
COURT OF APPEAL, CIVIL DIVISION
PETER GIBSON, TUCKEY AND KEENE LJJ
12, 13, 23 MAY 2003

Conversion – Auctioneer's liability – Return of goods to consignor – Whether auctioneer, acting in good faith and without notice, liable in conversion if not selling
c *true owner's goods but merely returning them to consignor.*

The claimant had at all material times been the owner of a painting painted by a Dutch master in about 1667. The painting was stolen in 1979. Its theft was reported to the police and it was registered as stolen on the Art Loss Register. In
d or about 1997, the defendant auctioneers obtained possession of the painting from S for the purposes of selling it at auction. They catalogued and advertised the painting and offered it for sale at a public auction in July 1997. The painting was unsold, and the defendants returned it to S. The claimant commenced proceedings against the defendants, claiming that they were liable to him in conversion or bailment. The defendant's application in the county court to strike
e out the statement of case was granted, on the ground that it disclosed no reasonable grounds for bringing the claim. The claimant's appeal to the High Court was dismissed. He appealed, contending that the defendants were strictly liable in conversion having regard to the extent of their encroachment on the claimant's rights as owner of the picture; and that they had breached their
f obligation as bailees to take such care as was reasonable in all the circumstances to ensure that the person who had delivered the goods had the right to do so, and that the person to whom they redelivered the goods had a right to receive them.

Held – (1) An auctioneer who received goods from their apparent owner, and merely redelivered them to him when they were unsold, was not liable in
g conversion, provided that he had acted in good faith and without knowledge of any adverse claim to the goods. If the auctioneer sold the goods, he would incur liability if he delivered them to the buyer. His intention to sell the goods did not, however, make him liable: it was what he did in relation to the goods which determined liability (see [24], [43], below).
h   (2) An agent who received goods from someone who was their apparent owner and later returned them to him did not owe a duty to their true owner to investigate title, in the absence of anything to put him on inquiry. The claim in bailment failed and the appeal would, accordingly, be dismissed (see [54]–[59], below).
    Decision of Jack J [2002] 4 All ER 1005 affirmed.

j **Notes**
For liability of auctioneers for conversion, see 2 *Halsbury's Laws* (4th edn reissue) para 926.

Cases referred to in judgments
Australian and New Zealand Banking Group Ltd v Curlett, Cannon and Galbell Pty Ltd
    [1992] 2 VR 647, Vic SC.

AVX Ltd v EGM Solders Ltd (1982) Times, 7 July.

Barclays Mercantile Business Finance Ltd v Sibec Developments Ltd [1993] 2 All ER 195,
    [1992] 1 WLR 1253.   *a*

Barker v Furlong [1891] 2 Ch 172, [1891–4] All ER Rep Ext 2030.

City Television v Conference and Training Office Ltd [2001] EWCA Civ 1770.

Cochrane v Rymill (1879) 40 LT 744, CA.

Consolidated Co v Curtis & Son [1892] 1 QB 495.   *b*

Fowler v Hollins (1872) LR 7 QB 616, Ex Ch; *affd sub nom Hollins v Fowler* (1875)
    LR 7 HL 757, [1874–80] All ER Rep 118, HL.

Heffron v Imperial Parking Co (1974) 46 DLR (3d) 642, Ont CA.

Jackson v Cochrane [1989] 2 Qd R 23, Qld Full Ct.

Kuwait Airways Corp v Iraqi Airways Co (No 3) [2002] UKHL 19, [2002] 3 All ER 209,   *c*
    [2002] 2 AC 883, [2002] 2 WLR 1353.

Lancashire Waggon Co Ltd v Fitzhugh (1861) 6 H & N 502, 158 ER 206.

Loeschman v Machin (1818) 2 Stark 311.

McCowan v McCullogh [1926] 1 DLR 312, NS SC.

Michael Gerson (Leasing) Ltd v Wilkinson [2001] 1 All ER 148, [2001] QB 514, [2000] *d*
    3 WLR 1645, CA.

Mitchell v Ealing London Borough [1978] 2 All ER 779, [1979] QB 1, [1978] 2 WLR
    999, QBD.

Moorgate Mercantile Co Ltd v Finch [1962] 2 All ER 467, [1962] 1 QB 701, [1962]
    3 WLR 110, CA.
                                                                                        e
National Mercantile Bank Ltd v Rymill (1881) 44 LT 767, CA.

Parker v British Airways Board [1982] 1 All ER 834, [1982] QB 1004, [1982] 2 WLR
    503, CA.

Pioneer Container, The, KH Enterprise (cargo owners) v Pioneer Containers (owners)
    [1994] 2 All ER 250, [1994] 2 AC 324, [1994] 3 WLR 1, PC.
                                                                                        f
Saleh Farid v Theodorou and Blacklake Securities [1992] CA Transcript 51.

Smith (Administrator of Cosslett (Contractors) Ltd) v Bridgend County BC [2001]
    UKHL 58, [2002] 1 All ER 292, [2002] 1 AC 336, [2001] 3 WLR 1347.

Southland Hospital Board v Perkins Estates [1986] 1 NZLR 373, NZ HC.

Tear v Freebody (1858) 4 CBNS 228, 140 ER 1071, CP.

Williams v Millington (1788) 1 Hy Bl 81, 126 ER 49, [1775–1802] All ER Rep 124.   *g*

Willis (RH) and Son (a firm) v British Car Auctions Ltd [1978] 2 All ER 392, [1978]
    1 WLR 438, CA.

Appeal
                                                                                        h
The claimant, Philippe Marcq, appealed from the decision of Jack J on 29 October
2002 ([2002] EWHC 2148 (QB), [2002] 4 All ER 1005) upholding the decision of
Judge Hallgarten QC at the Central London County Court on 25 January 2002
whereby he held that the defendant, Christie Manson & Woods Ltd (t/a
Christie's) was entitled to succeed on its application to strike out proceedings for
conversion and breach of duty as bailee brought against it by Mr Marcq. The   *j*
facts are set out in the judgment of Tuckey LJ.

Professor Norman Palmer and *Angus Piper* (instructed by *Ralph Davis*) for the claimant.
John McCaughran QC (instructed by *Stephenson Harwood*) for Christie's.

                                                                          Cur adv vult

23 May 2003. The following judgments were delivered.

TUCKEY LJ (delivering the first judgment at the invitation of Peter Gibson LJ).

[1] If a painting is unsold at auction and returned to the prospective seller who is not in fact its true owner, is the auctioneer, who has acted in good faith and without notice, liable in conversion or bailment to its owner? This question
b arises on appeal from Jack J who upheld on 29 October 2002 (see [2002] EWHC 2148 (QB), [2002] 4 All ER 1005) a decision by Judge Hallgarten QC made in the Central London County Court that the auctioneer was not liable.

THE FACTS

c [2] Judge Hallgarten's decision was made on an application to strike out the claimant's statement of case because it disclosed no reasonable grounds for bringing the claim. Conventionally such applications are decided on the assumption that the facts alleged by the claimant are true. In his judgment Jack J refers to a few additional facts which were not pleaded by the claimant. We were told that this information was given to Jack J orally at his request without
d objection from the claimant. However Professor Palmer, who appeared for the claimant below, complains that Jack J should not have taken this additional information into account, although this is not one of the grounds of appeal. To avoid further controversy about this, the facts I set out below are only those which appear in the draft amended particulars of claim which were before Jack J.

e [3] The claimant is now and has at all material times been the owner of an oil painting known as the Backgammon Players painted by the Dutch master Jan Steen in or about 1667. The painting was stolen from the claimant's London house over Easter 1979. Its theft was reported to the police and it was registered as stolen on the Art Loss Register before 1997. In or about July 1997 the defendants, Christie, Manson & Woods Ltd (Christie's), obtained possession of
f the painting from a Mr Schünemann for the purposes of selling it at auction on the terms of their conditions of business. Under this contract Christie's catalogued and advertised the painting and offered it for sale at a public auction of old masters on 4 July 1997. The painting was unsold and 'thereafter Christie's caused and/or procured and/or permitted' the removal of the painting from their London premises and its return to Mr Schünemann.
g [4] Before Judge Hallgarten and Jack J the claimant was able to keep open the possibility of being able to allege want of good faith and notice against Christie's although no such case had been pleaded. Both judges held that irrespective of where the burden of proof lay, the claimant had to plead any case he had on these issues. He was given a final chance to do this by Jack J's order which said:
h

'The claimant shall by 19 November 2002 make an application to the Central London County Court business list for permission to serve a reply out of time for the purpose of pleading want of good faith and notice annexing a draft reply to that application, failing which this action shall stand
j dismissed.'

No such application was made and on 28 November 2002 the claim was dismissed. Professor Palmer maintains that it is still open to the claimant to contend that Christie's had notice of the theft of the picture in answer to Christie's assertion that they did not. I do not agree. The claimant has had disclosure of all Christie's documents and more than ample opportunity to state

his case about notice and has not done so. We must proceed therefore on the
basis that Christie's acted in good faith and without notice.
　[5] Christie's terms of business cover their contractual relationship with
prospective sellers and buyers. Those relating to sellers include:

'2. **Christie's role as agent**
　Our sales at public auction are undertaken as agent, on behalf of the Seller …
4. **Expenses**
　The Seller will bear all costs relating to: (a) packing and shipping the Lot to
us for sale … (c) packing and shipping the Lot if it is returned to the Seller …
(d) insurance under Christie's Fine Arts Policy (explained below) …
(f) catalogue illustration … (k) a contribution to our general expenses if the
Lot is not sold equal to 5% of the Insured Value
5A. **Where Insurance is arranged by us**
　(a) Unless we agree otherwise, the Lot will be automatically insured under
Christie's Fine Arts Policy for the amount that we from time to time consider
to be its appropriate value. (b) We shall charge the Seller a sum to cover
insurance, at the rate of 1% of … if the Lot is unsold, its insured value …
6. **The Seller's undertakings regarding the Lot**
　We shall handle the Lot, and the Buyer will purchase, on the basis of the
Seller's undertakings that; (a) the Seller is the sole owner of the Lot with an
unrestricted right to transfer title to the buyer free from all third party rights
or claims … (c) the Seller has notified us in writing … of any concerns
expressed by third parties in relation to the ownership …. of the Lot.
7. **Sale Arrangements**
　… (c) The Seller may not withdraw the Lot from sale without our consent …
(d) If either we or the Seller withdraw the Lot, we shall charge the Seller a
fee equal to 10% of the Insured Value, plus an amount equal to our
commission if the Lot had been sold at the Insured Value, together with any
applicable VAT and insurance and other expenses …
9. **After the Sale**
　(a) Accounting … If for any reason we make payment to the Seller of the
amount due before payment by the Buyer, we shall acquire complete
ownership of and title in the Lot … (d) Unsold Lot If any Lot is unsold, or
is not included in a sale, or is withdrawn from sale for any reason, it must be
collected from us within 35 days after we send the Seller a notice requiring
the Seller to collect it. If any such Lot remains uncollected for a period
exceeding 35 days, a storage charge of £1 per item per day will apply and an
additional charge will be made for insurance. The Seller will not be entitled
to collect the Lot until all outstanding charges are met. If any such Lot is not
collected within 90 days after the date of the sale or the date of the notice
referred to above (whichever occurs first) it may be disposed of by us as we
see fit, which may involve its removal to a third party warehouse at the
Seller's expense and its sale by public auction on such terms as we consider
appropriate, including those relating to estimates and reserves. We shall
then account to the Seller for the proceeds of sale, having deducted all
amounts due. If any Lot is bought in or otherwise unsold by auction, we are
authorised as the exclusive agent for the Seller for a period of two months
following the auction to sell such Lot privately for a price that will result in
a payment to the Seller of not less than the net amount—i.e. after deduction
of all charges due from the Seller—to which the Seller would have been

entitled had the Lot been sold at a price equal to the Reserve, or for such
lesser amount as we and the Seller shall agree.   In such event the Seller's
obligations to us with respect to such a Lot are the same as if it had been sold
at auction ...'

THE JUDGMENTS BELOW

[6] I should start by paying tribute to both judges' judgments.   They are
models of industry and clarity.

[7] Professor Palmer argued that Christie's were strictly liable in conversion
having regard to the extent of their encroachment on the claimant's rights as
owner of the picture.   Jack J correctly noted that there was no reported case in
which a court has had to consider the liability of an auctioneer who had simply
put goods up for auction and then returned them unsold to the would-be seller.
After an extensive review of the authorities he concluded ([2002] 4 All ER 1005 at [41]):

'I deduce that there is a strong line of authority in the Court of Appeal that,
for an auctioneer to be liable where he receives in good faith and without
notice goods for auction from a non-owner, there must be a sale in which he
is sufficiently involved followed by delivery to the purchaser. I am therefore
so far against Professor Palmer's submission. So I would uphold the similar
conclusion of Judge Hallgarten ...'

[8] He then went on to consider whether Christie's terms of business,
particularly cl 7(c), which prevents the seller from withdrawing the lot, and cl 9(d),
which gives Christie's a lien, made any difference.   Firstly he pointed out that
auctioneers had always had a lien at common law and then said:

'[44] Secondly it is clear that the lien here was never exercised against
anyone, let alone against [the claimant]. Nor did a right to exercise the lien
arise. For the right would only arise after a notice had been sent requiring
collection. No such notice was sent by Christie's here. Even if a right of lien
had been exercised by Christie's against Mr Schunemann, I think it doubtful
whether that would amount to a conversion as against [the claimant] ...

[45] I do not consider that the fact that Christie's took a right as against
Mr Schunemann to refuse to permit the picture to be withdrawn prior to
auction can by itself, or if added to the other circumstances, convert what
would not otherwise be a conversion, into one.

[46] It was the view of Judge Hallgarten that what matters in conversion
is not the taking of powers by a bailee against his consignor but their exercise.
I agree.'

[9] Professor Palmer had also submitted that by taking a lien coupled with a
right of sale in cl 9(d) Christie's received the picture as a pledge.   This was
conversion because s 11(2) of the Torts (Interference with Goods) Act 1977
says: 'Receipt of goods by a way of pledge is conversion if delivery of the goods
is conversion.'

[10] Jack J said there was a short answer to this submission. The circumstances
in which Christie's were entitled to a right of sale had never come about.

[11] Jack J dealt with the claim in bailment quite shortly. He records Professor
Palmer's submission as being that Christie's were to be treated as the bailees of
the claimant. They were in the position of a finder or an unconscious bailee and
as such owed duties to the claimant.

[12] Jack J rejected these submissions because, like Judge Hallgarten, he could not accept that the law of bailment and conversion were quite different. He derived support for this view from a passage from Lord Goff of Chieveley's judgment in *The Pioneer Container, KH Enterprise (cargo owners) v Pioneer Containers (owners)* [1994] 2 All ER 250 at 262, [1994] 2 AC 324 at 342, to which I will refer later.

CONVERSION

[13] Professor Palmer started his submissions by reminding us of the ways in which conversion has been defined in a number of cases over the years. In those cases however there is a recognition that definition is difficult and none is exhaustive. Thus in the latest case, *Kuwait Airways Corp v Iraqi Airways Co (No 3)* [2002] UKHL 9 at [39], [2002] 3 All ER 209 at [39], [2002] 2 AC 883 Lord Nicholls of Birkenhead said: 'Conversion of goods can occur in so many different circumstances that framing a precise definition of universal application is well nigh impossible.' He went on to add however:

> 'In general, the basic features of the tort are threefold. First the defendant's conduct was inconsistent with the rights of the owner (or other person entitled to possession). Second, the conduct was deliberate, not accidental. Third, the conduct was so extensive an encroachment on the rights of the owner as to exclude him from use and possession of the goods. The contrast is with lesser acts of interference.'

In the instant case the first and second of these features are present. It is the third which gives rise to the argument. Was there a sufficient encroachment on the claimant's rights as owner to amount to conversion?

[14] Professor Palmer first submitted that any unauthorised possession of goods amounted to conversion with the possible exception of passive or minimal possession. But this submission flies in the face of a long line of authority which shows that possession of goods by an agent on the instructions of their apparent owner for the purpose of carrying out what have been described as ministerial acts such as storage or carriage does not amount to conversion. The possession in such cases is inconsistent with the rights of the true owner and is deliberate but does not encroach sufficiently on the owner's title to the goods. This principle was stated by Blackburn J in *Hollins v Fowler* (1875) LR 7 HL 757 at 766–767:

> 'I cannot find it anywhere distinctly laid down, but I submit to your Lordships that on principle, one who deals with goods at the request of the person who has the actual custody of them, in the *bonâ fide* belief that the custodier is the true owner, or has the authority of the true owner, should be excused for what he does if the act is of such a nature as would be excused if done by the authority of the person in possession, if he was a finder of the goods, or intrusted with their custody. I do not mean to say that this is the extreme limit of the excuse, but it is a principle that will embrace most of the cases which have been suggested as difficulties. Thus a warehouseman with whom goods had been deposited is guilty of no conversion by keeping them, or restoring them to the person who deposited them with him, though that person turns out to have had no authority from the true owner ... And the same principle would apply to ... persons "acting in a subsidiary character, like that of a person who has the goods of a person employing him to carry them, or a caretaker, such as a wharfinger."'

a [15] Auctioneers do not fall within this statement of principle since they are not simply entrusted with the custody of goods but also asked to sell them. Professor Palmer submits that this makes all the difference since a sale necessarily encroaches on the true owner's title. There is, he submits, no authority which compels this court to decide in favour of Christie's in this case and other authority which supports his main argument which is that if one looks at all the circumstances of this case and in particular what he described as the penetrative,
b invasive and retentive rights which Christie's assumed over the picture under their contract terms their conduct amounted to conversion.

[16] It is convenient to start by referring to the auctioneer cases which Professor Palmer submitted we should put on one side as being decisions on their own facts.

c [17] In *National Mercantile Bank Ltd v Rymill* (1881) 44 LT 767 the plaintiff was the owner of horses the subject of a bill of sale. The grantor of the bill sold the horses privately in the defendant's auction yard and following the sale, on the grantor's instructions, the auctioneer delivered the horses to the buyer. It was held that there had been no conversion. Bramwell LJ said that the auctioneer—

d
'has not claimed to transfer the title, and he has not purported to sell; all the dominion he exercised over the chattels was to re-deliver them to the person to whom the man from whom he had received them had told him to redeliver them.'

e Brett and Cotton LJJ agreed that on the evidence there had been no sale by the auctioneer. This case has been criticised, mainly for the conclusion that there had been no sale by the auctioneer.

[18] In *Barker v Furlong* [1891] 2 Ch 172 Romer J decided that an auctioneer who sold and delivered goods to the buyer at auction was liable. In that case the executor plaintiffs were entitled to furniture which was sent to auction without
f their knowledge or consent. Some of the furniture was returned unsold to the would-be seller and no claim was made against the defendant auctioneer in respect of that furniture. But he was held liable for the furniture he sold. Romer J said (at 181–182):

g
'... where, as here, the auctioneer receives the goods into his custody, and, on selling them, hands over the goods to the purchasers with a view to passing the property in them, then I think the auctioneer has converted the goods and is liable accordingly ... The general rule is that where an agent takes part in transferring the property in a chattel and it turns out that his principal has no title, his ignorance of this fact affords him no protection. I
h was referred to the cases of a carrier and packing agent as supporting the case of the auctioneers. But the carrier and packing agent are generally held not to have converted, because by their acts they merely purport to change the position of the goods, and not the property in them.'

[19] *Consolidated Co v Curtis & Son* [1892] 1 QB 495 was another case of an
j auctioneer who sold and delivered goods the subject of a bill of sale. Collins J held that an auctioneer who sells and delivers is liable because he is acting as more than a mere broker or intermediary. Earlier in his judgment however he said (at 497–498):

'... it is not easy to draw the line at the precise point where a dealing with goods by an intermediary becomes a conversion. The difficulty is

diminished by remembering that in trover the original possession was by a *a*
fiction deemed to be lawful ... and some act had therefore to be shewn
constituting a conversion by the defendant of the chattel *to his own use*, some
act incompatible with a recognition on his part of the continuous right of the
true owner to the dominion over it. All acts, therefore, as suggested by
Blackburn, J., in his opinion ... in *Hollins* v. *Fowler*, which are consistent with
the duty of a mere finder such as the safe guarding by warehousing or *b*
asportation for the like purpose, may well be looked upon as entirely
compatible with the right of the true owner, and, therefore, as not
constituting a conversion by the defendant. It may be, as suggested by
Brett, J., in the same case, that the test is whether there is an intent to
interfere in any manner with the title of or ownership in the chattel, not
merely with the possession. The difficulty is, I think, rather in drawing the *c*
true inference from facts in particular cases than in grasping the principle.
There are, however, happily many cases which fall clearly on one side or
other of the line. It is clear that there can be no conversion by a mere bargain
and sale without a transfer of possession. The act, unless in market overt, is
merely void, and does not change the property or the possession: [*Lancashire* *d*
Waggon Co Ltd v Fitzhugh (1861) 6 H & N 502, 158 ER 206], and per Brett, J.,
in *Fowler* v. *Hollins* ((1872) LR 7 QB 616 at 627). A fortiori, mere intervention
as broker or intermediary in a sale by others is not a conversion.'

This passage emphasises the point that it is interference with the title or
ownership of the chattel which counts for conversion. Thus it is the act of *e*
delivery following sale which makes the auctioneer liable in conversion since that
is what interferes with the title or ownership of the goods. A sale without
delivery does not have this effect and does not therefore amount to conversion.

[20] In *RH Willis and Son (a firm) v British Car Auctions Ltd* [1978] 2 All ER 392,
[1978] 1 WLR 438 a car on hire purchase was sold and delivered by auctioneers
on the instructions of the hirer. The main issue was whether the auctioneers' *f*
liability was affected by the fact that the car had been sold under their provisional
bid procedure. This court held the auctioneers liable. In his judgment Lord
Denning MR said ([1978] 2 All ER 392 at 396, [1978] 1 WLR 438 at 442):

'It is now, I think, well established that if an auctioneer sells goods by
knocking down his hammer at an auction and thereafter delivers them to the *g*
purchaser—then although he is only an agent—then if the vendor has no title
to the goods, both the auctioneer and the purchaser are liable in conversion
to the true owner, no matter how innocent the auctioneer may have been in
handling the goods or the purchaser in acquiring them: see *Barker v Furlong*
... and *Consolidated Co. v Curtis & Son* ... This state of the law has been *h*
considered by the Law Reform Committee ... in 1971 as to innocent
handlers. But Parliament has made no change in it; no doubt it would have
done so in the Torts (Interference with Goods) Act 1977 if it had thought fit
to do so.'

[21] The report (Law Reform Committee *Eighteenth Report on Conversion and* *j*
Detinue (Cmnd 4774) (September 1971)) to which Lord Denning MR refers was
prepared by a distinguished committee chaired by Lord Pearson. Commenting
on *National Mercantile Bank Ltd v Rymill* (1881) 44 LT 767 they say (para 41):

'If rightly decided, it is an authority for the proposition that a bailee escapes
liability for conversion, not only where he merely re-delivers to his bailor,

but where he delivers at the bailor's directions to a third party without knowledge of any adverse claim, though with knowledge that such delivery is in pursuance of a sale or other disposition.'

They then discuss (para 43) the rule that receipt under a purported sale would amount to conversion and justify its retention without the need for a demand 'subject to the principle that a bailee who has accounted for the goods to his bailor should be exempt from liability to any other person'. Turning to the problem of the innocent handler they say:

'46. It is clear ... that there are many cases in which the existing law imposes liability in conversion upon an "innocent handler" of goods ... But it is not entirely clear which acts of a handler will, and which will not, attract this liability. It has been said that a merely ministerial handling of goods at the request of an apparent owner having the actual control of them is not a conversion and that a handling is ministerial where it merely changes the position of the goods and not the property in them.'

After referring to Blackburn J's test in *Hollins v Fowler* (1875) LR 7 HL 757, [1874–80] All ER Rep 118 they conclude:

'47. Where the handler, having received goods from an apparent owner and without knowledge of any adverse claim, merely re-delivers them to the same person, we consider that all the above tests can fairly be said to have been satisfied, and we think that the same applies where the handler delivers the goods at the direction of the apparent owner to a third party without knowledge of any adverse claim or that any question of title is involved. But difficulties arise where the handler has knowledge that a question of title is involved, as where the act he is required to do is to his knowledge in pursuance of a sale or other disposition by the apparent owner to a third party. In such a case, on the authority of *National Mercantile Bank* v. *Rymill* no liability attaches unless the defendant himself effected the sale as agent for the apparent owner; and, although the facts of that case hardly satisfy the test propounded by Blackburn, J. (whether the act done by the defendant can fairly be said to have changed no more than the position of the goods), we do not, on a balance of the conflicting considerations involved, recommend a statutory reversal of this decision.'

[22] The auctioneer cases and the report of the Law Reform Committee led Jack J to the conclusion ([2002] 4 All ER 1005 at [41]) that for an auctioneer to be liable there must be a sale in which he is sufficiently involved followed by delivery to the buyer.

[23] Professor Palmer submits that this conclusion was too restrictive. An auctioneer, for example, will be liable in conversion for misdelivery (see *Jackson v Cochrane* [1989] 2 Qd R 23 at 25, 26 where the English cases are referred to). There is also a suggestion in *Cochrane v Rymill* (1879) 40 LT 744 (an earlier case where this auctioneer sold horses and carriages the subject of a bill of sale) that simply dealing with goods amounts to conversion. This was a case however where the auctioneer took the goods as security for a loan to the grantor. They were then sold and delivered at auction and the loan was repaid from the proceeds of sale. I do not see anything in this case which was subsequently distinguished on its facts in the *National Mercantile Bank* case which justifies any more extensive

liability for auctioneers than the later cases establish. Nor does the fact that an
auctioneer may be liable for misdelivery.

[24] Without reference to the particular facts of this case, I agree with Jack J
and Judge Hallgarten that the authorities indicate that an auctioneer who
receives goods from their apparent owner and simply redelivers them to him
when they are unsold is not liable in conversion provided he has acted in good
faith and without knowledge of any adverse claim to them. Although strictly the
cases do not compel this conclusion they cannot simply be put aside as Professor
Palmer suggests. The auctioneer intends to sell and if he does so will incur
liability if he delivers the goods to the buyer. But his intention does not make him
liable; it is what he *does* in relation to the goods which determines liability. Mere
receipt of the goods does not amount to conversion. In receiving the goods from
and redelivering them to their apparent owner the auctioneer in such a case has
only acted ministerially. He has in the event merely changed the position of the
goods and not the property in them. This I think is a just conclusion, although I
realise it may be dangerous to test issues of strict liability in this way.
Nevertheless I think it would be unduly harsh if auctioneers were to be held liable
in circumstances such as these.

[25] So I turn to the particular facts of this case. The first question is how
relevant are the contractual terms agreed between Mr Schünemann and
Christie's? They govern his (and any buyer's) relationship with Christie's but do
not and cannot affect the legal position between the claimant and Christie's.
What Christie's may *do* in exercising their contractual rights may impact upon
the claimant's title but the mere existence of those rights will not.

[26] Professor Palmer argues that this analysis is contrary to authority. He
relied on *Smith (Administrator of Cosslett (Contractors) Ltd) v Bridgend County BC*
[2001] UKHL 58, [2002] 1 All ER 292, [2002] 1 AC 336 where a company had plant
on a site owned by the council. When the company got into financial difficulties
the council were entitled to use the plant but entered into a continuation contract
with other contractors which, on completion of the contract, passed title to the
plant to the contractors and allowed them to remove it from the site. The case
principally involved issues about fixed and floating charges but the House also
had to decide whether the council had converted the plant. Professor Palmer
referred us to Lord Scott of Foscote's judgment ([2002] 1 All ER 292 at [73]–[75])
where he appears to have decided that the continuation contract itself amounted
to conversion. But Lord Scott was in the minority. The majority judgment was
given by Lord Hoffmann with whom Lord Bingham of Cornhill, Lord Browne-
Wilkinson and Lord Rodger of Earlsferry agreed. Lord Hoffmann said (at [39]):

'The council consented to the removal of the plant by [the other
contractor] in violation of the company's right to possession. The fact that
they gave such consent in advance, at a time when the company was not
entitled to possession, can make no difference. The consent remained
effective until the moment when [the other contractor] took the plant. This
was sufficient to amount to a conversion.'

This gives no support to Professor Palmer's submission. I read Lord Hoffmann
as saying that the conversion took place when the plant was removed and that
the council were liable because it happened with their consent which had been
given earlier in the continuation contract.

[27] If the contract terms between Christie's and Mr Schünemann are
irrelevant unless Christie's exercise of their contractual rights impacted on the

a claimant's title there is a simple answer to all or at least most of Professor Palmer's main argument: there is no allegation that Christie's exercised a lien or power of sale or any of their other contractual rights to the detriment of the claimant's title; so his submissions based simply on the contract terms get him nowhere.

b [28] But lest this analysis is wrong I shall consider Professor Palmer's submissions in more detail. Looking at the contract he says it permitted Christie's to catalogue, market and expose the painting for sale. The seller was not allowed to withdraw it from the sale without Christie's consent (see cl 7(c)) and when it was unsold they were entitled to keep it for two months to try and sell it privately (see cl 9(d)). All the while charges were being incurred for carriage, insurance and Christie's expenses (see cl 4) which they could require to *c* be paid before the picture could be collected, and if they were not they could sell it (see cl 9(d)). Such an intrusion on the claimant's right to immediate possession of his picture amounts to conversion.

[29] Professor Palmer referred us to three cases which he said supported these submissions by analogy. The first of these was *Saleh Farid v Theodorou and* *d* *Blacklake Securities* [1992] CA Transcript 51 where the first defendant had entered into an unauthorised sale and leaseback of the claimant's car to secure a loan. The second defendant finance company admitted that they had converted the car even though they had not physically possessed it. Their involvement had 'rendered them parties to the deprivation of the plaintiff's title to the car'. I do not see how this case helps Professor Palmer. Although they had not been in *e* possession of the car the finance company had admittedly been parties to the first defendant's conversion. The car was worth very substantially more than the amount it had been 'sold' for and in any event had been pledged as security for repayment of the loan.

[30] The second case *Michael Gerson (Leasing) Ltd v Wilkinson* [2001] 1 All ER *f* 148, [2001] QB 514 also involved an unauthorised sale and leaseback to a finance company. The question was whether the finance company could rely on s 24 of the Sale of Goods Act 1979 which protects buyers in good faith and without notice if the goods or their documents of title have been delivered or transferred to the buyer. Clarke LJ said [2001] 1 All ER 148 at 158, [2001] QB 514 at 526 (para 30)), with which the other two members of the court agreed, that the effect *g* of the sale and leaseback was that the goods must be taken to have been delivered to the finance company because otherwise they could not have leased them back. He said ([2001] 1 All ER 148 at 159, [2001] QB 514 at 527 (para 36)) it made 'commercial sense to hold that such arrangements involve a transfer of constructive possession to the finance company' as the purchase of goods was commonly *h* financed by sale and leaseback contracts. Professor Palmer says that this case shows that there may be a sale without actual delivery and by analogy offering ('hawking or touting' as he put it) for sale should also be considered as the equivalent of sale and delivery. I am perfectly prepared to accept that an auctioneer may be liable if following a sale his delivery of the goods to the *j* purchaser may be constructive, but I think the analogy which Professor Palmer seeks to make is impossible. Offering something for sale is not a sale; nor does it involve any delivery, constructive or otherwise.

[31] Professor Palmer's third case was *Moorgate Mercantile Co Ltd v Finch* [1962] 2 All ER 467, [1962] 1 QB 701. There the hirer of a car on hire purchase lent the car to the second defendant who used it to smuggle watches. He was caught and the car was forfeited by Customs and Excise. The court held that the second

defendant had converted the car because what he had done would in all
probability have resulted in the owners being deprived of it. He was to be taken
to have intended the likely consequences of his conduct. Professor Palmer says
that this case shows that you can convert goods by exposing them to risk and that
is what Christie's did by offering the picture for sale. I do not think this case, the
result of which is entirely unsurprising, justifies any such conclusion. The car was
converted when it was forfeited and the defendant was held liable because that
was the natural and probable consequence of what he had done.

[32] I turn then to the terms themselves. First is what Professor Palmer called
'the sealed maze' which may give Christie's possession of the goods for a
substantial period of time. He submits that a right to subtract and enjoy a
substantial possessory portion from the claimant's overall possessory right
without his consent amounts in effect to a non-statutory exception to the nemo
dat principle.

[33] I think the simple answer to this point is that the duration of Christie's
possession is of itself of no consequence. Mere possession, for however long, is
immaterial. It all depends upon what else, if anything, Christie's do and if that
encroaches on the claimant's title. If, for example, the claimant had made a
demand for the return of the picture which Christie's refused they would be
liable. But if such a demand was made by Mr Schünemann and Christie's, relying
on their terms, refused, this would be of no consequence to the claimant.

[34] The fact that Christie's catalogued and offered the picture for sale and did
so for reward adds nothing to the claimant's case; that is an auctioneer's business.

[35] At common law an auctioneer has a lien over the goods for his costs and
commission (see *Williams v Millington* (1788) 1 Hy Bl 81, 126 ER 49). Under cl 9(d)
the seller is not entitled to collect his goods until all outstanding charges are met.
As I have already said, in this case it is not alleged that Christie's exercised any lien
or similar right under cl 9(d) over the picture. The need for such a right to be
exercised was made clear by Millett J in *Barclays Mercantile Business Finance Ltd v
Sibec Developments Ltd* [1993] 2 All ER 195 at 199, [1992] 1 WLR 1253 at 1257–1258
when he said:

> 'Demand is not an essential precondition of the tort in the sense that what
> is required is an overt act of withholding possession of the chattel from the
> true owner. Such an act may consist of a refusal to deliver up the chattel on
> demand made, but it may be demonstrated by other conduct, for example by
> asserting a lien. Some positive act of withholding, however, is required; so
> that, absent any positive conduct on the part of the defendant, the plaintiff
> can establish a cause of action in conversion only by making demand.'

[36] If the lien was exercised in response to a demand for the picture by the
claimant there is no doubt that this would amount to conversion. In *Loeschman v
Machin* (1818) 2 Stark 311 at 312 Abbott J said:

> '... if he [the hirer of the goods] send them to an auctioneer to be sold, he
> is guilty of a conversion of the goods; and that if the auctioneer afterwards
> refuse to deliver them to the owner, unless he will pay a sum of money
> which he claims, he is also guilty of a conversion.'

This case is not however authority for the proposition that the exercise of a lien
against the would-be seller would amount to conversion against the true owner.
As Jack J said there must be some doubt about this.

a [37] The other case about lien to which Professor Palmer referred was *Tear v Freebody* (1858) 4 CBNS 228, 140 ER 1071 in which the surveyor to a parish was found to have taken possession of the plaintiff's materials so as to obtain an unfounded lien over them. This was therefore the overt assertion of a lien against the owner of the materials which not surprisingly was held to amount to conversion and so takes the matter no further.

b [38] I turn finally to consider the submission that Christie's received the picture by way of pledge because of the lien and the right to sell contained in cl 9(d).

[39] Volume 36(1) of *Halsbury's Laws* (4th edn reissue) paras 101–104 states:

c 'A "pawn" or "pledge" is a bailment of personal property as a security for some debt or engagement ... Pawn has been described as a security where, by contract, a deposit of goods is made a security for a debt and the right to the property vests in the pawnee so far as is necessary to secure the debt; in this sense it is intermediate between a simple lien and a mortgage which wholly passes the property in the thing conveyed ... The rights of the pawnee in the thing pawned are distinguishable from a common law lien in

d that he acquires a special property or special interest in the property pawned, whereas a person exercising a lien has only a right to detain the subject matter of the lien until he is paid, and a lien is not transferable to a third person.'

e [40] Professor Palmer relied on the Australian case of *Australian and New Zealand Banking Group Ltd v Curlett, Cannon and Galbell Pty Ltd* [1992] 2 VR 647 at 649 where customs agents refused to deliver up goods which they were holding because they had not been paid by their customers. Their contract entitled them to a 'special and general lien and pledge for moneys due' over all goods which came into their possession. The bank who had a charge over the customer's

f assets argued that this was not a pledge. Ormiston J in the Supreme Court of Victoria held that it was and in doing so rejected the bank's arguments that pledge was confined to securing a loan or other advance, that the debt had to exist at the time the goods were deposited and that the deposit had to be for the sole purpose of securing the obligation in question.

g [41] I have no difficulty in accepting these general propositions. But the first question is, whether looking at the contract as a whole, the parties have intended that the goods should be pledged. In the *Australian and New Zealand Banking Group* case the clearest indication of the parties' intentions was to be found in the contract which expressly pledged the goods. There is no such expressed intention in the instant case. The deposit of the picture with Christie's was for the purpose

h of their selling it as agents for Mr Schünemann. If one asks whether it was also deposited for the purpose of providing security for some future debt I think the answer must be no. The court should be slow to infer such a purpose because otherwise any custodian who takes a lien over goods with a residual right to sell (as most do) would be a pledgee. Some may wish to provide expressly for this,

j but it should not be readily inferred from contract terms such as cl 9(d).

[42] Those terms themselves provide a further reason for saying that there is no pledge here. Assuming that it is possible to spell out a pledge simply from the right to sell, cl 9(d) only confers that right if an unsold lot is uncollected 90 days after the sale or 35 days after notice to collect has been given. There is no right to sell before this time and no general right attaching to all goods as there was in the *Australian and New Zealand Banking Group* case. Looking at the language of

s 11(2) of the 1977 Act I do not think it can be said that Christie's receipt of the
picture from Mr Schünemann was a 'receipt of goods by way of pledge'. At the
time of receipt Christie's had no power of sale whatsoever.

[43] I concluded (in [24], above) that generally an auctioneer who has acted in
good faith and without notice is not liable in conversion if he returns unsold
goods to the prospective seller. For the reasons I have given I do not think the
particular facts of this case make Christie's liable to the claimant in conversion
either.

BAILMENT

[44] The draft amended particulars of claim allege that Christie's were in
breach of their obligations 'as a bailee of the claimant or as a person owing the
obligations of or equivalent to those of a finder, or as an involuntary or
unconscious bailee'. As such Christie's are alleged to have had a variety of duties
which Professor Palmer summarised in his final submissions to us as follows:

'A person taking possession of goods for a limited period or purpose owes
a duty to take such care as is reasonable in all the circumstances to ensure
that the person who delivers has the right to do so and the person to whom
he redelivers the goods has a right to receive them.'

[45] Professor Palmer supports these submissions with a broad plea to the
merits of the claimant's case. His picture has been stolen. It has passed through
the hands of international auctioneers who should at least have to explain why
they did not discover it had been stolen. Auctioneers should have a strong
interest in the provenance of high-value portable items and not simply rely on
their client's word. Such standards are now expected as, for example, the Return
of Cultural Objects Regulations 1994, SI 1994/501 and the British Art Market
Federation Code 2000 show.

[46] The critical question is whether any relationship of bailor and bailee or
the like existed between Christie's and the claimant. Such a relationship
undoubtedly existed between Christie's and Mr Schünemann. But how can it be
said to have existed with the claimant of whose interest in the painting Christie's
were wholly unaware?

[47] Professor Palmer relied on a number of cases to say that it could. First he
referred us to three cases of gratuitous bailment: *McCowan v McCullogh* [1926]
1 DLR 312 where a man mistakenly took the plaintiff's suitcase from a train,
Mitchell v Ealing London Borough [1978] 2 All ER 779, [1979] QB 1 where the council
stored the plaintiff's goods after they had evicted her and *City Television v
Conference and Training Office Ltd* [2001] EWCA Civ 1770 where the defendants
came into possession of equipment stolen from the plaintiffs. Next we were
referred to two cases of what Professor Palmer called constructive bailment
where the interest of the owner was reasonably foreseeable: *Southland Hospital
Board v Perkins Estates* [1986] 1 NZLR 373, where a hospital were held to be bailees
of a deceased patient's ring and *Heffron v Imperial Parking Co* (1974) 46 DLR (3d)
642 where the owners of a parking lot were held to be bailees of the contents of
a car which was stolen from the lot. Then we were referred to *Parker v British
Airways Board* [1982] 1 All ER 834, [1982] QB 1004 where the rights and
obligations of a finder were considered. After this flurry of citation Professor
Palmer submitted that there was no case since the war in which someone in the
position of bailee or the like had not been found subject to some duty.

a
[48] But this begs the question: duty to whom? None of these cases sheds light on the critical question in this case. Christie's were not a gratuitous or involuntary bailee. There was no doubt as to what they were bailees of and they were not finders. They believed they were bailees for reward of Mr Schünemann and no one else.

b
[49] Support for the view that a bailee must have some knowledge of the existence of his bailor is to be found in *The Pioneer Container, KH Enterprise (cargo owners) v Pioneer Containers (owners)* [1994] 2 All ER 250 at 262, [1994] 2 AC 324 at 342 where Lord Goff said:

c
'Their Lordships wish to add that this conclusion ... produces a result which in their opinion is both principled and just. They incline to the opinion that a sub-bailee can only be said for these purposes to have voluntarily taken into his possession the goods of another if he has sufficient notice that a person other than the bailee is interested in the goods so that it can properly be said that (in addition to his duties to the bailee) he has, by taking the goods into his custody, assumed towards that other person the responsibility for the goods which is characteristic of a bailee. This they believe to be the underlying principle.'

d

[50] Professor Palmer rightly submits that the House of Lords was not concerned with the position of a bailor who sub-bails the goods without the owner's authority. Nevertheless the statement emphasises the obvious, which is that if you are to owe duties to someone else you should know or at least have some means of knowing of his existence. We have not been referred to any authority to the contrary.

e
[51] Professor Palmer placed considerable reliance on the decision of Staughton J in *AVX Ltd v EGM Solders Ltd* (1982) Times, 7 July. In that case the defendants had agreed to the return of defective spheres of solder which they had manufactured for the plaintiffs. By mistake, as well as returning the defective solder in one box, the plaintiffs returned 21 boxes of capacitors which were as the judge said 'finished goods which could not, by any stretch of imagination, be said to look remotely like solder spheres'. The defendants set about scrapping the capacitors in the mistaken belief that they were their own property and mixed them with the rejected solder spheres so that it became uneconomic to retrieve them. The judge held that they were liable as unconscious bailees whose duty before dealing with the goods was to 'use what is in all the circumstances of the case a sufficient standard of care to ascertain that they were truly' their own goods.

f

g

h
[52] On the facts of that case I should have thought that there would have been no difficulty in establishing negligence without invoking any relationship of bailor and bailee. A person, who destroys goods which are self-evidently not his in the mistaken belief that they are, must be liable. In the instant case Christie's asserted no personal rights of ownership over the picture and after it went unsold simply returned it to Mr Schünemann from whom they had received it in the first place. So I do not think that the *AVX* case is authority for the proposition that an agent who receives goods from someone who is their apparent owner and later returns them to him owes any duty to their true owner to investigate title in the absence of anything to put him on inquiry.

j
[53] Professor Palmer's proposed duty has far-reaching implications, not only for auctioneers but also for other custodians such as warehousemen and carriers whose position has been clear since the decision in *Hollins v Fowler* (1875) LR 7 HL 757.

Professor Palmer tried to allay our concern about this by saying that in many
cases it might not be reasonable for such agents to have to make inquiries about   *a*
their customer's title. But this illustrates the problem. In what circumstances, for
example, should a warehouseman who is asked to store a high-value portable
item have to make his own inquiries about his customer's title and what inquiries
should he have to make of whom?

[54] If of course there are circumstances which should put the agent on   *b*
inquiry then a positive case of negligence on conventional grounds can be
alleged. But no such case is or, on the assumed facts, could be made here. I do
not accept that the law of bailment or something akin to it can be stretched so as
to found a duty of the kind alleged. Quite apart from anything else the law of
conversion, which attaches strict liability in certain circumstances, has been
developed over the years to provide the remedy, if any, in cases such as these.   *c*
Now to invoke different principles from the law of bailment is not justified.
Auctioneers such as Christie's must of course take care to avoid dealing with
works of doubtful title since they will be strictly liable if they sell on behalf of
anyone other than the true owner, but that is not a policy reason for making them
liable when they do not sell and simply return the goods to their client in good   *d*
faith and without notice of the true owner's interest.

[55] For these reasons I think Jack J and Judge Hallgarten were right to
conclude that the claim in bailment failed.

CONCLUSION

[56] I would therefore dismiss this appeal. There were no reasonable grounds   *e*
for bringing the claim in conversion or bailment and Judge Hallgarten and Jack J
were right to strike out the claimant's statement of case.

[57] The appellant's notice says that Jack J should not have ordered the
claimant to pay all Christie's costs, but this point was not pursued by Professor
Palmer, rightly in my view because there was nothing in it.   *f*

KEENE LJ.
[58] I agree.

PETER GIBSON LJ.
[59] I also agree.   *g*

Appeal dismissed.

Kate O'Hanlon   Barrister.

a

R (on the application of Carson) v Secretary of State for Work and Pensions

R (on the application of Reynolds) v Secretary of State for Work and Pensions

b

[2003] EWCA Civ 797

COURT OF APPEAL, CIVIL DIVISION

SIMON BROWN, LAWS AND RIX LJJ

24–26 MARCH, 17 JUNE 2003

c

Social security – Retirement pension – Inflation uprating – Claimant not entitled to inflation uprating of state pension because of residence in South Africa – Whether freeze on claimant's pension infringing her human rights – Human Rights Act 1998, Sch 1, Pt I, art 14, Pt II, art 1.

d

Social security – Jobseeker's allowance – Age-related amount – Highest age-related amount applicable to persons who had attained age of 25 years – Claimant aged 24 years old receiving contributions-based jobseeker's allowance calculated by reference to age-related amount for persons aged between 18 and 24 years – Whether receipt of lesser age-related amount infringing her human rights – Human Rights Act 1998, Sch 1, Pt I, art 14, Pt II, art 1.

e

In the first of two conjoined appeals, the claimant was a South African resident. She had spent most of her working life in England and had paid full national insurance contributions. On retirement, she received a United Kingdom state retirement pension. Domestic legislation disqualified her from receiving the annual increase based on price inflation which was received by pensioners who had paid like contributions but remained resident in the United Kingdom. Such increases were payable, however, to pensioners who lived in countries with which the United Kingdom government had entered into bilateral agreements providing for such uprating. South Africa was not such a country. The claimant brought proceedings for judicial review against the Secretary of State, contending, inter alia, that the failure to pay her the annual increases violated art 14[a] of the European Convention for the Protection of Human Rights and Fundamental Freedoms 1950 (as set out in Sch 1 to the Human Rights Act 1998) when read with art 1[b] of the First Protocol to the convention (the right to peaceful enjoyment of possessions) by discriminating between her and those pensioners, whether resident in the United Kingdom or abroad, who did receive the inflation uplift. The judge dismissed her application and she appealed.

f

g

h

In the second appeal, the claimant, who was then 24 years old, received a contributions-based jobseeker's allowance. As a person in the 18 to 24 years age range, she was paid a lesser allowance than she would have received if she had been 25 years or over. She applied for judicial review on the basis, inter alia, of art 14 and art 1 of the First Protocol, alleging discrimination in that she had been less favourably treated than persons aged over 25. The judge dismissed her

j

---

a   Article 14 is set out at [2], below

b   Article 1, so far as material, is set out at [2], below

application and she appealed. On both appeals, an issue arose as to whether
art 14, when read with art 1, was engaged at all.

Held – Article 14 of the convention, taken with art 1 of the First Protocol, was
engaged, since the payment of contributions gave rise to a species of pecuniary
right, such as to constitute a possession for the purposes of art 1. While states
were in general free to grant, amend or discontinue social security benefits and to
change the conditions for entitlement to them as they pleased without any
convention constraint, where contributions were exacted as a price of
entitlement the contributor should be awarded a measure of protection. It had
cost him something to acquire the benefit. A reduction or qualification of the
right to be paid thus engaged art 1, although it might not amount to a violation
of the article simpliciter because the convention conferred no right to receive any
particular amount. However, the reduction or qualification was subject to the
constraints of art 14: if it were done on discriminatory grounds, the
discrimination had to be justified. When a court was invited to consider
complaints of discrimination contrary to art 14, one of the questions to be asked
was whether the circumstances of the comparator and the putative victim of
discrimination were so similar as to call, in the mind of a rational and fair minded
person, for a positive justification for the less favourable treatment of one in
comparison with the other. In the first appeal, the circumstances of the claimant
and the chosen comparators were not so similar as to call for a positive
justification for the withholding of the pension increase in the cases where it was
withheld. In the second appeal, the circumstances of a person over 25 and a
person under 25 were so similar as to call for a positive justification for the less
favourable treatment of those under 25 in comparison with those over 25.
However, the Secretary of State had demonstrated a perfectly reasonable
justification for the differential payments of jobseeker's allowance. The appeals
would therefore be dismissed (see [47], [48], [61], [63], [75], [84]–[87], below).

Gaygusuz v Austria (1997) 23 EHRR 364 and *Wandsworth London BC v Michalak*
[2002] 4 All ER 1136 considered.

Decision of Stanley Burnton J [2002] 3 All ER 994 affirmed.

Notes

For the convention prohibition of discrimination and the right to property, see
8(2) *Halsbury's Laws* (4th edn reissue) paras 164, 165.

For the Human Rights Act 1998, Sch 1, Pt I, art 14, Pt II, art 1, see 7 *Halsbury's
Statutes* (4th edn) (2002 reissue) 556.

Cases referred to in judgments

Abdulaziz v UK (1985) 7 EHRR 471, [1985] ECHR 9214/80, ECt HR.
Andersson v Sweden (1986) 46 DR 251, E Com HR.
Aston Cantlow and Wilmcote with Billesley Parochial Church Council v Wallbank
[2001] EWCA Civ 713, [2001] 3 All ER 393, [2002] Ch 51, [2001] 3 WLR 1323;
rvsd [2003] UKHL 37, [2003] All ER (D) 360 (Jun).
Azinas v Cyprus [2002] ECHR 56679/00, ECt HR.
Belgian Linguistic Case (No 2) (1968) 1 EHRR 252, [1968] ECHR 1474/62, ECt HR.
Botta v Italy (1998) 4 BHRC 81, ECt HR.
Carlin v UK App no 27537/95 (3 December 1997, unreported), E Com HR.
Chapman v UK (2001) 10 BHRC 48, ECt HR.
Corner v UK App no 11271/84 (17 May 1985, unreported), E Com HR.

a *Gaygusuz v Austria* (1997) 23 EHRR 364, [1996] ECHR 17371/90, ECt HR.
Ghaidan v Mendoza [2002] EWCA Civ 1533, [2002] 4 All ER 1162, [2003] 2 WLR 478.
James v UK (1986) 8 EHRR 123, [1986] ECHR 8793/79, ECt HR.
Jankovic v Croatia App no 43440/98 (12 October 2000, unreported), ECt HR.
JW v UK (1983) 34 DR 153, E Com HR.
Marckx v Belgium (1979) 2 EHRR 330, [1979] ECHR 6833/74, ECt HR.
b *Matthews v UK* App no 40302/98 (28 November 2000, unreported), ECt HR.
Moustaquim v Belgium (1991) 13 EHRR 801, [1991] ECHR 12313/86, ECt HR.
Müller v Austria (1975) 3 DR 25, E Com HR.
Nasser v United Bank of Kuwait [2001] EWCA Civ 556, [2002] 1 All ER 401, [2002] 1 WLR 1868.
c *National Union of Belgian Police v Belgium* (1975) 1 EHRR 578, [1975] ECHR 4464/70, ECt HR.
Petrovic v Austria (2001) 33 EHRR 307, [1998] 20458/92, ECt HR.
R (on the application of Alconbury Developments Ltd) v Secretary of State for the Environment, Transport and the Regions [2001] UKHL 23, [2001] 2 All ER 929, [2001] 2 WLR 1389.
d *R (on the application of ProLife Alliance) v BBC* [2003] UKHL 23, [2003] 2 All ER 977, [2003] 2 WLR 1403.
R v DPP, ex p Kebeline, R v DPP, ex p Rechachi [1999] 4 All ER 801, [2000] 2 AC 326, [1999] 3 WLR 972, HL.
R v Secretary of State for Education, ex p Schaffter [1987] IRLR 53.
e *Shackell v UK* App no 45851/99 (27 April 2000, unreported), ECt HR.
Sporrong v Sweden (1982) 5 EHRR 35, [1982] ECHR 7151/75, ECt HR.
Stubbings v UK (1996) 23 EHRR 213, [1996] ECHR 22083/93, ECt HR.
Szrabjer v UK, Clarke v UK App nos 27004/95 and 27011/95 (23 October 1997, unreported), E Com HR.
f *Vaughan v UK* App no 12639/87 (12 December 1987, unreported), E Com HR.
Walden v Liechtenstein App no 33916/96 (16 March 2000, unreported), ECt HR.
Wandsworth London BC v Michalak [2002] EWCA Civ 271, [2002] 4 All ER 1136, [2003] 1 WLR 617.
Wessels-Bergervoet v Netherlands [2002] ECHR 34462/97, ECt HR.
Willis v UK [2002] ECHR 36042/97, ECt HR.
g *X v Italy* (1977) 11 DR 114, E Com HR.

Cases referred to in skeleton arguments
Advocate General v MacDonald 2002 SC 1, Ct of Sess; *affd* [2003] UKHL 34, [2003] All ER (D) 259 (Jun), (2003) Times, 20 June.
h *Aftab v Norway* App no 32365/96 (4 May 2000, unreported), ECt HR.
Bellet v France App no 40832/98 (27 April 1999, unreported), ECt HR.
Burton v UK (1996) 22 EHRR CD 134, E Com HR.
Coke v UK App no 38696/97 (9 September 1998, unreported), E Com HR.
Council of Civil Service Unions v Minister for the Civil Service [1984] 3 All ER 935, [1985] AC 374, [1984] 3 WLR 1174, HL.
j *Dove v Scottish Ministers* 2002 SC 257, Ct of Sess (OH); *affd* 2002 SLT 1296, Ct of Sess (Ex Div).
East African Asians v UK (1973) 3 EHRR 76, E Com HR.
Fredin v Sweden (1991) 13 EHRR 784, [1991] ECHR 12033/86, ECt HR.
Frette v France [2002] ECHR 36515/97, ECt HR.
Hadzic v Croatia App no 48788/99 (13 September 2001, unreported), ECt HR.

Hall (Arthur JS) & Co (a firm) v Simons, Barratt v Ansell (t/a Woolf Seddon (a firm)),
Harris v Scholfield Roberts & Hill (a firm) [2000] 3 All ER 673, [2002] 1 AC 615, *a*
[2000] 3 WLR 543, HL.
Havard v UK App no 38882/97 (22 October 1998, unreported), E Com HR.
Kjeldsen v Denmark (1976) 1 EHRR 711, [1976] ECHR 5095/71, ECt HR.
Krasner v Dennison, Lawrence v Lesser [2000] 3 All ER 234, [2001] Ch 76, [2000]
3 WLR 720, CA. *b*
Lindsay v UK (1987) 9 EHRR 555, E Com HR.
Massachusetts Board of Retirement v Murgia (1976) 427 US 307, US SC.
Matadeen v Pointu [1999] 1 AC 98, [1998] 3 WLR 18, PC.
Mellacher v Austria (1989) 12 EHRR 391, [1989] ECHR 10522/83, ECt HR.
Neill v UK App no 56721/00 (29 January 2002, unreported), ECt HR. *c*
New Zealand Maori Council v A-G of New Zealand [1994] 1 All ER 623, [1994] 1 AC
466, [1994] 2 WLR 254, PC.
P v UK App no 14751/89 (12 December 1990, unreported), E Com HR.
Pearce v Governing Body of Mayfield Secondary School [2001] EWCA Civ 1347, [2002]
ICR 198.
Poplar Housing and Regeneration Community Association Ltd v Donoghue [2001] *d*
EWCA Civ 595, [2001] 4 All ER 604, [2001] 3 WLR 183.
Pretty v UK [2002] 2 FCR 97, ECt HR.
R (Asif Javed) v Secretary of State for the Home Dept, R (Zulfiqar Ali) v Secretary of State
for the Home Dept, R (Abid Ali) v Secretary of State for the Home Dept [2001] EWCA
Civ 789, [2002] QB 129, [2001] 3 WLR 323. *e*
R (Montana) v Secretary of State for the Home Dept [2001] 1 FCR 358, [2001] 1 WLR
552, CA.
R (on the application of Bancoult) v Secretary of State for Foreign and Commonwealth
Affairs [2001] QB 1067, [2001] 2 WLR 1219, DC.
R (on the application of Gurung) v Ministry of Defence [2002] EWHC 2463 (Admin), *f*
(2003) 100(6) LSG 25.
R (on the application of Hooper) v Secretary of State for Work and Pensions [2002]
EWHC 191 (Admin), [2002] UKHRR 785.
R (on the application of Hussain) v Asylum Support Adjudicator (6 October 2001,
unreported).
R (on the application of Q) v Secretary of State for the Home Dept [2003] EWCA Civ *g*
364, [2003] 2 All ER 905.
R (on the application of Smeaton) v Secretary of State for Health (Costs) [2002] EWHC
886 (Admin), [2002] 2 FLR 146.
R (on the application of Tucker) v Secretary of State for Social Security [2001] EWHC
260 (Admin), [2001] ACD 397; affd [2001] EWCA Civ 1646, [2002] HLR 500. *h*
R (on the application of Williamson) v Secretary of State for Education and Employment
[2001] EWHC Admin 960, [2002] 3 FLR 493; affd [2002] EWCA Civ 1820,
[2003] 1 All ER 385.
R (Waite) v Hammersmith and Fulham London BC and Secretary of State for Social
Security [2002] EWCA Civ 482, [2003] HLR 24. *j*
R v Lord Chancellor, ex p Child Poverty Action Group, R v DPP, ex p Bull [1998] 2 All ER
755, [1999] 1 WLR 347.
R v Ministry of Defence, ex p Smith [1996] 1 All ER 257, [1996] QB 517, [1996] 2 WLR
305, CA.
R v Secretary of State for Foreign Affairs, ex p World Development Movement Ltd [1995]
1 All ER 611, [1995] 1 WLR 386, DC.

a   *R v Secretary of State for Foreign and Commonwealth Affairs, ex p Rees-Mogg* [1994]
    1 All ER 457, [1994] QB 552, [1994] 2 WLR 115, DC.

  *R v Secretary of State for the Environment, Transport and the Regions, ex p Spath
    Holme Ltd* [2001] 1 All ER 195, [2001] 2 AC 349, [2001] 2 WLR 15, HL.

  R v Secretary of State for the Home Dept, ex p Daly [2001] UKHL 26, [2001] 3 All ER
    433, [2001] 2 AC 532, [2001] 2 WLR 1622.

b   *R v Secretary of State for the Home Dept, ex p Saleem* [2000] 4 All ER 814, [2001]
    1 WLR 443, CA.

  Rasmussen v Denmark (1985) 7 EHRR 371, [1984] ECHR 8777/79, ECt HR.

  Shamoon v Chief Constable of the Royal Ulster Constabulary [2003] UKHL 11, [2003]
    2 All ER 26.

c   *Skorkiewicz v Poland* App no 39860/98 (1 June 1999, unreported), ECt HR.

  Southwark London BC v St Brice [2001] EWCA Civ 1138, [2002] 1 WLR 1537.

  T v Sweden (1985) 42 DR 229, E Com HR.

  Thlimmenos v Greece [2000] ECHR 34369/97, ECt HR.

d   *Wilson v First County Trust Ltd* [2001] EWCA Civ 633, [2001] 3 All ER 229, [2002]
    QB 74, [2001] 3 WLR 42; *rvsd* [2003] UKHL 40, [2003] All ER (D) 187 (Jul).

  Woolwich Equitable Building Society v IRC [1991] 4 All ER 92, [1990] 1 WLR 1400, HL.

  Zehnalova v Czech Republic App no 38621/97 (14 May 2002, unreported), ECt HR.

e **Appeals**

    R (on the application of Carson) v Secretary of State for Work and Pensions

The claimant, Annette Carson, appealed with permission of Stanley Burnton J
from his decision on 22 May 2002 ([2002] EWHC 978 (Admin), [2002] 3 All ER
994) dismissing her claim for judicial review against the defendant, the Secretary
f of State for Work and Pensions, in respect of the failure to pay her, on the
grounds of her residence in South Africa, the annual inflation uprating to her
United Kingdom state pension. The facts are set out in the judgment of Laws LJ.

    R (on the application of Reynolds) v Secretary of State for Work and Pensions

g The claimant, Joanne Reynolds, appealed with permission of Sedley LJ granted
on 1 July 2002 from the decision of Wilson J on 7 March 2002 ([2002] EWHC 426
(Admin), [2002] All ER (D) 64 (Mar)) dismissing her claim for judicial review
against the defendant, the Secretary of State for Work and Pensions, in respect of
the payment to her of jobseeker's allowance calculated with reference to her age.
h The facts are set out in the judgment of Laws LJ.

  Richard Drabble QC, Helen Mountfield and *Murray Hunt* (instructed by *Thomas Eggar*)
    for Ms Carson.

  John Howell QC and *James Eadie* (instructed by the *Solicitor for the Department for
    Work and Pensions and the Department of Health*) for the Secretary of State.
j

  Manjit Gill QC and *Ramby de Mello* (instructed by *JM Wilson*, Birmingham) for
    Ms Reynolds.

  John Howell QC and *Jason Coppel* (instructed by the *Solicitor for the Department for
    Work and Pensions and the Department of Health*) for the Secretary of State.

                                      Cur adv vult

17 June 2003. The following judgments were delivered.

a

LAWS LJ (giving the first judgment at the invitation of Simon Brown LJ).

INTRODUCTORY

[1] These two appeals raise important issues concerning the impact of provisions contained in the European Convention for the Protection of Human Rights and *b* Fundamental Freedoms 1950 (as set out in Sch 1 to the Human Rights Act 1998) upon our municipal legislation relating to certain state benefits. The relevant articles in the convention are arts 8, 14, and art 1 of the First Protocol (to which I will refer for convenience as 'art 1P'). The benefits in question are jobseeker's allowance and income support (*Reynolds'* case) and retirement pension (*Carson's* case). In circumstances which I shall shortly explain, the weekly rates at which *c* jobseeker's allowance and income support are paid are higher for persons aged 25 or over than for those between 18 and 25; and United Kingdom pensioners living abroad in certain countries (mainly but not entirely, the countries of the Old Commonwealth) do not receive the annual uprate to their pensions which is paid to pensioners living here and those living in certain other foreign jurisdictions. *d* These facts are said to give rise to violations of art 1P or art 14 read with art 1P, or (*Reynolds'* case) art 8 read with art 14.

[2] It is convenient at once to set out the material convention provisions. Article 8 provides:

e

'1. Everyone has the right to respect for his private and family life, his home and his correspondence.

2. There shall be no interference by a public authority with the exercise of this right except such as is in accordance with the law and is necessary in a democratic society in the interests of national security, public safety or the economic well-being of the country, for the prevention of disorder or crime, *f* for the protection of health or morals, or for the protection of the rights and freedoms of others.'

Article 14:

'The enjoyment of the rights and freedoms set forth in this Convention *g* shall be secured without discrimination on any ground such as sex, race, colour, language, religion, political or other opinion, national or social origin, association with a national minority, property, birth or other status.'

Article 1P:

h

'Every natural or legal person is entitled to the peaceful enjoyment of his possessions. No one shall be deprived of his possessions except in the public interest and subject to the conditions provided for by law and by the general principles of international law ...'

j

THE OUTLINE FACTS AND THE DOMESTIC LEGISLATION

[3] What follows here is an account of the basic primary facts in each case, and the applicable domestic legislation. There are other important factual matters which it will be more convenient to set out when I have described the nature of the legal challenge in each case, and come to confront its merits.

Reynolds' case

a

[4] The appeal is from the decision of Wilson J given in the Administrative Court on 7 March 2002 ([2002] EWHC 426 (Admin), [2002] All ER (D) 64 (Mar)), when he dismissed Ms Reynolds' claim for judicial review.   Sedley LJ granted permission to appeal, limited as I shall explain to certain grounds only, on 1 July 2002.

b

[5] Ms Reynolds was born on 9 November 1976. She has a son who was born on 9 June 2001. After leaving school she was in paid employment until she was made redundant on 12 October 2000, and during that period National Insurance contributions were paid by her employers on her behalf and by herself. On 24 October 2000 she applied for jobseeker's allowance, and was notified by letter of 14 November 2000 that she qualified by virtue of her class 1 National Insurance contributions. There are two kinds of jobseeker's allowance. 'JSA(C)' is contributions-based. 'JSA(IB)' is income-based. Ms Reynolds satisfied the conditions for both, but was paid JSA(C) only: in her particular circumstances she was not entitled to any greater sum by way of JSA(IB). As she was a single claimant in the age range 18 to 24, she was paid at the rate of £41·35 per week. Had she been 25 or over, she would have received £52·20 per week. It is important to notice that, as regards JSA(C), a person's contributions do not in whole or in part constitute a fund from which the benefit is later paid. It is a contributory benefit only in the sense that the payment of sufficient contributions is a condition of entitlement.

c

d

[6] As from 12 January 2001 Ms Reynolds was considered to be incapable of working because of difficulties which she suffered relating to her pregnancy. Accordingly from that date up to the birth of her baby (as I have said on 9 June 2001) she received income support rather than jobseeker's allowance, but at the same rate. Between 24 October 2000 and 9 June 2001 Ms Reynolds received housing benefit and council tax benefit in addition to the successive payments of jobseeker's allowance and income support.   She also received a maternity allowance for about the final three months of pregnancy. Her case on the facts was and is that she was subjected to severe hardship by virtue of the low rate of benefit which she got. Her evidence is that because she had to pay about £20 per week for gas and electricity and to repay a loan at the rate of £10 per week, she was constrained to borrow £4 or £5 per week from her mother and to eat twice a week at her mother's house in order to make ends meet at the most basic level. Moreover she suffered from an under-active thyroid gland and asthma; she had to take iron and vitamin tablets to help with her anaemic condition; when she was pregnant she discovered that she could not get free milk tokens; she was not entitled to claim social fund or other hardship payments.

e

f

g

[7] In relation to JSA(C), the difference in treatment on the basis of age is authorised by s 4(1) of the Jobseekers Act 1995 and by reg 79 of the Jobseeker's Allowance Regulations 1996, SI 1996/207. Section 4 provides:

h

'(1) In the case of contribution-based jobseeker's allowance, the amount payable in respect of a claimant ("his personal rate") shall be calculated by—(a) determining the age-related amount applicable to him; and (b) making prescribed deductions in respect of earnings and pension payments.

j

(2) The age-related amount applicable to a claimant, for the purposes of subsection (1)(a), shall be determined in accordance with regulations.'

Regulation 79 provides:

'(1) In the case of contribution-based jobseeker's allowance, the age-related amount applicable to a claimant for the purposes of section 4(1)(a) shall be—(a) in the case of a person who has not attained the age of 18, [£31·45] per week; (b) in the case of a person who has attained the age of 18 but not the age of 25, [£41·35] per week; (c) in the case of a person who has attained the age of 25, [£52·20] per week.'

[8] There is like provision relating to JSA(IB) which however I need not set out. As regards income support I can summarise the position as Wilson J did ([2002] All ER (D) 64 (Mar) at [9]). Sections 124(4), 135(1) and 137(1) of the Social Security Contributions and Benefits Act 1992 taken together provide that the amount of any income support should be such as was determined in accordance with regulations. Regulation 17(1) of and Sch 2 to the Income Support (General) Regulations 1987, SI 1987/1967 provide that a single claimant to income support aged not less than 18 but less than 25 should receive (in the absence of any income) a sum which in April 2000 rose to £41·35, whereas such a claimant aged not less than 25 should receive a sum which then rose to £52·20. Ms Reynolds' essential case is that in relation to the amount of her benefit she is a victim of discrimination contrary to art 14 of the convention read with art 1P, because she is less favourably treated than a benefit claimant, otherwise in like case with herself, who is over 25.

Carson's case

[9] The appeal is from the judgment of Stanley Burnton J given in the Administrative Court on 22 May 2002 ([2002] EWHC 978 (Admin), [2002] 3 All ER 994), when he dismissed Ms Carson's claim for judicial review. Permission to appeal was granted by the judge below, as I understand it without limitation to any particular issue or issues.

[10] Ms Carson spent most of her working life in England, and while she was employed she and her employer, and while she was self-employed she alone, paid full National Insurance contributions. I should say that just as with JSA(C), the contributions do not in whole or in part constitute a specific fund from which the pension is later paid: the benefits are paid out on what has been called a 'pay as you go' basis, from a notional fund topped up as required by grants from the Exchequer. Ms Carson has been resident in South Africa since 1990. When she was working in South Africa she paid voluntary contributions to protect her right to a United Kingdom state pension. She began to draw her pension in September 2000. She receives a British retirement pension of £103·62 per week. That is made up of a basic pension of £67·50, an additional pension (under the State Earnings Related Pension Scheme, or SERPS) of £32·17, and graduated pension of £3·95. She has not received the increase in the basic retirement pension of £5 (from £67·50 to £72·50) that has been paid since 9 April 2001 to those entitled to it; nor has she received the percentage increase in the additional pension and graduated pension which has been paid since that date. It is accepted on her behalf that she is not qualified for these increases by reason of the relevant provisions of United Kingdom legislation and delegated legislation, apart from the Human Rights Act 1998. While she remains in South Africa, her total British pension will remain frozen at £103·62. Pensioners who have paid like contributions to those made by Ms Carson but who remain resident in the United Kingdom receive an annual uplift based on price inflation. Others who live abroad, but in countries with which the United Kingdom government has

a entered into certain forms of bilateral agreement, also receive this uplift. I shall give the necessary details later. Ms Carson says that she faces severe financial hardship and a very insecure retirement in which she will be forced to continue to work in order to compensate for her British pension being so much lower than she expected. Her essential case is that in relation to the amount of her pension she is a victim of discrimination contrary to art 14 of the convention read with

b art 1P, because she is less favourably treated than those United Kingdom pensioners, whether living here or abroad, who receive the inflation uplift.

[11] The relevant domestic legislation is as follows. Section 20(1) of the 1992 Act provides so far as relevant:

c   'Contributory benefits under this Part of this Act are of the following descriptions, namely … (f) retirement pensions of the following categories— (i) Category A, payable to a person by virtue of his own contributions …'

Section 21:

d   '(1) Entitlement to any of the benefits specified in section 20(1) above … depends on contribution conditions being satisfied …
      (2) The class or classes of contribution which, for the purposes of subsection (1) above, are relevant in relation to each of those benefits are as follows … Category A retirement pension: Class 1, 2 or 3.'

Section 44 is important:

e   '(1) A person shall be entitled to a Category A retirement pension if—(a) he is over pensionable age; and (b) he satisfies the contribution conditions for a Category A retirement pension specified in Schedule 3, Part I, paragraph 5; and, subject to the provisions of this Act, he shall become so entitled on the day on which he attains pensionable age and his

f   entitlement shall continue throughout his life …
      (3) A Category A retirement pension shall consist of—(a) a basic pension payable at a weekly rate; and (b) an additional pension payable where there are one or more surpluses in the pensioner's earnings factors for the relevant years.

g   (4) The weekly rate of the basic pension shall be £72.50 …'

The conditions stated in Sch 3, Pt I, para 5 to the 1992 Act provide that the individual must, for a requisite number of years of his working life, have paid or been credited with contributions. The requisite number of years during which contributions must have been made is calculated according to the length of the

h individual's working life. Section 113 of the 1992 Act contains general provisions as to disqualification from receiving benefits, and for suspending payments. Section 113(1) provides, so far as relevant:

j   'Except where regulations otherwise provide, a person shall be disqualified for receiving any benefit under Parts II to V of this Act … for any period during which the person—(a) is absent from Great Britain; or (b) is undergoing imprisonment or detention in legal custody.'

Section 113(3) provides:

      'Regulations may provide for a person who would be entitled to any such benefit but for the operation of any provision of this Act … to be treated as if entitled to it for the purposes of any rights or obligations ... which depend on his entitlement, other than the right to payment of the benefit.'

The general statutory disqualification from receiving Category A retirement pension by reason of being absent from Great Britain is disapplied by reg 4(1) of the Social Security Benefit (Persons Abroad) Regulations 1975, SI 1975/563, which modifies the 1992 Act in relation to, inter alia, retirement pension. It provides, so far as material:

'Subject to the provisions of this regulation and of regulation 5 below, a person shall not be disqualified for receiving ... a retirement pension of any category ... by reason of being absent from Great Britain.'

Regulation 5 of the same regulations, however, provides for the re-application of the disqualification in regulations providing for the uprating of retirement pensions:

'(1) Where regulations made in consequence of an order under section 63 of the Social Security Act 1986 (up-rating of benefits ...) provide for the application of this regulation to any additional benefit becoming payable by virtue of that order, the following provisions of this regulation shall ... have effect in relation to the entitlement to that benefit of persons absent from Great Britain ...

(3) ... where a person is not ordinarily resident in Great Britain immediately before the appointed date the provisions of these regulations (except this regulation) shall not, unless and until he becomes ordinarily resident in Great Britain, affect his disqualification while he is absent from Great Britain for receiving ... (c) ... any additional retirement pension of any category ... if that person had ... become entitled to a retirement pension ... before the appointed date.'

Regulation 3 of the Social Security Benefits Up-rating Regulations 2001, SI 2001/910 provided for the application of the disqualification to the additional benefit payable by virtue of the Social Security Benefits Up-rating (No 2) Order 2000, SI 2001/207 including the uprating of the retirement pension introduced by art 4 of the 2001 order with effect from 9 April 2001:

'3. Regulation 5 of the Social Security Benefit (Persons Abroad) Regulations 1975 (application of disqualification in respect of up-rating of benefit) shall apply to any additional benefit payable by virtue of the Up-rating Order.'

[12] In each tax year the Secretary of State is obliged by virtue of s 150 of the 1992 Act to review the sums specified (inter alia) in s 44(4) 'in order to determine whether they have retained their value in relation to the general level of prices obtaining in Great Britain' and to lay an uprating order before Parliament where it appears to him that the general level of prices is greater at the end of the review than it was at the beginning of the period. The draft order must increase the sum specified in s 44(4) by a percentage which is no less than that increase.

[13] Her Majesty is empowered by Order in Council to make provision for modifying or adapting the relevant legislation in its application to cases affected by an agreement with a country outside the United Kingdom which provides for reciprocity in matters relating to payments for purposes similar or comparable to the purposes of the 1992 Act: see s 179 of the 1992 Act. There are extant agreements allowing for payment of pension increases with a number of

a
countries. United Kingdom pensioners living in these countries, unlike Ms Carson and many others who live in other foreign states, receive the uprate made year by year by the Secretary of State under s 150. The part played by these agreements—'bilaterals' in this appeal's vocabulary—in the debate before us was of no little importance. As I have said it will be convenient to describe the material details when I come to confront the merits of Ms Carson's case.

b
THE ISSUES IDENTIFIED

[14] As I have indicated, in *Reynolds'* case Sedley LJ gave permission to appeal on a limited basis. He considered there were no arguable grounds to suggest a violation of arts 3, 8, or art 1P taken on its own; but that art 14 read with art 1P and/or the common law might support a viable case of arbitrary discrimination
c
in the distribution of jobseeker's allowance and income support. After the grant of permission Mr Gill QC for Ms Reynolds and his junior supplied a note to the court signifying an intention also to argue (a) violation of art 1P simpliciter and (b) violation of art 14 read with art 8. It is plain that this court's permission would be required if these further points were to be entertained. At the hearing Mr Gill
d
disavowed any argument based on the common law aside from the convention.

[15] Mr Drabble QC for Ms Carson advanced two arguments to support the conclusion that withholding the retirement pension uprate from his client and others in her position was unlawful: more formally, that reg 3 of the 2001 regulations was ultra vires. He submitted first that reg 3 was repugnant to art 14 read with art 1P because it discriminated against Ms Carson on grounds of her
e
place of residence without any objective and reasonable justification. In the alternative, the regulation constituted a violation of art 1P taken on its own. I should say that Stanley Burnton J ([2002] 3 All ER 994) raised of his own motion a further point which if good would have disposed of Ms Carson's case in limine. This was whether, having regard to art 1 of the convention (which I will not set
f
out), a signatory state is only obliged to secure the convention rights for the benefit of persons residing within its territorial jurisdiction. The judge held that art 1 did not operate so as to bar Ms Carson's claim. That conclusion has not been contested by the Secretary of State; and although there are, I am sure, nice questions as to the reach of the convention rights in light of art 1 of the convention, it is not necessary to debate them in the *Carson* appeal.

g
[16] In both appeals the major issue is whether there was a violation of art 14 read with art 1P. Within this question there were various areas of debate which I will explain in due course. But it is convenient first to clear the other issues out of the way.

h
ARTICLE I OF THE FIRST PROTOCOL TAKEN ON ITS OWN (BOTH APPEALS)

[17] One of those areas of debate which I will have to confront when I come to deal with art 14 read with art 1P for the purposes of the *Reynolds* appeal is whether non-contributory social security benefits such as income support may constitute 'possessions' within the meaning of art 1P. However in addressing (as
j
I now do) the case made for violations of art 1P simpliciter, it is convenient to assume in Ms Reynolds' favour that income support indeed falls within the meaning of 'possessions'.

[18] In my judgment the starting point for this part of the case is the proposition, vouched by the Strasbourg court's judgment in *Marckx v Belgium* (1979) 2 EHRR 330, that art 1P applies only to a person's existing possessions: it does not guarantee a right to acquire possessions. It is then submitted for the

Secretary of State that domestic legislation which specifies the amount of any
state benefit, as has happened here in both appeals, cannot constitute an *a*
interference with the right given by art 1P: rather it merely *defines* the property
right in the particular case, whose security art 1P may then protect.

[19] This position taken by the Secretary of State is supported by a consistent
line of Strasbourg authority, some of it dealing in terms with complaints put
forward by United Kingdom pensioners resident abroad as to the government's *b*
failure or refusal to uprate their pensions. The first case is the decision of the
European Commission on Human Rights (the Commission) in *Müller v Austria*
(1975) 3 DR 25, in which the Commission held that art 1P does not guarantee a
right to a pension of any particular amount. Then in *X v Italy* (1977) 11 DR 114
the Commission rejected as manifestly ill-founded a claim of infringement of
art 1P because the applicant had not satisfied the requirements under his *c*
domestic law for the payment of a pension. *Müller v Austria* and *X v Italy* were
both referred to in *JW v UK* (1983) 34 DR 153, which was the first case in which
the Commission considered a complaint that the United Kingdom government's
failure to pay an uprated pension infringed the pensioner's convention rights.
There, the applicants were emigrating to Australia. The Commission rejected *d*
the complaint as inadmissible. In view of its particular relevance Stanley
Burnton J ([2002] 3 All ER 994 at [41]) set out the reported extract in full. I will
cite just these following passages ((1983) 34 DR 153 at 154–155):

'3. The Commission has considered the applicants' complaint under
Article 1 of the Protocol. It first recalls that it has previously held that *e*
although this provision does not as such guarantee a right to a pension, the
right to benefit from a social security system to which a person has
contributed may in some circumstances be a property right protected by it.
However the Commission also held that Article 1 does not guarantee a right
to a pension of any particular amount, but that the right safeguarded by *f*
Article 1 consists, at most, "in being entitled as a beneficiary of the social
insurance scheme to any payments made by the fund" [*Müller v Austria* (1975)
3 DR 25 at 31]. It has further held that before the right to benefit protected
by Article 1 can be established, it is necessary that the interested party should
have satisfied domestic legal requirements governing the right [*X v Italy*
(1977) 11 DR 114]. In the present case when the applicants emigrate to *g*
Australia their entitlement to benefit from the United Kingdom pension
scheme will come to be regulated by different rules of domestic law, under
which they will cease to qualify for payment of future pension increases
contemplated by the relevant legislation. To that extent they will not satisfy
domestic legal requirements to benefit from the United Kingdom pension
scheme. Even if the right to benefit from a scheme will normally also apply
to the regular increases this is not necessarily the case where a person leaves
the country where the specific scheme operates. The Commission notes that
in many countries specific restrictions as to the payment of social security
benefits to foreign countries exist or have existed ... In the Commission's
view such operation of domestic law does not amount to a deprivation of
possessions infringing Article 1 of the Protocol and there is thus no
appearance of any breach of this provision.'

The Commission in *JW v UK* proceeded also to reject the applicants' complaint of
violation of art 14 read with art 1P.

a

[20] Two years after its decision in *JW v UK*, the Commission considered another complaint as to the United Kingdom government's failure to pay uprated pension, this time by an applicant who had emigrated to South Africa. In *Corner v UK* App no 11271/84 (17 May 1985, unreported), the Commission rejected as manifestly ill-founded the applicant's complaint that the failure to pay the uprate infringed art 1P. It also held, again, that there was no violation of art 14 read with

b art 1P. The Commission said this:

> 'The Commission recalls that it has previously held that, although art 1 of Protocol No 1 does not, as such, guarantee a right to a pension, the right to benefit from a social security system to which a person has contributed may, in some circumstances, be a property right protected by it ... However, the
> c   Commission has also held that art 1 does not guarantee a right to a pension of a particular amount, but that the right safeguarded by art 1 consists, at most, "in being entitled as a beneficiary of the social insurance scheme to any payments made by the fund" ... in accordance with domestic legal requirements ... Further, the Commission has held that the "freezing" of a
> d   pension at a particular level when a person leaves the United Kingdom does not amount to a deprivation of possessions infringing art 1 of the First Protocol ...'

[21] The appellants seek between them to escape the coils of this learning by reference to other cases, namely *Gaygusuz v Austria* (1997) 23 EHRR 364, *Szrabjer v*

e *UK*, *Clarke v UK* App nos 27004/95 and 27011/95 (23 October 1997, unreported), and *Willis v UK* [2002] ECHR 36042/97. But *Gaygusuz v Austria* and *Willis v UK* were cases on art 14; indeed, as I shall show, *Gaygusuz v Austria* is an important authority for some of the points we shall have to consider in dealing with the principal art 14 issue arising in these appeals. *Szrabjer v UK* was rather different.

f There, the applicants were denied the earnings-related element of their pensions while they were in prison, pursuant to s 113(1)(d) of the 1992 Act which I have set out. They claimed violations both of art 1P, and of art 14 read with art 1P. The Commission declared the complaints inadmissible. It held (referring to *Gaygusuz v Austria*) that the earnings-related pension amounted to a pecuniary right for the purposes of art 1P; however its being withheld from the applicants while they were in prison could be considered (as the government contended) as being in the public interest. Accordingly the complaint of a violation of art 1P simpliciter was manifestly ill-founded. Mr Drabble in his skeleton argument sought to build out of this a positive holding to the effect that the disqualification imposed by s 113(1)(d) operated so as to amount to a deprivation of possessions for the purposes of art 1P. I do not believe that any such proposition can be got from the reasoning in *Szrabjer v UK*. All that can be said (as Mr Howell QC for the Secretary of State suggested) is that the Commission did not state, as a reason for holding the complaint inadmissible, that the disqualification could *not* amount to such a deprivation.

[22] I should notice also that in *Carlin v UK* App no 27537/95 (3 December 1997, unreported), decided as I understand it shortly after *Szrabjer v UK*, the Commission dismissed as manifestly unfounded a complaint that the suspension of industrial injuries disability benefit during a person's imprisonment involved any violation of art 1P. It reiterated that 'it is still necessary, in order for such a right to be established, that the person concerned should have satisfied domestic legal requirements'.

[23] I conclude that no violation of art 1P taken on its own is disclosed on the facts in either of these appeals. The argument to the contrary involves the proposition that art 1P, at least in some circumstances, confers a right to *acquire* property. But that is contradicted by the plain words of the article and by the learning in Strasbourg from the case of *Marckx v Belgium* (1979) 2 EHRR 330 onwards.

ARTICLE 14 READ WITH ART 8 (*REYNOLDS'* CASE)

[24] As I have indicated, permission is in my judgment needed for this point to be raised (though Mr Gill did not distinctly accept as much). I would give permission, only because it is convenient to treat all the issues that have been canvassed on the same procedural footing. However I should say at once that there is but limited space in the appeal's geography for this point to operate: it only has independent life if (the submission on art 1P taken on its own being rejected, as I would reject it) the court were to hold, in relation to art 14 read with art 1P: (a) that payments of income support do not constitute 'possessions' for the purposes of the argument; but (b) that unjustified discrimination was none the less established. In that case Ms Reynolds could only rely on art 14 vis-à-vis the period in which she was paid income support rather than jobseeker's allowance by asserting a breach of the article read with art 8. Since for my part I am satisfied for reasons which I will explain that Ms Reynolds' complaint of discrimination should fail on its merits, if Simon Brown and Rix LJJ agree it follows that this part of the case is moot. However, out of respect for the argument, I will deal with it shortly.

[25] It is common ground that art 14 confers no free-standing right, independent of the other substantive convention provisions. It requires only that the rights guaranteed by those provisions be enjoyed without discrimination of the kinds stated in the article. It may be violated though there is no violation of the substantive right (otherwise, of course, it would be otiose, or at best a rule of interpretation of the substantive rights). What has to be shown is that the act complained of: (a) falls within the 'ambit' of a substantive convention right; (b) involves discrimination against the complainant on a prohibited ground; which (c) is not objectively justified. All this is elementary and I will not take time citing authority to support it. Plainly all these propositions will have to be considered when I come to art 14 taken with art 1P.

[26] Mr Gill submits that the facts, which I have already outlined, disclose circumstances of such marked hardship suffered by Ms Reynolds that the levels of jobseeker's allowance and income support received by her fall readily within the ambit of art 8. While of course we must not lose sight of the fact that there is no complaint here of any violation of art 8 read on its own, it is in my judgment important to recognise that on the Strasbourg learning art 8 does not require the state to provide a home: see *Chapman v UK* (2001) 10 BHRC 48 at 72 (para 99); nor does it impose any positive obligation to provide financial assistance to support a person's family life or to ensure that individuals may enjoy family life to the full or in any particular manner: see *Vaughan v UK* App no 12639/87 (12 December 1987, unreported), *Anderson and Kullmann v Sweden* (1986) 46 DR 251, *Petrovic v Austria* (2001) 33 EHRR 307 at 319 (para 26).

[27] At the same time the European Court of Human Rights has accepted that there may be circumstances in which art 8 imposes a positive obligation upon states to take steps to secure or to further respect for the home or family life. In this territory, however, the states enjoy a wide margin of appreciation: see

a *Abdulaziz v UK* (1985) 7 EHRR 471 at 497 (para 67). It is also true that in establishing a system or regime to comply with a convention obligation, a state may include within the system elements that are not strictly required by the convention itself, as in the case of appeal rights in the context of art 6; and where that is done, the distribution of these supererogatory rights must comply with art 14: see *Belgian Linguistic Case (No 2)* (1968) 1 EHRR 252 at 283.

b [28] In the present case I am clear that the provision of jobseeker's allowance and income support has not been made by the United Kingdom legislature and executive out of compliance with any actual or perceived positive obligation arising under art 8. Such positive obligations may arise where there is a 'direct and immediate link between the measures sought by an applicant and the latter's private and/or family life': see *Botta v Italy* (1998) 4 BHRC 81 at 88 (para 34).

c Recognised instances include circumstances where the criminal law is required to offer protection for family life against particular dangers (see again *Botta v Italy* (at 88 (para 34)). But they cannot, in my judgment, extend to include whole swathes of a state's social security system without embracing that system within the general duty vouchsafed by art 8. That, however, would be contrary to the

d learning to which I have referred in [26], above.

[29] Mr Gill's argument as to the ambit of art 8 cannot in my judgment be limited to the particular circumstances of Ms Reynolds' case. I do not mean to belittle her undoubted difficulties, but it is clear that like difficulties are common to many people in receipt of benefit. Mr Gill's submission, if correct, would in principle subject the general welfare provisions made by the state to the

e requirements of art 8 and of art 14 read with art 8. That is not the law. There is nothing in this argument.

ARTICLE 14 READ WITH ART 1 OF THE FIRST PROTOCOL

[30] Mr Howell accepted that age (*Reynolds'* case) and place of residence

f (*Carson's* case) each constituted a 'status' for the purposes of art 14. But as I have foreshadowed this major issue raises a number of discrete areas of debate. (1) (*Reynolds'* case only.) Is a non-contributory benefit, in this case income support, within the meaning of 'possessions' in art 1P for the purpose of the art 14 argument? (2) (*Carson's* case only.) Was there discrimination at all? Ms Carson asserted that her situation should be viewed against two classes of comparators:

g pensioners living in the United Kingdom, and pensioners living in those foreign states where the uprate was paid. Stanley Burnton J held that neither class of comparator was in an analogous situation to that of the appellant, so that there was no discrimination upon which art 14 might bite. (It is not conceded that there was discrimination in *Reynolds'* case; but I regard the point as barren in the

h *Reynolds* appeal: see [75], below.) (3) (Both appeals, or *Reynolds'* case only if discrimination is not made out in *Carson's* case.) Was there on the facts in each case an objective and reasonable justification for the discrimination? For reasons which I will explain, questions (2) and (3) seem to me to overlap. A fourth question was raised by myself in the course of argument, which, if it possessed any force, logically would come first. This was whether art 14 was engaged in these cases at all; that is to say, whether the facts in each appeal actually touched the enjoyment of the right guaranteed by art 1P.

[31] Although with some considerable misgiving I have concluded that this last issue does not drive the case in the Secretary of State's favour, and Mr Howell was right to eschew any reliance on the suggestion that art 14 was not engaged in these appeals at all, I propose nevertheless to deal with it. The basis upon which

the point ultimately falls to be rejected is closely connected with the steps towards
the answer to question (1) above (is income support an art 1P 'possession'?); and   *a*
some discussion of the subject may serve to clarify the scope of art 14, or at least
expose its attendant difficulties. I turn to this point therefore first of all.

IS ART 14 (READ WITH ART 1P) ENGAGED AT ALL?

[32] I have already stated (see [25], above) that, as is common ground, art 14   *b*
confers no free-standing right, but requires only that the rights guaranteed by the
convention's substantive provisions be enjoyed without discrimination of the
kinds stated in the article. The point is put, if I may respectfully say so, with
particular clarity in *Petrovic v Austria* (2001) 33 EHRR 307 at 319 (para 28):

> 'The Court has said on many occasions that Article 14 comes into play   *c*
> whenever "the subject-matter of the disadvantage ... constitutes one of the
> modalities of the exercise of a right guaranteed", or the measures
> complained of are "linked to the exercise of a right guaranteed".'

[33] What troubled me at the outset of the argument was that I could not see,
on the facts of either appeal, how any exercise of the art 1P right was involved   *d*
such as might engage art 14. The right guaranteed by art 1P is to peaceful
enjoyment of one's possessions, and not to be deprived of one's possessions save
on a permitted justification. As it seemed to me, art 14 would come into play
only in certain limited sets of circumstances. One such would arise if there were
some apparent or potential interference with a substantive convention right
which could however be justified if the case were looked at in isolation (so that   *e*
there would be no violation of art 1P simpliciter), but which would fall to be
condemned under art 14 upon its being shown that the justification imposed, on
discriminatory grounds of a kind contemplated in the article, a heavier burden on
the complainant than was imposed on another person or class of persons in a
comparable situation.

[34] Such a state of affairs might most easily be illustrated by reference to what   *f*
are sometimes called the political rights guaranteed by arts 8–11. In each of these,
para 2 of the article states considerations upon which the right may be abrogated
or qualified, essentially on public interest grounds. Now, one might readily
construct an example where (say) free speech in some particular area is
proscribed by the state in various instances. Grounds to justify the prohibition   *g*
are then put forward by the state under art 10, para 2. In the example, let it be
said that in each given instance taken alone the proscription is well justified under
para 2 on the grounds put forward. However the grounds of justification thus
advanced are more, or less, intrusive or onerous between instances and the
difference is attributable to a prohibited discriminatory ground. In that case the
fact of such differential justifications between classes (or persons) will offend
art 14 unless the state can justify the difference or differences.

[35] Another circumstance which would expose a violation of art 14 might
arise in relation to the substantive rights guaranteed by art 6 of the convention.
Here, the case would not be constituted by the existence of a potential breach of
the substantive right which is however justified, where the art 14 complaint must
rest in discriminatory justifications. In this instance the art 14 complaint rests in
discrimination as regards what counts as breach of the primary right; there are no
issues of justification. Article 6 contains no analogue to para 2 as it appears in
each of arts 8–11. However, the standard which the law demands for compliance
with the requirement that a person's civil rights or obligations (or a criminal

a charge against him) be determined under art 6 at 'a fair and public hearing within a reasonable time by an independent and impartial tribunal' is not a unitary or singular standard or set of principles. In the broadest terms there will be a spectrum of standards within which the court will not interfere. It may be said that this is so by force of the Strasbourg court's doctrine of 'margin of appreciation'. I prefer to say that in the real world there are inevitably shades and

b degrees of every one of the variables in art 6: fairness, publicity, delay, independence, impartiality. So it is that in connection with art 6 a complaint under art 14 may arise where it is said that upon any of these variables the state has applied a different standard to one class of persons compared to another, and done so on a prohibited discriminatory ground. A crude instance of arts 6/14 discrimination would thus arise if a legal system adopted a different rule for the

c admission of confession evidence for members of one class of society (or for members of a particular racial group) compared with the rule adopted for another. In the courts of ancient Athens the evidence of a slave was inadmissible *unless* he had been tortured.

d [36] In each of these examples, and one could generate many others, the enjoyment of the substantive convention right is engaged on the facts of the case fair and square. My difficulty was in seeing how that could be so in these present appeals. In neither case was there any interruption of the appellant's peaceful enjoyment of her possessions. Nor is there any question of either appellant having been deprived—let alone unjustifiably deprived—of any of her possessions.

e Each appellant has had in full measure what the domestic law entitles her to have. The complaint of each, in contrast, is that the domestic law should have given her more. It is plain that art 1P provides no such entitlement whatever; I have dealt with the argument for a violation of art 1P taken on its own. In those circumstances I was unable to see how on the facts there could be any complaint of art 14 taken with art 1P. Such a complaint might arise if the state offered

f differential justifications as between persons or classes for measures of deprivation of property. That would be analogous to the first example given above relating to art 10; but nothing of that sort remotely arises in these appeals.

g [37] It is, however, plain that the Strasbourg court has not confined the scope of art 14 within limits of the kind I have described. Here, I should introduce the facts of *Gaygusuz v Austria* (1997) 23 EHRR 364, to which I have already referred in passing. The applicant was a Turkish national resident in Austria. While working there he had paid unemployment insurance contributions. At a stage when he was unemployed he applied for an advance on his pension in the form of emergency assistance. That was available under the material Austrian legislation, but

h one of the conditions was that the applicant should 'possess Austrian nationality', and so the applicant was refused. The court held, unanimously, that art 14 taken with art 1P applied to the case and had been violated. It said (at 380–381):

j '36. According to the Court's established case law, Article 14 of the Convention complements the other substantive provisions of the Convention and the Protocols. It has no independent existence since it has effect solely in relation to "the enjoyment of the rights and freedoms" safeguarded by those provisions. Although the application of Article 14 does not presuppose a breach of those provisions—and to this extent it is autonomous—there can be no room for its application unless the facts at issue fall within the ambit of one or more of them.

37. The applicant and the Turkish Government argued that Article 14 of
the Convention was applicable in conjunction with Article 1 of Protocol   *a*
No. 1. They referred to the reasoning of the Commission, which found that
the award of emergency assistance was linked to the payment of
contributions to the unemployment insurance fund.

38. The Austrian Government, however, submitted that emergency
assistance did not come within the scope of Article 1 of Protocol No. 1.   *b*
Entitlement thereto did not result automatically from the payment of
contributions to the unemployment insurance fund. It was an emergency
payment granted by the State to people in need. Consequently, Article 14 of
the Convention was not applicable either.

39. The Court notes that at the material time emergency assistance was
granted to persons who had exhausted their entitlement to unemployment   *c*
benefit and satisfied the other statutory conditions laid down in ... the ... Act.
Entitlement to this social benefit is therefore linked to the payment of
contributions to the unemployment insurance fund, which is a precondition
for the payment of unemployment benefit. It follows that there is no
entitlement to emergency assistance where such contributions have not   *d*
been made.

40. In the instant case it has not been argued that the applicant did not
satisfy that condition; the refusal to grant him emergency assistance was
based exclusively on the finding that he did not have Austrian nationality and
did not fall into any of the categories exempted from that condition.

41. The Court considers that the right to emergency assistance—in so far   *e*
as provided for in the applicable legislation—is a pecuniary right for the
purposes of Article 1 of Protocol No. 1. That provision is therefore
applicable without it being necessary to rely solely on the link between
entitlement to emergency assistance and the obligation to pay "taxes or
other contributions". Accordingly, as the applicant was denied emergency   *f*
assistance on a ground of distinction covered by Article 14, namely his
nationality, that provision is also applicable.'

[38] The court concluded that there had been a violation of art 14 taken with
art 1P. In doing so, as it seems to me, by necessary implication it held that
although the conditions of entitlement to a state benefit under a domestic legal   *g*
scheme (and an applicant's failure to fulfil them)—as opposed to any conditions
under which such a benefit might be *withdrawn*—could not in principle give rise
to a claim under art 1P taken on its own, yet they could yield a good claim under
art 14 taken with art 1P. On this footing the reach of art 14 is longer than it would
be if it were confined to instances of the kind I gave in [34], [35], above. However,   *h*
it is correctly submitted for the appellants that there is a consistent line of
Strasbourg authority which favours the longer reach. Reference is made to
Belgian Linguistic Case (No 2) (1968) 1 EHRR 252 (in particular at 283 (para 9)),
Walden v Liechtenstein App no 33916/96 (16 March 2000, unreported), *Matthews v
UK* App no 40302/98 (28 November 2000, unreported) and *Shackell v UK* App
no 45851/99 (27 April 2000, unreported), whose texts with respect I need not cite,   *j*
as well as *Gaygusuz v Austria*.

[39] With great respect, I am driven to confess to a good deal of unease at this
line of authority. It seems to me to represent an extension of the scope of art 14,
forged no doubt in the cause of liberal values, beyond what the high contracting
parties would by the language of the article appear plainly to have agreed. I have
the greatest difficulty in seeing how the attribution of so broad a reach can be

a conformed with art 14's actual words, '[t]he enjoyment of the rights and freedoms set forth in this Convention shall be secured without discrimination ...' Despite the court's protestations to the contrary, the approach taken in the cases begins to give art 14 a life of its own—*beyond* the enjoyment of the substantive convention rights as such. Yet art 14 must surely stand in contrast to art 1 of the new Twelfth Protocol, which has been opened for signature but which the *b* United Kingdom has not ratified. It clearly occupies much greater territory than art 14. It provides:

> *c* '1. The enjoyment of any right set forth by law shall be secured without discrimination on any ground such as sex, race, colour, language, religion, political or other opinion, national or social origin, association with a national minority, property, birth or other status.
>
> 2. No one shall be discriminated against by any public authority on any grounds such as those mentioned in paragraph 1.'

d Paragraph 1 of this provision remains adjectival, as is art 14, but now it is adjectival to '*any* right set forth by law', including, presumably, any provision of municipal law. If that is right, it represents a very much bigger anti-discrimination provision than that apparently contained in art 14. And para 2 creates a true free-standing right, applicable in relation to any action by a public authority. Now, I do not of course suggest that the Strasbourg cases have gone so far as to hold that art 14 as it presently stands possesses the reach of either *e* paragraph of art 1 of the Twelfth Protocol. But the contrast between the two sets of provisions is a focussed reminder of what must have been the intended limitations of art 14.

[40] In all these circumstances I have considered whether it would be right to depart from the Strasbourg learning on this question of the scope of art 14, and to hold that on that measure's true interpretation it is not engaged at all on the *f* facts of either of these appeals. Our duty under s 2(1) of the 1998 Act is to 'take into account' the Strasbourg case law. It is trite that we are not bound by it. However in *R (on the application of Alconbury Developments Ltd) v Secretary of State for the Environment, Transport and the Regions* [2001] UKHL 23 at [26], [2001] 2 All ER 929 at [26], [2001] 2 WLR 1389 at [26] Lord Slynn of Hadley said:

> *g* 'In the absence of some special circumstances it seems to me that the court should follow any clear and constant jurisprudence of the European Court of Human Rights.'

[41] As the argument developed it became clear that the integrity of this broad approach to the scope of art 14 was as I have already said (see [31], above) *h* intertwined with another issue arising in the *Reynolds* appeal, namely, the first question which I identified earlier (see [30], above): is a non-contributory benefit, in this case income support, within the meaning of 'possessions' in art 1P for the purpose of the art 14 argument? It is thus convenient to pass on to that question, whose resolution will show why—in addition to general reasons of comity, *j* certainty and finality of proceedings—I would not in the end depart from the Strasbourg learning on this issue of the scope of art 14.

REYNOLDS' CASE: IS A NON-CONTRIBUTORY BENEFIT (HERE INCOME SUPPORT) WITHIN THE MEANING OF 'POSSESSIONS' IN ART 1P FOR THE PURPOSE OF THE APPLICATION OF ART 14?

[42] Mr Howell submitted that not every social security benefit which a national legal system may for the time being provide constitutes a 'possession' for

the purpose of art 1P. A benefit may do so, but only if there is shown to be a link between the payment of contributions and entitlement to the benefit; in the *Reynolds* appeal, the link is made out in the case of contribution-based jobseeker's allowance, but not in the case of income support. The payment of contributions to a fund (whether by or in respect of an individual) may in certain circumstances create a property right in a portion of the fund which art 1P may protect. Mr Howell cited a succession of cases to make the submission good: *Müller v Austria* (1975) 3 DR 25, *JW v UK* (1983) 34 DR 153, *Corner v UK* App no 11271/84 (17 May 1985, unreported), *Carlin v UK* App no 27537/95 (3 December 1997, unreported) and *Gaygusuz v Austria* (1997) 23 EHRR 364, to all of which I have referred, and also *Jankovic v Croatia* App no 43440/98 (12 October 2000, unreported).

[43] There was, I think, no contest but that the Strasbourg jurisprudence pre-*Gaygusuz v Austria* supported Mr Howell's argument. But Mr Gill placed particular emphasis on *Gaygusuz v Austria* (1997) 23 EHRR 364 at 380 (para 41), which I will cite again for convenience:

> 'The Court considers that the right to emergency assistance—in so far as provided for in the applicable legislation—is a pecuniary right for the purposes of Article 1 of Protocol No. 1. That provision is therefore applicable without it being necessary to rely solely on the link between entitlement to emergency assistance and the obligation to pay "taxes or other contributions".'

Mr Gill referred also to decisions arrived at after *Gaygusuz v Austria* (see *Matthews v UK* App no 40302/98 (28 November 2000, unreported), *Willis v UK* [2002] ECHR 36042/97 and *Wessels-Bergervoet v Netherlands* [2002] ECHR 34462/97), as showing some implicit support for the view that the making of contributions was not a necessary precondition for the treatment of a benefit as a possession, or at least that since *Gaygusuz v Austria* the Strasbourg court has not spoken with an entirely clear voice on the subject. Wilson J accepted Mr Howell's argument ([2002] All ER (D) 64 (Mar) at [17]). In *Carson's* case, however, Stanley Burnton J also discussed the *Gaygusuz v Austria* decision and concluded ([2002] 3 All ER 994 at [46]):

> 'The second sentence of para 41 of the court's judgment is framed in not untypical Delphic terms. It is unnecessary for me to decide what the court intended to lay down, but I read it as holding that a state benefit may be a pecuniary right protected by art 1 of the First Protocol even if it is not a contributory benefit entitlement to which is conditional on compulsory payment of a tax or other contribution. This is logical. There would be some logic in restricting art 1 to pecuniary rights derived from a defined investment funded by individual contributions. In such a case the right is a true right of property. Where, however, the payment of contributions is no more than a condition for entitlement to a benefit (as I assume was the position in *Gaygusuz's* case), it is difficult to see why entitlement to a benefit resulting from satisfaction of that condition should create a pecuniary right protected by art 1, when entitlement to benefit resulting from satisfaction of some other condition should not. In a case such as the present, the payment of benefit does not create a right of property in any real sense.'

[44] At first glance it seemed to me that this reasoning was plainly correct. If a person fulfils the conditions set by domestic law for entitlement to benefit, he is as surely entitled to receive the benefit—in theory, to sue for it—where the

a conditions have not required him to make prior contributions as where they have. The entitlement is a 'possession' in both cases, or neither.

[45] It is clear, however (and uncontentious), that the term 'possessions' bears an autonomous meaning for the purposes of the convention; and in the field of social security the Strasbourg court has drawn a line, from the decision in *Müller v Austria* onwards, between contributory and non-contributory benefits. I do not
b accept Mr Gill's submission that the law of the convention took a different course in *Gaygusuz v Austria* (1997) 23 EHRR 364 at 380 (paras 38–41). The court there had to deal with the Austrian government's submission that emergency assistance did not come within the scope of art 1P because (to summarise the argument in my own words) the payment of contributions was only a necessary, not a sufficient, condition of entitlement to the benefit (para 38). That was
c rejected (paras 39 and 41). The court pointed out (para 39) that entitlement to the benefit was linked to the payment of contributions to the unemployment insurance fund. As I read these paragraphs that fact was in truth regarded as a *premise* of the conclusion that the right to the benefit was a pecuniary right for the purposes of art 1P. The use of the adverb 'solely' in para 41, which is really the
d linchpin of Mr Gill's argument, is I think no more than a reflection of the court's rejection of the view that art 1P would not bite unless the payment of contributions was a sufficient condition of entitlement to the benefit in question.

[46] Mr Gill is not assisted by later Strasbourg decisions; quite the contrary. I will not take time with all the cases. In *Szrabjer v UK, Clarke v UK* App nos 27004/95 and 27011/95 (23 October 1997, unreported) the Commission
e stated:

> '... the Commission recalls the case of *Gaygusuz v Austria* ... In that case the court noted that emergency assistance was linked to and dependent upon a payment of contributions and held that in these circumstances the right to emergency assistance was a "pecuniary right" under art [1P].'

f In *Azinas v Cyprus* [2002] ECHR 56679/00 the European Court of Human Rights said (para 33):

> '... in its judgment in the case of *Gaygusuz v Austria* (1997) 23 EHRR 364 at 380 (paras 39–41), the court held that entitlement to a social benefit is linked
g to the payment of contributions ...'

There is other learning to like effect. There is nothing in the authorities to suggest that the Strasbourg court perceives itself as having taken a new line in *Gaygusuz v Austria*, or that it has done so in any other case.

[47] It seems to me, then, that the law of the convention is settled on this point
h as to the scope of 'possessions' for the purpose of art 1P. The policy of the cases is, I think, that while states are in general free to grant, amend or discontinue social security benefits and to change the conditions for entitlement to them as they please without any convention constraint, yet where contributions are exacted as a price of entitlement the contributor should be afforded a measure of
j protection: it has, so to speak, cost him something to acquire the benefit.

[48] This approach throws much needed light on the scope of art 14 read with art 1P, which as I have explained has caused me considerable difficulty. We can now see that the Strasbourg court has treated the payment of contributions as giving rise to a species of pecuniary right, such as to constitute a 'possession' for the purpose of art 1P. A reduction or qualification of the right to be paid the benefit thus engages art 1P, although it may not amount to a violation of the

article simpliciter because the convention confers no right to receive any particular amount. However, the reduction or qualification is subject to the constraints of art 14: if it is done on discriminatory grounds, the discrimination must be justified.

[49] I am not sure that this line of reasoning lays my difficulty with the scope of art 14 entirely to rest. But it provides a clear enough basis for setting the edge of convention protection at the point at which, it seems, the court has undoubtedly set it. In these circumstances I think it would be quite wrong to depart from the Strasbourg learning on the subject. It follows that Ms Reynolds' complaint of a violation of art 14 read with art 1P can only bite on the payments of jobseeker's allowance made to her, and not income support. Wilson J was of the same view ([2002] All ER (D) 64 (Mar) at [17]).

[50] I should acknowledge, before leaving this part of the case, the submissions made by Mr Howell based on the 1961 European Social Charter (the 1961 charter) entered into by states members of the Council of Europe, and the revised charter which was opened for signature in May 1996 but has not been ratified by the United Kingdom. The argument is that these provisions made very substantial provision for social security, but conferred no right of individual application (and the 1961 charter contained no analogue of art 14); in those circumstances; if the scope of 'possessions' within art 1P were as wide as Mr Gill contends—as wide as provided in the 1961 charter—the latter document would actually constitute a retrograde step, since the convention regime confers rights of individual petition and of course includes art 14. A like argument, in the context of trade union rights under art 11 of the convention, found favour with the Strasbourg court in *National Union of Belgian Police v Belgium* (1979) 1 EHRR 578 at 590–591 (para 38). I need say only that this is grist to Mr Howell's mill.

CARSON'S CASE: WAS THERE DISCRIMINATION WITHIN THE MEANING OF ART 14?

[51] The question here is whether there are any true 'comparators' to pensioners living abroad like Ms Carson who do not receive the annual uprate to their United Kingdom pension. There can be no discrimination unless its alleged victim can point to other persons who are in an analogous or relevantly similar situation, yet are treated more favourably. If there is no such analogous situation, any difference in treatment between X and Y has no legal significance for the purposes of art 14 (or, I would add, any rational law of discrimination). Mr Drabble names two sets of comparators: (1) United Kingdom pensioners who like Ms Carson live abroad, but in countries where the uprate is paid; (2) United Kingdom pensioners living in the United Kingdom, all of whom are paid the uprate.

[52] I must explain rather more of the background than has so far appeared. First, it is right to say that the case has considerable implications for many pensioners and for the national finances. According to the Secretary of State, as at January 2002, of some 900,000 pensioners and widow beneficiaries who live abroad less than half (some 420,000) receive the annual uprate. The cost of extending uprating to all pensions from the time when each was awarded would cost an additional £3bn. There is some other material about the figures, but I need not set it out. This was stated in evidence filed on behalf of the Secretary of State:

'Successive Governments have taken the view that the level of increases in retirement pensions relates to conditions in the UK and that it would not be right to impose an additional burden on contributors and taxpayers in the *a*   UK in order to pay pension increases to people who have chosen to become resident elsewhere in the world.'

A number of attempts in Parliament to require the government to pay the uprate to those in Ms Carson's position have foundered in both Houses of Parliament: a DSS Memorandum of 1996 on the uprating of state retirement pensions payable
b   to people resident abroad, submitted to the Social Security Committee of the House of Commons, referred in particular to amendments tabled in both Houses in June and July 1995 during the passage of the Pensions Bill, calling for uprating to be paid. All were defeated by large majorities.

[53] Since the National Insurance Act 1946 came into force, the general position has always been that British pensioners who are not in Great Britain have
c   not received uprated pensions. Only those in the European Economic Area and in states with which the United Kingdom has entered into bilateral agreements requiring such payments receive them. Between 1948 and 1992 the United Kingdom entered into bilateral agreements, or reciprocal social security agreements, with a number of foreign states. With one minor exception,
d   the agreements entered into after 1979 fulfilled earlier commitments given by the United Kingdom government. Agreements with Australia, New Zealand and Canada came into force in 1953, 1956 and 1959 respectively; however they did not require payment of uprated pensions. The agreement with Australia was terminated by it with effect from 1 March 2001, because of the refusal of the United Kingdom government to pay uprated pensions to its pensioners living in
e   Australia. Uprating has never been applied to those living in South Africa, Australia, Canada and New Zealand. The EC regulations on social security for migrant workers require uprating of benefits throughout the European Union. In practice, the entry of the United Kingdom into the European Community had little effect on the provision for uprating pensions in the member states, because
f   there were pre-existing reciprocal agreements with all of them except Denmark providing for payment of uprate.

[54] There is no doubt but that the overall position as it stands today is a haphazard consequence of events, including not least the conclusion of the various bilateral agreements, happening over time. On 13 November 2000 the Minister of State (Mr Jeff Rooker) said this in the House of Commons (356 HC
g   Official Report (6th Series) col 628):

> 'I have already said I am not prepared to defend the logic of the present situation. It is illogical. There is no consistent pattern. It does not matter whether a country is in the Commonwealth or outside it. We have
h   arrangements with some Commonwealth countries and not with others. Indeed, there are differences among Caribbean countries. This is an historical issue and the situation has existed for years. It would cost some £300 million to change the policy for all concerned.'

j   I should notice also what was said in the Third Report (January 1997) of the House of Commons Social Security Committee (*Uprating of State Retirement Pensions Payable to People Resident Abroad*; HC Paper 143): 'It is impossible to discern any pattern behind the selection of countries with whom bilateral agreements have been made providing for uprating.'

[55] Some explanation of these bilateral agreements is given in the DSS Memorandum to which I have already referred (p 41):

'17. The main purpose of reciprocal agreements so far has been to provide a measure of social protection for workers, and the immediate members of their families, when moving from one country to the other during their working lives. In effect, they generally prevent such workers from having to contribute to both countries' Social Security schemes at the same time while ensuring that they retain benefit cover from either one country or the other. On reaching pensionable age, such workers who have been insured in two or more countries' schemes can receive a pension from each which reflects the amount of their insurance in each.

18. Whether a reciprocal Social Security agreement with another country is entered into depends on various factors, among them the numbers of people moving from one country to the other, the benefits available under the other country's scheme, how far reciprocity is possible and the extent to which the advantages to be gained by an agreement outweigh the additional expenditure likely to be incurred by the UK in negotiating and implementing it. Where an agreement is in place, the flow of funds may differ depending on the level of each country's benefits and the number of people going in each direction.

19. Since June 1996, the Government's policy has been that future reciprocal agreements should normally be limited to resolving questions of liability for social security contributions.'

In the same document (para 38) observations were made which foreshadowed the Minister of State's words on 13 November 2000:

'Surely no one would have deliberately designed a policy of paying pensions to people living abroad intending to end up in the position we are at today ... It is impossible to discern any pattern behind the selection of countries with whom bilateral agreements have been made providing for uprating.'

[56] Before turning to the question in hand, namely whether there are any true comparators in an analogous situation to that of Ms Carson, it is convenient to refer to the approach to be taken to complaints of discrimination contrary to art 14 as it was commended by Brooke LJ in *Wandsworth London BC v Michalak* [2002] EWCA Civ 271 at [20], [2002] 4 All ER 1136 at [20], [2003] 1 WLR 617 at [20]:

'It appears to me that it will usually be convenient for a court, when invited to consider an art 14 issue, to approach its task in a structured way. For this purpose I adopt the structure suggested by Stephen Grosz, Jack Beatson QC and the late Peter Duffy QC in their book *Human Rights: The 1998 Act and the European Convention* (2000). If a court follows this model it should ask itself the four questions I set out below. If the answer to any of the four questions is No, then the claim is likely to fail, and it is in general unnecessary to proceed to the next question. These questions are: (i) Do the facts fall within the ambit of one or more of the substantive convention provisions ... (ii) If so, was there different treatment as respects that right between the complainant on the one hand and other persons put forward for comparison ("the chosen comparators") on the other? (iii) Were the chosen comparators in an analogous situation to the complainant's situation? (iv) If so, did the difference in treatment have an objective and reasonable justification: in other words, did it pursue a legitimate aim and did the differential treatment a bear a reasonable relationship of proportionality to the aim sought to be achieved?'

(In fact, of course, the claim would only be 'likely to fail' in a case where question (iv) were reached if the answer to that question were Yes rather than No.) For reasons I have given question (i) falls to be answered affirmatively. There is no contest as to (ii). The structured approach commended by Brooke LJ plainly
b separates out (iii) and (iv) as distinct successive steps. However Mr Drabble submits that Stanley Burnton J confused these two steps, and I shall address that complaint first.

[57] Stanley Burnton J noted ([2002] 3 All ER 994 at [60]) the two sets of comparators put forward: pensioners resident in the United Kingdom and those
c resident abroad but in countries where the uprate is paid. He continued:

'[61] So far as the first class of comparators is concerned, persons who live in other countries have different costs of living from those in Great Britain, and live in economies that are subject to different rates of inflation. If a comparison were appropriate, it would be justifiable to compare the cost of
d living in sterling terms of a foreign pensioner with that in the United Kingdom. A pensioner resident abroad may be better off, in real terms, than a pensioner living in Great Britain, because of different local costs of living which are not fully reflected in exchange rates.

[62] While I have no evidence before me, it is notorious that the cost of living in this country is relatively high, and certainly higher than that in
e South Africa, partly as a result of the equally notorious depreciation of the rand as against, in particular, sterling. The depreciation of the rand has doubtless led to inflation in South Africa in terms of the local currency, and the claimant's evidence refers to the facts that inflation and interest rates are higher there than here. However, the purchasing power of her fixed United
f Kingdom pension is not fixed: it depends on the rate of inflation in South Africa and changes in the sterling/rand exchange rate. Importantly, the claimant does not state that the purchasing power in South Africa of her fixed sterling pension has declined because it has not been uprated; and as mentioned above the uprating so far refused to the claimant personally is a relatively small sum. Perhaps more fundamentally, she has not compared
g the cost of living in South Africa with that in the United Kingdom. Lastly, she obviously cannot provide a prediction as to whether her cost of living in South Africa will increase in sterling terms.

[63] Similar comments apply to the comparison between the claimant and those living in other countries.

h [64] There are other differences between the circumstances of those resident here and those resident abroad, of which the most obvious in the present context are differences in local social security provision and in local taxation. The claimant is unfortunate in that South Africa has limited social security provision, or at least did so at the time of the Social Security
j Committee Report. The position of pensioners in Australia is different: some of them benefit from Australian social security provision, at significant cost to the Australian exchequer. Of the (about) 220,000 United Kingdom pensioners in Australia, 158,000 qualify for an Australian pension, which is payable to those who have been resident in Australia for at least ten years and have reached retirement age, and have less than a specified income. The position of pensioners in New Zealand, as described in the 1996 DSS

Memorandum, is different again: under the reciprocal agreement between the United Kingdom and New Zealand, periods of residence in the United Kingdom are treated as periods of residence in New Zealand. As a result, United Kingdom pensioners living in New Zealand qualify for New Zealand pensions (called superannuation), less the amount of their United Kingdom pensions, by reason of their residence here or there. Increases in their United Kingdom pensions would result in an equivalent reduction in their New Zealand pensions.

[65] It seems to me that the comparison between the positions of persons living in different countries, in different social and economic circumstances, and under different tax and social security regimes, is complex, and cannot simply be restricted to a comparison of the sterling amounts of their United Kingdom pensions.'

[58] And so Stanley Burnton J concluded (at [67]) that Ms Carson's application must fail. Mr Drabble's argument is that all the factors which led the judge to hold that the proposed comparators were not in an analogous situation were functions or consequences of the difference in place of residence between them and Ms Carson; but place of residence was the 'impugned characteristic' for the purpose of the discrimination complaint, and so, on the authority of *Aston Cantlow and Wilmcote with Billesley Parochial Church Council v Wallbank* [2001] EWCA Civ 713, [2001] 3 All ER 393, [2002] Ch 51, it should have been left out of account in dealing with question (iii) in Brooke LJ's structured approach. In the *Aston Cantlow* case Ferris J at first instance had held that landowners within a particular category (lay impropriators, occupying former glebe land) who were required to pay what was said to amount to a particular form of tax which other landowners were not required to pay were not in an analogous situation with the others, because all lay impropriators had to pay the tax; hence there was no discrimination. On appeal this court stated (at [50]):

'The treatment complained of is not that of [the defendants] personally but that of lay impropriators generally, [the defendants] included. It is therefore necessary to compare the situation of lay impropriators with that of a larger class of which they form part—a class of persons "in an analogous or relevantly similar situation" (*Stubbings v UK* (1996) 23 EHRR 213 at 238 (para 70)). *This class has therefore to be identified by reference to shared material characteristics other than the impugned one.* The material characteristic in the present case is in our view the ownership of freehold land either in England at large or in the parish of Aston Cantlow.' (My emphasis.)

[59] We were told there is an outstanding appeal to the House of Lords in the *Aston Cantlow* case. Whatever the outcome before their Lordships, the reason why this court put the matter as it did in the sentence italicised is with great respect not far to seek. The proposition that lay impropriators were not discriminated against merely because all lay impropriators were treated in the same way may be said to amount to a refusal to recognise that there might be *other* comparators, not lay impropriators, in a materially analogous situation; and without consideration being given to that possibility, the discrimination complaint is stillborn. It is as if, in the present case, it were suggested that Ms Carson's appropriate comparators were all other United Kingdom pensioners resident in countries where the uprate is not paid, and that would be absurd.

a [60] Mr Howell says that this court's reasoning in the *Aston Cantlow* case cannot be applied in the present case. He submits that it cannot be assumed (as was the case in the *Aston Cantlow* case) that there will always be a class, of which the discrimination complainant is a member, all of whose members will be in a materially analogous situation to the complainant. Whether the chosen comparator is in an analogous or similar situation is a question of fact which the
b party alleging discrimination must establish on the facts, not by what Mr Howell referred to as 'definitional devices'. And for good measure Mr Howell submits further that in *Wandsworth London BC v Michalak* [2002] 4 All ER 1136 itself the court did not ignore 'the impugned characteristic', or differences in circumstances said to be consequences of it. In *Michalak*'s case it was contended (for the purposes of a discrimination argument) that Rent Act tenants were in a relevantly
c similar situation to local authority secure tenants. The Court of Appeal held (at [35]–[39], [55]) that the two were not in a relevantly similar situation 'because of the significant differences between the two types of tenancy'. Mr Howell further submits that the jurisprudence of the Strasbourg court itself discloses at least one plain instance where the 'impugned characteristic' (in that case, marriage) itself
d disqualified a proposed group (unmarried partners) from qualifying as comparators for the purpose of a case being made under art 14: see *Shackell v UK* App no 45851/99 (27 April 2000, unreported). It seems to me that we would generate both conceptual and practical difficulties if a studied ignorance of the 'impugned characteristic' were elevated into a general principle for the purpose of identifying relevant comparators in an art 14 case, and I do not believe that the
e court in the *Aston Cantlow* case intended any such outcome.

[61] But there is more to say as to the approach to be taken in such cases. Wilson J in *Reynolds'* case, without referring to *Michalak*'s case, made these observations (at [25]):

f   'The defendant does not accept that a person aged 25 or more would have been in a situation analogous to that of Ms Reynolds during that period. In other words his case is that the difference in age is reflective of other significant differences. He also seeks objectively to justify the demarcation at age 25. I use the word "also" because theoretically the inquiry into whether the situations are analogous precedes the inquiry into justification.
g   But I find the distinction elusive. I consider that it suffices for me to focus on the second inquiry and to ask whether the defendant establishes objective justification for the demarcation, as being in pursuit of a legitimate aim to which it is proportionate.'

h I have considerable sympathy with this approach expressed by Wilson J. A factor or circumstance which puts person X (the comparator) in a different case from person Y (the putative victim of discrimination) may be said to undermine any comparison or analogy between X and Y, and so promote a negative answer to Brooke LJ's question (iii); but the justification of discrimination—which only arises for consideration if question (iii) is answered affirmatively—will *also* often
j rest on the very demonstration of a factor or factors which put X in a different case from Y. There is, therefore, some fragility in the separation between (iii) and (iv) in *Michalak*'s case, and it is to be noted that Brooke LJ himself observed ([2002] 4 All ER 1136 at [22]):

    'It is important to stress that this is only a framework ... There is a potential overlap between the considerations that are relevant when determining, at

any rate, the last two, and possibly the last three questions. There may
sometimes, therefore, be a need for caution about treating the four questions
as a series of hurdles, to be surmounted in turn. In *Nasser v United Bank of
Kuwait* [2001] EWCA Civ 556 at [56], [2002] 1 All ER 401 at [56], [2002] 1 WLR
1868 Mance LJ observed, in effect, that questions (iii) and (iv) above tend to
merge into [one] another.'

However, it may be said that this leaves the true relation between questions (iii)
and (iv) unresolved. A possible approach, as it seems to me, is to ask a
compendious question in place of (iii): are the circumstances of X and Y so similar
as to call (in the mind of a rational and fair-minded person) for a positive
justification for the less favourable treatment of Y in comparison with X? This
provides a relation between questions (iii) and (iv) and avoids any tight adherence
to a rule requiring the 'impugned characteristic' to be ignored.

[62] If one approaches this part of the case by asking this compendious
question, it seems to me quite impossible to conclude that the factors addressed
by Stanley Burnton J ([2002] 3 All ER 994 at [61]–[65]) ought somehow to be
ignored. They are inevitably part of the picture against which a judgment must
be made as to whether such difference in treatment as is relied on stands in need
of a distinct justification. I should add (though perhaps it is self-evident) that in
my view there is no place, in the course of asking and answering this
compendious question, for the operation of any judicial deference to the
legislative or executive branches of government. Though the question is
obviously not limited to the ascertainment of facts, but involves an *evaluation*, the
evaluation does no more than rule out or in the requirement of justification; that
is to say, it is a test for the application of art 14, not a judgment whether the article
is violated. No amount of judicial deference, even in the sphere of macro-
economic policy, could rightly persuade the court to forsake its duty to decide
whether or not the article applies. The scope for such deference, so far as any is
due, is at the point of decision whether or not the article is breached.

[63] In my judgment, the circumstances of Ms Carson and her chosen
comparators are not so similar as to call (in the mind of a rational and fair-minded
person) for a positive justification for the withholding of the pension uprate in the
cases where it is withheld. I arrive at this conclusion in light of all the factors
discussed by Stanley Burnton J (at [61]–[65]). And if the right question is not the
compendious one which I have ventured to suggest, but (more conventionally)
whether the comparators put forward by Mr Drabble are in an analogous
position to that of Ms Carson, I consider that Stanley Burnton J gave the right
answer.

[64] It seems to me important to have in mind (and this well illustrates the link
or overlap between the issue of true comparators and the issue of justification)
that the Secretary of State's obligation under s 150 of the 1992 Act, as I have
already explained (see [12], above), is to review inter alia the sum specified in
s 44(4) for the weekly rate of the basic pension 'in order to determine whether [it
has] retained [its] value in relation to the general level of prices obtaining in Great
Britain', and to lay an uprating order before Parliament where it appears to him
that the general level of prices is greater at the end of the review than it was at the
beginning of the period. The draft order must increase the sum specified in
s 44(4) by a percentage which is no less than that increase. Thus the scheme of
the primary legislation is entirely geared to the impact on the pension of price
inflation in the United Kingdom. There is simply no inherent probability that

a price inflation in other countries where expatriate United Kingdom pensioners might have made their home (or, for that matter, any other economic factors) will have a comparable effect on the value of the pension to such pensioners. They may do better, they may do worse. There will also, of course, be the impact of variable exchange rates. There will be, if I may be forgiven a jejune metaphor, swings and roundabouts. While I certainly do not suggest there are no principled *b* arguments in favour of the annual uprate being paid to those in Ms Carson's position, it seems to me inescapable that its being awarded across the board to all such pensioners would have random effects. A refusal by government to put in place a measure which would produce such effects (which in the end is all that has happened here) cannot be said to stand in need of justification by reason if its being compared with the clear and certain effects of the uprate for United *c* Kingdom-resident pensioners.

CARSON'S CASE: IS THERE AN OBJECTIVE AND REASONABLE JUSTIFICATION FOR THE DISCRIMINATION RELIED ON?

[**65**] Like the judge below, I turn to this question lest I am wrong on the issue of comparators, whether as conventionally formulated or as I prefer to formulate *d* it. Mr Drabble submitted that this part of the case fell inevitably to be determined against the Secretary of State, and no question of judicial deference could arise to qualify the matter, because in truth no justification was offered; it was accepted by government (see the minister's statement cited at [54], above) that the present situation is 'illogical'. But this argument involves a non sequitur: even though the *e* overall effect of the successive bilateral agreements on the distribution of the uprate to foreign resident pensioners is not or may not be *intrinsically* supportable, it by no means follows that the government's refusal to date to ameliorate the position in favour of those in like case to Ms Carson is necessarily unjustifiable. Put another way, Mr Drabble's argument confuses the undoubted truth that the bilateral agreements have over time created a haphazard state of *f* affairs with the proposition, far from undoubted, that against that background a failure to award uprate to those in Ms Carson's position necessarily constitutes a violation of art 14.

[**66**] The judge below held ([2002] 3 All ER 994 at [76]) that—

g 'the remedy of the expatriate United Kingdom pensioners who do not receive uprated pensions is political, not judicial. The decision to pay them uprated pensions must be made by Parliament.'

Part of his reasoning towards this conclusion consisted (at [70]) in the proposition that, by virtue of the impact of the bilateral agreements, the case touched the *h* government's conduct of relations with foreign states, and this was generally a non-justiciable area: '[t]he court will not embark on questions whether it is or is not in the public interest for such agreements to be entered into'. But the question for decision in this case does not in truth engage the government's conduct of foreign relations at all. As I understand it, it would be open to the *j* government to uprate all or any pensions payable abroad irrespective of the bilateral agreements, because although in some instances the agreements *require* payment of uprate, in no case do they *forbid* it. The judicial taboo of foreign relations is a red herring. In fairness Stanley Burnton J went at any rate some distance (at [72]–[77]) to address the merits of the justification argument.

[**67**] I would also reject Mr Howell's argument—and this is linked to the point on foreign relations—to the effect that because states possess (as they surely do)

the right under international law to conclude bilateral treaties in relation to social security, the fact that, as a result, individuals obtain more favourable treatment in some cases than in others does not give rise to an issue under art 14. The conferment or withholding of the uprate is purely a matter for the Secretary of State's exercise of statutory powers conferred by domestic law in the ordinary way. For this reason Mr Howell is not in my judgment assisted by the Strasbourg decision in *Moustaquim v Belgium* (1991) 13 EHRR 801, which he cited in this context. I will not burden this already lengthy judgment by travelling into its details.

[68] I turn then myself to the merits. I should first make it clear that there is no question of any legitimate expectation, enjoyed by Ms Carson, that she would receive the uprate in South Africa. It is entirely plain that the literature distributed by the then Department of Social Security (and sent to her) was perfectly explicit as to the position of United Kingdom pensioners who chose to live in South Africa.

[69] I would accept this submission made by Mr Howell in his skeleton argument:

'There is no reason why a decision that resources can be found to uprate the pensions payable to those in Great Britain to maintain their value given inflation in the general level of prices obtaining in Great Britain should require the pensions payable to those not ordinarily resident in and absent from the United Kingdom to be increased by the same amount.'

The submission is, however, another demonstration of the overlap between the issues of comparators (or analogous situation) and justification. The true justification of the government's refusal to pay the uprate to Ms Carson and those in like case is that they have chosen to live in societies, more pointedly economies, outside the United Kingdom where the specific rationale for the uplift may by no means necessarily apply (see [64], above).

[70] There is no escape from the fact, implicitly demonstrated by materials which I have already cited, that a major factor in the decision of government, indeed as I understand it successive governments, not to extend the uprate to those in Ms Carson's position has been the daunting cost of doing so. Mr Drabble roundly submitted that cost could not constitute a legitimate justification. For reasons just given I consider that this decision or decisions are objectively justified without regard to cost. But Mr Drabble's submission is of some importance, not least for its reliance on the judgment of Schiemann J as he then was in *R v Secretary of State for Education, ex p Schaffter* [1987] IRLR 53. Ms Schaffter, a single parent who had not been married, complained (relying on the European Communities Equal Treatment Directive (EEC) 76/207 (OJ 1976 L39 p 40)) that a statutory scheme for the payment of hardship grants to single parents who were studying was discriminatory in its application because the grant was only payable to students who had been married but had lost their spouse, and was not available to lone parent students who had not been married. One of the justifications put forward (though not relied on by counsel at the hearing) was the cost of any extension of the scheme. Schiemann J said (at 57 (para 33)):

'Given a constant pool of available money the question is whether it should be distributed in a discriminatory or a non-discriminatory manner. I have found the existing manner to be, *prima facie*, discriminatory. The constant pool of money could undoubtedly be distributed differently a although this would, as a matter of arithmetic, inevitably mean that those who presently qualify would have (notionally) to suffer a reduction in order to leave some over for those who do not presently qualify.'

[71] I would repudiate altogether the suggestion that this reasoning (whose force in its context I respectfully acknowledge) can have the least application in this present case. If by this court's decision the law required the Secretary of State
b to uprate the pensions of Ms Carson and others he could not, *out of the same* 'pool of money', fulfil his duty under s 150 of the 1992 Act to lay an order providing for a percentage uprate for United Kingdom resident pensioners which would compensate them for United Kingdom price inflation. New money would have to be found. Section 150, whose effect I have described at [12], above, is in
c mandatory terms. Even if it were not, faced with a duty imposed by the courts to uprate Ms Carson's pension the Secretary of State would in my judgment at least be obliged, by the ordinary requirements of public law, to *consider* whether he should find new money so as to maintain the uprate for United Kingdom resident pensioners.

d [72] In my judgment the implications of an extended uprate for the public finances are in the context of this case a legitimate factor going in justification of the Secretary of State's position. The inevitable effect of Mr Drabble's argument is that the court would order the Secretary of State to deploy public funds in a way which would require the executive to decide, in turn, how public funds should or should not be deployed or distributed in other areas which are not
e before the court to consider. I recognise, of course, that once an issue of justification under art 14 arises—the fourth question in *Wandsworth London BC v Michalak* [2002] 4 All ER 1136—the public authority which carries the burden of demonstrating that its act is justified is faced with a weighty and substantial task, and 'it is simply not enough to claim that what has been done falls within the permissible ambit of Parliament's discretion' (see *Ghaidan v Mendoza* [2002]
f EWCA Civ 1533 at [18], [2002] 4 All ER 1162 at [18], [2003] 2 WLR 478 at [18] per Buxton LJ). But I am quite unable to accept that the courts' duty under the Human Rights Act 1998 to protect and vindicate the convention rights, or the jurisprudence of the European Court of Human Rights itself, mandates so stark a judicialisation of the political function as is implied by Mr Drabble's argument.
g If the judges are to confine and circumscribe the elected government's economic policies to the tune suggested here, it could only be upon a legal imperative far more pressing than anything we have listened to in this case.

[73] I have already referred (see [62], above) to the idea of judicial deference, a term which has found its way into the argot of the cases on convention rights.
h But its utility as a measure of the relation between the courts and the other branches of government may perhaps be doubted, not least given the observations of Lord Hoffmann in R (*on the application of ProLife Alliance*) v BBC [2003] UKHL 23 at [75], [2003] 2 All ER 977 at [75], [2003] 2 WLR 1403 at [75]:

j 'My Lords, although the word "deference" is now very popular in describing the relationship between the judicial and the other branches of government, I do not think that its overtones of servility, or perhaps gracious concession, are appropriate to describe what is happening. In a society based upon the rule of law and the separation of powers, it is necessary to decide which branch of government has in any particular instance the decision-making power and what the legal limits of that power are. That is a question of law and must therefore be decided by the courts.'

I hope it is consistent with this exposition to say that the powers of the courts and the powers of the other branches of government, if they do not overlap, at least may operate in the same field; they are not marked off by walls without windows; they are in constellation with each other, so that what government may settle as policy may be qualified by the constraint of law, settled by the judges. The teaching which Lord Hoffmann's observation provides, if I may say so, is that in any particular area the decision-making power of this or that branch of government may be greater or smaller, and where the power is possessed by the legislature or executive, the role of the courts to constrain its exercise may correspondingly be smaller or greater. In the field of what may be called macro-economic policy, certainly including the distribution of public funds upon retirement pensions, the decision-making power of the elected arms of government is all but at its greatest, and the constraining role of the courts, absent a florid violation by government of established legal principles, is correspondingly modest. I conceive this approach to be wholly in line with our responsibilities under the Human Rights Act 1998. In general terms I think it reflects a recurrent theme of the Strasbourg jurisprudence, the search for a fair balance between the demands of the general interest of the community and the protection of individual rights: see *Sporrong v Sweden* (1982) 5 EHRR 35. More particularly, it chimes with what the court said in *James v UK* (1986) 8 EHRR 123 at 142 (para 46), in which a challenge brought on behalf of the Duke of Westminster to certain aspects of the leasehold enfranchisement legislation was rejected:

'... the decision to enact laws expropriating property will commonly involve consideration of political, economic and social issues on which opinions within a democratic society may reasonably differ widely. The Court, finding it natural that the margin of appreciation available to the legislature in implementing social and economic policies should be a wide one, will respect the legislature's judgment as to what is "in the public interest" unless that judgment be manifestly without reasonable foundation.'

Lastly in this context it is helpful to recall this well-known passage in the speech of Lord Hope of Craighead in *R v DPP, ex p Kebeline, R v DPP, ex p Rechachi* [1999] 4 All ER 801 at 844, [2000] 2 AC 326 at 381:

'In some circumstances it will be appropriate for the courts to recognise that there is an area of judgment within which the judiciary will defer, on democratic grounds, to the considered opinion of the elected body or person whose act or decision is said to be incompatible with the convention ... [T]he area in which these choices may arise is conveniently and appropriately described as the "discretionary area of judgment". It will be easier for such an area of judgment to be recognised where the convention itself requires a balance to be struck, much less so where the right is stated in terms which are unqualified. It will be easier for it to be recognised where the issues involve questions of social or economic policy, much less so where the rights are of high constitutional importance or are of a kind where the courts are especially well placed to assess the need for protection.'

[74] Addressing the case in the light of all these matters, I conclude that there is no consideration which remotely constitutes so powerful a legal imperative as to deny the justifications I have discussed for the government's refusal to uprate the pensions of Ms Carson and those in like case. As I read the cases, this

a conclusion is entirely in line with a consistent series of decisions in Strasbourg. I have already said (see [19], above) that the Commission in *JW v UK* (1983) 34 DR 153 rejected the applicants' complaint of violation of art 14 read with art 1P. I will at this stage do no more than set out a passage from *Corner v UK* App no 11271/84 (17 May 1985, unreported), which I have already cited (see [20], above). In that case the Commission rejected as manifestly ill-founded an argument that the

b failure to pay uprate amounted to a breach of art 14 read with art 1P:

> c '... the Commission has held that the "freezing" of a pension at a particular level when a person leaves the United Kingdom does not amount to a deprivation of possessions infringing Article 1 of the Protocol. Moreover, the different treatment of persons entitled to pensions who remain in the country of payment compared with those who emigrate is justified on the grounds that the applicant will only lose the benefit of future increases in the pension, whose purpose broadly speaking is to compensate for rises in the cost of living in the United Kingdom and which the applicant will not have to endure. The Commission also considers that the economic state of third countries is not a matter which domestic pension authorities should be obliged to consider.'

d

REYNOLDS' CASE: IS THERE AN OBJECTIVE AND REASONABLE JUSTIFICATION FOR THE DISCRIMINATION RELIED ON?

[75] Although Mr Gill has referred to and relied upon a considerable body of evidence, I can without injustice to his client deal with this question rather more

e shortly, having already set out the substance of the relevant learning. By way of preliminary I should say that although in his skeleton argument Mr Howell for the Secretary of State did not accept that recipients of benefit under age 25 were in an analogous position to those of 25 and over for the purposes of art 14, it seems to me to be plain that the real issue here is justification. In this appeal I

f would answer my compendious question—are the circumstances of X (over 25) and Y (under 25) so similar as to call (in the mind of a rational and fair-minded person) for a positive justification for the less favourable treatment of Y in comparison with X?—in the affirmative, in contrast to my answer in *Carson*'s case. The selection, for the purpose of settling differential levels of payment of state benefit, of any particular break point in terms of age is in a sense (and not a

g pejorative sense) bound to be arbitrary, if only because there will be claimants either side of the line whose circumstances do not perceptibly differ. However the depth of the justification required, the reach of the court's scrutiny of what is advanced by way of justification, is quite another matter.

[76] It should be recalled that the justification question only arises in relation

h to the payment of jobseeker's allowance to Ms Reynolds and not income support, if Simon Brown and Rix LJJ concur with my conclusion (at [49], above) as to the scope of 'possessions' for the purposes of art 1P. However it is necessary to say a little about the history of income support, because the payment of a higher amount at age 25 was first introduced in relation to that benefit, and then applied to jobseeker's allowance, which came later.

j [77] Income support replaced supplementary benefit, following proposals contained in a Green Paper entitled *Reform of Social Security* (Cmnd 9517–9519) published in June 1985. It contained these passages (Cmnd 9518 (p 23)):

> '2.72 There will be a standard personal allowance for all claimants, varied only by age and marital status. That will end the present householder/

non-householder distinction and the structural distinction between ordinary
and long-term rates. [These were features of the supplementary benefit
scheme.] These will be replaced by age-related rates.

2.73 There is no one age dividing line relevant to all claimants. But it is
clear that at the age of 18 the majority of claimants are not fully independent
and that the great majority of claimants above age 25 are. This is already in
practice reflected in the present scheme. In 1983 nearly 90 per cent of all
claimants over 25 were getting the higher householder rate. By contrast the
clear majority of claimants under 25 were living in someone else's
household. This is particularly marked for single claimants, the great
majority of whom aged between 18 and 24 presently get a lower rate of help.
The Government have concluded that an appropriate dividing line is age 25.
There will therefore be different rates for adult claimants above and below
age 25, although, as explained below, account will be taken of claimants'
family responsibilities.'

The break point at age 25 was almost immediately the subject of criticism, and
indeed in its Fourth Report the government's own Social Security Advisory
Committee stated (para 3.10): 'If an age split is thought preferable for
administrative reasons, then 25 is certainly too high.' The government accepted
that all couples aged 18 and over should receive the same rate, but declined to
change its position as regards single claimants. A White Paper was published in
December 1985 in which it was stated:

'3.13 All age-dividing lines are of course open to argument at the margin.
Nonetheless, the fact is that the great majority of single claimants without
children under 25 now live in other people's households and they already
receive a lower rate of help. Overall, four-fifths of single claimants without
children in the 18 to 24 age group get the non-householder rate. It is also
reasonable to recognise that earnings levels are generally lower for this
group than for those in older age groups. The abolition of the householder
distinction and the introduction of the 25 age point have enabled the
Government to concentrate more resources on older people—including
pensioners and disabled persons living in other people's households.'

[78] Jobseeker's allowance was heralded by a White Paper published in
October 1994 (Cm 2687). There was no mention of age-related bands in the
White Paper but when in due course the relevant legislation was presented to
Parliament, it became clear that the government intended to import into the
structure of both types of jobseeker's allowance the same break point for
differential payments as applied to income support.

[79] In a statement of 5 September 2001 made in these proceedings Mr Taylor,
section head of the Working Age Financial Support Change Branch of the
Department of Work and Pensions, has set out the Secretary of State's
explanation for the change of payment rates at age 25 (para 17):

'(1) People in the 18–24 age-group in general earn less than those 25 or
over, and may legitimately be regarded as having lower earnings
expectations.

(2) The majority of those 18–24 do not live independently and may
legitimately be regarded as having lower living costs than the group of
claimants aged 25 or over.

a
(3) The payment of lower rates of JSA and IS to those between 18–24 may be expected to have the effect of discouraging them from living independently, and encouraging them to live together with others, notably parents or other family members, which may be seen to have wider social benefits.

b
(4) Other aspects of the social security system serve to prevent any resultant hardship to the minority of persons in the position which was that of the Claimant who are aged between 18–24 and do not live independently.

(5) It is important from the point of view of good administration for the social security system to be based upon clear, easily applicable rules, rather than attempting to cater for the individual situation of every claimant.'

c
[80] Mr Gill has sought to mount a comprehensive attack upon every one of these propositions, largely through the medium of evidence from Professor Smith, Emeritus Professor of Statistics at the University of Southampton. Professor Smith sets out the five propositions, asserts that they involve 'two key concepts: (i) earnings expectations, and (ii) living independently', and then produces a wealth of statistical detail to assault, in particular, the attachment of
d
any special significance to age 25 as a break point in terms of either of his 'key concepts'.

[81] In my judgment Professor Smith's arguments and materials do not demonstrate that the selection of age 25 as the break point for an increase in the level of benefit was not an available option to a reasonable Secretary of State.
e
Their highly specific focus might lead the theorist to this or that conclusion, but is quite inapt to compel any particular view of what the broad policy should be. It is obvious (and of itself, uncontentious) that at least within limits different reasonable views might be taken as to the age at which (if any) the payable benefit should increase. No less obviously, what may be called the demographic facts—levels of earnings related to age, living alone or with parents or
f
others—differ from place to place and time to time. And it seems to me in particular that Mr Taylor's third proposition (which I assume to be of no little importance as an engine of the policy) is not really capable of being demonstrated or disproved by statistical material.

[82] Beyond these brief observations I would decline altogether to enter into
g
the minutiae of the points put forward by Mr Gill to support his case that the age break point at 25 for the purposes of the levels of payment of jobseeker's allowance is unjustified. That is not out of any disrespect for the quality of his evidence. It is because the exercise would, in my judgment, be fundamentally misconceived. Wilson J observed ([2002] All ER (D) 64 (Mar) at [28]):

h
'... I regard it as unnecessary, indeed inappropriate, for me to address the arguments presented by the defendant by way of justification for the demarcation with the degree of detail into which, drawing upon a statement of an eminent statistician as well as a host of other material, Mr Gill would have me descend. Indeed, as his enthusiastic argument proceeded, I
j
increasingly sensed the incongruity that such a debate was proceeding in court instead of in Parliament.'

I entirely agree. I have already referred (at [73], above) to *James v UK* (1986) 8 EHRR 123 and to *R v DPP, ex p Kebeline, R v DPP, ex p Rechachi* [1999] 4 All ER 801, [2000] 2 AC 326. The reasoning in the passages there cited seems to me if anything to apply with greater force here than in the *Carson* appeal. The

consequence of Mr Gill's argument would be to require the Secretary of State to
re-order the social security budget in a way whose effects, both for claimants and
for the public purse, would be quite beyond the purview of this court to predict
or control, and in any event the court has no business controlling them. The case
is even farther distant from Schiemann J's 'constant pool of available money' than
is *Carson's* case.

[83] I have referred also (see [72], above) to the judicialisation of the political
function. As I see this case, Mr Gill has for all the world invited this court to make
government policy under the pretence—for that is what I think it is—of the
vindication of convention rights. The decision of the question, in Lord
Hoffmann's language, which branch of government has in any particular instance
the decision-making power and what the legal limits of that power are, may
sometimes call up a profound constitutional challenge which the courts must be
alert to confront. But not in this case. Mr Gill's argument allots a false role to the
judge and I for one would repudiate it altogether.

[84] In my view the Secretary of State has demonstrated a perfectly reasonable
justification for the differential payments of jobseeker's allowance.

[85] I would dismiss both appeals.

RIX LJ.

[86] I agree.

SIMON BROWN LJ.

[87] I also agree.

Appeals dismissed.

Dilys Tausz   Barrister.

Bagnall v Official Receiver

[2003] EWHC 1398 (Ch)

CHANCERY DIVISION

EVANS-LOMBE J

12, 18 JUNE 2003

Bankruptcy – Discharge – Automatic discharge – Application for suspension of automatic discharge – Appeal from dismissal of bankrupt's application to strike out application to suspend automatic discharge – Power of court to make interim ex parte order suspending automatic discharge – Insolvency Act 1986, s 279(3) – Insolvency Rules 1986, rr 6.215(4), 7.4(6).

A bankrupt would have obtained an automatic discharge from his bankruptcy, pursuant to the provisions of s 279[a] of the Insolvency Act 1986, on 6 August 2002, which was three years from the date of his bankruptcy order. However, on 23 July, at the request of the trustee in bankruptcy, the Official Receiver applied for a suspension of the automatic discharge pursuant to s 279(3) on the grounds that the bankrupt had failed to fulfil his statutory obligations to give certain information to his trustee. The Official Receiver was unable to give the bankrupt 21 days' notice of the application as required by r 6.215(4)[b] of the Insolvency Rules 1986 and he applied to the district judge ex parte on 2 August for suspension of the discharge. An application under s 279(3) was governed by Ch 1 of Pt 7 of the Rules. Rule 7.4(6)[c] provided that where the case was one of urgency, the court might hear the application immediately, either with or without notice, to the other parties. The district judge ordered that the application be adjourned until 11 September 2002 to allow for service on the debtor and the trustee as prescribed by the Rules and that the automatic discharge be suspended until the substantive hearing of the application. The bankrupt's application to strike out the proceedings was dismissed. The bankrupt appealed on the ground, inter alia, that the district judge had no power to make the order of 2 August ex parte since r 6.215 had not been complied with and it contained no provision for the making of interim ex parte orders of suspension before such compliance had taken place.

Held – An application for an order was urgent within r 7.4(6) of the 1986 Rules in circumstances where, if the order were not made, the situation of the relevant parties or one of them, would irretrievably alter. The provisions of r 7.4(6) conferred power on the court to make an interim order suspending a bankrupt's automatic discharge, ex parte and before the provisions of r 6.215 had been complied with, in a case where the court could properly regard the making of such an order as urgent and where, on the balance of convenience, it was appropriate that such an order should be made. Accordingly, the district judge had power to make the order of 2 August and there was material before him upon which he could conclude that it was appropriate to do so. The prejudice to the bankrupt in the prolongation of his status as a bankrupt was outweighed by the

---

a   Section 279 is set out at [4], below

b   Rule 6.215(4) is set out at [6], below

c   Rule 7.4(6) is set out at [16], below

prejudice to the creditors in irretrievably losing the coercive effect of the
continuation of the bankruptcy, without being able, through the Official
Receiver's application, to justify and so obtain an order of suspension. The appeal
would therefore be dismissed (see [19], [20], [24], [29], below).

Notes
For the power of the court to suspend the automatic discharge of a bankrupt, see
3(2) *Halsbury's Laws* (4th edn) (2002 reissue) paras 633, 634.

    For the Insolvency Act 1986, s 279 and the Insolvency Rules 1986, rr 6.125 and
7.4, see 4 *Halsbury's Statutes* (4th edn) (1998 reissue), 945 and 3 *Halsbury's Statutory
Instruments* (2001 issue) 590, 599 respectively.

Cases referred to in judgment
First Express Ltd, Re [1992] BCLC 824.
Hardy v Focus Insurance Co Ltd [1997] BPIR 77.
Jacobs v Official Receiver [1998] 3 All ER 250, [1999] 1 WLR 619.
Official Receiver v Murjani (1 March 1995, unreported).

Appeal
Kenneth Reginald Bagnall QC, a bankrupt, appealed from the order of Deputy
District Judge Robinson in the Eastbourne County Court made pursuant to his
judgment on 30 January 2003 dismissing the bankrupt's application to strike out
the Official Receiver's application under s 279(1)(2) of the Insolvency Act 1986 to
suspend his automatic discharge from bankruptcy on the date three years from
the date of the order making him bankrupt. The facts are set out in the judgment.

The bankrupt appeared in person.
Richard Ritchie (instructed by the *Treasury Solicitor*) for the Official Receiver.

Cur adv vult

18 June 2003. The following judgment was delivered.

EVANS-LOMBE J.
    [1] This is an appeal from the order of District Judge Robinson in the
Eastbourne County Court made pursuant to a judgment given on 30 January 2003
whereby he dismissed the appellant's application to strike out the Official
Receiver's proceedings to suspend his automatic discharge from bankruptcy
which otherwise would have taken effect on 6 August 2002. In effect the
application sought the discharge of interim orders made by Deputy District
Judge Radcliffe in his bankruptcy pursuant to s 279(3) of the Insolvency Act 1986,
suspending his automatic discharge pending a full hearing of the Official Receiver's
application to suspend that discharge until the bankrupt had co-operated more
fully in the disclosure of his affairs.
    [2] The procedural history of the case may be summarised as follows. In
February 1999 a bankruptcy petition was served on the bankrupt based on a
judgment for £705,000 obtained against him by a company of which he was the
controlling director, the cause of action being his misfeasance in that capacity. In
May 1999 the bankrupt initiated proceedings to obtain an individual voluntary
arrangement with his creditors. Pursuant to those proceedings an interim order
was made on 10 June 1999 but the proceedings failed in July. A bankruptcy order
was made on 6 August 1999. Thereafter the trustee undertook inquiries into the

a extent of the assets comprised in the bankrupt's estate including examination of
the bankrupt under s 366 of the 1986 Act. That examination concluded on
12 December 2000.

[3] The bankrupt would have obtained an automatic discharge pursuant to
the provisions of s 279(1) and (2) of the 1986 Act on 6 August 2002, namely three
years from the date of the bankruptcy order. On 23 July 2002 the Official Receiver
b applied for a suspension of the automatic discharge pursuant to sub-s (3) on
grounds set out in a report of the same date filed with the court. In that report
the Official Receiver stated that he was—

> 'of the opinion that the bankrupt has failed to fulfil his obligations under
> section 333 of the Insolvency Act 1986 and that the period until his automatic
c > discharge should be suspended until such time that the bankrupt has
> complied with the requirements of the trustee in bankruptcy.'

The report stated that the Official Receiver had been asked to make this
application by the trustee for reasons set out in a letter dated 19 July 2002 from
the trustee to the Official Receiver. That letter set out a number of complaints
d by the trustee as to information relating to his estate provided by the bankrupt
and inconsistencies between the various descriptions of his estate produced by
him.

[4] Before continuing with the procedural history it is convenient at this point
to set out the relevant statutory provisions. They are:

e > '**279.** *Duration.*—(1)   Subject as follows, a bankrupt is discharged from
> bankruptcy ... (b) in any other case, by the expiration of the relevant period
> under this section.
>
> (2) That period is as follows ... (b) in any other case the period of three
> years beginning with the commencement of the bankruptcy.
f > (3) Where the court is satisfied on the application of the official receiver
> that an undischarged bankrupt in relation to whom subsection (1)(b) applies
> has failed or is failing to comply with any of his obligations under this Part
> the court may order that the relevant period under this section shall cease to
> run for such period, or until the fulfilment of such conditions (including a
> condition requiring the court to be satisfied as to any matter), as may be
g > specified in the order.'

[5] It is common ground that in order to be effective to suspend an automatic
discharge the court's order must be made before that automatic discharge takes
place, in this case 6 August 2002. Once an automatic discharge has been obtained
that discharge cannot be revoked so as to reimpose the bankruptcy (see the
h passage quoted at [21], below from the judgment of Robert Walker J in *Hardy v
Focus Insurance Co Ltd* [1997] BPIR 77 at 81).

[6] Proceedings under s 279(3) of the 1986 Act are governed by r 6.215 of the
Insolvency Rules 1986, SI 1986/1925, which provides as follows:

j > '*Application for suspension of discharge.*—(1) The following applies where
> the official receiver applies to the court for an order under section 279(3)
> (suspension of automatic discharge) ...
>
> (2) The official receiver shall with his application file a report setting out
> the reasons why it appears to him such an order should be made.
>
> (3) The court shall fix a venue for the hearing of the application and give
> notice of it to the official receiver, the trustee and the bankrupt.

(4) Copies of the official receiver's report under this Rule shall be sent by *a* him to the trustee and the bankrupt, so as to reach them at least 21 days before the date fixed for the hearing.

(5) The bankrupt may, not later than 7 days before the date of the hearing, file in court a notice specifying any statements in the official receiver's report which he intends to deny or dispute. If he gives notice under this paragraph, he shall send copies of it, not less than 4 days before the *b* date of the hearing, to the official receiver and the trustee.

(6) If on the hearing the court makes an order suspending the bankrupt's discharge, copies of the order shall be sent by the court to the official receiver, the trustee and the bankrupt.'

[7] It will be apparent from these provisions that by 23 July the Official *c* Receiver was not able to give the bankrupt the necessary 21 days' notice under r 6.215(4) before 6 August. The Official Receiver therefore applied, ex parte, to the Eastbourne County Court and obtained an order from Deputy District Judge Radcliffe on 2 August. On that application the deputy district judge ordered that the application to suspend the discharge be adjourned until 11 September 2002 *d* (to allow for service on the debtor and the trustee as prescribed by the 1986 rules). He further ordered that 'the debtor's automatic discharge be suspended until the substantive hearing of the application'.

[8] Subsequently the Official Receiver became aware that the debtor had written a letter with enclosures seeking to rebut the suggestion that he had failed to co-operate with his trustee. He was concerned, therefore, that the order of *e* 2 August had been obtained without the court being aware of the bankrupt's case. Accordingly on 7 August he wrote to the Eastbourne County Court asking that Deputy District Judge Radcliffe review his order of 2 August in the light of the contents of that letter. The Official Receiver's letter concludes with the following postscript: *f*

'I have since spoken to Edwin Coe solicitors to Mr Bagnall appraised ed (sic) them of the above course of action and they have requested (and to which I would have no objection) that the review of the order be conducted by District Judge Griggs if not possible by Deputy District Judge Radcliffe as the former dealt with the Private Examination of the debtor in December 2000.' *g*

[9] On 8 August, Deputy District Judge Radcliffe without the attendance of any of the parties reviewed his order and made the following further order:

'IT IS ORDERED THAT:
(1) Order to stand; *h*
(2) Substantive application to be heard at adjourned hearing on 11 September 2002.'

[10] On 27 August 2002 the bankrupt made an application under s 303 of the 1986 Act with which I am not concerned. On 28 August District Judge Robinson ordered— *j*

'that: The Official Receiver's application to suspend discharge and Edwin Coe's application filed on 27 August 2002 be adjourned to 11 October 2002 at 11 am at Eastbourne County Court ...'

[11] On 11 October, to which date all the outstanding applications had been adjourned, they were further adjourned. On this occasion the bankrupt attended

a and no objection was taken to the fact that his automatic discharge had been suspended.

[12] The bankrupt's application to strike out came on for hearing on 30 January 2003 when that application was dismissed. I have a brief note of District Judge Robinson's judgment but no copy of the order that he made. It is difficult to discern from the note the basis upon which the district judge decided the case.

b The Official Receiver's application to suspend the discharge was heard by District Judge Robinson on 7 March 2003 and he handed down a written judgment on 16 May. I have a copy of that judgment but again I have not seen a copy of any order that he made and I am told that none has been drawn up. The concluding paragraphs of the judgment indicate that the district judge had decided to make an order for suspension but had left for further argument the exact form that that

c order should take.

[13] It is the bankrupt's submission that Deputy District Judge Radcliffe had no power to make the order of 2 August 2002, ex parte without giving him an opportunity to be heard. Rule 6.215 of the 1986 rules governs applications under s 279(3) of the 1986 Act. That rule had not been complied with at the time the

d order was made and it contains no provision for the making of interim ex parte orders of suspension before such compliance has taken place. If this submission is correct then the further order of Deputy District Judge Radcliffe on 8 August reviewing and confirming the order of 2 August was otiose as were all subsequent proceedings on the Official Receiver's application to suspend.

e [14] The bankrupt further submits in the alternative that if there was a power in the court to make the order of 2 August then that power and its exercise constituted a breach of his right to a fair trial under art 6 of the European Convention for the Protection of Human Rights and Fundamental Freedoms 1950 (as set out in Sch 1 to the Human Rights Act 1998).

[15] I will deal with those submissions in order.

f [16] It is clear that an application under s 279(3) of the 1986 Act is governed by Ch 1 of Pt 7 of the 1986 rules. Rules 7.4(6) and 7.5 provide:

> '7.4 ... (6) Where the case is one of urgency, the court may (without prejudice to its general power to extend or abridge time limits)—(a) hear the application immediately, either with or without notice to, or the attendance
> *g* of, other parties ...
>
> 7.5 *Other hearings ex parte.*—(1) Where the relevant provisions of the Act or Rules do not require service of the application on, or notice of it to be given to, any person, the court may hear the application ex parte.
>
> (2) Where the application is properly made ex parte, the court may hear
> *h* it forthwith, without fixing a venue as required by Rule 7.4(2) ...'

[17] Rule 7.5(1) appears to have a limited operative effect, if any. It would seem to follow that where relevant provisions do not require service of an application or notice of that application to be given to a party the court is able to

j deal with it without that party being present. Its effect however may be, when read with r 7.51, to exclude any inherent power or power under the CPR for the court to hear applications ex parte other than as provided for in the 1986 rules. In any event it seems to me that r 7.5(1) is a 'sweeping up' provision supplemental to the powers conferred on the court by r 7.4(6).

[18] There does not appear to be any authority on the operation of r 7.4(6) and in particular on what constitutes a case of 'urgency' within that rule. The

obtaining of a particular order may appear urgent to the applicant but not urgent at all to persons affected by the order when made.

[19] It seems to me that whether a particular order is to be treated as urgent within r 7.4(6) is a matter for the court in deciding whether or not to make the order. An application for an order is urgent within the rule in circumstances where, if the order is not made, the situation of the relevant parties or one of them will irretrievably alter. The court will then go on to consider whether in fact to make the order on familiar principles of balance of convenience.

[20] The decision of Mr Michael Burton QC in *Jacobs v Official Receiver* [1998] 3 All ER 250, [1999] 1 WLR 619 is authority for the proposition that a court considering an application under s 279(3) of the 1986 Act may make an interim order suspending a bankrupt's automatic discharge pending a full hearing of the Official Receiver's application for such suspension. In that case, however, the order appealed from, which was upheld, was made after there had been full compliance with r 6.215 of the 1986 rules and inter partes in the sense that it was made at a preliminary hearing where the bankrupt was present and able to argue against the making of the interim order in circumstances where he had not been able to put his own evidence before the court or to challenge that of the Official Receiver. It does not appear from the report that the court considered the provisions of rr 7.4(6) or 7.5(1).

[21] In *Hardy v Focus Insurance Co Ltd* [1997] BPIR 77 Robert Walker J was dealing with a case where it was being contended that a creditor was able to bring before the court an application under s 279(3). In the course of his judgment rejecting that contention he said (at 81):

'I must now go back to consider s 279(3). It refers to the court being satisfied in relation to an undischarged bankrupt. The well-known and reliable practitioner's book *Muir Hunter on Personal Insolvency* notes at 3/129: "There seems to be no power to undo this mode of discharge, once the relevant period has expired." It seems to me that that is plainly right in a case where no application under s 279(3) has been made before the expiry of the 3-year period. If an application has been made by the official receiver, I would be very doubtful whether a bankrupt could, simply by managing to obtain an adjournment for any reason, good or bad, defeat the court's power to adjudicate on an application which had been properly launched. I am, therefore, rather doubtful about the official receiver's suggestion in his official report that, in practice, it is impossible to make an application under s 279(3) within the last 21 days before the expiration of the 3-year period because of the requirement of notice under r 6.215. I should, however, note that that view obtains at least slight support from a comment by Sir Mervyn Davies made in his judgment in *Official Receiver v Murjani* (1 March 1995, unreported), although I do not regard that expression of view as a considered part of the decision.'

[22] I have not been able to obtain a transcript of Sir Mervyn Davies' judgment in *Murjani*'s case.

[23] In *Re First Express Ltd* [1992] BCLC 824, Hoffman J was considering an application by a liquidator to discharge an order that had been made against him under s 234 of the 1986 Act, ex parte, requiring him to hand over books and records of the company in his possession to administrative receivers. He is shown as saying (at 828):

'I am firmly of the view that it was wrong for the application to be made ex parte. It is a basic principle of justice that an order should not be made against a party without giving him an opportunity to be heard. The only exception is when two conditions are satisfied. First, that giving him such an opportunity appears likely to cause injustice to the applicant, by reason either of the delay involved or the action which it appears likely that the respondent or others would take before the order can be made. Secondly, when the court is satisfied that any damage which the respondent may suffer through having to comply with the order is compensatable under the cross-undertaking or that the risk of uncompensatable loss is clearly outweighed by the risk of injustice to the applicant if the order is not made. There is, I think, a tendency among applicants to think that a calculation of the balance of advantage and disadvantage in accordance with the second condition is sufficient to justify an ex parte order. In my view, this attitude should be discouraged. One does not reach any balancing of advantage and disadvantage unless the first condition has been satisfied. The principle audi alterem partem does not yield to a mere utilitarian calculation. It can be displaced only by invoking the overriding principle of justice which enables the court to act at once when it appears likely that otherwise injustice will be caused.'

[**24**] In my judgment the provisions of r 7.4(6) of the 1986 rules confer power on the court to make an interim order suspending a bankrupt's automatic discharge, ex parte and before the provisions of r 6.215 have been complied with in a case where the court can properly regard the making of such an order as urgent and has concluded that, on the balance of convenience between the Official Receiver, as representing the interests of the creditors, and the bankrupt, it is appropriate that such an order should be made. I am satisfied that when Deputy District Judge Radcliffe made the order of suspension of 2 August 2002 he had the power to make such an order and, subject to questions arising under art 6 of the convention, there was material before him upon which he could conclude that it was appropriate for him to do so. Suspension of discharge is one of the weapons available to those administering insolvent estates to coerce a bankrupt into duly performing his duty to co-operate with the trustee in bankruptcy in realising his assets for the benefit of his creditors. Had the order of 2 August not been made this weapon would have been removed before proper consideration could take place at a full hearing of whether the Official Receiver was justified in seeking an order of suspension. The prejudice to the bankrupt in the prolongation of his status as a bankrupt in the interim was outweighed by the prejudice to the creditors in irretrievably losing the coercive effect of the continuation of the bankruptcy, without being able, through the Official Receiver's application, to justify and so obtain an order of suspension.

[**25**] In the present case Deputy District Judge Radcliffe had before him on 2 August the Official Receiver's application with appended to it the trustee's letter of 19 July. That presented a strong prima facie case that the bankrupt had failed to co-operate properly with his trustee. The bankrupt would have achieved an irreversible discharge from bankruptcy within four days. I have no evidence of whether or not it was a practical proposition to convene an interlocutory hearing which the bankrupt could attend before 6 August but I am willing to assume that it was in fact impossible to do so. It seems to me that it would have been reasonable for the district judge to assume that the interim suspension of the

discharge would not be of particularly long duration. In fact the time between
the 2 August order and the delivery of the written judgment of District Judge
Robinson on 23 May 2003 was approximately nine months, of which two-and-
a-half months was the period between the hearing of the Official Receiver's
application and the handing down of the written judgment. To some extent at
least, that delay was within the control of the bankrupt in pressing for speedy
preparation and an early hearing date for the Official Receiver's application.

[26] The bankrupt's alternative argument is that the making of the 2 August
order by Deputy District Judge Radcliffe constituted a breach of his rights under
art 6 of the convention guaranteeing a right to fair trial. If this submission were
correct it would require the court to construe the relevant statutory provisions so
as to find that the court had no power to grant an interim order of suspension of
discharges in bankruptcy ex parte. Since it is clearly established by authority that
interlocutory orders of the court, pending a full hearing at which the rights of the
complainant are to be determined finally, do not result in a breach of art 6, even
if originally made ex parte, it seems to me that this alternative submission fails.
Even though the original order was made ex parte it was open to the bankrupt to
apply at any time subsequently to discharge it which is what in effect he has done.
The interim order had the effect of depriving the bankrupt of his right to be
discharged on 6 August 2002. In that sense it was determinative of a right of the
bankrupt. However, at that date, that right to be discharged was already under
challenge by the Official Receiver and defeasible if, as turned out to be the case,
the Official Receiver made good his case for suspension. In my view the fact that
the ex parte hearing of 2 August resulted in an order affecting the status of the
bankrupt does not make any difference to the applicability of art 6.

[27] The bankrupt pursued a second separate appeal based on a construction
of the two orders of 2 and 8 August 2002. The bankrupt contends that the effect
of the order of 8 August is to make the suspension of the discharge until a
substantive hearing of the Official Receiver's application a suspension only until
the date fixed by the 8 August order for that hearing, namely 11 September 2002.
Thus, if correct, the bankrupt achieved his discharge on that date.

[28] I need only to say that it seems to me these contentions are misconceived.
The terms of the 8 August order cannot be read as altering the final paragraphs of
the order of 2 August, indeed it confirms them.

[29] For these reasons these appeals must be dismissed.

Appeal dismissed.

Victoria Parkin   Barrister.

a # Glen and others v Korean Airlines Co Ltd
[2003] EWHC 643 (QB)

QUEEN'S BENCH DIVISION

SIMON J

b 17, 18, 28 MARCH 2003

Air traffic – Aircraft – Damage caused by aircraft – Statutory provision imposing strict liability for 'material loss or damage' caused by aircraft to person on land 'as if the loss or damage had been caused by the wilful act, neglect, or default' of aircraft owner –
c *Whether 'material loss or damage' limited to physical loss or damage – Whether recovery under statute subject to common law rules as to category of persons entitled to recover – Civil Aviation Act 1982, ss 76(2), 105.*

An aircraft of the defendant airline crashed at a site near to where the claimants lived. They issued proceedings to recover damages for psychiatric injury
d allegedly caused by seeing or hearing the crash and the events following it. The claimants relied on s 76(2)[a] of the Civil Aviation Act 1982 which provided, inter alia, that where 'material loss or damage' was caused to any person on land by an aircraft while in flight, taking off or landing, damages in respect of the 'loss or damage' were recoverable without proof of negligence or intention 'as if the loss or damage had been caused by the wilful act, neglect or default of the owner of
e the aircraft'. Section 76(2) was a re-enactment of a provision found in earlier statutes going back to the Air Navigation Act 1920, save that the 1920 Act had referred to 'material damage or loss' rather than 'material loss or damage'. The words 'damage or loss' had not been defined in the 1920 Act, but s 105[b] of the 1982 Act defined 'loss or damage' as including 'personal injury'. In its defence, the
f airline contended that claims for psychiatric injury were not recoverable under s 76(2) and that, if they were recoverable, they were limited to those categories of primary or secondary victims who would be entitled to recover damages in negligence for such injuries. The master ordered a trial of three preliminary issues, namely (i) whether 'material loss or damage' in s 76(2) was limited to
g physical loss or damage; (ii) whether 'personal injury' for the purposes of s 105 included mental injury where that injury was evidence of structural changes to the brain and/or central nervous system; and (iii) whether, if damages were otherwise recoverable under s 76(2), such recovery was subject to the common law rules as to categories of person who could recover damages.

h **Held** – The words 'loss or damage' in s 76(2) of the 1982 Act, as interpreted by s 105 of the Act, were wide enough to permit recovery for psychiatric or mental loss or damage. Psychiatric injury was a recognised form of personal injury in 1982, and the word 'material' would have been an inapt choice of word if there had been an intention to limit recovery to physical or bodily loss or damage. Even
j if the words 'material damage or loss' in the 1920 Act had been restricted to physical or bodily damage or loss, that meaning had not remained fixed in all subsequent enactments. Rather, the 1982 Act and its predecessors were 'always speaking' statutes, and the 1982 Act should be construed in the light of

---

a   Section 76, so far as material, is set out at [6], below
b   Section 105, so far as material, is set out at [7], below

contemporary circumstances. It followed that 'personal injury' in s 105 was not
to be treated as bodily injury, and that the 'loss or damage' referred to in s 76(2)
was not limited to physical loss or damage. However, the words 'as if the loss or
damage had been caused by the wilful act, neglect or default of the owner of the
aircraft' limited the categories of person that were entitled to recover under
s 76(2) to those who would be able to recover at common law. The effect of
s 76(2) was that the claimant was absolved from having to show either a
deliberate act or carelessness. In that context, 'wilful act' meant a deliberate act
and not 'intentional wrongdoing'. On that basis, there was no reason why the
normal rules of remoteness and foreseeability should not apply. Accordingly, the
questions set out in the preliminary issues would be answered as follows:
issue (i) No; issue (ii) Yes; and issue (iii) Yes (see [14], [16], [18], [20], [33]–[35],
[37], [39], [40], below).

    R v Ireland, R v Burstow [1997] 4 All ER 225 considered.

Notes
For statutory liability for material loss or damage caused by an aircraft to persons
on land and for common law liability for psychiatric injury, see respectively 2(3)
Halsbury's Laws (4th edn reissue) para 1109 and 33 *Halsbury's Laws* (4th edn
reissue) para 612.

    For the Civil Aviation Act 1982, ss 76, 105, see 4 *Halsbury's Statutes* (4th edn)
(1998 reissue) 178, 211.

Cases referred to in judgment
Morris v KLM Royal Dutch Airlines, King v Bristow Helicopters Ltd [2002] UKHL 7,
    [2002] 2 All ER 565, [2002] 2 AC 628, [2002] 2 WLR 578.
Pepper (Inspector of Taxes) v Hart [1993] 1 All ER 42, [1993] AC 593, [1992] 3 WLR
    1032, HL.
R v Ireland, R v Burstow [1997] 4 All ER 225, [1998] AC 147, [1997] 3 WLR 534, HL.
Royal College of Nursing of the UK v Dept of Health and Social Security [1981] 1 All ER
    545, [1981] AC 800, [1981] 2 WLR 279, QBD, CA and HL.
Steel-Maitland v British Airways Board 1981 SLT 110, Ct of Sess (OH).
White v Chief Constable of the South Yorkshire Police [1999] 1 All ER 1, [1999] 2 AC
    455, [1998] 2 WLR 1509, HL.
Wilkinson v Downton [1897] 2 QB 57, [1895–9] All ER Rep 267.

Cases also cited or referred to in skeleton arguments
A-G of the Province of Alberta v Huggard Assets Ltd [1953] 2 All ER 951, [1953] AC 420,
    [1952] 2 WLR 768, PC.
Allen v Gulf Oil Refining Ltd [1981] 1 All ER 353, [1981] AC 1001, [1981] 2 WLR 188, HL.
Canterbury City Council v Colley [1993] 1 All ER 591, [1993] AC 401, [1993] 2 WLR
    254, HL.
Fellowes (or Herd) v Clyde Helicopters Ltd [1997] 1 All ER 775, [1997] AC 534, [1997]
    2 WLR 380, HL.
Hay or Bourhill v Young [1942] 2 All ER 396, [1943] AC 92, HL.
Leith v Medhurst [1991] 2 VR 362, Vict SC.
London Brighton and South Coast Rly Co v Truman (1885) 11 App Cas 45, [1881–5]
    All ER Rep 134, HL.
R v Chan-Fook [1994] 2 All ER 552, [1994] 1 WLR 689, CA.
Sidhu v British Airways plc, Abnett (known as Sykes) v British Airways plc [1997] 1 All ER
    193, [1997] AC 430, [1997] 2 WLR 26, HL.
Stock v Frank Jones (Tipton) Ltd [1978] 1 All ER 948, [1978] 1 WLR 231, HL.

Preliminary issues

a By order of Master Whitaker made on 25 November 2002, the court was required to determine three preliminary issues, summarised at [4], below, in proceedings for recovery of damages for psychiatric injury brought by the claimants, Leonard James Glen, Nicholas Glen, Sarah Glen, Marc William Glen, Philippa Anne Glen, Carole Morris, Amanda Jane Spruce, Remy Amanda Spruce, Rhea Dawn Miller,

b Alison Howard-McLennan, Brian Howard-McLennan, Philippa Howard-McLennan and Daniel Patching, against the defendant, Korean Airlines Co Ltd. The facts are set out in the judgment.

Philip Shepherd (instructed by *Leigh Day & Co*, Manchester) for the claimants.
Charles Pugh and *Ben Cooper* (instructed by *Beaumont and Son*) for the defendant.

c
Cur adv vult

28 March 2003. The following judgment was delivered.

d **SIMON J.**

BACKGROUND

[1] In this action the claimants claim damages for personal injury, loss and damage arising out of the crash of the defendant's Boeing 747-2B5F aircraft, registration HL-7451 (the aircraft) on 22 December 1999.

e [2] The aircraft had arrived at Stansted Airport at 15.05 hrs from Tashkent. At 18.36 hrs it took off from runway 23/05 bound for Malpensa Airport, Milan, as Flight KAL 8509. According to the load sheet, the aircraft's weight for take-off was 548,352 lbs, which included 68,300 lbs of fuel. After take-off the aircraft maintained a track close to the extended runway line before turning left.

f According to the Stansted Watchman radar it reached a maximum altitude of 2,460 ft amsl (above mean sea level) and a maximum speed calculated as 228 knots. The aircraft then descended, flying low until, at 18.38 hrs, it crashed into the Hatfield Forest at a position 1.9 nautical miles from the centre point of the runway on a bearing of 204° (the crash site).

[3] The claimants all lived near the crash site at Great Hallingbury in

g Hertfordshire. On 21 December 2001 they began the present action. The claimants rely on s 76(2) of the Civil Aviation Act 1982. This section provides (in broad summary) that, where an aircraft crashes causing loss or damage to those on the ground, they may recover without the need to prove negligence. It is common ground that s 76(2) creates a statutory tort. However, in paras 5–6 of its

h defence, the defendant contends that the right to recover under s 76(2) is limited in two ways. First, claims for psychiatric injury are not recoverable and, secondly, if they are recoverable they are limited to those categories of primary or secondary victims who would be entitled to recover damages in negligence for such injuries.

j PRELIMINARY ISSUES

[4] On 25 November 2002 Master Whitaker ordered the trial of three preliminary issues in relation to s 76(2) of the 1982 Act. These issues can conveniently be expressed as follows: (1) whether 'material loss or damage', referred to in s 76(2), is limited to 'physical loss or damage'; (2) whether 'personal injury', in s 105 of the 1982 Act, includes mental injury where the mental injury is evidence of structural changes to the brain and/or central nervous system;

(3) whether, if damages are otherwise recoverable under s 76(2), such recovery is subject to the common law rules as to categories of people who may recover damages?

[5] For the purposes of the preliminary issue it is assumed that the crash occurred, that all the claimants witnessed the crash and the events following the crash either seeing them or hearing them and that, as a result of such experiences the claimants suffered sustained psychiatric injury.

THE 1982 ACT

[6] Section 76 of the 1982 Act is in the following terms:

'(1) No action shall lie in respect of trespass or in respect of nuisance, by reason only of the flight of an aircraft over any property at a height above the ground which, having regard to wind, weather and all the circumstances of the case is reasonable, or the ordinary incidents of such flight, so long as the provisions of any Air Navigation Order and of any orders under section 62 above have been duly complied with and there has been no breach of section 81 below.

(2) Subject to subsection (3) below, where material loss or damage is caused to any person or property on land or water by, or by a person in, or an article, animal or person falling from, an aircraft while in flight, taking off or landing, then unless the loss or damage was caused or contributed to by the negligence of the person by whom it was suffered, damages in respect of the loss or damage shall be recoverable without proof of negligence or intention or other cause of action, as if the loss or damage had been caused by the wilful act, neglect, or default of the owner of the aircraft.'

The terms of s 76(3) are not relevant to the preliminary issue.

[7] The general interpretation provisions of the 1982 Act are set out in s 105(1). This provides: 'In this Act, except where the context otherwise requires ... "loss or damage" includes, in relation to persons, loss of life and personal injury ...'

[8] The broad intent of s 76 is that: (1) provided aircraft comply with certain specified criteria, they will not be susceptible to claims for trespass and nuisance when they over-fly property; and (2) a freestanding right to claim damages arises where loss and damage has been caused to persons or property by the crash of an aircraft or by objects propelled from an aircraft in flight.

THE STATUTORY HISTORY

[9] The words of s 76(1) and (2) of the 1982 Act were originally enacted as s 9 of the Air Navigation Act 1920. The 1920 Act was described as: 'An Act to enable effect to be given to a Convention for regulating Air Navigation, and to make further provision for the control and regulation of aviation.' As this description suggests, there were two parts to the 1920 Act. Pt I created the power to apply the 1919 Paris Convention Relating to the Regulation of Air Navigation (Paris, 13 October 1919; UK TS 2 (1922); Cmd 1609), which had determined uniform rules with respect to air navigation. Pt II (in which s 9 appeared) was intended in the words of the preamble to control and regulate the navigation of aircraft within the jurisdiction.

[10] The relevant words in the 1920 Act were 'material damage or loss' and there was no definition of the words 'damage or loss'. A definition of those words was introduced by s 34(3) of the Air Navigation Act 1936. This provided, that the

a expression 'damage or loss' in s 9 of the 1920 Act included 'in relation to persons, loss of life and personal injury'.

[11] The words 'damage' and 'loss' were transposed to 'loss or damage' in the Civil Aviation Act 1949, which repealed and replaced the 1920 Act. The words 'loss or damage' were defined in s 63(3) of the 1949 Act. 'For the avoidance of doubt it is hereby declared that in this Act the expression "loss or damage" includes in relation to persons, loss of life and personal injury.'

b [12] The 1982 Act, to which I have already referred, was expressed to be 'An Act to consolidate certain enactments relating to civil aviation'.

[13] Two points arise from the statutory history. First, since the 1982 Act was a consolidation act, on normal principles of statutory construction, the words of the 1982 Act are to be treated as having the same meaning as they had in earlier c enactments. Secondly, the words of s 76(2) do not derive from an international convention. It follows that the court is not searching for 'a common construction' or an interpretation that is required to be consistent with the interpretation in the jurisdictions of other countries. The court's task in the present case is in contrast to the task faced by the House of Lords in *Morris v KLM Royal Dutch Airlines, King v* d *Bristow Helicopters Ltd* [2002] UKHL 7, [2002] 2 All ER 565, [2002] 2 AC 628 where the House was construing a provision of an international convention: art 17 of the Warsaw Convention 1929, incorporated into English law as Sch 1 to the Carriage by Air Act 1961.

ISSUE 1: THE CONSTRUCTION OF SECTION 76(2) OF THE 1982 ACT

e [14] If one is looking at the words 'loss or damage' in s 76(2), as interpreted by s 105 of the 1982 Act, it is my view that the words are wide enough to include psychiatric injury. First, psychiatric injury was a recognised form of personal injury in 1982. Secondly, the parties have not been able to find any statutes where 'personal injury' is defined as excluding mental impairment. Thirdly, it is difficult f to see why Parliament should have intended to exclude psychiatric injury from recoverable loss in a 1982 statute.

[15] In *Morris v KLM* [2002] 2 All ER 565 at [17] Lord Steyn drew a distinction between the restrictive words 'bodily injury' and the wider usage 'personal injury':

g 'In this context it is reasonable to expect that if it had been intended to cover mental injury or illness, it would have been provided for expressly. In the absence of such an express reference it is reasonable to interpret "bodily injury" and "lésion corporelle" as words of restriction, ie as referring to non-fatal injury which is physical rather than mental: contrast *the wide term* "personal injury" in the Guatemala Protocol which never came into force …'
h (My emphasis.)

The context that Lord Steyn was referring to was, (1) the fact that mental injury was not the subject of compensation in many of the contracting states at the time of the Warsaw Convention, and (2) the large number of circumstances implicit in air travel which might give rise to claims by passengers for mental injury: from j in-flight turbulence to delayed gate departure due to mechanical problems with aircraft. So far as the second point is concerned, the circumstances giving rise to a claim under s 76(2) are, fortunately, uncommon. I was told that this is the first case in which it has been necessary to decide the present point.

[16] Mr Pugh (counsel for the defendant) submits that the determination of this issue depends on the proper construction of the word 'material'. He submits that, in its 1920 context, the word means 'physical or bodily' damage or loss to

the exclusion of mental or physical damage or loss. He accepts that, looking at the matter in 1982, the word 'material' would not be used to mean 'physical' damage; but he submits that, once the word acquired that meaning, it was preserved in succeeding statutes, subject to one qualification. The qualification is that, if the 1982 Act and its legislative predecessors were 'always speaking' statutes, then the 1982 Act should be construed in the light of contemporary circumstances.

[17] Mr Shepherd (counsel for the claimants) relied on another meaning of the word 'material', as meaning 'legally significant' or 'relevant'.

[18] Looking at the terms of ss 76 and 105 of the 1982 Act as a whole, it is my view that the statutory tort in s 76(2) is drawn in sufficiently wide terms to permit the recovery of psychiatric or mental loss or damage. The word 'material' would have been an inapt choice of word to use if the intention had been to limit recovery to physical or bodily loss or damage.

[19] The proper interpretation of the 1920 Act is more problematic. There was no definition of 'damage or loss' until 1936. 'Material' in its context might mean 'legally significant' or 'relevant'; but, if this were so, it would be necessary to identify the contrast that is being drawn. If no contrast is being drawn then it seems to me that Mr Pugh is correct in his submission that the word 'material' would be superfluous. It may be that the draftsman was seeking to exclude disturbance and inconvenience damage from s 76(2). However, if that was the intention then it was clumsily executed since, as Mr Pugh submitted, s 76(1) and (2) of the 1982 Act are dealing with discrete issues. Section 76(1) is dealing with a limitation on a common law right to sue in nuisance and trespass, whereas s 76(2) is dealing with a self-standing statutory tort.

[20] Despite this uncertainty, I am prepared to assume for the purposes of the defendant's argument that they are right in their submission that the 'material damage or loss' in the 1920 Act meant physical or bodily damage or loss. The issue then is whether that meaning remained fixed in all subsequent enactments so as to provide the key to the proper construction of the 1982 Act.

[21] The defendant's submit that, since the statutory words in s 76(2) of the 1982 Act date back in substantially identical form to the 1920 Act, they should be taken to have retained the same meaning as they had in the 1920 Act. In advancing this submission Mr Pugh drew a distinction between statutes whose meaning is fixed and statutes that are, to use the infelicitous but well-established phrase, 'always speaking'.

[22] It is common ground that it is a principle of statutory construction that the meaning of statutes is not immutable and fixed, and that Acts must be construed in the light of contemporary circumstances, see *Morris v KLM* [2002] 2 All ER 565 at [25] per Lord Steyn and *Bennion on Statutory Interpretation* (4th edn, 2002) p 762. This principle is subject to an exception where the court concludes that, on proper analysis, the words of the Act were intended to be of unchanging effect.

[23] The general principle was described in the speech of Lord Steyn in *R v Ireland, R v Burstow* [1997] 4 All ER 225 at 233, [1998] AC 147 at 158:

'Bearing in mind that statutes are usually intended to operate for many years it would be most inconvenient if courts could never rely in difficult cases on the current meaning of statutes. Recognising the problem Lord Thring, the great Victorian draftsman of the second half of the last century, exhorted draftsmen to draft so that "An Act of Parliament should be deemed

a

to be always speaking" (see *Practical Legislation* (1902) p 83; see also Cross *Statutory Interpretation* (3rd edn, 1995) p 51 and Pearce and Geddes *Statutory Interpretation in Australia* (4th edn, 1996) pp 90–93).'

Lord Steyn (with whom the other members of the House of Lords agreed) set out how a court approaches the question as to whether a particular statute is within the general principle or the exception:

b

'In cases where the problem arises it is a matter of interpretation whether a court must search for the historical or original meaning of a statute or whether it is free to apply the current meaning of the statute to present day conditions. Statutes dealing with a particular grievance or problem may sometimes require to be historically interpreted. But the drafting technique of Lord Thring and his successors has brought about the situation that statutes will generally be found to be of the "always speaking" variety (see *Royal College of Nursing of the UK v Dept of Health and Social Security* [1981] 1 All ER 545, [1981] AC 800 for an example of an "always speaking" construction in the House of Lords).'

c

d

[24] In *R v Ireland,* the House of Lords treated the Offences against the Person Act 1861 as an 'always speaking' statute, and held that the words 'bodily harm' covered recognised psychiatric injury. As Lord Steyn said:

e

'The proposition that the Victorian legislator when enacting ss 18, 20 and 47 of the 1861 Act, would not have had in mind psychiatric illness is no doubt correct. Psychiatry was in its infancy in 1861. But the subjective intention of the draftsman is immaterial. The only relevant inquiry is as to the sense of the words in the context in which they are used. Moreover the 1861 Act is a statute of the "always speaking" type: the statute must be interpreted in the light of the best current scientific appreciation of the link between the body and psychiatric injury.' (See [1997] 4 All ER 225 at 233, [1998] AC 147 at 158–159.)

f

Developments in scientific understanding are not the only criteria for interpreting 'always speaking' statutes. Other changes in social conditions, technology, medical knowledge and in the meaning of particular words, may all affect the interpretation.

g

[25] Lord Steyn identified statutes dealing with a particular grievance or problem as requiring a fixed or 'historical interpretation'; but there are other types of statute that may call for this 'historical interpretation': for example, where the statute is in the nature of a contract or implements an international convention, see *Bennion* pp 779–780.

h

[26] In the present case, the defendant submits: (1) that the 1982 Act and its predecessors represented 'a trade-off between landowners and air carriers'; (2) such a trade-off was in the nature of a contract; and (3) the court should adopt an historical interpretation and should not adopt a construction which opens up an entirely new area of liability which cannot have been intended in 1920.

j

[27] In support of the first and second submission, the defendant relied on ministerial speeches reported in Hansard in the debate on the second reading of the bill; and submitted that these speeches were admissible as an aid to construction on the principle established by *Pepper (Inspector of Taxes) v Hart* [1993] 1 All ER 42, [1993] AC 593. That case relaxed the rule that excluded reference to parliamentary history as an aid to statutory construction. However,

Lord Oliver of Alymerton ([1993] 1 All ER 42 at 52, [1993] AC 593 at 620) made
clear that the relaxation of the rule was to be confined: *a*

> 'It is, however, important to stress the limits within which such a
> relaxation is permissible ... It can apply only where the expression of the
> legislative intention is genuinely ambiguous or obscure or where a literal or
> prima facie construction leads to a manifest absurdity and where the
> difficulty can be resolved by a clear statement directed to the matter in issue. *b*
> Ingenuity can sometimes suggest ambiguity or obscurity where none exists
> in fact, and, if the instant case were to be thought to justify the exercise of
> combing through reports of parliamentary proceedings in the hope of
> unearthing some perhaps incautious expression of opinion in support of an
> improbable secondary meaning, the relaxation of the rule might indeed lead *c*
> to the fruitless expense and labour which has been prayed in aid in the past
> as one of the reasons justifying its maintenance.'

On this basis reference to the parliamentary history can only be made where
there is genuine ambiguity, obscurity or potential absurdity; but, even in such
cases, only if parliamentary proceedings clearly disclose the legislative intention *d*
behind the ambiguous or obscure words (see also Lord Browne-Wilkinson [1993]
1 All ER 42 at 64, [1993] AC 593 at 634).

[28] Mr Pugh recognised that his reason for referring to the parliamentary
history was not to resolve ambiguity or obscurity; but rather to demonstrate that
the 1920 Act was in the nature of a bargain or contract so that its interpretation
was to be treated as fixed as at 1920. I am doubtful whether references to *e*
parliamentary proceedings is permissible for this purpose; but, in any event,
references to the debates on the 1920 Act do not support his submissions.

[29] The Secretary of State for Air (Mr WS Churchill MP) and the Under-
Secretary (Lord Londonderry) described the intention of the relevant part of the
bill as being the reconciliation of the rights of landowners in the super-incumbent *f*
air with the practical necessities of civil aviation. The reconciliation was to be
achieved by laying down the principle that no action would lie for aerial trespass
or nuisance simply by reason of the aerial flight through the column of air; but
that, where damage was done to any persons on the ground, the owner of the
offending aircraft would be liable without forcing the injured person to prove
negligence. *g*

[30] Two points should be noticed. First, a close examination of the ministerial
speeches shows that they were not giving particularly close attention to the
language they used; and what they said amounted to little more than a summary
of s 9 of the 1920 Act. No ambiguity or obscurity is resolved by reference to these
debates. Secondly and importantly, the parliamentary history does not establish *h*
a 'trade-off' or contract between landowners and air carriers. The ministers told
Parliament that the legislative intent was to reconcile potentially conflicting
rights. This is a commonplace legislative intent. In the modern world there will
frequently be a need to reconcile potentially conflicting interests; but this broad
legislative intent cannot bring a statute outside the general category of 'always *j*
speaking' Acts.

[31] Before leaving this point it is necessary to refer to an authority and a
textbook which the defendant relies on in support of this part of its argument. In
Steel-Maitland v British Airways Board 1981 SLT 110, the pursuer brought a claim
against various air carriers for physical damage allegedly caused to Gogar Castle
from over-flying aircraft. The case came before the Lord Ordinary (Lord Jauncey)

a   on an application to dismiss the pursuer's pleas. Those pleas included the plea
that, in view of s 40(1) of the 1949 Act (the equivalent of s 76(1) of the 1982 Act),
the pursuer could only have a claim under s 40(2) (the equivalent of s 76(2) of the
1982 Act); and that a claim under s 40(2) only applied to single instances of
damage and not to cumulative damage. The Lord Ordinary rejected that
contention and, in doing so, observed:

b   'In *McNair's Law of the Air* (3rd ed.), p 107, it is stated with reference to the
       two sub-sections of s 40 that "they represent a compromise or bargain which
       can be summed up as establishing no liability for technical legal injury (if
       any), but absolute liability for actual material injury". This statement in my
       view accurately summarises the effect of the two subsections. What the
c   section intended to achieve was the removal of certain activities from the
       realm of common law nuisance or trespass if they only resulted in
       disturbance or inconvenience but to afford to an aggrieved person a remedy,
       at least as effective as his abolished common law remedy in respect of the
       same activities if they caused material damage to him or his property.'

d   The 3rd edition of *McNair on the Law of the Air* was edited by Mr Michael Kerr QC
and Mr Anthony Evans (as then they were).
      [**32**] It is to be noted that, although reference is made to 'a compromise or
bargain', the contrast which is drawn is between aerial activities that caused
'technical legal injury' or 'disturbance and inconvenience' on the one hand, and
'actual material injury' on the other. Although these sources support the view
e   that disturbance and inconvenience damages are irrecoverable, they do not
directly assist the defendant in its contention that there was a bargain or contract
which precluded an award of damages in respect of psychiatric injury. There is
also a further and more general point that militates against treating statutes as
requiring a fixed or historical interpretation. Although the court may feel
f   confident in construing statutory language according to current meanings of the
words used, the search for historical or original meanings may prove more
elusive and require rather more than a dictionary based on historical principles.

CONCLUSION ON ISSUE 1
      [**33**] I have therefore concluded that the 'loss or damage' referred to in s 76(2)
g   of the 1982 Act is not limited to 'physical loss or damage' and (subject to my
conclusions on issue 3) includes psychiatric injury.

ISSUE 2: THE MEANING OF 'PERSONAL INJURY' IN SECTION 105 OF THE 1982 ACT
      [**34**] This matter is largely covered by my conclusions on issue 1, since I have
h   (implicitly) rejected the defendant's submission that 'personal injury' in s 105 of
the 1982 Act is to be treated as 'bodily injury'. But in any event, the defendant
very properly accepted that, in the light of the majority opinion in *Morris v KLM,*
a person can recover on the basis of a bodily injury if that person can establish that
the mental injury is evidence of structural change to the brain or central nervous
system.
j

ISSUE 3: WHETHER THE LOSS AND DAMAGE RECOVERABLE UNDER SECTION 76(2) IS
LIMITED TO DAMAGES RECOVERABLE AT COMMON LAW?
      [**35**] The defendant submits: (1) that, if personal injury in s 76(2) of the 1982
Act covers psychiatric injury, the words '*as if* the loss and damage had been
caused by the wilful act, neglect, or default of the owner of the aircraft' (my
emphasis) limits the categories of people who can recover damages in respect of

such injuries; (2) that, if negligence were proved, the law would restrict the
categories of persons who can recover damages in respect of psychiatric injury,
see for example *White v Chief Constable of the South Yorkshire Police* [1999] 1 All ER
1 at 41, 43, [1999] 2 AC 455 at 502, 504–505; (3) on this approach, the claimants
can only recover damages for psychiatric injury if they are primary victims or
secondary victims with sufficient proximity and ties of love and affection.

[36] The claimants submit that: (1) this approach places too much emphasis
on the word 'neglect' and ignores the other words in the phrase, in particular
'wilful act'; (2) there is no reason to restrict the right to recover damages for this
statutory tort on the basis of rules relating to the recovery of damages for
negligence; and (3) by referring to 'wilful act' the 1982 Act treats the defendant's
act as if it were the deliberate infliction of injury, see *Wilkinson v Downton* [1897]
2 QB 57, [1895–9] All ER Rep 267.

[37] I accept the defendant's submissions on this issue. Where there is damage
to land and an action for trespass the claimant would have to show an intentional
or wilful act of trespass. Where there is injury to a person, there might be an
action in negligence; and the claimant would have to show carelessness. In my
view, the effect of s 76(2) is that the claimant is absolved from having to show
either a deliberate act or carelessness. In this context, 'wilful act' means a
deliberate act and not 'intentional wrongdoing'. On this basis I can see no reason
why the normal rules as to foreseeability and remoteness should not apply.

[38] I am reinforced in this conclusion by three further points. First, as the
defendant points out, if the claimants' construction were correct, then there
would be potentially two different approaches to the recoverability of damages
(one arising from a 'wilful act', and the other from 'neglect or default') without
any statutory indication as to which approach applies in any particular case. This
is an inherently unlikely legislative intention. Secondly, the conclusion I have
reached is more easy to reconcile with the reference to contributory negligence.
Thirdly, if claimants can always proceed on the basis that there has been an
intentional wrongdoing as if there had been a deliberate assault, then they could
recover damages for injury to feelings, see *McGregor on Damages* (16th edn, 1997)
para 1844. This too seems an inherently unlikely legislative intention.

[39] It follows that I find that the answer to issue 3 is that loss or damage is
only recoverable under s 76(2) if such loss or damage would be recoverable at
common law.

CONCLUSION
[40] I therefore answer the questions set out in the preliminary issue as
follows:

Issue 1: No
Issue 2: Yes
Issue 3: Yes.

Order accordingly.

Aaron Turpin   Barrister.

Sayers and others v Merck SmithKline Beecham plc and others
X and others v Schering Health Care Ltd
Afrika and others v Cape plc
[2001] EWCA Civ 2017

COURT OF APPEAL, CIVIL DIVISION
MUMMERY, BUXTON AND LONGMORE LJJ
5, 6, 21 DECEMBER 2001

Costs – Order for costs – Cost-sharing order – Multi-party actions – Amendment of order – Whether cost-sharing order should provide for costs of common issues to follow determination of common issues – Whether cost-sharing order should provide for liability for common costs for discontinuing or settling claimants to be determined at trial of common issues – CPR 48.6A.

In three separate multi-party actions, cost-sharing orders were made under CPR 48.6A, a provision which related to costs where group litigation orders had been made. Each order, inter alia, defined 'individual costs' as those incurred in respect of any individual claimant in relation to matters which were personal to that claimant, excluding any costs incurred in respect of claims selected as lead cases; defined 'common costs' as all costs other than individual costs; and provided: (i) that common costs incurred in any quarter by claimants and defendants were to be divided by the number of claimants pursuing their claims on the first day of the quarter; (ii) that a claimant compromising his claim in any quarter on terms which provided for a defendant to pay his costs would be entitled to recover his individual costs and his share of the common costs incurred by the claimants up to the last day of that quarter; and (iii) that a claimant discontinuing his claim in any quarter (or where his claim was dismissed by order of the court under which the claimant was ordered to pay a defendant's costs) would be liable for his individual costs and his share of the common costs incurred by the defendant up to the last day of that quarter. The claimants appealed against each cost-sharing order and requested: (i) the insertion of a provision that the order for payment of common costs between the parties following any trial of the common issues whether by trial of the lead actions or otherwise should follow the event and not depend upon the outcome of individual cases or of issues individual to the lead actions; and (ii) the substitution of the provisions for costs in the case of compromise or discontinuance by a provision that in the event of any claimant discontinuing or settling his action any liability for common costs should be determined at the trial of the common issues in the lead actions.

Held – (1) While it was likely that, if common issues were directed to be tried, the costs of those issues would be ordered to follow the determination of those issues rather than await the individual fate of each claimant's action, it would be wrong to say at the outset that that should be the presumptive position. The court should be free to make whatever appeared to be the appropriate order in the circumstances. Accordingly, in so far as they sought a costs order by reference to the determination of common issues, the claimants' appeals would be dismissed (see [15], below).

(2) Claimants who settled their cases did not usually need any presumptive order as to the incidence of costs since costs would be part of the discussion leading to settlement in any event. If there were an agreement that any defendant was to pay any claimant's costs, then the existing terms of the order were entirely appropriate. Accordingly, there was no reason to interfere with that part of the order (see [16], below).

(3) In group actions certain common or generic issues would be tried on their own, before it was possible or sensible to apply the results to individual claimants. There were many different reasons why claimants might decide to leave the group once the action had started. To have a prima facie rule that any discontinuing claimant should have a crystallised inability to recover common costs and a potential liability for the common costs of defendants as at the end of the quarter in which he discontinued was too blunt an instrument and was unnecessarily favourable to defendants at a time when it would be unknown whether the claimants as a whole would be successful in the common issues which were to be tried. It was more sensible and more consonant with justice that both the recoverability of common costs and the liability (if any) of discontinuing claimants for costs of common issues should be determined at the same time as orders for common costs were made in respect of those common issues. The court then would have a full picture and could make whatever order was just in all the circumstances. Accordingly, in so far as they related to discontinuing claimants, the orders would be amended as sought by the claimants. To that extent, the appeals would be allowed (see [19], [20], [28], below).

Notes

For costs where the court has made a group litigation order, see 10 *Halsbury's Laws* (4th edn) (2002 reissue) para 207.

Cases referred to in judgment

British Coal Respiratory Disease Litigation, Re (23 January 1998, unreported).
Davies (Joseph Owen) v Eli Lilly & Co (8 May 1987, unreported) QBD; *affd* [1987] 3 All ER 94, [1987] 1 WLR 1136, CA.
Foster v Roussel Laboratories (29 October 1997, unreported).
Johnsey Estates (1990) Ltd v Secretary of State for the Environment, Transport and the Regions [2001] EWCA Civ 535, [2001] 2 EGLR 128, CA.
Phonographic Performance v AEI Rediffusion Music Ltd [1999] 2 All ER 299, [1999] 1 WLR 1507, CA
Ward v Guinness Mahon & Co Ltd, Koppel v Guinness Mahon & Co Ltd, Evans v Guinness Mahon & Co Ltd [1996] 4 All ER 112, [1996] 1 WLR 894, CA.

Cases also cited

AB v John Wyeth & Bro Ltd (1997) 8 Med LR 57, CA; *affg* (1996) 7 Med LR 267.
AB v John Wyeth & Bro Ltd (No 2) (1993) 18 BMLR 38, CA.
Brent London BC v Aniedobe (No 2) [1999] CA Transcript 2003.
Bridgewater v Griffiths [2000] 1 WLR 524.
Elgindata Ltd (No 2), Re [1993] 1 All ER 232, [1992] 1 WLR 1207, CA.
General of Berne Insurance Co v Jardine Reinsurance Management Ltd [1998] 1 WLR 1231, [1998] 2 All ER 301, CA.
Gwembe Valley Development Co Ltd v Koshy (No 2) [2000] TLR 247.

a   *Loveday v Renton* [1990] 1 Med LR 117.

McDonald v Horn [1995] 1 All ER 961, CA.

Nash v Eli Lilly & Co [1993] 4 All ER 383, [1993] 1 WLR 782, CA.

Ochwat v Watson Burton (a firm) [1999] All ER (D) 1407.

R v Lord Chancellor, ex p Child Poverty Action Group, R v DPP, ex p Bull [1998] 2 All ER 755, [1999] 1 WLR 347.

b   *Wallersteiner v Moir (No 2), Moir v Wallersteiner (No 2)* [1975] 1 All ER 849, [1975] QB 373, [1975] 2 WLR 389, CA

Appeals

c

Sayers and others v Merck SmithKline Beecham plc and others

Paul Sayers and a number of other claimants appealed from the decision of Bell J on 3 November 2000 dismissing their appeal from the order of Master Ungley on 8 February 2000 providing for cost-sharing in a multi-party action against the defendants, Merck SmithKline Beecham plc, SmithKline & French Laboratories, Merck & Co Inc, Aventis Pasteur MSD Ltd and other defendants. Various NHS

d   trusts and health authorities were joined as interested parties. The facts are set out in the judgment of the court.

X and others v Schering Health Care Ltd and others

X and a number of other claimants appealed from the decision of Smith J on

e   14 November 2000 dismissing their appeal from the orders of Master Tennant made on 9 January 1998 and 24 March 1998 providing for cost-sharing in a multi-party action against the defendant Schering Health Care Ltd, Organon Laboratories Ltd, John Wyeth & Bro Ltd and other defendants. Various NHS trusts and health authorities were joined as interested parties. The facts are set out in the judgment of the court.

f

Afrika and others v Cape plc

Hendrik Ismael Afrika and a number of other claimants appealed from the order made by Wright J on 4 December 2000 providing for cost-sharing in a multi-party action against the defendant, Cape plc. The facts are set out in the judgment of the

g   court.

Lord Brennan QC and *Robin Oppenheim* (instructed by *Freeth Cartwright*, Nottingham) for the claimants in the first case.

Andrew Prynne QC and *Prashant Popat* (instructed by *Lovells*) for the first three defendants in the first case.

h   *George Leggatt QC* (instructed by *CMS Cameron McKenna*) for the fourth defendant in the first case.

Lord Brennan QC and *Robin Oppenheim* (instructed by *Houghton & Co*, Hereford) for the claimants in the second case.

Michael Spencer QC and *Jonathan Waite* (instructed by *CMS Cameron McKenna*) for

j   the defendants in the second case.

Lord Brennan QC and *Robin Oppenheim* (instructed by *Leigh Day & Co*) for the claimants in the third case.

Charles Gibson QC (instructed by *Davies Arnold Cooper*) for the defendant in the third case.

Justin Fenwick QC and *Sue Carr* (instructed by *Reynolds Porter Chamberlain*) for the interested parties.

Cur adv vult

a

21 December 2001. The following judgment of the court was delivered.

LONGMORE LJ.

[1] Multi-party actions are a comparatively novel feature of English litigation
and the courts have attempted over recent years to fashion new types of order to   *b*
enable viable actions to be brought in situations where a single individual would
find it prohibitively expensive to bring proceedings on his or her own. The
present appeals arise in three separate multi-party actions: the first is what is
known as the MMR/MR litigation in which claims are made for injuries allegedly
suffered by children as a result of the administration of vaccine against measles,
mumps and rubella (or just measles and rubella); the second action is the oral   *c*
contraceptive litigation (OCP) in which claimants seek damages for injuries
sustained by the taking of oral contraceptives; the third action (Afrika) is brought
by workers in South Africa against the English holding company of the South
African subsidiary, which employed them, for injuries suffered as a result of
exposure to asbestos. Typically defendants are drug manufacturers, health trusts   *d*
on whose behalf drugs are prescribed, or other large corporations some of whom
(or whose insurers) have deep pockets. Claimants are typically individuals who
could not contemplate financing litigation themselves and obtain assistance for
that purpose from the Legal Service Commission or, perhaps, under a conditional
fee agreement.

e

[2] These actions are difficult, as well as expensive, to run and impose great
burdens on the practitioners who conduct them and judges who try them. They
can, however, be a service to many who suffer severe injuries and it is the policy
of the courts to facilitate such actions in appropriate cases and adapt traditional
procedures accordingly. These appeals arise only in relation to the details of
cost-sharing orders made in the actions but it is right that the court should be   *f*
guided by the considerations set out in the Woolf Report on *Access to Justice*
published in July 1996. In ch 17 of his report Lord Woolf said this in relation to
multi-party actions (para 2):

'It is now generally recognised, by judges, practitioners and consumer
representatives, that there is a need for a new approach both in relation to   *g*
court procedures and legal aid. The new procedures should achieve the
following objectives: (a) provide access to justice where large numbers of
people have been affected by another's conduct, but individual loss is so
small that it makes an individual action economically unviable; (b) provide
expeditious, effective and proportionate methods of resolving cases, where   *h*
individual damages are large enough to justify individual action but where
the number of claimants and the nature of the issues involved mean that the
cases cannot be managed satisfactorily in accordance with normal procedure;
(c) achieve a balance between the normal rights of claimants and defendants,
to pursue and defend cases individually, and the interests of a group of parties   *j*
to litigate the action as a whole in an effective manner.'

In relation to the costs of multi-party actions Lord Woolf said:

'57. If the treatment of costs is not examined from the outset, the result is
either subsidiary litigation or protracted problems when the matter comes to
taxation. My general proposals for information on costs to be made available

a
at every stage when the managing judge is involved are all the more important in relation to multi-party actions, where many claimants will be legally aided and have no direct control over costs and where costs can escalate dramatically. At every stage in the management of the MPS [multi-party situation] the judge should consider, with the help of the parties, the potential impact on costs of the directions that are contemplated, and

b
whether these are justified in relation to what is at issue. Parties and their legal representatives, as in other cases on the multi-track, should provide information on costs already incurred and be prepared to estimate the cost of proposed further work. It has been suggested that such examination should occur at intervals of three months. That must be for the managing judge to determine in each individual case.'

c
[3] As a result of the Woolf report CPR 19.3 makes provision for group litigation pursuant to a group litigation order and CPR 48.6A provides for costs where such an order has been made. We were told that each of the group actions (as we shall now call them) with which we are concerned is now being run in accordance with these rules. Pursuant to the rules cost-sharing orders have been

d
made; since the same points arise in each appeal it is sufficient to set out the order of Master Ungley as approved by Bell J in the MMR/MR litigation.

[4] The order provided, inter alia:

'15. Save as otherwise ordered: (a) The liability of each party for and each party's entitlement to recover costs shall be several and not joint.

e
(b) Individual costs are those costs and disbursements incurred for and/or in respect of any individual claimant in relation to matters which are personal to each such claimant, excluding costs and disbursements incurred for and/or in respect of any claims which may hereafter be selected as lead cases. (c) Common costs are all costs and disbursements other than

f
individual costs. (d) The common costs incurred in any quarter by the claimants and each of the defendants are to be divided by the number of claimants pursuing their claims on the first day of the quarter. (e) If in any quarter a claimant compromises his/her claim with any one or more of the defendants on terms which provide for such defendants to pay that claimant his/her costs then that claimant shall be entitled to recover his/her

g
individual costs and his/her several share of the common costs incurred by the claimants up to the last day of that quarter. (f) If in any quarter a claimant discontinues his/her claim against any one or more of the defendants or it is dismissed by an order of the court whereby that claimant is ordered to pay such defendants' costs, then he/she will be liable for

h
his/her individual costs together with his/her several share of the common costs incurred by such defendants up to the last day of that quarter. (g) The first quarter under this costs-sharing order shall run from 14 April 1999. (h) Each of the claimants shall for the purposes of this order be treated as if he/she had been a claimant in the actions as from 14 April 1999.'

j
It will be seen that the provision for quarterly costings mirrors the recommendations of para 57 of Lord Woolf's report.

[5] The claimants appeal against this order and ask for a provision in the following form to be inserted (between (c) and (d) in the order above):

'The order for payment of common costs and disbursements between the parties following any trial of the common issues whether by trial of the lead actions or otherwise shall follow the event and not depend upon the outcome of individual cases or of issues individual to the lead actions unless otherwise ordered.'—

and for a provision in the following form to be substituted for (e) and (f):

'In the event of any claimant discontinuing his/her action or settling his/her action any liability for common costs and disbursements of or in respect of such a claimant shall be determined at the trial of the common issues in the lead actions with permission to apply if such trial does not take place.'

We shall call them the 'costs by common issues order' and 'the discontinuers and settlers order' respectively.

[6] While the issues raised in this appeal are comparatively narrow ones, they are of importance to the parties and this is the first time that the detailed provisions of cost-sharing orders, commonly made at first instance, have been considered by this court. We had the advantage of assistance from witness statements of Mr Colin Stutt of the Legal Services Commission and of three solicitors, who have conducted group actions, as well as the assistance of submissions from no less than six leading counsel experienced in this type of litigation.

APPROACH OF THIS COURT

[7] Costs orders made at the end of a case are very much a matter for the discretion of the judge who has heard that case. It is only recently that such orders could be appealed at all without the permission of the judge himself. Such orders are now appealable provided that permission is obtained from either the judge or the Court of Appeal but this court is still notoriously reluctant to interfere with the judge's discretion (see *Johnsey Estates (1990) Ltd v Secretary of State for the Environment, Transport and the Regions* [2001] EWCA Civ 535 at [21], [22], [2001] 2 EGLR 128 at [21], [22] per Chadwick LJ).

[8] Despite a submission from the defendants to the contrary we look at the present appeals in a different way. The orders under appeal have been inaccurately called 'pre-emptive' orders. They are not pre-emptive since they allow for the judge to make a special order in a particular case or a different more general order, if circumstances change. Nevertheless they are orders that are intended to cater for (at least the generality of) future events. If it can be shown that some different order from that which the judge has made would be more appropriate, it would not be right for this court to attach any particular sanctity to the judge's order. That is all the more the case in a jurisdiction which is still a developing jurisdiction, as group litigation is. It is important that any general order as to cost-sharing should be the best available in the circumstances. That is not, of course, to say that the appellant should not bear the normal burden of persuading this court that the judge's order is wrong or, at least, inappropriate for the future conduct of the cases.

[9] We are, moreover, not persuaded that merely because in traditional litigation a discontinuing claimant will be required to pay a defendant's costs that that is, of itself, sufficient to justify the judge's order in these group actions. An action which has many claimants is inherently somewhat different from an action in which there is only one claimant, since the action will continue in the same form as currently constituted even after a claimant, for whatever reason, decides to settle or discontinue.

BRIEF HISTORY OF COST-SHARING ORDERS IN GROUP LITIGATION

a   [10] The courts have been developing the concept of cost-sharing orders since *Joseph Owen Davies v Eli Lilly & Co* (8 May 1987, unreported) (the Opren litigation). In that case Hirst J requested the appointment of an amicus to help the court; Mr George Pulman was instructed and he, together with the assistance of counsel for other parties, drafted a form of order which provided for all b plaintiffs to bear costs proportionately among themselves. This resolved an important practical difficulty that, if there was to be one or more legal actions, the claimants in those lead actions would otherwise have had to bear all the costs themselves. Even if such claimants won, the burden of irrecoverable costs would be too great for any claimant, who did not have legal aid, to bear them; moreover, even any legally aided claimant would be liable to find his damages c wiped out by the Law Society's charge for costs. The Court of Appeal upheld the order made by Hirst J as being within the provisions of the then rules of court (see [1987] 3 All ER 94, [1987] 1 WLR 1136). The order was further refined in *Ward v Guinness Mahon & Co Ltd, Koppel v Guinness Mahon & Co Ltd, Evans v Guinness Mahon & Co Ltd* [1996] 4 All ER 112, [1996] 1 WLR 894 where the concept of several liability on the part of the claimants was confirmed and applied to the d liability which claimants might have for costs of defendants.

    [11] It was May J in *Foster v Roussel Laboratories* (29 October 1997, unreported) who developed the concept of the cost-sharing order so as to require quarterly rests for the calculation of costs for the purpose of application to settlers and discontinuers; in that case at the instance of the defendants he made an order in e essentially the same form as that made by Master Ungley in the MMR/MR litigation in relation to settlers and discontinuers. In explaining it, he said:

> 'Cost Sharing
>   In principle the plaintiffs, individually and as a group, and the defendants need to know the basis upon which costs liabilities would be spread if an f order for costs were made or came into force. The underlying principle should be that costs which it is appropriate to apportion between or for the benefit of plaintiffs should be divided by the total number of relevant plaintiffs. Costs which it is appropriate to apportion could include (a) the defendants' costs, if one or more of the plaintiffs becomes liable to pay them, and (b) plaintiffs' central administration costs and other plaintiffs' costs g which are incurred for the benefit of plaintiffs as a whole, rather than for individual plaintiffs. Any plaintiff who joins the group in the future will acquire the benefit of work done in the past and should become potentially liable for apportionable costs liabilities going back to the beginning. Thus the defendant should be potentially liable to each individual plaintiff for that h plaintiff's proper individual costs and for a fraction of the plaintiffs' central costs whose denominator is the number of plaintiffs in the group. Each plaintiff should be potentially liable for a fraction of the defendants' costs whose denominator is the number of plaintiffs in the group. If plaintiffs leave the group by settlement or discontinuance before the conclusion of the j litigation when a general costs order is made, a calculation should be made to withdraw from the plaintiffs' central costs and from the defendants' costs a fraction of each of the then totals whose denominator is the number of plaintiffs then in the group before the departing plaintiff leaves. If the departing plaintiff is to pay the defendants' costs, the amount will be the amount of the defendants' costs so withdrawn. If the defendant is to pay the departing plaintiff's costs, the amount will be the amount withdrawn from

the plaintiffs' central costs plus the departing plaintiff's proper individual costs. All this would be subject to taxation. This means that costs calculations will need to be made on a quarterly basis, and both the plaintiffs centrally and the defendants need to keep records appropriately.'

[12] With this brief introduction to the background of cost-sharing orders, we can examine the submissions made by Lord Brennan QC on behalf of all the claimants in these appeals.

COSTS BY COMMON ISSUES ORDER

[13] Lord Brennan submitted that since the CPR have come into force, the courts were encouraged to make orders for costs in relation to individual issues and commonly did so. He referred us to dicta of Lord Woolf MR in *Phonographic Performance v AEI Rediffusion Music Ltd* [1999] 2 All ER 299, [1999] 1 WLR 1507 and said that this new approach should now be reflected in costs-sharing orders made in group actions.

[14] Mr Leggatt QC making the relevant submissions on behalf of the defendants on this aspect of the case submitted that the point of the costs-sharing order was not to say what order for costs should be made but to legislate for how costs should be apportioned once a costs order was made. Echoing Lord Brennan's own submissions on the discontinuers and settlers order, he submitted that it would be wrong now to make a presumptive order as to costs at the end of a trial of common issues (even if it was likely that the court would make an issue-based order after the trial of such common issues) since the circumstances at the end of a trial will be various and unpredictable.

[15] We agree with the submissions of Mr Leggatt. However likely it may be that, if common issues are directed to be tried, the costs of those issues will be ordered to follow the determination of those issues rather than await the individual fate of each claimant's action, it would, in our judgment, be wrong to say now that that should be the presumptive position. If, after all, the resolution of a common issue were to turn out to be entirely or largely academic the court should be free to make whatever appears to be the appropriate order in the circumstances. We therefore dismiss the claimants' appeal in so far as it seeks a costs order by reference to the determination of common issues.

DISCONTINUERS AND SETTLERS ORDER

(1) *Settlers*

[16] We consider that discontinuers and settlers cannot be considered together. As far as those that settle their cases are concerned, they do not usually need any presumptive order as to the incidence of costs since costs will be part of the discussion leading to settlement in any event. If there is an agreement that any defendant is to pay any claimant's costs, para (e) of Master Ungley's order is entirely appropriate and we see no reason to interfere with that part of the order.

(2) *Discontinuers*

[17] It is discontinuers that give rise to the more difficult problem and it was about them that most of the argument took place. In relation to them Lord Brennan submitted: (1) that group actions were almost inevitably issue-driven in the sense that the court would decide to try in the first instance common issues of fact and/or law as the only practicable way of achieving a fair outcome; (2) that orders for costs after the trial of common issues would usually (or often) follow

a the event of such issues; (3) that it was more consonant with overall justice that orders for costs in relation to common issues should await the determination of such issues rather than being prescribed in advance in the case of discontinuing claimants who might have any number of reasons for discontinuing; (4) that if the traditional form of order in relation to discontinuing claimants were to be the usual order, even though it was capable of being varied to meet a particular

b objection, it was an unfair advantage to defendants, who might lose on such common issues, that they should collect orders exempting them from paying costs of those who had discontinued (and indeed orders entitling them to costs in their favour) on the way to that defeat; (5) that the traditional order was also unfair to claimants, if the class of claimants was enlarged by late joiners, since the discontinuer would be paying a larger proportion of costs as calculated at the end

c of the relevant quarter than he would if the calculation was made when the trial was completed or the case were settled.

[18] The defendants submitted: (1) that the provisions for discontinuing claimants made in Master Ungley's order was in a standard form and had been approved by judges experienced in the field of personal injuries for many years;

d (2) that costs orders were always a matter for the judge's discretion and should not be reversed unless the judge had misdirected himself in law or was clearly wrong; (3) the fact that these actions were group actions was no reason for departing from the normal rule that a discontinuer should pay the appropriate costs of the action to date; (4) that claimants would, in any event, want to know the extent of their liability if they proposed to discontinue and should be able to

e leave the action, pay the costs incurred and forget about it; (5) that, if no decision as to the discontinuers' liability for common costs was made until common issues had been determined, there was no incentive on the claimants or their funders to weed out weak cases for early disposal; (6) that there would be a considerable risk of satellite litigation at the time when costs of common issues came to be

f determined; if for example it was negligent to market or prescribe a drug or to expose workers to asbestos products only after a certain date, it might be necessary for further issues (eg the degree to which the drug was taken or the workers were exposed before and after the date) to be resolved only for the purpose of determining the incidence of costs.

g CONCLUSION ON DISCONTINUERS

[19] We have already stated our negative reaction to the defendants' first three arguments. We have, further, concluded in the light of the parties' submissions that an inherent injustice to claimants and an inappropriate advantage to defendants is indeed liable to occur if the current form of order in relation to

h discontinuing claimants remains the norm. This is because a group action of the kind with which we are concerned in the present case is essentially different from the typical action where a single claimant (or a limited number of claimants) brings an action. Usually in such typical actions all issues of liability will be tried together whereas it is likely that in group actions certain common or generic

j issues will be tried on their own, before it is possible or sensible to apply the results to individual claimants. Meanwhile there may be many different reasons why claimants may decide to leave the group once the action has started. Of course, one reason may be that an individual claimant realises that his case is hopeless. But to have a prima facie rule that any discontinuing claimant should have a crystallised inability to recover common costs and a potential liability for the common costs of defendants at the end of the quarter in which he discontinues is too blunt an instrument and is unnecessarily favourable to defendants, when it is as yet unknown whether the claimants as a whole are to be successful in the common issues which are to be tried.

[20] A prima facie rule tends to become the accepted rule, especially if it is necessary to incur the expense of going to the judge and asking, against opposition, for a different order. It is therefore not merely more sensible but also more consonant with justice that both the recoverability of common costs and the liability (if any) of discontinuing claimants for costs of common issues should be determined at the same time as orders for common costs are made in respect of those common issues. The court then has a full picture and can make whatever order is just in all the circumstances. We were given a number of worked examples which we need not set out, but the striking feature of the order in its current form is that defendants who lose on general issues will never pay that proportion of common costs attributable to discontinuing claimants. Whereas that may, in the event, be a correct order, it is not right now to decide that it is, or even to say that it will be the right order unless the judge decides otherwise.

[21] It is also noteworthy that, in one of the few examples of group litigation which progressed to a final decision, *Re British Coal Respiratory Disease Litigation* (23 January 1998, unreported), Turner J ordered the defendants to pay the costs of claimants, who had not discontinued and persevered to the end of litigation, but lost their cases on their own individual facts. No doubt any such order as that would be highly exceptional but it shows the wisdom of not having any a priori rule for discontinuing claimants in group actions which takes effect before the outcome of common issues is known.

[22] Bell J recorded that, as at the date of his judgment (3 November 2000), there were only 16 discontinuers out of a total of 269 claimants who had sued the first defendants. The number in relation to the other defendants is much the same. It looks therefore that, at any rate in the MMR/MR litigation, the problem of discontinuers is not an enormous one. But we bear in mind Mr Stutt's written statement in which he says that it may be difficult for the Legal Services Commission to fulfil its statutory duty to obtain the best value for money if a significant proportion of costs expended will be irrecoverable regardless of success on common issues. We think Bell J (whose judgment was followed in the judgments in the other cases under appeal) was right to regard the problem as a matter of principle. He summed up his views in para 41 of his judgment, dealing with both discontinuers and settlers:

'In my view, with all these factors in mind, effective case management requires that the parties have, at this early stage, a clear idea of the costs that they will be liable for, subject to any later order, and that provision is made for those persons likely to discontinue or settle early. Master Ungley's costs order achieves this. Moreover it promotes discipline in the scrutiny and early abandonment of any weak claims. The order proposed on behalf of the claimants, on the other hand, would leave the liability of any claimant who discontinued or settled his action at large in respect of his liability (if any) for common costs and disbursements in respect of his claim. It would remain at large until trial of common issues, with liberty to apply if such a trial did not take place. In the circumstances of this case it might remain at large for a considerable period. Like Master Ungley, I regard that as highly undesirable.'

a   [23] The views of Bell J are entitled to great respect and, if we thought that the problems raised by discontinuers were just a matter of case management, we would not interfere. As it seems to us, however, the possible injustice to discontinuers and correspondingly premature advantage to defendants of the relevant paragraphs of Master Ungley's order go beyond mere case management considerations and should be addressed as a matter of principle. The judge says

b   that it is important that the parties have 'a clear idea of the costs that they will be liable for'. In the context of discontinuers, he is referring here to claimants who discontinue, but his concern is somewhat difficult to follow in the case of a legally aided claimant who is not himself going to be responsible for the defendants' costs at all. The judge's concern is more apt for a non-legally aided claimant (none of whom apparently exist in the MMR/MR litigation), but such a claimant

c   can always, if he wishes, offer to pay his appropriate proportion of common costs if he wants to leave the litigation and pay costs at once. The judge also says that it is highly undesirable that a claimant's potential liability for common costs should remain at large for a considerable period but this is just a more emphatic way of making the same point.

d   [24] More generally, the respondents argued that it was detrimental to the discontinuing claimants themselves to have their potential liability left unresolved and in doubt until the end of the trial, perhaps some years distant. To that, Lord Brennan reasonably replied that it was for claimants and their advisers to decide what was best for them. Whilst the court should of course withhold a solution sought by the claimants if it would be unfair to the defendants or

e   contrary to the requirements of public policy, it could hardly do so simply because it thought that the claimants were not acting in their own best interests. And so far as defendants are concerned, in practical terms an order for immediate payment obtained against legally aided claimants, who form the vast majority of those with whom we are concerned, will not in fact be immediately enforced.

f   [25] The judge also refers to a matter much emphasised by Mr Prynne QC and Mr Fenwick QC for the defendants that an immediate order for costs in respect of discontinuing claimants will promote 'discipline in the scrutiny and early abandonment of any weak claims'. We are not persuaded by this argument, attractive as counsel made it sound. To begin with, counsel and solicitors have no business advising that claimants with weak cases should join the register of the

g   relevant group in the first place. And as Lord Brennan reminded us, serious professional obligations rest on both solicitors and counsel who act in legally aided cases to ensure that the Legal Services Commission is kept informed of the state of the case, and that unmeritorious cases do not continue to receive support. But secondly no one suggests that a notice of discontinuance will have no

h   attraction for a claimant with a weak case. The proposed alteration to Master Ungley's order relates only to common costs. Claimants will still wish to discontinue in order to cease incurring individual costs which will not be recoverable from defendants and indeed to stop defendants continuing to incur costs in relation to individual issues, for which the claimant will or may be liable

j   at the end of the day. Moreover, service of notice of discontinuance will operate to draw a line at the end of the quarter in relation to common costs even if no decision is then made as to the liability for such costs. There will thus still be an incentive for claimants to discontinue weak cases in any event.

[26] The 'discipline' argument is, therefore, not persuasive as a matter of fact. We should, however, also add that, even if the argument were more convincing in itself, we would have needed also to be convinced of its real necessity before

acting on it. When an order is unfair to claimants, as we believe the order of Bell J to be, strong reasons of policy or case management would be required before that order is none the less maintained.

[27] Lastly, we consider Mr Prynne's concern about satellite litigation arising on questions of costs to be exaggerated. If costs cannot be determined after trial of common issues, that will usually be because the issues themselves need refining and not because costs need to be resolved.

[28] For these reasons we consider that para 15(f) of Master Ungley's order, in so far as it relates to discontinuers, needs amending by the deletion of the words 'together with his/her several share of the common costs' and the addition at the end of the paragraph of the words after a semi-colon:

> 'liability for common costs and disbursements to be determined following the trial of common issues, with permission to apply if such trial does not take place.'

To this extent the claimants' appeal will be allowed. The orders similar to Master Ungley's that were appealed in the Afrika and OCP claims need amending in like form. We make no decision about claims which are dismissed by order of the court and there is no reason why Master Ungley's order should not remain as it is in order to deal with such cases.

CLAIMANTS' ALTERNATIVE PROPOSAL

[29] At a very late date Lord Brennan put forward a suggestion to the effect that there should be an order that the claimants' solicitors in the lead actions (rather than all the claimants severally) should be entitled to recover the common costs of common issues incurred when such costs were ordered to be paid by the defendants. Whatever merits any such order might have, it seems to us that it offends against the indemnity principle whereby a party awarded costs of litigation cannot recover more than he is himself obliged to pay in respect of the costs of the litigation. This principle has been subject to criticism; indeed we understand that at the costs conference which took place on 30 November/ 1 December 2001 organised by the Civil Justice Council it was the almost unanimous view of those taking part (who included Lord Phillips of Worth Matravers MR and May LJ) that the indemnity principle should be abolished, provided that at the same time positive statutory provisions can be enacted identifying the basis upon which an award of costs can be made. It was also their view, with which we respectfully agree, that this can only be done by primary legislation. In these circumstances we do not think it right to give Lord Brennan's alternative proposal any further consideration.

Appeal allowed in part.

Melanie Martyn   Barrister.

Black and others v Sumitomo Corporation and others

[2001] EWCA Civ 1819

COURT OF APPEAL, CIVIL DIVISION
WARD, MAY AND RIX LJJ
3 OCTOBER, 3 DECEMBER 2001

Disclosure – Production of documents – Production before commencement of proceedings – Whether persons likely to be party to subsequent proceedings – Whether disclosure to be ordered when criteria of desirability met – Supreme Court Act 1981, s 33(2) – CPR 31.16.

B and his companies (the prospective claimants), were prospective claimants in proceedings against the prospective defendant companies for unlawful conspiracy to manipulate markets and/or anti-competitive behaviour. The potential proceedings arose out of the unauthorised trading activities of the chief copper trader and general manager of the non-ferrous metals division of one of the prospective defendant companies. B was a metal dealer and copper trader, who complained that after the manager's dismissal there had been a conspiracy involving, inter alia, the prospective defendants to manipulate the copper market by continuing with the strategy employed by the manager. The prospective claim was for failure to secure speculative profits. They sought pre-action disclosure under s 33(2)[a] of the Supreme Court Act 1981 which applied to persons who were 'likely' to be party to subsequent proceedings and CPR 31.16. The judge addressed himself to, inter alia, the following questions: (i) whether proceedings between the parties were likely; (ii) whether pre-action disclosure was within any of the three reasons set out in CPR 31.16(3)(d) which were that it was desirable in order to dispose fairly of the anticipated proceedings; assist the dispute to be resolved within proceedings; or save costs; and (iii) whether the court should order disclosure in the exercise of its discretion under CPR 31.16(3). He concluded that the test of proceedings being 'likely' was that the prospective claimant had a 'reasonable basis' for making the claim against the prospective defendant, and that in the instant case that test had been met. The judge apparently considered that each of the reasons in CPR 31.16(3)(d) had been met, giving him jurisdiction to order disclosure. He then decided to exercise his discretion in favour of disclosure, on the basis that once the test of desirability had been met, it was unlikely that an order for disclosure would be refused altogether. The prospective defendants appealed. The prospective claimants' contentions were based in part on documents and information obtained under United States freedom of information legislation.

Held – Section 33(2) of the 1981 Act meant no more than that the persons concerned were likely to be parties in proceedings if those proceedings were issued, and 'likely' meant no more than 'might well'. The jurisdictional and discretionary aspects of CPR 31.16(3) should not be confused. There was a two-stage process involved. For jurisdictional purposes the court was only

---

a   Section 33, so far as material, is set out at [4], below

permitted to consider the granting of pre-action disclosure where there was a real
prospect in principle of such an order being fair to the parties if litigation were
commenced, or of assisting the parties to avoid litigation, or of saving costs in any
event. If there were such a real prospect, then the court should go on to consider
the question of discretion, which had to be considered on all the facts in detail.
Whilst it was perhaps not vital to keep the two stages of the process separate, the
danger was that a court might be misled by the ease with which the jurisdictional
threshold could be passed into thinking that it had thereby decided the question
of discretion, when in truth it had not. In the instant case the judge had not, in
effect, stood back, having dealt with the jurisdictional thresholds, and asked
himself whether the case was one in which his discretion should be exercised in
favour of disclosure. The court was, therefore, entitled to exercise its discretion
anew. In the circumstances of the instant case the expressed determination of the
prospective claimants to litigate and the avenues open to them to obtain
documentation or information from other sources militated against them.
Accordingly, the appeal would be allowed and the judge's order set aside (see
[71], [72], [81], [82], [85]–[87], [97], [101]–[103], below).

Notes

For pre-action disclosure, see 37 *Halsbury's Laws* (4th edn reissue), paras 206, 207.
	For the Supreme Court Act 1981, s 33, see 11 *Halsbury's Statutes* (2000 reissue), 1071.

Cases referred to in judgments

Bermuda International Securities Ltd v KPMG (a firm) [2001] EWCA Civ 269, [2001]
	Lloyd's Rep PN 392.
Burns v Shuttlehurst Ltd [1999] 2 All ER 27, [1999] 1 WLR 1449, CA.
Dunning v Board of Governors of the United Liverpool Hospitals [1973] 2 All ER 454,
	[1973] 1 WLR 586, CA.
Hytrac Conveyors Ltd v Conveyors International Ltd [1982] 3 All ER 415, [1983] 1 WLR
	44, CA.
Post Office v Norwich Union Fire Insurance Society Ltd [1967] 1 All ER 577, [1967]
	2 QB 363, [1967] 2 WLR 709, CA.
RHM Foods Ltd v Bovril Ltd [1982] 1 All ER 673, [1982] 1 WLR 661, CA.
Shaw v Vauxhall Motors Ltd [1974] 2 All ER 1185, [1974] 1 WLR 1035, CA.
Sumitomo Corp v Credit Lyonnais Rouse Ltd [2001] EWCA Civ 1152, [2002] 4 All ER
	68, [2002] 1 WLR 479.

Appeal

Sumitomo Corporation, Sumitomo Corporation (UK) plc and Sumitomo
Corporation of America, the prospective defendants, appealed with permission
granted by Brooke LJ on 10 September 2001 from the decision of Michael
Brindle QC, sitting as a deputy high court judge, ordering pre-action disclosure
against the prospective defendants on an application by Hebert Black, American
Iron & Metal Company Inc and Lito Trade Inc concerning a possible claim for
unlawful conspiring to manipulate markets and/or breach of arts 81, 82 EC.

Geoffrey Vos QC, Joe Smouha and *Andrew Twigger* (instructed by *Teacher Stern Selby*)
	for Mr Black.
Charles Hollander QC and *Orlando Gledhill* (instructed by *Ashurst Morris Crisp*) for
	Sumitomo.

Cur adv vult

a 3 December 2001. The following judgments were delivered.

RIX LJ (giving the first judgment at the invitation of Ward LJ).

[1] This is an appeal about pre-action disclosure. It arises in the context of heavy prospective litigation in the Commercial Court concerning a possible claim for unlawful conspiracy to manipulate markets and/or breach of arts 81,

b 82 EC (formerly arts 85, 86 of the EC Treaty). The prospective claimants, Mr Herbert Black and his companies (Mr Black), say that they have suffered losses amounting to at least $126m.

[2] In the court below Michael Brindle QC, sitting as a deputy judge of the High Court, ordered nine categories of pre-action disclosure against prospective defendants Sumitomo Corporation and other companies in the Sumitomo group

c (Sumitomo). Sumitomo appeals.

[3] The power to order pre-action disclosure arises out of s 33(2) of the Supreme Court Act 1981, as amended by the Civil Procedure (Modification of Enactments) Order 1998, SI 1998/2940 pursuant to the Civil Procedure Act 1997 so as to extend the power from cases in respect of personal injury or death to all

d cases. The extension was recommended by Lord Woolf's *Access to Justice: Final Report to the Lord Chancellor on the Civil Justice System of England and Wales* (July 1996) (*Access to Justice*) pp 127–128 (paras 47–52) and came into force at the same time as the CPR regime in general on 26 April 1999. The procedure is now governed by CPR 31.16.

e
SECTION 33(2) OF THE SUPREME COURT ACT 1981

[4] Section 33(2) of the 1981 Act provides as follows:

'On the application, in accordance with rules of court, of a person who appears to the High Court to be likely to be a party to subsequent

f proceedings in that court … the High Court shall, in such circumstances as may be specified in the rules, have power to order a person who appears to the court to be likely to be a party to the proceedings and to be likely to have or to have had in his possession, custody or power any documents which are relevant to an issue arising or likely to arise out of that claim—(a) to disclose whether those documents are in his possession, custody or power; and (b) to

g produce such of those documents as are in his possession, custody or power to the applicant …'

CPR 31.16

[5] CPR 31.16 provides as follows:

h
'(1) This rule applies where an application is made to the court under any Act for disclosure before proceedings have started.

(2) The application must be supported by evidence.

(3) The court may make an order under this rule only where—(a) the

j respondent is likely to be a party to subsequent proceedings; (b) the applicant is also likely to be a party to those proceedings; (c) if proceedings had started, the respondent's duty by way of standard disclosure, set in rule 31.6, would extend to the documents or classes of documents of which the applicant seeks disclosure; and (d) disclosure before proceedings have started is desirable in order to—(i) dispose fairly of the anticipated proceedings; (ii) assist the dispute to be resolved without proceedings; or (iii) save costs.'

THE HAMANAKA AFFAIR

[6] The background to these proceedings is the Hamanaka affair. On 13 June 1996 *a* Sumitomo, the world's largest copper trader and a major user of copper in its own operations, announced that it had dismissed its chief copper trader, Mr Yasuo Hamanaka, the general manager of its non-ferrous metals division, on the ground of his unauthorised trading activities. Sumitomo said that over the previous ten years such activities had lost it $1.8bn. It is not clear whether that *b* figure represented only liquidated losses to date or included an estimate of the cost of unwinding Sumitomo's current copper positions, but probably the latter.

[7] Those positions were huge. Mr Hamanaka had in effect attempted to corner the world's copper market. There is evidence that as of that time Sumitomo was 'long' (ie was the net purchaser) of about one million tonnes (40,000 lots) of copper futures and warrants and had also sold put options for a *c* further one million tonnes. The sale of a put option gives its buyer the right but not the obligation to sell copper at the strike price. These totals, albeit they represented obligations running into the future, dwarfed the amount of physical stocks held in the warehouses of the world's leading copper markets such as the London Metal Exchange (LME). A subsequent report by the United States *d* Commodity Futures Trading Commission (CFTC) dated 11 May 1998 put the matter like this:

> 'Sumitomo through its agent or agents intentionally acquired and maintained a dominant and controlling position in both the physical supply of deliverable LME warehouse stocks and in maturing LME futures *e* positions. At various times within the period in question Sumitomo owned virtually all deliverable LME copper stocks. These positions were not intended to meet Sumitomo's legitimate commercial needs. The intent motivating the acquisition and control of both the cash market positions and the futures market positions was expressly to create artificially high absolute prices. Sumitomo deliberately exploited its market dominance in order to *f* profit when market prices became artificially high as Sumitomo had foreseen and planned.'

[8] Although Mr Hamanaka's dismissal was announced on 13 June 1996, the regulatory authorities, the CFTC and in the United Kingdom the Securities and Investment Board (SIB), had begun to investigate the manipulation of copper *g* prices in October 1995. Those investigations led to Sumitomo's suspension of Mr Hamanaka on 8 or 9 May 1996. In early June he confessed to his ten-year rogue trading scheme and revealed the positions which he had hidden from his management. On 13 June there was a meeting, convened at Sumitomo's request, in Washington DC with representatives of CFTC and SIB. Sumitomo's evidence *h* is that at that meeting Sumitomo explained 'the three pillars' of its policy: full co-operation with government authorities; the maintenance of orderly markets; and reduction of Sumitomo's positions without severe market disruption. The regulators were equally concerned to maintain orderly markets. The regulators recommended Sumitomo to seek professional guidance about liquidating its *j* positions. The press announcement of that day was agreed. It spoke of Sumitomo's intention to co-operate with the authorities and to help to ensure 'a stable and orderly copper market in consultation with the [LME]'. In a further press release made the same day Sumitomo confirmed, at CFTC's request, that it would honour all Mr Hamanaka's dealings, regardless of whether they were authorised. Sumitomo retained Goldman Sachs to assist in the liquidation

a process, and on 18–20 June transferred the majority of its open positions to a special Goldman Sachs account. At the regulators' further request, an open and direct line of communication was authorised between the regulators and LME on the one hand and Goldman Sachs on the other, so as to permit the former to monitor the liquidation process.

b **[9]** On 11 May 1998 Sumitomo and the Financial Services Authority (FSA), as SIB had by then become, entered into an agreement under which the FSA agreed not to proceed further against Sumitomo and Sumitomo agreed voluntarily to pay £5m 'towards the FSA's time, effort and expense'. The agreement annexed an agreed press statement which contained the following passage:

c 'In reaching today's agreement, the FSA recognises that Sumitomo has given prompt, valuable and extensive co-operation following Hamanaka's confession in June 1996. Sumitomo agrees to assist the FSA in the finalisation of its investigations. The FSA has also received substantial co-operation in investigating and dealing with the Hamanaka affair from relevant authorities on a world-wide basis, in particular from the [CFTC] in the USA and from the Tokyo District Public Prosecutor's Office in Japan; and in the UK from
d the Securities and Futures Authority ("SFA") and the [LME].'

[10] Also on 11 May 1998 the CFTC published its findings in relation to the Hamanaka affair in the form of an order. The order recorded that Sumitomo's conduct had satisfied all the requisite elements of the offence of price
e manipulation, and while acknowledging Mr Hamanaka's acts of deception and the losses suffered by Sumitomo amounting by then to $2.6bn, agreed with the Japanese court which had sentenced Mr Hamanaka to eight years' imprisonment that Sumitomo's inadequate management control had been one of the causes of the debacle. Sumitomo offered to pay and was ordered to pay a civil monetary penalty of $125m plus a further $25m to be available as restitution of damages
f caused to private claimants prior to 30 June 1996. The order also commended Sumitomo's substantial co-operation and provision of information.

[11] In a further order dated 20 May 1999 the CFTC made allegations concerning co-conspirators in the manipulation. They included a company based in New York called Global Minerals and Metals Corp (Global) and its principal
g Mr David Campbell. The order charged that the conspirators were knowingly assisted in their scheme by Merrill Lynch. The order set out detailed allegations as to the mechanisms of the manipulation. By an order dated 30 June 1999 Merrill Lynch settled the proceedings against it, without admission or denial, on payment of $15m.

h **[12]** The Hamanaka affair has led to many private suits against Sumitomo, numbering something more than 20. Sumitomo has also been a claimant in still further proceedings, eg in this country in *Sumitomo Corp v Credit Lyonnais Rouse Ltd* [2001] EWCA Civ 1152, [2002] 4 All ER 68, [2002] 1 WLR 479. A passage in this court's judgment in that case describes the state of Sumitomo's documentation and thus is relevant to the present appeal:

j '[6] From late December 1995 to mid-June 1996 PW [Sumitomo's United States attorneys] assembled a large amount of documentation to assist Sumitomo and its United States subsidiary in responding to the CFTC subpoena. This process continued following Mr Hamanaka's confession. It included what was described in evidence as "a comprehensive document collection exercise" at Sumitomo's offices in Tokyo and at its subsidiaries'

offices in New York, Hong Kong and London. This exercise resulted in the
assembling of some 6.9m pages of documentation, mostly in Japanese. The
next step was for a team of about 30 lawyers from PW, assisted by
translators, to carry out a review of each document in this collection to
determine whether and to what extent it was or might become relevant to
the current, or any future, investigations and proceedings arising out of
Mr Hamanaka's unauthorised activities. Based upon this review, PW
lawyers selected certain documents for inclusion in a computerised litigation
database (the PW database). About 4% of the totality of the documentation
was imaged onto the PW database.

[7] As part of this review process, which continued until 1998, PW
commissioned English translations of some 5,000 selected documents (about
30,000 pages, representing some 0.4% of the totality of the documentation).'

MR BLACK'S PROSPECTIVE CLAIM

[13] Mr Black is a Canadian metal dealer and copper trader and in this court is
the respondent. He controls one of the largest scrap metal recycling businesses
in Canada (his co-applicant, American Iron & Metal Company Inc). In 1996 he
was an active trader in the LME and COMEX copper markets. In early July 1996
he appears to have given an interview which is reported in Toronto's *Financial
Post* for 6 July and the Dallas *Morning News* for 7 July. He is said there to have sold
copper in December 1995 and March 1996 and to have suffered losses as the price
continued to rise. Then in May 1996 he sold again with greater success. It will be
recalled that Mr Hamanaka was suspended about 8 May. The spot price of
copper was then $2,840. Mr Black is reported to have made sales about 17 May.
After the announcement of 13 June he made further sales. 'I just felt copper was
heading for a fall. I've closed my positions now and I did well.' His profit was
'many millions'. (A report in *The Independent* for 29 June 1996 illustrates the
volatility at this time, stating that the price had collapsed to a 30-month low of
$1,745 on 25 June but had recovered to $1,943 by 28 June.) He is also reported as
saying that his belief was that the bulk of copper's decline was over for the present
and that he expected three-month copper to trade between $1,800 and $2,200
through to the end of 1996. In early October Mr Black was in London for its
annual 'Metals Week', where he addressed a trade lunch, reported in *The Guardian*
for 8 October. The price on 7 October was around $1,920. He is said to have
claimed to have made $30m selling copper following the announcement of
Mr Hamanaka's unauthorised trading in June and to have predicted that the price
of copper would continue to fall to around $1,600 in 1997 and $1,400 in 1998. I
bear in mind that such reporting is not necessarily accurate.

[14] If it is true that Mr Black was an unsuccessful short seller of copper in
December 1995 and March 1996, he has so far as I am aware brought no claim
against Sumitomo for such losses. His evidence is that following the emergence
of the Hamanaka affair he offered to buy copper from Sumitomo in June 1996,
but that it refused to deal with him. The court has no details of that allegation.
At any rate it gave rise to no claim against Sumitomo at that time.

[15] Over four years later on 21 December 2000 his solicitors wrote a long
letter out of the blue to Sumitomo. It has been referred to as a letter before
action. It refers to the Hamanaka affair and then complains that in the period of
June to September 1996 ('the relevant period'), by which I think is meant during
that period following the appointment of Goldman Sachs in mid-June, six named
individuals at Sumitomo and a further six named individuals at Goldman Sachs

a conspired together to devise and implement a 'Plan' amounting to a serious manipulation of the copper market. In brief what is said is that Sumitomo and Goldman Sachs continued with the Hamanaka strategy for controlling the market; by taking delivery of Sumitomo's near-term purchases so as to keep the market short of supply, and by withholding the vast majority of its positions and being prepared to lend to the market only distantly dated goods, it was able to

b maintain the market price at artificially high and manipulated levels, to Sumitomo's profit and the loss of others in the market such as Mr Black who had adopted a strategy based on short selling. The letter said that Goldman Sachs itself made $40m on its own account, plus its fees of $25m. It was 'a conspiracy intentionally to injure the business interests of all market participants who had short positions during the period'. The conspiracy was unlawful because it

c employed unlawful means in breach of s 47(2) of the Financial Services Act 1986 (which makes it a criminal offence to engage in 'any course of conduct which creates a false or misleading impression as to the market … for the purpose of creating that impression and of thereby inducing another' to act in the market in some way). In addition there were breaches of arts 81 and 82 EC (formerly

d arts 85 and 85 of the EC Treaty) because of abuse of the conspirators' dominant position and collusion to distort competition within the European Union. The letter then stated Mr Black's financial claim to damages in a sum of at least $126m. This was premised on the allegation that in the absence of manipulation the price of copper would have fallen to at least $1,400 by September 1996. The $126m was made up in the main of the loss of the profits of $130m which Mr Black would

e have made if the price had fallen to $1,400. In addition there was a claim of nearly $14m in respect of the losses actually made; but Mr Black was prepared to allow a credit of over $18m in respect of losses on 'option trading' which it is said that Mr Black would have incurred if the price had fallen to $1,400.

f [16] It follows that the claim is essentially for the failure to secure speculative profits rather than for realised losses. The reference to an unmanipulated price of $1,400 by September 1996 does not sit very easily with what is reported to have been Mr Black's public predictions as of early July and again as of early October 1996 (see [13], above).

[17] The letter ended with a request for discovery under CPR 31.16 for 'all documents' under various headings. One of those headings related to the so-called

g 'China Deal', a reference to an allegedly sham contract between Sumitomo and China for 'sale' to China of 90,000 tonnes ex LME warehouses but in reality for storage out of the way in Sumitomo's name in China. The requests in effect covered documentation relating to all Sumitomo's positions and dealings from 1 June to 30 September 1996. I shall have to refer to the China deal in further detail

h below, because it is put forward as Mr Black's best evidence of the continuation of market manipulation into the post-Hamanaka period.

[18] The last paragraph of the letter, headed 'Time Limit', requested a response by 31 January 2001 'failing which Mr Black will, without further notice, issue either an application for disclosure under Rule 31.16 … or a claim form'.

j [19] The question has arisen as to why it took Mr Black over four years to raise this complaint. It is said on his behalf that it was only in 2000 that he was able to obtain by means of the United States Freedom of Information Act (the United States Act) documents which have enabled him to formulate his case against Sumitomo. On its part, Sumitomo is concerned lest the timing of Mr Black's complaint has anything to do with the recruitment of Mr Dennis O'Keefe into Mr Black's employment as of about 12 December 2000 as general counsel of an

affiliate of American Iron & Metal. Up to that date Mr O'Keefe had been
employed as an attorney by CFTC, where he had been its lead investigator into   *a*
the Hamanaka affair. He was the main contact of Sumitomo's United States
lawyers throughout the period from June 1996 to late November 2000 pursuant
to Sumitomo's commitment to co-operate with the regulatory authorities.
Sumitomo and its lawyers are concerned about the possibility that Mr O'Keefe
has violated United States law or his obligations of confidentiality as a lawyer.   *b*
Mr O'Keefe has stated that he is well aware of his obligations and that the concern
raised is absolutely baseless. On the other hand the evidence filed on behalf of
Mr Black also confirms that Mr O'Keefe has been assisting in relation to potential
claims and that he 'is likely to be reliable and well informed'.

THE CHINA DEAL   *c*

[20] Deputy Judge Brindle said that he had detected a coyness on the part of
Sumitomo in giving any worthwhile details about the China deal; and that there
were non-fanciful grounds to suspect that the transaction may not have been a
genuine sale at the time it was entered into nor when subsequently adopted by
Sumitomo and Goldman Sachs. He said it seemed most peculiar and called for   *d*
explanation.

[21] Documentation concerning the China deal put forward on behalf of
Mr Black in support of his application before Deputy Judge Brindle appears to
date from the period just before Mr Hamanaka was suspended. A manuscript
document contemplates a 'Copper Transaction for China'. The significance of
the proposal is somewhat opaque but appears to be as follows. A total of   *e*
90,000 tonnes was to be shipped to Shanghai in May/June 1996, of which
65,200 tonnes were to be supplied initially by Global to Sumitomo. The delivery
to China was to be within the period of June to December 1996. The cost price
to Sumitomo from Global and the sales price to China would be the LME average
price for the relevant month of delivery or the price for a specified day, but   *f*
China's purchase was to be spread over the period from June to December 1996,
and it was to have no obligation to purchase unless the LME price for
three-month futures was $2,500 or less. In the meantime the shipment cost was
to be at China's expense on Chinese flag vessels, and the cost of warehousing in
Shanghai pending the take-up of the copper and the interest on the price were to
be at the sellers' risk unless and until China completed the purchase. If the   *g*
purchase was not completed, then the cost of reshipping the copper to Singapore,
the warehousing cost in Shanghai and the burden of interest would all fall on the
sellers, Global or Sumitomo, in proportion to the origin of the goods. The total
risk of such sums was calculated at $14.7m to Global and $5.6m to Sumitomo. In
addition there was the risk for the sellers that the price of copper would fall from   *h*
its present spot price of $2,800 to just above $2,500 without China being obliged
to purchase. It was suggested that the deal was a sham, 'an attempt to drive up
copper prices by reducing apparently available stocks'.

[22] It is not clear to me on the basis of this document why it was suggested in
the evidence adduced on Mr Black's behalf that the China deal there   *j*
contemplated had actually gone ahead. Presumably Mr Black had some further
information. At any rate, the response of Sumitomo's evidence came from
Mr Vigrass, a partner in its London solicitors. He said that the deal had its origin
in March 1996 when China had expressed an interest in purchasing a large
volume of refined copper in the form of LME warrants. There were market
rumours that in April 1995 China had sold 85,000 tonnes of copper to LME

a warehouses out of its stockpiles and that China therefore had a real need for copper. A sale had been concluded for 90,000 tonnes and physical delivery had been taken by China for the whole of that quantity.

[23] In response to Mr Vigrass' witness statement there was complaint that Sumitomo had not disclosed any documents to support his evidence that physical delivery had been taken by China. It was suggested that disclosure of such

b documents was desirable to save costs 'since, if the applicants' contentions in relation to the China deal are incorrect, that issue will not be pursued any further'. Moreover, China's need for copper was questioned on the basis of a fax dated 29 May 1996 (obtained through the United States Act) written to Global by a senior manager of Sumitomo: this referred to a forthcoming meeting with the Chinese set for 31 May and to the fact that 'we do not have a firm commitment

c from CNIEC [the Chinese entity involved] to take copper'. I am not sure that I follow the point being made: perhaps the inference intended was that the sale was a sham, or possibly that there was no sale.

[24] Among the documents put into evidence at this stage on behalf of Mr Black was a lengthy note of 22 pages of a meeting of 30 May 1996 held at the

d offices of SIB. The note was prepared by representatives of SIB present at the meeting. Also present was Mr O'Keefe. Among the items discussed was 'a projected sale of approximately 90,000 metric tons to China'. It is described as 'brought to Sumitomo' by Global. The note continues:

e 'Sumitomo is hoping (to) acquire from Global, for onward sale to the Chinese. However, [Martin London, a partner of Paul Weiss Rifkind Wharton & Garrison, Sumitomo's United States attorneys] stressed that Sumitomo was not guaranteeing any part of this deal. Rather, it is purely a purchaser and seller of the copper.'

[25] The note was briefly referred to in Mr Black's evidence. An additional
f request was made for disclosure of any documents disclosing the China deal to the regulatory authorities.

[26] In a second witness statement Mr Vigrass returned to the subject of the China deal. He said that it was entered into before June 1996, I suppose thereby indicating that it fell outside the 'relevant period'. He also said that, whether profitable or not, it was an important transaction for Sumitomo since it was eager
g to establish and develop a relationship with China and to gain an insight into its overall trading strategy. He repeated that China had taken physical delivery of all 90,000 tonnes.

[27] When Deputy Judge Brindle came to order pre-trial disclosure from Sumitomo he included three categories of documents specifically related to the
h China deal, viz (a) documents evidencing it, (b) documents disclosing it to the regulatory authorities and (c) documents evidencing physical delivery to CNIEC.

[28] There has been a further round of evidence concerning the China deal, starting on this occasion with Sumitomo, in the period between Deputy Judge Brindle's decision and the hearing of this appeal. Mr Kameoka, who on 9 May 1996
j had replaced Mr Hamanaka as general manager of Sumitomo's non-ferrous products and metals division and who had also been the author of the fax dated 29 May 1996 referred to in [23], above, made a detailed witness statement. He said that the deal had been under negotiation from March 1996, that although Sumitomo would not make a profit from it, it was a highly coveted opportunity to make a customer of China and to benefit from a broader relationship with it in the future. It was concluded in response to CNIEC's request to purchase copper,

to replenish its strategic reserves. It was a legitimate business transaction and not an attempt to manipulate prices. The contract was executed on 22 May 1996 and a copy of it was exhibited. Ninety-one thousand tonnes were actually delivered under it. The copper was shipped to Shanghai, where it was stored and called off by CNIEC in ten instalments between August and December 1996. The instalments were priced by reference to the LME price on various settlement dates (plus fixed premiums by reference to the source of the copper) varying between $1,959 and $2,235. Documents evidencing the calling off of these instalments were exhibited, and also documents evidencing the reconciliation of accounts between Sumitomo and Global.

[29] The China deal sales contract exhibited was for a quantity of 'approximately' 90,000 tonnes of LME grade and registered brand copper to be delivered in a Shanghai warehouse between 1 June and 31 December 1996 provided that CNIEC had first priced the quantity to be delivered (in quantities of any multiple of 25 tonnes) by reference to the LME cash settlement price (presumably on a specified day) plus the premium and had obtained customs clearance. The contract was subject to the prior receipt of CNIEC's letter of credit. Sumitomo was to bear the warehouse rent until the tenth day after presentation of negotiable documents and CNIEC was to bear such rent from 1 January 1997 in any event. There was an addendum also dated 22 May 1996 dealing with terms which it is not relevant to mention here.

[30] Mr Kameoka's evidence led to a further witness statement from Mr Rabinowicz, a partner in Mr Black's London solicitors. The main purpose of this evidence was to annex a further document obtained by Mr Black by means of the United States Act. This was a fax dated 16 June 1996 from CNIEC to Sumitomo headed 'Draft Text of Addendum' and annexing the draft in question. The draft, which was headed with the contract number and date (22 May 1996) of the China deal contract exhibited by Mr Kameoka, began with the following clauses:

'(1) Buyer must accept and pay for all tonnage delivered into bonded warehouse Shanghai and/or Bayuquan by no later than December 31, 1996, provided that the LME Grade A copper three month selling price averages US$2500.00 m/t or lower for any consecutive thirty (30) days period after August 1, 1996.

(2) In the event of a major, unforeseen disruption of supply that results in higher LME prices for Grade A copper, Buyer and Seller will discuss in good faith, but without any obligation, an adjustment in the price at which buyer must accept and pay for the actual quantity delivered into bonded warehouse in China by no later than December 31, 1996.'

[31] The covering fax from CNIEC proposed altered language for the draft, and indicates that critical elements of the contract were still under negotiation. That was also indicated by Mr Kameoka's fax to Global of 29 May 1996 which had pointed out that 'we do not have firm commitment from CNIEC to take copper' and from the SIB note of the meeting of 30 May 1996 which had referred to a 'projected sale' to China. Mr Rabinowicz made such points in his witness statement, and also referred the $2,500 price condition back to the manuscript note about the structure of the deal passing between Sumitomo and Global shortly before Mr Hamanaka's suspension. Mr Rabinowicz complained that Mr Kameoka had not produced 'proof' that the copper was in fact paid for by the

a Chinese, and submitted that it raised 'yet further suspicions' and had failed to establish that the China deal had had a legitimate commercial purpose.

[32] This further evidence since the hearing below has been admitted in this court by common consent of the parties.

[33] I would mention in passing that documents exhibited at various stages in the evidence produced on behalf of Mr Black as having been obtained by means *b* of the United States Act bear on them a legend beginning 'CFTC-FOIA-DOCS'. Examples are the note of the SIB meeting of 30 May 1996 and the CNIEC fax of 16 June 1996. I would infer that such documents have been in the possession of the CFTC.

[34] I have referred to the evidence relating to the China deal in some detail because the China deal appears to have been at the root of Deputy Judge Brindle's *c* decision to order disclosure, because on appeal it has been at the core of Mr Vos QC's submissions on behalf of Mr Black, and because there has been further evidence on the subject since the hearing below.

MR BLACK'S EVIDENCE

d [35] At the time of the opening of the hearing below Mr Black had not personally submitted any evidence to the court. Evidence had been produced on his behalf by his solicitor, Mr Rabinowicz. At the hearing Deputy Judge Brindle had required Mr Black to verify the letter before action and a witness statement was produced to which the deputy judge referred in his judgment. In it Mr Black verified both the letter of 21 December 1996 and Mr Rabinowicz's first two *e* witness statements. He also stated that had the market not been manipulated following Mr Hamanaka's dismissal in June 1996 then the price of copper would have fallen significantly: and that at the time everyone had believed that the manipulations of the Hamanaka period were no longer in the system.

f THE JUDGMENT BELOW

[36] Deputy Judge Brindle addressed himself to four questions in turn. (1) Are proceedings (between the parties) likely? (2) Do the documents sought fall within the scope of standard disclosure? (3) Is pre-action disclosure 'desirable' for any of the three reasons set out in CPR 31.16(3)(d)? (4) Should the court order disclosure in the exercise of its discretion?

g [37] CPR 31.16(3) begins: 'The court may make an order under this rule only where …'. What follows sets out the jurisdictional thresholds to an order under the rule, and when those thresholds have been crossed, there remains an exercise of discretion: see *Bermuda International Securities Ltd v KPMG (a firm)* [2001] EWCA Civ 269, [2001] Lloyd's Rep PN 392, a decision of this court cited by Deputy Judge *h* Brindle. Thus these four questions were intended to address the three jurisdictional thresholds mentioned (1) in CPR 31.16(3)(a) and (b), (2) in CPR 31.16(3)(c), and (3) in CPR 31.16(3)(d) respectively; and finally to address (4) the ultimate issue of discretion.

[38] Deputy Judge Brindle spent most of his judgment addressing the first *j* question. He concluded, on the guidance of authorities on s 33(2) of the 1981 Act in its pre-amended form, at the time when it was dealing with pre-action disclosure only in the case of personal injury claims, that the test of proceedings being 'likely' was that the prospective claimant has a 'reasonable basis' for making a claim against the prospective defendant: but that in this context such a claim meant *not* a prima facie claim nor even one that could resist being struck out, but rather a claim which was not merely based on irresponsible allegation or

speculation or hope, which was not a merely fishing claim. This much appears
to have been common ground below. He appears to have also accepted in the
light of the earlier authorities, that a claim might have a reasonable basis in the
sense required if—

> 'in cases where a prima facie cause of action does not yet exist ... there is a
> reasonable basis for believing that it might do if disclosure could first be
> ordered.'

[39] In this context he dealt with conflicting submissions on whether a case of
fraud fell to be considered any differently from any other case. For these
purposes he was treating a case of fraud as extending to any case in which
allegations of dishonest or criminal conduct were being made, such as the case
being advanced by Mr Black before him. He concluded that there was no
essential difference: a case of fraud might fall foul of the disapproval of speculative
or ill-founded allegations or of mere fishing, but if there was a reasonable basis for
the allegations, then the court should be cautious about letting possible fraudsters
escape down the 'black hole' of the absence of documentation which made it
impossible for the claimant to plead his case. Indeed, it might be said that 'the
inhibitions on pleading fraud in English law and practice militate in favour of
allowing pre-action disclosure ...'.

[40] He therefore turned to the facts to consider 'whether or not there is a
reasonable basis for an allegation of ... conspiratorial or anti-competitive
behaviour' and concluded that there was, but only because of the evidence
relating to the China deal. Thus he said:

> 'Plainly Sumitomo were dealing with very large copper positions in futures
> and options, almost any trading in which was bound to affect the market in
> some way or another ... I think that Mr Vos and his clients face real
> difficulties in framing an arguable claim against Sumitomo arising out of
> these activities ... Most of the facts and matters relied upon by Mr Vos seem
> to me at this stage to be at least capable of reasonable explanation by
> Sumitomo. When, however, the evidence relating to the "China deal" is
> added, it seems to me that a different picture is suggested.'

[41] As to that, he thought that Sumitomo was being coy, and that there
were—

> 'non-fanciful grounds to suspect that the transaction may not have been a
> genuine sale ... The deal seems most peculiar and calls for explanation ... I
> therefore conclude that it is "likely" that Mr Black and his companies on the
> one hand and Sumitomo on the other will both become parties to litigation,
> which litigation will have a reasonable basis along the lines of the authorities
> cited to me.'

It is to be observed that at this stage Deputy Judge Brindle had merely answered
the first question as to his jurisdiction, and had decided, on a narrow basis, that
litigation between the parties was 'likely'. He had not as yet undertaken an
exercise of discretion.

[42] Deputy Judge Brindle then proceeded to the second question, as to
standard disclosure. That was effectively dealt with by an agreement between
the parties that, if disclosure was ordered, it would simply be limited in the order
itself to standard disclosure. Therefore there was no consideration of the issues
which were likely to arise in any proceedings and whether standard disclosure

a would extend to the documents demanded. It may be noted that Deputy Judge Brindle stated: 'The order will be limited accordingly'. Of course, he had not yet determined that an order for disclosure would be made.

[43] Deputy Judge Brindle considered the third question and concluded that it would be desirable to order disclosure not only in relation to the China deal but also generally. 'I have also been persuaded that disclosure should not be limited
b to the China deal.' He appears to have thought that that each of the three limbs of CPR 31.16(3)(d) had been met. There was 'a real possibility' that early disclosure would dispose fairly of the anticipated proceedings or assist the dispute to be resolved without proceedings; as for the saving of costs, he was 'not convinced', but there was a very real prospect that it would occur in one way or another—either by Mr Black withdrawing without commencing proceedings, or
c by the resolution of such proceedings by agreement, or by Sumitomo being inclined not to contest the claim. This hurdle was dealt with in a single paragraph, without, it was submitted on behalf of Sumitomo, much if anything in the way of reasoning, and without any reasons for extending disclosure beyond the China deal.

d [44] Deputy Judge Brindle then dealt with the fourth and final stage, the ultimate exercise of his discretion. He covered this in a few lines:

'Once the test of desirability is met, it is unlikely (although possible) for an order to be refused altogether. It is clear from what I have said above that an order should be made and I exercise my discretion to do so, subject
e to issues of oppression.'

[45] Under the heading of oppression, Deputy Judge Brindle found that a real case had been made on behalf of Sumitomo, based on the enormous number of documents, not chronologically ordered, which would have to be looked through if an order were granted in the terms sought. He thought, however, that
f he could overcome this danger by limiting the disclosure that he was prepared to order even beyond concessions that had been made by Mr Vos in the course of the hearing.

THE ORDER MADE

g [46] Ultimately Deputy Judge Brindle made an order in the following terms:

'1. Statements showing copper warrants held by or on behalf of the respondents (or any of them) throughout or at any time during the period 1 June–1 October 1996.

h 2. Daily trading statements showing copper futures positions, copper options, or any other copper positions, held, granted, purchased and/or sold by or on behalf of the respondents (or any of them) throughout or at any time during the period from 1 June–1 October 1996 on or through the LME and/or COMEX.

j 3. Documents containing or evidencing any agreement between the respondents or any of them and Goldman Sachs (or any part of Goldman Sachs) relating to the advice given or action taken by Goldman Sachs (or any part of Goldman Sachs) in relation to Sumitomo's copper positions on the LME and/or COMEX during the period 1 June–1 October 1996.

4. Documents evidencing the China deal (referred to in Mr Vigrass' first statement) and made between Global, CNIEC and/or the respondents (or any of them).

5. Documents disclosing the China deal (referred to in para 4, above) to the regulatory authorities.

6. Documents evidencing the physical delivery of copper to CNIEC as referred to in Mr Vigrass' first statement.

7. Judgments or pleadings in civil or regulatory actions brought since June 1996 by or against the respondents (or any of them) relating to or involving allegations in respect of the China deal (referred to in para 4, above) and/or to manipulation of the copper market between 1 June 1996 and 1 October 1996.

8. Written communications from the respondents (or any of them or any person on their behalf) to CFTC, SIB, SFA or LME and/or notes of meetings between the respondents (or any of them or any person on their behalf) and CFTC, SIB, SFA or LME between 1 June 1996 and 1 October 1996 relating to the disclosure of Sumitomo's intentions and activities in relation to the unwinding of its copper positions.

9. Any transcripts and/or minutes of the meeting of 28 June 1996 referred to in Mr London's statement.'

THE SUBMISSIONS

[47] Detailed written and oral submissions were made on all aspects of the evidence, on the pre-CPR authorities which had influenced Deputy Judge Brindle, on the background to CPR 31.16, on the role of disclosure in the CPR era, and as to the breadth or narrowness of the disclosure ordered. In particular, Mr Vos continued to emphasise the loose ends in the evidence concerning the China deal. As to the circumstances of the case, the position remained what it had been before Deputy Judge Brindle, with Mr Hollander QC (who appeared for Sumitomo) describing this as an archetypal fishing exercise, and Mr Vos calling it a paradigm case for disclosure. Ultimately, the essential difference between the parties on this appeal was that Mr Hollander submitted that Deputy Judge Brindle had never really stood back to take account of the circumstances of the case for the purpose of an exercise of discretion, whereas Mr Vos submitted that Deputy Judge Brindle had taken everything into account and that his decision on what in the end was a matter for his discretion was unassailable.

[48] Mr Hollander also drew attention to a feature of the appeal which he submitted was in stark contrast to the position below. As appears from Deputy Judge Brindle's judgment, Mr Black's case had been regarded primarily as one about a dishonest conspiracy to manipulate markets, a case akin to fraud (with anti-competitive behaviour under arts 81, 82 EC as an alternative). I will also use 'fraud' as the handle for such a primary case. Moreover, Mr Black was determined to sue, unless perhaps pre-action disclosure satisfied him that he had no case. Deputy Judge Brindle said that he had 'a clear settled intention to sue', a description of which Mr Vos made some complaint, but in my judgment it reflects the evidence and I have no reason to think that it did not accurately reflect the way in which the matter was put before the deputy judge. On appeal, however, Mr Vos went a long way to suggest a very different scenario. He put anti-competitive behaviour under arts 81, 82 EC (formerly arts 85, 86 of the EC Treaty) rather than fraud at the forefront of his argument. He also suggested that, whatever his client's wishes, Mr Black might find it hard to obtain counsel's signature to a pleading of fraud on the current material available to Mr Black and in the absence of something more revealing emerging out of pre-action disclosure.

ACCESS TO JUSTICE

a   **[49]** In *Access to Justice*, Lord Woolf made his proposals on the subject of disclosure of documents. He recommended that the process of disclosure within litigation should be curtailed, save in the exceptional case, to what he called 'standard disclosure', a term which has been adopted in the CPR. That recommendation was made because (p 124 (para 37)) 'the process had become

b   disproportionate, especially in larger cases where large numbers of documents may have to be searched for and disclosed, though only a small number turn out to be significant'. On the other hand, in the context of pre-action disclosure, he recommended that the court's power to make such orders should no longer be confined to potential claims in respect of personal injury or death but should extend to all cases. He wrote (pp 127–128):

c
> '49. There may be some apprehension about the unforeseen consequences of such an extension. In relation to claims for injury or death, it was fairly clear against which categories of potential defendants such applications were likely to be made. When the jurisdiction to make pre-action orders was first introduced, applications for medical records tended to be hard-fought and
d   often acrimonious. I understand that it is now rarely necessary even to make such applications, since documents are usually provided directly in response to a reasonable request. I have no doubt that the recent protocol prepared by the Civil Litigation Committee of the Law Society for use in this context will have helped further to simplify the process. This involves the use of standard forms of request and response, and has been approved by the NHS
e   Management Executive.

> 50. Opening up the range of cases in which pre-action applications may be made obviously widens the range of potential defendants who might be subject to such applications. But it must be remembered, first, that any such application would have to be in respect of specific documents, which will
f   have to be shown to be in the possession of the respondent; secondly, that there is a likelihood that the respondent would indeed be a defendant if proceedings were initiated; and, thirdly, that the documents sought are relevant to a potential claim … [T]he court would apply a rigorous cost-benefit analysis … I believe that its effect would be that the court would
g   invariably not allow disclosure [beyond standard disclosure] at a stage when issues had not been fully elaborated between the parties.'

[50] In the event, CPR 31.16 is not limited to applications in respect of 'specific documents', because CPR 31.16(3)(c) speaks of 'documents or classes of documents'. Otherwise, Lord Woolf's recommendations are reflected in the
h   new rule.

PROTOCOLS AND FRAUD

[51] In the passage quoted above from *Access to Justice*, Lord Woolf referred to the protocol then recently prepared for use in personal injury litigation. The
j   existence of a protocol is not without relevance to the question of pre-action disclosure: it may indicate that documents of a certain class, such as the paradigm case of medical records in clinical disputes, should as a matter of course be disclosed before service of a claim form. But protocols have, at any rate so far, been developed in areas of litigation, such as personal injury claims, clinical disputes, construction and engineering disputes, and professional negligence disputes, where familiarity with the nature of such disputes and/or the

interrelationship of the parties indicate the way forward: see the discussion of
such protocols in *Bermuda International Securities Ltd v KPMG (a firm)* [2001]
Lloyd's Rep PN 392, since when the professional negligence protocol has been
formally published and has come into force in July 2001. Outside those areas and
CPR 31.16 itself the guiding principle of practice is that set out in the Practice
Direction—Protocols, White Book (*Civil Procedure* (2001)) vol 1, pp 1983–1987
(paras C1-001–C1-005), p 1984 (para C1-003) which reads as follows:

> '4.1 In cases not covered by any approved protocol, the court will expect
> the parties, in accordance with the overriding objective and the matters
> referred to in CPR 1.1(2)(a), (b) and (c), to act reasonably in exchanging
> information and documents relevant to the claim and generally in trying to
> avoid the necessity for the start of proceedings.'

[52] In this context it is necessary to stand back for a moment and ask oneself
what, if anything, the nature of the current dispute and the interrelationship of its
parties indicate as to the proper role of pre-action exchange of information and
documents. Mr Black's claim does not arise out of any contractual dispute or any
professional relationship. It does not arise out of the relationship inherent in a
situation where one party owes a duty of care to another (his 'neighbour', in Lord
Atkin's formula) breach of which has resulted in personal injury or death. If there
has been any fraud or manipulation, it has not been between parties to a contract
but affects Mr Black only in as much as he was part of a worldwide market. I
would accept Mr Hollander's submission that in terms of the current dispute
Mr Black and Sumitomo are in essence strangers. Mr Vos's response is that they
are not total strangers in that Mr Black is well known in the world of copper
trading; and he also relies on the unparticularised allegation that Sumitomo
refused to sell to Mr Black in the aftermath of the Hamanaka affair. Nevertheless,
for over four years Mr Black remained silent. His public utterances spoke only of
his gains and of anticipated price levels which are inconsistent with his present
claim. Thus unlike a personal injury claimant who has suffered some undoubted
misfortune, but needs disclosure to investigate the mechanism of his misfortune,
Mr Black's losses are themselves a matter of uncertainty and dispute. No
complaint was made to the regulatory authorities which he knew were
investigating the situation.

[53] Mr Black says that until his recent acquisition of documents by means of
the United States Act, he was unable to proceed. That raises the question of the
extent of material in or potentially in the public domain and available to
Mr Black. Mr Vos has submitted that pre-action disclosure is necessary in this
case to ensure that dishonesty is brought to light. But Mr Black's case is based on
documents which he has himself obtained from public sources. Mr Black,
perhaps for understandable tactical reasons, has not disclosed in one go all such
documents as he currently possesses. Thus he has responded to Sumitomo's first
round of evidence on the China deal by putting forward the fax dated 29 May 1996
from Sumitomo to Global and the note of the SIB meeting of 30 May 1996; and
he has responded to Sumitomo's post-judgment disclosure by putting in evidence
the fax dated 16 June 1996 from CNIEC to Sumitomo. Deputy Judge Brindle
thought that Sumitomo was being coy about the China deal; but this is not a case
in which Mr Black has started by putting all his cards on the table either. In this
connection Mr O'Keefe's role is uncertain: on the one hand he has been faithful
to his obligations, but on the other hand that has not prevented him from

a   assisting in relation to potential claims in respect of information where he is 'likely to be reliable and well informed'.

[54] Mr Vos has sought to play down the case of fraud raised in Mr Black's letter before action and in his evidence and to emphasise instead the case of anti-competitive behaviour under arts 81 and 82 EC. On the other hand Deputy Judge Brindle and this court were pressed by him with the problems which an

b   allegation of fraud presents at the pre-action stage. At a general level, there are clearly concerns that allegations of dishonesty are not lightly made, that a defendant to an allegation of dishonesty knows plainly what it is that is alleged against him, and also that dishonesty does not spread its cloak over the means by which it can be detected and revealed. It is not plain how these concerns are to be reconciled in any particular case in the context of pre-action disclosure, but it

c   would seem to me that a court which is asked to grant such disclosure should be careful to pay proper regard to each of them. In any event it cannot be right that an allegation of fraud should assist the potential claimant to obtain pre-action disclosure, unless his allegations carry both some specificity and some conviction and his request for disclosure is appropriately focused.

d   [55] Traditionally at any rate, English law has been cautious about the allegation of dishonesty. Thus Mr Hollander relied in this context on *Hytrac Conveyors Ltd v Conveyors International Ltd* [1982] 3 All ER 415, [1983] 1 WLR 44, where the plaintiffs, who wished to advance a case of conspiracy to infringe their copyright, applied for an extension of time to serve their statement of claim pending the obtaining of interlocutory injunctions. This court, in refusing the

e   application, said this ([1982] 3 All ER 415 at 418, [1983] 1 WLR 44 at 47 per Lawton LJ):

> 'It has to be remembered by all concerned that we do not have in this country an inquisitorial procedure for civil litigation. Our procedure is accusatorial. Those who make charges must state right at the beginning
f   what they are and what facts they are based on. They must not use Anton Piller orders as a means of finding out what sort of charges they can make.'

[56] In *RHM Foods Ltd v Bovril Ltd* [1982] 1 All ER 673, [1982] 1 WLR 661 the plaintiffs, in a passing-off action, sought disclosure in advance of pleading their statement of claim. They alleged a deliberate intent to deceive the public. The

g   judge acceded to the application. This court acknowledged the jurisdiction to make such an order, but considered that the exercise of that jurisdiction would require an exceptional case and that it would be unfair to the defendants to order disclosure against them before the plaintiffs had pleaded their serious allegations. Oliver LJ said ([1982] 1 All ER 673 at 680, [1982] 1 WLR 661 at 668–669):

h
> 'I do not say that there cannot be such a case, for the court has a wide power to order discovery where the justice of the case demands it, but it must be very rare. Like Lawton LJ, I remain, despite the powerful advocacy of counsel for the plaintiffs, wholly unconvinced that this case, on the unparticularised allegations of his deponents' individual beliefs, is a case where the discovery sought at this stage is necessary for fairly disposing of the matter and I too, therefore, would allow the appeal.'

[57] Those cases were decided under the former regime of the Rules of the Supreme Court 1965 and I do not consider them to be formally binding in the context of the CPR, a new code with its overriding objective, its greater flexibility, its statements of truth, and its new principles of disclosure, favouring

both more limited disclosure and earlier disclosure. Nevertheless, in my
judgment it is not to be supposed that in the modern context allegations of fraud   *a*
have become just like any other allegations. There is still the obligation on
counsel pleading fraud to satisfy himself that he can properly do so: Mr Vos has
himself relied on that obligation, to hint that without the pre-action disclosure
which his client seeks, he might find himself unable to sign a statement of
case which pleads fraud. There is still the obligation (see CPR PD 16, para 8.2) to   *b*
'specifically set out' any allegation of fraud.

[58] Moreover, if the opportunity provided by CPR 31.16 is set against the
background of the prospective parties' obligation in any case not covered by a
protocol 'to act reasonably in exchanging information and documents relevant to
the claim' (see White Book (*Civil Procedure* (2001)) vol 1, p 1984 (para C1-003) and
if consideration is given to the question of what the extent of that obligation is in   *c*
a case of alleged fraud, it is hard to think that a prospective claimant could easily
say that his allegedly fraudulent prospective defendant had failed to co-operate by
refusing widespread disclosure in response to unspecific and unverified (because
unpleaded) allegations.

d

THE PREVIOUS AUTHORITIES ON s 33(2) OF THE 1981 ACT

[59] Although Deputy Judge Brindle did not regard those authorities as
binding, he did nevertheless derive assistance from them on the question of the
application of the jurisdictional test that the applicant and the respondent were
'likely' to be parties to subsequent litigation. Mr Vos, who had relied on them   *e*
before Deputy Judge Brindle (without, it may be said, much opposition) to
support his submissions as to the meaning of 'likely', in the end himself accepted
that they were of doubtful value since they turned on the meaning of a phrase
('likely to be made') which has now dropped out of the subsection.

[60] In the circumstances it is unnecessary to consider those authorities on the
basis that they are binding precedents: but, since they provided support for   *f*
Deputy Judge Brindle 's approach and also because they illustrate a point of real
difficulty about the way in which the opportunity for pre-action disclosure is to
be applied, I will deal with them to see what if any value they have in the present
circumstances.

[61] Section 33(2) of the 1981 Act was originally enacted as s 31 of the
Administration of Justice Act 1970, and used to read as follows: *g*

> 'On the application, in accordance with rules of court, of a person who
> appears to the High Court to be likely to be a party to subsequent
> proceedings in that court *in which a claim in respect of personal injuries to a
> person or in respect of a person's death is likely to be made*, the High Court shall ...'   *r*

The words in italics were removed by the amendment. It will be observed that
the deleted phrase ends with the words 'likely to be made'. Those are the words
which the previous authorities had to construe.

[62] The first case on the meaning of those words was *Dunning v Board of
Governors of the United Liverpool Hospitals* [1973] 2 All ER 454, [1973] 1 WLR 586.
Mrs Dunning was admitted to hospital with a cough for investigation but was
otherwise in good health, but while there became gravely ill. The hospital
refused to release the hospital case notes. Mrs Dunning obtained legal aid to
bring proceedings against the hospital, *despite* her medical expert's report to the
effect that, while assessment had been hampered by the absence of the notes, the
hospital was probably *not* at fault. However, he also said that the failure to release

a   the notes had unreasonably prolonged the litigation and he urged their release so that he could determine whether or not they confirmed his opinion. The difficulty in the case was that because more than six years had passed since Mrs Dunning's stay in hospital, leave was needed to bring the proceedings for which legal aid had been granted. The application for leave was adjourned, for in the light of the expert's opinion and the hospital's continuing refusal to disclose *b*   the notes there was no basis for an action at a time when there was no provision for pre-action disclosure. Section 31 of the 1970 Act then came into force and Mrs Dunning applied under it for pre-action disclosure of the notes. The question was whether a claim was 'likely to be made': if it was, then of course Mrs Dunning and the hospital were likely to be parties. Stamp LJ dissented ([1973] 2 All ER 454 at 458, 459, [1973] 1 WLR 586 at 591, 592) on the ground that *c*   in the light of the expert's opinion proceedings were unlikely, since disclosure was unlikely to produce anything to justify it. Lord Denning MR, however, thought ([1973] 2 All ER 454 at 457, [1973] 1 WLR 586 at 590) that 'likely' merely meant 'may' or 'may well be made' dependent on the outcome of the disclosure. The object of the statute would be defeated if the applicant had to show in *d*   advance that he already had a good cause of action. James LJ thought ([1973] 2 All ER 454 at 460, [1973] 1 WLR 586 at 593–594) that a claim was 'likely' if there was a 'reasonable prospect' of one: and on the facts he pointed out the evidence of the sudden dramatic change in Mrs Dunning's health and the expert's report with its express need to see the hospital records.

e   [63] In the next case, *Shaw v Vauxhall Motors Ltd* [1974] 2 All ER 1185, [1974] 1 WLR 1035, the applicant was injured driving a truck at work. There was a dispute with his employers about whether the truck was defective. The applicant wanted disclosure of the maintenance records of the truck to see whether the braking system was defective. The application was made on the advice of counsel to enable him to advise the legal aid committee: it was made clear that if the *f*   records supported the complaint that the system was defective, litigation would ensue, otherwise it would not. The judge refused disclosure, but it was ordered by this court. The judgments make it clear that it was common ground that there was jurisdiction under s 31 of the 1970 Act to make the order sought, and the argument was whether it should be made as a matter of discretion. All three judgments were agreed that it should be. The rule of court in question was *g*   RSC Ord 24, r 8, which put on the respondent the burden of showing that discovery was 'not necessary either for disposing fairly of the cause or matter or for saving costs'. Lord Denning MR thought ([1974] 2 All ER 1185 at 1188, [1974] 1 WLR 1035 at 1039) that in such a case it should be the general practice to order disclosure as it enabled each side to know the strength or weakness of the case *h*   before embarking on litigation: 'It is particularly useful in a legal aid case ...' . Buckley LJ said ([1974] 2 All ER 1185 at 1188, [1974] 1 WLR 1035 at 1040) that the power to order pre-trial disclosure 'is certainly not one which should be used to encourage fishing expeditions to enable a prospective plaintiff to discover whether he has in fact got a case at all', but that there were two special grounds *j*   in favour of the order in that case (see [1974] 2 All ER 1185 at 1189, [1974] 1 WLR 1035 at 1040–1041): one was that it was in the public interest that advisers of legally aided parties should have early information on matters which may affect the parties' position in the litigation; and the other was that the applicant had conceded that if the records showed that the truck was not defective, the claim would be dropped. Ormrod LJ agreed with both those factors ([1974] 2 All ER 1185 at 1189, 1190, [1974] 1 WLR 1035 at 1041, 1042), and also stressed the

importance of a letter before action in which the applicant should commit himself
as to how the accident happened or else state that he did not know.

[64] Although *Shaw*'s case was a case on discretion, Lord Denning MR
repeated his view in *Dunning*'s case that the words 'likely to be made' mean 'may'
or 'may well be made' dependent on the outcome of the discovery and said
([1974] 2 All ER 1185 at 1187, [1974] 1 WLR 1035 at 1039) that that was what
Dunning's case had decided.

[65] The third case considered below and cited to this court was *Burns v
Shuttlehurst Ltd* [1999] 2 All ER 27, [1999] 1 WLR 1449. This was still concerned
with the unamended s 33(2) of the 1981 Act. The underlying facts were similar
to those in *Shaw*'s case, that is to say the applicant had been injured while driving
his employers' vehicle. He had already obtained judgment against his employers,
but now wanted to recover against their insurers under the Third Parties (Rights
against Insurers) Act 1930: he therefore sought pre-action disclosure against the
insurers of the employers' insurance policies. It was held that a claim under the
1930 Act against insurers was not a claim for personal injuries within s 33(2) of the
1981 Act; but also that in any event the applicant had no cause of action until his
claim against the employers had been quantified and therefore a claim against the
insurers was both premature and not 'likely'. The only reasoned judgment was
given by Stuart-Smith LJ. He interpreted *Dunning*'s case somewhat differently.
Having pointed out that Lord Denning MR had interpreted 'likely to be made' as
meaning 'may' or 'may well be made' dependent on the outcome of the discovery,
he went on to say ([1999] 2 All ER 27 at 35–36, [1999] 1 WLR 1449 at 1457
(paras 32–33)) that both James LJ and Stamp LJ had formulated the same test
'namely, at the time of the application there must be shown to be a worthwhile
action or a reasonable basis for the intended action', albeit they had differed on
what the facts had shown. He then said ([1999] 2 All ER 27 at 36, [1999] 1 WLR
1449 at 1458 (para 34)) that in *Burns*' case there was probably just enough to show
a reasonable basis for an intended action, if the applicant otherwise had a
complete cause of action; but he did not. He went on to accept that, once the
applicant's judgment against the employers had been quantified the documents
would clearly be discoverable (see [1999] 2 All ER 27 at 38, [1999] 1 WLR 1449 at
1459 (para 39)), but that in the meantime there was no cause of action and thus
([1999] 2 All ER 27 at 37, [1999] 1 WLR 1449 at 1459 (para 37)) 'I do not see how
it can be said that a claim is likely'. It would seem, therefore, that the temporary
absence of any legal basis for a claim (*Post Office v Norwich Union Fire Insurance
Society Ltd* [1967] 1 All ER 577, [1967] 2 QB 363 had made that established law)
prevented it being said that a claim was 'likely'.

[66] The phrase 'a claim ... is likely to be made' is no longer part of the
amended s 33(2) of the 1981 Act and therefore on any view these authorities are
no longer binding. If, however, it matters, my own interpretation of these
authorities is as follows. In *Dunning v Board of Governors of the United Liverpool
Hospitals* [1973] 2 All ER 454, [1973] 1 WLR 586 both Lord Denning MR and
James LJ agreed that the word 'likely' in that phrase did not mean 'more likely on
the balance of probability than not' in the absence of disclosure but meant 'may'
or 'may well' or 'reasonable prospect' if disclosure was granted. It is harder to say
what Stamp LJ thought 'likely' meant, for he did not gloss its meaning: but he too
agreed ([1973] 2 All ER 454 at 458, [1973] 1 WLR 586 at 591) that in deciding
whether a claim was likely it was permissible for the court to consider, on the
evidence before it, whether disclosure was likely to produce 'a worthwhile and
catchable fish'. He added:

a
'The word "likely" must in my view be read as connoting that the respondent to the application is likely to be a party to a worthwhile action by a litigant not acting irresponsibly'.

I do not myself believe that Stamp LJ was there construing the section—and certainly not the word 'likely' which is repeated in that sentence without being glossed—so much as laying down a principle as to the exercise of discretion. If,

b
however, he was construing the section, then in my respectful opinion, he was alone in doing so in this way. James LJ, in a passage picked up and cited by Stuart-Smith LJ in *Burns'* case, said ([1973] 2 All ER 454 at 460, [1973] 1 WLR 586 at 593):

c
'In order to take advantage of the section the applicant for relief must disclose the nature of the claim he intends to make and show not only the intention of making it but also that there is a reasonable basis for making it. Ill-founded, irresponsible and speculative allegations or allegations based merely on hope would not provide a reasonable basis for an intended claim in subsequent proceedings.'

d
That, however, as it seems to me, is clearly not an attempt to construe the section but a statement of principle as to the exercise of its discretion. That is shown by a similar discussion in *Shaw's* case, which was a case entirely about discretion, for jurisdiction was there common ground. As to construction, which was therefore not in issue, Lord Denning MR there stated his view that in *Dunning's* case this

e
court had held that the phrase meant 'may' or 'may well be made' dependent on the outcome of the disclosure. That was an obiter dictum, but it seems to me that it was entirely correct.

[67] As for *Burns'* case, it is possible that Stuart-Smith LJ (with the approval of the other members of the court) did intend to adopt, on his reading of *Dunning's*

f
case, the test of 'a worthwhile action or a reasonable basis for the intended action' as having been laid down by James and Stamp LJJ as the test for deciding whether a claim was 'likely to be made': but if so, it follows from what I have said above that I would respectfully disagree with that interpretation. If that was his intention, the question might arise, although the amendment to s 33(2) of the 1981 Act makes the possibility a theoretical one, whether the interpretation of

g
Dunning's case found in *Burns'* case is part of the ratio of the latter case and binding on this court, whatever *Dunning's* case said. Happily, however, that question need not trouble the determination of the present appeal.

[68] What, however, these authorities on the unamended section in my judgment reveal, and usefully so, is as follows. First, that at any rate in its origin

h
the power to grant pre-trial disclosure was not intended to assist only those who could already plead a cause of action to improve their pleadings, but also those who needed disclosure as a vital step in deciding whether to litigate at all or as a vital ingredient in the pleading of their case. Secondly, however, that (as what I would call a matter of discretion) it was highly relevant in those cases that the

j
injury was clear and called for examination of the documents in question, the disclosure requested was narrowly focused and bore directly on the injury complained of and responsibility for it, and the documents would be decisive on the conduct or even the existence of the litigation. Thirdly, that on the question of discretion, it was material that a prospective claimant in need of legal aid might be unable even to commence proceedings without the help of pre-action disclosure.

THE AMENDED s 33(2) OF THE 1981 ACT AND THE CURRENT RULE OF COURT

[69] I now turn to the amended s 33(2) of the 1981 Act and the current rule of court, and will consider first of all the jurisdictional thresholds which have to be passed ('only where' (see CPR 31.16(3))) in order to vest a court with discretion to make an order for pre-trial disclosure.

CPR 31.16(3)(A) AND (B): 'LIKELY TO BE A PARTY'

[70] The application has to be made by 'a person ... likely to be a party to subsequent proceedings' against 'a person ... likely to be a party to the proceedings' (s 33(2) of the 1981 Act) and those requirements are reflected (in reverse order) in CPR 31.16(3)(a) and (b). There is no longer any statutory requirement that 'a claim ... is likely to be made'.

[71] Of course, in one sense it might be said that a person is hardly likely to be a party to subsequent proceedings whether as a claimant or otherwise unless some form of proceedings is itself likely to be issued. Two questions, however, arise. One is whether the statute requires that it be likely that proceedings are issued, or only that the persons concerned are likely to be parties *if* subsequent proceedings are issued. The other is whether 'likely' means 'more probably than not' or 'may well'. As to the first question, in my judgment the amended statute means no more than that the persons concerned are likely to be parties in proceedings if those proceedings are issued. That was what Lord Woolf had in mind when he wrote of the requirement that 'there is a likelihood that the respondent would indeed be a defendant if proceedings were initiated' (*Access to Justice* p 127 (para 50) (see [46], above)). The omission of any language which expressly requires that the initiation of proceedings itself be likely, which could have been included in the amended section, appears to me to reflect the difficulties which the earlier authorities had explored in the sort of circumstances found in *Dunning v Board of Governors of the United Liverpool Hospitals* [1973] 2 All ER 454, [1973] 1 WLR 586. What the current language of the section appears to me to emphasise, as does the rule of court, is that the parties concerned in an application are parties who would be likely to be involved if proceedings ensued. The concern is that pre-action disclosure would be sought against a stranger to any possible proceedings, or by a party who would himself be unlikely to be involved. If the statute and rule are understood in this sense, then all difficulties, which might arise where the issue of proceedings might depend crucially on the nature of the disclosure sought and where it is impossible at the time of making the application to say whether the disclosure would critically support or undermine the prospective claim, disappear.

[72] As to the second question, it is not uncommon for 'likely' to mean something less than probable in its strict sense. It seems to me that if I am wrong about the first question, then it is plain that 'likely' must be given its more extended and open meaning (see Lord Denning MR in *Dunning*'s case), because otherwise one of the fundamental purposes of the statute will have been undermined. If, however, I am right about the first question, the second question is of less moment. Even so, however, I am inclined to answer it by saying that 'likely' here means no more than 'may well'. Where the future has to be predicted, but on an application which is not merely pre-trial but pre-action, a high test requiring proof on the balance of probability will be both undesirable and unnecessary: undesirable, because it does not respond to the nature and timing of the application; and unnecessary, because the court has all the power it needs in the overall exercise of its discretion to balance the possible uncertainties

a of the situation against the specificity or otherwise of the disclosure requested. Clearly, the narrower the disclosure requested and the more determinative it may be of the dispute in issue between the parties to the application, the easier it is for the court to find the request well founded; and vice versa.

b [73] On this basis, I think that Deputy Judge Brindle was led into error by the fact that before him there had been a large degree of common ground about seeking to derive from the earlier cases a complicated formula as to the meaning of 'likely'. In my view, apart from the two issues of principle which present themselves and which I have sought to answer in this section of my judgment, the word itself presents no difficulties. Temptations to gloss the statutory language should be resisted. The jurisdictional threshold is not, I think, intended to be a high one. The real question is likely to be one of discretion, and answering

c the jurisdictional question in the affirmative is unlikely in itself to give the judge much of a steer as to the correct exercise of his power.

CPR 31.16(3)(C): 'DUTY BY WAY OF STANDARD DISCLOSURE ... WOULD EXTEND TO THE DOCUMENTS'

d [74] Any dispute before Deputy Judge Brindle as to whether the duty of standard disclosure in any proceedings between Mr Black and Sumitomo would extend to the documents which ultimately might become the subject matter of Deputy Judge Brindle's order was surmounted by the agreement that disclosure of such documents would be limited to standard disclosure. That agreement tended to obscure and perhaps to obliterate any argument as to whether any of

e the categories of documents requested were inherently outside the regime of standard disclosure.

[75] In the circumstances it seems to me that no question of jurisdiction or principle can arise on this threshold in this case.

[76] In general, however, it should in my judgment be remembered that the

f extent of standard disclosure cannot easily be discerned without clarity as to the issues which would arise once pleadings in the prospective litigation had been formulated. This court touched on the question in *Bermuda International Securities Ltd v KPMG (a firm)* [2001] Lloyd's Rep PN 392 when Waller LJ there said (at [26]):

g 'The circumstances spelt out by the rule show that it will "only" be ordered where the court can say that the documents asked for will be documents that will have to be produced at the standard disclosure stage. It follows from that, that the court must be clear what the issues in the litigation are likely to be ie what case the claimant is likely to be making and what defence is likely to be being run so as to make sure the documents being asked for are ones which will adversely affect the case of one side or the other, or support the

h case of one side or the other.'

[77] It also seems to me to follow that if there would be considerable doubt as to whether the disclosure stage would ever be reached, that is a matter which the court can and should take into account as a matter of its discretion.

j [78] In any event, all issues of discretion remain. The fact that the jurisdictional threshold under CPR 31.16 (3)(c) was dealt with by agreement tended, in my judgment, to obscure the necessity for clarity as to the issues in the prospective litigation. The importance of such clarity was illustrated in this appeal when the focus of submissions were turned from fraud onto anti-competitive conduct.

CPR 31.16(3)(D): 'DESIRABLE'

[79] This is a difficult test to interpret, for it is framed both in terms of a *a* jurisdictional threshold ('only where') and in terms of the exercise of a discretionary judgment ('desirable').

[80] Three considerations are mentioned in CPR 31.16(3)(d): disposing fairly of the anticipated proceedings; assisting the dispute to be resolved without proceedings; and saving costs. The first of this trio obviously contemplates the *b* disposal of proceedings once they have been commenced—in that context the phrase 'dispose fairly' is a familiar one (see eg RSC Ord 24, r 8); the second as clearly contemplates the possibility of avoiding the initiation of litigation altogether; the third is neutral between both of these possibilities.

[81] It is plain not only that the test of 'desirable' is one that easily merges into an exercise of discretion, but that the test of 'dispose fairly' does so too. In the *c* circumstances, it seems to me that it is necessary not to confuse the jurisdictional and the discretionary aspects of the sub-rule as a whole. In the *Bermuda International* case Waller LJ contemplated (at [26]) that CPR 31.16(3)(d) may involve a two-stage process. I think that is correct. In my judgment, for jurisdictional purposes the court is only permitted to consider the granting of *d* pre-action disclosure where there is a real prospect in principle of such an order being fair to the parties if litigation is commenced, or of assisting the parties to avoid litigation, or of saving costs in any event. If there is such a real prospect, then the court should go on to consider the question of discretion, which has to be considered on all the facts and not merely in principle but in detail.

[82] Of course, since the questions of principle and of detail can merge into *e* one another, it is not easy to keep the two stages of the process separate. Nor is it perhaps vital to do so, *provided* however that the court is aware of the need for both stages to be carried out. The danger, however, is that a court may be misled by the ease with which the jurisdictional threshold can be passed into thinking that it has thereby decided the question of discretion, when in truth it has not. *f* This is a real danger because first, in very many if not most cases it will be possible to make a case for achieving one or other of the three purposes, and secondly, each of the three possibilities is in itself inherently desirable.

[83] The point can be illustrated in a number of ways. For instance, suppose the jurisdictional test is met by the prospect that costs will be saved. That may well happen whenever there are reasonable hopes *either* that litigation can be *g* avoided *or* that pre-action disclosure will assist in avoiding the need for pleadings to be amended after disclosure in the ordinary way. That alternative will occur in a very large number of cases. However, the crossing of the jurisdictional threshold on that basis tells you practically nothing about the broader and more particular discretionary aspects of the individual case or the ultimate exercise of *h* discretion. For that, you need to know much more: if the case is a personal injury claim and the request is for medical records, it is easy to conclude that pre-action disclosure ought to be made; but if the action is a speculative commercial action and the disclosure sought is broad, a fortiori if it is ill-defined, it might be much harder.

[84] In the present case, I think with respect that Deputy Judge Brindle fell into *j* this error. Thus he dealt with CPR 31.16(3)(d) in a single paragraph in which he decided that disclosure relating to the China deal and generally was desirable and should be made. He said that his reasoning or much of it was already dealt with under the heading of the 'likelihood of proceedings'. There, however, he had in turn applied the wrong test; and even though in doing so he had considered

a matters which properly belonged to the question of discretion, by dealing with them for the different purpose of asking himself whether proceedings were likely, he was led into thinking that having decided that proceedings were likely, therefore pre-action disclosure should be made. That is demonstrated by his very next paragraph (headed 'Discretion') where he simply says that 'It is clear from what I have said above that an order should be made …'

b [85] In effect, Deputy Judge Brindle never stood back, having dealt with the jurisdictional thresholds, and asked himself whether this was a case where his discretion should be exercised in favour of disclosure. It cannot be right to think that, wherever proceedings are likely between the parties to such an application and there is a real prospect of one of the purposes under CPR 31.16(3)(d) being met, an order for disclosure should be made of documents which would in due

c course fall within standard disclosure. Otherwise an order for pre-action disclosure should be made in almost every dispute of any seriousness, irrespective of its context and detail. Whereas outside obvious examples such as medical records or their equivalent (as indicated by pre-action protocols) in certain other kinds of disputes, by and large the concept of disclosure being ordered at other

d than the normal time is presented as something differing from the normal, at any rate where the parties at the pre-action stage have been acting reasonably.

[86] It is to be observed that because of the way in which he proceeded, Deputy Judge Brindle decided the question of discretion even before considering the breadth of the discovery requested or the allegation of oppression.

e DISCRETION

[87] Therefore it seems to me that this court is entitled to exercise its discretion anew.

[88] That discretion is not confined and will depend on all the facts of the case. Among the important considerations, however, as it seems to me, are the nature

f of the injury or loss complained of; the clarity and identification of the issues raised by the complaint; the nature of the documents requested; the relevance of any protocol or pre-action inquiries; and the opportunity which the complainant has to make his case without pre-action disclosure.

[89] In the present case, the loss complained of is a speculative market loss of $126m. Apart from one element in the claim which is put as costs of $14m

g actually incurred, almost the entire claim is made up of a lost opportunity for gain calculated at $130m. As a claim, it was unknown for four years during which Mr Black made no complaint about Sumitomo. When the letter before action of 21 December 2000 was written, it came out of the blue. This was despite the fact that throughout those years it was well known that Sumitomo was having to deal

h with its ongoing responsibility for Mr Hamanaka's market manipulation. Indeed the publicity regarding the Hamanaka affair was the very catalyst for Mr Black's copper speculations. The quantification of the loss is entirely dependent on Mr Black and his own documents. Prima facie its calculation is inconsistent with public expressions of Mr Black's own market predictions back in 1996.

j [90] That is the injury or loss for which Mr Black seeks a remedy. I am far from saying that there is no basis for a complaint that Mr Black has suffered such a loss, which remains to be seen. That, however, is not the question save in the sense that if it could be said that there was no real prospect of such a loss having been suffered then this application would fail at the very outset. This, therefore, is not a case where the prospective claimant has suffered some reasonably plain injury or loss, at any rate on the face of things—such as following medical treatment, or following an accident at work or on the roads, or because of the sale of unfit goods, or non-delivery, or some other breach of contract.

[91] The loss complained of is one thing; the cause or causes of action by which Mr Black seeks a remedy and the clarity with which the legal issues are raised by such a cause of action are the next matters for consideration. The complaint is one of dishonest market manipulation and/or anti-competitive behaviour in breach of arts 81, 82 EC. Again, the question is not whether such causes of action exist in the legal repertoire, for they do, nor whether there is a reasonable basis for the complaint, for Deputy Judge Brindle found that there was and I am prepared to assume for present purposes that he is right. Mr Black can point to the established and admitted background of the Hamanaka affair and to the possibility that in its immediate aftermath Sumitomo, although newly advised by Goldman Sachs, was unable or perhaps even unwilling to avoid doing things with its inherited market positions which might call for censure. That, however, with the possible exception of the China deal to which I will come below, is the essential limit of the complaint. The matter can be tested by considering the recitation of the issues allegedly 'made clear' in Mr Black's letter before action and application: see Mr Vos' skeleton argument before Deputy Judge Brindle. Eight questions are there raised, the essence of which is whether there was any legitimate commercial motivation for Sumitomo's market dealings in the relevant period, whether there was a conspiracy between Sumitomo and Goldman Sachs to injure market participants, whether that conspiracy used unlawful means, and whether such market dealings were in breach of arts 81 or 82 EC. There is no draft pleading. That is, it seems to me, an utterly jejune identification of the issues which might arise in any litigation. Again with the possible exception of the China deal, an exception if only because it is a specific transaction which has been identified and condemned by Mr Black, it seems to me that the complaint, its factual and legal basis, and the issues which it raises, are speculative in the extreme.

[92] In such circumstances, unless there is some real evidence of dishonesty or abuse which only early disclosure can properly reveal and which may, in the absence of such disclosure, escape the probing eye of the litigation process and thus possibly all detection, I think that the court should be slow to allow a merely prospective litigant to conduct a review of the documents of another party, replacing focused allegation by a roving inquisition.

[93] This then is the importance of the China deal, for it is Mr Black's attempt to make a focused attack on Sumitomo's honesty or anti-competitive conduct during the relevant period. Moreover the China deal appears to have been in very large part the sole basis of Deputy Judge Brindle's decision to order any disclosure at all. To a certain extent the position has moved on from what it was below, since in the meantime Sumitomo has given disclosure of the contract with CNIEC and of the delivery orders which CNIEC gave to Sumitomo pursuant to that contract. Those delivery orders appear prima facie to show that the contract was not a sham, and that the copper was delivered to CNIEC in the six months during which the contract allowed CNIEC to call the copper off. Further evidence on behalf of Mr Black and Mr Vos's submissions have since been devoted to raising further questions about this disclosure in the light of new material which Mr Black has obtained by means of the United States Act: but I am not particularly impressed by this. If Mr Black had such information or could obtain such information, it throws into doubt his need for disclosure from Sumitomo. It is wholly unclear to me to what extent Mr Black already has

a documentation, or could obtain documentation, or could legitimately obtain information from Mr O'Keefe, which would enable him either to plead his case that the China deal was dishonest manipulation or to recognise that the contract was genuine. Mr Black now complains that he has no Sumitomo documentation to prove that CNIEC paid for the copper: but he did not request and Deputy Judge Brindle did not order such disclosure. What Deputy Judge Brindle ordered

b was: '5. Documents evidencing the physical delivery of copper to CNIEC ...'; and that is what Sumitomo has disclosed. In any event, documents disclosed by Sumitomo relating to the reconciliation of payments as between Global and itself would seem to evidence the payment by CNIEC for the copper delivered.

[94] I come next to the nature of the documents requested. Mr Black's request for disclosure went extremely wide. It was not confined to documents, such as

c medical reports, or the maintenance reports of an item of equipment, or some other category of internal reports, which could be said at one and the same time to be reasonably narrowly focused and to relate directly to a loss or injury plainly sustained. It was not confined, as in *Bermuda International Securities Ltd v KPMG (a firm)* [2001] Lloyd's Rep PN 392, to documents which were directly related to

d professional work alleged to have been negligently performed by a prospective defendant for a prospective claimant. It was not confined to documents which a protocol had identified as the sort of material one party should be disclosing at an early stage to another. Even after Deputy Judge Brindle had limited the disclosure which he was willing to entertain, the categories stated in his order indicate the width of the disclosure required. Thus he ordered 'statements

e showing copper warrants held' by Sumitomo throughout the relevant period, as well as 'daily trading statements showing copper future positions, copper options or any other copper positions' throughout the same period. He also ordered disclosure of any documents containing or evidencing any agreement between Sumitomo and Goldman Sachs relating to the advice given or action taken by

f Goldman Sachs during the relevant period; any judgments or pleadings in any civil litigation brought against Sumitomo relating to or involving any allegations in respect of the China deal or to manipulation of the copper market during the relevant period; and any documents relating to the disclosure to the regulatory authorities of Sumitomo's intentions and activities in relation to the unwinding of its copper positions. Mr Vos submitted that such disclosure was not wide and

g represented the least that was necessary to police the allegations made. In my judgment, however, such disclosure was very wide indeed. I am sceptical that the disclosure of daily trading statements throughout the period fell within standard disclosure in any event: they seem to me to be in effect 'train of inquiry' or at any rate merely background documents. It would in any event be difficult

h to assess this question without a pleaded statement of case. Or, to put the matter another way: if such documents were to fall within standard disclosure, that fact would itself indicate the width of the allegations made.

[95] In my judgment, the more focused the complaint and the more limited the disclosure sought in that connection, the easier it is for the court to exercise

j its discretion in favour of pre-action disclosure, even where the complaint might seem somewhat speculative or the request might be argued to constitute a mere fishing exercise. In appropriate circumstances, where the jurisdictional thresholds have been crossed, the court might be entitled to take the view that transparency was what the interests of justice and proportionality most required. The more diffuse the allegations, however, and the wider the disclosure sought, the more sceptical the court is entitled to be about the merit of the exercise.

[96] In this connection, the difficulties which the retrieval of the documentation requested would cause to Sumitomo is also a relevant factor. Deputy Judge *a* Brindle accepted that a 'real case' of oppression had been made on Sumitomo's evidence. However, he thought that the tailoring of his order would avoid the danger of anything oppressive or unreasonable. It is of course relevant that the cost of such disclosure falls, as a general rule, upon the party requesting it (CPR 48.1(2)). Even so, it is evident that it is only because Deputy Judge Brindle *b* had already determined that in principle he would order disclosure that he was not deterred from doing so, at any rate to the extent that he did so, by the difficulties of the exercise. I can understand that conclusion. If, however, the court is yet to be persuaded of the justice of disclosure, a 'real case' of oppression hardly makes it any easier to order it. It is after all the applicant who bears the burden of persuasion, even if, once he has shouldered that successfully, he must *c* also bear the burden of the costs of disclosure. The burden of disclosure still rests on the respondent.

[97] In the present circumstances, the expressed determination of Mr Black to commence proceedings, and the avenues open to him to obtain documentation or (as it seems) information from other sources, militate against him. *d*

[98] In this connection, as this case demonstrates, there is considerable danger of a request for pre-action disclosure leading to what must be expensive satellite litigation in connection with proceedings which have not yet been initiated.

[99] It is possible that Sumitomo's reaction to Mr Black's request for disclosure could be criticised. In effect, having indicated in answer to the 21 December 2000 letter before action (which demanded a response by 31 January *e* 2001) that a considered answer would be forthcoming by 16 March 2001, it failed to meet that date. A letter dated 21 March 2001 from Mr Black's solicitors indicates that in a telephone conversation with Sumitomo's London solicitors it was said that Sumitomo was very busily involved in litigation in the United States and that Mr Black's request had not yet made it on to an agenda for discussion. *f* The result was Mr Black's almost immediate issue of this application, which is dated 30 March 2001. In subsequent evidence on behalf of Sumitomo, Mr London, a partner of Paul Weiss, Sumitomo's United States attorneys, explains that an additional difficulty is Sumitomo's concern over the role of Mr O'Keefe. It is difficult to evaluate these matters and this court has yet to be addressed on them in relation to a question of costs. In the circumstances I would revert to the *g* underlying situation: which is that Mr Black's claim emerged out of the blue after a period of four years; that he claimed damages of at least $126m based on lost opportunities for speculative profits; that Mr Black and Sumitomo are essentially 'strangers', not contract partners, nor 'neighbours'; that the claim was originally premised on a dishonest conspiracy with Goldman Sachs, who had not *h* previously been involved with Sumitomo during the Hamanaka affair; that the alleged conspiracy occurred in a period when Sumitomo was co-operating with the regulatory authorities in the full glare of the exposure and admission of Mr Hamanaka's manipulations; that in this court the focus on fraud has switched to a focus on anti-competitive behaviour, despite Mr Black's evidence verifying *j* the complaint of fraud and despite the complete baldness (and width) of the anti-competitive behaviour alleged; and that I am not persuaded that Mr Black will be deterred by the absence of pre-action disclosure from putting his claim to the test of the courts.

[100] If the matter had stood where it did before Deputy Judge Brindle, it is possible that a pre-action disclosure order limited to the China deal alone would

a have been justified. That would have been to take the China deal as representing Mr Black's 'best case' for testing the theory of unlawful market manipulation. Deputy Judge Brindle in fact ordered documents evidencing the China deal, documents evidencing physical delivery of copper to CNIEC pursuant to it, and documents disclosing it to the regulatory authorities. Of course, Deputy Judge Brindle also went well beyond that point in his overall order for disclosure.

b In the light of Sumitomo's disclosure of at any rate part of what Deputy Judge Brindle ordered in respect of the China deal, and in the light of Mr Black's evident ability to obtain documents relating to the China deal for himself without Sumitomo's assistance, I can see no virtue in maintaining a small part of the deputy judge's original order. Mr Black's evidence was that if disclosure showed that his contentions about the China deal being a sham were incorrect, the issue

c 'will not be pursued any further' (see [23], above). Disclosure has shown, prima facie, that the copper under the China deal was sold and delivered to the Chinese and was not a sham. It may well be that the documents at present before the court raise new questions which have yet to be answered. I suspect that more documents would raise more questions. I would prefer at this stage to know

d clearly what Mr Black is saying about the China deal: whether it was a sham; whether delivery never took place; or whether, despite being a genuine transaction (as it appears prima facie to be), it was nevertheless used in some way dishonestly or anti-competitively or otherwise unlawfully to manipulate the market, and if so, how.

[101] In the circumstances, I would allow this appeal and set aside Deputy
e Judge Brindle's order for pre-action disclosure.

MAY LJ.

[102] I agree that this appeal should be allowed for the reasons given by Rix LJ.

f **WARD LJ.**

[103] I also agree.

Appeal allowed.

Kate O'Hanlon   Barrister.

Note

R (on the application of M) v Secretary of State for Health

[2003] EWHC 1094 (Admin)

QUEEN'S BENCH DIVISION (ADMINISTRATIVE COURT)

MAURICE KAY J

7, 16 APRIL 2003

Mental health – Patient – Nearest relative – Removal or change of nearest relative – Compatibility with right to respect for private life – Mental Health Act 1983, ss 26, 29 – Human Rights Act 1998, Sch 1, Pt I, art 8.

Section 26 of the Mental Health Act 1983 specifies the 'nearest relative' of a patient detained under s 2 or s 3 of the Act by listing classes of relatives in order and providing that the person who is first described in the list should be appointed the nearest relative. The role accorded to the nearest relative is one of the safeguards provided for by the 1983 Act since ss 2 and 3 involve the restriction of personal liberty. Section 29 of the 1983 Act provides for the removal or change of the nearest relative by the court but a patient cannot apply for such removal or change. In proceedings for judicial review brought by M, who had been detained pursuant to s 3 and released on leave but remained liable to detention, **MAURICE KAY J** declared pursuant to s 4 of the Human Rights Act 1998 that ss 26(1) and 29 of the 1983 Act were incompatible with M's right to respect for her private life under art 8(1) of the European Convention for the Protection of Human Rights and Fundamental Freedoms 1950 (as set out in Sch 1 to the 1998 Act) in so far as she had no choice over the appointment, nor any legal means to change the appointment, of her nearest relative.

Alexander Horne   Barrister.

a
R (on the application of Hooper and others) v Secretary of State for Work and Pensions
[2003] EWCA Civ 813

b
COURT OF APPEAL, CIVIL DIVISION

LORD PHILLIPS OF WORTH MATRAVERS MR, MANTELL AND RIX LJJ

7–10 OCTOBER, 19 DECEMBER 2002, 14 MARCH, 18 JUNE 2003

c
Social security – Benefits – Widows' benefits – Widows' benefits not available to widowers – Prohibition of discrimination – Contributions and Benefits Act 1992, ss 36–38 – Human Rights Act 1998, ss 3, 6, 8, Sch 1, Pt I, arts 8, 14, Pt II, art 1.

d
The appeal involved four individual appellants, each of whom was a widower whose wife had died at a time when, under ss 36–38[a] of the Social Security Contributions and Benefits Act 1992, widows received certain benefits in circumstances in which widowers did not. Widow's payment was a lump sum payment of £1,000. Widowed mother's allowance was payable to widows with dependent children. Widow's pension was payable to widows, not entitled to widowed mother's allowance, over 45 and under 65. Article 14[b] of the European Convention for the Protection of Human Rights and Fundamental Freedoms
e
1950 (as set out in Sch 1 to the Human Rights Act 1998) prohibited discrimination on inter alia grounds of sex. Article 8[c] secured the right to respect for private and family life and art 1[d] of the First Protocol provided for the protection of property. The 1998 Act came into force on 2 October 2000. On 9 April 2001 the Welfare Reform and Pensions Act 1999 came into force, amending the 1992 Act and introducing a system of survivor's benefits payable to both men and women. The
f
appellants claimed that between 2 October 2000 and 9 April 2001 they should have received the same benefits that were available to widows under the previous regime. Three appellants with dependent children had claims for the equivalent of widowed mother's allowance, M claimed the equivalent of widow's payment and N claimed the equivalent of widow's pension. A number of similar
g
claims had been brought before the European Court of Human Rights and it was the policy of the Secretary of State to settle those claims declared to be admissible. The court identified, inter alia, the following issues: (i) whether s 3[e] of the 1998 Act, which provided for legislation to be read and given effect in a way compatible with convention rights, required ss 36–38 of the 1992 Act to be interpreted in such a way as to confer on widowers as well as widows the right to
h
receive the benefits in issue; (ii) whether there had been objective justification for the entitlement of women but not men to widow's pension until 9 April 2001; (iii) whether the state had been entitled to a reasonable period within which rectify discriminatory law; (iv) whether discrimination between widowers who brought proceedings at the European Court of Human Rights and had their
j

---

a   Sections 36–38 are set out in the annex to the judgment, below
b   Article 14, so far as material, is set out at [9], below
c   Article 8, so far as material, is set out at [8], below
d   Article 1, so far as material, provides: 'Every ... person is entitled to the peaceful enjoyment of his possessions. No one shall be deprived of his possessions except in the public interest and subject to the conditions provided for by law and by the general principles of international law.'
e   Section 3, so far as material, is set out at [11], below

claims settled and the appellants was a violation of art 14 of the convention read
with art 8 or art 1 of the First Protocol or of the principles of domestic public law; *a*
(v) whether extra-statutory payments preventing discrimination could be made
lawfully; and (vi) whether it was necessary to make payments of compensation
to the appellants in order to afford them just satisfaction within s 8[f] of the 1998 Act.

Held – The appeal would be allowed, in part, for the following reasons. *b*
(1) It was not possible, pursuant to s 3 of the 1998 Act, to read references to the
feminine gender in ss 36–38 of the 1992 Act as including the masculine. Those
sections drew a distinction between men and women and husbands and wives
(see [28], below).

(2) The difference in economic activity between men and women no longer
justified discriminating between them by paying, indiscriminately, pensions to *c*
widows aged between 45 and 65. There had been therefore no objective
justification for not taking steps to remove the discrimination involved in paying
pensions under s 38 of the 1992 Act (see [64], [69], below).

(3) The state was entitled not merely to a wide margin of appreciation when
considering whether and when a change was required to domestic law in order
to ensure that it remained convention compliant in changing circumstances, but *d*
also, having so decided, to such time as was reasonable to make the necessary
change. No criticism had been, or could be, made of the period taken to consult
on and then introduce the 1999 Act. The criticism, which was well-founded, had
been of the delay in deciding that a change in the law was necessary (see [78],
below); *Walden v Liechtenstein* (App No 33916/96) (16 March 2000, unreported) *e*
considered.

(4) The policy under which any pre-1998 Act victim who had brought a claim
before the European Court of Human Rights and had had that claim ruled
admissible would receive a friendly settlement did not constitute discrimination
such as to constitute an independent violation of art 14 of the convention read
with art 8 or art 1 of the First Protocol between those widowers with claims *f*
similar to the appellants and the appellants themselves. The policy did not create
two classes of victims, one of which was treated more favourably than the other.
The reason why the appellants were not able to benefit from the policy was
because they had not advanced a claim before the European Court of Human
Rights, and not because the policy discriminated between one class and another *g*
(see [101], below); *Abdulaziz v UK* (1985) 7 EHRR 471 considered.

(5) There was nothing demonstrably perverse, irrational or unfair about the
state's course of conduct which had brought about the result that the issues
which were concerned in the instant case had been preserved for litigation in the
domestic forum before contesting them at the European Court of Human Rights *h*
(see [108], below).

(6) It was plainly implicit that Parliament had intended the express statutory
provisions for payment of benefits to widows to occupy the entire field of
entitlement to payment of benefits as a result of the death of a spouse. After the
1998 Act came into effect there was a presumption that Parliament did not intend
legislation to infringe the convention. In so far as the 1998 Act placed upon the *j*
Secretary of State an obligation to make extra-statutory payments, no constitutional
impropriety or illegality could be involved in his putting in place a scheme to give
effect to that obligation. It followed that neither s 6(2)(a) nor (b) of the 1998 Act
afforded the Secretary of State a defence to the claim that by failing to make

f   Section 8, so far as material, is set out at [14], below *a* extra-statutory payments to the appellants he had infringed art 14 (see [135]–[137], below).

(7) By failing to make extra-statutory payments the Secretary of State had acted in a way incompatible with the appellants' convention rights. However, although the making of extra-statutory payments would have prevented discrimination, it was not irrational for the Secretary of State to have declined to adopt that course.

b If Parliament conferred on one class a benefit for which there was no rational justification, it might make more sense to leave those who did not receive that benefit to seek such remedy as the law allowed rather than to make to them also payments for which there was no rational justification (see [144], below).

(8) The discrimination that existed during the relevant transitional period from 2 October 2000 to 9 April 2001 resulted in the failure of widowers to receive lump

c sum payments to which in justice they should have been entitled. M and any others in his position should receive damages of £1,000 and interest by way of just satisfaction. The appellants who claimed payments equivalent to widowed mother's allowance had not demonstrated that the discrimination complained of had caused them any pecuniary loss so the principle of just satisfaction did not

d require any award in that respect. In relation to widow's pension there was no justification for making equivalent payments to widowers. Accordingly, the principle of just satisfaction did not entitle N to extra-statutory payments equivalent to widow's pension (see [155], [158], [162], [163], below); *Van Raalte v Netherlands* (1997) 24 EHRR 503 considered.

e **Notes**

For widow's benefits, see Supp to 44(2) *Halsbury's Laws* (4th edn reissue) paras 80–90.

For the Social Security Contributions and Benefits Act 1992, ss 36–38, see 40 *Halsbury's Statutes* (4th edn) (2001 reissue) 325.

f For the Human Rights Act 1998, ss 3, 8, Sch 1, Pt I, arts 8, 14, Pt II, art 1, see 7 *Halsbury's Statutes* (4th edn) (2002 reissue) 532, 538, 555, 556.

Cases referred to in judgment

Abdulaziz v UK (1985) 7 EHRR 471, [1985] ECHR 9214/80, ECt HR.

A-G v De Keyser's Royal Hotel Ltd [1920] AC 508, [1920] All ER Rep 80, HL.

Auckland Harbour Board v R [1924] AC 318, PC.

Buckley v UK (1996) 23 EHRR 101, [1996] ECHR 20348/92, ECt HR.

Burghartz v Switzerland (1994) 18 EHRR 101, ECt HR.

Cornwell v UK (2000) 27 EHRR CD 62, ECt HR.

Fielding v UK App No 36940/97 (8 June 1999, unreported), ECt HR.

Goodwin v UK [2002] 2 FCR 577, ECt HR.

JR v Germany App No 22651/93 (18 October 1995, unreported), E Com HR.

Kingsley v UK (2002) 35 EHRR 177, [2002] ECHR 35605/97, ECt HR.

Kjeldsen v Denmark (1976) 1 EHRR 711, [1976] ECHR 5095/71, ECt HR.

Lord Advocate v Dumbarton DC [1990] 1 All ER 1, [1990] 2 AC 580, [1989] 3 WLR 1346, HL.

Lustig-Prean and Beckett v UK (1999) 7 BHRC 65, ECt HR.

Marckx v Belgium (1979) 2 EHRR 330, [1979] ECHR 6833/74, ECt HR.

Mellacher v Austria (1989) 12 EHRR 391, [1989] ECHR 10522/83, ECt HR.

National and Provincial Building Society v UK (1998) 25 EHRR 127, [1997] ECHR 21319/93, ECt HR.

Papamichalopoulos v Greece (1996) 21 EHRR 439, [1995] ECHR 14556/89, ECt HR.

R (on the application of KB) v Mental Health Review Tribunal [2003] EWHC 193
(Admin), [2003] 2 All ER 209.

R v A (No 2) [2001] UKHL 25, [2001] 3 All ER 1, [2002] 1 AC 45, [2001] 2 WLR 1546.

R v Hertfordshire CC, ex p Cheung (1986) Times, 26 March, CA.

R v Lambert [2001] UKHL 37, [2001] 3 All ER 577, [2002] 2 AC 545, [2001] 3 WLR 206.

R v Secretary of State for Foreign Affairs, ex p World Development Movement Ltd [1995]
1 All ER 611, [1995] 1 WLR 386, DC.

R v Secretary of State for the Home Dept, ex p Fire Brigades Union [1995] 2 All ER 244,
[1995] 2 AC 513, [1995] 2 WLR 464, HL.

R v Secretary of State for the Home Dept, ex p Northumbria Police Authority [1988] 1 All ER
556, [1989] QB 26, [1988] 2 WLR 590, CA.

Smith v UK (2000) 29 EHRR 493, [1999] ECHR 33985/96, ECt HR.

Steele Ford & Newton (a firm) v CPS [1993] 2 All ER 769, [1994] 1 AC 22, [1993]
2 WLR 934, HL.

Stubbings v UK (1996) 1 BHRC 316, ECt HR.

Valmont v UK App No 36385/97 (23 March 1999, unreported), ECt HR.

Van Raalte v Netherlands (1997) 24 EHRR 503, [1996] ECHR 20060/92, ECt HR.

Walden v Liechtenstein (App No 33916/96) (16 March 2000, unreported), ECt HR.

Wandsworth London BC v Michalak [2002] EWCA Civ 271, [2002] 4 All ER 1136.

White v UK App No 53134/99 (7 June 2001, unreported), ECt HR.

Willis v UK [2002] 2 FCR 743, ECt HR.

Appeal

Thomas Hooper, Leslie Withey, Andrew Martin and Frank Naylor appealed
from the decision of Moses J on 14 February 2002 ([2002] EWHC 191 (Admin),
[2002] All ER (D) 193 (Feb)) granting a declaration of incompatibility with the
European Convention for the Protection of Human Rights and Fundamental
Freedoms 1950 (as set out in Sch 1 to the Human Rights Act 1998) in relation to
ss 36 and 37 of the Social Security Contributions and Benefits Act 1992 but
otherwise dismissing their claims for judicial review of the refusal of the Secretary
of State for Work and Pensions to allow their claims, following the death of their
wives, for payments equivalent to widow's payment, widowed mother's
allowance and widow's pension. The hearing of the appeal began on 7 October
2002, but the court found it necessary to invite the parties to return for further
argument, so that the hearing was not concluded until 14 March 2003. The facts
are set out in the judgment of the court.

James Goudie QC and *Jason Coppel* (instructed by *Loosemores*) for the first appellant.
Geoffrey Cox QC and *Edward Risso-Gill* (instructed by *Royds Treadwell*) for the
second, third and fourth appellants.
Neil Garnham QC (at the October hearing), *Philip Sales* (at the March hearing) and
Jemima Stratford (at both hearings) (instructed by the *Solicitor to the Department
of Work and Pensions*) for the Secretary of State.

Cur adv vult

18 June 2003. The following judgment of the court was delivered.

LORD PHILLIPS OF WORTH MATRAVERS MR.

INTRODUCTION

[1] There are before the court two conjoined appeals involving five individual
appellants. Each is a widower. The wife of each died at a time when a statutory

a regime prevailed under which widows received benefits or tax allowances in
circumstances in which widowers did not. This regime reflected a bygone era in
which the husband was the breadwinner of the family and the wife did not
usually go out to work. That regime has changed, and the state now recognises
that to provide such benefits to widows alone would constitute discrimination
based on gender which would infringe art 14, together with art 8, or, in the case
b of tax allowances, art 1 of the First Protocol, of the European Convention for the
Protection of Human Rights and Fundamental Freedoms 1950 (the convention).
On 2 October 2000, the convention was incorporated into English law by, and
subject to the provisions of, the Human Rights Act 1998.

[2] The appellants claim that they should have received the same benefits that
were available to widows under the old regime. They contend that they are the
c victims of discrimination which violates the convention. In advancing their
claims they rely upon the provisions of the 1998 Act. They do not, however, all
do so in the same manner. Some of the issues that their claims raise are novel and
far-reaching. These cases have been treated as test cases and many other cases
will turn on the result of these appeals.

d
THE APPELLANTS AND THE LEGISLATION UNDER WHICH THEY CLAIM

[3] Four of the appellants, Messrs Hooper, Withey, Martin and Naylor,
complain of discrimination in the matter of widow's benefits paid pursuant to
ss 36–38 of the Social Security Contributions and Benefits Act 1992, and the fifth,
Mr Wilkinson, complains of discrimination in the matter of the widow's
e bereavement allowance granted under s 262(1) of the Income and Corporation
Taxes Act 1988. The respondent in the case of the 1992 Act is the Secretary of
State for Work and Pensions, and the respondents in the case of the 1988 Act are
the IRC.

[4] Although similar issues arise in both appeals, we propose to deal with the
f appeals one at a time.

HOOPER, WITHEY, MARTIN AND NAYLOR'S APPEAL

The legislation
[5] We propose at this point to summarise the relevant statutory provisions
g that relate to benefits, which we set out in full as an Annex.

[6] Section 36 of the 1992 Act provided for a *widow's payment*, a lump sum
payment of £1,000, subject to conditions which included restriction to widows
under pensionable age whose late husbands had made national insurance
contributions. Section 37 provided for a *widowed mother's allowance* (WMA) payable
h weekly, subject to similar conditions, to widows with dependent children.
Section 38 provided for a *widow's pension*, payable weekly, subject to similar
conditions, to widows not entitled to a WMA over 45 and under 65 at the date of
their husband's death or at the date when they ceased to be entitled to a WMA.
Under applicable regulations (the Social Security (Claims and Payments)
Regulations 1987, SI 1987/1968) such benefits had to be applied for 'in writing on
i a form approved by the Secretary of State … or in such other manner, being in
writing, as the Secretary of State … may accept as sufficient in the circumstances
of any particular case' (reg 4(1)); and within three months 'beginning with any
day on which, apart from satisfying the condition of making a claim, the claimant
is entitled to the benefit concerned' (reg 19(2)). There were special forms for
making claim to widow's benefits, which not surprisingly were drafted in terms
which would not be appropriate for a claim by a widower. The effect of the three-

month time limitation was (i) that if the widow's payment was not claimed in time, it was wholly lost, and (ii) that arrears of the WMA and the widow's pension could not be recovered for more than three months prior to the date on which a valid claim for these was made.

The new regime

[7] On 9 April 2001 the Welfare Reform and Pensions Act 1999 came fully into force, amending the 1992 Act. Its provisions introduced a system of survivor's benefits payable to both men and women, but at the price that these were more limited forms of benefit, targeted most on those in need. For those already in receipt of widow's benefits under the 1992 Act, however, the 1999 Act preserved the distinction between widows and widowers, for existing rights were preserved. Section 54 substituted a new s 36 into the 1992 Act and replaced the widow's payment with a new *bereavement payment*, set at £2,000 (thus recognising an increase in expenses arising directly from bereavement) and payable to widows and widowers alike, whose spouses had died after 9 April 2001. Section 55 introduced a number of new sections into the 1992 Act: a new s 39A replaced the WMA with a new *widowed parent's allowance* (WPA) for widows or widowers with dependent children; and a new s 39B replaced the widow's pension with a *bereavement allowance* payable for only 52 weeks to those over 45 but under pensionable age. Existing rights to the WMA and the widow's pension were preserved by a new s 36A, and by s 36A(2) the new WPA was extended after 9 April 2001 to widowers whose wives had died before 9 April 2001 and who had dependent children as at 9 April 2001.

The convention

[8] Article 8 of the convention provides that 'Everyone has the right to respect for his private and family life, his home and his correspondence'.

[9] Article 14 provides:

'The enjoyment of the rights and freedoms set forth in this Convention shall be secured without discrimination on any ground such as sex, race, colour, language, religion, political or other opinion, national or social origin, association with a national minority, property, birth or other status.'

[10] Article 41 provides:

'If the Court finds that there has been a violation of the Convention or the Protocols thereto, and if the internal law of the High Contracting Party concerned allows only partial reparation to be made, the Court shall, if necessary, afford just satisfaction to the injured party.'

The Human Rights Act 1998

[11] Section 3 provides:

'(1) So far as it is possible to do so, primary legislation and subordinate legislation must be read and given effect in a way which is compatible with the Convention rights.

(2) This section—(a) applies to primary legislation and subordinate legislation whenever enacted; (b) does not affect the validity, continuing operation or enforcement of any incompatible primary legislation; and (c) does not affect the validity, continuing operation or enforcement of any

a

incompatible subordinate legislation if (disregarding any possibility of revocation) primary legislation prevents removal of the incompatibility.'

[12] Section 6, sub-ss (1) and (2) provide:

'(1) It is unlawful for a public authority to act in a way which is incompatible with a Convention right.

b

(2) Subsection (1) does not apply to an act if—(a) as the result of one or more provisions of primary legislation, the authority could not have acted differently; or (b) in the case of one or more provisions of, or made under, primary legislation which cannot be read or given effect in a way which is compatible with the Convention rights, the authority was acting so as to give effect to or enforce those provisions'

c

[13] Section 7 provides:

'(1) A person who claims that a public authority has acted (or proposes to act) in a way which is made unlawful by section 6(1) may—(a) bring proceedings against the authority under this Act in the appropriate court or tribunal, or (b) rely on the Convention right or rights concerned in any legal proceedings, but only if he is (or would be) a victim of the unlawful act …

d

(7) For the purposes of this section, a person is a victim of an unlawful act only if he would be a victim for the purposes of Article 34 of the Convention if proceedings were brought in the European Court of Human Rights in respect of that act.'

e

[14] Section 8 provides:

'(1) In relation to any act (or proposed act) of a public authority which the court finds is (or would be) unlawful, it may grant such relief or remedy, or make such order, within its powers as it considers just and appropriate.

f

(2) But damages may be awarded only by a court which has power to award damages, or to order the payment of compensation, in civil proceedings.

(3) No award of damages is to be made unless, taking account of all the circumstances of the case, including—(a) any other relief or remedy granted, or order made, in relation to the act in question (by that or any other court), and (b) the consequences of any decision (of that or any other court) in respect of that act, the court is satisfied that the award is necessary to afford just satisfaction to the person in whose favour it is made.

g

(4) In determining—(a) whether to award damages, or (b) the amount of an award, the court must take into account the principles applied by the European Court of Human Rights in relation to the award of compensation under Article 41 of the Convention …

h

(6) In this section—
"court" includes a tribunal;
"damages" means damages for an unlawful act of a public authority; and
"unlawful" means unlawful under section 6(1).'

j

The relief claimed and the issues raised

[15] Messrs Hooper, Withey and Martin's claims are founded on the fact that, had they been women, they would have received a widow's payment and a WMA upon the deaths of their spouses. Mr Naylor's claim is founded on the fact that, had he been a woman, he would have received a widow's payment and a widow's pension on the death of his spouse. Each appellant contends that he was

the victim of discrimination which violated art 14, when read with art 8, of the convention.

[16] Before Moses J, Messrs Withey, Martin and Naylor argued that, although, if given their natural meaning, the relevant statutory provisions appeared to discriminate against men, it was possible to interpret them in such a way as to confer on widowers as well as widows the right to receive the benefits in issue. They contended that s 3 of the 1998 Act required the provisions in question to be so interpreted, with the result that they were entitled to receive the benefits in question under the statute. Mr Hooper did not adopt this argument and Moses J did not accept it. It has not been actively pursued before us, but it has been 'kept open' for us to decide, as it is a point that has been taken in a number of other cases. We shall deal with this as the first issue.

[17] On the assumption that they do not succeed on the first issue, the three appellants who have espoused it join with Hooper in contending that the effect of the legislation is to discriminate against them contrary to art 14, when read with art 8, of the convention. In relation to some, an issue arises as to whether, or when, they became 'victims' of the alleged discrimination so as to be in a position to rely upon a breach of the convention. We shall deal with this as the second issue.

[18] The Secretary of State has now accepted that, in the period with which the claims are concerned, the statutory provisions which entitled women, but not men, to a widow's payment and a WMA constituted discrimination which violated art 14, when read with art 8. The Secretary of State has accepted the reasoning of Moses J on this point, and we consider that he was right to do so subject to the *Walden* point discussed below (see *Walden v Liechtenstein* (App No 33916/96) (16 March 2000, unreported)). Nor has the Secretary of State sought to contend that there was any objective justification for this discrimination. The same is not true of the entitlement of women, but not men, to a widow's pension. The Secretary of State contends that there was objective justification for this up to the moment that the law was changed. Whether this contention is well founded constitutes the third issue that we shall address.

[19] The Secretary of State accepts that, by November 1999, when the 1999 Act was enacted, wrongful discrimination in relation to a widow's payment, a WMA and, if he loses on the third issue, a widow's pension had been identified. The Secretary of State contends, however, that Strasbourg jurisprudence demonstrates that the state was entitled to a reasonable period within which to rectify the law, during which period no individual could found a claim on wrongful discrimination. This contention is founded on decisions of the Strasbourg court which include that of 16 March 2000 in *Walden*'s case, and has been described as the *Walden* point. We shall deal with this point as the fourth issue.

[20] Thus far, the claims that we have been describing have founded on discrimination between women and men. We now turn to an allegation of wrongful discrimination that has a different basis. A number of claims have been brought in Strasbourg by claimants founding on the same breaches of the convention as are relied upon in the four appeals before us. Amicable settlements have been reached in the case of some of these, and, in the case of benefit claimants, it was at all material times the policy of the Secretary of State to settle claims declared to be admissible at Strasbourg. The appellants contend that discrimination between those widowers who have brought proceedings at Strasbourg, who have had their claims settled, and the appellants themselves, whose claims under the 1998 Act are being resisted in these proceedings,

a constitutes an independent violation of art 14, when read with art 8, or with art 1 of the First Protocol to the convention. We shall deal with the validity of this contention as the fifth issue.

[21] By way of alternative to the fifth issue, all four appellants contend that discrimination between those who bring claims at Strasbourg and those who have not yet done so violates principles of our domestic public law. Whether this *b* contention is well-founded will constitute the sixth issue that we shall consider.

[22] The four appellants join in pursuing what is the most important issue raised by this appeal. They contend that the discrimination which has occurred could and should have been avoided. It was and is open to the Secretary of State to make extra-statutory payments to the claimants thereby putting them on an equal footing both with widows and with widowers whose claims have been *c* settled at Strasbourg. Such action would have prevented the discrimination which was bound otherwise to occur as a result of making the payments to which widows were statutorily entitled under the 1992 Act and as a result of settling claims brought at Strasbourg. Section 6(1) of the 1998 Act made it unlawful for the Secretary of State to decline to make such payments. The court should make *d* a mandatory order that such payments be made.

[23] Moses J held that this basis for claiming payments was unsound. Section 6(1) had no application because the case fell within the provisions of s 6(2)(b). He went on to make a declaration of incompatibility in relation to ss 36 and 37 of the 1992 Act. Whether the four appellants' claims to extra-statutory payments were unsound is the seventh issue that we shall address.

e [24] Questions arise as to whether any appellant can complain of the effects of discrimination insofar as these impacted prior to 2 October 2000. These we shall consider as the eighth issue.

[25] Finally, an issue arises as to whether it is necessary to make payments of compensation to the appellants in order to afford them 'just satisfaction'. This is *f* the ninth issue.

The first issue

[26] We agree with Moses J that the principles to be applied when considering the effect of s 3 of the 1998 Act are encapsulated in the following statements. In *g* *R v A (No 2)* [2001] UKHL 25 at [44], [2001] 3 All ER 1 at [44], [2002] 1 AC 45 Lord Steyn said:

> 'In accordance with the will of Parliament as reflected in s 3, it will sometimes be necessary to adopt an interpretation which linguistically may appear strained. The techniques to be used will not only involve the reading *h* down of express language in the statute, but also the implication of provisions. A declaration of incompatibility is a measure of last resort. It must be avoided unless it is plainly impossible to do so. If a clear limitation on convention rights is stated in terms, such an impossibility will arise.'

j However, in *R v Lambert* [2001] UKHL 37 at [79], [2001] 3 All ER 577 at [79], [2002] 2 AC 545, decided about one-and-a-half months after *R v A*, Lord Hope observed that s 3(1) preserves the sovereignty of Parliament: 'It does not give power to the judges to overrule decisions, which the language of the statute shows have been taken on the very point at issue by the legislature.' Later he observed (at [81]):

> 'But the interpretation of the statute by reading words in to give effect to the presumed intention must always be distinguished carefully from

amendment. Amendment is a legislative act. It is an exercise which must be reserved to Parliament.'

[27] Section 6 of the Interpretation Act 1978 provides:

'In any Act, unless the contrary intention appears,—(a) words importing the masculine gender include the feminine; (b) words importing the feminine gender include the masculine ...'

[28] In our judgment 'the contrary intention' appears emphatically from the provisions of ss 36–38 of the 1992 Act. As Moses J observed, the sections draw a distinction between men and women and husbands and wives. This distinction is particularly marked in s 37, which includes, in the conditions entitling a woman to a WMA, pregnancy by her late husband and artificial insemination with the semen of some person other than her husband. It is quite impossible to read references to the feminine gender in these sections as including the masculine. Moses J so held, and we agree with him.

The second issue

[29] Section 7(1) of the 1998 Act, which we have set out above, provides that only a 'victim' can make a claim under s 6(1). Under s 7(7) the test of a 'victim' is that applied by the Strasbourg court. In the present context identification of the test is assisted by the fact that the Strasbourg court has made a number of decisions on admissibility of claims which are close to carbon copies of those before us. Those decisions have greatly reduced the area of controversy between the parties. While they identify the relevant principles they have not, however, applied these in a manner which we find satisfactory.

[30] We have drawn attention to the regulations which require a widow to make her claim within three months of becoming entitled to a payment. Because a widow who has not made a claim has no entitlement to benefits, the Strasbourg court does not consider that a widower who has made no claim is in a position to complain of discrimination. Only when he has made a claim is he in a position to complain that he is not being treated in the same way as a woman.

[31] This approach was first manifested in *Cornwell v UK* (2000) 27 EHRR CD 62. Mr Cornwell's wife had died on 24 October 1989, leaving a dependent child. On 7 February 1997 his representative had 'contacted' the Benefits Agency to enquire about widow's benefits. On 14 February 1997 the agency 'answered' to say that legislation provided only for widows and not widowers. On 28 March 1997 the agency confirmed that if Mrs Cornwell's record had been that of a man, her survivor would have been entitled to a widow's payment and a WMA. The position of the government was set out in the decision as follows ((2000) 27 EHRR CD 62 at 65):

'The Government contests the admissibility of the application in so far as it relates to the period 24 October 1989 to 7 February 1996. It points out that the applicant did not attempt to claim widows' benefits until 7 February 1997 and that it was only from this date onwards that the legislation was applied to him. Had a woman claimed widows' benefits on 7 February 1997 in respect of the death of her husband in October 1989, she would have been told that she was out of time for claiming a widow's payment and that she could only claim widowed mothers' allowance with effect from 8 February 1996.'

This reflects the fact that, at the relevant time, a claim had to be made within 12 months of the benefit becoming payable.

a [32] The court went on to deal with the government's objection in the following passage:

b   'The Court recalls that under Article 34 of the Convention it may receive applications from individuals and others "claiming to be the victim of a violation by one of the High Contracting Parties of the rights set forth in the Convention or the protocols thereto". In order to claim to be a victim of a violation, a person must be directly affected by the impugned measure (see, for example, the *Buckley v UK* (1996) 23 EHRR 101 at 125 (paras 56–59) and *Valmont v UK* App no 36385/97 (23 March 1999, unreported)). In the present case, during the period between his wife's death on 24 October 1989 and his claim for benefits on 7 February 1997, the applicant cannot be said to have been directly affected by the discrimination of which he complains, since a woman in the same position who had made no claim would have had no entitlement to widows' benefits under domestic law. It follows that for the period 24 October 1989 to 7 February 1997 the applicant cannot claim to have been a victim of a violation of his rights under the Convention and First Protocol, and that the application, in so far as it relates to this period, is incompatible *ratione personae* with the provisions of the Convention and must be declared inadmissible in accordance with Article 35(3) and (4) of the Convention.'

e [33] The court then recited, incorrectly, that the government did not contest the admissibility of the application insofar as it related to the period after 7 February 1997 and declared the application inadmissible up to that date, but admissible thereafter.

[34] It is clear that the application should have been declared admissible in respect of the period beginning on 7 February 1996. The important point to note, however, is that the court required 'an attempt to claim' benefit as a precondition *f* to becoming a victim. No point was taken in that case as to the manner of the attempt to claim benefit, but evidence was placed before us which satisfied us that the attempt had been made in writing.

[35] In *White v UK* App No 53134/99 (7 June 2001, unreported) the United Kingdom government took the far from attractive point that the claimant, who *g* had advanced a claim in writing for benefit, had not done so on the official form, notwithstanding that this was designed specifically for widows. The court gave this short shrift:

h   'The court notes that in the present case the applicant made clear in the form notifying the social security office of the death of his wife that he wished to claim "widowers' benefits". The court further notes that on two occasions a minister of the Department of Social Security wrote to the applicant's Member of Parliament confirming that, as a man, the applicant was not entitled under the current law to claim widows' benefits.

j   The government contend that the applicant never made a claim for any benefits "in the proper form" and that, applying the court's reasoning in *Cornwell v UK*, the applicant cannot claim to be a victim of discrimination in violation of the Convention. The court is unable to accept this argument. As appears from *Cornwell v UK* itself, the precise form in which an applicant indicates his intention to claim benefits is not of importance, the central question being whether the applicant has made clear his wish to claim benefits. The court finds that in the present case the applicant made clear such intention and that he can accordingly claim to be a victim of a violation of the Convention for the purposes of art 34.'

[36] We have been asked to resolve one issue that remains unclear. Will it suffice as a precondition to becoming a 'victim' for a widower to make clear orally to the relevant authority that he is seeking benefit or must the claim be made in writing? As to this question, Moses J concluded as follows ([2002] All ER (D) 193 (Feb) at [63]): 'In my view, and I suspect in the view of the European Court of Human Rights, the claimant must make his claim to benefits clear in writing.'

[37] We do not agree with this conclusion. While it is plainly desirable that a claim should be made in writing, we cannot see why, if it is clear that a claim has been made orally to the appropriate authority, this should not suffice. Normally, such a claim is likely to be recorded in writing. If it is not, then it may be difficult to prove. But, subject to proof, we can see no reason in principle why an oral claim, made and rejected, should not suffice to constitute the claimant a victim. Let us take an extreme example. Imagine that an illiterate widower had arranged a meeting with a social security officer to claim benefit and had been told that he was entitled to none. It seems to us that discrimination would have begun at that moment. We note that in *Fielding v UK* App No 36940/97 (8 June 1999, unreported) the transcript shows that the government conceded victim status on the basis of a telephone enquiry to the Benefits Agency. This concession was appropriate. If an authority informs an oral claimant that he has no entitlement to claim, the authority should not be entitled, thereafter, to contend that a claim should have been advanced in writing.

[38] We turn to consider the position in relation to each of the four appellants who were denied benefits. It is important to distinguish between a number of different questions. (i) When, if at all, did the appellant make the claim that was necessary to render him a victim? (ii) In respect of what period of deprivation of benefits is the appellant entitled to found a claim under the 1998 Act? (iii) When did time start to run for the purpose of the three-month period for claiming judicial review? The second question is one that we shall consider as the eighth issue. No point has been taken that any application for judicial review was out of time. Thus, at this stage, we shall limit our consideration to the question of victim status.

Mr Hooper

[39] Mr Hooper has been widowed on two occasions. His claim relates to the second of these. Mr Hooper's (second) wife died on 27 March 1997, leaving three dependent children. In April 1997 he wrote to a local Department of Social Security (DSS) office asking that he be awarded benefits in the same way that a widow would have been. In May the DSS replied, refusing his claim on the ground that such benefits were only available to widows. On 1 June 1997 he wrote to the Prime Minister complaining about the rejection of his claim. His letter was referred to the DSS. As a result, he was visited by an employee of the Benefits Agency in August 1997, who again explained to him that he was not entitled to widow's benefits. Nearly three years later, on 10 May 2000, after hearing about payments being made to complainants in Strasbourg, he wrote to the DSS again, to pursue his claim. On 26 May 2000 the DSS replied declining his claim in terms that we shall have to consider when we come to consider the fifth and sixth issues.

a [40] On the same day the Benefits Agency also replied to Mr Hooper, refusing his renewed claim on the ground that there was currently no legislation which entitled a widower to widow's benefits. Mr Hooper pursued his correspondence, and a DSS letter dated 10 August 2000 informed him that 'It is, of course, a decision for those widowers concerned as to whether they follow their claims through to the European Court for a ruling on admissibility'.

b [41] A letter from Mr Hooper's solicitors dated 16 August 2000 informed the Benefits Agency that Mr Hooper intended to seek redress either by way of judicial review or by the seeking of an admissibility ruling in Strasbourg, and asked for confirmation that he would have met all the required conditions for benefit, had his wife been a husband and had he been a widow. It was subsequent to this stage, that the 1998 Act came into effect on 2 October 2000.

c [42] Moses J found:

> 'Letters, which he asserts he sent, have not been discovered. But I see no reason for doubting his assertions. It is plain that he was making written claims at least by July 1997 but it is not clear to me that he made a written claim within three months of the death of his second wife on 27 March 1997. *d* He is a victim in respect of Widowed Mother's Allowance from three months prior to the date of his first written claim to benefits, subject to the arguments as to the retrospectivity of the 1998 Act.'

[43] On the basis that he accepted Mr Hooper's evidence about his *e* correspondence, the judge appears to have overlooked the letters to the DSS of April 1997 and to the Prime Minister of 1 June 1997, both within three months of Mr Hooper's wife's death. Thus, so far as the convention is concerned, Mr Hooper became a 'victim' in respect of both his claim in relation to widow's payment and his claim in relation to a WMA, for he had claimed, in writing, in respect of both within three months of the death of his wife. The extent to which his claims are *f* defeated by reason of the fact that the 1998 Act did not come into force until 2 October 2000 we shall consider when we come to deal with the eighth issue.

Mr Withey

[44] Mr Withey's wife died on 26 November 1996, leaving two dependent *g* children. His evidence was that in January or February 1997 he made a telephone inquiry of his local Benefits Agency to ask how he should go about applying for widow's benefits. He was told that he had no entitlement. The judge found that this did not suffice to make him a 'victim'; he should have made a claim in writing. This demonstrates the injustice of imposing a requirement for a claim in writing, for Mr Withey can hardly be criticised for not making such a claim after having been *h* authoritatively informed that he had no entitlement to benefit. We hold that his telephone inquiry was enough to constitute him a 'victim'. Moses J held that, while he failed to make a timely claim in respect of widow's payment, his letter before action on 29 August 2000 sufficed to constitute him a victim in respect of WMA, with effect from three months before the date of that letter. On either *j* footing, we shall have to consider the effect of the fact that the 1998 Act was not in force on these dates when we come to address the eighth issue.

Mr Martin

[45] Mr Martin's wife died on 11 September 2000 leaving two dependent children. He made an oral claim in September 2000. This constituted him a victim in relation to both the widow's payment and the WMA. Once again a

question arises as to whether his claim can relate back to the period before 2 October 2000, which will fall for consideration in the context of the eighth issue.   *a*

Mr Naylor

[46] Mr Naylor's wife died on 2 July 1995, leaving no dependent children. He made no claim within three months of her death, and thus is not in a position to contend that he is a victim in relation to the widow's payment. On 14 September *b* 2000, however, he made a formal written claim on form BW1. This rendered him a victim in relation to the widow's pension. Once again there is a short period prior to 2 October 2000 to which we shall have to give consideration in the context of the eighth issue.

The third issue   *c*

[47] The third issue arises only in the context of a widow's pension and, on this, Mr Naylor's is the test case. The point can be stated simply. With effect from 9 April 2001, women whose husbands died ceased to be entitled to a widow's pension. As from this date it is common ground that there was insufficient justification for continuing to grant these pensions. Widows already *d* in receipt of pensions were to continue to receive them. Mr Naylor's wife died in 1995. He suffered discrimination in that he received no pension in consequence of his loss, though if he had died his wife would have received a pension. Because he did not make a claim until 14 September 2000, his claim relates to the period beginning three months before that date. His submission is that, by the year 2000, the discrimination between widows and widowers could not be justified. *e* Moses J was wrong to find to the contrary.

[48] A widow's pension was and, for those still entitled to it, is paid weekly to widows under 65 who were aged over 45 when their husband died (or when they ceased to be entitled to a WMA). The justification for singling out this large cohort for this benefit was that, as a general proposition, those who comprised it *f* had special financial needs. Widows in this age bracket were likely to have been unemployed, dependent upon the earnings of their husbands for subsistence and not readily able to obtain employment. The justification for ceasing to grant pensions to widows is that this is no longer the position. Over the years married women have increasingly gone out to work and, if widowed, have continued to work or have obtained employment if they were not then in employment. *g* Although statistics show that there is still some disparity between widows aged between 45 and 65 and men within the same age bracket so far as the benefits of employment are concerned, this does not justify the indiscriminate payment of widow's pensions. The change in the legislation grants to widows and widowers alike a bereavement allowance. This is, however, limited to a period of 52 weeks. *h* It is not a substitute for a 20-year pension.

[49] It follows that if, as Mr Naylor contends, the state has dragged its feet in legislating to bring the grant of a widow's pension to an end, the state has not thereby inflicted hardship on widowers in the same age bracket. What they complain of is not discrimination against men, but discrimination in favour of women, and there is a difference. *j*

[50] The legislature has now adopted means to remove this discrimination. The complaint is that it has not done so fast enough. In due course we shall have to consider what will constitute appropriate 'just satisfaction' if this complaint is made good. At this point we would simply observe that the nature of the discrimination complained of—excessive generosity to widows rather than oppressive deprivation of widowers—seems to us to be a relevant factor when

a scrutinising the speed with which the state has moved to remedy the disparity of treatment.

[51] Moses J observed ([2002] All ER (D) 193 (Feb) at [108]):

b 'The essential question seems to me to be not so much whether the position of women in the work-place had converged with that of men but, rather, when that position had been reached and when the government should have acted to recognise that convergence.'

Mr Cox submitted that the judge had correctly identified the issue, and we agree.

[52] It should occasion no surprise that the matrix of facts to which the state has had regard when taking decisions about widows' benefits is complex. Carol Freer, the Head of Work Rules 3 Section of the Working Age Group in the *c* Department of Social Security had, in March 2001, responsibility for policy in relation to widows' benefits. In a witness statement made in that month she traces the history of widows' benefits from 1925. She exhibits statistical tables, showing how the position of women in society, and more pertinently in the work place, has changed over the years. A short summary of these gives some *d* indication of the nature of these changes:

'11. Table 3 shows that in 2000, 84·3% of men were economically active, compared to 72·9% of women. By contrast, the figures for 1985 were 88·1% and 67% respectively. Table 5 sets out the percentage of inactive men and women with family responsibilities. In 2000, 0·9% of men and 12·7% of *e* women fell within this category, whereas in 1985 the figures were 0·4% and 16·4% respectively. These figures show that even during the past 15 years, there has been a marked rise in the number of economically active women, and a corresponding (but smaller) fall in the number of women with family responsibilities who are economically inactive.

f 12. Table 4 demonstrates that women still perform overwhelmingly more part-time work than men and this figure remains the same for women throughout the period 1985 to 2000 at 44%, whilst the figure for men has risen from 4% in 1985 to 9% in 2000. Tables 3 and 4 taken together therefore indicate that 84·3% of men are economically active and of these 91% work full-time, whereas 72·9% of women are economically active and of those *g* 44% work part-time (or 56% work full-time). Table 7 sets out the comparison of economic activity of mothers by age of child, and shows that the most marked change has occurred in relation to those with children aged 0–4 years (48·2% economically active in 1990 compared with 58.2% economically active ten years later in 2000).

h 13. Statistics regarding income levels are exhibited at "CEF1", p.200. These show that over time women have been closing the income gap, although the change is less marked for women working part time than for women working full time. In 1972 women working full time earned 64 pence for every £1 that a man earned, whereas by 1999 a woman was earning 84 pence for every £1 earned by men ...

j 14. The fact that substantially more married women return to work quickly after having children now than in the 1970s and 80s also points to younger married women's greater involvement in the labour market, with them combining work and caring. Reference is made to Table 7 in this regard. Overall, these statistics show that there has been a marked change in the position of younger married women compared with older women within society and the workforce over the past 15 years.'

[53] Carol Freer laid particular emphasis on the position of older women—those who would be the beneficiaries of widow's pensions. Again she illustrated *a*
her theme with statistics:

> '27. Furthermore, this change has taken place only gradually over time. Amongst existing widows there will still be a significant number of women who were wholly dependent on their late husband's income, and that group will include a particularly high proportion of those older widows whose *b*
> expectation on marrying was that their husband would provide a significant part if not all of the income of the household whilst they concentrated on bringing up any children and/or looked after the home. Some statistics which illustrate this point ... show that:
>
> (1) 44% of working women of all ages work part time, whereas 51% of *c*
> women aged between 55 and 59 work part time;
>
> (2) there is a larger rise of 8% in the number of women aged between 55 and 59 working part time compared to those aged 45 to 49;
>
> (3) there is a significant drop of 21% in women's economic activity for those aged between 55 and 59 as compared to those aged between 45 and 49; *d*
>
> (4) men are more economically active than women across all the age ranges; however, the % difference ranges from 11% in the 45 to 49 age group up to 17% in the 55 to 59 age group.
>
> Accordingly older women are less likely to work than both younger women and older men, and when they do work older women are more likely than the average woman to work part time.' *e*

[54] She summarised the state's case in the following paragraph:

> *'The Special Position of Older Women*
>
> 22. A significant number of older widows, particularly those who stayed at home to care for children, will until now quite reasonably have expected *f*
> to rely on their husband's income throughout their life. For very many older women, their and their husband's expectation on marrying was that their husband would provide a significant part, if not all, of the income of the household, whilst the wife concentrated on bringing up any children and/or looked after the home. For older women a return to the job market and the likelihood of finding full-time employment, although not impossible, would *g*
> have been more difficult in even the recent past than it is now, since there is today a greater propensity for women of all ages to work at least part-time. So although society's expectations relating to the role of men and women has been changing during the past 15–20 years, the shift has been a gradual one, and it was therefore reasonable and proportionate for the legislation to *h*
> continue to provide support by way of widows' pension to widows during this period of social change.'

[55] We have incorporated these rather lengthy passages from Carol Freer's evidence because they illustrate the difficulty of the task that the court faces when evaluating an argument that the granting of widow's pensions should have been *j*
discontinued by 2000, rather than April 2001. Moses J grappled with the figures which demonstrated, so he found, that there ought to have been a growing appreciation that affording benefits only to women was having a disproportionate impact on the allocation of resources. At the end of the day, however, he accepted the Secretary of State's contention that there was objective justification for continuing to pay widow's pensions until April 2001. He held that the

a government was entitled to wait until 1998 to produce a consultation paper on the subject and thereafter to wait until April 2001 before introducing measures designed to achieve equality. In so holding he applied the following principles: (i) it was appropriate for the court to scrutinise the evidence advanced by Carol Freer to see whether justification for discrimination was made out; (ii) the court should adopt a restrained approach to submissions that there were preferable
b alternative methods of meeting the needs for which widows' pensions were designed; such submissions directly engaged questions of social and economic policy with which the court was ill-equipped to deal; (iii) the government was entitled to a period for considering the effect of the increasing part that women had to play within the labour market; (iv) the government was entitled to a period to correct the effects of discrimination which was no longer justified; (v) in
c determining how to target resources to those in need, the legislature was entitled to impose 'bright line' rules which were easy to apply and which might not focus with precision on the merits of individual cases.

[56] Mr Cox challenged the judge's approach in a number of respects. He submitted that it was not appropriate to accord the government a wide margin of
d discretion or to pay considerable deference to the legislature having regard to the fact that discrimination on account of gender is in issue. Equality between the sexes was a fundamental principle of democracy and of European Community law. Only compelling reasons supported by convincing evidence would suffice to justify a distinction based on sex. Even if there were reasons for the discrimination, they would not suffice unless the discrimination was reasonably
e proportionate to the object that it was intended to achieve. It would not be reasonably proportionate unless it represented the minimum difference of treatment necessary to achieve that object. On all of these matters the burden of proof lay on the Secretary of State.

[57] Both the judge's approach and Mr Cox's attack upon it find support in the
f Strasbourg jurisprudence. The judge relied on *Mellacher v Austria* (1989) 12 EHRR 391. That case concerned restrictions on the rent that a property owner could charge, which brought into play the second paragraph of art 1 of the First Protocol to the convention. The court observed (at 408–409 (para 45)):

g   'The second paragraph reserves to States the right to enact such laws as they deem necessary to control the use of property in accordance with the general interest. Such laws are especially called for and usual in the field of housing, which in our modern societies is a central concern of social and economic policies. In order to implement such policies, the legislature must have a wide margin of appreciation both with regard to the existence of a
h   problem of public concern warranting measures of control and as to the choice of the detailed rules for the implementation of such measures. The Court will respect the legislature's judgement as to what is in the general interest unless that judgement be manifestly without reasonable foundation.'

j [58] Mr Cox argued that, while this principle applied to dealings with property, it did not extend to a situation that involved discrimination on the ground of gender. He relied on *Abdulaziz v UK* (1985) 7 EHRR 471; *Burghartz v Switzerland* (1994) 18 EHRR 101 and *Van Raalte v Netherlands* (1997) 24 EHRR 503.

[59] *Abdulaziz v UK* involved discrimination in the field of immigration. Non-national wives were permitted entry into the United Kingdom to join their husbands, more readily than husbands were permitted entry to join their wives. The government sought to justify this on the ground that it was necessary to

protect the labour market at a time of high unemployment, because men were more likely to seek work than women. The court held that the impact on the labour market was insufficiently significant to justify the discrimination. It is also worth recording the court's reaction to another argument, which has some relevance in the present context ((1985) 7 EHRR 471 at 503):

> '82. There remains a more general argument advanced by the Government, namely that the United Kingdom was not in violation of Article 14 by reason of the fact that it acted more generously in some respects—that is, as regards the admission of non-national wives and fiancées of men settled in the country—than the Convention required. The Court cannot accept this argument. It would point out that Article 14 is concerned with the avoidance of discrimination in the enjoyment of the Convention rights in so far as the requirements of the Convention as to those rights can be complied with in different ways. The notion of discrimination within the meaning of Article 14 includes in general cases where a person or group is treated, without proper justification, less favourably than another, even though the more favourable treatment is not called for by the Convention.'

[60] *Burghartz*'s case involved discrimination between husband and wife in relation to the entitlement to use family names. No substantive justification was put forward for this other than tradition. In these circumstances, the court commented ((1994) 18 EHRR 101 at 116 (para 27)):

> 'The Court reiterates that the advancement of the equality of the sexes is today a major goal in the Member States of the Council of Europe; this means that very weighty reasons would have to be put forward before a difference of treatment on the sole ground of sex could be regarded as compatible with the Convention.'

[61] In *Van Raalte*'s case Dutch law provided for an exemption for unmarried childless women over the age of 45 from the obligation to pay contributions under the General Child Benefits Act. The applicant was an unmarried childless man who objected that his obligation to pay such contributions from 1985 to 1988 was discriminatory and violated art 14 when read with art 1 of the First Protocol. The exemption had been enacted in 1962 and abolished in 1989. The Commission concluded that the principal reason for this discrimination was sympathy for the plight of childless women whose condition would be exacerbated if they had to contribute to child benefit. The Commission considered that such considerations had become outmoded. They conceded ((1997) 24 EHRR 503 at 514 (para 44)) that—

> 'it is difficult to establish exactly at what moment developments have attained a durability and general acceptance which require them to be incorporated into legislation.'

They concluded, however, that on the facts the continuation of the discrimination until 1989 could not be justified as being the inevitably belated reaction to developments in society. The court concurred.

[62] This decision comes closest to the facts with which we are concerned. There are, however, significant differences. In *Van Raalte*'s case there was, on analysis, no significant distinction between the position of women and men. On the facts before us there has, at all times, been a significantly larger proportion of widows between the ages of 45 and 65 without employment than of widowers in

a the same age group. The contrast between the two cohorts has, however, been steadily shrinking. At what point did the distinction between the two cohorts reduce to such an extent that art 14 required the state to take action to remove the favourable treatment accorded to widows?

b [63] Despite Mr Cox's submissions, we consider that in answering this question a very considerable margin of discretion must be accorded to the Secretary of State. Difficult questions of economic and social policy were involved, the resolution of which fell within the province of the executive and the legislature rather than the courts. In this context we revert to the fact that the issue was the point in time at which benefits which had long been enjoyed by widows should be withdrawn. No statistical formula or calculation could provide a precise answer to this question. At the end of the day, however, the c burden must lie on the Secretary of State to provide objective justification for what was, without question, discrimination in favour of women.

[64] We have concluded, contrary to the conclusion of Moses J, that the Secretary of State has failed to discharge this burden. Different strands of the evidence all lead to the same conclusion. By 1995, if not earlier, the difference in d economic activity between women and men no longer justified discriminating between them by paying, indiscriminately, pensions to widows aged between 45 and 65.

[65] The starting point must be the statistics. We have quoted above the passage from Carol Freer's statement in which she compares the economic activity of women in 1985 with that in 2000. It is informative to compare, in the e tables to which she refers, the position in 2000 with the position in 1995. We have extracted the relevant data:

Table 1—Older women compared to younger women

% of women economically active

f

	1995	2000
Age 18–24	69.8%	70.8%
Age 25–34	71.6%	75.3%
Age 35–39	76.6%	77.7%
Age 50–59	63.2%	65.9%

g

Table 2—Older men compared to older women

% of older men and women economically active

h

	1995	2000
Men aged 50–54	71.5%	72.5%
Women aged 50–59	63.2%	65.9%

j

Table 3—% of men and women economically active

	1995	2000
Men	84.7%	84.3%
Women	70.9%	72.9%

Table 4—Part time working by men and women

	1995	2000
Men	8%	9%
Women	44%	44%

Table 5—Comparison of economically inactive men and women looking after family/home

	1995	2000
Men	0.7%	0.9%
Women	15.4%	12.7%

Table 7—Comparison of economic activity of mothers by age of child

Age of child	1995	2000
0–4 years	51.9%	58.2%
5–10 years	71%	73.6%
11–15 years	77%	78.3%
16–18 years	81.8%	80%

[66] The change between 1995 and 2000 can be seen to be relatively modest. This, of course, would be nothing to the point if the figures spanned a watershed, but it does not seem to us that they do. The economic activity of women in 1995, including older women, makes it difficult to accept that there was still justification for the payment of pensions to all older widows as a class. By 1995, in 22·7% of all households where the woman was in some form of paid employment, she was also the main breadwinner.

[67] Our impression that 1995 to 2000 was not a watershed period receives support from comments made by those who had the conduct of the Welfare Reform and Pensions Bill on behalf of the government in Parliament. The Consultation Paper published by the government in November 1998, after stating that the current scheme was unfair because, among other reasons, 'It gives most help to people who do not need widows' benefits all their lives when they are earning a decent living or have large occupational pensions or life insurance', went on to describe the case for reform as 'overwhelming'. 'Equal treatment', it commented, 'can no longer be ignored'. In committee, Mr Stephen Timms MP described the benefits system as 'hugely out of date as regards bereavement' and 'woefully out of date'. Mr Stephen Bayley MP, Parliamentary Under-Secretary of State for Social Security, said:

'The current system is both unfair and outdated. It does not reflect today's society with 70% of married women now working and it openly discriminates against married men. We agree that widowers have been poorly treated by the system in the past and we want to change that for the *a* future.' (See HC Official Report, SC D (Welfare Reform and Pensions Bill), 25 March 1999.)

[68] Looking at the position in Europe, the following countries had established equal entitlement to survivors' benefits by 1995: Austria, Belgium, Denmark, Finland, France, Germany, Greece, Ireland, Italy, Luxembourg, the Netherlands, Norway, Spain, Sweden, Russia and Turkey. Moses J commented
b that it was difficult to accord overriding weight to this factor. The brief description of the position in other countries did not enable the court to assess the overall economic impact of the measures taken. As a general proposition we agree, but the overall picture cuts the ground from the submission, largely 'ex cathedra', that there were good reasons for the government to take no steps to
c bring this country into line with our neighbours until 1998.

[69] For these reasons we find that the Secretary of State has failed to establish that, after 1995, there was objective justification for not taking steps to remove the discrimination involved in paying pensions to widows aged between 45 and 65, when widowers had no similar entitlement.

d *The fourth issue*

[70] The best way of explaining this issue is to quote the paragraphs of the skeleton argument submitted on behalf of the state in which the *Walden* point is advanced:

e 'It is an established principle in the jurisprudence of the European Court of Human Rights that where there is a potential breach of the Convention, the relevant domestic legal authorities are afforded a reasonable period within which to change clear statutory provisions for the future, and are not be treated as having been in breach of the Convention in other cases, retrospectively: see *Marckx v Belgium* (1979) 2 EHRR 330 at para 58; *Walden v*
f *Liechtenstein* (App No 33916/96) (16 March 2000, unreported) at pp 6–7; *JR v Germany* App No 22651/93 (18 October 1995, unreported). The starting point for this reasonable period may be an authoritative ruling by the European Court of Human Rights or by a national constitutional court on the critical point.

The essence of this doctrine is that in circumstances where the legal
g position has been unclear and it is then authoritatively clarified, and where an entire administrative system (e g for the payment of welfare benefits) will have to be adjusted as a result to take account of the law as clarified, it is reasonable to afford a state a reasonable period to adjust—while in the meantime maintaining the application of the established rules in respect of
h persons affected. This is in the interests of promoting legal certainty, ensuring that changes can be properly funded, and ensuring that the system can continue to be properly administered without invidious or difficult choices having to be made by state officials responsible for administering the system (which would carry the risk of unjustified differential treatment of
j similar cases).'

[71] The Secretary of State submitted in his skeleton argument that the earliest point at which the state could be required to take action 'under the domestic regime' was 2 October 2000, when the 1998 Act came into force. By that time Parliament had already recognised, by passing the 1999 Act, that the differential treatment between widows and widowers needed to be corrected. The complexity of the changes required a reasonable period of delay before they

were implemented. The 1999 Act, in fact, came into force only six months after 2 October 2000. This period of delay was no more than reasonable. Thus it followed, so the state submitted, that no complaint could be made of breach of the convention during this period, or earlier. This submission received a degree of refinement in the course of oral argument, but remained the same in principle. We propose to look at the principle before relating it to the facts.

[72] In *Marckx's* case the Strasbourg court was concerned with a provision of Belgian law that restricted the capacity of a mother to give or bequeath property to her illegitimate child. The court held that this provision infringed art 8 and art 14, when taken in conjunction with both art 8 and art 1 of the First Protocol of the convention. The question was raised of the effect that the court's judgment might have on the many distributions of estates within Belgium shown to have been effected according to law which infringed the convention. In a ruling which was without precedent at Strasbourg, but which drew on the jurisprudence of the Luxembourg court, the court held:

> 'Having regard to all these circumstances, the principle of legal certainty, which is necessarily inherent in the law of the Convention as in Community Law, dispenses the Belgian State from re-opening legal acts or situations that antedate the delivery of the present Judgment. Moreover, a similar solution is found in certain Contracting States having a constitutional court: their public law limits the retroactive effects of those decisions of that court that annul legislation.'

[73] *Walden's* case was a case concerned with a Liechtenstein pension law that discriminated against women. After protracted civil litigation, in which the applicant was unsuccessful at all levels, including the Supreme Court, he obtained a ruling from the state court, sitting as a Constitutional Court, that the relevant legislation was unconstitutional as being contrary to the principle of non-discrimination on the ground of gender. Legislative procedures were already in train to reform the legislation in a manner which would make it convention-compliant. The legislation was, however, complex and the proposed changes might take time. In these circumstances, the state court decided not to set aside the legislation or to quash the decision of the Supreme Court.

[74] The Strasbourg court noted that the parties' submissions concentrated on the question of whether the state court should have set the contested legislative provisions aside. The applicant contended that it should have done so, with retroactive effect. The government contended that it was prevented from doing so for reasons of legal certainty. In fact, the amending legislation was introduced within about seven months of the state court's decision. The Strasbourg court ruled as follows:

> 'Taking all these circumstances into account, the court finds that the present case does not differ substantially from the case in which a Constitutional Court annuls an unconstitutional provision and sets a time limit for enacting new legislation. It, therefore, considers that the state court's decision, which had the effect that unconstitutional legislation remained applicable to the applicant for a limited period, served the interests of legal certainty. Given the brevity of this period which ended about seven months after the state court's decision, namely on 1 January 1997 when new legislation entered into force, the continued application of the pension provisions at issue can also be regarded as proportionate.'

a [75] Two related principles are to be derived from the two cases that we have just considered. (1) Where the Strasbourg court rules that a state's legislation violates the convention, the court can, in the interests of legal certainty, direct that its decision shall not have retrospective effect. (2) Where the Constitutional Court of a state rules that a law of that state is unconstitutional in a respect which violates the convention, that court will not itself infringe the convention if it

b refrains from annulling the legislation in order to permit its orderly amendment within a reasonable time.

[76] We cannot see how either of these principles impacts on the present case. As to the first principle, we understand that the Strasbourg court has only applied this once—in *Marckx*'s case itself. The complaint made against the Secretary of State is that he delayed too long in initiating reform, to which it can be no answer

c that it takes time to implement reform.

[77] So far as the second principle is concerned, this country has no Constitutional Court. The manner in which we have given effect to the convention preserves the supremacy of Parliament. The court can do no more than declare legislation incompatible with the convention, leaving it to

d Parliament to address the offending legislation. The *Walden* principle can have no direct application in this jurisdiction.

[78] Having said this, we consider that the *Walden* principle reflects the fact that the state is entitled not merely to a wide margin of appreciation when considering whether and when a change is required to the law in order to ensure that it remains convention compliant in changing circumstances, but that, having

e so decided, it is entitled to such time as is reasonable to make the necessary change. No criticism has been, or in our view could be, made of the period taken to consult on and then introduce the 1999 Act. The criticism, which we have held to be well founded, has been of the delay in deciding that a change in the law was necessary.

f
The fifth issue

[79] The submissions in relation to this issue were made by Mr Goudie QC on behalf of Mr Hooper and adopted by Mr Cox on behalf of Messrs Withey and Martin. It could not be advanced on behalf of Mr Naylor because no claim in

g respect of a widow's pension has been the subject of a settlement at Strasbourg.

[80] The submissions can be summarised as follows. Claimants have brought claims in Strasbourg which mirror those of the appellants. The state has followed a policy of settling Strasbourg claims as soon as they have been held to be admissible. The state has declined to settle the claims of the appellants. This, so

h it is alleged, constitutes discrimination in favour of the Strasbourg claimants which infringes art 14, in combination with art 8 and with art 1 of the First Protocol.

[81] We have had difficulty in identifying the precise nature of this issue. On reflecting on Mr Goudie's submissions after the October hearing it seemed to us that the case which he had advanced differed from that which Moses J had

j addressed. We sought clarification of his case at the March hearing and this made it clear that it does indeed differ from the case addressed in the judgment of Moses J. It is not clear to us whether this is because Moses J did not fully appreciate the nature of the appellants' case or because Mr Goudie has refined his case since the hearing at first instance. Certainly no objection was raised on behalf of the Secretary of State that Mr Goudie had changed his ground. We propose first to make some general comments about the nature of claims of

breach of art 14, then to consider the manner in which Moses J dealt with the
issue and finally to address the issue as it was presented before us.   *a*

Article 14 claims

[82] Article 14 forbids discrimination in securing convention rights and
obligations. The article makes plain the grounds of discrimination against which
it is primarily addressed, namely 'any ground such as sex, race, colour, language,   *b*
religion, political or other opinion, national or social origin, association with a
national minority, property, birth or other status'. Thus, typically, the article
addresses the situation where a state discriminates against a readily identifiable
class in the manner in which it respects, or fails to respect, convention rights. The
discrimination need not go so far as infringing the convention rights of the party
discriminated against—were that the case art 14 would be superfluous. More   *c*
generous treatment in securing the enjoyment of a convention right by one class
rather than the other can suffice to engage art 14, in conjunction with the right in
question. We repeat the principle stated by the Strasbourg court in *Abdulaziz v UK*
(1985) 7 EHRR 471 at 503 (para 82):

> 'The notion of discrimination within the meaning of Article 14 includes, in   *d*
> general, cases where a person or group is treated, without proper
> justification, less favourably than another, even though the more favourable
> treatment is not called for by the Convention.'

The nature of this nexus between art 14 and some other convention right is
usually described, not very helpfully, by the proposition that the facts must fall   *e*
'within the ambit' of a substantive convention right.

[83] Where it is alleged that art 14 has been infringed it is first necessary to
consider whether the claimant has been treated less favourably in relation to the
enjoyment of a convention right than others. If he has, the next task is to identify
why this is—on what grounds has he suffered discrimination? If there is no   *f*
rational explanation for the discrimination, art 14 will not be engaged. Equally,
if the discrimination has been for some idiosyncratic reason, such as a personal
dislike of the claimant on the part of a state official, art 14 will not be engaged.
The terms of art 14 suggest that what has to be demonstrated is that the claimant
is one of a class or group who share a distinguishing characteristic and that this
characteristic is the ground upon which the state distinguishes against the   *g*
members of the class or group. Racial discrimination is the paradigm example.

[84] It follows that the reason for the discrimination will be the touchstone of
the identification of the class. The identification of a common factor which results
in discrimination will at the same time result in the identification of the class or
group discriminated against. Care has to be taken to make sure that the common   *h*
factor is, indeed, the ground for discrimination. This will not be so if there are
other factors which explain treating the claimants differently from others. Thus
it is necessary to be sure that, apart from the alleged ground for discrimination,
the claimants are in an analogous situation to those who are more favourably
treated. Consideration of an art 14 claim usually involves comparing the class
into which the claimant falls with a comparator class that is treated more   *j*
favourably. An issue can arise, and does arise in this case, as to whether the
distinction between the two classes has to be a personal characteristic or status,
such as one of the examples listed in art 14.

[85] In the leading judgment in *Wandsworth London BC v Michalak* [2002]
EWCA Civ 271, [2002] 4 All ER 1136 Brooke LJ recommended the following
structured approach to consideration of an art 14 claim. The court should ask,

a sequentially, four questions. If any one is answered in the negative it will normally follow that the claim is ill-founded. The questions (at [20]) are:

> '(i) Do the facts fall within the ambit of one or more of the substantive Convention provisions (for the relevant Convention rights see s 1(1) of the 1998 Act)? (ii) If so, was there different treatment as respects that right between the complainant on the one hand and other persons put forward for
b comparison ("the chosen comparators") on the other? (iii) Were the chosen comparators in an analogous situation to the complainant's situation? (iv) If so, did the difference in treatment have an objective and reasonable justification: in other words, did it pursue a legitimate aim and did the differential treatment bear a reasonable relationship of proportionality to the
c aim sought to be achieved?'

We agree with Brooke LJ that this structured approach is helpful. It is one that was followed by Moses J.

The treatment of art 14 by Moses J

d [86] The foundation of the claim before Moses J was a policy followed by the Secretary of State which the claimants alleged infringed art 14. The policy was stated in a letter written on behalf of the Secretary of State to Mr Hooper on 26 May 2000 in the following terms:

> 'As you know, the Government has secured friendly settlement in two
e [Strasbourg] cases recently. Nevertheless there is no statutory basis to make payments of Widow's Benefits to men and the Government's obligation, following the European Court of Human Rights' finding that the cases are admissible, is to future widowers. There are no plans to make extra-statutory payments before the new bereavement benefits are introduced other than to those widowed fathers who take cases to the European Court of Human
f Rights and obtain an admissibility ruling.'

[87] As Moses J understood the position, the claimants identified themselves as belonging to a class of claimants in domestic proceedings and identified as the comparator and more favoured class, claimants before the Strasbourg Court. The discriminatory treatment complained of consisted of reaching friendly
g settlements with Strasbourg claimants whose claims had been ruled admissible but refusing to conclude similar settlements with domestic claimants.

[88] Moses J first considered whether the facts fell 'within the ambit' of art 8. He decided, very shortly, that they did. Before us the Secretary of State challenged that conclusion. We consider that Moses J was correct for the
h following simple reason.

[89] It is common ground that discrimination between widows who receive benefits and widowers who do not engages art 8. It seems to us to follow that discrimination between Strasbourg claimants whose art 8 claims are settled and domestic claimants whose art 8 claims are not settled must also engage art 8. Counsel for the Secretary of State sought to dissuade us from this conclusion by
j submitting that the Strasbourg claimants were claiming compensation in respect of breaches of their art 8 rights whereas the domestic claimants were seeking to enforce such rights. We failed to follow why this should make any difference.

[90] Moses J took it as read that there was different treatment in settling Strasbourg claims but not settling domestic claims. He then turned to the third question identified by Brooke LJ, namely whether Strasbourg claimants and domestic claimants were in an analogous situation. In order to answer this

question Moses J considered two matters, although not in this order: (1) would
discrimination in favour of claimants on the ground that they were claiming in
Strasbourg, rather than in England, engage art 14; and (2) were there grounds for
distinguishing between Strasbourg claimants and English claimants other than
simply the venue in which the claims were being pursued?

[91] Moses J answered the first question in the negative. The Secretary of
State submitted to Moses J, and submits to us, that the difference in treatment of
Strasbourg claimants and domestic claimants does not fall within art 14 because
art 14 only applies to discrimination on the ground of 'a personal characteristic
(status) by which persons or groups of persons are distinguishable from each
other' (see *Kjeldsen v Denmark* (1976) 1 EHRR 711). Moses J accepted this
submission. Mr Goudie submitted to us that *Kjeldsen's* case was outdated
jurisprudence and referred us to the very recent decision of this court in
Michalak's case in support of this submission. We share the view expressed by
Brooke LJ in that case ([2002] 4 All ER 1136 at [34]) that *Kjeldsen's* case appears to
have been superseded by more recent Strasbourg authority. We can see no
reason in principle why litigants in the English court should not be entitled to
complain under art 14 if, on the ground of their status as litigants in that court,
they are treated less favourably than litigants before the Strasbourg court in a
manner which engages one of the other convention rights.

[92] Accordingly, we do not agree with the reasoning of Moses J in relation to
this first question. It is, however, no longer relevant (if it ever was) for Mr Goudie
has made it plain that he does not rely upon the venue of litigation as being the
characteristic which distinguishes between the claimants and the Strasbourg
litigants, or as the ground upon which the adverse treatment of the claimants is
based.

[93] In dealing with the second question, Moses J concluded that it was not
simply the venue in which the claims were brought that was the ground for
distinguishing between Strasbourg and domestic litigants. There were substantive
differences between the relief available in the two jurisdictions. He cited
Stubbings v UK (1996) 1 BHRC 316 and *National and Provincial Building Society v UK*
(1998) 25 EHRR 127 as establishing that the forum in which the claimants litigate
may afford a valid ground for distinction between groups of litigants. It does not
seem to us that either of these decisions establishes that proposition, but we think
that the facts of this case are demonstration enough that the proposition is true.
To succeed in the domestic forum the claimants have to surmount the barriers
posed by s 22(4) of the 1998 Act. That section precludes a claimant from basing a
claim under the Act on any act that took place before 2 October 2000 when the
1998 Act came into force. Most of the claimants became 'victims' before
2 October 2000. Those who claim in Strasbourg will not be affected by the fact
that their claims relate to decisions taken before 2 October 2000. In this
jurisdiction the Secretary of State contends that the relevant decisions, or at least
some of them, were taken before 2 October 2000 and is invoking s 22(4) of the
1998 Act in answer to the claims—see the eighth issue below. There are thus
substantive grounds for resisting the claims in this jurisdiction which are not
available at Strasbourg. Litigants in this jurisdiction are patently not in an
analogous situation to litigants before the court in Strasbourg. Moses J was
correct so to conclude.

[94] Moses J held that, because claimants at Strasbourg were not in an
analogous position to claimants before the English court, it was unnecessary to
consider whether there was an objective justification for treating them
differently. He went on to do so none the less, because he held that a similar

a question arose under the plea that the differentiation of treatment was irrational and therefore unlawful under principles of domestic public law. He held that because claims brought in the English court raised 'major constitutional points in domestic law' it was rational and legitimate for the state to settle claims in Strasbourg but to leave itself free to pursue the issues that arose in domestic law.

b [95] The issues of objective justification and rationality considered by Moses J are similar to issues raised by the 'Strasbourg discrimination' issue as formulated, or re-formulated, before us. We propose to consider them in that context.

The Strasbourg discrimination issue as presented before us

c [96] The clue to the fact that the Strasbourg discrimination point was to be put before us on a different basis to that considered by Moses J was to be found in a passage in Mr Goudie's skeleton argument. This contended that the justification accepted by Moses J was directed at the wrong target in that it addressed the issue of why the state had not settled the present proceedings but did not address Mr Hooper's actual complaint that 'he should have received an extra-statutory payment without having to commence any litigation at all'. At the October

d hearing neither we, nor we believe counsel for the Secretary of State, fully appreciated the nature of the case being advanced. This was clarified by Mr Goudie at the resumed hearing in March. His argument on behalf of Mr Hooper runs as follows. The unlawful discrimination is between two classes of those who became 'victims' of discrimination by making claims for benefit.

e One class consists of those seeking compensation by bringing claims at Strasbourg whose claims have been ruled admissible. The other class consists of those who have not made claims at Strasbourg. The policy favours the former, by settling their claims, whereas no such accommodation is offered to the latter. Before 2 October 2000 the latter had no right to claim that this discrimination infringed art 14. That right arose when the state failed to change its policy on

f 2 October 2000. At that point Mr Hooper and those in like position acquired a right to complain that this continuing discrimination infringed art 14. Claimants at Strasbourg have been granted settlements which compensate them both for their failure to receive benefits before 2 October 2000 and for their failure to receive benefits during the period from 2 October 2000 to 9 April 2001, when the new regime came into force. In order to avoid discrimination the state is bound

g to make ex gratia payments of like amounts to victims who have not brought claims at Strasbourg.

[97] In this way Mr Goudie seeks to get on its feet a claim that will compensate Mr Hooper for failure to receive benefits during the period before the 1998 Act

h came into effect, thereby finessing the effect of s 22(4)(b) of the 1998 Act. Messrs Withey and Naylor are in the same position in relation to discrimination that they allege occurred before 2 October 2000.

[98] At the March hearing Mr Sales clarified the Secretary of State's policy. It applied only to claims commenced at Strasbourg before 2 October 2000, which claims necessarily covered a period before the 1998 Act came into force. In

j relation to those claims it was at all material times the policy of the state to reach a friendly settlement with the claimant once the claim had been ruled admissible by the Strasbourg court. This policy did not extend to claims commenced after 2 October 2000. As far as such claims are concerned, it has been the practice of the state to contend that they are inadmissible because the claimant has not exhausted the remedies that are, or may be, now available in this country under s 6(1) of the 1998 Act.

[99] It seems to us that, while Mr Hooper, Mr Withey and Mr Naylor are all in a position to contend that, as pre-2 October 2000 victims, they are in comparable positions to those whose cases have been the subject of friendly settlements at Strasbourg, Mr Martin is not in the same position as he did not become a victim until 2 October 2000.

[100] Before us Mr Sales understandably sought to rely upon a recent 'partial decision as to admissibility' by the Strasbourg court in relation to 26 applicants who have advanced claims similar to those with which we are concerned. Two applicants advanced claims similar to that of Mr Wilkinson, described as claims in respect of 'Bereavement Tax Allowance'. They contended that they had been discriminated against as compared with other widowers who had received payments under friendly settlements of their claims. The court ruled that this discrimination claim was 'manifestly ill-founded', remarking:

'The court notes that the men concerned have received those payments in friendly settlement of applications which have been communicated to the government by this court. The court considers that the applicants in the present cases are not in an analogous situation to those men ...'

[101] While this decision is plainly in point, we have been unable to follow the precise reasoning of the court. Quite apart from this decision, however, it seems to us that there is a fatal flaw in the Strasbourg discrimination claim as now formulated. The policy alleged to be discriminatory is one under which any pre-1998 Act victim who brought a claim at Strasbourg before 2 October 2000 and has that claim ruled admissible, will receive a friendly settlement. That policy does not create two classes of victims, one of which is treated more favourably than the other. It applies a single condition precedent to receipt of a friendly settlement by a member of a single class—namely pre-1998 Act victims. The reason why Mr Hooper and those in a like position are not able to benefit from this policy is because they have not advanced a claim at Strasbourg, not because there is a policy which discriminates between one class and another.

[102] For this reason, we consider that the fifth issue falls to be decided against the appellants. The issue of objective justification does not arise. However, a similar issue remains alive under domestic public law, and we now turn to consider it.

The sixth issue

[103] The irrationality challenge can be simply stated. Mr Goudie contended that the state's policy of declining to pay victims of discrimination unless and until a claim had been brought at Strasbourg and declared admissible was a policy of attrition that had no justification and was irrational and unfair. There could be no justification for requiring claimants to follow a course which involved treading a road which was 'long and hard' and which now included exhausting domestic remedies under the 1998 Act before finally settling at Strasbourg a claim which was certain to succeed. He contended that the state should have treated the friendly settlement reached in the Strasbourg proceedings in *Cornwell v UK* as if it were the determination of a test case, so that other claimants in the same position as Mr Cornwell should be treated in similar fashion. He relied, by analogy, on the approach of this court in *R v Hertfordshire CC, ex p Cheung* (1986) Times, 26 March.

[104] *Cheung's* case was not a test case. We do not consider that the suggested analogy is a fair one, or that a settlement without admission of liability, whether at Strasbourg or in any other proceedings, requires the state to make equivalent

a   payments to all in a like position to the claimant whose claim has been settled. A well-recognised motive for settling a case is to avoid the risk of an adverse decision and a settlement cannot be considered as carrying the same consequences as such a decision.

[105] Article 38 of the convention provides as follows:

b   '1. If the Court declares the application admissible, it shall ... (b) place itself at the disposal of the parties concerned with a view to securing a friendly settlement of the matter on the basis of respect for human rights as defined in the Convention and the protocols thereto.'

[106] Rule 62 of the Rules of the Strasbourg court make the following
c   provisions in relation to friendly settlements:

'1. Once an application has been declared admissible, the Registrar, acting on the instructions of the Chamber or its President, shall enter into contact with the parties with a view to securing a friendly settlement of the matter in accordance with Article 38(1)(b) of the Convention. The Chamber shall
d   take any steps that appear appropriate to facilitate such a settlement.

2. In accordance with Article 38(2) of the Convention, the friendly-settlement negotiations shall be confidential and without prejudice to the parties' argument in the contentious proceedings. No written or oral communication and no offer or concession made in the framework of the
e   attempt to secure a friendly settlement may be referred to or relied on in the contentious proceedings.

3. If the Chamber is informed by the Registrar that the parties have agreed to a friendly settlement, it shall, after verifying that the settlement has been reached on the basis of respect for human rights as defined in the Convention and the protocols thereto, strike the case out of the Court's list in accordance
f   with Rule 44(2).'

[107] We can see no basis for spelling out of these provisions a principle whereby a friendly settlement of a claim requires a state to treat all others in the same position as the claimant in the same way. No precedent has been cited to
g   us to support such a proposition, whether in the jurisprudence of the Strasbourg court, or in our domestic jurisprudence.

[108] Moses J accepted the contention of Mr Sales that it was legitimate and rational for the state to settle cases at Strasbourg in order, in effect, to keep its powder dry to fight the first battle before the domestic court once the 1998 Act
h   had come into force. Mr Goudie complained that this assertion was unsupported by any evidence and was unconvincing. In a footnote to its skeleton argument for the resumed hearing, the Secretary of State provided details of the battle that the United Kingdom is currently fighting before the Strasbourg court to ensure that, at the present time, no claim of the type with which we are concerned should be admitted until a remedy has first been sought in domestic proceedings
j   under the 1998 Act. We consider that this lends some support to the contention that the government's strategy has been all along to preserve for litigation in the domestic forum issues with which we are concerned before contesting these at Strasbourg. At the end of the day, however, we do not consider that this is something which the Secretary of State has to prove. It suffices that we can see nothing demonstrably perverse, irrational or unfair about a course of conduct which has brought about that result.

The seventh issue

[109] Moses J held that payment of a widow's payment and a WMA to widows, but not to widowers, involved infringement of art 14, in conjunction with art 8, which could not be justified. That finding has not been challenged before us. He held that the Secretary of State had objective justification for paying a widow's pension to widows but not to widowers. We have allowed the appeal against that finding. Moses J held that the appellants were entitled to a declaration that ss 36 and 37 of the 1992 Act were incompatible with their convention rights, but not to any monetary compensation. This was because he ruled that s 6(2)(b) of the 1998 Act provided the Secretary of State with a defence to the allegation that he had acted unlawfully. The appellants challenge that conclusion.

[110] The manner in which the appellants put their claim is as follows. (i) It is unlawful for a public authority to act in a way which is incompatible with a convention right—s 6(1) of the 1998 Act. (ii) 'Act' includes 'failure to act'—s 6(6) of the 1998 Act. (iii) Paying benefits to widows who had claimed payment, but not to widowers who had claimed payment, was discrimination which was incompatible with convention rights. (iv) Had the state made extra-statutory payments to widowers equivalent to the benefits paid to widows, there would have been no discrimination and therefore no violation of the convention. (v) It follows that it was and is unlawful for the state to refrain from making those extra-statutory payments. (vi) A mandatory order should be made requiring the state to make the extra-statutory payments in question. (vii) Alternatively, the appellants are entitled to damages for the breach of the Secretary of State's duty to make extra-statutory payments.

[111] Before Moses J the debate in relation to this issue focussed exclusively on the effect of s 6(2) of the 1998 Act. Moses J introduced his consideration of this issue with the following statement ([2002] All ER (D) 193 (Feb) at [170]):

'Mr Sales accepts that s 6(2)(a) has no application in the instant case. He makes the important concession that ss 36 and 37 [of the 1992 Act] do not expressly, or by implication, exclude the power of the Crown to make an extra-statutory payment. The source of such power … was not made clear to me.'

[112] At the October hearing we sought clarification from Mr Garnham as to the basis of the Secretary of State's concession. This led him to place before us a paper on Parliamentary control over expenditure to the effect that any payment to widowers on an extra-statutory basis would need to be accounted for within estimates presented to Parliament. This did not wholly answer our question—indeed it seemed to us, and we suspect to Mr Garnham, that this suggested, at the least, that parliamentary approval would be needed before the Secretary of State could make payments to widowers. Right at the end of the October hearing, however, Mr Garnham informed us, on instructions but without explanation, that the Secretary of State enjoyed extra-statutory power to make payments to all widowers of sums equivalent to the benefits received by widows.

[113] We have not been prepared to accept this concession without question and, at the resumed hearing, we asked the parties to present argument on the predicate that it was unsound. At that hearing Mr Sales provided, in a lengthy section of his skeleton argument, an explanation of the concession. He also emphasised that, while in the context of the present case, this was correctly described as a concession, the Secretary of State was concerned at the wider

a implications of a possible finding by this court that he enjoyed no common law power to make the payments in question.

[114] The issue of whether the Secretary of State enjoys the common law power in question need not be addressed if Moses J was correct to conclude, on the premise that he enjoyed such a power, that he committed no breach of duty in deciding not to exercise it. We turn first to that question.

b [115] The appellants' argument is a simple one. If the Secretary of State has a power to make extra-statutory payments, s 6(1) obliges him to exercise that power for, by so doing, he will avoid the breach of the appellants' convention rights which will otherwise occur. Moses J rejected this argument. He held:

c '[183] In the instant case, it seems to me that the fatal flaw in the claimants' argument is that its effect is to convert the power to make an extra-statutory payment into a duty. It destroys the power altogether. There are no circumstances in which the defendant could exercise a power not to give a benefit.

d [184] For that reason I conclude that the primary legislation is incompatible with the convention. Whatever the nature of the power, at least it can be said that the legislation imposes no duty to give benefits to widowers and cannot be read in a way which has that effect. The Secretary of State's refusal gives effect to those provisions and the power to make statutory allowances is irrelevant. He can rely upon s 6(2)(b).'

e [116] At the October hearing we had difficulty in understanding this passage from the judgment below and following the argument advanced on behalf of the Secretary of State to support it. With the benefit of further submissions made at the March hearing, we now believe that we understand this argument. We shall set out, in stages, the argument as we understand it. (i) Section 6(2)(a) provides an authority with a defence when a statute *requires* the authority to Act in a way *f* which is incompatible with a convention right; s 6(2)(b) provides an authority with a defence where a statute confers on an authority *a power* which, if exercised, will necessarily involve infringement of a convention right. (ii) The 1992 and 1999 Acts, on their true construction, leave unfettered the Secretary of State's common law power to pay benefits to widowers if he chooses so to do. (iii) Each *g* Act might, for the avoidance of doubt, have provided 'this Act is without prejudice to the Secretary of State's common law power to pay benefits to widowers, if he chooses so to do'. The position would still have been precisely the same as (ii). (iv) Each Act might have stated: '(i) The Secretary of State may pay benefits to widowers if he chooses so to do; (ii) The Secretary of State may *h* refrain from making payments to widowers if he chooses so to do …' The position would still have been precisely the same as in (ii) and (iii). (v) Had the Acts expressly authorised the Secretary of State to refrain from paying benefits to widowers, the exercise of that statutory power would necessarily have involved infringing their convention rights. In such circumstances s 6(2)(b) would have provided him with a defence. (vi) Parliament cannot have intended that, by *j* leaving implicit what could have been expressed, the Secretary of State's discretion should be fettered by the 1998 Act.

[117] We accept the starting point of this argument. If a statute confers an express power which can only be exercised in a manner which infringes a convention right, then Parliament has expressly authorised a breach of the convention. Section 6(2)(b) preserves the supremacy of Parliament by permitting an authority to exercise the power granted by Parliament.

[118] The chain of reasoning that follows is, however, fallacious. If the 1992 and 1999 Acts do not restrict a common law power enjoyed by the Secretary of States to make payments to whomsoever he pleases, it does not follow that Parliament has thereby authorised the Secretary of State to ignore the requirements of the 1998 Act when deciding whether or not to exercise that power. A duty in certain circumstances to make payments to widowers is in no way incompatible with a general common law power to make payments to anybody.

[119] The 1992 and 1999 Acts expressly require the Secretary of State to pay benefits to widows in accordance with their terms. If he retains a common law power to make payments to widowers, we cannot see how a decision not to exercise that power can be said to be necessary in order to give effect to the provisions, express or implied, of either Act. The decision of Moses J on this point was in error.

Does the Secretary of State have a common law power to pay benefits to widowers?

[120] The Secretary of State's primary case, albeit contrary to his interests in this litigation, has been that the 1992 and the 1999 Acts left him free, if he thought fit, to introduce an extra-statutory regime under which widowers would receive benefits commensurate to those to which widows were entitled under the two Acts. Alternatively he submitted that, if the two Acts preclude his common law power to make payments to widowers, they do so comprehensively, so that he has acted beyond his powers in settling with Strasbourg claimants and will not even have power to honour any judgments that may be given in favour of the litigants in these proceedings.

[121] Paradoxically, while the Secretary of State has been prepared to concede that he has common law powers that would enable him to make payments to all widowers, Mr Goudie, on behalf of Mr Hooper, has been prepared to concede that he has not. Mr Goudie has accepted that it would be inconsistent with the scheme of the legislation for the Secretary of State to pay to all widowers' benefits equivalent to those received by widows. He has argued that the Secretary of State none the less retains common law powers to make payments to those who have brought these proceedings and to those other claimants who are in the same position as the appellants.

[122] If the appellants are to succeed in their claims to monetary payments we think that they must demonstrate that the 1992 and 1999 Acts left the Secretary of State free to make extra-statutory payments to all widowers. If they did, then it can be argued that the Secretary of State should be ordered to exercise that power in favour of the appellants, or pay damages in lieu. If they did not, the Secretary of State will have a defence under s 6(2)(a) of the 1998 Act on the basis that the Acts required him to make payments to widows in circumstances where he had no power to make equivalent payments to widowers.

[123] It is unfortunate that we approach this important issue of the powers of the Secretary of State in circumstances where the two parties have made conflicting concessions against interest. The result is that the issue has not been fully explored in argument.

[124] The appellants' claim to an order for money payment is founded on the contention that the Secretary of State had and has the power to make ex gratia payments that will place widowers in the same position as widows. While the Secretary of State has purported to accept that this is indeed the position, much of the argument advanced on his behalf has been to the effect that it would be

a contrary to the will of Parliament to exercise that power in the manner suggested. Thus, in the skeleton argument for the October hearing, prepared by Mr Sales and Miss Stratford, the following contention is advanced:

> 'To seek an order from the court in relation to an extra-statutory, discretionary payment is, the respondent respectfully submits, misconceived.
> *b* In substance, the appellants are attempting to mount a collateral attack on Parliament's failure to legislate in a particular way in the 1992 and/or 1999 Acts, and its deliberate choice to confine widow's benefits to widows (with no entitlement for widowers). The necessary implication of the appellants' argument in this respect is that the Secretary of State is required under the 1998 Act to set up the very scheme for payment of benefits to widowers *c* which Parliament chose not to set up when it legislated by way of primary legislation in this field; according to the appellants the Secretary of State must treat himself as bound to make such payments, whereas Parliament specifically decided that he should not be so bound. Such a collateral attack upon Parliament's failure to legislate in this regard would be directly contrary to the provisions of the 1998 Act, to the scheme of that Act, and to *d* parliamentary sovereignty which the 1998 Act is careful to preserve.'

[125] After referring to the constitutional principle that there be full Parliamentary control over taxation and expenditure—see Dicey *Introduction to the Study of the Law of the Constitution* (10th edn, 1959) pp 315–318—the skeleton argument continues:
e
> 'It would not (with respect) be constitutionally legitimate for the courts, even with the benefit of the 1998 Act, to impose requirements as to extra-statutory payments to be made by the Crown to fill in a gap deliberately left by Parliament in legislation.'

f [126] These submissions are echoed by Moses J's observation ([2002] All ER (D) 193 (Feb) at [185]) that Mr Goudie's argument in relation to s 6 came 'perilously close to a submission that the court should impose a duty to grant benefits where Parliament has chosen not to do so'.

[127] Mr Sales accepted that where Parliament has legislated in such a way as *g* to occupy an entire field, any prerogative or common law right of the Crown to act within that field will be displaced. He contended, however, (against his interest in this appeal) that the 1992 and 1999 Acts did not occupy the field in relation to bereavement benefits so as to preclude the common law power of the Crown to pay these to widowers. We had difficulty in reconciling that submission *h* with the passages of argument that we have set out above and so, it seems, did Mr Goudie. We turn to consider the authorities to which Mr Sales referred us.

[128] The starting point is *A-G v De Keyser's Royal Hotel Ltd* [1920] AC 508, [1920] All ER Rep 80. In that case the House of Lords held that a statutory power to requisition property displaced the prerogative power to do this that the Crown would otherwise have enjoyed. Lord Dunedin observed ([1920] AC 508 at 526,
j [1920] All ER Rep 80 at 86) 'if the whole ground of something which could be done by the prerogative is covered by the statute, it is the statute that rules'. Lord Atkinson said 'after the statute has been passed, and while it is in force, the thing it empowers the Crown to do can thenceforth only be done under the statute' (see [1920] AC 508 at 540, [1920] All ER Rep 80 at 92–93).

[129] Mr Sales submitted, however, that this principle had no application on the facts of the present case. Statutes should not be treated as binding the Crown,

or fettering the powers of the Crown, unless they did so expressly or by necessary
implication—see *Lord Advocate v Dumbarton DC* [1990] 1 All ER 1, [1990] 2 AC 580;
R v Secretary of State for the Home Dept, ex p Northumbria Police Authority [1988] 1 All ER
556, [1989] QB 26. The general principle advanced by Mr Sales is not in doubt.
But we are here dealing with a suggestion that the court can grant relief against
the Crown on the basis that the Crown has both the power under common law
and the duty under s 6(1) of the 1998 Act, to put in place an ex gratia regime of
paying bereavement benefits to widowers when Parliament has made express
statutory provision as to the circumstances in which such benefits should be paid
to widows and, under the 1992 Act as amended by the 1999 Act, to widowers. In
this context it is necessary to have regard to this injunction of Lord Bridge in *Steele
Ford & Newton (a firm) v CPS* [1993] 2 All ER 769 at 774, [1994] 1 AC 22 at 33:

'But still more important, in the present context, is the special
constitutional convention which jealously safeguards the exclusive control
exercised by Parliament over both the levying and the expenditure of the
public revenue. It is trite law that nothing less than clear, express and
unambiguous language is effective to levy a tax. Scarcely less stringent is the
requirement of clear statutory authority for public expenditure. As it was
put by Viscount Haldane in *Auckland Harbour Board v R* [1924] AC 318 at 326:
"It has been a principle of the British Constitution now for more than two
centuries ... that no money can be taken out of the Consolidated Fund into
which the revenues of the state have been paid, excepting under a distinct
authorisation from Parliament itself."'

[130] The rules governing the circumstances in which ministers can properly
make payment out of public funds are rules of constitutional law of some
complexity. We shall try to provide a summary, simplified so far as is possible to
meet the needs of this judgment.

[131] The fundamental principle is that any expenditure of public funds must
be authorised by statute: 8(2) *Halsbury's Laws* (4th edn reissue) para 230; *Auckland
Harbour Board v R* [1924] AC 318; *R v Secretary of State for Foreign Affairs, ex p World
Development Movement Ltd* [1995] 1 All ER 611, [1995] 1 WLR 386—the *Pergau Dam*
case. The complication arises out of the fact that Parliament authorises
expenditure of public funds by two different types of statute. Statutes dealing
with a particular area of government make provision for specific expenditure for
a defined purpose. We shall here describe these as 'specific statutes'. The 1992
and the 1999 Acts are examples of such legislation. Such statutes do not,
however, of themselves provide ministers with access to the public funds.
Revenues raised by taxation or otherwise are, in general, paid into the Exchequer
Account at the Bank of England, where they constitute the Consolidated Fund.
Parliamentary authorisation is required for issues from the Consolidated Fund
and this is provided each year by the second type of statute. A series of
Consolidated Fund Bills are brought before Parliament founded upon supply
resolutions. The final such Bill is the Consolidated Fund (Appropriation) Bill,
which becomes the Appropriation Act. We shall describe this type of legislation
as appropriation legislation. Such legislation authorises the issue to government
departments of the funds that they have demonstrated that they require to
perform their executive functions. In some instances the funds will be required
to make the payments already authorised by specific statutes. In other instances
the funds will be required to enable the government departments to make
payments pursuant to prerogative or common law powers which are not the

subject of any specific statute. Whether expenditure should be authorised by specific statutes, or merely by appropriation statutes is a question of constitutional law on which the views of the Treasury and the Public Accounts Committee have differed. Footnote 4 to the paragraph of *Halsbury's Laws* to which we have already referred (8(2) *Halsbury's Laws* (4th edn reissue) para 230) records the following exchange:

'In 1932 the Committee of Public Accounts (as to which see para 719 post) and the Treasury reached a concordat concerning the requirement to obtain specific legislative authority for expenditure. The Committee of Public Accounts stated that "where it is desired that continuing functions should be exercised by a government department, particularly where such functions may involve financial liabilities extending beyond a given financial year, it is proper, subject to certain recognised exceptions, that the powers and duties to be exercised should be defined by specific statute." The Treasury said that "while they think the Executive government must continue to be allowed a certain measure of discretion in asking Parliament to exercise a power which undoubtedly belongs to it, they agree that practice should normally accord with the view expressed by the Committee [see supra]. The Treasury will, for their part, continue to aim at observance of this principle." Later in 1932 the Treasury restated their view that "while it is competent to Parliament, by means of an annual vote embodied in the Appropriation Acts, in effect to extend powers specifically limited by statute, constitutional propriety requires that such extensions should be regularised at the earliest possible date by amending legislation, unless they are of a purely emergency or non-continuing character".'

[132] On 2 November 1945 Mr Granville Ram, First Parliamentary Counsel, produced a memorandum setting out what has become known as 'The Ram Doctrine' and which is, we understand, still treated by ministers as setting out the position in respect of the question of 'how far legislation is necessary to authorise any extension of the existing powers of a Government Department'? Mr Ram commented that it was necessary to draw a sharp distinction between what was legally possible and what was permissible having regard to established practice. He referred to the exchange of views in 1932, to which we have referred above. He reached the following conclusions:

'a. Legislation is not legally necessary to authorise an extension of the existing powers of a Government Department except where such an extension is precluded by a previous statute either expressly or by necessary implication.
b. If the extended powers involve an annual charge extended over a period of years legislation though not required by law, is required by established practice formally recorded in the transactions between the Public Accounts Committee and the Treasury.'

[133] Where a minister proposes to make a payment that has been authorised by a specific statute the court can properly review his decision to see whether, on true interpretation of the statute, the payment falls within its authorisation. If it does not, the decision to make the payment will be unlawful—see the *Pergau Dam* case.

[134] Where a minister proposes to make payments in circumstances where this conflicts with the intention of Parliament, as manifested in a specific statute,

the decision will be unlawful as an abuse of power, even, it seems, if Parliament *a*
has authorised the issue of funds for that purpose in an appropriation statute—see
R v Secretary of State for the Home Dept, ex p Fire Brigades Union [1995] 2 All ER 244
at 256, [1995] 2 AC 513 at 554.

[135] We turn to consider whether it would conflict with the intention of
Parliament, as expressed in the 1992 and 1999 Acts to introduce a scheme of
making extra statutory payments to widowers to match those payable to widows. *b*
Before the 1998 Act came into force we are in no doubt that it would have done.
As we have shown it has been, at the least, an established practice for more than
half a century that the exercise of powers requiring an annual charge over a
period of years should receive specific statutory authorisation. The 1992 and 1999
Acts constituted such authorisation in relation to bereavement benefits. It seems
to us plainly implicit that Parliament intended the express statutory provisions *c*
for payment of benefits to widows to occupy the entire field of entitlement to
payment of benefits as a result of the death of a spouse. We endorse the
submission made in Mr Sales' skeleton argument that Parliament made 'a deliberate
choice to confine widow's benefits to widows (with no entitlement to widowers)'. In
these circumstances, prior to 2 October 2000, it would have been an abuse of *d*
power for the minister to introduce a scheme of making matching extra-statutory
payments to widowers.

[136] Does the introduction of the 1998 Act make a difference? In our
judgment it does. Section 3 of the Act requires that 'so far as it is possible to do
so, primary legislation … must be read and given effect in a way which is
compatible with the Convention rights'. This statutory requirement enforces the *e*
conclusion that we would have reached, even had the Act not contained this
provision. Once the 1998 Act came into effect it seems to us that its requirements
altered the restraint upon the Secretary of State which resulted from the principle
in *A-G v De Keyser's Royal Hotel Ltd*. There is a presumption that Parliament does
not intend legislation to infringe the convention. Acts of Parliament should be *f*
read, in so far as possible, as not precluding common law or prerogative powers
of the Crown to take any action that may be necessary to prevent infringement
of convention rights. In so far as the 1998 Act placed upon the Secretary of State
an obligation to make extra statutory payments, no constitutional impropriety or
illegality could be involved in his putting in place a scheme to give effect to that
obligation and, if necessary, seeking from Parliament appropriation of funds to *g*
implement the scheme.

[137] It follows that neither s 6(2)(a) nor s 6(2)(b) affords the Secretary of State
a defence to the claim that by failing to make extra-statutory payments to the
claimants he infringed art 14 of the convention. It remains to consider whether
the 1998 Act required the Secretary of State to make the payments claimed by the
appellants and, if it did, the relief that should be accorded by this court. This turns *h*
upon the answers to be given to the last two issues.

The eighth issue

[138] The discrimination between the appellants and widows occurred, in
large measure, prior to 2 October 2000, when the 1998 Act came into force.
Mr Hooper was denied payments equivalent to a widow's payment and a WMA
in 1997. Mr Withey was denied payments in respect of a widow's payment and a
WMA in 1997, and again denied payments equivalent to WMA in August 2000.
Mr Martin was denied payments equivalent to a widow's payment and a WMA
after 2 October 2000, but his claims relate back to his wife's death on
11 September 2000. Mr Naylor claimed payments equivalent to a widow's

a   pension on 14 September 2000, and thus the relevant period in respect of which he claims extends back three months before that date.

[139] No claim can be founded on the 1998 Act in respect of those incidents of discrimination, which occurred before the Act came into force. This is because s 22(4) of the Act provides that no proceedings may be brought under s 7(1)(a) of the Act in relation to any act or failure to act which occurred before the Act came

b   into force.

[140] Before Moses J, counsel for Mr Hooper argued that Mr Hooper's Strasbourg discrimination claim could properly embrace failure to settle that part of his claim which related to discrimination before 2 October 2000. Moses J rejected this contention on the ground that the decision not to extend a friendly settlement to Mr Hooper was taken before 2 October 2000. We question

c   whether he was correct to do so. Had the Strasbourg discrimination claim been well founded, the duty under the 1998 Act not to discriminate between Strasbourg claimants and others would have arisen when that Act came into force on 2 October 2000. We do not see how a refusal before that date by the Secretary of State to settle Mr Hooper's claim could have precluded a duty on the

d   part of the Secretary of State not to discriminate against Mr Hooper once the 1998 Act came into force, nor Mr Hooper's right to bring proceedings in relation to breach of that duty. The fact that the discrimination complained of related, in part, to events before 2 October 2000 would not have invalidated the claim in whole or in part. We have, however, as did Moses J, ruled the Strasbourg discrimination claim invalid. It is for this reason that no claims lie in relation to

e   discrimination which occurred prior to 2 October 2000.

[141] This leaves for consideration those incidents of discrimination which have occurred since 2 October 2000. Mr Goudie submitted, in our view correctly, that claimants, who had constituted themselves 'victims' under the convention by claiming before the 1998 Act came into force, were in a position

f   to bring proceedings under the Act in respect of continuing discrimination without the need to repeat their claims. We identify these as follows. (i) Failure to accept Mr Martin's demand for payment equivalent to a widow's payment. (ii) Failure to make payments equivalent to a WMA to Hooper, Withey and Martin. (iii) Failure to make payments equivalent to a widow's pension to Mr Naylor.

[142] If and in so far as making these payments would have prevented

g   breaches of art 14 coupled with art 8 of the convention, we have held that the Secretary of State had power to make the payments. By failing to make such payments the Secretary of State acted in a way incompatible with the appellants' convention rights. By reason of the provisions of s 6(1) of the 1998 Act we see no escape from the conclusion that he acted unlawfully in failing to make these

h   payments. We put the matter in this way because, although extra-statutory payments would have prevented discrimination against widowers, we do not consider that it was irrational for the Secretary of State to decline to adopt this course. If Parliament confers on one class a benefit for which there is no rational justification it may make more sense to leave those who do not receive that

j   benefit to seek such remedy as the law allows rather than to make to them also payments for which there is no rational justification. This is a matter to which we shall return when we consider the ninth issue.

The ninth issue

[143] The appellants seek a mandatory order that the Secretary of State make to them the extra-statutory payments which he has so far declined to make. Alternatively they claim damages for his breach of s 6(1) of the 1998 Act in failing

to make those payments. Widows who were entitled to pensions prior to 9 April
2001 remain entitled to receive these. Thus Mr Naylor has a continuing claim;
the claims of the other appellants all relate to periods prior to 9 April 2001, when
the new regime came into effect. We consider that, if the appellants have claims
to monetary compensation in respect of their failure to receive payments during
these periods, this should be by way of damages for breach of the 1998 Act.
Section 8 (1) of the 1998 Act entitles us to grant such relief or remedy or make
such order, within our powers, as we consider just and appropriate. We would
not consider it just or appropriate to make a mandatory order that the Secretary
of State make the payments sought in circumstances where his failure to do so
would not sound in damages under the Act. Thus the issue at this stage is the
extent to which, if at all, the appellants are entitled to damages.

Just satisfaction

[144] Section 8(3) of the Act precludes this court from awarding damages to
the appellants unless we are satisfied that such awards are necessary in order to
afford them just satisfaction. In considering this question we are required to take
into account the principles applied by the Strasbourg court. This was an area of
the case in respect of which we had to seek assistance from counsel on the second
hearing, as they had made scarcely any submissions in relation to 'just
satisfaction' at the first hearing.

[145] The appellants' case has a beguiling simplicity. The breaches of the 1998
Act of which they complain lie in failing to make payments to them equivalent to
the payments received by widows. They have thus suffered pecuniary loss in the
amount of the payments that they should have received. Just satisfaction requires
that they be paid these sums. In addition they claim a modest sum of
compensation for the distress that they have been caused by the discrimination
itself.

[146] Mr Sales challenged this approach. He submitted that the Strasbourg
court does not always award compensation, even where the applicant has
suffered damage which is in principle compensatable. Where the appropriate
response to discrimination is to 'level down' rather than 'level up', it is not
appropriate to award compensation on the basis of levelling up.

[147] It is notoriously difficult to deduce clear principles in relation to 'just
satisfaction' from the Strasbourg jurisprudence—see the comments of the Report
of the Law Commission and the Scottish Law Commission *Damages under the
Human Rights Act 1998* (Law Com No 266) (Cm 4853) paras 3.4 to 3.15. As that
report states at para 3.19, the general approach is to restore the applicant to the
position that he or she would have been in had there not been a breach of
convention rights. Where the breach has caused pecuniary loss, an award of
pecuniary compensation is the norm—see paras 3.23 to 3.25 of the Report. The
Strasbourg court has also made awards for non-pecuniary loss in respect of a wide
range of intangible injuries—see paras 3.26 and 3.27 of the Report. Particular
difficulties arise where the complaint is of breach of art 14, and decisions on this
situation are particularly sparse.

[148] Mr Goudie submitted that we should follow the approach of the
Strasbourg court in *Willis v UK* [2002] 2 FCR 743. Mr Willis' wife died on 7 June
1996. On 4 November 1996 he applied for benefits equivalent to a widow's
payment and a WMA. His application was refused. He complained of violation
of art 14, taken in conjunction with art 8 and art 1 of the First Protocol. The
government did not resist the claim (under arts 14 and 8). The court found that
a violation of art 14 and art 1 of the First Protocol had occurred. Mr Willis

a   claimed in relation to pecuniary damage a total of £21,804·07 plus interest in respect of loss of a widow's payment and a WMA, after giving credit for receipt of invalid care allowance and one parent benefit that had been paid to him. The government did not challenge these calculations but resisted the claim for interest. The court awarded £25,000, inclusive of interest, 'on an equitable basis'.

[149] For the other three appellants, Mr Cox submitted that the Strasbourg
b   court adopts the general aim of restoring the applicant to the position that he would have been in had there not been a breach of his convention rights: *Papamichalopoulos v Greece* (1996) 21 EHRR 439 at 451 (para 34); *Kingsley v UK* (2002) 35 EHRR 177 at 190 (para 40); *R (on the application of KB) v Mental Health Review Tribunal* [2003] EWHC 193 (Admin) at [28], [2003] 2 All ER 209 at [28] per Stanley Burnton J. He further submitted that in cases where there has been an
c   actual pecuniary loss, which has been clearly caused by the violation, the court will invariably award damages to compensate for the loss: *Kingsley v UK; Law Commission Report Damages under the Human Rights Act* (Law Com No 266) para 3.43. An award may be made for future and ongoing loss: *Lustig-Prean and Beckett v UK* (1999) 7 BHRC 65 and *Smith v UK* (2000) 29 EHRR 493.

d   [150] Mr Sales relied particularly on two decisions of the Strasbourg court. In *Goodwin v UK* [2002] 2 FCR 577 the court found that the United Kingdom was in breach of the rights of the applicant (who was a post-operative transsexual) under arts 8, 12 and 14 in failing to arrange its laws to recognise the applicant's acquired sexual identity in a range of areas. The applicant had claimed pecuniary damage including a sum of £31,200 in respect of the pension which she had been unable
e   to claim at age 60, as a woman in her acquired sexual identity. The court recognized that the government would have to introduce changes in legislation 'in due course' to take account of its judgment, and held in relation to art 41 of the convention that the finding of violation, with the changes in legislation for the future, could in the circumstances of the case be regarded as constituting just
f   satisfaction.

[151] The circumstances in question included (1) a finding by the court that the degree of financial detriment suffered, if any, was not clear cut and (2) a finding by the court that the lack of legal recognition of the gender re-assignment of post-operative transsexuals lay at the heart of the complaint. Having regard to these factors, we do not find this decision of assistance in resolving the issue of
g   just satisfaction in the present case.

[152] More pertinent is the other decision relied upon by Mr Sales. In *Van Raalte v Netherlands* (1997) 24 EHRR 503 the applicant was an unmarried childless man over the age of 45. Dutch legislation provided for an exemption for unmarried childless women over the age of 45 from the obligation to pay
h   contributions under the General Child Benefits Act. There was no similar exemption for men. The court held that art 14 of the convention taken together with art 1 of the First Protocol had been violated. However, the court rejected the applicant's request that he should be awarded compensation for pecuniary damage in the amount of the contribution which he had paid between 1985 and
i   1988. The Dutch government stated that 'had there not been the difference in treatment complained of, men and women would have been equally liable to pay contributions under the General Child Benefits Act, so that the applicant would have had to pay them in any case' (at 520 (para 48)). The court held (at 520–521 (para 50)):

'… the finding of a violation of Article 14 of the Convention taken together with Article 1 of Protocol No. 1 does not entitle the applicant to retrospective exemption from contributions under the scheme in question. Accordingly the applicant's claim for pecuniary damage has not been substantiated.'

[153] Under the relevant legislation everyone had to contribute to the cost of providing child benefits, whether or not they had children, with the exception of childless women over 45. Part of the rationale of this was that to make such women contribute to the cost of providing child benefits would rub salt in the wound of being childless. The court indicated its doubts about whether a desire to spare the feelings of such women could be a legitimate aim. We read the passage of its judgment quoted above as indicating the court's acceptance that the breach of art 14 consisted in granting the allowance to women rather than in not also granting it to men so that it was not appropriate to award pecuniary compensation.

[154] With the benefit of these authorities, we have reached the following conclusions. This appeal is concerned with the fruits of national insurance contributions. It is concerned with payments designed to mitigate particular adverse financial consequences to widows of the death of the husband who paid the contributions. Where those adverse financial consequences are also suffered by widowers who have lost wives who paid national insurance contributions, it is manifestly discriminatory and unfair that the widowers should not also receive similar payments to mitigate those consequences.

[155] This is the position as far as a widow's payment is concerned. The payment of a lump sum had and has rational justification, having regard to the additional financial demands attendant on that event. The justification applies, however, equally in the case of the death of a wife. This is now recognised by the payment of bereavement payments to widows and widowers alike. The discrimination that existed during the relevant transitional period—2 October 2000 to 9 April 2001—can properly be said to have resulted in the failure of widowers to receive payments to which, in justice, they should have been entitled. For this reason we consider that Mr Martin, and any others in his position, should receive damages of £1,000, together with interest, by way of just satisfaction.

[156] WMA was paid in recognition of the burden shouldered by a widow, who had to bring up children without the support of a husband. That, however, is a burden which falls upon a parent whose spouse dies, be the parent husband or wife. That fact is now recognised by the entitlement of both widows and widowers with dependent children to a WPA. On the face of it, the discrimination in the transitional period which saw a WPA being paid to widows but not to widowers can properly be said to have resulted in a failure on the part of widowers to receive payments to which, in justice, they should have been entitled. The picture is not, however, as simple as this so far as the appellants before us are concerned.

[157] For widows who were earning little or nothing, entitlement to a WMA and, indeed to a widow's pension was an irrelevance. This was because other social security benefits were provided—in particular income support—to the extent necessary to raise the widow's total income to a pre-calculated minimum, which exceeded both a WMA and a widow's pension. Receipt of a WMA simply reduced the amount which would otherwise have been received by way of income support, so that the widow's income remained the same.

[158] Before Moses J Mr Sales' skeleton argument asserted that each of Mr Hooper, Mr Withey and Mr Martin were in receipt of income support in excess of a WMA. Had they been paid sums equivalent to a WMA this would not

a have affected their total income. We understand that these assertions are accepted. In these circumstances, those three appellants have not demonstrated that the discrimination of which they complain in respect of a WMA has caused them any pecuniary loss, so the principle of just satisfaction does not require any award in respect of pecuniary loss. Indeed it might have led the Secretary of State to question whether, in truth, they have been discriminated against by the refusal
b to pay them a WMA. They have received the same amount of social security benefits that they would have received had they been widows in the same situation. It is only the form in which they have received those benefits that differs.

[159] Mr Cox, on behalf of Messrs Withey, Naylor and Martin, argued that receipt of WMA is more advantageous than receipt of income support in that a
c WMA is paid regardless of income, whereas if a person in receipt of income support works, Income Support is reduced by the amount that is earned. None of these three appellants has established that he was worse off as a result of receiving income support in place of a WMA and, accordingly, we see no basis for an award of pecuniary compensation. Had the claimants demonstrated that
d they were worse off as a result of failure to receive the equivalent of a WMA we would, to that extent, have held them entitled to damages.

[160] We turn to the question of whether the principle of just satisfaction entitles Mr Naylor to an award for failing to receive the equivalent of a widow's pension. Had he been a widow he would have been entitled to this until reaching the age of 65, so he claims not merely in respect of past receipt but in respect of
e his failure to receive payments in the future. As we understand the position Mr Naylor has been receiving income support in a sum exceeding the equivalent of a widow's pension, but, for the moment, we shall put that fact to one side and consider this question as one of principle.

[161] We have held that the justification for paying pensions to widows had
f ceased and should have been discontinued by 2000. It was not, in fact, discontinued until 9 April 2001. Furthermore, those who became entitled to a widow's pension before that date remained entitled to them thereafter. Mr Naylor argues that he should have been treated in the same way and should, under the principle of just satisfaction, be compensated for the fact that he has not been.

g [162] In 1999, before the 1998 Act came into force, Parliament had passed an Act which would abolish a widow's pension with effect from 9 April 2001 but, as from that date, grant a bereavement allowance for a period of 52 weeks to widows and widowers alike. This reflected the fact that there had ceased to be justification for paying pensions to widows. It also reflected the fact that there
h was no justification for paying a similar pension to widowers either. The fact that widows over 45 enjoyed a right to a pension until reaching the age of 65 was recognised as an anomaly. Parliament decided to allow a transitional period until 9 April 2001 before bringing in the new regime and to allow those in receipt of a widow's pension to continue to receive it, but it does not follow from this that there was any justification for making equivalent payments to widowers. To have done so would merely have increased the size of those to whom anomalous payments were being made. This would not have achieved any legitimate aim.

[163] For these reasons we do not consider that the principle of just satisfaction entitles Mr Naylor to extra-statutory payments equivalent to a widow's pension either in respect of the period from 2 October 2000 to 9 April 2001 or thereafter. The appropriate course in this case is that adopted by the Strasbourg court in *Van Raalte's* case.

[164] We have considered whether Mr Naylor is none the less entitled, by way
of just satisfaction, to payment equivalent to bereavement payment, on the
ground that this was introduced for widows and widowers alike in place of a
widow's pension. We have decided that he is not. We do not consider that this
payment to both sexes for a maximum of 52 weeks, can properly be considered
as similar in nature to pension rights that were previously enjoyed by widows
until reaching the age of 65. They are part of a new, and very different regime.
Furthermore, had such payment been made to Mr Naylor, it would simply have
reduced, by the same amount, the income support that he received, so that he is
not out of pocket as a result of not receiving such payment.

[165] We do not consider that the decision in *Willis v UK* requires us to reach
a decision to the contrary. Section 2 of the 1998 Act requires us to take this
decision into account, but it carries little weight. In the first place that case did
not concern a widow's pension. In the second place the United Kingdom did not
challenge its obligation to pay pecuniary compensation in that case, other than
interest, so that the principle of just satisfaction was not in issue. We have been
required by the 1998 Act to give consideration to that principle.

[166] All the claimants argued that they should be awarded by way of
damages additional sums in respect of injury to their feelings caused by the
obduracy of the Secretary of State in discriminating against them, relying on a
number of cases in which Strasbourg had made such awards in cases of sex
discrimination. These claims were parasitic on the other claims for damages and,
in particular, the Strasbourg discrimination claims. For this reason alone they fail
in all cases save that of Mr Martin. Quite apart from that there is no comparison
between the nature of the discrimination complained of in this case and that
which had occurred in the cases of sex discrimination relied upon. We do not
consider that the principle of just satisfaction requires any award to Mr Martin
under this head.

[167] For these reasons, with the exception of a payment of £1,000 to
Mr Martin, we reject the claims for money payments.

[168] We invite submissions from counsel as to the form of order that should
follow from our judgment.

Appeal allowed in part.

Kate O'Hanlon   Barrister.

ANNEX
Social Security Contributions and Benefits Act 1992 c 4:

'Benefits for widows and widowers

36. *Widow's payment.*—(1) A woman who has been widowed shall be
entitled to a widow's payment of the amount specified in Schedule 4, Part II
if—(a) she was under pensionable age at the time when her late husband
died, or he was then not entitled to a Category A retirement pension under
section 44 below; and (b) her late husband satisfied the contribution
condition for a widow's payment specified in Schedule 3, Part I, paragraph 4.

(2) The payment shall not be payable to a widow if she and a man to
whom she is not married are living together as husband and wife at the time
of her husband's death.

a

(3) A widow's payment is payable only in cases where the husband dies on or after 11 April 1988 (the coming into force of section 36(1) of the 1986 Act, which introduced the widow's payment by making provision corresponding to this section).

37. *Widowed mother's allowance.*—(1) A woman who has been widowed shall be entitled to a widowed mother's allowance at the rate determined in accordance with section 39 below if her late husband satisfied the contribution conditions for a widowed mother's allowance specified in Schedule 3, Part I, paragraph 5 and either—(a) the woman is entitled to child benefit in respect of a child falling within subsection (2) below; or (b) the woman is pregnant by her late husband; or (c) if the woman and her late husband were residing together immediately before the time of his death, the woman is pregnant as the result of being artificially inseminated before that time with the semen of some person other than her husband, or as the result of the placing in her before that time of an embryo, of an egg in the process of fertilisation, or of sperm and eggs.

b

c

(2) A child falls within this subsection if one of the conditions specified in section 81(2) below is for the time being satisfied with respect to the child and the child is either—(a) a son or daughter of the woman and her late husband; or (b) a child in respect of whom her late husband was immediately before his death entitled to child benefit; or (c) if the woman and her late husband were residing together immediately before his death, a child in respect of whom she was then entitled to child benefit.

d

(3) The widow shall not be entitled to the allowance for any period after she remarries, but, subject to that, she shall continue to be entitled to it for any period throughout which she satisfies the requirements of subsection (1)(a), (b) or (c) above.

e

(4) A widowed mother's allowance shall not be payable—(a) for any period falling before the day on which the widow's entitlement is to be regarded as commencing for that purpose by virtue of section 5(1)(k) of the Administration Act; or (b) for any period during which she and a man to whom she is not married are living together as husband and wife.

f

38. *Widow's pension.*—(1) A woman who has been widowed shall be entitled to a widow's pension at the rate determined in accordance with section 39 below if her late husband satisfied the contribution conditions for a widow's pension specified in Schedule 3, Part I, paragraph 5 and either—(a) she was, at the husband's death, over the age of 45 but under the age of 65; or (b) she ceased to be entitled to a widowed mother's allowance at a time when she was over the age of 45 but under the age of 65.

g

(2) The widow shall not be entitled to the pension for any period after she remarries, but, subject to that, she shall continue to be entitled to it until she attains the age of 65.

h

(3) A widow's pension shall not be payable—(a) for any period falling before the day on which the widow's entitlement is to be regarded as commencing for that purpose by virtue of section 5(1)(k) of the Administration Act; (b) for any period for which she is entitled to a widowed mother's allowance; or (c) for any period during which she and a man to whom she is not married are living together as husband and wife.

(4) In the case of a widow whose late husband died before 11 April 1988 and who either—(a) was over the age of 40 but under the age of 55 at the time of her husband's death; or (b) is over the age of 40 but under the age of 55 at the time when she ceases to be entitled to a widowed mother's

allowance, subsection (1) above shall have effect as if for "45" there were
substituted "40".

39. *Rate of widowed mother's allowance and widow's pension.*—(1) The
weekly rate of—(a) a widowed mother's allowance, (b) a widow's pension,
shall be determined in accordance with the provisions of sections 44 and 45
below as they apply in the case of a Category A retirement pension, but
subject, in particular, to the following provisions of this section and section
46(2) below.

(2) In the application of sections 44 and 45 below by virtue of subsection
(1) above—(a) where the woman's husband was over pensionable age when
he died, references in those sections to the pensioner shall be taken as
references to the husband, and (b) where the husband was under pensionable
age when he died, references in those sections to the pensioner and the tax
year in which he attained pensionable age shall be taken as references to the
husband and the tax year in which he died.

(3) In the case of a woman whose husband dies after 5 April 2000, the
additional pension falling to be calculated under sections 44 and 45 below by
virtue of subsection (1) above shall (before making any reduction required by
subsection (4) below) be one half of the amount which it would be apart
from this subsection.

(4) Where a widow's pension is payable to a woman who was under the
age of 55 at the time when the applicable qualifying condition was fulfilled,
the weekly rate of the pension shall be reduced by 7% of what it would be
apart from this subsection multiplied by the number of years by which her
age at that time was less than 55 (any fraction of a year being counted as a year).

(5) For the purposes of subsection (4) above, the time when the applicable
qualifying condition was fulfilled is the time when the woman's late husband
died or, as the case may be, the time when she ceased to be entitled to a
widowed mother's allowance.

(6) In the case of a widow whose late husband died before 11 April 1988
and who either—(a) was over the age of 40 but under the age of 55 at the
time of her husband's death; or (b) is over the age of 40 but under the age of
55 at the time when she ceases to be entitled to a widowed mother's
allowance, subsection (4) above shall have effect as if for "55" there were
substituted "50", in both places where it occurs.'

Welfare Reform and Pensions Act 1999 c 30:

'*Benefits for widows and widowers*
54. *Bereavement payment.*—(1) For section 36 of the Contributions and
Benefits Act there shall be substituted—

"*Bereavement payment*
36.—(1) A person whose spouse dies on or after the appointed day
shall be entitled to a bereavement payment if—(a) either that person was
under pensionable age at the time when the spouse died or the spouse
was then not entitled to a Category A retirement pension under section
44 below; and (b) the spouse satisfied the contribution condition for a
bereavement payment specified in Schedule 3, Part I, paragraph 4.

(2) A bereavement payment shall not be payable to a person if that
person and a person of the opposite sex to whom that person was not
married were living together as husband and wife at the time of the
spouse's death.

a

(3) In this section 'the appointed day' means the day appointed for the coming into force of sections 54 to 56 of the Welfare Reform and Pensions Act 1999."

(2) In Schedule 4 to the Contributions and Benefits Act (rates of benefits etc), for Part II there shall be substituted—

b

"Part II
Bereavement Payment
Bereavement payment   £2,000.00."

55.—(1) After section 36 of the Contributions and Benefits Act there shall be inserted—

c

"**36A.** *Cases in which sections 37 to 41 apply.*—(1) Sections 37 to 39 and section 40 below apply only in cases where a woman's husband has died before the appointed day, and section 41 below applies only in cases where a man's wife has died before that day.

d

(2) Sections 39A to 39C below apply in cases where a person's spouse dies on or after the appointed day, but section 39A also applies (in accordance with subsection (1)(b) of that section) in cases where a man's wife has died before that day.

(3) In this section, and in sections 39A and 39B below, 'the appointed day' means the day appointed for the coming into force of sections 54 to 56 of the Welfare Reform and Pensions Act 1999."

e

(2) After section 39 of the Contributions and Benefits Act there shall be inserted—

f

"**39A.** *Widowed parent's allowance.*—(1)   This section applies where—(a) a person whose spouse dies on or after the appointed day is under pensionable age at the time of the spouse's death, or (b) a man whose wife died before the appointed day—(i) has not remarried before that day, and (ii) is under pensionable age on that day.

g

(2) The surviving spouse shall be entitled to a widowed parent's allowance at the rate determined in accordance with section 39C below if the deceased spouse satisfied the contribution conditions for a widowed parent's allowance specified in Schedule 3, Part I, paragraph 5 and—(a) the surviving spouse is entitled to child benefit in respect of a child falling within subsection (3) below; or (b) the surviving spouse is a woman who either— (i) is pregnant by her late husband, or (ii) if she and he were residing together immediately before the time of his death, is pregnant in circumstances falling within section 37(1)(c) above.

h

(3) A child falls within this subsection if one of the conditions specified in section 81(2) below is for the time being satisfied with respect to the child and the child is either—(a) a son or daughter of the surviving spouse and the deceased spouse; or (b) a child in respect of whom the deceased spouse was immediately before his or her death entitled to child benefit; or (c) if the surviving spouse and the deceased spouse were residing together immediately before his or her death, a child in respect of whom the surviving spouse was then entitled to child benefit.

(4) The surviving spouse shall not be entitled to the allowance for any period after she or he remarries, but, subject to that, the surviving spouse shall continue to be entitled to it for any period throughout

which she or he—(a) satisfies the requirements of subsection (2)(a) or (b) above; and (b) is under pensionable age.

(5) A widowed parent's allowance shall not be payable—(a) for any period falling before the day on which the surviving spouse's entitlement is to be regarded as commencing by virtue of section 5(1)(k) of the Administration Act; or (b) for any period during which the surviving spouse and a person of the opposite sex to whom she or he is not married are living together as husband and wife.

39B. *Bereavement allowance where no dependent children.*—(1) This section applies where a person whose spouse dies on or after the appointed day is over the age of 45 but under pensionable age at the spouse's death.

(2) The surviving spouse shall be entitled to a bereavement allowance at the rate determined in accordance with section 39C below if the deceased spouse satisfied the contribution conditions for a bereavement allowance specified in Schedule 3, Part I, paragraph 5.

(3) A bereavement allowance shall be payable for not more than 52 weeks beginning with the date of the spouse's death or (if later) the day on which the surviving spouse's entitlement is to be regarded as commencing by virtue of section 5(1)(k) of the Administration Act.

(4) The surviving spouse shall not be entitled to the allowance for any period after she or he remarries, but, subject to that, the surviving spouse shall continue to be entitled to it until—(a) she or he attains pensionable age, or (b) the period of 52 weeks mentioned in subsection (3) above expires, whichever happens first.

(5) The allowance shall not be payable—(a) for any period for which the surviving spouse is entitled to a widowed parent's allowance; or (b) for any period during which the surviving spouse and a person of the opposite sex to whom she or he is not married are living together as husband and wife."'

R (on the application of Wilkinson) v Inland Revenue Commissioners

[2003] EWCA Civ 814

COURT OF APPEAL, CIVIL DIVISION

LORD PHILLIPS OF WORTH MATRAVERS MR, MANTELL AND RIX LJJ

7–10 OCTOBER, 19 DECEMBER 2002, 14 MARCH, 18 JUNE 2003

Income tax – Allowances – Widow's bereavement allowance – Allowance not available to widowers – Statutory provision discriminating against widowers – Taxes Management Act 1970, s 1 – Income and Corporation Taxes Act 1988, s 262 – Human Rights Act 1998, ss 6(2)(b), 8, Sch 1, Pt I, art 14, Pt II, art 1.

The appellant was a widower, whose wife had died in June 1999. After his wife's death, he became aware of the case of another widower who had made a claim in the European Court of Human Rights, alleging that the lack of any provision for a bereavement allowance for widowers under United Kingdom law, equivalent to the income tax reduction for widows under s 262[a] of the Income and Corporation Taxes Act 1988 known as widow's bereavement allowance, discriminated against him on the grounds of his sex, in breach of art 14[b] of the European Convention for the Protection of Human Rights and Fundamental Freedoms 1950 (as set out in Sch 1 to the Human Rights Act 1998) read with art 8[c] and art 1[d] of the First Protocol to the convention. That claim was declared admissible, and the United Kingdom government thereafter reached a friendly settlement with the widower. The appellant wrote to the Revenue claiming the equivalent of widow's bereavement allowance, and referring to the European Court of Human Rights case. His claim was refused; the Revenue stated that they considered that their care and management powers under s 1(1)[e] of the Taxes Management Act 1970 did not permit them to contradict unambiguous, primary legislation such as s 262 of the 1988 Act, and that their refusal to grant the appellant an allowance or to make him an equivalent extra-statutory payment was not therefore unlawful by reason of s 6(2)[f] of the 1998 Act which provided that it was not unlawful for a public authority to act in a way which was incompatible with a convention right if the authority was acting so as to give effect to or enforce provisions of primary legislation which could not be read or given effect in a way which was compatible with convention rights. The claimant applied for judicial review of that decision. The judge granted a declaration that

---

a   Section 262, so far as material, is set out at [11], below

b   Article 14, so far as material, is set out at [20], below

c   Article 8, so far as material, provides: '1. Everyone has the right to respect for his private and family life, his home and his correspondence. 2. There shall be no interference by a public authority with the exercise of this right except such as is in accordance with the law and is necessary in a democratic society in the interests of … the economic well-being of the country …'

d   Article 1, so far as material, is set out at [21], below

e   Section 1, so far as material, is set out at [16], below

f   Section 6, so far as material, provides: '(1) It is unlawful for a public authority to act in a way which is incompatible with a Convention right. (2) Subsection (1) does not apply to an act if—…(b) in the case of one or more provisions of … primary legislation which cannot be read or given effect in a way which is compatible with the Convention rights, the authority was acting so as to give effect to or enforce those provisions …'

s 262 of the 1988 Act was incompatible, but otherwise dismissed the application. The appellant appealed. By s 34 of the Finance Act 1999, s 262 of the 1988 Act ceased to have effect in relation to deaths occurring on or after 6 April 2000. The issues for determination by the court were: (i) the extent of the Revenue's powers under s 1(1) of the 1970 Act; (ii) the correct application of s 6(2)(b) of the 1998 Act; and (iii) whether the Revenue had acted unfairly. The Revenue submitted that, given that widow's bereavement allowance had been abolished prospectively before the 1998 Act came into force on 2 October 2000, under the principle in s 8[g] of the 1998 Act, which provided inter alia that no award of damages might be made unless the court was satisfied that the award was necessary to afford just satisfaction to the person in whose favour it was made, they were not required to make the appellant any payment.

Held – The appeal would be dismissed for the following reasons.

(1) It was not possible to interpret s 1 as permitting the Revenue to grant concessions to taxpayers if they were necessary in order to prevent discrimination in the imposition of taxes which violated art 14. There was no doubt that, when enacting s 262 of the 1988 Act and s 34 of the 1999 Act, Parliament had intended widow's bereavement allowance, for so long as it continued in existence, to be restricted to women. The Revenue had no power to make similar allowances to men. For that reason it was right to make a declaration of incompatibility (see [45], [48], [49], below).

(2) Section 6(2)(b) of the 1998 Act addressed the grant by Parliament of a statutory power which, regardless of the circumstances in which it was exercised, would inevitably be incompatible with convention rights. In such circumstances the power could not be given effect in a way which was compatible with the convention, and thus s 6(2)(b) enabled the exercise of the power without breach of s 6(1). Section 1 of the 1970 Act was a wide general power. In most circumstances either exercising it, or failing to exercise it, would involve no incompatibility with the convention. If circumstances arose under which it was necessary to exercise the power in order to avoid a breach of convention rights, there was no basis on which the Revenue could rely on s 6(2)(b) to justify a refusal to exercise the power (see [52], [53], below).

(3) The fact that the commissioners had chosen to settle the claim made to the Court of Human Rights did not preclude them from challenging similar claims in the domestic forum, now that the 1998 Act permitted convention issues to be raised in that forum. Before the 1998 Act had come into force, steps had been taken to remove the anomaly of awarding widow's bereavement allowance to women only by abolishing it prospectively with effect from 6 April 2000. To award the appellant, or other taxpayers in his position, an equivalent payment would be to swell the numbers of those who had received tax allowances for which there was no legitimate justification. The principle of just satisfaction did not require any such payment (see [59], [63], [65], [66], below).

---

g   Section 8, so far as material, provides: '(1) In relation to any act ... of a public authority which the court finds is ... unlawful, it may grant such relief or remedy ... within its powers as it considers just and appropriate ... (3) No award of damages is to be made unless, taking into account all the circumstances of the case ... the court is satisfied that the award is necessary to afford just satisfaction to the person in whose favour it is made.'

Notes
a For the powers of the Inland Revenue Commissioners generally, see 23(1) *Halsbury's Laws* (4th edn reissue) para 31.

For the Taxes Management Act 1970, s 1(1), see 42 *Halsbury's Statutes* (4th edn) (2002 reissue) 131.

For the Human Rights Act 1998, ss 6(2)(b), 8, see 7 *Halsbury's Statutes* (4th edn)
b (2002 reissue) 535, 538.

Section 262 of the Income and Corporation Taxes Act 1988 was repealed by ss 34 and 139 of and Pt III(5) of Sch 20 to the Finance Act 1999 for deaths occurring after 5 April 2000.

Cases referred to in judgment
c *Abdulaziz v UK* (1985) 7 EHRR 471, [1985] ECHR 9214/80, ECt HR.
Absalom v Talbot (Inspector of Taxes) [1943] 1 All ER 589, CA; *rvsd* [1944] 1 All ER 642, [1944] AC 204, HL.
Bates v IRC [1967] 1 All ER 84, [1968] AC 483, [1967] 2 WLR 60, HL.
Crossland v UK App No 36120/97 (8 June 1999, unreported), ECt HR.
d *Darby v Sweden* (1991) 13 EHRR 774, [1990] ECHR 11581/85, ECt HR.
Fielding v UK (2002) Times, 25 February, ECt HR.
IRC v National Federation of Self-Employed and Small Businesses Ltd [1981] 2 All ER 93, [1982] AC 617, [1981] 2 WLR 722, HL.
R (on the application of Alconbury Developments Ltd) v Secretary of State for the Environment, Transport and the Regions [2001] UKHL 23, [2001] 2 All ER 929,
e [2001] 2 WLR 1389.
R (on the application of British Sky Broadcasting Group) v Customs and Excise Comrs [2001] EWHC Admin 127, [2001] STC 437.
R (on the application of Hooper) v Secretary of State for Work and Pensions [2003] EWCA Civ 813, [2003] 3 All ER 673; *rvsg in part* [2002] EWHC 191 (Admin),
f [2002] All ER (D) 193 (Feb).
R v Hertfordshire County Council, ex p Cheung (1986) Times, 4 April, CA.
R v IRC, ex p Unilever plc [1996] STC 681, CA.
R v Kansal (No 2) [2001] UKHL 62, [2002] 1 All ER 257, [2002] 2 AC 69, [2001] 3 WLR 1562.
Vestey v IRC (No 2) [1979] 2 All ER 225, [1979] Ch 198, [1978] 3 WLR 693; *affd*
g [1979] 3 All ER 976, [1980] AC 1148, [1979] 3 WLR 915, HL.
Vestey v IRC [1977] 3 All ER 1073, [1979] Ch 177, [1978] 2 WLR 136; *affd* [1979] 3 All ER 976, [1980] AC 1148, [1979] 3 WLR 915, HL.

Cases referred to in skeleton arguments
h *Goodwin v UK* [2002] 2 FCR 577, ECt HR.
National & Provincial Building Society v UK [1997] STC 1466, ECt HR.
R v DPP, ex p Kebeline, R v DPP, ex p Rechachi [1999] 4 All ER 801, [2000] 2 AC 326, [1999] 3 WLR 972, HL.
R v IRC, ex p Commerzbank AG Case C-330/91 [1993] 4 All ER 37, [1994] QB 219,
j [1994] 2 WLR 128, [1993] ECR I-4017, ECJ.
R v IRC, ex p Fulford-Dobson [1987] STC 344, [1987] QB 978, [1987] 3 WLR 277.
R v Secretary of State for the Home Dept, ex p Simms [1999] 3 All ER 400, [2000] 2 AC 115, [1999] 3 WLR 328, HL.
Robinson v Secretary of State for Northern Ireland [2002] UKHL 32, [2002] NI 390, HL.
Steele Ford & Newton (a firm) v CPS [1993] 2 All ER 769, [1994] 1 AC 22, [1993] 2 WLR 934, HL.

Van Raalte v Netherlands (1997) 24 EHRR 503, [1997] ECHR 20060/92, ECt HR.

Appeal

Adrian John Wilkinson appealed with permission from the judgment of Moses J
on 14 February 2002 ([2002] EWHC 182 (Admin), [2002] STC 347) granting a
declaration of incompatibility with the European Convention for the Protection
of Human Rights and Fundamental Freedoms 1950 (as set out in Sch 1 to the
Human Rights Act 1998) in relation to s 262 of the Income and Corporation Taxes
Act 1988 but otherwise dismissing his claim for judicial review of the Revenue's
refusal to allow his claim, following the death of his wife, for a sum equivalent to
widow's bereavement allowance under s 262 or an equivalent allowance granted
by extra-statutory concession. The Revenue cross-appealed against the finding
that s 1(1) of the Taxes Management Act 1970 gave the Revenue power to grant
concessions to taxpayers which derogated from their obligation to pay tax. The
facts are set out in the judgment of the court.

Dinah Rose (instructed by *Liberty*) for Mr Wilkinson.
Timothy Brennan QC and *Ingrid Simler* (instructed by the *Solicitor of Inland Revenue*)
  for the Revenue.

Cur adv vult

18 June 2003. The following judgment was delivered.

LORD PHILLIPS OF WORTH MATRAVERS MR. This is the judgment of the
court.

[1] This is an appeal against the second judgment delivered by Moses J on
14 February 2002 ([2002] EWHC Admin 182, [2002] STC 347). The issues raised
are, to a degree, similar to some of the issues that we have addressed in the appeal
of *R (on the application of Hooper) v Secretary of State for Work and Pensions* [2003]
EWCA Civ 813, [2003] 3 All ER 673. They arise in the context of taxation. They
concern a legislative provision that granted to widows a tax allowance that was
not granted to widowers. The respondents, the Commissioners of Inland
Revenue, now concede and contend that this provision infringed art 14, when
read in conjunction with art 1 of the First Protocol of the European Convention
for the Protection of Human Rights and Fundamental Freedoms 1950 (as set out
in Sch 1 to the Human Rights Act 1998). Moses J so found and made a 'declaration
of incompatibility' pursuant to s 4 of the 1998 Act. Mr Wilkinson, who is
supported in this litigation by Liberty, contends that the legislation was not
incompatible with convention rights in as much as it lay within the statutory
powers of the commissioners to apply the legislation in a manner which would
not involve any discrimination. He claims that the commissioners are obliged by
s 6(1) of the 1998 Act to exercise those powers in his favour by making a money
payment to him which will place him in the same position as if he had been
granted the tax allowance made to widows.

[2] Mr Wilkinson has been represented by Miss Dinah Rose. Her skeleton
argument sets out the background facts and the legislative framework with
admirable lucidity and we shall draw upon it in our judgment.

THE BACKGROUND FACTS

[3] By s 262 of the Income and Corporation Taxes Act 1988 an income tax
reduction known as widow's bereavement allowance (WBA) was available to a

a widow for the year of assessment in which her husband died and the following year. The 1988 Act makes no express provision for any equivalent income tax reduction for widowers. By s 34 of the Finance Act 1999, the WBA has been abolished in relation to deaths occurring on or after 6 April 2000.

b [4] In 1997, Christopher Crossland, a widower who had been refused an allowance equivalent to WBA on the grounds of his sex, brought a complaint before the European Commission of Human Rights, alleging that the lack of any provision for a bereavement tax allowance for widowers under United Kingdom law discriminated against him on the grounds of his sex, in breach of art 14 read with art 8 and art 1 of the First Protocol of the convention. The United Kingdom government did not contest the admissibility of Mr Crossland's claim, which was referred to the court, and declared admissible on 8 June 1999 (*Crossland v UK* App No 36120/97 (8 June 1999, unreported)).

c [5] In September 1999, the government, having never at any stage contested the merits of Mr Crossland's claim, reached a friendly settlement with him. Under the settlement, the respondents paid to Mr Crossland the sum of £575, representing the full amount that he would have been paid had WBA been available to men at the date of his wife's death, and the sum of £3,962·48, representing his reasonable legal costs. As a result, Mr Crossland's case was struck out of the court's list on 9 November 1999.

d [6] A similar sequence of events occurred in the case of *Fielding v UK* (2002) Times, 25 February.

e [7] Mr Wilkinson, the claimant in these proceedings, is a widower whose wife died on 23 June 1999. After his wife's death, Mr Wilkinson became aware of Mr Crossland's case, and the settlement that the respondents had reached with him. By a letter dated 13 November 2000, Mr Wilkinson claimed from the Inland Revenue the equivalent of WBA (he requested a 'widower's bereavement payment'), referring to Mr Crossland's case.

f [8] By a letter dated 11 December 2000 (the decision challenged in these proceedings), the respondents replied as follows:

'You have made a claim for a Widow's Bereavement payment for the year ended 5 April 2000. This was on the basis of the Crossland case which our Head Office have considered carefully. I can confirm that the allowance was challenged by Mr Crossland under the European Convention on Human Rights (ECHR) because it was only available to Women, and that the challenge was resolved through a friendly settlement.

However, there is still no basis in UK law for allowing Widowers to claim the Widow's Bereavement Allowance, I am therefore unable to accept your claim for the year in question.'

[9] On 27 February 2001, Liberty wrote to the respondents on Mr Wilkinson's behalf, inviting them to allow his claim for a WBA, or an extra-statutory equivalent. By a letter dated 5 March 2001, the respondents denied that they had any power to grant an allowance to Mr Wilkinson, stating:

'The Board's care and management powers allow us to make relaxations which give taxpayers a reduction in liability to which they are not entitled under the strict letter of the law. Most concessions are made to deal with what are, on the whole, minor or transitory anomalies under the legislation and to meet cases of hardship at the margins of the code where a statutory remedy would be difficult to devise or would run to a length out of proportion to the intrinsic importance of the matter ...

The care and management powers do not allow the Inland Revenue to contradict unambiguous, primary legislation such as the provisions that govern entitlement to WBA. The Human Rights Act makes it unlawful for a public authority to act in a way that is incompatible with a Convention right *unless* it is required to do so by primary legislation. In applying the rules of the WBA legislation, the Inland Revenue was applying a provision of primary legislation, Section 262 Income and Corporation Taxes Act 1988. The intention of the legislation was clear: to help widows, not widowers. If the effect of the Human Rights Act was to require us to grant WBA to widowers under our care and management powers, notwithstanding the clear terms of the legislation, that would effectively undermine Parliamentary sovereignty which the Human Rights Act was careful to preserve.'

[10] An application for judicial review was lodged on 9 March 2001. On 14 February 2002, Moses J granted a declaration that s 262 of the 1998 Act was incompatible with the convention, but otherwise dismissed the application.

THE TAX LEGISLATION

Widow's Bereavement Allowance
[11] Section 262(1) of the 1988 Act (as amended) provided as follows:

'Where a married man whose wife is living with him dies, his widow shall be entitled—(a) for the year of assessment in which the death occurs, to an income tax reduction calculated by reference to an amount equal to the amount specified in section 257A(1) for that year; and (b) (unless she married again before the beginning of it) for the next following year of assessment, to an income tax reduction calculated by reference to an amount equal to the amount specified in section 257A(1) for that year.'

[12] The amount specified for the tax year 1999–2000 was £1,970, restricted to a 10% reduction of tax liability. The amount specified for the tax year 2000–2001 was £2,000, restricted to a 10% reduction of tax liability. Mr Wilkinson restricts his claim to the tax year 1999–2000.

[13] By s 34 of the Finance Act 1999, s 262 of the 1988 Act ceased to have effect in relation to deaths occurring on or after 6 April 2000.

Duties and powers of the Commissioners of Inland Revenue
[14] By s 1(1) of the Inland Revenue Regulation Act 1890, it is lawful for the Crown to appoint persons to be Commissioners for the collection and management of inland revenue.
[15] Section 13(1) of the 1890 Act provides:

'The Commissioners shall collect and cause to be collected every part of inland revenue, and all money under their care and management, and shall keep distinct accounts thereof at their chief office.'

[16] Section 1(1) of the Taxes Management Act 1970 provides (as far as material): 'Income tax, corporation tax and capital gains tax shall be under the care and management of the Commissioners of Inland Revenue ...'

THE HUMAN RIGHTS ACT 1998

a [17] By s 6(1) of the 1998 Act, it is unlawful for a public authority to act in a way which is incompatible with a convention right. It is not disputed that the commissioners are a public authority within the meaning of this provision.

[18] Section 6(2) of the 1998 Act provides:

b 'Subsection (1) does not apply to an act if—(a) as a result of one or more provisions of primary legislation, the authority could not have acted differently; or (b) in the case of one or more provisions of, or made under, primary legislation which cannot be read or given effect in a way which is compatible with the Convention rights, the authority was acting so as to give effect to or enforce those provisions.'

c

[19] By s 3(1) of the 1998 Act, primary legislation and subordinate legislation much be read and given effect in a way which is compatible with the convention rights, so far as it is possible to do so. By s 3(2)(a), this provision applies to legislation whenever enacted.

d THE HUMAN RIGHTS CONVENTION

[20] Article 14 of the convention provides:

'The enjoyment of the rights and freedoms set forth in this Convention shall be secured without discrimination on any ground such as sex, race, *e* colour, language, religion, political or other opinion, national or social origin, association with a national minority, property, birth or other status.'

[21] Article 1 of the First Protocol provides:

'Every natural or legal person is entitled to the peaceful enjoyment of his *f* possessions. No one shall be deprived of his possessions except in the public interest and subject to the conditions provided for by law and by the general principles of international law.

The preceding provisions shall not, however, in any way impair the right of a State to enforce such laws as it deems necessary to control the use of *g* property in accordance with the general interest or to secure the payment of taxes or other contributions or penalties.'

[22] Article 14 has no independent existence, but complements the other substantive provisions of the convention and its Protocols. Although the application of art 14 does not presuppose a breach of those provisions, in order *h* for it to be applied, the facts of the case must come within the ambit of one or more of them: *Abdulaziz v UK* (1985) 7 EHRR 471 at 499, 503 (paras 71 and 82).

THE ALLEGED INCOMPATIBILITY WITH CONVENTION RIGHTS

[23] In our judgment in *Hooper*'s case we have explained how art 14 of the *j* convention will be infringed where there is discrimination that falls 'within the ambit' of one of the other convention rights. In the present case it is common ground that s 262 of the 1988 Act was discriminatory in that it treated widows more favourably than widowers. Moses J held, and the commissioners now concede, that this discrimination fell within the ambit of art 1 of the First Protocol to the convention and thus infringed art 14—see *Darby v Sweden* (1991) 13 EHRR 774.

THE ISSUES

[24] Mr Wilkinson contends that s 1(1) of the 1970 Act gives to the *a* commissioners a wide statutory power to grant concessions to taxpayers which derogate from their obligations to pay tax in accordance with the letter of the applicable tax legislation. He contends that this power entitled the commissioners to grant to widowers an allowance equivalent to the WBA to which widows were entitled. The commissioners contend that when enacting s 262 of the 1988 Act *b* and, more pertinently, when abolishing that section prospectively by s 34 of the Finance Act 1999, it was Parliament's clear intention that entitlement to a WBA should be restricted to widows. The commissioners further contend that their powers under s 1(1) of the 1970 Act do not extend to granting concessions that will conflict with the intention of Parliament, as expressed in the relevant legislation. *c*

[25] Moses J ruled in favour of Mr Wilkinson on this issue. The commissioners cross-appeal against his ruling. If they succeed in their cross-appeal it will follow that s 262 of the 1988 Act obliged them to discriminate in favour of widows in breach of art 14. Section 6(2)(a) of the 1998 Act will then provide them with a defence to the allegation that they have acted in breach of s 6(1) of that Act. The *d* extent of the commissioners' powers under s 1(1) of the 1970 Act is the first issue that we shall address. This issue bears some similarity to the issue in the *Hooper* appeal of the extent of the Secretary of State's common law power to make extra-statutory payments to widowers to match benefits to which widows were entitled under statute. *e*

[26] The second issue will only arise if the commissioners' cross-appeal fails. It is common ground that the tax regime keeps open a taxpayer's fiscal position for a period of five years from the 31 January following the year of assessment (see s 43 of the 1970 Act). Mr Wilkinson contends that, when the 1998 Act came into force on 2 October 2000, s 6(1) of that Act imposed on the commissioners an obligation to exercise the powers that they enjoy under s 1 of the 1970 Act by *f* paying to him an allowance equivalent to the WBA to which he would have been entitled had he been a widow.

[27] Moses J held that s 6(2)(b) of the 1998 Act entitled the commissioners to decline to exercise their s 1 powers in this way, without committing any breach of s 6(1). Mr Wilkinson challenges this conclusion. Whether Moses J correctly *g* applied s 6(2)(b) of the 1998 Act is the second issue that we shall address. This issue bears some similarity to the issue in the *Hooper* appeal of the applicability of s 6(2)(b) of the 1998 Act.

[28] The third issue involves a comparison between the treatment of Mr Crossland, whose claim before the Strasbourg court was the subject of an *h* amicable settlement, and the treatment of Mr Wilkinson, whose claim before the English court the commissioners have declined to settle. In relation to this issue, and in contrast to the majority of the appellants in the *Hooper* appeal, Mr Wilkinson does not allege that the difference in treatment of which he complains infringes art 14. He contends that it constitutes a breach of the *j* commissioners' duty, under established principles of public law, to avoid discriminating between taxpayers without justification, and thus an abuse of power. Thus this issue is similar to the issue raised by the contention in the *Hooper* appeal that the Secretary of State's treatment of the majority of the appellants was in breach of established principles of public law. Moses J shortly rejected Mr Wilkinson's contentions in respect of this issue by cross-reference to

a his decision in *Hooper's* case. Whether he was correct in so doing is the third issue that we shall address.

The first issue

[29] The commissioners have long proceeded on the basis that the power and duty placed upon them by s 1 of the 1970 Act to take responsibility for the care *b* and management of income tax, corporation tax and capital gains tax vests in them a wide managerial discretion to refrain from recovering taxes which are payable under a strict application of the relevant legislation. Evidence in relation to this practice is given in the witness statement of Sarah Walker. As assistant director of personal tax she has had responsibility for policy matters concerning the structure of income tax rates and allowances, including the widow's *c* bereavement allowance. The commissioners publish a list of extra-statutory concessions that they are prepared to make when collecting taxation. By 31 August 1999 this list totalled no less than 294 concessions, not all of which are of current applicability. The list is introduced by the explanation:

d   'An extra statutory concession is a relaxation which gives taxpayers a reduction in tax liability to which they would not be entitled under the strict letter of the law. Most concessions are made to deal with what are, on the whole, minor or transitory anomalies under the legislation and to meet cases of hardship at the margins of the code where a statutory remedy would be difficult to devise or would run to a length out of proportion to the intrinsic *e*   importance of the matter.'

[30] Sarah Walker, in para 41 of her statement, adds the explanation:

     'The Board would consider it appropriate to use its power to make ESC's where the result would be consistent with the intention of Parliament in *f*   passing the relevant legislation.'

[31] In the *Hooper* litigation the Secretary of State was concerned to contend that he enjoyed a wide power to make extra-statutory payments, notwithstanding that this contention was adverse to his position in the particular litigation. Equally, in the present case, Mr Brennan QC for the commissioners *g* has argued from the premise that their practice of making extra-statutory concessions falls within their powers under s 1(1) of the 1970 Act. Miss Rose has, naturally, been more than happy to accept that premise. It was also accepted by Moses J. In these circumstances the argument in respect of this issue was confined within a narrow compass. What were the limits of the commissioners' *h* powers to make extra-statutory concessions? Mr Brennan argued that they could not extend to granting concessions which were contrary to the intention of Parliament in passing the relevant legislation. Miss Rose argued, by particular reference to four of the published concessions, that no such restriction existed. Clearly, she submitted, it was open to the commissioners to make a concession *j* where this was necessary to avoid an infringement of a convention right. Indeed, s 3 of the 1998 Act required the court so to interpret s 1(1) of the 1970 Act as to give the commissioners that power.

[32] Moses J accepted as appropriate the exercise of examining individual published concessions on the premise that they constituted legitimate exercises of the commissioners' powers. He accepted that two of the four examples relied upon by Miss Rose evidenced the grant of concessions which were contrary to

the intention of Parliament as expressed in the relevant legislation. He observed
([2002] STC 347 at [27]):

> 'The essential quest ought, in my view, to be targeted on finding some
> principled distinction between extra-statutory concessions and the
> concession sought in this case. I can find none. Once it is accepted that
> there are extra-statutory concessions which are not merely temporary, are
> not merely of minor effect, but directly contradict the intention of
> Parliament expressed in statutory provisions, it becomes impossible to find
> any principle according to which in some cases the Revenue will grant a
> concession and in others they will not.'

[33] Moses J went on to conclude in the following paragraph (at [28]):

> 'I conclude that there is no principle which would prevent the Revenue
> from issuing an extra-statutory concession which contradicted the intention
> of Parliament to restrict the allowances to women.'

[34] Before us Mr Brennan attacked the judge's approach. He started by
conceding that it was common ground—

> 'that the Revenue, with the duty of care and management of the tax
> system, has the power to issue and publish Extra Statutory Concessions—
> relaxations which give the taxpayers a reduction in tax liability to which they
> would not be entitled under the strict letter of the law.'

[35] He went on, however, to challenge the use of individual published
concessions as a touchstone for determining the extent of the commissioners'
power to make such concessions. In so far as an individual concession was
contrary to the intention of Parliament, as expressed in the relevant legislation,
the correct conclusion was that the concession was beyond the commissioners'
powers, not that the commissioners had power to disregard Parliament's
expressed intention. He went on, none the less, to challenge the judge's
conclusion that two of the published concessions were, in fact, contrary to—at
least—the spirit of the relevant legislation.

[36] Both Mr Brennan and Moses J referred to expressions of judicial concern
as to the legitimacy of the commissioners' practice of making extra-statutory tax
concessions, though neither suggested that the legitimacy of the practice was in
doubt. It seems to us that, before drawing conclusions from the way in which the
commissioners' practice has been exercised, it is pertinent to consider what the
courts have had to say about that practice.

[37] *Bates v IRC* [1967] 1 All ER 84, [1968] AC 483 concerned s 408 of the
Income Tax Act 1952 which, on its plain meaning, produced results in some cases
which were 'monstrous' and which Parliament can never have intended—see
[1967] 1 All ER 84 at 89, [1968] AC 483 at 504 per Lord Reid. The commissioners
had not sought to amend the legislation. Instead, as Lord Upjohn explained
([1967] 1 All ER 84 at 96, [1968] AC 483 at 516):

> '… realising the monstrous result of giving effect to the true construction
> of the section, have in fact worked out what they consider to be an equitable
> way of operating it which seems to them to result in a fair system of
> taxation.'

Lord Upjohn commented: 'I am quite unable to understand upon what principle
they can properly do so.'

[38] In *Vestey v IRC* [1977] 3 All ER 1073, [1979] Ch 177 Walton J was
concerned with another section of the 1952 Act, which had become s 478 of the
Income and Corporation Taxes Act 1970, which also had monstrous and
unintended results, if applied in accordance with its natural meaning. The
commissioners did not seek to apply the section in a manner which produced
such results. Walton J quoted with approval the comment of Lord Upjohn which
we have set out above, and added 'One should be taxed by law, and not be
untaxed by concession'.

[39] In *Vestey v IRC (No 2)* [1979] 2 All ER 225 at 233, [1979] Ch 198 at 202–203
Walton J expanded on this comment in a passage which deserves citation in full:

'It is at this point that there arises what counsel for the taxpayers has
denominated as a serious constitutional question; namely what rights the
Inland Revenue Commissioners have to pick and choose when recovering
tax. The Solicitor General says, and doubtless rightly says, that the
commissioners are under no duty to recover every halfpenny of tax which
may be due. One may say "Amen" to that very readily, because the costs of
recovery of extremely small amounts of tax would far outweigh the tax
recovered. One expects the tax authorities to behave sensibly. In this
connection I was referred to s 1 of the Inland Revenue Regulation Act 1890
and to s 1 of the Taxes Management Act 1970, but I do not think that either
of these provisions has any real bearing on the matter. What the revenue
authorities, through the Solicitor General, are here claiming is a general
dispensing power, no more and no less. He submitted that the system of
extra-statutory concessions was well known and well recognised, and that
what was happening in the present case was no more than the grant of an
additional extra-statutory concession. In the first place, I, in company with
many judges before me, am totally unable to understand upon what basis the
Inland Revenue Commissioners are entitled to make extra-statutory
concessions. To take a very simple example (since example is clearly called
for), upon what basis have the commissioners taken it upon themselves to
provide that income tax is not to be charged upon a miner's free coal and
allowances in lieu thereof? That this should be the law is doubtless quite
correct; I am not arguing the merits, or even suggesting that some other
result, as a matter of equity, should be reached. But this, surely, ought to be
a matter for Parliament, and not the commissioners. If this kind of
concession can be made, where does it stop; and why are some groups
favoured as against others?'

[40] The two *Vestey* decisions were appealed direct to the House of Lords.
Lord Wilberforce had this to say of the commissioners' submission that they had
a discretion as to how the section in issue should be applied, which enabled them
to mitigate the rigours of the section if applied literally ([1979] 3 All ER 976 at
984–985, [1980] AC 1148 at 1172):

'Taxes are imposed upon subjects by Parliament. A citizen cannot be taxed
unless he is designated in clear terms by a taxing Act as a taxpayer and the
amount of his liability is clearly defined. A proposition that whether a
subject is to be taxed or not, or, if he is, the amount of his liability, is to be
decided (even though within a limit) by an administrative body represents a
radical departure from constitutional principle. It may be that the revenue
could persuade Parliament to enact such a proposition in such terms that the

courts would have to give effect to it: but unless it has done so, the courts, *a* acting on constitutional principles, not only should not, but cannot, validate it. The Crown's contentions to the contrary, however moderate and persuasive their presentation by leading counsel, fail to support the proposition. The Crown say that the income tax legislation gives the commissioners a general administrative discretion as to the execution of the Acts, and it refers to particular instances, of which one is s 115(2) of the *b* Income and Corporation Taxes Act 1970 (power to decide period of assessment). The judge described the comparison of such limited discretions with that now contended for as "laughable". Less genially I agree. More generally, they say that s 412 imposes a liability upon each and every beneficiary for tax in respect of the whole income of the foreign transferees; that there is no duty on the commissioners to collect the whole of this from *c* any one beneficiary, that they are entitled, so long as they do not exceed the total, to collect from selected beneficiaries an amount decided on by themselves. My Lords, I must reject this proposition. When Parliament imposes a tax, it is the duty of the commissioners to assess and levy it on and from those who are liable by law. Of course they may, indeed should, act *d* with administrative commonsense. To expend a large amount of taxpayers' money in collecting, or attempting to collect, small sums would be an exercise in futility: and no one is going to complain if they bring humanity to bear in hard cases. I accept also that they cannot, in the absence of clear power, tax any given income more than once. But all of this falls far short of saying that so long as they do not exceed a maximum they can decide that *e* beneficiary A is to bear so much tax and no more, or that beneficiary B is to bear no tax. This would be taxation by self asserted administrative discretion and not by law. As the judge well said ([1977] 3 All ER 1073 at 1098, [1979] Ch 177 at 197): "One should be taxed by law, and not be untaxed by concession." The fact in the present case is that Parliament has laid down no *f* basis on which tax can be apportioned where there are numerous discretionary beneficiaries.'

[41] Viscount Dilhorne ([1979] 3 All ER 976 at 994, [1980] AC 1148 at 1185) also expressed the view that the commissioners had no power to mitigate the gross injustice that would result from the strict application of the section, as *g* interpreted by them. Lord Salmon ([1979] 3 All ER 976 at 998, [1980] AC 1148 at 1190) agreed with everything said by Lord Wilberforce.

[42] Beginning at [1979] 3 All ER 976 at 1001–1002, [1980] AC 1148 at 1194 Lord Edmund-Davies carried out a detailed review of the authorities dealing with the practice of the commissioners of making extra-statutory concessions, in the *h* course of which he referred to the provisions of s 1 of the 1970 Act. He observed that judicial comment was mixed, but aligned himself firmly with those who disapproved of the practice, including Scott LJ, who in *Absalom v Talbot (Inspector of Taxes)* [1943] 1 All ER 589 at 598 had stated: 'No judicial countenance can or ought to be given in matters of taxation to any system of extra-legal concessions.' Lord Edmund-Davies concluded ([1979] 3 All ER 976 at 1003, [1980] AC 1148 at *j* 1196) that the devices resorted to by the commissioners were unconstitutional.

[43] The extent of the powers of the commissioners under s 1 of the 1970 Act was directly in issue in *IRC v National Federation of Self-Employed and Small Businesses Ltd* [1981] 2 All ER 93, [1982] AC 617. The commissioners had been concerned at tax evasion to the tune of some £1m a year by casual workers

a employed in Fleet Street. They made an agreement with the employers and the unions that would enable them to collect tax in the future, but in achieving this agreed that they would not attempt to pursue those who had evaded taxes in the past. The Federation sought to challenge this concession and the principal issue was whether it had standing to do so. It was relevant, however, to consider the strength of the case that the commissioners were acting beyond their powers.

b Lord Diplock described their powers as follows ([1981] 2 All ER 93 at 101, [1982] AC 617 at 636–637):

> '... the Board are charged by statute with the care, management and collection on behalf of the Crown of income tax, corporation tax and capital gains tax. In the exercise of these functions the Board have a wide
c managerial discretion as to the best means of obtaining for the national exchequer from the taxes committed to their charge, the highest net return that is practicable having regard to the staff available to them and the cost of collection. The Board and the inspectors and collectors who act under their directions are under a statutory duty of confidentiality with respect to information about individual taxpayers' affairs that has been obtained in the
d course of their duties in making assessments and collecting the taxes; and this imposes a limitation on their managerial discretion. I do not doubt, however, and I do not understand any of your Lordships to doubt, that if it were established that the board were proposing to exercise or to refrain from exercising its powers not for reasons of "good management" but for some
e extraneous or ulterior reason, that action or inaction of the Board would be ultra vires and would be a proper matter for judicial review if it were brought to the attention of the court by an applicant with "a sufficient interest" in having the Board compelled to observe the law.'

[44] Lord Scarman approved the following statement ([1981] 2 All ER 93 at
f 111, [1982] AC 617 at 651):

> '... in the daily discharge of their duties inspectors are constantly required to balance the duty to collect "every part" of due tax against the duty of good management. This conflict of duties can be resolved only by good managerial decisions, some of which will inevitably mean that not all the tax known to
g be due will be collected.'

[45] It seems to us that the effect of these authorities is plain. One of the primary tasks of the commissioners is to recover those taxes which Parliament has decreed shall be paid. Section 1 of the 1970 Act permits the commissioners to set about this task pragmatically and to have regard to principles of good
h management. Concessions can be made where those will facilitate the overall task of tax collection. We draw attention, however, to Lord Diplock's statement that the commissioners' managerial discretion is as to the best manner of obtaining for the national exchequer the highest net return that is practicable.

[46] No doubt, when interpreting tax legislation, it is open to the
j commissioners to be as purposive as the most pro-active judge in attempting to ensure that effect is given to the intention of Parliament and that anomalies and injustices are avoided. But in the light of the authorities that we have cited above and of fundamental constitutional principle we do not see how s 1 of the 1970 Act can authorise the commissioners to announce that they will deliberately refrain from collecting taxes that Parliament has unequivocally decreed shall be paid, not because this will facilitate the overall task of collecting taxes, but because the

commissioners take the view that it is objectionable that the taxpayer should have to pay the taxes in question.

[47] We do not consider that there is any need to enter into the debate as to whether, as Moses J concluded, two of the published tax concessions contradicted the intention of Parliament. If they did, then it is arguable that the concessions fell outside the authority of the commissioners. What they could not do was justify Moses J's conclusion that—

> 'there is no principle which would prevent the Revenue from issuing an extra statutory concession which contradicted the intention of Parliament to restrict the allowances to women.'

[48] Miss Rose argued that s 3 of the 1998 Act enabled and required the court to read s 1 of the 1970 Act as permitting the commissioners to grant concessions to taxpayers if they are necessary in order to prevent discrimination in the imposition of taxes which violates art 14. We do not accept that it is possible to interpret s 1 in such a way.

[49] We are in no doubt that, when enacting s 262 of the 1988 Act and s 34 of the Finance Act 1999, Parliament intended the WBA, for so long as it remained in existence, to be restricted to women. The commissioners had no power to make similar allowances to men. For this reason, which was not the one that he gave, Moses J was correct to make a declaration of incompatibility.

[50] On the finding that we have made the second issue does not arise. We propose none the less to deal with it, albeit briefly.

The second issue

[51] Moses J held that s 1 of the 1970 Act gave the commissioners a discretionary power to grant allowances to widowers that matched the WBA. In these circumstances he held that s 6(2)(a) of the 1998 Act provided the commissioners with no defence to Mr Wilkinson's claim. He went on to hold, however, that the commissioners had a defence under s 6(2)(b). As we understand his reasoning, it was as follows. (i) Where a statute confers a power, the exercise of which will inevitably be incompatible with convention rights, s 6(2)(b) of the 1998 Act enables that power to be exercised without breach of s 6(1)—see *R v Kansal (No 2)* [2001] UKHL 62, [2002] 1 All ER 257, [2002] 2 AC 69 and *R (on the application of Alconbury Developments Ltd) v Secretary of State for the Environment, Transport and the Regions* [2001] UKHL 23, [2001] 2 All ER 929. (ii) The present case is the converse of those two cases. Failure by the commissioners to exercise their powers under s 1 of the 1970 Act will inevitably be incompatible with Mr Wilkinson's convention rights. (iii) To postulate that the commissioners must exercise their power under s 1 of the 1970 Act to give allowances to widowers is to convert that power into a duty, so that it ceases to be a power at all. This is not legitimate. (iv) Accordingly:

> '... in refusing to exercise its power to make an extra-statutory allowance, the Revenue was giving effect to primary legislation which cannot be read in a way which is compatible with the Convention.'

[52] We are no more able to accept this reasoning than we were the similar reasoning in *Hooper's* case. It seems to us that s 6(2)(b) addresses the grant by Parliament of a statutory power which, regardless of the circumstances in which it is exercised, will inevitably be incompatible with convention rights. In such circumstances the power cannot be given effect to in a way which is compatible

a with the convention, and thus s 6(2)(b) enables the exercise of the power without breach of s 6(1).

[53] We appreciate the argument that if a failure to exercise a statutory power will inevitably involve a breach of convention rights, s 6(2)(b) is engaged, because implicit in the statutory power is the right to refrain from exercising the power. We make no comment as to whether that argument is sound or unsound. We
b simply observe that it has no application to the facts of this case. Section 1 of the 1970 Act is a wide general power. In most circumstances exercising that power will involve no incompatibility with the convention. Equally, in most circumstances failing to exercise the power will involve no incompatibility with the convention. If circumstances arise under which it is necessary to exercise the power in order to avoid a breach of convention rights, we can see no basis upon
c which the commissioners can rely upon s 6(2)(b) to justify a refusal to exercise the power.

[54] For these reasons we disagree with the conclusion of Moses J on the second issue. Had we held that the commissioners had power under s 1 of the 1970 Act to grant extra-statutory allowances to widowers to match the WBA, we
d would not have held that s 6(2)(b) of the 1998 Act excused them from failing to exercise that power.

The third issue

[55] Miss Rose contends that the refusal of the commissioners to offer
e Mr Wilkinson a settlement on the same terms as those granted to Mr Crossland and Mr Fielding in their Strasbourg proceedings constitutes an abuse of power. She puts her case in two ways. (i) 'The respondents are under a common law duty to treat taxpayers fairly, and not to discriminate without justification between taxpayers: see *IRC v National Federation of Self-Employed and Small Businesses Ltd* [1981] 2 All ER 93 at 111, [1982] AC 617 at 651; *R v IRC, ex p Unilever*
f *plc* [1996] STC 681 at 692; *R (on the application of British Sky Broadcasting Group) v Customs and Excise Comrs* [2001] EWHC Admin 127 at [6]–[10], [2001] STC 437 at [6]–[10].' (ii) Mr Wilkinson is bound to obtain the compensation he seeks, together with his costs, if he pursues his claim to Strasbourg. To compel him, and others in his position, to go to those lengths will 'simply massively increase the financial burden of these claims on public funds' and is irrational.
g [56] Although we have held that s 1 of the 1970 Act did not empower the commissioners to introduce a scheme of making extra-statutory concessions to all widowers, we are prepared to accept for the purposes of the present issue that their powers extend to settling Mr Wilkinson's claim and that of any other taxpayer who sets out on the road of litigation that may end in Strasbourg.
h [57] Moses J applied to Miss Rose's arguments the reasoning that he had applied to the same issue in *Hooper's* case. He held that the commissioners were 'entitled to litigate the issue of reliance on s 6(2)(b) notwithstanding a settlement of Mr Crossland's application'. The commissioners have sought to support this reasoning.
j [58] In elaboration of the first way Miss Rose puts her case, she submitted in her skeleton argument:

> 'In accordance with good administration and fairness, having settled a test case in Strasbourg, and elected not to pursue any argument that refusing to grant the Allowance to widowers was compatible with the Convention, the Respondents ought to have treated other similarly-situated taxpayers in the

same way: see *R v Hertfordshire County Council, ex p Cheung* (1986) *Times*,
4 April, quoted by Moses J in *R (on the application of Hooper) v Secretary of State*
for Work and Pensions [2002] EWHC 191 (Admin) at [154], [2002] All ER (D)
193 (Feb) at [154].'

[59] We see no basis for the contention that *Crossland's* case was a test case,
nor do we see that the fact that the commissioners chose to settle the claims made
at Strasbourg by Mr Crossland and Mr Fielding precludes them from challenging
similar claims in the domestic forum, now that the 1998 Act permits convention
issues to be raised in that forum.

[60] So far as Miss Rose's argument based on irrationality is concerned, s 6(2)
of the Human Rights Act 1998 provides a defence in respect of acts or omissions
that infringe convention rights where Parliament has required or authorised the
acts or omissions in question. Where this occurs the claimant will almost
inevitably have a remedy if he pursues his claim to Strasbourg. If Miss Rose's
argument is correct, s 6(2) could almost always be finessed by a contention that it
was irrational to compel the claimant to incur the expense of going to Strasbourg
for his remedy. None the less, if the commissioners had conceded that there
would be no answer to Mr Wilkinson's claim for compensation once he got to
Strasbourg, we would have some sympathy with her argument. That is not,
however, the position.

JUST SATISFACTION

[61] The considerations in the *Hooper* appeal that led us to conclude that just
satisfaction did not require the payment to Mr Naylor of compensation for failure
to receive a widow's pension apply with even greater force in the present context.

[62] The history of the tax regime for married couples is complex. Moses J
attempted to summarise it ([2002] STC 347 at [7]) in order to set the dispute
before him in context. In essence WBA was an anachronistic relic of a tax regime
abandoned by 1994. Under the new regime there was no legitimate justification
for granting a widow this allowance on the death of her husband. The allowance
no longer reflected an adverse fiscal consequence of the husband's death. While
the WBA discriminated in favour of widows, it seems to us that the
discrimination provided widows with an unjustified advantage not merely over
widower taxpayers, but over all taxpayers.

[63] Before the 1998 Act had come into force, the Revenue had taken steps to
remove this anomaly, by abolishing the WBA prospectively, with effect from
6 April 2000. To award Mr Wilkinson, or other taxpayers in his position, an
equivalent payment would be to swell the numbers of those who have received
tax allowances for which there is no legitimate justification. The principle of just
satisfaction does not require any such payment.

[64] The facts of the present case are not to be compared with that of *Darby v*
Sweden. That case concerned a thoroughly justified exemption from a particular
tax, which was not allowed to Mr Darby on the ground that he was resident
outside Sweden. The court held that this fact did not provide legitimate
justification for not extending the exemption to him and ordered that he be
repaid the tax that had been wrongly exacted.

[65] Miss Rose submitted that it was inconceivable that the Strasbourg court
would not award compensation to Mr Wilkinson, having regard to the decisions
in *Crossland's* case and *Fielding v UK*. We do not agree. This is the first occasion
upon which the principle of just satisfaction has received judicial consideration in
the present context. We consider that the case for not making to widowers

a payments equivalent to a WBA is a cogent one and it is at least possible that the Strasbourg court will take the same view.

[**66**] For these reasons the commissioners cannot be said to have acted unfairly or irrationally in declining to settle Mr Wilkinson's claim.   This appeal is dismissed.

b *Appeal dismissed.*

Kate O'Hanlon   Barrister.

Bloomsbury Publishing Group Ltd and another v News Group Newspapers Ltd and others

[2003] EWHC 1205 (Ch)

CHANCERY DIVISION

SIR ANDREW MORRITT V-C

21, 23 MAY 2003

Practice – Parties – Description of parties – Description sufficiently certain to identify defendant – Whether requirement that defendant be named – CPR PD 7, para 4.1(1) – CPR 3.10.

The second claimant was the well-known writer of the Harry Potter books. Arrangements were made by the first claimant, the publisher, for the fifth book in the series to be printed under conditions of exceptional security. However, copies of the book were taken from the printers, without authority, and offered to the press at varying prices. The court made an order against 'the person (or persons) who have offered the publishers of the Sun, the Daily Mail, and the Daily Mirror newspapers a copy of the book ... requiring them to deliver up all copies of the book, any notes recording any part of it or any information derived from it and restraining them from disclosing to any person all or any part of the book or any information derived from it'. The issue was whether the orders against the second defendant should be continued until the date of the publication of the book notwithstanding that he, she and/or they were not described by name. At the hearing the claimants sought to amend the description of that defendant or defendants to include 'the person or persons who has or have physical possession of a copy of the said book or any part thereof without the consent of the claimants'. CPR 3.10[a] conferred on the court a general power of dispensation where there had been a procedural error and provided that such error did not invalidate any step taken in the proceedings unless the court so ordered. CPR PD 7, para 4.1(1)[b] indicated that the title of the proceedings 'should state ... the full name of each party'.

Held – The overriding objective and the obligations cast on the court were inconsistent with an undue reliance on form over substance. There was no requirement that a defendant had to be named, merely a direction that he should be. The proper application of CPR 3.10 was incompatible with a conclusion that the joinder of a defendant by description rather than by name was for that reason alone impermissible. However, the description used had to be sufficiently certain as to identify both those who were included and those who were not. If that test was satisfied then it did not matter that the description might apply to no one or more than one person nor that there was no further element of subsequent identification whether by service or otherwise. Accordingly, the court was

---

a CPR 3.10 provides: 'Where there has been an error of procedure ... (a) the error does not invalidate any step taken in the proceedings unless the court so orders; and (b) the court may make an order to remedy the error.'

b CPR PD 7, para 4.1(1), so far as material, is set out at [16], below

a entitled, if it thought fit, to make the order sought. In the circumstances there would be no injustice to anyone if the court made the order sought but considerable potential for injustice to the claimants if it did not (see [19], [21], [22], below).

Friern Barnet UDC v Adams [1927] 2 Ch 25 and Re Wykeham Terrace, Brighton, Sussex, ex p Territorial Auxiliary and Volunteer Reserve Association for the South East

b [1971] Ch 204 distinguished.

Notes

For the rule as to parties to proceedings and defendants generally, see 37 Halsbury's Laws (4th edn reissue), paras 251.

c ### Cases referred to in judgment

Acrow (Automation) Ltd v R Chainbelt Inc [1971] 3 All ER 1175, [1971] 1 WLR 1676, CA.

A-G v Times Newspapers Ltd [1991] 2 All ER 398, [1992] 1 AC 191, [1991] 2 WLR 994, HL.

Barnett v French [1981] 1 WLR 848, DC.

d Biguzzi v Rank Leisure plc [1999] 4 All ER 934, [1999] 1 WLR 1926, CA.

Blain (Tony) Pty Ltd v Splain [1993] 3 NZLR 185, NZ HC.

EMI Records Ltd v Kudhail [1985] FSR 36, CA.

Friern Barnet UDC v Adams [1927] 2 Ch 25, CA.

Golden Eagle Liberia Ltd v International Organization of Masters, Mates and Pilots
e [1974] 5 WWR 49, BC SC.

Jackson v Bubela [1972] 5 WWR 80, BC CA.

Levy v Levy (9 November 1979, unreported), CA.

McPhail v persons, names unknown [1973] 3 All ER 393, [1973] Ch 447, [1973] 3 WLR 71, CA.

Stewart v Engel [2000] 3 All ER 518, [2000] 1 WLR 2268, CA.

f Wykeham Terrace, Brighton, Sussex, Re, ex p Territorial Auxiliary and Volunteer Reserve Association for the South East [1971] Ch 204, [1970] 3 WLR 649.

Cases referred to in skeleton arguments

A-G v Newspaper Publishing plc [1987] 3 All ER 276, [1988] Ch 333, [1987] 3 WLR
g 942, CA.

Ewing v UK App No 14720/89 (6 May 1989, unreported), E Com HR.

Kent Free Press v NGA [1987] IRLR 267.

News Group Newspapers Ltd v Society of Graphical and Allied Trades '82 (No 2) [1987] ICR 181.

h Venables v News Group Newspapers Ltd [2001] 1 All ER 908, [2001] Fam 430, [2001] 2 WLR 1038.

Application

The claimants, Bloomsbury Publishing Group Ltd and JK Rowling, sought to amend the description of certain defendants, described as person or persons
j unknown, in an order of Laddie J made on 7 May 2003 ([2003] EWHC 1087 (Ch), [2003] All ER (D) 344 (May)) requiring the delivery of copies of an unpublished book and any notes and information derived from it and restraining them from disclosing to any person any part of the book or any information derived from it. The order was continued by Laddie J on 9 May, by Rimer J on 14 May and by Sir Andrew Morritt V-C on 21 May. The facts are set out in the judgment of Sir Andrew Morritt V-C.

David Kitchin QC and *Adrian Speck* (instructed by *Schillings*) for the claimants.
Bruce Carr (instructed by the *Treasury Solicitor*) as advocate to the court.

a

Cur adv vult

23 May 2003. The following judgment was delivered.

SIR ANDREW MORRITT V-C.

b

[1] The second claimant, JK Rowling, is the well-known writer of the Harry Potter books. The fifth book is eagerly awaited and is to be published by the first claimant, Bloomsbury Publishing Group Ltd (Bloomsbury), on 21 June 2003. In April 2003 Bloomsbury made arrangements for the book to be printed by Clays Ltd of Bungay, Suffolk under conditions of exceptional security.

c

[2] Those arrangements have not been wholly successful. The evidence clearly establishes that at least three copies of the book have been taken away from the printers without authority and offered to the press at varying prices. Thus, on 5 May 2003 a man telephoned the Daily Mail. He indicated that he had a copy of the new book and asked how much they would pay him for it. On 6 May Mr Webb found two somewhat damp copies in the grass on the Common at Bungay. It is unclear how they got there. They have now been returned to the claimants via the first defendant, the Sun newspaper. Later on the same day the Sun received two separate telephone calls from a man. In the first he offered to sell to them three chapters of the book for £25,000. In the second, he offered to sell four chapters for £20,000. On 7 May the Daily Mirror was offered the first three chapters for an unspecified price. On 13 May another copy of the book was found in the grass on the Common at Bungay.

d

e

[3] These events prompted a number of legal steps. On 7 May Laddie J made an order (([2003] EWHC 1087 (Ch), [2003] All ER (D) 344 (May)) against 'the person (or persons) who have offered the publishers of the Sun, the Daily Mail, and the Daily Mirror newspapers a copy of the book *Harry Potter and the Order of the Phoenix* by JK Rowling' requiring them to deliver up all copies of the book, any notes recording any part of it or any information derived from it and restraining them from disclosing to any person all or any part of the book or any information derived from it. In his judgment he explained the unusual nature of the order against defendants so described and recognised the need in due course to address the issue in more detail. That order was continued by Laddie J on 9 May and by Rimer J on 14 May. On 21 May I continued it again until today in order to put this judgment into writing.

f

g

[4] The application against the first defendant has been disposed of on the basis of certain undertakings. The third to sixth defendants were arrested on 7 May and charged with theft of copies of the book or receiving them knowing them to have been stolen. They were joined as defendants by name on 14 May and submitted to the orders I made against them on 21 May. Thus the only outstanding issue is whether the orders against the second defendant first made by Laddie J on 7 May should be continued until 21 June notwithstanding that he, she and/or they are not described by name. In the light of the argument the claimants seek to amend the description of that defendant or those defendants so as to read:

h

j

'... the person or persons who have offered the publishers of the Sun, the Daily Mail, and the Daily Mirror newspapers a copy of the book *Harry Potter and the Order of the Phoenix* by JK Rowling or any part thereof and the person or persons who has or have physical possession of a copy of the said book or any part thereof without the consent of the claimants.'

[5] The problem with regard to an order against persons so described was revealed by the decision of the Court of Appeal in *Friern Barnet UDC v Adams* [1927] 2 Ch 25. In that case the plaintiff sought to recover the cost of certain street works from the relevant frontagers. They did not know their names and issued a writ against 'the owners of' certain land clearly identified by name. It was pointed out that only owners of that land at the date of the completion of the works could be liable. In order to cover that point the plaintiff sought to amend the description by adding 'at the time of the completion of the works'. The judge refused leave to amend and his decision was upheld by the Court of Appeal. Lord Hanworth MR said (at 30):

> 'A writ cannot be issued in the terms proposed referring to the parties sought to be summoned in this vague way. I think that that is clear from the rules and the official forms. Tracing the matter a little further back the original official form of writ in use established by the Act of 2 Will. 4, c.39. That Act recited that "whereas the process for the commencement of personal actions is by reason of its great variety and multiplicity very inconvenient in practice," and proceeded to enact that the process in all such actions should be according to the form contained in the Schedule to the Act annexed marked No. 1, and which process should be called a writ of summons. In the form of the writ in the Schedule the writ is directed to C. D. of, etc., in the County of ... That form was followed in the Judicature Act, 1873, and it is to be found now in the forms directed to be used in Order II., r. 3, which directs that "the writ of summons for the commencement of an action shall, except in the cases in which any different form is hereinafter provided, be in one of the Forms Nos. 1, 2, 3, and 4 in Appendix A, Part 1, with such variations as circumstances may require," and the appendix shows that the writ must be directed to a particular defendant of a specified address. In my opinion, this writ does not comply with the form of writ which has the basis of statutory authority.'

[6] Similarly Atkin LJ said (at 31):

> 'It appears to me that the procedure established by the Judicature Act necessarily implies even if it does not expressly state—and I think it does so state—that it is necessary to an action that the defendants should be named. In some cases they may be described by the office which they hold, but apart from that, they must be named; and it seems to me to be contrary to the rules to issue a writ against defendants whom you do not know by describing them merely as owners of certain property. It is not right to describe the defendants in the vague way adopted in this writ.'

[7] Lawrence LJ added (at 32):

> 'This is a writ in personam, and in my opinion, the writ, in not naming the defendants, but merely describing them as the owners of adjoining property, is bad. The plaintiffs do not know, and the writ does not state, whether any one of the defendants is a lunatic, or an infant, or is residing abroad, or is under any kind of disability, in each of which cases some special directions or some special procedure might be required. There is no authority or

precedent for such a writ, and counsel was unable to tell us of any case where
a writ of this sort has been allowed.'   *a*

Thus the objections were twofold. First, the prescribed form required names and
addresses. Second the description was too vague.

[8] A similar problem arose in *Re Wykeham Terrace, Brighton, Sussex,
ex p Territorial Auxiliary and Volunteer Reserve Association for the South East* [1971]   *b*
Ch 204, [1970] 3 WLR 649. In that case squatters had broken into and were in
occupation of vacant premises. The plaintiff owner did not know their names.
He applied for an order for possession by means of an ex parte originating
summons to which there was no defendant. Service was effected by putting it
through the letter box. Stamp J refused to make an order for possession on such
an application. He concluded that there were two insuperable objections. The   *c*
first ([1971] Ch 204 at 208, [1970] 3 WLR 649 at 653) was:

> '... it is axiomatic that a person claiming an order of this court against
> another, except where a statute provides otherwise—and I shall have to
> consider whether the order and rules made under statute do provide
> otherwise—cannot obtain that relief except in proceedings to which that   *d*
> other person is a party and after that other person—the person against whom
> the relief is sought—has had the opportunity of appearing before this court
> and putting forward his answer to the claim. The accusatorial process by
> which the person against whom relief is sought is summoned to appear to
> answer the plaintiff's claim is the process by which justice has been done in   *e*
> England and Wales between man and man over the centuries.'

[9] The second was dealt with by Stamp J in these terms ([1971] Ch 204 at 209,
[1970] 3 WLR 649 at 653–654):

> 'The second objection, and it is in my judgment a fatal objection, to the
> procedure which the applicants invoke is that an order made upon an ex   *f*
> parte application in ex parte proceedings will bind nobody. It is a truism that
> an order or judgment of this court binds only those who are parties to or
> attending the proceedings in which the order or judgment is given or made.
> This principle is blurred where the action is an action for the recovery of land
> by reason of the process by which the judgment is executed. The sheriff   *g*
> acting pursuant to a writ of possession will be bound to turn out those he
> finds upon the land whether they are bound by the judgment or not. But
> judgment and the execution of the judgment are two different things, and
> much of the argument which has been addressed to me in this case, I think,
> ignores that distinction. It is no doubt correct that if I were to grant the relief   *h*
> which the applicants seek upon this present application and order that the
> persons in occupation do deliver possession of the premises and that the
> applicants be at liberty forthwith to issue a writ of possession the trespassers
> would be turned out and in that sense the order would be binding upon
> them. But as a matter of law an order that the plaintiffs do recover
> possession of the premises binds only the parties to the proceedings: which   *j*
> these trespassers are not.'

Thus the objections in this case were different to those in the *Friern Barnet* case,
namely, there was no defendant and the order, as sought, would have no effect.

[10] In *McPhail v persons, names unknown* [1973] 3 All ER 393, [1973] Ch 447 the
Court of Appeal was faced with a similar problem to that confronting Stamp J.

a   Lord Denning MR doubted the correctness of the decision of Stamp J ([1973] 3 All ER 393 at 398, [1973] Ch 447 at 458) but, as the rules had been altered, did not say why. Similar problems have arisen in the case of 'touts' and others selling pirate copies of copyright goods. In such cases if one of them is identified by name the court has been prepared to make an order against that defendant on his own behalf and as representing all other persons engaged in the activity of which

b   complaint is made. In *EMI Records Ltd v Kudhail* [1985] FSR 36 the Court of Appeal concluded that the common link afforded by that activity and the common interest in wishing to remain anonymous is sufficient to justify the order.

[11] Accordingly even before the introduction of the CPR the position in England was anomalous. A claimant could obtain an injunction against all infringers by description so long as he could identify one of them by name, but,

c   by contrast, if he could not name one of them then he could not get an injunction against any of them.

[12] Other common law countries took a different line. Thus in *Jackson v Bubela* [1972] 5 WWR 80 the British Columbia Court of Appeal allowed an amendment to correct the name of the defendant from 'John Doe' to the real

d   name of the driver involved in the relevant accident. It was held to be a misnomer not the substitution of one party for another. Bull JA said (at 82):

'However, I have reached the conclusion that the Local Judge was wrong in holding that a substitution for, or addition of, a party was involved and erred in not holding that the application was merely to correct a misnomer

e   of an existing party to the action. The words "John Doe" to my mind are not restricted in connotation to a "fictitious" person or one not in existence. Traditionally the words were used in that limited sense in early ejectment suits, but for generations they have come to be accepted, used and understood, both in legal and common parlance, as indicating a real person existing and identifiable but whose name is not known or available to the

f   person referring to him. That is the situation here. The appellant was not purporting to sue a fiction to maintain or acquire some property right as was done in ancient times. On the contrary, she was suing a living man whom she alleged was at a particular defined time and place operating a described motor vehicle in such a negligent manner as to cause her injuries then and

g   there. Her litigating finger was pointed at that driver and no one else, but she did not know his name. For the purposes of suit (and it was necessary to act quickly because of the imminent expiry of the limitation period) she gave that identifiable and identified man a name, using one that would clearly connotate to all that it did not purport to be his real name. And, further, in the endorsement it was clearly stated that the real name of the defendant

h   driver was not "John Doe" but was unknown except to the other defendant, the female respondent. Under these circumstances, I can see no elements of an addition of, or substitution for, a defendant. No new entity or person was involved. It was merely an application to change the name of a party from a patently incorrect one to his proper one.'

j
Thus the description 'John Doe' sufficiently identified the driver of the vehicle at the relevant time and place even though it was obviously not his name. The use of that description was both permitted and sufficiently certain. Such a description was also approved by the Court of Appeal in England in the case of *Levy v Levy* (9 November 1979, unreported), see *Barnett v French* [1981] 1 WLR 848 at 853 per Donaldson LJ.

[13] *Jackson's* case was followed by the British Columbia Supreme Court in *Golden Eagle v International Organization of Masters* [1974] 5 WWR 49. In that case *a* the plaintiff (see [1974] 5 WWR 49 at 50) sued 'persons unknown to the Plaintiffs picketing in the vicinity of ... carrying signs directed against the Plaintiffs' vessel ...' Four persons entered appearances in the name 'John Doe' and applied to have the proceedings struck out. The judge refused to strike out the action so as to frustrate a genuine claim on the ground that the plaintiff could not name the *b* defendant. After referring to the *Friern Barnet* case, *Re Wykeham Terrace* and *Jackson's* case, the judge said (at 52–53):

> 'The Court of Appeal of this province has endorsed the practice of the use of "John Doe" to describe a defendant who is a real person but whose name is not known. In the case of *Jackson v Bubela*, [1972] 5 W.W.R. 80, 20 D.L.R. *c* (3d) 500 (B.C. C.A.), the Court of Appeal permitted the plaintiff to amend his writ of summons to substitute for the name "John Doe" the proper name of the driver of the motor vehicle. The discussion in that case indicates very clearly that in this jurisdiction a plaintiff is not to be frustrated in his claim by a procedural requirement that the defendant be named where the *d* circumstances are such that the name is not known or ascertainable. A well-established practice of the court ought not to be changed without a convincing reason. None has been shown to me and moreover, by implication, the practice has the approval of the Court of Appeal.'

There is no indication in the reports of either *Jackson's* case or the *Golden Eagle* case *e* that the decisions turned on provisions peculiar to the law of British Columbia.

[14] The *Friern Barnet* case and *Re Wykeham Terrace* have not been followed in New Zealand either. In *Tony Blain Pty Ltd v Splain* [1993] 3 NZLR 185 the second defendant was sued as 'all persons who sell unlicensed ... merchandise at or about the ... stadium on 26th March 1993 who are served with this statement of claim'. *f* Anderson J granted the ex parte order sought. He said (at 187):

> 'It is an ancient maxim of the law that where there is a right there is a remedy; ubi jus, ibi remedium. In circumstances where it is plain that persons are infringing proprietary interests which the law recognises, or deceiving the public by way of trade in a manner which may indirectly affect *g* the commercial interests of others, the law should, if it reasonably can, provide a remedy. What is proposed in this case is that certain solicitors named in the application, who by virtue of their status are officers of this Court, should be authorised to accost bootleggers at the concert venues and require them to provide their current addresses, evidence of identity, and to *h* surrender up to the named solicitors all merchandise including t-shirts, headbands, badges or programmes in their possession or control. Persons required to respond to these oral interrogatories, which conceptually is what they are, will be such persons as are served with the orders for injunction also sought in this proceeding. The second and third defendants are identified as *j* persons who sell unlicensed merchandise at the relevant concert venues. It is expedient to refer to them in this judgment as "John Doe" and "Jane Doe". The fact that persons cannot be identified at this stage of the proceeding is no bar to relief against persons who may be identified at a relevant time. It is not the name but the identity and identification of infringing persons which is relevant. The identify may not be immediately established but persons

a   infringing will be identified by their act of infringement. Jane Doe and John Doe will be known by their works.'

[15] I should also refer to the relevant provisions of the CPR. CPR 1.1(1) proclaims that: 'These Rules are a new procedural code with the overriding objective of enabling the court to deal with cases justly.' What that involves is

b   amplified in CPR 1.1(2). CPR 1.2 requires the court to give effect to the overriding objective when it exercises any power given by the CPR. Such powers include the general powers of management set out in CPR 3.1 which include the power (see CPR 3.1(2)(m)) to 'take any other step or make any other order for the purpose of managing the case and furthering the overriding objective'. CPR 3.10 confers on the court a general power of dispensation where there has been a

c   procedural error and provides that such error does not invalidate any step taken in the proceedings unless the court so orders.

[16] Proceedings are started when the court issues a claim form at the request of the claimant (see CPR 7.2(1)). The form to be used is specified in CPR 4(1). CPR 4(2) authorises a variation in that form 'if ... required by the circumstances

d   of a particular case'. CPR PD 7, para 4.1(1) provides that the claim form must be headed with the title of the proceedings and indicates that the title 'should state ... the full name of each party'. The claim form must be served on the defendant within four months or such extended time as the court may allow (see CPR 7.5).

[17] Counsel for the claimants has properly been concerned throughout each stage of these proceedings with whether the court had the power to make orders

e   of the type he sought against a defendant described otherwise than by name. He emphasises that the evidence clearly indicates that at least four copies of the book have been taken from the printers, at least one of which is still at large. He points out that, given the elaborate security surrounding the printing it must have been obvious to any one who took or received a copy that such copy and its contents

f   were secret until publication on 21 June 2003. He suggests that an order in the form sought cannot cause confusion because anyone to whom it is shown will know immediately whether or not it is descriptive of and therefore directed to him or her.

[18] Thus there are two questions. (a) Am I entitled to make the order sought? And if so (b) should I do so? The answer to the first question depends on

g   whether and if so to what extent I am bound by the ratio decidendi of either the *Friern Barnet* case or *Re Wykeham Terrace*. I will consider them in turn.

[19] *Friern Barnet UDC v Adams* [1927] 2 Ch 25 was decided on two grounds, first that the prescribed form of writ required the defendant to be named, second that the description used was too vague. Both points were decided against the

h   background of the regime prescribed by the RSC. The regime introduced by the CPR is quite different. There is no requirement that a defendant must be named, merely a direction that he 'should' be. The failure to give the name of the defendant cannot now invalidate the proceedings both because they are started by the issue of the claim form at the request of the claimant and because, unless

j   the court thinks otherwise, CPR 3.10 so provides. The overriding objective and the obligations cast on the court are inconsistent with an undue reliance on form over substance. The proper application of CPR 3.10 is incompatible with a conclusion that the joinder of a defendant by description rather than by name is for that reason alone impermissible. For these reasons I conclude that the decision of the Court of Appeal in the *Friern Barnet* case is not applicable to proceedings brought under the CPR.

[20] The decision of Stamp J in *Re Wykeham Terrace, Brighton, Sussex, ex p Territorial Auxiliary and Volunteer Reserve Association for the South East* [1971] Ch 204, [1970] 3 WLR 649 is not binding on me in any event, though I would follow it unless it was distinguishable or I was satisfied that it was wrongly decided. I consider that it is distinguishable as being, like the *Friern Barnet* case, inapplicable to cases under the CPR. But it is also distinguishable on other grounds. First the objection in that case was that there was no defendant. In this case there is; the question is whether he or she has been properly described. Second, the objection in that case was that the order sought would not bind anyone to do or abstain from doing anything. That is not so in this case. A person falling within the description of the defendant could be liable for contempt of court if he acted inconsistently with it. Any other person who knowing of the order assists in its breach or nullifies the purpose of a trial may also be liable for contempt: *Acrow (Automation) Ltd v Rex Chainbelt Inc* [1971] 3 All ER 1175, [1971] 1 WLR 1676 and *A-G v Times Newspapers Ltd* [1991] 2 All ER 398, [1992] 1 AC 191.

[21] These conclusions are consistent with the decisions of the Court of Appeal in *Biguzzi v Rank Leisure plc* [1999] 4 All ER 934, [1999] 1 WLR 1926 and *Stewart v Engel* [2000] 3 All ER 518, [2000] 1 WLR 2268. Accordingly I conclude that the claimants are entitled to join as defendants and I am entitled, if I see fit, to make the order sought against persons described as quoted in [4], above. Mr Carr, as advocate to the court, for whose assistance I am most grateful, suggested that there might be a distinction to be drawn between cases such as *Jackson's* case and *Levy's* case, in which the description clearly referred to an identified person, the *Golden Eagle* case in which the defendants were identified in part by service of the statement of claim and the *Tony Blain* case in which the defendant was also identified in part by service of the order, and this case where the description may cover no one or, by contrast, more than one person. I accept that those distinctions may be drawn but I do not consider that they should lead to a different result. The crucial point, as it seems to me, is that the description used must be sufficiently certain as to identify both those who are included and those who are not. If that test is satisfied then it does not seem to me to matter that the description may apply to no one or to more than one person nor that there is no further element of subsequent identification whether by service or otherwise.

[22] I can see no injustice to anyone if I make an order in the form sought but considerable potential for injustice to the claimants if I do not. For these reasons I will make the order.

Order accordingly.

Celia Fox   Barrister.

a
Grady v Prison Service
[2003] EWCA Civ 527

b
COURT OF APPEAL, CIVIL DIVISION

THORPE, SEDLEY LJJ AND RICHARDS J

1, 11 APRIL 2003

Employment Appeal Tribunal – Jurisdiction – Unfair dismissal – Employee adjudicated bankrupt – Bankrupt's estate vesting in trustee in bankruptcy – Whether unfair
c *dismissal claim property right rather than personal right.*

The claimant's employment with the prison service was terminated, and she made a complaint to an employment tribunal, alleging unfair dismissal, wrongful dismissal and disability discrimination. In November 2001 the claims were all struck out for repeated non-compliance with procedural directions, and the
d employee gave notice of appeal to the Employment Appeal Tribunal. In January 2002 she was adjudged bankrupt. At the hearing of the appeal before the EAT, the employer submitted that the claimant lacked standing to pursue the appeal, because all her property, including things in action, such as the right to bring legal proceedings, had vested in her trustee in bankruptcy by reason of ss 283(1), 306
e and 436[a] of the Insolvency Act 1986. The EAT acceded to that submission and dismissed the appeal. The claimant appealed. Whilst she accepted that her claims for wrongful dismissal and disability discrimination, which were in substance money claims, had vested in her trustee in bankruptcy, she argued that the claim for unfair dismissal, being principally a claim for reinstatement in the
f lost job or re-engagement in a similar job, was a personal claim and as such did not vest in her trustee.

Held – Whilst the 1986 Act provided that a bankrupt's right to bring or pursue legal proceedings, which was a thing in action, vested in the trustee in bankruptcy, there was a distinction between proceedings which sought to
g recover money or property, in which the bankrupt's creditors would have an interest, and causes of action personal to the bankrupt, which did not vest in his trustee. A claim for reinstatement or re-engagement consequent on an unfair dismissal, and indeed a significant element of the compensation which could be awarded in lieu of those, was not a thing in action of the kind which formed part
h of a bankrupt's estate, even though the eventual fund, if an award were made, might be. It was a claim of a unique kind which offered the restoration to the claimant of something only the claimant could do. To vest it in the trustee in bankruptcy would be of no appreciable benefit to the creditors except to the extent that it might produce a money settlement. The appeal would accordingly
j be allowed, and the matter would be remitted to the EAT for determination on the merits (see [10], [11], [25], [27], [29], below).

---

a   Sections 283 and 436, so far as material, are set out at [10], below. Section 306, so far as material, provides: '(1) The bankrupt's estate shall vest in the trustee immediately on his appointment taking effect ... (2) Where any property which is ... comprised in the bankrupt's estate vests in the trustee ... it shall so vest without any conveyance, assignment or transfer.'

Notes

For causes of action vesting in a trustee in bankruptcy, see 3(2) *Halsbury's Laws* (4th edn) (2002 reissue) para 435.

Cases referred to in judgment

Beckham v Drake (1849) 2 HL Cas 579, 9 ER 1213, HL.
Gibson v Carruthers (1841) 8 M & W 321, 151 ER 1061, [1835–42] All ER Rep 565.
Heath v Tang, Stevens v Peacock [1993] 4 All ER 694, [1993] 1 WLR 1421, CA.
Hill v CA Parsons & Co Ltd [1971] 3 All ER 1345, [1972] Ch 305, [1971] 3 WLR 995, CA.
Ord v Upton (as trustee to the property of Ord) [2000] 1 All ER 193, [2000] Ch 352, [2000] 2 WLR 755, CA.
Wenlock v Moloney [1965] 2 All ER 871, [1965] 1 WLR 1238, CA.
Wilson v United Counties Bank Ltd [1920] AC 102, [1918–19] All ER Rep 1035, HL.
Wilson, Re, ex p Vine (1878) 8 Ch D 364, CA.

Cases referred to in skeleton arguments

Church of Scientology Advanced Organisation Saint Hill Europe and South Africa v Scott [1997] BPIR 418, CA.
De Keyser Ltd v Wilson [2001] IRLR 324, EAT.
Ellison v Petrie Tucker & Partners Ltd [2002] All ER (D) 536 (Jul), EAT.
Harris (suing as personal representative of Andrews (decd)) v Lewisham and Guy's Mental Health NHS Trust [2000] 3 All ER 769, CA.
Hurley v Mustoe (No 2) [1983] ICR 422, EAT.
Marshall v Southampton and South West Hampshire Area Health Authority (No 2) Case C-271/91 [1993] 4 All ER 586, [1994] QB 126, [1993] 3 WLR 1054, ECJ.
Mulkerrins v Pricewaterhouse Coopers (a firm) [2001] BPIR 106, CA.

Appeal

The claimant, Sharon Marie Grady, appealed with permission of the Employment Appeal Tribunal (Judge Mcmullen QC, Mr D Lambert and Mr A Manners) from the tribunal's decision on 5 December 2002 dismissing for want of jurisdiction the claimant's appeal against the Employment Tribunal's decison striking out, for non-compliance with procedural directions, her claims for unfair dismissal, wrongful dismissal and disability discrimination. The facts are set out in the judgment of the court.

Michael Mulholland (instructed by *Linder Myers*, Manchester) for Ms Grady.
Jeremy Johnson (instructed by the *Treasury Solicitor*) for the Prison Service.

Cur adv vult

11 April 2003. The following judgment of the court was delivered.

SEDLEY LJ.

[1] This is a judgment of the court.

THE ISSUE

[2] The appellant was for almost 15 years an administration officer in the Prison Service. Following the termination of her employment in November 2000 she brought proceedings before the employment tribunal sitting at Leeds alleging unfair dismissal, wrongful dismissal and disability discrimination. The employment tribunal has jurisdiction today, as it used not to have, in all three matters.

a [3] On the date scheduled for the hearing, 12 November 2001, her claims were all struck out for repeated non-compliance with procedural directions and she was ordered to pay costs. She gave notice of appeal to the Employment Appeal Tribunal (EAT) on 21 November. On 31 January 2002 she was adjudged bankrupt, and when her appeal came on for hearing before the EAT counsel for the respondent submitted that Ms Grady lacked standing to pursue it because all

b her rights of action had vested by law in her trustee in bankruptcy, who had not reassigned any of them to her. The EAT acceded to this argument and dismissed the appeal for want of jurisdiction ([2003] All ER (D) 49 (Feb), (2003) Times, 24 February). Because the point was not an easy or a clear one, they themselves granted permission to appeal to this court.

[4] Before going any further it is right to say that the EAT went on to indicate
c that the substantive appeal, if competent, might have had merit.

THE STATUTORY FRAMEWORK

[5] Since the answer to the issue before us depends in part on the framework of statute law, it is as well to set it out now. For reasons to which we will come,
d we are concerned only with the unfair dismissal provisions.

[6] By s 94(1) of the Employment Rights Act 1996 an employee has the right not to be unfairly dismissed. While dismissal is necessarily a matter of contract law, fairness in relation to it is a statutory construct. By s 98, provided that the employer can show that the dismissal was on a stipulated ground, the tribunal must decide whether or not it was reasonable in the circumstances to base the
e dismissal on it.

[7] By s 111 employment tribunals are given jurisdiction to hear complaints of unfair dismissal. If they find it established, the remedies are those set out in ss 112–117: reinstatement, re-engagement and compensation. By s 112 the tribunal must explain to the complainant what orders it can make under the first
f two heads and in what circumstances. If the complainant then asks for such an order, the tribunal has power to make it (see s 112(3)), and by s 116(1) it must begin by considering reinstatement in the same job (see s 114). If, but only if, it decides against reinstatement it must consider re-engagement (see s 115).

[8] By s 112(4) if no order is made either for reinstatement or for re-engagement, the tribunal is to make an award of compensation, calculated
g according to ss 118–127A. This consists in essence of a basic award, representing not consequential loss but the years of the employee's life invested in the lost job, and a compensatory award representing an equivalent of common law damages. By s 117(3), if an order for reinstatement or re-engagement has been made and not complied with, the tribunal is required to make a full award in lieu for unfair
h dismissal, plus 'an additional award of compensation of an amount not less than twenty-six nor more than fifty-two weeks' pay'.

[9] Section 206(2) and (3) provides that where an employee has died, tribunal proceedings for unfair dismissal may be instituted or continued by the employee's personal representative. No provision is made for transmission or
j discontinuance in the event of bankruptcy.

THE EFFECT OF BANKRUPTCY

[10] Section 306 of the Insolvency Act 1986 provides that the estate of a bankrupt shall vest in his trustee in bankruptcy at the moment of the trustee's appointment without the need of any formality. By s 283(1) the estate is defined as comprising 'all property belonging to or vested in the bankrupt at the

commencement of the bankruptcy', and by s 436 property is defined as including
'things in action'. A right to bring or pursue legal proceedings is a thing in action.

[11] The law has for many years distinguished, however, between
proceedings which seek to recover money or property in which the bankrupt's
creditors will have an interest and causes of action personal to the bankrupt
which do not vest in his trustee. Among these, as Hoffmann LJ explained in
Heath v Tang, Stevens v Peacock [1993] 4 All ER 694 at 697, [1993] 1 WLR 1421 at
1423, are—

> 'cases in which—"the damages are to be estimated by immediate reference
> to pain felt by the bankrupt in respect of his body, mind, or character, and
> without immediate reference to his rights of property." (See *Beckham v Drake*
> (1849) 2 HL Cas 579 at 604, 9 ER 1213 at 1222 per Erle J. See also *Wilson v
> United Counties Bank Ltd* [1920] AC 102, [1918–19] All ER Rep 1035.) Actions
> for defamation and assault are obvious examples. The bankruptcy does not
> affect his ability to litigate such claims.'

If, however, the damages from such a claim are invested, the investment can be
claimed by the trustee: see *Re Wilson, ex p Vine* (1878) 8 Ch D 364.

[12] If within a single claim both kinds of remedy are sought (in other words,
if the claim is hybrid), the claim falls outside the exception and vests in the trustee:
see *Ord v Upton (as trustee to the property of Ord)* [2000] 1 All ER 193 at 197, [2000]
Ch 352 at 360. But where one event gives rises to two or more claims, one for
damage to property and one for personal injury, the former alone vests in the
trustee and the latter remains with the bankrupt: see 3(2) *Halsbury's Laws*
(4th edn) (2002 reissue) para 436.

[13] *Halsbury's Laws* para 435, n 2, lists (with authority for each) the following
examples of causes of action which pass to the trustee: breach of contract to
deliver goods, or to repair; for commission or other money earned by the
bankrupt, other than 'personal earnings'; for earnings greater than are needed for
the maintenance of the bankrupt and his family; for trespass or negligence
causing damage to the bankrupt's property or involving him in pecuniary
liability; for misrepresentation or fraud; for relief against a usurious bargain or
against forfeiture. The list also includes, on the authority of *Beckham v Drake*
(1849) 2 HL Cas 579, 9 ER 1213, a claim for wrongful dismissal.

[14] The borderline is marked by such distinctions as that between a claim for
damages for a conspiracy which has caused mental and physical distress and loss
of reputation (which, if it relates in part to the bankrupt in the way of his business,
ranks as property passing to the trustee: see *Wenlock v Moloney* [1965] 2 All ER 871,
[1965] 1 WLR 1238), and a claim for damages for negligence or assault causing
personal injury, or for defamation (see *Beckham's* case). There is no bright line.

THE ARGUMENTS

[15] Mr Mulholland accepted before the EAT that in the light of these
authorities Ms Grady's claims for wrongful dismissal and disability discrimination,
being in substance money claims, had vested by operation of law in her trustee in
bankruptcy and could not be pursued except by the trustee or by means of
reassignment to her. But he has submitted that the claim for a remedy for unfair
dismissal is of a different and personal kind, falling within the exception in favour
of personal causes of action, because it is principally a claim for reinstatement in
the lost job or re-engagement in an equivalent one.

[16] Mr Johnson, for the Prison Service, in addition to a technical point to
which we will come in a moment, contends that a claim in respect of unfair

a   dismissal is not materially different from a claim in respect of unlawful dismissal. In the latter, reinstatement by way of specific performance is also possible: see *Hill v CA Parsons & Co Ltd* [1971] 3 All ER 1345, [1972] Ch 305. In the former, the claim is as much for compensation as for reinstatement or re-engagement. He also contends that Mr Mulholland, by admitting that the claim in respect of wrongful dismissal has gone, has debarred himself from arguing that the claim in

b   respect of unfair dismissal has not gone too. But his essential contention is that unfair dismissal is in its essence an action on a contract with the immaterial qualification that by statute the breach has to involve unreasonableness.

[17] For the appellant it is said that this is a false analysis: the action is a unique statutory tort in which termination is merely the gateway to the enforcement of a right to keep a job which the claimant has unfairly lost.

c

HOW MANY CLAIMS?

[18] Mr Johnson begins with a somewhat technical argument that because both tribunals below had before them a single application containing three claims, two of which were admitted to have vested in the trustee, the appeal

d   which was under way when Ms Grady became bankrupt was a hybrid claim the whole of which therefore vested in her trustee. We did not find it necessary to trouble Mr Mulholland about this. Not only is this manifestly a case falling within the class, set out in [11], above, of distinct claims arising out of a single set of facts. The submission, if right, would produce the pointless result that applicants could guard themselves against the risk of a supervening bankruptcy by issuing three

e   applications or notices of appeal instead of one (and no doubt that their lawyers could be sued for not advising them to do so).

DID THE UNFAIR DISMISSAL CLAIM VEST IN THE TRUSTEE?

[19] The principle underlying this seemingly metaphysical question is that a

f   bankrupt forfeits his assets, beyond the means of subsistence, to his creditors. The qualification that a viable legal claim does not pass to the trustee with the bankrupt's other assets if it represents redress for some wrong personal to the bankrupt is not, as Mr Johnson suggested it was, an exception to the statutory provision devised by the common law. It is the accepted construction, known to Parliament long before the passage of the 1986 Act, of a thing in action in the context of the insolvency legislation: see *Ord v Upton (as trustee to the property of Ord)* [2000] 1 All ER 193 at 197–198, [2000] Ch 352 at 360 per Aldous LJ. There is no dispute that, by the process described in [10], above, all things in action belonging to the bankrupt vest in her trustee. The question is whether the pending appeal to the EAT was a thing in action within the meaning of the legislation.

[20] There can in our judgment be no distinction for this purpose between the claim and the appeal. The appeal, brought as of right, was a continuation of the claim once it had failed at first instance. Either both fall or neither falls within the material meaning of a thing in action.

[21] It seems to us that the upshot of the many decided cases on this topic is that a claim which represents a transmissible asset of the bankrupt forms part of the estate on which the creditors have a claim, while one which reflects some aspect of the bankrupt's individuality does not. This is not to say that the end-product of the latter is also protected. Just as an investment of, say, libel damages will accrue to the estate and vest in the trustee (see [11], above), one would expect that earnings beyond those needed for subsistence from a job in

which the bankrupt was reinstated would form part of the estate, as those from a
bankrupt's continuing employment do.

[22] In our judgment the essential nature of a claim for unfair dismissal is
personal, not proprietary. Unlike a claim for wrongful dismissal, which (except
in the rare case where specific performance can be granted) is an action for
damages for breach of a contract, a claim for unfair dismissal only begins with the
employer's fundamental breach. It proceeds through the issues described in
paraphrase in [6] and [7], above. The purpose and effect of the sequential
provisions for judgment and redress can fairly be said to be the recognition of a
vested interest in a job—something of a different order from the common law's
view of a job as a simple contract which can be broken by a party willing to pay
the appropriate price for breach.

[23] Mr Johnson relies nevertheless on the reasoning of Lord Brougham in
Beckham v Drake (1849) 2 HL Cas 579 at 640, 9 ER 1213 at 1235:

> 'The law ... is shewn to be this, that even where there is no actual damage
> proved, or even where the damage is merely nominal for a breach of
> contract, still if that is in respect either of property or of a proprietary right,
> such as service or work and labour, as in the present case, even in that case it
> passes.'

While *Beckham*'s case is undoubtedly regarded as a continuing source of law, care
needs to be taken with it. It was in form a decision of the House of Lords in the
years before the Judicature Acts, and the speech of Lord Brougham was
concurred in by Lord Campbell alone. The report does not indicate which if any
other members of the House sat and voted. The report is for this reason more
valued for the extensive opinions of the judges which their Lordships had called
for upon the appeal from the Court of Exchequer Chamber, among them the
opinion of Erle J cited by Hoffmann LJ in *Heath v Tang, Stevens v Peacock* [1993]
4 All ER 694 at 697, [1993] 1 WLR 1421 at 1423 (see [11], above). The action was
for payment of a fixed contractual sum for the premature termination of the
plaintiff's seven-year contract of service, and the plea in bar was that the cause of
action had passed on his bankruptcy to the assignees. Erle J said ((1849) 2 HL Cas
579 at 606, 9 ER 1213 at 1223):

> 'As to that part of [the promise] respecting the continuance of this relation,
> it has no reference to the feelings of the bankrupt, so as to be analogous to
> the promises and causes of action which are decided to be excepted, and it is
> not the substance of the promise which is considered in the award of
> damage; but as to the other part, namely, the paying of the wages, it is the
> consideration for the promise of service ... [T]he first ground above
> mentioned, namely, that the contract relates to the person, is true only in
> respect of the consideration for the promise, which is personal skill and
> labour, and not in respect of the promise itself ...'

The reasoning of Williams J ((1849) 2 HL Cas 579 at 598–599, 9 ER 1213 at 1220)
picks up this point:

> '... it cannot be doubted that where a contract remains to be executed, and
> cannot be executed without the co-operation of the bankrupt, his assignees
> cannot enforce the contract, at all events unless they can procure him to
> co-operate.'

a

Williams J goes on to point out ((1849) 2 HL Cas 579 at 599, 9 ER 1213 at 1220) that, a breach having now occurred, the plaintiff 'is not bound by the contract to bestow any of his skill and labour in order to sustain the right of action'.

[24] None of this reasoning answers the present question, but all of it in our view tends to place on the non-vesting side of the line a claim which is primarily directed at the restoration of a contractual relationship in which the claimant's

b

skill and labour are the essential commodity. There is nothing frivolous in Mr Mulholland's question whether the Official Receiver could seriously seek reinstatement in Ms Grady's former job—for that is the principal remedy claimed in these proceedings which are said to have become his, and the first remedy which the tribunal is required by law to explore. It was in principle the question

c

posed by Lord Abinger CB (dissenting, it is true, but not on this aspect of the argument) in *Gibson v Carruthers* (1841) 8 M & W 321 at 343–344, 151 ER 1061 at 1070–1071. Lord Abinger CB recalled that at the time when Sir Walter Scott's publisher became bankrupt (he was probably referring to Constable, who in 1826 went down with over £250,000 in debts) he had contracted to pay Scott £4,000 for

d

his next novel. When his assignees claimed the benefit of the contract, Scott had objected that the quality and respectability of the publisher was so central to the contract that Constable's bankruptcy had discharged it. 'I must own' said Lord Abinger CB—

e

> 'that his reasoning appeared satisfactory to me; but a more obvious illustration of the principle on which it rested would have been afforded by reversing the case, and supposing that Sir Walter Scott had been the bankrupt and his booksellers solvent, would they have been content to pay their £4000, and take the risk of publishing a novel written by the assignees of the novelist?'

f

[25] In our judgment a claim for reinstatement or re-engagement consequent on an unfair dismissal, and indeed a significant element of the compensation which can be awarded in lieu of these, is not a thing in action of the kind which forms part of a bankrupt's estate, even though the eventual fund (if an award is made) may be. It is a claim of a unique kind which offers the restoration to the claimant of something which only the claimant can do. To vest it in the trustee in bankruptcy would be of no appreciable benefit to the creditors except to the extent that it might produce a money settlement (which would represent not a concession but a liquidation of the bankrupt's claim to her job). For the rest, the creditors will probably be better served if the bankrupt can get her job back or a similar job in its place, and that is something the trustee cannot do in her stead. Mr Johnson rightly does not fall back on the circular proposition that in that case the trustee can always reassign the claim to the bankrupt.

[26] The EAT (Judge McMullen QC, Mr Lambert and Mr Manners) ([2003] All ER (D) 49 (Feb), (2003) Times, 24 February) took the view that the difference between wrongful and unfair dismissal being chiefly one of remedies, and orders for re-engagement and reinstatement being 'very rare' (we do not in fact know the figures), there was no sufficient difference between the two to indicate a differential effect of bankruptcy. They concluded that in the light of the authorities a right to claim unfair dismissal was a property right and not a personal right.

CONCLUSIONS

[27] For reasons which we have given we respectfully take the contrary view. *a* We consider that an unfair dismissal claim, both in its nature and in its remedies, is personal to the claimant and not apt to vest in her trustee in bankruptcy as a thing in action.

[28] We have been invited, if we reach this stage, to determine the substantive issue which the EAT considered itself precluded from determining. We decline *b* to do so. The issue is one which depends heavily on the accumulated experience and knowledge of the EAT in respect of employment tribunal practice and procedure, and our judgment—at least in the absence of a reasoned decision from them—would be a poor substitute for theirs.

[29] We therefore allow the appeal as to Ms Grady's standing and remit the matter to the EAT for determination on its merits. *c*

POSTSCRIPT

[30] The Prison Service is not a legal entity. The true respondent is the Crown, which by virtue of the list issued pursuant to s 17 of the Crown Proceedings Act 1947 should be sued in the name of the Home Office.

d

Appeal allowed.

Melanie Martyn   Barrister.

a # Higgs v Brighton and Hove City Council
[2003] EWCA Civ 895

COURT OF APPEAL, CIVIL DIVISION

SIMON BROWN, WALLER AND KAY LJJ

b 21 MAY, 30 JUNE 2003

Housing – Homeless person – Duty of housing authority to provide accommodation –
Priority need – Sudden unexplained disappearance of caravan used as accommodation
– Whether disappearance an emergency such as flood, fire or other disaster – Housing
Act 1996, s 189(1)(d).
c

The appellant lived in a caravan placed on land owned by the respondent housing
authority. He had no lawful right to do so. The authority began enforcement
action but before the relevant hearing could take place the caravan vanished
without trace while the appellant was absent. It was never found. The appellant
d found temporary accommodation with friends. He made a formal application to
the authority for housing as a homeless person pursuant to Pt VII of the Housing
Act 1996. Section 189(1)(d)[a] provided that a person who was homeless as a result
of an emergency such as flood, fire or other disaster had a priority need for
accommodation. A housing authority had a duty to ensure that accommodation
was available for a person with a priority need who was not intentionally
e homeless. The authority accepted that the appellant was homeless and that he
was not intentionally homeless but concluded that he did not have a priority
need. The authority considered that in order to qualify as 'a disaster', the disaster
had to be in the nature of a flood or fire, and involve some form of physical
damage or threat of damage. The appellant requested a review of the decision,
f and upon its confirmation, he appealed to the county court. The judge concluded
that the disappearance of the caravan without explanation as to by whom, for
what motive, or what had become of it, did not fall within s 189 and that
therefore the authority was not under a duty to ensure that accommodation was
available. The appellant appealed. The authority submitted that the appellant's
homelessness was in any event not a result of the loss of the caravan since by
g virtue of s 175(2)(b)[b] of the 1996 Act a person was homeless if he had
accommodation which consisted of a moveable structure and had no place where
he was entitled to place and reside in it.

Held – The sudden disappearance without trace of a caravan in which a person
was making his home came within the description of 'an emergency such as
h flood, fire or other disaster' in s 189(1)(d) of the 1996 Act so as to give the owner
a priority need for accommodation. The loss of the appellant's home was an
emergency akin to those referred to expressly. It involved the sudden and wholly
unexpected loss of the appellant's home in circumstances wholly outside his
control by the loss of the structure in which he had made his home. However, in
j the instant case, the loss of the caravan had done nothing to change the
appellant's status as homeless. His homelessness was caused under s 175(2)(b) of
the 1996 Act by whatever circumstances had led him to live in a caravan, which
he had no right to park anywhere, not the subsequent loss of the caravan.

a   Section 189, so far as material, is set out at [8], below
b   Section 175, so far as material, is set out at [6], below

Accordingly, the appellant did not have a priority need and his appeal would therefore be dismissed (see [19], [20], [24], [25], [30], [31], [33]–[36], below).

R v Bristol City Council, ex p Bradic [1995] 3 FCR 189 distinguished.

Notes

For the duties of housing authorities to the homeless and for those with a priority need, see 22 *Halsbury's Laws* (4th edn reissue) paras 244, 245, 255.

For the Housing Act 1996, s 189, see 21 *Halsbury's Statutes* (4th edn) (1997 reissue) 189.

Cases referred to in judgments

Noble v South Herefordshire DC (1983) 17 HLR 80, CA.

R v Bristol City Council, ex p Bradic [1995] 3 FCR 189, CA.

Cases referred to in skeleton arguments

Azimi v Newham London BC (2000) 33 HLR 569, CA.

R v Kensington and Chelsea London BC, ex p Kihara (1996) 29 HLR 147, CA.

Appeal

The appellant, Scott Higgs, appealed with permission of Sedley LJ given on 13 March 2003, from the decision of Mr Recorder Morris-Coole on 5 February 2003 in the Brighton County Court upholding the decision of Brighton and Hove City Council (the authority) that the sudden disappearance without trace of the caravan in which the appellant had been living without permission on authority property was not an emergency such as flood, fire or other disaster within s 189(1)(d) of the Housing Act 1996. By a respondent's notice, for which permission was given at the hearing, the authority maintained that the appellant had not been made homeless as a result of his loss within s 189(1)(d). The facts are set out in the judgment of Kay LJ.

David Watkinson (instructed by *Brighton Housing Trust*) for the appellant.

Clare Roberts (instructed by *Abraham Ghebre-Ghiorghis*, Hove) for the respondent authority.

Cur adv vult

30 June 2003. The following judgments were delivered.

KAY LJ (giving the first judgment at the invitation of Simon Brown LJ).

[1] This appeal brought with permission from Sedley LJ raises a short point of statutory construction namely whether the sudden disappearance without trace of the caravan in which a person was making his home comes within the description of 'an emergency such as flood, fire or other disaster' in s 189(1)(d) of the Housing Act 1996 so as to give him a priority need for accommodation. The respondent's notice, for which we gave permission at the hearing, raises a further issue as to whether the appellant's homelessness was in any event 'as a result of' the loss of his caravan.

[2] On 5 February 2003 Mr Recorder Morris-Coole sitting at Brighton County Court concluded that the loss of the caravan was not such an emergency and accordingly dismissed an appeal brought by the appellant, Scott Higgs, against a decision of Brighton and Hove City Council (the respondent authority) that it was not under a duty to provide him with accommodation.

a

[3] From a date some time after Christmas 2001 the appellant lived in a caravan placed on council land in Hove Park. It is accepted that he had no lawful right to locate the caravan at that place. In March 2002, the respondent took enforcement action under the Criminal Justice and Public Order Act 1994 requiring the appellant to remove the caravan. A summons was served on the appellant for the matter to be heard on 2 April.

b

[4] Before that hearing could take place, the appellant went out with his dogs on 30 March and discovered on his return that his caravan containing all his possessions had vanished without trace. The caravan has never been found and there is no evidence as to what became of it.

[5] The appellant found temporary accommodation with friends and on 21 May 2002, he made a formal application to the respondent authority for

c

housing as a homeless person pursuant to Pt VII of the 1996 Act.

[6] Section 175 of the 1996 Act provides the relevant definition of homelessness:

d

'(1) A person is homeless if he has no accommodation available for his occupation, in the United Kingdom or elsewhere, which he—(a) is entitled to occupy by virtue of an interest in it or by virtue of an order of a court, (b) has an express or implied licence to occupy, or (c) occupies as a residence by virtue of any enactment or rule of law giving him the right to remain in occupation or restricting the right of another person to recover possession.

e

(2) A person is also homeless if he has accommodation but—(a) he cannot secure entry to it, or (b) it consists of a moveable structure, vehicle or vessel designed or adapted for human habitation and there is no place where he is entitled or permitted both to place it and to reside in it.'

[7] By s 192 of the 1996 Act a housing authority has a duty to provide advice and information to a homeless person in any attempts he might make to ensure

f

that accommodation becomes available for his occupation. If, however, a homeless person has 'a priority need for accommodation', and is not intentionally homeless the duty becomes one under s 193 to ensure that accommodation is available for him.

[8] Section 189(1) of the 1996 Act provided the following definition of a priority need for those purposes:

g

'The following have a priority need for accommodation—(a) a pregnant woman or a person with whom she resides or might reasonably be expected to reside; (b) a person with whom children reside or might be expected to reside; (c) a person who is vulnerable as a result of old age, mental illness or handicap or physical disability or other special reason, or with whom such a person resides or might reasonably be expected to reside; (d) a person who is homeless or threatened with homelessness as a result of an emergency such as flood, fire or other disaster.'

[9] The respondent authority accepted that the appellant was homeless and further that he was not intentionally homeless but concluded that he did not have a priority need. In the letter containing its decision, dated 7 September 2002, the relevant officer explained why he did not consider that the appellant came within category (d) of s 189(1) by reference to the *Homelessness Code of Guidance for Local Authorities* (July 2002). Paragraph 8 42 of the code provided:

'To qualify as an "other disaster" the disaster must be in the nature of a flood or fire, and involve some form of physical damage or threat of damage.

The volcanic activity on the island of Montserrat was treated as an example *a*
of an "other disaster". Applicants have a priority need by reason of such an
emergency whether or not they have dependent children or are vulnerable
for any reason.'

After considering that guidance the decision letter concluded that the appellant
did not come within the relevant provision. Thus the respondent authority was
prepared to offer advice and information but not to secure accommodation. *b*

[10] The appellant requested a review under s 202 of the 1996 Act. The
respondent authority notified him of its decision on 18 October 2002. The letter
stated:

> '... I am satisfied that the decision made on 7th September 2002 was correct *c*
> and although Mr Higgs is homeless, he is not in priority need ...
> Consideration was given to the circumstances in which Mr Higgs lost his
> caravan, and whether or not that constituted an emergency. Having
> consulted the code of guidance, it was decided that these circumstances did
> not amount to an emergency within the meaning of the Act. Mr Higgs has
> lost his accommodation in the same way that someone might if evicted *d*
> illegally, however this in itself does not constitute priority need.'

[11] The appellant exercised his right of appeal to the county court. At the
hearing the recorder's attention was drawn to the case of *R v Bristol City Council,
ex p Bradic* [1995] 3 FCR 189 in which this court had to consider precisely the same
provisions then contained in s 59(1)(d) of the Housing Act 1985. *e*

[12] In that case the court dealt with the case of a person rendered homeless
when his landlord unlawfully evicted him whilst he was away on holiday and the
landlord himself lost possession of the premises to a building society by court
order. The judge at first instance concluded that the loss of his home in such
circumstances was to be characterised as an emergency such as flood, fire or
other disaster and the local authority appealed that decision. *f*

[13] The Court of Appeal affirmed the view expressed by the court in
considering a similar provision in earlier legislation, s 2(1)(b) of the Housing
(Homeless Persons) Act 1977, in the case of *Noble v South Herefordshire DC* (1983)
17 HLR 80, where Waller LJ, with whom May LJ agreed, said (at 81):

> 'In my opinion that argument [that the word "emergency" was used in a
> wider sense than emergencies confined to emergencies arising from disaster]
> has no force in this case because in the phrase "any emergency such as flood,
> fire or any other disaster" the words "or any other disaster" are clearly
> indicating "any other disaster" similar to a flood or a fire.'

[14] Having accepted that proposition, Roch LJ in his judgment in *Ex p Bradic*,
with which the other two members of the court expressly agreed, said ([1995]
3 FCR 189 at 209):

> 'In my view the event that results in the homelessness of the person
> claiming a priority need must have the characteristics of being "an
> emergency" and "a disaster". The omission of the word "any" before the
> words "other disaster" in the 1985 Act reinforces, in my opinion, this reading
> of the subsection. I would therefore interpret the words of the subsection to
> mean an emergency such as flood, fire or other disaster of a similar nature.
> The line is not, in my judgment, to be drawn as narrowly as to confine the
> emergencies which can give rise to a priority need to those amounting to

a "force majeure". Parliament must have had in mind emergencies caused by
fires deliberately or accidentally started by human beings and floods
deliberately or accidentally caused by human beings. In my opinion the line
is to be drawn so as to embrace all emergencies which consist of physical
damage to the accommodation of the applicant which have made the
accommodation uninhabitable.'

b [15] The recorder in this case applying the construction of the section 'as laid
down in *Ex p Bradic*' concluded that 'the disappearance of this property without
any explanation as to by whom, for what motive, or what has become of it does
not fall within the construction of this priority section'.

[16] On behalf of the respondent, Miss Roberts contends that the recorder was
c right to so find. She argues that whilst the loss of the caravan was no doubt a
disaster from the point of view of the appellant, it was not a disaster similar to
flood or fire. She contends that what the section clearly envisages is a loss of
home through some physical disaster.

[17] Miss Roberts accepts that the intervention of some other person will not
prevent an emergency coming within the provision. Roch LJ gave the example
d of an arsonist deliberately setting fire to a home. But she argues that physical
damage is the essential element.

[18] I cannot accept these arguments. No one knows what became of this
caravan. It may for all that is known have been removed and destroyed. Can
Parliament really have intended that unless the appellant could trace his caravan
e or its remains and show that it had been rendered uninhabitable, he was not to
be treated as a priority need?

[19] It would be surprising to say the least if a person whose caravan was
removed without trace was in a fundamentally different position from someone
whose caravan was destroyed whether by deliberate fire or by vandalism. Most
other dwellings simply cannot be removed but if one considers a prefabricated
f structure that was dismantled and taken away it is difficult to see how such a
situation could be viewed as different from someone having just razed it to
the ground.

[20] Thus I am satisfied that this loss of the appellant's home was an
emergency akin to those expressly referred to in s 189(1)(d) of the 1996 Act. It
g involved the sudden and wholly unexpected loss of the appellant's home in
circumstances wholly outside his control by the loss of the structure in which he
made his home. The removal of the caravan was a form of physical interference
with the property that deprived the appellant of his home and this is to be
contrasted with the situation in *Ex p Bradic* where the home remained available
h as a home in which the respondent could have lived but for the operation of the
law that precluded him from regaining occupation of the premises.

[21] If it were not for the second point raised by the respondent's notice I
should feel bound to allow the appeal. However, Miss Roberts raises a further
difficulty in the path of the appellant which she contends meant that in any event
his claim was bound to fail.

j [22] Section 175(2)(b) of the 1996 Act means that a person is homeless if he
lives in a caravan and he has no place where he is entitled to locate his caravan
and to reside in it. That, Miss Roberts argues, was the position of the appellant
prior to the loss of his caravan. He was, therefore, homeless long before the
caravan went missing. In these circumstances she submits the homelessness was
not 'as a result' of the loss of his caravan as is required by s 189(1)(d) of the
1996 Act.

[23] Mr Watkinson, on behalf of the appellant, responds by saying that at the time *a* when a person claims to be homeless, it is necessary to look at the operating factor that has deprived him of his home at that stage and in this case that was the loss of the caravan. It is, he submits, of no consequence that prior to the loss of the caravan he might have been deemed to be homeless because it was only the disappearance of the caravan that caused the appellant to seek the assistance of the respondent.

[24] With every respect to Mr Watkinson, that argument simply cannot be *b* right. The appellant had not had a home for some time and the supervening event of the loss of the caravan did nothing to change his status as homeless. His homelessness was caused under the 1996 Act by whatever circumstances led him to live in a caravan which he had no right to park anywhere. Unless and until he had a home again, his homelessness continued and it resulted from that cause and not as in this case from the subsequent loss of the caravan. *c*

[25] For these reasons, I accept the respondent's argument that the decision below must be upheld, although not for the reasons given by the recorder but rather by reference to the matter raised in the respondent's notice. I would, therefore, dismiss this appeal.

d

SIMON BROWN LJ.

[26] This appeal centres on s 189(1)(d) of the Housing Act 1996 which provides:

'The following have a priority need for accommodation ... (d) a person who is homeless or threatened with homelessness as a result of an emergency such as flood, fire or other disaster.' *e*

[27] Two question arise: first, whether the sudden disappearance of the appellant's caravan in the circumstances described by Kay LJ constituted 'an emergency such as flood, fire or other disaster'; secondly, even supposing that it did, whether the appellant's homelessness was 'as a result of' that emergency.

[28] Mr Recorder Morris-Coole decided the first issue against the appellant *f* who now appeals to this court by permission of Sedley LJ who described the issue as 'a short and truly important point of principle'. The recorder noted but expressed no conclusion upon the second issue which now comes before us by way of a respondent's notice (for which we gave leave at the hearing).

ISSUE 1 *g*

[29] The most authoritative decision in point on this issue is *R v Bristol City Council, ex p Bradic* [1995] 3 FCR 189 in which this court held that a tenant's illegal eviction did not constitute an emergency within the relevant provision (then s 59(1)(d) of the Housing Act 1985). In the leading judgment Roch LJ said (at 209):

'In my view the event that results in the homelessness of the person *h* claiming a priority need must have the characteristics of being "an emergency" and "a disaster" ... I would therefore interpret the words of the subsection to mean an emergency such as flood, fire or other disaster of a similar nature. The line is not, in my judgment, to be drawn as narrowly as to confine the emergencies which can give rise to a priority need to those *j* amounting to "force majeure". Parliament must have had in mind emergencies caused by fires deliberately or accidentally started by human means and floods deliberately or accidentally caused by human beings. In my opinion the line is to be drawn so as to embrace all emergencies which consist of physical damage to the accommodation of the applicant which have made that accommodation uninhabitable.'

a The other members of the court agreed with that reasoning before adding short judgments of their own.

[30] Was the sudden disappearance of the appellant's caravan properly to be characterised both as 'an emergency' and a 'disaster' of a similar nature to the destruction of a building by flood or fire (recognising that such flood or fire may be caused deliberately as well as accidentally)? In my judgment it was. If a
b relevant emergency is constituted by someone hostile to the applicant setting fire to his accommodation, why not equally by such a person permanently removing it? If a tornado were to carry away a caravan, why should one treat its loss through malign human action as any less of an emergency and disaster? Most accommodation, of course, is to be found in permanent rather than moveable structures. Where, however, as here, it is moveable, it seems to me vulnerable
c to the additional hazard of disappearance (in the case of a vessel, for example a houseboat, by sinking), a disaster to my mind of a similar nature to the burning or flooding of a house.

[31] I respectfully disagree with the recorder's conclusions on this first issue.

d ISSUE 2

[32] Section 175(2)(b) of the 1996 Act provides:

> 'A person is also homeless if he has accommodation but ... (b) it consists of a moveable structure, vehicle or vessel designed or adapted for human habitation and there is no place where he is entitled or permitted both to
e place it and to reside in it.'

[33] In these proceedings it is conceded that at the date of the caravan's disappearance (indeed for some months previously) there was no place where the appellant was entitled or permitted both to place it and to reside in it. He was,
f therefore, at that time homeless within the meaning of the 1996 Act.

[34] In those circumstances it seems to me quite impossible to contend that he was homeless 'as a result of' the emergency constituted by the caravan's disappearance so as to establish a priority need for accommodation under s 189(1)(d) of the 1996 Act. He was already homeless. He was not made homeless by the caravan's disappearance.

g [35] I would accordingly uphold the decision below—the decision that the appellant has not made out a case for priority need—but solely by reference to the causation issue raised by the respondent's notice. On this basis, in common with Kay LJ whose judgment I have now read, and agree with, I too would dismiss the appeal.

h

WALLER LJ.

[36] I agree that for the reasons given in both judgments the loss of the appellant's caravan should properly have been characterised as an 'emergency' and a 'disaster' similar in nature to the destruction of a building by flood or fire.
j However I also agree again for the reasons given in both judgments that the appeal must be dismissed because the appellant was already homeless, and thus his homelessness was not as a result of that emergency or disaster.

Appeal dismissed.

Dilys Tausz   Barrister.

Jones v University of Warwick

[2003] EWCA Civ 151

COURT OF APPEAL, CIVIL DIVISION

LORD WOOLF CJ, HALE AND LATHAM LJJ

22 JANUARY, 4 FEBRUARY 2003

Evidence – Improperly obtained evidence – Relevant to matters in issue – Duty of court – Whether court concerned with method of obtaining evidence – CPR 32.1 – Human Rights Act 1998, Sch 1, Pt I, art 8.

The claimant commenced proceedings against the defendant employer, claiming damages for personal injury to her right hand, as a result of which she alleged that she was suffering continuing disability. The defendant admitted liability but disputed that the claimant was suffering continuing disability. An inquiry agent, acting for the defendant's insurers, obtained access to the claimant's home on two occasions by posing as a market researcher, and recorded the claimant, without her knowledge, using a hidden video camera. The defendant's expert, having viewed the video recordings, was of the opinion that the claimant had an entirely satisfactory function in her right hand. The defendant applied for directions as to whether the video recordings were admissible in evidence. The claimant, relying on the court's discretion under CPR 32.1(2)[a] and on the right to privacy in art 8(1)[b] of the European Convention for the Protection of Human Rights and Fundamental Freedoms 1950 (as set out in Sch 1 to the Human Rights Act 1998), contended that the recordings should not be admitted. The district judge concluded that the evidence should be excluded, because the court should not give approval to the methods used by the defendant's agent. The defendant appealed, and the judge held that the evidence was admissible, the primary question for the court being not whether or not to give approval to the method whereby evidence had been obtained, but rather whether justice and fairness required its admission. The claimant appealed.

Held – The judge's approach to the question whether the evidence was admissible was consistent with that which would have been adopted prior to the coming into force of the CPR and the 1998 Act, when the achieving of justice in the particular case before the court was the paramount consideration. That approach, however, did nothing to promote the observance of the law by those engaged or about to be engaged in legal proceedings, which was also a matter of real public concern. If the conduct of the insurers went uncensured, there would be a significant risk that practices of the type which they had adopted would be encouraged, and that would be highly undesirable. Proactive management of civil proceedings, which was at the heart of the CPR, was not only concerned with an individual piece of litigation which was before the court, but was concerned with litigation as a whole. Where, therefore, as in the instant case, a defendant's insurers had been responsible for trespass and for contravention of a

---

a CPR 32.1, so far as material, is set out at [18], below

b Article 8(1) provides: 'Everyone has the right to respect for his private and family life, his home and his correspondence.'

a claimant's privacy, in violation of art 8 of the convention, that was a relevant consideration for the court in the exercise of its discretion in making orders as to the management of the proceedings. In the instant case, the conduct of the insurers had not been so outrageous that the defence should be struck out, and it would be artificial and undesirable for evidence which was relevant and admissible not to be before the judge who had the task of trying the case.

b Accordingly, it would not be right to interfere with the decision of the judge below. The court could, however, reflect its disapproval of the insurers' conduct by ordering that the defendant pay the costs of the proceedings relating to the admissibility of the evidence before the district judge, the judge, and on the appeal (see [21]–[23], [25], [28]–[31], below).

c **Notes**
For the court's power to control evidence, see 17(1) *Halsbury's Laws* (4th edn reissue) para 427.

For the Human Rights Act 1998, Sch 1, Pt I, art 8, see 7 *Halsbury's Statutes* (4th edn) (2002 reissue) 555.

d **Cases referred to in judgment**
Kuruma Son of Kaniu v R [1955] 1 All ER 236, [1955] AC 197, [1955] 2 WLR 223, PC.
McNally v RG Manufacturing Ltd [2001] Lloyd's Rep IR 379.
PG and JH v UK App No 44787/98 (25 September 2001, unreported), ECt HR.
R v Khan (Sultan) [1996] 3 All ER 289, [1997] AC 558, [1996] 3 WLR 162, HL.
e *R v Loveridge* [2001] EWCA Crim 973, [2001] 2 Cr App R 591.
R v Mason [2002] EWCA Crim 385, [2002] 2 Cr App R 628.
R v Sang [1979] 2 All ER 1222, [1980] AC 402, [1979] 3 WLR 263, HL.
Rall v Hume [2001] EWCA Civ 146, [2001] 3 All ER 248.
Schenk v Switzerland (1988) 13 EHRR 242, [1988] ECHR 10862/84, ECt HR.
f *Venables v News Group Newspapers Ltd* [2001] 1 All ER 908, [2001] Fam 430, [2001] 2 WLR 1038.

Cases referred to in skeleton arguments
Daniels v Walker [2000] 1 WLR 1382n, CA.
Douglas v Hello! Ltd [2001] 2 All ER 289, [2001] QB 967, [2001] 2 WLR 992, CA.
g *G v G* [1985] 2 All ER 225, [1985] 1 WLR 647, HL.
Glaser v UK [2000] 3 FCR 193, ECt HR.
Grobbelaar Sun Newspapers Ltd (1999) Times, 12 August, CA.
Khan v UK (2000) 8 BHRC 310, ECt HR.
National Justice Cia Naviera SA v Prudential Assurance Co Ltd, The Ikarian Reefer [1993] 2 Lloyd's Rep 68; *rvsd* [1995] 1 Lloyd's Rep 455, CA.
h *Vernon v Bosley (No 2)* [1997] 1 All ER 614, [1999] QB 18, [1997] 3 WLR 683, CA.
X v Netherlands (1985) 8 EHRR 235, [1985] ECHR 8978/80, ECt HR.

Introduction
The claimant, Jean Jones appealed against the decision of Judge Charles
i Harris QC sitting as a deputy High Court judge on 16 May 2002 allowing the appeal of the defendant, the University of Warwick, from the decision of District Judge Wartnaby on 1 November 2001 that video evidence obtained at the claimant's home would not be admissible as evidence in proceedings brought by the claimant against the defendant for damages for personal injury. The facts are set out in the judgment of the court.

Robert Weir (instructed by *Irwin Mitchell*) for the claimant.
Robert Owen QC (instructed by *Bullers Jeffries*) for the defendant.

Cur adv vult

4 February 2003. The following judgment of the court was delivered.

LORD WOOLF CJ.

[1] The issue which this appeal raises is whether, and if so when, a defendant
to a personal injury claim is entitled to use as evidence a video of the claimant
which was obtained by filming the claimant in her home without her knowledge
after the person taking the film had obtained access to the claimant's home by
deception.

[2] As Mr Robert Weir, who appears on behalf of the claimant contends, the
issue on the appeal requires this court to consider two competing public interests:
the interests of the public that in litigation, the truth should be revealed and the
interests of the public that the courts should not acquiesce in, let alone
encourage, a party to use unlawful means to obtain evidence.

THE BACKGROUND TO THE APPEAL

[3] The claimant, Mrs Jean F Jones, appeals against an order of Judge Charles
Harris QC, sitting as a deputy High Court judge, who on 16 May 2002, allowed
an appeal from the decision of District Judge Wartnaby and made an order
allowing the University of Warwick, the defendant, to rely, at the trial of the
claimant's action against the defendant, on a video film which they had recorded
of the claimant in her home without her knowledge.

[4] The action arose out of an accident that occurred when the claimant
dropped a full cash box with a broken lid onto her right wrist causing a small cut
in the web between her fourth and fifth fingers of her right hand.

[5] The claimant was employed by the defendant. The claimant contended
that she had developed a focal dystonia. She alleged significant continuing
disability and claimed special damages in excess of £135,000.

[6] The defendant admits liability but disputes that the claimant has the
continuing disability she alleges. The defendant has expert medical evidence that
accepts that the claimant appears to have had an episode of extensor
tenosynovitis but contends she had virtually recovered by March 1998 and her
ongoing disability 'remains uncertain but it seems to be more related to habit
than need'.

[7] The video evidence, the admissibility of which is in dispute, was obtained
on two occasions by an inquiry agent, acting for the insurers of the defendant.
The first occasion was 19 November 1999 and the second 18 January 2000. The
inquiry agent obtained access to the claimant's home by posing as a market
researcher. The inquiry agent used a hidden camera and the claimant had no idea
that she was being filmed. The film which was made was disclosed on 11 June 2001.
This was after High Court proceedings had been issued on 30 August 2000 by the
claimant in which she claimed substantial damages. Nothing turns on the date
that the filming took place. It was, however, followed by the filming of the
claimant in public on 21 January and 30 March 2001. The admissibility of this
later filming is not in dispute but it is common ground that the later films are not
as helpful to the defendant as the films which were taken in the claimant's home.

[8] The defendant's expert, after seeing the films taken in her home, was of the
opinion that the claimant had an entirely satisfactory function in her right hand.

a The claimant's medical experts have come to a different conclusion. This is that the claimant still has a significant continuing disability but the films taken in her home can be explained because the extent of the disability in her hand varies. She has good and bad days.

[9] It is not in dispute that: (i) the inquiry agent was guilty of trespass and that she would not have been given permission to enter had she not misled the
b claimant as to her identity; (ii) as the medical experts have now seen what was recorded in the films taken at the claimant's home, if the film was not to be admitted in evidence, those experts would not be able to give evidence. New medical experts would have to be instructed and the existence of the recordings would have to be concealed from the court and the new experts.

c THE APPROACH OF THE JUDGES IN THE LOWER COURTS

[10] On 23 August 2001 the defendant made an application to the court for directions as to whether the video evidence obtained at the claimant's home should be admissible in evidence. At a hearing before District Judge Wartnaby on 19 October 2001, the claimant contended the disputed recordings should not
d be admitted, relying on the court's discretion under CPR 32.1(2) and art 8(1) of the European Convention for the Protection of Human Rights and Fundamental Freedoms 1950 (as set out in Sch 1 to the Human Rights Act 1998). On 1 November 2001 District Judge Wartnaby gave a reserved judgment in writing, in which he came to the conclusion that:

e   'The court has to carry out a balancing exercise between the benefit to the court of having all the evidence available and the consideration of the improper way in which the video evidence was obtained.
       The court should not in any way give approval to the methods used by the defendant's agent misleading the claimant and gaining improper entry to her home. In those circumstances I am not satisfied that the video evidence
f   should be available and I order that it is excluded.'

[11] In his reserved judgment of 16 May 2002, Judge Harris came to the opposite conclusion. Judge Harris drew attention to the fact that the claimant was alleging a substantial handicap and therefore that she was entitled to substantial compensation; that the disputed films revealed in the words of the
g defendant's orthopaedic expert 'that she has regained full function of her right hand'; that as copies of the film had been provided on 11 June 2001, this was not an ambush case; that in English criminal proceedings the fact that evidence has been illegally obtained does not render it inadmissible, subject to the power of the trial judge to exclude evidence in the exercise of its common law discretion or
h under the provisions of s 78 of the Police and Criminal Evidence Act 1984.

[12] Judge Harris was considerably influenced by the approach adopted by Lord Nolan in his speech in R v Khan (Sultan) [1996] 3 All ER 289, [1997] AC 558. Judge Harris pointed out that 'the overriding objective in a civil case tried in England is that court should deal with a case justly' and referred to his own
j judgment in McNally v RG Manufacturing Ltd [2001] Lloyd's Rep IR 379 at 382, where he had stated that if a party is making—

       'an inflated, exaggerated or unjustified claim then he is seeking other people's money to which he is not entitled. It is clearly both just and fair that he should be prevented from succeeding in this. In order to uncover his deception steps may have been taken which involved him in being misled or

his privacy being infringed. Misleading him may be the only practical means
of showing that he himself is misleading other people ...'

He added that in that case he had concluded—

'there were next to no physical signs as opposed to complaints of anything
wrong with him. I do not think that the deception involved in coming to his
house in the guise of a market researcher ... was of such gravity or
impropriety as to render evidence thus obtained inadmissible.'

[13] As to the reliance upon the convention, he contended that under the
Strasbourg jurisprudence questions of admissibility were matters of domestic
law. Referring to the CPR, he stated that:

'The overriding objective of those rules is to enable the court to deal with
cases justly. This includes, inter alia, ensuring that the parties are on an equal
footing, that the case is dealt with in ways which are proportionate to the
amount of money involved and that the case is dealt with "fairly" (see
CPR 1.1). The plaintiff knows very well what she can do with her hand, the
defendants do not. They are not, therefore, on an equal footing in this
respect.'

[14] Judge Harris added:

'So, the question for me to decide, in my review of District Judge
Wartnaby's decision is whether it was wrong. I think it plainly was. The
central passage of District Judge Wartnaby's reasoning was, "the courts
should not in any way give approval to the method used by the defendant's
agent. In those circumstances, I am not satisfied that the video evidence
should be available."'

[15] Judge Harris continued by saying:

'The primary question for the court is not whether or not to give approval
to the method whereby evidence was obtained. It is whether justice and
fairness require that this highly material evidence, which contradicts the
evidence which she has given to others, should be put to her before the trial
judge to enable him to reach a sound conclusion about the true extent of any
disability. True, the claimant was herself deceived but there is strong prima
facie evidence that she herself is deceiving or misleading the defendants to
enrich herself thereby. It is not easy for the defendants to protect themselves
against exaggerated claims. Anyone with much experience of personal
injury litigation will know that the defendants and their insurers are
frequently faced by claimants who suggest that their disabilities are far
greater than they are, and large sums of money may be unjustifiably sought.
Though such people are rarely, if ever prosecuted, in many cases what they
do or seek to do must amount to the crime of obtaining property or
pecuniary advantage by deception. In these circumstances I do not believe
that the courts should be too astute to prevent effective investigation by the
defendants of claimants against them. Clearly, there is a public interest that
unfair, tortious and illegal methods should not be used in general and where
they are unnecessary, but the conflicting considerations are on the one side
the claimant's privacy and on the other the legitimate need and public
interest that defendants or their insurers should be able to prevent and
uncover unjustified, dishonest and fraudulent claims. In the instant case I

a   have no doubt that the latter considerations do and should outweigh the
former.'

[16] Finally, Judge Harris commented in a critical manner about the fact that
up to that stage the claimant's solicitors had kept the films from their own
medical experts, 'thus not giving them all the available material to enable them
to make a disinterested assessment of the degree of her disability'. Having
b   acknowledged that he had not heard very extensive argument upon this 'perhaps
not wholly straightforward topic', he added, 'at first blush this seems, to put it
mildly, very unsatisfactory'.

THE CONTENTIONS OF THE PARTIES
c   [17] We can deal with Mr Robert Owen QC's submissions on behalf of the
defendant fairly succinctly because he naturally relied very strongly on the
forceful reasoning of Judge Harris. Mr Owen was, however, careful to make it
clear that in his submissions he was not inviting the court to give a green light to
insurers taking unlawful action, such as trespassing, in order to obtain evidence.
His submission was that the court had a discretion to exercise and the judge had
d   exercised his discretion properly, having come to the conclusion that the district
judge had exercised his discretion wrongly, and this being so, this court should
not intervene.

[18] Mr Weir was in agreement with Mr Owen that the judge had a discretion.
The discretion was contained in CPR 32.1 which provides, so far as relevant:

e   '(1) The court may control the evidence by giving direction as to … (c) the
way in which the evidence is to be placed before the court.
(2) The court may use its power under this rule to exclude evidence that
would otherwise be admissible.'

He also relies upon the overriding objective contained in CPR 1.1 which provides:
f
'(1) These Rules are a new procedural code with the overriding objective
of enabling the court to deal with cases justly.
(2) Dealing with a case justly includes, so far as practical—(a) ensuring
that the parties are on an equal footing … (d) ensuring that it is dealt with
expeditiously and fairly; and (e) allotting to it an appropriate share of the
g   court's resources, while taking into account the need to allot resources to
other cases.'

He could also have referred to the duty of the parties under CPR 1.3 'to help the
court to further the overriding objective'.

h   [19] When it comes to determining how a court should exercise its discretion
Mr Weir argues that the answer is provided by the relevant provisions of the
convention and in particular arts 6 and 8 thereof. The art 6 right to a fair hearing
he argues must be analysed in the context of the court's obligation to determine
whether the introduction of the video is in accordance with the law and necessary
for the protection of the defendant's rights. In saying this he relies on the fact that
j   the video recording was obtained as a result of the defendant's representative
having trespassed and infringed the claimant's right of privacy under art 8(1).
The reference to law and necessity he extracts from art 8(2) which provides:

'There shall be no interference by a public authority with the exercise of
this right except such as is in accordance with the law and is necessary in a
democratic society in the interests of national security …'

[20] Mr Weir accepts that he cannot rely upon art 8 directly because the insurers of the defendant were responsible for obtaining the evidence in this way and not a public authority. But he contends that this does not prevent him relying upon art 8. This is because of the fact that the court that has to exercise its discretion is a public authority (see s 6(3) of the 1998 Act) and it is 'unlawful for a public authority to act in a way which is incompatible with a Convention right' (see s 6(1)). He submits that for the court to ignore the manner in which the video evidence was obtained would involve the court acting in a way that is incompatible with the claimant's art 8 rights unless the evidence which was obtained in contravention of art 8 was necessary in order to achieve justice in the case.

SQUARING THE CIRCLE

[21] It is not possible to reconcile in a totally satisfactory manner, the conflicting public policies which District Judge Wartnaby and Judge Harris had to try and balance in this case. The approach of Judge Harris was consistent with the approach which would have been adopted in both criminal and civil proceedings prior to the coming into force of the CPR and the 1998 Act. The achieving of justice in the particular case which was before the court was then the paramount consideration for the judge trying the case. If evidence was available, the court did not concern itself with how it was obtained.

[22] While this approach will help to achieve justice in a particular case, it will do nothing to promote the observance of the law by those engaged or about to be engaged in legal proceedings. This is also a matter of real public concern.

[23] If the conduct of the insurers in this case goes uncensured there would be a significant risk that practices of this type would be encouraged. This would be highly undesirable, particularly as there will be cases in which a claimant's privacy will be infringed and the evidence obtained will confirm that the claimant has not exaggerated the claim in any way. This could still be the result in this case.

[24] Fortunately, in both criminal and civil proceedings, courts can now adopt a less rigid approach to that adopted hitherto which gives recognition to the fact that there are conflicting public interests which have to be reconciled as far as this is possible. The approach adopted in *Kuruma Son of Kaniu v R* [1955] 1 All ER 236, [1955] AC 197, *R v Sang* [1979] 2 All ER 1222, [1980] AC 402 and *R v Khan (Sultan)* [1996] 3 All ER 289, [1997] AC 558 which was applied by Judge Harris has to be modified as a result of the changes that have taken place in the law. The position in criminal proceedings is that now when evidence is wrongly obtained the court will consider whether it adversely affects the fairness of the proceedings and, if it does, may exclude the evidence (see s 78 of the Police and Criminal Evidence Act 1984). In an extreme case, the court will even consider whether there has been an abuse of process of a gravity which requires the prosecution to be brought to a halt (see *R v Loveridge* [2001] EWCA Crim 973, [2001] 2 Cr App R 591 and *R v Mason* [2002] EWCA Crim 385 at [50], [68] and [76], [2002] 2 Cr App R 628 at [50], [68] and [76]). In civil proceedings, Potter LJ recognised this in *Rall v Hume* [2001] EWCA Civ 146 at [19], [2001] 3 All ER 248 at [19]. He commenced by saying:

> 'In principle ... the *starting point* on any application of this kind must be that, where video evidence is available which, according to the defendant, undermines the case of the claimant to an extent that would substantially reduce the award of damages to which she is entitled, it will usually be in the overall interests of justice to require that the defendant should be permitted

a   to cross-examine the claimant and her medical advisors upon it ...' (My emphasis.)

[25] But Potter LJ then added that this does not apply if the conduct of the defendant amounts 'to trial by ambush'. The discretion on the court is not, however, confined to cases where the defendants have failed to make proper *b* disclosure. A judge's responsibility today in the course of properly managing litigation requires him, when exercising his discretion in accordance with the overriding objective contained in CPR Pt 1, to consider the effect of his decision upon litigation generally. An example of the wider approach is that the judges are required to ensure that a case only uses its appropriate share of the resources of the court (see CPR 1.1(2)(e)). Proactive management of civil proceedings, *c* which is at the heart of the CPR, is not only concerned with an individual piece of litigation which is before the court, it is also concerned with litigation as a whole. So the fact that in this case the defendant's insurers, as was accepted by Mr Owen, have been responsible for the trespass involved in entering the claimant's house and infringing her privacy contrary to art 8(1) of the convention *d* is a relevant circumstance for the court to weigh in the balance when coming to a decision as to how it should properly exercise its discretion in making orders as to the management of the proceedings.

[26] Mr Weir argues that unless it was *necessary* for the insurers to take the actions they did, the evidence must inevitably, at least in a case such as this, be held inadmissible. He submits that otherwise the court would be contravening *e* the duty that it is under, pursuant to s 6 of the 1998 Act, not to contravene art 8. While the court should not ignore the contravention of art 8, to adopt Mr Weir's approach would fail to recognise that the contravention would still remain that of the insurer's inquiry agent and not that of the court. The court's obligation under s 6 of the 1998 Act is to 'not itself act in a way which is incompatible with *f* a convention right' (see *Venables v News Group Newspapers Ltd* [2001] 1 All ER 908 at 917–918, [2001] Fam 430 at 445–446 (paras 24–27).

[27] As the Strasbourg jurisprudence makes clear, the convention does not decide what is to be the consequence of evidence being obtained in breach of art 8 (see *Schenk v Switzerland* (1988) 13 EHRR 242 and *PG and JH v UK* App No 44787/98 (25 September 2001, unreported), para 76). This is a matter, at *g* least initially, for the domestic courts. Once the court has decided the order, which it should make in order to deal with the case justly, in accordance with the overriding objectives set out in CPR 1.1 in the exercise of its discretion under CPR 32.1, then it is required or it is necessary for the court to make that order. Accordingly if the court could be said to have breached art 8(1) by making the *h* order which it has decided the law requires, it would be acting within art 8(2) in doing so.

[28] That leaves the issue as to how the court should exercise its discretion in the difficult situation confronting District Judge Wartnaby and Judge Harris. The court must try to give effect to what are here the two conflicting public interests. *j* The weight to be attached to each will vary according to the circumstances. The significance of the evidence will differ as will the gravity of the breach of art 8, according to the facts of the particular case. The decision will depend on all the circumstances. Here, the court cannot ignore the reality of the situation. This is not a case where the conduct of the defendant's insurers is so outrageous that the defence should be struck out. The case, therefore, has to be tried. It would be artificial and undesirable for the actual evidence, which is relevant and

admissible, not to be placed before the judge who has the task of trying the case. We accept Mr Owen's submission that to exclude the use of the evidence would *a* create a wholly undesirable situation. Fresh medical experts would have to be instructed on both sides. Evidence which is relevant would have to be concealed from them, perhaps resulting in a misdiagnosis; and it would not be possible to cross-examine the claimant appropriately. For these reasons we do not consider it would be right to interfere with Judge Harris's decision not to exclude the *b* evidence.

[29] Mr Weir's submission that we should determine the issue on the basis of the facts as they were before District Judge Wartnaby is not realistic. None the less, it is right that we should make clear that we do not accept that the criticism of the claimant's legal advisers for deciding not to reveal the contents of the video films in issue to their medical experts is justified. It was sensible to defer doing so *c* until it was known whether the evidence could be used. While not excluding the evidence it is appropriate to make clear that the conduct of the insurers was improper and not justified. We disagree with the indication by Judge Harris to the contrary. The fact that the insurers may have been motivated by a desire to achieve what they considered would be a just result does not justify either the *d* commission of trespass or the contravention of the claimant's privacy which took place. We come to this conclusion irrespective of whether Mr Weir is right in contending that in this particular case the evidence could be obtained by other means.

[30] Excluding the evidence is not, moreover, the only weapon in the court's armoury. The court has other steps it can take to discourage conduct of the type *e* of which complaint is made. In particular it can reflect its disapproval in the orders for costs which it makes. In this appeal, we therefore propose, because the conduct of the insurers gave rise to the litigation over admissibility of the evidence which has followed upon their conduct, to order the defendants to pay the costs of these proceedings to resolve this issue before District Judge *f* Wartnaby, Judge Harris and this court even though we otherwise dismiss the appeal. This is subject to Mr Owen having an opportunity to persuade us to do otherwise. In addition, we would indicate to the trial judge that when he comes to deal with the question of costs he should take into account the defendant's conduct which is the subject of this appeal when deciding the appropriate order for costs. He may consider the costs of the inquiry agent should not be recovered. *g* If he concludes, as the complainant now contends, that there is an innocent explanation for what is shown as to the claimant's control of her movements then this is a matter which should be reflected in costs, perhaps by ordering the defendants to pay the costs throughout on an indemnity basis. In giving effect to the overriding objective, and taking into account the wider interests of the *h* administration of justice, the court must while doing justice between the parties, also deter improper conduct of a party while conducting litigation. We do not pretend that this is a perfect reconciliation of the conflicting public interests. It is not; but at least the solution does not ignore the insurer's conduct.

[31] Subject to hearing further argument on costs, the appeal is dismissed. *j*

Appeal dismissed.

Kate O'Hanlon   Barrister.

a

R v Field

R v Young

[2002] EWCA Crim 2913

b

COURT OF APPEAL, CRIMINAL DIVISION

KAY LJ, GRIGSON AND OUSELEY JJ

4 JULY, 12 DECEMBER 2002

c
Sentence – Disqualification – Order disqualifying individual from working with children – Whether such an order could be made in respect of offence committed before implementation of statutory provisions creating order – Criminal Justice and Court Services Act 2000, s 28 – Human Rights Act 1998, Sch 1, Pt I, art 7.

d
In two cases raising the same point of law, the defendants, F and Y, were convicted of, or pleaded guilty to, various sexual offences. Those offences had been committed before the implementation of the Criminal Justice and Court Services Act 2000, but sentencing took place after the Act came into force. Section 28[a] of the Act required the court to make an order disqualifying an individual from working with children if either of two qualifying conditions were satisfied. The first qualifying condition, which both defendants satisfied,

e
required, inter alia, that the individual had been convicted of an offence against a child. There was no such requirement for a conviction in the second qualifying condition. The court could not make a s 28 order if it were satisfied that it was unlikely that the individual would commit any further offence against a child. In each case, the sentencing judge made a disqualification order under s 28. On an

f
appeal by F against sentence, he contended that a such an order was a 'penalty' within the meaning of art 7[b] of the European Convention for the Protection of Human Rights and Fundamental Freedoms 1950 (as set out in Sch 1 to the Human Rights Act 1998); that, if imposed in respect of an offence committed before s 28 had come into force, such an order would be in breach of art 7 of the convention as constituting a heavier penalty than the one applicable at the time

g
that the criminal offence had been committed; and that, in order to render s 28 compatible with convention rights, it had to be construed as applying only to convictions in respect of offences committed on or after the day that the relevant Part of the 2000 Act had come into force. The success of an application by Y for leave to appeal against sentence depended on the outcome of F's appeal.

h
Held – A disqualification order could be made under s 28 of the 2000 Act based on an offence committed before the Act came into force. Such an order did not constitute a penalty under art 7 of the convention. It was of considerable importance that a conviction was not a necessary condition for the making of a s 28 order. When consideration was given to the nature and purpose of such an

j
order, it pointed overwhelmingly to that being for preventative rather than punitive effect. The same order was made whether or not a person was convicted, and the making of the order had no regard to the extent or seriousness

---

a   Section 28 is set out at [11], below

b   Article 7, so far as material, is set out at [18], below

of the offending but rather to whether a repetition of the conduct was likely. It
followed that art 7 did not require the court to interpret s 28 in a way that would
make it apply only to convictions for offences committed after the 2000 Act had
come into force. Accordingly, F's appeal would be dismissed and Y's application
would be refused (see [58], [62], below).

R v M, R v Kerr, R v H [2002] 1 WLR 824, Gough v Chief Constable of the Derbyshire
Constabulary [2002] 2 All ER 985 and R (on the application of McCann) v Crown Court
at Manchester, R v Clingham v Kensington and Chelsea Royal London BC [2002] 4
All ER 593 applied.

Welch v UK (1995) 20 EHRR 247 distinguished.

Notes

For the prohibition of retrospective laws, see 8(2) Halsbury's Laws (4th edn
reissue) para 148.

For the Human Rights Act 1998, Sch 1, Pt I, art 7, see 7 Halsbury's Statutes (4th
edn) (2002 reissue) 554.

Cases referred to in judgment

B v Chief Constable of Avon and Somerset Constabulary [2001] 1 All ER 562, [2001] 1
WLR 340, DC.

Gough v Chief Constable of the Derbyshire Constabulary [2002] EWCA Civ 351, [2002]
2 All ER 985, [2002] 3 WLR 289; affg [2001] EWHC Admin 554, [2001] 4 All ER
289, [2002] QB 459, [2001] 3 WLR 1392, DC.

Ibbotson v UK (1998) 27 EHRR CD 332, E Com HR.

Jamil v France (1995) 21 EHRR 65, [1995] ECHR 15917/89, ECt HR.

R v Antoine [2000] 2 All ER 208, [2001] 1 AC 340, [2000] 2 WLR 703, HL; affg [2001]
1 AC 340, [1999] 3 WLR 1204, CA.

R v M, R v Kerr, R v H [2001] EWCA Crim 2024, [2002] 1 WLR 824; affd sub nom
R v H [2003] UKHL 1, [2003] 1 All ER 497, [2003] 1 WLR 411.

R (on the application of McCann) v Crown Court at Manchester, R v Clingham v
Kensington and Chelsea Royal London BC [2002] UKHL 39, [2002] 4 All ER 593,
[2002] 3 WLR 1313; affg [2001] EWCA Civ 281, [2001] 4 All ER 264, [2001] 1
WLR 1084.

Welch v UK (1995) 20 EHRR 247, [1995] ECHR 17440/90, ECt HR.

Cases referred to in skeleton arguments

Adamson v UK (1999) 28 EHRR CD 209, ECt HR.

Brindle v HW Smith (Cabinets) Ltd [1973] 1 All ER 230, [1973] ICR 12, [1972] 1 WLR
1653, CA.

DPP v B Lamb, DPP v A Lamb, DPP v R Lamb [1941] 2 All ER 499, [1941] 2 KB 89, DC.

Han v Customs and Excise Comrs, Martins v Customs and Excise Comrs, Morris v
Customs and Excise Comrs [2001] EWCA Civ 1040, [2001] 4 All ER 687, [2001] 1
WLR 2253.

M v Italy (1991) 70 DR 59, E Com HR.

Master Ladies Tailors Organisation v Minister of Labour and National Service [1950] 2
All ER 525.

R v G (offences against children) (2001) Times, 12 November 2001, CA.

R v Inhabitants of St Mary, Whitechapel (1848) 12 QB 120.

R v Oliver [1943] 2 All ER 800, [1944] KB 68, CCA.

R v Vine (1875) LR 10 QB 195, DC.

a *Securities and Investments Board and another v Financial Intermediaries Managers and Brokers Regulatory Association Ltd* [1991] 4 All ER 398, [1992] Ch 268, [1991] 3 WLR 889.
Solicitor's Clerk, Re A [1957] 3 All ER 617, [1957] 1 WLR 1219, DC.

Appeal against sentence and application for leave to appeal against sentence

b
R v Field

Brian John Field appealed from the order of Judge Simpson, made in the Crown Court at Maidstone on 11 May 2001 pursuant to s 28 of the Criminal Justice and Court Services Act 2000, disqualifying him from working with children. The order formed part of the sentence imposed on Field following his conviction on
c 6 April 2001 of five counts of indecent assault and one count of indecency with a child. The Secretary of State for the Home Department intervened in the appeal. The facts, so far as material, are set out in the judgment of the court.

R v Young

d Alfred Young applied for leave to appeal from the order of Judge Mitchell, made in the Crown Court at Wolverhampton on 16 November 2001 pursuant to s 28 of the Criminal Justice and Court Services Act 2000, disqualifying him from working with children. The order formed part of the sentence imposed on Young following his plea of guilty on 15 October 2001 to two offences of indecent assault. The facts, so far as material, are set out in the judgment of the court.
e

Richard Bendall (assigned by the *Registrar of Criminal Appeals*) for Field.
Jonathan Crow (instructed by the *Treasury Solicitor*) for the Secretary of State.
Young was not represented.

f
Cur adv vult

12 December 2002. The following judgment of the court was delivered.

KAY LJ.
g
[1] The court has before it two cases that raise the same point of law in relation to s 28 of the Criminal Justice and Court Services Act 2000. The question is whether a disqualification order can be made under s 28, disqualifying an adult from working with children, based on an offence committed before the 2000 Act came into force.

h [2] In the first case, on 6 April 2001 Brian John Field was convicted at the Crown Court at Maidstone on five counts of indecent assault and one count of indecency with a child. The offences had been committed between 1 July and 3 September 2000, which was before the 2000 Act came into force on 11 January 2001. On 11 May 2001, he was sentenced by Judge Simpson to four years' imprisonment on each count, such sentences to be concurrent with one another. In addition the judge made an order under s 28 of the 2000 Act disqualifying him from working with children indefinitely.

[3] He sought leave to appeal against conviction and sentence. Leave to appeal against conviction was refused by the single judge and on 17 January 2002 the court rejected his renewed application. The application for leave to appeal against sentence, which was confined to the order under s 28, was referred to the

court by the registrar and leave was granted. In view of the difficult issues raised, the court required assistance from the Crown and the matter was adjourned. The *a* Secretary of State for the Home Department sought and was granted leave to intervene, and it is the appeal against that aspect of the sentence with which we are now concerned.

[4] In the second case, on 15 October 2001 Alfred Young pleaded guilty at the Crown Court at Wolverhampton to two offences of indecent assault. He was *b* sentenced on 16 November by Judge Mitchell to an extended term of five years' imprisonment of which the custodial part was two years. He too was disqualified indefinitely under s 28 of the 2000 Act from working with children. In his case the two offences were committed between the 21 August 1999 and 20 August 2000, again before the coming into force of the relevant part of the 2000 Act.

[5] Alfred Young sought leave to appeal against his sentence. His grounds *c* challenged both the extended prison sentence and the disqualification order. The application was referred directly to the full court by the Registrar and on 14 March 2002 the court considered his application. It refused the application in respect of the extended sentence but adjourned consideration of the application relating to the disqualification order for it to be heard together with Field's case. *d* Arrangements were made for the skeleton arguments in Field's case to be made available to Young's counsel so that he could, if he wished, make representations to the court to add to the arguments advanced. No such representations have been made and since the point is an identical one, determination of Field's appeal will be determinative of the decision in Young's application.

[6] It is wholly unnecessary to record the facts of either case because nothing *e* turns upon the circumstances of the convictions already set out. In any event they are recorded in the earlier judgments of this court to which reference has already been made.

[7] Two issues arise: (1) whether a disqualification order under s 28 of the 2000 Act constitutes 'a penalty' such that art 7 of the European Convention on Human *f* Rights and Fundamental Freedoms 1950 (as set out in Sch 1 to the Human Rights Act 1998) precludes any such order being made in relation to an offence committed before the section came into force; and (2) whether on its true interpretation the 2000 Act was intended to apply to pre-enactment offences.

[8] As Mr Crow, on behalf of the Secretary of State comments, these issues are potentially of great significance. Largely because of the age and the vulnerability *g* of the victims, sexual offences relating to children are often reported and prosecuted many years after the offences in question were committed. Accordingly these questions will arise not merely in the short term but for many years to come.

[9] The arguments advanced on behalf of the appellant and the applicant are *h* acknowledged by the Secretary of State to be arguments that have received significant support in the past. When the 2000 Act was enacted, the Home Office view was that such a disqualification order could not be made relating to a pre-enactment offence. This view was thereafter expressed in circulars issued by the Crown Prosecution Service to prosecutors and by the Lord Chancellor's *j* Department to the Court Service. However, both the Home Office and the circulars recognised that interpretation of the statute was ultimately a matter for decision by the courts.

[10] *Archbold's Criminal Pleading, Evidence and Practice* (2001 edn) (Third Supplement) p 49 (para 5–562a) lent further support stating that the 2000 Act 'has been drafted in such a way as to make it clear that it has no application to an

a offence committed before the commencement date'. Both the 2002 and 2003 editions are in less emphatic terms but maintain the same standpoint saying, 'it appears that (s 28) can apply only to persons convicted of offences committed on or after' the commencement date. An article in Criminal Law Week (issue 41) reached a similar conclusion.

b THE RELEVANT LEGISLATION

[11] Section 28 of the 2000 Act provides:

'(1) This section applies where either of the conditions set out below is satisfied in the case of an individual.

c (2) The first condition is that—(a) the individual is convicted of an offence against a child committed when he was 18 or over, and (b) a qualifying sentence is imposed by a senior court in respect of the conviction.

(3) The second condition is that—(a) the individual is charged with an offence against a child committed when he was aged 18 or over, and (b) a relevant order is made by a senior court in respect of the act or omission

d charged against him as the offence.

(4) Subject to subsection (5), the court must order the individual to be disqualified from working with children.

(5) An order shall not be made under this section if the court is satisfied, having regard to all the circumstances, that it is unlikely that the individual

e will commit any further offence against a child.

(6) If the court does not make an order under this section, it must state its reasons for not doing so and cause those reasons to be included in the record of the proceedings.'

f [12] An 'offence against a child' is defined in s 26 and Sch 4 and includes various specified sexual and violent offences against children. A 'qualifying sentence' is defined by s 30 to be 'a sentence of imprisonment for a term of 12 months or more' in the case of an adult. A 'relevant order' for the purpose of the condition contained in s 28(3) is defined by s 30 as either 'an order made by the Crown Court ... that the individual in question be admitted to hospital' or 'a

g guardianship order'.

[13] By s 35, it is an offence for a person who has been disqualified under s 28 to seek or engage in a defined range of work with children. The areas of work are extensive covering not only those that might immediately come to mind but also such activities as baby-sitting and being on a school's governing body. The

h prohibition applies to both paid and unpaid work. It is further an offence for any other person to offer or provide work to a disqualified person.

[14] Section 31(1) provides for a right of appeal against the disqualification order imposed following conviction 'as if the order were a sentence'. Section 38(1) provides that a disqualification order 'is not a sentence for the

j purposes of' the Rehabilitation of Offenders Act 1974.

[15] An order under s 28 is of indefinite duration. Provision is made by s 32 for review of the disqualification. An adult who is subject to a disqualification order may apply after a minimum of ten years to the tribunal established by s 9 of the Protection of Children Act 1999 for the order to cease to have effect. Section 32(3) of the 2000 Act provides:

'If the Tribunal is satisfied that the individual is suitable to work with
children, it must direct that the order is to cease to have effect; otherwise it   *a*
must dismiss the application.'

[16] Section 34 provides for a chief officer of police or a director of social
services of a local authority to apply to the High Court for restoration of an order
that has ceased to have effect when—

b

'the individual has acted in such a way (whether before or after the order
ceased to be in force) as to give reasonable cause to believe that an order
under this section is necessary to protect children in general, or any children
in particular, from serious harm from him.'

[17] The relevant parts of the 2000 Act were brought into effect on 11 January   *c*
2001 by the Criminal Justice and Court Services Act 2000 (Commencement No 1)
Order 2000, SI 2000/3302. The order made no transitional provisions and
provides no assistance on the issues that the court has to determine.

THE ECHR ISSUE

[18] The argument advanced on behalf of the appellant and the applicant is   *d*
that a disqualification order is a penalty within the meaning of art 7 of the
convention and thus if imposed in respect of an offence committed before the
relevant statutory provisions came into effect would amount to a breach of
art 7(1) being the imposition of 'a heavier penalty ... than the one that was
applicable at the time the criminal offence was committed'. Since, under s 3 of
the 1998 Act, the court is required to read and give effect to primary and   *e*
subordinate legislation in a way which is compatible with convention rights so far
as it is possible so to do, it is submitted that s 28 of the 2000 Act should be
interpreted as only applying to convictions in respect of offences committed on
or after the day when the relevant part of the Act came into force.

[19] On behalf of the Secretary of State it is accepted that the argument is valid   *f*
provided that a disqualification order is a penalty for the purposes of art 7. Thus
the issue turns on the meaning of the word 'penalty' in art 7.

[20] It is common ground between the parties that this is an autonomous
concept under the convention defined by reference to criteria closely analogous
to those applicable to the concept of a 'criminal charge' under art 6. Both counsel
have drawn attention to the leading case in the European Court of Human Rights   *g*
concerning the determination of whether an order is or is not a penalty: *Welch v
UK* (1995) 20 EHRR 247. Mr Crow on behalf of the Secretary of State has distilled
from that judgment the following criteria. (i) The starting point is whether the
measure is imposed following a criminal conviction (see paras 28 and 29 of the
judgment). (ii) The nature and purpose of the measure are also relevant (paras 28   *h*
and 30). (iii) Its characterisation under national law is relevant (paras 28 and 31).
(iv) The procedures involved in the making and implementation of the measure
are relevant (para 28). (v) Its severity is relevant (paras 28 and 32). (vi) The
court will look at the substance, rather than the form, in determining whether the
measure forms part of a 'regime of punishment' (paras 27, 33 and 34).
[21] Mr Bendall for the appellant agrees that this list properly reflects the   *j*
considerations indicated by the court and thus the task facing this court is to apply
each of these criteria to s 28 of the 2000 Act.

[22] Mr Crow in his submissions to the court was minded to concede that a
disqualification order was an order which could only be imposed following a
criminal conviction. However, when the court invited his assistance on s 28(3),

a   he recognised that his argument in this respect was stronger than he suggested. Section 28(1) and (3) effectively require the making of an order, subject to s 28(5), where either a jury returns a special verdict of 'not guilty by reason of insanity' or where a person has been found to be under a disability under s 4 of the Criminal Procedure (Insanity) Act 1964 and it is determined on the available evidence that he did the act or made the omission charged against him pursuant to s 4A of the

b same Act, and in either case the court makes an order that he be admitted to hospital or a guardianship order. Whilst there are purposes for which such an order is treated as if it was a conviction (see s 25 of the Criminal Justice and Public Order Act 1994, restrictions on the grant of bail for serious offences), such a finding is not a conviction and cannot justify the imposition of a penalty although it may require the making of an order for the protection of the public. An order

c made because the condition under s 28(3) is satisfied is indistinguishable in its terms from an order made following conviction.

    [23] In *Gough v Chief Constable of the Derbyshire Constabulary* [2001] EWHC Admin 554, [2001] 4 All ER 289, [2002] QB 459, the Divisional Court considered whether football banning orders under s 14A of the Football Spectators Act 1989

d were a penalty. Section 14A provided for the making of an order where a person was convicted of a relevant offence. Section 14B made further provision for a chief officer of police to apply for such an order where a person had at any time 'caused or contributed to any violence or disorder in the United Kingdom or elsewhere'. There was no requirement that a conviction should precede the making of an order under s 14B.

e   [24] In his judgment, Laws LJ said ([2001] 4 All ER 289 at [42]):

    '(2) The order is not made as part of the process of distributive criminal justice. Under s 14B there is no requirement of a criminal conviction, so that the *Welch* starting point is not met. In s 14A, the existence of a relevant

f   conviction is in my judgment no more than a gateway criterion for the making of the order, equivalent to the provision in s 14B(4)(a) when no conviction is involved.'

    [25] Laws LJ went on to point to the fact that s 14A(4)(a) provided that a football banning order could only be made 'in addition' to a sentence thereby

g contrasting the banning order with the sentence. That is to an extent mirrored in the 2000 Act, which provides for an appeal against a disqualification order under s 28 'as if it were a sentence imposed following conviction'.

    [26] The conclusions of Laws LJ in this regard were specifically indorsed on appeal by the Court of Appeal (see [2002] EWCA Civ 351 at [89], [2002] 2 All ER

h 985 at [89], [2002] 3 WLR 289).

    [27] Under s 28 of the 2000 Act, a conviction is 'a gateway criterion' in the sense described by Laws LJ for the making of a disqualification order but it is not the only such criterion: a special verdict or a finding in respect of a person under a disability that they did the act or made the omission charged against them will

j require the making of a disqualification order subject to s 28(5).

    [28] Mr Bendall contended in argument that these other circumstances give rise to an 'analogous situation'. We do not accept that this is so. In neither of these other cases is there a conclusion that would merit the imposition of any penal provision even though restriction of the right of the individual may be demonstrated to be necessary in order to protect others. This view gains the strongest possible support from a decision which Mr Bendall very properly

thought ought to be drawn to the court's attention following the hearing as it bore upon these issues but had not been referred to in argument.   *a*

[**29**] In *R v M, R v Kerr, R v H* [2001] EWCA Crim 2024, [2002] 1 WLR 824, this court had to consider whether, following a finding that a defendant was unfit to plead, proceedings to determine whether he did the act charged against him were incompatible with art 6 of the convention. The court thus had to determine whether such proceedings were criminal proceedings within the meaning of   *b* art 6. The court concluded that they were not because they could not result in a conviction or the imposition of a penalty. Giving the judgment of the court, the Vice-President of the Criminal Division, Rose LJ, said ([2002] 1 WLR 824):

'[19] In our judgment, the criminal charge provisions of article 6 do not apply to proceedings which cannot result in a conviction. The object of the   *c* Convention is to protect the citizen against abuse of his rights by the state. The protection afforded by Article 6 is unnecessary if the proceedings in question cannot lead to the conviction and punishment of the accused. A procedure that can lead only to an acquittal of a criminal charge is not within article 6 … We find some support for this approach in that, as mentioned below, the European Court of Human Rights has never held proceedings to   *d* be criminal if they cannot result in the imposition of a penalty. Proceedings that can only result in an acquittal cannot result in a penalty. If, therefore, proceedings under sections 4 and 4A are to be held to be criminal, it must be some reason other than that an acquittal may result from them.

[20] … if an accused is found to have committed the act, the verdict is not   *e* one of guilty, but a finding that he did the act or made the omission charged against him … The finding of a jury that an accused person has committed the act lacks a finding as to intent. It cannot, therefore, be a finding of guilt of the offence. Expressions such as "guilty" and "convicted" are noticeably absent from these provisions. Significantly, if an accused is found to be unfit and to have committed the act charged against him, and subsequently   *f* recovers, he may be tried for the criminal offence in question … As was held in *R v Antoine* ([2000] 2 All ER 208, [2001] 1 AC 340), once it has been determined under section 4(5) that the accused person is under a disability, the trial terminates and he is no longer liable to be convicted.

[21] Furthermore, the orders available to the court under section 5(2) do   *g* not include any punishment or any order that can be seen as retributive or deterrent. With the exception of an absolute discharge, they are concerned with the treatment and care of the accused …

[26] Lastly, although proceedings under section 4A involve the determination of facts which may constitute a criminal offence, this, in our   *h* judgment, is irrelevant. Civil and disciplinary proceedings often involve allegations that a person has committed acts which constitute a criminal offence. That does not transform such proceedings into criminal proceedings …'

[**30**] The court in *R v M* thus concluded that such a finding was not a   *j* conviction and that an order made in consequence of the finding was not a penalty. For these reasons the court concluded that the proceedings were not criminal proceedings within the meaning of art 6. Since under s 28 of the 2000 Act, an identical order is made following such a finding to that made following conviction, it suggests strongly that this provision is not penal within the meaning of art 7.

a   [31] Mr Crow points to the fact that when an order has ceased to have effect
as a result of a review by the tribunal under s 32, it can be restored under s 34
without any requirement for a further conviction. It is sufficient that the court
concludes that the conduct of the person gives 'reasonable cause to believe that
an order ... is necessary to protect children in general, or any children in
particular, from serious harm from him'. Since the restriction can be re-imposed
b   without the necessity of there being any further conviction, it is suggested that
this again supports the view that it is not a penalty.

[32] The next element to be considered is the nature and purpose of the order.
Mr Bendall submits that the nature of the measure is an indefinite disqualification
from working with children which carries with it up to five years' imprisonment
or a fine for breach of the order. He accepts that the purpose is 'presumably the
c   protection of children' but submits that this is not conclusive. He points to the
fact that in *Welch v UK* (1995) 20 EHRR 247 the purpose of the Drug Trafficking
Offences Act 1986 was to prevent future trafficking but this did not prevent it
from being a penalty. He refers to the judgment and that part which reads (at 262
(para 30)):

d   'The preventive purpose of confiscating property that might be available
for use in future drug trafficking operations as well as the purpose of
ensuring that crime does not pay are evident from the ministerial statements
that were made to Parliament at the time of the introduction of the
legislation ... However, it cannot be excluded that legislation which confers
e   such broad powers of confiscation on the courts also pursues the aim of
punishing the offender. Indeed, the aims of prevention and reparation are
consistent with a punitive purpose and may be seen as constituent elements
of the very notion of punishment.'

[33] He also draws attention to *Jamil v France* (1995) 21 EHRR 65 where the
f   European Court of Human Rights rejected arguments that prison terms in
default of payment of customs fines were not punitive because they were not
intended to punish but to compel discharge of a civil obligation, and that they
were not classified as penalties under French law. The court reiterated that it
must remain free to go behind appearance and detect the substance of the
provision.
g   [34] Mr Crow submits that an order under s 28 is plainly not penal in its nature
since it neither restricts the offender's liberty, nor involves any fine or
confiscation of property. It merely involves a restriction on certain activities in
relation to children.

[35] It does not seem to us that a matter is not penal in nature merely because
h   it does not restrict liberty or impose a fine or other financial consequence. By
way of example, a disqualification from driving a motor car does no more than
restrict a person's right to a particular form of activity and it does have a
preventive element to it. None the less we should have thought that it was
clearly penal in its nature. It is imposed by reference to the conduct that led to
j   the conviction and without necessarily any relationship to the danger a person
may represent when driving a motor car.

[36] It is difficult to divorce the nature of the measure from its purpose and
Mr Crow submits that the purpose of an order under s 28 is plainly preventive
and not punitive. He points to the acceptance of this by Mr Bendall and suggests
that the factors which cause that concession are important to the overall
conclusion in this matter. He highlights the following specific points: (i) The

long title to the 2000 Act expressly recites that one of its purposes is 'to make
further provision for the protection of children'. (ii) Part II of the 2000 Act, in
which s 28 appears, is itself headed 'Protection of Children'. (iii) The effect of a
disqualification order is plainly to minimise an offender's ability to work with
children in certain defined circumstances, in order to reduce the risk of
re-offending. (iv) It is submitted that it also significant that, under s 28(5), the
court is not required to make an order if, having regard to all the circumstances,
it concludes that it is unlikely that the individual will commit any further offence
against a child. In other words, the grounds for making, or refraining from
making, a disqualification order are based not on the gravity of the offence for
which the individual has been sentenced, but on the risk of his re-offending in the
future. This, it is submitted, is the hallmark of a preventive, rather than a punitive
measure. (v) The effect of s 28(5) in relation to adults is complementary to the
provisions contained within s 29 which relates to juveniles who have been
convicted. In respect of a juvenile, under s 29(4) an order is only to be made if it
is likely that he will commit another offence against a child. Once again, it is
submitted the whole basis for making an order is the risk of re-offending, not
punishment for past offences. (vi) The power of the tribunal to direct the
disqualification order be set aside can only be exercised if it considers that the
individual 'is suitable to work with children'. Once again it is submitted that this
emphasises the preventive nature of the order. (vii) Finally, the duty of the court
to restore a disqualification order under s 34 is triggered if the individual has acted
in such a way as to give reasonable cause to believe that an order under the
section is 'necessary to protect children in general, or any children in particular,
from serious harm from him'. Yet again, the purely protective purposes of the
disqualification regime under the 2000 Act are said to be clear.

[37] Mr Crow suggests that a confiscation order under the Drug Trafficking
Offences Act 1986 is clearly distinguishable from an order under s 28. He submits
that the passage from the judgment quoted above merely illustrates a self-evident
truth, namely that a punitive sanction may also contain a protective element and
that a protective measure may also contain a punitive sanction. However this, he
suggests, does not assist the court in determining the specific issue in a particular
case.

[38] The decision in *Welch v UK* (1995) 20 EHRR 247 that the measure in
question was a penalty was, it is submitted, prompted by a number of
considerations not in any way present in the making of a disqualification order
under s 28: (i) the legislative presumption that all property passing through the
defendant's hands in a six-year period was the proceeds of drug trafficking unless
proved otherwise; (ii) the confiscation order was not limited to the element of
enrichment or profit; (iii) the discretion of the trial judge in fixing the amount of
confiscation to take into account the degree of culpability of the accused; (iv) the
possibility of automatic imprisonment in the event of a failure to pay.

[39] Next we consider characterisation under domestic law and the procedure
involved in the making and implementation of the order. Mr Bendall contends
that a disqualification order is characterised under domestic law as a criminal
measure because it can only be imposed by a criminal court.

[40] Mr Crow submits that the reason why it is initially imposed by a criminal
court is simply one of administrative convenience. He points to the fact that the
triggering event for making such an order is a criminal conviction or one of the
other orders that require the making of such an order. There would be no
administrative purpose to be served in referring the matter to some other

a tribunal at that stage since the criminal court has just made the necessary determination and is best placed to consider any issue under s 28(5). He submits that it is also for the same reason that a disqualification order is treated 'as if it were a part of the sentence passed on him' for the purposes of an appeal. He then contrasts the position to that stage later on when the setting aside of an order is to be considered by the tribunal rather than a criminal court and the possible

b restoration of the order once it has been set aside is to be considered by the High Court rather than a criminal court. In addition he points to the fact that for the purposes of the Rehabilitation of Offenders Act 1974 the order is not treated as part of the sentence. For these reasons he submits that a disqualification order is not characterised as a criminal sanction under domestic law.

[41] We are further bound to have regard to the severity of the order. There
c is no doubt that the order can have a major impact upon a person's life. It may prevent that person from pursuing the only employment for which they have been trained. The order runs indefinitely and no application can be made for ten years to discharge it.

[42] However many orders that are undoubtedly civil in nature and not a
d penalty can have severe consequences and whilst this element must be borne in mind in assessing the true nature of the order, it cannot be the only factor to be considered.

[43] In *R (on the application of McCann) v Crown Court at Manchester, R v Clingham v Kensington and Chelsea Royal London BC* [2001] EWCA Civ 281, [2001] 4 All ER 264, [2001] 1 WLR 1084 (quoted with approval on appeal to the House of
e Lords by Lord Steyn [2002] UKHL 39 at [25], [2002] 4 All ER 593 at [25], [2002] 3 WLR 1313) Lord Phillips of Worth Matravers MR observed ([2001] 4 All ER 264 at [39]):

f 'Many injunctions in civil proceedings operate severely upon those against whom they are ordered. In matrimonial proceedings a husband may be ordered to leave his home and not to have contact with his children. Such an order may be made as a consequence of violence which amounted to criminal conduct. But such an order is imposed not for the purpose of punishment but for protection of the family. This demonstrates that, when considering whether an order imposes a penalty or punishment, it is
g necessary to look beyond its consequence and to consider its purpose.'

[44] In addition to these submissions on the criteria as explained in *Welch's* case, our attention has been drawn to a number of authorities relating to other comparable legislative regimes. It is not suggested by either side that they can be determinative of this matter but Mr Crow submits that they provide strong
h support for the Secretary of State's argument that a s 28 disqualification order is a penalty.

[45] We have already made reference to *Gough's* case in which both the Divisional Court ([2001] 4 All ER 289, [2002] QB 459) and the Court of Appeal ([2002] 2 All ER 985, [2002] 3 WLR 289) concluded that a football banning order
j was not a penalty within the meaning of art 7 of the convention whether or not the order had been made following a conviction. Thus such an order can be made even where the conduct relied upon occurred before the relevant date.

[46] Mr Bendall seeks to distinguish a disqualification order under s 28 from a football banning order because a football banning order under s 14B of the Football Spectators Act 1989 can be imposed without any prior conviction. However, following *R v M* [2002] 1 WLR 824 this distinction cannot be

maintained because a s 28 disqualification order can be made in circumstances
where the Court of Appeal has clearly determined that there is no conviction   *a*
following a finding that a person who is not fit to stand trial did the act or made
the omission charged. In each of these cases where there is no conviction, there
will need to be a determination of the facts to satisfy the relevant condition and
hence no significant distinction is to be found between the two in this regard.

[47] Mr Bendall next suggests there is a distinction to be drawn because a   *b*
football banning order can only be made if there are reasonable grounds for
believing that the making of an order will help to prevent violence or disorder in
connection with regulated football matches. A s 28 disqualification order, he
suggests, is mandatory save in limited circumstances. However it is the
qualification that there are limited circumstances that has to be considered. An
order will not be made if the court is satisfied that the individual will not commit   *c*
further offences against a child. Thus the only distinction is that there is a
rebuttable presumption in favour of an order in the case of a disqualification
under s 28, which is not to be found in considering a football banning order. But,
as Mr Crow submits, the substance of the court's decision in each case is the
same, namely whether there is a risk of re-offending.

[48] In *B v Chief Constable of Avon and Somerset Constabulary* [2001] 1 All ER 562,   *d*
[2001] 1 WLR 340, the Divisional Court concluded that an application for a sex
offender order under s 2 of the Crime and Disorder Act 1998 was an application
in civil proceedings involving preventive measures rather than criminal
punishment. Lord Bingham of Cornhill CJ said ([2001] 1 All ER 562 at 571–572,
[2001] 1 WLR 340 at 352 (para 25)):   *e*

> 'There is no room for doubt about the mischief against which this
> legislation is directed, which is the risk of re-offending by sex offenders who
> have offended in the past and have shown a continuing propensity to offend.
> Parliament might have decided to wait until, if at all, the offender did offend
> again and then appropriate charges could be laid on the basis of that further   *f*
> offending. Before 1998 there was effectively no choice but to act in that way.
> But the obvious disadvantage was that, by the time the offender had
> offended again, some victim had suffered. The rationale of s 2 was, by means
> of an injunctive order, to seek to avoid the contingency of any further
> suffering by any further victim. It would also of course be to the advantage   *g*
> of a defendant if he were to be saved from further offending. As in the case
> of a civil injunction, a breach of the court's order may attract a sanction. But,
> also as in the case of a civil injunction, the order, although restraining the
> defendant from doing that which is prohibited, imposes no penalty or
> disability upon him. I am accordingly satisfied that, as a matter of English
> domestic law, the application is a civil proceeding, as Parliament   *h*
> undoubtedly intended it to be.'

[49] It is to be observed that the order in that case upheld by the Divisional
Court prohibited the appellant from: (1) seeking to communicate with a child or
young person under the age of 16 years, (2) associating with or befriending a child
or young person under the age of 16 years, (3) residing in any private dwelling   *j*
where a child or young person under the age of 16 years was present, or
(4) undertaking any activity (paid, voluntary or recreational) which by its nature
was likely to bring him into contact with a child or young person under the age
of 16 years. In terms of the severity of the restrictions imposed by the order, it
was at least as far-reaching as those under a s 28 disqualification order but the

a severity of the consequences for the appellant did not in any way translate it into a penalty.

[50] In *Ibbotson v UK* (1998) 27 EHRR CD 332, the European Commission of Human Rights has ruled that the requirement to register under the Sex Offenders Act 1997 does not involve the imposition of a penalty within the meaning of art 7 of the convention. Mr Bendall seeks to distinguish this decision on the basis that

b the obligation is imposed as a matter of law, not as a part of the sentencing process. In one sense that is correct: the requirement to register will take effect whether or not the court says anything about it. However, a s 28 disqualification order is mandatory unless the court concludes that it is unlikely that the person will commit any further offence against a child. It is not immediately obvious why this distinction should in itself lead to a different conclusion.

c
[51] Mr Bendall also seeks to distinguish *Ibbotson v UK* on the basis that the restrictions imposed under a disqualification order under s 28 are far greater than the requirements in respect of registration. That is undoubtedly right and it is a factor to be considered in the overall equation but, for reasons already explained, it cannot be determinative of the question.

d
[52] Finally we were referred to *R (on the application of McCann) v Crown Court at Manchester*. That case had been heard in the Court of Appeal at the time of the hearing but judgment was awaited in the House of Lords. We were asked to postpone our judgment pending the decision of the House of Lords and this explains the delay in our giving judgment. We invited counsel to make written

e representations on the decision and we have received such representations from Mr Crow. Mr Crow provided Mr Bendall with a copy of his representations and Mr Bendall has indicated that there is nothing that he feels he can add to his earlier submissions.

[53] In *McCann's* case, the Court of Appeal and the House of Lords had to

f consider antisocial behaviour orders made under s 1 of the Crime and Disorder Act 1998. The question raised in that case was whether such proceedings were to be classified as civil or criminal in domestic law and whether they constituted a 'criminal charge' within art 6 of the convention. It is accepted that what amounts to a penalty under art 7 is closely analogous to the concept of a 'criminal charge' under art 6.

g [54] In *McCann's* case [2002] 4 All ER 593, [2002] 3 WLR 1313 the House of Lords recognised that s 1 of the Crime and Disorder Act 1998 formed part of a wider raft of legislation in which Parliament employed the technique of the civil injunction to deal with novel social problems where the criminal law itself did not provide adequate protection for the public (see [2002] 4 All ER 593 at [17]–[18], [42], [85] per Lord Steyn, Lord Hope of Craighead and Lord Hutton, respectively). We have no doubt that s 28 of the 2000 Act has to be seen in much the same light and again employs injunctive remedies to supplement the normal criminal sanctions which are perceived as providing inadequate protection for children.

h [55] One of the principal reasons for concluding that the proceedings in *McCann's* case were classified in domestic law as civil and not criminal was that the nature of an antisocial behaviour order is not penal and its purpose is not punitive. It is designed to protect members of the public and prevent future misconduct not to punish past misconduct. (See in this regard Lord Steyn at [19]–[24] and Lord Hutton at [94]–[95].) Mr Crow submits that exactly the same purpose can be discerned in relation to the disqualification order in this case.

[56] In *McCann's* case, the House of Lords rejected the suggestion that, in
seeking to determine whether an antisocial behaviour order is civil or criminal,
the effect of the order itself must be considered in conjunction with the
consequences of any possible breach. (See Lord Steyn at [23].)

[57] Having thus recorded the arguments advanced and the authorities to
which we were referred, we have to determine whether a s 28 disqualification
order is a penalty within the meaning of art 7. We make clear that we have been
considerably helped by both counsels' clear and concise submissions in this
regard for which we are grateful.

[58] Having considered the matters though we have little difficulty in
concluding that the arguments advanced on behalf of the Secretary of State by
Mr Crow must prevail. It seems to us of considerable importance that a
conviction is not a necessary condition for the making of such an order. When
one considers the nature and purpose of such an order it points overwhelmingly
to this being for preventative rather than punitive effect. Precisely the same order
is made whether a person is convicted or not and the making of the order has no
regard to the extent or seriousness of the offending but rather to whether a
repetition of the conduct is likely. Save to the very limited extent we made clear
in setting out his submissions, we accept the force of the various arguments
advanced by Mr Crow. The various authorities to which we were referred seem
entirely consistent with the approach that he adopted and we believe lead to an
inevitable conclusion that a s 28 disqualification order is not a penalty within the
meaning of art 7. It follows that art 7 does not require the court to interpret s 28
in a way that would make it apply only to convictions for offences after the
coming into force of the 2000 Act.

THE INTERPRETATION ISSUE

[59] In the grounds of appeal in Field's case, it seemed that a second issue was
raised as to whether as a matter of statutory interpretation, s 28 could apply
where a conviction related to conduct that pre-dated the coming into force of the
2000 Act. Mr Bendall indicated that he was not taking any separate point over
and above the convention point but it is perhaps desirable that we make clear that
we have considered this aspect of the matter as well.

[60] On behalf of the Secretary of State, the following submissions in this
regard were made:

'1. Looking simply at the words of s 28(2)(a), its temporal effect is entirely
general. The only limitation is that the offender must have committed an
offence against a child when he was aged 18 years or over. There is no
suggestion from the wording of s 28 that the acts constituting the offence
must have been committed after the 2000 Act came into force.

2. Assuming that a disqualification order is not a criminal penalty, the
Secretary of State's interpretation does not offend against the presumption
against retrospective legislation. That presumption is based on concepts of
fairness and legal certainty, which dictate that accrued rights and the legal
status of past acts should not be altered by subsequent legislation. But the
effect of a disqualification order is entirely prospective, because it only affects
future conduct. In such circumstances, a statute does not offend against the
presumption against retrospective effect merely because it depends for its
future application upon events that may have occurred before it came into
force.

a   3. Finally, the purpose of s 28 is plainly to protect children. That purpose
would be severely undermined if a disqualification order could only be
imposed in relation to offences committed after the Section came into force.
The court should take a more relaxed approach to a potentially retro-active
element in legislation where its intended purpose is to protect the public.'

b   [61] We have no doubt that the Secretary of State's submissions are right and
that s 28 is to be construed as applying to a conviction whenever the offending
behaviour occurred.

CONCLUSION
[62] For these reasons the appeal of Field against sentence is dismissed. It
follows that there are no prospects of Young successfully appealing against the
c   disqualification order made in his case and his application for leave to appeal
against sentence is refused in this respect as it was in relation to the extended term
of imprisonment.

Field's appeal dismissed. Young's application for leave to appeal refused.

Sanchia Pereira   Barrister.

R (on the application of Rusbridger and another) v Attorney General

[2003] UKHL 38

HOUSE OF LORDS

LORD STEYN, LORD HUTTON, LORD SCOTT OF FOSCOTE, LORD RODGER OF EARLSFERRY
AND LORD WALKER OF GESTINGTHORPE

21 MAY, 26 JUNE 2003

Declaration – Jurisdiction – Jurisdiction of civil court to grant declaration regarding criminal law – Declaration regarding criminality of future conduct – Criteria to be applied when determining whether to grant such declaration – Treason Felony Act 1848, s 3 – Human Rights Act 1998.

The claimants were the editor of a newspaper and one of its journalists. They agreed to write and publish a series of articles urging the peaceful abolition of the monarchy. The editor was aware of s 3[a] of the Treason Felony Act 1848 which made it an offence, punishable by a maximum sentence of life imprisonment, for a person to compass by publication 'to deprive or depose' the Queen from the Crown. Although no prosecution had been brought under that provision since 1883, the editor invited the Attorney General to announce an intention to disapply the 1848 Act in respect of all published advocacy of the deposition of the monarchy other than by criminal violence. In accordance with his normal practice, the Attorney General declined to give an assurance regarding whether or not a prosecution or other action would be undertaken in respect of the proposed conduct. The newspaper published the articles and no prosecution was brought. In subsequent judicial review proceedings, the claimants sought a declaration as to the proper interpretation of s 3 of the 1848 Act read in the light of the Human Rights Act 1998, or a declaration that s 3 was incompatible with the right to freedom of expression guaranteed by the European Convention for the Protection of Human Rights and Fundamental Freedoms 1950 (as set out in Sch 1 to the 1998 Act). The Administrative Court, sitting as a Divisional Court, refused permission to apply for judicial review. The claimants applied to the Court of Appeal for permission to appeal. That court formally refused the application, but held that the claimants should be allowed to proceed with an amended claim for a declaration that s 3 of the 1848 Act was to be read and given effect to as if the words 'by acts of force or constraint or other unlawful means' followed and qualified the words 'to deprive or depose'. The Court of Appeal also allowed the claimants to proceed with their alternative claim for a declaration of incompatibility. On the Attorney General's appeal to the House of Lords, their Lordships considered, inter alia, the principles to be applied by a civil court when it was determining whether to entertain a claim for declaratory relief on a question of criminal law.

Held – Three criteria were to be applied to determine whether a particular case fell within the exceptional category where it would be proper for a member of the public to bring proceedings against the Crown for a declaration that certain

---

a   Section 3, so far as material, is set out at [3], below

333333

3

proposed conduct was lawful. The first was the absence of any genuine dispute about the subject matter. That had to be approached realistically. There would be a dispute if the Attorney General threatened to prosecute but not if, in accordance with present practice, he simply declined to indicate any view. That could not by itself conclude the matter, or be a weighty criterion if there were otherwise good reasons to allow the claim for a declaration to go forward. The second criterion was whether the case was fact sensitive or not. That was a factor of great importance. Most claims for a declaration that particular conduct was unlawful would founder on that ground. However, a question of pure law might more readily be made the subject matter of a declaration. The third criterion was whether there was a cogent public or individual interest which could be advanced by a grant of a declaration. Such an interest could include matters of constitutional importance. The instant case might fall within the exceptional category, but no purpose would be served by allowing it to go back to the Administrative Court. The part of s 3 of the 1848 Act which appeared to criminalise the advocacy of republicanism was part of a bygone age, and the idea that it could survive scrutiny under the 1998 Act was unreal. It had become a dead letter, and the issue which the claimants had brought before the courts could not be described as a live, practical question. It was not the function of the courts to bring the statute book up to date. Accordingly, the appeal would be allowed (see [16], [22]–[25], [28], [29], [33], [36]–[38], [40], [44], [45], [47], [48], [51], [53], [56], [58]–[61], below).

Munnich v Godstone Rural DC [1966] 1 All ER 930, *Imperial Tobacco Ltd v A-G* [1980] 1 All ER 866, *Airedale NHS Trust v Bland* [1993] 1 All ER 821 and *R (on the application of Pretty) v DPP* [2002] 1 All ER 1 considered.

Notes

For declarations by civil courts relating to the criminal law, see 10 *Halsbury's Laws* (4th edn reissue) para 310.

For the Treason Felony Act 1848, s 3, see 12 *Halsbury's Statutes* (4th edn) (2002 reissue) 90.

For the Human Rights Act 1998, see 7 *Halsbury's Statutes* (4th edn) (2002 reissue) 528.

Cases referred to in opinions

A-G v Able [1984] 1 All ER 277, [1984] QB 795, [1983] 3 WLR 845.

Airedale NHS Trust v Bland [1993] 1 All ER 821, [1993] AC 789, [1993] 2 WLR 316, Fam D, CA and HL.

Derbyshire CC v Times Newspapers Ltd [1993] 1 All ER 1011, [1993] AC 534, [1993] 2 WLR 449, HL.

Hadmor Productions Ltd v Hamilton [1982] 1 All ER 1042, [1983] 1 AC 191, [1982] 2 WLR 322, HL.

Imperial Tobacco Ltd v A-G [1980] 1 All ER 866, [1981] AC 718, [1980] 2 WLR 466, HL.

Macnaughton v Macnaughton's Trustees 1953 SC 387, Ct of Sess.

Munnich v Godstone Rural DC [1966] 1 All ER 930, [1966] 1 WLR 427.

Norris v Ireland (1991) 13 EHRR 186, [1988] ECHR 10581/83, ECt HR.

R (on the application of Pretty) v DPP [2002] UKHL 61, [2002] 1 All ER 1, [2002] 1 AC 800, [2001] 3 WLR 1598.

R v DPP, ex p Camelot plc (1997) 10 Admin LR 93, DC.

R v DPP, ex p Kebeline, R v DPP, ex p Rechachi [1999] 4 All ER 801, [2000] 2 AC 326,
     [1999] 3 WLR 972, HL.   *a*
R v Duffy (1848) 7 State Tr NS 795.
R v Gallagher (1883) 15 Cox CC 291.
R v Mitchel (1848) 6 State Tr NS 599.
Royal College of Nursing of the UK v Dept of Health and Social Security [1981] 1 All ER
     545, [1981] AC 800, [1981] 2 WLR 279, HL.   *b*
S (children: care plan), Re, Re W (children: care plan) [2002] UKHL 10, [2002] 2 All
     ER 192, sub nom *Re S (Minors) (Care Order: Implementation of Care Plan), Re W
     (Minors) (Care Order: Adequacy of Care Plan)* [2002] 2 AC 291, [2002] 2 WLR 720.

Cases referred to in list of authorities
A (children) (conjoined twins: surgical separation), Re [2000] 4 All ER 961, [2001] Fam   *c*
     147, [2001] 2 WLR 480, CA.
A-G v Guardian Newspapers Ltd (No 2) [1988] 3 All ER 545, [1990] 1 AC 109, [1988]
     3 WLR 776, HL.
Ahmed v UK (1998) 29 EHRR 1, [1998] ECHR 22954/93, ECt HR.
Ainsbury v Millington [1987] 1 All ER 929, [1987] 1 WLR 379n, HL.   *d*
Asiansky Television plc v Bayer-Rosin [2001] EWCA Civ 1792, [2002] CPLR 111.
Audergon v La Baguette Ltd [2002] EWCA Civ 10, [2002] CPLR 192.
Bellinger v Bellinger [2003] UKHL 21, [2003] 2 All ER 593, [2003] 2 WLR 1174.
Benmax v Austin Motor Co Ltd [1955] 1 All ER 326, [1955] AC 370, [1955] 2 WLR
     418, HL.
                                                                                                   e
Biguzzi v Rank Leisure plc [1999] 4 All ER 934, [1999] 1 WLR 1926, CA.
Bowman v UK (1998) 4 BHRC 25, ECt HR.
Buscarini v San Marino (1999) 6 BHRC 638, ECt HR.
Castells v Spain (1992) 14 EHRR 445, [1992] ECHR 11798/85, ECt HR.
Chassagnou v France (1999) 7 BHRC 151, ECt HR.
Dudgeon v UK (1981) 4 EHRR 149, [1981] ECHR 7525/76, ECt HR.   *f*
F v West Berkshire Health Authority (Mental Health Act Commission intervening) [1989]
     2 All ER 545, sub nom *Re F (Mental Patient: Sterilisation)* [1990] 2 AC 1, [1989]
     2 WLR 1025, HL.
Findlay v UK (1997) 24 EHRR 221, [1997] ECHR 22107/93, ECt HR.
Gillick v West Norfolk and Wisbech Area Health Authority [1985] 3 All ER 402, [1986]   *g*
     AC 112, [1985] 3 WLR 830, HL.
Goodwin v UK (1996) 1 BHRC 81, ECt HR.
Grayan Building Services Ltd (in liq), Re [1995] Ch 241, [1995] 3 WLR 1, CA.
Hector v A-G of Antigua and Barbuda [1990] 2 All ER 103, [1990] 2 AC 312, [1990] 2
     WLR 606, PC.   *h*
Kokkinakis v Greece (1993) 17 EHRR 397, [1993] ECHR 14307/88, ECt HR.
Kyriakides v Cyprus App no 53059/99 (11 December 2001, unreported), ECt HR.
Lingens v Austria (1986) 8 EHRR 407, [1986] ECHR 9815/82, ECt HR.
McKay v Essex Area Health Authority [1982] 2 All ER 771, [1982] QB 1166, [1982] 2
     WLR 890, CA.
                                                                                                   j
Pharmaceutical Society of Great Britain v Dickson [1968] 2 All ER 686, [1970] AC 403,
     [1968] 3 WLR 286, HL.
Pyx Granite Co Ltd v Ministry of Housing and Local Government [1959] 3 All ER 1,
     [1960] AC 260, [1959] 3 WLR 346, HL.
R v Secretary of State for the Home Dept, ex p Simms [1999] 3 All ER 400, [2000] 2 AC
     115, [1999] 3 WLR 328, HL.

a *R v Benjafield* [2001] 2 All ER 609, [2001] 3 WLR 75, CA; *affd on different grounds*
    [2002] UKHL 2, [2002] 1 All ER 815, [2002] 2 WLR 235.
   R v Horne Tooke (1794) 25 State Tr 725.
   R v Secretary of State for Health, ex p US Tobacco International Inc [1992] 1 All ER 212,
    [1992] QB 353, [1991] 3 WLR 529, DC.
   Scott v Scott [1913] AC 417, [1911–13] All ER Rep 1, HL.
b *Streletz v Germany* (2001) 33 EHRR 751, ECt HR.
   Sunday Times v UK (1979) 2 EHRR 245, [1979] ECHR 6538/74, ECt HR.
   Sunday Times v UK (No 2) (1992) 14 EHRR 229, [1991] ECHR 13166/87, ECt HR.
   SW v UK, CR v UK (1995) 21 EHRR 363, ECt HR.
   Thames Launches Ltd v Corp of the Trinity House of Deptford Strond [1961] 1 All ER 26,
    [1961] Ch 197, [1961] 2 WLR 16.
c *Theophanous v Herald and Weekly Times Ltd* (1994) 124 ALR 1, Aust HC.
   Wille v Liechtenstein (2000) 8 BHRC 69, ECt HR.

Appeal

The defendant, the Attorney General, appealed with permission of the Appeal
d Committee of the House of Lords given on 23 July 2002 from the order of the
Court of Appeal (Schiemann, May and Jonathan Parker LJJ) on 21 March 2002
([2002] EWCA Civ 397) remitting to the Administrative Court amended
proceedings brought by the claimants, Alan Rusbridger and Polly Toynbee,
against the Attorney General under s 7(1)(a) of the Human Rights Act 1998. The
Administrative Court, sitting as a Divisional Court (Rose LJ and Silber J), had
e refused the claimants permission to apply for judicial review on 22 June 2001
([2001] EWHC Admin 529). The facts are set out in the opinion of Lord Steyn.

Philip Sales, David Perry and *Ben Hooper* (instructed by the *Treasury Solicitor*) for the
    Attorney General.
f *Geoffrey Robertson QC, Martin Westgate* and *Laura Dubinsky* (instructed by *Jan
    Johannes*) for the claimants.

Their Lordships took time for consideration.

g 26 June 2003. The following opinions were delivered.

LORD STEYN.

[1] My Lords, behind the procedural questions brought before the House by
the Attorney General lies the question whether the editor of a newspaper, who
conducts a press campaign advocating the peaceful and constitutional
h replacement of the monarchy by a republican form of government, may be guilty
of an offence under s 3 of the Treason Felony Act 1848. The same question could
be asked about the rights of an individual. The Attorney General has invited the
House to concentrate on procedural issues with minimal reference to the
ultimate question. Judges, however, ought not to work in the dark.

(I) THE 1848 ACT

[2] 1848 was the year of revolutions on continental Europe, but there was only
one Chartist demonstration on 10 April 1848 in a relatively tranquil Britain. But
there was a fear that the contagion of revolution, with its associations with the
Terror after 1789, might spread to Britain. This was probably one of the reasons
why Parliament passed the 1848 Act. A further factor was that while the Treason

Act 1351 applied to the whole United Kingdom it was unclear whether later
statutes (such as the Treason Act 1795) extended to Ireland. Certainly Parliament
was told that this was the principal mischief to be addressed. There was another
objective. The 1351 Act was still in place as it is in part to this day. The 1795 Act
was passed to facilitate the prosecution of constructive treasons: it did so by
criminalising them as treasons. But juries were reluctant to convict defendants of
what were sometimes perceived to be political charges but carrying the death
penalty. The 1848 Act therefore provided that certain constructive treasons were
to be felonies, punishable by life imprisonment. It did, however, specifically
provide that conduct penalised by the 1848 Act could still be charged as treason.
This is the relevant historical setting of the statute.

[3] Section 3 of the 1848 Act provides:

'... if any person whatsoever ... shall, within the United Kingdom or
without, compass, imagine, invent, devise, or intend to deprive or depose
our Most Gracious Lady the Queen ... from the style, honour, or royal name
of the imperial crown of the United Kingdom, or of any other of her
Majesty's dominions and countries, or to levy war against her Majesty ...
within any part of the United Kingdom, in order by force or constraint to
compel her ... to change her ... measures or counsels, or in order to put any
force or constraint upon or in order to intimidate or overawe both Houses
or either House of Parliament, or to move or stir any foreigner or stranger
with force to invade the United Kingdom or any other of her Majesty's
dominions or countries under the obeisance of her Majesty ... and such
compassings, imaginations, inventions, devices, or intentions, or any of
them, shall express, utter, or declare, by publishing any printing or writing
... or by any overt act or deed, every person so offending shall be guilty of
felony, and being convicted thereof shall be liable ... to be transported
beyond the seas for the term of his or her natural life ...'

The gaps in the text reflect words repealed by the Statute Law (Repeals) Act 1891
and the Statute Law (Repeals) Act 1892. The old common law classification of
crimes as treasons, felonies and misdemeanours has been abolished: see s 1 of the
Criminal Law Act 1967. The reference in s 3 of the 1848 Act to 'felony' is to be
read as a reference to an offence. The penalty under s 3 is now imprisonment for
life or any shorter period: see the Penal Servitude Act 1857 and Criminal Justice
Act 1948. Subject to these statutory changes, s 3 remains in full force.

[4] The question has been raised whether s 3 makes punishable a press
campaign to seek to persuade the British people to make a peaceful change from
a monarchical form of government to a republican one. The way in which this
point arises on the wording of the section can be briefly explained. Despite the
quaintness of the language it is possible to divide the scheme of s 3 into: (1) the
compassing (contriving) etc, generally and (2) the compassing specifically by
publishing etc, in order: (a) to deprive the Sovereign of the Crown; (b) to levy war
against the Sovereign; (c) to encourage foreigners to invade the United Kingdom.
This is how the section is approached in 11(1) Halsbury's Laws (4th edn reissue)
para 86, and in Smith and Hogan Criminal Law (6th edn, 1988) pp 832–833, the
relevant section being omitted from subsequent editions of this book. For
present purposes the material part of s 3 is that directed against compassing by
publication to deprive or depose the Queen from the Crown. This provision had
as a prime target editors of newspapers and this was indeed the main use made of

a it in prosecutions in Victorian times. No prosecutions have, however, been brought under it since 1883.

[5] It will be noted that in parts (b) and (c) identified above the use of force is expressly made a necessary ingredient of the offence. The question is whether it is also an ingredient of the offence contained in part (a). At first glance the language is wide enough to cover a press campaign advocating the adoption of a
b republican form of government by constitutional processes. If that is so, peaceful political debate on the virtues of republicanism is criminalised. The question could be posed whether this is the correct reading. Interpretation is not infinitely expandable; there is a Rubicon which may not be crossed. On the other hand, counsel for the Attorney General accepted that the 1848 Act must be construed as an always speaking statute in a modern democracy. In this context it may well
c be that the strong operative words 'deprive or depose' import the idea of changing our form of government by unlawful force. If this interpretation is correct, the reason for the present litigation collapses at the threshold. For reasons which will become clear it is not necessary to express a view on this point.

d (II) THE HUMAN RIGHTS ACT 1998

[6] The United Kingdom became a party to the European Convention for the Protection of Human Rights and Fundamental Freedoms in 1950. Its provisions are well known. The establishment and recognition of fundamental individual rights was its main aim but its preamble envisaged that this aim could only be established by creating conditions of 'effective political democracy'. Plainly that
e involved the idea that peaceful political debate about constitutional and governmental structures should be encouraged. Political free speech, criticising an existing form of government, was regarded as central to the development of European liberal democracies.

[7] The Human Rights Act 1998 has potential implications for interpretation of s 3 of the 1848 Act if it makes punishable the advocacy of republicanism by
f individuals or the press by constitutional methods. The convention right at stake is freedom of expression. Article 10 of the convention provides:

> '1. Everyone has the right to freedom of expression. This right shall include freedom to hold opinions and to receive and impart information and ideas without interference by public authority and regardless of frontiers.
g > This Article shall not prevent States from requiring the licensing of broadcasting, television or cinema enterprises.
> 2. The exercise of these freedoms, since it carries with it duties and responsibilities, may be subject to such formalities, conditions, restrictions or penalties as are prescribed by law and are necessary in a democratic society,
h > in the interests of national security, territorial integrity or public safety, for the prevention of disorder or crime, for the protection of health or morals, for the protection of the reputation or rights of others, for preventing the disclosure of information received in confidence, or for maintaining the authority and impartiality of the judiciary.'

j Freedom of political speech is a core value of our legal system. Without it the rule of law cannot be maintained. Whatever may have been the position before the 1998 Act came into operation, it is difficult to think of any rational argument justifying the criminalisation of the conduct of citizens who wish to argue for a different form of government.

[8] Section 3(1) of the 1998 Act provides:

'So far as it is possible to do so, primary legislation and subordinate legislation must be read and given effect in a way which is compatible with the Convention rights.' a

Section 3(1) is not available where the suggested interpretation is contrary to express statutory words or is by implication necessarily contradicted by the statute: see *Re S (children: care plan), Re W (children: care plan)* [2002] UKHL 10 at [40], [2002] 2 All ER 192 at [40], [2002] 2 AC 291 at [40] per Lord Nicholls of b Birkenhead. If it is unavailable, incompatibility of legislation with a convention right brings s 4 into play. Section 4, so far as material, provides:

'(1) Subsection (2) applies in any proceedings in which a court determines whether a provision of primary legislation is compatible with a Convention right. c
(2) If the court is satisfied that the provision is incompatible with a Convention right, it may make a declaration of that incompatibility.
(3) Subsection (4) applies in any proceedings in which a court determines whether a provision of subordinate legislation, made in the exercise of a power conferred by primary legislation, is compatible with a Convention d right.
(4) If the court is satisfied—(a) that the provision is incompatible with a Convention right, and (b) that (disregarding any possibility of revocation) the primary legislation concerned prevents removal of the incompatibility, it may make a declaration of that incompatibility ...
(6) A declaration under this section ("a declaration of e incompatibility")—(a) does not affect the validity, continuing operation or enforcement of the provision in respect of which it is given; and (b) is not binding on the parties to the proceedings in which it is made.'

Any suggestion that a total legislative ban on republican discourse in print could be compatible with art 10 of the convention would stretch judicial gullibility to f breaking point. It, therefore, appears inevitable that any resultant incompatibility would have to be read down under the strong interpretative obligation under s 3(1).

(III) THE SHAPE OF THE APPEAL
[9] The Guardian is a daily newspaper with a circulation in excess of 400,000. g Mr Alan Rusbridger and Ms Polly Toynbee are respectively the editor and a well-known journalist of the Guardian. In November 2000 they and other employees of the Guardian agreed to write and publish a series of articles urging the abolition of the monarchy. They agreed that none of the articles would in any way encourage the use of force. Mr Rusbridger was aware of the 1848 Act. He h was concerned that his agreement to promote republicanism might constitute a treasonable campaign. He received legal advice that the interpretation of s 3 of the 1848 Act would be read down under s 3 of the 1998 Act on the grounds that s 3 of the 1848 Act, as interpreted in various nineteenth century decisions, was incompatible with art 10 of the convention: see *R v Mitchel* (1848) 6 State Tr NS j 599; and *R v Duffy* (1848) 7 State Tr NS 795. In a letter dated 28 November 2000 Mr Rusbridger informed the Attorney General of the Guardian's proposals to publish the articles. He asked for a clarification of his legal position in the light of the 1848 Act and invited the Attorney General to announce an intention to disapply the 1848 Act in respect of all published advocacy of the deposition of the monarchy other than by criminal violence. In the alternative, he suggested that

a the Attorney General might seek a declaration as to the proper interpretation of s 3 of the 1848 Act in the light of the 1998 Act. In his written reply of 4 December 2000, the Attorney General declined to give an assurance regarding whether or not a prosecution or other action would be taken in respect of the conduct proposed.

b [10] On 6 December 2000, the Guardian published articles which unambiguously advocated republicanism and Mr Rusbridger sent a copy of the newspaper to the Attorney General together with a reply to the Attorney General's letter of 4 December 2000. Mr Rusbridger asked to be informed, within 28 days, whether a prosecution would be brought and also stated that he would be commencing a claim under s 7 of the 1998 Act for a declaration on the construction of the 1848 Act. The Attorney General replied on 8 December 2000.

c In the event, no prosecutions were brought against Mr Rusbridger and Ms Toynbee.

[11] On 16 February 2001, the Guardian commenced a claim for: (1) a declaration that two decisions allegedly taken by the Attorney General during his exchange of correspondence with Mr Rusbridger were erroneous in law and in

d breach of s 6 of the 1998 Act; (2) a declaration that s 3 of the 1848 Act, when read in the light of the 1998 Act, does not apply to persons who evince in print or in writing an intent to depose the monarch or deprive her of her imperial status or to establish a republican form of government unless their intent is to achieve this by acts of force, constraint or other unlawful means; and (3) in the alternative, a declaration of incompatibility.

e [12] On 22 June 2001, the Administrative Court sitting as a Divisional Court (Rose LJ and Silber J) ([2001] EWHC Admin 529) held that there was no decision made by the Attorney General which was susceptible to challenge. In any event, the Administrative Court held that it was—

f   'not … appropriate for declarations as to the criminality or otherwise of conduct to be made, save in exceptional circumstances, and certainly not, generally speaking, before the conduct has itself occurred.'

The Administrative Court refused the Guardian's application for permission to pursue their claim in so far as it was properly to be characterised as a judicial

g review claim and, in the alternative, struck out the claim. Permission to appeal was refused.

[13] On 18 February 2002, the Guardian renewed the application for permission to appeal before the Court of Appeal. At an oral hearing the Guardian did not press its appeal against the refusal to grant permission for the judicial

h review of the Attorney General's two alleged decisions. The Guardian obtained an amendment of its claim for declaratory relief to a claim for a declaration that s 3 of the 1998 Act applies to s 3 of the 1848 Act and that in consequence the latter section must henceforth be read and given effect to as if the phrase 'by acts of force or constraint or other unlawful means' followed and qualified the words 'to

j deprive or depose'.

[14] In its judgment of 20 March 2002 ([2002] EWCA Civ 397), the Court of Appeal formally refused the application for permission to appeal against the Administrative Court's decision to refuse to grant permission for the judicial review claim to proceed. However, the Court of Appeal held that the Guardian should be allowed to proceed with both their claim for a declaration on the proper construction of s 3 of the 1848 Act and their alternative claim for a

declaration of incompatibility. Giving the judgment of the court Schiemann LJ
observed (at [27]):

> 'We of course express no view as to whether a declaration in the form now
> sought should be granted or as to the construction of the 1848 Act but we
> consider that it would not be in the interests of justice to prevent the matters
> raised in this application from being fully argued. We do not approach the
> matter as though we were reviewing the exercise of discretion by the
> Administrative Court since that court did not have before it the application
> for the declaration which we have before us and since the arguments
> apparently addressed to it were different from those which we heard.'

The Guardian's claim as amended was ordered to be remitted to the
Administrative Court. The Court of Appeal declined to grant leave to appeal to
the House of Lords.

[15] On 23 July 2002, the House granted leave to appeal to the Attorney
General. The questions which are now before the House are as follows.
(1) What are the principles that determine whether a civil court should entertain
a claim for declaratory relief on a question of criminal law? (2) Was the Court of
Appeal entitled to interfere with the Administrative Court's decision to dismiss
the Guardian's claim for a declaration? (3) In the light of the answers to issues (1)
and (2), should the Guardian's remaining claims for declaratory relief be allowed
to proceed?

(IV) ISSUE (1): THE PRINCIPLE

[16] The general principle has often been stated that, save in exceptional
circumstances, it is not appropriate for a member of the public to bring
proceedings against the Crown for a declaration that certain proposed conduct is
lawful and name the Attorney General as the formal defendant to the claim. This
principle was discussed in *Imperial Tobacco Ltd v A-G* [1980] 1 All ER 866, [1981] AC
718. That case, however, involved an attempt to obtain a declaration in the face
of pending criminal proceedings which were properly launched and were not
vexatious. Here there are no criminal proceedings pending or threatened. All
that need be said about the actual decision of the House in the *Imperial Tobacco*
case is that it was based on the paradigm for the application of the restrictive
principle. Viscount Dilhorne did, however, express himself more generally. He
observed ([1980] 1 All ER 866 at 876, [1981] AC 718 at 742):

> 'My Lords, it is not necessary in this case to decide whether a declaration
> as to the criminality or otherwise of future conduct can ever properly be
> made by a civil court. In my opinion it would be a very exceptional case in
> which it would be right to do so.'

Since 1951 it has become well established that there is jurisdiction for a civil court
to make such a declaration: compare Zamir and Woolf *The Declaratory Judgment*
(3rd edn, 2002) p 214 (para 4.201); *R v DPP, ex p Camelot plc* (1997) 10 Admin LR
93. But the exceptional nature of such a declaration by a civil court has on a
number of occasions been emphasised.

[17] In *Airedale NHS Trust v Bland* [1993] 1 All ER 821, [1993] AC 789 the House
granted a declaration that it would be lawful to discontinue life-sustaining
treatment to Mr Bland who was in a permanent vegetative state. This was, of
course, a truly exceptional case and the House held that the general principle does
not debar declaratory relief.

a
[18] The principle, and the exception to it, is in line with the ratio of the decision of the House of Lords in *R v DPP, ex p Kebeline, R v DPP, ex p Rechachi* [1999] 4 All ER 801, [2000] 2 AC 326, viz that, absent 'dishonesty or mala fide or an exceptional circumstance' decisions by the Director of Public Prosecutions to consent to a prosecution are not amenable to judicial review. In *R (on the application of Pretty) v DPP* [2002] UKHL 61, [2002] 1 All ER 1, [2002] 1 AC 800 the

b
applicant sought a declaration that it was lawful for Mrs Pretty to be assisted by her husband to commit suicide. Lord Hobhouse of Woodborough observed (at [116]):

c
'In exceptional circumstances it may be proper for a member of the public to bring proceedings against the Crown for a declaration that certain proposed conduct is lawful and name the Attorney General as the formal defendant to the claim. But that is not what occurred here and, even then, the court would have a discretion which it would normally exercise to refuse to rule upon hypothetical facts. Had the case raised by the appellant been one where it was appropriate to grant a declaration as to legality or compatibility, the court would no doubt have adopted that approach.'

d
[19] Counsel for the Attorney General has not argued that the principle summarised by Lord Hobhouse requires revision. His concern was rather with the fact that the Court of Appeal treated the present case as exceptional and with the way in which the reasoning was expressed. The Attorney General apparently fears that the decision of the Court of Appeal may be a slippery slope to the virtual

e
abandonment of the principle. Counsel for the Guardian also did not invite the House to consider any revision. For my part the principle as formulated is as necessary after the advent of the 1998 Act as it was before. It must be maintained. Normally, the seeking of a declaration in a civil case about the lawfulness of future conduct will not be permitted. But in truly exceptional cases the court

f
may allow such a claim to proceed.

[20] In a powerful speech counsel for the Attorney General observed that a more structured approach to what may constitute exceptional circumstances was required. He invited the House to examine the criteria which may be relevant to a decision whether a particular case falls within the exceptional category or not. Such a decision is not an entirely discretionary matter: rather it involves an

g
exercise of judgment. I agree that the applicable criteria ought to be examined.

[21] The starting point must be that the relief claimed may as a matter of jurisdiction be granted. The Guardian do not have to demonstrate that they are 'victims' under s 7 of the 1998 Act. That much is conceded and, in any event, obvious on proper view of the place of s 3 in the scheme of the 1998 Act. It is,

h
however, worth noting the broad approach which the European Court of Human Rights adopts to the concept of victim. Thus in *Norris v Ireland* (1991) 13 EHRR 186 a homosexual man complained that the criminalisation of homosexual conduct in Ireland violated his art 8 right to respect for his private life, although he accepted that the risk of being prosecuted was remote. The

j
court accepted that he was a victim. Even an administrative policy of not prosecuting for the offence in question would not have made a difference. For present purposes it is sufficient that the Guardian has an interest and standing. That is the threshold requirement.

[22] I now turn directly to the matters, which counsel for the Attorney General invited the House to spell out. He put forward three criteria. The first was the absence of any genuine dispute about the subject-matter. This objection

must be realistically approached. There would be a dispute if the Attorney General threatened to prosecute. In that event it would be said that no claim for *a* a declaration is possible because there is an imminent threat of prosecution. On the other hand, if in accordance with present practice the Attorney General simply declines to indicate any view, there is no dispute. But that cannot by itself conclude the matter or be a weighty criterion if there are otherwise good reasons to allow the claim for a declaration to go forward. It is not a significant factor *b* militating against placing the present case in an exceptional category. Unfortunately, the oral debate in the House concentrated on the wrong target. Counsel for the Guardian relied on what he termed the chilling effect of s 3 of the 1848 Act. Given that the editor *did* publish articles advocating a republic, the argument was threadbare. Clearly, the editor of the Guardian has not slept uneasily in his bed for fear of being prosecuted under s 3 of the 1848 Act. But the *c* Guardian may be entitled to seek certainty by pursuing its claim for declaratory relief. In that event the outcome may be that a declaration is unnecessary as was the case in *A-G v Able* [1984] 1 All ER 277, [1984] QB 795. The Court of Appeal has not foreclosed such a conclusion.

[23] The second criterion advanced is whether the case is fact-sensitive or not. *d* This is a factor of great importance and most claims for a declaration that particular conduct is unlawful will founder on this ground. In principle therefore I accept the approach of counsel for the Attorney General. But it has always been recognised that a question of pure law may more readily be made the subject-matter of a declaration: see *Munnich v Godstone Rural DC* [1966] 1 All ER 930, [1966] 1 WLR 427, cited with approval by Lord Lane (with whom Lord *e* Edmund-Davies and Lord Scarman agreed) in *Imperial Tobacco Ltd v A-G* [1980] 1 All ER 866 at 883–884, [1981] AC 718 at 751–752. It is clear as a pikestaff that there can be no issue of fact concerning either the incompatibility of s 3 of the 1848 Act with art 10 of the convention or the court's decision under s 3 of the 1998 Act. It is not a fact-sensitive case. In my view the Guardian has satisfied this criterion. *f*

[24] The third criterion advanced by counsel for the Attorney General focuses on the question whether there is a cogent public or individual interest which could be advanced by the grant of a declaration. *Airedale NHS Trust v Bland* [1993] 1 All ER 821, [1993] AC 789 was an example of an overwhelming interest of an individual in the grant of a declaration that the cessation of life-sustaining medical support was lawful. But the jurisdiction is in no way limited to life and death *g* issues: see *Royal College of Nursing of the UK v Dept of Health and Social Security* [1981] 1 All ER 545, [1981] AC 800. The Guardian alleges that some 25% of the population supports republicanism. The Guardian wishes to continue the debate. In words attributed to Voltaire the person on the Underground might say: 'I disapprove of what you say, but I will defend to death your right to say it.' *h* It may be a matter of constitutional importance. An historic anomaly in our political democracy could be examined by our courts. There is something to be said for the view that it ought not to be left to the court in Strasbourg to drag us to an obvious conclusion.

[25] I conclude that the present case may fall within the exceptional category. This does not, however, conclude the matter.

(V) ISSUE (2): THE DECISION OF THE ADMINISTRATIVE COURT

[26] Counsel for the Attorney General submitted that the Court of Appeal was not entitled to reverse the decision of the Administrative Court. He relied on the familiar principles summarised in *Hadmor Productions Ltd v Hamilton* [1982] 1 All

a ER 1042 at 1046, [1983] 1 AC 191 at 220. The difficulty is, however, that neither the Administrative Court—nor for that matter the Court of Appeal—approached the case in the structured way, with reference to specific criteria, which I have been persuaded must be adopted. Dealing with the decision of the Administrative Court, I concentrate on the judgment of Rose LJ with whom Silber J agreed. In truth the motivation of Rose LJ is conclusionary in nature and not altogether easy

b to follow. He did not examine the argument that the Guardian is entitled to certainty. He did not consider the fact that the issues are of pure law. He did not take into account the constitutional import of the case. In fairness one must add that the argument before the House probably dealt with the criteria in somewhat more detail than was the case before the Administrative Court. The criteria applicable to determining whether a case falls in the exceptional category have

c now been clarified to some extent for future guidance.

[**27**] But the House is not bound to follow the decision of the Administrative Court.

d [**28**] It is now necessary to look at the matter in the round. Ought the matter to be heard again by the Administrative Court? It would certainly be competent for the House to allow the case to go back. But what purpose would it serve? The part of s 3 of the 1848 Act which appears to criminalise the advocacy of republicanism is a relic of a bygone age and does not fit into the fabric of our modern legal system. The idea that s 3 could survive scrutiny under the 1998 Act

e is unreal. The fears of the editor of the Guardian were more than a trifle alarmist. In my view the courts ought not to be troubled further with this unnecessary litigation.

(VII) CONCLUSION

f [**29**] I would allow the appeal and quash the decision of the Court of Appeal. In the result the application of the Guardian is dismissed. I would further direct that there should be no order of costs below and that the Guardian must pay the costs of the appeal to the House.

LORD HUTTON.

g [**30**] My Lords, the freedom of the press to express views and opinions on political and constitutional matters is a fundamental and central element in the life of a democratic society and is enshrined in art 10 of the European Convention for the Protection of Human Rights and Fundamental Freedoms 1950 (as set out in Sch 1 to the Human Rights Act 1998).

h [**31**] It is upon this principle that the claimants, Mr Alan Rusbridger, the editor of the Guardian, and Ms Polly Toynbee, a prominent journalist of that newspaper, rely in these proceedings, the background to which has been fully described in the speech of my noble and learned friend Lord Steyn. They contend that there is uncertainty as to the meaning of s 3 of the Treason Felony Act 1848.

j They further contend that there is a risk that those who advocate in print the replacement of the monarchy by a republican form of government by peaceful and constitutional means might be prosecuted and be liable to imprisonment under that section and that this risk constitutes an infringement of their rights under art 10 of the convention. They seek to uphold the decision of the Court of Appeal ([2002] EWCA Civ 397) that the Administrative Court ([2001] EWHC Admin 529) should rule on their application for a declaration that, consequent on the application of s 3 of the 1998 Act, s 3 of the 1848 Act does not make it an offence to publish views advocating that the Queen should be deprived of or deposed from the Crown by peaceful and constitutional means.

[32] In reply to the claimants' argument the Attorney General submits that a civil court should not give a declaratory judgment on an issue of criminal law save in an exceptional case, and that the present proceedings are not such a case. The Attorney General cites *Imperial Tobacco Ltd v A-G* [1980] 1 All ER 866 at 876, [1981] AC 718 at 742 where Viscount Dilhorne stated:

> 'My Lords, it is not necessary in this case to decide whether a declaration as to the criminality or otherwise of future conduct can ever properly be made by a civil court. In my opinion it would be a very exceptional case in which it would be right to do so.'

And in *R (on the application of Pretty) v DPP* [2002] UKHL 61 at [116], [2002] 1 All ER 1 at [116], [2002] 1 AC 800 at [116] Lord Hobhouse of Woodborough stated:

> 'In exceptional circumstances it may be proper for a member of the public to bring proceedings against the Crown for a declaration that certain proposed conduct is lawful and name the Attorney General as the formal defendant to the claim. But that is not what occurred here and, even then, the court would have a discretion which it would normally exercise to refuse to rule upon hypothetical facts.'

[33] My Lords, whilst the claimants' submissions relate to principles of great importance in respect of the freedom of the press in a democratic society, I consider that when the actual facts of this case are considered it becomes apparent that those principles are not directly engaged and that the risk described by the claimants is, in the real world, non-existent. Nor is there any real possibility that 'the chilling effect' referred to by Lord Keith of Kinkel in *Derbyshire CC v Times Newspapers Ltd* [1993] 1 All ER 1011 at 1018, [1993] AC 534 at 548 would operate. This is clearly shown by the passage in the judgment of the Court of Appeal delivered by Schiemann LJ which states (at [21]):

> 'We do not understand the claimants to suggest that the uncertainty of our law as to treason has affected their decision to publish in the past or is likely to in the future. Their stance is that of the Duke of Wellington: publish and be damned. Nor is there any evidence to suggest that the existence of the 1848 Act causes them to sleep in their beds less soundly.'

Therefore it is clear that the freedom of the claimants to express views and opinions and to impart ideas has not been hindered or impeded and that their rights under art 10 of the convention have not been breached.

[34] The reasons why the Court of Appeal remitted the case to the Administrative Court to give further consideration to the respondents' application for a declaration are stated in their judgment (at [22]–[26]). Parts of these paragraphs read as follows:

> '[22] On the other side, there are powerful arguments in favour of free speech and also of having our criminal law formulated in such a way that the citizen can see what is prohibited and what is not. Of course there will always be borderline cases but it cannot seriously be contended that our many statutes dealing with treason which go back to 1351 but are still partly in force leave the law in a satisfactory state ...

a

[23] … No one has been prosecuted under the 1848 Act for over 100 years. Every few years Parliament passes a Statute Law (Repeals) Act which repeals outdated statutes. While bits of the 1848 Act were repealed in the nineteenth century other bits including the section with which we are concerned survive in part …

b

[24] In 1998, 150 years later, the Human Rights Act was passed. Parliament chose, for reasons which are readily understandable, not to amend all Acts which might require amendment in the light of our obligations under the convention but instead to leave the courts to do what they can with the help of s 3 of the 1998 Act …

[26] The Attorney General has chosen not to express his view as to the proper construction of the 1848 Act in the light of the 1998 Act. Indeed we

c

do not know if he has one. Neither he nor the Director of Public Prosecutions have indicated what prosecution policy is in relation to articles advocating republicanism in this country. The proper construction of the 1848 Act seems to us potentially relevant to the exercise by the court of any discretion to make a declaration. We see room for a possible argument to

d

the effect that s 3 of the 1848 Act is on its face incompatible with the 1998 Act even if read in the light of s 3 of the 1998 Act and that it is in the public interest that this incompatibility be declared so that the remedial action in s 10 may be considered by the Home Secretary.'

[35] I respectfully dissent from this view expressed by the Court of Appeal. It

e

is not the function of the courts to decide hypothetical questions which do not impact on the parties before them. This point was well put by Lord Justice-Clerk Thomson in *Macnaughton v Macnaughton's Trustees* 1953 SC 387 at 392:

'Our Courts have consistently acted on the view that it is their function in the ordinary run of contentious litigation to decide only live, practical

f

questions, and that they have no concern with hypothetical, premature or academic questions, nor do they exist to advise litigants as to the policy which they should adopt in the ordering of their affairs. The Courts are neither a debating club nor an advisory bureau. Just what is a live practical question is not always easy to decide and must, in the long run, turn on the

g

circumstances of the particular case.'

[36] As it is clear that any uncertainty as to the interpretation of s 3 of the 1848 Act has not affected the decision of the claimants to publish in the past and is not likely to affect their decision to publish in the future, I consider that the issue which the claimants have brought before the courts cannot be described as a live,

h

practical question. In addition I wish to express my full agreement with the views of my noble and learned friends Lord Rodger of Earlsferry and Lord Walker of Gestingthorpe that it is not the function of the courts to keep the statute book up-to-date and that ss 3 and 4 of the 1998 Act are not intended to be an instrument by which the courts can chivvy Parliament into spring-cleaning the statute book.

i

[37] Therefore for the reasons which I have given I would allow the appeal and quash the decision of the Court of Appeal.

LORD SCOTT OF FOSCOTE

[38] My Lords, I have had the advantage of reading in advance the opinion of my noble and learned friend Lord Steyn and am in complete and respectful agreement with everything he has said.

[39] The claimants have said that they fear that if they advocate the abolition *a* of the monarchy and its replacement by a republic, all by peaceful and constitutional means, they may be prosecuted for treason pursuant to s 3 of the Treason Felony Act 1848. They refer to the 'chilling effect' that section has upon the freedom of expression guaranteed by art 10 of the European Convention for the Protection of Human Rights and Fundamental Freedoms 1950 (as set out in Sch 1 to the Human Rights Act 1998). *b*

[40] My Lords, I do not believe a word of it. It is plain as a pikestaff to the claimants and everyone else that no one who advocates the peaceful abolition of the monarchy and its replacement by a republican form of government is at any risk of prosecution. Whatever may be the correct construction of s 3, taken by itself, it is clear beyond any peradventure first, that the section would now be 'read down' as required by s 3 of the 1998 Act so that the advocacy contemplated *c* by the respondents could not constitute a criminal offence, and second, that no Attorney General or Director of Public Prosecutions would or could authorise a prosecution for such advocacy without becoming a laughing stock. To do so would plainly be an unlawful act under s 6(1) of the 1998 Act.

[41] Moreover, if a private prosecution, complaining of advocacy for the *d* peaceful abolition of the monarchy and its replacement by a republic, were to be brought by some successor of the League of Empire Loyalists it would be the clear duty of the Attorney General, in order to honour the right to freedom of expression guaranteed by art 10 to issue a nolle prosequi—unless, of course, the Director of Public Prosecutions had exercised his power to take over and then discontinue the prosecution. It may be that if it were the claimants who were *e* prosecuted they would welcome the prosecution and be anxious for the proceedings to come before a judge with the maximum of publicity. They must know that the prosecution would be bound to fail. The judge would have no alternative but to dismiss the case as hopeless.

[42] The claimants will have received legal advice about the prospects of such *f* a prosecution being brought and about the prospects of its success. The advice is protected by the legal professional privilege to which they are entitled but, speaking for myself, I do not for one moment believe that they were advised that there was any risk of a prosecution or of a conviction.

[43] It was, in my opinion, instructive that Mr Sales, counsel for the Attorney General, told your Lordships that he had no instructions to make any submission *g* about the merits of the respondents' s 3 point. If he had made any submission it could only have been to accept that, at least since 2 October 2000 when the 1998 Act came into force, no one who advocates the abolition of the monarchy by peaceful and constitutional means has been at any risk of prosecution (other than a private prosecution) or of conviction. Mr Sales is a very good lawyer. So, too, *h* is Mr Robertson QC. But you do not have to be a very good lawyer to know that to advocate the abolition of the monarchy and its replacement by a republic by peaceful and constitutional means will lead neither to prosecution nor to conviction. All you need to be is a lawyer with common sense.

[44] The Administrative Court ([2001] EWHC Admin 529), in dealing with the *j* claimants' judicial review application, regarded the application, I rather think, as not worth taking seriously. I sympathise with them and do not criticise their dismissal of the application. They dismissed the application on the procedural ground that although civil courts have jurisdiction to make declarations as to the criminality or non-criminality of conduct, proposed or actual, it is a jurisdiction to be exercised only in exceptional circumstances. The claimants' s 3 point, said

a the Administrative Court, did not qualify. But they did not spell out that the reason why the point did not qualify was because it was so obviously and incontestably right that the time of the court should not have been wasted in having to deal with it. The Administrative Court should, in my view, have dealt with the application either by dismissing it on the ground I have mentioned or by making the declaration sought but ordering the claimants to pay the costs of the

b unnecessary court proceedings. To dismiss the application on the procedural ground that the case did not fall within the exceptional circumstances category without making clear that the Emperor had no clothes led to the case coming before the Court of Appeal on the quite unreal footing that the Emperor was wearing some sort of costume that did require to be recognised and dealt with. The Court of Appeal, for its part, recognised the high constitutional importance

c of freedom of speech in a political context and sent the case back to the Administrative Court in order, as I infer, for there to be a formal recognition by that court of what must have been obvious to the Court of Appeal, namely, that s 3 of the 1848 Act is a dead letter so far as advocacy of political change by peaceful and constitutional means is concerned.

d [45] And so the case comes to your Lordships' House. My Lords the valuable time of the courts should be spent on real issues. I have already expressed my non-belief in the reality of the claimants' alleged fear of prosecution. I repeat it. I do not suppose there is any school debating society that has not regularly debated the issue of monarchy versus republic. Everyone who reads newspapers or magazines will have read numerous articles and letters extolling the

e advantages of a republic over a monarchy and advocating a change—and vice versa, of course. These articles and letters have not led to prosecution or any threat of it. Nor have those responsible for school debating societies received visits from the Special Branch. This has been the state of affairs throughout my adult life but it is, I do not doubt, of longer standing than that. There has been no

f prosecution under the 1848 Act since 1883. The enactment and coming into force of the 1998 Act made the tolerance de facto of advocacy of peaceful political change a tolerance de jure.

[46] The Attorney General, in his responses to the letters written to him by the claimants, said nothing to give them any reason to suppose that he did not share the views expressed above. He took his stand on the theoretical impropriety of

g assurances being given in advance about the non-criminality of hypothetical conduct. It might have been better if he had simply said that the United Kingdom is a mature democracy and in a mature democracy people do not get prosecuted for advocating political change by peaceful and constitutional means. If he had said that there would surely have been no litigation.

h [47] Your Lordships in dealing with the appeal have unanimously endorsed the lawfulness of such advocacy. The claimants may regard that endorsement as representing a successful outcome to their litigation. But if unnecessary litigation is commenced in order to obtain obvious results, the claimant must expect to have to pay the costs of the exercise. In my opinion the appeal should be allowed

j and the dismissal of the claimants' application affirmed. The claimants should pay the costs of the appeal to this House but there should be no order as to the costs below.

LORD RODGER OF EARLSFERRY.
[48] My Lords, I agree with your Lordships that the appeal should be allowed and that the order proposed by my noble and learned friend Lord Steyn should

be made. Since he has fully described the background, I can state my reasons
quite shortly.   *a*

[49] At the hearing before the House Mr Sales, counsel for the Attorney
General, was careful to make no submissions as to the proper interpretation of s 3
of the Treason Felony Act 1848. I proceed on the basis, however, that a person
commits an offence if he 'shall ... compass, imagine, invent, devise, or intend' to do
the various things listed—   *b*

> 'and such compassings, imaginations, inventions, devices, or intentions, or
> any of them, shall express, utter, or declare, by publishing any printing or
> writing ... or by any overt act or deed ...'

In other words, the offender must not only compass etc the various things but
must express, utter or declare such compassings etc by publishing a printing or   *c*
writing or by an overt act or deed.

[50] One of the things that it is an offence to compass etc in these ways is 'to
deprive or depose our Most Gracious Lady the Queen ... from the style, honour,
or royal name of the imperial crown of the United Kingdom ...' If these words
are read in isolation, they appear to make it an offence, punishable with life   *d*
imprisonment, for anyone, including journalists and newspaper editors, to
publish articles advocating a peaceful change from a constitutional monarchy to
a republic in the United Kingdom. That is how the courts interpreted the words
shortly after the 1848 Act was passed. Relying on s 3 of the Human Rights Act
1998 and art 10 of the European Convention for the Protection of Human Rights
and Fundamental Freedoms 1950 (as set out in Sch 1 to the 1998 Act), however,   *e*
in these proceedings the claimants, Mr Rusbridger and Ms Toynbee, seek a
declaration that s 3 of the 1848 Act should be read as applying only to compassing
etc 'by acts of force or constraint or other unlawful means' to deprive the Queen
of her position. Alternatively, they seek a declaration under s 4 of the 1998 Act
that s 3 of the 1848 Act is incompatible with the right to freedom of expression in   *f*
art 10 of the convention.

[51] The 1848 Act was passed to meet a perceived threat, particularly in
Ireland, in the heated atmosphere of that year. Section 3 has not been used as the
basis of a prosecution since *R v Gallagher* (1883) 15 Cox CC 291. This is despite
the fact that across the intervening years many people of greater or lesser
prominence in public life, from members of Parliament, peers and other   *g*
politicians to academics, journalists and media personalities, have published
books, articles and interviews advocating a peaceful change from a monarchy to
a republic. Support for a republic was the declared editorial policy of at least one
national daily newspaper and one national Sunday newspaper long before the
Guardian decided to publish its articles at the end of 2000. Needless to say, there   *h*
has never been the slightest hint that any of these people would be prosecuted for
publishing their views. This part of s 3 of the 1848 Act has long been a dead letter.
Otherwise, it would surely have been amended so as to cover modern methods
of communication.

[52] In an ideal world the statute book would always be up-to-date and
contain only those Acts and provisions which are needed at present. In practice,   *j*
that has never been the case. At any given moment you can find statutes which
have become out-of-date and which should be repealed or amended but which
linger on untouched since, in a crowded Parliamentary timetable, governments
have had other priorities. Such statutes pose a familiar problem for those who
have to decide whether to prosecute, especially when social circumstances have

a changed. Recent history provides examples. Should breaches of the Sunday trading laws be prosecuted when the shops appear to meet a public demand? Should corner shop owners be prosecuted if, to their customers' satisfaction, they stay open long after the statutory closing time, that was introduced to save fuel during the First World War? Should people be prosecuted for participating in consensual homosexual acts in private? When these and similar issues have
b arisen, prosecutors have done what they always do: they have had regard to the public interest in deciding whether to prosecute. See, for instance, paras 6.1–6.3 of the Code for Crown Prosecutors issued by the Crown Prosecution Service. If the prosecutors mistake the public interest, any resulting prosecution is liable to provoke public criticism or even ridicule, while placing a martyr's crown on the defendant's head.

c   [53] This part of s 3 of the 1848 Act is another example of a provision whose time has long passed. Therefore, as one would expect, no prosecutions have been instituted under it for more than a century, despite the many publications advocating a peaceful change to a republican constitution. This inaction on the part of generations of prosecutors throughout the United Kingdom speaks louder
d than words. They long ago recognised that it would not be in the public interest to prosecute those who published such material. Indeed it seems unlikely that the possibility of prosecuting had even occurred to the relevant authorities for many years until Mr Rusbridger wrote to the Attorney General. Inevitably, no prosecution followed. Equally clearly, there is not the slightest prospect that the claimants will be prosecuted if they choose to publish similar articles in future.
e Nor is the threat of a rogue private prosecution any more substantial, since the reality is that, having regard to the public interest, the Director of Public Prosecutions would take it over and discontinue it or the Attorney General would enter a nolle prosequi.

  [54] Unlike, I suspect, the vast majority of the population, the claimants have
f actually heard of s 3 of the 1848 Act and know what it says. But they also know that they will not be prosecuted for publishing their articles and so, as rational individuals, they are not adversely affected by the mere existence of s 3. In the Court of Appeal ([2002] EWCA Civ 397) Schiemann LJ, giving a twist to the Duke of Wellington's famous challenge, described the claimants' attitude in this way (at [21]):
g
    'We do not understand the claimants to suggest that the uncertainty of our law as to treason has affected their decision to publish in the past or is likely to in the future. Their stance is that of the Duke of Wellington: publish and be damned. Nor is there any evidence to suggest that the existence of the 1848 Act causes them to sleep in their beds less soundly.'
h
In other words neither any decision that the claimants take in their professional lives nor their general well-being is adversely affected by the existence of s 3 of the 1848 Act. In argument on their behalf Mr Robertson QC accepted this but—with understandable diffidence—suggested that s 3 might have
j subconsciously affected them in deciding on the tone of the articles. But for s 3, they might not, for instance, have proposed that a referendum should be held before any change to a republic. Nothing supports that implausible suggestion. Section 3 has no 'chilling effect' on the claimants' freedom of expression.

  [55] The claimants are, therefore, unaffected either in their actions or in their well-being by the existence of s 3. In both respects they are in a very different position from the applicant in Norris v Ireland (1991) 13 EHRR 186 who claimed

that legislation penalising homosexual conduct infringed his art 8 rights. There
the European Court of Human Rights emphasised that art 25 (now art 34) of the   *a*
convention requires that an individual applicant should be able to claim to be
actually affected by the measure of which he complains. The convention article
may not be used to found an action in the nature of an actio popularis. The court
proceeded (at 195–196 (para 33)) to identify reasons why the existence of the
legislation actually affected Mr Norris' activities and well-being, even though the   *b*
more recent practice was for the Irish Attorney General not to authorise
prosecutions based on conduct in private between consulting adults. In that
situation a majority of the court were prepared to regard Mr Norris as a victim in
convention terms. By contrast, since there is no sign that the claimants have been
affected in any way by the existence of s 3 of the 1848 Act, the present proceedings
are in substance an actio popularis.   *c*

[56] Should these proceedings go ahead? The Divisional Court thought not,
while the Court of Appeal thought they should. I agree with the Divisional
Court. The claimants seek a declaration as to the interpretation of s 3 of the 1848
Act or as to its incompatibility with the right to freedom of expression under
art 10 of the convention. Before the House the parties agreed that these   *d*
declarations should be treated in the same way as a civil declaration as to the
criminality or otherwise of future conduct. A civil court can make such a
declaration, although it would be right to do so only in a very exceptional case:
see *Imperial Tobacco Ltd v A-G* [1980] 1 All ER 866 at 876, [1981] AC 718 at 742 per
Viscount Dilhorne. The authorities do not spell out what constitutes a very
exceptional case for these purposes. In ordinary cases people must take and act   *e*
on their own legal advice. So, broadly speaking, a very exceptional case must be
one where, unusually, the interests of justice require that the particular claimant
should be able to obtain the ruling of the civil court before embarking on, or
continuing with, a particular course of conduct which, on one view, might
expose him to the risk of prosecution.   *f*

[57] Approaching the matter in that way, I am satisfied that the present is not
a very exceptional case of that kind. The claimants have published articles
supporting a transition to a republic and, even though Mr Rusbridger specifically
drew the articles to the attention of the Attorney General, they have not been
prosecuted. They want to publish similar articles in the future and, if they do so,
they will not be prosecuted then either. Their decisions as to whether or not to   *g*
publish such articles are not affected in any way by the existence of s 3. The issue
of the compatibility or incompatibility of that section with art 10 of the
convention is therefore moot so far as the claimants are concerned. It is also
moot in respect of other people: the claimants themselves make the point that—

> 'It is most unlikely that the issue will ever be decided by the criminal courts   *h*
> in the course of an actual prosecution, given the absence of any such
> prosecution (despite some published republican advocacy) over the last
> century.'

The Divisional Court is therefore being asked to make a declaration about a point   *j*
of criminal law because a criminal court will never have to decide it. So far from
this being the kind of very exceptional case where the interests of justice require
that the claimants should be able to obtain a declaration from the Divisional
Court, it is exactly the kind of case where they should not.

[58] It is not the function of the courts to keep the statute book up-to-date.
That important responsibility lies with Parliament and the executive. As long ago

a as 1977 the Law Commission recommended reform of the law of treason and allied offences. Parliament has not so far found the time to enact legislation to give effect to that recommendation. Successive Home Secretaries have given a higher priority to other reforms. While that might seem unfortunate, it is ultimately a matter for the political judgment of the executive and Parliament. The claimants are, of course, free to use their influence in a campaign to try to *b* change that political judgment. But it would be wrong in principle for the courts to allow the claimants to go on with proceedings where the only favourable outcome of any practical use to them would be a declaration of incompatibility that they could use to further any such political campaign.

LORD WALKER OF GESTINGTHORPE.

c [59] My Lords, I have had the advantage of reading in draft the speech of my noble and learned friend Lord Steyn. I agree with Lord Steyn that this appeal should be allowed for the reasons set out in his speech, with the consequence that the Court of Appeal's order ([2002] EWCA Civ 397) would be quashed. I add a few remarks of my own.

d [60] Lord Steyn has described s 3 of the Treason Felony Act 1848 as a relic of a bygone age. I agree. It is inconceivable that it could be invoked in the twenty-first century in order to punish anyone who advocates that a republican form of government should be established by peaceful means. Mr Rusbridger himself (in his first letter to the Attorney General) said that the law had 'become in effect a dead letter'. In the statement of facts which Mr Rusbridger verified he *e* said no more than that he was 'concerned' about the law. Before this House his counsel did not challenge the Court of Appeal's observation that Mr Rusbridger was not losing sleep because of the 1848 Act.

[61] In my opinion it is most undesirable that obsolete statutes should remain unrepealed. Quaint language and interesting historical associations are no *f* justification for preserving obsolete statutes in a mummified state. But as the Attorney General replied to Mr Rusbridger, it is still the role of the legislature, rather than that of the courts, to decide whether to repeal or retain legislation. Sections 3 and 4 of the Human Rights Act 1998 are intended to promote and protect human rights in a practical way, not to be an instrument by which the courts can chivvy Parliament into spring-cleaning the statute book, perhaps to *g* the detriment of more important legislation. Such a spring-cleaning process might have some symbolic significance but I can see no other practical purpose which this litigation would achieve.

[62] However to conclude (as I do) that the litigation is unnecessary does not display the slightest enthusiasm for the continued existence of s 3 of the 1848 Act *h* if and so far as it could theoretically apply to the expression of political opinion advocating non-violent constitutional change.

Appeal allowed.

Dilys Tausz   Barrister.

EIC Services Ltd and another v Phipps and others

[2003] EWHC 1507 (Ch)

CHANCERY DIVISION

NEUBERGER J

4–7, 10–14, 21 FEBRUARY, 13 MARCH 2003

Company – Shares – Issue of shares – Bonus shares – Mistake – Proper approach to determining whether issue and allotment of bonus shares void for mistake.

Company – Dealing with company – Person dealing with company in good faith – Statutory provision operating in favour of 'a person dealing with a company' – Whether shareholder receiving bonus shares such a person – Companies Act 1985, s 35A(1).

(1) The issue and allotment of bonus shares, at least once they have been accepted by the shareholders to whom they have been allotted, is analogous to a contract, and accordingly the question whether the issue and allotment of such shares is void for mistake must be decided by reference to the principles governing the effect of a common mistake on a contract. Thus the court must not overlook the commercial common sense of the nature of the mistake or oversight, and it should be very reluctant to reach a conclusion which is plainly contrary to that which could conceivably have been intended by the parties. In particular, where the mistake consists in overlooking the need for consent to the transaction by one of the parties, it is wrong to conclude (at least in the absence of very unusual facts) that the mistake can be regarded as 'essential' or 'fundamental', so as to vitiate the contract or arrangement, if all the parties would have plainly rejected the notion that the mistake would have had that effect (see [159], [168], [170], [176], [181], below); *Associated Japanese Bank (International) Ltd v Crédit du Nord SA* [1988] 3 All ER 902 and *Great Peace Shipping Ltd v Tsavliris Salvage (International) Ltd, The Great Peace* [2002] 4 All ER 689 applied; dictum of Scott J in *Re Cleveland Trust plc* [1991] BCLC 424 at 434 followed.

(2) A shareholder receiving bonus shares from a company is 'a person dealing with a company' within the ambit of s 35A(1)[a] of the Companies Act 1985, and accordingly such a shareholder can in principle take advantage of s 35A(1) which provides that, in favour of a person dealing with a company in good faith, the power of the board of directors to bind the company, or authorise others to do so, shall be deemed to be free of any limitation under the company's constitution. The words 'a person dealing with a company' are not expressly fettered in any way. As a matter of ordinary language, a shareholder receiving bonus shares from the company is within the ambit of those wide words, and, in the absence of a powerful reason to the contrary, it is inappropriate to treat naturally wide words in a statute as subject to an implied limitation (see [196], [203], below); *Smith v Henniker-Major & Co* [2002] 2 BCLC 655 considered.

---

a   Section 35A, so far as material, is set out at [192], below

a
Notes
For powers of directors to bind the company and for mistake in contract, see respectively 7(2) *Halsbury's Laws* (4th edn) (1996 reissue) para 1108 and 9(1) *Halsbury's Laws* (4th edn reissue) para 895.
    For the Companies Act 1985, s 35A, see 8 *Halsbury's Statutes* (4th edn) (1999 reissue) 135.

b
Cases referred to in report
Associated Japanese Bank (International) Ltd v Crédit du Nord SA [1988] 3 All ER 902, [1989] 1 WLR 255.
Bell v Lever Bros Ltd [1932] AC 161, [1931] All ER Rep 1, HL.
Cleveland Trust plc, Re [1991] BCLC 424.
c   *Duomatic Ltd, Re* [1969] 1 All ER 161, [1969] 2 Ch 365, [1969] 2 WLR 114.
Great Peace Shipping Ltd v Tsavliris Salvage (International) Ltd, The Great Peace [2002] EWCA Civ 1407, [2002] 4 All ER 689, [2003] QB 679, [2002] 3 WLR 1617.
Messier-Dowty Ltd v Sabena SA (No 2) [2001] 1 All ER 275, [2000] 1 WLR 2040, CA.
Ooregum Gold Mining Co of India Ltd v Roper, Wallroth v Roper [1892] AC 125, HL.
d   *Patten v Burke Publishing Co Ltd* [1991] 2 All ER 821, [1991] 1 WLR 541.
Royal British Bank v Turquand (1856) 6 E & B 327, 119 ER 886, [1843–60] All ER Rep 435, Ex Ch.
Smith v Henniker-Major & Co [2002] EWCA Civ 762, [2002] 2 BCLC 655, [2003] Ch 182, [2002] 3 WLR 1848.
Towers v African Tug Co [1904] 1 Ch 558, CA.
e

Preliminary issues
By order of Master Moncaster made on 26 June 2002, the court was required to determine preliminary issues, summarised at [18], below, arising in proceedings brought by the claimants, EIC Services Ltd and European Internet Capital Ltd, f   against the defendants, Stephen Lawry Phipps, Jonathan Paul, Jeremy Lee Barber, Stella Sutton and Hambros Bank Nominees Ltd. The last two defendants took no part in the proceedings. The facts are set out in the judgment.

Phillip Gillyon (instructed by *Jones Day Gouldens*) for the claimants.
David Chivers QC (instructed by *Herbert Smith*) for Mr Phipps and Mr Paul.
g   *David Mabb QC* and *Leon Kuschke* (instructed by *SJ Berwin*) for Mr Lee Barber.

Cur adv vult

13 March 2003. The following judgment was delivered.

h   **NEUBERGER J.**

INTRODUCTION
    [1] This judgment concerns certain preliminary questions which are directed to the validity of bonus shares issued, paid up by appropriating a sum in the share j   premium account, by EIC Services Ltd (the company) on 15 December 1999. The argument that the bonus issue was wholly or partly invalid is based on the propositions that: (1) a very substantial number of the bonus shares were allotted to shareholders whose shares were not paid up, namely (a) 200 shares issued in April 1999 and (b) 110,320 shares issued in November 1999; (2) the issue of bonus shares was not approved by a resolution of, or otherwise authorised by, the shareholders of the company; (3) in these circumstances, the bonus issue and the

allotment of some or all of the bonus shares were invalid and void. These propositions encapsulate the issues to be decided.

[2] I shall begin by setting out the basic facts. Then, I shall turn to explain a little more fully the nature of the three issues, and how they arise. I shall then discuss issue 1(a), which primarily turns on findings of fact, and issue 1(b), which turns on findings of fact, although it additionally involves the determination of an application to amend. Issue 2 involves questions of fact and law (principally relating to the applicability of the so-called *Duomatic* principle (see *Re Duomatic Ltd* [1969] 1 All ER 161, [1969] 2 Ch 365)). Issue 3 only involves questions of law, namely the interrelationship of the law of mistake and the unauthorised decisions by directors, and the ambit of s 35A of the Companies Act 1985.

[3] The topics are dealt with in the following paragraphs:
- The facts: [4]–[20];
- The issues: [21]–[35];
- Issue 1(a): Payment for the 200 shares: [36]–[52];
- Issue 1 (b): Payment for the 110,320 shares:
  (i) Introductory: [53]–[58];
  (ii) The pleaded case: [59]–[100];
  (iii) The application to amend: [101]–[119];
- Issue 2: Approval of the bonus issue: [120]–[147];
- Issue 3: The status of the bonus shares:
  (i) Introductory: [148]–[151];
  (ii) The contention that the bonus shares are void for mistake: [152]–[190];
  (iii) The effect of the breach of the articles and s 35A: [191]–[208];
  (iv) The declaration as to voidness: [209]–[225];
- Conclusion: [226].

THE BASIC FACTS

[4] On 8 April 1999, the company was incorporated in England and Wales under the name of Miltentone Ltd with an authorised share capital of 1,000 shares of £1 each, two of which were issued to the original subscribers, who did not pay for them.

[5] On 20 May 1999, Mr James Spickernell and Mr Julian Bryson were appointed directors of the company in place of its first director. They were already directors of a number of other companies, including Enterprise Technology Development Ltd (ETD). The shareholders in that company were members of the family, or friends, of Mr Spickernell or Mr Bryson. ETD was intended to focus on healthcare technology investments. However, at the beginning of 1999, Mr Spickernell and Mr Bryson became interested in investments in Internet-related businesses, and investigated such opportunities, especially in the United States. They acquired the company for the purpose of investing in that type of business.

[6] On 21 July 1999, the two nil paid £1 shares in the company were transferred, one to Mr Spickernell and the other to Mr Bryson. On the same day, the authorised share capital of the company was divided into 100,000 ordinary shares of 1p each, so that Mr Spickernell and Mr Bryson each had 100 1p shares (the subscriber shares). Mr Spickernell and Mr Bryson each subsequently transferred his 100 shares to a company owned by him, namely Berdino International Ltd (Berdino) and Okimax International Ltd (Okimax) respectively.

[7] On 12 November 1999, there was a board meeting, which Mr Bryson attended by telephone. As a result of that meeting (which was interrupted by an

a EGM necessary for that purpose), the authorised capital of the company was increased from £1,000 to £300,000 by the creation of an additional 29,900,000 1p shares. At the board meeting, Mr Spickernell and Mr Bryson appointed Mr Simon Reid as a third director of the company. (Mr Reid actually started working for the company in January 2000.)

b [8] Also on 12 November 1999, Mr Spickernell and Mr Bryson decided to allot to Berdino, Okimax, Mr Reid, and 13 other parties a total of 110,320 new 1p shares (the November shares). These 13 other parties (the 13 shareholders) were all shareholders in ETD; they included the second defendant Mr Jonathan Paul. Accordingly, as at close of business on 12 November 1999, there were 110,520 issued 1p shares in the company, owned by 16 shareholders, ie the 13 shareholders, Okimax, Berdino and Mr Reid (the 16 shareholders). It was *c* recorded in the minutes of the board meeting that each of the 16 shareholders 'had already paid the company a total of 1p in respect of each share to be allotted to them'.

[9] At a board meeting held on 15 December 1999, the directors of the company resolved to allot a further 27,035 1p shares in the company, at a price of *d* £29 each, to a total of 33 shareholders, of whom five were among the 16 shareholders. Accordingly, with effect from 15 December 1999, there were 28 new shareholders (the 28 shareholders), including the first defendant, Mr Stephen Phipps. This meant that the total number of issued shares in the company was 137,555. At the same meeting on 15 December 1999, the directors resolved to make a 99 for 1 bonus issue. That share issue (the bonus issue) increased the *e* number of shares in issue by 13,617,945. This bonus issue involved capitalising £136,179·45 (representing the value of the 13,617,945 bonus 1p shares) of the amount standing to the credit of the share premium account.

[10] The decision to issue the bonus shares arose from the fact that Mr Spickernell and Mr Bryson were well on the way with implementing *f* proposals to float the company on the alternative investment market (AIM). The market for shares in Internet-related shares such as the company was very strong; indeed, one could fairly describe it as a bubble. The advice received by the company was that the shares might be worth around £250 each, and that such a high price might render them less marketable. Accordingly, a bonus issue of 99 for 1 would result in a more attractive projected share price of £2·50.
g
[11] The resolution of the directors passed at the board meeting of 15 December 1999 began by noting 'that there were now 137,555 ordinary shares in issue'. The resolution then went on to state that—

h '£136,179·45 of the sum standing to the credit of the share premium account ... be capitalised and appropriated to the holders of the Ordinary Shares on the register ... in the same proportion as they would be entitled to that sum were it distributed by way of dividend ... in paying up in full at par all the [bonus] shares to be issued and distributed credited as fully paid to those persons in the proportion of 99 Ordinary Shares for each Ordinary *j* Shares now registered in their names.'

[12] On 22 December 1999, the third defendant, Mr Jeremy Lee Barber, agreed to subscribe for 2,500,000 1p shares at a price of £1·25 each, and, shortly thereafter, he paid £3,125,000 for those shares. On 20 January 2000, the company issued these shares to Mr Lee Barber, and a further 220,000 shares to other persons who had also subscribed £1·25 per share. Subsequently, a further

5,542,000 1p shares were issued by the company at a price of £2·50 each between 4 February and 23 March 2000.

[13] On 22 March 2000, Mr Spickernell drew a cheque in favour of the company in the sum of £1,105·20. This sum represented the nominal value of the subscriber shares plus the November shares (the disputed shares). The reason he wrote out this cheque was because Mr Gop Menon of PricewaterhouseCoopers, the company's auditors, had said that there was no record of any payment having been made for the subscriber shares or the November shares, in the company's books and records, as far as he could see.

[14] On 24 March 2000, European Internet Capital Ltd, a Guernsey company (the Guernsey company), then named Vesuvius Ltd, made an offer to acquire all of the issued shares in the company, in exchange for shares in the Guernsey company. That offer was accepted, and it was completed on 9 April 2000. Accordingly, the company is, and has been since 9 April 2000, a wholly-owned subsidiary of the Guernsey company. Shortly thereafter, Mr Spickernell, Mr Bryson and Mr Reid ceased to be directors of the company.

[15] The company's name changed from time to time. On 30 July 1999, it was changed to ETD Infotech Ltd, and on 22 October 1999 to European Internet Capital Ltd. Finally, on 17 May 2000, after the take-over of the company in April 2000, it acquired its current name, EIC Services Ltd.

[16] The second half of 1999 and the first three months of 2000 was, as the evidence in this case vividly showed, the height of the Internet bubble. Since that time, shares in almost all companies concerned with Internet activities have fallen in value, mostly very substantially. As I understand it, the value of the shares in the company and the Guernsey company are no exception.

[17] It appears that Mr Lee Barber sought legal advice during the first half of 2001; in or shortly before September 2001, he and some other shareholders started to suggest that the bonus issue effected on 15 December 1999 was wholly or partially invalid. This point was formally taken on behalf of Mr Lee Barber in a letter from his solicitors dated 21 September 2001. The present proceedings were brought by the company and the Guernsey company on 18 December 2001. They seek a determination as to the validity of the bonus issue.

[18] On 26 June 2002, Master Moncaster directed the determination of three preliminary issues. The first part of the first issue is whether the subscriber shares were fully paid up at the time of the bonus issue, namely on 15 December 1999. The second part of the first issue is whether the November shares were fully paid at the time of the bonus issue. The second issue is whether the capitalisation of reserves and the issue and allotment of the bonus shares were effectively authorised by the members of the company. The third issue, which Master Moncaster directed should only be determined 'if the trial judge thinks fit', is whether, in light of the determination on the other issues, the bonus shares were themselves validly issued or allotted. The master also ordered that the first and second defendants, Mr Phipps and Mr Paul, should contend that the issues be answered in the affirmative, on behalf of all those interested in so arguing, and that the third defendant, Mr Lee Barber, should argue that the issues be answered in the negative, on behalf of those interested in so arguing.

[19] The company and the Guernsey company (the claimants) say that they are simply seeking guidance as to the correct answer or approach in relation to the preliminary issues. Accordingly, although appearing by counsel, Mr Philip Gillyon, they take no position on the issues in these proceedings with one exception. The contention that the disputed shares were not fully paid, and the

a contention that the capitalisation of reserves and bonus issues were not properly
authorised, are therefore advanced by Mr David Mabb QC, who appears (with
Mr Leon Kuschke) for Mr Lee Barber; Mr Mabb also argues that the bonus shares
were not validly issued or allotted. The contrary argument in relation to each of
the preliminary issues, is raised by Mr David Chivers QC, who appears on behalf
of Mr Phipps and Mr Paul. However, Mr Chivers also argues that I should not
b determine the third issue. The claimants want the third issue determined. It is
also right to record that the costs of Mr Phipps and Mr Paul on this preliminary
issue have been underwritten by Mr Spickernell, Mr Bryson and Mr Reid.

[20] It should also be mentioned that there have been proceedings in
Guernsey which have gone to the Guernsey Court of Appeal. Those proceedings
have little, albeit some, relevance to the determination of the issues which I have
c to determine.

THE ISSUES

[21] The importance of the first issue (namely whether the disputed shares
were fully paid up by 15 December 1999), and of the second issue (whether there
d has been a valid approval of the bonus issue) arises from the provisions of reg 110
and 104 of the 1985 version of table A, in the Schedule to the Companies (Tables
A to F) Regulations 1985, SI 1985/805, which were incorporated into the articles
of the company.

[22] Regulation 110 provides, so far as relevant:

e   'The directors may *with the authority of an ordinary resolution of the
company*—(a) ... resolve to capitalise ... any sum standing to the credit of the
company's share premium account ... [and] (b) appropriate the sum resolved
to be capitalised to the members who would have been entitled to it *if it were
distributed by way of dividend* and in the same proportions and *apply such sum*
f   *on their behalf* ... *in paying up in full unissued shares* ... of the company in
nominal amount equal to that sum, *and allot the shares ... credited as fully
paid* ...' (My emphasis.)

[23] The relevant part of reg 104 is to this effect: '... all dividends shall be
declared and paid *according to the amounts paid up on the shares* on which the
g dividend is paid.' (My emphasis.)

[24] Accordingly, regs 110 and 104 require that, in relation to any bonus issue,
(a) the amounts appropriated to members in paying up bonus shares must be in
proportion to the amount paid up on the shares in respect of which the bonus
shares are to be allotted, and (b) the appropriation of any sum in the share
h premium account in paying up bonus shares must be authorised by an ordinary
resolution of the company.

[In [25]–[35] his Lordship reviewed some of the submissions, and then
considered, in [36]–[119], whether the 200 subscriber 1p shares issued in April
1999 and the 110, 320 'November' 1p shares issued in November 1999 had been
j fully paid up by the date of the bonus issue on 15 December 1999. He concluded
that the subscriber shares had been fully paid up by that date, but that the
November shares were not paid up by then, and remained unpaid until March
2000. His Lordship then went on to decide, in [120]–[147], that, although all the
existing shareholders had been informed of the bonus issue, they could not be
treated as having authorised or approved it. In so concluding, he held that the
Duomatic principle did not apply. He then proceeded to consider the third issue.]

ISSUE 3: THE STATUS OF THE BONUS SHARES

a

Introductory

[148] The first submission by Mr Mabb on behalf of Mr Lee Barber, is that the bonus issue was void, and that the bonus shares should effectively be treated as never having been issued and allotted, on the ground of common mistake. On the facts I have found, he primarily identifies two mistakes, namely: (i) the bonus shares issued to the holders of the November shares were allotted to those shareholders contrary to regs 104 and 110 of the 1985 regulations, because the November shares were not paid up; (ii) all the 13,617,945 bonus shares were issued purportedly paid up to the 16 shareholders and the 28 shareholders (the 44 shareholders) in that they were issued and paid up without 'the authority of an ordinary resolution' contrary to reg 110. As a result, he contends, the issue of all the bonus shares, or of the bonus shares allotted to the 16 shareholders, is void.

b

c

[149] It is right to mention that Mr Mabb has what may be characterised as two variations on the first point, namely, that there are other vitiating mistakes, namely, that in their resolution to issue the bonus shares: (i) the directors did not purport to appropriate any sum to be capitalised from the share premium account to members holding unpaid shares (ie the 16 shareholders); and (ii) the directors did not purport to allot bonus shares to members holding unpaid shares. I shall refer to these aspects as 'the additional mistakes'.

d

[150] Mr Mabb's second submission is that the issue of the bonus shares was void because, in light of regs 104 and 110, the company, and/or the three directors, had no power to cause the bonus shares to be issued, paid up through the capitalisation of the share premium account, to the 16 shareholders in respect of the unpaid November shares and/or because of the absence of approval by the 16 shareholders. I put this argument second, because Mr Mabb advanced common mistake as his main point (to the extent that Mr Chivers apparently understood it to be his only point).

e

f

[151] I shall first consider Mr Lee Barber's case based on common mistake. I shall then deal with the case based on breach of the articles, which involves consideration of the ambit of s 35A. I shall then turn to the question of the grant of a declaration.

The contention that the bonus issue is void for mistake

g

[152] Mr Mabb relies on the decision of Scott J in *Re Cleveland Trust plc* [1991] BCLC 424. That case concerned three companies, McInnes, a wholly-owned subsidiary of Gunnergate, itself a wholly-owned subsidiary of Cleveland; all three companies had common directors. McInnes declared a substantial dividend, which it then paid to Gunnergate, which in turn declared the same sum by way of dividend, which it paid to Cleveland. Cleveland then made a bonus issue of fully paid shares to be capitalised out of its profit and loss account, ie out of the sum paid by way of dividend by McInnes and Gunnergate. It then transpired that McInnes had no capacity to declare the dividend. The argument accepted by the judge was that, in these circumstances, the bonus issue was void on grounds of common mistake.

h

j

[153] Scott J (at 434) accepted: 'The issue and acceptance of the bonus shares involved ... a relationship between Cleveland and the shareholders analogous to a contractual relationship.' He then went on to consider (at 435–436) the law relating to 'the basis on which a contract may be set aside as void on the ground of common mistake'.

a

[154] Scott J said (at 436):

> 'It was fundamental to the [bonus] issue that the dividend deriving from McInnes's capital profit could be used in paying up the bonus shares. The true state of affairs, in which the capital profit could not be so used and the Gunnergate dividend was repayable, did, in my judgment, "render essentially and radically different the subject matter which the parties believed to exist". I am, accordingly, satisfied that the bonus issue can probably be declared void on the ground of common mistake.'

b

[155] The law relating to the effect of common mistake on a contract is difficult, and has been most recently considered by the Court of Appeal in *Great Peace Shipping Ltd v Tsavliris Salvage (International) Ltd, The Great Peace* [2002] EWCA Civ 1407, [2002] 4 All ER 689, [2003] QB 679. Lord Phillips of Worth Matravers MR, giving the judgment of the court, considered the effect of a number of cases, most notably *Bell v Lever Bros Ltd* [1932] AC 161, [1931] All ER Rep 1 and *Associated Japanese Bank (International) Ltd v Crédit du Nord SA* [1988] 3 All ER 902, [1989] 1 WLR 255, both of which were cited by Scott J in *Re Cleveland*.

c

d

[156] The decision in *The Great Peace* represents significant development in the law, not only in so far as it rejected the doctrine of equitable rescission in relation to mistake (see [2002] 4 All ER 689 at [95]–[161]), but also in relation to the analysis of the common law, and in particular the famous speech of Lord Atkin in *Bell v Lever Bros*.

e

[157] In *The Great Peace* [2002] 4 All ER 689 at [76], the court indicated that authority suggested that there should be five 'elements [which] must be present if common mistake is to avoid a contract'. They are as follows:

> '… (i) there must be a common assumption as to the existence of a state of affairs; (ii) there must be no warranty by either party that that state of affairs exists; (iii) the non-existence of the state of affairs must not be attributable to the fault of either party; (iv) the non-existence of the state of affairs must render performance of the contract impossible; (v) the state of affairs may be the existence, or a vital attribute, of the consideration to be provided or circumstances which must subsist if performance of the contractual adventure is to be possible.'

f

g

[158] These tests are similar to those which can be extracted from the principles identified by Steyn J in the *Associated Japanese Bank* case [1988] 3 All ER 902 at 912–913, [1989] 1 WLR 255 at 268, which the court in *The Great Peace* [2002] 4 All ER 689 at [90], [91] quoted and approved. The passage cited from the judgment of Steyn J begins with this sentence: 'The first imperative must be that the law ought to uphold rather than destroy apparent contracts.' Steyn J went on to say that, in order to render the contract void, 'the mistake must render the subject matter of the contract essentially and radically different from the subject matter which the parties believed to exist'.

h

[159] I respectfully agree with the observations of Scott J in *Re Cleveland Trust plc* [1991] BCLC 424, to the effect that the issue and allotment of bonus shares, at least once they have been accepted by the shareholders to whom they have been allotted, is analogous to a contract, albeit that, as he suggested (at 435), it 'may not be strictly contractual'. I also am content to proceed on the basis that the law relating to common mistake in contract can be applied by analogy to the completed issued of bonus shares (as both counsel accept). However, because the case proceeds by analogy, it may be that a certain amount of adaptation of the principles is necessary, because they have been developed in relation to contracts, whereas a case such as the present involves something similar and analogous, but *a* not identical, to a contract.

[160] The two grounds (the defects) upon which voidness is alleged, namely the fact that the November shares were not paid up at the time of the allotment of the bonus shares, and the absence of an ordinary resolution, can each properly be characterised as common mistakes. Neither the company nor the 16 *b* shareholders, nor, indeed, the three directors, appreciated that the November shares should have been paid up before the bonus shares could properly be allotted to the 16 shareholders. That was a mistake which was common to all the parties concerned. (The 16 shareholders, or at least 13 of them, believed that the November shares were paid up because they had been told that Mr Spickernell would pay for them, but that was probably a unilateral mistake, as the three *c* directors at least ought to have known that those shares were not paid up.) However, the need for an ordinary resolution was not appreciated by any of the parties concerned: they made a common mistake in overlooking this requirement.

[161] In the case of each defect there was therefore 'a common assumption as *d* to the existence of a state of affairs', namely that the issue and allotment of the bonus shares were regular and proper. Although that formulation applies to both defects, they must, I think, be considered separately. Although they are each deficiencies which have arisen in relation to the bonus issue, and which are relied on to support the same or a similar argument, namely that the bonus shares were void in whole or in part, they are, as a matter of fact and law, separate and *e* unrelated points. That is well illustrated by the fact that, if Mr Mabb is correct, the failure to obtain a resolution would render the issue of all the bonus shares void, but the fact that the November shares were not paid up may render only those bonus shares allotted to the 16 shareholders void.

[162] The first defect whose effect I shall consider is the fact that the *f* November shares were not paid up at the date that the bonus shares were issued to the 16 shareholders, and whether this should lead to the conclusion that the allotment of the bonus shares to those shareholders was void.

[163] I accept that, when they decided to issue some of the bonus shares to the 16 shareholders, the three directors had overlooked the fact, indeed were wholly unaware of the fact, that the bonus shares should not have been allotted paid up *g* to the 16 shareholders, unless and until the November shares were paid up. I consider that the three directors, or at least two of them, namely Mr Spickernell and Mr Bryson, were aware of the facts that gave rise to the conclusion that the November shares were not fully paid up. That conclusion is almost inevitable, because, as at 15 December 1999, it was Mr Spickernell and Mr Bryson who had *h* been solely responsible for deciding on, and arranging for, the way in which the November shares would be paid for (apart from the advice received from Mr Connolly, the solicitor, and the involvement of Mrs Thomson, Mr Spickernell's secretary).

[164] It also is clear that the 13 shareholders (ie the holders of the November shares, with the exception of Berdino, Okimax and Mr Reid) were unaware that their November shares were not fully paid up. I think it substantially more likely than not that they were unaware of the requirement that those shares had to be fully paid up, before any bonus shares could properly be allotted in respect of them. However, I do not consider that, on the facts of this case, this justifies concluding that the issue of the bonus shares to the 13 shareholders on

a 12 November 1999 was void. I reach that conclusion on the basis of the combined effect of three factors.

[165] First, it appears to me that this is not a case where it can merely be said that the 13 shareholders were innocent of any responsibility for, or in connection with, the mistake. They were positively misled into believing that the November shares would be fully paid up, because they had been told, before the
b November shares were issued to them, by one of the three directors, that Mr Spickernell would ensure that their shares were fully paid up. That is the effect of the evidence of Mr Spickernell and Mr Bryson, supported by the evidence of Mr Paul, and it seems inherently probable, especially in light of the documentary evidence, and the evidence of Mrs Thomson.

c [166] By contrast, the position of the company was very different. It was, at best, merely innocent, but it was not misled. However, on one view, its directors had misled the 16 shareholders by telling them that their shares would be paid up by one of the directors, who then failed to pay up the shares. In these circumstances, the observation of Steyn J in the *Associated Japanese Bank* case [1988] 3 All ER 902 at 913, [1989] 1 WLR 255 at 268 is close to being in point:

d
> 'In my judgment a party cannot be allowed to rely on a common mistake when the mistake consists of a belief which is entertained by him without any reasonable grounds to such belief ...'

I would also refer to propositions (ii) and (iii) in *The Great Peace* [2002] 4 All ER 689
e at [76].

[167] Secondly, the case for rejecting the contention that the allotment of the bonus shares to the 13 shareholders was rendered void by this mistake is heavily reinforced by considering the consequence of that contention. The issue of the bonus shares to the 13 shareholders (and, indeed, to any other shareholders) in no
f way altered the size of their respective interests in the company; indeed, save to render their interests a little more marketable if and when the company was floated on AIM, the issue of the bonus shares did not alter the value of their respective holdings in the company. Accordingly, were the bonus shares issued to the 16 shareholders void, it would mean that the apparently innocuous, indeed apparently beneficial, issue of the bonus shares reduced the value of their interest
g in the company by a very substantial extent, possibly as against the 28 shareholders (whose shares were fully paid up on 15 December 1999), and certainly as against any subsequent shareholders. The 28 shareholders (if they retain their bonus shares), and any persons who subsequently acquired shares (such as Mr Lee Barber) believing the November shares allotted to the 16
h shareholders were valid, would enjoy a concomitant windfall. Particularly as the 16 shareholders were misled into the mistake by the directors, the conclusion that the bonus shares allotted to the 16 shareholders were void cannot, in my view, be the proper analysis.

[168] That commercially commonsense factor appears to me to be
j particularly important given that one is in the area of law relating to contract. The court should be very reluctant to reach a conclusion, which is plainly contrary to that which could conceivably have been intended by the parties. Further, it appears to me that this point is reinforced once one remembers 'the first imperative' identified by Steyn J, namely 'that the law ought to uphold rather than destroy apparent contracts'—see the passage cited in *The Great Peace* [2002] 4 All ER 689 at [90]. To put the point slightly differently, if Mr Mabb is right as to

the effect of this defect, the commercial consequences of the mistake bear no
relation to the nature of the mistake.

[169] Thirdly, it appears to me that the mistake was one which as at
15 December 1999, would have been perceived as one which obviously could
readily have been put right. Indeed it was put right around three months after
that date, by Mr Spickernell making out the March cheque, for a sum which
resulted in the November shares being fully paid up. Mr Mabb argues that that
is not enough to prevent the allotment of the bonus shares being void at least in
so far as they were allotted to the 16 shareholders, because the matter has to be
judged as at 15 December 1999. There is obvious logical force in that argument,
because 15 December 1999 is the date on which the bonus shares were issued and
allotted, and it is on the date of allotment that the shares in respect of which the
bonus shares were allotted should have been fully paid up.

[170] However, even accepting that point, I do not consider that the allotment
of the bonus shares to the 13 shareholders was rendered void by the mistake. In
so far as the allotment of bonus shares can be treated as analogous to a contract
(as Scott J held in *Re Cleveland*), and in so far as voidness on the ground of mutual
mistake is to be judged by reference to the question of whether the mistake
relates to a 'fundamental' or 'essential' aspect of the transaction, it appears to me
that one must not overlook the commercial common sense of the nature of the
mistake or oversight. Standing as at 15 December 1999, the November
shareholders had been told that their shares were paid up, and steps were being
taken to ensure that the November shares were paid up, although the matter was
not being given the sort of attention which it should have been given, because of
the very heavy pressures on Mr Spickernell and Mr Bryson, and because they
were unaware of the urgency of the need to make the November shares fully paid
up.

[171] Furthermore, the amount of money needed to make the shares fully
paid up was just over £1,000, which, in the context of the company's then
perceived value and potential, was virtually de minimis. On the assumption that
the November shares were worth £250 each (before the issue of the bonus
shares), their combined value was over £2·5m, whereas the amount needed to
make them paid up was just over £1,000. The notion that there would be any
difficulty about making those shares paid up would have been nothing short of
fanciful, as, indeed, is borne out by the ease with which the cheque was obtained
from Mr Spickernell on 22 March 2000. That is further reinforced by the fact that,
as the three directors would have known, Mr Spickernell was contractually
obliged (as against the 13 shareholders) to pay for their shares.

[172] It appears to me therefore that, so far as the common mistake argument
is concerned, rather than the allotment of the bonus shares to the 13 shareholders
being void, the position as at 15 December 1999 was that their allotment was
irregular, but was capable of being put right by rendering the November shares
paid up. This view derives a little indirect support from the decision of the House
of Lords in *Ooregum Gold Mining Co of India Ltd v Roper, Wallroth v Roper* [1892] AC
125. That case is authority for the proposition that a company cannot allot shares
as fully paid unless it receives at least par value for them, ie that a company
cannot issue shares at a discount (see in this context s 100(1) of the Companies
Act 1985). The conclusion reached by the House of Lords was that, although the
issue of such shares was beyond the powers of the company, the original allottees
of the shares were liable to pay to the company in cash the full amount unpaid on
the shares.

[173] As I see it, it would have been open to the allottees of the shares in the *Ooregum* case to contend that they were not liable to pay anything in respect of the shares concerned, because the issue, or at least the allotment, of the shares was void, as it was outside the powers of the company to allot shares on the basis that they were allotted. If such an argument had been maintained and had been upheld, then the conclusion reached by the House of Lords would presumably have been different. It would, however, be wrong to place too much weight on that point, partly because at least some of the shares in that case had been transferred to third parties, and partly because the argument that the allotment was void was not raised. However, it does appear to me to be consistent with the conclusion I have reached in the present case.

[174] I do not consider that the decision in *Re Cleveland Trust plc* [1991] BCLC 424 casts doubt on my conclusion. First, it does not appear to have been a case where any particular group of shareholders would have suffered or benefited by the bonus issue being avoided, because, unlike the present case, there had been no issue of shares equivalent to the issue of new shares to the 33 shareholders on 15 December 1999, and no increase in the number of shares since the allocation of the bonus shares, equivalent to the issue of new shares to Mr Lee Barber and others. Therefore, in *Re Cleveland*, each of the shareholders lost the same number of bonus shares relative to the number of shares he held. Secondly, *Re Cleveland* does not appear to have been a case where it could have been said that the company or its directors misled the shareholders in the way in which the three directors in the present case led at least 13 of the 16 shareholders to believe that their shares would be fully paid up. Thirdly, there was no question of *Re Cleveland* being able to recover from anyone a sum equal to the amount which had been wrongly paid to it by McInnes via Gunnergate, whereas, in the present case, it was clear, as at 15 December 1999, that the November shares could and would be fully paid up in due course. Fourthly, the mistake in *Re Cleveland* was conceptually, as well as commercially, far more 'essential' or 'fundamental' to the issue of the bonus shares than the mistake in this case.

[175] I turn to the second defect upon which Mr Mabb rests his case on common mistake, namely the failure of the directors to obtain the approval, whether at an ordinary meeting or otherwise, of the shareholders of the company to the issue and allotment of the bonus shares. Here too, I take the view that this mistake did not vitiate, so as to render void, the issue of the bonus shares. In the first place, this was, as it were, a procedural defect, rather than a substantive defect. There is no doubt that the company, through its directors, had power to issue the bonus shares, and that, subject to the first defect which I have considered, the bonus shares could properly have been allotted as they were allotted. The failure to obtain the approval of the shareholders could, I accept, be said to result in the directors having exceeded their powers, because those powers were limited by the articles.

[176] Once again, it seems to me that the question of whether the issue and allotment of the bonus shares was, as a result, void for mistake must be decided by reference to the principles laid down by Steyn J in the *Associated Japanese Bank* case and by the Court of Appeal in *The Great Peace* effectively by analogy as indicated by Scott J in *Re Cleveland*. In connection with this defect, while the mistake can be said to be entirely the fault of the three directors, there is no question, as there was in relation to the first defect, of their having misled the 13 shareholders, or indeed the 28 shareholders (who also received the bonus shares) on this issue.

[177] Applying the approach of Scott J in *Re Cleveland*, on which Mr Mabb rests his case, one must consider whether the failure to obtain the consent of the 16 shareholders should be treated as such a fundamental defect as to vitiate the entire issue and allotment of the bonus shares. As Mr Mabb contends, the question has primarily to be determined by reference to how matters stood at the date of the issue and allotment of the bonus shares, i e the date that the notional contract came into existence and was performed, namely 15 December 1999. As at that date, the notional contract in relation to the issue of the bonus shares was between the company (and, possibly, the three directors) and the relevant shareholders, i e probably the 16 shareholders, given that the decision to issue and allot the bonus shares was made before the 28 shareholders became shareholders. Following *The Great Peace* I consider that the failure to obtain the consent of the 16 shareholders to the issue of the bonus shares to them could not possibly have been regarded, whether subjectively by the parties or objectively, as such a fundamental or essential mistake that it rendered the issue and allotment of the bonus shares void.

[178] The implied term test was rejected by the Court of Appeal in *The Great Peace* [2002] 4 All ER 689 at [73] as the basis for determining whether a term was 'essential' in the context of a mutual mistake. However, it is not uninstructive to consider the position if, on 15 December 1999, the officious bystander had asked the directors and the 16 shareholders whether the issue and allotment of the bonus shares should be treated as vitiated by mistake because there had been a failure to obtain the consent of the 16 shareholders to the issue and allotment of the bonus shares. There could only have been one answer, namely, 'Of course, not'.

[179] The mistake concerned was the directors' failure to obtain the consent of the 16 shareholders to the issue of the bonus shares. The purpose of that issue was to improve the position of the 16 shareholders (and any future shareholders), by rendering their shares in the company more easily and profitably marketable, if and when the company was floated on AIM. It would be fanciful to suggest that, in answer to the officious bystander, it is even conceivable that any of the shareholders would have suggested that the failure to obtain their consent, in these circumstances, to the allotment of the bonus shares would vitiate that allotment. Similarly, given that the company, through the three directors, wished to issue and allot the bonus shares, it is not conceivable that any of the directors would have even attempted to suggest, in answer to the officious bystander, that the failure to obtain the consent of the 16 shareholders should vitiate the issue and allotment of shares. The notion that the effect of £136,000-odd being transferred from the share premium account to the share capital account would have given a moment's concern to any shareholder, or indeed to the directors, appears to me to be fanciful.

[180] That view is reinforced when one considers the disastrous commercial consequences for the 16 shareholders if the bonus shares allotted to them had been void, a factor to which I have already referred. Because the bonus shares issued to the 33 shareholders may not be void, and because future allottees of shares (such as Mr Lee Barber) would acquire their shares for a price which assumed that the bonus shares were valid, a subsequent cancellation of the bonus shares would very substantially reduce the value of the shareholding of each of the 16 shareholders.

[181] However, as I have said, the implied term test is not, of itself, appropriate for determining the effect of mutual mistake. But the present

a instance is a case where the mistake was overlooking the need for the consent to
a transaction by one of the parties, namely the 16 shareholders. In such a case, if
all the parties involved in the contract, or the analogous arrangement, would
have plainly rejected the notion that the mistake would have vitiated the contract
or the arrangement, it seems to me (at least in the absence of very unusual facts)
wrong to conclude that the mistake could be regarded as 'essential' or
b 'fundamental', so as to vitiate the contract or arrangement.

[182] If the party whose consent was required, but not obtained, is not merely
content to dispense with the consent, but is positively disadvantaged by the
absence of his consent leading to the result that the contract or arrangement
being avoided, it seems almost grotesque that he should be forced to that result.
Yet that is the effect of Mr Mabb's argument, as is illustrated by the fact that
c Mr Paul, the representative of the 16 shareholders, whose assent was required, is
arguing, through Mr Chivers, against the arrangement in question, the issue of
the bonus shares, being avoided.

[183] I do not consider that the additional mistakes (identified in [149], above)
take matters further. It is clear from the number of bonus shares, the specific sum
d to be capitalised, and the fact that the issue was to be 99 for 1, all of which were
mentioned in the 15 December 1999 resolution, that the three directors intended
to allot bonus shares to the 16 shareholders. Accordingly, on the basis of
commercial common sense, the oral evidence of the three directors, and the
contemporaneous facts (eg the discussions with each of the 13 shareholders), it is
clear that the three directors intended to allot bonus shares to the 16
e shareholders.

[184] The argument for avoiding the bonus issue (entirely or in so far as it
relates to bonus shares allotted to the 16 shareholders) on the basis of the
additional mistakes places unjustifiable weight on the fact that the 15 December
1999 resolution appropriated the capitalised sum from the share premium
f account to shareholders 'in the same proportion as they would be entitled to that
sum were it distributed by way of dividend'. The argument not only overlooks
commercial common sense, the oral evidence of the three directors and the
contemporaneous evidence. It also overlooks that part of the 15 December 1999
resolution which specifically allots bonus shares to the holders of 'each ordinary
share'. Further, if one takes such a blinkered approach to the question of
g concentrating on the company's formal records, one would have to take into
account the 12 November 1999 minutes, which specifically record that the
November shares were fully paid up.

[185] Accordingly, I conclude that the contention that the issue of the
allotment of the bonus shares was, in whole or in part, void on the grounds of
h mistake must be rejected, even though, in so far as the bonus shares were allotted
to the 16 shareholders, there was a defect in that the November shares had not
been paid up at all, and, in relation to the issue and allotment of all the bonus
shares, there was a failure to obtain the assent of the 16 shareholders.

[186] If this analysis of the consequences of the common mistakes in this case
j is not right, then, as at present advised, I would still have rejected the contention
that the bonus shares were void. Each of the two defects arises from the fact that
the bonus shares (or some of them) should not have been issued paid up through
the capitalisation of a sum in the share premium account. In other words, neither
the issue nor the allotment of the bonus shares as shares were of themselves
irregular owing to the defects: the irregularity lay in the fact that the bonus shares
(or some of them) were issued and allotted paid up. In those circumstances, I

would have concluded that, if there was a void aspect, it was the payment up of the bonus shares (or at least those allotted to the 16 shareholders) through the capitalisation of a sum in the share premium account, rather than the issue of the bonus shares. Thus the bonus shares would be valid as shares, but (at least those allotted to the 16 shareholders) they would not be treated as paid up (with the consequences which follow from the reasoning in the *Ooregum* case). As a matter of principle, it appears to me that where a common mistake results in voidness, the court should, where it accords with principle and is commercially sensible, seek to achieve an outcome which minimises the extent of the voidness. That view seems to me to accord with Steyn J's 'first imperative', but it is somewhat tentative, as the point was only touched on, but not fully argued, during the hearing.

[187] I suppose one reason that it was not fully argued may be that the point does not strictly arise on the preliminary issues ordered by the master. None the less, if there is an avoidable aspect of the bonus shares, the conclusion that it only attaches to the payment up of those shares (or some of them), rather than to the shares themselves, appears to me to accord far better with principle and commercial common sense. Such a conclusion, in relation to each of the two defects, does not run into the commercial common sense difficulties which face the conclusion that the bonus shares were themselves void.

[188] Finally, on this aspect, I should make three points. First, it might appear that my conclusion that the issue of the bonus shares was not void, despite the failure to obtain the consent of the 16 shareholders, is precious close to letting in the argument based on the *Duomatic* principle through the back door, having barred the front door. However, I do not consider that that is a valid point. If the *Duomatic* principle had applied, then (at least if the November shares had been fully paid up by 15 December 1999) the issue and allotment of the bonus shares would have been regular and unimpeachable. In light of my decision that the *Duomatic* principle does not apply, the issue and allotment of the bonus shares was irregular, and would, in light of the reasoning in *Re Cleveland*, have been capable of being void. As it is, because of the particular facts I have described, and in light of the reasoning in *The Great Peace* and the *Associated Japanese Bank* case, the issue and allotment of the shares, while in breach of the terms of the articles, is not void, and, indeed, appears to me to be unlikely to be assailable.

[189] Secondly, the voidness argument may be stronger in relation to the bonus shares allotted to Berdino, Okimax and Mr Reid, the three of the 16 shareholders being or owned by the three directors. Their state of knowledge, as to the defects, and, in relation to the first defect, because they were not misled into thinking that the November shares were paid up, puts them in a potentially different category from the 13 shareholders. At present, I doubt these distinctions justify a different result, but I have heard no argument on the point, and, indeed, any such argument may have been inappropriate because neither Berdino, Okimax or Mr Reid are parties to these proceedings.

[190] Thirdly, nobody has suggested that the logically anterior question of allocation of risk played any part in this case (see *The Great Peace* [2002] 4 All ER 689 at [80], [84]).

The effect of the breach of the articles and s 35A of the 1985 Act

[191] The second argument raised by Mr Mabb is that there was simply no power to issue the bonus shares on the facts I have found, because each of the two defects impinged the authority of the three directors, or of the company itself, to

a issue the bonus shares, either generally or in respect of the November shares. In answer to this, Mr Chivers does not rely on cases such as *Royal British Bank v Turquand* (1856) 6 E & B 327, [1843–60] All ER Rep 435. His contention is that the three directors have acted beyond their powers but the company has not acted beyond its powers, and that s 35A accordingly applies.

[192] Section 35A provides, so far as relevant:

b '(1) In favour of a person dealing with a company in good faith, the power of the board of directors to bind the company, or authorise others to do so, shall be deemed to be free of any limitation under the company's constitution.

(2) For this purpose—(a) a person "deals with" a company if he is a party to any transaction or other act to which the company is a party ...

c (5) [Subsection (1) does not] affect any liability incurred by the directors, or any other person, by reason of the directors' exceeding their powers.'

[193] Mr Chivers contends that each shareholder who received the bonus shares was a person who 'deal[t] with' the company, on the basis that the issue *d* and allotment of the bonus shares constituted a 'transaction or other act', 'to which the company [was] a party'. In this connection, I think it does not matter whether one regards the issue of the bonus shares as a single composite act, or whether one regards the issue of each parcel of bonus shares to particular shareholders as a separate act. That point was not gone into, and I suppose that it is conceivable that the decision to issue the bonus shares should be treated as *e* one act, and each decision to allot a specific parcel of bonus shares to shareholder is a separate act.

[194] In so far as Mr Reid, and Mr Spickernell and Mr Bryson, and their respective companies, are concerned, it is perhaps also relevant to refer to the provisions of s 35A(2)(b) and (c), which are to the following effect:

f '(b) a person shall not be regarded as acting in bad faith by reason only of his knowing that an act is beyond the powers of the directors under the company's constitution; and (c) a person shall be presumed to have acted in good faith unless the contrary is proved.'

It can be said with considerable force, and probably correctly (albeit that the point *g* was not discussed), that, as directors of the company, Mr Spickernell, Mr Bryson and Mr Reid should have known of the two breaches of the articles, and they knew the facts which gave rise to the two breaches. However, it seems to me pretty clear on the evidence that they did not 'know' that the issue and allotment of the bonus shares was 'beyond [their] powers', in the sense of being in breach *h* of the articles in the two respects I have found.

[195] I have not been specifically addressed on the issue of whether Mr Spickernell, Mr Bryson and Mr Reid acted 'in good faith' in connection with the issue and allotment of the bonus shares. In light of the findings I have made during the course of this judgment, my present, reasonably strong, inclination *j* would be to conclude that they did act in good faith. Although I have made criticisms of Mr Spickernell and Mr Bryson as witnesses, and although I have made a fairly damaging finding in relation to the disputed letter[b], none of the findings impinge directly on their conduct or state of mind as at 15 December 1999 in relation to the issue of the bonus shares. Further, at least at the moment,

---

b   Editor's note: this was a letter whose dating was in dispute.

I would be very unattracted by any suggestion that any detrimental findings I
have made would somehow even indirectly cast doubt on the good faith of   *a*
Mr Spickernell, Mr Bryson and Mr Reid in relation to the issue and allotment of
the bonus shares.

[196] I turn, then, to the central issue, namely whether the 44 shareholders to
whom the bonus shares were allotted can, in principle, take advantage of s 35A.
The words 'a person dealing with a company' in s 35A(1) are not expressly   *b*
fettered in any way. Thus, as a matter of ordinary language, a person (whether
or not already a shareholder) receiving shares (whether or not bonus shares) from
a company is 'a person dealing with a company'. Indeed, the reasoning and
approach of Scott J in *Re Cleveland*, which represents something of a sheet anchor
to Mr Mabb's case on voidness for mistake, appears to me to be consistent with
that view, as Mr Chivers points out. Both 'a person' and 'dealing with' are wide   *c*
expressions, which are not expressly limited in s 35A.

[197] It is true that s 35A was enacted to give effect to art 9 of the First Council
Directive (EEC) 68/151 (on the co-ordination of safeguards which, for the
protection of the interests of members and others, are required by member states
of companies within the meaning of the second paragraph of art 58 of the Treaty,   *d*
with a view to making such safeguards equivalent throughout the Community)
(OJ English Sp Edn 1968 (I) p 41) (see *Smith v Henniker-Major & Co* [2002] EWCA
Civ 762 at [19]–[20], [2002] 2 BCLC 655 at [19]–[20], [2003] Ch 182 at [19]–[20]),
and that art 9(2) limits reliance on the powers of the organs of the company 'as
against third parties'. However, I do not find that of much assistance to the third
defendant's case, essentially for two reasons. First, it is not entirely clear what is   *e*
meant by 'third parties' in art 9(2). Secondly, even if Directive 68/151 required
legislation along the lines of s 35A to protect persons dealing with the company,
who were not members of the company, there is no reason why the legislation
subsequently enacted should not have gone further—see what was said by
Schiemann LJ in *Smith's* case [2002] 2 BCLC 655 at [119]. Further, I note that   *f*
neither Carnwath LJ nor Schiemann LJ, who gave s 35A a slightly more restricted
effect, at least in relation to a director dealing with the company, than the wholly
unqualified meaning which the words might suggest, relied upon the directive.

[198] Mr Mabb suggests that the words 'to bind the company' and '[i]n favour
of a person' in s 35A(1) and the wording of s 35A(2)(a) suggest that members of
the company were not intended to be within the ambit of s 35A. I do not see how   *g*
those words assist that contention.

[199] In my view, there is no reason why s 35A should not apply to members
of the company dealing with the company, certainly in connection with matters
such as receiving shares, whether shares for which they pay, or bonus shares.
Apart from the natural meaning of s 35A, it seems to me that this conclusion   *h*
receives a degree of support from the judgment in *Smith's* case.

[200] Robert Walker LJ, who dissented on this issue, accepted (at [52]) that,
even the director involved in the unauthorised act, could be a 'person' within
s 35A, in light of the preceding paragraphs. It is fair to say that part of his
reasoning could not be directly invoked by Mr Chivers in the present case, in that   *j*
he relied in part on s 322A of the 1985 Act, which only applies to directors.
However, it seems to me that it would be surprising if s 35A could apply to the
very director involved in making the unauthorised decision, but could not apply
to a wholly innocent shareholder.

[201] So far as the judgment of Carnwath LJ is concerned, he held that, on the
facts of that case, the director concerned could not rely on s 35A, but emphasised

a (at [110]) that he preferred 'to express no view about the position of directors in other circumstances'. In the preceding paragraph, he accepted that s 35A—

> 'does not distinguish between insiders and outsiders. It applies to any "person dealing with the company". These words are wide enough to include a director of the company. There is nothing in law to prevent a director from being "a person dealing" with his own company.'

b

Like Robert Walker LJ, he derived some assistance in reaching that conclusion from s 322A, but it appears to me that, rather contrary to Mr Mabb's submission, Carnwath LJ's judgment tends, if anything, to support the view that a shareholder is not prevented from relying on s 35A in a case such as this.

c [**202**] Schiemann LJ agreed with Carnwath LJ. He asked (at [118]):

> 'Does that section [sc s 35A] enable a director, who has made an honest mistake as to the meaning of the provision in the articles of the company of which he is director, himself to rely on his own mistake in order to give validity to something which would lack validity were it not for that mistake?'

d

He accepted (at [125]) 'that the word "person" is on its face wide enough to include such a director', but ultimately rejected the contention that it did. The implication in his judgment, at least to me, is that as a matter of principle a director may not be excluded from s 35A, and that there is no reason why a shareholder should be excluded from that section, especially where he is 'dealing with' the company, in the ordinary sense of that expression.

e

[**203**] In these circumstances, I am of the view that a shareholder receiving bonus shares from the company is 'a person dealing with a company' within the ambit of s 35A(1). First, as a matter of ordinary language, such a shareholder would be within the ambit of those wide words, and, in the absence of a powerful reason to the contrary, it is inappropriate to treat naturally wide words in a statute as subject to an implied limitation. Secondly, the majority view in *Smith's* case was that the policy behind s 35A was such that the very director responsible for the mistake, even if an innocent mistake, should not be able to rely upon s 35A, but that does not, to my mind, cast doubt on my conclusion. Thirdly, the reasoning of each member of the Court of Appeal, as summarised above, appears to me, if anything, to support the conclusion I have reached.

f

g

[**204**] Fourthly, I believe that s 322A of the 1985 Act, to which reference was made in all three of the judgments in *Smith's* case, tends, albeit indirectly, to support this conclusion. Section 322A sets out the circumstances in which s 35A cannot be relied on (see sub-s (7)), and it is concerned with the voidability of certain transactions entered into between the company and either a director or a person connected with a director. As Mr Chivers contends, it would be strange if the benefit of s 35A was removed from one group of individuals, namely directors and persons connected with them, in express terms by the legislature, but the benefit of the section was removed from another group, namely shareholders, merely by implication.

h

j

[**205**] Fifthly, the policy behind s 35A was summarised by Carnwath LJ in *Smith's* case (at [108]), in these terms:

> 'The general policy seems to be that, if a document is put forward as a decision of the board by someone appearing to act on behalf of the company, in circumstances where there is no reason to doubt its authenticity, a person

dealing with the company in good faith should be able to take it at face
value ...'

It appears to me that, in relation to the bonus share certificates issued to the 16
shareholders (and indeed the 33 shareholders), this case plainly falls within that
policy.

[206] If s 35A is in principle capable of being relied on by a shareholder
receiving bonus shares, Mr Mabb further contends that reg 110 is not so much a
'limitation', the word used in s 35A(1), but an enabling power, and, even if it is to
be regarded as a limitation, it is a limitation on the power of the company, not on
the power of the board. I do not agree. It appears to me that the opening words
of reg 110 make it clear that the power to issue bonus shares is ultimately given
to the directors. I accept that reg 110 may be characterised as 'an enabling
power', but it is a power subject to limitations, and the defects in this case, namely
that the shares in respect of which the bonus shares were issued must be paid up,
and that the bonus shares should have been issued with the authority of an
ordinary resolution, arise from the fact that the limitations have been effectively
ignored in those respects.

[207] Finally, Mr Mabb argues that the question of whether s 35A applies to a
particular shareholder will depend upon the facts relating to the particular
shareholder, and the point is therefore covered by the limitation already imposed
on the declaration as to voidness which he seeks, namely 'without prejudice to
the right of any person who was previously a member of the company to raise
any defence arising out of his own particular circumstances'. While that point has
some force, it is a rather strange submission from a party who is seeking a
declaration as to voidness subject to that limitation. If I had concluded that the
issue of the bonus shares was void, it would then have been necessary to decide
whether or not to grant a declaration to that effect. One of Mr Chivers's
objections to such a declaration (which I shall consider below) would have been
that it would be of little use, because it would still be necessary to consider the
facts of each case, as the qualification I have quoted indicates. Mr Mabb's answer
to that point is that it would none the less be useful to have a decision in principle
on the issue of voidness. If that is right, then it would also be useful, as I see it, to
have a decision in principle as to the applicability of s 35A. In any event, at least
on the facts currently known to me, it is hard to see the grounds upon which any
shareholder who received bonus shares could be prevented from relying on
s 35A.

[208] If I am wrong as to the applicability of s 35A, then I would none the less
have concluded that the effect of the two defects would not have been to have
rendered the bonus shares, or some of them, invalid. It would have been to
render their having been paid up invalid. As I have observed in relation to the
mistake argument (see [186], [187], above), it seems right to minimise the effect
of the defects, in so far as it is possible to do so consistently with principle and
commercial common sense. Again, as with my similar view in relation to
mistake, this is a somewhat tentative view, but it would appear to produce a
more sensible result than the bonus shares themselves being avoided.

The declaration as to voidness

[209] If I had decided that the issue or allotment of the bonus shares was void,
that would have raised a further question, namely whether I should have granted
a declaration to that effect. The court has a discretion whether or not to grant a

a declaration. It seems to me that the effect of the observations of Millett LJ in *Patten v Burke Publishing Co Ltd* [1991] 2 All ER 821, [1991] 1 WLR 541 and of Lord Woolf MR in *Messier-Dowty Ltd v Sabena SA (No 2)* [2001] 1 All ER 275, [2000] 1 WLR 2040 is that, when considering whether to grant a declaration, the court should bear in mind justice to the parties, the extent to which a declaration would serve a useful purpose, and whether there are any special reasons, in favour or b against granting a declaration. In effect, the discretion is one whose exercise depends very much on the particular facts of the particular case.

[210] The arguments against granting a declaration in such circumstances would have been fairly formidable. First, even if the issue and allotment of the bonus shares had been void initially, it seems to me that the bonus shares could no longer have been treated as void once they had been acquired for value by the c Guernsey company. Whether that would have been on the basis of the Guernsey company being a bona fide purchaser for value of the shares without notice, or whether it is more properly based on estoppel, matters not. For authority on this point, one need look no further than observations, admittedly obiter, of Scott J in *Re Cleveland Trust plc* [1991] BCLC 424 at 437 to the following effect:

d 'Finally I should comment on the position of third parties who might have become assignees for value of the bonus shares. I am told that there are no such third parties. If there had been, they would, I think, have been entitled as against Cleveland to rely on the share certificates relating to the shares. Their title would derive not from the void bonus issue itself but from an estoppel based upon the content of the share certificates. A decision that the e bonus issue should be declared void for mistake does not, in my opinion, place innocent third party assignees in jeopardy.'

[211] If the bonus shares would now be valid, and indeed would have been valid for nearly three years, it would seem rather strange to declare that they had f been void.

[212] Secondly, the person arguing for a declaration that the bonus shares were void is the third defendant, Mr Lee Barber. He would seem to have no locus standi to argue the point, given that he is no longer a shareholder in the company, having ceased in April 2000 to be a shareholder when the company was taken over by the Guernsey company. Further, at least on the evidence I have heard, g he would seem to have no basis for complaint in any event. When he acquired his shares in the company, in January 2000, Mr Lee Barber was not misled in any way in connection with the bonus shares. Thus, he was not led to believe that the bonus shares did not exist: he bought his shares, as I understand it, knowing full well the total number of issued shares in the company. While I appreciate h that he did not understand that the bonus shares had been issued and allotted in breach of the articles, he in no way suffered as a result.

[213] Had the Guernsey company not taken over the company, then, as I have mentioned, it would have represented nothing other than a wholly uncovenanted windfall for Mr Lee Barber, and other persons who had acquired j shares in the company after 15 December 1999, if some or all of the bonus shares were effectively cancelled. It would have resulted in their owning a substantially greater proportion of the company than they had previously owned, or than they thought they were acquiring when they purchased their shares. Indeed, in his evidence he acknowledged that he had received the correct number of, and the correct proportion of the total issued shares for which he had negotiated. Even though he is a representative party, Mr Chivers points out that, if I conclude that

he is not entitled to a declaration, then it cannot be contended that any other a
person whom he represents would be entitled to a declaration (see *Towers v
African Tug Co* [1904] 1 Ch 558 at 566–567 per Vaughan Williams LJ).

[214] Thirdly, just as it would have represented an unfair windfall for
shareholders such as Mr Lee Barber, if the bonus shares were void, so would it
have represented an unfair penalty for shareholders who received bonus shares,
such as Mr Phipps and Mr Paul. b

[215] Fourthly, the declaration which would have been sought by
Mr Lee Barber on this issue would have been qualified in any event, because the
declaration of voidness would have been expressly subject to the proviso that it
was 'without prejudice to the right of any person who was previously a member
of the company to raise any defence arising out of his own particular
circumstances'. c

[216] Despite these arguments, if I had decided that the issue and allotment of
the bonus shares was void in whole or in part, I would have thought it right to
grant a declaration to that effect. It is not as if Mr Lee Barber is the only party to
the litigation who would have been seeking such a declaration if I had made such
a finding. The claimants, ie the company and the Guernsey company, would d
both have wanted a declaration to that effect. Secondly, the purpose of seeking
such a declaration would have been to have a determination by an English court,
as to the effect of the breaches of the articles on the validity of, issue and
allotment of, the bonus shares. This would then have assisted the Guernsey
court, which, as I have mentioned, is faced with litigation which involves some
of the parties alleging that the bonus shares were void. e

[217] As I understand it, the argument of some of the shareholders in the
Guernsey company, including Mr Lee Barber, is that many of the shares
in the Guernsey company which were allotted, on the takeover of the company,
to shareholders in the company who had bonus shares, should effectively be
reallocated to shareholders who did not have such bonus shares. This would f
presumably be on the basis that, at the time of the acquisition of the company,
the bonus shares were void, and therefore should have been cancelled, in
accordance with the reasoning of Scott J in *Re Cleveland*, and that therefore the
shares in the Guernsey company allotted in respect of the bonus shares should
not have been so allotted, and should have been allotted instead to the other
shareholders in the company. g

[218] I do not propose to comment on the strength or otherwise of this
argument (which I may have summarised somewhat ineptly), because it would
be for the Guernsey courts to determine in accordance with Guernsey law, as
it relates to a Guernsey company, and in any event it has not been developed
before me. However, if I understand it correctly, it is, or may be, a necessary h
foundation of this argument that the bonus shares were void when issued. I think
there is considerable force in Mr Gillyon's contention that it would be more
sensible for the English court to determine whether or not the bonus shares were
void, rather than leaving it to the Guernsey company to determine this point of
English law. Observations of the Guernsey Court of Appeal appear to support j
this conclusion—see the judgment of Sir John Nutting QC (paras 43, 46, 50).

[219] Furthermore, at the most recent meeting of the shareholders of the
Guernsey company, there was a dispute as to which shareholders were entitled
to vote, and in respect of how many shares each shareholder was entitled to vote.
That dispute was, as I understand it, essentially based on the arguments I have
been rehearsing. As a result, it is said that the meeting could not proceed. It is

a fair to say that there is some reason for thinking that this dispute may not have been the real reason for the meeting of the Guernsey company being adjourned, and therefore I prefer not to rest my decision on that aspect.

[**220**] It is true that the declaration would have had to be qualified so that any individual could raise his particular circumstances to show that, despite my conclusion, the voidness of a particular bonus share, or parcel of bonus shares, *b* was not void, at least as against him. An obvious example would be a purchase of the bonus shares. However, I do not see why that should prevent a declaration of the sort I would have made if satisfied that the issue was void, being of some value to the company, the Guernsey company and the Guernsey courts.

[**221**] In all the circumstances, had I decided that some or all of the bonus *c* shares were void, at least until they were acquired by the Guernsey company, I would have been prepared so to declare. As it is, the point does not arise.

[**222**] In view of my decision that the issue of the bonus shares was not void on either ground raised by Mr Mabb, there is no reason why I should not so declare. However, as I have held that the breaches of the articles are avoided by *d* s 35A, and there could be circumstances in which shareholders who received bonus shares might not be able to rely upon s 35A, the declaration should be framed to reflect this. None the less, even in that event, I do not think any of the bonus shares would have been treated as void: they would merely have been treated as not paid up (see [208], above).

[**223**] I should like to add two points with regard to my conclusion that, *e* despite the breaches of the articles in relation to the issue of the bonus shares, their issue and allotment were not void. First, it is a conclusion which, on the facts of this case, appears to me to be a sensible one. So far as the failure to obtain the approval of the 16 shareholders to the payment of the bonus shares by the capitalisation of moneys in the share premium account is concerned, I have *f* already observed that this appears to me to be nothing but a technical defect. To my mind, it would have been a foregone conclusion that a majority of the 16 shareholders, indeed, all of those shareholders who bothered to vote, would have supported the proposal. In those circumstances, it would have been an extraordinary result if what, on the facts of this case, amounted to no more than a technical oversight on the part of the three directors, which was itself *g* attributable to poor legal advice, would have had the extraordinarily far-reaching and penal result of the bonus shares being cancelled.

[**224**] The fact that the November shares, in respect of which bonus shares were issued fully paid, were unpaid at the time, also appears to me to be, at least on the facts of this case, little more than a technical point, which one would not *h* expect to have far-reaching and penal consequences. Quite apart from the fact that, at any rate 13 of the 16 shareholders, who would suffer if the bonus shares were cancelled, were misled into thinking that their shares were paid up, the amount involved in paying up the November shares was very small, and it is clear that the November shares were going to be paid up. The only problem was that, *i* as at the crucial date, namely the date of issue and allotment of the bonus shares, no firm decision had been reached as to how they were to be paid up. Even if I am wrong in concluding that the issue of the bonus shares to the 13 shareholders (or, indeed, as it currently appears to me, to the 16 shareholders) was not affected, so far as they were concerned, by the fact that their November shares were not paid up, it appears to me that the furthest the effect of that fact can go, is to result in the bonus shares allotted to them being treated as nil paid.

[225] The second point is that, my conclusion that the two defects did not
render the bonus shares void does not mean that no relief could be accorded to
anybody as a result of the defects. It may be that, for instance, the issue or
allotment of some of the bonus shares could be voidable at the instance of a
person with a relevant interest who could establish that he had suffered as a result
of the breaches of the articles. Alternatively, such a person may be entitled to
recover damages or some other relief against (in decreasing order of likely
liability) the directors, or (possibly) the shareholders to whom the bonus shares
were allotted, or the company. Such a claim is specifically contemplated by
s 35A(5). On the facts of this case, at least as at present advised, I find it difficult
to see how any such claim could be established. However, there are a number of
issues raised by Mr Lee Barber (and possibly other persons who acquired shares
in the company after December 1999) against the three directors, and I do not
know much about some of those issues. At the moment, I do not understand
how any loss or prejudice alleged in those proceedings could sensibly be said to
have been suffered as a result of the failure to comply with the articles in relation
to the issue and allotment of the bonus shares, but it should be emphasised that
that is little more than a matter of impression.

CONCLUSION

[226] In these circumstances, my conclusions are as follows in relation to the
issues to be determined at this stage: (i) the bonus issue and the allotment of the
bonus shares were irregular because they were effected in respect of some shares,
namely the November shares, which were not paid up, albeit that the subscriber
shares were paid up; (ii) the issue of the bonus shares and their allotment was
irregular, because it was not approved by a resolution of the shareholders of the
company; (iii) however, in the circumstances of this case, neither of these defects
rendered the issue or allotment of the bonus shares void, but if s 35A did not
apply to a particular allottee, his bonus shares would have been treated as not
paid up.

Order accordingly.

Celia Fox   Barrister.

a

R (on the application of Anufrijeva) v Secretary of State for the Home Department

[2003] UKHL 36

b

HOUSE OF LORDS

LORD BINGHAM OF CORNHILL, LORD STEYN, LORD HOFFMANN, LORD MILLETT AND LORD SCOTT OF FOSCOTE

30 APRIL, 1 MAY, 26 JUNE 2003

c

Social security – Income support – Urgent cases payments – Asylum seekers – Claimant asylum seeker entitled to benefit until date claim for asylum recorded by Secretary of State as having been determined – Secretary of State recording determination of claim for asylum – Deliberate delay in notifying claimant – Whether claimant entitled to benefit until date of actual notification – Income Support (General) Regulations 1987, reg 70(3A)(b)(i).

d

The claimant applied for asylum in August 1998, and then made a claim for income support as an asylum seeker within reg 70(3A)(a)[a] of the Income Support (General) Regulations 1987, which provided that persons were asylum seekers within the meaning of the regulations when they submitted a claim which was recorded by the Secretary of State. She was paid income support at the applicable rate. Regulation 70(3A)(b)(i) provided, inter alia, that a person ceased to be an asylum seeker, in the case of a claim for asylum which was recorded by the Secretary of State as having been determined (other than on appeal), on the date on which it was so recorded. On 20 November 1999 an internal file note was signed in the Home Office, reading: 'For the reasons given in the letter aside … Refusal is appropriate. Case hereby recorded as determined.' The content of that note was communicated to the Benefits Agency on 30 November. It was not communicated to the claimant, and the 'letter aside' addressed to the claimant containing the Secretary of State's reasons for refusal of asylum was not sent to her. The claimant's income support was stopped with effect from 9 December 1999; the Benefits Agency informed the claimant's solicitors later in the month that payments had been stopped because it had been notified that her asylum claim had been refused on 20 November. It was Home Office departmental policy not to communicate to an asylum seeker that their claim had been refused until an immigration officer had considered whether the asylum seeker's request for leave to enter should be granted on some ground other than that of refugee status. On 25 April 2000 an immigration officer's written notice of refusal was sent to the claimant, together with the letter of 20 November 1999. The claimant applied for judicial review of, inter alia, the Home Secretary's decision to treat her asylum claim as having been refused on 20 November 1999 and the Secretary of State for Social Security's decision to withdraw her income support on 9 December 1999. Her application was dismissed, as was her subsequent appeal to the Court of Appeal, because both courts regarded themselves as bound by a previous decision of the Court of Appeal to the effect that, for the purposes of

e

f

g

h

j

---

a   Regulation 70, so far as material, is set out at [3] and [6], below

reg 70(3A)(b)(i), a person ceased to be entitled to income support from the date *a* when his claim for asylum was recorded as determined on an internal file note in the Home Office, even though he had not yet been informed of the determination. The claimant appealed.

Held – (Lord Bingham dissenting) The right of access to justice was a fundamental and constitutional principle of the United Kingdom legal system. *b* That right meant that notice of a decision was required before it could have the character of a determination with legal effect because the individual concerned had to be in a position to challenge that decision in the courts if he or she wished to do so. The constitutional principle requiring the rule of law to be observed also required that a constitutional state had to accord to individuals the right to know of a decision before their rights could be adversely affected. It was an *c* unjust proposition that an uncommunicated administrative decision could bind an individual. Parliament had not expressly or by necessary implication legislated to displace the applicable constitutional principles. The claimant's appeal would accordingly be allowed (see [26], [28], [30], [31], [34], [36], [37], [43], [44], [57], [59], below); *R v Secretary of State for the Home Dept, ex p Salem* [1999] QB 805 overruled. *d*
   Decision of the Court of Appeal [2002] All ER (D) 365 (Mar) reversed.

Notes
For persons from abroad entitled to claim income support, see Supp, to 44(2) *Halsbury's Laws* (4th edn reissue) para 200.
   Regulation 70(3A) of the Income Support (General) Regulations 1987, was *e* revoked by reg 3(1), (7)(c) of the Social Security (Immigration and Asylum) Consequential Amendments Regulations 2000, with effect from 3 April 2000.

Cases referred to in opinions
Firma A Racke v Hauptzollamt Mainz Case 98/78 [1979] ECR 69, ECJ.
Hillingdon London BC v Commission for Racial Equality [1982] AC 779, [1982] 3 WLR *f* 159, HL.
HTV Ltd v Price Commission [1976] ICR 170, CA.
Laker Airways Ltd v Dept of Trade [1977] 2 All ER 182, [1977] QB 643, [1977] 2 WLR 234, CA.
Opel Austria GmbH (Austria intervening) v EU Council (European Commission *g* *intervening)* Case T-115/94 [1997] All ER (EC) 97, [1997] ECR II-39, CFI.
Preston v IRC [1985] 2 All ER 327, [1985] AC 835, [1985] 2 WLR 836, HL.
R v Secretary of State for Social Security, ex p Joint Council for the Welfare of Immigrants, R v Secretary of State for Social Security, ex p B [1996] 4 All ER 385, [1997] 1 WLR 275, CA. *h*
R v Secretary of State for the Home Department, ex p Salem [1999] QB 805, [1999] 2 WLR 1, CA; *affd* [1999] 2 All ER 42, [1999] AC 450, [1999] 2 WLR 483, HL.
R v Secretary of State for the Home Dept, ex p Leech [1993] 4 All ER 539, [1994] QB 198, [1993] 3 WLR 1125, CA.
R v Secretary of State for the Home Dept, ex p Simms [1999] 3 All ER 400, [2000] 2 AC 115, [1999] 3 WLR 328, HL. *j*
Raymond v Honey [1982] 1 All ER 756, [1983] 1 AC 1, [1982] 2 WLR 465, HL.

Cases referred to in list of authorities
R v Secretary of State for the Home Dept, ex p Paulo [2001] EWHC Admin 480, [2001] Imm AR 645.

a *R v Westminster City Council, ex p A* (1997) 9 Admin LR 504, CA.
R v Secretary of State for the Home Dept, ex p Karaoui, R v Secretary of State for the Home Dept, ex p Abbad (1997) Times, 27 March.
R v Westminster CC, ex p Ermakov [1996] 2 All ER 302, CA.
Rafiq v Secretary of State for the Home Dept [1998] 1 FCR 293, CA.
Secretary of State for the Home Dept v Thirukumar [1989] Imm AR 402, CA.

b

Appeal

The claimant, Nadezda Anufrijeva, appealed with permission of the Court of Appeal (Schiemann, Hale and Sedley LJJ) from its decision on 22 March 2002 ([2002] EWCA Civ 399, [2002] All ER (D) 365 (Mar)) dismissing the claimant's appeal from the order of Sir Christopher Bellamy QC, sitting as a deputy judge of *c* the High Court, on 25 October 2001 ([2001] EWHC Admin 895, [2001] All ER (D) 353 (Oct)) dismissing the claimant's application for judicial review of the decision of the Home Secretary to treat her claim for asylum as having been refused on 20 November 1999 and the decision of the Secretary of State for Social Security to withdraw her income support benefit on 9 December 1999. The facts are set out *d* in the opinions of Lord Bingham of Cornhill and Lord Steyn.

Richard Drabble QC and *Nicola Braganza* (instructed by *Ole Hanson & Partners*) for the claimant.
John Howell QC and *Dinah Rose* (instructed by the *Treasury Solicitor* and the *Solicitor for the Department of Work and Pensions*) for the Secretaries of State for the *e* Home Department and for Social Security.

Their Lordships took time for consideration.

f 26 June 2003. The following opinions were delivered.

LORD BINGHAM OF CORNHILL.

[1] My Lords, the issue in this appeal is whether income support should have been paid to Nadezda Anufrijeva (the appellant) as an asylum seeker between 10 December 1999 and 25 April 2000. The answer depends on whether, on or before the earlier of those dates, she had ceased to be an asylum seeker. That in *g* turn depends on whether, on or before the earlier of the dates, her claim for asylum had been 'recorded by the Secretary of State as having been determined (other than on appeal)' within the meaning of reg 70(3A)(b)(i) of the Income Support (General) Regulations 1987, SI 1987/1967.

h [2] On 31 August 1998 the appellant, then aged 20, arrived at Gatwick airport with her father and several other members of her family. They were Lithuanians of Russian origin and had flown to this country from Lithuania. Her father claimed asylum for himself and other dependent members of the family. The appellant claimed asylum on her own behalf. It seems clear (and it has not been questioned) that her claim for asylum was duly recorded by the Secretary of State *j* as having been made.

[3] On 4 September 1998 the appellant claimed payment of income support. This is an income-related benefit governed by Pt VII of the Social Security Contributions and Benefits Act 1992. The amount payable to a 'person from abroad' as defined in reg 21(3) of the 1987 regulations is ordinarily nil, entitling such person to no payment. But Pt VI of the 1987 regulations made special

provision for some urgent cases, in which there was an entitlement to payment
of 90% of the amount normally payable to those entitled. The class of urgent case *a*
relevant for present purposes is persons from abroad who were asylum seekers
for purposes of para (3A) of reg 70 of the regulations. That paragraph provided
(so far as relevant):

> 'For the purposes of this paragraph, a person—(a) is an asylum seeker *b*
> when he submits on his arrival (other than on his re-entry) in the United
> Kingdom from a country outside the Common Travel Area a claim for
> asylum to the Secretary of State that it would be contrary to the United
> Kingdom's obligations under the [Geneva Convention relating to the Status
> of Refugees (Geneva, 28 July 1951); TS 39 (1953); Cmnd 9171) and the 1967
> Protocol to that convention (New York, 31 January 1967; TS 15 (1969); *c*
> Cmnd 3906)] for him to be removed from, or required to leave, the United
> Kingdom and that claim is recorded by the Secretary of State as having been
> made ...'

The appellant was accepted as falling within that description. Income support
at the applicable rate (90% of the normal rate) was accordingly paid to her with *d*
effect from 4 September 1998. It continued to be paid for some 14 months until,
with effect from 9 December 1999, payment was stopped.

[4] At some time after her arrival in the United Kingdom the appellant was
interviewed by an immigration officer concerning the merits of her asylum
claim. Decisions on asylum, however, unlike decisions on leave to enter, are *e*
taken not by immigration officers but by the Secretary of State. This
long-standing rule is now found in r 328 of the Statement of Changes in
Immigration Rules (1994) (HC 395) laid before Parliament in accordance with
s 3(2) of the Immigration Act 1971 as a statement of 'the practice to be followed'
in the administration of the Immigration Acts. Rule 328 provides:
f
> 'All asylum applications will be determined by the Secretary of State in
> accordance with the United Kingdom's obligations under the United
> Nations Convention and Protocol relating to the Status of Refugees. Every
> asylum application made by a person at a port or airport in the United
> Kingdom will be referred by the Immigration Officer for determination by
> the Secretary of State in accordance with these Rules.' *g*

The immigration officer's record of the interview with the appellant has not
been produced in these proceedings, but it was produced to and considered by
an adjudicator who heard appeals by the appellant and her father in December
2000–January 2001 (appeal nos CC/17722/00 and CC 15675/00, March 2000 *h*
(para 75)) and it seems clear that the record was sent to the officials responsible
for making asylum decisions on behalf of the Home Secretary to enable them
to make that decision.

[5] On 20 November 1999 the responsible official in the Integrated
Casework Directorate of the Home Office made a note to the following effect *j*
in the file relating to the appellant's asylum claim:

> 'This woman has cited numerous mishaps throughout the 1990s and puts
> her woes down to an encounter her father had with a drunken solicitor in
> 1991. There is no credibility in any of this and no Convention reason
> anyway. For the reasons given in the letter aside, this applicant has failed

a   to establish a well founded fear of persecution. Refusal is appropriate.
Case hereby recorded as determined. Certified under 5(4)(a).'

The terms of this note, and the certification of the appellant's asylum claim
under para 5(4)(a) of Sch 2 to the Asylum and Immigration Appeals Act 1993
as not showing a fear of persecution for a convention reason, make plain that
in the opinion of the Home Office the claim was hopeless. This was not the
b   view later taken by the adjudicator who, although rejecting the asylum claim,
believed the appellant's account, recommended that the Home Secretary
consider granting her exceptional leave to remain and declined to uphold
the certificate under para 5(4)(a). But the Home Office did not regard the
appellant's claim as in any way borderline, as is evident from the terms of
c   the 'letter aside': this was a draft letter setting out the Home Secretary's
reasons for refusing the asylum claim which was dated 20 November 1999, the
same date as the file note, but was not at that stage sent to the appellant or her
solicitors.

[6] Upon the making of the file note just described, the Home Office
considered (whether rightly or wrongly, which is the issue in this appeal) that
d   the appellant was no longer an asylum seeker and so no longer entitled to
payment of income support. As already shown, the appellant's entitlement to
income support depended on her being an asylum seeker within the definition
in para (3A) of reg 70 of the 1987 regulations. But that paragraph also provided:

e   'For the purposes of this paragraph, a person … (b) ceases to be an
asylum seeker—(i) in the case of a claim for asylum which, on or after 5th
February 1996, is recorded by the Secretary of State as having been
determined (other than on appeal) or abandoned, on the date on which it
is so recorded …'

f   The Home Office treated the appellant as ceasing to be an asylum seeker on
20 November 1999 and communicated its decision to the Benefits Agency,
responsible for paying income support to the appellant, some days later. That
agency ceased to pay income support to the appellant with effect from
9 December 1999 and on the same day wrote to her asking for the return of her
income support order book and directing her to cash no further orders. A week
g   earlier the London Borough of Southwark had written to the solicitors acting
for the appellant and her father referring to refusal of 'the family's' asylum
application and indicating that there was no longer an entitlement to housing
assistance. The appellant's solicitors gathered from the Benefits Agency and
the local authority that her (and her father's) asylum claims had been refused,
h   and on 23 December 1999 the Benefits Agency confirmed that it had been told
by the Home Office that her asylum claim had been refused on 20 November
and that payments of income support had been stopped with effect from
9 December. It is, however, a very regrettable feature of this case that the
appellant was not informed directly that her asylum claim had been refused or
when, was given neither reasons for the refusal nor any promise that reasons
j   would be given at a later date, and was not told that her income support
payments were to be stopped or why or when.

[7] Upon the Home Secretary's determination (or purported determination)
of the appellant's asylum claim, responsibility for resolving her immigration
status returned to the immigration officer at Gatwick. Had the Home Secretary
decided to grant asylum and had the appellant not yet received leave to enter,

the immigration officer would have granted limited leave to enter pursuant to
r 330 of the Immigration Rules. But r 331 provides:

> 'If a person seeking leave to enter is refused asylum, the Immigration
> Officer ... will then resume his examination to determine whether or not
> to grant him leave to enter under any other provision of these Rules. If the
> person fails at any time to comply with a requirement to report to an
> Immigration Officer for examination, the Immigration Officer may direct
> that the person's examination shall be treated as concluded at that time.
> The Immigration Officer will then consider any outstanding applications
> for entry on the basis of any evidence before him.'

[8] In order to discharge the duty under this rule, the immigration officer at
Gatwick wrote to the appellant on 28 November 1999, inviting her to attend for
interview there on 11 January 2000. At this interview, had it taken place, it is
likely that the appellant would have been refused leave to enter and would have
been handed the letter of 20 November 1999 setting out the Home Secretary's
reasons for refusing asylum. Rule 333 of the rules prescribed the procedure to
be followed:

> 'A person who is refused leave to enter following the refusal of an asylum
> application will be provided with a notice informing him of the decision
> and of the reasons for refusal. The notice of refusal will also explain any
> rights of appeal available to the applicant and will inform him of the means
> by which he may exercise those rights ... the applicant will not be removed
> from the United Kingdom so long as any appeal which he may bring or
> pursue in the United Kingdom is pending.'

At the applicant's request the interview arranged for 11 January 2000 was
deferred to 7 March 2000, but the appellant (unable, as she claimed, to afford
the train fare) did not attend. Nor, for the same reason, did she attend a further
interview arranged for 17 April. That led the immigration officer to give her a
written notice of refusal of leave to enter. The notice was dated 18 April 2000
but was sent to her on 25 April. At the same time he sent to the appellant the
letter of 20 November setting out the Home Secretary's reasons for refusing
asylum. Copies of these documents were sent to her solicitors on the same
date. It is common ground that the appellant would not on any showing have
been entitled to income support after 25 April 2000, unless an appeal against the
refusal of asylum had succeeded, in which case reg 21ZA of the 1987
regulations would have entitled her to retrospective payment.

[9] The appellant unsuccessfully challenged the refusal of her asylum claim
before an adjudicator, was refused permission by the Immigration Appeal
Tribunal to appeal against that decision and applied unsuccessfully for judicial
review of that refusal (see [2002] EWHC Admin 383). She was also refused
permission to apply for judicial review of the Home Secretary's refusal of leave
to enter (see [2002] EWHC Admin 600). In the present proceedings she sought
judicial review of two decisions: the Home Secretary's decision to treat her
asylum claim as having been refused on 20 November 1999; and the Secretary
of State for Social Security's decision to withdraw her income support benefit
on 9 December 1999. Her application was heard by Sir Christopher
Bellamy QC sitting as a deputy judge: in a detailed and careful reserved
judgment given on 25 October 2001 ([2001] EWHC Admin 895, [2001] All

a ER (D) 353 (Oct)) he dismissed the application, recognising considerable force in the submissions made on her behalf but holding himself bound to reject it by the Court of Appeal's decision in *R v Secretary of State for the Home Department, ex p Salem* [1999] QB 805, [1999] 2 WLR 1. In a judgment of the court delivered by Schiemann LJ, the Court of Appeal (Schiemann, Hale and Sedley LJJ) ([2002] EWCA Civ 300, [2002] All ER (D) 365 (Mar)) also held itself bound by *Ex p Salem*
b to dismiss the appeal but saw force in her arguments and gave her permission to appeal to the House.

[10] In opening the appeal, Mr Drabble QC for the appellant submitted, first, that it was not open to the Home Secretary to record a claim as determined on a date earlier than that on which it had in fact been determined. This is plainly so. Regulation 70(3A)(b)(i) of the 1987 regulations provides that
c a person ceases to be an asylum seeker on (relevantly) the date on which it is recorded by the Secretary of State that his claim for asylum has been determined otherwise than on appeal. An event cannot be 'recorded' for purposes of the subparagraph unless it has taken place. Thus on 20 November 1999 the responsible official could validly record the appellant's asylum claim
d as determined only if it had been determined. The plain intention of the provision was that income support should be payable to a qualifying asylum seeker so long as the Home Secretary's determination of the claim was pending but not once he had determined the claim and his determination had been recorded.

[11] Mr Drabble's second main submission was based on r 348 of the
e Immigration Rules which at the material time provided:

'Special provisions governing appeals in asylum cases are set out in the Asylum and Immigration Appeals Act 1993, the Asylum and Immigration Act 1996 and the Asylum Appeals (Procedure) Rules 1996 [SI 1996/2070].
f Where asylum is refused, the applicant will be provided with a notice informing him of the decision and of the reasons for refusal. At the same time that asylum is refused, the applicant may be notified of removal directions, or served with a notice of the Secretary of State's intention to deport him, as appropriate. The notice of refusal of asylum will also explain any rights of appeal available to the applicant and will inform him
g of the means by which he may exercise those rights.'

This rule, it was argued, must be read with reg 70(3A)(b)(i). It governs the steps to be taken when asylum is refused, requiring provision of a notice informing the applicant of the refusal and the reasons for it, and also the giving of information about the applicant's right of appeal. The rule is quite inconsistent
h with an uncommunicated refusal of asylum, recorded only in a departmental file. Not until the steps required by the rule have been accomplished has an asylum application been refused or determined adversely to the applicant. Thus the Home Secretary could not, on 20 November 1999, validly record an adverse determination which had yet to be made.

j [12] There are, in my opinion, a number of reasons why this argument cannot be accepted. First, the language of reg 70(3A)(b)(i) is not in any way ambiguous. It defines a date by reference to the recording by the Secretary of State of the claim for asylum as having been determined. It makes no reference to notification of the claimant. The reference to 'recorded' is, as Hobhouse LJ pointed out in *Ex p Salem* [1999] QB 805 at 812, [1999] 2 WLR 1 at 7: '... a formal criterion which must be applied by looking at the records kept by the Secretary of State. It is used in contrast and contradistinction to any concept of notification.' Although the Court of Appeal was divided on the outcome in *Ex p Salem*, there was no disagreement on this point. Secondly, the absence of reference to notification in reg 70(3A)(b)(i) cannot be treated as inadvertent, since in reg 21ZA of the 1987 regulations, inserted by amendment later in the same year as para (3A), express reference was made in paras (1) and (3) to notification of the asylum claimant that he had been recorded as a refugee. In s 6 of the Asylum and Immigration Appeals Act 1993 (since repealed but re-enacted) it was similarly provided that:

'During the period beginning when a person makes a claim for asylum and ending when the Secretary of State gives him notice of the decision on the claim, he may not be removed from, or required to leave, the United Kingdom.'

Parliamentary draftsmen have no difficulty in distinguishing between the making of a determination or decision and giving notice of it to the party affected. Thirdly, there are compelling practical reasons why reg 70(3A)(b)(i) should not have provided for notification. As already noted in [7], above, the Home Secretary's decision on asylum is the first stage in a two-stage process in which, under rr 330 and 331 of the Immigration Rules, the second stage is performed by the immigration officer. Where the Home Secretary's decision is to grant asylum, the immigration officer's role may be something of a formality. But where the Home Secretary's decision is to refuse asylum, the immigration officer must none the less consider whether leave to enter should be given. Thus the Home Secretary's decision on asylum, even if favourable, does not finally resolve the applicant's immigration status, and if it is adverse it gives rise of itself to no ground of appeal, since under s 8 of the 1993 Act (since repealed but re-enacted) an appeal lay only against the refusal of leave to enter and not against the refusal of asylum as such. Rule 348 of the Immigration Rules is directed to the last formal stage of the immigration officer's involvement, as evidenced by the references to removal directions and notice of intention to deport. The Home Secretary's decision on asylum must necessarily have come earlier.

[13] A further ground for rejecting Mr Drabble's second submission is found in consideration of the perceived mischief at which reg 70(3A)(b)(i) was directed. The provisions contained in the Social Security (Persons from Abroad) Miscellaneous Amendments Regulations 1996, SI 1996/30, were the subject of a statement made by the Secretary of State to the Social Security Advisory Committee in accordance with s 174(2) of the Social Security Administration Act 1992. In this he recorded that in recent years the number of asylum applications made in the United Kingdom had increased very sharply, both absolutely and proportionately in relation to other countries. Well over 90% of those claiming were found not to be genuine refugees. Most of these were economic migrants, attracted to this country by the ready availability in this country of benefits which were relatively generous, in comparison both with wages in the applicants' countries of origin and with benefits available in some other European countries. The availability of such benefits during the process of appeal following initial rejection of an asylum claim provided a further inducement, since a high proportion of

a unsuccessful applicants appealed, although only 4% of appeals succeeded. The number of applicants and appellants made for further delay and, inevitably, greater cost to the taxpayer. The proposed solution (para 57 of the statement) was to withdraw benefits from 'asylum seekers who have been found by the immigration authorities not to be refugees' and also from those claiming asylum otherwise than on arrival in the country. In *R v Secretary of State for*

b *Social Security, ex p Joint Council for the Welfare of Immigrants, R v Secretary of State for Social Security, ex p B* [1996] 4 All ER 385, [1997] 1 WLR 275 the Court of Appeal, by a majority (Neill LJ dissenting), held the 1996 regulations to be ultra vires on the ground that:

c   'Parliament cannot have intended a significant number of genuine asylum seekers to be impaled on the horns of so intolerable a dilemma: the need either to abandon their claims to refugee status or alternatively to maintain them as best they can but in a state of utter destitution.' (See [1996] 4 All ER 385 at 402, [1997] 1 WLR 275 at 293 per Simon Brown LJ.)

d Parliament's response was to enact s 11 of the Asylum and Immigration Act 1996, which provided in sub-s (1):

      'Notwithstanding any enactment or rule of law, regulations may exclude any person who has made a claim for asylum from entitlement to any of the following benefits, namely—(a) income support ...'

e Regulation 70(3A)(b)(i) of the 1987 regulations applied to asylum applicants whose claims were granted by the Home Secretary as well as those whose claims were refused, but the latter were expected to be far more numerous. (In an earlier explanatory memorandum submitted to the Advisory Committee reference had been made, in para 12, to 'ending the benefit entitlement of all asylum applicants at the point where they receive a negative decision from the

f Home Office' and, in para 17, to removing entitlement 'at the point where the initial decision is made by the immigration authorities that the applicant is not a refugee and should not be granted exceptional leave to remain'. This language was not, however, repeated in the Secretary of State's later statement and is not to be found in the regulations as amended in 1996.) To read

g reg 70(3A)(b)(i) as intended to deny income support to an unsuccessful asylum applicant from the day that the Home Secretary's decision to refuse asylum was recorded, no matter how long it might thereafter take the immigration officer finally to resolve the applicant's immigration status, is not to defeat but to give effect to what I regard as a clear legislative intention. It is not of course for the House, sitting judicially, to express any view on the merits of this legislation.

h Mr Drabble pointed out that although a very small percentage of those claiming asylum were found to be refugees, a much larger number were granted exceptional leave to remain.

    [14] Mr Drabble's second major submission was that the statutory scheme imposed a public law duty on the Home Secretary to notify the appellant of the asylum decision, that a decision only recorded in an uncommunicated file note could not be other than provisional, since it could be altered at any time before notification was given to the appellant, and that accordingly there was no determination for purposes of reg 70(3A)(b)(i) until 25 April 2000. This submission drew on the revulsion naturally felt for an official decision, taken privately, recorded in an undisclosed file and not communicated to the person

to whom the decision relates. This somewhat Kafkaesque procedure was to some extent mitigated in this case by the fact that the appellant and her solicitors learned of the decision, although indirectly, relatively soon after it was made, that she would have received formal notice of the refusal with reasons two months earlier than she did if she had not cancelled the meeting fixed for 11 January 2000 and that her right of appeal would not have arisen until she had been refused leave to enter even if notice of the asylum decision had been given earlier. This is, however, an unhappy feature of the case and it is reassuring to learn that the practice has been changed.

[15] I would readily accept that the Home Secretary was subject to a public law duty to notify the appellant of his decision on her asylum application and, if it was adverse, his reasons for refusing it. Such an obligation is expressed explicitly in r 348 of the Immigration Rules and would in any event be implied. But there is inevitably, in a written procedure, some gap between the making and notifying of a decision. Rule 348 prescribes no time limit. Any implied duty would be to give notice within a reasonable time. Failure to give notice within a reasonable time would be a breach of the Home Secretary's public law duty but would not necessarily nullify or invalidate his decision. In any event, it was not argued that notice of the Home Secretary's reasons was not given within a reasonable time.

[16] Sir Christopher Bellamy QC cited *Firma A Racke v Hauptzollamt Mainz* Case 98/78 [1979] ECR 69 at 84 (para 15), for this proposition:

'A fundamental principle in the Community legal order requires that a measure adopted by the public authorities shall not be applicable to those concerned before they have the opportunity to make themselves acquainted with it.'

Reference was also made to *Opel Austria GmbH (Austria intervening) v EU Council (European Commission intervening)* Case T-115/94 [1997] All ER (EC) 97 at 118, [1997] ECR II-39 at 82 (para 124). Both these cases, however, concerned Community regulations, and even so it was recognised that there could exceptionally be departures from the principle (see the *Firma A Racke* case [1979] ECR 69 at 86 (para 20)). I do not think this principle can be readily applied in a domestic context to an official decision which, although undoubtedly affecting the rights of the individual, calls for no compliance by that individual and exposes him or her to no penalty. No domestic authority was cited to support such a rule, which would in any event be overridden by what I have found to be a clear legislative intention that payment of income support should stop on the day the Home Secretary's decision is recorded, irrespective of notification to the claimant.

[17] I would accept that, to be a determination within the meaning of reg 70(3A)(b)(i), a decision must have a sufficient quality of finality about it. There is no room for what Hobhouse LJ in *R v Secretary of State for the Home Department, ex p Salem* [1999] QB 805 at 823, [1999] 2 WLR 1 at 17–18, called 'the undeterminative determination'. In that case, however, all members of the court agreed—

'that as a matter of statutory construction, the asylum seeker's right to income support in a favoured category of "persons from abroad" stops immediately on the date the Secretary of State records his determination *a*   of the claim.' (See [1999] QB 805 at 824, [1999] 2 WLR 1 at 18 per Brooke LJ.)

The issue which divided the court was whether the Home Secretary had made a determination in May 1997, when an internal record of refusal was made. Hobhouse LJ, dissenting, held that there had been no determination at that date because later correspondence was wholly inconsistent with the Home
b   Secretary having already made a determination. The majority (Brooke LJ and Sir John Balcombe) held that the Home Secretary had made a determination in May when he was recorded as having done so, even though he continued to be willing to receive representations bearing on the applicant's claim for asylum. It is unnecessary to resolve that difference of opinion, which turned very
c   largely on how the exchanges between the parties were properly to be understood. The facts here permit no such difference of opinion. As pointed out in [5], above, the Home Office regarded this (wrongly, as the adjudicator held) as a very clear case. Relatively prompt steps were taken to stop the payment of benefit and the provision of housing assistance and to instruct the immigration officer to resume the examination. Only with reluctance did
d   the immigration officer agree to postpone the meeting arranged for 11 January 2000. At no stage did the Home Secretary or his officials invite or indicate willingness to consider further submissions on the appellant's asylum claim, and nothing suggests that they had second thoughts about the correctness of its rejection.

e   [18] I cannot accept that a decision or determination must necessarily be regarded as provisional and lacking the quality of finality necessary for recognition as a decision or determination because it is open to the decision-maker to alter it. I take one example. Section 47(2) of the Supreme Court Act 1981 provides that:

f   '... a sentence imposed, or other order made, by the Crown Court when dealing with an offender may be varied or rescinded by the Crown Court within the period of 28 days beginning with the day on which the sentence or other order was imposed or made ...'

The existence of that power could not, in my opinion, be said to render
g   provisional any sentence passed or order made, or to deny recognition of such sentence or order as a decision or determination. In that context, of course, the sentence or order would ordinarily be communicated to the defendant, but it has already been shown that notification or communication of a decision in this context is not, in law, a necessary condition of its recognition as having
h   been made.

[19] In my respectful opinion the legal principles stated by all three members of the court in *Ex p Salem* were correct, and I would endorse them. Applied to this case, for the reasons I have given, they compel the conclusion that this appeal should be dismissed.

i   [20] I am naturally concerned that my noble and learned friends have formed a different opinion. I would not for my part question the principle of legality, let alone the importance of maintaining the rule of law. It is however a cardinal principle of the rule of law, not inconsistent with the principle of legality, that subject to exceptions not material in this case effect should be given to a clear and unambiguous legislative provision. There is nothing in any way unclear or ambiguous about the words 'recorded by the Secretary of State

as having been determined ... on the date on which it is so recorded'. They
define the moment when a person ceases to be an asylum seeker and so
disentitled to income support. The words do not say and cannot be fairly
understood to mean 'recorded by the Secretary of State as having been
determined ... on the date on which it is so recorded and notice given to the
applicant'. To contrast this provision with other provisions in which express
reference is made to notification is not to rely on niceties of statutory language
but to undertake a conventional exercise of construction, seeking to give effect
to the meaning of the regulations. If, as I think, the meaning of reg 70(3A)(b)(i)
is plain, it cannot be overridden by the terms of the Immigration Rules, which
do not have legislative force and which in any event provide that refusal of
asylum by the Home Secretary will be followed by the immigration officer's
decision on leave to enter, at which stage (not before) notice of the refusal of
asylum and the reasons for it will be given. It is only then that the applicant's
right of appeal for the first time arises. While I share the distaste of my noble
and learned friends for the procedure followed in this case, that distaste should
not lead the House to give reg 70(3A)(b)(i) anything other than its clear and
obvious meaning.

LORD STEYN.

[21] My Lords, the question is how reg 70(3A)(b)(i) of the Income Support
(General) Regulations 1987, SI 1987/1962, should be interpreted. The question
is whether Parliament intended to authorise the withdrawing of income
support by an internal note on a departmental file with legal effect from a date
before notification of the decision. At first glance it may appear to be a rather
technical issue. But the decision by the House may have a more general
bearing on the development of our public law.

[22] The background is as follows. On 31 August 1998 the appellant applied
for asylum. On 4 September 1998 she claimed income support benefits, which
were paid with effect from that date. Regulation 70(3A) of the 1987 regulations
provides for the payment of income support at the rate applicable for urgent
cases (90% of the normal rate) to persons who are asylum seekers within the
meaning of the same regulation. Regulation 70(3A)(b)(i) provides that a person
ceases to be an asylum seeker (and thus loses the right to income support)—

'in the case of a claim for asylum which, on or after 5th February 1996, is
recorded by the Secretary of State as having been determined (other than
on appeal) or abandoned, on the date on which it is so recorded ...'

On 20 November 1999 a Mr Stuart Beaton signed an internal file note. It read:

'This woman has cited numerous mishaps throughout the 1990s and puts
her woes down to an encounter her father had with a drunken solicitor in
1991. There is no credibility in any of this and no Convention reason
anyway. For the reasons given in the letter aside, this application has failed
to establish a well founded fear of persecution. Refusal is appropriate.
Case hereby recorded as determined.'

On 30 November 1999 the content of this file note was communicated to the
Benefits Agency. It was not communicated to the appellant and the 'letter
aside' of 20 November 1999 containing the Home Secretary's reasons for
refusal of asylum was not sent to the appellant.

a   [23] By letter of 28 November 1999 the appellant was asked to attend an interview on 11 January 2000. On 9 December and 15 December 1999 the Benefits Agency asked for the return of the appellant's income support book. The appellant's income support was stopped without explanation with effect from 9 December 1999. On 17 December 1999 the solicitors now acting for the appellant asked the Home Office for a postponement of the interview fixed for

b 11 January 2000. On 23 December 1999 the Benefits Agency advised the appellant's solicitors that it had been informed by the Home Office that the appellant's claim for asylum had been refused on 20 November 1999. For this reason the Benefits Agency had stopped the income support payments with effect from 9 December 1999. On 24 December 1999 the appellant's solicitors lodged an appeal with the Benefits Agency against the withdrawal of the

c appellant's income support. A further interview was arranged by the Home Office for 7 March 2000, which was subsequently refixed for 17 April 2000. The appellant was unable to comply because she was unable to obtain funds for the train fare. Under cover of a letter dated 25 April 2000 the decision rejecting the appellant's application for asylum and refusing her leave to enter was sent to her. The notice of refusal of leave to the appellant to enter the United Kingdom

d was signed by an immigration officer on 18 April 2000 and sent to the appellant. The notice of 18 April 2000 was accompanied by the reasons for refusal letter dated 20 November 1999.

   [24] The hearing at first instance before Sir Christopher Bellamy QC ([2001] EWHC Admin 895, [2001] All ER (D) 353 (Oct))—to whose judgment I wish to

e pay tribute—took place under the shadow of the decision of the Court of Appeal in *R v Secretary of State for the Home Department, ex p Salem* [1999] QB 805, [1999] 2 WLR 1. In *Ex p Salem* the Court of Appeal (Hobhouse, Brooke LJJ and Sir John Balcombe) held that for the purposes of reg 70(3A)(b)(i) a person ceased to be entitled to income support from the date when his claim for

f asylum was recorded as determined on an internal file note in the Asylum Directorate in the Home Department, even though he had not yet been informed of the determination. The House granted leave to appeal the decision in *Ex p Salem*. In the event, the matter did not proceed as Mr Salem was granted refugee status (see [1999] 2 All ER 42, [1999] AC 450). Reluctantly, Sir Christopher felt compelled to dismiss the appellant's application for judicial

g review. The Court of Appeal also regarded itself as bound by *Ex p Salem*. Having so decided the Court of Appeal had to dismiss the appeal of the present appellant. But the Court of Appeal voiced its concerns about the policy of the Secretary of State and the decision in *Ex p Salem* in clear terms. Schiemann LJ ([2002] EWCA Civ 399 at [29], [2002] All ER (D) 365 (Mar) at [29]) (with the

h agreement of Hale and Sedley LJJ) trenchantly observed about the factual matrix:

    'We have also been told by leading counsel for the Home Secretary, Mr John Howell QC, that the delay of over four months between the preparation and the dispatch of the letter explaining why asylum has been

j refused was not accidental: it was a consistent practice. But for it, the present issue of law would have no significance. Mr Howell was wholly unable to explain it, let alone justify it. He was able to do no more than read us part of an affidavit which had been sworn in *Ex p Salem* which asserted that the implications of cost and effort if interim notifications were sent out were too great. When one bears in mind first that the

asylum-seeker's ability to contest the refusal of asylum is entirely
dependent on receipt of the Home Secretary's reasons for refusal, and
secondly that the letter containing full reasons is already on file and that
sooner or later the Home Office will have to put it in an envelope and post
it, even the flimsy explanation we were given falls away. Since Mr Howell
was able to tell us that the practice is now to send out a prompt notification
(though he could not tell us whether it included reasons, and Mr Gill's
instructions suggested that it did not), one is left wondering what the real
reason was. Ms Anufrijeva's inability, her benefit having been stopped, to
find £17 to travel to Gatwick for her "reasons for refusal" interview gives
little to be proud of.'

In oral argument before the House counsel stated that the Secretary of State did
not condone delay in notification of a decision on asylum. These were weasel
words. There was no unintended lapse. The practice of not notifying asylum
seekers of the fact of withdrawal of income support was consistently and
deliberately adopted. There simply is no rational explanation for such a policy.
Having abandoned this practice the Secretary of State still seeks to justify it as
lawful. It provides a peep into contemporary standards of public
administration. Transparency is not its hallmark. It is not an encouraging
picture.

[25] The Court of Appeal observed about the interpretation of the
regulation (at [30]):

'... once an asylum seeker knows that her application has been refused,
and that she is not to be given leave to enter the country on any other basis,
and has the reasons for those decisions, she can reasonably be expected to
make a choice: either to accept the decision and leave or to stay and fight
but without recourse to state benefits. But she cannot reasonably be
expected to make that choice before she knows of the decisions and the
reasons for them. There is nothing in the material before us to suggest that
it is consistent with the declared purpose of the regulation to expect her to
do so.'

I would respectfully endorse this observation.

[26] The arguments for the Home Secretary ignore fundamental principles of
our law. Notice of a decision is required before it can have the character of a
determination with legal effect because the individual concerned must be in a
position to challenge the decision in the courts if he or she wishes to do so. This
is not a technical rule. It is simply an application of the right of access to justice.
That is a fundamental and constitutional principle of our legal system (see
Raymond v Honey [1982] 1 All ER 756 at 758–759, [1983] 1 AC 1 at 10 per Lord
Wilberforce, R v Secretary of State for the Home Dept, ex p Leech [1993] 4 All ER 539
at 547, [1994] QB 198 at 209, R v Secretary of State for the Home Dept, ex p Simms
[1999] 3 All ER 400, [2000] 2 AC 115).

[27] What then is the relevance of this dimension for the present case? The
answer is provided by Lord Hoffmann's elegant explanation of the principle of
legality in Ex p Simms. He said:

'Parliamentary sovereignty means that Parliament can, if it chooses,
legislate contrary to fundamental principles of human rights. The Human
Rights Act 1998 will not detract from this power. The constraints upon its

a exercise by Parliament are ultimately political, not legal. But the principle of legality means that Parliament must squarely confront what it is doing and accept the political cost. Fundamental rights cannot be overridden by general or ambiguous words. This is because there is too great a risk that the full implications of their unqualified meaning may have passed unnoticed in the democratic process. In the absence of express language or necessary

b implication to the contrary, the courts therefore presume that even the most general words were intended to be subject to the basic rights of the individual. In this way the courts of the United Kingdom, though acknowledging the sovereignty of Parliament, apply principles of constitutionality little different from those which exist in countries where the power of the legislature is expressly limited by a constitutional

c document.' (See [1999] 3 All ER 400 at 412, [2000] 2 AC 115 at 131.)

This principle may find its primary application in respect of cases under the European Convention for the Protection of Human Rights and Fundamental Freedoms 1950 (as set out in Sch 1 to the Human Rights Act 1998). But the convention is not an exhaustive statement of fundamental rights under our

d system of law. Lord Hoffmann's dictum applies to fundamental rights beyond the four corners of the convention. It is engaged in the present case.

[28] This view is reinforced by the constitutional principle requiring the rule of law to be observed. That principle too requires that a constitutional state must accord to individuals the right to know of a decision before their rights can be

e adversely affected. The antithesis of such a state was described by Kafka: a state where the rights of individuals are overridden by hole in the corner decisions or knocks on doors in the early hours. That is not our system. I accept, of course, that there must be exceptions to this approach, notably in the criminal field, eg arrests and search warrants, where notification is not possible. But it is difficult

f to visualise a rational argument which could even arguably justify putting the present case in the exceptional category. If this analysis is right, it also engages the principle of construction explained by Lord Hoffmann in Ex p Simms.

[29] In European law the approach is possibly a little more formalistic but the thrust is the same. It has been held to be a 'fundamental principle in the Community legal order ... that a measure adopted by the public authorities shall

g not be applicable to those concerned before they have the opportunity to make themselves acquainted with it' (see Firma A Racke v Hauptzollamt Mainz Case 98/78 [1979] ECR 69 at 84 (para 15), Opel Austria GmbH (Austria intervening) v EU Council (European Commission intervening) Case T-115/94 [1997] All ER (EC) 97 at 118, [1997] ECR II-39 at 82 (para 124), Schwarze European Administrative Law

h (1992) pp 1416–1420, Council of Europe Publishing The administration and you—A handbook (1996) Ch 3 (para 49).

[30] Until the decision in Ex p Salem it had never been suggested that an uncommunicated administrative decision can bind an individual. It is an astonishingly unjust proposition. In our system of law surprise is regarded as the

j enemy of justice. Fairness is the guiding principle of our public law. In Hillingdon London BC v Commission for Racial Equality [1982] AC 779 at 787, [1982] 3 WLR 159 at 165 Lord Diplock explained the position:

'Where an Act of Parliament confers upon an administrative body functions which involve its making decisions which affect to their detriment the rights of other persons or curtail their liberty to do as they please, there

is a presumption that Parliament intended that the administrative body
should act fairly towards those persons who will be affected by their
decision.'

Where decisions are published or notified to those concerned accountability of
public authorities is achieved. Elementary fairness therefore supports a principle
that a decision takes effect only upon communication.

[31] If this analysis is correct, it is plain that Parliament has not expressly or by
necessary implication legislated to the contrary effect. The decision in question
involves a fundamental right. It is in effect one involving a binding determination
as to status. It is of importance to the individual to be informed of it so that he or
she can decide what to do. Moreover, neither cost nor administrative
convenience can in such a case conceivably justify a different approach. This is
underlined by the fact that the bizarre earlier practice has now been abandoned.
Given this context Parliament has not in specific and unmistakeable terms
legislated to displace the applicable constitutional principles.

[32] The contrary arguments can be dealt with quite briefly. Counsel for the
Home Secretary submits that before a 'determination' can be 'notified' there
must be a determination. This is legalism and conceptualism run riot. One can
readily accept that in this case there must have been a decision as reflected in the
file note. That does not mean that the statutory requirement of a 'determination'
has been fulfilled. On the contrary, the decision is provisional until notified.

[33] Counsel for the Home Secretary relied strongly on some niceties of
statutory language. He pointed out that reg 21ZA of the 1987 regulations, as well
as in s 6 of the Asylum and Immigration Appeals Act 1993, the draftsmen
provided expressly for notification. In contrast reg 70(3A)(b)(i) makes no
reference to notification. The fact, however, that other provisions made the
requirement of notification *explicit* does not rule out the possibility that
notification was all along *implicit* in the concept of 'the determination'. For my
part a stronger indication of Parliamentary intent is provided by the Statement of
Changes in Immigration Rules (1994) (HC 395), which were laid before
Parliament on 23 May 1994 under s 3(2) of the Immigration Act 1971. The
concept of a 'refusal' of asylum to be found in rr 331, 333 and 348 plainly
contemplates notification of an adverse decision. These rules are part of the
contextual scene of reg 70(3A)(b)(i). They support the argument that notification
of a decision is necessary for it to become a determination. But the major point
is that the semantic arguments of counsel for the Home Secretary cannot displace
the constitutional principles outlined above.

[34] For all these reasons I would reject the submissions of counsel for the
Home Secretary and hold that *Ex p Salem* was wrongly decided. It follows that in
my view the present appeal should be allowed.

[35] My noble and learned friend Lord Bingham of Cornhill has observed that
the Home Secretary was under a public law duty to give notice within a
reasonable time but that breach of this duty cannot nullify or invalidate his
decision. I would question this conclusion. It is important to bear in mind that
the breach involved a deliberate policy decision by the Home Office not to
comply with the public law duty. This amounts to an abuse of power and ought
to preclude the Home Secretary from relying on his unlawful conduct until
notification has taken place. While generally an estoppel cannot operate against
the Crown, it can be estopped when it is abusing its powers (see *HTV Ltd v Price
Commission* [1976] ICR 170 at 185 per Lord Denning MR, *Preston v IRC* [1985] 2

a All ER 327 at 340, [1985] AC 835 at 865 per Lord Templeman, *Laker Airways Ltd v Dept of Trade* [1977] 2 All ER 182 at 194, 195–196, [1977] QB 643 at 707, 709 per Lord Denning MR, Roskill LJ, respectively). For this further reason I would reject the submissions made on behalf of the Home Secretary.

[36] I recognise, of course, that in some ways the appellant's case does not merit great sympathy. But even in unprepossessing cases fundamental principles

b must be upheld. The rule of law requires it. In my view the appellant is entitled to recover income support until proper notification of the determination on 25 April 2000. I would therefore allow the appeal.

LORD HOFFMANN.

c [37] My Lords, I have had the advantage of reading in draft the speech of my noble and learned friend Lord Steyn. For the reasons he has given, I too would allow this appeal.

LORD MILLETT.

d [38] My Lords, I have had the advantage of reading in draft the powerful speech of my noble and learned friend, Lord Steyn. Until then I was of the opinion that the appeal should be dismissed; but I have been persuaded to change my mind.

[39] I agree that a determination must actually be made before it can properly be recorded; and that it is not necessarily merely provisional until it is notified to

e the person or persons adversely affected by it. But it does not follow that it has legal effect before it has been notified; and it is fallacious to suppose that an uncommunicated decision must be effective for all purposes or for none.

[40] I am satisfied that the appellant's asylum application was determined on 20 November 1999, that the determination was final and not provisional, and that it had immediate legal effect for some purposes. Thus it returned the

f responsibility for deciding the appellant's immigrant status to the immigration officer, so that he could consider whether she should be granted exceptional leave to remain. But she could not be removed from or required to leave the United Kingdom until she had been given notice of the decision on her claim: s 6 of the Asylum and Immigration Appeals Act 1993 expressly so provided. The question

g is whether the refusal of her application had immediate effect for the purpose of ending her entitlement to income support or took effect for this purpose only when she was notified of it.

[41] I was initially influenced by two considerations. One was the evidence that it was Parliament's intention to deprive asylum seekers of social security benefits even while the decision to refuse asylum is under challenge. On further

h reflection I do not think that this can be determinative of the present question: it does not follow that Parliament intended to deprive an asylum seeker of benefit before he or she is even told of the decision.

[42] The second consideration was textual. Benefit ends when the claimant 'ceases to be an asylum seeker'; and this depends on the date on which the claim

j to asylum 'is recorded by the Secretary of State as having been determined'. There is a conspicuous absence of any reference to the need to notify the claimant of the decision. The claimant ceases to be an asylum seeker, neither on the date when the decision is made nor on the date when it is notified to the claimant, but on the date on which it is recorded. This initially persuaded me that even the deliberate failure to inform the appellant at the same time as the benefit office of the

outcome of her application for asylum was merely an act of maladministration
which did not invalidate the decision or delay the time at which her entitlement to   *a*
benefit should cease.

[43] But I am persuaded that the omission was of more fundamental effect.
The presumption that notice of a decision must be given to the person adversely
affected by it before it can have legal effect is a strong one. It cannot be lightly
overturned. I do not subscribe to the view that the failure to notify the appellant   *b*
of the decision invalidated it, but I have come to the conclusion that it could not
properly be recorded so as to deprive her of her right to income support until it
was communicated to her; or at least until reasonable steps were taken to do so.
This does not require any violation to be done to para (3A) of reg 70 of the
Income Support (General) Regulations 1987, SI 1987/1967. It means only that   *c*
the word 'determined' in that paragraph should be read as meaning not merely
'actually determined' but as meaning 'determined in such manner as to affect the
claimant's legal rights'. The presumption against legal effect being given to
uncommunicated decisions does the rest. The determination must have been
made and appropriate steps must have been taken to communicate it to the
claimant before it can lawfully be recorded so as to have the effect contended for.   *d*

[44] I would allow the appeal.

LORD SCOTT OF FOSCOTE.

[45] My Lords, the appellant, Nadezda Anufrijeva, arrived in this country   *e*
from Lithuania on 31 August 1998 and made an application for asylum as a
Geneva convention refugee (see Geneva Convention relating to the Status of
Refugees (Geneva, 28 July 1951; TS 39 (1953); Cmnd 9171)). On 4 September
1998 she made a claim for income support. Entitlement to income support is
governed by Pt VII of the Social Security Contributions and Benefits Act 1992 and
the regulations made thereunder (or under one of the Act's legislative   *f*
predecessors). The regulations applicable to the appellant's claim were the
Income Support (General) Regulations 1987, SI 1987/1967.

[46] A 'person from abroad' (see reg 21(3) of the 1987 regulations) is not
entitled to income support unless he or she qualifies for such support as an urgent
case. Persons from abroad falling within an urgent case category are entitled to   *g*
90% of the normal amount of income support. Asylum seekers, who often, if not
usually, arrive in this country with no means of support, are recognised as falling
within an urgent case category. The appellant accordingly qualified for income
support as an asylum seeker and as from 4 September 1998 received income
support at 90% of the normal rate.

[47] The appellant continued to receive income support until 9 December
1999 when it ceased. It ceased because the Benefits Agency had been informed
by the Home Office that she had ceased to be an asylum seeker. The Home
Office was purporting to apply para (3A)(b)(i) of reg 70 of the 1987 regulations.
Paragraph (3A)(b)(i) says that:

   '... a person ... (b) ceases to be an asylum seeker—(i) in the case of a claim
   for asylum which, on or after 5th February 1996, is recorded by the Secretary
   of State as having been determined (other than on appeal) or abandoned, on
   the date on which it is so recorded ...'

a [48] The file entry which led the Home Office to inform the Benefits Agency that the appellant had ceased to be an asylum seeker was contained in a Home Office file note dated 20 November 1999 which said, inter alia, that—

> 'For the reasons given in the letter aside, this applicant has failed to establish a well founded fear of persecution. Refusal is appropriate. Case hereby recorded as determined. Certified under 5(4)(a).'

b

So 20 November 1999 is the date on which, the Home Office contend, it was recorded that the appellant's asylum claim had been determined.

[49] The 'letter aside' referred to in the note was a letter, also dated 20 November 1999, which set out the reasons for the refusal of the appellant's *c* asylum claim. The letter was addressed to the appellant but it was not sent to her until much later, nor was any other notification of the refusal of her asylum claim sent to her. This was not an oversight on the part of the Home Office; it appears to have been departmental policy not to communicate to an asylum seeker that his or her claim for asylum had been refused until an immigration officer had had the opportunity to consider whether the asylum seeker's request for leave to *d* enter the country should be granted on some other ground than that of refugee status. Once the immigration officer had reached a decision on the request for leave to enter, the asylum seeker would then be informed of it and at the same time would be sent the letter stating that his or her claim to refugee status had been refused and the reasons for the refusal.

e [50] In the present case the appellant was not sent the letter refusing her claim for asylum and telling her the reasons for the refusal until 25 April 2000 notwithstanding that the letter had been written as long before as 20 November 1999 and in the intervening period had simply been retained in the Home Office file.

f [51] The appellant must, of course, have come to understand in a roundabout way that her asylum claim had been refused but she did not know the reasons for the refusal until she received on 25 April 2000 the 'letter aside' dated 20 November 1999. The relevant sequence of events between those two dates is set out in [22], [23], above, and I need not repeat them.

g [52] The departmental policy that led to the long delay in notifying the appellant that her asylum claim had been refused, and why, has been the subject of adverse comments by the Court of Appeal, cited by Lord Steyn in his opinion, and by Lord Steyn on his own account (see [24], above). I would wish to associate myself fully with Lord Steyn's comments. There seem to have been no practical reasons why the refusal of an asylum claim and the reasons for it could not have *h* been promptly notified to the asylum seeker. It is true that the asylum seeker's request for leave to enter the country had to be dealt with by an immigration officer and that the immigration officer's role in dealing with the request for leave to enter was a role separate from although complementary to the Secretary of State's role in deciding whether to allow or refuse the asylum claim. But the immigration officer's role would not be in the least prejudiced or undermined by a prompt notification to the asylum seeker of the fate of the asylum claim. The connection, if there is one, between the immigration officer's role and the institutional delay by the Home Office in notifying asylum seekers of the fate of their asylum claims does not constitute a practical reason justifying the delay. That it was no such thing seems to me to be shown by the fact that the practice has apparently now been abandoned.

[53] Be that as it may, the issue for your Lordships on this appeal is whether the unnotified decision of the Secretary of State to refuse the appellant's asylum claim, 'recorded as determined' according to the 20 November 1999 note, effectively deprived her as from that date of her status as an asylum seeker for income support purposes, or whether she retained that status until she was notified on 25 April 2000, by her eventual receipt of the letter of 20 November 1999, of the refusal of her asylum claim.

[54] The issue is one of construction of reg 70(3A)(b)(i) of the 1987 regulations. Paragraph (3A) was added to reg 70 by an amendment made in 1996. Like any other provision of primary or secondary legislation, para (3A)(b)(i) must be construed in the context of the statutory scheme of which it forms part. The statutory scheme includes s 11(1) of the Asylum and Immigration Act 1996, cited in [13] of the opinion of my noble and learned friend Lord Bingham of Cornhill, which makes explicit Parliament's intention to give power to the Secretary of State to make regulations excluding asylum seekers from entitlement to income support. And there is no doubt that para (3A)(b)(i) was intended to exclude asylum seekers from income support once a particular stage in the progress of their asylum claims had been reached. But what was that stage? At what point are asylum claims to be regarded as 'having been determined'?

[55] The contextual background against which para (3A)(b)(i) must be construed consists also of the Statement of Changes in Immigration Rules (1994) (HC 395). The rules current in 1996, when para (3A)(b)(i) was added to reg 70, included r 333, cited in [8], above. Rule 333 makes clear that the refusal of an asylum claim is to be notified to the asylum seeker by a 'notice of refusal' which will inform him or her of the reasons for the refusal. Rules 331 and 348 underline the point. It is, indeed, inherent in the concept of a 'refusal' that it should be communicated to the person to whom it is directed. The communication of a refusal may be either by words or by conduct from which the requisite inference can be drawn, but without communication there will be no more than a non-acceptance, a quite different concept from that of a refusal. The Immigration Rules require a refusal and that the refusal is to be communicated by a 'notice of refusal'.

[56] It has been rightly accepted before your Lordships that, for the purposes of reg 70(3A)(b)(i), an asylum claim cannot be 'recorded as determined' until it has actually been 'determined'. The submissions of counsel for the Secretary of State draw a distinction between the refusal of the asylum claim for the purposes of the Immigration Rules, which requires a notice of the refusal to be sent to the asylum seeker, and the determination of the claim for the purposes of reg 70(3A)(b)(i), which does not. So the claim can be 'determined' before it has been 'refused'. This is an elegant linguistic conceptual distinction but it makes, to my mind, little practical sense and is redolent with unfairness to the asylum seeker.

[57] My noble and learned friend Lord Steyn has cogently explained why an uncommunicated decision terminating an asylum seeker's right to income support offends against well-established principles of legality and access to justice. I cannot improve on his exposition and agree with it. Parliament can, of course, override these principles. But in s 11(1) of the 1996 Act Parliament has not done so expressly. There is nothing in the empowering provision to suggest a Parliamentary intention that an asylum seeker's status as an asylum seeker entitled to income support can be terminated not only without the asylum

a seeker being told the reasons for the termination of the status but without the asylum seeker even being notified of the termination.

[**58**] There are, therefore, two reasons why, in my opinion, this appeal must succeed and *R v Secretary of State for the Home Department, ex p Salem* [1999] 2 All ER 42, [1999] AC 450 be overruled. First, I would construe the reference in reg 70(3A)(b)(i) to an asylum claim being 'determined' in a manner consistent

b with the Immigration Rules and hold that it cannot be 'determined' until it has been refused and that that requires notification. Second, and alternatively, I consider that s 11(1) of the 1996 Act did not empower the Secretary of State to make regulations which have the effect that an asylum seeker can be deprived of that status for income support purposes without notification.

[**59**] For these reasons, supplemental to those of my noble and learned friend Lord Steyn with which I am in complete agreement, I would allow this appeal.

Appeal allowed.

Kate O'Hanlon Barrister.

Maronier v Larmer

[2002] EWCA Civ 774

COURT OF APPEAL, CIVIL DIVISION

LORD PHILLIPS OF WORTH MATRAVERS MR, ROBERT WALKER AND CLARKE LJJ

15, 29 MAY 2002

Conflict of laws – Foreign judgment – Registration in England – Setting aside registration – Judgment obtained without notice to defendant – Whether judgment obtained in breach of right to fair trial – Whether registration contrary to public policy – Civil Jurisdiction and Judgments Act 1982, Sch 1, art 27(1), (2) – Human Rights Act 1998, Sch 1, Pt I, art 6(1).

In 1984 the applicant commenced negligence proceedings in the Netherlands against the respondent, a dentist then practising in that country. The proceedings were duly served on the respondent, whose lawyers filed a defence on his behalf. In 1986 the proceedings were stayed because of the applicant's bankruptcy. In 1991 the respondent moved to England and informed the local authorities and the Dutch dentists' association of his new address. Seven years later, the applicant instructed a new firm of lawyers to pursue the claim. The applicant's lawyers contacted the respondent's lawyers, who informed them that the respondent was living in England. The respondent's lawyers thereupon withdrew from the case because they could not obtain instructions. Judgment was entered in favour of the applicant. The respondent was still unaware of the reactivation of the proceedings when his right of appeal expired three months later. The applicant sought to register the judgment in England and Wales pursuant to the Brussels Convention on Jurisdiction and the Enforcement of Judgments in Civil and Commercial Matters 1968 (as set out in Sch 1 to the Civil Jurisdiction and Judgments Act 1982) (the Brussels Convention)[a], which application was granted by the master. Article 27(1) of the Brussels Convention provided that a judgment should not be recognised if recognition would be contrary to public policy in the state in which it was sought and art 27(2) provided that a judgment should not be recognised where it was given in default of appearance and the defendant was not duly served with the document which instituted the proceedings in sufficient time to enable him or her to arrange for a defence. On appeal, the judge held that the right to an effective opportunity to defend oneself in civil proceedings was an important public policy in England and Wales and throughout the European Union and that the respondent had been denied that right. The judge therefore declared himself satisfied that the recognition of the judgment of the Dutch court would be contrary to the public policy of England and Wales because the procedures of the Dutch court had made it possible for a stale claim to be revived and pursued to judgment in circumstances in which the respondent was not aware of the reactivation of proceedings and in which he was not personally at fault. The applicant appealed to the Court of Appeal, contending, inter alia, that the judge had erred in having carried out a review of whether the respondent had received a fair trial before the Dutch court. The respondent submitted that the protection of the right to a fair trial, which was a requirement of art 6 of the European Convention for the Protection of Human Rights and Fundamental

---

a The Brussels Convention, so far as material, is set out at [14], below

a Freedoms 1950 (as set out in Sch 1 to the Human Rights Act 1998), was a requirement of public policy in England and Wales and, as to the facts, that the judge had correctly concluded that no fault lay with him.

Held – One of the fundamental objectives of the Brussels Convention was to facilitate the free movement of judgments by providing for a simple and rapid
b enforcement procedure. That objective would be frustrated if the courts of an enforcing state could be required to carry out a detailed review of whether the procedures that had resulted in the judgment had complied with art 6 of the convention. The courts should therefore apply a strong presumption that the procedures of other signatory states to the convention were compliant with art 6. However, that did not mean that the court was to apply an irrebuttable
c presumption that a judgment given in another European Community member state could not have resulted from a breach of art 6: although the court of a state asked to enforce a judgment could not decline, on the ground of public policy, to enforce that judgment on the ground that it infringed Community law, there was a distinction in principle between a decision that resolved an issue of substantive
d law and a decision reached by a procedure that violated the fundamental human right to a fair trial. Moreover, the provisions of art 27(2) of the Brussels Convention expressly recognised the paramount importance of one aspect of the right to a fair trial; the trial process had to ensure that the defendant had a fair chance to defend himself. It was thus clear that in an exceptional case where the procedure of the court first seised had resulted in a defendant being prevented
e from putting his or her case to the court, art 27(1) of the Brussels Convention could justify a refusal to enforce the resultant judgment on grounds of public policy. In the instant case, the respondent had been unaware that proceedings in the Netherlands against him had been reactivated until even the time for an appeal had passed, and he had not been present or had any representation at the
f trial. The respondent had manifestly not received the fair trial required by art 6 and there could be no doubt that the judge had been correct to conclude that it would have been contrary to public policy to enforce the applicant's judgment. Accordingly, the appeal would be dismissed (see [23]–[30], [37], [38], below).
  Debaecker v Bouwman Case 49/84 [1985] ECR 1779 considered.

g **Notes**
For non-jurisdictional objections to recognition of a judgment, see 8(1) *Halsbury's Laws* (4th edn reissue) para 1046.
  For the Civil Jurisdiction and Judgments Act 1982, Sch 1, art 27, see 22 *Halsbury's Statutes* (4th edn) (2000 reissue) 582.
h For the Human Rights Act 1998, Sch 1, Pt 1, art 6, see 7 *Halsbury's Statutes* (4th edn) (2002 reissue) 554.

Cases referred to in judgment
Debaecker v Bouwman Case 49/84 [1985] ECR 1779, ECJ.
j *Hendrikman v Magenta Druck & Verlag GmbH* Case C-78/95 [1996] All ER (EC) 944, [1997] QB 426, [1997] 2 WLR 349, [1996] ECR I-4943, ECJ.
Krombach v Bamberski Case C-7/98 [2001] All ER (EC) 584, [2001] QB 709, [2001] 3 WLR 488, [2001] ECR I-1935, ECJ.
Régie Nationale des Usines Renault SA v Maxicar SpA Case C-38/98 [2000] ECR I-2973, ECJ.
Solo Kleinmotoren GmbH v Boch Case C-414/92 [1994] ECR I-2237, ECJ.

Cases also cited or referred to in skeleton arguments
Emesa Sugar (Free Zone) NV v Aruba Case C-17/98 [2000] ECR I-675, ECJ.
Klomps v Michel Case 166/80 [1981] ECR 1593, ECJ.
König v Germany (1978) 2 EHRR 170, [1978] ECHR 6232/73, ECt HR.
Vermeulen v Belgium (1996) 32 EHRR 313, [1996] ECHR 19075/91, ECt HR.

Appeal
Wim Harry Gerard Maronier appealed with the permission of Dyson LJ from the decision of Judge Richard Seymour QC sitting as a judge of the Queen's Bench Division on 22 May 2001 whereby he dismissed an appeal from the order of Deputy Master Chism made on 2 February 2001 setting aside registration of a judgment of the District Court of Rotterdam on 30 December 1999 made against the respondent, Bryan Larmer. The facts are set out in the judgment of the court.

Peter Ralls QC and *Gary Pryce* (instructed by *Howard Kennedy*) for Mr Maronier.
John Foy QC and *Laura Elfield* (instructed by *Bartlett Gooding & Weelen*, Shepton Mallett) for Mr Larmer.

Cur adv vult

29 May 2002. The following judgment of the court was delivered.

LORD PHILLIPS OF WORTH MATRAVERS MR.

INTRODUCTION
[1] Mr Maronier is a citizen of the Netherlands. He appeals against the decision of Judge Richard Seymour QC (sitting as a judge of the Queen's Bench Division). He dismissed an appeal against the order of Deputy Master Chism made on 2 February 2001. By that order the deputy master set aside registration of a judgment of the District Court of Rotterdam dated 30 December 1999. By that judgment Mr Maronier was awarded damages assessed at 17,864 Netherlands guilders, together with interest and costs. As we shall explain, the procedure followed in this case has gone awry, but it is accepted that this court has jurisdiction to entertain the appeal.

[2] This appeal raises an issue as to the manner of application of art 27(1) of the Convention on Jurisdiction and the Enforcement of Judgments in Civil and Commercial Matters 1968 (as set out in Sch 1 to the Civil Jurisdiction and Judgments Act 1982) (the Brussels Convention). With effect from 1 March 2002 a new regime for the enforcement of Community judgments was introduced under the Civil Jurisdiction and Judgments Order 2001, SI 2001/3929. Under the transitional provisions that order has no effect on this appeal and the wording of the new order raises similar issues to those arising on this appeal. Those issues arise in the context of facts which are quite extraordinary. Furthermore, the evidence before the court leaves unclear a number of matters which are or might be material.

EVENTS IN HOLLAND
[3] These facts are derived piecemeal from a series of witness statements provided by the parties and by Dutch lawyers instructed on their behalf. Sources of information and belief are not always clear, but no point has been taken on the admissibility of this evidence.

a [4] Mr Larmer, the respondent, is now aged 68. Since 1991 he has lived at an address in Kingston-upon-Thames. Between 1978 and 1991 he practised as a dentist in Rotterdam. One of his patients was the appellant, Mr Maronier. In 1983 Mr Maronier complained to the Rotterdam Dental Association, which is a local branch of the Dutch Association of Dentists, about treatment that he had received from Mr Larmer. This complaint led, after an informal hearing, to

b Mr Larmer being fined the equivalent of about £1,600 and subsequently being ordered to pay the costs of remedial treatment by another dentist.

[5] On 12 March 1984 Mr Maronier commenced proceedings in the District Court of Rotterdam in which he claimed damages in respect of the treatment that he had received, which he alleged was negligent, in the sum of 57,059 Netherlands guilders. That is the equivalent of approximately £17,000.

c The proceedings were duly served on Mr Larmer in the Netherlands. Mr Larmer consulted the firm of de Bliek Linssen, which appears to have been a partnership of Mr de Bliek and Mr Linssen. Mr Linssen filed a defence on Mr Larmer's behalf. There was then an exchange of pleadings and statements, ending with a statement filed by Mr Maronier on 2 May 1986.

d [6] A statement filed on behalf of Mr Maronier by Mr Jacobs, a lawyer whom he instructed later in the story, informs us that the proceedings brought against Mr Larmer were delayed due to the fact that Mr Maronier was working abroad for long periods and also suffered chronic health problems and that the proceedings in the District Court of Rotterdam were stayed. Surprisingly, Mr Jacobs omits to state why the proceedings were stayed. The reason is that on

e 20 May 1986 Mr Maronier went bankrupt. The bankruptcy was dissolved on 3 March 1987.

[7] Before leaving for England in 1991, Mr Larmer left his address in England with the City Hall in Rotterdam and the Dutch Association of Dentists.

[8] Nothing that is relevant then occurred until, in July 1998, Mr Maronier

f instructed a new firm of lawyers, of which Mr Jacobs was a partner, to pursue his claim. These lawyers, a firm called Kniestedt Jacobs & Duijs, wrote a letter dated 23 July 1998 to Mr Linssen, which was not put in evidence. Mr Linssen had by this time dissolved his partnership with Mr de Bliek. Mr Linssen's reply dated the 24 July 1998 read:

g 'In the above-mentioned matter we received your letter of 23 July 1998. This matter is unknown to me; the matter is not a current matter and does not show in our records. Apart from that, I have had no contact with the client for a number of years. According to my information, the client is presently living in England. I am sorry that I cannot inform you otherwise.'

h [9] What then occurred is described by Mr Jacobs as follows:

'When the proceedings were reactivated, the defendant was represented before the District Court of Rotterdam by his solicitor, Mr J de Bliek. At the point the proceedings recommenced, Mr de Bliek declared himself to be "incapable", which in Holland means a solicitor withdraws from a case due to problems encountered with his client. The withdrawal of Mr de Bliek from the proceedings was agreed by the District Court of Rotterdam as can be seen from the front page of the judgment dated the 30 December 1999 ... I believe, in this current matter, that Mr de Bliek withdrew from the case as he could not obtain any instructions from his client.'

[10] The judgment to which Mr Jacobs refers records Mr Larmer as 'residing in Rotterdam' and adds: 'Attorney initially Mr J de Bliek, presently *a* not represented anymore in law.' That judgment awarded Mr Maronier 17,864 Netherlands guilders together with 'statutory interest' and costs. Interest vastly exceeded the capital sum awarded, and the total amount of the judgment was 70,234 Netherlands guilders.

[11] Under Dutch procedure there was a right of appeal against this judgment. *b* That right expired, however, three months after the judgment, at a time when Mr Larmer was not yet aware of the reactivation of the action, let alone of its outcome. It is common ground that the judgment is now 'unassailable' in Holland.

MATTERS NOT IN EVIDENCE   *c*
[12] The following matters cannot be deduced from the evidence before us: (i) what Mr Larmer could reasonably expect to happen to the proceedings once the action was stayed; (ii) what Mr Larmer could reasonably expect to happen to the proceedings when he left for England approximately five years after the last step had been taken in the action; (iii) whether Mr Larmer should have instructed *d* de Bliek Linssen to continue to represent him in the action; (iv) what, if any, grounds were required for reactivating the action, after so long a delay; (v) what procedures had to be followed to reactivate the action; (vi) what duty, if any, either Mr Linssen or Mr de Bliek owed to Mr Larmer when the action was reactivated after 12 years of inactivity; (vii) what explanation Mr de Bliek advanced to the court when obtaining permission to withdraw from the case; *e* (viii) whether, as the judgment suggests, the court believed that Mr Larmer was resident in Rotterdam; (ix) the basis upon which the rules of the Rotterdam District Court permitted the claimant to proceed to obtain a judgment in the absence of Mr Larmer; (x) the nature of the time limit placed on the exercise of the right of appeal and in particular whether the District Court had any discretion to extend the period within which to appeal if Mr Larmer was *f* unaware of the judgment; (xi) how Mr Maronier obtained Mr Larmer's address in Kingston-upon-Thames, which he succeeded in doing for the purpose of enforcement.

PROVISIONS OF THE BRUSSELS CONVENTION   *g*
[13] In addition to its application under the transitional provisions of the 2001 order, the Brussels Convention remains applicable between member states and Denmark. We shall refer to its effects in the present tense, despite its limited field of application.

[14] The Brussels Convention has the force of law in the United Kingdom by virtue of the provisions of s 2 of the 1982 Act. The following provisions of the Brussels Convention are material:

> 'Article 26
> A judgment given in a Contracting State shall be recognised in the other Contracting States without any special procedure being required ...
> Article 27
> A judgment shall not be recognised:
> (1) if such recognition is contrary to public policy in the State in which recognition is sought;
> (2) where it was given in default of appearance, if the defendant was not duly served with the document which instituted the proceedings or with an

a   equivalent document in sufficient time to enable him to arrange for his defence ...

Article 31

A judgment given in a Contracting State and enforceable in that State shall be enforced in another Contracting State when, on the application of any interested party, it has been declared enforceable there. However, in the
b   United Kingdom, such a judgment shall be enforced in England and Wales, in Scotland, or in Northern Ireland when, on the application of any interested party, it has been registered for enforcement in that part of the United Kingdom.

Article 32

c   1. The application shall be submitted ...

(1) in England and Wales, to the High Court of Justice ...

Article 33

The procedure for making the application shall be governed by the law of the State in which enforcement is sought ...

d   *Article 34*

The court applied to shall give its decision without delay; the party against whom enforcement is sought shall not at this stage of the proceedings be entitled to make any submissions on the application.

The application may be refused only for one of the reasons specified in
e   Articles 27 and 28.

Under no circumstances may the foreign judgment be reviewed as to its substance ...

Article 36

If enforcement is authorised, the party against whom enforcement is
f   sought may appeal against the decision within one month of service thereof ...

Article 37

An appeal against the decision authorising enforcement shall be lodged in accordance with the rules governing procedure in contentious matters ...
J   (1) in England and Wales, with the High Court of Justice ... The judgment given on the appeal may be contested only ... in the United Kingdom, by a single further appeal on a point of law.'

THE ERROR OF PROCEDURE

[15] The procedure for recognition and enforcement of a judgment required by the Brussels Convention differs from that normal in this jurisdiction in the following respect. The application for enforcement is made to a master without notice to the judgment debtor. Under normal procedure the judgment debtor would be entitled to apply to have an order made in such circumstances set aside. The convention requires, however, that he is not allowed to make any submissions on the application, but is to have a right to appeal. When Mr Maronier's judgment was registered, the material provision of the CPR was in CPR Sch 1 RSC Ord 71 r 33, which provided: '(1) An appeal under article 37 ... must be made to a judge by application in accordance with CPR Pt 23.'

[16] The order obtained by Mr Maronier, which was made by Master Trench on 14 July 2000, provided:

'IT IS ORDERED that the judgment dated the 30 December 1999 of the District Court of Rotterdam be registered in the Queen's Bench Division of the High Court of Justice pursuant to the Civil Jurisdiction and Judgments Act 1982. AND IT IS FURTHER ORDERED that the said Bryan Larmer shall have liberty within two months after service upon them of notice of registration of the judgment to appeal against such registration and execution shall not issue to enforce the judgment until after the expiry of that period or until after any such appeal has been determined.'

[17] This order was served on Mr Larmer on 10 August 2000 at his home in Kingston-upon-Thames. This was the first notice that he received that the Rotterdam proceedings had been reactivated.

[18] What Mr Larmer should have done, in accordance with the procedure set out above, was to appeal against this order to a High Court judge. Instead, those acting for Mr Larmer 'appealed' to Deputy Master Chism. He, despite protest from those representing Mr Maronier that he had no jurisdiction, entertained the appeal and allowed it. He did so on the ground that it was contrary to public policy in this country for Mr Maronier's lawyers, in the circumstances described above, to revive his case without making any attempt to trace Mr Larmer in order to give notice of what they were doing.

[19] The appropriate course in these circumstances is to disregard the hearing before Deputy Master Chism as a procedural aberration and treat the judgment of Judge Seymour as if it had been delivered pursuant to a first appeal.

THE JUDGMENT BELOW

[20] Judge Seymour upheld the decision of Deputy Master Chism. He reviewed relevant European case precedent, which we consider below. He expressed his conclusion as follows:

'The right to an effective opportunity to defend oneself in civil as in criminal proceedings is thus, in my judgment, an important public policy in England and Wales as throughout the European Union. On the facts of the present case, Mr Larmer has been denied that right. I am satisfied on the evidence that he personally is not in any way to blame for that state of affairs arising. A suggestion by Mr Pryce, that in relation to an action in which no steps had been taken by the claimant for five years before Mr Larmer left the Netherlands, he should have kept the District Court of Rotterdam notified of his address, or kept in touch with his Dutch lawyers, I regard as fanciful. Mr Larmer's uncontradicted evidence is that he notified the City Hall in Rotterdam, and the Dutch Association of Dentists, of his address in England. In the result, I am satisfied that the recognition of the judgment of the District Court of Rotterdam is contrary to the public policy of England and Wales because the procedures of the Dutch court have made it possible for a very stale claim to be revived and pursued to judgment without the defendant ever being aware of what was going on and in circumstances in which he was not personally at fault, he having every reason to suppose that the claim had been abandoned.'

THE ISSUES

[21] On behalf of Mr Maronier, Mr Ralls QC advanced two submissions: (i) the judge had erred in carrying out a review of whether Mr Larmer had received a fair trial before the Rotterdam District Court; (ii) the judge erred in his

a finding as to absence of fault. He should have found that, though Mr Larmer might not be personally at fault, his lawyers were at fault for withdrawing from representing him without informing him that the action was being revived. In such circumstances there was no justification for denying recognition of the judgment.

b [22] For Mr Larmer, Mr Foy QC contended that protection of the right to a fair trial, which was a requirement under art 6 of the European Convention for the Protection of Human Rights and Fundamental Freedoms 1950 (as set out in Sch 1 to the Human Rights Act 1998) (the convention), was a requirement of public policy in England. If a defendant had not had a fair trial, then recognition of the judgment was contrary to public policy. As to the facts, Mr Foy submitted
c that the judge had correctly concluded that no fault lay with Mr Larmer. The same was true of his lawyers. To conduct the trial when Mr Larmer was in ignorance that it had been revived had violated his right to a fair trial under art 6. Quite apart from this, a delay in pursuing the claim for 12 years was an independent violation of that article.

d
PUBLIC POLICY AND THE RIGHT TO A FAIR TRIAL

[23] Mr Ralls submitted forcefully that Holland, as a party to the convention, is committed to ensuring that art 6 is observed. Dutch courts would automatically have regard for the requirements of art 6. It was contrary to the scheme of the recognition and enforcement provisions of the Brussels
e Convention for one member state to review or 'second guess' compliance with art 6 by the courts of another member state.

[24] We sympathise with the broad thrust of Mr Ralls' submissions. As the Court of Justice of the European Communities observed in *Solo Kleinmotoren GmbH v Boch* Case C-414/92 [1994] ECR I-2237 at 2256 (para 20), one of the fundamental
f objectives of the Brussels Convention is to 'facilitate, to the greatest extent possible, the free movement of judgments by providing for a simple and rapid enforcement procedure'. This objective would be frustrated if courts of an enforcing state could be required to carry out a detailed review of whether the procedures that resulted in the judgment had complied with art 6.

g [25] Court procedures differ from one state to another and the courts of this country should apply a strong presumption that the procedures of other signatories of the convention are compliant with art 6. What we cannot accept is that we must apply an irrebuttable presumption that a judgment given in another member state cannot have resulted from a violation of art 6.

h [26] Where the state first seised of a dispute reaches a decision of substantive law, even if it is a decision on its own jurisdiction, the court of a state asked to enforce the resultant judgment cannot decline, on grounds of public policy, to enforce the decision on the ground that it infringes Community law. As the Court of Justice observed in *Régie Nationale des Usines Renault SA v Maxicar SpA* Case C-38/98 [2000] ECR I-2973 at 3021–3022 (para 32): 'It is for the national court to ensure with equal diligence the protection of rights established in national law and rights conferred by Community law.' There is, however, a distinction in principle between a decision that resolves an issue of substantive law and a decision reached by a procedure that violates the fundamental human right to a fair trial.

[27] The provisions of art 27(2) of the Brussels Convention expressly
recognise the paramount importance of one aspect of the right to a fair trial. *a*
The trial process must ensure that the defendant has a fair chance to defend
himself. The court must hear both parties: see *Hendrikman v Magenta Druck &
Verlag GmbH* Case C-78/95 [1996] All ER (EC) 944 at 959, [1997] QB 426 at 441,
[1996] ECR I-4943 at 4966 (para 15) and cases there cited.

[28] In *Krombach v Bamberski* Case C-7/98 [2001] All ER (EC) 584, [2001] QB *b*
709, [2001] ECR I-1935 the Court of Justice considered an objection under
art 27(1) to the enforcement in Germany of an award of damages made
following the conviction of the defendant at a criminal trial in Paris. The
defendant declined to attend the relevant hearing in person, but sought to be
legally represented at the hearing. He was not allowed to do so. He challenged
enforcement of the subsequent award of damages on the ground that he had been *c*
denied a fair hearing in violation of his art 6 rights. The Bundesgerichtshof
sought a ruling on whether this was a matter to which it could legitimately have
regard under art 27(1). The court observed ([2001] All ER (EC) 584 at 604, [2001]
QB 709 at 728–729, [2001] ECR I-1935) that:

d
'25. The court has consistently held that fundamental rights form an
integral part of the general principles of law whose observance the court
ensures ... For that purpose, the court draws inspiration from the
constitutional traditions common to the member states and from the
guidelines supplied by international treaties for the protection of human
rights on which the member states have collaborated or of which they are *e*
signatories. In that regard, the Convention for the Protection of Human
Rights and Fundamental Freedoms (Rome, 4 November 1950; TS 71 (1953);
Cmd 8969) (the European Convention on Human Rights) has particular
significance ...

26. The court has thus expressly recognised the general principle of *f*
Community law that everyone is entitled to fair legal process, which is
inspired by those fundamental rights ...'

[29] The court went on to hold ([2001] All ER (EC) 584 at 607, [2001] QB 709
at 731, [2001] ECR I-1935):

g
'42. ... it follows from a line of case law developed by the court on the
basis of the principles referred to in paras 25 and 26, above, that observance
of the right to a fair hearing is, in all proceedings initiated against a person
which are liable to culminate in a measure adversely affecting that person, a
fundamental principle of Community law which must be guaranteed even in *h*
the absence of any rules governing the proceedings in question ...

43. The court has also held that, even though the [Brussels Convention]
is intended to secure the simplification of formalities governing the
reciprocal recognition and enforcement of judgments of courts or tribunals,
it is not permissible to achieve that aim by undermining the rights to a fair
hearing ... *j*

44. It follows from the foregoing developments in the case law that
recourse to the public policy clause must be regarded as being possible in
exceptional cases where the guarantees laid down in the legislation of the
state of origin and in the convention itself have been insufficient to protect
the defendant from a manifest breach of his right to defend himself before

a   the court of origin, as recognised by the European Convention on Human Rights.'

(We have omitted the authorities cited in support of these propositions.)

[30] It is thus clear that, in an exceptional case where the procedure of the court first seised has resulted in a defendant being prevented from putting his case to the court, art 27(1) of the Brussels Convention can justify a refusal to enforce *b*   the resultant judgment on grounds of public policy.

FAULT

[31] Mr Ralls submitted that Mr Larmer's predicament in this case was attributable to breach of duty on the part of de Bliek Linssen in failing to inform *c*   Mr Larmer that the Rotterdam proceedings had been reactivated. This submission was based on a complaint made by Mr Larmer in his first witness statement. He stated that he had been in correspondence with Mr Linssen about another matter in 1991. Thus Mr Linssen should have been aware of his English address. Alternatively he should have obtained this from the Rotterdam City Hall. Mr Larmer alleged of the firm 'being lawyers acting on my behalf and being *d*   on the court record in the matter they owed me a duty of care to undertake such inquiries'.

[32] We would not conclude on the evidence before us that the two partners of de Bliek Linssen retained, or were under a duty to retain, Mr Larmer's address over the 12 years that elapsed since the Rotterdam action was stayed, or that they *e*   were under a duty to seek out his address in order to inform him that the proceedings had been reactivated. We note that Mr Jacobs makes no such allegation. He simply comments that 'it is clear that if Mr Larmer believes Mr de Bliek wrongly withdrew from the case the defendant's recourse lies in an action against Mr de Bliek for damages sustained by him as a result'.

[33] As we have noted above, Mr Jacobs' understanding was that Mr de Bliek *f*   withdrew because he could not obtain any instructions from his client. He added:

> 'The matters referred to by Mr Larmer in relation to the lack of attention given to this matter by his own lawyers is not a matter which can concern the claimant. When a solicitor withdraws from proceedings on behalf of a party in Holland, this is entirely at the risk of the party represented. Dutch
g   > law does not demand any action from the other party, neither from the court. If no new solicitor is appointed on behalf of the party in question, the proceedings will continue without the party.'

CONCLUSIONS

[34] The facts of this case have some similarities to those considered by the Court of Justice in *Debaecker v Bouwman* Case 49/84 [1985] ECR 1779. That case concerned the application of art 27(2) of the Brussels Convention. A tenant of business premises in Antwerp suddenly left leaving no forwarding address. The landlords issued a summons, claiming damages for breach of the lease, which was duly served on the tenant in accordance with Belgian procedural rules by being delivered to the Antwerp police headquarters. The tenant then wrote repudiating the lease and leaving a contact address. The landlords did not contact the tenant, but entered judgment in default, relying on the fact that service had been validly effected under Belgian law. The landlords sought to enforce their judgment in Holland. The Hoge Raad sought the decision of the Court of Justice on a number of questions including whether, for the purposes

of art 27(2), the adequacy of service fell to be considered having regard to the
facts existing at the time of service, or whether it was legitimate to have regard
to subsequent events. In particular, the court was asked whether the plaintiff
could be required, as a result of events which took place after service, to take
further steps to inform the defendant of the pending action or whether the fact
that it was the defendant's own fault that he was not served personally
prevented the court from having regard to events after service was effected.

[35] The Court of Justice held (at 1800) that the Brussels Convention did not
impose any obligation on the plaintiffs to take steps to alert the defendant to the
proceedings once service had been effected. It continued, however:

'27. ... The failure to take such steps is in reality merely a factor which
must be taken into account in order to establish whether service was effected
in sufficient time.

28. Seen in that light, the fact that the plaintiff, after service, learns of the
defendant's new address does not compel him to take any further steps, but
renders his subsequent behaviour important for the purpose of determining
whether service was effected in sufficient time. By notifying the defendant
at his new address, the plaintiff ensures that the court in which enforcement
is sought cannot decide that the defendant's change of address is an
exceptional circumstance which prevents the service effected at his former
address from being regarded as having been effected in sufficient time.'

[36] There is much that we find surprising about the present case. We find it
surprising that the procedure of the Rotterdam court permitted Mr Maronier to
reactivate an action that had been stayed for 12 years without requiring fresh
service of an appropriate process to be effected on Mr Larmer. We find it
surprising that full interest was awarded to Mr Maronier for the whole of the
period of the delay, which appears to have been entirely of his own making. We
find it surprising that, having regard to the fact that Mr Larmer was unaware that
the action had been reactivated, the three-month limit for appealing renders the
judgment 'unassailable' without the court apparently having any discretion to
reopen the matter. We are, however, acutely aware that, as we demonstrated
early in this judgment, there are many matters which are unclear on the evidence
and nothing that we have said should be taken as criticism of the Rotterdam
District Court or the procedure that it was applying.

[37] It may well be that, in a normal case, a defendant to an action in Holland
should continue to retain lawyers to act on his behalf in relation to proceedings
which have been stayed. This is not, however, a normal case. We feel sure that
a stay lasting 12 years of a simple claim for medical negligence must be quite
extraordinary. On the basis of the facts before us, we are driven to the conclusion
that Mr Larmer was denied a fair trial in Rotterdam because he was unaware that
proceedings had been reactivated until even the time for an appeal had passed. It
may well be that Dutch procedure did not require Mr Maronier to ensure that
Mr Larmer received notice of the reactivation of the action. Mr Linssen's letter
of 24 July 1998 and Mr de Bliek's withdrawal from representing Mr Larmer put
Mr Maronier's lawyers on notice that Mr Larmer was probably unaware of the
fact that the action had been reactivated. Dutch procedure appears to have
permitted the action to proceed without the presence of Mr Larmer or anyone
representing him. The consequence is, none the less, that he has manifestly not
received the fair trial that art 6 of the convention required.

a   [**38**] On the, happily, unusual facts of this case we are in no doubt that the judge was correct to conclude that it would be contrary to the public policy of this country to enforce Mr Maronier's judgment. Accordingly, this appeal will be dismissed.

Appeal dismissed.

James Brooks   Barrister.

Re Trusts of X Charity

[2003] EWHC 1462 (Ch)

CHANCERY DIVISION

SIR ANDREW MORRITT V-C

12, 24 JUNE 2003

Practice – Application for directions – Right to a fair and public hearing – Trustees of charity applying in private for directions relating to pending proceedings – Whether court entitled to pronounce judgment in private – Human Rights Act 1998, Sch 1, Pt I, art 6.

In the course of the hearing in private of an application by the trustees of a charity for the directions of the court in relation to certain pending proceedings, the question arose whether the court was obliged by art 6(1) of the European Convention for the Protection of Human Rights and Fundamental Freedoms 1950 (as set out in Sch 1 to the Human Rights Act 1998) to give its judgment in public. Article 6(1)[a] provided, inter alia, that in the determination of his civil rights everyone was entitled to a fair and public hearing and that judgment should be pronounced publicly but the press and public might be excluded from all or part of the trial to the extent strictly necessary in the opinion of the court in special circumstances where publicity would prejudice the interests of justice. CPR 5.4(2)(c) provided that any person who paid the prescribed fee might search for, inspect and take a copy from the court records of, inter alia, any judgment or order given or made in public or any other document if the court gave permission.

Held – The court was entitled to pronounce its judgment in private since an application to the court by trustees for directions might well affect but did not normally determine the civil rights of anyone, but even if it did, in the circumstances of a hearing in private, justified by the restriction in relation to the interests of justice, the practical impossibility of producing an anonymised or abridged version of the judgment, and the fact that copies could be made available in accordance with the provisions of CPR 5.4(2)(c) it was permitted by art 6(1) (see [11], [12], below); *Sutter v Switzerland* (1984) 6 EHRR 272, *Campbell v UK* (1985) 7 EHRR 165 and *B v UK* [2001] 2 FCR 221 considered.

Notes

For the right to a fair trial and a public hearing, see 8(2) *Halsbury's Laws* (4th edn reissue) paras 134, 138.

For the Human Rights Act 1998, Sch 1, Pt I, art 6, see 7 *Halsbury's Statutes* (4th edn) (2002 reissue) 554.

Cases referred to in judgment

B v UK [2001] 2 FCR 221, ECt HR.

Campbell v UK (1985) 7 EHRR 165, [1984] ECHR 7819/77, ECt HR.

Håkansson v Sweden (1991) 13 EHRR 1, [1990] ECHR 11855/95, ECt HR.

---

a   Article 6, so far as material, is set out at [2], below

a *Hinckley Island Hotel Ltd, Re, Craig v Humberclyde Industrial Finance Ltd* [1998] 2
    BCLC 526, [1999] 1 WLR 129, CA.
    Sutter v Switzerland (1984) 6 EHRR 272, [1984] ECHR 8209/78, ECt HR.

Application

The trustees of the X charity applied for directions in relation to certain pending
b proceedings. The hearing of the application was listed to be heard in private. In
the course of the hearing the question arose whether the court was obliged by
virtue of art 6 of the European Convention for the Protection of Human Rights
and Fundamental Freedoms 1950 (as set out in Sch 1 to the Human Rights Act
1998) to give its judgment in public.

c 24 June 2003. The following judgment was delivered.

SIR ANDREW MORRITT V-C.

[1] In the course of the hearing in private of an application by the trustees of a
charity for the directions of the court in relation to certain pending proceedings,
d the question arose whether I was obliged by art 6(1) of the European Convention
for the Protection of Human Rights and Fundamental Freedoms 1950 (as set out
in Sch 1 to the Human Rights Act 1998) to give my judgment in public. I heard
argument from, amongst others, junior counsel for the Attorney General. I am
most grateful to all of them. I indicated that I was satisfied that I could and should
give my judgment in private and would give my reasons for that conclusion later.
e I have given judgment on the application. What follows are my reasons for
concluding that I was entitled to do so in private.

[2] Article 6(1) provides:

> 'In the determination of his civil rights and obligations or of any criminal
f charge against him, everyone is entitled to a fair and public hearing within a
> reasonable time by an independent and impartial tribunal established by law.
> Judgment shall be pronounced publicly but the press and public may be
> excluded from all or part of the trial in the interests of morals, public order
> or national security in a democratic society, where the interests of juveniles
> or the protection of the private life of the parties so require, or to the extent
g strictly necessary in the opinion of the court in special circumstances where
> publicity would prejudice the interests of justice.'

The problem arises from the apparent distinction in the second sentence between
the pronouncement of the judgment and the trial.

[3] The hearing of the application was listed to be heard in private as it was an
h application within the terms of CPR PD 39, para 1.5(10). No application was
made for the hearing to be held in public. I was and am satisfied that the nature
of the application was such that a hearing in private was 'strictly necessary [as]
publicity would prejudice the interests of justice'. In those circumstances it
would be surprising if my judgment, which in practice could not be anonymised,
j had to be given in public.

[4] I have been referred to three decisions of the European Court of Human
Rights which, as provided by s 2(1)(a) of the 1998 Act, I am bound to take into
account. The first chronologically is *Sutter v Switzerland* (1984) 6 EHRR 272. In that
case a Swiss national was convicted by the Divisional Court of insubordination and
failure to observe service regulations during his military service. He was sentenced
to ten days' imprisonment. His appeal on a point of law to the Court of Cassation

was dismissed. The relevant complaint was that the judgment of the Court of
Cassation had not been given in public and so infringed art 6(1).

[5] It is apparent (at 275–276, 279 (paras 20 and 34)) that the judgment was
available to any member of the public who could demonstrate an interest in
obtaining it and it was in fact published. Thus the argument appears to have been
that art 6(1) requires the court to read out its judgment in public. This contention
was rejected by a majority of 11 to 4. It is stated (at 279 (para 33)):

> 'The Court therefore does not feel bound to adopt a literal interpretation.
> It considers that in each case the form of publicity given to the "judgment"
> under the domestic law of the respondent State must be assessed in the light
> of the special features of the proceedings in question and by reference to the
> object and purpose of Article 6(1).'

It is unclear from that conclusion whether the majority considered that the
restrictions contained in the second sentence of art 6(1) apply to the obligation to
pronounce judgment in public as well as to the obligation to hold the trial in public.
However the concurring opinion of Judges Bernhardt, Bindschedler-Robert and
Matscher (at 281–282) shows that they considered that they do.

[6] The second decision is *Campbell v UK* (1985) 7 EHRR 165. In that case two
convicted prisoners were injured during a prison disturbance. The board of
visitors convicted them of breaches of disciplinary regulations and sentenced
them to substantial loss of remission. The decision of the board of visitors was
given in private. The European Court of Human Rights held that there had been
an infringement of art 6(1) in that respect. But the argument was not that the
express restrictions contained in the second sentence should be applied to the
obligation to pronounce judgment in public. The submission was that such
obligation was subject to some other implied restriction. This submission was
rejected. The court stated (at 202):

> '91. The Court has said in other cases that it does not feel bound to adopt
> a literal interpretation of the words "pronounced publicly": in each case the
> form of publication given to the "judgment" under the domestic law of the
> respondent State must be assessed in the light of the special features of the
> proceedings in question and by reference to the object pursued by
> Article 6(1) in this context, namely to ensure scrutiny of the judiciary by the
> public with a view to safeguarding the right to a fair trial.
> 92. However, in the present case it does not appear that any steps were
> taken to make public the Board of Visitors' decision. There has accordingly
> been a violation of Article 6(1) on this point.'

[7] The third decision of the European Court of Human Rights to which I was
referred is *B v UK* [2001] 2 FCR 221. That case concerned applications for
residence orders. Each of the applicants applied for the hearings to be in public.
The applications were refused and such refusal was upheld on appeal in each case
because private hearings were required by r 4.16(7) of the Family Proceedings
Rules 1991, SI 1991/1247. Accordingly the hearings were private and the
judgments were given in private too. A third party could obtain a copy of the
judgments but only with the permission of the court.

[8] The United Kingdom government submitted that if judgment had to be
given in public it would subvert the reasons for the hearing being conducted in
private. The applicants relied on the facts that the obligation is expressed in
unqualified terms and the court had rejected any implied restriction in *Campbell v*

a *UK* (1985) 7 EHRR 165. The court rejected the complaint by a majority of five to two. It recalled its case law (at 235 (para 45)) to the effect that the extent and nature of the requisite publicity depended on the nature of the proceedings and the objectives of art 6(1). It recalled (at 235 (para 46)) that it had upheld the decisions to conduct the hearings in private and expressly agreed with the United Kingdom government 'that to pronounce the judgment in public would, to a
b large extent, frustrate these aims'. The court noted (at 235 (para 47)) that copies of the judgment could be made available to third parties who could establish an interest and obtain the permission of the court. It concluded (at 235–236):

c
> '48. Having regard to the nature of the proceedings and the form of publicity applied by the national law, the Court considers that a literal interpretation of the terms of art 6(1) concerning the pronouncement of judgments would not only be unnecessary for the purposes of public scrutiny but might even frustrate the primary aim of art 6(1), which is to secure a fair hearing (see, *mutatis mutandis*, the above-mentioned (*Sutter v Switzerland* (1984) 6 EHRR 272 at 279 (para 34)).

d
> 49. The Court thus concludes that the Convention did not require making available to the general public the residence judgments in the present cases, and that there has been no violation of art 6(1) in this respect.'

[9] Bratza J (at 237–239) concurred in the conclusion but for reasons he set out in a separate opinion of his own. He accepted the proposition advanced by the applicants that the obligation to pronounce judgment in public, unlike that
e relating to the trial, is expressed in unqualified terms. He drew attention to the distinction in this respect between art 6(1) and art 14 of the International Covenant on Civil and Political Rights (New York, 16 December 1966 TS 6(1977) Cmnd 6702). He expressed sympathy for the dissenting opinion of Cremona J and others in *Sutter v Switzerland* (1984) 6 EHRR 272 to the effect that restricted
f access to judgments falls short of what the convention requires. Nevertheless he decided that there was in those cases sufficient compliance with the requirements of art 6(1). The essence of his conclusion is contained in para (2) (at 238–239) where he said:

g
> 'It is well established that art 6(1) of the Convention must be read as a whole. There is, as the majority judgment recognises, a logical relationship between the public nature of the proceedings and the public pronouncement of the judgment which is the result of those proceedings. If the public may legitimately be excluded from the hearing for the purpose of protecting the interests of children or the private lives of parties to a matrimonial dispute,
h the requirement that the judgment should be pronounced publicly should not be interpreted in such a way as to undermine that protection. It seems to me that it is not a satisfactory answer to this point to argue that the judgment could be entirely anonymised so that it contained no details capable of identifying the parties or the children concerned and/or abridged to the point where only the operative part of the court's decision was made
j public. Even if such a course could be said to be adequate to protect the interests of the children or the parties concerned, it is difficult to see how the publication of a judgment so anonymised and abridged could be said to serve the aim of public scrutability of judicial proceedings.'

[10] Bratza J (at 239) drew attention to the case law of the court to the effect that notwithstanding the apparently unqualified requirement it had been interpreted with 'some flexibility' so that the form of publicity was to be assessed in the light of the nature of the proceedings. He concluded that on the facts of the case the fact that the judgment would be made available to one who could demonstrate a legitimate interest in obtaining a copy and who obtained the permission of the court was enough to satisfy the requirement.

[11] As I have already indicated I was satisfied that the hearing should be held in private because the interests of justice so required. I was also satisfied that it was not a practical possibility to produce an anonymised or abridged version. Copies can be made available in accordance with CPR 5.4(2)(c). In those circumstances there is nothing in the decisions to which I must have regard to suggest that I should have given my judgment in public. It is, I think, clear that the flexible interpretation of art 6(1) to which Bratza J referred does not entitle the court simply to apply by analogy to the obligation to pronounce judgment in public the same restrictions as are available in relation to the obligation to hold the trial in public. This is no doubt for the good reason that the judgment of a court of justice cannot be a wholly private document. Its ultimate availability to the public can no doubt be hedged around with restrictions in appropriate cases but should not be excluded altogether.

[12] There is however another ground on which the pronouncement of my judgment in private was justified. As the opening words of art 6(1) make plain it only applies to 'the determination of civil rights'. An application to the court by trustees for directions may well affect but does not normally determine the civil rights of anyone. Similar procedures exist for the protection of other fiduciaries such as liquidators or receivers. Cf *Re Hinckley Island Hotel Ltd, Craig v Humberclyde Industrial Finance Ltd* [1998] 2 BCLC 526 at 532–534, [1999] 1 WLR 129 at 135–136 (paras 15–19). This, essentially administrative, jurisdiction is designed to provide guidance to the fiduciary as to the proper exercise of his powers in the problematic circumstances with which he is faced. Only rarely could it be said to determine the rights of anyone.

[13] Counsel for the Attorney General also submitted that the obligation to pronounce judgment in public may be overridden by the consent of all parties to the proceedings. He relied on the decision of the European Court of Human Rights in *Håkansson v Sweden* (1991) 13 EHRR 1 to the effect that an individual may waive his right to a public hearing. In view of my conclusions on the applicability and ambit of art 6(1) I do not have to reach a final conclusion on this submission. Suffice it to say that I should take a good deal of persuasion to conclude that it is right. To uphold it would seem to me to introduce into art 6(1) an implied restriction contrary to the decision in *Sutter v Switzerland* (1984) 6 EHRR 272 and to undermine the policy both domestic and European which requires hearings to be held in public.

[14] In summary I conclude that I was entitled to pronounce my judgment in private because: (a) it did not determine the civil rights of anyone, but even if it did (b) in the circumstances of a hearing in private, justified by the restriction in relation to the interests of justice, the practical impossibility of producing an anonymised or abridged version and the provisions of r 5.4(2)(c) it was permitted by art 6(1).

Order accordingly.

Celia Fox   Barrister.

a
Arsenal Football Club plc v Reed
[2003] EWCA Civ 696

COURT OF APPEAL, CIVIL DIVISION
ALDOUS, CLARKE AND JONATHAN PARKER LJJ
b
30 APRIL, 1, 21 MAY 2003

European Community – European Court of Justice – Jurisdiction – Reference to European Court of Justice – Application of guidance given by European Court of Justice on law to findings of fact made by national court.
c
Trade mark – Infringement – Use of identical trade mark – Non-trade mark use – Whether use affected function of trademark – Trade Marks Act 1994, s 10 – First Council Directive (EEC) 89/104, art 5(1).

d
The claimant, an internationally-known football club, commenced proceedings against the defendant, in which it alleged, inter alia, that he had infringed certain of its registered trade marks under s 10[a] of the Trade Marks Act 1994 (which implemented art 4[b] of First Council Directive (EEC) 89/104 approximating the laws of the member states relating to trade marks). Section 10(1) provided that a person infringed a registered trade mark if he used in the course of trade a sign which was identical with the trade mark in relation to goods or services identical
e
with those for which it was registered. The defendant sold souvenirs and memorabilia likely to appeal to the fans of the claimant, including articles bearing the trade marks Arsenal, Arsenal Gunners and certain device marks. The defendant contended that there could be no infringement if the use complained of was not 'trade mark use'. He argued that his products would be perceived as
f
a badge of support, loyalty or affiliation by those to whom they were directed, and not as indicating trade origin. In his first judgment, the judge concluded that the defence raised an issue of construction of the Directive which could not be decided without a reference to the Court of Justice of the European Communities (ECJ). The ECJ held that the material consideration was whether the use complained of was liable to jeopardise the guarantee of origin, not whether the
g
use was trade mark use. It concluded that where a third party used in the course of trade a sign which was identical to a validly registered trade mark on goods which were identical to those for which it was registered, the trade mark proprietor was entitled, in circumstances such as those in the instant case, to rely on art 5(1)(a) of the Directive to prevent that use, and that it was immaterial that,
h
in the context of that use, the sign was perceived as a badge of support for or loyalty or affiliation to the trade mark proprietor. The case came back before the judge. In his second judgment the judge concluded that the ECJ had disagreed with findings of fact made by him in his first judgment, and that that being so the ECJ had exceeded its jurisdiction, with the result that he was not bound by its

j

a   Section 10, so far as material, is set out at [14], below
b   Article 5, so far as material, provides: '1. The registered trade mark shall confer on the proprietor exclusive rights therein. The proprietor shall be entitled to prevent all third parties not having his consent from using in the course of trade: (a) any sign which is identical with the trade mark in relation to goods or services which are identical with those for which the trade mark is registered …'

final conclusion. He then applied the ECJ's guidance on the law, as he
understood it, to the findings of fact made in his first judgment, and concluded
that there had been no infringement, a different conclusion from that reached by
the ECJ. The claimant appealed.

Held – Upon a reference for a preliminary ruling on the interpretation of acts of
Community institutions the purpose of the ECJ was to decide a question of law,
and that ruling was binding on the national court as to the interpretation of the
Community acts in question; it was for the national court alone to find the facts.
In the instant case, therefore, the judge would have been entitled to disregard any
conclusion reached by the ECJ in so far as it was based upon a factual background
inconsistent with his judgment. However, the ECJ had not disregarded the
conclusions of fact made by the judge in his first judgment. The ECJ had not been
concerned with whether the use complained of was trade mark use, but rather
whether the third party's use affected or was likely to affect the functions of the
trade mark, namely guarantee of origin. The judge had not come to any
conclusion on that issue. Whilst the ECJ had concluded as a fact that, in the
circumstances found by the judge, use by the defendant was likely to jeopardise
the guarantee of origin which constituted the essential function of the trade mark
rights owned by the claimant, that finding of fact was inevitable in the
circumstances. Unchecked use of the mark by a third party, which was not
descriptive use, was likely to damage the function of the trade mark right because
the registered trade mark could no longer guarantee origin, that being an
essential function of a trade mark. As found by the judge, the trade marks, when
applied to the goods, were purchased and worn as badges of support, loyalty and
affiliation to Arsenal, but that did not mean that the use by a third party would
not be liable to jeopardise the function of the trade marks, namely, to guarantee
origin. To the contrary, the wider and more extensive the use, the less likely the
trade marks would be able to perform their function. The actions of the
defendant meant that goods, not coming from the claimant but bearing the trade
marks, were in circulation. That affected the ability of the trade marks to
guarantee the origin of the goods. It followed that the judge should have
followed the ECJ's ruling and decided the case in the claimant's favour.
Accordingly, the appeal would be allowed (see [25], [26], [33], [37], [43], [45],
[47]–[49], [73], [74], below).

Decision of Laddie J [2003] 1 All ER 137 reversed.

Notes
For identical marks to trade marks for identical goods and services and for
questions of interpretation of Community law, see 48 *Halsbury's Laws* (4th edn)
(2000 reissue) para 81 and 51 *Halsbury's Laws* (4th edn) para 3.80 respectively.

For the Trade Marks Act 1994, s 10, see 48 *Halsbury's Statutes* (4th edn) (2001
reissue) 120.

Cases referred to in judgments
Benedetti v Munari Flli SAS Case 52/76 [1977] ECR 163, ECJ.
Bollinger (J) v Costa Brava Wine Co Ltd [1959] 3 All ER 800, [1960] Ch 262, [1959] 3
     WLR 966.
Bollinger (J) v Costa Brava Wine Co Ltd (No 2) [1961] 1 All ER 561, [1961] 1 WLR 277.
Bosch (Robert) GmbH v Hauptzollamt Hildesheim Case 135/77 [1978] ECR 855, ECJ.
British Sugar plc v James Robertson & Sons Ltd [1996] RPC 281.

a   *European Commission v Camar Srl* Case C-312/00 (2002) Transcript (judgment), 10 December 2002, ECJ.

Hoffmann-La Roche & Co AG v Centrafarm Vertriebsgesellschaft Pharmazeutischer Erzeugnisse mbH Case 102/77 [1978] ECR 1139, ECJ.

Hölterhoff v Freiesleben Case C-2/00 [2002] All ER (EC) 665, [2002] ECR I-4187, ECJ.

b   *Kutz-Bauer v Freie und Hansestadt Hamburg* Case C-187/00 (2003) Transcript (judgment), 20 March 2003, ECJ.

Lloyd Schuhfabrik Meyer & Co GmbH v Klijsen Handel BV Case C-342/97 [1999] All ER (EC) 587, [1999] ECR I-3819, ECJ.

Loendersloot (t/a F Loendersloot Internationale Expeditie) v George Ballantine & Son Ltd Case C-349/95 [1997] ECR I-6227, ECJ.

c   *Philips Electronics NV v Remington Consumer Products Ltd* [1999] RPC 809, CA.

Philips Electronics NV v Remington Consumer Products Ltd Case C-299/99 [2002] All ER (EC) 634, [2003] Ch 159, [2003] 2 WLR 294, [2002] ECR I-5475, ECJ.

R v Secretary of State for Transport, ex p Factortame Ltd [1999] 4 All ER 906, [2000] 1 AC 524, [1999] 3 WLR 1062, HL.

d   *Reddaway (Frank) & Co Ltd v George Banham & Co Ltd* [1896] AC 199, [1895–9] All ER Rep 313, HL.

Vine Products Ltd v Mackenzie & Co Ltd [1969] RPC 1.

Appeal

e   The claimant, Arsenal Football Club plc, brought proceedings for infringement of trade mark and passing off against the defendant, Matthew Reed. In his first judgment on 6 April 2001 ([2001] IP & T 810) Laddie J referred two questions upon the construction of First Council Directive (EEC) 89/104 (to approximate the laws of the member states relating to trade marks) (OJ 1989 L40 p 1) to the Court of Justice of the European Communities (ECJ) under art 234 EC.

f   Following the ruling of the ECJ ([2003] All ER (EC) 1) the matter came back before the judge. In his second judgment on 12 December 2002 ([2002] EWHC 2695 (Ch), [2003] 1 All ER 137) Laddie J dismissed the claim. The claimant appealed. The facts are set out in the judgment of Aldous LJ.

g   *Simon Thorley QC, Mark Brealey QC* and *Thomas Mitcheson* (instructed by *Lawrence Jones*) for the claimant.

Roger Wyand QC, Nicholas Green QC and *Ashley Roughton* (instructed by *Duffield Stunt*, Chelmsford) for the defendant.

Cur adv vult

h   21 May 2003. The following judgments were delivered.

ALDOUS LJ.

i   [1] In January 1999 Arsenal Football Club plc (Arsenal) started proceedings against Mr Matthew Reed in which they alleged that Mr Reed had infringed certain of their registered trade marks and had carried out acts of passing off. Those proceedings came before Laddie J in March 2001.

[2] The judge in his first judgment ([2001] IP & T 810), handed down on 6 April 2001, held that the allegations of passing off had not been established. The judge went on to conclude that the defence raised an issue of construction of the First Council Directive (EEC) 89/104 (to approximate the laws of the member states

relating to trade marks) (OJ 1989 L40 p 1) (the Trade Mark Directive) which could
not be decided without a reference to the Court of Justice of the European
Communities (ECJ). He therefore referred the following questions to the ECJ.

'1. Where a trade mark is validly registered and (a) a third party uses in the
course of trade a sign identical with that trade mark in relation to goods which
are identical with those for which the trade mark is registered; and (b) the third
party has no defence to infringement by virtue of art 6(1) of the Trade Mark
Directive; does the third party have a defence to infringement on the ground
that the use complained of does not indicate trade origin (ie a connection in the
course of trade between the goods and the trade mark proprietor)?
2. If so, is the fact that the use in question would be perceived as a badge of
support, loyalty or affiliation to the trade mark proprietor a sufficient
connection?'

[3] The ECJ ([2003] All ER (EC) 1 at 31) did not answer those questions in the
form posed. They concluded:

'62. In the light of the foregoing, the answer to the national court's questions
must be that, in a situation which is not covered by art 6(1) of the [Trade Mark
Directive], where a third party uses in the course of trade a sign which is
identical to a validly registered trade mark on goods which are identical to
those for which it is registered, the trade mark proprietor is entitled, in
circumstances such as those in the present case, to rely on art 5(1)(a) of the
[Trade Mark Directive] to prevent that use. It is immaterial that, in the context
of that use, the sign is perceived as a badge of support for or loyalty or affiliation
to the trade mark proprietor.'

[4] They therefore ruled (at 31–32 (para 63)):

'In a situation which is not covered by art 6(1) of the [Trade Mark Directive]
where a third party uses in the course of trade a sign which is identical to a
validly registered trade mark on goods which are identical to those for which
it is registered, the trade mark proprietor of the mark is entitled, in
circumstances such as those in the present case, to rely on art 5(1)(a) of that
directive to prevent that use. It is immaterial that, in the context of that use,
the sign is perceived as a badge of support for or loyalty or affiliation to the
trade mark proprietor.'

[5] The case came back before the judge in December 2002. In his judgment of
12 December 2002 ([2002] EWHC 2695 (Ch), [2003] 1 All ER 137) (the second
judgment) the judge concluded that the ECJ had disagreed with findings of fact
made by him in his first judgment. That being so, the ECJ had 'exceeded its
jurisdiction' with the result that he was not bound by its final conclusion. He then
applied the ECJ's guidance on the law, as he understood it, to the findings of fact
made in his first judgment and concluded that infringement of the trade marks had
not taken place. That resulted in the judge coming to a different conclusion from
that reached by the ECJ.

[6] Arsenal have not appealed against the findings of the judge that passing off
had not been established. Mr Reed also contended that Arsenal's trade mark was
invalid. That contention was rejected by the judge and there is no appeal against
that conclusion. Thus this appeal is only concerned with the issue of trade mark
infringement.

THE BACKGROUND

a   [7] The factual background was fully set out by the judge and is not in dispute. I can therefore take from the judgment the salient facts to enable my judgment to be understood.

[8] Arsenal is the internationally-known football club. It is known as 'Arsenal' or 'the Gunners'. Part of the business carried on by Arsenal involves the sale of

b products bearing the words 'Arsenal', 'Arsenal Gunners' and the device marks reproduced below:

The Crest Device:

c

d

The Cannon Device:

e

f

[9] Arsenal alleged infringement of the following trade marks:

'(a) Registered trade mark number 1383343 for "ARSENAL" in class 25
g (registered 9th May 1989); (b) Registered trade mark number 1387461 for the
Arsenal Cannon device in class 25 (registered 8th June 1989); (c) Registered
trade mark number 1387589 for the Arsenal Crest Device in class 25 (registered
13th June 1989) (d) Registered trade mark number 1393203 for "ARSENAL
GUNNERS" in class 25 (registered 27th July 1989).'

h [10] Mr Reed is the self-employed proprietor of a wholesale and retail football merchandise business. Amongst the articles that he sells are souvenirs and memorabilia likely to appeal to Arsenal fans. Such include articles bearing the trade marks Arsenal, Arsenal Gunners and the device marks illustrated above. He accepted that he had, without Arsenal's consent, used in the course of trade signs

j identical to the registered trade marks relied on by Arsenal in relation to the goods for which they were registered. He denied infringement. No positive case was pleaded in the defence, but in voluntary particulars it was made clear that he was asserting that there could be no infringement if the use complained about was not trade mark use, and his use was not trade mark use. It was that point which caused the reference to the ECJ.

THE STATUTORY BACKGROUND

[11] The Trade Marks Act 1994 swept away the old law and implemented the *a* Trade Mark Directive. It follows that the provisions of the 1994 Act must be construed so as to reflect the terms of the Trade Mark Directive.

[12] Section 1(b) defines a 'trade mark' as meaning 'any sign capable of being represented graphically which is capable of distinguishing goods or services of one undertaking from those of other undertakings'. There is no doubt that Arsenal's *b* registered trade marks are signs which have the character required.

[13] A registered trade mark is a property right (see s 2) which is personal property (see s 22). It can be assigned either in connection with the goodwill of a business or independently (see s 24). Once obtained a registration is prima facie valid (see s 72). It need not be used for the initial five years after registration, but thereafter it is liable to be revoked in whole or in part for non-use under s 46. *c*

[14] Section 2(1) states that the proprietor of a registered trade mark 'has the rights and remedies provided by this Act'. For the purpose of this case the relevant rights are those contained in s 10 (art 5 of the Trade Mark Directive). The applicable parts of that section are as follows:

'*Infringement of registered trade mark.*—(1) A person infringes a registered *d* trade mark if he uses in the course of trade a sign which is identical with the trade mark in relation to goods or services which are identical with those for which it is registered.

(2) A person infringes a registered trade mark if he uses in the course of trade a sign where because—(a) the sign is identical with the trade mark and is used *e* in relation to goods or services similar to those for which the trade mark is registered, or (b) the sign is similar to the trade mark and is used in relation to goods or services identical with or similar to those for which the trade mark is registered, there exists a likelihood of confusion on the part of the public, which includes the likelihood of association with the trade mark.

(3) A person infringes a registered trade mark if he uses in the course of trade *f* a sign which—(a) is identical with or similar to the trade mark, and (b) is used in relation to goods or services which are not similar to those for which the trade mark is registered, where the trade mark has a reputation in the United Kingdom and the use of the sign, being without due cause, takes unfair advantage of, or is detrimental to, the distinctive character or the repute of the *g* trade mark.

(4) For the purposes of this section a person uses a sign if, in particular, he—(a) affixes it to goods or the packaging thereof; (b) offers or exposes goods for sale, puts them on the market or stocks them for those purposes under the sign, or offers or supplies services under the sign; (c) imports or exports goods under the sign; or (d) uses the sign on business papers or in advertising ... *h*

(6) Nothing in the preceding provisions of this section shall be construed as preventing the use of a registered trade mark by any person for the purpose of identifying goods or services as those of the proprietor or a licensee. But any such use otherwise than in accordance with honest practices in industrial or commercial matters shall be treated as infringing the registered trade mark if *j* the use without due cause takes unfair advantage of, or is detrimental to, the distinctive character or repute of the trade mark.'

[15] It is important to note the difference between sub-ss (1) and (2) of that section. This case is concerned with identicality of registered trade mark and sign and identicality of goods. Thus infringement will occur if the alleged infringer 'uses

a in the course of trade' the sign. Subsection (2) deals with use when the goods and/or the signs are not identical. In those circumstances a likelihood of confusion must be shown. That requires the proprietor to establish that there is a risk that the public might believe that the goods in question came from the same undertaking or an economically linked undertaking (see *Lloyd Schuhfabrik Meyer & Co GmbH v Klijsen Handel BV* Case C-342/97 [1999] All ER (EC) 587, [1999] ECR I-3819).

b   [16] Section 11 contains exceptions to s 10. It is in this form:

> '*Limits on effect of registered trade mark.*—(1) A registered trade mark is not infringed by the use of another registered trade mark in relation to goods or services for which the latter is registered (but see section 47(6) (effect of declaration of invalidity of registration)).
c
> (2) A registered trade mark is not infringed by—(a) the use by a person of his own name or address, (b) the use of indications concerning the kind, quality, quantity, intended purpose, value, geographical origin, the time of production of goods or of rendering of services, or other characteristics of goods or services, or (c) the use of the trade mark where it is necessary to indicate the
d intended purpose of a product or service (in particular, as accessories or spare parts), provided the use is in accordance with honest practices in industrial or commercial matters.
>
> (3) A registered trade mark is not infringed by the use in the course of trade in a particular locality of an earlier right which applies only in that locality. For
e this purpose an "earlier right" means an unregistered trade mark or other sign continuously used in relation to goods or services by a person or a predecessor in title of his from a date prior to whichever is the earlier of—(a) the use of the first-mentioned trade mark in relation to those goods or services by the proprietor or a predecessor in title of his, or (b) the registration of the first-mentioned trade mark in respect of those goods or services in the name of
f the proprietor or a predecessor in title of his; and an earlier right shall be regarded as applying in a locality if, or to the extent that, its use in that locality is protected by virtue of any rule of law (in particular, the law of passing off).'

THE FIRST JUDGMENT
g   [17] As I have said Mr Reed did not dispute that he had used signs identical to Arsenal's registered trade marks in the course of his trade. His defence was that the words 'uses in the course of trade a sign' required the use to be trade mark use. By that he meant that the use had to be in a manner that indicated the origin of the goods. It was his case that he used the word 'Arsenal' and other trade marks as
h badges of allegiance, not in a manner that indicated a connection in the course of trade between the goods and Arsenal. The judge held ([2001] IP & T 810 at [58]) that Mr Reed's use was not trade mark use. He said:

> 'In my view, and consistent with the views expressed at para 42 above, the
j Arsenal signs on Mr Reed's products would be perceived as a badge of support, loyalty or affiliation to those to whom they are directed. They would not be perceived as indicating trade origin. Therefore I reject Mr Thorley's first answer to Mr Roughton's argument. It follows that for AFC to succeed on trade mark infringement, it has to rely on the non-trade mark use of those signs, that is to say the wide construction of s 10.'

[18] The judge went on to consider the submission of Arsenal that 'non-trade mark' use fell within s 10(1) of the 1994 Act. He referred to other sections of the 1994 Act and the Trade Mark Directive and concluded (at [60]):

> 'All of these points and others based on the recitals in the Trade Marks Directive might suggest that only use as a trade mark can infringe the rights secured by registration ...'

[19] The judge then noted that Jacob J in *British Sugar plc v James Robertson & Sons Ltd* [1996] RPC 281 had expressed a contrary view as had the Court of Appeal in *Philips Electronics NV v Remington Consumer Products Ltd* [1999] RPC 809. That view was a provisional view expressed prior to the Court of Appeal seeking guidance from the ECJ. It was therefore not binding on the judge. With that background in mind the judge referred to the ECJ the questions set out in [2], above.

THE SECOND JUDGMENT (12 DECEMBER 2002)

[20] The judge went through the judgment of the ECJ and concluded ([2003] 1 All ER 137 at [20]):

> 'It appears from the above analysis that the ECJ held that where the defendant's use of a mark is not intended by him, or understood by the public, to be a designation of origin, there can be no infringement because such use does not prejudice the essential function of the registered mark. If that is so, then the first question in the reference should have been answered in the affirmative. However, it will be seen that the ECJ did not answer that question in the affirmative or the negative but only stated that "in the circumstances" of this case, the claimant should succeed.'

[21] The judge then came to the submissions advanced on behalf of the parties. Mr Wyand QC, on behalf of Mr Reed, submitted that the ECJ had interpreted the Trade Mark Directive in the way that he had submitted it should be interpreted, but had then come to a conclusion ([2003] All ER (EC) 1 at 31 (para 62)) (see [3], above) in favour of Arsenal and had so ruled (see [4], above). That, he submitted, was the result of the ECJ embarking on an impermissible determination of fact. In any case the conclusion reached by the ECJ was incompatible with the findings of fact made at the trial.

[22] Mr Thorley QC, who appeared for Arsenal, submitted that Mr Wyand had misconstrued and misunderstood the judgment of the ECJ.

[23] The judge accepted the submissions of Mr Wyand. He said ([2003] 1 All ER 137 at [27]):

> 'It appears to me that Mr Wyand's analysis is correct. The ECJ has disagreed with the conclusions of fact reached at the trial and indicated that the claimant should win because Mr Reed's use was such as would be perceived by some customers or users as a designation of origin. If this is so, the ECJ has exceeded its jurisdiction and I am not bound by its final conclusion. I must apply its guidance on the law to the facts as found at the trial.'

[24] The judge went on to consider what should be done. He rejected the idea that there should be a further reference and concluded that he should apply the guidance on the law given by the ECJ to the facts as found by him. That he decided meant that there was no infringement. As I understand his judgment, he believed that the ECJ had upheld Mr Reed's contention that there could not be infringement

a   unless the use complained about was trade mark use in the sense that it indicated trade origin. He therefore dismissed Arsenal's claim for trade mark infringement.

THE JURISDICTION OF THE ECJ

[25] There was no dispute between the parties that on a reference under art 234 EC (formerly art 177 of the EC Treaty), the purpose of the ECJ is 'to decide a question of law and that the ruling is binding on the national court as to the

b   interpretation of the community provisions and acts in question' (see *Benedetti v Munari Flli SAS* Case 52/76 [1977] ECR 163). Even so, the ECJ has jurisdiction to review the legal characterisation of facts found by the national court (see *European Commission v Camar Srl* Case C-312/00 (2002) Transcript (judgment), 10 December 2002). Also the ECJ has in the past provided guidance in order to enable the

c   national court to give judgment (see *Kutz-Bauer v Freie und Hansestadt Hamburg* Case C-187/00 (2003) Transcript (judgment), 20 March 2003). On occasions it has 'steered' the national court for the purpose of unified application of the law. However, as the House of Lords made clear in *R v Secretary of State for Transport, ex p Factortame Ltd* [1999] 4 All ER 506 at 927, [2000] 1 AC 524 at 550, the English court is not bound by that steer and therefore, with hesitation, could conclude the

d   case in a different way. It is the national court alone that must find the facts.

[26] It follows that the judge was entitled to disregard any conclusion reached, in so far as it was based upon a factual background inconsistent with his judgment. Thus, upon his perception of the ECJ's judgment, he was entitled to disregard the conclusion in the ruling and decide the case upon the legal principles stated in the

e   judgment of the ECJ.

THE SUBMISSIONS OF THE PARTIES

[27] In outline, Arsenal put forward three submissions. First, the ruling (see [3], above) was a ruling as to the law and was binding on the court. Thus the judge's conclusion was wrong. Second, the judge had misunderstood the reasoning of the

f   ECJ judgment. Arsenal accept that the jurisdiction of the ECJ was interpretation, but the ECJ could and do reformulate questions referred. That was what had happened in this case. That was necessary as Yes or No answers could not be given to the questions referred. The court had interpreted the word 'uses' in the Trade Mark Directive (as in s 10(1) of the 1994 Act) as not requiring that the use must

g   indicate trade origin. It was sufficient if the use complained of was liable 'to jeopardise the guarantee of origin which constitutes the essential function of the mark'. That being so, upon the findings of fact made by the judge, no reasonable court could come to a conclusion that differed from the ruling of the ECJ. It was immaterial that the trade mark was perceived as a badge of loyalty as the use complained of was liable to jeopardise the guarantee of origin of the Arsenal trade

h   marks.

[28] Arsenal also submitted that the judge had in his first judgment wrongly held that the use of signs identical to the registered trade marks by Mr Reed were not such as to indicate trade origin ie a connection in the course of trade between the goods and the trade mark proprietor. It did not follow from the fact that goods

j   bearing the signs were used by fans of Arsenal as badges of allegiance that the use was not use in a trade mark sense and the judge was wrong to believe that it did.

[29] Mr Reed supported the conclusion and reasoning of the judge. He submitted that the ruling was not binding upon the court as it contained within it conclusions of fact contrary to those found by the judge. In any case, it needed to be interpreted in the light of the reasoning that preceded it. He submitted that the

judgment of the ECJ provided three principles. First, not every use of a sign
identical to the trade mark in respect of identical goods to those for which the mark
is registered can be prohibited by the proprietor of the trade mark. Second, only
such use as affects or is likely to affect the functions of the trade mark is prohibited.
Third, the fact that the use is of a sign which is perceived as a badge of support for
or loyalty or affiliation to the proprietor of the mark is immaterial to the issue of
infringement. The judge had correctly understood the law as set out in the ECJ
judgment and upon his findings of fact in his first judgment was bound to come to
the conclusion he did.

[30] In any case, Arsenal had failed to show that Mr Reed's use was likely to
affect the functions of the trade marks. That was clear as they failed to produce any
evidence that anybody believed there was a connection in the course of trade
between Mr Reed's goods and Arsenal. There was no evidence of confusion. The
judge was correct to come to the conclusions of fact that he did.

IS THE RULING OF THE ECJ BINDING?

[31] Of course the ruling of the ECJ is binding in so far as it is a ruling upon
interpretation. However I reject the submission of Mr Thorley that the national
court should confine its attention solely to the ruling. Strictly speaking the
judgment is the explanation of the ruling, but as Advocate General Warner
explained in *Robert Bosch GmbH v Hauptzollamt Hildesheim* Case 135/77 [1978] ECR
855 at 861: '... the operative part of a Judgment of this Court should always be
interpreted in the light of the reasoning that precedes it.' That is particularly apt in
the present case as the ruling uses the words 'in circumstances such as those in the
present case'. To ascertain what the ECJ believed the circumstances were, it is
necessary to have recourse to the preceding paragraphs of the judgment. I
therefore turn to consider the ECJ judgment with the submissions of the parties in
mind.

THE ECJ'S JUDGMENT

[32] The ECJ concluded ([2003] All ER (EC) 1 at 29 (para 42)):

'To answer the High Court's questions, it must be determined whether
art 5(1)(a) of the [Trade Mark Directive] entitles the trade mark proprietor to
prohibit any use by a third party in the course of trade of a sign identical to the
trade mark for goods identical to those for which the mark is registered, or
whether that right of prohibition presupposes the existence of a specific
interest of the proprietor as trade mark proprietor, in that use of the sign in
question by a third party must affect or be liable to affect one of the functions
of the mark.'

[33] The ECJ (at 29 (para 42)) do not set out to answer the questions referred.
Their reason becomes clear from the rest of the judgment. The referred questions
were based upon the view that the issue of infringement would depend upon
whether the use complained about was trade mark use, in the sense that the use
indicated the origin of the goods. That the ECJ concluded was not the relevant
consideration. In summary the ECJ held that registration of a trade mark gave to
the proprietor a property right (see s 2 of the 1994 Act). The relevant consideration
was whether the use complained about was likely to damage that property right or,
as the ECJ put it, is likely to affect or jeopardise the guarantee of origin which
constitutes the essential function of the mark. That did not depend on whether the
use complained of was trade mark use.

a [34] The judge in his second judgment ([2003] 1 All ER 137 at [66]) stated that the first of the two alternatives in the ECJ's judgment (at 29 (para 42)) was Arsenal's submission and the second was in substance Mr Reed's argument. That was not correct. The crucial difference between Mr Reed's argument and the second alternative in the reformulated question was that the reformulated question looks at the interest of the proprietor's trade mark right and whether that interest is liable

b to be affected: whereas Mr Reed's submission looks at whether his use was of a particular type, namely, did it denote a connection in the course of trade between the goods and the proprietor.

 [35] The ECJ judgment proceeds to determine which of the alternatives (at 29 (para 42)) is correct. Upon the basis of the reasoning (at 29 (paras 43–47)), the ECJ set out (at 29–30 (para 48)) the essential function of a trade mark in these terms:

c

> 'In that context, the essential function of a trade mark is to guarantee the identity of origin of the marked goods or services to the consumer or end user by enabling him, without any possibility of confusion, to distinguish the goods or services from others which have another origin. For the trade mark to be able to fulfil its essential role in the system of undistorted competition which
d > the Treaty seeks to establish and maintain, it must offer a guarantee that all the goods or services bearing it have been manufactured or supplied under the control of a single undertaking which is responsible for their quality (see, inter alia, *Hoffmann-La Roche & Co AG v Centrafarm Vertriebsgesellschaft Pharmazeutischer Erzeugnisse mbH* Case 102/77 [1978] ECR 1139 (para 7) and
e > *Philips Electronics NV v Remington Consumer Products Ltd* Case C-299/99 [2002] All ER (EC) 634 at 649, [2002] ECR I-5475 (para 30)).'

 [36] The judgment then gives guidance (at 30) as to how that essential function can be ensured.

f

> '50. For that guarantee of origin, which constitutes the essential function of a trade mark, to be ensured, the proprietor must be protected against competitors wishing to take unfair advantage of the status and reputation of the trade mark by selling products illegally bearing it (see, inter alia, the *Hoffmann-La Roche* case (para 7) and *Loendersloot (t/a F Loendersloot Internationale Expeditie) v George Ballantine & Son Ltd* Case C-349/95 [1997]
g > ECR I-6227 (para 22)). In this respect, the tenth recital of the preamble to the [Trade Mark Directive] points out the absolute nature of the protection afforded by the trade mark in the case of identity between the mark and the sign and between the goods or services concerned and those for which the mark is registered. It states that the aim of that protection is in particular to
h > guarantee the trade mark as an indication of origin.
> 51. It follows that the exclusive right under art 5(1)(a) of the [Trade Mark Directive] was conferred in order to enable the trade mark proprietor to protect his specific interests as proprietor, that is, to ensure that the trade mark can fulfil its functions. The exercise of that right must therefore be reserved to
j > cases in which a third party's use of the sign affects or is liable to affect the functions of the trade mark, in particular its essential function of guaranteeing to consumers the origin of the goods.'

 [37] It is important to note that the ECJ is not concerned with whether the use complained about is trade mark use. The consideration is whether the third party's use affects or is likely to affect the functions of the trade mark. An instance of where

that will occur is given, namely where a competitor wishes to take unfair advantage
of the reputation of the trade mark by selling products illegally bearing the mark.   *a*
That would happen whether or not the third party's use was trade mark use or
whether there was confusion.

[38] The ECJ explains (at 30 (para 54)) that certain uses for descriptive purposes
will not infringe because they cannot affect the registered proprietary rights. That
meant that the first alternative posed in para 42 of the ECJ judgment (see [32],   *b*
above) could not be the law. The judge went further. Having cited para 54 of the
ECJ judgment he said ([2003] 1 All ER 137 at [20]):

> 'It appears from the above analysis that the ECJ held that where the
> defendant's use of a mark is not intended by him, or understood by the public,
> to be a designation of origin, there can be no infringement because such use   *c*
> does not prejudice the essential function of the registered mark. If that is so,
> then the first question in the reference should have been answered in the
> affirmative. However, it will be seen that the ECJ did not answer that question
> in the affirmative or the negative but only stated that "in the circumstances" of
> this case, the claimant should succeed.'
>
> *d*

[39] Paragraph 54 of the ECJ judgment has to be read in the context of the
judgment in *Hölterhoff v Freiesleben* Case C-2/00 [2002] All ER (EC) 665 at 682, [2002]
ECR I-4187 (para 16)). The descriptive use in that case was held not to affect the
proprietor's trade mark interest. At no stage did the ECJ suggest that use which was
not understood by the public to be a designation of origin could not infringe. The
ECJ indicated that the Trade Mark Directive required consideration as to whether   *e*
the function of the trade mark right was liable to be harmed. That becomes more
apparent from the paragraphs of the ECJ judgment that follow.

[40] Two reasons are given ([2003] All ER (EC) 1 at 30–31 (paras 56–59)) as to
why Mr Reed's use of signs identical to the registered trade marks is liable to affect
one of the functions of Arsenal's registered trade marks. The first is contained in   *f*
paras 56 and 57 which are as follows:

> '56. Having regard to the presentation of the word "Arsenal" on the goods
> at issue in the main proceedings and the other secondary markings on them
> (see para 39, above), the use of that sign is such as to create the impression that
> there is a material link in the course of trade between the goods concerned and   *g*
> the trade mark proprietor.
>
> 57. That conclusion is not affected by the presence on Mr Reed's stall of the
> notice stating that the goods at issue in the main proceedings are not official
> Arsenal FC products (see para 17, above). Even on the assumption that such a
> notice may be relied on by a third party as a defence to an action for trade mark
> infringement, there is a clear possibility in the present case that some   *h*
> consumers, in particular if they come across the goods after they have been
> sold by Mr Reed and taken away from the stall where the notice appears, may
> interpret the sign as designating Arsenal FC as the undertaking of origin of the
> goods.'

[41] The judge read paras 56 and 57 as containing a finding of fact by the ECJ   *j*
contrary to his findings of fact in his first judgment ([2001] IP & T 810) which were
in this form:

> '[42] It seems to me that the use of the Arsenal signs on Mr Reed's products
> carries no message of trade origin. Although I accept that some fans will want

a   to purchase official Arsenal memorabilia so as to support their club, it is a non-sequitur to say that this means all Arsenal memorabilia or memorabilia displaying one or more of the Arsenal signs will be taken by them to have come from or be licensed by AFC. Choosing to give your custom to one company by buying goods from it does not mean that that type of goods only comes from that company. What is necessary is some additional sign or circumstance

b   of trading which says to the customer that the goods come from or are commercially connected with the source he likes and not some other source ...

[58] In my view, and consistent with the views expressed at para 42 above, the Arsenal signs on Mr Reed's products would be perceived as a badge of support, loyalty or affiliation to those to whom they are directed. They would not be perceived as indicating trade origin. Therefore I reject Mr Thorley's

c   first answer to Mr Roughton's argument. It follows that for AFC to succeed on trade mark infringement, it has to rely on the non-trade mark use of those signs, that is to say the wide construction of s 10.'

[42] Paragraph [42] came in the part of the judgment where the judge dealt with

d   passing off. The issue was whether Mr Reed had misrepresented that goods sold by him were goods that came from Arsenal. The judge held that he had not done so. There was a finding by the judge (at [58]) that Mr Reed's use was not trade mark use in that it did not indicate the origin of the goods. However the judge did not come to any conclusion as to whether Mr Reed's use was liable to affect or jeopardise the guarantee of origin which was the essential feature of Arsenal's trade

e   mark rights. No doubt this was not argued as an issue and because of that he did not consider it to be relevant.

[43] Paragraphs 56 and 57 ([2003] All ER (EC) 1 at 30–31) appear to contain conclusions of fact reached by the ECJ. As such they cannot be binding on the national court. However, the conclusions reached are not inconsistent with the

f   findings of fact reached by the judge. The crucial sentence in understanding the ECJ reasoning is the last one in para 57. There the court states that there is a clear possibility in the present case that consumers may interpret the sign as designating Arsenal as the undertaking of origin in a case where the goods are taken away from Mr Reed and therefore not subject to Mr Reed's explanation that they do not come from Arsenal. The judge's findings of fact were based upon the balance of

g   probabilities. He was concerned with the effect of the signs upon Mr Reed's customers, not upon consumers who might not know anything about Mr Reed.

[44] The second reason is contained in paras 58 and 59:

'58. Moreover, in the present case, there is also no guarantee, as required by the court's case law cited in para 48, above, that all the goods designated by the

h   trade mark have been manufactured or supplied under the control of a single undertaking which is responsible for their quality.

59. The goods at issue are in fact supplied outside the control of Arsenal FC as trade mark proprietor, it being common ground that they do not come from

j   Arsenal FC or from its approved resellers.' (See [2003] All ER (EC) 1 at 31.)

[45] Mr Wyand submitted that those paragraphs also contained findings of fact contrary to those made by the judge in his first judgment. I reject that submission. The paragraphs contain reasoning and explanation based upon agreed facts. The ECJ looks at the function of a trade mark not whether the use is trade mark use. Unchecked use of the mark by a third party, which is not descriptive use, is likely to

damage the function of the trade mark right because the registered trade mark can no longer guarantee origin, that being an essential function of a trade mark.

[46] There follows in the ECJ judgment the conclusion ([2003] All ER (EC) 1 at 31 (para 61)):

> 'Once it has been found that, in the present case, the use of the sign in question by the third party is liable to affect the guarantee of origin of the goods and that the trade mark proprietor must be able to prevent this, it is immaterial that in the context of that use the sign is perceived as a badge of support for or loyalty or affiliation to the proprietor of the mark.'

[47] The judge held that the ECJ had indicated that Arsenal should win because Mr Reed's use *was* such as would be perceived by some customers or users as a designation of origin. That in my view was not the basis of the ECJ judgment. The judgment of the ECJ makes it clear that the important consideration is whether the right given by registration is likely to be affected by a third party's use. That occurs when the use complained about is likely to jeopardise the guarantee of origin which constitutes the essential function of the trade mark right. That was a matter never considered by the judge in his first judgment. He concentrated on whether Mr Reed's use was trade mark use.

THE CONCLUSION

[48] For the reasons given, I do not believe that the ECJ disregarded the conclusions of fact made by the judge in his first judgment. However I accept that they did conclude as a fact that, in the circumstances found by the judge, use by Mr Reed was liable to jeopardise the guarantee of origin which constituted the essential function of the trade mark rights owned by Arsenal. That was, I believe, a finding of fact that was inevitable in the circumstances. As found by the judge, the trade marks, when applied to the goods, were purchased and worn as badges of support, loyalty and affiliation to Arsenal, but that did not mean that the use by a third party would not be liable to jeopardise the functions of the trade marks, namely the ability to guarantee origin. To the contrary, the wider and more extensive the use, the less likely the trade marks would be able to perform their function. As the ECJ pointed out, the actions of Mr Reed meant that goods, not coming from Arsenal but bearing the trade marks, were in circulation. That affected the ability of the trade marks to guarantee the origin of the goods. I therefore conclude that the result reached by the ECJ was inevitable once their judgment had made it clear that the material consideration was whether the use complained of was liable to jeopardise the guarantee of origin, not whether the use was trade mark use. The judge should have followed the ruling and decided the case in Arsenal's favour.

[49] For those reasons I would allow the appeal and give judgment for Arsenal. That being so, it is not strictly necessary to deal with the second issue, whether the judge was correct that Mr Reed's use was not trade mark use, but I will do so as it was argued in full.

WAS MR REED'S USE TRADE MARK USE?

[50] Mr Thorley referred us to the evidence and submitted that there was no basis for the conclusion reached by the judge. I will come to Mr Wyand's submissions, but before doing so will summarise the relevant evidence.

[51] Mr Hazell had been the commercial manager of Arsenal since 1989. He explained how Arsenal's marketing had expanded and had played an important part

a in the club's activities. He said that it was apparent from the turnover that had been generated that demand by members of the public for licensed goods bearing the Arsenal trade mark was high. He believed that people wished to buy Arsenal merchandise partly because they were contributing towards the activities and success of the club. He said that from time to time the club's retail outlets received complaints about counterfeit merchandise displaying one or more of the Arsenal *b* trade marks and he was pressed upon that in cross-examination. He said that since 1989 he had had half a dozen instances of confusion brought to his attention. He was asked by the judge:

> '*Laddie J*: … You said perhaps about half a dozen instances of confusion you've heard about, because everybody is terribly busy, and what you are
> *c* talking about is what people in your shop report to you? *A*: I think all, if not all, six or seven or whatever, but all of those customers that came back into the shop were most annoyed, they probably brought a garment the week before and bought it back the following home game. Most of those people have asked to see the commercial manager. I've been brought on match day to speak to those people personally.
> *d* *Q*: You said it was a bit vague because the shop was so busy? *A*: Yes.
> *Q*: You also said in answer to an earlier question "I think there is an element of confusion out there. Some customers bought back goods they were under the impression came from us"? *A*: Yes.
> *Q*: How—you have never spoken to any of these customers? *A*: Yes, about *e* half a dozen of them.
> *Q*: You personally? *A*: They would have called me on a match day to say they wanted to speak to the commercial manager.
> *Q*: You spoke to the customer? *A*: Yes.
> *Q*: You say you thought they were under the impression. How did they get *f* that impression? *A*: Because it had a club crest on. The garment, I think one or more were T-shirts, one or two were sweat shirts.
> *Q*: How do you know it was their impression? *A*: Because they told me.'

[52] Mr Ireland had held the position of company secretary for Tottenham Hotspur. He explained to the judge that the club's merchandising activities were a *g* major commercial success and the demand for official Spurs' merchandise bearing their trade marks was very high. He said their fans had come to expect the club to market its own range of goods and he believed that the success of Spurs' merchandising activities was partly due to the high quality of the materials being sold. He said that by buying Spurs' branded clothing the fans knew that they were *h* contributing to the club's finances. In cross-examination he was asked about unofficial goods being sold bearing the Tottenham Hotspur trade marks and whether the fans understood the difference between official and unofficial goods. He said:

> *i* 'They understand if they buy something with one of our trade marks, that that indicates that it is a Tottenham Hotspur item of merchandise, because no-one else is allowed to use our trade marks. There is an unofficial market in stalls outside the ground on match days where people sell a blue and white scarf, or they sell T-shirts with images of Sol Campbell, or they sell T-shirts, sadly quite distasteful T-shirts, making comments about Arsenal Football Club.'

[53] He went on to refute the suggestion that fans knew that both official and unofficial goods were on the market. In his view 'any use of our trade marks on any clothing means it's from the club'.

[54] Mr O'Donovan was the national and international trade mark manager of Manchester United. He had held that position since 1990. He explained how the merchandising of Manchester United goods had expanded over the years and stated that it had become increasingly important to the success of the club. He said that Manchester United supporters were very aware that the success of the merchandising efforts generated the funds available to improve the stadium and its approaches, to provide car parking facilities, to provide academy and training facilities and to provide funds to enable the club to expend money on players as necessary. In cross-examination he was asked whether people wearing Manchester United clothing did so to show that they were supporters. He said that he assumed that to be the position, but also said that it was to show that the person had 'bought the items manufactured by Manchester United'.

[55] Miss Bouchard had been at Arsenal and was at the time that she gave evidence with West Ham. She was asked by the judge why warnings were given to supporters that there were inferior products about. She said:

'A: The problem we had, and to some degree still have, is that people assume that something if it is carrying the official club crest or logo on it, it is produced by the club. We have had an instance where people have purchased items outside the shop and have brought them into the official club shop and said this is rubbish we want it replaced. We have said, but it is not an official club product, and they say it is bearing your logo. We say that may be but it is not official club merchandise. The public assume that anything bearing the club logo is often official ...

Laddie J: Do you keep a log of these complaints? A: We do at West Ham now.

Q: At West Ham you do? A: Yes.

Q: Can you say what is the turn over at West Ham of their club shop? A: Currently between £4·5 and £5m.

Q: Per annum? A: Yes, per annum.

Q: How many complaints like this, wrongly ascribing non-licensed goods to you, how many of those do you get a year? A: On an average probably about 20.

Q: Did you keep a similar log when you were with Arsenal? A: No. I mean I was relatively a junior member of staff at that time, and my then shop manager, Jack Kelsey, who is unfortunately deceased now, I do not believe he kept a record.

Q: Maybe things have changed, but did you receive complaints in those days when you were with Arsenal? A: Yes, we did.

Q: In the same sort of frequency we're talking about? A: Possibly more so. Supporters, somewhat in their naivety do sometimes assume when they are buying something from a market, because it bears the official club crest believe that it is an official club product. Often they are of inferior quality. The clubs do feel that it is not a good reflection.'

[56] Mr Reed made it clear in his evidence that he sold his goods as badges of allegiance and that everybody who purchased items from him knew full well that if it was marked official then it was a product that originated from Arsenal or an

a approved source and if not, it was not an official product. That was made clear in cross-examination when he identified the difference between official and unofficial goods as being that the official goods had labels or swing tickets whereas the unofficial goods had nothing. He accepted that absent such a label there was no way that consumers could differentiate between his products and those which were official.

b [57] Mr Adams gave evidence that a particular instance of alleged passing off had not occurred as there had been no misrepresentation. He accepted in cross-examination that 'an official product is something produced and sold by the Arsenal Football Club'. When asked how he distinguished between what was an official and unofficial product he explained that he was told which was which by Mr Reed. If he was unsure, he would go and ask, then he would put a sign on the various goods saying which were official. He explained that the official goods, *c* being those coming from Arsenal, were stated to be official and that a sign was put on them stating that fact. That was the only way that consumers could tell the difference. He knew that Mr Reed would be angry if he sold something as official which was not and that on every occasion a sign was put up to differentiate *d* between the two.

[58] Mr Matthews also dealt with the alleged instance of passing off. He said in his witness statement that sometimes people did ask if goods on the stall were official. In the main it was foreigners who asked the question, and that it was probably half a dozen times a year that the question was asked. His standard answer was that nothing was official unless it actually said so on the product. He *e* also made it clear that if he was in doubt he asked Mr Reed which were official goods and which were not. He would always ask if he was not sure, whether there were tags or not. It was his view that official goods had tags on and they were the means by which they were differentiated.

[59] Mr Stephens also gave evidence as to the alleged incidence of passing off. In *f* cross-examination he was shown two hats bearing an Arsenal trade mark and was asked which one was official. He accepted that a hat which just had the club crest on it might be official and that if he was working for Mr Reed he would ask him whether it was official or not.

[60] Mr Reed and those who helped him were in no doubt that there was a market for what they referred to as official goods. Such goods bore the trade marks. *g* In their view what differentiated those goods from the alleged infringing goods were tags or swing tickets which stated that the official goods emanated from Arsenal.

[61] Mr Wyand submitted that the evidence established that the use by Mr Reed did not indicate a connection in the course of trade between Mr Reed's goods and *h* Arsenal. He submitted that that was the result of the acts of Arsenal over 30 years. As Arsenal had started to expand their merchandising, they needed to distinguish their goods from those of others, in particular those of Mr Reed. It was Arsenal who had educated consumers that if they wished to support the club they should buy their goods from Arsenal. Arsenal themselves had told the public that they *j* could not rely upon the word 'Arsenal' on the goods as indicating that they came from Arsenal.

[62] That submission is correct in part. No doubt Arsenal have been at pains to tell the public to purchase goods from them and not to purchase copies. However that message cannot have reached consumers at large. It is those who attend matches who could get the message, not the thousands of others who support or

are interested in Arsenal and goods bearing the trade marks. Further the fact that consumers know that there are copies about does not mean that the word 'Arsenal' on goods does not indicate origin. It could do so, but with the worry that it might be a wrong indication.

[63] As to the instances of confusion, Mr Wyand supported the judge's conclusion that they were de minimis. He also submitted that such instances could have been the result of a false description of a scarf as an official scarf by somebody other than Mr Reed.

[64] No attempt was made to differentiate between the use of the word 'Arsenal' and the other trade marks. That seems to have been the result of the reputation of the other trade marks. It is therefore acceptable to consider whether Mr Reed's use was trade mark use, taking as an example use of the word 'Arsenal' on a scarf or other item of clothing.

[65] The use of the word 'Arsenal' on a scarf or other item of clothing could in theory denote three things. First that the owner was a supporter of Arsenal; second that the goods came from Arsenal or third a combination of the two. I suspect that to certain persons the first meaning would be the correct one. Mr Reed is an example of such a person. The crucial question is whether the other two meanings would occur to a substantial number of consumers.

[66] As Mr Reed's goods are in substance identical to those of Arsenal's, there is nothing to differentiate them from Arsenal's goods once the swing ticket or tag is removed. That was accepted by the witnesses called on behalf of Mr Reed. It was for that reason that they went to the length that they did to differentiate Mr Reed's goods from those coming from Arsenal.

[67] It is apparent from the evidence that a substantial number of consumers want to purchase goods bearing the sign 'Arsenal' from Arsenal. That was the evidence of Mr Hazell which was supported by analogy by the evidence of Mr Ireland and Mr O'Donovan. Further, there was evidence of instances of confusion. Those instances of confusion were thought by the judge to be de minimis. But it is reasonable to conclude that the instances were just the tip of an iceberg as those that are confused will not complain without ground for complaint. However the importance of the evidence is not that there was confusion, but that consumers seeing the signs identical to the Arsenal registered trade mark on the goods turned to Arsenal to complain. As Mr Hazell said, they complained to Arsenal because the goods had on them the Arsenal crest. Miss Bouchard's evidence was that people assumed that goods carrying the trade marks were produced by Arsenal. That appears to have been the position at Tottenham and Manchester United and there is nothing in the evidence that suggests that their fans think differently to fans of Arsenal as to the meaning of the trade marks on goods.

[68] Mr Reed takes considerable care to inform his customers that his goods are not official in the sense that they do not come from Arsenal. If the use of the word 'Arsenal' did not carry with it such an indication of origin, there would be no need for Mr Reed to do anything at all. Clearly Mr Reed is suspicious that persons purchasing from him would, absent an explanation, believe that the goods came from Arsenal. Why? The answer must be that they bear the name Arsenal and that it denotes origin. His suspicion supports the evidence of the witnesses called by Arsenal.

[69] I accept the judge's finding that the trade marks upon the goods are considered to be badges of allegiance, but all the evidence suggests that the trade marks do also designate origin of the goods to a substantial number of consumers. As to Mr Reed's use I accept that he does differentiate his goods from official goods,

a but his goods marked with the trade marks were identical to those emanating from Arsenal and therefore his use of the word Arsenal would, absent an explanation carry the same inference as similar use of the trade mark by Arsenal. Certainly the evidence suggests that that would be the inference that consumers would draw, particularly those that received the goods as a present. In my view the evidence is all one way, namely that use of the trade mark on goods such as scarves and hats,
b whether by Arsenal or others does denote origin.

PASSING OFF

[70] I realise that there was no appeal on the conclusion reached by the judge on the cause of action traditionally called passing off, perhaps best referred to as unfair competition. However I am not convinced that his reasoning was correct. The
c traditional form of passing off as enunciated in such cases as *Frank Reddaway & Co Ltd v George Banham & Co Ltd* [1896] AC 199, [1895–9] All ER Rep 313 is no longer definitive of the ambit of the cause of action.

[71] As Cross J said in *Vine Products Ltd v Mackenzie & Co Ltd* [1969] RPC 1 at 23 of the decision in the Spanish Champagne cases (*J Bollinger v Costa Brava Wine Co Ltd*
d [1959] 3 All ER 800, [1960] Ch 262 and *J Bollinger v Costa Brava Wine Co Ltd (No 2)* [1961] 1 All ER 561, [1961] 1 WLR 277).

e 'A man who does not know where Champagne comes from can have not the slightest reason for thinking that a bottle labelled "Spanish Champagne" contains a wine produced in France. But what he may very well think is that he is buying the genuine article—real Champagne—and that, I have no doubt, was the sort of deception which the judge had in mind. He thought, as I read his judgment, that if people were allowed to call sparkling wine not produced in Champagne "Champagne," even though preceded by an adjective denoting the country of origin, the distinction between genuine Champagne and "champagne type" wines produced elsewhere would become blurred; that the word "Champagne"
f would come gradually to mean no more than "sparkling wine;" and that the part of the plaintiffs' goodwill which consisted in the name would be diluted and gradually destroyed. If I may say so without impertinence I agree entirely with the decision in the *Spanish Champagne* case—but as I see it it uncovered a piece of common law or equity which had till then escaped notice—for in such a case there is not, in any ordinary sense, any representation that the goods of the
g defendant are the goods of the plaintiffs, and evidence that no-one has been confused or deceived in that way is quite beside the mark. In truth the decision went beyond the well-trodden paths of passing off into the unmapped area of "unfair trading" or "unlawful competition".'

h [72] I would allow the appeal and give judgment in favour of Arsenal and hear counsel as to the order that should be made.

CLARKE LJ.

[73] I agree.

j **JONATHAN PARKER LJ.**

[74] I also agree.

Appeal allowed. Permission to appeal to the House of Lords refused.

Kate O'Hanlon   Barrister.

R v Johnstone

a

[2003] UKHL 28

HOUSE OF LORDS

LORD NICHOLLS OF BIRKENHEAD, LORD HOPE OF CRAIGHEAD, LORD HUTTON, LORD
RODGER OF EARLSFERRY AND LORD WALKER OF GESTINGTHORPE

b

12, 13 FEBRUARY, 22 MAY 2003

*Trade mark – Infringement – Unauthorised use of registered trade mark – Criminal
offence – Whether essential ingredient of offence use of registered trade mark as
indication of trade origin – Whether reasonable belief no relevant trade mark registered
a defence – Trade Marks Act 1994, s 92.*

c

The respondent had been involved in making and copying bootleg recordings of
performances by well known performers onto compact discs. The compact discs
were labelled with the names of the performers. All the performers had
registered their names as trade marks under the Trade Marks Act 1994. Sections
9ᵃ and 10 of the 1994 Act provided that the proprietor of a registered trade mark
had the exclusive rights in it which were infringed by the use of trade mark
without his consent and set out the acts amounting to infringement. Section
11(2)(b)ᵇ provided that a registered trade mark was not infringed by, inter alia,
the use of indications concerning the characteristics of goods. Section 92ᶜ created
criminal offences of unauthorised use of signs identical to or likely to be mistaken
for registered trade marks and sub-s (5) provided a defence of belief on reasonable
grounds that the use of the sign in the manner in which it had been used was not
an infringement of the registered trade mark. The respondent was charged with
offences of the false application or use of trade marks contrary to s 92(1). At trial
he submitted that before the Crown could establish one of the offences under s
92 it had to prove a civil infringement of the trade mark in question, in accordance
with ss 9–11. He wished to rely on s 11(2)(b) and contend that the performers'
names had not been used as indications of trade origin, but merely to identify the
artists. Alternatively, he wished to use the defence in s 92(5). The judge held that
s 92 was a 'stand alone' provision, and that it was not necessary to prove a civil
infringement. The respondent then pleaded guilty to all the offences. His appeal
was allowed by the Court of Appeal, which held that s 92(5) presupposed that the
illegal unauthorised use amounted to civil infringement; that to establish an
offence under s 92(1) the Crown need not prove a defendant's conduct
constituted a civil infringement unless the defendant raised a defence under, inter
alia, s 11, in which case it would be for the Crown to disprove such a defence; and
that the judge's ruling had deprived the respondent the opportunity to have his
defence under s 11(2)(b) considered by the jury. The Crown appealed.

d

e

f

g

h

Held – (1) Section 92 should be interpreted as applying only when the offending
sign was used as an indication of trade origin. That was one of the ingredients of
each of the offences created by s 92. It had, therefore, to be proved by the

j

---

a   Sections 9 and 10, so far as material, are set out at [8]–[11], below
b   Section 11, so far as material, is set out at [12], below
c   Section 92, so far as material, is set out at [18], [19], below

a prosecution. Whether a sign had been so used was a question of fact in each case, the test being how the use of the sign would be perceived by the average consumer of the type of goods in question. The respondent would clearly have committed an offence under s 92(1) if he had sold compact discs under a brand name which was the name of a performer who had registered his name as a trade mark for compact discs. Used in that way, the sign would be an indication of trade origin. That was not, however, what the respondent had done. He had

b included on the labels the names of the artists whose performances had been recorded on the compact discs. As a matter of principle, the position in such a case was that if the name of the artist affixed to the compact disc and displayed on the packaging was exclusively an indication of the name of the performer whose performance was recorded on the compact disc, and if that use of the name of the

c performer was not likely to be understood as indicating any other connection between the performer and the compact disc, then such use would be descriptive only. It would not be an indication of the trade origin of the compact disc itself. Whether labelling and packaging satisfied that test, and consequently were innocuous for trade mark purposes, was a question of fact in each case (see [31],

d [35], [36], [56]–[58], [88], below).

(2) Section 92(5) should be interpreted as furnishing a defence where the reason why a defendant believed his use of the sign did not infringe a registered trade mark was that he reasonably believed no relevant trade mark was registered, as well as where the defendant believed on reasonable grounds that his use of the sign did not infringe a registered trade mark of whose existence he

e was aware. Accordingly, the Crown's appeal would be dismissed (see [43], [55]–[58], [89], below).

Per curiam. The burden of proving the relevant facts on the balance of probability placed on an accused person by the s 92(5) defence is compatible with art 6(2) of the Convention for the Protection of Human Rights and Fundamental

f Freedoms 1950 (as set out in Sch 1 to the Human Rights Act 1998) (see [54], [56]–[58], [90], below).

Notes

For infringement of registered trade marks, see 48 *Halsbury's Laws* (4th edn) (2000

g reissue) paras 79–85.

For the Trade Marks Act 1994, s 92, see 48 *Halsbury's Statutes* (4th edn) (2001 reissue) 174.

Cases referred to in opinions

h *A-G of Hong Kong v Lee Kwong-kut, A-G of Hong Kong v Lo Chak-man* [1993] 3 All ER 939, [1993] AC 951, [1993] 3 WLR 329, PC.

Arsenal Football Club plc v Reed [2001] IP & T 810; [2002] EWHC 2695 (Ch), [2003] 1 All ER 137; *rvsd* [2003] EWCA Civ 696, [2003] 3 All ER 865.

Arsenal Football Club plc v Reed Case C-206/01 [2003] All ER (EC) 1, [2003] 3 WLR 450, ECJ.

j *Bravado Merchandising Services Ltd v Mainstream Publishing (Edinburgh) Ltd* [1996] FSR 205, Ct of Sess.

British Sugar plc v James Robertson & Sons Ltd [1996] RPC 281.

Davidoff & Cie SA v Gofkid Ltd Case C-292/00 [2003] 1 WLR 1714, ECJ.

Hölterhoff v Freiesleben Case C-2/00 [2002] All ER (EC) 665, [2002] ECR I-4187, ECJ.

Marleasing SA v La Comercial Internacional de Alimentacion SA Case C-106/89 [1990]
ECR I-4135.

a

Mothercare UK Ltd v Penguin Books Ltd [1988] RPC 113, CA.

Musidor BV v Tansing (trading as Apple Music House) (1994) 123 ALR 593,
Aust Fed Ct.

Philips Electronics NV v Remington Consumer Products Ltd [1998] RPC 283; [1999]
RPC 809, CA.

b

Philips Electronics NV v Remington Consumer Products Ltd Case C-299/99 [2002] All
ER (EC) 634, [2003] Ch 159, [2003] 2 WLR 294, [2002] ECR I-5475, ECJ.

R v DPP, ex p Kebeline, R v DPP, ex p Rechachi [1999] 4 All ER 801, [2000] 2 AC 326,
[1999] 3 WLR 972, HL.

R v Keane [2001] FSR 63, CA.

R v Lambert [2001] UKHL 37, [2001] 3 All ER 577, [2002] 2 AC 545, [2001] 3 WLR
206.

c

R v Rhodes [2002] EWCA 1390, [2003] FSR 147.

R v Whyte (1988) 51 DLR (4th) 481, Can SC.

S v London Borough of Havering [2002] EWCA Crim 2558, [2003] 1 Cr App Rep 602.

Sabel BV v Puma AG Case C-251/95 [1997] ECR I-6191.

d

Salabiaku v France (1988) 13 EHRR 379, [1988] ECHR 10589/83, ECt HR.

Scandecor Development AB v Scandecor Marketing AB [2001] UKHL 21, [2001] IP & T
676.

Silhouette International Schmied GmbH & Co KG v Hartlauer Handelsgesellschaft mbH
Case C-355/96 [1998] All ER (EC) 769, [1999] Ch 77, [1998] 3 WLR 1218, [1998]
ECR I-4799, ECJ.

e

State v Coetzee [1997] 2 LRC 593, SA Const Ct.

Torbay Council v Singh [1999] IP & T 54, DC

*Zino Davidoff SA v A & G Imports Ltd, Levi Strauss & Co v Tesco Stores Ltd, Levi
Strauss & Co v Costco Wholesale UK Ltd* Joined cases C-414/99–C-416/99 [2002]
All ER (EC) 55, [2002] Ch 109, [2002] 2 WLR 321, [2001] ECR I-8691, ECJ.

f

Cases also referred to in list of authorities

Anklagemyndigheden v Handsen & Son I/S Case 326/88 [1990] ECR I-2911, [1992]
ICR 277, ECJ.

Factortame Ltd v Secretary of State for Transport (No 2) Case C-213/89 [1991] 1 All ER
70, [1991] 1 AC 603, [1990] 3 WLR 818, [1990] ECR I-2433, ECJ and HL.

g

Gallotti, Criminal proceedings against Joined cases C-58/95, C-75/95, C-112/95,
C-119/95, C-123/95, C-135/95, C-140/95, C-141/95, C-154/95 and C-157/95
[1996] ECR I-4345.

Hermès International v FHT Marketing Choice BV Case C-53/96 [1998] ECR I-3603.

h

L v DPP [2001] EWHC Admin 882, [2002] 2 All ER 854, [2003] QB 137, [2003]
3 WLR 863, DC.

Proctor & Gamble Ltd v Registrar of Trade Marks [1999] CA Transcript 83, CA.

R v Carass [2001] EWCA Crim 2845, [2002] 1 WLR 1714.

R v Daniel [2002] EWCA Crim 959, [2002] All ER (D) 354 (Mar).

j

R v Gookey (Michael) (24 April 1996, unreported).

R v Hinks [2000] 4 All ER 833, [2001] 2 AC 241, [2000] 3 WLR 1590, HL.

R v Hudson (Steven) (21 April 1999, unreported).

R v Reed (Matthew) (1 December 1997, unreported).

R v Simon (Nigel) (29 March 1999, unreported).

R v Tymen Case 269/80 [1981] ECR 3079.

a *Schieving-Nijstad v Groeneveld* Case C-89/99 [2002] IP & T 353, [2001] ECR I-5851, ECJ.

Appeal

The Crown appealed with permission of the Appeal Committee of the House of Lords given on 17 October 2002 from the order of the Court of Appeal
b (Tuckey LJ, Pumfrey and Burton JJ) on 31 January 2002 ([2002] EWCA Crim 194, [2002] All ER (D) 34 (Feb)) allowing the appeal by the respondent, Robert Alexander Johnstone, against his conviction in the Crown Court at Kingston on 28 October 1999, when he had first entered not guilty pleas and then, following a ruling of law by Judge Mitchell which was adverse to him, entered guilty pleas to
     12 counts of false application or use of trade marks, contrary to s 92(1)(c) of the
c Trade Marks Act 1994. The court certified that a point of law of general public importance, set out at [25], below, was involved in its decision. The British Phonographic Industry was granted leave to intervene by the Appeal Committee on 15 January 2003. The facts are set out in the opinion of Lord Nicholls of Birkenhead.
d

David Lane QC and *John Boumphrey* (instructed by *Audu*) for Johnstone.

David Perry and *Brian O'Neill* and *George Hayman* (instructed by the *Crown Prosecution Service*) for the Crown.

e *Geoffrey Hobbs QC* and *David Groome* (instructed by *Richards Butler*) for The British Phonographic Industry.

Their Lordships took time for consideration.

f 22 May 2003. The following opinions were delivered.

LORD NICHOLLS OF BIRKENHEAD.

[1] My Lords, counterfeit goods and pirated goods are big business. They account for between 5% and 7% of world trade. They are estimated to cost the economy of this country some £9bn each year. Counterfeit goods comprise
g cheap imitations of the authentic article, sold under the trade mark of the authentic article, as with imitation 'Rolex' watches. Pirated goods comprise illicit copies of the authentic article which are not sold under the trade mark of the authentic article. This would happen, for instance, when a person makes and sells unauthorised copies of computer software which is the subject of copyright.
h Thus, in the context of music recordings, a counterfeit compact disc is an unlawful copy of, say, a Virgin compact disc, sold ostensibly as a Virgin product. A pirated compact disc is an unlawful copy of, in my example, a Virgin compact disc which is sold, not as a Virgin product, but under a different brand name.

[2] Another type of unlawful trading is 'bootlegging'. Like counterfeit records
j and pirated records, bootleg records are also big business. They comprise copies of an unlawful recording of a performance at a live concert. The recording is made at an auditorium or taken from a radio or television broadcast.

[3] Most bootleg products sold in this country are in compact disc format. They are mainly manufactured abroad and imported into this country without cases or paperwork. The importer then packages the discs, with created paperwork, into locally obtained cases.

[4] So it was with the subject matter of the present appeal. The present appeal relates to copies, in the form of compact discs, of bootleg recordings made of performances by well-known performers. The case concerns the use, in connection with these compact discs, of the criminal sanctions contained in the trade marks legislation. Questions about trade marks arise in this context in the following way. When sold to the public each of these compact discs bears, in the usual manner, the name of the performer whose performance is recorded on the disc: Rolling Stones, or Beatles, or whoever it may be. This name also appears on the accompanying paperwork inside the disc's case. Nowadays leading performers register their professional names as trade marks in respect of recordings. So, it is said, sales of the discs labelled in this way constitute infringements of the performers' registered trade marks.

[5] The case arises out of the 'bootlegging' activities of Mr Robert Johnstone, the respondent to this appeal. His activities only came to light because of a misdirected parcel. Mrs Luddington lives in Hemel Hempstead. In October 1997 she was surprised to receive a large box. It contained 519 compact discs and associated artwork. The box had been mistakenly posted to her by Mr Johnstone from his home address in New Malden. Mrs Luddington notified Polygram Records, whose head of security retrieved the box and contacted the police.

[6] Police officers then searched Mr Johnstone's home. They were accompanied by a representative of the trade body, British Phonographic Industry (BPI). Some 500 compact discs and audio cassettes were seized during the search. The investigator from BPI considered that most of the compact discs found, as well as those sent by error to Mrs Luddington, were bootleg recordings. Mr Johnstone was charged with having committed criminal offences under s 92 of the Trade Marks Act 1994.

THE STATUTORY PROVISIONS

[7] Before elaborating further, and in order to explain the point of law which has arisen, I should refer briefly to the relevant statutory provisions. Part I of the 1994 Act concerns registered trade marks. Section 1 defines a trade mark as any sign capable of being represented graphically which is capable of distinguishing goods or services of one undertaking from those of other undertakings. A trade mark may consist of words, including personal names. The proprietor of a registered trade mark has the rights and remedies provided by the Act (see s 2).

[8] Sections 9–13 comprise a fasciculus of sections setting out the effect of a registered trade mark. Section 9(1) provides that the proprietor of a registered trade mark has the exclusive rights in the trade mark 'which are infringed by use of the trade mark in the United Kingdom without his consent'. The acts amounting to infringement if done without the consent of the proprietor are stated in s 10.

[9] Section 10 deals with several different situations. Section 10(1) concerns the case where a person in the course of trade uses a sign identical with a registered trade mark in relation to goods identical with those for which it is registered. Such use constitutes infringement:

'(1) A person infringes a registered trade mark if he uses in the course of trade a sign which is identical with the trade mark in relation to goods or services which are identical with those for which it is registered.'

[10] Section 10(2) addresses cases where either (a) a sign identical with a registered trade mark is used in relation to goods similar to those for which the

a trade mark is registered or (b) a sign similar to a registered trade mark is used in relation to goods identical with or similar to those for which the trade mark is registered. In such cases user constitutes infringement if there exists a likelihood of confusion on the part of the public. Section 10(3) concerns cases where a sign identical with or similar to a registered trade mark is used in relation to goods not similar to those for which the trade mark is registered. Then, in short, user *b* constitutes infringement where the trade mark has a reputation within the United Kingdom and the sign takes unfair advantage of, or is detrimental to, the distinctive character or the repute of the trade mark.

[11] One of the ingredients of infringement as described in s 10(1)–(3) is the 'use' of a sign by a person. Section 10(4) gives some examples of what this means. A person uses a sign if he affixes the sign to goods or its packaging, or if he offers *c* goods for sale under the sign.

[12] Section 11 specifies some limits on the effect of a registered trade mark. Section 11(2) provides:

> *d* 'A registered trade mark is not infringed by—(a) the use by a person of his own name or address, (b) the use of indications concerning the kind, quality, quantity, intended purpose, value, geographical origin, the time of production of goods or of rendering of services, or other characteristics of goods or services, or (c) the use of the trade mark where it is necessary to indicate the intended purpose of a product or service (in particular, as accessories or spare parts), provided the use is in accordance with honest *e* practices in industrial or commercial matters.'

TRADE MARK USE: INDICATION OF TRADE ORIGIN

[13] The message conveyed by a trade mark has developed over the years, with changing patterns in the conduct of business (see the discussion in *Scandecor* *f* *Development AB v Scandecor Marketing AB* [2001] UKHL 21, [2001] I & PT 676). But the essence of a trade mark has always been that it is a badge of origin. It indicates trade source: a connection in the course of trade between the goods and the proprietor of the mark. That is its function. Hence the exclusive rights granted to the proprietor of a registered trade mark are limited to use of a mark likely to be taken as an indication of trade origin. Use of this character is an essential *g* prerequisite to infringement. Use of a mark in a manner not indicative of trade origin of goods or services does not encroach upon the proprietor's monopoly rights. Dillon LJ observed trenchantly in *Mothercare UK Ltd v Penguin Books Ltd* [1988] RPC 113 at 118–119:

> *h* '... it stands to reason that a Trade Marks Act would only be concerned to restrict the use of a mark as a trademark or in a trademark sense, and should be construed accordingly. If descriptive words are legitimately registered [as a trademark], there is still no reason why other people should not be free to use the words in a descriptive sense, and not in any trademark sense.'

j In this regard I cannot forbear adding the extreme hypothetical example beloved of trade mark lawyers. If a magazine publisher were to register an ordinary question mark, '?', as a trade mark for magazines this would not prevent the grammatical use of question marks on the covers of other magazines.

[14] This fundamental principle, limiting the scope of the rights of the proprietor of a registered trade mark, was well established under the early trade marks legislation. It was carried forward expressly into s 4(1)(a) of the

Trade Marks Act 1938 ('being used as a trade mark'). Section 4(1)(b) muddied the
waters a little. The wording of s 4(1)(b) gave rise to an unresolved controversy *a*
over whether, and to what extent, this paragraph further extended the rights of a
proprietor (see the discussion in *Kerly's Law of Trade Marks* (12th edn, 1986)
pp 263–265 and the authorities cited there). This controversy is now of no more
than historic interest.

[15] Against this background I turn to the 1994 Act. Section 10(1)–(3) specifies *b*
the acts which constitute infringement, but there is no express statement that the
offending use must be use as a trade mark. I would not regard this as sufficient
reason to suppose that Parliament intended to depart from such a basic principle.
But on this, as so much else in the law of trade marks, it is necessary to look for
guidance beyond the confines of the 1994 Act. One of the main purposes of this
statute was to implement Council Directive (EEC) 89/104 to approximate the *c*
laws of member states relating to trade marks (OJ 1989 L40 p 1). This directive,
which I shall call 'the trade mark directive', was concerned with harmonising the
trade mark laws of member states. Articles 5 and 6 of the directive made
provision regarding the rights conferred by a trade mark and the limits of those
rights. Sections 10 and 11 of the 1994 Act give effect to these two articles. So *d*
authoritative guidance on the interpretation of s 10 now comes from the Court
of Justice of the European Communities.

[16] For some time questions were raised on whether, given its derivation
from art 5 of the trade mark directive, non-trade mark use could be caught by
ss 10(1)–(3) (see *British Sugar plc v James Robertson & Sons Ltd* [1996] RPC 281 at 291 *e*
per Jacob J, *Philips Electronics NV v Remington Consumer Products Ltd* [1998] RPC
283 at 311–312 per Jacob J, and in the Court of Appeal, [1999] RPC 809, 823 per
Aldous LJ). These doubts must now be regarded as laid to rest by the decision of
the European Court in the 'football souvenirs' case of *Arsenal Football Club plc v
Reed* Case C-206/01 [2003] All ER (EC) 1 at 23, [2003] 3 WLR 450 at 473. The
court reaffirmed its characterisation of the purpose of a trade mark in terms *f*
which accord with the approach of English law ([2003] All ER (EC) 1 at 29, [2003]
3 WLR 450 at 479 (para 48)):

> '... the essential function of a trade mark is to guarantee the identity of
> origin of the marked goods or services to the consumer or end user by *g*
> enabling him, without any possibility of confusion, to distinguish the goods
> or services from others which have another origin. For the trade mark to be
> able to fulfil its essential role in the system of undistorted competition which
> the Treaty seeks to establish and maintain, it must offer a guarantee that all
> the goods or services bearing it have been manufactured or supplied under
> the control of a single undertaking which is responsible for their quality ...' *h*

[17] The court then considered ([2003] All ER (EC) 1 at 30, [2003] 3 WLR 450
at 480 (paras 51–54)) the scope of the exclusive right conferred on the proprietor
of a trade mark under art 5(1)(a) of the trade mark directive, which corresponds
to s 10(2)(a) of the 1994 Act. The court held that the scope of this right is *j*
co-terminous with the function of registered trade marks:

> '51 ... the exclusive right under art 5(1)(a) of the ... Directive was conferred
> in order to enable the trade mark proprietor to protect his specific interests
> as proprietor, that is, to ensure that the trade mark can fulfil its functions.
> *The exercise of that right must therefore be reserved to cases in which a third party's*

a   *use of the sign affects or is liable to affect the functions of the trade mark, in particular its essential function of guaranteeing to consumers the origin of the goods.*

52. The exclusive nature of the right conferred by a registered trade mark on its proprietor under art 5(1)(a) of the ... Directive can be justified only within the limits of the application of that article ...

b   54. The proprietor may not prohibit the use of a sign identical to the trade mark for goods identical to those for which the mark is registered if that use cannot affect his own interests as proprietor of the mark, having regard to its functions. Thus certain uses for purely descriptive purposes are excluded from the scope of art 5(1)(a) of the ... Directive because they do not affect any of the interests which that provision aims to protect, *and do not therefore fall within the concept of use within the meaning of that provision ...'* (My

c   emphasis.)

Plainly, s 10 of the 1994 Act is capable of being so construed. In accordance with the *Marleasing* principle (see *Marleasing SA v La Comercial Internacional de Alimentacion SA* Case C-106/89 [1990] ECR I-4135), it should therefore be so construed. Non-trade mark use is not within s 10(1)–(3).

d

SECTION 92 AND MR JOHNSTONE'S CONVICTION

[18] Part II of the 1994 Act relates to Community trade marks and international matters. Community trade marks were brought into effect by Council Regulation (EC) 40/94 on the Community trade mark (OJ 1994 L11 p 1),

e   which is directly applicable to this country without the need for legislation by Parliament. Part II of the Act makes provision for consequential provisions and other matters. Part III of the Act, ss 62–97, contains administrative and supplemental provisions. Tucked away towards the end of these provisions are four sections which create criminal offences. The material section for the purposes of this appeal is s 92, bearing the heading: 'Unauthorised use of trade

f   mark, &c. in relation to goods.' Section 92(1) provides:

'A person commits an offence who with a view to gain for himself or another, or with intent to cause loss to another, and without the consent of the proprietor—(a) applies to goods or their packaging a sign identical to, or likely to be mistaken for, a registered trade mark, or (b) sells or lets for hire,

g   offers or exposes for sale or hire or distributes goods which bear, or the packaging of which bears, such a sign, or (c) has in his possession, custody or control in the course of a business any such goods with a view to the doing of anything, by himself or another, which would be an offence under paragraph (b).'

h   [19] Section 92(2) creates a comparable offence relating to material intended to be used for labelling or packaging goods, or as a business paper in relation to goods, or for advertising goods. Section 92(3) creates a comparable offence relating to making or possessing what can loosely be described as printer's plates. The opening rubric of s 92(2) and (3) is the same as in s 92(1). The activities must

j   be done with a view to gain or with intent to cause loss and, in either case, without the consent of the proprietor. Section 92(4) prescribes two limiting conditions. No offence is committed under the section unless one or other of these conditions is satisfied. I need mention only condition (a): that the goods are goods in respect of which the trade mark is registered. Section 92(5) provides a defence of reasonable belief of non-infringement:

'It is a defence for a person charged with an offence under this section to show that he believed on reasonable grounds that the use of the sign in the manner in which it was used, or was to be used, was not an infringement of the registered trade mark.'

[20] I can now return to the narrative. Mr Johnstone was arraigned at the Crown Court at Kingston on an indictment containing 12 specimen counts. Each count related to one compact disc. In each count the offence comprised the false application or use of trade marks, contrary to s 92(1)(c) of the 1994 Act. The particulars of offence under count 1 read as follows:

'Robert Alexander JOHNSTONE on or before the 24th day of October 1997 with a view to gain for himself or another or with intent to cause loss to another and without the lawful consent of the proprietor had in his possession, custody or control in the course of a business, a compact disc entitled "The B Sides Collection—Volumes One and Two" bearing the trademark Bon Jovi, with a view to the commission of an act by himself or another which would be an offence under s 92(1)(b) of the Trade Marks Act 1994.'

[21] At trial on 25 October 1999 Mr Lane QC submitted on behalf of Mr Johnstone that before the Crown could establish an offence under s 92 the Crown must prove a civil infringement of the registered trade mark in question, in accordance with the provisions of ss 9–11 of the 1994 Act. The defence wished to rely on s 11(2)(b) and contend that the use of the performer's name on each of the compact discs was not as an indication of trade origin. It was merely to indicate who was the performer. Alternatively, Mr Johnstone wished to rely on the honest and reasonable belief defence under s 92(5).

[22] Judge Mitchell, in a preliminary ruling, rejected these submissions. In doing so he followed several other decisions in the Crown Court. Section 92 was a 'stand alone' provision. It was a complete code so far as criminal offences were concerned, and it was not necessary to prove a civil infringement. 'Infringement' in s 92(5) meant unauthorised use as defined in the earlier provisions of the section. Mr Johnstone then pleaded guilty to the offences with which he was charged. He was subsequently sentenced to six months' imprisonment concurrent on each count. A confiscation order in the amount of £130,181·24 was made, together with forfeiture orders.

THE COURT OF APPEAL

[23] Mr Johnstone appealed. On 31 January 2002 the Court of Appeal ([2002] EWCA Crim 194, [2002] FSR 840), comprising Tuckey LJ and Pumfrey and Burton JJ, allowed the appeal. In disagreeing with the judge, the court considered that unless the defences available to a claim for civil infringement of a trade mark were available in criminal proceedings s 92 would embrace behaviour which could not be the subject of a successful civil claim. This is not what Parliament intended. Section 92(5) presupposes that the illegal unauthorised use amounts to infringement as defined in ss 9(1), (2) and 10 (see the definition in s 104).

[24] The Court of Appeal said that to establish an offence under s 92(1) the prosecution need not prove the defendant's conduct constituted a civil infringement unless the defence raises a defence under ss 10–12. Then it will be for the prosecution to disprove such a defence. The court allowed Mr Johnstone's appeal because the judge's ruling had denied him the opportunity to have his defence under s 11(2)(b) considered by the jury. The court did not

a order a re-trial. Mr Johnstone had served his sentence of imprisonment, and the alleged offences occurred four-and-a-half years ago.

SECTION 92 AND USE AS A TRADE MARK

[25] The certified question on this appeal to your Lordships' House is whether it is a defence to a criminal charge under s 92 of the 1994 Act that the defendant's
b acts do not amount to a civil infringement of the trade mark. On this, although he substantially modified his stance in the course of his reply, Mr Perry's opening submissions to the House were to the following effect. The 1994 Act provides for two separate regimes for the protection of trade marks and consumers. One regime is concerned with civil infringement, the other with criminal unauthorised use of trade marks in relation to goods. As a matter of construction
c s 92 does not require proof of civil infringement. In keeping with other offence-creating provisions, the ingredients of the offences created by s 92 appear on the face of the section. Parliament intended to create offences which would be simple for local weights and measures authorities to enforce and for magistrates and jurors to understand. Parliament did not intend to introduce
d questions of civil infringement into the criminal courts, save to the limited extent that an accused's belief he was not infringing a registered trade mark might amount to a defence.

[26] I agree that the ingredients of the offences created by s 92 are to be found within the section itself. Where I part company with Mr Perry's opening submissions is on the interpretation of s 92. Section 92 is concerned to prohibit
e the wrongful exploitation of registered trade marks. It replaced s 58A of the Trade Marks Act 1938. Section 58A made the fraudulent use of a trade mark an offence. Difficulties arose in practice in proving the necessary intent in cases where at point of sale the trader disclaimed the authenticity of his goods. The trader would describe his counterfeit products as 'brand copies' or 'genuine
f fakes'. Section 92 avoids this problem. In particular, intention to infringe a registered trade mark is not an ingredient of the offence. Instead, s 92 focuses simply on unauthorised use of 'a sign identical to, or likely to be mistaken for, a registered trade mark' (see s 92(1)(a), (2)(a) and (3)(a)).

[27] In my view it is implicit in these provisions that the offending use of the sign must be use as a trade mark. Take, as an illustration, s 92(1)(a). This
g prohibits the application to goods of a sign identical to, or likely to be mistaken for, a registered trade mark. Apply this to a case where the registered trade mark consists of words capable of being used descriptively. Use of these words in their descriptive sense would be, in terms of trade mark law, unobjectionable. The registration of the word 'Alabaster' as a trade mark would not preclude others
h from lawfully stating that their product was 'made from alabaster'. Section 92 cannot have been intended to criminalise such conduct.

[28] This is my starting point. Within the section there are two clear indications confirming this interpretation. First, a prescribed ingredient of each offence is that the conduct in question is done 'without the consent of the proprietor' of the registered trade mark. This assumes the proprietor could object to the acts in question. Without his consent the acts could not lawfully be done. The section is aimed at criminalising conduct of this character, namely, conduct to which the proprietor could object. This is as one would expect. Parliament cannot have intended to criminalise conduct which could lawfully be done without the proprietor's consent. Parliament cannot have intended to make it an offence to use a sign in a way which is innocuous because it does not

infringe the proprietor's rights. That would be to extend, by means of a criminal sanction, the scope of the rights of the proprietor.

[29] Secondly, s 92(5) presupposes that the conduct of the person charged was an infringement of a registered trade mark. It would make no sense for reasonable belief in non-infringement to provide a defence if infringement was irrelevant so far as the criminal offences are concerned.

[30] Further, and looking more widely, the 1994 Act as a whole must be interpreted so far as possible to give effect to the trade mark directive. This obligation applies to provisions such as s 92, whose terms do not derive from the trade mark directive, as it does to provisions, such as s 10, which derive directly from the directive. Articles 5–7 of the directive embody a 'complete harmonisation' of the rules relating to the rights conferred by a trade mark (see *Silhouette International Schmied GmbH & Co KG v Hartlauer Handelsgesellschaft mbH* Case C-355/96 [1998] All ER (EC) 769 at 788, [1998] ECR I-4799 at 4831 (para 25)). They define the rights of trade mark proprietors in the Community (see *Zino Davidoff SA v A & G Imports Ltd, Levi Strauss & Co v Tesco Stores Ltd, Levi Strauss & Co v Costco Wholesale UK Ltd* Joined cases C-414/99–C-416/99 [2002] All ER (EC) 55 at 91, [2001] ECR I-8691 (para 39)). If s 92 were to be interpreted as applying in circumstances beyond those within ss 9–11, there might well be inconsistency with the trade mark directive.

[31] For these reasons s 92 is to be interpreted as applying only when the offending sign is used as an indication of trade origin. This is one of the ingredients of each of the offences created by s 92. It must therefore be proved by the prosecution. Whether a sign is so used is a question of fact in each case. The test is how the use of the sign would be perceived by the average consumer of the type of goods in question (see *Sabel BV v Puma AG* Case C-251/95 [1997] ECR I-6191 at 6224 (para 23)).

[32] This should not give rise to practical difficulties for weights and measures authorities or for magistrates or jurors. Despite Mr Perry's submissions, I see no reason to doubt that all those concerned are well able to grasp and apply the notion of a sign being used as an indication of trade origin as distinct, for instance, from a sign comprising words being used descriptively. In the overwhelming majority of cases there should be little difficulty. Ironically, the present case is not so straightforward. I shall mention later why this is so.

[33] It will be seen, therefore, that I have reached much the same conclusion as the Court of Appeal although by a more confined process of interpretation. On the interpretation of s 92 which commends itself to me the pieces of this little jigsaw, some home-grown, such as s 92, and others imported from the trade marks directive, although not fitting perfectly, fit together tolerably well. In particular, on this interpretation the circumstances in which criminal liability arises are for the most part either the same as, or narrower than, the circumstances in which civil liability arises under ss 9–11. This is as one would expect. Consistently with this, the s 92(5) defence can operate according to its tenor, with infringement bearing the meaning defined in s 104.

[34] I should mention one possible exception. Civil liability under s 10(1)–(3) arises only in respect of use of a sign 'in the course of trade'. The equivalent phrase 'in the course of a business' appears in s 92 in respect of some, but not all, of the alternative sets of factual ingredients of the offences. For instance, this equivalent phrase appears in s 92(1)(c), (2)(b) and (c). But it is not stated as a necessary ingredient in, for example, s 92(1)(a) or (2)(a). I doubt whether this dissonance between ss 10(1)–(3) and 92(1)–(3) is of practical importance. An

a essential ingredient of all the criminal offences created by s 92(1)–(3) is that a person commits an offence where 'with a view to gain for himself or another, or with intent to cause loss to another' he does the act in question. With this in mind it is hard to think of a realistic example of conduct which would attract criminal liability and yet be excluded from civil liability because it would not be 'in the course of trade'.

b

A QUESTION OF FACT

[35] I turn to apply s 92(1)(c) to the facts of the present case, taking count 1 for ease of reference. 'Bon Jovi' is, it seems, registered as a trade mark for compact discs. Clearly Mr Johnstone would commit an offence under s 92(1) if he sold *c* compact discs under the brand name 'Bon Jovi'. Used in this way the sign 'Bon Jovi' would be an indication of trade origin, in the same way as household names such as EMI or Sony are used to indicate the trade origin of compact discs marketed under those brand names. This use of the sign 'Bon Jovi' would be as an indication that the discs themselves all came from a source known as 'Bon Jovi'.

d [36] That is not what Mr Johnstone did. What he did was to include on the compact disc labels and, I assume, the accompanying packaging, the name of the group or artist whose performance was recorded on the compact disc in question: Bon Jovi in the case of count 1, U2 in the case of count 2, Rolling Stones in the case of count 3, and so on. Considered as a matter of principle, the position in this *e* type of case is as follows. If the name of the artist or group affixed to the compact disc and displayed on the packaging is *exclusively* an indication of the name of the performer whose performance is recorded on the compact disc, and if this use of the name of the performer is not likely to be understood as indicating any other connection between the performer and the compact disc, then such use would be descriptive only. By identifying the performer it would be descriptive of the *f* contents of the disc and nothing more. It would not be an indication of the trade 'origin' of the disc itself. Whether particular labelling and packaging satisfy this test, and consequently are innocuous for trade mark purposes, is a question of fact in each case.

[37] On this question of fact different minds may sometimes reach different *g* conclusions. This is illustrated by the decision of the Federal Court of Australia, sitting as a Full Court, in *Musidor BV v Tansing (trading as Apple Music House)* (1994) 123 ALR 593. Tansing manufactured and sold compact discs bearing bootleg recordings of live performances by the Rolling Stones group in the 1960s. The packaging bore a photograph of the Rolling Stones and the name Rolling Stones in prominent lettering. The compact discs also bore the name Rolling Stones. *h* 'Rolling Stones' was registered as a trade mark for compact discs. The majority of the court, comprising Gummow and Heerey JJ, held that this use did not infringe the trade mark because it was not use as a trade mark. Use of the words 'Rolling Stones' on the packaging and discs would convey to the prospective purchaser that if he bought the disc and played it there would emerge music of *j* the well-known group Rolling Stones. There is no other way of readily identifying the group whose performance was recorded on the disc.

[38] In his dissenting judgment Davies J reached a different conclusion on how this use of the words Rolling Stones would be understood. He expressed himself in quite general terms. If a trade mark is used in relation to sound recordings, and the name is that of a musical group—

'the use of the mark will ordinarily inform the public that the article is a
recording of a performance by the group *and that its release has been authorised*   *a*
by them or their organisation.' (My emphasis.) (See (1994) 123 ALR 593 at 594.)

[39] In the present case the Court of Appeal preferred the minority opinion of
Davies J, while emphasising that whether a mark is used as a trade mark is a
question of fact in every case. I do not understand the Court of Appeal to have
been saying that the test applicable when deciding this question of fact is different   *b*
from what I have set out above. If they were, I respectfully disagree.

[40] The crucial issue here, as I have said, is one of fact. I add a general
comment. Difficulties can be expected to arise if trade mark law is utilised as a
means of enforcing performers' rights in respect of recordings of their
performances. Trade mark law, as already emphasised, is concerned essentially   *c*
with the trade origin of goods. Protection for the rights of performers as such is
properly found elsewhere: nowadays, in Pt II of the Copyright, Designs and
Patents Act 1988, as amended by the Duration of Copyright and Rights in
Performances Regulations 1995, SI 1995/3297, the Copyright and Related Rights
Regulations 1996, SI 1996/2967 and the Copyright, etc and Trade Marks
(Offences and Enforcement) Act 2002. This legislation contains an elaborate code   *d*
concerning the rights of performers, together with remedies and criminal
sanctions for infringements of performers' rights by making, possessing or selling
illicit recordings. The code includes like provision for persons having recording
rights. I recognise that, given the control performers have over recordings of
their performances, a buyer of a compact disc may expect the recording has been   *e*
approved by or on behalf of the performer. But that expectation, where it exists,
is not necessarily indicative that the performer's name is being used on the
compact disc as a trade mark or that the average buyer so understands.

[41] For completeness I add that the decision of the Court of Justice in *Arsenal
Football Club plc v Reed* Case C-206/01 [2003] All ER (EC) 1, [2003] 3 WLR 450,
already mentioned, does not assist either way on this point in the present case.   *f*
There the defendant sold football club souvenirs and memorabilia, including
scarves bearing the name 'Arsenal'. The plaintiff football club had registered the
trade mark 'Arsenal' for classes of goods which included scarves. The club
claimed the defendant's activities infringed its registered trade marks. Having
stated the applicable legal principles as quoted above, the court expressed its view   *g*
on the facts of the case. Use of the Arsenal logo was not intended for purely
descriptive purposes. The use was such as to create the impression 'that there is
a material link in the course of trade between the goods concerned and the trade
mark proprietor' (see at 30–31 (para 56)). Whether it was open to the court to
reach this factual conclusion has proved controversial (see [2002] EWHC 2695
(Ch), [2003] 1 All ER 137, [2003] EWCA Civ 696, [2003] 3 All ER 865). The rights   *h*
and wrongs of this particular controversy are not material to the outcome of the
present case.

THE REASONABLE BELIEF DEFENCE: S 92(5)

[42] Mr Johnstone's alternative defence was based on s 92(5). His case was
that he relied upon advice given by a reputable trade marks attorney that
possession of the goods in question was lawful. Two points arise here. The first
concerns the availability of the s 92(5) defence where the defendant does not
know of the existence of the registered trade mark in question. In *Torbay Council
v Singh* [1999] IP & T 54 the Divisional Court of the Queen's Bench Division held
that the defence was not available in such a case. The court noted that s 92(5)

a speaks of a reasonable belief that the 'manner' of use of the sign did not infringe 'the registered trade mark'. Auld LJ held that this presupposes an awareness by the defendant of the existence of the registration against which he can match his manner of use of the allegedly infringing sign. The Court of Appeal followed this interpretation in *R v Keane* [2001] FSR 63. More recently, a differently constituted Court of Appeal, comprising Kay LJ and Andrew Smith J, doubted the correctness

b of this interpretation (see *R v Rhodes* [2002] EWCA 1390 at [21], [22], [2003] FSR 147 at [21], [22]).

[43] I share these doubts. The interpretation adopted in *Singh*'s case draws a distinction Parliament cannot have intended. The language of the subsection gives no support to this distinction. Section 92(5) is concerned to provide a defence where the person charged has a reasonable belief in the lawfulness of

c what he did. Those who act honestly and reasonably are not to be visited with criminal sanctions. It makes no sense to confine this defence to cases where the defendant is aware of the existence of the registered trade mark and exclude altogether those cases where the defendant is not. Section 92(5) provides a defence where the defendant believes on reasonable grounds his use of the sign

d does not infringe a registered trade mark of whose existence he is aware. It would be extraordinary if the subsection does not equally furnish a defence in the stronger case where the reason why the defendant believes his use of the sign does not infringe a registered trade mark is that he reasonably believes no relevant trade mark is registered. Section 92(5) is to be interpreted as including the latter case as well as the former.

e

BURDEN OF PROOF

[44] The opening words of s 92(5) are that it 'is a defence for a person charged with an offence under this section to show that he believed ...'. This wording gives rise to the second point arising in respect of the s 92(5) defence. It concerns

f the burden of proof. On this there are conflicting decisions of the Court of Appeal. In the present case the Court of Appeal held that, having regard to the presumption of innocence in art 6(2) of the European Convention for the Protection of Human Rights and Fundamental Freedoms 1950 (as set out in Sch 1 to the Human Rights Act 1998), the burden cast upon the accused is what is often called an evidentiary burden. He must raise an issue sufficient to require the

g prosecution to disprove it as part of the burden of proof resting on the prosecution. If the accused raises such an issue, and the prosecution fails to disprove the facts raised by the issue, the defence succeeds. It is not necessary for the accused person himself to prove the facts set out in s 92(5).

[45] In the present case the prosecution did not argue the contrary view in the

h Court of Appeal. In the later case of *S v London Borough of Havering* [2002] EWCA Crim 2558, [2003] 1 Cr App Rep 602 the prosecution took a different line. There the point was not conceded. After what was clearly a much fuller citation of authority and examination of the issue, the Court of Appeal, comprising Rose LJ and Hughes and Davis JJ, reached the contrary conclusion on the proper

j interpretation of s 92(5). Before your Lordships' House the prosecution submitted that the decision of the Court of Appeal in the present case was wrong and the views expressed in *S*'s case were to be preferred.

[46] In the events which have happened this issue does not call for decision in the present case. But the House should not leave the law on this point in its present state, with differing views expressed by the Court of Appeal. I shall, therefore, state my views as shortly as may be. First, I entertain no doubt that,

unless this interpretation is incompatible with art 6(2) of the convention, s 92(5)
should be interpreted as imposing on the accused person the burden of proving   *a*
the relevant facts on the balance of probability. Unless he proves these facts he
does not make good the defence provided by s 92(5). The contrary interpretation
of s 92(5) involves substantial re-writing of the subsection. It would not be
sufficient to read the subsection as meaning that it is a defence for a person
charged to raise an issue on the facts in question. That would not be sufficient,   *b*
because raising an issue does not provide the person charged with a defence. It
provides him with a defence only if, he having raised an issue, the prosecution
then fails to disprove the relevant facts beyond reasonable doubt. I do not believe
s 92(5) can be so read. I do not believe that is what Parliament intended.

[47] The question which next arises is whether this interpretation, namely,
that s 92(5) imposes a 'legal' or 'persuasive' onus on the person charged, is   *c*
compatible with the presumption of innocence contained in art 6(2) of the
convention. Prima facie this interpretation derogates from that principle. That
much is clear. On this interpretation s 92(5) sets out facts a defendant must
establish if he is to avoid conviction. These facts are presumed against him unless
he establishes the contrary.   *d*

[48] That is not the end of the matter. The European Court of Human Rights
has recognised that the convention does not, in principle, prohibit presumptions
of fact or law. What art 6(2) requires is that they must be confined within
reasonable limits which take into account the importance of what is at stake and
maintain the rights of the defence (see *Salabiaku v France* (1988) 13 EHRR 379 at
388 (para 28)). Thus, as elsewhere in the convention, a reasonable balance has to   *e*
be held between the public interest and the interests of the individual. In each
case it is for the state to show that the balance held in the legislation is reasonable.
The derogation from the presumption of innocence requires justification.

[49] Identifying the requirements of a reasonable balance is not as easy as it
might seem. One is seeking to balance incommensurables. At the heart of the   *f*
difficulty is the paradox noted by Sachs J in *State v Coetzee* [1997] 2 LRC 593 at 677
(para 220): the more serious the crime and the greater the public interest in
securing convictions of the guilty, the more important the constitutional
protection of the accused becomes. In the face of this paradox all that can be said
is that for a reverse burden of proof to be acceptable there must be a compelling
reason why it is fair and reasonable to deny the accused person the protection   *g*
normally guaranteed to everyone by the presumption of innocence.

[50] The relevant factors to be take into account when considering whether
such a reason exists have been considered in several recent authorities, in
particular the decisions of the House in *R v DPP, ex p Kebeline, R v DPP, ex p
Rechachi* [1999] 4 All ER 801, [2000] 2 AC 326 and *R v Lambert* [2001] UKHL 37,   *h*
[2001] 3 All ER 577. And there is now a lengthening list of decisions of the Court
of Appeal and other courts in respect of particular statutory provisions. A sound
starting point is to remember that if an accused is required to prove a fact on the
balance of probability to avoid conviction, this permits a conviction in spite of the
fact-finding tribunal having a reasonable doubt as to the guilt of the accused (see
Dickson CJC in *R v Whyte* (1988) 51 DLR (4th) 481 at 493). This consequence of   *j*
a reverse burden of proof should colour one's approach when evaluating the
reasons why it is said that, in the absence of a persuasive burden on the accused,
the public interest will be prejudiced to an extent which justifies placing a
persuasive burden on the accused. The more serious the punishment which may
flow from conviction, the more compelling must be the reasons. The extent and

a nature of the factual matters required to be proved by the accused, and their importance relative to the matters required to be proved by the prosecution, have to be taken into account. So also does the extent to which the burden on the accused relates to facts which, if they exist, are readily provable by him as matters within his own knowledge or to which he has ready access.

b [51] In evaluating these factors the court's role is one of review. Parliament, not the court, is charged with the primary responsibility for deciding, as a matter of policy, what should be the constituent elements of a criminal offence. I echo the words of Lord Woolf in *A-G of Hong Kong v Lee Kwong-kut, A-G of Hong Kong v Lo Chak-man* [1993] 3 All ER 939 at 955, [1993] AC 951 at 975:

c 'In order to maintain the balance between the individual and the society as a whole, rigid and inflexible standards should not be imposed on the legislature's attempts to resolve the difficult and intransigent problems with which society is faced when seeking to deal with serious crime.'

The court will reach a different conclusion from the legislature only when it is apparent the legislature has attached insufficient importance to the fundamental

d right of an individual to be presumed innocent until proved guilty.

[52] I turn to s 92. (1) Counterfeiting is fraudulent trading. It is a serious contemporary problem. Counterfeiting has adverse economic effects on genuine trade. It also has adverse effects on consumers, in terms of quality of goods and, sometimes, on the health or safety of consumers. The Commission of the European Communities has noted the scale of this 'widespread phenomenon

e with a global impact'. Urgent steps are needed to combat counterfeiting and piracy (see the Green Paper, Combating Counterfeiting and Piracy in the Single Market (COM(98) 569 final) and its follow up (COM(2000) 789 final)). Protection of consumers and honest manufacturers and traders from counterfeiting is an important policy consideration. (2) The offences created by s 92 have rightly

f been described as offences of 'near absolute liability'. The prosecution is not required to prove intent to infringe a registered trade mark. (3) The offences attract a serious level of punishment: a maximum penalty on indictment of an unlimited fine or imprisonment for up to ten years or both, together with the possibility of confiscation and deprivation orders. (4) Those who trade in brand products are aware of the need to be on guard against counterfeit goods. They

g are aware of the need to deal with reputable suppliers and keep records and of the risks they take if they do not. (5) The s 92(5) defence relates to facts within the accused person's own knowledge: his state of mind, and the reasons why he held the belief in question. His sources of supply are known to him. (6) Conversely, by and large it is to be expected that those who supply traders with counterfeit

h products, if traceable at all by outside investigators, are unlikely to be co-operative. So, in practice, if the prosecution must prove that a trader acted dishonestly, fewer investigations will be undertaken and fewer prosecutions will take place.

[53] In my view factors (4) and (6) constitute compelling reasons why the

j s 92(5) defence should place a persuasive burden on the accused person. Taking all the factors mentioned above into account, these reasons justify the loss of protection which will be suffered by the individual. Given the importance and difficulty of combating counterfeiting, and given the comparative ease with which an accused can raise an issue about his honesty, overall it is fair and reasonable to require a trader, should need arise, to prove on the balance of probability that he honestly and reasonably believed the goods were genuine.

[54] For these reasons, which are substantially the same as those given by
Rose LJ in *S v London Borough of Havering* [2003] 1 Cr App Rep 602, I consider the
persuasive burden placed on an accused person by the s 92(5) defence is
compatible with art 6(2). This being so, it becomes unnecessary to consider
whether, if this interpretation of s 92(5) were incompatible with art 6(2), s 92(5)
might be open to a different interpretation pursuant to s 3(1) of the 1998 Act.

[55] I would dismiss this appeal. The answer to the certified question is that
use of the offending sign as an indication of trade origin is an ingredient of the
offences created by s 92 of the 1994 Act.

LORD HOPE OF CRAIGHEAD.

[56] My Lords, I have had the advantage of reading in draft the speeches of my
noble and learned friends Lord Nicholls of Birkenhead and Lord Walker of
Gestingthorpe. I agree with them, and for the reasons which they give I too
would dismiss this appeal.

LORD HUTTON.

[57] My Lords, I have had the advantage of reading in draft the speeches of my
noble and learned friends Lord Nicholls of Birkenhead and Lord Walker of
Gestingthorpe. I agree with them and for the reasons which they give I too
would dismiss this appeal.

LORD RODGER OF EARLSFERRY.

[58] My Lords, I have had the privilege of reading in draft the speech delivered
by my noble and learned friend Lord Nicholls of Birkenhead, as well as the speech
to be delivered by my noble and learned friend Lord Walker of Gestingthorpe. I
respectfully agree with both of them and, for the reasons that they give, I too
would dismiss the appeal.

LORD WALKER OF GESTINGTHORPE.

[59] My Lords, counterfeiting, piracy and bootlegging of consumer goods
(including video and audio recordings, computer equipment, toys and perfume)
are big business and have a significant effect on the economies of many countries.
A recent Green Paper from the Commission of the European Communities
(Combating Counterfeiting and Piracy in the Single Market (COM(98) 569 final))
estimated that counterfeiting and piracy accounted for between 5% and 7% of
world trade, with the estimated figure being as high as 25% in the audio-visual
industry. Counterfeiting, piracy and bootlegging are not exact terms but all
involve deliberate, and generally fraudulent, infringement of various intellectual
property rights—notably trade marks, copyright, design right and performing
rights. Counterfeiting is generally used to include unauthorised sale, under a
well-known trade mark, of goods not made or authorised by the proprietor of the
trade mark. Piracy is generally used to include infringement of copyright
(including copyright in computer software). Bootlegging is generally used to
describe the sale of sound recordings made, without authority, either at live
concerts or from broadcasts. Typically, bootleg sound recordings are sold under
a manufacturer's name which is unobjectionable but with unauthorised use, on
the compact disc and its packaging, of the name of the performers (for instance,
the Rolling Stones) despite the fact that their name may be a registered
trade mark.

a [60] The international community has a strong interest in suppressing these dishonest activities by both civil and criminal sanctions. This case is concerned with this country's criminal sanctions against misuse of trade marks used in the popular music industry. Your Lordships have in a sense been looking at only a small part of the total picture of sanctions against these activities, since your Lordships have not been concerned with civil or criminal sanctions against
b copyright infringements, or with the far-reaching civil and criminal sanctions provided under the Trade Descriptions Act 1968 and the Consumer Protection Act 1987.

[61] Section 92 of the Trade Marks Act 1994 creates a number of criminal offences punishable (on conviction on indictment) by up to ten years' imprisonment. The principal issue raised on this appeal is whether a person can
c be convicted of an offence under s 92 for acts which do not amount to a civil infringement of a registered trade mark. There are also some subsidiary and related issues. In order to explain how they arise it is necessary to say something about the background to the 1994 Act and its legislative scheme and purpose.

[62] The law of trade marks has ancient origins which are preserved in the
d non-statutory law of passing off. Statutory regulation of trade marks, including a system of registration, was introduced by the Trade Marks Act 1875 and the Trade Marks Registration Act 1875. For much of the twentieth century the operative statute was the Trade Marks Act 1938. In recent times the whole of trade mark law has been re-shaped by the 1994 Act, which was enacted (as its long title states)—
e

> 'to make new provision for registered trade marks, implementing Council Directive No. 89/104/EEC of 21st December 1988 to approximate the laws of the Member States relating to trade marks; to make provision in connection with Council Regulation (EC) No. 40/94 of 20th December 1993
f > on the Community trade mark; to give effect to the Madrid Protocol Relating to the International Registration of Marks of 27th June 1989, and to certain provisions of the Paris Convention for the Protection of Industrial Property of 20th March 1883, as revised and amended; and for connected purposes.'

g [63] In construing the 1994 Act your Lordships have to approach it as a new statute, the main purpose of which is to implement the directive. Council Directive (EEC) 89/104 to approximate the laws of the member states relating to trade marks (OJ 1989 L40 p 1) (the directive) aims at the partial approximation (but not the complete harmonisation) of the trade mark laws of the member
h states. The 1994 Act must be construed accordingly (see *Marleasing SA v La Comercial Internacional de Alimentacion SA* Case C-106/89 [1990] ECR I-4135 at 4159 (para 8)). But many of the basic concepts in the directive appear to be the same as, or closely similar to, those which have informed the previous domestic law. That is natural enough, since the basic purpose of a trade mark is the same in any national economic system. The purpose is as a guarantee of commercial
i origin. As it was recently put by the Court of Justice of the European Communities in *Philips Electronics NV v Remington Consumer Products Ltd* Case C-299/99 [2002] All ER (EC) 634 at 649, [2002] ECR I-5475 (para 30):

> '… according to the case law of the court, the essential function of a trade mark is to guarantee the identity of the origin of the marked product to the consumer or end-user by enabling him, without any possibility of confusion,

a

to distinguish the product or service from others which have another origin, and for the trade mark to be able to fulfil its essential role in the system of undistorted competition which the [EC Treaty] seeks to establish, it must offer a guarantee that all the goods or services bearing it have originated under the control of a single undertaking which is responsible for their quality ...'

b

[64] In order to fulfil this function, a trade mark must be distinctive. That has always been a requirement under English law (although under the 1938 Act two levels of distinctiveness were required for so-called Pt A and Pt B registrations, a complication which has now disappeared). Distinctiveness is in this context to be contrasted with descriptiveness. Words which would be absurdly inappropriate as a description (such as North Pole for bananas: see *British Sugar plc v James* *c* *Robertson & Sons Ltd* [1996] RPC 281 at 306) may for precisely that reason be particularly distinctive. The contrast is closely connected with the issue of trade mark use (that is, use of a registered trade mark for its statutory purpose, rather than for some other purpose) to which it will be necessary to return.

[65] Section 92 must be set in its context of the general scheme of the 1994 Act. *d* Its scheme is that Pt I (ss 1–50) deals with registered trade marks. Part II (ss 51–60) deals with Community trade marks and international matters. Part III (ss 62–98) contains administrative and other supplementary provisions. Part IV (ss 99–110) contains miscellaneous and general provisions. For present purposes the most important sections in Pt I are ss 1–3 and 9–12. Section 1 defines 'trade mark' as 'any sign capable of being represented graphically which is capable of *e* distinguishing goods or services of one undertaking from those of other undertakings'. Section 2 provides that a registered trade mark is a property right which gives the proprietor rights and remedies under the Act. Section 3 lists absolute grounds for refusal of registration, including (in sub-s (1)):

'(b) trade marks which are devoid of any distinctive character; (c) trade *f* marks which consist exclusively of signs or indications which may serve, in trade, to designate the kind, quality, quantity, intended purpose, value, geographical origin, the time of production of goods or of rendering of services, or other characteristics of goods or services ...'

g

The general effect of para (c) is to indicate that a proposed trade mark may not perform a purely descriptive function, and its language is echoed by that of s 11(2)(b).

[66] Section 9(1) provides:

'The proprietor of a registered trade mark has exclusive rights in the trade *h* mark which are infringed by use of the trade mark in the United Kingdom without his consent.

The acts amounting to infringement, if done without the consent of the proprietor, are specified in section 10.'

j

So what amounts to an infringement (sometimes referred to in the course of argument in the appeal as civil infringement) is to be gathered from s 10, as supplemented by ss 11 and 12. These sections are something of an intricate mosaic (no doubt reflecting the difficulties facing the draftsman in amalgamating the old law under the 1938 Act with the directive, and in particular arts 5 and 6 of the directive).

a

[67] The text of ss 10 and 11 is set out either verbatim or in detailed summary in the speech of my noble and learned friend Lord Nicholls of Birkenhead, which I have had the advantage of reading in draft (and from which I also gratefully adopt the summary of the facts). I will merely repeat the general effect of ss 10 and 11 (s 12 deals with exhaustion of rights and is not relevant to this appeal). (1) Infringement occurs only if there is unauthorised use in the course of trade

b

(defined in s 103 as including any business or profession). (2) If use is of the same mark for the same goods (referred to in argument as double identity) liability is (subject to the question of trade mark use) automatic (see s 10(1), reflecting art 5(1)(a)). (3) If the allegedly infringing use is a case of identity of mark (only) or of goods (only) with mere similarity in the other element, liability is not automatic but depends on likelihood of confusion (see s 10(2), reflecting

c

art 5(1)(b)). (4) If the mark used is the same or similar, but the goods are not similar, there is liability if the trade mark has a reputation in the United Kingdom, and the alleged infringement takes unfair advantage of, or is detrimental to, the distinctive character or the repute of the trade mark (see s 10(3), reflecting the permissive provision in art 5(2) (which has recently been given a liberal

d

interpretation by the Court of Justice of the European Communities in *Davidoff & Cie SA v Gofkid Ltd* Case C-292/00 [2003] 1 WLR 1714 at 1719 (paras 17–30)). (5) Use is defined (non-exhaustively) in s 10(4), reflecting art 5(3); s 10(5) extends liability to accomplices; and s 10(6) covers comparative advertising (and similar special uses) provided that they are fair and honest. (6) All these provisions are subject to the specific restrictions and exceptions in ss 11 and 12. For present

e

purposes the most important exception is in s 11(2):

> 'A registered trade mark is not infringed by—(a) the use by a person of his own name or address, (b) the use of indications concerning the kind, quality, quantity, intended purpose, value, geographical origin, the time of production of goods or of rendering of services, or other characteristics of

f

> goods or services, or (c) the use of the trade mark where it is necessary to indicate the intended purpose of a product or service (in particular, as accessories or spare parts), provided the use is in accordance with honest practices in industrial or commercial matters.'

g

This provision reproduces, almost word for word, art 6(1) of the directive.

[68] Section 92, in Pt III of the 1994 Act, represents the third generation of statutory provisions creating trade mark offences. From the earliest days it was an offence to falsify the register or falsely represent a trade mark as being registered (see now ss 94 and 95 of the 1994 Act) but those provisions are not now in point. Section 58A of the 1938 Act (introduced by the Copyright, Designs and

h

Patents Act 1988) first made fraudulent application or use of a trade mark a criminal offence. Your Lordships are not concerned with the detail of s 58A but it may be noted that it had a relatively demanding test of mens rea and it proved unsatisfactory in practice.

[69] It is necessary to set out s 92 in full:

j

> '(1) A person commits an offence who with a view to gain for himself or another, or with intent to cause loss to another, and without the consent of the proprietor—(a) applies to goods or their packaging a sign identical to, or likely to be mistaken for, a registered trade mark, or (b) sells or lets for hire, offers or exposes for sale or hire or distributes goods which bear, or the packaging of which bears, such a sign, or (c) has in his possession, custody or

control in the course of a business any such goods with a view to the doing of anything, by himself or another, which would be an offence under paragraph (b).

(2) A person commits an offence who with a view to gain for himself or another, or with intent to cause loss to another, and without the consent of the proprietor—(a) applies a sign identical to, or likely to be mistaken for, a registered trade mark to material intended to be used—(i) for labelling or packaging goods, (ii) as a business paper in relation to goods, or (iii) for advertising goods, or (b) uses in the course of a business material bearing such a sign for labelling or packaging goods, as a business paper in relation to goods, or for advertising goods, or (c) has in his possession, custody or control in the course of a business any such material with a view to the doing of anything, by himself or another, which would be an offence under paragraph (b).

(3) A person commits an offence who with a view to gain for himself or another, or with intent to cause loss to another, and without the consent of the proprietor—(a) makes an article specifically designed or adapted for making copies of a sign identical to, or likely to be mistaken for, a registered trade mark, or (b) has such an article in his possession, custody or control in the course of a business, knowing or having reason to believe that it has been, or is to be, used to produce goods, or material for labelling or packaging goods, as a business paper in relation to goods, or for advertising goods.

(4) A person does not commit an offence under this section unless—(a) the goods are goods in respect of which the trade mark is registered, or (b) the trade mark has a reputation in the United Kingdom and the use of the sign takes or would take unfair advantage of, or is or would be detrimental to, the distinctive character or the repute of the trade mark.

(5) It is a defence for a person charged with an offence under this section to show that he believed on reasonable grounds that the use of the sign in the manner in which it was used, or was to be used, was not an infringement of the registered trade mark.

(6) A person guilty of an offence under this section is liable—(a) on summary conviction to imprisonment for a term not exceeding six months or a fine not exceeding the statutory maximum, or both; (b) on conviction on indictment to a fine or imprisonment for a term not exceeding ten years, or both.'

[70] There is no special definition of 'infringement' in s 92(5). Under the index in s 104 it is to be construed in accordance with ss 9(1), (2) and 10. It was not argued that that does not necessarily include ss 11 and 12.

[71] Section 92 was enacted by Parliament in conformity with international obligations (under art 61 of the Agreement on Trade-Related Aspects of Intellectual Property Rights, or 'TRIPS' (Marrakesh, 15 April 1994; TS 10 (1996); Cm 3046)) which take effect as part of Community law. Mr Hobbs QC (for the intervener, The British Phonographic Industry) gave a detailed explanation of the background but it is not necessary to go further into it.

[72] Much of the argument before your Lordships has focused on sub-s (5) of s 92. It provides a defence if the accused shows that he believed on reasonable grounds that he was not infringing the registered trade mark. This very strongly suggests (but the section does not in terms state) that it must also be a defence if

a the accused was not actually infringing the registered trade mark under ss 9–11. The Court of Appeal ([2002] EWCA Crim 194, [2002] FSR 840) found that argument conclusive. Tuckey LJ put the point strongly (at [46]):

'Put another way, it would provide a defence when a defendant has a reasonable belief that there is no civil infringement, when in fact the absence of civil infringement would be no defence. This is a nonsense.'

b

[73] Both sides agreed that it is hard to find an example of conduct which would be a criminal offence under s 92(1)–(4), but would not amount to a civil infringement. It was also common ground that if an exceptional case were to be found (such as a single sale of a limited number of articles, such as T-shirts, arguably not amounting to trading) it would in practice be most unlikely to *c* attract prosecution under s 92. Mr Perry (for the appellant) identified six points of substantial difference between s 92 and what I will call the civil infringement sections, and it is useful to examine these. But it must be recognised at once that if the scope or 'footprint' of s 92 is smaller than, and wholly contained within, the 'footprint' of the civil infringement sections, it is at first blush surprising that the *d* linguistic differences between them are so extensive. Their superficial disparity must be explained, I think, by Parliament's natural anxiety to frame the offence-creating provisions of the 1994 Act so as to be as self-contained and as simple a code as possible. Prosecutions under s 92 are heard either in the magistrates' court or in the Crown Court. It would be burdensome if lay magistrates and juries regularly had to go into the intricacies of the law of civil *e* infringement, especially in its present state of flux following the decision of the European Court of Justice in *Arsenal Football Club plc v Reed* Case C-206/01 [2003] All ER (EC) 1, [2003] 3 WLR 450 (to which I shall return). I respectfully agree with the view of Lord Nicholls that this House should so far as possible adhere to the language of s 92, treating it as being as self-contained as possible, and avoiding *f* any unnecessary elaboration of trade mark law as it falls to be applied in criminal courts.

[74] As the arrangement and language of the two sets of provisions is so different it may be helpful to summarise Mr Perry's six points. (1) Under s 92 the prosecution must prove the special mens rea of 'with a view to gain' (including causing loss to another). There is no civil equivalent. (2) The offence-creating *g* provisions apply only in respect of goods (whereas the civil provisions cover goods or services). (3) The offence-creating provisions refer to a sign 'identical to, or likely to be mistaken for' the registered mark. This is a simpler and narrower formulation than that in s 10(2). (4) Section 92(4) combines the functions of parts of s 10(2) and (3) but differs in substance only if the form of words in sub-s (4) *h* ('goods in respect of which the trade mark is registered') is narrower than that in s 10(2)(a) ('identical with ... or similar to'). (5) Section 92(5) has no civil equivalent: a defendant's belief in his innocence is irrelevant to civil liability. (6) Criminal liability may arise from acts although they are not done in the course of trade (this is, as already noted, the only respect in which the scope of s 92 may *i* be wider, and it seems to be of little practical importance).

[75] In summary, s 92 is clearly narrower on points (1), (2) and (5) above; it may be narrower (and is certainly not wider) on points (3) and (4); point (6) tends to lead to an unprofitable debate as to whether fraudulent activities should be regarded as a trade, and it is easy to see why Parliament avoided language which raised that issue. However Mr Perry's points do not include the issues which lie at the heart of this appeal, that is (i) whether 'trade mark use' is a necessary

ingredient of criminal liability under s 92; (ii) if so, what are its proper limits; and
(iii) how it should be dealt with in practice, in terms of directions to a jury or
self-direction to magistrates, in prosecutions under s 92. To those issues I now
turn.

[76] 'Trade mark use' is a convenient shorthand expression for use of a
registered trade mark for its proper purpose (that is, identifying and guaranteeing
the trade origin of the goods to which it is applied) rather than for some other
purpose. It is easy to recognise those cases which fall squarely on one side or
other of the line. If a counterfeiter sells a cheap imitation watch under the
trade mark OMEGA, he is fraudulently engaging in trade mark use (as he is, as
Mr Hobbs suggested, if he uses the mark HOMEGAS but prints the first and last
letters very faintly). But if a publisher publishes a book named *Mother Care/Other
Care* (a serious study of the upbringing of young children of working mothers)
there is no infringement of the registered trade mark of Mothercare UK Ltd,
despite the fact that the trade mark is registered for many classes of goods,
including books (see *Mothercare UK Ltd v Penguin Books Ltd* [1988] RPC 113).

[77] That was a decision of the Court of Appeal on a Pt A registration under
the 1938 Act, but the essential point holds good. Dillon LJ said (at 118–119):

'it stands to reason that a Trade Marks Act would only be concerned to
restrict the use of a mark as a trademark or in a trademark sense, and should
be construed accordingly. If descriptive words are legitimately registered in
Part A of the register, there is still no reason why other people should not be
free to use the words in a descriptive sense, and not in any trademark sense.
[Counsel for the respondent] took the further point, on the trademark aspect
of the case, that Mothercare suffers damage because the value and
exclusivity of its mark is diminished, by any use by anyone else of the words
"mother care", but that, in my judgment, can only be so if those words are
used by the offender as a trademark or in a trademark sense; if descriptive
words are merely used descriptively, the mark is unaffected. In the present
case the words "Mother Care" in the title of the book are not, in my
judgment, used as a trademark or in any trademark sense. They are merely
used descriptively as describing, with the words "Other Care", what the
book is about.'

Similarly Bingham LJ said (of s 4(1)(b) of the 1938 Act (at 123)):

'To conclude otherwise would be to hold (where a trademark consists of
an English word or words) that Parliament intended to grant the proprietor
of the trademark what would in effect be commercial copyright in that word
or those words. Had that been the intention, the drafting of the section could
have been a great deal simpler.'

[78] In *Bravado Merchandising Services Ltd v Mainstream Publishing (Edinburgh)
Ltd* [1996] FSR 205, a comparable question arose under the 1994 Act. The
petitioner was the proprietor of the trade mark Wet Wet Wet (the name of a
popular music group). It was registered for (among other classes of goods) books.
The defendant intended to publish a book about the group using 'Wet Wet Wet'
as part of the title. In the Court of Session Lord McCluskey found (distinguishing
the *Mothercare* case) that that would be trade mark use, but that it would
nevertheless be within s 11(2)(b) (as amounting to an indication of the
characteristics of the goods to which the mark was applied) and so would not
amount to an infringement. So Lord McCluskey might be thought to have given

a   with one hand and to have taken away with the other; but that depends on
whether ss 10 and 11 of the 1994 Act should be seen as contingent or intersecting
circles, a point on which there was a good deal of discussion in the course of
argument.

[79] Your Lordships were also referred to the decision of the Federal Court of
Australia in *Musidor BV v Tansing (trading as Apple Music House)* (1994) 123 ALR
b   593. The Federal Court was divided as to whether the trade mark Rolling Stones
(registered in respect of compact discs as well as other goods) was infringed by
bootleg discs (using recordings made at live concerts in the 1960s) which used the
words Rolling Stones on each disc and its case insert. The insert also stated that
the recordings had not been authorised. The majority (Gummow and Heerey JJ)
concluded (at 605) that this was not trade mark use:
c

'... the words "The Rolling Stones" are not used for the purpose of
indicating a connection in the course of trade between him and the discs or
any other goods in respect of which the trade marks are registered. Rather,
they are used here to identify a recording made many years ago of a live
d   performance by those persons in the United States, which has been
reproduced and embodied in the discs manufactured by the respondent.'

Davies J, dissenting, thought that there had been trade mark use, and that the
disclaimer of authorisation made no difference:

e   'To exemplify the infringement, assume that "Pierre Cardin" and "Gucci"
are registered trade marks and that the Pierre Cardin organisation or the
Gucci organisation manufactured goods but declined to put them on sale
being not satisfied with their quality. It would, in my opinion, be an
infringement for some other person without authority to put the goods on
the market with the description that they were manufactured by Pierre
f   Cardin or by Gucci but that the sale had not been authorised. Yet that is
what the respondent seeks to do in the present case'. (See (1994) 123 ALR
593 at 598.)

Davies J also expressed the view that the respondent had not used the words
'Rolling Stones' in good faith.
g
[80] Comparable problems have recently been considered by the Court of
Justice of the European Communities in *Arsenal Football Club plc v Reed* Case
C-206/01 [2003] All ER (EC) 1, [2003] 3 WLR 450. Arsenal Football Club (AFC)
is the proprietor of four trade marks, including two word marks ('Arsenal' and
'Arsenal Gunners') registered for (among other goods) clothing and sports
h   footwear. Mr Reed had since 1970 been selling clothing (especially scarves)
marked 'Arsenal'. He displayed prominent notices disavowing 'any affiliation or
relationship with the manufacturers or distributors of any other product'. AFC
sued him for passing off and trade mark infringement. The claim in passing off
failed. The trade mark claim led to a reference to the Court of Justice by the High
j   Court (Laddie J ([2001] IP & T 810)) of the following questions:

'(1) Where a trade mark is validly registered and (a) a third party uses in the
course of trade a sign identical with that trade mark in relation to goods
which are identical with those for which the trade mark is registered; and (b)
the third party has no defence to infringement by virtue of art 6(1) of [the
directive]: does the third party have a defence to infringement on the ground

that the use complained of does not indicate trade origin (ie a connection in
the course of trade between the goods and the trade mark proprietor)?   a

(2) If so, is the fact that the use in question would be perceived as a badge
of support, loyalty or affiliation to the trade mark proprietor a sufficient
connection?'

[81] As already noted, art 6(1) (like s 11(2)) makes an exception for descriptive   b
use, but only if it is use 'in accordance with honest practices in industrial or
commercial matters'. It is not entirely clear whether the terms of the reference
made by the High Court assumed that art 6(1) provided no defence because of the
need for descriptiveness, or because of the proviso as to honest practices.

[82] In making the reference Laddie J made what he described as findings of
fact which are recorded in the judgment of the Court of Justice ([2003] All ER   c
(EC) 1 at 26, [2003] 3 WLR 450 at 476):

'21 ... the High Court rejected [AFC's] argument that the use by Mr Reed
of the signs registered as trade marks was perceived by those to whom they
were addressed as a badge of origin, so that the use was a "trade mark use".

22. According to the High Court, the signs affixed to Mr Reed's goods   d
were in fact perceived by the public as "badges of support, loyalty or
affiliation".'

[83] The Court of Justice recognised (at 30 (para 54)) that—

'... uses for purely descriptive purposes are excluded from the scope of   e
art 5(1) of the ... Directive because they do not affect any of the interests
which that provision aims to protect, and do not therefore fall within the
concept of use within the meaning of that provision (see, with respect to a
use for purely descriptive purposes relating to the characteristics of the
product offered, Hölterhoff v Freiesleben Case C-2/00 [2002] All ER (EC) 665 at
682, [2002] ECR I-4187 (para 16)).'   f

The court distinguished Hölterhoff's case (where a trade mark had been used to
describe a method of cutting precious stones, rather than to identify their
producer) as being concerned with a transaction in the course of wholesale trade.
The court stated that Mr Reed's use of the Arsenal sign took place in the context
of sales to consumers and was obviously not intended for purely descriptive   g
purposes. The use was such as to create the impression that there was a material
link in the course of trade between Mr Reed's goods and AFC. AFC could
therefore rely on what Mr Reed had done as trade mark use.

[84] Laddie J has since ([2002] EWHC 2695 (Ch), [2003] 1 All ER 137) held that
the Court of Justice exceeded its jurisdiction by determining issues of fact which   h
were for the national court to decide (and which he had, as he saw it, already
decided in a manner favourable to Mr Reed). An appeal to the Court of Appeal
seems likely [see [2003] 3 All ER 865].

[85] The law is therefore in something of a state of disarray. But even if the
Court of Justice exceeded its jurisdiction in the Arsenal case (a point on which I
would express no view), its exposition of the general principles is still highly   j
material. The court has excluded use of a trade mark for 'purely descriptive
purposes' (and the word 'purely' is important) because such use does not affect
the interests which the trade mark proprietor is entitled to protect. But there will
be infringement if the sign is used, without authority, 'to create the impression
that there is a material link in the course of trade between the goods concerned

a and the trade mark proprietor' (see [2003] All ER (EC) 1 at 30–31, [2003] 3 WLR 450 at 480–481 (para 56)). There may be such a link, in the view of the European Court of Justice, even though the consumer treats the mark as a badge of support for or loyalty to the trade mark proprietor. As the Advocate General (Ruiz-Jarabo Colomer) put it in a footnote to his opinion:

b   'However much Mr Reed may announce that the goods which he sells neither come from [AFC] nor are authorised by it, he is able to market them—and his customers buy them—precisely because they bear the signs which, under registered protection, identify the club.' (See [2003] All ER (EC) 1 at 17 (n 52), [2003] 3 WLR 450 at 467 (para 66).)

c [86] The difficulty arises, I think, because between cases which are clearly at the opposite extremes of 'distinctiveness' and 'descriptiveness' there is something of a no man's land of debatable cases, and the problem of analysis varies with the character of the mark and the character of the goods to which it is affixed. Disputes about books, and scarves, and compact discs, cannot easily be resolved by a single test. Most people would have an intuitive feeling that to label a *d* compact disc with the words 'Rolling Stones' is less purely descriptive than entitling a biography 'Wet Wet Wet'. That is no doubt because a group of musicians are in some sense the authors (or at least the performers) of what is on the disc, but are not the authors of an unauthorised book about themselves. But in that case is not their real grievance infringement of their copyright or their performing rights, rather than of their trade mark? Was not Mr Hölterhoff's real *e* complaint infringement of his design right in two new methods of cutting precious stones (if indeed he had invented those methods) rather than of his trade mark?

[87] These are difficult questions which it is not necessary for your Lordships to determine in order to dispose of this appeal. Whatever uncertainties there are *f* about the decision of the Court of Justice in the *Arsenal* case, its likely effect is that the province of trade mark use has annexed a significant part of the no man's land in which elements of distinctiveness and descriptiveness overlap. But it would be idle to speculate whether the view taken by the Court of Justice in the *Arsenal* case is reconcilable with the majority view in the *Musidor* case (1994) 123 ALR 593 because (as Lord Nicholls of Birkenhead has emphasised in his speech, and as I *g* respectfully agree) trade mark use is essentially a question of fact (of a fairly complex sort). The *Musidor* case can indeed be seen as turning on whether it was right for the Federal Court to differ from the trial judge on an issue of that sort. The judgments mention some of the factors which may contribute to the eventual conclusion: the prominence and apparent purpose with which the *h* group's name (and registered trade mark) is used on the disc and its packaging; what other brand marks (registered or unregistered) are used on the disc and its packaging; the terms and prominence of any disclaimer (although a disclaimer, by itself, cannot be conclusive); and any other matters going to the alleged infringer's good faith and honesty.

[88] I come back to what I described as the issues which lie at the heart of this appeal. First, is trade mark use a necessary ingredient of criminal liability under s 92? On this point I am in respectful agreement with the reasoning and conclusions in the speech of Lord Nicholls. It is a necessary ingredient, and there is no need to go on a circuitous route through art 6(1)(b) or s 11(2)(b) in order to arrive at that conclusion. It is adequately (if not pellucidly) expressed in the language of s 92, which in its three offence-creating subsections requires the

defendant, for the purpose of gain, to have applied a sign to goods (or their packaging), or to have engaged in other acts or conduct in relation to goods (or business materials) which bear that sign. I would hold that such acts or conduct must be restricted to acts or conduct amounting to trade mark use. Facts such as those of *Mothercare UK Ltd v Penguin Books Ltd* [1988] RPC 113 or *Hölterhoff v Freiesleben* Case C-2/00 [2002] All ER (EC) 665, [2002] ECR I-4187 would not fall within any of sub-ss (1)–(3) of s 92.

[89] On the second issue (the proper limits of trade mark use) I would not go so far as the Court of Appeal went in preferring the minority view in the *Musidor* case and in inclining to the view that every bootlegging case of this sort would involve trade mark use. It seems likely that Mr Johnstone would have had a difficult task in making good the defences on which he wished to rely. However, he should have been permitted to run them. I agree with the Court of Appeal that his conviction (on his pleading guilty after not being allowed to put forward the defences on which he wished to rely) must be regarded as unsafe. I would therefore dismiss this appeal.

[90] That is sufficient to dispose of the appeal itself, but there remain the issue of the burden of proof placed on the defendant by s 92(5), and further issues, on which your Lordships heard argument, whether *R v Keane* [2001] FSR 63 and *S v London Borough of Havering* [2003] 1 Cr App Rep 602 were rightly decided. On all these issues I am in complete and respectful agreement with the speech of Lord Nicholls.

Appeal dismissed.

Kate O'Hanlon   Barrister.

a

Price v Price (trading as Poppyland Headware)

[2003] EWCA Civ 888

b

COURT OF APPEAL, CIVIL DIVISION

BROOKE, SEDLEY AND HALE LJJ

4, 26 JUNE 2003

Particulars of claim – Service – Extension of time for service – Factors to be considered in deciding whether to grant extension of time – Grant of extension of time subject to
c *conditions – CPR 3.1, 3.9.*

The claimant commenced proceedings against the defendant, claiming over £500,000 damages for personal injury. The claim form was issued on 4 April 2001, without any accompanying particulars of claim, medical report or schedule of
d loss. No particulars of claim were served, and no application for an extension of time in which to serve them was made until 16 July 2002. The main reason behind the delay was that the claimant's solicitors were seeking a second medical opinion, without communicating that fact to the other side, because they did not like the advice given by the expert who had been agreed by the parties. In August 2002 the deputy district judge allowed the claimant an extension of time, having
e considered whether there was an adequate explanation for the delay and whether the defendant had been significantly prejudiced by the delay. The defendant appealed to the judge, who struck out the claim, taking the view that the claim was plainly one where there had been disgraceful, long delay, all the way through. The judge said that to permit an extension of time in all the
f circumstances of the case would be an affront to civil justice and to the administration of justice under the CPR. The claimant appealed.

Held – The necessity for a judge to follow the checklist in CPR 3.9[a] when considering an application in a complex case for an extension of time applied
g equally whether the application was for an extension of time in which to appeal or in which to serve particulars of claim. In the instant case, neither the deputy district judge nor the judge had followed the checklist. Although the judge had actually taken many of the matters set out in CPR 3.9 into account, his approach was flawed in that he did not appear to have taken account of the fact that the claimant would be barred from prosecuting what was represented as a valid claim
h for over £500,000 if he was denied the relief sought. In those circumstances, the judge having left out of account an important feature of the case which he should have considered, the court would have to exercise its discretion afresh. The real question was whether, despite other considerations tending strongly in favour of

---

i   a   Rule 3.9, so far as material, provides: '... the court will consider all the circumstances including—(a) the interests of the administration of justice; (b) whether the application for relief has been made promptly; (c) whether the failure to comply was intentional; (d) whether there is a good explanation for the failure; (e) the extent to which the party in default has complied with other rules, practice directions, court orders and any relevant pre-action protocol; (f) whether the failure to comply was caused by the party or his legal representative; (g) whether the trial date or the likely trial date can still be met if relief is granted; (h) the effect which the failure to comply had on each party; and (i) the effect which the granting of relief would have on each party.'

the defendant, the fact that the claimant was being denied access to the court could drive the balance the other way. In all the circumstances of the instant case, the extension sought would have been refused, but for the fact that, pursuant to CPR 3.1(2)(a) and 3.1(3)(a)[b], there was a route available (which needed to be more widely used on appropriate occasions) by which the court could do effective justice to both sides, ie by extending time for compliance subject to conditions. The appeal would accordingly be allowed by extending the time for the service of particulars of claim for 28 days from the date of the judgment, on condition that no claim were made for special or general damages, other than what might be substantiated by any pre-April 2001 report written by the original expert, which the claimant might care to disclose in support of his claim.

Sayers v Clarke Walker (a firm) [2002] 3 All ER 490, *Walsh v Misseldine* [2002] All ER (D) 261 applied.

Notes

For the extension of time for serving a claim form, see 37 *Halsbury's Laws* (4th edn reissue) para 306.

Cases referred to in judgment

Ashingdane v UK (1985) 7 EHRR 528, [1985] ECHR 8225/78, ECt HR.
Biguzzi v Rank Leisure plc [1999] 4 All ER 934, [1999] 1 WLR 1926, CA.
Carlson v Townsend [2001] EWCA Civ 511, [2001] 3 All ER 663, [2001] 1 WLR 2415.
Costellow v Somerset CC [1993] 1 All ER 952, [1993] 1 WLR 256, CA.
Phonographic Performance v AEI Rediffusion Music Ltd [1999] 2 All ER 299, [1999] 1 WLR 1507, CA.
Sayers v Clarke Walker (a firm) [2002] EWCA Civ 645, [2002] 3 All ER 490, [2002] 1 WLR 3095, CA.
Tanfern Ltd v Cameron-Macdonald [2000] 2 All ER 801, [2000] 1 WLR 1311, CA.
Tinnelly & Sons Ltd v UK (1998) 4 BHRC 393, ECt HR.
Totty v Snowden, Hewitt v Wirral and West Cheshire Community NHS Trust [2001] EWCA Civ 1415, [2001] 4 All ER 577, [2002] 1 WLR 1384.
Walsh v Misseldine (29 February 2000, unreported), CA.
Woodhouse v Consignia plc, Steliou v Compton [2002] EWCA Civ 275, [2002] 2 All ER 737, [2002] 1 WLR 2558.

Appeal

The claimant, Paul Terence Price, appealed from the order of Judge O'Brien made at the Norwich County Court on 19 October 2002 allowing the appeal of the defendant, Rosalind Price (trading as Poppyland Headware), from an order of Deputy District Judge Pugh on 15 August 2002 granting the claimant an extension of time for serving particulars of claim in his personal injury action against the defendant. The facts are set out in the judgment of the court.

---

b   Rule 3.1, so far as material, provides: '(2) ... the court may—(a) extend or shorten the time for compliance with any rule, practice direction or court order (even if an application for extension is made after the time for compliance has expired) ... (3) When the court makes an order, it may—(a) make it subject to conditions, including a condition to pay a sum of money into court ...'

a *Anne Studd* (instructed by *Hansells*, Norwich) for the claimant.
Nicholas Heathcote Williams (instructed by *Plexus Law*) for the respondent.

Cur adv vult

26 June 2003. The following judgment of the court was delivered.

b

BROOKE LJ.
[1] This is an appeal by the claimant Paul Terence Price against an order by Judge O'Brien at the Norwich County Court on 19 October 2002 whereby he allowed the defendant's appeal against an order of Deputy District Judge Pugh on 15 August 2002. The deputy district judge had granted the claimant an extension
c of time for serving the particulars of claim in this personal injuries action. In allowing the defendant's appeal, the judge struck out the action. Permission was granted for this second appeal on the grounds that it gave rise to an important point of practice.

[2] The accident which gave rise to these proceedings is said to have taken
d place on 5 May 1998. The claimant and the defendant are husband and wife, and at the material time the defendant was employing the claimant as a shop assistant in her hat shop in Cromer at a salary of £60 per week. The claim form was issued on 4 April 2001, without any accompanying particulars of claim, medical report or schedule of loss. It was served on 14 April 2001. The particulars of claim ought to have been served on the defendant on or before 28 April 2001 pursuant to CPR
e 7.4(1)(b) which provides, so far as is material, that: '(1) Particulars of claim must ... (b) ... be served on the defendant by the claimant within 14 days after service of the claim form.'

[3] At that time there was an unresolved dispute as to whether a court had power in any circumstances to extend the time for serving particulars of claim
f pursuant to the general power to extend time which is contained in CPR 3.1. In *Totty v Snowden, Hewitt v Wirral and West Cheshire Community NHS Trust* [2001] EWCA Civ 1415, [2001] 4 All ER 577, [2002] 1 WLR 1384 it was held that this power did exist. However, CPR 7.4(1)(b) contains the mandatory word 'must', from which it can readily be inferred that the longer the period a claimant allows to elapse before he/she applies for an extension of time, the slower a court may
g be to exercise a favourable discretion. In the event no application for an extension of time was made until 16 July 2002, over 14 months out of time.

[4] By this time this court had made it clear in *Sayers v Clarke Walker (a firm)* [2002] EWCA Civ 645, [2002] 3 All ER 490, [2002] 1 WLR 3095 that in a case of any complexity, when a court was considering an application for an extension of
h time made after the time prescribed for the taking of a step in proceedings had expired, the court should follow the checklist given in CPR 3.9. Although the present case is concerned with an extension of time for serving particulars of claim, and not with an extension of time for appealing, the underlying logic is the same. If the court is not willing to extend time, the action will be at an end
i because the claimant will not be able to proceed with it any further.

[5] Although this judgment had been fully reported in the All England Law Reports on 17 July 2002, the deputy district judge did not, as this court had adjured, approach his task within the structured framework set out in CPR 3.9. He seems to have thought that it was sufficient for him to consider whether there was an adequate explanation of the delay and whether the defendant had been significantly prejudiced by the delay. His approach was reminiscent of the

approach forced on the courts in pre-CPR days when an application was made to strike out a claim for want of prosecution. He appears, among other things, to have been influenced by a dictum of Chadwick LJ in *Totty v Snowden* [2001] 4 All ER 577 at [46] to the effect that once a defendant had been served with a claim form he would be in a position to invoke the assistance of the court if particulars of claim were not forthcoming within due time.

[6] On the defendant's appeal Judge O'Brien, too, did not adopt the CPR 3.9 framework. He overruled the deputy district judge because he took the view that this was plainly a claim where there had been disgraceful, long delay all the way through it. He said that a great deal of the delay was unexplained, and insofar as it was explained it was in circumstances where the conduct of the claimant's solicitors was reprehensible. He therefore found that the delay was deliberate, long and without explanation.

[7] When he came to consider matters of prejudice, he considered what Bingham MR had said in a pre-CPR context in *Costellow v Somerset CC* [1993] 1 All ER 952 at 960, [1993] 1 WLR 256 at 264:

'Save in special cases or exceptional circumstances it can rarely be appropriate on an overall assessment of what justice requires to deny the plaintiff an extension where the denial will stifle his action because of a procedural default, which even if unjustifiable, had caused the defendant no prejudice for which he cannot be compensated by an order for costs.'

[8] The judge said that for the reasons he had given he did not regard what had been going on, on the claimant's side of the action, as being capable of the description of 'a procedural default'. Having regard to the degree, extent and gravity of the delay in this case and the real reason for that delay he thought it was right that justice did not require the defendant to prove an enormous amount of prejudice to her. It seemed to him that there was prejudice, and that the deputy district judge had somewhat underrated it. He also founded his decision on matters relating to the administration of justice. He said that to permit an extension of time in all the circumstances of this case would be an affront to civil justice and an affront to the administration of justice under the CPR, which he was not going to permit. He therefore held that the deputy district judge was wrong.

[9] The claimant is legally-aided, and it is noteworthy that the deputy district judge and the judge in turn directed that the claimant's solicitors should show cause why they should not pay the defendant's costs of the original application for an extension and the defendant's appeal.

[10] The reasons why the two judges took such a jaundiced view of the behaviour of the claimant's solicitors are not difficult to seek. The first notification the defendant's insurers received about the claimant's accident was when they received a letter on 9 April 1999, 11 months after the accident. A period of six months then elapsed before they agreed to provide indemnity in principle for this claim. On 5 November 1999 they obtained a short statement from the defendant, and on the same day the claimant's solicitors wrote to them for the first time. This letter did not comply with the Pre-Action Protocol for Personal Injury Cases in that it did not contain a clear summary of the facts on which the claim was based, nor any indication of the nature of any injuries suffered nor, most importantly, of any financial loss incurred (Protocol, para 3.2). In these circumstances there was nothing within the letter to enable the insurers to put a broad valuation on the 'risk' (Protocol, para 3.5). Instead, the solicitors

a merely said that they were acting for Mr Price, identified the date of his injury at
   work, and referred to their understanding that the insurers already had full details
   of the circumstances of the accident from Mr Price and that an identified firm of
   loss adjusters had been investigating the circumstances of the accident. At this
   stage the insurers had received no notice of any claim for loss of earnings. Their
   initial investigation had revealed that Mr Price had returned to work after the
b accident and had suffered no loss of earnings as a result of it.

   [11] On 17 November 1999 a legal aid certificate was granted to Mr Price,
   limited to obtaining further evidence and counsel's opinion thereafter.

   [12] On 4 January 2000 the claimant's solicitors particularised their allegations
   of negligence for the first time. They also told the insurers that they wished to
   instruct a local consultant rheumatologist, Dr Gaffney, to prepare a medical
c report. Their letter was phrased in such a way as to make it clear that they were
   familiar with the provisions of the Pre-Action Protocol Relating to the Instruction
   of Experts (Protocol, paras 3.14–3.19). The defendant's insurers agreed to
   Dr Gaffney being instructed, and on 2 February 2000 they wrote to the effect that
   negligence was accepted 'subject to the sight of medical evidence which will
d confirm causation'. In the ordinary course of things it would have been expected
   that this admission of liability would have resulted in the disclosure of
   Dr Gaffney's medical report, once it was ready (Protocol, para 3.21). The
   defendant's solicitor has said that at this stage up to £10,000 was being allowed by
   the insurers for the cost of a claim for a moderate back injury, and that their belief
   that there was no loss of earnings claim influenced their decision on the value of
e the claim and the extent of any investigations that were required.

   [13] The defendant's insurers knew nothing more about the matter for over
   14 months, when the claim form, issued on 4 April 2001, was served by the court.
   This stated, unexpectedly, that the value of the claim was expected to exceed
   £50,000. As I have already said, the particulars of claim were not served with the
   claim form. Nor were they served 14 days afterwards, as required by CPR
f 7.4(1)(b). It now appears that the claimant's legal aid certificate had not been
   extended to cover the issue of proceedings, and that his solicitors had no medical
   evidence to substantiate a claim by their client on the scale which he wished to
   present. On 8 May 2001 the defendant's insurers wrote to the claimant's solicitors
   in the following terms:

g
       'I note that medical evidence was being obtained by Dr Carl Gaffney,
       Consultant Rheumatologist, and await this report by return now please.

       If the report is still not available, please confirm when you anticipate being
       in a position to disclose it, and please provide us with an update as to the
       Claimant's recovery from his injuries.
h
       We would also be grateful if you could detail without prejudice if
       necessary, what Special Damages are being claimed in respect of this claim,
       although we note that you have issued proceedings on this case.

       What is the situation regarding your Client's employment? If still off work,
       when is a return to employment likely? From the enquiries we were able to
j   undertake via our insured, it appears that your Client was earning £60 per
       week, and if this is indeed the case we cannot see how we are concerned with
       a claim where losses are likely to exceed £50,000 as per your Claim Form, but
       would appreciate clarification.

       We look forward to hearing from you as soon as possible please.'

   No reply was received, and on 3 July 2001 the insurers sent a chasing letter.

[14] It now appears that all the necessary notes and records had been made available to Dr Gaffney by 24 May 2000. He then asked for further records, and in September 2000 he recommended a MRI scan, which was performed in November 2000. The claimant's solicitor has said that he did not receive a copy of the scan until January 2001, and, without giving any details at all, he asserts that there followed a further lengthy delay because of the doctor's failure to respond to a request for further comment. The procedure envisaged by the Pre-Action Protocol had completely broken down, presumably because Dr Gaffney was giving unwelcome advice. The claimant's solicitors did not tell the defendant's insurers (or their solicitors, who were first instructed when the claim was served) what was going on. Instead, they told them, by a letter dated 11 July 2001, that counsel had now been instructed to advise the Legal Services Commission as a preliminary to receiving authority to settle particulars of claim. It appears that they had received this advice by 2 August, because they told the defendant's solicitors by a letter of that date that they were now seeking authority for the extension of the legal aid certificate.

[15] There followed a short exchange of correspondence in which the defendant's solicitors were contending, wrongly as it turned out, that it was not possible to obtain an extension of time for service of particulars of claim. This dispute had been cleared up by mid-October, however, and they certainly did not at any time agree expressly or impliedly to any extension. The judge was extremely critical, moreover, of the contents of a letter from the claimant's solicitors dated 4 September 2001 in which they said:

'Having protected the position for limitation purposes we are not yet in a position to serve particulars containing medical evidence and a schedule but we are working towards that end.'

[16] The judge said:

'... it seems to me that giving that reason was not consistent with the present requirements of being open and above board in conducting litigation. The main reason, of course, the reason behind the delay was seeking a second medical opinion. That was not communicated to the other side. In my judgment it plainly should have been. If they were seeking to instruct another doctor, consistent with the way the protocol operates (and I appreciate that the action has now started), it would seem to be the proper course would be to notify the other side, and to notify the name of the doctor and possibly as well give some explanation as to why a second doctor was being instructed, but certainly to provide the name of the doctor proposed to be instructed. That was not done.'

[17] In my judgment, the judge's comments were justified. His thinking coincided with the approach of this court in *Carlson v Townsend* [2001] EWCA Civ 511, [2001] 3 All ER 663, [2001] 1 WLR 2415, another case in which a claimant's solicitor did not like the advice given by a medical expert whose identity had been agreed with the other side and then sought to instruct a different expert without obtaining the other side's agreement first.

[18] On 12 October 2001 the claimant's solicitors told the defendant's solicitors that as soon as they received the necessary authority from the Legal Services Commission they would issue an application for an extension of time to serve the particulars of claim. After further correspondence the defendant's solicitors inquired on 13 November 2001 why particulars of claim had not been

a served with the claim form and whether the claimant's solicitors were still
   attempting to obtain legal aid to cover their application. They received no reply,
   and had to send a chasing letter five weeks later. This chasing letter appears, at
   long last, to have prompted the claimant's solicitors to make the requisite
   application to the Legal Services Commission on 20 December 2001, and the
   necessary extension of the certificate was granted eight days later. The certificate
b was formally amended to cover all steps up to trial on 21 January 2002.

   [19] At some unspecified date counsel advised in consultation that 'it was
   deemed essential to commission an up to date medical report'. On 24 January
   2002 the claimant's solicitors wrote:

c   'Our client now has legal aid to enable him to commission a full up to date
         medical report. Particulars of claim were not served with the claim form
         because of the absence of medical evidence, and we intend to ask the court
         to give permission for service of the particulars out of time with medical
         evidence to be served at a later stage when the reports become available. We
         confirm we have instructed Counsel to draft the particulars. Your clients
         have not been prejudiced in any way. There has been a provisional
d   admission of liability subject only to proof of causation, and your clients have
         been well aware of the circumstances at an early stage.'

   [20] The judge commented in these terms:

         'Although there is reference to a medical report and medical evidence, and
e   the application being made for medical evidence apparently to be served
         even later than the particulars, there is not a breath of a hint that what is
         really going on is that they are not satisfied with the evidence of the doctor
         whom the defendants have agreed should be instructed, but are in fact
         instructing another doctor; indeed, the letter would tend to suggest that the
         delay is that they simply require a further report—an up-to-date
f   report—presumably from Dr Gaffney, if that is the only doctor that was
         known about.'

   [21] The letter dated 24 January provoked an understandable response on
   30 January 2002:

g   'According to our client's file you were proposing to instruct Dr Gaffney to
         prepare a medical report as long ago as January 2000. Our clients confirmed
         that they had no objections to you instructing that expert on 6 January 2000.
         Was a report obtained? If not, why not?
         We note that you state that our clients have not been prejudiced in any
h   way. Please confirm how you know that to be the case.
         You will be aware that if this is a multi-track case that our clients are
         entitled to retract an admission of liability. In view of the close relationship
         between the owner of the business and the employee, that may well be the
         case. You should not therefore rely on the pre-proceedings admission when
         drafting the particulars of claim. Mr Price appears to have been in all respects
j   a joint owner of the business and would therefore be as responsible for safety
         as Mrs Price.
         We note that you are preparing an application for permission for service of
         the particulars of claim out of time. We are not prepared to deal with that
         permission ex parte. Please ask for a hearing date with a time estimate of at
         least one hour.'

[22] The letter received no response. A chasing letter ten weeks later received the following terse reply on 16 April:

'We confirm a report was obtained from Dr Gaffney but our medical evidence is not yet finalised and for that reason we are still not ready to proceed. We note your observations regarding liability and the time to be allowed for a hearing of any application.'

[23] On 22 March 2002, nearly three months after receiving the extension to the legal aid certificate and without notifying the defendant's solicitors, the claimant's solicitors had instructed a different consultant rheumatologist (Dr Hazleman) in place of Dr Gaffney. Against this background the judge made the following comment on their letter dated 16 April: 'I am afraid I have to say that that letter comes as close to a blatant lie as one would ever fear to see in litigation correspondence.'

[24] On 29 April Dr Hazleman issued his report, in which he attributed the claimant's continuing back problem, which he described as chronic and disabling, to the accident four years earlier. The claimant's solicitors did not serve his report on the defendant's solicitors when they received it. Instead the latter had to write a further chasing letter on 28 May. This received a stalling reply on 6 June 2002. Eventually on 29 July 2002 the defendant's solicitors accepted service of an application for an extension of time to serve the particulars of claim, accompanied by a witness statement, Dr Hazleman's medical report and a schedule of special damages, which revealed a claim for £548,170.

[25] The service of these documents, four years and three months after the relevant accident, constituted the first notification that the defendant's solicitors had received. (i) That the claimant was saying that he had sustained a chronic and disabling back problem as a result of the accident. (ii) That he had obtained a report from Dr Hazleman in addition to Dr Gaffney. (iii) That Dr Hazleman supported the claimant's claim. (iv) That the claimant was maintaining that but for the accident he would have returned to the kind of management consultancy work he was doing up to 1994 (when he had moved to Cromer with his wife at the age of 40) and would probably have earned at a gross rate of £60,000 a year (instead of £60 a week) for the rest of his working life.

[26] This, then, was the material round which the claimant's application for an extension of time was centred. In my judgment Judge O'Brien was correct to take the view that the order of the deputy district judge should not stand, even if not for the reasons he gave. It is not sufficient for an appeal court in a case of this kind simply to say that the order made in a lower court was wrong, if the case turned on the exercise of a discretion. I explained the governing principles in my judgment in *Tanfern Ltd v Cameron-Macdonald* [2000] 2 All ER 801 at 808–809, [2000] 1 WLR 1311 at 1317 (paras 32–33). Another helpful way of describing the appellate function in relation to judicial discretion is to be found in the judgment of Lord Woolf MR in *Phonographic Performance v AEI Rediffusion Music Ltd* [1999] 2 All ER 299 at 314, [1999] 1 WLR 1507 at 1523:

'Before the court can interfere it must be shown that the judge has either erred in principle in his approach or has left out of account or has taken into account some feature that he should, or should not, have considered, or that his decision was wholly wrong because the court is forced to the conclusion that he has not balanced the various factors fairly in the scale.'

[27] The defect in the approach of the deputy district judge was that he did not address his mind to a number of the most important considerations set out in the checklist in CPR 3.9, so that he exercised his discretion without taking very material matters into account.

[28] Mr Heathcote Williams, who appeared for the defendant, sought to show us that Judge O'Brien did take a lot of the matters set out in CPR 3.9 into account, although he did not structure his judgment, which was given immediately the hearing ended, around that framework. In my judgment, however, there was considerable force in the submission made by Miss Studd, who appeared for the claimant, that his approach to items (h) and (i) on the checklist was either superficial or plainly wrong. These items read: '(h) the effect which the failure to comply has on each party; and (i) the effect which the granting of relief would have on each party.'

[29] It is unnecessary to examine too rigorously the question whether 'the effect of the failure to comply' refers narrowly to the immediate effect of failing to serve particulars of claim within 14 days. The main point which Miss Studd made was that the effect of granting relief would be to allow her client to have access to the court for the trial of his very large claim, which would otherwise be denied to him, whereas the effect on the defendant's side would merely be that her insurers would have the inconvenience of mounting a defence to the claim on issues which were still susceptible of a fair trial, notwithstanding the huge delay. She also argued that any prejudice which might face the defendant's advisers in having to defend this claim once they knew its details would not be significantly greater than those that would have faced them if they had received these details 15 months earlier.

[30] In my judgment the judge's approach was indeed flawed in this respect. He does not appear to have taken into account the fact that the claimant would be barred from prosecuting what was represented as a valid claim for over £½m if he denied him the relief he sought. Although he weighed in the balance the prejudice to the defendant, he did not clearly weigh in the balance the prejudice to the claimant. In these circumstances he left out of account an important feature of the case which he ought to have considered. In the circumstances this court will have to exercise its discretion afresh.

[31] On most of the factors enumerated in the CPR 3.9 checklist, the argument tends strongly in favour of the defendant but not sufficiently to warrant the claimant being denied access to the court completely if this was his first default following the institution of proceedings. Thus—(b) The application for relief was not made promptly. It was made disgracefully late. (c) The failure to serve particulars of claim within the prescribed time was intentional: it was not an inadvertent oversight. (d) There was no good reason for the failure to serve particulars of claim within the prescribed time. The claimant's solicitor told the deputy district judge that the trouble with Dr Gaffney's report was not that it did not support a claim for damages for personal injuries but that it did not support a claim on the scale the claimant wished to present. (e) There had been two flagrant breaches of the pre-action protocol. No particulars of the financial loss nor the claimant's injuries were notified in the letter before action, and the claimant's solicitor entirely departed from the protocol once he or his client were dissatisfied by Dr Gaffney's report. (f) We do not know the extent to which the failure to comply was dictated to the claimant's solicitor by his client.

[32] No point arises about the trial date (g), and I have already explained why it is item (i) rather than item (h) on which our attention should really be focused.

So far as item (h) is concerned, the failure to comply meant that the claimant *a* could no longer proceed with his claim without obtaining the defendant's agreement or a ruling of the court granting him an extension of time, while the defendant was in the converse position that the claim could not proceed against her unless one or other of these events (in reality the second of them) occurred. This is why it is item (i) which is so much more important.

[33] The real tension here, therefore, is between the interests of the *b* administration of justice and the effect which the granting of relief would have on each party. Other relevant considerations tend strongly in favour of the defendant. Can the fact that the claimant is being denied access to the court (with all its art 6(1) implications (art 6(1) of the European Convention for the Protection of Human Rights and Fundamental Freedoms 1950, as set out in Sch 1 to the Human Rights Act 1998)) drive the balance down the other way? *c*

[34] I summarised the effect of relevant Strasbourg jurisprudence in this area when delivering the judgment of the court in *Woodhouse v Consignia plc, Steliou v Compton* [2002] EWCA Civ 275, [2002] 2 All ER 737, [2002] 1 WLR 2558. I said:

'[43] Provided that judges make their decisions in these cases within the general framework provided by rr 3.9 and 1.1, they are unlikely to fall foul of *d* the ECHR in this regard. In *Ashingdane v UK* (1985) 7 EHRR 528 at 546 (para 57), the European Court of Human Rights said:

"Certainly, the right of access to the courts is not absolute but may be subject to limitations; these are permitted by implication since the right of access 'by its very nature calls for regulation by the State, regulation which *e* may vary in time and place according to the needs and resources of the community and of individuals'."

[44] More recently the court emphasised the need for proportionality when it said in *Tinnelly & Sons Ltd v UK* (1998) 4 BHRC 393 at 415 (para 72):

"... a limitation will not be compatible with art 6(1) if it does not pursue a legitimate aim and if there is not a reasonable relationship of proportionality *f* between the means employed and the aim sought to be achieved."'

[35] It follows that if this court considers that a refusal of an extension of time in this case would be a proportionate response to the claimant's failure to state clearly what he is claiming and the reasons underlying his claim, despite so many requests by the defendant's insurers, his convention rights would not thereby be *g* imperilled because the concept of a fair trial betokens fairness to both sides.

[36] The interests of the administration of justice can best be identified in the present context by reference to CPR Pt 1. CPR 1.1(2) carries within it the ideas that justice will best be achieved if: (a) the parties are on an equal footing; (b) unnecessary expense is avoided; (c) a case is handled in a way that is *h* proportionate to the matters listed; (d) a case is dealt with expeditiously and fairly; and (e) an appropriate share of the court's resources is allocated to it.

[37] By CPR 1.3 a claimant is required to help the court to further the overriding objective of being able to deal with his case justly. By CPR 1.4 the court is under a duty to further the overriding objective by managing the case *j* actively.

[38] In his seminal judgment in *Biguzzi v Rank Leisure plc* [1999] 4 All ER 934, [1999] 1 WLR 1926 Lord Woolf MR made it clear that the new Civil Procedure Rules had ushered in a new regime, and that it was no longer useful to look back at decisions under the pre-CPR regime because that was a different regime. We no longer have to succumb feebly to the argument that a defendant was already

a so prejudiced that any further prejudice caused by a further long delay could not
be regarded as significant. On an occasion like this we have to look objectively at
the extent to which the defendant would be prejudiced if the case was allowed to
continue, whether on the enlarged basis for which the claimant is now
contending or at all, and then consider whether and the extent to which the
claimant's cumulative defaults have caused that prejudice. Our final duty is to
b decide whether it would be a disproportionate response to stop the case now by
refusing the extension of time outright, or whether it may be possible to fashion
a more proportionate response.

[39] In her respondent's notice the defendant (in reality her insurers)
articulated clearly the ways in which they would be prejudiced if the claim would
be allowed to proceed. They say that the claimant's conduct has deprived them
c of the opportunity to investigate at an early stage matters where documents may
well be incomplete, lost or inapplicable, and where the recollection of former
employers, colleagues and administrators may be crucial. They split their
arguments into two parts. In the first they identified not only the issue whether
the claimant had complained of back trouble prior to the incident at work
d (bearing in mind that complaints are not always made to doctors) but also how
successful he had been in his management consultancy type work, and why he
had left it, allegedly to take a job as his wife's shop assistant at £60 per week. In
the second they identified questions relating to the conduct of the Poppyland
Headwear business: who was its true proprietor (and the employer), why this
business failed (if it did), and whether the claimant had ever expressed any
e intention or plan of returning to management consultancy type work in due
course.

[40] It is obvious that the parties are not on an equal footing now. All these
matters are within the knowledge of the claimant. The defendant's insurers have
to start investigating them now, long after the claimant should have explained his
f claim to them. It is also obvious that the case cannot now be dealt with
expeditiously. Nor will it be so easy to deal with it fairly in the light of the delay
that has occurred.

[41] The claimant is in serious default in relation to his duty to help the court
to deal with his case fairly. He has also made it impossible for it to manage the
case actively because until he served his particulars of claim and the defendant
g responded to it, there was nothing for the court to manage. Although it would
have been open to the defendant's solicitors to incur the expense of seeking
directions from the court, as suggested by Chadwick LJ in *Totty*'s case, they were
certainly not obliged to incur this expense, especially where the claimant's
solicitors were holding them at bay with statements which turned out to be some
h way distant from the whole truth.

[42] In my judgment this is a case in which this court has to say 'enough is
enough', and like the judge (though for different reasons) to refuse the extension
of time sought, unless it were possible to impose conditions on any order for an
extension. There are just too many considerations pointing in favour of the
j defendant to allow the claimant's right of access to a court for the purpose of
prosecuting his enlarged claim to trump those considerations on the facts of this
case. It is not only that he (or his advisers) failed to comply with the pre-action
protocol, and that he (or they) failed to serve the particulars of claim within the
time prescribed by the rules or to answer the questions asked of them often more
than once. It is also that the defendant's insurers (and, in turn, their solicitors)
acted impeccably throughout this history in seeking the information they needed

to evaluate the claim properly with a view to resolving it, if possible, without the
need for the expense of court proceedings at all. In other words, they complied
with their CPR 1.3 duty: the claimant did not. The result was that the court was
deprived of the opportunity of managing the case actively in pursuance of the
overriding objective by reason of the claimant's defaults, and it would not now
be possible to deal with the case in a manner that is fair to both sides if the court
simply extended time unconditionally.

[43] There is, however, a route available by which the court could do effective
justice to both sides. The operation of CPR 3.1(2)(a) and 3.1(3)(a) give the court
power to extend time for compliance with a rule subject to conditions. In *Walsh v
Misseldine* (29 February 2000, unreported) this court made effective use of this
power, which needs to be more widely used on appropriate occasions.

[44] In that case the claimant was claiming damages for injuries suffered in
1989 in a very serious road traffic accident. His claim was pursued effectively, if
very slowly, until 1994, but a four-year delay then ensued. The claimant then
sought to enlarge his claim greatly by introducing a lot of new issues of which the
defendant's insurers had no notice when they calculated the value of the claim in
the early 1990s for the purposes of a payment into court. Four paragraphs in my
judgment (with which Stuart-Smith LJ agreed) are relevant in the present
context:

> '86. It is also quite clear that it would not be possible or fair to conduct a
> trial of the additional issues Mr Walsh's advisers sought to introduce into his
> case in August 1999. Their predecessors had had their opportunity to set out
> his case in 1993 and early 1994, and they did not take it. It would be wrong
> to allow them to amend their schedule of loss now to include a whole lot of
> new issues dating back over the previous seven years. In my judgment the
> defendant's insurers were entitled to say that it would be unjust to expose
> them now to an inquiry into the reasons why Mr Walsh was made redundant
> in June 1992 and to a claim that any loss of income he sustained after that
> time must be ascribed to the effects of his 1989 accident ...
>
> 89. In deciding what order to make on the defendant's application, we now
> apply a new procedural code which was designed with the overriding
> objective of enabling us to deal with the case justly. So far as practicable, we
> must ensure that it is dealt with fairly.
>
> 90. It would not be fair to expose the defendant now to a claim which
> incorporates all the additional items the claimant sought to introduce into it
> for the first time in August 1999. On the other hand, since his claim, as
> formulated at the time the court gave directions in January 1994, could still
> be justly assessed today, it would not be fair to dismiss his action altogether.
> This would entail permitting the negligent defendant to retrieve all the
> money his insurers paid into court, ordering repayment of the interim
> payments made between 1991 and 1993, and directing the claimant to pay
> the defendant his costs of the entire action, as District Judge Rhodes ordered
> on 22 June 1999. This type of order had to be made under the former "all or
> nothing" regime. It is no longer obligatory to make such an order today, if
> it would be unjust to do so.
>
> 91. In my judgment, it would not be just to strike out this statement of case
> under CPR 3.4(2) in these circumstances. By the same token, it would not
> be just to allow the claimant to enlarge his pleading or his schedule of special
> damages in any way, or to allow him to serve a witness statement or to give

a   any evidence which goes in any way beyond what he is reported to have told his doctors and the other medical experts in the reports which culminated in Mr Shepherd's report in 1994 (if the defendant wishes to rely on that undisclosed report). He may of course rely on his pleaded case, which will sound in general damages, that by reason of his injuries he is at a disadvantage on the open labour market. The action should be allowed to
b   proceed to trial on that basis, and subject to the condition, which will form part of the order of this court, that the judge assesses the compensation which would have been payable to Mr Walsh at a trial conducted on 15 March 1995 and that he is not entitled to any interest on those damages between that date and the date of this court's order allowing his appeal.'

c   [45] It appears to me that it is possible to adopt a similar approach in the present case. It is very important that this court should not relax the disciplinary framework created by the CPR in a case like this. On the other hand to bar the claimant from pursuing his claim as it stood in April 2001, when the particulars of claim should have been served, would be a disproportionate response and would give the defendant's insurers an unjustified windfall.

d   [46] I would therefore allow this appeal by extending the time for the service of the particulars of claim on condition that no claim is made for special or general damages other than what may be substantiated by any pre-April 2001 written report by Dr Gaffney which the claimant may care to disclose in support of his claim. The court will hear counsel as to the precise wording of the requisite
e   condition. The order for costs made by the circuit judge should stand, and I would direct that the claimant pay the defendant the costs of this appeal (on the usual public funding terms), such costs to be available for set-off against any damages the claimant may recover in this action. If the claimant wishes to proceed with his claim on this condition, the particulars of claim must be filed by 24 July 2003 (28 days from the date this judgment is handed down).

f

Appeal allowed.

Kate O'Hanlon   Barrister.

Hourigan v Secretary of State for Work and Pensions

[2002] EWCA Civ 1890

COURT OF APPEAL, CIVIL DIVISION

AULD, BROOKE AND SEDLEY LJJ

18 NOVEMBER, 19 DECEMBER 2002

Social security – Income support – Capital limit – Calculation of capital – Income support claimant and another sharing beneficial interest in property as tenants in common in unequal shares – Whether claimant should be treated in calculating value of her capital assets as entitled to beneficial half share in property – Income Support (General) Regulations 1987, reg 52.

The claimant was the legal owner of her house and she and her son were tenants in common in equity in shares of one-sixth and five-sixths respectively. Regulation 52[a] of the Income Support (General) Regulations 1987 provided that where a person claiming income support and one or more other persons were beneficially entitled in possession to any capital asset, they should be treated for the purposes of valuing capital for income support as if they were entitled to the beneficial interest in the capital asset in equal shares. In 1993, when the claimant moved into a residential home, the value of the house was £27,000. Shortly after her move, her income support was terminated on the basis that she possessed capital in excess of £8,000 and therefore did not qualify for income support. On appeal, the Social Security Appeal Tribunal determined that for the purposes of her claim for income support she had an equal half-share in the value of the house. The social security commissioner allowed the claimant's appeal from the tribunal's decision, holding that at all material times the value of her capital had been less than £8,000. The Secretary of State appealed. The issue on the appeal was whether, on the proper interpretation of reg 52, the claimant was to be deemed, artificially, to have been the beneficial owner of half the property.

Held – The natural effect of reg 52 was to treat that unity of interest which was a necessary feature of a joint tenancy as severed, and to treat a claimant as if he or she were entitled to an equal share (with the others) of the whole beneficial interest. With a tenancy in common, however, there was no need to treat a claimant's unity of interest as if it had been severed. A beneficial interest which a claimant owned as a tenant in common was an asset separately disposable by him or her. In the instant case, the son's five-sixths beneficial interest in his mother's house, and her one-sixth interest, represented separate capital assets of which each had been free to dispose in those shares. It was easy to see why Parliament had used the language of reg 52 to enable the Secretary of State to make sensible arrangements governing the treatment of capital held in a joint tenancy. It was unnecessary to conclude that by the use of those words an intention had to be attributed to Parliament to the effect that it contemplated the making of regulations that were manifestly unfair. The Secretary of State's appeal would, therefore, be dismissed (see [16]–[18], [24]–[26], [28], [31], below).

---

a Regulation 52, so far as material, is set out at [12], below

a **Notes**
For the capital limit for income support and capital jointly held, see 44(2)
Halsbury's Laws (4th edn reissue), paras 194, 197.

Cases referred to in judgments
Chief Adjudication Officer v Palfrey [1995] 11 LS Gaz R 39, CA.
b *R v Chesterfield BC, ex p Fullwood* [1994] 2 FCR 158, CA.
Social Security Decision CIS 7097/95, Tribunal of Comrs.
Social Security Decision CIS 3283/97, Tribunal of Comrs.

Cases referred to in skeleton arguments
Dennis v McDonald [1982] 1 All ER 590, [1982] Fam 63, [1982] 2 WLR 275, CA.
c *Gartside v IRC* [1968] 1 All ER 121, [1968] AC 553, [1968] 2 WLR 277, HL.
Leeves v Chief Adjudication Officer [1999] ELR 90, CA.
Pearson v IRC [1980] 2 All ER 479, [1981] AC 753, [1980] 2 WLR 872, HL.
*R (on the application of Alconbury Developments Ltd) v Secretary of State for
    Environment, Transport and the Regions* [2001] UKHL 23, [2001] 2 All ER 929, 2
d   WLR 1389.
Wilkinson v Chief Adjudication Officer [2000] 2 FCR 82, CA.

Appeal
The Secretary of State for Work and Pensions appealed from the decision of
A Lloyd-Davies, sitting as a social security commissioner, on 15 October 2001,
e allowing the appeal of James Hourigan, on behalf of his mother, Mary Hourigan
(deceased) (the claimant) from the decision of a Social Security Appeal Tribunal
on 8 June 1998 determining that the claimant had had an equal half share in the
value of her house, which exceeded the capital limit of £8,000 and that she
therefore did not qualify for income support. The facts are set out in the
f judgment of Brooke LJ.

John Howell QC and *Kate Gallafent* (instructed by *Child Poverty Action Group*) for the
    claimant.
Nathalie Lieven (instructed by the *Solicitor to the Department of Work and Pensions*)
    for the Secretary of State.

g   *Cur adv vult*

19 December 2002. The following judgments were delivered.

BROOKE LJ.
h [1] This is an appeal by the Secretary of State from a decision of
Mr Commissioner Lloyd-Davies, sitting as a social security commissioner, on 15
October 2001 whereby he allowed the claimant's appeal from a decision of a
Social Security Appeal Tribunal on 8 June 1998 which had determined that the
deceased claimant Mrs Mary Hourigan had an equal half-share in the value of her
j house at 53 Lake Road, Stalybridge and therefore did not qualify for income
support. The commissioner substituted a determination that at all material times
the value of her capital was less than £8,000.
[2] The underlying facts of the case are very straightforward. Mrs Hourigan
had bought her home from the local authority with the help of her son James
who contributed five-sixths of the purchase price. In 1993 the value of the house
was £27,000. In March of that year she moved from her home to a residential

home because she was becoming increasingly frail, and she stayed at that _a_
residential home until her death in August 1997.

[3] At all material times her son James has acted as his mother's appointee, and
he has continued to pursue her appeal after her death. Her income support was
terminated in June 1993, soon after her move, on the basis that she possessed
capital in excess of £8,000. A lengthy series of appeals culminated in the matter
being remitted to the appeal tribunal which on 8 June 1998 made the findings of _b_
fact which I have incorporated into this judgment. It is the appeal tribunal's
finding of law which has been the subject of the appeals first to the commissioner
and then to this court.

[4] The effect of the appeal tribunal's decision was that Mrs Hourigan was the
legal owner of 53 Lake Road and that she and her son James owned the beneficial
interest in that property as tenants in common in a ratio of 1:5. The question of _c_
law we have to determine is whether on the proper interpretation of reg 52 of the
Income Support (General) Regulations 1987, SI 1987/1967 Mrs Hourigan is to be
deemed, artificially, to have been the beneficial owner of half the property. If she
is, then her capital at the material time would have exceeded £8,000 and it would
have been correct to refuse her income support after her move to the residential _d_
home.

[5] Miss Lieven, who appears for the Secretary of State, argues that this is the
correct result. Mr John Howell QC, who appears for the claimant, submits that
reg 52 of the 1987 regulations does not have this artificial effect when the
beneficial interests in property are owned by tenants in common. Alternatively, _e_
he submits that reg 52 is ultra vires.

[6] For the purposes of resolving this dispute it is necessary only to consider a
few sections of the Social Security Contribution and Benefits Act 1992 which are
all included in Pt VII of that Act (entitled 'Income-Related Benefits'), and a few of
the 1987 regulations.

[7] Section 124 of the 1992 Act provides, so far as is material: _f_

'(1) A person in Great Britain is entitled to income support if—(a) he is of
or over the age of 16; (b) he has no income or his income does not exceed the
applicable amount; (c) he is not engaged in remunerative work ...

(4) ... where a person is entitled to income support, then—(a) if he has no
income, the amount shall be the applicable amount; and (b) if he has income, _g_
the amount shall be the difference between his income and the applicable
amount.'

[8] Section 134(1) provides: 'No person shall be entitled to an income-related
benefit if his capital or a prescribed part of it exceeds the prescribed amount.' _h_

[9] Section 135(1) provides:

'The applicable amount, in relation to any income-related benefit, shall be
such amount or the aggregate of such amounts as may be prescribed in
relation to that benefit.'
_j_

[10] Section 136 provides, so far as is material:

'(2) Regulations may provide that capital not exceeding the amount
prescribed under section 134(1) above but exceeding a prescribed lower
amount, shall be treated, to a prescribed extent, as if it were income of a
prescribed amount.

a
(3) Income and capital shall be calculated or estimated in such manner as may be prescribed ...

(5) Circumstances may be prescribed in which—(a) a person is treated as possessing capital or income which he does not possess; (b) capital or income which a person does possess is to be disregarded ...'

b
[11] The basic rules for valuing capital for the purposes of income support are contained in regs 49 and 50 of the 1987 regulations. In particular reg 49 provides:

'Capital which a claimant possesses in the United Kingdom shall be calculated—(a) except in [the case of a National Savings Certificate], at its current market or surrender value, less—(i) where there would be expenses attributable to sale, 10 per cent; and (ii) the amount of any encumbrance secured on it ...'

c

[12] Regulation 52, which is at the centre of this appeal, provides:

'Except where a claimant possesses capital which is disregarded under regulation 51(4) (notional capital) where a claimant and one or more persons are beneficially entitled in possession to any capital asset they shall be treated as if each of them were entitled in possession to the whole beneficial interest therein in an equal share and the foregoing provisions of this Chapter shall apply for the purposes of calculating the amount of capital which the claimant is treated as possessing as if it were actual capital which the claimant does possess.'

d

e
[13] Regulation 51 provides that a claimant is to be treated as possessing capital of which he has deprived himself for the purposes of obtaining income support. Regulation 53 provides for a claimant to be ascribed a tariff income for each amount of capital taken into account.

f
[14] In *Chief Adjudication Officer v Palfrey* [1995] 11 LS Gaz R 39 this court interpreted reg 52 as meaning that a claimant to whom the regulation applied was to be treated as possessing a particular amount of capital (namely, an entitlement in possession to an equal share in the whole beneficial interest), and that the value of that share was to be calculated at its current market value in accordance with reg 49. The court rejected a contention by the Secretary of State

g
to the effect that reg 52 required the whole beneficial interest to be valued, disregarding the existence of the shares in it and their consequences, and for the claimant to be treated as possessing an equal share of that value.

[15] The critical words in reg 52 which fall for interpretation on this appeal are the words—

h
'*where a claimant and one or more persons are beneficially entitled in possession to any capital asset they shall be treated as if each of them were entitled in possession to the whole beneficial interest therein in an equal share* ...' (My emphasis.)

j
It was common ground on the hearing of the appeal that the words 'entitled in possession' were to be contrasted with 'entitled in expectancy' or 'entitled in reversion'. They can therefore be ignored for the purposes of the problem we have been asked to resolve.

[16] The language of reg 52 lends itself naturally to a situation in which two or more people are jointly entitled to the equitable interest in the same capital asset. They do not each possess a separate share in the equitable interest. They are

jointly invested with the whole of that interest together with the other joint tenants. If there are two joint tenants and one dies, the other is solely entitled by survivorship to the whole beneficial interest. Unity of interest is a necessary feature of a joint tenancy. The natural effect of reg 52 is therefore to treat that unity of interest as severed, and to treat the claimant as if he/she was entitled to an equal share (with the others) of the whole beneficial interest. Thus he/she is to be treated as possessing what he/she does not in fact possess (see s 136(5)(b) of the 1992 Act).

[17] With tenancies in common, there is no need to treat a claimant's unity of interest as if it had been severed for the purpose of computing fairly the capital he/she owns for the purposes of Pt VII of the 1992 Act. As Mr Commissioner PL Howell QC observed (in *Social Security Decision CIS 7097/95*), a beneficial interest which a claimant owns as a tenant in common is an asset separately disposable by him/her, both in English and Scots law. In that case the claimant was not beneficially entitled to nearly 75% of the money, derived from her husband's National Savings, which had only been paid into their joint bank account as a convenience in order to enable their daughter to pay his nursing home bills by direct debit. If this money of his had been paid into a building society account, or a bank account, in his own name, there could have been no suggestion that his wife was entitled to a beneficial interest in half of it.

[18] Similarly, on the facts of the present case, the son's five-sixth beneficial interest in his mother's house, and his mother's one-sixth interest, represented separate capital assets of which each was free to dispose in those shares. It would be a misuse of language to say that the two of them were beneficially entitled to the house within the meaning of reg 52: they were not.

[19] Miss Lieven, in her admirable submissions on behalf of the Secretary of State, called in aid administrative convenience in support of the interpretation for which she contended. She told us that the Department of Work and Pensions' staff do not necessarily have legal acumen, and administrative convenience demands a statutory code which is reasonably simple to administer. When a court has to identify the ownership of beneficial interests between competing parties, it has some hope of reaching a 'true' solution because each party is keen that the court should attribute the maximum interest to their own share. Inside the statutory scheme created by Pt VII of the 1992 Act, on the other hand, there is no such incentive, and experience, she tells us, has showed that the members of a family habitually attribute as low a value as is realistically possible for a claimant's share in shared property in order to maximise the chances of him/her qualifying for an income-related benefit.

[20] Miss Lieven told us that social security benefits staff are not customarily concerned with divided shares in corn or oil or in the other commodities which the members of the court, drawing on their memories of the Roman law concepts of commixtio or confusio, put to her during the course of argument. In the real world of social security she said that it is the ownership of shares in a business, or a house, or money that gives rise to questions of this kind. Those instructing her thought that no difficulties had arisen under this aspect of reg 52 until the *Social Security Decision CIS 7097/95* in February 1997. Claimants and their representatives had seemingly been content to allow a claimant's share to be treated for the purposes of this regulation as a half, or a third, or a quarter, or as the case may be, depending on the number of other parties also entitled to a share.

[21] However that may be, the issue has now been raised and a just answer to

a it must be found.   Justice is not always the handmaiden of administrative convenience.   In my judgment it would need very much clearer words in the regulation if a court were to be constrained to interpret it in the unfair way for which the Secretary of State contends.   There is, in my judgment, great force in the submission by Mr John Howell, who appeared for Mr Hourigan, in his

b skeleton argument:

> '22. Regulation 52 may only apply to require a person to be treated as if he is entitled in possession to an equal share of the whole beneficial interest when in fact he is not so entitled. The obvious case (if the regulation applies to a tenancy in common as the Secretary of State contends) is where
>
> *c* individuals have different shares in the beneficial interest.   For example, whether a claimant owned only 5% or 95% of the equitable interest, in either case he would be treated as owning 50% of the whole equitable interest if there is only one other person also beneficially entitled in possession to a share.   But he would be treated as owning 33% if two others are involved; 25% if three other are; 20% if four other are; and so on.   There is no rational
>
> *d* reason in the context of income support why a claimant should be deemed to possess so much more than he actually has and no rational reason why, given the same actual share, the amount that the claimant is deemed to have should depend on the number of others with a share regardless of their actual interest.   Indeed the latter would be a standing invitation to abuse.   Nor is it
>
> *e* rational, if the number of others involved may be relevant, for those who have an interest in the same equitable interest otherwise than beneficially in possession (such as those interested in it in reversion) to be ignored.
>
> 23. As Mr Commissioner Howell observed [in *Social Security Decision CIS 7097/95*], the result of the Secretary of State's interpretation would be to make the system "a lottery ... producing arbitrary answers (on some facts
>
> *f* unjustly in favour of claimants, on others against)" and that "the injustice and absurdity" was "obvious".'

[22] We have had the opportunity of considering the decision of Mr Commissioner Goodman in *Social Security Decision CIS 3283/97* (Appendix to linked cases, at paras 16–18).   At the end of this decision he adopted the

g interpretation of reg 52 for which the Secretary of State is now contending. He considered that the regulation applied to all kinds of co-ownership because its language was broad enough to cover both joint tenants and tenancies in common.   He called in aid of this interpretation the heading to reg 52 ('Capital jointly held') and the reference to 'the other joint owners' of a dwelling which

h appeared, fleetingly, in a 1995 amendment to reg 52.   (He was to declare the regulation, as amended, to be ultra vires, and it has now reverted to its original form.)   He said he did not think it necessary, desirable or practicable to try to distinguish between the various kinds of co-ownership, and if this meant that an owner of an undivided share was regarded as possessing a greater share than in

j fact he did, then that was in his view an inescapable result of the application of reg 52.

[23] For my part, I do not consider that such an interpretation of reg 52 is inescapable.   In *R v Chesterfield BC, ex p Fullwood* [1994] 2 FCR 158 at 161 Hoffmann LJ observed that there was no ordinary and generally understood meaning of the words 'jointly occupied', and that the ordinary speaker of English would probably say that he thought one should ask a lawyer to ascertain what

these words meant in the context of a statutory regulation. So, too, with the words 'capital jointly held'. A lawyer would furnish the answer given by Mr Commissioner Howell.

[24] Miss Lieven argued that Parliament must have contemplated such a potentially unfair and unreasonable result when it empowered the Secretary of State to prescribe circumstances in which a person was to be treated as possessing capital which he did not possess. It is easy to see why Parliament used that language to enable the Secretary of State to make sensible arrangements governing the treatment of capital held in a joint tenancy. It is unnecessary to conclude that by the use of these words an intention must be attributed to Parliament to the effect that it contemplated the making of regulations which were manifestly unfair. The intention of this statutory scheme is that people should be expected to dip into their capital rather than be reliant on the state for income support. Why should Parliament have expected people to dip into capital which they did not in fact possess? Miss Lieven did not give us any answer other than that encapsulated in the words 'administrative convenience'.

[25] For these reasons I would dismiss this appeal. It is not therefore necessary to consider Mr John Howell's alternative argument for Mr Hourigan, namely that reg 52 is ultra vires if it has to be interpreted in the manner for which the Secretary of State contends.

SEDLEY LJ.

[26] I agree with Brooke LJ's conclusion that this appeal should be dismissed. But since a fresh regulation may well follow our judgment, I will set out my reasons, which are not quite the same as his.

[27] First, I am not persuaded that reg 52 of the Income Support (General) Regulations 1987, SI 1987/1967 even meets the purpose of administrative convenience which is the foundation of Miss Lieven's case. It does not relieve officials of the Department of Work and Pensions of the sometimes extremely difficult task of deciding whether property is held in shares at all, for if it is not, the regulation does not apply. What it does is cut out the often relatively easy sequel of deciding what the respective shares are.

[28] Secondly, it replaces the true share with a crude calculation which, as Brooke LJ has shown, can be both a source of real unfairness and an incentive to create multiple shares, perhaps spuriously, in order to drive up the divisor and so drive down the imputed value of the claimant's interest. Even in relation to honest arrangements, in fact, the regulation can be counter-productive—notably where the claimant's true share is greater than her deemed share. Thus if a house worth £45,000 is shared as to 50% by the claimant and as to 10% by each of her five children, her real share of £22,500 will be deemed to be a one-sixth share worth £7,500, making her artificially eligible for income support. Such an outcome is unfair not only to other claimants, including people like the present respondent, but to the public who provide the funds.

[29] We have been shown no real need for such an erratic device. Where the Secretary of State is satisfied that there is a genuine division of shares, there can be no difficulty in giving effect to it. Where he is not, it may well be that a default allocation of deemed equal shares is reasonable and practicable. But nothing like this has been attempted in reg 52 of the 1987 regulations as it now stands.

[30] The relevance of the foregoing considerations is not that reg 52 could be a much sharper and fairer instrument than it is. That is a question solely for the Secretary of State. It is that Miss Lieven cannot, in spite of her admirable

a endeavours, establish the breadth of meaning for which she contends on grounds either of administrative convenience (since the regulation largely misses out on this) or of abuse prevention (since it draws in honest as well as devious arrangements). We are left with a power granted by Parliament which, for the reasons set out by Brooke LJ, cannot be held to have contemplated such an arbitrary form of implementation. To read it down as the commissioner has *b* done is enough to protect Mrs Hourigan. The question of vires remains unaddressed.

AULD LJ.

[**31**] I agree that the appeal should be dismissed for the reasons given by Brooke and Sedley LJJ.

c [**32**] Regulation 52 of the Income Support (General) Regulations 1987, SI 1987/1967 does not apply to this case—one of a tenancy in common where the tenant has no unity of beneficial interest with another or others in the capital in question. It applies only to a joint tenancy where there is such unity of interest *and* where the entitlement of the claimant is, or may, not be equal to that of the *d* other joint tenant or tenants. In such a case it operates to sever the unity of interest and to treat the claimant as if he were entitled to an equal share with the other or others of the whole beneficial interest.

[**33**] Such an interpretation accords with the plain legal meaning of the words used by the Parliamentary draftsman, who must be taken to have had in mind the distinction between a tenancy in common and a joint tenancy. I see no reason *e* why, in this context, the words should be given any other meaning. The clear intention of the provision was to simplify the administrative task of assessing the value of a claimant's interest in jointly held property for the purpose of determining his entitlement to income support. No doubt, it was considered that the exercise of identifying the relative sizes of shares for this purpose would be *f* less difficult in the case of tenancies in common.

[**34**] As Sedley LJ has pointed out, reg 52 of the 1987 regulations, in deeming an equal apportionment in cases of joint tenancy, can produce injustice either way—as it also could in cases of a tenancy in common if it applied to it. Whatever the strengths and failings of the device as an aid to administrative convenience, prevention of abuse or overall fairness in application, they do not, in my view, *g* support the interpretation for which the Secretary of State contends.

Appeal dismissed.

Kate O'Hanlon   Barrister.

Wong v Parkside Health NHS Trust and another

[2001] EWCA Civ 1721

COURT OF APPEAL, CIVIL DIVISION

BROOKE, HALE LJJ AND DAVID STEEL J

25, 26 OCTOBER, 16 NOVEMBER 2001

Tort – Intentional infliction of harm – Claimant having brought private prosecution for assault – Whether claimant entitled to rely on assault to found claim for intentional infliction of harm – Offences Against the Person Act 1861, s 45.

Tort – Harassment – Whether intentional infliction of harassment tort at common law.

The claimant was employed by the first defendant NHS Trust from January 1995. She worked in the same office as the second defendant and another worker. Her fellow workers were rude and unfriendly; they criticised her, locked her out of the office, interfered with her desk and personal effects and hid things that she needed. In February the second defendant threatened the claimant with reprisals from an ex-convict if she told their employer about the second defendant's absences from work. The second defendant was involved in setting off the claimant's car alarm and frightening her by throwing an object against her office window. In March the second defendant assaulted the claimant. The claimant went on sick leave after the assault and remained absent until her employment was terminated. She brought a private prosecution against the second defendant who was convicted of common assault in October 1995. The claimant was diagnosed as suffering physical and psychiatric injuries due to harassment and stress at her place of work. In March 1998 she brought proceedings against both defendants. Her claim against the first defendant was based on negligence and upon its vicarious liability for the torts of its employees. The claim against the second defendant was based upon 'the tort of intentional harassment'. The second defendant applied to strike out the claim against her. The judge granted her application, and adjourned the claim against the first defendant, holding (i) that before the enactment of the Protection from Harassment Act 1997, which had put the law of harassment on a statutory basis, there had been no common law tort of harassment; and (ii) that the complaints made against the second defendant could not amount to the tort of intentional infliction of harm. In reaching that decision he had excluded the assault on the claimant from consideration because s 45[a] of the Offences against the Person Act 1861 provided, inter alia, that a person who had been convicted of assault should be released from all further or other proceedings, civil or criminal, for the same cause. The judge had also excluded the threat of reprisals made by the second defendant because the claimant had conceded to him that it had not been the cause of her trauma. The claimant appealed.

Held – (1) The effect of s 45 of the 1861 Act was that a victim of an assault who had brought a private prosecution could not rely upon the assault in any other

---

a   Section 45, so far as material, is set out at [14], below

a proceedings. The judge had therefore been right to exclude it from his consideration of whether the second defendant's conduct was of a nature which was sufficiently likely to result in harm to the claimant that an intention to produce harm could be imputed to her. The claimant had conceded that the threat made by the second defendant had not caused her illness. The remaining catalogue of rudeness and unfriendliness was not behaviour so calculated to
b infringe her legal right to personal safety that an intention to do so should be imputed to the second defendant (see [13], [16], [17], below).

(2) Before the 1997 Act came into force the common law had not reached the point of recognising a tort of intentional harassment going beyond the tort of intentional infliction of harm. The appeal would accordingly be dismissed (see [29]–[31], below).

c

Notes
For the tort of intentional physical harm and the effect of conviction for common assault, see 45(2) *Halsbury's Laws* (4th edn reissue) para 456 and 11(1) *Halsbury's Laws* (4th edn reissue) para 502 respectively.
d   For the Offences against the Person Act 1861, s 45, see 12 *Halsbury's Statutes* (4th edn) (2002 reissue) 117.

Cases referred to in judgment
Burnett v George [1993] 1 FCR 1012, CA.
Burris v Azadani [1995] 4 All ER 802, [1995] 1 WLR 1372, CA.
e *Davis v Johnson* [1978] 1 All ER 1132, [1979] AC 264, [1978] 2 WLR 553, HL.
Donoghue v Stevenson [1932] AC 562, [1932] All ER Rep 1, HL.
Horner v Horner [1982] 2 All ER 495, [1982] Fam 90, [1982] 2 WLR 914, CA.
Hunter v Canary Wharf Ltd [1997] 2 All ER 426, [1997] AC 655, [1997] 2 WLR 684, HL.
f *Janvier v Sweeney* [1919] 2 KB 316, [1918–19] All ER Rep 1056, CA.
Khorasandjian v Bush [1993] 3 All ER 669, [1993] QB 727, [1993] 3 WLR 476, CA.
Masper v Brown (1876) 1 CPD 97.
News Group Newspapers Ltd v Society of Graphical and Allied Trades '82 (No 2) [1987] ICR 181.
Patel v Patel [1988] 2 FLR 179, CA.
g *Pidduck v Molloy* [1992] 1 FCR 418, CA.
Thomas v National Union of Mineworkers (South Wales Area) [1985] 2 All ER 1, [1986] Ch 20, [1985] 2 WLR 1081.
Wilkinson v Downton [1897] 2 QB 57, [1895–9] All ER Rep 267.

h ### Cases referred to in skeleton arguments
Clark v Canada [1994] 3 FC 323, Can Fed Ct.
Hicks v Chief Constable of the South Yorkshire Police [1992] 2 All ER 65, HL.
Lau v DPP [2000] Crim LR 580, DC.
Motherwell v Motherwell (1976) 73 DLR (3d) 62, Alta SC.
j *Page v Smith* [1995] 2 All ER 736, [1996] AC 155, [1995] 2 WLR 644, HL.

Appeal
The claimant, Minna Wong, an employee of the first defendant, Parkside Health NHS Trust, appealed with permission of the Court of Appeal (Brooke and Rix LJJ) granted on 21 December 2000 from the order of Mr Recorder Talbot QC on 14 December 1999 in the Mayor's and City of London County Court striking

out her claim against the second defendant, Susan Mullins, an employee of the
first defendant, for harassment and intentional infliction of harm. The facts are *a*
set out in the judgment of the court.

Matthew Chapman (instructed through the *Bar Pro Bono Unit*) for the appellant.
John Greenbourne (instructed by *Hammond Bale*) for the defendants.

Cur adv vult *b*

16 November 2001. The following judgment of the court was delivered.

HALE LJ.
[1] This is the judgment of the court in an appeal against the order of *c*
Mr Recorder Talbot QC, made on 14 December 1999 in the Mayor's and City of
London County Court, striking out the appellant's claim against the second
defendant. The appellant complained of a campaign of harassment against her in
1995 by three fellow employees and an inadequate response by the first defendant
employers. The second defendant is one of those three employees. The issues *d*
raised are: (1) the precise scope of the tort of intentionally causing harm under the
principle in *Wilkinson v Downton* [1897] 2 QB 57, [1895–9] All ER Rep 267 and
(2) whether there was a tort of harassment at common law before the Protection
from Harassment Act 1997 came into force.
[2] The appellant was employed as a wheelchair administrator by the first
defendant NHS Trust from 3 January 1995. She worked in the same office as the *e*
second defendant, Susan Mullins, and another employee, Josie Lucas. Also there
at the beginning was a temporary worker, Carmel Woods, who had applied
unsuccessfully for the appellant's position but was now charged with explaining
the work to the appellant. The appellant's case was that Susan Mullins and Josie
Lucas believed that Carmel Woods should have got the job and were extremely
rude and unfriendly to her from the start. Carmel Woods did not explain the *f*
work properly to her. They criticised her for arriving on time, told her that she
had not mastered the job and should leave, locked her out of the office, interfered
with her desk and personal effects, and hid things that she needed. On
20 February 1995 the second defendant threatened her with reprisals from an
ex-convict if she told their employers about the second defendant's absences. On *g*
9 March 1995 she was assaulted by the second defendant, who had also been
responsible, with Josie Lucas, for setting off her car alarm and frightening her by
throwing something against the office window. In all, out of 22 particulars of
harassment, 13 applied to the second defendant, although in three further
incidents of interference with the appellant's property the perpetrator was *h*
unknown.
[3] The appellant went on sick leave after the assault and remained absent
until her employment was terminated in August 1996. She brought a private
prosecution for assault against the second defendant. On 9 October 1995, in
Ealing Magistrates' Court, the second defendant was convicted of common
assault, conditionally discharged and ordered to pay £75 compensation and £250 *j*
costs.
[4] These proceedings were brought on 6 March 1998. The claim against the
first defendant employers was based on negligence and upon their vicarious
liability for the torts of their employees. The claim against the second defendant
was based upon the 'tort of intentional harassment, for which she is liable for the

a foreseeable consequences' (see the amended particulars of claim). It was claimed that the appellant had suffered both physical and psychiatric injuries. Appended to the claim was a report from Dr Elizabeth Tylden, a retired consultant psychiatrist, diagnosing—

b 'chronic post-traumatic stress reaction due to harassment and stress at her place of work with a series of stressful incidents culminating in an assault. Severe disability in arm function due to residual physical and dissociative effects of trauma as specified in F43 and F44 of ICD–10 (the World Health Organisation's *International Statistical Classification of Diseases and Related Health Problems* (10th rev, 1992–1994)).'

The defendants deny these allegations.

c [5] The case against both defendants was listed for trial beginning on 14 December 1999. At the outset, the second defendant renewed an application to strike out the claim against her, which had been made earlier but not determined. The recorder granted that application and adjourned the claim against the first defendant employers. He held that there was no tort of

d harassment at common law before the enactment of the 1997 Act, which does not have retrospective effect; he further held that the complaints made against the second defendant could not amount to the tort of intentional infliction of harm under the principle in *Wilkinson v Downton* [1897] 2 QB 57, [1895–9] All ER Rep 267. In reaching that decision, he excluded the assault on 9 March, because of s 45 of the Offences Against the Person Act 1861; he also excluded the threat on 20

e February because the appellant conceded to him that it had not been the cause of her trauma.

[6] At that stage, the appellant was acting in person, legal aid having been withdrawn. Before us, she has been represented under the pro bono scheme run by the Royal Courts of Justice Citizens' Advice Bureau, by Mr Matthew

f Chapman of counsel. He has argued her case before us as well as it could possibly be argued and we are most grateful to him, and to the bureau and the scheme, for their help with some difficult but important issues of law.

WILKINSON v DOWNTON
[7] As every law student knows, the common law distinguished between an

g action in trespass and an action upon the case. Trespass to the person consisted in the direct infliction of harm (or the threat of the immediate infliction of such harm) upon the claimant. But the law recognised that physical harm might be inflicted indirectly. If intentional, this was the tort recognised by the High Court in *Wilkinson v Downton* and confirmed by the Court of Appeal in *Janvier v Sweeney*

h [1919] 2 KB 316, [1918–19] All ER Rep 1056. If negligent, it was eventually recognised as the tort of negligence in *Donoghue v Stevenson* [1932] AC 562, [1932] All ER Rep 1.

[8] In *Wilkinson v Downton*, the defendant did not intend to cause physical harm to the claimant. He intended to play a particularly nasty practical joke upon her. He told her, knowing that it was not true but meaning her to believe them,

j that her husband had had an accident returning from the races in a wagonette, had broken both his legs, was lying in a public house in Leytonstone, and wished the claimant to go at once with a cab and some pillows to fetch him home. She suffered a violent shock to her nervous system, producing vomiting and other more serious and permanent physical consequences at one time threatening her reason, and entailing weeks of suffering for her and expense to her husband.

Wright J found in her favour ([1897] 2 QB 57 at 58–59, [1895–9] All ER Rep 267 at 269):

> 'The defendant has ... wilfully done an act calculated to cause physical harm to the plaintiff—that is to say, to infringe her legal right to personal safety, and has in fact thereby caused physical harm to her. That proposition without more appears to me to state a good cause of action, there being no justification alleged for the act. This wilful injuria is in law malicious, although no malicious purpose to cause the harm which was caused nor any motive of spite is imputed to the defendant. It remains to consider whether the assumptions involved in the proposition are made out. One question is whether the defendant's act was so plainly calculated to produce some effect of the kind which was produced that an intention to produce it ought to be imputed to the defendant, regard being had to the fact that the effect was produced on a person proved to be in an ordinary state of health and mind. I think that it was. It is difficult to imagine that such a statement, made suddenly and with apparent seriousness, could fail to produce grave effects under the circumstances upon any but an exceptionally indifferent person, and therefore an intention to produce such an effect must be imputed, and it is no answer in law to say that more harm was done than was anticipated, for that is commonly the case with all wrongs.'

[9] This was approved in the later, and 'much stronger', *Janvier*'s case. In order to persuade the plaintiff to hand over letters belonging to her employer, the second defendant, an employee of the first defendant, pretended to be from Scotland Yard, representing the military authorities who wanted the plaintiff for corresponding with a German spy. The plaintiff suffered a severe shock, resulting in neurasthenia, shingles and other ailments. Although these cases were concerned with words, the same principle would obviously apply to the intentional infliction of physical harm by other indirect means, such as digging a pit into which it is intended that another should fall.

[10] It follows from Wright J's formulation that, although the tort is commonly labelled 'intentional infliction of harm', it is not necessary to prove that the defendant actually wanted to produce such harm. If the conduct complained of was 'calculated' to do so, and does so, then that is enough. Much depends, therefore, on what is meant by 'calculated'.

[11] Professor Fleming states in *The Law of Torts* (9th edn, 1998) p 38:

> 'Cases will be rare where nervous shock involving physical injury was fully intended (desired). More frequently, the defendant's aim would have been merely to frighten, terrify or alarm his victim. But this is quite sufficient, provided his conduct was of a kind reasonably capable of terrifying a normal person, or was known or ought to have been known to the defendant to be likely to terrify the plaintiff for reasons special to him. Such conduct could be described as reckless.'

This might be read to mean that the tort is committed if there is deliberate conduct which will foreseeably lead to alarm or distress falling short of the recognised psychiatric illness which is now considered the equivalent of physical harm, provided that such harm is actually suffered. We do not consider that English law has gone so far.

a [12] For the tort to be committed, as with any other action on the case, there has to be actual damage. The damage is physical harm or recognised psychiatric illness. The defendant must have intended to violate the claimant's interest in his freedom from such harm. The conduct complained of has to be such that that degree of harm is sufficiently likely to result that the defendant cannot be heard to say that he did not 'mean' it to do so. He is taken to have meant it to do so by

b the combination of the likelihood of such harm being suffered as the result of his behaviour and his deliberately engaging in that behaviour. This view is consistent with that taken by Dillon LJ in *Khorasandjian v Bush* [1993] 3 All ER 669 at 676, [1993] QB 727 at 735–736:

c '... false words or verbal threats calculated to cause, and uttered with the knowledge that they are likely to cause and actually causing physical injury to the person to whom they are uttered are actionable: see the judgment of Wright J in *Wilkinson v Downton* [1897] 2 QB 57 at 59, [1895–9] All ER Rep 267 at 269 cited by Bankes LJ in *Janvier v Sweeney* [1919] 2 KB 316 at 321–322, [1918–19] All ER Rep 1056 at 1059. There was a wilful false statement, or unfounded threat, which was in law malicious, and which was likely to cause

d and did in fact cause physical injury, viz illness of the nature of nervous shock.'

[13] There is no allegation in this case that the second defendant intended to cause the harm that Dr Tylden diagnosed. The question therefore is whether her conduct was of a nature which was sufficiently likely to result in such harm that

e an intention to produce it could be imputed to her. The recorder held that it was not. But in doing so he left out of account the two most important allegations made against this defendant, the threat and the assault.

[14] The assault was excluded because of s 45 of the 1861 Act. This provides:

f 'If any person against whom any such complaint as is mentioned in s 44 of this Act [ie of assault or battery] shall have been preferred by or on the behalf of the party aggrieved shall have obtained such certificate [ie of dismissal because not proved, or justified or so trifling as not to merit any punishment], or, having been convicted, shall have paid the whole amount adjudged to be paid, or shall have suffered the imprisonment awarded, in

g every such case he shall be released from all further or other proceedings, civil or criminal, for the same cause.'

[15] The claimant brought a private prosecution against the second defendant, which resulted in a conviction, and orders for compensation and costs,

h all of which have been paid. Mr Chapman argues that this precludes bringing a civil action for assault or battery relying upon the same allegation, but it does not prevent that allegation being used for the purpose of proving a completely different tort. It is all part of the picture of behaviour 'calculated' to cause the claimant physical harm. However, in the case of *Masper v Brown* (1876) 1 CPD 97, this court held that 'cause' in s 45 of the 1861 Act meant 'assault': an action by a

j husband in respect of the consequential damage to him by reason of an assault upon his wife (presumably the old action per quod servitium or consortium amisit) was therefore prohibited. The fact that it was a completely different cause of action, brought by a different claimant, made no difference. Lord Coleridge CJ referred to the earlier provision in the Criminal Procedure Act 1853 relating to aggravated assaults, which had barred future proceedings for the same 'assault'.

He pointed out that it would be a very strange thing if the legislature, when
dealing with aggravated assaults only, should have intended to make the *a*
conviction a bar to all further proceedings against the offender for the same
assault, and then, when dealing with non-aggravated assaults as well as
aggravated assaults, should have intended the conviction to be only a bar to
proceedings for the same cause of action.

[16] Thus the victim of an assault has a choice. If the authorities choose to *b*
prosecute, there is no problem. But if they do not, she must choose between
bringing a private prosecution or a civil action. The former will destroy her right
to bring the latter, irrespective of the outcome. The alleged perpetrator is not to
be put in double jeopardy for the same cause. This may be an anomalous
approach in today's world, given the differences in the burden of proof and
sometimes in the level of compensation awarded by criminal and civil courts. But *c*
for as long as s 45 of the 1861 Act is on the statute book, the effect in a case such
as this is clear: the claimant cannot rely upon the assault in any other proceedings.
The recorder was therefore right to exclude it from his consideration.

[17] The threat is different. It is the most serious of the other allegations made
against the second defendant. But the claimant herself conceded to the judge that *d*
it had not caused her illness. The trigger had been the earlier incidents which had
led to her two-day absence in January. Without it, all that is left is a catalogue of
rudeness and unfriendliness, behaviour not to be expected of grown-up
colleagues in the workplace, but not behaviour so calculated 'to infringe her legal
right to personal safety' (see *Wilkinson v Downton* [1897] 2 QB 57 at 59, [1895–9] *e*
All ER Rep 267 at 269) that an intention to do so should be imputed to the second
defendant.

A TORT OF HARASSMENT
[18] There was growing public concern and media debate about harassment,
at least in the form popularly known as 'stalking', before the 1997 Act. The
context was usually obsessive behaviour towards a person with whom the stalker *f*
had had or wished to have an intimate relationship. Remedies had been
developed within family law but these only gave protection to a limited class of
people. Others had to rely upon the law of tort. The case law was developing in
such a way that some considered that a new tort of harassment had already been
created. However, in all of the cases the question was whether an injunction *g*
should be granted to prevent particular kinds of behaviour: there was no case in
which damages were awarded to compensate for such behaviour in the past.

[19] Remedies against molestation were first developed in pending
matrimonial causes. This was before actions in tort became possible between
spouses following the Law Reform (Husband and Wife) Act 1962. The object *h*
was to protect the integrity of the legal process, by preventing a wife petitioner
for divorce being 'kicked or kissed' out of her remedy. The concept of
molestation embraced some behaviour, such as violence and threats of violence,
which was obviously tortious, but other behaviour which was not. The classic
definition is that of Ormrod LJ in *Horner v Horner* [1982] 2 All ER 495 at 497, [1982] *j*
Fam 90 at 93:

'For my part I have no doubt that the word "molesting" in s 1(1)(*a*) of the
1976 Act does not imply necessarily either violence or threats of violence. It
applies to any conduct which can properly be regarded as such a degree of
harassment as to call for the intervention of the court.'

a [20] This was a reference to the Domestic Violence and Matrimonial Proceedings Act 1976. Section 1 had given county courts jurisdiction to grant injunctions against molestation, not only between husband and wife, but also between 'a man and a woman who are living with each other in the same household as husband and wife', whether or not any other relief was sought in the proceedings. The House of Lords in *Davis v Johnson* [1978] 1 All ER 1132, *b* [1979] AC 264 confirmed that this was not merely a procedural provision. There remained many gaps, for example, where the couple were no longer married or living together, or where they had never lived together, or were related in some other way.

[21] Many of the gaps in the statutory scheme were filled by the new scheme introduced by Pt IV of the Family Law Act 1996. Some of them had already been *c* filled by the cases decided before then. In *Burnett v George* [1993] 1 FCR 1012, the plaintiff complained of a series of molestations and assaults by a former cohabitant. An injunction was granted in the then standard form restraining him from assaulting, molesting or otherwise interfering with her. On appeal it was argued that molestation and interference were not actionable wrongs. Sir John *d* Arnold P agreed (at 1014–1015):

> '... I regard that as a conclusive argument unless there be evidence that the health of the plaintiff is being impaired by molestation or interference calculated to create such impairment, in which case relief would be granted by way of an injunction to the extent that it would be necessary to avoid that *e* impairment of health. That exception is, in my judgment, validly grounded on *Wilkinson* v. *Downton* [1897] 2 QB 57 ...'

As there was evidence that the defendant's behaviour was causing injury to the plaintiff's health, an injunction was substituted prohibiting him from 'assaulting, molesting or otherwise interfering with the plaintiff by doing acts calculated to *f* cause her harm'.

[22] The Court of Appeal may have gone a little further in *Pidduck v Molloy* [1992] 1 FCR 418 at 421. This was another case between former cohabitants, where an injunction against speaking to the plaintiff was replaced by one against speaking to her 'in an intimidatory, threatening or abusive manner' on the basis that these were all *capable of* amounting to crimes or torts.

[23] Then came *Khorasandjian v Bush* [1993] 3 All ER 669, [1993] QB 727. The parties had never married or lived together but had been friends. The defendant was unable to accept that the plaintiff wanted nothing more to do with him. She complained of violence, threats of violence, damage to her property, and persecution by telephone calls. The current injunction restrained him from 'using violence to, harassing, pestering or communicating' with her. Dillon LJ ([1993] 3 All ER 669 at 679–680, [1993] QB 727 at 739–740), with whom Rose LJ agreed, upheld the injunction without qualification, because—

> '(i) the campaign of harassment has to be regarded as a whole without consideration of each ingredient in isolation, and viewed as a whole it is plainly calculated to cause the plaintiff harm, and can be restrained quia timet because of the danger to her health from a continuation of the stress to which she has been subjected (ii) threats of violence can be restrained per se, whether or not the threat, without the subsequent violence, is calculated to cause the plaintiff harm; and (iii) telephone harassment is, in my judgment ... an actionable interference with her ordinary and reasonable use and

enjoyment of property where she is lawfully present, and thus, on the past history, can be restrained quia timet without further proof or damage.'   a

[24] Point (iii) was based upon extending the tort of private nuisance so as to protect a mere licensee. Peter Gibson J, as he then was, disagreed ([1993] 3 All ER 669 at 684, [1993] QB 727 at 745):

'I know of no authority which would allow a person with no interest in   b
land or right to occupy land to sue in private nuisance. Given that the purpose of an action in nuisance is to protect the right to use and enjoyment of land ... it seems to me to be wrong in principle if a mere licensee or someone without such right could sue in private nuisance.'

In this view he was entirely vindicated by the House of Lords in *Hunter v Canary*   c
Wharf Ltd [1997] 2 All ER 426, [1997] AC 655. To that extent the decision of the majority of the Court of Appeal in *Khorasandjian v Bush* [1993] 3 All ER 669, [1993] QB 727 was overruled. But *Hunter's* case was about the scope of the tort of private nuisance; it had nothing to do with harassment. There is nothing in the speeches in their Lordships' House to cast doubt upon that part of the decision which was based upon the principle in *Wilkinson v Downton*.   d

[25] However, there was also a difference of opinion in the Court of Appeal (*Khorasandjian's* case [1993] 3 All ER 669, [1993] QB 727) on that point. Dillon and Rose LJJ did not limit the injunction to conduct calculated to cause harm, because taken as a whole, the conduct complained of was clearly so calculated. Peter Gibson J, on the other hand, would have followed the decision in *Burnett's* case in   e
including such a limitation. In so far as *Pidduck's* case had gone further in restraining conduct which was merely capable of amounting to a crime or a tort rather than conduct which would amount to a crime or a tort, he preferred *Burnett's* case, 'because in principle only conduct amounting to an actionable wrong (including conduct facilitating such a wrong) should be restrained' (see [1993] 3 All ER 669 at 682, [1993] QB 727 at 742).   f

[26] The Court of Appeal took the broader view in *Burris v Azadani* [1995] 4 All ER 802, [1999] 1 WLR 1372. There had been no relationship between the parties, but the defendant had wanted one. He had indulged in 'an intolerable history of harassment and molestation'. An injunction was granted against (a) assaulting, molesting, harassing, threatening, pestering or otherwise   g
interfering with the plaintiff, her children or her friend, or (b) communicating with any of them, or (c) coming or remaining within 250 yards of her home. He was committed for breach of para (c). Bingham MR, said ([1995] 4 All ER 802 at 807, [1999] 1 WLR 1372 at 1377):

'If an injunction may only properly be granted to restrain conduct which is in itself tortious or otherwise unlawful, that would be a conclusive objection to term (c) ... I do not, however, think that the court's power is so limited. A Mareva injunction granted in the familiar form restrains a defendant from acting in a way which is not, in itself, tortious or otherwise unlawful. The order is made to try to ensure that the procedures of the court are in practice effective to achieve their ends. The court recognises a need to protect the legitimate interests of those who have invoked its jurisdiction.'

He concluded that there was power to make an 'exclusion zone' order. But such order should not be made readily or without very good reason. The liberty of the defendant should be respected up to the point at which his conduct infringed or a threatened to infringe the rights of the plaintiff. He said ([1995] 4 All ER 802 at 811, [1999] 1 WLR 1372 at 1380–1381):

'Ordinarily, the victim will be adequately protected by an injunction which restrains the tort which has been or is likely to be committed, whether trespass to the person or to land, interference with goods, harassment,
b intimidation or as the case may be. But it may be clear on the facts that if the defendant approaches the vicinity of the plaintiff's home he will succumb to the temptation to enter it, or to abuse or harass the plaintiff; or that he may loiter outside the house, watching and besetting it, in a manner which might be highly stressful and disturbing to a plaintiff.'

c [27] The basis of the decision is therefore that an interlocutory injunction may be granted to prohibit conduct which is not in itself unlawful if it is necessary to prevent such unlawful conduct taking place or to protect the claimant's right to bring the matter before the court. Understandably, Mr Chapman relies strongly upon the reference in the passage just quoted to a tort of harassment. Earlier,
d Bingham MR had discussed the case of *Patel v Patel* [1988] 2 FLR 179, in which an exclusion zone order had been removed from an injunction granted to a father-in-law against his son-in-law. May LJ had observed (at 180) that an injunction 'can only be an appropriate remedy where an actual tortious act has been or is likely to be committed'. Waterhouse J had said (at 182) that 'in the present state of the law there is no tort of harassment'. Bingham MR commented
e in *Burris v Azadani* [1995] 4 All ER 802 at 809, [1995] 1 WLR 1372 at 1378: 'Nor, in the light of later authority, can the view be upheld that there is no tort of harassment.'

[28] The later authority was *Khorasandjian v Bush* [1993] 3 All ER 669, [1993] QB 727. Dillon LJ found it difficult to give much weight to what Waterhouse J
f had said, because the reformulated injunction in *Patel's* case had continued to prohibit molestation. Peter Gibson J, however, agreed with his statement, while pointing out ([1993] 3 All ER 669 at 683, [1993] QB 727 at 744) that 'many forms of molestation, in the wide sense in which it has been interpreted by the courts … are tortious, but in my view not every form of molestation is a tort'. Both Dillon LJ and Peter Gibson J considered the decision of Scott J, as he then was, in
g *Thomas v National Union of Mineworkers (South Wales Area)* [1985] 2 All ER 1, [1986] Ch 20. He had held that the plaintiffs were entitled to enjoy their right to use the highway to go to work without unreasonable harassment and that picketing by 50 to 70 striking miners shouting abuse was a tortious interference with that right. This decision has been criticised, as interference with the right to use the highway is only actionable in public nuisance on proof of special damage. In *News Group Newspapers Ltd v Society of Graphical and Allied Trades '82 (No 2)* [1987] ICR 181, Stuart-Smith J, as he then was, saw force in the criticism but did not find it necessary to express a view. Nor did Dillon LJ in *Khorasandjian's* case [1993] 3 All ER 669 at 679, [1993] QB 727 at 738. Peter Gibson J ([1993] 3 All ER 669 at 683, [1993] QB 727 at 744) expressly disagreed with Scott J, to the extent that he was holding that there was now a tort of unreasonable harassment. It is, however, quite clear that neither the majority nor the minority in *Khorasandjian's* case were creating a new tort. They were merely developing existing torts to cover the behaviour complained of and, in the case of the majority, to prohibit conduct which was likely to result in harm being suffered even though it had not yet done so.

[29] *Burris'* case was decided before the House of Lords' decision in *Hunter v Canary Wharf Ltd* [1997] 2 All ER 426, [1997] AC 655. The speeches there do not lend support to the view that there is now a general tort of harassment at common law. Lord Goff of Chieveley said ([1997] 2 All ER 426 at 438, [1997] AC 655 at 691–692):

'In truth, what the Court of Appeal appears to have been doing was to exploit the law of private nuisance in order to create by the back door a tort of harassment which was only partially effective in that it was artificially limited to harassment which takes place in her home. I myself do not consider that this is a satisfactory manner in which to develop the law ... In any event, a tort of harassment has now received statutory recognition (see the Protection from Harassment Act 1997). We are therefore no longer troubled with the question whether the common law should be developed to provide such a remedy.'

Lord Hoffmann said ([1997] 2 All ER 426 at 452, [1997] AC 655 at 707):

'The perceived gap in *Khorasandjian's* case was the absence of a tort of intentional harassment causing distress without actual bodily or psychiatric illness. This limitation is thought to arise out of cases like *Wilkinson v Downton* [1897] 2 QB 57, [1895–9] All ER Rep 267 and *Janvier v Sweeney* [1919] 2 KB 316, [1918–19] All ER Rep 1056. The law of harassment has now been put on a statutory basis ... and it is unnecessary to consider how the common law might have developed.'

This gives no warrant for concluding that the common law had by then reached the point of recognising a tort of intentional harassment going beyond the tort of intentional infliction of harm. It is a clear indication that matters should now be left to Parliament.

[30] Lord Hoffmann went on to comment:

'I see no reason why a tort of intention should be subject to the rule which excludes compensation for mere distress, inconvenience or discomfort in actions based on negligence ... The policy considerations are quite different.'

Indeed they are, and Parliament has provided a civil remedy, which includes damages for anxiety, as well as a criminal remedy in the 1997 Act. No doubt the concept of 'a course of conduct ... which amounts to harassment' (see s 1 of the 1997 Act) will be developed in decisions under that Act. Until that Act came into force, there was power to restrain by injunction conduct which might result in the tort of intentional infliction of harm or otherwise threaten the claimant's right of access to the courts, but there was no right to damages for conduct falling short of an actual tort.

[31] As the allegations in this case do not amount to that or any other tort recognised at common law at the time when these events took place, the recorder was right to strike out the claim and this appeal must be dismissed.

Appeal dismissed.

Kate O'Hanlon   Barrister.

a Wainwright and another v Home Office
[2001] EWCA Civ 2081

COURT OF APPEAL, CIVIL DIVISION

LORD WOOLF CJ, MUMMERY AND BUXTON LJJ

b 20, 21 NOVEMBER, 20 DECEMBER 2001

Intentional infliction of harm – Invasion of privacy – Visitors to prison who were strip searched suffering distress and humiliation – Whether intentional infliction of harm – Whether invasion of privacy – Whether human rights legislation applicable despite events taking place before implementation of legislation – Human Rights Act 1998, s 3(1).

c

In 1997, the first claimant and her 21 year old son, the second claimant, went to visit another son of the first claimant in prison. There was a pressing drug problem in the prison and the claimants were told by prison officers that they *d* were to be strip searched because they were suspected of bringing drugs into the prison, and that if they refused they might be denied their visit. The statutory authority to conduct searches provided, inter alia, that any person entering a prison might be stopped, examined, and searched. During the searches both claimants signed consent forms. The searches did not comply with the prison's own procedures for the strip searching of visitors. The circumstances of the *e* searches were such that both claimants felt distressed and humiliated; the first claimant believed that she could be seen by people outside the building while she was semi-naked and the second claimant was physically handled during his search while he was naked. He developed post-traumatic stress syndrome. They brought proceedings against the defendant, the Home Office, claiming damages. *f* The second claimant claimed for battery. The judge found that, even though the first claimant had suffered no physical injury, but only distress and humiliation, her right to privacy had been infringed, basing his conclusion in part on common law and in part on the Human Rights Act 1998. He held that the tort of trespass to the person, consisting of wilfully causing a person to do something to himself which infringed his right to privacy, had been committed against both claimants *g* and that the tort of trespass to the person, consisting of wilfully causing a person to do something calculated to cause harm to him, namely infringing his legal right to personal safety, had been committed against the second claimant. The judge awarded damages and aggravated damages in each case. The defendant appealed. On the appeal there was no dispute that the defendant was liable to the *h* second claimant for battery. The court considered the requirements of a claim in the tort of intentional infliction of harm; the existence of remedies for invasion of privacy at common law; and whether the claimants were entitled to rely on s 3[a] of the 1998 Act, which provided that legislation had to be read and given effect in a way which was compatible with the rights contained in the European Convention for the Protection of Human Rights and Fundamental Freedoms 1950 (as set out in Sch 1 to the 1998 Act), either to qualify the interpretation of the statutory authority to conduct searches, or to introduce a right of privacy, notwithstanding that the searches had occurred before the 1998 Act came into force.

---

a Section 3, so far as material, is set out at [24], below

Held – (1) Damages could be recovered for the tort of intentional infliction of harm if actual recognised psychiatric illness or bodily injury resulted. A limiting factor was, however, the intention to cause harm, which harm was in fact then caused, or recklessness as to whether that harm would be caused. The judge had not been asked to make, nor had he made any finding that the prison officers were intending to cause or were reckless as to whether they caused harm, and the findings he had made were inconsistent with such a conclusion (see [47]–[49], [51], [55], [56], [84], [85], [124], below); *Wilkinson v Downton* [1897] 2 QB 57 distinguished.

(2) There was no existing common law remedy for invasion of privacy; therefore the claimants could not be granted relief on that basis (see [56]–[58], [102], [107], [115], [124], below); *Douglas v Hello! Ltd* [2001] 2 All ER 289 considered.

(3) Section 3(1) of the 1998 Act did not apply retrospectively to the cause of action in the instant case which arose in 1997. It therefore could not assist on the construction of the statutory authority to conduct searches or by introducing a right of privacy. Accordingly, the appeal would be allowed (see [40], [61], [89], below); *R v Lambert* [2001] 3 All ER 577 followed.

Notes

For the tort of intentional physical harm, the scope of the right to personal privacy, and the right to respect for personal privacy under the European Convention for the Protection of Human Rights and Fundamental Freedoms 1950, see 45(2) *Halsbury's Laws* (4th edn reissue) para 456 and 8(2) *Halsbury's Laws* (4th edn reissue) paras 110, 149–150, respectively.

For the Human Rights Act 1998, s 3, see 7 *Halsbury's Statutes* (4th edn) (2002 reissue) 532.

Cases referred to in judgments

Associated Provincial Picture Houses Ltd v Wednesbury Corp [1947] 2 All ER 680, [1948] 1 KB 223, CA.

Brind v Secretary of State for the Home Dept [1991] 1 All ER 720, [1991] 1 AC 696, [1991] 2 WLR 588, HL.

Burnett v George [1993] 1 FCR 1012, CA.

Burris v Azadani [1995] 4 All ER 802, [1995] 1 WLR 1372, CA.

Douglas v Hello! Ltd [2001] 2 All ER 289, [2001] QB 967, [2001] 2 WLR 992, CA.

DPP v K (a minor) [1990] 1 WLR 1067, DC.

Hellewell v Chief Constable of Derbyshire [1995] 4 All ER 473, [1995] 1 WLR 804.

Hunter v Canary Wharf Ltd, Hunter v London Docklands Development Corp [1997] 2 All ER 426, [1997] AC 655, [1997] 2 WLR 684, HL.

Janvier v Sweeney [1919] 2 KB 316, [1918–19] All ER Rep 1056, CA.

Kaye v Robertson [1991] FSR 62, CA.

Khorasandjian v Bush [1993] 3 All ER 669, [1993] QB 727, [1993] 3 WLR 476, CA.

Letang v Cooper [1964] 2 All ER 929, [1965] 1 QB 232, [1964] 3 WLR 573, CA.

Maclaine Watson & Co Ltd v Dept of Trade and Industry, Maclaine Watson & Co Ltd v International Tin Council [1989] 3 All ER 523, sub nom *Rayner (JH) (Mincing Lane) Ltd v Dept of Trade and Industry* [1990] 2 AC 418, [1989] 3 WLR 969, HL.

Malone v Comr of Police of the Metropolis (No 2) [1979] 2 All ER 620, [1979] Ch 344, [1979] 2 WLR 700.

a *Pearce v Governing Body of Mayfield Secondary School* [2001] EWCA Civ 1347, [2001] IRLR 669, [2002] ICR 198.

Peters v Prince of Wales Theatre (Birmingham) Ltd [1942] 2 All ER 533, [1943] KB 73.

Platform Home Loans Ltd v Oyston Shipways Ltd [1999] 1 All ER 833, [2000] 2 AC 190, [1999] 2 WLR 518, HL.

b *Pye (J A) (Oxford) Ltd v Graham* [2001] EWCA Civ 117, [2001] Ch 804, [2001] 2 WLR 1293; *rvsd* [2002] UKHL 30, [2002] 3 All ER 865, [2003] 1 AC 419, [2002] 3 WLR 221.

R (on the application of Pretty) v DPP [2001] UKHL 61, [2002] 1 All ER 1, [2002] 1 AC 800, [2001] 3 WLR 1598.

R v Benjafield [2001] 2 All ER 609, [2001] 3 WLR 75, CA.

c *R v Kansal (No 2)* [2001] UKHL 62, [2002] 1 All ER 257, [2002] 2 AC 69, [2001] 3 WLR 1562.

R v Lambert [2001] UKHL 37, [2001] 3 All ER 577, [2002] 2 AC 545, [2001] 3 WLR 206.

R v Martin (1881) 8 QBD 54, [1881–5] All ER Rep 699, CCR.

d *Spencer (Earl) v UK* (1998) 25 EHRR CD 105, E Com HR.

Victorian Railways Comrs v Coultas (1888) 13 App Cas 222, PC.

Warner v Riddiford (1858) 4 CBNS 180.

Wilkinson v Downton [1897] 2 QB 57, [1985–9] All ER Rep 267.

Wilson v First County Trust Ltd [2001] EWCA Civ 633, [2001] 3 All ER 229, [2002] QB 74, [2001] 3 WLR 42; *rvsd* [2003] UKHL 40, [2003] 3 WLR 568.

e *Wilson v Pringle* [1986] 2 All ER 440, [1987] QB 237, [1986] 3 WLR 1, CA.

Wong v Parkside Health NHS Trust [2001] EWCA Civ 1721, [2003] 3 All ER 932.

Cases also cited or referred to in skeleton arguments

f *Hague v Deputy Governor of Parkhurst Prison, Weldon v Home Office* [1991] 3 All ER 733, [1992] 1 AC 58, [1991] 3 WLR 340, HL.

Laskey v UK (1997) 24 EHRR 39, [1997] ECHR 21627/93, ECt HR.

Latter v Braddell (1881) 44 LT 369, CA.

R (on the application of Daly) v Secretary of State for the Home Dept [2001] UKHL 26, [2001] 3 All ER 433, [2001] 2 AC 532, [2001] 2 WLR 1622.

g *R (on the application of Mahmood) v Secretary of State for the Home Dept* [2001] 2 FCR 63, [2001] 1 WLR 840, CA.

R v DPP, ex p Kebeline [1999] 4 All ER 801, [2000] 2 AC 326, [1999] 3 WLR 972, HL.

Appeal

The Home Office appealed, with the permission of Judge McGonigal, from his judgment given at the Leeds County Court on 23 May 2001 awarding basic and aggravated damage in compensation for the manner in which the claimants, Mary Wainwright and Alan Wainwright (suing as a patient by Mary Wainwright, his litigation friend) were strip searched by prison officers at HM Prison Leeds on 2 January 1997. The facts are set out in the judgment of Lord Woolf CJ.

Robin Tam (instructed by the *Treasury Solicitor*) for the Home Office.

David Wilby QC and *Ashley Serr* (instructed by *David A Reston*, York) for Mrs Wainwright and Mr Wainwright.

Cur adv vult

20 December 2001. The following judgments were delivered.   *a*

LORD WOOLF CJ.

[1]   This appeal relates to a judgment of Judge McGonigal, given at the Leeds County Court on 23 April 2001. The claimants were a mother, Mrs Mary Wainwright, and her son, Alan Wainwright. The judge awarded basic and aggravated damages which were, in total, for the mother the sum of £2,600 and *b* for the son the sum of £4,500. The damages were compensation for the manner in which they were strip-searched by prison officers when they went to HM Prison Leeds in order to visit another son (Patrick O'Neill) of Mrs Wainwright.

[2]   The case raises difficult issues of law and the judge gave leave to appeal. The most important of those issues are identified by Mr Tam for the appellant, *c* the Home Office, as being whether a person is liable in tort if he: (i) wilfully causes a person to do something calculated to cause harm to him, namely to infringe his legal right to personal safety; (ii) wilfully causes a person to do something to himself which infringes his right of privacy?

[3]   Additional issues were: (i) if such conduct was tortious, whether, on the *d* facts of this case (a) it was negatived by consent or (b) protected by statutory authority; (ii) whether the complainants were entitled to rely on s 3 of the Human Rights Act 1998 notwithstanding that the conduct complained of occurred on 2 January 1997, before the 1998 Act came into force.

[4]   Judge McGonigal gave a detailed and clear judgment both as to his findings of fact and the legal principles which he applied in this difficult case. It is *e* therefore possible to rely on the judgment in order to explain the factual background and the issues.

FACTUAL BACKGROUND

[5]   At the time of the visit Alan Wainwright was 21 years of age. He suffers *f* from cerebral palsy with a degree of mental impairment. He therefore sues as a patient by Mrs Wainwright, his litigation friend.

[6]   On the 2 January 1997 Mrs Wainwright and Alan arrived at the prison at about 6 pm. They went through normal security checks and then waited with the other visitors prior to seeing Patrick. They were then approached by a number of prison officers and asked to accompany them. They then proceeded to the *g* north gatehouse of the prison. On the way there, they were told they were to be strip-searched because they were suspected of bringing drugs in to the prison and if they refused they might be denied a visit to Patrick. At the gatehouse they were taken up to the first floor where they were separated.

[7]   Mrs Wainwright was strip-searched by two female prison officers in one *h* room while Alan was searched by two male prison officers in another room. They were then allowed to visit Patrick.

[8]   Before a strip-search takes place, the person who is to be strip-searched is required to sign a consent form. There is no dispute that both claimants signed the form which is known as F2141. There was a dispute as to *when* they signed the form. The form reads as follows:

'Notice for the information of visitors or other persons entering an establishment
Strip-search
Please read carefully
The Governor has directed that, for the reasons explained to you, you should be strip-searched.

a
The police have been informed but cannot come to deal with the matter. The search will therefore be carried out by prison staff.

The procedure for the search is explained overleaf.

Please sign below if the search is taking place with your consent.

I have read this notice (or it has been read to me) and I understand it.

I agree to be strip-searched by prison staff.'

b

[9]   The prison officers who gave evidence said that the forms would have been signed prior to the search being undertaken in accordance with proper practice. Mrs Wainwright and Alan both said that they were asked to sign the forms after the search had been substantially completed. The judge preferred their evidence on this issue. He regarded Mrs Wainwright 'as an honest witness
c   who was doing her best to tell the truth as she remembered it'. He felt the circumstances surrounding Alan's search supported his story.

[10]   The search was conducted at a time when it was dark outside and Mrs Wainwright believed that she could be seen by those who were in a single storey flat roofed administration block which was on the opposite side of the road
d   or from that road. There were roller blinds on the windows of the room that she was in but the judge accepted her evidence that the blinds were not pulled down. Mrs Wainwright does not allege that she was touched by either of the female officers who searched her, but says that she felt threatened and that she was upset and worried. Alan said (and this the judge accepted) that during his search he was naked, a finger was poked into his armpits and that one prison officer went all
e   round his body, lifted up his penis and pulled back the foreskin. The judge also found that Mrs Wainwright was correct in saying that there was a point when she was naked apart from knickers around her ankle and a vest held above her breasts. The judge also accepted that the officers had *not* known of Alan's learning difficulties before they had completed the strip-search of him—see para
f   56 of his judgment. Paragraph 10 as currently drafted might, through ambiguity, give the erroneous impression that they were aware throughout the search procedure of Alan's learning difficulties. We would respectfully ask that consideration be given to clarifying this point. Mrs Wainwright describes how she was crying during the search and there is no doubt that she and Alan were very upset by what happened.

g
[11]   The judge also made the following relevant findings of fact: (i) there was a pressing problem involving the prevalence of illicit drugs within the prison; (ii) visitors in general were a major source of such drugs and that all visitors were suspected of bringing in drugs until it was proved otherwise because all sorts of unlikely visitors had been known to bring in drugs; (iii) there were reasonable
h   grounds for believing that Mrs Wainwright's son, Patrick, had been obtaining illicit drugs; (iv) the claimants each consented to being strip-searched before they were searched although in each case they signed the consent forms after the search was complete or substantially complete; (v) the search of each of the complaints was not conducted in as seemly a manner as was consistent with discovering anything concealed; (vi) the officers honestly believed that they had a legal right to strip-search the claimants; (vii) Mrs Wainwright understood and was intended to understand that the officers had a legal right to strip-search the claimants; (viii) notwithstanding that each claimant consented to the strip-search, such consent was not a real consent because they were expressly told that if they did not consent the defendant would deny the claimants the proposed visit; (ix) further, such consent was not a real consent because it was represented to

them that the officers had a legal right to strip-search them, which was untrue, although honestly believed; (x) any search under a power given by r 86 of the Prison Rules 1964, SI 1964/388 was lawful only if it was conducted in as seemly a manner as was consistent with discovering anything concealed; (xi) the strip-search of the claimants was not a proportionate response to the objective of preventing that person from obtaining drugs from visitors and was therefore not permitted by that rule; and (xii) the prison officers had no right to conduct a search.

[12] The judge on these findings came to the conclusion that a tort of trespass to the person, consisting of wilfully causing a person to do something to himself which infringes his right to privacy had been committed against both claimants. In addition he concluded that the tort of trespass to the person, consisting of wilfully causing a person to do something calculated to cause harm to him, namely infringing his legal right to personal safety, had been committed against the second claimant.

[13] There is no dispute now that the Home Office is liable to Alan for the physical handling which took place and that this amounted to battery. Nothing was found during the course of the searches.

[14] As to injuries, the findings of the judge are not so clear. It appears that he accepted in the case of Mrs Wainwright there was exacerbation of existing depression and unpleasant memories of the incident. In the case of Alan, it appears that the judge found that he was suffering from post-traumatic stress disorder.

[15] Both claimants sought exemplary and aggravated damages. The judge did not consider that it was an appropriate case for exemplary damages. He considered that it was an appropriate case in which to award aggravated damages. As aggravated damages, he awarded each claimant £1,000.

THE STATUTORY AUTHORITY TO CONDUCT SEARCHES

[16] The 1964 rules are made pursuant to s 47 of the Prison Act 1952. The parties accept that these rules applied to the search. The rule which is directly applicable is r 86(1). This rule provides: 'Any person or vehicle entering or leaving a prison may be stopped, examined and searched.'

[17] The very general terms of r 86 have to be contrasted with the terms of r 39(1) which applies to prisoners. This states:

'(1) Every prisoner shall be searched when taken into custody by an officer on his reception into a prison and subsequently as the Governor thinks necessary or as the Secretary of State may direct.
(2) A prisoner shall be searched in as seemly a manner as is consistent with discovering anything concealed.
(3) No person shall be stripped and searched in sight of another prisoner, or in the sight or presence of an officer not of the same sex.'

[18] Leeds prison has its own strategy and procedure relating to searches. Part of the strategy applies to visitors to prisons. The following statements are important. Section 1.2.1:

'Searches will be conducted in as seemly and sensitive manner as is consistent with discovering anything concealed.
No person will be strip-searched in the sight of anyone not directly involved in the search.

a   A person who refuses to be searched will be denied access to the prison or detained in accordance with s 1.2.7.'

Section 1.2.5:

'Strip-searching of visitors is not permitted except in the circumstances specified in section 1.2.7 and then only if police attendance is not possible. In *b*   cases where strip-searches of visitors are necessary it is preferable that this is done by the police.'

Section 1.2.6:

'A visitor who refuses to co-operate with the search procedures will be advised that the failure to comply will result in exclusion from the prison.'
c
Section 1.2.7:

'If the duty governor sanctions a strip-search, the visitor should be taken to a room which is completely private and informed of the general nature of the suspected article.'

d   [19]   After the conclusion of the oral argument our attention was drawn to two recent decisions. At our invitation the parties submitted further written submissions on those decisions.

THE HUMAN RIGHTS ACT ISSUE

e   [20]   It is convenient to take this issue first. It relates to the judge's finding that the Home Office was under a liability to Mrs Wainwright based on the infringement of her right to privacy, notwithstanding that she suffered no physical injury, but only distress and humiliation. The existence of such a right at common law has never been clearly established but the judge found that she was entitled to the protection of such a right, basing his conclusion in part on the *f*   judgment of Sedley LJ in *Douglas v Hello! Ltd* [2001] 2 All ER 289, [2001] QB 967 that such a right could exist at common law and in part on the 1998 Act. However, as the judge recognised, in that case the acts complained of occurred after the 1998 Act had come into force on 2 October 2000, (Sedley LJ in his most instructive judgment was dealing with the question 'Is there today a right of privacy in English Law?' (see [2001] 2 All ER 289 at 316, [2001] QB 967 at 997 (para *g*   109)), while here the matters of complaint occurred prior to that date.

[21]   On this appeal Mr Wilby relies on the 1998 Act for a different purpose, namely to qualify the interpretation of r 86 so that it accords with art 8 of the European Convention for the Protection of Human Rights and Fundamental Freedoms 1950 (as set out in Sch 1 to the 1998 Act).

h   [22]   There has been considerable uncertainty as to whether the 1998 Act can apply retrospectively in situations where the conduct complained of occurred before the Act came into force. The position was considered by the House of Lords in *R v Lambert* [2001] UKHL 37, [2001] 3 All ER 577, [2002] 2 AC 545. After the hearing of this appeal the decision was given by the House of Lords in *R v* *j*   *Kansal (No 2)* [2001] UKHL 62, [2002] 1 All ER 257, [2002] 2 AC 69. In *R v Kansal* the actual decision in *R v Lambert* was subject to considerable criticism but because *R v Lambert* had only been recently decided and the decision only concerned a transitional situation the case of *R v Lambert* was not overruled.

[23]   Mr Wilby QC, on behalf of the claimants, concedes that *R v Lambert* made clear that convictions by courts before the 1998 Act had come into force cannot be impugned after the 1998 Act came into force on the grounds that the

court acted in a way which would be incompatible with convention rights. He
therefore accepts, for example, that the Court of Appeal could not on an appeal
coming before it after 2 October 2000 differ from a decision of the Employment
Appeal Tribunal prior to the Act coming into force as to the construction of the
Sex Discrimination Act 1975, if the construction of the Employment Appeal
Tribunal would have been regarded as correct before the 1998 Act came into
force. *Pearce v Governing Body of Mayfield Secondary School* [2001] EWCA Civ 1347,
[2001] IRLR 669 was cited in support of this concession.

[24]   However, Mr Wilby argues that this does not apply to s 3 of the 1998
Act. Section 3(1) provides:

'(1)   So far as it is possible to do so, primary legislation and subordinate
legislation must be read and given effect in a way which is compatible with
the Convention rights.

(2)   This section applies to primary legislation and subordinate legislation
whenever enacted ...'

[25]   It is not necessary to refer to s 3(2) as Mr Wilby does not rely on s 3(2) to
support his contention. He accepts the only relevance of that subsection is to
make it clear that once s 3 is in force it applies to legislation prior to the 1998 Act
coming into force.

[26]   Mr Wilby says looking at the language of s 3(1), it is clear from its
unqualified wording that once the 1998 Act was in force the judge and this court
are obliged to comply with s 3(1). Mr Wilby stresses that there has been no case
in which there is a judgment which is inconsistent with his submissions that once
the 1998 Act is in force a court is required to give effect to s 3(1) even though
matters complained of (as here) took place before the Act came into force. He
submits to do so does not involve giving retrospective effect to s 3 as long as the
court, as here, is trying the case after the 1998 Act is in force.

[27]   *R v Lambert* and *R v Kansal* do not directly decide this point. They did not
concern s 3. In those cases, unlike the position here, the decision under appeal
was given before the 1998 Act came into force. In addition there was no appeal
by a public authority as there is here by the Home Office. However the decision
in both cases is consistent with the general presumption that legislation should
not be treated as changing the substantive law in relation to events taking place
prior to legislation coming into force. But the whole purpose of this part of the
claimants' argument is to rely on s 3 to assist in establishing a liability on the
Home Office for causing humiliation and distress where without s 3 it would not
exist. This is therefore an attempt by Mr Wilby to rely on s 3 to achieve an
interpretation of r 86 which is then to be applied retrospectively to a situation
when the 1998 Act was not in force.

[28]   Of course, legislation can expressly provide that it is to apply
retrospectively and if it does so the legislation is retrospective in accordance with
the terms of the legislation. This is the position with regard to s 22(4) of the 1998
Act. Section 22(4) provides:

'Paragraph (b) subsection (1) of section 7 applies to proceedings brought by
or at the instigation of a public authority whenever the act in question took
place; but otherwise that subsection does not apply to an act taking place
before the coming into force of that section.'

[29]   Section 22(4) has no application to s 3. However, this does not mean that s 22(4) is not relevant. On the contrary, it is highly significant since it demonstrates that when Parliament wanted the 1998 Act to operate retrospectively it says so.

[30]   The speeches in *R v Lambert* as to the general approach to the 1998 Act commence with that of Lord Slynn ([2001] 3 All ER 577 at [6]):

> 'It is clear that the 1998 Act must be given its full import and that long or well entrenched ideas may have to be put aside, sacred cows culled. Since, however, the 1998 Act did not come into force (apart from limited provisions) until the Secretary of State had appointed a day or days for the Act or parts of it to come into force, and since there is a presumption against retrospectivity in legislation, it is not to be assumed a priori that convention rights, however commendable, are to be enforceable in national courts in respect of past events. The question is whether the 1998 Act has provided for rights to be enforceable in respect of such past events or more precisely whether a court reviewing the legality of a direction to a jury at a criminal trial given before the 1998 Act came into force, which was in accordance with the law at the time, has to be judged by the standards of the convention.'

[31]   Lord Slynn was concerned to look at the reality of the situation, as I would suggest we must do here, in order to see whether we are being asked to apply the 1998 Act retrospectively. Lord Slynn's approach is indicated in this passage from his speech (at [12]):

> 'Moreover, even if there is a basis for the contention that the appellant's argument based on ss 7 and 22 do not involve retrospectivity, it seems to me that the obvious effect of s 6 as interpreted by the appellant is to impose on the House the current duty of quashing retrospectively a conviction which was good as the law stood at the time.'

[32]   The speech of Lord Hope is also relevant. Lord Hope says (at [115]):

> '... there is nothing in the 1998 Act to indicate that that subsection is to be applied retrospectively to acts of courts or tribunals which took place before the coming into force of s 3(1).'

[33]   Furthermore Lord Hope cited what Sir Andrew Morritt V-C had said in *Wilson v First County Trust Ltd* [2001] EWCA Civ 633, [2001] 3 All ER 229, [2002] QB 74 and then goes on to say:

> 'I agree with Sir Andrew Morritt V-C that the answer to this argument is to be found in s 22(4). Parliament made its choice as to the extent to which the 1998 Act should have effect retrospectively. It did so by express enactment, and in my opinion no other reading of s 22(4) than that which I have indicated is possible.'

[34]   What had been said by Sir Andrew Morritt V-C is ([2001] 3 All ER 229 at [20]):

> 'The effect of s 22(4) is not in doubt. It provides (by the second limb of the section) that, in general, s 7(1) does not apply to an act taking place before 2 October 2000. So, for example, a person who claims that a public authority has acted in a way which is incompatible with a convention right (contrary to s 6(1) of the 1998 Act) cannot bring proceedings against the authority

under the 1998 Act (pursuant to s 7(1)(a)) if the unlawful act took place before 2 October 2000.'

[35] Lord Clyde also dealt with the issue but his approach is neutral so far as the present issue is concerned. He said ([2001] 3 All ER 577 at [142]):

'In my view s 3 only became obligatory on courts on 2 October 2000. The rule of construction which it expresses applies to all legislation whenever enacted.'

[36] However later (at [143]) Lord Clyde indicates his general approach when he adds:

'In general Acts of Parliament should not be read as operating so as to affect things done prior to their coming into effect. I see no reason why that principle should not apply to the 1998 Act. If a departure from the usual course was intended I would expect that to have been clearly stated.'

[37] In R v Kansal Lord Hope again refers expressly to s 3 after referring to my judgment in R v Benjafield [2001] 2 All ER 609 at 625, [2001] 3 WLR 75 at 92. He states ([2002] 1 All ER 257 at [84]): 'In my opinion however the usual presumption that statutes are not intended to be retrospective in effect applies to s 3(1).'

[38] And at the end of [84] he adds: 'So I would not extend retrospectivity to s 3(1), in the absence of an express provision to that effect.'

[39] In their additional written submissions, counsel on behalf of Mrs Wainwright and Alan submit R v Lambert should be given a very narrow application and confined to its facts. However, the major part of the criticism of the decision in R v Lambert relates to the artificial distinction which was drawn between proceedings involving the trial and the appeal. This distinction has no relevance to the present appeal. The point is also made that not to apply the 1998 Act to what happened to the claimants, will only result in their having to take proceedings in the European Court of Human Rights so as to obtain an effective remedy. This contention would have more force if the claimants were not seeking to rely on the convention to change English substantive law. Where this is what is in issue it is by no means clear that the European Court will provide a remedy when our courts do not do so.

[40] I would reject Mr Wilby's argument that the 1998 Act can affect the outcome of this appeal. It certainly cannot be relied on to change substantive law by introducing a retrospective right to privacy which did not exist at common law. The convention, contrary to the conclusion of the judge, is only relevant here as background against which the appeal is to be decided. This undermines one of the foundations for the judge's conclusions that the claimants were entitled to succeed on an extended form of trespass designed to protect the privacy of the individual.

WILKINSON V DOWNTON

[41] The other prop on which the judge relied to find that there was an extended tort of trespass containing the ingredients to which I have referred, is the judgment of Wright J in Wilkinson v Downton [1897] 2 QB 57, [1895–9] All ER Rep 267. The facts of Wilkinson v Downton are different from those here. The case involved a practical joke by the defendant. He falsely represented to the claimant, a married woman, that her husband had met with a serious accident in which his legs had been broken. The defendant made the statement with intent that it should be believed to be true. The plaintiff believed it to be true and in

a consequence suffered a violent nervous shock which rendered her ill. Why reliance is placed on this decision by the claimants is because at the time of the decision *Victorian Railways Comrs v Coultas* (1888) 13 App Cas 222, as was acknowledged, would have made it difficult, if not impossible, to recover damages for 'illness which was the effect of shock caused by fright'. Such injury was regarded as being too remote in an action for negligence.

b [42]   Wright J decided for the claimant and in doing so set out as 'the real ground' of action as being that 'a person who makes a false statement intended to be acted on must make good the damage naturally resulting from it being acted on'. Of this he said ([1897] 2 QB 57 at 58–59, [1895–9] All ER Rep 267 at 269):

c 'The defendant has, as I assume for the moment, wilfully done an act calculated to cause physical harm to the plaintiff—that is to say, to infringe her legal right to personal safety, and has in fact thereby caused physical harm to her. That proposition without more appears to me to state a good cause of action, there being no justification alleged for the act. This wilful injuria is in law malicious, although no malicious purpose to cause the harm which was caused nor any motive of spite is imputed to the defendant.'

[43]   And later Wright J added ([1897] 2 QB 57 at 59, [1895–9] All ER Rep 267 at 269):

e 'It remains to consider whether the assumptions involved in the proposition are made out. One question is whether the defendant's act was so plainly calculated to produce some effect of the kind which was produced that an intention to produce it ought to be imputed to the defendant, regard being had to the fact that the effect was produced on a person proved to be in an ordinary state of health and mind. I think that it was. It is difficult to f imagine that such a statement, made suddenly and with apparent seriousness, could fail to produce grave effects under the circumstances upon any but an exceptionally indifferent person, and therefore an intention to produce such an effect must be imputed, and it is no answer in law to say that more harm was done than was anticipated, for that is commonly the case with all wrongs. The other question is whether the effect was, to use the g ordinary phrase, too remote to be in law regarded as a consequence for which the defendant is answerable.'

[44]   To understand the approach of Wright J it is important to note the emphasis which Wright J places on the act being 'wilfully done'. For this to be h the position, the act has to be either one which is done with the intention of causing harm or done in circumstances where it was so likely that the harm would be incurred that an intention to produce harm has to be imputed. Certainly nothing less than recklessness would do.

[45]   Until the very recent decision of this court in *Wong v Parkside Health NHS* j *Trust* [2001] EWCA Civ 1721, [2003] 3 All ER 932, *Wilkinson v Downton* had not been considered extensively. Wright J's judgment was approved in *Janvier v Sweeney* [1919] 2 KB 316, [1918–19] All ER Rep 1056. In *Janvier's* case there was an actual intention to terrify the plaintiff for the purpose of obtaining an unlawful object in which both the defendants were jointly concerned. *Wilkinson v Downton* was more recently relied on in this court in *Burnett v George* [1993] 1 FCR 1012. However, that was a case involving the jurisdiction to grant an injunction and is

not of any real assistance in determining the ambit or the validity of the principle enunciated by Wright J.

[46] Our attention was drawn by Mr Wilby to Mullany and Handford *Tort Liability for Psychiatric Damage* (1993). In ch 14 of that book *Wilkinson v Downton* is considered in some detail. It points out that *Wilkinson v Downton* has been followed in a number of Commonwealth jurisdictions and in the United States. In that jurisdiction the approach is confined by the need for the conduct to be 'extreme and outrageous conduct' (see p 299). The editors consider that the argument for the *Wilkinson v Downton* action, being distinct from the tort of negligence, is that cases based on this principle do involve the intentional or reckless causing of shock 'in that the defendant intends to cause or is reckless as to, the immediate consequences—fright or horror—and that the physical harm which results can be regarded as intended or likely, rather than as merely foreseeable' (see p 290).

[47] In *Wong's* case the judgment of the court was given by Hale LJ. She considered the 'tort' created by *Wilkinson v Downton*. She did not doubt that there was a tort commonly labelled 'intentional infliction of harm'. She rejected the suggestion that the tort would be committed if there was deliberate conduct which 'foreseeably [led] to alarm or distress falling short of the recognised psychiatric illness which is now considered the equivalent of physical harm, provided that such harm is actually suffered' ([2003] 3 All ER 932 at [11]). She added (at [12]):

'For the tort to be committed, as with any other action on the case, there has to be actual damage. The damage is physical harm or recognised psychiatric illness. The defendant must have intended to violate the claimant's interest in his freedom from such harm. The conduct complained of has to be such that that degree of harm is sufficiently likely to result that the defendant cannot be heard to say that he did not "mean" it to do so. He is taken to have meant it to do so by the combination of the likelihood of such harm being suffered as the result of his behaviour and his deliberately engaging in that behaviour.'

[48] I happily adopt this definition of the 'tort' though I am not sure I would regard it as an action on the case but this is only of historic interest. I accept that an actual recognised psychiatric illness or bodily injury is required in order for damages to be recovered.

[49] The limiting factor to the 'tort' is the intention to cause harm which harm is in fact then caused or recklessness as to whether that harm would be caused. While the tort is not conventional trespass it is closer to trespass than negligence. I personally have no difficulty with the statement in *Salmond and Heuston on Torts* (21st edn, 1996) p 215 that 'one who by extreme and outrageous conduct intentionally or recklessly causes severe emotional distress to another is liable for such emotional distress, provided that bodily harm resulted from it'. This passage accepts that emotional distress by itself does not suffice. It requires bodily harm to have resulted. It presumably is intended to recognise that emotional distress although severe may not be classifiable by psychiatrists as a psychiatric illness. It therefore requires, in lay terms, that the severe emotional distress has caused bodily harm. It also requires that this is what the defendant intended to be the consequence or was reckless as to whether this would be the consequence.

a [50]   Both as a matter of principle and authority I regard it appropriate that there should be a right to compensation in these circumstances. We are here concerned with an intentional tort and intended harm. In such a situation, unlike negligence, problems as to forseeability do not arise. If the conduct is actionable then compensation should be payable for the intended harm. For this general approach there is general support in *Winfield and Jolowicz on Tort* (15th edn, 1998)
b pp 86–87.

[51]   In this jurisdiction I consider that *Wilkinson v Downton* should be so limited. This provides the proper justification for distinguishing the cause of action from negligence. On that basis I would not seek to doubt the correctness of the decision in *Wilkinson v Downton*. However, so understood *Wilkinson v Downton* cannot be relied upon by the claimants in the present case. The judge
c made no finding that the prison officers were intending to cause or were reckless as to whether they caused harm. Furthermore the findings which he did make were inconsistent with such a conclusion. Had the facts been otherwise and harm had been intended or if there had been recklessness then I would have upheld the decision of the judge. I would have concluded that on the judge's
d findings the complainants had suffered the necessary damage.

JUSTIFICATION
[52]   Mr Tam, on behalf of the Home Office, argued that because of the width of r 86, in any event what the prison officers did was justified. Mr Tam argued that because of the language of r 86, the Home Office was not bound by
e either what appears on the consent form or what is stated in the policy strategy document which applies specifically to HM Prison Leeds. This cannot be the position. If there are clearly laid down restrictions on how a particular activity is to be conducted, then the conduct of the prison officers cannot be excused merely because those restrictions may not have been observed. The conduct may not be
f actionable but as we will see the rule cannot justify their conduct if it were otherwise actionable. I would therefore reject this part of the argument on behalf of the Home Office if it had been necessary to do so.

CONSENT
[53]   Mr Tam also argued the judge was wrong to conclude there had been
g no real consent here. Again I disagree but do so on the grounds that the consent which was given was given on the basis that the search would be conducted in accordance with proper practice. It was not and so the consent does not provide the Home Office with a defence.

PROPORTIONALITY
h [54]   As the 1998 Act was not in force, the judge should not have become involved in issues as to proportionality. However, as he expressed the view that to conduct the search in the circumstances which were then existent at the prison was disproportionate, I should make it clear that we would not agree with that view. Each case, of course, depends on its facts but when one has the sort of
j problem with which the prison service is faced in relation to drugs, clearly it is not sufficient to search the prisoner. There are numerous ways in which drugs can be smuggled into the prison and the most vigorous regime of searching *prisoners* will not in itself suffice. On the findings of the judge, searching, if it had been properly conducted, was perfectly appropriate. The visitor who is treated in accordance with the instructions laid down was reasonably given the choice of having a visit and submitting to being searched or not being searched.

[55]   It follows that the appeal has to be allowed except for the finding of battery which was not subject to appeal.   This has the effect that Mrs Wainwright's claim is dismissed and Alan's claim for damages has to be reduced. Unfortunately the parties were unable to agree what should be the proper measure of damages. We are not in a position to do more than give the most limited consideration to this subject and without the figure which we have determined being regarded as any precedent for other cases, I would reduce the damages that Alan receives to £3,750 including £1,000 aggravated damages.

MUMMERY LJ.

[56]   I agree that this appeal should be allowed for the reasons given by Lord Woolf CJ and Buxton LJ. I shall confine my brief additional comments to the issue of invasion of privacy at common law and in equity and to the applicability of s 3(1) of the Human Rights Act 1998.

(1) INVASION OF PRIVACY AT COMMON LAW AND IN EQUITY

[57]   This claim fails, as there is no tort of invasion of privacy. Instead there are torts protecting a person's interests in the privacy of his body, his home, and his personal property. There is also available the equitable doctrine of breach of confidence for the protection of personal information, private communications and correspondence.

[58]   The common law position remains as stated in the Justice Report on Privacy and the Law (1970) para 30: '... it is generally recognised that at the present time there is no existing common law remedy for invasion of privacy as such.'

[59]   According to a more recent statement of the legal position in Clayton and Tomlinson The Law of Human Rights (2000) para 12.06: 'It is well established that English law does not recognise a right of privacy as such.'

[60]   As to the future I foresee serious definitional difficulties and conceptual problems in the judicial development of a 'blockbuster' tort vaguely embracing such a potentially wide range of situations. I am not even sure that anybody—the public, Parliament, the press—really wants the creation of a new tort, which could give rise to as many problems as it is sought to solve. A more promising and well trod path is that of incremental evolution, both at common law and by statute (eg s 3 of the Protection from Harassment Act 1997), of traditional nominate torts pragmatically crafted as to conditions of liability, specific defences and appropriate remedies, and tailored to suit significantly different privacy interests and infringement situations.

(2) SECTION 3(1) OF THE HUMAN RIGHTS ACT 1998

[61]   With the benefit of the recent decisions of the House of Lords (R v Lambert [2001] UKHL 37, [2001] 3 All ER 577, [2002] 2 AC 545 and R v Kansal (No 2) [2001] UKHL 62, [2002] 1 All ER 257, [2002] 2 AC 69) and of this court (Wilson v First County Trust Ltd [2001] EWCA Civ 633, [2001] 3 All ER 229, [2002] QB 74 and Pearce v Governing Body of Mayfield Secondary School [2001] EWCA Civ 1347, [2001] IRLR 669), I am now convinced that I was wrong in the remarks made by me obiter in JA Pye (Oxford) Ltd v Graham [2001] EWCA Civ 117 at [59], [2001] 2 WLR 1293 at [59] on the applicability of the principle of interpretation in s 3(1) to causes of action arising before the section came into effect. Section 3(1) does not apply retrospectively to the cause of action in this case which arose in 1997.

a It cannot therefore assist on the construction of r 86 of the Prison Rules 1964, SI 1964/388.

BUXTON LJ.

INTRODUCTION

b [62] I gratefully adopt the account set out by Lord Woolf CJ of the facts of this worrying and difficult case. If the deplorable treatment meted out to Mrs Wainwright and her son had occurred not in January 1997 but in August 1997, after the coming into effect of the Protection from Harassment Act 1997, they would have had a strong case, subject to as yet unresolved difficulties about the definition of 'course of conduct', for relief under s 3 thereof. If the
c events had occurred in October 2000, they would equally have had a strong case for relief under s 7 of the Human Rights Act 1998, by reason of a public authority's lack of regard for art 8 of the European Convention for the Protection of Human Rights and Fundamental Freedoms 1950 (as set out in Sch 1 to the 1998 Act). Whether, in either case, that would have led to recovery in respect of the damage claimed is another matter, to which I will in due course have to return.
d But the issue in this case is whether, before those two alterations in the law, English law provided any private law relief at all in respect of conduct of the type with which we are concerned.

[63] I have reached the clear conclusion that the judge, in a difficult and unusual case, was in error in finding that the conduct complained of fell within a
e tort recognised by English law, subject only to the potential defences of consent and justification. It will first be necessary to examine in some detail the basis on which the judge felt able to proceed, and then set out what in my judgement is the true state of the law, and how that law should be applied to the facts of the present case.

f
AN ANALYSIS OF THE JUDGE'S REASONING

[64] In the hope of better explaining some parts of this judgment that follows, I feel constrained to set out the relevant parts of the judge's reasoning verbatim. The judge found that Alan Wainwright had been stripped naked and Mrs Wainwright virtually so, dealt with the additional allegation of battery in
g relation to Alan Wainwright, and then continued:

'70. It is clear that the original tort of trespass to the person, namely battery, has been extended in a number of ways beyond its original scope of protecting the interest of the victim in freedom from bodily harm. In the form of trespass to the person known as assault the interest of the victim
h which is protected is the victim's interest in freedom from a particular form of anxiety, namely the apprehension of bodily harm. The form of trespass to the person involve in false imprisonment protects the interest in freedom from confinement or freedom of movement. The tort of trespass to the person protects, therefore, a wider range of interests than protection from
j bodily harm.

71. Another element in the law of torts generally and trespass to the person in particular is the conduct of the defendant. Again the original tort focused on some physical act of the defendant, namely touching the plaintiff or doing something which causes the plaintiff to apprehend physical contact. In *Wilkinson v Downton* [1897] 2 QB 57, [1985–9] All ER Rep 267 and the subsequent Court of Appeal decision in *Janvier v Sweeney* [1919] 2 KB 316,

[1918–19] All ER Rep 1056 the courts extended the types of conduct which *a* could constitute the tort of trespass to the person to include words intentionally uttered which caused physical harm. In *Burnett v George* [1993] 1 FCR 1012 the principle derived from these two cases, namely that there is a good cause of action if A wilfully does something calculated to cause harm to B, namely infringing B's right to personal safety, and does in fact cause physical harm to B, was extended to a case of harassment. The conduct *b* involved in trespass to the person includes conduct which involves no bodily contact with the victim but nevertheless has an effect on the victim by infringing some interest of the victim which the law protects.

72. In this case the essence of the complaint is that the prison officers caused Mrs Wainwright and her son to take their clothes off and thereby suffer distress and humiliation in the case of both claimants and damage to *c* health in the case of Alan Wainwright. The law of torts already recognises causes of action where the defendant induces the claimant to act to the claimant's detriment. Misrepresentation is one example and intimidation another. It does not, therefore, seem to me to be a significant extension of the principle in *Wilkinson v Downton* to hold that if A wilfully causes B to do *d* something which is calculated to cause harm to B, namely infringe B's legal right to personal safety, and does in fact cause physical harm to B, that constitutes a valid cause of action unless it can be justified in some way. I would hold, therefore, that if the prison officers caused Alan Wainwright to take his clothes off and that was calculated to cause a physical harm, namely illness, to Alan Wainwright there is a valid cause of action in trespass to the *e* person unless their conduct can be justified ...

74. The same principle would apply to Mrs Wainwright but in her case the strip-search did not cause any physical illness. This raises the question whether this particular form of trespass to the person should be limited to protecting the victim's right to personal safety or whether it should be *f* extended to other rights, including in particular the right of privacy. In the case of assault the law of trespass protects the victim's interest in being protected from mental distress caused by the apprehension of physical harm. Other forms of trespass to the person protect a victim's interest in freedom of movement or even freedom from harm caused by verbal practical jokes in bad taste. It seems difficult to justify a situation in which the same act *g* (inducing someone to take their clothes off) gives the victim a cause of action if the victim succumbs to some form of illness but denies a remedy to a more robust victim who merely suffers distress and humiliation.

75. In *Douglas v Hello! Ltd* [2001] 2 All ER 289, [2001] QB 967 the Court of Appeal discharged an injunction granted against Hello! Magazine from *h* publishing unauthorized photographs of a wedding. Another magazine had the exclusive rights to photograph the wedding. Sedley LJ said that a point had been reached where it could be said with confidence that the law recognised and would appropriately protect a right of personal privacy for two reasons. The first reason was that there was a powerfully arguable case *j* that the bride and groom had a right of privacy which English Law would recognise and, where appropriate, protect. The second reason was that the Human Rights Act 1998 required courts to give appropriate effect to the right of respect for private and family life set out in art 8 of the convention. Keene LJ said that it seemed unlikely that *Kaye*'s case, which held that that there was no actionable right of privacy in English Law, would be decided

a   the same way on that aspect today. These dicta show how the attitude of the courts to invasions of someone's privacy have developed in recent years. There seems to me to be no valid objection to extending the tort of trespass to the person to protect an interest in privacy ...

77. ... [Counsel for the claimants] pointed out that in *Brind v Secretary of State for the Home Dept* [1991] 1 All ER 720, [1991] 1 AC 696 the House of
b   Lords had held in 1991 that any provision in domestic legislation which was capable of a meaning which either conformed to or conflicted with the convention would be construed in conformity with the convention on the basis that Parliament was to be presumed to have intended to legislate in accordance with the convention. On analogous reasoning it appears to me that it was right to apply and, so far as appropriate, extend the common law
c   so that it is also in conformity with the convention even before the passing of the 1998 Act. Sections 2 and 3 of that Act strengthen the force of that reasoning.

78.   I conclude therefore that the tort of trespass of the person extends to situations where A causes B to do something to himself which infringes B's
d   right of privacy. The defendant is liable to Mrs Wainwright and Alan Wainwright unless the defendant can set up a valid defence. The two defences put forward are those of consent and legal justification.'

[65]   This reasoning contains the following elements. (i)   The tort of trespass to the person extends to interests other than protection from bodily harm. (ii)   One example of such extension is to 'words intentionally uttered
e   which caused physical harm', as in *Wilkinson v Downton* (para 71). (iii)   However, 'physical harm' in that formulation means illness, which was proved in the case of Alan Wainwright but not in the case of Mrs Wainwright. Alan Wainwright could therefore recover under this head of tort, but Mrs Wainwright could not (para 72). (iv)   English law however recognises a tort of breach of privacy,
f   independent of any change introduced by the 1998 Act, and therefore applicable to events occurring in January 1997. That tort, described as an aspect of trespass to the person, had been committed in relation to Mrs Wainwright, and also, in addition to the *Wilkinson v Downton* tort, in relation to Alan Wainwright (para 78).

g
THE INAPPROPRIATENESS OF TRESPASS

[66]   Whatever torts the Wainwrights may be able to complain of, none of them are, or are properly derivatives of, the tort of trespass to the person, and only confusion was caused by the attempt to force what occurred in this case into that straitjacket. That objection is not merely an obsolete recourse to the forms
h   of action, nor a reflection of a mediaeval distinction between trespass and case. As I shall demonstrate, it reflects fundamental principles by which modern English law, rightly or wrongly, limits the ambit of tortious liability.

[67]   Leaving aside false imprisonment, which is sometimes, though not very happily, categorised as a trespass to the person, trespass in this sense consists of
j   battery and of assault. Battery is physical interference with the person of the plaintiff. That will normally consist of direct touching of the person, but has also been extended to acts directly likely to cause such interference, such as hitting the plaintiff's horse, causing him to fall off; and more controversially, in the criminal understanding of battery, to the creating of a dangerous situation from which physical interference naturally results, such as putting sulphuric acid into a hot air dryer that when used by others blew out and caused them injury (*DPP v K (a*

minor) [1990] 1 WLR 1067); or locking the doors of a theatre and then causing a
panic, with injury occurring to persons in the resulting crush (*R v Martin* (1881)
8 QBD 54, [1881–5] All ER Rep 699). The unifying factor in all these cases is an
invasion of the physical person of the plaintiff.

[68]   An assault has long been defined as an overt action, by word or by deed,
indicating an immediate intention to commit a battery and with the capacity to
carry the threat into action: see *Clerk and Lindsell on Torts* (18th edn, 2000)
para 13-13; or, as it is sometimes expressed, to put the plaintiff in fear of an
immediate assault. This tort is therefore parasitic upon, and protects the interests
protected by, battery.

[69]   The importance that the law attaches to protecting citizens from direct
physical interference with their persons is demonstrated by two particular
features of the tort of battery, both of which sharply distinguish it from the tort
of negligence. The first, expounded in further detail in the judgment of this court
in *Wilson v Pringle* [1986] 2 All ER 440, [1987] QB 237, is that any intended 'hostile'
touching founds an action for battery, even if there is no intention thereby to
cause injury or actual physical harm. The second is that battery is actionable per
se. That in turn implies two things: first, damages are recoverable for the act of
interference itself, even if it causes no injury and no loss; but, secondly, if damage
is caused by a trespass it is recoverable simply on the basis of causation, and does
not additionally require foreseeability to be established.

[70]   These rules show the basis of the tort of trespass, in the protection of
interference with the person of the plaintiff by direct contact with him. Once the
defendant causes such contact, without justification, he is not only liable for
damages even if no quantifiable loss results; but also liable for any loss that is in
fact caused by the interference. These rules are strikingly different from those
obtaining in negligence. Liability in negligence is limited to the type of damage
that the defendant should have foreseen as liable to result from his acts: authority
is hardly needed for that proposition, but I would venture to refer to the recent
exposition by Lord Hobhouse of Woodborough, speaking with the agreement of
a majority of the House, in *Platform Home Loans Ltd v Oyston Shipways Ltd* [1999]
1 All ER 833 at 847, [2000] 2 AC 190 at 209.

[71]   There are therefore powerful reasons why a claimant will be well
advised to seek to categorise his claim as sounding in trespass. Once he has passed
through that door, he not only is able to recover for unforeseeable damage, but
also is relieved of the issues of duty of care and of fairness, justice and
reasonableness that are applied to limit recovery in negligence. And on the other
side of the coin there are strong policy reasons why the tort of trespass to the
person should be limited to its proper sphere. It was these considerations that
Lord Denning MR had in mind when he said in *Letang v Cooper* [1964] 2 All ER 929
at 932, [1965] 1 QB 232 at 239 that an unintentional but negligent battery must be
pleaded in negligence and not in trespass.

[72]   But our case goes further than that. It is not a case of direct interference,
battery, at all, but of causing the claimants to do something to themselves that led
to humiliation and illness. Nor was the case argued to be a case of trespass, nor
was it seen as such by the judge. Rather it was presented as an extension of the
tort of trespass into the areas covered by *Wilkinson v Downton* and privacy. Such
an extension of trespass is unsupported by authority, entirely unprincipled, and if
adopted would severely undermine the policy reasons for limiting the ambit of
trespass that are referred to above.

a [73] It does not, however, follow from that that the appeal must necessarily succeed. It is possible to read the judgment as a decision that the Home Office is liable on the basis of separate and independent torts, outside the law of trespass, of 'Wilkinson v Downton' in the case of Alan Wainwright, and of breach of privacy in respect of both of the Wainwrights. If, as the judge thought, the requirements of those torts were in fact fulfilled, I would not permit the argument to fail just

b because of the inappropriate pleading in terms of trespass. I therefore turn to those torts.

WILKINSON V DOWNTON
[74] In *Wilkinson v Downton* [1897] 2 QB 57 at 58–59, [1985–9] All ER Rep 267 at 269 Wright J said:

c
'The defendant has, as I assume for the moment, wilfully done an act calculated to cause physical harm to the plaintiff—that is to say, to infringe her legal right to personal safety, and has in fact thereby caused physical harm to her. That proposition without more appears to me to state a good cause of action, there being no justification alleged for the act. This wilful

d injuria is in law malicious, although no malicious purpose to cause the harm which was caused nor any motive of spite is imputed to the defendant ... One question is whether the defendant's act was so plainly calculated to produce some effect of the kind which was produced that an intention to produce it ought to be imputed to the defendant, regard being had to the fact

e that the effect was produced on a person proved to be in an ordinary state of health and mind.'

[75] The greatest respect is always paid to anything that fell from Wright J: see for instance Goddard LJ in *Peters v Prince of Wales Theatre (Birmingham) Ltd* [1942] 2 All ER 533 at 537–538, [1943] KB 73 at 77. However, one cannot escape

f from the observation that *Wilkinson v Downton* has puzzled generations of tort lawyers. No little part of the difficulty has sprung from a tendency to quote Wright J's reference to acts 'calculated to cause physical harm' divorced from the rest of his formulation of the cause of action: as indeed the judge did in our case, in para 72 of his judgment. That is particularly unfortunate, because the word 'calculated' is ambiguous between acts subjectively intended to cause harm and

g acts objectively very likely to cause harm. And Wright J's extension of 'physical harm' into infringement of the 'legal right to personal safety' carries difficulties of its own, since it again is ambiguous between the actuality of physical harm and a threat of such harm.

[76] Wright J provided further explanation by his later reference, in a passage

h much less often quoted, to an 'act so plainly calculated to produce some effect of the kind which was produced that an intention to produce it ought to be imputed to the defendant'. That, however, raises further difficulties, since although using the concept of intention it stops short of requiring actual intention, and rather speaks of 'imputed' intention, in terms that would nowadays be analysed as

j referring to gross (objective) negligence.
[77] This court took up the matter in *Janvier v Sweeney* [1919] 2 KB 316. Much of the judgments is addressed to the question in issue in that case of whether it was possible to recover at all for 'nervous shock'. That had been doubted in the Privy Council case of *Victorian Railways Comrs v Coultas* (1888) 13 App Cas 222, but the Court of Appeal recognised that if they were to accept that argument they would have to differ from *Wilkinson v Downton*, which they declined to do. The

judgments are, however, less clear as to the acts and intentions leading to the nervous shock that are sufficient to found the tort. While not differing from, *a* indeed adopting, the formulation of Wright J, both Bankes LJ and Duke LJ laid stress on the fact that the plaintiff in *Janvier v Sweeney* had put the plaintiff in a state of terror, Duke LJ saying in terms that the defendant had intended to produce that condition.

[78] The learned editor of the Law Reports report of *Janvier v Sweeney* *b* synthesised the effect of the judgments thus:

> 'False words and threats calculated to cause, uttered with the knowledge that they are likely to cause, and actually causing physical injury to the person to whom they are uttered are actionable.'

c

This statement is important, because in *Khorasandjian v Bush* [1993] 3 All ER 669 at 676, [1993] QB 727 at 735 the majority in this court accepted it as a correct expression of the doctrine of *Wilkinson v Downton* and *Janvier v Sweeney*; and would have granted quia timet relief against such words that could be expected, if continued, to result in a recognisable psychiatric illness: which is how the majority ([1993] 3 All ER 669 at 676–677, [1993] QB 727 at 735 at 736) considered *d* that 'nervous shock' should now be understood. These observations were obiter, in view of the majority's placing of liability on the basis of private nuisance; but they were fully considered and, because of their obiter nature have, as Mr Wilby QC urged upon us, escaped the condemnation by the House of Lords in *Hunter v Canary Wharf Ltd, Hunter v London Docklands Development Corp* [1997] 2 All ER 426, *e* [1997] AC 655 of the nuisance aspects of *Khorasandjian's* case.

[79] I respectfully consider that the headnote in *Janvier v Sweeney*, adopted in *Khorasandjian's* case, comes as close as it is possible to do to a general statement of the rule in *Wilkinson v Downton*. If that is not correct, then the rule must be limited to the statement in the latter part of Wright J's observations cited in [13], above, that the defendant's act was so clearly likely to produce a result of the kind *f* that occurred that an intention to produce it should be imputed to him: that is to say, objective recklessness. I do not find helpful in this connection the only other Court of Appeal case shown to us, *Burnett v George* [1993] 1 FCR 1012, since there the court simply read the 'calculated' formula of *Wilkinson v Downton* into the form of an injunction, without further investigating the implications of that *g* language.

[80] It follows that I cannot agree with the formulation adopted in *Salmond and Heuston on Torts* (21st edn, 1996) p 215 from the American Law Institute *Restatement of the Law, Torts* 2d (1965) para 46 that—

h
> 'one who by extreme and outrageous conduct intentionally or recklessly causes severe emotional distress to another is liable for such emotional distress, provided that bodily harm results from it.'

No doubt the outrageous nature of the defendant's conduct was not far from the minds of the judges in *Wilkinson v Downton* and, in particular, *Janvier v Sweeney*. *j* However, moral condemnation is not enough. What is required by the *Khorasandjian* formulation is knowledge that the words are likely to cause, that is to say subjective recklessness as to the causation of, physical injury in the sense of recognisable psychiatric illness. Intention or recklessness merely as to severe emotional distress, from which bodily harm happens in fact to result, is not enough.

a

[81] It also follows that, with equal respect, I am unable to adopt as a complete statement of the law the observation in *Clerk and Lindsell on Torts* (para 13-17) that—

> 'It would appear that any act deliberately designed to "infringe [the] legal right to personal safety", albeit falling outside the torts of assault and battery, will now readily be classified as tortious.'

b

The authority cited for this proposition is *Burris v Azadani* [1995] 4 All ER 802, [1995] 1 WLR 1372. Since that case largely relied on that part of *Khorasandjian* that was disapproved in the *Canary Wharf* case; and in any event was an injunction case in which this court was of the view that conduct could be enjoined even if it was not in itself tortious; its authority in the present context

c must be open to question. And while it is correct that *Clerk and Lindsell's* formulation does quote the ipsissima verba of Wright J, it leaves unresolved the uncertainties as to the ambit of the 'right to personal safety' to which I have ventured to draw attention in [75]–[76], above.

[82] After the close of argument in the present appeal, and after the

d substance of the foregoing paragraphs of this judgment had been drafted, there came to our attention the judgment of this court in *Wong v Parkside Health NHS Trust* [2001] EWCA Civ 1721, [2003] 3 All ER 932, in which another division of this court was, like ourselves, called upon to consider the correct ambit of *Wilkinson v Downton*.

[83] This court said in *Wong*'s case (at [12])—

e

> 'The damage is physical harm or recognised psychiatric illness. The defendant must have intended to violate the claimant's interest in his freedom from such harm. The conduct complained of has to be such that that degree of harm is sufficiently likely to result that the defendant cannot be heard to say that he did not "mean" it to do so. He is taken to have meant

f

> it to do so by the combination of the likelihood of such harm being suffered as the result of his behaviour and his deliberately engaging in that behaviour'

and then referred in support of that formulation to the observations of Dillon LJ in *Khorasandjian*'s case [1993] 3 All ER 669 at 676, [1993] QB 727 at 735. The court accordingly saw as equivalent in their effect the two formulations between which

g a distinction was drawn in the first two sentences of [79], above.

[84] The decision in *Wong*'s case, to the extent to which it differs from the analysis earlier in this judgment, binds us as an earlier decision of this court. However, in the present case it does not matter which of these various detailed formulations is adopted, because it is plain that the claimants can bring

h themselves within none of them. Because the case proceeded on the basis of the formulaic expression of 'calculated to cause physical harm', without further examination of what that meant, the judge was not asked to make, and did not make, any finding as to actual intention to cause, or imputed intention to cause, or recklessness, either objective or subjective, as to physical injury, recognisable

j psychiatric illness, or even severe emotional distress. Mr Wilby gallantly sought to argue that some such findings could be extracted from the last two sentences of para 72 of the judgment, but with respect to him all that the judge did there was to recite in abstract terms what he considered the law to be, rather than analyse the facts of the case in the light of that law.

[85] A claim based on *Wilkinson v Downton* must therefore fail. I should however perhaps make it clear that, although the claim fails because of the

absence of findings necessary to support it, I do not regard that as a merely
technical or formalistic objection. Had the judge been asked to make any of the *a*
findings referred to in [84], above it seems to me that he would have found it
difficult or impossible to do so: however much the prison officers ought to have
realised, and perhaps did realise, that what they asked the Wainwrights to do
would and did cause them offence and distress.

[86]   It is therefore necessary to turn to the alternative basis on which the *b*
judge decided the case in favour of Alan Wainwright, and the only basis on
which, because the search did not cause her physical illness, he decided the case
in favour of Mrs Wainwright: the tort of invasion of privacy.

PRIVACY: INTRODUCTION
[87]   The present case is important, not only because it appears to be the first *c*
case in which recovery has been achieved simply for a breach of the right to
privacy; but also because, as Brooke LJ pointed out in the important case of
Douglas v Hello! Ltd [2001] 2 All ER 289 at 307–308, [2001] QB 967 at 988 (para 71),
previous investigations of this area have all been in cases where, in one way or
another, confidence can be said to have been broken. That was of course the case *d*
in *Douglas*'s case itself. The difficulty arises, as Brooke LJ foresaw, in a case where
privacy alone is in issue; and that is this case, since whatever else the Wainwrights
may be able to complain of, they cannot and do not say that any right of *confidence*
has been infringed.

[88]   It will therefore be necessary to examine whether there was in 1997 a
tort of breach of privacy, and if so what was its ambit. That will require attention *e*
both to authority and, since this is an area in which it has been suggested that the
judges should take the initiative in extending the law, also to some issues of
policy. First, however, it is necessary to dispose of a series of issues that relate to
the convention.

f

PRIVACY: THE EUROPEAN COURT OF HUMAN RIGHTS
[89]   First, since the events complained of took place in 1997, the tort of
privacy that is relied on, if it exists, must have an existence independent of the
1998 Act. I respectfully agree with what is said by Lord Woolf CJ at [39]–[40],
above:

g
    'the claimants [are] seeking to rely on the convention to change English
    substantive law ... [the 1998 Act] certainly cannot be relied on to change
    substantive law by introducing a retrospective right to privacy which did not
    exist at common law.'

[90]   Second, that implies that the tort must indeed be a tort, that is, sounding *h*
in damages in private law, and available against any kind of defendant: however
much in the present case the complaint is about the conduct of a public authority
in the performance of its public functions.

[91]   Third, however, is the judge's reasoning in para 77 of his judgment that,
by analogy with the approach to legislative construction that was adopted in *j*
Brind v Secretary of State for the Home Dept [1991] 1 All ER 720, [1991] 1 AC 696, the
common law should be read as being 'in conformity with the convention' even
before the passing of the 1998 Act. While courts before the 1998 Act were alert
to the importance of the United Kingdom's treaty obligations, there was never
any suggestion of an approach as broad as that of the judge, and positive authority
against it, specifically in the context of privacy, in the judgment of Megarry V-C

a in *Malone v Comr of Police of the Metropolis (No 2)* [1979] 2 All ER 620, [1979] Ch 344.
And that is quite apart from the more general principle, enunciated for instance
by Lord Templeman, speaking for a majority of the House, in *Maclaine Watson &
Co Ltd v Dept of Trade and Industry, Maclaine Watson & Co Ltd v International Tin
Council* [1989] 3 All ER 523 at 526–527, sub nom *Rayner (JH) (Mincing Lane) Ltd v
Dept of Trade and Industry* [1990] 2 AC 418 at 476–477, that international treaties,
b such as was the status of the convention in England before 2 October 2000,
cannot confer rights enforceable in English courts. Indeed, if the judge were
right, it would be difficult to understand why Parliament thought it necessary to
pass the 1998 Act at all.

[92] And further, quite apart from that fundamental difficulty, the judge's
approach does not face up to the fact that the convention by its terms creates
c obligations only against the state, and not against other private individuals. That
point was plainly in the mind of Megarry V-C in *Malone's* case [1979] 2 All ER 620
at 648, [1979] Ch 344 at 379:

d   'It seems to me that where Parliament has abstained from legislating on a
point that is plainly suitable for legislation, it is indeed difficult for the court
to lay down new rules of common law or equity that will carry out the
Crown's treaty obligations, or to discover for the first time that such rules
have always existed.'

Some have argued that, with the advent of the 1998 Act, it is possible to use the
e recognition of the courts as 'public authorities' by s 6(3)(a) thereof to create
private law rights broadly in the same verbal terms as the wording of the articles
of the convention. There are many difficulties about that contention: I readily
adopt the observation of Sedley LJ in *Douglas's* case [2001] 2 All ER 289 at 320,
[2001] QB 967 at 1001 (para 128) that this also is not the place, at least without
much fuller argument, in which to resolve such a large question. But the present
f importance of that issue is that it is seen to be the terms of the 1998 Act, and not,
as the judge thought, the direct application of the terms of the convention, that
render it even arguable that the convention creates new torts in English private
law.

[93] Fourth, it may be convenient to say that, if the events in question had
occurred after 2 October 2000, they would in my view have grounded a right to
g relief for the Wainwrights under s 7(1)(a) of the 1998 Act, by reason of the prison
authorities' breach of art 8 of the convention. That does not, however, engage a
private law right in tort, such as the Wainwrights must establish in relation to
events occurring before 2 October 2000, because s 7(1)(a) makes the defendants
liable on the basis of, and only on the basis of, their status as public authorities. I
h would consider that the right to privacy in art 8(1) had been infringed, and that
that breach could not be offset under art 8(2). That would not be because, as the
judge seems to have thought, at paras 107–108 of his judgment, that something
like a 'blanket' policy of searching visitors to suspected drug dealers was not
justified: in the context of the threat of drug abuse in prisons that policy was well
j within the reasonable, and if it is relevant the proportionate, actions of the prison
authorities. Rather, the failure was in the manner in which this particular search
was conducted, a matter to which I return when considering the defence of
consent.

[94] It does not, however, follow from that that the Wainwrights could
recover in respect of the injuries on which their present claim is based, as
opposed to recovering some amount, perhaps not dissimilar to the aggravated

damages awarded in this case, to mark the unlawful invasion of their privacy. That is because it is wholly unclear what are the rules of remoteness attaching to a claim under s 7; whether breaches of the convention by public authorities are actionable per se; and if they are, what heads of damage and amounts of damages are recoverable. I mention these matters because they are difficulties that equally attach to the private law tort of breach of privacy that is asserted in this case.

[95]   I have ventured to address these matters in some detail because, when considering the implications for private law torts of a case such as *Douglas*'s case that was decided after 2 October 2000, it is necessary to be clear as to what springs from the effect of the 1998 Act, and what from the application of the common law as it stood before that date. To the latter question I now turn.

PRIVACY: AUTHORITY

[96]   Mr Wilby relied very heavily upon an observation of Sedley LJ in *Douglas*'s case [2001] 2 All ER 289 at 320, [2001] QB 967 at 1001 (para 126). This observation was obiter, since the court was satisfied that recovery was available in respect of breach of *confidence*, in which circumstances it is unnecessary to go on to the wider category of acts argued to ground liability for breach of privacy. Nevertheless, the passage indubitably demands the closest attention. Sedley LJ said:

> 'What a concept of privacy does, however, is accord recognition to the fact that the law has to protect not only those people whose trust has been abused but those who simply find themselves subjected to an unwanted intrusion into their personal lives. The law no longer needs to construct an artificial relationship of confidentiality between intruder and victim: it can recognise privacy itself as a legal principle drawn from the fundamental value of personal autonomy.'

It will be noted that this formulation of the basis of recovery is distinctly different from that adopted by the judge, and discussed in [91]–[92], above. Sedley LJ saw the tort as one existing in English private law, independently of the convention. True it is that he referred to the 1998 Act as 'arguably [giving] the final impetus to the recognition of a right of privacy in English law' (see [2001] 2 All ER 289 at 317, [2001] QB 967 at 998 (para 111)): which may of course raise some questions about the status of the tort in 1997. But in truth the process is seen as one of judicial development of the common law, with the convention serving as, at most, a catalyst for that development.

[97]   This is at first sight an attractive prospect and, if I may very respectfully say so, it could not have been put more attractively than it was by my brother in *Douglas*'s case. However, authority in this court precludes our taking that course; and in addition there are serious difficulties of principle in the way of the judges creating a tort in the terms now suggested.

[98]   With one exception, all of the previous cases that are seen as providing the germ of a tort of breach of privacy were decided on the basis of breach of confidence. That is clear from the exposition by Brooke LJ in *Douglas*'s case [2001] 2 All ER 289 at 305–308, [2001] QB 967 at 985–988 (paras 64–71), as indeed from the exposition of Sedley LJ ([2001] 2 All ER 289 at 317–319, [2001] QB 967 at 998–1000 (paras 116–122)). And that is true even of the well known observation of Laws LJ in *Hellewell v Chief Constable of Derbyshire* [1995] 4 All ER 473 at 476,

a [1995] 1 WLR 804 at 807, which was strongly relied on by Sedley LJ in *Douglas's* case:

> 'If someone with a telephoto lens were to take from a distance and with no authority a picture of another engaged in some private act, his *subsequent disclosure of the picture* would ... as surely amount to *a breach of confidence* as if
b he had found or stolen a letter or diary in which the act was recounted *and proceeded to publish it ...*'

[99] These cases therefore do nothing to assist the crucial move now urged, that the courts in giving relief should step outside the limits imposed by a requirement of a relationship of confidence, artificial or otherwise. This court
c was called on to consider making that move in *Kaye v Robertson* [1991] FSR 62. It declined to do so.

[100] The conduct of the defendants in that case, in breaking into the plaintiff's hospital ward, taking a photograph of him in a distressed state, and then seeking to publish it in their newspaper, was, in the words of Bingham LJ (at 70)
d a monstrous invasion of his privacy. Glidewell LJ said however that there was no right of action in English law for breach of a person's privacy, and both Bingham LJ and Leggatt LJ expressed, in extremely strong terms, their profound regret that English law provided no remedy on that basis. In *Douglas's* case [2001] 2 All ER 289 at 317, [2001] QB 967 at 998 (para 113) Sedley LJ argued that *Kaye* did not in fact decide that point, since the court 'adopted—for it plainly
e shared—counsel's assumption that there was [no tort of breach of privacy]'. However, first, if a court not only adopts but says that it actively shares a concession or assumption by counsel, that assumption then becomes part of its reasoning, whatever may have been the origin of the point. And, second, even if, on a very narrow view of ratio, it is possible to say that the court's observations
f about privacy were obiter, the language of Bingham and Leggatt LJJ shows, in what Brooke LJ characterised in *Douglas's* case [2001] 2 All ER 289 at 304–305, [2001] QB 967 at 984 (para 61) as uncompromising terms, that they had directed their minds to the possibility of relief for breach of privacy, and had rejected that possibility. Even if, which I doubt, it is in technical terms open to us to do so, it would be a very strong thing indeed for a subsequent division of this court to say
g that they were wrong.

[101] *Kaye's* case was consistent with the only other clear authority in this field, the judgment of Megarry V-C in *Malone's* case. The issue that *Kaye's* case addressed was reverted to again in *Khorasandjian's* case. Counsel argued in that case that the defendant's behaviour was an actionable interference with privacy.
h That, if correct, would have provided the court with a ready-made basis for achieving the result that they plainly, and rightly, sought, of protecting the plaintiff from the unwanted attentions of the defendant, without becoming entangled either in the obscurities of *Wilkinson v Downton* or in an unprincipled extension of the law of private nuisance. However, Dillon and Rose LJJ did not
j even mention this potential right of action. The assumption that that was because they thought the claim was without foundation in law is given force when one turns to the judgment of Peter Gibson J. He said ([1993] 3 All ER 669 at 684, [1993] QB 727 at 744):

> '[Counsel] submitted that the respondent has a right of privacy with which the appellant was unreasonably interfering. But that argument is not open

to him in the light of the decision of this court in *Kaye v Robertson* [1991] FSR
62, confirming that English law has recognised no such right.'

[102]   In my respectful view, the combination of the judgments in
Khorasandijan's case comes very close indeed to establishing as a matter of ratio
that there is no English law tort of breach of privacy.   Certainly, they are a
formidable barrier to this court now declaring that such a tort had in some way
come into existence by 1997.

[103]   That view is reinforced by a number of further considerations.

[104]   First, one of the situations that was, rightly, thought to be most in need
of protection on the ground of privacy was the causing of distress by harassment,
besetting and intrusive telephoning, often in a sexual context: the very conduct
that engaged the concern of this court in *Khorasandsjian*'s case.   After an
exhaustive analysis of the authorities before 1997 this court concluded in *Wong v
Parkside Health NHS Trust* [2003] 3 All ER 932 at [30], that before the passing of s 3
of the Protection from Harassment Act 1997 there had been no tort of harassment
in English law.   Two comments follow.   First, nowhere in any of the cases
reviewed in *Wong*'s case was it suggested that the matter might be regulated on
the basis of a tort of invasion of privacy which, if it had existed, would have been
an obvious solution to the problems of harassment.   Second, if the tort of invasion
of privacy now contended for had always been in existence the statutory tort of
harassment, introduced in 1997, would appear to be substantially redundant:
granted in particular that by s 7(2) of the 1997 Act 'harassment' includes the
causing of distress, the very circumstance that most attracts demands for the
protection of privacy.

[105]   Second, in *Douglas*'s case [2001] 2 All ER 289 at 319–320, [2001] QB 967
at 1001 (para 124) Sedley LJ drew attention to the ruling of the European
Commission on Human Rights in *Earl Spencer v UK* (1998) 25 EHRR CD 105;
commented that that ruling had been the considered view of a body of
distinguished jurists; and said that it would not be a happy thing if the national
courts were to go back without cogent reason on the United Kingdom's
successful exegesis of its own law.   I respectfully agree.   But the law expounded
by the United Kingdom and accepted by the commission was indeed that there is
no law of privacy, as such, in England and Wales, citing *Kaye*'s case.   That
submission cannot of course affect us if it was wrong; but at the lowest it
represents a respectable strand of construction of the current state of English law.

[106]   Third, and further in that respect, I have not been able to find any
commentator who thought, at least before the coming into effect of the 1998 Act,
that there was a tort of invasion of privacy in English law, as opposed to thinking
that there should be such a tort.   Paragraph 1–34 of *Clerk and Lindsell* the leading
authority, says of the law in 2001, and thus a fortiori of the law before 1998:

'Privacy remains an interest unprotected by the English law of torts.
However gross the invasion of the claimant's privacy, that violation of
privacy is not itself a tort.'

That English law provides no direct action for invasion of privacy is also the view
of the learned editor of the fifteenth edition of *Winfield and Jolowicz on Tort* (15th
edn, 1998) pp 464–465; and of Sir Brian Neill in his essay in the important
collection *Protecting Privacy* (ed Markesinis) (1999) p 17.

[107]   I am therefore plainly of the opinion that it is not open to us to grant
relief to the claimants on the basis of an invasion of their privacy.   Since, however,

a the protection of privacy has been seen by some as nonetheless a proper field for the exercise of judicial activism, I venture to go further and draw attention to some difficulties that stand in our way.

PRIVACY: POLICY

[108] 'Privacy' covers a very wide range of cases, which are affected by a very
b wide range of policy considerations. What occurred in our case is perhaps one of the simpler examples. The right not to have another stare at one's naked body, save by consent or in clearly defined situations of necessity, would be unambiguously regarded as a matter of privacy. But what of the obtaining of information that (on the assumptions made to justify the extension of the law of tort into new situations of privacy) is not covered by the law of confidence? What
c of the making of true statements about others, hitherto rigorously excluded from the law of defamation? What of the whistle-blower? And, indeed, what of a preference to have photographs of your wedding in one publication rather than another?

[109] As is well accepted, in none of these cases can a right to privacy be
d absolute. But that is only the start. What needs to be worked out is the delicate balance, particularly in the area of the publication of information, between the interests on the one hand of the subject and on the other of someone entering his private space, or of the publisher and the latter's audience. It also has to be borne in mind that what is necessarily proposed is a general tort, available not only to private citizens who simply want to get on with their own lives, like the
e Wainwrights; but also to corporate bodies that want to keep their affairs private. That plainly adds a further dimension of considerable difficulty to attempts to formulate the proper ambit and balance of the tort.

[110] That even without those complications, and while remaining within the ambit of private individuals, differing views can be held on the issue of
f protection of privacy, and that such views can change over time, can perhaps be illustrated from the classic article that first investigated a right to privacy, and which is still viewed as a significant intellectual source of the proposed tort: see the judgment in *Douglas*'s case [2001] 2 All ER 289 at 318–319, [2001] QB 967 at 999–1000 (para 120). The article is by Samuel Warren and Louis Brandeis 'The Right to Privacy' (1890) 4 Harv L Rev 193. Its point of departure is believed to
g have been the behaviour of the press in Boston on the occasion of the wedding of Mr Warren's sister. The learned authors commented (at 196):

'Gossip is no longer the resource of the idle and of the vicious, but has become a trade, which is pursued with industry as well as effrontery. To
h satisfy a prurient taste the details of sexual relations are spread broadcast in the columns of the daily papers. To occupy the indolent, column upon column is filled with idle gossip, which can only be provided by intrusion upon the domestic circle ... When personal gossip attains the dignity of print, and crowds the space available for matters of real interest to the community, what wonder that the ignorant and thoughtless mistake its relative
j importance.'

It may be doubted whether a judge in 2001 would feel able to advance quite that justification for awarding damages for breach of privacy.

[111] All these considerations indicate that not only is the problem a difficult one, but also that on grounds not merely of rationality but also of democracy the difficult social balance that the tort involves should be struck by Parliament and

not by the judges: as Megarry V-C urged in *Malone*'s case, in the passage quoted in [92], above, and Legatt LJ urged in *Kaye*'s case. And that is rendered the more, *a* not the less, the case by reason of the fact that Parliament, and those who advise it, have themselves found the problem of the limits of tort of invasion of privacy to be one of profound difficulty. The Law Commission has had the issue of a tort of invasion of privacy on its agenda since the 1960s. No proposals have emerged. The Younger Committee on Privacy (1972) (Cmnd 5012), considered in detail *b* whether there should be 'a general right of privacy' protected by law, and rejected that proposal, on grounds, amongst others, of uncertainty: see in particular the discussion at paras 660–666 of the report. Subsequent initiatives, summarised by Brooke LJ in *Douglas*'s case [2001] 2 All ER 289 at 312, [2001] QB 967 at 993 (paras 89–90), have borne no further fruit.

[112]   Whatever sympathy may be felt for the particular position of the *c* Wainwrights, we have to remember that laws are not made for particular cases but for men in general: *R (on the application of Pretty) v DPP* [2001] UKHL 61 at [29], [2002] 1 All ER 1 at [29], [2002] 1 AC 800, per Lord Bingham of Cornhill. And I have no doubt that in being invited to recognise the existence of a tort of breach of privacy we are indeed being invited to make the law, and not merely to apply *d* it. Diffidence in the face of such an invitation is not, in my view, an abdication of our responsibility, but rather a recognition that, in areas involving extremely contested and strongly conflicting social interests, the judges are extremely ill-equipped to undertake the detailed investigations necessary before the proper shape of the law can be decided. It is only by inquiry outside the narrow boundaries of a particular case that the proper ambit of such a tort can be *e* determined. The interests of democracy demand that such inquiry should be conducted in order to inform, and the appropriate conclusions should be drawn from the inquiry by, Parliament and not the courts. It is thus for Parliament to remove, if it thinks fit, the barrier to the recognition of a tort of breach of privacy that is at present erected by *Kaye*'s case and *Khorasandjian*'s case.   *f*

PRIVACY: REMOTENESS OF DAMAGE

[113]   Mr Wilby said confidently that once a tort of breach of privacy was established, all damage caused by that breach was recoverable simply on the basis of causation. There may have been some echo in that formulation of the original claim in trespass: see [70], above. However, the claim, and in particular the claim *g* on the basis of the facts of the present case, illustrates a further uncertainty about a tort of breach of privacy. It is entirely unclear why the illness that in the event overtook Alan Wainwright should be recoverable just because it followed upon a breach of privacy: a tort whose values do not include prevention of physical injury. And even more difficult questions can easily be hypothesised: for *h* instance, if non-confidential and true, but private, information is published about someone, with the result that he loses his job, or his marriage.

PRIVACY: CONCLUSIONS

[114]   Even, therefore, if the Wainwrights could bring themselves under the *j* protection of a tort of invasion of privacy, I would find it difficult to see how they could recover for special damage claimed in this case. But in the event that issue does not arise, since it is still the law of England that there is no tort of invasion of privacy.

[115]   That suffices to reverse the finding of the judge and to allow the appeal. However, in deference to the arguments that we received, and also to the

a importance of the issue, I do go on and consider the two defences upon which the
Home Office sought to rely, on the assumption that otherwise it would have
been liable. Those defences are consent and justification. I do not consider that
either of them could be made out in this case.

CONSENT

b [116]   The judge held, at para 82 of his judgment, that the Wainwrights
'consented to the strip-search' because they were told that, if they did not, they
could not visit Mr O'Neill; but because the consent was obtained by a show of
authority it was not real consent in law.

[117]   The question of the distinction between consent and submission, and
of the concepts of 'social' or 'forced' consent, is a subject of considerable
c difficulty in relation to crimes involving offences against the person, and for the
same reasons difficult also in the law of tort. Some account of the subject in the
former context is given in Law Commission Consultation Paper *Consent and
Offences Against the Person* (1993) (Law Com No 134) paras 24.1–31.1. It may be
mentioned in passing that the authority relied on by the judge, the judgment of
d Willes J in *Warner v Riddiford* (1858) 4 CBNS 180 at 206, is not a case on consent.
These issues do not however arise in the present case, because the Home Office's
argument, and the judge's acceptance of it, was mistaken on the facts.

[118]   What the Wainwrights, and all other visitors to Armley Gaol, were
asked to consent to was not 'a strip-search' in general terms; with the result, as
the Home Office appeared to argue, that they had forfeited their right to
e complain about anything that was done as part of an activity that could be so
described. Rather, the search that was proposed and for which consent was
sought was that described in the prison's procedure document, and set out on the
back of the consent form. The relevant procedures have already been set out by
Lord Woolf CJ, but it will be convenient to repeat the prison's own public
f statement of the limits of the search:

'1.   Two officers will be present. No person of the opposite sex will be
present.
2.   You will not be required to be fully undressed at any stage.
3.   You will be asked to remove clothes from one half of your body, and
pass them to an officer so that they may be examined. Your body will then
be examined briefly so that the officers can see if anything is concealed. The
clothes will then be returned to you without delay and you will be given time
to put them on.
4.   The procedure will then be repeated for the other half of your body.
5.   The soles of your feet will be checked.
6.   When your upper body is undressed, you may be required to hold your
arms up.
7.   When your lower body is undressed, you may be required to position
yourself in such a way as to enable staff to observe whether anything is
hidden in the genital and anal areas. Your body will not be touched during
the process.
8.   If you have long hair, it may be necessary for an officer to search it. It
may also be necessary for an officer to check your ears, and mouth. You will
not be touched otherwise.'

[119]   Since Alan Wainwright was required wholly to undress, and
Mrs Wainwright effectively so, items 2 and 3 of these rules were flagrantly

departed from. So effectively was item 1 in the case of Mrs Wainwright, to the extent that she may have been visible from outside the office. If the Wainwrights had been shown the consent forms before the procedure and had them explained to them, then it would have been impossible thereafter to contend that they had consented to what in the event occurred. I reject as entirely unreal Mr Tam's contention that they could nonetheless have caused the search to be interrupted; and in any event the point does not arise on the facts, because the Wainwrights had not been told what the rules of the search were. The Home Office cannot be in a better position because it did not follow its own procedure that required it to present the forms before the search began. I would therefore hold that no consent was given to what actually occurred; so the defence would fail on that ground alone.

JUSTIFICATION

[120] This defence was based on a comparison between r 86(1) of the 1964 rules, which says, but says no more than, that 'Any person or vehicle entering or leaving a prison may be stopped, examined and searched' and r 39(2), relating to searches of prisoners, which provides that 'a prisoner shall be searched in as seemly a manner as is consistent with discovering anything concealed'. Expressio unius, said the Home Office, exclusio alterius. The search of a visitor does not have to be seemly.

[121] I regret that this point was ever taken. A rule as broad as r 86, giving power over persons who have committed no crime, and who attend as part of the accepted social policy that prisoners' families are entitled to contact with them, cannot have been intended by Parliament, and cannot be justified, in terms that give largely unlimited powers to the prison authorities. And, as Mr Wilby acutely pointed out, the prison authorities themselves did not think that to be the case, as evidenced by their own rulebook, already quoted, and by their internal strategy document that is set out by Lord Woolf CJ at [18], above. This is not a question of limitation on *Wednesbury* grounds, as the Home Office submitted and the judge accepted; rather, it is a question, to be determined by the court, of what the legislation is to be taken as authorising. In company with the rulebook, I hold that it did not authorise the search that in fact took place.

[122] The judge did not take that view. Rather, the case became involved before him in a long inquiry into whether the form of the search could be justified in terms of art 8(2) of the convention. The basis for this inquiry was the contention that r 86, even in its application before 2 October 2000, had by reason of s 3(1) of the 1998 Act to be read by a court after that date in terms that if possible complied with the convention. I respectfully agree with what Lord Woolf CJ says on that subject in [29], above and following. I would also venture to add that in my view any liberty for this court to hold that s 3(1) of 1998 Act has retrospective force has been put to rest by the decision in *Pearce v Governing Body of Mayfield Secondary School* [2001] EWCA Civ 1347, [2001] IRLR 669, as expressed in the judgment of Judge LJ (at [79]). Nothing in *R v Kansal* undermines the binding authority for this court of *Pearce*'s case.

[123] None of this, however, affect the result of this appeal. A defence of justification would fail for the reason set out in [121], above, and not because of any implication of the convention.

DISPOSAL OF THE APPEAL

a   [124]   I would allow the appeal, because the claimants cannot make out any claim in either trespass, '*Wilkinson v Downton*' or breach of privacy. If a prima facie claim had been made out, it would not have been defeated by a defence either of consent or of justification.

     [125]   I respectfully agree with Lord Woolf CJ as to the disposal of the further

b   outstanding matter of the measure of damages to be awarded to Alan Wainwright in relation to the separate battery committed upon him.

Appeal allowed. Permission to appeal to the House of Lords granted.

Kate O'Hanlon   Barrister.

Practice Note

CHANCERY DIVISION

Trust and trustee – Judicial trustee – Remuneration – Common form of order – Judicial Trustees Act 1896, s 1(5) – Judicial Trustees Rules 1983, r 11.

[1] When dealing with the assignment of remuneration to a judicial trustee under s 1(5) of the Judicial Trustees Act 1896 and r 11 of the Judicial Trustee Rules 1983, SI 1983/370, the court will consider directions as to remuneration based on the common form of order set out below, subject to such modifications as may be required in any particular case.

[2] In general the court when considering reasonable remuneration for the purposes of r 11(1)(a) will need to be satisfied as to the basis upon which the remuneration is claimed, that it is justified and that the amount is reasonable and proportionate and within the limit of 15% of the capital value of the trust property specified in the rule.

[3] The court may, before determining the amount of remuneration, require the judicial trustee to provide further information, alternatively refer the matter to a costs judge for him to assess remuneration.

[4] When an application is made to the court for the appointment of a judicial trustee or when the court gives directions under r 8 practitioners should produce to the court a draft order which should take account of the common form of order.

DRAFT PARAGRAPHS OF ORDER

'[IT IS ORDERED]

… that the remuneration of the Judicial Trustee shall be in such amount as may be approved from time to time by this court upon application for payment on examination of his accounts.

… that the Judicial Trustees accounts shall be endorsed by him with a certificate of the approximate capital value of the trust property at the commencement of the year of account.

… that every application for payment by the Judicial Trustee shall be in the form of a letter to the court (with a copy to the beneficiaries) which shall (a) set out the basis of the claim to remuneration, the scales or rates of any professional charges, the work done and time spent, any information concerning the complexity of the trusteeship that may be relied on and any other matters which the court shall be invited by the Judicial Trustee to take account and (b) certify that he considers that the claim for remuneration is reasonable and proportionate.'

MASTER WINEGARTEN
Chief Chancery Master
1 July 2003   With the authority of Sir Andrew Morritt V-C

Shalson v Keepers and Governors of the Free Grammar School of John Lyon

[2003] UKHL 32

HOUSE OF LORDS

LORD BINGHAM OF CORNHILL, LORD STEYN, LORD HOFFMANN, LORD MILLETT AND LORD SCOTT OF FOSCOTE

29 APRIL, 12 JUNE 2003

Landlord and tenant – Leasehold enfranchisement – Valuation – Improvement – Former lessee converting property from single house into flats – Current lessee converting property back into single house and thereby increasing value of property – Whether lessee's works an 'improvement' for purposes of leasehold valuation if merely reversing work done by previous lessee that had depressed value of property – Leasehold Reform Act 1967, s 9(1A)(d).

The Leasehold Reform Act 1967 gave a qualifying tenant a statutory right to buy the freehold of the house of which he was the leaseholder. Section 9(1A)[a] of the Act provided that, in the case of houses over a certain rateable value, the price was to be the amount which, at the time when the tenant gave notice of his desire to purchase, the freehold of the house and premises might be expected to realise on the open market. Section 9(1A)(d) required that the price be diminished by the extent to which the value of the house and premises had been increased by 'any improvement' carried out by the tenant or his predecessors in title at their own expense. The appellant was the tenant of a large house. It had originally been one dwelling for family occupation, but had been converted into five flats in 1947. While the 1947 works had originally increased the value of the house, the converted state made it worth less in the 1980s than it would have been in its original state. In 1987 the tenant's predecessor converted the house into two dwellings. In 1991 the tenant made further alterations. By 1997, when he gave notice of his desire to buy the freehold, the house was again arranged for single family occupation, more or less as it had originally been constructed. In subsequent proceedings, the Lands Tribunal held that both the conversion and the reconversion were improvements, but that the reconversion works did not entitle the tenant to pay a diminished price because their effect was to reverse the conversion works carried out and return the house to its original configuration. That decision was upheld by the Court of Appeal. On the tenant's appeal to the House of Lords, their Lordships considered the correct approach to s 9(1A)(d).

Held – For the tenant to secure a reduction under s 9(1A)(d) of the 1967 Act, he had, first, to identify improvements which he or his predecessors had carried out at their own expense and, secondly, satisfy the tribunal that, but for those improvements, the house and premises would have been worth less. In general terms, the word 'improvement' meant additions or alterations to the house and premises which were not mere repairs or renewals. It referred to the works themselves and not to the effect, if any, which they had had on the value of the premises. In considering whether an improvement had added to the value of

---

a   Section 9, so far as material, is set out at [3], below

the house, the comparison was between the value of the house as it stood and
what its value would have been if the improvement had not been made. The
words 'any improvement' meant that each improvement relied upon by the
tenant had to be separately considered in comparison with what the house would
otherwise have been worth. If it had added nothing to the value, it was
disregarded. In the instant case, the Lands Tribunal had correctly held that the
conversion and the subsequent reconversion were both improvements, even
though the 1947 improvements had been stripped out before the valuation date
and, even if they had remained intact, would have reduced rather than
increased the value. However, the 1947 improvements made no difference to
the value of the house at the valuation date because they had ceased to exist.
On the other hand, if the reconversion had not taken place, the
1947 improvements would still have existed and the house would have been
worth less. To the extent that it was worth more, the tenant was entitled to a
reduction in the open market value. Accordingly, the appeal would be allowed
(see [1], [7], [8], [17]–[20], [24], [28], [45], [46], below).

    Decision of the Court of Appeal [2002] 3 All ER 1119 reversed.

Notes

For the purchase price in leasehold enfranchisement for houses within the higher
range of values, see 27(2) *Halsbury's Laws* (4th edn reissue) para 1297.

    For the Leasehold Reform Act 1967, s 9, see 23 *Halsbury's Statutes* (4th edn) (1997
reissue) 224.

Cases referred to in opinions

Balls Brothers Ltd v Sinclair [1931] 2 Ch 325, [1931] All ER Rep 803.
Rosen v Trustees of Camden Charities [2001] 2 All ER 399, [2002] Ch 69, [2001] 3 WLR
    1470, CA.

Case referred to in list of authorities

King (decd), Re, Robinson v Gray [1963] 1 All ER 781, [1963] Ch 459, [1963] 2 WLR
    629, CA.

Appeal

Peter Shalson, the tenant of a property known as 98 Hamilton Terrace, St John's
Wood, London, NW8, appealed with permission of the Appeal Committee of the
House of Lords given on 14 October 2002 from the decision of the Court of Appeal
(Thorpe, Buxton LJJ and Moses J) on 15 April 2002 ([2002] EWCA Civ 538, [2002] 3
All ER 1119, [2003] Ch 110) dismissing his appeal from the decision of the Lands
Tribunal (NJ Rose FRICS) on 19 April 2001 dismissing his appeal from the decision
of the Leasehold Valuation Tribunal (J McGrandle B Sc (Est Man), ARICS, MRTPI
(chairman), SE McGrath and DZ Myer-Smith LLB) on 2 November 1999 that
certain works carried out by Mr Shalson and his predecessors in title did not
constitute an 'improvement' to the property for the purposes of s 9(1A)(d) of the
Leasehold Reform Act 1967 and were therefore not to be disregarded in
determining the price to be paid for the freehold by Mr Shalson to the respondent
landlord, the Keepers and Governors of the Free Grammar School of John Lyon.
The facts are set out in the opinion of Lord Hoffmann.

Edwin Johnson (instructed by *David Conway & Co*) for Mr Shalson.
Kenneth Munro (instructed by *Pemberton Greenish*) for the landlord.

a

Their Lordships took time for consideration.

12 June 2003. The following opinions were delivered.

LORD BINGHAM OF CORNHILL.

[1] My Lords, I am in complete agreement with the opinion of my noble and
b learned friend Lord Hoffmann, and I gratefully adopt his account of the facts
and issues in this appeal.

[2] The Leasehold Reform Act 1967 as amended gives to a qualifying tenant a
statutory right to buy the freehold of the house of which he is the leaseholder.
The effect is that the owner, instead of recovering his property on the expiry of
the lease in the ordinary way, receives a capital sum representing the value of the
c house at the date when the tenant gave notice of his wish to buy. The calculation
of that value is governed by a statutory formula clearly intended to yield a fair
result as between tenant and owner, conferring no undue benefit on either. Thus
the value is based (s 9(1A)) on the amount which at the relevant time the house,
if sold in the market by a willing seller, might be expected to realise on certain
d assumptions, among them (s 9(1A)(a)) that the vendor is selling for an estate in
fee simple subject to the unexpired term of the existing tenancy.

[3] A further assumption, with which alone this appeal is concerned, is
(s 9(1A)(d))—

> 'that the price be diminished by the extent to which the value of the house
e   and premises has been increased by any improvement carried out by the
>   tenant or his predecessors in title at their own expense.'

This statutory language makes plain that the price will be diminished under this
head if and only if it is found: (i) that works of improvement (meaning works
other than renewals and repairs) have been carried out by the tenant or his
f predecessors in title; (ii) that the tenant or his predecessors in title have carried
out these works at their own expense; and (iii) that these works have increased
the value of the house. To the extent of the increase attributable to those works
the price payable for the house is diminished. The fairness of this provision is
obvious. It would not be fair if the tenant were obliged to pay an enhanced price
to the extent that such enhancement was attributable to works done by him or
g his predecessors in title (probably voluntarily) at their own expense: the tenant
would in effect be paying twice. It would not be fair if the owner received a
price inflated as a result of works done by the tenant or his predecessors in title
(probably voluntarily) at their own expense: the owner would be reaping an
adventitious gain as a result of works which he had had no right to require.
h Thus in each case where this assumption is in issue the question must be asked:
has the value of this house been increased by any improvement carried out by the
tenant or his predecessors in title at their own expense? If the answer to this
question is Yes, the market price must be reduced so as to discount the increase
attributable to that improvement (or improvements, if there are more than one).

j [4] It has been common ground between the parties to this appeal that when
this question is asked with reference to the extra storey and mansard roof built in
the 1920s, the answer is Yes, and they are agreed on the extent to which the price
should be reduced on account of those works. The controversy has centred on
the works, admittedly done by the appellant (Mr Shalson) and his predecessors in
title, and admittedly done at their own expense, to reconvert the house from five
flats to a single dwelling as it was when originally let.

[5] It seems to me plain that these works were improvements within the statutory language, since they were not works of repair and renewal and the statutory language makes plain that whether such works cause an increase of value raises a separate question; it is not a defining characteristic of an improvement that it has the effect of increasing the value of the house. In the present case it is common ground that the improvements in question (the reconversion works) increased the value of the house as compared with its value had those works not been done. Thus the question posed in [3], above, must be answered Yes, and there is agreement on the extent to which the price must be diminished on that basis.

[6] The Leasehold Valuation Tribunal and the Lands Tribunal held that the reconversion works did not entitle Mr Shalson to pay a diminished price because their effect was to reverse the conversion works carried out in the 1940s and return the house to its original configuration. The Court of Appeal upheld those decisions ([2002] EWCA Civ 538, [2002] 3 All ER 1119, [2003] Ch 110). I would accept that those conversion works were, within the statutory language, improvements. It seems very questionable whether they were improvements carried out by Mr Shalson's predecessor in title at his own expense, since the 1947 tenant was contractually bound to carry out the works and it seems likely (although there is no finding on this) that the rent payable under the lease was abated to reflect the expense to which he was committing himself. But even if it were accepted that the conversion works were improvements carried out by Mr Shalson's predecessor in title at his own expense, it is quite plain that they did not (as of the valuation date, which is the only date that matters) increase the value of the house. The effect of the reconversion works voluntarily undertaken by Mr Shalson and his predecessors in title was to undo the conversion works and so render them wholly irrelevant for purposes of the statutory calculation, as having no effect on the market value of the house.

[7] I would accordingly allow the appeal and make the order which Lord Hoffmann proposes.

LORD STEYN.

[8] My Lords, I have read the opinions of my noble and learned friends Lord Bingham of Cornhill, Lord Hoffmann and Lord Millett. For the reasons they have given I would also make the order which Lord Hoffmann has proposed.

LORD HOFFMANN.

[9] My Lords, this appeal concerns the principle upon which the price which a tenant has to pay pursuant to s 9 of the Leasehold Reform Act 1967 for the freehold interest in a house should be adjusted to reflect any increase in its value attributable to improvements which he or his predecessors in title have made at their own expense.

[10] Section 9(1A) of the 1967 Act provides that, in the case of houses over a certain rateable value, the price shall be 'the amount which at the relevant time the house and premises, if sold in the open market by a willing seller, might be expected to realise' on various assumptions. The 'relevant time' means the time at which the tenant gives notice of his desire to buy the freehold: see s 37(1)(d). For present purposes, the only relevant statutory assumption is para (d) of s 9(1A):

a

'on the assumption that the price be diminished by the extent to which the value of the house and premises has been increased by any improvement carried out by the tenant or his predecessors in title at their own expense …'

[11] The appellant Mr Shalson was tenant of a large house in St John's Wood under a lease dated 19 May 1947 for a term of 99 years from 25 March 1947 at a yearly rent of £140. The lease had been granted in consideration of the covenants

b

which it contained and the surrender of a 50-year lease of the same premises granted in 1921. That lease in turn had been granted in consideration of the surrender of a 95-year lease granted in 1843. The history is relevant because s 3(3) of the 1967 Act provides that if a tenant of property under a long tenancy, on the coming to an end of that tenancy, becomes tenant under another long tenancy,

c

the 1967 Act is to apply as if there had been a single tenancy for a term beginning with the commencement of the earlier tenancy and expiring with the term of the later tenancy. Mr Munro, who appeared for the landlord, wanted to keep open the question of whether this provision could apply more than once and unify all three long tenancies. But, subject to that point (which need not be decided) all tenants since 1843 count as predecessors in title of Mr Shalson.

d

[12] The house was originally a villa constructed for family occupation. At some time in the 1920s it was enlarged by the addition of an extra storey with a mansard roof. Under the 1947 lease, the tenant covenanted to carry out certain alterations to convert the house into five self-contained flats. It may be assumed that this reflected the weak demand for big Victorian houses in London just after

e

the Second World War. The work was done and for the next 40 years or so the house was in multiple occupation. The lease also contained a tenant's covenant (cl 2(21)) not to make any further alterations without the landlord's licence in writing. During the 1980s the market changed. There was a demand for big family houses in good areas of London. The result was that while the 1947 works had originally increased the value of the house, the converted state of the house

f

made it worth rather less in the 1980s than it would have been in its original state. Pursuant to a licence granted in 1983, the upper part of the house was converted into one dwelling with a self-contained basement flat beneath. In 1991 Mr Shalson acquired the lease and made further alterations, pursuant to a further licence, to convert the basement flat into a swimming pool, sauna, gym and maid's quarters. By the time Mr Shalson gave notice of his desire to buy the

g

freehold on 19 November 1997, the house was once more arranged for family occupation, more or less as it had originally been constructed.

[13] There is no dispute that Mr Shalson is entitled to a deduction for the extent to which the value of the house was increased by the addition of the mansard storey. The issue is over whether he is entitled to a deduction for the value which

h

he and his predecessors in title have added to the house by reconverting it from five flats into a single dwelling, or whether the comparison should be with what the house would have been worth if it had remained in the state in which it had been let in 1843, 1921 or 1947. It is agreed that on the first assumption, the price produced by the statutory calculation is £275,298. On the second, it is £398,200.

j

[14] The Leasehold Valuation Tribunal, which has jurisdiction under s 21(1)(a) of the 1967 Act to determine the price payable under s 9, considered that the correct comparison was with the house as originally let. This decision was upheld by the Lands Tribunal (Mr NJ Rose FRICS). He said:

'Both the original conversion from a house to flats and the subsequent re-conversion from flats to a house were equally tenant's improvements and there is no requirement for the valuer to restrict his analysis to the effect of only one of them.'

    a

[15] The Court of Appeal (Thorpe, Buxton LJJ and Moses J) upheld this decision ([2002] EWCA Civ 538, [2002] 3 All ER 1119, [2003] Ch 110). But the reasoning of Buxton LJ, who gave a judgment with which the other two members agreed, was not quite the same as that of the Lands Tribunal. He said ([2002] 3 All ER 1119 at [9]) that works done to the house cannot constitute an improvement increasing its value if they consist—

    b

'only of reversing work done by a predecessor in title (or even, more remarkably, by the instant tenant) that depressed the value of the house and premises; which, as at the valuation date, the conversion into five flats indeed would have so done.'

    c

[16] Buxton LJ was unwilling to accept that in principle the increase in value must be by reference to the state of the house and premises at the time of the grant. That might give rise to practical difficulties in discovering exactly what the state of the house then was. In the present case, it might require an inquiry going back to 1843. So Buxton LJ (at [16]) limited the principle to a case in which—

    d

'the alleged works of improvement are doing no more than altering previous works to the property that, in the market as it existed at the valuation date, would have been a depressing rather than an increasing factor in the market price.'

    e

[17] In my opinion the language of s 9(1A)(d) is clear. A diminution in the open market value is to be allowed only by the extent to which that value has been increased by 'any improvement' which has been carried out by the tenant or a predecessor at their own expense. For the tenant to secure a reduction, he must therefore, first, identify improvements which he or his predecessors have carried out at their own expense, and secondly, satisfy the tribunal that but for those improvements the house and premises would have been worth less.

    f

[18] The first of these two conditions requires consideration of any changes which have been made to the premises during the term of the lease, or the period which s 3(3) deems to have been the term of the lease. 'Improvement' is a word of ancient lineage in the law of landlord and tenant and land law generally: see, for example, s 25 of the Settled Land Act 1882. In general terms it means additions or alterations to the house and premises which are not mere repairs or renewals: see *Hague on Leasehold Enfranchisement* (3rd edn, 1999) pp 198–199 (para 9-30). It is important to bear in mind that an improvement is a physical and not an economic concept. It refers to the works themselves and not to the effect, if any, which they have upon the value of the premises. It is the second condition which deals with the effect on value. So the Lands Tribunal was in my opinion quite right to say that the 1947 conversion and the subsequent reconversion were both improvements, even though the 1947 improvements had been stripped out before the valuation date and, even if they had remained intact, would have reduced rather than increased the value of the house and premises.

    g

    h

    j

[19] The issue in this appeal turns upon what I have called the second condition. What does it mean to say that the value of the house and premises has been increased by the improvement? In my opinion, it signifies a simple causal relationship: but for the improvement, the house and premises would have been

a worth less. The comparison is between the value of the house as it stands and what its value would have been if the improvement had not been made.

[20] The hypothetical house envisaged by this comparison is in my opinion one which has all the features of the real house, including its history, save for one: that the improvement in question had not been made. By that test, the 1947 improvements made no difference to the value of the house at the valuation
b date, because they had ceased to exist. On the other hand, if the reconversion had not taken place, the 1947 improvements would still have existed and the house would have been worth less. To the extent that it was worth more, the tenant was entitled to a reduction in the open market value.

[21] I can see no room in the statutory language for a comparative hypothesis which assumes, as the Court of Appeal did, that the improvement in question had
c not been done and also that there had been no earlier changes which the improvement reversed. In considering whether an improvement has added to the value of the house, the comparison is simply with the house as it would otherwise have been. This seems to me fair to both parties. If the tenant had not carried out the reconversion, the landlord's interest would have been the
d reversion on a house converted into five flats. The tenant was under no obligation to reinstate. If the tenant increases the value of the landlord's interest by expenditure on reconversion, it would not seem fair that he should have to pay a second time when the landlord's interest is valued for the purposes of a sale of the freehold.

[22] It seems to me no answer to this unfairness that the value of the landlord's
e interest had been depreciated by the improvements made by the tenant's predecessor in title in 1947. The landlord cannot complain of those changes. As it happens, he actually covenanted that they should be made. But even if he had not done so, he would have been in no position to complain; for example, if the lease had simply contained no covenant against alterations or the landlord had
f granted a licence. If the tenant had waited to serve his notice desiring the freehold before commencing the reconversion, he would have had to pay only for the landlord's interest in the unimproved house. It seems to me contrary to the purpose of para (d) that the price should be increased because he does the improvements first.

[23] The position might have been different if the 1947 lease had contained a
g covenant to reinstate the premises as a single dwelling before the end of the tenancy. It is unnecessary to express a concluded view, but it would seem to me arguable that in such a case the reinstatement was pursuant to the bargain for which the tenant had received consideration by the grant of the lease and was therefore not at his own expense for the purposes of para (d): compare *Rosen v*
h *Trustees of Camden Charities* [2001] 2 All ER 399, [2002] Ch 69.

[24] Similarly, I see no justification for taking the approach of the Lands Tribunal and aggregating the net effect of all improvements made during the course of the lease, so as to compare the house as it stands at the valuation date with the house as it was let in 1843 or 1921 or 1947. If that was what Parliament
j had meant, it would have said that the price was to be diminished by the extent to which its value had been increased by 'all the improvements' carried out by the tenant or his predecessors at their own expense and not 'any improvement' so carried out. The words 'any improvement' mean that each improvement relied upon by the tenant must be separately considered in comparison with what the house would otherwise have been worth. If it has added nothing to the value, it is disregarded; it does not play a ghostly role in the calculation of the value added

by a later improvement by assuming its absence as part of the hypothetical unimproved property.

[25] Both sides produced examples, of varying degrees of realism, of how the construction favoured by the other would produce unfair results. On one side was the case, mentioned by Buxton LJ, in which the tenant made radical alterations which reduced the value of the premises and soon afterwards restored them to their original state. On the other was the tenant who built an expensive conservatory in 1995 only to find that the site had been occupied from the grant of the lease in 1830 until 1870 by an elaborate conservatory which the then tenant had demolished (with the consent of the landlord) but would, if it still existed, have made the house worth even more than with the new one.

[26] In the case mentioned by Buxton LJ, it seems to me that a landlord who has allowed his tenant to make alterations which reduce the value of his reversion without any covenant for reinstatement has only himself to blame if he finds that the value of his reversion has been reduced. I do not think that he can recoup the consequences of his folly by making the tenant (or a new tenant) pay a price for the reversion which is higher than he would have had to pay if he had enfranchised while the house was still in its ruined state. On the other hand, taking the other example, it does not seem to me fair that an accident of history which has left no trace upon the property or the obligations of landlord or tenant should result in the tenant having to pay the landlord for an increase in the value of the reversion which his own expenditure has created.

[27] There may of course have been more than one improvement which has increased the value of the house. In the present case, both the mansard storey and the reconversion had increased the value and the Lands Tribunal, when valuing the property on the assumption that the tenant's contentions were right, took both into account. In making this calculation, there cannot be any double counting. The amount by which improvement A (made in 1981) has increased the value of the house over what it would have been worth only with improvement B (made in 1991) and the amount by which improvement B has increased the value over what it would have been worth only with improvement A cannot add up to more than the increase in what the house would have been worth without either A or B. But that presents no problem in the present case, because the 1947 improvements added nothing to the value at the relevant date and fell to be altogether disregarded.

[28] I would therefore allow the appeal and determine that the amount payable by the tenant is the agreed figure of £275,298. The landlord must pay the costs of the tenant in this House, the Court of Appeal and the Lands Tribunal.

LORD MILLETT.

[29] My Lords, this appeal is concerned with the determination of the price payable by a tenant of a house held on a long tenancy for the right to enfranchise his property. Some time before the relevant date for valuation the tenant had at his own expense converted the property from a house divided into flats to a single house. This significantly increased the value of the property at the valuation date. The question is whether that increase should be left out of account in determining the enfranchisement price. Normally it should. The problem in the present case is due to the fact that the property was formerly a single house which had been converted into flats by a previous tenant, so that the enfranchising tenant had merely reconverted the property to its former condition as a single house.

a
[**30**] The tenant's right to acquire the freehold of his house arises under the Leasehold Reform Act 1967. The purchase price payable for the freehold interest is ascertained in accordance with s 9. The subject matter to be valued is 'the house and premises' as at the relevant time, that is to say the time when the tenant gave notice of his desire to acquire the freehold. At that time 'the house and premises' consisted of a single undivided house. Section 9 requires the

b
property to be valued at the amount which it might be expected to realise if sold subject to the tenancy in the market by a willing seller to a willing purchaser. In arriving at the amount of the price, however, the valuer must make a number of assumptions. The present appeal is concerned with the assumption required by sub-s (1A)(d) (the subsection):

c
> '… that the price be diminished by the extent to which the value of the house and premises has been increased by any improvement carried out by the tenant or his predecessors in title at their own expense.'

The Court of Appeal held ([2002] EWCA Civ 538, [2002] 3 All ER 1119, [2003] Ch 110) that works which merely reversed work done by a previous tenant and

d
restored the property to its former condition were not works of 'improvement' within the meaning of the subsection.

[**31**] My Lords, there is no warrant for this conclusion in the wording of the subsection. In order to lead to a diminution in the price the works must: (i) consist of an 'improvement'; (ii) be carried out by the tenant or a predecessor in title at his expense; and (iii) increase the value of the house and premises at the

e
relevant time. Nothing more is required. All three conditions were satisfied by the work of reconverting the property to a single undivided house. The work was an improvement, that is to say it was not merely a work of repair or renewal. It was carried out by the tenant at his expense. And it increased the value of the property at the relevant time, in that the property would have been worth less if

f
the work had not been carried out and the house had remained divided into flats. There is no further condition that the work should not consist only of reversing some earlier work or merely restore the property to an earlier state.

[**32**] Such a condition would frustrate the purpose of the subsection. It is designed to avoid the tenant having to pay a price which reflects a value in the property for which he has already paid: see *Hague on Leasehold Enfranchisement*

g
(3rd edn, 1999) pp 198–199 (para 9-30). If the tenant carries out alterations to the property which enhance its value he thereby increases the value of the landlord's reversionary interest which he afterwards claims to acquire. The subsection prevents his own expenditure resulting in an increase in the price he has to pay. This would be the case whether or not the work consisted of merely reversing the

h
effect of some earlier work. If the tenant in the present case had served his notice before commencing the work of reconversion, he could not have been required to pay a price which represented more than the current value of a house divided into flats. There is nothing in s 9 to enable the landlord to require the depreciatory consequences of the subdivision to be ignored; nor would this be

j
appropriate when the reduction in the value of the property was due to works to which he had consented or at least not objected (and in the present case for which he had stipulated). It would make no sense to require the tenant to pay a higher price for the property because he served the notice after completing the work of reconversion instead of before commencing it. It would also be unfair when the increase in the value of the property was the result of works which he had carried out at his own expense.

[33] The Lands Tribunal and the Court of Appeal were troubled by examples given in argument of cases where it was said that it would be unfair to take *a* account of work to the extent to which it merely restored the property to its former state. Most of such cases were cases of demolition and reconstruction. An example was given of a house with an Edwardian conservatory in a conservation area. The tenant demolishes the conservatory and, after a lapse of some time spent in obtaining planning permission and listed building consent, erects a *b* modern home extension in its place. It would be unfair to the landlord to reduce the price to reflect the value of the house with neither the conservatory nor the home extension. I agree. The price must be diminished by the extent to which the house with the home extension is more valuable than the house with a conservatory. But this is not because part of the value attributable to the construction of the home extension is to be ignored on the ground that it merely *c* reversed the demolition of the conservatory. It is because the relevant improvement consisted of works of demolition and reconstruction. Whether works carried out independently at different times consist of a single improvement or two separate improvements is a question of fact. It is not one which is likely to cause difficulty in practice. The answer will often be found in the terms of the landlord's consent *d* or a relevant planning permission. In the example given, it is highly unlikely that the tenant would ask for or that the landlord be prepared to grant consent to the demolition of the conservatory without its replacement by the home extension.

[34] In my opinion, the reconversion of the property to a single undivided house was unquestionably an improvement carried out at the expense of the *e* tenant which increased the value of the property and which should therefore result in a diminution of the enfranchisement price. But the subsection refers to '*any* improvement carried out by the tenant or his predecessors in title' (my emphasis). It is not sufficient to have regard only to the most recent improvement. The tenant is entitled to have account taken of any relevant improvement which *f* satisfies the statutory criteria. The real question is whether the earlier work of subdividing the house into flats also constituted an improvement; and if so what effect if any it should have on the price.

[35] My Lords, the concept of an 'improvement' is a very familiar one in the law of landlord and tenant. It connotes additions or alterations which are not merely repairs or renewals. Whether an 'improvement' really improves the *g* property is considered from the point of view of the tenant alone, so that work may constitute an improvement although it does not increase the value of the property at all or even reduces it: see *Balls Brothers Ltd v Sinclair* [1931] 2 Ch 325, [1931] All ER Rep 803. As my noble and learned friend Lord Hoffmann observes, the concept is a physical and not an economic one. *h*

[36] Accordingly the works by which the house was divided into flats constituted an 'improvement' within the meaning of the subsection. And they were carried out by a predecessor in title of the enfranchising tenant. But they do not fall to be taken into account in determining the amount of the enfranchisement price for two separate and independent reasons: (i) they were not carried out at the *j* tenant's expense; and (ii) had the house still been divided into flats at the valuation date they would not have increased the value of the property as at that date but reduced it.

[37] The subdivision of the house into flats was carried out by the tenant as a term of the grant of the 1947 lease. It was, therefore, carried out not merely pursuant to a contractual obligation in that behalf but in consideration for the

a
grant of the tenancy. Had the work been carried out by the landlord, he would
either have charged a premium or an increased rent. Thus the work must be
taken to have been carried out by the tenant in return for the grant of the tenancy
at a reduced rent and without a premium, in other words at the expense of the
landlord: see *Rosen v Trustees of Camden Charities* [2001] 2 All ER 399, [2002] Ch 69.

b
[**38**] Even if this had not been the case, however, and the work had been
carried out by the tenant at his own expense, the result would have been the
same. It may be assumed that, when the work of subdivision was originally
carried out, it did increase the value of the property. As the years passed,
however, market conditions changed; and the extent to which the subdivision
increased the value of the property gradually dwindled and eventually vanished
altogether. By the valuation date, it would have reduced the value of the
c
property.

[**39**] Had the tenant served an enfranchisement notice at any time when the
property was still worth more subdivided into flats than as a single house, he
would have obtained a reduction of the price to reflect the remaining value
attributable to the work of subdivision. But by the time he began the work of
d
reconversion to a single house, the property was worth less as a house subdivided
into flats than it would have been as a single house. He could not have obtained
the benefit of a diminution of the enfranchisement price by virtue of the
subsection, since his predecessor's expenditure was no longer reflected in an
increase in the value of the property at the relevant time. He would still have
e
obtained a diminution of the price as the result of the expenditure, of course, but
by a different means; had it not been carried out the house would have remained
undivided and worth more, so that the price would have been higher.

[**40**] The Lands Tribunal compared the property at the valuation date with the
property as it was when originally let. But there is no warrant for this approach
in the wording of the subsection either. The 'extent to which the value of the
f
house and premises has been increased' by an improvement is simply the difference
between the value of the property with the improvement in question and the value
of the property without it. The problem to which the approach of the Lands
Tribunal gives rise is that it may take account of improvements in the distant past
which have long since ceased to have any effect on the value of the property, and
g
accordingly do not satisfy the conditions of the subsection. If the tenant
constructs a home extension on a part of the lawn backing onto the rear wall of
his house, for example, it will not help the landlord to show that a conservatory
had originally stood on the site but had long since been pulled down.

[**41**] On the other hand, the tenant is entitled to take advantage of any
h
improvement, however ancient, which satisfies the conditions of the subsection. It
must have the effect directly or indirectly of increasing the value of the property
at the valuation date, but it need not have physically survived to that date. If a
former tenant had increased the value of the house by adding a conservatory, and
the enfranchising tenant increased the value of the house still further by
j
demolishing the conservatory and erecting a home extension in its place, he would
be entitled to a reduction in price which reflected the combined effect of both
improvements. His own improvement would consist of works of demolition and
reconstruction; but it would not be fair to reduce the price by an amount which
reflected only the difference between the value of the house with a conservatory
and the house with the benefit of the home extension. Had he not demolished the
conservatory and built the home extension, he would still have been entitled to a

diminution in the price to reflect the increase in the value of the house brought about by the construction of the conservatory.

[42] This, of course, presupposes that the earlier work also increased the value of the property and did not reduce it. There is no question of netting off an increase against an earlier reduction. The landlord gets the worst of both worlds; he receives a lower price if the tenant carries out alterations which reduce the value of the property, and does not receive the benefit if the tenant carries out alterations which increase it. The Court of Appeal were troubled by this. They took the case of a tenant who, for his own eccentric reasons, significantly altered the property in a way which materially reduced its value. They did not think that it would be sensible for a later tenant, let alone the same tenant, to obtain a reduction in the enfranchisement price merely by 'putting that right'.

[43] But with respect it is not a question of putting anything right. The landlord must have consented or at least not objected to the earlier works which reduced the value of the property. Any diminution in the price which he receives is the result of the tenant's having lawfully carried out works which reduced the value of his reversionary interest. The landlord can avoid this result by taking a covenant in the lease that the tenant should obtain his prior consent to any works of improvement, and either refusing his consent or imposing a condition that the tenant restore the property to its former state at the termination of the tenancy. Even if the works of restoration should still fall to be treated as being carried out at the tenant's expense, as to which I prefer to express no opinion, the obligation would severely limit and perhaps eliminate any effect the works would have on the value of the landlord's reversionary interest.

[44] The Court of Appeal expressed caution about taking account of works carried out in the distant past, on the ground that this would only be possible if a reliable history of the property was available. This is true, but it does not, with respect, affect the principle that every improvement, however ancient, which satisfies the statutory criteria and has the effect of increasing the value of the property at the valuation date may be taken into account. It must be remembered that the landlord is prima facie entitled to the full value of his interest in the property as it stands at the valuation date. If the tenant claims a diminution in the price he must establish the facts which entitle him to it.

[45] For these reasons, and also for the reasons given by my noble and learned friend Lord Hoffmann whose speech I have had the advantage of reading in draft, I would allow the appeal.

LORD SCOTT OF FOSCOTE.

[46] My Lords, I have had the advantage of reading in advance the opinion of my noble and learned friend Lord Hoffmann and am in agreement both with his conclusion that this appeal should be allowed and with his reasons for reaching that conclusion. I, too, would make the order that he has proposed.

Appeal allowed.

Celia Fox   Barrister.

Insured Financial Structures Ltd v Elektrocieplownia Tychy SA

[2003] EWCA Civ 110

COURT OF APPEAL, CIVIL DIVISION
LORD WOOLF CJ, HALE AND LATHAM LJJ
28 JANUARY 2003

Conflict of laws – Jurisdiction – Challenge to jurisdiction – Agreement between English company and Polish company providing for non-exclusive jurisdiction of Polish courts – English company commencing proceedings against Polish company in England – Whether Polish courts having exclusive jurisdiction – Civil Jurisdiction and Judgments Act 1982, Sch 3C, art 17(1).

By a written agreement, the claimant, an English-registered company which was domiciled in the United Kingdom, agreed to supply certain services to the defendant, a company domiciled in Poland. Under the agreement, each party agreed to the 'non-exclusive jurisdiction' of the courts of Poland in connection with any disputes arising out of it. The agreement also provided that it should be interpreted according to English law. Both the United Kingdom and Poland were contracting states of the Lugano Convention on Jurisdiction and the Enforcement of Judgments in Civil and Commercial Matters 1988 (as set out in Sch 3C to the Civil Jurisdiction and Judgments Act 1982). Article 17(1)[a] of the convention provided that if the parties, one or more of whom was domiciled in a contracting state, had agreed that the court or courts of a contracting state were to have jurisdiction to settle any disputes which had arisen or which might arise in connection with a particular legal relationship, that court or those courts were to have 'exclusive jurisdiction'. After the Polish company failed to meet its obligations to make payments under the agreement, the English company commenced proceedings against it in England. The Polish company successfully applied to the master for an order that the English courts had no jurisdiction to try the claim, but the English company's appeal against that order was allowed by the judge. On its appeal to the Court of Appeal, the Polish company relied on art 17(1) in contending that the Polish courts had exclusive jurisdiction.

Held – The Polish courts did not have exclusive jurisdiction. The interpretation of the agreement between the parties had to be the starting point. That agreement had to be construed against the provisions of the convention; however, if the matter were approached as one of English interpretation (which was what the contract expressly required), it seemed that the parties had intended that Polish courts were to have jurisdiction, but that that jurisdiction was not to be exclusive. The agreement should be regarded as expressly conferring jurisdiction on a number of contracting states, the identity of those contracting states, apart from Poland, being provided by the convention itself. The express reference to Poland meant that the Polish courts were to have jurisdiction, even if they would not have had jurisdiction under the provision of the convention in the absence of an express reference to Poland. There was no difficulty in fitting

---

a   Article 17, so far as material, is set out at [4], below.

that interpretation into the language of art 17(1). The agreement by implication
conferred jurisdiction upon more than one contracting state. It identified one   *a*
state expressly, but the other states were brought into consideration because of
the very important words included, making the Polish jurisdiction non-exclusive.
The language of art 17(1) had to be given effect in a manner which took into
account the intentions of the parties and should not be construed in a way which
involved the courts having to come to a conclusion which would be directly   *b*
contrary to that which the parties intended. Accordingly, the appeal would be
dismissed (see [8], [9], [13], [14], [20]–[22], below).

Kurz v Stella Musical Veranstaltungs Gmbh [1992] 1 All ER 630 approved.

Notes

For jurisdictional provisions of the Lugano Convention generally and jurisdiction   *c*
derived from a choice of court agreement in particular, see 8(1) *Halsbury's Laws*
(4th edn reissue) paras 618, 633.

For the Civil Jurisdiction and Judgments Act 1982, Sch 3C, art 17, see
11 *Halsbury's Statutes* (4th edn) (2000 reissue) 1210.

d

Cases referred to in judgments

Ets A de Bloos SPRL v Société en commandite par actions Bouyer Case 14/76 [1976]
    ECR 1497, ECJ.
GPA Group plc v Governor and Company of the Bank of Ireland and the European
    Organisation for the Safety of Air Navigation (EURO-CONTROL) [1992] 2 IR 408.
e
Hantarex SpA v SA Digital Research [1993] IL Pr 501, Paris CA.
Kurz v Stella Musical Veranstaltungs Gmbh [1992] 1 All ER 630, [1992] Ch 196, [1991]
    3 WLR 1046.
Meeth v Glacetal SARL Case 23/78 [1978] ECR 2133, ECJ.

Cases also cited or referred to in skeleton arguments   *f*

Anterist v Crédit Lyonnais Case 22/85 [1986] ECR 1951, ECJ.
Arab Bank Ltd v Barclays Bank (Dominion, Colonial and Overseas) [1954] 2 All ER 226,
    [1954] AC 495, [1954] 2 WLR 1022, HL.
Bank of Scotland v Seitz 1990 SLT 584, Ct of Sess.
Benincasa v Dentalkit Srl Case C-269/95 [1998] All ER (EC) 135, [1997] ECR I-3767,   *g*
    ECJ.
Continental Bank NA v Aeakos Cia Naviera SA [1994] 2 All ER 540, [1994] 1 WLR
    588, CA.
Dresser UK Ltd v Falcongate Freight Management Ltd, The Duke of Yare [1992] 2 All ER
    450, [1992] QB 502, [1992] 2 WLR 319, CA.
h
Eider, The [1893] P 119, CA.
Fessard v Mugnier [1865] 18 CBNS 286, 144 ER 453.
Gamlestaden plc v Casa de Suecia SA [1994] 1 Lloyd's Rep 433.
GIE Groupe Concorde v The Suhadiwarno Panjan (master) Case C-440/97 [1999] 2 All
    ER (Comm) 700, [1999] ECR I-6307, ECJ.
j
Hough v P & O Containers Ltd (Blohm + Voss Holding AG and ors, third parties) [1998]
    2 All ER 978, [1999] QB 834, [1998] 3 WLR 851.
Industrie Tessili Italiana Como v Dunlop AG Case 12/76 [1976] ECR 1473, ECJ.
IP Metal Ltd v Ruote Oz SpA (No 2) [1993] 2 Lloyd's Rep 60; *affd* [1994] 2 Lloyd's
    Rep 560, CA.
Ivenel v Schwab Case 133/81 [1982] ECR 1891, ECJ.

a   *Lafi Office and International Business SL v Meriden Animal Health Ltd* [2001] 1 All ER
       (Comm) 54.
    Malik v Narodni Banka Ceskoslovenska [1946] 2 All ER 663, CA.
    Mercury Communications Ltd v Communication Telesystems International [1999] 2 All
       ER (Comm) 33.
    Rein v Stein [1892] 1 QB 753, CA.
b   *Robey v Snaefell Mining Co Ltd* (1887) 20 QBD 152, DC.
    Shenavai v Kreischer Case 266/85 [1987] ECR 239, ECJ.

Appeal

The appellant, Elektrocieplownia Tychy SA, appealed with permission of
Aldous LJ granted on 19 August 2002 from the order of Sir Oliver Popplewell,
c   sitting as a judge of the Queen's Bench Division, on 21 June 2002 allowing an
appeal by the respondent, Insured Financial Structures Ltd, from the order of
Master Eyre on 3 May 2002 declaring that the courts of England and Wales had
no jurisdiction to try the claim brought by the respondent against the appellant.
The facts are set out in the judgment of Lord Woolf CJ.

d
    Guy Philipps QC (instructed by *Nicholson Graham & Jones*) for the appellant.
    John Higham QC of *Stephenson Harwood* for the respondent.

LORD WOOLF CJ.

    [1] This is a second appeal by the appellant, Elektrocieplownia Tychy SA,
e   against an order of Sir Oliver Popplewell, sitting as a judge of the High Court of
Justice of the Queen's Bench Division, of 21 June 2002. The judge allowed the
appeal of the respondent against the order of Master Eyre dated 3 May 2002. The
master had declared that the English courts had no jurisdiction to try the claim
which had been brought by the respondent.
f   [2] On the appeal the sole issue is whether a contract which provides that the
parties agree on the non-exclusive jurisdiction of the courts of Poland have
thereby, because of the provisions of art 17(1) of the Lugano Convention on
Jurisdiction and the Enforcement of Judgments in Civil and Commercial Matters
1988 (as set out in Sch 3C to the Civil Jurisdiction and Judgments Act 1982), in fact
conferred exclusive jurisdiction on Poland.

g
    THE FACTS
    [3] The respondent company is registered and carries on business in England
and Wales. The appellant is a state-owned Polish company. On 23 October 2000,
by an agreement in writing between the parties, it was agreed that the respondent
h   was to provide corporate financial advisory services to the appellant in
connection with the financing of electricity generating plants in Poland.
Clause 11 of the agreement states: 'Each party agrees to the non-exclusive
jurisdiction of the courts [of Poland] in connection with any disputes arising out
of this agreement.' The appellant failed to meet its obligations to make payments
under the agreement. On 20 April 2001, it gave notice of termination.
j   [4] Article 17 of the Lugano Convention provides, so far as material:

       '1. If the parties, one or more of whom is domiciled in a Contracting State,
    have agreed that a court or the courts of a Contracting State are to have
    jurisdiction to settle any disputes which have arisen or which may arise in
    connection with a particular legal relationship, that court or those courts
    shall have exclusive jurisdiction ...

2. The court or courts of a Contracting State on which a trust instrument has conferred jurisdiction shall have exclusive jurisdiction in any proceedings brought against a settlor, trustee or beneficiary, if relations between these persons or their rights or obligations under the trust are involved.

3. Agreements or provisions of a trust instrument conferring jurisdiction shall have no legal force if they are contrary to the provisions of Article 12 or 15, or if the courts whose jurisdiction they purport to exclude have exclusive jurisdiction by virtue of Article 16.

4. If an agreement conferring jurisdiction was concluded for the benefit of only one of the parties, that party shall retain the right to bring proceedings in any other court which has jurisdiction by virtue of this Convention.'

[5] It is common ground that both parties are domiciled in contracting states and that they have agreed that the court of a contracting state, namely Poland, is to have jurisdiction to settle any disputes which may arise in connection with the contract between them. It is not common ground, so far as the respondent is concerned, that Poland has exclusive jurisdiction. For reasons which will become apparent hereafter, in indicating what is not common ground I refer only to the respondent.

[6] Given the parties' express agreement that the jurisdiction of the Polish courts should be non-exclusive, Sir Oliver Popplewell came to the conclusion that the jurisdiction of the Polish courts was, as the agreement states, in fact non-exclusive. That is not a surprising conclusion. However, Mr Guy Philipps QC, in his very clear submissions to this court, argues that the proper application of art 17 of the Lugano Convention requires this court to come to the conclusion that the only courts which have jurisdiction in respect of a claim by the respondent are indeed the Polish courts.

[7] Initially, before I received assistance from Mr Philipps, it occurred to me that the simple explanation for the apparent tension on which Mr Philipps relies is that art 17(1), when it refers to a 'Contracting State', meant a contracting state and not more than one contracting state. However, such a view of art 17(1) was not advocated by Mr Higham QC for the respondent, and Mr Philipps has satisfied me that that is not the proper approach to art 17(1). Furthermore, if it were the right interpretation, it could lead to undesirable consequences because it would have the effect that the parties could not agree to two states having exclusive jurisdiction. At first sight the expression that a contracting state has exclusive jurisdiction implies that no other state has jurisdiction. It is therefore necessary to inquire further into the effect of art 17 of the Lugano Convention on the simple facts that have been placed before this court.

[8] The starting point, in my judgment, must be the interpretation of the agreement which was made by the parties. I accept Mr Philipps' contention that the agreement has to be construed against the provisions of the Lugano Convention. However, if the matter is approached as one of English interpretation (which is the appropriate approach to adopt because that is what the contract expressly requires), then it seems to me that the parties undoubtedly intended by the words that they used that Poland was to have jurisdiction, but that that jurisdiction was not to be exclusive. Its effect was to be that Poland was to have jurisdiction in any event, but under the rules governing jurisdiction, where there was no express conferment of jurisdiction, jurisdiction should be applied in accordance with the provisions contained in the Lugano Convention which identify the relevant jurisdiction. In other words, the agreement should be

a regarded as expressly conferring jurisdiction on a number of contracting states, the identity of those contracting states (apart from Poland) being provided by the Lugano Convention itself.

[9] The benefit of the express reference to Poland meant that that country was to have jurisdiction, even if it was not one which would have jurisdiction under the provision of the Lugano Convention in the absence of an express reference to
b Poland.

[10] In coming to that view, I am helped by the authorities to which we were referred in the course of argument. The general intention of the convention appears from the decision in *Ets A de Bloos SPRL v Société en commandite par actions Bouyer* Case 14/76 [1976] ECR 1497 at 1508, where the European Court of Justice said, in relation to the Brussels Convention on Jurisdiction and the Enforcement
c of Judgments in Civil and Commercial Matters 1968 (as set out in Sch 1 to the 1982 Act), which is in the same terms as the Lugano Convention:

> '8. As stated in its preamble, the Convention is intended to determine the international jurisdiction of the courts of the contracting States, to facilitate the recognition and to introduce an expeditious procedure for securing the
d enforcement of judgments.
>
> 9. These objectives imply the need to avoid, so far as possible, creating a situation in which a number of courts have jurisdiction in respect of one and the same contract.'

e That decision of the European Court of Justice specifies the general purpose of the Brussels Convention, which is commendable.

[11] In *Meeth v Glacetal SARL* Case 23/78 [1978] ECR 2133 at 2141–2142, the European Court of Justice said:

> '5. According to the first paragraph of Article 17 [of the Brussels
f Convention] "if the parties ... have agreed that a court or the courts of a Contracting State are to have jurisdiction to settle any disputes which have arisen or which may arise in connexion with a particular legal relationship, that court or those courts shall have exclusive jurisdiction". With regard to an agreement conferring reciprocal jurisdiction in the form in which it appears in the contract whose implementation forms the subject-matter of
g the dispute, the interpretation of that provision gives rise to difficulty because of the fact that Article 17, as it is worded, refers to the choice by the parties to the contract of a single court or the courts of a single State. That wording, which is based on the most widespread business practice, cannot, however, be interpreted as intending to exclude the right of the parties to agree on two or more courts for the purpose of settling any disputes which
h may arise. This interpretation is justified on the ground that Article 17 is based on a recognition of the independent will of the parties to a contract in deciding which courts are to have jurisdiction to settle disputes falling within the scope of the [Brussels Convention], other than those which are expressly excluded pursuant to the second paragraph of Article 17. This applies
j particularly where the parties have by such an agreement reciprocally conferred jurisdiction on the courts specified in the general rule laid down by Article 2 of the [Brussels Convention].'

[12] I find those passages of assistance. First, they indicate that there can be more than one state that has jurisdiction for the purposes of art 17. Second, they clearly convey to me the fact that when it is possible to do so it is necessary to give

effect to the intention of the parties when applying art 17, even though this may
create a tension with the language of art 17.

[13] If the interpretation of the agreement to which I have referred earlier is
the correct interpretation, how can that fit in with the language of art 17(1)? I find
no difficulty in fitting it into the language of art 17(1). The agreement by
implication confers jurisdiction upon more than one contracting state. It
identifies expressly one state, but the other states are brought into consideration
because of the very important words that are included in the agreement, making
the Polish jurisdiction non-exclusive.

[14] Mr Philipps says that that approach is not appropriate because art 17(1)
expressly refers to an exclusive jurisdiction, so making inclusive what is stated
to be an exclusive jurisdiction is contrary to the language of art 17(1). Once it
is appreciated that more than one state can have exclusive jurisdiction, I do not
accept that that consequence follows. It seems to me that the language of
art 17(1) has to be given effect in a manner which takes into account the
intentions of the parties, and certainly should not be construed in a way which
involves the courts having to come to a conclusion which would be directly
contrary to that which the parties intended.

[15] The interpretation of art 17 which Mr Philipps submits the court should
apply, depends upon the language of art 17(4). He recognises that some effect
must be given to the use of the words 'non-exclusive jurisdiction'. He submits
that that can be accommodated by regarding Poland as having exclusive
jurisdiction so far as the respondent is concerned, but not exclusive jurisdiction
so far as the appellant is concerned. He submits that art 17(4), together with the
reference to 'non-exclusive jurisdiction', means that the appellant is in the
fortunate position of being entitled to bring proceedings either in Poland or in
any other appropriate state identified by the Lugano Convention, but that the
respondent is confined to Poland because it should be inferred that the reference
to 'non-exclusive' is for the appellant's benefit alone. With the greatest respect to
the elegant manner in which Mr Philipps advanced that argument, I find it
difficult to believe that that is an appropriate approach to adopt in relation to a
commercial matter. I cannot conceive that any party to an agreement of this sort
would be agreeable to the state of the other party being able to be selected when
that is what the party from that state wishes, but that the party who is not from
that contracting state has no such flexibility and has always to use the jurisdiction
of the specified state. I prefer the interpretation that I have already indicated to
that argued for by Mr Philipps.

[16] I am encouraged to adopt the interpretation that I have adopted because
it accords with a judgment of Hoffmann J (as he then was) in *Kurz v Stella Musical
Veranstaltungs Gmbh* [1992] 1 All ER 630, [1992] Ch 196. This is a case which has
been followed at first instance in a series of authorities to which it is not necessary
to refer. I do not propose to refer to the facts of that case. The following passages
point clearly to the conclusion which I regard as being the correct one here.
Hoffmann J said ([1992] 1 All ER 630 at 637, [1992] Ch 196 at 203–204):

'This argument in my judgment misinterprets what art 17 means when it
says that the chosen or "prorogated" jurisdiction is to be *exclusive*. It does not
mean "unique", that the parties are limited to choosing a single jurisdiction.
It means only that their choice, whatever it is, shall (subject to the exceptions
made in sentence 5) have effect to the exclusion of the jurisdictions which
would otherwise be imposed on the parties by the earlier articles of the

a

[Brussels Convention]. Once the parties have availed themselves of art 17 by the prescribed method, jurisdiction becomes a question of the intention of the parties. But (subject always to sentence 5) the article does not limit their choice or the language in which it can be expressed. Nor does it prevent them from including in their choice, expressly or by implication, courts which would otherwise have had jurisdiction under the [Brussels

b

Convention]. Jurisdiction thus conferred is still based exclusively on the intention of the parties rather than imposed by the general law and is therefore within the terms of art 17. Although one of the objects of the [Brussels Convention] is to harmonise the jurisdiction rules of the contracting states, one cannot discern a strong general policy in favour of having only a single jurisdiction available to the parties for any particular

c

dispute. There are many cases in which concurrent jurisdictions may exist under different articles and this possibility is expressly contemplated by art 21. There is of course such a policy in the exceptional cases mentioned in sentence 5, but, outside of these, the desirability of a single jurisdiction cannot in my judgment override the principle of freedom of contract.'

d

Later, Hoffmann J said ([1992] 1 All ER 630 at 638, [1992] Ch 196 at 205):

'But the important principles are, first, that art 17 should be interpreted to give effect to the intention of the parties, and secondly, that the parties may if they choose confer jurisdiction upon two or more courts and their choice

e

may include or exclude courts which would otherwise have had jurisdiction under the earlier articles of the convention. Let us assume that the place of performance of the payment obligations under the subscription agreement was Germany, so that either party could have sued the other in Germany under art 5(1) but only Stella M could have brought an action in England under art 2. If the parties wanted Mr Kurz to be able to sue in England as

f

well, [Meeth v Glacetal SARL Case 23/78 [1978] ECR 2133] shows that they could have expressly provided that the courts of England and Germany were to have jurisdiction in any proceedings brought by either party. But (in the courts of a convention country) this has exactly the same effect as a provision that the English courts are to have non-exclusive jurisdiction. The latter formula is simply another way of saying that the parties confer general

g

jurisdiction on the English courts *in addition* to the jurisdictions which would have existed under the convention if there had been no art 17 choice.'

[17] That approach does achieve, as I see it, the purpose of the Lugano Convention. It is true that in many situations the identification of the state with jurisdiction will not be as clear or obvious as it would be if a specific state was

h

identified without the qualification that exists here and art 17(1) clearly applies. However, the Lugano Convention recognises that clarity cannot always be achieved. There will be many situations where the principles which are set out in the Lugano Convention have to be applied, as here, to the particular facts before the court. The approach which I have adopted has also the advantage that

j

it accords with the approach which was adopted by Keane J in *GPA Group plc v Governor and Company of the Bank of Ireland and the European Orgnisation for the Safety of Air Navigation (EURO-CONTROL)* [1992] 2 IR 408.

[18] The only other authority to which it is necessary to refer is a decision of the Paris Court of Appeal in *Hantarex SpA v SA Digital Research* [1993] IL Pr 501, on which Mr Philipps rested considerable weight. That case, however, is one

which it is necessary to approach with a degree of caution when applying it to the
situation with which we are faced here. First of all, as is submitted by *a*
Mr Higham, we have the disadvantage that we do not know the actual terms of
the jurisdiction clause. It is true that in the judgment it is referred to as a clause
which confers 'non-exclusive jurisdiction'. But those words can have a number
of meanings; they may be saying no more than that the courts did not expressly
say that the jurisdiction of the Paris courts was to be exclusive. It could have said *b*
that it was non-exclusive, but the position is not clear. Furthermore, having set
out the contentions of the parties, the court went on to say:

> '[15] The jurisdiction clause enables Digital Research [the respondent], if
> it is the plaintiff, to bring an action before "the Paris courts", or any other
> competent court under the rules of the [Brussels Convention]. *c*
> [16] The clause, which in this way gives one of the parties a wider choice
> of courts, is in conformity with Article 17(4) of the [Brussels Convention].'

In view of those remarks, it may be, depending upon the language of the clause,
that this is no more than a case where art 17(4) of the Lugano Convention applies
in accordance with the tenor of its terms. Without in any way seeking to suggest *d*
that the decision of the Court of Appeal of Paris was incorrect, I find nothing in
that judgment, having regard to our limited knowledge as to the circumstances,
which interferes with the views that I have expressed so far.

[19] Finally, the parties are agreed that in this case it is not possible to obtain
any benefit in directly construing art 17 of the Lugano Convention from Council
Regulation (EC) 44/2001 (on jurisdiction and the recognition and enforcement of *e*
judgments in civil and commercial matters (OJ 2001 L12 p1)), which has replaced
the Brussels Convention. The two conventions are in parallel, and it is obviously
desirable that the courts should not strain to come to a different interpretation of
the Lugano Convention from that which applies in the case of the Brussels
Convention. Article 23 in its current form, which came into effect last year but *f*
which was agreed in 2000, provides:

> '1. If the parties, one or more of whom is domiciled in a Member State,
> have agreed that a court or the courts of a Member State are to have
> jurisdiction to settle any disputes which have arisen, or which may arise in
> connection with a particular legal relationship, that court or those courts *g*
> shall have jurisdiction. Such jurisdiction shall be exclusive unless the parties
> have agreed otherwise. Such an agreement conferring jurisdiction shall be
> either ...'

It then goes on to set out the choices.

[20] As it seems to me, the approach which I regard as being appropriate to *h*
art 17 of the Lugano Convention happily coincides with the clear language
of art 23 of Regulation 44/2001. I would therefore dismiss this appeal. I consider
that the judge was right in the conclusion to which he came. This court has
jurisdiction, as he indicates.

 j

HALE LJ.

[21] I agree. This began as a case on the interpretation of art 17(1) of the
Lugano Convention on Jurisdiction and the Enforcement of Judgments in Civil
and Commercial Matters 1988 (as set out in Sch 3C to the Civil Jurisdiction and
Judgments Act 1982), but in the course of argument it has turned into a case about
the interpretation of this particular contract. It is common ground that the

a parties may agree to confer jurisdiction on more than one contracting state for
the purpose of art 17(1). It is also accepted by Mr Philipps that they could agree
to confer jurisdiction on, for example, Poland and any other contracting state
having jurisdiction under the terms of the Lugano Convention. In other words,
they do not have to exclude any such jurisdiction for their agreement to fall
within the terms of art 17(1). Once that has been conceded, it becomes a pure
b question of what was meant by the terms of this particular contract and by the
words 'non-exclusive'. Did they mean that only one party could benefit from the
other jurisdictions, or did they mean that both parties could do so? As the clause
in the contract concerned starts 'each party agrees' the answer to that question
seems to me to be tolerably obvious. I, too, would dismiss this appeal.

c **LATHAM LJ.**
[22] I agree with both judgments.

Appeal dismissed.

d   Kate O'Hanlon   Barrister.

Douglas and others v Hello! Ltd and others (No 3)

[2003] EWHC 786 (Ch)

CHANCERY DIVISION

LINDSAY J

3–5, 7, 10–14, 17–21, 24–26 FEBRUARY, 3–7, 10–12 MARCH, 11 APRIL 2003

Equity – Breach of confidence – Confidential information – Publication of unauthorised photographs – Celebrity couple entering into agreement with magazine for authorised wedding photographs – Rival magazine publishing unauthorised wedding photographs – Freedom of expression – Respect for private and family life – Whether publication in breach of confidence – Human Rights Act 1998, s 12, Sch 1, Pt I, arts 8, 10.

The first and second claimants, well-known film stars, were married in New York. Extensive security arrangements were put in place for the wedding intended to confine the event to family and friends, to ensure that only authorised photographs were taken, and to preserve the exclusivity of the photographic rights, which had been sold to the third claimant, the publisher of OK! magazine. However, a photographer eluded security and surreptitiously took photographs which were then bought for publication in OK!'s rival magazine, Hello! Hello! published the unauthorised photographs, knowing them to be unauthorised, on the same day as that on which OK!, having had to bring its arrangements forward, published the first set of the authorised photographs, which had had to be hurriedly approved by the first and second claimants. The first and second defendants published and distributed Hello! in the United Kingdom and the third defendant was a director of and controlling shareholder in the second defendant and editor-in-chief of Hello! (the Hello! defendants). There were three other defendants. The claimants brought proceedings against the defendants alleging, inter alia, breach of confidence and breach of privacy. Under s 6[a] of the Human Rights Act 1998 it was unlawful for a public authority, which included a court, to act in a way incompatible with a right contained in the European Convention for the Protection of Human Rights and Fundamental Freedoms 1950 (as set out in Sch 1 to the 1998 Act). The issue arose as to the relation between the right of the first and second claimants to respect for private and family life under art 8[b] of the convention and the right of the media to freedom of expression under art 10[c] of the convention. Section 12[d] of the 1998 Act provided that when the court was considering whether to grant any relief which might affect the right to freedom of expression, and the proceedings related to journalistic material, it had to have

---

a   Section 6, so far as material, provides: 'It is unlawful for a public authority to act in a way which is incompatible with a Convention right ... '

b   Article 8, so far as material, provides: 'Everyone has the right to respect for private and family life.'

c   Article 10, so far as material, provides: '(1) Everyone has the right to freedom of expression. This right shall include freedom to receive and impart information ... (2) The exercise of these freedoms, since it carries with it duties and responsibilities, may be subject to such ... conditions, restrictions or penalties as are prescribed by law ... '

d   Section 12, so far as material, provides: '(1) This section applies if a court is considering whether to grant any relief which ... might affect the exercise of the ... right to freedom of expression ... (4) The court must have particular regard ... where the proceedings related to ... journalistic ... material ... to ... (b) any relevant privacy code ...'

a   regard to any relevant privacy code. The relevant code was the Press Complaints Commission code which stated, inter alia, that a publication would be expected to justify intrusions into any individual's private life without consent and that the use of photography to take pictures of people in private places without their consent was unacceptable.

b   **Held** – The equitable jurisdiction in confidence was based on the duty to be of good faith and on the moral principle of fair dealing. But while breach of confidence was an established cause of action, its scope had to be evaluated in the light of obligations falling upon the court under s 6(1) of the 1998 Act. That could be achieved by regarding the often opposed rights conferred respectively by c   arts 8 and 10 of the convention as absorbed into the action for breach of confidence. The right to freedom of expression described in art 10(1) was expressly made subject not only to the right under art 8 for respect to private and family life but also to rights recognised by the law as to confidence, even where those latter rights were not themselves convention rights. Freedom of expression d   on the media's part, as a counter-force to privacy, was not invariably the ace of trumps but it was a powerful card to which the court had to pay appropriate respect. There was no presumptive priority given to freedom of expression when it was in conflict with another convention right, or rights under the law of confidence. The effect of s 12 of the 1998 Act was that the court had to have particular regard to any relevant privacy code, in the instant case that of the Press e   Complaints Commission. In the absence of any public interest the court was bound to pay particular regard to the code and a newspaper which flouted the code might have its claim to freedom of expression trumped by art 10(2) considerations of privacy. In the instant case, the claimants had a valuable trade asset, a commodity the value of which depended upon its content at first being f   kept a secret and then being made public in a controlled manner. Moreover, OK!'s right to exclusivity of photographic coverage was even more plainly a right in the nature of a trade secret: what the first and second claimants looked like at the exceptional occasion of their wedding had the quality of commercial confidentiality. The private character of the event and the elaborate security g   arrangements all conduced to that conclusion. Further, the Hello! defendants had not acted in good faith nor by way of fair dealing, the publication of the unauthorised photographs was unconscionable and the claimants had thereby suffered detriment. There had been an unjustified intrusion into individuals' private lives without consent of which the Hello! defendants knew or ought to h   have known. It followed that, regarding the case as one of either commercial confidence, the claimants being in a position akin to that of holders of a trade secret, or a hybrid in which, by reason of it having become a commodity, elements that would otherwise have been merely private became commercial, the Hello! defendants had acted unconscionably and by reason of breach of confidence were liable to all three claimants to the extent of the detriment which j   was thereby caused to them. The claims under the law of confidence would, accordingly, be allowed (see [181], [186], [196]–[198], [205], [227], [228], [279], [280], bclow).

    Douglas v Hello! Ltd [2001] 2 All ER 289, *Venables v News Group Newspapers Ltd* [2001] 1 All ER 908, *A v B (a company)* [2002] 2 All ER 545 and *Campbell v Mirror Group Newspapers Ltd* [2003] 1 All ER 224 applied.

Per curiam. The subject of privacy is better left to Parliament which can consult interests far more widely than can be taken into account in the course of ordinary inter partes litigation (see [229], below).

Notes
For the equitable jurisdiction in breach of confidence, the essential features of confidentiality, and the relation to freedom of expression, see 8(1) *Halsbury's Laws* (4th edn) (2003 reissue) paras 406, 410, and 418 respectively.

For the Human Rights Act 1998, s 12, Sch 1, Pt I, arts 8, 10, see 7 *Halsbury's Statutes* (4th edn) (2002 reissue) 542, 555.

Cases referred to in judgment
A v B (a company) [2002] EWCA Civ 337, [2002] 2 All ER 545, [2003] QB 195, [2002] 3 WLR 542.
A-G v Guardian Newspapers Ltd (No 2) [1988] 3 All ER 545, [1990] 1 AC 109, [1988] 3 WLR 776, Ch D, CA and HL.
Albert (Prince) v Strange (1849) 1 Mac & G 25, 41 ER 1171, LC.
American Cyanamid Co v Ethicon Ltd [1975] 1 All ER 504, [1975] AC 396, [1975] 2 WLR 316, HL.
Argyll (Duchess of) v Duke of Argyll [1965] 1 All ER 611, [1967] Ch 302, [1965] 2 WLR 790.
Australian Broadcasting Corp v Lenah Game Meats Pty Ltd (2001) 185 ALR 1, Aust HC.
Campbell v Mirror Group Newspapers Ltd [2002] EWCA Civ 1373, [2003] 1 All ER 224, [2003] QB 633, [2003] 2 WLR 80; *rvsg* [2002] EWHC 499 (QB), [2002] IP & T 612.
Coco v AN Clark (Engineers) Ltd [1969] RPC 41.
Cream Holdings Ltd v Banerjee [2003] EWCA Civ 103, [2003] 2 All ER 318.
Creation Records Ltd v News Group Newspapers Ltd [1997] EMLR 444.
Crofter Hand Woven Harris Tweed Co Ltd v Veitch [1942] 1 All ER 142, [1942] AC 435, HL.
Douglas v Hello! Ltd [2001] 2 All ER 289, [2001] QB 967, [2001] 2 WLR 992, CA.
Francome v Mirror Group Newspapers Ltd [1984] 2 All ER 408, [1984] 1 WLR 892, CA.
Fraser v Evans [1969] 1 All ER 8, [1969] 1 QB 349, [1968] 3 WLR 1172, CA.
Fraser v Thames Television Ltd [1983] 2 All ER 101, [1984] QB 44, [1983] 2 WLR 917.
Gilbert v Star Newspaper Co Ltd (1894) 11 TLR 4.
Kuddus v Chief Constable of Leicestershire Constabulary [2001] UKHL 29, [2001] 3 All ER 193, [2002] 2 AC 122, [2001] 2 WLR 1789.
Merkur Island Shipping Corp v Laughton [1983] 1 All ER 334, [1983] 2 AC 570, [1983] 2 WLR 45, CA; *affd* [1983] 2 All ER 189, [1983] 2 AC 570, [1983] 2 WLR 778, HL.
Mustad (O) & Son v S Allcock & Co Ltd and Dosen (1928) [1963] 3 All ER 416, [1964] 1 WLR 109n, HL.
Peck v UK (2003) 13 BHRC 669, ECt HR.
Pollard v Photographic Co (1888) 40 Ch D 345.
R v Dept of Health, ex p Source Informatics Ltd [2000] 1 All ER 786, [2001] QB 424, [2000] 2 WLR 940, CA.
RCA Corp v Pollard [1982] 3 All ER 771, [1983] Ch 135, CA.
Rickless v United Artists Corp [1987] 1 All ER 679, [1988] QB 40, [1987] 2 WLR 945, CA; *affg* [1986] FSR 502.
Rookes v Barnard [1964] 1 All ER 367, [1964] AC 1129, [1964] 2 WLR 269, HL.
Saltman Engineering Co Ltd v Campbell Engineering Co Ltd [1963] 3 All ER 413n, CA.
Shelley Films Ltd v Rex Features Ltd [1994] EMLR 134.

a   Smith Kline & French Laboratories (Australia) Ltd v Secretary to the Dept of
     Community Services and Health, Alphafarm Pty Ltd v Secretary to the Dept of
     Community Services and Health (1990) 95 ALR 87, Aust Fed Ct; affd (1991) 99
     ALR 679, Aust Fed Ct.
     Sports & General Press Agency Ltd v Our Dogs Publishing Co Ltd [1917] KB 125, CA.
     Stephens v Avery [1988] Ch 449, [1988] 2 All ER 477, [1988] 2 WLR 1280.
b   Times Newspapers Ltd v MGN Ltd [1993] EMLR 443, CA.
     Venables v News Group Newspapers Ltd [2001] 1 All ER 908, [2001] 2 WLR 1038.
     Wainwright v Home Office [2001] EWCA Civ 2081, [2003] 3 All ER 943, [2002] QB
     1334, [2002] 3 WLR 405.
     Woodward v Hutchins [1977] 2 All ER 751, [1977] 1 WLR 760, CA.

c **Claim**
   The claimants, Michael Douglas, Catherine Zeta-Jones and Northern & Shell plc,
   the publisher of OK! magazine, brought proceedings for, inter alia, breach of
   confidence against the first defendant, Hello! Ltd, the second defendant, Hola SA,
   of which the first defendant was a subsidiary, the third defendant, Eduardo
d Sanchez Junco, director and controlling shareholder of the second defendant and
   editor-in-chief of Hello! magazine (the Hello! defendants), the sixth defendant,
   the Marquesa de Varela, the fifth defendant, Neneta Overseas Ltd, a company
   owned by the fourth defendant and the sixth defendant, Philip Ramey, a
   photographer, in respect of photographs published in Hello! magazine taken of
   the first and second claimants' wedding. A split trial was ordered and accordingly
e the instant proceedings were on liability only. The facts are set out in the
   judgment.

   Michael Tugendhat QC and David Sherborne (instructed by Theodore Goddard) for
   the claimants.
f James Price QC and Giles Fernando (instructed by Charles Russell) for the Hello!
   defendants.
   Helen Mulcahy of Reed Smith for the fourth and fifth defendants.
   The sixth defendant did not appear.

                                                                      Cur adv vult

g
   11 April 2003. The following judgment was delivered.

   LINDSAY J.

   AN OUTLINE
h   [1] The well-known film stars Mr Michael Douglas and Miss Zeta-Jones
   married at the Plaza Hotel in New York on 18 November 2000. It was, said one
   witness, the event of the year. Extensive security arrangements had therefore
   been made, intended to ensure that access to the ceremony and reception would
   be denied to all but the family members and friends who had been invited and the
j attendant staff, who had been put on terms to keep the wedding confidential.
   The bride and groom hired their own selected photographers and it was made
   plain that other photography was not to be permitted. In making such
   arrangements the bride and groom were doing as they were bound by contract
   to do as they had sold exclusive photographic rights of the event to OK!
   magazine, although they had retained control over the selection of such pictures,
   taken by their own photographers, as they should choose to release to OK!. The

security arrangements thus were intended to serve the three-fold purposes of
confining the event to family and friends, of ensuring that only authorised
photographs were taken and of preserving the exclusivity of the photographic
rights for which OK! had paid £1m.

[2] The wedding passed off as a great success, enjoyed by all present but,
unknown to any as the events unfolded, it soon thereafter transpired that one
intruder, a photographer, had eluded security and had surreptitiously taken
relatively poor photographs which were then bought for publication in OK!'s
rival magazine, Hello!. The Douglases and OK!, then, as now, represented by
Mr Tugendhat QC and Mr Sherborne, quickly moved in England for an
injunction to restrain publication and they obtained that relief. However, the
Court of Appeal acceded to Hello!'s arguments and lifted the injunction, leaving
the claimants to claim in damages.

[3] In the result, Hello! published the unauthorised photographs on the same
day as that on which OK!, having had to bring its arrangements forward,
published parts of the full authorised portfolio of photographs covering the event,
approved by the Douglases, for which it had paid.

[4] As the litigation developed other parties were added as defendants and
other causes of action beyond the initial claims were added. The parties to the
action now, as claimants, are, as they were from the outset, Mr Douglas and
Miss Zeta-Jones (now Mrs Douglas) as first and second claimants and the
publishers of OK!, Northern & Shell plc, as third claimant. It will be convenient
to refer to the third claimant simply as OK!.

[5] On the defendants' side, Hello! Ltd, the first defendant, is a subsidiary of
the second defendant, Hola SA; the second defendant publishes Hello! magazine
and the first defendant distributes it in the United Kingdom. The third defendant
is Eduardo Sanchez Junco, a director of and controlling shareholder in Hola SA
and editor-in-chief of Hello! magazine. I will call the first three defendants the
Hello! defendants. They appear by Mr James Price QC and Mr Fernando. The
fourth defendant, the Marquesa de Varela, is a person who has frequently
supplied features for use in Hello! magazine and in Hola, its Spanish sister
publication. The fifth defendant is a company owned by the Marquesa de Varela.
They appear by Miss Mulcahy. The sixth defendant, Philip Ramey, is a paparazzo
photographer who also has a photographic agency in California. He was not the
photographer of the unauthorised photographs but it was he who sold them to
the Hello! defendants. He has not been represented and has taken no part before
me. The claimants propose to move against him later and do not seek relief
against him at this stage.

[6] A split trial was ordered so at this stage I am concerned only with whether
there is liability in one or more of the first five defendants to one or more of the
claimants. If I find there to be such a liability I shall not be concerned with
attempting to ascribe some monetary figure to that liability or even with
determining how that should be done.

THE PROCEDURAL HISTORY

[7] The procedural history is more complicated than one might expect as,
quite apart from collateral skirmishes, there have been, as I shall relate below,
two interlocutory hearings at first instance followed by one abortive appeal to a
two-man Court of Appeal and then a successful appeal to a three-man Court of
Appeal ([2001] 2 All ER 289, [2001] QB 967). Then, a good deal later and only
shortly before the trial began, there was an unsuccessful application to

a Sir Andrew Morritt V-C ([2003] EWHC 55 (Ch), [2003] 1 All ER 1087n) for the striking out of the defences of the Hello! defendants, an application on which Senor Sanchez Junco and three witnesses for the Hello! defendants were cross-examined.

PAPARAZZI

b   [8] As I shall explain in the course of the narrative, the photographer who took the unauthorised photographs, a Mr Rupert Thorpe, was in some form of loose association, the details of which are not known, not only with the sixth defendant, Mr Ramey, but also with two others, Frank Griffin and Randy Bauer. All carry on business as paparazzi, a term especially used and which I shall use to include those photographers whose business it is to take photographs of events *c* and celebrities where access to photographers generally to the event is forbidden or limited and where the consent of the celebrities to be photographed is known or likely to be refused and is thus dispensed with by the paparazzi concerned. In varying degrees, as may become necessary for them to obtain the photographs they seek, they turn to deception, to intrusion and, occasionally, to unlawful *d* behaviour. Mr Ramey, in particular, has a reputation of being able to get in where others were unlikely to be able to.

INTRUSION, IN CONTEXT

   [9] These proceedings have already attracted a good deal of public and press attention such that there are two points that I should mention as to be borne in *e* mind. The first is the extent to which celebrities of the status of Mr Douglas and Miss Zeta-Jones, whilst, of course, welcoming much of the publicity that surrounds them, can also find their privacy or ordinary life severely curtailed. Thus the undisputed evidence before me includes, for example, that Miss Zeta-Jones has been frightened by a photographer jumping out of a *f* doorway at night to photograph her, that on another occasion she swerved her car into a lamp post trying to escape from a paparazzo and that the press got hold of and published the fact of her pregnancy even before she had had all the medical tests she had wanted to take and before even she had told her close family of it, including her mother. When she was in hospital after the birth of her son, journalists tricked their way into the hospital by pretending to be members of her *g* family. When she was wheeled from the delivery room back to her room in the hospital she was covered by a sheet to avoid being photographed by the photographers who had tricked their way in. In one remarkable incident when her son was only one week old he, with his nanny, was in a car driven in California by Miss Zeta-Jones. Photographers for a British tabloid newspaper *h* deliberately ran into the car. Under Californian law Miss Zeta-Jones had to get out of the car to exchange details. Her evidence continues, of the photographers:

> 'They immediately jumped out of their car and took photographs of me looking furious at the side of the road. They then published them in an article about me being consumed by road rage.'

j Hardly surprisingly, her evidence continued: 'This incident made me very angry.' It is easy to see, against such a background, how celebrities may become especially defensive, though I add that this case is nothing to do with photography of either Mr Douglas or Miss Zeta-Jones in public.

   [10] The other point I make is that whilst the claimants' case is now chiefly for money it was not always so and it was not by their choice that it became so. What

all claimants first moved for was an injunction to restrain publication. The case
only became chiefly for monetary compensation after the three-man Court of
Appeal had ruled that the existing injunction was to be undone and that the
claimants would have to be satisfied with claims in damages.

THE MAGAZINES

[11] Hola has been published in Spain for over 50 years and the three versions,
'Hola' in Spanish, 'Hello!' in English and 'Oh La' in French are sold in almost
60 countries. Hello! has been circulated weekly in the United Kingdom for some
12 years and is bought by an average of some 456,000 people per week, leading,
it is said, to a readership of some 2·2 million people per week. It is sold through
about 55,000 outlets in the United Kingdom, going on sale on Tuesdays in
London and on Wednesdays in the rest of the country. It is printed in Spain and
published by Hola SA. The cover price in 2000 was £1·55.

[12] OK! is printed in England and published weekly by the third claimant. It
is a more recently-established magazine than Hello!, that being broadly reflected
in the issue numbers at the time of the Douglas wedding, namely no 639 for
Hello! and no 241 for OK!. Its cover price in 2000 was £1·85. It normally comes
out on Thursdays in London and on Fridays throughout the rest of the United
Kingdom. In November 2000 OK! sold about 455,000 copies per issue on average.

[13] Whilst, no doubt, each magazine has especial characteristics which
commend it to particular prospective customers, less discerning readers will find
much that is common to both. Indeed, there is some strong feeling amongst
London staff at Hello! that OK! is a copycat. Both magazines are of similar size
and shape and provide a regular diet of photographs and text of and about Royal
but, more usually, entertainment, sporting and social celebrities, with
photographs taking precedence over text. Many of the main features are in the
highest degree posed and show, for example, the celebrity's yacht or home or
show his or her engagement or wedding. Many such features will have been
commissioned by arrangement with the subjects and paid for by the magazine in
question, the more celebrated or newsworthy celebrities being able to command,
should they wish, higher fees than the less celebrated. Other photographs, whilst
such that the subjects can be seen to be very aware of and, as it would seem,
content with the camera, are far less formal and record, for example, arrivals at a
party or at the opening of a film. Each magazine includes from time to time
photographs taken, so far as one can judge, without the subject's knowledge or
consent but they represent a minority overall.

[14] There are brief passages about travel, cooking, 'lifestyle' and health
advice and as to current television programming. There are short features on
particular celebrities in the news in the current week. The texts generally are, if
not unquestioning or flattering, at least warm as to the celebrities featured, no
doubt for the practical reason that if that were not so the supply of willing
celebrities might dry up.

[15] The two magazines are plainly keen rivals in the same market and were
so in 2000.

EVIDENCE

[16] On the claimants' side I heard oral evidence from Miss Zeta-Jones,
Mr Michael Douglas, Mr Allen Burry (Mr Douglas' executive assistant and
publicist), Miss Simone Martel Levinson (the event planner engaged by the
Douglases to organise their wedding), Ms Cece Yorke (Miss Zeta-Jones'

a publicist), Mr Martin Townsend (formerly editor of OK! magazine, in office at the time of the wedding) and Mr Paul Anderson (picture editor of OK! magazine). The evidence of Miss Levinson and Ms Yorke was given by video link to and from the United States.

[17] So far as the claimants' expert evidence was concerned, I heard oral evidence as to New York law by video link from Professor Arthur J Jacobson, Max *b* Freund Professor of Litigation and Advocacy at the Benjamin N Cardozo School of Law in New York City. The claimants' evidence as to Spanish law was given orally by Senor Enric Enrich, senior partner of the Barcelona firm of advocates, Enrich Amat I Vidal-Quedras, former co-chairman of the Committee of Intellectual Property of the International Bar Association and currently the chairman of the Copyright and Image Rights' section of the Barcelona Bar *c* Association.

[18] All of the above-described witnesses were cross-examined, each having supplied one or more witness statements or reports.

[19] On the defendants' side the main body of evidence came from the Hello! defendants. Senor Eduardo Sanchez Junco gave his oral evidence by way of an *d* interpreter as he speaks little or no English. Senor Javier Riera, managing director of Hola SA, did the same; he has sufficient command of *written* English to comprehend untechnical and straightforward documents. His personal assistant, Senora Elisa Sanchez-Ferragut Arnau (conveniently and, as I hope, without offence, usually referred to during the hearing as Senora Elisa) gave her oral evidence through the interpreter. Mr Anthony Luke, co-ordinating editor of *e* Hello! magazine, who works in Madrid and has fluent Spanish, spoke in English. Hello!'s publishing director, Sally Amanda Cartwright, who also has good Spanish, gave oral evidence, as did Maria José Doughty, a native Spanish speaker but whose English is impeccable. She is administration and financial controller at Hello! Ltd in London. Mr Christopher Mark Hutchings, solicitor, a partner in *f* Charles Russell, solicitors to the Hello! defendants, also gave oral evidence, as did Margaret Koumi, the editor of Hello! in 2000. All of these witnesses had supplied one or more witness statements and all were cross-examined.

[20] The Hello! defendants' expert evidence consisted of the evidence of Professor Diane L Zimmerman on New York law and of Senor Miguel Engel Rodriguez on Spanish law. Professor Zimmerman, Professor of Law at New *g* York University, gave oral evidence by video link and Senor Rodriguez, a member of the Madrid Bar and until recently Associate Professor of Constitutional Law at Universidad Autonomia at Madrid, gave his oral evidence here in London through an interpreter. Both had put in one or more written reports.

h [21] Oral evidence on behalf of the fourth and fifth defendants consisted of the evidence of the fourth defendant herself, Maria J Marin, also known as the Marquesa de Varela (the Marquesa), and her personal assistant, Pirjetta Mildh, both of whom had a complete command of English despite it being the mother tongue of neither. No expert evidence was put in on behalf of the fourth and fifth defendants. Each of the Marquesa and Miss Mildh put in one witness statement; a second was prepared for the Marquesa but did not find its way into evidence.

[22] In a category of her own amongst those who gave oral evidence was Sue Neal, no longer an employee of Hello! or Hola SA but formerly a picture editor working in London for Hello!. She had prepared two witness statements; one was prepared by the solicitors for the fourth and fifth defendants, one by the solicitors to the claimants. Neither the fourth and fifth defendants nor the

claimants chose either to call Miss Neal or to put in either or both of her witness statements but at a late stage in his case Mr Price chose to put in her witness statements as hearsay evidence under CPR 32.5(5). That led Mr Tugendhat to apply to cross-examine on her statements under CPR 33.4(1). I ruled that he could do so and the Court of Appeal, in an interlocutory ruling, upheld that decision. Accordingly Miss Sue Neal was cross-examined by Mr Tugendhat and re-examined by Mr Price.

[23] Mr Philip Ramey, the sixth defendant, a photographer well-known as a paparazzo and who also conducts a photographic agency, has put in a defence (with a statement as to its truth) and a witness statement but otherwise, as I have mentioned, has taken no part in the proceedings. Much of his witness statement is uncontroversial or is confirmed by other evidence but in the absence of his having submitted himself for cross-examination I do not feel able to attach weight to his assertions that he offered European rights to the unauthorised pictures to the Marquesa or that she bought them from him, either on arms' length commercial terms or at all.

[24] There have been several other witness statements by or on behalf of individuals who have not given oral evidence, some on topics which do not yet need to be pursued, and notice as to hearsay evidence has been given in respect of some but I have not felt that any either displaces or adds significantly to conclusions formed on the basis of the other documentary evidence and the evidence given by witnesses whose evidence has been tested by cross-examination.

THE NARRATIVE BEGINS

[25] A chronological order will occasionally have to be departed from but I shall attempt, as far as practicable, to set out the facts I find in that order.

[26] Miss Zeta-Jones and Mr Douglas met in September 1998. A relationship developed. Later they had a holiday together. Articles began to appear in the press about them as a couple. That they might become engaged and marry began to occur to OK! as, doubtless, it did to Hello!. Such events would be exactly the kind each would want to cover. On 6 September 1999, before any engagement had been announced, OK! offered £1m 'subject to contract' for exclusive photographic rights for the engagement, wedding, honeymoon and for Miss Zeta-Jones' thirtieth birthday party.

[27] In September 1999 OK! acquired exclusive photographic rights by contract to the wedding in California and honeymoon of the television presenter Jenny McCarthy and John Asher for $100,000. A term of the contract was that the bride and groom should, at their own expense, provide such reasonable security at the wedding as was reasonably necessary to ensure that unauthorised photographers, journalists and members of the public would be unable to gain access to the grounds and premises so as to minimise the risk of photographs of the wedding being made available to the media. OK! was to make a full feature of the events. None the less, Hello! acquired and published photographs of the wedding, one at least of which has the appearance of being an out-of-focus shot, surreptitiously taken from a low level by a camera of which the bride and groom appear ignorant. Invoices sent to Hello! in respect of the pictures it used were from, respectively, Messrs Ramey, Griffin, Bauer and Thorpe, all photographers to whose names I shall need to return. The invoices bear words, added in handwriting at Hello!'s office, such as 'Ordered by Marquesa and Eduardo' and 'Commissioned by Marquesa and Eduardo'. Mr Ramey makes reference to a

a 'Day Rate' in his invoice and does not identify the event photographed, referring instead to a 'Special Project'. The others openly refer to the McCarthy wedding. Mr Bauer's invoice refers to '2 days'. The invoices bear marks indicating that they were processed in London. These details came to light only in the course of the trial, after the Marquesa's evidence was concluded. There was no application for her recall. That she had (with Senor Sanchez Junco) an involvement in the

b arrangements made for the unauthorised photographs is plain not only from the superscriptions on the invoices but also from the fact that Hello! paid her a 'fee for Jenny McCarthy wedding' of £5,000. Although such photographs of paparazzi type were not her usual style, that she could and would take a hand in arrangements for them is plain. OK!'s big feature on the wedding in their issue of 24 September 1999 had some, at least, of its exclusiveness diminished by the

c unauthorised photographs in Hello!'s issue 579. The Marquesa was able to crow to Anthony Luke, the co-ordinating editor in Madrid: 'My paparazzi spoiled OK!'s Jenny McCarthy wedding.' In respect of aspects of the handling of the Douglas wedding, both sides made reference back to the McCarthy wedding, to emphasise similarities (as did the claimants) or differences (as did the Hello!

d defendants).

DECEMBER 1999

[28] In December 1999 Miss Zeta-Jones became pregnant with Mr Douglas' child. At a millennium party they agreed they would marry. They started to plan their wedding. They picked New York as a venue roughly central between the

e United Kingdom to the east and California to the west. The Plaza Hotel was chosen as it had a proven track record for hosting large-scale events which required security. It was also a place where guests could stay and, as Miss Zeta-Jones planned to stay there, she could procure that her arrival at the wedding would not (as she put it) be turned into a media circus.

f [29] Miss Zeta-Jones did not want to be forced to have her wedding in secret. She had always wanted it, she said, to be a very special day and it was important to her that her family, in particular, would be there to share it with her. There was concern that media intrusion might destroy the intimacy and joy of the event. Miss Simone Martel Levinson was brought in, an experienced event planner. She was told that the bride and groom wanted the wedding to be

g personal, romantic, intimate and unforgettable.

[30] Miss Zeta-Jones' pregnancy was thought to be a closely-guarded secret but in January 2000, only some seven to eight weeks into the pregnancy and, as I have touched on already, before Miss Zeta-Jones had either had all of the medical tests which she wished to have or had told her close family, she found that the

h Sun newspaper had learned of the pregnancy and was going to publish the story. She was forced into announcing the pregnancy to her family before she was ready to do so. As this was to be her first child she had particularly wanted to have every possible test before giving the news to her family. Her inquiries suggested that paparazzi had obtained the information from an assistant in the office of the lawyers then acting for her. Her pregnancy became public knowledge.

[31] OK!'s offer for an exclusive was accordingly modified to include a sum for photographs of both parents and the baby. From about March 2000 Hello! was also in contact with Mr Allen Burry, Mr Douglas' publicist, but Mr Burry had not found it easy to deal with Senor Sanchez Junco's calls because of the language difficulties. The prospective bride and groom had not yet decided whether to permit a feature to be published either of the baby or of the wedding.

APRIL 2000

[32] The Marquesa entered the lists in April 2000. Her personal assistant, *a*
Pirjetta Mildh, was in contact with Mr Burry, from whom she heard of his
dissatisfaction with his dealings with Madrid. Mr Burry was not averse, though,
to dealing with the Marquesa, who made contact with him. The Madrid office of
Hello! and Senor Sanchez Junco continued to approach Mr Burry but to no effect
save that Mr Burry's displeasure with Madrid grew. The Marquesa felt strongly *b*
that Senor Sanchez Junco was mishandling matters, that Hello!'s bid would be far
better conducted by her and that, left to itself, Madrid was likely to drive any
'exclusive' into the hands of OK!. The thing that Mr Burry had not been able to
get Madrid to grasp, as he put it to Miss Mildh and as she related to the Marquesa,
was:

c
    'Money is not the point! The point is doing it with the magazine they like
    and trust and have a good working relationship with so they can have a
    lovely wedding without any worries.'

Both OK! and Hello! continued to make offers but Miss Zeta-Jones and
Mr Douglas remained undecided not only as between those offerors but as to *d*
coverage of the prospective events at all, the events, by May, being, of course, not
only the wedding but the earlier birth of Miss Zeta-Jones' first child, expected in
August 2000.

[33] On 3 May 2000 the Marquesa, for Hello!, wrote to Mr Burry to say that
Senor Sanchez Junco offered $500,000 for exclusive pictures of the mother and
father with their baby and £1m for the wedding. Mr Burry, though, had wanted *e*
clear written proposals from Hello!. That elicited a further offer from Senor
Sanchez Junco, now put at $1·5m for the wedding alone. His proposals, which he
described as '[t]he biggest investment ever made by our magazine', included that
Hello!'s own photographers should cover the event as well as those selected by
the bride and groom. He was also keen to ensure that the one approved picture, *f*
which the couple were going to release generally and gratis to the media on the
day, should not be released until Hello! had appeared on the market. He also
wanted that free picture to be 'a medium shot' rather than a close-up or
full-length photograph. Neither of those provisions was likely to commend itself
to the couple.

[34] At Hello! it was felt, rightly as it transpired, that negotiations were going *g*
OK!'s way. The Marquesa felt that if the exclusive for the baby was lost to Hello!,
it would be likely to lose the wedding as well. Hello!, by way of the Marquesa,
on 21 July increased its offer to $600,000 for the baby pictures and £1m for the
wedding but to no avail.

AUGUST 2000

[35] On 8 August 2000 Senor Sanchez Junco, disappointed and feeling that
Hello! would not get the exclusive, telephoned the Marquesa, who was in New
York trying to encourage Mr Burry to deal with Hello!. She told Senor Sanchez
Junco that if the couple would not deal with Hello! then the only option was to
contact, and buy pictures from, paparazzi. There was nothing new about that as
a possibility to Senor Sanchez Junco; he has bought pictures from paparazzi
including the two I shall next mention, for years. Senor Sanchez Junco told her
that Sue Neal, the Hello! pictures editor in London, was already in contact with
two paparazzi, Phil Ramey and Frank Griffin. In so holding I have preferred the
evidence of the Marquesa to that of Senor Sanchez Junco. Of the two

a photographers, both had wide reputations as paparazzi. Mr Ramey, in particular, a difficult man to deal with, was renowned as an aggressive photographer; as the Marquesa put it: 'You know, he can get into anyone's house and do the pictures.' Sue Neal described him as a confident gatecrasher. Senor Sanchez Junco knew of his reputation. The Marquesa volunteered to get in touch with the paparazzi and did so. It suited both Senor Sanchez Junco and the Marquesa that it should be the
b Marquesa who should contact the paparazzi. Senor Sanchez Junco might well have felt disappointed at his own handling so far of the Douglas wedding and would in any event have been willing to pass it to the Marquesa but more probable was it that he, in this respect a cautious or even fearful man, saw it to be unwise to be seen to be in direct contact with paparazzi whose means of obtaining photographs, certainly any inside the wedding, might well be at best
c dubious or at worst unlawful. The Marquesa, whose star had been waning at Hello!, was not unwilling to have the chance of emerging as the 'fixer' who could come up with some solution where all others had failed, thus hoping to restore herself more fully to Senor Sanchez Junco's favour.

d [36] The Marquesa told each of Ramey and Griffin that Senor Sanchez Junco was keen to get first refusal on any pictures that might be obtained of the Douglas wedding. Each said that he already dealt with Sue Neal and that the wedding had already been discussed with her.

THE $10,000
e [37] Mr Ramey asked the Marquesa whether Senor Sanchez Junco would be prepared to pay $10,000 as a sign of goodwill, because expenses would be incurred. In her witness statement the Marquesa says: 'I assured Mr Ramey that I did not think this would be a problem but I would ask Eduardo if he was willing to accept Phil Ramey's request.'

f [38] It has since suited Mr Ramey to describe that conversation to Hello!, including to Sue Neal, as a promise of $10,000 in any event and it is likely that the Marquesa did express herself to him with some assurance as to the $10,000 being paid. In an e-mail much later, of 17 December 2000, she wrote, of the $10,000, 'that I could assure him of that'. But I accept also that when she spoke to Senor Sanchez Junco on the point he told her it would not be paid and that she passed the message on to Mr Ramey, but coupled with the encouraging addition that Senor Sanchez Junco would pay (meaning pay well) for good pictures. If there had been a clear promise of $10,000 in advance either for pictures or for a right of first refusal it was, I hold, soon supplanted by Mr Ramey being left in no doubt, instead, that Hello! was very keen to acquire pictures, however they might be taken, and, as the Marquesa put it, 'there's nobody who has paid like Mr Sanchez'.

g [39] On 16 August 2000 the Marquesa sent a draft contract to Mr Burry under which the deal would not be with Hello! but with a company of hers, Marquesa Productions Ltd of the British Virgin Islands. She had not appreciated that Mr Burry would not recommend any contract other than directly with a magazine publisher.

[40] Hello! further harmed its cause when it bought paparazzo pictures of the mother, father and baby after the birth of Dylan Douglas to the couple in August 2000. OK! had succeeded in obtaining exclusive picture rights to photographs of the parents with their new baby. The 'shoot' went well and the parents developed a trust in Martin Townsend, OK!'s editor. The money for the photographs was put into a trust for the infant Dylan Douglas.

[41] By contrast, as the couple, the three-week-old baby and their nurse left *a* the hospital, paparazzi managed to take photographs without the parents' consent nor, so far as one can tell, with their even being aware that they were being photographed. Similar photographs were taken of the mother, father and baby without the nurse. Hello! bought those pictures and published them. When the Marquesa pressed Hello!'s case by referring to how vulgar, she said, had been OK!'s coverage of another celebrity wedding, Mr Burry's response was: *b* 'At least OK! was smart enough to turn down the hospital departure pictures when they were offered to them.'

[42] Hello! was not prepared to give up. It attempted to make fresh contact by other intermediaries; desperation was setting in, with Senor Sanchez Junco not only having in mind, of course, payment to the bride and groom but even payment of substantial sums to an intermediary who might restore contact with *c* them. It was to no avail; on 6 November Mr Burry indicated that the couple had decided that they would offer the wedding for publication, but to OK!. Mr Burry turned to giving Mr Townsend details of the event.

AUTUMN 2000 *d*

[43] The plan, in outline, was for a wedding in New York at the Plaza Hotel with a dinner the night before at the Russian Tea Room for the guests from out of town. The ceremony itself was to be conducted by a judge and was to be non-denominational. There were to be some 360 or so guests, of whom 84 were to be the bride's relatives and friends flying in from the United Kingdom and the rest were the groom's family and mutual friends of bride and groom. *e*

[44] That was the plan but, for the moment, it lay in the future. In the meantime, Sue Neal, in London had almost daily contact with Phil Ramey and Frank Griffin, part of a clique which included Rupert Thorpe and Randy Bauer. Sometime around August 2000 Mr Ramey told Miss Neal that 'Your Marquesa' had told him that Senor Sanchez Junco had asked her to see if it was possible to *f* get photographs of the Douglas wedding. Mr Ramey told Miss Neal that he preferred to deal with someone he knew. By that he meant Miss Neal. Miss Neal got the impression that the Marquesa had had only one or two conversations with Mr Ramey. Mr Luke told Miss Neal that Senor Sanchez Junco was seeking to obtain pictures of the wedding from *any* source. Miss Neal told Mr Ramey that *g* if he wanted to send pictures of the wedding to Hello! that that was up to him but she did tell him that Senor Sanchez Junco was extremely interested in obtaining them. She left it on the basis that Mr Ramey was not obliged to supply any, nor was Hello! to accept any. Her understanding was that Senor Sanchez Junco was dealing with the Douglas wedding himself instead of the Marquesa.

[45] In his frequent calls to Miss Neal on other subjects Mr Ramey would try *h* to find out whether Hello! had managed to get exclusive rights to the wedding. He wanted to know so as to target whichever magazine had not got the exclusive. Sue Neal at that stage knew nothing and told him nothing; it was left as a subject to be reverted to nearer the time of the wedding.

[46] Miss Martel Levinson did her best in the course of her arrangements for *j* the wedding, to ensure that the venue of the wedding was kept secret. Suppliers or prospective suppliers of goods and services were asked to sign confidentiality agreements. Many are in the evidence. After the wedding it was found that a few people had not signed such agreements but her evidence, which I accept, was that—

a

'[e]veryone whom I hired to deal with some aspects of the wedding knew from my discussions with them that the plans for the wedding were confidential and were not to reach the public arena.'

b

[47] Unfortunately one of the florists who had tendered for the work, albeit unsuccessfully, told the New York Post, who then published, that the wedding was going to be held at the Plaza Hotel. The original plan had been to tell invitees only that the wedding was to be in New York City on 18 November 2000, the precise venue and time then to be given only at the last minute. The florist's breach required a change of plan. The invitations went out in their original form but on acceptance a second notice was sent indicating that the wedding was to be at the Plaza at 7.00 pm, coupled with a request from the bride and groom that no

c

photographic equipment should be brought. The message—'We would appreciate no photography or video devices at the ceremony or reception'—whilst not an outright prohibition, was as nearly so as one might reasonably address to family and friends. An entry card was required to be produced at the entrance to the Rose Room on the evening of the wedding.

d

Entrance to the hotel was to be by way of the Rose Room.

A STRATEGY FOR THE WEDDING

[48] Whilst reflecting on their possible arrangements for the wedding, Miss Zeta-Jones and Mr Douglas looked back on the successful event that had been the presentation to the public of their baby, Dylan. The exclusive rights sold

e

to OK! had led to excellent photographs being published without any real media intrusion. Miss Zeta-Jones' witness statement says, and I accept, as follows:

f

'When considering how to deal with the inevitable media interest in our wedding we ultimately decided to go down the same route that we had chosen in respect of Dylan's birth. We decided that, with a view to reducing the media frenzy for photographs of the wedding and protecting our wedding day from the inevitable media intrusion, we would reach an agreement with a magazine which we would allow to publish a limited number of our wedding photographs. We hoped that once the rest of the media found out that we had entered into such an arrangement they would

g

be less interested in trying to infiltrate our wedding. This would leave us and our guests free to enjoy the day without worrying about the media. Both Michael and I also accept that as celebrities we have an obligation not to ignore those people who make us celebrities, the people who pay money to watch our movies. One of the reasons that we decided to reach a deal with

h

a magazine was to make contact with our fans and to avoid the accusation that we had shunned them or were too aloof. We wanted to do so in a context where the choice was ours as to what was and was not published about our wedding, not left to a media free-for-all.'

[49] Mr Douglas' evidence in the same area was to similar effect though more

j

emphasising control. He said:

'Eventually, we decided that the best way to control the media and to protect our privacy would be to reach an agreement with a single magazine or newspaper who would have the rights to publish photographs of, and text about, our child and our wedding, and to syndicate the photographs and text to specified and pre-agreed publications around the world.'

[50] Miss Cece Yorke, Miss Zeta-Jones' publicist, thought the strategy a good one. She said:

'I really felt that if other publications knew that one magazine was going to have an exclusive story with beautiful photographs and access to Michael and Catherine they would think there was no point in publishing poor quality photographs with no quotes from the bride and groom or the family. It seemed to me that the public would want to see the beautiful photos and to hear the real story and that would be the calculation that the media would also make. I believed that the exclusive arrangement with OK! was the best option in the circumstances. We decided that we would also release one official photograph to everyone else on the actual day of the wedding (since the official photographs would not be published in OK! for a little while).'

[51] An initial view, that there should be no press involvement at all and that the media would have to be satisfied with one released authorised photograph, was thought to be unrealistic. The media would try to get their own photographs. Other celebrity weddings had been spoilt by intrusions. Having the wedding at the Plaza eliminated the risk of helicopters that had intruded in other cases but Mr Burry said:

'Having seen the determination and lack of scruples of the media at earlier celebrity weddings, we became more and more convinced that we should provide, on an exclusive basis, official photographs of the wedding personally selected by the bride and groom to a single media organisation who would then syndicate those photographs to other publications of our choice. It was our hope that the rest of the world's media would be discouraged from trying to infiltrate the wedding as they would know that the official photographs would be published and syndicated exclusively elsewhere. We thought that by providing a limited number of "authorised" pictures of the wedding we would reduce the price that illicitly-obtained photographs of the wedding could command and therefore reduce the incentive of any photographer to take such photographs. In the past I have found that if you give an exclusive to one magazine its rivals tend to be philosophical, hoping that they will get the next exclusive. They will act accordingly, not wanting to damage their chances of an exclusive in the future. We all thought that this would be the best way for Catherine and Michael to retain their privacy and the intimate and private nature of the wedding.'

[52] Mr Price cross-examined as to this strategy, broadly suggesting that it was more for money than for privacy, could not be expected or be believed to work and was aimed at control of the media. That it involved control was plain. But, as to money, Mr Douglas pointed out that neither bride nor groom nor publicist approached the magazines but the magazines had approached them. Nor had the bride and groom or their agents negotiated about price. Indeed, they could very readily have organised transactions so as to have received more than they did. As for the strategy, it worked (as will transpire) for all but one paparazzo and, as Mr Douglas said:

'... it was not that we did not think that the public would not be interested, we thought that the paparazzi's desire would be lowered because they would not have very many outlets, and therefore they personally would not a be able to make as much money selling them individually, so that they said, "Oh well, I don't think its worth it".'

On the evidence I hold that the notion of an exclusive contract as a means of reducing the risk of intrusion by unauthorised members of the media and hence of preserving the privacy of a celebrity occasion is a notion that can reasonably be believed in as a potentially workable strategy to achieve such ends and was
b honestly believed in by Miss Zeta-Jones, Mr Douglas and their advisers. The fact that, because of one lapse, the strategy failed does not disprove its reasonableness, still less that it was believed in. Whilst I would not hold the £1m on offer to be other than a real blandishment even to a couple as rich as Mr Douglas and Miss Zeta-Jones, I see their expectation that an exclusive contract to one selected
c publisher offered the best strategy for obtaining a wedding of the kind they both wanted and offered also the certainty of fair coverage of it as their chief reason for making such a contract.

THE CONTRACT WITH OK!; 10 NOVEMBER 2000

[53] On 10 November 2000 basic terms of a contract under Californian law
d between OK! and Mr Burry on behalf of the bride and groom were agreed in writing. £500,000 was to be paid to each of 'MKD' and 'CZJ' not later than a week before the wedding. OK! was given exclusive rights to publish photographs selected for the purpose by 'MKD' and 'CZJ'. Each of 'MKD' and 'CZJ' was given 'copy caption and headline approval over any syndication of the photographs', such approval not to be unreasonably withheld. The photographs were to be in
e colour and were to be taken by photographers chosen and paid for by 'MKD' and 'CZJ', who were required (cl 6) to—

> '[u]se their best efforts to ensure that no other media ... shall be permitted access to the wedding and that no guests or anyone else present at the wedding (including staff at the venues) shall be allowed to take photographs.'

f
[54] Copyright in the photographs was to be in 'MKD' and 'CZJ', who were to approve such photographs as they chose to release not later than 22 November 2000. Text approval was also given to 'MKD' and 'CZJ'. The Douglases could, had they wished, have chosen to release no photographs or too few to make a feature, but on pain of repayment to OK! (cl 9). If syndication brought in more
g than £1m the excess was to be split 50% to OK! and 25% each to 'MKD' and 'CZJ', but OK! was to have the first £1m. Clause 16 provided:

> 'MKD and CZJ will take all reasonable means to provide such security (approved by OK magazine) during the entirety of the wedding proceedings at the wedding venues as is necessary to ensure that third party media ...
h and/or members of the public and/or staff hired or employed for the wedding are unable to gain access to the relevant wedding grounds and the venues in order to minimise the risk of photographs and/or footage of the wedding (including but not limited to photographs/footage of the wedding dress, the ceremony and the party) may be made available to third party
j media.'

[55] In the week beginning 13 November, the week before the wedding, Hello! was alive to a prospect of getting photographs from inside the wedding. Mr Luke told Sue Neal: 'We might be getting something.' Senor Sanchez Junco said so to Mr Luke, as did Maggie Koumi, the London editor. Both Phil Ramey and Frank Griffin told Sue Neal: 'Don't forget the weekend.' On Thursday 16 or

Friday 17 November Mr Ramey told Miss Neal that he was trying to get someone
into the wedding to take pictures. She told that to Mr Luke, who asked her to go   *a*
into work over the weekend. That was so that technical incompatibility
problems could be overcome by pictures from the United States of America going
to Madrid via London. There was confidence that at the very least there would
be pictures from *outside* the wedding, of the guests arriving.

THE RUSSIAN TEA ROOM; 17 NOVEMBER 2000   *b*

[56] As planned, a dinner was held the night before the wedding at the Russian
Tea Room. The photographs of this event, later spread over some eight or nine
pages in Hello!'s issue 639, show the press to have been there in massive strength.
Mr Douglas and Miss Zeta-Jones paused to pose frequently for photographs, as
did members of the respective families and their friends.   *c*

HELLO! MAKES ARRANGEMENTS

[57] In the meantime, Hello! was planning the issue (no 639) of Hello! due to
appear next after the wedding, on Saturday 18 November 2000. It was scheduled
to be distributed in London on Tuesday 21 November and in the rest of the
United Kingdom on Wednesday 22 November. It was not unknown in 2000 and   *d*
earlier for the greater part of the magazine to be printed (in Spain, as then was the
case), section by section, over the Thursday and Friday of a given week but with
the final centre pages and, if appropriate, the cover and back page to be either
re-cast or left to the last convenient time, either so as to cover an unexpected
event or some event likely to happen at the weekend concerned. Late changes to   *e*
the magazine shortly before or even after first going to print had been made on
occasions such as the deaths of Jackie Kennedy Onassis and Princess Diana and
upon John Kennedy Jr and his wife going missing. A late special edition added
photographs of Madonna's wedding and her baby's christening. The Tuesday
distribution date could not be postponed. Hello! had begun to plan for an
issue 639 which would have on its cover Mr Douglas and Miss Zeta-Jones outside   *f*
the Russian Tea Room in New York on the Friday evening of 17 November.
Neither OK! nor anyone else had exclusive rights as to that and it could be
expected that there would be ample opportunity for photographs of the couple,
their family and friends, as they arrived and left. At least photographs for the
cover showing the couple could be expected to be obtained (leaving the centre to   *g*
be filled with a different feature) but even that would leave a tight timetable
because of the time difference between Madrid and New York and the time
necessarily taken up with processing, selection, printing and movement to
London for distribution by the Tuesday. Such movement was, in ordinary
course, by lorry.

[58] The photographs of the Russian Tea Room event arrived in Spain on   *h*
Saturday 18 November. Mr Luke said at first that they arrived on Saturday
morning but he settled into saying that they arrived late on Saturday. On that
basis, printing of the cover and final section (leaving aside any prospect of later
paparazzo photographs taken at the wedding itself) would probably not have
started until Sunday 19 November. On the question of whether, on that basis,   *j*
lorries could not be used but recourse would have had to have been made to
aircraft, Mr Luke said:

'Yes it would have to have flown I think at that stage, because we were
getting really late, and being in direct competition with OK! we could not
lose any days on the [news] stand.'

a On that basis (which I accept) special arrangements would have needed to be made for airfreight even if only the Russian Tea Room photographs had been awaited.

[59] Airfreight was arranged, additional copies of Hello! were ordered to be printed and staff were called in, both in London and Madrid, to deal with the preparation of the magazine over the weekend. Mr Tugendhat argues that all *b* this shows that Hello! was anticipating a high-selling issue and that it points to Hello!'s having commissioned in advance a breach of OK!'s exclusivity and an intrusion upon the Douglases' privacy. He argued that Hello! had been assured of obtaining unauthorised photographs of the wedding. There is, I would accept, some documentary support for such a view. The Hello! print records show that the print order was greatly increased; an invoice shows that a freight aircraft was *c* chartered on 17 November for 173,950 Euros (part of which sum had to be paid whether the plane transpired to be used or not) and there is no doubt but that staff had been called in or retained to work at the weekend. There is, though, a good deal of contrary evidence indicating that there had been no assurance that paparazzo photographs would be available from inside the wedding or even that *d* a right of first refusal had been given to Hello!. Senor Sanchez Junco in cross-examination was emphatic that there had been no prior commitment to any paparazzi to buy any photographs. I have already indicated that there was no unsupplanted agreement even that Hello! should have a right of first refusal (though it would be an obvious course for a paparazzo to approach Hello! first). Mr Luke's evidence was that Senor Sanchez Junco was 'a very visual man'; he *e* would not pay anything, he said, for a picture before he had seen it and never paid paparazzi advance fees. Mr Luke also described the Douglas wedding as 'an amazing event' for people who read magazines such as Hello! and OK!. It was, he said, the event of the year. Even if no photographs had been obtained from inside the wedding itself and Hello! had had to rely on the Russian Tea Room *f* pictures or ones of guests arriving at the wedding, the publishers could thus be expected to arrange for greater sales than usual. Moreover, as I have indicated, an aircraft and weekend working would have been necessary even if only the Russian Tea Room photographs had been used. Nor have I any evidence that even an aggressive paparazzo such as Mr Ramey could be *sure* that the elaborate security surrounding the wedding could be overridden and that photographs *g* within the wedding would assuredly become available. These events do not, in my judgment, indicate that Hello! had commissioned the breach and intrusion which I shall come on to describe. The fact that a second freight aircraft was chartered on Monday 20 November, only after the unauthorised pictures had arrived, does nothing to support a view that even before they arrived it was *h* known that they would.

[60] To the same end a comparison was made with the material relating to the McCarthy wedding. That material, not put to the Marquesa for an explanation, seems to show the Marquesa in a closer relationship with the very same paparazzi as were used in the Douglas case than her own evidence suggested. It also shows *j* creditors' descriptions and the debtor's written additions on the McCarthy invoices to be in some respects like those found on one invoice in the Douglas case. But there are differences; the McCarthy invoices include daily rates payable to the photographers, a system more likely to be indicative of a true pre-commissioning of the paparazzi than is shown on the invoices as to the Douglas wedding, which have no daily rates. Indeed, so little was said in evidence about the role of the paparazzi or of the Marquesa in the McCarthy case

that I cannot hold that in that case the paparazzi were commissioned in advance
and, in turn, cannot hold that, because of the similarities in the two cases, the
paparazzi were therefore also so commissioned in the Douglas case.

ARRANGEMENTS FOR SECURITY AT THE PLAZA HOTEL

[61] On 17 November 2000, the day before the wedding, entry cards were
hand-delivered to all guests staying in New York and were sent by courier to
guests out of town, to arrive on 17 November. This late delivery was to reduce
the risk of their being copied. Miss Martel Levinson had marked each card with
a code that indicated to her (but only to her) the identity of the guest related to
that card and with an invisible ink design on the back which only she knew. The
entry cards indicated whether they were for one or two guests.

[62] There was a fear that the Plaza's fire alarm system might be tampered
with (driving everyone into the street, where they then could be photographed
at will) so a specialist fire firm that worked in conjunction with the New York Fire
Department was brought in and a technician monitored the fire alarm system of
the hotel throughout the wedding.

[63] Three private security companies were employed and there was
consultation with the New York Police Department and the Fire Department.
The Plaza's own security staff had the task of ensuring that other guests staying
at the hotel did not stray from the public areas of the hotel into those reserved for
the wedding. The rooms used for the wedding were regularly 'swept' until an
hour before the ceremony to ensure there were no hidden sound or video
devices. Special arrangements were made for exclusive use of the lifts in the
hotel. Guests arriving by car were required to enter a special car tent where
the invisible ink on the entry card could be inspected. The car tent was secured
at all access points by police. Barriers were erected so that the press could take
photographs of guests entering the hotel but could not get too near the entrance.

[64] Guests had to enter the Rose Room of the hotel. There was a sign there
reminding them that photography was not permitted. Entry cards were then
checked against the code to ensure that appearances corresponded with the
invitation. If all was well, on the entry card being handed in a gold wedding pin
was given to the guests, the design of which had been commissioned by the bride
and groom and had, so far as practical, been kept secret.

[65] Arrangements were made so that if it was found at entry that any guest
had brought a camera, it would be required to be checked in at the cloakroom
and the guest would be reminded that there was to be no photography. If the
camera was discovered inside the wedding, security staff were to remove the
film, develop it at the Douglases' expense and return all photographs save for any
of the wedding. A computer was on hand so that digital films could be processed
so as to obliterate any shots of the wedding but not any other pictures on the film.
In some six or eight cases a guest or other person present, without having
tried to conceal it, had been found to have a camera or video with him or her
and the arrangements I have described were then implemented. In one of the
cases the camera had been held quite openly by a member of the Welsh choir
which was to entertain the guests and that led to the whole choir being 'frisked'.
No other camera was found on them. Comprehensive arrangements were also
made to ensure that the copyright in the photographs taken by the official
photographers (selected and paid for by the Douglases) belonged to the bride and
groom and that no unauthorised copies could be made from their films, which
were taken off for processing and processed under the eyes of security staff.

[66] Miss Martel Levinson gave oral evidence of how every corridor on the relevant floor in the hotel was, as she put it, 'locked down'; to ensure that other hotel guests could not stray into the wedding she blocked off some 30 to 40 rooms and put security staff in for the entire weekend beginning on the Friday night, even in stairwells. It was arranged that only one bank of elevators would serve the floor in question and that was reserved for the bride and groom to move from the suite which they were occupying to the ceremony and, after it, to the reception in the ballroom immediately above. Her evidence in her cross-examination by Mr Price included:

> 'Everyone felt confident that it would be as locked down as we could and that with the presence of security people at all of these posts, it was very clear that this was a private function.'

To which Mr Price replied: 'Oh, I am sure it was.' She had been careful to look at all possible situations, she said, having had security teams and meetings looking at every possible situation and scenario. To Mr Tugendhat's question as to whether Mr Thorpe (the one paparazzo who got in and took photographs, as I shall come on to describe) could have got in to any of the rooms where the wedding or reception was taking place without his realising that he was forbidden to be there, she replied: 'Absolutely not.' I accept her evidence. To the extent that privacy consists of the inclusion only of the invited and the exclusion of all others, the wedding was as private as was possible consistent with its being a socially pleasant event. Equally, the arrangements made to ensure that only authorised photographs could emerge, after their approval by the bride and groom, of the ceremony and reception, were as comprehensive in design and execution as could be made in relation to such an event. The security bill alone was for $66,006. Mr Thorpe, it transpires, was not the only person to have succeeded in making some unauthorised visual or sound recording of the events on the day but no one else's record has led, as it would seem, to any form of publication and, perhaps for that reason, little was said about these other forms of record and I do not hold their existence to be indicative of the security arrangements not having been reasonable.

THE WEDDING; THE EVENING OF 18 NOVEMBER 2000

[67] There are undoubtedly some events not otherwise of interest to the public that become of such interest by reason of the celebrities who attend. Minor celebrities may thus aggrandise their events by inviting major ones. When that is done an intrinsically private event might come to be regarded and be intended to be regarded as a public one. But the Douglas wedding was not such an event. The guest list, which was not publicised at the time, has been made available and there, amongst or alongside the 120 or so members of either the bride's or groom's family, are many names that anyone would recognise as famous or celebrated. However, it was not successfully shown to me that anyone who was not truly family or friend was invited (although, inevitably, there were some cases, where a guest and his or her partner were invited, in which only the guest could be truly described as a direct friend). In that sense the wedding was not a celebrity event and I accept Miss Zeta-Jones' evidence that it was not intended to be one.

[68] Further, the Douglases had no need to and did not themselves take any steps to stir up publicity for the event. Even without any 'hype' it was going to be, as Hello! later described it, 'the showbiz wedding of the year'. I accept

Mr Douglas' evidence that '[w]e issued absolutely no press releases at all
concerning the wedding and none of the pre-wedding press coverage was
initiated by us'.

[69] In the Court of Appeal, Brooke LJ ([2001] 2 All ER 289 at 304, [2001] QB
967 at 984 (para 57)), after referring to the wedding as a private occasion, later said
of the bride and groom ([2001] 2 All ER 289 at 314, [2001] QB 967 at 995 (para 95))
that—

'[t]hey did not choose to have a private wedding, attended by a few
members of their family and a few friends, in the normal sense of the words
"private wedding".'

I would be uneasy at characterising a wedding as not private simply on the basis
of numbers, especially where the means of the parties were so ample that even a
lavish wedding for 350 to 360 would not make real inroads, where the couple was
popular enough to have many friends and where elaborate security arrangements
were in place. But, amongst the evidence which I have had but which was not
available before the Court of Appeal, is not only Miss Martel Levinson's as to
security arrangements and the guest list itself but also Mr Douglas' which
includes:

'Out of our guest list, approximately 125 of our guests were family
members. Both Catherine and I have very extensive families. My mother,
for instance, has six brothers and sisters. My father has six sisters. It was
therefore impossible for us to invite all the members of my family that I
would have liked to have invited. If we had invited all the members of our
families that we had wanted to then we would have needed a considerably
larger venue or would not have been able to invite any of our friends.'

It was, in my judgment, a private wedding.

[70] The wedding, a 'black tie' event, began on 18 November at around
7.30–8 pm New York time. It was a great success. It went off, as it seemed,
without a hitch. The cake was cut at about midnight and the reception ran on
until 5 or 6 am in the morning of Sunday 19 November. Miss Zeta-Jones'
evidence is that—

'[i]t was exactly the wedding I wanted—a homely wedding not
withstanding the fact that it was on a large scale. We had managed to have
a private wedding for our family and friends without suffering the intrusion
of the media into our special day. We spent the first day of our
"honeymoon" reminiscing about what a wonderful time we and our guests
had had.'

There had been speeches, entertainers, music and dancing. The bride, as one
might expect, danced with the groom. Mr Douglas' evidence is that—

'[t]he wedding was a great success. I believe that all of our guests had a
wonderful time and the atmosphere was tremendously warm and
family-oriented. We could not have asked for a more wonderful wedding.'

A PAPARAZZO GOT IN

[71] Although this was not known at the time, a paparazzo photographer,
Rupert Thorpe, had infiltrated the wedding and, without anyone's consent or
knowledge, had surreptitiously taken photographs that included the bride, the

a groom, the wedding dress and the cake. Whilst, as will appear, it soon became
apparent that unauthorised pictures had been taken, Thorpe's identity was not
discovered until shortly before trial. When all the *authorised* pictures were duly
examined, a man standing in a dinner jacket was seen in one photograph holding
a small camera cupped in his hands, below waist level. The camera is tilted,
presumably in the hope (as no viewfinder could be used) that it was pointed in
b the intended direction. The photograph of him does not reliably show whether
or not he was wearing one of the small identifying gold pins, if only because the
photographs of guests who would undoubtedly have had pins do not invariably
show that the pin has caught the light and so had shown up on the photographs.
The man in the photograph was later identified as Rupert Thorpe, who is
normally based in California. Later still inquiries have suggested that he attended
c with his then fiancée, Michelle Day, and that both had stayed at the Plaza. How
he got into the wedding has not been established. As I shall show, he seems to
have been working in some loose association with Phil Ramey and others but
whether some others tried to get in but failed or got in but failed to be able to take
any photographs is unknown. The trial has proceeded on the tacit assumption
d that Mr Thorpe was the only paparazzo intruder and that the unauthorised
photographs were taken by him.

THE UNAUTHORISED PHOTOGRAPHS ARE PURCHASED

[72] At about 11 pm, London time, on 18 November photographs connected
with the Douglas wedding began to arrive by ISDN line from the United States
e to Sue Neal in London. Some were from agencies but, later, some were from
paparazzi including Frank Griffin, who had received them in Los Angeles in
digital form from New York. Sue Neal called them up on her screen in London
and then forwarded them by ISDN line to Mr Luke in Madrid for him to show
them to Senor Sanchez Junco. Mr Luke had spoken to Mr Ramey to be sure the
f latter had the appropriate address for Hello! so that he would be able to send the
photographs in electronic form. Some of these photographs were presumably of
guests arriving *outside* the wedding, as to which no complaint is made, but these
first photographs to arrive could not yet have included the cutting of the cake at
midnight New York time.

[73] At some stage photographs on the *inside* of the wedding, so to speak, of
g the bride walking down the aisle to the ceremony and then at the reception must
have begun to come through. Sue Neal called them up on her screen in London
and Mr Luke printed them out in Spain to show them to Senor Sanchez Junco.
Mr Ramey telephoned Sue Neal to ask whether she had received the
photographs. Running into the early hours of Sunday 19 November she had as
h many as some 10 to 15 telephone calls. At some point, I assume when as many
of the 'inside' photographs had been passed to Madrid as there were likely to be,
the telephone calls turned to how much would be paid for them. Mr Ramey in
California was on one line to Sue Neal in London; she was at the same time on
another telephone to Mr Luke on his mobile in Madrid and, standing alongside
j Mr Luke, only a couple of feet or so away, was Senor Sanchez Junco, who could
speak and understand little English. Ramey spoke to Neal, Neal spoke to Luke,
Luke translated into Spanish for Sanchez Junco. The process was then reversed.

[74] Ramey began by demanding £200,000 but after a number of calls Senor
Sanchez Junco, by the means I have described, agreed to pay Ramey £125,000, the
Dollar equivalent of which was then $188,000. By now it was well into Sunday
19 November. Sue Neal had been able to hear Luke speaking to Sanchez Junco

and he speaking to Luke. In the last of the calls Ramey asked Sue Neal to confirm
the fee in writing, which she did by fax to Ramey Photograph Agency from 'Sue *a*
Neal—Picture Editor' on Hello! writing paper. Her fax records agreement at
£125,000 for exclusive rights 'to the above pictures' (not otherwise identified):
'For Hello! UK, Hola Spain and Oh La France; it is agreed that you will invoice in
US Dollars for US $188,000.' Sue Neal signed the fax. She expected to receive an
invoice for $188,000, an expectation which confirms that the invoice was to be *b*
directed to Hello! and that Hello! and not the Marquesa was the purchaser.

[75] There is no suggestion in the evidence that the Marquesa knew of, took
any part in or even had her name mentioned in these dealings with Ramey, nor
could anyone party to the dealings have thought that she was any part of them.
She was asleep in Sotogrande.

[76] The photographs received, of the order of some 15 in all, included the six *c*
whose publication is complained of. The composition is generally poor and two
are well out of focus. None shows any awareness on the part of the subject that
a photograph was being taken and it can be assumed none used flash. The
photograph of the bride going down the aisle towards the wedding ceremony on
the arm of her father cuts off all of him but his arm. Two show the bride eating, *d*
one of which has the groom holding a fork down into her mouth. In one she
playfully holds up a cake knife at her husband. In one taken from a very low level
she dances, but not with the groom. Another, hopelessly out of focus, shows the
bride and groom kissing. The bride's dress is shown to a greater or lesser extent
in all six and parts of the very elaborate wedding cake are visible in three. In one
the foreground seems to consist of the arm of, and lighting held by, an authorised *e*
photographer.

[77] Having received the photographs Senor Sanchez Junco set about
arranging a layout, his usual task. The ISDN line at Hello!'s office in Madrid had
been installed prior to 1998. In Madrid some thin lines appearing on the
unauthorised photographs as they had arrived were processed out by the printers, *f*
using a computer program. The photographs had been sent to the printers in
Spain from Hello!'s Madrid office in electronic form. Senor Sanchez Junco
telephoned the Marquesa at about 4 am Spanish time on the Sunday morning to
tell her that he had got some wedding pictures after all. He was very pleased. He
mentioned that Mr Ramey had taken them. She had incurred telephone call
charges in connection with her earlier unsuccessful efforts on Hello!'s behalf and *g*
she took the opportunity to raise with him whether she could raise an invoice for
them. He said she could.

[78] Senor Sanchez Junco completed the layout; the front cover was changed
to include an amalgam of one of the unauthorised pictures and an insert of a
Russian Tea Room picture; parts of an earlier layout were discarded and the *h*
revised format was sent to the printers some time on Sunday morning.

[79] As he set about arranging the unauthorised photographs into a layout for
an issue of Hello!, Senor Sanchez Junco well knew that OK! had obtained an
exclusive contract for coverage of the Douglas wedding. He knew of Ramey's
reputation and the kind of work that Ramey handled and the intrusive systems *j*
which paparazzi such as Ramey employed. It was a kind of journalism he and
Hello! did not like, he said, and usually tried to avoid. At least a part of the
reasons for Senor Sanchez Junco's insistence that Ramey should not be
commissioned in advance, was in my judgment, that he, as a cautious man, was
uncomfortable in being seen, as a commission would involve, to be procuring the
sort of unpredictable and possibly unlawful activity that a paparazzo of Ramey's

a reputation might get up to. Whilst he would not have known of the specific language used, Senor Sanchez Junco knew that a feature of OK!'s 'exclusive' would have been that security arrangements were required by contract so far as was reasonable to ensure that only those invited or duly employed would be present at the wedding and that no photographs were to be taken other than the authorised ones. For example, Hello!'s own pleaded exclusive contract for

b coverage of the wedding of Gloria Hunniford required reasonable security to be enforced. Such arrangements had to be contemplated by those in the trade as an inevitable concomitant of an 'exclusive', certainly where as much as £1m was at stake.

[80] It was obvious to him that the photographs were unauthorised. He said in cross-examination that he had no doubt but that the person who did the

c photographs was trying to hide himself. He was then asked:

> '*Mr Tugendhat*: Did you ask Mr Ramey any questions about how the photographs were taken? *Witness*: No.
> *Mr Tugendhat*: Is that because you did not care whether they were taken
d legally or illegally? *Witness*: No, it was because I didn't want any information. I didn't want to know anything about it. I wasn't curious about it. I didn't want to know.'

Similarly, to Mr Luke, co-ordinating editor in Madrid, it was a matter of indifference how the photographs had been obtained. Senor Sanchez Junco knew from his contacts with Mr Burry that the Douglases had been insisting on

e control over what photographs would be released and his own proposals to Mr Burry of May 2000 had accordingly offered the Douglases full picture approval rights.

[81] In my judgment Senor Sanchez Junco knew and ought to have known, as he selected the unauthorised photographs for publication, that what he was

f doing would or might significantly diminish the benefits which OK! would otherwise derive from its exclusive contract with the Douglases, that it would deny the Douglases the picture approval which he knew they wanted and which he would have expected them to have procured in their contract with OK! and that the taking of the unauthorised photographs, which he had been careful not

g to commission, would have involved at least a trespass or some deceit or misrepresentation on the photographer's part in order for the photographer to overcome the security arrangements which, in outline, he knew or must be taken to have known to have been in place at a wedding which he had no reason to think was other than private. It was obvious, agreed Sue Neal, Hello!'s picture editor at the time, that the photographs had been taken by someone 'who had no

h business to be there'. Mrs Cartwright's evidence was that they had to have been taken surreptitiously.

THE CLAIMANTS LEARN OF THE UNAUTHORISED PHOTOGRAPHS

[82] At some time on Monday morning (London time), 20 November, OK!'s

j editor, Mr Martin Townsend, and picture editor, Mr Paul Anderson, learned, in London, that unauthorised photographs of the wedding were on the market. Nine low resolution photographs, understood at that time to have been taken by Mr Ramey, were faxed to OK! by an agency in Holland. Mr Anderson telephoned Mr Ramey who called back in the afternoon. Mr Ramey said that he was merely Eduardo Sanchez's agent for selling the photographs in the United States. Mr Anderson had been told to buy the photographs if he could so as to

take them off the market. Later still—evening, London time—Mr Ramey
telephoned Mr Anderson to say that he was withdrawing the photographs from
all the United States magazines to which he had distributed them. He said it was
not worth his sticking his neck out for Eduardo Sanchez. Mr Anderson was left
with a clear impression that Senor Sanchez Junco owned the unauthorised
pictures taken inside the Douglas wedding. Mr Townsend telephoned Mr Allen
Burry to tell him all this, only to find that he was with Michael Douglas and
Catherine Zeta-Jones and all four then had a conversation on a speaker
telephone. Michael Douglas and Catherine Zeta-Jones were, said Mr Townsend,
devastated by the news. Miss Zeta-Jones uses the same word; she says:

> 'It was an appalling and very upsetting shock to discover that our wedding
> had been invaded in that way. Our peace and happiness evaporated. I felt
> violated and that something precious had been stolen from me. Our distress
> and anger at what Hello! did to us continues to this day.'

[83] Mr Douglas says:

> 'We were devastated and shocked by the news. We felt as if our home had
> been ransacked and everything taken out of it and spread in the street. It was
> a truly gut-wrenching and very disturbing experience which left both of us
> deeply upset.'

[84] It is easy to regard such language as exaggerated but it has to be
remembered that the Douglases were speaking of a time when their joy at how
successful their wedding plans had proved to be was at its height. They crashed
down from a relatively euphoric height. Mr Price cross-examined Mr Douglas to
the effect that, in comparison with, say, the loss of a limb, their distress was minor
and Mr Douglas accepted, against such a comparison, that that was so but he also
said:

> 'When we spent as much time as we had preparing this wedding, and
> making all the efforts that we had, one of which was deciding between the
> two publications that are here today, and when that wedding turned out as
> wonderful as we ever could have anticipated, it was a magical, magical night,
> and it was great, so when you go from that euphoric high of having such a
> special, special event turn out as well as it did for all of our family and friends,
> and then to find that somehow somebody, either one of the members of our
> wedding party or, as it turned out, a spy, a paparazzi person snuck into to
> take pictures which were going to be released, we thought it was one of the
> most vindictive and mean-spirited acts we could have imagined and were
> deeply deeply offended. Again I think it has to do with the diametrics of
> coming so soon after our wedding.'

I have no doubt but that Mr Douglas and Miss Zeta-Jones both suffered real
distress, though it is no present task of mine to attempt to put some
compensatory cash value upon it. An aspect of their distress, which led
Miss Zeta-Jones to tears, was their wondering, if it was a guest, which of their
guests it was that had betrayed them.

[85] On the same day, 20 November, the Marquesa's assistant at the Marquesa's
request sent an invoice to Hello! in London for £1,000 plus VAT described as
'invoice for telephone expenses for arranging photographs of Douglas/Zeta-Jones
wedding'. This was the claim which the Marquesa had cleared with Senor
Sanchez Junco in their 4 am telephone call. At that stage, before any problems

a had arisen, the Marquesa was only too happy to enlarge her role in the apparently successful use of paparazzi which she had suggested back in August but it is not possible to infer from this invoice, modest in amount relative to the Marquesa's usual operations, that she had played any greater role so far than as already described. It is, though, possible that the invoice, addressed to Mrs Doughty, did later conduce to acceptance in London that the unauthorised photographs (and,

b perhaps, the accompanying text) represented a Marquesa feature, perhaps with the main invoices being intended to follow this opening one.

[86] The printing of the centre section of Hello!'s issue 639, now featuring the unauthorised photographs, as did the cover, was completed and the magazines, in greater numbers than usual to cope with the expected unusually heavy demand, were bundled, loaded into the specially chartered aircraft and flown on

c Monday 20 November to England for distribution in the usual way on the Tuesday and the Wednesday.

[87] Until the news arrived of Hello!'s acquisition of unauthorised pictures OK! had planned not to put wedding pictures in issue 241, due to go on general sale on Friday 24 November, but to spread Douglas wedding items over to later

d issues, no 242 for publication on 30 November (London) and 1 December (the rest of the United Kingdom) and no 243 a week later. Now, simultaneously, two decisions were made; one was to bring forward *some* wedding coverage into issue 241. That meant that the Douglases would have to select which photographs they approved for publication very quickly.

[88] The Douglases set about that task. It had been thought that it would be

e a leisurely unhurried and pleasant process; now it had to take place in priority to everything else and in some haste. They spent hours and hours sitting on the floor going through photographs in a mad rush, said Miss Zeta-Jones. Eventually the agreed photographs were taken by Mr Burry to London. Expenses were incurred by reason of the need for expedition, expenses that would not have been

f incurred otherwise.

AN INJUNCTION IS GRANTED; 20 NOVEMBER 2000

[89] The other decision was to move the court in England for an injunction. On the evening of Monday 20 November Buckley J, the Queen's Bench duty judge, was moved ex parte and (despite attempts to tell Hello!) without notice,

g by telephone. At that stage there were already all three claimants but only Hello! Ltd was a defendant. The relief sought was an injunction to restrain publication by Hello! of any photographs of the wedding and reception. Buckley J granted relief over the following day with a view to there then being an inter partes hearing on short notice on 21 November.

h

20–21 NOVEMBER 2000

[90] It was about midnight on the night of 20–21 November that Mrs Cartwright, Hello!'s publishing director in London, learned of the injunction. She rang Mrs Doughty, administration and financial controller of Hello! in London, to get the number of Mr Christopher Hutchings, solicitor, of Charles Russell, and then told him what she knew. She speaks Spanish and hence was able to speak to Senor Sanchez Junco after getting his number from Javier Riera. It was agreed that an attempt should be made to get the injunction lifted. The following day, Tuesday 21 November, she made a written note which read:

'I rang our owner, Eduardo Sanchez in Spain and alerted him to what had happened. He told me we had bought 10 or 11 photos of ceremony and reception through normal channels in which the Press work, and photographer who took them did not wish his name revealed. Hola SA who bought the pix, bought them for three countries, UK, Spain and France. It is our understanding that they will be sold throughout the world ... I rang Phil Ramey in LA. Sue Neal involved. Ramey very cagey, said dealt with Marquesa. Did not want to be involved.'

[91] Although the note speaks of acquisition of the photos 'through normal channels in which the Press work' and although Senor Sanchez Junco may at first have used some such expression, the note only makes sense if he had gone on to mention Mr Ramey by name and to ask her to phone Mr Ramey as otherwise Mrs Cartwright would have had no reason to telephone him, as she did. Indeed, in her oral evidence Mrs Cartwright said that Senor Sanchez Junco had told her to ring Ramey 'as the supplier of the pictures' as opposed to his being the photographer. When she spoke to Ramey he was guarded; he did not know Mrs Cartwright and wanted to be sure to whom he was speaking. He suggested that Sue Neal, whom he well knew, should identify Mrs Cartwright to him. Sue Neal was awakened in the middle of the night. A three-way telephone conference call ensued during which Sue Neal could hear what was being said and in which she first identified Mrs Cartwright to Mr Ramey. Mrs Cartwright's evidence was that Ramey said 'I dealt with the Marquesa', as her note recorded. Quite why Ramey was to be telephoned and what he was to be told is unclear. Miss Neal, who heard the conversation, was able to give no reason why Ramey, who was agitated, should have been phoned. She did not think there had been any speaking about the Marquesa during the conversation. However, in her supplementary evidence-in-chief Mrs Cartwright said that Ramey had said 'I dealt with the Marquesa' and, continuing the quotation from her evidence, she went on to say:

'And I just assumed, which if one had been in the company for some time, was a very reasonable assumption, that it was a Marquesa feature, which she had done the fixing.'

It is possible that Sue Neal was not on the line or within earshot for the whole of the conversation and may have been drowsy as she was broken from her sleep. I accept Mrs Cartwright's evidence that Ramey had said that he had dealt with the Marquesa. I accept also that she 'just assumed' that the Douglas wedding photographs amounted to 'a Marquesa feature'.

[92] By that time it would already have become apparent that it might not be inconvenient to put some distance between Hello! and Ramey, who was himself exhibiting signs that some distance between himself and the photographs would not be unwelcome. If Mrs Cartwright had thought about what 'a Marquesa feature' usually consisted of and if she had raised direct questions with either Senor Sanchez Junco, Mr Ramey or the Marquesa she would soon have had to accept that the wedding had not been 'a Marquesa feature'. However, Ramey's description that he had dealt with the Marquesa gave her a peg just sufficient to support the assumption she then made and upon which she thereafter acted.

[93] On Tuesday 21 November Mr Tugendhat and Mr Sherborne (as they had on 20 November) represented the claimants as they sought an extension of the injunction from Hunt J. The single defendant was represented by Mr Silverleaf QC and Mr Fernando. Hunt J, after a short hearing, extended the injunction over trial or earlier further order.

a [94] Hello! immediately appealed and the hearing of the appeal began on the afternoon of 21 November before Ward and Walker LJJ. Mr Silverleaf and Mr Fernando again represented the (then) sole defendant, Hello! Ltd. At the close of argument the court indicated that its members could not agree and arrangements were made for a hearing before a three-man court the very next day, Wednesday 22 November.

b [95] Hello!, having learned of the injunction of 20 November, took immediate and largely successful steps to ensure that the injunction was not breached. Only a relatively few copies—some 15,750 out of a total print run of 755,900—were put on sale. How many were sold to members of the public is not known. The rest were embargoed to await the outcome of the litigation.

c THE THREE-MAN COURT OF APPEAL; MRS CARTWRIGHT'S SECOND WITNESS STATEMENT

[96] Mr Silverleaf had been unable to represent the defendant at the hearing on 22 November and its representation was by Mr Henry Carr QC and Mr Fernando. On the Hello! side evidence was collected for the appeal hearing. That included a draft second witness statement of Mrs Cartwright. After dealing *d* with evidence as to attempts by OK! earlier to spoil Hello!'s 'exclusives' (a subject referred to during the trial as for tit for tat evidence) Mrs Cartwright continued, in the unsigned draft faxed to the claimants' solicitors at 1.57 pm on 22 November during the short adjournment on the first day of the three-man appeal hearing as follows:

e   '10. On a separate matter it has been alleged that Hello! knew well in advance that the pictures complained of would be available for publication in the issue of the magazine subject to this injunction. In fact they were offered on the open market around the world on Sunday 19 November and that is when Hello! purchased them and we were able to fit them in the magazine which was by then substantially ready.

f   11. Hello! had no previous knowledge whatsoever that these pictures were going to be taken or offered. I believe that the facts stated in this witness statement are true.'

[97] A signed but undated version of this witness statement exists, still containing paras 10 and 11, but the last page of it, which bears Mrs Cartwright's signature, says nothing save that she believed the facts in the statement to be true. Mrs Cartwright was unable to shed any light on how, in the circumstances I next describe, the page had come to be signed.

[98] An unsigned version of that witness statement containing those paras 10 and 11 was handed in to the three-man Court of Appeal. When that version of her draft second witness statement had been put to Mrs Cartwright for her signature she says that she had indicated that she could not sign as it was not true. Whilst it was literally true that it was not known in advance that the very pictures complained of would become available and that those particular pictures ('these pictures') would be taken or offered, Mrs Cartwright had rightly felt that to assert the truth of paras 10 and 11 would mislead. Accordingly the draft was at her request, she said, amended to take out paras 10 and 11 to which she felt unable to subscribe. She signed but did not date the last page of a version from which the offending paragraphs had been omitted. Unfortunately, as I have mentioned, that did not stop a signed version still containing paras 10 and 11 from being used in court. Paragraphs 10 and 11 were later referred to in the judgments of the Court of Appeal, which had plainly relied on them.

[99] The Hello! defendants waived privilege in connection with the preparation and service of Mrs Cartwright's second witness statement but despite that and despite intense study by Mr Tugendhat of word-processing and associated costing records and the availability of Mrs Cartwright and Mr Hutchings to give oral evidence, it was, through no fault of the claimants, never established in the evidence who had framed the words that became paras 10 and 11 of that unsigned second witness statement which I have cited above. Nor, apart from a somewhat desperate plea that all that been done at speed, was it ever explained how it came about that the incorrect version, including paras 10 and 11, had come to be handed to the Court of Appeal rather than the corrected and signed version.

[100] A particular difficulty in the way of the credibility of Mrs Cartwright's evidence (that she was not willing to sign the misleading version) is that no version of the corrected version exists which has, as its last page, only a statement as to truth. On the face of things her signature to a sheet merely having a statement of truth on it could therefore only be an acceptance of the misleading version. Unfortunately, though, the collection of evidence was not being carefully or properly handled and it is at least possible that Mrs Cartwright was asked to sign a backsheet whilst understanding that it would come to be affixed to the corrected front sheets and was then asked to sign afresh once it was found that the corrected version had more than a statement of truth on its last page.

[101] It is, of course, possible to devise a scenario in which Mrs Cartwright paradoxically affected a strict regard for the truth in order to mask that she had lied, by creating the corrected version of her second witness statement to explain away the presentation to the court of the uncorrected version. That, though, seems to me to be improbable. Anyone devious enough to do that would surely have ensured that the corrected version was edited so as to have had a last sheet that had nothing but a statement of truth on it and the plan would have depended on the claimants not promptly spotting that there were two different versions despite their being sent both. Further, as to Mrs Cartwright's state of mind at the time, I have had no evidence that paras 10 or 11 were read aloud to the Court of Appeal either at all or in Mrs Cartwright's hearing or that she had reason during the hearing to know that it was not the corrected version which was in the court's hands.

[102] Whatever else the incident shows it shows that whoever was given the task of collecting the views of the witness was content to *assume* what Mrs Cartwright would say rather than first questioning her to find out to what she could subscribe.

[103] Mr Hutchings, speaking of the fact that the Court of Appeal had had before them a version of her evidence which included paragraphs Mrs Cartwright would not have wished to have laid before them, said:

'It certainly was very regrettable. I believe it was a terrible clerical error, but I think that obviously the first version should have been torn up, and it did not happen. There were obviously various versions floating around.'

He described it as 'very much an administrative blunder rather than anything else'. On balance I accept that that was the case. Mr Hutchings, although the solicitor having the conduct of the case on behalf of the Hello! defendants, escapes direct personal blame as he was in court whilst the impugned document was being prepared but, whilst I accept, having heard and seen Mrs Cartwright giving her evidence, that there was, lying behind the production of the document, no intent to mislead the court, the unfortunate incident reflects poorly on the *a* broad class of Hello! defendants and their advisers without my being able to pin blame more particularly within that broad class.

[**104**] Nor, despite it being quite visible in the three judgments of the Court of Appeal that reliance had been put on the misleading paras 10 and 11 and despite that the judgments were then read, no doubt with some care, by and on behalf of the Hello! defendants, was it ever volunteered by them that something had gone

b wrong and that it might, at lowest, be prudent so to inform the claimants or the court.

[**105**] As to that, I would exculpate the lay individuals such as Mrs Cartwright and Mrs Doughty, who might well have not focused sufficiently on the mistake in evidence and, even if they had, might not have realised that, procedurally, the matter could be corrected. In particular Mrs Cartwright has grounds on which

c she is to be exonerated as there is evidence both from her and from Mr Hutchings that she raised the question with Mr Hutchings in the New Year. As to others, it was urged upon me that by the time the Hello! defendants had put in their defence (para 30) in May 2001, it was made plain by then that *some* degree of prior knowledge on the part of the Hello! defendants had existed and that thereby the

d defence had undone whatever misrepresentation the witness statement had caused. That, though, fails to explain the inactivity on the issue on the Hello! defendants' part between the giving of the judgment in the Court of Appeal in late December 2000 and the service of the defence in May 2001. The whole incident was lamentable, as also is the fact that, despite privilege having been waived, material questions remain incapable of answer.

e

THE MARQUESA IS ASKED TO HELP; 23 NOVEMBER 2000

[**106**] Also on 22 November 2000 Senor Sanchez Junco telephoned the Marquesa. He told her there was a problem with the magazine. He said something about an injunction. He told her he wanted her to help him but did

f not say how. She said: 'Well, you know, if I can help, I will be of help, and he answered: "Well thank you very much. I will not forget this one."' I accept that things were left generally in that way; I do not hold that Senor Sanchez Junco indicated that a letter would be required of her or that she would be asked to compromise herself or lie. She held strong views, especially on the subject of how beneficial would be the tit for tat evidence which she would be able to give to assist in Hello!'s case for the lifting of the injunction. Nor was she averse to ingratiating herself with Senor Sanchez Junco as Hello!'s editor-in-chief, with whom her relations had been erratic and were not then as good as they had earlier been.

[**107**] In his oral evidence Senor Sanchez Junco at first said that he could not remember asking the Marquesa for help; then he turned to avoiding a direct answer by questioning in what way she could in any event have helped him. Finally he became firmly of the view that he had not asked her to help him. I prefer the Marquesa's evidence which, from her witness statement on, was constant on the point. 'I will help you in any way that you need' said the Marquesa to Senor Sanchez Junco and she added: 'You can count on me always.'

[**108**] On the same day Mr Hutchings telephoned the Marquesa. He explained to her that he was asking for a statement from her which might help clarify what had taken place. He explained that he understood that she had arranged and purchased the Douglas wedding feature. That is a view which was consistent with the loose assumption of the wedding having been 'a Marquesa feature' which Mrs Cartwright had made and which it is likely Mr Hutchings formed after

speaking either to Mrs Cartwright or to Mrs Doughty, who was of the same view. Mr Hutchings said to the Marquesa that if it was the case that she had arranged and purchased the feature it would be helpful to have this explained in a letter. His eleventh witness statement, not made until 20 February 2003, continues:

> 'The Marquesa confirmed that this was correct and agreed to provide a letter to this effect. Had she said anything at all to cause me to question my understanding or raised any concerns whatsoever, I most certainly would have discussed these with her, until I was satisfied as to the actual position.'

[109] He was not cross-examined on that lately-given evidence.

[110] Because that important evidence arrived so late it was never put to the Marquesa that she had confirmed to Mr Hutchings that she had arranged and purchased the feature but, given the lack of challenge to his evidence on the point, I accept that she did confirm as Mr Hutchings indicates. It was not asked of the Marquesa, either, again because of the lateness of the evidence that Mr Hutchings gave, whether she realised that his request was, unknown to Mr Hutchings and unmentioned by him, the first step in a working-through of her indication to Senor Sanchez Junco that she would give to him such help as she could. However, given her later behaviour, it is hard to see how her failure to deny that she had arranged and purchased the feature can otherwise be explained. Mr Hutchings was, innocently on his part, asking her to provide a letter which she would have known would be untrue. Consistently with her willingness to help, she would have not protested to him that she was being required to lie. She would not, I expect, have felt safe indicating to a solicitor that he was procuring false evidence.

[111] The Marquesa then tried to telephone Senor Riera, managing director of Hola SA, with whom her relations were poor. Not getting through to him, she sent an e-mail. She described herself, in relation to the Douglas wedding, as 'the one person who has been involved in the matter from the beginning'. In the sense that she had long before tried to gain an 'exclusive' for Hello! and, after Senor Sanchez Junco's intervention and upon that failing, had spoken to Senor Sanchez Junco about paparazzi, that description was true but it ignored the absence of any real active role of hers since August 2000 or thereabouts and that it was Senor Sanchez Junco who had bought the pictures on 19 November. Her e-mail both criticised the past handling by Hello! of the Douglas wedding opportunity and suggested that she had a role to play for the future. She did not mention that Senor Sanchez Junco had asked for her help.

[112] Senor Riera did not telephone the Marquesa but his secretary, Senora Elisa, began frequently to telephone the Marquesa or the latter's assistant, Miss Mildh, indicating what it was that was required from the Marquesa. The Marquesa's understanding of that and Miss Mildh's led to Miss Mildh typing out a letter which was never sent but which read:

> 'I confirm that this company [Marquesa's Production Ltd] was offered the photographs relating to the wedding of Michael Douglas and Catherine Zeta-Jones. This company accepted the offer and payment was made accordingly for such photographs.'

Miss Mildh was an impressive and intelligent witness and I do not doubt but that that draft letter was an accurate reflection of what Madrid, by way of Senora Elisa, had been indicating it required, namely a letter showing that the Marquesa's company had bought and paid for the unauthorised photographs, a a complete fiction. Miss Mildh knew that the function of the letter that was being requested was to help in a lifting of the injunction. As she knew that I do not doubt that the Marquesa knew that too.

[113] The Marquesa felt she was in a difficult position. Miss Mildh's witness statement said:

b 'I remember a great deal of telephone traffic that day, back and forth. The Marquesa felt very strongly she could not decline to "help" Senor Sanchez Junco in this way if she wished to retain his good opinion of her and, more importantly, her job! I felt she was being unfairly pressurised. She was very upset.'

c The Marquesa, hoping that the position might resolve itself without her finally being obliged to lie, left her office early on 22 November, despite what were, said Miss Mildh, 'frantic phone calls' from Madrid.

THE MARQUESA'S LETTER

d [114] In the meantime, in London, Mr Hutchings discussed with Hello!'s counsel, Mr Carr and Mr Fernando, as to what, in the light of the confirmation which the Marquesa had given to Mr Hutchings, a letter from the Marquesa should state. At one point it had seemed that Mr Fernando had been thought to have proposed a form of words but it was not written down on paper and quite how the form was finally arrived at was never resolved in the formal evidence.

e Leaving aside how the words came to be composed (another subject on which privilege was waived), Mr Hutchings then spoke to Mrs Cartwright, who put the words by telephone to Senor Riera with the intent that he should then write to the Marquesa. Why it was Senor Riera who was selected to play this part and who made the selection of him for the task has not been satisfactorily explained. The Marquesa could have been approached directly or by way of Senor Sanchez

f Junco. Instead the managing director, with whom her relations were poor, was invited to contact her. There is a very real suspicion that he was used as he, above others, represented in person the ability of Hello! to deny the Marquesa any work for the group in the future. He could not be charmed by her; unless he chose, he could not be contacted by telephone except by way of his secretary and the

g Marquesa could not negotiate with him or protest to him. He was the embodiment of the pressure that was put upon her.

[115] The form of words proposed by London was then sent by Senor Riera to the Marquesa. The suggested form of words was in English, the rest in Spanish; putting the whole in English it read as follows:

h 'We need to receive by tomorrow at [10] a.m. at our Barrister's Mr. Giles Fernando fax number 0207 742 4282, a document signed by you in a headed paper with the name of your company with the following text: I confirm that my company sold exclusive UK rights in the photographs of the wedding of Michael Douglas and Catherine Zeta-Jones to Hola SA for use in Hello!

j magazine. The agreement was concluded on the telephone between me and Eduardo Sanchez, the proprietor of Hola SA, on Sunday November the 19th.'

The letter was signed by Senor Riera. The letter went by fax late on the evening of 22 November. The reference to [10 am] was to ensure her letter could be produced at the hearing before the Court of Appeal.

[116] On the next day, 23 November, the second day of the hearing before the three-man Court of Appeal in London, the Marquesa saw for the first time the fax from Senor Riera. By the time Miss Mildh arrived late at her office she said:

'I found the Marquesa in high dudgeon as she had earlier found in her office a fax from Madrid, containing the exact proposed wording of this sought-after document. Furthermore, she told me that she had already received several semi-hysterical phone calls from Madrid, demanding that the document be written and faxed to the High Court before 10 am. The Marquesa had by now resolved to sign this document.'

Miss Mildh typed out the required form of words on the writing paper of Neneta Overseas Ltd, another Marquesa company. The Marquesa, having fervently hoped overnight that the requirement that she should sign a letter would go away, had found that it had not; at the very last minute she signed it and it was faxed to the number that had been given by the Madrid office. Both the Marquesa and Miss Mildh recognised that no such transaction as the letter described had ever taken place.

[117] Mr Hutchings exhibited the letter from Neneta Overseas Ltd to a witness statement of his and it was produced to the Court of Appeal.

[118] Also on the morning of 23 November Mr Hutchings telephoned the Marquesa and asked her whether she had prepared a letter to confirm her involvement. By then the Marquesa would have had Senor Riera's draft before her. Mr Hutchings says: 'I recall very clearly that the Marquesa said absolutely nothing to the effect that the letter she was providing to us was in any way incorrect.'

[119] Senora Elisa's evidence was that in the course of the several telephone calls that were made between her and the Marquesa before, finally, the Marquesa faxed off to London, at the last possible moment, the letter which Senor Riera had asked for (the Marquesa's letter), the Marquesa had protested about her being asked to provide it but that she had never said the letter was untrue. The point is finely balanced as, given, as Senora Elisa accepted, the Marquesa did not protest about any of the component parts into which the letter could be broken, on her evidence the Marquesa would seem to have had nothing to protest about save for the untruth of the letter. However, in her oral evidence the Marquesa, after some hesitation, said that she had also told Mr Hutchings that what was being required of her was an untruth. Given that Mr Hutchings' evidence that she had said absolutely nothing to the effect that the letter was incorrect was not challenged, I prefer the evidence of Senora Elisa and Mr Hutchings on this issue to that of the Marquesa. I hold that she did not complain of the untruth of the Marquesa's letter either to Senora Elisa or to Mr Hutchings. It is, of course, not inconsistent with her willingness to help Senor Sanchez Junco and to help Hello! procure the lifting of the injunction that she should have kept from Senora Elisa and Mr Hutchings the fact that her letter was untrue.

[120] I turn to Senor Riera's state of mind in respect of the Marquesa's letter. He knew it was very important. One might therefore have expected him to speak directly to the Marquesa about it. However, so far from doing so, and despite the Marquesa's having asked Senora Elisa to get him to telephone her, he did not do so. It is difficult to resist the conclusion that he had deliberately made himself unavailable to her. His evidence was that he had received the form of words from either Mrs Cartwright or Mrs Doughty in London and had no reason to believe it was untrue. On the other hand, he was the senior man in Madrid as to

a administrative matters. He was the person consulted, he said, on economic matters and commercial and legal ones. He was content to describe himself as a stickler for good order, a fairly rigorous sort of person. He knew that the Marquesa's letter was to be used in court and that it had to be truthful and very accurate. None the less, he did not inquire, in relation to the letter, as to which of her companies was being asked to say that it had sold the rights, nor what title

b it had to the rights, nor did he make any inquiry of the Marquesa or, he said, of Senor Sanchez Junco.

[121] So far one would have to conclude that he was so incurious as to have been indifferent to the truth or falsity of the letter but had he spoken to Senor Sanchez Junco before sending it to the Marquesa for her signature he would inescapably have learned that it was false; the least discussion with Senor

c Sanchez Junco would have disclosed to him that it was not the Marquesa who had made any agreement with Senor Sanchez Junco on 19 November. It is thus important to look into whether, despite his denial of this, he had in fact spoken to Senor Sanchez Junco in relation to the letter. I am driven to holding that he had. A good deal later, on 18 September 2002, he sent a fax to the Marquesa that said:

d 'Following the instructions from Mr Sanchez Junco I sent you the fax dated 22nd November 2002 ...' a reference to the Marquesa's letter. In oral supplementary evidence-in-chief he said that that passage was incorrect. When Mr Price asked him why, then, had he sent it he said: 'The Marquesa does not really pay any attention to me and, in any event, this is not true.' As an explanation that is quite hopeless. He had a further opportunity to explain himself on the point when

e Mr Tugendhat cross-examined him on it but his answer did not improve. When asked 'Why did you write it if it was untrue?' he answered: 'If I'm sincere, I don't know. Probably it was possible to emphasise my own letter.'

[122] I am left with no reason to disbelieve what Senor Riera had said in his fax of 18 September 2002; he had, indeed, spoken to Senor Sanchez Junco and it

f was on the latter's instructions that the request for the Marquesa's letter was made. Although they worked in different offices in Madrid, in ordinary course they spoke together nearly every day. Senor Riera knew, too, that, in relation to the letter, the Marquesa had been complaining to Senora Elisa. Moreover, as Mr Luke said, Senor Sanchez Junco was a 'hands-on' proprietor; 'he likes to get a grasp of everything'. He was a strong figure; as Mr Luke said: 'I promise you, if

g you've been on the wrong side of Mr Eduardo Sanchez, its an experience you will never forget.'

[123] It was inherently likely, on the important questions that arose in relation to the Marquesa's assistance in the lifting of the injunction, that Senor Riera would have consulted Senor Sanchez Junco. Senor Riera's denial of having made

h contact with Senor Sanchez Junco is not true. In all the circumstances Senor Riera must have known that the letter being required of the Marquesa was untrue.

[124] That conclusion invites me to look into Senor Sanchez Junco's position in relation to the Marquesa's letter. He said at the trial that he had not seen it before. He said Senor Riera had not spoken to him beforehand but he added: 'It

j may have happened.' He thought Senor Riera had made a reasonable assumption that he, Senor Sanchez Junco, had come to an agreement with the Marquesa on the day of the wedding. He said of that that it was 'what Mr Riera believed was the reality of the matter'. In an attempt to explain how he knew what Senor Riera had believed he relied on the Marquesa having been known to have handled the feature from August 2000 on. But her role had not been akin to her normal role

and she had had little or no contact with the Douglas wedding feature after
August 2000. There were no grounds for a reasonable assumption by Senor Riera   *a*
save, perhaps, one derived from the message that he had received through either
Mrs Cartwright or Mrs Doughty in London, but those were grounds on which
Senor Sanchez Junco, claiming to have had no discussion with Senor Riera on the
point, could not rely. Senor Sanchez Junco's answers provide no reason not to
accept the truth of Senor Riera's own written assertion, albeit one that he later   *b*
resiled from, that he had sent the request to the Marquesa for her to complete the
Marquesa's letter on the instructions of Senor Sanchez Junco. I do not accept
Senor Sanchez Junco's evidence that he had no prior knowledge of the
Marquesa's letter and no knowledge that it was untrue. Still less was I impressed
with his assertions, firstly, that the Marquesa's letter was not false and then,
secondly, '[i]t is closer to the truth than [to] an untruth'.   *c*

SENOR SANCHEZ JUNCO'S STATEMENT
    [125] Another piece of evidence which was used by the Hello! defendants
before the Court of Appeal was a witness statement of Mrs Maria José Doughty,
Hello!'s administration and financial controller. Mr Anderson, picture editor for
OK!, had put in a witness statement as to his telephone calls to Mr Ramey in   *d*
which the paparazzo had left the impression on Mr Anderson that Senor Sanchez
Junco owned the unauthorised pictures. Mrs Doughty, whose first language is
Spanish, was given the task of getting Senor Sanchez Junco's observations on the
point. She telephoned him and took down his reply which, in English, was:

    '1. I have never commissioned the disputed photographs, nor have I   *e*
    financed them or agreed a price for them in advance. I have never had any
    contacts with the provider of these photographs except on Sunday the 19th
    November to agree a price for them once the photographs were delivered to
    me that day. This was done through one of my employees.
    2. I do not have any agents representing me or my company in the United   *f*
    States or anywhere else and anyone pretending to do so does it under false
    pretences.
    3. Neither I nor my company have ever owned the copyright in the
    photographs with the exception of the exclusive rights of publication in the
    United Kingdom, Spain or France.'
    g
    [126] In the light of the Marquesa's letter, also produced to the court, 'the
provider of these photographs' would have been read, by anyone reading both it
and Senor Sanchez Junco's statement, as intended to refer to the Marquesa but
whilst the claimants would have known that it was nonsense to suggest that
Senor Sanchez Junco had not had previous contact with the Marquesa, the Court   *h*
of Appeal would not have known that and the claimants had no immediate proof
to the contrary. After hearing cross-examination of Senor Sanchez Junco on the
issue, as I shall explain, in January 2003 Sir Andrew Morritt V-C concluded that
Senor Sanchez Junco's statement was false and misleading. He said ([2003]
EWHC 55 (Ch) at [25], [2003] 1 All ER 1087n at [25]):
    j
    'First, it is clear that he had contact with Mr Ramey on a regular basis
    through members of the staff of his companies, notably Ms Neal. Second, he
    had contact specifically with regard to the wedding photographs through the
    Marquesa and Ms Neal. In each case the contact was indirect. But contact
    does not have to be direct. The third sentence of para 2 of his statement
    suggests that his reference to contact included indirect contact. If he sought

a to confine the preceding sentence of his statement to direct and personal contact then he should have said so. Third, his statement was misleading in implying, in the context of the statement of Mr Anderson, that Mr Ramey was not the provider of the photographs. In my judgment Senor Sanchez-Junco knew that his statement was false and misleading in these respects.'

b [127] I have had a good deal more evidence than had Sir Andrew Morritt V-C. I am unable to find fault with the first sentence of para 1 of Senor Sanchez Junco's statement. As for contacts with Mr Ramey, Sir Andrew Morritt V-C pointed out that the third sentence suggested that Senor Sanchez Junco's reference to contact included indirect contact. For what it is worth, Sir Andrew Morritt V-C had had

c different evidence as to the telephone calls during which the price was agreed with Mr Ramey; he was told of a three-person call involving Mr Ramey on the line to Mr Luke with Mr Luke then translating to Senor Sanchez Junco. The evidence I have heard and which I have accepted is of a four-person call, Ramey to Sue Neal on one line, and Neal to Luke's mobile, with Luke translating to Sanchez Junco only a couple of feet away. In the context of the four-person call

d it is, in my view, a not unfair reading of Senor Sanchez Junco's statement that the phrase 'this was done through one of my employees' was intended to refer not to vicarious contact through an employee of the usual kind of which a director or manager of a company might have no direct personal knowledge but was, in effect, saying that even such contact as he had had with Mr Ramey on

e 19 November was, albeit by way of another, none the less direct, within his personal knowledge, by way of the four-person dealings which he had through Sue Neal and Mr Luke. In evidence before me Senor Sanchez Junco said:

f 'I imagine that at that time, because what I was being accused of was having bought photographs from Senor Ramey as a commission, I wanted to give the clear impression that I have never had any contact with Mr Ramey *in that sense*.' (My emphasis.)

g [128] It is with diffidence that I come to a different conclusion than Sir Andrew Morritt V-C but I acquit Senor Sanchez Junco of knowing that his statement was false and misleading *as to contact*. By the use of the word 'contact' he was, I hold, intending to refer only to such contact with Mr Ramey relating to the Douglas wedding of a kind of which he was able to speak to from his own personal knowledge. He was intending to say that *such* contact occurred only once, on 19 November. So limited, both his first and second sentences in his para 1 were not, I hold, known by him to be misleading. However, given that I have held that

h he had spoken to Senor Riera about the Marquesa's letter and had instructed him to request it of her, and given that he knew both were for production to the court in England, I cannot acquit Senor Sanchez Junco of intentionally misleading the court by his reference to 'the provider of these photographs' rather than, if he meant Mr Ramey, saying so. There was no sufficient reason for not identifying

j Mr Ramey, certainly once Mr Anderson had done so. On this issue, Sir Andrew Morritt V-C's third count, I hold that Senor Sanchez Junco did know that his statement was misleading.

[129] Given that Mrs Cartwright's paras 10 and 11 did not represent what she wished to have as any part of her evidence and were misleading, that the Marquesa's letter was untrue and that Senor Sanchez Junco's statement to Mrs Doughty as put before the Court of Appeal was, as to part, misleading, I can

only echo Sir Andrew Morritt V-C's conclusion that the case advanced by Hello!
to that court was a false one.   *a*

THE INJUNCTION IS LIFTED; 23 NOVEMBER 2000
    [130] After argument had concluded before the Court of Appeal on Thursday
23 November the court indicated that the appeal would be allowed and the
injunction lifted. Although the evidence before the court had included that   *b*
Mr Douglas and Miss Zeta-Jones had been upset to learn of the possible
publication of the unauthorised photographs, Hello! elected to go forward and
publish. It informed the distributors that the embargo was lifted and its issue 639
went on full sale to the public on Friday 24 November without any further
changes to text or photographs.
                                                                              c
ISSUE 639 OF HELLO!
    [131] The text in issue 639 relating to the wedding itself, as opposed to the
Russian Tea Room event the night before and to descriptions of arrivals before
the wedding, has been said to have been composed by way of brief interviews
with guests as they left the wedding. It was inaccurate in many respects as,
indeed, had been the description of the Russian Tea Room event and the arrivals *d*
there but Mr and Mrs Douglas complain, in particular, of a reference to
Mr Douglas having given Miss Zeta-Jones a £1m yacht as a wedding present and
to a caption to a photograph of Miss Zeta-Jones dancing which read: 'The
vivacious bride took to the dance floor but not, at any time, with her groom.'
    [132] There had been no gift of a £1m yacht and the bride and groom had not *e*
only led the dance but had danced several times. As Mr Douglas, whom Hello!
described as a rich man with a fortune to protect, was marrying a woman less rich
and some 25 years younger, the combination of Hello!'s untruthful comments
was hurtful to the Douglases. Exactly who had arranged with whom and when
as to the text and by whom the various passages of it were written were questions
only partly and unsatisfactorily explored in evidence but when Mr Luke was   *f*
questioned as to innuendi in the text he sought to explain them away by reference
to the sub-editors, called in at the weekend and required to work long hours,
having been overtired. I cannot accept that evidence; I see no likely link between
tiredness and the mean-spiritedness of Hello!'s comments. If anything, one
would expect tiredness to lead to an adoption of Hello!'s familiar eulogistic and *g*
flattering tone, the usual nature of which served only to mark a contrast with the
comments I have described. However, the evidence, whilst giving rise to real
doubt, has not, in my view, been sufficient to amount to proof of an instruction
having gone out that snide or hurtful comment would, unusually, be welcomed
in the text in order to repay the Douglases for having given the exclusive to OK!.
                                                                              h
HELLO! AND OK! BOTH PUBLISH
    [133] OK! had successfully striven to bring forward Douglas wedding
coverage into its issue 241 (bearing date 1 December 2000) and it went on public
sale on the very same day as Hello!'s issue 639. Issue 241, with a full family
wedding group on the cover and boasting that OK! was first for celebrity   *j*
weddings, bore the banner 'the first *real* wedding pictures'. Issue 242 (dated
2 December), with a close-up of bride and groom on the cover, came out later
and together issues 241 and 242 completed the whole coverage of the wedding by
OK!. The authorised photographs of the wedding were very widely syndicated
by OK! and some or all appeared in many publications at many points throughout
the world.

a
[134] As she left court on 23 November Mrs Cartwright telephoned Hello!'s London editor, Maggie Koumi, to tell her that the injunction had been lifted. She said that, following a common practice, the national and daily press could be authorised to use the whole of the cover of issue 639 but not pictures from its inside pages. News of the overturning of the injunctions spread fast and within 15 minutes or so Ms Koumi was telephoned on behalf of the Daily Mirror, the

b
Daily Mail, the Mail on Sunday and the Daily Telegraph. Ms Koumi told them that it was alright for them to use the cover of issue 639 but not the pictures inside. The editor of the Sun also telephoned her. He had earlier asked whether, if the injunction were to be lifted, he could use pictures from the inside of issue 639. She had earlier said that that *might* be possible. Now she told him that the lawyers had advised that it was not to be done. He said: 'But I've already laid

c
out four pages.' She reiterated that inside pictures were not to be used but only the cover and then in its entirety (thus, of course, advertising Hello!). It was not then too late for the Sun to have withdrawn from its print run any pictures from the inside of Hello! which the Sun had proposed to use.

[135] By the time Mrs Cartwright and Mrs Doughty arrived, after court, at
d
Hello!'s offices, the legal advice had changed; not even the cover was now to be authorised. Ms Koumi rang to tell those to whom she had earlier spoken that not even the cover could be used. At some stage between 6–8 pm she tried to ring the Sun's editor. She was told he was in a meeting. She made clear that the cover was not to be used and insisted that the message should be taken to him immediately. A 'picture kill' had been circulated by the Press Association and
e
Hello!'s solicitors had circulated newspapers to like effect.

[136] At about 10.45 pm on Thursday 23 November Ms Koumi was telephoned on behalf of the picture desk at the Daily Mirror. She was asked if Hello! had made a deal with the Sun. She said that that was not the case. She was told that she had better get a copy of tomorrow's Sun. The man at the Mirror by
f
then had a copy of the following day's issue of the Sun in front of him and told her that the whole of the front page barring one column featured photographs published in Hello!.

[137] Mrs Koumi bought a copy of the Sun on the following morning, Friday 24 November. She says in her witness statement:

g
'I then realised why the Mirror had assumed we had made a deal with the Sun. This was because of the following phrasing used by them: "But yesterday a judge overturned the ruling, allowing Hello!—*and the Sun*—to show the sensational snaps."'

h
[138] She telephoned Mr Hutchings of Charles Russell. Ms Koumi's evidence, which I accept, was that it was totally untrue that permission had been given to the Sun to republish the Douglas wedding pictures.

OTHERS PUBLISH THE UNAUTHORISED PHOTOGRAPHS
j
[139] The issue of the Sun published on 24 November contained five of the unauthorised pictures. It included also, but compressed into a very small size, a reproduction of the cover of Hello!, including the magazine's name. The unauthorised pictures of Miss Zeta-Jones eating or being fed wedding cake had attracted the headline 'Catherine Eater Jones'. The Daily Mail on the same day published a formal authorised picture of the couple and also reproduced Hello!'s cover in legible form. That picture of the couple had been the picture that the

couple had released to the press generally. The Daily Mail also published four of
the unauthorised photographs on Saturday 25 November.

[140] After a hesitant start Hello! had, in my judgment, acted with reasonable
speed to stop publication by others either of the cover or of the inside of Hello!.
I hold that the publication that I have described in the Sun and the Daily Mail had
not been authorised by Hello!. It has not been shown, either, that the newspapers
ever paid Hello! for any right to publish as they had.

INVOICES ARRIVE

[141] On or about 28 November 2000 Sue Neal, as Hello!'s picture editor,
received four invoices addressed to her. They were respectively from Mr Ramey
for $75,200 and marked 'Agreed Fee Special Project Eduardo Sanchez', from
Rupert Thorpe marked 'Agreed Fee—Royals on holiday' for $56,400, from Frank
Griffin Photography marked 'Photo Sales—November 2000' for $29,000 and
from Randy Bauer Photo marked 'Special Project—New York (as per Frank)
$29,000'. All, despite anonymous and false descriptions, were for the
unauthorised photographs or work in connection therewith but they totalled
$189,600 and not the $188,000 which had been agreed. Consistently with the only
agreement made with respect to the unauthorised photographs, it was to Hello!
and not to the Marquesa that they were addressed. Sue Neal had no reason not
to approve them for payment and thus, as she had been asked by Mrs Doughty
to do, she quickly passed them to Mrs Doughty, which was the ordinary course
of dealings with invoices. Mrs Doughty spotted that they did not add up to the
$188,000 and Sue Neal, after speaking to Mr Ramey, with his agreement adjusted
his down to $73,600.

[142] At the same time as the four invoices I have described above there also
arrived an invoice for $10,000 addressed to 'Hello! Magazine Picture Desk,
Marquessa De Varella' (sic) from Mr Ramey. It was for 'Story—Agreed Fee
Special Project $10,000'. Sue Neal wrote upon it 'Zeta/Douglas Wedding
Guarantee Fee Issue 639'. Mr Ramey had told her that that was what it
represented. Her evidence is difficult to understand on this issue. At one stage
she agreed that Mr Ramey had said words to the effect: 'The 10,000 is what the
Marquesa promised me.' Her witness statement had also asserted that the sum
had been promised. However, in oral evidence there was the following
exchange:

'Mr Tugendhat: Did he say that the Marquesa had agreed to pay it? Ms Neal:
No, he did not say that. He did not say the Marquesa had agreed to pay it.

Mr Tugendhat: What did he say, then, to justify the invoice? Ms Neal: He
said that he had said to the Marquesa that he wanted a fee of $10,000.

Mr Tugendhat: [Correctly] But in your statement you say he said he had
been promised the $10,000 ... by the Marquesa. Ms Neal: That is what he
said.

Mr Tugendhat: Yes and that is right, is it? Ms Neal: Yes.'

[143] Ms Neal was in my judgment a truthful witness despite such internal
contradictions and I hold the case to have been that on occasions both before and
after the wedding Mr Ramey had asserted to her that a guarantee fee had been
indicated by the Marquesa to be payable, as Ms Neal put it:

a   '... if they had not taken as good a photograph as they were hoping to take, and did not come up with material which would warrant a higher sales figure. A guarantee would be to offset some of their expenses.'

Even that was, in my judgment, a more firm indication of prospective payment than the Marquesa had actually given to Mr Ramey (see [38], above) but it was in such terms that Ms Neal understood the position from Mr Ramey. Of course, by

b   this time, Mr Ramey had 'come up with material' that had fetched a good price so the $10,000 on such a contingency would not have been payable. Ms Neal said that she had suggested to Mr Ramey that he should '[j]ust forget about the invoice' and that he had accepted that. As far as it goes, his accepting that supports a conclusion that the $10,000 was never promised or at any rate never

c   promised unconditionally as the evidence about Mr Ramey has not suggested that he would easily give up $10,000 to which he was entitled.

[144] I accept Ms Neal's evidence that she handed all five invoices to Mrs Doughty, who asked her to ask the photographers to readdress them to the Marquesa's company, Neneta Overseas Ltd. That she did.

d   [145] When all five invoices were passed to Mrs Doughty (and not the four only, as she asserted), her understanding was that they were not payable by Hello!. She faxed copies of them to Senor Riera and he rang her back to say that she was right and that they should be readdressed to the Marquesa, which, as I have just mentioned, Mrs Doughty then asked Sue Neal to set about.

e   [146] Mrs Doughty is susceptible to an attack on the lines that she knew full well that the Marquesa had had only little to do with the unauthorised photographs, that they could not be described as a typical Marquesa feature or indeed any Marquesa feature but that in asking, as she did, for the invoices to be readdressed, she was attempting to bolster the untruthful tale, that the Marquesa had sold the pictures to Hello!, that Hello! was now asserting.

f   [147] However, at that time, whilst she did know of the Marquesa's letter, she had no certain reason to believe that it was untrue or that the Marquesa would have put her name to it if it had been. As invoices were in ordinary course passed to her she would probably have had the Marquesa's invoice of 20 November, the heading of which suggested that the Marquesa had arranged photographs of the Douglas wedding. She would have spoken to Mrs Cartwright who was of the view that it was the Marquesa who had dealt with Mr Ramey. She may well have heard counsel on the Hello! side asserting that in court. She would have known from the McCarthy case that, although such work was outside her usual run, the Marquesa would quite gleefully stoop to paparazzi work to help Hello! against its rival. It was Mrs Doughty's habit to clear the Marquesa's and other large invoices with Madrid so a telephone call to Senor Riera was quite natural. She had taken down Senor Sanchez Junco's statement that he had not had any contact with '[t]he provider of these photographs' save to agree a price once they had been delivered but she, in her mind, drew a distinction between the photographer and the provider of the unauthorised photographs. She did not understand an agreement between Senor Sanchez Junco and Mr Ramey, perhaps as photographer, as excluding that the photographs represented a Marquesa feature of which the Marquesa was provider. When she telephoned Senor Riera, with whom practically all her dealings with Madrid were conducted, he confirmed, as I have mentioned, that the invoices were for the Marquesa.

[148] My impression is that she was and is a loyal employee. 'If I am to believe somebody, I believe my own company' she said. She was content to act

on what Senor Riera told her to do without testing her belief as to the
Marquesa's involvement by, say, telephoning the Marquesa or Miss Mildh.   *a*
There was in any event little love lost between the senior figures at Hello!'s
London office and the Marquesa. I have heard and seen her give evidence and,
on balance I do not hold Mrs Doughty to have knowingly embarked upon a
course intended to put false and extra distance between Hello! and the
paparazzo incursion in New York.   *b*

[149] On 15 December 2000 Senor Riera sent a fax to the Marquesa. He told
her that Hello! had received invoices for a total of $188,000 from the four
photographers. The fax continued:

> 'For us there is no intermediary other than you, as it was your company
> who offered to us and managed this matter. Therefore, we are puzzled by   *c*
> these invoices and I would be grateful if you take control of them as we are
> not going to pay them. In this regard either you get in touch with them or
> we will ask them to contact your company, whose name I would ask you
> to let me know. You will, of course, invoice us for your fees.'

[150] Senor Riera's own evidence was that on 14 December he had been told   *d*
by Senor Sanchez Junco that the agreement to acquire the unauthorised
photographs had been with Mr Ramey and had been made by Senor Sanchez
Junco. He sought to say that none the less it was for the Marquesa to pay the
photographers. He also said that on 14 December he had told Senor Sanchez
Junco that he was going to bill the Marquesa but that Senor Sanchez Junco had
said: 'No, the agreement was with Mr Ramey.' Despite that and, as he put it, to   *e*
stick to the rules, it was, he thought, for the Marquesa to pay the photographers.
Hence the fax of 15 December. Except as part of a conscious and false pretence
on his part as to a deeper involvement of the Marquesa in the unauthorised
photographs than had been the case, the fax is inexplicable. The word translated
as 'intermediary' had, in Spanish, been 'interlocutor'.

[151] The Marquesa, still willing at that stage to help, faxed back twice the
same day to Senor Riera saying, ruefully, 'I am obviously a "todo terreno"', an   *f*
all-terrain vehicle, meaning that she was being called upon to do anything
demanded of her. But she gave him the name and address of her company and
inquired what invoice was it that she had to pay, hardly a question that would
have been likely to have needed to be asked had her company been the person
who had contracted to buy the photographs. She also asked Mrs Doughty at
Hello! to send her copies of the invoices. Mrs Doughty did fax the Hello! invoices
to the Marquesa who, on seeing that they were addressed to Hello!, telephoned
Mrs Doughty to ask for it to be arranged that fresh invoices should be prepared
addressed to Neneta Overseas Ltd.

[152] The Marquesa was puzzled by the fact that there were as many as five
invoices, including ones other than from Mr Ramey, but she telephoned
Senor Sanchez Junco on the evening of 15 December and he told her that the
whole $188,000 should be paid to Mr Ramey. She did not care for that advice and
said that she would pay each invoice separately.

[153] On 17 December the Marquesa faxed Senor Riera and in the course of a
long and rather meandering fax made, in effect, five points. Firstly, that
Senor Sanchez Junco had told her to pay the whole sum to Mr Ramey; secondly,
that that was not possible as he would be unlikely to share the money with the
other three photographers who had sent her invoices but who needed to be dealt
with; thirdly: 'It is true that Phil Ramey asked me to assure $10,000 for the

a photographs that might be taken at the Douglas wedding and I told him that I could assure him that' and, fourthly, that that had not been compromising because the photographs she had referred to could equally have been photographs outside the wedding and that she had been careful to tell him to do as he wanted. Ramey had sent her an invoice for the $10,000, she said, presumably a reference to the one addressed to her at 'Hello! Magazine Desk b Marquessa De Varella' at Hello!'s London office. Fifthly, she said she would like to pay that invoice.

[154] The next day her assistant Miss Mildh, pointing out that the Marquesa was about to leave for Uruguay, e-mailed Mr Luke saying that she must speak to him, adding, in reference to Hello! and the photographers: 'They are now sending invoices to us re: the photographers—stuff we never had anything to do c with, things that were actually arranged by Sue Neal.' No one called back. On 21 December Miss Mildh faxed Senor Sanchez Junco's secretary asking her to get in touch with the Marquesa, saying: 'You cannot just drop the lawyers onto her and then leave her with it as in fact she never had anything to do with these pictures in the first place.' There was no answer.

d
FRESH INVOICES

[155] Around this time, in December 2000 or early January 2001, the photographers submitted fresh invoices, now addressed to Neneta Overseas Ltd at its address in the British Virgin Islands. They had adjusted the respective sums so that the aggregate was $188,000 but had done so in a different way than had e Sue Neal when they had been received by Hello!. Amongst the invoices addressed to Neneta Overseas Ltd was a fresh one from Mr Ramey for $10,000, still bearing the description 'Agreed Fee Special Project of the Marquesa De Varela', now with her title correctly spelt.

THE COURT OF APPEAL'S REASONED JUDGMENTS

[156] On 21 December 2000 the Court of Appeal ([2001] 2 All ER 289, [2001] f QB 967) gave the reasons for its earlier decision to lift the injunction. I shall be citing passages from the decision later but, in outline, the court held that despite there being sound arguments for confidence or even for a case in privacy, the balance of convenience tipped the matter in favour of there being no prior restraint.

THE $10,000 AGAIN

[157] On 29 December the Marquesa e-mailed Senora Elisa saying that Phil Ramey wanted to be paid the $10,000 'which we promised no matter what happened'. She was asking that so that when Hello! came to pay her in order that she, in turn, could pay the photographers, the invoice for $10,000 from Phil Ramey should be added 'otherwise he is going to continue pestering with the subject'.

[158] It might be thought that the contemporary indications from the Marquesa that the $10,000 had been promised 'no matter what happened' and that she 'could assure him of that' are reliable indications that that had, indeed, been the case. However, on balance I am unpersuaded that that is so; it suited the Marquesa to say so to Hello! in order that she would be put in funds to pay the $10,000 so that she would not be 'pestered' by Mr Ramey on that score. But when she spoke of her dealings in August 2000, when were given whatever promises or indications as were given, she had told Mr Ramey that he could be sure that if he got good pictures Senor Sanchez Junco would pay him more than

the $10,000 so that expenses he had incurred would be covered. She had said:
'You will have your expenses back because probably if you get the pictures it
would be more valuable than $10,000.'

[159] Senor Sanchez Junco had said to her, as to $10,000 being paid in advance
or in any event: 'Absolutely not. I am not going to fund anyone going to New
York. I don't want to know.' The Marquesa had had no authority to offer the
$10,000 from Hello! and had retracted such assurances that she had given but had
added the consolation that, if pictures were obtained, Hello! would pay well.

[160] Still the photographers had not been paid. Hello! had passed the subject
of their payment to the Marquesa and the Marquesa had not been put in funds to
pay them. The photographers were in frequent contact with Sue Neal. She
pressed the case for their payment upon Mrs Doughty. They had, she said, done
a good job under difficult circumstances and if a squabble developed regarding
their payment it would damage the very good relationship which the Hello!
picture department had with them.

[161] The Marquesa, in the meantime, was getting cold feet. She got in touch
with the lawyers who administered her British Virgin Islands company and told
them that she had had to declare that the unauthorised photographs had been
bought by Neneta Overseas Ltd and that that company therefore had to issue an
invoice to Hola in Madrid. She asked for advice. On a practical level, Miss Mildh
told Senora Elisa on 10 January that the Marquesa could not pay the
photographers until Hello! had paid her and that an invoice to Hello! from
Neneta Overseas Ltd was being prepared. She indicated that the Marquesa
would be adding $5,000 to it to cover expenses and asked for clarification as to the
amount of the larger Ramey invoice.

INVOICES AND THE MARQUESA ARE PAID

[162] On the same day Neneta Overseas Ltd sent to Senor Riera at Hola, an
invoice headed 'Douglas/Zeta-Jones Project New York; $205,000'. The
photographers' invoices sent to the Marquesa had totalled either $189,600
(uncorrected down to $188,000) or $188,000, to which could be added the
disputable $10,000 'Guarantee Fee' and the $5,000 indicated as the Marquesa's
expenses. The total thus would either have been $204,600 or $203,000. On either
footing the Marquesa's request for $205,000 was including the $10,000
'Guarantee Fee' and was rounding up her expenses. Yet Hello! paid the full
$205,000 to Neneta Overseas Ltd without further ado on 15 January 2001 under
the signature of Senor Sanchez Junco.

[163] The $205,000 paid was in addition to the £1,175 paid to the Marquesa for
telephone expenses on 27 November. Senor Riera never accepted that a $10,000
'Guarantee' had ever been paid; he said he had no knowledge of that $10,000.
Senora Elisa told him that the sums did not tally but none the less he passed a
bank transfer for the full $205,000 to Senor Sanchez Junco for him to sign it, as he
did. Senor Riera claimed that the difference or inclusion of the $10,000, was
commission for the Marquesa but there is no hint that that was ever suggested or
agreed. The Marquesa, having been put in funds, promptly paid Mr Thorpe,
Mr Griffin and Randy Bauer but a difficulty arose as to the payment to
Mr Ramey. He asked for his amount to be paid into a bank account not in his
own name but in the name of someone else. Miss Mildh sensibly insisted that a
letter should be received from Mr Ramey authorising the payment of the amount
to the other account. She explained that to Senora Elisa. Senora Elisa's response
was that it was for the Marquesa to get in touch with Mr Ramey and that

Senor Riera had insisted that it was the Marquesa that must pay him. Miss Mildh found a way out; she spoke with Sue Neal and Sue Neal had said that she would talk to Mr Ramey on the subject. By this time it would seem that the Hello! defendants were almost paranoid (Sue Neal apart) about avoiding being seen to be in contact with Mr Ramey. But when Mr Ramey telephoned Sue Neal he indicated that he did not want to cause any trouble, he just wanted his money. He made an extraordinary suggestion.

[164] It was that Hello! should create a fictitious job for him, paying him a retainer of, say, $5,000 a month until the sum he was claiming, $75,200, should be paid. From the sale of them on 19 November onwards, Mr Ramey had been anxious to conceal or not to reveal his connection with the unauthorised photographs and his willingness to be paid over so long a time again illustrates his defensive, if not guilty, state of mind. The proposal for the retainer was, said Sue Neal, Mr Ramey's idea; he did not wish to be identified with the unauthorised pictures in any way. Miss Mildh, after speaking to Sue Neal, reported the proposal to the Marquesa although describing the plan (mistakenly, as I hold) as Sue Neal's idea. Sue Neal told Mr Ramey she would consult the new editor on his idea but did so in a tone that suggested that it was doubtful that Mr Hall, the incoming editor of Hello!, would adopt it. Nothing further came of the proposal but the Marquesa, without in terms saying that the Marquesa's letter had been a lie, began to warn Senora Elisa of the difficulties inherent in Hello!'s position, plainly intending the message to be passed on to Senor Riera. Mr Ramey had told her (and she had believed) that he had taped his conversation with Senor Sanchez Junco. She warned Senora Elisa: 'I do not think it will be a good idea to go to court to lie. The truth will prevail.'

[165] On 7 March 2001 there was received from Mr Ramey a note authorising payment of his invoices that had been sent to the Marquesa to the account of 'John Phillipp'. The Marquesa or her company paid $US 75,200 to Mr Ramey in that indirect way on or about 30 March 2001. She did not pay the $US 10,000 invoice, nor repay it to Hello!, nor was she asked to refund the $10,000.

THE PROCEEDINGS DEVELOP

[166] In the meantime the claimants had served particulars of claim on 22 February 2001 and a defence was then served on 16 May 2001. Paragraph 30 of the defence asserted that Senor Sanchez Junco had bought the unauthorised pictures from Mr Ramey in the early hours of 20 November 2000. Differences between Charles Russell for Hello! and Theodore Goddard for the claimants began to appear in relation to the adequacy or otherwise of disclosure. Mr Hutchings turned to the Marquesa for help in the production of the invoice for $188,000. Senor Riera faxed her to say that he would be grateful if she would comply with the request. The Marquesa, again without in terms saying that the Marquesa's letter had been a lie or that Mr Hutchings knew that it was, warned Mr Hutchings that it would be useless to deny that a conversation between Senor Sanchez Junco and Mr Ramey had taken place. She did not identify, either, which particular conversation between them she had in mind.

[167] On 2 May 2002 Jacob J gave leave for an amendment to the claim form to add Senor Sanchez Junco, the Marquesa, Neneta Overseas Ltd and Philip Ramey as defendants. At first it was contemplated, at least by the Marquesa, that Charles Russell would act for the Marquesa and they went on the record in that regard but instructions were given from Madrid that brought to an end any further representation of the Marquesa by Charles Russell and such papers as she

had given that firm were returned. Mr Hutchings warned her on 22 May that time for her defence was close to expiring. On 18 July the Marquesa, using her nickname Neneta, faxed Senor Sanchez Junco saying:

> 'Thanks to the mess that Riera has put me into I am spending the whole day from lawyer to another one!! And on top of it nobody pays them?? This is too much ... I hope everybody will say the truth of how Hello! bought the M. Douglas pictures. I am fed up of problems and of nastiness.'

[168] In para 13.9 of her defence of 22 July 2002 she admitted and averred, for the avoidance of doubt, that the contents of the Marquesa's letter were untrue. By 23 August 2002 she was faxing Senor Riera saying:

> 'The jam you have put me in with the Zeta-Jones/Douglas trial when you asked me to sign a letter knowing that I could not possibly have bought these photographs, is something that is akin to evil. Anthony Luke knows the truth, like Eduardo Sanchez knows the truth, like Sue knows the truth, like the photographers know the truth. I did not buy those pictures. I just spoke a few times in August 2000 with Mr Ramey and once with F. Griffin and then, in December, I spoke to the writer who lives in New York about the text which was not even published in the end. If the case goes to Court the truth will come out and it will be damaging to Hello!'s reputation. One day the truth will be known and it will come out that in all these years I have been the victim of several injustices and of a continuous persecution.'

A little later she adds: 'I cannot continue telling lies, I am sorry.'

[169] It was in answer to that fax that Senor Riera made the important response, to which I have earlier referred, that it was '[f]ollowing instructions from Senor Sanchez Junco' that he had sent the fax of 22 November 2000 to her. Senor Riera in this fax continued in a self-serving way. He said, of the Marquesa's participation in the purchase of the photographs of the Douglas wedding:

> 'This participation was to a lesser or greater degree the same as your other collaborations with Hello! for more than 15 years. Meaning that you offered to Mr Sanchez Junco the possibility of a story, you negotiated its execution with the means you consider appropriate, you choose the photographer and the journalist that will execute it and in most of the cases you take responsibility for their expenses in order to later invoice Hello! for all your services, including the total of the story itself. As far as all of us in this company, including myself and all our lawyers, understand this was your involvement, the same as in all other features, and that's the reason for your note, even though we later came to know the photographer, in this case Mr Ramey, chosen by you to co-ordinate the delivery of the feature, contacted Mr Sanchez Junco in the last moments, who with Mr Anthony Luke acting as translator, agreed on a final fee for this story. Fee that was told to you later via phone.'

[170] I cannot accept that Mr Riera thought that was the truth. It is impossible to see the agreement of the price for the unauthorised pictures between Mr Ramey and Senor Sanchez Junco, Sue Neal's acknowledgment of the price of $188,000 and the photographer's invoices sent direct to Hello! in the first instance, coupled with the absence of any fee for the feature payable to the Marquesa as even 'to a lesser ... degree' the same as her usual collaborations with Hello! over 15 years or so. Moreover to speak of Mr Ramey's contact and

a agreement with Senor Sanchez Junco as merely being something which '[w]e later came to know' is absurd. Further, Senor Riera's assertion later in the fax that '[w]hen we asked you to certify your actions regarding this feature … you gave freely your help' is not possible to square with his oral evidence that he knew that the Marquesa had been complaining about being required to sign the Marquesa's letter. The Marquesa in a fax of 20 September 2002 told Senor Riera:

b 'I had nothing to do with the relationship between Phil Ramey and Griffin and Hello! or the purchase of the photographs or their publication. Hola and Hello! have published their pictures for so long that it is childish to believe that I was the one to discover them or that I dealt with the matter. Phil Ramey has been selling his features for over 15 years through agencies like *c* Keystone Nemes. The night of the wedding all the photographs were sent electronically to Hello!. How could I buy something if I was in Sotogrande, where I do not even have a fax. Why was Eduardo going to allow me to buy these pictures? It is ridiculous and it is not true.'

[171] A little later she said:

d 'I would love to be able to continue helping Hello! (but now I know that the truth has to be told). I only signed that letter you sent me to help Hello! and I cannot go on lying. I signed in such a hurry that I had no time to realise what I was signing. Elisa hurried me because they had to send it in order to lift the injunction.'

e I do not accept that she did not realise that what she was signing was untrue but I do accept that she had little to do with the unauthorised photographs and nothing to do with their purchase.
[172] Her fax continued:

f 'I felt coerced into signing something that was not true and now I can be in contempt of Court for having lied. A few days ago Eduardo asked me "And why did you sign it?". I told him "I signed it because otherwise Riera would have told you that I failed you when you most needed me".'

BEFORE SIR ANDREW MORRITT V-C; JANUARY 2003
[173] As the proceedings unfolded (Hola SA having been added and then, in May 2002, the third, fourth and fifth defendants) the claimants became increasingly concerned at what they regarded as the inadequacy of disclosure on the part of the Hello! defendants, which had been given on 18 February, 19 March, 30 May and 29 October 2002. They also had very real doubts about Mrs Cartwright's second witness statement, Senor Sanchez Junco's statement as given to Mrs Doughty and the Marquesa's letter as evidence handed to the Court of Appeal. On 13 December 2002 they applied for an order that the defences of the Hello! defendants should be struck out. That application came on, with others, before Sir Andrew Morritt V-C, on 16 January 2003. He heard oral evidence from Senor Sanchez Junco, Senor Riera, Mrs Cartwright and Mrs Doughty.
[174] That hearing concluded on 21 January 2003 and Sir Andrew Morritt V-C gave judgment on 27 January ([2003] 1 All ER 1087). He held (at [25]) that Senor Sanchez Junco's statement was false and misleading and that he had known that it was, that it was admitted that the Marquesa's letter was false (at [26]) and that on her own admission, Mrs Cartwright's second witness statement was false

as to the paras 10 and 11 included within it. As I have already noted, Sir Andrew Morritt V-C concluded (at [34]) that the case advanced by Hello! before the Court of Appeal, based, as it was, on those false statements, was itself false. Of the three makers of the false documents Sir Andrew Morritt V-C said: 'Each of them knew that his or her statement was false or misleading in the respects I have mentioned.' I accept that Mrs Cartwright knew that paras 10 and 11 in her second witness statement were likely to mislead but I am not satisfied that she knew before the court gave its judgment that a form of her witness statement with those paragraphs in it was going to be used or had been used.

[175] Sir Andrew Morritt V-C also dealt with an allegation of inadequate disclosure. He gave (at [36], [37]) details of documents missing from the Hello! defendants' disclosure or destroyed by them (see also [38], [39], [41] and [42]). The Hello! defendants (at [43]) did not dispute the claimants' table of the respects in which, the claimants said, the disclosure had been defective. Sir Andrew Morritt V-C held (at [87]) that he had no evidence that any pre-action documents had been destroyed in an attempt to pervert the course of justice. He said:

'[88] Thus the material disposals or destructions are those made after the effective commencement of proceedings on 20 November 2000. These comprise, the photographs sent by Mr Ramey in electronic form, all the documents later disclosed by the Marquesa and the transmission data relating to the faxed memorandum from Ms Neal to Mr Ramey sent on 19 November 2000 and referred to in [16], above. Such destruction was plainly deliberate in the sense that it is not suggested to have been accidental. But was it more than that?

[97] … What is not available are the originals or copies of the documents destroyed which had been in the possession of the Hello! defendants. Such documents may or may not have had notes on them made by the recipient or sender respectively. Equally, there is not now available any other document destroyed or disposed of. But what evidence is there that there were any?

[98] This is the conundrum. I have given anxious consideration to whether I should, on a balance of probability, infer from the conduct of the Hello! defendants to which I have referred that there were further material undisclosed documents. I consider that I should.'

[176] However, Sir Andrew Morritt V-C continued (at [101]):

'… I do not consider that there is a real risk that there cannot be a fair trial on those issues, given the documentary evidence and the ability of the judge to draw inferences.'

He held, notwithstanding conduct attributable to the Hello! defendants which had left a very great deal to be desired with regard to the veracity of their evidence and the adequacy of their disclosure, that he was not persuaded that a fair trial was no longer possible. Re-amendment was at the same time permitted of the particulars of claim.

[177] A draft defence was put in on behalf of sixth defendant, Mr Ramey, and, as I have mentioned, a witness statement was received from him but he has taken no further part in the action. As between the claimants and the Hello! defendants, after further amendments, the hearing proceeded on the basis of re-re-amended particulars of claim from the claimants and a re-amended defence on the part of the Hello! defendants.

SE OG HØR

a
[178] At a very late stage Mr Price produced, but not by way of formal evidence verified by anyone, a copy of a Danish magazine, Se Og Hør of 14–18 December 2000, which included a number of the authorised pictures of the wedding. It was an unseemly attempt, by reference to the unedifying surroundings in which the wedding photographs were to be found in Se Og Hør,

b to lower any estimation of the quality of the publicity for the wedding which the claimants were willing to authorise. As it was not put into evidence and was produced so late, there was no opportunity to the claimants to inquire into whether Se Og Hør had duly acquired photographic rights from OK! or whether, if they had, that had been done in compliance with OK!'s obligations to Mr and Mrs Douglas. In the circumstances I pay no attention to Se Og Hør; it should not

c have been produced as and when it was.

[179] Whilst there have been several procedural skirmishes and many allegations of fact which I have not found it necessary to deal with, that suffices as the factual background against which the claimants raise their several causes of action.

d
THE PARTICULARS OF CLAIM

[180] Although the re-re-amended particulars of claim are at points, unclear as to whether a claim already mentioned is being repeated or a fresh claim is being made, in broad outline the particulars of claim appear to me to raise claims of the following kind: (i) on the basis that the wedding ceremony and reception was

e private, Mr and Mrs Douglas claim in confidence, a duty, in that circumstance, owed only to them (paras 6, 15, 18 and 19 of the re-re-amended particulars of claim); (ii) further, or alternatively, on the basis that the wedding had become an event which was exploited for gain, then all three claimants raise claims in confidence, the case being that photographic representation of the events was, in effect, a commercial or trade secret (paras 6(a) and 30); (iii) breaches of the Data

f Protection Act 1998 by which Mr and Mrs Douglas suffered damage (para 27); (iv) a claim under the laws as to privacy, a claim available only to Mr and Mrs Douglas (para 28); (v) infringement of Mr and Mrs Douglas's rights under Spanish law (para 29(a)); (vi) deliberate interference by all defendants with the rights or businesses of all three claimants, by unlawful means; (vii) conspiracy by

g all defendants save Mr Ramey to injure all the claimants by unlawful means; (viii) conspiracy by the Hello! defendants to injure all claimants by unlawful means; (ix) conspiracy by the Hello! defendants with the predominant purpose of injuring all claimants (para 32(b)); (x) that the judgment of the Court of Appeal should be set aside as having been procured by false evidence; (xi) exemplary damages for all claimants (para 33(a)); (xii) aggravated damages for the distress

h caused to Mr and Mrs Douglas (para 35); (xiii) injunctive and ancillary relief (para 37). I shall deal first with the law of confidence.

THE LAW OF CONFIDENCE

[181] At the broadest level of generality it can be said that equity offers

j remedies where a breach of an appropriate confidence, personal or commercial, is threatened or has occurred. There is nothing new about the availability of remedies in either type of confidence—see, for example, *Prince Albert v Strange* (1849) 1 Mac & G 25, 41 ER 1171, a case as to personal confidence but in which authorities on commercial confidence are cited. The jurisdiction in confidence 'is based, not so much on property or on contract, but rather on the duty to be of good faith' (see *Fraser v Evans* [1969] 1 All ER 8 at 11, [1969] 1 QB 349 at 361 per

Lord Denning MR). It is based 'on the moral principles of loyalty and fair dealing' (see *A-G v Guardian Newspapers Ltd (No 2)* [1988] 3 All ER 545 at 649, [1990] 1 AC 109 at 269 per Lord Griffiths. There is a public interest in the maintenance of confidences—per Lord Goff of Chieveley in the *Guardian Newspapers* case [1988] 3 All ER 545 at 658, [1990] 1 AC 109 at 281 where he said:

> 'I start with the broad general principle (which I do not intend in any way to be definitive) that a duty of confidence arises when confidential information comes to the knowledge of a person (the confidant) in circumstances where he has notice, or is held to have agreed, that the information is confidential, with the effect that it would be just in all the circumstances that he should be precluded from disclosing the information to others. I have used the word "notice" advisedly, in order to avoid the (here unnecessary) question of the extent to which actual knowledge is necessary, though I of course understand knowledge to include circumstances where the confidant has deliberately closed his eyes to the obvious.'

And see the passage from the judgment of Bingham LJ in the *Guardian Newspapers* case [1988] 3 All ER 545 at 624–625, [1990] 1 AC 109 at 215–216 emphasising, upon a wide basis of citation, that the law of confidence rests on an obligation of conscience—see also *R v Dept of Health, ex p Source Informatics Ltd* [2000] 1 All ER 786 at 793–796, [2001] QB 424 at 436–439 (paras 24–31). Lord Griffiths, in relation to the case where not the confidant but a third party is the defendant said, in the *Guardian Newspapers* case ([1988] 3 All ER 545 at 649, [1990] 1 AC 109 at 268):

> 'The duty of confidence is, as a general rule, also imposed on a third party who is in possession of information which he knows is subject to an obligation of confidence: see *Prince Albert v Strange* (1849) 1 Mac & G 25, 41 ER 1171 and [*Duchess of Argyll v Duke of Argyll* [1965] 1 All ER 611, [1967] Ch 302]. If this was not the law, the right would be of little practical value; there would be no point in imposing a duty of confidence in respect of the secrets of the marital bed if newspapers were free to publish those secrets when betrayed to them by the unfaithful partner in the marriage. When trade secrets are betrayed by a confidant to a third party it is usually the third party who is to exploit the information and it is the activity of the third party that must be stopped in order to protect the owner of the trade secret.'

And ([1988] 3 All ER 545 at 652, [1990] 1 AC 109 at 272 respectively):

> 'In a case of commercial secrets with which the development of the law of confidence has been mostly concerned, a third party who knowingly receives the confidential information directly from the confidant, which is the usual case, is tainted and identified with the confidant's breach of duty and will be restrained from making use of the information.'

[182] The necessary components of a successful claim in confidence were conveniently collected by Megarry J in *Coco v AN Clark (Engineers) Ltd* [1969] RPC 41 in a passage which has been repeatedly used ever since although occasionally refined in the light of particular considerations, see *Smith Kline & French Laboratories (Australia) Ltd v Secretary to the Dept of Community Services and Health, Alphafarm Pty Ltd v Secretary to the Dept of Community Services and Health* (1990) 95 ALR 87 at 102 per Gummow J in the Federal Court of Australia. After tracing the

a origins of equity's concern with confidence back to a couplet attributed to Sir Thomas More, Megarry J continued to say:

> 'In my judgment, three elements are normally required if, apart from contract, a case of breach of confidence is to succeed. First, the information itself, in the words of Lord Greene, M.R. in [*Saltman Engineering Co Ltd v Campbell Engineering Co Ltd* [1963] 3 All ER 413n at 415], must "have the *b* necessary quality of confidence about it." Secondly, that information must have been imparted in circumstances importing an obligation of confidence. Thirdly, there must be an unauthorised use of that information to the detriment of the party communicating it.' (See [1969] RPC 41 at 47.)

c It is important to note, though, that the citation from Lord Greene MR as to the information having to have 'the necessary quality of confidence about it' is a citation that stops mid-sentence. Lord Greene MR's sentence in full read:

> 'The information, to be confidential must, I apprehend, apart from contract, have the necessary quality of confidence about it, *namely, it must not be something which is public property and public knowledge.'* (See [1963] 3 All ER *d* 413n at 415). (My emphasis.)

[183] The 'necessary quality of confidence' which Megarry J contemplated, by his adoption of Lord Greene MR's dictum, was and was only therefore a quality of that particular kind—see also Lord Griffiths in the *Guardian Newspapers* case [1988] 3 All ER 545 at 648–649, [1990] 1 AC 109 at 268. I mention this as there is *e* a suspicion that in some later cases the phrase the 'necessary quality of confidence' has been regarded as including factors other than such as Lord Greene MR had had in mind. Instead, at the point at which Megarry J was considering it, in the first of his three requirements, the question, to adopt the neat phrase from Gurry *Breach of Confidence* (1984) p 70 which attracted the notice *f* of Bingham LJ in the *Guardian Newspapers* case in the Court of Appeal ([1988] 3 All ER 545 at 624, [1990] 1 AC 109 at 215) is whether the information has 'the basic attribute of inaccessibility'.

[184] As for the second component, that the information must have been imparted in circumstances importing an obligation of confidence, Megarry J in *Coco v AN Clark (Engineers) Ltd* [1969] RPC 41 at 48 said:
g
> 'It seems to me that if the circumstances are such that any reasonable man standing in the shoes of the recipient of the information would have realised that upon reasonable grounds the information was being given to him in confidence, then this should suffice to impose upon him the equitable *h* obligation of confidence.'

Included within that description are cases in which a third party defendant has received information with notice that he received it by way of a breach of confidence by the confidant to whom it was given and includes also cases where that third party has deliberately closed his eyes to the obvious (see the *Guardian j Newspapers* case [1988] 3 All ER 545 at 658, [1990] 1 AC 109 at 281 per Lord Goff of Chieveley and [1988] 3 All ER 545 at 649, 652, [1990] 1 AC 109 at 268, 272 per Lord Griffiths respectively in the passages cited above, and see also *Campbell v Mirror Group Newspapers Ltd* [2002] EWCA Civ 1373 at [66], [2003] 1 All ER 224 at [66], [2003] QB 633 at [66]).

[185] As for the third element, detriment, I need say nothing further on it at this stage before turning to four recent cases, three in the Court of Appeal, which

have all included significant consideration of the modern law of confidence in relation to personal confidence. The cases are the interlocutory stage in this case in the Court of Appeal, namely *Douglas v Hello! Ltd* [2001] 2 All ER 289, [2001] QB 967, a judgment delivered on 21 December 2000, *Venables v News Group Newspapers Ltd* [2001] 1 All ER 908, [2001] 2 WLR 1038, a judgment delivered on 8 January 2001 by Dame Elizabeth Butler-Sloss P, *A v B (a company)* [2002] EWCA Civ 337, [2002] 2 All ER 545, [2003] QB 195, a judgment delivered on 11 March 2002 and *Campbell's* case, a judgment delivered on 14 October 2002.

[186] These cases, as it seems to me, represent a fusion between the pre-existing law of confidence and rights and duties arising under the Human Rights Act 1998. The relevant general principles which I derive, chiefly from these recent cases, are as follows.

(i) Breach of confidence is an established cause of action but its scope now needs to be evaluated in the light of obligations falling upon the court under s 6(1) of the Human Rights Act 1998 (see *Douglas'* case [2001] 2 All ER 289 at 330, [2001] QB 967 at 1011–1012 (para 166) per Keene LJ). That can be achieved by regarding the often opposed rights conferred respectively by arts 8 and 10 of the European Convention for the Protection of Human Rights and Fundamental Freedoms 1950 (as set out in Sch 1 to the Human Rights Act 1998) as absorbed into the action for breach of confidence and as thereby to some extent giving it new strength and breadth (see *A v B* [2002] 2 All ER 545 at [4], [6]). The convention thus comes into play even in private law cases (see *Venables'* case [2001] 1 All ER 908 at 917–918, [2001] 2 WLR 1038 at 1049 (para 25)). It will be necessary for the courts to identify, on a case by case basis, the principles by which the law of confidentiality must accommodate arts 8 and 10 (see *Campbell's* case [2003] 1 All ER 224 at [43]). The weaker the claim for privacy, the more likely it will be outweighed by a claim based on freedom of expression (see *A v B* [2002] 2 All ER 545 at [11](vii)). A balance between the conflicting interests has to be struck (see *A v B* at [12]).

(ii) The right to freedom of expression described in art 10(1) of the convention is, by art 10(2), 'subject to such ... conditions ... as are prescribed by law and are necessary in a democratic society ... for the protection of the ... rights of others [and] for preventing the disclosure of information received in confidence ...' The art 10(1) right to freedom of expression is thus expressly made subject not only to the art 8 right for respect to private and family life but also to rights recognised by the law as to confidence, even where those latter rights are not themselves convention rights. In consequence, privacy rights under art 8 may not, as such, require to be considered in a particular case but none the less there can be an internal conflict within art 10 between the art 10(1) freedom and the art 10(2) rights under the law of confidence to which art 10(1) is made subject.

(iii) The Council of Europe Resolution 1165 of 1998 gives some guidance which includes a recognition that information about some people's lives has become a highly lucrative commodity for certain sections of the media and that protection is to be given against interference by the media (see *A v B* [2002] 2 All ER 545 at [11](xii)). Thus even a public figure, which includes those in the arts, is entitled to a private life although he or she may expect and accept that his or her circumstances will be more carefully scrutinised by the media (see *A v B* at [11](xii)). That is not to say, though, that the fact that an individual has achieved prominence on the public stage means that his private life can be laid bare by the media (see *Campbell's* case [2003] 1 All ER 224 at [41]).

a   (iv) If public attention has been courted by a claimant then that may lead that claimant to have less ground upon which to object to intrusion (see *A v B* [2002] 2 All ER 545 at [11](xii)).

(v) Freedom of expression on the media's part, as a counter-force to, for example, privacy is not invariably the ace of trumps but it is a powerful card to which the court must always pay appropriate respect (see *Douglas'* case [2001] 2

b All ER 289 at 302, [2001] QB 967 at 982 (para 49) per Brooke LJ). Put another way, there is no 'presumptive priority' given to such freedom of expression when it is in conflict with another convention right—see *Douglas'* case [2001] 2 All ER 289 at 323–324, [2001] QB 967 at 1004–1005 (paras 135 and 136) per Sedley LJ. Nor, as it seems to me, is there any such presumptive priority where the conflict is with rights under the law of confidence; it would be pointless of art 10(2) to make

c freedom of expression subject to such rights if it invariably overrode them.

(vi) Where the court is considering whether to grant *any* relief which, if granted, might affect the exercise of the convention right to freedom of expression, then the court, where the proceedings relate to material which is claimed or appears to be journalistic, *must* have particular regard, inter alia, to any

d relevant privacy code (see s 12(1) and (4) of the Human Rights Act 1998 and *Douglas'* case [2001] 2 All ER 289 at 313, [2001] QB 967 at 994 (para 92), *A v B* [2002] 2 All ER 545 at [11](v)).

(vii) There is such a code in place, that of the Press Complaints Commission (the PCC code), the relevant edition of which is that last modified in December 1999. Under the heading 'Privacy' one finds:

e

> '3.—(i) Everyone is entitled to respect for his or her private and family life, home, health and correspondence. A publication will be expected to justify intrusions into any individual's private life without consent. (ii) The use of long lens photography to take pictures of people in private places without their consent is unacceptable. Note—Private places are public or private

f   property where there is a reasonable expectation of privacy.'

Under the heading 'Misrepresentation' one finds:

> '11.—(i) Journalists must not generally obtain or seek to obtain information or pictures through misrepresentation or subterfuge. ... (iii)

g   Subterfuge can be justified only in the public interest and only when material cannot be obtained by any other means.'

Under the heading 'The Public Interest' the PCC code provides that there may be exceptions to, inter alia, the provisions as to privacy and as to misrepresentation where they can be demonstrated to be in the public interest. The public interest

h is defined to include:

> '(i) Detecting or exposing crime or a serious misdemeanour, (ii) Protecting public health and safety, (iii) Preventing the public from being misled by some statement or action of an individual or organisation.'

j Under the same heading at (iii) one finds:

> 'There is a public interest in freedom of expression itself. The Commission will therefore have regard to the extent to which material has, or is about to, become available to the public.'

It has not been said by Mr Price that, for the purposes of that code, any material public interest existed in relation to the publication of the unauthorised pictures

by Hello! and, no doubt, in not contending for any such public interest he is likely
to have had in mind that in any event even fuller coverage of the wedding was   *a*
intended to be published by OK! within a matter of days. In the absence of any
public interest the court is especially bound to pay particular regard to the PCC
code and a newspaper which flouts the code may have its claim to freedom of
expression trumped by art 10(2) considerations of privacy (see *Douglas'* case
[2001] 2 All ER 289 at 313–314, [2001] QB 967 at 994 (para 94) per Brooke LJ and   *b*
A v B [2002] 2 All ER 545 at [11](xiv)). Given the shape of art 10(2) I take the
relevant considerations to include also such as are protected by the law of
confidence although I recognise that a right of confidence on a subject not
protected as a convention right is likely to have less weight than a convention
right.

(viii) The regard which the PCC code requires to be had to whether the   *c*
material is about to become available to the public is an echo of s 12(4)(a)(ii) of
the Human Rights Act 1998, where that is a feature to which the court, in a
journalistic matter, is to pay particular regard. However, that someone else—for
example a complainant—is about to publish is not to be taken as necessarily
justifying publication by the defendant; that authorised publication is due in a   *d*
moment may, on the contrary, make it harder for the unauthorised publisher to
justify his breach—see e g *Times Newspapers Ltd v MGN Ltd* [1993] EMLR 443
(where authorised publication of the full Thatcher memoirs was due in ten days'
time).

(ix) If there is an intrusion in a situation in which a person can reasonably
expect his privacy to be respected then that intrusion will be capable of giving rise   *e*
to liability in an action for breach of confidence unless the intrusion can be
justified (see *A v B* [2002] 2 All ER 545 at [11](x)).

(x) It is still the case that a duty of confidence arises whenever the party subject
to the duty is in a situation where he either knows or ought to know that the
other person can reasonably expect his privacy to be protected (see *A v B* at   *f*
[11](ix)).

(xi) The existence of a relation such as may create a duty of confidence may,
and in personal confidence cases commonly will, have to be inferred from the
facts (see *A v B* at [11](ix) and (x)).

(xii) The fact that the information at issue is obtained by unlawful activity does   *g*
not mean that its publication will necessarily be restrained but that unlawful
means have been used to obtain the information may be a compelling factor
when a discretion comes to be exercised (see *A v B* at [11](x)).

(xiii) It can be right to regard unauthorised photographs as 'information' for
the purposes of the law of confidence. In the case before me the unauthorised   *h*
photographs have been said to convey the information 'This is what the wedding
and the happy couple looked like' (see *Douglas'* case [2001] 2 All ER 289 at 324,
[2001] QB 967 at 1005 (para 138) per Sedley LJ). The law of confidence can well
encompass photographs of such an event and no less so because the event could
have been described in words or by drawings. The photographs—

    j

> 'conveyed to the public information not otherwise truly obtainable, that is
> to say, what the event and its participants looked like. It is said that a picture
> is worth a thousand words. Were that not so, there would not be a market
> for magazines like Hello! and OK! The same result is not obtainable through
> the medium of words alone, nor by recollected drawings with their
> inevitable inaccuracy. There is no reason why these photographs inherently

a   could not be the subject of a breach of confidence.' (See *Douglas'* case [2001]
     2 All ER 289 at 329–330, [2001] QB 967 at 1011 (para 165) per Keene LJ.)

     (xiv) It is a familiar course for chancery judges to grant injunctions to restrain
     the publication of photographs taken surreptitiously in circumstances such that
     the photographer is to be taken to have known that the occasion was a private
     one and that the taking of photographs by outsiders was not permitted (see
b   *Douglas'* case [2001] 2 All ER 289 at 306–307, [2001] QB 967 at 986–987
     (paras 68–69) citing *Creation Records Ltd v News Group Newspapers Ltd* [1997] EMLR
     444 and *Shelley Films Ltd v Rex Features Ltd* [1994] EMLR 134).
     (xv) It is well settled that equity may intervene to prevent a publication of
     photographic images taken in breach of confidence. If, on some private occasion,
c   the prospective claimant makes it clear, expressly or impliedly, that no
     photographic images are to be taken of them, then all those present will be bound
     by the obligation of confidence created by their knowledge (or imputed
     knowledge) of that restriction (see *Douglas'* case [2001] 2 All ER 289 at 307–308,
     [2001] QB 967 at 988 (para 71) per Brooke LJ).

d   [187] So far, the general principles I have been concerned to set out have
     mainly related to cases of personal or individual confidence but as I shall need to
     consider also commercial confidence I need to add some further matters. Thus:
     (i) The Hello! defendants accept, of course, that trade secrets can be sold and it
     is common enough in commercial confidence cases for the benefit of the
     confidentiality to pass to be shared with others. The confidentiality of a trade
e   secret, for example, may be shared between, and be enforceable by, the inventor
     and the manufacturer to whom he had granted licence for the secret to be turned
     to account. Thus in *Gilbert v Star Newspaper Co Ltd* (1894) 11 TLR 4, WS Gilbert
     had found that, in breach of the implied obligation upon cast members and
     theatre employees not to disclose the plot of the play in respect of which they
f   were engaged, the plot of his comic opera 'His Excellency' had been disclosed to
     the newspaper. Without proof, as it seems, of any particular document of
     assignment or as to joint ownership but simply relying upon the factual situation
     Chitty J required the joinder of the theatre manager as a co-plaintiff and granted
     an appropriate injunction in favour of both plaintiffs. (ii) So also in *O Mustad &*
     Son v S Allcock & Co Ltd and Dosen, a case of 1928 not reported until [1964] 1 WLR
g   109 and then only as a note. There the confidence had originally been owed by
     Dosen to his employer, Thoring & Co, which went into liquidation. The benefit
     of that company's trade secrets was bought by the plaintiffs, O Mustad & Son.
     The report is not entirely clear as it sometimes speaks of Dosen having acquired
     information whilst in 'their service', ie that of Mustad, yet speaks also of what
h   Dosen had learned in the service of his 'former Master', a reference to Thoring
     & Co. The better view, as it seems to me, is that Dosen was never in Mustad's
     employ and never acquired the relevant knowledge whilst in Mustad's employ.
     On that footing the case shows that the benefit of a confidence can pass, in that
     case by purchase from the liquidator of Thoring, and, if that is so, then it is hard
j   to see why it should not be shared between and be enforceable by co-owners or
     by a successor in title, at any rate where the defendant knew or could be taken to
     have known of the co-ownership or sharing before acting in breach and where all
     entitled to the confidence assert it. It remains the case, of course, that it is only
     the person or persons to whom confidence is owed that can assert the
     confidence—see e g *Fraser v Evans* [1969] 1 All ER 8 at 11, [1969] 1 QB 349 at 361
     per Lord Denning MR. Despite the Hello! defendants' argument, I find nothing

in *Rickless v United Artists Corp* [1987] 1 All ER 679, [1988] QB 40 that suggests that, while surrounding circumstances can create the enforceability of a confidence by *a* the original confider, they cannot also create an enforceability shared between more than one, the original confider and another or others, where the facts require that such others should be protected.

[188] In my approach to the law I have had to consider a passage from the judgment of Gleeson CJ in *Australian Broadcasting Corp v Lenah Game Meats Pty Ltd* *b* (2001) 185 ALR 1, a passage cited by the Court of Appeal both in *A v B (a company)* [2002] 2 All ER 545, [2003] QB 195 and in *Campbell v Mirror Group Newspapers Ltd* [2003] 1 All ER 224, [2003] QB 633. The passage reads (at 13 (para 42)):

> 'There is no bright line which can be drawn between what is private and what is not. Use of the term "public" is often a convenient method of *c* contrast, but there is a large area in between what is necessarily public and what is necessarily private. An activity is not private simply because it is not done in public. It does not suffice to make an act private that, because it occurs on private property, it has such measure of protection from the public gaze as the characteristics of the property, the nature of the activity, the *d* locality, and the disposition of the property owner combine to afford. Certain kinds of information about a person, such as information relating to health, personal relationships, or finances, may be easy to identify as private; as may certain kinds of activity, which a reasonable person, applying contemporary standards of morals and behaviour, would understand to be meant to be unobserved. The requirement that disclosure or observation of *e* information or conduct would be highly offensive to a reasonable person of ordinary sensibilities is in many circumstances a useful practical test of what is private.'

[189] In *Campbell's* case at first instance ([2002] EWHC 499 (QB), [2002] IP & T *f* 612) Morland J had turned to this dictum whilst considering (for the purposes of the first limb of the three-part test suggested by *Coco v AN Clark (Engineers) Ltd* [1969] RPC 41) whether the details published about the model Naomi Campbell had 'the necessary quality of confidence about them' (see *Campbell's* case in the Court of Appeal [2003] 1 All ER 224 at [19], [20]). She was claiming only in confidence ([2003] 1 All ER 224 at [7]). Morland J held, in the light of Gleeson CJ's *g* dictum, that that test was satisfied. It is not clear to me whether the Court of Appeal in *Campbell's* case also used the dictum as a yardstick appropriate for judging whether the first test in *Coco's* case was satisfied—consider *Campbell's* case ([2003] 1 All ER 224 at [48] and [51])—but when one looks at the matter more closely it seems to me that cannot have been intended. The first limb in *Coco's* *h* case as to the necessary quality of confidence is to do and to do only, as the full citation from *Saltman Engineering Co Ltd v Campbell Engineering Co Ltd* [1963] 3 All ER 413n shows (see [182], above), with whether the information is already public property and public knowledge. It is not concerned with whether or not the information is 'private' in the sense that its disclosure would be significantly *j* harmful. The law at that first stage of the *Coco* test does not, for example, in a trade secret case, raise what would be corresponding issues such as whether the trade secret in question is truly such as might be turned to great commercial advantage or with whether its disclosure would be thoroughly damaging to the claimant's trade. It is not, as I see it, appropriate in a case of personal or individual confidence to look into any corresponding question *at this first stage*. Nor, on

a looking in more detail at the Australian case, does one find that the dictum was intended for any such use.

[**190**] The case did not concern personal or individual confidence or, indeed, in Gleeson CJ's view of the facts, the law of confidence at all (see *Australian Broadcasting Corp v Lenah Game Meats Pty Ltd* (2001) 185 ALR 1 at 17 (para 55). The case concerned the surreptitious filming for television of the respondent's

b brush-tailed possum processing operations, in particular the stunning and killing of such possums at its licensed abattoir. It was not suggested that the operations filmed were secret or that the requirements of confidentiality had been imposed upon those who might see the operations. The fact that the operations were and had to be licensed by a public authority suggested that information about the nature of the operations was not confidential (at 9 (para 25) per Gleeson CJ). It

c was, indeed, conceded (at 10 (para 30)) that information about the nature of the processing was not confidential and not imparted in confidence. The activities filmed were carried out on private property but were not private in any other sense (at 12 (para 35)). It was against that background that the respondent and the Attorney-General of the Commonwealth, intervening, asserted not confidence

d but a very broad kind of unconscionability and privacy (at 10–11, 12 (paras 31 and 38)). But Gleeson CJ was cautious about 'declaring a new tort of the kind for which the respondent contends' (at 13 (para 41)).

[**191**] It was in the context of difficulties in constructing such a tort that the passage cited above appeared (at 13 (para 42)), the difficulties including a reflection by Gleeson CJ on whether notions of privacy deriving from the

e concept of human dignity could, under Australian law, in any event be invoked by a corporation. The last sentence of the citation was concerned with what might be regarded as *private* for a possible law of privacy or unconscionability; it did not purport to be a description of what may be confidential for the purposes of the law of confidence, still less was it addressing the first limb of the three-part

f test in *Coco v AN Clark (Engineers) Ltd* [1969] RPC 41. Moreover the dictum does not even purport to be an exclusive definition of what is private; that matters the disclosure of which would be highly offensive to a reasonable person of ordinary sensibilities may, on that account, be regarded as private does not, of itself, suggest that no other matters can be so regarded.

[**192**] On this basis I do not feel it necessary, whilst considering the law of

g confidence, to subject the unauthorised photographs to any test such as whether a reasonable person of ordinary sensibilities would, in the circumstances of the Douglases, have regarded them or their publication by Hello! as highly offensive. However, had I been required to apply that test, I would not have held the photographs themselves to be highly offensive or offensive at all but that their

h taking and their publication, in all the surrounding circumstances, was likely to offend the Douglases.

[**193**] It is not the case, where all three components of the *Coco* test are satisfied, that substantive relief necessarily follows. That would be to confuse the fundamental nature of the legal right with the question of whether equity affords

j a remedy in the particular case—see *Stephens v Avery* [1988] 2 All ER 477 at 481, [1988] Ch 449 at 454 per Browne-Wilkinson V-C. It is thus, for example, that no confidence 'in iniquity' will be protected, nor does equity extend itself to protect mere trivial tittle-tattle, however confidential it might be. It is also, as it seems to me, that it is at the remedy or relief stage that equity can and should take into account such features as whether, on conducting a balance between confidentiality and freedom of expression, substantive relief (eg an injunction or

damages or equitable compensation beyond the nominal) should be
granted—see Lord Griffiths in *A-G v Guardian Newspapers Ltd (No 2)* [1988] 3
All ER 545 at 649–650, [1990] 1 AC 109 at 268–269 as to the court refusing, in
appropriate cases, to uphold the right to confidence and as to judges being
required to balance the public interest in upholding a right to confidence against
some other public interest, an approach only the more appropriate now that the
Human Rights Act 1998 and the recent authorities to which I have referred
require conflicting issues such as confidentiality on the one hand and freedom of
expression on the other to be weighed and a balance struck. It is at this stage that
the degree of offensiveness of the activity complained of and its propensity to
injure may be put in the scale.

A PROVISIONAL APPLICATION OF THE LAW TO THE FACTS

[194] Before I examine the Hello! defendants' arguments on the law of
confidence I shall attempt to apply the law, as I have described it so far, to the
facts, those I have already found and those I shall describe as I proceed.

[195] I shall first look to see whether it can be right to regard the Douglas
wedding generally, and, in particular, the reception coupled with rights to the
photography of the event, as a commercial entity attracting such aspects of the
law of confidence as can be deployed to protect trade secrets. I have already
noted the Council of Europe Resolution 1165 of 1998 and the recognition in *A v
B (a company)* [2002] 2 All ER 545, [2003] QB 195 (see [186](iii), above) that
information about private lives has become a lucrative commodity for certain
sections of the media. Here it is difficult to deny the title of commodity to that
which the two rival magazines each bid a £1m or more to obtain. Moreover, to
bride and groom, actor and actress, the public representation of their respective
appearances was and is an important part of a successful career and business.
Thus in evidence that was not disputed Miss Zeta-Jones said:

'Both Michael and I are in the business of "name and likeness". Any
photographs of us that are published are important to us, not just personally
but professionally as well. People go to see movies specifically because
either Michael or I are in them and they have expectations, amongst other
things, of the way we will look. Those expectations are created to a
significant degree by the images they see of us in the media. Directors take
into account the public's perception of actors and actresses when casting for
films. The hard reality of the film industry is that preserving my image,
particularly as a woman, is vital to my career. I had a lesson in Britain of the
way in which poor publicity can stunt your career prospects. I have always
been determined not to allow this to happen to me in the United States
where I do virtually all my work. For this reason, there is a clause in every
performance contract I sign giving me full photo approval. This means that
no still photographs of the movie may be published or distributed without
my prior consent. This is not a right that all actors manage to obtain and is
only granted to those with sufficient "star" power. It is a right that I have had
to work hard to obtain and I work hard to enforce and control it. I spend a
great deal of time sifting through the hundreds of photographs that are taken
of me during a film shoot and selecting those which I know will benefit my
career.'

Mr Douglas says:

a   'On a professional level, because my name and likeness is a valuable asset
       to me, it has always been important for me, professionally, to protect my
       name and likeness and to prevent unauthorised use of either and I have taken
       steps to do so.'

b
[196] Given that and given also the lengths to which Miss Zeta-Jones and
Mr Douglas went to ensure the privacy of their wedding, I see it as appropriate to
examine the applicability of the law of confidence on the basis that the claimants
had here a valuable trade asset, a commodity the value of which depended, in
part at least, upon its content at first being kept secret and then of its being made
public in ways controlled by Miss Zeta-Jones and Mr Douglas for the benefit of
them and of the third claimant. I quite see that such an approach may lead to a
c distinction between the circumstances in which equity affords protection to those
who seek to manage their publicity as part of their trade or profession and whose
private life is a valuable commodity and those whose is not but I am untroubled
by that; the law which protects individual confidences and a law of privacy may
protect the latter class and provide no reason to diminish protection for the
d former. So far as concerns OK!, the right to exclusivity of photographic coverage
of the wedding was, in contrast with the nature of the confidence as to the first
and second claimants, even more plainly a right in the nature of a trade secret.

[197] I thus regard photographic representation of the wedding reception as
having had the quality of confidence about it. Of course, the general appearance
of both Mr Douglas and Miss Zeta-Jones was no secret; what they looked like was
e well known to the public. But that does not deny the quality of commercial
confidentiality to what they looked like on the exceptional occasion of their
wedding. As I have said, the very facts that Hello! and OK! competed for
exclusivity as they did and that each was ready to pay so much for it points to the
commercial confidentiality of coverage of the event. The event was private in
f character and the elaborate steps to exclude the uninvited, to include only the
invited, to preclude unauthorised photography, to control the authorised
photography and to have had the claimants' intentions in that regard made clear
all conduce to that conclusion. Such images as were, so to speak, radiated by the
event were imparted to those present, including Mr Thorpe and his camera, in
circumstances importing an obligation of confidence. Everyone there knew that
g was so. In the circumstances as I have held them to be, Mr Thorpe knew (or at
the very least ought to have known) that the claimants reasonably expected the
private character of the event and photographic representation of it to be
protected.

[198] As for the Hello! defendants, their consciences were, in my view,
h tainted; they were not acting in good faith nor by way of fair dealing. Whilst their
position might have been worse had I held that the taking of unauthorised
pictures for use by them had been truly commissioned in advance, even without
that there is in my view enough to afflict their conscience. They knew that OK!
had an exclusive contract; as persons long engaged in the relevant trade, they
j knew what sort of provisions any such contract would include and that it would
include provisions intended to preclude intrusion and unauthorised photography.
Particularly would that be so where, as they knew, a very considerable sum
would have had to have been paid for the exclusive rights which had been
obtained. As to their knowledge of steps taken to protect the secrecy of the event,
their own written text in their issue 639 spoke of 'elaborate security procedures'.
The surrounding facts were such that a duty of confidence should be inferred

from them. The Hello! defendants had indicated to paparazzi in advance that they would pay well for photographs and they knew the reputation of the paparazzi for being able to intrude. The unauthorised pictures themselves plainly indicated they were taken surreptitiously. Yet these defendants firmly kept their eyes shut lest they might see what they undeniably knew would have become apparent to them. Breach of confidence apart, had the Hello! defendants opened their eyes they would have seen that the taking of the photographs which they bought had involved at least a trespass. The fact, as I have held it to be, that they did not in advance and in terms require or authorise on their behalf trespass and surreptitious photography by Thorpe or by any other paparazzo does not disprove the unconscionability, as I hold it to be, under English law, of their publication of the unauthorised photographs in England and Wales.

[199] It cannot be doubted but that the claimants suffered detriment from the publication by the Hello! defendants. Distress was caused to Mr and Mrs Douglas who also had to re-arrange their plans for approval of the authorised photographs. They incurred expenses that would otherwise have been unnecessary. They may also have suffered financial loss if it transpires that syndication receipts that would otherwise have become payable to them were lost upon syndication being either less extensive or less profitable than it would have been had not wedding photographs being published by Hello!.

[200] As for OK!, it not only had costs in the re-arranging of its schedule so as to get out some of the authorised images as soon as possible to mitigate loss but it lost also the kudos of being and being seen to be the only one of the two leading rivals to be able to offer authorised coverage of the 'showbiz wedding of the year'. They may well have sold fewer copies of their magazine and have received less in respect of syndication rights than would have been the case had Hello! not published the unauthorised pictures.

[201] A wedding is an exceptional event to any bride and groom and I do not hold Mr and Mrs Douglas' position as public figures or as persons who had, as to other events, no doubt been tolerant of or even welcoming to publicity, as lessening their right, as any might have, to complain of intrusion at their wedding or of the consequences of that intrusion. It was an intrusion against which elaborate steps had been taken. I have in mind, too, that the steps taken by the Douglases were not taken solely for reward or as 'hype' but were taken in a genuine and reasonable belief that thereby an offensive media frenzy would be avoided.

[202] However, it does not follow from the mere presence of all the elements of a successful case in breach of confidence that substantive relief will follow. The Hello! defendants' right to freedom of expression and provisions of s 12 of the Human Rights Act 1998 here come into play, as I have indicated. Section 12(1) provides:

'This section applies if a court is considering whether to grant any relief which, if granted, might affect the exercise of the Convention right to freedom of expression.'

[203] Section 12(5) makes it clear that 'relief' includes any remedy or order. The term thus includes an award of damages or of equitable compensation. Whilst any award of damages against the Hello! defendants and in favour of the claimants does not, in one sense, affect the Hello! defendants' right to freedom of expression as to the unauthorised photographs because they have already been published, any conclusion of mine that conduces to awards of

a
damages generally can be said to affect the exercise of the convention right to freedom of expression because a possible exposure to a substantial monetary award can deter or inhibit expression almost as completely as would an injunction. I thus proceed on the basis that s 12 applies to the case before me.

[204] Striking a balance between freedom of expression and confidentiality as directed by s 12 and the authorities to which I have referred, I have in mind that
b
no public interest is claimed for the unauthorised pictures, either within the understanding of the phrase in the general law or within the terms of 'the relevant privacy code', the PCC code to which I earlier referred. I have in mind that photographic representation of the wedding (though not by way of the unauthorised photographs) was, in November 2000, about to become available to the public by way of the intended editions of OK! and that the unauthorised
c
photographs, journalistic material but of poor quality, did become available to the public at the same time as the authorised pictures. I do not regard these features as sufficiently persuasive to exclude a grant of relief to the claimants. More significant, in my view, are the terms of the PCC code.

[205] Looking at that code, there was an intrusion into individuals' private
d
lives without consent; that intrusion was known or must be taken to have been known to the Hello! defendants, as was also that it amounted to a failure to respect the Douglases' private and family lives. I have not understood any justification for the intrusion to have been advanced except Hello!'s wish to include as early as practicable some coverage of the event, an event which they were confident their readers would wish it to cover. I do not hold the intrusion
e
to have been justified. The very same principle in the PCC code that provides that the use of long lenses to take pictures of people in private places without their consent was unacceptable must, as I read it, inescapably also make the surreptitious use of short lenses to take pictures of people in private places without their consent at least equally unacceptable. Moreover, on the day and in
f
the surrounding circumstances, the parts of the Plaza Hotel in New York where the wedding ceremony and reception took place were private places in the sense, used by the PCC code, that they were places in respect of which there was a reasonable expectation of privacy. Given that Mr Thorpe, not an invitee, managed to effect an entry and took the trouble to wear a 'tuxedo' in order to hold himself out as if a guest at the wedding, I hold also that the unauthorised
g
photographs were obtained by misrepresentation or subterfuge. The PCC code was broken and the Hello! defendants either knew or, had they not closed their eyes to the truth, would have known and hence must be taken to have known, that that was the case.

[206] So far, then, and without yet having looked at the particular arguments
h
on the law which the Hello! defendants press upon me, I provisionally see the rights to freedom of expression of the Hello! defendants to have been subject to and, in the circumstances, to have been overborne by the rights of all the claimants respectively under the law of confidence.

THE HELLO! DEFENDANTS' DEFENCES UNDER THE LAW OF CONFIDENCE

[207] In response to the claimants' claims under the law of confidence Mr Price and Mr Fernando raise a formidable battery of arguments. They say that the information as to which confidence is claimed is not sufficiently identified and that the protection of equity is to be denied because events of the wedding day could have been made public other than photography by, for example, a verbal description or by drawings. That argument is denied force by

the observations in the Court of Appeal to which I have referred in [186](xiii), above and which I adopt. In any event, where the relevant principles are broad ones operating in conscience I doubt the wisdom of attempting to split hairs.

[208] Next it is said that it was generally understood that the unauthorised pictures, once taken, could be fairly sold, bought and published. That is true in the sense only that there *could* have come about a situation in which someone whose conscience was wholly untainted by notice or knowledge of the circumstances that gave rise to the claim in confidence could have acquired the pictures, a person who would, on that account, have been able to publish them without risk of restraint from, or of having to provide compensation to, the claimants. The point, however, has nothing whatsoever to do with the factual position of the Hello! defendants.

[209] Next it is said that as the unauthorised pictures and Hello!'s authorised ones, as it transpired, on the Court of Appeal's lifting of the injunction, both came out on the same day, any rights of the claimants were thereby lost; I cannot see that the giving or withholding of the protection of equity is to be denied by reason only of a defendant, otherwise liable, having been able to rush into print. It would be extraordinary if, by accelerating his otherwise unconscionable publication, a defendant could say that he had done no wrong.

[210] Next the Hello! defendants say that any confidence that otherwise would or might have existed evaporated upon the contract being made by the Douglases for sale of authorised pictures of the same event. No authority is given for the proposition save for s 12(4) of the Human Rights Act 1998 which, as I read it, does not support the proposition even as to a personal or individual confidence. But, of course, when the claim is regarded as one of commercial confidence, so far from its sale being destructive of confidence, it is a common form whereby the protected information should be turned to account, as, for example, might be the plot of an opera or of a proposed television series (see *Gilbert v Star Newspaper Co Ltd* (1894) 11 TLR 4 and *Fraser v Evans* [1969] 1 All ER 8, [1969] 1 QB 349.

[211] Next it is said that the Hello! defendants bought the information, the unauthorised photographs, rather than taking them themselves. That, of itself, is no defence where the successor in title, so to speak, to the original breaker of confidence has or is taken to have a conscience which is tainted. Were it otherwise, as Lord Griffiths pointed out (see [181], above) the protection of the law of confidence would be entirely worthless. Then these defendants say there was no wrong done by the law of the place, New York, but, firstly, I cannot see how Mr Thorpe can fail to be regarded as other than having been at least a trespasser by the law of New York and it has certainly not been demonstrated to me that he was not. Secondly, so long as the conscience of the publishers of Hello! is tainted, as I have held it to be, I fail to see how Thorpe's innocence of any breach of local law, even had that been proved to me, should assist them.

[212] Then these defendants say, rightly in my view, that their rights under art 10 are engaged. But that is no trump card; a balance has to be struck and, as I have attempted to do by reference to the relevant code, the balance falls against the Hello! defendants' art 10's rights. These defendants also assert, again rightly, that the countervailing rights of confidence can only overcome an art 10(1) right to freedom of expression if they are 'prescribed by law'. In my judgment they are; I am not conscious of having extended but merely of having applied the law.

[213] Next, as I have understood the argument, it is said that a right to confidence that would otherwise have existed is lost upon a claimant himself

a making the information public. I accept that that may in some cases be so but I do not see that the argument denies relief at trial to a claimant on the ground that he had *intended* to make the information public. If it were otherwise then whenever an injunction were to be declined and where, therefore, the defendant was free to and did publish ahead of or at the same time as the claimant, the refusal of the injunction would, in effect, be a denial of all relief. Damages could

b never be an adequate remedy, yet here the Court of Appeal has held that they can be.

[214] Then these defendants say that the information contained in the unauthorised pictures was so generally available as that it could not be regarded as confidential. That, in my view, flies in the face of the facts as to the considerable lengths gone to in order to keep the appearance of the dress and the

c cake and of the bride and groom on the day all secret, to keep the event to invitees to the exclusion of others and to ensure that only approved photographs were to be able to be both taken and published.

[215] Next it is said that what the claimants are truly claiming is a non-existent intellectual property right corresponding to copyright in the visual aspect of the

d wedding. That the rights claimed by the claimants are in some respects capable of being likened to or to overlap with a claim in copyright does not, in my judgment, deny the claims validity. There are crucial differences, of which the fact that the claim in confidence operates by reference to the conscience of the defendant is perhaps the most significant. That there may be an overlap does not disable a claimant from the ability to assert the separate right, not in copyright,

e which the claimants here assert.

[216] A recurring theme on the part of these defendants is that what the Douglases, in particular, were seeking was not privacy or confidentiality but control. They wanted to be sure that the only visual representations of the wedding that were to be available to the media were such as had been approved

f by them. In that way control over the media would be exercised. That, though, overlooks that control is not an improper objective of the law of confidence; that certain information should not be published or that copies of certain documents should be destroyed or returned or that abuse of a trade secret should be barred to a person are all both familiar aspects of the law of confidentiality and aspects of control. I do not see the fact that control was sought to be exercised as of itself

g denying the attempt the characteristics of an application of the law of confidence; it is, rather another factor in the overall balance between confidence and freedom of expression.

[217] Then it is said that by intending to make public *some* visual aspects of the wedding (namely photographs selected by them) the Douglases lost the right to

h claim in confidence as to *any* such representations (and therefore lost the right to complain of the unauthorised pictures). But I cannot see that that should follow, especially if one regards the confidence here as a commercial one. It is common, with respect to commercial confidences, that turning them to account involves making them public; the fact that there is an intention to make them public does

j not deny that rights of confidence can exist with respect to them. Moreover, though these may not be complete analogies, it would be absurd if, for example, a playwright, intending his play later to be performed in public, upon his disclosing to a prospective supporter in confidence only that his play was about, say, a Prince of Denmark or if a television screen-writer, intending his series to be put on television, upon his disclosure only that his idea was for a series about three girls sharing a flat in Kensington, should in either case thereby lose rights to the confidentiality of the play or of the idea for a series. Mr Tugendhat, as an example showing that disclosure to the public of a chosen part can still leave rights in confidence in an unpublicised remainder, points to the Royal Family in the nineteenth century having permitted to be published engravings of an 1841 Landseer oil. The painting showed Her Majesty Queen Victoria, HRH Prince Albert, their eldest daughter, the Princess Royal, Victoria, their dogs and dead game and other birds in the green drawing room at Windsor. Mr Tugendhat asks rhetorically whether it could possibly be that by permitting that family scene to be made public the Royal Family thereby lost such rights as the law of confidence otherwise would have conferred on them to restrain publication of *other* representations of their private and family life. I see the force of the example. Indeed, if anything, the claimants here are in a better position because at the very point at which the Hello! defendants intended to publish, unless enjoined, the claimants had allowed the publication of nothing but one close-up of the bride and groom showing neither the bride's dress nor the wedding cake.

[218] Then Mr Price and Mr Fernando referred me to *Pollard v Photographic Co* (1888) 40 Ch D 345. Mrs Pollard had contracted with the defendant photographic company for photographs to be taken of herself for her own purposes. She found that the defendant was using the photograph for quite different purposes. The case was argued on the footing that, she having contracted for the photograph to be taken for one purpose, there was an implied term that it should not be used for any other. North J held that such an implied term did exist. There was no citation of authorities upon or any examination of, the law of confidence. Before me counsel argued that publication of a photograph of Mrs Pollard taken by a paparazzo outside the photographic company's premises would not have been a breach of confidence. That, as it seems to me, is very likely but it is nothing to do with this case. If the portrait photograph of Mrs Pollard had been taken for publication by her and was published then, say these defendants, there could, *apart from copyright and contract*, be no cause of action against the photographer were he separately to publish the photograph. That example supposes that the unauthorised publication took place after the authorised one. That is not the case before me.

[219] Then these defendants comment on *Shelley Films Ltd v Rex Features Ltd* [1994] EMLR 134 saying that it was important in that case to the producers' marketing and commercial strategy that the appearance of the latex Frankenstein creature mask in that case was kept secret pending the release of the film in which the mask was to be worn. I do not see that the comment assists these defendants; it was similarly important to the marketing and commercial strategy of all the claimants that the appearance of the bride, groom, wedding cake and other features of the wedding should be kept secret pending release of the approved photographs. In the *Shelley Films* case Mr M E Mann QC said (at 151):

> 'I do not ignore, of course, that there will come a time, possibly before the action comes on for trial, which I am told by Counsel I should assume it will, when Shelley's right to the protection it now seeks will be lost because Shelley will by then have released its confidential information to the public in a manner of its own choosing.'

[220] There is nothing about that passage which suggests that a claimant loses any of his remedies when his release to the public is not earlier than that, by the defendant, of which he complains.

a
[221] Next these defendants are critical of the decision in *Creation Records Ltd v News Group Newspapers Ltd* [1997] EMLR 444 but the extensive citation from it by Brooke LJ in the Court of Appeal hearing in *Douglas v Hello! Ltd* [2001] 2 All ER 289, [2001] QB 967 contains no criticism of the case and I do not accept that the case contains any relevant confusion between the scene itself which the observer saw and a photographic record of it. The law of confidence may there have been
b
used to create an exclusive right to photography but I do not understand the Court of Appeal to have disapproved of that.

[222] Then these defendants rely upon *Sports & General Press Agency Ltd v Our Dogs Publishing Co Ltd* [1917] KB 125. The plaintiff there had sold the press photographic rights to a dog show. An independent photographer took pictures and sold them to the defendant, who published them. The plaintiff sought to
c
restrain further publication. An injunction was refused on the ground that the dog show organisers and the plaintiff could, by contract, have laid down, but had failed to lay down, conditions of entry or as to banning the use of unauthorised cameras. The authority does not assist in a case where (as before me) conditions of entry (albeit not by contract) were laid down and where there had been a
d
well-understood ban on cameras. No questions as to confidentiality were argued.

[223] These defendants then referred to *Times Newspapers Ltd v MGN Ltd* [1993] EMLR 443. Bingham MR complained that the court would have welcomed, but was denied, the opportunity of considering the plaintiffs' application for an injunction at greater length. Another difficulty in the case was that the plaintiffs (oddly, in my view) were not able satisfactorily to frame an
e
injunction that did not go too far. However, Bingham MR did say that the unauthorised extracts from Lady Thatcher's memoirs, acquired by the defendant 'by means that are unknown' and parts of which the defendant had already published, were '[c]ertainly not information which is confidential in a sense that the public is not intended to learn of it, because this is material which is intended
f
to be published, no doubt, as widely as an efficient publisher can procure'.

[224] I respectfully doubt whether, even as to a wholly personal or individual confidence, an intention to publish should of itself invariably deny a claimant relief but it cannot sensibly deny relief in the case of a commercial secret. An inventor (to return to a point I have touched upon) might, for example, confide to a prospective manufacturer secret details of his invention which he hoped soon
g
to make public by way of an application for a patent. So also in the case of the plot of a comic opera (see *Gilbert v Star Newspaper Co Ltd* (1894) 11 TLR 4), or the idea for a television series (see *Fraser v Thames Television Ltd* [1983] 2 All ER 101, [1984] QB 44). In such cases it would be absurd, as I have already mentioned, if an intention to make the subject matter of the confidence public should destroy
h
confidentiality. It is to be noted, too, that in considering whether 'to take the extreme step of restraining publication of material which a newspaper wishes to publish', the Court of Appeal in 1993 did not then have the guidance of s 12(4) of the Human Rights Act 1998 and its reference to 'any relevant privacy code'. Had that been a relevant consideration in 1993 and had the circumstances of the
j
defendants' acquisition of the material accordingly been investigated, questions might well, one would think, have arisen as to whether the material had been acquired through misrepresentation, subterfuge or worse. I do not regard the *Times Newspapers* case as authoritative in the post-Human Rights Act 1998 age.

[225] Then these defendants argue that *Woodward v Hutchins* [1977] 2 All ER 751, [1977] 1 WLR 760 illustrates that a claimant who has deliberately sought publicity loses the right to insist upon confidentiality in respect of publicity. That,

as it seems to me, goes too far and I do not see the case as establishing that proposition; what the case does illustrate is that where a claimant has fostered an image which is not a true one, there can be a public interest in correcting it (see also *Campbell v Mirror Group Newspapers Ltd* [2003] 1 All ER 224, [2003] QB 633 (where the claimant could be described as a role model). The public, said Lord Denning MR, should not be misled ([1977] 2 All ER 751 at 754, [1977] 1 WLR 760 at 764). The defendant's case in *Woodward*'s case was that the image which the plaintiffs had created was one of fallacies and half-truths ([1977] 2 All ER 751 at 756, [1977] 1 WLR 760 at 765 per Bridge LJ). No such allegation is made against Mr and Mrs Douglas, nor is it even said that the unauthorised photographs were intended to correct a false image which the authorised ones were about to create. To hold that those who have sought *any* publicity lose all protection would be to repeal art 8's application to very many of those who are likely most to need it. I would accept that a claimant who has himself publicised a certain area of his private life (for example his sexual proclivities and activity) might well lose the protection otherwise available to him *in that area* or, possibly, even more generally, but I have not seen how that argument could serve to diminish the protection to be afforded to the unique event, not 'hyped' by them, of the Douglas wedding.

[226] I hope I have now dealt with at least the principal submissions of the Hello! defendants on the English law as to confidence. For the reasons I have given their arguments do not deflect me from the view I expressed earlier.

CONCLUSIONS AS TO CONFIDENCE

[227] In my judgment, and first regarding the claimants' case as one of either commercial confidence or of a hybrid kind in which, by reason of it having become a commodity, elements that would otherwise have been merely private became commercial, I find the Hello! defendants to have acted unconscionably and that, by reason of breach of confidence, they are liable to all three claimants to the extent of the detriment which was thereby caused to the claimants respectively.

[228] Were I to be wrong in having regarded the first and second claimants' positions as akin to that of holders of a trade secret and had the confidence in question therefore to be regarded as wholly personal and individual, then, as I see it, the defence against them (but only them) that they intended by sale to release photographs of the event to the public, albeit ones selected by them, has greater force. Even so, I have difficulties. I do not understand Mr Price to say that there would have been no right under the law of confidence and in turn no right to injunctive or other relief if the bride and groom, having taken steps to keep the event private by way of security as they did, then made no agreement with any magazine and chose to allow no photographs at all to be published. If in such a case equity would have protected them, why should a sale of the photographic rights under which publication of photographs of the event were *intended* to be published itself deny that protection ahead of their actual publication? The Court of Appeal knew, of course, that the Douglases had sold exclusive photographic coverage of the wedding to OK! with the knowledge that authorised photographs would thus be published but no member of the court held that the Douglases thereby lost *all* rights and had destroyed their whole causes of action. Instead, at most, the court held that they had thereby confined their relief under their causes of action to damages. Even in a contest between, on the one hand, a claim to personal confidence weakened by sale and the intention to publish, and, on the

a other, the Hello! defendants' rights to freedom of expression, I would still have been affected by the circumstances I have described, including Hello!'s breach of the PCC code. I would have come to the same decision as that given in [227], above. I fail to see why the fact that publication of authorised photographs was *intended* makes it any less unconscionable on the part of the Hello! defendants to seek, as they did, to anticipate that publication.

b
PRIVACY

[229] It is notorious that, as our law was before the Human Rights Act 1998, there was no effective law of privacy; there was nothing to fill such gaps as might exist when neither the law of confidence nor any other law protected a claimant. That other jurisdictions, in general terms no less free or democratic than this one,

c have apparently workable laws of privacy which neither oppress nor stifle is at least arguable; Mr Tugendhat refers me to examples in Germany, Canada and France. Senor Enrich in his clear and impressive evidence as to Spanish law showed how such a law operates in Spain. That a strong case can be made, by way of the convention and the Human Rights Act 1998 coupled with decisions of

d the European Court of Human Rights, that in some respects we do now have a law of privacy is apparent from the judgment of Sedley LJ in *Douglas v Hello! Ltd* [2001] 2 All ER 289, [2001] QB 967. I am invited to hold that there is an existing law of privacy under which the first and second claimants are entitled to relief. I decline that invitation for five reasons. (i) Whilst Sedley LJ's judgment provides a powerful case for the existence, already, of a law of privacy, that another view

e is tenable can be seen from the judgments in *Wainwright v Home Office* [2001] EWCA Civ 2081, [2003] 3 All ER 943, [2002] QB 1334, judgments delivered on 20 December 2001, after *Douglas'* case. There the events complained of occurred before the Human Rights Act 1998 came into effect and were such that no case in confidence could be made. The hearing before the judge below and, of course,

f in the Court of Appeal, was after the Human Rights Act 1998 had come into force. The Court of Appeal held there had been no general law of privacy before the Human Rights Act 1998 and that the Act had had no retrospective effect. Thus even had the court held either that there had been or that there had not been a law of privacy created by the Human Rights Act 1998, it could only have been obiter. None the less there was reference made to the decision in *Douglas'* case.

g Lord Woolf CJ, beyond describing Sedley LJ's judgment as 'most instructive' ([2003] 3 All ER 943 at [20]) did nothing further to espouse it. Mummery LJ (at [60]), looking to the future, foresaw difficulties in the judicial development of a comprehensive or 'blockbuster' tort and Buxton LJ set out a strong case from [97] on as to the difficulties in the way of creating any such broad tort. (ii) Sedley LJ's

h case for a general tort depends, on my reading of his judgment, on our law otherwise being so inadequate in relation to the protection and enforcement of individual rights to private and family life as to fall short of compliance with the convention, the Human Rights Act 1998 and the requirements of decisions of European Court of Human Rights. Even accepting the attractive argument so

j raised, it does not point to any need for the creation of new law in areas in which (for example, by way of reference to the law of confidence) protection and enforcement are already not only available in theory but in practice even in the particular case. As I have held Mr and Mrs Douglas to have been protected by the law of confidence, no relevant hole exists in English law such as, on the facts of the case before me, a due respect for the convention requires should be filled. (iii) So broad is the subject of privacy and such are the ramifications of any

free-standing law in the area that the subject is better left to Parliament which
can, of course, consult interests far more widely than can be taken into account
in the course of ordinary inter partes litigation. A judge should therefore be chary
of doing that which is better done by Parliament. That Parliament has failed so
far to grasp the nettle does not prove that it will not have to be grasped in the
future. The recent judgment in *Peck v UK* (2003) 13 BHRC 669 in the European
Court of Human Rights, given on 28 January 2003, shows that in circumstances
where the law of confidence did not operate our domestic law has already been
held to be inadequate. That inadequacy will have to be made good and if
Parliament does not step in then the courts will be obliged to. Further
development by the courts may merely be awaiting the first post-Human Rights
Act 1998 case where neither the law of confidence nor any other domestic law
protects an individual who deserves protection. A glance at a crystal ball of, so to
speak, only a low wattage suggests that if Parliament does not act soon the less
satisfactory course, of the courts creating the law bit by bit at the expense of
litigants and with inevitable delays and uncertainty, will be thrust upon the
judiciary. But that will only happen when a case arises in which the existing law
of confidence gives no or inadequate protection; this case now before me is not
such a case and there is therefore no need for me to attempt to construct a law of
privacy and, that being so, it would be wrong of me to attempt to do so. (iv) I
have in mind also the judgment of the court delivered by Lord Woolf in *A v B (a
company)* [2002] 2 All ER 545, [2003] QB 195 where, amongst the guidelines laid
down, one finds (at [11](vi)):

'It is most unlikely that any purpose will be served by a judge seeking to
decide whether there exists a new cause of action in tort which protects
privacy. In the great majority of situations, if not all situations, where the
protection of privacy is justified, relating to events after the [Human Rights
Act 1998] came into force, an action for breach of confidence now will,
where this is appropriate, provide the necessary protection.'

(v) Finally, it has not been suggested that, even were there to be a law of privacy,
the Douglases would be able to make any recovery greater than that which is
open to them under the law of confidence as I have held it to be. For those
reasons I say nothing further as to any law of privacy.

THE DATA PROTECTION ACT 1998

[230] There is a full analysis of the relevant provisions of the Data Protection
Act 1998 in *Campbell v Mirror Group Newspapers Ltd* [2003] 1 All ER 224 at
[72]–[138], which, fortunately, make an understanding of the Act easier than do
the unvarnished provisions of the Act itself. At the risk of my construing the
authority rather than the Act, I find, after reading *Campbell*'s case, that all three
Hello! defendants can be taken to be a data controller, that the unauthorised
pictures represent personal data and that publication of them in England is to be
treated as part of the operations covered by the requirements of the Data
Protection Act 1998. That is because when a data controller is responsible for the
publication of hard copies that reproduce data that has previously been processed
by means of equipment operated automatically, the publication forms part of the
process and falls within the scope of the Act. The hard copies here were, of
course, the copies of Hello! magazine (see *Campbell*'s case (at [75]–[76], [78], [107])
and the sections of the Data Protection Act 1998 there referred).

a [231] That there had been such processing by equipment operating automatically appears because such processes were used in the transmission by ISDN line from California to London, in the calling up of the pictures on to a screen in London by Sue Neal, in her transmission of them to Madrid by ISDN line, in the taking out from unauthorised photographs of the defects that one or more of the earlier processes had introduced into them, in the transmission from

b Hola's office in Madrid to the printers and in the processes used in the course of preparation for and in the course of printing. I am told there was also publication of the unauthorised photographs on a Hello! website. The exemption given in respect of the processing of personal data for journalistic purposes, the exemption which the Court of Appeal held to apply in *Campbell*'s case, does not apply in the case before me because it depends, inter alia, on the data controller reasonably

c believing that publication would be in the public interest. I have had no credible evidence as to such a belief nor, given the nature of the unauthorised photographs, the manner of their obtaining and that the Hello! defendants well knew that authorised photographs were shortly to be published by OK!, do I see any room for any conclusion that publication could reasonably be so regarded.

d That the public would be interested is not to be confused with there being a public interest.

[232] Lest the s 32 exemption should not be available to his clients, Mr Fernando, who alone addressed argument for the Hello! defendants under the Data Protection Act 1998, argued also that they could claim the exemption conferred by the transitional provisions in Sch 8 to the Act. The only relevant

e kind of exemption is that of Sch 8, Pt II relating to the period between the commencement of the schedule and 24 October 2001—defined as 'the first transitional period'. During that period, which began on 24 October 1998, 'eligible automated data' were made exempt from certain provisions—Sch 8, para 13(1). But to be eligible automated data, the data has first to be 'eligible

f data'—Sch 8, para 1(2). And, where the data is personal data (such as the unauthorised photographs) the data will only be eligible at any time 'if, and to the extent that, they are at that time subject to processing which was already under way immediately before 24th October 1998' (see Sch 8, para 1(1)).

[233] That seems to require an examination of whether, when the proceedings began or now ('at that time') the unauthorised pictures were subject

g to 'processing which was already under way immediately before 24th October 1998'. As the unauthorised photographs were not taken until November 2000, that appears to be impossible. Mr Fernando alternatively says that if any photographs of Mr Douglas and Miss Zeta-Jones were processed by the Hello! defendants before 24 October 1998 then, although that processing was of

h different photographs, that suffices. But 'already under way' seems to suggest a continuous process from 24 October 1998 as would be the case where, for example, a running bank account was processed both before and after that date. I fail to see how it assists that *other* photographs than the unauthorised photographs but relating to Mr Douglas or Miss Zeta-Jones were processed

j before that date; photographs even of the same subjects are quite separate items of personal data in a way that, say, operations on a running bank account, where the balance at any time is dependent upon the cumulative effect of earlier transactions, are not.

[234] Mr Fernando then says that it is enough that some processing of personal data in the form of photographs (even not of Mr Douglas or Miss Zeta-Jones at all) has continuously been a feature of the work of the Hello!

defendants since 24 October 1998. That seems to prove too much; had there been but one photograph by way of personal information of anyone in process before 24 October 1998, the transitional provision would, if this argument is right, exempt the, say, 5,000 photographs by way of personal data processed after that date to the extent of the exemption, an exemption which would be so wide as to be surprising and such as, had it been attended at all, would have been likely to have been spelled out in terms much clearer than one finds in the difficult terms of Sch 8, para 1(1). I do not find the Hello! defendants to be able to claim any of the exemptions by way of transitional relief offered by Sch 8 to the Act.

[235] That being so the Hello! defendants as data controllers were, without exemption, under a duty to comply with the data protection principles as to the unauthorised photographs (see s 4(4) and (1)). Their processing therefore had to be done 'fairly and lawfully' and in such a way that at least one of the conditions in Sch 2 was met (see Sch 1, Pt I, para 1(a)).

[236] As for the fairness of the processing, regard has to be had as to how the data were obtained (see Sch 1, Pt II, para 1(1)). Given the circumstances, as I have held them to be, in which the unauthorised photographs were obtained, that regard points to the processing (in particular the publication) as having not been fair. Nor are the other prerequisites of fair processing as set out in Sch 1, Pt II met.

[237] As for Sch 2, concerned with the processing of personal data, no consent to the processing (including publication) of the unauthorised photographs was given by 'the data subjects'—Mr and Mrs Douglas—Sch 2, para 1. The processing was not necessary for any of the purposes of Sch 2, paras 2–5 inclusive. As for para 6, it provides:

'(1) The processing is necessary for the purposes of legitimate interests pursued by the data controller ... except where the processing is unwarranted in any particular case by reason of prejudice to the rights and freedoms or legitimate interests of the data subject.'

[238] The Hello! defendants did, in my view, have a relevant legitimate interest—the publication of their magazine to include coverage of the Douglas wedding—but para 6 denies legitimacy to the processing to that end if it is unwarranted by reason of prejudice to the rights and legitimate interests of the data subjects. The provision is not, it seems, one that requires some general balance between freedom of expression and rights to privacy or confidence; where there is a real public interest in relation to the material in issue then in the case of the press such a general approach will have been considered under s 32. Here (in the events which I have held occurred) the question is more simply whether the publication is unwarranted by reason of the prejudice to Mr and Mrs Douglas' legal rights. Paragraph 6 does not provide, as it so easily could have done, how serious has to be the prejudice before the processing becomes unwarranted and in point of language any prejudice beyond the trivial would seem to suffice. Here the prejudice to each of Mr and Mrs Douglas by reason of the publication was in my judgment above the trivial and indeed was substantial. I therefore do not see para 6 as assisting the Hello! defendants. Nor do I see that the fact that the Douglases had by contract authorised processing by OK! as working some general waiver such that anyone else, including Hello!, might process by way of publication photographs of the wedding on the footing that the Douglases' rights had evaporated.

a [239] I thus see no defence to Mr and Mrs Douglas' claims, as individuals, to compensation under s 13(1) of the Act; had their consents to the publication of the unauthorised photographs been asked for, as the Act requires, it would, I am confident, have been refused. But can it be said that such damage or distress as was suffered was 'by reason of any contravention by a data controller' of any of the requirements of this Act. If the obligations under the Act had been performed

b would it truly have made any difference? As it seems to me, it is only if deployment by Mr and Mrs Douglas of the data protection argument would have caused the Hello! defendants, on consent being refused to them, to elect not to publish the unauthorised pictures or if such an argument would have caused the Court of Appeal to leave Hunt J's injunction in place, that it could reasonably be said that the damage and distress occasioned to the Douglases was *by reason of a*

c *contravention* of the Act—s 13. The data processing argument was not in fact laid before the Court of Appeal but, in what is inevitably a speculative exercise, my reading of what the situation would have been is that the Hello! defendants would have elected to go ahead and publish and that the Court of Appeal would still have held that damages would be a sufficient remedy. Thus, although I hold

d there to have been a breach of the requirements of the Data Protection Act 1998, I do not see it as adding a separate route to recovery for damage or distress beyond a nominal award, which I shall make.

INTERFERENCE WITH BUSINESS; BREACH OF CONFIDENCE AND OF THE DATA PROTECTION ACT 1998

e [240] If I have been right in seeing OK! to be a person entitled to invoke the law of confidence against the Hello! defendants then this claim and many of the others I shall deal with add nothing. However, lest I am wrong, I will deal with further causes of action.

[241] It cannot be said that Mr and Mrs Douglas are in breach of their contract with OK!. The fact that Mr Thorpe eluded or deceived the security at the

f wedding does not suggest, still less prove, that the Douglases had failed, within cl 16 of their contract (see [54], above) to take all *reasonable* means to provide such security as was necessary to ensure the exclusion of unauthorised media. The presence of the word 'reasonable' indicates the obligation was not absolute, as also does the obligation not to eliminate but to '*minimise*' the risk of unauthorised

g photography. Under cl 6 it was only 'best efforts' that were required to be used. Hence the Hello! defendants' purchase and publication of the unauthorised photographs did not bring about any breach by the Douglases of their contract, nor did it even impede its performance. Indeed, as the security to be provided was in relation to a wedding on 18 November, as the purchase of the unauthorised photographs was on 19 November and as their publication by

h Hello! was on 24 November, the timing alone suggests that that was so.

[242] In a passage in *RCA Corp v Pollard* [1982] 3 All ER 771, [1983] Ch 135, adopted by Hobhouse J in *Rickless v United Artists Corp* [1987] 1 All ER 679, [1988] QB 450 and [1986] FSR 502, Slade LJ said ([1982] 3 All ER 771 at 784, [1983] Ch 135 at 156):

j
'... as I understand the facts of all these cases where liability has been established under this particular head of tort, there has been an interference or attempt to interfere with the *performance* by a third party of his contractual obligations. There is nothing in *this* line of authority which I have been able to discover which suggests that A may be liable to B under this head of tort merely because A does an act (even an illegal act) which he knows is likely to

render less valuable certain contractual rights of B as against C, without
actually interfering with the performance by C of the contractual obligations   *a*
owed by him to B.'

In that case the defendant, Pollard, was a 'bootlegger' and, as such, he did not
interfere with the performance of the artists' contracts with the plaintiff recording
company even though he made the latter's rights under their exclusive contract   *b*
less valuable; so also, as it seems to me, Hello! did not interfere with OK!'s
contract with the Douglases, although it may be argued that what Hello! did
rendered OK!'s rights under the contract less valuable than otherwise they would
have been.

[243] That being so, OK! can succeed under this tort only if a further
component is present, the one relevant for immediate consideration being   *c*
whether there was an intent to injure by unlawful means.

[244] Lord Wedderburn's chapter on economic torts in *Clerk & Lindsell on
Torts* (18th edn, 2000) describes a tort 'which consists in one person using
unlawful means with the object of and effect of causing damage to another'. The
role of intent in the tort is not always described in the same terms in the   *d*
authorities—compare *Merkur Island Shipping Corp v Laughton* [1983] 2 All ER 189
at 196–197, [1983] 2 AC 570 at 609—but it is appropriate for me to accept the *Clerk
& Lindsell* formulation as it is by reference to that description that the claimants
make their claim and that is the formulation which the defendants have been
required to answer.

[245] As for the relevant intent of the Hello! defendants, in practical terms it is   *e*
either to be found in Senor Sanchez Junco or it does not exist. As to his intent,
his written evidence said:

> 'I want to state categorically that there was never an intention to cause
> damage to any of the claimants—to the first two claimants because we have
> always treated them in Hello! with deference and sympathy, in accordance   *f*
> with the magazine style. In our 60-year history we have never tried to
> damage anyone. Therefore, we would not want to do it to people whom we
> have always treated fairly and objectively in our reports portraying them in
> the best possible light. With respect to OK! we took it for granted that,
> without a doubt, they would have a great editorial success, as they had a   *g*
> great exclusive and consequently, the magazine would be sold under
> excellent conditions as was the case. Our main purpose was to inform our
> readers about an event which had been publicised all over the media for
> weeks before the wedding, which shows that this wedding was of interest for
> the United Kingdom. We did not wish to disappoint our readers. It was   *h*
> never our aim or intention to damage the third claimant, our prime
> motivation was only to give our readers information on the wedding of two
> celebrities, about whom, without doubt, our readers expected to read in
> Hello!. Other consideration was to defend the interests of our magazine and
> keep our place in the market. There was little or no monetary incentive in
> publishing these photographs because the increase in sales was not likely to   *j*
> compensate the costs incurred in purchasing the photographs, changing the
> edition and airlifting a proportion of the copies from Spain into the United
> Kingdom. However, this is something that every publisher must be
> prepared to do from time to time and it is a matter of professional pride and
> an investment in the goodwill of the publication's readership.'

[246] In his oral evidence Senor Sanchez Junco disavowed having acted in revenge against the Douglases for his not getting the exclusive he so wished; rather he wanted, despite losing the exclusive, to publish an edition that would interest his readers, the event being one which had captured the imagination of the public. His act, he said, was not of revenge but of salvage. He denied having the intention of spoiling OK!'s sales adding: '... my motive was never to spoil the exclusive of OK!. I repeat, I wanted to defend as far as I could my publication ...' Mr Tugendhat put this to him:

> 'What I am suggesting to you is that in all of this you were driven by your anger and you were intending to do as much damages as you could both to the Douglases and to the publishers of OK!'

Senor Sanchez Junco:

> 'No. My priority was to save my publication after having, in the light of a very important big loss, and that is that of the exclusive, and I didn't think of the possible damage that I could inflict on OK! or the Douglases because the photographs, I never thought that these photographs could be considered to damaging for the Douglases and that is because photographs published in that way were unlikely to damage the authorised exclusive.'

[247] Then, referring to an argument which I hold to be not unreasonable, namely that poor photographs in one of the rival magazines could in fact increase the sales of the other which covered the event in a better way, he added, of such a case:

> 'In some cases it encourages it. It has happened to me many times and I've never considered it to be that it was a damage which—certainly not a serious one. This supposed damage which I was supposed to have wanted to inflict on OK! wasn't even, in my opinion, clear damage. Maybe it could even help out its exclusive. In any event, I sold a few more, and I believe that OK! sold its exclusive very well.'

Ms Koumi, too, gave evidence that poor photographs of an event in one of the rival magazines could increase the sales of the rival that has better ones (though I am not to be taken to be holding that was in fact the case here).

[248] Mr Luke, in close contact with Senor Sanchez Junco in Madrid was asked the question: 'How common, to your recollection, are spoilers by Hello! of OK! exclusives?' Mr Luke:

> 'It is a bit of a misnomer. I would not call it a spoiler because in the case of ... If we go back to the Zeta-Jones wedding, it was the event of the year. It is like one had to cover the outbreak of war because—or would not cover it because Churchill had given his exclusive interview to the Express. We had to cover it in some way. I think "spoiler" is a bit of a misnomer. It is something we have to cover, and if photographs become available you publish them. This is not an attack on your competition, this is because our readers want to know about these events so you go ahead and publish them. If those photographs are made available by an orang utan with a polaroid, well you publish them.'

[249] I have not found Senor Sanchez Junco or Mr Luke to be reliable as witnesses but I do accept the evidence they gave on this subject. Whilst I recognise that for a defendant to act out of self-interest does not, of itself, disprove that he had no intent to injure another, here I find on the evidence that there was no intent to injure by unlawful means because there was no intent to injure at all. Had I found such intent in the Hello! defendants I would have gone on to have found the intent to be to injure by the unlawful means of publishing in breach of obligation of confidence owed to all claimants and by way of contravention of the Data Protection Act 1998.

[250] As for the interest of the Marquesa and her company, Neneta Overseas Ltd, the latter had no intent other than through her. She was very loyal to Senor Sanchez Junco and was annoyed that, through no fault of hers, Hello! had failed to get an exclusive of the wedding as to which she had played only a limited role, namely in suggesting the possibility of paparazzi photographers to Senor Sanchez Junco and in identifying Mr Ramey to him. She had been careful not to compromise anyone in that it was not paparazzi photographs *inside* the wedding to which she had referred. As for the Marquesa's letter and its part in the lifting of the injunction, she did not regard the unauthorised photographs (such bad photographs, in her view) as being capable of spoiling OK!'s far better coverage. She was willing to accept that the publication of the unauthorised pictures by Hello! was a spoiling operation by Hello! aimed at OK! but that answer, without more, did not prove any such intent in her. The Marquesa's letter was in any case brought about by a combination of a wish to ingratiate herself with Senor Sanchez Junco, a wish to preserve her prospects of further employment by Hello! and a response to severe pressure, as she took it to be, from Senor Riera and, on his behalf, from Senora Elisa. I do not find the presence in her, either, of the necessary component, an intention to injure OK!.

[251] The claimants' case under this heading therefore fails.

INTERFERENCE WITH BUSINESS; ABUSE OF PROCESS

[252] Here the unlawful means asserted consist of the deployment of a false case in the Court of Appeal in order to procure the lifting of the injunction.

[253] I refer back to the *Clerk & Lindsell* formulation which requires there not only to be the object but the *effect* of causing damage to another if this tort is to be proven.

[254] That the injunction was lifted cannot be doubted but was its lifting the effect of the falsity of the case put forwarded by Hello! Ltd, then the only defendant? Despite such strength as was conferred upon the defendant's case in the Court of Appeal by Senor Sanchez Junco's statement, Miss Cartwright's second witness statement (in the form in which the court saw it) and the Marquesa's letter, the Court of Appeal held that some or all of the claimants had a sound case in breach of confidence or privacy (see [2001] 2 All ER 289 at 314 and 320, 324, [2001] QB 967 at 995 and 1001, 1005 (paras 96 and 125, 137) per Brooke and Sedley LJJ respectively), but the court went on to lift the injunction chiefly, as it seems to me, on the grounds that damages would be a sufficient remedy for OK! but an insufficient one for Hello! (see [2001] 2 All ER 289 at 314–315, 325, 331, [2001] QB 967 at 995–996, 1006, 1013 (paras 96, 97, 99, 142, 171) per Brooke, Sedley and Keene LJJ respectively). In the circumstances it is difficult to suppose that the Court of Appeal would have held other than they did as to the respective adequacy and inadequacy of damages as a remedy had the falsity of the defendant's case been seen for what it was. There is, in my view, no causal link between the falsity and the lifting of the injunction; the effect cannot be attributed to the alleged cause. On this ground this head of claim fails.

CONSPIRACY OF ALL OR FIVE OF THE DEFENDANTS TO INJURE THE CLAIMANTS BY
UNLAWFUL MEANS

a

[**255**] There are, as it would seem from the re-re-amended particulars of claim,
a number of conspiracies alleged in this regard.   One asserts the necessary
combination as being of the Hello! defendants, the Marquesa, her company
Neneta Overseas Ltd and Mr Ramey (para 32 of the re-re-amended particulars of
claim). There is no alternative plea that some only of those six conspired together

b

and the target of this alleged conspiracy consists of all three claimants without
any alternative plea that some only might have been the intended target.
However the pleading is not entirely clear as in para 32 the conspiracy is of all
defendants, with the unlawful acts '(as set out in paragraph 33 below)', whereas
para 33 alleges a conspiracy only of the Hello! defendants. In another conspiracy

c

of this kind (para 32A) the combination alleged is of all defendants except
Mr Ramey. Again there is no alternate plea as to a combination of only some of
the five defendants and again the target is and is only all claimants. I have already
set out some findings as to the intentions of the alleged conspirators.

[**256**] As to the combination alleged to include Mr Ramey, he must have

d

known of Thorpe's trespass and that the unauthorised photographs had been
taken deliberately and surreptitiously and in breach of rules sought to be imposed
upon guests and staff and that they had been taken despite stringent security
arrangements intended to make unauthorised photographs impossible. I can
assume that he knew that OK! had obtained an 'exclusive' for the wedding.
However, there is nothing before me to suggest any relevant intent on his part

e

except, by inference, that he should gain as much financial reward as possible for
the unauthorised photographs and, perhaps also, further to bolster his reputation
as the paparazzo who could overcome any obstacles. Had he reflected on the
matter (and I have no evidence to suggest that he did) he would have seen that
his activity would be likely to distress the Douglases and reduce the fruits gained

f

by OK! from its exclusive contract but his concern, as I see it, was to sell to the
highest bidder. The fact that the unauthorised photographs had found their way
to a Dutch agency suggests that it was not only to Hello! that the unauthorised
photographs were offered. He could have expected Hello! to be the highest
bidder but I am unable to hold him to have been part of any concert to injure the
Douglases or OK! or all three of the claimants.

g

[**257**] As for a conspiracy said to involve all defendants except Mr Ramey,
there are difficulties for the claimants in relation to the Marquesa's role. She was
asked by Senor Sanchez Junco to help but was not directly asked by him to lie.
However, Senor Riera, on Senor Sanchez Junco's instructions, did directly ask her
to lie and lie she did. I must take it that she appreciated that one, at least, of the

h

functions of the lie was to assist Hello! in having the injunction lifted. But, even
if I could find a combination between Hola SA, Hello!, Senor Sanchez Junco and
the Marquesa and even were I to hold that a target of the conspirators was injury
to OK! as opposed to promoting Hello!'s ability to give its readers that which they
would wish to see, I still have a difficulty about attributing to the Marquesa, in

j

relation to her signature to the Marquesa's letter, any intent alone or in concert
with others to harm the Douglases. Her intent, as I have said, was to improve her
relations with Hello! and in particular with Senor Sanchez Junco and thereby to
preserve or enhance the likelihood of her gaining further work from Hello!.
Good relations with celebrities and a reputation for good relations with
celebrities was the very lifeblood of her trade. Moreover, whilst this, of itself,
does not deny her entry into any combination, what was put to her in

cross-examination by Mr Tugendhat was that she was 'set up' or 'used' as a screen between the paparazzi and Senor Sanchez Junco. A similar description of her role was put to Senor Sanchez Junco. I accept Miss Mulcahy's argument that such a description of her paints her more as a victim than a conspirator.

[258] There was, in my judgment, no common plan or intent between the four or five said to be involved, to harm all claimants. I add that a further difficulty in treating the Marquesa as a separate conspirator is that, before Sir Andrew Morritt V-C, the claimants were at pains, and were successful, in arguing that, in relation to the creation of the Marquesa's letter, her actions were to be attributed to the Hello! defendants.

[259] Accordingly, in my judgment both these claims in conspiracy fail.

CONSPIRACY BETWEEN THE HELLO! DEFENDANTS ONLY; UNLAWFUL MEANS

[260] The alleged target of this conspiracy is *all* claimants (para 33 of the re-re-amended particulars of claim). This is not an area of the law where it can be *assumed* that a person intends the natural and probable consequences of his actions or omissions (see *Crofter Hand Woven Harris Tweed Co Ltd v Veitch* [1942] 1 All ER 142 at 149, [1942] AC 435 at 444 per Viscount Simon LC) so that for this conspiracy to succeed an intent to harm the Douglases on the part of the Hello! defendants is required to be proved. However, like the Marquesa, Senor Sanchez Junco is not in the business of upsetting celebrities. He genuinely did not think the unauthorised photographs were unpleasant or offensive or such as to give offence to the Douglases and he attributed the bringing of proceedings for an injunction to OK!'s commercial needs rather than any wish on the part of the Douglases. I have already cited answers that he gave. No intent attributable to any of the Hello! defendants otherwise than the intent of Senor Sanchez Junco was proved and I do not hold him to have had any intent to injure the Douglases. Accordingly, neither, therefore, had Hola or Hello! any such intent. This head of claim therefore fails.

CONSPIRACY BETWEEN THE HELLO! DEFENDANTS WITH THE PREDOMINANT PURPOSE OF INJURING THE CLAIMANTS

[261] A key argument of the claimants in respect of this allegation in para 32(B) of the re-re-amended particulars of claim is that the Hello! defendants could never have expected that the extra sales likely to be generated by issue 639 in which the unauthorised photographs were incorporated would ever repay the extra expenses—printing and freight—which, in addition to the purchase price of the photographs themselves, were inescapable if the issue was to be on sale as early as they intended it to be. That being so, say the claimants, it follows that the Hello! defendants were motivated by a predominant purpose to injure OK!, their commercial rival. Leaving aside that that would not prove a predominant intent to injure the Douglases, it is in any case based on a fallacy. I accept Senor Sanchez Junco's evidence that it was not unknown for Hello! to proceed with an issue on the basis that even expected extra sales would not avoid a loss on a particular issue. Average sales, it would be hoped, he said, would increase and the prestige of the magazine, too, would be an objective. It often happened, he said, that one would never recover extra costs. The impossibility of recovering extra costs therefore, in my judgment, does not, of itself, suggest the existence of predominant intent to injure. I do not here repeat what I have earlier said as to the intentions which motivated the Hello! defendants but I do not find the predominant purpose which is necessary for this tort to succeed. This claim therefore fails.

THE HELLO! DEFENDANTS' IMPROPRIETY AS TO DISCLOSURE OF DOCUMENTS

a [262] There is an allegation that there were documents in the hands of one or more of the Hello! defendants that had come into existence in the period from 20 November–22 December 2000 but which were deliberately destroyed or disposed of with a view to avoiding their disclosure or were deliberately not disclosed.

b [263] I cannot see how any impropriety as to disclosure would have affected the result in the Court of Appeal as no one could have expected any completed disclosure by 23 November 2000, the last day of the proceedings before the three-man Court of Appeal and only two days after the issue of the claimants' claim form. Any complaint as to disclosure at that stage would have been met with the response that there were then no pleadings, that the issues between the parties had not by then sufficiently emerged and that everyones' time was fully engaged with the conduct of the appeal so that disclosure would have to await its due turn.

[264] As to Hello!'s dealings with documents, I confess to some doubts, in particular as to whether any business efficiently conducted could countenance d the destruction of invoices as early as Mrs Doughty's evidence suggested had been the case. The Hello! defendants did not produce the originals of the five invoices they received from Ramey, Griffin, Thorpe and Bauer. The originals *may* have had (but were not proved to have had) handwritten additions on them that *could* have been material. Mrs Doughty's evidence was that once *she* was e sure the invoice was not meant for Hello! there was no point in keeping it and, that (her evidence implied) it was then promptly destroyed. Building on that, her evidence was that once she had seen that the invoices relating to the unauthorised photographs were not for Hello! and once the Marquesa had faxed her on 15 December 2000 asking for copies of them to be sent to her there was, in effect, no further need to keep the originals and that she was thus able to and f did dispense with keeping them any further. The disposal of the invoices in that way was thus, as far as she was concerned, in ordinary course but, whilst it should not have occurred, it was not done with a view to avoid disclosure. I have preferred evidence other than Mrs Doughty's on a number of points but I do accept her evidence on that. Whilst the Hello! defendants' handling of documents g was far from satisfactory, having heard the evidence I am not satisfied that any material documents were deliberately not disclosed or were deliberately destroyed or disposed of after proceedings had begun with the view to avoiding their disclosure.

[265] That finding, coupled with the facts that Sir Andrew Morritt V-C had h held there had been no mishandling of documents before the proceedings had begun, that the outcome in the Court of Appeal was (in my view) unaffected by poor disclosure and that Sir Andrew Morritt V-C held that a fair trial was possible notwithstanding such shortcomings as he identified, together, as it seems to me, dispose of matters as to documents, given, too, that I have found in the claimants' j favour without resorting to inferences as to the content of any known or likely documents on the basis that they had been improperly undisclosed.

SETTING ASIDE THE JUDGMENT OF THE COURT OF APPEAL

[266] So far as concerns the setting aside of the lifting of the injunction, the claim is pointless; publication of the unauthorised photographs has taken place. But can the Court of Appeal's order as to costs be varied?

[267] Whilst the usual means of seeking the setting aside of an order made in proceedings was previously to start a new action seeking that relief, Mr Tugendhat argues that under the new procedures there is no necessity for that where the impugned proceedings were interlocutory and are followed by a trial in the same proceedings. I see some force in that. To my suggestion that the obvious place for the variation of an order for costs made by the Court of Appeal was, surely, the Court of Appeal, Mr Tugendhat replies that it would be wrong to inflict upon his clients the need for a fresh hearing in that court when the question can be economically dealt with before me and that to require him to go direct to the Court of Appeal would deny him a tier of appeals that he would have if I were to decide the issue or if (albeit after disproportionate expense in time and costs) he was obliged to begin a second action to set aside a costs order made in the first.

[268] Further argument on this part of the re-re-amended particulars of claim was left over for consideration in the light of such facts as I should find but I should mention two subjects.

[269] Firstly, if, during the hearing of the case before the Court of Appeal, Senor Sanchez Junco's statement, Mrs Cartwright's second witness statement (in the form in which that court saw it) and the Marquesa's letter were all seen to be false, there would, of course, have been very powerful criticism of the way in which the defendants had acted, but would the outcome still have been a lifting of the injunction?

[270] The claimants allege that it is no part of their primary case to speculate on what might have been but I will wish to be addressed on whether some such speculation is inevitable. Unless the court in the second process is required to find that the matter complained of in the earlier process had probably had a real effect on the outcome of that first process, would not courts be inundated with applications to set aside decisions on the grounds of lies or combinations which had been unlikely to have had any effect on the outcome?

[271] Secondly, that there were arguments that could have been presented to the Court of Appeal to do otherwise than they did is plain. The law of confidence was only or primarily argued, it would seem, in relation to confidentiality of a private kind rather than such as can arise in a commercial context. Paragraph 6(a) of the re-re-amended particulars of claim did not raise the analogy with trade secrets until 3 May 2002. The fact that a confidence of the privacy kind had been sold by the Douglases with a view to publication by OK! weighed heavily against the claimants, whereas had the claim been presented as one akin to a trade secret the sale may have been seen as the natural way of turning the commodity to account. Nor was it urged that by refusing an injunction because damages sufficed the Court of Appeal would, in effect, be allowing a compulsory purchase by Hello! of a right to breach the exclusiveness for which its trade rival had paid so much and to do so despite the court regarding the claimants as having sound claims in confidence—compare *Francome v Mirror Group Newspapers Ltd* [1984] 2 All ER 408 at 412–413, [1984] 1 WLR 892 at 897 per Sir John Donaldson MR. Nor, either, was it argued that it was wrong to apply an *American Cyanamid* approach (one designed, in any case where at least a serious question could be seen to require to be tried, to avoid any evaluation of the merits save as a very last resort) (see *American Cyanamid Co v Ethicon Ltd* [1975] 1 All ER 504, [1975] AC 396) to a case in which, under s 12(3) of the Human Rights Act 1998, an evaluation of who would win was *to some extent* required by statute (see *Cream Holdings Ltd v Banerjee* [2003] EWCA Civ 103, [2003] 2 All ER 318). Subject to the answer as to the

a propriety of speculation, I will wish to be addressed on whether, had the defendants been caught out in their misbehaviour, it would have been probable that the injunction would have remained in place.

EXEMPLARY DAMAGES

[272] This vexed corner of the law has recently been visited by the House of
b Lords in *Kuddus v Chief Constable of Leicestershire Constabulary* [2001] UKHL 29, [2001] 3 All ER 193, [2002] 2 AC 122. The law was not as fully explored in the case as it might have been as the appeal was against a striking out rather than in a case which had been fully resolved on the merits. However, *Kuddus'* case, as I read it, points to three considerations in particular. The first is that the question whether or not to award exemplary damages should be determined more by reference to
c the nature of the behaviour complained of than by reference to the nature of cause of action to which that behaviour has given rise. The second is that a powerful case can be made that such damages should be considered where, and perhaps only where, the behaviour complained of gives rise to a sense of outrage: see Lord Nicholls of Birkenhead's speech (at [65]). The third is that a recognised
d category in which such damages may be awarded is where damages on an ordinary compensatory basis can be seen not to be sufficient to do justice. Lord Devlin in *Rookes v Barnard* [1964] 1 All ER 367 at 410, [1964] AC 1129 at 1226 spoke of a category in which the defendant's conduct had been calculated by him to make a profit for himself which might well exceed the compensation payable to the plaintiff.

e [273] As to those three features, I am content to assume, without deciding, that exemplary damages (or equity's equivalent) are available in respect of breach of confidence. However, I do not find it possible to describe my judicial reaction to the conduct of the Hello! defendants as one of outrage, especially so far as it relates to the position as between Hello! and OK!. Both of them are participants
f in an industry—the press as part of the media—in which intrusion upon privacy and little regard for each other's business rights have, at any rate before the Human Rights Act 1998, been not unknown. Whilst I would not take either OK! or Hello! to have been as frequently intrusive or as disrespectful of other's rights as may have incurred in other sectors, neither of them is wholly without blemish. In that circumstance the word 'outrage' would be to overstate the matter.
g Senor Sanchez Junco stooped to a kind of journalism he professed not to like and did thereby disregard the rights of each of the claimants but to describe his conduct as contumelious would be to exaggerate. Moreover, I am not satisfied that none of the various ways in which damages or equitable compensation can be computed in response to the breach of the law of confidence which I have held
h to have existed will yield a figure such that Hello!'s profit for itself would exceed the compensation due to the claimants, nor even that any Hello! defendant had ever calculated that that might be so.

[274] For these reasons I do not award exemplary damages.

j AGGRAVATED DAMAGES

[275] Mr and Mrs Douglas claim aggravated damages for distress, relying on three factors; the alleged flagrancy of the defendants' conduct, the fact that on the lifting of the injunction the defendants promptly went ahead and published the unauthorised photographs, knowing of the distress that that would cause and on the publications in the Sun and Daily Mail to which I have referred. As to that last factor, the Hello! defendants did act reasonably, although unsuccessfully, to stop

publication by those newspapers. As for the puns which the newspapers
published ('Catherine Eater Jones' and 'That takes the cake') they would not have
appeared had the newspapers done as Hello! requested and, surely, conduce
more to a groan than to offence. As to publishing once the injunction was lifted,
it is difficult to regard that as high-handed or oppressive or otherwise such as to
require aggravated damages; the Court of Appeal had just ruled, in effect, that a
remedy in damages sufficed to meet the Douglases' claims and there is no
suggestion that the Hello! defendants will be unable to meet any likely award in
damages. Given that there was, in any event, to be very extensive photographic
coverage of the wedding, albeit as selected by the Douglases, I do not see the
behaviour of the Hello! defendants as so flagrant or offensive as to justify an
award of aggravated damages.

LIABILITY OF THE MARQUESA TO ALL OR ANY CLAIMANTS

[276] The claims made against the Marquesa were for interference with
business by unlawful means and conspiracy by unlawful means with the intent
and purpose of causing damage to the claimants. No such claim succeeds against
her and I do not find her liable in damages to any claimant. She is not in any
position to re-publish the unauthorised pictures, nor has it been argued that she
has or might acquire any intention to do so. She has nothing relevant to deliver
up to the claimants on oath. But this is not to say that her writing of the
Marquesa's letter has not left her vulnerable to an argument that her costs in this
action should not follow the event, an argument and any counter to it which I can
leave over until later. I accept, though, that her expressions of regret at ever
having written her letter were not merely self-serving but are genuine and it is to
be remembered that she had freely owned up to the falsity of the letter by her
defence of 22 July 2002 and her witness statement of 22 November 2002.

NEW YORK AND SPANISH LAW

[277] As the evidence came out, no defendant or non-expert witness for a
defendant credibly asserted a belief that what he, she, or it had done should not
be complained of because it was not offensive under the local law. In that
circumstance and on the basis of my other conclusions of fact and of law I do not
see it as necessary to say anything as to the law of New York or as to Spanish law.
In particular, as to the only claim in respect of which I have held any defendant
as other than nominally liable, I do not see that publication of Hello! by the Hello!
defendants in England would, in all the circumstances, have been any less
unconscionable in the view of an English court had publication in New York been
lawful.

AN INJUNCTION

[278] It does not follow from the fact that an item has passed into the public
domain that it must be taken to have remained there in such a way that its
confidentiality has been irretrievably lost. The fact that the unauthorised or
authorised photographs were published in November 2000 does not, of itself,
therefore deny the claimants a perpetual injunction. Whilst these proceedings
have brought back into the public eye the fact that there were unauthorised
photographs, I think it likely, given that the far better authorised pictures were
also, of course, put into the public domain, that the look of the unauthorised
photographs has passed out of the public mind. I thus see the claimants as in a
position to ask for an injunction restraining the defendants such as is sought by
the claimants in para 1 of the prayer to their re-re-amended particulars of claim.

a I indicate immediately, though, that I shall be willing to accept an undertaking of the Hello! defendants in lieu. Such an injunction or undertaking will, in practical terms, make delivery-up unnecessary.

CONCLUSION

b [**279**] For the reasons I have given, I hold the Hello! defendants to be liable to all three claimants under the law as to confidence. It will have been noted that an important step in my coming to that conclusion has been that, on balancing rights to confidence against freedom of expression for the purpose of granting or withholding relief, I have been required by statute to pay, and have paid, regard to the PCC code. The Hello! defendants broke their own industry's code.

c [**280**] Save for the above liability in confidence, the undertaking or injunction I have described and a nominal award under the Data Protection Act 1998, I dismiss all other claims made by the claimants against the first to fifth defendants. Unless the parties agree, there will have to be a further hearing to establish the amount for which the Hello! defendants are liable to the claimants. Whilst there has been a little discussion as to the assessment of a notional licence fee as an appropriate approach to the quantification of compensation for OK!, at this stage *d* I say nothing as to that being apt or inapt but it is already clear that OK! has elected not to seek any account of the profits which Hello! may be said to have derived from the impugned publication. That aside, all issues as to quantum are left over, should it be necessary, for a later hearing.

e *Order accordingly.*

Celia Fox   Barrister.

Chappell v Somers & Blake (a firm)   *a*

[2003] EWHC 1644 (Ch)

CHANCERY DIVISION

NEUBERGER J   *b*

27 JUNE, 8 JULY 2003

Executor and administrator – Liability – Liability to estate or beneficiaries – Whether person appointed executor under will could be liable for losses suffered by estate or beneficiaries because of prolonged delay before will proved.

c

Solicitor – Will – Duty of care – Testatrix leaving properties to beneficiary – Solicitors allegedly failing to progress administration of estate for five years – Executrix suing to recover loss of income on properties during five-year period – Whether executrix having cause of action.

d

The testatrix died in December 1995. By her will, she appointed the claimant as executrix, and left her residuary estate to a single beneficiary. The residue included two properties, neither of which, according to the executrix, had been let at the time of the testatrix's death. In early January 1996 the executrix instructed the defendant solicitors to act on her behalf in the administration of the estate. Over *e* the next five years, according to the executrix, the solicitors did nothing at all to progress the administration of the estate. The executrix therefore terminated the solicitors' retainer in April 2001 and went elsewhere for advice. As a result of that advice, she applied for, and was granted, probate, and in due course she distributed the estate in accordance with the terms of the will. The properties *f* which formed part of the residuary estate remained unlet until after they were transferred to the beneficiary. The executrix, acting as such, brought proceedings against the solicitors, alleging breach of the contractual and tortious duties owed by them to her. She alleged, inter alia, that, if the solicitors had acted in accordance with their duty, the properties would have been assented to the beneficiary five years earlier than they were actually assented to; that income would have been *g* earned from them during that period either by renting them out, or by selling them and enjoying interest on the proceeds of sale; and that the loss of income for that period was the liability of the solicitors owing to their failure to advise properly, promptly or at all. The solicitors applied to strike out that part of the claim, contending that any alleged loss had been suffered by the beneficiary, in its *h* capacity as devisee of the properties, and not by the executrix in her capacity as such. Although the circuit judge apparently accepted that contention, he dismissed the application, holding that a claim by the executrix against the solicitors might succeed on the basis that she should be able to obtain an indemnity from them in respect of any liability she might have to the beneficiary *j* if it brought proceedings against her for failing to administer the estate efficiently or properly. On the solicitors' appeal, the High Court considered whether that reasoning was sustainable and, if not, whether, on the assumption that her allegations were correct, the executrix was entitled, as executrix, to sue for the recovery of the loss of income on the properties, accounting to the beneficiary for any damages received.

a   **Held** – A person appointed executor under a will could not be held liable for any losses which accrued to the estate, or to the beneficiaries under the will, as a result of prolonged delay before the will was proved. Although that result might appear surprising, it was explained by the fact that a person was not under a duty to accept an appointment as executor. Indeed, many persons appointed executors in wills were unaware of their appointment until after the testator had died. In

b   those circumstances, some basis for the principle could be seen. Moreover, a beneficiary who thought that an executor was not moving swiftly enough to obtain a grant of probate could either apply to the Principal Probate Registry for the issue of a citation to accept or refuse a grant, or apply to the High Court to pass over the executor. It followed in the instant case that the circuit judge's decision could not

c   stand on the basis of his reasoning. However, the action was properly constituted in that there was a cause of action vested in the executrix, in her capacity as such, in relation to the disputed claim. It was appropriate to treat the executrix as representing the interest of the owner of the property, and therefore the person entitled to recover damages. Due to the breach of duty owed by the solicitors to the claimant as executrix of the will and owner of the properties throughout the

d   time that the duty had been breached, the person who was or should have been the owner of the properties had lost the income attributable to them. In those circumstances, it was hard to see why the executrix should be disentitled from recovering damages for such loss from the solicitors, and accounting for them to the beneficiary, to whom the properties had been devised as part of the very

e   estate which she was responsible for administering. If to hold otherwise would involve the solicitors escaping any liability in damages, the result would be inconsistent with the policy consideration that solicitors should not be able to escape liability merely because they could identify a dichotomy between the person who could claim against them for a breach of duty, namely the executrix, and the

f   person who could be said to have suffered the damage, namely the beneficiary. Accordingly, the appeal would be dismissed (see [12]–[14], [16], [19]–[21], [33], [36], below).

    Re Stevens, Cooke v Stevens [1898] 1 Ch 162, *White v Jones* [1995] 1 All ER 691 and *Carr-Glynn v Frearsons (a firm)* [1998] 4 All ER 225 considered.

g

Notes

For a personal representative's liability in negligence and for a solicitor's liability for negligence generally, see respectively 17(2) *Halsbury's Laws* (4th edn reissue) para 794 and 44(1) *Halsbury's Laws* (4th edn reissue) para 152.

h

Cases referred to in judgment

Cancer Research Campaign v Ernest Brown & Co (a firm) [1997] STC 1425.

Carr-Glynn v Frearsons (a firm) [1998] 4 All ER 225, [1999] Ch 326, [1999] 2 WLR 1046, CA.

j   *Johnson v Gore Wood & Co (a firm)* [2001] 1 All ER 481, [2002] 2 AC 1, [2001] 2 WLR 72, HL.

Marshall (Inspector of Taxes) v Kerr [1994] 3 All ER 106, [1995] 1 AC 148, [1994] 3 WLR 299, HL.

Stevens, Re, Cooke v Stevens [1898] 1 Ch 162, CA.

White v Jones [1995] 1 All ER 691, [1995] 2 AC 207, [1995] 2 WLR 187, HL.

Appeal

The defendant, Somers & Blake, a firm of solicitors, appealed with permission of
Patten J granted on 10 April 2003 from the decision of Judge Cowell in the Central
London County Court on 21 February 2003 dismissing their application to strike
out part of an action for negligence brought against them by the claimant,
Marceline Ann Chappell, suing in her capacity as executrix of the estate of Nellie
Ivy Price (deceased). The facts are set out in the judgment.

Elspeth Talbot-Rice (instructed by *Withers LLP*) for the solicitors.
Giles Harrap (instructed by *Blake Lapthorn Linnell*) for Mrs Chappell.

Cur adv vult

8 July 2003. The following judgment was delivered.

NEUBERGER J.

[1] This is an appeal brought by the defendant, Somers & Blake, a firm of
solicitors (the solicitors), against the refusal of Judge Cowell to strike out part of
the claim brought against them by Mrs Marceline Chappell, in her capacity as the
executrix of the will of Nellie Price (the deceased).

[2] The facts of the case are as follows. The deceased died on 24 December
1995. By cl 1 of her will (the will), dated 5 April 1995, the deceased appointed
Mrs Chappell as her sole executrix. By cl 2 of the will, the deceased made specific
bequests totalling just over £20,000, and cll 3 and 4 of her will involved other
specific bequests. In cl 7 of the will, the deceased bequeathed and devised the
residue of her estate to the Parochial Church Council of the Parish of St Mary's
Church, St Mary's Road, South Ealing (the PCC).

[3] According to her pleaded case in these proceedings, it was in early January
1996 that Mrs Chappell instructed the solicitors 'to act on her behalf in the
administration of the estate of the deceased'.

[4] Mrs Chappell's pleaded case goes on to allege that she spoke to the solicitors
on a number of occasions between 1996 and 2001 about the administration of the
estate (the estate). In her particulars of claim, Mrs Chappell alleges that between
the time that they were first instructed, in January 1996, and early April 2001 the
solicitors were in breach of their contractual and tortious duties to Mrs Chappell
in that, to put it shortly, they did absolutely nothing. In particular, she alleges
that they failed to give her any advice, to ascertain the assets and liabilities of
the estate, to obtain a grant of probate, to make inquiries with regard to title
deeds, to respond to her requests for information and advice regarding
properties in the estate, to pay legacies within the executor's year or at all, and
to progress the administration of the estate at all.

[5] In these circumstances, in early April 2001, Mrs Chappell terminated the
solicitors' retainer and went elsewhere for advice. As a result of this advice,
Mrs Chappell applied for, and was granted, probate, and in due course she
distributed the estate in accordance with the terms of the will. The residue of
the estate included two properties, namely 37 Netherbury Road, London W5
and the Top Floor, 7 Winchester Street, London W3 (the properties). At the
date of the deceased's death, according to Mrs Chappell's pleaded case, these
properties were unlet, and they remained unlet until after they were
transferred to the PCC, pursuant to the provisions of cl 7 of the will.

a   [6] In the schedule of losses appended to Mrs Chappell's particulars of claim, the loss alleged to have been suffered as a result of the solicitors' alleged breach of duty, so far as it relates to the properties, is expressed in these terms:

b   'The continuing delay [in applying for probate, and consequential administering and devolving of the deceased's estate] deprived the estate of income from part of its capital namely [the properties] ... The net loss claimed is put forward as a figure that enables a court to make a fair appraisal of the loss of income from the delay in a situation in which in the absence of any breach the estate would have been duly wound up and the properties assented to the residuary beneficiary by 1 January 1997 or in any event before 1 July 1997 or sold with the entire proceeds yielding investment income by 1

c   January 1997 or in any event before 1 July 1997.'

   [7] Mrs Chappell's claim for damages against the solicitors, in so far as it relates to the properties, is based on the following proposition. First, had the solicitors acted in accordance with their duty, the properties would have been assented to the PCC by 1 January (or at any rate by 1 July) 1997, which is

d   approximately five years earlier than they were actually assented to the PCC. Secondly, income would then have been earned from the properties (either by renting them out, or by selling them and enjoying interest on the proceeds of sale) for that period of five years. Thirdly, the loss of income suffered for that period is properly the liability of the solicitors, owing to their failure to advise properly, promptly, or at all, over the period that they were instructed by

e   Mrs Chappell.

   [8] As this is an application to strike out the claim (albeit only in so far as it relates to the damages relating to the properties), I proceed on the basis that the allegations made in the particulars of claim are correct. Further, as it is not suggested (nor, I think, could it be suggested) by the solicitors that the claim

f   against them based on breach of contract and negligence is bound to fail, I must also assume that the factual allegations of breach of duty are justified.

   [9] Mrs Elspeth Talbot-Rice, who appears for the solicitors, contends that, both as a matter of principle, and in light of the way in which it is pleaded, Mrs Chappell's claim against the solicitors, in so far as it is based on loss of income from the properties, is bound to fail, and should accordingly be struck out. This

g   contention is based on the proposition that any alleged loss must have been suffered by the PCC, in its capacity as the devisee of the properties, and not by Mrs Chappell, in her capacity as executrix of the deceased's estate. Such a contention is supported by the fact that, if the solicitors had not been in breach of duty as alleged, with the consequence of the deceased's estate being wound up

h   five years earlier than it was, then the properties would have become vested in the PCC five years earlier than actually occurred. Thus, it is said that it is the PCC, and not Mrs Chappell, who would have received any income from those properties over the five years, either by renting them out, or by selling them and investing the proceeds.

j   [10] Judge Cowell appears to have accepted this argument, but he none the less refused to strike out the relevant part of the pleading on the grounds that a claim somewhat along the lines pleaded might none the less succeed. He said that the PCC might seek to claim damages from Mrs Chappell, arising from her failure to administer the estate efficiently or properly, with the result that the properties were not vested in the PCC until 2002, and in those circumstances the PCC might seek to recover damages for its loss of income from the properties during the very period pleaded in the present particulars of claim. Judge Cowell considered that, on this basis, a claim by Mrs Chappell against the solicitors could succeed, because she should be able to obtain an indemnity from the solicitors in respect of any such liability as she might have to the PCC.

[11] Mr Giles Harrap, who appears for Mrs Chappell, does not seek to support this reasoning. In my opinion, he is correct. First, as a matter of fact, there was and is no suggestion that the PCC is even contemplating bringing proceedings against Mrs Chappell. On the contrary. Since the decision of Judge Cowell, the only involvement of the PCC has been to indicate that it is prepared to be joined as a party in these proceedings, if that is necessary for Mrs Chappell's claim to be properly constituted. Quite apart from this, as Mrs Talbot-Rice points out, Mrs Chappell's claim as pleaded does not rely on any liability which she has, or might have, to the PCC; nor does it seek any indemnity in relation to such potential liability. Further, it is clear from the correspondence between the parties that it is common ground that no claim could be, or is being, brought by Mrs Chappell on this basis.

[12] Over and above this, it appears to me that, as a matter of law, a person who is appointed executor under a will cannot be held liable for any losses which accrue to the estate or to the beneficiaries under the will, as a result of a prolonged delay before the will is proved. That this is the law appears to me to receive support from the decision of the Court of Appeal in *Re Stevens, Cooke v Stevens* [1898] 1 Ch 162. The point is most clearly made by Vaughan Williams LJ (at 177); I believe the same point is made, albeit not so clearly, and perhaps a little more tentatively, in the last paragraph of the judgment of Chitty LJ (at 174); in the last paragraph of his judgment (at 170), Lindley MR left the point open. It seems to me that Harman J took the same view in *Cancer Research Campaign v Ernest Brown & Co (a firm)* [1997] STC 1425.

[13] Although this result may appear at first sight to be surprising, it is explained, as Mrs Talbot-Rice submits, by the fact that a person is not under a duty to accept an appointment as an executor, indeed, many persons appointed executors in wills are unaware of their appointment until after the testator has died. In those circumstances, one can see some basis for the principle. As Mrs Talbot-Rice also points out, a beneficiary, who thinks that an executor is not moving swiftly enough to obtain a grant of probate, can either apply to the Principal Probate Registry under r 47 of the Non-Contentious Probate Rules 1987, SI 1987/2024 for the issue of a citation to accept or refuse a grant, or apply to the High Court under r 52 of the 1987 rules to pass over the executor under s 116 of the Supreme Court Act 1981.

[14] Accordingly, it seems to me that Judge Cowell's decision cannot stand on the basis of his reasoning. The question is whether it can be justified on the way in which Mr Harrap puts his case, namely that, even though the income from the properties, which would have been enjoyed if the solicitors had not been in breach of duty, would have been paid to the PCC, as devisee, it is none the less Mrs Chappell who is entitled to sue for the recovery of this loss of income, as executrix of the estate, albeit that she will have to account for any damages she receives to the PCC.

[15] The issue raised by that argument is not entirely easy. Assuming, which appears to me to be correct and as is common ground in light of the authorities to which I have referred, that there can be no question of the solicitors having to indemnify Mrs Chappell in respect of any liability she may have to the PCC, it appears to me that there are, at least as a matter of logic, three possible answers

a to the present conundrum. The first, supported by Mr Harrap, is, as I have indicated, that the executrix is entitled to sue the solicitors, but has to account for any damages received to the beneficiary. The problem with that argument, as Mrs Talbot-Rice points out, is that the claimant, namely the executrix, is not the person who has suffered any loss as a result of the solicitors' breach of duty. The second possibility is that the beneficiary is entitled to sue the solicitors for any loss *b* suffered. The problem with that argument is that the solicitors plainly owed no contractual duty to the beneficiary, and there must be considerable doubt as to whether it would be right, as a matter of principle, to impose any tortious duty to the beneficiary on the solicitors. The third possibility is that, as the solicitors' duty was owed to the executrix, and any loss resulting from the breach of duty was suffered by the beneficiary, there is what has been referred to in argument as *c* a 'black hole', and the solicitors, in effect, escape from having to pay any damages.

[16] Considering this issue by reference to general policy, as opposed to legal principle, I am of the view that there are two main points. The first is that it would be wrong if the solicitors escaped any liability for damages in a case such as this, merely because they could identify a dichotomy between the person who *d* can claim against them for a breach of duty, namely the executrix, and the person who can be said to have suffered the damage, namely the beneficiary. I believe that this principle, which is there identified as 'the impulse to do practical justice', is supported by the speech of Lord Goff of Chieveley in *White v Jones* [1995] 1 All ER 691 at 702–703, [1995] 2 AC 207 at 259–260. In that case, the majority of the House of Lords held that a solicitor who had been negligent in drafting a will *e* could be sued by the disappointed beneficiary, because otherwise the solicitor could escape liability, as the client, the deceased, had suffered no loss. The speech of Lord Goff contains the ratio of the decision of the House of Lords—see *Carr-Glynn v Frearsons (a firm)* [1998] 4 All ER 225 at 233, [1999] Ch 326 at 335 per Chadwick LJ (with whom Thorpe and Butler-Sloss LJJ agreed). Indeed, the same *f* policy point was articulated in Chadwick LJ's judgment ([1998] 4 All ER 225 at 231–232, [1999] Ch 326 at 334), citing Lord Browne-Wilkinson's observations in *White*'s case [1995] 1 All ER 691 at 718, [1995] 2 AC 207 at 276, to the effect that it would be 'unacceptable' if a solicitor escaped liability in that case.

[17] The second policy principle appears to me to be that, given that any damages would ultimately come to the beneficiary, irrespective of who has the *g* right to sue, the question of whether it is the executrix or the beneficiary who can bring the proceedings is not of great significance. The essential point is to ensure that there cannot be double recovery (ie that the same damages cannot be recovered twice, once by the beneficiary and once by the executor). In that connection, I would refer to the decision of the House of Lords in *Johnson v Gore* *h* *Wood & Co (a firm)* [2001] 1 All ER 481, [2002] 2 AC 1, especially per Lord Cooke of Thorndon ([2001] 1 All ER 481 at 514, [2002] 2 AC 1 at 47) and per Lord Millett ([2001] 1 All ER 481 at 528, [2002] 2 AC 1 at 62). Again, the judgment of Chadwick LJ in *Carr-Glynn*'s case provides support for this point—see especially [1998] 4 All ER 225 at 231, 234, [1999] Ch 326 at 333–334, 336–337.

j [18] However, considerations of policy cannot, at least on their own especially for a first instance judge, justify a decision which is contrary to established legal principle or binding authority. The minority speeches of Lord Keith of Kinkel and Lord Mustill in *White*'s case demonstrate that legal principle may sometimes require a court to reach a conclusion which is hard, or even impossible, to reconcile with policy considerations such as those I have just articulated. In the same case, Lord Goff ([1995] 1 All ER 691 at 710, [1995] 2 AC 207 at 268) was anxious to find a solution which was not an 'unacceptable circumvention of established principles'. The importance of a legally principled approach was also underlined in *Johnson's* case [2001] 1 All ER 481 at 503, 529, [2002] 2 AC 1 at 35–36, 62–63 per Lord Bingham of Cornhill and Lord Millett respectively.

[19] However, I consider that, in this case, legal principle does justify a conclusion consistent with the first of the two policy considerations, and that the second of the two policy considerations does not really arise. In my judgment, the present action is properly constituted, in that there is a cause of action vested in Mrs Chappell, as the executrix of the estate, in relation to the instant disputed claim.

[20] It seems to me that Mr Harrap is right in his contention that it is appropriate to treat the executrix as representing the interest of the owner of the property, and therefore the person entitled to recover damages. As is explained in Williams, Mortimer and Sunnucks *Executors, Administrators and Probate* (18th edn, 2000) p 471 (para 42-10):

> 'The interests vesting in the personal representative do not vest in him beneficially. Although he is not necessarily a trustee he is said to hold "in auter droit" so that his interest is different from the absolute and ordinary interest which everyone has in his own property.'

In *Marshall (Inspector of Taxes) v Kerr* [1994] 3 All ER 106 at 112, [1995] 1 AC 148 at 157, Lord Templeman approved the following formulation:

> '[T]he entire ownership of the property comprised in the estate of a deceased person which remains unadministered is in the deceased's legal personal representatives for the purposes of administration without any differentiation between legal and equitable interests ...'

In the same case Lord Browne-Wilkinson said ([1994] 3 All ER 106 at 119, [1995] 1 AC 148 at 165) that 'during the period of administration the legatee has no legal or equitable interest in the assets comprised in the estate'.

[21] Owing to the solicitors' breach of duty owed to Mrs Chappell, as the executrix of the will and the owner of the properties throughout the time that the duty was breached, the person who was or should have been the owner of the properties lost the income attributable to the properties. It is hard to see why, in those circumstances, Mrs Chappell should be disentitled from recovering damages for such loss from the solicitors, and accounting for them to the beneficiary, to whom the properties were devised as part of the very estate which she was responsible for administering. If to hold otherwise would involve the solicitors escaping any liability in damages, then it seems to me that the result would be inconsistent with the reasoning of the majority of the House of Lords in *White v Jones* [1995] 1 All ER 691, [1995] 2 AC 207, and of the Court of Appeal in *Carr-Glynn v Frearsons (a firm)* [1998] 4 All ER 225, [1999] Ch 326. Furthermore, to hold that the executrix could recover in such circumstances does not seem to me even to fall foul of the reasoning or conclusions of Lord Keith or Lord Mustill, who dissented, in *White's* case.

[22] The only sensible alternative, as I have mentioned, would be that it is the beneficiary, in this case the PCC, who would be entitled to recover. There is no question of the beneficiary having been a client of the solicitors: the client was the executrix. In those circumstances, the notion of the beneficiary having a claim would be inconsistent with the speeches of Lord Keith and Lord Mustill in *White's* case, although it would not, at least on the face of it, be inconsistent with the

a speeches of Lord Browne-Wilkinson or Lord Nolan. Lord Goff, whose speech represents the ratio of *White*'s case, accepted that there were 'conceptual difficulties' in such a notion, and he identified those difficulties (see [1995] 1 All ER 691 at 698–701, [1995] 2 AC 207 at 255–258). In my judgment, the objections which impressed Lord Goff apply equally here. It is clear from the speech of Lord Goff that it was only with considerable difficulty that he was persuaded that a claim

b against a solicitor who had negligently drafted (or failed to draft) a will could be brought by a disappointed potential beneficiary thereunder. Unlike in the present case, there was, in *White*'s case, no conceivable basis upon which the solicitors' client (or his executors) could possibly maintain a claim for substantial damages against the solicitor. Accordingly, the majority of the House of Lords held, to quote Chadwick LJ in *Carr-Glynn*'s case [1998] 4 All ER 225 at 234, [1999] Ch 326

c at 336, that it was 'entitled—indeed, bound—to fashion a remedy to meet the need' to satisfy the requirements of justice, rather than to adopt a relatively conservative attitude, with the unjust result that the solicitor escaped liability for any substantial damages.

[23] In the present case, given that there is a basis upon which it can fairly be

d said that the executrix can maintain a claim for the loss that has actually been suffered, it seems inappropriate to strain to find another lacuna and then to fill it by further extending the exceptional and somewhat controversial, if just, extension of the law established in *White*'s case.

[24] To hold that the executrix can recover in the present case does not seem to me to be inconsistent with the fact that no claim (other than for nominal

e damages for breach of contract) could have been maintained by the executor in *White*'s case. First, unlike in *White*'s case, the loss in the present case was suffered during the time that the properties were vested in the executrix. The damages would be calculated on the basis that the properties should have been available for letting or sale from about a year after the solicitors were instructed until they

f were assented to the beneficiary. During the whole of that period, the properties were vested in the executrix.

[25] It is true that the damages claim is calculated by reference to the loss of income over a later period owing to the time needed to find tenants (or to sell the properties) after the properties were, or would have been, vested in the beneficiary. However, for virtually the whole of that period, the properties were

g vested in the executrix. Furthermore, it is important to distinguish between the basis upon which the loss is identified, and the way in which damages are calculated. The basis upon which the loss in the present case is identified and assessed depends on the assertion that, while, from about one year after the death of the deceased, the properties were vested in the executrix, they were not let,

h and the executrix was under no obligation to let them, and it was only when they became vested in the beneficiary that there was any impetus and opportunity in practice to let them. Accordingly, the period in respect of which loss is claimed is, in effect, the period during which the properties wrongly remained in the hands of the executrix owing to the breach of duty by the solicitors.

j [26] The second important difference between the present case and *White*'s case is that, had the executor in *White*'s case been awarded substantial damages, there could have been no sensible basis upon which such an executor could be said to hold the damages for the ultimate benefit of the disappointed beneficiary in that case. That point is made by Chadwick LJ in *Carr-Glynn*'s case [1998] 4 All ER 225 at 234, [1999] Ch 326 at 336. In the present case, it is quite rightly accepted by Mrs Talbot-Rice that if, contrary to her contention, the executrix is entitled to

sue the solicitors in respect of the loss in question, she would be obliged to
account to the beneficiary for any damages she received.

[27] I believe that my conclusion is supported if one turns to consider a rather
different factual situation. An example which was raised during argument was
that of a bare trustee who seeks advice from a solicitor as to whether to
distribute trust property, where the right advice is that the property should
be distributed as soon as possible, because its income would attract a much
lower rate of tax in the hands of the beneficiary than in the hands of the
trustee, for some reason. If the solicitor delayed giving this advice for five years,
it seems to me that it would be the trustee, and not the beneficiary, who would
be entitled to sue the solicitor for the extra tax paid during that period. In such a
case, it would be the trustee who was the client of the solicitor, and it would be
the trustee who had had to pay the extra tax.

[28] The fact that it would be the beneficiary who, in practical terms, lost the
tax which was paid, and it was the beneficiary who, but for the negligence of the
solicitors, would have legally owned the trust property during the period when
the loss was incurred, would not alter the fact that the appropriate claimant
would be the trustee. I believe that it would be the trustee who should claim
even in a case where the last instalment of extra tax was payable by the
beneficiary after distribution, but it is not necessary to decide the point. As here,
of course, the trustee would have to account to the beneficiary for any damages
recovered from the solicitor.

[29] At least in some respects, it could be said that Mrs Chappell's case is
stronger than that of the trustee in the example I have given. In that example, the
beneficiary had some interest (albeit not a legal interest) in the trust property at
the relevant time, whereas, as the observations quoted above show, a beneficiary
under a will, such as the PCC in this case, does not even have an equitable interest
in a property devised to it in a will, during the period of administration.

[30] Mrs Talbot-Rice suggested that, in the case of a will whose provisions
were more complex than those in the present case, the conclusion that a claim
such as the present would properly vest in the executrix could lead to difficulties.
She postulated a case where a property was devised to A, and the residue of the
estate was left to B, and where the executrix consulted a solicitor with the same
consequences as those which are alleged to have arisen in the present case.
Mrs Talbot-Rice said that if the executrix was entitled to recover damages to
compensate for the loss of income during the relevant period of delay, the damages
would be calculated on the basis of what had been suffered by A, the devisee of the
particular property, but the executrix would have to pay them over to B, because
they would form part of the residue of the estate.

[31] In the absence of having been referred to any principle or any authority
which unequivocally justified that conclusion, I am of the view that the argument
should be rejected. It seems to me that, in such a case, the executrix's claim
would be in her capacity not only as the executrix client of the solicitor, but also
as the owner of the property. In those circumstances, I consider that the executrix
would hold any damages which she recovered as representing the loss of income
on the property for the benefit of A, and not of B. I believe my view is consistent
with the fact that the executrix would, in the normal way, be expected to account
for any income from the property which accrued during the administration to A,
not to B—see *Theobald on Wills* (16th edn, 2001) p 281. In any event, the person to
whom the account had to be effected would be a matter between the executrix and
the beneficiaries, and it is not a matter as between the executrix and the solicitor.

a
[32] I have not so far discussed the applicability of the second policy issue, namely the need to avoid double recovery. In the light of my conclusion that it is Mrs Chappell, the executrix, and not the PCC, the beneficiary, who has the right of action, no question of double recovery arises. However, as I have mentioned, the PCC is prepared to be joined as a party to this action, and, at least as at present advised, it seems to me that, unless it would cause any delay or any significant

b
increase in costs, the PCC should be so joined. First, it would avoid any risk of double recovery (in case, at a later date, the PCC brings proceedings against the solicitors and successfully contends that it is not bound by this judgment, an event which I regard to be very unlikely indeed). Secondly, it would obviate the necessity or benefit of any appeal, unless there was a prospect of the solicitors successfully arguing that they could avoid liability against either party (which

c
seems very improbable in light of the reasoning in *White v Jones* [1995] 1 All ER 691, [1995] 2 AC 207 and *Carr-Glynn v Frearsons (a firm)* [1998] 4 All ER 225, [1999] Ch 326), or the court could be persuaded that an appeal could be justified in relation to the issue of the costs of the present application and appeal.

d
[33] In my judgment, therefore, it is competent for Mrs Chappell, as executrix of the deceased's will, to bring proceedings against the solicitors for damages arising out of the income lost on the properties as a result of any breach of duty of care on the part of the solicitors as alleged in the particulars of claim.

[34] As already mentioned, Mrs Talbot-Rice also contends that the claim was not properly pleaded, even if it could be justified in principle. I accept that, like

e
almost any pleading, the way in which the particulars of claim in this case have been expressed could be improved. In particular, the passage I have quoted from the schedule of losses is in fairly broad terms, and it is not entirely clear, for instance, whether or not it is part of Mrs Chappell's case that the properties would have been let, and if so when, had the solicitors not been negligent as

f
alleged.

[35] Having said that, it seems to me that there are two points which, when taken together, provide a satisfactory answer to the point. The first is that it is tolerably clear to any fair-minded person what is being alleged in terms of damages, namely that the owner of the properties has been deprived of the

g
opportunity to earn income on them during the period of the solicitors' inaction. The purpose of particulars of claim is to ensure that the defendant understands the nature of the claimant's case, and is not taken by surprise. However, and secondly, in so far as it can be said that there are any gaps or uncertainties in the particulars of claim, it is always open to a defendant to ask for further information, either formally or informally. Where it is arguable, for instance, that the claimant

h
might be impliedly alleging something, or should be alleging something, or where it is not clear whether he is alleging something, the more sensible course for a defendant to take is to ask the claimant for clarification, rather than taking the aggressive and potentially time-consuming and expensive course of applying to strike out the claim.

j
[36] In these circumstances, albeit for somewhat different reasons from Judge Cowell, I would dismiss this appeal.

Appeal dismissed.

Victoria Parkin   Barrister.

Director of Public Prosecutions v Stoke-on-Trent Magistrates' Court and another

[2003] EWHC 1593 (Admin)

QUEEN'S BENCH DIVISION (DIVISIONAL COURT)

AULD LJ AND GOLDRING J

16 JUNE 2003

Public order – Football – Designated football match – Indecent or racialist chanting – Whether chanting including use of word 'Paki' of a racialist nature – Football (Offences) Act 1991, s 3(2)(b).

A designated football match took place between Port Vale and Oldham Athletic at the Port Vale football ground. The defendant attended the match and was a member of a group of Port Vale supporters who were chanting, 'You're just a town full of Pakis', at the Oldham supporters. The defendant was arrested and charged with taking part at a designated football match in chanting of a racialist nature contrary to s 3(1)[a] of the Football (Offences) Act 1991. Section 3(2)(b) of that Act provided that 'of a racialist nature' meant matter which was threatening, abusive or insulting to a person, by reason of his colour, race, nationality or ethnic or national origins. The district judge acquitted the defendant being of the opinion, inter alia, that the phrase was 'mere doggerel' and amounted to no more than aimlessly stating that 'our town is better than your town'; that it contained no swearing or offensive language per se; and that 'Paki' was no more insulting or racialist than terms such as 'Brit', or 'Aussie'. The prosecution appealed by way of case stated.

Held – The use of the word 'Paki', certainly in the context of the 1991 Act, but more generally nowadays, was racialist in the sense defined by the 1991 Act since the modern common understanding of the word 'Paki' was that it was a slang expression which was racially offensive. Indeed it was a word which was often used as a prelude to violence, whether provoking or offering it. There was no doubt that in most contexts the purpose of its use went beyond a convenient and/or affectionate abbreviation of a description of a nationality, such as an Aussie or a Brit. Furthermore, it was immaterial for the purposes of the offence whether persons of the racial group referred to in the offending words were present so as to hear them, or, if so present, were offended or affected in any way by them. The purpose of the 1991 Act was to discourage conduct of a racially insulting nature which could have that effect. Although, it was necessary to look at the use of the word on a case-by-case basis, on the facts found in the instant case, it was plain that the chanting in which the defendant was alleged to have taken part was 'of a racialist nature' as defined by s 3(2)(b). Moreover, it was behaviour which fell squarely within the mischief at which the statutory

---

a   Section 3, so far as material provided: '(1) It is an offence to ... take part in chanting of ... a racialist nature. (2) For this purpose ... "of a racialist nature" means consisting of or including matter which is threatening, abusive or insulting to a person by reason of his colour, race, nationality (including citizenship) or ethnic or national origins.'

a provision was aimed. It followed that the matter would be remitted to the district judge with a direction to convict (see [14], [15], [24]–[26], [28], below).

R v Reader [2000] 2 Cr App R (S) 442; R v Webb [2001] 1 Cr App R (S) 112, and R v Salihu [2001] All ER (D) 32 (Mar) considered.

Notes

b For offences at football matches, see 45(2) Halsbury's Laws (4th edn reissue) para 113.

For the Football (Offences) Act 1991, s 3, see 45 Halsbury's Statutes (4th edn) (1999 reissue) 940.

Cases referred to in judgment

c R v Reader [2000] 2 Cr App R (S) 442, CA.

R v Salihu [2001] EWCA Crim 483, [2001] All ER (D) 32 (Mar).

R v Webb [2001] 1 Cr App R (S) 112, CA.

Case stated

d The Director of Public Prosecutions appealed by way of case stated against the acquittal, by a district judge sitting at Stoke-on-Trent Magistrates' Court on 28 January 2003, of Sean Ratcliffe on a charge of taking part at a designated football match in chanting of a racialist nature contrary to ss 3(1) and 5 of the Football (Offences) Act 1991. The question for the opinion of the High Court

e was: 'Whether the evidence which was properly adduced before the learned judge entitled him to find that the chanting in which the defendant was alleged to have taken part was not "of a racialist nature" as defined by s 3(2)(b) of the Football (Offences) Act 1991.' The facts are set out in the judgment of Auld LJ.

Edward Coke (instructed by the Crown Prosecution Service) for the prosecution.

f The respondents did not appear.

Cur adv vult

16 June 2003. The following judgments were delivered.

g **AULD LJ.**

[1] This is an appeal by the Director of Public Prosecutions (DPP) by way of case stated against an acquittal by the district judge at Stoke-on-Trent Magistrates' Court on 28 January 2003 of Sean Ratcliffe on a charge of taking part at a designated football match in chanting of a racialist nature, contrary to s 3 of

h the Football (Offences) Act 1991. The first respondent has indicated that he does not intend to take any part in the proceedings, and Sean Ratcliffe, the second respondent, who has been duly served with them, does not appear.

[2] On 12 October 2002, a designated football match took place between Port Vale and Oldham Athletic at the Port Vale football ground, Stoke-on-Trent in

j Staffordshire. Sean Ratcliffe attended the match. At it, a number of persons were chanting: 'You're just a town full of Pakis.' The chant was directed at the Oldham Athletic supporters, who were in the adjacent section of the ground, known as Hamil Row. The evidence was that it was audible to those supporters.

[3] On 26 October 2002, Ratcliffe was arrested for the offence. In interview, he admitted using the phrase at the football match on 12 October, along with many others. He was charged with the offence.

[4] His trial took place before the district judge on 28 January of this year, as I have said, at Stoke-on-Trent Magistrates' Court. Ratcliffe did not give evidence. On a submission that the words used were not of a racialist nature, he was acquitted at the close of the prosecution case.

[5] The district judge, in his case stated of 4 April 2003, set out the following facts:

'(a) On 12 October 2002, at 4.10 pm Port Vale were playing a nationwide league game against Oldham Athletic at Vale Park, Burslem, Stoke-on-Trent. (b) The defendant was present at the game as a paying spectator situated in the front eastern end of the area known as the Railway Stand. (c) Certain of the spectators in that area, between 50–100 in number, began and continued to chant the words: "You're just a town full of Pakis." (d) Those words were audible to the supporters of Oldham Athletic who were situated in the adjacent Hamil Row end of Vale Park. (e) There were no Pakistani, Asian or black persons in the crowd or on the playing field.

5. The defendant elected not to give evidence, but, in his police interview on 26 October 2002, he had agreed that he had used the ... phrase.

6. The prosecution ... contended [that] the ... phrase that was uttered by the defendant was insulting and was therefore "of a racialist nature" within the meaning of s 3 of the 1991 Act.

7. The defendant contended and submitted that the phrases were not insulting [in that sense].'

[6]–[11] The district judge gave five reasons for his acquittal of Ratcliffe, namely: 1. The phrase was 'mere doggerel' and amounted to no more than aimlessly stating that 'our town is better than your town'. 2. It contained no swearing or offensive language per se. 3. The word 'Paki' was no more insulting or racialist than the use of the words 'Pom', 'Brit', 'Yank', 'Aussie' or 'Kiwi'. 4. The word 'Paki' is not insulting, whereas 'Frog' or 'Kraut' could be termed insulting. 5. The word 'Paki' is no more than a shortened form of 'Pakistani', which is an adjectival word meaning 'of the Pakistan nation'.

[12] The question that the district judge has posed for this court is in the following terms:

'Whether the evidence which was properly adduced before the learned judge entitled him to find that the chanting in which the defendant was alleged to have taken part was not "of a racialist nature" as defined by s 3(2)(b) of the 1991 Act.'

[13] Chanting of a racialist nature at a designated football match is an offence under s 3 of the 1991 Act. The words 'of a racialist nature' mean, as provided by s 3(2)(b), that the chant consists of or includes matter which is threatening, abusive or insulting to a person, by reason of his colour, race, nationality or ethnic or national origins.

[14] I should note that it is immaterial for the purposes of the offence whether persons of the racial group referred to in the alleged offending words are present so as to hear them, or, if so present, are offended or affected in any way by them. The purpose of the 1991 Act is to discourage conduct of a racially insulting nature which could have that effect.

[15] Mr Edward Coke, in his helpful submissions on behalf of the DPP, has submitted that it is obvious that the use of the very word 'Paki', certainly in this

a context, but more generally nowadays, is racialist in the sense defined by the 1991 Act.

[16] As to the district judge's description of it as 'mere doggerel', Mr Coke submitted that, doggerel or no, the chant was intended to insult those coming from Oldham, whatever their origin, and that it was implicit in the chant that Oldham was inferior because of the nationality or ethnic or national origin of a *b* number of its citizens. He said that the use of the word 'Paki' in that context demonstrated that it was those of Pakistani origin who were implicitly the cause of the inferiority. The effect, submitted Mr Coke, was that the chant was insulting within the meaning of the section.

[17] He also challenged the district judge's finding that the chanting contained no offensive language, taking as the starting point of his submissions a reference *c* to the *Shorter Oxford English Dictionary* (5th edn, 2002), where the word 'Paki' is defined as 'slang which is racially offensive'.

[18] As to the comparison drawn by the district judge between the word 'Paki' and the words 'Brit', 'Aussie' or 'Kiwi', Mr Coke submitted that, however it has come about historically, the normal usage of those words is not taken as being *d* derogatory—often the contrary—and words like 'Pom' or 'Yank' may or may not be derogatory or complimentary, depending on the context.

[19] 'Paki', Mr Coke suggested, is more to be bracketed with the words 'Frog' or 'Kraut', which were also referred to by the district judge in his case stated. It is wrong to suggest, he submitted, that the word 'Paki' is nowadays merely the *e* shortened form of 'Pakistani'.

[20] If legal support is needed for those submissions, Mr Coke provided it by reference to three cases. Under the general submission that the word 'Paki' has been recognised by the courts as something in the nature of racialist abuse, the first case to which he referred the court is *R v Reader* [2000] 2 Cr App R (S) 442. It involved offences of wounding with intent to cause grievous bodily harm, *f* contrary to s 18 of the Offences Against the Person Act 1861, and actual bodily harm, contrary to s 47 of that Act, and criminal damage. The words used in the course of the violence, the subject of those charges, were: 'What are you doing standing up for a Paki?'

[21] As Mr Coke observed, there was never any suggestion that the words *g* were anything other than words of a racialist nature; and the Court of Appeal treated them, as the sentencing judge had done, as an aggravating factor.

[22] The second case to which Mr Coke referred the court was *R v Webb* [2001] 1 Cr App R (S) 112. In that case, the words in question were: 'Paki bastard.' It was part of the prosecution case that the attack had been racially motivated *h* when those words were used. Again, there was no suggestion before the court that the words were not of a racialist nature. Indeed, the matter was dealt with as a racially aggravated assault for that reason.

[23] Third is the case of *R v Salihu* [2001] EWCA Crim 483, [2001] All ER (D) 32 (Mar), another case of racially aggravated assault in which the words 'fucking *j* Paki' and 'Paki wanker' were treated by the court as racially aggravated.

[24] On the strength of those submissions and those authorities, Mr Coke maintained that the word 'Paki' is in itself a derogatory expression and a racialist one now, and certainly was in the context in which it was used in this case.

[25] In my view, Mr Coke's submission is well founded. The *Shorter Oxford English Dictionary*, in its definition in 2002 of the word 'Paki' as a slang expression which is racially offensive reflects the modern, common understanding of the

word; it is also, unfortunately, all too familiar an expression to the courts, used,
as it so often is, as a prelude to violence, whether provoking or offering it.

[26] There is no doubt that in most contexts the purpose of its use goes
beyond a convenient and/or affectionate abbreviation of a description of a
nationality, such as an Aussie or a Brit. It is odd and a shame that that is so in this
country, but the unpleasant context in which it is so often used has left it with a
derogatory or an insulting racialist connotation.

[27] Of course, as Mr Coke submitted, the use of the word 'Paki' must, on a
case-by-case basis, be looked at in its context. Here, there can be no doubt on the
facts found by the district judge as set out in his case stated that Ratcliffe and his
fellow Port Vale supporters, in using it as part of their chant against the opposing
Oldham supporters, were using it in a racially derogatory or insulting sense. That
is plain, if nothing else, from the presence of the word 'just' in the chant: 'You're
just a town full of Pakis.'

[28] In my view, Ratcliffe's admitted behaviour fell squarely within the
definition in the 1991 Act of chanting of a racialist nature at a designated football
match and within the mischief at which the statutory provision was aimed. I
would, therefore, answer 'No' to the question in the case stated, allow the DPP's
appeal and remit the case to the district judge with a direction that he should on
that evidence convict Ratcliffe of the offence.

GOLDRING J.
[29] I agree.

Appeal allowed.

Dilys Tausz   Barrister.

a
Savings and Investment Bank Ltd v Fincken
[2003] EWHC 719 (Ch)

b
CHANCERY DIVISION
PATTEN J
19 FEBRUARY 2003

c
Statement of claim – Leave to amend – Statements made in 'without prejudice' discussions inconsistent with statements made in affidavit – Whether within 'unambiguous impropriety' exception to 'without prejudice' rule.

The claimant company was in liquidation. At the time of its winding up the defendant was substantially indebted to it. The claimant commenced proceedings in order to recover the moneys due to it. Discussion between the
d parties resulted in their entering into a deed of settlement in relation to the indebtedness and a further supplemental deed. The defendant failed to fulfil a substantial part of his obligations under those deeds of settlement. He subsequently swore an affidavit of means in which he set out his material assets. The parties then entered into a third deed of settlement, expressed to be in full and final settlement of all claims, under which the defendant warranted that he
e had made full disclosure of his material assets in his affidavit. The claimant subsequently alleged that it had discovered that the defendant owned certain property which he had not disclosed. On the basis of that alleged non-disclosure and consequential misrepresentation in the defendant's affidavit, the claimant commenced proceedings seeking, inter alia, rescission of the third deed of
f settlement. In an attempt to settle the proceedings, a 'without prejudice' meeting was arranged between the parties. The claimant alleged that at that meeting the defendant had admitted to ownership of shares in a company. The claimant later made further inquiries and discovered a director's loan from the company to the defendant. Consequently, the claimant applied to reamend its statement of claim
g to add those non-disclosures to its particulars of claim on the grounds that the defendant's inconsistencies as revealed by that meeting fell within the 'unambiguous impropriety' exception to the 'without prejudice' rule. The defendant submitted that the only circumstances in which the 'without prejudice' rule could be avoided within the 'unambiguous impropriety' exception was in a case where the admissions against interest, made at a without prejudice meeting
h or in without prejudice communications, were accompanied by a threat.

Held – There were a number of established exceptions to the 'without prejudice' rule designed to restrict the operation of the rule to what it was intended to protect and to prevent abuse. One party might be allowed to give evidence of
j what the other said or wrote in 'without prejudice' negotiations if the exclusion of the evidence would act as a cloak for perjury, blackmail or other unambiguous impropriety. Where the protection afforded by the rule had been unequivocally abused the veil imposed by public policy might have to be pulled aside, even so as to disclose admissions. No discernible difference could be seen, having regard to the policy of the privilege, between a case where there was an admission against interest accompanied by a threat and the instant case where a person

unambiguously asserted the truth of a particular set of facts and in subsequent
proceedings sought to deny it. Circumstances of that kind amounted to an abuse
and the exclusion of such evidence by virtue of the rule would act as a cloak for
perjury. Accordingly, the claimant's application to amend its statement of claim
would be allowed (see [35]–[38], [40], [42], [52], below).

    Rush & Tompkins Ltd v Greater London Council [1988] 3 All ER 737 and
Unilever plc v The Proctor & Gamble Co [2001] 1 All ER 783 applied.

Notes
For the rule as to 'without prejudice' communications, see 17(1) *Halsbury's Laws*
(4th edn reissue) paras 887, 888.

Cases referred to in judgment
Cobbold v Greenwich London BC [1999] CA Transcript 1406.
Fazil-Alizadeh v Nikbin [1993] CA Transcript 205, (1993) Times, 19 March.
Forster v Friedland [1992] CA Transcript 1052.
Greenwood v Fitts (1961) 29 DLR (2d) 260, BC CA.
Hawick Jersey International Ltd v Caplan (1988) Times, 11 March.
Merrill Lynch, Pierce Fenner & Smith Inc v Raffa [2001] IL Pr 31.
Muller v Linsley & Mortimer (a firm) [1996] PNLR 74, CA.
Rush & Tompkins Ltd v Greater London Council [1988] 3 All ER 737, [1989] AC 1280,
    [1988] 3 WLR 939, HL.
Unilever plc v The Proctor & Gamble Co [2001] 1 All ER 783, [2000] 1 WLR 2436, CA.

Application
The claimant, Savings and Investment Bank Ltd, applied for permission to
reamend its statement of claim in proceedings against the defendant, Kenneth
Fincken, seeking rescission of a compromise agreement reached in relation to the
liabilities of the defendant to the claimant. The facts are set out in the judgment.

David Ashton (instructed by *D J Freeman*) for the claimant.
Adrian Francis (instructed by *RadcliffesLeBrasseur*) for Mr Fincken.

PATTEN J.
[1] This is an application by the claimant in these proceedings, the Savings and
Investment Bank Ltd (SIB), which is a company in liquidation, for permission to
re-reamend the statement of claim. The principal relief sought in this action is the
rescission of a compromise agreement reached in relation to the liabilities of the
defendant, Mr Fincken, to the claimant company.

[2] At the time of the winding up of the claimant company it is alleged, and I
think common ground, that the defendant was substantially indebted to SIB,
either as principal debtor or in relation to various guarantees. In order to recover
those moneys, and I take these facts from the re-reamended statement of claim,
SIB issued proceedings on 23 February 1988 in action CH/1988/S/1540.

[3] There were then discussions which resulted first in a deed of settlement in
relation to the indebtedness executed on 13 October 1988 by Mr Fincken and his
wife. Under the terms of that agreement Mr Fincken acknowledged the existence
of various debts and agreed to deliver by 30 November of that year a bill of
exchange in the sum of some £19,266,000 odd.

[4] It was also agreed that no later than 13 October 1989 Mr Fincken would
pay the sum of £250,000 to SIB, whereupon the company would return to him

a the bill of exchange unpresented and unnegotiated. That first deed of settlement was said to be in full and final settlement of all disputes between the parties. The bill of exchange was duly delivered on approximately 18 November 1988, but by 13 October 1989 Mr Fincken had paid only the sum of £50,000 and the obligation to return the bill did not therefore arise.

b [5] The parties then entered into a supplemental deed of settlement on 25 July 1990, which contained terms under which it was to be effective from 18 October 1989. It provided that in lieu of the terms of the prior agreement under which a single bill of exchange would be delivered, Mr Fincken agreed to deliver five bills of exchange, each in the sum of £19,216,276·02, payable respectively on 18 April 1990, 18 October 1990, 18 April 1991, 18 October 1991 and 18 April 1992.

c [6] The second deed also provided that Mr Fincken would make payments of £50,000 on each of those dates up to and including 18 October 1991 and a further £20,000 on 18 April 1992. On the payment of those moneys in accordance with that timetable the various bills of exchange would be returned to Mr Fincken unpresented and unnegotiated, but in default of such payments the claimant

d would be entitled to present and sue upon the appropriate bills of exchange.

[7] It is alleged, and again I think common ground, that Mr Fincken failed to make the payments due on 18 April 1990 and on 18 October 1990 as a result of which the claimant presented the bill of exchange payable on 18 October 1990 which was subsequently dishonoured. There then followed the presentation in

e April 1991 of a bankruptcy petition against Mr Fincken in the Aylesbury County Court. The petition was dismissed and there was a subsequent appeal to the High Court.

[8] On 9 December 1991, Mr Fincken swore an affidavit of means exhibiting a statement of personal assets, liabilities and business interests as at 9 December 1991.

f That statement which Mr Fincken deposed to as being true contained a number of statements, including a statement that he possessed or owned no land or buildings or other property save his residence at Field House in Chalfont St Giles and that he possessed or had no other investments or collections save two shotguns worth £2,500.

[9] On 6 May 1992, the claimant and Mr Fincken entered into a third deed of

g settlement, under cl 2 of which Mr Fincken warranted that in the affidavit of means I have referred to he had made full disclosure of all material assets worldwide beneficially owned by him or in which he had an interest, whether alone or jointly with others. As a term of that agreement the claimant agreed to discontinue its appeal and it was agreed that the third deed would be in full and

h final settlement of all claims.

[10] It is now said prior to the amendment which this application is concerned with that the defendant, Mr Fincken, failed to disclose two material assets. The first was a beneficial interest in or ownership of a property called Field House Barn in Chalfont St Giles which is said to have a value of at least £25,000.

j Secondly, his beneficial interest in or ownership of a 20 bore shotgun worth at least £7,500.

[11] On the basis of those alleged non-disclosures and consequently the misrepresentations contained in the 1991 affidavit of means the claimant now seeks rescission of the third settlement agreement and, therefore, the right to enforce the provisions of the second deed of settlement or alternatively, to enforce and continue proceedings for the recovery of the original debt.

[12] The present application seeks to add to the particulars of *a*
misrepresentation and non-disclosure two further items. The first is alleged
non-disclosure of beneficial interests in 47,500 fully paid ordinary shares of £1
each and 250,000 fully paid preference shares of £1 each in a company called
Westminster Property Holdings plc, which for convenience I will refer to as
Westminster. It is said that at the relevant time those shares were worth at least
£228,785. The second item is an alleged indebtedness by way of director's loan *b*
to the defendant from Westminster in the sum of some £291,480.

[13] The first item, that is to say the shares, is said to have come to the
attention of the claimant as a result of a meeting which took place on
13 December 2002 between Mr Fincken and Mr Michael Jordan, who is one of
the claimant's joint liquidators. Paragraph 19.27 of the proposed amended
pleading states that in the course of that meeting: *c*

'Mr Fincken told Mr Jordan that all the Hallam shares were held by Hallam
as his nominee and later in the meeting he again confirmed that he was the
owner of all the Hallam shares.'

[14] The Hallam shares are the shares in Westminster that I have referred to. *d*
In relation to the director's loan, reliance is not placed on any alleged admissions
made by Mr Fincken in the meeting with Mr Jordan. Rather, it is said by
Mr Ashton that his clients, having been alerted to the position in relation to the
shares, then caused further inquiries to be made and a further examination of the
available material at Companies House and elsewhere as a result of which they
were able to plead that there was this additional asset in the form of the *e*
indebtedness by way of director's loan.

[15] The application for permission to reamend is opposed by Mr Fincken on,
essentially, three grounds. The first two are connected. Those grounds are that
the meeting in December last year, which is pleaded in para 19.27, was a
privileged occasion in the sense that it was a without prejudice meeting and the *f*
claimant is not therefore entitled to rely on and to adduce evidence as to what
was said at that meeting in support of his claim to recover the shares, or rather to
rely on the non-disclosure of the shares in support of his claim for rescission.

[16] Secondly, and this is the allied point, it is said that even if the plea in
para 19.27 is removed and instead, as Mr Ashton has indicated, there is
substituted a mere assertion that Mr Fincken was at all material times the *g*
beneficial owner of the Hallam shares, the position still remains that that claim
can only be substantiated by the court receiving evidence of what took place at
the without prejudice meeting and, therefore, I ought not to allow that claim into
the pleadings if it is apparent from the outset that the evidence to support it will
not be available. *h*

[17] Thirdly, and more generally, Mr Francis, on behalf of Mr Fincken, says
that these claims are far too late, that his client has had to endure these
proceedings over a very considerable period of time and at considerable cost and
expense to himself, both financial and in terms of the strain which litigation
necessarily places upon an individual and that a line should now be drawn so that *j*
the action can proceed to trial on 17 March, when the trial is due to take place on
the basis of the existing pleading.

[18] I will come back to those issues later in this judgment, but the position at
the moment is that the action has been set down for trial in March as a result of
an order in a case management conference made by Master Bragge as long ago as
May 2002. It is common ground between the parties that if I allow these

a proposed amendments into the pleadings a trial on that date will not be possible. There is an element of dispute, I think, between the parties as to whether a trial on that date is feasible even if the amendments are not allowed and the claim is restricted to the current allegations on the pleadings.

[19] I turn first of all to the principal ground of objection, which is the question of the admissibility of what took place at the meeting on 13 December. The b privilege attaching to without prejudice communications between parties to litigation is designed to encourage settlement in litigation and to prevent admissions against interest being received in evidence in subsequent proceedings.

[20] The dangers of discouraging settlement that would flow from the general relaxation of the without prejudice rule are obvious, but it is equally clear on the authorities that the without prejudice rule and the privilege that attaches to such c discussions is subject to a number of established exceptions designed on the one hand to restrict the operation of the rule to what it was intended to protect, and secondly, to prevent abuse.

[21] The purpose of the rule was described in some detail by Hoffmann LJ in *Muller v Linsley & Mortimer (a firm)* [1996] PNLR 74. Hoffmann LJ in his judgment d in that case explained (at 77) that the rule has two justifications—

> 'Firstly, the public policy of encouraging parties to negotiate and settle their disputes out of court and, secondly, an implied agreement arising out of what is commonly understood to be the consequences of offering or agreeing to negotiate without prejudice. In some cases both of these
> e justifications are present; in others, only one or the other.'

[22] Hoffmann LJ then went on to analyse the way in which the rule operates and said (at 79):

> 'If one analyses the relationship between the without prejudice rule and the other rules of evidence, it seems to me that the privilege operates as an
> f exception to the general rule on admissions (which can itself be regarded as an exception to the rule against hearsay) that the statement or conduct of a party is always admissible against him to prove any fact which is thereby expressly or impliedly asserted or admitted. The public policy aspect of the rule is not in my judgment concerned with the admissibility of statements
> g which are relevant otherwise than as admissions, *i.e.* independently of the truth of the facts alleged to have been admitted.'

[23] Hoffmann LJ went on to give examples of such exceptions. Without prejudice communications may be admitted in evidence when, for example, the issue is whether they resulted in an agreement or alternatively whether there was h some misrepresentation actually practised in the course of those negotiations or whether, for example, a without prejudice letter containing a statement amounted to an act of bankruptcy. That is not an exhaustive list of the exceptions but is sufficient, I think, to establish and identify the principle.

[24] But, in the present case I am concerned not with exceptions of that kind j but with a submission made by the claimant that to allow the defendant to take advantage of the privilege attaching to the December meeting would constitute an abuse because it would conceivably allow Mr Fincken to advance a case in subsequent proceedings to the effect that the shares do not belong to him when little over a month ago he was prepared to concede that they did.

[25] The relevant exception to the without prejudice rule relied on to support the admission of that evidence is what is referred to in the authorities as the

unambiguous impropriety exception. That phrase was first coined by
Hoffmann LJ in the unreported decision of *Forster v Friedland* [1992] CA
Transcript 1052. That was a case where there was an allegation that the
defendants had agreed to purchase shares in a company by 31 October 1989. The
defendants denied the existence of any legally binding agreement, saying it was
merely an agreement in principle. No completion took place in accordance with
the alleged agreement and there followed a threat of proceedings.

[26] During the course of various meetings and telephone conversations
between the parties, all of which the claimant secretly tape recorded, the first
defendant was said to have made clear his position that if the matter went to a
trial he would deny that there was any legally binding agreement but was, none
the less, prepared to assure the claimant that he regarded himself as honour
bound to go through with the deal. All that he really wanted was time to arrange
matters so as to avoid the need to offer 73p in the pound to the other shareholders
in accordance with the City Takeover Code.

[27] The claimant sought to adduce that evidence in the subsequent
proceedings on the basis that the defendant should not be allowed to assert the
claim that there was no legally binding agreement when, as he had conceded at
the meeting, he was prepared to honour the agreement. The Court of Appeal
held that the facts of that case did not fall within what is now referred to as the
unambiguous impropriety exception.

[28] That result was hardly surprising, bearing in mind that the defendants
never conceded even in the without prejudice negotiations that there was a
legally binding agreement. For my own part, I am unable to see how the judge
would have been assisted merely by knowing that the defendants were prepared
to treat the agreement as binding in honour. But the case is important for the
principle which it establishes. Hoffmann LJ who gave the leading judgment in
the Court of Appeal, began by analysing two earlier cases in which the without
prejudice privilege had been avoided in favour of allowing the evidence of the
communications to be presented to the court.

[29] The first of those cases was the Canadian case of *Greenwood v Fitts* (1961)
29 DLR (2d) 260, in which the defendant told the plaintiffs in the course of
without prejudice negotiations that unless they withdrew their claim for
fraudulent misrepresentation he would give perjured evidence and bribe other
witnesses to perjure themselves, and that even if they succeeded he would leave
Canada rather than pay damages.

[30] The court held that the without prejudice rule was never intended to give
protection to that sort of thing. In the English decision in *Hawick Jersey
International Ltd v Caplan* (1988) Times, 11 March, Anthony May QC, then sitting
as a deputy judge of the Queen's Bench Division, had to deal with a case where
the plaintiff is said to have asserted during the course of without prejudice
negotiations that he did not dispute and, indeed, accepted that a transaction was
not a loan but one involving an exchange for some £10,000 in cash.

[31] During the course of those exchanges the defendant said to the plaintiff:
'You are not going to force my hand by blackmailing me.' To which the plaintiff
replied: 'But I have got to, what would you do if you had been me?' Hoffmann LJ
analysed these cases in the following way:

'These are clear cases of improper threats, but the value of the without
prejudice rule would be seriously impaired if its protection could be
removed from anything less than unambiguous impropriety. The rule is

a   designed to encourage parties to express themselves freely and without inhibition. I think it is quite wrong for the tape recorded words of a layman, who has used colourful or even exaggerated language, to be picked over in order to support an argument that he intends to raise defences which he does not really believe to be true.'

b   [32] Although it is clear from that passage that Hoffmann LJ had identified the two earlier cases as ones in each of which there had been, to use his words, improper threats, his principal concern was to avoid an artificial and unrealistic dissection of the exchanges between the parties with a view to extracting unambiguous admissions that might form the basis of an application for their reception in evidence in the event that in subsequent proceedings the party *c*   making them intended to run a contrary case. That, I think, is clear from the concluding words of the quotation that I have just made.

[33] Similarly, in the subsequent decision of the Court of Appeal in *Fazil-Alizadeh v Nikbin* [1993] CA Transcript 205, (1993) Times, 19 March, Simon Brown LJ rejected a submission that certain alleged admissions to the effect that an agreement had been altered at a later date than had been originally suggested *d*   should be admitted in evidence. He held that those statements were ambiguous and therefore did not represent an unambiguous impropriety within the meaning of that term. As Simon Brown LJ said in that case:

e   'There are ... powerful policy reasons for admitting in evidence as exceptions to the without prejudice rule only the very clearest of cases. Unless this highly beneficial rule is most scrupulously and jealously protected, it will all too readily become eroded.'

[34] That, I think, is a reflection of part of the speech of Lord Griffiths in *Rush & Tompkins Ltd v Greater London Council* [1988] 3 All ER 737, [1989] AC 1280, in *f*   which the basis of the privilege was established and confirmed by the House of Lords. In his speech in that case Lord Griffiths said ([1988] 3 All ER 737 at 740, [1989] AC 1280 at 1300) that it was important not to allow the whittling down of the protection given to the parties—

g   'to speak freely about all issues in the litigation both factual and legal when seeking compromise and, for the purpose of establishing a basis of compromise, admitting certain facts.'

[35] In *Unilever plc v The Proctor & Gamble Co* [2001] 1 All ER 783 at 796, [2000] 1 WLR 2436 at 2449 that point was picked up in his judgment by Robert Walker LJ who said that parties cannot speak freely at a without prejudice *h*   meeting if they must constantly monitor every sentence with lawyers or patent agents sitting at their shoulders as minders. But he recognised the exception to this rule. He said ([2001] 1 All ER 783 at 796, [2000] 1 WLR 2436 at 2449):

j   'Lord Griffiths in the *Rush & Tompkins* case noted, and more recent decisions illustrate, that even in situations to which the without prejudice rule undoubtedly applies, the veil imposed by public policy may have to be pulled aside, even so as to disclose admissions, in cases where the protection afforded by the rule has been unequivocally abused.'

[36] This is a reference back to an earlier part of his judgment ([2001] 1 All ER 783 at 792, [2000] 1 WLR 2436 at 2444) where he referred to *Forster v Friedland*

[1992] CA Transcript 1052 and *Hawick Jersey International Ltd v Caplan* (1988) Times, 11 March as establishing the following principle:

> 'Apart from any concluded contract or estoppel, one party may be allowed to give evidence of what the other said or wrote in without prejudice negotiations if the exclusion of the evidence would act as a cloak for perjury, blackmail or other "unambiguous impropriety" ...'

[37] It seems to me, therefore, that it is not right and I cannot accept Mr Francis's primary submission that the only circumstances in which the without prejudice rule can be avoided is in a case where at the without prejudice meeting itself, or in the course of the without prejudice communications, the admission against interest is accompanied by some kind of threat.

[38] For my own part, I can see no discernible difference, having regard to the policy of the privilege, between the case where a threat of that kind is present and a case where somebody merely asserts in unambiguous and unequivocal terms the truth of a particular set of facts and then in subsequent proceedings seeks to deny it.

[39] The concerns of Lord Griffiths and Robert Walker LJ, and to that I add Hoffmann LJ, in the cases that I have referred to are largely concerned with ensuring that what may be complicated without prejudice negotiations should not subsequently be scrutinised with a view to constructing admissions which when made, and particularly in the context in which they were made, were never intended to be and were not in truth unequivocal and unambiguous admissions of liability.

[40] It seems to me that the exception identified by Robert Walker LJ can extend, in appropriate cases, not only to instances where the without prejudice occasion is abused by the making of threats but also cases where there is an unambiguous admission of facts which is intended to be followed by an equally unambiguous denial of those facts by the same party. Circumstances of that kind amount to an abuse and the exclusion of such evidence by virtue of the rule would act as a cloak for perjury.

[41] I am also satisfied, for what it is worth, that circumstances of that kind constitute unambiguous impropriety of the kind envisaged by Hoffmann LJ. That is not to say, as I hope I have indicated, that every admission, legal or factual, can be open to the court in subsequent proceedings regardless of the circumstances. The sort of cases that I have in mind are cases where in an uncomplicated situation and not for the purpose of establishing a negotiating position on a hypothetical basis the party has made a clear admission of relevant facts which he or she then subsequently chooses to deny.

[42] My decision on what I readily accept is not a straightforward point is, I believe, consistent with Anthony May's decision in the *Hawick Jersey International* case, and also with a later decision of Judge Jack QC in *Merrill Lynch, Pierce Fenner & Smith Inc v Raffa* [2001] IL Pr 31. For those reasons I reject Mr Francis's primary ground of objection to the proposed amendment.

[43] His second point is that even if the claimant is prepared to omit para 19.27 from the proposed amendment and to leave it to either a reply or the trial to seek to admit the evidence of the without prejudice meeting, that does not overcome the difficulty, and indeed creates the difficulty, that there is currently no evidence on which the allegation that Mr Fincken owns the shares can be based.

[44] Given the way I have decided the first issue, that point I think does not really arise. On the basis of the material before me and in particular the witness

a statement of Mr Richard Colman made in support of this application, there is evidence before the court that at the meeting on 13 December 2002, Mr Fincken freely admitted to Mr Jordan that the shares in Westminster were his and that is sufficient to overcome the objection to the amendment that it cannot as currently formulated be substantiated at the trial.

b [45] That leaves, then, the more general objection to these amendments, namely that they are late and cause undue prejudice, particularly in relation to the possible vacation of the trial date. The court's power to permit amendments to statements of case is a general discretion which has to be exercised having regard to a number of well-established factors. In *Cobbold v Greenwich London BC* [1999] CA Transcript 1406, Peter Gibson LJ summed up the position in this way:

c   'The overriding objective [for the CPR] is that the court should deal with cases justly. That includes, so far as practical, ensuring that each case is dealt with not only expeditiously but also fairly. Amendments in general ought to be allowed so that the real dispute between the parties can be adjudicated upon provided that any prejudice to the other party or parties caused by the

d   amendment can be compensated for in costs, and the public interest in the official administration of justice is not significantly harmed.'

[46] The present amendments, although made late, are explicable in terms of timing by virtue of the late admission relied on at the December meeting. Undoubtedly, the amendments, if permission is granted, will generate additional

e costs but some of those within the ordinary course of events will be costs for which the claimant will be responsible. Therefore, as I see it, there are two serious factors to be considered in terms of weighing up the general discretion in this particular case.

[47] The first is the rather difficult to assess criterion of the general effect and

f additional worry that this may cause to Mr Fincken in terms of having to cope with these matters very late in the day. The second matter is the effect granting the amendment, and therefore having to put off the trial, will have on other court users. I will deal with the second first.

[48] Although this application is made very late, the position in relation to the action as a whole is itself far from satisfactory. Although the master made

g directions back in May last year for disclosure and for the provision of experts' reports, none of those orders has been complied with, mainly, as I understand it, because the parties have very sensibly been engaged in discussions designed, although in the event unsuccessfully, to compromise these proceedings.

[49] But the fact remains, perhaps through no fault of their own on either side,

h that as things stand this afternoon none of the case management conference directions about disclosure and the provision of witness statements, including experts statements, have been adhered to and, although I think the true position is that both parties have approached the court today on the footing that they could be ready by 17 March on the basis of the existing pleading, there must be a

j real doubt as to whether that is in fact achievable.

[50] But, even if it is achievable, I am of the view that if I adjourn the trial now there will not be a significant impact on other court users. It will be possible for the judicial time that would have been engaged by the hearing of this case to be used in relation to some other case and I have no reason to suppose that the case will not be accommodated at some later time this year without any undue inconvenience to other parties. Therefore, I do not regard the effect of allowing

the amendment on other court users as sufficient in itself to refuse permission to amend.

[51] That leaves, then, the position of Mr Fincken. I know very little about his personal circumstances beyond what Mr Francis has told me and there is no evidence from him in relation to this application, but I suppose it must be the position that when somebody has had to deal with litigation for a period now of at least 14 years it must necessarily have been a strain. On the other hand, these are serious claims. Although they have been reduced in scale by a decision of the Court of Appeal, the basic claim that there is a case for rescission of the settlement agreements remains viable; there has been no attempt that I am aware of, certainly no successful attempt, to strike out the existing pleading. And, if it is right that there should be a trial in relation to that pleading, it is, in my judgment, right that there should be a trial in relation to that pleading which includes all relevant issues.

[52] The position in relation to the shares and the loans on the proposed amended pleading is that they are clearly relevant to a consideration of whether or not there has been a material misrepresentation and, in my judgment, the need to do justice between the parties by allowing those issues properly to be litigated outweighs what I am aware of in terms of the effect that allowing the amendment with the further consequent delay will have on Mr Fincken. In those circumstances, with the proposed alteration and substitution of para 19.27, suggested by Mr Ashton, I will give permission to reamend.

Application allowed.

Neneh Munu   Barrister.

Donoghue v Folkestone Properties Ltd

a

[2003] EWCA Civ 231

COURT OF APPEAL, CIVIL DIVISION

LORD PHILLIPS OF WORTH MATRAVERS MR, BROOKE AND LAWS LJJ

b   11, 27 FEBRUARY 2003

Occupier's liability – Trespasser – Duty of care – Whether test of existence of duty of care to be determined having regard to circumstances prevailing at time of accident – Occupiers' Liability Act 1984, s 1(3)(b).

c

The claimant decided to go for a night swim shortly after midnight on 27 December 1997. He dived from a slipway into Folkestone harbour, struck his head on a submerged pile, broke his neck and was rendered tetraplegic. At the head of each of the two staircases leading down to landing stages in the harbour, notices stated that jumping into the harbour and swimming were prohibited.
d   There was no such notice at the top of the slipway. It was known that children and the occasional adult swam from the slipway in the summer, and security guards would try to stop children swimming in the harbour. The claimant brought proceedings against the defendant, the owner and occupier of the harbour, claiming that it was in breach of duty owed to him under the Occupiers'
e   Liability Act 1984. Section 1(3)(b)[a] of the 1984 Act provided that an occupier owed a duty to a person other than a visitor if, inter alia, he knew or had reasonable grounds to believe that the person was coming or might come into the vicinity of a danger of which the occupier was aware. The judge upheld the claim, although with a finding of 75% contributory negligence. The defendant
f   appealed, contending that while it accepted that it owed a duty of care to those who, as it was well aware, swam and dived in the vicinity of the slipway in the summer, that duty did not extend to the claimant, of whose swimming expedition in mid-winter in the middle of the night it had neither known nor could reasonably have been expected to know.

g   **Held** – The test whether a duty of care existed under the 1984 Act had to be determined having regard to the circumstances prevailing at the time that it was alleged that the breach of duty had resulted in injury to the claimant. At the time that the claimant in the instant case sustained his grievous injuries, the defendant had had no reason to believe that he, or anyone else, would be swimming from
h   the slipway. The criterion in s 1(3)(b) was not, therefore, satisfied. The defendant had owed no duty to the claimant and should not have been held to be under any liability for his accident. The appeal would accordingly be allowed (see [58], [77], [79], below).

    White v Council of the City and District of St Albans (1990) Times, 12 March and
j   *Ratcliff v McConnell* [1999] 1 WLR 670 applied.

Notes

For an occupier's duty of care to persons other than visitors, see *33 Halsbury's Laws* (4th edn reissue) para 640.

a   Section 1, so far as material, is set out at [13], below

For the Occupiers' Liability Act 1984, s 1, see 31 *Halsbury's Statutes* (4th edn)
(2000 reissue) 488.

Cases referred to in judgments

Addie (Robert) & Sons (Collieries) Ltd v Dumbreck [1929] AC 358, [1929] All ER Rep 1,
    HL.

British Railways Board v Herrington [1972] 1 All ER 749, [1972] AC 877, [1972] 2 WLR
    537, HL.

Comr for Railways v Quinlan [1964] 1 All ER 897, [1964] AC 1054, [1964] 2 WLR 817,
    PC.

Donoghue (or M'Alister) v Stevenson [1932] AC 562, [1932] All ER Rep 1, HL.

Fairchild v Glenhaven Funeral Services Ltd [2001] EWCA Civ 1881, [2002] IRLR 129,
    [2002] 1 WLR 1052; *rvsd* [2002] UKHL 22, [2002] 3 All ER 305, [2003] 1 AC 32,
    [2002] 3 WLR 89.

Haley v London Electricity Board [1964] 3 All ER 185, [1965] AC 778, [1964] 3 WLR
    479, HL.

Hardy v Central London Rly Co [1920] 3 KB 459, [1920] All ER Rep 205, CA.

Hughes v Lord Advocate [1963] 1 All ER 705, [1963] AC 837, [1963] 2 WLR 779, HL.

Indermaur v Dames (1866) LR 1 CP 274, [1861–73] All ER Rep 15; *affd* (1867) LR 2
    CP 311, [1861–73] All ER Rep 15, Ex Ch.

Ratcliff v McConnell [1999] 1 WLR 670, CA.

Smith v Leech Brain & Co Ltd [1961] 3 All ER 1159, [1962] 2 QB 405, [1962] 2 WLR
    148.

Tomlinson v Congleton BC [2002] EWCA Civ 309, [2003] 3 All ER 1122, [2003] 2 WLR
    1120; *rvsd* [2003] UKHL 47, [2003] 3 All ER 1122.

Videan v British Transport Commission [1963] 2 All ER 860, [1963] 2 QB 650, [1963] 3
    WLR 374, CA.

White v St Albans City and District Council (1990) Times, 12 March, CA.

Case also cited or referred to in skeleton argument

Swain v Puri [1996] PIQR P 442, CA.

Appeal

The defendant, Folkestone Properties Ltd, appealed with permission of
Brooke LJ granted on 15 October 2002 from the decision of Judge Bowers, sitting
as a judge of the High Court in Newcastle upon Tyne, on 2 September 2002
holding that Folkestone Properties was liable to the claimant, John Simon
Donoghue, for damages for breach of its duty of care under s 1 of the Occupiers'
Liability Act 1984. The facts are set out in the judgment of Lord Phillips of Worth
Matravers MR.

Lawrence West (instructed by *Eversheds*, Cardiff) for Folkestone Properties.

Bill Braithwaite QC and *Alan Saggerson* (instructed by *Cunningham John*, Thetford)
    for Mr Donoghue.

Cur adv vult

a   27 February 2003. The following judgments were delivered.

LORD PHILLIPS OF WORTH MATRAVERS MR.

INTRODUCTION

[1] This is an appeal against the judgment given on 2 September 2002 by Judge
b Bowers, sitting as an additional judge of the High Court. It arises out of a tragic
accident. On Saturday, 27 December 1997, shortly after midnight, the
respondent, Mr Donoghue, decided to go for a swim in Folkestone Harbour. He
dived into the sea from a slipway, struck his head on an underwater obstruction,
broke his neck and was rendered tetraplegic.

[2] The appellants, Folkestone Properties Ltd (Folkestone Properties), own
c and occupy the harbour. Mr Donoghue claimed that they had been in breach of
duty owed to him under the Occupiers' Liability Act 1984 and were responsible
for his injuries. The judge upheld this claim, but found that Mr Donoghue had
contributed to the accident by his own negligence to the extent that he could only
recover 25% of his damages. He does not appeal against that finding. Folkestone
d Properties appeal. They contend that the judge erred in finding that they owed
any duty of care to Mr Donoghue. They do not challenge his finding that they
owed a duty of care to those who, as they were well aware, swam and dived in
the vicinity of the slipway in the summer. They contend, however, that this duty
did not extend to Mr Donoghue, of whose swimming expedition in mid-winter
in the middle of the night they neither knew nor could reasonably have been
e expected to know.

THE HARBOUR

[3] The judge has given a careful and detailed description of Folkestone inner
harbour where the accident occurred. Because the issue raised on this appeal is a
f narrow one, and essentially an issue of law, I can describe it much more briefly.

[4] The slipway, off which the accident occurred, lies in the north-west corner
of the inner harbour. Initially it slopes down parallel and adjacent to the north
wall of the inner harbour, but it then angles away from that wall, forming a dog's
leg and continuing to slope down until it reaches the bed of the harbour.

[5] Protruding into the harbour at right angles to the lower limb of the dog's
g leg are seven substantial horizontal wooden beams, each set on a concrete base.
These are grid piles forming a 'grid bed' upon which a boat can be placed as the
tide ebbs away, so that access can be gained to her hull. The grid piles stand
proud of the harbour bed to the extent of some 80 cm. As the tide rises the grid
bed is progressively submerged until it is wholly under water for a period of
h between four and seven hours, depending upon whether the tides are spring or
neap.

[6] The object of the slipway is to enable the launching or recovery of boats
and jet-skis and members of the public were licensed by Folkestone Properties to
use the slipway for this purpose. The judge found that they probably had an
j implied licence to walk down the slipway to the water's edge, and that they had
a licence to walk up and down the path at the top of the harbour walls.

[7] Members of the public did not have a licence to use the inner harbour for
the purpose of swimming or jumping or diving in the water. On the contrary,
Folkestone Properties tried to prevent this. Eastward of the slipway, in two
places, steps descended from the north harbour wall to a landing stage. In the
summer these landing stages were popular places from which children, and the

occasional adult, entered the water to swim. At the head of each staircase, but
not the slipway, a notice was placed stating 'jumping in the harbour and
swimming is prohibited'.

[8] Children and the occasional adult also swam from the slipway in the
summer, although in smaller numbers. They would sometimes jump or dive
into the water from the slipway, and Folkestone Properties were aware of this.
Security guards would try to stop the children from swimming in the harbour
and, on occasion, the police were called, but to no marked effect.

MR DONOGHUE

[9] Mr Donoghue was aged 31 at the time of his accident. He was about 6 ft
2 in tall, weighed 16 stone and was very fit. He was a professional scuba diver.
He was trained in the Royal Navy and had served as a diver. His service records
show the extent of his very considerable experience, which included on a number
of occasions the recovery of bodies. After leaving the Navy, he continued to
work as a diver. As a diving supervisor it had been his responsibility to ascertain
water depths and freedom from obstructions before authorising a dive. As the
judge found, years of professional training and experience reinforced in his case
the common sense rule that you should not dive into water unless sure of
sufficient depth and the absence of obstructions.

[10] Mr Donoghue had lived in Folkestone since 1994. He had visited the
harbour once every month or two and occasionally launched a rigid inflatable
from the slipway. He had seen children and adults swimming in the harbour in
the summer, but had never observed the grid piles or the notices at the top of the
stairways, which prohibited swimming. The judge rejected his evidence that he
thought the harbour was a recognised place to swim. He found that
Mr Donoghue realised perfectly well that swimming was probably unauthorised
but difficult to prevent.

THE ACCIDENT

[11] Mr Donoghue spent the latter part of the evening of Boxing Day drinking
in Scruffy Murphy's public house with his partner Samia and with a number of
friends. These included David Watkins, another professional diver who had been
in the Navy with Mr Donoghue and who had taught him to dive. While in the
public house Mr Donoghue consumed at least five pints of beer, so that he was
'merry drunk', but not incapable or unable to know what he was doing or saying.
He had already had it in mind to go for a Boxing Day swim, and he discussed
going for a night swim with the others in the public house. When they left, some
of the party, including Samia, went home by taxi while Mr Donoghue,
Mr Watkins and another man and woman walked to the slipway.

[12] Mr Donoghue and Mr Watkins both intended to swim. Mr Donoghue
undressed the faster and, having removed all his clothes, walked down the
slipway until he reached the water. The state of the tide was such that there was
about two feet or so of water over the grid bed. Mr Donoghue dived in and hit
his head on a grid pile and broke his neck. He then floated face down on the
water. Mr Watkins jumped in and rescued him.

THE OCCUPIERS' LIABILITY ACT 1984

[13] Section 1 of the 1984 Act provides, so far as material, as follows:

> 'Duty of occupier to persons other than his visitors.—(1) The rules enacted by
> this section shall have effect, in place of the rules of the common law, to

determine—(a) whether any duty is owed by a person as occupier of premises to persons other than his visitors in respect of any risk of their suffering injury on the premises by reason of any danger due to the state of the premises or to things done or omitted to be done on them; and (b) if so, what that duty is.

(2) For the purposes of this section, the persons who are to be treated respectively as an occupier of any premises (which, for those purposes, include any fixed or movable structure) and as his visitors are—(a) any person who owes in relation to the premises the duty referred to in section 2 of the Occupiers' Liability Act 1957 (the common duty of care), and (b) those who are his visitors for the purposes of that duty.

(3) An occupier of premises owes a duty to another (not being his visitor) in respect of any such risk as is referred to in subsection (1) above if—(a) he is aware of the danger or has reasonable grounds to believe that it exists; (b) he knows or has reasonable grounds to believe that the other is in the vicinity of the danger concerned or that he may come into the vicinity of the danger (in either case, whether the other has lawful authority for being in that vicinity or not); and (c) the risk is one against which, in all the circumstances of the case, he may reasonably be expected to offer the other some protection.

(4) Where, by virtue of this section, an occupier of premises owes a duty to another in respect of such a risk, the duty is to take such care as is reasonable in all the circumstances of the case to see that he does not suffer injury on the premises by reason of the danger concerned.

(5) Any duty owed by virtue of this section in respect of a risk may, in an appropriate case, be discharged by taking such steps as are reasonable in all the circumstances of the case to give warning of the danger concerned or to discourage persons from incurring the risk.

(6) No duty is owed by virtue of this section to any person in respect of risks willingly accepted as his by that person (the question whether a risk was so accepted to be decided on the same principles as in other cases in which one person owes a duty of care to another).'

[14] For the purposes of the 1984 Act, Folkestone Properties were the occupiers of the slipway. The judge found that Mr Donoghue did not go onto the slipway as a licensee. He was a trespasser and thus a person 'other than a visitor'. There is no appeal against that finding.

THE JUDGMENT

[15] The facts that I have set out above are based upon findings made by the judge which are not challenged. I now turn to the judge's application of the 1984 Act to these facts.

[16] The judge saw as his starting point the need to 'identify in precise terms the danger which creates a risk of personal injury due to the state of the premises'. He did so in these terms: 'the danger is from the presence of the grid piles immediately adjacent to the slipway which are submerged for substantial periods of each day.'

[17] The judge went on to consider the three criteria that give rise to a duty of care by reason of the provisions of s 1(3) of the 1984 Act. The critical issue in this appeal relates to his approach to this subsection. I shall explain the nature of that issue.

[18] Section 1(3) of the 1984 Act lays down the test of whether a duty of care is owed to an individual—'the other'. It was and is the case advanced by Mr Lawrence West, on behalf of Folkestone Properties, that each of the criteria in s 1(3) must be considered having regard to the characteristics and attributes of the individual claimant and the circumstances prevailing when that individual suffered his injury. Thus the question raised by s 1(3) of whether the grid bed posed a danger had to be answered by considering whether it posed a danger to Mr Donoghue, a mature adult with great experience as a professional diver. The question raised by s 1(3)(b) of whether Folkestone Properties had reasonable grounds to believe that Mr Donoghue might be in, or come into, the vicinity of the danger had to be answered having regard to the time of year and the time of day when the accident occurred. The question raised by s 1(3)(c) of whether Folkestone Properties might reasonably be expected to offer some protection against the risk of suffering injury by reason of the presence of the grid bed had to be considered having regard to Mr Donoghue's personal characteristics and attributes.

[19] On behalf of Mr Donoghue, Mr Braithwaite QC submitted to the judge, as he did to us, that the correct approach was that laid down by Ward LJ in *Tomlinson v Congleton BC* [2002] EWCA Civ 309, [2003] 3 All ER 1122, [2003] 2 WLR 1120. This demonstrated, so he submitted, that the approach when applying s 1(3) of the 1984 Act differed from the approach to be adopted when applying s 1(4). Section 1(3) imposed a duty on an occupier to offer some protection when he could reasonably believe that a class of persons, usually trespassers, might come into the vicinity of a danger that carried the risk of causing injury or death. Section 1(4) was concerned with the precise nature of the precautions that should be taken to protect the particular individual bringing the claim for breach of duty. If the appropriate precaution was, as in the present case, a warning sign, and failure to put up such a sign caused the individual to sustain injury, all the elements to establish liability would be present even though the accident occurred at a time other than that when the presence of the class of trespassers was reasonably to be anticipated.

[20] The judge accepted Mr Braithwaite's submissions as to the way to determine if a duty exists—see the following passage of his judgment (at [32]):

'... the claimant points, in particular, to the approach of Ward LJ in *Tomlinson*'s case who, when considering the issue of the existence of the duty (at [23]–[29]) did so in general terms rather than specifically to the individual claimant. Furthermore he points out that it is only when Ward LJ comes to look at the standard of care under s 1(4) that he states (at [30]): "By now the focus has to be on the duty owed to the individual claimant whereas at the earlier stages of the inquiry it was probably more accurate to think of the duty owed to the claimant as a member of a class of persons, young or old, nefariously on the premises or using them to the occupier's knowledge, if not with his permission." Comments drawing a similar distinction between on the one hand the duty being owed to the claimant personally but as a member of a class at risk and on the other hand the nature and extent of that duty (which are entirely personal to the claimant) are stated by Stuart-Smith LJ in *Ratcliff v McConnell* [1999] 1 WLR 670 at 683 (para 44). In looking at s 1(3) it is interesting to note that the expression used is "another (not being his visitor)" and thereafter "the other" is clearly a reference back to a notional person ie someone other than a visitor. In s 1(4) by contrast the

a standard of care relates not to "the" (notional) "other" but to see that "he" does not suffer injury. Even therefore, if I did not feel bound by the authority of *Tomlinson* and the interpretation of Ward LJ (which I do) I would arrive at the same interpretation. I am quite satisfied that the existence of the duty is to be looked at in more general terms as a class of trespasser whereas the standard of care to be exercised is specifically set by reference to the
b individual trespasser.'

[21] The judge, applying this approach to the facts, concluded (at 33) that Folkestone Properties had owed a duty to offer some protection by virtue of the provisions of s 1(3) of the 1984 Act:

c 'Thus in my judgment the danger is from the presence of the grid piles immediately adjacent to the slipway which are submerged for substantial periods of each day. The defendants clearly knew of their existence, whether from the 1920s (their evidence) or the 1970s (Mr Gale). Equally clearly, the defendants knew or had reasonable grounds to believe that trespassers swam, jumped or dived in the harbour and some of them did so off the
d slipway in the vicinity of the grid piles. At certain times of the year (and of the day) the numbers could be substantial. There are self-evident risks in a tidal harbour regarding the depth of water and the possibility of submerged obstructions which might well be regarded as obvious to an adult and in respect of which no warning is required. However this is a permanent obstruction adjacent to the slipway from which an adult and/or child may
e attempt to jump or dive—indeed on the only side of the slipway from which one could jump or dive. The water is always murky according to the evidence and the grid piles are covered with water for significant periods in each day. Those periods when the grid piles are covered are the very times when swimming jumping or diving could take place and whilst at high tide
f the piles are well covered there are significant periods when the depth of water is relatively shallow. Thus in all the circumstances I consider that the occupier could reasonably be expected to offer some protection.'

[22] The judge held (at [35]) that the precaution that Folkestone Properties should have taken was to display at the top of the slipway a notice stating words
g to the effect 'Danger; No swimming, jumping or diving; Hidden objects; Shallow water'. He later held that, had such a notice been displayed, it would have dissuaded Mr Donoghue from diving off the slipway.

[23] While the judge commented (at [33]) that the numbers of trespassers swimming, jumping and diving could be substantial at certain times of the year
h (and of the day), he made no express finding as to whether there were other times of the year (or day) when it would not be reasonable to expect any members of the class in question to be in the vicinity of the danger. It seems to me that he cannot have considered that this question was relevant. His approach to duty 'in general terms' involved the application of a test that was satisfied once it was shown that Folkestone Properties had reason to believe that on some occasions
j a class of persons would be swimming, jumping and diving in the vicinity of the grid bed.

[24] The judge did, however, make the following finding in relation to the particular facts of this case:

'It goes without saying that if I had accepted the defendants' interpretation then clearly they could not possibly have known or had reasonable grounds

to believe that the claimant would come onto the slipway in drink, after
midnight, in mid-winter to dive naked into the harbour in the vicinity of the   *a*
grid piles which were inadequately covered with water. Equally they would
not reasonably be expected to offer him some protection from that risk.'

[25] Mr Braithwaite conceded that it was implicit from this finding that
Folkestone Properties did not have reason to believe that anyone would be
swimming, jumping or diving in the vicinity of the grid piles in mid-winter. He   *b*
accepted that there was no basis upon which the judge could have found
otherwise.

THE ISSUE
[26] Mr West has not abandoned his contention that the question of whether   *c*
a danger existed and of whether a duty was owed under s 1(3) had to be decided
by reference to a man with the attributes of Mr Donoghue. He has accepted,
however, that, on the findings made by the judge, had Mr Donoghue been
among those who to the knowledge of Folkestone Properties were accustomed
to swim in the vicinity of the slipway in the summer, they would in the summer
have owed a duty to protect him by posting a warning of the kind formulated by   *d*
the judge. His appeal is founded solely upon the requirement of s 1(3)(b). He
submits that the duty that is owed to offer some protection to a trespasser against
a danger only extends to the time or times at which the occupier has reasonable
grounds to believe that the trespasser may be in the vicinity of and at risk from
the danger. As there were no reasonable grounds to believe that anyone would   *e*
be swimming in the vicinity of the slipway in the middle of the night in
mid-winter, no duty was owed to Mr Donoghue at the time that he had his
accident.

[27] In reaching his conclusion in relation to duty, the judge was influenced by
the approach that he understood to have been laid down by Ward LJ in
Tomlinson's case. In so far as that case turned on any holding of legal principle we   *f*
must follow it. I propose to make some general observations about the manner
in which the 1984 Act appears to operate, and to refer to the sparse authority
before *Tomlinson*'s case that bears on this, before turning to consider the effect of
that decision.

THE 1984 ACT   *g*
[28] The starting point is the Occupiers' Liability Act 1957. The 1957 Act
imposes on an occupier 'the common duty of care' to all his visitors—that is his
invitees or licensees. Section 2(2) provides:

> 'The common duty of care is a duty to take such care as in all the   *h*
> circumstances of the case is reasonable to see that the visitor will be
> reasonably safe in using the premises for the purposes for which he is invited
> or permitted by the occupier to be there.'

[29] The 1957 Act did not impose any duty towards trespassers. In the
decisions reflected in *Robert Addie & Sons (Collieries) Ltd v Dumbreck* [1929] AC 358,   *j*
[1929] All ER Rep 1 and in *British Railways Board v Herrington* [1972] 1 All ER 749,
[1972] AC 877 the common law moved some way to fill the gap. In *Ratcliff v
McConnell* [1999] 1 WLR 670 Stuart-Smith LJ, in a judgment with which the other
two members of the court agreed, considered the effect of the 1984 Act on the
principles laid down by the speech of Lord Diplock in *Herrington*'s case. First he
cited the following passage from Lord Diplock's speech ([1972] 1 All ER 749 at

a   796, [1972] AC 877 at 941–942), emphasising one phrase in the manner shown below:

> 'First, the duty does not arise until the occupier has actual knowledge either of the presence of the trespasser on his land or of facts which make it likely that the trespasser will come on to his land; and has also actual
> b   knowledge of facts as to the condition of his land or of activities carried out on it which are likely to cause personal injury to a trespasser who is unaware of the danger. He is under no duty to the trespasser to make any enquiry or inspection to ascertain whether or not such facts do exist. His liability does not arise until he actually knows of them. Secondly, once the occupier has actual knowledge of such facts, his own failure to appreciate the likelihood
> c   of the trespasser's presence or the risk to him involved, does not absolve the occupier from his duty to the trespasser if a reasonable man possessed of the actual knowledge of the occupier would recognise that likelihood and that risk. Thirdly, the duty when it arises is limited to taking reasonable steps to enable the trespasser to avoid the danger. Where the likely trespasser is a
> d   child too young to understand or heed a written or a previous oral warning, this may involve providing reasonable physical obstacles to keep the child away from the danger. Fourthly, the relevant likelihood to be considered is of the trespasser's presence at the actual time and place of danger to him. The degree of likelihood needed to give rise to the duty cannot, I think, be more closely defined than as being such as would *impel a man of ordinary*
> e   *humane feelings to take some steps to mitigate the risk* of injury to the trespasser to which the particular danger exposes him. It will thus depend on all the circumstances of the case: the permanent or intermittent character of the danger; the severity of the injuries which it is likely to cause; in the case of children, the attractiveness to them of that which constitutes the dangerous object or condition of the land; the expense involved in giving effective
> f   warning of it to the kind of trespasser likely to be injured, in relation to the occupier's resources in money or in labour.'

[**30**] Stuart-Smith LJ then commented ([1999] 1 WLR 670 at 680 (para 34)):

> g   'Although the court must now obviously apply the words of the statute, it seems to me that the considerations enunciated by Lord Diplock in *Herrington's* case [1972] AC 877, 941, with the exception of the words emphasised in his fourth proposition, are still apposite. Those words which I have emphasised are no longer correct in the light of section 1(3)(c) and (5) of the 1984 Act.'
> h

I concur in this analysis.

[**31**] The duty of care identified by Lord Diplock and imposed under the 1984 Act is significantly less exacting than the common duty of care imposed under the 1957 Act, as a comparison of the two statutes readily demonstrates.

j   [**32**] The 1984 Act imposes a duty on an occupier where: (1) the state of the premises poses a danger; (2) the danger is one that poses a risk of causing injury to a trespasser (it is convenient, though not always accurate, so to describe the 'non visitor') if he comes into the vicinity of the danger; (3) there are reasonable grounds for believing that the trespasser is or may come into the vicinity of the danger; and (4) in all the circumstances of the case it is reasonable to afford the trespasser some protection against the risk.

[33] The obvious situation where a duty under the 1984 Act is likely to arise is
where the occupier knows that a trespasser may come upon a danger that is
latent. In such a case the trespasser may be exposed to the risk of injury without
realising that the danger exists. Where the state of the premises constitutes a
danger that is perfectly obvious, and there is no reason for a trespasser observing
it to go near it, a duty under the 1984 Act is unlikely to arise for at least two
reasons. The first is that because the danger can readily be avoided, it is unlikely
to pose a risk of injuring the trespasser whose presence on the premises is
envisaged.

[34] There are, however, circumstances in which it may be foreseeable that a
trespasser will appreciate that a dangerous feature of premises poses a risk of
injury, but will nevertheless deliberately court the danger and risk the injury. It
seems to me that, at least where the individual is an adult, it will be rare that those
circumstances will be such that the occupier can reasonably be expected to offer
some protection to the trespasser against the risk.

[35] There are some features of land that are not inherently dangerous but
which may tempt a person on the land to indulge in an activity which carries a
risk of injury. Such activities include cliff climbing, mountaineering, skiing, and
hang-gliding by way of example. It does not seem to me that a person carrying
on such an activity can ascribe to the 'state of the premises' an injury sustained as
a result of a mishap in the course of carrying on the activity—provided of course
that the mishap is not caused by an unusual or latent feature of the landscape. I
do not consider that the 1984 Act imposes any duty on an occupier to protect a
trespasser from making use of a particular feature of the premises in order to
carry on an activity simply because that activity carries with it an inherent risk of
injury.

[36] This brings me to swimming and diving. An expanse of water, be it a lake,
pond, river or the sea, does not normally pose any danger to a person on land. If
a trespasser deliberately enters the water to swim, then the trespasser chooses to
indulge in an activity which carries a degree of inherent risk. If the trespasser gets
cramp or becomes exhausted and drowns, it cannot properly be said that this
tragedy is attributable to the 'state of the premises'. Where a trespasser suffers
injury as a result of diving onto the bottom, or onto an obstruction that stands
proud of the bottom, the position is less simple.

[37] If a trespasser jumps down a bank and injures himself by contact with the
ground, his injury cannot properly be said to be attributable to the 'state of the
premises'. If the bank is on the edge of a lake, and the ground is beneath the
water, I still have difficulty in seeing how his injury can be said to be attributable
to the 'state of the premises'. If, however, there is a concealed obstruction
beneath what appears to be deep water, it then becomes arguable that an injury
suffered by a trespasser who dives upon it is attributable, in part, to the 'state of
the premises'. It will not, of course, necessarily follow that the occupier will be
liable under the 1984 Act. This will depend upon the application of the other
criteria laid down by the Act.

[38] I now return to *Ratcliff v McConnell* [1999] 1 WLR 670. In that case a
student had gained access to a swimming pool by climbing over a locked gate at
night and dived into the shallow end, sustaining severe injuries. He claimed that
the defendants were liable under the 1984 Act in that they should have taken
greater precautions to prevent such an accident. The Court of Appeal held that
no duty was owed to him under the 1984 Act because he was aware of the risk
involved and willingly accepted it.

a   [39] In holding that the majority of Lord Diplock's principles were applicable under the statutory regime, it is particularly significant in the context of the present case that Stuart-Smith LJ indorsed the proposition that the existence of the duty had to be determined by reference to the likelihood of the trespasser's presence in the vicinity of the danger *at the actual time and place of danger to him.*

   [40] I turn to Stuart-Smith LJ's judgment (at 683 (para 44)), which the judge
b considered supported the approach of identifying whether a duty arises under s 1(3) of the 1984 Act by reference to a 'class at risk'. What Stuart-Smith LJ said was this:

> 'The duty, if any, is owed to the individual trespasser, though he may be a member of a class that the occupier knows or has reasonable grounds to
> *c*   believe is in the vicinity of the danger. But the nature and extent of what it is reasonable to expect of the occupier varies greatly depending on whether the trespasser is very young or very old and so may not appreciate the nature of the danger which is or ought to be apparent to an adult.'

   [41] These observations do not support the proposition that, when applying
d s 1(3), it is appropriate to ask the question of whether a duty is owed to a class. Consideration of a class of trespasser may be helpful when approaching the question raised by s 1(3)(b) of whether the occupier has reasonable grounds to believe that the trespasser may come into the vicinity of the danger. Plainly this does not restrict those who are the subject of the duty to individuals of whom the occupier has personal knowledge. It will be enough if the trespasser can show
e that he was one of a class of persons whom the occupier had reason to believe might be in the vicinity of the danger. Once, however, s 1(3)(b) is satisfied, it then becomes necessary to consider whether any duty was owed to the particular member of that class who suffered the injury. That was the very point made by Stuart-Smith LJ when he observed that what it is reasonable to expect of the
f occupier varies greatly depending upon the age of the trespasser. A duty to offer some protection to children known to be present in the vicinity of the danger may well exist in circumstances where the occupier cannot reasonably be required to offer any protection to an adult.

   [42] There is an earlier decision of the Court of Appeal, which affords some further guidance to the approach to s 1 of the 1984 Act. *White v St Albans City and*
g *District Council* (1990) Times, 12 March involved a claim by a trespasser who had suffered injury by falling into a gap when taking a short cut to a car park. In the leading judgment, after setting out sub-ss (3), (4) and (5) of s 1, Neill LJ commented:

> *h*   'We can see, therefore, the scheme of those last three subsections. Subsection (3) contains the provisions which are relevant for the purpose of determining whether the occupier of the premises owes any duty at all to the person who is described as "another (not being his visitor)". Subsection (4) sets out the nature and extent of the duty once it has been established that the person on the premises is a person to whom a duty is owed.
> *j*   Subsection (5) contains provisions which may, in certain circumstances, apply whereby the occupier may be able to discharge his duty by taking such steps as are reasonable in all the circumstances, either to give warning of the danger or, alternatively, to discourage persons from incurring the risk.'

These comments draw no distinction between the subsections in respect of the approach to be adopted when considering whether a duty is owed to a trespasser.

[43] A subsequent passage in Neill LJ's judgment is particularly relevant to the present case. Mr West, in that case appearing for the claimant, argued that the fact that the defendants had placed a chain link fence to inhibit access to the gap demonstrated that the likelihood of trespassers approaching the gap had been appreciated by them. He contended that, when considering whether a duty of care existed, it was necessary to consider the position before any precautions had been taken. Neill LJ rejected this submission. He held:

'It seems to me that the question to be considered under sub-s (3)(b) must be answered by looking at the actual state of affairs on the ground at the time when the injury is suffered. The question is: had the occupier of the premises reasonable grounds to believe that somebody such as Mr White might come into the vicinity of the danger ... To my mind, the judge was wholly justified in coming to the conclusion that the council had no reasonable grounds for believing that Mr White on that occasion might come into the vicinity of this gap or channel into which, unhappily, he fell.'

TOMLINSON

[44] Having considered the prior authorities which are relevant I now turn to *Tomlinson v Congleton BC* [2003] 3 All ER 1122, [2003] 2 WLR 1120. Mr Tomlinson, the claimant, suffered injuries which rendered him a paraplegic as a consequence of hitting his head on the bottom when he dived into a lake that was situated on land owned and occupied by the defendant council. He had dived from a position standing in the water and hit his head on the bed of the lake, not on any obstruction. The council permitted the public to have access to the lake and the land around it for various leisure activities, but these did not include swimming. The prohibition on swimming was made clear by notices at the shore of the lake reading 'DANGEROUS WATER; NO SWIMMING'.

[45] The trial judge ruled that, by ignoring this notice, Mr Tomlinson became a trespasser so that the applicable statute was the 1984 Act. That proposition was not challenged, though in his dissenting judgment Longmore LJ expressed reservations about it. I share those reservations. What was at issue in the case was whether the council should have taken steps which would have prevented Mr Tomlinson from entering the lake, that is, whether a duty of care was owed to him before he did the unauthorised act. In those circumstances it seems to me that it was arguable that the relevant statute was the 1957 Act. However for present purposes what is relevant is what the Court of Appeal had to say about the operation of the 1984 Act.

[46] The trial judge held that the council was under no liability to Mr Tomlinson. He held that the danger and risk of injury from diving in the lake where it was shallow were obvious. Applying previous decisions under the 1957 Act, he held that an occupier was not under a duty to warn against a risk which was obvious. In any event, he held that the signs prohibiting swimming were reasonable and sufficient steps to give warning of the danger. The council were aware that these signs were widely disregarded, but the judge rejected the argument that in these circumstances the council owed a duty to fence off the beaches and to plant vegetation that would discourage the public from entering the water. He held that the decision to enter the water was one that members of the public were free to make; they could choose to accept the risk.

[47] The Court of Appeal reversed the trial judge. Ward LJ gave the leading judgment. He was impressed by documentary evidence showing hundreds of

a people swam in the lake on warm summer days, that there had been a history of accidents in the lake, including near drownings, and that the council had been advised that it was only a question of time before somebody drowned. In these circumstances he held (at [38]) that the council had been under a duty to prevent members of the public from suffering injury 'by reason of the dangers which awaited those who entered the water for a swim'. Those dangers he had earlier
b identified as follows (at [21]):

'In this case there was a risk of injury being suffered by anyone entering the water because of the dangers due to the state of the premises, the premises being constituted by the configuration and contents of this pond created as it was from a disused sand-extraction pit. There was a risk of injury through
c drowning because of the dangers, among others, of the effect of cold water, being caught in weed, being stuck in the mud or plunging unexpectedly into deep water. There was the risk of injury through diving because of the dangers of diving too steeply in shallow water or into an obstruction. There may have been risks of other injury from other dangers, eg Weil's disease.
d These risks of injury arose as soon as one entered the water because one did not know what danger lurked, or where it lay hidden. The exact nature of the hazard may not much matter in the particular circumstances of this case.'

[48] Ward LJ held that the 1984 Act had to be used as a 'template' for judgment and that it was necessary to look to the Act for the relevant principles.
e It was a staged process. The first stage was to identify the risk and the danger. This he did in the manner set out in the paragraph above. The second stage was to determine whether or not a duty was owed by the occupier. This depended solely on whether the criteria in s 1(3) were satisfied. In applying this test the judge drew no distinction between Mr Tomlinson and the many other
f trespassers who were known to enter the lake. He held that s 1(3)(b) was satisfied because it was known to the council that many entered the water and were in the vicinity of the dangers concerned.

[49] When addressing s 1(3)(c) Ward LJ held that a different approach was required from that which was applicable when considering s 1(4). He said (at [26]):
g

'The third, and in this case crucial, requirement laid down by s 1(3)(c) is whether the risk was one against which, in all the circumstances of the case, the occupiers might reasonably be expected to offer the trespasser some protection. Analysing that, the protection is against any such risk as is
h referred to in sub-s (1), the risk, that is, of the trespasser suffering injury by reason of the dangers lurking in the mere. The protection we are looking for is "*some* protection". The question is whether *some* protection might reasonably be expected to be offered. The question is *not* whether *reasonable* protection is to be expected. To frame the question that way is to fail to
j distinguish between the establishing of the duty under s 1(3) and the standard of care necessary to satisfy the duty which is provided by s 1(4). These are distinct and separate requirements and I am concerned that the judge may have failed to keep them separate and distinct when he said (at [28]–[29]): "In the circumstances of this case at least, consideration of the third requirement under s 1(3) and the consideration of the duty under s 1(4) cover much the same ground … In my view the danger and risk of injury

from diving in the lake where it was shallow were obvious ... an occupier is
not under a duty to warn against a risk which is obvious."'

[50] Ward LJ went on to review the evidence of the history of accidents and
near drownings over the years and concluded that the occupiers were reasonably
to be expected to offer some protection against the risks of entering the water and
that it followed that the council was under a duty to Mr Tomlinson. He then
turned to s 1(4) and said (at [30]):

> 'The standard of care is defined by s 1(4). It is—"to take such care as is
> reasonable in all the circumstances of the case to see that he does not suffer
> injury on the premises by reason of the danger concerned." By now the
> focus has to be on the duty owed to the individual claimant whereas at the
> earlier stages of the inquiry it was probably more accurate to think of the
> duty owed to the claimant as a member of a class of persons, young or old,
> nefariously on the premises or using them to the occupier's knowledge, if
> not with his permission.'

This is the passage that led Judge Bowers to approach the question of whether
Folkestone Properties owed a duty of care 'in general terms' without reference to
the particular experience that Mr Donoghue had as a diver or to the time of year
and of day when he had his accident.

[51] Ward LJ went on to consider the nature of the steps that the council should
have taken to protect Mr Tomlinson and concluded that the council should have
carried out landscaping and planting that would have transformed the lakeside
beach into a barrier.

[52] Sedley LJ agreed that the appeal should be allowed. He added some brief
reasoning of his own, the essence of which was as follows (at [43]–[45]):

> 'It is, I agree, an apparent oddity that a person who is injured by diving into
> shallow water—a pretty obvious hazard—should be able to claim the benefit
> of precautions which in reality were needed in order to stop people losing
> their footing where the lake bed shelved steeply or becoming entangled in
> thick weeds. But there are two separate answers, one relating to the
> obviousness of the hazard, the other to its nature ... As to the nature of the
> hazard, it was rightly not argued by the respondents that this could make the
> difference between liability and no liability in the present case. It is well
> settled by authority that if there is a duty to protect people against
> foreseeable injury, it does not matter if the accident which happens was not
> itself foreseeable, so long as it is not in an entirely different league: see *Hughes
> v Lord Advocate* [1963] 1 All ER 705, [1963] AC 837 and *Smith v Leech Brain
> & Co Ltd* [1961] 3 All ER 1159, [1962] 2 QB 405 ... If primary liability is
> established, the obviousness of the hazard goes to contributory negligence;
> for it is only where the risk is so obvious that the occupier can safely assume
> that nobody will take it that there will be no liability.'

Longmore LJ gave a short but powerful dissenting judgment.

[53] There are aspects of each of the majority judgments in *Tomlinson*'s case
with which I have difficulty. I have been unable to identify in either judgment the
'state of the premises' which posed a danger which carried with it the risk of the
injury suffered by Mr Tomlinson. It seems to me that Mr Tomlinson suffered
his injury because he chose to indulge in an activity which had inherent dangers,
not because the premises were in a dangerous state. Nor can I readily reconcile

a
Sedley LJ's statement (at [45]) that 'it is only where the risk is so obvious that the occupier can safely assume that nobody will take it that there will be no liability' with the terms under which the 1984 Act, and particularly s 1(5), imposes a limited duty of care in respect of trespassers.

[54] Turning to the distinction that Ward LJ made between the approach to s 1(3) and the approach to s 1(4), this does not form part of the majority ratio, nor
b   indeed was it critical to the result reached by Ward LJ himself. I am not bound to follow it and shall not attempt to do so, for I do not consider that the distinction is a valid one. On the natural meaning of s 1(3) and s 1(4) it seems to me that 'the other' in s 1(3) is the same person as 'another' in s 1(4), namely the very individual who has sustained the injury and in respect of whom the issue under consideration has arisen. Quite apart from the natural meaning of the words, I
c   cannot see how one can logically reach the question of what action it is reasonable for an occupier to take to protect an individual trespasser against a risk pursuant to s 1(4) unless one has first decided that the risk is such that it is reasonable for the occupier to offer *that person* some protection pursuant to s 1(3).

[55] If I am correct, the basis underlying the judge's decision on duty is
d   unsound. Even if I am not correct, it does not seem to me that Ward LJ's approach should have led the judge to the conclusion that, when considering whether a duty of care existed pursuant to s 1(3), it was unnecessary to apply the statutory criteria to the circumstances prevailing at the time that the accident occurred. In *Tomlinson's* case it was common ground that the council had reasonable grounds to believe that members of the public such as Mr Tomlinson
e   were likely to be in the vicinity of the lake when the accident occurred. No issue under s 1(3)(b) arose. Ward LJ's approach did not involve the conclusion that if a duty of care exists in the summer, an identical duty will exist in the winter. The circumstances which are material to the existence of the duty may change with the seasons or the time of day. That was the position in the present case.

f   [56] In the course of argument we invited Mr Braithwaite to consider what the position would have been if Folkestone Properties had decided to adopt a more effective way of preventing members of the public from swimming from the slipway than merely posting a notice. What if they had posted a security guard on the slipway to prevent people from swimming? If they withdrew the guard during hours of darkness in circumstances where there were
g   no reasonable grounds to believe that anyone would wish to swim from the slipway, could they possibly be held to be in breach of duty under the 1984 Act? Mr Braithwaite was hard pressed to argue that they could, but contended that the facts of this case were different in that the reasonable steps that the judge held should have been adopted involved putting up a notice, which would have
h   remained day and night, summer and winter.

[57] I did not find this response convincing. It does not seem to me that the period during which a duty of care extends can depend upon the means that may be used to discharge the duty. Furthermore, we asked Mr Braithwaite whether Folkestone Properties would have been in breach of duty had they posted a
j   notice in the summer, but taken away all notices prohibiting swimming shortly before Christmas to repaint them, in the reasonable belief that no one would attempt to go swimming in the harbour in mid-winter. Mr Braithwaite conceded that he would have been unable to establish a breach of duty in such circumstances

[58] The observations of members of this court, which I have cited, in *Ratcliff v McConnell* [1999] 1 WLR 670 and *White v St Albans City and District Council* (1990)

Times, 12 March suggest that the test of whether a duty of care exists under the
1984 Act must be determined having regard to the circumstances prevailing at the   *a*
time that it is alleged that the breach of duty resulted in injury to the claimant.
That is my own reading of the relevant provisions of the 1984 Act. At the time
that Mr Donoghue sustained his grievous injuries, Folkestone Properties had no
reason to believe that he, or anyone else, would be swimming from the slipway.
The criterion of s 1(3)(b) of the 1984 Act was not satisfied. Folkestone Properties   *b*
owed no duty to Mr Donoghue and should not have been held under any liability
for his accident. It is never a pleasant task to snatch from a grievously injured
claimant compensation that might provide a measure of mitigation of his
ill-fortune but for the reasons that I have given I would allow this appeal.

                                                                                     c
BROOKE LJ.

[59] This case is all about the duty an occupier of premises owes to a
trespasser. In *Fairchild v Glenhaven Funeral Services Ltd* [2001] 1 EWCA Civ 1881 at
[118]–[121], [2002] IRLR 129 at [118]–[121], [2002] 1 WLR 1052 at [118]–[121]
I explained in section 8(iii) of the judgment of the court certain features of the
common law relating to occupiers' liability prior to the enactment of the   *d*
Occupiers' Liability Act 1957. In particular I quoted (at [116]) the well-known
dictum of Willes J in *Indermaur v Dames* (1866) LR 1 CP 274 at 288, [1861–73] All
ER Rep 15 at 21 in which he set out what I described as an occupier's occupancy
duty towards his invitees:

                                                                                     e
    'And, with respect to such a visitor at least, we consider it settled law, that
    he, using reasonable care on his part for his own safety, is entitled to expect
    that the occupier shall on his part use reasonable care to prevent damage
    from unusual danger, which he knows or ought to know; and that, where
    there is evidence of neglect, the question whether such reasonable care has
    been taken, by notice, lighting, guarding, or otherwise, and whether there   *f*
    was contributory negligence in the sufferer, must be determined by a jury as
    matter of fact.'

[60] The 1957 Act abolished the old Byzantine distinctions between an invitee
and a licensee. It clarified by statute the nature of the common duty of care which
an occupier owes to all his visitors in consequence of the invitation or permission   *g*
he gave to them to enter or use his premises. But it left untouched the question
whether an occupier owed a duty, and if so what duty, to trespassers (being
people whom he did not invite or permit to enter or use his premises for the
purposes for which they chose to enter them, and who used them without any
such invitation or permission).   *h*

[61] In general the old common law judges had little sympathy with
trespassers. In his speech in *British Railways Board v Herrington* [1972] 1 All ER 749
at 763–764, [1972] AC 877 at 905–906, however, Lord Morris of Borth-y-Gest
referred to a trilogy of early nineteenth-century cases in which plaintiffs had
claimed damages after being shot by spring guns which landowners placed on   *j*
their land to deter trespassers. Two strands of thought flowed from the decisions
in these cases. The first was that the law should not sanction conduct towards
trespassers that was inconsistent with common humanity. The second was that
the law should not sanction conduct whereby an occupier of land intentionally
set out to cause physical harm to trespassers. In the fullness of time an occupier
who conducted himself with a reckless disregard for the safety of trespassers also

a   came within this rubric. This was the state of the law when *Robert Addie & Sons (Collieries) Ltd v Dumbreck* [1929] AC 358, [1929] All ER Rep 1 was decided.

[**62**] Mr Dumbreck's four-year-old son, like many others of all ages, trespassed in a field which was being used as a dump for the deposit of ashes from the pithead of a colliery. The boy was killed while sitting on the cover of an unprotected iron wheel. He was caught and drawn into the operating machinery. Lord Hailsham LC

b   said ([1929] AC 358 at 367, [1929] All ER Rep 1 at 6) that English law had been accurately summarised by Scrutton LJ in an earlier case in these terms:

> 'If the children were trespassers, the landowner was not entitled intentionally to injure them, or to put dangerous traps for them intending to injure them, but was under no liability if in trespassing they injured
c   > themselves on objects legitimately on his land in the course of his business. Against those he was under no obligation to guard trespassers.' (See *Hardy v Central London Rly Co* [1920] 3 KB 459 at 473–474.)

[**63**] In his speech in the same case Viscount Dunedin widened the scope of potential liability to a trespasser to include reckless conduct ([1929] AC 358 at
d   376–377, [1929] All ER Rep 1 at 10):

> '... if the person is a trespasser, then the only duty the proprietor has towards him is not maliciously to injure him: he may not shoot him; he may not set a spring gun, for that is just to arrange to shoot him without personally firing the shot. Other illustrations of what he may not do might
e   > be found, but they all come under the same head – injury either directly malicious or an acting so reckless as to be tantamount to malicious acting.'

[**64**] As a consequence Mr Dumbreck's claim failed. These two dicta dominated any discussion of the common law duty to trespassers in this jurisdiction for the next 40 years.

f   [**65**] In the years after *Addie's* case the development of the modern law of negligence proceeded apace following the breakthrough decision in *Donoghue v Stevenson* [1932] AC 562, [1932] All ER Rep 1, but the law governing an occupier's duty to trespassers stood still, at least so far as the House of Lords was concerned. As I have indicated it was omitted from the law reform project that led up to the enactment of the 1957 Act, and on this side of the border there was nothing
g   resembling the statutory scheme introduced into the law of Scotland by the Occupiers' Liability (Scotland) Act 1960 which Lord Reid mentions in his speech in *British Railways Board v Herrington* [1972] 1 All ER 749 at 757, [1972] AC 877 at 898.

[**66**] It is unnecessary for the purposes of this judgment to discuss such cases
h   as *Videan v British Transport Commission* [1963] 2 All ER 860, [1963] 2 QB 650 or *Comr for Railways v Quinlan* [1964] 1 All ER 897, [1964] AC 1054 in which efforts were made to confer on trespassers greater rights, and to impose on occupiers greater obligations, than were consistent with the decision in *Addie's* case. They are fully discussed in *Herrington's* case and in the Law Commission's publications
j   which followed *Herrington*. I can go straight to *Herrington's* case in which the five members of the House of Lords unanimously dismissed an appeal by the British Railways Board against an order directing them to pay compensation to a child trespasser who had strayed across a dilapidated fence onto their electrified railway line.

[**67**] The trouble with *Herrington's* case, from the point of view of the smooth administration of justice, was that the five members of the House of Lords

expressed themselves in different terms. The contents of their speeches, and the nature of the difficulties they created, are well-summarised by the Law Commission in their working paper on *Liability for Damage or Injury to Trespassers and Related Questions of Occupiers' Liability* (1973) (Consultation Paper no 52 (paras 15–22)). The five Law Lords spoke with different voices when they tried to identify the occasions on which an occupier's duty to a trespasser might arise. They also spoke with different voices when they sought to identify the content of that duty.

[68] This, then, is the background against which the Occupiers' Liability Act 1984 falls to be interpreted. The House of Lords had rejected the harshness of *Addie*'s case. They considered that humanity required a softer approach to the law relating to trespassers (and particularly child trespassers), but they could not agree what that approach should be. The situation was tailor-made for the statutory reference the Lord Chancellor made to the Law Commission in April 1972 (two months after *Herrington*'s case was decided) in these terms:

> 'To consider, in the light of the decision of the House of Lords in *British Railways Board v Herrington* ([1972] 1 All ER 749, [1972] AC 877) the law relating to liability for damage or injury suffered by trespassers.'

[69] This reference led in due course to the publication of the Law Commission's report on *Liability for Damage or Injury to Trespassers and Related Questions of Occupiers' Liability* (Law Com no 75) (1976) and the enactment eight years later of the Occupiers' Liability Act 1984. That Act by s 1(1) expressly replaced the common law rules relating to the existence and nature of the duty owed by an occupier of premises to persons other than his visitors with a new statutory code.

[70] The mischief which this legislation was enacted to remedy is clear from paras 4–11 of the Law Commission's report. It said that the decision of the House of Lords in *Herrington*'s case represented a considerable development of the principles laid down by the House in *Addie*'s case. It was difficult, however, to conclude that the question as to *when* special facts gave rise to a duty to the trespasser had received an entirely consistent answer in that case, nor to give a simple answer as to *the content* of the occupier's duty once it could be said, on the facts, to have arisen.

[71] The language of the Law Commission's suggested legislative solution differed to a considerable extent from the language eventually adopted by Parliament, although there are certain similarities. For instance the new statutory duty will only arise if the danger/risk was 'one against which in all the circumstances of the case, the [occupier/he] can reasonably be expected to offer [him/the other] some protection'. Once the duty arises, it is described in each case as—

> 'a duty to take such care as is reasonable in all the circumstance of the case to see that [the entrant/he] does not suffer [personal injury or death/injury] by reason of the danger [concerned].'

[72] In an important passage of its report, after explaining the duty in this way, the Law Commission said:

> '28. It will be evident that the duty towards the trespasser under our recommendations is of a quite different character from the "common duty of care" under the Occupiers' Liability Act 1957. Under the latter that duty

is, in short, owed to all visitors and the occupier has to take reasonable care to see that they are reasonably safe. Under the former, while the duty is one which is owed potentially to all trespassers, the question of the extent of the duty does not arise at all unless, in the first place, the court decides as a question of fact that the danger is one against which, in all the circumstances, it is reasonable for the occupier to offer some protection. In consequence, given identical circumstances, the fulfilment of the common duty of care towards a visitor may be expected in many instances to produce results entirely dissimilar from the fulfilment of our recommended duty of care towards the trespasser. To take a few very obvious examples: if one of the steps upon the stairs in his house is temporarily missing while it is being repaired, an occupier may be expected to warn his visitor making use of the stairs of this fact in order to render him reasonably safe. But it would, in our view, be entirely unreasonable in the circumstances to expect the occupier to offer a burglar at night any protection at all in respect of this danger; and under our recommendations, therefore, no duty would be owed if the burglar were injured in consequence of this danger. Again, a farmer selling livestock might be expected to keep a path reasonably safe for a customer who visits him to view the stock and to give him warning of, or protection in respect of, any dangers he might meet with in the course of his inspection. But he could not reasonably be expected to take the same precautions in respect of a thief engaged in stealing the stock. Such a person may enter at night by places other than the usual entrance and might injure himself on farm implements left lying off the path or on rusty nails on gates which he is unable to see; or he may even encounter dangers of an entirely natural character, such as a stream in which he falls and is injured or even drowned. In those circumstances it might very well be unreasonable to expect the farmer to offer any protection; and if so, again no duty at all would arise. Finally, it may well be that in some circumstances it will be reasonable to offer some protection to the trespasser who is a child. This does not, however, mean that all child trespassers will be owed a duty: each case will depend upon its facts as to whether it would be reasonable in the circumstances to expect some protection to be given. Examples could, of course, be multiplied; but we give here sufficient only to indicate that the duty we are recommending is far less onerous than the common duty of care owed to the visitor, in that a positive answer must be given to the first element of the proposed duty before any consideration at all is given to the extent of the duty owed.

29. When a court has decided as a question of fact that an occupier did in the particular circumstances of a case owe some protection to a trespasser, the question then to be decided, in accordance with our recommendations, is whether the occupier has discharged the duty on him by taking such care as is reasonable in all the circumstances of the case to see that the trespasser did not suffer personal injury or death by reason of the danger upon the premises. In the range of circumstances to which the courts will have regard in deciding whether the occupier has acted reasonably, the application of the duty towards trespassers may again be expected to differ markedly from the common duty of care.'

[73] On the facts of the present case, the question we have to answer is whether, in the language of s 1(1) of the 1984 Act, Folkestone Properties Ltd, as

the occupiers of this working port, owed any duty to Mr Donoghue (being a person other than a visitor for these purposes: see s 1(2)) in respect of his having suffered a broken neck by reason of the danger posed by the presence of the grid piles below the waterline. That question is to be answered by applying the tests set out in s 1(3). It is only if the answer is 'Yes, Folkestone Properties did owe him a duty in respect of the risk posed by the submerged grid piles' that one must then move on to s 1(4) to ascertain, in the language of s 1(1), what that duty is.

[74] Like Lord Phillips of Worth Matravers MR, I have not been able to detect with any clarity any common ratio in the judgments of the majority of this court in *Tomlinson v Congleton BC* [2002] EWCA Civ 309, [2003] 3 All ER 1122, [2003] 2 WLR 1120. If Sedley LJ had said that he agreed with the analysis contained in Ward LJ's judgment, we would have been bound by that analysis, however much we might disagree with it. But I do not know the route by which Sedley LJ concluded that the defendants owed Mr Tomlinson a duty in the circumstances of that case, or why he considered that they were in breach of that duty. His short judgment was concerned with other matters.

[75] The law protects people from foreseeable harm in at least two distinct ways. For instance it may, by regulation, require the occupier of dangerous premises or the owner of dangerous machinery to provide fencing or guardrails or warning notices or other safety devices to protect people from risk of injury. Or it may, according to the genius of the common law, ask whether a particular defendant owed a particular injured person a legal duty in the circumstances in which he met with his injury. If he did, it will ask what that duty was, and whether it was breached before going on to consider questions of causation and foreseeability and the amount of any recoverable damages.

[76] Usually judges and lawyers do not have to pause very long in the early stages of this analysis. The driver of a motor car, for example, owes a duty of care to those who may be foreseeably injured by his driving of the car, and if he drives his car carelessly and someone gets injured as a result, then there are the makings of a legal claim. But in more unusual contexts, where these questions are to be answered by reference to common law tests, the inquiry will always be fact specific. In *Haley v London Electricity Board* [1964] 3 All ER 185, [1965] AC 778 the House of Lords held that electricity undertakers owed a duty of care to blind persons as a class when they excavated a trench along a pavement in a London suburb because blind people foreseeably walk along pavements. The content of the duty was also fact specific, founded on the principle that such undertakers were entitled to assume that blind people would take reasonable care to protect themselves, for example by using a stick to ascertain if there was anything in the way. Unlike the maker of a statutory regulation, who legislates to provide protection against a number of different risks, the common law examines the factual situation in the particular case before undertaking the necessary inquiry as to liability.

[77] In the present case Mr Donoghue dived into the inner harbour in the early hours of Saturday, 27 December 1997. Section 1(3) of the 1984 Act compels us to focus on that factual situation, which has nothing to do with the circumstances in which children swam or dived in the harbour at high tide on a sunny August bank holiday weekend. Although the defendants were aware of the danger posed by the presence of the grid piles under the waterline, the judge made the unchallenged findings, adverse to Mr Donoghue, which Lord Phillips MR has recited (at [24], above). On these facts, therefore, the claim fails

a at the hurdle imposed by s 1(3)(b) of the 1984 Act and I, too, would allow the appeal.

[78] In the circumstances it is not necessary to say much about s 1(3)(c). In the modern law of negligence, which postdates the enactment of the 1984 Act, we are accustomed to ask ourselves whether it is fair, just and reasonable for the law to impose the duty contended for. In the context of this statutory scheme

b Parliament has in essence declared that it is fair and just to impose a duty if the requirements of s 1(3)(a) and (b) are satisfied. When courts decide, on the facts of a particular case, whether the risk is one against which, in all the circumstances of the case, an occupier might reasonably be expected to offer a trespasser some protection, they would do well to refer to the passage in the 1976 Law Commission report which I have quoted at [72], above. I can see no evidence that

c in 1984 Parliament intended to alter the general philosophy of the law relating to trespassers which the House of Lords articulated in differing terms in *Herrington's* case. The mischief the 1984 Act was enacted to remedy was the one identified by the Law Commission at the start of its report (see [70], above), and nothing more.

d **LAWS LJ.**

[79] I agree with both judgments.

Appeal allowed.

Kate O'Hanlon   Barrister.

Tomlinson v Congleton Borough Council and another

[2002] EWCA Civ 309, [2003] UKHL 47

COURT OF APPEAL, CIVIL DIVISION
WARD, SEDLEY AND LONGMORE LJJ
16 JANUARY, 14 MARCH 2002

HOUSE OF LORDS
LORD NICHOLLS OF BIRKENHEAD, LORD HOFFMANN, LORD HUTTON, LORD HOBHOUSE
OF WOODBOROUGH AND LORD SCOTT OF FOSCOTE
23, 24 JUNE, 31 JULY 2003

Occupier's liability – Common duty of care – Nature of duty – Reasonable care – Lake open to the public – Occupier posting notices prohibiting swimming – Occupier aware of further steps which could minimise likelihood of swimming – Claimant running into lake, diving, and suffering injury – Whether occupier having taken such care as in all the circumstances was reasonable to see that claimant would be reasonably safe – Occupiers' Liability Act 1957, s 2.

The defendants owned, occupied and managed a public park. In the park was a lake formed from a disused sand extraction pit. The lake had sandy beaches and was a popular recreational venue where yachting, sub-aqua diving and other regulated activities were permitted, but swimming was not. Notices reading 'Dangerous water: no swimming' were posted but they had little or no effect. The unauthorised use of the lake and the increasing possibility of an accident was of concern to the defendants. A plan to landscape the shores and plant over the beaches from which people swam had been approved, but work had begun only shortly before 6 May 1995. On that date the claimant went to the lake. He ran into the water and dived, striking his head on the sandy bottom with sufficient force to cause him an injury which resulted in paralysis from the neck downward. He brought proceedings for damages claiming that the defendants, as occupiers, owed him the common duty of care set out in s 2(2)[a] of the Occupiers' Liability Act 1957, which was a duty to take such care as in all the circumstances was reasonable to see that a visitor would be reasonably safe in using the premises for the purposes for which he was permitted to be there. At trial it was conceded that he had seen and ignored the warning signs so that when he entered the water he had ceased to be at the park for purposes for which he had been invited and permitted by the defendants to be there, and had accordingly ceased to be a visitor and had become a trespasser. As such he was owed a lesser duty of care under the Occupiers' Liability Act 1984. The judge found against the claimant, holding inter alia that the danger and risk of injury were obvious, and that an occupier was not under a duty to warn against such a risk. The claimant appealed. The majority of the Court of Appeal allowed his appeal, holding that the gravity of the risk of injury, the frequency with which park users came to be exposed to the risk, the failure of warning signs to curtail the extent to which the risk was being run and the attractiveness of the location led to the conclusion that

---

a   Section 2, so far as material, is set out at [6], below

a   the occupiers were reasonably to be expected to offer some protection against the risks of entering the water. The posting of notices, shown to be ineffective, had therefore not been enough to discharge the duty. The authorities should have carried out the landscaping and planting which had been recommended to them. The defendants appealed.

b   **Held** – The majority of the Court of Appeal appeared to have proceeded on the oversimplified basis that if there had been a foreseeable risk of serious injury the defendants had been under a duty to do what was necessary to prevent it. Even assuming that the circumstances of the instant case were such that a duty had been owned to a lawful visitor under s 2(2) of the 1957 Act, and that there had been a risk attributable to the state of the premises rather than to the acts of the
c   claimant, the question of what amounted to 'such care as in all the circumstances of the case is reasonable' depended not only on the likelihood that someone might be injured and the seriousness of the injury which might occur, but also on the social value of the activity which gave rise to the risk and the cost of preventative measures. Those factors had to be balanced against each other. It
d   would be extremely rare for an occupier of land to be under a duty to prevent people from taking risks which were inherent in the activities they freely chose to undertake upon the land. He would be entitled to impose conditions prohibiting risky activities, as the defendants had done in the instant case by prohibiting swimming. But the law did not require him to do so. There was an important question of freedom at stake. It would be unjust if the harmless recreation of
e   responsible people upon the beaches were prohibited in order to comply with what was thought to be a legal duty to safeguard irresponsible visitors against dangers which were perfectly obvious. That such people took no notice of warnings could not create a duty to take other steps to protect them. Local authorities and other occupiers of land were ordinarily under no duty to incur
f   such social and financial costs as had been incurred in the instant case to protect a minority, or even a majority, against obvious dangers. Accordingly, in the instant case, even if swimming had not been prohibited, and the defendants had owed a duty under s 2(2) of the 1957 Act, that duty would not have required them to have taken any steps to prevent the claimant from diving or warning him against dangers that were perfectly obvious. It followed that there could have
g   been no duty owed under the 1984 Act. The appeal would therefore be allowed (see [1], [34], [40]–[42], [45], [46], [48], [50]–[52], [65], [83], [84], [94], below (House of Lords judgment)).
    Dictum of Lord Phillips of Worth Matravers MR in *Donoghue v Folkestone Properties Ltd* [2003] 3 All ER 1101 at [53] approved.

h   **Notes**
    For the common duty of care to visitors and an occupier's duty of care to persons other than visitors, see *33 Halsbury's Laws* (4th edn reissue) paras 631–634, 640.
    For the Occupiers' Liability Act 1957, s 2, see *31 Halsbury's Statutes* (4th edn)
j   (2000 reissue) 466.

Cases referred to in judgments and opinions
Addie (Robert) & Sons (Collieries) Ltd v Dumbreck [1929] AC 358, [1929] All ER Rep 1, HL.
Bartrum v Hepworth Minerals and Chemicals Ltd (29 October 1999, unreported), QBD.
Bolton v Stone [1951] 1 All ER 1078, [1951] AC 850, HL.

British Railways Board v Herrington [1972] 1 All ER 749, [1972] AC 877, [1972] 2   *a*
   WLR 537, HL.
Bucheleres v Chicago Park District (1996) 171 Ill 2d 435, Ill SC.
Calgarth, The, The Otarama [1927] P 93, CA.
Coggs v Bernard (1703) 2 Ld Raym 909, 92 ER 107, [1558–1774] All ER Rep 1, DC.
Corp of the City of Glasgow v Taylor [1922] 1 AC 44, HL.
Cotton v Derbyshire Dales DC [1994] CA Transcript 753, (1994) Times, June 20.   *b*
Darby v National Trust [2001] EWCA Civ 189, [2001] PIQR P372.
Donoghue v Folkestone Properties Ltd [2003] EWCA Civ 231, [2003] 3 All ER 1101,
   [2003] 2 WLR 1138.
Donoghue v Stevenson [1932] AC 562, [1932] All ER Rep 1, HL.
Hastie v Magistrates of Edinburgh 1907 SC 1102, Ct of Sess.
Hillen v ICI (Alkali) Ltd [1936] AC 65, [1935] All ER Rep 555, HL.   *c*
Hughes v Lord Advocate [1963] 1 All ER 705, [1963] AC 837, [1963] 2 WLR 779, HL.
Jebson v Ministry of Defence [2000] 1 WLR 2055, CA.
Jolley v Sutton London BC [2000] 3 All ER 409, [2000] 1 WLR 1082, HL.
Overseas Tankship (UK) Ltd v Miller Steamship Co Pty, The Wagon Mound (No 2)
   [1966] 2 All ER 709, [1967] 1 AC 617, [1966] 3 WLR 498, PC.   *d*
Ratcliff v McConnell [1999] 1 WLR 670, CA.
Reeves v Metropolitan Police Comr [1999] 3 All ER 897, [2000] 1 AC 360, [1999] 3
   WLR 363, HL.
Scott v Associated British Ports, Swainger v Associated British Ports [2000] All ER (D)
   1937, CA.
Smith v Leech Brain & Co Ltd [1961] 3 All ER 1159, [1962] 2 QB 405, [1962] 2 WLR 148.   *e*
Staples v West Dorset DC (1995) 93 LGR 536, CA.
Stevenson v Corp of Glasgow 1908 SC 1034, Ct of Sess.
Vancouver-Fraser Park District v Olmstead (1974) 51 DLR (3d) 416, Can SC.
Whyte v Redland Aggregates Ltd [1997] CA Transcript 2034, CA.

                                                        f

Cases also cited or referred to in skeleton arguments and in list of authorities
Fairchild v Glenhaven Funeral Services Ltd, Dyson v Leeds City Council, Pendleton v
   Stone & Webster Engineering Ltd, Babcock International Ltd, National Grid Co, Fox
   v Spousal (Midland) Ltd, Matthews v Associated Portland Cement Manufacturers
   (1978) Ltd [2001] EWCA Civ 1881, [2002] IRLR 129, [2002] 1 WLR 1052; rvsd
   [2002] UKHL 22, [2002] 3 All ER 305, [2003] 1 AC 32, [2002] 3 WLR 89.   *g*
Ferguson v Welsh [1987] 3 All ER 777, [1987] 1 WLR 1553, HL.
Glasgow Corp v Muir [1943] 2 All ER 44, [1943] AC 448, HL.
Heaven v Pender (1883) 11 QBD 503, CA.
Indermaur v Dames (1865–66) LR 1 CP 274, CCP; affd (1866–67) LR 2 CP 311, Ex
   Cham.   *h*
Letang v Ottawa v Electric Railway Co [1926] AC 725, PC.
Nagle v Rottnest Island Authority (1993) 177 CLR 423, HC Aust.
Osborne v London and North Western Rly Co (1888) 21 QBD 220, DC.
Parker v PFC Flooring Supplies Ltd [2001] PIQR P115.
Romeo v Conservation Commission of the Northern Territory (1998) 151 ALR 263, Aust HC.   *j*
White v Blackmore [972] 3 All ER 158, [1972] 2 QB 651, [1972] 3 WLR 296, CA.

Appeal
The claimant, John Peter Tomlinson, appealed from the decision of Jack J on 21
March 2001 in the Manchester District Registry holding (i) that the defendants,
Congleton Borough Council and Cheshire County Council, were not liable for

a damages for breach of their duty of care under s 1 of the Occupiers' Liability Act 1984 to the claimant who had suffered accidental injury as a trespasser in a park which the defendants together owned, occupied and managed; and (ii) that the claimant's contributory negligence amounted to a proportion of two-thirds. The facts are set out in the judgment of Ward LJ.

b *Bill Braithwaite QC* and *Gerard Martin QC* (instructed by *Paul Ross & Co,* Manchester) for the claimant.

Raymond Machell QC (instructed by *James Chapman & Co,* Manchester) for the councils.

Cur adv vult

c

14 March 2003. The following judgments were delivered.

WARD LJ.

d [1] This appeal concerns an accident with very severe consequences which happened on 6 May 1995 to the claimant, John Tomlinson. He was 18 years old at the time and he was one of many hundreds of people who regularly went to Brereton Heath Park near Congleton in Cheshire. The park was owned and occupied by the borough council (the first defendant) and managed for them by the county council (the second defendant). They have resolved their initial *e* differences and now defend jointly as occupiers.

[2] The centrepiece of the park is a lake. It is not a natural mere but a disused quarry, about 40 feet deep at its deepest point towards which the shore shelves at varying degrees. It was an extremely popular venue where yachting, sub-aqua diving and other regulated activities were permitted, but swimming and diving *f* were not. The prohibition was made clear by notices reading 'DANGEROUS WATER: NO SWIMMING', which had little or no effect. A succession of disclosed internal documents, to which I shall have to refer in detail later, shows the local authorities to have been fully alive to this and the need to do what they could about it. A scheme was in fact developed to plant the shores from which people swam with vegetation which would make them inaccessible, but by the *g* date of the accident the budgetary bids for the relatively modest cost of doing this work had been repeatedly turned down. Since the accident, planting has been carried out and has proved effective.

[3] May 6 1995 was the Saturday of a bank holiday weekend and a hot day. The claimant went there after work with some friends in the early afternoon. He *h* went in and out of the water, like others, to cool off, diving or plunging within his depth. At one point of the afternoon Mr Tomlinson dived from a standing position in water which came no higher than his mid-thigh. Somehow—it has never become clear how, but the judge saw no reason to attribute it to a submerged object—Mr Tomlinson struck his head with sufficient force to drive *j* his fifth cervical vertebra into the spinal canal. The injury paralysed him from the neck down, and in the time since he has made only a limited recovery of the use of his hands and arms.

[4] His case against the local authorities is that as occupiers it was their breach of their duty of care towards him which was the cause of his accident. Their case is that the risk of danger was, as he knew, an obvious one and he willingly accepted it.

[5] Jack J, who tried the issue of liability in Manchester on 21 March 2001, set
out the history in careful detail. At the end of it he said:

> 'I conclude this section by noting that there was nothing about the mere at
> Brereton Heath which made it any more dangerous than any other ordinary
> stretch of open water in England. Swimming and diving carry their own
> risks. So, if the mere at Brereton was to be described as a danger, it was only
> because it attracted swimming and diving, which activities carry a risk.'

[6] As to the occurrence of the accident, the judge found:

> 'Mr Tomlinson waded into the water until it was a little above his knees,
> probably at or no deeper than mid-thigh level. He could not see the bottom.
> He then threw himself forward in a dive or plunge. He intended it to be a
> shallow dive. But it went wrong. He went deeper than he intended. His
> head struck the sandy bottom ... I am satisfied that he did not dive towards
> the shore, and I am satisfied that he did not jump into the air and then
> jack-knife to do a vertical dive ... Mr Tomlinson said that he was a strong
> swimmer. It appeared from his evidence that he did not have much
> experience of diving. Somehow on this occasion he just got it wrong, with
> tragic results. He might have been saved by his arms, had they been
> outstretched in from of him, but somehow he was not.'

[7] The judge's findings, which have not been challenged on this appeal, that
the claimant had seen and ignored the signs meant that when he entered the
water, he ceased to be at the park for the purposes for which he was invited and
permitted by the defendants to be there. He accordingly ceased to be a visitor and
became a trespasser. As such, he was owed not the common duty of care under
the Occupiers' Liability Act 1957 but the duty contained in s 1 of the Occupiers'
Liability Act 1984. That Act, replacing the accretion of common law rules,
provides by s 1:

> 'Duty of occupier to persons other than his visitors.—(1) The rules enacted by
> this section shall have effect, in place of the rules of the common law, to
> determine—(a) whether any duty is owed by a person as occupier of
> premises to persons other than his visitors in respect of any risk of their
> suffering injury on the premises by reason of any danger due to the state of
> the premises or to things done or omitted to be done on them; and (b) if so,
> what that duty is.
>
> (2) For the purposes of this section, the persons who are to be treated
> respectively as an occupier of any premises (which, for those purposes,
> include any fixed or movable structure) and as his visitors are—(a) any
> person who owes in relation to the premises the duty referred to in section 2
> of the Occupiers' Liability Act 1957 (the common duty of care), and (b) those
> who are his visitors for the purposes of that duty.
>
> (3) An occupier of premises owes a duty to another (not being his visitor)
> in respect of any such risk as is referred to in subsection (1) above if—(a) he
> is aware of the danger or has reasonable grounds to believe that it exists;
> (b) he knows or has reasonable grounds to believe that the other is in the
> vicinity of the danger concerned or that he may come into the vicinity of the
> danger (in either case, whether the other has lawful authority for being in
> that vicinity or not); and (c) the risk is one against which, in all the

a   circumstances of the case, he may reasonably be expected to offer the other some protection.

(4) Where, by virtue of this section, an occupier of premises owes a duty to another in respect of such a risk, the duty is to take such care as is reasonable in all the circumstances of the case to see that he does not suffer injury on the premises by reason of the danger concerned.

b   (5) Any duty owed by virtue of this section in respect of a risk may, in an appropriate case, be discharged by taking such steps as are reasonable in all the circumstances of the case to give warning of the danger concerned or to discourage persons from incurring the risk.

(6) No duty is owed by virtue of this section to any person in respect of risks willingly accepted as his by that person (the question whether a risk was *c*   so accepted to be decided on the same principles as in other cases in which one person owes a duty of care to another) ...'

[8] Jack J found against the claimant. His essential conclusions were these:

d   '[27] In his cross-examination Mr Tomlinson accepted that he knew that he should not dive in shallow water where he might hit the bottom. He accepted that he could not see the lake bed, that he assumed that it was sufficiently deep to dive without hitting the bed, and that he should have checked. These were important answers but in reality they were a necessary acceptance of the obvious. In short, Mr Tomlinson took a risk.

e   [28] A duty arises by reason of s 1(3) of the 1984 Act if three matters are satisfied. First, there must be a risk of which the occupier was aware (or had reasonable grounds to believe existed). The risk here was not the risk of drowning through, for example, exhaustion or cramp, but the risk of injury through diving—which might include drowning consequent on a direct injury. The defendants were aware of this danger: I refer in particular to the *f*   two head injuries in 1992. The second is satisfied if the occupier knows that the claimant may come into the vicinity of the danger. That was the case here. The third is that, in all the circumstances of the case, the risk was one against which the occupier may reasonably be expected to offer the claimant some protection. It was submitted on behalf of the defendants that this was not satisfied. Where there is a duty, s 1(4) provides that it is to take such steps *g*   as are reasonable in all the circumstances to give warning of the danger concerned or to discourage persons from incurring that risk. In the circumstances of this case at least, consideration of the third requirement under s 1(3) and consideration of the duty under s 1(4) cover much the same ground.

h   [29] In my view the danger and risk of injury from diving in the lake where it was shallow were obvious. That is my conclusion on the evidence in the case. It concurs with the conclusions reached in the cases which I have cited. On the basis of *Darby v National Trust* [2001] EWCA Civ 189, [2001] PIQR P372 that is really the end of the matter. For the essence of that *j*   case—a 1957 Act case—and others is, in my view, that an occupier is not under a duty to warn against a risk which is obvious. But, if I take a step further and say that the history showed some protection was required because of the attractions of the lake, then I would hold that the signs were reasonable and sufficient steps to give warning of the danger and to discourage persons from incurring the risk. It can be said that despite the signs people continued to go into the water. That was a decision which they

were free to make: they could choose to accept the risk. I do not think that
the defendants' legal duty to the claimant in the circumstances required
them to take the extreme measures which were completed after the accident
involving the fencing off of the areas where people went into the water and
the planting of the beaches with trees. I should add that I reject the
submission that by putting the warning signs on the beaches the defendants
were inviting swimming elsewhere. That is lacking in realism. If the water
was dangerous off the beaches, it was plainly at least as dangerous elsewhere.

[30] I also consider that an alternative route to the answer in this case is
under s 1(6). For, by diving as he did, Mr Tomlinson willingly accepted the
risk involved ...

[34] Finally, if I am wrong and the defendants were in breach of duty to
the claimant, the question of contributory negligence would arise. In my
view, on the facts and circumstances which I have set out it would be
appropriate to apportion the responsibility for the injury as to one-third to
the defendants and two-thirds to the claimant. I do so on the basis that
Mr Tomlinson dived in very shallow water, knowing of the notices warning
of the danger.'

[9] Mr Braithwaite QC, having taken this court through the authorities which
Jack J had considered in detail, and having drawn attention to the way the dangers
had been considered by the authorities, submitted that if Jack J's decision was
right, an occupier's liability is discharged simply by the display of notices even
where the locus is a public resort, where it is perceptible that the notices do not
have the required effect, and where alternative measures which will be effective
are manifest but are not undertaken. The duty, he submits, was to do what was
practicable to prevent the occurrence of accidents, not merely to warn people
that they might occur. As to contributory negligence, he submits that no more
than one third of the blame can properly rest upon the claimant.

[10] Mr Machell QC submits that in the circumstances found by the judge the
defendants owed the claimant no duty; or that if they did, it was discharged by
the display of warning notices. He relies in particular upon the judge's finding
that there was nothing about this lake which made it more dangerous than any
other stretch of open water, and that the risk of injury from diving where the lake
was shallow was obvious. This was not a case where an unpredictable declivity
in the lake bed had caused a child to lose its footing and drown (which,
Mr Machell accepted, would have attracted liability): this was a case of an adult
choosing to dive into shallow water.

[11] Mr Braithwaite meets this argument initially by submitting that the judge
has adopted two erroneous premises in reaching his conclusion. He has expressly
treated the lake as no more dangerous than any other ordinary open stretch of
water, when the chief reason for keeping swimmers out was precisely that it was
treacherous underfoot. And he has taken the risk to be not the generalised risk
that anybody entering the water might, albeit in a possibly unpredictable way,
have a nasty accident, but as the specific risk of injury through diving. If so, he
argues, the conclusion must be arrived at afresh by this court on a correct factual
and legal basis.

[12] Like the judge, we have reviewed various authorities. I must deal with
them, albeit shortly. The first is *Staples v West Dorset DC* (1995) 93 LGR 536. There
the plaintiff was crouching on a plainly visible dark layer of the algae-covered
slope of the harbour wall to which the public had access as a promenade. He

a slipped and suffered serious injury. His claim was brought under the Occupier's Liability Act 1957 and he contended that the council ought to have erected a sign warning that the cobb was slippery particularly when wet. Kennedy LJ with whom the other members of the court agreed held (at 541):

b
'It is, in my judgment, of significance that the duty is a duty owed by the occupier to the individual visitor, so that it can only be said that there was a duty to warn if without a warning the visitor in question would have been unaware of the nature and extent of the risk. As the statute makes clear, there may be circumstances in which even an explicit warning will not absolve the occupier from liability (see section 4(*a*) above); but if the danger is obvious, the visitor is able to appreciate it, he is not under any kind of
c pressure and he is free to do what is necessary for his own safety, then no warning is required.'

One should, however, not pass from the judgment without noting Kennedy LJ's further comment (at 544):

d
'Of course, after the accident the position was different. The district council then knew that a visitor had slipped off the edge into the sea, and, as responsible occupiers, they had to do what they could to prevent a recurrence, so they posted warning notices. The fact that they took that action after the accident does not enable me to draw the inference that, in order to discharge the common duty of care to the plaintiff, they should have
e done so before the accident occurred.'

[13] *Whyte v Redland Aggregates Ltd* [1997] CA Transcript 2034 is an unreported decision of this court handed down on 27 November 1997. The plaintiff hit his head when diving into the water in a disused gravel pit owned by the defendants. Again it was a case on the common duty of care under the 1957 Act. The
f plaintiff's complaints were that the occupiers had failed to find out about the uneven state of the bottom of the pit and had failed to give proper warnings as to the danger. There had been no previous accidents. Hirst LJ dismissed the appeal after an analysis of the facts. Henry LJ agreed but added this:

g
'In my judgment, the occupier of land containing or bordered by the river, the seashore, the pond or the gravel pit, does not have to warn of uneven surfaces below the water. Such surfaces are by their nature quite likely to be uneven. Diving where you cannot see the bottom clearly enough to know that it is safe to dive is dangerous unless you have made sure, by reconnaissance or otherwise that diving is safe ie that there is adequate depth
h at the place where you choose to dive. In those circumstances, the dangers of there being an uneven surface in an area where you cannot plainly see the bottom are too plain to require a specific warning and, accordingly, there is no such duty to warn ...'

j Harman J added pungently:

'There is far too much open water in this island where riparian owners are private citizens for a duty of such a wide general nature to be easily imposed by the law.'

[14] *Ratcliff v McConnell* [1999] 1 WLR 670 concerned an inebriated student ignoring all clear warnings, climbing over a locked gate and diving more steeply

into the shallow end of the pool than he intended. Giving a judgment with which
the other members of the court agreed Stuart-Smith LJ said (at 681 (para 37)):

'Even if the defendants knew or had reasonable grounds to believe that
students might defy the prohibition on use of the pool and climb over the not
insignificant barrier of the wall or gate, it does not seem to me that they were
under any duty to warn the plaintiff against diving into too shallow water, a
risk of which any adult would be aware and which the plaintiff, as one would
expect, admitted that he was aware. Had there been some hidden
obstruction in the form of an extraneous object in the pool or a dangerous
spike, of which the defendants were aware, the position might have been
different.'

Stuart-Smith LJ added two other pertinent comments. First he said (at 680
(para 35)): '... it is important to identify the risk or danger concerned since the
occupier had to have knowledge of it, or reasonable grounds to believe it exists:
section 1(3)(a).' He later said (at 683 (para 44)):

'The duty, if any, is owed to the individual trespasser, though he may be a
member of a class that the occupier knows or has reasonable grounds to
believe is in the vicinity of the danger. But the danger of and extent of what
it is reasonable to expect of the occupier varies greatly depending on whether
the trespasser is very young or very old and so may not appreciate the nature
of the danger which is or ought to be apparent to an adult.'

[15] *Bartrum v Hepworth Minerals and Chemicals Ltd* (29 October 1999,
unreported) is a decision of Turner J. The claimant dived from a ledge on a cliff
and struck his head on the bottom of an old quarry. There was a history of
swimming accidents and signs warning against swimming were being ignored.
Turner J held that the danger of not diving far enough out from the cliff to enter
the deep water was so obvious to any adult that it was not reasonably to be
expected of the defendants that they would offer any protection. Even if there
was a duty, a sign warning 'NO SWIMMING' was—

'authoritative for the proposition that people were not expected to swim
in that lake, whether they entered it by walking or wading, or by jumping or
diving; the greater must, it seems to me, include the less.'

[16] The latest swimming case is *Darby v National Trust* [2001] EWCA Civ 189,
[2001] PIQR P372. The claim was brought under the 1957 Act. There were no
warning signs. A little unusually leading counsel and junior counsel for the
claimant put forward different propositions. Leading counsel accepting the
difficulty that the risk of death by drowning was foreseeable submitted that the
warning should have included a warning against the possibility of contracting
Weil's disease. Junior counsel submitted there was no proper correlation
between the risk of swimming in the sea and of swimming in that particular pond.
The Court of Appeal did not agree with him. May LJ said (at [27]):

'It cannot be the duty of the owner of every stretch of coastline to have
notices warning of the dangers of swimming in the sea. If it were so, the
coast would have to be littered with notices in places other than those where
there are known to be special dangers which are not obvious. The same
would apply to all inland lakes and reservoirs. In my judgment there was no
duty on the National Trust on the facts of this case to warn against

a swimming in this pond where the dangers of drowning were no other or greater than those which were quite obvious to any adult such as the unfortunate deceased.'

[17] When giving permission to appeal Henry LJ drew attention to some obiter comments of Simon Brown LJ in *Scott v Associated British Ports, Swainger v Associated British Ports* [2000] All ER (D) 1937 at [20], a decision of the Court of Appeal, to the effect that:

b

> '... let us postulate (contrary to the facts) that the defendants here had known full well that dozens of youngsters in the 13 to 15 age group routinely surfed on their rails in the manner of these appellants, and that a simple fence would have been wholly effective in eliminating this practice. Could it really
>
> c then be said that they were under no duty to erect such a fence; or, indeed, that a youth who came to be injured whilst surfing had accepted the risk and therefore was owed no duty of care? I hardly think so. For my part, indeed, I would recognise that on certain facts a comparable duty would be owed by occupiers to trespassers who they know are consciously imperilling
>
> d themselves on their land to that owed by police or prison officers to those known to be of suicidal tendency in their care: see *Reeves v Metropolitan Police Comr* [1999] 3 All ER 897, [2000] 1 AC 360. All that, however, is for another day and another case.'

Mr Braithwaite submits that today is the day and this is the case.

e [18] Mr Braithwaite did rely also on *Jebson v Ministry of Defence* [2000] 1 WLR 2055 but I do not find the authority helpful as it concerns a duty of care as carriers to passengers being carried in an army lorry. The case is, however, convenient for its citation of a passage in the speech of Lord Steyn in *Jolley v Sutton London BC* [2000] 3 All ER 409 at 416, [2000] 1 WLR 1082 at 1089:

f

> 'Two general observations are, however, appropriate. First, in this corner of the law the results of decided cases are inevitably very fact sensitive. Both counsel nevertheless at times invited your Lordships to compare the facts of the present case with the facts of other decided cases. That is a sterile exercise. Precedent is a valuable stabilising influence in our legal system.
>
> g But, comparing the facts of an outcomes of cases in this branch of the law is a misuse of the only proper use of precedent, namely to identify the relevant rule to apply to the facts as found.'

I respectfully agree.

[19] In that search for principle, I have found it useful to trace the
h development of the law. The extreme position was taken by *Robert Addie & Sons (Collieries) Ltd v Dumbreck* [1929] AC 358 at 365, [1929] All ER Rep 1 at 4 which established the rule that an occupier was only liable to a trespasser if he did 'some act ... with the deliberate intention of doing harm to the trespasser, or at least some act done with reckless disregard of the presence of the trespasser'. The
j harshness of that rule was ameliorated by *British Railways Board v Herrington* [1972] 1 All ER 749, [1972] AC 877 which discarded the *Addie* test and substituted a test, variously expressed, but usually summed up as the test of 'common humanity'. That prompted the Law Commission's inquiries and their report on *Liability for Damage or Injury to Trespassers and Related Questions of Occupiers' Liability* (Law Com no 75) (Cmnd 6428) was presented in March 1976. The Law Commission proposed steering a path between extending the common duty of

care to trespassers and treating trespassing as an activity to be undertaken at the trespasser's risk with there being no duty on the occupier to make his land safe for persons whom the occupier did not desire to be present on his land at all. The result was the 1984 Act, the terms of which I have already recited.

[20] Since the 1984 Act defines when an occupier of premises owes a duty to another, and if so what the standard of care is, it is in my view essential to use the Act as a template for judgment in each and every case. I do not wish to suggest that the decisions in the cases I have recited are wrong but I have found it useful to warn myself that a finding that a risk was obvious is a statement of a conclusion, not the application of a principle. For the principle one must look to the 1984 Act. It is a staged process.

[21] The first stage under s 1(1) is to identify the risk and the danger. The risk is expressed to be to persons other than visitors suffering injury on the premises by reason of any danger due to the state of the premises (or to things done or omitted to be done on them). In this case there was a risk of injury being suffered by anyone entering the water because of the dangers due to the state of the premises, the premises being constituted by the configuration and contents of this pond created as it was from a disused sand-extraction pit. There was a risk of injury through drowning because of the dangers, among others, of the effect of cold water, being caught in weed, being stuck in the mud or plunging unexpectedly into deep water. There was the risk of injury through diving because of the dangers of diving too steeply in shallow water or into an obstruction. There may have been risks of other injury from other dangers, e g Weil's disease. These risks of injury arose as soon as one entered the water because one did not know what danger lurked, or where it lay hidden. The exact nature of the hazard may not much matter in the particular circumstances of this case.

[22] The next stage is to determine whether or not a duty was owed by the occupier. That question depends solely upon whether the three criteria of s 1(3) are satisfied.

[23] The first is whether the occupier was aware of the danger. Here that is beyond question. But a few of the records will suffice to indicate the extent of the defendants' knowledge. The Brereton Heath Management Advisory Group was established in January 1983. At the end of its first year the minutes of 21 November 1983 record that: 'The risk of a fatality to swimmers was stressed and agreed by all.' A water safety site visit of 11 May 1990 recorded:

'Many instances of swimming during hot spells. During such times up to 2,000 people are present with as many as 100 in the water ... Extensive "beach" areas are popular with families ... Not unnaturally many will venture into the water for a swim.
Hazards.
(iii) Long history of swimming activity here (a "known" spot for swimming).'

An accident was recorded on 19 May 1992 when a man dived into the lake and 'hit head on something'. The following week a person was pulled unconscious from the lake and had to be resuscitated. The management committee reported on 9 June 1992:

'The lake acts as a magnet to the public and has become heavily used for swimming in spite of a no swimming policy due to safety considerations. As a   a result of the general flaunting [sic]of the policy [to ban swimming] there have been a number of near fatalities in the lake with three incidents requiring hospital treatment in the week around Whitsun. Whilst the rangers are doing all they can to protect the public it is likely to be only a matter of time before someone drowns.'

b   [24] On 23 July 1992 the leisure services department wrote:

'To provide a facility that is open to the public and which contains beach and water areas is, in my view, an open invitation and temptation to swim and engage in other waters-edge activities despite the cautionary note that is struck by deterrent notices etc., and in that type of situation accidents become inevitable.'

c

The Cheshire Water Safety Committee meeting on 5 October 1993 noted that: 'The site has a history of near drownings.' In a resolution put to the borough council on 21 November 1999 it was noted that: 'We have on average three or four near drownings every year and it is only a matter of time before someone dies.' The claimant suffered his injuries six months later.

d   [25] The second criterion to establish whether a duty is owed is provided by s 1(3)(b), namely that the occupier knows or has reasonable grounds to believe that the other person is in the vicinity of the danger concerned. Again this has not been in dispute. The minutes I have cited establish that and there is more to like effect. It is quite clear that the park was a very popular venue and despite all

e   efforts to impose the ban on swimming, it was known to the defendants that many entered the water and were in the vicinity of the dangers concerned.

[26] The third, and in this case crucial, requirement laid down by s 1(3)(c) is whether the risk was one against which, in all the circumstances of the case, the occupiers might reasonably be expected to offer the trespasser some protection.

f   Analysing that, the protection is against any such risk as is referred to in sub-s (1), the risk, that is, of the trespasser suffering injury by reason of the dangers lurking in the mere. The protection we are looking for is 'some protection'. The question is whether some protection might reasonably be expected to be offered. The question is not whether reasonable protection is to be expected. To frame the question that way is to fail to distinguish between the establishing of the duty

g   under s 1(3) and the standard of care necessary to satisfy the duty which is provided by s 1(4). These are distinct and separate requirements and I am concerned that the judge may have failed to keep them separate and distinct when he said:

h   '[28] ... In the circumstances of this case at least, consideration of the third requirement under s 1(3) and the consideration of the duty under s 1(4) cover much the same ground ...

[29] In my view the danger and risk of injury from diving in the lake where it was shallow were obvious ... an occupier is not under a duty to warn against a risk which is obvious.'

j

[27] There is a further important phrase in s 1(3)(c): the question is whether some protection might reasonably be expected to be offered 'in all the circumstances of the case'. This serves to emphasise Lord Steyn's observation that cases are 'inevitably very fact sensitive' (see [18], above).

[28] The circumstances of this case are that Brereton Heath Park has for years been a well-known and well-used leisure attraction. The minutes show that in

1992 160,000 people used the park during the year. During a hot spell
2,000 people were present with as many as 100 in the water. The lake was a   *a*
magnet to the public and the sandy beaches an invitation to swim. Of major
concern to the occupiers was the unauthorised use of the lake and the increasing
possibility of an accident. As minutes of the advisory group held as long ago as
17 March 1988 record:

> 'On busy days the overwhelming numbers make it impossible to control   *b*
> this use (swimming and the use of rubber boats) of the lake, and it is difficult
> to see how the situation can change unless the whole concept of managing
> the park and the lake is revised.'

[29] In discharge of the common duty of care owed to the visitors under the
Occupiers' Liability Act 1957, the authorities placed prominently signs which   *c*
forbade swimming and warned of the 'dangerous water'. In entering the water
against that prohibition, the claimant made himself a trespasser to whom a
different duty was now owed. If the words on the noticeboard 'NO SWIMMING'
qualified the use he was permitted to make of the facility, do the other words
above or below that, 'DANGEROUS WATER' constitute some protection   *d*
against the risk of injury if the person decides to take a swim? I think that maybe
too narrow a view of a warning notice which serves a composite purpose of
turning a visitor into a trespasser and also warning him of a danger. But this case
does not rest there. The misuse of the facility, the extent of the unauthorised
swimming, the history of accidents and the perceived risk of fatality was noted
and acted upon by the occupiers over many years. They did not, as may have   *e*
been the fact in some of the other decided cases, treat the notice as sufficient to
discharge any duty that might be owed. Here the authorities employed rangers
whose duty it was to give oral warnings against swimming albeit that this met
with mixed success and sometimes attracted abuse for their troubles. In addition
to the oral warnings, the rangers would hand out safety leaflets which warned of   *f*
the variable depth in the pond, the cold, the weeds, the absence of rescue services,
waterborne diseases and the risk of accidents occurring. It seems to me that the
rangers' patrols and advice and the handing out of these leaflets reinforced the
ineffective message on the sign and constituted 'some protection' in fact given
and reasonably expected to be offered in the circumstances of this case.
Congleton Beach, as the place was also known, was as alluring to 'macho' young   *g*
men as other dangerous places were to young children. In my judgment the
gravity of the risk of injury, the frequency with which those using the park came
to be exposed to the risk, the failure of warning signs to curtail the extent to which
the risk was being run, indeed the very fact that the attractiveness of the beach
and the lake acted as a magnet to draw so many into the cooling waters, all that   *h*
leads me to the conclusion that the occupiers were reasonably to be expected to
offer some protection against the risks of entering the water. It follows that in my
judgment the defendants were under a duty to the claimant.

[30] The standard of care is defined by s 1(4). It is—

> 'to take such care as is reasonable in all the circumstances of the case to see   *j*
> that he does not suffer injury on the premises by reason of the danger
> concerned.'

By now the focus has to be on the duty owed to the individual claimant whereas
at the earlier stages of the inquiry it was probably more accurate to think of the
duty owed to the claimant as a member of a class of persons, young or old,

a nefariously on the premises or using them to the occupier's knowledge, if not with his permission. The Law Commission rejected the invitation to give guidelines for determining what may reasonably be expected of an occupier. I should do likewise. Whilst, therefore, this does not pretend to be a checklist, it is obvious that among the facts and circumstances which inevitably will have to be taken into account—and this is not an exhaustive list by any means—the court
b will have regard to the age and character of the claimant, the nature and purpose of the trespassory entry on the premises, the extent to which any protective steps which were taken had proved to have been inadequate, the difficulty or ease with which steps could be taken to reduce or eliminate the danger and the question of the cost of taking those precautions balanced against the gravity of the risks of injury. Once again the key words are 'reasonable in all the circumstances of the
c case'.

[31] Before looking at the matter generally, the question under s 1(5) arises first. Is this an appropriate case where the duty can be said to have been discharged by the warnings given of the danger concerned and the discouragement to persons from incurring the risk of injury from that danger? Subsection (5)
d expressly recognises that the giving of a warning 'may, in an appropriate case' discharge the duty. It follows that a warning does not necessarily or inevitably discharge the duty. In the time-honoured phrase, it must all be a matter of fact and degree. That, in my judgment, is the weakness of the judgment under appeal. The judge found that the risk was obvious, which means no more than that the claimant acknowledged the inevitable, namely that diving into water
e where one cannot see the bottom creates the risk that one will dive too steeply and so suffer injury. That may be a sufficient answer in many cases, perhaps even most cases. But here the history both of the danger and of the exposure to it drove the authorities inevitably, and rightly, to the conclusion that warnings were not working. The authorities were inviting public use of this amenity
f knowing that the water was a siren call strong enough to turn stout men's minds. In my judgment the posting of notices, shown to be ineffective, was not enough to discharge the duty.

[32] The next question is whether the claimant willingly accepted as his the risk of his suffering injury from the dangers concerned. There are, in my judgment, two answers to this. The first is that the claimant did not freely and
g voluntarily accept the risk. For the defence to succeed it must be shown that he had full knowledge of the nature and extent of the risk he ran and impliedly agreed to incur it. I accept the submission made on the claimant's behalf that he made an assumption which was erroneous that it was safe to dive. He did not know that the water where he dived was so shallow and the dive he made so
h steep that he would be injured. There were risks in general but he thought that what he did was safe. He did not freely and voluntarily wish the injury on himself. The second point is that if the duty on the defendants was to take reasonable steps to prevent the claimant from diving into the mere, then the defendants concede that they could not seek to argue that in diving into the mere
j the claimant voluntarily assumed the risk of injury attendant upon such act. I have identified the risk of injury to be the risk of entering the water but, in agreement with Turner J (at [15], above), the greater includes the less and consequently upon entering the water there is a risk of diving into it.

[33] The crucial question is, therefore, whether there was a breach by the defendants of the duty owed to the claimant. What care was it reasonable in all the circumstances of this case for the authorities to take to see that the claimant

did not suffer injury on the premises by reason of the danger concerned? The defendants' own documents provide the answer. The recommendation after a water safety site visit on 11 May 1990 was: *a*

'The creation of beach areas is a great encouragement for people to indulge in beach-type activities and this includes swimming. Suggest cutting down on beach area by increasing reed zones.' *b*

[34] Dealing with water safety in Cheshire, a meeting on 25 May 1990 noted that precautions against the hazards of swimming included introducing reed beds in littoral zones and planting shrubs on the littoral zone. It was said that precautions which could easily be implemented should be undertaken with immediate effect. *c*

[35] On 7 December 1992 the minutes of the Congleton countryside progress meeting reveal that the estates department was being asked for a plan and costings for covering the beach areas.

[36] When the rangers met on 19 January 1994 the borough council's area service manager stated that a decision had been taken by the council to remove the beaches; that £10,000 had been allocated for that purpose but that the *d* proposal had not been activated because of financial restraint. At the same time Mr Tyler-Jones, the chairman of the Cheshire Water Safety Committee was reporting that his major recommendation to remove the beaches had not been carried out. Later in March he recommended a reputable landscape architect to advise on suitable plant species to reclaim the water margins. The Brereton *e* Heath Park Management Advisory Group were told in July 1994 that the 1994/95 bid for landscaping the beaches had been rejected but there was the possibility of money being left at the end of the year to do one beach at a time. The following month, on 10 August, 'all agreed on the urgency to take action to landscape the beaches to deter swimming'. In putting forward a recommendation to cover the beach with soil and planting the margin of the water with reeds and other aquatic *f* plants at a capital cost of £15,000 it was stated that:

'We have on average three or four near drownings every year and it is only a matter of time before someone dies. The recommendation from the National Water Safety Committee, endorsed by County Councils is that *g* something must now be done to reduce the "beach areas" both in size and attractiveness. If nothing is done about this and someone dies the borough council is likely to be held liable and would have to accept responsibility.'

At a meeting of the community services committee of the borough council on 21 November the general capital programme for 1995/1996 allocated £5,000 for *h* safety improvements to the Brereton Heath Country Park. The work of covering the beach with topsoil and planting the beaches began shortly before this accident.

[37] In my judgment the defendants, prudent and responsible as they showed themselves to be, came under a duty to the claimant to carry out the landscaping *j* and planting that was recommended in the minutes I have recited. The carrying out of the work presented no practical problems and if carried out was likely to prove to be and in fact did turn out to be an effective deterrent to swimming in the mere. The expense, be it £5,000 or £15,000, was not excessive, especially having regard to the serious risk of injury from the accident that was waiting to happen.

a

[38] It follows that in my judgment the defendants were in breach of a duty they owed the claimant to take reasonable care to see that he did not suffer injury at the country park by reason of the dangers which awaited those who entered the water for a swim.

[39] The final question is the extent to which the court thinks it just and equitable that the damages recoverable be reduced having regard to the

b claimant's share in the responsibility for the damage. The judge would have assessed his contribution at two-thirds, an apportionment Mr Machell supports whereas Mr Braithwaite submits the proportions be reversed: one-third to the claimant, two-thirds to the defendants. The claimant knew he should not enter the water and he took some risk. The defendants knew that someone was bound to do just that sooner or later and that comparatively simple remedial steps

c would absolve them from responsibility. If the matter had been left to my judgment, I would have held that the relative share of blameworthiness and the relative importance of the acts and omissions in causing this damage fell equally on claimant and defendants. However, this court is always loath to interfere with an assessment of contributory negligence even where the judge expressed his

d conclusions from the difficult position that he had already found against the claimant. Since Sedley and Longmore LJJ, whose judgments I have been able to read in draft, would not interfere with the judge's apportionment, I recognise that my views should not be imposed.

[40] I do not pretend to have found this case easy. My views have swung one way and the other. That admitted, I am satisfied now that the appeal must be

e allowed and the matter must be remitted to the High Court for the assessment of damages to be reduced by two-thirds for the claimant's contributory negligence.

SEDLEY LJ.

[41] I agree with Ward LJ that this appeal should be allowed. But because I

f have read Longmore LJ's judgment in favour of dismissing the appeal, I add some brief reasoning of my own.

[42] I do not consider that it is appropriate to reason out a claim like the present one from its consequences. If the logic of our decision is that other public lakes and ponds require similar precautions to those which were lacking at Brereton Heath, so be it. But negligence is fact-specific, and we are able neither

g to determine what the occupiers' duties are in other places nor to predicate our decision on what its effect on those occupiers might be. We are creating no duty and no standard of care which is not already laid down by Parliament. Our task, like that of the trial judge, is simply to apply a general law to specific facts.

[43] The other matter to which Longmore LJ draws attention is the

h particularity of the hazard to which the claimant fell prey. It is, I agree, an apparent oddity that a person who is injured by diving into shallow water—a pretty obvious hazard—should be able to claim the benefit of precautions which in reality were needed in order to stop people losing their footing where the lake bed shelved steeply or becoming entangled in thick weeds. But there are two

j separate answers, one relating to the obviousness of the hazard, the other to its nature.

[44] As to the nature of the hazard, it was rightly not argued by the defendants that this could make the difference between liability and no liability in the present case. It is well settled by authority that if there is a duty to protect people against foreseeable injury, it does not matter if the accident which happens was not itself foreseeable, so long as it is not in an entirely different league: see *Hughes v Lord*

Advocate [1963] 1 All ER 705, [1963] AC 837 and *Smith v Leech Brain & Co Ltd* [1961]
3 All ER 1159, [1962] 2 QB 405.

[45] If primary liability is established, the obviousness of the hazard goes to
contributory negligence; for it is only where the risk is so obvious that the
occupier can safely assume that nobody will take it that there will be no liability.
Even so, in a gross case contributory negligence can approach one hundred per
cent. This is not such a case, but it is a case in which the claimant did something
which he was old enough to realise was stupid—not so much by entering the
mere (everyone was doing that, and the defendants had failed to take reasonable
measures to stop it) but by diving steeply from a standing position in a couple of
feet of water. I see no reason to differ from Jack J's contingent assessment of the
claimant's share of responsibility for his consequent misfortune as two-thirds.

[46] The nub of the defendants' case was that the mere did not present any
unusual or special risks at all. As to this, the logic of Ward LJ's judgment seems
to me compelling, and I do not need to add to it. I would accordingly allow the
appeal and direct entry of judgment for one-third of the damages to be assessed.

LONGMORE LJ.

[47] One of the dangers of going for a swim in any stretch of water other than
a dedicated swimming pool is that the swimmer may slip and injure himself. He
may also quickly find himself out of his depth and be unable to cope; he may get
cramp or be assailed by the coldness of the water and be unable to recover. All
these are obvious dangers to anyone except a small and unaccompanied child.
Another danger is that a swimmer may decide to dive into the water and hit his
head on the bottom, if the water is too shallow; in my judgment that is an equally
obvious danger and cannot provide a reason for saying that the owner or
occupier of the water should be under any duty to take reasonable steps to
prevent people swimming or diving in the relevant stretch of water.

[48] The position would, of course, be different if the occupier knew of some
concealed danger or some danger that was not obvious to people using the water.
But in this case Jack J has held in terms that there was nothing about the mere at
Brereton Heath which made it any more dangerous than any other ordinary
stretch of open water in England. The judge thought (and I agree) that if there
was a duty to take reasonable steps to prevent public access for the purpose of
swimming at Brereton Heath, similar steps would have to be taken in relation to
other stretches of open water in the country.

[49] Mr John Tomlinson has suffered appalling injuries as a result of his
unfortunate dive while enjoying the water on a warm May bank holiday
weekend in 1995. Mr Braithwaite QC on his behalf has submitted that the mere
at Brereton Heath was a special case different from other stretches of water
because: (1) the heath was a managed site where the defendants encouraged the
public to go to spend their leisure time; (2) the defendants knew that accidents
were liable to happen (and, indeed, had happened on three previous occasions);
and (3) the defendants were in the process of taking steps to eliminate injuries
from swimming accidents in that they: (a) put up signs prohibiting swimming;
and (b) when it became clear that the signs were being ignored, they were advised
that the beaches on the mere should be fenced off and covered in vegetation but
had not got round to doing this by the time of Mr Tomlinson's accident.

[50] I do not consider that these factors either singly or together make the
mere at Brereton Heath different from other stretches of open water. The fact
that the defendants arranged and even promoted the site for leisure activity does

a not mean that they should have taken reasonable steps to prevent swimming unless they knew of any particular hazard. Even then it would probably be sufficient to give a warning in relation to that hazard. There was here no allegation or evidence of any particular hazard, beyond the ordinary hazards of swimming in open water.

b [51] The fact that during the defendants' management of the site three accidents had occurred to people swimming in the mere cannot of itself impose a duty of care since swimming in open stretches of water is often an inherently dangerous activity. It would only be if the number of accidents was significantly above the norm that any duty could arise and that would then be because it would be possible to conclude that there was a particular hazard in relation to the stretch of water (even if the hazard might not at first be easily identifiable).

c Likewise, the fact that a local authority may responsibly seek to deter or prevent swimming does not to my mind give rise to any duty to an individual member of the public or the public at large to take steps to prevent people swimming, unless there is a particular hazard (over and above the ordinary risks of swimming) about which the public should know.

d [52] I should add that, for myself, I would have reached the same conclusion even if the claimant had not conceded that he was a trespasser. I find it odd that if there is a general licence to the public to come to a park for leisure activities but there are notices which prohibit swimming, someone who enters the water intending to swim becomes a trespasser. At what point does he become a trespasser? When he starts to paddle, intending thereafter to swim? There was

e no evidence that Mr Tomlinson in fact swam at all. He dived from a position in which swimming was difficult, if not impossible. I would be troubled if the defendants' duty of care differed depending on the precise moment when a swim could be said to have begun.

f [53] For these reasons which are much the same as those given by this court in *Darby v National Trust* [2001] EWCA Civ 189, [2001] PIQR P372 it seems to me that this appeal should fail. It is noteworthy that the Supreme Court of Canada seems to have come to a similar conclusion in relation to a similar stretch of water in British Columbia (see *Vancouver-Fraser Park District v Olmstead* (1974) 51 DLR (3d) 416).

j [54] On contributory negligence, I would not interfere with the judge's apportionment.

Appeal allowed in part.

Kate O'Hanlon   Barrister.

Appeal

The defendants appealed with permission of the Appeal Committee of the House of Lords given on 23 July 2002. The claimant cross-appealed, with permission of the Appeal Committee given on 9 October 2002, as to quantum of contributory negligence.

Raymond Machell QC and *Peter Burns* (instructed by *James Chapman & Co,* Manchester) for the councils.

Bill Braithwaite QC and *Gerard Martin QC* (instructed by *Paul Ross & Co,* Manchester) for the claimant.

31 July 2003. The following opinions were delivered.

LORD NICHOLLS OF BIRKENHEAD.

[1] My Lords, I have had the advantage of reading in draft the speech of my noble and learned friend Lord Hoffmann. For the reasons he gives, with which I agree, I would allow this appeal.

LORD HOFFMANN.

THE ACCIDENT

[2] My Lords, in rural south-east Cheshire the early May Bank Holiday weekend in 1995 was unseasonably hot. John Tomlinson, aged 18, had to work until midday on Saturday 6 May but then met some of his friends and drove them to Brereton Heath Country Park, between Holmes Chapel and Congleton. The park covers about 80 acres. In about 1980 Congleton Borough Council acquired the land, surrounding what was then a derelict sand quarry, and laid it out as a country park. Paths now run through woods of silver birch and in summer bright yellow brimstone butterflies flutter in grassy meadows. But the attraction of the park for John Tomlinson and his young friends was a 14-acre lake which had been created by flooding the old sand quarry. The sandy banks provided some attractive beaches and in hot weather many people, including families with children, went there to play in the sand, sunbathe and paddle in the water. A beach at the far end of the lake from the car park was where in fine weather groups of teenagers like John Tomlinson would regularly hang out. He had been going there since he was a child.

[3] After sitting in the hot sun for a couple of hours, John Tomlinson decided that he wanted to cool off. So he ran out into the water and dived. He had done the same thing many times before. But this time the dive was badly executed because he struck his head hard on the sandy bottom. So hard that he broke his neck at the fifth vertebra. He is now a tetraplegic and unable to walk.

[4] It is a terrible tragedy to suffer such dreadful injury in consequence of a relatively minor act of carelessness. It came nowhere near the stupidity of Luke Ratcliff, a student who climbed a fence at 2.30 am on a December morning to take a running dive into the shallow end of a swimming pool (*Ratcliff v McConnell* [1999] 1 WLR 670) or John Donoghue, who dived into Folkestone Harbour from a slipway at midnight on 27 December after an evening in the pub (*Donoghue v Folkestone Properties Ltd* [2003] EWCA Civ 231, [2003] 3 All ER 1101, [2003] 2 WLR 1138). John Tomlinson's mind must often recur to that hot day which irretrievably changed his life. He may feel, not unreasonably, that fate has dealt with him unfairly. And so in these proceedings he seeks financial compensation: for the loss of his earning capacity, for the expense of the care he will need, for the loss of the ability to lead an ordinary life. But the law does not provide such compensation simply on the basis that the injury was disproportionately severe in relation to one's own fault or even not one's own fault at all. Perhaps it should, but society might not be able to afford to compensate everyone on that principle, certainly at the level at which such compensation is now paid. The law provides compensation only when the injury was someone else's fault. In order to succeed in his claim, that is what Mr Tomlinson has to prove.

OCCUPIERS' LIABILITY

a   [5] In these proceedings Mr Tomlinson sues the Congleton Borough Council and the Cheshire County Council, claiming that as occupiers of the park they were in breach of their duties under the Occupiers' Liability Acts 1957 and 1984. If one had to decide which of the two councils was the occupier, it might not be easy. Although the park belongs to the borough council, it is managed on their

b behalf by the countryside management service of the county council. The borough council provides the funds to enable the countryside management service to maintain the park. It is the county which employs the rangers who look after it. But the two councils very sensibly agreed that one or other or both was the occupier. Unless it is necessary to distinguish between the county council and the borough council for the purpose of telling the story, I shall call them both

c the council.

VISITOR OR TRESPASSER?

    [6] The 1957 Act was passed to amend and codify the common law duties of occupiers to certain persons who came upon their land. The common law had

d distinguished between invitees, in whose visit the occupier had some material interest, and licensees, who came simply by express or implied permission. Different duties were owed to each class. The Act, on the recommendation of the Law Reform Committee (*Third Report: Occupiers' Liability to Invitees, Licensees and Trespassers* (1954) Cmd 9305), amalgamated (without redefining) the two common law categories, designated the combined class 'visitors' (s 1(2)) and

e provided that (subject to contrary agreement) all visitors should be owed a 'common duty of care'. That duty is set out in s 2(2), as refined by sub-ss (3)–(5):

'(2) The common duty of care is a duty to take such care as in all the circumstances of the case is reasonable to see that the visitor will be

f   reasonably safe in using the premises for the purposes for which he is invited or permitted by the occupier to be there.

(3) The circumstances relevant for the present purpose include the degree of care, and of want of care, which would ordinarily be looked for in such a visitor, so that (for example) in proper cases—(a) an occupier must be prepared for children to be less careful than adults; and (b) an occupier may

g expect that a person, in the exercise of his calling, will appreciate and guard against any special risks ordinarily incident to it, so far as the occupier leaves him free to do so.

(4) In determining whether the occupier of premises has discharged the common duty of care to a visitor, regard is to be had to all the circumstances,

h so that (for example)—(a) where damage is caused to a visitor by a danger of which he had been warned by the occupier, the warning is not to be treated without more as absolving the occupier from liability, unless in all the circumstances it was enough to enable the visitor to be reasonably safe; and (b) where damage is caused to a visitor by a danger due to the faulty

j execution of any work of construction, maintenance or repair by an independent contractor employed by the occupier, the occupier is not to be treated without more as answerable for the danger if in all the circumstances he had acted reasonably in entrusting the work to an independent contractor and had taken such steps (if any) as he reasonably ought in order to satisfy himself that the contractor was competent and that the work had been properly done.

(5) The common duty of care does not impose on an occupier any
obligation to a visitor in respect of risks willingly accepted as his by the visitor
(the question whether a risk was so accepted to be decided on the same
principles as in other cases in which one person owes a duty of care to
another).'

[7] At first Mr Tomlinson claimed that the council was in breach of its
common duty of care under s 2(2). His complaint was that the premises were not
reasonably safe because diving into the water was dangerous and the council had
not given adequate warning of this fact or taken sufficient steps to prevent or
discourage him from doing it. But then a difficulty emerged. The county council,
as manager of the park, had for many years pursued a policy of prohibiting
swimming or the use of inflatable dinghies or mattresses. Canoeing and
windsurfing were allowed in one area of the lake and angling in another. But not
swimming; except, I suppose, by capsized canoeists or windsurfers. Notices had
been erected at the entrance and elsewhere saying 'DANGEROUS WATER. NO
SWIMMING'. The policy had not been altogether effective because many
people, particularly rowdy teenagers, ignored the notices. They were sometimes
rude to the rangers who tried to get them out of the water. Nevertheless, it was
hard to say that swimming or diving was, in the language of s 2(2), one of the
purposes 'for which [Mr Tomlinson was] invited or permitted by the occupier to
be there'. The council went further and said that once he entered the lake to
swim, he was no longer a 'visitor' at all. He became a trespasser, to whom no
duty under the 1957 Act is owed. The council cited a famous bon mot of
Scrutton LJ in *The Calgarth, The Otarama* [1927] P 93 at 110: 'When you invite a
person into your house to use the staircase, you do not invite him to slide down
the banisters ...' This quip was used by Lord Atkin in *Hillen v ICI (Alkali) Ltd*
[1936] AC 65 at 69, [1935] All ER Rep 555 at 558 to explain why stevedores who
were lawfully on a barge for the purpose of discharging it nevertheless became
trespassers when they went onto an inadequately supported hatch cover in order
to unload some of the cargo. They knew, said Lord Atkin ([1936] AC 65 at 69–70,
[1935] All ER Rep 555 at 558) that they ought not to use the covered hatch for this
purpose 'for them for such a purpose it was out of bounds; they were trespassers'.
So the stevedores could not complain that the barge owners should have warned
them that the hatch cover was not adequately supported. Similarly, says the
council, Mr Tomlinson became a trespasser and took himself outside the 1957
Act when he entered the water to swim.

[8] Mr Tomlinson's advisers, having reflected on the matter, decided to
concede that he was indeed a trespasser when he went into the water. Although
that took him outside the 1957 Act, it did not necessarily mean that the council
owed him no duty. At common law the only duty to trespassers was not to cause
them deliberate or reckless injury, but after an inconclusive attempt by the House
of Lords to modify this rule in *British Railways Board v Herrington* [1972] 1 All ER
749, [1972] AC 877, the Law Commission recommended the creation of a
statutory duty to trespassers (see its *Report on Liability for Damage or Injury to
Trespassers and Related Questions of Occupiers' Liability* (1976) (Law Com no 75)
(Cmnd 6428)). The recommendation was given effect by the Occupiers' Liability
Act 1984. Section 1(1) describes the purpose of that Act:

'(1) The rules enacted by this section shall have effect, in place of the rules
of the common law, to determine—(a) whether any duty is owed by a person
as occupier of premises to persons other than his visitors in respect of any risk

a of their suffering injury on the premises by reason of any danger due to the state of the premises or to things done or omitted to be done on them; and (b) if so, what that duty is.'

[9] The circumstances in which a duty may arise are then defined in sub-s (3) and the content of the duty is described in sub-ss (4)–(6):

b '(3) An occupier of premises owes a duty to another (not being his visitor) in respect of any such risk as is referred to in subsection (1) above if—

(a) he is aware of the danger or has reasonable grounds to believe that it exists;

(b) he knows or has reasonable grounds to believe that the other is in the
c vicinity of the danger concerned or that he may come into the vicinity of the danger (in either case, whether he has lawful authority for being in that vicinity or not); and

(c) the risk is one against which, in all the circumstances of the case, he may reasonably be expected to offer the other some protection.

(4) Where, by virtue of this section, an occupier of premises owes a duty
d to another in respect of such a risk, the duty is to take such care as is reasonable in all the circumstances of the case to see that he does not suffer injury on the premises by reason of the danger concerned.

(5) Any duty owed by virtue of this section in respect of a risk may, in an appropriate case, be discharged by taking such steps as are reasonable in all
e the circumstances of the case to give warning of the danger concerned or to discourage persons from incurring the risk.

(6) No duty is owed by virtue of this section to any person in respect of risks willingly accepted as his by that person (the question whether a risk was so accepted to be decided on the same principles as in other cases in which
f one person owes a duty of care to another).'

[10] Mr Tomlinson says that the conditions set out in sub-s (3) were satisfied. The council was therefore under a duty under sub-s (4) to take reasonable care to see that he did not suffer injury by reason of the danger from diving. Subsection (5) shows that although in appropriate circumstances it may be
g sufficient to warn or discourage, the notices in the present case had been patently ineffectual and therefore it was necessary to take more drastic measures to prevent people like himself from going into the water. Such measures, as I shall later recount in detail, had already been considered by the council.

[11] The case has therefore proceeded upon a concession that the relevant
h duty, if any, is that to a trespasser under s 1(4) of the 1984 Act and not to a lawful visitor under s 2(2) of the 1957 Act. On one analysis, this is a rather odd hypothesis. Mr Tomlinson's complaint is that he should have been prevented or discouraged from going into the water, that is to say, from turning himself into a trespasser. Logically, it can be said, that duty must have been owed to him (if at all) while he was still a lawful visitor. Once he had become a trespasser, it could
j not have meaningful effect. In the Court of Appeal ([2002] EWCA Civ 309, [2003] 3 All ER 1122, [2003] 2 WLR 1120), Longmore LJ was puzzled by this paradox:

'[52] … At what point does he become a trespasser? When he starts to paddle, intending thereafter to swim? There was no evidence that Mr Tomlinson in fact swam at all. He dived from a position in which swimming was difficult, if not impossible. I would be troubled if the defendants' duty of care differed depending on the precise moment when a swim could be said to have begun.'

[12] In the later case of *Donoghue v Folkestone Properties Ltd* [2003] EWCA Civ 231 at [45], [2003] 3 All ER 1101 at [45], [2003] 2 WLR 1138 Lord Phillips of Worth Matravers MR said that he shared these reservations about the concession:

'What was at issue in the case was whether the council should have taken steps which would have prevented Mr Tomlinson from entering the lake, that is, whether a duty of care was owed to him before he did the unauthorised act.'

[13] As a matter of logic, I see the force of these observations. But I have nevertheless come to the conclusion that the concession was rightly made. The duty under the 1984 Act was intended to be a lesser duty, as to both incidence and scope, than the duty to a lawful visitor under the 1957 Act. That was because Parliament recognised that it would often be unduly burdensome to require landowners to take steps to protect the safety of people who came upon their land without invitation or permission. They should not ordinarily be able to force duties upon unwilling hosts. In the application of that principle, I can see no difference between a person who comes upon land without permission and one who, having come with permission, does something which he has not been given permission to do. In both cases, the entrant would be imposing upon the landowner a duty of care which he has not expressly or impliedly accepted. The 1984 Act provides that even in such cases a duty may exist, based simply upon occupation of land and knowledge or foresight that unauthorised persons may come upon the land or authorised persons may use it for unauthorised purposes. But that duty is rarer and different in quality from the duty which arises from express or implied invitation or permission to come upon the land and use it.

[14] In addition, I think that the concession is supported by the high authority of Lord Atkin in *Hillen's* case. There too, it could be said that the stevedores' complaint was that they should have been warned not to go upon the hatch cover and that logically this duty was owed to them, if at all, when they were lawfully on the barge.

[15] I would certainly agree with Longmore LJ that the incidence and content of the duty should not depend on the precise moment at which Mr Tomlinson crossed the line between the status of lawful visitor and that of trespasser. But there is no dispute that the act in respect of which Mr Tomlinson says that he was owed a duty, namely, diving into the water, was to his knowledge prohibited by the terms upon which he had been admitted to the park. It is, I think, for this reason that the council owed him no duty under the 1957 Act and that the incidence and content of any duty they may have owed was governed by the 1984 Act. But I shall later return to the question of whether it would have made any difference if swimming had not been prohibited and the 1957 Act had applied.

[16] It is therefore necessary to consider the conditions which s 1(3) of the 1984 Act requires to be satisfied in order that any duty under s 1(4) should exist. But before looking at the statutory requirements, I must say something more about the history of the lake, upon which Mr Braithwaite QC, who appeared for Mr Tomlinson, placed great reliance in support of his submission that the council owed him a duty with which it failed to comply.

THE HISTORY OF THE LAKE

a   [17] The working of the sand quarry ceased in about 1975 and for some years
thereafter the land lay derelict. People went there for barbecues, camp fires,
open-air parties and swimming. The borough council bought the land in 1980
and most of the work of landscaping and planting was finished by 1983. The land
was reclaimed for municipal recreation. But the traditions established in the
b   previous anarchic state of nature were hard to eradicate. From the beginning, the
county council's management plan treated swimming as an 'unacceptable water
activity'. The minutes of the county council's advisory group of interested
organisations (anglers, windsurfers and so forth) record that on 21 November
1983 the managers proposed to put up more signs to dissuade swimmers: 'The
risk of a fatality to swimmers was stressed and agreed by all.' The windsurfers in
c   particular were concerned about swimmers getting in their way; perhaps being
injured by a fast-moving board. The chairman summed up by saying that
although the lake with its sandy beaches was a great attraction to visitors, it was
also a management problem because of misuse and dangerous activities on the
water.

d   [18] In the following year, 1984, the management reported that larger notice
boards had prevented the swimming problem from getting any worse: 'Every
reasonable precaution had now been taken, but it was recognised that some
foolhardy persons would continue to put their lives at risk.'

[19] The management report for 1988 stated that a major concern was—

e   'the unauthorised use of the lake and the increasing possibility of an
accident; this is swimming and the use of rubber boats. Warnings are
ignored by large numbers who see Brereton as easy, free access to open
water. On busy days the overwhelming numbers make it impossible to
control this use of the lake, and it is difficult to see how the situation can
change unless the whole concept of managing the park and the lake is
f   revised.'

[20] In 1990 there was an inspection by Mr Victor Tyler-Jones, the county
council's water safety officer. He reported that the swimming problem
continued, due to the ease of access, the grassy lakeside picnic areas and the
beaches and the long history of swimming in the lake. His recommendation was
g   to reduce the beach areas by planting them with reeds. His guidelines for the
entire county said that swimming in lakes, rivers and ponds should be
discouraged:

'We do not recommend swimming as a suitable activity for any of our
managed sites. Potential swimmers could be dissuaded by noticeboard
h   reference to less pleasant features e.g. soft muddy bottom, danger of
contracting Weil's Disease, presence of blue-green algae.'

If this did not have the desired effect, ballast should be dumped on beaches and
banks to make them muddy and unattractive and reeds and shrubs should be
j   planted.

[21] The money to implement these recommendations had to be provided by
the borough council, which was under some financial pressure. But impetus was
provided in the summer of 1992 by a number of incidents. Over Whitsuntide
there were three cases of 'near drowning resulting in hospital visits'. The only
such incident of which more details are available concerned a man who 'was
swimming in lake, after drinking, and got into difficulty'. He was rescued by a

relative, resuscitated by an off-duty paramedic and taken to hospital. Two men
cut their heads by hitting them on something when diving into the lake; there is
no information about where they dived. Mr Kitching, the county council's
countryside manager, prepared a paper for the borough council at the end of the
first week in June. He said that the park had become very popular:

'... the total number of visitors now exceeds 160,000 per annum ... The
lake acts as a magnet to the public and has become heavily used for
swimming in spite of a no swimming policy due to safety considerations ...
Advice has been sought from the County Council's water safety officer as to
how the problem should be addressed and this has been carefully followed.
Notices are posted warning of the dangers and leaflets are handed to visitors
to emphasise the situation. Life belts and throwing lines are provided for use
in emergencies. In spite of these actions the public continue to ignore the
advice and the requests of the rangers not to swim. The attitude is that they
will do what they want to do and that rangers should not interfere with their
enjoyment. There have been several occasions when small children have
been out in the middle of the lake and their parents have been extremely
rude to staff when approached about this. As a result of the general flaunting
of the policy there have been a number of near fatalities in the lake with three
incidents requiring hospital treatment in the week around Whitsun. Whilst
the rangers are doing all they can to protect the public it is likely to be only
a matter of time before someone drowns.'

[22] In July 1992 the borough council's leisure officer visited the park and
concluded that the notices and leaflets were not having the desired effect. On 23
July 1992 he proposed to other officers the preparation of a report to the borough
council recommending the adoption of Mr Tyler-Jones' scheme for making the
beaches less hospitable to visitors:

'... I want the water's edge to be far less accessible, desirable and inviting
than it currently is for children's beach/water's edge type of play activities.
I personally find this course of action a regrettable one but I have to remind
myself that Council policy was to establish a Country Park and not
specifically to provide a swimming facility, no matter how popular this may
have become in consequence. To provide a facility that is open to the public
and which contains beach and water areas is, in my view, an open invitation
and temptation to swim and engage in other water's edge activities despite
the cautionary note that is struck by deterrent notices etc., and in that type
of situation accidents become inevitable. We must therefore do everything
that is reasonably possible to deter, discourage and prevent people from
swimming or paddling in the lake or diving into the lake ... Work should be
prepared for the report with a view to implementation of a scheme at the
earliest opportunity, bearing in mind that we shall require a supplementary
estimate for the exercise ...'

[23] As a result of this proposal, the borough leisure officer was asked to
prepare a feasibility report with costings. £5,000 was provided in the draft
estimates for the borough's amenities and leisure services committee, but it was
one of many items deleted at the committee's meeting on 1 March 1993 to
achieve a total saving of £200,000. In 1994, the officers tried again. It was listed
as a 'desirable' growth bid in the budget (below 'essential' and 'highly desirable').

a   But the bid failed. When it came to the 1995 budget round, the officers presented a strongly-worded proposal:

'Cheshire Countryside Management Service has now taken all reasonable steps with regard to providing information and attempting to educate the public about the dangers of bathing in the lake. This has had a limited effect

b   on the numbers entering the water for short periods but there are still numbers of people, including young children, swimming, paddling and using inflatable rafts and dinghies whenever the weather is warm and sunny. We have on average three or four near drownings every year and it is only a matter of time before someone dies. The recommendation from the

c   National Safety Water Committee, endorsed by County Councils is that something must now be done to reduce the "beach areas" both in size and attractiveness. If nothing is done about this and someone dies the Borough Council is likely to be held liable and would have to accept responsibility.'

d   [24] The borough council found this persuasive and in 1995 £5,000 was allocated to the scheme. But the work had not yet begun when Mr Tomlinson had his accident. At that time, the beach to which he and his friends had been accustomed to go since childhood was still there. The diggers, graders and planters arrived to destroy it a few months later.

e   THE SCOPE OF THE DUTY UNDER THE 1984 ACT
[25] The conditions in s 1(3) of the 1984 Act determine whether or not a duty is owed to 'another' in respect of 'any such risk as is referred to in subsection (1)'. Two conclusions follow from this language. First, the risks in respect of which the Act imposes a duty are limited to those mentioned in sub-s (1)(a)—risks of

f   injury 'by reason of any danger due to the state of the premises or to things done or omitted to be done on them'. The Act is not concerned with risks due to anything else. Secondly, the conditions have to be satisfied in respect of the claimant as 'another'; that is to say, in respect of a class of persons which includes him and a description of risk which includes that which caused his injury.

g   A DANGER 'DUE TO THE STATE OF THE PREMISES'
[26] The first question, therefore, is whether there was a risk within the scope of the statute; a danger 'due to the state of the premises or to things done or omitted to be done on them'. The judge found that there was 'nothing about the

h   mere at Brereton Heath which made it any more dangerous than any other ordinary stretch of open water in England'. There was nothing special about its configuration; there were no hidden dangers. It was shallow in some places and deep in others, but that is the nature of lakes. Nor was the council doing or permitting anything to be done which created a danger to persons who came to the lake. No power boats or jet skis threatened the safety of either lawful

j   windsurfers or unlawful swimmers. So the council submits that there was no danger attributable to the state of premises or things done or omitted on them. In *Donoghue v Folkestone Properties Ltd* [2003] 3 All ER 1101 at [53] Lord Phillips MR expressed the same opinion. He said that he had been unable to identify the 'state of the premises' which carried with it the risk of the injury suffered by Mr Tomlinson:

'It seems to me that Mr Tomlinson suffered his injury because he chose to
indulge in an activity which had inherent dangers, not because the premises *a*
were in a dangerous state.'

[27] In making this comment, Lord Phillips MR was identifying a point which
is in my opinion central to this appeal. It is relevant at a number of points in the
analysis of the duties under the 1957 and 1984 Acts. Mr Tomlinson was a person
of full capacity who voluntarily and without any pressure or inducement engaged *b*
in an activity which had inherent risk. The risk was that he might not execute his
dive properly and so sustain injury. Likewise, a person who goes mountaineering
incurs the risk that he might stumble or misjudge where to put his weight. In
neither case can the risk be attributed to the state of the premises. Otherwise any
premises can be said to be dangerous to someone who chooses to use them for *c*
some dangerous activity. In the present case, Mr Tomlinson knew the lake well
and even if he had not, the judge's finding was that it contained no dangers which
one would not have expected. So the only risk arose out of what he chose to do
and not out of the state of the premises.

[28] Mr Braithwaite was inclined to accept the difficulty of establishing that
the risk was due to the state of the premises. He therefore contended that it was *d*
due to 'things done or omitted to be done' on the premises. When asked what
these might be, he said that they consisted in the attraction of the lake and the
council's inadequate attempts to keep people out of the water. The council, he
said, were 'luring people into a deathtrap'. Ward LJ ([2003] All ER 1122 at [31])
said that the water was 'a siren call strong enough to turn stout men's minds'. In *e*
my opinion this is gross hyperbole. The trouble with the island of the sirens was
not the state of the premises. It was that the sirens held mariners spellbound until
they died of hunger. The beach, give or take a fringe of human bones, was an
ordinary mediterranean beach. If Odysseus had gone ashore and accidentally
drowned himself having a swim, Penelope would have had no action against the
sirens for luring him there with their songs. Likewise in this case, the water was *f*
perfectly safe for all normal activities. In my opinion 'things done or omitted to
be done' means activities or the lack of precautions which cause risk, like
allowing speedboats among the swimmers. It is a mere circularity to say that a
failure to stop people getting into the water was an omission which gave rise to
a duty to take steps to stop people from getting into the water. *g*

[29] It follows that in my opinion, there was no risk to Mr Tomlinson due to
the state of the premises or anything done or omitted upon the premises. That
means that there was no risk of a kind which gave rise to a duty under the 1957
or 1984 Acts. I shall nevertheless go on to consider the matter on the assumption
that there was. *h*

THE CONDITIONS FOR THE EXISTENCE OF A DUTY

(i) *Knowledge or foresight of the danger*
[30] Section 1(3) of the 1984 Act has three conditions which must be satisfied.
First, under para (a), the occupier must be aware of the danger or have reasonable *j*
grounds to believe that it exists. For this purpose, it is necessary to say what the
relevant danger was. The judge thought it was the risk of suffering an injury
through diving and said that the council was aware of this danger because two
men had suffered minor head injuries from diving in May 1992. In the Court of
Appeal, Ward LJ described the relevant risk much more broadly. He regarded all
the swimming incidents as indicative of the council's knowledge that a danger

a existed. I am inclined to think that this is too wide a description. The risk of injury from diving off the beach was in my opinion different from the risk of drowning in the deep water. For example, the council might have fenced off the deep water or marked it with buoys and left people to paddle in the shallows. That would have reduced the risk of drowning but would not have prevented the injury to Mr Tomlinson. We know very little about the circumstances in which

b two men suffered minor cuts to their heads in 1992 and I am not sure that they really provide much support for an inference that there was knowledge, or reasonable grounds to believe, that the beach posed a risk of serious diving injury. Dr Penny, a consultant occupational health and safety physician with long experience of advising organisations involved in aquatic sports (and himself a diver) said that the *Code of Safety for Beaches*, published in 1993 by the Royal Life

c Saving Society and the Royal Society for the Prevention of Accidents, made no mention of diving risks, no doubt assuming that, because there was little possibility of high diving from a beach, the risk of serious diving injuries was very small compared with the risk of drowning. I accept that the council must have known that there was a possibility that some boisterous teenager would injure himself by horseplay in the shallows and I would not disturb the concurrent

d findings that this was sufficient to satisfy para (a). But the chances of such an accident were small. I shall return later, in connection with para (c), to the relevance of where the risk comes on the scale of probability.

e (ii) *Knowledge or foresight of the presence of the trespasser*
    [31] Once it is found that the risk of a swimmer injuring himself by diving was something of which the council knew or which they had reasonable grounds to believe to exist, para (b) presents no difficulty. The council plainly knew that swimmers came to the lake and Mr Tomlinson fell within that class.

f (iii) *Reasonable to expect protection*
    [32] That leaves para (c). Was the risk one against which the council might reasonably be expected to offer Mr Tomlinson some protection? The judge found that 'the danger and risk of injury from diving in the lake where it was shallow were obvious'. In such a case the judge held, both as a matter of common sense and following consistent authority (*Staples v West Dorset DC* (1995)

g 93 LGR 536, *Ratcliff v McConnell* [1999] 1 WLR 670, *Darby v National Trust* [2001] PIQR P372), that there was no duty to warn against the danger. A warning would not tell a swimmer anything he did not already know. Nor was it necessary to do anything else. 'I do not think', said the judge, 'that the defendants' legal duty to the claimant in the circumstances required them to take the extreme measures

h which were completed after the accident'. Even if Mr Tomlinson had been owed a duty under the 1957 Act as a lawful visitor, the council would not have been obliged to do more than they did.
    [33] The Court of Appeal disagreed. Ward LJ said that the council was obliged to do something more. The gravity of the risk, the number of people who

j regularly incurred it and the attractiveness of the beach created a duty. The prohibition on swimming was obviously ineffectual and therefore it was necessary to take additional steps to prevent or discourage people from getting into the water. Sedley LJ said ([2003] 3 All ER 1122 at [45]): '... it is only where the risk is so obvious that the occupier can safely assume that nobody will take it that there will be no liability.' Longmore LJ dissented. The majority reduced the damages by two-thirds to reflect Mr Tomlinson's contributory negligence,

although Ward LJ said that he would have been inclined to reduce them only by
half. The council appeals against the finding of liability and Mr Tomlinson
appeals against the apportionment, which he says should have been in
accordance with the view of Ward LJ.

THE BALANCE OF RISK, GRAVITY OF INJURY, COST AND SOCIAL VALUE.

[34] My Lords, the majority of the Court of Appeal appear to have proceeded
on the basis that if there was a foreseeable risk of serious injury, the council was
under a duty to do what was necessary to prevent it. But this in my opinion is an
oversimplification. Even in the case of the duty owed to a lawful visitor under
s 2(2) of the 1957 Act and even if the risk had been attributable to the state of the
premises rather than the acts of Mr Tomlinson, the question of what amounts to
'such care as in all the circumstances of the case is reasonable' depends upon
assessing, as in the case of common law negligence, not only the likelihood that
someone may be injured and the seriousness of the injury which may occur, but
also the social value of the activity which gives rise to the risk and the cost of
preventative measures. These factors have to be balanced against each other.

[35] For example, in *Overseas Tankship (UK) Ltd v Miller Steamship Co Pty, The
Wagon Mound (No 2)* [1966] 2 All ER 709, [1967] 1 AC 617, there was no social
value or cost saving in the defendant's activity. Lord Reid said:

'In the present case there was no justification whatever for discharging the
oil into Sydney Harbour. Not only was it an offence to do so, but also it
involved considerable loss financially. If the ship's engineer had thought
about the matter there could have been no question of balancing the
advantages and disadvantages. From every point of view it was both his duty
and his interest to stop the discharge immediately.' (See [1966] 2 All ER 709
at 718, [1967] 1 AC 617 at 643.)

[36] So the defendants were held liable for damage which was only a very
remote possibility. Similarly in *Jolley v Sutton London BC* [2000] 3 All ER 409,
[2000] 1 WLR 1082 there was no social value or cost saving to the council in
creating a risk by leaving a derelict boat lying about. It was something which they
ought to have removed whether it created a risk of injury or not. So they were
held liable for an injury which, though foreseeable, was not particularly likely.
On the other hand, in *The Wagon Mound (No 2)* [1966] 2 All ER 709 at 718, [1967]
1 AC 617 at 642 Lord Reid drew a contrast with *Bolton v Stone* [1951] 1 All ER 1078,
[1951] AC 850 in which the House of Lords held that it was not negligent for a
cricket club to do nothing about the risk of someone being injured by a cricket
ball hit out of the ground. The difference was that the cricket club were carrying
on a lawful and socially useful activity and would have had to stop playing cricket
at that ground.

[37] This is the kind of balance which has to be struck even in a situation in
which it is clearly fair, just and reasonable that there should in principle be a duty
of care or in which Parliament, as in the 1957 Act, has decreed that there should
be. And it may lead to the conclusion that even though injury is foreseeable, as
it was in *Bolton v Stone*, it is still in all the circumstances reasonable to do nothing
about it.

THE 1957 AND 1984 ACTS CONTRASTED

[38] In the case of the 1984 Act, there is the additional consideration that
unless in all the circumstances it is reasonable to expect the occupier to do

a something, that is to say, to 'offer the other some protection', there is no duty at
all. One may ask what difference there is between the case in which the claimant
is a lawful visitor and there is in principle a duty under the 1957 Act but on the
particular facts no duty to do anything, and the case in which he is a trespasser
and there is on the particular facts no duty under the 1984 Act. Of course in such
a case the result is the same. But Parliament has made it clear that in the case of
b a lawful visitor, one starts from the assumption that there is a duty whereas in the
case of a trespasser one starts from the assumption that there is none.

THE BALANCE UNDER THE 1957 ACT

[39] My Lords, it will in the circumstances be convenient to consider first the
question of what the position would have been if Mr Tomlinson had been a
c lawful visitor owed a duty under s 2(2) of the 1957 Act. Assume, therefore, that
there had been no prohibition on swimming. What was the risk of serious injury?
To some extent this depends upon what one regards as the relevant risk. As I
have mentioned, the judge thought it was the risk of injury through diving while
the Court of Appeal thought it was any kind of injury which could happen to
d people in the water. Although, as I have said, I am inclined to agree with the
judge, I do not want to put the basis of my decision too narrowly. So I accept that
we are concerned with the steps, if any, which should have been taken to prevent
any kind of water accident. According to the Royal Society for the Prevention of
Accidents, about 450 people drown while swimming in the United Kingdom
every year (see *Darby v National Trust* [2001] PIQR P372 at 374). About 25–35
e break their necks diving and no doubt others sustain less serious injuries. So there
is obviously some degree of risk in swimming and diving, as there is in climbing,
cycling, fell walking and many other such activities.

[40] I turn then to the cost of taking preventative measures. Ward LJ
described it (£5,000) as 'not excessive'. Perhaps it was not, although the outlay
f has to be seen in the context of the other items (rated 'essential' and 'highly
desirable') in the borough council budget which had taken precedence over the
destruction of the beaches for the previous two years.

[41] I do not however regard the financial cost as a significant item in the
balancing exercise which the court has to undertake. There are two other related
considerations which are far more important. The first is the social value of the
g activities which would have to be prohibited in order to reduce or eliminate the
risk from swimming. And the second is the question of whether the council
should be entitled to allow people of full capacity to decide for themselves
whether to take the risk.

[42] The Court of Appeal made no reference at all to the social value of the
h activities which were to be prohibited. The majority of people who went to the
beaches to sunbathe, paddle and play with their children were enjoying
themselves in a way which gave them pleasure and caused no risk to themselves
or anyone else. This must be something to be taken into account in deciding
whether it was reasonable to expect the council to destroy the beaches.

j [43] I have the impression that the Court of Appeal felt able to brush these
matters aside because the council had already decided to do the work. But they
were held liable for having failed to do so before Mr Tomlinson's accident and the
question is therefore whether they were under a legal duty to do so. Ward LJ
placed much emphasis upon the fact that the council had decided to destroy the
beaches and that its officers thought that this was necessary to avoid being held
liable for an accident to a swimmer. But the fact that the council's safety officers

thought that the work was necessary does not show that there was a legal duty
to do it. In *Darby's* case the claimant's husband was tragically drowned while *a*
swimming in a pond on the National Trust estate at Hardwick Hall.
Miss Rebecca Kirkwood, the water and leisure safety consultant to the Royal
Society for the Prevention of Accidents, gave uncontradicted evidence, which the
judge accepted, that the pond was unsuitable for swimming because it was deep
in the middle and the edges were uneven. The National Trust should have made *b*
it clear that swimming in the pond was not allowed and taken steps to enforce the
prohibition. But May LJ said robustly that it was for the court, not
Miss Kirkwood, to decide whether the Trust was under a legal duty to take such
steps. There was no duty because the risks from swimming in the pond were
perfectly obvious.
c

FREE WILL

[44] The second consideration, namely the question of whether people should
accept responsibility for the risks they choose to run, is the point made by Lord
Phillips MR in *Donoghue v Folkestone Properties Ltd* [2003] 3 All ER 1101 at [53] and
which I said was central to this appeal. Mr Tomlinson was freely and voluntarily *d*
undertaking an activity which inherently involved some risk. By contrast,
Miss Bessie Stone, to whom the House of Lords held that no duty was owed, was
innocently standing on the pavement outside her garden gate at 10 Beckenham
Road, Cheetham when she was struck by a ball hit for six out of the Cheetham
Cricket Club ground. She was certainly not engaging in any activity which *e*
involved an inherent risk of such injury. So compared with *Bolton v Stone*, this is
an a fortiori case.

[45] I think it will be extremely rare for an occupier of land to be under a duty
to prevent people from taking risks which are inherent in the activities they freely
choose to undertake upon the land. If people want to climb mountains, go hang
gliding or swim or dive in ponds or lakes, that is their affair. Of course the *f*
landowner may for his own reasons wish to prohibit such activities. He may be
think that they are a danger or inconvenience to himself or others. Or he may
take a paternalist view and prefer people not to undertake risky activities on his
land. He is entitled to impose such conditions, as the council did by prohibiting
swimming. But the law does not require him to do so. *g*

[46] My Lords, as will be clear from what I have just said, I think that there is
an important question of freedom at stake. It is unjust that the harmless
recreation of responsible parents and children with buckets and spades on the
beaches should be prohibited in order to comply with what is thought to be a
legal duty to safeguard irresponsible visitors against dangers which are perfectly *h*
obvious. The fact that such people take no notice of warnings cannot create a
duty to take other steps to protect them. I find it difficult to express with
appropriate moderation my disagreement with the proposition of Sedley LJ
([2003] 3 All ER 1122 at [45]) that it is 'only where the risk is so obvious that the
occupier can safely assume that nobody will take it that there will be no liability'. *j*
A duty to protect against obvious risks or self-inflicted harm exists only in cases
in which there is no genuine and informed choice, or in the case of employees, or
some lack of capacity, such as the inability of children to recognise danger (see
British Railways Board v Herrington [1972] 1 All ER 749, [1972] AC 877) or the
despair of prisoners which may lead them to inflict injury on themselves (see
Reeves v Metropolitan Police Comr [1999] 3 All ER 897, [2000] 1 AC 360).

a   [47] It is of course understandable that organisations like the Royal Society for the Prevention of Accidents should favour policies which require people to be prevented from taking risks. Their function is to prevent accidents and that is one way of doing so. But they do not have to consider the cost, not only in money but also in deprivation of liberty, which such restrictions entail. The courts will naturally respect the technical expertise of such organisations in drawing

b   attention to what can be done to prevent accidents. But the balance between risk on the one hand and individual autonomy on the other is not a matter of expert opinion. It is a judgment which the courts must make and which in England reflects the individualist values of the common law.

     [48] As for the council officers, they were obviously motivated by the view that it was necessary to take defensive measures to prevent the council from

c   being held liable to pay compensation. The borough leisure officer said that he regretted the need to destroy the beaches but saw no alternative if the council was not to be held liable for an accident to a swimmer. So this appeal gives your Lordships the opportunity to say clearly that local authorities and other occupiers of land are ordinarily under no duty to incur such social and financial costs to

d   protect a minority (or even a majority) against obvious dangers. On the other hand, if the decision of the Court of Appeal were left standing, every such occupier would feel obliged to take similar defensive measures. Sedley LJ was able to say that if the logic of the Court of Appeal's decision was that other public lakes and ponds required similar precautions, 'so be it'. But I cannot view this prospect with the same equanimity. In my opinion it would damage the quality

e   of many people's lives.

     [49] In the particular case of diving injuries, there is little evidence that such defensive measures have had much effect. Dr Penny, the council's expert, said that over the past decade there had been little change in the rate of serious diving accidents. Each year, as I have mentioned, there are about 25–35 fracture-

f   dislocations of the neck. Almost all those affected are males and their average age is consistently around 25 years. In spite of greatly increased safety measures, particularly in swimming pools, the numbers (when Dr Penny gave evidence) had remained the same for a decade:

g   'This is probably because of the sudden, unpredictable nature of these dangerous dives, undertaken mostly by boisterous young men ... hence the common description the "Macho Male Diving Syndrome".'

     [50] My Lords, for these reasons I consider that even if swimming had not been prohibited and the council had owed a duty under s 2(2) of the 1957 Act, that duty would not have required them to take any steps to prevent Mr Tomlinson

h   from diving or warning him against dangers which were perfectly obvious. If that is the case, then plainly there can have been no duty under the 1984 Act. The risk was not one against which he was entitled under s 1(3)(c) to protection. I would therefore allow the appeal and restore the decision of Jack J. It follows that the cross-appeal against the apportionment of damages must be dismissed.

j   **LORD HUTTON.**
     [51] My Lords, I have had the advantage of reading in draft the speech of my noble and learned friend Lord Hoffmann and I gratefully adopt his account of the background facts to the tragic injury which Mr Tomlinson suffered in the lake in Brereton Heath Country Park in Cheshire. I agree with your Lordships that the appeal brought by Congleton Borough Council and Cheshire County Council

(together the council) should be allowed, but as I was attracted for a considerable
time during the hearing of the appeal by Mr Tomlinson's argument supporting
the reasoning of Ward LJ in the Court of Appeal (with which Sedley LJ agreed)
([2002] EWCA Civ 309, [2003] 3 All ER 1122, [2003] 2 WLR 1120) that
Mr Tomlinson was entitled to recover damages, I wish to add some observations
of my own.

[52] I approach the case on the basis that Mr Tomlinson was, in strict law, a
trespasser at the time he dived and struck his head on the bottom of the lake. It
is clear that he was invited by the council to come to the country park but it is
also clear that swimming in the lake was expressly prohibited by the council and,
as the trial judge found, Mr Tomlinson was fully aware of this prohibition.
Therefore when he began to dive he became a trespasser because, as Lord Atkin
stated in *Hillen v ICI (Alkali) Ltd* [1936] AC 65 at 69, [1935] All ER Rep 555 at 558:

'So far as he sets foot on so much of the premises as lie outside the invitation
or uses them for purposes which are alien to the invitation he is not an invitee
but a trespasser, and his rights must be determined accordingly.'

However I agree with Lord Hoffmann that even if Mr Tomlinson had not been a
trespasser at the time of his dive but had been a visitor within the meaning of the
Occupiers' Liability Act 1957, he would still not have been entitled to recover
damages.

[53] In relation to s 1(1)(a) of the Occupiers' Liability Act 1984 I recognise that
there is force in the argument that the injury was not due to the state of the
premises but was due to Mr Tomlinson's own lack of care in diving into shallow
water. But the trial judge found that Mr Tomlinson could not see the bottom of
the lake and, on balance, I incline to the view that dark and murky water which
prevents a person seeing the bottom of the lake where he is diving can be viewed
as 'the state of the premises' and that if he sustains injury through striking his
head on the bottom which he cannot see this can be viewed as a danger 'due to
the state of the premises'. If water were allowed to become dark and murky in
an indoor swimming pool provided by a local authority and a diver struck his
head on the bottom I consider that the danger could be regarded as 'due to the
state of the premises', and whilst there is an obvious difference between such
water and water in a lake which in its natural state is dark and murky, I think that
the term 'the state of the premises' can be applied both to the swimming pool and
to the lake.

[54] Section 1(3) and (4) of the 1984 Act provide:

'(3) An occupier of premises owes a duty to another (not being his visitor)
in respect of any such risk as is referred to in subsection (1) above if—
    (a) he is aware of the danger or has reasonable grounds to believe that it
exists;
    (b) he knows or has reasonable grounds to believe that the other is in the
vicinity of the danger concerned or that he may come into the vicinity of the
danger (in either case, whether the other has lawful authority for being in
that vicinity or not); and
    (c) the risk is one against which, in all the circumstances of the case, he
may reasonably be expected to offer the other some protection.
    (4) Where, by virtue of this section, an occupier of premises owes a duty
to another in respect of such a risk, the duty is to take such care as is

a reasonable in all the circumstances of the case to see that he does not suffer injury on the premises by reason of the danger concerned.'

[55] There is no doubt from the reports and proposals of the council's officials to the borough's amenities and leisure services committee and to the borough council which Lord Hoffmann has described that paras (a), (b) of s 1(3) are satisfied. If s 1(3) were satisfied and the risk was one against which, in all the circumstances of the case, the council might reasonably be expected to offer Mr Tomlinson some protection, I consider that there would be an argument of some force that they were in breach of the duty specified in s 1(4), because the minutes of the meetings showed that they knew that there were dangers to persons swimming or diving in the lake (there had been two cases of swimmers sustaining head injuries) and they knew that the dangers might lead to death or serious injury, but they had decided not to take the recommended steps such as planting reeds on the beach, which would probably have stopped swimming, because of financial constraints, although the cost of these precautionary measures would have been only in the region of £15,000.

d [56] Therefore I think the crucial question is whether Mr Tomlinson has established that the risk was one to which s 1(3)(c) applies. On this point the reasoning of Ward LJ was contained in [2003] 3 All ER 1122 at [29]:

'Here the authorities employed rangers whose duty it was to give oral warnings against swimming albeit that this met with mixed success and sometimes attracted abuse for their troubles. In addition to the oral warnings, the rangers would hand out safety leaflets which warned of the variable depth in the pond, the cold, the weeds, the absence of rescue services, waterborne diseases and the risk of accidents occurring. It seems to me that the rangers' patrols and advice and the handing out of these leaflets reinforced the ineffective message on the sign and constituted "some protection" in fact given and reasonably expected to be offered in the circumstances of this case.'

[57] I thought for a time that this reasoning was persuasive, but I have concluded that it should not be accepted because I consider that it is contrary to a principle stated in the older authorities which is still good law. In *Stevenson v Corp of Glasgow* 1908 SC 1034 at 1039 Lord M'Laren stated:

'... in a town, as well as in the country, there are physical features which may be productive of injury to careless persons or to young children against which it is impossible to guard by protective measures. The situation of a town on the banks of a river is a familiar feature; and whether the stream be sluggish like the Clyde at Glasgow, or swift and variable like the Ness at Inverness, or the Tay at Perth, there is always danger to the individual who may be so unfortunate as to fall into the stream. But in none of these places has it been found necessary to fence the river to prevent children or careless persons from falling into the water. Now, as the common law is just the formal statement of the results and conclusions of the common sense of mankind, I come without difficulty to the conclusion that precautions which have been rejected by common sense as unnecessary and inconvenient are not required by the law.'

[58] In *Corp of the City of Glasgow v Taylor* [1922] 1 AC 44 at 61 Lord Shaw of Dunfermline stated:

'Grounds thrown open by a municipality to the public may contain objects of natural beauty, say precipitous cliffs or the banks of streams, the dangers of the resort to which are plain.'

Lord Shaw then cited with approval the words of Lord M'Laren in *Stevenson's* case that 'in a town, as well as in the country, there are physical features which may be productive of injury to careless persons or to young children against which it is impossible to guard by protective measures'. I think that when Lord M'Laren referred to physical features against which 'it is impossible to guard by protective measures' he was not referring to protective measures which it is physically impossible to put in place; rather he had in mind measures which the common sense of mankind indicates as being unnecessary to take. This statement echoed the observation of the Lord President (Lord Dunedin) in *Hastie v Magistrates of Edinburgh* 1907 SC 1102 at 1106 that there are certain risks against which the law, in accordance with the dictates of common sense, does not give protection—such risks are 'just one of the results of the world as we find it'.

[59] *Stevenson's* and *Hastie's* cases (which were not concerned with trespassers) were decided almost a century ago and the judgments are couched in old-fashioned language, but I consider that they express a principle which is still valid today, namely, that it is contrary to common sense, and therefore not sound law, to expect an occupier to provide protection against an obvious danger on his land arising from a natural feature such as a lake or a cliff and to impose a duty on him to do so. In my opinion this principle, although not always explicitly stated, underlies the cases relied on by the council where it has been held that the occupier is not liable where a person has injured himself or drowned in an inland lake or pool or in the sea or on some natural feature.

[60] In *Cotton v Derbyshire Dales DC* [1994] CA Transcript 753 the Court of Appeal upheld the decision of the trial judge dismissing the plaintiff's claim for damages for serious injuries sustained from falling off a cliff. Applying the judgment of Lord Shaw in *Taylor's* case the Court of Appeal held that the occupiers were under no duty to provide protection against dangers which are themselves obvious.

[61] In *Whyte v Redland Aggregates Ltd* [1997] CA Transcript 2034 the appellant dived into a disused gravel pit and alleged that he had struck his head on an obstruction on the floor of the pit. The Court of Appeal dismissed his appeal against the judgment of the trial judge who held that he was not entitled to damages. Henry LJ stated:

'In my judgment, the occupier of land containing or bordered by the river, the seashore, the pond or the gravel pit, does not have to warn of uneven surfaces below the water. Such surfaces are by their nature quite likely to be uneven. Diving where you cannot see the bottom clearly enough to know that it is safe to dive is dangerous unless you have made sure, by reconnaissance or otherwise, that the diving is safe ie that there is adequate depth at the place where you choose to dive. In those circumstances, the dangers of there being an uneven surface in an area where you cannot plainly see the bottom are too plain to require a specific warning and, accordingly, there is no such duty to warn (see Lord Shaw in *Corp of the City of Glasgow v Taylor* [1922] 1 AC 44 at 60). There was no trap here on the judge's finding. There was just an uneven surface, as one would expect to find in a disused gravel pit.'

a
[62] In *Bartrum v Hepworth Minerals and Chemicals Ltd* (29 October 1999, unreported), the claimant dived from a ledge on a cliff. In order to avoid shallow water he knew that he had to dive out into the pool but he failed to do so and fractured his neck. Turner J dismissed his claim for damages and stated:

b
'So far as the Act is concerned, by s 1(3) of the Occupiers' Liability Act 1984 the defendants were under a duty to those whom they had reasonable grounds to believe would be in the vicinity of the danger, that is on the cliff for the purpose of diving, and the risk was one which, in all the circumstances, [they] may be reasonably expected to offer some protection. In my judgment the danger here was so obvious to any adult that it was not reasonably to be expected of the defendants that they would offer any
c   protection.'

[63] In *Darby v National Trust* [2001] EWCA Civ 189, [2001] PIQR P372 the claimant's husband was drowned whilst swimming in a pond on National Trust property. The Court of Appeal allowed an appeal by the National Trust against the trial judge's finding of liability and May LJ stated (at [27]):
d
'It cannot be the duty of the owner of every stretch of coastline to have notices warning of the dangers of swimming in the sea. If it were so, the coast would have to be littered with notices in places other than those where there are known to be special dangers which are not obvious. The same would apply to all inland lakes and reservoirs. In my judgment there was no
e   duty on the National Trust on the facts of this case to warn against swimming in this pond where the dangers of drowning were no other or greater than those which were quite obvious to any adult such as the unfortunate deceased. That, in my view, applies as much to the risk that a swimmer might get into difficulties from the temperature of the water as to
f   the risk that he might get into difficulties from mud or sludge on the bottom of the pond.'

[64] I also think that the principle stated by Lord M'Laren in *Stevenson*'s case is implicit in the judgment of Lord Phillips of Worth Matravers MR in *Donoghue v Folkestone Properties Ltd* [2003] EWCA Civ 231 at [34], [2003] 3 All ER 1101 at [34],
g   [2003] 2 WLR 1138. In that case the claimant dived from a slipway into Folkestone harbour after midnight in mid-winter. He struck his head on a grid pile under the water adjacent to the harbour wall and broke his neck. The Court of Appeal allowed an appeal by the defendant against the trial judge's finding of liability. Lord Phillips MR stated:

h
'[33] The obvious situation where a duty under the 1984 Act is likely to arise is where the occupier knows that a trespasser may come upon a danger that is latent. In such a case the trespasser may be exposed to the risk of injury without realising that the danger exists. Where the state of the premises constitutes a danger that is perfectly obvious, and there is no reason
j   for a trespasser observing it to go near it, a duty under the 1984 Act is unlikely to arise for at least two reasons. The first is that because the danger can readily be avoided, it is unlikely to pose a risk of injuring the trespasser whose presence on the premises is envisaged.
[34] There are, however, circumstances in which it may be foreseeable that a trespasser will appreciate that a dangerous feature of premises poses a risk of injury, but will nevertheless deliberately court the danger and risk the

injury. It seems to me that, at least where the individual is an adult, it will be
rare that those circumstances will be such that the occupier can reasonably
be expected to offer some protection to the trespasser against the risk.'

Lord Phillips MR then went on to state that where a person was tempted by some
natural feature of the occupier's land to engage in some activity such as
mountaineering which carried a risk of injury, he could not ascribe to 'the state
of the premises' an injury sustained in carrying on that activity. However in the
present case, as I have stated, I incline to the view that the dark and murky water
can be viewed as 'the state of the premises'.

[65] Therefore I consider that the risk of Mr Tomlinson striking his head on
the bottom of the lake was not one against which the council might reasonably
have been expected to offer him some protection, and accordingly they are not
liable to him because they owed him no duty. I would add that there might be
exceptional cases where the principle stated in Stevenson's and Taylor's case
should not apply and where a claimant might be able to establish that the risk
arising from some natural feature on the land was such that the occupier might
reasonably be expected to offer him some protection against it, for example,
where there was a very narrow and slippery path with a camber beside the edge
of a cliff from which a number of persons had fallen. But the present is not such
a case and, for the reasons which I have given, I consider that the appeal should
be allowed.

LORD HOBHOUSE OF WOODBOROUGH.

[66] My Lords, in this case the trial judge after having heard all the evidence
made findings of fact which are now accepted by Mr Tomlinson:

> 'There was nothing about the mere which made it any more dangerous
> than any other stretch of open water in England. Swimming and diving held
> their own risks. So if the mere was to be described as a danger, it was only
> because it attracted swimming and diving, which activities carry a risk.
> Despite having seen signs stating "DANGEROUS WATER: NO
> SWIMMING", the claimant ignored them. The danger and risk of injury
> from diving in the lake where it was shallow was obvious. At the time of the
> accident, the claimant was 18 years of age and had regularly been going to
> the park since he was a small child. He knew it well. The accident occurred
> when he waded into the water until the water was a little above his knees and
> threw himself forward in a dive or plunge. He knew that he shouldn't. He
> could not see the bottom. In fact it was a smooth sandy surface without any
> obstruction or hazard. He dived deeper than he had intended and his head
> hit the sandy bottom causing his injury. Besides the notices already referred
> to, visitors were handed leaflets warning them of the dangers of swimming
> in the mere. Wardens patrolled the park and told people further that they
> should not swim in the mere. However it was the fact that visitors often
> took no notice and very many people did bathe in the mere in summer.'

[67] Mr Tomlinson has made his claim for personal injuries under the
Occupiers' Liability Act 1984 on the basis that at the time that he suffered his
injury he was a trespasser in that he was swimming in the mere and swimming
was, as he was aware, forbidden. This seems to me to be a somewhat artificial
approach to the case; since paddling was apparently allowed but not swimming
and Mr Tomlinson was at the material time in water which only came a little

a above his knees. However, under the Occupiers' Liability Act 1957 (and at common law) when an invitee or licensee breaches the conditions upon which he has entered the premises, he ceases to be a visitor and becomes a trespasser (s 2(2)). Mr Tomlinson was permitted to enter the park on the condition that (inter alia) he did not swim in the mere. If he should swim in the mere, he broke this condition and as a result ceased to be a visitor. However, like all of your

b Lordships, I consider that whether he makes his claim under the 1984 Act or the 1957 Act, he does not succeed.

[68] The two Acts apply the same general policy and the 1984 Act is a supplement to the 1957 Act. The earlier Act was the result of a re-examination of the common law relating to occupiers' liability. Its primary purpose was to

c simplify the law. It had previously been based upon placing those coming on another's land into various different categories and then stipulating different standards of care from the occupier in respect of each category. This was the historical approach of the common law to the question of negligence and found its inspiration in Roman law concepts (as was the case in the law of bailment (see *Coggs v Bernard* (1703) 2 Ld Raym 909, [1558–1774] All ER Rep 1)). By 1957, the

d dominant approach had become the 'good neighbour' principle enunciated in *Donoghue v Stevenson* [1932] AC 562, [1932] All ER Rep 1. But special rules still applied to relationships which were not merely neighbourly. One such was occupiers' liability. The relevant, indeed, principal simplification introduced in the 1957 Act was to introduce the 'common duty of care' as a single standard covering both invitees and licensees (see s 2(2)). The 1957 Act applied only to

e visitors, ie persons coming onto the land with the occupier's express or implied consent. It did not apply to persons who were not visitors including trespassers. The 1984 Act made provision for when a duty of care should be owed to persons who were not visitors (I will for the sake of convenience call such persons 'trespassers') and what the duty should then be, that is, a duty of care in the terms

f of s 1(3), more narrow than that imposed by the 1957 Act. Thus the duty owed to visitors and the lesser duty which may be owed to trespassers was defined in appropriate terms. But, in each Act, there are further provisions which define the content of the duty and, depending upon the particular circumstances, its scope and extent.

g [69] The first and fundamental definition is to be found in both Acts. The duty is owed 'in respect of dangers due to the state of the premises or to things done or omitted to be done on them'. In the 1957 Act it is s 1(1). In the 1984 Act it is in s 1(1)(a) which forms the starting point for determining whether any duty is owed to the trespasser (see also s 1(3)) and provides the subject matter of any duty

h which may be owed. It is this phrase which provides the basic definition of 'danger' as used elsewhere in the Acts. There are two alternatives. The first is that it must be due to the state of the premises. The state of the premises is the physical features of the premises as they exist at the relevant time. It can include footpaths covered in ice and open mine shafts. It will not normally include parts

j of the landscape, say, steep slopes or difficult terrain in mountainous areas or cliffs close to cliff paths. There will certainly be dangers requiring care and experience from the visitor but it normally would be a misuse of language to describe such features as 'the state of the premises'. The same could be said about trees and, at any rate, natural lakes and rivers. The second alternative is dangers due to things done or omitted to be done on the premises. Thus if shooting is taking place on the premises, a danger to visitors may arise from that fact. If speed boats are allowed to go into an area where swimmers are, the safety of the swimmers may be endangered.

[70] In the present case, the mere was used for a number of activities—angling, board-sailing, sub-aqua, canoeing and sailing model yachts—but none of these was suggested to have given rise to any danger to Mr Tomlinson or others. Therefore Mr Tomlinson has to found his case upon a danger due to the 'state of the premises'. His difficulty is that the judge has found that there was none and he has accepted that finding. Therefore his case fails in limine. If there was no such danger the remainder of the provisions of the Acts all of which depend upon the existence of such a danger cannot assist him. Mr Tomlinson clearly appreciated this when he brought his claim since his statement of claim specifically pleaded that there had been 'an obstruction under the surface of the water' on which he struck his head. The judge found that there was no such obstruction.

[71] Section 2 of the 1957 Act deals with the content of the duty (if any). Thus s 2(2) defines the common duty of care as one—

> 'to take such care as in all the circumstances of the case is reasonable to see that the visitor will be reasonably safe in using the premises for the purposes for which he is invited or permitted by the occupier to be there.'

If swimming is not one of those purposes, the duty of care does not extend to him while he is swimming. Section 2(3) deals with what circumstances are relevant to assessing any duty owed. They include 'the degree of care, and of want of care, which would ordinarily be looked for in such a visitor'. Examples are given: '(a) an occupier must be prepared for children to be less careful than adults ...' A skilled visitor can be expected to appreciate and guard against risks ordinarily incident to his skilled activities (see s 2(2)(b)). An obvious instance of the second example is a steeple jack brought in to repair a spire or an electrician to deal with faulty wiring. Here, Mr Tomlinson was an 18-year-old youth who ought to be well able to appreciate and cope with the character of an ordinary lake. He can take care of himself; he does not need to be looked after in the same way as a child.

[72] Turning to the 1984 Act, one can observe the same features. The basic requirement of a 'danger due to the state of the premises' is there. Section 1(2) contains a cross-reference to s 2(2) of the earlier Act. Section 1(3) depends upon the existence, and knowledge, of a danger coming within s 1(1). The risk of personal injury arising from that danger must further be one against which, in all the circumstances, it is reasonable to expect the occupier 'to offer the [trespasser] some protection'. The equivalent phrase 'reasonable in all the circumstances' is used in sub-ss (4), (5). Subsection (5) specifically permits the use of warnings and discouragements against incurring the relevant risk.

[73] It is an irony of the present case that Mr Tomlinson has found it easier to put his case under the 1984 Act than under the 1957 Act and argue, in effect, that the occupier owed a higher duty to a trespasser than to a visitor. This is because the inclusion of the words in s 2(4), duty 'to see that he does not suffer injury on the premises by reason of the danger concerned'. Mr Tomlinson did suffer injury whilst on the premises; the councils failed to see that he did not. Whilst this argument in any event fails on account of the fundamental point that the state of the premises did not give rise to any danger, it would be perverse to construe these two Acts of Parliament so as to give the 1984 Act the effect which Mr Tomlinson contends for. (See also the quotation from the Law Commission

a report by Brooke LJ in his judgment in *Donoghue v Folkestone Properties Ltd* [2003] EWCA Civ 231 at [72], [2003] 3 All ER 1101 at [72], [2003] 2 WLR 1138.) The key is in the circumstances and what it is reasonable to expect of the occupier. The reference to warnings and discouragements in sub-s (5) and the use of the words 'some protection' in sub-s (3)(c) both demonstrate that the duty is not as onerous as Mr Tomlinson argues. Warnings can be disregarded (as was the case here);

b discouragements can be evaded; the trespasser may still be injured (or injure himself) while on the premises. There is no guarantee of safety any more than there is under the 1957 Act. The question remains what is it reasonable to expect the occupier to do for unauthorised trespassers on his land. The trespasser by avoiding getting the consent of the occupier, avoids having conditions or restrictions imposed upon his entry or behaviour once on the premises. By

c definition, the occupier cannot control the trespasser in the same way as he can control a visitor. The Acts both lay stress upon what is reasonable in all the circumstances. Such circumstances must be relevant to the relative duties owed under the two Acts.

d [74] Returning to the facts of this case, what more was it reasonable to expect of the councils beyond putting up the notices and issuing warnings and prohibitions? It will not have escaped your Lordships that the putting up of the notices prohibiting swimming is the peg which Mr Tomlinson uses to acquire the status of trespasser and the benefit of the suggested more favourable duty of care under the 1984 Act. But this is a case where, as held by the judge, all the relevant characteristics of this mere were already obvious to Mr Tomlinson. In these

e circumstances, no purpose was in fact served by the warning. It told Mr Tomlinson nothing he did not already know. (See *Staples v West Dorset DC* (1995) 93 LGR 536, *Whyte v Redland Aggregates Ltd* [1997] CA Transcript 2034, *Ratcliff v McConnell* [1999] 1 WLR 670, *Darby v National Trust* [2001] EWCA Civ 189, [2001] PIQR P372.) The location was not one from which one could dive

f into water from a height. There was a shallow gradually sloping sandy beach. The bather had to wade in and Mr Tomlinson knew exactly how deep the water was where he was standing with the water coming up to a little above his knees. Mr Tomlinson's case is so far from giving a cause of action under the statute that it is hard to discuss coherently the hypotheses upon which it depends. There was no danger; any danger did not arise from the state of the premises; any risk of

g striking the bottom from diving in such shallow water was obvious; Mr Tomlinson did not need to be warned against running that risk; it was not reasonable to expect the occupier to offer the claimant (or any other trespasser) any protection against that obvious risk.

h [75] Faced with these insuperable difficulties and with the fact that they had failed to prove the pleaded case, counsel for Mr Tomlinson put the argument in a different way. They pointed to the internal reports and minutes disclosed by the defendant councils. Passing over a minute of 22 November 1984 which under the heading 'Swimming' accurately stated:

j 'Probably as a result of the larger notice boards the problems of swimming were no worse than in previous years and perhaps marginally better. Every reasonable precaution had now been taken, but it was recognised that some foolhardy persons would continue to put their lives at risk.'

They referred to an undated report of some time in 1992 concerning swimming in the mere. It reported many instances of swimming during hot spells with up to 2,000 people present and as many as 100 in the water. It referred to the

popularity of the extensive beach areas with families where children paddled and
made sandcastles and groups picnicked, adding 'not unnaturally many [people]
will venture into the water for a swim'. The 'hazards' pointing to the likelihood
of future problems were stated to include 'lakeside grassy picnic area'. The
recommendations were directed at the beach areas: 'Suggest cutting down on
beach area by increasing reed zones'. 'Signs should indicate the nature of the
hazard e g "Danger—Water 5m deep".' It is clear that accidents such as that
suffered by Mr Tomlinson were not in the writer's mind. Other similar reports
are referred to in the opinion of my noble and learned friend Lord Hoffmann and
it is otiose to quote from them again.

[76] In July of the same year a departmental memorandum referred to the
council's policy to stop all swimming. It therefore called upon the council to
engage on a scheme of landscaping to make 'the water's edge to be far less
accessible, desirable and inviting than it currently is for children's beach/water's
edge type of play activities'. The solution called for was to remove or cover over
the beaches and replace them by muddy reed beds. Part of the reasoning was that
with attractive beaches 'accidents become inevitable' and 'we must therefore do
everything that is reasonably possible to deter, discourage and prevent people
from swimming or paddling in the lake or diving into the lake'. An estimate of
cost was asked for.

[77] Funds were short but in 1994 a request for finance was presented. It was
based upon the public's disregard of the embargo on bathing in the lake despite
having 'taken all reasonable steps' to educate the public. The request states that
'we have on average three or four near drownings every year and it is only a
matter of time before someone dies'. 'If nothing is done about [the landscaping]
and someone dies the Borough Council is to be held liable and would have to
accept responsibility.' This was the nub of Mr Tomlinson's case. The situation
was dangerous. The councils realised that they should do something about
it—remove the beaches and make the water's edge unattractive and not so easily
accessible. They recognised that they would be liable if they did not do so. This
reasoning needs to be examined.

[78] The first point to be made is that the councils were always at liberty,
subject to the Local Government Acts, to have and enforce a no swimming
policy. Indeed this had all along been one of the factors which had driven their
management of this park. Likewise, subject to the same important qualification,
they were at liberty to take moral responsibility for and pay compensation for any
accident that might occur in the park. It is to be doubted that this was ever, so
stated, their view. But neither of these factors create any legal liability which is
what is in question in the present case. If they mistakenly misunderstood what
the law required of them or what their legal liabilities were, that does not make
them legally liable.

[79] The second point is the mistreatment of the concept of risk. To suffer a
broken neck and paralysis for life could hardly be a more serious injury; any loss
of life is a consequence of the greatest seriousness. There was undoubtedly a risk
of drowning for inexperienced, incompetent or drunken swimmers in the deeper
parts of the mere or in patches of weed when they were out of their depth
although no lives had actually been lost. But there was no evidence of any
incident where anyone before Mr Tomlinson had broken his neck by plunging
from a standing position and striking his head on the smooth sandy bottom on
which he was standing. Indeed, at the trial it was not his case that this was what
had happened; he had alleged that there must have been some obstruction.

a There had been some evidence of two other incidents where someone suffered a minor injury (a cut or a graze) to their head whilst diving but there was no evidence that these two incidents were in any way comparable with that involving Mr Tomlinson. It is then necessary to put these few incidents in context. The park had been open to the public since about 1982. Some 160,000 people used to visit the park in a year. Up to 200 would be bathing in the mere

b on a fine summer's day. Yet the number of incidents involving the mere were so few. It is a fallacy to say that because drowning is a serious matter that there is therefore a serious risk of drowning. In truth the risk of a drowning was very low indeed and there had never actually been one and the accident suffered by Mr Tomlinson was unique. Whilst broken necks can result from incautious or reckless diving, the probability of one being suffered in the circumstances of

c Mr Tomlinson were so remote that the risk was minimal. The internal reports before his accident make the common but elementary error of confusing the seriousness of the outcome with the degree of risk that it will occur.

[80] The third point is that this confusion leads to the erroneous conclusion that there was a significant risk of injury presented to Mr Tomlinson when he

d went into the shallow water on the day in question. One cannot say that there was no risk of injury because we know now what happened. But, in my view, it was objectively so small a risk as not to trigger s 1(1) of the 1984 Act, otherwise every injury would suffice because it must imply the existence of some risk. However, and probably more importantly, the degree of risk is central to the

e assessment of what reasonably should be expected of the occupier and what would be a reasonable response to the existence of that degree of risk. The response should be appropriate and proportionate to both the degree of risk and the seriousness of the outcome at risk. If the risk of serious injury is so slight and remote that it is highly unlikely ever to materialise, it may well be that it is not reasonable to expect the occupier to take any steps to protect anyone against it.

f The law does not require disproportionate or unreasonable responses.

[81] The fourth point, one to which I know that your Lordships attach importance, is the fact that it is not, and should never be, the policy of the law to require the protection of the foolhardy or reckless few to deprive, or interfere with, the enjoyment by the remainder of society of the liberties and amenities to

g which they are rightly entitled. Does the law require that all trees be cut down because some youths may climb them and fall? Does the law require the coastline and other beauty spots to be lined with warning notices? Does the law require that attractive water-side picnic spots be destroyed because of a few foolhardy individuals who choose to ignore warning notices and indulge in

h activities dangerous only to themselves? The answer to all these questions is, of course, No. But this is the road down which your Lordships, like other courts before, have been invited to travel and which the councils in the present case found so inviting. In truth, the arguments for Mr Tomlinson have involved an attack upon the liberties of the citizen which should not be countenanced. They

j attack the liberty of the individual to engage in dangerous, but otherwise harmless, pastimes at his own risk and the liberty of citizens as a whole fully to enjoy the variety and quality of the landscape of this country. The pursuit of an unrestrained culture of blame and compensation has many evil consequences and one is certainly the interference with the liberty of the citizen. The discussion of social utility in the Illinois Supreme Court is to the same effect (see *Bucheleres v Chicago Park District* (1996) 171 Ill 2d 435 at 457–458).

[82] I cannot leave this case without expressing my complete agreement with
the reasoning of the judgment of Lord Phillips MR in *Donoghue v Folkestone
Properties Ltd* [2003] 3 All ER 1101.

[83] For these reasons and those given by my noble and learned friend Lord
Hoffmann, and in agreement with the judgment of Longmore LJ, I too would
allow this appeal.

LORD SCOTT OF FOSCOTE.

[84] My Lords, I have had the advantage of reading in draft the opinion of my
noble and learned friend Lord Hoffmann. Subject to one reservation I am in
complete agreement with the reasons he gives for allowing this appeal. But I find
myself in such fundamental disagreement with the approach to this case by the
majority in the Court of Appeal ([2002] EWCA Civ 309, [2003] 3 All ER 1122,
[2003] 2 WLR 1120) that I want to add, also, a few comments of my own.

[85] My reservation is that the Act which must be applied to the facts of this
case in order to decide whether the council is under any liability to Mr Tomlinson
is, in my opinion, the Occupiers' Liability Act 1957, not the Occupiers' Liability
Act 1984.

[86] The 1957 Act regulates the duty of care which an occupier of premises
owes to visitors to the premises (see s 1(1)). 'Visitors' are persons who would, at
common law, be invitees or licensees (see s 1(2)). The 1984 Act, on the other
hand, applies to persons on the premises who are not visitors but are trespassers.
It lays down the criteria for deciding whether the occupier of the premises owes
any duty of care at all to the trespasser in question in relation to the type of injury
he has suffered (see s 1(3)). If a duty of care is owed, the Act describes the duty
(see s 1(4)).

[87] Mr Tomlinson's case against the council is based on an alleged breach of
the duty of care they owed him. There is no doubt at all that he was a visitor at
the park. The park was open to the public and he was entitled to be there.
Wearing the shoes of a visitor, he was owed the duty of care prescribed by the
1957 Act.

[88] The notices prominently displayed at various places in the park forbade
swimming in the lake. But entry into the water was not forbidden. Visitors to
the park were entitled to paddle and splash in the shallows of the lake. Many did
so, particularly children. They were entitled to run into the water and splash one
another. They were entitled to lie in the shallows and let the cool water lap over
them. In doing these things they were visitors and were owed the 1957 Act duty
of care. All they were forbidden to do was to swim. If they had started
swimming, using the lake for a purpose which was forbidden, they would have
lost their status as visitors and become trespassers. The 1984 Act would then
have applied.

[89] Mr Tomlinson did not suffer his tragic accident while swimming in the
lake. He ran into the water and, when the depth of the water was at mid thigh
level, executed the disastrous 'dive' and suffered the accident. At no stage did he
swim. It may be that his 'dive' was preparatory to swimming. But swimming in
water not much above knee level, say 2 feet 6 inches deep, is difficult. There
might be some element of flotation but I do not think the activity would normally
justify the use of the verb 'swim'. In any event, Mr Tomlinson's injury was not
caused while he was swimming and cannot be attributed in any way to the
dangers of swimming. His complaint against the council is that the council did
not take reasonable care to discourage him while in the shallows of the lake from

a   executing a 'dive'. If the 'dive' was, which I regard as doubtful for the reasons given, a preliminary to an attempt to swim, the complaint may be regarded as a complaint that the council failed to prevent him from becoming a trespasser. But this must necessarily, in my view, have been a duty owed to him while he was a visitor.

[90] An analogous situation might arise in relation to the trees in the park.
b   Suppose there were notices forbidding the climbing of trees. None the less a visitor to the park climbs a tree, falls from it, injures himself and sues the council. He would have been a trespasser vis-à-vis the tree. But a claim under the 1984 Act would be hopeless. The proposition that the council owed him a duty to make the tree easier or safer to climb would be ridiculous. But the injured climber might contend that the presence of the tree posed an enticing, exciting
c   and irresistible challenge to those visitors to the park who, like himself, were addicted to the adrenalin surge caused by climbing high trees and that, consequently, the council owed a duty to make it impossible for him, and others like him, to succumb to the temptation, to prevent him from becoming a trespasser vis-à-vis the tree. This duty, if it were owed at all, would be a duty
d   owed to him, a visitor, under the 1957 Act. The contention would, of course, be rejected. The council's 1957 Act duty of care to its visitors would not require the trees to be cut down or the trunks and lower branches to be festooned with barbed wire in order to prevent visitors to the park from disobeying the notices and turning themselves into trespassers by climbing the trees. For present purposes, however, the point I want to make is that the climber's contention
e   would engage the 1957 Act, not the 1984 Act.

[91] In the present case it seems to me unreal to regard Mr Tomlinson's injury as having been caused while he was a trespasser. His complaint, rejected by the trial judge but accepted by the majority in the Court of Appeal, was that the council ought to have taken effective steps to discourage entry by visitors into the
f   waters of the lake. The notices were held to be inadequate discouragement. But, if there was this duty, it was a duty owed to visitors. The people who read the notices, or who could have read them but failed to do so, would have been visitors. These were the people to be discouraged. The alleged duty was a 1957 Act duty.

[92] The council's duty under the 1957 Act to its visitors was a duty 'to take
g   such care as in all the circumstances of the case is reasonable to see that the visitor will be reasonably safe in using the premises for the purposes for which he is invited or permitted ... to be there' (see s 2(2)). The purpose for which visitors were invited or permitted to be in the park was general recreation. This included paddling and playing about in the water. The proposition that in order to
h   discharge their 1957 Act duty to visitors the council had to discourage them from any entry into the water and, in effect, to prevent the paddling and playing about that so many had for so long enjoyed is, in my opinion, for the reasons so cogently expressed by Lord Hoffmann, wholly unacceptable. There was no breach by the council of its 1957 Act duty. The question whether it owed any 1984 Act duty did
j   not, in my opinion, arise. If, wrongly in my opinion, the 1984 Act were to be regarded as applicable, the case would be a fortiori.

[93] There are two respects, in my opinion, in which the approach of the courts below to the facts of this case have been somewhat unreal. First, the action of Mr Tomlinson that brought about his tragic injury has been described as a 'dive'. I think it is misdescribed. A dive into water, as normally understood, involves a hands-arms-head-first movement from a standpoint above the water

down into the water. A dive is dangerous if the depth of the water is unknown
for the obvious reason that if the depth is inadequate the head may strike the   *a*
bottom of the pool or the lake before the diver is able to check his downwards
trajectory and curve out of the dive. There had, apparently, been two previous
occasions over the past five years or so on which a person diving into the lake had
suffered head injuries. The evidence did not disclose the details but it seems
reasonable to assume that these occasions had involved dives properly so-called.   *b*
Mr Tomlinson did not execute a dive in the ordinary sense. He ran into the lake
and, when he thought he was far enough in to do so, he threw himself forward.
His forward plunge may, for want of a better word, be called a 'dive' but it should
not be confused with the normal and usual dive. Mr Tomlinson was not diving
from a standpoint above the lake down into water of uncertain depth. His feet
were on the bottom of the lake immediately before he executed his forward   *c*
plunge. He knew how deep the water was when he began the plunge. He must
have expected the downward shelving of the bottom of the lake to continue and
there is no evidence that it did not. The accident happened because the trajectory
of his forward plunge was not sufficiently shallow. This was not a diving accident
in the ordinary sense and there was no evidence that an accident caused in the   *d*
manner in which Mr Tomlinson's was caused had ever previously occurred at the
lake.

[94] Second, much was made of the trial judge's finding that the dangers of
diving or swimming in the lake were obvious, at least to adults. No one has
contested that finding of fact. But I think its importance has been overstated.
Mr Tomlinson was not diving in the normal sense, nor was he swimming. He   *e*
simply ran into the water and when he could not run any further, because the
water was above his knees and the galloping action that we all adopt when
running into water on a shelving beach had become too difficult, he plunged
forward. This is something that happens on every beach in every country in the
world, temperature and conditions permitting. Mr Tomlinson would not have   *f*
stopped to think about the dangers of swimming or diving in the lake. He was
not taking a pre-meditated risk. It would not have occurred to him, if he had
thought about it, that he was taking a risk at all. He was a high-spirited young
man enjoying himself with his friends in a pleasant park with a pleasant water
facility. If he had set out to swim across the lake, it might have been relevant to
speak of his taking an obvious risk. If he had climbed a tree with branches   *g*
overhanging the lake and had dived from a branch into the water he would have
been courting an obvious danger. But he was not doing any such thing. He was
simply sporting about in the water with his friends, giving free rein to his
exuberance. And why not? And why should the council be discouraged by the
law of tort from providing facilities for young men and young women to enjoy   *h*
themselves in this way? Of course there is some risk of accidents arising out of
the joie de vivre of the young. But that is no reason for imposing a grey and dull
safety regime on everyone. This appeal must be allowed.

Appeal allowed. Cross-appeal dismissed.

Kate O'Hanlon   Barrister.

a
AD v East Kent Community NHS Trust
[2002] EWCA Civ 1872

COURT OF APPEAL, CIVIL DIVISION

b JUDGE, LONGMORE LJJ AND SULLIVAN J

3, 17 DECEMBER 2002

Damages – Unwanted pregnancy – Negligence – Assessment of damages – Patient detained under Mental Health Act 1983 – Patient becoming pregnant while in care of
c *NHS Trust and giving birth to healthy child – Patient unable to care for child – Whether damages recoverable by patient for costs incurred by grandmother in rearing child.*

The claimant was a patient detained under the Mental Health Act 1983 in the care of the defendant NHS trust. She suffered from mental instability as a result of
d brain damage caused by a childhood illness. She was transferred to a mixed psychiatric ward where she became pregnant as a result of having sexual intercourse with an unknown patient. She gave birth to a healthy daughter although she was unable to care for her. The child's grandmother applied for and was granted a residence order and took on all responsibility for looking after the child. The claimant issued proceedings against the defendant alleging that the
e pregnancy and resultant birth were caused by the defendant's negligence while it was responsible for her psychiatric care, and seeking damages for, inter alia, the costs of the child's upbringing, maintenance and education. At a preliminary hearing the judge decided that the claimant was not entitled to claim loss and damage in respect of those costs. The claimant appealed contending, inter alia,
f that there was no basis for distinguishing between a severely incapacitated mother, whose disability added expense, which was claimable, to the costs of rearing a healthy child born as a result of medical negligence, and herself, who was totally disabled from caring for her child.

g **Held** – Even if the birth of a child resulted from medical negligence, damages were not recoverable to compensate for the cost of rearing a healthy child. In the instant case, the costs of rearing the child were not 'additional' or 'extra' in the sense that they arose from the child's or the mother's disability. They were costs, being borne by someone other than the mother, which would have been borne
h by the child's mother if she had been fit. As a head of damages, those costs were not recoverable as part of the mother's claim. Accordingly, the appeal would be dismissed (see [14], [17], [19], [20], below).

McFarlane v Tayside Health Board [1999] 4 All ER 961, *Parkinson v St James and Seacroft University Hospital NHS Trust* [2001] 3 All ER 97 and *Rees v Darlington*
j *Memorial Hospital NHS Trust* [2002] 2 All ER 177 applied.

Decision of Cooke J [2002] 3 FCR 658 affirmed.

Notes

For damages and the policy informing the assessment of damages, see 12(1) *Halsbury's Laws* (4th edn reissue) paras 802, 822.

Cases referred to in judgments

Caparo Industries plc v Dickman [1990] 1 All ER 568, [1990] 2 AC 605, [1990] 2 WLR 358, HL.

Donnelly v Joyce [1973] 3 All ER 475, [1974] QB 454, [1973] 3 WLR 514, CA.

Greenfield v Flather [2001] EWCA Civ 113, (2001) 59 BMLR 43, [2001] WLR 1279.

Groom v Selby [2001] EWCA Civ 1522, (2002) 64 BMLR 47.

Hunt v Severs [1994] 2 All ER 385, [1994] 2 AC 350, [1994] 2 WLR 602, HL.

McFarlane v Tayside Health Board [1999] 4 All ER 961, [2000] 2 AC 59, [1999] 3 WLR 1301, HL.

Parkinson v St James and Seacroft University Hospital NHS Trust [2001] EWCA Civ 530, [2001] 3 All ER 97, [2002] QB 266, [2001] 3 WLR 376.

Rees v Darlington Memorial Hospital NHS Trust [2002] EWCA Civ 88, [2002] 2 All ER 177, [2003] 1 QB 20, [2002] 2 WLR 1483.

Appeal

The claimant, A, a patient detained under s 3 of the Mental Health Act 1983 and in the care of the defendant, the East Kent Community NHS Trust, brought proceedings against the defendant, alleging that her pregnancy and the resultant birth of her child were caused by the defendant's negligence while it was responsible for her psychiatric care. The claimant appealed, with permission granted by Cooke J, against his decision on 24 May 2002 ([2002] EWHC 2256 (QB), [2002] 3 FCR 658) on the trial of a preliminary issue, that the claimant was not entitled to claim damage and loss in respect of the child's upbringing, maintenance and education. The facts are set out in the judgment of the court.

Nicholas Yell (instructed by *Dominic Goward & Co*, Canterbury) for the claimant.
Robert Francis QC and *Bridget Dolan* (instructed by *Brachers*, Maidstone) for the defendant.

Cur adv vult

17 December 2002. The following judgment of the court was delivered.

JUDGE LJ.

[1] This litigation arises from the birth of a child, C, on 27 July 1998. Her father is unknown. Her mother, the claimant, A, was born on 16 March 1971. Her maternal grandmother, Mrs A, was born on 3 October 1950.

[2] C is a healthy little girl. Her grandmother, now aged 52 years, is also fit and well. Unfortunately, the claimant suffers from mental instability, the result of brain damage caused by encephalopathic illness when she was five years old.

[3] A has been intellectually impaired ever since, and her behaviour is 'characterised by manic mood swings, aggression, temper tantrums, promiscuity and disinhibition'. She is 'sectioned' under s 3 of the Mental Health Act 1983, and in March 1997, after a series of placements, she was transferred to a mixed psychiatric ward at St Martin's Hospital, Canterbury, which was run by the defendant NHS Trust.

[4] According to the pleaded case, towards the end of October 1997, the claimant became pregnant 'as a result of having sexual intercourse with an unknown patient'. Although the word rape was mentioned in argument, nothing is known of the circumstances. When the claimant discovered her pregnancy, a 'scan was carried out on 19 January 1998 [which] showed her to

a be eleven weeks and five days pregnant. The claimant decided not to have a termination, and her daughter was born on July 27 1998'.

[5] Shortly before the child's birth, after a case conference convened by social services, she was designated as a 'child in need'. Rather than arrangements for fostering or adoption, immediately after her birth, her grandmother applied to Canterbury County Court for a residence order. This *b* was made on 31 July. Since then the child has been brought up by her grandmother, who has accepted responsibility for looking after her for the 'foreseeable future'.

[6] It is not contended that A's inability to care for C was caused by the defendants. Her long-term problem preceded her admission to the hospital for which they were responsible. What is alleged is that the pregnancy and *c* resultant birth of the child were caused by the defendants' negligence, while they were responsible for her psychiatric care. The factual matters alleged are in dispute, but for present purposes must be assumed to be correct:

d 'The defendants: (a) Placed the claimant in a mixed psychiatric ward, when it was obviously unsuitable for her; (b) Failed to place the claimant in a single-sex ward; (c) Failed to arrange for the claimant to be sterilised or given some form of contraception to prevent her from becoming pregnant; (d) Failed to solicit and obtain the claimant's consent to be sterilised or given some form of contraception to prevent her from becoming pregnant and / or, if it was refused, to seek the assistance of the court authorising *e* her sterilisation or the provision of a suitable method of contraception; (e) Failed to heed and act upon Mrs A's express concerns about the claimant's vulnerability, including the risk of her becoming pregnant; (f) Failed to provide an adequate level of supervision of the claimant and in the ward generally, and (g) Failed to prevent the claimant from becoming pregnant.'

f [7] For completeness, we must add that the defendants have denied negligence. They contend that the claimant 'was capable of deciding whether or not to engage in sexual intercourse and ... whether or not to consent to contraceptive treatment', and that she was fully aware of the risks of pregnancy and the benefits of contraceptive measures, which she had elected not to use. *g* The defendants also draw attention to the absence from the claimant's case of any assertion that she had no desire to become pregnant, or that the child was unwanted, or that she was unaware of the risk of pregnancy if contraception was not used. These are all matters which will be decided in due course at a full hearing. At the risk of repetition, we must proceed on the basis that the claimant's allegations are factually correct.
h [8] The loss consequent on the alleged negligence has two distinct ingredients. First, by para 9, the claimant 'suffered injury, namely the physical and psychological effects of the pregnancy, and the psychiatric trauma caused by her separation from and inability to bring up the child'. Second, by para 10, she 'sustained loss and damage, namely the costs of the child's upbringing, *j* maintenance and education', on the basis that effectively the mother is carrying out all these necessary functions for and on behalf of her daughter.

[9] This is an appeal from a decision by Cooke J dated 24 May 2002 ([2002] EWHC 2256 (QB), [2002] 3 FCR 658) at the trial of the preliminary issue which was confined to the second ingredient of the alleged loss: 'Whether the claimant is entitled to claim in respect of the child's upbringing, maintenance

and education.' Cooke J decided that the claimant was not so entitled, and gave   *a* her permission to appeal.

[10] In reaching his decision, Cooke J was bound by the decisions and principles set out in three authorities. They are equally binding on us. These were: *McFarlane v Tayside Health Board* [1999] 4 All ER 961, [2000] 2 AC 59, *Parkinson v St James and Seacroft University Hospital NHS Trust* [2001] EWCA Civ 530, [2001] 3 All ER 97, [2002] QB 266 and *Rees v Darlington Memorial Hospital* *b* *NHS Trust* [2002] EWCA Civ 88, [2002] 2 All ER 177, [2003] 1 QB 20. We understand that permission to appeal this third decision has been granted by the House of Lords.

[11] The starting point is *McFarlane*'s case. By a majority, the House of Lords held that, in view of the negligence which had attended a vasectomy operation carried out on the father, the mother, who gave birth to a healthy, *c* normal child, was entitled to general damages for pain and suffering, and the inconvenience of pregnancy and childbirth, together with associated special damages. The House also held, unanimously, that the cost of caring for and bringing up the baby were not recoverable.

[12] The skeleton arguments before us carefully analysed the reasoning *d* process by which each member of the House of Lords came to a conclusion. We do not think it necessary to examine the different judgments: the principle is clear. If A were capable of bringing up her child, based on *McFarlane*'s case, the claim pleaded in para 10 would be unsustainable.

[13] Since *McFarlane*'s case, however, these issues have been reconsidered *e* in this court. First, we must note *Greenfield v Flather* [2001] EWCA Civ 113, (2001) 59 BMLR 43, [2001] WLR 1279. Following the birth of a healthy child, the mother made a claim for the loss of earnings sustained when she gave up work to care for and bring up her child. Although for the purposes of argument, the Court of Appeal was prepared to accept that the House in *McFarlane*'s case was not consciously directing its attention to such a claim, the *f* claim for these losses was held to fall within the *McFarlane* principle, and hence was unsustainable. For example, May LJ ((2001) 59 BMLR 43 at [44]) could discern no 'material distinction between the costs of caring for and bringing up a child held to be irrecoverable in *McFarlane*'s case, and the mother's claim for loss of earnings'. Laws LJ thought it sufficient for the decision to reflect that *g* the existence of a healthy child could not be categorised as a detriment sounding in damages. The argument before us makes it unnecessary to deal with the further distinction sought to be drawn with *McFarlane*'s case, that the claim there was decided on the basis of economic loss resulting from negligent advice, rather than physical injury caused by negligent omission, as in *h* *Greenfield v Flather*.

[14] As we are here concerned with the birth of a healthy child, we need not consider the problems which might have arisen if C had been disabled at birth. In *Parkinson*'s case and *Groom v Selby* [2001] EWCA Civ 1522, (2002) 64 BMLR 47, and a number of cases at first instance, a distinction was drawn between *McFarlane*'s case, where a healthy child was born, and such cases. That said, *j* *Parkinson*'s case lends emphasis to the principle that the ordinary costs of rearing a child cannot be recovered: the admissible claim was directed to the 'additional' costs arising from the child's disability.

[15] In the present case, of course, unlike *McFarlane*'s case and indeed *Parkinson*'s case, the mother herself was disabled: so we must consider a further

a distinction with *McFarlane*'s case. Inevitably, and rightly, therefore, our particular attention was focused on *Rees'* case, where the mother's vision was substantially impaired. Mr Nicolas Yell pointed out to us that, notwithstanding the residence order, in this case the mother herself was not divested of her statutory parental responsibility for her child under the Children Act 1989, and the Child Support Act 1991. This responsibility may indeed have survived the

b residence order, but no one has suggested that in practical terms this responsibility is, or may become more than technical or theoretical, and, in any event, it extends to the normal obligation of maintenance and support of the child. Moreover, it is expressly pleaded that C will be brought up by her grandmother, who will be 'looking after her for the foreseeable future', and the

c claimant herself claims damages for the psychiatric trauma 'caused by her separation from and inability to bring up' her daughter. It is not alleged that the mother's disability will involve additional expense, beyond the cost inevitably involved in rearing a healthy child. Given that the House of Lords will be examining *Rees'* case, we shall not complicate the debate by adding any observations of our own. It is sufficient to record that, although the disability

d in this case arose from the mother's mental, rather than any physical infirmity, if she had been going to bring up her own child, and if further, her disability would have required her to incur additional cost while doing so, we should have been required to apply *Rees'* case.

[16] To overcome the difficulty presented by the principle in *McFarlane*'s

e case, Mr Yell submitted that there was no logical basis for distinguishing between the severely incapacitated mother and the claimant, who is totally disabled from caring for her child. It was not 'fair, just and reasonable', within the ambit of the *Caparo* principle (see *Caparo Industries plc v Dickman* [1990] 1 All ER 568, [1990] 2 AC 605), to hold that the prohibition created by *McFarlane*'s

f case extended as far as this case, in which the grandmother had assumed the burden of care and support. He submitted that the birth of the child to this mother provided no benefit whatever to her: to the contrary, she was seeking an award of damages to compensate her for psychiatric illness caused by deprivation of the joys of motherhood. In this context, Hale LJ's metaphor of 'deemed equilibrium' (see *Parkinson*'s case [2001] 3 All ER 97 at [90] and *Rees'*

g case [2002] 2 All ER 177 at [10]) was apposite, because the birth of her child produced no benefits for the mother. Accordingly, and in summary, taking this mother as they found her (that is, unable through mental infirmity to care for her child), the costs of bringing the child up were 'additional' or 'extra' costs for the grandmother arising from the mother's total disability. During the course

h of his reply, Mr Yell suggested that the claim should be seen as the valuation of substituted care provided by another carer. However, he did not seek to amend para 10(v), and suggested that this new approach to the claim was subsumed in the original pleading.

[17] Despite Mr Yell's persuasive submissions, in reality, this mother is

j claiming as damages the entire cost of bringing up and supporting her healthy child on the basis that, although she could not recover such damages herself if she were fit and healthy (see *McFarlane*'s case), and could recover only the 'extra' costs occasioned by her disability if she were partly disabled (see *Rees'* case), she should now recover all these costs because her mother has fully accepted the responsibilities which would otherwise have fallen on her. In effect, her mother has replaced her in the life of her child, carrying both the emotional and financial burdens.

[18] This is not a claim for damages either by the child herself, nor indeed by her grandmother. The principles which govern cases where a relative gratuitously provides care for an injured claimant are well understood. Damages are recoverable from the tortfeasor to the injured claimant for the reasonable value of such services, and are then held in trust for the benefit of the person providing the voluntary care (see *Hunt v Severs* [1994] 2 All ER 385, [1994] 2 AC 350). Notwithstanding some of the difficulties about the concept of a trust created in these circumstances, for present purposes it is enough, but crucial, to notice that Lord Bridge of Harwich ([1994] 2 All ER 385 at 389, [1994] 2 AC 350 at 358), giving the judgment with which the other members of the House agreed, made clear that the person providing the voluntary services has no cause of action of her own.

[19] As a matter of principle, therefore, we are required to focus on the sustainability of a claim by the mother for the cost of rearing her healthy child. It is illuminating to contrast the position of the mother, who has lost earnings as a result of giving up work to care for her injured child (the situation in *Donnelly v Joyce* [1973] 3 All ER 475, [1974] QB 454) with that of the mother, similarly losing earnings, in order to be at home to care for the healthy child born to her as a result of the defendant's negligence (as in *Greenfield v Flather* (2001) 59 BMLR 43, [2001] WLR 1279). Although some of Megaw LJ's observations in *Donnelly*'s case about the basis of the mother's claim are no longer authoritative, no one doubts that the tortious defendant would be liable to pay damages to the injured child if his mother were to suffer loss of earnings in order to be at home to care for him. Nevertheless, as we have already seen, in *Greenfield v Flather,* losses sustained on the same basis (loss of earnings to be at home to care for a healthy child) were not recoverable by the mother who had been the victim of negligence by a hospital authority. The difference is not accidental: it reflects the principle that even if the birth of the child resulted from medical negligence, damages are not recoverable to compensate for the cost of rearing a healthy child, notwithstanding that identifiable expense can be established.

[20] The cost of rearing C is not 'additional' or 'extra' in the sense envisaged in *Parkinson*'s case and *Rees*' case. For all practical purposes, they are the same costs, now being borne by someone other than the mother, Mrs A, gratuitously providing for her granddaughter in the same way as the child's mother would have done, if she had been fit. As a head of damages, on the authorities, these costs are not recoverable as part of the mother's claim.

[21] We must add that we do not accept that this child cannot and never will provide any possible benefit to her mother. It is not inconceivable that in years to come C will discover within herself a well-spring of affection for the mother who bore her, who, even in her continuing mental infirmity, will derive unanticipated comfort and strength from it. And if the claim could be advanced by Mrs A herself (which, for the reasons we have given, it has not and cannot) it would be invidious to attempt to put a money value on the benefit that she will derive from the joy of having her healthy granddaughter living with her and growing up in her home.

a

[22] We naturally have great sympathy for Mrs A as well as considerable admiration for the way in which she has come to C's rescue and provided her with the love and care that she needs. We must, however, dismiss this appeal.

Appeal dismissed.

Melanie Martyn   Barrister.

R (on the application of Ullah) v Special Adjudicator

a

Do v Secretary of State for the Home Department

[2002] EWCA Civ 1856

b

COURT OF APPEAL, CIVIL DIVISION

LORD PHILLIPS OF WORTH MATRAVERS MR, KAY AND DYSON LJJ

25, 26 NOVEMBER, 16 DECEMBER 2002

c

Immigration – Deportation – Refugee – Asylum – Right to freedom of thought, conscience and religion – Asylum seekers without well-founded fear of persecution – Deportation of asylum seekers not leading to torture or inhuman or degrading treatment or punishment – Whether deportation of asylum seekers leading to breach of right to freedom of thought, conscience and religion lawful – Human Rights Act 1998, Sch 1, Pt I, arts 3, 9.

d

In the first of two conjoined appeals, the claimant, an active member of the Ahmadhiya faith who carried out preaching and teaching, entered the United Kingdom from Pakistan and applied for asylum on the basis of persecution he had suffered as a result of practising his religion, and for permission to remain by virtue of the rights contained in the European Convention for the Protection of Human Rights and Fundamental Freedoms 1950 (as set out in Sch 1 to the Human Rights Act 1998) (the convention). The Secretary of State did not accept that the claimant had shown that he had a well-founded fear of persecution under the Convention and Protocol relating to the Status of Refugees 1951 (the refugee convention) and dismissed his claim for asylum. He also concluded that the claimant had not shown that he qualified for permission to remain under any of the articles of the convention. The special adjudicator dismissed the claimant's appeal, holding that he did not fall within the refugee convention and that while art 9[a] of the convention, guaranteeing the freedom of religion, was engaged, the Secretary of State had acted lawfully and proportionately in pursuance of the legitimate aim of immigration control. The claimant's application for judicial review was refused and permission to appeal granted only in relation to the claimant's reliance on art 9.

e

f

g

In the second appeal, the claimant, a Vietnamese Roman Catholic who had been teaching the Catholic religion to children in Vietnam, made similar claims under the refugee convention and arts 3[b] and 9 of the convention. Article 3 provided that no one should be subjected to torture or to inhuman or degrading treatment or punishment. The immigration appeal tribunal upheld the refusal of the immigration adjudicator to grant her asylum and her claims under arts 3 and 9. The evidence showed that there was local variation in Vietnam in the restrictive treatment of persons practising religion. The claimant appealed. At the hearing of the conjoined appeals the court identified the following issues:

h

j

---

a   Article 9, so far as material, is set out at [2], below.
b   Article 3 provides: 'No one shall be subjected to torture or to inhuman or degrading treatment or punishment.'

a

(i) whether the 1998 Act, together with art 9 of the convention, required the United Kingdom to give refuge to immigrants who were prevented from freely practising, and in particular from preaching or teaching, their religion in their own countries; and (ii) the extent to which the 1998 Act inhibited the United Kingdom from expelling asylum seekers who fell short of demonstrating a well-founded fear of persecution.

b

Held – (1) The underlying rationale for the application of the convention to the act of expulsion was that it was an affront to fundamental humanitarian principles to remove an individual to a country where there was a real risk of serious ill-treatment, even though such ill-treatment might not satisfy the criteria of persecution under the refugee convention. Article 3 of the convention provided the test. The European Court of Human Rights (ECHR) had not yet taken the step of extending the scope of the convention to articles other than art 3 where the apprehended treatment of a deportee in the receiving state would fall short of that covered by art 3. Sections 3 and 6 of the 1998 Act did not require United Kingdom courts to take that further step. There was no domestic authority requiring the court to hold that where an alien was removed to a country where his right to practice his religion was inhibited, art 9 would, or could, be engaged. Accordingly, a decision to remove an asylum seeker to a country that did not respect his rights under art 9 of the convention would not infringe the 1998 Act where the nature of the interference with the right to practice religion that was anticipated in the receiving state fell short of ill-treatment within the terms of art 3. The refugee convention and art 3 of the convention already catered for the more severe categories of ill-treatment on the ground of religion. It was not for the courts, but for the executive, or for Parliament, to decide whether to offer refuge to persons who were not in a position to claim refuge under the refugee convention, or the convention as currently applied by the ECHR (see [39], [47],

f [58], [60]–[63], below).

(2) Where the treatment to which an alien, refused the right to enter or remain, was likely to be subjected to by the receiving state fell outside art 3, there might be cases which justified the grant of exceptional leave to remain on humanitarian grounds. The decision of the Secretary of State in such cases would be subject to the ordinary principles of judicial review, but not to the constraints of the convention (see [64], below).

(3) In the instant appeals it was unnecessary to consider further the facts of the claimant in the first appeal's case, since it had already been determined that they did not engage art 3. In the claimant in the second appeal's case, the inhibition that might be placed on her right to practice her religion by the possibility that she might have to move from her home to a different part of the country fell far short of persecution under the refugee convention or ill-treatment that violated art 3 of the convention. Nor was art 9 of the convention engaged by her proposed removal. The appeals, would, accordingly be dismissed (see [3], [65], [67], [68], [70], below).

j
Decision of Harrison J [2002] All ER (D) 235 (Jul) affirmed.

Notes

For the convention prohibition of torture; inhuman and degrading treatment or punishment and the right to freedom of conscience, see 8(2) *Halsbury's Laws* (4th edn reissue) paras 124 and 156, 157.

For the Human Rights Act 1998, Sch 1, Pt I, arts 3, 9, see 7 *Halsbury's Statutes* (4th edn) (2002 reissue) 553, 555.

Cases referred to in judgment
Abdulaziz v UK (1985) 7 EHRR 471, [1985] ECHR 9214/80, ECt HR.
Ahmed v Secretary of State for the Home Dept [2000] INLR 1, CA.
Bensaid v UK (2001) 33 EHRR 205, [2001] ECHR 44599/98, ECt HR.
Chahal v UK (1996) 1 BHRC 405, ECt HR.
Dehwari v Netherlands (2001) 29 EHRR CD 74, ECt HR.
Devaseelan v Secretary of State for the Home Dept (13 March 2002, unreported), IAT.
Drozd v France (1992) 14 EHRR 745, ECt HR.
Foreign Students (15) v UK (1977) 9 DR 185, E Com HR.
Hilal v UK (2001) 11 BHRC 354, ECt HR.
Kacaj v Secretary of State for the Home Dept [2002] Imm AR 213, IAT; rvsd [2002] EWCA Civ 314, [2002] All ER (D) 203 (Mar).
Kokkinakis v Greece (1994) 17 EHRR 397, ECt HR.
R (on the application of Ahmadi) v Secretary of State for the Home Dept [2002] EWHC 1897 (Admin), [2002] All ER (D) 52 (Sep), [2003] ACD 14.
R (on the application of Farrakhan) v Secretary of State for the Home Dept [2002] EWCA Civ 606, [2002] 4 All ER 289, [2002] QB 1391, [2002] 3 WLR 481.
R (on the application of Holub) v Secretary of State for the Home Dept [2001] 1 WLR 1359, CA.
R (on the application of Mahmood) v Secretary of State for the Home Dept [2001] 1 WLR 840, CA.
Salazar v Sweden App No 28987/95 (7 March 1996, unreported), E Com HR.
Secretary of State for the Home Dept v S and K (3 December 2002, unreported), IAT.
Secretary of State for the Home Dept v Z [2001] EWCA Civ 952, [2002] Imm AR 560.
Soering v UK (1989) 11 EHRR 439, [1989] ECHR 10438/88, ECt HR.
Tyrer v UK (1978) 2 EHRR 1, [1978] ECHR 5856/72, ECt HR.

Cases referred to in skeleton arguments
Bankovic v Belgium (2001) 11 BHRC 435, ECt HR.
Loizidou v Turkey (1995) 20 EHRR 99, ECt HR.

Appeals

R (on the application of Ullah) v Special Adjudicator
The claimant, Ahsan Ullah, appealed with permission granted by Harrison J on 16 July 2002 from his judgment on that date ([2002] All ER (D) 235 (Jul)) refusing the claimant's application to quash the decision of the defendant special adjudicator, promulgated on 17 September 2001, dismissing his appeal against the refusal of the Secretary of State for the Home Department of his claim for asylum and rejection of his claim that it would be contrary to the Human Rights Act 1998 to remove him to his home country, Pakistan. The facts are set out in the judgment of the court.

Do v Secretary of State for the Home Department
The claimant, Thi Lien Do, appealed, with permission granted by Tuckey LJ on 22 May 2002, from the determination of the immigration appeal tribunal (Judge Holden, M Padfield and SS Ramsumair) on 7 January 2002 upholding the decision of a special adjudicator (HS Coleman), promulgated on 5 September 2001,

a upholding the refusal of the defendant Secretary of State to grant the claimant asylum and rejecting her claim that it would be contrary to the Human Rights Act to remove her to her home country, Vietnam. The facts are set out in the judgment of the court.

Nicholas Blake QC and *Martin Soorjoo* (instructed by *Thompson & Co*) for Mr Ullah.

b *Monica Carss-Frisk QC* and *Lisa Giovannetti* (instructed by the *Treasury Solicitor*) for the special adjudicator.
Manjit Gill QC and *Christa Fielden* (instructed by *Sheikh & Co*) for Miss Do.
Monica Carss-Frisk QC and *Kassie Smith* (instructed by the *Treasury Solicitor*) for the Secretary of State.

c   *Cur adv vult*

16 December 2002. The following judgment of the court was delivered.

LORD PHILLIPS OF WORTH MATRAVERS MR.

d INTRODUCTION
[1] There are before the court two conjoined appeals. Common to each is the following question. Does the Human Rights Act 1998, together with art 9 of the European Convention for the Protection of Human Rights and Fundamental Freedoms 1950 (as set out in Sch 1 to the 1998 Act) (the human rights convention), require this country to give a refuge to immigrants who are
e prevented from freely practising, and in particular from preaching or teaching, their religion in their own countries? This question reflects a wider issue. To what extent does the 1998 Act inhibit the United Kingdom from expelling asylum seekers who fall short of demonstrating a well-founded fear of persecution?
[2] Article 9 of the human rights convention provides:

f
> *'Freedom of thought, conscience and religion*
>   1. Everyone has the right to freedom of thought, conscience and religion; this right includes freedom to change his religion or belief and freedom, either alone or in community with others and in public or private, to
g manifest his religion or belief, in worship, teaching, practice and observance.
>   2. Freedom to manifest one's religion or beliefs shall be subject only to such limitations as are prescribed by law and are necessary in a democratic society in the interests of public safety, for the protection of public order, health or morals, or for the protection of the rights and freedoms of others.'

h
THE FACTS

Mr Ullah's appeal
[3] This is an appeal from a judgment of Harrison J dated 16 July 2002 in which
j he refused Mr Ullah's application to quash the decision of an immigration adjudicator, promulgated on 17 September 2001. The adjudicator dismissed Mr Ullah's appeal against the Secretary of State's refusal to grant him asylum and rejected a claim that it would be contrary to the 1998 Act to remove him to his home country, Pakistan. Permission to seek judicial review was granted by Mr Jack Beatson QC, sitting as a deputy judge of the High Court on 12 April 2002. Permission was, however, restricted to a single point—Mr Ullah's reliance on

art 9 of the human rights convention. Harrison J, in his turn, gave permission to
appeal 'on the basis of the importance of some of the points involved in the case'.

[4] Mr Ullah is a citizen of Pakistan. He is an active member of the Ahmadiyya
faith.   In particular, on 28 December 1998 he was appointed 'secretary of
teaching' in order to spread the beliefs of the Ahmadiyya faith and thereafter
carried on what he has described as 'preaching duties' and 'preaching activities'
in Pakistan.

[5] On 15 January 2001 Mr Ullah arrived at Heathrow on a plane
from Karachi. He entered the country on false documents that he had
purchased in Karachi. He applied for asylum two days later. He claimed to have
a well-founded fear of persecution as a result of persecution that he had suffered
as a result of practising his faith.   In particular, he alleged that he had been
harassed, intimidated and, on two occasions, attacked by members of a religious
terrorist group called Khatme Nabuwait, in whose activities the local police were
complicit. On one occasion he said that he had been beaten and left for dead. On
the other occasion he said that his house was burnt down. Faced with further
death threats he fled to England.

[6] The Secretary of State found some aspects of Mr Ullah's account to be
implausible. He did not accept that Mr Ullah had demonstrated that he had a
well-founded fear of persecution under the terms of the Geneva Convention
relating to the Status of Refugees (Geneva, 28 July 1951; TS 39 (1954); Cmd 9171)
(as amended by the 1967 Protocol relating to the Status of Refugees (New York,
31 January 1967; TS 15 (1969); Cmnd 3906)) (the refugee convention). He
dismissed the claim for asylum. He further concluded that Mr Ullah had not
demonstrated that he qualified for permission to remain in this country by reason
of any of the articles of the human rights convention.

[7] Mr Ullah appealed against the Home Secretary's decision. With the
assistance of Thompson & Co, solicitors, he filed detailed grounds of appeal.
Most of these were in terms that applied to the position of all Ahmadis in
Pakistan. They alleged that Ahmadis were subject to persistent and organised
persecution and that the government of Pakistan failed to provide protection to
Ahmadis against religious extremists.

[8] We set out in Annex A to our judgment the relevant findings of the
adjudicator, Mrs Nichols, in relation to Mr Ullah's asylum application. We set
out in Annex B her findings in relation to Mr Ullah's claim under the 1998 Act. In
summary, the adjudicator did not find credible much of Mr Ullah's evidence and
concluded that he did not have a well-founded fear of persecution. So far as his
claim under the human rights convention is concerned, the adjudicator found
that arts 9, 10 and 11 of the convention were engaged. She found that Ahmadis
were a religious minority and that if Mr Ullah returned to Pakistan he would not
enjoy the same rights as the majority. He would none the less be able to practise
his religion. The articles invoked gave qualified rights. In refusing to permit
Mr Ullah to remain in this country the Secretary of State was acting lawfully in
pursuance of the legitimate aim of immigration control. The act of removing
Mr Ullah to Pakistan was proportionate to any difficulties he might face on his
return.

[9] On the application to Harrison J for judicial review, counsel for Mr Ullah
submitted that the adjudicator had been wrong to find that, by reason of art 9(2)
of the human rights convention, immigration control was a legitimate aim which
could justify interference with the art 9 rights. Counsel for the Secretary of State
challenged this assertion, but argued that the adjudicator had erred in finding that

a art 9 was engaged at all. She submitted that, where art 9 was invoked as a bar to removal from the jurisdiction, it could only be engaged if the alleged violation was 'flagrant'. This it was not.

[10] Harrison J accepted the submissions made on behalf of the Secretary of State. He ruled that the alleged violation of art 9 was not flagrant. He further ruled that immigration control fell within the legitimate aims that were *b* recognised by art 9(2).

Miss Do's appeal

[11] This is an appeal from the final determination of the Immigration Appeal Tribunal dated 7 January 2002. The tribunal had upheld the decision of an *c* immigration adjudicator, promulgated on 5 September 2001. The adjudicator had upheld the refusal of the Secretary of State to grant Miss Do asylum. She also rejected a claim that it would be contrary to arts 3 and 5 of the human rights convention to remove Miss Do to her home country, Vietnam. The tribunal considered also whether Miss Do had a case under art 9, and concluded that she did not. Permission to appeal to this court was granted by Tuckey LJ, who *d* remarked 'the art 9 point may be of some importance'.

[12] Miss Do is a citizen of Vietnam, where she was born in 1979. On 20 November 2000 she arrived in the United Kingdom clandestinely and without travel documents. On 13 December 2000 she claimed asylum. The basis of her claim was that she had a well-founded fear of persecution in Vietnam as a result *e* of her religious beliefs as a Catholic. The Secretary of State rejected her claim to asylum. He remarked that when questioned she had showed ignorance of the basic beliefs of the Catholic Church. She had never been arrested, detained or charged by the police in Vietnam. The Secretary of State considered whether Miss Do qualified for protection under any of the articles of the human rights convention and decided that she did not.

f [13] Miss Do supported her appeal to the adjudicator with an appeal statement, prepared with the assistance of Sheikh & Co, solicitors. This included the following statements:

> 'It is correct that recently the Vietnamese government has eased its control
> *g* over church activities. There might be a certain freedom of religion in
> Vietnam in comparison with the past, but this is only the case for big cities.
> In the villages and in the countryside, Catholic Christians are still harassed by
> the Vietnamese authorities. For example in my village the church never got
> permission from the local authorities to be refurbished. The local authorities
> also confiscated the building where we were teaching catechism. When I
> *h* was teaching Catholicism I was harassed by the authorities and suffered
> discrimination. The police came to my house many times and took me to
> the police station. In June 2001 I was taken twice to the police station. The
> police told me to stop teaching Catholicism or I would be arrested. I carried
> on teaching as my faith was stronger and because I thought that they could
> *j* not find out what I was doing. I did not feel safe anywhere in Vietnam and
> that is why I decided to leave the country. The Communist government
> wants children to be raised and taught according to Communist beliefs.
> Teaching Catholicism is believed to be acting against the government. If I
> were to be returned to Vietnam I could not practice my religion freely and I
> could not teach Catholicism, as it is my wish. The Vietnamese authorities
> would eventually arrest me and put me in prison. This happened to a lot of

Christians in Vietnam and is still happening ... I suffered discrimination and threat to my life in my country of origin. If I was to be returned to Vietnam *a* I could not practice my religion freely and I will not be allowed to teach Catholicism to the children, as it is my wish. Furthermore the Vietnamese authorities are suspicious towards people coming from abroad. I would be watched by the police even more closely. I fear for my safety and my freedom as I could be put into prison if I am required to return to Vietnam. *b* I therefore request that I should be allowed to remain in the United Kingdom as a refugee recognised under the convention.'

[14] We set out in Annex C the relevant findings of the adjudicator. In summary, the adjudicator accepted Miss Do's evidence that she had practised the Catholic religion in Vietnam. That evidence included the statement that Miss Do *c* taught the Catholic religion to children. The adjudicator found that, as a practising Catholic, Miss Do had suffered from discrimination and harassment, but that this fell short of persecution or violation of the human rights invoked by Miss Do. Miss Do could still practise her religion 'albeit under reduced circumstances'.

d

[15] Before the tribunal Miss Do was represented by counsel. The tribunal recorded her counsel's submission that, because Miss Do's ability to teach children about the Catholic faith was curtailed, there was a substantial interference with her right to practise a religion of her choice. In short, but adequate, reasons the tribunal expressed the view that the adjudicator had reached the correct decision for the reasons that she had given. In relation to art 9 *e* the tribunal commented that the 'reduced circumstances' identified by the adjudicator appeared to relate to Miss Do's suggested difficulties in teaching young children. The tribunal was not satisfied that these were sufficient to amount to a violation of Miss Do's art 9 rights.

f

ISSUES AND SUBMISSIONS

[16] Mr Gill QC, who appeared for Miss Do, argued briefly that the treatment that she had received in Vietnam was sufficient to cause her a well-founded fear of persecution. For reasons that will become apparent in due course, we are in no doubt that the adjudicator and the tribunal were right to dismiss Miss Do's claim to asylum under the refugee convention. The important issue raised by her *g* appeal relates to the application of art 9 of the human rights convention. On this issue, Mr Gill's submissions were in harmony with those of Mr Blake QC, who appeared for Mr Ullah.

'TERRITORIALITY'   *h*

[17] Article 1 of the human rights convention requires the contracting states to secure to everyone *within their jurisdiction* (my emphasis) the convention rights and freedoms. Section 6 of the 1998 Act provides that it is unlawful for a public authority to act in a way which is incompatible with a convention right. The courts of this country have proceeded on the basis that the obligation *j* imposed by s 6 is subject to the same limitation as that which results from the words that we have emphasised in art 1 of the human rights convention. It applies only in relation to persons *within the jurisdiction* of the United Kingdom. So far as we are aware, this interpretation of s 6 has never been challenged, and certainly neither Mr Blake nor Mr Gill has challenged it in the present case. The issue that has been explored on this appeal is the manner in which the words

a 'within their jurisdiction' limit the obligations of the contracting parties to the convention and of public authorities under the 1998 Act.

[18] Both Mr Ullah and Miss Do are within this jurisdiction. The act of removing either will, if it takes place, be an act of a public authority done to a person within the jurisdiction. If the consequence of this act will be that the person will be removed to a country where his or her art 9 rights will not be

b respected, will this infringe the human rights convention and the 1998 Act? To this question Mr Blake suggested a qualified answer. Yes, provided that the restriction on religious freedom is *severe*. Mr Gill was not prepared to accept such a qualification. His primary submission was that all that Miss Do had to demonstrate was that there was 'real risk' that, if she were removed to Vietnam, her art 9(1) rights would be infringed.

c [19] For the Secretary of State Miss Carss-Frisk QC's primary submission was that removal of a person from this country pursuant to our immigration laws was not capable of engaging art 9 of the human rights convention. Alternatively, she submitted that art 9 would only be engaged if removal would be likely to lead to a 'flagrant' breach of the individual's art 9 rights.

d [20] The debate in relation to these contentions focused both on Strasbourg and domestic jurisprudence. Each counsel submitted that, if the test were apprehension of 'flagrant' violation of art 9, his client could readily satisfy that test. We propose first to consider the law before turning to the facts of the individual cases.

e STRASBOURG JURISPRUDENCE

[21] The human rights convention was opened for signature in November 1950. Most signatories to that convention also subscribed to the refugee convention. It is notable that art 33(2) of the latter convention permitted a state to remove someone convicted of a particularly serious crime, or constituting a

f danger to the community, notwithstanding that removal would be to a country where that person's life would be threatened. We do not believe that the signatories to the human rights convention conceived that it would impact on their rights under international law to refuse entry to or to remove aliens from their territory.

g [22] Our belief receives support from the terms of the human rights convention itself. The right of immigration control is recognised by art 5(1)(f) which qualifies the right to liberty by permitting arrest or detention of a person 'to prevent his effecting an unauthorised entry into the country or of a person against whom action is being taken with a view to deportation or extradition'. Nowhere else in the qualifications to those convention rights which are not

h absolute is there any reference to the right of a state to control immigration. We do not believe that this was because this right would, or would arguably, be covered by express limitations, such as 'the interests of national security, public safety or the economic well-being of the country', which justify derogation from art 8 rights. We believe that it was because the contracting states had no

j intention of restricting their rights of immigration control. The human rights convention was not designed to impact on the rights of states to refuse entry to aliens or to remove them. The convention was designed to govern the treatment of those living within the territorial jurisdiction of the contracting states.

[23] The human rights convention is, however, a living instrument. If, initially, it was not designed to impact on the right to control immigration it has, to a degree, been interpreted by the Strasbourg court in a manner which does

have that effect. The task of identifying the principles which govern the
application of the convention in this context is not an easy one.

[24] In cases involving expulsion or refusal of entry the Strasbourg court has
repeatedly emphasised the following principle (see, for instance, *Bensaid v UK*
(2001) 33 EHRR 205 at 216 (para 32)):

> 'Contracting States have the right, as a matter of well-established
> international law and subject to their treaty obligations including the
> convention, to control the entry, residence and expulsion of aliens.'

As we consider the authorities, it will become apparent that the court does not
consider that the human rights convention will be engaged simply because the
effect of the exercise of immigration control will be to remove an individual to a
country where the convention rights are not fully respected. Equally, where the
court finds that removal or refusal of entry engages the human rights convention,
the court will often treat the right to control immigration as one that outweighs,
or trumps, the convention right.

[25] The first case to which we turn is, perhaps, the most significant, and we
propose to analyse it at some length. In *Soering v UK* (1989) 11 EHRR 439 the
applicant was a German national, detained in the United Kingdom pending
extradition to the United States of America to face charges of murder in the
Commonwealth of Virginia. If extradited and convicted he would face the death
penalty and the stresses and rigours associated with prolonged detention on
'death row'. He alleged that this prospect was so severe that extradition would
violate his art 3 right not to be subjected to inhuman or degrading treatment or
punishment. He further contended that he would not be entitled to legal
representation in Virginia and that this meant that extradition would violate his
art 6 rights to a fair trial.

[26] The United Kingdom contended that the human rights convention was
not engaged. An extraditing state could not be held responsible for acts which
occurred outside its territorial jurisdiction. To surrender a fugitive criminal was
not to 'subject' him to any treatment that he might thereafter receive in the
receiving state.

[27] The court made the following statement of general principle (at 466
(para 86)):

> 'Article 1 of the Convention, which provides that "the High Contracting
> Parties shall secure to everyone within their jurisdiction the rights and
> freedoms defined in Section I," sets a limit, notably territorial, on the reach
> of the Convention. In particular, the engagement undertaken by a
> Contracting State is confined to "securing" ("*reconnâitre*" in the French text)
> the listed rights and freedoms to persons within its own "jurisdiction".
> Further, the Convention does not govern the actions of States not Parties to
> it, nor does it purport to be a means of requiring the Contracting States to
> impose Convention standards on other States. Article 1 cannot be read as
> justifying a general principle to the effect that, notwithstanding its
> extradition obligations, a Contracting State may not surrender an individual
> unless satisfied that the conditions awaiting him in the country of destination
> are in full accord with each of the safeguards of the Convention.'

[28] Despite this general principle, the court held that, where extradition
exposes an individual to a real risk of being subjected to inhuman or degrading

a treatment or punishment proscribed by art 3, that article will be violated. The reasoning of the court appears in the following passages (at 467–469):

'88. Article 3 makes no provision for exceptions and no derogation from it
b is permissible under Article 15 in time of war or other national emergency.
This absolute prohibition on torture and on inhuman or degrading
treatment or punishment under the terms of the Convention shows that
Article 3 enshrines one of the fundamental values of the democratic societies
making up the Council of Europe. It is also to be found in similar terms in
other international instruments such as the 1966 International Covenant on
Civil and Political Rights and the 1969 American Convention on Human
Rights and is generally recognised as an internationally accepted standard.
c The question remains whether the extradition of a fugitive to another State
where he would be subjected or be likely to be subjected to torture or to
inhuman or degrading treatment or punishment would itself engage the
responsibility of a Contracting State under Article 3 ... It would hardly be
compatible with the underlying values of the Convention, that "common
heritage of political traditions, ideals, freedom and the rule of law" to which
d the Preamble refers, were a Contracting State knowingly to surrender a
fugitive to another State where there were substantial grounds for believing
that he would be in danger of being subjected to torture, however heinous
the crime allegedly committed. Extradition in such circumstances, while not
explicitly referred to in the brief and general wording of Article 3, would
e plainly be contrary to the spirit and intendment of the Article, and in the
Court's view this inherent obligation not to extradite also extends to cases in
which the fugitive would be faced in the receiving State by a real risk of
exposure to inhuman or degrading treatment or punishment proscribed by
that Article ...

f 91. In sum, the decision by a Contracting State to extradite a fugitive may
give rise to an issue under Article 3, and hence engage the responsibility of
that State under the Convention, where substantial grounds have been
shown for believing that the person concerned, if extradited, faces a real risk
of being subjected to torture or to inhuman or degrading treatment or
punishment in the requesting country. The establishment of such
g responsibility inevitably involves an assessment of conditions in the
requesting country against the standards of Article 3 of the Convention.
Nonetheless, there is no question of adjudicating on or establishing the
responsibility of the receiving country, whether under general international
law, under the Convention or otherwise. In so far as any liability under the
Convention is or may be incurred, it is liability incurred by the extraditing
h Contracting State by reason of its having taken action which has as a direct
consequence the exposure of an individual to proscribed ill-treatment.'

[29] It is often said that the effect of the passages that we have quoted is to give
to art 3 'extra-territorial effect'. This phrase is not wholly apposite. The act
j which infringes art 3 is the act of extradition which takes place within the
jurisdiction in relation to an individual who is within the jurisdiction. But the act
of removal does not itself constitute inhuman treatment. It is the foreseeable
consequences of the act which the court held engaged art 3. It seems to us that
this reasoning involved a significant extension of the ambit of the human rights
convention. Had Mr Soering been extradited, tried and acquitted by the Virginia
court we do not find it easy to see how art 3 would have been infringed. The

principle applied by the Strasbourg court appears to have been that it is a breach of the human rights convention to take action in relation to someone within the jurisdiction which carries with it the real risk that it will expose that person to infringement of his art 3 rights outside the jurisdiction.

[30] Such a principle is readily intelligible. What is less easy to see is why it should not be applied to any convention right. Yet we think that Miss Carss-Frisk was plainly right to submit that the approach of the court in *Soering v UK* (1989) 11 EHRR 439 was exceptional. What is the basis of the exception and what are its parameters? In considering the application in *15 Foreign Students v UK* (1977) 9 DR 185 the European Commission of Human Rights declined to extend the approach in *Soering*'s case to a complaint that removal would deprive the applicants of the right to education under art 2 of the First Protocol to the convention. The Commission held (at 187 (para 6)) that the applicants' complaints could not be compared with complaints under art 3 which 'concerns alleged violations of human rights of a particularly serious nature'.

[31] Some passages in *Soering*'s case itself lend support to the thesis that the basis of the exception is the severity of the foreseeable consequences of extradition. Apart from the passages which we have already cited, we would draw attention to the manner in which the court dealt with the application under art 6 (at 479 (para 113)):

'The right to a fair trial in criminal proceedings, as embodied in Article 6, holds a prominent place in a democratic society. The Court does not exclude that an issue might exceptionally be raised under Article 6 by an extradition decision in circumstances where the fugitive has suffered or risks suffering a flagrant denial of a fair trial in the requesting country. However, the facts of the present case do not disclose such a risk. Accordingly, no issue arises under Article 6(3)(c) in this respect.'

[32] The possibility that expulsion to Iran might infringe art 6 if this involved a *flagrant* risk of deprivation of a fair trial was recognised by the Commission in *Dehwari v Netherlands* (2001) 29 EHRR CD 74 at 78 (para 86), citing *Soering*'s case. The 'flagrancy' test in *Soering*'s case was also cited 'mutatis mutandis' by the court in *Drozd v France* (1992) 14 EHRR 745 at 793 (para 110). It held that art 5 might be engaged by imprisoning an individual within the jurisdiction pursuant to conviction in a trial outside the jurisdiction 'if it emerges that the conviction is the result of a *flagrant* denial of justice'.

[33] These decisions are, as we understand it, the basis of Miss Carss-Frisk's submission that, if art 9 is engaged, this can only be on the basis that removal will involve a risk of a flagrant breach of art 9 in the receiving state. Her primary submission is, however, that expulsion can only engage a convention right where, as in the case of art 3, the right is absolute.

[34] Before leaving *Soering*'s case we should draw attention to two passages in which the court suggested that the importance of extradition fell to be weighed in the balance when deciding whether the treatment to be anticipated in the receiving state was sufficiently severe to engage art 3. The court endorsed (at 466 (para 86)) the submission of the United Kingdom that the beneficial purpose of extradition in preventing fugitive offenders from evading justice cannot be ignored in determining the scope of application of the human rights convention and of art 3 in particular.

[35] The court reverted to this theme (at 468 (para 89)):

'What amounts to "inhuman or degrading treatment or punishment" depends on all the circumstances of the case. Furthermore, inherent in the whole of the Convention is a search for a fair balance between the demands of the general interest of the community and the requirements of the protection of the individual's fundamental rights. As movement about the world becomes easier and crime takes on a larger international dimension, it is increasingly in the interest of all nations that suspected offenders who flee abroad should be brought to justice. Conversely, the establishment of safe havens for fugitives would not only result in danger for the State obliged to harbour the protected person but also tend to undermine the foundations of extradition. These considerations must also be included among the factors to be taken into account in the interpretation and application of the notions of inhuman and degrading treatment or punishment in extradition cases.'

[36] In *Chahal v UK* (1996) 1 BHRC 405 the court considered whether deportation of a Sikh separatist leader to India would violate art 3. The United Kingdom argued that if he remained in this country he would be a threat to national security, so that the human rights convention posed no bar to his deportation, even if he would be at risk of torture or inhuman or degrading treatment in India. The threat to national security fell to be balanced against the risk of ill-treatment. The court rejected this argument, holding that the national interests of the state could not be invoked to override the interests of the individual where substantial grounds had been shown for believing that he would be subjected to ill-treatment if expelled.

[37] The court continued (at 424):

'79. Article 3 enshrines one of the most fundamental values of democratic society ... The Court is well aware of the immense difficulties faced by states in modern times in protecting their communities from terrorist violence. However, even in these circumstances, the convention prohibits in absolute terms torture or inhuman or degrading treatment or punishment, irrespective of the victim's conduct. Unlike most of the substantive clauses of the convention and of Protocols Nos 1 and 4, art 3 makes no provision for exceptions and no derogation from it is permissible under art 15 even in the event of a public emergency threatening the life of the nation ...

80. The prohibition provided by art 3 against ill-treatment is equally absolute in expulsion cases. Thus, whenever substantial grounds have been shown for believing that an individual would face a real risk of being subjected to treatment contrary to art 3 if removed to another state, the responsibility of the contracting state to safeguard him or her against such treatment is engaged in the event of expulsion ... In these circumstances, the activities of the individual in question, however undesirable or dangerous, cannot be a material consideration. The protection afforded by art 3 is thus wider than that provided by arts 32 and 33 of the 1951 convention ...

81. The Court's judgment in *Soering v UK* 11 EHRR 439 at 467–468 (para 88), which concerned extradition to the United States of America, clearly and forcefully expresses the above view. It should not be inferred from the Court's remarks (para 89) concerning the risk of undermining the foundations of extradition that there is any room for balancing the risk of ill-treatment against the reasons for expulsion in determining whether a state's responsibility under art 3 is engaged.'

[38] We find it hard to reconcile this passage with the court's judgment in
Soering v UK (1989) 11 EHRR 439 at 468 (para 89). It seems to us that the court
was resiling from that paragraph. Clayton and Tomlinson *The Law of Human
Rights* (2000) p 387 (para 8.15) observed that art 3 provides protection 'only
against the most serious ill-treatment'. If the risk of such treatment is to prevail
absolutely over the right of a state to extradite a criminal pursuant to a treaty, or
to deport an alien who is a threat to national security, then it seems to us that the
ill-treatment in question must necessarily be serious. In *Tyrer v UK* (1978)
2 EHRR 1 the court held that three strokes with a birch constituted degrading
punishment for a 15-year-old boy which violated art 3, having regard to the
particular circumstances in which it was administered. We find it hard to accept
that the risk of such treatment could suffice to override the right of a state to
deport an alien guilty of a serious crime. It seems to us that the court had reason
in *Soering's* case for concluding that the interest in an effective system of
extradition was a relevant factor when considering the severity of ill-treatment in
the receiving state that would preclude the extradition of a suspected criminal.

[39] As we read *Soering's* case and *Chahal's* case, the underlying rationale for
the application of the convention to the act of expulsion is that it is an affront to
fundamental humanitarian principles to remove an individual to a country where
there is a real risk of serious ill-treatment, even though such ill-treatment may not
satisfy the criteria of persecution under the refugee convention.   Article 3
provides the test of such treatment.   The issue then arises of whether this
rationale extends to preventing removal of aliens where there is a real risk that
the receiving country will treat them in a way that infringes other articles, and in
particular art 9.

[40] While in *Soering's* case the court recognised that expulsion might engage
art 6, we know of no case where the court has held that it has done so.

[41] There is a line of Strasbourg authority that suggests that where an
individual is removed, or, having landed, is denied entry, with the specific motive
of preventing the enjoyment of a convention right such as, for instance, a right
protected by arts 9 or 10, the right in question will be engaged—see the cases
cited in *R (on the application of Farrakhan) v Secretary of State for the Home Dept* [2002]
EWCA Civ 606, [2002] 4 All ER 289, [2002] QB 1391 and the discussion of these
at [52]–[56]. That situation has, however, no relevance in the present context.

[42] Article 8 has been quite often invoked in support of a submission that an
immigration restriction infringes the human rights convention. We believe,
however, that it has only successfully been invoked where removal or refusal of
entry has impacted on the enjoyment of family life of those already established
within the jurisdiction. The Strasbourg cases in this field were reviewed by Lord
Phillips of Worth Matravers MR in *R (on the application of Mahmood) v Secretary of
State for the Home Dept* [2001] 1 WLR 840 at 858–861 (paras 43–56).

[43] In the leading case of *Abdulaziz v UK* (1985) 7 EHRR 471 applicants living
within this jurisdiction complained that their art 8 rights were infringed because
their husbands were not permitted entry in order to join them. The United
Kingdom argued that neither art 8, nor any other article of the human rights
convention applied to immigration control. In rejecting this argument the court
remarked that the applicants were not the husbands but the wives and that they
were not complaining of being refused leave to enter or remain in the United
Kingdom, but as persons lawfully settled in the country of being deprived or
threatened with deprivation of the company of their spouses.

a [44] In *Abdulaziz's* case, as in all similar art 8 cases, the court has been astute to recognise the right under international law of a state to control immigration into its territory. This right has been weighed against the degree of interference with the enjoyment of family life caused by the immigration restriction often, as we see it, not because this served a legitimate aim under art 8(2) but because it acted as a free-standing restriction on the art 8 right.

b [45] A recent case in which art 8 was invoked as a bar to expulsion was *Bensaid v UK* (2001) 33 EHRR 205. The applicant was a schizophrenic, faced, as an illegal immigrant, with removal to Algeria. He claimed that the proposed move would deprive him of essential medical treatment and sever ties that he had developed in England that were essential to his well-being. He claimed that his art 3 and art 8 rights would be infringed and his complaint focused, in part, on the

c treatment that he would receive, or fail to receive, in Algeria. The court held that his case under art 3 was not made out. It went on (at 219–220) to deal with his art 8 claim:

d '46. Not every act or measure which adversely affects moral or physical integrity will interfere with the right to respect to private life guaranteed by Article 8. However, the Court's case-law does not exclude that treatment which does not reach the severity of Article 3 treatment may nonetheless breach Article 8 in its private life aspect where there are sufficiently adverse effects on physical and moral integrity.

e 47. Private life is a broad term not susceptible to exhaustive definition. The Court has already held that elements such as gender identification, name and sexual orientation and sexual life are important elements of the personal sphere protected by Article 8. Mental health must also be regarded as a crucial part of private life associated with the aspect of moral integrity. Article 8 protects a right to identity and personal development, and the right to establish and develop relationships with other human beings and the

f outside world. The preservation of mental stability is in that context an indispensable precondition to effective enjoyment of the right to respect for private life.

48. Turning to the present case, the Court recalls that it has found above that the risk of damage to the applicant's health from return to his country

g of origin was based on largely hypothetical factors and that it was not substantiated that he would suffer inhuman and degrading treatment. Nor in the circumstances has it been established that his moral integrity would be substantially affected to a degree falling within the scope of Article 8 of the Convention. Even assuming that the dislocation caused to the applicant by removal from the United Kingdom where he has lived for the last eleven

h years was to be considered by itself as affecting his private life, in the context of the relationships and support framework which he enjoyed there, the Court considers that such interference may be regarded as complying with the requirements of the second paragraph of Article 8, namely as a measure "in accordance with the law", pursuing the aims of the protection of the

j economic well-being of the country and the prevention of disorder and crime, as well as being "necessary in a democratic society" for those aims.'

[46] Part of the reasoning of the court suggests that the treatment that a deportee is at risk of experiencing in the receiving state might so severely interfere with his art 8 rights as to render his deportation contrary to the convention. The more significant art 8 factor was, however, the disruption of

private life within this country. There is a difference in principle between the
situation where art 8 rights are engaged in whole or in part because of the effect
of removal in disrupting an individual's established enjoyment of those rights
within this jurisdiction and the situation where art 8 rights are alleged to be
engaged solely on the ground of the treatment that the individual is likely to be
subjected to in the receiving state. In *Bensaid*'s case the court considered that the
right to control immigration constituted a valid ground under art 8(2) for
derogating from the art 8 rights of the applicant in that case.

[47] We shall now set out our conclusions in relation to the Strasbourg
jurisprudence that deals with the apprehended treatment of a deportee in the
receiving state. The application of art 3 in expulsion cases is an extension of the
scope of the convention and one that is at odds with the principle of territoriality
expressed in art 1. That extension has occurred because the human rights
convention is a living instrument. The extension no doubt reflects the fact that it
would affront the humanitarian principles that underlie the human rights
convention and the refugee convention for a state to remove an individual to a
country where he or she is foreseeably at real risk of being seriously ill-treated.
To date, with the possible exception of *Bensaid*'s case, the application of this
extension has been restricted to art 3 cases. To apply the principle to other
articles where the apprehended treatment would fall short of that covered by
art 3 would be likely to constitute a further extension. While the Strasbourg
court has contemplated the possibility of such a step, it has not yet taken it. The
obligations in ss 3 and 6 of the 1998 Act do not require this court to take that
further step. We turn now to consider the approach that has been taken by the
English courts.

THE DOMESTIC JURISPRUDENCE

[48] The possibility that an immigration decision may engage the human
rights convention is recognised by ss 65 and 77(3) of the Immigration and Asylum
Act 1999. The latter subsection provides:

'In considering—(a) any ground mentioned in section 69, or (b) any
question relating to the appellant's rights under Article 3 of the Human
Rights Convention, the appellate authority may take into account any
evidence which it considers to be relevant to the appeal (including evidence
about matters arising after the date on which the decision appealed against
was taken).'

This demonstrates that Parliament has accepted that immigration decisions can
engage art 3 of the human rights convention. It also demonstrates that
Parliament has not accepted that immigration decisions can engage other articles
of the convention. We do not consider that it demonstrates that Parliament has
accepted that immigration decisions *cannot* engage other articles of the
convention—see the discussion in *Secretary of State for the Home Dept v S and K*
(3 December 2002, unreported) considered at [57], below.

[49] *Secretary of State for the Home Dept v Z* [2001] EWCA Civ 952, [2002] Imm
AR 560 was an appeal from a decision of the Immigration Appeal Tribunal which
had ruled unlawful the removal of the respondent to Zimbabwe. It was common
ground that the decision of the tribunal in the case of Z could not stand. The
appeal in Z's case was heard with two others that raised similar issues. Each
involved an application by a man who claimed to be a homosexual. Apart from
claims to asylum under the refugee convention, each claimed that removal to

a   Zimbabwe would violate both arts 3 and 8 of the human rights convention. This was because in Zimbabwe 'living the sort of sexual life which he would wish to live has been subjected to various social and statutory inhibitions' (see [2002] Imm AR 560 at 564 (para 8) per Schiemann LJ). Schiemann LJ, with whose judgment the other two members of the court agreed, did not have to do more than consider whether it was arguable that art 3 or art 8 was engaged. So far as

b   art 3 was concerned, he held (at 566 (para 16)):

> 'Circumstances can undoubtedly exist in which the treatment which awaits a claimant in a destination state is of a severity which would cause a state to be in breach of a claimant's art 3 rights if it expelled him to that destination State. I would not rule out the possibility that amongst those
> c   circumstances might be treatment which was aimed at a particular sexual group. However, I do not consider that the mere existence of a law in the destination state prohibiting particular types of sexual conduct in private amongst adults has the automatic result that an expelling state which wishes to expel a person who wishes to indulge in that type of sexual conduct is breaching his rights under article 3.'

d
[50] So far as art 8 is concerned, Schiemann LJ concluded that the question was fact-specific and should not be decided in the abstract. In the case of both Z and A the matter was remitted to the tribunal. Schiemann LJ clearly considered that it was possible that art 8 was engaged by the decision to remove each of them, but we do not consider that his judgment is conclusive of this question.

e
[51] In R (on the application of Holub) v Secretary of State for the Home Dept [2001] 1 WLR 1359 the Court of Appeal had to consider a claim that the removal of a schoolgirl to Poland would interfere with her right to education under art 2 of the First Protocol. In giving the judgment of the court, Tuckey LJ made this observation (at 1366 (para 21)):

f
> 'We are not bound to follow the decisions of the European Court of Human Rights but simply to take them into account. Nevertheless the jurisprudence of the court does point clearly to the fact that rights which are not absolute, such as the right to education, are not engaged where a state is exercising legitimate immigration control. Accordingly we think
> g   Mr Pleming's submissions on this issue are right. A child's right to education whilst it is in the United Kingdom does not carry with it the right to stay here. The Secretary of State has obviously to take account of any educational difficulties which it is alleged the child will suffer if returned to the country of origin as part of the compassionate grounds for granting exceptional leave to remain, but is not obliged to take a view as to whether the child's article 2
> h   right will be infringed there. However, in the spirit of restraint to which we have referred, we do not think it is necessary to decide this point authoritatively in this case, in view of our decision on the other issues to which we now turn.'

j   He went on to consider whether art 2 was infringed and held that it was not.
[52] In R (on the application of Ahmadi) v Secretary of State for the Home Dept [2002] EWHC 1897 (Admin), [2002] All ER (D) 52 (Sep), [2003] ACD 14 Scott Baker J had to consider the issue of whether removal to Germany of a family of refugees from Afghanistan was contrary to the human rights convention. Germany was the country responsible for entertaining their application for asylum under the Convention determining the State responsible for examining Applications for

Asylum lodged in one of the Member States of the European Communities
(Dublin; TS 72 (1997); Cm 3806). They claimed, however, that removal to *a*
Germany would infringe arts 3, 8 and 14 of the human rights convention. The
evidence relied upon in the case of Mrs Ahmadi sought to demonstrate that the
contrast between the family's living conditions in this country and in Germany
would damage her fragile mental health and, thus, infringe her art 8 rights.
Reliance was placed on, among other matters, evidence that, in the words of her *b*
consultant psychiatrist (at [44]–[45]):

> 'She has been allowed to develop a social network that has helped to
> support her ... she has now been in the UK long enough to develop a positive
> and supportive social network ... I do believe that if returned she will
> deteriorate markedly if only because of the loss of her social network.' *c*

[53] No issue was raised as to whether, in principle, art 8 could be engaged.
The issue was simply as to whether, on the facts, the claim under the convention
was 'manifestly unfounded'. Scott Baker J decided that in the case of Mrs Ahmadi
it was not—there was a case to go before the adjudicator.

[54] So far as the children were concerned, greater emphasis appears to have *d*
been placed on the effect on them of the conditions in Germany, and Scott
Baker J expressly held that this was material. He held that, in considering the
art 8 claim, it was necessary to 'look at this family as a whole' and ruled that the
children also had an arguable case under art 8.

[55] It remains to consider three starred appeals to the tribunal. The first, *e*
Kacaj v Secretary of State for the Home Dept [2002] Imm AR 213, was reversed by the
Court of Appeal on the facts ([2002] EWCA Civ 314, [2002] All ER (D) 203 (Mar)),
but without comment on the tribunal's analysis of the law. The applicant
claimed asylum under the refugee convention and the right to remain on the
ground that return to her native country of Albania would infringe arts 3, 4 and
8 of the human rights convention. The Secretary of State contended that only *f*
art 3 was capable of being engaged by an immigration decision, relying in part on
the observation of this court in *R (on the application of Holub) v Secretary of State for
the Home Dept* [2001] 1 WLR 1359 that we have quoted at [51], above. In the
judgment of the tribunal, Collins J ([2002] Imm AR 213 at 228) analysed the
position as follows: *g*

> '25. With great respect to the Court of Appeal, we are not persuaded that
> the rights are not engaged in immigration cases. That in our view is contrary
> to [*Soering v UK* (1989) 11 EHRR 439]. The true analysis is that, although the
> rights may be engaged, legitimate immigration control will almost certainly
> mean that derogation from the rights will be proper and will not be *h*
> disproportionate. There may be exceptions, as the reference in *Soering* to
> flagrant breaches of article 6 indicate. This is because the court has
> recognised that a country is entitled, "as a matter of well-established
> international law and subject to their treaty obligations including the
> Convention, to control the entry, residence and expulsion of aliens". (See *j*
> *Hilal v United Kingdom* ((2001) 11 BHRC 354) at paragraph 59). In *Salazar v
> Sweden* (App No 28987/95 (7 March 1996, unreported)) the Commission
> observed: "In the field of immigration Contracting States enjoy a wide
> margin of appreciation in determining the steps to be taken to ensure
> compliance with the Convention, with due regard to the needs and
> resources of the community and of individuals." Among other cases, it cites

Abdulaziz v United Kingdom (1985) 7 EHRR 471, which concerned an alleged breach of article 8 in the refusal to permit the applicant to join his family in the United Kingdom. The Court decided that article 8 could apply where immigration control was being enforced but that in the circumstances of that case there was no breach.

26. We therefore see no reason to exclude the possible application of any relevant article (save, perhaps article 2 if the reasoning in [*Dehwari v Netherlands* (2001) 29 EHRR CD 74] is to be followed) in deportation cases, but it will be virtually impossible for an applicant to establish that control on immigration was disproportionate to any breach. In particular, if article 3 is not established, it is difficult to see how article 8 could be if, as in this instant case, the alleged breach will occur in the receiving state when the applicant is removed. In the context of this case, the adjudicator was in error in concluding that article 4 could not be relied on because it did not, as he put it, have extra-territorial effect. That definition is misleading since there is no question of extra-territorial effect in the true sense of that word since the breach, if any, will have occurred within the jurisdiction by the decision to remove which will have the effect of exposing the individual to whatever violation of his human rights is in issue. We have used the word as a convenient label for the argument, but, for the reasons given, we reject the argument.'

[56] Shortly after this decision, the appeal in *Devaseelan v Secretary of State for the Home Dept* (13 March 2002, unreported) was heard by a tribunal presided over by Mr Mark Ockelton. The appellant, a Tamil, contended that removal to Sri Lanka would infringe his rights under arts 3, 5, 6 and 8 of the human rights convention. The tribunal ruled out any danger of infringement of arts 3 and 8 on the facts. So far as the alleged engagement of arts 5 and 6 were concerned, the tribunal said this:

'110. ... It is clear that the Court does not attempt to impose the duties of the Convention on States that are not party to it. It is also clear that the fact that a person may be treated in a manner that would, in a signatory State, be a breach of the Convention does not of itself render his expulsion to another country unlawful, unless *either* the breach will be of Article 3, *or* the consequences of return will be so extreme a breach of another Article that the returning State, as one of its obligations under the Convention, is obliged to have regard to them. Following the jurisprudence on Articles 5 and 6, this consequence will only arise if the situation in the receiving country is that there will be a flagrant denial or gross violation of the rights secured by the Convention. For this reason we have not needed to consider in this determination the precise implications of Articles 5 and 6 within signatory States.

111. The reason why flagrant denial or gross violation is to be taken into account is that it is only in such a case—where the right will be completely denied or nullified in the destination country—that it can be said that removal will breach the treaty obligations of the signatory State however those obligations might be interpreted or whatever might be said by or on behalf of the destination State.'

[57] In *Secretary of State for the Home Dept v S and K* (3 December 2002, unreported), the tribunal presided over by Collins J considered, among other

issues, the effect of the 1998 Act on the proposed removal to Croatia of a number
of ethnic Serbs. The tribunal made the following comments in relation to s 77 of   a
the 1999 Act:

> '21. Section 6 of the 1998 Act requires the appellate authority as a public
> authority (see s 6(3)(a)) to act in a way which is compatible with a
> convention right. This obligation does not apply if "as a result of one or
> more provisions of primary legislation, the authority could not have acted   b
> differently" (see s 6(2)(a)). Section 3 of the 1998 Act requires us to read and
> give effect to legislation so far as possible in a way which is compatible with
> the convention rights. To make a determination which upholds a decision
> to return in breach of human rights could, subject to the impact of primary
> legislation, breach s 6. It is important to note the language of and relationship   c
> between s 77(3) and (4). In s 77(3) a distinction is drawn between a "ground
> mentioned in s 69" and a question relating to rights under art 3. Section 77(4)
> refers to consideration of "any other ground" not to consideration of other
> questions arising. The differences in wording must be taken to have been
> deliberate. We are well aware that the Home Office view was (and the
> argument has been raised by Mr Wilken in his skeleton but not developed   d
> because of our decision in [*Kacaj v Secretary of State for the Home Dept* [2002]
> Imm AR 213]) that only art 3 could be relied on in removal cases. It is
> therefore not surprising that Parliament should have wanted to leave the
> matter open, particularly in the light of indications in *Soering v UK* (1989) 11
> EHRR 439 that art 6 certainly might be relied on in such cases. Parliament   e
> no doubt recognised the absurdities and contradictions of its "one-stop"
> policy which would arise otherwise and it is incidentally to be noted that the
> matter is put beyond doubt in the [Nationality, Immigration and Asylum Act
> 2002] which has just been passed.
> 22. In our judgment s 77(4) does not in appeals concerned with potential
> removals from the United Kingdom prevent consideration of any question   f
> relating to an appellant's rights under any article of the human rights
> convention as at the date of hearing.'

[58] The two decisions of the Court of Appeal that we have cited are
inconclusive on the question of whether an expulsion decision can engage articles   g
other than art 3 on the ground of the treatment to be anticipated in the receiving
state. In *R (on the application of Ahmadi) v Secretary of State for the Home Dept* [2002]
All ER (D) 52 (Sep), [2003] ACD 14 no issue was raised as to whether on the facts,
which bore similarities to those in *Bensaid v UK* (2001) 33 EHRR 205, art 8 was
capable of being engaged. The decisions of the tribunal accept that other articles
can be engaged in principle, although, in *Devaseelan v Secretary of State for the Home*   h
Dept (13 March 2002, unreported), only where a flagrant violation is anticipated.
In *Kacaj v Secretary of State for the Home Dept* [2002] Imm AR 213, Collins J
considered that the right to control immigration would almost inevitably
outweigh any interference with a convention right other than one arising under
art 3. These decisions are not binding on this court. There is no domestic   j
authority which requires us to hold that where an alien is removed to a country
where his right to practise his religion is inhibited, art 9 will, or can, be engaged.

ARTICLE 9
[59] Both Mr Blake and Mr Gill urged the importance of art 9 rights. They
submitted that they were 'fundamental' or 'core' rights under the human rights

a convention. In support of this submission they referred us to the following statement of principle by the court in *Kokkinakis v Greece* (1994) 17 EHRR 397 at 418 (para 31):

> *b* 'As enshrined in Article 9, freedom of thought, conscience and religion is one of the foundations of a "democratic society" within the meaning of the Convention. It is, in its religious dimension, one of the most vital elements that go to make up the identity of believers and of their conception of life, but it is also a precious asset for atheists, agnostics, sceptics and the unconcerned. The pluralism indissociable from a democratic society, which has been dearly won over the centuries, depends on it. While religious freedom is primarily a matter of individual conscience, it also implies, *inter* *c* *alia*, freedom to "manifest [one's] religion." Bearing witness in words and deeds is bound up with the existence of religious convictions. According to Article 9, freedom to manifest one's religion is not only exercisable in community with others, "in public" and within the circle of those whose faith one shares, but can also be asserted "alone" and "in private"; furthermore, it includes in principle the right to try to convince one's *d* neighbour, for example through "teaching", failing which, moreover, "freedom to change [one's] religion or belief," enshrined in Article 9, would be likely to remain a dead letter.'

[60] Counsel emphasised that art 9 rights are, to a degree, absolute. It is only the freedom to manifest one's religion or beliefs that can, in pursuance of the *e* prescribed aims, be limited. They referred us to Professor Hathaway's *The Law of Refugee Status* (1991) p 109. There the author identifies 'basic and inalienable rights' and comments: 'the failure to ensure these rights in any circumstances is ... appropriately considered to be tantamount to persecution'. The rights identified include 'freedom of thought, conscience and religion'.

f [61] We recognise that ill-treatment of a member of a religious minority is capable of amounting to persecution under the refugee convention or to infringement of art 3 rights—see, for instance, *Ahmed v Secretary of State for the Home Dept* [2000] INLR 1. Mr Ullah's contention that his case fell into this category did not succeed and is not the subject of this appeal. We have yet to explain why Miss Do's claim under the refugee convention is not made out. *g* What we are currently considering is, in effect, a submission that the 1998 Act and the convention require this country to grant asylum to anyone who can demonstrate that his freedom to practise his religion is not respected in his home country, though Mr Blake adds the proviso that the interference with that freedom must be 'severe'.

h [62] Mr Blake accepted that the Strasbourg court has not gone this far. He submitted, however, that this court should take the lead in recognising that removal in the interests of immigration control can engage art 9. In our judgment there are compelling reasons why this court should not do so. The refugee convention and art 3 of the human rights convention already cater for the *j* more severe categories of ill-treatment on the ground of religion. The extension of grounds for asylum that Mr Blake and Mr Gill seek to establish would open the door to claims to enter this country by a potentially very large new category of asylum seeker. It is not for the court to take such a step. It is for the executive, or for Parliament, to decide whether to offer refuge in this country to persons who are not in a position to claim this under the refugee convention, or the human rights convention as currently applied by the Strasbourg court. There may be strong humanitarian grounds for offering refuge in this country to individuals whose human rights are not respected in their own country, and it is open to the Secretary of State to grant exceptional leave to remain where he concludes that the facts justify this course. There are, however, practical and political considerations which weigh against any general extension of the grounds upon which refuge may be sought in this country. It is not for the courts to make that extension.

[63] For these reasons we hold that a removal decision to a country that does not respect art 9 rights will not infringe the 1998 Act where the nature of the interference with the right to practise religion that is anticipated in the receiving state falls short of art 3 ill-treatment. It may be that this does not differ greatly, in effect, from holding that interference with the right to practise religion in such circumstances will not result in the engagement of the human rights convention unless the interference is 'flagrant'.

OTHER ARTICLES

[64] This appeal is concerned with art 9. Our reasoning has, however, wider implications. Where the human rights convention is invoked on the sole ground of the treatment to which an alien, refused the right to enter or remain, is likely to be subjected by the receiving state, and that treatment is not sufficiently severe to engage art 3, the English court is not required to recognise that any other article of the human rights convention is, or may be, engaged. Where such treatment falls outside art 3, there may be cases which justify the grant of exceptional leave to remain on humanitarian grounds. The decision of the Secretary of State in such cases will be subject to the ordinary principles of judicial review but not to the constraints of the human rights convention.

[65] Our conclusion renders it unnecessary to consider further the facts of Mr Ullah's case, for it has already been determined that these do not engage art 3. We would simply observe that most of the matters urged by Mr Blake in relation to the facts applied to all Ahmadis in Pakistan. Mr Ullah's special position as a preacher added little to his case in the light of the adjudicator's finding that his preaching 'did not result in any serious problems for him'. In Miss Do's case, her claim under the refugee convention as well as her claim under art 3 remain to be considered, in addition to her claim under art 9. We turn to the facts of her case.

MISS DO'S APPEAL

[66] Miss Do's more extreme allegations of harassment and arrest by the police were not accepted. Before the tribunal it was submitted on her behalf that the adjudicator's finding that Miss Do could only practise her religion 'under reduced circumstances' was enough to make good her case. This was because this constituted an infringement of a 'basic' or 'first category' right from which there could be no derogation. The grounds of appeal to this court focused largely on the allegation that Miss Do would have to curtail that part of her religious activities which consisted of teaching her faith to children if she returned to Vietnam. It was submitted that this was an inhibition on her core right to practise her religion, which infringed art 9(1) and could not be justified under art 9(2). If apprehension of a 'flagrant' violation of her right was the correct test, then that test was satisfied.

[67] The evidence does not indicate that there is a total embargo on teaching the Catholic faith in Vietnam. It does establish that, if Miss Do wishes to continue to do this, she may have to move from her home to a different part of the country.

a Such inhibition as this might place on her right to practise her religion falls far short of persecution under the refugee convention or ill-treatment that violates art 3 of the human rights convention. There is evidence of other restrictions on the practice of Catholicism as a minority religion in Vietnam, but these are applicable to all of that minority, which has the sizeable total of some eight million. Mr Gill was wise not to press these points. That part of Miss Do's *b* case was not, and could not be, made out.

[68] Miss Do's case based on art 9 fails in consequence of our finding that art 9 is not engaged by her proposed removal. We wish, however, to draw attention to a paradox in her case which struck us from the outset. In so far as she was prevented from teaching Christianity to children in Vietnam, she did nothing to improve her position by coming to this country. Had she been an English *c* missionary and had the Vietnamese authorities deported her to this country, she would have had a stronger case of interference with her right to teach Catholicism than that which she advances. We put this paradox to Mr Gill at the start of the hearing. It was not one which appeared to have occurred to those instructing him. They at once set about inquiring whether there was an answer *d* to it. If it transpired that Miss Do had a burning desire to proselytise the Catholic faith no matter where she found herself the paradox would be shown to be illusory. This proved not to be the case. Miss Do has been in this country about two years. She attends mass at a church in Tottenham every Sunday. She asked the assistant priest whether she could help in any way with the parish's teaching of young children. He declined on the basis that her English was not good *e* enough for her to be of any real use to him. She did not persist in attempting to teach, although she provided the assistant priest with some general assistance in the parish. This picture is at odds with the suggestion that Miss Do came to England in order to be able to continue to teach her faith. The paradox remains.

[69] We do not see that the 'reduced circumstances' under which Miss Do was *f* practising her faith in Vietnam differ significantly from those encountered by the other eight million Catholics in that country. This merely underlines the implications that would follow were it correct that the decision to remove her to Vietnam engaged art 9 of the human rights convention.

[70] As it is, for the reasons that we have given, the appeals of both Mr Ullah and Miss Do must be dismissed.
g

Appeals dismissed. Permission to appeal to the House of Lords granted.

Kate O'Hanlon   Barrister.

h

ANNEX A

*Relevant findings of the immigration adjudicator, Mrs Nichols, in relation to
Mr Ullah's asylum application*

j 35. In summary therefore I find that although the appellant's family may well have been subjected to general harassment and verbal abuse in recent years, perhaps because it has become known in the community the appellant preaches, there is no credible evidence that he has in fact suffered from serious incidents of violence which the police have been unwilling to investigate. The appellant and his family remained living in Karachi during the whole of this period. The appellant's family are still living in Karachi and do not appear to be experiencing

any serious problems, although I accept that his children may continue to be
abused at school. His father lives in Karachi as does his wife's family and there is
no evidence that they suffer any particular problems. The appellant has never
been subjected to any state investigation as a result of his preaching; he has never
been arrested nor detained for any reason at all. He claims to have been a
successful businessman, even to the extent of being able to restart a business in
Karachi with no apparent difficulty and yet he produces no evidence about his
business activities. He had no problems at all until the age of 42 and has been able
to carry on his faith all of his life without serious hindrance. This evidence must
be viewed against the background evidence of serious discrimination against
some followers of the Ahmadi faith in their work and daily lives and serious
interference in their ability to follow and practise their faith. There is no credible
evidence that this has been the position in relation to this appellant. Having
regard to the evidence in totality, I have come to the conclusion that the appellant
has come to the United Kingdom for reasons other than the need to seek
international protection.

36. The appellant has therefore not established that he has in fact been
persecuted in the past on account of his faith and neither has he established that
he would face a serious risk of persecution, in his particular circumstances, if he
returns to Pakistan now. I see no reason why the appellant cannot return to
Karachi to his wife and children where on his own account it is open to him to
continue his business activities and, importantly, in his case, the evidence
strongly supports the finding that he will be able to carry on his faith as before, as
his family appear to do so currently. Even accepting that he began to preach in
1998, for the reasons I have already given, I do not find that in his case that did
result in any serious problems for him. He is an ordinary member of the
Ahmadiyya faith; he has not come to the attention of the authorities on account
of his faith; has no credible evidence that he has been targeted by religious
extremists for that reason and no evidence on which to properly conclude that he
would face such problems in the future.

ANNEX B

*Relevant findings of the immigration adjudicator, Mrs Nichols, in relation to
Mr Ullah's claim under the Human Rights Act 1998*

In relation to arts 9, 10 and 11 (freedom of thought, conscience and religion and
expression and freedom of assembly and association) it is clear from the
background evidence that the ability of Ahmadis to exercise their free rights
under these articles are constrained by the law and by societal attitudes towards
them and that state action is generally ineffective. In relation to the appellant
however, these rights do have to be regarded in the context of the evidence
before me, which as I have said, has led to my finding that he has not personally
experienced to any serious degree some of the problems which are faced by many
Ahmadis in Pakistan. I have referred to the background evidence included in the
appellant's bundle and to two further fairly recent reports in late 2000 from
Amnesty International concerning the stepping up of campaigns against
minorities in the country. The background evidence also supports the conclusion
that the government continues to express its opposition to discrimination against
religious minorities although, I accept, that this may just be words as opposed to
action. I have concluded that in the context of these articles, that is that they
enshrine an individual's right to express his beliefs in public or private and to

a   manifest his beliefs in worship, teaching practice and observance and to share ideas and information concerning his or her opinions and also to have the freedom of peaceful assembly, that returning the appellant to Pakistan where those rights are curtailed, does engage those articles under the convention in the appellant's case. These articles are qualified articles and I must therefore consider whether or not the United Kingdom government's action in returning the

b   appellant would be in breach of those articles by a reference to a three-stage test, that is: whether or not the respondent's action is in accordance with the law; whether it pursues a legitimate aim; and whether or not it is proportionate in relation to the prospective breach. It is my finding that the respondent's action is in accordance with the law in that he has made his decisions in accordance with immigration legislation and the decisions he has made comply with statutory

c   requirements. I also find that the respondent is pursuing a legitimate aim, that is immigration control which is a state's right. The appellant will be returned to a society where he is regarded as a religious minority and he is not afforded the same rights as the majority. Nevertheless, for the reasons I have already given in his particular circumstances, that has not prevented him from carrying on his

d   faith nor has it prevented his family. He has been preaching since 1998 and the authorities have taken no action against him. He has been a life-long Ahmadi, he was born into an Ahmadi family and neither he nor his family appear to have suffered any direct discrimination from the state. He has been successful in business; his children have been educated and apart from incidents of verbal abuse in the streets and minor violence there is no credible evidence of any

e   serious problems. His family remain in Karachi and there is no evidence that they are experiencing any real difficulties. I have therefore come to the conclusion that the United Kingdom government's action in seeking to remove the appellant to Pakistan in pursuance of the need for proper immigration control, and in the light of my findings in this case, will not breach the appellant's right under these

f   articles as that action is proportionate to any difficulties the appellant may face as a result of his faith on return to Pakistan.

ANNEX C

g   *Relevant findings of the immigration adjudicator, Mrs Coleman, in relation to Miss Do's asylum application*

     14. The respondent refused the claim saying that he did not believe that the appellant was a Roman Catholic. This was based on the fact that the appellant appeared to have little knowledge of Roman Catholicism and her replies to technical questions were inadequate. That evidence has now been rebutted in

h   three ways. The first way is the fact that a lot of the evidence was simply based on mistranslation. I can say from my own experience at the hearing that this is a problem. Clearly the Vietnamese interpreters available in this country are all Buddhist with little or no knowledge of Christian terminology. They were unable to translate what she was saying either in interview or at the hearing. For

j   this reason I put little weight on some of the answers. Further the appellant has now produced two important pieces of evidence that strongly support her claim. The first is the photographic evidence. And clear evidence that the appellant was given first Holy Communion in the Catholic Church and confirmed into that Church. I find that unassailable evidence of her membership of the Catholic Church. Finally her evidence is supported by the Vietnamese priest being the Reverend Simon Thag Duc Nguyen who submitted a witness statement. That

witness statement indicates that the appellant is a strong supporter of the
Catholic faith and her lack of knowledge of Catholic tenets would be expected
from someone brought up in Vietnam under the repressive regime which did not
allow good religious instruction. On that basis I accept that the appellant has
proved to the necessary standard that she was a member of the Catholic Church
and that she practised the Catholic religion in Vietnam.

15. The appellant has also claimed that she found it difficult to practice her
religion because of the attitude of the authorities in Vietnam. I have described
above the ways in which she said she was disadvantaged. I have considered that
evidence in the light of the objective evidence. The objective evidence does show
that there are problems with certain religions. Up until recently religions were
banned but that has been changed and the constitution now provides for freedom
of worship. However the United States Department of State report says:
'Government regulations control religious hierarchies and organised religious
activities in part because the Community Party fears that organised religion may
weaken its authority and influence.' The report also says:

> 'Many of these restrictive powers lie principally with provincial city
> people's committees and local treatment of religious persons varied widely
> ... In other areas such as the north-west provinces local officials allowed
> believers little discretion in practising their faith. In general religious groups
> face difficulties in obtaining teaching materials, expanding training facilities,
> publishing religious materials, and expanding the clergy in training in
> response to the increased demand from the congregation.'

In those circumstances the appellant's evidence of difficulties in following her
faith and discrimination are supported by the evidence and I accept the same.

16. The appellant has also belatedly claimed that the police had questioned her
and taken her to the station on a number of occasions. Although I have generally
accepted the appellant's evidence I do not accept this evidence. This evidence is
in direct contradiction to her original interview and statement. Her statement
never mentioned any question of a problem with the police. The statement was
detailed and such an omission seems to me surprising, to say the least, if it were
true. Further in interview she very specifically said that she had never been
arrested although she did say that there were difficulties with the police over the
religion. However, that reference was only to discriminatory steps being taken.
I therefore find it highly suspicious that suddenly just before the hearing, and after
the criticism of her claim in the refusal letter relating to lack of arrests, she adds a
claim that she has been harassed by the police and taken to the police station.
Further I cannot understand the distinction she is trying to make between being
arrested and being invited to go to the police station and being taken there. The
evidence itself was contradictory as to whether she ever went to a police station
or not. I simply believe that this is an embellishment to the claim and I do not
accept the appellant's evidence in that regard at all ...

18. I have considered the objective evidence in the light of the arguments
before me. I do not find that the objective evidence supports the appellant's
claim. The Home Office Country Information and Policy Unit report, the United
States Department of State International Religious Freedom report and the
United States Department of State report all indicate that Roman Catholicism is
a recognised religion by the government of Vietnam. Although there certainly is
some discrimination against religious practices and efforts to minimise their
effect, there is absolutely no evidence that persons are actually persecuted.

a Certainly there is no evidence of widespread arrests. There is evidence of arrests of certain political and religious dissidents but the objective evidence makes it clear that those religious dissidents are not Roman Catholic. There are some Buddhists, Protestants and something called a Hoa Hoa Sect which have been targeted. However, there is no evidence at all that Roman Catholics are at risk of persecution. The sort of behaviour the appellant specified in her statement is

b discrimination. It does not affect her basic rights. She can still practice her religion albeit under reduced circumstances and her rights to earning a living, physical safety and her right to shelter are not compromised. In those circumstances such disadvantages as she does suffer because of her faith do not cross the line from discrimination to persecution. For all these reasons therefore I find that the appellant has not proved to the necessary standard that she is likely

c to be persecuted or arrested if she were returned to Vietnam because of her religion. I therefore dismiss the asylum appeal.

Flightline Ltd v Edwards and another

[2003] EWCA Civ 63

COURT OF APPEAL, CIVIL DIVISION
WARD, LAWS AND JONATHAN PARKER LJJ
16 JANUARY, 5 FEBRUARY 2003

Practice – Order – Consent order – Claimant obtaining freezing order against defendant – Debt owed to defendant by third party being paid into account held by parties' solicitors – Court discharging freezing order by consent on undertaking by defendant not to withdraw or dispose of money in account – Whether terms of consent order giving claimant charge over money in account.

On commencing an action to recover £4,200,000, the claimant obtained a freezing order restraining the defendant company from dealing with its assets up to the value of the sum claimed. The company sought the discharge of that order, but the hearing was adjourned, and the freezing order continued, on agreed terms that were embodied in a consent order. Those terms included a provision that, pending the adjourned hearing, a debtor of the company was to be at liberty to pay a sum of £4,200,000 out of the moneys owed by it to the company into an account in the joint names of the parties' solicitors, and that no sums were to be withdrawn from that account pending further order of the court or the written consent of the parties' solicitors. After the £4,200,000 had been paid into the account, the parties compromised the interlocutory dispute on terms which were incorporated in another consent order (the discharge order) discharging the freezing order. Those terms included an undertaking by the company not to withdraw, dispose of, deal with or encumber its interest in the moneys in the account up to a limit of £3,325,000 pending further order of the court or the written consent of the parties' solicitors. Subsequently, provisional liquidators of the company were appointed. That appointment precluded the claimant from continuing its action without the leave of the court. The claimant duly sought leave. The success of that application depended on the claimant having, as against the liquidators, a valid charge over the moneys in the account. The judge allowed the application, holding that the claimant had such a charge to secure any judgment which it might obtain in the action up to a maximum of £3,325,000. On the liquidators' appeal, the Court of Appeal considered whether the discharge order had in fact created such a charge or whether it had simply provided continuing interim protection in the nature of a freezing order—a form of relief which created no proprietary rights in the assets that were subject to it.

Held – A consent order, embodying a term agreed between the parties that the debtor would not withdraw or dispose of or deal with its interest in moneys in an account, did not give rise to a security right in relation to that fund unless it contained an obligation in favour of the creditor to pay the debt out of the fund. A freezing order created no such right over the assets from time to time subject to it precisely because such an order, without more, did not impose an obligation on the part of a respondent to satisfy any judgment debt out of those assets. In the instant case, it was impossible to spell out of the terms of the discharge order a provision to the effect that the company had to satisfy any judgment obtained by the claimant (up to the specified maximum of £3,325,000). There was nothing a on the face of the discharge order to indicate anything other than an intention to provide continuing interim protection of a 'freezing' nature. Accordingly, the discharge order did not confer any security right on the claimant, and the appeal would therefore be allowed (see [43], [47]–[49], [53], below).

Palmer v Carey [1926] All ER Rep 650 applied.

b **Notes**

For money paid into an account for a special purpose, see 3(1) *Halsbury's Laws* (4th edn reissue) para 156.

Cases referred to in judgment

c *Agnew v Comr of Inland Revenue* [2001] UKPC 28, [2001] 2 BCLC 188, [2001] 2 AC 710, [2001] 3 WLR 454.

Cretanor Maritime Co Ltd v Irish Marine Management Ltd [1978] 3 All ER 164, [1978] 1 WLR 966, CA.

Ford, Re, ex p the trustee [1900] 2 QB 211.

d *Halvanon Insurance Co Ltd v Central Reinsurance Corp* [1988] 3 All ER 857, [1988] 1 WLR 1122.

Investors Compensation Scheme v West Bromwich Building Society, Investors Compensation Scheme Ltd v Hopkin & Sons (a firm), Alford v West Bromwich Building Society, Armitage v West Bromwich Building Society [1998] 1 All ER 98, [1998] 1 WLR 896, HL.

e *Mordant, Re, Mordant v Halls* [1997] 2 FCR 378.

Multi Guarantee Co Ltd, Re [1987] BCLC 257, CA.

Palmer v Carey [1926] AC 703, [1926] All ER Rep 650, PC; *rvsg sub nom Carey v Palmer* (1924) 34 CLR 380, Aust HC.

f *Rodick v Gandell* (1852) 1 De GM & G 763, 42 ER 749, LC.

Sherratt (WA) Ltd v John Bromley (Church Stretton) Ltd [1985] 1 All ER 216, [1985] QB 1038, [1985] 2 WLR 742, CA.

Swiss Bank Corp v Lloyds Bank Ltd [1981] 2 All ER 449, [1982] AC 584, [1981] 2 WLR 893, HL.

g **Appeal**

Nicholas Guy Edwards and James Robert Drummond Smith, the liquidators of Swissair Schweizerische Luftverkehr-Aktiengesellschaft (the company), appealed with permission of Neuberger J from his decision on 2 August 2002 ([2002] EWHC 1648 (Ch), [2003] 1 BCLC 427, [2002] 1 WLR 2535) granting the respondent, Flightline Ltd, leave to continue an action that it had brought against the company. The facts are set out in the judgment of the court.

Martin Pascoe QC and *Lucy Frazer* (instructed by *Lovells*) for the appellants.

j *Gabriel Moss QC* and *Jeremy Goldring* (instructed by *Field Fisher Waterhouse*) for Flightline.

At the conclusion of argument, the court announced that the appeal would be allowed for reasons to be given later.

5 February 2003. The following judgment was delivered.

JONATHAN PARKER LJ.

INTRODUCTION

[1] This is the judgment of the court.

[2] This is an appeal by Mr Nicholas Edwards and Mr James Smith (the appellants), as provisional liquidators of Swissair Schweizerische Luftverkehr-Aktiengesellschaft (the company), against an order made by Neuberger J in the Chancery Division, Companies Court, on 2 August 2002 granting leave to Flightline Ltd (Flightline) pursuant to s 130(2) of the Insolvency Act 1986 to continue an action which it had commenced against the company in the Queen's Bench Division on 16 January 2002. In the action, Flightline claims some £4·2m as money owed to it by the company, alternatively it claims damages. The judge granted permission to appeal.

[3] The judge's judgment ([2002] EWHC 1648 (Ch)) is reported at [2003] 1 BCLC 427, [2002] 1 WLR 2535, and for the purposes of this judgment we shall take it as read.

[4] The substantive issue before the judge, as before us, is whether (as Flightline contends) Flightline has, as against the appellants, a valid charge over moneys standing to the credit of an account at the Bishopsgate branch of the National Westminster Bank plc in the joint names of Allen & Overy and Field Fisher Waterhouse, respectively the former solicitors for the company and the solicitors for Flightline, limited to £3·325m of those moneys. If Flightline has such a charge, with the consequence that it is a secured creditor in respect of any judgment which it may obtain in the action up to a maximum of £3·325m, then it is accepted by the appellants that leave to continue the action should be granted. Conversely, if it has not, then Flightline accepts that such leave should be refused.

[5] The judge concluded that Flightline has a charge over the moneys in the joint account to secure any judgment which it may obtain in the action up to a maximum of £3·325m, and he accordingly granted Flightline leave pursuant to s 130(2) of the 1986 Act to continue the action.

[6] Before the judge, argument was directed solely to the question whether the effect of what took place in relation to the setting up of the joint account was to create the charge for which Flightline contends. On this appeal, however, the appellants seek to raise a further argument, viz that even if a charge was created, such charge is nevertheless void as against the appellants for non-registration pursuant to ss 395 and 396 of the Companies Act 1985.

[7] After hearing full argument on the primary issue as to whether a charge was created, we concluded that that issue should be decided in favour of the appellants and that the appeal should accordingly be allowed. We therefore indicated to Mr Martin Pascoe QC (for the appellants) and Mr Gabriel Moss QC (for Flightline) that we did not need to hear argument on the secondary issue as to non-registration, and that we would give our reasons for allowing the appeal on the primary issue in writing and hand down our judgments in due course. This judgment is accordingly concerned only with the primary issue as to whether a charge was created.

THE FACTUAL BACKGROUND

[8] The company was incorporated in Switzerland. It formed part of the Swissair Group (the group), which provided commercial air services in

a Switzerland and elsewhere. Flightline operated certain routes on behalf of the company.

[9] In October 2001 the group collapsed, and the company repudiated its arrangements with Flightline. Flightline then commenced two actions against the company. The first action related to the period prior to October 2001, and has since been compromised. The second action, which relates to the period after
b October 2001, is the action with which these proceedings are concerned. As already noted, this action was commenced on 16 January 2002, and seeks recovery of a sum of £4·2m. The claim is primarily in debt, but with an alternative claim for damages.

[10] In the meantime, in October 2001 insolvency proceedings were taken against the group in Switzerland. On 5 October 2001 the Swiss court appointed
c a provisional administrator of the group, and in December 2001 it granted a debt restructuring moratorium, the effect of which (under Swiss law) was to restrict the bringing or continuing of actions against companies in the group. We are told that that moratorium is still in place, and that unless some kind of debt restructuring scheme is put in place, the eventual liquidation of the group is
d inevitable.

[11] On the commencement of the action on 16 January 2002, Flightline applied without notice for, and was granted, a freezing order until 6 February 2002 restraining the company from dealing with its assets in England and Wales, up to the value of £4·2m. The order was expressed to extend to the company's interest in any account held by the International Air Transport Association
e (IATA), which at that time owed substantial sums of money to the company. Notwithstanding that the standard form of freezing order as set out in the annex to CPR PD 25 (see now the White Book (*Civil Procedure* (Autumn 2002) vol 1, p 552) provides expressly (para 11(4)) that the freezing order shall cease to have effect if the respondent provides security in a sum to be specified in the order, either by means of a payment into court or by some other agreed method, the
f freezing order as granted (and as subsequently continued) contained no such express provision.

[12] The company indicated that on the return date (6 February 2002) it intended not only to oppose any continuation of the freezing order but also to apply to discharge the order. The application to discharge, if successful, would of
g course have exposed Flightline to liability under its cross-undertakings in the freezing order.

[13] On 6 February 2002 the matter was adjourned to 14 February 2002 with an estimated length of hearing of half a day.

[14] On 14 February 2002 the matter came before McCombe J, but there was
h not time to complete the argument on that day. Accordingly, by his order dated 14 February 2002 (the February order) McCombe J, by consent, adjourned the matter to a date to be fixed and continued the freezing order in the meantime, on agreed terms.

[15] As at 14 February 2002 the company was expecting to receive from the
j IATA, within the next few days, a payment in excess of £4·2m. The company was concerned that the entirety of the IATA moneys should not be frozen, pending the adjourned hearing. In the event it was agreed that, pending the adjourned hearing, the IATA should be at liberty to pay a sum of £4·2m out of moneys owed by it to the company into an account in the joint names of the parties' solicitors, and having done so to release to the company the balance of any moneys owed to the company, and that thereupon the freezing order should immediately cease

to have effect. These terms were duly incorporated in paras 3 and 4 of the
February order. Paragraph 5 of the February order was in the following terms:

'If the sum of [£4·2m] is paid into such joint bank account as referred to in
para 3 of this order, it shall be retained in such account and no sums shall be
withdrawn therefrom pending further order of the court or the written
consent of both [firms of solicitors].'

[16] Shortly after the making of the February order the two firms of solicitors
opened the joint account, which was designated by the bank as a 'Solicitors'
Reserve Account'. It was entitled 'Allen & Overy and Field Fisher Waterhouse
Joint Escrow General Client Account'. On 18 February 2002 £4·2m was paid by
the IATA to Allen & Overy and held by Allen & Overy in its client account. On
20 February 2002 Allen & Overy paid that sum into the joint account.

[17] The date fixed for the adjourned hearing of the matter was 13 March
2002. In the meantime, however, the parties had reached agreement on terms of
compromise of the interlocutory dispute. These terms were incorporated in a
further consent order made by McCombe J on 13 March 2002 (the March order).

[18] The March order was expressed to be made on undertakings by the
parties. Flightline undertook not to apply for a further freezing order over the
company's assets without giving two clear days' written notice of the application.
The company's undertaking was in the following terms (set out in the second
schedule to the March order):

'Not to withdraw or in any way dispose of or deal with or encumber its
interest in the moneys in the [joint account] up to a limit of £3,325,000
pending further order of the court or the written consent of [the two firms
of solicitors].'

[19] The body of the March order (which was expressed to be made by
consent) provided merely that the freezing order be discharged; that the
company's application to discharge it be dismissed; and that there be no order as
to costs. It also contained general liberty to apply.

[20] On 4 April 2002 the appellants were appointed provisional liquidators of
the company. On 16 October 2002 the company was compulsorily wound up
and the appellants were appointed liquidators of the company by the Secretary of
State. It is common ground that at all material times the company was in serious
financial difficulties, and that such difficulties were known to Flightline.

[21] On 28 May 2002 Flightline issued its application pursuant to s 130(2) of
the 1986 Act for leave to continue its action against the company.

SECTION 130(2) OF THE 1986 ACT

[22] Section 130(2) of the 1986 Act provides as follows:

'When a winding-up order has been made or a provisional liquidator has
been appointed, no action or proceeding shall be proceeded with or
commenced against the company or its property, except by leave of the
court and subject to such terms as the court may impose.'

THE JUDGE'S JUDGMENT

[23] After setting out the factual and procedural background, the judge
referred to the two distinct lines of authority which had been cited to him. One
such line of authority (exemplified by *Re Ford, ex p the trustee* [1900] 2 QB 211,

a *WA Sherratt Ltd v John Bromley (Church Stretton) Ltd* [1985] 1 All ER 216, [1985] QB
   1038, *Halvanon Insurance Co Ltd v Central Reinsurance Corp* [1988] 3 All ER 857,
   [1988] 1 WLR 1122 and *Re Mordant, Mordant v Halls* [1997] 2 FCR 378) establishes
   that where money is paid into court by a defendant as a condition of the grant of
   permission to defend the action or as an offer of compromise under the relevant
   procedural rules, or where it is paid into an account out of court but with the
b intention that the same consequences shall follow as if it had been paid into court,
   the claimant has a charge on the money so paid to secure any judgment obtained
   by him in the action. The other line of authority (exemplified by *Cretanor
   Maritime Co Ltd v Irish Marine Management Ltd* [1978] 3 All ER 164, [1978] 1 WLR
   966 and *Re Multi Guarantee Co Ltd* [1987] BCLC 257) establishes that a freezing
   order is relief in personam and creates no proprietary rights in the assets from
c time to time subject to it.

   [24] The judge continued ([2003] 1 BCLC 427, [2002] 1 WLR 2535):

      '[26] The present case is something of a hybrid. On the one hand, as in all
      the cases where the money (whether in court or in a bank account) has been
d   held to be security for the claim, it is, subject to the parties agreeing
      otherwise, under the control of the court, which must mean the court which
      is seised of the action in relation to which the payment has been made. In all
      those cases the money has been treated as security. On the other hand,
      unlike those cases, in this case the money has been paid to discharge, or in
e   substitution for, an order which is non-proprietary. That can therefore be
      said to support the contention that, in accordance with part of the reasoning
      in [the *Multi Guarantee* case], the money should not be treated as security for
      the claimant.

      [27] It would therefore be idle to suggest that the argument raised by
      Mr Pascoe on behalf of the [provisional liquidators], to the effect that
f   [Flightline] cannot claim that the money in the joint account is to be treated
      as security for its claim, has no force. On the contrary: it is an attractive
      argument, which was attractively advanced. None the less, I have reached
      the conclusion that [Flightline's] case is correct, and that the money held in
      the joint account pursuant to the March order is indeed security for any
g   judgment which the applicant may obtain, whether by consent or otherwise,
      in the claim.'

   [25] The judge went on to express his reasons for reaching this conclusion.
   [26] In the first place, the judge noted that the effect of the March order was
   that the money was to be held in the account subject only to what the court
h might order (the judge took the view that the reference to the parties' consent
   added nothing in this respect, since it is always open to the parties to agree how
   to deal with money paid in connection with an action). The judge went on
   (at [28]):

j   'The effect of the March order is, therefore, that the £3.325m is sterilised
      and is beyond the reach of the company, unless and until the court orders
      otherwise. On the face of it, therefore, as with a payment into court (or into
      a joint bank account) in circumstances such as those in [*Re Ford, ex p the
      trustee* [1900] 2 QB 211, *WA Sherratt Ltd v John Bromley (Church Stretton) Ltd*
      [1985] 1 All ER 216, [1985] QB 1038] or [*Re Mordant, Mordant v Halls* [1997] 2
      FCR 378], the money will remain in the joint account until the claim is

disposed of. One would therefore expect it to be available to satisfy any
judgment in the applicant's favour ...'

[27] The judge said:

'[29] The retention of the £3.325m in the joint account pursuant to the
company's undertaking in the March order was agreed in order to discharge
the freezing order. The purpose of the freezing order was to protect
[Flightline] from the risk of being unable to obtain satisfaction of any
judgment it obtained on the claim, owing to dissipation of the company's
assets. It seems to me that, on a sensible, commercial view, what the parties
intended by agreeing the March order was that the freezing order was no
longer necessary because [Flightline] had security for its claim, in the form of
the money in court. The perceived danger of the company dissipating its
assets remained, but, following the March order (and indeed following the
February order) [Flightline] had no ground for maintaining the freezing
order because it was protected by the payment of the money into the joint
account.

[30] It is true that there is nothing in the company's undertaking in the
March order which indicates how the court is to exercise its power to control
the money in the joint account. There is therefore obviously substantial
room for argument that the fact that the money is to be effectively controlled
by the court means that the court should regard it in the same way as it
would regard assets frozen by the freezing order, particularly as the money
was paid into the joint account effectively in substitution for, or to discharge,
the freezing order. However, if that is what the parties had intended, then,
particularly in light of the authorities which I have referred to dealing with
payments into court or into accounts which were in some way to be
controlled by the court, in the context of cases which are already underway,
one would have expected them to spell it out. Thus, it does not seem likely
that, after the March order, [Flightline] or the company would have intended
the court to be able to permit the company to use the moneys in court to
discharge its legal costs and expenses in connection with the claim: if that had
been their intention, it would have been only too easy to say so.'

[28] The judge's second reason for concluding that the money in the joint
account stands as security for Flightline's claim was the existence in the standard
form of freezing order of a provision that the freezing order shall cease to have
effect if the respondent provides 'security' by paying money into court or by
some other agreed method. The judge accepted, however, that this point was
weakened by the fact that the freezing order in question did not contain such a
provision. The judge went on (at [31]):

'As the freezing injunction will, ex hypothesi, have been discharged as a
result of the payment of such "security", it appears to me that the natural
inference is that such payment would be security for the claimant's claim.
Accordingly, I consider that the notion that a payment into court or into a
joint account in the name of both parties' solicitors to discharge or buy off a
freezing injunction should then be treated as security for any judgment
which the claimant subsequently obtains, is not by any means inherently
inconsistent with the notion of a freezing order.'

a
[29] The judge's third reason for his conclusion was that he considered that, on analysis, the decision of this court in *Re Multi Guarantee Co Ltd* [1987] BCLC 257 provided no significant support for the appellants' argument, since in the *Multi Guarantee* case at the time when the money was paid into a joint account proceedings had not yet been commenced, albeit they had been threatened. The judge considered (at [32]) that there was 'a very substantial difference' between a

b payment into a joint account when there were no legal proceedings pending, and one which is made in the context of litigation which is already under way. Further, in so far as Nourse LJ (who gave the leading judgment in the *Multi Guarantee* case) relied on the fact that the payment was made in the context of a possible application for a freezing order, the judge noted that the Court of Appeal did not appear to have considered the provision in the standard form of freezing

c order to which reference has already been made, and that the fact that the background in that case included the possibility of a freezing order was merely one of the factors which weighed with the Court of Appeal. The judge suggested that equal, if not more, weight appeared to have been placed by the Court of Appeal on the negotiations between the parties, and the absence of any express

d agreement as to the basis upon which the money in the joint account in that case was to be held.

[30] Fourthly, the judge considered that the fact that a payment of money into court or into a joint bank account in order to discharge a freezing order converts the claimant pro tanto into a secured creditor in respect of his claim was not such a surprising result as might at first appear. The judge went on to point to what

e he regarded as similarities between the position of a claimant in such a case and that of a claimant who has obtained the benefit of a payment into court. The judge took the view that there was no intrinsic reason why a claimant who has obtained a freezing order, and in the process has incurred risk and expense, should not be in a better position than other creditors, either by being paid or by

f having the benefit of security. However, the judge went on (at [35]) to acknowledge—

'that it is arguable that a creditor who applies for summary judgment and, as it were, only fails by a short head, as a result of which there is a payment into court, has by his action, justified his secured creditor status rather more
g obviously than a creditor who achieves that status through a payment into court to discharge a freezing injunction.'

[31] Finally, the judge referred to three other matters relied on by Flightline which, in the judge's view, provided some further support for the conclusion which he had reached: first, the fact that the joint account was described as an
h 'escrow' account; secondly, the 20% or so reduction in the amount to be paid into the joint account; and thirdly the fact that at the material time the company was in serious financial difficulties. In connection with this last matter, the judge commented that it must have been reasonably foreseeable that the company would go into some form of liquidation in the near future. He considered that in

j those circumstances it was rather more likely that the parties would have agreed the provision of security rather than merely a mechanism for the replacement of the freezing order.

THE ARGUMENTS
[32] Mr Pascoe submits that having concluded (at [30]) that the terms embodied in the March order—including the company's undertaking—were

'effectively in substitution for, or to discharge, the freezing order', the judge
ought to have gone on to conclude that just as the freezing order created no *a*
security rights neither did the March order.

[33] Whilst accepting, as he must (see *Investors Compensation Scheme v West
Bromwich Building Society, Investors Compensation Scheme Ltd v Hopkin & Sons (a
firm), Alford v West Bromwich Building Society, Armitage v West Bromwich Building
Society* [1998] 1 All ER 98 at 114, [1998] 1 WLR 896 at 913 per Lord Hoffmann), *b*
that in determining the effect of the March order regard may not be had to 'the
previous negotiations of the parties and their declarations of subjective intent',
Mr Pascoe submits that it is not only legitimate but essential for the court to
consider the effect of the March order against the background of the February
order. He submits that the terms and effect of the February order afford strong
support for the conclusion that the effect of the March order was merely to *c*
provide an alternative form of freezing relief pending trial. Thus he submits
firstly that there is nothing on the face of the February order to suggest that the
parties intended to do more than provide an alternative mechanism of a 'freezing'
nature. Secondly, he points out that the February order was to continue only
until the adjourned hearing of the interlocutory proceedings—proceedings in *d*
which the company was not only opposing any continuation of the freezing order
but was also intending to seek the discharge of the freezing order ab initio, with
consequential exposure of Flightline to liability under its cross-undertakings.
Viewing the February order in that context, it is (he submits) inherently
extremely improbable that the parties would have intended to create security
rights in favour of Flightline. *e*

[34] Turning to the March order, Mr Pascoe submits that (as in the case of the
February order) there in nothing on the face of the March order to indicate that
in compromising the interlocutory proceedings the parties intended to do more
than substitute an alternative mechanism of a 'freezing' nature, albeit (in contrast
to the February order) a mechanism which was intended to continue until trial or *f*
further order. He submits that the words 'pending further order of the court' in
the company's undertaking in the March order are entirely consistent with an
arrangement for the freezing of the moneys in the joint account (up to the
specified limit), as is the grant in the body of the March order of liberty to apply.
Secondly, he submits that that conclusion is reinforced when the March order is
viewed against the background of the February order, which (as he submits, see *g*
above) plainly created no security rights.

[35] Mr Pascoe submits that it is nothing to the point that the freezing order
as granted on 16 January 2002 and as subsequently extended did not include the
provision as to security which appears in the standard form of freezing order.

[36] In the course of argument we invited Mr Pascoe to comment on the *h*
well-known passage in the judgment of the Privy Council in *Palmer v Carey* [1926]
AC 703 at 706–707, [1926] All ER Rep 650 at 651–652, to which we drew his
attention (and to which further reference will be made at [43], below), to the
effect that in order for an equitable charge to be created over a specific fund it is
necessary to find not merely a restriction on disposal of the fund by the debtor *j*
but also an obligation on the debtor to pay the debt out of the fund. In response
to that invitation, Mr Pascoe submitted that in the instant case there was nothing
in the March order to support the existence of such an obligation.

[37] Mr Moss submits that the resolution of the issue whether the March order
created security rights involves the two-stage process identified by Lord Millett in
Agnew v Comr of Inland Revenue [2001] UKPC 28 at [32], [2001] 2 BCLC 189 at [32],

a [2001] 2 AC 710 at [32]. The first stage is to ascertain from the language which the parties have used the nature of the rights and obligations which they intended to create: the second stage is to consider whether, as a matter of law, those rights and obligations give rise to a charge. So, he submits, the question to be addressed in the instant case is not 'Did the parties intend that the March order should create a security?', but rather 'As a matter of law, does the March order have the effect of

b creating a security?'

[38] As to the first stage in the two-stage process, Mr Moss submits that as a matter of construction of the March order it was intended that the moneys in the joint account be available to Flightline to satisfy any judgment which it might obtain in the action, up to the specified limit of £3·325m. He relies in this connection (more strongly here than below, it would appear) on the fact that the

c title to the joint account includes the word 'escrow'. He referred us to one of the dictionary meanings of the word as 'a deposit held in trust or as security'. He also referred us to a passage in 13 *Halsbury's Laws* (4th edn reissue) para 36 where the technical conveyancing meaning of the word is explained. Thus a deed which is delivered 'in escrow' will not become binding on the party delivering it unless

d and until some specified event happens or some specified condition is fulfilled. Mr Moss submits that notwithstanding that the word 'escrow' in the title to the joint account is plainly not used in its strict technical sense, nevertheless the flavour of word points towards the existence of some kind of security rights and the fact that the parties have seen fit to include that word in the title to the joint account is an indicator that they regarded the March order as having created a

e security.

[39] Mr Moss submits that it is of central importance that under the March order (as under the February order) the moneys in the joint account were placed under the control of the court. He accepts that that is not in itself sufficient to take the instant case out of the category of freezing order cases and to place it in

f the same category as cases where money is paid into court, since the control of the court is present in each category of case; but he submits that what is crucial in the instant case is that under the terms of the March order the court may direct that the moneys in the joint account (up to the specified maximum) be paid out to Flightline in or towards satisfaction of any judgment which it may obtain in the action. That additional feature, he submits, is sufficient to place the instant case

g in the same category as cases where money is paid into court.

[40] As to *Palmer v Carey*, Mr Moss submits that the security created by the March order is not a security in the nature of an equitable assignment but is rather in the nature of what Professor Roy Goode in *Commercial Law* (2nd edn, 1995) pp 671–673 categorises as 'procedural securities'. Professor Goode includes in

h that category the payment of money into court, whether in fulfilment of a condition of leave to defend or in satisfaction of the claimant's claim, or in compliance with an order for security for costs. Professor Goode goes on to contrast an order, such as a freezing order, which merely restrains the defendant from dealing with his assets without attaching them in any way and which creates

j no proprietary rights.

[41] Mr Moss submits that the effect of the March order, as a matter of law, is to be determined without reference to the February order. Alternatively, if it be legitimate for this purpose to have regard to the terms of the February order, Mr Moss submits that it is by no means clear that the February order was not intended to create rights and obligations extending beyond the date of the adjourned hearing. He submits that, from a commercial point of view, there is

good reason to suppose that in agreeing the terms of the February order the
parties were intending that the moneys in the account should be available to
satisfy any judgment which Flightline might obtain in the action. At all events,
he submits that that is the only sensible commercial interpretation of the terms
of the March order, and that the judge was right so to conclude.

[42] Mr Moss also points to the absence from both the February order and the
March order of many of the detailed, but essential, provisions of the freezing
order as originally granted on 16 January 2002, including in particular the power
for the respondent to vary or discharge the order. He submits that the judge was
right to conclude that had it been intended that the March order was intended to
do no more than provide a substitute for the freezing order, the parties would
have been likely to say so in clear terms.

CONCLUSIONS

[43] In *Palmer v Carey* [1926] AC 703, [1926] All ER Rep 650 a lender agreed to
finance the activities of a trader in goods, on terms that the proceeds of sale of the
goods be paid into an account in the name of the lender, and that the lender
recoup himself on a monthly basis in respect of sums advanced, with the balance
being released to the trader subject to a right for the lender to retain a sum
representing an agreed share of the trader's profit. The trader subsequently
became bankrupt. At the date of the bankruptcy, a substantial sum was owing to
the lender in respect of sums advanced. The lender claimed security over goods
and proceeds of sale in the hands of the trader. The Privy Council, reversing the
decision of the High Court of Australia ((1924) 34 CLR 380) (Knox CJ dissenting),
held that the lender had no such security. In the course of its judgment (delivered
by Lord Wrenbury), the Privy Council said ([1926] AC 703 at 706–707, [1926] All
ER Rep 650 at 651–652):

'The law as to equitable assignment, as stated by Lord Truro in *Rodick v.
Gandell* ((1852) 1 De GM & G 763, 42 ER 749), is this: "The extent of the
principle to be deduced is that an agreement between a debtor and a creditor
that the debt owing shall be paid out of a specific fund coming to the debtor,
or an order given by a debtor to his creditor upon a person owing money or
holding funds belonging to the giver of the order, directing such person to
pay such funds to the creditor, will create a valid equitable charge upon such
fund, in other words, will operate as an equitable assignment of the debts or
fund to which the order refers." An agreement for valuable consideration
that a fund shall be applied in a particular way may found an injunction to
restrain its application in another way. But if there be nothing more, such a
stipulation will not amount to an equitable assignment. *It is necessary to find,
further, that an obligation has been imposed in favour of the creditor to pay the debt
out of the fund.* This is but an instance of a familiar doctrine of equity that a
contract for valuable consideration to transfer or charge a subject matter
passes a beneficial interest by way of property in that subject matter if the
contract is one of which a Court of equity will decree specific performance.'
(Our emphasis.)

[44] The above statement of principle was adopted verbatim by the House of
Lords in *Swiss Bank Corp v Lloyds Bank Ltd* [1981] 2 All ER 449 at 453, [1982] AC
584 at 613 per Lord Wilberforce.

[45] The judgment in *Palmer v Carey* then turns to the provisions of the
agreement between the lender and the trader in that case, and in particular the

a provision in art 3 of the agreement that the proceeds of sale of the goods be paid
into an account in the name of the lender. The judgment continues ([1926] AC
703 at 707, [1926] All ER Rep 650 at 652):

b 'Under art. 3, however, the proceeds are to be paid to the lender's credit at
his bank. This gives the lender a most efficient hold to prevent the
misapplication of the proceeds, but there is nothing in that article to give him
a property by way of security or otherwise in the moneys of the borrower
before or after he, the lender, has them in his charge.'

[46] The judgment goes on to express the agreement of the Privy Council
with the following passage from the dissenting judgment of Knox CJ in the court
c below ((1924) 34 CLR 380 at 388):

'The words of the agreement on which the appellant relies are apt to
express a contract by the bankrupt to apply the money in the purchase of
goods, to sell those goods, and to pay the proceeds of the sale into the
appellant's bank account, but I can see nothing in them to indicate that the
d intention was to assign any interest in goods purchased by the bankrupt or
to create either a charge over or a trust of such goods in favour of the
appellant.'

[47] Although *Palmer v Carey* concerned contractual arrangements made
between the parties out of court, in our judgment Lord Wrenbury's statement of
e principle applies directly to consent orders, such as the February order and the
March order, which embody terms agreed between the parties; and also
indirectly, by analogy, to other court orders. Thus, the reason why a freezing
order does not create a security right over the assets from time to time subject to
it is, in my judgment, that a freezing order—without more—does not impose an
obligation on the part of the respondent to satisfy any judgment debt out of those
f assets. Rather, a freezing order provides what Lord Wrenbury described (in the
passage quoted at [45], above) as 'a most efficient hold to prevent the
misapplication [of those assets]'. As Lord Wrenbury makes clear, that is not
enough to create a security right. On the other hand, cases in Professor Goode's
category of 'procedural securities' are cases in which the clear purpose of the
order is to afford a claimant an element of security in the satisfaction of his claim.
g Hence, by analogy with the principle stated by Lord Wrenbury, a security right
is created.

[48] The question in the instant case, then, is whether one can spell out of the
terms of the March order a provision (albeit not expressed in terms) to the effect
that the company must satisfy any judgment obtained by Flightline (up to the
h specified maximum of £3·325m) out of the moneys in the joint account; or, to put
it the other way round, a provision to the effect that if Flightline is successful in
obtaining a judgment in the action it is entitled to payment out of such moneys
(or of so much thereof as is required to satisfy the judgment) as a matter of right.

[49] We find ourselves wholly unable to spell out of the March order any such
j provision. Firstly, we can see nothing on the face of the March order (without at
this stage bringing into account any background facts) to indicate that anything
other than continuing interim protection of a 'freezing' nature was intended to
be provided. In particular, the terms of the company's undertaking, as contained
in the second schedule to the March order, seem to me to be entirely consistent
with the continuance of interim protection of a 'freezing' nature until trial or
further order. As Mr Moss accepted, the mere fact that the moneys in the

account were under the control of the court does not serve to take the case out
of the freezing order category. Secondly, when one takes account by way of
background of the terms of the February order, the conclusion that the March
order confers no security rights is in my judgment reinforced. We agree with
Mr Pascoe that the February order plainly did not achieve anything more than
the continuation of interim protection of a 'freezing' nature until the date of the
adjourned hearing.

[50] Nor are we persuaded that Mr Moss' reliance on the inclusion of the word
'escrow' in the title of the joint account has the significance which he seeks to give
it. In our judgment there is no satisfactory basis for inferring (because there is no
direct evidence about it) that the use of that word indicates that the parties for
their part understood the March order to create a security right. In any event, as
Mr Moss himself asserts, the question whether the March order created a security
right is ultimately a question of law.

[51] Equally, it seems to us to be nothing to the point that the freezing order
as granted on 16 January 2002 does not contain the subparagraph in the standard
form relating to the provision of security.

[52] As to the figure of £3·325m which appears in the company's undertaking
in the March order, as compared with the figure of £4·2m which appears in the
February order, given that the March order represented a compromise of the
interlocutory dispute (including the company's application to discharge the
freezing order ab initio) we find it impossible to draw any relevant inference from
the fact that the £4·2m was reduced to £3·325m. Nor does the background of the
company's serious financial difficulties seem to us to afford any reliable indication
as to whether the March order created a security right.

[53] In respectful disagreement with the judge, therefore, we conclude that
the March order did not confer any security right on Flightline and that the appeal
should accordingly be allowed on the primary issue.

Appeal allowed.

Kate O'Hanlon   Barrister.

Aston Cantlow and Wilmcote with Billesley Parochial Church Council v Wallbank and another

[2003] UKHL 37

HOUSE OF LORDS

LORD NICHOLLS OF BIRKENHEAD, LORD HOPE OF CRAIGHEAD, LORD HOBHOUSE OF WOODBOROUGH, LORD SCOTT OF FOSCOTE AND LORD RODGER OF EARLSFERRY

3–5 MARCH, 26 JUNE 2003

Ecclesiastical law – Parochial church council – Public authority – Whether parochial church council constituting for purposes of human rights legislation a public authority per se or a public authority when enforcing liability for chancel repairs – Chancel Repairs Act 1932 – Human Rights Act 1998, s 6.

Human rights – Public authority – 'Core' public authority – Whether non-governmental organisation could be regarded as 'core' public authority for purposes of human rights legislation – Human Rights Act 1998, s 6.

The defendants were, as freehold owners of certain rectorial land, the lay rectors of a parish. As such, they were under a common law obligation to repair the chancel of the parish church. The statutory power to enforce that obligation lay with the claimant parochial church council (PCC), a body corporate which formed part of the Church of England and whose functions included co-operating with the minister in promoting the Church's mission within the parish. After the chancel fell into disrepair, the PCC served notices on the lay rectors under the Chancel Repairs Act 1932, calling on them to repair the chancel. They disputed their liability, and the PCC therefore brought proceedings against them to recover the estimated cost of the repairs. On the determination of a preliminary issue, the judge held that the lay rectors were liable. They appealed, relying on s 6(1)[a] of the Human Rights Act 1998 which made it unlawful for a 'public authority' to act in a way that was incompatible with a right under the European Convention for the Protection of Human Rights and Fundamental Freedoms 1950 (as set out in Sch 1 to the 1998 Act). Section 6(3)(b) provided that 'public authority' included any person certain of whose functions were functions of a public nature, but that extension did not apply to a person if the nature of the act in question was 'private'. The Court of Appeal held that the PCC was a 'core' public authority (ie an authority which fell within s 6 without reference to sub-s (3)) since it formed part of the church by law established, and that in any event it was performing a function of a public nature when it was enforcing the lay rectors' liability for the chancel repairs. The court further held that the PCC's act in serving the notice was incompatible with convention rights of the lay rectors. Accordingly, their appeal was allowed. On the PCC's appeal to the House of Lords, the issue arose, inter alia, as to whether a PCC could be a 'core' public authority given that (i) only the 'victim' of an infringement of convention rights could bring proceedings before the European Court of Human Rights or against a public

---

authority under the 1998 Act, and (ii) both the convention and the Act defined 'victim' as any person, 'non-governmental organisation' or group of individuals. *a*

Held – A PCC was not a 'core' public authority for the purposes of s 6 of the 1998 Act, and (Lord Scott dissenting) it did not become a public authority by virtue of sub-s (3)(b) when enforcing a lay rector's liability for chancel repairs. A person who would be regarded as a 'non-governmental organisation' within *b* the meaning of the convention ought not to be regarded as a 'core' public authority for the purposes of s 6. That would deprive such an organisation of the rights enjoyed by the victims of acts which were incompatible with convention rights and had been made unlawful by s 6(1). The Church of England itself could not be said to be part of the government, and its legal framework as a church by law established did not lead to the conclusion that a *c* PCC was a public authority. The PCC's general function was to carry out the religious mission of the Church in the parish, rather than to exercise any governmental power. Nor was it in any sense under the supervision of the state. Furthermore, the enforcement of liability for chancel repairs was a private rather than a public act. The nature of the act was to be found in the *d* nature of the obligation that the PCC was seeking to enforce, namely a civil debt. The function which it was performing had nothing to do with the responsibilities owed to the public by the state. Accordingly (Lord Scott concurring), the appeal would be allowed (see [8], [13]–[17], [47], [58]–[64], [75], [86], [87], [89], [94], [129], [136], [156], [161], [166], [171], [173], below).

Holy Monasteries v Greece (1995) 20 EHRR 1 and *Hautanemi v Sweden* (1996) 22 *e* EHRR CD 155 considered.

Decision of the Court of Appeal [2001] 3 All ER 393 reversed.

Notes

For public authority and for liability to repair chancels, see respectively 1(1) *f* *Halsbury's Laws* (4th edn) (2001 reissue) para 87 n2 and 14 *Halsbury's Laws* (4th edn) para 1100.

For the Chancel Repairs Act 1932, see 14 *Halsbury's Statutes* (4th edn) (2003 reissue) 350.

For the Human Rights Act 1998, s 6, see 7 *Halsbury's Statutes* (4th edn) (2002 reissue) 535. *g*

Cases referred to in opinions

Ayuntamiento de Mula v Spain App No 55346/00 (1 February 2001, unreported), ECt HR.

Barnes, Re, Simpson v Barnes (1922) [1930] 2 Ch 80n. *h*

Chivers & Sons Ltd v Secretary of State for Air (Queens' College, Cambridge, Third Party) [1955] 2 All ER 607, [1955] Ch 585, [1955] 3 WLR 154.

Doughty v Rolls-Royce plc [1992] 1 CMLR 1045, CA.

ECSC v Acciaierie e Ferriere Busseni SpA (in liq) Case C-221/88 [1990] ECR I-495, ECJ. *j*

Ely (Bishop of) v Gibbons & Goody (1833) 4 Hag Ecc 156, 162 ER 1405.

Foster v British Gas plc Case C-188/89 [1990] 3 All ER 897, [1991] 1 QB 405, [1991] 2 WLR 258, [1990] ECR I-3313, ECJ.

General Assembly of Free Church of Scotland v Lord Overtoun, Macalister v Young [1904] AC 515, HL.

Gilbert v Trinity House Corp (1886) 17 QBD 795, DC.

a   *Hautanemi v Sweden* (1996) 22 EHRR CD 155, E Com HR.
    Holy Monasteries v Greece (1995) 20 EHRR 1, [1994] ECHR 13029/87, ECt HR.
    Hong Kong Polytechnic University v Next Magazine Publishing Ltd [1996] 2 HKLR 260.
    James v UK (1986) 8 EHRR 123, [1986] ECHR 8795/79, ECt HR.
    Johnston v Chief Constable of the Royal Ulster Constabulary Case 222/84 [1986] 3 All
        ER 135, [1987] QB 129, [1986] 3 WLR 1038, [1986] ECR 1651, ECJ.
b   *Marckx v Belgium* (1979) 2 EHRR 330, [1979] ECHR 6833/74, ECt HR.
    Marshall v Graham, Bell v Graham [1907] 2 KB 112, DC.
    Pepper (Inspector of Taxes) v Hart [1993] 1 All ER 42, [1993] AC 593, [1992] 3 WLR
        1032, HL.
    R v Benjafield [2002] UKHL 2, [2002] 1 All ER 815, [2002] 2 WLR 235.
c   *R v Chief Rabbi of the United Hebrew Congregations of Great Britain and the
        Commonwealth, ex p Wachmann* [1993] 2 All ER 249, [1992] 1 WLR 1036.
    R v Kansal (No 2) [2001] UKHL 62, [2002] 1 All ER 257, [2002] 2 AC 69, [2001] 3
        WLR 1562.
    R v Lambert [2001] UKHL 37, [2001] 3 All ER 577, [2002] 2 AC 545, [2001] 3 WLR
        206.
d   *Representative Body of the Church in Wales v Tithe Redemption Commission, Plymouth
        Estates Ltd v Tithe Redemption Commission* [1944] 1 All ER 710, [1944] AC 228,
        HL.
    Rothenthurm Commune v Switzerland (1988) 59 DR 251, E Com HR.
    Sporrong v Sweden (1983) 5 EHRR 35, [1982] ECHR 7151/75, ECt HR.
e   *Wainwright v Home Office* [2001] EWCA Civ 2081, [2003] 3 All ER 943, [2002] QB
        1334, [2002] 3 WLR 405.
    Walwyn v Awberry (1677) 2 Mod 254.
    Wickhambrook Parochial Church Council v Croxford [1935] 2 KB 417, CA.
    Young v UK (1982) 4 EHRR 38, ECt HR.

f   **Cases referred to in list of authorities**
    Bahamas Methodist Church v Symonette [2000] 5 LRC 196, PC.
    Darby v Sweden (1991) 13 EHRR 774, [1990] ECHR 11581/85, ECt HR.
    Former King of Greece v Greece App No 25701/94 (23 November 2000, unreported),
        ECt HR.
g   *Håkansson v Sweden* (1991) 13 EHRR 1, [1990] ECHR 11855/85, ECt HR.
    Hauxton Parochial Church Council v Stevens [1929] P 240.
    Hentrich v France (1994) 18 EHRR 440, [1994] ECHR 13616/88, ECt HR.
    Kjeldsen v Denmark (1976) 1 EHRR 711, [1976] ECHR 5095/71, ECt HR.
    National & Provincial Building Society v UK (1998) 25 EHRR 127, [1997] ECHR
h   21319/93, ECt HR.
    Poplar Housing and Regeneration Community Association Ltd v Donoghue [2001]
        EWCA Civ 595, [2001] 4 All ER 604, [2002] QB 48.
    Pye (JA) (Oxford) Ltd v Graham [2002] UKHL 30, [2002] 3 All ER 865, [2002] 3 WLR
        221.
j   *R (Molinaro) v Kensington and Chelsea Royal London BC* [2001] EWHC Admin 896,
        [2002] LGR 336.
    R (on the application of Heather) v Leonard Cheshire Foundation [2002] EWCA Civ
        366, [2002] 2 All ER 936.
    R v Archbishop of Canterbury, ex p Reverend Williamson (1 March 1994, unreported),
        [1994] CA Transcript 0341.
    R v Bolsover DC, ex p Pepper [2001] LGR 43.

R v Ecclesiastical Committee of Both Houses of Parliament and the Archbishops of Canterbury and York, ex p Church Society (1993) 6 Admin LR 670, DC.
R v Panel on Take-overs and Mergers, ex p Datafin plc (Norton Opax plc intervening) [1987] 1 All ER 564, [1987] QB 815, [1987] 2 WLR 699, CA.
R v Provincial Court of the Church in Wales, ex p Williams (1998) 5 Ecc LJ 217.
Rhone v Stephens [1994] 2 All ER 65, [1994] 2 AC 310, [1994] 2 WLR 429, HL.
St Brice v Southwark London BC [2001] EWCA Civ 1138, [2002] LGR 117, [2002] 1 WLR 1537, CA.
Stubbings v UK (1997) 23 EHRR 213, [1996] ECHR 22083/93, ECt HR.
Sunday Times v UK (1979) 2 EHRR 245, ECt HR.
Thamesmead Town Ltd v Allotey [1998] 3 EGLR 97, CA.
Wandsworth London BC v Michalak [2002] EWCA Civ 271, [2002] 4 All ER 1136, [2003] 1 WLR 617.

Appeal
The claimant, the Parochial Church Council of Aston Cantlow and Wilmcote with Billesley, Warwickshire, appealed with permission of the Appeal Committee of the House of Lords given on 11 February 2002 from the decision of the Court of Appeal (Sir Andrew Morritt V-C, Robert Walker and Sedley LJJ) on 17 May 2001 ([2001] EWCA Civ 713, [2001] 3 All ER 393, [2002] Ch 51) allowing an appeal by the defendants, Gail R Wallbank and Andrew David Wallbank, from the decision of Ferris J on 28 March 2000 ([2000] All ER (D) 419) whereby, on the determination of a preliminary issue, he held that the Wallbanks were liable for the cost of repairs to the chancel of the church of St John the Baptist, Aston Cantlow. The facts are set out in the opinion of Lord Hope of Craighead.

Charles George QC and *Mark Hill* (instructed by *Winckworth Sherwood* as agents for *Rotherham & Co*, Coventry) for the parochial church council.
Michael Beloff QC and *Ian Partridge* (instructed by *Eddowes Perry & Osbourne*, Sutton Coldfield) for the Wallbanks.

Their Lordships took time for consideration.

26 June 2003. The following opinions were delivered.

LORD NICHOLLS OF BIRKENHEAD.
[1] My Lords, I have had the advantage of reading in draft the speeches of all your Lordships. I too would allow this appeal. On some of the issues your Lordships have expressed different views. I shall state my own views without repeating the facts.
[2] This case concerns one of the more arcane and unsatisfactory areas of property law: the liability of a lay rector, or lay impropriator, for the repair of the chancel of a church. The very language is redolent of a society long disappeared. The anachronistic, even capricious, nature of this ancient liability was recognised some years ago by the Law Commission: *Liability for Chancel Repairs* (Law Com No 152 (1985)). The Commission said (p 2 (para 1.5)): '... this relic of the past is ... no longer acceptable.' The Commission recommended its phased abolition.
[3] In these proceedings Mr and Mrs Wallbank admitted that, apart from the Human Rights Act 1998, they have no defence to the claim made against them by

a the Parochial Church Council (PCC) of the parish of Aston Cantlow and Wilmcote with Billesley, Warwickshire. The House was not asked to consider whether the case of *Wickhambrook Parochial Church Council v Croxford* [1935] 2 KB 417 was correctly decided.

[4] At first sight the Human Rights Act might seem to have nothing to do with the present case. The events giving rise to the litigation occurred, and the decision of Ferris J ([2000] All ER (D) 419) was given, before the Human Rights *b* Act came into force. But the decision of the Court of Appeal ([2001] EWCA Civ 713, [2001] 3 All ER 393, [2002] Ch 51) was based on the provisions of the Human Rights Act, and this decision has wide financial implications for the Church of England, going far beyond the outcome of this particular case. The decision affects numerous PCCs and perhaps as many as one third of all parish churches. *c* The Church of England needs to know whether, as the Court of Appeal held, it is unlawful now for a PCC to enforce a lay rector's obligation to meet the cost of chancel repairs. Accordingly, in order to obtain the decision of the House on this point, the PCC conceded that the Human Rights Act applies in this case. This concession having been made by the PCC, no argument was addressed to *d* your Lordships' House on the question of law thus conceded. I express no view on this question.

[5] Assuming the Human Rights Act is applicable in this case, the overall question is whether the PCC's prosecution of proceedings against Mr and Mrs Wallbank is rendered unlawful by s 6 of the Human Rights Act as an act by *e* a public authority which is incompatible with a right under the European Convention for the Protection of Human Rights and Fundamental Freedoms 1950 (as set out in Sch 1 to the Human Rights Act). In answering this question the initial step is to consider whether the PCC is 'a public authority'.

[6] The expression 'public authority' is not defined in the Human Rights Act, *f* nor is it a recognised term of art in English law, that is, an expression with a specific recognised meaning. The word 'public' is a term of uncertain import, used with many different shades of meaning: public policy, public rights of way, public property, public authority (in the Public Authorities Protection Act 1893), public nuisance, public house, public school, public company. So in the present case the statutory context is all important. As to that, the broad purpose sought *g* to be achieved by s 6(1) is not in doubt. The purpose is that those bodies for whose acts the state is answerable before the European Court of Human Rights shall in future be subject to a domestic law obligation not to act incompatibly with convention rights. If they act in breach of this legal obligation victims may henceforth obtain redress from the courts of this country. In future victims *h* should not need to travel to Strasbourg.

[7] Conformably with this purpose, the phrase 'a public authority' in s 6(1) is essentially a reference to a body whose nature is governmental in a broad sense of that expression. It is in respect of organisations of this nature that the government is answerable under the convention. Hence, under the Human *j* Rights Act a body of this nature is required to act compatibly with convention rights in everything it does. The most obvious examples are government departments, local authorities, the police and the armed forces. Behind the instinctive classification of these organisations as bodies whose nature is governmental lie factors such as the possession of special powers, democratic accountability, public funding in whole or in part, an obligation to act only in the public interest, and a statutory constitution: see the valuable article by Professor

Dawn Oliver 'The Frontiers of the State: Public Authorities and Public Functions
under the Human Rights Act' [2000] PL 476.   *a*

[8] A further, general point should be noted. One consequence of being a
'core' public authority, namely, an authority falling within s 6 without reference
to s 6(3), is that the body in question does not itself enjoy convention rights. It is
difficult to see how a core public authority could ever claim to be a victim of an
infringement of convention rights. A core public authority seems inherently   *b*
incapable of satisfying the convention description of a victim: 'any person,
non-governmental organisation or group of individuals' (see art 34; my emphasis).
Only victims of an unlawful act may bring proceedings under s 7 of the Human
Rights Act, and the convention description of a victim has been incorporated
into the Act, by s 7(7). This feature, that a core public authority is incapable of
having convention rights of its own, is a matter to be borne in mind when   *c*
considering whether or not a particular body is a core public authority. In itself
this feature throws some light on how the expression 'public authority' should be
understood and applied. It must always be relevant to consider whether
Parliament can have intended that the body in question should have no
convention rights.   *d*

[9] In a modern developed state governmental functions extend far beyond
maintenance of law and order and defence of the realm. Further, the manner in
which wide-ranging governmental functions are discharged varies considerably.
In the interests of efficiency and economy, and for other reasons, functions of a
governmental nature are frequently discharged by non-governmental bodies.
Sometimes this will be a consequence of privatisation, sometimes not. One   *e*
obvious example is the running of prisons by commercial organisations. Another
is the discharge of regulatory functions by organisations in the private sector, for
instance, the Law Society. Section 6(3)(b) gathers this type of case into the
embrace of s 6 by including within the phrase 'public authority' any person
whose functions include 'functions of a public nature'. This extension of the   *f*
expression 'public authority' does not apply to a person if the nature of the act in
question is 'private'.

[10] Again, the statute does not amplify what the expression 'public' and its
counterpart 'private' mean in this context. But, here also, given the statutory
context already mentioned and the repetition of the description 'public',
essentially the contrast being drawn is between functions of a governmental   *g*
nature and functions, or acts, which are not of that nature. I stress, however, that
this is no more than a useful guide. The phrase used in the Act is public function,
not governmental function.

[11] Unlike a core public authority, a 'hybrid' public authority, exercising both
public functions and non-public functions, is not absolutely disabled from having   *h*
convention rights. A hybrid public authority is not a public authority in respect
of an act of a private nature. Here again, as with s 6(1), this feature throws some
light on the approach to be adopted when interpreting s 6(3)(b). Giving a
generously wide scope to the expression 'public function' in s 6(3)(b) will further
the statutory aim of promoting the observance of human rights values without   *j*
depriving the bodies in question of the ability themselves to rely on convention
rights when necessary.

[12] What, then, is the touchstone to be used in deciding whether a function
is public for this purpose? Clearly there is no single test of universal application.
There cannot be, given the diverse nature of governmental functions and the
variety of means by which these functions are discharged today. Factors to be

a taken into account include the extent to which in carrying out the relevant function the body is publicly funded, or is exercising statutory powers, or is taking the place of central government or local authorities, or is providing a public service.

[13] Turning to the facts in the present case, I do not think PCCs are 'core' public authorities. Historically the Church of England has discharged an

b important and influential role in the life of this country. As the established Church it still has special links with central government. But the Church of England remains essentially a religious organisation. This is so even though some of the emanations of the Church discharge functions which may qualify as governmental. Church schools and the conduct of marriage services are two instances. The legislative powers of the General Synod of the Church of England

c are another. This should not be regarded as infecting the Church of England as a whole, or its emanations in general, with the character of a governmental organisation.

[14] As to PCCs, their constitution and functions lend no support to the view that they should be characterised as governmental organisations or, more

d precisely, in the language of the statute, public authorities. PCCs are established as corporate bodies under a Church measure, now the Parochial Church Councils (Powers) Measure 1956. For historical reasons this unique form of legislation, having the same force as a statute, is the way the Church of England governs its affairs. But the essential role of a PCC is to provide a formal means, prescribed by the Church of England, whereby ex officio and elected members of

e the local church promote the mission of the Church and discharge financial responsibilities in respect of their own parish church, including responsibilities regarding maintenance of the fabric of the building. This smacks of a Church body engaged in self-governance and promotion of its affairs. This is far removed from the type of body whose acts engage the responsibility of the state under the

f convention.

[15] The contrary conclusion, that the Church authorities in general and PCCs in particular are 'core' public authorities, would mean these bodies are not capable of being victims within the meaning of the Human Rights Act. Accordingly they are not able to complain of infringements of convention rights. That would be an extraordinary conclusion. The Human Rights Act goes out of

g its way, in s 13, to single out for express mention the exercise by religious organisations of the convention right of freedom of thought, conscience and religion. One would expect that these and other convention rights would be enjoyed by the Church of England as much as other religious bodies.

[16] I turn next to consider whether a PCC is a hybrid public authority. For

h this purpose it is not necessary to analyse each of the functions of a PCC and see if any of them is a public function. What matters is whether the particular act done by the PCC of which complaint is made is a private act as contrasted with the discharge of a public function. The impugned act is enforcement of Mr and Mrs Wallbank's liability, as lay rectors, for the repair of the chancel of the church

j of St John the Baptist at Aston Cantlow. As I see it, the only respect in which there is any 'public' involvement is that parishioners have certain rights to attend church services and in respect of marriage and burial services. To that extent the state of repair of the church building may be said to affect rights of the public. But I do not think this suffices to characterise actions taken by the PCC for the repair of the church as 'public'. If a PCC enters into a contract with a builder for the repair of the chancel arch, that could be hardly be described as a public act.

Likewise when a PCC enforces, in accordance with the provisions of the Chancel
Repairs Act 1932, a burdensome incident attached to the ownership of certain *a*
pieces of land: there is nothing particularly 'public' about this. This is no more a
public act than is the enforcement of a restrictive covenant of which Church land
has the benefit.

[17] For these reasons this appeal succeeds. A PCC is not a core public
authority, nor does it become such by virtue of s 6(3)(b) when enforcing a lay *b*
rector's liability for chancel repairs. Accordingly the Human Rights Act affords
lay rectors no relief from their liabilities. This conclusion should not be allowed
to detract from the force of the recommendations, already mentioned, of the Law
Commission. The need for reform has not lessened with the passage of time.

[18] On this footing the other issues raised in this case do not call for decision.
I prefer to express no view on the application of art 1 of the First Protocol to the *c*
convention or, more specifically, on the compatibility of the 1932 Act with
Mr and Mrs Wallbank's convention right under that article. The latter was not
the subject of discrete argument.

[19] I add only that even if s 6(1) of the Human Rights Act is applicable in this
type of case, and even if the provisions of the 1932 Act are incompatible with *d*
Mr and Mrs Wallbank's convention rights under art 1 of the First Protocol, even
so the PCC would not be acting unlawfully in enforcing Mr and Mrs Wallbank's
liability as lay rectors. Like ss 3(2) and 4(6), s 6(2) of the Human Rights Act is
concerned to preserve the primacy, and legitimacy, of primary legislation. This
is one of the basic principles of the Act. As noted in Grosz, Beatson and Duffy
Human Rights: the 1998 Act and the European Convention (2000) p 72 (para 4-22) a *e*
public authority is not obliged to neutralise primary legislation by treating it as a
dead letter. If a statutory provision cannot be rendered convention compliant by
application of s 3(1), it remains lawful for a public authority, despite the
incompatibility, to act so as to 'give effect to' that provision: see s 6(2)(b). Here,
s 2 of the 1932 Act provides that if the defendant would have been liable to be *f*
admonished to repair the chancel by the appropriate ecclesiastical court, the
court shall give judgment for the cost of putting the chancel in repair. When a
PCC acts pursuant to that provision it is acting within the scope of the exception
set out in s 6(2)(b).

LORD HOPE OF CRAIGHEAD.   *g*

[20] My Lords, the village of Aston Cantlow lies about three miles to the
north west of Stratford-upon-Avon. It has a long history. The parish church,
St John the Baptist, stands on an ancient Saxon site. Two images of its
exterior can be seen on the website Pictorial Images of Warwickshire,
www.genuki.org.uk/big/eng/WAR/images. It is the church where *h*
Shakespeare's mother, Mary Arden, who lived at Wilmcote within the parish,
married John Shakespeare. The earliest part of the present structure is the
chancel which has been there since the late thirteenth century. It was built in
the decorated style and contains a fine example of the use of flowing tracery:
see Pevsner and Wedgewood *The Buildings of England: Warwickshire* (1965) *j*
pp 19, 75. As time went on the condition of the structure began to deteriorate,
and it is now in need of repair. It has been in that state since at least 1990.

[21] In January 1995, when this action began, it was estimated that the cost of
the repairs to the chancel was £95,260·84. By that date the Parochial Church
Council (PCC) had served a notice under the Chancel Repairs Act 1932 in the
prescribed form on Mrs Wallbank in her capacity as lay rector calling upon her to

a   repair the chancel. She disputed liability, so the PCC brought proceedings against her under s 2(2) of the 1932 Act. When the notice was served on 12 September 1994 it was thought that Mrs Wallbank was the sole freehold owner of Glebe Farm. In fact, as a result of her conveyance of the farm into their joint names in 1990, she is its joint owner together with Mr Wallbank. So a further notice was served on 23 January 1996 on both Mr and Mrs Wallbank and an application was

b   made for Mr Wallbank to be joined as a defendant in the proceedings. Several years have gone by. The dispute between the parties has still not been resolved. The cost of the repairs must now greatly exceed the amount of the original estimate.

     [22] On 17 February 2000 Ferris J heard argument on the question whether the liability of the lay rector to repair the chancel or otherwise to meet the cost of

c   the repairs was unenforceable by reason of the Human Rights Act 1998 or otherwise. He had been asked to determine this question as a preliminary issue. On 28 March 2000 he answered the question in the negative. At the end of his judgment ([2000] All ER (D) 419) he observed that it had been posed in terms which would only be appropriate if the Act was already in force. The only

d   provisions which were in force then were ss 18, 20 and 21(5): see s 22(2) of the Human Rights Act. By the time of the hearing in the Court of Appeal on 19 March 2001 the position had changed. The remaining provisions of the Human Rights Act were brought into force on 2 October 2000: see the Human Rights Act (Commencement No 2) Order 2000, SI 2000/1851. Mr and Mrs Wallbank were allowed to amend their notice of appeal so that the issues

e   which they wished to raise could be properly pleaded. On 17 May 2001 the Court of Appeal ([2001] EWCA Civ 713, [2001] 3 All ER 393, [2002] Ch 51) held that the PCC was a public authority for the purposes of s 6 of the Human Rights Act. The court also held that the PCC's action in serving the notice on Mr and Mrs Wallbank was unlawful by reason of art 1 of the First Protocol of the

f   European Convention for the Protection of Human Rights and Fundamental Freedoms 1950 (as set out in Sch 1 to the Human Rights Act), read either alone or with art 14 of the convention.

     [23] The circumstances in which Mr and Mrs Wallbank are said to be liable for the cost of the repairs have been helpfully described by my noble and learned friend Lord Scott of Foscote. I gratefully adopt what he has said about them. It

g   is clear from his account that the liability of the lay impropriator to pay the cost of repairing the chancel has been part of ecclesiastical law for many centuries. As Wynn-Parry J explained in *Chivers & Sons Ltd v Secretary of State for Air (Queens' College, Cambridge, Third Party)* [1955] 2 All ER 607 at 609, [1955] Ch 585 at 593, it rests on the maxim, which has long been recognised, that he who has the profits

h   of the benefice should bear the burden. But the questions about the scope and effect of the Human Rights Act which your Lordships have been asked to decide in this appeal, and on which I wish to concentrate, are of current interest and very considerable public importance. They raise issues whose significance extends far beyond the boundaries of the parish of Aston Cantlow.

j   [24] The principal human rights issues which arise are: (a) whether Mr and Mrs Wallbank can rely upon an alleged violation of their convention rights as a ground of appeal when both the act complained of and the decision which went against them at first instance took place before 2 October 2000 (the retrospectivity issue); (b) whether the PCC is a public authority for the purposes of s 6(1) of the Human Rights Act (the public authority issue); and (c) whether the act of the PCC in serving the notice under the 1932 Act on Mr and Mrs Wallbank

was incompatible with their rights under art 1 of the First Protocol read either
alone or in conjunction with art 14 of the convention (the incompatibility issue). *a*

THE RETROSPECTIVITY ISSUE

[25] When the case came before the Court of Appeal the PCC conceded that
it was open to Mr and Mrs Wallbank to raise the question whether its act in
serving the notice was unlawful under s 6(1) of the Human Rights Act by virtue   *b*
of ss 7(1)(b) and 22(4) of that Act, notwithstanding that service of the notice
predated the coming into force of those sections. The Court of Appeal accepted
this concession, which they considered to have been rightly made ([2001] 3 All ER
393 at [7]). Those were, of course, early days in the life of the Act. The cases of
R v Lambert [2001] UKHL 37, [2001] 3 All ER 577, [2002] 2 AC 545, R v Kansal (No 2)
[2001] UKHL 62, [2002] 1 All ER 257, [2002] 2 AC 69 and R v Benjafield [2002]   *c*
UKHL 2, [2002] 1 All ER 815, [2002] 2 WLR 235 had yet to come before your
Lordships' House. In the light of what was said in those cases about the issue of
retrospectivity the PCC gave notice in the statement of facts and issues of its
intention to apply for leave to dispute the issue in the course of the hearing of this
appeal. But in the PCC's written case it is stated that this contention is no longer   *d*
being pursued. In the result, although the parties were told at the outset of the
hearing that it should not be assumed that the House would necessarily proceed
on the basis of this concession, the issue was not the subject of argument.

[26] I have, nevertheless, given some thought to the question whether it
would be appropriate to examine the issue whether the service of the notice was
incompatible with Mr and Mrs Wallbank's convention rights. The question   *e*
whether, and if so in what circumstances, effect should be given to the Human
Rights Act where relevant events occurred before it came into force is far from
easy. So I should like to take a moment or two to explain why I have come to
the conclusion that the concession was properly made and that in this case
Mr and Mrs Wallbank are entitled to claim in these proceedings that the PCC   *f*
has acted in a way that is made unlawful by s 6(1) of the Act.

[27] As Lord Woolf CJ observed in Wainwright v Home Office [2001] EWCA
Civ 2081 at [22], [2003] 3 All ER 943 at [22], [2002] QB 1334 at [22], there has been
considerable uncertainty as to whether the Human Rights Act can apply
retrospectively in situations where the conduct complained of occurred before
the Act came into force. The position which we have reached so far can, I think,   *g*
be summarised in this way.

[28] The only provision in the Human Rights Act which gives retrospective
effect to any of its provisions is s 22(4). It directs attention exclusively to that part
of the Act which deals with the acts of public authorities: see ss 6–9. It has been
said that its effect is to enable the Act to be used defensively against public   *h*
authorities with retrospective effect but not offensively: see the annotations to
the Act by the late Peter Duffy QC in Current Law Statutes (1998) vol 3.
Section 22(4) states that s 7(1)(b) applies to proceedings brought by or at the
instigation of a public authority whenever the act in question took place, but
that otherwise sub-s (1)(b) does not apply to an act taking place before the   *j*
coming into force of s 7. Section 7(1)(b) enables a person who claims that a
public authority has acted in a way which is made unlawful by s 6(1) to rely on
his convention rights in proceedings brought by or at the instigation of the
public authority. Section 6(2)(a) provides that s 6(1) does not apply if as a result
of one or more provisions of primary legislation the authority could not have
acted differently.

a
[29] It has been held that acts of courts or tribunals which took place before 2 October 2000 which they were required to make by primary legislation and were made according to the meaning which was to be given to the legislation at that time are not affected by s 22(4): see *R v Kansal (No 2)* [2002] 1 All ER 257 at [84], *Wainwright's* case [2003] 3 All ER 943 at [29]–[36]. Section 3(2) states that the obligation in s 3(1) to interpret legislation in a way that is compatible with convention rights applies to primary and secondary legislation whenever
b enacted. But the interpretative obligation in s 3(1) cannot be applied to invalidate a decision which was good at the time when it was made by changing retrospectively the meaning which the court or tribunal previously gave to that legislation. The same view has been taken where the claim relates to acts of public authorities other than courts or tribunals. Here too it has been held that
c the Act cannot be relied upon retrospectively by introducing a right of privacy to make unlawful conduct which was lawful at the time when it took place: see *Wainwright's* case [2003] 3 All ER 943 at [40].

[30] In this case the act which s 6(1) is said to have made unlawful is the enforcement by the PCC of the liability for the cost of the repairs to the chancel.
d It is the enforcement of that liability that is said to be an unlawful interference with the personal property rights of Mr and Mrs Wallbank contrary to art 1 of the First Protocol. Service by the PCC of the notice on Mr and Mrs Wallbank under s 2(1) of the 1932 Act took place in September 1994, well before the coming into effect of the Human Rights Act. But the service of the notice under that subsection was just the first step in the taking of proceedings under
e the 1932 Act to enforce the liability to repair. If, as has happened here, the chancel is not put in proper repair within a period of one month from the date when the notice to repair was served proceedings must be taken by the responsible authority to recover the sum required to put the chancel in proper repair by means of an order of the court: see s 2(2) of the 1932 Act. The final step
f in the process is the giving by the court of judgment for the responsible authority for such sum as appears to it to represent the cost of putting the chancel in proper repair: see s 2(3). The arguments before Ferris J and in the Court of Appeal arose out of a direction that there should be trial of preliminary issues. The question which is before your Lordships relates to one of those issues. The proceedings are, in that sense, still at the preliminary stage. The stage of giving judgment
g under s 2(3) has not yet been reached.

[31] If the only act of the PCC which was in issue in this case had been the service of the notice on Mr and Mrs Wallbank it would have difficult, in the light of what was decided in *R v Lambert* and *R v Kansal*, to say that that act, which was lawful at the time when the notice was served and was still lawful when the
h preliminary issue was decided by Ferris J at first instance, had become unlawful following the coming into effect of the Human Rights Act. But the proceedings to give effect to that notice are still on foot. In this situation there is, in my opinion, no issue of retrospectivity. Mr and Mrs Wallbank do not need to rely on s 22(4). It is sufficient for their purpose to say that they wish to rely on their
j convention right in the proceedings which the PCC are still taking against them with a view to having the notice enforced. This is something that they are entitled to do under s 7(1)(b).

[32] It should be emphasised that the situation which I have outlined avoids the problems which were discussed in *R v Lambert* and *R v Kansal* about extending s 22(4) to appeals. We are, of course, dealing in this case with an appeal against the decision of a court or tribunal: see s 7(6)(a). But the fact is that the appeal

relates to a preliminary issue only. This means that the court has yet to reach the stage in these proceedings when effect can be given to the notice which the PCC have served. That still lies in the future. Section 7(6)(a) states that the expression 'legal proceedings' in s 7(1)(b) includes 'proceedings brought by or at the instigation of a public authority'. The preliminary issue has been examined as part of these proceedings.

[33] The question whether the proceedings of which an examination of the preliminary issue forms part are 'legal proceedings' as so defined brings me to the next issue, which is whether the PCC is a public authority for the purposes of s 6(1) of the Human Rights Act.

THE PUBLIC AUTHORITY ISSUE

(a) *Introduction*

[34] Section 6(1) provides that it is unlawful for a public authority to act in a way which is incompatible with a convention right. The expression 'public authority' is not fully defined anywhere in the Human Rights Act. What the Act does instead is to address itself to some particular issues. In all other respects the expression has been left to bear its ordinary meaning according to the context in which it is used. Section 6(3) provides:

'In this section "public authority" includes—(a) a court or tribunal, and (b) any person certain of whose functions are functions of a public nature, but does not include either House of Parliament or a person exercising functions in connection with proceedings in Parliament.'

Section 6(5) provides: 'In relation to a particular act, a person is not a public authority by virtue only of subsection (3)(b) if the nature of the act is private.'

[35] It is clear from these provisions that, for the purposes of this Act, public authorities fall into two distinct types or categories. Courts and tribunals, which are expressly included in the definition, can perhaps be said to constitute a third category but they can be left on one side for present purposes. The first category comprises those persons or bodies which are obviously public or 'standard' public authorities: see Clayton and Tomlinson *The Law of Human Rights* (2000) pp 189 (para 5.08). They were referred to in the course of the argument as 'core' public authorities. It appears to have been thought that no further description was needed as they obviously have the character of public authorities. In the *Notes on Clauses* which are quoted in *Clayton and Tomlinson* p 188 (para 5.06), it was explained that the legislation proceeds on the basis that some authorities are so obviously public authorities that it is not necessary to define them expressly. In other words, they are public authorities through and through. So s 6(5) does not apply to them. The second category comprises persons or bodies some of whose functions are of a public nature. They are described in *Clayton and Tomlinson* as 'functional' public authorities and were referred to in the argument as 'hybrid' public authorities. Section 6(5) applies to them, so in their case a distinction must be drawn between their public functions and the acts which they perform which are of a private nature.

[36] Skilfully drawn though these provisions are, they leave a great deal of open ground. There is room for doubt and for argument. It has been left to the courts to resolve these issues when they arise. It is plain that the Court of Appeal were being invited to enter into largely uncharted territory. As a result of their efforts we are better equipped as we set out on the same journey. We have the

a benefit of their decision and of the criticisms that have been made of it. We must now see where all this leads us. First, it is necessary to examine what they did.

[37] The Court of Appeal ([2003] 1 All ER 393 at [29]) declined, rightly in my opinion, to look to Hansard for assistance. They rejected the argument that there was an ambiguity which brought this case within the scope of the limited exception which was described in *Pepper (Inspector of Taxes) v Hart* [1993] 1 All ER

b 42, [1993] AC 593. It is true that various attempts were made by ministers in both Houses to explain their approach to the application of the Bill to what it described as public authorities. That was understandable, as some concern was expressed about the implications of this aspect of the legislation. But it is not the ministers' words, uttered as they were on behalf of the executive, that must be referred to in order to understand what Parliament intended. It is the words

c used by Parliament that must be examined in order to understand and apply the legislation that it has enacted.

[38] The Court of Appeal were invited to hold that the test of what is a public authority for the purposes of s 6 was function-based. They rejected this proposition too. As Sir Andrew Morritt V-C delivering the judgment of the

d court pointed out, this may well be determinative as regards the 'hybrid' class of public authorities as defined by s 6(3)(b). But it does not follow that it governs the principal category of 'core' public authorities ([2001] 3 All ER 393 at [33]). In the following paragraph he said that for this reason the decided cases on the amenability of bodies to judicial review, while plainly relevant, will not necessarily be determinative of a body's membership either of the

e principal or hybrid class of public authority. He noted that the authorities on judicial review, as they now stand, draw a conceptual line between functions of public governance and functions of mutual governance. He said that there was no surviving element of mutuality or mutual governance as between the impropriator and the church in the lay rector's modern liability for chancel

f repairs.

[39] Sir Andrew Morritt V-C set out the conclusions of the Court of Appeal on the public authority issue (at [35]):

g 'In our judgment it is inescapable, in these circumstances, that a PCC is a public authority. It is an authority in the sense that it possesses powers which private individuals do not possess to determine how others should act. Thus, in particular, its notice to repair has statutory force. It is public in the sense that it is created and empowered by law; that it forms part of the church by law established; and that its functions include the enforcement through the courts of a common law liability to maintain its chancels resting upon

h persons who need not be members of the church. If this were to be incorrect, the PCC would nevertheless, and for the same reasons, be a legal person certain of whose functions, chancel repairs among them, are functions of a public nature. It follows on either basis by virtue of s 6 that its acts, to be lawful, must be compatible with the rights set out in Sch 1 to the [Human Rights Act 1998].'

j [40] The Court of Appeal, in reaching the conclusion that the PCC is a 'core' public authority, appears to have proceeded in this way: (1) the PCC is an authority because it possesses powers which private individuals do not possess to enforce the lay rector's liability; and (2) it is public because it is created and empowered by law, it forms part of the Church of England as the established Church and its functions include the enforcement of the liability on persons

who need not be members of the Church. By a similar process of reasoning the
Court of Appeal concluded that the PCC is in any event a person some of whose *a*
functions, including chancel repairs, are functions of a public nature. In their
view the fact that the PCC has the power and duty to enforce the obligation on
persons with whom it has no other relationship showed that it has the character
of a public authority, or at least that it is performing a function of a public
nature when it is enforcing this liability (see also [2001] 3 All ER 393 at [36]).   *b*

[41] This approach has the obvious merit of concentrating on the words of the
statute. The words 'public' and 'authority' in s 6(1), 'functions of a public nature'
in s 6(3)(b) and 'private' in s 6(5) are, of course, important. The word 'public'
suggests that there are some persons which may be described as authorities that
are nevertheless private and not public. The word 'authority' suggests that the
person has regulatory or coercive powers given to it by statute or by the common *c*
law. The combination of these two words in the single unqualified phrase 'public
authority' suggests that it is the nature of the person itself, not the functions
which it may perform, that is determinative. Section 6(1) does not distinguish
between public and private functions. It assumes that everything that a 'core'
public authority does is a public function. It applies to everything that a *d*
person does in that capacity. This suggests that some care needs to be taken
to limit this category to cases where it is clear that this overarching treatment
is appropriate. The phrase 'functions of a public nature' in s 6(3), on the other
hand, does not make that assumption. It requires a distinction to be drawn
between functions which are public and those which are private. It has a much
wider reach, and it is sensitive to the facts of each case. It is the function that the *e*
person is performing that is determinative of the question whether it is, for the
purposes of that case, a 'hybrid' public authority. The question whether s 6(5)
applies to a particular act depends on the nature of the act which is in question in
each case.

[42] The absence of a more precise definition of the expression 'public *f*
authority' for the purposes of s 6(1) of the Human Rights Act may be contrasted
with the way that expression is used in the devolution legislation for Scotland
and Northern Ireland. Sections 88–90 of the Scotland Act 1998 deal with what
that Act calls 'cross-border public authorities'. 'Scottish public authorities' are
dealt with in Pt III of Sch 5. Definitions of these expressions are provided in
s 88(5), which requires 'a cross-border public authority' to be specified by Order *g*
in Council and in s 126(1) which states that 'Scottish public authority' means any
public body, public office or holder of such an office whose functions are
exercisable only in or as regards Scotland. A list of public bodies was appended
to the White Paper *Scotland's Parliament* (Cm 3658 (1997)): see also the note to
s 88 of the Human Rights Act in *Current Law Statutes* (1998) vol 3. It included *h*
three nationalised industries, a group of tribunals, three statutory water
authorities, health bodies and a large number of miscellaneous executive and
advisory bodies. Sections 75 and 76 of the Northern Ireland Act 1998 impose a
duty on public authorities to promote equality of opportunity and prohibit
discrimination in the carrying out of their functions. The expression 'public *j*
authority' for the purposes of each of these sections is defined in a way that
appears to leave no room for doubt as to which departments, corporations or
other bodies are included: see ss 75(3), 76(7).

[43] The Court of Appeal did not explore the significance of the distinction
which is drawn in s 6 between 'core' and 'hybrid' public authorities. In their
view the PCC, for the same reasons, fell into either category (see [2001] 3 All

a ER 393 at [35]). But the width that can be given to the 'hybrid' category suggests that the purpose of the legislation would not be impeded if the scope to be given to the concept of a 'core' public authority were to be narrowed considerably from that indicated by the Court of Appeal.

[44] There is one vital step that is missing from the Court of Appeal's analysis. It is not mentioned expressly in the Human Rights Act, but it is crucial

b to a proper understanding of the balance which ss 6–9 of the Act seek to strike between the position of public authorities on the one hand and private persons on the other. The purpose of these sections is to provide a remedial structure in domestic law for the rights guaranteed by the convention. It is the obligation of states which have ratified the convention to secure to everyone within their jurisdiction the rights and freedoms which it protects: see *Young v UK* (1981) 4

c EHRR 38 at 52 (para 49). The source of this obligation is art 13. It was omitted from the articles mentioned in s 1(1) which defines the meaning of the expression 'the Convention rights', as the purpose of ss 6–9 was to fulfil the obligation which it sets out. But it provides the background against which one must examine the scheme which these sections provide.

d [45] The principle upon which the scheme proceeds is that actions by public authorities are unlawful if they are in breach of convention rights: see s 6(1). Effect is given to that principle in s 7. It enables anyone who is a victim of an act made unlawful by s 6(1) to obtain a remedy. The extent to which the scheme derives its inspiration from the convention is revealed by the definition of the word 'victim' which is set out in s 7(7). It provides:

e
> 'For the purposes of this section, a person is a victim of an unlawful act only if he would be a victim for the purposes of Article 34 of the Convention if proceedings were brought in the European Court of Human Rights in respect of that act.'

f Article 34 of the convention is in these terms:

> 'The Court may receive applications from any person, non-governmental organisation or group of individuals claiming to be the victim of a violation by one of the High Contracting Parties of the rights set forth in the Convention or the protocols thereto. The High Contracting Parties
g undertake not to hinder in any way the effective exercise of this right.'

[46] The reference to non-governmental organisations in art 34 provides an important guide as to the nature of those persons who, for the purposes of s 6(1) of the Human Rights Act and the remedial scheme which flows from it, are to be taken to be public authorities. Non-governmental organisations have

h the right of individual application to the European Court of Human Rights as victims if their convention rights have been violated. If the scheme to give effect to art 13 is to be followed through, they must be entitled to obtain a remedy for a violation of their convention rights under s 7 in respect of acts made unlawful by s 6.

j [47] The test as to whether a person or body is or is not a 'core' public authority for the purposes of s 6(1) is not capable of being defined precisely. But it can at least be said that a distinction should be drawn between those persons who, in convention terms, are governmental organisations on the one hand and those who are non-governmental organisations on the other. A person who would be regarded as a non-governmental organisation within the meaning of art 34 ought not to be regarded as a 'core' public authority for

the purposes of s 6. That would deprive it of the rights enjoyed by the victims
of acts which are incompatible with convention rights that are made unlawful   *a*
by s 6(1). Professor Dawn Oliver 'The Frontiers of the State: Public Authorities
and Public Functions under the Human Rights Act' [2000] PL 476 at 491–493
has observed that this would have serious implications. It would undermine
the protections against state control which are the hallmarks of a liberal
democracy.   *b*

[48] In *Rothenthurm Commune v Switzerland* (1988) 59 DR 251 the European
Commission held that local government organisations such as the applicant
commune which exercise public functions are clearly 'governmental
organisations' as opposed to 'non-governmental organisations' within the
meaning of art 25 (now art 34) of the convention, with the result that the
commune which was complaining that proceedings for the expropriation of land   *c*
for a military training area were in breach of their rights under art 6(1) could not
bring an application under that article. In *Ayuntamiento de Mula v Spain*
App No 55346/00 (1 February 2001, unreported), the European Court of
Human Rights held that under the settled case law of the convention
institutions local government organisations are public law bodies which   *d*
perform official duties assigned to them by the constitution and by
substantive law and are therefore quite clearly governmental organisations.
It added this comment:

> 'In that connection, the court reiterates that in international law the
> expression "governmental organisations" cannot be held to refer only to   *e*
> the government or the central organs of the state. When powers are
> distributed along decentralised lines, it refers to any national authority
> which exercises public functions.'

[49] The phrase 'public functions' in this context is thus clearly linked to the
functions and powers, whether centralised or distributed, of government. This   *f*
point was developed more fully in *Holy Monasteries v Greece* (1995) 20 EHRR 1.
The government of Greece argued that the applicant monasteries, which were
challenging legislation which provided for the transfer of a large part of the
monastic property to the Greek state, were not non-governmental organisations
within the meaning of art 25 (now art 34) of the convention. It was pointed out *g*
that the monasteries were hierarchically integrated into the organic structure
of the Greek Orthodox Church, that legal personality was attributed to the
Church and its constituent parts in public law and that the Church and its
institutions, which played a direct and active part in public administration, took
administrative decisions whose lawfulness was subject to judicial review by the *h*
Supreme Administrative Court like those of any other public authority.
Rejecting this argument, the court said (at 41 (para 49)):

> 'Like the Commission in its admissibility decision, the Court notes at the
> outset that the applicant monasteries do not exercise governmental powers.
> Section 39(1) of the Charter of the Greek Church describes the monasteries   *j*
> as ascetic religious institutions. Their objectives—essentially ecclesiastical
> and spiritual ones, but also cultural and social ones in some cases—are not
> such as to enable them to be classed with governmental organisations
> established for public administration purposes. From the classification as
> public law entities it may be inferred only that the legislature—on account of
> the special links between the monasteries and the State—wished to afford

a them the same legal protection *vis-à-vis* third parties as was accorded to other public law entities. Furthermore, the monastery councils' only power consists in making rules concerning the organisation and furtherance of spiritual life and the internal administration of each monastery.'

b [50] The phrase 'governmental organisations established for public administration purposes' in the third sentence of the passage which I have quoted from the *Holy Monasteries* case is significant. It indicates that test of whether a person or body is a 'non-governmental organisation' within the meaning of art 34 of the convention is whether it was established with a view to public administration as part of the process of government. That too was the approach which was taken by the European Commission in *Hautanemi v Sweden*
c (1996) 22 EHRR CD 155. At the relevant time the Church of Sweden and its member parishes were to be regarded as corporations of public law in the domestic legal order. It was held nevertheless that the applicant parish was a victim within the meaning of what was then art 25, on the ground that the Church and its member parishes could not be considered to have been exercising
d governmental powers and the parish was a non-governmental organisation.

[51] It can be seen from what was said in these cases that the convention institutions have developed their own jurisprudence as to the meaning which is to be given to the expression 'non-governmental organisation' in art 34. We must take that jurisprudence into account in determining any question which has arisen in connection with a convention right: see s 2(1) of the Human
e Rights Act.

[52] The Court of Appeal left this jurisprudence out of account. They looked instead for guidance to cases about the amenability of bodies to judicial review, although they recognised that they were not necessarily determinative ([2001] 3 All ER at [34]). But, as Professor Oliver has pointed out
f in her commentary on the decision of the Court of Appeal in this case, 'Chancel repairs and the Human Rights Act' [2001] PL 651, the decided cases on the amenability of bodies to judicial review have been made for purposes which have nothing to do with the liability of the state in international law. They cannot be regarded as determinative of a body's membership of the class of 'core' public authorities: see also Grosz, Beatson, Duffy *Human Rights: The 1998*
g *Act and the European Convention* (2000) p 61 (para 4-04). Nor can they be regarded as determinative of the question whether a body falls within the 'hybrid' class. That is not to say that the case law on judicial review may not provide some assistance as to what does, and what does not, constitute a 'function of a public nature' within the meaning of s 6(3)(b). It may well be
h helpful. But the domestic case law must be examined in the light of the jurisprudence of the Strasbourg court as to those bodies which engage the responsibility of the state for the purposes of the convention.

[53] At first sight there is a close link between the question whether a person is a non-governmental organisation for the purposes of art 34 and the question
j whether a person is a public authority against which the doctrine of the direct effect of directives operates under Community law: see art 249 EC (formerly art 189). Both concepts lie at the heart of the obligations of the state under international law. Individual applications for a violation of convention rights may be received under art 34 from 'any person, non-governmental organisation or group of individuals'. Direct effect exists only against the member state concerned 'and other public authorities': see *ECSC v Acciaierie e Ferriere*

Busseni SpA (in liq) Case C-221/88 [1990] ECR I-495 at 525 (para 23); Brent *Directives: Rights and Remedies in English and Community Law* (2001) pp 198–199 (para 15.11).

[54] The types of organisations and bodies against whom the provisions of a directive could be relied on were discussed in *Foster v British Gas plc* Case C-188/89 [1990] 3 All ER 897 at 921–922, [1991] 1 QB 405 at 427, [1990] ECR I-3313 at 3348 (para 18). The court noted that it had been held in a series of cases that provisions of a directive could be relied on against organisations and bodies which were subject to the authority or control of the state or had special powers beyond those which result from the normal rules applicable to relations between individuals. Reference was made to a number of its decisions to illustrate this point. Its conclusions were set out ([1990] 3 All ER 897 at 922, [1991] 1 QB 405 at 427, [1990] ECR I-3313 at 3348–3349 (para 20)):

> 'It follows from the foregoing that a body, whatever its legal form, which has been made responsible, pursuant to a measure adopted by the state, for providing a public service under the control of the state and which has for that purpose special powers beyond those which result from the normal rules applicable in relations between individuals is included in any event among the bodies against which the provisions of a directive capable of having direct effect may be relied on.'

[55] This is a broad definition of the concept by which such bodies have come to be referred to as 'emanations of the State': e g *Johnston v Chief Constable of the Royal Ulster Constabulary* Case 222/84 [1986] 3 All ER 135 at 161, [1987] QB 129 at 154, [1986] ECR 1651 at 1691 (para 56). It has been described as a starting point: see *Doughty v Rolls-Royce plc* [1992] 1 CMLR 1045 at 1058 per Mustill LJ. As Brent p 199, para 15.11, note 101 points out, the phrase 'emanation of the State' is an English legal concept derived from *Gilbert v Trinity House Corp* (1886) 17 QBD 795 which was later criticised by the courts as inappropriate and undefined. Whatever its value may be in the context of European Community law, however, it would be neither safe nor helpful to use this concept as a shorthand way of describing the test that must be applied to determine whether a person or body is a non-governmental organisation for the purposes of art 34 of the convention. There is no right of individual application to the European Court of Justice in European Community law. The phrase 'non-governmental organisation' has an autonomous meaning in convention law.

(b) Is the PCC a public authority?

[56] The general functions and powers of PCCs in the Church of England are set out in the Parochial Church Councils (Powers) Measure 1956. That was a measure passed by the National Assembly of the Church of England under the powers which were conferred on the National Assembly by the Church of England Assembly (Powers) Act 1919. The National Assembly was renamed and reconstituted as the General Synod of the Church of England by the Synodical Government Measure 1969. Section 7 of the 1969 measure provides that the rules contained in Sch 3, which may be cited as the Church Representation Rules, are to have effect for the purpose of providing for the constitution and proceedings of diocesan and deanery synods and making further provision for the synodical government of the church. Part II of the Church Representation Rules provides for the holding of annual parochial

a church meetings at which parochial representatives of the laity to the PCC and
the deanery synod are to take place. Rule 14 sets out the membership of the
PCC. It includes the clergy, churchwardens, any persons on the roll of the parish
who are members of any deanery or diocesan synod or the General Synod,
elected representatives of the laity and co-opted members.

b [57] Section 2(1) of the 1956 measure provides that it shall be the duty of the
minister, as defined in r 44(1) of the Church Representation Rules, and the PCC
to consult together on matters of general concern and importance to the parish.
Section 2(2) states that the functions of PCCs shall include, among other things,
co-operation with the minister in promoting in the parish the whole mission of
the Church, pastoral, evangelistic, social and ecumenical and the consideration
and discussion of matters concerning the Church of England or any other matters
c of religious or public interest other than the declaration of the doctrine of the
Church on any question. Among the powers, duties and liabilities vested in PCCs
by s 4 are those relating to the financial affairs of the church and the care,
maintenance and preservation of its fabric. Section 2 of the Chancel Repairs
Act 1932 provides that, where a chancel is in need of repair, proceedings to
d enforce the liability to repair are to be taken by the responsible authority.
Section 4(1) of the 1932 Act provides that the expression '[r]esponsible authority'
in relation to a chancel means the PCC of the parish in which the chancel is
situate.

[58] There is no doubt that PCCs are an essential part of the administration,
on the authority of the General Synod, of the affairs of the Church of England.
e The parish itself has been described as the basic building block of the Church and
the PCC as the central forum for decision-making and discussion in relation to
parish affairs: Mark Hill *Ecclesiastical Law* (2nd edn, 2001) pp 48–49 and 74
(paras 3.11 and 3.74). It is constituted by s 3 of the 1956 measure as a body
corporate. It has statutory powers which it may exercise under s 2 of the 1932
f Act against any person who appears to it to be liable to repair the chancel,
irrespective of whether that person is resident in the parish and is a member of
the Church of England. In that context, perhaps, it may be said in a very loose
sense to be a public rather than a private body.

[59] But none of these characteristics indicate that it is a governmental
organisation, as that phrase is understood in the context of art 34 of the
g convention. It plainly has nothing whatever to do with the process of either
central or local government. It is not accountable to the general public for
what it does. It receives no public funding, apart from occasional grants from
English Heritage for the preservation of its historic buildings. In that respect
it is in a position which is no different from that of any private individual. The
h statutory powers which it has been given by the 1932 Act are not exercisable
against the public generally or any class or group of persons which forms part
of it. The purpose of that Act, as its long title indicates, was to abolish
proceedings in ecclesiastical courts for enforcing the liability to repair. The only
person against whom the liability may be enforced is the person who, in that
j obscure phrase, 'would, but for the provisions of this Act, have been liable to be
admonished to repair the chancel by the appropriate Ecclesiastical Court in a
cause of office promoted against him in that Court on the date when the notice
was served' (see s 2(3); *Wickhambrook Parochial Church Council v Croxford* [1935] 2
KB 417 at 429 per Lord Hanworth MR).

[60] Then there is the fact that the PCC is part of the Church of England.
The Court of Appeal said that it exemplifies the special status of the Church of

which it forms part ([2001] 3 All ER 393 at [32]). The fact that it forms part of
the Church by law established showed, it was said (at [35]), that the PCC is a
public authority. The implication of these observations is that other bodies
such as diocesan and deanery synods and the General Synod itself fall into the
same category. In my opinion however the legal framework of the Church of
England as a Church by law established does not lead to this conclusion.

[61] The Church of England as a whole has no legal status or personality.
There is no Act of Parliament that purports to establish it as the Church of
England: Sir Lewis Dibdin *Establishment in England: Essays on Church and State*
(1932) p 111. What establishment in law means is that the state has incorporated
its law into the law of the realm as a branch of its general law. In *Marshall v
Graham, Bell v Graham* [1907] 2 KB 112 at 126 Phillimore J said:

> 'A Church which is established is not thereby made a department of the
> State. The process of establishment means that the State has accepted the
> Church as the religious body in its opinion truly teaching the Christian faith,
> and given to it a certain legal position, and to its decrees, if rendered under
> certain legal conditions, certain civil sanctions.'

The Church of England is identified with the state in other ways, the monarch
being head of each: see Norman Doe *The Legal Framework of the Church of
England* (1996) p 9. It has regulatory functions within its own sphere, but it
cannot be said to be part of government. The state has not surrendered or
delegated any of its functions or powers to the Church. None of the functions
that the Church of England performs would have to be performed in its place
by the state if the Church were to abdicate its responsibility: see *R v Chief Rabbi
of the United Hebrew Congregations of Great Britain and the Commonwealth,
ex p Wachmann* [1993] 2 All ER 249 at 254, [1992] 1 WLR 1036 at 1042 per Simon
Brown J. The relationship which the state has with the Church of England is
one of recognition, not of the devolution to it of any of the powers or functions
of government.

[62] The decisions of the Strasbourg court in *Holy Monasteries v Greece* (1995)
20 EHRR 1 and *Hautanemi v Sweden* (1996) 22 EHRR CD 155 support this
approach. It is also worth noting that, while the two main churches in Germany
(Roman Catholic and Lutheran) have public legal personality and are public
authorities bound by the provisions of art 19(4) of the German constitution
(Grundgesetz) or Basic Law which guarantees recourse to the court should any
person's basic rights be violated by public authority, they are in general
considered to be 'non-governmental organisations' within the meaning of art 34
of the convention. As such, they are entitled to avail themselves of, for example,
the right to protection of property under art 1 of the First Protocol: Frowein and
Peukert *Kommentar zur Europäishen Menschenrechtskonvention* (2nd edn, 1996)
art 25, para 16. Maunz and Dürig *Kommentar zum Grundgesetz* (looseleaf) art 33,
para 38 explain the position in this way:

> 'Keine hoheitsrechtlichen Befugnisse nehmen die Amtsträger der Kirchen
> wahr, soweit sie nicht kraft staatlicher Ermächtigung (etwa in
> Kirchensteurangelegenheiten) tätig werden; die Kirchen sind, auch soweit
> sie öffentlich-rechtlichen Status haben, nicht Bestandteile der staatlichen
> Organisation.'

[Church officeholders do not exercise sovereign power so long as they are not
acting by virtue of state empowerment (for example, in matters concerning

a church taxes); the churches do not, even though they have public law status, form an integral part of the organisation of the state.] This reflects the view of the German Constitutional Court in its 1965 decision (BVerfGE 18, 385) that measures taken by a church relating to purely internal matters which do not reach out into the sphere of the state do not constitute acts of sovereign power. The churches are not, as we would put it, 'core' public authorities although

b they may be regarded as 'hybrid' public authorities for certain purposes.

[63] For these reasons I would hold that the PCC is not a 'core' public authority. As for the question whether it is a 'hybrid' public authority, I would prefer not to deal with it in the abstract. The answer must depend on the facts of each case. The issue with which your Lordships are concerned in this case relates to the functions of the PCC in the enforcement of a liability

c to effect repairs to the chancel. Section 6(5) of the Human Rights Act provides that a person is not a public authority by virtue only of sub-s (3) if the nature of the act which is alleged to be unlawful is private. The Court of Appeal said that the function of chancel repairs is of a public nature ([2001] 3 All ER 393 at [35]). But the liability of the lay rector to repair the chancel is a

d burden which arises as a matter of private law from the ownership of glebe land.

[64] It is true, as Wynn-Parry J observed in *Chivers & Sons Ltd v Secretary of State for Air (Queens' College, Cambridge, Third Party)* [1955] 2 All ER 607 at 609, [1955] Ch 585 at 593, that the burden is imposed for the benefit of the parishioners. It may be said that, as the church is a historic building which is

e open to the public, it is in the public interest that these repairs should be carried out. It is also true that the liability to repair the chancel rests on persons who need not be members of the church and that there is, as the Court of Appeal observed (at [34]), no surviving element of mutuality or mutual governance between the church and the impropriator. But none of these factors leads to the

f conclusion that the PCC's act in seeking to enforce the lay rector's liability on behalf of the parishioners is a public rather than a private act. The nature of the act is to be found in the nature of the obligation which the PCC is seeking to enforce. It is seeking to enforce a civil debt. The function which it is performing has nothing to do with the responsibilities which are owed to the public by the state. I would hold that s 6(5) applies, and that in relation to this act the PCC is

g not for the purposes of s 6(1) a public authority.

THE INCOMPATIBILITY ISSUE

[65] This issue does not arise if, as I would hold, the PCC is not for present purposes a public authority. But I should like to offer these brief comments on it,

h as I do not agree with the Court of Appeal's finding (at [38]–[46]) that Mr and Mrs Wallbank's right to peaceful enjoyment of their possessions under art 1 of the First Protocol, read either alone or with art 14 of the convention, has been violated.

[66] Article 1 of the First Protocol provides:

j

'Every natural or legal person is entitled to the peaceful enjoyment of his possessions. No one shall be deprived of his possessions except in the public interest and subject to the conditions provided for by law and by the general principles of international law. The preceding provisions shall not, however, in any way impair the right of a State to enforce such laws as it deems necessary to control the use of property in accordance with the general interest or to secure the payment of taxes or other contributions or penalties.'

Article 14 of the convention prohibits discrimination in the enjoyment of the rights and freedoms which the convention sets forth.

[67] Article 1 of the First Protocol contains three distinct rules: see *Sporrong v Sweden* (1983) 5 EHRR 35 at 50 (para 61), *James v UK* (1986) 8 EHRR 123 at 139–140 (para 37). The first rule is set out in the first sentence, which is of a general nature and enunciates the principle of the peaceful enjoyment of property. It then deals with two forms of interference with a person's possessions by the state: deprivation of possessions which it subjects to certain conditions, and control of the use of property in accordance with the general interest. In each case a balance must be struck between the rights of the individual and the public interest to determine whether the interference was justified. These rules are not unconnected as, before considering whether the first rule has been complied with, the court must first determine whether the last two rules are applicable. As it was put in *James v UK* (at 139–140 (para 37)), the second and third rules are concerned with particular instances of interference with the right to peaceful enjoyment of property. They should be construed in the light of the general principle enunciated in the first rule.

[68] The Court of Appeal appear to have overlooked this guidance. They did not address the question whether Mr and Mrs Wallbank were being deprived of their possessions according to the second rule, and they did not deal with the question whether there was an interference with the first rule. They held that the liability to defray the cost of chancel repairs was levy upon the personal funds of Mr and Mrs Wallbank, that this was a form of taxation within the third rule in the second paragraph of art 1, and that it was arbitrary and disproportionate. They rejected the PCC's argument the source of the liability was their ownership of Glebe Farm. They held ([2001] 3 All ER 393 at [40]) that there was in this case an outside intervention by the general law which made ownership of the land a fiscal liability.

[69] Ferris J said in his judgment that, if the law relating to chancel repairs was as he understood it to be (which he described as 'the supposed rule'), it did not involve a deprivation of possessions. As he put it:

'The argument for Mr and Mrs Wallbank seems to assume that the starting point is that they are to be regarded as the owners of Glebe Farm free from incumbrances or other burdensome incidents attached to the ownership of the land. But this is not in fact correct if the supposed rule represents the law. The liability to repair the chancel is, on that basis, one of the incidents of ownership of that part of Glebe Farm which consists of land allotted under the inclosure award in lieu of tithe or other rectorial property. It is, of course, an unusual incident because it does not amount to a charge on the land, is not limited to the value of the land and imposes a personal liability on the owner of the land. But in principle I do not find it possible to distinguish it from the liability which would attach to the owner of land which is purchased subject to a mortgage, restrictive covenant or other incumbrance created by a predecessor in title.'

He said that the case was quite different from that in which there was some kind of outside intervention in the form of taxation, compulsory purchase or control over the way in which the property can be used.

a   [70] I prefer Ferris J's analysis to that of the Court of Appeal. The principle which we must follow was described in *James v UK* (at 139 (para 36)). We must confine our attention, as far as possible, to the concrete case which is before us. It must not be directed to the impact of the law relating to the enforcement of the chancel repair liability in the abstract, but to its impact as it affects Mr and Mrs Wallbank.

b   [71] How then does the liability arise? It cannot be considered in isolation from the obligation that gives rise to it. That is the obligation which rests on the owner of rectorial land, not as a result of any outside intervention with the possession of the land by the state but as a matter of private law. The conveyance of Glebe Farm to Mrs Wallbank's parents in 1970 described the land as subject to the liability for the repair of the chancel mentioned in previous
c   conveyances. Their deeds of gift to Mrs Wallbank in 1974 and 1986 also referred to the chancel repair liability. This is a burden on the land, just like any other burden that runs with the lands. It is, and has been at all times, within the scope of the property right which she acquired and among the various factors to be taken into account in determining its value. She could have
d   divested herself of it at any time by disposing of the land to which it was attached. The enforcement of the liability under the general law is an incident of the property right which is now vested jointly in Mr and Mrs Wallbank. It is not, as the Court of Appeal said (at [40]), an outside intervention by way of a form of taxation.

e   [72] I recognise that Mr and Mrs Wallbank may well need to draw on their personal funds to discharge the liability. But they are not being deprived of their possessions or being controlled in the use of their property, as those expressions must be understood in the light of the general principle of peaceful enjoyment set out in the first sentence of art 1 of the First Protocol. The liability is simply an incident of the ownership of the land which gives rise to it.
f   The peaceful enjoyment of land involves the discharge of burdens which are attached to it as well as the enjoyment of its rights and privileges. I do not think that in this case the right which art 1 of the First Protocol guarantees, read alone or in conjunction with art 14 of the convention, is being violated.

CONCLUSION

g   [73] The law relating to the liability for chancel repairs is open to criticism on various grounds. The liability has been described by the Law Commission as anachronistic and capricious in its application and as highly anomalous: *Liability for Chancel Repairs* (Law Com No 152 (1985)) p 7 (para 3.1); *Land Registration for the Twenty-First Century: A Consultative Document* (1998) (Law Com No 254;
h   Cm 4027) pp 81–82 (para 5.37). The existence of the liability can be difficult to discover, as most lay rectories have become fragmented over the years as a result of the division and separate disposals of land: *Transfer of Land, Liability for Chancel Repairs* (1983) (Law Commission Working Paper No 86) pp 20–21 (para 2.29). The fact that it is a several liability may operate unfairly in cases where there is
j   more than one lay rector and the person who is found liable is unable to recover a contribution from others who ought to have been found liable.

    [74] On the other hand it was noted in the 1983 Law Commission Working Paper that there were some 5,200 chancels for which there is a chancel repair liability. Not all of these cases involve individual landowners. About 800 are the liability of the Church Commissioners, 200 the liability of cathedrals and 200 the liability of educational foundations. Charitable donations may provide relief in

some cases, while in others grants may be available from English Heritage. But
there is no other source of private funding that can be relied upon, and there is
no right of access to public funds. Unsatisfactory though the system may appear
to be, there is no obvious alternative. Ferris J recognised in his judgment that the
law relating to chancel repairs is capable of operating arbitrarily, harshly and
unfairly. But he did not find any basis for declaring the law to be otherwise than
it appeared to be on the authorities.

[75] It is not open to us to resolve these problems judicially. All one can say
is that the Human Rights Act does not provide a vehicle for doing so. I would
allow the appeal and restore the order and determination made by Ferris J.

LORD HOBHOUSE OF WOODBOROUGH.

[76] My Lords, it is admitted by the defendants that, apart from the Human
Rights Act 1998, they are, as the joint owners of Glebe Farm, Aston Cantlow,
and have been at all material times personally responsible for the repair of the
chancel of the church of St John the Baptist Aston Cantlow and that, they
having failed to repair the chancel, the Parochial Church Council (PCC) is
entitled to a judgment against them under s 2(3) of the Chancel Repairs
Act 1932 for such sum as represents the cost of putting the chancel into a proper
state of repair. This is because the defendants, Mr and Mrs Wallbank, being
liable to repair the chancel, would, but for the 1932 Act, have been liable to be
admonished to repair the chancel by an ecclesiastical court. The obligation of
the defendants is the obligation to repair. Under the 1932 Act the remedy of an
order that the obligation be performed is no longer to be available and the
monetary remedy is provided in lieu but the character of the obligation was left
unchanged.

[77] The obligation to repair is one which derives from the ownership of land
to which the obligation is attached. The obligation runs with the land. The
fifteenth and sixteenth century origins of this are helpfully explained in the
opinion of my noble and learned friend Lord Scott of Foscote. In the present
case the obligation arose not from the receipt of tithes but as a result of an
inclosure award of 1743 made under the private Act of Parliament of 1742. It is
a personal obligation but only exists so long as the person in question is the
owner of the land. Thus he acquires it by a voluntary act—the acquisition of
the title to the land of which the obligation is an incident. He can divest himself
of the obligation by a further voluntary act—the disposal of the land or, under
s 52 of the Ecclesiastical Dilapidations Measure 1923, by redemption. At all the
times material to this case, the obligation was categorised by s 70 of the Land
Registration Act 1925 as an overriding interest. The person or persons who are
under such an obligation are described, using the historical terminology, as the
'lay rectors' or the 'lay impropriators'.

[78] In fact the defendants knew that ownership of the land was believed to
carry with it the obligation. It was referred to in all the title deeds and, in at
least one conveyance, an express indemnity had been taken by the vendor. In
other cases some special consideration might arise from the fact that the
relevant landowner had acquired the title to the land without any notice of
the existence, or possible existence, of the obligation. But that is not this case
and it need not be discussed further.

[79] The only defence now raised by the defendants to the claim of the PCC
under the 1932 Act is based upon the Human Rights Act 1998 and/or the
convention. The Human Rights Act had not come into force at the time when

a the defendants failed to carry out the relevant repairs, nor when the PCC served the notice required by s 2(1) of the 1932 Act, nor at the time when Ferris J ([2000] All ER (D) 419) tried the case and gave judgment for the PCC. He was formally trying two preliminary issues ordered by Master Bragge but, when he decided the human rights issue against the defendants, the defendants, having abandoned their case on the other issue, admitted that they had no defence to
b the claim except as to quantum. He accordingly made a declaration of liability, ordered an inquiry as to quantum and ordered the defendants to pay to the claimants the sum found due on the inquiry. The question of quantum arose under s 2(3) of the 1932 Act: '[the] court ... shall give judgment ... for such sum as appears to the court to represent the cost of putting the chancel in proper repair'. The points which the defendants were taking on quantum were pleaded
c in para 1 of the outline defence. The judgment of Ferris J was in English procedural law a final judgment. The defendants appealed to the Court of Appeal. By the time that the defendants' appeal was heard, the Human Rights Act had however come into force.

[80] This timetable raises again the question of the extent to which the
d Human Rights Act has a retrospective effect, a question on which the Court of Appeal ([2001] 3 All ER 393) did not express an opinion since no point was taken in that regard by the PCC. Your Lordships were not satisfied that this was necessarily correct; however it was clearly convenient and in the interest of both of the parties that the House should first hear the parties' arguments upon the points which the Court of Appeal did decide. I stress that the House has not heard
e any argument upon the question of the extent, if at all, to which the Act has retrospective effect. It is not appropriate that any view should be expressed on it in the present case. Anything said will not be authoritative. The retrospectivity point will arise for decision in other unrelated appeals and will then fall to be decided after full argument and due consideration. It is in any event not correct
f to approach that question on the basis that the judgment of Ferris J was undeterminative or merely interlocutory. In English procedural law, it was a final judgment which, unless reversed on appeal, determined the parties' rights and liabilities, subject only to quantum. I will accordingly proceed on the basis of assuming that the Human Rights Act applies to this case in accordance with the provisions of ss 22(4), 7(1)(b) and 6.

g [81] The structure of the defendants' argument under the Human Rights Act is that they have to establish three propositions. If they fail on any one of these, their defence fails. They are: (a) that the PCC is a public authority, the s 6(1), (3) and (5) point; and (b) that there has been a breach of art 1 of the First Protocol, the arts 1 and 14 point; and (c) that the exclusion in s 6(2) does not apply. Before
h Ferris J only point (b) arose and he decided it in favour of the claimants. In the Court of Appeal all three points were decided in favour of the defendants.

[82] These were the questions of law raised on this appeal. They are questions which are of relevance not only to the present case but to many other cases or potential cases concerning the enforcement under the 1932 Act of the obligation
j to repair chancels. Other cases may, on their facts, raise special considerations not found in this case and, similarly, legal questions not dependent upon the Human Rights Act may arise. Your Lordships' decision of this appeal does not touch upon any of them. But I must expressly disassociate myself from any suggestion that there is a cap upon the monetary liability under s 2(3) of the 1932 Act or that any such point is presently open to the defendants upon the inquiry ordered by Ferris J as discussed in the opinion of my noble and learned friend

Lord Scott of Foscote, which I have had the privilege of reading in draft after I had
prepared this opinion, together with his questioning of the correctness of the
decision in *Wickhambrook Parochial Church Council v Croxford* [1935] 2 KB 417. The
question was neither raised nor argued. There are contentious points which will
arise if it ever is: does the cap apply where the express words of the 1932 Act are
applicable? How does it apply to successive or continuing and cumulative
breaches of the obligation to repair? Does the cap apply where the liability is not
attributable to the ownership of a tithe rentcharge but simply to the ownership
of land? If so, how does one assess what the cap should be? It is by no means clear
that any of these questions should be answered in a way that could assist the
defendants. But they have not been argued and I will say no more about them.

IS THE PCC A PUBLIC AUTHORITY?

[83] Historically PCCs did not exist. They were introduced by the Parochial
Church Councils Measure 1921 as a body at parish level which would better
enable the lay members of the congregation to be represented. It was agreed that
at the material times the powers and functions of PCCs were defined by the
Parochial Church Councils (Powers) Measure 1956. Section 2 (as amended)
provided:

'*General Functions of Council.*—(1) It shall be the duty of the minister and
the [PCC] to consult together on matters of general concern and importance
to the parish.
(2) The functions of [PCCs] shall include—(a) co-operation with the
minister in promoting in the parish the whole mission of the Church,
pastoral, evangelistic, social and ecumenical; (b) the consideration and
discussions of matters concerning the Church of England or any other
matters of religious or public interest, but not the declaration of the doctrine
of the Church on any question; (c) making known and putting into effect any
provision made by the diocesan synod or the deanery synod, but without
prejudice to the powers of the council on any particular matter; (d) giving
advice to the diocesan synod and the deanery synod on any matter referred
to the council; (e) raising such matters as the council consider appropriate
with the diocesan synod or deanery synod.
(3) In the exercise of its functions the [PCC] shall take into consideration
any expression of opinion by any parochial church meeting.'

Section 3 provided that the PCC was to be a body corporate with perpetual
succession. Section 4 made provision for the PCC as successor to certain other
bodies to have the relevant powers of those bodies:

'(1) ... the council of every parish shall have ... (ii) The like powers duties
and liabilities as, immediately before [1 July 1921], the churchwardens of
such parish had with respect to—(a) The financial affairs of the church
including the collection and administration of all moneys raised for church
purposes and the keeping of accounts in relation to such affairs and moneys;
(b) The care maintenance preservation and insurance of the fabric of the
church and the goods and ornaments thereof; (c) The care and maintenance
of any churchyard (open or closed), and the power of giving a certificate
under the provisions of section eighteen of the Burial Act 1855 with the like
powers as, immediately before [1 July 1921], were possessed by the
churchwardens to recover the cost of maintaining a closed churchyard ...'

a Of these powers, the most relevant to the present case are those in s 4(1)(ii)(b) but it is important to note that these are only those powers and duties which the churchwardens had and that the churchwardens did not have a duty to repair the fabric but only a duty to report its disrepair. As stated by Chancellor Richard Burn in the ninth edition of his work *Ecclesiastical Law* (1842) edited by Robert Phillimore (vol I, p 357):

b   'And although churchwardens are not charged with the repairs of the chancel, yet they are charged with the supervisal thereof, to see that it be not permitted to dilapidate and fall into decay; and when any such dilapidations shall happen, if no care be taken to repair the same, they are to make presentation thereof at the next visitation.'

c It was no doubt following this logic that the PCC were given the power (and correlative duty) in 1932 to bring the action to obtain a remedy for the failure of a lay rector to repair the chancel. (The changes later introduced by s 39 of the Endowment and Glebe Measure 1976 relating to incumbents of a benefice are not relevant to this case.)

d [84] The PCC is thus the creature of a statutory provision by what was then the National Assembly of the Church of England. It has only those functions, duties and powers which have been conferred on it by that or other legislation. It is part of the structure known as the Church of England but the Church of England is not itself a legal entity. The legal entities are the various office-holders and various distinct bodies set up within that structure.

e [85] The Human Rights Act and s 6 do not contain any complete or general definition of the term 'a public authority'. Section 6 does however contain a secondary definition in sub-ss (3)(b) and (5) as including, in respect of acts which are not of a private nature, persons (or bodies) certain of whose functions are functions of a public nature. This secondary category has been described as

f 'hybrid' public authorities. It requires a twofold assessment, first of the body's functions, and secondly of the particular act in question. The body must be one of which at least some, but not all, of its functions are of a public nature. This leaves what by inference from sub-s (3)(b) is the primary category, ie a person or body *all* of whose functions are of a public nature. This category has conveniently been called by the commentators a 'core' public authority. For this

g category, there is no second requirement; the section potentially applies to everything that they do regardless of whether it is an act of a private or public nature.

[86] Is a PCC a 'core' public authority? The answer I would give to this question is that it is clearly not. Its functions, as identified above from the

h relevant statutory provisions, clearly include matters which are concerned only with the pastoral and organisational concerns of the diocese and the congregation of believers in the parish. It acts in the sectional not the public interest. The most that can be said is that it is a creature of a Church measure having the force of a statute—but that is not suggested to be conclusive—and that some aspects

j of the Church of England which is the 'established Church' are of wider general interest and not of importance to the congregation alone. Thus the priest ministering in the parish may have responsibilities that are certainly not public, such as the supervision of the liturgies used or advising about doctrine, but may have other responsibilities which are of a public nature, such as a responsibility for marriages and burials and the keeping of registers. But the PCC itself does not have such public responsibilities nor are its functions public; it is essentially a domestic religious body. The fact that the Church of England is the established Church of England may mean that various bodies within that Church may as a result perform public functions. But it does not follow that PCCs themselves perform any such functions. Even the monasteries of the established Church in Greece, which has strong legal links with the state, such as the presence of representatives of the state on its governing body and direct financial links with the state, has been held not to be an emanation of the state for the purposes of the convention: see *Holy Monasteries v Greece* (1995) 20 EHRR 1.

[87] The Court of Appeal reached a different conclusion. I do not find their reasoning satisfactory. Neither Parliamentary material nor references to the law of judicial review assist on this question. The relevant underlying principles are to be found in human rights law not in Community law nor in the administrative law of England and Wales. The Strasbourg jurisprudence has already been deployed in the opinion of my noble and learned friend Lord Hope of Craighead and I need not repeat it. The relevant concept is the opposition of the 'victim' and a 'governmental body'. The former can make a complaint; the latter can only be the object of a complaint. The difference between them is that the latter has a governmental character and discharges governmental functions. If there is a need to find additional assistance in construing s 6 of the Human Rights Act, this is where it is to be found. The structure of the Act also supports the same conclusion. It is through s 7 and its reference to victims in s 7(1) and (7) that one gets from s 22(4) to s 6(1). Section 7 is drafted having regard to the Strasbourg jurisprudence; it would be inconsistent to construe s 6 in a manner opposed to that jurisprudence. The Court of Appeal's approach cannot be supported.

[88] In my opinion it has not been established that PCCs in general nor this PCC in particular perform any function of a public or governmental nature. If it is to be said that they do, I am unaware what specifically it can be said is that function. The Court of Appeal ([2001] 3 All ER at [34]) said that the recovery of money under s 2 of the 1932 Act was the function which made the PCC a public authority. This is to be contrasted with the statement (at [37]) that the 'power and, no doubt duty' to do so is a 'common law' power. The nature of the person's functions are not to be confused with the nature of the act complained of, as s 6 makes clear. But in neither case are they governmental in nature nor is the body itself inherently governmental. It follows that in my opinion the PCC was neither a 'core' nor a 'hybrid' public authority. On that basis the defence of Mr and Mrs Wallbank must fail.

[89] But, if I am wrong, and the PCC was a 'hybrid' public authority, the further question arises under s 6(5): is the nature of the relevant act private? The act is the enforcement of a civil liability. The liability is one which arises under private law and which is enforceable by the PCC as a civil debt by virtue of the 1932 Act. The 1932 Act did not alter the pre-existing law as to the obligations of lay impropriators. It is simply remedial (as the Court of Appeal recognised at [37]). Its purpose is to enable repairs to be done which the lay rector ought to have, but has not, himself carried out. It is argued that it is akin to a power of taxation. Whether or not it was once true in the sixteenth century that such a power existed, it was certainly not true in the twentieth century. Whatever the former obligations of lay impropriators may once have been, by the eighteenth century they were or had been converted into civil obligations. In the present case this occurred in 1743 as a result of an inclosure award made under a private

a Act of Parliament of 1742 entitled: 'An Act for Dividing and Inclosing, Setting out and Allotting, certain Common Fields and Inclosures within the Manor and Parish of Aston Cantlow, in the County of Warwick.' In return for financial and proprietorial advantages then conferred upon them, the impropriators accepted the obligation to repair the chancel as and when the need arose. That is the private law obligation which is being enforced in the present action using

b the remedy provided in the 1932 Act.

[90] The 1932 Act is irrelevant unless and until the lay impropriator fails to perform his obligation to repair the chancel, a failure which may have occurred on a single occasion or may, as in the present case, have been a continuing and cumulative failure over a long period of time. The responsibility for repairing the chancel was since 1743 an incident of the ownership of certain particular

c parcels of land. When Mr and Mrs Wallbank acquired the title to that land they assumed that responsibility to repair and the consequent liability in default if they should fail to discharge it. This was not a responsibility and liability which they shared with the public in general; it was something which they had personally assumed voluntarily by a voluntary act of acquisition which at the

d time they apparently thought was advantageous to them. From the point of view of both the PCC and the Wallbanks, the transaction and its incident were private law, non-governmental, non-public activities and not of a public nature. Again, this conclusion is adverse to the Wallbanks' defence.

HAS THERE BEEN A BREACH OF ART 1 (AND ART 14)?

e [91] Article 14 (discrimination) is not a free-standing provision but has to be read in conjunction with the recognition of the rights conferred by other articles. Therefore the material article is art 1 of the First Protocol which endorses the entitlement to the peaceful enjoyment of a person's possessions and prohibits depriving a person of his possessions, subject to certain qualifications. The word

f 'possessions' has been considered by the European Court of Human Rights, in particular in the cases of *Marckx v Belgium* (1979) 2 EHRR 330 and *Sporrong v Sweden* (1983) 5 EHRR 35. It applies to all forms of property and is the equivalent of 'assets'. But what is clear is that it does not extend to grant relief from liabilities incurred in accordance with the civil law. It may be that there are cases where the liability is merely a pretext or mechanism for depriving someone of their

g possessions by expropriation but that is not the case here. The liability is a private law liability which has arisen from the voluntary acts of the persons liable. They have no convention right to be relieved of that liability. Nor do they have a convention right to be relieved from the consequences of a bargain made, albeit some 200 years earlier, by their predecessors in title. They do not make any

h complaint under art 6 or complain about the fairness of these legal proceedings. They cannot complain that they are being discriminated against. The only reason why they are being sued is because they are the parties liable. This defence also fails. The submission that there should be a declaration of incompatibility likewise fails.

j [92] For the sake of completeness, it was clear that at all material times both they and their predecessors in title knew of the responsibility to repair or at least that it was asserted that they would be responsible if they acquired the title to the relevant land, an assertion which they have now admitted to be correct subject only to the Human Rights Act. Further, they originally ran a case of waiver by the PCC which they have now accepted was rightly rejected. If they had had a legal defence it would have been recognised by the court and the action would have been dismissed. Their financial liability under the 1932 Act is not arbitrary. It arises from their failure to perform a civil private law obligation which they had voluntarily assumed.

THE SECTION 6(2) POINT

[93] This point would only arise if I was wrong on all the preceding points. One therefore has to assume that the PCC is a public authority and the demand for payment is not of a private nature. In such circumstances, sub-s (2) creates an exception to the application of sub-s (1). The words of exception relevant to this case are 'the authority was acting so as to give effect to or enforce' provisions of primary legislation. The primary legislation is the 1932 Act. Incontrovertibly the PCC were seeking to give effect to and enforce provisions of that Act. On the above-stated assumption, the PCC's act in suing the Wallbanks comes squarely within the exception. Paragraph (b) of the subsection is to be contrasted with para (a) which is manifestly intended to cover cases where the public authority did not have any alternative but to act as it did (ie it was compelled to do so). Paragraph (b), on the other hand, covers situations where the public authority was empowered by legislation to act as it did and the intention of the legislation, whilst leaving open a measure of discretion, was that it should use the power provided. For some unstated reason, the Court of Appeal treated only para (a) as being relevant and this accounts for their mistaken decision on this point.

CONCLUSION

[94] It follows that, far from making out all three of the necessary constituents in their defence, the defendants have made out none. Their defence accordingly fails and the appeal must be allowed. There is no need to consider the retrospectivity question.

LORD SCOTT OF FOSCOTE.

INTRODUCTION

[95] My Lords, the respondents, Mr and Mrs Wallbank, are the freehold owners of Glebe Farm, Aston Cantlow in Warwickshire. Glebe Farm, which consists of a farmhouse and about 179 acres of land, includes five fields amounting to just over 52 acres known, or formerly known, as Clanacre. The Clanacre fields, it is contended, were and remain rectorial property thereby constituting its owners for the time being lay rectors and subjecting them to the liability of paying for all and any necessary repairs to the chancel of St John the Baptist church, the parish church of Aston Cantlow.

[96] The appellants, the Parochial Church Council (PCC) of Aston Cantlow are responsible for supervising the care, maintenance, preservation and insurance of the fabric of the church (see s 4(1)(ii)(b) of the Parochial Church Councils (Powers) Measure 1956) and have served notices on Mr and Mrs Wallbank requiring them to put the chancel in proper repair. The notices were served on 12 September 1994 and 23 January 1996 pursuant to s 2 of the Chancel Repairs Act 1932. The cost of the necessary repairs is put in the notices at £95,260 odd. Mr and Mrs Wallbank dispute their liability. This litigation has resulted.

THE LAW ON CHANCEL REPAIRS

[97] A description, even a brief one, of the law on chancel repairs must, if it is to be comprehensible, start with mediaeval times when every parish had its parish priest, the 'rector'. The rector had, by virtue of his office, a number of

a
valuable proprietary rights which, collectively, constituted his 'rectory'. These rights included the profits of glebe land and tithes, usually one-tenth of the produce of land in the parish. Responsibility for the repair of the parish church was, absent some special custom to the contrary (see *Bishop of Ely v Gibbons & Goody* (1833) 4 Hag Ecc 156, 162 ER 1405), shared between the rector and the parishioners. The parishioners were responsible for repairing the part of the

b church where they sat, the western end of the church. The rector was responsible for repairing the chancel, the eastern end of the church. The rector's glebe land and tithes, the 'rectory', provided both for his maintenance and a fund from which he could pay for chancel repairs.

[98] The right of appointment to a rectory, the advowson, was an item of property transferable by conveyance and often in the hands of a lay person,

c typically the landowner who had built and endowed the church or his successors. But the appointee had to be a spiritual rector and, on appointment, would become entitled to the rectorial rights and subject to the chancel repair liability.

[99] In the 300 years or so prior to the dissolution of the monasteries under Henry VIII a great number of advowsons were acquired by monasteries. A

d monastery, having acquired an advowson, would almost invariably appoint itself the rector and thereby appropriate to itself the valuable rectorial rights, the rectory. It would, of course, be a spiritual rector. The parish would, however, need a parish priest. So the monastery would appoint a deputy, a vicar, to fulfil that role, usually allocating to the vicar some part of the rectorial tithes or glebe. It seems, interestingly, never to have been suggested that the vicar, by

e virtue of the allocation to him of some part of the rectory thereby became liable for chancel repairs. Vicarial tithes or vicarial glebe did not carry that liability which remained with the rector.

[100] On the dissolution of the monasteries under Henry VIII the property of religious houses, including their advowsons and the rectories they had

f appropriated, were compulsorily sold, impropriated, to lay institutions, such as Oxford and Cambridge colleges, and individuals. The lay institutions and individuals who acquired the rectories became lay rectors, or lay impropriators (the terms are synonymous) and, as such, subject to the chancel repair liability. The lay rector may have, and usually had, also acquired the advowson and thereby become the patron and entitled to appoint the vicar of the parish. A

g vicar, thus appointed, was no longer a deputy but held office in his own right. The obligation to repair the chancel lay on the lay rector in that capacity and not as owner of the advowson.

[101] The proprietary rights acquired by lay rectors would have included the rectorial glebe and the rectorial tithes. These rights could be alienated and

h divided up. Many rectorial tithes were extinguished under inclosure awards made pursuant to Inclosure Acts. Under these awards plots forming part of the common lands to be enclosed were allotted to lay rectors in lieu of their rectorial tithes. It is generally assumed that the allotted lands then took the place of the tithes as the lay rector's rectorial property (see the Law Commission's Working

j Paper No 86 *Transfer of land, Liability for Chancel Repairs* (1983) pp 8–9 (para 2.11)).

[102] Tithes, other than those extinguished under inclosure awards, were converted into tithe rentcharges under the Tithe Act 1836. Tithe rentcharges, unlike their predecessor tithes, were charged on the land in respect of which the tithe had been payable and attracted the same chancel repair liability as had been attracted by the predecessor tithes: see s 71 of the 1836 Act which subjected the rentcharges to 'the same liabilities and incidents as the like estate in the tithes

commuted'. Over the next hundred years various further statutory changes were made until, finally, the Tithe Act 1936 abolished tithe rentcharges and replaced *a* them with tithe redemption annuities. The annuities were payable to the government and the owners of the rentcharges received government stock in compensation for the extinction of their rights.

[103] Section 31 of and Sch 7 to the 1936 Act dealt specifically with chancel repairs. As to liability for chancel repair arising from the ownership of tithe *b* rentcharges (evidently on the footing that the tithe rentcharge had taken the place of the tithes as rectorial property) a part of the government stock to be issued in respect of that rentcharge was to go to the diocesan authority to provide for the cost of future repairs to the chancel and the cost of insuring against damage by fire (see s 31(2)). Subsections (3) and (4) of s 31 merit mention. They provided, in conjunction with s 21 of the 1936 Act and s 1 of the Tithe Act 1839, *c* that where the tithe rentcharge and the land on which it was charged were in the same ownership, the rentcharge would be treated as abolished by merger but the land would be subject to the chancel repair liability 'to the extent of the value of ... the rent-charge' (see s 1 of the 1839 Act). The chancel repair liability of the lay rector became thereby limited to the value of the rectorial property, the *d* rentcharge, from which his office of lay rector was derived.

[104] It is clear that a lay rectorship and liability for chancel repair could attach to a person who had become owner of a part only of the rectorial property. That that is so is implicit in the decision of this House in *Representative Body of the Church in Wales v Tithe Redemption Commission, Plymouth Estates Ltd v Tithe Redemption Commission* [1944] 1 All ER 710, [1944] AC 228, the Welsh *e* Commissioners case. The issue, which arose out of the disestablishment in 1914 of the Welsh Church, was whether tithe rentcharges which, until abolished by the 1936 Act, had become temporally vested in the Commissioner of Church Temporalities in Wales (the Welsh Commissioners) pending their transfer to the University of Wales under provisions in the Welsh Church Acts 1914 and 1919 *f* had, while so vested, subjected the Welsh Commissioners to chancel repair liability. If the answer was Yes, government stock needed to be issued to the appropriate Welsh authority pursuant to the 1936 Act. Their Lordships held that the Welsh Commissioners, so long as they held the tithe rentcharges, were lay impropriators and accordingly under a chancel repair liability. The issue, which applied to a number of parishes in Wales, was examined by reference to a *g* particular parish, Llanwit Major in Glamorgan. Tithe rentcharges valued at £481 7s 11d, representing rectorial property of the parish, were held by the Dean and Chapter of Gloucester. Other tithe rentcharges, valued at £64 4s 2d and also representing rectorial property of the parish were held by a limited company, Plymouth Estates Ltd. Viscount Simon LC said ([1944] 1 All ER 710 at 713, [1944] *h* AC 228 at 239) that 'Plymouth Estates, Ltd ... plainly and admittedly remain liable for chancel repair'. He described the obligation of a rector to repair the chancel as 'an obligation imposed by common law' ([1944] 1 All ER 710 at 713, [1944] AC 228 at 240 and see also [1944] 1 All ER 710 at 717, [1944] AC 228 at 247 per Lord Wright). Lord Porter expressed himself to the same effect. He said *j* ([1944] 1 All ER 710 at 718, [1944] AC 228 at 249): '*Prima facie*, therefore, if the tithe rentcharge gets into the hands of a lay impropriator at any time it is held subject to the liability to repair' and that 'impropriation exists where the property is in lay hands' (see [1944] 1 All ER 710 at 719, [1944] AC 228 at 250).

[105] But although it must now be regarded as settled law that an individual who becomes the owner of rectorial property of a parish becomes liable for

a chancel repair, there remain subsidiary issues which, in my opinion, are not
settled. For example, the extent of the liability is not settled. Is the liability
limited to the value of the rectorial profits the ownership of which has attracted
the office of lay rector and the consequent chancel repair liability or is it unlimited
in amount? I have already referred to the effect of s 31(3) and (4) of the 1936 Act
whereby, by reference to s 21 of that Act and s 1 of the 1839 Act, the chancel
b repair liability of a lay rector attributable to his ownership of a tithe rentcharge
which had merged in the land on which it was charged was limited to the value
of the rentcharge. In *Walwyn v Awberry* (1677) 2 Mod 254 a lay rector brought an
action for trespass because the local bishop had sequestered his tithes on account
of his failure to obey an admonition to repair the chancel of the parish church.
The issue was whether sequestration was an available remedy. It was held that
c it was not. Atkins J (at 258) who disagreed on the sequestration point, said that—

> 'it was agreed by all, that an impropriator is chargeable with the repairs of
> the chancel; but the charge was not personal but in regard of the profits of
> the impropriation ...'

d This suggests that the liability is limited to the amount of the profits. A similar
suggestion appears in the Report of the Chancel Repairs Committee presented by
the Lord Chancellor to Parliament in May 1930 (Cmd 3571). The chancel repair
liability was described (p 5 (para 4(a))) as—

e > 'an obligation imposed by the Common Law of England, which annexes to
> the ownership of the rectory the duty of the rector to maintain the chancel
> of the church *out of the profits of the rectory.*' (My emphasis.)

As to the position where the rectorial property has passed to several owners, the
paragraph said: '... every several owner is, *to the extent of the profits derived by him*
f *from his piece of the property,* under the duty of maintaining the chancel ...' (My
emphasis.)

[106] In *Wickhambrook Parochial Church Council v Croxford* [1935] 2 KB 417,
however, the Court of Appeal decided otherwise. The defendants were lay
rectors of the parish of Wickhambrook by virtue of ownership of rentcharge of
£39 11s 9d per year, a sub-divided part of a tithe rentcharge of £120 per year. The
g cost of the necessary chancel repairs was estimated to be £123 12s 6d. It was this
sum that the PCC sought to recover from the defendants. It was proved at trial
that the total sum actually received by the defendants from their ownership of the
rentcharge was £50 odd. The trial judge, relying on passages in *Phillimore's
Ecclesiastical Law* (2nd edn, 1895), held (at 423) that it was necessary to prove that
h the impropriator had received tithes or other profits belonging to the rectory
sufficient to cover the cost of repair and, accordingly, that the PCC's claim failed.
He was reversed on appeal. Lord Hanworth MR after examining various reports
of *Walwyn v Awberry* expressed the view (at 437) that the case was an
unsatisfactory authority on which to found a limitation of a lay rector's chancel
j repair liability and concluded that 'the liability of a lay impropriator is personal,
and is not limited to the amount of his receipts from the tithe'. But he held that
the defendants had a right of contribution from other owners of parts of the tithe
rentcharge. Romer LJ agreed with Lord Hanworth MR, as too did Eve J who
added (at 445) that 'the result ... does not appear to me to be reasonable or just'.

[107] In *Representative Body of the Church in Wales v Tithe Redemption
Commission, Plymouth Estates Ltd v Tithe Redemption Commission* [1944] 1 All ER 710

at 713, [1944] AC 228 at 239, Viscount Simon LC, having referred to the chancel
repair liability of Plymouth Estates Ltd, said that—

> '[i]t is not necessary for the purposes of the present appeal to discuss the
> difficult question as to the extent of their possible responsibility, or as to
> whether *Wickhambrook Parochial Church Council* v. *Croxford* was rightly
> decided.'

[108] Counsel before your Lordships have not argued whether the
Wickhambrook case was or was not rightly decided. But if Mr and Mrs Wallbank
are liable as lay rectors, the question whether their liability should be limited to
the profits they have received from the rectorial property may be open to them.
The point is certainly still open in this House.

[109] A further point of law that cannot, in my opinion, yet be regarded as
settled is whether each and every alienation by a lay rector of impropriatorial
assets of the rectory necessarily makes the alienee a co-lay rector and liable for
chancel repairs. The point arose in *Chivers & Sons Ltd v Secretary of State for Air
(Queens' College, Cambridge, Third Party)* [1955] 2 All ER 607 at 609, [1955] Ch 585
at 594 where Wynn-Parry J held that the liability to repair the chancel 'is not a
charge on the rectorial property, but a personal liability imposed on the owner or
owners for the time being of the rectorial property' and that '[i]f there is more
than one owner, each is severally liable'. For reasons which will appear, this is
not a point which can have any bearing on the present case but, none the less, the
conclusion to which Wynn-Parry J came may be open to question. Is it really the
case that on every disposition of any part of former rectorial property, no matter
how small and no matter what may be the intentions of the parties, express or
implied, regarding the assumption by the transferee of chancel repair liabilities,
the transferee becomes willy-nilly by dint of inflexible legal principle a lay
impropriator liable to chancel repairs? I doubt it.

THE CONVEYANCING HISTORY OF CLANACRE

[110] At the time of the Inclosure Act 1742 and the award of 1743, under
which the common lands of Aston Cantlow were enclosed, Lord Brooke was the
lay impropriator of the rectory of the parish church of Aston Cantlow. A recital
to the Act so states. It appears from another recital to the Act that Lord Brooke
was the owner of tithes and it appears from the terms of the award that the
impropriated property included glebe land.

[111] Under the award Lord Brooke was allotted Clanacre. It was described
as 'one plot lying in Aston Cantlow … called Clanacre combining (containing) …
fifty two Acres two roods and twenty one perches'. Details of its boundaries
were given so that there could be no doubt as to the identity of what had been
allotted.

[112] It is unclear from the extract of the award contained in the papers before
your Lordships on account of what rectorial rights Clanacre was allotted. It may
have been allotted on account of Lord Brooke's tithes or it may have been
allotted on account of glebe comprised in the common lands that were being
enclosed. But it is not in dispute that one way or another Clanacre became, by
substitution, rectorial property. Certainly all Lord Brooke's tithes over the
common lands were extinguished by the Act and the award.

[113] At some time between 1743 and 1875 Lord Brooke, or his successors,
sold Clanacre together with the rest of what later became Glebe Farm. Whether

a the sale was of all Lord Brooke's impropriated property or of only part of it is not apparent from the papers in evidence in the case.

   [114] The first readable conveyance dealing with Clanacre is a conveyance of 21 October 1918 under which the vendor, Thomas Wood, conveyed to two purchasers, both with the surname Terry, Glebe Farm and its 179-odd acres including the 52-odd Clanacre acres. The habendum to the conveyance says that
b the purchasers were to hold the land—

       'in fee simple in equal shares as tenants in common subject primarily and in priority to the other hereditaments charged therewith to the repairs of the Chancel of Aston Church.'

c The 'subject to' provision indicates the strong likelihood that the vendor, Thomas Wood, who must have been a lay impropriator, was selling part of the rectorial property but retaining other parts. It seems to me unlikely, given the content of this provision, that Mr and Mrs Wallbank could succeed in claiming from Thomas Wood or his successors a contribution towards any chancel repairing liability that rests on them by virtue of their ownership of Clanacre.

d [115] In 1970 Mr and Mrs Coulton, Mrs Wallbank's parents, purchased Glebe Farm and the 179 acres from Herbert Terry & Sons Ltd, no doubt the successors of the 1918 Terry purchasers. Clause 2 of the conveyance to the Coultons said that the property was conveyed—

       'subject to the liability for the repair of the Chancel of Aston Church ... so
e   far as the same affects the property hereby conveyed and is still subsisting and capable of being enforced.'

   And under two deeds of gift dated respectively 21 March 1974 and 1 May 1986 Glebe Farm and the bulk of the 179 acres, including all the Clanacre fields, were conveyed to Mrs Wallbank by her parents. Mrs Wallbank later placed the
f property in the joint names of herself and her husband.

   [116] It is plain from this conveyancing history that Mr and Mrs Wallbank acquired Glebe Farm, including Clanacre, with the knowledge that ownership might carry with it a liability to pay for repairs to the chancel of the parish church.

g THE CHANCEL REPAIRS ACT 1932
   [117] The 1932 Act was passed in consequence of the inadequacies of enforcement procedure revealed by litigation between Hauxton PCC and a Mr Stevens. Pre-1932 the enforcement of chancel repair liability was primarily a matter for ecclesiastical courts. Proceedings for the issue of an admonition requiring the alleged lay rector to carry out the repairs had to be issued in the
h consistory court. It had been established by dicta in, if not by the ratio of, Walwyn v Awberry (1677) 2 Mod 254 that ordinary civil law enforcement procedures were not available. If the consistory court issued the admonition and it was not obeyed, the next step would be either a decree of excommunication or a transfer of the proceedings to the High Court in order for proceedings for
j committal for contempt of court to be brought, or both. The unfortunate Mr Stevens, having unsuccessfully disputed his liability, ignored the admonition issued by the consistory court. He ended up in prison for contempt under a committal order made in the King's Bench Division. He obtained his release only on undertaking to carry out the requisite repairs.

   [118] Such a disproportionate remedy was obviously unsatisfactory and s 2 of the 1932 Act authorised PCCs to serve notices to repair on individuals alleged to

be liable for chancel repairs. If such a notice is not complied with, the PCC can commence proceedings in the ordinary courts to recover the sum required to put the chancel in proper repair. The court, if satisfied that the defendant would, but for the 1932 Act, 'have been liable to be admonished to repair the chancel by the appropriate ecclesiastical court', can give judgment against the defendant for the sum representing the cost of the necessary repairs. The judgment would be enforceable like any other money judgment. Hence the notices served by the PCC on Mr and Mrs Wallbank and the litigation that followed Mr and Mrs Wallbank's denial of liability.

THE LITIGATION

[119] The pleadings in the case confirmed that there was a dispute as to Mr and Mrs Wallbank's liability to bear the cost of the chancel repairs. On 29 September 1999 the case came before Master Bragge on what I take to have been a summons for directions. On this summons Master Bragge directed that two preliminary issues be tried. Each related to contentions by Mr and Mrs Wallbank as to why they were not liable. One of these contentions was abandoned at trial. The other is the issue that has found its way to your Lordships' House. But before reciting its terms it is important to notice an important concession made by Mr Wallbank, who appeared in person, and on the basis of which the master directed the trial of the preliminary issues. The concession is recorded in the order in the following terms:

'And upon the second defendant on his own behalf and on that of the first defendant stating that he agreed and accepted that the defendants (and each of them) as the joint freeholders of Glebe Farm Aston Cantlow Warwickshire are and at all material times have been the lay rector and are personally liable for the repair of the chancel of the Church of St John the Baptist Aston Cantlow Warwickshire ("the Church") if and to the extent that the liability is enforceable and/or exists by reason of the preliminary issues particularised below.'

This concession very greatly reduced the number of issues relating to chancel repair liability that Mr and Mrs Wallbank could raise.

[120] The preliminary issue that was, and is, persisted in was subsequently amended and in its amended form is as follows:

'Whether having regard to the provisions of the European Convention on Human Rights, a co-rector is liable to repair the chancel of the church or otherwise to meet the costs of the said repairs by reason of the provisions of the 1932 Act and the common law.'

[121] The preliminary issue was tried before Ferris J ([2000] All ER (D) 419). It was tried after the Human Rights Act 1998 had been passed but before 2 October 2000, the date on which the Act was to come into effect. In his judgment Ferris J described the argument addressed to him by counsel for Mr and Mrs Wallbank as having two main elements, namely:

'(i) that English law is not yet settled in deciding that a lay rector is liable for chancel repairs, at any rate where the rectorial property owned by that lay rector consists of part only of a larger parcel of land allotted under an inclosure award in lieu of tithes or other rectorial property; and (ii) that it should be decided that such a lay rector is not liable because to hold to the a contrary would involve a contravention of one or more of the rights declared by the convention.'

[122] I find some difficulty in reconciling the first argument with Mr Wallbank's concession as recited in Master Bragge's order. That, perhaps, does not matter because Ferris J, following *Wickhambrook Parochial Church Council v Croxford* [1935] 2 KB 417 and *Chivers & Sons Ltd v Secretary of State for Air*
b *(Queens' College, Cambridge, Third Party)* [1955] 2 All ER 607, [1955] Ch 585 held that it was settled law that an individual who had come into ownership of part only of the rectorial property became liable to the full burden of the chancel repair liability. In the Court of Appeal ([2001] 3 All ER 393 at [15]), Sir Andrew Morritt V-C, relying on the same authorities, agreed and held, in addition, that
c the liability 'is not limited or proportioned to the value or fruits of the benefice: its sole measure is the cost of necessary repairs'. This was what had been held in the *Wickhambrook* case, a case by which the Court of Appeal in the present case was bound. This is not a point which has been argued before your Lordships in the present appeal nor, in my opinion, is it a point which arises under the
d preliminary issue. It is a point that may re-emerge if the quantum of the cost of repairs for which the Wallbanks are liable has to be litigated. For the present I want to say no more about it than Viscount Simon LC said in *Representative Body of the Church in Wales v Tithe Redemption Commission, Plymouth Estates Ltd v Tithe Redemption Commission* [1944] 1 All ER 710, [1944] AC 228, namely, that it is a difficult question and that whether the *Wickhambrook* case was rightly decided is
e open to debate at least in this House.

[123] As to the *Chivers & Sons* point (see [2001] 3 All ER 393 at [16] per Sir Andrew Morritt V-C) it cannot avail the Wallbanks. The 1918 conveyance plainly intended to make the Terrys, the transferees, co-rectors. Otherwise there would have been no mention of the chancel repair liability.

f [124] As to the second argument for the Wallbanks to which Ferris J referred, the argument based on the Human Rights Act, the judge held that there was no breach of art 1 of the First Protocol. The Wallbanks' liability to repair the chancel was an incident of their ownership of the Clanacre fields and the enforcement of that liability by those entitled to enforce it could not be regarded as a deprivation of their possessions. Their possessions, he pointed out, were always liable to such
g enforcement. Ferris J, therefore, answered in the negative the question posed in the preliminary issue.

[125] The Court of Appeal disagreed with Ferris J on the Human Rights Act point. They held, first, that the PCC was a core 'public authority' within the meaning of that expression in s 6 of the Act. Section 6(1) provides: 'It is unlawful
h for a public authority to act in a way which is incompatible with a Convention right.' They held, alternatively, that the PCC's function in enforcing against the Wallbanks their chancel repair liability was a function 'of a public nature'. Section 6(3)(b) provides that the expression 'public authority' includes 'any person certain of whose functions are functions of a public nature' and s 6(5) says:
j 'In relation to a particular act, a person is not a public authority by virtue only of subsection (3)(b) if the nature of the act is private.'

[126] Having reached conclusions under which the PCC's attempts to enforce the chancel repair liability against the Wallbanks were acts of a public authority for s 6 purposes, the question was whether the enforcement was incompatible with a convention right. The Court of Appeal first addressed itself to art 1 of the First Protocol and held that the liability to defray the cost of chancel repairs was

'inescapably' a form of taxation. The reasoning ([2001] 3 All ER 393 at [40]) was
that 'a private individual who has no necessary connection with the church [was
being] required by law to pay money to a public authority for its upkeep'. The
Court of Appeal (at [44]) identified in Strasbourg jurisprudence a requirement
that 'the legitimate aim of taxation in the public interest must be pursued by
means which are not completely arbitrary or out of all proportion to their
purpose', held (at [45]) that the liability for chancel repair was a tax which
operated entirely arbitrarily 'first because the land to which it attaches, now
shorn of any connection with the rectory, does not differ relevantly from any
other freehold land, and secondly because the liability may arise at any time and
be … in almost any amount', and held that the 'tax' accordingly violated art 1 of
the First Protocol.

[127] The Court of Appeal held, also, that the way in which the chancel repair
liability operated discriminated, impermissibly and in breach of art 14, between
the Wallbanks, who were subject to the liability, and other landowners in the
parish who were not.

[128] The following issues therefore arise for decision on this appeal. (1) Is
the PCC a 'core' public authority for the purposes of s 6 of the Human Rights Act?
(2) If the PCC is not a core public authority, is its function in enforcing chancel
repair liability a function 'of a public nature'? (3) If the PCC's enforcement of
chancel repair liability is a function of a public nature, does the enforcement
infringe art 1 of the First Protocol to the convention? (4) Or does it infringe
art 14 of the convention?

IS THE PCC A CORE PUBLIC AUTHORITY?

[129] I have had the advantage of reading in advance the opinions of my noble
and learned friends, Lord Hope of Craighead and Lord Rodger of Earlsferry.
Each has concluded that a PCC is not a core public authority. I am in complete
agreement with their reasons for coming to that conclusion and cannot usefully
add to them. I, too, would hold that a PCC is not a core public authority.

IS THE ENFORCEMENT OF CHANCEL REPAIR LIABILITY A FUNCTION OF A PUBLIC NATURE?

[130] On this issue my noble and learned friends have come to the conclusion
that the nature of enforcement of chancel repair liability is private. I have found
this a difficult question but at the end have come to the opposite conclusion. I
agree with Lord Hope that the answer to the question, whether an authority, not
being a 'core' public authority, is, when exercising a particular function,
exercising a function of a public nature, must depend upon the facts of the
particular case (see [63], above). The important facts and matters relevant to the
question in the present case seem to me, in no particular order of importance, to
be the following. (1) The parish church is a church of the Church of England, a
church by law established. (2) It is a church to which the Anglican public are
entitled to have recourse, regardless of whether they are practising members of
the church, for marriage, for baptism of their children, for weddings, for funerals
and burial, and perhaps for other purposes as well. (3) Members of other
denominations, or even other religions, are, if parishioners, entitled to burial in
the parish churchyard. (4) The church is, therefore, a public building. It is not a
private building from which the public can lawfully be excluded at the whim of
the owner. (5) The PCC is corporate and its functions are charitable. Its
members have the status of charity trustees. Charitable trusts are public trusts,
not private ones. (6) A decision by a PCC to enforce a chancel repairing liability

a is a decision taken in the interests of the parishioners as a whole. It is not taken in pursuit of any private interests. If it were so taken, it would I think be impeachable by judicial review.

[131] Lord Hope has said that the liability of the lay rector to repair the chancel arises as a matter of private law from the ownership of glebe land (see [35], above). I would respectfully question whether the adjective 'private' is apt.

b In *Representative Body of the Church in Wales v Tithe Redemption Commission, Plymouth Estates Ltd v Tithe Redemption Commission* [1944] 1 All ER 710, [1944] AC 228 at 234 Sir Walter Monckton KC for the appellants in his submissions to their Lordships commented on the fact that the Welsh Church Act 1914 had made no express provision for a tribunal to take the place of the consistory court in enforcing chancel repair and put to their Lordships that '[p]erhaps the

c Attorney-General might have dealt with the matter as a public right'. There was no recorded dissent and I respectfully suggest that Sir Walter's comment was soundly based. The liability of a lay rector is a personal liability arising from his ownership of impropriated property and is imposed by common law (see [1944] 1 All ER 710 at 713, [1944] AC 228 at 240 per Viscount Simon LC). But obligations

d imposed by common law are not necessarily private law obligations. Whether they are so or not must depend on those to whom they are owed. The chancel repair obligations are not owed to private individuals. Private individuals cannot release them. Section 52 of the Ecclesiastical Dilapidations Measure 1923 provided a procedure whereby lay rectors liable for chancel repairs could compound their liability and thereby obtain a release from it. The procedure

e required there to be consultation with the PCC of the parish, the obtaining of approval from the diocesan dilapidations board and payment of the requisite sum to the diocesan authority. The sum paid becomes trust money (see sub-s (5)). These provisions have an unmistakable public law flavour to them. The chancel repair obligations resting on a lay rector are not, in my opinion, private law

f obligations.

[132] In my opinion, therefore, the question posed under this issue should be answered in the affirmative. It follows, if that is right, that in enforcing chancel repair liability, a PCC must not act in a manner incompatible with a convention right. Is enforcement of chancel repair liability against Mr and Mrs Wallbank an infringement of their rights under art 1 of the First Protocol?

g [133] The terms of art 1 have been set out by Lord Hope in [66], above. I need not repeat that exercise. The question is whether the enforcement of the chancel repair liability constitutes a deprivation of the lay rector's possessions. The Court of Appeal prayed in aid the analogy of taxation in order to justify the proposition that the relevant deprivation was of the Wallbanks' funds. It was their personal

h funds of which they were to be deprived, not Glebe Farm. For my part, although I disagree with the categorisation of the liability as a form of taxation (see [2001] 3 All ER 393 at [40]) I would accept the analysis. The enforcement of the liability is indeed an attack on the Wallbanks' personal funds but it does not on that account infringe art 1 any more than a claim to enforce any other pecuniary

j liability does so. It is here, perhaps, that the taxation analogy does become relevant. Taxation is a levy imposed by a state, or perhaps by some core public authority authorised by the state to impose the levy, either on the public generally or on some identified section of the public. In *Black's Law Dictionary* (6th edn, 1990) p 1457, 'tax' is described as '[a] charge by the government', as '[a] pecuniary burden laid upon individuals or property to support the government, and [being] a payment exacted by legislative authority' and whose '[e]ssential characteristics ... are that it is not a voluntary payment or donation, but an enforced contribution, exacted pursuant to legislative authority'. It may be that the obligation imposed on parishioners by the common law to pay tithes to the rector of the parish could, although not imposed by government or by the legislature, reasonably be regarded as an obligation to pay a tax. But the obligation of the recipient of the tithes to repair the chancel of the parish church could not, in my opinion, be so described. When tithe rentcharge took the place of tithes, the obligation to pay the tithe rentcharge might similarly have been regarded as an obligation of a taxation character. But the obligation to repair the chancel of the church resting on the recipient of the tithe rentcharge could not be so described. It remained a quid pro quo for the receipt of the tithe rentcharge. The substitution under an inclosure award of land for tithes could no more have changed the nature of the obligation to repair the church chancel than the substitution of tithe rentcharge for tithes could have done. The taxation analogy drawn by the Court of Appeal is, in my respectful opinion, misplaced.

[134] The chancel repair liability satisfies, in my opinion, the requirements of the art 1 exception: it is a liability created by the common law, it operates in the narrow public interest of the parishioners in the parish concerned and in the general public interest in the maintenance of churches. It is created by common law and is subject to the incidents attached to it by common law. And in the case of Mr and Mrs Wallbank they acquired the rectorial property and became lay rectors with full knowledge of the potential liability for chancel repair that that acquisition would carry with it. I can see no infringement of (or incompatibility with) art 1 produced by the actions of the PCC in enforcing that liability.

[135] Nor, in my opinion, do Mr and Mrs Wallbank have any case of infringement of art 14. The comparators for art 14 purposes cannot possibly be persons who are not lay rectors. A person who is sued for £1000 that he owes is not discriminated against for art 14 purposes because people who do not owe £1000 are not similarly sued. A person who builds in breach of planning permission and has proceedings taken against him by the local planning authority is not discriminated against for art 14 purposes because a person who builds and has obtained planning permission is not sued. The comparators are not apt. The apt comparator in the present case would be a co-lay rector who was liable for chancel repairs to the Aston Cantlow church but on whom no 1932 Act notice had been served. There is no case here of art 14 discrimination.

[136] For these reasons I would allow the appeal and restore the declaration and order made by Ferris J.

[137] A final point before your Lordships was whether, if the PCC's enforcement of the chancel repair liability had constituted an infringement of Mr and Mrs Wallbank's convention rights, the PCC could have relied on s 6(2)(a) or (b) of the Human Rights Act. As to (a), it was contended that, as a result of s 2 of the 1932 Act, the PCC could not have done otherwise than enforce the chancel repair liability. In my opinion, this contention could not be sustained. Section 2 confers a power. It does not impose a mandatory duty. The PCC could have decided not to enforce the repairing obligation. They could have so decided for a number of different reasons which, in particular factual situations, might have had weight. They might, for example, have recommended the deconsecration of the church and its sale for conversion into a dwelling. They might have taken into account excessive hardship to Mr and Mrs Wallbank in having to find £95,000. Trustees are not always obliged to be Scrooge. Section 2 is not, in my opinion, a provision of primary legislation capable of engaging s 6(2)(a) of the

a Human Rights Act. As to (b), it is not s 2 of the 1932 Act that produces the alleged incompatibility with convention rights. Section 2 merely provides enforcement machinery for the obligation created by the common law. If s 2 had never been enacted the allegedly convention-infringing obligation to pay for chancel repairs would still have been present. None the less, if the imposition by the common law of the obligation constitutes an infringement of convention rights so, too, the *b* use of s 2 for the purpose of enforcement would constitute an infringement. So I respectfully agree with my learned friends Lord Nicholls of Birkenhead and Lord Hobhouse of Woodborough that the PCC would be entitled to rely on s 6(2)(b).

LORD RODGER OF EARLSFERRY.

c [138] My Lords, in 1986 Mrs Gail Wallbank became the owner of the freehold of Glebe Farm near the village of Aston Cantlow in Warwickshire. Four years later she conveyed the property into the joint names of herself and her husband. As owners of Glebe Farm Mr and Mrs Wallbank are the lay rectors or impropriators of the parish church and, as such, potentially liable to pay the cost *d* of repairs to the chancel. By 1990 the chancel was in disrepair. At that time the Parochial Church Council (PCC) did not know about the conveyance into joint names and accordingly it simply asked Mrs Wallbank to pay for the repairs. She disputed the liability. In 1994 the PCC, as the responsible authority, served notice on Mrs Wallbank under s 2(1) of the Chancel Repairs Act 1932, calling on her to repair the chancel. When she still refused to do so, the PCC began these *e* proceedings under s 2(2) of the 1932 Act to recover over £95,000, the estimated cost of the repairs. Subsequently, the PCC joined Mr Wallbank as a defendant.

[139] My noble and learned friend Lord Scott of Foscote has described the origins and development of the liability for chancel repairs as well as the way in which that liability attaches to the owners of Glebe Farm. The law as it applies *f* today can scarcely be regarded as satisfactory and may well cause real hardship to lay rectors who are called on to pay the cost of repairs to the chancel. Not surprisingly, the Law Commission have made proposals for the abolition of the liability over a period of time: *Liability for Chancel Repairs* (Law Com No 152 (1985)). Not altogether surprisingly either, Parliament has not yet acted on those proposals since abolition without compensation would cause significant financial *g* harm to many ancient parish churches throughout England. This case highlights both aspects of the problem.

[140] Mr and Mrs Wallbank do not now dispute that, absent the Human Rights Act 1998, they would be liable to pay the reasonable cost of the necessary repairs to the chancel. They defend the proceedings, however, on the basis that *h* the PCC is a 'public authority' which has acted unlawfully in terms of s 6(1) of the Human Rights Act by requiring them to pay the sum in question and so interfering with their peaceful enjoyment of their possessions in contravention of art 1 of the First Protocol to the European Convention for the Protection of Human Rights and Fundamental Freedoms 1950 (as set out in Sch 1 to the *j* Human Rights Act).

[141] The demand for payment was made and the action begun long before the Human Rights Act was even thought of. And indeed Ferris J heard argument and delivered judgment at first instance some months before the Act came into force ([2000] All ER (D) 419). By the time of the hearing in the Court of Appeal the Act was in force and the PCC conceded that, by virtue of ss 7(1)(b) and 22(4), Mr and Mrs Wallbank were entitled to rely on their convention right. In their

judgment delivered by Sir Andrew Morritt V-C, the Court of Appeal accepted the
concession ([2001] EWCA 713 at [7], [2001] 3 All ER 393 at [7], [2002] Ch 51 at [7]). *a*
In its written case in this House the PCC indicated an intention to withdraw the
concession. When the appeal opened, however, Mr George QC indicated that he
did not intend to argue the point. This may have been, in part at least, because
the Church authorities are anxious to have the substantial issue resolved. In these
circumstances the House heard no argument on what the cases show to be a *b*
difficult area of the law. I therefore prefer to express no view on the point.

[142] Differing from the decision of Ferris J, the Court of Appeal disposed of
the case by holding that the liability of Mr and Mrs Wallbank, as lay rectors, to
meet the cost of the chancel repairs was unenforceable by reason of the Human
Rights Act. In that way the Court of Appeal lifted the burden from lay rectors like
Mr and Mrs Wallbank, albeit at the expense of PCCs like the one at Aston *c*
Cantlow. The question for the House is whether the Court of Appeal were right
to take this momentous step on the basis of the Human Rights Act.

[143] In reaching their conclusion the Court of Appeal held that the PCC was
indeed a 'public authority' in terms of s 6 of the Human Rights Act. While a
number of other issues were argued in the hearing of the appeal to your *d*
Lordships' House, none of them arises unless the PCC is indeed to be regarded as
a public authority for this purpose.

[144] Section 6 provides inter alia:

'(1) It is unlawful for a public authority to act in a way which is
incompatible with a Convention right … *e*
(3) In this section "public authority" includes … (b) any person certain of
whose functions are functions of a public nature …
(5) In relation to a particular act, a person is not a public authority by
virtue only of subsection 3(b) if the nature of the act is private.'

The use of the word 'includes' in sub-s (3) shows that there are public authorities *f*
other than persons only certain of whose functions are of a public nature. So
there must be persons who are public authorities because all their functions are
of a public nature. These are sometimes referred to as 'core' public authorities,
as opposed to 'hybrid' authorities, only certain of whose functions are public and
some of whose acts may be private in nature. In view of my overall conclusion *g*
on the appeal I have not found it necessary on this occasion to explore the
significance of the distinction between the two kinds of public authorities.

[145] In deciding that the PCC was to be regarded as a public authority, the
Court of Appeal first noted that in the area of judicial review the cases at present
draw a conceptual line between functions of public governance and functions of *h*
mutual governance. But the Court of Appeal ([2001] 3 All ER 393 at [34]) could
detect no surviving element of mutuality or mutual governance as between the
impropriator and the church in the modern liability for chancel repairs: the
relationship in which the function arose was created by a rule of law and a state
of fact which were independent of the volition of either of them. In the hearing
before the House Mr George did not argue the contrary. The Court of Appeal *j*
continued (at [35]):

'In our judgment it is inescapable, in these circumstances, that a PCC is a
public authority. It is an authority in the sense that it possesses powers which
private individuals do not possess to determine how others should act. Thus,
in particular, its notice to repair has statutory force. It is public in the sense

a   that it is created and empowered by law; that it forms part of the church by
law established; and that its functions include the enforcement through the
courts of a common law liability to maintain its chancels resting upon
persons who need not be members of the church. If this were to be
incorrect, the PCC would nevertheless, and for the same reasons, be a legal
person certain of whose functions, chancel repairs among them, are
b   functions of a public nature. It follows on either basis by virtue of s 6 that its
acts, to be lawful, must be compatible with the rights set out in Sch 1 to the
[Human Rights Act 1998].'

The Court of Appeal's main conclusion therefore was that the PCC was a core
public authority. Alternatively, it was a hybrid authority, some of whose
c   functions were public—among them enforcing the impropriators' obligation to
pay for chancel repairs.

[146] There is no doubt that, in terms of s 2(1) of the 1932 Act, the PCC is an
authority—more precisely, 'the responsible authority'. For present purposes,
however, the question is whether the PCC should be regarded as a public
d   authority in terms of s 6. Parliament has chosen to use a composite phrase
'public authority'. There are therefore distinct dangers in interpreting it by
breaking it down and examining the two components separately. Be that as it
may, the Court of Appeal considered each of the two elements in turn.

[147] They first held that the PCC was an 'authority' for purposes of s 6
e   because it had powers which private individuals do not possess to determine how
others should act—the relevant example being its power to serve a notice to
repair which has statutory force. That is a somewhat imprecise criterion for
identifying an authority, however. When a police officer arrests an offender, his
act is that of a public 'authority' irrespective of whether or not the arrest is one
that a private citizen could have effected. Moreover Parliament can, if it wishes,
f   invest private individuals with quite remarkable powers over their fellow
citizens. For instance, s 391 of the Burgh Police (Scotland) Act 1892, now
repealed, provided:

g   'It shall be lawful for any householder, personally or by his servant, or by a
constable of police, to require any street musician or singer to depart from
the neighbourhood of the house of such householder; and every person who
shall continue to sound or play any instrument, or sing in any street, at any
time after being so required to depart, shall be liable to a penalty not
exceeding twenty shillings.'

h   A paterfamilias standing in evening dress at the entrance to his New Town
residence could address an order to an organ-grinder to depart from the vicinity,
or his butler could issue it from the top of the area steps. In either event, the
organ-grinder would commit an offence under the section if he continued to play
in the street. But if, instead, they had summoned a constable who had issued the
j   same instruction with exactly the same effect, he would unquestionably have
been an 'authority'—and indeed a 'public authority'. The existence or
non-existence of the equivalent statutory power in the householder and his
servant would not be germane to the constable's status. So the fact that no
individual possesses the power to issue a statutory repair notice with specific
effects on the lay rector cannot in itself be sufficient to show that the PCC is to be
regarded as an authority for the purposes of s 6.

[148] The Court of Appeal drew attention to three features which they *a* thought pointed to the PCC being a 'public' authority for purposes of s 6: the PCC is created and empowered by law; it forms part of the church by law established and its functions include the enforcement through the courts of a common law liability to maintain the chancel resting upon persons who need not be members of the Church.

[149] It is necessary to look a little more closely at the Court of Appeal's *b* observation that the PCC 'is created and empowered by law'. The origins of PCCs can be traced back to the movement that began in the nineteenth century for greater self-government and better representation of the laity in the Church of England. Part of the problem was that, while the Convocations of Canterbury and York could pass canons which were binding on the clergy, any wider legislation had to be by Act of Parliament and Parliament passed only relatively *c* few of the Acts for which the Church asked. In 1916 a special committee set up to look into the question recommended the formation of a Church Council with power to legislate on ecclesiastical matters. Eventually, after further work by another committee, the necessary scheme was approved by the Convocations of Canterbury and York. Both Convocations adopted identical addresses which *d* were presented to King George V on 10 May 1919. The text is to be found in the Acts of the Upper and Lower Houses, Convocation of Canterbury, 6 May 1919, Upper House, *Official Year Book of the Church of England 1920*, p 193. Attached to the addresses was an appendix (*Official Year Book of the Church of England 1921*, p 16) setting out the constitution of what was now called the National Assembly of the Church of England. Paragraph 17 of the constitution provided that, before *e* entering on any other legislative business, the National Assembly should make further provision for the self-government of the Church by passing through the assembly two measures, the second being to confer 'upon the Parochial Church Councils constituted under the Schedule to this Constitution such powers as the Assembly may determine'.

[150] The necessary machinery for giving assembly measures legal effect was *f* created later that year when Parliament passed the Church of England Assembly (Powers) Act 1919. Under s 4, measures passed by the National Assembly and submitted to the Ecclesiastical Committee of Parliament would, on being approved and receiving the Royal Assent, have the force and effect of an Act of Parliament. In accordance with that procedure, the National Assembly *g* proceeded to pass the Parochial Church Councils (Powers) Measure 1921. The preamble duly records that the measure was passed to fulfil a requirement of the constitution of the assembly to—

'make further provision for the self-government of the Church by passing *h* through the Assembly Measures inter alia for conferring on the Parochial Church Councils constituted under the Schedule to such Constitution such powers as the Assembly may determine.'

[151] As the preamble shows, just like the National Assembly itself, the PCCs were actually constituted when the scheme, comprising the constitution of the *j* assembly and the schedule of rules for the representation of the laity, was approved by the Convocations of Canterbury and York. The function of the 1921 measure was, accordingly, not to constitute or 'create' the PCCs but to confer powers on them. The same division survives today. The rules for the representation of the laity, including those relating to PCCs, are to be found in Sch 3 to the Synodical Government Measure 1969, while the powers of PCCs are

a now in the Parochial Church Councils (Powers) Measure 1956. Like s 3 of the 1921 measure, s 3 of the 1956 measure provides for the PCC to be a body corporate. Section 2 of the 1921 measure made it 'the primary duty of the council in every parish to co-operate with the incumbent in the initiation and development of Church work both within the parish and outside', while s 2 of the 1956 measure, which was inserted by s 6 of the 1969 measure, confers rather
b more elaborate general functions on the PCC. I come back to that section shortly.

[152] On closer examination, therefore, the process by which the PCCs were constituted and received their powers is really very different from the way in which a public body such as the Equal Opportunities Commission is created and given its powers by statute. In a case of that kind, the fact that the body owes both
c its existence and its powers to statute may well indicate that it has been called into existence to carry out some function that relates to the government of the country in a broad sense. By contrast, the PCCs were not constituted by statute but by the Church. They then became bodies corporate and received their powers not by virtue of an Act of Parliament but by virtue of an assembly
d measure, having the force and effect of an Act of Parliament. These factors suggest that, in reality, PCCs were constituted by the Church to carry out functions to be determined by the National Assembly, later the General Synod, of the Church.

[153] The Court of Appeal pointed next to the PCC being part of the Church by law established. In his submissions on behalf of Mr and Mrs Wallbank
e Mr Beloff QC embellished this argument. The Church of England—with Her Majesty the Queen at its head, with bishops appointed by the Queen on the recommendation of the Prime Minister, with the legislation of General Synod receiving the Royal Assent and having the force and effect of an Act of Parliament and with the civil power being available to enforce the judgments of its
f courts—was so woven into the fabric of the state that it should be regarded as a core public authority for purposes of s 6. Then, since 'the parish is the basic building block of the church' (Mark Hill *Ecclesiastical Law* (2nd edn, 2001) p 74), the PCC too should be regarded as a core public authority—whatever might be its precise functions in terms of s 2 of the 1956 measure.

g [154] I would reject that argument. In this case the House is not concerned with any theological doctrine of establishment such as gave rise to one of the issues in *General Assembly of Free Church of Scotland v Lord Overtoun, Macalister v Young* [1904] AC 515. Mr Beloff's argument centred, rather, on the general position of the Church of England in English law. The juridical nature of the Church is, notoriously, somewhat amorphous. The Church has been described
h as 'an organised operative institution' or as 'the quasi corporate institution which carries on the work' of the Church of England: see *Re Barnes, Simpson v Barnes* (1922) [1930] 2 Ch 80n at 81. Whether or not such an institution itself could ever count as a public authority in terms of s 6, I see no basis upon which a body within the Church, which would not otherwise be regarded as a public authority, could
j be impliedly invested with that character simply by reason of being part of the wider institution.

[155] On the other hand, the 1956 measure passed by the National Assembly of the Church casts light on the nature of the functions of a PCC. Under s 2(1) its duty is to consult with the minister on matters of general concern and importance to the parish. By s 2(2) the PCC's general functions include:

'(a) co-operation with the minister in promoting in the parish the whole
mission of the Church, pastoral, evangelistic, social and ecumenical; (b) the *a*
consideration and discussions of matters concerning the Church of England
or any other matters of religious or public interest, but not the declaration of
the doctrine of the Church on any question; (c) making known and putting
into effect any provision made by the diocesan synod or the deanery synod,
but without prejudice to the powers of the council on any particular matter; *b*
(d) giving advice to the diocesan synod and the deanery synod on any matter
referred to the council; (e) raising such matters as the council consider
appropriate with the diocesan synod or deanery synod.'

In addition to these general functions, by virtue of s 4 the PCC is given powers,
duties and liabilities which formerly vested in the churchwardens. These focus *c*
very much on the parish church and its affairs. In particular, under s 4(1)(b) the
PCC has powers, duties and liabilities with respect to the care, maintenance,
preservation and insurance of the fabric of the church and of its goods and
ornaments. By s 7(ii) the PCC has power to levy and collect a voluntary church
rate for any purpose connected with the affairs of the parish church. *d*

[156] The key to the role of the PCC lies in the first of its general functions:
co-operation with the minister in promoting in the parish the whole mission of
the Church. Its other more particular functions are to be seen as ways of carrying
out this general function. The mission of the Church is a *religious* mission, distinct
from the secular mission of government, whether central or local. Founding on
scriptural and other recognised authority, the Church seeks to serve the purposes *e*
of God, not those of the government carried on by the modern equivalents of
Caesar and his proconsuls. This is true even though the Church of England has
certain important links with the state. Those links, which do not include any
funding of the Church by the government, give the Church a unique position but
they do not mean that it is a department of state: see *Marshall v Graham, Bell v* *f*
Graham [1907] 2 KB 112 at 126 per Phillimore J. In so far as the ties are intended
to assist the Church, it is to accomplish the Church's own mission, not the aims
and objectives of the government of the United Kingdom. The PCC exists to
carry forward the Church's mission at the local level.

[157] Against that background the adjective 'private' is not perhaps the one
that springs most readily to mind to describe the functions of a PCC in the Church *g*
of England either generally or as compared, for instance, with those of a church
council in the Methodist Church. It might therefore be tempting to conclude that
the PCC's functions must be 'public' and that the PCC must itself be a 'public'
authority for the purposes of the Human Rights Act. At this point it becomes
necessary to look more closely at the meaning of the composite expression *h*
'public authority' in s 6. This in turn takes one back behind the Act to the
convention itself.

[158] The 'High Contracting Parties' to the convention were 'the
governments signatory' to the convention, more particularly 'the governments
of European countries' having certain common characteristics. In the fourth *j*
recital to the convention they reaffirmed their profound belief in those rights and
freedoms which are the foundation of justice and peace in the world and which
are best maintained by a common understanding and observance of the human
rights upon which they depend. The governments gave concrete expression to
the beliefs and aspirations recorded in the recitals by undertaking in art 1 to
secure to everyone within their jurisdiction the rights and freedoms set out in s 1

a of the convention. It can reasonably be inferred from the terms of the recitals and art 1 that the freedoms, and the rights on which they depend, relate to the powers and responsibilities of the governments which are parties to the convention.

[159] That inference is confirmed by art 34 which provides that the European Court of Human Rights—

b 'may receive applications from any person, non-governmental organisation or group of individuals claiming to be the victim of a violation by one of the High Contracting Parties of the rights set forth in the Convention or the protocols thereto. The High Contracting Parties undertake not to hinder in any way the effective exercise of this right.'

c I respectfully agree with the Court of Appeal ([2001] 3 All ER 393 at [33]), that, taken together, arts 1 and 34 assume the existence of a state which stands distinct from persons, groups and non-governmental organisations. I would go further: the reference in art 1 to the rights and freedoms defined in s 1 of the convention only makes sense if the state in question is exercising a range of functions which are, in a broad sense, governmental—and to which the rights and freedoms in s 1 *d* can therefore relate. Long ago, the functions of government were usually confined to defending the realm and keeping the peace. Nowadays, in addition, they commonly cover such matters as education, health and the environment. The exact range of governmental power will vary, of course, from state to state, depending on the history of the particular state and the political philosophy of its *e* government. Similarly, the distribution of governmental power will depend on the constitutional arrangements of the individual states. In some, the central government will retain most functions, in others power will be shared on some kind of federal system, while, in most at least, some functions will be allotted to local or community bodies. Irrespective of these and other possible permutations, under art 1 of the convention the states parties are responsible for *f* securing that all bodies exercising governmental power within their jurisdiction respect the relevant rights and freedoms. This approach underlies the admissibility decision of the Fourth Chamber of the European Court of Human Rights in *Ayuntamiento de Mula v Spain* App No 55346/00 (1 February 2001, unreported).

g [160] The obligation under art 1 has bound the United Kingdom ever since the convention came into force. Since 1966 individuals have been able to bring proceedings in Strasbourg to ensure that the United Kingdom complies with that obligation. Prima facie, therefore, when Parliament enacted the Human Rights Act 'to give further effect to rights and freedoms guaranteed under the European Convention on Human Rights', the intention was to make provision in our *h* domestic law to ensure that the bodies carrying out the functions of government in the United Kingdom observed the rights and freedoms set out in the convention. Parliament chose to bring this about by enacting inter alia s 6(1), which makes it unlawful for 'a public authority' to act in a way that is incompatible with a convention right. A purposive construction of that section *j* accordingly indicates that the essential characteristic of a public authority is that it carries out a function of government which would engage the responsibility of the United Kingdom before the Strasbourg organs.

[161] Mr Beloff accepted, of course, that, in order to achieve the government's declared aim of bringing rights home, in the legislation which it placed before Parliament the term 'public authority' must have been intended to include all bodies that carry out a function of government that would engage the

responsibility of the United Kingdom in Strasbourg. But, he said, that was simply a minimum. The government and, more particularly, Parliament could well have intended to go further and to include other public bodies, even though their acts would not engage the international responsibility of the United Kingdom. It would therefore be wrong to limit the scope of 'public authority' in s 6 to bodies exercising a governmental function of the state, however loosely defined. Mr Beloff could not point to any authoritative statement showing that Parliament had intended the Human Rights Act to have this wider effect. But he argued that, if Parliament had meant to limit the legislation to bodies carrying out a function of government, the natural thing would have been to use some such term as 'a governmental authority' or 'a governmental organisation'—which would mirror the term 'non-governmental organisation' to be found in art 34 of the convention. That was how the draftsman of the Act had proceeded in s 7(7) when he provided that a person was to be a 'victim' of an unlawful act for the purposes of the section only if he would have been a victim for the purposes of art 34 in proceedings before the European Court of Human Rights in respect of that act. Not only had the draftsman not adopted a similar approach in s 6(1): when an attempt had been made to amend the Bill so as to align the domestic test with the test adopted by the European Court in interpreting the convention, the government had opposed it and the amendment had failed.

[162] I see no proper basis for referring to Hansard as an aid to construing the term 'public authority' in s 6. But it appears that, in advancing this particular argument, Mr Beloff had in mind the amendments moved by Mr Edward Leigh MP and discussed by the Home Secretary during the Commons committee stage of the Bill (314 HC Official Report (6th series) cols 400, 418–425, 432–433). Since the convention is concerned with the obligations of the governments of the states parties, it does not define the domestic bodies whose acts engage the liability of those governments. Moreover, the jurisprudence of the Strasbourg court on the point is not extensive. A definition of the relevant public bodies in the Human Rights Act by reference to the approach of the Strasbourg court would therefore not have been particularly workable. Keith J made much the same point in relation to the Hong Kong Bill of Rights in *Hong Kong Polytechnic University v Next Magazine Publishing Ltd* [1996] 2 HKLR 260 at 264. According to the Home Secretary, because of these problems and in an attempt to replicate the situation under the convention, the government chose the term 'public authority' to indicate that the body concerned was to be sufficiently public to engage the responsibility of the United Kingdom. If—contrary to my view—the House could properly derive assistance from the fate of these amendments, it would lie in the confirmation that, in promoting the Bill, the government intended to give people rights in domestic law against the same bodies as would engage the liability of the United Kingdom before the Strasbourg court.

[163] In the present case the question therefore comes to be whether a PCC is a public authority in the sense that it carries out, either generally or on the relevant occasion, the kind of public function of government which would engage the responsibility of the United Kingdom before the Strasbourg organs. It so happens that there are two cases from Strasbourg dealing with the position of churches in this regard. They suggest that, in general, church authorities should not be treated as public authorities in this sense.

[164] The first case is *Holy Monasteries v Greece* (1995) 20 EHRR 1. On the basis of various provisions of the convention, including art 1 of the First Protocol, the

applicant monasteries challenged a Greek statute which changed the rules of
administration of their patrimony and provided for the transfer of a large part of
their estate to the Greek state. The links between the Greek Orthodox Church
and the Greek state were particularly close. In Greek law the Holy Monasteries
were public law entities that could be founded, merged or dissolved by means of
a decree of the President of Greece. Another public law entity, under the
b supervision of the ministry of education and religious affairs, was responsible for
managing the property belonging to the monasteries. In these circumstances the
Greek government stated, as a preliminary objection to the Holy Monasteries'
application, that they were not a non-governmental organisation which could
make an application as a victim in terms of art 25(1) (now art 34) of the
convention. Repelling that objection, the European Court of Human Rights held
c (at 41 (para 49)):

> 'Like the Commission in its admissibility decision, the Court notes at the
> outset that the applicant monasteries do not exercise governmental powers.
> Section 39(1) of the Charter of the Greek Church describes the monasteries
> as ascetic religious institutions. Their objectives—essentially ecclesiastical
d> and spiritual ones, but also cultural and social ones in some cases—are not
> such as to enable them to be classed with governmental organisations
> established for public administration purposes. From the classification as
> public law entities it may be inferred only that the legislature—on account of
> the special links between the monasteries and the State—wished to afford
e> them the same legal protection vis-à-vis third parties as was accorded to other
> public law entities. Furthermore, the monastery councils' only power
> consists in making rules concerning the organisation and furtherance of
> spiritual life and the internal administration of each monastery. The
> monasteries come under the spiritual supervision of the local archbishop,
> not under the supervision of the State, and they are accordingly entities
f> distinct from the State, of which they are completely independent. The
> applicant monasteries are therefore to be regarded as non-governmental
> organisations within the meaning of Article 25 of the Convention.'

While the positions of the Holy Monasteries and of a PCC are scarcely
g comparable, the judgment of the European Court is important for its reasoning
that the nature of the objectives of the monasteries was not such that they could
be classed with 'governmental organisations established for public administration
purposes'. The court also attached importance to the fact that the monasteries
came under the spiritual supervision of the local archbishop rather than under the
supervision of the state, as an indication that they were entities distinct from the
h state.

[165] In *Hautanemi v Sweden* (1996) 22 EHRR CD 155 the applicants were
members of a parish of the Church of Sweden who complained of a violation of
art 9 of the convention because the Assembly of the Church of Sweden had
prohibited the use of the liturgy of the Finnish Evangelical-Lutheran Church in
j their parish. Under reference to the judgment in the *Holy Monasteries* case, the
European Commission recalled art 25(1) (now art 34) of the convention and
observed (at 155):

> 'at the relevant time the Church of Sweden and its member parishes were
> to be regarded as corporations of public law. Since these religious bodies
> cannot be considered to have been exercising governmental powers, the

Church of Sweden and notably the applicant parish can nevertheless be regarded as "non-governmental organisations" within the meaning of Article 25(1).' a

Having held that, as members of the parish, the applicants could be regarded as victims in terms of art 25(1), the Commission added (at 156):

'The Commission has just found that, for the purposes of Article 25 of the b Convention, the Church of Sweden and its member parishes are to be regarded as "non-governmental organisations". It follows that the respondent State cannot be held responsible for the alleged violation of the applicants' freedom of religion resulting from the decision of the Church Assembly ... There has thus been no State interference with that freedom.' c

[166] In the light of these decisions what matters is that the PCC's general function is to carry out the religious mission of the Church in the parish, rather than to exercise any governmental power. Moreover, the PCC is not in any sense under the supervision of the state: under s 9 of the 1956 measure it is the bishop who has certain powers in relation to the PCC's activities. In these circumstances d the fact that the PCC is constituted as a body corporate under the 1956 measure is irrelevant. For these reasons, in respectful disagreement with the Court of Appeal, I consider that the PCC is not a core public authority for purposes of s 6 of the Act.

[167] This conclusion finds further support in the treatment of certain e churches in relation to art 19(4) of the German constitution or Grundgesetz. That article provides that, if any person's rights are infringed by 'public power' ('öffentliche Gewalt'), recourse to the courts is open to him. The history of relations between Church and state in Germany is, of course, very different from the history of that relationship in any part of the United Kingdom. In Germany f it has culminated in a declaration that there is to be no state Church (art 137(1) of the Weimar constitution incorporated by art 140 of the constitution). This important difference must not be overlooked. Nevertheless, as permitted by art 137, certain churches are constituted as public law corporations. In general, domestic public law entities are regarded as exercising public power in terms of art 19(4), whereas natural persons and private law associations are not. Despite g this, because of their particular (religious) mission which does not derive from the state, the churches that are public law corporations are treated differently from other public law corporations that are organically integrated into the state. 'Church power is indeed public, but not state power' ('ist kirchliche Gewalt zwar öffentliche, aber nicht staatliche Gewalt'): see BVerwGE 18, 385, 386–387; h BVerwGE 25, 226, 228–229. So, in relation to these churches, the Administrative Court interprets the phrase 'public power' in art 19(4) as being equivalent to 'state power'. Since within their own sphere the churches do not exercise state power, even if they exercise public power, the art 19(4) guarantee does not apply. Despite the rather different context, this interpretation of 'public power' tends to j confirm the interpretation of 'public authority' in s 6 which I prefer. Moreover, due allowance having been made for the particular position of the Church of England, the reasoning of the Administrative Court also tends to confirm that the mere fact that s 3 of the 1956 measure makes every PCC a body corporate does not carry with it any necessary implication that the PCC should, on that account alone, be regarded as a public authority for the purposes of s 6.

a [168] Of course, if the churches in Germany go outside their own unique sphere and undertake state functions, for example, in running schools, the constitutional guarantee in art 19(4) applies to them: BVerfGE 18, 385, 387—388; BVerfGE 25, 226, 229. In much the same way, for example, a Church of England body which was entrusted, as part of its responsibilities, with running a school or other educational establishment might find that it had stepped over into the

b sphere of governmental functions and was, in that respect, to be regarded as a public authority for purposes of s 6(1).

[169] The Court of Appeal did indeed consider that, even if they were wrong in holding that PCCs are core public authorities, a PCC should be regarded as a public authority when enforcing the common law obligation of lay rectors, who need not be members of the Church, to maintain the chancel of the parish

c church. Mr Beloff reinforced this argument by pointing both to the duty of the minister under the relevant canons to hold certain services in the parish church and to the widespread belief, whether particularly well-founded or not, that any resident of a parish was entitled to be married in the church. These were indications of the public role of the parish church and, accordingly, of the public

d nature of the PCC's function in relation to the maintenance of the fabric of the church so that the minister could perform those public duties there. Enforcing the lay rectors' obligation was part of that public function.

[170] For the most part, in performing his duties and conducting the prescribed services, the minister is simply carrying out part of the mission of the Church, not any governmental function of the state. On the other hand, when

e in the course of his pastoral duties the minister marries a couple in the parish church, he may be carrying out a governmental function in a broad sense and so may be regarded as a public authority for purposes of the Human Rights Act. In performing its duties in relation to the maintenance of the fabric of the church so that services may take place there, the PCC is doing its part to help the minister

f discharge his pastoral and evangelistic duties. The PCC may be acting in the public interest, in a general sense, but it is still carrying out a church rather than a governmental function. That remains the case even although, from time to time, when performing one of his pastoral duties—conducting a marriage service in the church—the minister himself may act as a public authority.

[171] Moreover, the fact that, as part of its responsibilities in relation to the

g maintenance of the church fabric, the PCC may have to enforce a common law obligation against a lay rector who happens not to be a member of the Church can hardly transform the PCC into a public authority. Indeed, the very term 'lay rector' is a reminder that the common law obligation which the PCC is enforcing is the last remnant of a set of more complex rights and liabilities that were

h ecclesiastical in origin. As Ferris J held, today the liability to repair the chancel can be regarded as one of the incidents of ownership of rectorial property:

> 'It is, of course, an unusual incident because it does not amount to a charge on the land, is not limited to the value of the land and imposes a personal liability on the owner of the land. But in principle I do not find it possible to
>
> j distinguish it from the liability which would attach to the owner of land which is purchased subject to a mortgage, restrictive covenant or other incumbrance created by a predecessor in title.'

I respectfully agree. There is nothing in the nature of the obligation itself, or in the means or purpose of its enforcement, that would lead to the conclusion that the PCC of Aston Cantlow is exercising a governmental function, however broadly defined, when it enforces the lay rectors' obligation to pay for chancel repairs. Therefore, even when it is enforcing that obligation, the PCC is not to be regarded as a public authority for the purposes of s 6 of the Human Rights Act.

[172] I should add that I agree with the observations of my noble and learned friend, Lord Nicholls of Birkenhead, in the final paragraph of his speech.

[173] For these reasons I would allow the appeal and make the order proposed by Lord Scott of Foscote.

Appeal allowed.

Celia Fox   Barrister.

a # Edore v Secretary of State for the Home Department
[2003] EWCA Civ 716

b COURT OF APPEAL, CIVIL DIVISION
SIMON BROWN, WALLER AND KAY LJJ
19, 23 MAY 2003

c *Immigration – Appeal – Decision relating to person's entitlement to enter or remain in United Kingdom – Approach to appeal in which proportionality in issue – Immigration and Asylum Act 1999, s 65.*

The appellant was a citizen of Nigeria who had entered the United Kingdom in 1990 and remained after her visa had expired. She had two children, born in 1999 and 2000, whose father was a British citizen. He was married with three other *d* children. The appellant's children were maintained by their father who saw them regularly. They were emotionally dependent upon him and he was a stable influence in their lives. If the appellant and her children were returned to Nigeria their relationship with him would end. The Secretary of State decided to issue and serve removal directions on the appellant. She appealed under s 65[a] of the *e* Immigration and Asylum Act 1999 which provided that a person alleging that an authority had, in taking any decision under the Immigration Acts relating to that person's entitlement to enter or remain in the United Kingdom, acted 'in breach of his human rights' might appeal to an adjudicator against that decision. Paragraph 21[b] of Sch 4 to the 1999 Act provided, inter alia, that on an appeal to him the adjudicator had to allow the appeal if he considered that the decision or *f* action against which the appeal was brought was 'not in accordance with the law. In 2002 the adjudicator allowed her appeal, finding that the removal of the appellant and her two dependent children was an interference with her right to family life under art 8[c] of the Convention for the Protection of Human Rights and Fundamental Freedoms 1950 (as set out in Sch 1 to the Human Rights Act 1998) which was disproportionate to the legitimate aim of preserving the integrity of *g* immigration control. The Secretary of State appealed to the Immigration Appeal Tribunal, who reinstated his decision to issue and serve removal directions. The appellant appealed. On appeal two issues arose: (i) what was the correct approach to an appeal under s 65 of the 1999 Act; and (ii) whether the tribunal had been entitled to have regarded the decision to return the appellant and her *h* children to Nigeria as striking a fair balance between the relevant interests.

Held – Where the essential facts were not in doubt or dispute, the adjudicator's task on a human rights appeal under s 65 of the 1999 Act was to determine

---

j a   Section 65, so far as material, is set out at [11], below
    b   Paragraph 21, so far as material, is set out at [13], below
    c   Article 8, so far as material, provided: '(1) Everyone has the right to respect for his private and family life … (2) There shall be interference by a public authority with the exercise of this right except such as is in accordance with the law and is necessary in a democratic society in the interests of national security, public safety or the economic well-being of the country, for the prevention of disorder or crime, for the protection of health or morals, or for the protection of the rights and freedoms of others.'

whether the decision under appeal was properly one within the decision-maker's discretion, namely that it was a decision which could reasonably be regarded as proportionate and as striking a fair balance between the competing interests in play. If it were, then the adjudicator could not characterise it as a decision 'not in accordance with the law' and so, even if he personally would have preferred the balance to have been struck differently, he could not substitute his preference for the decision in fact taken. However, there would be occasions where it could properly be said that the decision reached by the Secretary of State was outside the range of permissible responses open to him, in that the balance struck was simply wrong. The instant case was such an occasion. The tribunal had not been entitled to have regarded the Secretary of State's decision to return the appellant and her children to Nigeria as striking a fair balance between the competing interests in play. Accordingly, the appeal would be allowed, the decision of the tribunal set aside and the decision of the adjudicator reinstated (see [20], [25], [27]–[30], below).

R (on the application of Ala) v Secretary of State for the Home Dept [2003] All ER (D) 283 (Mar) applied.

Notes

For appeals against a decision under the Immigration Acts in breach of a person's human rights, see 4(2) *Halsbury's Laws* (4th edn) (2002 reissue) para 179.

Section 65 of the Immigration and Asylum Act 1999 has been repealed by the Nationality, Immigration and Asylum Act 2002, ss 114(1), (2), 161, Sch 9 with effect from 1 April 2003.

Cases referred to in judgments

Associated Provincial Picture Houses Ltd v Wednesbury Corp [1947] 2 All ER 680, [1948] 1 KB 223, CA.
B v Secretary of State for the Home Dept [2000] Imm AR 478, CA.
Baah [2002] UK IAT 05998, IAT.
Noruwa v Secretary of State for the Home Dept (3 July 2001, unreported), IAT.
R (on the application of Ala) v Secretary of State for the Home Dept [2003] EWHC 521 (Admin), [2003] All ER (D) 283 (Mar).
R v Secretary of State for the Home Dept, ex p Isiko [2001] 1 FCR 633, CA.
R (on the application of Mahmood) v Secretary of State for the Home Dept [2001] 1 WLR 840, CA.
R (on the application of Samaroo) v Secretary of State for the Home Dept, R (on the application of Sezek) v Secretary of State for the Home Dept [2001] EWCA Civ 1139, [2001] UKHRR 1150.
Sporrong v Sweden (1982) 5 EHRR 35, [1982] ECHR 7151/75, ECt HR.

Appeal

The appellant, Blessing Edore, appealed with permission granted by Latham LJ from the decision of the Immigration and Appeal Tribunal on 29 January 2003 allowing the appeal of the Secretary of State for the Home Department from the decision of Mrs Frudd, a special adjudicator, allowing the appeal of the appellant from the decision of the Secretary of State to return her with her dependent children to her country of citizenship. The facts are set out in the judgment of Simon Brown LJ.

a Sibghat Ullah Kadri QC and Satvinder Juss (instructed by Ikie Solicitors) for the appellant.

Ashley Underwood QC (instructed by the Treasury Solicitor) for the Secretary of State.

Cur adv vult

b 23 May 2003. The following judgments were delivered.

SIMON BROWN LJ.

[1] Ms Blessing Edore, the appellant, is a citizen of Nigeria now aged 39. She c has been in this country since her illegal entry here in 1990. She has two young children fathered by a married man, Mr Okadiegbo, a British citizen with a wife and three older children, also living here. It is the appellant's case that to return her to Nigeria as the Secretary of State proposes would infringe her (and her children's) right to family life under art 8 of the European Convention on Human Rights and Fundamental Freedoms 1950 (as set out in Sch 1 to the Human Rights d Act 1998). The Secretary of State contends to the contrary that the appellant's return is necessary and proportionate in the interests of effective immigration control.

[2] On 20 June 2002, on the appellant's appeal under s 65 of the Immigration and Asylum Act 1999, a special adjudicator, Mrs Frudd, allowed the appeal: she e found that 'removal of the appellant and her two dependent children would be disproportionate to the aim of preserving the integrity of immigration control pursuant to art 8 of the [European Convention for the Protection of Human Rights and Fundamental Freedoms 1950 (as set out in Sch 1 to the Human Rights Act 1998)]'.

[3] On 29 January 2003 the Immigration Appeal Tribunal (the IAT) allowed f the Secretary of State's appeal and reinstated his decision to issue and serve removal directions.

[4] The appellant now appeals to this court with permission granted by Latham LJ in these terms:

g   'It seems to me that this court should take the opportunity to consider the starred appeal of *Noruwa v Secretary of State for the Home Dept* (3 July 2001, unreported) and the way in which adjudicators and the tribunal should approach appeals in which proportionality is in issue.'

[5] Essentially two questions arise on the appeal: first, as suggested by h Latham LJ, what approach should the independent appellate authorities bring to bear on a s 65 appeal arising, as commonly such appeals do, in circumstances such as exist here. More particularly, if there is room for two views as to whether, in ordering the appellant's removal, the Secretary of State has acted proportionately and struck a fair balance between the competing interests in play, are the j appellate authorities bound to dismiss the appeal or can they, if they prefer, substitute for the Secretary of State's decision one more favourable to the appellant? This first question is plainly one of some general importance. The second question arising is whether, whatever may be held to be the correct approach to its jurisdiction, the IAT was right on the facts of this particular case to have upheld the Secretary of State's decision to return the appellant and her children to Nigeria.

[6] Before addressing either question it is convenient first to sketch in the facts of the case, noting as I do so that these have never been the subject of dispute.

[7] The appellant entered the UK on 11 September 1990 on a visa valid for only 24 hours. In 1996 she met Mr Okadiegbo, an accountant by profession. He had just been naturalised and, as she knew, was a married man with three children, the eldest, Michael, being profoundly deaf. The appellant and Mr Okadiegbo planned a family and began to spend virtually every weekend together. After miscarrying several times in 1997 and 1998, on 29 May 1999 she bore him a son; and on 11 October 2000, a daughter. He supports the family by giving her £200 per week for her council house rent and for the children's upkeep. He also buys them clothes and toys. She herself works as a cleaner, claiming family allowance but no other benefits. The children see their father every Saturday without fail. The love between them is mutual. He telephones the appellant every day and sometimes sees her and the children during the week. Were the appellant and her children to be returned to Nigeria their relationship with Mr Okadiegbo would end. He could not and would not leave his marriage to live with the appellant. He loves all his five children equally. He feels particularly responsible for Michael. His wife is aware of his relationship with the appellant and has indicated that if he were ever to seek a divorce she would make it as difficult as possible for him to see the three children of the marriage.

[8] Having recorded the facts essentially as I have just sought to summarise them, the adjudicator continued:

'38. The two children are maintained by Mr Okadiegbo in the United Kingdom, but more importantly they appear to be dependent upon him emotionally as their father. He sees them regularly every week, at least once a week and is part of their lives. Even though they are still a tender age, he is a stable influence remaining in daily contact with them and their mother ... I find as a fact that there are substantial "family ties" in this case and these children should not suffer because their father is in a complicated position with his wife and three children from his marriage.

39. Consequently I am satisfied that there would be an interference with the right to respect of private life and family life were the appellant and her children sent to Nigeria ...

42. I am conscious of the fact that the appellant has flouted immigration control and has had a relationship with a man who still lives with his wife and three children which has led to the birth of two children whilst her immigration status was uncertain. Against this I have to balance the facts of this particular case in terms of the interests of the appellant and her family. There is clearly a balance of public interest and private interest to be considered.

43. Having considered all of the evidence in this matter I find that it would be disproportionate in this particular instance to return the appellant to Nigeria together with her two dependent young children because of the severe effects which it would have upon the appellant and more particularly her two children who were born in the United Kingdom.'

[9] I turn now to the IAT's determination by which it concluded, first, that the interference with family life involved in returning the appellant and her children to Nigeria flowed rather from the father's decision not to live with them there rather than the Secretary of State's decision to return them and, secondly, that in any event the removal of the appellant and her two children to Nigeria would be

a proportionate. Let me at once set out the most directly relevant passages from the IAT's decision:

> '19. ... [T]here is an interference if the children's father will not go to Nigeria but there is not if he is prepared to go. We do not accept in these circumstances that the interference follows automatically from the Secretary of State's decision; it follows naturally from the father's decision.
b
> 20. Given that what the adjudicator found were substantial family ties, she also found that there would be an interference of the right to private life and family life were the appellant and her children sent to Nigeria. This finding was only open to the adjudicator if she took no proper account of the father's choice, and we consider this was an error. We find on the particular
c facts of this unusual case that what would be the operative interference with family life in Nigeria is the father's choice to remain in the United Kingdom. Absent the father's decision, there is no free-standing insurmountable obstacle to family life in Nigeria ...
> 29. We differ from the adjudicator in her assessment of proportionality. In our view proportionality is not solely a question of fact, but is essentially
d a question of law, based on the facts.
> 30. In this particular case the applicant came to the United Kingdom illegally and has made an application for asylum which has failed. Late in the day she makes an application to stay on the basis of a potential breach of her human rights and at all stages she has known of the precarious nature of her
e immigration status.
> 31. There is no proper reasoning in the adjudicator's determination for the conclusion that the applicant's children's would be adversely affected by removal, but we accept what must be inherent in looking at the facts that the children would be going to a country where they were not born and have, we assume, never visited ...
f
> 33. There is a lack of any proper evidence before the adjudicator relating to the actual impact upon the children if they did have to live in Nigeria.
> 34. The family unit in question is not long-established in the United Kingdom.
> 35. We take the view that the removal of the applicant and her two
g children to Nigeria would be proportionate.'

[10] I turn now to the first issue arising here: what is the correct approach to an appeal under s 65 of the 1999 Act?
[11] Clearly the starting point must be the statutory language in which the
h appeal jurisdiction is conferred on the adjudicator. So far as material s 65 provides:

> '(1) A person who alleges that an authority has, in taking any decision under the Immigration Acts relating to that person's entitlement to enter or remain in the United Kingdom, acted in breach of his human rights may
j appeal to an adjudicator against that decision ...
> (2) For the purposes of this Part ... (b) an authority acts in breach of a person's human rights if he acts, or fails to act, in relation to that other person in a way which is made unlawful by section 6(1) of the Human Rights Act 1998.
> (3) Subsections (4) and (5) apply if, in proceedings before an adjudicator or the Immigration Appeal Tribunal on an appeal, a question arises as to

whether an authority has, in taking any decision under the Immigration Acts relating to the appellant's entitlement to enter or remain in the United Kingdom ... acted in breach of the appellant's human rights ...

(5) If the ... adjudicator, or the Tribunal, decides that the authority concerned ... (b) acted in breach of the appellant's human rights, the appeal may be allowed on that ground.'

[12] Section 6(1) of the Human Rights Act 1998 provides:

'It is unlawful for a public authority to act in a way which is incompatible with a Convention right.'

[13] Paragraph 21 of Sch 4 to the 1999 Act, under the heading 'Determination of Appeals', provides (so far as material):

'(1) On an appeal to him under [the relevant Part], an adjudicator must allow the appeal if he considers—(a) that the decision or action against which the appeal is brought was not in accordance with the law or with any immigration rules applicable to the case, or (b) if the decision or action involved the exercise of a discretion by the Secretary of State or an officer, that the discretion should have been exercised differently, but otherwise must dismiss the appeal ...

(3) For the purposes of sub-paragraph (1), the adjudicator may review any determination of a question of fact on which the decision or action was based.'

[14] Paragraph 22(2) of Sch 4 provides that:

'The Tribunal may affirm the determination or make any other determination which the adjudicator could have made.'

[15] The effect of these provisions taken together is that a person may appeal to the adjudicator in respect of an immigration decision which he alleges is incompatible with his convention rights and, if the adjudicator finds the alleged breach established, his appeal will be allowed, otherwise it will be dismissed. The fundamental question, therefore, is: does the decision under appeal infringe a convention right?

[16] Latham LJ referred in his grant of permission to 'the starred appeal of *Noruwa'*—a decision of the IAT (no 00/TH/2345) (3 July 2001, unreported) (presided over by Mr Ockleton, the deputy president)). Rather, however, than attempt any prolonged examination of that rather difficult determination, I am able instead to turn immediately to a recent decision of Moses J in *R (on the application of Ala) v Secretary of State for the Home Dept* [2003] EWHC 521 (Admin), [2003] All ER (D) 283 (Mar) which for my part I have found enormously helpful on the very question we are now addressing, the nature of the adjudicator's jurisdiction on a s 65 appeal. So helpful is it, indeed, that I propose to cite the relevant part of the judgment in its entirety, pausing only to note, first, that the proposal there was to remove the applicant to Germany under the Convention determining the State responsible for examining Applications for Asylum lodged in one of the Member States of the European Communities (Dublin; TS 72 (1997); Cm 3806) for the determination of his asylum claim (and any entry clearance application he might then make) and, secondly, that the challenge was in fact to the Secretary of State's decision to certify the alleged art 8 breach as manifestly unfounded under s 72(2)(a) of the 1999 Act:

a
'[37] ... If the only question is whether the balance between the need for effective immigration control and the undisputed family circumstances of a claimant should have been struck in favour of the claimant, is it open to an adjudicator to substitute his own decision for that of the Secretary of State?

[38] The solution to the question is to be found, not in the nature of an adjudicator's jurisdiction but in the nature of the issue to be determined on

b
appeal. The issue before an adjudicator would be whether the Secretary of State has acted in breach of the appellant's human rights (see s 65(3) and (5)(b) of the 1999 Act). In the instant case the statutory question posed to the adjudicator by s 65(2)(b), (3) and (5)(b) of the 1999 Act is whether the Secretary of State has, in ordering the removal of the claimant, acted in breach of the claimant's rights enshrined in art 8 of the European

c
Convention on Human Rights.

[39] The Secretary of State's decision that the claimant should be returned to Germany for the determination of his asylum claim is an interference with his rights under art 8(1). There is no dispute but that the Secretary of State's decision was taken in pursuance of a legitimate aim,

d
namely effective immigration control. The issue is whether the Secretary of State's decision was a proportionate response to the question whether such removal was justified in this particular case. The obligation upon the Secretary of State to act in a proportionate manner required him to strike a fair balance between the legitimate aim of immigration control and the claimant's rights under art 8. In *R (on the application of Samaroo) v Secretary of*

e
State for the Home Dept, R (on the application of Sezek) v Secretary of State for the Home Dept [2001] EWCA Civ 1139 at [24], [2001] UKHRR 1150 at [24]. Dyson LJ emphasised (at [26]):

"The striking of a fair balance lies at the heart of proportionality. In

f
Sporrong v Sweden (1982) 5 EHRR 35 (para 69), the court said: 'The court must determine whether a fair balance was struck between the demands of the general interest of the community and the requirements of the protection of the individual's fundamental right ... The search for this balance is inherent in the whole of the Convention.'"

g
[40] The jurisprudence of the European Court of Human Rights recognises that art 8 affords the decision maker, the Secretary of State, a "discretionary area of judgment" in striking the balance fairly between the conflicting interests of a claimant's right to respect for family life and effective immigration control. The Court of Appeal cited (at [29]) with approval Thomas J's recognition of the discretionary area of judgment in the

h
context of art 8. Dyson LJ said (at [35]):

"... the function of the court in a case such as this is to decide whether the Secretary of State has struck the balance fairly between the conflicting interests of Mr Samaroo's right to respect of his family life on the one hand and the prevention of crime and disorder on the other. In reaching its

j
decision the court must recognise and allow to the Secretary of State a discretionary area of judgment."

He continued:

"In my judgment, in a case such as this, the Court should undoubtedly give a significant margin of discretion to the decision of the Secretary of State.

The convention right engaged is not absolute. The right to respect for family life is not regarded as a right which requires a high degree of constitutional protection. It is true that the issues are not technical as economic and social issues often are. But the court does not have expertise in judging how effective a deterrent is a policy of defaulting foreign nationals who have been convicted of serious drug trafficking offences once they have served their sentences."

[41] It is true that this is not a case of deportation following a conviction (in *Samaroo's* case of drug offences). But it is a case where the Secretary of State is bound to be better placed to take a wider overall view as to what is needed to ensure that immigration control is effective.

[42] It must be recalled that in *Samaroo's case* the Court of Appeal was concerned, not with the appellate jurisdiction of an adjudicator but with the role of the court on an application for judicial review. The adjudicator is not exercising the residual jurisdiction of judicial review. Still less is he in the position of the European Court of Human Rights which affords member states a margin of appreciation when considering whether a high contracting party is in breach of its treaty obligations under the convention. The essential question is whether an adjudicator is entitled to substitute his own decision as to where the balance fairly lies.

[43] The answer is to be found, in my view, in the recognition, acknowledged both by the European Court of Human Rights and the Court of Appeal, that the convention itself, in the context of art 8, affords the decision-maker, the Secretary of State, a discretionary area of judgment. The test of proportionality posed by art 8(2) is whether the decision-maker has struck a fair balance. That test is not affected by the concept of margin of appreciation to be applied by the European Court of Human Rights nor by the nature of the Administrative Court's jurisdiction. As Dyson LJ pointed out (at [24]):

"The court has clearly said that the issue for it is to determine whether the deportation struck a fair balance between the relevant interests. That is what proportionality requires. In my view, the margin of appreciation does not affect the nature of the test to be applied or the question to be asked."

Similarly the question to be asked by an adjudicator, the test to be applied by him, in determining whether the Secretary of State has acted in breach of the claimant's rights under art 8, remains the same as the test to be deployed by the Administrative Court or the European Court of Human Rights itself.

[44] It is the convention itself and, in particular, the concept of proportionality which confers upon the decision-maker a margin of discretion in deciding where the balance should be struck between the interests of an individual and the interests of the community. A decision-maker may fairly reach one of two opposite conclusions, one in favour of a claimant the other in favour of his removal. Of neither could it be said that the balance had been struck unfairly. In such circumstances, the mere fact that an alternative but favourable decision could reasonably have been reached will not lead to the conclusion that the decision maker has acted in breach of the claimant's human rights. Such a breach will only occur where the decision is outwith the range of reasonable responses to the question as to where a fair balance lies between the conflicting interests.

a

Once it is accepted that the balance could be struck fairly either way, the Secretary of State cannot be regarded as having infringed the claimant's art 8 rights by concluding that he should be removed.

[45] So to conclude is not to categorise the adjudicator's appellate function as limited to review. It merely recognises that the decision of the Secretary of State in relation to art 8 cannot be said to have infringed the

b

claimant's rights merely because a different view as to where the balance should fairly be struck might have been reached.

[46] This is not a recognition of an exercise of a discretion by the Secretary of State within the meaning of para 21(1)(b) of Sch 4 to the 1999 Act. The ground of appeal under s 65 is not that the Secretary of State's discretion should have been exercised differently but that the Secretary of State has

c

acted in breach of the claimant's human rights enshrined in art 8. The concept of a discretionary area of judgment describes no more than an area within which two reasonable albeit opposite conclusions may fairly be reached.

[47] Accordingly I conclude that an adjudicator, on an appeal based upon

d

art 8, where there is no issue of fact, is concerned only with the question whether the Secretary of State has struck a fair balance between the need for effective immigration control and the claimant's rights under art 8. In order to answer that question he is concerned only with the issue whether the decision of the Secretary of State is outwith the range of reasonable responses. This conclusion has the merit of support from a starred decision

e

of the Immigration Appeal Tribunal in *Noruwa v Secretary of State for the Home Dept* (3 July 2001, unreported). There was much debate before me as to what appeared to be two conflicting paragraphs within that decision in paras 47 and 54. But it is plain from another decision, not cited before me in *Baah* [2002] UK IAT 05998 (para 39) chaired by the same deputy president, that the

f

IAT's conclusion was the same as my own.'

[17] I have already described the IAT's decision in *Noruwa*'s case as somewhat difficult. The following brief citations will illustrate why:

'47 ... So far as the human rights element of the claim is concerned, the appellate authority will be concerned with whether the decision is shown to

g

have been one which was outside the range of permissible responses ...

54. If an appellant claims that a decision was disproportionate, that is a matter which he is entitled to bring to the appellate authority and which the authority must determine. In doing so the authority will examine all relevant material (going both to law and to the facts) and will reach its own

h

conclusion. This is a genuine appeal, not merely a review of whether the respondent's conclusion on proportionality was open to him. If the authority reaches the conclusion that the decision was disproportionate, that is the end of the matter: the decision was unlawful and the appeal must be allowed ...

j

56. In particular, the fact that an argument based on proportionality has been raised and has failed (because the decision was not outside the allowable area of discretion) does not of itself allow an adjudicator or the tribunal to intervene in the exercise of a discretion. Nor does it of itself allow the adjudicator or the tribunal to substitute its own discretion for that of the respondent. That power only arises where the original decision involves the exercise of a discretion.'

[18] With regard to that final paragraph, the IAT had already stated in para 49, rightly to my mind: 'The issue of proportionality is a matter of judgment and balance, but not of itself a matter of discretion.'

[19] In so far as some tension may be thought to arise between paras 47 and 56 on the one hand and para 54 on the other, Mr Ockleton's view was subsequently made plain, as Moses J pointed out in the IAT's decision in *Baah* [2002] UK IAT 05998 (para 39):

'The question for us is whether or not the respondent's decision is lawful under s 6(1): that is to say whether it is proportionate. It is not open to us to substitute our own decision if the decision was within the allowable area of discretion allowed to the respondent.'

[20] For my part I find Moses J's analysis in *R (on the application of Ala) v Secretary of State for the Home Dept* [2003] EWHC 521 (Admin), [2003] All ER (D) 283 (Mar) entirely convincing and in the result conclude that, in cases like the present where the essential facts are not in doubt or dispute, the adjudicator's task on a human rights appeal under s 65 is to determine whether the decision under appeal (ex hypothesi a decision unfavourable to the appellant) was properly one within the decision-maker's discretion, ie was a decision which could reasonably be regarded as proportionate and as striking a fair balance between the competing interests in play. If it was, then the adjudicator cannot characterise it as a decision 'not in accordance with the law' and so, even if he personally would have preferred the balance to have been struck differently (ie in the appellant's favour), he cannot substitute his preference for the decision in fact taken.

[21] In *B v Secretary of State for the Home Dept* [2000] Imm AR 478 at 486 (para 36) Sedley LJ, giving the leading judgment in this court, said:

'I have no doubt that the Home Secretary's view that deportation was nevertheless merited was legitimately open to him ... But our public law ... now has to accommodate and give effect to the requirements of EU law and, through EU law [this was before the coming into force of the Human Rights Act 1998] of the European Convention. It means making up our own minds about the proportionality of a public law measure—not simply deciding whether the Home Secretary's or the Tribunal's view of it is lawful and rational.'

[22] I myself said (at 488 (para 47)):

'It was common ground before us that proportionality involves a question of law and that, on a statutory appeal of this nature, the court is required to form its own view on whether the test is satisfied, although, of course, in doing so it will give such deference to the Tribunal's decision as appropriately recognises their advantage in having heard the evidence. This task is, of course, both different from and more onerous than that undertaken by the court when applying the conventional *Wednesbury* approach [see *Associated Provincial Picture Houses Ltd v Wednesbury Corp* [1947] 2 All ER 680, [1948] 1 KB 223]. It would not be proper for us to say that we disagree with the Tribunal's conclusion on proportionality but that, since there is clearly room for two views and their view cannot be stigmatised as irrational, we cannot interfere. Rather, if our view differs from the Tribunal's, then we are bound to say so and to allow the appeal, substituting our decision for theirs.'

a Ward LJ expressly agreed with both judgments.

[23] In *Noruwa v Secretary of State for the Home Dept* (3 July 2001, unreported) the IAT considered B's case in the light of three later Court of Appeal authorities concerning the judicial review of decisions by the Secretary of State to remove individuals from the United Kingdom: *R (on the application of Mahmood) v Secretary of State for the Home Dept* [2001] 1 WLR 840, *R v Secretary of State for the Home Dept,*

b *ex p Isiko* [2001] 1 FCR 633 and *R (on the application of Samaroo) v Secretary of State for the Home Dept, R (on the application of Sezek) v Secretary of State for the Home Dept* [2001] EWCA Civ 1139, [2001] UKHRR 1150 (although the latter case had not by then reached the Court of Appeal) and concluded that B's case had proceeded on the basis of a concession and should not be followed in so far as it indicated that the question of proportionality was a question of law. For my part I now readily

c accept that it is unhelpful to characterise the question of proportionality as one of law and certainly the approach which we adopted in B's case appears to me irreconcilable with that which by the terms of s 65 Parliament has now dictated independent appellate authorities must take towards appeals from removal directions made by the Secretary of State and his officers. It is perhaps worth

d pointing out that B's case was decided at a time when, under s 15(1)(a) and (7)(a) of the Immigration Act 1971, a decision to deport, as there, on the ground that such deportation was conducive to the public good was appealable directly to the IAT *on the merits.*

[24] Having resolved the first issue in favour of the respondent I turn now to

e the second question arising on the appeal: was the IAT entitled on the facts of this case to have regarded the Secretary of State's decision to return the appellant and her children to Nigeria as striking a fair balance between the competing interests in play?

[25] This question I can deal with altogether more briefly. In my judgment it

f was not. Although the IAT allowed the appeal against the adjudicator's decision on two separate grounds, Mr Underwood QC very fairly recognises that neither ground is sustainable, at any rate by reference to the reasoning given. That the removal of the appellant and her children to Nigeria would interfere with their art 8(1) rights is surely plain and indisputable and Mr Underwood does not seek to support the approach taken in paras 19 and 20 of the IAT's determination (see

g [9], above). As for the IAT's view that removal here would be proportionate, the tribunal seems to have allowed the appeal from the adjudicator's contrary view on the basis (see para 31 of its determination) that '[t]here is no proper reasoning in the adjudicator's determination for the conclusion that the applicant's children would be adversely affected by removal'. I simply cannot follow that reasoning.

h On the contrary, the adjudicator seems to me to have explained perfectly plainly how the children would be adversely affected: they are 'emotionally dependent' upon their father who provides 'a stable influence' in their lives; if sent to Nigeria they would be permanently deprived of his love and support. What clearer or more convincing reasoning could one have for not imposing this separation upon

j them?

[26] I recognise, of course, the flagrancy of the appellant's breach of immigration control and the precariousness of her presence in the UK whilst she was creating this new 'family'. So too did the adjudicator: see para 42 of her determination set out at [8], above. I recognise also the need for effective immigration control. In the highly unusual circumstances of this case, however, it seems to me that there really is only room for one view as to how the balance

between these competing interests should be struck and that is the view taken by
the adjudicator who, of course, heard all the evidence in the case.

[27] Mr Kadri QC asked rhetorically during the course of his submissions on
the first part of the case what was the point of having a right of appeal under s 65
if the appellate authorities' jurisdiction is as relatively restricted as Moses J found
in *R (on the application of Ala) v Secretary of State for the Home Dept* [2003] EWHC
521 (Admin), [2003] All ER (D) 283 (Mar) and as I for my part would hold it to be.
The outcome to the present appeal surely provides the answer to that question.
There will be occasions when it can properly be said that the decision reached
by the Secretary of State was outside the range of permissible responses open
to him, when in other words the balance struck by the Secretary of State is simply
wrong. There may not be many such occasions but to my mind this certainly was
one of them.

[28] I would accordingly allow the appeal, set aside the decision of the IAT
and reinstate that of the adjudicator.

WALLER LJ.

[29] I agree.

KAY LJ.

[30] I also agree.

Appeal allowed.

Dilys Tausz   Barrister.

a # R (on the application of C) v Lewisham London Borough Council
[2003] EWCA Civ 927

b COURT OF APPEAL, CIVIL DIVISION
WARD, WALLER AND DYSON LJJ
6 MARCH, 4 JULY 2003

Housing – Homeless person – Duty of housing authority to provide accommodation –
c *Appeals procedure – Scope of discretion of housing authority to extend time for request*
for review of decision as to duty owed to applicant – Whether applicant entitled to make
repeated applications for extension of time – Housing Act 1996, s 202(3).

In response to an application by the claimant, under Pt VII of the Housing Act
1996, for housing assistance as a homeless person, the defendant local housing
d authority concluded that she was intentionally homeless on the basis of eviction
for persistent rent arrears (the initial decision). Under s 202[a] of the 1996 Act, the
claimant had the right to request a review of that decision. Subsection (3)
provided that such a request had to be made within 21 days or such longer
period as the authority might allow. The claimant made no request for a
review within the 21-day period, but some months later made a formal request
e for an extension of time for a review. After that request was rejected, she made
a request for a further review of the initial decision, relying on a medical report
which concluded that she had not made herself intentionally homeless because
her disturbed mental state had rendered her unable to manage her affairs in any
meaningful way. The authority rejected that request, stating, inter alia, that the
f new material had not persuaded it that any review would have good prospects
of success. The claimant sought permission to apply for judicial review of that
decision, but the judge refused permission. She applied to the Court of Appeal
for permission to appeal, contending, inter alia, that the officer charged with
deciding whether to extend time should only have regard to whether new
information was material. In dealing with that submission, the Court of Appeal
g considered the scope of an authority's discretion, under s 202(3), to extend time
for review. It also considered whether the claimant had been entitled to make
repeated applications for an extension of time.

Held – (1) The discretion to extend time for a review conferred by s 202(3)
h of the 1996 Act was unfettered in the sense that Parliament had not stipulated,
as it often did, the factors to be taken into account in the exercise of the discretion
which it conferred. In the absence of such a statutory checklist, the discretion was
wide, but it could only be validly exercised for reasons relevant to the
achievement of the purpose which the discretion was intended to serve. In
j Pt VII of the 1996 Act, Parliament had laid down a clear scheme which
provided the means of ensuring that a local housing authority fulfilled its duty
to homeless persons. The purpose was, therefore, to lay down the procedures
and time limits to enable the orderly management by the authority of its
precious supply of housing, but also to enable it, if appropriate, to grant an

---

a   Section 202, so far as material, is set out at [39], below

indulgence to the homeless person on as important a matter as his or her *a* housing, where a claim for review might be deserving enough to override the failure to act in time, and so keep the door open for further assistance. Even though the length of the delay and reasons for it were often balanced against the prospect of success, it was possible to envisage circumstances in which an authority could rationally and properly conclude that even a short delay for which there was a good explanation was not good enough to justify an *b* extension of time for a review. Conversely, the authority could rationally and properly decide to grant an extension of time where there had been a long delay for which no explanation had been provided. Delay and prospects of success did not always have to be balanced against each other. An authority was entitled to reach a decision without forming a provisional view of the underlying merits of the case if, in all the circumstances, it thought it *c* reasonable to do so. Given the wide ambit of the discretion, the decision of the authority in the instant case could not be impugned on the basis that no authority, acting reasonably, could have taken the prospects of success to be a relevant and appropriate factor for their consideration, nor was the decision perverse or irrational (see [46], [48], [49], [51], [52], below). *d*

(2) A housing authority was not bound to entertain a succession of applications for review or for extensions of time for review given that Parliament had circumscribed the applicant's right to seek them, but it could choose to entertain such requests as a matter of its discretion. That extra-statutory discretion, however, was likely to be held to be close to absolute. In so far as the local authority in the instant case had been exercising such a discretion, it was *e* even further beyond challenge by judicial review than a decision taken under s 202(3) of the 1996 Act. Accordingly, though permission to appeal would be granted, the appeal itself would be dismissed (see [36], [59], [60], below); *R v Westminster City Council, ex p Ellioua* (1998) 31 HLR 440 and *Demetri v Westminster City Council* [2000] 1 WLR 772 applied. *f*

Notes

For the right to request a review, see 22 *Halsbury's Laws* (4th edn reissue) para 263.

For the Housing Act 1996, s 202, see 21 *Halsbury's Statutes* (4th edn) (1997 *g* reissue) 910.

Cases referred to in the judgment

Associated Provincial Picture Houses Ltd v Wednesbury Corp [1947] 2 All ER 680, [1948] 1 KB 223, CA. *h*

Demetri v Westminster City Council [2000] 1 WLR 772, CA.

Lumley v Gye (1853) 2 E&B 216, [1843–60] All ER Rep 208.

Lumley v Wagner (1852) 1 De GM & G 604, 42 ER 687, [1843–60] All ER Rep 368, LC.

R v Brighton and Hove BC, ex p Nacion (1999) 11 Admin LR 472, CA. *j*

R v London Borough of Tower Hamlets, ex p Saber (1991) 24 HLR 611.

R v Panel on Take-overs and Mergers, ex p Guinness plc [1989] 1 All ER 509, [1990] 1 QB 146, [1989] 2 WLR 863, CA.

R v Westminster City Council, ex p Ellioua (1998) 31 HLR 440, CA.

Tesco Stores Ltd v Secretary of State for the Environment [1995] 2 All ER 636, [1995] 1 WLR 759, HL.

a *Tower Hamlets London BC v Chetnik Developments Ltd* [1988] 1 All ER 961, [1988] 1 AC 858, [1988] 2 WLR 654, HL.

Application for permission to appeal

The claimant, C, applied for permission to appeal from the decision of Maurice Kay J on 12 August 2002 refusing her permission to apply for judicial review of *b* the decision of the defendant local housing authority, Lewisham London Borough Council, on 4 March 2002 declining to exercise its discretion to extend time for her to request a review of the authority's decision of 24 January 2001 that she was intentionally homeless. The facts are set out in the judgment of the court.

c *Jan Luba QC* and *Jamie Burton* (instructed by *Straker Holford & Co*) for the claimant. *Ranjit Bhose* (instructed by *Kath Nicholson*) for the authority.

Cur adv vult

d 4 July 2003. The following judgment of the court was delivered.

WARD LJ.

[1] This is the judgment of the court to which each of the members of the court has contributed.

e THE CLAIMANT'S UNHAPPY CIRCUMSTANCES

[2] The claimant whom we shall identify under her initials, MC, is a young woman aged 24 years. She has had a sad and troubled life. When aged only 15 she was forced by a boyfriend to have sexual intercourse with him against her will. It was a traumatic event. It was compounded about a year later when she suffered a brutal attack at the hands of a so-called family friend who raped her *f* in her parents' home. This time the police were involved but she was too unwell to give evidence. She had begun to suffer depression and in May 1996 attempted suicide by taking an overdose of paracetamol leading to her admission to the Lewisham Hospital as a result. She received some psychiatric care but only for a short period. All of these events led to a deterioration of her relationship with her parents and she determined to leave home.

g [3] Thus it was that in about August 1997 the respondent local authority granted her a tenancy of a bed-sit flat in Catford, London SE6. Arrears of rent began to build up during the first year of that tenancy. From time to time she was in employment but it was not regular. She was unable to pay her gas, electricity and telephone bills and incurred debt to catalogue companies. When not *h* employed she failed to claim housing benefit and the arrears began to grow and she was warned that the local authority would be forced to serve notice seeking possession but she took no action upon that warning.

[4] Meanwhile in 1998 she had met a young man and hoped to have a stable relationship with him. When she became pregnant, he left her and she was very *j* distressed. During this time attempts were made to resolve the housing problem but all efforts made by the local authority came to nought because the claimant failed to attend meetings and failed to comply with arrangements to pay her rent. Eventually proceedings were taken against her in the county court leading to a suspended order for possession being made in February 1999 but she failed to make the rent payments and payments towards arrears which the court ordered.

[5] Her baby was born on 22 September 1999. At the end of November 1999
she was given a date for eviction which was postponed to give her a last
opportunity to submit claims for income support and housing benefit. She did
not do so and on 13 April 2000 she was evicted from her flat.

[6] Initially she stayed with her parents then moved in with a sister.
Eventually she was granted accommodation at a hostel with a mother and baby
unit where she prospered.

[7] She applied under Pt VII of the Housing Act 1996 as a homeless person
and the local authority embarked upon their statutory duty to make such
inquiries as were necessary to satisfy themselves whether she was eligible for
assistance.

[8] Nearly a year had elapsed after her eviction when on 24 January 2001 the
Homeless Persons Unit of the London Borough of Lewisham informed the
applicant in writing that they had concluded that she was eligible for assistance
and had priority need but concluded under s 191 of the 1996 Act that she had
become homeless intentionally. In coming to that conclusion the acting senior
housing adviser wrote:

> 'I have taken into consideration other information you provided about
> your well-being, you stated that you were drinking and that you were
> suffering depression. Investigations have shown that there is no evidence
> that you were depressed or being treated for this and there is no evidence to
> suggest that your overdose was a suicide attempt. By your own mitigation
> you did not seek any treatment for your drinking problem and you stated
> that this is where your money was being spent, again on investigation we
> have no evidence of your alcohol problem. You also stated that you were
> raped, while I appreciate this traumatic assault on you must have been
> devastating, all of this took place when you were 16 years old in 1994, well
> before your being given a tenancy, and at the time of the rape you were
> referred for counselling and to the Child Guidance Unit of which you never
> kept to the appointment. Your case has now been concluded that you are
> intentionally homeless ... on the basis of eviction for persistent rent arrears.
> This is seen to be a deliberate act, and causation of homelessness.'

The letter concluded:

> 'You have the right to request a review of this decision. If you wish to do
> so, please forward your appeal or representations in writing to the Advice
> Service Manager Mr Peter Jones within 21 days of this notification stating
> your reasons for requesting a review.'

[9] The applicant was vague as to her response to that letter and it is not at
all clear what approaches she made to the local authority or what she said when
she did approach them. She did see her general practitioner who wrote a letter
dated 8 February 2001 setting out the history of the two assaults upon her and
saying:

> 'Since then she has been more vulnerable and emotionally labile. From the
> records I can see that on 13th May 1996 she attend Casualty at Lewisham
> Hospital having taken an overdose of Paracetamol tablets. The blood test
> did show an abnormal level of Paracetamol and therefore she was kept under
> observation and given a follow up appointment later on and was also
> referred to see a psychiatrist for her emotional problems. Both these

a   incidents have left a scar on her life and periodically she gets depressed and a feeling of guilt complex. I do not think she will ever recover fully to her normal self.'

For some reason or other, possibly lack of money to pay the doctor's fee, she did not collect that report for months. On 25 April she wrote to Mr Jones sending him a copy of that letter and asking to make an urgent appointment 'to
b   see you as my situation is now desperate'. For one reason or another it took until 16 July for her to attend on the Homeless Persons Unit seeking help because she had been asked to leave her parents' home. Her plea for help, which was treated as a fresh application for housing assistance, not a review, was rejected.

c   [10] In their letter dated 18 July 2001 the local authority explained:

'During the interview you were advised that since the date of your initial application and our decision letter dated 24th January 2001 there has been no material change to your circumstances as the information you provided had already been assessed in your homeless application of 10th April 2000
d   neither had there been any intervening period of settled accommodation therefore the original decision still stood. Your decision letter advised you of your right to request a review within 21 days from the date of that letter however, you did not exercise your right to a review within the time period advised. You were advised at our interview that as the homelessness service were unable to assist that you should contact the Children and Families
e   Team within the Social Services Department for further assistance ... Please be advised that at this time the Homelessness Unit cannot be of any further assistance.'

[11] The applicant consulted solicitors and they wrote on her behalf on 31 August 2001 making a formal request to extend the time for a review of the
f   decision of 24 January 2001 on the ground that her age and mental state were such that she was not able properly to deal with her affairs such as completing housing benefit claim forms. In that letter the solicitors explained that the applicant was still unwell and extremely vulnerable, having 'great difficulty in coping with everyday life'. Her failure to explain the lapse in time between her
g   consulting her general practitioner and forwarding his report to the local authority was said to show that her inability to deal with matters was continuing. The solicitors reserved the right to submit further medical evidence once notified that the council agreed to an out-of-time review. No doubt with that in mind they also arranged an appointment for her with Dr Michael Browne, a consultant psychiatrist.
h

THE CLAIM FOR JUDICIAL REVIEW AND THE UNUSUAL ENSUING EVENTS
[12] On 18 October 2001 the claimant issued her claim for judicial review. The nature of her challenge was expressed to be against—

j   'the decision of the respondent dated 18 July 2001 not to extend the time limit for the applicant to request a review of the respondent's decision dated 24 January 2001 that she is intentionally homeless (pursuant to s 191 of the Housing Act 1996), pursuant to its power to do so, s 202(3) of the 1996 Act.'

[13] The local authority eventually responded to the applicant's solicitor's letter of 31 August. There is confusion about the date of that response which

inexplicably is sometimes referred to as having been dated 15 October, and
sometimes as dated 25 October 2001, even though the copy before us bears the
date 'November 9'. In it Mr Jones wrote:

> 'I have now gone through the papers and given fresh consideration to the
> matters raised in your letter of 31st August, and I regret to inform you that
> the authority here will not be conducting a review out of time of the
> decision of 24th January 2001, and adheres to the view expressed in the
> letter of 18th July 2001 that the authority has discharged its duty to Ms C.,
> and is under no further duty, either to make enquiries, or to review the
> original decision in your client's current circumstances.'

Several reasons were given. The first was that there was no proper explanation
for the delay in requesting a review and no proper explanation for the delay in
not submitting the further medical report until 25 April. Secondly Mr Jones
explained that their own inquiries made of the applicant's case did not support
her contentions. Consideration was given to the general practitioner's letter—

> 'but it is in no way compelling evidence that Ms C has problems attending
> to the administrative affairs in her life. Given the events that occurred in Ms
> C's teens, I would have thought it self evident that Ms C may not "recover
> fully to her normal self", but there is no causal link drawn between these
> events and an inability to cope with financial and administrative matters, and
> the doctor's letter does not link these matters in any way.'

[14] On 2 January 2002 Mr Jack Beatson QC sitting as an additional judge of
the High Court dismissed the application for permission to apply for judicial
review of 18 July decision observing that:

> 'No arguable case that Lewisham's decision not to extend the time limit for
> the claimant to request a review of its decision that she was intentionally
> homeless is impugnable on public law grounds.'

On the next day the applicant sought an oral hearing and the matter was listed for
11 February 2002.

[15] On 24 January 2002 the applicant's solicitors wrote to the legal
department of the local authority enclosing a copy of the report prepared by
Dr Browne. This report had in fact been written three months earlier on
19 October 2001. He recounted the history he had taken from the applicant. He
expressed the opinion that:

> 'This young woman though not mentally ill in the clinical or formal sense
> has in my opinion quite significant personality problems in that she is
> unusually anxious and to some extent unstable. Some of these problems
> undoubtedly stem from the two unfortunate episodes related above, i.e. the
> two rapes. It seems fair to say that these have cast a dark shadow on her
> life and have caused a psychiatric/psychological mental state amounting to
> something near to post-traumatic stress disorder. It is my opinion that this
> led to her leading a disjointed and chaotic lifestyle during which she drank
> to excess and because of which she was unable to think straight and to keep
> her affairs in order ... As a result of my examination and having thought
> carefully about the matter, I am of the opinion that this young woman did
> not make herself intentionally homeless as alleged by Lewisham Council.

a
I believe that her disturbed mental state rendered her unable to manage her affairs in any meaningful way over that period.'

The solicitors emphasised the causal link between her psychiatric/psychological problems and her inability to manage her own affairs. The applicant's solicitors wrote formally to request a review of the decision of 24 January 2001 'in the light of the new evidence provided, i.e. Doctor Browne's report'. They invited the local authority to treat it either as a review under s 202 of the 1996 Act or as a new application. They wrote: 'If your clients are prepared to agree to the above course of action, we are instructed to agree to withdraw the application for judicial review with no order for costs.'

b

[16] The legal department wrote the next day, 25 January 2002 that the housing department would consider the report but that their initial response was that the fresh evidence did not justify a fresh application. They observed that the evidence did not seem to touch the decision under review, namely that of 18 July, because Dr Browne gave no particular information about the applicant's state of mind after the January decision and leading up to the July decision. In any event it was said that the history had already been taken into consideration. There was some challenge to Dr Browne's expertise as to what does or does not constitute 'intentionality' for the purposes of the homelessness rules and they sought further information about this.

c

d

[17] Ms C's solicitors' response is interesting in the light of the submissions developed before us. They wrote on 1 February 2002:

e

'In our submission the two most important factors that a local authority should have regard to when considering the exercise of their discretion whether to permit an out of time review are (i) the merits of the original decision, having regard to the degree to which it is undermined by any fresh evidence/representations, and (ii) the reasons why the conducting of a review was not agreed within the 21 day time period.'

f

They expressed the view that Dr Browne's report constituted fresh evidence of sufficient probity to cast serious doubt over the local authority's decision of 24 January 2001, especially because it did establish the causal link between the loss of the accommodation and her psychological problems.

g

[18] The applicant then amended her claim to add a challenge to the decision of '25th October 2001' and to suggest that the letter of 25 January 2002 was reviewable on the basis that it was an omission to take a relevant decision.

[19] It was that amended application which came before Maurice Kay J on the afternoon of 11 February and for some 20 minutes on the following morning. In his skeleton argument on behalf of the applicant, Mr Jamie Burton submitted as follows:

h

'25. Under s 202(3) of the Housing Act 1996 the respondent has a discretion to extend the time for requesting a review of a decision beyond 21 days. When exercising its discretion the authority must take account of all material considerations and must not act irrationally.

j

26. It is submitted that when considering a request for a late review a local authority should have regard to both: (i) the reasons why the review request has been made out of time; and (ii) the merits of the applicant's case in relation to the validity of the decision under review, having regard to any further representations/evidence the applicant may or may not provide.

27. Furthermore it is submitted that where the challenge on the merits is strong the lesser the requirement that any delay in requesting a review be incurred reasonably, as the authority should be loath to permit a clearly erroneous decision to stand. Equally where the explanation for any delay is suitably exculpatory then the merits should not overly concern the authority as prima facie every applicant has the right to a review of the decision irrespective of the merits.'

Mr Ranjit Bhose submitted in his written argument that s 202(3) created a very broad procedural discretion and save for the most obvious of cases the court should not intervene (cf *R v Brighton and Hove BC, ex p Nacion* (1999) 11 Admin LR 472). He also dealt with the amended case that no decision had been taken in response to the request of 24 January 2002 and he submitted:

'13. It is accepted (for the purposes of this application) that where a local authority has decided not to extend time under s 202(3) it may nevertheless be called upon to reconsider that decision, in the light of further representations made. Any challenge to its decision would be a matter for this court, but again on grounds of perversity (assessed in the light of the fact that it had already fully considered the s 202(3) exercise).'

He went on, however, to set out on his client's express instructions, the reasons why the council did not consider that the report of Dr Browne should cause it to conclude any differently on whether or not to extend time and he set out their thinking.

[20] On 12 February 2002 Maurice Kay J ordered that:

'(i) Permission be refused in relation to the decisions of 18 July 2001 and 15 October. (ii) Deferred consideration of the local authority's position post Dr Browne's report for 28 days. (iii) The local authority reach and formulate its decision and provide reasons for it within 21 days. (iv) At the end of the 28-day period written submissions should be sent to Maurice Kay J at this court confined to the issue of whatever is decided and reasoned. Written submissions to begin with the counsel for the claimant putting in writing what he has to say about the situation followed within 48 hours by submissions from counsel for the defendant.'

We have no transcript of those proceedings and no transcript of the judgment. What is significant, however, is the fact that there is no appeal against that order and there is, thus, no longer any challenge to the decision either of 18 July or of 15/25 October 2001.

[21] The local authority duly considered the request made to them in the light of Dr Browne's report. On 4 March 2002 Mr Jones wrote:

'As stated at the hearing, having considered all of the new material presented, the council is not willing to reverse its decision not to extend the time within which Ms C might seek a s. 202 review of the original decision of 24th January 2001 that Ms C is intentionally homeless. Nor is the council willing to undertake any other sort of extra statutory review. Many of the reasons for my conclusion are set out in the council's skeleton argument, which was compiled on my instructions. However for the purposes of completeness I set out my reasoning in full which should be read in conjunction with my first decision not to extend time of 25th October 2001.'

a

[22] He continued:

> 'I remain of the view that no proper explanation has been provided for the
> failure to seek a review, nor the failure to supply [the general practitioner's]
> letter until 25th April 2001 (when on Ms C's account she had it in early March
> 2001). I have approached your request by seeing whether any of the new
> matters put forward are sufficiently compelling in your client's favour to
> suggest any review would have a good chance of success and that that should
> take precedence over my conclusion of there being no good reason for the
> failure to review in time. I have first considered the report of Doctor
> Browne. I do not find the report particularly compelling. I have found it to
> be generalised, non-date specific, and based almost entirely on what Ms C
> has told him.'

b

c

He went on to point out that the relevant period was when the rent arrears arose,
principally in 1999 to April 2000. He took the view that whereas incapacity, for
example old age, mental illness or handicap, would be a good reason that word
suggested that more was required than 'being simply depressed or having
difficulties coping. The test is a high one'. He pointed out Dr Browne did not
focus on the particular periods during which the arrears arose. He agreed that
the applicant was having 'a very difficult time' in the aftermath of the assaults
upon her leading to her being admitted to hospital in May 1996 but he pointed
out that was more than a year before the tenancy was even granted. He
pointed out that she did pay the rent from time to time and that things really
began to go wrong only in 1999. She obtained housing benefit and had to hold
down employment for long periods suggesting some ability to manage her
affairs. He concluded:

d

e

> 'Overall, in assessing the merits aspect of this decision, nothing that Doctor
> Browne has said causes me to consider that any review would have good
> prospects of success. Whilst I would naturally have regard to his report on
> any review, the amount of weight to be placed upon it would be limited. I
> also note that he does not deal with Ms C's mental state in the period when
> she should have applied for the review, or put forward any opinion to explain
> her failure.'

f

g

[23] He went on to deal with detailed complaints about her earnings and her
ability to pay the rent. He pointed out that the council had contacted her GP but
was referred to his partner in his absence on holiday. The council had also
telephoned Lewisham Hospital. In the result:

h

> 'Overall, I regret to inform you that I stand by my decision of 25th October
> 2001. I do not consider that anything you have now put forward should
> cause me to reach a different conclusion. I continue to conclude that the
> original s. 184 decision was correct, and that any review as might take place
> would not stand a good prospect of success. Indeed, even if I had concluded
> that there were good prospects I would still have borne very much in mind
> the wholesale failure to review in time, the delay there had been, and the fact
> that I have already once given the application for extension a full
> consideration. Therefore I decline to exercise my discretion in your client's
> favour.'

j

[24] As directed by the judge, Mr Jamie Burton put in further lengthy
submissions to counter each of the reasons given by the local authority for

example as to her late request for a review of the January 2001 decision, the
calculation in her earnings and the criticisms made of Dr Browne's report. As to   *a*
the approach taken by the local authority counsel submitted that:

> '... medical evidence stating that C was incapable of managing her affairs
> presents a prima facie case that she was so incapable and can only be rejected
> by reference to other medical evidence and reasons why it is preferable to
> that disclosed by C ... Therefore in the absence of evidence which   *b*
> contradicts that of Dr Browne it is not open to D to lawfully conclude that C
> would not have strong prospects of success on a review.'

[25] In addition to advancing his submissions on the decision letter,
Mr Burton sought to introduce fresh evidence from Dr Browne set out in a report
dated 14 March 2002. In that skeleton argument Mr Burton said: *c*

> 'In order to assist the defendant reach the correct decision on the merits of
> the claimant's request the claimant has been to see Dr Browne for a second
> time in order that he could address some of the concerns raised by the
> defendant in its decision letter. He has produced a report dated 14 March
> 2002. Had these issues been explored within the defendant's duty to conduct   *d*
> inquiries pursuant to s 184 of the Housing Act 1996 then it is submitted that
> its concerns would have been met in this way, namely by further reference
> to the opinion of Dr Browne.'

In that report he dealt with her difficulties over the whole period saying among   *e*
other things:

> 'Irrespective of whether she worked or not, it remains a fact in my opinion
> that she has instabilities and frailties of personality which surfaced over the
> period in question and which make her clearly in my eyes a person in need
> of help with her daily affairs ... Again, in the period in early 2001, when she   *f*
> was late in making an appeal, the information I have is that this was due to
> her state of acute distress due to losing her place in a hostel but more
> importantly as a reflection of her enduring frail mental capacity to deal with
> such crises.'

[26] In his response Mr Ranjit Bhose set out 'the relevant principles' as   *g*
follows:

> '6. The defendant continues to rely on the submissions made in the
> skeleton argument (dated 11 February 2002) at paras 2–6, which demonstrate
> that the discretion to consider a review out of time is a procedural discretion
> of exceptional width, the exercise of which this court should very rarely   *h*
> intervene in. So long as there is some consideration of material factors, any
> decision is unimpeachable (save on *Wednesbury* grounds) [see *Associated
> Provincial Picture Houses Ltd v Wednesbury Corp* [1947] 2 All ER 680, [1948] 1
> KB 223].
> 7. Furthermore, this court, in assessing the lawfulness of the defendant's   *j*
> (second) decision not to extend time, is not conducting for itself any s 202
> review. Nor is it required to analyse whether the original s 184
> determination was flawed in the *Lumley* sense. That, however, is precisely
> what the claimant's further submissions invite the court to do.
> 8. *In reality* it would really only be if this court concluded—on a perusal
> of the papers—that (i) any review was highly likely to succeed and (ii) the

a
reasons for not seeking a review were entirely explicable, that it might intervene. That is not this case.'

[27] We add the emphasis because Mr Bhose was anxious to point out that he was not suggesting that the test to be applied was that (i) the review had to be highly likely to succeed or (ii) the reason had to be explicable. As the discretion was wide and unfettered, it was only in those circumstances that the court would
b
interfere with the decision.

[28] As for Dr Browne's further report Mr Bhose said:

'The defendant has not considered the further report of Dr Browne, and nor should the court. The defendant's position on her further application for an extension of time is as set out in the letter of 4 March 2002. There must
c
come a time when there is some finality to litigation, and a finality to what the defendant may, in its discretion need to consider. That time has been reached.'

[29] On 12 August 2002 Maurice Kay J gave his reasons in writing as follows:

d
'I have considered the written submissions of the parties in relation to the decision of London Borough of Lewisham set out in the letter dated 4 March 2002. I refuse permission to apply for judicial review. When I deferred further consideration of 12 February 2002 it was solely to enable Lewisham to provide a reasoned decision in writing. That they have done, and, in my view, it is not arguably susceptible to challenge. In this application, which I
e
have allowed to extend beyond the date of the lodging of the claim form, I am not willing to extend it further to embrace evidence subsequent to 4 March 2002. Essentially, I am refusing permission in relation to the decision of 4 March 2002 for the reasons set out in the respondent's written submissions which were received in the Administrative Court office on 19
f
March 2002.'

THE APPLICATION FOR PERMISSION TO APPEAL
[30] When rejecting the application for permission to appeal on paper, Buxton LJ said:

g
'The judge was concerned with the standard to be applied by the court before it intervenes in a procedural decision by the local authority involving a high degree of discretion in relation to a matter in respect of which the applicant is in mercy. He was right to accept a demanding standard in relation to prospects of success, not least in order to avoid investigation of a
h
preliminary and procedural issue degenerating into a trial of the original decision. The council's ruling on the application for an extension could have been different, but it cannot be said that it was not open to it on the material. It was also open to it to refuse to take into account the second report of Dr Browne in view of the time at which it was filed. No separate point arises under the convention. Article 6 of the European Convention for the
j
Protection of Human Rights and Fundamental Freedoms 1950 (as set out in Sch 1 to the Human Rights Act 1998) provides for reasonable procedural control of access to the court or tribunal, provided it is exercised in a judicial manner, which condition was fulfilled here.'

[31] On renewing the application for permission before Mummery and Rix LJJ, Mr Burton submitted that there was an error of law by the council in

requiring that the review requested out of time should have a 'good prospect of
success'. His submission, which was illustrated by reference to a number of a
authorities, was that there was a lower threshold test for the exercise of that
discretion, a test which Mr Burton described as that of 'materiality'. Material
matters were put forward for the consideration of the council, which had
previously not received consideration. He also submitted the decision was
Wednesbury unreasonable. Mummery LJ concluded that: b

> '... although I am not in a position to say that this application has a real
> prospect of success, I am satisfied that there is a matter here which should be
> argued before the full court. As Mr Burton pointed out, there has been no
> decided case on the exercise of this discretion. There is a possible point of
> principle as to what is the proper threshold for deciding whether or not to c
> exercise the discretion.'

Rix LJ agreed and the matter was stood over for a hearing before us on notice to
the respondent.

COUNSELS' SUBMISSIONS d
[32] Mr Jan Luba QC now appears for the applicant and we are indebted to
him as ever for his cogent submissions. His first and main submission is that
the application raises an important issue which he defines in these terms:

> 'What is the correct approach to be taken by a local housing authority, in
> the exercise of its discretion, when presented with a request from a homeless e
> person that it review an adverse original decision where (i) the 21-day period
> for seeking a review "as of right" under s 202(2) of the Housing Act 1996 has
> expired and (ii) the homeless person relies on new material relevant to an
> important issue in the original decision.'

We should add that a similar question arises in a third situation, which is the f
actual situation before us, namely where the homeless person makes a further
request for a review of the original decision out of time, his or her first request
under s 202(3) already having been refused.

[33] Mr Luba submits in summary that the exercise of discretion must be
conducted in a principled way. He accepts that if the applicant is late and the
nature of the request is that he or she wishes the original decision to be g
reconsidered on the same or essentially the same material, then it may well be an
appropriate approach to require that (i) some good explanation for the delay is
advanced and/or (ii) some plain or obvious error in the original decision be
identified *before* an authority agrees to undertake the review. He submits,
however, that the position is different where the applicant is submitting fresh h
evidence which 'shakes the foundation of' or even 'goes to' the original decision.
Since a review is conducted by another officer under an established procedure
which requires all the material before him to be considered afresh, it is wrong for
whomsoever has to decide whether to extend time and permit that review to
form any appraisal of the merit of the fresh evidence. The decision-maker must j
not usurp the function of the reviewer and must always bear in mind that the
review will be conducted on the basis of any evidence including any further
evidence that is then put before the reviewer. The sole test for the
decision-maker is whether the fresh evidence is material to the original decision.
The 1996 Act is there to protect the homeless and must be construed and
implemented in a benign way.

a [34] As the second issue in the appeal he submits that if the approach of the decision-maker is held to be correct, his conclusion reached on the available material was perverse in the *Wednesbury* sense. The third and quite discrete issue is that the judge was wrong to reject Dr Browne's second report.

[35] In response Mr Bhose whose submissions were presented with equally admirable conciseness, argued that where the decision-maker had to decide
b whether or not to extend time for a review then it was always incumbent upon him or her to have regard on the one hand to the length of and reasons for the delay and, on the other hand, to the prospects of success of the review. He submits that there is a balance to be struck so that if delay is short and excusable, then the merits need not be great whereas if the delay is lengthy and inexcusable, then a good case on the merits needs to be established. As to the alternative
c submissions, he simply says the decision was well reasoned and the further report tendered far too late.

GRANTING PERMISSION TO APPEAL

[36] Having heard those arguments for a day, we conclude that it is proper to
d grant permission to appeal and to deal with the appeal on the basis of those submissions.

THE STATUTORY BACKGROUND

[37] The statutory framework imposed by Pt VII of the 1996 Act must be
e borne in mind. Section 184 places the local housing authority under a duty to make such inquiries as are necessary to satisfy themselves whether an applicant for housing assistance is eligible for that assistance and if so what duty if any is owed to him. Only a limited duty is owed to whomsoever has become homeless intentionally as defined in s 191 to be—

f   'if he deliberately does or fails to do anything in consequence of which he ceases to occupy accommodation which is available for his occupation and which it would have been reasonable for him to continue to occupy.'

It was and is the applicant's case that her state of mind during the period of her tenancy had been such that her failure to pay her rent could not fairly be
g described as 'deliberate'.

[38] Before the 1996 Act a dissatisfied applicant could either seek a judicial review of the unfavourable decision or invite the housing authority voluntarily to reconsider their earlier decision. As McCullough J observed in *R v London Borough of Tower Hamlets, ex p Saber* (1991) 24 HLR 611 at 621:
h

'It is not uncommon, after a decision has been reached that an applicant for housing under Part III of the Act became intentionally homeless, for a request to be made to reconsider the decision in the light of additional material or argument. Such a request is not the equivalent of a reapplication
j   and does not cast on the housing authority the duties imposed when an application under Part III is made. It is otherwise if there has meanwhile been a material change of circumstances ... The housing authority has, however, a discretion to accede to the request. A decision not to reconsider the original decision is clearly reviewable on ordinary *Wednesbury* principles. I do not accept that some more stringent criteria (referred to in argument as super *Wednesbury*) can apply ... It may well therefore be that a challenge to

a decision not to reconsider will infrequently succeed. Each case will of course fall to be considered on its own facts.'

[39] A plethora of applications for judicial review was no doubt perceived to be a mischief in need of cure. The 1996 Act for the first time provided by s 202 a statutory right to require an authority to review an earlier adverse decision. Section 202, so far as is material, provides as follows:

'(1) An applicant has the right to request a review of ... (b) any decision of a local housing authority as to what duty (if any) is owed to him ...
(2) There is no right to request a review of the decision reached on an earlier review.
(3) A request for review must be made before the end of the period of 21 days beginning with the day on which he is notified of the authority's decision or such longer period as the authority may in writing allow.
(4) On a request being duly made to them, the authority or authorities concerned shall review their decision.'

[40] Section 203 sets out the procedure on a review. It is prescribed by regulations and quite elaborate safeguards are in place to ensure that the dissatisfied applicant has a fair consideration of his or her review. The decision on the review must be reasoned and notified in writing which must include notice to the applicant of his right to appeal to a county court on a point of law and of the period within which such an appeal must be made.

[41] Section 204 provides for that appeal as follows:

'(1) If an applicant who has requested a review under section 202—(a) is dissatisfied with the decision on the review, or (b) is not notified of the decision on the review within the time prescribed under section 203, he may appeal to the county court on any point of law arising from the decision or, as the case may be, the original decision.'
(2) An appeal must be brought within 21 days of his being notified of the decision ...'

The full rigour of this stark time limit has been modified by an amendment made by the Homelessness Act 2002 which has inserted sub-s (2A) as follows:

'(2A) The court may give permission for an appeal to be brought after the end of the period allowed by subsection (2), but only if it is satisfied—
(a) where permission is sought before the end of that period, that there is a good reason for the applicant to be unable to bring the appeal in time;
(b) where permission is sought after that time, that there was a good reason for the applicant's failure to bring the appeal in time and for any delay in applying for permission ...'

[42] It is plain from the clear terms of s 202(4) that if the application for a review is made within the 21-day time limit, the applicant is entitled to the fresh consideration of his or her case whether or not fresh evidence is available to bolster it, or whether or not there has been any material change in the circumstances since the decision was taken. The entitlement is for a fresh consideration by a more senior officer and it can bring advantages of an oral hearing and representation at it. It can be a significant protection for the homeless.

a [43] If the 21-day time limit has expired, then the applicant is at mercy and the local housing authority have a discretion whether or not to extend time. This appeal raises questions as to how that discretion was exercised.

THE MAIN ISSUE: EXERCISE OF A DISCRETION TO EXTEND TIME FOR REVIEW PURSUANT TO SECTION 202(3)

b [44] Having posed the question for our consideration to be to rule on the proper approach to be taken by a local housing authority in exercising that discretion, Mr Luba submits that the discretion must be exercised in a principled way. We would agree, but that, of course, begs the question of what the proper principles are. One can say this with confidence. The decision must not be made in bad faith or capriciously for improper motives. The decision

c must not be taken only in rigidly defined situations since that would involve an unlawful fetter on the discretionary power given by the 1996 Act. The decision must be taken responsibly in furtherance of, and not in excess of, the statutory power having regard to the statutory purpose and policy. It must be taken reasonably as explained in *Associated Provincial Picture Houses Ltd v Wednesbury Corp* [1947] 2 All ER 680, [1948] 1 KB 223.

d [45] It is not necessary to go further than that. The questions before us boil down to (i) whether the decision-maker had regard to matters which were irrelevant and, (ii) whether, assuming the local housing authority have kept within the four corners of the matters they ought to have considered, they have come to a conclusion which was irrational or perverse being so unreasonable that

e no reasonable authority could ever have come to it.

[46] The discretion conferred by s 202(3) is unfettered in the sense that Parliament has not stipulated, as it often does, the factors to be taken into account in the exercise of the discretion which it confers. In the absence of such a statutory checklist, the discretion is wide. The question is: how wide? The

f answer is given by Lord Bridge of Harwich in *Tower Hamlets London BC v Chetnik Developments Ltd* [1988] 1 All ER 961 at 967, [1988] 1 AC 858 at 873:

'Thus, before deciding whether a discretion has been exercised for good or bad reasons, the court must first construe the enactment by which the discretion is conferred. Some statutory discretions may be so wide that they

g can, for practical purposes, only be challenged if shown to have been exercised irrationally or in bad faith. But if the purpose which the discretion is intended to serve is clear, the discretion can only be validly exercised for reasons relevant to the achievement of that purpose.'

[47] That calls for an examination of Pt VII of the 1996 Act. The main building

h blocks of the statutory scheme are these. (1) The local housing authority *must* inquire into the application for housing assistance and *must* notify their decision in writing informing the applicant of his right to request a review and the time within which to seek it (see s 184(1), (3) and (5)). (2) If a review is requested in time and therefore 'duly made', a review *must* be afforded in accordance with the

j prescribed procedure (see ss 202(4) and 203). (3) If the request is not made within 21 days, then the local housing authority *may* allow a longer time (see s 202(3)) and, by inference, if time is extended, the authority *must* review their original decision. (4) The authority *must* inform the applicant of the decision, of his right of appeal and the time for the appeal (see s 203(4) and (5)). (5) There is an appeal but there is no right to request a review of an earlier review (see s 202(2)). (6) The right of appeal is given against the decision which was taken on the statutory review provided for by ss 202 and 203. (7) As originally devised, the appeal had to be brought within 21 days with no power to extend time but the 2002 amendment now gives the county court discretion to do so if good reason is shown for the failure to apply in time and for the ensuing delay. (8) The appeal is on a point of law only.

[48] It seems to us that Parliament was laying down a clear scheme which provided the means of ensuring that the local housing authority fulfils its duty to the homeless persons. The purpose was, therefore, to lay down the procedures and time limits to enable the orderly management by the local housing authority of its precious supply of housing but also to enable it, if it is appropriate, to grant an indulgence to the homeless person on as important a matter as his or her housing where a claim for review may be deserving enough to override the failure to act in time and so keep the door open for further assistance. Even within those parameters, one must always remember, as Lord Donaldson of Lymington MR said in *R v Panel on Take-overs and Mergers, ex p Guinness plc* [1989] 1 All ER 509 at 512, [1990] 1 QB 146 at 159:

> 'Irrationality, at least in the sense of failing to take account of relevant factors or taking account of irrelevant factors, is a difficult concept in the context of a body which is itself charged with the duty of making a judgment on what is and what is not relevant, although clearly a theoretical scenario could be constructed in which the panel acted on the basis of considerations which on any view must have been irrelevant or ignored something which on any view must have been relevant.'

[49] When the decision-maker comes to balance the factors he is entitled to place in the scales, it is well settled, as Lord Keith of Kinkel said in *Tesco Stores Ltd v Secretary of State for the Environment* [1995] 2 All ER 636 at 642, [1995] 1 WLR 759 at 764:

> '... it is entirely for the decision-maker to attribute to the relevant consideration such weight as he thinks fit, and the courts will not interfere unless he has acted unreasonably in the *Wednesbury* sense (see *Associated Provincial Picture Houses Ltd v Wednesbury Corp* [1947] 2 All ER 680, [1948] 1 KB 223).'

Thus, even though the length of delay and reasons for it are often balanced against the prospect of success, it is possible to envisage circumstances in which an authority can rationally and properly conclude that even short delay for which there is a good explanation is not good enough to justify an extension of time for review. The authority might, for example, conclude that the case is so hopeless that a review would serve no useful purpose. Conversely, the authority could rationally and properly decide to grant an extension of time where there has been a long delay for which no explanation has been provided. Thus, the authority might take the view that the applicant has a powerful case on the merits and that it is able to take a relatively relaxed view when dealing with applications for an extension of time. Delay and prospects of success do not always have to be balanced against each other. An authority is entitled to reach a decision without forming a provisional view of the underlying merits of the case if, in all the circumstances, it thinks it reasonable for it to do so. It may, for example, reasonably take the view that, in the light of the length of the extension of time that is required and the poverty of the explanation, if any, for the delay, it can *a* reasonably and properly refuse the application without any consideration of the merits at all.

THE FACTORS TREATED AS RELEVANT TO THIS DECISION

[50] In our case the principal factors taken into account were twofold. First the lack of proper explanation both for the failure to seek a review in time and for *b* the late supply of medical evidence. Mr Luba does not seek to suggest this was an improper factor to take into account. It was plainly a most relevant consideration. Secondly, and this is the subject of Mr Luba's attack, the new material was not thought to be sufficiently compelling to suggest a good chance of success. Mr Luba contends that since the decision on review is taken by a wholly different officer, the officer charged with deciding whether to extend time *c* or not should only have regard to whether or not the new information was material. We reject this argument for three reasons. (1) Forming a provisional view of the eventual outcome of the case is a regular feature of the exercise of judicial discretion in allied circumstances and it cannot be unreasonable for an administrative discretion to treat prospects of success as a relevant consideration *d* to be put into the scales before striking the ultimate balance. It may reasonably be thought to be a proper counterweight to delay. It may perfectly properly be thought to be important to assess whether the case sought to be advanced on review has no real prospects of success and is hopeless, or that it is arguable even if the prospect of success is less than 50%, or that it has a seriously good chance of prevailing. (2) The reasonableness of taking account of prospects of success *e* is all the stronger given the margin of appreciation enjoyed by the decision-maker to determine the criteria by which he approaches his task. (3) The materiality of the fresh evidence can, therefore, perfectly reasonably be treated as an aspect of assessing the prospects of success. The decision-maker may bear in mind that if time is extended the ultimate decision is taken by *f* another person in accordance with the regulated procedure for review but that does not mean that the decision-maker may not assess the strength of the case that will be laid before the reviewing officer if, in all the circumstances of the case, it is appropriate to do so.

[51] Given the wide ambit of discretion conferred on the local housing authority, we are, totally satisfied that the decision of 4 March 2002 cannot be *g* impugned on the basis that no authority, acting reasonably, could have taken the prospects of success to be a relevant and appropriate factor for their consideration. Mr Luba's main submission must fail.

THE SECOND ISSUE: THE RATIONALITY OF THE DECISION TO REFUSE TO EXTEND TIME

h [52] The decision reached by Mr Jones on 4 March 2002 was well and sufficiently reasoned and, given the wide scope he had for weighing matters in the scales he had to hold, and given our judgment that he did not have regard to irrelevant factors, the conclusion he reached was an eminently reasonable one. The argument that it was perverse or irrational is simply unsustainable.

j
THE THIRD ISSUE: ADMITTING FRESH EVIDENCE

[53] Maurice Kay J was right to refuse to extend the indulgence of the court any further to embrace evidence subsequent to 4 March 2002 and in effect force the housing department to entertain a third application to extend time for review. There was no adequate explanation for the failure to produce Dr Browne's second report any earlier. It was too late to seek to introduce matters which in

many cases were well over a year old. Too many bites had already been taken out of this cherry. Enough was enough.

[54] That might be enough to dispose of this appeal save that during the course of the argument it became apparent to us that s 202(3) of the 1996 Act might no longer be in play, in which case quite different considerations might prevail. It seemed to us arguable that the statutory scheme set out in Pt VII permitted only one application for review and only one application to extend time.

EXTRA-STATUTORY DISCRETION

[55] Since the facts are quite complicated it is worth summarising what has happened. The s 184 decision was taken on 24 January 2001. The applicant failed to seek a review in time. Her July application was treated as a fresh application. She formally requested an extension of time for a review on 31 August but that was rejected on 15/25 October and the correctness of that decision is no longer challenged. That was the application to which s 202(3) applied. The letter of 24 January 2002 was a request for a further review of the January 2001 decision. That fell outside the statutory scheme. The decision taken on 4 March 2002 in response to that application has to be judged in that light.

[56] If and in so far as the applicant was seeking to review the October decision as a decision 'reached on an earlier review', she had no right to do so (see s 202(2)). We accept, however, that a refusal to extend time might arguably be something different from a decision reached on an earlier review on the basis that the refusal to extend time has precluded any decision by way of review. Thus what she was seeking was a second chance to seek a review of the January 2001 decision. Although this is not expressly covered by s 202, we wondered in the course of the argument whether she was in fact entitled to make repeated applications for extensions of time. It was not a matter which counsel had come prepared to argue but we have been greatly assisted by Mr Luba's placing before us two decisions of this court which bear somewhat upon the point.

[57] In R v Westminster City Council, ex p Ellioua (1998) 31 HLR 440, this court refused a renewed application to move for judicial review of a refusal by the local housing authority to conduct a review of their decision. There had been a full and proper review of the s 184 decision but no appeal against the decision taken on review. Instead the applicant on advice sought a further review of the original decision because it had been based on a mistaken view of the facts. Judge LJ held (at 444):

'In my judgment the express exclusion [by s 202(2)] of any such right [to request a review of the decision reached on an earlier review] does not have the effect of precluding the authority from reconsidering the decision if it is minded to do so … although it was open to the authority to do so, they were not required to carry out this further re-review, and they refused to accede to the application.'

On the facts of that case he held that a judicial review based entirely on errors of law was inappropriate given the existing remedy of an appeal to the county court where the same errors could have been canvassed. Robert Walker and Peter Gibson LJJ agreed.

[58] In Demetri v Westminster City Council [2000] 1 WLR 772 the Court of Appeal was considering an appeal from the decision of the county court judge striking out the appeal made to him under s 204 of the 1996 Act. There, there had

a been a review followed by a request to reconsider that decision taken on that
review. The housing authority agreed to reconsider but then confirmed its
previous decision. The unsuccessful applicant was out of the then strict 21-day
time limit for appealing against the first review decision and so sought to appeal
the reconsidered decision within time. Douglas Brown J held (at 778):

b   'In my judgment, this appeal must fail. There is no doubt that a council in
      its discretion can decide to reconsider or review a review decision formerly
      given under section 202(1). This was an appropriate case for this council to
      do so where it was being represented to it that on the original review some
      material argument had not been considered.'

c He held, however, that the appeal to the county court lay only against the
original decision made on review, not against the reconsideration of that
decision.

[59] Whilst reminding ourselves that we have not heard full argument on
these matters, we none the less feel able to say that we are in agreement with
d those judgments. It seems to us to follow that a housing authority is not bound
to entertain a succession of applications for review or for extensions of time for
review given that Parliament has circumscribed the applicant's right to seek
them. The scheme envisages only one review, or, if the 21-day time limit has
expired, one application to extend time for review. That is not to say that a local
e authority may not choose as a matter of their discretion to entertain such a
request for a further review or a further extension of time. This may be granted
for sound pragmatic policy reasons to prevent the kind of roundabout
applications to which Mr Luba referred, where the disappointed applicant simply
goes to the neighbouring housing authority with the result that, if successful, the
f matter is referred back to the first authority. The authority may choose to
reconsider matters of fact or new matters of fact which would lie outside the
scope of an appeal to the county court. These are, however, decisions of good
housing management and this extra-statutory discretion of the local housing
authority is likely to be held to be close to being absolute. An attempt judicially
to review a refusal to consider such a further indulgence is likely to receive the
g same treatment as was meted out in *R v Brighton and Hove BC, ex p Nacion* (1999)
11 Admin LR 472 at 475–476 where Tuckey LJ held:

      'It is only in a very exceptional case that there will really be any reasonable
      prospect of interesting the court by way of judicial review to interfere with
h   the exercise of the very broad discretion which the council have, bearing in
      mind that they exercise it, knowing the circumstances of the applicants, the
      range and availability of accommodation in their area ...'

Lord Woolf MR (at 477) was of like mind, saying: '... I have difficulty in
envisaging cases where application for judicial review will be appropriate.'
j   [60] Upon a proper view of the facts this is exactly such a case. In so far as the
local housing authority was exercising such an extra-statutory discretion—and
Mr Jones contemplated that he was—he was fully entitled to cry, 'Hold, enough'.
In fact, as we have seen, he gave full reasons why his department was not
prepared to accede to the request. This decision is even further beyond challenge
by judicial review than a decision taken under s 202(3).

CONCLUSION

[61] We all have some sympathy for this unhappy young lady but we are
bound to dismiss her appeal. So much time has passed since the crucial decision
of 24 January 2001 that she may now perhaps be able to make a fresh application
for assistance based upon her present circumstances. That, of course, is a matter
between her and the housing department.

Permission to appeal granted, but appeal dismissed.

Kate O'Hanlon   Barrister.

a # Ali Reza-Delta Transport Co Ltd v United Arab Shipping Co SAG (No 2)
[2003] EWCA Civ 811

b COURT OF APPEAL, CIVIL DIVISION
PETER GIBSON, TUCKEY LJJ AND NELSON J
2 MAY, 17 JUNE 2003

c *Costs – Order for costs – Indemnity costs – Power to award indemnity costs where defendant failing to beat claimant's Pt 36 offer – Offer including terms as to costs – Offer waiving interest uplift on damages and costs – Whether part of Pt 36 offer relating to waiver to be taken into account when deciding whether judgment was more advantageous than proposals contained in offer – Whether refusal of offer attracting exercise of court's discretion to make order on indemnity basis – CPR 36.21, 44.3.*

d When judgment was given in the Court of Appeal awarding the claimant $US 227,400 in a claim for damages (the court below having awarded only $US 115,800), the claimant was awarded its costs of the trial on the indemnity basis and interest at 3% over the prime rate, in the light of two offers under CPR Pt 36 made before trial. It fell to be determined whether the court should accede to the claimant's submission that, in the light of a third Pt 36 offer *e* made before the hearing of the appeal, whereby the claimant offered to accept $US 227,400 plus the costs of the trial on the indemnity basis but waiving any interest uplift on both the damages and the costs awarded, it should be awarded its costs of the appeal on the indemnity basis pursuant to CPR 36.21[a] or, if that were inapplicable, pursuant to the court's general discretion on costs under *f* CPR 44.3. The claimant submitted that costs should be awarded on the indemnity basis under CPR 36.21 because the defendant had been held liable for more than the claimant had proposed in its third Pt 36 offer, or that it had secured a judgment which was more advantageous to it than its proposal in that offer, and that in each case the concession offered relating to interest represented a discount agreed to be about $US 12,000 on the footing of the uplift of 3% over *g* the prime rate. It further contended that an award of interest, unlike costs, related directly to the substantive liability claimed, and that the award of interest formed part of the measure of the claimant's loss.

Held – (1) Although the award of interest formed part of the defendant's *h* liability in a way that the award of costs did not, the relevant concession offered by the claimant related solely to uplift interest, ie interest over the ordinary rate. The court could award uplift interest only if the conditions of CPR 36.21(1) were satisfied. Thus, while the provisions of Pt 36 expressly contemplated that a Pt 36 offer might include an offer as to interest, and while the court was *j* directed by CPR 36.21(4) to make an order as to interest in accordance with CPR 36.21(2) unless it considered it unjust to do so, the draftsman of the rule could not have contemplated that uplift interest should be any part of the offer to be taken into account in determining the applicability of the rule (see [9], below); *Mitchell v James* [2003] 2 All ER 1064 applied.

---

a   Rule 36.21 is set out at [4], below

(2) The court had a wide discretion under CPR 44.3, though that discretion *a*
had to be exercised taking account of the matters to which the court was required
to have regard. The fact that the claimant had offered by a Pt 36 offer to accept
as much as it was awarded was plainly an important factor, but so was the fact
that the offer had been made on appeal, the court below having awarded a
lesser sum. The defendant had not acted unreasonably in seeking to resist the
appeal nor had its conduct of the appeal been in any way improper. The instant *b*
case was not one of those rare cases in which the refusal of a settlement offer
would attract, under CPR Pt 44, not merely an adverse order for costs, but an
order on the indemnity rather than the standard basis. Accordingly, the
defendant would be directed to pay the claimant's costs of the appeal on the
standard basis (see [12], [13], below); *Kiam v MGN Ltd (No 2)* [2002] 2 All ER 242
applied. *c*

Notes
For circumstances to be taken into account when exercising the court's discretion
over costs, and for costs and other consequences where the claimant does better
than proposed in a Pt 36 offer, see respectively 10 *Halsbury's Laws* (4th edn *d*
reissue) para 17 and 37 *Halsbury's Laws* (4th edn reissue) para 826.

Cases referred to in judgment
Dredger Liesbosch (owners) v Steamship Edison (owners) [1933] AC 449, sub nom *The
    Edison* [1933] All ER Rep 144, HL.
Kiam v MGN Ltd (No 2) [2002] EWCA Civ 66, [2002] 2 All ER 242, [2002] 1 WLR *e*
    2810.
Mitchell v James [2002] EWCA Civ 997, [2003] 2 All ER 1064.
Petrotrade Inc v Texaco Ltd [2001] 4 All ER 853, [2002] 1 WLR 947, CA.

Application for costs
The appellants, Ali Reza-Delta Transport Co Ltd, applied for costs of their appeal *f*
following the award by the Court of Appeal on 2 May 2003 ([2003] EWCA Civ
684, [2003] 2 All ER (Comm) 269) of damages of $US 227,400 in place of the
original award of $US 115,800 made against the respondents, United Arab
Shipping Co SAG. The facts are set out in the judgment of the court.

g

Chirag Karia (instructed by *Jackson Parton*) for the appellants.
Ricky Diwan (instructed by *Hill Taylor Dickinson*) for the respondents.

Cur adv vult

17 June 2003. The following judgment of the court was delivered. *h*

PETER GIBSON LJ.
[1] When judgment was given in this court on 2 May 2003 ([2003] EWCA Civ
684, [2003] 2 All ER (Comm) 269) awarding the successful appellants $US 227,400
in place of the judge's award of $US 115,800, we were informed by Mr Karia for *j*
the appellants that they had made three Pt 36 offers. It is common ground that
in the light of this court's judgment the appellants did better than both their
first two offers made before trial, and accordingly this court awarded the
appellants their costs of the trial on the indemnity basis and interest at 3%
over the prime rate. The third offer was made on 10 March 2003, when the
appellants offered to accept $US 227,400 plus the costs of the trial on the

a indemnity basis but waiving any interest uplift on both the damages and the costs awarded.

[2] The only question outstanding is whether this court should accede to the appellants' submission that it is on the indemnity basis that they should be awarded their costs of the appeal pursuant to CPR 36.21, or, if that is inapplicable, pursuant to r 44.3. That submission is opposed by the respondents.

b They say that this court should award the appellants their costs of the appeal only on the standard basis.

[3] We drew the attention of counsel to the decision of this court in *Mitchell v James* [2002] EWCA Civ 997, [2003] 2 All ER 1064 and allowed them to make submissions in writing on the applicability, if any, of what was said in that case to the present case. This judgment is written in the light of the helpful written

c submissions which we have received from each side.

[4] Rule 36.21 is in this form:

'Costs and other consequences where claimant does better than he proposed in his Part 36 offer

d (1) This rule applies where at trial—(a) a defendant is held liable for more; or (b) the judgment against a defendant is more advantageous to the claimant, than the proposals contained in a claimant's Part 36 offer.

(2) The court may order interest on the whole or part of any sum of money (excluding interest) awarded to the claimant at a rate not exceeding 10% above base rate for some or all of the period starting with the latest date on

e which the defendant could have accepted the offer without needing the permission of the court.

(3) The court may also order that the claimant is entitled to—(a) his costs on the indemnity basis from the latest date when the defendant could have accepted the offer without needing the permission of the court; and

f (b) interest on those costs at a rate not exceeding 10% above base rate.

(4) Where this rule applies, the court will make the orders referred to in paragraphs (2) and (3) unless it considers it unjust to do so.'

g [5] In *Mitchell's* case the relevant offer was one whereby the claimants offered to accept payment of a specified sum and, amongst other terms, each party was to bear his own costs. Park J had held at the end of the trial that the claimants' case succeeded and that the defendants should pay the claimants' costs. He further held that the requirements of r 36.21(1) were not satisfied and so he ordered costs to be paid on the standard basis. On appeal this court concluded that terms as to costs were not intended to be included in Pt 36 offers. In a

h judgment with which Potter LJ and Sir Murray Stuart-Smith agreed, Peter Gibson LJ gave the following reasons for that conclusion:

'[30] First, r 36.14 is worded as applicable whenever a claimant's Pt 36 offer is accepted without needing the permission of the court. It does not say

j "unless a claimant's Part 36 offer indicates to the contrary" (r 36.22(1)) or other wording to indicate that the parties can agree otherwise. Similarly, para 7.2 of the Practice Direction indicates that on acceptance of the Pt 36 offer "the costs consequences set out in rule ... 36.14 will then come into effect." So too in a case where the court's permission is needed for the defendants to accept a Pt 36 offer, if permission is given, para 7.5 envisages that the court may order that the costs consequences set out in r 36.14 will

apply. These provisions are inconsistent with a term as to costs being part of
the Pt 36 offer.

[31] Second, r 36.21 is applicable where at trial either a defendant is "held
liable" for more, or "the judgment" against a defendant is more
advantageous to the claimant, than the offer. The words "held liable" and
"the judgment" both appear to me to connote what the trial judge holds or
decides on the substantive issues in the case as distinct from the ancillary
issue of costs to be determined after the substantive issues are decided.
Mr Brunner accepted that that was so in relation to "held liable", though not
in relation to "judgment". For my part, I cannot see why there should be
such a difference.

[32] Third, the rule is intended to apply universally at the end of the trial
when the judge is required to make an order for costs. Save in a case where
the judge can make a summary assessment or the rare case where the costs
at that point are agreed, there will have been no assessment of the costs, the
figure for which would therefore be uncertain. Yet the rule contemplates
that merely by reference to that for which the defendant is held liable or by
reference to the judgment the judge will be able to decide whether r 36.21
applies because the defendant has been held liable for more, or the judgment
against a defendant is more advantageous, than the offer. I find it hard to
believe that the draftsman contemplated that a Pt 36 offer is one which
includes a term as to costs, so that the judge might have to evaluate the
quantum of his costs order. That is normally the function of a costs judge,
not the trial judge.

[33] Fourth, there would be a real risk of abuse if a term as to costs could
be included in a Pt 36 order. Every well-advised claimant would make a
Pt 36 offer containing the terms sought in his claim plus an offer as to costs
in the hope that if he succeeded in his substantive claim he would obtain
indemnity costs in place of the ordinary award of costs on the standard
basis. Merely to win on his substantive claim and to obtain an order for
costs under the general rule (see CPR 44.3(2)) will cause r 36.21 to be
applicable, so that the court "will" make the orders referred to in r 36.21(2)
and (3) unless it considers it unjust to do so. Injustice in the eyes of the
court is therefore the only basis on which the court could refuse to make
an order for indemnity costs and interest. That does not confer a general
discretion on the court.'

[6] Mr Karia's primary submission is that costs should be awarded on the
indemnity basis under r 36.21 because the respondents have been held liable for
more than the appellants proposed in their offer of 10 March 2003 or the
appellants have secured a judgment which is more advantageous to them than
they proposed in that offer. In each case, he says, the concession offered relating
to interest represents a discount now agreed to be about $US 12,000 on the
footing of the uplift of 3% over the prime rate.

[7] Mr Karia distinguishes *Mitchell's* case on the ground that it related to an
offer on costs, whereas the present case relates to an offer on interest. He points
out that the award of interest, unlike costs, relates directly to the substantive
liability claimed and he prays in aid of the remarks of Lord Wright in *Dredger
Liesbosch (owners) v Steamship Edison (owners)* [1933] AC 449 at 468, sub nom *The
Edison* [1933] All ER Rep 144 at 162 that interest represents 'damages for the loss
of the use of the money representing the lost vessel'—in the present case the

a equivalent is the equipment the subject of the appellants' claim—'as from the date of the loss until payment'. He therefore says that the award of interest forms part of the measure of the appellants' loss. Further, he argues that none of the reasons which impelled this court to its conclusion in *Mitchell's* case apply to the present case. He draws attention to the fact that some of the provisions of the rules and the Pt 36 Practice Direction on which this court

b relied do not apply to the award of interest, and he submits that the financial effect of concessions involving interest will be immediately apparent at the time the court determines the principal sum and interest rate to be awarded. He also says that there is no real risk of abuse. Finally, he relies on some general policy considerations, arguing that parties should be encouraged to accept reasonable settlement offers when to do so would result in them being better off

c and in saving court time. He urges us to take a broad commercial view and to apply a purposive approach to construing r 36.21.

[8] Mr Diwan for the respondents submits that the offer did not satisfy the requirements of r 36.21(1), because the appellants only offered to accept what they were claiming, and the offer of a concession on the interest uplift was

d irrelevant. He says that in the same way that concessions as to costs are not to be taken into account in assessing whether or not a claimant has done better than his Pt 36 offer, so concessions as to uplift interest should also be left out of account. Accordingly he contends that the respondents have been held liable for as much as, but not more than, what the appellants proposed in their offer and the judgment against the respondents is the same as, but not more advantageous

e than, those proposals. He argues that parts of the reasoning of this court in *Mitchell's* case are directly applicable to the question of uplift interest for the following reasons: (1) the words 'held liable' and 'the judgment' in r 36.21(1) relate to what the court decides on the substantive issue as distinct from ancillary issues such as costs; a fortiori the issue of whether to award uplift

f interest is an ancillary matter entirely within the discretion of the court and consequent upon comparing the liability or judgment with the Pt 36 offer and is no part of the court's determination of the substantive issue; (2) there is a risk of abuse in claimants making concessions not on the substantive claim but on ancillary matters such as uplift interest, and by offering to accept ordinary interest claimants bargain with something to which they are not entitled and which is

g entirely within the court's discretion; (3) this court's reasoning in *Mitchell's* case was that r 36.21 was intended to apply universally at the end of the trial when the court is required to make an order for costs and that the rule contemplates that the court, merely by reference to that for which the defendant is held liable or by reference to the judgment of the court, will be able to discern whether r 36.21

h applies; that cannot be done in the case of uplift interest the award of which depends on whether the claimant has done better than he proposed in his Pt 36 offer.

[9] In our judgment, the submissions of Mr Diwan are to be preferred. We accept that the award of interest forms part of the defendant's liability in a way

j that the award of costs does not; but the relevant concession offered by the appellants related solely to uplift interest, that is to say interest over the ordinary rate. The court can award uplift interest only if the conditions of r 36.21(1) are satisfied. Thus while the provisions of Pt 36 expressly contemplate that a Pt 36 offer may include an offer as to interest (see r 36.22), and while the court is directed by r 36.21(4) to make an order as to interest in accordance with r 36.21(2) unless it considers it unjust to do so, the draftsman of the rule cannot have contemplated that uplift interest should be any part of the offer to be taken into account in determining the applicability of the rule.

[10] We turn next to Mr Karia's alternative submission that the court should exercise its discretion under r 44.3 to award costs of the appeal on the indemnity basis, having regard to paras (4) and (5) of that rule. By r 44.3(4) the court is required to have regard to all the circumstances, including the conduct of the parties and any admissible offer to settle made by a party and drawn to the court's attention, whether or not made in accordance with Pt 36. Mr Karia suggests that as a matter of substance and reality the appellants won and did better than their offer, and he argues that the respondents misinterpreted the evidence of the expert, Mr Gibbons, and did so as a way of seeking to avoid the inevitable success of the appellants' appeal. He relies on the view expressed in Foskett *The Law and Practice of Compromise* (5th edn, 2002) n 30 to para 23.11, on r 36.21(1):

> 'The word "more" is used in sub-paragraphs (a) and (b) of this rule. It follows that, strictly speaking r. 36.21 would not become engaged if the claimant merely *matched* his offer at trial. However, such an offer would clearly be seen to have been a reasonable one in the light of the result of the trial and one that the defendant ought to have accepted. Given that the court has power to award indemnity costs where a party has behaved unreasonably, and has the power to award interest at such a rate as it considers just (see *Petrotrade Inc v Texaco Ltd* ([2001] 4 All ER 853, [2002] 1 WLR 947)), there would be no reason why orders similar to those contemplated in paragraphs (2) and (3) should not be made in this situation.'

[11] Mr Diwan submits that in resisting the appeal the respondents' conduct does not deserve the court's disapproval and was not so unreasonable as to justify costs being awarded against them on the indemnity basis.

[12] It is not in dispute that we have a wide discretion under r 44.3, though one which we must exercise taking account of the matters to which we are required to have regard. The fact that the appellants offered by a Pt 36 offer to accept as much as they were awarded is plainly an important factor, but so is the fact that the offer was made on the appeal, the court below having awarded a lesser sum. We do not think that the respondents acted unreasonably in seeking to resist the appeal nor was their conduct of the appeal in any way improper. In *Kiam v MGN Ltd (No 2)* [2002] EWCA Civ 66, [2002] 2 All ER 242, [2002] 1 WLR 2810 Simon Brown LJ, with whom Waller and Sedley LJJ agreed, after citing from the *Petrotrade* case, said:

> '[12] I for my part understand the court there to have been deciding no more than that conduct, albeit falling short of misconduct deserving of moral condemnation, *can* be so unreasonable as to justify an order for indemnity costs. With that I respectfully agree. To my mind, however, such conduct would need to be unreasonable to a high degree; unreasonable in this context certainly does not mean merely wrong or misguided in hindsight. An indemnity costs order made under Pt 44 (unlike one made under Pt 36) does, I think, carry at least some stigma. It is of its nature penal rather than exhortatory.
>
> [13] It follows from all this that in my judgment it will be a rare case indeed where the refusal of a settlement offer will attract under Pt 44 not

a   merely an adverse order for costs, but an order on an indemnity rather than standard basis.'

[13] In our judgment, having regard to all the circumstances, we do not regard this case as one of those rare cases. We therefore direct that the respondents pay the appellants' costs of the appeal on the standard basis.

b   *Order accordingly.*

Kate O'Hanlon   Barrister.

Thames Water Utilities Ltd v Hampstead Homes (London) Ltd

[2002] EWCA Civ 1487

a

COURT OF APPEAL, CIVIL DIVISION

b

MAY LJ AND BODEY J

8 OCTOBER 2002

Water supply – Supply of water for domestic purposes – Premises never previously connected to supply of water for domestic purposes – Two buildings connected to supply c *of water converted into 109 flats – Whether flats premises never previously connected to supply of water for domestic purposes – Water Industry Act 1991, s 146(2).*

The defendant developers owned two office blocks which were connected to the water mains and public sewers. Each received a supply of water for domestic d purposes. The developers converted the buildings into 109 flats, and asked the claimant water and sewerage undertaker to supply service pipe connections for each of the flats. The undertaker installed two new water service pipe connections, one at each of the two premises. Those were main supplies to the buildings as a whole rather than supplies to the individual flats. Although there was no physical change to the main connection with the public sewer, each of the e flats was connected internally to the existing main sewer into the public sewage system. Under s 146(2)(a)[a] of the Water Industry Act 1991, an undertaker was entitled to charge for the connection to a water supply of 'premises' which had never at any previous time been connected to a supply of water provided for domestic purposes by a water undertaker. Subsection (2)(b) contained a similar f provision in respect of connection to a public sewer. The undertaker made a charge, but the developers refused to pay. In subsequent proceedings brought by the undertaker for recovery of the charge, the judge regarded the premises as the two buildings as a whole rather than each of the individual new flats, and held that the two buildings were premises that had previously been connected to a water supply and a sewer. Accordingly, he dismissed the claim. On the g undertaker's appeal, the Court of Appeal considered the purpose and scope of s 146(2).

Held – Section 146(2) of the 1991 Act was concerned with the connection to the water and sewerage systems of premises which had not previously been so h connected, and included new premises which were likely to place an additional burden on the system as a whole. Where existing buildings were converted, it was a question of fact and degree whether the result was, or included, the construction and connection of premises which had never previously been connected, or whether the conversion retained the identity of premises which j existed and were connected before the conversion took place. In the instant case, the 109 flats were new premises which had never previously been connected, and the undertaker had been entitled to make a charge for each of them under s 146(2). The appeal would therefore be allowed (see [37]–[40], below).

---

a Section 146, so far as material, is set out at [16], below

Notes

a   For a statutory water or sewerage undertaker's powers to make infrastructure charges, see 49(2) *Halsbury's Laws* (4th edn reissue) para 556.

For the Water Industry Act 1991, s 146, see 49 *Halsbury's Statutes* (4th edn) (1999 reissue) 544.

b   **Cases referred to in judgments**

Pepper (Inspector of Taxes) v Hart [1993] 1 All ER 42, [1993] AC 593, [1992] 3 WLR 1032, HL.

Thames Water Utilities Ltd v Bursar, Magdalen College, Oxford (30 June 1999, unreported).

Thames Water Utilities Ltd v Shepherd Bush Housing Association (5 November 1996,
c   unreported), CC.

United Utilities Water plc v Albany Homes Ltd (9 November 2001, unreported), CC.

Cases also cited or referred to in skeleton arguments

Daymond v South West Water Authority [1976] 1 All ER 39, [1976] AC 609, [1975] 3
d   WLR 865, HL.

Hanlon v Law Society [1980] 2 All ER 199, [1981] AC 124, [1980] 2 WLR 756, HL.

Higgins v Silverston [1956] 2 All ER 893, [1956] 2 QB 525, [1956] 3 WLR 448, CA.

Maunsell v Olins [1975] 1 All ER 16, [1975] AC 373, [1974] 3 WLR 835, HL.

Appeal

e   The claimants, Thames Water Utilities Ltd, appealed with permission of Judge Catlin from his decision in the Reading County Court on 17 October 2001 dismissing their claim against the defendants, Hampstead Homes Ltd, for statutory fixed charges of £42,790·32, allegedly payable under s 146(2) of the Water Industry Act 1991 as a result of the connection of water and sewerage
f   services made at the defendants' request. The facts are set out in the judgment of May LJ.

James Watson QC (instructed by *Peter Taylor*, Reading) for the claimants.
The defendants were not represented.

g   **MAY LJ.**

[1] This is an appeal from a decision of Judge Catlin sitting in the Reading County Court on 17 October 2001, when he gave his decision, and subsequently handed down written reasons on 23 November 2001. He dismissed the appellants' claim for £42,790·32 under s 146(2)(a) and (b) of the Water Industry
h   Act 1991. The issue which the appeal raises is of some importance to the water industry and to building developers. Judge Catlin, recognising this, gave permission to appeal.

[2] The claimants, Thames Water Utilities Ltd, are a water undertaker and sewerage undertaker appointed under s 6 of the 1991 Act. The defendants are
j   building developers. The claimants' claim form simply states that their claim was for infrastructure charges to the value of £42,790·32. The particulars of claim stated that the claim was for the statutory fixed charges payable as a result of the connection of water and sewerage services made at the defendants' request, details of which it was said had been delivered.

[3] A short form defence asserted that infrastructure charges can only be levied on premises that were never previously connected to a water main or to a

public sewer. Boss House, it was said, was a warehouse with ancillary offices
which received water and sewerage services for domestic purposes. The entire *a*
building was a single demise. The disputed charges were being levied on
premises that were previously connected and therefore exempt from the
statutory charging provision. Therefore the charges which the claimants sought
to recover were invalid. The defence went on to make subsidiary lesser
submissions, including contesting the level of infrastructure charges claimed. *b*

[4] The claim was heard by Judge Catlin on an agreed statement of facts,
supported by the unchallenged witness statement of Robert Movell. The facts,
so far as it is necessary to relate them, are as follows. The claim relates to land
owned by the defendants and known as 227–229 Tooley Street and Boss House,
Lafone Street, Southwark, London SE1. In 1996 or 1997 the defendants *c*
converted two office blocks, one at each of these addresses, into 109 flats. The
Tooley Street block originally comprised ground floor and first, second, third and
fourth floors. The Boss House block was similar but with a basement floor. The
defendants added one floor to the Tooley Street block and two floors to Boss
House. The original buildings were connected to the water mains. Each received
a supply of water for domestic purposes. The Boss House building fronting on to *d*
Queen Street was connected by a 4-inch diameter service pipe. A 6-inch diameter
supply pipe connected the building fronting Tooley Street. Each of the original
buildings were connected to the public sewers.

[5] On 15 September 1995 the defendants' agent wrote to the claimants
making an application for the supply of service connections for each of these *e*
buildings. The application form for Tooley Street stated that the number of
service pipe connections required was 59. The application form for Boss House
stated that the number of service pipe connections required was 50. That in total
made the 109 flats with which the appeal is concerned. The claimants, having
received the application forms, provided a quotation. The quotation had three
sums of money, making up a total of £52,898·88. The first two of those sums *f*
were each amounts of £23,432 for what was referred to as infrastructure charge
for sewerage and water respectively. The third amount was under the heading
'design estimate' and the amount quoted was £6,034·88. Although design
estimate was not particularly well explained in the quotation, it was understood
to be a charge for making service pipe connections for the water supply. What in *g*
fact happened was that the claimants put in two 125-mm new water service pipe
connections, one at each of the two premises. Those, needless to say, were mains
supplies to the buildings as a whole and not in that form supplies to the individual
flats. Mr Watson QC tells us that there was no physical change to the main
connection with the public sewer, but that what in practice happened was that *h*
each of the new 109 flats was connected internally to the existing main sewer into
the public sewage system. The amount of the quotation for infrastructure
charges was subsequently reduced by negotiation and became the £42,790·32
which was claimed in these proceedings.

[6] Robert Movell explained in his witness statement the industry *j*
understanding of infrastructure charges and their purpose. He explained how in
principle they are calculated and explained how they were calculated in the
present case. He said:

'The principle of infrastructure charges is to obtain a contribution from
builders and developers to the capital investment that is required by water

a and sewerage undertakers to develop the public water and sewerage systems to meet the demands placed on those systems from new development.'

[7] Section 146 of the 1991 Act has to be seen and understood in its context. The 1991 Act has in s 1 provision for the appointment of an officer known as the Director General of Water Services who has functions to perform under the Act. *b* Sections 2, 3, 4 and 5 are general sections making provision for general duties in respect of the water industry, for general environmental and recreational duties, for environmental duties with respect to sites of special interest, and for codes of practice with respect to environmental and recreational duties. Part II of the Act, which begins with s 6, concerns the appointment of relevant undertakers. Section 6(1) provides that a company may be appointed by the Secretary of State *c* or with his authorisation by the Director to be the water undertaker or sewerage undertaker for any area of England and Wales. It was under that provision that the claimants in these proceedings were appointed. Section 6(2) provides:

d 'Without prejudice to the obligation of a company holding an appointment under this Chapter to comply with the conditions of its appointment, the appointment of a company to be the water undertaker or sewerage undertaker for any area shall have the effect, while the appointment remains in force—of ...'

e requiring that company to undertake certain specified obligations in relation to water and sewerage, which I need not set out in detail. It will be seen that there is reference there to the obligation of an appointed company to comply with conditions of its appointment. It will be necessary to return later to those conditions.

[8] Part III is concerned with water supply. Chapter II is concerned with supply duties, and relevantly to this appeal s 45 contains a duty to make a *f* connection with a water main. Subsection (1) provides:

'Subject to the following provisions of this section and to sections 46 and 47 below, it shall be the duty of a water undertaker (in accordance with section 51 below) to make a connection under this section where the owner or occupier of any premises which—(a) consists in the whole or any part of *g* a building; or (b) are premises on which any person is proposing to erect any building or part of a building, serves a notice on the undertaker requiring it, for the purpose of providing a supply of water for domestic purposes to that building or part of a building, to connect a service pipe to those premises with one of the undertaker's water mains.'

h [9] Subsection (2):

'Where a notice has been served for the purposes of this section, the duty imposed by subsection (1) above shall be a duty, at the expense of the person serving the notice, to make the connection required by the notice if ...'

j [10] There are certain conditions set out. Subsection (6) provides:

'Where a water undertaker carries out any works which it is its duty under this section to carry out at another person's expense, the undertaker shall be entitled to recover from that person an amount equal to the expenses reasonably incurred by the undertaker in carrying out the works.'

[11] So in that section one finds a duty in appropriate circumstances upon the water undertaker to make a water connection and the power to charge for doing so. Similar, if rather more complicated provisions, appear later in the statute in relation to sewerage undertakers, in particular in ss 98, 106 and 107. It is not necessary to refer to the detail of those sections for the purpose of this judgment.

[12] We then come to Pt V of the 1991 Act. Chapter I is concerned with charges. Section 142(1), under the side heading 'Powers of undertakers to charge', provides:

> 'Subject to the following provisions of this Chapter, the powers of every relevant undertaker shall include power—(a) to fix charges for any services provided in the course of carrying out its functions and, in the case of a sewerage undertaker, charges to be paid in connection with the carrying out of its trade effluent functions; and (b) to demand and recover charges fixed under this section from any persons to whom the undertaker provides services or in relation to whom it carries out trade effluent functions.'

[13] Subsection (4) provides:

> 'Except in so far as this Chapter otherwise provides, a relevant undertaker may fix charges under this section by reference to such matters, and may adopt such methods and principles for the calculation and imposition of the charges, as appear to the undertaker to be appropriate.'

[14] Pausing there for one moment, that is evidently a subsection which gives the undertakers a fairly wide discretion as to the fixing and calculation of their charges. It is a subsection which, as will appear, is qualified by at least one subsequent section of the Chapter. It is also qualified in practice by the Office of Water Services and the Director General insisting on compliance with conditions of appointment which the undertakers have been subjected to by virtue of s 6 of the 1991 Act to which I have referred.

[15] Section 143 makes provision for charges schemes. Section 143A provides for regulations as to the provisions to be included in charges schemes. Section 144 provides for liability of occupiers for charges. Section 144A provides for the right of the consumer to elect charging by reference to volume. Section 144B places restrictions on the undertakers' powers to require fixing of charges by reference to volume. Section 145 was repealed in 1999 and is not relevant to this appeal. Then we come to s 146. Subsection (1) provides:

> 'Subject to subsection (2) below, nothing in this Chapter or in any other enactment shall entitle any relevant undertaker to fix, demand or recover an initial charge for its becoming, or for its taking steps for the purpose of becoming—(a) the person who provides a supply of water for domestic purposes to any premises; or (b) the person who provides sewerage services for the purposes of the drainage for domestic sewerage purposes of any premises.'

[16] Subsection (2)—the critical subsection for the purpose of this appeal:

> 'Subject to subsection (3) below, nothing in subsection (1) above or in any other enactment shall be construed as prohibiting the fixing, demand or recovery by a relevant undertaker of—(a) a charge for the connection to a water supply of premises which have never at any previous time (whether before or after the coming into force of the restriction contained in this

a section) been connected to a supply of water provided for domestic purposes by a water undertaker or by any other authority or body which at that time provided supplies of water in the course of carrying out functions under any enactment; or (b) a charge for the connection to a public sewer of premises which have never at any previous time (whether before or after the coming into force of the restriction contained in this section) been connected to a

b sewer used for the drainage for domestic sewerage purposes of those premises by a sewerage undertaker or by any other authority or body which at that time provided sewerage services in the course of carrying out functions under any enactment.'

[17] Speaking in general therefore, undertakers may make charges which
c include: (a) charges for the cost of making physical connections (s 45(6) is an example of this); (b) periodic charges for supply (those are obvious charges with which we are all familiar); and (c) charges under s 146(2) whose ambit is the subject of these proceedings.

[18] Judge Catlin considered a number of authorities. These included *Thames Water Utilities Ltd v Shepherd Bush Housing Association* (5 November 1996,
d unreported), a decision of Judge Holden, to which I shall refer briefly later in this judgment; and a decision of Mr John Goldring QC sitting as a deputy judge of the High Court in *Thames Water Utilities Ltd v Bursar, Magdalen College, Oxford* (30 June 1999, unreported). I shall refer to that case later in this judgment. Judge Catlin reckoned that the *Magdalen College* case was distinguishable from the
e present case but he considered that details of the statutory framework, regulatory background and infrastructure charges set out in Mr Goldring's judgment were correct.

[19] Having set out the facts of the present case and referred to the principal statutory provisions, Judge Catlin made his finding in these terms:

f   'I find that the buildings which contained offices were connected to water and sewerage and that the existing building containing flats is connected to water and sewerage. Both these buildings are within the meaning of the word "premises" in s 146(2). Again I accept and adopt the reasons set out in the *Magdalen College* case. Where that case is to be distinguished on its facts to the present case is that in my judgment the present buildings cannot be
g   regarded as new buildings, these buildings have in my judgment previously been connected to a water supply and a sewer.'

[20] Judge Catlin went on to find, although the relevance of this finding is not entirely clear to his judgment, that the claimants did not make the connections to
h the individual 109 flats. I do not think that it has been suggested that they did. In essence, Judge Catlin decided that these were not premises which came within the exception in s 146(2) to the charging exemption because they had been previously connected to water and sewerage services. In doing so, he was plainly regarding the premises as the two buildings as a whole, the existing office buildings, and was not, as had been submitted to him on behalf of the claimant,
j regarding the premises as each of the individual 109 new flats.

[21] The main ground of appeal in substance is that Judge Catlin misinterpreted the word 'premises' in s 146(2) and misapplied that section to the facts of this case. He should have regarded each of the 109 flats as premises within the subsection, those premises never previously having been connected to a supply of water or to a sewer used for domestic drainage purposes.

[22] The defendants originally opposed the appeal. They supported Judge *a*
Catlin's judgment with a written skeleton argument prepared by counsel and a
respondent's notice seeking to uphold the decision on the additional ground that
the charges made were not within what was authorised in the statute anyway.
This morning the court was told that the parties had in part reached a
compromise. The effect of the compromise is that they have compromised the
financial consequences of this judgment, both as to payment and as to costs, *b*
whatever the outcome of the appeal. In these circumstances, the defendants have
not been represented before the court today. The appeal in that sense is
unopposed but the claimants seek a reasoned decision reversing, as they submit,
the decision of Judge Catlin on the ground that it is an important point for the
claimant and for the industry as a whole.

[23] The decision of Mr Goldring QC, as he was, in the *Magdalen College* case *c*
concerned again a claim by Thames Water Utilities in relation to buildings
constructed within the grounds of Magdalen College, Oxford on land which had
previously been used for squash courts and a building called the Back Lodge.
Each of those buildings had been connected for domestic purposes to the
claimants' water supply and public sewer. The college demolished the squash *d*
courts and the lodge and replaced them with two halls of residence. It applied for
water and sewerage connections but contested the claimants' claim for
infrastructure charges or, more accurately, for a charge under s 146(2).
Mr Goldring set out the statutory provisions in rather greater detail than I have.
He then said, under the heading 'Infrastructure charge':
e

> 'The phrase does not appear in the Act. It does appear in a number of
> documents which have been drawn to my attention. Although helpful in
> understanding the general position, none of the documents has statutory
> force. If the 1991 Act does not provide for infrastructure charges, none of the
> documents I am about to refer to can provide a basis to claim them.'
f

[24] He went on to refer to the claimants' deed of appointment under what
was then the Water Act 1989. He made reference to conditions of appointment,
including condition C, which has been referred to again in the context of the
present appeal. Mr Goldring had a section in his judgment about the debate in
the House of Lords and made references to *Pepper (Inspector of Taxes) v Hart* [1993] *g*
1 All ER 42, [1993] AC 593. He did not think it necessary to take the Hansard
references into account. Under the heading 'The first issue. Is Thames Water
entitled to infrastructure charges?', he said:

> '(1) Sections 45 and 46 entitle Thames Water to claim expenses incurred
> in making connections. In addition, Parliament gave the water and sewerage *h*
> undertaking the power, within specified circumstances, to make charges. It
> gave the undertaker a broad discretion in setting them. (2) Section 142(1)
> gives the undertaker the power to fix, demand and recover charges.
> Section 142(2)(a) provides that the power shall be exercised, among other
> things, in accordance with a charges scheme under s 143. Section 143(4) *j*
> permits the undertaker to take into account the circumstances of a particular
> case. Section 142(4) provides the undertaker with a very wide discretion in
> setting those charges. Section 146 limits the circumstances in which the
> charges can be made. They cannot be made for taking steps to become or
> becoming an undertaker (s 146(1)). They can be made for connection of
> premises which have never previously been connected (s 146(2)). (3) The

a   limits set upon the undertaker in fixing the charges are specified in the provisions. Provided the undertaker acts within those limits, it can set charges and decide the factors it wishes to take into account. Although infrastructure issues are not specifically mentioned as a factor, I can see no reason at all why they should not be. The provisions do not prevent it. There is nothing surprising in a water undertaking wishing, in setting its

b   charges, to take into account such matters as capital investment and its general capacity to provide connections. (4) Parliament intended that the consumer should be protected by the regulatory framework set out in the Act. This is to provide the balance between the undertaker's need to impose charges to enable it adequately to finance its statutory functions and the protection of the consumer. This case has demonstrated an example of the

c   Director General acting to protect the consumer. He required undertakings to lower their charges. (5) It comes to this. Parliament conferred and must have intended to confer a wide discretion on the water undertaker in setting its charges. It intended to protect the consumer by regulation. The undertaker can take such issues as the infrastructure into account when

d   setting those charges. Thames Water did that here. It has followed the charges scheme approved by the Director. If the charges claimed are in accordance with s 146(2) of the 1991 Act, they are recoverable.'

[25] He went on to deal with the second issue which was whether the infrastructure charges sought in that case were recoverable. He set out briefly the

e   opposing cases of the parties. Thames Water's case was that the construction of the word 'premises' is perfectly simple. It is a matter of common sense. It is to be construed having regard to the context in which it is found. Here, it was submitted that the new buildings were plainly premises which have never been connected to a water supply or sewer. They could not have been. They were not built. The College's case included that 'premises' within the 1991 Act meant

f   more than buildings. It meant the premises shown and described in the rating list; that is to say, the university college and premises. There was no subdivision of that. The word 'premises' is capable of meaning a building or part of a building when the Act specifically so provides. Otherwise it should be given its natural meaning. On the basis of that definition these premises, it was submitted, had

g   previously been connected.

[26] Mr Goldring considered those submissions in some detail and in conclusion he rejected the case on behalf of the College. He said:

'(1) The meaning of "premises" in s 146(2) is on its face and in its context quite straightforward. It is being used, not in a technical sense, but a natural

h   and ordinary way. It relates to buildings in the way Miss Baxendale submits. (2) The halls of residence are new buildings. By definition, they are premises which have never previously been connected to a water supply or a sewer. (3) What Parliament intended is clear. It was to permit the undertaker to charge in respect of buildings never previously connected.'

j   [27] It was the first two sentences at least of that brief conclusion to which Judge Catlin referred in the present case in support of his conclusion that in the present case the buildings were premises which had previously been connected to the water and the sewerage services.

[28] The decision to which Judge Catlin also referred of *United Utilities Water plc v Albany Homes Ltd* (9 November 2001, unreported) was a decision in the

West London County Court by Judge Cowell. Its facts bear some similarities to those in the present case. Judge Cowell introduced his judgment in these terms: *a*

> 'United Utilities Water plc, a water and sewerage undertaker for the North West, claims in this action an "infrastructure charge" of £23,072·16 from the defendant, Albany Homes Ltd, which in about 1998 purchased property in Cobourg Street, Manchester, known as Stonebridge House. It was an old textile mill or warehouse; but, whichever it was, the water supplied to it was *b* not used in any manufacturing process, but was used for domestic purposes within the meaning of the legislation I shall mention.'

[29] Judge Cowell went on to recount that the building was gutted inside and some of the peripheral walls remained. The building as it now was after the *c* development was a block of 42 flats which contained 30% more floor space than the original building. The defendant had made an application for water supply, asking for a new supply for 42 flats with a preferred size of connection of 110 mm. During the works pipe works, soil pipes and gutters were removed from the original building and then a water pipe was put through the wall into the pavement. The claimants, the water undertaking, made the connection and *d* installed a meter inside the building to serve the whole building and approved all of that by its inspector. Nothing was done outside the building to connect into the sewerage system. The new system installed inside the building was connected to the old system at some point inside. On those facts a former textile mill or warehouse, having water and sewerage services for domestic purposes, *e* was converted into 42 flats and a new water supply main was installed to connect to the building. The judge referred to the *Magdalen College* case. He found Mr Goldring's judgment very helpful. He said that he was bound to follow it. But if he was not bound to do so, he had no reason to disagree with it. He observed that s 146(2) does not refer to a building but to premises never at any previous time connected. He said that the use of the word 'premises' in ss 41 *f* and 45 showed that 'premises' may in the context of the Act consist of a part of a building. He then said:

> 'Therefore even if the word might in some contexts have a wider meaning I do not think the word in s 146(2) should have a different meaning from that in ss 41 and 45. It seems to me therefore that each one of the flats, being a *g* part of a building, is something, properly to be described as "premises", never at any previous time connected. Each flat, the premises, was simply not there in 1998 and before. The purpose of the development was to create 42 of them so that each could be separately sold or let as individual premises, and not to sell or let identifiable parts of the old mill building as it used to *h* stand with its floor and rooms before it was gutted. I am therefore satisfied that the claimant has established that the 42 flats are each premises never at any previous time connected.'

[30] He then said of the *Magdalen College* case that it seemed to him that it was *j* sufficient for the purpose of deciding that case for the judge to have stated that Parliament intended to permit the undertaker to charge in respect of buildings never previously connected.

[31] Judge Cowell was referred to Judge Catlin's decision in the present case. He referred to written submissions before him made by the defendants that premises must be equated with buildings. He did not accept that submission. He

said: 'Premises in the sections of the Act I have referred to cannot exist without a
a   building, but are not in my judgment to be equated with buildings.'

[32] He went on:

'It seems to me therefore that the existence of the same building is not
conclusive of the question whether the premises are new so as never
previously to have been connected, and that it is only a factor in deciding
b   whether the premises after works have been done to the building are new so
as never previously to have been connected. For example, if the building is
not demolished and the existing floors are simply let out separately as
self-contained units it would probably not be correct to regard any one floor
as premises never at any previous time connected. The more each floor was
c   altered in layout or design or in its capacity to use the water and sewerage
systems the more readily could it be said that new premises had been created
which had never at any previous time been connected.'

[33] The one other previous decision to which I shall refer is a decision of
d   Judge Holden sitting in the Brentford County Court in *Thames Water Utilities Ltd v
Shepherd Bush Housing Association* (5 November 1996, unreported). It is not
necessary to recount the facts of that case. Suffice it to refer to a single paragraph
in the judge's judgment. He said:

'Section 146(2)(b) inter alia allows ... an undertaking to make a connection
e   charge ie a charge "for" the connection to a public sewer of premises which
have never at any previous time been connected to a sewer for the drainage
of domestic sewerage purposes. A connection charge arises notwithstanding
the fact that connection might be made by the developers and not the
defendants. It is the acceptance of that sewerage into the undertaking system
which is material. In my judgment a connection of the services is in itself the
f   provision of services. I do not see that it matters if such a service is described
as being an "infrastructure charge". Such an expression is not used in the
primary legislation.'

[34] I say straightaway that in my judgment Mr Goldring's analysis of the
structure of the Act, so far as relevant for present purposes, was correct. I agree
g   with the analysis undertaken by Judge Cowell and with his application of it to the
facts of his case. I agree with the paragraph from Judge Holden's judgment that
I have just read.

[35] Mr Watson on behalf of the claimants submits that Judge Catlin in the
present case misinterpreted s 146(2). He submits that he appears to have read the
h   passage in Mr Goldring's judgment out of context as defining the word 'premises'
as synonymous with and limited to buildings. He submits that the statute uses
the word 'premises' in a flexible way in various places, thus illustrating that its
meaning has to be derived from its particular context. The meaning may not be
inflexibly the same every time that it is used. He submits that Judge Cowell was
j   correct and that Judge Catlin in the present case was not.

[36] I take into account the written submissions lodged on behalf of the
defendants in support of Judge Catlin's judgment but it is not necessary, I think,
to refer to them in detail. In my judgment, the interpretation of s 146(2) has to
be considered not only by reference to the word 'premises' but also by reference
to the use there of the word 'connection'. 'Premises' is an ordinary word whose
precise meaning is to be derived from its context. It is to be noted that neither

'premises' nor 'connection' or 'connected' are defined in the definition section of this Act, s 219. 'Premises', it seem to me, will usually include buildings but may not be limited to buildings and might in some circumstances refer to a place with few or no buildings on it. Premises may in its context also consist of a part of a larger building. A garden centre or a builder's merchant may have premises which include one or more buildings but the premises may extend to the larger site used for the keeping of plants or bricks and sand. A garden centre might conceivably have premises with no buildings on it at all. The premises of a farming business might consist of a group of farm buildings but it would be a somewhat strange context perhaps, though not impossible, which included 100 acres of fields as part of the farm premises. The premises of a large corporation might in context consist of the entirety of a large office block. The premises of a small firm or company might consist of one or two rooms on an upper floor of a much larger building. In the general context of the supply of water and sewerage services premises are likely to include buildings or parts of buildings to which the water is supplied and from which the sewage is taken away. There are a number of references to premises in various other sections of this statute. Those include, but are not perhaps limited to, ss 41, 45, 52 and 64. These show that in this statute the expression 'premises' is used in various contexts with various contextual shades of meaning.

[37] In my judgment, as I have said, the relevant meaning of s 146(2)(a) and (b) is to be derived not only from the use of the word 'premises' but from its use in the context of the word 'connection'. The full relevant expression is—

> 'a charge for the connection to a water supply of premises which have never at any previous time ... been connected to a supply of water provided for domestic purposes by a water undertaker ...'

I think that the heading of s 146 may be misleading. At first blush, it appears to refer to the making of a physical connection so that the charge would be a charge for doing so. But the undertaker does not have to go to s 146(2) to be able to charge the costs of the physical connection. Section 45(6) provides the power to make such charge for water and ss 106 and 107 do so also for sewerage. Section 146(2) is concerned, I think, with the connection to the water and sewerage systems of premises which have not previously been so connected and must include new premises which are likely to place an additional burden on the system as a whole. If the premises are in this sense new premises, there is I think no need to establish positively that there will be a volumetric additional burden. It may be taken that in the round there will be. The section applies to a new housing development on what was formerly an unoccupied site. It would probably not apply to a modest alteration to an existing house which did not constitute the building of new premises. Where existing buildings are converted, it will be a question of fact and degree whether the result is or includes the construction and connection of premises which have never previously been connected, or whether the conversion retains the identity of premises which existed and were connected before the conversion took place. Judge Cowell gave an example of such in his decision to which I have referred.

[38] On the facts of the present case the 109 flats were new premises which had never previously been connected and the claimants were entitled to make a charge for each of them under s 146(2). Although the expression 'infrastructure charge' does not appear in the statute, I am satisfied that the charge to which s 146(2) refers is in the nature of a contribution to the capital and maintenance

a cost of providing services, subject to the additional demand which the connection of premises not previously connected must in general generate. I reach this conclusion without reference to Hansard or to condition C of the claimants' conditions of appointment. Mr Watson did not persuade me that condition C was properly available as an aid to construing s 146(2) but it is not necessary for me to decide.

b [39] For these reasons I would allow the appeal and invite Mr Watson to address us as to the form of any order that should be made.

BODEY J.

[40] I agree with the judgment just delivered. There is nothing which I can usefully add.

c

Appeal allowed.

James Brooks   Barrister.

Pennycook v Shaws (EAL) Ltd

[2002] EWHC 2769 (Ch)

CHANCERY DIVISION

PUMFREY J

28 NOVEMBER 2002

Landlord and tenant – Business premises – Notice by landlord to terminate tenancy –
Tenant giving counter-notice erroneously indicating willingness to give up possession –
Tenant giving second counter-notice within prescribed period correctly indicating
unwillingness to give up possession – Whether first counter-notice binding – Landlord
and Tenant Act 1954, ss 25, 29(2).

The claimant tenant's lease was governed by the provisions of the Landlord and
Tenant Act 1954. His landlord served him with a notice under s 25[a] of the 1954
Act as a prerequisite to terminating the tenancy. Section 25(5) provided that such
a notice was not to have effect unless it required the tenant, within two months
after the giving of the notice, to notify the landlord in writing whether or not at
the date of termination the tenant would be willing to give up possession. If a
tenant applied to the court for a new tenancy in consequence of a landlord's s 25
notice, s 29(2)[b] precluded the court from entertaining the application unless the
tenant had 'duly' notified the landlord that he would not be willing to give up
possession. The tenant served a positive counter-notice on the landlord,
indicating his willingness to give up possession of the premises on the
termination date. However, the notice, which was in pre-printed form, had been
filled in wrongly by the tenant's solicitor, and the tenant had instead intended to
give a negative counter-notice, stating that he would not be willing to give up
possession. The error was detected, and the tenant served a negative
counter-notice within two months of the receipt of the landlord's notice. Relying
on that second counter-notice, he issued proceedings in the county court
claiming a new tenancy. The judge struck out his claim on the basis that a
positive counter-notice to a landlord's s 25 notice was irrevocable and that
accordingly the tenant was bound by his first counter-notice. The tenant
appealed.

Held – A positive counter-notice to a landlord's notice under s 25 of the 1954 Act
was not always irrevocable. Section 29(2) of the Act was satisfied if, within the
two-month period, thus giving proper emphasis to the word 'duly', a notice had
been given, stating that a tenant would not be willing at the date of termination
to give up possession. However, in any case where the tenant had made a
positive representation, it would be a question whether he was in fact entitled to
resile from the positive notice which had been given in answer to the landlord's
s 25 notice. It was open to the court to determine that in all the circumstances it
was wrong for a tenant to seek to substitute a new statement of his intention for
the purposes of s 29(2), but each such case was to be dealt with on its own merits.
In the instant case, the tenant had been entitled to give a second notice, and

---

a   Section 25, so far as material, is set out at [6], [7], below
b   Section 29, so far as material, is set out at [8], below

a s 29(2) was potentially satisfied. Accordingly, the appeal would be allowed (see [16], [18], [20], below).

Dicta of Brightman J in *Re 14 Grafton Street, London W1, De Haviland (Antiques) Ltd v Centrovincial Estates (Mayfair) Ltd* [1971] 2 All ER 1 at 6–7 not followed.

b **Notes**
For the right of tenants under business tenancies to apply for a new tenancy, see 27(1) *Halsbury's Laws* (4th edn reissue) para 574.

For the Landlord and Tenant Act 1954, ss 25, 29, see 23 *Halsbury's Statutes* (4th edn) (1997 reissue) 147, 151.

c **Case referred to in judgment**
Grafton Street (14), London W1, Re, De Haviland (Antiques) Ltd v Centrovincial Estates (Mayfair) Ltd [1971] 2 All ER 1, [1971] Ch 935, [1971] 2 WLR 159.

Cases referred to in skeleton arguments
d *Bramelid v Sweden* (1982) 5 EHRR 249, E Com HR.
Family Housing Association v Donnellan [2002] 1 P&CR 449.
Ghaidan v Mendoza [2002] EWCA Civ 1533, [2002] 4 All ER 1162, [2003] 2 WLR 478.
James v UK (1986) 8 EHRR 123, [1986] ECHR 8793/79, ECt HR.
Mellacher v Austria (1989) 12 EHRR 391, [1989] ECHR 10522/83, ECt HR.
e *Osman v UK* (1998) 5 BHRC 293, ECt HR.
Poplar Housing and Regeneration Community Association Ltd v Donoghue [2001] EWCA Civ 595, [2001] 4 All ER 604, [2002] QB 48, [2001] 3 WLR 183.
Pressos Cia Naviera SA v Belgium (1995) 21 EHRR 301, [1995] 17849/91, ECt HR.
Pye (JA) (Oxford) Ltd v Graham [2001] EWCA Civ 117, [2001] Ch 804, [2001] 2 WLR
f 1293; *rvsd* [2002] UKHL 30, [2002] 3 All ER 865, [2002] 3 WLR 221.
R v Carass [2001] EWCA Crim 2845, [2002] 1 WLR 1714.
Wilson v First County Trust Ltd [2001] EWCA Civ 633, [2001] 3 All ER 229, [2002] QB 74, [2001] 3 WLR 42; *rvsd* [2003] UKHL 40, [2003] 3 WLR 568.

g **Appeal**
The claimant, Walbert Pennycook, appealed with the permission of Judge Cox from his decision in the Lambeth County Court on 9 July 2002 striking out his claim under s 24(1) of the Landlord and Tenant Act 1954 seeking the grant of a new tenancy of business premises at 130 Railton Road, London SE24 by the defendant landlord, Shaws (EAL) Ltd. The facts are set out in the judgment.
h
William Geldart (instructed by *Hallmark Atkinson Wynter*) for Mr Pennycook.
Neil Vickery (instructed by *Belmont Hansford*) for the landlord.

PUMFREY J.
j [1] This is an appeal from an order by Judge Cox sitting at the Lambeth County Court whereby he struck out proceedings for a new tenancy commenced by Mr Walbert Pennycook in respect of premises at 130 Railton Road, London SE24. The premises in question are principally a barber shop and, I believe, a floor over.

[2] Mr Pennycook was the tenant under a lease for ten years of the premises granted by the then landlord, Mayshore Property Co Ltd, on 27 March 1991. The

demise was for a period of ten years from 25 March 1989. Towards the end of the
contractual term, Mr Pennycook entered into some inconclusive negotiations
with the landlord in respect of a purchase of the freehold of the premises, and
even gave a tenant's notice under Pt II of the Landlord and Tenant Act 1954 in
respect of which the necessary proceedings were not commenced in time. The
history which gives rise to the present proceedings starts with a landlord's notice
which was served on Mr Pennycook on 8 November 2001 pursuant to s 25 of the
1954 Act. On 4 December 2001, Mr Pennycook served a counter-notice. This
counter-notice was served on a form printed by the well-known law stationers,
Oyez, headed 'Landlord and Tenant Act 1954 sections 25(5) and 29(2)' and is
entitled 'Tenant's counter-notice as to willingness to give up possession of
business premises'. After reciting the essential features of the landlord's notice,
the pro forma continues, against a marginal note 6, 'Delete if tenant does not
wish to apply for a new tenancy, see note 3' with the following: 'Take notice that
I/We will [not] be willing to give up possession of the property comprised in the
tenancy on that date.'

[3] Mr Pennycook's solicitor, Mr Alfonso Constantine Wynter, sets out in his
witness statement the circumstances in which this notice came to be given. He
says that he perused the papers when he was instructed by Mr Pennycook on
4 December 2002 and he prepared the counter-notice, and he says that he typed
it, and at the same time he instructed a surveyor to act for Mr Pennycook in
negotiations of the terms for a new lease. It was the surveyor who detected the
error in the counter-notice, since he received a letter from Mr Wynter telling him
that Mr Pennycook wished to renew the lease and was going to instruct
Mr Wynter to apply to the court for a new lease unless terms could be agreed
with the landlord.

[4] This evidence, at its lowest, strongly suggests that Mr Wynter made a
grave error in the completion of the form and completed it contrary to his
instructions (but I say no more about that at this stage), since the two-month
period for a counter-notice to the landlord's notice had, when Mr Wynter gave
the defective notice, another month to run. As soon as the surveyor detected the
error and notified Mr Wynter of it on 2 January 2002, Mr Wynter on 4 January
2002 gave a further notice, this time in the correct form. Purportedly pursuant to
that notice, Mr Pennycook issued his claim in the Lambeth County Court for a
new tenancy and the claim was struck out by Judge Cox on 9 July 2002.

[5] The relevant provisions of the Landlord and Tenant Act 1954 are, as
follows. By s 24(1):

'A tenancy to which this Part of this Act applies shall not come to an end
unless terminated in accordance with the provisions of this Part of this Act;
and, subject to the provisions of section twenty-nine of this Act, the tenant
under such a tenancy may apply to the court for a new tenancy—(a) if the
landlord has given notice under section 25 of this Act to terminate the
tenancy, or (b) if the tenant has made a request for a new tenancy in
accordance with section twenty-six of this Act.'

[6] Section 25, as is well known, sets out the prerequisites for the termination
of a tenancy by the landlord. The notice to be given by the landlord to the tenant
must be in the prescribed form and must specify the date at which the tenancy is
to come to an end, which is defined as the date of termination. The section
concerns itself both with the permitted range of dates of termination and
prescribes by sub-s (4) that subject to the provisions of sub-s (3)—

a 'a notice under the section shall not specify a date of termination earlier than the date on which apart from this part of this Act the tenancy would have come to an end by effluxion of time.'

[7] By sub-s (5)—

b 'A notice under this section shall not have effect unless it requires the tenant, within two months after the giving of the notice, to notify the landlord in writing whether or not, at the date of termination, the tenant will be willing to give up possession of the property comprised in the tenancy.'

The landlord's notice being on a pre-printed form, as one would expect, complied with this requirement and Mr Pennycook availed himself of the opportunity *c* provided to notify the landlord, first that he would be willing to give up possession, and second that he would not.

[8] By s 29—

d '(1) Subject to the provisions of this Act, on an application under subsection (1) of section twenty-four of this Act for a new tenancy the court shall make an order for the grant of a tenancy comprising such property, at such rent and on such other terms, as are hereinafter provided.

(2) Where such an application is made in consequence of a notice given by the landlord under section twenty-five of this Act, it shall not be entertained unless the tenant has duly notified the landlord that he will not *e* be willing at the date of termination to give up possession of the property comprised in the tenancy.

(3) No application under subsection (1) of section twenty-four of this Act shall be entertained unless it is made not less than two nor more than four months after the giving of the landlord's notice under section twenty-five of *f* this Act or, as the case may be, after the making of the tenant's request for a new tenancy.'

[9] There is no doubt that Mr Pennycook's application to the county court satisfied sub-s (3) of s 29; the question is whether it satisfied the requirements of sub-s (2). In approaching this question, the learned judge relied upon the decision of Brightman J in *Re 14 Grafton Street, London W1, De Haviland (Antiques) Ltd v* *g* *Centrovincial Estates (Mayfair) Ltd* [1971] 2 All ER 1, [1971] Ch 935. This was a case in which the tenant sought compensation under the Part of the 1954 Act as amended by the Law of Property Act 1969, an amendment which came into effect during the currency of the two-month period permitted for the tenant's notice. The headnote sets out the determinations of Brightman J as follows ([1971] Ch *h* 935):

'... that in order to be entitled to compensation for disturbance a tenant must, first, have served a counter notice on the landlord under section 29(2) of the Act of 1954, stating that he was unwilling to vacate the premises and secondly, under section 37(1) of the Act (before amendment), he must have *j* applied to the court for a new tenancy; that a counter notice which expressed willingness to quit was irrevocable; and that, accordingly, after October 13, the tenants could not give a notice of unwillingness to quit and had lost their right to apply to the court and the landlords, in turn, had acquired an indefeasible right to obtain possession on April 1, 1970, without paying compensation.'

[10] It is important in this case to observe the material dates. The notice to terminate the tenancy was given on 1 April 1970, the notice being given on 27 September 1969. The tenants gave what was subsequently described as a positive counter-notice, that is to say, a notice indicating their intention to vacate the premises, on 13 October 1969. On 22 October 1969, the royal assent was given to the amending statute which came into effect on 1 January 1970 and the tenants inquired about compensation on 11 February 1970. The two-month period from service of the notice therefore expired somewhere around about 27 November 1969.

[11] Brightman J first interpreted the expression 'duly notified' in s 29(2), which I have read, as meaning a notification within two months after the giving by the landlord of a s 25 notice. He said that that is made clear by the wording of s 25(5), which I have also read, and if I may respectfully say so, I respectfully agree.

[12] He then turned to the scheme of the statutory provisions, in a passage which I should read out in full ([1971] 2 All ER 1 at 5–7, [1971] Ch 935 at 942–944):

'It appears to be the scheme of the Act that a landlord's notice under s 25 shall be followed by a notification by the tenant either that he *is* willing or that he is *not* willing to give up possession on the date of termination specified in the landlord's notice. For convenience, I refer to such a notification by the tenant as a positive or a negative counter-notice, according to whether the tenant is or is not agreeable to the landlord's demand. A negative counter-notice is a condition precedent to an application by the tenant to the court: see s 29(2). An application by the tenant to the court was, prior to the 1969 Act, a condition precedent to the tenant's becoming entitled to compensation for disturbance. It is therefore hard to see how it can ever have been to a tenant's financial advantage to serve a *positive* counter-notice. Before the 1969 Act the result can only have been to deprive the tenant of the chance of obtaining compensation. Indeed, no counsel was able to suggest what practical function is performed by a positive counter-notice, except an act of courtesy to the landlord. On 22 October 1969 the Law of Property Act 1969 received the royal assent. Part I of the Act is headed: "AMENDMENT OF PART II OF THE LANDLORD AND TENANT ACT 1954". Section 11 of the Act amends s 37(1) of the 1954 Act by inserting new words. Section 37(1) as amended is set out in Sch 1 to the 1969 Act; the additional words follow the words "of that subsection" and provide: "or where no other ground is specified in the landlord's notice under section 25 of this Act or, as the case may be under section 26(6) thereof, than those specified in the said paragraphs (e), (f) and (g) and either no application under the said section 24 is made or such an application is withdrawn." The effect, therefore, of the amendment was to entitle the tenant to obtain compensation notwithstanding the absence of an application to the court. Section 31(2) of the 1969 Act provided that the parts of the Act relevant to this application should come into force on 1 January 1970. On 11 February 1970 the tenants' solicitors wrote to the landlords' solicitors: "Further to the Notice to Determine [the tenants'] Lease of the above premises [the tenants] now [propose] to leave approximately at the end of February. In the circumstances, will you kindly let us know what arrangements are being made regarding compensation payable under the Landlord and Tenant Act 1954 as amended by the Law of Property Act

1969." The landlords' s 25 notice had been sent with a letter dated 26 September and it is common ground that this notice should be treated as "given" on 27 September. The position therefore, on that day, was that 26 or 27 November (I assume 27 November without so deciding) was the last day available to the tenants for serving a negative counter-notice as a prelude to an application by the tenants to the court for an order for the grant of a new tenancy. In fact, as I have mentioned, the tenants' solicitors on 13 October had written a letter which the landlords accepted as, and which I hold to have been, a notification by the tenants within the meaning of s 25(5) of the 1954 Act that on 1 April 1970 they would be willing to give up possession of the property. There was some discussion, unsupported by authority as I was told none existed, whether the tenants could, on or before 27 November, have revoked their positive counter-notice and given the negative counter-notice required by s 29(2) to enable proceedings to be taken. In my view the purpose of s 25(5) is to introduce an element of certainty into the relationship between the landlord and the tenant. A tenant is not bound to serve a negative counter-notice before the end of the two month period allowed to him. He may pause for that period of time while he makes up his mind. If however he does serve a positive counter-notice during the two month period, I think that he must abide by what he has done. If that were not the case, the positive counter-notice would serve no purpose whatever compared with complete inaction, for in either case the landlord would not know where he stood until the end of the two month period. If a positive counter-notice is revocable, the tenant serving the same would be able to serve a negative counter-notice right up to the end of the two month period. If on the other hand the tenant does nothing, he may likewise serve a negative counter-notice right up to the end of the two month period. It follows that a positive counter-notice would be wholly devoid of any function, even that of courtesy, if it were revocable at the will of the tenant. I therefore conclude that a positive counter-notice is irrevocable; and that in this case the tenants ceased to be able to serve a negative counter-notice after 13 October 1969 and that they then lost their right to apply to the court for an order for the grant of a new tenancy. I have not overlooked the fact that the Act of 1954 is not expressed to impose on the tenant an obligation to serve a notice of either description within the two month period. All that the Act does is to impose on the landlord, as a condition of a valid s 25 notice, the obligation of informing the tenant that he is required to serve a notice one way or the other within the two month period, and to place the tenant under a disability if he fails to serve a negative counter-notice. In my view, however, it is a necessary implication from s 25(5) that a tenant is under a statutory obligation to serve notice one way or the other within the two month period, although I accept that there is no sanction imposed on him for ignoring that obligation, except his inability to apply to the court. In these circumstances the position in my view was as follows. On 14 October 1969, ie about eight days before the Law of Property Act 1969 received the royal assent, the landlords had an indefeasible right to recover possession on 1 April 1970 without payment of compensation, if I am correct in my conclusion that the tenants were precluded from withdrawing their letter of 13 October and from serving a negative counter-notice.'

[13] The learned judge, having quoted the material passage in Brightman J's judgment relating to the revocability of the positive counter-notice, said: *a*

> 'On the face of it, that passage from the judgment of Brightman J, concludes the issue in this case. If that passage is binding upon me and is good law, then it is perfectly clear in the circumstances of the case that whatever the circumstances in which the positive notice was given it is binding upon the tenant and it has brought to an end the tenancy.   *b* Mr Geldart, who has said everything that could be said on behalf of the claimant in these proceedings, has sought to distinguish *Re 14 Grafton Street* on a number of bases.'

And he sets out the arguments of counsel and it appears from the transcript that the learned county court judge concluded that the judgment of Brightman J was   *c* binding upon him and that he had no hesitation in following it. He accordingly struck out these proceedings.

[14] I think that it may be helpful, in considering the judgment of Brightman J, to examine the passage which I have quoted at length, in a little more detail than did the learned judge. Brightman J was unable to identify any practical function   *d* which was performed by a positive counter-notice except to act as an act of courtesy to the landlord. That being so, it is at first sight surprising that the effect of serving such notice is to preclude the tenant in all circumstances from giving a negative counter-notice within the two-month statutory period. I say in all the circumstances, since it is easy to envisage circumstances in which it would be wrong to permit a tenant to resile from a positive counter-notice. But I am   *e* concerned with the question whether in every case it is impossible to do that. Brightman J's reasoning on this question is found in the passage beginning with the words: 'The landlords' s 25 notice had been sent with a letter dated 26 September [1969] …' (see [1971] 2 All ER 1 at 6, [1971] Ch 935 at 943).

[15] The stages in the argument commence with the words: *f*

> 'There was some discussion, unsupported by authority as I was told none existed, as to whether the tenants could, on or before November 27 [which, it will be recalled is the expiry date of the two-month period], have revoked their positive counter-notice and given the negative counter-notice required by s 29(2) to enable proceedings to be taken.'   *g*

The crucial passage then follows ([1971] 2 All ER 1 at 6, [1971] Ch 935 at 943–944):

> 'In my view the purpose of s 25(5) is to introduce an element of certainty into the relationship between the landlord and the tenant. A tenant is not bound to serve a negative counter-notice before the end of the two month   *h* period allowed to him. He may pause for that period of time while he makes up his mind. If however he does serve a positive counter-notice during the two month period, I think that he must abide by what he has done. If that were not the case, the positive counter-notice would serve no purpose whatever compared with complete inaction, for in either case the landlord   *j* would not know where he stood until the end of the two month period. If a positive counter-notice is revocable, the tenant serving the same would be able to serve a negative counter-notice right up to the end of the two month period. If on the other hand the tenant does nothing, he may likewise serve a negative counter-notice right up to the end of the two month period. It follows the positive counter-notice would be wholly devoid of any function,

a even that of courtesy, if it were revocable at the will of the tenant. I therefore conclude that a positive counter-notice is irrevocable ...'

[16] I approach this passage with all the respect which is owing from me to a judge of great experience and authority in this field. I would, however, respectfully doubt whether the 'therefore' in the words, 'I therefore conclude that
b a positive counter-notice is irrevocable' in fact indicates a logical conclusion from the premises. It seems to me that it is a possible view that a positive counter-notice is not devoid of any function including that of courtesy if the tenant gives it, and thereafter it is acted upon by the landlord. If, however, there is no (to use a shorthand expression) 'change of position' on the part of the landlord in reliance upon the serving of a positive counter-notice, I do not, as
c presently advised, understand why it is necessary to conclude that the counter-notice is irrevocable. Mr Vickery, who appeared on behalf of the landlord in the present case, suggested a number of reasons why that should be so. He pointed to the symmetrical nature of the provisions of the statute relating first of all to landlord's notices under s 25 and secondly to the tenant's notice
d under s 26. He pointed out, correctly, that if a landlord gives a counter-notice, as is permitted under s 26(6), it is well settled that the grounds of opposition set out in such a notice are, like the grounds of opposition specified in the landlord's notice under s 25, unamendable and irrevocable. He submits that to treat the tenant's counter-notice under s 25(5), albeit it appears to have no other legal effect, as revocable, introduces an anomaly in the scheme of the 1954 Act which
e must be doubtful in view of the irrevocability of the other notices.

[17] Mr Vickery submitted further that there is a good reason for treating a tenant's positive counter-notice as irrevocable. If the only question, he says, is whether in all the circumstances it is fair to allow the tenant to resile from a positive counter-notice, then an undesirable species of satellite litigation is
f introduced into a well-understood, well-circumscribed, kind of application made all the time in the county court and well understood by all involved. He says that it is thoroughly undesirable to introduce into this well-understood system a possibility of satellite disputes as to the validity of tenants' negative notices if previously positive notices have been given and the tenant has for some reason or other changed its mind.

g [18] I see the force of these submissions. However, I am not satisfied that in point of fact the circumstances arising here are likely as a practical matter to arise at all frequently. There can be little doubt that there is no question of a change of mind here, but a simple error on the part of the solicitor. Second, I cannot see why, in the ordinary course, a tenant will give a positive notice unless quite
h satisfied that it does indeed intend to give up possession at the end of the notice period. I am not satisfied that positive counter-notices are such a common phenomenon in any event that it is necessary to consider the risks involved from the point of view of the proper administration of justice in permitting, in a proper case, a negative counter-notice to be substituted for a positive counter-notice
j already given. So although I freely accept the possibilities to which Mr Vickery referred, I doubt very much whether in point of fact they amount to a cogent objection to the construction of the relevant provisions, which I prefer. The construction which I prefer is that s 29(2) is satisfied if in point of fact within the two-month period, thus giving proper emphasis to the word 'duly', a notice stating that the tenant will not be willing at the date of termination to give up possession, has in point of fact been given.

[19] I do not believe that this construction is precluded by the judgment of Brightman J, since in that case although Brightman J says in the passage which I *a* have quoted that the landlords had an indefeasible right to recover possession on 1 April 1970 without payment of compensation, Brightman J is considering the indefeasible right of landlords having regard to the ability of the tenants to give a negative counter-notice after 13 October. It is to be observed that in that case no negative counter-notice was in fact given. The point, therefore, did not arise and *b* the tenants took no steps to raise the question until after the expiry of the two-month period. I do not think it can be seriously contended that the two-month period is in any way extensible, and it would follow, therefore, that after the expiry of the two-month period the landlord's right became indefeasible whether or not during the period from 13 October to 27 November there had been a contingent right in the tenants to revoke their original positive notice. *c* Accordingly, it does not seem to me that this determination was essential to the decision of Brightman J, but if that is a wrong analysis I would, to the extent that I have indicated, very respectfully disagree with the generality of what he said.

[20] It follows that in my view this appeal ought to succeed on the grounds that the tenant was entitled to give a second notice and that s 29(2) was *d* potentially satisfied. However, it seems to me that in any case where the tenant has made a positive representation, it will be a question whether it is in fact entitled to resile from the positive notice which is given in answer to a s 25 notice given by the landlord. I say no more about that in this case, save to say that it must be open to the court to determine that in all the circumstances it is wrong for a tenant to seek to substitute a new statement of his intention for the purposes *e* of s 29(2), but each such case must be dealt with on its own merits. I would accordingly allow this appeal on this ground.

[21] I should add that the learned judge granted permission to appeal only upon certain arguments which were addressed to him and addressed to me in far greater detail in writing by Mr Geldart and Mr Vickery, on points arising under *f* the Human Rights Act 1998, under the European Convention for the Protection of Human Rights and Fundamental Freedoms 1950, and in particular the First Protocol to the convention. These arguments raised points of what seemed to me to be very great difficulty. I have deliberately abstained from hearing the oral argument and from considering these points in detail. I have come to the conclusion without considering the human rights points. The learned judge gave *g* permission to appeal only upon the human rights points, but Mr Vickery has realistically accepted that, first of all it would be difficult to resist an application for permission to appeal out of time on the ground upon which I have decided the appeal also, and also I think that the investigation of the effect of Brightman J's decision is a necessary prerequisite to the application of the *h* principles articulated in the 1998 Act. For these reasons therefore I shall allow this appeal.

Appeal allowed.

j

Neneh Munu   Barrister.